W9-BIK-110

Features

New Tables *p.xi*

Guide to Tabular Presentation *p. xiv*

Telephone and Internet Contacts *p. xvi*

Guide to Sources of Statistics *p. 857*

Guide to State Statistical Abstracts *p. 871*

Guide to Foreign Statistical Abstracts *p. 875*

Metropolitan and Micropolitan Area
Concepts and Components *p. 877*

Index by Subject *p. 925*

Visit us on the Web at
http://www.census.gov/statab/www/

ACKNOWLEDGMENTS

Ian R. O'Brien was responsible for the technical supervision and coordination of this volume under the direction of **Lars B. Johanson**, Chief, Statistical Compendia Branch. Assisting in the research and analytical phases of assigned sections and in the development aspects of new tables were **Richard P. Kersey**, **Jean F. Mullin**, and **Michael Sellner**. **Catherine Lavender** provided primary editorial assistance. Other editorial assistance was rendered by **April C. Harris**, **Connie Nadzadi**, and **Virginia Zamaitis**.

Maps were designed and produced by **Connie Beard** and **Jessica Dobrowolski** of the Cartographic Products Management Branch within the Geography Division.

Catherine M. Raymond, **Theodora Forgione**, **Linda Chen**, and **Diane Oliff-Michael** of the Administrative and Customer Services Division, **Francis Grailand Hall**, Chief, provided publications and printing management, graphics design and composition, and editorial review for print and electronic media. General direction and production management were provided by **Claudette E. Bennett**, Assistant Division Chief, and **Wanda Cevis**, Chief, Publications Services Branch.

The cooperation of many contributors to this volume is gratefully acknowledged. The source note below each table credits the various government and private sector agencies that have collaborated in furnishing the information for the *Statistical Abstract*.

Statistical Abstract
of the United States: 2009

Issued October 2008

U.S. Department of Commerce
Carlos M. Gutierrez,
Secretary

John J. Sullivan,
Deputy Secretary

Economics and Statistics
Administration
Cynthia A. Glassman,
Under Secretary for Economic Affairs

U.S. CENSUS BUREAU
Steve H. Murdock,
Director

SUGGESTED CITATION

U.S. Census Bureau,
*Statistical Abstract of the
United States: 2009*
(128th Edition)
Washington, DC,
2008

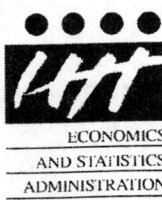

ECONOMICS
AND STATISTICS
ADMINISTRATION

**Economics
and Statistics
Administration**

Cynthia A. Glassman,
Under Secretary
for Economic Affairs

U.S. CENSUS BUREAU

Steve H. Murdock,
Director

Thomas L. Mesenbourg,
Acting Deputy Director and
Chief Operating Officer

Ted A. Johnson, Associate Director
for Administration
and Chief Financial Officer

Francis Grailand Hall, Chief,
Administrative
and Customer Services Division

ISBN 10: 1-59888-284-8
ISBN 13: 978-1-59888-284-1

Published in the United States of America by Bernan, a wholly owned subsidiary of
The Rowman and Littlefield Publishing Group, Inc.
4501 Forbes Boulevard, Suite 200
Lanham, Md. 20706
800-865-3457
info@bernan.com
www.bernan.com

Preface

The *Statistical Abstract of the United States,* published since 1878, is the standard summary of statistics on the social, political, and economic organization of the United States. It is designed to serve as a convenient volume for statistical reference and as a guide to other statistical publications and sources. The latter function is served by the introductory text to each section, the source note appearing below each table, and Appendix I, which comprises the Guide to Sources of Statistics, the Guide to State Statistical Abstracts, and the Guide to Foreign Statistical Abstracts.

This volume includes a selection of data from many statistical sources, both government and private. Publications cited as sources usually contain additional statistical detail and more comprehensive discussions of definitions and concepts. Data not available in publications issued by the contributing agency but obtained from the Internet or unpublished records are identified in the source notes. More information on the subjects covered in the tables so noted may generally be obtained from the source.

Except as indicated, figures are for the United States as presently constituted. Although emphasis in the *Statistical Abstract* is primarily given to national data, many tables present data for regions and individual states and a smaller number for metropolitan areas and cities. Appendix II, Metropolitan and Micropolitan Statistical Areas: Concepts, Components, and Population, presents explanatory text, a complete current listing and population data for metropolitan and micropolitan areas defined as of December 2006. Statistics for the Commonwealth of Puerto Rico and for island areas of the United States are included in many state tables and are supplemented by information in Section 29. Additional information for states, cities, counties, metropolitan areas, and other small units,

as well as more historical data are available in various supplements to the *Abstract* (see inside back cover).

Statistics in this edition are generally for the most recent year or period available by summer 2008. Each year over 1,400 tables and charts are reviewed and evaluated; new tables and charts of current interest are added, continuing series are updated, and less timely data are condensed or eliminated. Text notes and appendices are revised as appropriate. In addition, three special features—*Historical Statistics, State Rankings,* and *USA Statistics in Brief*—can be found on our Web site: <http://www.census.gov /compendia/statab/>.

Changes in this edition—This year we have introduced 49 new tables covering a wide range of subject areas. These cover a variety of topics including: religious composition of U.S. population, assisted reproductive technology, military retirement system, labor violations, aquaculture products sold, homeowner and rental vacancy rates by state, and expenditures for wildlife-related recreation. For a complete list of new tables, see section titled "New Tables," p. xi.

Statistical Abstract on other media— The *Abstract* is available on the Internet and on CD-ROM. Both versions contain the same material as the book, except for a few copyrighted tables for which we did not receive permission to release in these formats. Our Internet site <http://www .census.gov/compendia/statab/> contains this 2009 edition plus earlier editions in Adobe Acrobat .pdf format. Spreadsheet files for each table in the book are also available on the Web site and CD-ROM (free distribution of single copies on request). In many cases, the spreadsheet files show more years and/or subject/geographical detail.

Statistics for states and metropolitan areas—Extensive data for states and metropolitan areas of the United States can be found in the *State and Metropolitan Area Data Book: 2006.* This publication minus some data items, as well as selected rankings of the states and metropolitan areas, is available on our Internet site at <http://www.census.gov/compendia/smadb>.

Statistics for counties and cities— Extensive data for counties can be found in the *County and City Data Book: 2007.* It features 175 data items covering everything from age and agriculture to retail trade and water use for all states and counties with U.S. totals for comparison. Also included are approximately 80 data items for cities with populations of 25,000 or more. Six tables present nearly 80 additional data items from the 2005 American Community Survey for 242 incorporated places with populations of 100,000 or more.

This publication is available on our Internet site at <http://www.census.gov/compendia/ccdb> (tentative). For a database with over 6,000 county items, check out USA Counties at <http://censtats.census.gov/usa/usa.shtml>.

Limitations of the data—The contents of this volume were taken from many sources. All data from censuses and surveys or from administrative records are subject to error arising from a number of factors: Sampling variability (for statistics based on samples), reporting errors in the data for individual units, incomplete coverage, nonresponse, imputations, and processing error. (See also Appendix III, p. 897.) The Census Bureau cannot accept the responsibility for the accuracy or limitations of the data presented here, other than those for which it collects. The responsibility for selection of the material and for proper presentation, however, rests with the Census Bureau.

For additional information on data presented—Please consult the source publications available in local libraries or write to the agency indicated in the source notes. Write to the Census Bureau only if it is cited as the source.

Suggestions and comments—Users of the Statistical Abstract and its supplements (see inside back cover) are urged to make their data needs known for consideration in planning future editions. Suggestions and comments for improving coverage and presentation of data should be sent to the Director, U.S. Census Bureau, Washington, DC 20233.

Contents

[Numbers following subjects are page numbers]

	Page
New Tables	xi
Guide to Tabular Presentation	xiv
Telephone and Internet Contacts	xvi
Sec. 1. Population (Tables 1–76)	1
Estimates and projections by age, sex, race, and Hispanic origin	9
States, metropolitan areas, cities	17
Mobility status	35
Profiles of elderly, racial, and Hispanic-origin populations	37
Native and foreign-born populations	42
Immigration	45
Ancestry, languages	48
Marital status and households	50
Religion	60
Sec. 2. Births, Deaths, Marriages, and Divorces (Tables 77–123)	61
Births	63
Life expectancy	74
Deaths	77
Marriages and divorces	92
Sec. 3. Health and Nutrition (Tables 124–210)	93
National Health Expenditure Accounts	95
Medicare, Medicaid, and SCHIP	100
Health insurance	105
Employment	109
Hospitals	113
Health measures	127
Food consumption, nutrition	133
Sec. 4. Education (Tables 211–294)	137
School enrollment	139
Educational attainment	145
Technology in schools	163
Degrees conferred	181
Sec. 5. Law Enforcement, Courts, and Prisons (Tables 295–343)	185
Crime rates	188
Courts	201
Juveniles, child abuse	204
Prisoners and inmates	207
Sec. 6. Geography and Environment (Tables 344–379)	211
Land and water	213
Air quality	220
Municipal hazardous waste	221
Weather	225
Sec. 7. Elections (Tables 380–409)	235
Vote results	237
Campaign finances	255

U.S. Census Bureau, Statistical Abstract of the United States: 2009

Sec. 8. State and Local Government Finances and Employment
(Tables 410–450) 257
Governmental units 259
Aid to state and local governments 261
State and local governments 265
State government finances 278
Local government finances 284
Employment and payroll 292

Sec. 9. Federal Government Finances and Employment (Tables 451–484) . . . 299
Budget receipts, outlays, debt 302
Income taxes 309
Federal employment and payroll 318

Sec. 10. National Security and Veterans Affairs (Tables 485–518) 321
National defense outlays 324
Military manpower 326
Veterans 332
Homeland security 334

Sec. 11. Social Insurance and Human Services (Tables 519–566) 339
Government transfer payments 343
Social security 346
Public aid, federal food programs 356
Child care, child support 358

Sec. 12. Labor Force, Employment, and Earnings (Tables 567–644) 365
Labor force status 369
Multiple jobholding 381
Occupations 384
Projections 389
Employees and earnings 399
Benefits 414
Injuries 416
Union membership 419

Sec. 13. Income, Expenditures, Poverty, and Wealth (Tables 645–701) 421
Gross domestic product 425
Personal income 433
Consumer expenditures 438
Money income 442
State income and poverty 450
Poverty status 452
Wealth 458

Sec. 14. Prices (Tables 702–721) 461
Consumer price index 465
Cost of living index 469
Producer price index 474

Sec. 15. Business Enterprise (Tables 722–768) 481
Sole proprietors, partnerships, corporations 483
Establishments, employees, payroll 491
Women- and minority-owned businesses 498
Bankruptcy, patents 499
Investment, capital expenditures 501
Economic indicators 504
Corporate profits 506
Multinationals 507

Sec. 16. Science and Technology (Tables 769–792). 509
R&D funds, outlays. 510
Science and engineering degrees 515
Science and engineering employment 518
Space program. 520

Sec. 17. Agriculture (Tables 793–835) 521
Farms and farmland. 523
Farm balance sheet, income. 525
Foreign trade 529
Crops, livestock 532

Sec. 18. Natural Resources (Tables 836–880) 541
Timber, lumber. 544
Fishery. 549
Petroleum, natural gas, coal. 557

Sec. 19. Energy and Utilities (Tables 881–918) 563
Energy consumption, expenditures 566
Crude oil 573
Nuclear 575
Electric power 576
Gas utilities 582

Sec. 20. Construction and Housing (Tables 919–963) 585
Construction spending. 588
Home sales 595
Homeownership. 604
Home remodeling. 611

Sec. 21. Manufactures (Tables 964–1003) 613
Manufacturing summary 616
Industry reports by subject and subsector. 627
Consumer electronics. 632

Sec. 22. Wholesale and Retail Trade (Tables 1004–1023). 637
Wholesale trade 640
Retail trade. 643

Sec. 23. Transportation (Tables 1024–1085) 651
Transportation system 656
Air transportation. 661
Port traffic 666
Motor vehicle registration 673
Motor vehicle accidents 677
Transit ridership. 685

Sec. 24. Information and Communications (Tables 1086–1124) 691
Information industries 693
Media usage. 695
Newspapers. 697
Books. 699
Recording media 702
Telecommunications. 705
Internet access and use 709

Sec. 25. Banking, Finance, and Insurance (Tables 1125–1187) 713
Establishments, receipts. 715
Flow of funds, financial assets, and liabilities. 716
Financial institutions 719

Sec. 25. Banking, Finance, and Insurance—Con.
Payment instruments, credit and debit cards 723
Consumer credit, mortgage debt 725
Money stock, interest rates 728
Stocks and bonds, equity ownership, mutual funds 729
Insurance, real estate 738

Sec. 26. Arts, Recreation, and Travel (Tables 1188–1232) 741
Employees, establishments, and payroll 742
Performing arts 745
Leisure activities 747
Sports 750
Parks and wildlife activities 755
Travel 759

Sec. 27. Accommodation, Food Services, and Other Services
(Tables 1233–1245) 763
Professional, scientific, and technical services 768
Administrative and support and waste management 770

Sec. 28. Foreign Commerce and Aid (Tables 1246–1271) 773
International transactions 776
Foreign investments 780
Foreign grants and credits 784
Exports and imports 787

Sec. 29. Puerto Rico and the Island Areas (Tables 1272–1284) 797

Sec. 30. International Statistics (Tables 1285–1361) 803
World maps 806
World population; vital statistics 813
Economic measures 825
Labor force 833
Agriculture 836
Energy 840
Finance 848

Appendix I.
Guide to Sources of Statistics 857
Guide to State Statistical Abstracts 871
Guide to Foreign Statistical Abstracts 875

Appendix II.
Metropolitan and Micropolitan Statistical Areas: Concepts, Components,
and Population 877

Appendix III.
Limitations of the Data 897

Appendix IV.
Weights and Measures 921

Appendix V.
Tables Deleted From the 2008 Edition of the Statistical Abstract 923

Index 925

New Tables

Table number		Page number

Sec. 1. POPULATION 1

45 Refugee Arrivals and Individuals Granted Asylum by Country of Nationality: 2005 to 2007 45

72 Group Quarters Population by Type of Group Quarter and Selected Characteristics: 2006 58

74 Religious Composition of U.S. Population: 2007 59

Sec. 2. BIRTHS, DEATHS, MARRIAGES, AND DIVORCES 61

88 Infants Who Were Ever Breastfed by Maternal Age and Race-Ethnicity: 1999–2006 68

96 Outcomes of Assisted Reproductive Technology (ART) Procedures: 2000 to 2005 72

99 Abortions—Number and Rate by State: 2000 to 2005 73

Sec. 3. HEALTH AND NUTRITION 93

155 Osteopathic Physicians: 2001 to 2008 109

180 Children and Youth With Disabilities Served by Selected Programs: 1995 to 2006 121

181 Children Under 18 Years of Age Receiving Special Education or Early Intervention Services: 2006 122

Sec. 4. EDUCATION 137

240 Public Schools Using Selected Safety and Security Measures, by School Characteristics: 2000 to 2006 156

256 Percentage of Students Participating in After-School Activities, by School Activity and Student Characteristics: 2005 165

257 Percentage of Students Participating in Weekly Nonparental After-School Care Arrangements, by Activities, Arrangement Type, and Student Characteristics: 2005 165

Sec. 5. LAW ENFORCEMENT, COURTS, AND PRISONS 185

332 Detainees Under the Jurisdiction of the Bureau of Immigration and Customs Enforcement (ICE): 2000 to 2006 206

SEC. 6. GEOGRAPHY AND ENVIRONMENT 211

345 U.S.-Canada and U.S.-Mexico Border Lengths 214

346 Coastline and Shoreline of the United States by State 214

347 Largest Lakes in the United States 215

SEC. 8. STATE AND LOCAL GOVERNMENT FINANCES AND EMPLOYMENT 257

423 State and Local Governments—Total Revenue and Expenditures by State: 2000 to 2005 269

SEC 10. NATIONAL SECURITY AND VETERANS AFFAIRS 321

497 Military Retirement System: 2007 330

Table number		Page number

SEC. 11. SOCIAL INSURANCE AND HUMAN SERVICES 339

519   Selected Payments to Individuals by Function: 1960 to 2006 342
536   Characteristics of U.S. Households Owning IRAs: 2007 352
537   Percent Distribution of Assets in IRAs, by Type of IRA: 2007 353

SEC. 12. LABOR FORCE, EMPLOYMENT, AND EARNINGS 365

616   Employed Adults in Selected Work-Related Formal Learning Activities by Form of Employer Support: 2004–2005 404
630   Labor Force Violations: 2003 to 2007 413

SEC. 14. PRICES 461

719   Import and Export Price Indexes by End-Use Category: 1990 to 2007 479

SEC. 16. SCIENCE AND TECHNOLOGY 509

776   Academic and Industrial Research and Development (R&D) Performed by State: 2005 514
783   Science and Engineering (S&E) Doctorates by State: 2005 and 2006 516
784   Scientists and Engineers by Selected Demographic Characteristics: 2006 517
787   Employment and Earnings in Science & Engineering (S&E) Occupations by Industry: 2006 518

SEC. 18. NATURAL RESOURCES 541

855   Marketable Aquaculture Sales by Species: 2005 550
856   Sales of Aquaculture Products by Type, by State: 2005 550
870   Supply, Disposition, and Ending Stocks of Crude Oil and Petroleum Products: 2006 557

SEC. 20. CONSTRUCTION AND HOUSING 585

944   Homeownership and Rental Vacancy Rates by State: 2007 600
945   Homeownership and Rental Vacancy Rates by Metropolitan Area: 2007 600

SEC. 24. INFORMATION AND COMMUNICATIONS 691

1111   Average Annual Telephone Service Expenditures by All Consumer Units: 2001 to 2006 706
1118   Household Internet Usage In and Outside of the Home, by Selected Characteristics: 2007 709
1119   Household Internet Usage by Type of Internet Connection and State: 2007 710
1124   Online News Consumption, by Selected Characteristics: 2000 to 2008 712

SEC. 25. BANKING, FINANCE, AND INSURANCE 713

1144   Noncash Payments by Method of Payment and ATM Cash Withdrawals: 2003 and 2006 723

SEC. 26. ARTS, RECREATION, AND TRAVEL 741

1197   Total State Arts Agency Legislative Appropriations: 2007 to 2008 746
1217   Expenditures for Wildlife-Related Recreation Activities: 2006 757
1226   Chain-Type Price Indexes for Direct Tourism Output: 1998 to 2007 760

SEC. 29. PUERTO RICO AND THE ISLAND AREAS 797

1278   Tenure by Household Type in Puerto Rico: 2006 800
1279   Selected Social, Demographic, and Housing Characteristics in Puerto Rico: 2006 800

Table number		Page number
	SEC. 30. **INTERNATIONAL STATISTICS**	803
1306	Real GDP per Capita and per Employed Persons, by Country: 1980 to 2006 ...	826
1313	Indexes of Living Costs Abroad: 2008	830
1316	Percent of Women in National Parliaments by Country: 2008	832
1347	Research and Development (R&D) Expenditures, by Country	847
1356	Household Expenditure on Recreation and Culture as a Percentage of GDP: 1970 to 2006	854
1357	Development Assistance, by Country: 2005 and 2006	854

U.S. Census Bureau, Statistical Abstract of the United States: 2009

Guide to Tabular Presentation

Example of Table Structure

Table 518. **Seizure Statistics for Intellectual Property Rights (IPR): 2003 to 2007**

[In thousands of dollars (94,019 represents $94,019,000, except as indicated). Customs and Border Protection (CBP) is dedicated to protecting against the importation of goods which infringe/violate Intellectual Property Rights (IPR) by devoting substantial resources toward identifying and seizing shipments of infringing articles]

Item	2003	2004	2005	2006	2007
Number of IPR Seizures	6,500	7,255	8,022	14,675	13,657
Total domestic value of IPR seizures[1]	94,019	138,768	93,235	155,369	196,754
Selected IPR commodities seized by value ($1,000):					
Footwear.	2,555	2,049	8,941	63,446	77,781
Wearing apparel	13,889	51,737	16,100	24,321	27,006
Handbags/wallets/backpacks	11,458	23,190	14,955	14,750	14,214
Computers/hardware	(NA)	1,684	4,799	14,288	9,337
Consumer electronics [2]	3,780	8,880	8,794	7,057	16,042
Watches/parts.	3,384	2,543	3,071	2,832	13,356
Media [3]	7,358	5,050	(NA)	6,965	7,884
All others	51,595	43,636	36,576	21,710	31,134

NA Not available. [1] Domestic value is the cost of the seized goods, plus the costs of shipping and importing the goods into the U.S. and an amount for profit. [2] Consumer electronics includes cell phones and accessories, radios, power strips, electrical tools, and appliances. [3] Includes motion pictures on tape, laser disc, and DVD; interactive and computer software on CD-ROM and floppy discs; and music on CD or tape.

Source: U.S. Department of Homeland Security, Customs and Border Protection, Import, Commercial Enforcement, Intellectual Property Rights, Seizure Statistics; <http://www.cbp.gov/xp/cgov/trade/priority_trade/ipr/seizure/>.

Headnotes immediately below table titles provide information important for correct interpretation or evaluation of the table as a whole or for a major segment of it.

Footnotes below the bottom rule of tables give information relating to specific items or figures within the table.

Unit indicators show the *specified quantities* in which data items are presented. They are used for two primary reasons. Sometimes data are not available in absolute form and are estimates (as in the case of many surveys). In other cases we round the numbers in order to save space to show more data, as in the case above.

EXAMPLES OF UNIT INDICATOR INTERPRETATION FROM TABLE

Year	Item	Unit Indicator	Number shown	Multiplier
2003	Value of seizures	$ Thousands	94,019	1,000

To Determine the Figure it is Necessary to Multiply the Number Shown by the Unit Indicator:

Value of seizures by Customs and Border Patrol – 94,019 x $1,000 = $94,019,000 ($94 million)

When a table presents data with more than one unit indicator, they are found in the headnotes and column headings (Tables 2 and 25), spanner (Table 38), stub (Table 24), or unit column (Table 151). When the data in a table are shown in the same unit indicator, it is shown in boldface as the first part of the headnote (Table 2). If no unit indicator is shown, data presented are in absolute form (Table 1).

Vertical rules are used to separate independent sections of a table (Table 1), or in tables where the stub is continued into one or more additional columns (Table 2).

Averages—An average is a single number or value that is often used to represent the "typical value" of a group of numbers. It is regarded as a measure of "location" or "central tendency" of a group of numbers.

The *arithmetic mean* is the type of average used most frequently. It is derived by summing the individual item values of a particular group and dividing the total by the number of items. The arithmetic mean is often referred to as simply the "mean" or "average."

The *median* of a group of numbers is the middle number or value when each item in the group is arranged according to size (lowest to highest or visa versa); it generally has the same number of items above it as well as below it. If there is an even number of items in the group, the median is taken to be the average of the two middle numbers.

Per capita (or per person) quantities—a per capita figure represents an average computed for every person in a specified group (or population). It is derived by taking the total for an item (such as income, taxes, or retail sales) and dividing it by the number of persons in the specified population.

Index numbers—An index number is the measure of difference or change, usually expressed as a percent, relating one quantity (the variable) of a specified kind to another quantity of the same kind. Index numbers are widely used to express changes in prices over periods of time, but may also be used to express differences between related subjects for a single point in time.

To compute a price index, a base year or period is selected. The base year price (of the commodity or service) is then designated as the base or reference price to which the prices for other years or periods are related. Many price indexes use the year 1982 as the base year; in tables this is shown as "1982 = 100." A method of expressing the price relationship is: The price of a set of one or more items for a related year (e.g. 1990) **divided by** the price of the same set of items for the base year (e.g. 1982). The result multiplied by 100 provides the index number. When 100 is subtracted from the index number, the result equals the percent change in price from the base year.

Average annual percent change—Unless otherwise stated in the *Abstract* (as in Section 1, Population), average annual percent change is computed by use of a *compound interest formula.* This formula assumes that the rate of change is constant throughout a specified compounding period (1 year for average annual rates of change). The formula is similar to that used to compute the balance of a savings account that receives compound interest. According to this formula, at the end of a compounding period the amount of accrued change (e.g., school enrollment or bank interest) is added to the amount that existed at the beginning of the period. As a result, over time (e.g., with each year or quarter), the same rate of change is applied to a larger and larger figure.

The *exponential formula,* which is based on continuous compounding, is often used to measure population change. It is preferred by population experts, because they view population and population-related subjects as changing without interruption, ever ongoing. Both exponential and compound interest formulas assume a constant rate of change. The former, however, applies the amount of change continuously to the base rather than at the end of each compounding

period. When the average annual rates are small (e.g., less than 5 percent) both formulas give virtually the same results. For an explanation of these two formulas as they relate to population, see U.S. Census Bureau, *The Methods and Materials of Demography,* Vol. 2, 3d printing (rev.), 1975, pp. 372–381.

Current and constant dollars—Statistics in some tables in a number of sections are expressed in both current and constant dollars (see, e.g., Table 659 in Section 13, Income, Expenditures, Poverty, and Wealth). Current dollar figures reflect actual prices or costs prevailing during the specified year(s). Constant dollar figures are estimates representing an effort to remove the effects of price changes from statistical series reported in dollar terms. In general, constant dollar series are derived by dividing current dollar estimates by the appropriate price index for the appropriate period (e.g., the Consumer Price Index). The result is a series as it would presumably exist if prices were the same throughout, as in the base year—in other words, as if the dollar had constant purchasing power. Any changes in this constant dollar series would reflect only changes in real volume of output, income, expenditures, or other measure.

Explanation of Symbols

The following symbols, used in the tables throughout this book, are explained in condensed form in footnotes to the tables where they appear:

— Represents zero or rounds to less than half the unit of measurement shown.

B Base figure too small to meet statistical standards for reliability of a derived figure.

D Figure withheld to avoid disclosure pertaining to a specific organization or individual.

NA Data not enumerated, tabulated, or otherwise available separately.

S Figure does not meet publication standards for reasons other than that covered by symbol B, above.

X Figure not applicable because column heading and stub line make entry impossible, absurd, or meaningless.

Z Entry would amount to less than half the unit of measurement shown.

In many tables, details will not add to the totals shown because of rounding.

Telephone & Internet Contacts

To help *Abstract* users find more data and information about statistical publications, we are issuing this list of contacts for federal agencies with major statistical programs. The intent is to give a single, first-contact point-of-entry for users of statistics. These agencies will provide general information on their statistical programs and publications, as well as specific information on how to order their publications. We are also including the Internet (World Wide Web) addresses for many of these agencies. These URLs were current in July 2008.

Executive Office of the President

Office of Management and Budget

Administrator
Office of Information and Regulatory Affairs
Office of Management and Budget
725 17th Street, NW
Washington, DC 20503
Information: 202-395-3080
Internet address:
http://www.whitehouse.gov/omb

Department of Agriculture

Economic Research Service

Information Center
U.S. Department of Agriculture
1800 M Street, NW
Washington, DC 20036-5831
Information and Publications:
202-694-5050
Internet address:
http://www.ers.usda.gov/

National Agricultural Statistics Service

National Agricultural Statistics Service
USDA-NASS
1400 Independence Ave., SW
Washington, DC 20250
Information hotline: 1-800-727-9540
Internet address:
http://www.nass.usda.gov/

Department of Commerce

U.S. Census Bureau

Customer Services Branch
U.S. Census Bureau
4600 Silver Hill Road
Washington, DC 20233
Information and Publications:
1-800-923-8282
Internet address:
http://www.census.gov/

Bureau of Economic Analysis

Bureau of Economic Analysis
1441 L Street, NW
Washington, DC 20230
Information and Publications:
202-606-9900
Internet address: http://www.bea.gov/

Department of Commerce—Con.

International Trade Administration

International Trade Administration
1401 Constitution Ave., NW
Washington, DC 20230
Information: 1-800-872-8723
Internet address: http://trade.gov/

National Oceanic and Atmospheric Administration

National Oceanic and Atmospheric Administration Central Library
U.S. Department of Commerce
1315 East-West Highway
SSMC3, 2nd Floor
Silver Spring, MD 20910
Library: 301-713-2600 x.124
Internet address:
http://www.lib.noaa.gov/

Department of Defense

Department of Defense
Directorate of Communications
Room 3A750
601 N. Fairfax Street
Alexandria, VA 22314
Information: 703-428-0711
Internet address:
http://www.defenselink.mil

Department of Education

National Library of Education

U.S. Department of Education
400 Maryland Avenue, SW
Washington, DC 20202
Education Information and Statistics:
1-800-872-5327
Education Publications: 1-877-433-7827
Internet address: http://www.ed.gov/

Department of Energy

Energy Information Administration

National Energy Information Center
Energy Information Administration
1000 Independence Ave., SW
Washington, DC 20585
Information and Publications:
202-586-8800
Internet address:
http://www.eia.doe.gov/

Department of Health and Human Services

Health Resources and Services Administration
HRSA Information Center
P.O. Box 2910
Merrifield, VA 22116
Information Center: 1-888-275-4772
Internet address: http://www.hrsa.gov/

Substance Abuse and Mental Health Services Administration
Substance Abuse and Mental Health Services Administration
1 Choke Cherry Road
Rockville, MD 20857
Information: 240-276-2130
Publications: 1-877-726-4727
Internet address:
http://www.samhsa.gov/

Centers for Disease Control and Prevention
Public Inquiries/MASO
1600 Clifton Road
Atlanta, GA 30333
Public Inquiries: 1-800-311-3435
Internet address: http://www.cdc.gov/

Centers for Medicare and Medicaid Services (CMS)
U.S. Department of Health and Human Services
7500 Security Boulevard
Baltimore, MD 21244
1-877-267-2323
Internet address:
http://www.cms.hhs.gov/

National Center for Health Statistics
National Center for Health Statistics
3311 Toledo Road
Hyattsville, MD 20782 1-800-232-4636
Internet address:
http://www.cdc.gov/nchs

Department of Homeland Security

Office of Public Affairs
245 Murray Lane, SW
Washington, DC 20528
Information and Publications:
202-282-8010
Internet address: http://www.dhs.gov

Department of Housing and Urban Development

Office of the Assistant Secretary for Community Planning and Development
451 7th St., SW
Washington, DC 20410
Information: 202-708-1112
Publications: 1-800-767-7468
Internet address: http://www.hud.gov/

Department of the Interior

U.S. Geological Survey
USGS National Center
12201 Sunrise Valley Drive
Reston, VA 20192
Information and Publications:
1-888-275-8747
Internet address for minerals:
http://minerals.usgs.gov/
Internet address for other materials:
http://ask.usgs.gov/

Department of Justice

Bureau of Justice Statistics
Bureau of Justice Statistics
Statistics Division
810 7th Street, NW
Washington, DC 20531
Information and Publications:
1-800-851-3420
Internet address:
http://www.ojp.usdoj.gov/bjs/

National Criminal Justice Reference Service
P.O. Box 6000
Rockville, MD 20849-6000
Publications: 1-800-851-3420
Internet address: http://www.ncjrs.gov/

Federal Bureau of Investigation
Federal Bureau of Investigations
J. Edgar Hoover Building
935 Pennsylvania Avenue, NW
Washington, DC 20535-0001
Information: 202-324-3000
Internet address: http://www.fbi.gov/

Department of Labor

Bureau of Labor Statistics
Office of Publications and Special Studies Services
Bureau of Labor Statistics
Postal Square Building
2 Mass. Ave., NE
Washington, DC 20212-0001
Information and Publications:
202-691-5200
Internet address: http://www.bls.gov/

Employment and Training Administration
U.S. Department of Labor
Francis Perkins Building
200 Constitution Ave., NW
Washington, DC 20210
Information and Publications:
1-877-872-5627
Internet address: http://www.doleta.gov/

U.S. Census Bureau, Statistical Abstract of the United States: 2009

Department of Transportation

Federal Aviation Administration
Federal Aviation Administration
800 Independence Ave., SW
Washington, DC 20591
Information and Publications:
1-866-835-5322
Internet address: http://www.faa.gov/

Bureau of Transportation Statistics
Bureau of Transportation Statistics
1200 New Jersey Avenue, SE
Washington, DC 20590
Products and Statistical Information:
1-800-853-1351
Internet address: http://www.bts.gov/

Federal Highway Administration
Office of Public Affairs
U.S. Department of Transportation
1200 New Jersey Avenue, SE
Washington, DC 20590
Information: 202-366-0660
Internet address:
http://www.fhwa.dot.gov/

National Highway Traffic Safety Administration
Office of Public & Consumer Affairs
1200 New Jersey Avenue, SE - West Building
Washington, DC 20590
Information and Publications:
1-888-327-4236
Internet address:
http://www.nhtsa.dot.gov/

Department of the Treasury

Internal Revenue Service
Statistics of Income Division
Internal Revenue Service
P. O. Box 2608
Washington, DC 20013-2608
Information and Publications:
202-874-0410
Internet address:
http://www.irs.gov/taxstats/

Department of Veterans Affairs

Department of Veterans Affairs
Office of Public Affairs
810 Vermont Ave., NW
Washington, DC 20420
Information: 202-273-6000
Internet address: http://www.va.gov/

Independent Agencies

Administrative Office of the U.S. Courts
Office of Public Affairs
1 Columbia Circle, NE
Washington, DC 20544
Information: 202-502-2600
Internet address:
http://www.uscourts.gov/

Board of Governors of the Federal Reserve System
Division of Research and Statistics
Federal Reserve System
20th & Constitution Avenue, NW
Washington, DC 20551
Information: 202-452-3000
Publications: 202-452-3245
Internet address:
http://www.federalreserve.gov/

Environmental Protection Agency
Environmental Protection Agency
Ariel Rios Building
1200 Pennsylvania Ave., NW
Washington, DC 20460
Publications: 1-800-490-9198
Internet address: http://www.epa.gov/

National Science Foundation
Office of Legislation and Public Affairs
National Science Foundation
4201 Wilson Boulevard
Arlington, Virginia 22230
Information: 703-292-5111
Publications: 703-292-8134
Internet address: http://www.nsf.gov/

Securities and Exchange Commission
Office of Public Affairs
Securities and Exchange Commission
100 F Street, NE
Washington, DC 20549
Information: 202-942-8088
Publications: 202-551-4040
Internet address: http://www.sec.gov/

Social Security Administration
Social Security Administration
Office of Public Inquiries
6401 Security Boulevard
Baltimore, MD 21235
Information and Publications:
1-800-772-1213
Internet address:
http://www.socialsecurity.gov/

Population

This section presents statistics on the growth, distribution, and characteristics of the U.S. population. The principal source of these data is the U.S. Census Bureau, which conducts a decennial census of population, a monthly population survey, a program of population estimates and projections, and a number of other periodic surveys.

Decennial censuses—The U.S. Constitution provides for a census of the population every 10 years, primarily to establish a basis for apportionment of members of the House of Representatives among the states. For over a century after the first census in 1790, the census organization was a temporary one, created only for each decennial census. In 1902, the Census Bureau was established as a permanent federal agency, responsible for enumerating the population and also for compiling statistics on other population and housing characteristics.

Historically, the enumeration of the population has been a complete (100 percent) count. That is, an attempt is made to account for every person, for each person's residence, and for other characteristics (sex, age, family relationships, etc.). Since the 1940 census, in addition to the complete count information, some data have been obtained from representative samples of the population. In the 1990 and 2000 censuses, variable sampling rates were employed. For most of the country, 1 in every 6 households (about 17 percent) received the long form or sample questionnaire; in governmental units estimated to have fewer than 2,500 inhabitants, every other household (50 percent) received the sample questionnaire to enhance the reliability of sample data for small areas. Exact agreement is not to be expected between sample data and the 100-percent count. Sample data may be used with confidence where large numbers are involved and assumed to indicate trends and relationships where small numbers are involved.

Current Population Survey (CPS)—This is a monthly nationwide survey of a scientifically selected sample representing the noninstitutionalized civilian population. The sample is located in 824 areas with coverage in every state and the District of Columbia and is subject to sampling error. At the present time, about 60,000 occupied households are eligible for interview every month; of these, about 8 percent are, for various reasons, unavailable for interview.

While the primary purpose of the CPS is to obtain monthly statistics on the labor force, it also serves as a vehicle for inquiries on other subjects. Using CPS data, the Census Bureau issues a series of publications under the general title of *Current Population Reports,* which cover population characteristics (P20), consumer income (P60), special studies (P23), and other topics.

Estimates of population characteristics based on the CPS will not agree with the counts from the census because the CPS and the census use different procedures for collecting and processing the data for racial groups, the Hispanic population, and other topics. Caution should also be used when comparing estimates for various years because of the periodic introduction of changes into the CPS. Beginning in January 1994, a number of changes were introduced into the CPS that effect all data comparisons with prior years. These changes included the results of a major redesign of the survey questionnaire and collection methodology and the introduction of 1990 census population controls, adjusted for the estimated undercount. Beginning with the 2001 CPS Annual Demographic Supplement, the independent estimates used as control totals for the CPS are based on civilian population benchmarks consistent with Census 2000. In March 2002, the sample size of the Annual Demographic Supplement was increased to approximately 78,000. In 2003 the name of the March supplement was changed to Annual Social

U.S. Census Bureau, Statistical Abstract of the United States: 2009

and Economic Supplement. These changes in population controls had relatively little impact on derived measures such as means, medians, and percent distribution, but did have a significant impact on levels.

American Community Survey (ACS)—This is a nationwide survey to obtain data about demographic, social, economic, and housing information of people, households, and housing units. The survey collects the same type of information that has been collected every 10 years from the long-form questionnaire of the census, which the American Community Survey will replace. Beginning 2006, the estimates include the household population and the population living in institutions, college dormitories, and other group quarters.

Population estimates and projections—Estimates of the United States population are derived by updating the resident population enumerated in Census 2000 with information on the components of population change: births, deaths, and net international migration. The April 1, 2000, population used in these estimates reflects modifications to the Census 2000 population as documented in the Count Question Resolution program.

Registered births and deaths are estimated from data supplied by the National Center for Health Statistics. The net international migration component consists of four parts: (1) the net international migration of the foreign born, (2) the net migration of natives to and from the United States, (3) the net migration between the United States and Puerto Rico, and (4) the net overseas movement of the Armed Forces population. Data from the ACS are used to estimate the annual net migration of the foreign-born population. Estimates of the net migration of natives and net migration between Puerto Rico and the United States are derived from the Demographic Analysis and Population Estimates (DAPE) project (see Population Division Working Paper Series, No. 63 and No. 64). Estimates of the net overseas movement of the Armed Forces are derived from data collected by the Defense Manpower Data Center.

Estimates for state and county areas are based on the same components of change data and sources as the national estimates with the addition of net internal migration. Estimates of net internal migration are derived from federal income tax returns from the Internal Revenue Service, group quarters data from the Federal-State Cooperative Program, and Medicare data from the Centers for Medicare and Medicaid Services.

The population by age for April 1, 1990, reflects modifications to the 1990 census data counts. The review of detailed 1990 information indicated that respondents tended to report age as of the date of completion of the questionnaire, not as of April 1, 1990. In addition, there may have been a tendency for respondents to round up their age if they were close to having a birthday. A detailed explanation of the age modification procedure appears in 1990 Census of Population and Housing, Data Paper Listing CPH-L74.

Population estimates and projections are available on the Census Bureau Internet site <http://www.census.gov>. These estimates and projections are consistent with official decennial census figures with no adjustment for estimated net census coverage. However, the categories for these estimates and projections by race have been modified and are not comparable to the census race categories (see section below under "Race"). For details on methodology, see the sources cited below the individual tables.

Immigration—Immigration (migration *to* a country) is one component of international migration; the other component is emigration (migration *from* a country). In its simplest form, international migration is defined as any movement across a national border. In the United States, federal statistics on international migration are produced primarily by the U.S. Census Bureau and the Office of Immigration Statistics of the U.S. Department of Homeland Security (DHS).

The Census Bureau collects data used to estimate international migration through its decennial censuses and numerous surveys of the U.S. population.

The Office of Immigration Statistics publishes immigration data in annual flow reports and the *Yearbook of Immigration*

Statistics. Data for these publications are collected from several administrative data sources including the DS-230 Application for Immigrant Visa and Alien Registration (U.S. Department of State) for new arrivals, and the I-485 Application to Register Permanent Residence or Adjust Status (U.S. Citizenship and Immigration Services—USCIS) for persons adjusting immigrant status.

An immigrant, or legal permanent resident, is a foreign national who has been granted lawful permanent residence in the United States. New arrivals are foreign nationals living abroad who apply for an immigrant visa at a consular office of the Department of State, while individuals adjusting status are already living in the United States and file an application for adjustment of status to lawful permanent residence with USCIS. Individuals adjusting status include refugees, asylees, and various classes of nonimmigrants. A refugee is an alien outside the United States who is unable or unwilling to return to his or her country of origin because of persecution or a well-founded fear of persecution. Asylees must meet the same criteria as refugees, but are located in the United States or at a port of entry. After 1 year of residence, refugees and asylees are eligible to adjust to legal permanent resident status. Nonimmigrants are foreign nationals granted temporary entry into the United States. The major activities for which nonimmigrant admission is authorized include temporary visits for business or pleasure, academic or vocational study, temporary employment, and to act as a representative of a foreign government or international organization. DHS collects information on the characteristics of a proportion of nonimmigrant admissions, those recorded on the I-94 Arrival/Departure Record.

U.S. immigration law gives preferential immigration status to persons with a close family relationship with a U.S. citizen or legal permanent resident, persons with needed job skills, persons who qualify as refugees or asylees, and persons who are from countries with relatively low levels of immigration to the United States. Immigration to the United States can be divided into two general categories: (1) classes of admission subject to the annual worldwide limitation and (2) classes of admission exempt from worldwide limitations. Numerical limits are imposed on visas issued and not on admissions. In 2007, the annual limit for preference visas subject to limitation was 373,148, which included a family-sponsored preference limit of 226,000 and an employment-based preference limit of 147,148. Classes of admission exempt from the worldwide limitation include immediate relatives of U.S. citizens, refugees and asylees adjusting to permanent residence, and other various classes of special immigrants (see Table 47).

Metropolitan and micropolitan areas—The U.S. Office of Management and Budget (OMB) defines metropolitan and micropolitan statistical areas according to published standards that are applied to Census Bureau data. The general concept of a metropolitan or micropolitan statistical area is that of a core area containing a substantial population nucleus, together with adjacent communities having a high degree of economic and social integration with that core. Currently defined metropolitan and micropolitan statistical areas are based on application of 2000 standards to 2000 decennial census data as updated by application of those standards to more recent Census Bureau population estimates. The term "metropolitan area" (MA) was adopted in 1990 and referred collectively to metropolitan statistical areas (MSAs), consolidated metropolitan statistical areas (CMSAs), and primary metropolitan statistical areas (PMSAs). The term "core-based statistical area" (CBSA) became effective in 2003 and refers collectively to metropolitan and micropolitan statistical areas. For descriptive details and a list of titles and components of metropolitan and micropolitan statistical areas, see Appendix II.

Urban and rural—For Census 2000, the Census Bureau classified as urban all territory, population, and housing units located within urbanized areas (UAs) and urban clusters (UCs). A UA consists of densely settled territory that contains 50,000 or more people, while a UC consists of densely settled territory with at least 2,500 people but fewer than 50,000

U.S. Census Bureau, Statistical Abstract of the United States: 2009

people. From the 1950 census through the 1990 census, the urban population consisted of all people living in UAs and most places outside of UAs with a census population of 2,500 or more.

UAs and UCs encompass territory that generally consists of:

- A cluster of one or more block groups or census blocks each of which has a population density of at least 1,000 people per square mile at the time.

- Surrounding block groups and census blocks each of which has a population density of at least 500 people per square mile at the time.

- Less densely settled blocks that form enclaves or indentations, or are used to connect discontiguous areas with qualifying densities.

They also may include an airport located adjacent to qualifying densely settled area if it has an annual enplanement (aircraft boarding) of at least 10,000 people.

"Rural" for Census 2000 consists of all territory, population, and housing units located outside of UAs and UCs. Prior to Census 2000, rural consisted of all territory, population, and housing outside of UAs and outside of other places designated as "urban." For Census 2000, many more geographic entities, including metropolitan areas, counties, and places, contain both urban and rural territory, population, and housing units.

Residence—In determining residence, the Census Bureau counts each person as an inhabitant of a usual place of residence (i.e., the place where one lives and sleeps most of the time). While this place is not necessarily a person's legal residence or voting residence, the use of these different bases of classification would produce the same results in the vast majority of cases.

Race—For the 1990 census, the Census Bureau collected and published racial statistics as outlined in Statistical Policy Directive No. 15 issued by the OMB. This directive provided standards on ethnic and racial categories for statistical reporting to be used by all federal agencies. According to the directive, the basic racial categories were American Indian or Alaska Native, Asian or Pacific Islander, Black, and White. (The directive identified

Hispanic origin as an ethnicity.) The question on race for Census 2000 was different from the one for the 1990 census in several ways. Most significantly, respondents were given the option of selecting one or more race categories to indicate their racial identities. Because of these changes, the Census 2000 data on race are not directly comparable with data from the 1990 census or earlier censuses. Caution must be used when interpreting changes in the racial composition of the United States population over time. Census 2000 adheres to the federal standards for collecting and presenting data on race and ethnicity as established by the OMB in October 1997. Starting with Census 2000, the OMB requires federal agencies to use a minimum of five race categories: White, Black or African American, American Indian or Alaska Native, Asian, and Native Hawaiian or Other Pacific Islander. Additionally, to collect data on individuals of mixed race parentage, respondents were allowed to select one or more races. For respondents unable to identify with any of these five race categories, the OMB approved and included a sixth category— "Some other race" on the Census 2000 questionnaire. The Census 2000 question on race included 15 separate response categories and three areas where respondents could write in a more specific race group. The response categories and write-in answers can be combined to create the five minimum OMB race categories plus "Some other race." People who responded to the question on race by indicating only one race are referred to as the *race alone* population, or the group that reported only one race category. Six categories make up this population: White alone, Black or African American alone, American Indian and Alaska Native alone, Asian alone, Native Hawaiian and Other Pacific Islander alone, and Some other race alone. Individuals who chose more than one of the six race categories are referred to as the *Two or More Races* population, or as the group that reported more than one race. Additionally, respondents who reported one race together with those who reported the same race plus one or more other races are combined to create the *race alone or in combination* categories. For example, the *White alone or in combination group* consists of those respondents who reported only White or who reported White combined with one or more other race groups, such as "White and Black or African American," or "White and Asian and American Indian and Alaska Native." Another way to think of the group who reported White alone or in combination is as the total number of people who identified entirely or partially as White. This group is also described as people who reported White, whether or not they reported any other race.

The *alone or in combination* categories are tallies of *responses* rather than *respondents*. That is, the alone or in combination categories are not mutually exclusive. Individuals who reported two races were counted in two separate and distinct alone or in combination race categories, while those who reported three races were counted in three categories, and so on. Consequently, the sum of all alone or in combination categories equals the number of races reported, which exceeds the total population.

The concept of race, as used by the Census Bureau, reflects self-identification by people according to the race or races with which they most closely identify. These categories are sociopolitical constructs and should not be interpreted as being scientific or anthropological in nature. Furthermore, the race categories include both racial and national-origin groups. Additionally, data are available for the American Indian and Alaska Native tribes. A detailed explanation of race can be found at <http://www.census.gov/prod /cen2000/doc/sf1.pdf>.

Data for the population by race for April 1, 2000, (shown in Tables 6, 8, and 9) are modified counts and are not comparable to Census 2000 race categories. These numbers were computed using Census 2000 data by race that had been modified to be consistent with the 1997 OMB's "Revisions to the Standards for the Classification of Federal Data on Race and Ethnicity," (Federal Register Notice, Vol. 62, No 210, October 1997). A detailed explanation of the race modification procedure appears on the Census Web page <http://www.census.gov/popest /archives/files/MRSF-01-US1.html>.

In the CPS and other household sample surveys in which data are obtained through personal interview, respondents are asked to classify their race as: (1) White; (2) Black, African American, or Negro; (3) American Indian or Alaska Native; (4) Asian; (5) Native Hawaiian or Other Pacific Islander. Beginning January 2003, respondents were allowed to report more than one race to indicate their mixed racial heritage.

Hispanic population—The Census Bureau collected data on the Hispanic-origin population in the 2000 census by using a self-identification question. Persons of Spanish/Hispanic/Latino origin are those who classified themselves in one of the specific Hispanic origin categories listed on the questionnaire—Mexican, Puerto Rican, Cuban, as well as those who indicated that they were of Other Spanish/ Hispanic/Latino origin. Persons of Other Spanish/Hispanic/Latino origin are those whose origins are from Spain, the Spanish-speaking countries of Central or South America, or the Dominican Republic.

In the CPS, information on Hispanic persons is gathered by using a self-identification question. The respondents are first asked whether or not they are of Hispanic, Spanish, or Latino origin and based on their response are further classified into the following categories: Mexican or Mexican American or Chicano; Puerto Rican; Cuban; Central or South American; or Other Hispanic, Spanish, or Latino origin group.

Traditional and current data collection and classification treat race and Hispanic origin as two separate and distinct concepts in accordance with guidelines from the OMB. Race and Hispanic origin are two separate concepts in the federal statistical system. People who are Hispanic may be any race and people in each race group may be either Hispanic or Not Hispanic. Also, each person has two attributes, their race (or races) and whether or not they are Hispanic. The overlap of race and Hispanic origin is the main comparability issue. For example, Black Hispanics (Hispanic Blacks) are included in both the number of Blacks and in the number of Hispanics. For further information, see Census Web page <http://www.census .gov/population/www/socdemo /compraceho.html>.

Foreign-born and native populations—The Census Bureau separates the

U.S. Census Bureau, Statistical Abstract of the United States: 2009

U.S. resident population into two groups based on whether or not a person was a U.S. citizen or U.S. national at the time of birth. Anyone born in the United States, Puerto Rico, or a U.S. Island Area (such as Guam) or born abroad to a U.S. citizen parent is a U.S. citizen at the time of birth and consequently included in the *native population*. The term *foreign-born population* refers to anyone who is not a U.S. citizen or U.S. national at birth. This includes naturalized U.S. citizens, legal permanent resident aliens (immigrants), temporary migrants (such as foreign students), humanitarian migrants (such as refugees), and people illegally present in the United States. The Census Bureau provides a variety of demographic, social, economic, geographic, and housing information on the foreign-born population in the United States at <http://www.census.gov/population/www/socdemo/foreign/>.

Mobility status—The U.S. population is classified according to mobility status on the basis of a comparison between the place of residence of each individual at the time of the survey or census and the place of residence at a specified earlier date. Nonmovers are all persons who were living in the same house or apartment at the end of the period as at the beginning of the period. Movers are all persons who were living in a different house or apartment at the end of the period than at the beginning of the period. Movers are further classified as to whether they were living in the same or different county, state, region, or were movers from abroad. Movers from abroad include all persons whose place of residence was outside the United States (including Puerto Rico, other U.S. Island Area, or a foreign country) at the beginning of the period.

Living arrangements—Living arrangements refer to residency in households or in group quarters. A "household" comprises all persons who occupy a "housing unit," that is, a house, an apartment or other group of rooms, or a single room that constitutes "separate living quarters." A household includes the related family members and all the unrelated persons, if any, such as lodgers, foster children, or employees who share the housing unit. A person living alone or a group of unrelated persons sharing the same housing unit is also counted as a household. See text, Section 20, Construction and Housing, for definition of housing unit.

All persons not living in housing units are classified as living in group quarters. These individuals may be institutionalized, e.g., under care or custody in juvenile facilities, jails, correctional centers, hospitals, or nursing homes; or they may be residents in noninstitutional group quarters such as college dormitories, group homes, or military barracks.

Householder—The householder is the person in whose name the home is owned or rented. If a home is owned or rented jointly by a married couple, either the husband or the wife may be listed first.

Family—The term family refers to a group of two or more persons related by birth, marriage, or adoption and residing together in a household. A family includes among its members the householder.

Subfamily—A subfamily consists of a married couple and their children, if any, or one parent with one or more never-married children under 18 years old living in a household. Subfamilies are divided into "related" and "unrelated" subfamilies. A related subfamily is related to, but does not include, the householder or the spouse of the householder. Members of a related subfamily are also members of the family with whom they live. The number of related subfamilies, therefore, is not included in the count of families. An unrelated subfamily may include persons such as guests, lodgers, or resident employees and their spouses and/or children; none of whom is related to the householder.

Married couple—A married couple is defined as a husband and wife living together in the same household, with or without children and other relatives.

Statistical reliability—For a discussion of statistical collection and estimation, sampling procedures, and measures of statistical reliability applicable to Census Bureau data, see Appendix III.

Table 1. Population and Area: 1790 to 2000

[Area figures represent area on indicated date including in some cases considerable areas not then organized or settled, and not covered by the census. Area data include Alaska beginning in 1870 and Hawaii beginning in 1900. Total area figures for 1790 to 1970 have been recalculated on the basis of the remeasurement of states and counties for the 1980 census, but not on the basis of the 1990 census. The land and water area figures for past censuses have not been adjusted and are not strictly comparable with the total area data for comparable dates because the land areas were derived from different base data, and these values are known to have changed with the construction of reservoirs, draining of lakes, etc. Density figures are based on land area measurements as reported in earlier censuses]

Census date	Resident population				Area (square miles)		
	Number	Per square mile of land area	Increase over preceding census		Total	Land	Water [1]
			Number	Percent			
1790 (Aug. 2)	3,929,214	4.5	(X)	(X)	891,364	864,746	24,065
1800 (Aug. 4)	5,308,483	6.1	1,379,269	35.1	891,364	864,746	24,065
1810 (Aug. 6)	7,239,881	4.3	1,931,398	36.4	1,722,685	1,681,828	34,175
1820 (Aug. 7)	9,638,453	5.5	2,398,572	33.1	1,792,552	1,749,462	38,544
1830 (June 1)	12,866,020	7.4	3,227,567	33.5	1,792,552	1,749,462	38,544
1840 (June 1)	17,069,453	9.8	4,203,433	32.7	1,792,552	1,749,462	38,544
1850 (June 1)	23,191,876	7.9	6,122,423	35.9	2,991,655	2,940,042	52,705
1860 (June 1)	31,443,321	10.6	8,251,445	35.6	3,021,295	2,969,640	52,747
1870 (June 1)	[2]39,818,449	[2]11.2	8,375,128	26.6	3,612,299	3,540,705	68,082
1880 (June 1)	50,189,209	14.2	10,370,760	26.0	3,612,299	3,540,705	68,082
1890 (June 1)	62,979,766	17.8	12,790,557	25.5	3,612,299	3,540,705	68,082
1900 (June 1)	76,212,168	21.5	13,232,402	21.0	3,618,770	3,547,314	67,901
1910 (Apr. 15)	92,228,496	26.0	16,016,328	21.0	3,618,770	3,547,045	68,170
1920 (Jan. 1)	106,021,537	29.9	13,793,041	15.0	3,618,770	3,546,931	68,284
1930 (Apr. 1)	123,202,624	34.7	17,181,087	16.2	3,618,770	3,554,608	60,607
1940 (Apr. 1)	132,164,569	37.2	8,961,945	7.3	3,618,770	3,554,608	60,607
1950 (Apr. 1)	151,325,798	42.6	19,161,229	14.5	3,618,770	3,552,206	63,005
1960 (Apr. 1)	179,323,175	50.6	27,997,377	18.5	3,618,770	3,540,911	74,212
1970 (Apr. 1)	203,302,031	57.5	23,978,856	13.4	3,618,770	3,536,855	78,444
1980 (Apr. 1)	[3]226,542,199	64.0	23,240,168	11.4	3,618,770	3,539,289	79,481
1990 (Apr. 1)	[4]248,718,302	70.3	22,176,103	9.8	[5]3,717,796	3,536,278	[5]181,518
2000 (Apr. 1)	[6]281,424,603	79.6	32,706,301	13.1	3,794,083	3,537,438	256,645

X Not applicable. [1] Data for 1790 to 1980 cover inland water only. Data for 1990 comprise Great Lakes, inland, and coastal water. Data for 2000 comprise Great Lakes, inland, territorial, and coastal water. [2] Revised to include adjustments for underenumeration in southern states; unrevised number is 38,558,371 (10.9 per square mile). [3] Total population count has been revised since the 1980 census publications. Numbers by age, race, Hispanic origin, and sex have not been corrected. [4] The April 1, 1990, census count includes count question resolution corrections processed through December 1997, and does not include adjustments for census coverage errors. [5] Data reflect corrections made after publication of the results. [6] Reflects modifications to the Census 2000 population as documented in the Count Question Resolution program.

Source: U.S. Census Bureau, 2000 Census of Population and Housing, *Population and Housing Counts*, Series PHC-3-1, United States Summary; *Notes and Errata, 2000* SF/01-ER ; <http://www.census.gov/prod/cen2000/notes/errata.pdf>; *Areas of the United States: 1940*; Area data for 1990: unpublished data from TIGER®; and Davis, Warren; personal correspondence; U.S. Census Bureau; 23 June 2006.

Table 2. Population: 1960 to 2007

[In thousands, except percent (180,671 represents 180,671,000). Estimates as of July 1. Civilian population excludes Armed Forces. For basis of estimates, see text of this section]

Year	Resident population, including Armed Forces overseas		Resident population	Civilian population	Year	Resident population, including Armed Forces overseas		Resident population	Civilian population
	Population	Percent change [1]				Population	Percent change [1]		
1960	180,671	1.60	179,979	178,140	1984	236,348	0.87	235,825	234,110
1961	183,691	1.67	182,992	181,143	1985	238,466	0.90	237,924	236,219
1962	186,538	1.55	185,771	183,677	1986	240,651	0.92	240,133	238,412
1963	189,242	1.45	188,483	186,493	1987	242,804	0.89	242,289	240,550
1964	191,889	1.40	191,141	189,141	1988	245,021	0.91	244,499	242,817
1965	194,303	1.26	193,526	191,605	1989	247,342	0.95	246,819	245,131
1966	196,560	1.16	195,576	193,420	1990	250,132	1.13	249,623	247,983
1967	198,712	1.09	197,457	195,264	1991	253,493	1.34	252,981	251,370
1968	200,706	1.00	199,399	197,113	1992	256,894	1.34	256,514	254,929
1969	202,677	0.98	201,385	199,145	1993	260,255	1.31	259,919	258,446
1970	205,052	1.17	203,984	201,895	1994	263,436	1.22	263,126	261,714
1971	207,661	1.27	206,827	204,866	1995	266,557	1.18	266,278	264,927
1972	209,896	1.08	209,284	207,511	1996	269,667	1.17	269,394	268,108
1973	211,909	0.96	211,357	209,600	1997	272,912	1.20	272,647	271,394
1974	213,854	0.92	213,342	211,636	1998	276,115	1.17	275,854	274,633
1975	215,973	0.99	215,465	213,789	1999	279,295	1.15	279,040	277,841
1976	218,035	0.95	217,563	215,894	2000	282,407	1.11	282,194	280,950
1977	220,239	1.01	219,760	218,106	2001	285,339	1.04	285,112	283,876
1978	222,585	1.06	222,095	220,467	2002	288,189	1.00	287,888	286,621
1979	225,055	1.11	224,567	222,969	2003	290,941	0.95	290,448	289,228
1980	227,726	1.19	227,225	225,621	2004	293,609	0.92	293,192	291,931
1981	229,966	0.98	229,466	227,818	2005	296,329	0.93	295,896	294,705
1982	232,188	0.97	231,664	229,995	2006	299,157	0.95	298,755	297,575
1983	234,307	0.91	233,792	232,097	2007	302,045	0.97	301,621	300,466

[1] Percent change from immediate preceding year.

Source: U.S. Census Bureau, 1960 to 1979: *Current Population Reports* P25-802 and P25-917; 1980 to 1989: "Monthly Estimates of the United States Population: April 1, 1980, to July 1, 1999, with Short-Term Projections to November 1, 2000"; published 2 January 2001; <http://www.census.gov/popest/archives/1990s/nat-total.txt>; 1990 to 1999: "national intercensal estimates (1990–2000)"; published 13 August 2004; <http://www.census.gov/popest/archives/EST90INTERCENSAL/US-EST90INT -datasets.html>; 2000 to 2007: "Monthly Population Estimates for the United States: April 1, 2000, to December 1, 2007"; published 27 December 2007; <http://www.census.gov/popest/national/NA-EST2007-01.html>.

U.S. Census Bureau, Statistical Abstract of the United States: 2009

Table 3. **Resident Population Projections: 2008 to 2050**

[304,228 represents 304,228,000. **As of July 1**. Projections are based on assumptions about future births, deaths, and net international migration. More information on methodology and assumptions is available at <http://www.census.gov/population /www/projections/methodstatement.html>]

Year	Number (1,000)	Percent change [1]	Year	Number (1,000)	Percent change [1]	Year	Number (1,000)	Percent change [1]
2008	304,228	1.0	2023	351,018	0.9	2038	399,184	0.8
2009	307,212	1.0	2024	354,235	0.9	2039	402,415	0.8
2010	310,233	1.0	2025	357,452	0.9	2040	405,655	0.8
2011.	313,232	1.0	2026	360,667	0.9	2041	408,906	0.8
2012	316,266	1.0	2027	363,880	0.9	2042	412,170	0.8
2013	319,330	1.0	2028	367,090	0.9	2043	415,448	0.8
2014	322,423	1.0	2029	370,298	0.9	2044	418,743	0.8
2015	325,540	1.0	2030	373,504	0.9	2045	422,059	0.8
2016	328,678	1.0	2031	376,708	0.9	2046	425,395	0.8
2017	331,833	1.0	2032	379,912	0.9	2047	428,756	0.8
2018	335,005	1.0	2033	383,117	0.8	2048	432,143	0.8
2019	338,190	1.0	2034	386,323	0.8	2049	435,560	0.8
2020	341,387	0.9	2035	389,531	0.8	2050	439,010	0.8
2021	344,592	0.9	2036	392,743	0.8			
2022	347,803	0.9	2037	395,961	0.8			

[1] Percent change from immediate preceding year. 2008, change from 2007.

Source: U.S. Census Bureau, "2008 National Population Projections," released August 2008, <http://www.census.gov/population /www/projections/2008projections.html>.

Table 4. **Components of Population Change: 2000 to 2007**

[**In thousands (281,425 represents 281,425,000), except as indicated**. Resident population]

Period	Population as of beginning of period	Net increase		Births	Deaths	Net international migration [2]	Population as of end of period
		Total	Percent [1]				
April 1, 2000 to July 1, 2000 [3] . . .	281,425	770	0.3	989	561	342	282,194
July 1, 2000 to July 1, 2001	282,194	2,918	1.0	4,047	2,419	1,290	285,112
July 1, 2001 to July 1, 2002	285,112	2,776	1.0	4,007	2,430	1,199	287,888
July 1, 2002 to July 1, 2003	287,888	2,560	0.9	4,053	2,423	930	290,448
July 1, 2003 to July 1, 2004	290,448	2,744	0.9	4,113	2,450	1,081	293,192
July 1, 2004 to July 1, 2005	293,192	2,704	0.9	4,121	2,433	1,017	295,896
July 1, 2005 to July 1, 2006	295,896	2,859	1.0	4,201	2,431	1,090	298,755
July 1, 2006 to July 1, 2007	298,755	2,866	1.0	4,279	2,450	1,038	301,621

[1] Percent of population at beginning of period. [2] Includes (a) the net international migration of the foreign born, (b) the net migration between the United States and Puerto Rico, (c) the net migration of natives to and from the United States, and (d) the net overseas movement of the Armed Forces population. [3] The April 1, 2000, Population Estimates base reflects changes to the Census 2000 population from the Count Question Resolution program.

Source: U.S. Census Bureau, "Population, Population change and estimated components of population change: April 1, 2000, to July 1, 2007"; release date: December 27, 2007; <http://www.census.gov/popest/national/files/NST-EST2007-alldata.csv>.

Table 5. **Components of Population Change by Race and Hispanic Origin: 2000 to 2007**

[**In thousands (20,197 represents 20,197,000,000)**. Resident population. **Covers period April 1, 2000, to July 1, 2007.** The April 1, 2000, Population Estimates base reflects changes to the Census 2000 population from the Count Question Resolution program]

Race and Hispanic origin	Net increase	Natural increase			Net international migration [1]
		Total	Births	Deaths	
Total	**20,197**	**12,212**	**29,809**	**17,597**	**7,984**
One race.	19,238	11,348	28,835	17,487	7,890
White	13,060	7,662	22,647	14,985	5,398
Black or African American	3,051	2,460	4,583	2,123	592
American Indian and Alaska Native. . .	275	213	298	84	61
Asian	2,777	968	1,253	286	1,809
Native Hawaiian and Other Pacific Islander	75	45	54	9	29
Two or more races	959	864	974	110	94
Race alone or in combination: [2]					
White	13,938	8,469	23,547	15,077	5,468
Black or African American	3,639	3,015	5,169	2,153	623
American Indian and Alaska Native. . .	312	233	379	146	79
Asian	3,158	1,290	1,609	319	1,869
Native Hawaiian and Other Pacific Islander	113	69	91	22	44
Hispanic [3]	10,198	5,981	6,793	812	4,217
White alone, not Hispanic.	3,515	2,113	16,337	14,224	1,401

[1] See footnote 2, Table 4. [2] In combination with one or more other races. The sum of the five race groups adds to more than the total population because individuals may report more than one race. [3] Persons of Hispanic origin may be any race.

Source: U.S. Census Bureau, "Cumulative Estimates of the Components of Population Change by Race and Hispanic Origin for the United States: April 1, 2000, to July 1, 2007 (NC-EST2007-05)"; release date: May 1, 2008; <http://www.census.gov/popest /national/asrh/NC-EST2007/NC-EST2007-05.xls>.

Table 6. Resident Population by Sex, Race, and Hispanic-Origin Status: 2000 to 2007

[281,425 represents 281,425,000. As of July, except as noted. Data shown are modified race counts; see text, this section]

Characteristic	Number (1,000)					Percent change, 2000 to 2007
	2000 [1] (April 1)	2004	2005	2006	2007	
BOTH SEXES						
Total	**281,425**	**293,192**	**295,896**	**298,755**	**301,621**	**7.2**
One race	277,527	288,756	291,325	294,043	296,765	6.9
White	228,107	235,748	237,483	239,322	241,167	5.7
Black or African American	35,705	37,434	37,852	38,306	38,756	8.5
American Indian and Alaska Native	2,664	2,821	2,859	2,899	2,938	10.3
Asian	10,589	12,248	12,615	12,990	13,366	26.2
Native Hawaiian and Other Pacific Islander	463	504	515	526	537	16.1
Two or more races	3,898	4,436	4,571	4,712	4,856	24.6
Race alone or in combination: [2]						
White	231,436	239,570	241,429	243,397	245,374	6.0
Black or African American	37,105	39,163	39,664	40,204	40,744	9.8
American Indian and Alaska Native	4,225	4,404	4,447	4,492	4,537	7.4
Asian	12,007	13,879	14,300	14,731	15,165	26.3
Native Hawaiian and Other Pacific Islander	907	971	987	1,003	1,019	12.4
Not Hispanic	246,118	251,989	253,293	254,700	256,117	4.1
One race	242,712	248,135	249,326	250,616	251,912	3.8
White	195,577	197,657	198,092	198,589	199,092	1.8
Black or African American	34,314	35,889	36,253	36,646	37,037	7.9
American Indian and Alaska Native	2,097	2,205	2,231	2,259	2,287	9.0
Asian	10,357	11,988	12,347	12,712	13,080	26.3
Native Hawaiian and Other Pacific Islander	367	396	403	410	417	13.6
Two or more races	3,406	3,854	3,967	4,084	4,205	23.4
Race alone or in combination: [2]						
White	198,477	200,965	201,503	202,107	202,720	2.1
Black or African American	35,499	37,351	37,784	38,251	38,717	9.1
American Indian and Alaska Native	3,456	3,570	3,598	3,628	3,658	5.9
Asian	11,632	13,450	13,856	14,271	14,688	26.3
Native Hawaiian and Other Pacific Islander	752	798	809	821	832	10.6
Hispanic [3]	35,306	41,202	42,603	44,054	45,504	28.9
One race	34,815	40,620	41,999	43,427	44,853	28.8
White	32,530	38,091	39,391	40,734	42,075	29.3
Black or African American	1,391	1,545	1,599	1,660	1,719	23.6
American Indian and Alaska Native	566	617	628	640	652	15.1
Asian	232	259	268	277	287	23.3
Native Hawaiian and Other Pacific Islander	95	108	112	116	120	25.8
Two or more races	491	582	604	628	651	32.6
Race alone or in combination: [2]						
White	32,959	38,605	39,926	41,291	42,654	29.4
Black or African American	1,606	1,812	1,880	1,954	2,027	26.2
American Indian and Alaska Native	770	834	849	864	879	14.2
Asian	375	429	444	461	477	27.3
Native Hawaiian and Other Pacific Islander	155	173	178	183	188	21.1
MALE						
Total	**138,056**	**144,224**	**145,649**	**147,160**	**148,659**	**7.7**
One race	136,146	142,042	143,398	144,838	146,263	7.4
White	112,478	116,612	117,556	118,558	119,549	6.3
Black or African American	16,972	17,826	18,034	18,262	18,487	8.9
American Indian and Alaska Native	1,333	1,412	1,431	1,451	1,471	10.4
Asian	5,128	5,935	6,115	6,298	6,482	26.4
Native Hawaiian and Other Pacific Islander	235	256	262	268	273	16.2
Two or more races	1,910	2,183	2,251	2,323	2,396	25.4
Race alone or in combination: [2]						
White	114,116	118,499	119,505	120,573	121,632	6.6
Black or African American	17,644	18,665	18,916	19,188	19,458	10.3
American Indian and Alaska Native	2,088	2,178	2,199	2,222	2,245	7.5
Asian	5,834	6,749	6,956	7,168	7,381	26.5
Native Hawaiian and Other Pacific Islander	456	488	496	504	512	12.3
Not Hispanic	119,894	122,957	123,645	124,395	125,135	4.4
Hispanic [3]	18,162	21,267	22,004	22,765	23,524	29.5
FEMALE						
Total	**143,368**	**148,967**	**150,247**	**151,595**	**152,962**	**6.7**
One race	141,381	146,714	147,927	149,205	150,502	6.5
White	115,628	119,136	119,928	120,764	121,617	5.2
Black or African American	18,733	19,608	19,818	20,044	20,269	8.2
American Indian and Alaska Native	1,331	1,409	1,428	1,447	1,467	10.2
Asian	5,461	6,313	6,500	6,692	6,884	26.1
Native Hawaiian and Other Pacific Islander	227	248	253	258	264	16.0
Two or more races	1,987	2,253	2,320	2,389	2,460	23.8
Race alone or in combination: [2]						
White	117,321	121,071	121,924	122,824	123,742	5.5
Black or African American	19,461	20,498	20,748	21,017	21,286	9.4
American Indian and Alaska Native	2,137	2,226	2,248	2,270	2,292	7.3
Asian	6,173	7,130	7,344	7,563	7,784	26.1
Native Hawaiian and Other Pacific Islander	451	483	491	499	507	12.5
Not Hispanic	126,224	129,032	129,648	130,305	130,982	3.8
Hispanic [3]	17,144	19,935	20,599	21,290	21,981	28.2

[1] See footnote 3, Table 7. [2] In combination with one or more other races. The sum of the five race groups adds to more than the total population because individuals may report more than one race. [3] Persons of Hispanic origin may be any race.
Source: U.S. Census Bureau, "Annual Estimates of the Population by Sex, Race, and Hispanic Origin for the United States: April 1, 2000 to July 1, 2007 (NC-EST2007-03)"; release date: May 1, 2008; <http://www.census.gov/popest/national/asrh/NC-EST2007/NC-EST2007-03.xls>.

Population 9

Table 7. Resident Population by Age and Sex: 1980 to 2007

[In thousands, except as indicated (226,546 represents 226,546,000). 1980, 1990, and 2000 data are enumerated population as of April 1; data for other years are estimated population as of July 1. Excludes Armed Forces overseas. For definition of median, see Guide to Tabular Presentation]

Age group	1980 [1]			1990 [2]			2000 [3]			2001, total	2002, total	2003, total	2004, total	2005, total	2006, total	2007		
	Total	Male	Female	Total	Male	Female	Total	Male	Female							Total	Male	Female
Total	226,546	110,053	116,493	248,791	121,284	127,507	281,425	138,056	143,368	285,112	287,888	290,448	293,192	295,896	298,755	301,621	148,659	152,962
Under 5 years	16,348	8,362	7,986	18,765	9,603	9,162	19,176	9,811	9,365	19,350	19,537	19,774	20,060	20,300	20,452	20,724	10,603	10,121
5 to 9 years	16,700	8,539	8,161	18,042	9,236	8,806	20,550	10,523	10,026	20,235	19,976	19,754	19,599	19,526	19,674	19,850	10,149	9,701
10 to 14 years	18,242	9,316	8,926	17,067	8,742	8,325	20,528	10,520	10,008	20,892	21,108	21,193	21,117	20,845	20,587	20,314	10,400	9,914
15 to 19 years	21,168	10,755	10,413	17,893	9,178	8,714	20,219	10,391	9,828	20,305	20,362	20,468	20,703	21,020	21,275	21,474	11,007	10,467
20 to 24 years	21,319	10,663	10,655	19,143	9,749	9,394	18,963	9,688	9,275	19,797	20,299	20,636	20,870	20,947	20,994	21,032	10,853	10,179
25 to 29 years	19,521	9,705	9,816	21,336	10,708	10,629	19,382	9,799	9,583	18,938	18,896	19,051	19,458	19,945	20,575	21,058	10,776	10,282
30 to 34 years	17,561	8,677	8,884	21,838	10,866	10,973	20,511	10,322	10,189	20,732	20,802	20,673	20,408	20,010	19,607	19,533	9,906	9,627
35 to 39 years	13,965	6,862	7,104	19,851	9,837	10,014	22,707	11,319	11,388	22,280	21,830	21,373	21,007	20,952	21,119	21,176	10,655	10,522
40 to 44 years	11,669	5,708	5,961	17,593	8,679	8,914	22,442	11,130	11,313	22,843	22,941	22,964	23,022	22,824	22,436	21,985	10,964	11,021
45 to 49 years	11,090	5,388	5,702	13,747	6,741	7,006	20,093	9,890	10,203	20,709	21,272	21,752	22,103	22,462	22,767	22,861	11,303	11,559
50 to 54 years	11,710	5,621	6,089	11,315	5,494	5,821	17,586	8,608	8,978	18,662	18,695	19,034	19,486	19,986	20,459	21,013	10,292	10,721
55 to 59 years	11,615	5,482	6,133	10,489	5,009	5,480	13,469	6,509	6,961	13,934	15,082	15,719	16,479	17,341	18,206	18,236	8,847	9,389
60 to 64 years	10,088	4,670	5,418	10,627	4,947	5,679	10,806	5,137	5,669	11,104	11,501	12,109	12,583	12,993	13,350	14,476	6,928	7,548
65 to 74 years	15,581	6,757	8,824	18,048	7,908	10,140	18,391	8,303	10,088	18,322	18,282	18,349	18,472	18,639	18,910	19,352	8,887	10,465
75 to 84 years	7,729	2,867	4,862	10,014	3,745	6,268	12,361	4,879	7,482	12,590	12,760	12,885	12,978	13,052	13,057	13,024	5,313	7,711
85 years and over	2,240	682	1,559	3,022	841	2,181	4,240	1,227	3,013	4,417	4,546	4,715	4,847	5,055	5,286	5,512	1,777	3,735
5 to 13 years	31,159	15,923	15,237	31,839	16,301	15,538	37,026	18,964	18,062	37,080	36,972	36,752	36,345	36,064	36,009	35,971	18,399	17,572
14 to 17 years	16,247	8,298	7,950	13,345	6,860	6,485	16,093	8,285	7,808	16,184	16,353	16,497	16,813	17,068	17,207	17,207	8,816	8,391
18 to 24 years	30,022	15,054	14,969	26,961	13,744	13,217	27,141	13,873	13,268	27,966	28,420	28,801	29,131	29,206	29,313	29,492	15,194	14,299
18 years and over	162,791	77,473	85,321	184,841	88,519	96,322	209,130	100,996	108,133	212,498	215,026	217,425	219,973	222,464	225,087	227,719	110,841	116,878
55 years and over	47,253	20,458	26,796	52,200	22,450	29,748	59,267	26,055	33,212	60,368	62,171	63,776	65,360	67,080	68,810	70,600	31,752	38,849
65 years and over	25,550	10,306	15,245	31,084	12,494	18,589	34,992	14,410	20,582	35,330	35,588	35,949	36,297	36,746	37,253	37,888	15,976	21,912
75 years and over	9,969	3,549	6,421	13,036	4,586	8,449	16,601	6,106	10,495	17,008	17,306	17,600	17,825	18,107	18,343	18,536	7,089	11,446
Median age (years)	30.0	28.8	31.3	32.8	31.6	34.0	35.3	34.0	36.5	35.6	35.7	35.9	36.1	36.2	36.4	36.6	35.3	37.9

[1] Total population count has been revised since the 1980 census publications. Numbers by age and sex have not been corrected.   [2] The data shown have been modified from the official 1990 census counts. See text of this section for explanation. The April 1, 1990, estimates base (248,790,925) includes count resolution corrections processed through August 1997. It generally does not include adjustments for census coverage errors. However, it includes adjustments estimated for the 1995 Test Census in various localities in California, New Jersey, and Louisiana; and the 1998 census dress rehearsals in localities in California and Wisconsin. These adjustments amounted to a total of 81,052 persons.   [3] The April 1, 2000, population estimates base reflects changes to the Census 2000 population from the Count Question Resolution program.

Source: U.S. Census Bureau, Current Population Reports, P25-1095; "Table US-EST90INT-04 - Intercensal Estimates of the United States Resident Population by Age Groups and Sex, 1990–2000: Selected Months"; published 13 September 2002; <http://www.census.gov/popest/archives/EST90INTERCENSAL/US-EST90INT-04.html>; and "Annual Estimates of the Population by Sex and Five-Year Age Groups for the United States: April 1, 2000 to July 1, 2007 (NC-EST2007-01)", release date: May 1, 2008 <http://www.census.gov/popest/national/asrh/NC-EST2007/NC-EST2007-01.xls>.

Table 8. Resident Population by Race, Hispanic Origin, and Age: 2000 and 2007

[In thousands (281,425 represents 281,425,000); except as indicated. 2000, as of April and 2007, as of July. For definition of median, see Guide to Tabular Presentation]

Age group	Total 2000[1]	Total 2007	White alone 2000[1]	White alone 2007	Black or African American alone 2000[1]	Black or African American alone 2007	American Indian, Alaska Native alone 2000[1]	American Indian, Alaska Native alone 2007	Asian alone 2000[1]	Asian alone 2007	Native Hawaiian, Other Pacific Islander alone 2000[1]	Native Hawaiian, Other Pacific Islander alone 2007	Two or more races 2000[1]	Two or more races 2007	Hispanic origin[2] 2000[1]	Hispanic origin[2] 2007	Not Hispanic White alone 2000[1]	Not Hispanic White alone 2007
Total	281,425	301,621	228,107	241,167	35,705	38,756	2,664	2,938	10,589	13,366	463	537	3,898	4,856	35,306	45,504	195,577	199,092
Under 5 years . .	19,176	20,724	14,657	15,717	2,925	3,153	233	209	708	914	41	40	613	691	3,718	4,916	11,288	11,175
5 to 9 years	20,550	19,850	15,688	15,156	3,320	2,984	258	218	716	820	44	39	524	633	3,624	4,219	12,392	11,255
10 to 14 years . .	20,528	20,314	15,843	15,485	3,221	3,155	264	246	715	820	42	45	443	564	3,163	3,969	12,961	11,866
15 to 19 years . .	20,219	21,474	15,745	16,426	3,024	3,413	251	274	776	825	44	46	380	489	3,172	3,746	12,836	13,006
20 to 24 years . .	18,963	21,032	14,826	16,325	2,729	3,108	218	266	848	875	46	46	297	412	3,409	3,690	11,681	12,930
25 to 29 years . .	19,382	21,058	15,217	16,364	2,645	2,972	204	243	1,019	1,077	42	51	254	351	3,385	3,993	12,077	12,497
30 to 34 years . .	20,511	19,533	16,349	15,140	2,710	2,610	202	211	980	1,253	39	46	231	273	3,125	3,642	13,451	11,425
35 to 39 years . .	22,707	21,176	18,372	16,657	2,910	2,749	217	207	937	1,267	38	43	233	254	2,825	3,200	15,753	13,272
40 to 44 years . .	22,442	21,985	18,346	17,567	2,772	2,828	202	212	870	1,104	33	40	219	234	2,304	2,675	16,213	14,597
45 to 49 years . .	20,093	22,861	16,615	18,589	2,330	2,801	169	209	770	997	27	36	183	230	1,775	2,075	14,973	16,109
50 to 54 years . .	17,586	21,013	14,794	17,284	1,846	2,429	135	181	641	891	21	30	149	199	1,361	1,569	13,530	15,363
55 to 59 years . .	13,469	18,236	11,479	15,191	1,332	1,963	95	145	443	753	15	24	106	160	960	1,122	10,582	13,736
60 to 64 years . .	10,806	14,476	9,214	12,340	1,082	1,361	70	104	350	534	11	17	78	120	750	809	8,511	11,294
65 to 69 years . .	9,534	10,752	8,238	9,165	895	1,017	52	73	279	403	8	12	61	82	599	621	7,675	8,408
70 to 74 years . .	8,858	8,600	7,799	7,368	742	801	38	53	224	309	6	9	49	60	477	479	7,348	6,786
75 to 79 years . .	7,416	7,325	6,634	6,411	557	593	27	38	159	233	4	6	36	45	327	322	6,325	5,959
80 to 84 years . .	4,945	5,699	4,466	5,056	350	424	15	25	90	158	2	4	22	31	180	175	4,296	4,751
85 to 89 years . .	2,790	3,477	2,525	3,116	200	240	8	14	43	86	1	2	12	18	98	73	2,432	2,950
90 to 94 years . .	1,113	1,502	1,007	1,345	82	107	3	6	15	35	1	1	4	8	39	25	970	1,276
95 to 99 years . .	287	452	254	399	27	38	1	2	4	10	–	–	1	3	11	6	243	374
100 years and over . .	50	81	41	68	7	10	–	1	1	2	–	–	–	1	3		39	62
5 to 13 years . . .	37,026	35,971	28,381	27,454	5,923	5,462	471	412	1,288	1,477	78	74	885	1,091	6,186	7,402	22,754	20,652
14 to 17 years . .	16,093	17,207	12,523	13,115	2,426	2,768	205	218	590	657	33	37	315	412	2,438	3,101	10,290	10,286
18 to 24 years . .	27,141	29,492	21,197	22,822	3,944	4,430	315	374	1,178	1,207	64	64	444	596	4,744	5,122	16,827	18,119
16 years and over . .	217,151	236,468	178,790	191,560	25,633	28,780	1,857	2,211	8,304	10,649	328	404	2,237	2,865	24,204	31,618	156,352	162,259
18 years and over . .	209,130	227,719	172,546	184,880	24,431	27,373	1,755	2,099	8,003	10,319	311	385	2,084	2,663	22,964	30,085	151,245	156,979
16 to 64 years . . .	182,159	198,580	147,826	158,633	22,773	25,550	1,713	1,998	7,489	9,413	305	369	2,051	2,617	22,471	29,106	127,023	131,693
55 years and over . .	59,267	70,600	51,656	60,458	5,274	6,554	310	462	1,608	2,523	48	75	371	527	3,444	5,203	48,422	55,597
65 years and over . .	34,992	37,888	30,964	32,927	2,860	3,230	144	213	815	1,235	23	35	186	248	1,734	2,512	29,329	30,567
75 years and over . .	16,601	18,536	14,927	16,394	1,223	1,413	55	87	312	523	8	14	77	106	657	1,081	14,306	15,373
85 years and over . .	4,240	5,512	3,827	4,927	316	395	13	24	63	133	2	3	18	30	151	280	3,685	4,663
Median age (years)	35.3	36.6	36.6	38.0	30.0	31.1	27.7	30.3	32.5	35.4	26.8	30.2	19.8	20.6	25.8	27.6	38.6	40.8

– Represents or rounds to zero. [1] April 1, 2000, population estimates base reflects changes to the Census 2000 population from the Count Question Resolution program. [2] Persons of Hispanic origin may be any race.

Source: U.S. Census Bureau, "Annual Estimates of the Population by Race, Hispanic Origin, Sex and Age for the United States: April 1, 2000 to July 1, 2007 (NC-EST2007-04)"; release date: May 1, 2008; <http://www.census.gov/popest/national/asrh/NC-EST2007-asrh.html>.

Table 9. Resident Population by Race, Hispanic Origin, and Single Years of Age: 2007

[In thousands, except as indicated (301,621 represents 301,621,000). As of July 1. For derivation of estimates, see text of this section]

Age	Total	Race						Hispanic origin [1]	Not-Hispanic White alone
		White alone	Black or African American alone	American Indian, Alaska Native alone	Asian alone	Native Hawaiian and Other Pacific Islander alone	Two or more races		
Total........	301,621	241,167	38,756	2,938	13,366	537	4,856	45,504	199,092
Under 5 years old...	20,724	15,717	3,153	209	914	40	691	4,916	11,175
Under 1 year old..	4,257	3,211	660	44	186	9	147	1,033	2,266
1 year old......	4,182	3,154	651	43	184	8	142	1,025	2,215
2 years old	4,110	3,110	629	42	184	8	138	983	2,206
3 years old	4,111	3,134	612	41	182	8	135	952	2,247
4 years old	4,063	3,108	600	40	179	7	129	923	2,241
5 to 9 years old	19,850	15,156	2,984	218	820	39	633	4,219	11,255
5 years old	4,032	3,084	606	39	171	7	125	899	2,235
6 years old	4,089	3,124	622	39	174	7	124	886	2,289
7 years old	3,936	3,005	588	45	159	8	130	838	2,238
8 years old	3,892	2,970	580	47	157	9	130	801	2,243
9 years old	3,901	2,973	588	47	160	9	124	795	2,250
10 to 14 years old ..	20,314	15,485	3,155	246	820	45	564	3,969	11,866
10 years old.....	3,927	2,997	592	47	164	9	119	793	2,275
11 years old.....	4,010	3,066	604	48	167	9	117	800	2,337
12 years old.....	4,075	3,109	631	48	164	9	113	799	2,380
13 years old.....	4,109	3,125	652	50	163	9	109	790	2,405
14 years old.....	4,193	3,187	676	52	163	9	106	787	2,469
15 to 19 years old ..	21,474	16,426	3,413	274	825	46	489	3,746	13,006
15 years old.....	4,265	3,249	685	54	163	9	104	781	2,536
16 years old.....	4,334	3,307	697	55	163	9	102	770	2,605
17 years old.....	4,415	3,372	710	56	167	9	100	763	2,676
18 years old.....	4,258	3,262	672	54	167	9	94	718	2,606
19 years old.....	4,202	3,235	649	54	165	9	90	713	2,583
20 to 24 years old ..	21,032	16,325	3,108	266	875	46	412	3,690	12,930
20 years old.....	4,169	3,224	632	53	164	9	87	708	2,576
21 years old.....	4,205	3,260	628	53	170	9	85	716	2,603
22 years old.....	4,237	3,293	624	53	174	9	83	731	2,620
23 years old.....	4,172	3,240	610	53	180	9	80	746	2,553
24 years old.....	4,249	3,307	614	53	188	9	78	788	2,578
25 to 29 years old ..	21,058	16,364	2,972	243	1,077	51	351	4,176	12,497
25 years old.....	4,286	3,333	615	51	200	10	77	823	2,572
26 years old.....	4,332	3,369	615	51	212	10	75	838	2,593
27 years old.....	4,321	3,353	617	50	220	11	71	859	2,558
28 years old.....	4,116	3,193	578	47	222	10	66	829	2,426
29 years old.....	4,002	3,115	547	45	223	10	62	827	2,348
30 to 34 years old ..	19,533	15,140	2,610	211	1,253	46	273	3,993	11,425
30 years old.....	3,949	3,068	536	44	232	10	58	822	2,305
31 years old.....	3,851	2,986	515	43	242	10	56	814	2,229
32 years old.....	3,958	3,070	525	42	258	9	55	810	2,316
33 years old.....	3,842	2,976	507	41	257	9	52	776	2,253
34 years old.....	3,933	3,039	528	41	264	9	52	771	2,322
35 to 39 years old ..	21,176	16,657	2,749	207	1,267	43	254	3,642	13,272
35 years old.....	4,119	3,204	546	42	265	9	53	761	2,496
36 years old.....	4,346	3,411	569	43	260	9	54	753	2,712
37 years old.....	4,426	3,487	573	43	262	9	53	752	2,789
38 years old.....	4,182	3,311	529	41	245	8	49	696	2,664
39 years old.....	4,103	3,244	531	40	234	8	46	681	2,611
40 to 44 years old ..	21,985	17,567	2,828	212	1,104	40	234	3,200	14,597
40 years old.....	4,113	3,273	529	40	218	8	45	654	2,665
41 years old.....	4,227	3,356	556	41	220	8	46	654	2,749
42 years old.....	4,512	3,597	590	44	225	8	48	659	2,985
43 years old.....	4,576	3,672	582	44	222	8	48	633	3,085
44 years old.....	4,557	3,669	571	43	219	8	47	600	3,113
45 to 49 years old ..	22,861	18,589	2,801	209	997	36	230	2,675	16,109
45 years old.....	4,569	3,703	565	43	203	8	47	580	3,165
46 years old.....	4,612	3,753	564	42	199	7	46	555	3,238
47 years old.....	4,691	3,797	587	43	208	8	47	559	3,279
48 years old.....	4,495	3,662	548	40	193	7	45	503	3,196
49 years old.....	4,495	3,674	537	40	193	7	44	478	3,231

See footnote at end of table.

U.S. Census Bureau, Statistical Abstract of the United States: 2009

[In thousands, except as indicated (301,621 represents 301,621,000). As of July 1. For derivation of estimates, see text of this section]

Age	Total	Race						Hispanic origin [1]	Not-Hispanic White alone
		White alone	Black or African American alone	American Indian, Alaska Native alone	Asian alone	Native Hawaiian and Other Pacific Islander alone	Two or more races		
50 to 54 years old ..	21,013	17,284	2,429	181	891	30	199	2,075	15,363
50 years old.....	4,438	3,636	528	39	186	6	43	460	3,210
51 years old.....	4,263	3,494	501	37	184	6	41	435	3,090
52 years old.....	4,278	3,511	499	37	184	6	41	427	3,116
53 years old.....	4,087	3,373	465	35	171	6	38	389	3,013
54 years old.....	3,947	3,271	436	33	165	5	36	364	2,934
55 to 59 years old ..	18,236	15,191	1,963	145	753	24	160	1,569	13,736
55 years old.....	3,811	3,167	416	31	157	5	34	341	2,852
56 years old.....	3,706	3,075	412	30	152	5	33	329	2,771
57 years old.....	3,687	3,047	412	30	161	5	32	326	2,745
58 years old.....	3,535	2,953	373	28	146	5	31	294	2,680
59 years old.....	3,497	2,949	350	27	137	4	30	280	2,689
60 to 64 years old ..	14,476	12,340	1,361	104	534	17	120	1,122	11,294
60 years old.....	3,666	3,146	332	26	128	4	31	266	2,899
61 years old.....	2,720	2,295	268	21	110	4	23	234	2,078
62 years old.....	2,704	2,285	266	20	106	3	23	222	2,078
63 years old.....	2,651	2,260	249	19	99	3	21	206	2,068
64 years old.....	2,734	2,353	246	18	92	3	21	195	2,172
65 to 69 years old ..	10,752	9,165	1,017	73	403	12	82	809	8,408
65 years old.....	2,399	2,051	222	16	89	3	19	177	1,885
66 years old.....	2,215	1,886	210	15	84	3	17	167	1,729
67 years old.....	2,143	1,815	211	15	83	3	17	166	1,660
68 years old.....	2,024	1,729	189	13	75	2	15	153	1,586
69 years old.....	1,972	1,685	185	13	72	2	15	146	1,548
70 to 74 years old ..	8,600	7,368	801	53	309	9	60	621	6,786
70 years old.....	1,840	1,573	173	12	68	2	13	137	1,445
71 years old.....	1,790	1,530	169	11	65	2	13	131	1,407
72 years old.....	1,777	1,522	167	11	63	2	12	130	1,399
73 years old.....	1,604	1,376	148	10	57	2	11	115	1,269
74 years old.....	1,588	1,367	144	9	56	2	11	109	1,266
75 to 79 years old ..	7,325	6,411	593	38	233	6	45	479	5,959
75 years old.....	1,548	1,345	132	9	51	1	10	105	1,246
76 years old.....	1,510	1,322	121	8	49	1	9	101	1,227
77 years old.....	1,510	1,317	125	8	49	1	9	100	1,223
78 years old.....	1,394	1,225	110	7	43	1	8	90	1,140
79 years old.....	1,363	1,202	105	6	41	1	8	84	1,123
80 to 84 years old ..	5,699	5,056	424	25	158	4	31	322	4,751
80 years old.....	1,295	1,144	99	6	37	1	7	76	1,072
81 years old.....	1,208	1,068	92	5	34	1	7	71	1,002
82 years old.....	1,164	1,032	87	5	32	1	6	66	970
83 years old.....	1,068	952	77	5	29	1	6	58	897
84 years old.....	965	860	69	4	26	1	5	52	811
85 to 89 years old ..	3,477	3,116	240	14	86	2	18	175	2,950
90 to 94 years old ..	1,502	1,345	107	6	35	1	8	73	1,276
95 to 99 years old ..	452	399	38	2	10	–	3	25	374
100 years old and over..........	81	68	10	1	2	–	1	6	62
Median age (years)..	36.6	38.0	31.1	30.3	35.4	30.2	20.6	27.6	40.8

– Represents or rounds to zero.   [1] Persons of Hispanic origin may be any race.

Source: U.S. Census Bureau, "Monthly Population Estimates by Age, Sex, Race and Hispanic Origin for the United States: April 1, 2000 to July 1, 2007"; release date: May 1, 2008; <http://www.census.gov/popest/national/asrh/2007-nat-res.html>.

Table 10. **Resident Population Projections by Sex and Age: 2010 to 2050**

[In thousands, except as indicated (310,233 represents 310,233,000). **As of July 1.** Projections are based on assumptions about future births, deaths, and net international migration. More information on methodology and assumptions is available at <http://www.census.gov/population/www/projections/methodstatement.html>. For definition of median, see Guide to Tabular Presentation]

Age	2010 Total	2010 Male	2010 Female	2015 Total	2015 Male	2015 Female	2020	2025	2030	2035	2040	2045	2050	Percent distribution 2010	2015	2020	2025	2050
Total	310,233	152,753	157,479	325,540	160,424	165,116	341,387	357,452	373,504	389,531	405,655	422,059	439,010	100.0	100.0	100.0	100.0	100.0
Under 5 years	21,100	10,779	10,320	22,076	11,278	10,798	22,846	23,484	24,161	25,056	26,117	27,171	28,148	6.8	6.8	6.7	6.6	6.4
5 to 9 years	20,886	10,654	10,232	21,707	11,074	10,633	22,732	23,548	24,232	24,953	25,893	26,998	28,096	6.7	6.7	6.7	6.6	6.4
10 to 14 years	20,395	10,421	9,975	21,658	11,049	10,609	22,571	23,677	24,567	25,319	26,105	27,108	28,274	6.6	6.7	6.6	6.6	6.4
15 to 19 years	21,770	11,159	10,611	21,209	10,844	10,365	22,554	23,545	24,723	25,682	26,501	27,354	28,422	7.0	6.5	6.6	6.6	6.5
20 to 24 years	21,779	11,100	10,680	22,342	11,378	10,963	21,799	23,168	24,191	25,408	26,408	27,272	28,171	7.0	6.9	6.4	6.5	6.4
25 to 29 years	21,418	10,873	10,545	22,400	11,353	11,048	22,949	22,417	23,804	24,855	26,102	27,138	28,039	6.9	6.9	6.7	6.3	6.4
30 to 34 years	20,400	10,308	10,092	22,099	11,182	10,917	23,112	23,699	23,216	24,647	25,745	27,040	28,126	6.6	6.8	6.8	6.6	6.4
35 to 39 years	20,267	10,191	10,076	20,841	10,506	10,335	22,586	23,645	24,279	23,848	25,321	26,462	27,799	6.5	6.4	6.6	6.6	6.3
40 to 44 years	21,010	10,509	10,500	20,460	10,247	10,214	21,078	22,851	23,944	24,612	24,224	25,726	26,897	6.8	6.3	6.2	6.4	6.1
45 to 49 years	22,596	11,165	11,430	21,001	10,447	10,553	20,502	21,154	22,943	24,061	24,759	24,411	25,933	7.3	6.5	6.0	5.9	5.9
50 to 54 years	22,109	10,827	11,282	22,367	10,977	11,390	20,852	20,404	21,087	22,884	24,025	24,750	24,445	7.1	6.9	6.1	5.7	5.6
55 to 59 years	19,517	9,450	10,067	21,682	10,524	11,158	21,994	20,575	20,186	20,903	22,703	23,867	24,621	6.3	6.7	6.4	5.8	5.6
60 to 64 years	16,758	8,024	8,733	18,861	9,023	9,838	21,009	21,377	20,080	19,760	20,513	22,305	23,490	5.4	5.8	6.2	6.0	5.4
65 to 69 years	12,261	5,747	6,514	15,812	7,449	8,364	17,861	19,957	20,381	19,230	18,989	19,776	21,543	4.0	4.9	5.2	5.6	4.9
70 to 74 years	9,202	4,191	5,011	11,155	5,109	6,046	14,452	16,399	18,404	18,879	17,906	17,754	18,570	3.0	3.4	4.2	4.6	4.2
75 to 79 years	7,282	3,159	4,123	7,901	3,480	4,421	9,656	12,598	14,390	16,249	16,771	16,016	15,964	2.3	2.4	2.8	3.5	3.6
80 to 84 years	5,733	2,302	3,431	5,676	2,342	3,334	6,239	7,715	10,173	11,735	13,375	13,925	13,429	1.8	1.7	1.8	2.2	3.1
85 to 89 years	3,650	1,297	2,353	3,786	1,409	2,376	3,817	4,278	5,383	7,215	8,450	9,767	10,303	1.2	1.2	1.1	1.2	2.3
90 to 94 years	1,570	473	1,097	1,856	591	1,265	1,976	2,047	2,360	3,044	4,180	5,007	5,909	0.5	0.6	0.6	0.6	1.3
95 to 99 years	452	108	344	546	142	404	669	739	795	952	1,270	1,803	2,229	0.1	0.2	0.2	0.2	0.5
100 years and over	79	15	65	105	21	84	135	175	208	239	298	409	601	(Z)	(Z)	(Z)	(Z)	0.1
5 to 13 years	37,123	18,945	18,178	39,011	19,900	19,111	40,792	42,490	43,858	45,170	46,743	48,664	50,697	12.0	12.0	11.9	11.9	11.5
14 to 17 years	16,994	8,713	8,281	17,019	8,699	8,320	18,048	18,892	19,796	20,496	21,126	21,834	22,728	5.5	5.2	5.3	5.3	5.2
18 to 24 years	30,713	15,675	15,037	30,885	15,746	15,139	30,817	32,555	34,059	35,695	37,038	38,234	39,538	9.9	9.5	9.0	9.1	9.0
16 years and over	243,639	118,739	124,900	255,864	124,858	131,006	268,722	282,014	295,595	309,084	322,265	335,328	348,811	78.5	78.6	78.7	78.9	79.5
18 years and over	235,016	114,316	120,700	247,434	120,547	126,887	259,702	272,585	285,688	298,809	311,669	324,389	337,437	75.8	76.0	76.1	76.3	76.9
16 to 64 years	203,410	101,447	101,963	209,027	104,316	104,711	213,917	218,107	223,503	231,540	241,027	250,872	260,264	65.6	64.2	62.7	61.0	59.3
55 years and over	76,504	34,766	41,737	87,381	40,090	47,291	97,807	105,860	112,358	118,206	124,455	130,628	136,658	24.7	26.8	28.6	29.6	31.1
65 years and over	40,229	17,292	22,937	46,837	20,542	26,295	54,804	63,907	72,092	77,543	81,238	84,456	88,547	13.0	14.4	16.1	17.9	20.2
75 years and over	18,766	7,354	11,412	19,870	7,985	11,885	22,492	27,551	33,308	39,435	44,343	46,926	48,434	6.0	6.1	6.6	7.7	11.0
85 years and over	5,751	1,893	3,859	6,292	2,163	4,130	6,597	7,239	8,745	11,450	14,198	16,985	19,041	1.9	1.9	1.9	2.0	4.3
Median age (years)	36.9	35.5	38.2	37.1	35.9	38.4	37.7	38.2	38.7	39.0	38.9	38.9	39.0	(X)	(X)	(X)	(X)	(X)

X Not applicable.   Z Less than 0.05 percent.

Source: U.S. Census Bureau, "2008 National Population Projections," released August 2008, <http://www.census.gov/population/www/projections/2008projections.html>.

Table 11. Resident Population by Race, Hispanic-Origin Status, and Age—Projections: 2010 and 2015

[In thousands (310,233 represents 310,233,000), except as indicated. As of July 1. Projections are based on assumptions about future births, deaths, and net international migration. More information on methodology and assumptions is available at <http://www.census.gov/population/www/projections/methodstatement.html> For definition of median, see Guide to Tabular Presentation]

Age group	Total		White alone		Black alone		American Indian and Alaska Native alone		Asian alone		Native Hawaiian, Other Pacific Islander alone		Two or more races		Hispanic origin [1]		Not Hispanic, White alone	
	2010	2015	2010	2015	2010	2015	2010	2015	2010	2015	2010	2015	2010	2015	2010	2015	2010	2015
Total	310,233	325,540	246,630	256,306	39,909	42,137	3,188	3,472	14,415	16,527	592	662	5,499	6,435	49,726	57,711	200,853	203,208
Under 5 years	21,100	22,076	15,944	16,563	3,034	3,191	286	311	943	1,004	53	56	840	951	5,053	5,622	11,375	11,487
5 to 9 years	20,886	21,707	15,888	16,412	3,011	3,084	264	292	927	1,018	49	55	746	845	4,888	5,452	11,448	11,465
10 to 14 years	20,395	21,658	15,560	16,467	3,021	3,080	244	271	894	1,034	45	52	631	754	4,513	5,401	11,440	11,540
15 to 19 years	21,770	21,209	16,570	16,143	3,410	3,096	268	252	932	1,030	48	48	541	639	4,473	5,040	12,472	11,524
20 to 24 years	21,779	22,342	16,731	16,976	3,330	3,449	275	273	938	1,047	47	50	459	546	4,010	4,873	13,049	12,499
25 to 29 years	21,418	22,400	16,544	17,125	3,107	3,374	261	279	1,063	1,106	48	49	395	467	3,887	4,311	12,959	13,160
30 to 34 years	20,400	22,099	15,711	16,915	2,845	3,158	228	264	1,245	1,305	52	52	319	405	4,039	4,166	11,974	13,068
35 to 39 years	20,267	20,841	15,674	15,946	2,691	2,872	210	230	1,376	1,413	47	54	269	325	3,868	4,236	12,078	12,023
40 to 44 years	21,010	20,460	16,610	15,763	2,713	2,690	205	211	1,199	1,476	42	48	241	272	3,431	3,979	13,423	12,062
45 to 49 years	22,596	21,001	18,202	16,561	2,838	2,679	216	204	1,064	1,272	40	43	236	242	3,002	3,491	15,415	12,316
50 to 54 years	22,109	22,367	18,049	17,998	2,650	2,765	200	214	957	1,115	34	40	219	234	2,425	3,036	15,800	15,177
55 to 59 years	19,517	21,682	16,134	17,691	2,170	2,545	165	196	840	1,001	27	34	181	216	1,862	2,450	14,409	15,417
60 to 64 years	16,758	18,861	14,087	15,582	1,671	2,042	130	160	704	875	21	27	145	176	1,417	1,867	12,769	13,849
65 to 69 years	12,261	15,812	10,446	13,285	1,130	1,528	87	123	483	717	15	21	99	138	974	1,387	9,534	11,994
70 to 74 years	9,202	11,155	7,867	9,511	845	990	61	80	350	469	10	14	69	91	710	920	7,201	8,650
75 to 79 years	7,282	7,901	6,331	6,780	619	690	41	53	236	310	7	9	48	60	514	637	5,848	6,183
80 to 84 years	5,733	5,676	5,093	4,957	427	458	26	32	151	186	4	5	33	38	354	424	4,759	4,558
85 to 89 years	3,650	3,786	3,290	3,374	247	271	14	17	78	99	2	3	19	22	195	257	3,106	3,131
90 to 94 years	1,570	1,856	1,423	1,674	106	125	5	7	27	39	1	1	8	10	78	117	1,350	1,564
95 to 99 years	452	546	407	492	35	40	1	2	7	9	–	–	2	3	26	35	383	459
100 years and over	79	105	69	92	8	10	–	–	1	1	–	–	1	1	6	9	63	83
5 to 13 years	37,123	39,011	28,273	29,577	5,412	5,529	459	511	1,636	1,844	85	97	1,259	1,454	8,501	9,786	20,536	20,678
14 to 17 years	16,994	17,019	12,941	12,937	2,619	2,478	205	204	741	818	38	39	450	543	3,595	4,112	9,648	9,175
18 to 24 years	30,713	30,885	23,536	23,483	4,741	4,703	387	374	1,315	1,468	66	70	668	787	5,788	6,869	18,225	17,173
16 years and over	243,639	255,864	196,026	203,643	30,201	32,171	2,343	2,547	11,466	13,267	435	489	3,168	3,747	34,372	40,202	164,202	166,441
18 years and over	235,016	247,434	189,473	197,229	28,844	30,940	2,237	2,446	11,095	12,861	416	470	2,950	3,487	32,576	38,192	159,295	161,868
16 to 64 years	203,410	209,027	161,100	163,478	26,783	28,059	2,108	2,232	10,132	11,437	397	436	2,890	3,384	31,515	36,416	131,959	129,819
55 years and over	76,504	87,381	65,147	73,437	7,258	8,698	531	671	2,877	3,706	87	114	604	755	6,136	8,104	59,421	65,888
65 years and over	40,229	46,837	34,926	40,164	3,418	4,111	235	314	1,333	1,831	39	53	278	363	2,858	3,786	32,243	36,623
75 years and over	18,766	19,870	16,613	17,368	1,442	1,594	87	111	500	645	14	18	110	133	1,173	1,479	15,509	15,978
85 years and over	5,751	6,292	5,189	5,632	397	445	20	26	113	149	3	4	29	36	305	418	4,902	5,238
Median age (yrs.)	36.9	37.1	38.4	38.6	31.7	32.8	29.9	31.1	36.0	37.5	30.5	32.0	19.9	20.2	27.5	27.8	41.3	42.1

– Represents or rounds to zero.   [1] Persons of Hispanic origin may be any race.

Source: U.S. Census Bureau, "2008 National Population Projections," released August 2008, <http://www.census.gov/population/www/projections/2008projections.html>.

Figure 1.1
Center of Population: 1790 to 2000

[Prior to 1960, excludes Alaska and Hawaii. The median center is located at the intersection of two median lines, a north-south line constructed so that half of the nation's population lives east and half lives west of it, and an east-west line selected so that half of the nation's population lives north and half lives south of it. The mean center of population is that point at which an imaginary, flat, weightless, and rigid map of the United States would balance if weights of identical value were placed on it so that each weight represented the location of one person on the date of the census]

Year	Median center		Mean center		
	Latitude-N	Longitude	Latitude-N	Longitude-W	Approximate location
1790 (August 2)	(NA)	(NA)	39 16 30	76 11 12	In Kent County, MD, 23 miles E of Baltimore MD
1850 (June 1)..	(NA)	(NA)	38 59 00	81 19 00	In Wirt County, WV, 23 miles SE of Parkersburg, WV[1]
1900 (June 1)..	40 03 32	84 49 01	39 09 36	85 48 54	In Bartholomew County, IN, 6 miles SE of Columbus, IN
1950 (April 1)..	40 00 12	84 56 51	38 50 21	88 09 33	In Richland County, IL, 8 miles NNW of Olney, IL
1960 (April 1)..	39 56 25	85 16 60	38 35 58	89 12 35	In Clinton County, IL, 6.5 miles NW of Centralia, IL
1970 (April 1)..	39 47 43	85 31 43	38 27 47	89 42 22	In St. Clair County, IL, 5.3 miles ESE of Mascoutah, IL
1980 (April 1)..	39 18 60	86 08 15	38 08 13	90 34 26	In Jefferson County, MO, .25 mile W of DeSoto, MO
1990 (April 1)..	38 57 55	86 31 53	37 52 20	91 12 55	In Crawford County, MO, 10 miles SE of Steelville, MO
2000 (April 1)..	38 45 23	86 55 51	37 41 49	91 48 34	In Phelps County, MO, 3 miles E of Edgar Springs, MO

NA Not available.   [1]West Virginia was set off from Virginia, Dec. 31, 1862, and admitted as a state, June 19, 1863.

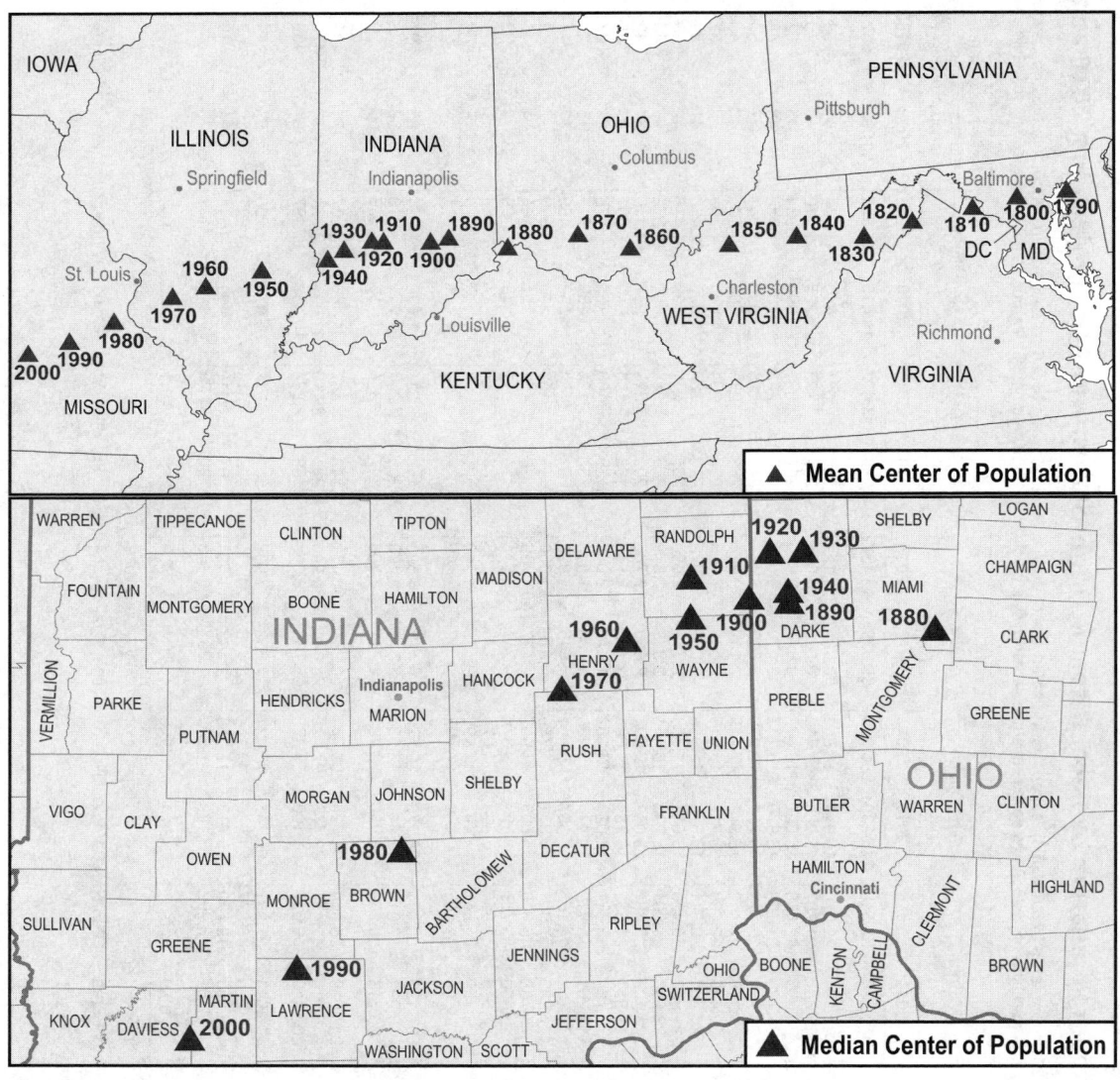

U.S. Census Bureau, Statistical Abstract of the United States: 2009

Table 12. **Resident Population—States: 1980 to 2007**

[In thousands (226,546 represents 226,546,000). 1980, 1990, and 2000 data as of April 1, data for other years as of July 1. Insofar as possible, population shown for all years is that of present area of state. See Appendix III]

State	1980 [1]	1990, estimates base [2]	2000, estimates base [3]	2002	2003	2004	2005	2006	2007
United States	**226,546**	**248,791**	**281,425**	**287,888**	**290,448**	**293,192**	**295,896**	**298,755**	**301,621**
Alabama.	3,894	4,040	4,447	4,471	4,488	4,509	4,540	4,590	4,628
Alaska	402	550	627	643	651	662	669	677	683
Arizona.	2,718	3,665	5,131	5,445	5,579	5,744	5,952	6,166	6,339
Arkansas	2,286	2,351	2,673	2,703	2,720	2,743	2,772	2,809	2,835
California	23,668	29,811	33,872	34,964	35,377	35,722	35,990	36,250	36,553
Colorado.	2,890	3,294	4,302	4,508	4,555	4,609	4,674	4,766	4,862
Connecticut.	3,108	3,287	3,406	3,452	3,473	3,482	3,486	3,496	3,502
Delaware	594	666	784	805	816	828	841	853	865
District of Columbia	638	607	572	579	577	580	582	585	588
Florida	9,746	12,938	15,983	16,668	16,959	17,343	17,736	18,058	18,251
Georgia	5,463	6,478	8,187	8,591	8,740	8,921	9,108	9,342	9,545
Hawaii	965	1,108	1,212	1,229	1,240	1,254	1,268	1,279	1,283
Idaho	944	1,007	1,294	1,342	1,364	1,392	1,426	1,464	1,499
Illinois	11,427	11,431	12,420	12,578	12,625	12,680	12,720	12,777	12,853
Indiana.	5,490	5,544	6,081	6,151	6,185	6,219	6,257	6,303	6,345
Iowa	2,914	2,777	2,926	2,931	2,936	2,946	2,956	2,973	2,988
Kansas.	2,364	2,478	2,689	2,712	2,722	2,731	2,742	2,756	2,776
Kentucky	3,661	3,687	4,042	4,089	4,114	4,140	4,171	4,204	4,241
Louisiana	4,206	4,222	4,469	4,465	4,474	4,488	4,496	4,243	4,293
Maine.	1,125	1,228	1,275	1,294	1,303	1,309	1,312	1,315	1,317
Maryland	4,217	4,781	5,297	5,434	5,494	5,538	5,573	5,602	5,618
Massachusetts.	5,737	6,016	6,349	6,432	6,439	6,434	6,429	6,434	6,450
Michigan.	9,262	9,295	9,938	10,044	10,075	10,103	10,108	10,102	10,072
Minnesota.	4,076	4,376	4,919	5,021	5,052	5,086	5,114	5,155	5,198
Mississippi	2,521	2,575	2,845	2,859	2,868	2,887	2,900	2,899	2,919
Missouri	4,917	5,117	5,597	5,676	5,706	5,745	5,788	5,838	5,878
Montana.	787	799	902	910	917	927	936	947	958
Nebraska	1,570	1,578	1,711	1,726	1,735	1,744	1,754	1,764	1,775
Nevada	800	1,202	1,998	2,168	2,238	2,330	2,409	2,492	2,565
New Hampshire	921	1,109	1,236	1,272	1,283	1,294	1,303	1,312	1,316
New Jersey.	7,365	7,748	8,414	8,558	8,605	8,641	8,657	8,666	8,686
New Mexico	1,303	1,515	1,819	1,851	1,870	1,892	1,916	1,942	1,970
New York	17,558	17,991	18,977	19,133	19,208	19,258	19,263	19,282	19,298
North Carolina	5,882	6,632	8,046	8,319	8,421	8,538	8,679	8,869	9,061
North Dakota.	653	639	642	634	633	637	636	637	640
Ohio	10,798	10,847	11,353	11,415	11,436	11,453	11,460	11,464	11,467
Oklahoma.	3,025	3,146	3,451	3,486	3,500	3,517	3,536	3,578	3,617
Oregon.	2,633	2,842	3,421	3,522	3,557	3,583	3,630	3,691	3,747
Pennsylvania.	11,864	11,883	12,281	12,306	12,327	12,349	12,367	12,403	12,433
Rhode Island.	947	1,003	1,048	1,067	1,073	1,073	1,067	1,062	1,058
South Carolina.	3,122	3,486	4,012	4,105	4,147	4,201	4,255	4,330	4,408
South Dakota.	691	696	755	762	767	774	780	788	796
Tennessee	4,591	4,877	5,689	5,802	5,853	5,912	5,989	6,075	6,157
Texas.	14,229	16,986	20,852	21,730	22,086	22,455	22,844	23,408	23,904
Utah	1,461	1,723	2,233	2,337	2,373	2,431	2,505	2,580	2,645
Vermont	511	563	609	615	617	619	620	621	621
Virginia.	5,347	6,189	7,079	7,282	7,371	7,464	7,558	7,640	7,712
Washington.	4,132	4,867	5,894	6,062	6,119	6,190	6,271	6,375	6,468
West Virginia.	1,950	1,793	1,808	1,800	1,803	1,805	1,806	1,809	1,812
Wisconsin	4,706	4,892	5,364	5,445	5,475	5,510	5,540	5,573	5,602
Wyoming	470	454	494	497	499	503	507	513	523

[1] See footnote 3, Table 1.   [2] The April 1, 1990, census counts include corrections processed through August 1997, results of special censuses and test censuses, and do not include adjustments for census coverage errors.   [3] Reflects modifications to the Census 2000 population as documented in the Count Question Resolution program and geographic program revisions.

Source: U.S. Census Bureau, Current Population Reports, P25-1106; "Table CO-EST2001-12-00 - Time Series of Intercensal State Populaton Estimates: April 1, 1990 to April 1, 2000"; published 11 April 2002; <http://www.census.gov/popest/archives/2000s /vintage2001/CO-EST2001-12/CO-EST2001-12-00.html>; and "Table 1: Annual Estimates of the Population for the United States, Regions, and States, and for Puerto Rico: April 1, 2000 to July 1, 2007 (NST-EST2007-01)" published 27 December 2007; <http://www.census.gov/popest/states/NST-ann-est.html>.

Population   17

Table 13. State Population—Rank, Percent Change, and Population Density: 1980 to 2007

[**As of April 1, except 2007, as of July 1.** Insofar as possible, population shown for all years is that of present area of state. For area figures of states, see Table 344. Minus sign (–) indicates decrease. See Appendix III]

State	Rank				Percent change			Population per square mile of land area [1]		
	1980	1990	2000	2007	1980–1990	1990–2000	2000–2007	1990	2000	2007
United States.	(X)	(X)	(X)	(X)	9.8	13.1	7.2	70.3	79.6	85.3
Alabama	22	22	23	23	3.8	10.1	4.1	79.6	87.6	91.2
Alaska	50	49	48	47	36.9	14.0	9.0	1.0	1.1	1.2
Arizona.	29	24	20	16	34.8	40.0	23.5	32.3	45.2	55.8
Arkansas.	33	33	33	32	2.8	13.7	6.0	45.1	51.3	54.4
California.	1	1	1	1	26.0	13.6	7.9	191.1	217.2	234.4
Colorado	28	26	24	22	14.0	30.6	13.0	31.8	41.5	46.9
Connecticut	25	27	29	29	5.8	3.6	2.8	678.5	702.9	722.9
Delaware.	47	46	45	45	12.1	17.6	10.4	341.0	401.1	442.7
District of Columbia. . .	(X)	(X)	(X)	(X)	–4.9	–5.7	2.8	9,884.4	9,316.4	9,581.3
Florida	7	4	4	4	32.7	23.5	14.2	239.9	296.4	338.4
Georgia	13	11	10	9	18.6	26.4	16.6	111.9	141.4	164.8
Hawaii	39	41	42	42	14.9	9.3	5.9	172.6	188.6	199.8
Idaho	41	42	39	39	6.7	28.5	15.9	12.2	15.6	18.1
Illinois.	5	6	5	5	(Z)	8.7	3.5	205.6	223.4	231.2
Indiana	12	14	14	15	1.0	9.7	4.4	154.6	169.5	176.9
Iowa.	27	30	30	30	–4.7	5.4	2.1	49.7	52.4	53.5
Kansas.	32	32	32	33	4.8	8.5	3.2	30.3	32.9	33.9
Kentucky.	23	23	25	26	0.7	9.6	4.9	92.8	101.7	106.8
Louisiana	19	21	22	25	0.4	5.9	–3.9	96.9	102.6	98.6
Maine	38	38	40	40	9.2	3.8	3.3	39.8	41.3	42.7
Maryland.	18	19	19	19	13.4	10.8	6.1	489.1	541.9	574.8
Massachusetts	11	13	13	14	4.9	5.5	1.6	767.4	809.8	822.7
Michigan	8	8	8	8	0.4	6.9	1.3	163.6	175.0	177.3
Minnesota	21	20	21	21	7.4	12.4	5.7	55.0	61.8	65.3
Mississippi.	31	31	31	31	2.2	10.5	2.6	54.9	60.6	62.2
Missouri	15	15	17	18	4.1	9.4	5.0	74.3	81.2	85.3
Montana	44	44	44	44	1.6	12.9	6.2	5.5	6.2	6.6
Nebraska	35	36	38	38	0.5	8.4	3.7	20.5	22.3	23.1
Nevada	43	39	35	35	50.1	66.3	28.4	10.9	18.2	23.4
New Hampshire	42	40	41	41	20.5	11.4	6.5	123.7	137.8	146.7
New Jersey	9	9	9	11	5.2	8.6	3.2	1,044.5	1,134.4	1,171.0
New Mexico.	37	37	36	36	16.3	20.1	8.3	12.5	15.0	16.2
New York	2	2	3	3	2.5	5.5	1.7	381.0	401.9	408.7
North Carolina	10	10	11	10	12.8	21.3	12.6	136.2	165.2	186.0
North Dakota	46	47	47	48	–2.1	0.5	–0.4	9.3	9.3	9.3
Ohio.	6	7	7	7	0.5	4.7	1.0	264.9	277.3	280.0
Oklahoma	26	28	27	28	4.0	9.7	4.8	45.8	50.3	52.7
Oregon	30	29	28	27	7.9	20.4	9.5	29.6	35.6	39.0
Pennsylvania	4	5	6	6	0.2	3.4	1.2	265.1	274.0	277.4
Rhode Island	40	43	43	43	5.9	4.5	0.9	960.3	1,003.2	1,012.3
South Carolina	24	25	26	24	11.7	15.1	9.9	115.8	133.2	146.4
South Dakota.	45	45	46	46	0.8	8.5	5.5	9.2	9.9	10.5
Tennessee.	17	17	16	17	6.2	16.7	8.2	118.3	138.0	149.4
Texas	3	3	2	2	19.4	22.8	14.6	64.9	79.6	91.3
Utah.	36	35	34	34	17.9	29.6	18.5	21.0	27.2	32.2
Vermont	48	48	49	49	10.0	8.2	2.0	60.8	65.8	67.2
Virginia	14	12	12	12	15.8	14.4	8.9	156.3	178.8	194.8
Washington	20	18	15	13	17.8	21.1	9.7	73.1	88.6	97.2
West Virginia	34	34	37	37	–8.0	0.8	0.2	74.5	75.1	75.3
Wisconsin	16	16	18	20	4.0	9.6	4.4	90.1	98.8	103.1
Wyoming.	49	50	50	50	–3.4	8.9	5.9	4.7	5.1	5.4

X Not applicable. Z Less than 0.05 percent. [1] Persons per square mile were calculated on the basis of land area data from the 2000 census.

Source: U.S. Census Bureau, Current Population Reports, P25-1106; "ST-99-3 State Population Estimates: Annual Time Series, July 1, 1990 to July 1, 1999"; published 29 December 1999; <http://www.census.gov/population/estimates/state /st-99-3.txt>; *Population Change and Distribution: 1990 to 2000, Census 2000 Brief*, (C2KBR/01-2), April 2001; and "Table 2: Cumulative Estimates of Population Change for the United States, Regions, States, and Puerto Rico and Region and State Rankings: April 1, 2000 to July 1, 2007"; release date: December 27, 2007; <http://www.census.gov/popest/states/tables /NST-EST2007-02.xls>.

Table 14. **State Resident Population—Projections: 2010 to 2030**

[**As of July 1. 4,596 represents 4,596,000**. These state projections were produced in correspondence with the U.S. interim projections released in March 2004. Projections in this table were developed for each of the 50 states and the District of Columbia by age and sex for the years 2000 to 2030, based on Census 2000 results. These projections differ from forecasts in that they represent the results of the mathematical projection model given that current state-specific trends in fertility, mortality, domestic migration, and net international migration continue. The projections to 2007 have been superseded by population estimates which are shown in Table 12. Minus sign (–) indicates decrease]

State	Number (1,000)					Change, **2000–2030**		Rank	
	2010	**2015**	**2020**	**2025**	**2030**	Number (1,000)	Percent	Total population, **2030**	Percent change, **2000–2030**
Alabama	4,596	4,663	4,729	4,800	4,874	427	9.6	24	35
Alaska.	694	733	774	821	868	241	38.4	46	12
Arizona	6,637	7,495	8,456	9,532	10,712	5,582	108.8	10	2
Arkansas.	2,875	2,969	3,060	3,151	3,240	567	21.2	32	21
California.	38,067	40,123	42,207	44,305	46,445	12,573	37.1	1	13
Colorado	4,832	5,049	5,279	5,523	5,792	1,491	34.7	22	14
Connecticut	3,577	3,635	3,676	3,691	3,689	283	8.3	30	38
Delaware.	884	927	963	991	1,013	229	29.2	45	18
District of Columbia . .	530	506	481	455	433	–139	–24.2	(X)	(X)
Florida.	19,252	21,204	23,407	25,912	28,686	12,703	79.5	3	3
Georgia.	9,589	10,231	10,844	11,439	12,018	3,831	46.8	8	8
Hawaii.	1,341	1,386	1,412	1,439	1,466	255	21.0	41	22
Idaho	1,517	1,630	1,741	1,853	1,970	676	52.2	37	6
Illinois	12,917	13,097	13,237	13,341	13,433	1,014	8.2	5	39
Indiana	6,392	6,518	6,627	6,721	6,810	730	12.0	18	31
Iowa	3,010	3,026	3,020	2,993	2,955	29	1.0	34	48
Kansas	2,805	2,853	2,891	2,919	2,940	252	9.4	35	36
Kentucky	4,265	4,351	4,424	4,490	4,555	513	12.7	27	30
Louisiana.	4,613	4,674	4,719	4,762	4,803	334	7.5	26	41
Maine	1,357	1,389	1,409	1,414	1,411	136	10.7	42	32
Maryland	5,905	6,208	6,498	6,763	7,022	1,726	32.6	16	16
Massachusetts	6,649	6,759	6,856	6,939	7,012	663	10.4	17	33
Michigan	10,429	10,599	10,696	10,714	10,694	756	7.6	11	40
Minnesota	5,421	5,668	5,901	6,109	6,306	1,387	28.2	20	20
Mississippi	2,971	3,014	3,045	3,069	3,092	248	8.7	33	37
Missouri.	5,922	6,070	6,200	6,315	6,430	835	14.9	19	27
Montana	969	999	1,023	1,037	1,045	143	15.8	44	25
Nebraska.	1,769	1,789	1,803	1,813	1,820	109	6.4	38	42
Nevada	2,691	3,058	3,452	3,863	4,282	2,284	114.3	28	1
New Hampshire	1,386	1,457	1,525	1,586	1,646	411	33.2	40	15
New Jersey	9,018	9,256	9,462	9,637	9,802	1,388	16.5	13	24
New Mexico.	1,980	2,042	2,084	2,107	2,100	281	15.4	36	26
New York.	19,444	19,547	19,577	19,540	19,477	501	2.6	4	46
North Carolina	9,346	10,011	10,709	11,449	12,228	4,178	51.9	7	7
North Dakota	637	635	630	621	607	–36	–5.5	49	50
Ohio	11,576	11,635	11,644	11,606	11,551	197	1.7	9	47
Oklahoma	3,592	3,662	3,736	3,821	3,913	463	13.4	29	29
Oregon	3,791	4,013	4,260	4,536	4,834	1,413	41.3	25	10
Pennsylvania	12,584	12,711	12,787	12,802	12,768	487	4.0	6	45
Rhode Island	1,117	1,140	1,154	1,158	1,153	105	10.0	43	34
South Carolina	4,447	4,642	4,823	4,990	5,149	1,137	28.3	23	19
South Dakota	786	797	802	802	800	46	6.0	47	43
Tennessee	6,231	6,502	6,781	7,073	7,381	1,691	29.7	15	17
Texas	24,649	26,586	28,635	30,865	33,318	12,466	59.8	2	4
Utah	2,595	2,783	2,990	3,226	3,485	1,252	56.1	31	5
Vermont	653	673	691	703	712	103	16.9	48	23
Virginia	8,010	8,467	8,917	9,364	9,825	2,747	38.8	12	11
Washington	6,542	6,951	7,432	7,996	8,625	2,731	46.3	14	9
West Virginia	1,829	1,823	1,801	1,766	1,720	–88	–4.9	39	49
Wisconsin	5,727	5,883	6,005	6,088	6,151	787	14.7	21	28
Wyoming	520	528	531	529	523	29	5.9	50	44

X Not applicable.

Source: U.S. Census Bureau, "Table A1: Interim Projections of the Total Population for the United States and States: April 1, 2000 to July 1, 2030"; published 21 April 2005; <http://www.census.gov/population/www/projections/projectionsagesex.html>.

Population   19

Table 15. State Resident Population—Components of Change: 2000 to 2007

[Covers period April 1, 2000, to July 1, 2007. Minus sign (–) indicates net decrease or net outflow]

State	Numeric population change [1]	Births	Deaths	Natural increase (births minus deaths)	Net migration Total	Net migration International [2]	Net migration Internal
United States	**20,196,555**	**29,809,472**	**17,597,188**	**12,212,284**	**7,984,271**	**7,984,271**	**(X)**
Alabama	180,500	437,898	335,018	102,880	90,493	30,650	59,843
Alaska.	56,547	74,878	21,712	53,166	–889	4,236	–5,125
Arizona	1,208,140	671,105	318,103	353,002	869,368	214,014	655,354
Arkansas	161,399	279,228	200,926	78,302	90,101	27,119	62,982
California	2,681,560	3,944,853	1,712,456	2,232,397	583,434	1,807,426	–1,223,992
Colorado	559,496	499,880	208,563	291,317	274,296	141,730	132,566
Connecticut	96,707	306,540	214,530	92,010	19,631	97,695	–78,064
Delaware	81,164	82,506	51,349	31,157	53,497	13,924	39,573
District of Columbia . . .	16,233	56,509	40,913	15,596	–17,648	25,783	–43,431
Florida.	2,268,419	1,578,928	1,217,956	360,972	1,960,446	674,271	1,286,175
Georgia.	1,357,934	1,001,287	479,305	521,982	725,733	240,814	484,919
Hawaii.	71,851	130,786	64,005	66,781	10,308	30,891	–20,583
Idaho	205,446	161,485	73,002	88,483	117,935	17,520	100,415
Illinois	432,901	1,324,293	760,202	564,091	–131,259	420,052	–551,311
Indiana	264,768	631,323	401,809	229,514	53,405	69,836	–16,431
Iowa	61,664	280,703	199,214	81,489	–14,031	36,217	–50,248
Kansas	87,173	286,874	177,032	109,842	–21,001	46,314	–67,315
Kentucky	199,193	401,673	290,796	110,877	94,672	30,881	63,791
Louisiana	–175,754	460,782	304,187	156,595	–312,739	22,477	–335,216
Maine	42,286	100,801	90,157	10,644	36,665	5,275	31,390
Maryland	321,836	543,744	315,834	227,910	81,385	135,800	–54,415
Massachusetts	100,650	574,867	402,613	172,254	–99,252	206,438	–305,690
Michigan	133,340	948,153	628,764	319,389	–204,072	155,686	–359,758
Minnesota	278,129	509,246	271,135	238,111	54,639	89,636	–34,997
Mississippi	74,129	311,575	205,552	106,023	–19,610	10,429	–30,039
Missouri.	281,732	563,796	394,940	168,856	92,888	51,809	41,079
Montana	55,666	83,417	59,570	23,847	32,545	2,099	30,446
Nebraska.	63,306	187,564	109,569	77,995	–9,319	27,398	–36,717
Nevada	567,125	251,500	127,010	124,490	449,261	84,578	364,683
New Hampshire	80,042	107,694	72,233	35,461	49,610	13,928	35,682
New Jersey	271,573	819,551	528,291	291,260	–640	376,519	–377,159
New Mexico	150,869	204,913	105,298	99,615	58,745	33,790	24,955
New York.	320,908	1,820,204	1,121,233	698,971	–589,175	859,994	–1,449,169
North Carolina	1,014,541	880,162	527,263	352,899	679,832	188,925	490,907
North Dakota	–2,485	58,630	42,022	16,608	–16,347	3,184	–19,531
Ohio	113,772	1,088,880	786,868	302,012	–207,387	94,461	–301,848
Oklahoma	166,662	372,792	251,811	120,981	54,047	42,146	11,901
Oregon	326,019	336,646	222,770	113,876	228,050	91,629	136,376
Pennsylvania	151,738	1,050,424	935,629	114,795	83,889	128,305	–44,416
Rhode Island	9,513	91,870	71,316	20,554	–6,375	23,874	–30,249
South Carolina	395,893	409,724	276,833	132,891	269,092	40,959	228,133
South Dakota	41,370	80,804	49,742	31,062	6,977	4,461	2,516
Tennessee	467,457	579,255	410,498	168,757	278,058	60,929	217,129
Texas	3,052,581	2,759,655	1,124,640	1,635,015	1,424,673	842,595	582,078
Utah	412,132	367,188	95,054	272,134	93,987	63,278	30,709
Vermont	12,427	47,131	36,718	10,413	4,667	5,046	–379
Virginia	633,061	740,719	416,604	324,115	314,832	159,627	155,205
Washington	574,284	597,061	330,009	267,052	320,442	164,951	155,491
West Virginia	3,685	150,776	151,717	–941	12,048	4,246	7,802
Wisconsin	237,925	510,107	334,748	175,359	52,748	58,366	–5,618
Wyoming	29,048	49,092	29,669	19,423	11,661	2,060	9,601

X Not applicable.   [1] The estimated components of population change will not sum to the numerical population change due to the process of controlling to national totals.   [2] Net international migration includes the international migration of both native and foreign-born populations. Specifically, it includes: (a) the net international migration of the foreign born, (b) the net migration between the United States and Puerto Rico, (c) the emigration of natives from the United States, and (d) the net overseas movement of the Armed Forces population.

Source: U.S. Census Bureau, "Cumulative Estimates of the Components of Population Change for the United States, Regions, and States: April 1, 2000 to July 1, 2007 (NST-EST2007-04);" release date: December 27, 2007; <http://www.census.gov /popest/states/tables/NST-EST2007-04.xls>.

Table 16. **Resident Population by Age and State: 2007**

[In thousands, except percent (301,621 represents 301,621,000). **As of July**. Includes Armed Forces stationed in area]

State	Total	Under 5 years	5 to 17 years	18 to 24 years	25 to 34 years	35 to 44 years	45 to 54 years	55 to 64 years	65 to 74 years	75 to 84 years	85 years and over	Percent 65 years and over
U.S.	301,621	20,724	53,178	29,492	40,591	43,161	43,875	32,712	19,352	13,024	5,512	12.6
AL.	4,628	308	815	447	606	630	668	528	333	210	82	13.5
AK.	683	51	131	73	101	98	110	72	29	14	5	7.0
AZ.	6,339	500	1,170	591	917	863	824	654	421	287	113	12.9
AR.	2,835	199	502	264	379	378	392	324	207	133	57	14.0
CA.	36,553	2,660	6,724	3,832	5,235	5,438	5,100	3,561	2,049	1,370	585	11.0
CO.	4,862	350	843	460	735	724	735	523	265	163	65	10.1
CT.	3,502	211	609	323	403	528	555	401	229	166	78	13.5
DE.	865	59	147	85	108	124	126	99	62	41	15	13.6
DC.	588	36	78	74	108	85	76	62	36	23	11	11.9
FL.	18,251	1,148	2,895	1,595	2,289	2,543	2,578	2,104	1,479	1,126	494	17.0
GA.	9,545	737	1,794	904	1,382	1,463	1,346	976	524	300	118	9.9
HI	1,283	87	199	123	179	178	183	150	87	68	29	14.3
ID	1,499	119	289	147	209	194	206	161	92	58	25	11.7
IL.	12,853	891	2,308	1,292	1,779	1,841	1,860	1,332	785	530	234	12.1
IN	6,345	437	1,149	605	852	884	931	690	408	273	115	12.5
IA	2,988	196	515	305	365	391	443	334	207	154	77	14.7
KS.	2,776	196	500	290	361	367	406	296	174	125	61	13.0
KY.	4,241	278	726	384	588	603	625	488	295	182	72	13.0
LA.	4,293	298	781	466	570	569	622	464	277	177	69	12.2
ME.	1,317	71	209	112	150	189	219	173	99	68	28	14.8
MD.	5,618	377	982	540	721	848	865	624	350	222	89	11.8
MA.	6,450	377	1,056	641	824	974	989	729	415	304	140	13.3
MI	10,072	633	1,814	974	1,262	1,430	1,537	1,142	655	443	182	12.7
MN.	5,198	354	906	507	687	743	804	560	317	215	105	12.2
MS.	2,919	219	549	302	382	384	406	312	193	121	51	12.5
MO.	5,878	393	1,032	558	776	804	870	656	402	268	118	13.4
MT.	958	59	160	94	117	119	153	121	69	45	20	14.0
NE.	1,775	130	316	187	229	230	257	189	114	83	40	13.3
NV.	2,565	195	465	210	385	382	356	286	163	92	30	11.1
NH.	1,316	75	223	119	151	201	220	160	85	56	24	12.6
NJ	8,686	557	1,507	766	1,070	1,349	1,342	960	569	397	169	13.1
NM.	1,970	145	355	205	264	256	278	217	132	85	34	12.7
NY.	19,298	1,197	3,217	1,975	2,523	2,844	2,854	2,142	1,282	880	385	13.2
NC.	9,061	638	1,580	855	1,219	1,341	1,301	1,023	592	369	143	12.2
ND.	640	40	103	83	79	77	95	69	43	33	17	14.6
OH.	11,467	736	2,015	1,075	1,461	1,592	1,745	1,297	781	542	222	13.5
OK.	3,617	261	638	372	493	467	508	398	251	161	68	13.3
OR.	3,747	236	627	336	528	513	562	457	249	166	73	13.1
PA.	12,433	730	2,057	1,197	1,455	1,734	1,920	1,451	896	692	302	15.2
RI	1,058	61	172	115	130	154	161	119	68	53	25	13.9
SC.	4,408	296	764	431	573	614	632	525	311	189	72	13.0
SD.	796	56	140	82	99	99	117	89	54	40	20	14.3
TN.	6,157	410	1,062	552	846	883	898	714	429	261	102	12.9
TX.	23,904	1,989	4,634	2,433	3,528	3,430	3,234	2,261	1,278	798	318	10.0
UT.	2,645	256	561	328	430	319	304	213	124	79	31	8.9
VT	621	32	99	61	70	88	104	82	44	29	12	13.6
VA	7,712	518	1,308	761	1,052	1,160	1,145	858	490	302	117	11.8
WA	6,468	423	1,113	598	907	939	986	745	394	252	111	11.7
WV	1,812	104	283	159	232	242	276	235	146	98	37	15.5
WI	5,602	356	965	550	712	790	867	625	365	256	115	13.1
WY	523	36	89	53	70	66	83	62	34	21	9	12.2

Source: U.S. Census Bureau, "Annual Estimates of the Population by Sex and Age for States and for Puerto Rico: April 1, 2000 to July 1, 2007"; release date: May 1, 2008; <http://www.census.gov/popest/states/asrh/SC-EST2007-02.html>.

Table 17. **Resident Population by Age and State—Projections: 2010 and 2015**

[**As of July 1. 1,092 represents 1,092,000**. These projections were produced in correspondence with the U.S. interim projections released in March 2004. Projections in this table were developed for each of the 50 states and the District of Columbia by age and sex for the years 2000 to 2030, based on Census 2000 results. These projections differ from forecasts in that they represent the results of the mathematical projection model given that current state-specific trends in fertility, mortality, domestic migration and net international migration continue. The projections to 2007 have been superseded by population estimates which are shown in Table 16]

| State | Population (1,000) | | | | | | | | | | Percent of population, 2015 | |
| | Under 18 years old | | 18 to 44 years old | | 45 to 64 years old | | 65 to 74 years old | | 75 years old and over | | Under 18 years old | 65 years old and over |
	2010	2015	2010	2015	2010	2015	2010	2015	2010	2015		
AL.	1,092	1,089	1,605	1,575	1,251	1,259	354	427	295	312	23.4	15.9
AK.	184	199	270	280	184	178	35	49	21	26	27.2	10.2
AZ.	1,688	1,892	2,349	2,529	1,678	1,892	516	711	406	470	25.2	15.8
AR.	703	721	996	998	765	782	227	274	185	194	24.3	15.8
CA.	9,497	9,820	14,787	15,240	9,391	9,835	2,333	2,972	2,060	2,256	24.5	13.0
CO	1,189	1,256	1,863	1,886	1,263	1,280	282	369	235	258	24.9	12.4
CT.	814	807	1,257	1,251	990	1,001	253	308	262	270	22.2	15.9
DE.	202	210	309	305	249	264	68	87	57	61	22.6	16.0
DC	114	112	237	225	118	108	32	34	29	27	22.1	12.2
FL.	4,086	4,455	6,315	6,614	5,431	6,002	1,773	2,345	1,646	1,789	21.0	19.5
GA	2,502	2,679	3,724	3,822	2,382	2,543	564	723	417	464	26.2	11.6
HI	316	330	477	479	357	350	101	131	90	96	23.8	16.3
ID	400	427	554	583	381	400	99	129	82	91	26.2	13.5
IL	3,197	3,215	4,842	4,798	3,277	3,307	826	979	774	799	24.5	13.6
IN	1,596	1,614	2,328	2,333	1,656	1,664	425	508	386	398	24.8	13.9
IA	711	707	1,049	1,031	800	794	217	259	233	236	23.4	16.3
KS.	699	708	1,004	1,001	727	724	185	225	190	194	24.8	14.7
KY.	1,002	1,007	1,540	1,526	1,165	1,181	309	376	249	262	23.1	14.6
LA	1,172	1,176	1,665	1,642	1,194	1,192	313	379	270	285	25.2	14.2
ME	269	269	462	455	413	415	110	142	102	108	19.3	18.0
MD	1,406	1,487	2,212	2,283	1,568	1,601	386	478	332	359	23.9	13.5
MA	1,484	1,474	2,440	2,402	1,817	1,857	454	567	454	458	21.8	15.2
MI	2,487	2,479	3,822	3,799	2,785	2,814	699	852	635	654	23.4	14.2
MN	1,290	1,349	2,027	2,069	1,433	1,475	343	429	327	346	23.8	13.7
MS	759	753	1,052	1,028	781	801	209	254	170	179	25.0	14.4
MO	1,411	1,436	2,111	2,123	1,578	1,589	432	518	390	404	23.7	15.2
MT	212	216	324	326	287	284	77	100	68	74	21.6	17.4
NE.	446	454	619	608	460	455	119	145	125	126	25.4	15.2
NV.	665	752	961	1,033	735	851	199	264	131	158	24.6	13.8
NH	304	313	494	508	408	418	97	129	82	88	21.5	14.9
NJ.	2,088	2,104	3,252	3,239	2,446	2,528	632	760	600	625	22.7	15.0
NM	479	485	669	654	553	560	153	201	126	142	23.7	16.8
NY.	4,421	4,353	7,227	7,077	5,144	5,173	1,346	1,589	1,306	1,354	22.3	15.1
NC	2,269	2,438	3,471	3,586	2,445	2,611	641	810	520	565	24.4	13.7
ND	142	139	223	219	174	169	46	56	51	51	21.8	17.0
OH	2,744	2,723	4,123	4,054	3,121	3,093	816	980	771	786	23.4	15.2
OK	895	915	1,264	1,260	938	933	266	316	229	238	25.0	15.1
OR	863	916	1,412	1,470	1,022	1,036	263	348	231	242	22.8	14.7
PA.	2,748	2,741	4,385	4,334	3,496	3,487	960	1,159	997	990	21.6	16.9
RI	249	248	410	412	300	304	76	94	82	81	21.8	15.4
SC.	1,036	1,061	1,579	1,581	1,226	1,271	343	439	263	290	22.9	15.7
SD.	194	196	269	264	209	209	55	67	60	61	24.6	16.1
TN.	1,479	1,539	2,249	2,275	1,673	1,720	461	570	368	399	23.7	14.9
TX.	6,785	7,376	9,417	9,848	5,859	6,248	1,426	1,826	1,162	1,287	27.7	11.7
UT.	819	872	1,021	1,073	520	556	127	162	108	119	31.3	10.1
VT.	132	132	232	235	195	193	50	67	43	46	19.6	16.9
VA.	1,880	1,982	2,997	3,085	2,139	2,207	554	703	441	490	23.4	14.1
WA	1,488	1,561	2,481	2,591	1,777	1,833	429	567	367	399	22.5	13.9
WV	382	373	618	595	536	525	156	190	136	140	20.4	18.1
WI.	1,319	1,343	2,076	2,067	1,561	1,591	392	487	380	395	22.8	15.0
WY	116	115	177	174	154	150	40	52	33	37	21.9	16.8

Source: U.S. Census Bureau, "File 2. Annual projections by 5-year and selected age groups by sex"; published 21 April 2005; <http://www.census.gov/population/www/projections/projectionsagesex.html>.

U.S. Census Bureau, Statistical Abstract of the United States: 2009

Table 18. **Resident Population by Race, Hispanic Origin, and State: 2007**

[**In thousands (301,621 represents 301,621,000). As of July**. Persons of Hispanic origin may be any race. Due to the complexities associated with the production of detailed characteristics' estimates at the state level, the values of the estimates at lower levels of geography may not necessarily sum to estimates at higher levels of geography]

State	Total population	One race					Two or more races	Hispanic origin	Not Hispanic White alone
		White alone	Black or African American alone	American Indian/ Alaska Native alone	Asian alone	Native Hawaiian and Other Pacific Islander alone			
U.S....	**301,621**	**241,167**	**38,756**	**2,938**	**13,366**	**537**	**4,856**	**45,504**	**199,092**
AL........	4,628	3,287	1,224	24	44	2	46	125	3,176
AK........	683	484	28	104	31	4	32	40	452
AZ........	6,339	5,513	252	297	157	13	106	1,878	3,743
AR........	2,835	2,293	448	23	30	3	37	150	2,154
CA........	36,553	28,082	2,450	423	4,544	153	901	13,221	15,624
CO........	4,862	4,370	206	57	130	7	92	966	3,468
CT........	3,502	2,959	361	13	120	3	48	403	2,604
DE........	865	644	180	3	25	1	12	56	594
DC........	588	232	325	2	20	1	9	49	191
FL........	18,251	14,604	2,897	84	412	17	239	3,756	11,099
GA........	9,545	6,259	2,864	33	269	8	112	741	5,584
HI........	1,283	374	37	7	512	114	239	105	317
ID........	1,499	1,421	13	22	18	2	24	147	1,283
IL........	12,853	10,177	1,927	42	549	9	149	1,920	8,353
IN........	6,345	5,593	572	19	86	3	73	315	5,301
IA........	2,988	2,820	77	12	47	1	31	120	2,708
KS........	2,776	2,467	169	28	62	2	49	244	2,240
KY........	4,241	3,817	327	11	42	2	43	95	3,732
LA........	4,293	2,793	1,369	27	62	2	40	137	2,674
ME........	1,317	1,271	13	8	12	(Z)	13	16	1,257
MD........	5,618	3,571	1,655	19	282	4	87	356	3,263
MA........	6,450	5,576	448	19	315	5	86	528	5,142
MI........	10,072	8,175	1,442	61	238	4	152	403	7,813
MN........	5,198	4,640	233	61	182	3	78	206	4,456
MS........	2,919	1,771	1,087	14	24	1	23	60	1,719
MO........	5,878	5,001	678	29	86	4	81	178	4,839
MT........	958	868	6	61	6	1	16	27	845
NE........	1,775	1,625	79	18	30	1	22	134	1,500
NV........	2,565	2,087	204	36	158	13	67	644	1,487
NH........	1,316	1,258	16	4	25	1	13	33	1,228
NJ........	8,686	6,624	1,260	28	652	7	114	1,382	5,400
NM........	1,970	1,664	56	186	28	3	33	875	834
NY........	19,298	14,194	3,347	106	1,339	20	291	3,162	11,633
NC........	9,061	6,704	1,967	112	171	6	101	638	6,121
ND........	640	586	7	34	5	(Z)	7	12	575
OH........	11,467	9,731	1,378	28	181	4	146	284	9,483
OK........	3,617	2,833	287	286	63	4	145	262	2,598
OR........	3,747	3,383	74	52	137	11	91	396	3,016
PA........	12,433	10,640	1,338	25	300	6	124	556	10,168
RI........	1,058	938	67	6	29	1	16	119	839
SC........	4,408	3,025	1,266	18	53	2	43	169	2,878
SD........	796	704	9	66	6	(Z)	11	18	688
TN........	6,157	4,948	1,039	20	82	3	65	215	4,755
TX........	23,904	19,742	2,857	171	814	29	291	8,600	11,444
UT........	2,645	2,465	32	35	52	19	41	307	2,177
VT........	621	599	5	2	7	(Z)	7	8	592
VA........	7,712	5,642	1,538	27	371	6	127	508	5,187
WA........	6,468	5,473	235	106	431	30	195	610	4,920
WV........	1,812	1,714	64	4	12	1	16	19	1,697
WI........	5,602	5,034	337	53	113	2	62	272	4,784
WY........	523	492	6	13	4	(Z)	7	38	457

Z Less than 500.

Source: U.S. Census Bureau, "Annual State Population Estimates by Demographic Characteristics with 6 Race Groups (5 Race Alone Groups and One Group with Two or more Race Groups): April 1, 2000 to July 1, 2007"; release date: May 1, 2008; <http://www.census.gov/popest/states/asrh/files/SC-EST2007-alldata6.csv>.

U.S. Census Bureau, Statistical Abstract of the United States: 2009

Table 19. **Large Metropolitan Statistical Areas—Population: 1990 to 2007**

[1990 and 2000, as of April 1; beginning 2005 as of July 1 (658 represents 658,000). Covers metropolitan statistical areas with 250,000 and over population in 2007, as defined by the U.S. Office of Management and Budget as of December 2006. All geographic boundaries for 2000 to 2007 population estimates are defined as of January 1, 2007. For definitions and components of all metropolitan and micropolitan areas, see Appendix II. Minus sign (−) indicates decrease]

Metropolitan statistical area	Number (1,000)					Percent change		Rank, 2007
	1990	2000, estimates base [1]	2005	2006	2007	1990 to 2000	2000 to 2007 [1]	
Akron, OH	658	695	701	700	699	5.7	0.6	71
Albany-Schenectady-Troy, NY	810	826	847	851	853	2.0	3.3	57
Albuquerque, NM	599	730	799	818	835	21.7	14.5	60
Allentown-Bethlehem-Easton, PA-NJ	687	740	786	795	804	7.8	8.6	62
Anchorage, AK	266	320	352	359	362	20.1	13.4	137
Ann Arbor, MI	283	323	345	348	350	14.1	8.4	141
Asheville, NC	308	369	391	398	404	19.9	9.5	122
Atlanta-Sandy Springs-Marietta, GA	3,069	4,248	4,957	5,128	5,279	38.4	24.3	9
Atlantic City, NJ	224	253	269	270	271	12.6	7.2	165
Augusta-Richmond County, GA-SC	436	500	518	523	529	14.7	5.8	95
Austin-Round Rock, TX	846	1,250	1,469	1,532	1,598	47.7	27.9	37
Bakersfield, CA	545	662	751	773	791	21.4	19.5	64
Baltimore-Towson, MD	2,382	2,553	2,650	2,663	2,668	7.2	4.5	20
Baton Rouge, LA	624	706	730	764	770	13.2	9.1	67
Beaumont-Port Arthur, TX	361	385	381	374	376	6.6	−2.3	131
Birmingham-Hoover, AL	957	1,051	1,088	1,100	1,108	10.0	5.4	47
Boise City-Nampa, ID	320	465	545	568	588	45.4	26.4	86
Boston-Cambridge-Quincy, MA-NH	4,134	4,392	4,455	4,466	4,483	6.2	2.1	10
Boulder, CO [2]	209	270	283	286	290	29.1	7.6	157
Bridgeport-Stamford-Norwalk, CT	828	883	895	894	895	6.6	1.4	56
Brownsville-Harlingen, TX	260	335	373	380	387	28.9	15.5	128
Buffalo-Niagara Falls, NY	1,189	1,170	1,141	1,133	1,128	−1.6	−3.6	46
Canton-Massillon, OH	394	407	408	407	407	3.3	0.1	120
Cape Coral-Fort Myers, FL	335	441	542	570	591	31.6	33.9	85
Cedar Rapids, IA	211	237	247	250	253	12.6	6.6	174
Charleston, WV	308	310	305	304	304	0.6	−1.8	151
Charleston-North Charleston, SC	507	549	602	617	630	8.3	14.8	81
Charlotte-Gastonia-Concord, NC-SC	1,025	1,330	1,522	1,585	1,652	29.8	24.1	35
Chattanooga, TN-GA	433	477	503	510	515	10.0	8.0	97
Chicago-Naperville-Joliet, IL-IN-WI	8,182	9,099	9,407	9,458	9,525	11.2	4.7	3
Cincinnati-Middletown, OH-KY-IN	1,845	2,010	2,103	2,121	2,134	8.9	6.2	24
Clarksville, TN-KY	189	232	252	253	262	22.6	12.8	169
Cleveland-Elyria-Mentor, OH	2,102	2,148	2,119	2,105	2,096	2.2	−2.4	25
Colorado Springs, CO	409	537	589	602	609	31.3	13.3	83
Columbia, SC	549	647	692	704	716	17.9	10.6	69
Columbus, GA-AL	266	282	284	290	283	5.7	0.4	161
Columbus, OH	1,405	1,613	1,715	1,735	1,754	14.8	8.8	32
Corpus Christi, TX	368	403	411	413	414	9.7	2.8	115
Dallas-Fort Worth-Arlington, TX	3,989	5,162	5,807	5,983	6,145	29.4	19.1	4
Davenport-Moline-Rock Island, IA-IL	368	376	373	374	376	2.1	(Z)	132
Dayton, OH	844	848	841	838	836	0.5	−1.5	59
Deltona-Daytona Beach-Ormond Beach, FL	371	443	486	496	500	19.6	12.9	100
Denver-Aurora, CO [2]	1,667	2,179	2,365	2,412	2,465	30.7	13.1	21
Des Moines-West Des Moines, IA	416	481	524	536	547	15.6	13.5	91
Detroit-Warren-Livonia, MI	4,249	4,453	4,504	4,495	4,468	4.8	0.3	11
Duluth, MN-WI	269	275	274	274	274	2.3	−0.4	164
Durham, NC	345	424	460	469	480	23.7	13.2	103
El Paso, TX	592	680	712	726	735	14.9	8.1	68
Erie, PA	276	281	279	280	279	1.9	−0.6	162
Eugene-Springfield, OR	283	323	336	340	344	14.2	6.4	144
Evansville, IN-KY	325	343	348	349	350	5.5	2.0	142
Fayetteville, NC	298	337	345	349	349	13.1	3.7	143
Fayetteville-Springdale-Rogers, AR-MO	239	347	409	424	436	44.9	25.5	110
Flint, MI	430	436	440	438	435	1.3	−0.3	111
Fort Collins-Loveland, CO	186	251	276	282	288	35.1	14.3	159
Fort Smith, AR-OK	234	273	283	287	290	16.7	6.0	158
Fort Wayne, IN	354	390	403	406	410	10.1	5.1	117
Fresno, CA	667	799	873	886	899	19.8	12.5	55

See footnotes at end of table.

U.S. Census Bureau, Statistical Abstract of the United States: 2009

[1990 and 2000, as of April 1; beginning 2005 as of July 1 (658 represents 658,000). Covers metropolitan statistical areas with 250,000 and over population in 2007, as defined by the U.S. Office of Management and Budget as of December 2006. All geographic boundaries for 2000 to 2007 population estimates are defined as of January 1, 2007. For definitions and components of all metropolitan and micropolitan areas, see Appendix II. Minus sign (–) indicates decrease]

Metropolitan statistical area	Number (1,000)					Percent change		Rank, 2007
	1990	2000, estimates base [1]	2005	2006	2007	1990 to 2000	2000 to 2007 [1]	
Gainesville, FL	191	232	248	254	257	21.5	10.6	172
Grand Rapids-Wyoming, MI	646	740	769	773	777	14.6	4.9	66
Green Bay, WI	244	282	296	299	301	16.0	6.6	153
Greensboro-High Point, NC	540	643	675	687	698	19.1	8.6	72
Greenville-Mauldin-Easley, SC	472	560	590	601	614	18.6	9.6	82
Hagerstown-Martinsburg, MD-WV	193	223	250	256	261	15.6	17.2	170
Harrisburg-Carlisle, PA	474	509	520	525	529	7.3	3.9	94
Hartford-West Hartford-East Hartford, CT	1,124	1,149	1,181	1,185	1,189	2.2	3.5	45
Hickory-Lenoir-Morganton, NC	292	342	354	357	360	16.9	5.5	138
Holland-Grand Haven, MI	188	238	255	257	259	26.9	8.8	171
Honolulu, HI	836	876	902	907	906	4.8	3.4	54
Houston-Sugar Land-Baytown, TX	3,767	4,715	5,322	5,508	5,628	25.2	19.4	6
Huntington-Ashland, WV-KY-OH	288	289	285	284	284	0.2	–1.6	160
Huntsville, AL	293	343	369	378	387	16.8	12.8	130
Indianapolis-Carmel, IN	1,294	1,525	1,645	1,670	1,695	17.8	11.1	33
Jackson, MS	447	497	522	531	534	11.2	7.4	93
Jacksonville, FL	925	1,123	1,250	1,279	1,301	21.4	15.9	40
Kalamazoo-Portage, MI	293	315	321	322	323	7.3	2.7	148
Kansas City, MO-KS	1,637	1,836	1,940	1,962	1,985	12.2	8.1	29
Killeen-Temple-Fort Hood, TX	269	331	355	358	370	23.0	11.9	134
Kingsport-Bristol-Bristol, TN-VA	276	298	300	302	304	8.3	1.7	152
Knoxville, TN	535	616	658	670	682	15.2	10.6	75
Lafayette, LA	209	239	247	255	256	14.5	7.4	173
Lakeland, FL	405	484	539	558	575	19.4	18.8	87
Lancaster, PA	423	471	489	494	498	11.3	5.9	101
Lansing-East Lansing, MI	433	448	457	457	456	3.5	1.9	106
Las Vegas-Paradise, NV	741	1,376	1,709	1,777	1,836	85.6	33.5	30
Lexington-Fayette, KY	348	408	433	441	447	17.2	9.5	109
Lincoln, NE	229	267	285	288	292	16.5	9.5	156
Little Rock-North Little Rock-Conway, AR	535	611	646	657	666	14.1	9.2	78
Los Angeles-Long Beach-Santa Ana, CA	11,274	12,366	12,874	12,867	12,876	9.7	4.1	2
Louisville/Jefferson County, KY-IN	1,056	1,162	1,209	1,220	1,234	10.0	6.1	42
Lubbock, TX	230	250	262	265	267	8.6	7.0	167
Madison, WI	432	502	541	548	556	16.1	10.7	89
Manchester-Nashua, NH	336	381	399	401	402	13.4	5.6	124
McAllen-Edinburg-Mission, TX	384	569	670	689	711	48.5	24.8	70
Memphis, TN-MS-AR	1,067	1,205	1,254	1,272	1,281	12.9	6.3	41
Miami-Fort Lauderdale-Pompano Beach, FL	4,056	5,008	5,386	5,415	5,413	23.5	8.1	7
Milwaukee-Waukesha-West Allis, WI	1,432	1,501	1,535	1,541	1,544	4.8	2.9	38
Minneapolis-St. Paul-Bloomington, MN-WI	2,539	2,969	3,138	3,172	3,208	16.9	8.1	16
Mobile, AL	379	400	398	402	404	5.6	1.1	121
Modesto, CA	371	447	501	507	511	20.6	14.4	99
Montgomery, AL	305	347	356	363	366	13.6	5.6	135
Naples-Marco Island, FL	152	251	307	313	316	65.3	25.6	150
Nashville-Davidson–Murfreesboro–Franklin, TN	1,048	1,312	1,450	1,487	1,521	25.1	16.0	39
New Haven-Milford, CT	804	824	842	843	845	2.5	2.6	58
New Orleans-Metairie-Kenner, LA	1,264	1,317	1,310	990	1,030	4.1	–21.7	51
New York-Northern New Jersey-Long Island, NY-NJ-PA	16,846	18,323	18,757	18,783	18,816	8.8	2.7	1
Norwich-New London, CT	255	259	266	268	267	1.6	3.2	166
Ocala, FL	195	259	302	314	325	32.9	25.5	147
Ogden-Clearfield, UT	352	443	492	504	518	25.8	17.1	96
Oklahoma City, OK	971	1,095	1,157	1,176	1,193	12.8	8.9	44
Omaha-Council Bluffs, NE-IA	686	767	812	821	830	11.8	8.2	61
Orlando-Kissimmee, FL	1,225	1,645	1,940	1,998	2,032	34.3	23.6	27
Oxnard-Thousand Oaks-Ventura, CA	669	753	791	794	798	12.6	6.0	63
Palm Bay-Melbourne-Titusville, FL	399	476	527	532	536	19.4	12.6	92
Pensacola-Ferry Pass-Brent, FL	344	412	445	451	453	19.7	10.0	108
Peoria, IL	359	367	367	369	371	2.3	1.2	133
Philadelphia-Camden-Wilmington, PA-NJ-DE-MD	5,436	5,687	5,793	5,811	5,828	4.6	2.5	5
Phoenix-Mesa-Scottsdale, AZ	2,238	3,252	3,884	4,047	4,179	45.3	28.5	13
Pittsburgh, PA	2,468	2,431	2,375	2,363	2,356	–1.5	–3.1	22

See footnotes at end of table.

[1990 and 2000, as of April 1; beginning 2005 as of July 1 (658 represents 658,000). Covers metropolitan statistical areas with 250,000 and over population in 2007, as defined by the U.S. Office of Management and Budget as of December 2006. All geographic boundaries for 2000 to 2007 population estimates are defined as of January 1, 2007. For definitions and components of all metropolitan and micropolitan areas, see Appendix II. Minus sign (–) indicates decrease]

Metropolitan statistical area	Number (1,000)					Percent change		Rank, 2007
	1990	2000, estimates base [1]	2005	2006	2007	1990 to 2000	2000 to 2007 [1]	
Portland-South Portland-Biddeford, ME	441	488	512	512	513	10.5	5.2	98
Portland-Vancouver-Beaverton, OR-WA	1,524	1,928	2,093	2,134	2,175	26.5	12.8	23
Port St. Lucie, FL.	251	319	376	389	400	27.2	25.3	126
Poughkeepsie-Newburgh-Middletown, NY . . .	567	622	663	666	670	9.6	7.8	77
Providence-New Bedford-Fall River, RI-MA . . .	1,510	1,583	1,610	1,604	1,601	4.8	1.1	36
Provo-Orem, UT	269	377	464	481	493	39.9	30.9	102
Raleigh-Cary, NC.	544	797	956	1,001	1,048	46.5	31.4	49
Reading, PA	337	374	394	399	402	11.0	7.6	125
Reno-Sparks, NV.	257	343	395	402	410	33.3	19.7	116
Richmond, VA	949	1,097	1,174	1,195	1,213	15.6	10.6	43
Riverside-San Bernardino-Ontario, CA.	2,589	3,255	3,880	3,995	4,081	25.7	25.4	14
Roanoke, VA.	269	288	292	294	297	7.4	2.9	154
Rochester, NY.	1,002	1,038	1,033	1,031	1,030	3.5	–0.7	50
Rockford, IL	284	320	340	345	352	12.9	10.0	140
Sacramento–Arden-Arcade–Roseville, CA . . .	1,481	1,797	2,038	2,063	2,091	21.3	16.4	26
St. Louis, MO-IL [3]	2,581	2,699	2,775	2,794	2,804	4.6	3.9	18
Salem, OR	278	347	373	380	387	24.9	11.4	129
Salinas, CA	356	402	409	406	408	13.0	1.5	119
Salt Lake City, UT	768	969	1,049	1,078	1,100	26.1	13.5	48
San Antonio, TX	1,408	1,712	1,883	1,937	1,991	21.6	16.3	28
San Diego-Carlsbad-San Marcos, CA	2,498	2,814	2,942	2,948	2,975	12.6	5.7	17
San Francisco-Oakland-Fremont, CA.	3,684	4,124	4,147	4,164	4,204	11.9	1.9	12
San Jose-Sunnyvale-Santa Clara, CA	1,534	1,736	1,754	1,775	1,804	13.1	3.9	31
San Luis Obispo-Paso Robles, CA	217	247	258	260	262	13.6	6.4	168
Santa Barbara-Santa Maria-Goleta, CA	370	399	403	402	404	8.0	1.2	123
Santa Cruz-Watsonville, CA.	230	256	250	251	252	11.3	–1.5	175
Santa Rosa-Petaluma, CA.	388	459	464	463	464	18.1	1.3	104
Sarasota-Bradenton-Venice, FL	489	590	669	681	687	20.5	16.5	73
Savannah, GA	258	293	314	321	329	13.6	12.3	146
Scranton–Wilkes-Barre, PA	575	561	549	549	549	–2.6	–2.0	90
Seattle-Tacoma-Bellevue, WA	2,559	3,044	3,205	3,262	3,309	18.9	8.7	15
Shreveport-Bossier City, LA	360	376	382	387	388	4.5	3.1	127
South Bend-Mishawaka, IN-MI	297	317	316	316	317	6.8	(Z)	149
Spartanburg, SC	227	254	266	270	276	11.9	8.6	163
Spokane, WA	361	418	440	447	456	15.7	9.1	107
Springfield, MA	673	680	684	683	683	1.0	0.4	74
Springfield, MO	299	368	401	411	420	23.3	14.0	114
Stockton, CA	481	564	658	665	671	17.3	19.1	76
Syracuse, NY	660	650	648	647	645	–1.5	–0.7	80
Tallahassee, FL	259	320	342	348	352	23.6	10.0	139
Tampa-St. Petersburg-Clearwater, FL	2,068	2,396	2,643	2,694	2,724	15.9	13.7	19
Toledo, OH.	654	659	655	653	651	0.8	–1.2	79
Trenton-Ewing, NJ	326	351	364	365	365	7.7	4.2	136
Tucson, AZ	667	844	927	949	967	26.5	14.6	52
Tulsa, OK.	761	860	882	893	906	12.9	5.4	53
Utica-Rome, NY	317	300	296	295	295	–5.3	–1.7	155
Vallejo-Fairfield, CA	339	395	408	408	409	16.2	3.6	118
Virginia Beach-Norfolk-Newport News, VA-NC.	1,451	1,577	1,650	1,661	1,659	8.7	5.2	34
Visalia-Porterville, CA	312	368	406	414	422	18.0	14.5	112
Washington-Arlington-Alexandria, DC-VA-MD-WV	4,122	4,796	5,223	5,261	5,307	16.3	10.6	8
Wichita, KS.	511	571	585	589	596	11.7	4.4	84
Wilmington, NC	200	275	317	329	340	37.2	23.7	145
Winston-Salem, NC	361	422	447	455	463	16.7	9.8	105
Worcester, MA	710	750	777	780	781	5.8	4.2	65
York-Hanover, PA	340	382	407	415	421	12.4	10.3	113
Youngstown-Warren-Boardman, OH-PA	614	603	581	577	571	–1.7	–5.4	88

Z Less than 0.05 percent.   [1] The April 1, 2000, estimates base reflects changes to the Census 2000 population resulting from legal boundary updates as of January 1 of the estimates year, other geographic program changes, and Count Question Resolution actions.   [2] Broomfield County, CO, was formed from parts of Adams, Boulder, Jefferson, and Weld Counties, CO, on November 15, 2001, and is coextensive with Broomfield city. For purposes of defining and presenting data for metropolitan statistical areas, Broomfield city is treated as if it were a county at the time of the 1990 and 2000 censuses.   [3] The portion of Sullivan city in Crawford County, Missouri, is legally part of the St. Louis, MO-IL MSA. Data shown here do not include this area.

Source: U.S. Census Bureau, "Table 1: Annual Estimates of the Population of Metropolitan and Micropolitan Statistical Areas: April 1, 2000 to July 1, 2007 (CBSA-EST2007-01)"; published 27 March 2008; <http://www.census.gov/population/www/estimates /CBSA-est2007-annual.html>.

Table 20. 50 Largest Metropolitan Statistical Areas in 2007— Components of Population Change: 2000 to 2007

[Covers period April 1, 2000, to July 1, 2007, (1,031 represents 1,031,000). Covers metropolitan statistical areas as defined by the U.S. Office of Management and Budget as of December 2006. All geographic boundaries for 2000 to 2007 population estimates are defined as of January 1, 2007. For definitions and components of all metropolitan and micropolitan areas, see Appendix II. Minus sign (–) indicates decrease or outmigration]

Metropolitan statistical area	Number (1,000)							Percent change
	Total change [1]	Natural increase			Net migration			
		Total	Births	Deaths	Total	Inter-national	Internal migration	
Atlanta-Sandy Springs-Marietta, GA	1,031	350	556	206	557	187	370	24.3
Austin-Round Rock, TX	348	119	169	50	234	61	173	27.9
Baltimore-Towson, MD	115	81	250	169	9	33	–23	4.5
Birmingham-Hoover, AL	57	28	108	80	30	9	21	5.4
Boston-Cambridge-Quincy, MA-NH	91	149	407	258	–95	169	–264	2.1
Buffalo-Niagara Falls, NY	–42	5	93	88	–41	10	–51	–3.6
Charlotte-Gastonia-Concord, NC-SC	321	93	169	76	235	44	191	24.1
Chicago-Naperville-Joliet, IL-IN-WI	426	520	1,026	506	–96	396	–491	4.7
Cincinnati-Middletown, OH-KY-IN	124	84	213	129	1	18	–16	6.2
Cleveland-Elyria-Mentor, OH	–52	38	193	155	–90	25	–115	–2.4
Columbus, OH	141	92	185	93	53	31	22	8.8
Dallas-Fort Worth-Arlington, TX	984	472	712	240	531	301	230	19.1
Denver-Aurora, CO [2]	286	170	270	100	119	96	23	13.1
Detroit-Warren-Livonia, MI	15	148	430	282	–175	94	–268	0.3
Hartford-West Hartford-East Hartford, CT	40	26	100	74	20	26	–7	3.5
Houston-Sugar Land-Baytown, TX	913	423	645	222	432	274	158	19.4
Indianapolis-Carmel, IN	170	90	181	91	79	21	58	11.1
Jacksonville, FL	178	52	126	74	130	11	119	15.9
Kansas City, MO-KS	149	99	209	111	53	30	23	8.1
Las Vegas-Paradise, NV	461	99	186	86	367	68	300	33.5
Los Angeles-Long Beach-Santa Ana, CA	510	871	1,432	561	–310	838	–1,148	4.1
Louisville/Jefferson County, KY-IN	71	36	116	80	37	12	25	6.1
Memphis, TN-MS-AR	75	63	141	78	16	13	3	6.3
Miami-Fort Lauderdale-Pompano Beach, FL	405	162	507	344	255	432	–177	8.1
Milwaukee-Waukesha-West Allis, WI	44	62	155	94	–45	24	–69	2.9
Minneapolis-St. Paul-Bloomington, MN-WI	239	194	331	136	56	75	–19	8.1
Nashville-Davidson–Murfreesboro–Franklin, TN	210	68	148	80	123	26	97	16.0
New York-Northern New Jersey-Long Island, NY-NJ-PA	493	827	1,863	1,036	–559	1,125	–1,685	2.7
Oklahoma City, OK	98	55	126	71	47	20	27	8.9
Orlando-Kissimmee, FL	388	90	190	100	302	68	234	23.6
Philadelphia-Camden-Wilmington, PA-NJ-DE-MD	141	155	546	391	8	97	–88	2.5
Phoenix-Mesa-Scottsdale, AZ	928	269	458	188	664	173	491	28.5
Pittsburgh, PA	–75	–25	181	205	–40	16	–56	–3.1
Portland-Vancouver-Beaverton, OR-WA	247	99	208	108	157	71	86	12.8
Providence-New Bedford-Fall River, RI-MA	18	32	140	108	–7	29	–37	1.1
Raleigh-Cary, NC	251	69	106	36	178	35	143	31.4
Richmond, VA	116	40	111	71	81	13	68	10.6
Riverside-San Bernardino-Ontario, CA	827	259	443	184	580	100	481	25.4
Rochester, NY	–7	24	88	65	–24	14	–37	–0.7
Sacramento–Arden-Arcade–Roseville, CA	294	101	205	104	200	66	134	16.4
St. Louis, MO-IL [3]	105	82	265	183	–8	27	–36	3.9
Salt Lake City, UT	131	106	146	40	8	41	–33	13.5
San Antonio, TX	279	122	218	96	164	30	134	16.3
San Diego-Carlsbad-San Marcos, CA	161	185	328	143	–10	103	–113	5.7
San Francisco-Oakland-Fremont, CA	80	195	407	213	–101	257	–358	1.9
San Jose-Sunnyvale-Santa Clara, CA	68	137	202	66	–64	167	–232	3.9
Seattle-Tacoma-Bellevue, WA	265	151	304	153	115	107	8	8.7
Tampa-St. Petersburg-Clearwater, FL	328	18	225	207	320	60	260	13.7
Virginia Beach-Norfolk-Newport News, VA-NC	82	82	171	89	3	–1	5	5.2
Washington-Arlington-Alexandria, DC-VA-MD-WV	511	338	558	220	154	253	–99	10.6

[1] The estimated components of population change will not sum to the total population change due to the process of controlling to national totals.   [2] Broomfield County, CO, was formed from parts of Adams, Boulder, Jefferson, and Weld Counties, CO, on November 15, 2001, and is coextensive with Broomfield city. For purposes of defining and presenting data for metropolitan statistical areas, Broomfield city is treated as if it were a county at the time of the 2000 census.   [3] The portion of Sullivan city in Crawford County, Missouri, is legally part of the St. Louis, MO-IL MSA. Data shown here do not include this area.

Source: U.S. Census Bureau, "Table 10: Cumulative Estimates of the Components of Population Change for Metropolitan and Micropolitan Statistical Areas: April 1, 2000 to July 1, 2007 (CBSA-EST2007-10)"; published 27 March 2008; <http://www.census.gov /population/www/estimates/CBSA-est2007-comp-chg.html>.

Table 21. Metropolitan Statistical Areas With More Than 750,000 Persons in 2007—Population by Race and Hispanic Origin: 2007

[In thousands (853 represents 853,000). As of July 1. Covers metropolitan statistical areas as defined by the U.S. Office of Management and Budget as of December 2006. All geographic boundaries are defined as of January 1, 2007. For definitions and components of all metropolitan and micropolitan areas, see Appendix II]

Metropolitan statistical area	Total persons	White alone	Black or African American alone	American Indian and Alaska Native alone	Asian alone	Native Hawaiian and Other Pacific Islander alone	Two or more races	Hispanic origin [1]
Albany-Schenectady-Troy, NY	853	750	64	2	25	(Z)	12	27
Albuquerque, NM	835	721	30	50	16	1	17	369
Allentown-Bethlehem-Easton, PA-NJ	804	737	36	2	19	(Z)	9	85
Atlanta-Sandy Springs-Marietta, GA	5,279	3,309	1,662	19	217	4	68	496
Austin-Round Rock, TX	1,598	1,363	126	11	72	2	24	476
Bakersfield, CA	791	677	51	14	32	2	16	366
Baltimore-Towson, MD	2,668	1,749	770	8	101	2	38	84
Baton Rouge, LA	770	472	277	2	12	(Z)	6	19
Birmingham-Hoover, AL	1,108	771	312	4	12	(Z)	9	34
Boston-Cambridge-Quincy, MA-NH	4,483	3,798	345	12	266	3	59	348
Bridgeport-Stamford-Norwalk, CT	895	746	97	3	38	1	10	133
Buffalo-Niagara Falls, NY	1,128	949	139	8	19	(Z)	13	38
Charlotte-Gastonia-Concord, NC-SC	1,652	1,194	387	8	43	1	18	139
Chicago-Naperville-Joliet, IL-IN-WI	9,525	7,151	1,725	34	499	8	109	1,858
Cincinnati-Middletown, OH-KY-IN	2,134	1,811	259	4	36	1	23	38
Cleveland-Elyria-Mentor, OH	2,096	1,611	416	5	38	1	26	85
Columbus, OH	1,754	1,419	248	5	55	1	27	50
Dallas-Fort Worth-Arlington, TX	6,145	4,831	887	43	290	9	85	1,654
Dayton, OH	836	684	123	2	13	(Z)	12	14
Denver-Aurora, CO	2,465	2,162	141	25	85	4	48	545
Detroit-Warren-Livonia, MI	4,468	3,216	1,032	15	141	2	61	162
Fresno, CA	899	733	52	17	79	2	17	433
Grand Rapids-Wyoming, MI	777	685	61	4	14	1	13	61
Hartford-West Hartford-East Hartford, CT	1,189	998	132	3	39	1	16	129
Honolulu, HI	906	230	34	5	408	76	154	67
Houston-Sugar Land-Baytown, TX	5,628	4,228	975	33	320	7	66	1,880
Indianapolis-Carmel, IN	1,695	1,389	249	5	30	1	21	79
Jacksonville, FL	1,301	944	292	5	38	1	20	74
Kansas City, MO-KS	1,985	1,657	243	11	40	2	32	138
Las Vegas-Paradise, NV	1,836	1,435	188	18	132	10	52	511
Los Angeles-Long Beach-Santa Ana, CA	12,876	9,683	1,001	120	1,785	44	241	5,675
Louisville/Jefferson County, KY-IN	1,234	1,032	167	4	16	1	15	33
Memphis, TN-MS-AR	1,281	659	583	4	22	1	12	48
Miami-Fort Lauderdale-Pompano Beach, FL	5,413	4,078	1,128	22	118	6	62	2,110
Milwaukee-Waukesha-West Allis, WI	1,544	1,219	253	9	40	1	22	127
Minneapolis-St. Paul-Bloomington, MN-WI	3,208	2,754	210	25	158	2	59	148
Nashville-Davidson–Murfreesboro–Franklin, TN	1,521	1,228	237	5	31	1	19	80
New Haven-Milford, CT	845	692	109	3	29	1	12	108
New Orleans-Metairie-Kenner, LA	1,030	652	334	5	27	1	12	64
New York-Northern New Jersey-Long Island, NY-NJ-PA	18,816	12,985	3,683	91	1,753	22	282	4,011
Oklahoma City, OK	1,193	942	129	46	36	1	39	111
Omaha-Council Bluffs, NE-IA	830	730	66	5	17	1	12	61
Orlando-Kissimee, FL	2,032	1,588	325	10	75	3	33	456
Oxnard-Thousand Oaks-Ventura, CA	798	699	17	9	53	2	18	297
Philadelphia-Camden-Wilmington, PA-NJ-DE-MD	5,828	4,260	1,224	15	253	3	72	373
Phoenix-Mesa-Scottsdale, AZ	4,179	3,686	195	99	120	9	72	1,271
Pittsburgh, PA	2,356	2,095	196	4	36	1	23	26
Portland-Vancouver-Beaverton, OR-WA	2,175	1,905	66	20	118	7	58	219
Providence-New Bedford-Fall River, RI-MA	1,601	1,442	87	8	39	2	23	145
Raleigh-Cary, NC	1,048	777	213	5	38	1	13	91
Richmond, VA	1,213	794	367	5	31	1	15	46
Riverside-San Bernardino-Ontario, CA	4,081	3,356	326	56	233	15	95	1,835
Rochester, NY	1,030	871	118	3	23	(Z)	15	51
Sacramento–Arden-Arcade–Roseville, CA	2,091	1,586	159	24	232	13	77	386
St. Louis, MO-IL [2]	2,804	2,196	513	8	52	1	34	59
Salt Lake City, UT	1,100	1,007	18	11	32	14	19	168
San Antonio, TX	1,991	1,767	135	19	38	3	29	1,050
San Diego-Carlsbad-San Marcos, CA	2,975	2,368	165	29	308	15	89	901
San Francisco-Oakland-Fremont, CA	4,204	2,699	383	27	925	30	139	844
San Jose-Sunnyvale-Santa Clara, CA	1,804	1,143	51	14	542	8	46	478
Seattle-Tacoma-Bellevue, WA	3,309	2,600	185	38	347	21	119	240
Tampa-St. Petersburg-Clearwater, FL	2,724	2,281	318	12	72	2	38	388
Tucson, AZ	967	855	35	33	25	2	17	316
Tulsa, OK	906	706	83	65	13	1	38	64
Virginia Beach-Norfolk-Newport News, VA-NC	1,659	1,034	529	7	52	2	34	67
Washington-Arlington-Alexandria, DC-VA-MD-WV	5,307	3,312	1,413	21	452	5	104	633
Worcester, MA	781	712	29	2	28	1	9	62

Z Less than 500.   [1] Persons of Hispanic origin may be any race.   [2] The portion of Sullivan city in Crawford County, Missouri, is legally part of the St. Louis, MO-IL MSA. Data shown here do not include this area.

Source: U.S. Census Bureau, USA Counties; <http://censtats.census.gov/usa/usa.shtml>; accessed 18 August 2008.

U.S. Census Bureau, Statistical Abstract of the United States: 2009

Table 22. Metropolitan Statistical Areas With More Than 750,000 Persons in 2007—Population by Age: 2007

[In thousands (853 represents 853,000). As of July 1. Covers metropolitan statistical areas as defined by the U.S. Office of Management and Budget as of December 2006. All geographic boundaries are defined as of January 1, 2007. For definitions and components of all metropolitan and micropolitan areas, see Appendix II]

Metropolitan statistical area	Number (1,000)						Percent under 18 years	Percent 65 years and over
	Total	Under 18 years	18 to 44 years	45 to 64 years	65 to 74 years	75 years and over		
Albany-Schenectady-Troy, NY	853	184	325	229	55	60	21.5	13.5
Albuquerque, NM	835	209	316	212	51	47	25.0	11.8
Allentown-Bethlehem-Easton, PA-NJ	804	184	285	217	55	64	22.8	14.7
Atlanta-Sandy Springs-Marietta, GA	5,279	1,427	2,123	1,302	248	179	27.0	8.1
Austin-Round Rock, TX	1,598	413	713	353	65	54	25.9	7.4
Bakersfield, CA	791	237	325	159	38	32	30.0	8.8
Baltimore-Towson, MD	2,668	640	992	713	168	156	24.0	12.1
Baton Rouge, LA	770	197	308	187	43	36	25.5	10.2
Birmingham-Hoover, AL	1,108	271	403	292	74	67	24.5	12.8
Boston-Cambridge-Quincy, MA-NH	4,483	999	1,718	1,201	282	283	22.3	12.6
Bridgeport-Stamford-Norwalk, CT	895	225	305	248	59	58	25.1	13.1
Buffalo-Niagara Falls, NY	1,128	247	398	309	81	93	21.9	15.4
Charlotte-Gastonia-Concord, NC-SC	1,652	434	648	414	86	69	26.3	9.4
Chicago-Naperville-Joliet, IL-IN-WI	9,525	2,461	3,655	2,371	543	495	25.8	10.9
Cincinnati-Middletown, OH-KY-IN	2,134	537	789	555	131	122	25.2	11.9
Cleveland-Elyria-Mentor, OH	2,096	499	710	584	149	155	23.8	14.5
Columbus, OH	1,754	446	701	429	96	81	25.4	10.1
Dallas-Fort Worth-Arlington, TX	6,145	1,714	2,508	1,421	285	216	27.9	8.2
Dayton, OH	836	195	299	223	61	58	23.3	14.2
Denver-Aurora, CO	2,465	628	961	642	127	106	25.5	9.4
Detroit-Warren-Livonia, MI	4,468	1,120	1,586	1,220	274	268	25.1	12.1
Fresno, CA	899	269	356	187	44	43	29.9	9.7
Grand Rapids-Wyoming, MI	777	206	295	192	42	41	26.6	10.7
Hartford-West Hartford-East Hartford, CT	1,189	270	429	326	79	84	22.7	13.7
Honolulu, HI	906	201	344	226	62	72	22.1	14.9
Houston-Sugar Land-Baytown, TX	5,628	1,592	2,225	1,353	263	195	28.3	8.1
Indianapolis-Carmel, IN	1,695	453	641	423	94	84	26.7	10.5
Jacksonville, FL	1,301	323	481	350	82	64	24.8	11.3
Kansas City, MO-KS	1,985	514	728	518	117	108	25.9	11.3
Las Vegas-Paradise, NV	1,836	485	717	444	111	80	26.4	10.4
Los Angeles-Long Beach-Santa Ana, CA	12,876	3,349	5,129	3,036	709	652	26.0	10.6
Louisville/Jefferson County, KY-IN	1,234	299	446	336	80	73	24.2	12.4
Memphis, TN-MS-AR	1,281	352	472	326	72	58	27.5	10.2
Miami-Fort Lauderdale-Pompano Beach, FL	5,413	1,228	1,914	1,392	403	476	22.7	16.2
Milwaukee-Waukesha-West Allis, WI	1,544	389	548	417	95	96	25.2	12.3
Minneapolis-St. Paul-Bloomington, MN-WI	3,208	814	1,231	845	168	150	25.4	9.9
Nashville-Davidson–Murfreesboro–Franklin, TN	1,521	376	594	393	88	71	24.7	10.4
New Haven-Milford, CT	845	197	310	222	54	62	23.3	13.7
New Orleans-Metairie-Kenner, LA	1,030	240	373	290	67	60	23.3	12.4
New York-Northern New Jersey-Long Island, NY-NJ-PA	18,816	4,421	7,113	4,860	1,233	1,189	23.5	12.9
Oklahoma City, OK	1,193	302	459	294	74	64	25.3	11.6
Omaha-Council Bluffs, NE-IA	830	222	313	205	47	43	26.7	10.8
Orlando-Kissimee, FL	2,032	490	780	502	137	124	24.1	12.8
Oxnard-Thousand Oaks-Ventura, CA	798	209	296	205	47	42	26.2	11.1
Philadelphia-Camden-Wilmington, PA-NJ-DE-MD	5,828	1,405	2,117	1,547	376	382	24.1	13.0
Phoenix-Mesa-Scottsdale, AZ	4,179	1,140	1,622	944	244	229	27.3	11.3
Pittsburgh, PA	2,356	488	785	679	183	220	20.7	17.1
Portland-Vancouver-Beaverton, OR-WA	2,175	529	831	588	121	106	24.3	10.4
Providence-New Bedford-Fall River, RI-MA	1,601	358	600	423	103	118	22.3	13.8
Raleigh-Cary, NC	1,048	275	430	259	48	36	26.2	8.0
Richmond, VA	1,213	290	463	320	73	67	23.9	11.5
Riverside-San Bernardino-Ontario, CA	4,081	1,180	1,669	834	201	198	28.9	9.8
Rochester, NY	1,030	234	377	281	68	70	22.7	13.4
Sacramento–Arden-Arcade–Roseville, CA	2,091	520	828	502	123	118	24.8	11.6
St. Louis, MO-IL [1]	2,804	684	1,009	751	182	178	24.4	12.8
Salt Lake City, UT	1,100	325	444	239	50	42	29.5	8.4
San Antonio, TX	1,991	551	769	457	111	102	27.7	10.7
San Diego-Carlsbad-San Marcos, CA	2,975	741	1,214	688	160	171	24.9	11.1
San Francisco-Oakland-Fremont, CA	4,204	911	1,624	1,149	265	256	21.7	12.4
San Jose-Sunnyvale-Santa Clara, CA	1,804	435	722	454	104	87	24.1	10.6
Seattle-Tacoma-Bellevue, WA	3,309	769	1,285	912	182	161	23.2	10.4
Tampa-St. Petersburg-Clearwater, FL	2,724	596	936	724	217	251	21.9	17.2
Tucson, AZ	967	230	354	240	70	73	23.8	14.8
Tulsa, OK	906	232	327	235	59	53	25.7	12.3
Virginia Beach-Norfolk-Newport News, VA-NC	1,659	418	653	403	98	86	25.2	11.1
Washington-Arlington-Alexandria, DC-VA-MD-WV	5,307	1,300	2,084	1,405	293	225	24.5	9.8
Worcester, MA	781	187	290	208	46	50	23.9	12.3

[1] The portion of Sullivan city in Crawford County, Missouri, is legally part of the St. Louis, MO-IL MSA. Data shown here do not include this area.

Source: U.S. Census Bureau, USA Counties; <http://censtats.census.gov/usa/usa.shtml>; accessed 18 August 2008.

U.S. Census Bureau, Statistical Abstract of the United States: 2009

Table 23. Population by Core-Based Statistical Area Status and State: 2000 to 2007

[2000, as of April 1; beginning 2005 as of July 1 (262,135 represents 262,135,000). Covers core-based statistical areas (metropolitan and micropolitan statistical areas) as defined by the U.S. Office of Management and Budget as of December 2006. All geographic boundaries for 2000 to 2007 population estimates are defined as of January 1, 2007. For definitions and components of all metropolitan and micropolitan areas, see Appendix II. Minus sign (–) indicates decrease]

| State | Core-Based Statistical Area (metropolitan and micropolitan) population | | | | | | Population outside Core-Based Statistical Area | | | | | |
| | Number (1,000) | | | Percent of total | | Percent change, 2000–2007 | Number (1,000) | | | Percent of total | | Percent change, 2000–2007 |
	2000 [1]	2005	2007	2000	2007		2000 [1]	2005	2007	2000	2007	
U.S. . . .	262,135	276,625	282,270	93.1	93.6	7.7	19,290	19,271	19,351	6.9	6.4	0.3
AL	3,945	4,055	4,145	88.7	89.6	5.1	503	485	483	11.3	10.4	–4.0
AK	461	503	517	73.6	75.6	12.1	166	166	167	26.4	24.4	0.6
AZ	4,944	5,757	6,137	96.4	96.8	24.1	187	195	201	3.6	3.2	7.9
AR	2,082	2,190	2,254	77.9	79.5	8.3	591	582	581	22.1	20.5	–1.8
CA	33,628	35,735	36,295	99.3	99.3	7.9	243	255	259	0.7	0.7	6.3
CO	[2]3,922	4,282	4,460	91.2	91.8	13.7	380	392	401	8.8	8.2	5.4
CT	3,406	3,486	3,502	100.0	100.0	2.8	–	–	–	–	–	–
DE	784	841	865	100.0	100.0	10.4	–	–	–	–	–	–
DC	572	582	588	100.0	100.0	2.8	–	–	–	–	–	–
FL	15,620	17,348	17,852	97.7	97.8	14.3	363	388	399	2.3	2.2	10.0
GA	7,411	8,295	8,710	90.5	91.3	17.5	776	813	835	9.5	8.7	7.7
HI	1,211	1,267	1,283	100.0	100.0	5.9	–	–	–	–	–	–19.0
ID	1,103	1,232	1,302	85.2	86.8	18.0	191	194	198	14.8	13.2	3.4
IL	11,796	12,109	12,247	95.0	95.3	3.8	624	610	606	5.0	4.7	–2.9
IN	5,715	5,893	5,982	94.0	94.3	4.7	366	364	363	6.0	5.7	–0.7
IA	2,090	2,148	2,188	71.4	73.2	4.7	836	808	800	28.6	26.8	–4.3
KS	2,248	2,328	2,369	83.6	85.3	5.4	440	414	407	16.4	14.7	–7.6
KY	3,036	3,162	3,227	75.1	76.1	6.3	1,006	1,009	1,015	24.9	23.9	0.8
LA	4,156	4,192	3,987	93.0	92.9	–4.1	313	303	306	7.0	7.1	–2.2
ME	893	927	930	70.0	70.6	4.2	382	386	387	30.0	29.4	1.3
MD	5,218	5,492	5,536	98.5	98.5	6.1	79	81	83	1.5	1.5	4.7
MA	6,325	6,403	6,424	99.6	99.6	1.6	25	26	26	0.4	0.4	6.2
MI	9,153	9,321	9,292	92.1	92.3	1.5	785	787	780	7.9	7.7	–0.7
MN	4,266	4,464	4,547	86.7	87.5	6.6	654	650	650	13.3	12.5	–0.5
MS	2,196	2,260	2,276	77.2	78.0	3.7	648	640	642	22.8	22.0	–0.9
MO	4,810	4,998	5,087	85.9	86.5	5.8	787	790	792	14.1	13.5	0.6
MT	574	612	632	63.7	65.9	10.0	328	324	326	36.3	34.1	–0.5
NE	1,339	1,402	1,429	78.2	80.5	6.7	373	352	346	21.8	19.5	–7.3
NV	1,950	2,362	2,517	97.6	98.1	29.1	48	47	48	2.4	1.9	0.8
NH	1,192	1,256	1,268	96.5	96.4	6.4	44	47	47	3.5	3.6	8.5
NJ	8,414	8,657	8,686	100.0	100.0	3.2	–	–	–	–	–	–
NM	1,737	1,839	1,893	95.5	96.1	9.0	82	78	77	4.5	3.9	–6.5
NY	18,547	18,835	18,870	97.7	97.8	1.7	430	428	428	2.3	2.2	–0.5
NC	7,352	7,968	8,340	91.4	92.0	13.4	695	712	721	8.6	8.0	3.7
ND	435	443	451	67.7	70.5	3.8	208	193	189	32.3	29.5	–9.1
OH	10,849	10,952	10,960	95.6	95.6	1.0	504	508	507	4.4	4.4	0.6
OK	2,891	2,982	3,060	83.8	84.6	5.9	560	554	557	16.2	15.4	–0.5
OR	3,281	3,491	3,608	95.9	96.3	9.9	140	139	140	4.1	3.7	–0.1
PA	11,899	11,986	12,051	96.9	96.9	1.3	382	381	381	3.1	3.1	–0.2
RI	1,048	1,067	1,058	100.0	100.0	0.9	–	–	–	–	–	–
SC	3,735	3,984	4,137	93.1	93.9	10.8	277	271	271	6.9	6.1	–2.3
SD	527	561	578	69.8	72.6	9.7	228	219	218	30.2	27.4	–4.2
TN	5,080	5,371	5,530	89.3	89.8	8.9	610	619	626	10.7	10.2	2.8
TX	19,486	21,473	22,526	93.5	94.2	15.6	1,366	1,371	1,378	6.5	5.8	0.9
UT	2,107	2,379	2,515	94.4	95.1	19.3	126	126	130	5.6	4.9	3.7
VT	449	457	458	73.8	73.8	2.0	159	162	163	26.2	26.2	2.2
VA	6,269	6,739	6,884	88.6	89.3	9.8	810	819	828	11.4	10.7	2.2
WA	5,678	6,050	6,243	96.3	96.5	10.0	216	221	225	3.7	3.5	4.1
WV	1,348	1,356	1,365	74.5	75.3	1.3	461	449	447	25.5	24.7	–2.9
WI	4,604	4,769	4,830	85.8	86.2	4.9	759	771	771	14.2	13.8	1.6
WY	352	364	376	71.3	71.9	6.8	142	142	147	28.7	28.1	3.6

– Represents or rounds to zero.   [1] The April 1, 2000, estimates base reflects changes to the Census 2000 population resulting from legal boundary updates as of January 1 of the estimates year, other geographic program changes, and the Count Question Resolution program.   [2] Includes Broomfield city.

Source: U.S. Census Bureau, "Annual Estimates of the Population for Counties: April 1, 2000 to July 1, 2007"; published 20 March 2008; <http://www.census.gov/popest/counties/CO-EST2007-01.html>; and unpublished data.

Table 24. Population in Coastal Counties: 1980 to 2007

[Population as of April 1, except as indicated (3,537 represents 3,537,000). Areas as defined by U.S. National Oceanic and Atmospheric Administration, 1992. Covers 673 counties and equivalent areas with at least 15 percent of their land area either in a coastal watershed (drainage area) or in a coastal cataloging unit (a coastal area between watersheds). See Appendix III]

| Year | Total | Counties in coastal regions | | | | | Balance of United States |
		Total	Atlantic	Gulf of Mexico	Great Lakes	Pacific	
Land area, 2000 (1,000 sq. mi.)	3,537	889	148	115	115	511	2,649
POPULATION							
1980 (mil.).	226.5	119.8	53.7	13.1	26.0	27.0	106.7
1990 (mil.).	248.7	133.4	59.0	15.2	25.9	33.2	115.3
2000 (mil.).	281.4	148.3	65.2	18.0	27.3	37.8	133.1
2007 (July 1) (mil.)	301.6	156.6	68.8	19.9	27.4	40.5	145.0
1980 (percent).	100	53	24	6	11	12	47
1990 (percent).	100	54	24	6	10	13	46
2000 (percent).	100	53	23	6	10	13	47
2007 (July 1) (percent)	100	52	23	7	9	13	48

Source: U.S. Census Bureau, 1980 Census of Population, Vol. 1, Chapter A (PC80-1-A-1), *U.S. Summary*; 1990 Census of Population and Housing (CPH1); and unpublished data.

Table 25. States with Coastal Counties—Population, Housing Units, Establishments, and Employees by Coastal Region and State: 2000 and 2007

[281,425 represents 281,425,000. Population and housing as of July 1, except 2000 as of April 1. See headnote, Table 24. Minus sign (–) indicates decrease]

| Coastal region and state | Population | | | | | Housing units | | | Private nonfarm [3]— | |
| | | 2007 | | Per-cent change, 2000–2007 | Per square mile 2007 [2] | Number | | Per-cent change, 2000–2007 | Estab-lish-ments, 2007 (1,000) | Employ-ees, 2007 (1,000) |
	2000 [1] (1,000)	Number (1,000)	Per-cent of state total			2000 [1] (1,000)	2007 (1,000)			
United States, total . .	281,425	301,621	(X)	7.2	85	115,904	127,902	10.4	7,601	119,917
Interior U.S.	133,103	145,020	(X)	9.0	55	55,918	62,691	12.1	3,549	57,510
Coastal counties, total . .	148,322	156,601	(X)	5.6	176	59,986	65,211	8.7	4,052	62,408
Atlantic.	65,198	68,772	(X)	5.5	465	26,821	29,062	8.4	1,886	28,309
Maine.	1,184	1,228	93.2	3.7	61	599	643	7.3	39	479
New Hampshire	1,007	1,077	81.9	7.0	256	432	471	9.2	32	459
Massachusetts	6,125	6,225	96.5	1.6	942	2,531	2,628	3.8	170	2,943
Rhode Island	1,048	1,058	100.0	0.9	1,012	440	451	2.5	30	440
Connecticut	3,406	3,502	100.0	2.8	723	1,386	1,438	3.8	93	1,578
New York	13,573	13,950	72.3	2.8	1,800	5,285	5,478	3.7	394	5,505
New Jersey	8,312	8,576	98.7	3.2	1,215	3,269	3,454	5.7	240	3,560
Pennsylvania	5,750	5,922	47.6	3.0	860	2,334	2,448	4.8	145	2,602
Delaware.	784	865	100.0	10.4	443	343	389	13.3	26	388
Maryland.	4,865	5,146	91.6	5.8	679	1,970	2,120	7.6	128	2,031
District of Columbia.	572	588	100.0	2.8	9,581	275	284	3.4	21	447
Virginia	4,794	5,233	67.8	9.1	376	1,912	2,158	12.9	135	2,241
North Carolina	1,985	2,110	23.3	6.3	108	905	1,031	14.0	49	650
South Carolina	1,653	1,839	41.7	11.2	121	750	890	18.7	46	631
Georgia.	822	895	9.4	8.9	74	346	389	12.4	20	281
Florida	9,320	10,557	57.8	13.3	564	4,043	4,790	18.5	317	4,075
Gulf of Mexico	18,003	19,876	(X)	10.4	174	7,718	8,859	14.8	461	6,875
Florida	6,249	7,229	39.6	15.7	230	3,074	3,720	21.0	189	2,429
Georgia.	95	99	1.0	4.4	62	40	44	9.8	2	30
Alabama	712	743	16.1	4.3	85	319	362	13.5	18	262
Mississippi	588	593	20.3	0.8	87	246	260	5.6	12	162
Louisiana	3,510	3,333	77.6	–5.0	130	1,439	1,424	–1.0	80	1,247
Texas	6,850	7,879	33.0	15.0	196	2,599	3,049	17.3	160	2,745
Great Lakes	27,325	27,404	(X)	0.3	237	11,405	12,032	5.5	664	11,321
New York	3,650	3,582	18.6	–1.8	167	1,586	1,626	2.6	83	1,384
Pennsylvania	281	279	2.2	–0.6	348	114	118	3.2	7	118
Ohio.	4,418	4,345	37.9	–1.7	412	1,869	1,950	4.3	109	1,883
Michigan	8,859	8,986	89.2	1.4	176	3,782	4,042	6.9	212	3,401
Indiana	1,378	1,421	22.4	3.1	349	556	603	8.6	33	601
Illinois	6,021	5,995	46.6	–0.4	4,303	2,322	2,425	4.4	151	2,691
Wisconsin	2,469	2,549	45.5	3.2	166	1,055	1,139	8.0	62	1,145
Minnesota	248	247	4.7	–0.7	23	121	128	6.1	7	98
Pacific	37,796	40,550	(X)	7.3	79	14,042	15,257	8.7	1,041	15,903
Washington	4,587	5,046	78.0	10.0	204	1,919	2,158	12.4	144	1,976
Oregon	1,808	1,931	51.5	6.8	92	794	859	8.2	60	816
California.	29,660	31,718	86.8	6.9	408	10,650	11,498	8.0	786	12,394
Alaska	530	571	83.6	7.9	1	219	236	7.4	17	209
Hawaii	1,212	1,283	100.0	5.9	200	461	507	10.0	33	506

X Not applicable.   [1] Reflects modifications to the Census 2000 population as documented in the Count Question Resolution program and geographic program revisions.   [2] Calculated on the basis of land area data from the 2000 census.   [3] Covers establishments with payroll. Excludes most government employees, railroad employees, self-employed persons. Employees are for the week including March 12.

Source: U.S. Census Bureau, USA Counties; <http://censtats.census.gov/usa/usa.shtml>; accessed 27 August 2008; and "County Business Patterns," <http://www.census.gov/epcd/cbp/index.html>.

Table 26. Incorporated Places With 150,000 or More Inhabitants in 2007— Population: 1990 to 2007

[In thousands, except as indicated (223 represents 223,000). As of April 1, except beginning 2005 as of July 1. Beginning with 2000 estimates base, data refer to boundaries in effect on January 1, 2007; 1990 and 2000 census data, boundaries in effect on January 1, 2000; Minus sign (–) indicates decrease. See Appendix III]

Incorporated place	Number (1,000)					Percent change		Rank, 2007
	1990	2000, estimates base [1]	2005	2006	2007	1990 to 2000 [2]	2000 to 2007 [1]	
Akron, OH.	223	217	211	209	208	–2.7	–4.2	95
Albuquerque, NM	387	449	499	510	518	15.9	15.3	34
Amarillo, TX.	158	174	183	185	186	10.0	7.2	120
Anaheim, CA	267	329	332	332	333	23.0	1.4	55
Anchorage, AK	226	260	277	280	280	15.0	7.4	65
Arlington, TX	262	333	362	367	371	27.1	11.4	50
Arlington, VA [3]	171	189	200	201	205	10.9	8.0	98
Atlanta, GA	394	418	483	499	519	5.8	24.2	33
Augusta-Richmond County, GA [4] . . .	186	195	192	192	192	4.8	–1.6	115
Aurora, CO	222	276	297	303	312	24.6	12.8	58
Aurora, IL	100	143	167	169	171	42.6	19.2	135
Austin, TX	497	660	704	725	743	32.1	12.6	16
Bakersfield, CA	188	244	293	306	316	31.4	29.6	57
Baltimore, MD	736	651	640	641	637	–11.5	–2.1	20
Baton Rouge, LA	223	229	223	231	227	2.2	–0.7	84
Birmingham, AL	266	242	232	231	230	–8.7	–5.2	81
Boise City, ID	142	195	200	200	203	30.8	4.0	101
Boston, MA	575	589	597	596	599	2.5	1.7	23
Brownsville, TX	114	142	165	169	173	22.6	21.3	130
Buffalo, NY	328	293	278	275	273	–10.8	–6.8	68
Cape Coral, FL.	75	102	140	151	157	36.1	53.2	145
Chandler, AZ	91	177	232	241	246	94.7	39.1	76
Charlotte, NC	428	567	633	654	672	26.4	18.5	19
Chattanooga, TN	153	156	166	168	170	1.8	8.7	138
Chesapeake, VA.	152	199	217	219	219	31.1	10.0	85
Chicago, IL	2,783	2,896	2,840	2,829	2,837	4.1	–2.1	3
Chula Vista, CA	135	174	212	214	217	28.3	25.3	89
Cincinnati, OH	365	331	331	332	332	–9.1	0.4	56
Cleveland, OH	506	477	450	443	438	–5.5	–8.3	40
Colorado Springs, CO	282	361	371	375	376	28.0	4.2	47
Columbus, GA	[4]179	186	189	192	187	[4]4.0	0.4	119
Columbus, OH	639	713	739	743	748	11.3	4.9	15
Corona, CA.	76	128	148	149	150	64.0	17.6	154
Corpus Christi, TX	258	277	282	284	286	7.4	2.9	63
Dallas, TX	1,007	1,189	1,214	1,228	1,240	18.1	4.4	9
Dayton, OH	182	166	158	157	155	–8.9	–6.5	147
Denver, CO	468	554	566	576	588	18.6	6.3	26
Des Moines, IA.	193	199	195	196	197	2.8	–1.0	110
Detroit, MI	1,028	951	921	919	917	–7.5	–3.6	11
Durham, NC	149	188	207	212	218	25.5	16.0	87
El Paso, TX.	516	564	591	601	607	9.3	7.6	21
Fayetteville, NC	117	175	173	173	172	3.4	–2.0	132
Fontana, CA	88	142	176	181	184	46.7	29.4	124
Fort Lauderdale, FL	150	171	184	184	184	1.6	7.6	122
Fort Wayne, IN.	206	252	248	249	251	–0.1	–0.2	71
Fort Worth, TX	449	542	623	652	682	19.1	25.9	17
Fremont, CA	173	203	200	201	201	17.3	–1.0	102
Fresno, CA	355	430	460	464	471	20.3	9.5	35
Garden Grove, CA	144	165	166	165	166	15.0	0.2	142
Garland, TX.	181	216	216	217	219	19.3	1.4	86
Gilbert, AZ.	30	114	182	196	208	265.6	82.3	96
Glendale, AZ	151	220	245	248	253	45.0	15.2	70
Glendale, CA.	180	195	199	198	197	8.3	1.0	111
Grand Prairie, TX	100	127	144	154	158	27.4	24.6	144
Grand Rapids, MI	189	198	194	193	194	4.7	–2.1	113
Greensboro, NC	192	228	237	241	247	16.9	8.2	74
Henderson, NV.	65	175	232	241	249	169.4	42.3	72
Hialeah, FL	188	226	219	215	212	20.5	–6.3	93
Honolulu, HI [3]	376	372	376	377	376	–1.2	1.1	49
Houston, TX	1,697	1,974	2,076	2,169	2,208	15.1	11.8	4
Huntington Beach, CA	181	190	194	193	193	4.7	1.7	114
Huntsville, AL.	161	160	166	168	171	–1.7	7.1	133
Indianapolis, IN [4]	732	782	789	792	795	6.9	1.7	13
Irvine, CA	111	144	187	193	201	28.4	39.6	103
Irving, TX	155	192	193	196	200	23.5	4.1	107
Jackson, MS	197	184	178	178	176	–6.3	–4.6	127
Jacksonville, FL	635	736	788	799	806	15.8	9.5	12
Jersey City, NJ.	229	240	239	241	242	4.8	1.0	77
Kansas City, MO.	435	442	444	447	450	1.5	2.0	39
Knoxville, TN	174	175	180	182	184	–0.1	4.7	123
Laredo, TX	126	178	206	212	218	40.1	22.5	88
Las Vegas, NV	259	480	545	553	559	84.7	16.4	28
Lexington-Fayette, KY	225	261	272	276	279	15.6	7.1	66
Lincoln, NE	193	226	243	245	249	17.0	9.9	73
Little Rock, AR	177	183	186	187	187	3.4	2.3	118
Long Beach, CA	430	462	472	469	467	7.4	1.1	36
Los Angeles, CA.	3,486	3,695	3,828	3,824	3,834	6.0	3.8	2
Louisville/Jefferson County, KY [4] . . .	[5]269	551	558	556	558	[5]–4.7	1.2	29
Lubbock, TX	187	200	212	215	217	6.9	8.8	90
Madison, WI	191	209	224	226	229	9.0	9.2	82

See footnotes at end of table.

U.S. Census Bureau, Statistical Abstract of the United States: 2009

[See headnote, page 32]

Incorporated place	Number (1,000)					Percent change		Rank, 2007
	1990	2000, estimates base [1]	2005	2006	2007	1990 to 2000 [2]	2000 to 2007 [1]	
Memphis, TN	664	691	677	677	674	-2.1	-2.4	18
Mesa, AZ	291	398	444	449	453	36.2	13.8	38
Miami, FL	359	362	383	400	410	1.0	13.0	43
Milwaukee, WI	629	597	601	603	602	-5.1	0.9	22
Minneapolis, MN	368	383	375	375	377	3.9	-1.4	46
Mobile, AL	198	199	190	192	191	0.3	-3.9	116
Modesto, CA	166	189	205	204	204	13.5	7.9	100
Montgomery, AL	191	202	201	204	204	5.6	1.2	99
Moreno Valley, CA	119	142	177	182	189	19.9	32.7	117
Nashville-Davidson, TN [4]	488	546	580	586	591	11.7	8.3	25
New Orleans, LA	497	485	454	210	239	-2.5	-50.7	78
New York, NY	7,323	8,009	8,214	8,251	8,275	9.4	3.3	1
Newark, NJ	275	273	278	279	280	-0.6	2.8	64
Newport News, VA	171	181	181	180	179	5.1	-0.9	126
Norfolk, VA	261	234	237	239	236	-10.3	0.6	79
North Las Vegas, NV	48	116	177	198	212	140.8	83.6	94
Oakland, CA	372	399	395	396	401	7.4	0.5	44
Oceanside, CA	128	161	167	167	169	25.8	4.7	141
Oklahoma City, OK	445	506	533	540	547	13.8	8.1	31
Omaha, NE	373	391	415	420	424	4.6	8.5	42
Ontario, CA	135	158	171	172	171	17.0	8.2	134
Orlando, FL	166	193	215	224	228	12.0	18.4	83
Overland Park, KS	111	149	165	167	169	34.3	13.3	139
Oxnard, CA	142	171	182	183	185	19.6	8.3	121
Philadelphia, PA	1,586	1,518	1,460	1,453	1,450	-4.3	-4.5	6
Phoenix, AZ	989	1,322	1,473	1,517	1,552	33.6	17.4	5
Pittsburgh, PA	370	335	317	314	311	-9.6	-7.0	59
Plano, TX	128	222	250	254	261	73.5	17.3	69
Pomona, CA	132	148	153	153	153	13.0	3.2	150
Port St. Lucie, FL	56	89	130	142	151	59.2	70.3	153
Portland, OR	486	529	537	542	550	8.9	4.0	30
Providence, RI	161	174	174	173	172	7.8	-0.7	131
Raleigh, NC	221	286	346	361	376	24.9	31.6	48
Rancho Cucamonga, CA	101	128	168	169	170	26.0	33.3	136
Reno, NV	139	183	206	211	215	29.8	17.2	92
Richmond, VA	203	198	198	199	200	-2.4	1.1	105
Riverside, CA	227	256	288	291	294	12.6	15.1	61
Rochester, NY	230	220	209	208	207	-4.4	-5.9	97
Rockford, IL	144	151	153	154	157	4.3	3.4	146
Sacramento, CA	370	407	451	453	460	10.0	13.1	37
Salem, OR	109	137	147	150	152	25.8	10.8	151
Salt Lake City, UT	160	182	178	180	181	13.6	-0.6	125
San Antonio, TX	998	1,160	1,263	1,296	1,329	14.7	14.6	7
San Bernardino, CA	171	188	200	200	199	8.3	5.8	108
San Diego, CA	1,111	1,223	1,259	1,259	1,267	10.1	3.5	8
San Francisco, CA	724	777	751	756	765	7.3	-1.5	14
San Jose, CA	783	896	913	925	940	14.2	4.9	10
Santa Ana, CA	294	338	340	338	340	14.8	0.5	53
Santa Clarita, CA	123	155	171	171	170	22.8	9.7	137
Santa Rosa, CA	121	149	153	153	154	22.0	3.9	149
Scottsdale, AZ	130	203	228	232	236	55.8	16.3	80
Seattle, WA	516	563	578	585	594	9.1	5.5	24
Shreveport, LA	199	201	198	201	200	0.6	-0.6	106
Sioux Falls, SD	102	125	145	148	152	21.5	21.6	152
Spokane, WA	178	197	198	199	201	9.8	2.0	104
Springfield, MO	141	152	153	154	155	7.4	1.7	148
St. Louis, MO	397	348	353	354	351	-12.2	0.7	52
St. Paul, MN	272	287	277	276	277	5.5	-3.3	67
St. Petersburg, FL	240	248	248	248	246	3.3	-0.8	75
Stockton, CA	212	243	284	286	287	15.0	18.1	62
Tacoma, WA	177	194	195	196	197	9.1	1.5	112
Tallahassee, FL	126	152	163	167	169	19.5	11.0	140
Tampa, FL	280	303	327	334	337	8.4	11.0	54
Tempe, AZ	142	159	167	170	174	11.7	9.8	128
Toledo, OH	333	314	301	298	295	-5.8	-6.0	60
Tucson, AZ	418	487	517	520	526	16.4	7.8	32
Tulsa, OK	367	393	381	383	384	7.0	-2.3	45
Vancouver, WA	104	145	158	159	161	38.0	11.5	143
Virginia Beach, VA	393	425	438	438	435	8.2	2.2	41
Washington, DC	607	572	582	585	588	-5.7	2.8	27
Wichita, KS	311	352	355	357	361	10.7	2.7	51
Winston–Salem, NC	168	201	208	212	215	10.6	6.9	91
Worcester, MA	170	173	175	174	174	1.8	0.8	129
Yonkers, NY	188	196	198	199	199	4.2	1.7	109

[1] Based on the April 1, 2000, population estimates base which reflects changes to the Census 2000 population from the Count Question Resolution program and geographic program revisions. [2] Based on 2000 census numbers as tabulated. [3] The population shown is for the census designated place (CDP). [4] Represents the portion of a consolidated city that is not within one or more separately incorporated places. [5] Data are for the incorporated place of Louisville city before consolidation of the city and county governments.

Source: U.S. Census Bureau, 2000 Census of Population and Housing, *Population and Housing Unit Counts* PHC-3; and "Annual Estimates of the Population for Incorporated Places Over 100,000, Ranked by July 1, 2007 Population: April 1, 2000 to July 1, 2007 (SUB-EST2007-01)"; release date: July 10, 2008 <http://www.census.gov/popest/cities/tables/SUB-EST2007-01.xls>.

Table 27. **Incorporated Places by Population Size: 1990 to 2007**

[**152.9 represents 152,900,000.** See Appendix III]

Population size	Number of incorporated places				Population (mil.)				Percent of total			
	1990	2000	2005	2007	1990	2000 [1]	2005	2007	1990	2000 [1]	2005	2007
Total	19,262	19,494	19,494	19,494	152.9	177.0	184.8	188.3	100.0	100.0	100.0	100.0
1,000,000 or more. . . .	8	9	9	9	20.0	23.0	23.6	24.0	13.0	13.0	12.8	12.7
500,000 to 999,999 . . .	15	21	23	25	10.1	13.5	15.0	16.3	6.6	7.6	8.1	8.7
250,000 to 499,999 . . .	41	38	38	37	14.2	13.7	13.7	13.0	9.3	7.8	7.4	6.9
100,000 to 249,999 . . .	131	176	184	191	19.1	26.1	28.0	29.1	12.5	14.8	15.1	15.4
50,000 to 99,999.	309	374	417	430	21.2	25.7	28.9	29.7	13.9	14.5	15.6	15.8
25,000 to 49,999.	567	657	674	684	20.0	23.0	23.4	23.7	13.0	13.0	12.7	12.6
10,000 to 24,999.	1,290	1,460	1,497	1,510	20.3	23.0	23.6	23.8	13.3	13.0	12.7	12.6
Under 10,000	16,901	16,759	16,652	16,608	28.2	28.9	28.7	28.7	18.4	16.4	15.5	15.2

[1] The April 1, 2000, population estimates base reflects modifications to the Census 2000 population as documented in the Count Question Resolution program and geographic program revisions.

Source: U.S. Census Bureau, *1990 Census of Population and Housing, Population and Housing Unit Counts* (CPH-2-1); and "Annual Estimates of the Population for Incorporated Places Over 100,000, Ranked by July 1, 2007 Population: April 1, 2000 to July 1, 2007 (SUB-EST2007-01)"; release date: July 10, 2008; <http://www.census.gov/popest/cities/tables/SUB-EST2007 -01.xls>.

Table 28. **Urban and Rural Population by State: 1990 and 2000**

[**222,361 represents 222,361,000. As of April 1.** Resident population. For urban definitions; see text, this section]

State	Urban population		2000, current definition		Rural population, 2000 (1,000)	State	Urban population		2000, current definition		Rural population, 2000 (1,000)
	1990 Former definition (percent)	1990 Current definition (percent)	Number (1,000)	Percent			1990 Former definition (percent)	1990 Current definition (percent)	Number (1,000)	Percent	
US, total . .	**75.2**	**78.0**	**222,361**	**79.0**	**59,061**	MS.	47.1	49.1	1,387	48.8	1,457
						MO	68.7	69.6	3,883	69.4	1,712
						MT.	52.5	56.4	488	54.1	414
AL	60.4	56.8	2,466	55.4	1,981	NE.	66.1	67.2	1,194	69.8	518
AK	67.5	61.0	411	65.6	216	NV.	88.3	87.4	1,829	91.5	170
AZ	87.5	86.5	4,524	88.2	607	NH.	51.0	57.2	732	59.3	503
AR	53.5	52.0	1,404	52.5	1,269	NJ	89.4	93.5	7,939	94.4	475
CA	92.6	93.7	31,990	94.4	1,882	NM.	73.0	75.0	1,364	75.0	456
CO.	82.4	83.8	3,633	84.5	668	NY.	84.3	87.4	16,603	87.5	2,374
CT.	79.1	87.0	2,988	87.7	418	NC.	50.4	57.8	4,849	60.2	3,200
DE.	73.0	79.2	628	80.1	156	ND.	53.3	53.4	359	55.9	283
DC.	100.0	100.0	572	100.0	–						
FL	84.8	88.0	14,270	89.3	1,712	OH.	74.1	77.5	8,782	77.4	2,571
						OK.	67.7	65.2	2,255	65.3	1,196
GA.	63.2	68.7	5,864	71.6	2,322	OR.	70.5	74.9	2,694	78.7	727
HI	89.0	90.5	1,108	91.5	103	PA.	68.9	76.8	9,464	77.1	2,817
ID	57.4	62.2	859	66.4	434	RI	86.0	89.9	953	90.9	95
IL.	84.6	86.4	10,910	87.8	1,510	SC.	54.6	61.5	2,427	60.5	1,585
IN	64.9	69.1	4,304	70.8	1,776	SD.	50.0	50.3	391	51.9	363
IA	60.6	59.4	1,787	61.1	1,139	TN.	60.9	62.7	3,620	63.6	2,069
KS	69.1	69.5	1,921	71.4	768	TX.	80.3	81.2	17,204	82.5	3,648
KY.	51.8	55.9	2,254	55.8	1,788	UT.	87.0	86.8	1,970	88.2	263
LA	68.1	72.9	3,246	72.6	1,223						
ME.	44.6	42.6	513	40.2	762	VT	32.2	40.2	232	38.2	376
						VA	69.4	71.5	5,170	73.0	1,909
MD.	81.3	85.0	4,559	86.1	738	WA	76.4	79.9	4,831	82.0	1,063
MA.	84.3	90.5	5,801	91.4	548	WV	36.1	46.9	833	46.1	976
MI	70.5	75.2	7,419	74.7	2,519	WI	65.7	67.3	3,664	68.3	1,700
MN	69.9	69.0	3,490	70.9	1,429	WY	65.0	67.1	321	65.1	172

– Represents zero.

Source: U.S. Census Bureau, 2000 Census of Population and Housing, *Population and Housing Unit Counts* PHC-3.

Table 29. Mobility Status of the Population by Selected Characteristics: 1981 to 2007

[As of March (221,641 represents 221,641,000). For persons 1 year old and over. Based on comparison of place of residence in immediate prior year and year shown. Excludes members of the Armed Forces except those living off post or with their families on post. Based on Current Population Survey, Annual Social and Economic Supplement; see text of this section and Appendix III. For composition of regions, see map, inside front cover]

Mobility period and characteristic	Total (1,000)	Non-movers	Percent distribution					Movers from abroad
			Movers (different house in United States)					
			Total	Same county	Different county			
					Total	Same state	Different state	
1981	221,641	83	17	10	6	3	3	1
1991	244,884	83	16	10	6	3	3	1
2001	275,611	86	14	8	6	3	3	1
2007, total	292,749	87	13	9	4	3	2	–
1 to 4 years old	16,455	80	19	13	6	4	2	–
5 to 9 years old	19,830	84	16	11	5	3	2	–
10 to 14 years old	20,444	88	12	8	4	2	1	–
15 to 19 years old	21,170	87	13	9	4	2	1	–
20 to 24 years old	20,532	73	26	18	8	5	3	1
25 to 29 years old	20,666	74	25	16	8	5	3	1
30 to 44 years old	61,964	85	14	9	5	3	2	1
45 to 64 years old	75,653	93	7	5	2	1	1	–
65 to 74 years old	18,998	96	4	2	2	1	1	–
75 to 84 years old	13,079	97	3	2	1	1	1	–
85 years old and over	3,958	96	4	3	1	1	1	–
Northeast	53,491	91	8	6	3	2	1	–
Midwest	64,672	87	13	8	5	3	2	–
South	106,406	86	14	9	5	3	2	–
West	68,181	85	14	10	4	2	2	–
Persons 16 years old and over	231,800	87	12	8	4	2	2	–
Civilian labor force	152,307	86	14	9	4	3	2	–
Employed	145,112	86	13	9	4	3	2	–
Unemployed	7,196	77	22	15	8	4	4	1
Armed Forces	767	70	26	13	12	4	8	5
Not in labor force	78,726	90	9	6	3	2	1	–
Employed civilians, 16 years old and over	145,112	86	13	9	4	3	2	–
Management, business, and financial	21,390	89	11	7	4	2	2	–
Professional	30,347	87	12	7	5	3	2	1
Service	23,843	84	16	12	4	3	2	1
Sales	16,653	86	14	9	5	3	2	–
Office and administrative support	19,524	87	13	9	4	2	2	–
Farming, fishing, and forestry	910	90	9	7	2	1	1	1
Construction and extraction	9,403	83	17	11	5	4	2	1
Installation, maintenance, and repair	5,024	88	12	8	4	2	1	–
Production	9,427	87	13	10	3	2	1	–
Transportation and material moving	8,591	87	13	9	4	2	1	–
Tenure:								
Owner-occupied units	207,774	93	6	4	2	1	1	–
Renter-occupied units	84,975	71	28	20	9	5	3	1

– Represents or rounds to zero.

Source: U.S. Census Bureau, "Geographical Mobility: 2006 to 2007, Detailed Tables"; <http://www.census.gov/population/www/socdemo/migrate.html>.

Table 30. Movers by Type of Move and Reason for Moving: 2007

[As of March (38,681 represents 38,681,000). For persons 1 year old and over. Based on comparison of place of residence in 2006 and 2007. Excludes members of the Armed Forces except those living off post or with their families on post. Based on Current Population Survey, Annual Social and Economic Supplement; see text of this section and Appendix III]

Reason for move	All movers	Intra-county	Inter-county	From abroad	Reason for move	All movers	Intra-county	Inter-county	From abroad
Total (1,000)	**38,681**	**25,192**	**12,299**	**1,191**	Housing-related reasons	42.0	52.8	23.2	6.5
PERCENT DISTRIBUTION					Wanted to own home/not rent	5.9	7.3	3.8	0.2
Total	100.0	100.0	100.0	100.0	New/better house/apartment	15.8	20.4	7.4	2.8
Family-related reasons	30.1	31.3	28.1	26.5	Better neighborhood/less crime	5.5	6.6	3.5	2.1
Change in marital status	5.9	6.2	5.3	5.7	Cheaper housing	8.0	9.9	4.9	0.1
To establish own household	9.8	12.0	5.9	5.0	Other housing	6.8	8.6		1.4
Other family reasons	14.4	13.0	16.9	15.8	Other reasons	7.0	5.2	10.2	14.5
Work-related reasons	20.8	10.7	38.5	52.4	Attend/leave college	1.9	1.0	3.3	6.8
New job/job transfer	9.8	2.5	23.2	25.8	Change of climate	0.4	0.1	1.0	0.2
To look for work/lost job	1.7	0.7	3.1	8.6	Health reasons	1.4	1.1	2.2	–
Closer to work/easier commute	4.8	4.5	5.5	3.1	Natural disaster	0.5	0.4	0.7	–
Retired	0.6	–	1.1	0.5	Other reason	2.9	2.6	3.1	7.6
Other job-related reason	4.0	2.8	5.5	14.4					

– Represents or rounds to zero.

Source: U.S. Census Bureau, "Geographical Mobility: 2006 to 2007, Detailed Tables"; <http://www.census.gov/population/www/socdemo/migrate.html>.

U.S. Census Bureau, Statistical Abstract of the United States: 2009

Table 31. Mobility Status of Households by Household Income: 2007

[As of March (116,041 represents 116,041,000). Covers householders 15 years old and over. Based on comparison of place of residence in 2006 and 2007. Excludes members of the Armed Forces except those living off post or with their families on post. Based on Current Population Survey, Annual Social and Economic Supplement; see text of this section and Appendix III]

Household income in 2006	Total (1,000)	Non-movers	Movers (different house in United States) Total	Same county	Different county Total	Same state	Different state	Movers from abroad
Householders, 15 years old and over	116,041	87	12	8	4	3	2	–
Less than $5,000	3,563	75	22	16	6	4	3	2
$5,000 to $9,999	5,129	82	18	13	5	3	2	–
$10,000 to $14,999	6,883	85	15	11	4	3	1	–
$15,000 to $24,999	13,743	85	15	10	5	3	2	–
$25,000 to $34,999	13,359	86	14	10	4	3	2	–
$35,000 to $49,999	16,931	86	14	10	4	3	2	–
$50,000 to $69,999	17,421	88	12	8	4	3	2	–
$70,000 to $99,999	16,860	91	9	6	3	2	1	–
$100,000 and over	22,152	92	8	5	3	2	2	–

– Represents or rounds to zero.

Source: U.S. Census Bureau, "Geographical Mobility: 2006 to 2007, Detailed Tables"; <http://www.census.gov/population/www/socdemo/migrate.html>.

Table 32. Mobility Status of Resident Population by State: 2006

[In percent, except as indicated (295,345 represents 295,345,000). Based on comparison of place of residence in 2005 and 2006. The American Community Survey universe includes the household population and the population living in institutions, college dormitories, and other group quarters. Based on a sample and subject to sampling variability; see text this section and Appendix III]

State	Population 1 year old and over [1] (1,000)	Same house in 2005	Different house in United States in 2005 — Same county	Different house in United States in 2005 — Different county	State	Population 1 year old and over [1] (1,000)	Same house in 2005	Different house in United States in 2005 — Same county	Different house in United States in 2005 — Different county
U.S. . .	295,345	83.2	9.9	6.3	MO	5,768	82.2	10.0	7.5
AL	4,543	83.6	9.8	6.3	MT	933	82.2	9.6	7.8
AK	660	78.1	12.0	9.2	NE	1,741	81.5	11.0	7.0
AZ	6,071	78.9	13.5	6.6	NV	2,458	77.3	14.8	7.2
AR	2,772	80.8	10.9	7.9	NH	1,301	85.9	7.8	5.8
CA	35,933	83.3	11.0	4.8	NJ	8,617	88.2	6.6	4.4
CO	4,685	79.6	10.4	9.2	NM	1,927	82.5	10.4	6.4
CT	3,466	86.4	8.8	4.3	NY	19,059	87.8	7.4	4.1
DE	842	85.7	9.3	4.7	NC	8,739	82.0	9.8	7.7
DC	573	79.8	10.2	8.5	ND	629	82.4	9.3	7.9
FL	17,858	81.8	10.5	6.8	OH	11,330	84.0	10.6	5.0
GA	9,221	80.5	9.5	9.3	OK	3,532	80.3	11.6	7.6
HI	1,269	84.2	9.3	5.2	OR	3,653	79.2	12.2	8.0
ID	1,443	78.3	11.4	9.6	PA	12,297	87.0	7.9	4.7
IL	12,659	84.5	10.0	4.9	RI	1,055	86.0	8.8	4.5
IN	6,229	82.8	10.5	6.3	SC	4,264	83.0	9.4	7.1
IA	2,944	82.6	10.1	6.9	SD	772	83.0	9.4	7.3
KS	2,725	80.7	10.8	7.9	TN	5,956	83.1	10.2	6.3
KY	4,153	82.9	10.0	6.8	TX	23,135	80.1	11.7	7.4
LA	4,227	80.8	10.6	8.3	UT	2,499	78.3	12.9	7.8
ME	1,307	85.4	8.7	5.7	VT	618	85.1	8.1	6.4
MD	5,538	84.7	7.8	6.7	VA	7,541	83.0	6.8	9.5
MA	6,360	85.7	8.3	5.2	WA	6,314	79.7	12.2	7.3
MI	9,972	85.5	9.2	5.0	WV	1,798	87.1	7.4	5.3
MN	5,097	85.3	7.6	6.5	WI	5,489	84.4	9.7	5.6
MS	2,865	82.6	10.2	7.0	WY	508	80.6	10.6	8.1

[1] Includes persons moving from abroad, not shown separately.

Source: U.S. Census Bureau, 2006 American Community Survey; B07003. Residence 1 Year Ago by Sex; using American FactFinder®; <http://factfinder.census.gov/>; (14 January 2008).

Table 33. Persons 65 Years Old and Over—Characteristics by Sex: 1990 to 2007

[As of March, except as noted (29.6 represents 29,600,000). Covers civilian noninstitutional population. Excludes members of Armed Forces except those living off post or with their families on post. Data for 1990 are based on 1980 census population controls; 2000 data based on 1990 census population controls; beginning 2005, data based on 2000 census population controls and an expanded sample of households. Based on Current Population Survey; see text, this section and Appendix III]

Characteristic	Total				Male				Female			
	1990	2000	2005	2007	1990	2000	2005	2007	1990	2000	2005	2007
Total (million)	29.6	32.6	35.2	36.0	12.3	13.9	15.1	15.4	17.2	18.7	20.0	20.6
PERCENT DISTRIBUTION												
Marital status:												
Never married	4.6	3.9	4.1	3.8	4.2	4.2	4.4	4.0	4.9	3.6	3.9	3.7
Married	56.1	57.2	57.7	57.7	76.5	75.2	74.9	75.4	41.4	43.8	44.7	44.5
Spouse present	54.1	54.6	54.8	55.3	74.2	72.6	71.7	72.8	39.7	41.3	42.0	42.2
Spouse absent	2.0	2.6	2.9	2.4	2.3	2.6	3.2	2.6	1.7	2.5	2.7	2.3
Widowed	34.2	32.1	30.3	29.7	14.2	14.4	13.7	13.1	48.6	45.3	42.9	42.2
Divorced	5.0	6.7	7.9	8.7	5.0	6.1	7.0	7.5	5.1	7.2	8.5	9.6
Educational attainment:												
Less than ninth grade	28.5	16.7	13.4	11.9	30.0	17.8	13.2	12.2	27.5	15.9	13.5	11.7
Completed 9th to 12th grade, but no high school diploma	[1]16.1	13.8	12.7	12.0	[1]15.7	12.7	11.9	11.4	[1]16.4	14.7	13.3	12.5
High school graduate	[2]32.9	35.9	36.3	37.4	[2]29.0	30.4	31.6	33.5	[2]35.6	39.9	39.9	40.3
Some college or associate's degree . .	[3]10.9	18.0	18.7	19.5	[3]10.8	17.8	18.4	18.2	[3]11.0	18.2	19.0	20.5
Bachelor's or advanced degree	[4]11.6	15.6	18.9	19.2	[4]14.5	21.4	24.9	24.8	[4]9.5	11.4	14.3	15.0
Labor force participation: [5]												
Employed	11.5	12.4	14.5	15.5	15.9	16.9	19.1	19.8	8.4	9.1	11.1	12.2
Unemployed	0.4	0.4	0.5	0.5	0.5	0.6	0.7	0.7	0.3	0.3	0.4	0.4
Not in labor force	88.1	87.2	84.9	84.0	83.6	82.5	80.2	79.5	91.3	90.6	88.5	87.4
Percent below poverty level [6]	11.4	9.7	9.8	9.4	7.8	6.9	7.0	6.6	13.9	11.8	11.9	11.5

[1] Represents those who completed 1 to 3 years of high school. [2] Represents those who completed 4 years of high school. [3] Represents those who completed 1 to 3 years of college. [4] Represents those who completed 4 years of college or more. [5] Annual averages of monthly figures. Source: U.S. Bureau of Labor Statistics, *Employment and Earnings*, January issues. See footnote 2, Table 567. [6] Poverty status based on income in preceding year.

Source: Except as noted, U.S. Census Bureau, *Current Population Reports*, P20-546, and earlier reports; "Educational Attainment"; <http://www.census.gov/population/www/socdemo/educ-attn.html>; "Families and Living Arrangements"; <http://www.census .gov/population/www/socdemo/hh-fam.html>; and "Detailed Poverty Tabulations from the CPS"; <http://www.census.gov/hhes /www/poverty/detailedpovtabs.html>.

Table 34. Persons 65 Years Old and Over—Living Arrangements and Disability Status: 2006

[In thousands (37,191 represents 37,191,000), except as indicated. The American Community Survey universe includes the household population and the population living in institutions, college dormitories, and other group quarters. Based on a sample and subject to sampling variability; see text, this section and Appendix III]

Relationship by household type	Number	Percent distri- bution	Type of disability	Total	65 to 74 years old	75 years old and over
Total	**37,191**	**100.0**	**Persons with a disability**	**14,567**	**5,624**	**8,943**
In households	35,304	94.9				
In family households	24,129	64.9	With a sensory disability	5,885	1,864	4,022
Householder	12,019	32.3	With a physical disability	11,143	4,344	6,799
Spouse	8,547	23.0	With a mental disability	4,406	1,438	2,968
Parent	2,074	5.6	With a self-care disability	3,719	1,132	2,587
Other relatives	1,341	3.6	With a go-outside-home disability . . .	6,302	1,742	4,559
Nonrelatives	148	0.4				
In nonfamily households . . .	11,175	30.0				
Householder	10,701	28.8				
Living alone	10,209	27.5				
Not living alone	492	1.3				
Nonrelatives	474	1.3				
In group quarters	1,887	5.1				

Source: U.S. Census Bureau, 2006 American Community Survey; B09017. Relationship by Household Type (Including Living Alone) for the Population 65 Years and Over; B18002. Sex by Age by Disability Status for the Civilian Noninstitutionalized Population 5 Years and Over; B18003. Sex by Age by Sensory Disability for the Civilian Noninstitutionalized Population 5 Years and Over; B18004. Sex by Age by Physical Disability for the Civilian Noninstitutionalized Population 5 Years and Over; B18005. Sex by Age by Mental Disability for the Civilian Noninstitutionalized Population 5 Years and Over; B18006. Sex by Age by Self-Care Disability for the Civilian Noninstitutionalized Population 5 Years and Over; B18007. Sex by Age by Go-Outside-Home Disability for the Civilian Noninstitutionalized Population 16 Years and Over; using American FactFinder®; <http://factfinder.census.gov/>; accessed: 16 January 2008.

Table 35. **Selected Characteristics of Racial Groups and Hispanic/Latino Population: 2006**

[**In thousands (195,933 represents 195,933,000), except as indicated**. The American Community Survey universe includes the household population and the population living in institutions, college dormitories, and other group quarters. Based on a sample and subject to sampling variability; see text of this section and Appendix III. For definition of median, see Guide to Tabular Presentation]

Characteristic	Total population	White alone	Black or African American alone	American Indian and Alaska Native alone	Asian alone
EDUCATIONAL ATTAINMENT					
Persons 25 years old and over, total	**195,933**	**150,606**	**21,877**	**1,403**	**8,902**
Less than 9th grade	12,744	7,782	1,303	134	745
9th to 12th grade, no diploma	18,503	12,529	3,196	200	538
High school graduate (includes equivalency)	59,124	45,771	7,474	475	1,549
Some college, no degree	38,186	30,074	4,636	304	1,067
Associate's degree	14,486	11,449	1,579	112	619
Bachelor's degree	33,496	27,168	2,444	117	2,636
Graduate degree	19,395	15,834	1,246	61	1,747
Percent high school graduate or higher	84.1	86.5	79.4	76.2	85.6
Percent bachelor's degree or higher	27.0	28.6	16.9	12.7	49.2
OCCUPATION					
Employed civilian population, 16 years old and over, total	**141,501**	**108,354**	**14,982**	**925**	**6,526**
Management, professional, and related occupations	48,058	38,893	3,962	230	3,049
Management, business, and financial operations occupations	19,415	16,116	1,432	87	1,009
Professional and related occupations	28,643	22,777	2,530	143	2,040
Service occupations	23,361	15,995	3,582	207	1,018
Sales and office occupations	36,616	28,474	3,996	212	1,520
Farming, fishing, and forestry occupations	1,007	748	47	15	15
Construction, extraction, and maintenance occupations	14,094	11,141	934	122	241
Construction and extraction occupations	9,133	7,118	549	88	105
Installation, maintenance, and repair occupations	4,961	4,023	385	34	136
Production, transportation, and material moving occupations	18,365	13,103	2,461	140	683
Production occupations	9,614	6,899	1,091	68	476
Transportation and material moving occupations	8,751	6,203	1,370	72	207
FAMILY INCOME IN THE PAST 12 MONTHS					
Total families	**74,564**	**57,424**	**8,421**	**540**	**3,083**
Less than $10,000	3,564	2,007	987	60	117
$10,000 to $19,999	5,886	3,738	1,208	80	187
$20,000 to $29,999	7,236	5,048	1,149	72	226
$30,000 to $39,999	7,528	5,555	998	65	236
$40,000 to $49,999	7,204	5,510	823	56	248
$50,000 to $59,999	6,721	5,303	691	45	228
$60,000 to $74,999	8,873	7,152	800	51	348
$75,000 to $99,999	10,640	8,752	855	54	456
$100,000 to $124,999	6,590	5,509	435	27	353
$125,000 to $149,999	3,605	3,044	209	12	216
$150,000 to $199,999	3,415	2,891	170	11	247
$200,000 or more	3,303	2,915	97	8	221
Median family income in the past 12 months (dol.)	58,526	62,712	38,385	38,800	72,305
POVERTY STATUS IN THE PAST 12 MONTHS [2]					
Persons below poverty level	38,757	22,657	8,969	607	1,381
Percent below poverty level	13.3	10.5	25.3	26.6	10.7
Families below poverty level	7,283	4,134	1,815	121	253
Percent below poverty level	9.8	7.2	21.6	22.5	8.2
HOUSING TENURE					
Total householders	**111,617**	**86,952**	**13,074**	**790**	**4,142**
Owner-occupied	75,086	62,908	6,056	442	2,499
Renter-occupied	36,531	24,044	7,018	348	1,643

See footnotes at end of table.

U.S. Census Bureau, Statistical Abstract of the United States: 2009

Table 35. **Selected Characteristics of Racial Groups and Hispanic/Latino Population: 2006**—Con.

[See headnote, page 38]

Characteristic	Native Hawaiian and Other Pacific Islander alone	Some other race alone	Two or more races	Hispanic/ Latino [1]	White alone, not Hispanic or Latino
EDUCATIONAL ATTAINMENT					
Persons 25 years old and over, total	252	10,435	2,458	24,066	137,803
Less than 9th grade	17	2,612	151	5,756	4,773
9th to 12th grade, no diploma	23	1,756	260	3,824	10,590
High school graduate (includes equivalency)	102	3,082	671	6,767	42,307
Some college, no degree	53	1,451	601	3,510	28,195
Associate's degree	21	505	201	1,257	10,754
Bachelor's degree	26	731	375	2,020	25,957
Graduate degree	9	298	199	932	15,227
Percent high school graduate or higher	84.1	58.1	83.3	60.2	88.9
Percent bachelor's degree or higher	13.9	9.9	23.3	12.3	29.9
OCCUPATION					
Employed civilian population, 16 years old and over, total	201	8,519	1,994	19,270	98,266
Management, professional, and related occupations	41	1,276	607	3,316	36,989
Management, business and financial operations occupations	16	530	224	1,400	15,297
Professional and related occupations	24	745	383	1,915	21,692
Service occupations	47	2,107	405	4,544	13,718
Sales and office occupations	56	1,806	553	4,226	26,233
Farming, fishing, and forestry occupations	1	167	13	447	485
Construction, extraction, and maintenance occupations	25	1,450	182	3,180	9,480
Construction and extraction occupations	18	1,139	116	2,496	5,811
Installation, maintenance, and repair occupations	7	310	65	684	3,669
Production, transportation, and material moving occupations	31	1,713	234	3,556	11,361
Production occupations	14	956	110	1,939	5,964
Transportation and material moving occupations	17	757	125	1,618	5,397
FAMILY INCOME IN THE PAST 12 MONTHS					
Total families	93	4,080	923	9,372	52,453
Less than $10,000	6	320	67	714	1,645
$10,000 to $19,999	8	573	92	1,282	3,074
$20,000 to $29,999	11	626	103	1,410	4,306
$30,000 to $39,999	12	560	103	1,270	4,884
$40,000 to $49,999	8	465	95	1,030	4,980
$50,000 to $59,999	7	364	84	823	4,870
$60,000 to $74,999	12	410	100	920	6,673
$75,000 to $99,999	11	390	121	918	8,260
$100,000 to $124,999	7	189	69	475	5,243
$125,000 to $149,999	5	85	34	223	2,913
$150,000 to $199,999	4	64	28	181	2,778
$200,000 or more	2	34	26	124	2,829
Median family income in the past 12 months (dol.)	52,104	39,156	50,089	40,074	65,180
POVERTY STATUS IN THE PAST 12 MONTHS [2]					
Persons below poverty level	67	4,084	992	9,293	17,890
Percent below poverty level	16.1	22.0	16.8	21.5	9.3
Families below poverty level	13	818	127	1,806	3,216
Percent below poverty level	14.3	20.1	13.8	19.3	6.1
HOUSING TENURE					
Total householders	120	5,106	1,433	12,025	80,493
Owner-occupied	55	2,339	787	5,933	59,526
Renter-occupied	65	2,766	646	6,092	20,967

[1] Persons of Hispanic/Latino origin may be of any race.　[2] For explanation of poverty level, see text, Section 13.

Source: U.S. Census Bureau, 2006 American Community Survey; B15002. Sex by Educational Attainment for the Population 25 Years and Over, B24010. Sex by Occupation for the Employed Civilian Population 16 Years and Over, B19101. Family Income in the Past 12 Months (In 2005 Inflation-Adjusted Dollars), B19113. Median Family Income in the Past 12 Months (In 2005 Inflation-Adjusted Dollars), B17001. Poverty Status in the Past 12 Months by Sex by Age, B17010. Poverty Status in the Past 12 Months of Families by Family Type by Presence of Related Children Under 18 Years by Age of Related Children, B25003. Tenure; using American FactFinder®; <http://factfinder.census.gov/>.

Table 36. American Indian and Alaska Native Population by Tribe: 2000

[**As of April**. This table shows data for American Indian and Alaska Native tribes alone or in combination of tribes or races. Respondents who identified themselves as American Indian or Alaska Native were asked to report their enrolled or principal tribe. Therefore, data shown here reflect the written tribal entries reported on the questionnaire. Some of the entries (for example, Iroquois, Sioux, Colorado River, and Flathead) represent nations or reservations. The information on tribe is based on self-identification and includes federally or state-recognized tribes, as well as bands and clans]

American Indian and Alaska Native tribe	Number	American Indian and Alaska Native tribe	Number
Total persons [1]	**4,119,301**	Osage	15,897
Apache	96,833	Ottawa	10,677
Blackfeet	85,750	Paiute	13,532
Cherokee	729,533	Pima	11,493
Cheyenne	18,204	Potawatomi	25,595
Chickasaw	38,351	Pueblo	74,085
Chippewa	149,669	Puget Sound Salish	14,631
Choctaw	158,774	Seminole	27,431
Colville	9,393	Shoshone	12,026
Comanche	19,376	Sioux	153,360
Cree	7,734	Tohono O'odham	20,087
Creek	71,310	United Houma Nation	8,713
Crow	13,394	Ute	10,385
Delaware	16,341	Yakama	10,851
Iroquois	80,822	Yaqui	22,412
Kiowa	12,242	Yuman	8,976
Latin American Indian	180,940	Alaskan Athabascan	18,838
Lumbee	57,868	Aleut	10,548
Menominee	9,840	Eskimo	54,761
Navajo	298,197	Tlingit-Haida	22,365

[1] Includes other tribes not shown separately.

Source: U.S. Census Bureau, *The American Indian and Alaska Native Population: 2000*, Census 2000 Brief (C2KBR/01-15), February 2002.

Table 37. Population Living on Selected Reservations and Trust Lands: 2000

[**As of April**. OTSA = Oklahoma Tribal Statistical Area; SDAISA = State Designated American Indian Statistical Area; ANRC = Alaska Native Regional Corporation]

Reservation, Trust Land, or Other Area	Total population	American Indian and Alaska Native population alone	American Indian and Alaska Native population alone or in combination with one or more races
Navajo Nation Reservation and Off-Reservation Trust Land, AZ–NM–UT	180,462	173,987	175,228
Cherokee OTSA, OK	462,327	76,041	104,482
Creek OTSA, OK	704,565	51,296	77,253
Lumbee SDAISA, NC	474,100	58,238	62,327
Choctaw OTSA, OK	224,472	29,521	39,984
Cook Inlet ANRC, AK	364,205	24,923	35,972
Chickasaw OTSA, OK	277,416	22,946	32,372
Calista ANRC, AK	23,032	19,617	20,353
United Houma Nation SDAISA, LA	839,880	11,019	15,305
Sealaska ANRC, AK	71,507	11,320	15,059
Pine Ridge Reservation and Off-Reservation Trust Land, SD–NE	15,521	14,304	14,484
Doyon ANRC, AK	97,190	11,182	14,128
Kiowa-Comanche-Apache-Fort Sill Apache OTSA, OK	193,260	9,675	13,045
Fort Apache Reservation, AZ	12,429	11,702	11,854
Citizen Potawatomi Nation-Absentee Shawnee OTSA, OK	106,624	6,733	10,617
Gila River Reservation, AZ	11,257	10,353	10,578
Cheyenne-Arapaho OTSA, OK	157,869	7,402	10,310
Tohono O'odham Reservation and Off-Reservation Trust Land, AZ	10,787	9,718	9,794
Osage Reservation, OK	44,437	6,410	9,209
Rosebud Reservation and Off-Reservation Trust Land, SD	10,469	9,040	9,165
San Carlos Reservation, AZ	9,385	8,921	9,065
Blackfeet Reservation and Off-Reservation Trust Land, MT	10,100	8,507	8,684
Yakama Reservation and Off-Reservation Trust Land, WA	31,799	7,411	8,193
Turtle Mountain Reservation and Off-Reservation Trust Land, MT–ND–SD	8,331	8,009	8,043
Flathead Reservation, MT	26,172	6,999	7,883
Zuni Reservation and Off-Reservation Trust Land, NM–AZ	7,758	7,426	7,466
Bering Straits ANRC, AK	9,196	6,915	7,274
Sac and Fox OTSA, OK	55,690	5,334	7,232
Eastern Cherokee Reservation, NC	8,092	6,665	6,898
Wind River Reservation and Off-Reservation Trust Land, WY	23,250	6,544	6,864
Hopi Reservation and Off-Reservation Trust Land, AZ	6,946	6,573	6,633
Fort Peck Reservation and Off-Reservation Trust Land, MT	10,321	6,391	6,577
Cheyenne River Reservation and Off-Reservation Trust Land, SD	8,470	6,249	6,346
NANA ANRC, AK	7,208	5,944	6,181
Standing Rock Reservation, SD–ND	8,250	5,964	6,054
Bristol Bay ANRC, AK	7,892	5,336	5,749
Arctic Slope ANRC, AK	7,385	5,050	5,453
Crow Reservation and Off-Reservation Trust Land, MT	6,894	5,165	5,275
Red Lake Reservation, MN	5,162	5,071	5,087

Source: U.S. Census Bureau, 2000 Census of Population and Housing, *Profiles of General Demographic Characteristics*. See also <http://factfinder.census.gov/home/aian/index.html>.

Table 38. Social and Economic Characteristics of the Hispanic Population: 2007

[As of March, except labor force status, annual average (44,854 represents 44,854,000). Excludes members of the Armed Forces except those living off post or with their families on post. Based on Current Population Survey; see text of this section and Appendix III]

Characteristic	Number (1,000)					Percent distribution				
	His-panic, total [1]	Mexi-can	Puerto Rican	Cuban	Cen-tral, South Ameri-can	His-panic, total [1]	Mexi-can	Puerto Rican	Cuban	Cen-tral, South Ameri-can
Total persons	44,854	29,145	3,868	1,661	7,822	100.0	100.0	100.0	100.0	100.0
Under 5 years old	4,781	3,451	359	120	614	10.7	11.8	9.3	7.2	7.9
5 to 14 years old	8,180	5,640	750	196	1,180	18.2	19.4	19.4	11.8	15.1
15 to 44 years old	22,179	14,466	1,743	730	4,254	49.5	49.7	45.1	43.9	54.3
45 to 64 years old	7,286	4,295	738	372	1,388	16.3	14.8	19.1	22.4	17.7
65 years old and over.	2,428	1,293	278	243	385	5.4	4.4	7.2	14.6	4.9
EDUCATIONAL ATTAINMENT										
Persons 25 years old and over.	24,551	15,260	2,167	1,134	4,650	100.0	100.0	100.0	100.0	100.0
High school graduate or more	14,810	8,226	1,593	905	3,043	60.3	53.9	73.5	79.8	65.4
Bachelor's degree or more	3,127	1,380	355	308	831	12.7	9.0	16.4	27.2	17.9
LABOR FORCE STATUS [2]										
Civilians 16 years old and over.	31,383	19,770	2,711	1,421	(NA)	100.0	100.0	100.0	100.0	(NA)
Civilian labor force.	21,602	13,672	1,684	898	(NA)	68.8	69.2	62.1	63.2	(NA)
Employed	20,382	12,908	1,551	862	(NA)	64.9	65.3	57.2	60.7	(NA)
Unemployed	1,220	764	133	36	(NA)	3.9	3.9	4.9	2.5	(NA)
Unemployment rate [3]	5.6	5.6	7.9	4.0	(NA)	(X)	(X)	(X)	(X)	(X)
Male	5.3	5.0	8.5	4.1	(NA)	(X)	(X)	(X)	(X)	(X)
Female	6.1	6.5	7.3	3.9	(NA)	(X)	(X)	(X)	(X)	(X)
Not in labor force.	9,781	6,098	1,027	523	(NA)	31.2	30.8	37.9	36.8	(NA)
HOUSEHOLDS										
Total	12,973	7,818	1,374	607	2,467	100.0	100.0	100.0	100.0	100.0
Family households.	10,152	6,355	981	437	1,905	78.3	81.3	71.4	72.0	77.2
Married-couple families [4]	6,762	4,411	513	331	1,194	52.1	56.4	37.3	54.5	48.4
Male householder, no spouse present	945	626	75	27	177	7.3	8.0	5.5	4.4	7.2
Female householder, no spouse present	2,445	1,318	393	80	534	18.8	16.9	28.6	13.2	21.6
Nonfamily households	2,821	1,464	393	170	561	21.7	18.7	28.6	28.0	22.7
Male householder.	1,590	888	203	78	311	12.3	11.4	14.8	12.9	12.6
Female householder	1,231	576	190	92	250	9.5	7.4	13.8	15.2	10.1
Size:										
One person.	2,082	1,046	323	144	387	16.0	13.4	23.5	23.8	15.7
Two people	2,895	1,567	357	203	558	22.3	20.0	26.0	33.5	22.6
Three people.	2,521	1,475	282	112	520	19.4	18.9	20.5	18.5	21.1
Four people.	2,655	1,684	234	102	526	20.5	21.5	17.1	16.8	21.3
Five people.	1,613	1,159	97	18	286	12.4	14.8	7.1	2.9	11.6
Six people.	752	525	56	22	134	5.8	6.7	4.0	3.6	5.4
Seven people or more.	455	362	25	6	56	3.5	4.6	1.8	1.0	2.3
FAMILY INCOME IN 2006										
Total families [5]	10,155	6,358	981	437	1,861	100.0	100.0	100.0	100.0	100.0
Less than $5,000.	342	197	48	14	67	3.3	3.1	4.9	3.1	3.5
$5,000 to $14,999	1,036	637	147	31	182	10.2	10.0	15.0	7.1	9.8
$15,000 to $24,999	1,566	1,062	143	31	259	15.4	16.7	14.6	7.1	13.9
$25,000 to $34,999	1,486	979	124	59	257	14.6	15.4	12.7	13.6	13.8
$35,000 to $49,999	1,822	1,204	132	85	335	17.9	18.9	13.4	19.5	18.0
$50,000 to $74,999	1,805	1,131	164	70	345	17.8	17.8	16.7	16.0	18.5
$75,000 and over	2,096	1,148	224	147	417	20.6	18.1	22.8	33.6	22.4
POVERTY STATUS IN 2006										
Families below poverty level [6]	1,922	1,276	214	45	311	18.9	20.1	21.8	10.2	16.7
Persons below poverty level [6]	9,243	6,318	934	226	1,370	20.6	21.7	24.2	13.6	17.5
HOUSEHOLD TENURE										
Total occupied units	12,973	7,818	1,374	607	2,401	100.0	100.0	100.0	100.0	100.0
Owner-occupied [7]	6,396	4,026	564	370	957	49.3	51.5	41.1	61.0	39.9
Renter-occupied [7]	6,577	3,792	810	237	1,444	50.7	48.5	58.9	39.0	60.1

NA Not available.   X Not applicable.   [1] Includes other Hispanic groups not shown separately.   [2] Source: U.S. Bureau of Labor Statistics, *Employment and Earnings*, January 2008; <http://stats.bls.gov/opub/ee/home.htm>.   [3] Total unemployment as percent of civilian labor force.   [4] In married-couple families, Hispanic origin refers to the householder.   [5] Includes families in group quarters.   [6] For explanation of poverty level, see text, Section 13.   [7] Includes no cash rent.

Source: Except as noted, U.S. Census Bureau, "Educational Attainment"; <http://www.census.gov/population/www/socdemo/educ-attn.html>; "Families and Living Arrangements"; <http://www.census.gov/population/www/socdemo/hh-fam.html>; "Detailed Income Tabulations from the CPS"; <http://www.census.gov/hhes/www/income/dinctabs.html>; "Detailed Poverty Tabulations from the CPS"; <http://www.census.gov/hhes/www/poverty/detailedpovtabs.html>, and unpublished data.

Table 39. Native and Foreign-Born Population by State: 2006

[261,851 represents 261,851,000. The American Community Survey universe includes the household population and the population living in institutions, college dormitories, and other group quarters. Based on a sample and subject to sampling variability; see text of this section and Appendix III. See headnote, Table 43]

State	Native popu-lation (1,000)	Foreign-born population Number (1,000)	Foreign-born population Percent of total popu-lation	Foreign-born population Percent entered 2000 or later	State	Native popu-lation (1,000)	Foreign-born population Number (1,000)	Foreign-born population Percent of total popu-lation	Foreign-born population Percent entered 2000 or later
U.S., total . .	261,851	37,548	12.5	25.3					
AL	4,469	130	2.8	42.5	MO	5,649	194	3.3	32.4
AK	623	47	7.0	28.4	MT	927	18	1.9	27.4
AZ	5,237	929	15.1	30.8	NE	1,669	100	5.6	32.9
AR	2,704	107	3.8	35.1	NV	2,020	476	19.1	27.7
CA	26,555	9,902	27.2	19.7	NH	1,244	71	5.4	27.2
CO	4,264	489	10.3	30.4	NJ	6,970	1,754	20.1	24.5
CT	3,052	452	12.9	25.3	NM	1,757	197	10.1	29.3
DE	785	69	8.1	33.3	NY	15,127	4,179	21.6	20.7
DC	508	74	12.7	32.8	NC	8,242	614	6.9	37.2
FL	14,664	3,426	18.9	26.1	ND	622	13	2.1	42.5
GA	8,504	860	9.2	35.2	OH	11,066	412	3.6	30.0
HI	1,075	210	16.3	24.2	OK	3,403	176	4.9	31.9
ID	1,384	82	5.6	27.5	OR	3,341	360	9.7	29.6
IL	11,058	1,774	13.8	23.2	PA	11,804	637	5.1	28.3
IN	6,050	264	4.2	36.7	RI	933	134	12.6	23.1
IA	2,870	112	3.8	32.4	SC	4,145	176	4.1	37.3
KS	2,591	173	6.3	31.3	SD	765	17	2.2	38.8
KY	4,094	112	2.7	43.5	TN	5,802	237	3.9	40.8
LA	4,163	125	2.9	27.8	TX	19,767	3,741	15.9	27.1
ME	1,280	42	3.2	23.1	UT	2,340	211	8.3	30.9
MD	4,933	683	12.2	31.9	VT	600	24	3.9	24.2
MA	5,529	908	14.1	27.0	VA	6,869	774	10.1	31.5
MI	9,497	599	5.9	27.3	WA	5,602	794	12.4	26.8
MN	4,828	339	6.6	33.1	WV	1,797	22	1.2	29.5
MS	2,859	51	1.8	39.5	WI	5,312	245	4.4	29.8
					WY	501	14	2.7	34.4

Source: U.S. Census Bureau, 2006 American Community Survey; C05002. Place of Birth by Citizenship Status; and C05005. Year of Entry by Citizenship Status; using American FactFinder®; <http://factfinder.census.gov/>; (accessed: 16 January 2008).

Table 40. Nativity and Place of Birth of Resident Population—25 Largest Cities: 2006

[717 represents 717,000. The American Community Survey universe includes the household population and the population living in institutions, college dormitories, and other group quarters. Based on a sample and subject to sampling variability; see text of this section and Appendix III. See headnote, Table 43]

City	Total population (1,000)	Native population Total (1,000)	Native population Born in United States (1,000)	Native population Born outside United States (1,000)	Foreign-born population Total Number (1,000)	Foreign-born population Total Percent of total population	Foreign-born population Entered 2000 or later Number (1,000)	Foreign-born population Entered 2000 or later Percent of foreign-born population
Austin, TX	717	572	563	9	145	20.3	59	40.3
Baltimore, MD	631	593	586	6	39	6.1	17	42.9
Boston, MA	575	419	400	19	157	27.2	45	28.8
Charlotte, NC	648	560	552	7	89	13.7	33	37.0
Chicago, IL	2,749	2,149	2,102	47	600	21.8	140	23.4
Columbus, OH	718	651	645	6	67	9.4	30	45.1
Dallas, TX	1,193	871	861	10	321	26.9	98	30.5
Denver, CO	567	470	463	7	97	17.1	27	28.2
Detroit, MI	834	796	791	5	38	4.5	10	26.4
El Paso, TX	596	436	425	11	160	26.9	31	19.1
Fort Worth, TX	637	526	521	6	111	17.4	33	29.5
Houston, TX	2,075	1,499	1,483	16	576	27.8	178	30.9
Indianapolis, IN [1]	789	738	734	4	51	6.5	23	45.5
Jacksonville, FL	800	734	719	15	66	8.2	22	32.8
Las Vegas, NV	570	437	431	6	132	23.2	40	30.4
Los Angeles, CA	3,774	2,267	2,234	33	1,507	39.9	308	20.5
Memphis, TN	643	608	605	4	35	5.4	17	49.4
New York, NY	8,214	5,176	4,859	318	3,038	37.0	629	20.7
Philadelphia, PA	1,448	1,291	1,248	43	158	10.9	54	34.3
Phoenix, AZ	1,430	1,095	1,080	16	334	23.4	117	35.0
San Antonio, TX	1,273	1,109	1,085	23	165	12.9	41	24.6
San Diego, CA	1,261	926	902	23	335	26.6	74	22.1
San Francisco, CA	744	474	463	11	270	36.3	52	19.2
San Jose, CA	916	562	553	10	354	38.6	80	22.5
Washington, DC	582	508	500	7	74	12.7	24	32.8

[1] Represents the portion of a consolidated city that is not within one or more separately incorporated places.

Source: U.S. Census Bureau, 2006 American Community Survey; C05002. Place of Birth by Citizenship Status; and C05005. Year of Entry by Citizenship Status; using American FactFinder®; <http://factfinder.census.gov/>; (accessed: 16 January 2008).

U.S. Census Bureau, Statistical Abstract of the United States: 2009

Table 41. Native and Foreign-Born Populations by Selected Characteristics: 2007

[In thousands (296,824 represents 296,824,000). As of March. The foreign-born population includes anyone who is not a U.S. citizen at birth. This includes legal permanent residents (immigrants), temporary migrants (such as students), humanitarian migrants (such as refugees), and persons illegally present in the United States. Based on Current Population Survey, Annual Social and Economic Supplement which includes the civilian noninstitutional population plus Armed Forces living off post or with their families on post; see text, this section, and Appendix III]

Characteristic	Total population	Native population	Foreign-born population			
			Total	Natural-ized citizen	Not U.S. citizen	Year of entry: 2000 to March 2007
Total	**296,824**	**259,545**	**37,279**	**14,538**	**22,741**	**10,268**
Under 5 years old...............	20,530	20,171	359	97	262	359
5 to 14 years old.............	40,274	38,417	1,857	254	1,603	1,296
15 to 24 years old.............	41,702	37,243	4,459	922	3,537	2,127
25 to 34 years old.............	39,868	31,691	8,176	1,852	6,325	3,277
35 to 44 years old.............	42,762	34,382	8,380	3,097	5,283	1,776
45 to 54 years old.............	43,461	37,291	6,170	3,210	2,960	773
55 to 64 years old.............	32,191	28,339	3,853	2,307	1,546	383
65 to 74 years old.............	18,998	16,717	2,281	1,550	731	179
75 to 84 years old.............	13,079	11,765	1,314	939	376	72
85 years old and over...........	3,958	3,529	430	312	118	28
Median age (years).............	36.4	35.7	39.3	48.2	34.5	28.9
Male...................	145,689	126,924	18,766	6,693	12,072	5,427
Female...................	151,135	132,621	18,514	7,845	10,669	4,841
MARITAL STATUS						
Persons 15 years old and over	**236,020**	**200,956**	**35,063**	**14,187**	**20,876**	**8,613**
Married........................	124,862	103,054	21,807	9,401	12,406	4,862
Widowed.......................	13,920	12,314	1,606	999	607	156
Divorced.......................	22,867	20,769	2,098	1,147	951	228
Separated......................	5,047	4,078	969	361	608	178
Never married..................	69,324	60,741	8,583	2,280	6,304	3,191
EDUCATIONAL ATTAINMENT						
Persons 25 years old and over	**194,318**	**163,714**	**30,604**	**13,265**	**17,339**	**6,487**
Not high school graduate..........	27,742	17,986	9,756	2,740	7,017	2,209
High school graduate/some college	110,733	98,435	12,299	5,972	6,327	2,275
Bachelor's degree...............	36,658	31,315	5,343	2,822	2,521	1,261
Advanced degree...............	19,184	15,977	3,206	1,732	1,474	741
EARNINGS IN 2006 [1]						
Persons 15 years old and over with earnings..............	**107,717**	**90,019**	**17,699**	**7,327**	**10,371**	**4,023**
Under $15,000...............	7,788	5,777	2,011	457	1,554	698
$15,000 to $24,999.............	18,916	14,366	4,550	1,308	3,242	1,336
$25,000 to $34,999.............	20,057	16,725	3,331	1,322	2,009	740
$35,000 to $49,999.............	22,968	19,881	3,088	1,500	1,588	517
$50,000 to $74,999.............	20,982	18,587	2,395	1,311	1,084	439
$75,000 and over.............	17,006	14,682	2,324	1,428	895	293
Median earnings (dollars) [2].........	38,489	40,346	31,078	40,351	26,218	24,683
HOUSEHOLD SIZE [3]						
Total households..............	**116,011**	**100,603**	**15,408**	**7,210**	**8,198**	**2,969**
One person......................	31,132	28,417	2,715	1,474	1,241	463
Two persons....................	38,580	34,707	3,873	2,037	1,836	767
Three persons..................	18,808	15,965	2,843	1,245	1,598	658
Four persons...................	16,172	13,132	3,041	1,293	1,747	620
Five persons...................	7,202	5,527	1,675	704	971	272
Six persons....................	2,702	1,931	770	286	485	117
Seven persons or more...........	1,415	924	492	170	321	72
INCOME IN 2006 [3]						
Total family households.........	**78,425**	**66,529**	**11,895**	**5,513**	**6,382**	**2,191**
Under $15,000................	5,899	4,827	1,073	373	700	264
$15,000 to $24,999.............	6,973	5,522	1,451	497	954	318
$25,000 to $34,999.............	8,025	6,507	1,517	593	924	328
$35,000 to $49,999.............	11,471	9,484	1,987	794	1,192	390
$50,000 to $74,999.............	15,859	13,695	2,163	1,051	1,112	413
$75,000 and over.............	30,198	26,494	3,705	2,205	1,500	477
Median income (dollars) [2]..........	59,894	61,565	44,706	60,733	41,650	49,241
POVERTY STATUS IN 2006 [4]						
Persons at or below poverty level....	**36,459**	**30,790**	**5,669**	**1,345**	**4,324**	**2,149**
Persons above poverty level.........	259,990	228,409	31,581	13,189	18,392	8,097

[1] Covers only year-round full-time workers. [2] For definition of median, see Guide to Tabular Presentation. [3] Based on citizenship of householder. [4] Persons for whom poverty status is determined. Excludes unrelated individuals under 15 years old.

Source: U.S. Census Bureau, unpublished data.

Table 42. Foreign-Born Population—Selected Characteristics by Region of Origin: 2007

[In thousands (37,279 represents 37,279,000). As of March. The term foreign-born refers to anyone who is not a U.S. citizen at birth. This includes naturalized U.S. citizens, legal permanent residents (immigrants), temporary migrants (such as foreign students), humanitarian migrants (such as refugees), and persons illegally present in the United States. Based on Current Population Survey, Annual Social and Economic Supplement; see text, this section and Appendix III]

Characteristic	Total foreign-born	Europe	Asia	Latin America Total	Carib-bean	Central America [1]	South America	Other areas
Total	**37,279**	**4,635**	**9,746**	**20,267**	**3,378**	**14,383**	**2,506**	**2,632**
Under 5 years old	359	39	103	191	21	158	12	27
5 to 14 years old	1,857	167	452	1,072	147	814	111	166
15 to 24 years old	4,459	434	885	2,809	330	2,133	345	331
25 to 34 years old	8,176	558	2,009	5,120	477	4,132	511	489
35 to 44 years old	8,380	801	2,178	4,791	796	3,431	563	611
45 to 54 years old	6,170	730	1,801	3,187	701	2,038	449	452
55 to 64 years old	3,853	712	1,213	1,652	419	954	279	275
65 to 74 years old	2,281	577	640	883	265	464	154	181
75 to 84 years old	1,314	459	365	411	167	178	65	80
85 years old and over	430	159	98	151	54	82	16	22
EDUCATIONAL ATTAINMENT								
Persons 25 years old and over	**30,604**	**3,995**	**8,305**	**16,195**	**2,879**	**11,279**	**2,037**	**2,109**
Less than ninth grade	6,100	392	643	4,881	365	4,321	194	184
9th to 12th grade (no diploma)	3,656	209	448	2,883	371	2,343	170	116
High school graduate	7,577	1,088	1,649	4,334	982	2,730	622	505
Some college or associate's degree	4,722	813	1,245	2,177	582	1,141	454	486
Bachelor's degree	5,343	862	2,542	1,457	431	595	431	482
Advanced degree	3,206	630	1,778	462	148	148	166	336
High school graduate or more	20,848	3,394	7,214	8,431	2,144	4,615	1,673	1,809
Bachelor's degree or more	8,549	1,493	4,319	1,919	579	744	596	818
INCOME IN 2006								
Total family households	**11,895**	**1,446**	**3,152**	**6,381**	**1,200**	**4,429**	**752**	**917**
Under $15,000	1,073	69	209	726	163	498	65	69
$15,000 to $24,999	1,451	126	206	1,043	142	839	63	76
$25,000 to $34,999	1,517	173	247	1,003	154	763	85	95
$35,000 to $49,999	1,987	208	355	1,295	234	919	141	129
$50,000 to $74,999	2,163	274	574	1,143	203	788	151	172
$75,000 and over	3,705	596	1,561	1,171	303	621	247	376
Median income (dol.) [2]	44,706	61,811	74,297	39,169	41,762	36,249	52,464	60,538

[1] Includes Mexico. [2] For definition of median, see Guide to Tabular Presentation.

Source: U.S. Census Bureau, unpublished data.

Table 43. Foreign-Born Population by Place of Birth and Citizenship Status: 2006

[In thousands, except percent (37,548 represents 37,548,000). The term foreign-born refers to anyone who is not a U.S. citizen at birth. This includes naturalized U.S. citizens, legal permanent residents (immigrants), temporary migrants (such as foreign students), humanitarian migrants (such as refugees), and persons illegally present in the United States. The American Community Survey universe includes the household population and the population living in institutions, college dormitories, and other group quarters. Based on a sample and subject to sampling variability; see text, this section and Appendix III]

Region	Foreign-born population, total	Naturalized citizen	Not U.S. citizen Number	Percent of foreign-born
Total [1]	**37,548**	**15,768**	**21,780**	**58**
Latin America	20,088	6,073	14,016	70
Caribbean	3,356	1,788	1,568	47
Central America	14,190	3,259	10,932	77
Mexico	11,541	2,480	9,062	79
Other Central America	2,649	779	1,870	71
South America	2,543	1,026	1,516	60
Asia	10,053	5,702	4,351	43
Europe	4,993	2,986	2,008	40
Africa	1,376	(NA)	(NA)	(NA)
Northern America	855	(NA)	(NA)	(NA)
Oceania	182	(NA)	(NA)	(NA)

NA Not available. [1] Includes persons born at sea.

Source: U.S. Census Bureau, 2006 American Community Survey; B05002. Place of Birth by Citizenship Status; C05006. Place of Birth for the Foreign-Born Population; and B05007. Place of Birth by Year of Entry by Citizenship Status for The Foreign-Born Population, using American FactFinder®; <http://factfinder.census.gov>; (accessed: 16 January 2008).

Table 44. Persons Obtaining Legal Permanent Resident Status: 1901 to 2007

[8,795 represents 8,795,000. For fiscal years ending in year shown; see text, Section 8. Rates based on Census Bureau estimates as of July 1 for resident population through 1929 and for resident population, including Armed Forces overseas, thereafter (excluding Alaska and Hawaii prior to 1959)]

Period	Number (1,000)	Rate [1]	Year	Number (1,000)	Rate [1]
1901 to 1910	8,795	10.4	1990	1,536	6.1
1911 to 1920	5,736	5.7	1995	720	2.7
1921 to 1930	4,107	3.5	1996	916	3.4
			1997	798	2.9
1931 to 1940	528	0.4	1998	653	2.4
1941 to 1950	1,035	0.7	1999	645	2.3
			2000	841	3.0
1951 to 1960	2,515	1.5	2001	1,059	3.7
1961 to 1970	3,322	1.7	2002	1,059	3.7
1971 to 1980	4,399	2.0	2003	704	2.4
			2004	958	3.3
1981 to 1990	7,256	3.0	2005	1,122	3.8
1991 to 2000	9,081	3.4	2006	1,266	4.2
2001 to 2007	7,220	3.5	2007	1,052	3.5

[1] Annual rate per 1,000 U.S. population. Rate computed by dividing sum of annual immigration totals by sum of annual U.S. population totals for same number of years.

Source: U.S. Department of Homeland Security, Office of Immigration Statistics, *2007 Yearbook of Immigration Statistics*. See also <http://www.dhs.gov/ximgtn/statistics/publications/yearbook.shtm>.

Table 45. Refugee Arrivals and Individuals Granted Asylum by Country of Nationality: 2005 to 2007

[**For year ending September 30**. Data shown provide information on the number of persons admitted to the United States as refugees or granted asylum in the United States in the year shown. In cases with no country of nationality, refers to country of last residence. For definitions of refugee and asylee, see text this section. Based on data from the Bureau of Population, Refugees, and Migration of the U.S. Department of State and the Executive Office for Immigration Review of the U.S. Department of Justice]

Country of nationality	Refugee arrivals			Country of nationality	Asylees		
	2005	2006	2007		2005	2006	2007
Total	53,738	41,150	48,217	Total	25,171	26,207	25,270
Burma	1,447	1,612	13,896	China	5,228	5,575	6,361
Somalia	10,405	10,357	6,969	Colombia	3,363	2,968	2,180
Iran	1,856	2,792	5,481	Haiti	2,938	2,998	1,660
Burundi	214	466	4,545	Venezuela	1,104	1,363	1,170
Cuba	6,360	3,143	2,922	Ethiopia	728	775	846
Russia	5,982	6,003	1,773	Indonesia	470	742	777
Iraq	198	202	1,608	Iraq	286	366	685
Liberia	4,289	2,402	1,606	Guatemala	386	637	681
Ukraine	2,889	2,483	1,605	El Salvador	244	596	569
Vietnam	2,009	3,039	1,500	Cameroon	645	587	505
Other countries [1] . . .	18,089	8,651	6,312	Other countries [1] . . .	9,779	9,600	9,836

[1] Includes unknown.

Source: U.S. Department of Homeland Security, Office of Immigration Statistics, Annual Flow Report, *Refugees and Asylees: 2007*, July 2008. See also <http://www.dhs.gov/xlibrary/assets/statistics/publications/oisrfafr2007.pdf>.

Table 46. Estimated Unauthorized Immigrants by Selected States and Countries of Origin: 2000 and 2006

[In thousands (8,460 represents 8,460,000). As of January. Unauthorized immigrants refers to foreign-born persons who entered the United States without inspection or who were admitted temporarily and stayed past the date they were required to leave. Unauthorized aliens who have applied for but have not yet received approval to lawfully remain in the United States are considered to be unauthorized. These estimates were calculated using a "residual method," whereby estimates of the legally resident foreign-born population were subtracted from the total foreign-born population in order to derive the unauthorized immigrant population. All of these component populations were resident in the United States on January 1, 2006, and entered during the 1980–2005 period. Persons who entered the United States prior to 1980 were assumed to be legally resident. Estimates of the legally resident foreign-born were based primarily on administrative data of the Department of Homeland Security, while estimates of the total foreign-born population were obtained from the American Community Survey of the U.S. Census Bureau. Estimates for 2000 are based on the same methodology, assumptions, and definitions with the exception that data from Census 2000 were used to estimate the foreign-born population in 2000 that entered the United States from January 1, 1980, through December 31, 1999]

State of residence	2000	2006	Country of birth	2000	2006
United States, total	8,460	11,550	Total	8,460	11,550
California	2,510	2,830	Mexico	4,680	6,570
Texas	1,090	1,640	El Salvador	430	510
Florida	800	980	Guatemala	290	430
Illinois	440	550	Philippines	200	280
New York	540	540	Honduras	160	280
Arizona	330	500	India	120	270
Georgia	220	490	Korea	180	250
New Jersey	350	430	Brazil	100	210
North Carolina	260	370	China	190	190
Washington	170	280	Vietnam	160	160
Other states	1,750	2,950	Other countries	1,950	2,410

Source: U.S. Department of Homeland Security, Office of Immigration Statistics, "Estimates of the Unauthorized Immigrant Population Residing in the United States: January 2006"; published August 2007; <http://www.dhs.gov/xlibrary/assets/statistics/publications/illpe2006.pdf>.

U.S. Census Bureau, Statistical Abstract of the United States: 2009

Table 47. Persons Obtaining Legal Permanent Resident Status by Class of Admission: 2000 to 2007

[For years ending September 30]

Class of admission	2000	2003	2004	2005	2006	2007
Total	**841,002**	**703,542**	**957,883**	**1,122,257**	**1,266,129**	**1,052,415**
New arrivals	407,279	358,333	373,962	383,955	446,881	431,368
Adjustments	433,723	345,209	583,921	738,302	819,248	621,047
Family-sponsored preferences	235,092	158,796	214,355	212,970	222,229	194,900
Unmarried sons/daughters of U.S. citizens and their children	27,635	21,471	26,380	24,729	25,432	22,858
Spouses, unmarried sons/daughters of alien residents and their children	124,540	53,195	93,609	100,139	112,051	86,151
Married sons/daughters of U.S. citizens [1]	22,804	27,287	28,695	22,953	21,491	20,611
Brothers or sisters of U.S. citizens [1]	60,113	56,843	65,671	65,149	63,255	65,280
Employment-based preferences	106,642	81,727	155,330	246,877	159,081	162,176
Priority workers [1]	27,566	14,453	31,291	64,731	36,960	26,697
Professionals with advanced degrees or aliens of exceptional ability [1]	20,255	15,406	32,534	42,597	21,911	44,162
Skilled workers, professionals, unskilled workers [1]	49,589	46,415	85,969	129,070	89,922	85,030
Special immigrants [1]	9,014	5,389	5,407	10,133	9,539	5,481
Employment creation (investors) [1]	218	64	129	346	749	806
Immediate relatives of U.S. citizens	346,350	331,286	417,815	436,115	580,348	494,920
Spouses [2]	196,405	183,796	252,193	259,144	339,843	274,358
Children [2]	82,638	77,948	88,088	94,858	120,064	103,828
Parents	67,307	69,542	77,534	82,113	120,441	116,734
Refugees	56,091	34,362	61,013	112,676	99,609	54,942
Asylees	6,837	10,402	10,217	30,286	116,845	81,183
Diversity [3]	50,920	46,335	50,084	46,234	44,471	42,127
Cancellation of removal	12,154	28,990	32,702	20,785	29,516	14,927
Parolees	3,162	4,196	7,121	7,715	4,569	1,999
Nicaraguan Adjustment and Central American Relief Act (NACARA)	20,364	2,498	2,292	1,155	661	340
Haitian Refugee Immigration Fairness Act (HRIFA)	435	1,406	2,451	2,820	3,375	2,448
Other	2,955	3,544	4,503	4,624	5,425	2,453

[1] Includes spouses and children. [2] Includes orphans. [3] Includes categories of immigrants admitted under three laws intended to diversify immigration: P.L. 99-603, P.L. 100-658, and P.L. 101-649.

Source: U.S. Dept. of Homeland Security, Office of Immigration Statistics, *2007 Yearbook of Immigration Statistics*. See also <http://www.dhs.gov/ximgtn/statistics/publications/yearbook.shtm>.

Table 48. Persons Obtaining Legal Permanent Resident Status by Selected Country of Birth and Selected Characteristics: 2007

[For year ending September 30]

Age, marital status, class of admission	Total [1]	Mexico	China	Philippines	India	Colombia	Haiti	Cuba	Vietnam
Total	**1,052,415**	**148,640**	**76,655**	**72,596**	**65,353**	**33,187**	**30,405**	**29,104**	**28,691**
Under 18 years old	210,626	30,132	14,389	16,280	9,755	6,124	7,673	5,033	6,552
18 to 24 years old	139,847	23,782	8,181	7,961	5,732	4,260	4,924	3,489	4,079
25 to 34 years old	257,522	35,386	12,608	14,325	20,170	7,586	5,881	5,817	6,268
35 to 44 years old	199,643	25,122	19,275	11,990	12,771	6,871	4,980	6,936	5,000
45 to 54 years old	113,717	13,098	11,006	7,433	7,374	5,049	2,657	3,491	3,561
55 to 64 years old	72,550	10,515	5,631	7,655	5,523	2,173	1,754	2,590	2,106
65 years old and over	58,504	10,604	5,565	6,952	4,028	1,124	2,535	1,748	1,125
Unknown	6	1	–	–	–	–	1	–	–
Single	387,252	51,630	23,981	28,424	16,286	11,583	18,743	12,176	10,186
Married	610,134	89,908	49,366	39,617	46,189	19,734	10,451	12,749	17,075
Other	50,318	6,396	3,122	4,383	2,734	1,654	1,021	3,926	1,362
Unknown	4,711	706	186	172	144	216	190	253	68
Family-sponsored preferences	194,900	45,422	15,261	13,535	15,551	3,177	8,028	1,794	12,430
Employment-based preferences	162,176	11,900	13,886	17,182	28,703	2,641	102	14	(D)
Immediate relatives of U.S. citizens	494,920	87,466	27,115	41,416	18,205	17,174	13,569	2,737	13,974
Diversity programs	42,127	10	22	4	57	11	–	229	(D)
Refugee and asylee adjustments	136,125	396	20,352	372	2,680	10,091	6,261	24,261	1,768
Other	22,167	3,446	19	87	157	93	2,445	69	317

– Represents zero. D Data withheld to avoid disclosure. [1] Includes other countries not shown separately.

Source: U.S. Department of Homeland Security, Office of Immigration Statistics, unpublished data.

Table 49. Persons Obtaining Legal Permanent Resident Status by Country of Birth: 1981 to 2007

[In thousands (7,256.0 represents 7,256,000). For years ending Sept. 30. Persons by country prior to 1996 are unrevised]

Country of birth	1981–1990, total	1991–2000, total	2001–2006, total	2007	Country of birth	1981–1990, total	1991–2000, total	2001–2006, total	2007
All countries [1] ..	**7,256.0**	**9,080.5**	**6,168.1**	**1,052.4**	Syria	20.6	26.1	15.9	2.4
Europe	**705.6**	**1,309.1**	**922.3**	**120.8**	Taiwan [5]........	([6])	106.3	55.1	9.0
Albania	(NA)	26.2	29.2	5.7	Thailand........	64.4	48.4	33.1	8.8
Armenia........	(X)	[2]26.6	15.6	4.4	Turkey........	20.9	26.3	23.0	4.4
Belarus	(X)	[2]28.9	16.5	2.3	Vietnam........	401.4	420.8	186.1	28.7
Bosnia and					**Africa** [1].........	**192.3**	**382.5**	**431.4**	**94.7**
Herzegovina	(X)	[2]38.8	83.5	1.6	Egypt.........	31.4	46.7	37.3	9.3
France..........	23.1	27.4	23.0	3.4	Ethiopia........	27.2	49.3	54.3	12.8
Germany	70.1	67.6	48.5	7.6	Ghana........	14.9	35.6	33.9	7.6
Ireland..........	32.8	58.9	9.4	1.5	Nigeria........	35.3	67.2	57.7	12.4
Italy............	32.9	22.5	15.9	2.6	Somalia........	(NA)	20.1	29.2	6.3
Poland..........	97.4	169.5	81.7	10.4	South Africa	15.7	22.6	21.3	3.0
Portugal........	40.0	22.7	7.3	1.0	**Oceania**	**(NA)**	**47.9**	**35.9**	**6.1**
Romania	38.9	57.5	34.0	5.8	**North America** [1].....	**3,125.0**	**3,910.1**	**2,160.7**	**339.4**
Russia..........	(X)	[2]127.8	103.6	9.4	Canada........	119.2	137.2	108.1	15.5
Serbia and					Mexico.........	1,653.3	2,250.5	1,050.6	148.6
Montenegro [3, 4] ..	19.2	25.8	34.0	3.6	Cuba..........	159.2	178.7	167.3	29.1
Soviet Union [3]	84.0	103.8	16.2	5.1	Dominican				
Ukraine	(X)	[2]141.0	107.8	11.0	Republic........	251.8	340.8	165.9	28.0
United Kingdom....	142.1	135.6	96.0	14.5	Haiti	140.2	181.7	110.5	30.4
Uzbekistan	(X)	[2]22.9	14.7	4.7	Jamaica........	213.8	173.4	101.3	19.4
Asia [1]...........	**2,817.4**	**2,890.2**	**2,089.6**	**383.5**	Trinidad and				
Bangladesh	15.2	66.0	51.4	12.1	Tobago........	39.5	63.2	37.3	6.8
Cambodia.........	116.6	18.5	20.9	4.2	El Salvador......	214.6	217.3	173.3	21.1
China [5]	[6]388.8	424.4	370.7	76.7	Guatemala	87.9	103.0	103.9	17.9
Hong Kong.......	63.0	74.0	28.9	3.5	Honduras	49.5	66.7	38.3	7.6
India	261.9	383.0	407.3	65.4	Nicaragua.......	44.1	94.6	45.8	3.7
Iran...........	154.8	112.5	68.9	10.5	Panama........	29.0	24.0	10.4	1.9
Iraq...........	19.6	40.7	24.5	3.8	**South America** [1]	**455.9**	**539.3**	**510.8**	**106.5**
Israel..........	36.3	31.9	26.2	4.5	Argentina........	25.7	24.3	29.3	5.6
Japan	43.2	61.4	48.5	6.7	Brazil..........	23.7	52.2	70.3	14.3
Jordan [7]........	32.6	39.7	22.7	3.9	Colombia	124.4	130.8	137.7	33.2
Korea	338.8	171.1	124.4	22.4	Ecuador........	56.0	76.3	65.0	12.2
Laos	145.6	43.5	8.8	2.6	Guyana	95.4	73.8	50.2	5.7
Lebanon........	41.6	43.4	23.7	4.3	Peru	64.4	105.6	81.6	17.7
Pakistan........	61.3	124.5	83.9	13.5	Venezuela	17.9	29.9	42.6	10.7
Philippines	495.3	505.3	342.4	72.6					

NA Not available. X Not applicable. [1] Includes countries not shown separately. [2] Covers years 1992–2000. [3] Prior to 1992, data include independent republics; beginning in 1992, data are for unknown republic only. [4] Yugoslavia (unknown republic) prior to February 7, 2003. [5] See footnote 2, table 1288. [6] Data for Taiwan included with China. [7] Prior to 2003, includes Palestine; beginning in 2003, Palestine included in Unknown.

Source: U.S. Department of Homeland Security, Office of Immigration Statistics, *2007 Yearbook of Immigration Statistics*. See also <http://www.dhs.gov/ximgtn/statistics/publications/yearbook.shtm>.

Table 50. Refugees and Asylees Obtaining Legal Permanent Resident Status by Country of Birth: 1991 to 2007

[For years ending September 30]

Country of birth	1991–2000, total	2001–2006, total	2007	Country of birth	1991–2000, total	2001–2006, total	2007
Total [1]........	**1,016,820**	**709,189**	**136,125**	India	2,538	14,355	2,680
Europe [1]..........	**425,047**	**242,876**	**19,894**	Iran.............	24,251	24,941	2,570
Albania	3,250	5,590	2,255	Iraq.............	22,488	14,144	1,422
Armenia.........	1,794	6,316	2,637	Laos............	37,203	3,249	1,472
Azerbaijan	[2]10,566	4,338	741	Pakistan	1,649	4,938	1,087
Belarus	[2]21,592	7,005	680	Thailand	22,716	7,549	3,631
Bosnia and				Vietnam........	206,530	29,251	1,768
Herzegovina......	[2]37,251	80,183	707	**Africa** [1]	**51,469**	**110,409**	**26,178**
Croatia.........	1,786	9,211	81	Ethiopia [6].......	17,829	16,917	3,851
Kazakhstan	[2]3,799	2,944	290	Kenya	1,438	5,461	2,187
Moldova	[2]10,150	8,057	555	Liberia	3,836	13,437	1,949
Poland	7,451	294	34	Sierra Leone	272	6,253	901
Romania	15,682	901	175	Somalia.........	16,737	26,864	5,721
Russia..........	[2]54,488	23,613	3,065	Sudan..........	5,174	15,514	1,944
Serbia and				**Oceania**	**291**	**831**	**315**
Montenegro [3, 4]	6,242	22,094	1,226	**North America** [1]	**183,251**	**164,663**	**33,100**
Soviet Union [3]	117,783	5,184	476	Cuba...........	142,571	144,510	24,261
Ukraine	[2]96,974	48,360	2,322	El Salvador	4,072	2,273	493
Uzbekistan........	[2]17,991	5,470	2,792	Haiti	9,354	9,724	6,261
Asia [1]	**350,702**	**164,399**	**42,384**	Nicaragua.......	22,468	1,445	133
Afghanistan	9,711	10,012	960	**South America** [1]	**5,840**	**24,981**	**14,000**
Burma..........	721	5,265	1,774	Colombia	1,129	15,293	10,091
Cambodia.........	6,358	979	281	Peru	2,500	4,117	919
China [5]	7,577	35,960	20,352				

[1] Includes other countries and unknown not shown separately. [2] Covers years 1992–2000. [3] Prior to 1992, data include independent republics; beginning in 1992, data are for unknown republic only. [4] Yugoslavia (unknown republic) prior to February 7, 2003. [5] See footnote 2, Table 1288. [6] Prior to 1993, data include Eritrea.

Source: U.S. Department of Homeland Security, Office of Immigration Statistics, *2007 Yearbook of Immigration Statistics*. See also <http://www.dhs.gov/ximgtn/statistics/publications/yearbook.shtm>.

Population 47

Table 51. Population by Selected Ancestry Group and Region: 2006

[In thousands (299,398 represents 299,398,000). Covers single and multiple ancestries. Ancestry refers to a person's ethnic origin or descent, roots, or heritage; or the place of birth of the person, the person's parents, or ancestors before their arrival in the United States. The American Community Survey universe includes the household population and the population living in institutions, college dormitories, and other group quarters. Based on a sample and subject to sampling variability; see text this section and Appendix III. For composition of regions, see map, inside front cover]

Ancestry group	Total (1,000)	North-east	Mid-west	South	West	Ancestry group	Total (1,000)	North-east	Mid-west	South	West
Total population [1]	**299,398**	**18**	**22**	**36**	**23**	Irish	35,976	26	24	32	18
Afghan	66	17	4	24	56	Israeli	142	42	8	23	27
Albanian	158	58	24	13	5	Italian	17,829	45	17	21	16
American	20,372	11	21	55	13	Latvian	94	29	27	18	25
Arab [1]	1,467	26	24	27	23	Lithuanian	723	39	29	18	14
Egyptian	178	39	12	23	26	Northern European	213	14	17	22	47
Iraqi	58	7	48	17	28	Norwegian	4,670	6	49	12	33
Jordanian	67	21	20	32	27	Pennsylvania German	350	55	25	12	7
Lebanese	482	25	26	29	20	Polish	10,025	33	37	18	12
Moroccan	74	36	14	33	18	Portuguese	1,442	45	3	12	39
Palestinian	68	18	23	33	27	Romanian	462	25	27	21	26
Syrian	156	37	17	25	21	Russian	3,106	37	17	21	25
Arab	258	19	33	26	22	Scandinavian	616	7	31	18	44
Armenian	428	22	10	9	59	Scotch-Irish	5,394	15	18	45	22
Assyrian/Chaldean/Syriac	89	3	59	6	32	Scottish	6,007	17	20	37	26
Australian	89	20	19	25	37	Serbian	170	20	45	18	18
Austrian	804	33	22	23	23	Slavic	135	29	27	23	21
Basque	62	4	3	13	80	Slovak	838	44	34	14	8
Belgian	389	11	54	16	19	Slovene	178	14	58	13	14
Brazilian	346	49	5	32	14	Subsaharan African [1]	2,541	22	17	45	16
British	1,346	16	17	39	28	Cape Verdean	88	87	2	7	4
Bulgarian	93	18	31	26	25	Ethiopian	151	8	18	41	32
Cajun	114	3	5	85	7	Ghanian	80	46	11	33	10
Canadian	736	28	17	27	28	Nigerian	238	23	16	47	13
Celtic	57	18	13	40	29	Somalian	91	9	45	15	30
Croatian	418	25	40	14	21	African	1,589	18	17	50	14
Czech	1,637	12	46	26	16	Swedish	4,417	13	39	16	32
Czechoslovakian	328	22	33	26	20	Swiss	1,019	16	35	19	31
Danish	1,516	8	33	14	46	Turkish	169	40	10	32	19
Dutch	5,188	16	35	27	22	Ukrainian	961	41	20	18	22
Eastern European	367	45	12	21	21	Welsh	1,960	20	23	30	27
English	28,290	17	21	37	25	West Indian [1,2]	2,419	48	3	44	5
European	2,667	13	20	32	34	Barbadian	56	68	3	25	5
Finnish	690	12	47	13	28	British West Indian	80	66	2	28	4
French (except Basque)	9,651	25	24	32	20	Dutch West Indian	65	3	6	80	11
French Canadian	2,241	41	21	23	15	Haitian	763	41	2	54	2
German	50,764	16	39	26	19	Jamaican	911	50	4	43	4
Greek	1,380	34	23	23	20	Trinidadian and Tobagonian	182	64	2	31	4
Guyanese	196	75	2	21	2	West Indian	280	63	4	27	5
Hungarian	1,563	32	31	20	17	Yugoslavian	351	21	30	21	28
Iranian	414	13	8	24	54						

[1] Includes other groups not shown separately. [2] Excludes Hispanic-origin groups.

Source: U.S. Census Bureau, 2006 American Community Survey; B04006. People Reporting Ancestry; using American FactFinder®; <http://factfinder.census.gov/>; (accessed: 16 January 2008).

Table 52. Languages Spoken at Home by Language: 2006

[279,013 represents 279,013,000. The American Community Survey universe includes the household population and the population living in institutions, college dormitories, and other group quarters. Based on a sample and subject to sampling variability; see text of this section and Appendix III]

Language	Number (1,000)	Language	Number (1,000)
Total population 5 years old and over	**279,013**	Other Indic languages	613
Speak only English	224,154	Other Indo-European languages	394
Spanish or Spanish Creole	34,045	Chinese	2,493
French (incl. Patois, Cajun)	1,396	Japanese	475
French Creole	602	Korean	1,061
Italian	829	Mon-Khmer, Cambodian	184
Portuguese or Portuguese Creole	683	Hmong	187
German	1,136	Thai	140
Yiddish	153	Laotian	147
Other West Germanic languages	255	Vietnamese	1,208
Scandinavian languages	130	Other Asian languages	609
Greek	353	Tagalog	1,416
Russian	823	Other Pacific Island languages	356
Polish	640	Navajo	176
Serbo-Croatian	271	Other Native North American languages	205
Other Slavic languages	312	Hungarian	97
Armenian	217	Arabic	733
Persian	349	Hebrew	225
Gujarathi	299	African languages	697
Hindi	505	Other and unspecified languages	122
Urdu	325		

Source: U.S. Census Bureau, 2006 American Community Survey; B16001. Language Spoken at Home by Ability to Speak English for the Population 5 Years and Over; using American FactFinder®; <http://factfinder.census.gov/>; (accessed: 17 January 2008).

Table 53. Language Spoken at Home by State: 2006

[**279,013** represents 279,013,000. The American Community Survey universe includes the household population and the population living in institutions, college dormitories, and other group quarters. Based on a sample and subject to sampling variability; see text this section and Appendix III]

State	Population 5 years and over (1,000)	English only (1,000)	Language other than English Number (1,000)	Percent of population 5 years and over	State	Population 5 years and over (1,000)	English only (1,000)	Language other than English Number (1,000)	Percent of population 5 years and over
U.S. . . .	**279,013**	**224,154**	**54,858**	**19.7**	MO	5,452	5,147	305	5.6
AL.	4,305	4,124	181	4.2	MT.	887	845	42	4.7
AK.	623	527	96	15.4	NE.	1,640	1,491	149	9.1
AZ.	5,687	4,094	1,593	28.0	NV.	2,312	1,691	621	26.9
AR.	2,616	2,456	160	6.1	NH.	1,241	1,139	102	8.2
CA.	33,785	19,415	14,370	42.5	NJ.	8,165	5,907	2,258	27.6
CO.	4,414	3,653	761	17.2	NM.	1,813	1,151	662	36.5
CT.	3,303	2,639	663	20.1	NY.	18,085	12,875	5,210	28.8
DE.	796	700	96	12.1	NC.	8,254	7,466	788	9.6
DC.	547	463	84	15.3	ND.	597	566	31	5.2
FL.	16,972	12,611	4,361	25.7	OH.	10,742	10,080	662	6.2
GA.	8,665	7,634	1,031	11.9	OK.	3,327	3,050	277	8.3
HI	1,198	917	281	23.5	OR.	3,471	2,979	492	14.2
ID	1,354	1,217	137	10.1	PA.	11,716	10,639	1,077	9.2
IL.	11,943	9,341	2,602	21.8	RI	1,006	800	206	20.4
IN	5,880	5,435	445	7.6	SC.	4,037	3,795	241	6.0
IA	2,791	2,613	178	6.4	SD.	728	681	47	6.5
KS.	2,569	2,305	264	10.3	TN.	5,640	5,330	309	5.5
KY.	3,929	3,769	160	4.1	TX.	21,586	14,289	7,296	33.8
LA.	3,987	3,650	337	8.4	UT.	2,303	1,974	329	14.3
ME.	1,251	1,155	97	7.7	VT.	591	559	31	5.3
MD.	5,247	4,467	780	14.9	VA.	7,139	6,202	938	13.1
MA.	6,050	4,828	1,222	20.2	WA	5,989	4,995	994	16.6
MI	9,456	8,607	849	9.0	WV	1,714	1,675	39	2.3
MN.	4,820	4,357	463	9.6	WI	5,205	4,782	423	8.1
MS.	2,704	2,619	85	3.1	WY	481	449	32	6.6

Source: U.S. Census Bureau, 2006 American Community Survey; C16005. Nativity by Language Spoken at Home by Ability to Speak English for the Population 5 Years and Over; using American FactFinder®; <http://factfinder.census.gov/>; (accessed 17 January 2008).

Table 54. Language Spoken at Home—25 Largest Cities: 2006

[**657** represents 657,000. The American Community Survey universe includes the household population and the population living in institutions, college dormitories, and other group quarters. Based on a sample and subject to sampling variability; see text this section and Appendix III]

City	Population 5 years and over (1,000)	English only (1,000)	Language other than English, total [1] Number (1,000)	Percent of population 5 years and over	Speak English less than "very well" (1,000)	Spanish (1,000)	Other Indo-European languages (1,000)	Asian and Pacific Island languages (1,000)
Austin, TX	657	426	231	35.2	101	183	17	26
Baltimore, MD	587	537	49	8.4	20	17	14	8
Boston, MA	539	352	187	34.7	93	73	69	36
Charlotte, NC.	597	494	103	17.2	55	58	22	16
Chicago, IL	2,540	1,612	927	36.5	454	640	173	83
Columbus, OH	661	581	81	12.2	36	28	18	19
Dallas, TX	1,083	613	470	43.4	269	424	16	19
Denver, CO	516	364	152	29.5	75	124	12	12
Detroit, MI	775	704	71	9.1	35	47	9	5
El Paso, TX	538	138	400	74.3	148	387	6	5
Fort Worth, TX	579	398	181	31.3	92	156	10	13
Houston, TX	1,892	1,041	851	45.0	456	713	52	66
Indianapolis, IN [2]	723	648	75	10.3	36	49	13	8
Jacksonville, FL	739	652	87	11.7	33	36	25	18
Las Vegas, NV	525	351	174	33.1	85	133	15	23
Los Angeles, CA.	3,493	1,384	2,109	60.4	1,070	1,539	244	277
Memphis, TN	592	543	49	8.3	27	34	5	7
New York, NY	7,638	3,982	3,656	47.9	1,792	1,884	998	596
Philadelphia, PA	1,342	1,075	267	19.9	115	126	68	57
Phoenix, AZ	1,305	796	508	39.0	261	439	33	17
San Antonio, TX	1,169	615	554	47.4	174	518	18	15
San Diego, CA.	1,173	710	463	39.5	214	263	49	135
San Francisco, CA . . .	703	377	326	46.4	169	84	47	186
San Jose, CA.	844	375	470	55.6	222	205	54	200
Washington, DC	547	463	84	15.3	31	45	22	9

[1] Includes other language groups not shown separately. [2] Represents the portion of a consolidated city that is not within one or more separately incorporated places.

Source: U.S. Census Bureau, 2006 American Community Survey; C16005. Nativity by Language Spoken at Home by Ability to Speak English for the Population 5 Years and Over; using American FactFinder®; <http://factfinder.census.gov/>; (accessed 22 January 2008).

Table 55. **Marital Status of the Population by Sex, Race, and Hispanic Origin: 1990 to 2007**

[**In millions, except percent (181.8 represents 181,800,000).** As of **March. Persons 18 years old and over**. Excludes members of Armed Forces except those living off post or with their families on post. Beginning 2005, population controls based on Census 2000 and an expanded sample of households. Based on Current Population Survey, see text of this section, and Appendix III]

Marital status, race, and Hispanic origin	Total				Male				Female			
	1990	2000	2005	2007	1990	2000	2005	2007	1990	2000	2005	2007
Total [1]	**181.8**	**201.8**	**217.2**	**222.6**	**86.9**	**96.9**	**104.8**	**107.8**	**95.0**	**104.9**	**112.3**	**114.8**
Never married	40.4	48.2	53.9	56.1	22.4	26.1	29.6	30.9	17.9	22.1	24.3	25.3
Married [2]	112.6	120.1	127.4	129.7	55.8	59.6	63.3	64.6	56.7	60.4	64.0	65.1
Widowed	13.8	13.7	13.8	13.9	2.3	2.6	2.7	2.7	11.5	11.1	11.1	11.2
Divorced	15.1	19.8	22.1	22.8	6.3	8.5	9.2	9.6	8.8	11.3	12.9	13.2
Percent of total	100.0	100.0	100.0	100.0	100.0	100.0	100.0	100.0	100.0	100.0	100.0	100.0
Never married	22.2	23.9	24.8	25.2	25.8	27.0	28.2	28.6	18.9	21.1	21.6	22.0
Married [2]	61.9	59.5	58.6	58.2	64.3	61.5	60.4	59.9	59.7	57.6	56.9	56.7
Widowed	7.6	6.8	6.4	6.2	2.7	2.7	2.6	2.5	12.1	10.5	9.9	9.8
Divorced	8.3	9.8	10.2	10.3	7.2	8.8	8.8	8.9	9.3	10.8	11.5	11.5
White, total [3]	**155.5**	**168.1**	**177.5**	**181.3**	**74.8**	**81.6**	**86.6**	**88.7**	**80.6**	**86.6**	**90.9**	**92.5**
Never married	31.6	36.0	39.7	41.2	18.0	20.3	22.6	23.5	13.6	15.7	17.0	17.6
Married [2]	99.5	104.1	108.3	109.8	49.5	51.8	54.0	54.9	49.9	52.2	54.2	54.9
Widowed	11.7	11.5	11.5	11.5	1.9	2.2	2.3	2.3	9.8	9.3	9.2	9.3
Divorced	12.6	16.5	18.1	18.8	5.4	7.2	7.6	8.1	7.3	9.3	10.4	10.7
Percent of total	100.0	100.0	100.0	100.0	100.0	100.0	100.0	100.0	100.0	100.0	100.0	100.0
Never married	20.3	21.4	22.3	22.7	24.1	24.9	26.1	26.5	16.9	18.1	18.7	19.1
Married [2]	64.0	62.0	61.0	60.5	66.2	63.5	62.4	61.8	61.9	60.3	59.7	59.3
Widowed	7.5	6.8	6.5	6.4	2.6	2.7	2.6	2.5	12.2	10.8	10.2	10.0
Divorced	8.1	9.8	10.2	10.4	7.2	8.8	8.8	9.1	9.0	10.7	11.5	11.6
Black, total [3]	**20.3**	**24.0**	**25.2**	**26.1**	**9.1**	**10.7**	**11.2**	**11.7**	**11.2**	**13.3**	**13.9**	**14.3**
Never married	7.1	9.5	10.2	10.5	3.5	4.3	4.7	4.9	3.6	5.1	5.5	5.6
Married [2]	9.3	10.1	10.3	10.8	4.5	5.0	5.0	5.3	4.8	5.1	5.2	5.5
Widowed	1.7	1.7	1.7	1.7	0.3	0.3	0.3	0.3	1.4	1.4	1.4	1.4
Divorced	2.1	2.8	2.9	3.1	0.8	1.1	1.1	1.1	1.3	1.7	1.8	1.9
Percent of total	100.0	100.0	100.0	100.0	100.0	100.0	100.0	100.0	100.0	100.0	100.0	100.0
Never married . . . . ,	35.1	39.4	40.6	40.4	38.4	40.2	42.0	41.9	32.5	38.3	39.5	39.1
Married [2]	45.8	42.1	41.0	41.4	49.2	46.7	45.5	45.5	43.0	38.3	37.4	38.1
Widowed	8.5	7.0	6.6	6.6	3.7	2.8	2.7	2.9	12.4	10.5	10.0	9.6
Divorced	10.6	11.5	11.7	11.5	8.8	10.3	9.8	9.7	12.0	12.8	13.3	13.0
Asian, total [3]	**(NA)**	**(NA)**	**9.4**	**10.2**	**(NA)**	**(NA)**	**4.5**	**4.9**	**(NA)**	**(NA)**	**4.9**	**5.4**
Never married	(NA)	(NA)	2.3	2.7	(NA)	(NA)	1.3	1.5	(NA)	(NA)	1.0	1.2
Married [2]	(NA)	(NA)	6.2	6.7	(NA)	(NA)	2.9	3.2	(NA)	(NA)	3.3	3.5
Widowed	(NA)	(NA)	0.4	0.4	(NA)	(NA)	0.1	0.1	(NA)	(NA)	0.3	0.4
Divorced	(NA)	(NA)	0.5	0.4	(NA)	(NA)	0.2	0.1	(NA)	(NA)	0.3	0.3
Percent of total	100.0	100.0	100.0	100.0	100.0	100.0	100.0	100.0	100.0	100.0	100.0	100.0
Never married	(NA)	(NA)	24.8	26.5	(NA)	(NA)	29.7	31.0	(NA)	(NA)	20.3	22.5
Married [2]	(NA)	(NA)	65.6	65.5	(NA)	(NA)	64.7	65.2	(NA)	(NA)	66.5	65.6
Widowed	(NA)	(NA)	4.3	4.0	(NA)	(NA)	1.3	1.2	(NA)	(NA)	6.7	6.6
Divorced	(NA)	(NA)	5.3	4.0	(NA)	(NA)	4.1	2.7	(NA)	(NA)	6.4	5.2
Hispanic, total [4]	**13.6**	**21.1**	**27.5**	**29.6**	**6.7**	**10.4**	**14.1**	**15.3**	**6.8**	**10.7**	**13.4**	**14.3**
Never married	3.7	5.9	8.6	9.3	2.2	3.4	5.2	5.6	1.5	2.5	3.4	3.7
Married [2]	8.4	12.7	15.6	17.0	4.1	6.2	7.8	8.5	4.3	6.5	7.8	8.4
Widowed	0.5	0.9	1.0	1.0	0.1	0.2	0.2	0.2	0.4	0.7	0.8	0.8
Divorced	1.0	1.6	2.2	2.3	0.4	0.7	0.9	0.9	0.6	1.0	1.3	1.4
Percent of total	100.0	100.0	100.0	100.0	100.0	100.0	100.0	100.0	100.0	100.0	100.0	100.0
Never married	27.2	28.0	31.3	31.4	32.1	32.3	36.7	36.7	22.5	23.4	25.6	25.7
Married [2]	61.7	60.2	57.0	57.3	60.9	59.7	55.6	55.7	62.4	60.7	58.7	58.8
Widowed	4.0	4.2	3.7	3.5	1.5	1.6	1.5	1.5	6.5	6.5	6.1	5.7
Divorced	7.0	7.6	7.9	7.8	5.5	6.4	6.3	6.1	8.5	9.3	9.7	9.7
Non-Hispanic White, total [3, 4]	**(NA)**	**(NA)**	**151.9**	**153.7**	**(NA)**	**(NA)**	**73.4**	**74.4**	**(NA)**	**(NA)**	**78.5**	**79.3**
Never married	(NA)	(NA)	31.8	32.7	(NA)	(NA)	17.8	18.4	(NA)	(NA)	13.9	14.3
Married [2]	(NA)	(NA)	93.5	93.8	(NA)	(NA)	46.6	46.8	(NA)	(NA)	47.0	47.1
Widowed	(NA)	(NA)	10.6	10.6	(NA)	(NA)	2.1	2.0	(NA)	(NA)	8.5	8.5
Divorced	(NA)	(NA)	16.0	16.7	(NA)	(NA)	6.8	7.2	(NA)	(NA)	9.2	9.4
Percent of total	100.0	100.0	100.0	100.0	100.0	100.0	100.0	100.0	100.0	100.0	100.0	100.0
Never married	(NA)	(NA)	20.9	21.3	(NA)	(NA)	24.3	24.7	(NA)	(NA)	17.7	18.1
Married [2]	(NA)	(NA)	61.5	61.0	(NA)	(NA)	63.5	62.9	(NA)	(NA)	59.7	58.9
Widowed	(NA)	(NA)	6.9	6.9	(NA)	(NA)	2.8	2.7	(NA)	(NA)	10.8	10.8
Divorced	(NA)	(NA)	10.6	10.8	(NA)	(NA)	9.3	9.7	(NA)	(NA)	11.7	11.9

NA Not available. [1] Includes persons of other races not shown separately. [2] Includes persons who are married with spouse present, married with spouse absent, and separated. [3] Beginning 2005, data represent persons who selected this race group only and exclude persons reporting more than one race. The CPS in 1990 and 2000 only allowed respondents to report one race group. See also comments on race in the text for this section. [4] Hispanic persons may be any race.

Source: U.S. Census Bureau, *Current Population Reports*, P20-537 and earlier reports; and "Families and Living Arrangements"; <http://www.census.gov/population/www/socdemo/hh-fam.html>.

Table 56. **Marital Status of the Population by Sex and Age: 2007**

[As of March (107,750 represents 107,750,000). Excludes members of Armed Forces except those living off post or with their families on post. Population controls based on Census 2000 and an expanded sample of households. Based on Current Population Survey, see text, this section, and Appendix III]

Sex and age	Number of persons (1,000)					Percent distribution				
	Total	Never married	Married¹	Widowed	Divorced	Total	Never married	Married¹	Widowed	Divorced
Male	**107,750**	**30,857**	**64,588**	**2,693**	**9,611**	**100.0**	**28.6**	**59.9**	**2.5**	**8.9**
18 to 19 years old	4,003	3,919	72	–	12	100.0	97.9	1.8	–	–
20 to 24 years old	10,406	9,041	1,271	10	84	100.0	86.9	12.2	0.1	0.8
25 to 29 years old	10,433	6,009	4,122	5	296	100.0	57.6	39.5	–	2.8
30 to 34 years old	9,569	3,100	5,844	10	616	100.0	32.4	61.1	0.1	6.4
35 to 39 years old	10,398	2,389	7,069	40	901	100.0	23.0	68.0	0.4	8.7
40 to 44 years old	10,774	1,827	7,572	55	1,320	100.0	16.9	70.3	0.5	12.3
45 to 54 years old	21,283	2,898	15,084	220	3,079	100.0	13.6	70.9	1.0	14.5
55 to 64 years old	15,460	1,056	11,929	335	2,140	100.0	6.8	77.2	2.2	13.8
65 to 74 years old	8,727	372	6,845	674	837	100.0	4.3	78.4	7.7	9.6
75 years old and over . . .	6,697	245	4,782	1,344	325	100.0	3.7	71.4	20.0	4.9
Female	**114,807**	**25,262**	**65,128**	**11,208**	**13,210**	**100.0**	**22.0**	**56.7**	**9.8**	**11.5**
18 to 19 years old	3,858	3,635	204	1	18	100.0	94.2	5.3	–	0.5
20 to 24 years old	10,118	7,727	2,207	16	167	100.0	76.4	21.8	0.2	1.7
25 to 29 years old	10,218	4,430	5,218	34	535	100.0	43.4	51.1	0.3	5.2
30 to 34 years old	9,610	2,307	6,460	62	781	100.0	24.0	67.2	0.6	8.1
35 to 39 years old	10,502	1,600	7,634	76	1,191	100.0	15.2	72.7	0.7	11.3
40 to 44 years old	11,075	1,427	7,799	166	1,683	100.0	12.9	70.4	1.5	15.2
45 to 54 years old	22,147	2,281	15,422	656	3,788	100.0	10.3	69.6	3.0	17.1
55 to 64 years old	16,708	1,102	11,026	1,512	3,067	100.0	6.6	66.0	9.0	18.4
65 to 74 years old	10,251	406	5,835	2,681	1,331	100.0	4.0	56.9	26.2	13.0
75 years old and over . . .	10,321	347	3,323	6,004	647	100.0	3.4	32.2	58.2	6.3

– Represents or rounds to zero.   ¹ Includes persons who are married with spouse present, married with spouse absent, and separated.

Source: U.S. Census Bureau, "America's Families and Living Arrangements: 2007, Table A1. Marital Status of People 15 Years and Over by Age, Sex, Personal Earnings, Race, and Hispanic Origin, 2007"; published July 2008; <http://www.census.gov/population/www/socdemo/hh-fam/cps2007.html>.

Table 57. **Living Arrangements of Persons 15 Years Old and Over by Selected Characteristics: 2007**

[In thousands (235,848 represents 235,848,000). As of March. See headnote, Table 56]

Living arrangement	Total	15 to 19 years old	20 to 24 years old	25 to 34 years old	35 to 44 years old	45 to 54 years old	55 to 64 years old	65 to 74 years old	75 years old and over
Total ¹	**235,848**	**21,152**	**20,524**	**39,830**	**42,749**	**43,430**	**32,168**	**18,978**	**17,018**
Alone	31,132	135	1,462	3,930	3,726	5,395	5,618	4,354	6,513
With spouse.	121,352	214	3,011	19,908	27,856	28,527	21,928	12,172	7,734
With other persons	83,364	20,803	16,051	15,992	11,167	9,508	4,622	2,452	2,771
White ²	191,422	16,257	16,034	31,117	34,096	35,551	27,133	16,195	15,039
Alone	25,280	100	1,121	2,924	2,839	4,263	4,573	3,634	5,825
With spouse.	103,961	193	2,662	16,837	23,200	24,207	19,117	10,757	6,989
With other persons	62,181	15,964	12,251	11,356	8,057	7,081	3,443	1,804	2,225
Black ²	28,117	3,310	2,895	5,229	5,306	5,088	3,210	1,833	1,248
Alone	4,467	24	264	690	671	888	828	576	527
With spouse.	8,950	13	172	1,412	2,329	2,354	1,503	801	365
With other persons	14,700	3,273	2,459	3,127	2,306	1,846	879	456	356
Asian ²	10,679	759	921	2,332	2,348	1,888	1,249	649	533
Alone	791	2	34	232	119	133	97	75	101
With spouse.	6,223	1	82	1,195	1,801	1,439	969	435	300
With other persons	3,665	756	805	905	428	316	183	139	132
Hispanic origin ³	31,874	3,664	3,672	8,105	6,724	4,646	2,637	1,445	983
Alone	2,082	12	163	363	292	378	362	285	226
With spouse.	14,764	80	828	4,156	4,123	2,797	1,564	806	411
With other persons	15,028	3,572	2,681	3,586	2,309	1,471	711	354	346
Non-Hispanic White ²,³ .	161,775	12,875	12,644	23,610	27,840	31,168	24,685	14,852	14,103
Alone	23,383	88	979	2,610	2,569	3,911	4,242	3,380	5,604
With spouse.	89,991	117	1,891	12,914	19,314	21,535	17,621	9,999	6,600
With other persons	48,401	12,670	9,774	8,086	5,957	5,722	2,822	1,473	1,899

¹ Includes other races and persons not of Hispanic origin not shown separately.   ² See footnote 3, Table 55.   ³ Persons of Hispanic origin may be any race.

Source: U.S. Census Bureau, "America's Families and Living Arrangements: 2007, Table A2. Family Status and Household Relationship of Persons 15 Years and Over, by Marital Status, Age, and Sex: 2007; published July 2008; <http://www.census.gov/population/www/socdemo/hh-fam/cps2007.html> and unpublished data.

Population   51

Table 58. Households, Families, Subfamilies, and Married Couples: 1980 to 2007

[In thousands, except as indicated (80,776 represents 80,776,000). As of March. Excludes members of Armed Forces except those living off post or with their families on post. Beginning 2005, population controls based on Census 2000 and an expanded sample of households. Based on Current Population Survey, see text of this section, and Appendix III. Minus sign (–) indicates decrease]

Type of unit	1980	1990	1995	2000	2005	2006	2007	Percent change 1980–1990	Percent change 1990–2000	Percent change 2000–2007
Households	**80,776**	**93,347**	**98,990**	**104,705**	**113,343**	**114,384**	**116,011**	**16**	**12**	**11**
Persons per household.	2.76	2.63	2.65	2.62	2.57	2.57	2.56	(X)	(X)	(X)
White [1]	70,766	80,163	83,737	87,671	92,880	93,588	94,705	13	9	8
Black [1]	8,586	10,486	11,655	12,849	13,809	14,002	14,354	22	23	12
Hispanic [2]	3,684	5,933	7,735	9,319	12,178	12,519	12,973	61	57	39
Family households	59,550	66,090	69,305	72,025	76,858	77,402	78,425	11	9	9
Married couple	49,112	52,317	53,858	55,311	57,975	58,179	58,945	7	6	7
Male householder [3]	1,733	2,884	3,226	4,028	4,901	5,130	5,063	66	40	26
Female householder [3]	8,705	10,890	12,220	12,687	13,981	14,093	14,416	25	17	14
Nonfamily households	21,226	27,257	29,686	32,680	36,485	36,982	37,587	28	20	15
Male householder	8,807	11,606	13,190	14,641	16,543	16,753	17,338	32	26	18
Female householder	12,419	15,651	16,496	18,039	19,942	20,230	20,249	26	15	12
One person	18,296	22,999	24,732	26,724	30,137	30,453	31,132	26	16	17
Families	**59,550**	**66,090**	**69,305**	**72,025**	**76,858**	**77,402**	**78,425**	**11**	**9**	**9**
Persons per family.	3.29	3.17	3.19	3.17	3.13	3.13	3.13	(X)	(X)	(X)
With own children [4]	31,022	32,289	34,296	34,605	36,211	36,466	36,757	4	7	6
Without own children [4]	28,528	33,801	35,009	37,420	40,647	40,936	41,668	18	11	11
Married couple	49,112	52,317	53,858	55,311	57,975	58,179	58,945	7	6	7
With own children [4]	24,961	24,537	25,241	25,248	25,919	25,982	26,158	–2	3	4
Without own children [4]	24,151	27,780	28,617	30,062	32,056	32,197	32,787	15	8	9
Male householder [3]	1,733	2,884	3,226	4,028	4,901	5,130	5,063	66	40	26
With own children [4]	616	1,153	1,440	1,786	2,021	2,095	2,015	87	55	13
Without own children [4]	1,117	1,731	1,786	2,242	2,880	3,035	3,049	55	30	36
Female householder [3]	8,705	10,890	12,220	12,687	13,981	14,093	14,416	25	17	14
With own children [4]	5,445	6,599	7,615	7,571	8,270	8,389	8,585	21	15	13
Without own children [4]	3,261	4,290	4,606	5,116	5,711	5,703	5,832	32	19	14
Unrelated subfamilies	360	534	674	571	515	504	567	48	7	–1
Married couple	20	68	64	37	62	36	89	(B)	(B)	(B)
Male reference persons [3] . . .	36	45	59	57	61	59	52	(B)	(B)	(B)
Female reference persons [3] . . .	304	421	550	477	392	409	429	39	13	–10
Related subfamilies	1,150	2,403	2,878	2,984	3,427	3,265	3,829	109	24	28
Married couple	582	871	1,015	1,149	1,336	1,312	1,645	50	32	43
Father-child [3]	54	153	195	201	387	347	331	(B)	31	65
Mother-child [3]	512	1,378	1,668	1,634	1,704	1,606	1,852	169	19	13
Married couples	**49,714**	**53,256**	**54,937**	**56,497**	**59,373**	**59,528**	**60,676**	**7**	**6**	**7**
With own household	49,112	52,317	53,858	55,311	57,975	58,179	58,945	7	6	7
Without own household	602	939	1,079	1,186	1,398	1,348	1,731	56	26	46
Percent without	1.2	1.8	2.0	2.1	2.4	2.3	2.9	(X)	(X)	(X)

B Not shown; base less than 75,000.   X Not applicable.   [1] Beginning with the 2003 Current Population Survey (CPS), respondents could choose more than one race. Beginning 2005, data shown represent persons who selected this race group only and exclude persons reporting more than one race. The CPS prior to 2003 only allowed respondents to report one race group. See also comments on race in the text for this section.   [2] Persons of Hispanic origin may be any race.   [3] No spouse present.   [4] Under 18 years old.

Source: U.S. Census Bureau, "Families and Living Arrangements"; <http://www.census.gov/population/www/socdemo/hh-fam.html>.

Table 59. Married Couples by Race and Hispanic Origin of Spouses: 1980 to 2007

[In thousands (49,714 represents 49,714,000). As of March. Persons 15 years old and over. Persons of Hispanic origin may be any race. Based on Current Population Survey; see headnote, Table 58 and Appendix III]

Race and origin of spouses	1980	1990	2000	2007
Married couples, total [1]	**49,714**	**53,256**	**56,497**	**60,676**
Interracial married couples, total	651	964	1,464	2,281
White [2]/Black [2]	167	211	363	464
Black husband/White wife	122	150	268	338
White husband/Black wife	45	61	95	126
White [2]/other race [3]	450	720	1,051	1,688
Black [2]/other race [3]	34	33	50	129
HISPANIC ORIGIN				
Hispanic/Hispanic	1,906	3,085	4,739	6,261
Hispanic/other origin (not Hispanic).	891	1,193	1,743	2,241
All other couples (not of Hispanic origin)	46,917	48,979	50,015	52,173

[1] Includes other married couples not shown separately.   [2] See footnote 1, Table 58.   [3] "Other race," is any race other than White or Black, such as American Indian, Japanese, Chinese, etc. This total excludes combinations of other races by other races.

Source: U.S. Census Bureau, Table MS-3. Interracial Married Couples: 1980 to 2002; published 15 September 2004; <http://www.census.gov/population/www/socdemo/hh-fam.html>; and unpublished data.

Table 60. Households and Persons Per Household by Type of Household: 1990 to 2007

[As of March (93,347 represents 93,347,000). See headnote, Table 58]

Type of household	Households						Persons per household		
	Number (1,000)			Percent distribution					
	1990	2000	2007	1990	2000	2007	1990	2000	2007
Total households	93,347	104,705	116,011	100	100	100	2.63	2.62	2.56
Family households	66,090	72,025	78,425	71	69	68	3.22	3.24	3.19
Married couple family	52,317	55,311	58,945	56	53	51	3.25	3.26	3.20
Male householder, no spouse present	2,884	4,028	5,063	3	4	4	3.04	3.16	3.12
Female householder, no spouse present. . .	10,890	12,687	14,416	12	12	12	3.10	3.17	3.15
Nonfamily households.	27,257	32,680	37,587	29	31	32	1.22	1.25	1.24
Living alone	22,999	26,724	31,132	25	26	27	1.00	1.00	1.00
Male householder.	11,606	14,641	17,338	12	14	15	1.33	1.34	1.33
Living alone	9,049	11,181	13,528	10	11	12	1.00	1.00	1.00
Female householder	15,651	18,039	20,249	17	17	17	1.14	1.17	1.16
Living alone	13,950	15,543	17,604	15	15	15	1.00	1.00	1.00

Source: U.S. Census Bureau, Current Population Reports, P20-537 and earlier reports; and "America's Families and Living Arrangements: 2007"; published July 2008; <http://www.census.gov/population/www/socdemo/hh-fam/cps2007.html>.

Table 61. Households by Age of Householder and Size of Household: 1990 to 2007

[In millions (93.3 represents 93,300,000). As of March. Based on Current Population Survey; see headnote, Table 58]

Age of householder and size of household	1990	2000	2005	2007					
				Total [1]	White [2]	Black [2]	Asian [2]	Hispanic [3]	Non-Hispanic White [3]
Total.	**93.3**	**104.7**	**113.3**	**116.0**	**94.7**	**14.4**	**4.5**	**13.0**	**82.7**
Age of householder:									
15 to 24 years old	5.1	5.9	6.7	6.7	5.1	1.1	0.2	1.1	4.1
25 to 29 years old	9.4	8.5	9.2	9.7	7.6	1.4	0.5	1.7	6.0
30 to 34 years old	11.0	10.1	10.1	9.8	7.5	1.4	0.6	1.8	5.9
35 to 44 years old	20.6	24.0	23.2	22.8	18.0	3.1	1.1	3.2	15.0
45 to 54 years old	14.5	20.9	23.4	24.1	19.6	3.1	0.9	2.3	17.5
55 to 64 years old	12.5	13.6	17.5	19.3	16.2	2.1	0.6	1.5	14.8
65 to 74 years old	11.7	11.3	11.5	11.9	10.1	1.3	0.3	0.8	9.4
75 years old and over . . .	8.4	10.4	11.6	11.8	10.5	0.9	0.3	0.5	10.0
One person	23.0	26.7	30.1	31.1	25.3	4.5	0.8	2.1	23.4
Male	9.0	11.2	12.8	13.5	11.0	1.9	0.4	1.1	10.0
Female.	14.0	15.5	17.3	17.6	14.3	2.6	0.4	1.0	13.4
Two persons	30.1	34.7	37.4	38.6	32.5	4.0	1.3	2.9	29.9
Three persons.	16.1	17.2	18.3	18.8	14.9	2.6	0.9	2.5	12.6
Four persons	14.5	15.3	16.4	16.2	13.1	1.8	0.9	2.7	10.6
Five persons.	6.2	7.0	7.2	7.2	5.8	1.0	0.3	1.6	4.3
Six persons	2.1	2.4	2.5	2.7	2.1	0.4	0.1	1.0	1.4
Seven persons or more. . . .	1.3	1.4	1.4	1.4	1.0	0.2	0.1	0.5	0.6

[1] Includes other races, not shown separately.   [2] Beginning with the 2003 Current Population Survey (CPS), respondents could choose more than one race. 2007 data represent persons who selected this race group only and exclude persons reporting more than one race. The CPS prior to 2003 only allowed respondents to report one race group. See also comments on race in the text for this section.   [3] Hispanic persons may be any race.

Source: U.S. Census Bureau, Current Population Reports, P20-537 and earlier reports; "America's Families and Living Arrangements: 2007"; published July 2008; <http://www.census.gov/population/www/socdemo/hh-fam/cps2007.html> and unpublished data.

Table 62. Unmarried-Partner Households by Sex of Partners: 2006

[The American Community Survey universe includes the household population and the population living in institutions, college dormitories, and other group quarters. Based on a sample and subject to sampling variability; see text, this section and Appendix III]

Item	Number
Total households	**111,617,402**
Unmarried-partner households.	6,017,462
Male householder and male partner	417,044
Male householder and female partner	2,705,513
Female householder and female partner	362,823
Female householder and male partner.	2,532,082
All other households	105,599,940

Source: U.S. Census Bureau, 2006 American Community Survey; B11009. Unmarried-Partner Households and Household Type by Sex of Partner; using American FactFinder®; <http://factfinder.census.gov/>; (accessed: 22 January 2008).

Population   53

Table 63. Families by Number of Own Children Under 18 Years Old: 2000 to 2007

[**As of March (72,025 represents 72,025,000).** Based on Current Population Survey; see headnote, Table 66]

Race, Hispanic origin, and year	Number of families (1,000)					Percent distribution				
	Total	No children	One child	Two children	Three or more children	Total	No children	One child	Two children	Three or more children
ALL FAMILIES [1]										
2000	72,025	37,420	14,311	13,215	7,080	100	52	20	18	10
2005	76,858	40,647	15,069	13,741	7,400	100	53	20	18	10
2007, total	**78,425**	**41,668**	**15,651**	**13,815**	**7,292**	**100**	**53**	**20**	**18**	**9**
Married couple	58,945	32,787	10,127	10,497	5,534	100	56	17	18	9
Male householder [2]	5,063	3,049	1,243	553	218	100	60	25	11	4
Female householder [2]	14,416	5,832	4,280	2,765	1,540	100	40	30	19	11
WHITE FAMILIES [3]										
2000	60,251	32,144	11,496	10,918	5,693	100	53	19	18	9
2005	63,079	34,255	11,872	11,127	5,825	100	54	19	18	9
2007, total	**64,091**	**34,993**	**12,231**	**11,115**	**5,752**	**100**	**55**	**19**	**17**	**9**
Married couple	50,729	28,741	8,419	8,866	4,704	100	57	17	17	9
Male householder [2]	3,806	2,236	977	434	159	100	59	26	11	4
Female householder [2]	9,556	4,017	2,835	1,815	890	100	42	30	19	9
BLACK FAMILIES [3]										
2000	8,664	3,882	2,101	1,624	1,058	100	45	24	19	12
2005	8,902	4,077	2,059	1,641	1,125	100	46	23	18	13
2007, total	**9,272**	**4,215**	**2,282**	**1,686**	**1,089**	**100**	**45**	**25**	**18**	**12**
Married couple	4,358	2,225	868	784	480	100	51	20	18	11
Male householder [2]	864	535	200	89	40	100	62	23	10	5
Female householder [2]	4,050	1,454	1,214	813	568	100	36	30	20	14
ASIAN FAMILIES [3]										
2005	3,142	1,535	730	646	230	100	49	23	21	7
2007, total	**3,346**	**1,676**	**722**	**721**	**226**	**100**	**50**	**22**	**22**	**7**
Married couple	2,754	1,277	618	655	204	100	46	22	24	7
Male householder [2]	223	181	23	14	5	100	81	10	6	2
Female householder [2]	369	218	81	53	17	100	59	22	14	5
HISPANIC FAMILIES [4]										
2000	7,561	2,747	1,791	1,693	1,330	100	36	24	22	18
2005	9,521	3,528	2,130	2,163	1,699	100	37	22	23	18
2007, total	**10,152**	**3,796**	**2,354**	**2,401**	**1,601**	**100**	**37**	**23**	**24**	**16**
Married couple	6,762	2,370	1,451	1,768	1,173	100	35	21	26	17
Male householder [2]	945	627	172	94	51	100	66	18	10	5
Female householder [2]	2,445	798	731	539	377	100	33	30	22	15
NON-HISPANIC WHITE FAMILIES [3, 4]										
2005	54,257	30,965	9,924	9,151	4,217	100	57	18	17	8
2007, total	**54,632**	**31,418**	**10,091**	**8,871**	**4,252**	**100**	**58**	**18**	**16**	**8**
Married couple	44,327	26,478	7,076	7,188	3,584	100	60	16	16	8
Male householder [2]	2,921	1,641	820	345	114	100	56	28	12	4
Female householder [2]	7,384	3,298	2,195	1,337	553	100	45	30	18	7

[1] Includes other races not shown separately.   [2] No spouse present.   [3] Beginning with the 2003 Current Population Survey (CPS), respondents could choose more than one race. Beginning 2005, data represent persons who selected this race group only and exclude persons reporting more than one race. The CPS prior to 2003 only allowed respondents to report one race group. See also comments on race in the text for this section.   [4] Hispanic persons may be any race.

Source: U.S. Census Bureau, Current Population Reports, P20-537; and "Families and Living Arrangements"; <http://www.census.gov/population/www/socdemo/hh-fam.html>.

Table 64. Family Households With Own Children Under Age 18 by Type of Family, 1990 to 2007, and by Age of Householder, 2007

[**As of March (32,289 represents 32,289,000).** See headnote, Table 66]

Family type			2007						
	1990	2000	Total	15 to 24 years old	25 to 34 years old	35 to 44 years old	45 to 54 years old	55 to 64 years old	65 years old and over
NUMBER (1,000)									
Family households with children	**32,289**	**34,605**	**36,757**	**1,902**	**10,346**	**14,756**	**8,277**	**1,274**	**203**
Married couple	24,537	25,248	26,158	810	6,888	10,970	6,370	991	129
Male householder, no spouse present	1,153	1,786	2,015	169	581	709	447	86	23
Female householder, no spouse present	6,599	7,571	8,585	923	2,877	3,077	1,460	197	52
PERCENT OF ALL FAMILY HOUSEHOLDS									
Family households with children, total . .	**49**	**48**	**47**	**54**	**76**	**82**	**46**	**10**	**2**
Married couple	47	46	44	60	73	82	46	9	1
Male householder, no spouse present	40	44	40	20	51	69	42	16	5
Female householder, no spouse present	61	60	60	69	92	84	50	13	3

Source: U.S. Census Bureau, Current Population Reports, P20-537 and earlier reports; and "America's Families and Living Arrangements: 2007"; published July 2008; <http://www.census.gov/population/www/socdemo/hh-fam/cps2007.html>.

Table 65. Families by Type, Race, and Hispanic Origin: 2007

[In thousands (78,425 represents 78,425,000). As of March. Excludes members of Armed Forces except those living off post or with their families on post. Population controls based on Census 2000 and an expanded sample of households. Based on Current Population Survey, see text of this section and Appendix III]

Characteristic	All families	Married couple families						Female family householder[4]						Male family householder,[4] all races
		All races[1]	White[2]	Black[2]	Asian[2]	Hispanic[3]	Non-Hispanic White[2,3]	All races[1]	White[2]	Black[2]	Asian[2]	Hispanic[3]	Non-Hispanic White[2,3]	
All families	78,425	58,945	50,729	4,358	2,754	6,762	44,327	14,416	9,556	4,050	369	2,445	7,384	5,063
Age of householder:														
Under 25 years old	3,534	1,354	1,210	84	23	333	895	1,329	831	421	33	255	604	852
25 to 34 years old	13,668	9,381	8,000	686	478	1,890	6,221	3,143	1,855	1,091	80	642	1,300	1,144
35 to 44 years old	18,053	13,371	11,140	1,099	861	1,932	9,311	3,651	2,436	1,018	76	705	1,802	1,030
45 to 54 years old	17,809	13,813	11,752	1,189	617	1,336	10,486	2,929	2,010	759	81	419	1,636	1,066
55 to 64 years old	12,976	10,910	9,566	715	454	743	8,854	1,530	1,040	391	61	229	845	535
65 to 74 years old	7,283	6,155	5,463	404	185	346	5,137	912	640	225	25	111	536	216
75 years old and over	5,102	3,960	3,599	180	136	183	3,423	922	743	145	13	85	661	220
Without own children under 18	41,668	32,787	28,741	2,225	1,277	2,370	26,478	5,832	4,017	1,454	218	798	3,298	3,049
With own children under 18	36,757	26,158	21,989	2,133	1,477	4,392	17,849	8,585	5,540	2,596	151	1,647	4,085	2,015
One own child under 18	15,651	10,127	8,419	868	618	1,451	7,076	4,280	2,835	1,214	81	731	2,195	1,243
Two own children under 18	13,815	10,497	8,866	784	655	1,768	7,188	2,765	1,815	813	53	539	1,337	553
Three or more own children under 18	7,292	5,534	4,704	480	204	1,173	3,584	1,540	890	568	17	377	553	218
Average per family with own children under 18	1.81	1.87	1.88	1.98	1.71	2.02	1.84	1.71	1.65	1.87	1.71	1.82	1.57	1.48
Age of own children:														
Of any age	47,698	32,316	27,113	2,657	1,876	5,112	22,281	12,445	8,297	3,525	248	2,130	6,396	2,936
Under 25 years old	42,549	29,971	25,217	2,424	1,707	4,826	20,656	10,099	6,563	3,012	194	1,863	4,916	2,478
Under 12 years old	26,970	19,483	16,413	1,522	1,138	3,560	13,038	6,115	3,869	1,938	102	1,233	2,790	1,372
Under 6 years old	16,306	12,130	10,224	906	720	2,352	7,996	3,373	2,076	1,129	52	720	1,442	803
Under 3 years old	9,469	7,175	6,118	508	390	1,364	4,821	1,790	1,121	579	19	390	782	503
Under 1 year old	3,483	2,619	2,279	148	143	433	1,864	662	411	219	10	125	306	202
Members 65 and older:														
Without members 65 and older	62,808	46,748	40,013	3,592	2,235	5,973	34,360	11,923	7,736	3,518	283	2,109	5,876	4,136
With members 65 and older	15,617	12,197	10,717	766	519	790	9,968	2,493	1,820	532	86	336	1,508	927
Marital status of householder:														
Married, spouse present	58,945	58,945	50,729	4,358	2,754	6,762	44,327	(X)	(X)	(X)	(X)	(X)	(X)	(X)
Married, spouse absent	2,832	(X)	(X)	(X)	(X)	(X)	(X)	2,193	1,426	632	67	592	900	639
Separated	1,999	(X)	(X)	(X)	(X)	(X)	(X)	1,641	1,080	489	30	436	692	358
Other	833	(X)	(X)	(X)	(X)	(X)	(X)	552	346	143	37	156	208	281
Widowed	2,606	(X)	(X)	(X)	(X)	(X)	(X)	2,186	1,622	450	55	237	1,400	419
Divorced	6,632	(X)	(X)	(X)	(X)	(X)	(X)	5,032	3,887	879	110	646	3,305	1,600
Never married	7,410	(X)	(X)	(X)	(X)	(X)	(X)	5,006	2,622	2,089	137	971	1,779	2,404

X Not applicable.   [1] Includes other races not shown separately.   [2] Beginning with the 2003 Current Population Survey (CPS), respondents could choose more than one race. Data represent persons who selected this race group only and exclude persons reporting more than one race. See also comments on race in the text for this section.   [3] Persons of Hispanic origin may be any race.   [4] No spouse present.

Source: U.S. Census Bureau, "America's Families and Living Arrangements: 2007"; published July 2008; <http://www.census.gov/population/www/socdemo/hh-fam/cps2007.html> and unpublished data.

Table 66. Family Groups With Children Under 18 Years Old by Race and Hispanic Origin: 1990 to 2007

[In thousands. As of March (34,670 represents 34,670,000). Family groups comprise family households, related subfamilies, and unrelated subfamilies. Excludes members of Armed Forces except those living off post or with their families on post. Beginning 2005, population controls based on Census 2000 and an expanded sample of households. Based on Current Population Survey, see text of this section and Appendix III]

Race and Hispanic origin of householder or reference person	Number (1,000)				Percent distribution			
	1990	2000	2005	2007	1990	2000	2005	2007
All races, total [1]	**34,670**	**37,496**	**39,317**	**39,983**	**100**	**100**	**100**	**100**
Two-parent family groups [2]	24,921	25,771	26,482	28,276	72	69	67	71
One-parent family groups	9,749	11,725	12,835	11,707	28	31	32	29
Maintained by mother	8,398	9,681	10,366	9,965	24	26	26	25
Maintained by father	1,351	2,044	2,469	1,742	4	5	6	4
White, total [3]	**28,294**	**30,079**	**30,960**	**31,357**	**100**	**100**	**100**	**100**
Two-parent family groups [2]	21,905	22,241	22,319	23,646	77	74	72	75
One-parent family groups	6,389	7,838	8,641	7,711	23	26	28	25
Maintained by mother	5,310	6,216	6,747	6,359	19	21	22	20
Maintained by father	1,079	1,622	1,894	1,353	4	5	6	4
Black, total [3]	**5,087**	**5,530**	**5,495**	**5,761**	**100**	**100**	**100**	**100**
Two-parent family groups [2]	2,006	2,135	2,065	2,404	39	39	38	42
One-parent family groups	3,081	3,396	3,430	3,357	61	61	62	58
Maintained by mother	2,860	3,060	3,037	3,067	56	55	55	53
Maintained by father	221	335	393	289	4	6	7	5
Asian, total [3]	**(NA)**	**1,469**	**1,757**	**1,794**	**100**	**100**	**100**	**100**
Two-parent family groups [2]	(NA)	1,184	1,472	1,568	(NA)	81	84	87
One-parent family groups	(NA)	285	285	226	(NA)	19	16	12
Maintained by mother	(NA)	236	222	185	(NA)	16	13	10
Maintained by father	(NA)	49	63	42	(NA)	3	4	2
Hispanic, total [4]	**3,429**	**5,503**	**6,752**	**7,193**	**100**	**100**	**100**	**100**
Two-parent family groups [2]	2,289	3,625	4,346	4,984	67	66	64	69
One-parent family groups	1,140	1,877	2,406	2,209	33	34	36	31
Maintained by mother	1,003	1,565	1,964	1,987	29	28	29	28
Maintained by father	138	313	442	221	4	6	7	3
Non-Hispanic White, total [3, 4] . . .	**(NA)**	**24,847**	**24,730**	**24,697**	**100**	**100**	**100**	**100**
Two-parent family groups [2]	(NA)	18,750	18,253	18,956	(NA)	75	74	77
One-parent family groups	(NA)	6,096	6,476	5,741	(NA)	25	26	23
Maintained by mother	(NA)	4,766	4,984	4,585	(NA)	19	20	19
Maintained by father	(NA)	1,331	1,492	1,155	(NA)	5	6	5

NA Not available.   [1] Includes other races not shown separately.   [2] Beginning 2007, includes children living both with married and unmarried parents.   [3] Beginning with the 2003 Current Population Survey (CPS), respondents could choose more than one race. Beginning 2005, data represent persons who selected this race group only and exclude persons reporting more than one race. The CPS prior to 2003 allowed respondents to report only one race group. See also comments on race in the text for this section.   [4] Hispanic persons may be any race.

Source: U.S. Census Bureau, Current Population Reports, P20-537, and earlier reports; and "Families and Living Arrangements"; <http://www.census.gov/population/www/socdemo/hh-fam.html>.

Table 67. Parents and Children in Stay-At-Home Parent Family Groups: 1995 to 2007

[In thousands (22,973 represents 22,973,000). Family groups with children include those families that maintain their own household (family households with own children); those that live in the home of a relative (related subfamilies); and those that live in the home of a nonrelative (unrelated subfamilies). Stay-at-home family groups are married-couple family groups with children under 15 where one parent is in the labor force all of the previous year and their spouse is out of the labor force for the entire year with the reason 'taking care of home and family.' Only married couples with children under 15 are included. Based on Current Population Survey; see Appendix III]

Year	Married-couple family groups with children under 15 years old			Children under 15 years old in married-couple family groups		
	Total	With stay-at-home mothers	With stay-at-home fathers	Total in married-couple family groups	With stay-at-home mothers	With stay-at-home fathers
1995	22,973	4,440	64	41,008	9,106	125
1996	22,808	4,633	49	40,739	9,693	115
1997	22,779	4,617	71	40,798	9,788	140
1998	22,881	4,555	90	41,038	9,432	196
1999	22,754	4,731	71	41,003	9,796	143
2000	22,953	4,785	93	41,860	10,087	180
2001	22,922	4,934	81	41,862	10,194	148
2002	23,339	5,206	106	41,802	10,573	189
2003	23,209	5,388	98	41,654	11,028	175
2004	23,160	5,571	147	41,409	11,205	268
2005	23,305	5,584	142	41,111	11,224	247
2006	23,232	5,646	159	41,259	11,372	283
2007	23,507	5,563	165	41,558	11,193	303

Source: U.S. Census Bureau, Table SHP-1. Parents and Children in Stay-At-Home Parent Family Groups: 1994 to Present; published July 2008; <http://www.census.gov/population/www/socdemo/hh-fam.html>.

Table 68. Children Under 18 Years Old by Presence of Parents: 2000 to 2007

[As of **March** (72,012 represents 72,012,000). Excludes persons under 18 years old who maintained households or family groups. Based on Current Population Survey; see headnote, Table 58]

Race Hispanic origin, and year	Number (1,000)	Both parents [1]	Percent living with— Mother only Total	Divorced	Married, spouse absent	Never married	Widowed	Father only	Neither parent
ALL RACES [2]									
2000	72,012	69.1	22.4	7.9	4.5	9.2	1.0	4.2	4.2
2005	73,494	67.3	23.4	7.9	4.6	10.1	0.8	4.8	4.5
2006	73,664	67.4	23.3	7.8	4.5	10.1	0.8	4.7	4.6
2007	73,746	70.7	22.6	7.7	4.7	9.4	0.8	3.2	3.5
WHITE [3]									
2000	56,455	75.3	17.3	(NA)	(NA)	(NA)	(NA)	4.3	3.1
2005	56,234	73.5	18.4	7.9	4.0	5.8	0.7	4.7	3.4
2006	56,332	73.8	17.9	7.7	3.7	5.8	0.7	4.6	3.6
2007	56,223	76.8	17.3	7.6	3.8	5.2	0.6	3.2	2.7
BLACK [3]									
2000	11,412	37.6	49.0	(NA)	(NA)	(NA)	(NA)	4.2	9.2
2005	11,293	35.0	50.2	8.7	8.1	32.0	1.3	5.0	9.8
2006	11,225	34.6	51.2	9.1	9.0	31.7	1.4	4.8	9.4
2007	11,310	39.5	50.2	8.5	9.3	31.0	1.4	3.6	6.8
ASIAN [3]									
2005	2,843	83.6	10.2	4.0	2.3	2.7	1.3	3.6	2.5
2006	2,869	83.8	9.7	3.4	2.9	2.8	0.6	3.6	3.0
2007	2,953	87.2	9.0	1.8	3.5	2.9	0.7	1.6	2.1
HISPANIC [4]									
2000	11,613	65.1	25.1	(NA)	(NA)	(NA)	(NA)	4.4	5.4
2005	14,241	64.7	25.4	6.1	7.1	11.4	0.8	4.8	5.2
2006	14,697	65.9	25.0	6.3	6.5	11.4	0.8	4.1	5.0
2007	15,113	69.9	24.5	6.4	7.0	10.4	0.7	2.1	3.6
NON-HISPANIC WHITE [3, 4]									
2005	43,106	75.9	16.4	8.5	3.1	4.2	0.7	4.8	2.9
2006	42,744	75.9	16.0	8.2	2.8	4.2	0.7	4.8	3.2
2007	42,261	78.6	15.3	8.1	2.8	3.7	0.6	3.6	2.5

NA Not available.   [1] Beginning in 2007, includes children living both with married and unmarried parents.   [2] Includes other races not shown separately.   [3] Beginning with the 2003 Current Population Survey (CPS), respondents could choose more than one race. Beginning 2005, data represent persons who selected this race group only and exclude persons reporting more than one race. The CPS prior to 2003 allowed respondents to report only one race group. See also comments on race in the text for this section.   [4] Hispanic persons may be any race.

Source: U.S. Census Bureau, "Families and Living Arrangements"; <http://www.census.gov/population/www/socdemo /hh-fam.html>.

Table 69. Grandparents Living With Grandchildren by Race and Sex: 2006

[6,062 represents 6,062,000. Covers both grandparents living in own home with grandchildren present and grandparents living in grandchildren's home. The American Community Survey universe includes the household population and the population living in institutions, college dormitories, and other group quarters. Based on a sample and subject to sampling variability; see text, this section and Appendix III]

Race, Hispanic origin, and sex	Grandparents living with grandchildren, total	Grandparents responsible for grandchildren Total	30 to 59 years old	60 years old and over
Grandparents living with own grandchildren under 18 years old (1,000)	**6,062**	**2,455**	**1,663**	**792**
PERCENT DISTRIBUTION				
Total	100.0	100.0	100.0	100.0
White alone	59.2	60.2	60.0	60.6
Black or African American alone	19.9	25.0	24.9	25.1
American Indian and Alaska Native alone	1.4	1.9	2.0	1.8
Asian alone	7.4	2.9	2.0	4.7
Native Hawaiian and Other Pacific Islander alone	0.3	0.3	0.3	0.4
Some other race alone	10.4	8.1	9.1	5.9
Two or more races	1.5	1.6	1.7	1.5
Hispanic or Latino [1]	22.4	17.9	19.5	14.7
White alone, not Hispanic or Latino	47.6	51.0	50.4	52.3
Male	35.3	36.5	34.4	40.8
Female	64.7	63.5	65.6	59.2

[1] Persons of Hispanic origin may be any race.

Source: U.S. Census Bureau, American Community Survey 2006, Subject Table S1002; using American FactFinder® <http://factfinder.census.gov/>; (accessed: 24 January 2008).

Population   57

Table 70. **Nonfamily Households by Sex and Age of Householder: 2007**

[In thousands (17,338 represents 17,338,000). As of March. See headnote, Table 64]

Item	Male householder					Female householder				
	Total	15 to 24 yrs. old	25 to 44 yrs. old	45 to 64 yrs. old	65 yrs. old and over	Total	15 to 24 yrs. old	25 to 44 yrs. old	45 to 64 yrs. old	65 yrs. old and over
Total	**17,338**	**1,637**	**6,593**	**5,928**	**3,181**	**20,249**	**1,491**	**3,901**	**6,694**	**8,163**
One person (living alone) . . .	13,528	799	4,717	5,079	2,934	17,604	799	2,939	5,933	7,932
Nonrelatives present	3,810	838	1,877	850	246	2,644	692	961	760	231
Never married.	8,738	1,551	4,772	1,954	460	6,456	1,414	2,748	1,814	479
Married [1]	1,598	40	576	683	301	1,112	37	299	497	280
Widowed	1,849	2	42	306	1,502	7,261	2	110	1,102	6,048
Divorced	5,152	44	1,204	2,986	919	5,420	37	744	3,282	1,358

[1] No spouse present.

Source: U.S. Census Bureau, "America's Families and Living Arrangements: 2007"; published July 2008; <http://www.census.gov/population/www/socdemo/hh-fam/cps2007.html>.

Table 71. **Persons Living Alone by Sex and Age: 1990 to 2007**

[As of March (22,999 represents 22,999,000). Excludes members of Armed Forces except those living off post or with their families on post. Beginning 2005, population controls based on Census 2000 and an expanded sample of households. Based on Current Population Survey, see text of this section and Appendix III]

Sex and age	Number of persons (1,000)						Percent distribution				
				2007					2007		
	1990	2000	2005	Total	Male	Female	1990	2000	Total	Male	Female
Total	**22,999**	**26,724**	**30,137**	**31,132**	**13,528**	**17,604**	**100**	**100**	**100**	**100**	**100**
15 to 24 years old	1,210	1,144	1,521	1,597	799	799	5	4	5	6	5
25 to 34 years old	3,972	3,848	3,836	3,930	2,351	1,579	17	14	13	17	9
35 to 44 years old	3,138	4,109	3,988	3,726	2,366	1,360	14	15	12	17	8
45 to 64 years old	5,502	7,842	10,180	11,013	5,079	5,933	24	29	35	38	34
65 to 74 years old	4,350	4,091	4,222	4,354	1,459	2,894	19	15	14	11	16
75 years old and over . . .	4,825	5,692	6,391	6,513	1,475	5,038	21	21	21	11	29

Source: U.S. Census Bureau, Current Population Reports, P20-537 and earlier reports; and "Families and Living Arrangements"; <http://www.census.gov/population/www/socdemo/hh-fam/html>.

Table 72. **Group Quarters Population by Type of Group Quarter and Selected Characteristics: 2006**

[In percent, except as indicated (8,066 represents 8,066,000). The American Community Survey universe includes the household population and the population living in institutions, college dormitories, and other group quarters. Based on a sample and subject to sampling variability; see text, this section and Appendix III]

Characteristic	Total group quarters population [1]	Adult correctional facilities	Nursing facilities/ skilled nursing facilities	College/ university housing	Characteristic	Total group quarters population [1]	Adult correctional facilities	Nursing facilities/ skilled nursing facilities	College/ university housing
Total population (1,000) .	**8,066**	**2,050**	**1,835**	**2,269**	One race (1,000)	7,863	1,978	1,822	2,209
PERCENT DISTRIBUTION					PERCENT DISTRIBUTION				
Male.	58.5	90.4	30.8	46.7	White	69.3	46.3	83.9	78.1
Female	41.5	9.6	69.2	53.3	Black or African American .	21.7	41.3	12.8	11.9
					American Indian and				
Under 15 years old	1.0	(X)	(X)	(X)	Alaska Native	1.2	2.2	0.5	0.6
15 to 17 years old.	1.9	0.4	(X)	1.6	Asian.	3.0	0.8	1.2	6.5
18 to 24 years old.	37.6	18.7	0.1	96.3	Native Hawaiian and Other				
25 to 34 years old	11.9	33.1	0.4	1.7	Pacific Islander	0.1	0.2	–	0.1
35 to 44 years old	10.8	27.9	1.5	0.2	Some other race	4.7	9.2	1.6	2.7
45 to 54 years old	8.4	14.9	3.9	0.1	Two or more races (1,000) . .	202	72	13	60
55 to 64 years old	4.9	4.1	7.7	0.1					
65 to 74 years old	4.1	0.8	12.5	–	Hispanic or Latino [2]	10.3	18.8	3.8	6.2
75 to 84 years old	8.3	0.1	31.1	(X)	Not Hispanic or Latino	89.7	81.2	96.2	93.8
85 years old and over	11.0	–	42.8	(X)	White alone, Not Hispanic or Latino.	62.9	36.7	81.2	73.2

– Represents zero.   X Not available or applicable.   [1] Includes other types of group quarters not shown separately.
[2] Persons of Hispanic origin may be any race.

Source: U.S. Census Bureau, 2006 American Community Survey; S2601A. Characteristics of the Group Quarters Population; and S2601B. Charcteristics of the Group Quarters Population by Group Quarters Type; using American FactFinder®; <http://factfinder.census.gov/>; (accessed: 22 January 2008).

Table 73. Population in Group Quarters by State: 2000 to 2007

[In thousands (7,780 represents 7,780,000). 2000, as of April; beginning 2005, as of July. For definition of group quarters, see text, this section]

State	2000 [1]	2005	2006	2007	State	2000 [1]	2005	2006	2007
U.S.	7,780	8,060	8,125	8,121	MO	164	168	168	168
AL	115	118	119	119	MT	25	26	27	27
AK	19	23	22	22	NE	51	52	52	53
AZ	110	110	109	109	NV	34	33	33	33
AR	74	78	80	80	NH	36	39	40	40
CA	820	845	858	862	NJ	195	195	196	196
CO	103	108	109	109	NM	36	42	42	43
CT	108	113	117	117	NY	581	603	606	606
DE	25	25	25	25	NC	254	271	274	274
DC	36	35	35	35	ND	24	26	28	28
FL	389	411	416	416	OH	299	305	305	305
GA	234	260	268	262	OK	112	111	116	116
HI	36	38	37	36	OR	77	82	82	82
ID	31	34	34	34	PA	433	456	466	466
IL	322	324	323	323	RI	39	38	40	40
IN	178	184	186	186	SC	135	141	144	144
IA	104	104	105	105	SD	28	30	31	31
KS	82	82	82	82	TN	148	152	152	152
KY	115	115	115	115	TX	561	597	595	595
LA	136	133	123	123	UT	40	44	44	45
ME	35	37	38	38	VT	21	21	21	21
MD	134	139	143	143	VA	231	241	246	244
MA	221	216	216	216	WA	136	142	140	139
MI	250	257	259	259	WV	43	46	46	46
MN	136	142	143	143	WI	156	160	160	160
MS	95	96	95	95	WY	14	14	14	14

[1] The April 1, 2000, Population Estimates base reflects changes to the Census 2000 population from the Count Question Resolution program and geographic program revisions.

Source: U.S. Census Bureau, "Annual Population Estimates, Estimated Components of Population Change, and Rates of the Components of Population Change for Counties: April 1, 2000 to July 1, 2007"; Release date: March 20, 2008; <http://www.census.gov/popest/counties/files/CO-EST2007-alldata.csv>.

Table 74. Religious Composition of U.S. Population: 2007

[In percent. Covers persons 18 years old and over. Based on the Religious Landscape Survey, a survey conducted in the summer of 2007 among a representative sample of 35,556 adults living in the continental United States. For details of survey methodology, see report cited below. Percents shown below represent respondents' answers to the question, "What is your present religion, if any?" and several follow-up questions]

Religious denomination/belief	Percent of adult population
Total [1]	100.0
Protestant [1]	51.3
Baptist [1]	17.2
Southern Baptist Convention	6.7
National Baptist Convention	1.8
American Baptist Churches in the USA	1.2
Methodist [1]	6.2
United Methodist Church	5.1
Lutheran [1]	4.6
Evangelical Lutheran Church in America	2.0
Lutheran Church, Missouri Synod	1.4
Nondenominational	4.5
Pentecostal [1]	4.4
Assemblies of God	1.4
Church of God in Christ	0.6
Presbyterian [1]	2.7
Presbyterian Church USA	1.1
Restorationist [1]	2.1
Church of Christ	1.5
Anglican/Episcopal [1]	1.5
Episcopal Church in the USA	1.0
Congregationalist [1]	0.8
United Church of Christ	0.5
Adventist	0.5
Catholic	23.9
Mormon [1]	1.7
Church of Jesus Christ of Latter-Day Saints	1.6
Jehovah's Witness	0.7
Orthodox	0.6
Jewish	1.7
Buddhist	0.7
Muslim	0.6
Hindu	0.4
Unitarians and other liberal faiths	0.7
New Age [2]	0.4
Unaffiliated [3]	16.1
Don't know	0.8

[1] Includes other denominations/beliefs not shown separately.   [2] Includes Wica (Wiccan), pagan, and other New Age groups.   [3] Atheist, agnostic, and nothing in particular.

Source: The Pew Forum on Religion & Public Life, Washington, DC, "U.S. Religious Landscape Survey"; released February 2008; <http://religions.pewforum.org/reports> (copyright).

Table 75. **Religious Bodies—Selected Data**

[**Membership data: 2,500 represents 2,500,000.** Includes the self-reported membership of religious bodies with 750,000 or more as reported to the *Yearbook of American and Canadian Churches.* Groups may be excluded if they do not supply information. The data are not standardized so comparisons between groups are difficult. The definition of "church member" is determined by the religious body]

Religious body	Year reported	Churches reported	Membership (1,000)
African Methodist Episcopal Church	1999	4,174	2,500
African Methodist Episcopal Zion Church	2006	3,310	1,443
American Baptist Churches in the USA	2006	5,659	1,371
Assemblies of God	2006	12,311	2,836
Baptist Bible Fellowship International	1997	4,500	1,200
Catholic Church	2006	19,044	67,515
Christian Churches and Churches of Christ	1988	5,579	1,072
Christian Methodist Episcopal Church	2006	3,500	850
Church of God in Christ	1991	15,300	5,500
Church of God (Cleveland, Tennessee)	2006	6,569	1,033
Church of Jesus Christ of Latter-day Saints	2006	13,010	5,779
Churches of Christ	2006	13,000	1,639
Episcopal Church	2006	7,095	2,155
Evangelical Lutheran Church in America	2006	10,470	4,774
Greek Orthodox Archdiocese of America	2006	560	1,500
Jehovah's Witnesses	2006	12,487	1,070
Lutheran Church—Missouri Synod	2006	6,155	2,418
National Baptist Convention of America Inc.	2000	(NA)	3,500
National Baptist Convention, U.S.A., Inc.	2004	9,000	5,000
National Missionary Baptist Convention of America	1992	(NA)	2,500
Orthodox Church in America	2004	737	1,064
Pentecostal Assemblies of the World, Inc.	2006	1,750	1,500
Presbyterian Church (U.S.A.)	2006	11,903	3,026
Progressive National Baptist Convention, Inc.	1995	2,000	2,500
Seventh Day Adventist Church	2006	4,820	981
Southern Baptist Convention	2006	44,223	16,306
United Church of Christ	2006	5,452	1,219
United Methodist Church	2005	34,397	7,995

NA Not available.

Source: National Council of Churches USA, New York, NY, *2008 Yearbook of American & Canadian Churches,* annual (copyright). (For more church-related information visit <http://www.ncccusa.org> or call 888-870-3325).

Table 76. **Christian Church Adherents, 2000, and Jewish Population, 2007— States**

[**133,377 represents 133,377,000.** Christian church adherents were defined as "all members, including full members, their children and the estimated number of other regular participants who are not considered as communicant, confirmed, or full members." The Jewish population includes Jews who define themselves as Jewish by religion as well as those who define themselves as Jewish in cultural terms. Data on Jewish population are based primarily on a compilation of individual estimates made by local Jewish federations. Additionally, most large communities have completed Jewish demographic surveys from which the Jewish population can be determined]

State	Christian adherents 2000 Number (1,000)	Christian adherents 2000 Percent of population [1]	Jewish population 2007 Number (1,000)	Jewish population 2007 Percent of population [1]	State	Christian adherents 2000 Number (1,000)	Christian adherents 2000 Percent of population [1]	Jewish population 2007 Number (1,000)	Jewish population 2007 Percent of population [1]
U.S.	**133,377**	**47.4**	**6,444**	**2.2**	MO	2,813	50.3	59	1.0
AL	2,418	54.4	9	0.2	MT	401	44.4	1	0.1
AK	210	33.6	3	0.5	NE	995	58.2	7	0.4
AZ	1,946	37.9	106	1.7	NV	604	30.2	70	2.8
AR	1,516	56.7	2	0.1	NH	571	46.2	10	0.8
CA	14,328	42.3	1,194	3.3	NJ	4,262	50.7	479	5.5
CO	1,604	37.3	88	1.8	NM	1,041	57.2	11	0.6
CT	1,828	53.7	113	3.2	NY	9,569	50.4	1,618	8.4
DE	299	38.2	15	1.8	NC	3,598	44.7	28	0.3
DC	331	57.8	28	4.8	ND	468	72.9	(Z)	0.1
FL	5,904	36.9	655	3.6	OH	4,912	43.3	145	1.3
GA	3,528	43.1	127	1.4	OK	2,079	60.3	5	0.1
HI	431	35.6	7	0.5	OR	1,029	30.1	32	0.9
ID	624	48.3	1	0.1	PA	6,751	55.0	285	2.3
IL	6,457	52.0	279	2.2	RI	646	61.7	19	1.8
IN	2,578	42.4	17	0.3	SC	1,874	46.7	11	0.3
IA	1,698	58.0	6	0.2	SD	510	67.6	(Z)	(Z)
KS	1,307	48.6	18	0.7	TN	2,867	50.4	19	0.3
KY	2,141	53.0	11	0.3	TX	11,316	54.3	130	0.6
LA	2,599	58.2	10	0.2	UT	1,659	74.3	4	0.2
ME	450	35.3	14	1.1	VT	230	37.8	6	0.9
MD	2,012	38.0	235	4.2	VA	2,807	39.7	98	1.3
MA	3,725	58.7	258	4.0	WA	1,872	31.8	43	0.7
MI	3,970	39.9	87	0.9	WV	646	35.7	2	0.1
MN	2,974	60.5	47	0.9	WI	3,198	59.6	28	0.5
MS	1,549	54.5	2	0.1	WY	229	46.4	(Z)	0.1

Z Fewer than 500 or .05 percent.   [1] Based on U.S. Census Bureau data for resident population enumerated as of April 1, 2000, and estimated as of July 1, 2007.

Source: Christian church adherents—Dale E. Jones, Sherri Doty, Clifford Grammich, James E. Horsch, Richard Houseal, John P. Marcum, Kenneth M. Sanchagrin, and Richard H. Taylor, *Religious Congregations and Membership in the United States: 2000,* Glenmary Research Center, Nashville, TN <www.glenmary.org/grc>, 2002 (copyright); Jewish population—American Jewish Committee, New York, NY, *American Jewish Year Book* (copyright).

Section 2
Births, Deaths, Marriages, and Divorces

This section presents vital statistics data on births, deaths, abortions, fetal deaths, fertility, life expectancy, marriages, and divorces. Vital statistics are compiled for the country as a whole by the National Center for Health Statistics (NCHS) and published in its annual report, *Vital Statistics of the United States,* in certain reports of the *Vital and Health Statistics* series, and in the *National Vital Statistics Reports.* Reports in this field are also issued by the various state bureaus of vital statistics. Data on fertility and selected characteristics of women who had a child in the last year, and on marital status and marital history are compiled by the U.S. Census Bureau from its Current Population Survey (CPS; see text, Section 1) and published in *Current Population Reports,* P20 Series. Data on abortions are published by the Alan Guttmacher Institute, New York, NY, in selected issues of *Perspectives on Sexual and Reproductive Health* online at <www.guttmacher.org /sections/abortion.php>.

Registration of vital events—The registration of births, deaths, fetal deaths, and other vital events in the United States is primarily a state and local function. There are 57 vital registration jurisdictions in the U.S.: the fifty states, five territories (Puerto Rico, etc.) District of Columbia, and New York City. Each of the 57 jurisdictions has a direct statistical reporting relationship with NCHS. Vital events occurring to U.S. residents outside the United States are not included in the data.

Births and deaths—The live-birth, death, and fetal-death statistics prepared by NCHS are based on vital records filed in the registration offices of all states, New York City, and the District of Columbia. The annual collection of death statistics on a national basis began in 1900 with a national death-registration area of ten states and the District of Columbia; a similar annual collection of birth statistics for a national birth-registration area began in 1915, also with ten reporting states and the District of Columbia. Since 1933, the birth- and death-registration areas have comprised the entire United States, including Alaska (beginning 1959) and Hawaii (beginning 1960). National statistics on fetal deaths were first compiled for 1918 and annually since 1922.

Prior to 1951, birth statistics came from a complete count of records received in the Public Health Service (now received in NCHS). From 1951 through 1971, they were based on a 50-percent sample of all registered births (except for a complete count in 1955 and a 20- to 50-percent sample in 1967). Beginning in 1972, they have been based on a complete count for states participating in the Vital Statistics Cooperative Program (VSCP) (for details, see the technical appendix in *Vital Statistics of the United States*) and on a 50-percent sample of all other areas. Beginning in 1986, all reporting areas participated in the VSCP. Mortality data have been based on a complete count of records for each area (except for a 50-percent sample in 1972). Beginning in 1970, births to and deaths of nonresident aliens of the United States and U.S. citizens outside the United States have been excluded from the data. Fetal deaths and deaths among Armed Forces abroad are excluded. Data based on samples are subject to sampling error; for details, see annual issues of *Vital Statistics of the United States.*

Mortality statistics by cause of death are compiled in accordance with World Health Organization regulations according to the *International Classification of Diseases* (ICD). The ICD is revised approximately every 10 years. The tenth revision of the ICD was employed beginning in 1999. Deaths for prior years were classified according to the revision of the ICD in use at the time. Each revision of the ICD introduces a number of discontinuities in mortality statistics; for a discussion of those between the ninth and tenth revisions of the ICD, see *National Vital Statistics*

U.S. Census Bureau, Statistical Abstract of the United States: 2009

Reports, Vol. 56, Nos. 2 and 10. Preliminary mortality data are based on a percentage of death records weighted up to the total number of deaths reported for the given year; for a discussion of preliminary data, see *National Vital Statistics Reports,* Vol. 56, No. 16. Information on tests of statistical significance, differences between death rates, and standard errors can also be found in the reports mentioned above.

Some of the tables present age-adjusted death rates in addition to crude death rates. Age-adjusted death rates shown in this section were prepared using the direct method, in which age-specific death rates for a population of interest are applied to a standard population distributed by age. Age adjustment eliminates the differences in observed rates between points in time or among compared population groups that result from age differences in population composition.

Fertility and life expectancy—The total fertility rate, defined as the number of births that 1,000 women would have in their lifetime if, at each year of age, they experienced the birth rates occurring in the specified year, is compiled and published by NCHS. Other data relating to social and medical factors that affect fertility rates, such as contraceptive use and birth expectations, are collected and made available by both NCHS and the Census Bureau. NCHS figures are based on information in birth and fetal death certificates and on the periodic National Surveys of Family Growth; Census Bureau data are based on decennial censuses and the CPS.

Data on life expectancy, the average remaining lifetime in years for persons who attain a given age, are computed and published by NCHS. For details, see *National Vital Statistics Reports,* Vol. 56, No. 9 and <http://www.cdc.gov/nchs/fastats/lifeexpec.htm>.

Marriage and divorce—In 1957 and 1958 respectively, the National Office of Vital Statistics established marriage- and divorce-registration areas. Beginning in 1957, the marriage-registration area comprised 30 states, plus Alaska, Hawaii, Puerto Rico, and the Virgin Islands; it currently includes 42 states and the District of Columbia. The divorce-registration area, starting in 1958 with 14 states, Alaska, Hawaii, and the Virgin Islands, currently includes a total of 31 states and the Virgin Islands. Procedures for estimating the number of marriages and divorces in the registration states are discussed in *Vital Statistics of the United States,* Vol. III—Marriage and Divorce. Total counts of events for registration and nonregistration states are gathered by collecting already summarized data on marriages and divorces reported by state offices of vital statistics and by county offices of registration. The collection and publication of detailed marriage and divorce statistics was suspended beginning in January 1996. For additional information, contact the National Center for Health Statistics online at <http://www.cdc.gov/nchs/datawh/datasite/frnotice.htm>.

Vital statistics rates—Except as noted, vital statistics rates computed by NCHS are based on decennial census population figures as of April 1 for 1960, 1970, 1980, 1990, and 2000; and on midyear population figures for other years, as estimated by the Census Bureau (see text, Section 1).

Race—Data by race for births, deaths, marriages, and divorces from NCHS are based on information contained in the certificates of registration. The Census Bureau's Current Population Survey obtains information on race by asking respondents to classify their race as (1) White, (2) Black, (3) American Indian or Alaska Native, (4) Native Hawaiian or Other Pacific Islander, and (5) Asian.

Beginning with the 1989 data year, NCHS is tabulating its birth data primarily by race of the mother. In 1988 and prior years, births were tabulated by race of the child, which was determined from the race of the parents as entered on the birth certificate.

Trend data by race shown in this section are by race of mother beginning with the 1980 data. Hispanic origin of the mother is reported and tabulated independently of race. Thus, persons of Hispanic origin may be any race. In 1994, 91 percent of women of Hispanic origin were reported as White.

Statistical reliability—For a discussion of statistical collection, estimation, and sampling procedures and measures of reliability applicable to data from NCHS and the Census Bureau, see Appendix III.

Table 77. **Live Births, Deaths, Marriages, and Divorces: 1960 to 2006**

[**4,258 represents 4,258,000**. Beginning 1970, excludes births to and deaths of nonresidents of the United States. See Appendix III]

Year	Number					Rate per 1,000 population				
		Deaths					Deaths			
	Births (1,000)	Total (1,000)	Infant [1] (1,000)	Marriages [2] (1,000)	Divorces [3] (1,000)	Births	Total	Infant [1]	Marriages [2]	Divorces [3]
1960	4,258	1,712	111	1,523	393	23.7	9.5	26.0	8.5	2.2
1965	3,760	1,828	93	1,800	479	19.4	9.4	24.7	9.3	2.5
1970	3,731	1,921	75	2,159	708	18.4	9.5	20.0	10.6	3.5
1971	3,556	1,928	68	2,190	773	17.2	9.3	19.1	10.6	3.7
1972	3,258	1,964	60	2,282	845	15.6	9.4	18.5	10.9	4.0
1973	3,137	1,973	56	2,284	915	14.8	9.3	17.7	10.8	4.3
1974	3,160	1,934	53	2,230	977	14.8	9.1	16.7	10.5	4.6
1975	3,144	1,893	51	2,153	1,036	14.6	8.8	16.1	10.0	4.8
1976	3,168	1,909	48	2,155	1,083	14.6	8.8	15.2	9.9	5.0
1977	3,327	1,900	47	2,178	1,091	15.1	8.6	14.1	9.9	5.0
1978	3,333	1,928	46	2,282	1,130	15.0	8.7	13.8	10.3	5.1
1979	3,494	1,914	46	2,331	1,181	15.6	8.5	13.1	10.4	5.3
1980	3,612	1,990	46	2,390	1,189	15.9	8.8	12.6	10.6	5.2
1981	3,629	1,978	43	2,422	1,213	15.8	8.6	11.9	10.6	5.3
1982	3,681	1,975	42	2,456	1,170	15.9	8.5	11.5	10.6	5.1
1983	3,639	2,019	41	2,446	1,158	15.6	8.6	11.2	10.5	5.0
1984	3,669	2,039	40	2,477	1,169	15.6	8.6	10.8	10.5	5.0
1985	3,761	2,086	40	2,413	1,190	15.8	8.8	10.6	10.1	5.0
1986	3,757	2,105	39	2,407	1,178	15.6	8.8	10.4	10.0	4.9
1987	3,809	2,123	38	2,403	1,166	15.7	8.8	10.1	9.9	4.8
1988	3,910	2,168	39	2,396	1,167	16.0	8.9	10.0	9.8	4.8
1989	4,041	2,150	40	2,403	1,157	16.4	8.7	9.8	9.7	4.7
1990	4,158	2,148	38	2,443	1,182	16.7	8.6	9.2	9.8	4.7
1991	4,111	2,170	37	2,371	1,187	16.2	8.6	8.9	9.4	4.7
1992	4,065	2,176	35	2,362	1,215	15.8	8.5	8.5	9.3	4.8
1993	4,000	2,269	33	2,334	1,187	15.4	8.8	8.4	9.0	4.6
1994	3,953	2,279	31	2,362	1,191	15.0	8.8	8.0	9.1	4.6
1995	3,900	2,312	30	2,336	1,169	14.6	8.7	7.6	8.9	4.4
1996	3,891	2,315	28	2,344	1,150	14.4	8.6	7.3	8.8	4.3
1997	3,881	2,314	28	2,384	1,163	14.2	8.5	7.2	8.9	4.3
1998 [4] . . .	3,942	2,337	28	2,244	1,135	14.3	8.5	7.2	8.4	4.2
1999 [4] . . .	3,959	2,391	28	2,358	(NA)	14.2	8.6	7.1	8.6	4.1
2000 [4] . . .	4,059	2,403	28	2,329	(NA)	14.4	8.5	6.9	8.3	4.1
2001 [4] . . .	4,026	2,416	28	2,345	(NA)	14.1	8.5	6.8	8.2	4.0
2002 [5] . . .	4,022	2,443	28	2,254	(NA)	13.9	8.5	7.0	7.8	3.9
2003 [5] . . .	4,090	2,448	28	2,245	(NA)	14.1	8.4	6.9	7.7	3.8
2004 [5] . . .	4,112	2,398	28	2,279	(NA)	14.0	8.2	6.8	7.8	3.7
2005 [5] . . .	4,138	2,448	28	[6]2,249	(NA)	14.0	8.3	6.9	[6,7]7.6	[6]3.6
2006 [5, 7] . .	4,266	2,426	29	[6, 8]2,160	(NA)	14.2	8.1	6.7	[6, 8]7.5	[6]3.6

NA Not available. [1] Infants under 1 year, excluding fetal deaths; rates per 1,000 registered live births. [2] Includes estimates for some states through 1965 and also for 1976 and 1977, and marriage licenses for some states for all years except 1973 and 1975. Beginning 1978, includes nonlicensed marriages in California. [3] Includes reported annulments and some estimated state figures for all years. [4] Divorce rate excludes data for California, Colorado, Indiana, and Louisiana; population for this rate also excludes these states. [5] Divorce rates exclude data for California, Georgia, Hawaii, Indiana, Louisiana, and Minnesota in 2005 and 2006; California, Georgia, Hawaii, Indiana, and Louisiana in 2004; California, Hawaii, Indiana, Louisiana, and Oklahoma in 2003; and California, Indiana, and Oklahoma in 2002. Populations for these rates also exclude these states. [6] Provisional data. Includes nonresidents. [7] Preliminary data. For births and deaths. [8] Excludes Louisiana.

Source: U.S. National Center for Health Statistics, *Vital Statistics of the United States,* and *National Vital Statistics Reports (NVSR).* See also <http://www.cdc.gov/nchs/births.htm>.

Table 78. **Live Births, Birth Rates, and Fertility Rates by Hispanic-Origin Status: 1990 to 2006**

[**4,093 represents 4,093,000**. Represents registered births. Excludes births to nonresidents of the United States. Data are based on Hispanic origin and race of mother. Persons of Hispanic origin may be any race. See Appendix III]

Hispanic-origin status and race of mother	Number of births (1,000)				Birth rate per 1,000 population				Fertility rate [2]			
	1990 [1]	2000	2005	2006, prel.	1990 [1]	2000	2005	2006, prel.	1990 [1]	2000	2005	2006, prel.
Total [3]	4,093	4,059	4,138	4,266	16.7	14.4	14.0	14.2	71.0	65.9	66.7	68.5
Hispanic origin	595	816	986	1,039	26.7	23.1	23.1	23.4	107.7	95.9	99.4	101.5
Mexican	386	582	693	(NA)	28.7	25.0	24.7	(NA)	118.9	105.1	107.7	(NA)
Puerto Rican	59	58	63	(NA)	21.6	18.1	17.2	(NA)	82.9	73.5	72.1	(NA)
Cuban	11	13	16	(NA)	10.9	9.7	10.2	(NA)	52.6	49.3	50.4	(NA)
Central and South American [4]	83	113	151	(NA)	27.5	21.8	22.8	(NA)	102.7	85.1	93.2	(NA)
Other and unknown Hispanic	56	49	62	(NA)	[4]	[4]	[4]	(NA)	[4]	[4]	[4]	(NA)
Non-Hispanic [5]	3,457	3,200	3,123	(NA)	15.7	13.2	12.4	(NA)	67.1	61.1	60.4	(NA)
White	2,627	2,363	2,280	2,310	14.4	12.2	11.5	11.6	62.8	58.5	58.3	59.5
Black	662	604	584	617	23.0	17.3	15.7	16.5	89.0	71.4	67.2	70.6

NA Not available. [1] Excludes data for New Hampshire and Oklahoma, which did not report Hispanic origin. [2] Live births per 1,000 women age 15 to 44 years in specified group. [3] Includes all races and Hispanic-origin status not stated. [4] Rates for the Central and South American population include other and unknown Hispanic. [5] Includes other races not shown separately.

Source: U.S. National Center for Health Statistics, *National Vital Statistics Reports (NVSR), Births: Final Data for 2005,* Volume 56, Number 6, December 5, 2007 and *Births: Preliminary Data for 2006,* Volume 56, Number 7, December 5, 2007.

Births, Deaths, Marriages, and Divorces   63

Table 79. Births and Birth Rates by Race, Sex, and Age: 1980 to 2006

[Births in thousands (3,612 represents 3,612,000). Births by race of mother. Excludes births to nonresidents of the United States. For population bases used to derive these data, see text this section, and Appendix III]

Item	1980	1985	1990	1995	2000	2001	2002	2003	2004	2005	2006, prel.
Live births [1]	3,612	3,761	4,158	3,900	4,059	4,026	4,022	4,090	4,112	4,138	4,266
White	2,936	3,038	3,290	3,099	3,194	3,178	3,175	3,226	3,223	3,229	(NA)
Black	568	582	684	603	623	606	594	600	616	633	(NA)
American Indian, Eskimo, Aleut	29	34	39	37	42	42	42	43	44	45	47
Asian or Pacific Islander	74	105	142	160	201	200	211	221	229	231	240
Male	1,853	1,928	2,129	1,996	2,077	2,058	2,058	2,094	2,105	(NA)	(NA)
Female	1,760	1,833	2,029	1,903	1,982	1,968	1,964	1,996	2,007	(NA)	(NA)
Males per 100 females	105	105	105	105	105	105	105	105	105	(NA)	(NA)
Age of mother:											
Under 20 years old	562	478	533	512	478	454	433	421	422	421	442
20 to 24 years old	1,226	1,141	1,094	966	1,018	1,022	1,022	1,032	1,034	1,040	1,081
25 to 29 years old	1,108	1,201	1,277	1,064	1,088	1,058	1,060	1,086	1,104	1,132	1,182
30 to 34 years old	550	696	886	905	929	943	951	976	966	951	950
35 to 39 years old	141	214	318	384	452	452	454	468	476	483	499
40 to 44 years old	(NA)	(NA)	(NA)	(NA)	90	93	96	101	104	105	105
45 to 49 years old	(NA)	(NA)	(NA)	(NA)	4	5	5	6	6	6	7
Mean age of mother at first birth (years)	22.7	23.7	24.2	24.5	24.9	25.0	25.1	25.2	25.2	25.2	(NA)
Birth rate per 1,000 population	15.9	15.8	16.7	14.6	14.4	14.1	13.9	14.1	14.0	14.0	14.2
White	15.1	15.0	15.8	14.1	13.9	13.7	13.5	13.6	13.5	13.4	(NA)
Black	21.3	20.4	22.4	17.8	17.0	16.3	15.7	15.7	16.0	16.2	(NA)
American Indian, Eskimo, Aleut	20.7	19.8	18.9	15.3	14.0	13.7	13.8	13.8	14.0	14.2	14.8
Asian or Pacific Islander	19.9	18.7	19.0	16.7	17.1	16.4	16.5	16.8	16.8	16.5	16.5
Age of mother:											
10 to 14 years old	1.1	1.2	1.4	1.3	0.9	0.8	0.7	0.6	0.7	0.7	0.6
15 to 19 years old	53.0	51.0	59.9	56.0	47.7	45.3	43.0	41.6	41.1	40.4	41.9
20 to 24 years old	115.1	108.3	116.5	107.5	109.7	106.2	103.6	102.6	101.7	102.2	105.9
25 to 29 years old	112.9	111.0	120.2	108.8	113.5	113.4	113.6	115.6	115.5	115.5	116.8
30 to 34 years old	61.9	69.1	80.8	81.1	91.2	91.9	91.5	95.1	95.3	95.8	97.7
35 to 39 years old	19.8	24.0	31.7	34.0	39.7	40.6	41.4	43.8	45.4	46.3	47.3
40 to 44 years old	3.9	4.0	5.5	6.6	8.0	8.1	8.3	8.7	8.9	9.1	9.4
45 to 49 years old [2]	0.2	0.2	0.2	0.3	0.5	0.5	0.5	0.5	0.5	0.6	0.6
Fertility rate per 1,000 women [3]	68.4	66.2	70.9	64.6	65.9	65.3	64.8	66.1	66.3	66.7	68.5
White [3]	65.6	64.1	68.3	63.6	65.3	65.0	64.8	66.1	66.1	66.3	(NA)
Black [3]	84.9	78.8	84.8	71.0	70.0	67.6	65.8	66.3	67.6	69.0	(NA)
American Indian, Eskimo, Aleut [3]	82.7	78.6	76.2	63.0	58.7	58.1	58.0	58.4	58.9	59.9	62.8
Asian or Pacific Islander [3]	73.2	68.4	69.6	62.6	65.8	64.2	64.1	66.3	67.1	66.6	67.2

NA Not available. [1] Includes other races not shown separately. [2] Beginning 2000, rates computed by relating births to women aged 45 to 54 years old to women 45 to 49 years old. [3] Number of live births per 1,000 women, 15 to 44 years old in specified group.

Source: U.S. National Center for Health Statistics, *National Vital Statistics Reports (NVSR), Births: Final Data for 2005*, Vol. 56, No. 6, December 5, 2007; and *Births: Preliminary Data for 2006*, Vol. 56, No. 7, December 5, 2007; and earlier reports.

Table 80. Births and Birth Rates by Plurality of Birth and Race and Hispanic-Origin Status of Mother: 1990 to 2005

[Persons of Hispanic origin may be of any race. See headnote, Table 78. See Appendix III]

Birth order	1990 [1]	2000	2002	2003	2004	2005
All births, total number [2]	4,158,212	4,058,814	4,021,726	4,089,950	4,112,052	4,138,349
Twin births	93,865	118,916	125,134	128,665	132,219	133,122
Triplet and higher order multiple births	3,028	7,325	7,401	7,663	7,275	6,694
Multiple birth rate [3]	23.3	31.1	33.0	33.3	33.9	33.8
Twin birth rate [4]	22.6	29.3	31.1	31.5	32.2	32.2
Triplet and higher order multiple birth rate [5]	72.8	180.5	184.0	187.4	176.9	161.8
Non-Hispanic White births, total number	2,626,500	2,362,968	2,298,156	2,321,904	2,296,683	2,279,768
Twin births	60,210	76,018	79,949	81,691	83,346	82,223
Triplet and higher order multiple births	2,358	5,821	5,754	5,922	5,590	4,966
Multiple birth rate [3]	23.8	34.6	37.3	37.7	38.7	38.2
Twin birth rate [4]	22.9	32.2	34.8	35.2	36.3	36.1
Non-Hispanic Black births, total number	661,701	604,346	578,335	576,033	578,772	583,759
Twin births	17,646	20,173	20,064	20,010	20,605	21,254
Triplet and higher order multiple births	306	506	591	631	577	616
Multiple birth rate [3]	27.1	34.2	35.7	35.8	36.6	37.5
Twin birth rate [4]	26.7	33.4	34.7	34.7	35.6	36.4
Hispanic births, total number	595,073	815,868	876,642	912,329	946,349	985,505
Twin births	10,713	16,470	18,128	19,472	20,351	21,723
Triplet and higher order multiple births	235	659	737	784	723	761
Multiple birth rate [3]	18.4	21.0	21.5	22.2	22.3	22.8
Twin birth rate [4]	18.0	20.2	20.7	21.3	21.5	22.0

[1] Data by Hispanic-origin status exclude data for New Hampshire and Oklahoma, which did not report Hispanic origin. [2] Includes other races not shown separately. [3] Number of live births in all multiple deliveries per 1,000 live births. [4] Number of live births in twin deliveries per 1,000 live births. [5] Number of live births in triplet and other higher-order deliveries per 100,000 live births.

Source: U.S. National Center for Health Statistics, *National Vital Statistics Reports (NVSR), Births: Final Data for 2005*, annual, Vol. 56, Number 6, December 5, 2007.

Table 81. **Live Births by State and Island Areas: 2006**

[Number of births, except rate. Registered births. Excludes births to nonresidents of the United States. By race and Hispanic origin of mother. Data for Non-Hispanic Black were not available. Data are preliminary. See Appendix III]

State and island area	All races [1]	Non-Hispanic White	Asian or Pacific Islander	American Indian, Eskimo, Aleut	Hispanic [2]	Birth rate [3]	Fertility rate [4]
United States	**4,265,996**	**2,309,833**	**239,829**	**47,494**	**1,039,051**	**14.2**	**68.5**
Alabama.	63,235	38,144	829	192	4,695	13.7	67.0
Alaska	10,991	6,285	897	2,716	752	16.4	76.7
Arizona.	102,475	43,378	3,221	6,605	45,534	16.6	81.6
Arkansas	40,973	27,686	647	272	4,400	14.6	72.3
California	562,431	158,424	70,812	3,425	293,320	15.4	71.8
Colorado.	70,750	42,127	2,421	612	22,813	14.9	70.2
Connecticut.	41,807	25,648	2,223	227	8,482	11.9	58.8
Delaware	11,988	6,579	489	30	1,882	14.0	67.3
District of Columbia	8,529	2,142	184	7	1,327	14.7	58.5
Florida	236,882	107,503	7,531	789	70,060	13.1	67.3
Georgia	148,619	69,491	5,129	319	23,675	15.9	72.4
Hawaii	18,982	4,585	12,764	75	3,039	14.8	73.9
Idaho	24,184	19,496	349	416	3,792	16.5	80.9
Illinois	180,583	95,327	9,315	309	44,341	14.1	66.8
Indiana	88,674	67,983	1,561	152	8,458	14.0	68.3
Iowa	40,610	34,516	962	240	3,227	13.6	69.1
Kansas.	40,964	29,670	1,364	400	6,586	14.8	73.3
Kentucky	58,291	49,256	980	87	2,777	13.9	67.2
Louisiana	63,399	35,544	996	426	2,233	14.8	70.6
Maine.	14,151	13,298	241	84	218	10.7	54.5
Maryland	77,478	37,000	4,735	176	10,086	13.8	64.2
Massachusetts.	77,769	53,712	5,654	173	10,755	12.1	57.0
Michigan.	127,476	87,151	4,656	722	8,682	12.6	61.7
Minnesota.	73,559	54,075	5,036	1,732	6,038	14.2	68.7
Mississippi	46,069	22,628	439	323	1,555	15.8	75.8
Missouri	81,388	62,116	1,915	402	4,556	13.9	67.9
Montana.	12,506	9,820	121	1,620	401	13.2	69.5
Nebraska	26,733	19,980	699	574	4,000	15.1	75.1
Nevada	40,085	17,284	2,954	435	15,621	16.1	78.0
New Hampshire	14,380	12,835	536	18	585	10.9	53.4
New Jersey	115,006	56,943	11,151	192	29,202	13.2	64.4
New Mexico	29,937	8,590	548	3,974	16,514	15.3	74.7
New York	250,091	125,297	22,036	636	59,331	13.0	61.1
North Carolina	127,841	71,361	3,737	1,731	21,214	14.4	69.0
North Dakota.	8,622	7,110	105	1,026	249	13.6	68.7
Ohio	150,590	115,912	3,216	329	6,736	13.1	64.7
Oklahoma.	54,018	34,911	1,105	6,054	7,065	15.1	74.7
Oregon.	48,717	33,876	2,720	922	9,947	13.2	65.5
Pennsylvania	149,082	107,610	5,953	457	13,294	12.0	60.6
Rhode Island.	12,379	6,123	576	154	2,558	11.6	54.6
South Carolina.	62,271	34,492	1,278	256	5,888	14.4	69.7
South Dakota	11,917	9,169	141	2,048	401	15.2	78.4
Tennessee	84,345	57,166	2,012	270	7,938	14.0	67.5
Texas.	399,612	139,913	14,748	1,134	198,291	17.0	78.8
Utah	53,499	42,222	1,660	709	8,224	21.0	94.1
Vermont	6,509	6,198	108	17	74	10.4	52.2
Virginia.	107,817	62,492	7,423	156	14,463	14.1	66.3
Washington.	86,848	56,242	8,634	2,268	15,785	13.6	65.2
West Virginia	20,928	19,757	177	22	219	11.5	59.4
Wisconsin.	72,335	54,541	2,735	1,233	6,870	13.0	64.0
Wyoming	7,670	6,224	104	347	897	14.9	75.9
Puerto Rico	48,590	1,328	–	–	47,143	12.4	57.2
Virgin Islands	1,431	101	–	51	253	13.2	64.6
Guam.	(NA)	(NA)	(NA)	(NA)	(NA)	(NA)	(NA)
American Samoa	1,442	(NA)	1,440	–	(NA)	25.0	110.4
Northern Marianas . . .	1,422	(NA)	1,403	–	(NA)	17.2	42.4

– Represents or rounds to zero.   NA Not available.   [1] Includes persons of other groups not shown separately.   [2] Persons of Hispanic origin may be any race.   [3] Per 1,000 estimated population.   [4] Number of births per 1,000 women age 15 to 44 years estimated.

Source: U.S. National Center for Health Statistics, *National Vital Statistics Reports (NVSR), Births: Preliminary Data for 2006,* annual, Vol. 56, No. 7, December 5, 2007.

Table 82. Total Fertility Rate by Race and Hispanic Origin: 1980 to 2006

[Based on race of mother. Excludes births to nonresidents of United States. The *total fertility rate* is the number of births that 1,000 women would have in their lifetime if, at each year of age, they experienced the birth rates occurring in the specified year. A total fertility rate of 2,110 represents "replacement level" fertility for the total population under current mortality conditions (assuming no net immigration). See Appendix III]

Race and Hispanic origin	1980	1990	2000	2002	2003	2004	2005	2006 [1]
Total [2]	**1,840**	**2,081**	**2,056**	**2,013**	**2,043**	**2,046**	**2,054**	**2,101**
White.	1,773	2,003	2,051	2,028	2,061	2,055	2,056	(NA)
Black.	2,177	2,480	2,129	1,991	1,999	2,033	2,071	(NA)
American Indian, Eskimo, Aleut. . .	2,165	2,185	1,773	1,735	1,732	1,735	1,750	1,820
Asian or Pacific Islander	1,954	2,003	1,892	1,820	1,873	1,898	1,889	1,908
Hispanic [3].	(NA)	2,960	2,730	2,718	2,786	2,825	2,885	2,959

NA Not available.   [1] Preliminary data.   [2] For 1980 and 1990, includes births to races not shown separately. Beginning 2000, unknown race of mother is imputed.   [3] Persons of Hispanic origin may be any race.

Source: U.S. National Center for Health Statistics, *National Vital Statistics Reports (NVSR), Births: Final Data for 2005, annual,* Volume 56, Number 6, December 5, 2007, and *Births: Preliminary Data for 2006, annual,* Volume 56, Number 7, December 5, 2007.

Table 83. Teenagers—Births and Birth Rates by Age, Race, and Hispanic Origin: 1990 to 2006

[**Birth rates per 1,000 women in specified group**, see text, this section. Based on race and Hispanic origin of mother]

Age, race, and Hispanic origin	Number of births					Birth rate				
	1990	1995	2000	2005	2006 [1]	1990	1995	2000	2005	2006 [1]
All races, total	[2]**521,826**	**499,873**	**468,990**	**414,593**	**435,427**	**59.9**	**56.0**	**47.7**	**40.5**	**41.9**
15 to 17 years old	183,327	192,508	157,209	133,191	138,920	37.5	35.5	26.9	21.4	22.0
18 and 19 years old	338,499	307,365	311,781	281,402	296,507	88.6	87.7	78.1	69.9	73.0
White.	354,482	349,635	333,013	295,265	(NA)	50.8	49.5	43.2	37.0	(NA)
Black.	151,613	133,694	118,954	103,905	(NA)	112.8	94.4	77.4	61.9	(NA)
American Indian, Eskimo, Aleut	(NA)	7,764	8,055	7,807	8,222	81.1	72.9	58.3	52.7	54.7
Asian or Pacific Islander . . .	(NA)	8,780	8,968	7,616	7,672	26.4	25.5	20.5	17.0	16.7
Hispanic [3]	(NA)	118,449	129,469	136,906	145,651	100.3	99.3	87.3	81.7	83.0
Non-Hispanic White	(NA)	230,024	204,056	165,005	169,837	42.5	39.3	32.6	25.9	26.6
Non-Hispanic Black	(NA)	130,907	116,019	96,813	103,692	116.2	97.2	79.2	60.9	63.7

NA Not available.   [1] Preliminary data.   [2] Includes races other than White and Black not shown separately.   [3] Persons of Hispanic origin may be any race.

Source: U.S. National Center for Health Statistics, *National Vital Statistics Reports (NVSR), Births: Final Data for 2005*, Volume 56, Number 6, December 5, 2007, and *Births: Preliminary Data for 2006, annual,* Volume 56, Number 7, December 5, 2007.

Table 84. Births to Unmarried Women by Race, Hispanic Origin, and Age of Mother: 1990 to 2005

[**1,165 represents 1,165,000.** Excludes births to nonresidents of United States. Persons of Hispanic origin may be any race. Marital status is inferred from a comparison of the child's and parents' surnames on the birth certificate for those states that do not report on marital status. No estimates included for misstatements on birth records or failures to register births. Based on race and Hispanic origin of mother. See also Appendix III]

Race and age of mother	Number (1,000)					Percent distribution				Birth rate [1]			
	1990	1995	2000	2004	2005	1990	1995	2000	2005	1990	1995	2000	2005
Total live births [2]	**1,165**	**1,254**	**1,347**	**1,470**	**1,527**	**100.0**	**100.0**	**100.0**	**100.0**	**43.8**	**44.3**	**44.1**	**47.5**
White.	670	785	866	983	1,023	57.5	62.6	64.3	67.0	32.9	37.0	38.2	43.0
Black.	455	421	427	424	439	39.1	33.6	31.7	28.7	90.5	74.5	70.5	67.8
American Indian, Eskimo, Aleut	(NA)	(NA)	(NA)	27	28	(NA)	(NA)	(NA)	1.9	(NA)	(NA)	(NA)	(NA)
Asian or Pacific Islander . .	(NA)	(NA)	(NA)	35	37	(NA)	(NA)	(NA)	2.4	(NA)	(NA)	20.9	24.9
Hispanic.	[3]219	278	348	440	473	[3]18.8	22.1	25.8	31.0	[3]89.6	88.8	87.3	100.3
Non-Hispanic White	[3]443	504	522	563	578	[3]38.0	40.2	38.7	37.8	[3]24.4	28.1	28.0	30.1
Non-Hispanic Black	(NA)	(NA)	415	401	408	(NA)	(NA)	30.8	26.7	(NA)	(NA)	(NA)	(NA)
Under 15 years	11	11	8	7	7	0.9	0.9	0.6	0.4	(NA)	(NA)	(NA)	(NA)
15 to 19 years.	350	376	369	342	345	30.0	30.0	27.4	22.6	42.5	43.8	39.0	34.5
20 to 24 years.	404	432	504	566	585	34.7	34.5	37.4	38.3	65.1	68.7	72.2	74.9
25 to 29 years.	230	229	255	308	332	19.7	18.2	18.9	21.7	56.0	54.3	58.5	71.1
30 to 34 years.	118	133	130	155	162	10.1	10.6	9.7	10.6	37.6	38.9	39.3	50.0
35 to 39 years.	44	60	65	72	76	3.8	4.8	4.8	5.0	17.3	19.3	19.7	24.5
40 years and over	9	13	16	20	21	0.7	1.0	1.2	1.4	3.6	4.7	5.0	6.2

NA Not available.   [1] Rate per 1,000 unmarried women (never-married, widowed, and divorced) estimated as of July 1. Total rate and rates by race/Hispanic origin cover women 15 to 44 years old. Rate for unmarried women 40 years and over relate births to women 40 years and over to unmarried women 40 to 44 years old.   [2] Includes races other than White and Black not shown separately.   [3] Excludes data for New Hampshire and Oklahoma, which did not report Hispanic origin.

Source: U.S. National Center for Health Statistics, *National Vital Statistics Reports (NVSR), Births: Final Data for 2005, annual,* Volume 56, Number 6, December 5, 2007; and earlier reports.

Table 85. Births to Teens and Unmarried Women, and Births with Low Birth Weight, by Race and Hispanic Origin: 1990 to 2006

[Represents registered births. Excludes births to nonresidents of the United States. Data are based on race and Hispanic origin of mother. See Appendix III]

Race and Hispanic origin	1990	1995	2000	2003	2004	2005	2006, prel.
Percent of births to teenage mothers	**12.8**	**13.1**	**11.8**	**10.3**	**10.3**	**10.0**	**10.4**
White	10.9	11.5	10.6	9.4	9.3	9.2	(NA)
Black	23.1	23.1	19.7	17.3	17.1	16.8	(NA)
American Indian, Eskimo, Aleut	19.5	21.4	19.7	18.2	17.9	17.4	17.3
Asian or Pacific Islander	5.7	5.6	4.5	3.5	3.4	3.3	3.2
Hispanic origin [1]	16.8	17.9	16.2	14.3	14.3	13.9	14.0
Mexican	17.7	18.8	17.0	15.3	15.3	(NA)	(NA)
Puerto Rican	21.7	23.5	20.0	17.9	17.6	(NA)	(NA)
Cuban	7.7	7.7	7.5	7.9	7.8	(NA)	(NA)
Central and South American	9.0	10.6	9.9	8.3	8.4	(NA)	(NA)
Percent of births to unmarried women	**26.6**	**32.2**	**33.2**	**34.6**	**35.8**	**36.9**	**38.5**
White	16.9	25.3	27.1	29.4	30.5	31.7	(NA)
Black	66.7	69.9	68.5	68.2	68.8	69.3	(NA)
American Indian, Eskimo, Aleut	53.6	57.2	58.4	61.3	62.3	63.5	64.6
Asian or Pacific Islander	13.2	16.3	14.8	15.0	15.5	16.2	16.3
Hispanic origin [1]	36.7	40.8	42.7	45.0	46.4	48.0	49.9
Mexican	33.3	38.1	40.7	43.7	45.2	(NA)	(NA)
Puerto Rican	55.9	60.0	59.6	59.8	61.0	(NA)	(NA)
Cuban	18.2	23.8	27.3	31.4	33.2	(NA)	(NA)
Central and South American	41.2	44.1	44.7	46.0	47.6	(NA)	(NA)
Percent of births with low birth weight [2]	**7.0**	**7.3**	**7.6**	**7.9**	**8.1**	**8.2**	**8.3**
White	5.7	6.2	6.5	6.9	7.1	7.2	(NA)
Black	13.3	13.1	13.0	13.4	13.4	13.6	(NA)
American Indian, Eskimo, Aleut	6.1	6.6	6.8	7.4	7.5	7.4	7.5
Asian or Pacific Islander	(NA)	6.9	7.3	7.8	7.9	8.0	8.1
Hispanic origin [1]	6.1	6.3	6.4	6.7	6.8	6.9	7.0
Mexican	5.5	5.8	6.0	6.3	6.4	6.5	(NA)
Puerto Rican	9.0	9.4	9.3	10.0	9.8	9.9	(NA)
Cuban	5.7	6.5	6.5	7.0	7.7	7.6	(NA)
Central and South American	5.8	6.2	6.3	6.7	6.7	6.8	(NA)

NA Not available.   [1] Hispanic persons may be any race. Includes other types not shown separately.   [2] Births less than 2,500 grams (5 lb.-8 oz.).

Source: U.S. National Center for Health Statistics, *National Vital Statistics Reports (NVSR)*, *Births: Final Data for 2005*, Volume 56, Number 6, December 5, 2007, and *Births: Preliminary Data for 2006*, Volume 56, Number 7, December 5, 2007.

Table 86. Births by Race, Hispanic-Origin Status, and Method of Delivery: 1990 to 2005

[In thousands (4,111 represents 4,111,000), except rate. 1990 excludes data for Oklahoma, which did not report method of delivery on the birth certificate. Persons of Hispanic origin may be any race. See Appendix III]

Method of delivery	1990	2000	2004	2005 Total [1]	2005 Hispanic	2005 Non-Hispanic White	2005 Non-Hispanic Black
Births, total	**4,111**	**4,059**	**4,112**	**4,138**	**986**	**2,280**	**584**
Vaginal	3,111	3,108	2,903	2,874	698	1,580	392
After previous caesarean	84	90	46	(NA)	(NA)	(NA)	(NA)
Caesarean deliveries	914	924	1,190	1,249	285	690	189
Primary	575	578	740	(NA)	(NA)	(NA)	(NA)
Repeat	339	346	450	(NA)	(NA)	(NA)	(NA)
Not stated	85	27	19	16	2	10	2
Caesarean delivery rate [2]	22.7	22.9	29.1	30.3	29.0	30.4	32.6
Primary [3]	16.0	16.1	20.6	(NA)	(NA)	(NA)	(NA)
Rate of vaginal birth after previous caesarean [4]	19.9	20.6	9.2	(NA)	(NA)	(NA)	(NA)

NA Not available.   [1] Includes other races not shown separately.   [2] Caesarean rates are the number of caesarean deliveries per 100 total deliveries for specified category.   [3] Number of primary caesareans per 100 live births to women who have not had a previous caesarean.   [4] Number of vaginal births after previous caesarean delivery per 100 live births to women with a previous cesarean delivery.

Source: U.S. National Center for Health Statistics, *National Vital Statistics Reports (NVSR)*, *Births: Final Data for 2005*, Volume 56, Number 6, December 5, 2007; and earlier reports.

U.S. Census Bureau, Statistical Abstract of the United States: 2009

Table 87. Births to Teenage Mothers and Unmarried Women and Births With Low Birth Weight—States and Island Areas: 2000 to 2006

[Represents registered births. Excludes births to nonresidents of the United States. Based on 100 percent of births in all states and the District of Columbia. 2006 data are preliminary and based on a substantial proportion of vital records for that year. See Appendix III]

State and island area	Births to teenage mothers, percent of total [1]		Births to unmarried women, percent of total		Percent of births with low birth weight [2]		State and island area	Births to teenage mothers, percent of total [1]		Births to unmarried women, percent of total		Percent of births with low birth weight [2]	
	2000	2006	2000	2006	2000	2006		2000	2006	2000	2006	2000	2006
United States	**11.8**	**10.4**	**33.2**	**38.5**	**7.6**	**8.3**	Nevada	12.7	10.9	36.4	41.2	7.2	8.3
Alabama	15.7	13.8	34.3	36.6	9.7	10.5	New Hampshire.	6.8	6.1	24.7	29.4	6.3	6.9
Alaska.	11.8	10.1	33.0	36.8	5.6	6.0	New Jersey	7.1	6.3	28.9	33.0	7.7	8.6
Arizona	14.3	12.7	39.3	44.0	7.0	7.1	New Mexico	17.4	15.7	45.6	51.2	8.0	8.9
Arkansas	17.3	14.7	35.7	41.8	8.6	9.2	New York	8.2	7.1	36.6	40.0	7.7	8.3
California	10.6	9.5	32.7	37.6	6.2	6.8	North Carolina.	13.0	11.7	33.3	40.1	8.8	9.1
Colorado	11.7	9.7	25.0	27.6	8.4	8.9	North Dakota	9.2	7.4	28.3	31.7	6.4	6.7
Connecticut	7.8	6.9	29.3	34.0	7.4	8.1	Ohio	12.1	10.7	34.6	40.5	7.9	8.8
Delaware	12.3	10.7	37.9	45.6	8.6	9.3	Oklahoma	15.9	13.6	34.3	40.9	7.5	8.3
District of Columbia . .	14.2	12.0	60.3	57.6	11.9	11.5	Oregon	11.3	8.9	30.1	34.3	5.6	6.1
Florida	12.6	10.9	38.2	44.5	8.0	8.7	Pennsylvania	9.9	9.3	32.7	38.3	7.7	8.4
Georgia	13.9	12.1	37.0	42.4	8.6	9.6	Rhode Island	10.2	9.2	35.5	40.5	7.2	8.0
Hawaii.	10.3	8.6	32.2	36.0	7.5	8.1	South Carolina	15.3	13.4	39.8	45.5	9.7	10.1
Idaho.	11.6	8.9	21.6	24.3	6.7	6.9	South Dakota	11.6	9.5	33.5	37.1	6.2	7.0
Illinois	11.4	10.0	34.5	38.7	7.9	8.6	Tennessee	14.7	13.0	34.5	41.4	9.2	9.6
Indiana	12.5	10.9	34.7	41.4	7.4	8.2	Texas	15.3	13.5	30.5	39.4	7.4	8.4
Iowa	10.0	8.7	28.0	33.8	6.1	6.9	Utah	8.9	6.6	17.3	18.8	6.6	6.9
Kansas	12.0	10.2	29.0	35.2	6.9	7.2	Vermont.	8.0	7.2	28.1	34.5	6.1	6.9
Kentucky	14.1	12.9	31.0	35.4	8.2	9.1	Virginia	9.9	8.6	29.9	33.8	7.9	8.3
Louisiana	17.0	13.8	45.6	49.1	10.3	11.3	Washington	10.2	8.3	28.2	31.8	5.6	6.5
Maine	9.4	8.1	31.0	37.1	6.0	6.8	West Virginia	15.9	12.5	31.7	37.9	8.3	9.7
Maryland	9.9	8.8	34.6	39.7	8.6	9.4	Wisconsin.	10.2	8.4	29.3	34.1	6.5	6.9
Massachusetts	6.6	6.2	26.5	32.2	7.1	7.9	Wyoming	13.5	11.2	28.8	33.0	8.3	8.9
Michigan	10.5	9.8	33.3	38.3	7.9	8.3							
Minnesota	8.3	7.0	25.8	31.7	6.1	6.5	Puerto Rico.	(NA)	18.4	49.7	57.6	10.8	13.0
Mississippi	18.8	16.4	46.0	52.8	10.7	12.4	Virgin Islands.	(NA)	13.0	66.7	70.8	9.1	10.5
Missouri.	13.1	11.4	34.6	39.3	7.6	8.1	Guam.	(NA)	(NA)	54.8	(NA)	7.6	(NA)
Montana	11.6	10.3	30.8	36.0	6.2	7.3	American Samoa . .	(NA)	7.7	35.5	34.7	2.7	2.8
Nebraska	10.2	8.0	27.2	32.3	6.8	7.1	Northern Marianas .	(NA)	7.5	(NA)	58.8	8.9	8.5

NA Not available. [1] Defined as mothers who are 19 years of age or younger. [2] Less than 2,500 grams (5 pounds-8 ounces).

Source: U.S. National Center for Health Statistics, *National Vital Statistics Reports (NVSR), Births: Preliminary Data for 2006*, Volume 56, Number 7, December 5, 2007.

Table 88. Infants Who Were Ever Breastfed by Maternal Age and Race-Ethnicity: 1999–2006

[**In percent**. Covers period from 1999 through 2006. Breastfeeding was defined as ever having been breastfed or received breast milk. Based on data from National Health and Nutrition Examination Surveys (NHANES)]

Race and ethnicity	Under 20 years old	20 to 29 years old	30 years old and older
Total	**43**	**65**	**75**
Non-Hispanic White	40	65	77
Non-Hispanic Black	30	44	56
Mexican American	66	75	76

Source: U.S. National Center for Health Statistics, "Breastfeeding in the United States Findings from the National Health and Nutrition Examination Surveys: 1999–2006," NCHS Data Brief, No. 5, April 2008. See <http://www.cdc.gov/nchs/data/databriefs /db05.htm>.

Table 89. Women Who Have Had a Child in the Last Year by Age: 1990 to 2006

[**3,913 represents 3,913,000. As of June**. See headnote, Table 90]

Age of mother	Women who had a child in last year (1,000)			Total births per 1,000 women			First births per 1,000 women		
	1990	2000	2006	1990	2000	2006	1990	2000	2006
Total	**3,913**	**3,934**	**3,974**	**67.0**	**64.6**	**64.4**	**26.4**	**26.7**	**25.1**
15 to 29 years old	2,568	2,432	2,399	90.8	85.9	79.0	43.2	43.1	37.1
15 to 19 years old. . .	338	586	417	39.8	59.7	40.6	30.1	38.7	23.7
20 to 24 years old. . .	1,038	850	935	113.4	91.8	92.8	51.8	47.1	47.9
25 to 29 years old. . .	1,192	996	1,046	112.1	107.9	104.6	46.2	43.7	40.1
30 to 44 years old	1,346	1,502	1,576	44.7	46.1	50.3	10.6	12.5	13.5
30 to 34 years old. . .	892	871	888	80.4	87.9	92.0	21.9	27.5	28.7
35 to 39 years old. . .	377	506	579	37.3	45.1	55.4	6.5	9.6	11.6
40 to 44 years old. . .	77	125	109	8.6	10.9	9.7	1.2	2.3	2.3

Source: U.S. Census Bureau, *Current Population Reports,* P20-543RV and unpublished data.

Table 90. **Women Who Had a Child in the Last Year by Selected Characteristics: 1990 to 2006**

[58,381 represents 58,381,000. **As of June**. Covers civilian noninstitutional population. Since the number of women who had a birth during the 12-month period was tabulated and not the actual numbers of births, some small underestimation of fertility for this period may exist due to the omission of: (1) Multiple births, (2) Two or more live births spaced within the 12-month period (the woman is counted only once), (3) Women who had births in the period and who did not survive to the survey date, (4) Women who were in institutions and therefore not in the survey universe. These losses may be somewhat offset by the inclusion in the CPS of births to immigrants who did not have their children born in the United States and births to nonresident women. These births would not have been recorded in the vital registration system. Based on Current Population Survey (CPS); see Appendix III]

| Characteristic | Total women (1,000) | Percent childless | Women who had a child in the last year | | | |
| | | | Total births | | First births | |
			Number (1,000)	Per 1,000 women	Number (1,000)	Per 1,000 women
1990	58,381	41.6	3,913	67.0	1,540	26.4
2000	60,873	42.8	3,934	64.6	1,626	26.7
2006, total [1]	**61,683**	**45.1**	**3,974**	**64.4**	**1,551**	**25.1**
15 to 19 years old.	10,269	93.3	417	40.6	243	23.7
20 to 24 years old.	10,079	68.6	935	92.8	483	47.9
25 to 29 years old.	10,004	45.6	1,046	104.6	401	40.1
30 to 34 years old.	9,647	26.2	888	92.0	277	28.7
35 to 39 years old.	10,450	18.9	579	55.4	121	11.6
40 to 44 years old.	11,235	20.4	109	9.7	26	2.3
White alone	47,846	45.6	3,155	65.9	1,216	25.4
White alone, non-Hispanic.	38,532	47.5	2,383	61.8	923	24.0
Black alone	8,896	41.4	513	57.7	201	22.6
Asian alone	3,145	47.7	178	56.6	75	23.8
Hispanic [2]	10,099	38.1	830	82.2	309	30.6
Married, husband present.	26,499	18.6	2,469	93.2	886	33.4
Married, husband absent [3]	2,534	24.5	148	58.4	32	12.6
Widowed or divorced.	4,920	21.3	129	26.2	41	8.3
Never married	27,730	76.6	1,228	44.3	592	21.3
Educational attainment:						
Not a high school graduate	13,377	61.4	867	64.8	293	21.9
High school, 4 years	15,420	33.6	989	64.1	392	25.4
Some college, no degree	12,760	48.2	713	55.9	252	19.7
Associate's degree	5,155	33.5	335	65.0	126	24.4
Bachelor's degree	10,771	44.2	746	69.3	332	30.8
Graduate or professional degree	4,199	43.1	324	77.2	156	37.2
Labor force status:						
Employed	39,961	44.5	2,054	51.4	914	22.9
Unemployed.	2,728	54.0	167	61.2	61	22.4
Not in labor force.	18,994	45.2	1,754	92.3	576	30.3
Family income:						
Under $10,000	3,878	39.4	337	86.9	110	28.4
$10,000 to $19,999	4,984	41.4	386	77.4	122	24.5
$20,000 to $24,999	2,903	41.7	223	76.8	81	27.9
$25,000 to $29,999	2,989	44.7	185	61.9	93	31.1
$30,000 to $34,999	3,236	42.8	202	62.4	78	24.1
$35,000 to $49,999	7,571	44.6	484	63.9	216	28.5
$50,000 to $74,999	10,724	45.0	705	65.7	277	25.8
$75,000 and over	15,421	47.9	949	61.5	387	25.1

[1] Includes women of other races and women with family income not reported, not shown separately.   [2] Persons of Hispanic origin may be any race.   [3] Includes separated women.

Source: U.S. Census Bureau, *Current Population Reports*, P20-543RV and unpublished data.

Table 91. **Women Who Have Had a Child in the Last Year by Age and Labor Force Status: 1990 to 2006**

[3,913 represents 3,913,000. See headnote, Table 90. See Appendix III]

| Year | Total, 15 to 44 years old | | | 15 to 29 years old | | | 30 to 44 years old | | |
| | Number (1,000) | In the labor force | | Number (1,000) | In the labor force | | Number (1,000) | In the labor force | |
		Number (1,000)	Percent		Number (1,000)	Percent		Number (1,000)	Percent
1990	3,913	2,068	53	2,568	1,275	50	1,346	793	59
1995	3,696	2,034	55	2,252	1,150	51	1,444	884	61
1998	3,671	2,155	59	2,274	1,275	56	1,397	880	63
2000	3,934	2,170	55	2,432	1,304	54	1,502	866	58
2002	3,766	2,056	55	2,318	1,175	51	1,448	881	61
2004	3,746	2,045	55	2,205	(NA)	(NA)	1,542	(NA)	59
2006	3,974	2,221	56	2,399	1,273	53	1,576	948	60

NA Not available.

Source: U.S. Census Bureau, *Current Population Reports,* P20-555; and earlier reports and unpublished data.

Births, Deaths, Marriages, and Divorces   69

Table 92. Persons Who Have Ever Had Sexual Contact by Selected Characteristics: 2002

[In percent except as indicated (61,147 represents 61,147,000). Based on the National Survey of Family Growth. See Appendix III]

Characteristic	Number (1,000)	Number of opposite-sex partners in lifetime							Any same-sex sexual contact[2]
		Any	One	Two	3 to 6	7 to 14	15 or more	Median number[1]	
Males, 15 to 44 years old[3]	**61,147**	**90.3**	**12.8**	**8.1**	**27.5**	**19.3**	**22.6**	**5.4**	**6.0**
15 to 19 years old	10,208	61.6	23.0	9.2	20.7	6.2	2.5	1.9	4.5
20 to 24 years old	9,883	91.1	15.9	11.7	33.5	14.1	15.9	3.8	5.5
25 to 44 years old	41,056	97.3	9.6	7.0	27.8	23.7	29.2	6.7	6.5
25 to 29 years old	9,226	95.2	10.0	8.8	29.4	23.2	23.8	5.9	5.7
30 to 34 years old	10,138	97.2	10.7	6.9	28.5	21.9	29.2	6.4	(NA)
35 to 39 years old	10,557	98.2	8.9	7.0	28.0	25.5	28.8	6.9	(NA)
40 to 44 years old	11,135	98.2	8.8	5.4	25.6	24.2	34.2	8.2	(NA)
White only, non-Hispanic	38,738	90.3	13.4	8.3	27.1	19.2	22.3	5.3	(NA)
Black only, non-Hispanic	6,940	91.8	5.8	5.9	24.1	22.2	33.8	8.3	(NA)
Hispanic or Latino origin	10,188	91.8	13.7	8.6	32.8	18.6	18.1	4.5	(NA)
Currently married	25,808	100.0	15.4	8.5	30.5	22.3	23.3	5.2	3.4
Currently cohabiting	5,653	100.0	4.7	6.4	34.1	26.6	28.3	6.6	5.3
Never married, not cohabiting	25,412	76.8	13.9	8.7	24.0	13.8	16.4	4.3	8.6
Formerly married, not cohabiting	4,274	100.0	0.7	3.6	22.5	24.6	48.6	11.9	7.1
Females, 15 to 44 years old[3]	**61,561**	**91.4**	**22.5**	**10.8**	**32.6**	**16.3**	**9.2**	**3.3**	**11.2**
15 to 19 years old	9,834	62.2	27.2	9.0	19.1	5.0	1.9	1.4	10.6
20 to 24 years old	9,840	91.1	24.6	13.0	32.2	14.4	6.9	2.8	14.2
25 to 44 years old	41,887	98.4	20.9	10.7	36.0	19.4	11.4	3.8	10.7
25 to 29 years old	9,249	97.5	22.5	11.7	31.3	20.1	11.9	3.5	14.1
30 to 34 years old	10,272	98.0	20.5	9.4	38.8	18.0	11.3	3.8	(NA)
35 to 39 years old	10,853	98.9	20.2	11.2	35.8	20.5	11.2	3.9	(NA)
40 to 44 years old	11,512	98.6	20.4	10.5	37.4	19.1	11.2	3.8	(NA)
White only, non-Hispanic	39,498	92.1	21.0	10.6	32.1	18.2	10.2	3.6	(NA)
Black only, non-Hispanic	8,250	92.4	12.4	8.4	44.8	18.0	8.8	4.1	(NA)
Hispanic or Latino origin	9,107	89.5	34.6	14.9	27.2	8.2	4.6	1.7	(NA)
Currently married	28,327	100.0	30.8	12.2	34.0	15.6	7.4	2.7	7.2
Currently cohabiting	5,570	100.0	13.7	12.2	39.2	20.4	14.5	4.3	17.6
Never married, not cohabiting	21,568	75.4	18.3	9.4	27.7	12.8	7.2	3.1	13.5
Formerly married, not cohabiting	6,096	100.0	6.5	8.1	37.8	28.5	19.1	5.6	16.3

NA Not available. [1] Excludes those who have never had sexual intercourse with a person of the opposite sex. For definition of median, see Guide to Tabular Presentation. [2] Same-sex sexual contact was measured using significantly different questions for males and females. [3] Includes person of other or multiple race and origin groups, not shown separately.

Source: U.S. National Center for Health Statistics, *Advance Data*, No. 362; "Sexual Behavior and Selected Health Measures: Men and Women 15–44 Years of Age, United States, 2002," September 15, 2005, and unpublished data.

Table 93. Males and Females Who Have Had Sexual Contact in Last 12 Months by Number and Sex of Partners: 2002

[In percent except as indicated (61,147 represents 61,147,000). Based on the National Survey of Family Growth. See Appendix III]

Sex and age	Number (1,000)	Percent distribution							
		Total	No partners in last 12 months	One partner		Two or more partners			Number of partners not ascertained
				Same sex[1]	Opposite sex	Same sex only[1]	Opposite sex only	Both same and opposite sex[1]	
Males 15 to 44 years old	**61,147**	**100.0**	**14.8**	**0.7**	**62.2**	**0.9**	**17.6**	**1.0**	**2.6**
15 to 19 years old	10,208	100.0	45.1	0.8	29.7	(S)	21.8	0.9	1.4
20 to 24 years old	9,883	100.0	14.2	0.4	48.8	0.9	30.9	1.5	3.2
25 to 44 years old	41,056	100.0	7.4	0.7	73.6	1.1	13.4	1.0	2.8
25 to 29 years old	9,226	100.0	10.0	0.5	66.6	0.9	18.4	1.1	2.5
30 to 34 years old	10,138	100.0	5.6	0.9	74.3	1.0	14.5	1.3	2.4
35 to 39 years old	10,557	100.0	7.1	0.9	76.5	1.2	11.4	0.5	2.5
40 to 44 years old	11,135	100.0	7.0	0.7	75.9	1.3	10.1	1.0	3.8
Females 15 to 44 years old	**61,561**	**100.0**	**13.9**	**1.1**	**66.8**	**0.2**	**12.7**	**3.1**	**2.2**
15 to 19 years old	9,834	100.0	42.9	1.7	30.5	(S)	16.8	5.8	2.1
20 to 24 years old	9,840	100.0	12.5	0.4	58.9	(S)	21.1	4.8	1.9
25 to 44 years old	41,887	100.0	7.4	1.1	77.2	0.2	9.8	2.0	2.2
25 to 29 years old	9,249	100.0	6.1	0.5	74.1	0.4	14.1	2.8	2.0
30 to 34 years old	10,272	100.0	7.1	0.5	78.5	(S)	9.7	2.1	1.9
35 to 39 years old	10,853	100.0	7.3	1.8	76.8	(S)	9.4	2.5	2.0
40 to 44 years old	11,512	100.0	9.0	1.4	78.8	(S)	6.7	0.9	3.0

S Does not meet standards for reliability or precision. [1] Same-sex sexual contact was measured using significantly different questions for males and females.

Source: U.S. National Center for Health Statistics, *Advance Data*, No. 362; Sexual *Advance Data*, No. 362; "Sexual Behavior and Selected Health Measures: Men and Women 15–44 Years of Age, United States, 2002," September 15, 2005, and unpublished data.

Table 94. Select Family Planning and Medical Service Use by Women, 15 to 44 Years of Age: 2002

[61,561 represents 61,561,000. Based on the National Survey of Family Growth, see Appendix III]

Characteristic	Number (1,000)	Percent using—							
		Family planning services			Medical services				
		At least one family planning service	Birth control method	Birth control checkup or test	At least one medical service	Preg-nancy test	Pap smear	Pelvic exam	Counseling/ test/ treatment for STD [1]
All women [2]	**61,561**	**41.7**	**33.9**	**23.6**	**69.1**	**19.7**	**64.4**	**59.7**	**12.6**
15 to 19 years old	9,834	39.9	31.1	22.0	40.6	18.3	34.6	27.0	15.2
15 to 17 years old	5,819	31.8	22.2	15.8	28.0	11.4	23.2	17.9	11.1
18 to 19 years old	4,016	51.6	43.9	31.0	58.9	28.2	51.2	40.2	21.1
20 to 24 years old	9,840	63.3	54.0	35.7	75.7	31.5	69.7	60.6	22.3
25 to 29 years old	9,249	55.4	46.3	30.2	75.9	30.2	70.7	66.0	16.6
30 to 34 years old	10,272	47.0	39.1	27.2	78.1	22.2	72.7	69.7	12.2
35 to 39 years old	10,853	30.5	23.9	18.6	71.5	13.6	68.3	65.9	6.9
40 to 44 years old	11,512	19.5	14.0	10.8	71.8	5.9	69.4	67.0	4.4
Currently married.	28,327	39.5	31.5	21.3	77.2	21.1	73.1	69.8	8.1
Currently cohabiting	5,570	50.4	43.2	30.2	77.2	31.0	72.2	64.7	20.3
Never married, not cohabiting	21,568	44.4	36.4	25.4	55.8	16.5	50.7	43.9	15.9
Formerly married, not cohabiting. . .	6,096	34.5	28.0	22.0	71.0	14.1	66.0	64.0	14.4
White only, Non-Hispanic	39,498	43.1	36.4	25.4	70.1	17.3	66.1	63.2	11.8
Black only, Non-Hispanic.	8,250	39.4	30.6	21.8	74.4	23.7	69.1	58.1	15.7
Hispanic [3]	9,107	39.7	28.9	20.6	63.4	24.3	57.1	48.5	12.5

[1] STD stands for sexually transmitted disease. [2] Includes other races not shown separately. [3] Persons of Hispanic origin may be any race.

Source: U.S. National Center for Health Statistics, *Advance Data*, Number 350, "Use of Contraception and Use of Family Planning Services in the United States: 1982–2002," December 10, 2004.

Table 95. Current Contraceptive Use by Women, by Race and Marital Status: 2002

[In percent, except total (61,561 represents 61,561,000). Based on the National Survey of Family Growth; see Appendix III]

Contraceptive status and method	All women, [1,2]	Race/ethnicity			Marital status		
		White only, Non-Hispanic	Black only, Non-Hispanic	Hispanic [3]	Never married, not cohabiting	Currently married	Formerly married, not cohabiting
All women (1,000).	**61,561**	**39,498**	**8,250**	**9,107**	**21,568**	**28,327**	**6,096**
PERCENT DISTRIBUTION							
Using contraception (contraceptors) [4]	61.9	64.6	57.6	59.0	44.0	72.9	64.4
Female sterilization	16.7	15.4	22.6	19.9	4.4	21.7	35.3
Male sterilization	5.7	7.6	1.3	2.6	0.4	11.2	2.2
Pill	18.9	22.2	13.1	13.0	21.8	17.2	12.3
Implant, Lunelle™	0.8	0.5	0.6	1.8	0.4	1.0	0.5
3-month injectable (Depo-Provera™). . .	3.3	2.7	5.4	4.3	4.2	2.2	1.7
Intrauterine device (IUD).	1.3	1.0	0.8	3.2	0.2	1.9	1.9
Diaphragm.	0.2	0.2	0.1	–	0.2	0.2	–
Condom	11.1	10.7	11.4	10.9	10.3	12.0	8.0
Periodic abstinence—calendar rhythm. .	0.7	0.8	0.3	0.6	0.2	1.3	0.3
Periodic abstinence—natural family planning.	0.2	0.3	0.1	0.3	0.0	0.4	–
Withdrawal.	2.5	2.6	1.5	2.2	1.6	3.0	1.3
Other methods [5]	0.6	0.7	0.5	0.3	0.2	0.7	0.9
Not using contraception	38.1	35.4	42.4	41.0	56.0	27.1	35.6
Surgically sterile-female (noncontraceptive)	1.5	1.6	1.6	0.9	0.4	2.1	3.0
Nonsurgically sterile-female or male [6] . .	1.6	1.7	1.4	1.7	1.0	2.0	2.5
Pregnant or postpartum	5.3	4.7	5.7	6.9	2.3	7.5	2.2
Seeking pregnancy	4.2	4.0	4.3	5.2	0.8	6.9	2.0
Other nonuse	25.5	23.6	29.5	26.4	51.4	8.6	26.0
Never had intercourse or no intercourse in 3 months before interview.	18.1	17.0	19.0	18.7	42.9	2.3	17.7
Had intercourse in 3 months before interview	7.4	6.5	10.4	7.7	8.5	6.3	8.2
All other nonusers	–	0.1	0.1	–	–	–	0.1

– Represents or rounds to zero. [1] Includes other races not shown separately. [2] Includes women who are currently cohabiting not shown separately. [3] Persons of Hispanic origin may be any race. [4] Percents may not add to the total who were using contraception because more than one method could have been used in the month of interview. [5] Includes implants, injectables, morning-after pill, suppository, Today™ sponge, and less frequently used methods. [6] Persons sterile from illness, accident, or congenital conditions.

Source: U.S. National Center for Health Statistics, *Advance Data*, Number 350, "Use of Contraception and Use of Family Planning Services in the United States: 1982–2002," December 10, 2004.

U.S. Census Bureau, Statistical Abstract of the United States: 2009

Table 96. **Outcomes of Assisted Reproductive Technology (ART) Procedures: 2000 to 2005**

[In 1996, Centers for Disease Control (CDC) initiated data collection regarding (ART) procedures performed in the United States, as mandated by the Fertility Clinic Success Rate and Certification Act. ARTs include those infertility treatments in which both eggs and sperm are handled in the laboratory for the purpose of establishing a pregnancy (i.e. in vitro fertilization and related procedures)]

Year	Procedures started	Number of pregnancies	Live birth deliveries [1]	Live born infants
2000	99,629	30,557	25,228	35,025
2001	107,587	35,726	29,344	40,687
2002	115,392	40,046	33,741	45,751
2003	122,872	43,503	35,785	48,756
2004	127,977	44,774	36,760	49,458
2005	134,260	47,651	38,910	52,041

[1] A live-birth delivery is defined as the delivery of one or more live-born infants.

Source: U.S. Centers for Disease Control and Prevention, Atlanta, GA, MMWR Surveillance Summary Reports, Assisted Reproductive Technology Surveillance; annual <http://www.cdc.gov/mmwr/preview/mmwrhtml/ss5606a1.htm?s_cid=ss5606a1_e>.

Table 97. **Abortions—Number and Rate by Race: 1990 to 2004**

[58,700 represents 58,700,000]

Year	All races — Women 15 to 44 years old (1,000)	All races — Abortions Number (1,000)	All races — Abortions Rate per 1,000 women	White — Women 15 to 44 years old (1,000)	White — Abortions Number (1,000)	White — Abortions Rate per 1,000 women	Black — Women 15 to 44 years old (1,000)	Black — Abortions Number (1,000)	Black — Abortions Rate per 1,000 women	Other — Women 15 to 44 years old (1,000)	Other — Abortions Number (1,000)	Other — Abortions Rate per 1,000 women
1990 [1]	58,700	1,609	27.4	48,224	1,039	21.5	7,905	505	63.9	2,571	65	25.1
1991	59,305	1,557	26.2	48,560	982	20.2	8,053	507	62.9	2,692	68	26.2
1992	59,417	1,529	25.7	48,435	943	19.5	8,170	517	63.3	2,812	69	24.4
1993 [1]	59,712	1,495	25.0	48,497	908	18.7	8,282	517	62.4	2,933	70	23.9
1994 [1]	60,020	1,423	23.7	48,592	856	17.6	8,390	492	58.6	3,039	76	23.7
1995	60,368	1,359	22.5	48,719	817	16.8	8,496	462	54.4	3,153	80	25.3
1996	60,704	1,360	22.4	48,837	797	16.3	8,592	483	56.2	3,275	81	24.6
1997 [1]	61,041	1,335	21.9	48,942	777	15.9	8,694	479	55.1	3,405	79	23.1
1998 [1]	61,326	1,319	21.5	49,012	762	15.5	8,785	476	54.2	3,528	81	23.1
1999	61,475	1,315	21.4	48,974	743	15.2	8,851	485	54.8	3,650	87	24.0
2000	61,631	1,313	21.3	48,936	733	15.0	8,907	488	54.8	3,788	92	24.4
2001	61,673	1,291	20.9	48,868	717	14.7	8,962	476	53.1	3,843	99	25.7
2002 [1]	62,044	1,269	20.5	48,998	706	14.4	9,026	468	51.8	4,020	96	23.8
2003 [1]	61,911	1,250	20.2	48,782	695	14.2	9,054	458	50.6	4,075	97	23.8
2004 [1]	62,033	1,222	19.7	48,758	674	13.8	9,116	453	49.7	4,160	95	22.9

[1] Total numbers of abortions in 1990, 1993, 1994, 1997, and 1998 have been estimated by interpolation. Data for 2001 through 2004 have been estimated using trends in Centers for Disease Control data.

Source: R.K. Jones, M.R.S. Zolna, S.K. Henshaw, and L.B. Finer, "Abortion in the United States: *Incidence and Access to Services, 2005," Perspectives on Sexual and Reproductive Health*, 2008, 40(1):6–16, and unpublished data from Guttmacher Institute (copyright).

Table 98. Abortions by Selected Characteristics: 1990 to 2004

[1,609 represents 1,609,000. Number of abortions from surveys conducted by source; characteristics from the U.S. Centers for Disease Control's (CDC) annual abortion surveillance summaries, with adjustments for changes in states reporting data to the CDC each year]

Characteristic	Number (1,000)			Percent distribution			Abortion rate per 1,000 women [1]		
	1990	2000	2004	1990	2000	2004	1990	2000	2004
Total abortions	**1,609**	**1,313**	**1,222**	**100**	**100**	**100**	**27.4**	**21.3**	**19.7**
Age of woman:									
Less than 15 years old [1]	13	9	7	0.8	0.7	0.6	7.9	4.4	3.3
15 to 19 years old	351	235	200	21.8	17.9	16.3	40.6	24.0	19.8
20 to 24 years old	532	430	406	33.1	32.7	33.2	56.7	45.9	39.9
25 to 29 years old	360	303	285	22.4	23.0	23.3	34.0	31.8	29.7
30 to 34 years old	216	190	184	13.4	14.5	15.1	19.7	18.6	18.2
35 to 39 years old	108	110	103	6.7	8.4	8.4	10.7	9.7	9.8
40 years old and over [2]	29	37	38	1.8	2.8	3.1	3.2	3.2	3.3
Race and ethnicity of woman:									
White	1,039	733	674	64.6	55.8	55.1	21.5	15.0	13.8
Black	505	488	453	31.4	37.2	37.1	63.9	54.8	49.7
Other	65	92	95	4.0	7.0	7.8	25.1	24.4	22.9
Hispanic	195	261	269	12.1	19.8	22.0	35.1	30.3	27.8
Non-Hispanic White	852	479	418	52.9	36.5	34.2	19.7	11.7	10.5
Marital status of woman: [3]									
Married	341	246	212	21	19	17.3	10.6	7.9	7.0
Unmarried	1,268	1,067	1,011	79	81	82.7	47.7	34.9	31.7
Number of prior live births:									
None	780	533	494	49	41	40	32.0	20.2	17.8
One	396	361	336	25	28	28	36.9	32.5	31.5
Two	280	260	237	17	20	19	20.5	18.9	17.5
Three	102	104	100	6	8	8	15.6	14.8	14.9
Four or more	50	56	54	3	4	4	14.7	16.5	16.1
Number of prior induced abortions:									
None	891	699	652	55	53	53	(NA)	(NA)	(NA)
One	443	355	327	28	27	27	(NA)	(NA)	(NA)
Two or more	275	259	243	17	20	20	(NA)	(NA)	(NA)
Weeks of gestation:									
Less than 9 weeks	825	749	750	51.3	57.1	61.3	(NA)	(NA)	(NA)
9 to 10 weeks	416	269	217	25.8	20.5	17.8	(NA)	(NA)	(NA)
11 to 12 weeks	195	138	117	12.1	10.5	9.6	(NA)	(NA)	(NA)
13 weeks or more	173	156	138	10.8	11.9	11.3	(NA)	(NA)	(NA)

NA Not available. [1] Denominator of rate is women aged 14. [2] Denominator of rate is women aged 40–44. [3] Separated women are included with married.

Source: R.K. Jones, M.R.S. Zolna, S.K. Henshaw, and L.B. Finer, "Abortion in the United States: Incidence and Access to Services, 2005," *Perspectives on Sexual and Reproductive Health*, 2008, 40(1):6–16; and unpublished data from Guttmacher Institute (copyright).

Table 99. Abortions—Number and Rate by State: 2000 to 2005

[Number of abortions by state of occurrence from surveys of hospitals, clinics, and physicians identified as providers of abortion services conducted by the Guttmacher Institute. Abortion rates are computed per 1,000 women 15 to 44 years of age on July 1 of specified year]

State	Number			Rate [1]			State	Number			Rate [1]		
	2000	2004	2005	2000	2004	2005		2000	2004	2005	2000	2004	2005
U.S.	**1,312,990**	**1,222,100**	**1,206,200**	**21.3**	**19.7**	**19.4**	MO	7,920	8,740	8,400	6.6	7.2	6.9
AL	13,830	11,400	11,340	14.2	12.0	11.9	MT	2,510	2,370	2,150	13.5	12.9	11.7
AK	1,660	1,920	1,880	11.7	13.8	13.6	NE	4,250	3,710	3,220	11.6	10.2	8.9
AZ	17,940	17,930	19,480	16.5	15.2	16.0	NV	13,740	13,210	13,530	32.4	27.2	27.0
AR	5,540	4,620	4,710	9.8	8.2	8.3	NH	3,010	3,160	3,170	11.2	11.6	11.7
CA	236,060	208,180	208,430	31.2	26.9	27.1	NJ	65,780	58,050	61,150	36.3	32.3	34.3
CO	15,530	15,550	16,120	16.0	15.6	16.1	NM	5,760	6,260	6,220	14.7	15.8	15.7
CT	15,240	16,810	16,780	21.1	23.5	23.6	NY	164,630	160,140	155,960	39.1	38.9	38.2
DE	5,440	4,990	5,150	31.3	28.0	28.8	NC	37,610	36,220	34,500	21.1	20.0	18.8
DC	9,800	7,130	7,230	68.2	52.3	54.2	ND	1,340	1,360	1,230	9.9	10.5	9.6
FL	103,050	96,680	92,300	32.0	28.4	26.8	OH	40,230	35,050	35,060	16.5	14.8	14.9
GA	32,140	34,100	33,180	16.9	17.2	16.3	OK	7,390	7,140	6,950	10.1	9.8	9.5
HI	5,630	5,190	5,350	22.2	21.0	21.8	OR	17,010	13,320	13,200	23.6	18.0	17.7
ID	1,950	2,000	1,810	7.0	6.9	6.1	PA	36,570	35,760	34,150	14.3	14.3	13.8
IL	63,690	52,870	50,970	23.2	19.5	18.9	RI	5,600	5,730	5,290	24.1	24.7	23.2
IN	12,490	11,010	11,150	9.4	8.5	8.6	SC	8,210	6,650	7,080	9.3	7.5	7.9
IA	5,970	6,160	6,370	9.8	10.2	10.6	SD	870	820	790	5.5	5.2	5.1
KS	12,270	11,330	10,410	21.4	19.9	18.4	TN	19,010	18,490	18,140	15.2	14.7	14.4
KY	4,700	3,670	3,870	5.3	4.2	4.4	TX	89,160	85,210	85,760	18.8	17.3	17.3
LA	13,100	12,760	11,400	13.0	13.0	11.7	UT	3,510	3,610	3,630	6.7	6.6	6.4
ME	2,650	2,910	2,770	9.9	10.9	10.5	VT	1,660	1,720	1,490	12.7	13.6	11.7
MD	34,560	38,020	37,590	29.0	31.7	31.5	VA	28,780	26,340	26,520	18.1	16.5	16.5
MA	30,410	26,330	27,270	21.4	18.9	19.9	WA	26,200	24,060	23,260	20.3	18.2	17.5
MI	46,470	43,590	40,600	21.6	20.6	19.4	WV	2,540	2,420	2,360	6.8	6.8	6.7
MN	14,610	13,980	13,910	13.5	12.8	12.7	WI	11,130	9,870	9,800	9.6	8.5	8.5
MS	3,780	3,500	3,090	6.0	5.6	4.9	WY	100	80	70	1.0	0.8	0.7

[1] Rate per 1,000 women, 15 to 44 years old.

Source: R.K. Jones et al., "Abortion in the United States: Incidence and Access to Services, 2005," Perspectives on Sexual and Reproductive Health, 2008, 40(1):6–16; and unpublished data from Guttmacher Institute (copyright).

Births, Deaths, Marriages, and Divorces   73

Table 100. Expectation of Life at Birth, 1970 to 2005, and Projections, 2010 to 2020

[**In years.** Excludes deaths of nonresidents of the United States. See Appendix III]

Year	Total			White			Black		
	Total	Male	Female	Total	Male	Female	Total	Male	Female
1970............	70.8	67.1	74.7	71.7	68.0	75.6	64.1	60.0	68.3
1975............	72.6	68.8	76.6	73.4	69.5	77.3	66.8	62.4	71.3
1980............	73.7	70.0	77.4	74.4	70.7	78.1	68.1	63.8	72.5
1981............	74.1	70.4	77.8	74.8	71.1	78.4	68.9	64.5	73.2
1982............	74.5	70.8	78.1	75.1	71.5	78.7	69.4	65.1	73.6
1983............	74.6	71.0	78.1	75.2	71.6	78.7	69.4	65.2	73.5
1984............	74.7	71.1	78.2	75.3	71.8	78.7	69.5	65.3	73.6
1985............	74.7	71.1	78.2	75.3	71.8	78.7	69.3	65.0	73.4
1986............	74.7	71.2	78.2	75.4	71.9	78.8	69.1	64.8	73.4
1987............	74.9	71.4	78.3	75.6	72.1	78.9	69.1	64.7	73.4
1988............	74.9	71.4	78.3	75.6	72.2	78.9	68.9	64.4	73.2
1989............	75.1	71.7	78.5	75.9	72.5	79.2	68.8	64.3	73.3
1990............	75.4	71.8	78.8	76.1	72.7	79.4	69.1	64.5	73.6
1991............	75.5	72.0	78.9	76.3	72.9	79.6	69.3	64.6	73.8
1992............	75.8	72.3	79.1	76.5	73.2	79.8	69.6	65.0	73.9
1993............	75.5	72.2	78.8	76.3	73.1	79.5	69.2	64.6	73.7
1994............	75.7	72.4	79.0	76.5	73.3	79.6	69.5	64.9	73.9
1995............	75.8	72.5	78.9	76.5	73.4	79.6	69.6	65.2	73.9
1996............	76.1	73.1	79.1	76.8	73.9	79.7	70.2	66.1	74.2
1997............	76.5	73.6	79.4	77.2	74.3	79.9	71.1	67.2	74.7
1998............	76.7	73.8	79.5	77.3	74.5	80.0	71.3	67.6	74.8
1999............	76.7	73.9	79.4	77.3	74.6	79.9	71.4	67.8	74.7
2000............	77.0	74.3	79.7	77.6	74.9	80.1	71.9	68.3	75.2
2001............	77.2	74.4	79.8	77.7	75.0	80.2	72.2	68.6	75.5
2002............	77.3	74.5	79.9	77.7	75.1	80.3	72.3	68.8	75.6
2003............	77.4	74.7	80.0	77.9	75.3	80.4	72.6	68.9	75.9
2004............	77.8	75.2	80.4	78.3	75.7	80.8	73.1	69.5	76.3
2005............	77.8	75.2	80.4	78.3	75.7	80.8	73.2	69.5	76.5
Projections [1]:									
2010..........	78.3	75.7	80.8	78.9	76.5	81.3	73.8	70.2	77.2
2015..........	78.9	76.4	81.4	79.5	77.1	81.8	75.0	71.4	78.2
2020..........	79.5	77.1	81.9	80.0	77.7	82.4	76.1	72.6	79.2

[1] Based on middle mortality assumptions; for details, see source. Source: U.S. Census Bureau, 2008 National Population Projections, released August 2008; <http://www.census.gov/population/www/projections/2008projections.html>.

Source: Except as noted, U.S. National Center for Health Statistics, National Vital Statistics Reports (NVSR), *Deaths: Final Data for 2005*, Vol. 56, No. 10, April 24, 2008.

Table 101. Average Number of Years of Life Remaining by Sex and Age: 1989 to 2005

[Excludes deaths of nonresidents of the United States. See Appendix III]

Age (years)	Total			Male			Female		
	1989–1991	1999–2001	2005	1989–1991	1999–2001	2005	1989–1991	1999–2001	2005
0.................	75.4	76.8	77.8	71.8	74.1	75.2	78.8	79.5	80.4
1.................	75.1	76.4	77.4	71.6	73.7	74.7	78.5	79.0	79.9
5.................	71.2	72.5	73.5	67.7	69.8	70.8	74.6	75.0	76.0
10................	66.3	67.5	68.5	62.8	64.8	65.9	69.7	70.1	71.0
15................	61.4	62.6	63.6	57.9	59.9	61.0	64.7	65.2	66.1
20................	56.6	57.8	58.8	53.3	55.2	56.2	59.9	60.3	61.2
25................	51.9	53.1	54.1	48.7	50.5	51.6	55.0	55.4	56.4
30................	47.2	48.3	49.3	44.1	45.9	47.0	50.2	50.6	51.5
35................	42.6	43.5	44.6	39.6	41.2	42.3	45.4	45.7	46.7
40................	38.0	38.9	39.9	35.1	36.6	37.7	40.7	41.0	41.9
45................	33.4	34.3	35.3	30.7	32.1	33.2	36.0	36.3	37.3
50................	29.0	29.9	30.9	26.4	27.8	28.9	31.4	31.7	32.7
55................	24.8	25.6	26.7	22.3	23.6	24.8	27.1	27.3	28.3
60................	20.9	21.5	22.6	18.5	19.7	20.8	22.9	23.1	24.0
65................	17.3	17.8	18.7	15.1	16.1	17.2	19.0	19.1	20.0
70................	14.0	14.3	15.2	12.1	12.8	13.8	15.4	15.4	16.3
75................	11.0	11.1	12.0	9.4	9.9	10.8	12.1	12.0	12.8
80................	8.4	8.4	9.2	7.1	7.4	8.2	9.1	9.1	9.7
85................	6.2	6.2	6.8	5.3	5.5	6.1	6.7	6.6	7.2
90................	4.5	4.5	5.0	3.9	4.0	4.4	4.7	4.7	5.2
95................	3.3	3.2	3.6	2.9	2.8	3.2	3.4	3.3	3.7
100...............	2.5	2.3	2.6	2.3	2.0	2.3	2.5	2.3	2.6

Source: U.S. National Center for Health Statistics, National Vital Statistics Reports (NVSR), *U.S. Decennial Life Tables for 1999–2001, United States Life Tables, Vol. 57, No. 1, August 5, 2008*, and, unpublished data.

Table 102. Selected Life Table Values: 1979 to 2005

[See Appendix III]

Age and sex	Total[1]								White								Black							
	1979–1981	1990	1995	2000	2002	2003	2004	2005	1979–1981	1990	1995	2000	2002	2003	2004	2005	1979–1981	1990	1995	2000	2002	2003	2004	2005
AVERAGE EXPECTATION OF LIFE IN YEARS																								
At birth: Male	70.1	71.8	72.5	74.3	74.5	74.7	75.2	75.2	70.8	72.7	73.4	74.9	75.1	75.3	75.7	75.7	64.1	64.5	65.2	68.3	68.8	68.9	69.5	69.5
Female	77.6	78.8	78.9	79.7	79.9	80.0	80.4	80.4	78.2	79.4	79.6	80.1	80.3	80.4	80.8	80.8	72.9	73.6	73.9	75.2	75.6	75.9	76.3	76.5
Age 20: Male	51.9	53.3	53.8	55.5	55.6	55.8	56.2	56.2	52.5	54.0	54.5	55.8	56.1	56.2	56.6	56.6	46.4	46.7	47.3	50.0	50.5	50.6	51.2	51.2
Female	59.0	59.8	59.9	60.5	60.7	60.8	61.2	61.2	59.4	60.3	60.3	60.9	61.0	61.1	61.5	61.5	54.9	55.3	55.5	56.6	57.0	57.2	57.7	57.8
Age 40: Male	33.6	35.1	35.6	36.7	37.0	37.2	37.6	37.7	34.0	35.6	36.1	37.1	37.4	37.6	37.9	38.0	29.5	30.1	30.6	32.3	32.8	32.9	33.4	33.4
Female	39.8	40.6	40.7	41.2	41.4	41.5	41.9	41.9	40.2	41.0	41.0	41.5	41.6	41.8	42.1	42.2	36.3	36.8	37.0	37.8	38.1	38.4	38.8	38.9
Age 50: Male	25.0	26.4	27.0	27.9	28.3	28.5	28.8	28.9	25.3	26.7	27.3	28.2	28.5	28.7	29.1	29.1	22.0	22.5	23.1	24.2	24.6	24.7	25.1	25.2
Female	30.7	31.3	31.4	32.0	32.2	32.3	32.7	32.7	31.0	31.6	31.7	32.2	32.4	32.5	32.9	32.9	27.8	28.2	28.5	29.1	29.5	29.8	30.1	30.2
Age 65: Male	14.2	15.1	15.6	16.2	16.6	16.8	17.1	17.2	14.3	15.2	15.7	16.3	16.6	16.8	17.2	17.2	13.3	13.2	13.7	14.2	14.6	14.8	15.2	15.2
Female	18.4	18.9	18.9	19.3	19.5	19.7	20.0	20.0	18.6	19.1	19.0	19.4	19.5	19.7	20.0	20.0	17.1	17.2	17.2	17.7	18.0	18.3	18.6	18.7
EXPECTED DEATHS PER 1,000 ALIVE AT SPECIFIED AGE[2]																								
At birth: Male	13.9	10.3	8.3	7.5	7.6	7.6	7.5	7.6	12.3	8.6	7.0	6.2	6.4	6.4	6.2	6.3	23.0	19.7	16.2	15.6	15.4	15.6	15.3	15.2
Female	11.2	8.2	6.8	6.2	6.3	6.1	6.1	6.2	9.7	6.6	5.6	5.1	5.1	5.1	5.1	5.1	19.3	16.3	13.8	12.7	13.2	12.4	12.4	12.3
Age 20: Male	1.8	1.6	(NA)	1.3	1.4	1.3	1.3	1.3	1.8	1.4	(NA)	1.2	1.3	1.2	1.2	1.2	2.2	2.7	(NA)	2.0	2.1	1.9	1.8	1.9
Female	0.6	0.5	(NA)	0.5	0.5	0.5	0.5	0.5	0.6	0.5	(NA)	0.4	0.4	0.5	0.4	0.4	0.7	0.7	(NA)	0.6	0.6	0.6	0.6	0.5
Age 40: Male	3.0	3.1	(NA)	2.6	2.7	2.6	2.4	2.4	2.6	2.7	(NA)	2.4	2.5	2.4	2.3	2.3	6.9	7.1	(NA)	4.6	4.3	4.3	3.9	3.9
Female	1.6	1.4	(NA)	1.5	1.5	1.5	1.5	1.4	1.4	1.2	(NA)	1.3	1.4	1.4	1.3	1.3	3.2	3.1	(NA)	2.8	2.6	2.7	2.6	2.5
Age 50: Male	7.8	6.2	(NA)	5.7	5.7	5.7	5.6	5.7	7.1	5.6	(NA)	5.2	5.2	5.2	5.2	5.3	14.9	12.8	(NA)	11.2	10.4	10.5	10.1	10.0
Female	4.2	3.5	(NA)	3.3	3.2	3.3	3.2	3.3	3.8	3.2	(NA)	2.9	2.8	2.9	2.9	3.0	7.7	6.6	(NA)	6.2	6.2	6.1	5.9	6.0
Age 65: Male	28.2	22.9	(NA)	20.0	18.9	18.5	17.8	17.6	27.4	23.0	(NA)	19.2	18.2	17.8	17.1	16.9	38.5	36.8	(NA)	29.6	29.3	29.1	28.4	28.0
Female	14.3	13.5	(NA)	12.7	12.1	11.9	11.5	11.4	13.6	12.8	(NA)	12.2	11.7	11.4	11.0	10.9	21.6	21.4	(NA)	18.2	17.8	17.7	16.9	16.8
NUMBER SURVIVING TO SPECIFIED AGE PER 1,000																								
Age 20: Male	973	979	981	984	984	985	985	985	975	981	981	986	986	986	987	986	961	963	967	973	974	974	974	974
Female	982	986	987	989	989	989	989	990	984	988	987	990	991	991	991	991	972	976	978	981	981	982	982	982
Age 40: Male	933	938	940	953	954	954	955	955	940	946	940	958	958	958	959	959	885	880	885	918	920	923	925	924
Female	965	971	975	975	975	975	976	976	969	975	971	978	978	978	978	978	941	944	944	955	957	958	958	959
Age 50: Male	890	899	899	917	918	918	921	920	901	912	899	925	925	925	927	926	801	801	803	855	862	864	869	869
Female	941	950	950	954	954	954	954	954	947	957	950	960	959	959	959	959	896	904	902	915	918	919	921	923
Age 65: Male	706	741	750	779	786	787	792	791	724	760	750	794	799	800	805	803	551	571	581	640	657	659	668	667
Female	835	851	855	863	867	867	870	871	848	864	855	874	876	877	879	879	733	751	758	780	785	786	792	794

NA Not available.   [1] Includes other races not shown separately.   [2] See footnote 1, Table 103.

Source: U.S. National Center for Health Statistics, National Vital Statistics Reports (NVSR), U.S. Life Tables, 2004, Vol. 56, No. 8, December, 28, 2007; Deaths: Final Data for 2005, Vol. 56, No. 10, April 24, 2008; and unpublished data.

Births, Deaths, Marriages, and Divorces   75

Table 103. Expectation of Life and Expected Deaths by Race, Sex, and Age: 2005

[See Appendix III]

Age (years)	Expectation of life in years					Expected deaths per 1,000 alive at specified age [2]				
	Total [1]	White		Black		Total [1]	White		Black	
		Male	Female	Male	Female		Male	Female	Male	Female
At birth	77.8	75.7	80.8	69.5	76.5	6.88	6.33	5.11	15.20	12.32
1	77.4	75.2	80.2	69.6	76.4	0.46	0.48	0.37	0.72	0.60
2	76.4	74.2	79.2	68.7	75.5	0.31	0.34	0.24	0.45	0.32
3	75.4	73.3	78.3	67.7	74.5	0.22	0.22	0.17	0.45	0.26
4	74.5	72.3	77.3	66.7	73.5	0.18	0.20	0.14	0.25	0.30
5	73.5	71.3	76.3	65.7	72.5	0.17	0.17	0.14	0.27	0.23
6	72.5	70.3	75.3	64.8	71.6	0.16	0.16	0.13	0.25	0.21
7	71.5	69.3	74.3	63.8	70.6	0.15	0.15	0.13	0.23	0.19
8	70.5	68.3	73.3	62.8	69.6	0.13	0.13	0.12	0.21	0.18
9	69.5	67.3	72.3	61.8	68.6	0.11	0.10	0.10	0.17	0.17
10	68.5	66.3	71.3	60.8	67.6	0.10	0.08	0.09	0.15	0.16
11	67.5	65.3	70.3	59.8	66.6	0.11	0.09	0.09	0.17	0.17
12	66.5	64.3	69.4	58.8	65.6	0.14	0.14	0.11	0.24	0.18
13	65.6	63.4	68.4	57.9	64.6	0.22	0.26	0.16	0.39	0.21
14	64.6	62.4	67.4	56.9	63.7	0.33	0.41	0.21	0.60	0.25
15	63.6	61.4	66.4	55.9	62.7	0.45	0.58	0.28	0.83	0.29
16	62.6	60.4	65.4	55.0	61.7	0.56	0.73	0.34	1.06	0.34
17	61.7	59.5	64.4	54.0	60.7	0.67	0.88	0.39	1.29	0.39
18	60.7	58.5	63.4	53.1	59.7	0.75	1.01	0.42	1.50	0.44
19	59.7	57.6	62.5	52.2	58.8	0.82	1.12	0.43	1.70	0.49
20	58.8	56.6	61.5	51.2	57.8	0.89	1.23	0.44	1.92	0.54
21	57.8	55.7	60.5	50.3	56.8	0.96	1.33	0.45	2.12	0.60
22	56.9	54.8	59.6	49.4	55.9	1.00	1.39	0.46	2.28	0.65
23	56.0	53.9	58.6	48.6	54.9	1.02	1.39	0.47	2.35	0.70
24	55.0	52.9	57.6	47.7	53.9	1.00	1.36	0.47	2.37	0.74
25	54.1	52.0	56.6	46.8	53.0	0.98	1.31	0.47	2.36	0.78
26	53.1	51.1	55.7	45.9	52.0	0.97	1.27	0.47	2.35	0.83
27	52.2	50.1	54.7	45.0	51.1	0.96	1.25	0.49	2.36	0.88
28	51.2	49.2	53.7	44.1	50.1	0.97	1.24	0.51	2.41	0.95
29	50.3	48.3	52.7	43.2	49.1	0.99	1.25	0.54	2.48	1.03
30	49.3	47.3	51.8	42.3	48.2	1.03	1.28	0.57	2.56	1.12
31	48.4	46.4	50.8	41.4	47.3	1.07	1.31	0.62	2.64	1.22
32	47.4	45.4	49.8	40.5	46.3	1.11	1.34	0.66	2.71	1.31
33	46.5	44.5	48.9	39.6	45.4	1.15	1.39	0.71	2.78	1.40
34	45.5	43.6	47.9	38.8	44.4	1.21	1.44	0.76	2.84	1.50
35	44.6	42.6	46.9	37.9	43.5	1.27	1.50	0.82	2.92	1.60
36	43.6	41.7	46.0	37.0	42.6	1.35	1.59	0.88	3.03	1.72
37	42.7	40.8	45.0	36.1	41.6	1.46	1.71	0.97	3.19	1.87
38	41.8	39.8	44.1	35.2	40.7	1.60	1.88	1.07	3.39	2.07
39	40.8	38.9	43.1	34.3	39.8	1.77	2.09	1.19	3.63	2.29
40	39.9	38.0	42.2	33.4	38.9	1.94	2.30	1.31	3.88	2.52
41	39.0	37.1	41.2	32.6	38.0	2.12	2.52	1.44	4.16	2.76
42	38.0	36.2	40.3	31.7	37.1	2.31	2.74	1.57	4.52	3.01
43	37.1	35.3	39.3	30.8	36.2	2.52	2.98	1.71	5.00	3.30
44	36.2	34.4	38.4	30.0	35.3	2.75	3.24	1.87	5.57	3.62
45	35.3	33.5	37.5	29.2	34.4	2.99	3.50	2.04	6.19	3.96
46	34.4	32.6	36.5	28.3	33.6	3.24	3.79	2.22	6.83	4.30
47	33.5	31.7	35.6	27.5	32.7	3.51	4.10	2.40	7.51	4.67
48	32.7	30.8	34.7	26.7	31.9	3.80	4.45	2.58	8.26	5.07
49	31.8	30.0	33.8	26.0	31.0	4.12	4.84	2.76	9.07	5.49
50	30.9	29.1	32.9	25.2	30.2	4.46	5.27	2.97	9.97	5.96
51	30.0	28.3	32.0	24.4	29.4	4.84	5.73	3.19	10.94	6.46
52	29.2	27.4	31.1	23.7	28.6	5.22	6.19	3.45	11.91	6.93
53	28.3	26.6	30.2	23.0	27.8	5.59	6.62	3.74	12.83	7.34
54	27.5	25.8	29.3	22.3	27.0	5.96	7.05	4.05	13.69	7.71
55	26.7	24.9	28.4	21.6	26.2	6.35	7.48	4.39	14.58	8.08
56	25.8	24.1	27.5	20.9	25.4	6.77	7.96	4.75	15.54	8.51
57	25.0	23.3	26.7	20.2	24.6	7.26	8.52	5.16	16.57	9.03
58	24.2	22.5	25.8	19.5	23.8	7.87	9.23	5.66	17.71	9.70
59	23.4	21.7	25.0	18.9	23.0	8.60	10.11	6.24	19.00	10.54
60	22.6	20.9	24.1	18.2	22.3	9.47	11.16	6.94	20.51	11.54
61	21.8	20.2	23.3	17.6	21.5	10.45	12.32	7.73	22.19	12.64
62	21.0	19.4	22.4	17.0	20.8	11.46	13.52	8.54	23.90	13.79
63	20.2	18.7	21.6	16.4	20.1	12.41	14.65	9.32	25.44	14.86
64	19.5	17.9	20.8	15.8	19.4	13.32	15.72	10.09	26.79	15.84
65	18.7	17.2	20.0	15.2	18.7	14.30	16.87	10.94	28.04	16.82
70	15.2	13.8	16.2	12.4	15.3	21.89	26.23	17.33	38.34	23.88
75	12.0	10.7	12.8	10.0	12.3	34.08	41.47	27.71	55.33	35.90
80	9.2	8.1	9.7	7.9	9.7	54.28	65.96	46.30	79.61	54.60

[1] Includes other races not shown separately.   [2] Based on the proportion of the cohort who are alive at the beginning of the indicated age who will die before reaching the age shown plus 1. For example, out of every 1,000 people alive and exactly 50 years old at the beginning of the period, between 4 and 5 (4.46) will die before reaching their 51st birthdays.

Source: U.S. National Center for Health Statistics, unpublished data.

Table 104. Deaths and Death Rates by Sex, Race, and Hispanic Origin: 1980 to 2005

[1,990 represents 1,990,000. Rates are per 1,000 population for specified groups. Excludes deaths of nonresidents of the United States and fetal deaths. For explanation of age adjustment, see text, this section. The standard population for age adjustment is the projected year 2000 population of the United States. See Appendix III. Data for Hispanic origin and specified races other than White and Black should be interpreted with caution because of inconsistencies between reporting Hispanic origin and race on death certificates and censuses and surveys]

Sex, race, and Hispanic origin	1980	1990	1995	1998	1999	2000	2001	2002	2003	2004	2005
Deaths [1] (1,000)	**1,990**	**2,148**	**2,312**	**2,337**	**2,391**	**2,403**	**2,416**	**2,443**	**2,448**	**2,398**	**2,448**
Male [1] (1,000)	1,075	1,113	1,173	1,157	1,175	1,178	1,183	1,199	1,202	1,182	1,208
Female [1] (1,000)	915	1,035	1,139	1,180	1,216	1,226	1,233	1,244	1,246	1,216	1,240
White (1,000)	1,739	1,853	1,987	2,016	2,061	2,071	2,080	2,103	2,104	2,057	2,098
Male (1,000)	934	951	997	990	1,005	1,007	1,011	1,025	1,026	1,007	1,028
Female (1,000)	805	902	990	1,026	1,056	1,064	1,068	1,077	1,078	1,049	1,070
Black (1,000)	233	265	286	278	285	286	288	290	291	287	293
Male (1,000)	130	145	154	143	146	145	146	147	148	146	149
Female (1,000)	103	120	132	135	139	141	142	143	143	141	144
Asian or Pacific Islander (1,000)	11	21	28	32	34	35	37	38	40	41	43
Male (1,000)	7	12	16	18	18	19	20	20	21	21	23
Female (1,000)	4	9	12	14	15	16	17	18	19	19	20
American Indian, Eskimo, Aleut (1,000)	7	8	10	11	11	11	12	12	13	13	14
Male (1,000)	4	5	6	6	6	6	6	7	7	7	8
Female (1,000)	3	3	4	5	5	5	6	6	6	6	6
Hispanic origin [2] (1,000)	(NA)	(NA)	(NA)	98	104	107	113	117	122	122	131
Male (1,000)	(NA)	(NA)	(NA)	56	58	60	63	66	68	69	74
Female (1,000)	(NA)	(NA)	(NA)	43	46	47	50	51	54	54	57
Non-Hispanic, White (1,000)	(NA)	(NA)	(NA)	1,913	1,953	1,960	1,963	1,982	1,979	1,933	1,967
Male (1,000)	(NA)	(NA)	(NA)	932	945	945	946	958	956	938	954
Female (1,000)	(NA)	(NA)	(NA)	981	1,008	1,015	1,017	1,024	1,023	995	1,013
Death rates [1]	**8.8**	**8.6**	**8.7**	**8.5**	**8.6**	**8.5**	**8.5**	**8.5**	**8.4**	**8.2**	**8.3**
Male [1]	9.8	9.2	9.0	8.6	8.6	8.5	8.5	8.5	8.4	8.2	8.3
Female [1]	7.9	8.1	8.4	8.4	8.5	8.6	8.5	8.5	8.4	8.2	8.2
White	8.9	8.9	9.0	8.9	9.0	9.0	9.0	9.0	8.9	8.6	8.7
Male	9.8	9.3	9.3	8.9	9.1	8.9	8.8	8.8	8.8	8.5	8.6
Female	8.1	8.5	8.9	8.9	9.2	9.1	9.1	9.1	9.0	8.7	8.8
Black	8.8	8.7	8.5	7.8	7.9	7.8	7.7	7.7	7.6	7.4	7.5
Male	10.3	10.1	9.8	8.5	8.8	8.3	8.2	8.2	8.1	7.9	8.0
Female	7.3	7.5	7.6	7.2	7.6	7.3	7.3	7.2	7.2	7.0	7.0
Asian or Pacific Islander	3.0	2.8	2.9	2.9	3.0	3.0	3.0	3.0	3.0	3.0	3.1
Male	3.8	3.3	3.4	3.4	3.3	3.3	3.4	3.3	3.3	3.2	3.3
Female	2.2	2.3	2.5	2.5	2.6	2.6	2.7	2.7	2.8	2.7	2.8
American Indian, Eskimo, Aleut	4.9	4.0	4.1	4.0	4.0	3.8	3.9	4.0	4.2	4.2	4.4
Male	6.0	4.8	4.6	4.4	4.3	4.2	4.2	4.4	4.6	4.5	4.8
Female	3.8	3.3	3.6	3.5	3.7	3.5	3.6	3.7	3.9	3.8	4.0
Hispanic origin [2]	(NA)	(NA)	(NA)	3.0	3.1	3.0	3.1	3.0	3.1	3.0	3.1
Male	(NA)	4.1	(NA)	3.3	3.7	3.3	3.3	3.3	3.3	3.2	3.3
Female	(NA)	2.9	(NA)	2.7	2.9	2.7	2.8	2.7	2.8	2.7	2.8
Non-Hispanic, White	(NA)	(NA)	(NA)	9.7	9.9	9.9	9.9	10.0	9.9	9.7	9.8
Male	(NA)	9.9	(NA)	9.7	9.8	9.8	9.8	10.0	9.8	9.6	9.7
Female	(NA)	9.0	(NA)	9.8	10.0	10.1	10.1	10.1	10.1	9.8	9.9
Age-adjusted death rates [1]	**10.4**	**9.4**	**9.2**	**8.7**	**8.8**	**8.7**	**8.5**	**8.5**	**8.3**	**8.0**	**8.0**
Male [1]	13.5	12.0	11.5	10.7	10.7	10.5	10.3	10.1	9.9	9.6	9.5
Female [1]	8.2	7.5	7.5	7.2	7.3	7.3	7.2	7.2	7.1	6.8	6.8
White	10.1	9.1	8.9	8.5	8.5	8.5	8.4	8.3	8.2	7.9	7.9
Male	13.2	11.7	11.1	10.4	10.4	10.3	10.1	9.9	9.7	9.4	9.3
Female	8.0	7.3	7.3	7.1	7.2	7.2	7.1	6.9	6.9	6.7	6.7
Black	13.1	12.5	12.2	11.3	11.4	11.2	11.0	10.8	10.7	10.3	10.2
Male	17.0	16.4	15.8	14.3	14.3	14.0	13.8	13.4	13.2	12.7	12.5
Female	10.3	9.8	9.7	9.2	9.3	9.3	9.1	9.0	8.9	8.6	8.5
Asian or Pacific Islander	5.9	5.8	6.2	5.2	5.2	5.1	4.9	4.7	4.7	4.4	4.4
Male	7.9	7.2	7.9	6.5	6.4	6.2	6.0	5.8	5.6	5.3	5.3
Female	4.3	4.7	4.9	4.3	4.3	4.2	4.1	4.0	3.9	3.8	3.7
American Indian, Eskimo, Aleut	8.7	7.2	7.2	7.7	7.8	7.1	6.9	6.8	6.9	6.5	6.6
Male	11.1	9.2	8.6	9.4	9.3	8.4	8.0	7.9	8.0	7.6	7.8
Female	6.6	5.6	5.9	6.4	6.7	6.0	5.9	5.8	5.9	5.6	5.7
Hispanic origin [2]	(NA)	(NA)	(NA)	6.7	6.8	6.7	6.6	6.3	6.2	5.9	5.9
Male	(NA)	8.9	(NA)	8.3	8.3	8.2	8.0	7.7	7.5	7.1	7.2
Female	(NA)	5.4	(NA)	5.4	5.6	5.5	5.4	5.2	5.2	4.9	4.9
Non-Hispanic, White	(NA)	(NA)	(NA)	8.5	8.6	8.6	8.4	8.4	8.3	8.0	8.0
Male	(NA)	11.7	(NA)	10.5	10.5	10.4	10.1	10.0	9.8	9.5	9.5
Female	(NA)	7.3	(NA)	7.1	7.2	7.2	7.1	7.1	7.0	6.8	6.8

NA Not available. [1] Includes other races, not shown separately. [2] Persons of Hispanic origin may be any race.

Source: U.S. National Center for Health Statistics, *National Vital Statistics Reports (NVSR), Deaths: Final Data for 2005*; Vol. 56, No. 10, April 24, 2008.

U.S. Census Bureau, Statistical Abstract of the United States: 2009

Table 105. Death Rates by Age, Sex, and Race: 1950 to 2005

[**Rates per 100,000 population**. Rates calculated by U.S. Census Bureau based on number of deaths and estimated population provided by National Center for Health Statistics. See headnote, Table 104 and Appendix III]

Characteristic	All ages [1]	Under 1 year	1-4 years	5-14 years	15-24 years	25-34 years	35-44 years	45-54 years	55-64 years	65-74 years	75-84 years	85 years and over
MALE												
1950	1,106	3,728	152	71	168	217	429	1,067	2,395	4,931	10,426	21,636
1960	1,105	3,059	120	56	152	188	373	992	2,310	4,914	10,178	21,186
1970	1,090	2,410	93	51	189	215	403	959	2,283	4,874	10,010	17,822
1980	977	1,429	73	37	172	196	299	767	1,815	4,105	8,817	18,801
1990	918	1,083	52	29	147	204	310	610	1,553	3,492	7,889	18,057
2000	853	807	36	21	115	139	255	543	1,231	2,980	6,973	17,501
2002	847	762	35	20	117	142	258	548	1,184	2,855	6,761	16,255
2003	840	777	35	20	117	141	255	552	1,166	2,772	6,642	15,794
2004	818	754	32	19	115	140	244	544	1,129	2,645	6,394	15,031
2005	827	762	33	18	119	144	242	560	1,182	2,644	6,424	14,889
White:												
1990	931	896	46	26	131	176	268	549	1,467	3,398	7,845	18,268
2000	888	668	33	20	106	124	234	497	1,163	2,906	6,933	17,716
2004	854	632	29	18	108	127	229	504	1,066	2,584	6,385	15,251
2005	865	640	31	17	111	131	227	519	1,113	2,576	6,404	15,157
Black:												
1990	1,008	2,112	86	41	252	431	700	1,261	2,618	4,946	9,130	16,955
2000	834	1,568	55	28	181	261	453	1,018	2,080	4,254	8,486	16,791
2004	793	1,414	49	26	164	252	397	955	1,961	3,818	7,710	14,453
2005	799	1,437	46	27	176	258	394	977	2,066	3,827	7,814	13,810
Asian or Pacific Islander [2]:												
1990	334	605	45	21	76	80	131	287	789	2,041	5,009	12,446
2000	333	529	23	13	55	55	105	250	642	1,661	4,328	12,125
2004	321	443	21	15	54	51	91	242	545	1,363	3,766	10,118
2005	334	464	21	14	57	56	97	252	585	1,485	3,978	9,839
American Indian, Eskimo, Aleut [2]:												
1990	476	1,057	77	33	220	256	365	620	1,211	2,462	5,389	11,244
2000	416	700	45	20	136	179	295	520	1,090	2,478	5,351	10,726
2004	454	1,076	55	24	136	189	321	543	1,067	2,197	4,584	7,924
2005	482	882	72	22	147	210	334	603	1,181	2,326	4,576	8,419
FEMALE												
1950	824	2,855	127	49	89	143	290	642	1,405	3,333	8,400	19,195
1960	809	2,321	98	37	61	107	229	527	1,196	2,872	7,633	19,008
1970	808	1,864	75	32	68	102	231	517	1,099	2,580	6,678	15,518
1980	785	1,142	55	24	58	76	159	413	934	2,145	5,440	14,747
1990	812	856	41	19	49	74	138	343	879	1,991	4,883	14,274
2000	855	663	29	15	43	64	143	313	772	1,921	4,815	14,719
2002	848	625	27	15	44	64	149	317	738	1,865	4,758	14,210
2003	843	619	28	14	44	65	149	318	733	1,823	4,676	14,063
2004	815	613	27	14	44	64	144	314	707	1,761	4,522	13,280
2005	825	619	25	14	43	64	143	326	729	1,749	4,533	13,298
White:												
1990	847	690	36	18	46	62	117	309	823	1,924	4,839	14,401
2000	912	551	26	14	41	55	126	281	731	1,868	4,785	14,891
2004	872	514	24	13	42	57	130	285	672	1,724	4,514	13,451
2005	883	515	23	13	42	58	129	296	690	1,708	4,518	13,498
Black:												
1990	748	1,736	68	28	69	160	299	639	1,453	2,866	5,688	13,310
2000	733	1,280	45	20	58	122	272	588	1,227	2,690	5,697	13,941
2004	700	1,150	41	21	54	112	256	564	1,129	2,386	5,300	12,897
2005	704	1,179	37	19	52	111	249	585	1,164	2,384	5,339	12,790
Asian or Pacific Islander [2]:												
1990	234	518	32	13	29	38	70	183	483	1,089	3,128	10,254
2000	262	434	20	12	22	28	66	156	391	996	2,882	9,052
2004	275	392	22	10	24	27	54	146	340	933	2,558	8,126
2005	283	395	18	12	26	29	60	147	381	944	2,697	7,793
American Indian, Eskimo, Aleut [2]:												
1990	330	689	38	26	69	102	156	381	806	1,679	3,073	8,201
2000	346	492	40	18	59	85	172	285	772	1,900	3,850	9,118
2004	380	715	53	20	65	103	192	340	704	1,701	3,533	7,094
2005	399	752	46	16	69	91	191	376	735	1,833	3,706	7,065

[1] Figures for age not stated are included in "All ages" but not distributed among age groups.   [2] The death rates for specified races other than White and Black should be interpreted with caution because of inconsistencies between reporting race on death certificates and censuses and surveys.

Source: U.S. National Center for Health Statistics, *National Vital Statistics Reports (NVSR), Deaths: Final Data for 2005*, Vol. 56, No. 10, April 24, 2008, and earlier reports.

Table 106. Age-Adjusted Death Rates by Sex, Race, and Hispanic Origin: 1960 to 2005

[Age-adjusted rates per 100,000 population; see headnote, Table 104. Populations enumerated as of April 1 for census years and estimated as of July 1 for all other years. Beginning 1970, excludes deaths of nonresidents of the United States. Data for Hispanic origin and specified races other than White and Black should be interpreted with caution because of inconsistencies reporting race on death certificates and on censuses and surveys. See Appendix III]

Sex, race, and Hispanic origin	1960	1970	1980	1990	2000	2001	2002	2003	2004	2005
ALL RACES [1]										
Total	1,339	1,223	1,039	939	869	855	845	833	801	799
Male	1,609	1,542	1,348	1,203	1,054	1,029	1,014	994	956	951
Female.	1,105	971	818	751	731	722	715	706	679	678
WHITE										
Total	1,311	1,193	1,013	910	850	837	829	817	786	785
Male	1,586	1,514	1,318	1,166	1,029	1,006	993	974	937	933
Female.	1,074	944	796	729	715	707	701	693	667	667
BLACK										
Total	1,578	1,518	1,315	1,250	1,121	1,101	1,083	1,066	1,027	1,017
Male	1,811	1,874	1,698	1,645	1,404	1,375	1,341	1,319	1,269	1,253
Female.	1,370	1,229	1,033	975	928	913	902	886	855	846
ASIAN OR PACIFIC ISLANDER										
Total	(NA)	(NA)	590	582	506	492	474	466	444	440
Male	(NA)	(NA)	787	716	624	597	578	563	535	534
Female.	(NA)	(NA)	426	469	417	412	396	393	376	369
AMERICAN INDIAN, ESKIMO, ALEUT										
Total	(NA)	(NA)	867	716	709	687	677	685	650	663
Male	(NA)	(NA)	1,112	916	842	799	794	797	758	775
Female.	(NA)	(NA)	662	562	605	594	581	592	558	568
HISPANIC ORIGIN [2]										
Total	(NA)	(NA)	(NA)	(NA)	666	659	629	621	587	591
Male	(NA)	(NA)	(NA)	886	818	803	767	748	707	717
Female.	(NA)	(NA)	(NA)	537	546	544	518	516	486	485
NON-HISPANIC, WHITE										
Total	(NA)	(NA)	(NA)	(NA)	856	843	838	826	797	797
Male	(NA)	(NA)	(NA)	1,171	1,035	1,013	1,002	984	949	945
Female.	(NA)	(NA)	(NA)	735	722	714	710	702	678	678

NA Not available. [1] For 1960 to 1990 includes deaths among races not shown separately. [2] Persons of Hispanic origin may be any race.

Source: U.S. National Center for Health Statistics, *National Vital Statistics Reports (NVSR), Deaths: Final Data for 2005;* Vol. 56, No. 10, April 24, 2008.

Table 107. Death Rates by Hispanic-Origin Status, Sex, and Age: 1990 to 2005

[Rates per 100,000 population. Rates are based on populations enumerated as of April 1 for census years and estimated as of July 1 for all other years. Excludes deaths of nonresidents of the United States. Data for Hispanic origin should be interpreted with caution because of inconsistencies between reporting Hispanic origin and race on death certificates and censuses and surveys]

Age	Hispanic male			Hispanic female			Non-Hispanic White male			Non-Hispanic White female		
	1990	2000	2005	1990	2000	2005	1990	2000	2005	1990	2000	2005
Age-adjusted [1]	886	818	717	537	546	485	1,171	1,035	945	735	722	678
Crude	412	331	334	285	275	278	986	979	971	904	1,007	993
Under 1 year	922	637	670	747	554	555	865	659	626	655	531	497
1 to 4 years	54	32	33	42	28	25	44	32	30	34	24	22
5 to 14 years	26	18	15	17	13	12	26	20	17	18	14	13
15 to 24 years	159	108	120	41	32	37	123	104	106	46	43	42
25 to 34 years	234	120	116	63	43	41	165	123	134	61	57	62
35 to 44 years	342	211	182	109	101	91	257	234	236	117	128	137
45 to 54 years	534	439	417	253	224	216	545	498	517	312	285	299
55 to 64 years	1,124	966	876	608	548	494	1,480	1,171	1,080	835	742	677
65 to 74 years	2,368	2,288	2,029	1,454	1,423	1,292	3,435	2,931	2,585	1,940	1,891	1,730
75 to 84 years	5,369	5,395	4,857	3,351	3,625	3,366	7,920	6,978	6,420	4,887	4,819	4,580
85 years and over . . .	12,272	13,086	10,141	10,099	11,203	9,068	18,505	17,853	15,401	14,533	14,972	13,683

[1] See headnote, Table 104.

Source: U.S. National Center for Health Statistics, *National Vital Statistics Reports (NVSR), Deaths: Final Data for 2005;* Vol. 56, No. 10, April 24, 2008.

Births, Deaths, Marriages, and Divorces   79

Table 108. **Deaths and Death Rates by State and Island Areas: 1990 to 2006**

[2,148 represents 2,148,000. By state of residence. Except as noted, excludes deaths of nonresidents of the United States. Caution should be used in comparing death rates by state; rates are affected by the population composition of the area. For explanation of age adjustment, see text this section, Table 104, and also Appendix III]

State and island area	Number of deaths (1,000)						Crude rate per 1,000 population [2]						Age-adjusted rate, 2006
	1990	1995	2000	2004	2005	2006 [1]	1990	1995	2000	2004	2005	2006 [1]	
United States......	**2,148**	**2,312**	**2,403**	**2,398**	**2,448**	**2,426**	**8.6**	**8.7**	**8.5**	**8.2**	**8.3**	**8.1**	**7.8**
Alabama...........	39	42	45	46	47	47	9.7	10.0	10.1	10.2	10.3	10.2	9.5
Alaska	2	3	3	3	3	3	4.0	4.2	4.6	4.7	4.8	5.0	7.7
Arizona...........	29	35	41	43	46	46	7.9	8.4	7.9	7.5	7.7	7.5	7.2
Arkansas.........	25	27	28	28	28	28	10.5	10.8	10.6	10.0	10.1	9.9	8.9
California..........	214	224	230	233	237	237	7.2	7.1	6.8	6.5	6.6	6.5	7.0
Colorado..........	22	25	27	28	30	30	6.6	6.7	6.3	6.2	6.4	6.2	7.2
Connecticut.......	28	29	30	29	29	29	8.4	9.0	8.8	8.4	8.4	8.4	7.2
Delaware.........	6	6	7	7	7	7	8.7	8.8	8.8	8.6	8.9	8.4	7.8
District of Columbia....	7	7	6	5	5	5	12.0	12.4	10.5	9.9	10.0	9.2	8.9
Florida	134	153	164	169	171	170	10.4	10.8	10.3	9.7	9.6	9.4	7.1
Georgia	52	58	64	66	67	68	8.0	8.1	7.8	7.5	7.4	7.2	8.6
Hawaii	7	8	8	9	9	9	6.1	6.4	6.8	7.2	7.2	7.4	6.3
Idaho	7	9	10	10	11	11	7.4	7.3	7.4	7.2	7.4	7.2	7.5
Illinois...........	103	108	107	103	104	102	9.0	9.2	8.6	8.1	8.1	8.0	7.8
Indiana...........	50	53	55	54	56	56	8.9	9.2	9.1	8.7	8.9	8.8	8.5
Iowa.............	27	28	28	27	28	27	9.7	9.9	9.6	9.1	9.4	9.2	7.3
Kansas...........	22	24	25	24	25	25	9.0	9.3	9.2	8.7	9.0	8.9	7.9
Kentucky.........	35	37	40	39	40	40	9.5	9.6	9.8	9.3	9.6	9.5	9.1
Louisiana	38	40	41	42	44	40	8.9	9.1	9.2	9.3	9.8	9.3	9.3
Maine............	11	12	12	12	13	12	9.0	9.5	9.7	9.4	9.7	9.3	7.7
Maryland..........	38	42	44	43	44	44	8.0	8.3	8.3	7.8	7.8	7.8	7.9
Massachusetts.......	53	55	57	55	54	53	8.8	9.1	8.9	8.5	8.4	8.3	7.2
Michigan..........	79	84	87	85	87	86	8.5	8.8	8.7	8.4	8.6	8.5	8.1
Minnesota.........	35	38	38	37	38	37	7.9	8.1	7.7	7.3	7.3	7.2	6.7
Mississippi.........	25	27	29	28	29	29	9.8	10.0	10.1	9.6	10.0	9.8	9.6
Missouri..........	50	54	55	54	55	55	9.8	10.2	9.8	9.4	9.4	9.4	8.5
Montana..........	7	8	8	8	9	8	8.6	8.8	9.0	8.7	9.1	9.0	7.8
Nebraska.........	15	15	15	15	15	15	9.4	9.3	8.8	8.4	8.5	8.4	7.4
Nevada...........	9	13	15	18	19	18	7.8	8.2	7.6	7.7	7.9	7.4	8.2
New Hampshire	8	9	10	10	10	10	7.7	8.0	7.8	7.8	7.8	7.6	7.2
New Jersey........	70	74	75	71	72	70	9.1	9.3	8.9	8.2	8.3	8.1	7.4
New Mexico........	11	13	13	14	15	15	7.0	7.4	7.4	7.5	7.8	7.8	7.7
New York	169	168	158	153	152	149	9.4	9.3	8.3	7.9	7.9	7.7	7.0
North Carolina	57	65	72	72	75	75	8.6	9.0	8.9	8.5	8.6	8.4	8.4
North Dakota........	6	6	6	6	6	6	8.9	9.3	9.1	8.8	9.0	9.2	7.3
Ohio..............	99	106	108	106	109	107	9.1	9.5	9.5	9.3	9.5	9.3	8.4
Oklahoma..........	30	33	35	34	36	35	9.7	10.0	10.2	9.8	10.2	9.9	9.2
Oregon...........	25	28	30	30	31	32	8.8	9.0	8.6	8.4	8.5	8.5	7.7
Pennsylvania.......	122	128	131	128	130	126	10.3	10.6	10.7	10.3	10.4	10.1	8.0
Rhode Island........	10	10	10	10	10	10	9.5	9.8	9.6	9.0	9.3	9.1	7.5
South Carolina	30	34	37	37	39	39	8.5	9.1	9.2	8.9	9.1	9.0	8.7
South Dakota.......	6	7	7	7	7	7	9.1	9.5	9.3	8.9	9.1	9.1	7.4
Tennessee.........	46	51	55	56	57	57	9.5	9.8	9.7	9.5	9.6	9.4	9.1
Texas............	125	138	150	153	156	157	7.4	7.4	7.2	6.8	6.8	6.7	7.8
Utah.............	9	11	12	13	13	14	5.3	5.6	5.5	5.6	5.4	5.4	7.1
Vermont	5	5	5	5	5	5	8.2	8.5	8.4	8.0	8.1	8.1	7.2
Virginia...........	48	53	56	57	58	58	7.8	8.0	8.0	7.6	7.6	7.5	7.8
Washington........	37	41	44	45	46	46	7.6	7.5	7.5	7.2	7.3	7.2	7.2
West Virginia	19	20	21	21	21	21	10.8	11.1	11.7	11.5	11.4	11.4	9.4
Wisconsin	43	45	46	46	47	46	8.7	8.8	8.7	8.3	8.4	8.3	7.5
Wyoming..........	3	4	4	4	4	4	7.1	7.7	7.9	7.8	8.0	8.4	8.2
Puerto Rico	26	30	28	29	30	28	7.3	8.1	7.2	7.4	7.5	7.2	7.3
Virgin Islands	(Z)	1	1	1	1	1	4.6	5.8	5.3	5.8	6.1	5.8	6.5
Guam	1	1	1	1	1	1	3.9	4.1	4.2	4.1	4.0	4.0	6.2
American Samoa....	(NA)	(NA)	(Z)	(NA)	(NA)	(NA)	(NA)	(NA)	3.3	4.9	4.4	4.6	13.1
Northern Marianas...	(NA)	(NA)	(Z)	(NA)	(NA)	(NA)	(NA)	(NA)	1.9	2.1	2.3	2.1	10.0

NA Not available.   Z Less than 500.   [1] Preliminary data. U.S. totals include only events occuring within the 50 states and the District of Columbia.   [2] Rates based on enumerated resident population as of April 1 for 1990 and 2000; estimated resident population as of July 1 for all other years.

Source: U.S. National Center for Health Statistics, *National Vital Statistics Reports (NVSR), Deaths: Final Data for 2005,* Vol. 56, No. 10, April 24, 2008; and *Deaths: Preliminary Data for 2006,* Vol. 56, No. 16, June 11, 2008.

Table 109. **Fetal and Infant Deaths: 1990 to 2004**

[See Appendix III]

Year	Fetal deaths Total [1]	Fetal deaths 20 to 27 weeks [2]	Fetal deaths 28 weeks or more [2]	Infant deaths Less than 7 days	Infant deaths Less than 28 days	Fetal mortality rate [3] Total [1]	Fetal mortality rate [3] 20 to 27 weeks [2]	Fetal mortality rate [3] 28 weeks or more [2]	Perinatal mortality rate Defini-tion I [4]	Perinatal mortality rate Defini-tion II [5]
1990 . . .	31,386	13,427	17,959	19,439	23,591	7.49	3.22	4.30	8.95	13.12
1995 . . .	27,294	13,043	14,251	15,483	19,186	6.95	3.33	3.64	7.60	11.84
1996 . . .	27,069	12,990	14,079	14,947	18,556	6.91	3.33	3.60	7.43	11.64
1997 . . .	26,486	12,800	13,686	14,827	18,507	6.78	3.29	3.51	7.32	11.51
1998 . . .	26,702	13,229	13,473	15,061	18,915	6.73	3.35	3.41	7.21	11.50
1999 . . .	26,884	13,457	13,427	14,874	18,700	6.74	3.39	3.38	7.12	11.44
2000 . . .	27,003	13,497	13,506	14,893	18,733	6.61	3.31	3.32	6.97	11.19
2001 . . .	26,373	13,122	13,251	14,622	18,275	6.51	3.25	3.28	6.90	11.02
2002 . . .	25,943	13,072	12,871	15,020	18,791	6.41	3.24	3.19	6.91	11.05
2003 . . .	25,653	13,168	12,485	15,152	18,935	6.23	3.21	3.04	6.71	10.78
2004 . . .	25,655	12,895	12,760	14,836	18,602	6.20	3.13	3.09	6.69	10.70

[1] Fetal deaths with stated or presumed gestation of 20 weeks or more. [2] Not stated gestational age proportionally distributed. [3] Rate per 1,000 live births and fetal deaths in specified group. [4] Infant deaths of less than 7 days and fetal deaths with stated or presumed period of gestation of 28 weeks or more, per 1,000 live births and fetal deaths. [5] Infant deaths of less than 28 days and fetal deaths with stated or presumed period of gestation of 20 weeks or more per 1,000 live births and fetal deaths.

Source: U.S. National Center for Health Statistics, *National Vital Statistics Reports (NVSR), Fetal and Perinatal Mortality, U.S., 2004*, Vol. 56., No. 3, October 11, 2007.

Table 110. **Infant, Neonatal, and Maternal Mortality Rates by Race: 1980 to 2005**

[**Deaths per 1,000 live births, except as noted.** Excludes deaths of nonresidents of U.S. infant and maternal deaths are based on race of the decedent. Fetal deaths and live births are based on race of mother. See also Appendix III]

Race and year	Infant mortality [1]	Neonatal mortality [1] Under 28 days	Neonatal mortality [1] Under 7 days	Post-neonatal mortality [1]	Fetal mortality rate [2]	Late fetal mortality rate [3]	Perinatal mortality rate [4]	Maternal mortality rate [5]
ALL RACES								
1980	12.6	8.5	7.1	4.1	9.1	6.2	13.2	9.2
1990	9.2	5.8	4.8	3.4	7.5	4.3	9.1	8.2
1995	7.6	4.9	4.0	2.7	7.0	3.6	7.6	7.1
2000	6.9	4.6	3.7	2.3	6.6	3.3	7.0	9.8
2001	6.8	4.5	3.6	2.3	6.5	3.3	6.9	9.9
2002	7.0	4.7	3.7	2.3	6.4	3.2	6.9	8.9
2003	6.9	4.6	3.7	2.2	6.2	3.0	6.7	[6]12.1
2004	6.8	4.5	3.6	2.3	6.2	3.1	6.7	[6]13.1
2005	6.9	4.5	3.6	2.3	(NA)	(NA)	(NA)	[6]15.1
WHITE								
1980	10.9	7.4	6.1	3.5	8.1	5.7	11.8	6.7
1990	7.6	4.8	3.9	2.8	6.4	3.8	7.7	5.4
1995	6.3	4.1	3.3	2.2	5.9	3.3	6.5	4.2
2000	5.7	3.8	3.0	1.9	5.6	2.9	5.9	7.5
2001	5.7	3.8	3.0	1.9	5.5	2.9	5.9	7.2
2002	5.8	3.9	3.1	1.9	5.5	2.8	5.9	6.0
2003	5.7	3.9	3.1	1.8	5.2	2.7	5.8	[6]8.7
2004	5.7	3.8	3.0	1.9	5.3	(NA)	(NA)	[6]9.3
2005	5.7	3.8	3.0	1.9	(NA)	(NA)	(NA)	[6]11.1
BLACK								
1980	22.2	14.6	12.3	7.6	14.7	9.1	21.3	21.5
1990	18.0	11.6	9.7	6.4	13.3	6.7	16.4	22.4
1995	15.1	9.8	8.2	5.3	12.7	5.7	13.8	22.1
2000	14.1	9.4	7.6	4.7	12.4	5.4	13.0	22.0
2001	14.0	9.2	7.6	4.8	12.1	5.3	12.8	24.7
2002	14.4	9.5	7.8	4.8	11.9	5.2	12.8	24.9
2003	14.0	9.4	7.5	4.6	12.0	5.1	12.4	[6]30.5
2004	13.8	9.1	7.3	4.7	11.5	(NA)	(NA)	[6]34.7
2005	13.7	9.1	7.3	4.7	(NA)	(NA)	(NA)	[6]36.5

NA Not available. [1] Infant (under 1 year of age), neonatal (under 28 days), early neonatal (under 7 days), and postneonatal (28 days–11 months). [2] Number of fetal deaths of 20 weeks or more gestation per 1,000 live births plus fetal deaths. [3] Number of fetal deaths of 28 weeks or more gestation (late fetal deaths) per 1,000 live births plus late fetal deaths. [4] Number of late fetal deaths plus infant deaths within 7 days of birth per 1,000 live births plus late fetal deaths. [5] Per 100,000 live births from deliveries and complications of pregnancy, childbirth, and the puerperium. Beginning 2000, deaths are classified according to the tenth revision of the *International Classification of Diseases;* earlier years classified according to the revision in use at the time; see text, this section. [6] Increase partially reflects the use of a separate item on the death certificate on pregnancy status by an increasing number of states.

Source: U.S. National Center for Health Statistics, *Health, United States 2007; National Vital Statistics Reports (NVSR), Deaths: Final Data for 2005*, Vol. 56, No. 10, April 24, 2008; and unpublished data.

Table 111. **Infant Mortality Rates by Race—States: 1980 to 2005**

[**Deaths per 1,000 live births, by place of residence.** Represents deaths of infants under 1 year old, exclusive of fetal deaths. Excludes deaths of nonresidents of the United States. See headnote, Table 110, and Appendix III]

State	Total [1]				White				Black			
	1980	1990	2000	2005	1980	1990	2000	2005	1980	1990	2000	2005
United States......	**12.6**	**9.2**	**6.9**	**6.9**	**10.9**	**7.6**	**5.7**	**5.7**	**22.2**	**18.0**	**14.1**	**13.7**
Alabama..........	15.1	10.8	9.4	9.4	11.6	8.1	6.6	7.2	21.6	16.0	15.4	14.7
Alaska...........	12.3	10.5	6.8	5.9	9.4	7.6	5.8	4.7	19.5	(B)	(B)	(B)
Arizona..........	12.4	8.8	6.7	6.9	11.8	7.8	6.2	6.6	18.4	20.6	17.6	12.6
Arkansas.........	12.7	9.2	8.4	7.9	10.3	8.4	7.0	6.4	20.0	13.9	13.7	14.9
California........	11.1	7.9	5.4	5.3	10.6	7.0	5.1	5.0	18.0	16.8	12.9	13.6
Colorado.........	10.1	8.8	6.2	6.4	9.8	7.8	5.6	6.0	19.1	19.4	19.5	16.3
Connecticut.......	11.2	7.9	6.6	5.8	10.2	6.3	5.6	4.9	19.1	17.6	14.4	13.5
Delaware.........	13.9	10.1	9.2	9.0	9.8	9.7	7.9	6.0	27.9	20.1	14.8	18.9
District of Columbia....	25.0	20.7	12.0	14.1	17.8	(B)	(B)	8.8	26.7	24.6	16.1	17.0
Florida	14.6	9.6	7.0	7.2	11.8	6.7	5.4	5.7	22.8	16.8	12.6	12.0
Georgia	14.5	12.4	8.5	8.2	10.8	7.4	5.9	5.9	21.0	18.3	13.9	12.6
Hawaii	10.3	6.7	8.1	6.5	11.6	6.1	6.5	6.3	(B)	(B)	(B)	(B)
Idaho	10.7	8.7	7.5	6.1	10.7	8.6	7.5	6.1	(NA)	(B)	(B)	(B)
Illinois..........	14.8	10.7	8.5	7.4	11.7	7.9	6.6	5.7	26.3	22.4	17.1	16.4
Indiana..........	11.9	9.6	7.8	8.0	10.5	7.9	6.9	7.0	23.4	17.4	15.8	17.0
Iowa............	11.8	8.1	6.5	5.3	11.5	7.9	6.0	5.1	27.2	21.9	21.1	13.9
Kansas..........	10.4	8.4	6.8	7.4	9.5	8.0	6.4	6.6	20.6	17.7	12.2	17.6
Kentucky.........	12.9	8.5	7.2	6.6	12.0	8.2	6.7	6.0	22.0	14.3	12.7	13.2
Louisiana........	14.3	11.1	9.0	10.1	10.5	8.1	5.9	7.0	20.6	16.7	13.3	14.9
Maine...........	9.2	6.2	4.9	6.9	9.4	6.7	4.8	6.9	(B)	(B)	(B)	(B)
Maryland.........	14.0	9.5	7.6	7.3	11.6	6.8	4.8	5.1	20.4	17.1	13.2	11.6
Massachusetts.......	10.5	7.0	4.6	5.2	10.1	6.1	4.0	4.8	16.8	11.9	9.9	8.2
Michigan.........	12.8	10.7	8.2	7.9	10.6	7.4	6.0	5.8	24.2	21.6	18.2	18.3
Minnesota........	10.0	7.3	5.6	5.1	9.6	6.7	4.8	4.5	20.0	23.7	14.6	10.6
Mississippi........	17.0	12.1	10.7	11.4	11.1	7.4	6.8	6.6	23.7	16.2	15.3	17.2
Missouri.........	12.4	9.4	7.2	7.5	11.1	7.9	5.9	6.4	20.7	18.2	14.7	14.6
Montana	12.4	9.0	6.1	7.0	11.8	6.0	5.5	6.7	(NA)	(B)	(B)	(B)
Nebraska	11.5	8.3	7.3	5.6	10.7	6.9	6.4	5.2	25.2	18.9	20.3	(B)
Nevada..........	10.7	8.4	6.5	5.8	10.0	8.2	6.0	5.2	20.6	14.2	12.7	13.7
New Hampshire	9.9	7.1	5.7	5.3	9.9	6.0	5.5	5.0	22.5	(B)	(B)	(B)
New Jersey	12.5	9.0	6.3	5.2	10.3	6.4	5.0	4.0	21.9	18.4	13.6	11.0
New Mexico........	11.5	9.0	6.6	6.1	11.3	7.6	6.3	5.6	23.1	(B)	(B)	(B)
New York	12.5	9.6	6.4	5.8	10.8	7.4	5.4	5.0	20.0	18.1	10.9	9.3
North Carolina	14.5	10.6	8.6	8.8	12.1	8.0	6.3	6.5	20.0	16.5	15.7	16.4
North Dakota	12.1	8.0	8.1	6.0	11.7	7.2	7.5	5.8	27.5	(B)	(B)	(B)
Ohio............	12.8	9.8	7.6	8.3	11.2	7.8	6.3	6.7	23.0	19.5	15.4	16.9
Oklahoma	12.7	9.2	8.5	8.1	12.1	9.1	7.9	7.3	21.8	14.3	16.9	15.4
Oregon..........	12.2	8.3	5.6	5.9	12.2	7.0	5.5	5.9	15.9	(B)	(B)	(B)
Pennsylvania	13.2	9.6	7.1	7.3	11.9	7.4	5.8	6.2	23.1	20.5	15.7	14.1
Rhode Island	11.0	8.1	6.3	6.5	10.9	7.0	5.9	5.8	(B)	(B)	(B)	(B)
South Carolina.......	15.6	11.7	8.7	9.4	10.8	8.1	5.4	7.1	22.9	17.3	14.8	13.8
South Dakota.......	10.9	10.1	5.5	7.2	9.0	8.0	4.3	6.0	(NA)	(B)	(B)	(B)
Tennessee.........	13.5	10.3	9.1	8.9	11.9	7.3	6.8	7.4	19.3	17.9	18.0	14.0
Texas...........	12.2	8.1	5.7	6.6	11.2	6.7	5.1	5.7	18.8	14.7	11.4	14.1
Utah............	10.4	7.5	5.2	4.5	10.5	6.0	5.1	4.4	27.3	(B)	(B)	(B)
Vermont	10.7	6.4	6.0	6.5	10.7	5.9	6.1	6.2	(B)	(B)	(B)	(B)
Virginia..........	13.6	10.2	6.9	7.5	11.9	7.4	5.4	5.8	19.8	19.5	12.4	14.1
Washington	11.8	7.8	5.2	5.1	11.5	7.3	4.9	4.8	16.4	20.6	9.4	10.9
West Virginia	11.8	9.9	7.6	8.1	11.4	8.1	7.4	7.9	21.5	(B)	(B)	(B)
Wisconsin.........	10.3	8.2	6.6	6.6	9.7	7.7	5.5	5.4	18.5	19.0	17.2	17.7
Wyoming..........	9.8	8.6	6.7	6.8	9.3	7.5	6.5	6.9	25.9	(B)	(B)	(B)
Puerto Rico	(NA)	(NA)	9.7	9.2	(NA)	(NA)	10.2	10.0	(NA)	(NA)	(B)	(B)
Virgin Islands	(NA)	(NA)	13.4	(B)	(NA)	(NA)	(B)	(B)	(B)	(B)	(B)	(B)
Guam	(NA)	(NA)	5.8	10.7	(NA)	(NA)	(B)	(B)	(B)	(B)	(B)	(B)
American Samoa....	(NA)	(NA)	(B)	(B)	(B)	(B)	(B)	(B)	(B)	(B)	(B)	(B)
Northern Marianas...	(NA)	(NA)	(B)	(B)	(B)	(B)	(B)	(B)	(B)	(B)	(B)	(B)

B Base figure too small to meet statistical standards for reliability.   NA Not available.   [1] Includes other races, not shown separately.

Source: U.S. National Center for Health Statistics, *Vital Statistics of the United States,* annual; and *National Vital Statistics Reports (NVSR), Deaths: Final Data for 2005* Vol. 56, No. 10, April 21, 2008; and earlier reports.

Table 112. Age-Adjusted Death Rates by Major Causes: 1960 to 2005

[Rates per 100,000 population; see headnote, Table 104. Beginning 1999, deaths classified according to tenth revision of International Classification of Diseases; for earlier years, causes of death were classified according to the revisions then in use. Changes in classification of causes of death due to these revisions may result in discontinuities in cause-of-death trends. See Appendix III]

Year	Diseases of heart	Malignant neoplasms (cancer)	Cerebrovascular diseases	Chronic lower respiratory diseases	Accidents [1]	Diabetes mellitus	Influenza and pneumonia	Nephritis, nephrotic syndrome, and nephrosis	Septicemia	Intentional self-harm (suicide)
1960	559.0	193.9	177.9	12.5	63.1	22.5	53.7	10.6	1.2	12.5
1961	545.3	193.4	173.1	12.6	60.6	22.1	43.4	10.0	1.2	12.2
1962	556.9	193.3	174.0	14.2	62.9	22.6	47.1	9.6	1.3	12.8
1963	563.4	194.7	173.9	16.5	64.0	23.1	55.6	9.2	1.5	13.0
1964	543.3	193.6	167.0	16.3	64.1	22.5	45.4	8.9	1.5	12.7
1965	542.5	195.6	166.4	18.3	65.8	22.9	46.8	8.3	1.5	13.0
1966	541.2	196.5	165.8	19.2	67.6	23.6	47.9	7.9	1.6	12.7
1967	524.7	197.3	159.3	19.2	66.2	23.4	42.2	7.3	1.6	12.5
1968	531.0	198.8	162.5	20.7	65.5	25.3	52.8	6.1	1.7	12.4
1969	516.8	198.5	155.4	20.9	64.9	25.1	47.9	6.0	1.7	12.7
1970	492.7	198.6	147.7	21.3	62.2	24.3	41.7	5.5	2.0	13.1
1971	492.9	199.3	147.6	21.8	60.3	23.9	38.4	5.2	2.2	13.1
1972	490.2	200.3	147.3	22.8	60.2	23.7	41.3	5.2	2.4	13.3
1973	482.0	200.0	145.2	23.6	59.3	23.0	41.2	5.0	2.6	13.1
1974	458.8	201.5	136.8	23.2	52.7	22.1	35.5	4.7	3.0	13.2
1975	431.2	200.1	123.5	23.7	50.8	20.3	34.9	4.7	3.1	13.6
1976	426.9	202.5	117.4	24.9	48.7	19.5	38.8	4.9	3.5	13.2
1977	413.7	203.5	110.4	24.7	48.8	18.2	31.0	4.8	3.8	13.7
1978	409.9	204.9	103.7	26.3	48.9	18.3	34.5	4.8	4.2	12.9
1979	401.6	204.0	97.1	25.5	46.5	17.5	26.1	8.6	4.3	12.6
1980	412.1	207.9	96.4	28.3	46.4	18.1	31.4	9.1	5.0	12.2
1981	397.0	206.4	89.5	29.0	43.4	17.6	30.0	9.1	5.4	12.3
1982	389.0	208.3	84.2	29.1	40.1	17.2	26.5	9.4	5.9	12.5
1983	388.9	209.1	81.2	31.6	39.1	17.6	29.8	9.6	6.7	12.4
1984	378.8	210.8	78.7	32.4	38.8	17.2	30.6	10.0	7.4	12.6
1985	375.0	211.3	76.6	34.5	38.5	17.4	34.5	10.4	8.3	12.5
1986	365.1	211.5	73.1	34.8	38.6	17.2	34.8	10.4	9.0	13.0
1987	355.9	211.7	71.6	35.0	38.2	17.4	33.8	10.4	9.3	12.8
1988	352.5	212.5	70.6	36.5	38.9	18.0	37.3	10.4	9.7	12.5
1989	332.0	214.2	66.9	36.6	37.7	20.5	35.9	9.6	8.8	12.3
1990	321.8	216.0	65.3	37.2	36.3	20.7	36.8	9.3	8.6	12.5
1991	312.5	215.2	62.9	37.9	34.7	20.7	34.7	9.3	8.6	12.3
1992	304.0	213.5	61.5	37.7	33.2	20.7	32.8	9.4	8.4	12.0
1993	308.1	213.5	62.7	40.7	34.2	21.9	35.0	9.7	8.6	12.1
1994	297.5	211.7	62.6	40.3	34.2	22.6	33.6	9.4	8.3	11.9
1995	293.4	209.9	63.1	40.1	34.4	23.2	33.4	9.5	8.4	11.8
1996	285.7	206.7	62.5	40.6	34.5	23.8	32.9	9.6	8.4	11.5
1997	277.7	203.4	61.1	41.1	34.2	23.7	33.3	9.8	8.6	11.2
1998	267.4	202.1	62.8	43.8	35.6	24.2	24.2	9.8	8.9	11.1
1999	266.5	200.8	61.6	45.4	35.3	25.0	23.5	13.0	11.3	10.5
2000	257.6	199.6	60.9	44.2	34.9	25.0	23.7	13.5	11.3	10.4
2001	247.8	196.0	57.9	43.7	35.7	25.3	22.0	14.0	11.4	10.7
2002	240.8	193.5	56.2	43.5	36.9	25.4	22.6	14.2	11.7	10.9
2003	232.3	190.1	53.5	43.3	37.3	25.3	22.0	14.4	11.6	10.8
2004	217.0	185.8	50.0	41.1	37.7	24.5	19.8	14.2	11.2	10.9
2005	211.1	183.8	46.6	43.2	39.1	24.6	20.3	14.3	11.2	10.9

[1] Unintentional injuries.

Source: U.S. National Center for Health Statistics, *Health, United States, 2007* annual. See <http://www.cdc.gov/nchs/hus.htm> and *National Vital Statistics Reports (NVSR), Deaths: Final Data for 2005, annual;* Vol. 56, No. 10, April 24, 2008; and unpublished data.

U.S. Census Bureau, Statistical Abstract of the United States: 2009

Table 113. **Deaths and Death Rates by Selected Causes: 2004 and 2005**

[**Rates per 100,000 population.** Figures are weighted data rounded to the nearest individual, so categories may not add to total or subtotal. Excludes deaths of nonresidents of the United States. Deaths classified according to tenth revision of International Classification of Diseases. See also Appendix III]

Cause of death	2004			2005		
	Number	Rate	Age-adjusted rate [1]	Number	Rate	Age-adjusted rate [1]
All causes [2]	**2,397,615**	**816.5**	**800.8**	**2,448,017**	**825.9**	**798.8**
Major cardiovascular diseases [2]	861,190	293.3	286.5	856,030	288.8	277.3
Diseases of heart	652,486	222.2	217.0	652,091	220.0	211.1
Acute rheumatic fever and chronic rheumatic heart disease	3,254	1.1	1.1	3,365	1.1	1.1
Hypertensive heart disease	28,585	9.7	9.5	29,282	9.9	9.4
Hypertensive heart and renal disease	3,046	1.0	1.0	3,172	1.1	1.0
Ischemic heart disease	451,326	153.7	150.2	445,687	150.4	144.4
Acute myocardial infarction	156,816	53.4	52.2	151,004	50.9	49.1
Essential (primary) hypertension and hypertensive renal disease	23,076	7.9	7.7	24,902	8.4	8.0
Cerebrovascular diseases	150,074	51.1	50.0	143,579	48.4	46.6
Atherosclerosis	11,861	4.0	3.9	11,841	4.0	3.8
Malignant neoplasms [2]	553,888	188.6	185.8	559,312	188.7	183.8
Malignant neoplasms of lip, oral cavity, and pharynx	7,826	2.7	2.6	7,773	2.6	2.5
Malignant neoplasms of esophagus	13,023	4.4	4.3	13,499	4.6	4.4
Malignant neoplasms of stomach	11,859	4.0	4.0	11,514	3.9	3.8
Malignant neoplasms of colon, rectum, and anus	53,772	18.3	18.0	53,252	18.0	17.5
Malignant neoplasms of liver and intrahepatic bile ducts	15,321	5.2	5.1	16,076	5.4	5.2
Malignant neoplasms of pancreas	31,772	10.8	10.6	32,760	11.1	10.8
Malignant neoplasms of trachea, bronchus, and lung	158,091	53.8	53.2	159,292	53.7	52.6
Malignant melanoma of skin	7,952	2.7	2.7	8,345	2.8	2.7
Malignant neoplasm of breast	41,316	14.1	13.8	41,491	14.0	13.5
Malignant neoplasm of ovary	14,716	5.0	4.9	14,787	5.0	4.8
Malignant neoplasm of prostate	29,004	9.9	9.8	28,905	9.8	9.5
Malignant neoplasms of kidney and renal pelvis	12,313	4.2	4.1	12,517	4.2	4.1
Malignant neoplasms of bladder	13,030	4.4	4.4	13,253	4.5	4.3
Malignant neoplasms of meninges, brain, and other parts of central nervous system	12,829	4.4	4.3	13,152	4.4	4.3
Malignant neoplasms of lymphoid, hematopoietic, and related tissue [2]	54,645	18.6	18.4	55,028	18.6	18.2
Non-Hodgkins' lymphoma	20,938	7.1	7.0	20,873	7.0	6.9
Leukemia	21,395	7.3	7.2	21,623	7.3	7.1
Accidents (unintentional injuries) [2]	112,012	38.1	37.7	117,809	39.7	39.1
Motor vehicle accidents	44,933	15.3	15.2	45,343	15.3	15.2
Falls	18,807	6.4	6.3	19,656	6.6	6.4
Accidental drowning and submersion	3,308	1.1	1.1	3,582	1.2	1.2
Accidental exposure to smoke, fire, and flames	3,229	1.1	1.1	3,197	1.1	1.1
Accidental poisoning and exposure to noxious substances	20,950	7.1	7.1	23,618	8.0	7.9
Chronic lower respiratory diseases	121,987	41.5	41.1	130,933	44.2	43.2
Emphysema	13,639	4.6	4.6	14,002	4.7	4.6
Asthma	3,816	1.3	1.3	3,884	1.3	1.3
Other chronic lower respiratory diseases	103,759	35.3	35.0	112,181	37.8	37.0
Influenza and pneumonia [2]	59,664	20.3	19.8	63,001	21.3	20.3
Pneumonia	58,564	19.9	19.4	61,189	20.6	19.7
Septicemia	33,373	11.4	11.2	34,136	11.5	11.2
Human immunodeficiency virus (HIV) disease	13,063	4.4	4.5	12,543	4.2	4.2
Anemias	4,575	1.6	1.5	4,624	1.6	1.5
Diabetes mellitus	73,138	24.9	24.5	75,119	25.3	24.6
Parkinson's disease	17,989	6.1	6.1	19,544	6.6	6.4
Alzheimer's disease	65,965	22.5	21.8	71,599	24.2	22.9
Chronic liver disease and cirrhosis	27,013	9.2	9.0	27,530	9.3	9.0
Cholelithiasis and other disorders of gallbladder	3,086	1.1	1.0	3,072	1.0	1.0
Nephritis, nephrotic syndrome, and nephrosis [2]	42,480	14.5	14.2	43,901	14.8	14.3
Renal failure	41,732	14.2	13.9	42,868	14.5	14.0
Intentional self-harm (suicide)	32,439	11.0	10.9	32,637	11.0	10.9
Intentional self-harm (suicide) by discharge of firearms	16,750	5.7	5.6	17,002	5.7	5.7
Intentional self-harm (suicide) by other and unspecified means and their sequelae	15,689	5.3	5.3	15,635	5.3	5.2
Assault (homicide)	17,357	5.9	5.9	18,124	6.1	6.1
Events of undetermined intent	4,976	1.7	1.7	4,742	1.6	1.6
Injury by firearms [3]	29,569	10.1	10.0	30,694	10.4	10.2
Drug-induced deaths [3]	30,711	10.5	10.4	33,541	11.3	11.3
Alcohol-induced deaths [3]	21,081	7.2	7.0	21,634	7.3	7.0
Injury at work	5,157	2.2	2.2	5,113	2.2	2.1

[1] See headnote, Table 104.   [2] Includes other causes not shown separately.   [3] Included in selected categories.

Source: U.S. National Center for Health Statistics, *National Vital Statistics Reports (NVSR), Deaths: Final Data for 2005*, Vol. 56, No. 10, April 24, 2008.

Table 114. Deaths by Age and Selected Causes: 2005

[Deaths are classified according to the Tenth Revision of the International Classification of Diseases. See Appendix III]

Cause of death	All ages[1]	Under 1 year	1 to 4 years	5 to 14 years	15 to 24 years	25 to 34 years	35 to 44 years	45 to 54 years	55 to 64 years	65 to 74 years	75 to 84 years	85 years and over
All causes[2]	2,448,017	28,440	4,756	6,602	34,234	41,925	84,785	183,530	275,301	398,355	686,665	703,169
Septicemia	34,136	302	85	81	148	311	840	2,211	3,912	6,073	10,626	9,544
Human immunodeficiency virus (HIV) disease	12,543	2	2	13	159	1,318	4,363	4,516	1,612	438	104	15
Malignant neoplasms[2]	559,312	75	377	1,000	1,717	3,601	14,566	50,405	99,240	138,446	166,421	83,455
Malignant neoplasm of esophagus	13,499	-	-	1	3	35	316	1,510	3,100	3,682	3,581	1,271
Malignant neoplasms of colon, rectum, and anus	53,252	1	-	4	47	305	1,297	4,343	8,153	11,792	16,254	11,054
Malignant neoplasms of liver and intrahepatic bile ducts	16,076	8	21	16	30	89	380	2,515	3,438	3,747	4,176	1,655
Malignant neoplasm of pancreas	32,760	1	-	2	3	64	565	2,744	5,984	8,288	10,147	4,962
Malignant neoplasms of trachea, bronchus, and lung	159,292	-	3	1	16	133	2,323	12,624	31,363	48,390	49,032	15,404
Malignant neoplasm of breast	41,491	1	-	-	12	356	2,497	6,232	8,646	8,113	9,382	6,252
Malignant neoplasm of ovary	14,787	-	-	-	18	3	413	1,682	3,048	3,569	4,031	1,940
Malignant neoplasm of prostate	28,905	-	-	-	-	-	24	395	2,154	5,764	11,666	8,897
Malignant neoplasm of bladder	13,253	-	1	3	1	15	122	523	1,482	2,772	4,859	3,480
Malignant neoplasms of lymphoid, hematopoietic and related tissue[2]	55,028	24	128	335	655	811	1,498	3,687	7,623	12,487	18,109	9,671
Non-Hodgkins lymphoma	20,873	1	6	48	127	222	566	1,410	2,925	4,626	7,111	3,831
Leukemia	21,623	22	120	275	466	461	680	1,419	2,662	4,673	6,832	4,013
In situ neoplasms, benign neoplasms, and neoplasms of uncertain or unknown behavior	13,710	59	52	76	93	162	368	729	1,318	2,350	4,594	3,909
Diabetes mellitus	75,119	1	2	38	202	617	2,045	5,691	11,301	16,183	23,136	15,903
Parkinson's disease	19,544	-	-	-	3	4	7	66	434	2,414	9,294	7,322
Alzheimer's disease	71,599	-	-	-	-	-	10	80	648	3,813	23,139	43,906
Major cardiovascular diseases[2]	856,030	503	217	367	1,391	4,041	15,852	46,928	79,896	124,366	256,362	326,066
Diseases of heart	652,091	358	151	252	1,119	3,249	12,688	38,103	65,208	96,729	190,693	243,504
Hypertensive heart disease	29,282	2	7	3	36	328	1,368	3,293	3,954	3,806	6,370	10,119
Ischemic heart diseases	445,687	13	7	14	151	1,014	6,860	25,310	46,799	70,121	134,435	160,935
Acute myocardial infarction	151,004	11	2	7	68	392	2,734	10,070	18,553	26,674	45,449	47,041
Essential (primary) hypertension and hypertensive renal disease	24,902	2	-	3	22	84	406	1,166	1,954	3,306	7,256	10,703
Cerebrovascular diseases	143,579	126	62	95	196	546	2,260	6,381	10,028	18,839	46,859	58,183
Influenza and pneumonia	63,001	265	110	106	172	354	934	2,183	3,422	6,623	18,563	30,267
Chronic lower respiratory diseases[2]	130,933	33	56	104	148	258	890	3,977	12,747	29,910	50,333	32,473
Emphysema	14,002	2	1	-	-	8	77	444	1,677	3,749	5,400	2,643
Pneumonitis due to solids and liquids	17,279	17	8	13	43	66	172	476	833	1,741	5,558	8,352
Chronic liver disease and cirrhosis	27,530	10	1	2	23	311	2,688	7,517	7,126	5,066	3,781	1,002
Nephritis, nephrotic syndrome, and nephrosis[2]	43,901	159	16	23	91	285	742	2,028	4,141	7,320	14,403	14,693
Renal failure	42,868	151	13	19	79	261	705	1,973	4,025	7,165	14,102	14,375
Certain conditions originating in the perinatal period[2]	14,549	14,423	58	26	18	18	6	6	2	-	1	-
Accidents (unintentional injuries)[2]	117,809	1,083	1,664	2,415	15,753	13,997	16,919	18,339	10,853	8,632	13,854	14,243
Motor vehicle accidents	45,343	146	617	1,447	10,908	7,239	6,748	6,397	4,454	3,110	2,991	1,280
Falls	19,656	16	34	32	236	295	607	1,181	1,451	2,319	5,957	7,526
Accidental poisoning and exposure to noxious substances	23,618	20	21	51	2,484	4,386	6,729	6,983	2,007	435	317	179
Intentional self-harm (suicide)	32,637	(X)	(X)	272	4,212	4,990	6,550	6,991	4,210	2,344	2,200	860
By discharge of firearms	17,002	(X)	(X)	84	1,962	2,269	2,855	3,472	2,470	1,669	1,649	571
By other and unspecified means and their sequelae	15,635	(X)	(X)	188	2,250	2,721	3,695	3,519	1,740	675	551	289
Assault (homicide)	18,124	306	375	341	5,466	4,752	3,109	2,060	862	440	283	109

- Represents zero.   X Not applicable.   [1] Includes persons with age not stated, not shown separately.   [2] Includes other causes, not shown separately.

Source: U.S. National Center for Health Statistics, National Vital Statistics Reports (NVSR), Deaths: Final Data for 2005, Vol. 56, No. 10, April 24, 2008.

Births, Deaths, Marriages, and Divorces   85

Table 115. Deaths and Death Rates by Leading Causes of Death and Age: 2005

[**Rates per 100,000 population in specified group**. Data are based on the tenth revision of the International Classification of Diseases (ICD). Numbers are based on weighted data rounded to the nearest individual, so categories may not add to totals. See Appendix III]

Age and cause of death	Number	Rate	Age and cause of death	Number	Rate
ALL AGES [1]			Malignant neoplasms	14,566	33.2
			Diseases of heart	12,688	28.9
All causes	**2,448,017**	**825.9**	Intentional self-harm (suicide)	6,550	14.9
Diseases of heart	652,091	220.0	Human immunodeficiency virus (HIV)		
Malignant neoplasms	559,312	188.7	disease	4,363	9.9
Cerebrovascular diseases	143,579	48.4	Assault (homicide)	3,109	7.1
Chronic lower respiratory diseases . . .	130,933	44.2	Chronic liver disease and cirrhosis . . .	2,688	6.1
Accidents (unintentional injuries)	117,809	39.7	Cerebrovascular diseases	2,260	5.2
Diabetes mellitus	75,119	25.3	Diabetes mellitus	2,045	4.7
Alzheimer's disease	71,599	24.2	Chronic lower respiratory diseases . . .	890	2.0
Influenza and pneumonia	63,001	21.3			
Nephritis, nephrotic syndrome, and			**45 TO 54 YEARS**		
nephrosis	43,901	14.8	**All causes . . . .**	**183,530**	**432.0**
Septicemia	34,136	11.5	Malignant neoplasms	50,405	118.6
			Diseases of heart	38,103	89.7
1 TO 4 YEARS			Accidents	18,339	43.2
All causes	**4,756**	**29.4**	Chronic liver disease and cirrhosis . . .	7,517	17.7
Accidents (unintentional injuries)	1,664	10.3	Intentional self-harm (suicide)	6,991	16.5
Congenital malformations,			Cerebrovascular diseases	6,381	15.0
deformations, and chromosomal			Diabetes mellitus	5,691	13.4
abnormalities	522	3.2	Human immunodeficiency virus (HIV)		
Malignant neoplasms	377	2.3	disease	4,516	10.6
Assault (homicide)	375	2.3	Chronic lower respiratory diseases . . .	3,977	9.4
Diseases of heart	151	0.9	Viral hepatitis	2,314	5.4
Influenza and pneumonia	110	0.7			
Septicemia	85	0.5	**55 TO 64 YEARS**		
Certain conditions originating in the			**All causes . . . .**	**275,301**	**906.9**
perinatal period [2]	58	0.4	Malignant neoplasms	99,240	326.9
In situ neoplasms [2]	52	0.3	Diseases of heart	65,208	214.8
Chronic lower respiratory diseases . . .	56	0.3	Chronic lower respiratory diseases . . .	12,747	42.0
			Diabetes mellitus	11,301	37.2
5 to 14 YEARS			Cerebrovascular diseases	10,853	35.8
All causes	**6,602**	**16.3**	Accidents (unintentional injuries)	10,028	33.0
Accidents (unintentional injuries)	2,415	6.0	Chronic liver disease and cirrhosis . . .	7,126	23.5
Malignant neoplasms	1,000	2.5	Intentional self-harm (suicide)	4,210	13.9
Congenital malformations,			Nephritis, nephrotic syndrome, and		
deformations, and chromosomal			nephrosis	4,141	13.6
abnormalities	396	1.0	Septicemia	3,912	12.9
Assault (homicide)	341	0.8			
Intentional self-harm (suicide)	272	0.7	**65 TO 74 YEARS**		
Diseases of heart	252	0.6	**All causes . . . .**	**398,355**	**2,137.1**
Influenza and pneumonia	106	0.3	Malignant neoplasms	138,446	742.7
Chronic lower respiratory diseases . . .	104	0.3	Diseases of heart	96,729	518.9
Cerebrovascular diseases	95	0.2	Chronic lower respiratory diseases . . .	29,910	160.5
			Cerebrovascular diseases	18,839	101.1
15 TO 24 YEARS			Diabetes mellitus	16,183	86.8
All causes	**34,234**	**81.4**	Accidents (unintentional injuries)	8,632	46.3
Accidents (unintentional injuries)	15,753	37.4	Nephritis, nephrotic syndrome, and		
Assault (homicide)	5,466	13.0	nephrosis	7,320	39.3
Intentional self-harm (suicide)	4,212	10.0	Influenza and pneumonia	6,623	35.5
Malignant neoplasms	1,717	4.1	Septicemia	6,073	32.6
Diseases of heart	1,119	2.7	Chronic liver disease and cirrhosis . . .	5,066	27.2
Congenital malformations,					
deformations, and chromosomal			**75 TO 84 YEARS**		
abnormalities	504	1.2	**All causes . . . .**	**686,665**	**5,260.0**
Cerebrovascular diseases	196	0.5	Diseases of heart	190,693	1,460.8
Influenza and pneumonia	172	0.4	Malignant neoplasms	166,421	1,274.8
Human immunodeficiency virus (HIV)			Cerebrovascular diseases	50,333	385.6
disease	159	0.4	Chronic lower respiratory diseases . . .	46,859	359.0
Chronic lower respiratory diseases . . .	148	0.4	Alzheimer's disease	23,139	177.3
			Diabetes mellitus	23,136	177.2
25 TO 34 YEARS			Influenza and pneumonia	18,563	142.2
All causes	**41,925**	**104.4**	Nephritis, nephrotic syndrome, and		
Accidents	13,997	34.9	nephrosis	14,403	110.3
Intentional self-harm (suicide)	4,990	12.4	Accidents (unintentional injuries)	13,854	106.1
Assault (homicide)	4,752	11.8	Septicemia	10,626	81.4
Malignant neoplasms	3,601	9.0			
Diseases of heart	3,249	8.1	**85 YEARS AND OVER**		
Human immunodeficiency virus (HIV)			**All causes . . . .**	**703,169**	**13,798.6**
disease	1,318	3.3	Diseases of heart	243,504	4,778.4
Diabetes mellitus	617	1.5	Malignant neoplasms	83,455	1,637.7
Cerebrovascular diseases	546	1.4	Cerebrovascular diseases	58,183	1,141.8
Congenital malformations,			Alzheimer's disease	43,906	861.6
deformations, and chromosomal			Chronic lower respiratory diseases . . .	32,473	637.2
abnormalities	436	1.1	Influenza and pneumonia	30,267	593.9
Chronic liver disease and cirrhosis . . .	311	0.8	Diabetes mellitus	15,903	312.1
			Nephritis, nephrotic syndrome, and		
35 TO 44 YEARS			nephrosis	14,693	288.3
All causes	**84,785**	**193.3**	Accidents (unintentional injuries)	14,243	279.5
Accidents	16,919	38.6	Septicemia	9,544	187.3

[1] Includes deaths under 1 year of age.   [2] Includes benign neoplasms and neoplasms of uncertain or unknown behavior.

Source: U.S. National Center for Health Statistics, *National Vital Statistics Reports (NVSR), Deaths: Final Data for 2005* Vol. 56, No. 10, April 24, 2008.

Table 116. Death Rates for Major Causes of Death—States and Island Areas: 2005

[**Deaths per 100,000 resident population estimated as of July 1.** By place of residence. Excludes nonresidents of the United States. Causes of death classified according to tenth revisions of International Classification of Diseases. See Appendix III]

State and island area	Total	Diseases of heart	Malignant neo-plasms (cancer)	Cerebro-vascular diseases	Chronic lower respira-tory diseases	Accidents Total	Accidents Motor vehicle acci-dents	Diabetes mellitus	Alz-hei-mer's dis-ease	Influ-enza and pneu-monia	Nephritis, nephrotic syndrome and nephrosis
U.S.	825.9	220.0	188.7	48.4	44.2	39.7	15.3	25.3	24.2	21.3	14.8
AL.	1,033.2	282.4	217.5	64.8	52.3	52.5	26.1	31.4	32.9	22.2	22.7
AK.	477.4	94.5	110.3	26.8	23.8	47.2	14.0	14.0	9.2	6.6	5.7
AZ.	771.6	184.6	165.3	39.8	47.5	53.0	20.2	20.3	30.8	21.8	10.2
AR.	1,009.5	272.6	228.9	66.5	56.1	47.8	25.0	29.6	24.7	31.9	22.5
CA.	656.0	179.7	151.5	43.1	36.5	30.8	12.3	21.3	21.3	20.9	6.9
CO	635.1	135.2	137.1	34.3	41.0	41.7	14.4	16.1	22.8	14.3	10.1
CT.	839.4	217.9	200.9	43.5	41.9	32.3	8.3	23.1	22.1	27.2	16.5
DE.	885.8	240.8	213.3	45.5	48.7	34.7	14.1	27.6	21.3	19.2	15.2
DC.	996.0	275.7	209.1	42.0	24.0	37.6	6.9	34.9	20.3	17.8	12.4
FL.	960.0	260.1	228.2	52.6	53.3	49.8	19.8	29.2	25.9	15.8	13.6
GA	735.6	185.0	158.3	42.5	37.6	41.5	18.6	19.2	19.2	17.6	16.8
HI	716.4	181.9	170.1	54.0	22.5	34.2	11.1	17.1	15.1	18.9	11.8
ID	738.6	171.4	165.7	50.2	50.2	42.4	19.8	20.9	28.5	20.2	7.7
IL	814.6	221.1	190.0	49.0	39.7	32.8	11.5	23.8	22.1	23.1	18.8
IN	887.7	231.9	204.0	52.6	55.3	39.5	15.5	27.4	26.3	21.0	20.5
IA	937.6	250.7	217.5	64.1	57.4	40.5	15.8	24.5	36.5	30.2	8.4
KS.	899.3	217.1	197.8	57.2	57.1	41.9	18.1	25.9	33.2	26.6	18.8
KY.	963.8	258.4	227.8	51.9	61.8	57.6	24.0	28.4	27.5	24.5	21.9
LA.	980.5	243.3	204.5	54.6	42.1	67.9	22.7	37.5	31.1	22.0	26.2
ME	973.7	222.5	243.5	52.4	62.8	43.8	14.5	29.1	36.0	26.6	18.9
MD	783.7	207.0	185.2	44.2	34.1	24.6	11.2	24.8	17.1	21.3	13.4
MA	841.9	207.5	206.0	46.5	41.4	29.8	7.6	19.9	25.6	30.2	22.0
MI	858.3	248.3	198.5	50.0	44.1	34.1	12.2	28.1	23.3	19.3	16.6
MN	731.3	154.4	171.9	46.3	38.3	37.4	12.5	24.5	25.7	16.5	13.0
MS	999.5	295.7	207.6	55.5	50.4	66.3	33.0	23.2	24.7	22.1	22.8
MO	942.3	258.2	214.1	57.7	53.2	49.1	20.7	26.7	28.2	26.3	19.9
MT	911.4	198.3	209.0	55.8	62.0	56.0	25.2	30.5	28.5	22.8	11.6
NE.	850.8	207.0	190.8	56.1	54.0	40.0	16.3	25.5	26.9	21.0	13.9
NV.	788.0	210.9	175.5	39.1	50.8	45.7	19.0	13.9	12.8	18.8	18.1
NH	778.2	193.1	194.6	37.9	48.1	36.4	12.4	23.7	28.7	20.8	13.2
NJ.	825.5	236.9	197.0	41.5	36.1	29.4	8.7	29.1	20.8	18.8	18.3
NM	777.0	178.1	162.9	37.9	44.3	65.7	23.9	30.9	17.0	18.3	12.4
NY.	791.6	270.0	184.7	34.4	35.4	24.1	7.9	21.0	10.7	28.7	12.3
NC	859.6	204.6	192.6	56.0	47.8	47.5	19.2	26.0	27.8	21.1	18.0
ND	902.2	237.5	204.5	57.8	42.7	45.1	20.4	32.0	45.1	27.0	10.5
OH	951.1	253.0	215.5	54.8	57.4	38.7	12.2	33.1	30.3	21.1	16.6
OK	1,019.8	283.1	209.9	63.0	66.7	56.5	23.5	34.3	28.5	26.7	15.9
OR	853.9	186.5	201.2	62.9	50.5	40.3	14.1	31.6	34.0	16.9	8.1
PA.	1,042.1	291.3	238.3	61.5	49.5	43.8	14.2	28.6	27.6	24.7	25.0
RI	929.9	279.2	213.0	49.5	48.6	31.0	8.1	26.2	27.7	23.5	14.5
SC.	909.7	219.9	203.3	57.8	46.5	53.4	25.2	27.9	30.9	18.1	19.3
SD.	913.2	228.9	207.7	65.9	56.7	51.8	22.7	31.1	37.4	31.1	7.1
TN.	960.3	250.6	217.9	61.4	53.4	52.8	21.9	30.9	34.1	26.6	12.1
TX.	684.4	175.6	150.0	41.0	34.9	37.6	16.5	24.5	20.2	16.0	11.9
UT.	543.9	116.3	102.0	32.2	24.0	30.1	12.9	21.9	14.9	13.5	7.2
VT.	813.1	198.1	192.9	41.7	61.2	43.7	13.2	27.8	29.5	15.6	8.3
VA.	764.5	187.5	183.4	48.6	38.3	34.9	12.8	21.7	20.5	19.3	16.9
WA	734.8	174.7	175.7	46.0	42.9	40.4	12.1	24.7	36.7	14.7	7.2
WV	1,143.7	304.8	254.1	63.4	74.3	51.7	22.2	42.2	27.7	25.2	24.3
WI	843.7	213.9	197.7	53.5	44.2	45.0	15.7	23.0	27.3	22.9	16.8
WY	804.8	186.9	174.0	43.4	57.1	59.3	30.4	25.5	21.6	23.4	13.0
PR	754.9	156.2	123.6	39.0	31.1	28.6	10.9	71.3	35.7	27.6	24.1
VI	609.9	188.6	114.1	34.0	(S)	22.1	(S)	38.6	(S)	(S)	(S)
GU.	401.6	123.4	56.4	36.8	12.5	26.7	14.8	20.2	(S)	(S)	(S)
AS	436.1	72.1	57.7	36.9	33.7	(S)	(S)	51.3	(S)	(S)	(S)
MP.	231.5	52.3	33.6	(S)	(S)	(S)	(S)	(S)	(S)	(S)	(S)

S Figure does not meet standards of reliability or precision.

Source: U.S. National Center for Health Statistics, *National Vital Statistics Reports (NVSR), Deaths: Final Data for 2005*, Vol. 56, No. 10, April 24, 2008.

U.S. Census Bureau, Statistical Abstract of the United States: 2009

Table 117. Death Rates from Heart Disease by Selected Characteristics: 1980 to 2005

[Rates per 100,000 population. See headnote, Tables 104 and 112. See Appendix III]

Characteristic	1980	1990	1995	2000	2001	2002	2003	2004	2005
Total, age adjusted.......	412.1	321.8	293.4	257.6	247.8	240.8	232.3	217.0	211.1
Total, crude............	336.0	289.5	277.0	252.6	245.8	241.7	235.6	222.2	220.0
Under 1 year.............	22.8	20.1	17.4	13.0	11.9	12.4	11.0	10.3	8.7
1 to 4 years..............	2.6	1.9	1.6	1.2	1.5	1.1	1.2	1.2	0.9
5 to 14 years.............	0.9	0.9	0.8	0.7	0.7	0.6	0.6	0.6	0.6
15 to 24 years............	2.9	2.5	2.8	2.6	2.5	2.5	2.7	2.5	2.7
25 to 34 years............	8.3	7.6	8.2	7.4	8.0	7.9	8.2	7.9	8.1
35 to 44 years............	44.6	31.4	31.8	29.2	29.6	30.5	30.7	29.3	28.9
45 to 54 years............	180.2	120.5	109.6	94.2	92.9	93.7	92.5	90.2	89.7
55 to 64 years............	494.1	367.3	320.1	261.2	246.9	241.5	233.2	218.8	214.8
65 to 74 years............	1,218.6	894.3	795.4	665.6	635.1	615.9	585.0	541.6	518.9
75 to 84 years............	2,993.1	2,295.7	2,050.5	1,780.3	1,725.7	1,677.2	1,611.1	1,506.3	1,460.8
85 years and over	7,777.1	6,739.9	6,391.5	5,926.1	5,664.2	5,446.8	5,278.4	4,895.9	4,778.4
Male, age adjusted	**538.9**	**412.4**	**371.0**	**320.0**	**305.4**	**297.4**	**286.6**	**267.9**	**260.9**
White......................	539.6	409.2	367.0	316.7	301.8	294.1	282.9	264.6	258.0
Black......................	561.4	485.4	451.3	392.5	384.5	371.0	364.3	342.1	329.8
American Indian, Alaska Native...	320.5	264.1	256.4	222.2	200.7	201.2	203.2	182.7	173.2
Asian, Pacific Islander..........	286.9	220.7	214.5	185.5	169.8	169.8	158.3	146.5	141.1
Hispanic origin [1]............	(NA)	270.0	260.8	238.2	232.6	219.8	206.8	193.9	192.4
Non-Hispanic, White [1].........	(NA)	413.6	369.1	319.9	304.8	297.7	286.9	268.7	262.2
Male, crude.............	**368.6**	**297.6**	**278.5**	**249.8**	**242.5**	**240.7**	**235.0**	**222.8**	**221.1**
Under 1 year...............	25.5	21.9	17.7	13.3	11.8	12.9	12.1	10.9	9.4
1 to 4 years..............	2.8	1.9	1.7	1.4	1.5	1.1	1.1	1.1	1.0
5 to 14 years.............	1.0	0.9	0.8	0.8	0.7	0.7	0.7	0.6	0.6
15 to 24 years............	3.7	3.1	3.5	3.2	3.2	3.3	3.4	3.2	3.6
25 to 34 years............	11.4	10.3	11.0	9.6	10.3	10.5	10.5	10.5	10.8
35 to 44 years............	68.7	48.1	46.9	41.4	41.7	43.1	42.8	40.9	40.7
45 to 54 years............	282.6	183.0	166.1	140.2	136.6	138.4	136.2	132.3	131.5
55 to 64 years............	746.8	537.3	460.1	371.7	349.8	343.4	331.7	312.8	306.9
65 to 74 years............	1,728.0	1,250.0	1,095.3	898.3	851.3	827.1	785.3	723.8	692.3
75 to 84 years............	3,834.3	2,968.2	2,622.9	2,248.1	2,177.3	2,110.1	2,030.3	1,893.6	1,829.4
85 years and over	8,752.7	7,418.4	6,993.5	6,430.0	6,040.5	5,823.5	5,621.5	5,239.3	5,143.4
Female, age adjusted.......	**320.8**	**257.0**	**236.6**	**210.9**	**203.9**	**197.2**	**190.3**	**177.3**	**172.3**
White......................	315.9	250.9	230.8	205.6	198.7	192.1	185.4	172.9	168.2
Black......................	378.6	327.5	304.0	277.6	269.8	263.2	253.8	236.5	228.3
American Indian, Alaska Native...	175.4	153.1	164.8	143.6	127.0	123.6	127.5	119.9	115.9
Asian, Pacific Islander..........	132.3	149.2	137.6	115.7	112.9	108.1	104.2	96.1	91.9
Hispanic origin [1]............	(NA)	177.2	173.8	163.7	161.0	149.7	145.8	130.0	129.1
Non-Hispanic, White [1].........	(NA)	252.6	231.5	206.8	200.0	193.7	187.1	175.1	170.3
Female, crude.............	**305.1**	**281.8**	**275.5**	**255.3**	**249.0**	**242.7**	**236.2**	**221.6**	**218.9**
Under 1 year...............	20.0	18.3	17.0	12.5	12.0	11.8	9.8	9.7	8.0
1 to 4 years..............	2.5	1.9	1.5	1.0	1.4	1.0	1.3	1.2	0.9
5 to 14 years.............	0.9	0.8	0.7	0.5	0.7	0.6	0.5	0.6	0.6
15 to 24 years............	2.1	1.8	2.1	2.1	1.8	1.7	2.1	1.7	1.7
25 to 34 years............	5.3	5.0	5.4	5.2	5.6	5.2	5.7	5.2	5.3
35 to 44 years............	21.4	15.1	17.0	17.2	17.6	18.0	18.6	17.7	17.1
45 to 54 years............	84.5	61.0	55.4	49.8	50.7	50.6	50.2	49.6	49.2
55 to 64 years............	272.1	215.7	192.6	159.3	151.8	147.2	141.9	131.5	129.1
65 to 74 years............	828.6	616.8	554.9	474.0	455.9	440.1	417.5	388.6	372.7
75 to 84 years............	2,497.0	1,893.8	1,692.7	1,475.1	1,428.9	1,389.7	1,331.1	1,245.6	1,210.5
85 years and over	7,350.5	6,478.1	6,159.6	5,720.9	5,506.8	5,283.3	5,126.7	4,741.5	4,610.8

NA Not available. [1] Persons of Hispanic origin may be any race. Data for 1995 exclude data from states lacking an Hispanic-origin item on their death certificates.

Source: U.S. National Center for Health Statistics, *Health, United States, 2007*, <http://www.cdc/gov/nchs/hus.htm>.

Table 118. Death Rates from Cerebrovascular Diseases by Sex and Age: 1990 to 2005

[Rates per 100,000 population. See headnote, Tables 104 and 112. See Appendix III]

Age	Total				Male				Female			
	1990	1995	2000	2005	1990	1995	2000	2005	1990	1995	2000	2005
All ages, age adjusted .	**65.3**	**63.1**	**60.9**	**46.6**	**68.5**	**65.9**	**62.4**	**46.9**	**62.6**	**60.5**	**59.1**	**45.6**
All ages, crude	**57.8**	**59.2**	**59.6**	**48.4**	**46.7**	**47.2**	**46.9**	**38.8**	**68.4**	**70.7**	**71.8**	**57.8**
Under 1 year	3.8	5.9	3.3	3.1	4.4	6.4	3.8	3.5	3.1	5.3	2.7	2.6
1 to 4 years..........	0.3	0.4	0.3	0.4	0.3	0.4	(B)	0.5	0.3	0.3	0.4	0.3
5 to 14 years	0.2	0.2	0.2	0.2	0.2	0.2	0.2	0.3	0.2	0.1	0.2	0.2
15 to 24 years	0.6	0.5	0.5	0.5	0.7	0.5	0.5	0.4	0.6	0.4	0.5	0.5
25 to 34 years	2.2	1.7	1.5	1.4	2.1	1.8	1.5	1.5	2.2	1.6	1.5	1.2
35 to 44 years	6.4	6.5	5.8	5.2	6.8	7.0	5.8	5.2	6.1	6.0	5.7	5.1
45 to 54 years	18.7	17.4	16.0	15.0	20.5	19.5	17.5	16.5	17.0	15.3	14.5	13.6
55 to 64 years	47.9	45.6	41.0	33.0	54.3	52.7	47.2	38.5	42.2	39.1	35.3	27.9
65 to 74 years	144.2	136.2	128.6	101.1	166.6	154.7	145.0	113.6	126.7	121.4	115.1	90.5
75 to 84 years	498.0	477.1	461.3	359.0	551.1	517.7	490.8	372.9	466.2	451.8	442.1	349.5
85 years and over......	1,628.9	1,607.2	1,589.2	1,141.8	1,528.5	1,522.1	1,484.3	1,023.3	1,667.6	1,640.0	1,632.0	1,196.1

B Base figure too small to meet statistical standards for reliability.

Source: U.S. National Center for Health Statistics, *Health, United States, 2007*, <http://www.cdc.gov/nchs/hus.htm>.

Table 119. Death Rates from Malignant Neoplasms, by Selected Characteristics: 1990 to 2005

[Rates per 100,000 population. Beginning 2000, cause of death is coded according to ICD-10; for explanation, see text, this section. For explanation of age adjustment, see headnote, Table 104. See Appendix III]

Characteristic	1990	2000	2001	2002	2003	2004	2005
Total, age adjusted	216.0	199.6	196.0	193.5	190.1	185.8	183.8
Total, crude	203.2	196.5	194.4	193.2	191.5	188.6	188.7
Under 1 year old	2.3	2.4	1.6	1.8	1.9	1.8	1.8
1 to 4 years old	3.5	2.7	2.7	2.6	2.5	2.5	2.3
5 to 14 years old	3.1	2.5	2.5	2.6	2.6	2.5	2.5
15 to 24 years old	4.9	4.4	4.3	4.3	4.0	4.1	4.1
25 to 34 years old	12.6	9.8	10.1	9.7	9.4	9.1	9.0
35 to 44 years old	43.3	36.6	36.8	35.8	35.0	33.4	33.2
45 to 54 years old	158.9	127.5	126.5	123.8	122.2	119.0	118.6
55 to 64 years old	449.6	366.7	356.5	351.1	343.0	333.4	326.9
65 to 74 years old	872.3	816.3	802.8	792.1	770.3	755.1	742.7
75 to 84 years old	1,348.5	1,335.6	1,315.8	1,311.9	1,302.5	1,280.4	1,274.8
85 years old and over	1,752.9	1,819.4	1,765.6	1,723.9	1,698.2	1,653.3	1,637.7
AGE-ADJUSTED RATES							
Male	280.4	248.9	243.7	238.9	233.3	227.7	225.1
Female	175.7	167.6	164.7	163.1	160.9	157.4	156.6
White male	272.2	243.9	239.2	235.2	230.1	224.4	222.3
Black male	397.9	340.3	330.9	319.6	308.8	301.2	293.7
American Indian, Alaska Native male	145.8	155.8	155.3	141.9	139.9	147.1	147.6
Asian, Pacific Islander male	172.5	150.8	147.0	137.9	137.2	136.3	133.0
Hispanic male, [1]	174.7	171.7	168.2	161.4	156.5	151.2	152.7
Non-Hispanic, White male, [1]	276.7	247.7	243.1	239.6	234.6	229.2	227.3
White female	174.0	166.9	163.9	162.4	160.2	157.0	155.2
Black female	205.9	193.8	191.3	190.3	187.7	182.5	179.6
American Indian, Alaska Native female	106.9	108.3	114.1	112.9	105.6	108.6	105.9
Asian, Pacific Islander female	103.0	100.7	99.3	95.9	96.7	92.0	94.5
Hispanic female, [1]	111.9	110.8	108.6	106.1	105.9	101.4	101.9
Non-Hispanic, White female, [1]	177.5	170.0	167.2	165.9	163.8	160.9	159.1
DEATH RATES FOR MALIGNANT NEOPLASM OF BREASTS FOR FEMALES							
All ages, age adjusted	33.3	29.4	28.2	27.6	26.6	24.4	24.1
All ages, crude	34.0	31.3	30.1	29.7	28.9	27.5	27.3
Under 25 years old	(B)	(B)	(B)	(B)	(B)	(B)	(B)
25 to 34 years old	2.9	2.6	2.5	2.5	2.2	2.0	1.8
35 to 44 years old	17.8	14.1	13.9	13.4	12.0	11.3	11.3
45 to 54 years old	45.4	38.3	37.3	35.3	32.9	29.3	28.7
55 to 64 years old	78.6	66.8	63.8	61.6	59.2	55.8	54.5
65 to 74 years old	111.7	98.3	93.3	92.4	88.9	81.6	79.2
75 to 84 years old	146.3	137.6	129.8	129.3	128.9	119.5	119.2
85 years old and over	196.8	201.7	195.3	193.4	200.8	178.6	177.9
DEATH RATES FOR MALIGNANT NEOPLASM OF TRACHEA, BRONCHUS, AND LUNG							
All ages, age adjusted	37.1	41.3	41.0	41.6	41.3	40.9	40.5
All ages, crude	39.4	45.4	45.3	46.0	46.1	45.9	45.9
Under 25 years old	(Z)	(Z)	(Z)	(Z)	(Z)	(Z)	(Z)
25 to 34 years old	0.5	0.5	0.4	0.4	0.4	0.3	0.3
35 to 44 years old	5.2	5.3	5.7	5.8	5.1	5.2	5.1
45 to 54 years old	34.5	25.0	24.3	24.3	24.4	24.2	24.5
55 to 64 years old	105.0	93.3	90.5	88.8	87.1	83.9	80.7
65 to 74 years old	177.6	206.9	204.9	207.7	204.8	205.0	199.6
75 to 84 years old	190.1	265.6	267.5	277.8	279.4	277.0	280.9
85 years old and over	138.1	212.8	215.0	217.0	221.0	221.3	226.2

B Base figure too small to meet statistical standards for reliability of a derived figure.   Z Less than 0.05.   [1] Excludes data from states lacking an Hispanic-origin item on their death certificates. See text, this section. Persons of Hispanic origin may be any race.

Source: U.S. National Center for Health Statistics, *Health, United States, 2007.* See <http:www.cdc.gov/nchs/data/hus/hus07 .pdf#listtables>.

Table 120. **Death Rates From Suicide, by Selected Characteristics: 1990 to 2005**

[**Rates per 100,000 population.** Beginning 2000, cause of death is coded according to ICD-10; for explanation, see text this section. For explanation of age adjustment, see headnote, Table 104. See Appendix III]

Characteristic	1990	2000	2001	2002	2003	2004	2005
All ages, age adjusted	**12.5**	**10.4**	**10.7**	**10.9**	**10.8**	**10.9**	**10.9**
All ages, crude	**12.4**	**10.4**	**10.8**	**11.0**	**10.8**	**11.0**	**11.0**
Under 1 year	(X)	(X)	(X)	(X)	(X)	(X)	(X)
1 to 4 years	(X)	(X)	(X)	(X)	(X)	(X)	(X)
5 to 14 years	0.8	0.7	0.7	0.6	0.6	0.7	0.7
15 to 24 years	13.2	10.2	9.9	9.9	9.7	10.3	10.0
25 to 34 years	15.2	12.0	12.8	12.6	12.7	12.7	12.4
35 to 44 years	15.3	14.5	14.7	15.3	14.9	15.0	14.9
45 to 54 years	14.8	14.4	15.2	15.7	15.9	16.6	16.5
55 to 64 years	16.0	12.1	13.1	13.6	13.8	13.8	13.9
65 to 74 years	17.9	12.5	13.3	13.5	12.7	12.3	12.6
75 to 84 years	24.9	17.6	17.4	17.7	16.4	16.3	16.9
85 years and over	22.2	19.6	17.5	18.0	16.9	16.4	16.9
AGE ADJUSTED							
Male	21.5	17.7	18.2	18.4	18.0	18.0	18.0
Female	4.8	4.0	4.0	4.2	4.2	4.5	4.4
White male	22.8	19.1	19.6	20.0	19.6	19.6	19.6
Black male	12.8	10.0	9.8	9.8	9.2	9.6	9.2
American Indian, Alaska Native male	20.1	16.0	17.4	16.4	16.6	18.7	18.9
Asian, Pacific Islander male	9.6	8.6	8.4	8.0	8.5	8.4	7.3
Hispanic male [1]	13.7	10.3	10.1	9.9	9.7	9.8	9.4
Non-Hispanic, White male [1]	23.5	20.2	21.0	21.4	21.0	21.0	21.2
White female	5.2	4.3	4.5	4.7	4.6	5.0	4.9
Black female	2.4	1.8	1.8	1.6	1.9	1.8	1.9
American Indian, Alaska Native female	3.6	3.8	4.0	4.1	3.5	5.9	4.6
Asian, Pacific Islander female	4.1	2.8	2.9	3.0	3.1	3.5	3.3
Hispanic female [1]	2.3	1.7	1.6	1.8	1.7	2.0	1.8
Non-Hispanic, White female [1]	5.4	4.7	4.9	5.1	5.0	5.4	5.3

X Not applicable.   [1] Data for 1990 exclude data from states lacking an Hispanic-origin item on their death certificates. Persons of Hispanic origin may be any race.

Source: U.S. National Center for Health Statistics, *Health, United States, 2007*, <http://www.cdc.gov/nchs/hus.htm>.

Table 121. **Death Rates from Human Immunodeficiency Virus (HIV) Disease by Selected Characteristics: 1990 to 2005**

[**Rates per 100,000 population.** Beginning 2000, cause of death is coded according to ICD 10; for explanation, see text this section. For explanation of age adjustment, see headnote, Table 102. See Appendix III]

Characteristic	1990	2000	2001	2002	2003	2004	2005
All ages, age adjusted	**10.2**	**5.2**	**5.0**	**4.9**	**4.7**	**4.5**	**4.2**
All ages, crude	**10.1**	**5.1**	**5.0**	**4.9**	**4.7**	**4.4**	**4.2**
Under 1 year	2.7	(B)	(B)	(B)	(B)	(B)	(B)
1 to 4 years	0.8	(B)	(B)	(B)	(B)	(B)	(B)
5 to 14 years	0.2	0.1	0.1	0.1	0.1	0.1	(B)
15 to 24 years	1.5	0.5	0.6	0.4	0.4	0.5	0.4
25 to 34 years	19.7	6.1	5.3	4.6	4.0	3.7	3.3
35 to 44 years	27.4	13.1	13.0	12.7	12.0	10.9	9.9
45 to 54 years	15.2	11.0	10.5	11.2	10.9	10.6	10.6
55 to 64 years	6.2	5.1	5.2	5.1	5.4	5.4	5.3
65 to 74 years	2.0	2.2	2.1	2.2	2.4	2.4	2.3
75 to 84 years	0.7	0.7	0.7	0.8	0.7	0.8	0.8
85 years and over	(B)	(B)	(B)	(B)	(B)	(B)	(B)
AGE ADJUSTED							
Male	18.5	7.9	7.5	7.4	7.1	6.6	6.2
Female	2.2	2.5	2.5	2.5	2.4	2.4	2.3
White male	15.7	4.6	4.4	4.3	4.2	3.8	3.6
Black male	46.3	35.1	33.8	33.3	31.3	29.2	28.2
American Indian, Alaska Native male	3.3	3.5	4.2	3.4	3.5	4.3	4.0
Asian or Pacific Islander male	4.3	1.2	1.2	1.5	1.1	1.2	1.0
Hispanic male [1]	28.8	10.6	9.7	9.1	9.2	8.2	7.5
Non-Hispanic, White male [1]	14.1	3.8	3.6	3.5	3.4	3.1	3.0
White female	1.1	1.0	0.9	0.9	0.9	0.9	0.8
Black female	10.1	13.2	13.4	13.4	12.8	13.0	12.0
American Indian, Alaska Native female	(B)	1.0	(B)	(B)	1.5	1.5	1.5
Asian or Pacific Islander female	(B)	0.2	(B)	(B)	(B)	(B)	(B)
Hispanic female [1]	3.8	2.9	2.7	2.6	2.7	2.4	1.9
Non-Hispanic, White female [1]	0.7	0.7	0.6	0.6	0.6	0.6	0.6

B Base figure too small to meet statistical standards for reliability of a derived figure.   [1] Data for 1990 exclude data from states lacking an Hispanic-origin item on their death certificates. Persons of Hispanic origin may be any race.

Source: U.S. National Center for Health Statistics, *Health, United States, 2007*, <http://www.cdc.gov/nchs/hus.htm>.

Table 122. Deaths—Life Years Lost and Mortality Costs by Age, Sex, and Cause: 2000 and 2004

[2,403 represents 2,403,000. **Life years lost:** Number of years person would have lived in absence of death. **Mortality cost:** value of lifetime earnings lost by persons who die prematurely]

Characteristic	Number of deaths (1,000)	Life years lost [1]		Mortality cost [2]	
		Total (1,000)	Per death	Total (mil. dol.)	Per death (dol.)
2000, total	**2,403**	**38,843**	**16.2**	**431,992**	**179,772**
Under 5 years old	33	2,522	76.4	30,421	921,471
5 to 14 years old	7	513	69.2	8,331	1,123,778
15 to 24 years old	31	1,835	58.6	43,039	1,374,751
25 to 44 years old	130	5,604	43.1	144,409	1,108,713
45 to 64 years old	346	10,555	30.5	168,201	486,146
65 years old and over	1,855	17,815	9.6	37,591	20,265
Heart disease	711	8,917	12.5	72,224	101,623
Cancer	553	10,028	18.1	107,501	194,367
Cerebrovascular diseases	168	1,934	11.5	12,103	72,187
Accidents and adverse effects	98	3,303	33.8	69,429	709,801
Other	874	14,661	16.8	170,736	195,408
Male	**1,177**	**20,415**	**17.3**	**316,850**	**269,135**
Under 5 years old	19	1,373	74.0	19,287	1,040,197
5 to 14 years old	4	295	67.0	5,540	1,258,796
15 to 24 years old	23	1,319	57.2	34,230	1,483,692
25 to 44 years old	85	3,549	41.7	107,638	1,263,555
45 to 64 years old	244	6,098	25.0	123,301	505,917
65 years old and over	802	7,781	9.7	26,853	33,467
Heart disease	345	4,709	13.7	56,883	164,989
Cancer	286	5,333	18.6	75,819	265,036
Cerebrovascular diseases	65	777	12.0	7,861	121,377
Accidents and adverse effects	64	2,259	35.4	55,756	874,831
Other	418	7,336	17.6	120,531	288,386
Female	**1,226**	**18,428**	**15.0**	**115,142**	**93,939**
Under 5 years old	14	1,149	79.4	11,134	769,356
5 to 14 years old	3	218	72.4	2,791	926,495
15 to 24 years old	8	516	62.6	8,809	1,069,584
25 to 44 years old	45	2,054	45.6	36,770	815,994
45 to 64 years old	102	4,457	43.6	44,899	439,031
65 years old and over	1,053	10,034	9.5	10,738	10,201
Heart disease	366	4,208	11.5	15,341	41,923
Cancer	267	4,695	17.6	31,681	118,653
Cerebrovascular diseases	103	1,157	11.2	4,241	41,223
Accidents and adverse effects	34	1,044	30.6	13,673	401,183
Other	456	7,325	16.1	50,205	110,150
2004, total [3]	**2,397**	**40,757**	**17.0**	**521,097**	**217,371**
Under 5 years old	33	2,533	77.4	33,848	1,034,435
5 to 14 years old	7	479	70.1	8,602	1,258,716
15 to 24 years old	33	1,989	59.5	51,159	1,530,741
25 to 44 years old	126	5,557	44.0	159,671	1,264,921
45 to 64 years old	383	12,057	31.4	221,232	576,889
65 years old and over	1,815	18,143	10.0	46,585	25,673
Heart disease	652	8,725	13.4	85,397	130,886
Cancer	554	10,499	19.0	130,136	234,953
Cerebrovascular diseases	150	1,853	12.3	14,187	94,537
Accidents and adverse effects	112	3,788	33.8	87,565	782,362
Other	929	15,892	17.1	203,812	219,401
Male	**1,181**	**21,477**	**18.2**	**369,785**	**313,008**
Under 5 years old	18	1,380	75.1	20,991	1,142,847
5 to 14 years old	4	272	67.9	5,536	1,384,437
15 to 24 years old	25	1,428	58.1	40,084	1,630,277
25 to 44 years old	82	3,506	42.7	115,982	1,413,796
45 to 64 years old	269	6,983	25.9	155,517	577,711
65 years old and over	783	7,908	10.1	31,675	40,443
Heart disease	322	4,677	14.5	65,320	202,895
Cancer	287	5,616	19.6	88,992	310,268
Cerebrovascular diseases	59	760	12.9	8,962	152,426
Accidents and adverse effects	72	2,544	35.4	68,109	946,275
Other	442	7,879	17.8	138,401	313,228
Female	**1,216**	**19,280**	**15.9**	**151,311**	**124,446**
Under 5 years old	14	1,153	80.3	12,857	895,714
5 to 14 years old	3	208	73.2	3,066	1,081,376
15 to 24 years old	9	560	63.4	11,075	1,253,712
25 to 44 years old	44	2,051	46.4	43,689	988,569
45 to 64 years old	114	5,073	44.4	65,715	574,951
65 years old and over	1,031	10,235	9.9	14,909	14,456
Heart disease	331	4,048	12.2	20,076	60,744
Cancer	267	4,883	18.3	41,143	154,063
Cerebrovascular diseases	91	1,093	12.0	5,225	57,246
Accidents and adverse effects	40	1,243	31.1	19,456	487,034
Other	487	8,013	16.4	65,410	134,288

[1] Based on life expectancy at year of death.   [2] Cost estimates based on the person's age, sex, life expectancy at the time of death, labor force participation rates, annual earnings, value of homemaking services, and a 3 percent discount rate by which to convert to present worth the potential aggregate earnings lost over the years.   [3] Total excludes 346 deaths for which age is unknown.

Source: Wendy Max and Yanling Shi, Institute for Health & Aging, University of California San Francisco, CA, unpublished data.

Table 123. **Marriages and Divorces—Number and Rate by State: 1990 to 2006**

[**2,443.5 represents 2,443,500.** By place of occurence. See Appendix III]

State	Marriages [1]						Divorces [3]					
	Number (1,000)			Rate per 1,000 population [2]			Number (1,000)			Rate per 1,000 population [2]		
	1990	2000	2006	1990	2000	2006	1990	2000	2006	1990	2000	2006
U.S. [4]	2,443.5	2,329.0	2,160.0	9.8	8.3	7.5	1,182.0	(NA)	(NA)	4.7	4.1	3.6
Alabama	43.1	45.0	39.6	10.6	10.3	8.6	25.3	23.5	22.1	6.1	5.4	4.8
Alaska	5.7	5.6	5.3	10.2	8.9	7.8	2.9	2.7	3.0	5.5	4.4	4.4
Arizona [5]	36.8	38.7	39.0	10.0	7.9	6.3	25.1	21.6	24.3	6.9	4.4	3.9
Arkansas	36.0	41.1	34.3	15.3	16.0	12.2	16.8	17.9	16.2	6.9	6.9	5.7
California.	237.1	196.9	216.0	7.9	5.9	6.0	128.0	(NA)	(NA)	4.3	(NA)	(NA)
Colorado	32.4	35.6	36.1	9.8	8.6	7.6	18.4	(NA)	21.1	5.5	(NA)	4.4
Connecticut	26.0	19.4	17.4	7.9	5.9	5.0	10.3	6.5	9.8	3.2	2.0	2.8
Delaware.	5.6	5.1	5.2	8.4	6.7	6.0	3.0	3.2	3.8	4.4	4.2	4.5
District of Columbia.	5.0	2.8	2.3	8.2	5.4	3.9	2.7	1.5	1.3	4.5	3.0	2.1
Florida	141.8	141.9	155.5	10.9	9.3	8.6	81.7	81.9	87.8	6.3	5.3	4.9
Georgia	66.8	56.0	66.5	10.3	7.1	7.1	35.7	30.7	(NA)	5.5	3.9	(NA)
Hawaii	18.3	25.0	28.7	16.4	21.2	22.4	5.2	4.6	(NA)	4.6	3.9	(NA)
Idaho	14.1	14.0	14.8	13.9	11.0	10.1	6.6	6.9	7.5	6.5	5.4	5.1
Illinois.	100.6	85.5	78.0	8.8	7.0	6.1	44.3	39.1	32.2	3.8	3.2	2.5
Indiana	53.2	34.5	50.9	9.6	5.8	8.1	(NA)	(NA)	(NA)	(NA)	(NA)	(NA)
Iowa.	24.9	20.3	20.0	9.0	7.0	6.7	11.1	9.4	8.0	3.9	3.3	2.7
Kansas.	22.7	22.2	18.9	9.2	8.3	6.8	12.6	10.6	9.2	5.0	4.0	3.3
Kentucky.	49.8	39.7	36.9	13.5	10.0	8.8	21.8	21.6	21.5	5.8	5.4	5.1
Louisiana	40.4	40.5	(NA)	9.6	9.3	(NA)	(NA)	(NA)	(NA)	(NA)	(NA)	(NA)
Maine.	11.9	10.5	9.7	9.7	8.3	7.4	5.3	5.8	4.8	4.3	4.6	3.6
Maryland.	46.3	40.0	36.5	9.7	7.7	6.5	16.1	17.0	17.0	3.4	3.3	3.0
Massachusetts . . .	47.7	37.0	38.5	7.9	6.0	6.0	16.8	18.6	14.6	2.8	3.0	2.3
Michigan	76.1	66.4	59.2	8.2	6.7	5.9	40.2	39.4	35.6	4.3	4.0	3.5
Minnesota	33.7	33.4	30.9	7.7	6.9	6.0	15.4	14.8	(NA)	3.5	3.1	(NA)
Mississippi.	24.3	19.7	16.9	9.4	7.1	5.8	14.4	14.4	13.7	5.5	5.2	4.7
Missouri	49.1	43.7	40.7	9.6	7.9	7.0	26.4	26.5	22.9	5.1	4.8	3.9
Montana	6.9	6.6	6.8	8.6	7.4	7.1	4.1	2.1	3.4	5.1	2.4	3.6
Nebraska	12.6	13.0	12.0	8.0	7.8	6.8	6.5	6.4	6.2	4.0	3.8	3.5
Nevada	120.6	144.3	131.8	99.0	76.7	52.9	13.3	18.1	16.7	11.4	9.6	6.7
New Hampshire . .	10.5	11.6	9.3	9.5	9.5	7.1	5.3	7.1	5.3	4.7	5.8	4.0
New Jersey	58.7	50.4	42.4	7.6	6.1	4.9	23.6	25.6	25.8	3.0	3.1	3.0
New Mexico [5] . . .	13.3	14.5	13.4	8.8	8.3	6.9	7.7	9.2	8.4	4.9	5.3	4.3
New York [5]	154.8	162.0	127.4	8.6	8.9	6.6	57.9	62.8	55.6	3.2	3.4	2.9
North Carolina . . .	51.9	65.6	55.3	7.8	8.5	6.2	34.0	36.9	36.4	5.1	4.8	4.1
North Dakota	4.8	4.6	4.3	7.5	7.3	6.8	2.3	2.0	1.7	3.6	3.2	2.6
Ohio.	98.1	88.5	73.1	9.0	7.9	6.4	51.0	49.3	41.0	4.7	4.4	3.6
Oklahoma	33.2	15.6	26.3	10.6	4.6	7.3	24.9	12.4	19.0	7.7	3.7	5.3
Oregon	25.3	26.0	26.9	8.9	7.8	7.3	15.9	16.7	14.2	5.5	5.0	3.9
Pennsylvania	84.9	73.2	68.6	7.1	6.1	5.5	40.1	37.9	27.4	3.3	3.2	2.2
Rhode Island	8.1	8.0	6.9	8.1	8.0	6.5	3.8	3.1	3.1	3.7	3.1	2.9
South Carolina . . .	55.8	42.7	32.8	15.9	10.9	7.6	16.1	14.4	12.8	4.5	3.7	3.0
South Dakota. . . .	7.7	7.1	6.3	11.1	9.6	8.0	2.6	2.7	2.5	3.7	3.6	3.2
Tennessee.	68.0	88.2	64.0	13.9	15.9	10.5	32.3	33.8	25.9	6.5	6.1	4.3
Texas	178.6	196.4	175.0	10.5	9.6	7.5	94.0	85.2	78.1	5.5	4.2	3.3
Utah.	19.4	24.1	23.7	11.2	11.1	9.2	8.8	9.7	9.9	5.1	4.5	3.8
Vermont	6.1	6.1	5.4	10.9	10.2	8.7	2.6	5.1	2.2	4.5	8.6	3.5
Virginia	71.0	62.4	60.8	11.4	9.0	8.0	27.3	30.2	31.1	4.4	4.3	4.1
Washington	46.6	40.9	41.0	9.5	7.0	6.4	28.8	27.2	24.0	5.9	4.7	3.8
West Virginia	13.0	15.7	13.1	7.2	8.7	7.3	9.7	9.3	8.5	5.3	5.2	4.7
Wisconsin	38.9	36.1	32.6	7.9	6.8	5.8	17.8	17.6	16.0	3.6	3.3	2.9
Wyoming.	4.9	4.9	5.0	10.7	10.3	9.8	3.1	2.8	2.7	6.6	5.9	5.4

NA Not available. [1] Data are counts of marriages performed, except as noted. [2] Based on total population residing in area; population enumerated as of April 1 for 1990 and 2000; estimated as of July 1 for all other years. [3] Includes annulments. [4] U.S. total for the number of divorces is an estimate which includes states not reporting. Beginning 2000, divorce rates based solely on the combined counts and populations for reporting states and the District of Columbia. [5] Some figures for marriages are marriage licenses issued.

Source: U.S. National Center for Health Statistics, *Births, Marriages, Divorces, and Deaths: Provisional Data for 2006*, annual; Volume 55, Number 20, August 28, 2007; and prior reports.

Section 3
Health and Nutrition

This section presents statistics on health expenditures and insurance coverage, including Medicare and Medicaid, medical personnel, hospitals, nursing homes and other care facilities, injuries, diseases, disability status, nutritional intake of the population, and food consumption. Summary statistics showing recent trends on health care and discussions of selected health issues are published annually by the U.S. National Center for Health Statistics (NCHS) in *Health, United States.* Data on national health expenditures, medical costs, and insurance coverage are compiled by the U.S. Centers for Medicare & Medicaid Services (CMS) (formerly Health Care Financing Administration), and appear on the CMS Web site at <http://www.cms.hhs.gov /NationalHealthExpendData/> and in the annual *Medicare and Medicaid Statistical Supplement* to the *Health Care Financing Review.* Statistics on health insurance are also collected by NCHS and are published in Series 10 of *Vital and Health Statistics.* NCHS also conducts periodic surveys of nutrient levels in the population, including estimates of food and nutrient intake, overweight and obesity, hypercholesterolemia, hypertension, and clinical signs of malnutrition. Data are published in Series 10 and 11 of *Vital and Health Statistics.* Statistics on hospitals are published annually by the Health Forum, L.L.C.; an American Hospital Association (AHA) company, in AHA Hospital Statistics. The primary source for data on nutrition is *Diet Quality and Food Consumption*, issued by the U.S. Department of Agriculture.

National health expenditures—CMS compiles estimates of national health expenditures (NHE) to measure spending for health care in the United States. The NHE accounts are structured to show spending by type of expenditure (i.e., hospital care, physician and clinical care, dental care, and other professional care; home health care; retail sales of prescription drugs; other medical nondurables; vision products and other medical

durables; nursing home care and other personal health expenditures; plus other health expenditures such as public health activities, administration, and the net cost of private health insurance; plus medical sector investment, the sum of noncommercial medical research and capital formation in medical sector structures and equipment; and by source of funding (e.g., private health insurance, out-of-pocket payments, and a range of public programs including Medicare, Medicaid, and those operated by the U.S. Department of Veterans Affairs (VA)).

Data used to estimate health expenditures come from existing sources, which are tabulated for other purposes. The type of expenditure estimates rely upon statistics produced by such groups as the AHA, the Census Bureau, and the U.S. Department of Health and Human Services (HHS). Source of funding estimates are constructed using administrative and statistical records from the Medicare and Medicaid programs, the U.S. Department of Defense and VA medical programs, the Social Security Administration, Census Bureau's *Governmental Finances,* state and local governments, other HHS agencies, and other nongovernment sources.

Medicare, Medicaid, and SCHIP—Since July 1966, the federal Medicare program has provided two coordinated plans for nearly all people age 65 and over: (1) a hospital insurance plan, which covers hospital and related services and (2) a voluntary supplementary medical insurance plan, financed partially by monthly premiums paid by participants, which partly covers physicians' and related medical services. Such insurance also applies, since July 1973, to disabled beneficiaries of any age after 24 months of entitlement to cash benefits under the social security or railroad retirement programs and to persons with end stage renal disease. On January 1, 2006, Medicare began to provide coverage for prescription drugs as mandated by the Medicare Prescription

Drug, Improvement, and Modernization Act of 2003 (MMA). This benefit is available on a voluntary basis to everyone with Medicare, and beneficiaries pay a monthly premium to enroll in one of Medicare's prescription drug plans.

Medicaid is a health insurance program for certain low-income people. These include: certain low-income families with children; aged, blind, or disabled people on supplemental security income; certain low-income pregnant women and children; and people who have very high medical bills. Medicaid is funded and administered through a state/federal partnership. Although there are broad federal requirements for Medicaid, states have a wide degree of flexibility to design their program. Congress created the State Children's Health Insurance Program (SCHIP) to address the growing problem of children without health insurance. SCHIP was designed as a federal/state partnership, similar to Medicaid, with the goal of expanding health insurance to children whose families earn too much money to be eligible for Medicaid, but not enough money to purchase private insurance.

Health resources—Hospital statistics based on data from AHA's yearly survey are published annually in *AHA Hospital Statistics* and cover all hospitals accepted for registration by the Association. To be accepted for registration, a hospital must meet certain requirements relating to number of beds, construction, equipment, medical and nursing staff, patient care, clinical records, surgical and obstetrical facilities, diagnostic and treatment facilities, laboratory services, etc. Data obtained from NCHS cover all U.S. hospitals that meet certain criteria for inclusion. The criteria are published in *Vital and Health Statistics* reports, Series 13.

Statistics on the demographic characteristics of persons employed in the health occupations are compiled by the U.S. Bureau of Labor Statistics and reported in *Employment and Earnings* (monthly) (see Table 596, Section 12, Labor Force, Employment, and Earnings). Data based on surveys of health personnel and utilization of health facilities providing long-term care, ambulatory care, emergency room care, and hospital care are presented in NCHS Series 13, *Data on Health Resources Utilization* and "National Health Statistics Reports." Statistics on patient visits to health care providers, as reported in health interviews, appear in NCHS Series 10, *National Health Interview Survey Data.*

The CMS's *Health Care Financing Review* and its annual *Medicare and Medicaid Statistical Supplement* present data for hospitals and nursing homes as well as extended care facilities and home health agencies. These data are based on records of the Medicare program and differ from those of other sources because they are limited to facilities meeting federal eligibility standards for participation in Medicare.

Disability and illness—General health statistics, including morbidity, disability, injuries, preventive care, and findings from physiological testing are collected by NCHS in its National Health Interview Survey and its National Health and Nutrition Examination Surveys and appear in *Vital and Health Statistics,* Series 10 and 11, respectively. The Department of Labor compiles statistics on occupational injuries (see Section 12, Labor Force, Employment, and Earnings). Annual incidence data on notifiable diseases are compiled by the Public Health Service (PHS) at its Centers for Disease Control and Prevention in Atlanta, Georgia, and are published as a supplement to its *Morbidity and Mortality Weekly Report (MMWR).* The list of diseases is revised annually and includes those which, by mutual agreement of the states and PHS, are communicable diseases of national importance.

Nutrition—Statistics on annual per capita consumption of food and its nutrient value are estimated by the Department of Agriculture. Data are available online at <http://www.ers.usda.gov/data/foodconsumption>.

Statistical reliability—For discussion of statistical collection, estimation, and sampling procedures and measures of reliability applicable to data from NCHS and CMS, see Appendix III.

Table 124. **National Health Expenditures—Summary, 1960 to 2006, and Projections, 2007 to 2017**

[In billions of dollars (28 represents $28,000,000,000). Excludes Puerto Rico and island areas]

Year	Total expenditures [1]	Private expenditures			Public expenditures			Health services and supplies				
		Total [2]	Out-of-pocket	Insurance	Total	Federal	State and local	Total [3]	Hospital care	Physician and clinical services	Prescription drugs	Nursing home care
1960	28	21	13	6	7	3	4	25	9	5	3	1
1961	29	22	13	6	7	3	4	26	10	6	3	1
1962	32	24	14	7	8	4	4	29	11	6	3	1
1963	35	26	15	8	9	4	5	31	12	7	3	1
1964	39	29	17	9	10	4	5	34	13	8	3	1
1965	42	32	18	10	10	5	6	37	14	8	4	1
1966	46	32	18	10	14	8	6	41	16	9	4	2
1967	52	33	18	10	19	12	7	47	18	10	4	2
1968	59	37	21	12	22	14	8	53	21	11	5	3
1969	66	41	23	13	25	16	9	59	24	12	5	3
1970	75	47	25	15	28	18	10	67	28	14	5	4
1971	83	51	26	18	32	21	12	74	31	16	6	5
1972	93	57	29	21	36	23	13	83	34	17	6	5
1973	103	63	32	23	40	25	15	93	38	19	7	6
1974	117	69	34	26	48	30	17	106	45	22	7	7
1975	133	77	37	30	56	36	20	121	52	25	8	8
1976	152	89	41	37	63	43	20	139	60	28	9	10
1977	173	102	45	45	71	47	23	159	67	33	9	12
1978	195	114	48	52	80	54	26	179	76	35	10	14
1979	220	129	53	60	91	61	30	203	87	41	11	16
1980	254	148	59	69	106	72	35	234	101	47	12	19
1981	294	172	66	81	123	83	40	271	118	55	13	21
1982	331	195	72	94	136	92	44	305	134	61	15	23
1983	365	216	79	105	150	103	47	336	145	68	17	26
1984	402	239	87	119	163	113	50	372	155	77	20	29
1985	440	263	96	131	177	123	54	409	165	90	22	32
1986	472	278	104	136	194	133	61	440	177	100	24	34
1987	513	301	109	149	212	144	68	478	190	112	27	36
1988	574	344	119	175	230	155	75	535	207	127	31	40
1989	639	383	125	205	256	174	82	596	227	142	35	46
1990	714	427	136	234	287	194	93	667	252	158	40	53
1991	782	456	140	255	325	223	102	731	277	175	44	58
1992	849	485	143	275	364	253	111	794	300	190	48	62
1993	913	512	145	296	400	279	121	853	317	201	51	65
1994	962	526	143	308	436	304	132	900	330	210	54	68
1995	1,017	552	146	325	465	327	138	953	341	221	61	74
1996	1,069	580	152	343	488	348	140	1,003	352	229	69	80
1997	1,125	614	162	359	511	365	146	1,054	365	241	78	84
1998	1,191	663	175	385	528	372	156	1,112	376	256	89	90
1999	1,265	710	184	418	555	390	165	1,180	395	270	105	91
2000	1,353	757	193	455	596	417	179	1,264	417	289	121	95
2001	1,470	808	200	499	661	464	197	1,376	451	313	139	102
2002	1,603	881	211	551	722	509	213	1,499	489	338	158	106
2003	1,732	955	225	603	777	551	227	1,621	525	367	174	110
2004	1,852	1,015	235	646	837	597	240	1,731	564	394	189	115
2005	1,973	1,077	247	686	897	639	258	1,844	606	423	200	121
2006	2,106	1,135	257	723	970	705	265	1,966	648	448	217	125
2007, proj. . . .	2,246	1,207	269	769	1,039	753	286	2,096	697	473	231	130
2008, proj. . . .	2,394	1,285	283	822	1,109	807	303	2,234	747	502	247	136
2009, proj. . . .	2,555	1,369	298	879	1,186	864	321	2,386	800	533	264	144
2010, proj. . . .	2,726	1,457	314	936	1,269	926	343	2,546	855	567	285	151
2011, proj. . . .	2,905	1,548	332	995	1,357	992	365	2,714	915	601	307	159
2012, proj. . . .	3,098	1,643	351	1,058	1,455	1,065	389	2,896	978	637	333	167
2013, proj. . . .	3,305	1,745	370	1,124	1,560	1,145	416	3,091	1,044	675	362	176
2014, proj. . . .	3,524	1,850	391	1,192	1,674	1,230	444	3,296	1,114	714	394	185
2015, proj. . . .	3,757	1,960	414	1,263	1,797	1,323	474	3,516	1,188	754	430	195
2016, proj. . . .	4,008	2,076	438	1,338	1,932	1,424	507	3,753	1,265	796	470	206
2017, proj. . . .	4,277	2,198	464	1,415	2,079	1,536	543	4,008	1,346	840	516	217

[1] Includes medical research and medical facilities construction not shown separately.   [2] Includes other private expenditures not shown separately.   [3] Includes other objects of expenditure not shown separately.

Source: U. S. Centers for Medicare & Medicaid Services, Office of the Actuary, "National Health Statistics Group"; <http://www.cms.hhs.gov/NationalHealthExpendData/>.

U.S. Census Bureau, Statistical Abstract of the United States: 2009

Table 125. National Health Expenditures by Type: 1990 to 2006

[In billions of dollars (714.0 represents $714,000,000,000), **except percent.** Excludes Puerto Rico and island areas]

Type of expenditure	1990	2000	2001	2002	2003	2004	2005	2006
Total	**714.0**	**1,353.3**	**1,469.6**	**1,603.4**	**1,732.4**	**1,852.3**	**1,973.3**	**2,105.5**
Annual percent change [1]	11.8	7.0	8.6	9.1	8.0	6.9	6.5	6.7
Percent of gross domestic product	12.3	13.8	14.5	15.3	15.8	15.9	15.9	16.0
Private expenditures	**427.3**	**757.1**	**808.5**	**882.3**	**955.1**	**1,014.8**	**1,076.6**	**1,135.2**
Health services and supplies	400.9	706.1	756.3	823.4	892.5	946.9	1,003.1	1,054.1
Out-of-pocket payments	136.1	192.9	200.0	211.4	224.9	234.9	247.1	256.5
Insurance premiums [2]	233.7	455.2	498.7	552.5	602.8	645.8	685.6	723.4
Other	31.1	58.0	57.6	59.5	64.8	66.2	70.4	74.1
Medical research	1.0	2.5	2.8	3.1	3.3	3.4	3.7	4.0
Medical structures and equipment [3]	25.4	48.5	49.4	55.9	59.3	64.5	69.8	77.1
Public expenditures	**286.7**	**596.1**	**661.1**	**721.1**	**777.3**	**837.5**	**896.8**	**970.3**
Percent federal of public	67.6	70.0	70.2	70.5	70.8	71.3	71.3	72.6
Health services and supplies	265.8	558.3	619.9	676.0	728.1	783.7	840.6	912.1
Medicare [4]	109.5	224.3	247.7	265.1	281.5	309.3	338.0	401.3
Public assistance medical payments [5]	78.7	207.5	233.2	258.3	282.0	303.2	325.2	323.7
Temporary disability insurance [6]	0.1	–	0.1	0.1	0.1	0.1	0.1	0.1
Workers' compensation (medical) [6]	17.4	24.9	28.1	30.1	31.8	32.4	32.2	33.0
Defense Dept. hospital, medical	10.4	13.7	15.4	18.7	21.8	24.5	26.2	28.8
Maternal, child health programs	1.7	2.7	2.7	2.7	2.7	2.6	2.6	2.6
Public health activities	20.0	43.4	46.8	52.1	53.8	53.9	56.3	58.7
Veterans' hospital, medical care	10.8	18.9	20.9	22.6	26.3	27.7	29.5	31.4
Medical vocational rehabilitation	0.3	0.4	0.4	0.5	0.5	0.5	0.5	0.5
State and local hospitals [7]	13.2	13.7	14.7	15.5	16.7	17.9	18.5	20.6
Other [8]	3.8	8.8	9.9	10.4	11.1	11.5	11.5	11.5
Medical research	11.7	23.1	26.0	29.5	32.2	35.4	36.9	37.8
Medical structures and equipment [3]	9.2	14.7	15.3	15.6	17.0	18.4	19.3	20.4

– Represents zero. [1] Change from immediate prior year. [2] Covers insurance benefits and amount retained by insurance companies for expenses, additions to reserves, and profits (net cost of insurance). [3] Represents expenditures for total medical sector acquisitions of structures and equipment including structures that house medical professionals' offices. [4] Represents expenditures for benefits and administrative cost from federal hospital and medical insurance trust funds under old-age, survivors, disability, and health insurance programs; see text this section. [5] Payments made directly to suppliers of medical care (primarily Medicaid). [6] Includes medical benefits paid under public law by private insurance carriers, state governments, and self-insurers. [7] Expenditures not offset by other revenues. [8] Covers expenditures for Substance Abuse and Mental Health Services Administration, Indian Health Service, school health, and other programs.

Source: U. S. Centers for Medicare & Medicaid Services, Office of the Actuary, "National Health Statistics Group"; See also <http://www.cms.hhs.gov/NationalHealthExpendData/>.

Table 126. National Health Expenditures by Object, 1990 to 2006, and Projections, 2007

[In billions of dollars (714.0 represents $714,000,000,000). Excludes Puerto Rico and outlying areas]

Object of expenditure	1990	2000	2001	2002	2003	2004	2005	2006	2007, proj.
Total	**714.0**	**1,353.3**	**1,469.6**	**1,603.4**	**1,732.4**	**1,852.3**	**1,973.3**	**2,105.5**	**2,245.6**
Spent by—									
Consumers	369.8	648.1	698.7	763.9	827.7	880.7	932.7	980.0	1,038.7
Out-of-pocket	136.1	192.9	200.0	211.4	224.9	234.9	247.1	256.5	269.3
Private insurance	233.7	455.2	498.7	552.5	602.8	645.8	685.6	723.4	769.4
Public	286.7	596.1	661.1	721.1	777.3	837.5	896.8	970.3	1,038.8
Other [1]	57.5	109.0	109.7	118.4	127.4	134.1	143.9	155.3	168.1
Spent for—									
Health services and supplies	666.7	1,264.4	1,376.2	1,499.4	1,620.7	1,730.6	1,843.6	1,966.2	2,095.5
Personal health care expenses	607.5	1,139.9	1,239.0	1,340.8	1,445.9	1,547.7	1,653.7	1,762.0	1,877.6
Hospital care	251.6	417.0	451.4	488.6	525.4	564.4	605.5	648.2	696.7
Physician and clinical services	157.5	288.6	313.2	337.9	366.7	393.6	422.6	447.6	473.0
Dental services	31.5	62.0	67.5	73.3	76.9	81.5	86.6	91.5	96.9
Other professional services [2]	18.2	39.1	42.8	45.6	49.0	52.4	56.2	58.9	61.7
Home health care	12.6	30.5	32.2	34.2	38.0	42.7	47.9	52.7	57.6
Prescription drugs	40.3	120.8	138.6	157.6	174.2	188.8	199.7	216.7	231.3
Other nondurable medical products	22.5	30.2	30.3	30.8	32.4	33.1	34.4	35.6	36.7
Durable medical equipment [3]	11.2	19.3	19.6	20.7	22.4	22.8	23.2	23.7	24.5
Nursing home care	52.6	95.3	101.5	105.7	110.5	115.2	120.7	124.9	129.7
Other personal health care	9.6	37.1	41.9	46.3	50.3	53.2	56.8	62.2	69.6
Public administration and net cost of private health insurance [4]	39.2	81.2	90.4	106.5	121.0	129.0	133.6	145.4	155.1
Public health activities	20.0	43.4	46.8	52.1	53.8	53.9	56.3	58.7	62.8
Medical research [5]	12.7	25.6	28.8	32.5	35.5	38.8	40.6	41.8	42.9
Medical structures and equipment [6]	34.7	63.2	64.7	71.5	76.3	83.0	89.1	97.6	107.2

[1] Includes nonpatient revenues, privately funded construction, and industrial inplant. [2] Includes services of registered and practical nurses in private duty, podiatrists, optometrists, physical therapists, clinical psychologists, chiropractors, naturopaths, and Christian Science practitioners. [3] Includes expenditures for eyeglasses, hearing aids, orthopedic appliances, artificial limbs, crutches, wheelchairs, etc. [4] Includes administrative expenses of federally financed health programs. [5] Research and development expenditures of drug companies and other manufacturers and providers of medical equipment and supplies are excluded from research expenditures, but are included in the expenditure class in which the product falls. [6] Represents expenditures for total medical sector acquisitions of structures and equipment including structures that house medical professionals' offices.

Source: U. S. Centers for Medicare & Medicaid Services, Office of the Actuary, "National Health Statistics Group"; See also <http://www.cms.hhs.gov/NationalHealthExpendData/>.

Table 127. **Health Services and Supplies—Per Capita Consumer Expenditures by Object: 1990 to 2006**

[In dollars, except percent. Based on U.S. Census Bureau estimates of total U.S. population as of July 1, excluding Armed Forces and federal employees abroad and civilian population of outlying areas. Excludes medical research, medical structures and equipment]

Object of expenditure	1990	2000	2001	2002	2003	2004	2005	2006
Total, national	**2,627**	**4,476**	**4,821**	**5,199**	**5,568**	**5,887**	**6,212**	**6,561**
Annual percent change [1]	10.6	6.1	7.7	7.9	7.1	5.7	5.5	5.6
Hospital care	991	1,476	1,581	1,694	1,804	1,920	2,040	2,163
Physician and clinical services	621	1,021	1,097	1,172	1,259	1,339	1,424	1,493
Dental services	124	219	237	254	264	277	292	305
Other professional services [2]	72	138	150	158	168	178	189	196
Home health care	50	108	113	119	131	145	162	176
Prescription drugs	159	427	485	547	600	642	673	723
Other nondurable medical products	88	107	106	107	111	113	116	119
Durable medical equipment [2]	44	68	69	72	77	77	78	79
Nursing home care	207	337	356	367	379	392	407	417
Other personal health care	38	131	147	161	173	181	191	208
Public administration and net cost of private health insurance	155	289	317	369	421	439	450	485
Public health activities	79	154	164	181	181	183	190	196
Total, private consumer [3]	**1,457**	**2,293**	**2,448**	**2,649**	**2,844**	**2,996**	**3,143**	**3,270**
Hospital care	430	559	600	651	698	753	792	855
Physician and clinical services	384	598	640	688	737	786	843	887
Dental services	120	209	223	239	248	260	274	287
Other professional services [2]	49	88	94	97	104	111	117	122
Home health care	20	44	39	35	34	37	37	40
Prescription drugs	130	329	370	410	441	464	487	476
Other nondurable medical products	86	102	101	101	105	106	109	111
Durable medical equipment [2]	36	52	51	51	53	54	54	54
Nursing home care	87	129	130	133	134	134	136	141
Net cost of private health insurance	115	184	201	243	289	291	293	296

[1] Change from immediate prior year.   [2] See footnotes for corresponding objects in Table 126.   [3] Represents out-of-pocket payments and private health insurance.

Source: U. S. Centers for Medicare and Medicaid Services, Office of the Actuary, "National Health Statistics Group." See also <http://www.cms.hhs.gov/NationalHealthExpendData/>.

Table 128. **Public Expenditures for Health Services and Supplies: 2006**

[In millions of dollars (912,107 represents $912,107,000,000). Excludes Puerto Rico and island areas. Excludes medical research, medical structures, and equipment]

Type of selected service	Total [1]	Federal	State and local	Medicare [2] (OASDHI)	Public assistance [3]	Other health services Veterans	Other health services Defense Dept. [4]	Other health services Workers' compensation [5]
Total [1]	**912,107**	**664,446**	**247,661**	**401,291**	**323,690**	**31,388**	**28,835**	**33,032**
Hospital care	362,624	290,193	72,431	187,153	115,161	20,856	14,727	6,155
Physician and clinical services . . .	153,085	126,438	26,647	92,147	33,965	2,861	5,493	12,594
Prescription drugs	74,016	58,744	15,272	39,453	23,784	2,789	4,312	3,499
Nursing home care	78,077	53,739	24,338	20,798	54,613	2,666	–	–
Public administration and net cost of private health insurance . .	55,207	36,707	18,499	20,249	23,916	65	2,849	7,860
Public health activities	58,702	9,668	49,034	–	–	–	–	–

– Represents zero.   [1] Includes other items not shown separately.   [2] Covers hospital and medical insurance payments and administrative costs under old-age, survivors, disability, and health insurance program (OASDHI).   [3] Covers Medicaid and other medical public assistance. Excludes funds paid into Medicare trust fund by states to cover premiums for public assistance recipients and medically indigent persons.   [4] Includes care for retirees and military dependents.   [5] Medical benefits.

Source: U. S. Centers for Medicare and Medicaid Services, Office of the Actuary, "National Health Statistics Group"; See also <http://www.cms.hhs.gov/NationalHealthExpendData/>.

Table 129. **Personal Health Care—Third Party Payments and Private Consumer Expenditures, 1990 to 2006, and Projections, 2007**

[In billions of dollars (607.5 represents $607,500,000,000), except percent. See headnote, Table 130]

Item	1990	2000	2001	2002	2003	2004	2005	2006	2007, proj.
Personal health care expenditures	607.5	1,139.6	1,238.7	1,340.8	1,445.9	1,547.7	1,653.7	1,762.0	1,877.6
Third party payments, total	**471.3**	**946.7**	**1,038.9**	**1,129.3**	**1,221.0**	**1,312.8**	**1,406.6**	**1,505.5**	**1,608.4**
Percent of personal health care	77.6	83.1	83.9	84.2	84.4	84.8	85.1	85.4	85.7
Private insurance payments	204.6	403.1	441.4	482.4	521.2	560.2	598.6	634.6	676.4
Public expenditures	236.2	486.7	541.1	588.7	636.2	687.7	739.0	798.2	855.0
Other [1]	30.5	57.0	56.4	58.3	63.6	64.9	69.0	72.7	77.0
Private consumer expenditures [2]	**340.7**	**596.0**	**641.2**	**693.8**	**746.1**	**795.1**	**845.7**	**891.1**	**945.7**
Percent met by private insurance	60.1	67.6	68.8	69.5	69.9	70.5	70.8	71.2	71.5
Hospital care	109.1	157.9	171.7	187.7	204.8	221.3	235.1	256.2	276.9
Percent met by private insurance	89.6	91.4	91.7	91.7	91.6	91.6	91.6	91.6	91.6
Physician and clinical services	97.5	168.9	182.4	198.3	215.2	231.1	250.3	265.8	281.1
Percent met by private insurance	69.0	80.9	81.6	82.2	82.6	82.7	82.7	82.6	82.7
Prescription drugs	33.0	93.0	105.3	118.4	127.7	136.3	144.5	142.7	151.1
Percent met by private insurance	32.2	64.0	65.8	65.9	65.4	66.1	66.2	66.6	66.7

[1] Includes nonpatient revenues and industrial inplant health services.   [2] Includes expenditures not shown separately. Represents out-of-pocket payments and private health insurance benefits. Excludes net cost of insurance.

Source: U. S. Centers for Medicare and Medicaid Services, Office of the Actuary, "National Health Statistics Group." See also <http://www.cms.hhs.gov/NationalHealthExpendData/>.

Health and Nutrition   97

Table 130. Personal Health Care Expenditures by Object and Source of Payment: 2006

[In millions of dollars (1,762,037 represents $1,762,037,000,000). Excludes Puerto Rico and island areas. Covers all expenditures for health services and supplies, except net cost of insurance and administration, public health activities, and administration for government and philanthropic agencies for fund-raising activities]

Object of expenditure	Total	Private payments						Public	Third party payments [2]
		Total	Consumer				Other [1]		
			Total	Out-of-pocket payments	Private health insurance				
Total	1,762,037	963,839	891,105	256,538	634,566		72,735	798,198	1,505,499
Hospital care	648,225	285,601	256,244	21,421	234,822		29,357	362,624	626,803
Physician and clinical services	447,571	294,486	265,849	46,174	219,675		28,636	153,085	401,396
Dental services	91,498	86,047	85,986	40,648	45,338		61	5,451	50,850
Other professional services [3]	58,881	39,609	36,613	15,071	21,542		2,996	19,272	43,810
Home health care	52,705	13,039	11,938	5,927	6,011		1,101	39,665	46,777
Prescription drugs	216,705	142,689	142,689	47,639	95,050		–	74,016	169,066
Other nondurable medical products	35,622	33,392	33,392	33,392	–		–	2,230	2,230
Durable medical equipment [3]	23,709	16,196	16,196	13,341	2,854		–	7,514	10,368
Nursing home care	124,911	46,834	42,197	32,924	9,273		4,637	78,077	91,987
Other personal health care	62,211	5,947	–	–	–		5,947	56,265	62,212

– Represents zero.   [1] Includes nonpatient revenues and industrial inplant.   [2] Covers private health insurance, other private payments (excluding out-of-pocket payments), and government.   [3] See footnotes for corresponding objects on Table 126.

Source: U. S. Centers for Medicare and Medicaid Services, Office of the Actuary National Health Statistics Group. See also <http://www.cms.hhs.gov/NationalHealthExpendData/>.

Table 131. Hospital Care, Physician and Clinical Service, Nursing Home Care, and Prescription Drug Expenditures by Source of Payment: 1990 to 2006

[In billions of dollars (251.6 represents $251,600,000,000). Excludes Puerto Rico and island areas]

Source of payment	1990	2000	2001	2002	2003	2004	2005	2006
Hospital care, total	**251.6**	**417.0**	**451.4**	**488.6**	**525.4**	**564.4**	**605.5**	**648.2**
Out-of-pocket payments	11.3	13.6	14.2	15.5	17.0	18.7	19.8	21.4
Third-party payments	240.2	403.5	437.2	473.1	508.4	545.8	585.8	626.8
Private health insurance	97.8	143.6	156.7	171.3	186.2	202.6	215.3	234.8
Other private funds	10.4	21.8	20.8	21.4	24.4	25.3	26.9	29.4
Public	132.0	238.1	259.7	280.3	297.8	317.9	343.6	362.6
Federal	101.7	192.9	210.9	227.2	241.8	257.9	276.7	290.2
State and local	30.3	45.2	48.9	53.2	56.0	60.0	66.9	72.4
Medicare [1]	67.8	125.5	137.6	146.7	153.8	163.5	178.1	187.2
Medicaid [2]	26.7	71.1	76.5	84.4	90.3	96.8	105.5	110.6
Physician and clinical services, total	**157.5**	**288.6**	**313.1**	**337.9**	**366.7**	**393.6**	**422.6**	**447.6**
Out-of-pocket payments	30.2	32.2	33.5	35.2	37.4	40.0	43.3	46.2
Third-party payments	127.3	256.4	279.6	302.7	329.3	353.6	379.3	401.2
Private health insurance	67.3	136.8	149.1	162.7	177.2	191.1	207.0	219.7
Other private funds	11.3	22.2	23.2	24.4	26.1	26.2	28.0	28.6
Public	48.7	97.4	107.3	115.6	126.0	136.3	144.3	153.1
Federal	38.0	79.0	86.9	93.9	102.9	112.0	118.7	126.4
State and local	10.7	18.4	20.4	21.6	23.0	24.3	25.6	26.6
Medicare [1]	29.4	58.3	63.6	67.7	73.8	80.9	86.4	92.1
Medicaid [2]	7.0	19.1	21.6	23.8	25.4	27.8	29.9	31.3
Nursing home care, total	**52.6**	**95.3**	**101.5**	**105.7**	**110.5**	**115.2**	**120.7**	**124.9**
Out-of-pocket payments	19.0	28.6	28.8	29.5	30.5	30.8	31.5	32.9
Third-party payments	33.6	66.7	72.7	76.2	80.0	84.3	89.3	92.0
Private health insurance	2.9	7.9	8.1	8.6	8.7	8.7	8.8	9.3
Other private funds	3.8	4.5	4.0	4.0	4.2	4.2	4.4	4.6
Public	26.9	54.3	60.6	63.6	67.2	71.5	76.1	78.1
Federal	16.3	36.5	42.2	44.6	46.1	49.3	52.1	53.7
State and local	10.6	17.8	18.4	18.9	21.1	22.2	24.0	24.3
Medicare [1]	1.7	10.3	12.6	14.1	14.7	17.0	19.2	20.8
Medicaid [2]	24.1	42.0	45.8	47.1	49.7	51.5	53.7	54.2
Prescription drugs, total	**40.3**	**120.8**	**138.6**	**157.9**	**174.6**	**188.8**	**199.7**	**216.7**
Out-of-pocket payments	22.4	33.4	36.2	40.0	44.4	46.2	48.8	47.6
Third-party payments	17.9	87.4	102.4	117.9	130.2	142.5	150.9	169.1
Private health insurance	10.6	59.7	69.3	78.7	84.1	90.1	95.7	95.1
Other private funds	–	–	–	–	–	–	–	–
Public	7.3	27.6	33.0	39.2	46.1	52.5	55.2	74.0
Federal	3.2	15.8	19.2	23.1	27.7	31.3	32.6	58.7
State and local	4.0	11.8	13.8	16.2	18.4	21.2	22.6	15.3
Medicare [1]	0.2	2.1	2.4	2.4	2.4	3.3	3.9	39.5
Medicaid [2]	5.1	20.2	23.8	27.8	32.5	36.3	37.3	19.2

– Represents zero.   [1] Medicare expenditures come from federal funds.   [2] Medicaid expenditures come from federal, state, and local funds.

Source: U. S. Centers for Medicare and Medicaid Services, Office of the Actuary, "National Health Statistics Group." See also <http://www.cms.hhs.gov/NationalHealthExpendData/>.

Table 132. **Consumer Price Indexes of Medical Care Prices: 1980 to 2007**

[1982–1984 = 100. Indexes are annual averages of monthly data based on components of consumer price index for all urban consumers; for explanation, see text, Section 14 and Appendix III]

Year	Medical care, total	Medical care services					Medical care commodities		Annual percent change [3]		
		Total [1]	Professional services			Hospital and related services	Total [2]	Prescription drugs and medical supplies	Medical care, total	Medical care services	Medical care commodities
			Total [1]	Physicians	Dental						
1980....	74.9	74.8	77.9	76.5	78.9	69.2	75.4	72.5	11.0	11.3	9.3
1985....	113.5	113.2	113.5	113.3	114.2	116.1	115.2	120.1	6.3	6.1	7.2
1990....	162.8	162.7	156.1	160.8	155.8	178.0	163.4	181.7	9.0	9.3	8.4
1995....	220.5	224.2	201.0	208.8	206.8	257.8	204.5	235.0	4.5	5.1	1.9
2000....	260.8	266.0	237.7	244.7	258.5	317.3	238.1	285.4	4.1	4.3	3.2
2001....	272.8	278.8	246.5	253.6	269.0	338.3	247.6	300.9	4.6	4.8	4.0
2002....	285.6	292.9	253.9	260.6	281.0	367.8	256.4	316.5	4.7	5.1	3.6
2003....	297.1	306.0	261.2	267.7	292.5	394.8	262.8	326.3	4.0	4.5	2.5
2004....	310.1	321.3	271.5	278.3	306.9	417.9	269.3	337.1	4.4	5.0	2.5
2005....	323.2	336.7	281.7	287.5	324.0	439.9	276.0	349.0	4.2	4.8	2.5
2006....	336.2	350.6	289.3	291.9	340.9	468.1	285.9	363.9	4.0	4.1	3.6
2007....	351.1	369.3	300.8	303.2	358.4	498.9	290.0	369.2	4.4	5.3	1.4

[1] Includes other services not shown separately. [2] Includes other commodities not shown separately. [3] Percent change from the immediate prior year.
Source: Bureau of Labor Statistics, *CPI Detailed Report,* monthly, and at <http://www.bls.gov/cpi/cpidr.htm>. See also *Monthly Labor Review* at <http://www.bls.gov/opub/mlr/welcome.htm>.

Table 133. **Average Annual Expenditures Per Consumer Unit for Health Care: 2004 to 2006**

[In dollars, except percent. See text, Section 13, and headnote, Table 664. For composition of regions, see map, inside front cover]

Item	Health care, total		Health insurance	Medical services	Drugs and medical supplies [1]	Percent distribution		
	Amount	Percent of total expenditures				Health insurance	Medical services	Drugs and medical supplies [1]
2004.....................	2,574	5.9	1,332	648	594	51.7	25.2	23.1
2005.....................	2,664	5.7	1,361	677	626	51.1	25.4	23.5
2006.....................	**2,766**	**5.7**	**1,465**	**670**	**631**	**53.0**	**24.2**	**22.8**
Age of reference person:								
Under 25 years old..........	706	2.5	367	193	146	52.0	27.3	20.7
25 to 34 years old	1,652	3.5	883	469	301	53.5	28.4	18.2
35 to 44 years old	2,284	4.0	1,214	634	435	53.2	27.8	19.0
45 to 54 years old	2,757	4.8	1,310	798	650	47.5	28.9	23.6
55 to 64 years old	3,556	7.0	1,676	978	902	47.1	27.5	25.4
65 to 74 years old	4,379	10.7	2,718	636	1,025	62.1	14.5	23.4
75 years old and over........	4,282	14.8	2,511	692	1,079	58.6	16.2	25.2
Race of reference person:								
White and other............	2,940	5.8	1,538	728	674	52.3	24.8	22.9
Black...................	1,497	4.3	927	248	321	61.9	16.6	21.4
Origin of reference person:								
Hispanic.................	1,659	3.9	780	504	374	47.0	30.4	22.5
Non-Hispanic	2,910	5.9	1,554	692	665	53.4	23.8	22.9
Region of residence:								
Northeast................	2,591	5.3	1,462	596	534	56.4	23.0	20.6
Midwest.................	2,816	6.2	1,505	697	614	53.4	24.8	21.8
South	2,775	6.2	1,459	614	703	52.6	22.1	25.3
West	2,853	5.0	1,437	798	618	50.4	28.0	21.7
Size of consumer unit:								
One person	1,827	6.2	948	424	454	51.9	23.2	24.8
Two or more persons	3,161	5.6	1,683	774	705	53.2	24.5	22.3
Two persons	3,641	7.2	1,976	809	856	54.3	22.2	23.5
Three persons	2,868	5.1	1,492	700	676	52.0	24.4	23.6
Four persons	2,824	4.4	1,513	771	541	53.6	27.3	19.2
Five persons or more	2,516	3.9	1,254	782	480	49.8	31.1	19.1
Income before taxes:								
Quintiles of income:								
Lowest 20 percent	1,485	7.3	817	290	378	55.0	19.5	25.5
Second 20 percent	2,456	8.1	1,347	504	605	54.8	20.5	24.6
Third 20 percent..........	2,647	6.4	1,446	602	599	54.6	22.7	22.6
Fourth 20 percent........	3,154	5.7	1,677	776	701	53.2	24.6	22.2
Highest 20 percent	4,086	4.3	2,036	1,179	871	49.8	28.9	21.3
Education:								
Less than a high school graduate..	1,991	6.9	1,123	368	499	56.4	18.5	25.1
High school graduate	2,575	6.6	1,446	531	598	56.2	20.6	23.2
High school graduate with some college.............	2,498	5.4	1,323	627	548	53.0	25.1	21.9
Associate's degree..........	2,923	5.6	1,473	690	760	50.4	23.6	26.0
Bachelor's degree..........	3,349	5.2	1,690	937	722	50.5	28.0	21.6
Master's, professional, doctoral degree	3,781	5.0	1,912	1,078	792	50.6	28.5	20.9

[1] Includes prescription and nonprescription drugs.
Source: U.S. Bureau of Labor Statistics, *Consumer Expenditure Survey,* annual; <http://www.bls.gov/cex/>.

Health and Nutrition 99

Table 134. **Medicare Benefits by Type of Provider: 1990 to 2007**

[**In millions of dollars (65,721 represents $65,721,000,000). For years ending Sept. 30.** Distribution of benefits by type is estimated and subject to change. The Medicare program has two components: Hospital Insurance (HI) or Medicare Part A and Supplementary Medical Insurance (SMI) consisting of Medicare Part B and Part D. See text in this section for details]

Type of provider	1990	1995	2000	2003	2004	2005	2006	2007
Hospital insurance benefits, total (Part A)	**65,721**	**113,395**	**125,992**	**153,144**	**163,764**	**181,460**	**185,005**	**207,461**
Inpatient hospital	57,012	81,095	86,561	108,570	114,375	122,288	122,035	129,586
Skilled nursing facility	2,761	8,684	10,269	14,938	16,673	18,631	19,651	22,293
Home health agency	3,295	15,715	4,880	4,940	5,213	5,861	5,861	6,343
Hospice	318	1,854	2,818	5,428	6,572	7,678	8,791	10,008
Managed care	2,335	6,047	21,463	19,267	20,932	27,001	28,668	39,230
Supplementary medical insurance benefits, total (Part B)	**41,498**	**63,490**	**88,876**	**119,455**	**131,357**	**147,923**	**154,477**	**169,227**
Physician fee schedule	(NA)	31,110	35,958	47,486	52,224	57,213	57,863	58,561
Durable medical equipment	(NA)	3,576	4,577	7,429	7,687	7,888	8,308	8,169
Carrier lab [1]	(NA)	2,819	2,194	2,946	3,206	3,521	3,672	3,982
Other carrier [2]	(NA)	4,513	7,154	12,432	13,794	15,197	15,277	16,003
Hospital [3]	(NA)	8,448	8,516	14,692	16,931	19,216	19,878	20,736
Home health	(NA)	223	4,281	5,158	5,577	6,749	7,440	9,115
Intermediary lab [4]	(NA)	1,437	1,748	2,408	2,670	2,866	2,860	2,845
Other intermediary [5]	(NA)	5,110	6,099	9,700	10,459	11,537	11,966	12,092
Managed care	(NA)	6,253	18,348	17,203	18,809	23,735	27,213	37,724
Supplementary medical insurance benefits, total (Part D) [6]	**(X)**	**(X)**	**(X)**	**(X)**	**216**	**1,198**	**33,745**	**51,219**

NA Not available.   X Not applicable.   [1] Lab services paid under the lab fee schedule performed in a physician's office lab or an independent lab.   [2] Includes free-standing ambulatory surgical center's facility costs, ambulance, and supplies.   [3] Includes the hospital facility costs for Medicare Part B services which are predominantly in the outpatient department. The physician reimbursement associated with these services is included on the "Physician Fee Schedule" line.   [4] Lab fee services paid under the lab fee schedule performed in a hospital outpatient department.   [5] Includes ESRD (End Stage Renal Disease) free-standing dialysis facility payments and payments to rural health clinics, outpatient rehabilitation facilities, psychiatric hospitals, and federally qualified health centers.   [6] Starting with 2006, Part D provides subsidized access to drug insurance coverage on a voluntary basis for all beneficiaries and premium and cost-sharing subsidies for low-income enrollees. Benefits prior to 2006 were for transitional assistance to beneficiaries with low income.

Source: U.S. Centers for Medicare and Medicaid Services, unpublished data. See also <http://www.cms.hhs.gov/ReportsTrustFunds/>.

Table 135. **Medicare—Enrollment by State and Other Areas: 2000 to 2005**

[**In thousands (39,620 represents 39,620,000). Hospital (HI) and/or supplementary medical insurance (SMI) enrollment as of July 1**]

State and area	2000	2003	2004	2005	State and area	2000	2003	2004	2005
All areas [1]	**39,620**	**41,087**	**41,729**	**42,395**	MT	137	142	145	146
					NE	254	257	259	259
U.S.	**38,762**	**40,173**	**40,792**	**41,003**	NV	240	274	286	294
AL	685	719	733	740	NH	170	180	183	185
AK	42	48	50	51	NJ	1,203	1,220	1,225	1,215
AZ	675	729	755	777	NM	234	250	257	261
AR	439	453	460	464	NY	2,715	2,763	2,775	2,758
CA	3,901	4,078	4,150	4,158	NC	1,133	1,205	1,235	1,255
CO	467	493	506	513	ND	103	103	103	103
CT	515	522	524	520	OH	1,701	1,727	1,739	1,731
DE	112	119	123	125	OK	508	521	529	531
DC	75	74	73	72	OR	489	513	527	532
FL	2,804	2,921	2,982	3,008	PA	2,095	2,110	2,118	2,108
GA	916	974	998	1,016	RI	172	172	173	171
HI	165	175	178	180	SC	568	606	624	637
ID	165	178	184	188	SD	119	122	123	123
IL	1,635	1,661	1,676	1,674	TN	829	872	891	903
IN	852	878	889	893	TX	2,265	2,390	2,451	2,491
IA	477	482	486	484	UT	206	220	227	231
KS	390	394	397	397	VT	89	93	94	95
KY	623	648	660	668	VA	893	946	967	981
LA	602	620	627	630	WA	736	775	799	807
ME	216	227	231	233	WV	338	347	351	351
MD	645	674	685	687	WI	783	804	814	818
MA	961	966	968	961	WY	65	69	70	70
MI	1,403	1,445	1,464	1,468					
MN	654	676	686	691	Outlying areas [2]	537	575	613	622
MS	419	437	446	449	Pending state designations [3]	321	340	324	769
MO	861	884	896	901					

[1] Includes outlying areas and pending state designation.   [2] Includes American Samoa, Federated States of Micronesia, Guam, Marshall Islands, Northern Marianas, Puerto Rico, Virgin Islands, and Wake Island.   [3] Include foreign countries and unknown places of residence.

Source: U.S. Centers for Medicare and Medicaid Services, Medicare Enrollment Reports. See also <http://www.cms.hhs.gov /MedicareEnrpts/>.

Table 136. **Medicare Enrollees: 1990 to 2007**

[**In millions (34.3 represents 34,300,000). As of July 1.** Includes Puerto Rico and island areas and enrollees in foreign countries and unknown place of residence. SMI is Supplemental Medical Insurance. See headnote, Table 134]

Item	1990	1995	2000	2003	2004	2005	2006	2007
Total	**34.3**	**37.6**	**39.7**	**41.2**	**41.9**	**42.6**	**43.2**	**44.2**
Aged	31.0	33.2	34.3	35.0	35.4	35.8	36.3	37.0
Disabled	3.3	4.4	5.4	6.2	6.5	6.8	7.0	7.1
Hospital insurance, Part A	**33.7**	**37.2**	**39.3**	**40.7**	**41.5**	**42.2**	**42.9**	**43.8**
Aged	30.5	32.7	33.8	34.6	35.0	35.4	35.9	36.6
Disabled	3.3	4.4	5.4	6.2	6.5	6.8	7.0	7.1
SMI, Part B	**32.6**	**35.6**	**37.3**	**38.6**	**39.1**	**39.7**	**40.3**	**40.7**
Aged	29.6	31.7	32.6	33.2	33.5	33.8	34.1	34.4
Disabled	2.9	3.9	4.8	5.4	5.7	5.9	6.1	6.3
SMI, Part D	**(X)**	**(X)**	**(X)**	**(X)**	**1.2**	**1.8**	**27.9**	**30.7**
Medicare Advantage [1]	1.3	2.7	6.2	4.7	4.7	5.1	6.5	7.9

X Not applicable.   [1] Prior to 2004, Medicare Advantage was referred to as Medicare + Choice.

Source: U.S. Centers for Medicare and Medicaid Services, Office of the Actuary, CMS Statistics Medicare Enrollment <http://www.cms.hhs.gov/MedicareEnrpts/>.

Table 137. **Medicare Disbursements by Type of Beneficiary: 1990 to 2007**

[**In millions of dollars (109,709 represents $109,709,000,000). For years ending Sept. 30.** Distribution of benefits by type is estimated and subject to change. See headnote, Table 134]

Selected type of beneficiary	1990	1995	2000	2003	2004	2005	2006	2007
Total disbursements	**109,709**	**180,096**	**219,276**	**277,846**	**301,488**	**336,877**	**380,433**	**434,701**
HI, Part A disbursements [1]	**66,687**	**114,883**	**130,284**	**153,792**	**166,998**	**184,629**	**188,444**	**210,502**
Benefits	65,722	113,394	125,992	153,144	163,764	181,460	185,005	207,461
Aged	58,503	100,107	110,261	132,415	140,704	155,469	157,347	175,696
Disabled	7,218	13,288	15,731	20,729	23,060	25,990	27,658	31,765
SMI, Part B disbursements [1]	**43,022**	**65,213**	**88,992**	**124,055**	**134,274**	**151,050**	**158,104**	**171,976**
Benefits	41,498	63,490	88,875	119,455	131,357	147,923	154,477	169,227
Aged	36,837	54,830	76,340	100,505	109,890	123,258	127,854	140,282
Disabled	4,661	8,660	12,535	18,940	21,467	24,665	26,623	28,946
Part D Transitional Assistance	(X)	(X)	(X)	(X)	153	566	366	28
SMI, Part D disbursements [1]	**(X)**	**(X)**	**(X)**	**(X)**	**216**	**1,198**	**33,884**	**52,223**
Benefits	(X)	(X)	(X)	(X)	–	73	33,481	51,209
Transitional assistance benefit payments	(X)	(X)	(X)	(X)	216	1,125	229	10

– Represents or rounds to zero.   X Not applicable.   [1] Other types not shown separately.

Source: U.S. Centers for Medicare and Medicaid Services, Trustees Report and Trust Funds, and unpublished data. See also <http://www.cms.hhs.gov/ReportsTrustFunds/>.

Table 138. **Medicare Insurance Trust Funds: 1990 to 2007**

[**In billions of dollars (126.3 represents $126,300,000,000)** SMI is Supplemental Medical Insurance. See headnote, Table 134]

Type of trust fund	1990	1995	2000	2002	2003	2004	2005	2006	2007
TOTAL MEDICARE									
Total income	126.3	175.3	257.1	284.8	291.6	317.7	357.5	437.1	461.9
Total expenditures	111.0	184.2	221.8	265.7	280.8	308.9	336.4	408.4	431.5
Assets, end of year	114.4	143.4	221.5	269.1	280.0	288.8	309.8	338.5	368.9
HOSPITAL INSURANCE (Part A)									
Net contribution income [1]	72.1	103.3	154.5	162.7	159.2	167.2	182.6	194.2	205.3
Interest received [2]	8.5	10.8	11.7	15.1	15.8	16.0	16.1	16.4	17.4
Benefit payments [3]	66.2	116.4	126.8	148.8	154.3	167.6	180.0	189.0	200.2
Assets, end of year	98.9	130.3	177.5	234.8	256.0	269.3	285.8	305.4	326.0
SMI (Part B)									
Net premium income	11.3	19.7	20.6	25.1	27.4	31.4	37.5	42.9	46.8
Transfers from general revenue	33.0	39.0	65.9	78.3	86.4	100.4	118.1	132.7	139.6
Interest received [2]	1.6	1.6	3.5	2.8	2.0	1.5	1.4	1.8	2.2
Benefit payments [3]	42.5	65.0	88.9	111.0	123.8	135.0	149.2	165.9	176.4
Assets, end of year	15.5	13.1	44.0	34.3	24.0	19.4	24.0	32.3	42.1
SMI (Part D)									
Net premium income	(X)	(X)	(X)	(X)	(X)	–	–	3.5	3.9
Transfers from general revenue [4]	(X)	(X)	(X)	(X)	(X)	0.4	1.1	39.2	38.8
Interest received	(X)	(X)	(X)	(X)	(X)	–	–	–	–
Benefit payments [4]	(X)	(X)	(X)	(X)	(X)	0.4	1.1	47.1	48.6
Assets, end of year	(X)	(X)	(X)	(X)	(X)	–	–	0.8	0.8

– Represents zero.   X Not applicable.   [1] Includes income from taxation of benefits beginning in 1994. Includes premiums from aged ineligibles enrolled in Hospital Insurance (HI).   [2] Includes recoveries of amounts reimbursed from the trust fund.   [3] Beginning 1998, monies transferred to the SMI trust fund for home health agency costs, as provided for by P.L. 105-33, are included in HI benefit payments but excluded from SMI benefit payments.   [4] These amounts for 2004 and 2005 include amounts transferred for transitional assistance for Part D of Medicare.

Source: U.S. Centers for Medicare and Medicaid Services, Annual Report of the Board of Trustees of the Federal Hospital Insurance Trust Fund and Annual Report of the Board of Trustees of the Federal Supplementary Medical Insurance Trust Fund. See also <http://www.cms.hhs.gov/ReportsTrustFunds/>.

Health and Nutrition   101

Table 139. **Medicaid—Selected Characteristics of Persons Covered: 2006**

[In thousands, except percent (38,088 represents 38,088,000). Represents number of persons as of March of following year who were enrolled at any time in year shown. Excludes unrelated individuals under age 15. Persons did not have to receive medical care paid for by Medicaid in order to be counted. See headnote, Table 548]

Poverty status	Total [1]	White alone [2]	Black alone [3]	Asian alone [4]	His-panic [5]	Under 18 years old	18–44 years old	45–64 years old	65 years old and over
Persons covered, total . . .	**38,088**	**26,372**	**8,491**	**1,474**	**9,621**	**19,874**	**9,603**	**5,247**	**3,364**
Below poverty level	15,409	9,653	4,928	374	4,034	8,399	4,092	2,039	880
Above poverty level	22,679	16,719	3,563	1,100	5,587	11,475	5,511	3,208	2,484
Percent of population covered	12.8	11.1	22.8	11.2	21.5	27.0	8.6	6.9	9.3
Below poverty level	42.3	39.5	54.5	27.6	43.6	65.5	29.2	32.8	25.9
Above poverty level	8.7	7.8	12.6	9.3	15.7	18.8	5.7	4.6	7.6

[1] Includes other races not shown separately.   [2] White alone refers to people who reported White and did not report any other race category.   [3] Black alone refers to people who reported Black and did not report any other race category.   [4] Asian alone refers to people who reported Asian and did not report any other race category.   [5] Persons of Hispanic origin may be of any race.

Source: U.S. Census Bureau, Current Population Reports, Income, Poverty, and Health Insurance Coverage in the United States: 2006, P60-233; and "Table HI02. Health Insurance Coverage Status and Type of Coverage by Selected Characteristics for People in the Poverty Universe: 2006"; and "Table HI03. Health Insurance Coverage Status and Type of Coverage by Selected Characteristics for Poor People in the Poverty Universe: 2006"; issued August 2007; <http://www.census.gov/hhes/www/hlthins/hlthin06.html>.

Table 140. **Medicaid—Beneficiaries and Payments: 2000 to 2005**

[For year ending September 30 (42,887 represents 42,887,000)]

Basis of eligibility and type of service	Beneficiaries (1,000) [1]				Payments (mil. dol.)			
	2000	2003	2004	2005 [2]	2000	2003	2004	2005 [2]
Total	**42,887**	**51,971**	**55,002**	**57,643**	**168,443**	**233,206**	**257,748**	**275,569**
Age 65 and over	3,730	4,041	4,318	4,396	44,560	55,271	59,541	63,358
Blind/Disabled	6,890	7,669	7,933	8,210	72,772	102,014	111,614	119,647
Children	19,018	23,992	25,613	26,337	23,490	35,080	39,194	42,012
Adults	8,671	11,679	12,225	12,529	17,671	26,689	30,522	32,385
Foster care children	761	839	846	875	3,309	4,791	5,011	5,337
Unknown	3,817	3,739	4,048	5,267	6,639	9,251	11,668	12,547
BCCA WOMEN [3]	(NA)	12	19	29	(NA)	110	199	283
Capitated care [4]	21,292	27,574	29,528	33,496	25,026	37,405	42,601	46,421
Clinic services	7,678	10,162	11,102	11,913	6,138	7,312	8,336	8,986
Dental services	5,922	8,510	9,037	9,328	1,413	2,595	2,867	3,045
Home health services	1,007	1,184	1,146	1,195	3,133	4,404	4,566	5,361
ICF/MR services [5]	119	114	114	109	9,376	10,861	11,193	11,730
Inpatient hospital services	4,913	5,217	5,425	5,488	24,131	31,549	34,914	35,347
Lab and X-ray services	11,439	14,687	15,875	16,020	1,292	2,365	2,695	2,927
Mental health facility services [6] . . .	100	105	117	120	1,769	2,143	2,326	2,333
Nursing facility services	1,706	1,691	1,709	1,712	34,528	40,381	42,008	44,675
Other care [7]	9,022	11,742	12,387	12,347	14,755	21,809	24,951	26,624
Outpatient hospital services	13,170	15,511	15,888	16,314	7,082	9,252	10,261	10,228
Other practitioner services	4,758	5,746	5,933	5,904	664	882	951	1,182
PCCM services [8]	5,649	7,542	8,548	8,750	177	208	500	235
Prescribed drugs	20,325	26,075	27,549	28,385	19,898	33,714	39,476	42,830
Physician services	18,965	22,857	23,612	24,204	6,809	9,210	10,061	11,278
Personal support services [9]	4,559	6,022	6,254	6,809	11,629	17,245	18,494	20,729
Sterilizations	137	160	174	179	128	166	207	212
Unknown	74	88	81	73	496	1,702	1,344	1,428

NA Not available.   [1] Beneficiaries data do not add due to number of beneficiaries that are reported in more than one category.   [2] 2005 beneficiary data is not available for Maine; 2004 data is reported.   [3] Women-Breast and Cervical Cancer Assistance.   [4] HMO payments and prepaid health plans.   [5] Intermediate care facilities for mentally retarded.   [6] Inpatient mental health-aged and inpatient mental health-under 21.   [7] Includes beneficiaries of, and payments for, other care not shown separately.   [8] Primary Care Case Management Services.   [9] Includes personal care services, rehabilitative services, physical occupational targeted case management services, speech therapies, hospice services, nurse midwife services, nurse practitioner services, private duty nursing services, and religious nonmedical health care institutions.

Source: U.S. Centers for Medicare and Medicaid Services, "Medicaid Program Statistics, Medicaid Statistical Information System"; <http://www.cms.hhs.gov/MedicaidDataSourcesGenInfo/02_MSISDATA.asp#TopOfPage>.

Table 141. **Medicaid—Summary by State: 2000 and 2005**

[(42,887 represents 42,887,000). For year ending September 30. See headnote, Table 140]

State	Beneficiaries [1] (1,000)		Payments [2] (mil. dol.)		State	Beneficiaries [1] (1,000)		Payments [2] (mil. dol.)	
	2000	2005	2000	2005		2000	2005	2000	2005
U.S.	**42,887**	**57,643**	**168,443**	**275,569**	MO	890	1,156	3,274	5,263
AL	619	839	2,393	4,154	MT	104	116	422	621
AK	96	125	473	1,004	NE	229	248	960	1,450
AZ	681	1,203	2,112	4,449	NV	138	257	516	1,090
AR	489	977	1,543	2,662	NH	97	121	651	818
CA	7,918	10,509	17,105	28,638	NJ	822	966	4,714	7,010
CO	381	593	1,809	2,595	NM	376	491	1,249	2,415
CT	420	521	2,839	3,787	NY	3,420	4,938	26,148	39,348
DE	115	165	529	885	NC	1,214	1,549	4,834	8,415
DC	139	158	793	1,316	ND	63	74	358	557
FL	2,373	3,166	7,433	13,154	OH	1,305	1,955	7,115	12,114
GA	1,369	2,038	3,624	6,821	OK	507	686	1,604	2,561
HI	194	224	600	931	OR	558	547	1,714	2,444
ID	131	201	594	1,072	PA	1,492	1,990	6,366	11,902
IL	1,519	2,239	7,807	10,788	RI	179	209	1,070	1,638
IN	706	984	2,977	4,780	SC	689	870	2,765	4,248
IA	314	400	1,477	2,350	SD	102	131	402	627
KS	263	385	1,227	2,080	TN	1,568	1,610	3,491	7,698
KY	764	857	2,921	4,044	TX	2,633	3,753	9,277	14,365
LA	761	1,146	2,632	4,420	UT	225	314	960	1,501
ME [3]	194	294	1,310	2,366	VT	139	151	480	859
MD	626	750	3,003	4,949	VA	627	778	2,479	4,061
MA	1,060	1,110	5,413	8,308	WA	896	1,178	2,435	5,335
MI	1,352	1,856	4,881	7,654	WV	342	374	1,394	2,339
MN	558	708	3,280	5,234	WI	577	949	2,968	4,580
MS	605	716	1,808	3,470	WY	46	69	215	398

[1] Persons who had payments made on their behalf at any time during the fiscal year. [2] Payments are for fiscal year and reflect federal and state contribution payments. Data exclude disproportionate share hospital payments. Disproportionate share hospitals receive higher medicaid reimbursement than other hospitals because they treat a disproportionate share of Medicaid patients. [3] 2005 beneficiary data are not available for Maine; 2004 data are reported.

Source: U.S. Centers for Medicare and Medicaid Services, "Medicaid, Program Statistics, Medicaid Statistical Information System"; <http://www.cms.hhs.gov/MedicaidDataSourcesGenInfo/02_MSISData.asp#TopOfPage>.

Table 142. **State Children's Health Insurance Program (SCHIP)—Enrollment and Expenditures by State: 2000 and 2007**

[(3,357.4 represents 3,357,400) For year ending September 30. This program provides health benefits coverage to children living in families whose incomes exceed the eligibility limits for Medicaid. Although it is generally targeted to families with incomes at or below 200 percent of the federal poverty level, each state may set its own income eligibility limits, within certain guidelines. States have three options: they may expand their Medicaid programs, develop a separate child health program that functions independently of Medicaid, or do a combination of both]

State	Enrollment [1] (1,000)		Expenditures [2] (mil. dol.)		State	Enrollment [1] (1,000)		Expenditures [2] (mil. dol.)	
	2000	2007	2000	2007		2000	2007	2000	2007
US	**3,357.4**	**7,144.8**	**1,928.8**	**5,931.57**	MO	72.8	81.8	41.2	79.4
AL	37.6	106.7	31.9	95.2	MT	8.3	20.1	4.3	18.2
AK	13.4	17.6	18.1	16.2	NE	11.4	46.2	6.1	33.2
AZ	59.6	104.2	29.4	117.7	NV	15.9	41.9	9.0	30.3
AR	1.9	89.6	1.5	68.8	NH	4.3	12.1	1.6	11.1
CA	484.4	1,538.4	187.3	980.7	NJ	89.0	150.3	46.9	280.0
CO	34.9	84.6	13.9	65.9	NM	8.0	16.5	3.4	49.9
CT	19.9	23.6	12.8	30.1	NY	769.5	651.9	401.0	324.4
DE	4.5	11.1	1.5	8.6	NC	103.6	240.2	65.5	166.6
DC	2.3	6.6	5.8	7.2	ND	2.6	5.5	1.8	10.5
FL	227.5	323.5	125.7	261.7	OH	118.3	231.5	53.1	186.9
GA	120.6	356.3	48.7	328.1	OK	57.7	117.1	51.3	96.4
HI	(Z)	24.0	0.4	18.7	OR	37.1	63.1	12.5	66.6
ID	12.4	33.1	7.5	27.4	PA	119.7	227.4	70.7	190.0
IL	62.5	345.6	32.7	448.5	RI	11.5	26.1	10.4	47.7
IN	44.4	130.4	53.7	92.1	SC	60.4	59.9	46.6	31.4
IA	20.0	50.2	15.5	51.3	SD	5.9	15.0	3.1	9.8
KS	26.3	49.5	12.8	45.1	TN	14.9	41.4	41.7	4.1
KY	55.6	68.8	60.0	81.2	TX	131.1	710.7	41.4	385.7
LA	50.0	153.7	25.3	119.9	UT	25.3	44.8	12.8	38.9
ME	22.7	31.0	11.4	31.2	VT	4.1	6.1	1.4	5.9
MD	93.1	132.9	92.2	138.4	VA	37.7	144.2	18.6	110.7
MA	113.0	184.5	44.2	211.5	WA	2.6	17.7	0.6	36.8
MI	55.4	114.0	36.2	171.6	WV	21.7	38.6	9.7	35.4
MN	(Z)	5.4	(Z)	64.4	WI	47.1	62.5	21.4	84.5
MS	12.2	81.6	21.1	107.5	WY	2.5	8.6	1.0	7.8

Z Less than 50 or $50,000. [1] Number of children ever enrolled during the year in SCHIP. [2] Expenditures for which states are entitled to federal reimbursement under Title XXI.

Source: U.S. Centers for Medicare & Medicaid Services, and the Statement of Expenditures for the SCHIP Program (CMS-21). See also <http://www.cms.hhs.gov/NationalSCHIPPolicy/SCHIPER/list.asp> and <http://www.cms.hhs.gov/medicaid/mbes/default.asp>.

Health and Nutrition   103

Table 143. **Medicaid Managed Care Enrollment by State and Other Areas: 1995 to 2007**

[For year ending June 30. (33,373 represents 33,373,000)]

State and other areas	Total enroll-ment [1] (1,000)	Managed care enrollment [2] Number (1,000)	Managed care enrollment [2] Per-cent of total	State and other areas	Total enroll-ment [1] (1,000)	Managed care enrollment [2] Number (1,000)	Managed care enrollment [2] Per-cent of total	State and other areas	Total enroll-ment [1] (1,000)	Managed care enrollment [2] Number (1,000)	Managed care enrollment [2] Per-cent of total
1995	33,373	9,800	29.4	HI	202	161	79.9	NY	4,120	2,559	62.1
2000	33,690	18,786	55.8	ID	180	152	84.8	NC	1,317	848	64.4
2003	42,741	24,406	58.4	IL	2,003	568	28.4	ND	52	29	56.0
2004	44,356	26,914	60.7	IN	826	600	72.6	OH	1,719	1,194	69.5
2005	45,392	28,576	63.0	IA	366	283	77.4	OK	592	412	69.5
2006	45,653	29,830	65.3	KS	272	139	51.1	OR	396	359	90.8
				KY	714	448	62.8	PA	1,773	1,439	81.2
2007, total..	**45,962**	**29,463**	**64.1**	LA	935	636	68.1	RI	181	114	63.1
				ME	254	172	67.4	SC	655	150	22.9
U.S...	**44,888**	**28,541**	**63.6**	MD	693	502	72.4	SD	101	99	98.6
AL	724	472	65.1	MA	1,082	642	59.3	TN	1,182	1,182	100.0
AK	96	–	–	MI	1,520	1,343	88.4	TX	3,002	2,021	67.3
AZ	990	890	89.9	MN	594	367	61.8	UT	201	165	82.3
AR	626	511	81.7	MS	548	–	–	VT	146	123	84.3
CA	6,465	3,286	50.8	MO	823	345	41.9	VA	695	446	64.2
CO	381	359	94.1	MT	80	45	55.7	WA	993	849	85.5
CT	405	299	73.7	NE	210	170	81.2	WV	304	135	44.6
DE	144	96	66.9	NV	170	144	84.8	WI	852	411	48.2
DC	142	92	64.7	NH	109	84	77.2	WY	61	–	–
FL	2,195	1,355	61.7	NJ	878	620	70.6	PR	1,067	922	86.5
GA	1,502	965	64.2	NM	414	256	61.9	VI	7	–	–

– Represents zero. [1] The unduplicated Medicaid enrollment figures include individuals in state health care reform programs that expand eligibility beyond traditional Medicaid eligibility standards. [2] The unduplicated managed care enrollment figures include enrollees receiving comprehensive and limited benefits.

Source: U.S. Centers for Medicare and Medicaid Services, *2007 Medicaid Managed Care Enrollment Report;* see also <http://www.cms.hhs.gov/MedicaidDataSourcesGenInfo/04_MdManCrEnrllRep.asp>.

Table 144. **Health Maintenance Organizations (HMOs): 1990 to 2007**

[As of January 1 (33.0 represents 33,000,000). An HMO is a prepaid health plan delivering comprehensive care to members through designated providers, having a fixed periodic payment for health care services, and requiring members to be in a plan for a specified period of time (usually 1 year). A group HMO delivers health services through a physician group that is controlled by the HMO unit or contracts with one or more independent group practices to provide health services. An individual practice association (IPA) HMO contracts directly with physicians in independent practice, and/or contracts with one or more associations of physicians in independent practice, and/or contracts with one or more multispecialty group practices. Data are based on a census of HMOs]

Model type	Number of plans 1990	2000	2004 [2]	2005 [4]	2006 [3,4]	2007 [3,4]	Enrollment [1] (mil.) 1990	2000	2004 [2]	2005 [4]	2006 [3,4]	2007 [3,4]
Total...	572	568	412	420	548	531	33.0	80.9	68.8	69.2	73.9	73.9
IPA	360	278	176	171	191	174	13.7	33.4	24.6	23.5	22.4	23.3
Group [5]	212	102	96	98	122	116	19.3	15.2	15.3	16.4	20.7	19.7
Mixed	(NA)	188	140	141	134	103	(NA)	32.3	28.9	29.0	25.5	21.5

NA Not available. [1] 1990–1995 exclude enrollees participating in open-ended plans; beginning 1999, includes open-ended enrollment. [2] Starting with 2004 data, Puerto Rico and Guam included in the total. [3] 2006 and 2007 data include "HMO Medicaid only plans." [4] 2005–2007 totals include plans that did not provide enough information to be classified as a model type. [5] 2006 and 2007 data include data for "Network, Staff and Group" types categorized under the "Group" model type.
Source: HealthLeaders-InterStudy, Nashville, TN, *The Competitive Edge*, (copyright). See also <http://www.interstudypublications.com/>.

Table 145. **Persons Enrolled in Health Maintenance Organizations (HMOs) by State: 2006 and 2007**

[As of January 1 (64,494 represents 64,494,000). Data are based on a census of health maintenance organizations]

State	Number 2007 (1,000)	Percent of population 2006	Percent of population 2007	State	Number 2007 (1,000)	Percent of population 2006	Percent of population 2007	State	Number 2007 (1,000)	Percent of population 2006	Percent of population 2007
US...	**64,494**	**23.8**	**21.5**	KS	362	14.8	13.1	ND	1	0.4	0.2
				KY	271	6.2	6.4	OH	2,080	23.2	18.1
AL	120	3.1	2.6	LA	282	9.5	6.6	OK	227	7.0	6.3
AK	–	–	–	ME	366	36.6	27.7	OR	875	24.8	23.6
AZ	1,522	34.2	24.7	MD	1,428	29.1	25.4	PA	3,214	26.9	25.8
AR	85	3.5	3.0	MA	2,265	44.2	35.2	RI	220	25.0	20.6
CA	15,992	49.2	43.9	MI	2,796	26.6	27.7	SC	295	7.4	6.8
CO	1,004	25.9	21.1	MN	704	23.4	13.6	SD	66	7.5	8.4
CT	1,053	31.3	30.1	MS	3	0.8	0.1	TN	1,510	25.8	25.0
DE	153	15.5	18.0	MO	1,050	18.6	18.0	TX	2,364	12.1	10.1
DC	332	55.4	57.0	MT	48	7.3	5.1	UT	719	26.1	28.2
FL	3,584	24.5	19.8	NE	97	7.9	5.5	VT	95	24.5	15.3
GA	2,157	15.4	23.0	NV	541	24.7	21.7	VA	1,341	19.5	17.5
HI	601	46.8	46.7	NH	216	21.5	16.4	WA	1,186	18.3	18.5
ID	64	2.9	4.4	NJ	1,884	24.4	21.6	WV	197	8.9	10.8
IL	1,626	15.2	12.7	NM	374	23.7	19.1	WI	1,224	26.3	22.0
IN	1,441	25.7	22.8	NY	5,784	27.5	30.0	WY	13	2.0	2.6
IA	238	11.5	8.0	NC	423	9.8	4.8				

– Represents zero.
Source: HealthLeaders-InterStudy, Nashville, TN, *The Competitive Edge*, (copyright); See also <http://www.interstudypublications.com/>.

[**(293,834 represents 293,834,000).** Persons as of following year for coverage in the year shown. Government health insurance includes Medicare, Medicaid, and military plans. Based on Current Population Survey, Annual Social and Economic Supplement; see text, Section 1, and Appendix III]

Characteristic	Number (1,000)							Percent			
	Total persons	Covered by private or government health insurance					Not covered by health insurance	Covered by private or government health insurance			Not covered by health insurance
		Total[1]	Private		Government			Total[1]	Private	Medi-caid	
			Total	Group health[2]	Medi-care	Medi-caid					
2005[3]	293,834	249,020	201,167	176,924	40,177	38,104	44,815	84.7	68.5	13.0	15.3
2006	296,824	249,829	201,690	177,152	40,343	38,281	46,995	84.2	67.9	12.9	15.8
Age:											
Under 18 years	74,101	65,440	47,906	44,257	411	20,067	8,661	88.3	64.6	27.1	11.7
Under 6 years	24,558	21,786	14,847	13,996	155	7,885	2,771	88.7	60.5	32.1	11.3
6 to 11 years	23,789	21,157	15,560	14,544	120	6,390	2,632	88.9	65.4	26.9	11.1
12 to 17 years	25,755	22,497	17,499	15,717	136	5,792	3,258	87.4	67.9	22.5	12.6
18 to 24 years	28,405	20,081	17,030	13,768	154	3,252	8,323	70.7	60.0	11.4	29.3
25 to 34 years	39,868	29,154	25,814	24,009	472	3,374	10,713	73.1	64.7	8.5	26.9
35 to 44 years	42,762	34,744	31,531	29,463	806	2,977	8,018	81.2	73.7	7.0	18.8
45 to 54 years	43,461	36,819	33,250	30,868	1,739	2,885	6,642	84.7	76.5	6.6	15.3
55 to 64 years	32,191	28,096	24,255	21,701	2,956	2,362	4,095	87.3	75.3	7.3	12.7
65 years and over	36,035	35,494	21,904	13,086	33,806	3,364	541	98.5	60.8	9.3	1.5
Sex: Male	145,689	120,158	98,760	87,790	17,427	17,201	25,531	82.5	67.8	11.8	17.5
Female	151,135	129,671	102,930	89,362	22,916	21,080	21,464	85.8	68.1	13.9	14.2
Race: White alone[4]	237,892	202,405	167,640	146,285	34,416	26,507	35,486	85.1	70.5	11.1	14.9
Black alone[4]	37,369	29,717	20,034	18,401	4,059	8,531	7,652	79.5	53.6	22.8	20.5
Asian alone[4]	13,194	11,149	9,339	8,201	1,187	1,480	2,045	84.5	70.8	11.2	15.5
Hispanic origin[5]	44,854	29,558	19,434	17,934	2,757	9,646	15,296	65.9	43.3	21.5	34.1
Household income:											
Less than $25,000	55,856	41,923	18,346	11,501	15,737	18,536	13,933	75.1	32.8	33.2	24.9
$25,000–$49,999	72,582	57,262	42,868	35,918	12,955	11,344	15,319	78.9	59.1	15.6	21.1
$50,000–$74,999	58,555	50,096	44,775	40,706	5,321	4,523	8,459	85.6	76.5	7.7	14.4
$75,000 or more	109,831	100,548	95,701	89,028	6,330	3,877	9,283	91.5	87.1	3.5	8.5
Persons below poverty	36,460	24,936	8,479	5,408	4,699	15,409	11,523	68.4	23.3	42.3	31.6

[1] Includes other government insurance not shown separately. Persons with coverage counted only once in total, even though they may have been covered by more than one type of policy. [2] Related to employment of self or other family members. [3] The estimates are revised from the originally published data. [4] Refers to people who reported specified race and did not report any other race category. [5] Persons of Hispanic origin may be any race.

Source: U.S. Census Bureau, Current Population Reports; Income, Poverty, and Health Insurance Coverage in the United States: 2006, P60-233; issued August 2007. Table HI01 Health Insurance Data, Health Insurance Coverage Status and Type of Coverage by Selected Characteristics: 2006. Table HI02. Health Insurance Coverage Status and Type of Coverage by Selected Characteristics for People in the Poverty Universe: 2006; <http://www.census.gov/hhes/www/hlthins/hlthin06.html>.

Table 147. **Persons With and Without Health Insurance Coverage by State: 2006**

[**249,829 represents 249,829,000**. Based on the Current Population Survey, Annual Social and Economic Supplement (ASEC), see text, Section 1, and Appendix III]

State	Total persons covered (1,000)	Total persons not covered		Children not covered		State	Total persons covered (1,000)	Total persons not covered		Children not covered	
		Number (1,000)	Percent of total	Number (1,000)	Percent of total			Number (1,000)	Percent of total	Number (1,000)	Percent of total
U.S.[1]	249,829	46,995	15.8	8,661	11.7	MO	5,028	772	13.3	127	9.1
AL	3,843	689	15.2	82	7.4	MT	772	160	17.1	31	14.5
AK	550	109	16.5	19	10.3	NE	1,549	217	12.3	45	10.1
AZ	4,958	1,311	20.9	283	17.0	NV	2,039	496	19.6	122	18.8
AR	2,237	521	18.9	65	9.3	NH	1,159	150	11.5	22	7.5
CA	29,417	6,791	18.8	1,225	12.8	NJ	7,319	1,341	15.5	277	13.3
CO	3,977	826	17.2	176	14.6	NM	1,498	445	22.9	93	17.9
CT	3,137	325	9.4	49	6.0	NY	16,378	2,662	14.0	380	8.4
DE	757	105	12.1	24	11.7	NC	7,266	1,585	17.9	307	14.0
DC	503	66	11.6	10	8.7	ND	541	75	12.2	15	10.3
FL	14,233	3,828	21.2	771	18.9	OH	10,181	1,138	10.1	157	5.7
GA	7,688	1,659	17.7	314	12.8	OK	2,831	661	18.9	114	12.5
HI	1,144	110	8.8	19	6.3	OR	3,051	665	17.9	114	13.1
ID	1,248	227	15.4	52	13.0	PA	11,108	1,237	10.0	203	7.3
IL	10,867	1,776	14.0	302	9.5	RI	963	91	8.6	10	4.1
IN	5,590	748	11.8	123	7.8	SC	3,553	672	15.9	112	10.7
IA	2,612	307	10.5	44	6.3	SD	679	91	11.8	18	9.2
KS	2,387	335	12.3	51	7.3	TN	5,111	809	13.7	94	6.4
KY	3,467	639	15.6	98	9.7	TX	17,533	5,704	24.5	1,392	21.2
LA	3,291	921	21.9	170	15.9	UT	2,094	442	17.4	120	15.0
ME	1,192	122	9.3	18	6.4	VT	557	63	10.2	11	8.0
MD	4,836	776	13.8	137	9.9	VA	6,532	1,006	13.3	185	10.1
MA	5,678	657	10.4	103	7.0	WA	5,572	746	11.8	105	6.9
MI	8,928	1,043	10.5	116	4.7	WV	1,570	245	13.5	34	8.5
MN	4,675	475	9.2	104	8.3	WI	4,995	481	8.8	63	4.9
MS	2,292	600	20.8	146	18.9	WY	441	75	14.6	10	8.2

[1] The estimates are revised from the originally published data.

Source: U.S. Census Bureau, Current Population Reports; Income, Poverty, and Health Insurance Coverage in the United States: 2006, P60-233; issued August 2007. Table HI05. Health Insurance Coverage Status and Type of Coverage by State for All People: 2006. See also <http://www.census.gov/hhes/www/hlthins/hlthin06.html>.

Health and Nutrition   105

Table 148. **People Without Health Insurance for the Entire Year by Selected Characteristics: 2005 and 2006**

[**In thousands, except as noted (293,834 represents 293,834,000)**. Based on the Current Population Survey; Annual Social and Economic Supplement (ASEC); see text, Section 1 and Appendix III]

Characteristic	2005			2006		
		Uninsured persons			Uninsured persons	
	Total persons	Number	Percent distribution	Total persons	Number	Percent distribution
Total [1,2]	293,834	44,815	100.0	296,824	46,995	100.0
Under 18 years	73,985	8,050	18.0	74,101	8,661	18.4
18 to 24 years	27,965	8,201	18.3	28,405	8,323	17.7
25 to 34 years	39,480	10,161	22.7	39,868	10,713	22.8
35 to 44 years	43,121	7,901	17.6	42,762	8,018	17.1
45 to 64 years	73,778	10,053	22.4	75,652	10,737	22.8
65 years and over	35,505	449	1.0	36,035	541	1.2
Male	144,188	24,166	53.9	145,689	25,531	54.3
Female.	149,647	20,648	46.1	151,135	21,464	45.7
White alone [3]	235,903	33,946	75.7	237,892	35,486	75.5
White alone or in combination . .	240,909	34,750	77.5	242,592	36,248	77.1
Black alone [3].	36,965	7,006	15.6	37,369	7,652	16.3
Black alone or in combination . .	38,729	7,239	16.2	39,083	7,921	16.9
Asian alone [3].	12,599	2,161	4.8	13,194	2,045	4.4
Asian alone or in combination . .	13,758	2,286	5.1	14,348	2,160	4.6
Hispanic [4].	43,168	13,954	31.1	44,854	15,296	32.5
White alone, not Hispanic.	195,893	20,909	46.7	196,252	21,162	45.0

[1] Includes other races not shown separately.   [2] The estimates are revised from the originally published data.   [3] Refers to people who reported specified race and did not report any other race category.   [4] Persons of Hispanic origin may be of any race.

Source: U.S. Census Bureau, Current Population Reports, Income, Poverty, and Health Insurance Coverage in the United States: 2006, P60-233. *Health Insurance Coverage Status and Type of Coverage by Selected Characteristics: 2006*. See also <http://www.census.gov/hhes/www/hlthins/hlthin06.html/>.

Table 149. **Medical Care Benefits of Workers by Type and Amount of Employee Contribution: 2007**

[**In percent.** Starting with the 2007 data, the range of dollars for the "flat monthly amounts" have changed. See headnote, Table 150]

Type and amount of contribution	Individual coverage [1]				Type and amount of contribution	Family coverage [1]			
	All employees	Management professional	Service	Production		All employees	Management professional	Service	Production
Total with contributory coverage	100	100	100	100	Total with contributory coverage	100	100	100	100
Flat monthly amount . .	77	77	71	80	Flat monthly amount. .	79	79	75	83
Less than $20.00 . .	4	4	4	5	Less than $100.00 . . .	9	8	8	12
$20.00–$29.99	5	6	4	5	$100.00–$149.99. . . .	7	7	5	11
$30.00–$39.99	6	5	5	7	$150.00–$199.99. . . .	11	11	8	15
$40.00–$49.99	6	7	5	8	$200.00–$249.99. . . .	10	10	10	10
$50.00–$59.99	9	8	7	11	$250.00–$299.99. . . .	10	11	8	9
$60.00–$69.99	8	7	7	9	$300.00–$349.99. . . .	7	7	7	8
$70.00–$79.99	7	8	6	6	$350.00–$399.99. . . .	5	5	5	4
$80.00–$89.99	6	5	5	7	$400.00–$449.99. . . .	4	4	3	2
$90.00–$99.99	5	5	4	4	$450.00–$499.99. . . .	3	2	3	3
$100.00–$109.99 . .	5	5	6	4	$500.00–$549.99. . . .	3	3	2	1
$110.00–$119.99 . .	4	4	4	3	$550.00–$599.99. . . .	2	2	5	1
$120.00–$129.99 . .	2	2	3	3	$600.00–$649.99. . . .	2	2	4	1
$130.00–$139.99 . .	2	2	2	2	$650.00–$699.99. . . .	2	2	1	1
$140.00–$149.99 . .	1	1	1	1	$700.00–$749.99. . . .	1	1	2	(Z)
$150.00 or more . . .	7	7	9	6	$750.00 or more	4	4	5	3
Composite rate [2]	1	2	1	1	Composite rate [1]	1	1	(Z)	(Z)
Varies [3]	5	6	5	4	Varies [2]	4	5	4	3
Flexible benefits [4]	1	2	1	1	Flexible benefits [3] . . .	1	2	1	1
Percent of earnings. . .	(Z)	(Z)	1	(Z)	Percent of earnings . .	(Z)	(Z)	1	(Z)
Exists, but unknown . .	14	12	20	14	Exists, but unknown . .	14	12	18	12
Other	1	1	2	1	Other.	1	1	2	1

Z Less than 0.5 percent.   [1] Other occupational groups not shown. See Table 150 for complete listing of groups.   [2] A composite rate is a set contribution covering more than one benefit area; for example, health care and life insurance. Cost data for individual plans cannot be determined.   [3] Based on worker attributes. For example, employee contributions may vary based on earnings, length of service, or age.   [4] Amount varies by options selected under a "cafeteria plan" or employer-sponsored reimbursement account.

Source: U.S. Bureau of Labor Statistics, *National Compensation Survey: Employee Benefits in Private Industry in the United States, March, 2007* (issued August 2007). See also <http://www.bls.gov/ncs/ebs/sp/ebsm0006.pdf>.

Table 150. Percent of Workers Participating in Health Care Benefit Programs and Percent of Participants Required to Contribute: 2007

[Based on National Compensation Survey, a sample survey of 12,821 private industry establishments of all sizes, representing about 108 million workers; see Appendix III. See also Table 634. The data below marks the first release of data on employee benefits under new industry and occupational classifications. For more information, see <http://www.bls.gov/ncs/ebs/ebsm0006.pdf>]

Characteristic	Percent of workers participating—				Single coverage medical care		Family coverage medical care	
	Medical care	Dental care	Vision care	Out-patient prescrip-tion drug coverage	Employee contri-butions required (percent)	Average monthly contri-bution [1] (dol.)	Employee contri-bytions required (percent)	Average monthly contri-bution [1] (dol.)
Total..............	**52**	**36**	**22**	**49**	**76**	**81.37**	**87**	**312.78**
Management, professional, and related..................	67	51	30	64	79	79.97	91	313.42
Service.................	28	20	14	27	81	88.89	92	342.92
Sales and office.............	48	33	19	46	79	83.63	91	333.44
Natural resources, construction, and maintenance...........	61	36	26	58	62	82.21	74	314.33
Production, transportation, and material moving...........	60	38	24	57	74	75.38	82	263.68
Full-time [2].............	64	44	27	61	76	80.67	87	311.94
Part-time [2].............	12	9	7	12	77	93.04	88	327.75
Union [3].............	78	62	47	75	50	62.45	57	211.91
Nonunion.................	49	33	19	46	81	83.51	93	323.80

[1] The average is presented for all covered workers and excludes workers without the plan provision. Averages are for plans stating a flat monthly cost.   [2] Employees are classified as working either a full-time or part-time schedule based on the definition used by each establishment.   [3] Union workers are those whose wages are determined through collective bargaining.

Source: U.S. Bureau of Labor Statistics, *National Compensation Survey: Employee Benefits in Private Industry in the United States, March, 2007* (issued August 2007). See also <http://www.bls.gov/ncs/ebs/publications.htm>.

Table 151. Retail Prescription Drug Sales: 1995 to 2007

[2,125 represents 2,125,000,000]

Sales outlet	Unit	1995	2000	2001	2002	2003	2004	2005	2006	2007
Number of prescriptions	Mil.......	2,125	2,865	3,009	3,139	3,215	3,274	3,279	3,420	3,515
Traditional chain............	Mil.......	908	1,335	1,408	1,463	1,483	1,500	1,518	1,605	1,660
Independent	Mil.......	672	698	710	719	736	738	714	732	745
Mass merchant.............	Mil.......	238	293	311	339	345	353	359	375	390
Supermarkets	Mil.......	221	394	418	444	462	470	465	476	478
Mail order	Mil.......	86	146	161	174	189	214	223	232	242
Percent distribution of brand/generic mix:										
Brand drugs.............	Percent ...	59.8	57.6	59.0	57.9	55.0	54.1	50.6	46.8	41.8
Generic drugs	Percent ...	40.2	42.4	41.0	42.1	45.0	47.5	51.3	53.2	58.2
Retail sales	Bil. dol. ...	72.2	145.6	161.3	182.7	204.2	220.1	232.0	250.6	259.4
Traditional chain............	bil. dol. ...	27.8	59.1	65.3	73.3	82.6	87.5	91.8	100.6	104.8
Independent	bil. dol. ...	22.0	33.4	36.2	38.0	41.2	43.3	44.6	46.2	47.2
Mass merchant.............	bil. dol. ...	7.7	13.5	15.2	18.0	20.0	21.5	22.5	24.3	25.7
Supermarkets	bil. dol. ...	7.4	17.4	19.8	23.1	25.2	26.9	27.6	28.9	28.5
Mail order	bil. dol. ...	7.4	22.1	24.8	30.2	35.0	40.8	45.5	50.5	53.1
Average prices [1]										
All prescriptions	Dollars ...	30.01	45.79	50.06	55.37	59.52	62.64	63.87	66.97	69.91
Brand drugs.............	Dollars ...	40.22	65.29	69.75	77.49	85.57	91.80	97.65	107.48	119.51
Generic drugs	Dollars ...	14.84	19.33	21.72	24.89	27.69	28.23	29.21	31.39	34.34
Average prescription cost [1] ..	Dollars ...	(NA)	(NA)	(NA)	(NA)	(NA)	(NA)	(NA)	66.97	69.91
Manufacturer receives	Dollars ...	(NA)	(NA)	(NA)	(NA)	(NA)	(NA)	(NA)	51.97	54.30
Wholesaler receives	Dollars ...	(NA)	(NA)	(NA)	(NA)	(NA)	(NA)	(NA)	2.07	2.44
Retailer receives...........	Dollars ...	(NA)	(NA)	(NA)	(NA)	(NA)	(NA)	(NA)	12.93	13.17

NA Not available.   [1] Excludes mail order.

Source: National Association of Chain Drug Stores, Alexandria, VA, *NACDS Foundation Chain Pharmacy Industry Profile, 2007* (copyright); <http://www.nacds.org>.

Table 152. **Annual Receipts/Revenue for Health Care Industries: 2000 to 2006**

[In millions of dollars (1,033,029 represents $1,033,029,000,000). Based on the North American Industry Classification System, 2002 (NAICS); see text, Section 15. All firms in NAICS 6211, 6212, 6213, and 6215 are defined as taxable. Estimates for the nonemployer portion are derived from administrative records data provided by other federal agencies. These data are available only at the total revenue level. See Appendix III]

Selected kind of business	2002 NAICS code	Total, all firms [1]			Taxable employer firms		
		2000	2005	2006	2000	2005	2006
Health care and social assistance	**62**	**1,033,029**	**1,478,316**	**1,568,166**	**500,932**	**730,588**	**778,862**
Ambulatory health care services [2]	621	419,402	610,290	647,892	376,095	549,376	583,985
Offices of physicians	6211	213,806	310,546	330,889	213,806	310,546	330,889
Offices of dentists	6212	60,931	83,688	87,405	60,931	83,688	87,405
Offices of other health practitioners	6213	32,037	45,185	46,779	32,037	45,185	46,779
Offices of chiropractors	62131	7,570	9,868	10,267	7,570	9,868	10,267
Offices of optometrists	62132	7,639	9,793	10,205	7,639	9,793	10,205
Offices of mental health practitioners	62133	3,516	4,066	4,316	3,516	4,066	4,316
Offices of PT/OT/speech therapy & audiology [3]	62134	8,486	14,273	14,583	8,486	14,273	14,583
Outpatient care centers	6214	(S)	69,541	73,966	(S)	31,448	34,361
Medical & diagnostic laboratories	6215	23,450	34,712	37,253	23,450	34,712	37,253
Home health care services	6216	26,841	43,443	47,007	16,879	29,733	32,126
Other ambulatory health care services	6219	15,565	23,175	24,593	9,421	14,064	15,172
Hospitals [2]	622	423,889	611,184	654,492	42,908	70,979	79,385
General medical & surgical hospitals	6221	397,526	572,948	613,098	36,926	58,511	64,989
Psychiatric & substance abuse hospitals	6222	13,422	13,901	15,260	2,189	2,304	2,726
Other specialty hospitals	6223	12,941	24,335	26,134	3,793	10,164	11,670
Nursing and residential care facilities [2]	623	112,706	145,717	148,716	66,245	85,381	88,226
Nursing care facilities	6231	67,238	83,552	85,229	49,816	61,277	63,087
Residential mental retardation/health facilities	6232	16,718	22,904	23,609	4,726	6,666	7,162
Residential mental retardation facilities	62321	11,570	15,606	16,112	3,297	4,638	4,959
Community care facilities for the elderly	6233	22,104	30,741	31,338	10,812	16,147	16,710
Continuing care retirement communities. . . .	623311	12,948	17,676	18,021	3,576	5,686	5,981
Homes for the elderly	623312	9,156	13,065	13,317	7,236	10,461	10,729
Other residential care facilities.	6239	6,646	8,520	8,540	891	1,291	1,267
Social assistance [2]	624	77,032	111,125	117,066	15,684	24,852	27,266
Individual and family services	6241	37,311	53,047	57,766	3,824	7,388	8,818
Community food and housing, and emergency and other relief services..	6242	12,281	18,983	18,887	46	(S)	(S)
Vocational rehabilitation services	6243	9,458	13,937	13,916	1,593	2,657	2,756
Child day care services	6244	17,982	25,158	26,497	10,221	14,584	15,484

S Figure does not meet publication standards.   [1] Includes taxable nonemployer firms, not shown separately.   [2] Includes other kinds of business not shown separately.   [3] Offices of physical, occupational, and speech therapists, and audiologists.

Source: U.S. Census Bureau, "Service Annual Survey, 2006"; <http://www.census.gov/econ/www/servmenu.html>.

Table 153. **Receipts for Selected Health Service Industries by Source of Revenue: 2001 and 2006**

[In millions of dollars (219,492 represents $219,492,000,000). Based on the 2002 North American Industry Classification System (NAICS), see text, Section 15. Based on a sample of taxable employer firms only and does not include nonemployer revenue. See Appendix III]

Source of revenue	Offices of physicians (NAICS 6211)		Offices of dentists (NAICS 6212)		Hospitals (NAICS 622)		Nursing and residential care facilities (NAICS 623)	
	2001	2006	2001	2006	2001	2006	2001	2006
Total	**219,492**	**330,889**	**62,599**	**87,405**	**462,216**	**654,492**	**111,855**	**148,246**
Medicare	52,649	71,201	(S)	768	147,841	176,843	14,857	24,344
Medicaid.	15,109	16,906	1,790	3,316	56,193	67,895	45,875	56,511
Other government [1]	2,347	4,415	(S)	507	24,745	33,261	8,227	11,265
Worker's compensation	8,050	7,556	(S)	80	5,117	7,005	(S)	(S)
Private insurance	105,846	165,769	33,201	40,241	169,885	267,931	6,617	7,171
Patient (out-of-pocket).	23,617	33,581	27,174	39,019	23,844	32,987	[2]26,339	[2]35,440
Other patient care sources, n.e.c [3] . . .	8,128	18,297	434	2,944	11,453	27,568	3,223	4,681
Nonpatient care revenue	3,746	13,164	(S)	530	23,138	41,002	6,717	8,834

S Figure does not meet publication standards.   [1] Veterans, National Institute of Health, Indian Affairs, etc.   [2] Represents payment from patients and their families plus patients' assigned social security benefits.   [3] n.e.c. represents not elsewhere classified.

Source: U.S. Census Bureau, "Service Annual Survey, 2006"; <http://www.census.gov/econ/www/servmenu.html>.

Table 154.
Table 154. Employment in the Health Service Industries: 1990 to 2007

[In thousands (9,296 represents 9,296,000). See headnote, Table 612. Based on the North American Industry Classification System 2007 code; see text, Section 15. For more information on the NAICS changes, please see <http://stats.bls.gov/ces/cescaics07.htm>]

Industry	2002 NAICS code [1]	1990	2000	2002	2003	2004	2005	2006	2007
Health care and social assistance [1]	62	9,296	12,718	13,556	13,893	14,190	14,536	14,925	15,378
Ambulatory health care services [1]	621	2,842	4,320	4,633	4,786	4,952	5,114	5,286	5,477
Offices of physicians	6211	1,278	1,840	1,968	2,003	2,048	2,094	2,148	2,204
Offices of dentists	6212	513	688	725	744	760	774	784	812
Offices of other health practitioners	6213	276	438	486	503	527	549	571	599
Medical and diagnostic laboratories	6215	129	162	175	182	190	198	202	212
Home health care services	6216	288	633	680	733	777	821	866	913
Hospitals [1]	622	3,513	3,954	4,160	4,245	4,285	4,345	4,423	4,517
General medical and surgical hospitals	6221	3,305	3,745	3,930	4,005	4,042	4,096	4,167	4,245
Psychiatric and substance abuse hospitals	6222	113	86	90	92	92	93	98	100
Other hospitals	6223	95	123	140	148	151	156	162	173
Nursing and residential care facilities [1]	623	1,856	2,583	2,743	2,786	2,818	2,855	2,893	2,952
Nursing care facilities	6231	1,170	1,514	1,573	1,580	1,577	1,577	1,581	1,601

[1] Includes other industries not shown separately.

Source: U.S. Bureau of Labor Statistics, "Employment and Earnings," March issues; <http://stats.bls.gov/ces/home.htm>.

Table 155. Osteopathic Physicians: 2001 to 2008

[As of May 31. Osteopathic physicians are fully qualified physicians licensed to practice medicine and to perform surgery. Osteopathic medicine has a strong emphasis on the interrelationship of the body's nerves, muscles, bones and organs. Doctors of osteopathic medicine, or D.O.s, apply the philosophy of treating the whole person to the prevention, diagnosis and treatment of illness, disease and injury]

Characteristic	2001	2005	2008	Characteristic	2001	2005	2008
Total number of D.O.s	46,990	56,512	64,000	Self-identified practice specialty [1]	31,996	38,442	43,896
Sex				Family and general practice	14,102	17,800	18,680
Female	10,875	15,147	19,138	General internal medicine	2,592	3,107	4,171
Male	36,115	41,365	44,862	General pediatrics/adolescent medicine	958	1,176	1,525
Age				Obstetrics and gynecology	1,219	1,465	1,858
Less than 35 years old	9,866	12,983	13,251	Pediatric specialties	320	348	470
35 to 44 years old	14,798	16,179	18,638	Osteopathic specialties [2]	414	464	656
45 to 54 years old	12,754	13,845	15,931	Other specialties	12,001	13,431	16,178
55 to 64 years old	4,706	7,998	9,819	Unknown	390	651	358
65 years old and over	4,838	5,189	6,120				
Unknown	28	318	241				

[1] D.O.s are assumed to be in active practice if they are under age 65 and have not informed the AOA that they have retired or are inactive. D.O.s are assumed to be in postdoctoral training (internship, residency, or fellowship) if they are within 4 years of graduation or if the AOA has received information that they are in a postdoctoral program. [2] Osteopathic self-identified practice specialties include OMT (osteopathic manipulative treatment) and OMM (osteopathic manipulative medicine). OMT is the therapeutic application of manually guided forces by an osteopathic physician to improve physiologic function and/or support homeostasis that has been altered by somatic dysfunction. OMM is the application of osteopathic philosophy, structural diagnosis, and use of OMT in the patient's diagnosis and management.

Source: American Osteopathic Association, Chicago, IL.; *AOA Annual Statistics;* See also <http://www.osteopathic.org/index.cfm?PageID=aoa_annualrprt>.

Table 156. Active Physicians and Nurses by State: 2006

[As of December. Excludes doctors of osteopathy, physicians with addresses unknown, and inactive status. Includes all physicians not classified according to activity status. Nurses' data come from the Bureau of Labor Statistics]

State	Physicians Total	Physicians Rate [1]	Nurses Total	Nurses Rate [1]	State	Physicians Total	Physicians Rate [1]	Nurses Total	Nurses Rate [1]
United States	800,586	267	2,417,150	807	Missouri	14,118	242	55,470	949
Alabama	9,893	215	40,010	870	Montana	2,086	221	7,290	772
Alaska	1,547	231	5,260	785	Nebraska	4,273	242	16,840	952
Arizona	12,797	208	31,890	517	Nevada	4,611	185	14,050	563
Arkansas	5,703	203	21,020	748	New Hampshire	3,463	263	12,440	946
California	95,676	262	234,260	643	New Jersey	27,091	311	80,330	921
Colorado	12,296	259	34,520	726	New Mexico	4,681	239	11,680	598
Connecticut	12,901	368	34,710	990	New York	75,743	392	164,970	854
Delaware	2,133	250	7,830	917	North Carolina	22,406	253	74,400	840
District of Columbia	4,646	799	7,930	1,364	North Dakota	1,544	243	6,900	1,085
Florida	43,884	243	146,290	809	Ohio	30,321	264	111,840	974
Georgia	20,350	217	60,850	650	Oklahoma	6,164	172	24,720	691
Hawaii	3,996	311	9,610	748	Oregon	10,004	270	28,090	759
Idaho	2,479	169	9,100	621	Pennsylvania	36,956	297	126,120	1,014
Illinois	35,311	275	103,100	803	Rhode Island	3,911	366	10,550	988
Indiana	13,567	215	52,910	838	South Carolina	9,887	229	31,810	736
Iowa	5,567	187	31,040	1,041	South Dakota	1,719	220	9,420	1,205
Kansas	6,104	221	23,590	853	Tennessee	15,925	264	52,780	874
Kentucky	9,671	230	38,120	906	Texas	49,740	212	156,590	666
Louisiana	11,429	267	37,940	885	Utah	5,401	212	16,510	647
Maine	3,569	270	13,690	1,036	Vermont	2,263	363	5,870	941
Maryland	23,331	415	47,560	847	Virginia	20,631	270	55,300	724
Massachusetts	29,756	462	76,350	1,186	Washington	16,965	265	48,190	753
Michigan	24,742	245	84,880	841	West Virginia	4,166	229	15,380	846
Minnesota	14,813	287	49,580	960	Wisconsin	14,257	257	48,460	872
Mississippi	5,149	177	25,100	862	Wyoming	950	184	4,010	779

[1] Per 100,000 resident population. Based on U.S. Census Bureau estimates as of July 1.

Source: Physicians: American Medical Association, Chicago, IL, *Physician Characteristics and Distribution in the U.S.,* annual (copyright); Nurses: Bureau of Labor Statistics, Occupational Employment Statistics, Occupational Employment and Wages; *Wage and Employment Statistics,* accessed February 2008.

Health and Nutrition   109

Table 157. **Physicians by Sex and Specialty: 1980 to 2006**

[In thousands (467.7 represents 467,700). As of Dec. 31, except 1990 as of Jan. 1, and as noted. Includes Puerto Rico and island areas]

Activity	1980 Total	1980 Office-based	1990 Total	1990 Office-based	2000 Total	2000 Office-based	2006 Total	2006 Office-based
Doctors of medicine, total [1]	467.7	272.0	615.4	361.0	813.8	490.4	921.9	560.4
Place of medical education:								
U.S. medical graduates	370.0	226.2	483.7	286.2	616.8	376.5	685.2	423.3
International medical graduates [2]	97.7	45.8	131.8	74.8	197.0	113.9	236.7	137.1
Sex: Male	413.4	251.4	511.2	311.7	618.2	382.3	665.6	407.9
Female	54.3	20.6	104.2	49.2	195.5	108.1	256.3	152.5
Allergy/immunology	1.5	1.4	3.4	2.5	4.0	3.1	4.2	3.3
Anesthesiology	16.0	11.3	26.0	17.8	35.7	27.6	41.2	31.7
Cardiovascular diseases	9.8	6.7	15.9	10.7	21.0	16.3	22.4	17.5
Child psychiatry	3.3	2.0	4.3	2.6	6.2	4.3	7.3	5.3
Dermatology	5.7	4.4	7.6	6.0	9.7	8.0	10.7	8.9
Diagnostic radiology	7.0	4.2	15.4	9.8	21.1	14.6	24.6	17.6
Emergency medicine	5.7	3.4	14.2	8.4	23.1	14.5	30.0	20.1
Family practice	27.5	18.4	47.6	37.5	71.6	54.2	82.9	66.0
Gastroenterology	4.0	2.7	7.5	5.2	10.6	8.5	12.3	9.9
General practice	32.5	29.6	22.8	20.5	15.2	13.0	10.5	8.9
General surgery	34.0	22.4	38.4	24.5	36.7	24.5	37.7	25.7
Internal medicine	71.5	40.6	98.3	58.0	134.5	89.7	155.7	107.3
Neurological surgery	3.3	2.5	4.4	3.1	5.0	3.7	5.4	4.1
Neurology	5.7	3.3	9.2	5.6	12.3	8.6	14.6	10.4
Obstetrics and gynecology	26.3	19.5	33.7	25.5	40.2	31.7	42.3	34.2
Ophthalmology	13.0	10.6	16.1	13.1	18.1	15.6	18.1	15.8
Orthopedic surgery	14.0	10.7	19.1	14.2	22.3	17.4	24.3	19.2
Otolaryngology	6.6	5.3	8.1	6.4	9.4	7.6	10.0	8.2
Pathology	13.6	6.1	16.6	7.5	18.8	10.6	19.8	11.9
Pediatrics	29.5	18.2	41.9	27.1	63.9	43.2	75.1	53.1
Physical med./rehab.	2.1	1.0	4.1	2.2	6.5	4.3	7.7	5.6
Plastic surgery	3.0	2.4	4.6	3.8	6.2	5.3	7.1	6.0
Psychiatry	27.5	16.0	35.2	20.1	39.5	25.0	41.4	27.4
Pulmonary diseases	3.7	2.0	6.1	3.7	8.7	5.9	10.2	7.4
Radiology	11.7	7.8	8.5	6.1	8.7	6.7	8.9	7.0
Urological surgery	7.7	6.2	9.4	7.4	10.3	8.5	10.5	8.9
Unspecified	12.3	5.0	8.1	1.6	8.3	3.8	7.5	4.0
Not classified	20.6	(X)	12.7	(X)	45.1	(X)	46.3	(X)
Other categories [3]	32.1	(X)	55.4	(X)	75.2	(X)	108.8	(X)

X Not applicable.   [1] Includes other categories not shown.   [2] International medical graduates received their medical education in schools outside the United States and Canada.   [3] Includes inactive and address unknown.

Source: Except as noted, American Medical Association, Chicago, IL, *Physician Characteristics and Distribution in the U.S.* annual (copyright).

Table 158. **Percent Distribution of Number of Visits to Health Care Professionals by Selected Characteristics: 2000 and 2006**

[Covers ambulatory visits to doctor's offices and emergency departments, and home health care visits during a 12-month period. Based on the redesigned National Health Interview Survey, a sample survey of the civilian noninstitutionalized population]

Characteristic	None 2000	None 2006	1–3 visits 2000	1–3 visits 2006	4–9 visits 2000	4–9 visits 2006	10 or more visits 2000	10 or more visits 2006
All persons [1, 2]	16.6	17.2	45.4	46.9	24.7	23.1	13.3	12.8
SEX [2]								
Male	21.5	22.8	46.0	46.8	22.4	20.0	10.1	10.4
Female	11.9	11.8	44.8	46.8	27.0	26.2	16.4	15.2
AGE								
Under 18 years old	12.2	10.9	53.7	57.2	26.4	24.6	7.7	7.3
18 to 44 years old	23.2	25.3	45.3	45.8	19.2	17.8	12.2	11.0
45 to 64 years old	15.0	16.4	43.4	44.3	25.7	23.6	15.8	15.7
65 to 74 years old	9.0	6.7	34.5	34.6	34.4	36.6	22.1	22.1
75 years old and over	5.8	5.3	29.3	31.5	39.3	35.7	25.6	27.6
RACE [2, 3]								
Race alone:								
White	16.0	17.2	45.1	46.2	25.3	23.4	13.7	13.2
Black or African American	17.3	16.0	46.7	49.2	23.4	23.3	12.6	11.5
American Indian or Alaska Native	21.2	13.5	42.9	44.2	20.0	27.6	15.8	14.7
Asian	20.2	21.9	49.2	51.3	20.9	18.1	9.7	8.7
Two or more races	12.1	16.3	41.6	44.8	28.3	21.3	17.9	17.6
HISPANIC ORIGIN AND RACE [2, 3, 4]								
Hispanic or Latino	26.5	27.1	41.8	43.0	20.0	19.6	11.7	10.3
Mexican	30.7	31.1	40.9	40.8	18.0	18.3	10.4	9.8
Not Hispanic or Latino	15.2	15.4	45.9	47.6	25.3	23.7	13.6	13.2
White, non-Hispanic	14.5	15.0	45.4	46.9	26.0	24.2	14.1	13.9
Black, non-Hispanic	17.2	15.7	46.9	49.5	23.4	23.4	12.6	11.4

[1] Includes other categories not shown separately.   [2] Estimates are age adjusted to the year 2000 standard using six age groups: Under 18 years, 18–44 years, 45–54 years, 55–64 years, 65–74 years, and 75 years and over.   [3] Estimates by race and Hispanic origin are tabulated using the 1997 standards for federal data on race and ethnicity. Estimates for specific race groups are shown when they meet requirements for statistical reliability and confidentiality. The categories "White only," "Black or African American only," "American Indian and Alaska Native (AI/AN) only," and "Asian only" include persons who reported only one racial group; and the category "2 or more races" includes persons who reported more than one of the five racial groups in the 1997 Standards or one of the five racial groups and "Some other race."   [4] Persons of Hispanic or Latino origin may be of any race or combination of races.

Source: U.S. National Center for Health Statistics, *Health, United States*, annual. See also <www.cdc.gov/nchs/hus.htm>.

Table 159. **Ambulatory Care Visits to Physicians' Offices and Hospital Outpatient and Emergency Departments: 2006**

[(1,123.4 represents 1,123,400,000.) Based on the annual National Ambulatory Medical Care Survey and National Hospital Ambulatory Medical Care Survey and subject to sampling error; see source for details]

Characteristic	Number of visits (mil.)				Visits per 100 persons			
	Total	Physi-cian offices	Outpa-tient dept.	Emer-gency dept.	Total	Physi-cian offices	Outpa-tient dept.	Emer-gency dept.
Total	1,123.4	902.0	102.2	119.2	381.9	306.6	34.7	40.5
Age:								
Under 15 years old	199.7	157.9	19.9	21.9	328.9	260.1	32.7	36.0
15 to 24 years old	104.0	72.4	12.0	19.5	250.9	174.8	29.0	47.1
25 to 44 years old	245.4	185.3	25.1	35.0	299.0	225.8	30.6	42.7
45 to 64 years old	310.7	256.5	28.7	25.5	417.8	345.0	38.6	34.3
65 to 74 years old	124.1	108.1	8.9	7.1	664.5	578.7	47.8	38.0
75 years old and over	139.6	121.8	7.6	10.2	823.5	718.6	44.8	60.2
Sex:								
Male	463.2	368.7	40.3	54.2	321.7	256.0	28.0	37.7
Female	660.2	533.3	62.0	65.0	439.6	355.1	41.3	43.3
Race:								
White	923.7	764.6	73.8	85.3	391.3	323.9	31.3	36.1
Black/African American	140.1	87.0	23.5	29.6	378.8	235.4	63.5	79.9
Asian	43.7	38.7	2.7	2.4	334.2	295.5	20.4	18.2
Native Hawaiian/Other Pacific Islander	3.9	3.0	0.5	[1]0.5	756.8	580.4	90.1	[1]86.3
American Indian/Alaska Native . . .	7.7	6.2	0.4	[1]1.1	270.3	216.6	14.0	[1]39.7
More than one race reported	4.2	2.4	1.4	0.4	89.7	51.5	29.7	8.4
Expected sources of payment [2]:								
Private insurance	636.2	545.7	43.2	47.3	(X)	(X)	(X)	(X)
Medicare	251.1	212.5	17.9	20.7	(X)	(X)	(X)	(X)
Medicaid	188.5	126.4	31.8	30.4	(X)	(X)	(X)	(X)
Worker's compensation	18.3	15.5	0.8	2.1	(X)	(X)	(X)	(X)
Self pay	61.1	35.5	6.5	19.0	(X)	(X)	(X)	(X)
No charge	12.0	[1]4.9	4.0	2.6	(X)	(X)	(X)	(X)
Other	35.1	26.3	4.6	4.2	(X)	(X)	(X)	(X)
Unknown	35.5	28.2	3.0	4.3	(X)	(X)	(X)	(X)

X Not applicable. [1] Figures do not meet standard of reliability or precision. [2] Starting with 2006 data, more than one source of payment could be reported per visit. Prior years showed "primary source of payments."

Source: U.S. National Center for Health Statistics, National Health Statistics Reports, Nos. 3, 4, and 7; August 06, 2008. <http://www.cdc.gov/nchs/namcs.htm>.

Table 160. **Visits to Office-Based Physicians and Hospital Outpatient Departments by Diagnosis: 2001 and 2006**

[(393.6 represents 393,600,000.) See headnote, Table 159]

Leading diagnosis [1]	Number (mil.)		Rate per 1,000 persons [2]		Leading diagnosis [1]	Number (mil.)		Rate per 1,000 persons [2]	
	2001	2006	2001	2006		2001	2006	2001	2006
MALE					FEMALE				
All ages	393.6	408.9	2,883	2,840	All ages	570.6	595.2	3,975	3,963
Under 15 years old [3]	86.7	91.8	2,803	2,958	Under 15 years old [3]	78.3	85.9	2,654	2,897
Routine infant or child health check	19.9	21.0	642	677	Routine infant or child health check	18.0	19.4	610	654
Acute upper respiratory infections [4]	7.5	7.5	243	241	Acute upper respiratory infections [4]	7.0	8.4	239	283
Otitis media & Eustachian tube disorders	5.8	6.6	188	211	Otitis media & Eustachian tube disorders	6.4	5.1	216	171
Attention deficit disorder . .	2.8	3.5	89	113	Acute pharyngitis	2.4	3.2	81	107
Acute pharyngitis	1.8	3.2	59	104	Chronic sinusitis	1.5	2.2	52	75
15 to 44 years old [3]	102.5	97.7	1,697	1,585	15 to 44 years old [3]	194.2	197.2	3,159	3,186
General medical exam . . .	3.8	4.3	63	70	Normal pregnancy	20.1	22.7	327	367
Acute respiratory infections [4]	4.2	3.1	70	51	Gynecological exam	6.1	8.9	99	143
Essential hypertension . .	3.2	3.1	53	50	Complications of preg-nancy, childbirth, and the puerperium	4.1	6.4	66	104
Spinal disorders	3.7	3.1	62	50	Acute respiratory infections [4]	6.0	6.3	97	103
Rheumatism, excluding back	3.5	2.8	59	45	Chronic sinusitis	3.8	4.5	61	72
45 to 64 years old [3]	105.0	118.5	3,384	1,185	45 to 64 years old [3]	155.7	166.7	4,714	4,360
Essential hypertension . .	7.5	8.4	243	232	Essential hypertension . .	8.1	9.1	246	239
Diabetes mellitus	6.4	5.6	206	154	Arthropathies and related disorders	8.1	8.1	245	212
Spinal disorders	4.5	5.5	145	152	Diabetes mellitus	5.7	6.9	173	180
Arthropathies and related disorders	3.1	4.8	100	134	Spinal disorders	5.5	6.8	166	177
Malignant neoplasms . . .	2.7	3.9	88	109	Gynecological exam	4.8	6.4	144	168
65 years old and over [3] . . .	99.4	100.9	7,010	6,633	65 years old and over [3] . . .	142.5	145.4	7,291	7,128
Malignant neoplasms . . .	4.5	7.2	319	471	Essential hypertension . .	10.8	10.6	555	518
Essential hypertension . .	6.3	5.8	444	379	Arthropathies and related disorders	7.5	7.1	384	348
Diabetes mellitus	5.1	5.1	361	337	Diabetes mellitus	8.0	6.6	412	323
Heart disease, excluding ischemic	5.2	4.2	365	279	Malignant neoplasms . . .	4.9	5.8	248	284
Ischemic heart disease . .	5.1	4.2	359	275	Heart disease, excluding ischemic	5.9	5.4	300	264

[1] Based on the International Classification of Diseases, 9th Revision, clinical modification, (ICD-9-CM). [2] Based on U.S. Census Bureau estimated civilian population as of July 1. [3] Includes other first-listed diagnoses not shown separately. [4] Excluding pharyngitis.

Source: U.S. National Center for Health Statistics, National Health Statistics Reports, Nos. 3 and 4; August 06, 2008. <http://www.cdc.gov/nchs/namcs.htm>.

Health and Nutrition   111

Table 161. Visits to Hospital Emergency Departments by Diagnosis: 2006

[(54,230 represents 54,230,000.) See headnote, Table 159]

Leading diagnosis [1]	Number (1,000)	Rate per 1,000 persons [2]	Leading diagnosis [1]	Number (1,000)	Rate per 1,000 persons [2]
MALE			FEMALE		
All ages	**54,230**	**377**	**All ages**	**64,962**	**433**
Under 15 years old [3]	**11,548**	**372**	**Under 15 years old** [3]	**10,328**	**348**
Acute upper respiratory infections [4] . .	1,146	37	Acute respiratory infections [4]	874	29
Otitis media and Eustachian			Otitis media and Eustachian		
tube disorders	761	25	tube disorders	671	23
Contusions with intact skin surfaces .	673	22	Pyrexia of unknown origin	651	22
Pyrexia of unknown origin	616	20	Contusions with intact skin surfaces .	509	17
Open wound of head	512	16	Acute pharyngitis	387	13
15 to 44 years old [3]	**23,372**	**379**	**15 to 44 years old** [3]	**31,188**	**504**
Open wound, excluding head	1,500	24	Abdominal pain	2,033	33
Contusions with intact skin surfaces .	1,306	21	Complications of pregnancy,		
Spinal disorders	960	16	childbirth, and the puerperium	1,411	23
Sprains and strains, excluding			Contusions with intact skin surfaces .	1,233	20
ankle and back	841	14	Spinal disorders	965	16
Cellulitis and abscess	827	13	Urinary tract infection, site not		
45 to 64 years old [3]	**12,271**	**340**	specified	915	15
Chest pain	875	24	**45 to 64 years old** [3]	**13,195**	**345**
Spinal disorders	543	15	Abdominal pain	708	19
Abdominal pain	469	13	Spinal disorders	551	14
Open wound, excluding head	452	13	Contusion with intact skin surface . . .	443	12
Contusion with intact skin surface . . .	427	12	Open wound, excluding head	400	10
65 years old and over [3]	**7,040**	**463**	**65 years old and over** [3]	**10,250**	**502**
Chest pain	447	29	Chest pain	538	26
Heart disease, excluding ischemic . . .	404	27	Contusion with intact skin surface . . .	518	25
Pneumonia	239	16	Heart disease, excluding ischemic . . .	494	24
Open wound, excluding head	235	15	Abdominal pain	342	17
Syncope and collapse	202	13	Urinary tract infection, site not		
			specified	310	15

[1] Based on the International Classification of Diseases, 9th Revision, Clinical Modification (ICD-9-CM). [2] Based on U.S. Census Bureau estimated civilian noninstitutional population as of July 1. [3] Includes other first-listed diagnoses not shown separately. [4] Excluding pharyngitis.

Source: U.S. National Center for Health Statistics, *National Health Statistics Reports,* No. 7, August 06, 2008. <http://www.cdc.gov/nchs/namcs.htm>.

Table 162. Procedures for Inpatients Discharged From Short-Stay Hospitals: 1990 to 2006

[(23,051 represents 23,051,000.) Procedure categories are based on the International Classification of Diseases, 9th Revision, Clinical Modification. See headnote, Table 167]

Sex and type of procedure	Number of procedures (1,000)				Rate per 1,000 population[1]			
	1990	1995	2000	2006	1990	1995	2000	2006
Surgical procedures, total [2]	**23,051**	**22,530**	**23,244**	**28,036**	**92.4**	**86.2**	**83.6**	**94.0**
Coronary artery bypass graft [3]	392	573	519	444	1.6	2.2	1.9	1.5
Cesarean section	945	785	855	1,295	3.8	3.0	3.1	4.3
Repair of current obstetric laceration	795	964	1,136	1,308	3.2	3.7	4.1	4.4
Cardiac catheterization	995	1,068	1,221	1,115	4.0	4.1	4.4	3.7
Reduction of fracture [4]	609	577	628	672	2.4	2.2	2.3	2.3
Male, total [2]	**8,538**	**8,388**	**8,689**	**11,199**	**70.6**	**65.9**	**63.9**	**76.4**
Reduction of fracture [4]	312	292	285	326	2.6	2.3	2.1	2.2
Cardiac catheterization	620	660	732	666	5.1	5.2	5.4	4.5
Coronary artery bypass graft [3]	286	423	371	320	2.4	3.3	2.7	2.2
Female, total [2]	**14,513**	**14,142**	**14,556**	**16,837**	**113.0**	**105.3**	**102.4**	**111.0**
Cesarean section	945	785	855	1,295	7.4	5.8	6.0	8.5
Repair of current obstetric laceration	795	964	1,136	1,308	6.2	7.2	8.0	8.6
Hysterectomy	591	583	633	569	4.6	4.3	4.5	3.8
Diagnostic and other nonsurgical								
procedures [5]	**17,455**	**17,278**	**16,737**	**17,927**	**70.0**	**66.1**	**60.2**	**60.1**
Angiocardiography and arteriography [6]	1,735	1,834	2,005	1,698	7.0	7.0	7.2	5.7
Respiratory therapy	1,164	1,127	991	1,088	4.7	4.3	3.6	3.6
Manual assisted delivery	750	866	898	1,207	3.0	3.3	3.2	4.0
Diagnostic ultrasound	1,608	1,181	886	888	6.4	4.5	3.2	3.0
Fetal electrocardiogram and fetal monitoring . .	1,377	935	750	797	5.6	3.6	2.7	2.7
Male, total [5]	**7,378**	**7,261**	**6,965**	**7,283**	**61.0**	**57.1**	**51.2**	**49.7**
Angiocardiography and arteriography [6]	1,051	1,076	1,157	938	8.7	8.5	8.5	6.4
Respiratory therapy	586	572	507	561	4.9	4.5	3.7	3.8
Computerized Axial Tomographic scan	736	473	345	366	6.1	3.7	2.5	2.5
Female, total [5]	**10,077**	**10,016**	**9,772**	**10,645**	**78.5**	**74.6**	**68.8**	**70.2**
Manual assisted delivery	750	866	898	1,207	5.9	6.5	6.3	8.0
Fetal EKG and fetal monitoring	1,377	935	750	797	10.8	7.0	5.5	5.3
Respiratory therapy	578	555	484	527	4.5	4.1	3.4	3.5
Diagnostic ultrasound	941	682	501	477	7.3	5.1	3.5	3.1

[1] Based on Census Bureau estimated civilian population as of July 1. Population estimates based on the 1990 census were used to calculate rates for 1990 through 2000. Population estimates based on the 2000 census were used to calculate rates for 2001 through 2006. [2] Includes other types of surgical procedures not shown separately. [3] It is possible for a discharge to have more than one of these recorded. [4] Excluding skull, nose, and jaw. [5] Includes other nonsurgical procedures not shown separately. [6] Using contrast material.

Source: U.S. National Center for Health Statistics, *Vital and Health Statistics,* series 13; and unpublished data. <http://www.cdc.gov/nchs/products/pubs/pubd/series/ser.htm>.

Table 163. Hospitals—Summary Characteristics: 1990 to 2006

[For beds, (1,213 represents 1,213,000). Covers hospitals accepted for registration by the American Hospital Association; see text, this section. Short-term hospitals have an average patient stay of less than 30 days; long-term, an average stay of longer duration. Special hospitals include obstetrics and gynecology; eye, ear, nose, and throat; rehabilitation; orthopedic; and chronic and other special hospitals except psychiatric, tuberculosis, alcoholism, and chemical dependency hospitals]

Item	1990	1995	2000	2001	2002	2003	2004	2005	2006
Number:									
All hospitals	6,649	6,291	5,810	5,801	5,794	5,764	5,759	5,756	5,747
With 100 beds or more	3,620	3,376	3,102	3,084	3,032	3,007	2,972	2,942	2,928
Nonfederal [1]	6,312	5,992	5,565	5,558	5,554	5,525	5,520	5,530	5,526
Community hospitals [2]	5,384	5,194	4,915	4,908	4,927	4,895	4,919	4,936	4,927
Nongovernmental nonprofit	3,191	3,092	3,003	2,998	3,025	2,984	2,967	2,958	2,919
For profit	749	752	749	754	766	790	835	868	889
State and local government	1,444	1,350	1,163	1,156	1,136	1,121	1,117	1,110	1,119
Long-term general and special	131	112	131	136	124	126	108	115	127
Psychiatric	757	657	496	491	477	477	466	456	462
Tuberculosis	4	3	4	4	4	4	4	3	2
Federal	337	299	245	243	240	239	239	226	221
Beds (1,000) [3]:									
All hospitals	1,213	1,081	984	987	976	965	956	947	947
Rate per 1,000 population [4]	4.9	4.1	3.5	3.5	3.4	3.3	3.3	3.2	3.2
Beds per hospital	182	172	169	170	168	167	166	165	164
Nonfederal [1]	1,113	1,004	931	936	926	917	908	901	901
Community hospitals [2]	927	873	824	826	821	813	808	802	802
Rate per 1,000 population [4]	3.7	3.3	2.9	2.9	2.8	2.8	2.8	2.7	2.7
Nongovernmental nonprofit	657	610	583	585	582	575	567	561	559
For profit	102	106	110	109	108	110	112	114	115
State and local government	169	157	131	132	130	120	127	128	128
Long-term general and special	25	19	18	19	18	18	15	15	16
Psychiatric	158	110	87	89	85	85	86	82	84
Tuberculosis	(Z)	(Z)	(Z)	(Z)	(Z)	(Z)	(Z)	(Z)	(Z)
Federal	98	78	53	53	50	47	58	46	46
Average daily census (1,000): [5]									
All hospitals	844	710	650	658	662	657	658	656	653
Community hospitals [2]	619	548	526	533	540	539	541	540	538
Nongovernmental nonprofit	455	393	382	385	391	389	388	388	384
For profit	54	55	61	63	64	65	68	68	67
State and local government	111	100	83	85	84	84	84	85	86
Expenses (bil. dol.): [6]									
All hospitals	234.9	320.3	395.4	426.8	462.2	498.1	533.8	570.5	607.3
Nonfederal [1]	219.6	300.0	371.5	399.3	432.5	467.2	499.0	533.7	569.8
Community hospitals [2]	203.7	285.6	356.6	383.7	416.6	450.1	481.2	515.7	551.8
Nongovernmental nonprofit	150.7	209.6	267.1	287.3	312.7	337.7	359.4	386.0	412.8
For profit	18.8	26.7	35.0	37.3	40.1	44.0	48.9	51.8	54.9
State and local government	34.2	49.3	54.5	59.1	63.8	68.4	72.8	77.9	83.9
Long-term general and special	2.7	2.2	2.8	3.3	3.6	3.6	3.6	3.6	4.0
Psychiatric	12.9	11.7	11.9	13.2	12.1	13.1	13.8	13.9	15.0
Tuberculosis	0.1	0.4	(Z)	(Z)	(Z)	(Z)	(Z)	(Z)	(Z)
Federal	15.2	20.2	23.9	27.5	29.7	30.9	34.8	36.8	37.5
Personnel (1,000): [7]									
All hospitals	4,063	4,273	4,454	4,535	4,610	4,650	4,695	4,790	4,907
Nonfederal [1]	3,760	3,971	4,157	4,236	4,312	4,350	4,379	4,479	4,569
Community hospitals [2]	3,420	3,714	3,911	3,987	4,069	4,108	4,147	4,260	4,343
Nongovernmental nonprofit	2,533	2,702	2,919	2,971	3,039	3,058	3,076	3,154	3,207
For profit	273	343	378	379	380	391	405	421	423
State and local government	614	670	614	637	651	658	665	681	713
Long-term general and special	55	38	41	44	46	45	42	38	43
Psychiatric	280	215	200	201	193	194	185	182	193
Tuberculosis	1	1	1	1	1	1	1	1	1
Federal	303	301	297	299	299	300	315	311	338
Outpatient visits (mil.)	368.2	483.2	592.7	612.0	640.5	648.6	662.1	673.7	690.4
Emergency	92.8	99.9	106.9	109.8	114.2	115.1	116.9	118.9	122.6

Z Less than 500 beds or $50 million. [1] Includes hospital units of institutions. [2] Short-term (average length of stay less than 30 days) general and special (e.g., obstetrics and gynecology; eye, ear, nose and throat; rehabilitation, etc. except psychiatric, tuberculosis, alcoholism, and chemical dependency). Excludes hospital units of institutions. [3] Number of beds at end of reporting period. [4] Based on Census Bureau estimated resident population as of July 1, 1990, and 2000 based on enumerated resident population as of April 1. Estimates reflect revisions based on the 2000 census of population. [5] The average number of people served on an inpatient basis on a single day during the reporting period. [6] Excludes new construction. [7] Includes full-time equivalents of part-time personnel.

Source: Health Forum, An American Hospital Association Company, Chicago, IL, *AHA Hospital Statistics 2008 Edition*, and prior years (copyright); <http://www.ahadata.com/>.

Table 164. **Average Cost to Community Hospitals Per Patient: 1990 to 2006**

[**In dollars, except percent.** Covers nonfederal short-term general or special hospitals (excluding psychiatric or tuberculosis hospitals and hospital units of institutions). Total cost per patient based on total hospital expenses (payroll, employee benefits, professional fees, supplies, etc.). Data have been adjusted for outpatient visits]

Type of expense and hospital	1990	1995	1999	2000	2001	2002	2003	2004	2005	2006
Average cost per day, total	687	968	1,103	1,149	1,217	1,290	1,379	1,450	1,522	1,612
Annual percent change [1]	7.8	4.0	3.3	4.2	5.9	6.0	6.9	5.1	5.0	5.9
Nongovernmental nonprofit	692	994	1,140	1,182	1,255	1,329	1,429	1,501	1,585	1,686
For profit	752	947	999	1,057	1,121	1,181	1,264	1,362	1,412	1,472
State and local government	635	878	1,007	1,064	1,114	1,188	1,238	1,291	1,329	1,400
Average cost per stay, total	4,947	6,216	6,512	6,649	6,980	7,346	7,796	8,166	8,793	8,970
Nongovernmental nonprofit	5,001	6,279	6,608	6,717	7,052	7,458	7,905	8,266	8,670	9,190
For profit	4,727	5,425	5,350	5,642	5,972	6,161	6,590	7,139	7,351	7,422
State and local government	4,838	6,445	6,923	7,106	7,400	7,773	8,205	8,473	8,793	9,147

[1] Change from immediate prior year.

Source: Health Forum, An American Hospital Association Company, Chicago, IL, *AHA Hospital Statistics 2008 Edition*, and prior years (copyright); <http://www.ahadata.com/>.

Table 165. **Community Hospitals—States: 2000 and 2006**

[**In thousands, (823.6 represents 823,600).** For definition of community hospitals see footnote 2, Table 163]

State	Number of hospitals		Beds (1,000)		Patients admitted (1,000)		Average daily census [1] (1,000)		Outpatient visits (mil.)		Average cost per day (dol.)	
	2000	2006	2000	2006	2000	2006	2000	2006	2000	2006	2000	2006
United States. . . .	4,915	4,927	823.6	802.6	33,089	35,377	525.7	538.4	521.4	599.5	1,149	1,612
Alabama	108	109	16.4	15.6	680	683	9.8	9.7	8.0	8.0	980	1,274
Alaska	18	22	1.4	1.5	47	52	0.8	0.8	1.3	1.7	1,495	2,455
Arizona	61	66	10.9	11.9	539	664	6.8	8.0	5.3	6.5	1,311	1,930
Arkansas	83	84	9.8	9.3	368	373	5.7	5.3	4.4	5.0	908	1,304
California	389	357	72.7	70.0	3,315	3,428	47.8	50.0	44.9	53.9	1,438	2,056
Colorado	69	73	9.4	9.5	397	420	5.4	5.9	6.7	7.2	1,280	1,864
Connecticut	35	35	7.7	7.9	349	406	5.8	6.3	6.7	7.7	1,373	1,839
Delaware	5	6	1.8	2.1	83	105	1.4	1.8	1.5	1.8	1,311	1,634
District of Columbia . .	11	11	3.3	3.6	129	139	2.5	2.6	1.3	1.6	1,512	2,131
Florida	202	203	51.2	51.4	2,119	2,373	31.0	34.1	21.8	22.7	1,161	1,595
Georgia	151	147	23.9	24.7	863	956	15.0	17.0	11.2	13.7	978	1,243
Hawaii	21	24	3.1	2.9	100	111	2.3	2.3	2.5	1.8	1,088	1,383
Idaho	42	38	3.5	3.3	123	141	1.8	1.8	2.2	2.7	1,003	1,511
Illinois	196	190	37.3	34.1	1,531	1,583	22.4	22.1	25.1	29.5	1,278	1,676
Indiana	109	114	19.2	18.0	700	726	10.8	10.4	14.1	16.5	1,132	1,699
Iowa	115	117	11.8	10.5	360	363	6.8	6.2	9.2	10.2	740	1,093
Kansas	129	129	10.8	10.0	310	332	5.7	5.5	5.3	6.1	837	1,155
Kentucky	105	104	14.8	14.5	582	612	9.1	8.8	8.7	8.8	929	1,318
Louisiana	123	132	17.5	15.8	654	623	9.8	9.8	10.0	9.8	1,075	1,288
Maine	37	37	3.7	3.4	147	150	2.4	2.3	3.2	4.2	1,148	1,627
Maryland	49	50	11.2	11.4	587	690	8.2	8.6	6.0	7.0	1,315	2,009
Massachusetts	80	80	16.6	16.3	740	834	11.7	12.1	16.7	19.5	1,467	1,895
Michigan	146	142	26.1	25.9	1,106	1,205	16.9	17.1	24.9	28.1	1,211	1,608
Minnesota	135	131	16.7	15.8	571	633	11.2	10.8	7.3	10.1	932	1,379
Mississippi	95	94	13.6	12.9	425	415	8.0	7.4	3.7	4.2	719	1,100
Missouri	119	119	20.1	18.8	773	830	11.7	11.8	14.8	16.3	1,185	1,687
Montana	52	52	4.3	4.0	99	106	2.9	2.6	2.6	2.9	579	924
Nebraska	85	85	8.2	7.3	209	215	4.8	4.5	3.4	4.0	743	1,180
Nevada	22	33	3.8	4.8	199	245	2.7	3.5	2.2	2.3	1,285	1,544
New Hampshire	28	28	2.9	2.8	111	118	1.7	1.7	2.8	3.8	1,201	1,714
New Jersey	80	79	25.3	22.0	1,074	1,111	17.3	15.9	16.3	16.9	1,299	1,910
New Mexico	35	36	3.5	3.5	174	160	2.0	2.0	3.1	4.3	1,388	1,738
New York	215	203	66.4	63.5	2,416	2,571	52.1	50.7	46.4	54.0	1,118	1,602
North Carolina	113	114	23.1	23.4	971	1,015	16.0	16.7	12.4	17.2	1,061	1,362
North Dakota	42	41	3.9	3.5	89	88	2.3	2.0	1.7	1.7	747	966
Ohio	163	171	33.8	32.8	1,404	1,542	20.6	21.2	26.9	32.6	1,198	1,773
Oklahoma	108	112	11.1	10.7	429	454	6.2	6.3	4.7	5.3	1,031	1,379
Oregon	59	58	6.6	6.6	330	341	3.9	4.1	7.3	8.2	1,461	2,202
Pennsylvania	207	188	42.3	39.5	1,796	1,866	28.8	27.7	31.8	35.7	1,080	1,601
Rhode Island	11	11	2.4	2.3	119	127	1.7	1.8	2.1	2.4	1,313	1,824
South Carolina	63	66	11.5	11.7	495	521	8.0	8.4	7.8	6.0	1,101	1,487
South Dakota	48	52	4.3	4.3	99	96	2.8	2.8	1.7	1.7	476	774
Tennessee	121	130	20.6	20.3	737	853	11.5	13.1	10.3	10.8	1,078	1,349
Texas	403	417	55.9	58.9	2,367	2,528	33.1	35.7	29.4	31.9	1,274	1,752
Utah	42	43	4.3	4.5	194	220	2.4	2.6	4.5	4.9	1,375	1,914
Vermont	14	14	1.7	1.3	52	50	1.1	0.8	1.2	2.5	888	1,355
Virginia	88	88	16.9	17.2	727	778	11.4	12.0	9.5	13.6	1,057	1,491
Washington	84	88	11.1	10.9	505	556	6.6	6.8	9.6	10.3	1,511	2,298
West Virginia	57	56	8.0	7.1	288	281	4.8	4.3	5.2	6.2	844	1,152
Wisconsin	118	124	15.3	14.1	558	609	9.1	8.7	10.9	12.5	1,055	1,566
Wyoming	24	24	1.9	2.0	48	52	1.1	1.1	0.9	0.9	677	906

[1] The average number of people served on an inpatient basis on a single day during the reporting period.

Source: Health Forum, An American Hospital Association Company, Chicago, IL, *AHA Hospital Statistics 2008 Edition*, and prior years (copyright); <http://www.ahadata.com/>.

Table 166. **Hospital Use Rates by Type of Hospital: 1990 to 2006**

Type of hospital	1990	1995	2000	2002	2003	2004	2005	2006
Community hospitals: [1]								
Admissions per 1,000 population [2]	125	116	117	120	120	119	119	118
Admissions per bed	34	35	40	42	43	43	44	44
Average length of stay (days) [3]	7.2	6.5	5.8	5.7	5.7	5.6	5.6	5.5
Outpatient visits per admission	9.7	13.4	15.8	16.1	16.2	16.3	16.5	16.9
Outpatient visits per 1,000 population [2]	1,207	1,556	1,852	1,932	1,937	1,946	1,976	2,002
Surgical operations (million) [4]	21.9	23.2	26.1	27.6	27.1	27.4	27.5	28.1
Number per admission	0.7	0.7	0.8	0.8	0.8	0.8	0.8	0.7
Nonfederal psychiatric:								
Admissions per 1,000 population [2]	2.9	2.7	2.4	2.5	2.6	2.7	2.5	2.3
Days in hospital per 1,000 population [2]	190	122	93	92	91	88	89	82

[1] Short term (average length of stay less than 30 days) general and special (e.g., obstetrics and gynecology; eye, ear, nose and throat; rehabilitation, etc. except psychiatric, tuberculosis, alcoholism and chemical dependency). Excludes hospital units of institutions.   [2] Based on U.S. Census Bureau estimated resident population as of July 1. Estimates reflect revisions based on the 2000 census of population. 1990 and 2000 based on enumerated resident population as of April 1.   [3] Number of inpatient days divided by number of admissions.   [4] 21.9 represents 21,900,000.

Source: Health Forum, An American Hospital Association Company, Chicago, IL, *AHA Hospital Statistics 2008 Edition*, and prior years (copyright). <http://www.healthforum.com/>.

Table 167. **Hospital Utilization Rates by Sex: 1990 to 2006**

[**(30,788 represents 30,788,000.)** Represents estimates of inpatients discharged from noninstitutional, short-stay hospitals, exclusive of federal hospitals. Excludes newborn infants. Based on sample data collected from the National Hospital Discharge Survey, a sample survey of hospital records of patients discharged in year shown; subject to sampling variability]

Item and sex	1990	1995	2000	2001	2002	2003	2004	2005	2006
Patients discharged (1,000)	30,788	30,722	31,706	32,653	33,727	34,738	34,864	34,667	34,854
Patients discharged per 1,000 persons, total [1]	122	116	114	115	118	120	119	117	117
Male	100	94	92	93	95	98	97	96	95
Female	143	136	135	137	139	141	141	138	138
Days of care per 1,000 persons, total [1]	784	620	560	562	572	578	574	562	558
Male	694	551	491	490	506	507	505	498	495
Female	869	686	627	631	635	646	641	624	619
Average stay (days)	6.4	5.4	4.9	4.9	4.9	4.8	4.8	4.8	4.8
Male	6.9	5.8	5.3	5.3	5.3	5.2	5.2	5.2	5.2
Female	6.1	5.0	4.6	4.6	4.6	4.6	4.5	4.5	4.5

[1] Rates are computed using Census Bureau estimates of the civilian population as of July 1. Rates for 1990 and 1995 were based on population estimates adjusted for the net underenumeration in the 1990 census. Rates for 2000 and later were calculated using 2000-based postcensal estimates.

Source: U.S. National Center for Health Statistics, *Vital and Health Statistics,* Series 13; and unpublished data; <http://www.cdc.gov/nchs/products/pubs/pubd/series/ser.htm>.

Table 168. **Hospital Utilization Measures for HIV Patients: 1990 to 2006**

[HIV represents human immunodeficiency virus. See headnote, Table 167]

Measure of utilization	Unit	1990	1995	2000	2004	2005	2006
Number of patients discharged	1,000	146	249	173	204	185	223
Male	1,000	114	183	115	132	113	145
Female	1,000	32	66	58	73	72	78
Rate of patient discharges [1]	Rate	5.8	9.4	6.2	7.0	6.3	7.5
Number of days of care	1,000	2,188	2,326	1,257	1,477	1,244	1,418
Male	1,000	1,777	1,649	895	876	751	907
Female	1,000	411	677	362	601	493	511
Rate of days of care [1]	Rate	86.9	87.6	45.2	50.5	42.2	47.6
Average length of stay	Days	14.9	9.3	7.3	7.2	6.7	6.3
Male	Days	15.5	9.0	7.8	6.7	6.7	6.2
Female	Days	12.9	10.3	6.3	8.3	6.8	6.5

[1] Per 10,000 population. Based on Census Bureau estimated civilian population as of July 1. Populations for 1990 and 1995 were adjusted for the net underenumeration in the 1990 census. Populations for 2000 and later were 2000-based postcensal estimates.

Source: National Center for Health Statistics, *Vital and Health Statistics,* Series 13; and unpublished data; <http://www.cdc.gov/nchs/products/pubs/pubd/series/ser.htm>.

U.S. Census Bureau, Statistical Abstract of the United States: 2009

Table 169. **Hospital Discharges and Days of Care: 2002 and 2006**

[**(33,727 represents 33,727,000.)** See headnote, Table 167. For composition of regions, see map, inside front cover]

Age, race, and region	Discharges Number (1,000) 2002	2006	Discharges Per 1,000 persons [1] 2002	2006	Days of care per 1,000 persons [1] 2002	2006	Average stay (days) 2002	2006
Total [2]	**33,727**	**34,854**	**118**	**117**	**572**	**558**	**4.9**	**4.8**
Age:								
Under 1 year old.	810	751	201	182	1,134	1,162	5.6	6.4
1 to 4 years old	713	682	46	42	159	141	3.5	3.4
5 to 14 years old	1,016	865	25	21	109	97	4.4	4.5
15 to 24 years old.	3,083	3,132	77	75	266	264	3.5	3.5
25 to 34 years old.	3,897	4,045	99	101	328	346	3.3	3.4
35 to 44 years old.	3,757	3,623	84	84	368	358	4.4	4.3
45 to 64 years old.	7,723	8,686	116	116	575	579	5.0	5.0
65 to 74 years old.	4,642	4,793	254	253	1,412	1,317	5.6	5.2
75 years old and over	8,085	8,278	467	451	2,795	2,541	6.0	5.6
Race:								
White	20,806	20,907	90	88	436	414	4.9	4.7
Black	3,995	4,241	109	111	584	621	5.3	5.6
Asian/Pacific Islander.	538	619	45	45	243	244	5.4	5.4
American Indian/Eskimo/ Aleut.	173	103	63	36	330	151	5.2	4.2
Region:								
Northeast	6,990	7,277	129	133	727	703	5.6	5.3
Midwest	7,503	7,951	115	120	512	508	4.4	4.2
South	12,994	13,140	127	121	618	595	4.9	4.9
West.	6,239	6,486	96	94	430	432	4.5	4.6

[1] Rates were calculated using U.S. Census Bureau 2000-based postcensal estimates of the civilian population as of July 1.
[2] Includes other races not shown separately.

Source: U.S. National Center for Health Statistics, *Vital and Health Statistics,* Series 13; and unpublished data; <http://www.cdc.gov/nchs/products/pubs/pubd/series/ser.htm>.

Table 170. **Hospital Discharges and Days of Care by Selected Diagnosis: 2006**

[**(13,990 represents 13,990,000.)** Represents estimates of inpatients discharged from noninstitutional, short-stay hospitals, exclusive of federal hospitals. Excludes newborn infants. Diagnostic categories are based on the International Classification of Diseases, 9th Revision, Clinical Modification. See headnote, Table 167]

Sex, age, and selected first-listed diagnosis [1]	Discharges Number [2] (1,000)	Per 1,000 persons [3]	Average stay [2] (days)	Sex, age, and selected first-listed diagnosis [1]	Discharges Number [2] (1,000)	Per 1,000 persons [3]	Average stay [2] (days)
Male				Female			
All ages [4]	**13,990**	**100.1**	**5.2**	**All ages, crude [4]** . . .	**20,864**	**137.5**	**4.5**
Under 18 years [4]	1,515	40.2	4.9	Under 18 years [4]	1,389	38.6	4.5
Injury	167	4.4	[5]3.9	Injury	82	2.3	[5]3.9
Pneumonia	101	2.7	[5]3.3	Pneumonia	79	2.2	3.5
Asthma	[5]99	[5]2.6	[5]2.1	Acute bronchitis and bronchiolitis	[5]69	[5]1.91	[5]2.9
18–44 years [4]	2,701	47.7	5.0	18–44 years [4]	7,492	134.4	3.2
Injury	398	7.0	4.8	Childbirth	3,980	71.4	2.6
Serious mental illness (psychoses) [6]	336	5.9	8.2	Serious mental illness (psychoses) [6]	370	6.6	7.1
Alcohol and drug [7]	186	3.3	[5]4.4	Injury	176	3.2	3.7
Heart disease.	173	3.1	3.7	Uterine fibroids	103	1.8	2.4
45–64 years [4]	4,287	117.6	5.1	45–64 years [4]	4,399	114.7	4.9
Heart disease.	803	22.0	3.7	Heart disease.	481	12.6	4.2
Injury	252	6.9	6.6	Serious mental illness (psychoses) [6]	243	6.3	8.9
Cancer, all	222	6.1	6.6	Cancer, all	217	5.7	5.8
Serious mental illness (psychoses) [6]	179	4.9	8.8	Osteoarthritis	191	5.0	3.8
65–74 years [5]	2,241	258.4	5.1	65–74 years [4]	2,552	249.1	5.3
Heart disease.	519	59.8	4.3	Heart disease.	406	39.7	4.7
Cancer, all	151	17.4	6.7	Osteoarthritis	169	16.5	3.7
Stroke	105	12.1	4.7	Cancer, all	160	15.6	6.9
Pneumonia	101	11.6	5.1	Pneumonia	112	10.9	5.8
75–84 years [4]	2,236	422.0	5.7	75–84 years [4]	3,016	389.3	5.6
Heart disease.	496	93.7	4.8	Heart disease.	570	73.5	4.9
Pneumonia	141	26.6	5.4	Injury	222	28.6	5.4
Cancer, all	114	21.5	8.0	Pneumonia	140	18.1	5.8
Stroke	113	21.4	4.5	Stroke	134	17.2	4.8
85 years and over [4] . . .	1,010	598.4	5.4	85 years and over [4] . . .	2,015	558.4	5.7
Heart disease.	209	123.9	4.7	Heart disease.	424	117.4	4.8
Pneumonia	82	48.7	5.6	Injury	203	56.3	5.4
Injury	71	41.9	5.2	Pneumonia	134	37.2	5.9

[1] The first-listed diagnosis is the one specified as the principal diagnosis or the first diagnosis listed on the face sheet or discharge summary of the medical record. It is usually the main cause of the hospitalization. The number of first-listed diagnoses is the same as the number of discharges. [2] Crude estimates. [3] Estimates are age adjusted to the year 2000 standard population using six age groups: under 18 years, 18–44 years, 45–54 years, 55–64 years, 65–74 years, and 75 years and over. [4] Includes discharges with first-listed diagnoses not shown in table. [5] Estimates are considered unreliable. [6] These estimates are for nonfederal short-stay hospitals only and do not include serious mental illness discharges. [7] Includes abuse, dependence, and withdrawal. These estimates are for nonfederal short-stay hospitals only and do not include alcohol and drug discharges from other types of facilities or programs such as the Department of Veterans Affairs or day treatment programs.

Source: Centers for Disease Control and Prevention, National Center for Health Statistics, National Hospital Discharge Survey; <http://www.cdc.gov/nchs/about/major/hdasd/nhds.htm>.

Table 171. Selected Cosmetic Plastic Surgery Procedures: 2001 to 2007

[In thousands (8,470.4 represents 8,470,400). As of December 31. The final data are projected to reflect nationwide statistics and are based on a survey of doctors who have been certified by the American Board of Medical Specialties recognized boards. The final data as reported by the American Society for Aesthetic Plastic Surgery (ASAPS) including but not limited to the American Board of Plastic Surgery. ASAPS members are plastic surgeons certified by the American Board of Plastic Surgery who specialize in cosmetic surgery of the face and the entire body. Procedures are ranked by total number in the most current year]

Procedure	2001	2002	2003	2004	2005	2006	2007
Total all procedures	**8,470.4**	**6,889.5**	**8,252.0**	**11,855.0**	**11,428.8**	**11,456.8**	**11,701.0**
Total surgical procedures	**1,609.6**	**1,620.7**	**1,819.5**	**2,120.0**	**2,131.0**	**1,922.8**	**2,079.0**
Lipoplasty (Liposuction)	385.4	372.8	384.6	478.3	455.5	403.7	456.8
Breast augmentation	216.8	249.6	280.4	334.1	364.6	383.9	399.4
Blepharoplasty (eyelid surgery)	246.3	229.1	267.6	290.3	231.5	210.0	240.8
Abdominoplasty (tummy tuck)	71.1	83.0	117.7	151.0	169.3	172.5	185.3
Breast reduction	114.9	125.6	147.2	144.4	160.5	145.8	153.1
Total nonsurgical procedures	**6,860.8**	**5,268.8**	**6,432.5**	**9,735.0**	**9,297.7**	**9,534.0**	**9,622.0**
Botox injection	1,600.3	1,658.7	2,272.1	2,837.3	3,294.8	3,181.6	2,775.2
Hyaluronic acid [1]	(X)	(X)	116.2	882.5	1,194.2	1,593.6	1,448.7
Laser hair removal	854.6	736.5	923.2	1,411.9	1,566.9	1,475.3	1,412.7
Microdermabrasion [2]	915.3	1,032.4	858.3	1,098.3	1,023.9	993.1	829.7
IPL laser treatment [3]	(X)	(X)	(X)	(X)	(X)	(X)	647.7
Laser skin resurfacing	122.6	72.5	127.5	589.7	475.7	576.5	509.9
Total female procedures	**7,447.8**	**6,081.9**	**7,177.9**	**10,681.4**	**10,443.8**	**10,516.7**	**10,602.5**
Total surgical procedures	**1,363.2**	**1,407.7**	**1,559.4**	**1,887.3**	**1,918.1**	**1,730.5**	**1,877.1**
Breast augmentation	216.8	249.6	280.4	334.1	364.6	383.9	399.4
Lipoplasty (Liposuction)	307.3	316.5	323.0	416.6	402.9	350.4	398.8
Blepharoplasty (eyelid surgery)	204.8	192.8	216.8	249.3	198.1	182.4	208.2
Abdominoplasty (tummy tuck)	67.7	79.7	112.7	145.3	164.1	164.8	180.5
Breast reduction	114.9	125.6	147.2	144.4	160.5	145.8	153.1
Total nonsurgical procedures	**6,083.1**	**4,674.2**	**5,618.6**	**8,794.1**	**8,525.7**	**8,786.2**	**8,725.4**
Botox injection	1,379.9	1,424.9	1,963.0	2,525.4	2,990.7	2,881.1	2,445.7
Hyaluronic acid [1]	(X)	(X)	104.7	838.9	1,149.2	1,519.9	1,364.5
Laser hair removal	715.1	588.5	695.2	1,215.1	1,334.7	1,308.7	1,227.0
Microdermabrasion [2]	820.5	936.2	774.3	999.1	939.5	922.0	743.7
IPL laser treatment [3]	(X)	(X)	(X)	(X)	(X)	(X)	584.5
Sclerotherapy (spider veins)	530.5	291.1	431.3	479.2	548.0	541.3	467.8
Total male procedures	**1,021.8**	**807.7**	**1,074.1**	**1,173.6**	**984.9**	**940.0**	**1,098.6**
Total surgical procedures	**246.4**	**213.1**	**260.1**	**232.7**	**212.9**	**192.3**	**202.0**
Lipoplasty (Liposuction)	78.0	56.3	61.6	61.6	52.5	53.3	58.0
Blepharoplasty (eyelid surgery)	41.5	36.3	50.8	41.1	33.4	27.6	32.6
Rhinoplasty (nose reshaping)	54.4	39.0	53.4	39.0	45.9	33.1	31.7
Gynecomastia (male breast reduction)	16.5	16.6	22.0	19.6	17.7	23.7	20.3
Facelift	11.8	11.1	13.6	11.8	13.0	14.1	12.4
Total nonsurgical procedures	**777.7**	**594.6**	**814.0**	**932.6**	**772.0**	**747.7**	**896.6**
Botox injection	220.4	233.8	309.1	311.9	304.1	300.5	329.5
Laser hair removal	139.5	147.9	228.0	196.8	232.2	166.6	185.7
Microdermabrasion [2]	94.3	96.2	84.0	99.2	84.4	71.1	85.9
Hyaluronic acid [1]	(X)	(X)	11.5	43.6	45.0	73.6	84.2
IPL laser treatment [3]	(X)	(X)	(X)	(X)	(X)	(X)	63.2
Laser skin resurfacing	17.5	4.2	11.0	69.4	43.1	48.5	30.1

X Not applicable. [1] In 2003, the FDA has approved hyaluronan injections for filling soft tissue defects such as facial wrinkles. [2] Procedure for reducing fine lines, "crow's feet," age spots, and acne scars. [3] IPL is intense pulse light. One of the procedures available for facial rejuvenation.

Source: The American Society for Aesthetic Plastic Surgery, Statistics, annual. See also, <http://www.surgery.org/press/statistics.php> (copyright).

Table 172. Organ Transplants and Grafts: 1990 to 2007

[As of end of year. Based on reports of procurement programs and transplant centers in the United States, except as noted]

Procedure	Number of procedures						Number of centers		Number of people waiting, 2007	1-year patient survival rates, 2006 (percent)
	1990	1995	2000	2005	2006	2007	1990	2007		
Transplant: [1]										
Heart	2,095	2,342	2,172	2,125	2,192	2,210	148	130	2,613	87.1
Heart-lung	52	69	47	35	31	30	79	52	101	74.3
Lung	203	869	955	1,406	1,405	1,469	70	65	2,102	82.4
Liver	2,631	3,818	4,816	6,443	6,650	6,493	85	127	16,311	86.0
Kidney	9,358	10,957	13,258	16,481	17,094	16,624	232	245	76,081	97.9
Kidney-pancreas	459	915	910	903	924	862	(NA)	(NA)	2,282	95.2
Pancreas	60	103	420	541	463	469	84	146	1,617	95.4
Intestine	1	21	29	178	175	198	(NA)	45	230	77.8
Multiorgan	71	124	213	518	(NA)	(NA)	(NA)	(NA)	(NA)	(NA)
Cornea grafts [2]	40,631	44,652	50,197	48,298	45,035	50,122	[3]107	[3]84	(NA)	(NA)
Bone grafts (1,000)	350	450	800	1,620	(NA)	(NA)	30	62	(NA)	(NA)
Skin grafts [4]	5,500	5,500	13,000	20,000	(NA)	(NA)	25	59	(NA)	(NA)

NA Not available. [1] Kidney-pancreas and heart-lung transplants are each counted as one procedure. All other multiorgan transplants, excluding kidney-pancreas and heart-lung, are included in the multiorgan row. Based on the Organ Procurement and Transplant Network (OPTN) as of May 30, 2008. The data have been supplied by UNOS under contract with HHS. This work was supported in part by Health Resources and Services Administration contract 231-00-0015. The authors alone are responsible for the reporting and interpretation of these data. Data subject to change based on future data submission or correction. [2] 1990–1992, number of procedures and eye banks include Canada. From 1995 on, the data is for the U.S. only. [3] Eye banks. [4] Procedure data are shown in terms of square feet.

Source: U.S. Department of Health and Human Services, Health Resources and Services Administration, Office of Special Programs, Division of Transplantation, Rockville, MD; United Network for Organ Sharing (UNOS), Richmond, VA; University Renal Research and Education Association, Ann Arbor, MI; American Association of Tissue Banks, McLean, VA; and Eye Bank Association of America, Washington, DC; and unpublished data. See also <http://www.optn.org/>.

U.S. Census Bureau, Statistical Abstract of the United States: 2009

Table 173. Cancer—Estimated New Cases, 2008, and Survival Rates: 1987–1989 to 1996–2004

[**1,437 represents 1,437,000**. The 5-year relative survival rate, which is derived by adjusting the observed survival rate for expected mortality, represents the likelihood that a person will not die from causes directly related to their cancer within 5 years. Survival data shown are based on those patients diagnosed while residents of an area listed below during the time periods shown. Data are based on information collected as part of the National Cancer Institute's Surveillance, Epidemiology, and End Results (SEER) program, a collection of population-based registries in five states (Connecticut, Hawaii, Iowa, New Mexico, Utah) and four metropolitan areas (Atlanta, Detroit, San Francisco-Oakland, and Seattle-Puget Sound)]

| Site | Estimated new cases, [1] 2008 (1,000) | | | 5-year relative survival rates (percent) | | | | | | | |
| | | | | White | | | | Black | | | |
	Total	Male	Female	1987–1989	1990–1992	1993–1995	1996–2004	1987–1989	1990–1992	1993–1995	1996–2004
All sites [2]	1,437	745	692	**57.8**	**62.4**	**63.4**	**67.5**	**43.7**	**48.2**	**52.9**	**57.5**
Lung	215	115	100	13.8	14.5	15.1	15.9	11.2	10.8	13.0	12.7
Breast [3]	184	2	182	85.3	86.7	88.0	90.5	71.3	71.8	72.8	77.8
Colon and rectum	149	77	72	61.1	63.2	61.5	66.3	53.4	53.8	52.9	56.0
Colon	108	54	54	61.7	64.0	61.4	66.0	53.3	54.2	52.3	55.0
Rectum	41	23	17	59.7	61.3	61.7	67.2	53.6	52.2	54.8	58.9
Prostate	186	186	(X)	85.4	95.3	96.2	99.4	72.2	85.5	91.5	95.9
Bladder	69	51	18	81.4	81.9	82.2	81.6	63.3	64.7	61.7	66.2
Corpus uteri	40	(X)	40	85.6	87.2	86.5	86.9	59.2	57.0	61.7	62.7
Non-Hodgkin's lymphoma [4]	66	35	31	52.8	52.9	54.5	65.9	47.4	42.0	42.0	57.6
Oral cavity and pharynx	35	25	10	56.6	58.7	60.9	62.4	34.4	33.3	38.2	41.7
Leukemia [4]	44	25	19	45.5	48.0	49.5	52.2	36.7	37.4	42.3	42.4
Melanoma of skin	62	35	28	88.3	89.6	89.7	92.1	79.9	60.3	66.8	77.9
Pancreas	38	19	19	3.4	4.7	4.2	4.9	5.9	3.7	3.7	4.6
Kidney	54	33	21	58.5	62.1	63.1	66.6	55.8	57.7	58.6	66.1
Stomach	22	13	8	19.1	19.3	20.6	23.1	20.0	23.8	19.8	24.5
Ovary	22	(X)	22	39.9	42.4	42.7	45.3	35.2	37.8	43.3	38.3
Cervix uteri [5]	11	(X)	11	73.6	71.9	74.7	73.7	58.2	58.8	64.0	65.3

X Not applicable. [1] Estimates provided by American Cancer Society (<www.cancer.org>) are based on rates from the National Cancer Institute's SEER program. [2] Includes other sites not shown separately. [3] Survival rates for female only. [4] All types combined. [5] Invasive cancer only.

Source: U.S. National Institutes of Health, National Cancer Institute; <http://seer.cancer.gov/csr/1975_2004/>.

Table 174. Cancer—Estimated New Cases and Deaths by State: 2008

[**In thousands (1,437.2 represents 1,437,200)**. Excludes basal and squamous cell skin cancers and in situ carcinomas except urinary bladder]

| State | New cases [1] | | | Deaths | | | State | New cases [1] | | | Deaths | | |
	Total [2]	Female breast	Lung & bron-chus	Total [2]	Female breast	Lung & bron-chus		Total [2]	Female breast	Lung & bron-chus	Total [2]	Female breast	Lung & bron-chus
U.S.	**1,437.2**	**182.5**	**215.0**	**565.7**	**40.5**	**161.8**							
							MO	29.4	3.8	5.6	12.6	0.9	4.1
AL	22.3	2.8	3.9	9.9	0.7	3.3	MT	5.1	0.6	0.7	2.0	0.1	0.6
AK	2.7	0.4	0.3	0.8	0.1	0.2	NE	8.7	1.2	1.2	3.3	0.2	0.9
AZ	25.5	3.2	3.9	10.3	0.7	2.8	NV	11.4	1.3	1.9	4.7	0.3	1.3
AR	14.8	1.8	2.6	6.4	0.4	2.2	NH	7.0	1.0	1.0	2.6	0.2	0.8
CA	156.5	20.1	18.1	55.6	4.2	13.1							
							NJ	45.9	6.3	6.2	16.8	1.4	4.3
CO	18.9	2.5	2.2	6.7	0.5	1.7	NM	8.3	1.1	0.9	3.3	0.2	0.7
CT	19.2	2.6	2.7	7.0	0.5	1.9	NY	97.1	13.3	13.5	34.9	2.7	9.0
DE	4.6	0.6	0.8	1.9	0.1	0.6	NC	40.4	5.0	6.5	17.5	1.3	5.5
DC	2.6	0.3	0.4	1.0	0.1	0.3	ND	3.1	0.4	0.4	1.2	0.1	0.3
FL	101.9	11.9	17.4	41.7	2.8	12.5							
							OH	56.8	7.0	9.5	24.4	1.8	7.4
GA	37.0	4.9	6.0	15.0	1.1	4.6	OK	17.9	2.3	3.2	7.4	0.5	2.4
HI	6.3	0.8	0.7	2.3	0.1	0.6	OR	19.2	2.4	2.6	7.5	0.5	2.2
ID	6.4	0.8	0.8	2.5	0.2	0.6	PA	70.1	9.4	10.3	29.4	2.2	8.2
IL	59.1	7.2	9.3	23.7	1.8	6.6	RI	6.1	0.8	0.9	2.3	0.1	0.6
IN	29.6	3.7	5.1	12.8	0.8	4.0							
							SC	20.7	2.5	3.6	8.9	0.6	2.9
IA	16.2	2.0	2.6	6.5	0.4	1.8	SD	4.1	0.5	0.5	1.6	0.1	0.5
KS	12.5	1.7	1.9	5.4	0.4	1.6	TN	29.4	3.7	5.1	13.3	0.9	4.5
KY	23.3	2.6	4.6	9.5	0.6	3.5	TX	96.3	12.2	13.8	35.0	2.5	9.9
LA	23.4	2.8	3.7	9.4	0.8	3.0	UT	7.8	1.0	0.6	2.7	0.2	0.5
ME	8.1	1.0	1.3	3.3	0.2	1.0							
							VT	3.5	0.5	0.5	1.1	0.1	0.4
MD	27.4	3.7	4.1	10.4	0.8	2.9	VA	35.6	4.7	5.3	14.0	1.1	4.6
MA	34.5	4.5	4.9	13.1	0.9	3.6	WA	32.4	4.1	4.1	11.4	0.8	3.2
MI	51.2	6.1	8.0	21.2	1.3	5.9	WV	10.3	1.2	2.0	4.6	0.3	1.5
MN	23.2	3.1	3.3	9.1	0.6	2.4	WI	27.6	3.4	3.9	11.2	0.8	2.9
MS	13.4	1.6	2.3	6.0	0.4	2.0	WY	2.6	0.3	0.3	1.0	0.1	0.3

[1] Estimates are offered as a rough guide and should be interpreted with caution. [2] Includes other types of cancer not shown separately.

Source: American Cancer Society, Inc., Atlanta, Georgia, *Cancer Facts and Figures—2008* (copyright); <http://www.cancer.org/docroot/STT/stt_0.asp>.

Table 175. **Selected Notifiable Diseases—Cases Reported: 1980 to 2006**

[(**190.9 represents 190,900.**) Figures should be interpreted with caution. Although reporting of some of these diseases is incomplete, the figures are of value in indicating trends of disease incidence. Includes cases imported from outside the United States]

Disease	1980	1990	1995	2000	2002	2003	2004	2005	2006
AIDS [1]	(2)	41,595	71,547	40,758	42,745	44,232	44,108	41,120	(NA)
Botulism [3]	89	92	97	138	118	129	133	135	48
Brucellosis (undulant fever)	183	85	98	87	125	104	114	120	121
Chickenpox (Varicella) [4] (1,000)	190.9	173.1	120.6	27.4	22.8	20.9	32.9	32.2	48.4
Coccidoidomycosis	(2)	(2)	(2)	2,867	4,968	4,870	6,449	6,542	8,917
Cryptosporidiosis	(2)	(2)	(NA)	3,128	3,016	3,506	3,577	5,659	6,071
Domestic arboviral diseases [5]									
West Nile: Neuroinvasie	(2)	(2)	(2)	(2)	2,840	2,866	1,142	1,309	1,495
Nonneuroinvasie	(2)	(2)	(2)	(2)	(2)	(2)	(2)	1,691	2,774
Enterohemorrhagic Escherichia coli 0157:H7	(2)	(2)	2,139	4,528	3,840	2,671	2,544	2,621	(2)
Giardiasis	(2)	(2)	(2)	(2)	21,206	19,709	20,636	19,733	18,953
Haemophilus influenza	(2)	(2)	1,180	1,398	1,743	2,013	2,085	2,304	2,496
Hansen disease (Leprosy)	223	198	144	91	96	95	105	87	66
Hepatitis: A (infectious) (1,000)	29.1	31.4	31.6	13.4	8.8	7.7	5.7	4.5	3.6
B (serum) (1,000)	19.0	21.1	10.8	8.0	8.0	7.5	6.2	5.1	4.7
C/Non-A, non-B (1,000) [6]	(2)	2.6	4.6	3,197	1,835	1,102	720	652	766
Legionellosis	(2)	1,370	1,241	1,127	1,321	2,232	2,093	2,301	2,834
Lyme disease	(2)	(2)	11,700	17,730	23,763	21,273	19,804	23,305	19,931
Malaria	2,062	1,292	1,419	1,560	1,430	1,402	1,458	1,494	1,474
Meningococcal infections	2,840	2,451	3,243	2,256	1,814	1,756	1,361	1,245	1,194
Mumps (1,000)	8.6	5.3	0.9	0.3	0.3	0.2	0.3	0.3	6.6
Pertussis [7] (1,000)	1.7	4.6	5.1	7.9	9.8	11.6	25.8	25.6	15.6
Psittacosis	124	113	64	17	18	12	12	16	21
Rabies, animal	6,421	4,826	7,811	6,934	7,609	6,846	6,345	5,915	5,534
Rocky Mountain spotted fever	1,163	651	590	495	1,104	1,091	1,713	1,936	2,288
Rubella [8]	3,904	1,125	128	176	18	7	10	11	11
Salmonellosis [9] (1,000)	33.7	48.6	46.0	39.6	44.3	43.7	42.2	45.3	45.8
Shigellosis [10] (1,000)	19.0	27.1	32.1	22.9	23.5	23.6	14.6	16.2	15.5
Streptococcal disease, invasive, Group A	(2)	(2)	(2)	3,144	4,720	5,872	4,395	4,715	5,407
Streptococcus pneumoniae, invasive:									
Drug-resistant	(2)	(2)	(2)	4,533	2,546	2,356	2,590	2,996	3,308
Age less than 5 years	(2)	(2)	(2)	(2)	513	845	1,162	1,495	1,861
Tetanus	95	64	41	35	25	20	34	27	41
Toxic-shock syndrome	(2)	322	191	135	109	133	95	90	101
Trichinosis	131	129	29	16	14	6	5	16	15
Tuberculosis [11] (1,000)	27.7	25.7	22.9	16.4	15.1	14.9	14.5	14.1	13.8
Typhoid fever	510	552	369	377	321	356	322	324	353
Sexually transmitted diseases:									
Chlamydia (1,000)	(2)	(2)	478	702	835	877	929	976	1,031
Gonorrhea (1,000)	1,004	690	393	359	352	335	330	340	358
Syphilis (1,000)	69	134	69	32	34	34	33	33	37

NA Not available. [1] Acquired immunodeficiency syndrome was not a notifiable disease until 1984. Figures are shown for years in which cases were reported to the CDC. Beginning 1995, based on revised classification system and expanded surveillance case definition. 2006 data are not available; see source for details. [2] Disease was not notifiable. [3] Includes foodborne, infant, wound, and unspecified cases. [4] Chickenpox was taken off the nationally notifiable list in 1991 but many states continue to report. [5] The national surveillance case definitions for the arboviral diseases was revised in 2005, and nonneuroinvasive arboviral diseases were added to the list of nationally notifiable infectious diseases. [6] Includes some persons positive for antibody to hepatitis C virus. [7] Whooping cough. [8] German measles. Excludes congenital syndrome. [9] Excludes typhoid fever. [10] Bacillary dysentery. [11] Newly reported active cases.

Source: *Summary of Notifiable Diseases, United States, 2006, Morbidity and Mortality Weekly Report,* Vol. 55, No. 53, March 21, 2008; <http://www.cdc.gov/mmwr/PDF/wk/mm5553.pdf>.

Table 176. **AIDS, 2005, Clamydia, and Lyme Diease, 2006, Cases Reported by State**

State	2005 [1] AIDS	2006 Clamydia	2006 Lyme diease	State	2005 [1] AIDS	2006 Clamydia	2006 Lyme diease	State	2005 [1] AIDS	2006 Clamydia	2006 Lyme diease
U.S.	**41,120**	**1,030,911**	**19,931**	KS	110	7,829	4	ND	10	1,820	7
				KY	267	8,940	7	OH	796	40,106	43
AL	523	22,915	11	LA	976	17,885	1	OK	284	12,992	–
AK	29	4,525	3	ME	22	2,306	338	OR	220	9,577	7
AZ	645	24,090	10	MD	1,596	21,859	1,248	PA	1,524	39,487	3,242
AR	242	8,259	–	MA	716	15,394	1,432	RI	90	3,142	308
CA	4,117	135,827	85	MI	829	36,753	55	SC	621	22,351	20
CO	364	16,313	–	MN	223	12,935	914	SD	19	2,633	1
CT	674	10,946	1,788	MS	390	19,002	3	TN	851	25,320	15
DE	177	3,615	482	MO	384	22,982	5	TX	3,152	75,543	29
DC	708	3,368	62	MT	20	2,650	1	UT	66	5,092	5
FL	5,055	48,955	34	NE	49	5,428	11	VT	7	1,191	105
GA	2,396	38,972	8	NV	296	8,398	4	VA	649	24,087	357
HI	110	5,548	(2)	NH	37	1,997	617	WA	486	17,819	8
ID	26	3,345	7	NJ	1,276	20,194	2,432	WV	76	2,910	28
IL	1,938	53,586	110	NM	139	9,829	3	WI	125	20,190	1,466
IN	414	19,859	26	NY	6,350	68,720	4,460	WY	6	1,422	1
IA	95	8,390	97	NC	945	33,615	31				

– Represents zero. [1] 2006 data are not available; see source for details. [2] Not notifiable.

Source: *Summary of Notifiable Diseases, United States, 2006, Morbidity and Mortality Weekly Report,* Vol. 55, No. 53, March 21, 2008; <http://www.cdc.gov/mmwr/PDF/wk/mm5553.pdf>.

Health and Nutrition 119

Table 177. **Reported AIDS Cases for Adults and Adolescents by Transmission Category and Sex: 2006**

[**Provisional.** For cases reported in the year shown. Includes Puerto Rico, Virgin Islands, Guam, and U.S. Pacific Islands. Acquired immunodeficiency syndrome (AIDS) is a specific group of diseases or conditions which are indicative of severe immunosuppression related to infection with the human immunodeficiency virus (HIV). Data are subject to retrospective changes and may differ from those data in Table 175. For information on HIV death rates, go to Table 121]

Transmission category	2006			Cumulative through 2006[1]		
	Total	Male	Female	Total	Male	Female
Persons 13 years old and over, total	**38,916**	**28,378**	**10,537**	**983,343**	**791,626**	**191,714**
Male-to-male sexual contact	13,775	13,775	(X)	429,897	429,897	(X)
Injection drug use.	5,239	3,413	1,826	230,763	163,070	67,693
Male-to-male sexual contact and injection drug use. . . .	1,603	1,603	(X)	65,524	65,524	(X)
Hemophilia/coagulation disorder	54	43	11	5,524	5,176	348
High-risk heterosexual contact.	7,836	2,997	4,839	134,796	49,610	85,186
Sex with injection drug user.	1,036	330	706	37,756	11,683	26,073
Sex with bisexual male.	234	(X)	234	5,162	(X)	5,162
Sex with person with hemophilia	12	1	11	586	84	502
Sex with HIV-infected person, transfusion recipient . .	43	22	21	1,346	553	793
Sex with HIV-infected person, risk factor not specified	6,511	2,644	3,867	89,946	37,290	52,656
Receipt of blood transfusion, blood components, or tissue	131	63	68	9,389	5,213	4,176
Other/risk not reported or identified	10,278	6,484	3,793	107,450	73,136	34,311

X Not applicable.   [1] Includes persons with a diagnosis of AIDS, reported from the beginning of the epidemic through 2006. Cumulative total includes persons with characteristics unknown.

Source: U.S. Centers for Disease Control and Prevention, Atlanta, GA, *HIV/AIDS Surveillance Report, 2006*, Volume 18; <http://www.cdc.gov/hiv/topics/surveillance/resources/reports/2006report/default.htm> (revised 1 April 2008).

Table 178. **Estimated Numbers of Persons Living With Acquired Immunodeficiency Syndrome (AIDS) by Year, Age, and Selected Characteristics: 2000 to 2006**

[These numbers do not represent reported case counts. Rather, these numbers are point estimates, which result from adjustments of reported case counts. The reported case counts are adjusted for reporting delays and for redistribution of cases in persons initially reported without an identified risk factor. The estimates do not include adjustment for incomplete reporting. Data for years 2003 to 2005 have been revised. See the Commentary section in the report. For information on HIV death rates, go to Table 121]

Age and characteristic	2000	2003	2004	2005	2006
Total [1, 2]	**320,177**	**383,024**	**404,849**	**425,646**	**448,871**
AGE AS OF END OF YEAR					
Less than 13 years old	2,843	2,006	1,684	1,394	1,115
13 and 14 years old	513	747	784	762	711
15 to 24 years old.	4,944	5,986	6,603	7,276	7,854
25 to 34 years old.	54,473	46,613	45,102	43,454	43,183
35 to 44 years old.	143,920	154,400	156,411	156,256	154,823
45 to 54 years old.	85,445	118,131	130,750	143,409	157,251
55 to 64 years old.	22,089	35,438	41,661	48,902	57,086
65 years old and over	5,950	8,946	10,604	12,430	14,669
RACE/ETHNICITY					
White, not Hispanic.	119,420	135,278	141,508	147,426	154,495
Black, not Hispanic	132,090	161,326	171,654	181,056	191,590
Hispanic	63,894	67,895	72,024	76,334	80,815
Asian/Pacific Islander	2,612	3,426	3,759	4,121	4,526
American Indian/Alaska Native	1,099	1,356	1,458	1,562	1,651
TRANSMISSION CATEGORY MALE ADULT/ADOLESCENT					
Males 13 years old and over, total	248,726	286,091	301,585	316,440	333,244
Male-to-male sexual contact	142,069	168,233	178,551	188,622	199,693
Injection drug use.	57,778	58,436	59,940	61,229	62,998
Male-to-male sexual contact and injection drug use. . . .	22,603	25,457	26,144	26,785	27,523
High-risk heterosexual contact.	22,568	30,300	33,181	35,916	39,004
Other [3]	3,708	3,665	3,769	3,888	4,026
FEMALE ADULT/ADOLESCENT					
Females 13 years old and over, total	67,601	82,395	88,236	93,653	99,671
Injection drug use.	26,656	28,874	29,828	30,646	31,575
Heterosexual contact.	39,121	51,489	56,229	60,693	65,631
Other [3]	1,824	2,033	2,178	2,315	2,465
CHILD (LESS THAN 13 YEARS OLD AT DIAGNOSIS)					
Total.	3,848	3,778	3,774	3,786	3,775
Perinatal	3,706	3,654	3,651	3,664	3,660
Other [4]	142	124	123	122	115

[1] Includes persons of unknown or multiple race and of unknown sex. Because column totals were calculated independently of the values for the subpopulations, the values in each column may not sum to the column total.   [2] Persons who reported multiple racial categories or whose race was unknown are included in the total numbers.   [3] Includes hemophilia, blood transfusion, perinatal, and risk not reported or not identified.   [4] Includes hemophilia, blood transfusion, and risk not reported or not identified.

Source: U.S. Centers for Disease Control and Prevention, Atlanta, GA, *HIV/AIDS Surveillance Report, 2006*, Volume 18. <http://www.cdc.gov/hiv/topics/surveillance/resources/reports/2006report/default.htm> (revised 1 April 2008).

Table 179. Learning Disability or Attention Deficit Hyperactivity Disorder for Children 3–17 Years of Age by Selected Characteristics: 2006

[In thousands, except percent (61,354 represents 61,354,000). Learning Disability is based on the question, "Has a representative from a school or a health professional ever told you that (child's name) has a learning disability?" Attention Deficit Hyperactivity Disorder is based on the question, "Has a doctor or health professional ever told you that (child's name) had Attention Hyperactivity Disorder or Attention Deficit Disorder?"]

| Selected characteristic | Total | Ever told had— | | | |
| | | Learning disability | | Attention deficit hyperactivity disorder | |
		Number	Percent	Number	Percent
Total [1,2]	61,354	4,748	7.7	4,545	7.4
SEX [2]					
Male	31,497	3,002	9.6	3,352	10.7
Female	29,857	1,746	5.9	1,193	4.0
AGE					
3 to 4 years old	8,271	172	2.1	[4]46	[4]0.6
5 to 11 years old	27,776	2,001	7.2	2,055	7.4
12 to 17 years old	25,307	2,575	10.2	2,443	9.7
RACE					
Race alone [2,3]	59,480	4,547	7.6	4,320	7.3
White	46,885	3,736	8.0	3,553	7.6
Black or African American	9,571	739	7.7	705	7.4
American Indian or Alaska Native	593	(B)	(B)	(B)	(B)
Asian	2,318	[4]54	[4]2.3	[4]34	[4]1.5
Native Hawaiian or Other Pacific Islander	114	–	–	–	–
Two or more races [2,5]	1,874	201	10.9	224	12.4
HISPANIC ORIGIN AND RACE: [2,6]					
Hispanic or Latino	12,014	753	6.4	602	5.1
Mexican or Mexican American	8,179	478	6.1	374	4.7
Not Hispanic or Latino	49,340	3,995	8.0	3,943	8.0
White, single race	36,023	3,103	8.6	3,059	8.4
Black or African American, single race	9,136	685	7.5	662	7.2

– Represents zero. B Base figure too small to meet statistical standards for reliability of a derived figure. [1] Includes other races not shown separately. [2] Percents are age-adjusted to the 2000 projected U.S. standard population using age groups 3–4 years, 5–11 years, and 12–17 years. [3] Refers to persons who indicated only a single race group. [4] Figures do not meet standard of reliability or precision. [5] Refers to all persons who indicated more than one race group. [6] Persons of Hispanic or Latino origin may be any race or combination of races.

Source: National Center for Health Statistics, *Vital and Health Statistics, Series 10, Number 234, Summary Health Statistics for U.S. Children: National Health Interview Survey, 2006*; <http://www.cdc.gov/nchs/data/series/sr_10/sr10_234.pdf>.

Table 180. Children and Youth With Disabilities Served by Selected Programs: 1995 to 2006

[In thousands (5,078.8 represents 5,078,800). As of Fall. For children and youth ages 6 to 21 served under the Individuals with Disabilities Education Act (IDEA) Part B. Includes outlying areas]

Disability	1995	2000	2001	2002	2003	2004	2005	2006
Total	5,078.8	5,773.9	5,861.4	5,959.1	6,045.4	6,116.4	6,113.5	6,081.9
Specific learning disabilities	2,601.8	2,881.6	2,878.3	2,878.6	2,867.1	2,839.3	2,782.8	2,710.5
Speech or language impairments	1,026.9	1,093.4	1,093.2	1,110.9	1,128.1	1,149.6	1,156.9	1,160.9
Mental retardation	585.6	613.4	605.0	591.7	582.6	567.6	546.0	523.2
Emotional disturbance	439.2	474.3	477.8	482.0	484.5	484.5	472.5	458.9
Multiple disabilities	94.5	122.9	128.7	130.8	132.7	133.4	134.0	134.2
Hearing impairments	68.0	70.8	71.2	72.0	72.0	72.6	72.4	72.6
Orthopedic impairments	63.2	73.0	73.7	74.0	68.2	65.4	63.1	61.9
Other health impairments	134.2	294.0	341.3	393.0	452.7	512.2	561.6	599.5
Visual impairments	25.5	26.0	25.8	26.1	25.9	26.1	26.0	26.4
Autism	29.1	79.6	98.6	118.8	141.1	166.5	193.8	224.6
Deaf-blind	1.4	1.3	1.6	1.6	1.7	1.7	1.6	1.5
Traumatic brain injury	9.6	14.9	20.8	21.5	22.5	23.3	23.5	23.9
Developmental delay [1]	(X)	28.6	45.3	58.3	66.3	74.4	79.1	83.9

X Not applicable. [1] States had the option of reporting children ages 3 to 9 under developmental delay beginning 1997.

Source: U.S. Department of Education, Office of Special Education Programs, Data Analysis System (DANS). See Internet site <http://www.ideadata.org/index.html>.

Table 181. Children Under 18 Years of Age Receiving Special Education or Early Intervention Services: 2006

[In thousands, except percent (73,492 represents 73,492,000). Receiving special education or early intervention services is based on the question, "Do any of the following (family members under 18 years of age) receive special education or early intervention services?"]

Selected characteristic	Total	Persons under 18 years who were receiving special education early intervention services	
		Number	Percent
Total [1,2]	**73,492**	**4,544**	**6.2**
SEX [2]			
Male	37,568	3,048	8.1
Female	35,924	1,496	4.2
AGE			
Under 12 years old	48,216	2,667	5.5
12 to 17 years old	25,276	1,876	7.5
RACE			
Race Alone [2,3]	71,043	4,374	6.2
White	55,866	3,539	6.3
Black or African American	11,496	707	6.1
American Indian or Alaska Native	737	[4]56	[4]7.5
Asian	2,850	68	2.4
Native Hawaiian or Other Pacific Islander	94	(B)	(B)
Two or more races [2,5]	2,449	169	6.8
HISPANIC ORIGIN AND RACE: [2,6]			
Hispanic or Latino	14,815	706	4.8
Mexican or Mexican American	10,125	396	4.0
Not Hispanic or Latino	58,677	3,837	6.5
White, single race	42,454	2,927	6.9
Black or African American, single race	10,914	648	5.9

B Base figure too small to meet statistical standards for reliability of a derived figure.   [1] Includes other races not shown separately.   [2] Percents are age-adjusted to the 2000 projected U.S. standard population using age groups 3–4 years, 5–11 years, and 12–17 years.   [3] Refers to persons who indicated only a single race group.   [4] Figures do not meet standard of reliability or precision.   [5] Refers to all persons who indicated more than one race group.   [6] Persons of Hispanic or Latino origin may be any race or combination of races.

Source: National Center for Health Statistics, *Vital and Health Statistics, Series 10, Number 236, Summary Health Statistics for the U.S. Population: National Health Interview Survey, 2006;* <http://www.cdc.gov/nchs/data/series/sr_10/sr10_236.pdf>.

Table 182. Disabilities Tallied by Age Group and by State: 2006

[In thousands (41,260 represents 41,260,000). Based on data from American Community Survey (ACS). See text, Section 1 and Appendix III]

State	Total	5 to 15 years [1]	16 to 64 years [2]	65 years and over [3]	State	Total	5 to 15 years [1]	16 to 64 years [2]	65 years and over [3]
U.S.	41,260	2,830	23,863	14,567	MO	911	60	531	320
AL	850	52	516	283	MT	151	9	90	52
AK	91	6	64	21	NE	217	16	121	81
AZ	796	57	437	302	NV	288	14	169	105
AR	557	39	332	187	NH	172	12	102	58
CA	4,283	275	2,443	1,565	NJ	987	68	527	392
CO	546	36	334	176	NM	293	19	173	101
CT	418	28	229	161	NY	2,480	166	1,385	929
DE	120	8	69	43	NC	1,361	93	823	445
DC	75	5	44	26	ND	82	6	41	35
FL	2,680	148	1,400	1,132	OH	1,699	126	996	578
GA	1,227	83	750	393	OK	635	40	384	211
HI	152	8	77	67	OR	560	34	336	190
ID	199	14	119	66	PA	1,860	125	1,035	700
IL	1,509	109	824	575	RI	156	11	91	54
IN	896	71	518	307	SC	687	41	414	233
IA	390	29	215	146	SD	97	6	51	40
KS	370	29	207	134	TN	1,043	62	645	336
KY	820	51	524	244	TX	3,081	262	1,810	1,009
LA	729	52	438	239	UT	279	25	169	85
ME	240	18	147	75	VT	98	7	60	31
MD	660	50	376	234	VA	951	66	549	335
MA	827	58	465	304	WA	937	61	576	300
MI	1,487	111	888	488	WV	395	21	245	129
MN	592	46	342	204	WI	687	54	389	244
MS	564	37	348	178	WY	74	5	44	24

[1] Persons aged 5–15 were classified as having a disability if they reported any one of the four conditions; sensory, physical, mental, or self-care disability.   [2] Persons aged 16–64 were classified as having a disability if they reported any one of the six conditions; sensory, physical, mental, self-care disability, go-outside-home, or employment disability.   [3] Persons 65 years and over were classified as having a disability if they reported any one of the five conditions; sensory, physical, mental, self-care disability, or go-outside-home disability.

Source: U.S. Census Bureau, "American Factfinder®, 2006 American Community Survey, Summary Table, Sex by Age by Disability Status for the Civilian Noninstitutionalized Population 5 Years and Over"; <http://www.factfinder.census.gov/>.

Table 183. **Children Immunized Against Specified Diseases: 1995 to 2006**

[In percent. Covers civilian noninstitutionalized population ages 19 months to 35 months. Based on estimates from the National Immunization Survey. The health care providers of the children are contacted to verify and/or complete vaccination information. Results are based on race/ethnic status of the child]

Vaccination	1995, total	2000, total	2006 [1]					
			Total	White, non-Hispanic	Black, non-Hispanic	His-panic [2]	American Indian/ Alaska Native [3]	Asian [3]
Diphtheria-tetanus-pertussis (DTP) diphtheria-tetanus:								
3+ doses	95.0	94.0	95.8	96.4	93.6	95.9	95.1	96.9
4+ doses	79.0	82.0	85.2	86.6	81.4	84.7	81.9	85.8
Polio: 3+ doses	88.0	90.0	92.9	93.3	90.7	93.4	91.3	92.4
Measles, mumps, rubella vaccine	90.0	91.0	92.4	92.8	91.0	92.1	89.1	94.6
Hib: 3+ doses [4]	92.0	93.0	93.4	94.0	91.1	94.0	93.9	89.4
Hepatitis B: 3+ doses	68.0	90.0	93.4	93.9	91.5	93.6	95.3	91.5
Varicella [5]	(NA)	68.0	89.3	88.8	89.2	89.8	84.9	92.9
PCV: 3+ doses [6]	(X)	(X)	87.0	87.2	83.3	89.1	86.8	81.1
4+ DTP/3+ polio/1+ MCV [7]	76.0	78.0	83.2	84.7	79.1	82.3	80.0	84.9
4+ DTP/3+ polio/1+ MCV/3+ Hib	74.0	76.0	82.3	83.9	78.6	81.7	79.5	80.4
4+ DTP/3+ polio/1+ MCV/3+ Hib/3+ HepB	55.1	72.8	80.6	82.2	76.8	80.1	78.6	78.4

NA Not available. X Not Applicable. [1] Children in the Q1/2006–Q4/2006 National Immunization Survey were born between January 2003 and June 2005. [2] Children of Hispanic ethnicity may be any race. [3] Non-Hispanic. [4] Haemophilus influenzae type B. [5] Data collection for varicella (chicken pox) began in July 1996. [6] PCV = Pneumococcal conjugate vaccine. [7] MCV = Measles containing vaccine.

Source: U.S. Centers for Disease Control and Prevention, Atlanta, GA, National Immunization Program, Data and Statistics, *Immunization Coverage in the U.S.*; <http://www.cdc.gov/vaccines/stats-surv/imz-coverage.htm#nis>.

Table 184. **Asthma Incidence Among Children Under 18 Years of Age by Selected Characteristics: 2006**

[In thousands, except percent (73,493 represents 73,493,000). Based on the National Health Interview Survey, a sample survey of the civilian noninstitutionalized population; see Appendix III]

Selected characteristic	Total	Ever told had asthma		Had asthma attack in past 12 months	
		Number	Percent	Number	Percent
Total [1, 2]	**73,493**	**9,876**	**13.6**	**6,819**	**9.4**
SEX [2]					
Male	37,569	5,875	15.8	4,122	11.1
Female	35,924	4,001	11.2	2,697	7.6
AGE					
0 to 4 years old	20,410	1,521	7.5	1,178	5.8
5 to 11 years old	27,776	4,455	16.1	3,191	11.5
12 to 17 years old	25,307	3,900	15.4	2,451	9.7
RACE					
Race Alone [2, 3]	70,976	9,422	13.4	6,493	9.2
White	55,881	7,100	12.8	4,816	8.7
Black or African American	11,455	1,921	16.9	1,461	12.9
American Indian or Alaska Native	691	[4]52	[4]7.2	[4]32	[4]4.3
Asian	2,835	334	11.9	177	6.4
Native Hawaiian or Other Pacific Islander	114	(B)	(B)	(B)	(B)
Two or more races [2, 5]	2,518	454	19.9	326	13.9
HISPANIC ORIGIN AND RACE: [2, 6]					
Hispanic or Latino	14,815	1,901	13.2	1,328	9.2
Mexican or Mexican American	10,186	1,052	10.8	673	6.9
Not Hispanic or Latino	58,678	7,975	13.7	5,492	9.5
White, single race	42,480	5,428	12.8	3,649	8.7
Black or African American, single race	10,899	1,800	16.6	1,383	12.8

B Figure too small to meet statistical standards for reliability of a derived figure. [1] Includes other races not shown separately. [2] Estimates are age-adjusted to the 2000 projected U.S. standard population using age groups 0–4 years, 5–11 years, and 12–17 years. [3] Refers to persons who indicated only a single race group. [4] Figures do not meet standard of reliability or precision. [5] Refers to all persons who indicated more than one race group. [6] Persons of Hispanic or Latino origin may be of any race or combination of races.

Source: National Center for Health Statistics, *Vital and Health Statistics, Series 10, Number 234, Summary Health Statistics for U.S. Children: National Health Interview Survey, 2006;* <http://www.cdc.gov/nchs/data/series/sr_10/sr10_234.pdf>.

Table 185. Persons With Limitation of Activity Caused by Chronic Conditions: 2000 to 2006

[In percent. Limitation of activity is assessed by asking respondents a series of questions about limitations in their ability to perform activities usual for their age group because of a physical, mental, or emotional problem. Based on the National Health Interview Survey, a sample survey of the civilian noninstitutionalized population; see Appendix III]

Characteristic	2000	2004	2005	2006	Characteristic	2000	2004	2005	2006
Total [1, 2]	**11.7**	**11.9**	**11.7**	**11.6**	Male [2]	11.7	11.8	11.7	11.6
Under 18 years old	6.0	7.0	7.0	7.3	Female [2]	11.5	11.9	11.6	11.5
18 to 44 years old	5.8	6.0	5.7	5.5					
45 to 54 years old	12.4	12.5	11.9	12.5	White, non-Hispanic [2] . . .	11.5	12.1	11.5	11.8
55 to 64 years old	19.7	19.9	19.9	20.0	Black, non-Hispanic [2] . . .	14.3	15.3	14.1	14.1
65 to 74 years old	26.1	25.5	25.2	24.8	Hispanic [2, 3]	10.3	10.2	10.5	10.0
75 years and over old . . .	45.1	43.9	43.5	41.6	Mexican	10.4	10.1	11.4	9.8

[1] Includes all other races not shown separately.   [2] Estimates for all persons are age adjusted to the year 2000 standard using six age groups: Under 18 years, 18–44 years, 45–54 years, 55–64 years, 65–74 years, and 75 years and over.   [3] Persons of Hispanic origin may be any race.

Source: U.S. National Center for Health Statistics, *Health, United States, annual*; <http://www.cdc.gov/nchs/hus.htm>.

Table 186. Persons 65 Years Old and Over With Limitation of Activity Caused by Chronic Conditions: 2000 to 2006

[In percent. Covers noninstitutionalized persons 65 years old and over. To determine activities of daily living (ADL) limitations, respondents were asked "Because of a physical, mental, or emotional problem, does (this person) need the help of other persons with personal care needs, such as eating, bathing, dressing, or getting around inside this home?" Instrumental activities of daily living (IADL) were determined by asking respondents "Because of a physical, mental, or emotional problem, does (this person) need the help of other persons in handling routine needs, such as everyday household chores, doing necessary business, shopping, or getting around for other purposes?" See also headnote, Table 185]

Characteristic	Percent with ADL limitation				Percent with IADL limitation			
	2000	2004	2005	2006	2000	2004	2005	2006
Total [1, 2]	**6.3**	**6.1**	**6.2**	**5.8**	**12.7**	**11.5**	**12.0**	**11.2**
65 to 74 years old	3.3	2.9	3.2	3.2	6.6	5.5	6.4	5.6
75 years old and over	9.5	9.5	9.4	8.6	19.3	18.1	18.3	17.3
Male [2]	5.1	4.8	4.6	4.6	9.2	8.4	8.1	7.9
Female [2]	7.0	6.9	7.2	6.6	15.1	13.6	14.8	13.6
Not Hispanic or Latino [2]	6.1	5.8	5.9	5.7	12.6	11.3	11.8	11.1
White	5.7	5.5	5.4	5.2	12.1	10.7	11.2	10.2
Black or African American	10.1	8.7	10.1	11.1	19.1	17.1	17.7	19.7
Hispanic or Latino [2, 3]	8.6	10.4	10.7	7.7	13.4	14.8	16.9	12.8
Mexican	9.4	10.7	12.0	7.6	16.3	15.3	19.6	12.2

[1] Includes other races not shown separately.   [2] Estimates are age adjusted to the year 2000 standard using two age groups: 65–74 years and 75 years and over.   [3] Persons of Hispanic origin may be of any race.

Source: U.S. National Center for Health Statistics, *Health, United States, annual*; <http://www.cdc.gov/nchs/hus.htm>.

Table 187. Nursing Homes—Selected Characteristics: 2004

[Beds: 1,730 represents 1,730,000. Covers licensed and/or certified nursing homes in the conterminous United States that had three or more beds. Based on the 2004 National Nursing Home Survey, a two-stage survey sample of nursing homes and their residents. Subject to sampling variability.]

Characteristic	Nursing homes	Beds		Current residents		Full-time equivalent employees [2]	
		Number (1,000)	Per nursing home	Number (1,000)	Occupancy rate [1]	Number (1,000)	Rate per 100 beds
Total	**16,100**	**1,730**	**107.6**	**1,492**	**86.3**	**1,053**	**60.9**
Ownership:							
Proprietary	9,900	1,074	108.6	918	85.5	615	57.2
Voluntary nonprofit	5,000	504	101.6	440	87.4	326	64.6
Government and other	1,200	152	123.6	134	87.9	113	74.1
Certification: [3]							
Medicare and medicaid certified . . .	14,100	1,600	113.5	1,380	86.2	972	60.8
Medicare only	[4]700	[4]33	[4]50.6	28	85.0	20	59.7
Medicaid only	1,100	76	69.0	68	89.1	41	53.7
Bed size:							
Fewer than 50 beds	2,200	76	33.8	62	82.1	43	56.6
50–99 beds	6,000	455	75.7	423	92.9	254	55.8
100–199 beds	6,800	903	132.0	789	87.3	563	62.4
200 beds or more	1,000	296	298.2	219	73.9	193	65.3
Region:							
Northeast	2,800	382	136.0	331	86.8	263	68.9
Midwest	5,300	527	99.4	448	85.1	286	54.2
South	5,400	586	108.2	502	85.6	353	60.3
West	2,600	236	92.1	211	89.5	151	64.1
Affiliation:							
Chain	8,700	939	107.9	812	86.5	540	57.4
Independent	7,400	791	107.2	680	86.0	514	65.0

[1] Number of residents divided by number of available beds multiplied by 100.   [2] Includes only those employees providing direct health-related services to residents. Includes nurses, nurses' aides, orderlies, dental hygienists, physical therapists, speech pathologists and/or audiologists, dieticians or nutritionists, podiatrists, and social workers.   [3] Estimates for nursing homes that are "not certified" are not shown because the sample size was less than 30 and figures are unreliable.   [4] Figure does not meet standards of reliability or precision.

Source: U.S. National Center for Health Statistics, National Nursing Home Survey; see also <http://www.cdc.gov/nchs/about/major/nnhsd/Facilitytables.htm>.

Table 188. Persons 18 Years and Over With Selected Diseases and Conditions by Selected Characteristics: 2006

[In thousands (217,774 represents 217,774,000). Based on National Health Interview Survey, a sample survey of the civilian noninstitutionalized population; see Appendix III]

Selected characteristic	Total persons	Persons with selected diseases and conditions					
		Diabetes [1, 2]	Ulcers [1]	Kidney disease [3, 4]	Liver disease [3]	Arthritis diagnosis [5]	Chronic joint symptoms [5]
Total [6]	217,774	17,110	14,474	3,347	3,294	46,502	56,364
SEX							
Male	106,252	8,204	6,969	1,621	1,782	18,737	25,188
Female	114,014	8,906	7,505	1,726	1,512	27,765	31,176
AGE							
18 to 44 years old	110,391	2,924	4,524	797	826	7,646	15,958
45 to 64 years old	74,203	7,752	6,125	1,339	1,948	21,269	24,981
65 to 74 years old	19,081	3,469	1,821	464	288	9,121	8,131
75 years old and over	16,593	2,965	2,004	747	231	8,465	7,294
RACE							
Race alone [7]	217,760	16,900	14,255	3,292	3,217	46,044	55,673
White	179,456	13,124	12,313	2,691	2,732	39,790	48,058
Black or African American	26,223	2,848	1,431	476	281	4,968	5,810
American Indian or Alaska Native	1,784	[8]219	[8]158	(B)	(B)	382	581
Asian	10,066	695	312	105	182	897	1,196
Native Hawaiian or other Pacific Islander	231	(B)	(B)	–	(B)	(B)	(B)
Two or more races [9]	2,506	210	220	[8]54	[8]77	458	691
HISPANIC ORIGIN AND RACE [10]							
Hispanic or Latino	28,664	2,147	1,192	370	436	3,058	4,564
Mexican or Mexican American	18,116	1,412	666	221	262	1,693	2,855

– Represents zero.   B Figure too small to meet statistical standards for reliability of a derived figure.   [1] Respondents were asked if they had ever been told by a health professional that they had an ulcer or diabetes. A person may be represented in more than one column.   [2] Excludes borderline diabetes.   [3] Respondents were asked if they had been told in the last 12 months by a health professional that they had weak or failing kidneys or any kind of liver condition.   [4] Excludes kidney stones, bladder infections, or incontinence.   [5] Respondents were asked if they had ever been told by a health professional that they had some form of arthritis, rheumatoid arthritis, gout, lupus or fibromyalgia. Respondents with joint symptoms (excluding back and neck) that began more than 3 months prior to interview; were classified as having chronic joint symptoms.   [6] Total includes other races not shown separately.   [7] Refers to persons who indicated only a single race group.   [8] Figures do not meet standard of reliability or precision.   [9] Refers to all persons who indicated more than one race group.   [10] Persons of Hispanic or Latino origin may be of any race or combination of races.

Source: U.S. National Center for Health Statistics, *Vital and Health Statistics, Series 10, Number 235, Summary Health Statistics for U.S. Adults: National Health Interview Survey, 2006;* <http://www.cdc.gov/nchs/data/series/sr_10/sr10_235.pdf>.

Table 189. Persons 18 Years of Age and Over With Selected Circulatory Diseases by Selected Characteristics: 2006

[In thousands (220,267 represents 220,267,000). In separate questions, respondents were asked if they had ever been told by a doctor or other health professional that they had: hypertension (or high blood pressure); coronary heart disease, angina (or angina pectoris); heart attack (or myocardial infarction); any other heart condition or disease not already mentioned; or a stroke. A person may be represented in more than one column. Based on National Health Interview Survey, a sample survey of the civilian noninstitutionalized population; see Appendix III]

Characteristic	Total persons	Selected circulatory diseases			
		Heart disease		Hypertension [3]	Stroke
		All types [1]	Coronary [2]		
Total [4]	220,267	24,107	14,063	51,562	5,642
SEX					
Male	106,252	12,135	7,877	24,380	2,822
Female	114,014	11,972	6,185	27,182	2,819
AGE					
18 to 44 years old	110,391	4,013	985	8,552	532
45 to 64 years old	74,203	9,094	5,346	24,073	1,809
65 to 74 years old	19,081	4,985	3,504	10,062	1,445
75 years old and over	16,593	6,015	4,228	8,875	1,855
RACE					
Race alone [5]	217,760	23,871	13,930	51,034	5,563
White	179,456	20,784	12,163	41,565	4,394
Black or African American	26,223	2,300	1,364	7,471	995
American Indian or Alaska Native	1,784	227	[6]99	385	[6]36
Asian	10,066	534	288	1,580	139
Native Hawaiian or Other Pacific Islander	231	B	B	[6]34	–
Two or more races [7]	2,506	236	132	528	[6]79
HISPANIC ORIGIN AND RACE [8]					
Hispanic or Latino	28,664	1,538	910	4,227	351
Mexican or Mexican American	18,116	813	459	2,354	193
Not Hispanic or Latino	191,603	22,569	13,153	47,335	5,291
White, single race	153,235	19,420	11,350	37,670	4,078
Black or African American, single race	25,145	2,243	1,317	7,361	984

– Represents zero.   B Figure too small to meet statistical standards for reliability of a derived figure.   [1] Heart disease includes coronary heart disease, angina pectoris, heart attack, or any other heart condition or disease.   [2] Coronary heart disease includes coronary heart disease, angina pectoris, or heart attack.   [3] Persons had to have been told on two or more different visits that they had hypertension, or high blood pressure, to be classified as hypertensive.   [4] Includes other races not shown separately.   [5] Refers to persons who indicated only a single race group.   [6] Figures do not meet standard of reliability or precision.   [7] Refers to all persons who indicated more than one race group.   [8] Persons of Hispanic or Latino origin may be any race or combination of races.

Source U.S. National Center for Health Statistics, *Vital and Health Statistics, Series 10, Number 235, Summary Health Statistics for U.S. Adults: National Health Interview Survey, 2006;* <http://www.cdc.gov/nchs/data/series/sr_10/sr10_235.pdf>.

Table 190. Selected Respiratory Diseases Among Persons 18 Years of Age and Over by Selected Characteristics: 2006

[In thousands (220,267 represents 220,267,000). Respondents were asked in two separate questions if they had ever been told by a doctor or other health professional that they had emphysema or asthma. Respondents who had been told they had asthma were asked if they still had asthma. Respondents were asked in three separate questions if they had been told by a doctor or other health professional in the past 12 months that they had hay fever, sinusitis, or bronchitis. Based on the National Health Interview Survey, a sample survey of the civilian noninstitutionalized population; see Appendix III]

Selected characteristic	Total persons	Selected respiratory condition [1]					
		Emphysema	Asthma		Hay fever	Sinusitis	Chronic bronchitis
			Ever	Still			
Total [2]	220,267	4,069	24,256	16,057	17,579	30,693	9,463
SEX							
Male	106,252	2,481	10,078	5,904	7,265	10,734	2,912
Female	114,014	1,587	14,178	10,152	10,314	19,959	6,551
AGE							
18 to 44 years old	110,391	290	12,668	7,990	7,756	13,254	3,182
45 to 64 years old	74,203	1,765	7,806	5,576	7,154	12,499	4,108
65 to 74 years old	19,081	945	2,238	1,481	1,670	2,987	1,063
75 years old and over	16,593	1,069	1,544	1,010	998	1,953	1,110
RACE							
Race alone: [3]	217,760	4,045	23,804	15,717	17,347	30,288	9,268
White	179,456	3,726	19,476	12,940	14,413	25,537	7,805
Black or African American	26,223	188	3,124	1,996	1,914	3,791	1,110
American Indian or Alaska Native	1,784	(B)	330	211	198	276	[4]114
Asian	10,066	[4]73	833	535	775	654	228
Native Hawaiian or other Pacific Islander	231	(B)	(B)	(B)	(B)	(B)	(B)
Two or more races [5]	2,506	(B)	451	339	232	405	195
HISPANIC ORIGIN AND RACE [6]							
Hispanic or Latino	28,664	112	2,345	1,447	1,542	2,317	644
Mexican or Mexican American	18,116	[4]67	1,119	745	859	1,279	340
Not Hispanic or Latino	191,603	3,957	21,911	14,609	16,037	28,376	8,819
White, single race	153,235	3,619	17,397	11,679	13,052	23,474	7,262
Black or African American, single race	25,145	186	2,981	1,884	1,846	3,650	1,085

B Figure too small to meet statistical standards for reliability of a derived figure. [1] A person may be represented in more than one column. [2] Total includes other races not shown separately. [3] Refers to persons who indicated only a single race group. [4] Figure does not meet standard of reliability or precision. [5] Refers to all persons who indicated more than one race group. [6] Persons of Hispanic or Latino origin may be any race or combination of races.
Source: U.S. National Center for Health Statistics, *Vital and Health Statistics, Series 10, Number 235, Summary Health Statistics for U.S. Adult: National Health Interview Survey, 2006*; <http://www.cdc.gov/nchs/data/series/sr_10/sr10_235.pdf>.

Table 191. Persons 18 Years of Age and Over With Migraines and Pains in the Neck, Lower Back, Face or Jaw, by Selected Characteristics: 2006

[In thousands (220,267 represents 220,267,000). Based on National Health Interview Survey, a sample survey of the civilian noninstitutionalized populaion, Appendix III]

Selected characteristic	Total persons	Migraines and pains [1]			
		Migraines or severe headaches [2]	Pain in neck [3]	Pains in lower back [3]	Pains in face or jaw [3]
Total [4]	220,267	33,099	32,002	60,607	9,893
SEX					
Male	106,252	10,340	12,972	27,300	3,058
Female	114,014	22,759	19,030	33,307	6,835
AGE					
18 to 44 years old	110,391	19,598	12,934	26,309	4,913
45 to 64 years old	74,203	10,913	13,756	23,036	3,662
65 to 74 years old	19,081	1,611	3,010	5,942	768
75 years and over	16,593	977	2,302	5,319	550
RACE					
Race alone [5]	217,760	32,559	31,489	59,623	9,679
White	179,456	26,977	27,487	50,988	8,471
Black or African American	26,223	4,236	2,769	6,264	872
American Indian or Alaska Native	1,784	355	275	588	[6]104
Asian	10,066	966	936	1,719	233
Native Hawaiian or other Pacific Islander	231	(B)	(B)	[6]64	–
Two or more races [7]	2,506	540	512	984	213
HISPANIC ORIGIN AND RACE [8]					
Hispanic or Latino	28,664	4,253	3,459	6,684	975
Mexican or Mexican American	18,116	2,548	1,871	3,878	508
Not Hispanic or Latino	191,603	28,846	28,543	53,923	8,917
White, single race	153,235	23,126	24,406	45,019	7,586
Black or African American, single race	25,145	4,056	2,621	5,989	841

– Represents zero. B Figure too small to meet statistical standards for reliability of a derived figure. [1] A person may be represented in more than one column. [2] Respondents were asked, "During the past 3 months, did you have a severe headache or migraine?" Respondents were instructed to report pain that had lasted a whole day or more and, conversely, not to report fleeting or minor aches or pains. [3] Respondents were asked, "During the past 3 months, did you have a neck pain; or low back pain; or facial ache or pain in the jaw muscles or the joint in front of the ear?" Respondents were instructed to report pain that had lasted a whole day or more and, conversely, not to report fleeting or minor aches or pains. [4] Total includes other races not shown separately. [5] Refers to persons who indicated only a single race group. [6] Figure does not meet standard of reliability or precision. [7] Refers to all persons who indicated more than one race group. [8] Persons of Hispanic or Latino origin may be any race or combination of races.
Source: *Vital and Health Statistics, Series 10, Number 235, Summary Health Statistics for U.S. Adults: National Health Interview Survey, 2006*; <http://www.cdc.gov/nchs/data/series/sr_10/sr10_235.pdf>.

Table 192. **Injury and Poisoning Episodes and Conditions by Age and Sex: 2006**

[**(33,256 represents 33,256,000).** Covers all medically attended injuries and poisonings occurring during the 5-week period prior to the survey interview. Age adjustment is used to adjust for differences in the age distribution of populations being compared. There may be more than one condition per episode. Based on the National Health Interview Survey, a sample survey of the civilian noninstitutionalized population; see Appendix III]

External cause and nature of injury	Both sexes							Male, total	Female, total
	Total	Total, age-adjusted[1]	Under 12 years old	12 to 21 years old	22 to 44 years old	45 to 64 years old	65 years old and over		
EPISODES									
Number (1,000)	33,256	(X)	4,642	5,641	9,956	7,642	5,376	17,107	16,149
Annual rate per 1,000 population, total[2]	113.2	113.5	96.3	135.6	105.8	102.9	151.1	118.9	107.7
Fall	44.5	44.8	46.1	46.0	25.3	35.0	111.0	38.8	49.9
Struck by or against a person or an object	13.4	13.5	20.2	21.5	11.5	11.2	[4]4.1	14.5	12.3
Transportation[3]	11.6	11.5	[4]7.0	17.1	11.5	13.4	[4]7.4	13.7	9.5
Overexertion	15.6	15.4	[4]3.7	14.8	20.6	18.5	[4]13.1	16.3	14.8
Cutting, piercing instruments	8.9	9.0	[4]5.8	[4]9.1	14.0	[4]7.2	[4]3.5	11.0	7.0
Poisoning[5]	[4]2.2	[4]2.2	[4]4.1	[4]3.8[4]	1.0	[4]1.5	[4]2.1	[4]1.9	[4]2.5
CONDITIONS									
Annual rate per 1,000 population, total[2]	154.9	154.7	110.3	176.7	145.9	156.4	210.9	158.6	151.5
Sprains/strains	45.7	45.2	19.5	36.7	51.4	59.3	48.5	41.4	49.9
Open wounds	20.8	21.1	30.4	26.3	22.0	12.1	[4]16.1	29.2	12.7
Fractures	25.3	25.4	15.6	38.5	16.5	21.4	54.4	28.9	21.8
Contusions	27.2	27.1	[4]16.9	24.6	22.1	29.0	53.8	23.7	30.5

X Not applicable.   [1] Data were age-adjusted using the 2000 standard population.   [2] Includes other items not shown separately.   [3] Includes the categories "Motor vehicle traffic"; "Pedal cycle, other"; "Pedestrian, other"; and "Transport, other."   [4] Figure does not meet standard of reliability or precision.   [5] Poisoning episodes are assumed to have a single condition resulting from the episode.

Source: U.S. National Center for Health Statistics, *Vital and Health Statistics*, unpublished data.

Table 193. **Injuries Associated With Selected Consumer Products: 2006**

[Estimates calculated from a representative sample of hospitals with emergency treatment departments in the United States. Data are estimates of the number of emergency-room treated cases nationwide associated with various products. Product involvement does not necessarily mean the product caused the accident. Products were selected from the U.S. Consumer Product Safety Commission's National Electronic Injury Surveillance System (NEISS)]

Product	Number	Product	Number
Home workshop equipment:		Stairs or steps	1,143,751
Saws (hand or power)	95,317	Other doors[2]	317,825
Hammers	34,829	Ceilings and walls	308,501
Household packaging and containers:		Home entertainment equipment:	
Household containers and packaging	215,537	Televisions	53,824
Bottles and jars	74,148	Personal use items:	
Housewares:		Footwear	136,156
Knives	434,331	Wheelchairs	115,743
Tableware and flatware	97,531	Crutches, canes, walkers	85,346
Drinking glasses	75,803	Yard and garden equipment:	
Home furnishing		Lawn mowers	78,740
Beds	526,331	Sports and recreation equipment:	
Chairs	317,888	Bicycles	490,434
Tables[1]	317,795	Skateboards	125,713
Household cabinets, racks, and shelves	279,322	Trampolines	109,522
Home structures, construction:		Playground climbing equipment	79,332
Floors or flooring materials	1,191,161	Swings or swing sets	55,349

[1] Excludes baby-changing and television tables or stands.   [2] Excludes glass doors and garage doors.

Source: National Safety Council, Itasca, IL, *Injury Facts, Annual* (copyright); <http://www.nsc.org/lrs/statstop.htm>.

Table 194. **Costs of Unintentional Injuries: 2006**

[**(652.1 represents $652,100,000,000).** Covers costs of deaths or disabling injuries together with vehicle accidents and fires]

Cost	Amount (bil. dol.)					Percent distribution				
	Total[1]	Motor vehicle	Work	Home	Other	Total[1]	Motor vehicle	Work	Home	Other
Total	**652.1**	**258.6**	**164.7**	**150.1**	**101.8**	**100.0**	**100.0**	**100.0**	**100.0**	**100.0**
Wage and productivity losses[2]	329.8	89.7	78.5	97.7	68.3	50.6	34.7	47.7	65.1	67.1
Medical expense	116.3	33.4	30.1	32.8	21.8	17.8	12.9	18.3	21.9	21.4
Administrative expenses[3]	134.5	91.5	42.4	7.9	7.5	20.6	35.4	25.7	5.3	7.4
Motor vehicle damage	41.7	41.7	1.7	(NA)	(NA)	6.4	16.1	1.0	(NA)	(NA)
Employer uninsured cost[4]	18.5	2.3	9.4	4.5	2.7	2.8	0.9	5.7	3.0	2.7
Fire loss	11.3	(NA)	2.6	7.2	1.5	1.7	(NA)	1.6	4.8	1.5

NA Not available.   [1] Excludes duplication between work and motor vehicle; $23.1 billion in 2006.   [2] Actual loss of wages and household production, and the present value of future earnings lost.   [3] Home and other costs may include costs of administering medical treatment claims for some motor-vehicle injuries filed through health insurance plans.   [4] Estimate of the uninsured costs incurred by employers, representing the money value of time lost by noninjured workers.

Source: National Safety Council, Itasca, IL, *Injury Facts, Annual* (copyright). <http://www.nsc.org/lrs/statstop.htm>.

Table 195. **Use of Mammography for Women 40 Years Old and Over by Patient Characteristics: 1990 to 2005**

[Percent of women having a mammogram within the past 2 years. Covers civilian noninstitutional population. Based on National Health Interview Survey; see Appendix III]

Characteristic	1990	2000 [1]	2005 [2]	Characteristic	1990	2000 [1]	2005 [2]
Total [3]	**51.4**	**70.4**	**66.8**	Years of school completed:			
40 to 49 years old	55.1	64.3	63.5	No high school diploma or GED .	36.4	57.7	52.8
50 years old and over.	49.7	73.6	68.4	High school diploma or GED . . .	52.7	69.7	64.9
50 to 64 years old	56.0	78.7	71.8	Some college or more	62.8	76.2	72.7
65 years old and over	43.4	67.9	63.8				
White, non-Hispanic	52.7	72.2	68.4	Poverty status: [5]			
Black, non-Hispanic	46.0	67.9	65.2	Below poverty	28.7	54.8	48.5
Hispanic origin [4]	45.2	61.2	58.8	At or above poverty	54.8	72.1	68.8

[1] Adjusted data—data for 2000 have been reweighted using the 2000 census population controls.   [2] Data for 2005 are weighted using the 2000 Census Population controls.   [3] Includes other races not shown separately and unknown education level and poverty status.   [4] Persons of Hispanic origin may be of any race or combination of races.   [5] For explanation of poverty level, see text, Section 13.

Source: U.S. National Center for Health Statistics, *Health, United States*, annual. See also <http://www.cdc.gov/nchs/hus.htm>.

Table 196. **Current Cigarette Smoking: 1990 to 2006**

[**In percent**. Prior to 1992, a current smoker is a person who has smoked at least 100 cigarettes and who now smokes. Beginning 1995, definition includes persons who smoke only "some days." Excludes unknown smoking status. Based on National Health Interview Survey; for details, see Appendix III]

Sex, age, and race	1990 [1]	1995 [1]	2000	2006	Sex, age, and race	1990 [1]	1995 [1]	2000	2006
Total smokers, age-adjusted [2]	**25.3**	**24.6**	**23.1**	**20.8**	Black, total	32.5	28.5	26.1	27.0
					18 to 24 years	21.3	[4]14.6	20.8	31.2
					25 to 34 years	33.8	25.1	23.3	26.3
Male	28.0	26.5	25.2	23.6	35 to 44 years	42.0	36.3	30.8	22.2
Female	22.9	22.7	21.1	18.1	45 to 64 years	36.7	33.9	32.2	32.6
					65 years and over . .	21.5	28.5	14.2	16.0
White male.	27.6	26.2	25.5	23.5					
Black male.	32.8	29.4	25.7	26.1	Female, total	22.8	22.6	21.0	18.0
					18 to 24 years	22.5	21.8	25.1	19.3
White female	23.5	23.4	22.0	18.8	25 to 34 years	28.2	26.4	22.5	21.5
Black female	20.8	23.5	20.7	18.5	35 to 44 years	24.8	27.1	26.2	20.6
					45 to 64 years	24.8	24.0	21.6	19.3
Total smokers [3] . . .	**25.5**	**24.7**	**23.2**	**20.8**	65 years and over	11.5	11.5	9.3	8.3
Male, total	28.4	27.0	25.7	23.9	White, total	23.4	23.1	21.6	18.4
18 to 24 years.	26.6	27.8	28.5	28.5	18 to 24 years	25.4	24.9	28.7	20.7
25 to 34 years.	31.6	29.5	29.0	27.4	25 to 34 years	28.5	27.3	25.1	23.7
35 to 44 years.	34.5	31.5	30.2	24.8	35 to 44 years	25.0	27.0	26.6	21.7
45 to 64 years.	29.3	27.1	26.4	24.5	45 to 64 years	25.4	24.3	21.4	18.8
65 years and over	14.6	14.9	10.2	12.6	65 years and over . .	11.5	11.7	9.1	8.4
White, total	28.0	26.6	25.8	23.6	Black, total	21.2	23.5	20.8	18.8
18 to 24 years	27.4	28.4	30.9	28.9	18 to 24 years	[4]10.0	[4]8.8	14.2	14.8
25 to 34 years	31.6	29.9	29.9	27.9	25 to 34 years	29.1	26.7	15.5	15.4
35 to 44 years	33.5	31.2	30.6	25.3	35 to 44 years	25.5	31.9	30.2	21.0
45 to 64 years	28.7	26.3	25.8	23.4	45 to 64 years	22.6	27.5	25.6	25.5
65 years and over . .	13.7	14.1	9.8	12.6	65 years and over . .	11.1	13.3	10.2	9.3

[1] Data prior to 1997 are not strictly comparable with data for later years due to the 1997 questionnaire redesign.   [2] Data are age adjusted to the year 2000 standard using five age groups: 18–24 years, 25–34 years, 35–44 years, 45–64 years, 65 years and over.   [3] Crude estimates, not age adjusted.   [4] Data have a relative standard error of 20 to 30 percent.

Source: U.S. National Center for Health Statistics, *Health, United States*, annual. See also <http://www.cdc.gov/nchs/hus.htm>.

Table 197. **Current Cigarette Smoking by Sex and State: 2006**

[**In percent**. Current cigarette smoking is defined as persons 18 years and older who reported having smoked 100 or more cigarettes during their lifetime and who currently smoke every day or some days. Based on the Behavioral Risk Factor Surveillance System, a telephone survey of health behaviors of the civilian, noninstitutionalized U.S. population, 18 years old and over; for details, see source]

State	Total	Male	Female	State	Total	Male	Female	State	Total	Male	Female
U.S. [1] . .	**20.2**	**22.2**	**18.5**	KS	20.0	22.2	18.0	ND	19.6	21.0	18.1
				KY	28.6	29.1	28.1	OH	22.5	24.9	20.2
AL	23.3	26.3	20.6	LA	23.4	28.6	20.5	OK	25.1	27.9	22.5
AK	24.2	25.3	22.9	ME	20.9	21.8	20.0	OR	18.5	19.7	17.2
AZ	18.1	21.7	14.7	MD	17.8	19.1	16.7	PA	21.5	22.3	20.8
AR	23.7	25.9	21.7	MA	17.8	19.4	16.4	RI	19.3	19.7	18.9
CA	14.9	18.5	11.4	MI	22.4	24.8	20.1	SC	22.3	25.7	19.2
CO	17.9	19.3	16.4	MN	18.3	18.5	18.2	SD	20.4	21.6	19.2
CT	17.0	18.9	15.3	MS	25.1	27.9	22.5	TN	22.6	23.8	21.5
DE	21.7	23.3	20.2	MO	23.3	24.7	22.1	TX	18.1	20.6	15.6
DC	17.9	21.4	14.9	MT	19.0	18.5	19.6	UT	9.8	10.4	9.2
FL	21.0	23.6	18.7	NE	18.6	19.6	17.7	VT	18.0	19.4	16.7
GA	20.0	22.4	17.7	NV	22.2	22.9	21.4	VA	19.3	20.1	18.5
HI	17.5	19.2	16.0	NH	18.7	19.3	18.2	WA	17.1	18.9	15.3
ID	16.8	18.7	15.0	NJ	18.1	20.8	15.6	WV	25.7	25.4	26.0
IL	20.5	24.2	17.0	NM	20.2	22.6	17.8	WI	20.8	23.4	18.3
IN	24.1	26.3	21.9	NY	18.3	19.0	17.6	WY	21.6	23.8	19.4
IA	21.5	23.2	19.9	NC	22.1	25.3	19.0				

[1] Represents median value among the states and DC. For definition of median, see Guide to Tabular Presentations.

Source: U.S. Centers for Disease Control and Prevention, Atlanta, GA, *Morbidity and Mortality Weekly Report,* Vol. 56, No. 38, (released 28 September 2007; <http://www.cdc.gov/mmwr>.

Table 198. Substance Abuse Treatment Facilities and Clients: 1995 to 2007

[As of October 2 (1995); as of October 1 (1998–2000), as of March 29 (2002), as of March 31 (2003–2006), and March 30, 2007. Based on the Uniform Facility Data Set (UFDS) National Survey of Substance Abuse Treatment Services (N-SSATS) survey, a census of all known facilities that provide substance abuse treatment in the United States and associated jurisdictions. Selected missing data for responding facilities were imputed]

Primary focus	Number	Primary focus	Number	Type of care and type of problem	Number of clients
FACILITIES		CLIENTS		2007, total [1,2]	1,135,425
1995	10,746	1995	1,009,127	Outpatient rehabilitation . . .	1,004,208
1998	13,455	1998	1,038,378	Outpatient detoxification. . .	12,705
2000	13,428	2000	1,000,896	24-hour rehabilitation.	104,657
2002	13,720	2002	1,136,287	24-hour detoxification	13,855
2003	13,623	2003	1,092,546		
2004	13,454	2004	1,072,251		
2005	13,371	2005	1,081,049	2007, total [1,2]	1,133,436
2006	13,771	2006	1,130,881	Drug only	412,418
				Alcohol only.	211,094
2007, total [2]	13,648	2007, total [2]	1,135,425	Both alcohol & drug.	509,924
Substance abuse treatment services	8,360	Substance abuse treatment services	768,047		
Mental health services . . .	949	Mental health services . . .	47,803		
General health care . . .	189	General health care . . .	12,747	Total with a drug problem [3]	922,342
Both substance abuse and mental health	3,957	Both substance abuse and mental health	297,907	Total with an alcohol problem [4]	721,018
Other.	193	Other.	8,921		

[1] Excludes clients at facilities that did not provide data on type of substance abuse problem treated.   [2] Data for 2007 are based on preliminary data and are subject to change.   [3] The sum of clients with a drug problem and clients with both diagnoses.   [4] The sum of clients with an alcohol problem and clients with both diagnoses.

Source: U.S. Substance Abuse and Mental Health Services Administration, Uniform Facility Data Set (UFDS): Annual surveys for 1995–1999, and Office of Applied Studies, Substance Abuse and Mental Health Services Administration, National Survey of Substance Abuse Treatment Services (N-SSATS), 2000–2007; <http://oas.samhsa.gov/oasftp.cfm#Data>.

Table 199. Drug Use by Type of Drug and Age Group: 2002 and 2006

[In percent. Data comes from the National Survey on Drug Use and Health (NSDUH). Current users are those who used drugs at least once within month prior to this study. Based on a representative sample of the U.S. population age 12 years and older, including persons living in households and in some group quarters such as dormitories and homeless shelters. Estimates are based on computer-assisted interviews of about 68,000 respondents. Subject to sampling variability; see source]

Age and type of drug	Ever used 2002	Ever used 2006	Current user 2002	Current user 2006	Age and type of drug	Ever used 2002	Ever used 2006	Current user 2002	Current user 2006
12 YEARS OLD AND OVER					**18 TO 25 YEARS OLD**				
Any illicit drug [1]	46.0	45.4	8.3	8.3	Any illicit drug [1]	59.8	59.0	20.2	19.8
Marijuana and hashish	40.4	39.8	6.2	6.0	Marijuana and hashish	53.8	52.4	17.3	16.3
Cocaine	14.4	14.3	0.9	1.0	Cocaine	15.4	15.7	2.0	2.2
Crack	3.6	3.5	0.2	0.3	Hallucinogens	24.2	20.2	1.9	1.7
Heroin	1.6	1.5	0.1	0.1	Inhalants	15.7	12.5	0.5	0.4
Hallucinogens	14.6	14.3	0.5	0.4	Any psychotherapeutic [2] . . .	27.7	30.3	5.4	6.4
LSD	10.4	9.5	–	0.1	Alcohol	86.7	86.5	60.5	61.9
PCP	3.2	2.7	–	–	"Binge" alcohol use [3]	(NA)	(NA)	40.9	42.2
Inhalants	9.7	9.3	0.3	0.3	Cigarettes	71.2	66.6	40.8	38.4
Any psychotherapeutic [2] . . .	19.8	20.3	2.6	2.8	Smokeless tobacco	23.7	20.2	4.8	5.2
Pain relievers.	12.6	13.6	1.9	2.1	Cigars	45.6	43.1	11.0	12.1
Tranquilizers	8.2	8.7	0.8	0.7	**26 TO 34 YEARS OLD**				
Stimulants	9.0	8.2	0.5	0.5	Any illicit drug [1]	58.3	57.7	10.5	11.9
Sedatives	4.2	3.6	0.2	0.2	Marijuana and hashish	52.2	50.7	7.7	8.5
Alcohol	83.1	82.7	51.0	50.9	Cocaine	17.6	18.2	1.2	1.7
"Binge" alcohol use [3]	(NA)	(NA)	22.9	23.0	Hallucinogens	20.6	22.1	0.5	0.5
Cigarettes	69.1	66.3	26.0	25.0	Inhalants	14.1	14.5	0.1	0.4
Smokeless tobacco	19.9	18.6	3.3	3.3	Any psychotherapeutic [2] . . .	24.4	28.3	3.6	4.3
Cigars	37.4	36.1	5.4	5.6	**35 YEARS OLD AND OVER**				
Pipe tobacco	17.0	15.6	0.8	0.9	Any illicit drug [1]	42.7	42.7	4.6	4.7
					Marijuana and hashish	38.0	38.3	3.1	3.2
12 TO 17 YEARS OLD					Cocaine	15.4	15.2	0.6	0.6
Any illicit drug [1]	30.9	27.6	11.6	9.8	Hallucinogens	12.6	13.0	0.1	–
Marijuana and hashish	20.6	17.3	8.2	6.7	Inhalants	7.2	7.3	0.1	0.1
Cocaine	2.7	2.2	0.6	0.4	Any psychotherapeutic [2] . . .	18.0	17.6	1.6	1.7
Hallucinogens	5.7	3.9	1.0	0.7	**26 YEARS OLD AND OVER**				
Inhalants	10.5	10.1	1.2	1.3	Alcohol	88.0	87.7	53.9	53.7
Any psychotherapeutic [2] . . .	13.7	12.4	4.0	3.3	"Binge" alcohol use [3]	(NA)	(NA)	21.4	21.4
Alcohol	43.4	40.4	17.6	16.6	Cigarettes	73.7	71.7	25.2	24.7
"Binge" alcohol use [3]	(NA)	(NA)	10.7	10.3	Smokeless tobacco	20.9	19.9	3.2	3.2
Cigarettes	33.3	25.8	13.0	10.0	Cigars	39.0	37.9	4.6	4.6
Smokeless tobacco	8.0	7.1	2.0	4.2					
Cigars	16.3	13.7	4.5	5.5					

– Represents or rounds to zero.   NA Not available.   [1] Illicit drugs include marijuana/hashish, cocaine (including crack), heroin, hallucinogens, inhalants, or prescription-type psychotherapeutics used nonmedically.   [2] Nonmedical use of prescription-type psychotherapeutics includes the nonmedical use of pain relievers, tranquilizers, stimulants, or sedatives and does not include over-the-counter drugs.   [3] Binge alcohol use is defined as drinking five or more drinks on the same occasion (i.e., at the same time or within a couple of hours of each other) on at least 1 day in the past 30 days. Heavy alcohol use is defined as drinking five or more drinks on the same occasion on each of 5 or more days in the past 30 days; all heavy alcohol users are also binge alcohol users.

Source: U.S. Substance Abuse and Mental Health Services Administration, National Survey on Drug Use and Health, 2002 and 2006; <http://oas.samhsa.gov/nhsda.htm>.

Health and Nutrition   129

Table 200. Estimated Use of Selected Drugs by State: 2005–2006

[**20,040 represents 20,040,000**. Data in this table cover a 2-year period. Data is based on the National Survey on Drug Use and Health (NSDUH). Current users are those persons 12 years old and over who used drugs at least once within month prior to this study. Based on national sample of respondents (see also headnote, Table 199). The state estimates were produced by combining the prevalence rate based on the state sample data and the prevalence rate based on a national regression model applied to local-area county and census block group/tract-level estimates from the state (i.e., a survey-weighted hierarchical Bayes estimation approach). The parameters of the regression model are estimated from the entire national sample. For comparison purposes, the data shown here display estimates for all 50 states and the District of Columbia utilizing the modeled estimates for all 51 areas]

State	Estimated current users (1,000)					Current users as percent of population				
	Any illicit drug [1]	Mari- juana	Any illicit drug other than mari- juana [1]	Ciga- rettes	Binge alcohol [2]	Any illicit drug [1]	Mari- juana	Any illicit drug other than mari- juana [1]	Ciga- rettes	Binge alcohol [2]
U.S.	**20,040**	**14,720**	**9,289**	**61,044**	**55,835**	**8.2**	**6.0**	**3.8**	**25.0**	**22.8**
AL.	279	181	152	1,045	710	7.4	4.8	4.0	27.6	18.7
AK.	58	46	22	127	113	11.1	8.8	4.2	24.3	21.6
AZ.	395	254	218	1,159	1,118	8.1	5.2	4.5	23.7	22.9
AR.	192	131	103	668	475	8.4	5.7	4.5	29.1	20.7
CA.	2,675	1,970	1,149	5,846	6,124	9.1	6.7	3.9	19.9	20.8
CO	384	295	162	851	949	10.0	7.7	4.2	22.2	24.7
CT.	268	222	113	623	734	9.2	7.6	3.9	21.3	25.1
DE.	57	42	25	172	150	8.1	5.9	3.6	24.5	21.3
DC	53	40	21	122	135	11.1	8.4	4.5	25.6	28.3
FL.	1,218	850	615	3,557	3,349	8.1	5.7	4.1	23.7	22.3
GA	578	436	245	1,723	1,457	7.8	5.9	3.3	23.2	19.7
HI	83	57	34	203	221	8.0	5.5	3.3	19.6	21.4
ID	84	62	41	274	256	7.2	5.3	3.5	23.5	21.9
IL	772	562	349	2,713	2,671	7.4	5.4	3.3	25.9	25.5
IN	417	286	216	1,455	1,089	8.1	5.5	4.2	28.2	21.1
IA	157	116	76	630	674	6.3	4.7	3.1	25.4	27.1
KS.	177	131	91	598	571	7.9	5.8	4.0	26.6	25.4
KY.	242	171	121	1,064	754	7.0	4.9	3.5	30.8	21.8
LA.	299	198	164	968	840	8.4	5.6	4.6	27.1	23.5
ME	113	102	35	306	254	10.0	9.0	3.1	27.0	22.4
MD	287	221	142	1,017	933	6.2	4.8	3.1	22.0	20.2
MA	537	429	249	1,277	1,349	10.0	8.0	4.6	23.7	25.0
MI	734	539	350	2,347	2,128	8.8	6.4	4.2	28.0	25.4
MN	349	307	135	1,071	1,193	8.2	7.2	3.2	25.0	27.9
MS	177	120	88	638	433	7.5	5.1	3.8	27.1	18.4
MO	385	261	181	1,427	1,148	8.0	5.4	3.8	29.7	23.9
MT	84	73	28	218	226	10.7	9.2	3.5	27.6	28.6
NE.	102	75	48	371	385	7.1	5.2	3.3	25.7	26.7
NV.	188	136	85	539	476	9.4	6.8	4.3	26.9	23.8
NH	98	85	34	254	265	8.9	7.6	3.1	22.9	23.8
NJ	537	379	247	1,522	1,610	7.4	5.3	3.4	21.1	22.3
NM	132	96	61	384	322	8.3	6.1	3.8	24.2	20.3
NY.	1,508	1,139	618	3,895	3,774	9.4	7.1	3.9	24.2	23.5
NC	549	399	285	1,876	1,390	7.7	5.6	4.0	26.3	19.5
ND	30	23	13	134	161	5.7	4.4	2.5	25.2	30.3
OH	754	584	328	2,709	2,326	7.9	6.1	3.5	28.5	24.5
OK	244	153	117	908	613	8.4	5.3	4.0	31.3	21.1
OR	295	242	116	700	665	9.6	7.9	3.8	22.8	21.6
PA	798	605	333	2,753	2,411	7.7	5.8	3.2	26.4	23.1
RI	101	83	41	223	244	11.2	9.2	4.5	24.7	27.1
SC	255	191	122	1,050	735	7.3	5.4	3.5	29.8	20.9
SD	44	33	18	168	179	6.9	5.2	2.8	26.5	28.1
TN	442	303	234	1,581	1,021	8.9	6.1	4.7	31.8	20.5
TX	1,247	800	721	4,696	4,421	6.8	4.4	3.9	25.5	24.1
UT.	133	85	75	377	339	6.8	4.3	3.9	19.3	17.4
VT.	59	52	21	134	140	11.0	9.7	4.0	25.1	26.0
VA.	448	341	210	1,535	1,344	7.3	5.5	3.4	24.9	21.8
WA	528	434	206	1,225	1,199	10.0	8.3	3.9	23.3	22.8
WV	123	92	65	501	292	8.0	6.0	4.2	32.5	18.9
WI	333	259	148	1,289	1,363	7.2	5.6	3.2	27.8	29.4
WY	37	29	16	119	108	8.7	6.8	3.6	27.8	25.2

[1] Illicit drugs include marijuana/hashish, cocaine (including crack), heroin, hallucinogens, inhalants, or prescription-type psychotherapeutics used nonmedically. Illicit drugs other than marijuana include cocaine (including crack), heroin, hallucinogens, inhalants, or prescription-type psychotherapeutics used nonmedically.   [2] Binge alcohol use is defined as drinking five or more drinks on the same occasion (i.e., at the same time or within a couple of hours of each other) on at least 1 day in the past 30 days.

Source: U.S. Substance Abuse and Mental Health Services Administration, *National Survey on Drug Use and Health, 2005 and 2006*; <http://www.oas.samhsa.gov/nhsda.htm>.

Table 201. Cumulative Percent Distribution of Population by Height and Sex: 2003–2006

[Data are based on National Health and Nutrition Examination Survey (NHANES), a sample of the civilian noninstitutional population. For this survey, the respondent participates in an interview and a physical examination. For persons 20 years old and over. Height was measured without shoes. Based on sample and subject to sampling variability; see source]

Height	Males 20–29 years	30–39 years	40–49 years	50–59 years	60–69 years	70–79 years	Females 20–29 years	30–39 years	40–49 years	50–59 years	60–69 years	70–79 years
Percent under—												
4'10"	–	–	–	–	–	–	1.1	¹0.9	(B)	2.0	1.7	¹2.6
4'11"	–	–	–	–	–	(B)	2.2	2.1	¹2.0	3.1	3.0	5.9
5'	–	(B)	–	–	(B)	(B)	5.5	5.2	6.3	8.2	6.1	13.5
5'1"	(B)	(B)	(B)	(B)	(B)	(B)	10.6	12.1	11.7	13.6	14.3	23.1
5'2"	(B)	(B)	¹0.3	(B)	(B)	(B)	18.5	19.6	19.6	20.8	23.9	37.3
5'3"	¹1.2	2.6	¹1.2	(B)	¹2.0	¹1.1	32.1	30.4	31.1	36.6	40.9	55.4
5'4"	2.8	4.8	2.8	¹2.7	4.1	5.3	47.4	45.2	46.3	53.6	54.1	68.7
5'5"	6.0	8.7	3.7	4.9	8.3	12.5	60.7	61.4	63.1	65.4	70.3	82.2
5'6"	10.8	13.6	8.5	10.8	14.0	20.2	74.2	74.1	75.6	79.1	82.7	90.0
5'7"	16.7	20.3	15.4	19.6	21.9	28.8	85.6	83.4	85.3	90.1	90.5	96.1
5'8"	25.8	30.8	24.9	30.6	36.4	42.4	94.0	91.3	91.5	95.8	96.0	99.0
5'9"	37.8	42.7	38.8	43.5	48.6	54.1	97.2	96.1	95.7	98.9	96.9	99.7
5'10"	49.7	57.7	54.3	56.2	61.7	71.1	98.8	98.6	98.4	99.5	98.2	100.0
5'11"	62.4	71.1	65.9	71.3	72.0	84.0	99.6	99.6	99.8	99.7	99.7	100.0
6'	73.5	80.7	78.0	80.7	84.9	89.0	99.8	99.9	100.0	99.9	99.7	100.0
6'1"	85.0	88.5	88.1	87.6	91.5	94.0	99.8	99.9	100.0	100.0	100.0	100.0
6'2"	91.4	92.1	94.6	93.2	95.3	97.1	100.0	100.0	100.0	100.0	100.0	100.0
6'3"	95.5	95.9	97.6	96.8	98.3	98.6	100.0	100.0	100.0	100.0	100.0	100.0
6'4"	98.7	97.7	99.3	98.8	99.3	99.5	100.0	100.0	100.0	100.0	100.0	100.0
6'5"	99.0	99.0	99.4	99.2	100.0	100.0	100.0	100.0	100.0	100.0	100.0	100.0
6'6"	99.8	99.7	99.9	99.8	100.0	100.0	100.0	100.0	100.0	100.0	100.0	100.0

– Represents zero.   B Base figure too small to meet statistical standards of reliability of a derived figure.   ¹ Figure does not meet standard of reliability or precision.

Source: U.S. National Center for Health Statistics, unpublished data; <http://www.cdc.gov/nchs/nhanes.htm>.

Table 202. Cumulative Percent Distribution of Population by Weight and Sex: 2003–2006

[See headnote, Table 201. Data are based on National Health and Nutrition Examination Survey (NHANES). Weight was measured without shoes. Pregnant females were excluded from the analyses. Based on sample and subject to sampling variability; see source]

Weight	Males 20–29 years	30–39 years	40–49 years	50–59 years	60–69 years	70–79 years	Females 20–29 years	30–39 years	40–49 years	50–59 years	60–69 years	70–79 years
Percent under—												
100 lbs.	(B)	(B)	–	–	(B)	(B)	2.6	(B)	(B)	(B)	(B)	(B)
110 lbs.	(B)	(B)	(B)	–	(B)	(B)	7.2	2.4	¹1.9	¹2.9	¹3.3	4.9
120 lbs.	¹1.5	(B)	(B)	(B)	(B)	(B)	18.9	10.8	8.9	9.1	7.1	12.4
130 lbs.	4.5	¹1.4	¹1.5	3.1	¹2.2	3.2	32.3	22.7	15.6	17.8	15.1	22.2
140 lbs.	10.1	6.0	3.1	4.6	4.6	7.9	46.6	35.7	26.5	25.9	24.5	34.3
150 lbs.	16.5	11.5	6.2	9.0	8.0	13.5	55.0	45.2	39.7	35.7	34.8	47.3
160 lbs.	28.2	20.9	12.3	15.2	13.3	22.0	63.1	55.1	49.6	47.0	46.1	59.7
170 lbs.	39.6	31.0	20.1	24.9	22.7	32.0	71.8	62.7	58.1	58.4	57.4	69.5
180 lbs.	52.4	41.3	30.3	37.0	30.9	44.4	77.9	71.9	65.4	65.7	66.6	79.8
190 lbs.	62.8	50.8	42.3	46.3	43.2	54.2	82.1	77.6	70.4	72.0	74.8	86.9
200 lbs.	70.4	60.6	52.5	55.8	52.6	65.5	86.5	81.0	77.2	77.6	80.1	88.7
210 lbs.	76.5	68.6	63.3	64.8	64.8	75.3	88.3	85.8	82.1	82.0	85.1	92.5
220 lbs.	80.8	76.7	72.3	73.2	73.5	85.5	90.5	88.5	84.5	85.5	88.8	94.8
230 lbs.	84.9	84.8	77.7	79.7	80.0	89.5	93.2	90.8	88.5	88.4	91.7	96.7
240 lbs.	88.6	89.2	83.9	85.7	86.2	91.7	94.8	93.1	90.7	91.3	93.4	97.9
250 lbs.	92.0	91.6	88.8	89.9	90.9	93.5	95.3	94.6	93.5	93.2	95.8	98.7
260 lbs.	93.9	93.9	92.5	91.2	93.7	95.6	96.3	96.0	95.1	95.1	97.2	99.2
270 lbs.	95.3	94.9	93.8	93.5	96.0	97.6	97.2	97.2	95.8	96.3	98.2	99.4
280 lbs.	96.2	95.6	95.8	95.7	97.0	98.0	98.4	97.9	97.2	97.3	98.6	99.4
290 lbs.	96.6	96.2	96.2	97.2	98.1	99.0	98.7	98.3	98.1	97.6	98.6	99.5
300 lbs.	96.8	97.2	97.1	98.5	98.2	99.4	98.8	98.6	98.5	98.4	98.9	99.6
320 lbs.	98.0	98.5	98.5	99.3	99.0	99.8	99.7	99.1	99.2	98.9	99.4	100.0
340 lbs.	98.7	99.1	99.1	99.6	99.5	100.0	99.7	99.6	99.6	99.3	99.4	100.0
360 lbs.	99.3	99.2	99.5	99.8	99.7	100.0	99.9	99.8	100.0	99.7	99.6	100.0
380 lbs.	99.5	99.6	99.6	100.0	100.0	100.0	99.9	99.9	100.0	99.7	99.6	100.0
400 lbs.	99.6	99.8	99.9	100.0	100.0	100.0	99.9	99.9	100.0	100.0	100.0	100.0
420 lbs.	99.6	99.8	99.9	100.0	100.0	100.0	99.9	100.0	100.0	100.0	100.0	100.0
440 lbs.	99.8	99.9	99.9	100.0	100.0	100.0	100.0	100.0	100.0	100.0	100.0	100.0

– Represents zero.   B Base figure too small to meet statistical standards of reliability of a derived figure.   ¹ Figure does not meet standard of reliability or precision.

Source: U.S. National Center for Health Statistics, unpublished data; <http://www.cdc.gov/nchs/nhanes.htm>.

U.S. Census Bureau, Statistical Abstract of the United States: 2009

Table 203. Age-Adjusted Percent Distributions of Body Mass Index (BMI) Among Persons 18 Years Old and Over by Selected Characteristics: 2003–2006

[See headnote, Table 201. Body Mass Index (BMI) is a measure that adjusts body weight for height. It is calculated as weight in kilograms divided by height in meters squared. For both men and women, underweight is indicated by a BMI under 18.5; healthy weight is indicated by a BMI greater than or equal to 18.5 and less than 25.0; overweight is greater than or equal to 25.0 and less than 30.0; obesity is indicated by a BMI greater than or equal to 30.0. BMI is calculated from the measurement of the participants' weight and height during the examination. Based on the National Health and Nutrition Examination Survey (NHANES)]

Selected characteristic	Under-weight	Healthy weight	Above healthy weight		
			Total	Overweight	Obese
Total [1] (age-adjusted)	**1.9**	**32.5**	**65.6**	**32.9**	**32.6**
Total [1] (crude).	**1.9**	**32.1**	**66.0**	**33.1**	**33.0**
Age: [2]					
18 to 44 years old	2.6	37.4	60.0	29.7	30.3
45 to 64 years old	1.1	25.5	73.4	35.0	38.4
65 to 74 years old	[3]0.9	25.1	73.9	39.1	34.8
75 years old and over	1.7	34.5	63.9	39.7	24.1
Sex:					
Male.	1.5	27.9	70.6	39.1	31.5
Female	2.3	37.2	60.5	26.9	33.7
Race/ethnicity and sex:					
Not Hispanic or Latino:					
White, male	1.6	27.9	70.5	38.8	31.6
White, female	2.6	40.2	57.2	26.1	31.1
Black alone or African American, male.	1.7	28.8	69.5	35.1	34.4
Black alone or African American, female	[3]1.2	20.3	78.4	26.0	52.4
Mexican or Mexican American, male	[3]0.5	26.4	73.1	45.0	28.1
Mexican or Mexican American, female	(B)	26.4	72.3	31.3	41.0
Education: [4]					
Less than a high school diploma	1.5	29.4	69.1	33.8	35.3
High school diploma or GED	1.3	26.9	71.8	34.1	37.7
Some college, bachelor's degree, or higher . . .	1.4	31.7	66.9	34.9	32.0

B Base figure too small to meet statistical standards for reliability of a derived figure. [1] Total includes other race/ethnicities not shown separately and persons with unknown race/ethnicity. [2] Estimates for age groups are not age adjusted. [3] Figure does not meet standard of reliability or precision. [4] Education is shown only for persons 25 years old and over.

Source: U.S. National Center for Health Statistics, unpublished data. <http://www.cdc.gov/nchs/nhanes.htm>.

Table 204. Percentage of Adults Engaging in Leisure-Time, Transportation-Related and Household-Related Physical Activity: 2005

[**In percent**. Covers persons 18 years old and over. Based on responses to questions about physical activity in prior month from the Behavioral Risk Factor Surveillance System. Estimates are age-adjusted to the year 2000 standard population. Based on a survey sample of approximately 350,000 persons in 50 states and the District of Columbia in 2005. The following lifestyle activities are used to help measure level of activity (see footnotes below). Leisure-time physical activity is exercise, sports, recreation, or hobbies that are not associated with activities as part of one's regular job duties, household, or transportation. Transportation-physical activity is walking, biking or wheeling (for wheelchair users), or similar activities to and from places such as: work, school, place of worship, and stores. Household physical activity includes, but is not limited to, activities such as sweeping floors, scrubbing, washing windows, and raking the lawn]

Characteristic	Persons who meet recommended activity [1]	Persons not meeting recommended activity [2]	Persons who are physically inactive [3]
Total	**48.3**	**51.7**	**25.1**
Male.	49.9	50.1	22.9
Female	47.0	53.0	27.1
White, non-Hispanic . . .	50.9	49.1	21.4
Black, non-Hispanic. . . .	40.2	59.8	32.8
Hispanic	42.1	57.9	37.4
Other	46.2	53.8	25.5
Males:			
18 to 29 years old . . .	58.5	41.5	18.8
30 to 44 years old . . .	50.1	49.9	21.0
45 to 64 years old . . .	46.6	53.4	24.6
65 to 74 years old . . .	47.7	52.3	26.0
75 years old and over	40.3	59.7	32.0
Females:			
18 to 29 years old . . .	52.1	47.9	23.2

Characteristic	Persons who meet recommended activity [1]	Persons not meeting recommended activity [2]	Persons who are physically inactive [3]
30 to 44 years old . . .	50.3	49.7	24.3
45 to 64 years old . . .	45.8	54.2	27.3
65 to 74 years old . . .	41.2	58.8	31.7
75 years old and over	31.8	68.2	41.8
School years completed:			
Less than 12 years . .	37.2	62.8	45.4
12 years	45.6	54.4	31.4
Some college (13 to 15 years)	49.2	50.8	22.5
College (16 or more years)	54.2	45.8	13.8
Household income:			
Less than $10,000. . .	36.9	63.1	44.6
$10,000 to $19,999 . .	38.7	61.3	39.8
$20,000 to $34,999 . .	45.3	54.7	30.6
$35,000 to $49,999 . .	49.1	50.9	22.9
$50,000 and over . . .	55.0	45.0	15.0

[1] Recommended activity is physical activity at least 5 times a week for 30 minutes at a time or vigorous physical activity for 20 minutes at a time at least 3 times/week. This can be accomplished through lifestyle activities (i.e., household, transportation, or leisure-time activities). [2] Doing more than 10 minutes total per week of moderate- or vigorous-intensity lifestyle activities (i.e., household, transportation, or leisure-time activities), but less than the recommended level of activity. [3] Persons with no reported physical activities in the previous month.

Source: U.S. National Center for Chronic Disease Prevention and Health Promotion, "Nutrition and Physical Activity"; and unpublished data. <http://www.cdc.gov/nccdphp/dnpa>.

Table 205. **High School Students Engaged in Physical Activity by Sex: 2005**

[In percent. For students in grades 9 to 12. Based on the Youth Risk Behavior Survey, a school-based survey and subject to sampling error; for details see source]

| Characteristic | Met currently recom- mended levels of physical activity [1] | Met previously recom- mended levels of physical activity [2] | No vigorous or moderate physical activity [3] | Enrolled in physical education class | | | Played on a sports team | Watched 3 or more hours/day of TV |
				Total	Attended daily	Exercised 20 minutes or more per class [4]		
All students	**35.8**	**68.7**	**9.6**	**54.2**	**33.0**	**84.0**	**56.0**	**37.2**
Male	43.8	75.8	7.9	60.0	37.1	87.2	61.8	38.0
Grade 9	42.8	78.4	7.2	72.8	46.5	86.3	64.7	42.4
Grade 10	46.8	77.8	7.5	65.4	39.0	88.0	63.4	42.7
Grade 11	43.8	74.2	8.4	51.1	33.5	87.5	61.0	34.1
Grade 12	41.9	71.9	8.4	45.9	26.1	87.3	57.3	30.3
Female	27.8	61.5	11.3	48.3	29.0	80.3	50.2	36.3
Grade 9	30.8	68.4	8.2	70.3	43.1	80.3	56.1	42.4
Grade 10	30.0	63.0	10.3	53.0	31.5	81.0	52.3	37.4
Grade 11	25.1	60.7	12.4	32.9	19.4	79.5	48.9	31.7
Grade 12	24.0	51.7	15.2	32.0	18.8	79.7	41.3	32.4

[1] Were physically active doing any kind of physical activity that increased their heart rate and made them breathe hard some of the time for a total of at least 60 minutes/day for at least 5 or more days out of the 7 days preceding the survey. [2] Participated in at least 20 minutes of vigorous physical activity on at least 3 or more days of the 7 days preceding the survey and/or at least 30 minutes of moderate physical activity (physical activity that did not make them sweat and breathe hard) on a least 5 or more days of the 7 days preceding the survey. [3] During the seven days preceding the survey. [4] For students enrolled in physical education classes.

Source: U.S. Centers for Disease Control and Prevention, Atlanta, GA, Youth Risk Behavior Surveillance—United States, 2005, *Morbidity and Mortality Weekly Report*, Vol. 55, No. SS-1, June 9, 2006. See also <http://www.cdc.gov/mmwr/preview/mmwrhtml /ss5505a1.htm>.

Table 206. **Households and Persons Having Problems With Access to Food: 2002 to 2006**

[**108,601 represents 108,601,000.** Food-secure means that a household had access at all times to enough food for an active healthy life for all household members, with no need for recourse to socially unacceptable food sources or extraordinary coping behaviors to meet their basic food needs. Food-insecure households had limited or uncertain ability to acquire acceptable foods in socially acceptable ways. Households with very low food security (a subset of food-insecure households) were those in which food intake of one or more household members was reduced and normal eating patterns disrupted due to inadequate resources for food. The severity of food insecurity in households is measured through a series of questions about experiences and behaviors known to characterize households that are having difficulty meeting basic food needs. These experiences and behaviors generally occur in an ordered sequence as the severity of food insecurity increases. As resources become more constrained, adults in typical households first worry about having enough food, then they stretch household resources and juggle other necessities, then decrease the quality and variety of household members' diets, then decrease the frequency and quantity of adults' food intake, and finally decrease the frequency and quantity of children's food intake. All questions refer to the previous 12 months and include a qualifying phrase reminding respondents to report only those occurrences that resulted from inadequate financial resources. Restrictions to food intake due to dieting or busy schedules are excluded. The omission of homeless persons may be a cause of underreporting. Data are from the Food Security Supplement to the Current Population Survey (CPS); for details about the CPS, see text, Section 1, Population, and Appendix III]

| Household food security level | Number (1,000) | | | | | Percent distribution | | | | |
	2002	2003	2004	2005	2006	2002	2003	2004	2005	2006
Households, total	**108,601**	**112,214**	**112,967**	**114,437**	**115,609**	**100.0**	**100.0**	**100.0**	**100.0**	**100.0**
Food-secure	96,543	99,631	99,473	101,851	102,961	88.9	88.8	88.1	89.0	89.1
Food-insecure	12,058	12,583	13,494	12,586	12,648	11.1	11.2	11.9	11.0	10.9
With low food security [1] . . .	8,259	8,663	9,045	8,158	8,031	7.6	7.7	8.0	7.1	6.9
With very low food security [2]	3,799	3,920	4,449	4,428	4,617	3.5	3.5	3.9	3.9	4.0
With very low food security among children [3]	265	207	274	270	221	0.7	0.5	0.7	0.7	0.6
Adult members.	**206,493**	**213,441**	**215,564**	**217,897**	**220,423**	**100.0**	**100.0**	**100.0**	**100.0**	**100.0**
In food-secure households	184,718	190,451	191,236	195,172	197,536	89.5	89.2	88.7	89.6	89.6
In food-insecure households	21,775	22,990	24,328	22,725	22,887	10.5	10.8	11.3	10.4	10.4
With low food security . . . . [1]	15,486	16,358	16,946	15,146	15,193	7.5	7.7	7.9	7.0	6.9
With very low food security [2]	6,289	6,632	7,382	7,579	7,694	3.0	3.1	3.4	3.5	3.5
Child members.	**72,542**	**72,969**	**73,039**	**73,604**	**73,587**	**100.0**	**100.0**	**100.0**	**100.0**	**100.0**
In food-secure households	59,415	59,704	59,171	61,201	60,959	81.9	81.8	81.0	83.1	82.8
In food-insecure households	13,127	13,265	13,868	12,403	12,628	18.1	18.2	19.0	16.9	17.2
With low food security among adults or children	12,560	12,845	13,323	11,797	12,198	17.3	17.6	18.2	16.0	16.6
With very low food security among children [3]	567	420	545	606	430	0.8	0.6	0.7	0.8	0.6

[1] Prior to 2006, USDA described these households as food insecure without hunger. [2] Food intake of one or more members in these households was reduced and normal eating patterns disrupted at some time during the year because of the household's food insecurity. Prior to 2006, USDA described these households as food insecure with hunger. [3] The food security survey measures food security status at the household level. Not all children residing in food-insecure households were directly affected by the households food insecurity. Similarly, not all children in households classified as having very low food security among children were subject to the reductions in food intake and disruptions in eating patterns that characterize this condition. Young children, in particular, are often protected from effects of the households food insecurity.

Source: U.S. Dept. of Agriculture, Economic Research Service, *Household Food Security in the United States, 2006, Economic Research Report Number 49*; November 2007; <http://www.ers.usda.gov/publications/err49/>.

Health and Nutrition   133

Table 207. Per Capita Consumption of Selected Beverages by Type: 1980 to 2006

[**In gallons.** See headnote, Table 209. Per capita consumption uses U.S. resident population, July 1, for all beverages except coffee, tea, and fruit juices which use U.S. total population (Resident plus Armed Forces overseas), July 1]

Commodity	1980	1990	1995	2000	2002	2003	2004	2005	2006
Nonalcoholic	105.5	134.6	138.0	150.9	149.3	151.0	152.8	152.8	154.0
Milk (plain and flavored)	27.6	25.7	23.9	22.5	21.9	21.6	21.3	21.0	21.0
Whole	17.0	10.5	8.6	8.1	7.7	7.6	7.3	6.9	6.7
Reduced-fat, light, and skim	10.5	15.2	15.3	14.4	14.2	14.0	14.0	14.1	14.3
Tea	7.3	6.9	7.9	7.8	7.8	7.5	7.9	7.9	8.4
Coffee	26.7	26.8	20.2	26.3	23.6	24.2	24.6	24.2	24.3
Bottled water	2.7	8.8	11.6	16.7	20.1	21.6	23.2	25.5	27.6
Carbonated soft drinks	33.6	47.1	50.6	53.2	52.8	52.5	52.4	51.6	50.6
Diet	(NA)	14.0	13.8	13.8	14.4	15.0	15.9	16.1	15.9
Regular	(NA)	33.1	36.8	39.4	38.5	37.5	36.6	35.6	34.6
Fruit juices	7.6	6.9	8.0	9.0	8.0	8.6	8.6	8.2	8.2
Fruit drinks, cocktails, and ades	(NA)	12.3	15.0	14.8	14.6	14.5	14.3	13.9	13.5
Canned iced tea	(NA)	0.1	0.7	(NA)	(NA)	(NA)	(NA)	(NA)	(NA)
Vegetable juices	(NA)	(NA)	(NA)	0.5	0.5	0.5	0.5	0.5	0.5
Alcoholic	28.3	27.5	24.7	25.0	25.1	25.1	25.2	25.1	25.3
Beer	24.3	23.9	21.8	21.7	21.8	21.6	21.7	21.5	21.6
Wine [1]	2.1	2.0	1.7	2.0	2.0	2.1	2.2	2.2	2.3
Distilled spirits	2.0	1.5	1.2	1.3	1.3	1.3	1.4	1.4	1.4

NA Not available.   [1] Beginning 1983, includes wine coolers.

Source: U.S. Department of Agriculture, Economic Research Service, *Food Consumption, Prices, and Expenditures, 1970–1997*; Food Consumption (Per Capita) Data System; <http://www.ers.usda.gov/data/foodconsumption/>.

Table 208. Nutrition—Nutrients in Foods Available for Civilian Consumption Per Capita Per Day: 1970 to 2005

[Computed by the Center for Nutrition Policy and Promotion (CNPP). Based on Economic Research Service (ERS) estimates of per capita quantities of food available for consumption from "Food Consumption, Prices, and, Expenditures," on imputed consumption data for foods no longer reported by ERS, and on CNPP estimates of quantities of produce from home gardens. Food supply estimates do not reflect loss of food or nutrients from further marketing or home processing. Enrichment and fortification levels of iron, zinc, thiamin, riboflavin, niacin, folate, vitamin A, vitamin B_6, vitamin B_{12}, and Vitamin C are included]

Nutrient	Unit	1970–79	1980–89	1990–99	2000	2005
Food energy	Kilocalories	3,200	3,400	3,600	3,900	4,000
Carbohydrate	Grams	395	420	481	498	479
Fiber	Grams	20	21	24	25	25
Protein	Grams	97	101	109	112	115
Total fat [1]	Grams	145	152	150	173	190
Saturated	Grams	49	50	48	54	59
Monounsaturated	Grams	58	61	64	76	85
Polyunsaturated	Grams	27	31	31	36	37
Cholesterol	Milligrams	440	420	400	420	430
Vitamin A	Micrograms RAE [2] . . .	1,260	1,230	1,270	1,260	1,040
Carotene	Micrograms	580	630	750	730	670
Vitamin E	Milligrams a-TE [3]	14	16	17	20	21
Vitamin C	Milligrams	112	119	127	131	116
Thiamin	Milligrams	2	3	3	3	3
Riboflavin	Milligrams	3	3	3	3	3
Niacin	Milligrams	25	29	32	33	33
Vitamin B_6	Milligrams	2	2	2	3	3
Folate [4]	Micrograms DFE [5] . . .	343	386	518	927	893
Vitamin B_{12}	Micrograms	9	8	8	8	9
Calcium	Milligrams	940	940	980	990	950
Phosphorus	Milligrams	1,530	1,580	1,690	1,720	1,730
Magnesium	Milligrams	340	360	400	410	410
Iron	Milligrams	17	20	23	24	24
Zinc	Milligrams	13	14	15	15	16
Copper	Milligrams	2	2	2	2	2
Potassium	Milligrams	3,610	3,640	3,850	3,920	3,820
Sodium [6]	Milligrams	1,270	1,260	1,290	1,280	1,270
Selenium	Micrograms	129	139	163	179	184

[1] Includes other types of fat not shown separately.   [2] Retinol activity equivalents.   [3] Alpha-Tocopherol equivalents.
[4] Reflects new terminology from Institute of Medicine's Dietary Reference Intakes reports.   [5] Dietary Folate Equivalents (DFE).
[6] Does not include amount from processed foods; underestimates actual availability.

Source: U.S. Dept. of Agriculture, Center for Nutrition Policy and Promotion, *Nutrient Content of the U.S. Food Supply, 1909–2005,* (released 28 March 2008) Data also published by Economic Research Service in *Food Consumption, Prices, and Expenditures,* annual. See also <http://www.usda.gov/cnpp/>.

Table 209. Per Capita Consumption of Major Food Commodities: 1980 to 2006

[**In pounds, retail weight, except as indicated**. Consumption represents the residual after exports, nonfood use and ending stocks are subtracted from the sum of beginning stocks, domestic production, and imports. Based on Census Bureau estimated resident population]

Commodity	Unit	1980	1990	1995	2000	2004	2005	2006
Red meat, total (boneless, trimmed weight) [1, 2]	Pounds	126.4	112.2	113.6	113.7	112.0	110.2	109.9
Beef	Pounds	72.1	63.9	63.5	64.5	62.9	62.4	62.7
Veal	Pounds	1.3	0.9	0.8	0.5	0.4	0.4	0.4
Lamb and mutton	Pounds	1.0	1.0	0.9	0.8	0.8	0.8	0.8
Pork	Pounds	52.1	46.4	48.4	47.8	47.8	46.5	46.0
Poultry (boneless, trimmed weight) [2]	Pounds	40.8	56.2	62.1	67.9	72.7	73.6	74.7
Chicken	Pounds	32.7	42.4	48.2	54.2	59.2	60.5	61.3
Turkey	Pounds	8.1	13.8	13.9	13.7	13.4	13.2	13.3
Fish and shellfish (boneless, trimmed weight)	Pounds	12.4	14.9	14.8	15.2	16.5	16.1	16.5
Eggs	Number	271	234	232	251	256	255	251
Shell	Number	236	186	172	178	180	176	177
Processed	Number	35	48	60	73	76	79	73
Dairy products, total [3]	Pounds	543.1	568.0	576.2	592.2	591.8	597.7	606.3
Fluid milk products [4]	Gallons	27.9	26.2	24.6	23.2	22.3	22.2	22.3
Beverage milks	Gallons	27.6	25.7	23.9	22.5	21.2	21.0	21.0
Plain whole milk	Gallons	16.5	10.2	8.3	7.7	6.9	6.6	6.4
Plain reduced-fat milk (2%)	Gallons	6.3	9.1	8.0	7.1	6.9	6.9	6.9
Reduced fat milk (1%) and skim milk	Gallons	3.1	4.9	6.1	6.1	5.5	5.6	5.8
Flavored whole milk	Gallons	0.6	0.3	0.3	0.4	0.3	0.3	0.3
Flavored milks other than whole	Gallons	0.6	0.8	0.8	1.0	1.4	1.4	1.4
Buttermilk	Gallons	0.5	0.4	0.3	0.3	0.2	0.2	0.2
Yogurt (excl. frozen)	1/2 pints	4.6	7.8	11.4	12.0	17.0	19.1	20.4
Fluid cream products [5]	1/2 pints	10.5	14.3	15.6	18.3	23.5	24.0	24.1
Cream [6]	1/2 pints	6.3	8.7	9.4	11.6	14.8	14.9	15.4
Sour cream and dips	1/2 pints	3.4	4.7	5.4	6.1	7.9	8.3	7.9
Condensed and evaporated milks	Pounds	7.0	7.9	6.8	5.8	5.5	5.9	6.4
Whole milk	Pounds	3.8	3.1	2.3	2.0	2.2	2.2	2.2
Skim milk	Pounds	3.3	4.8	4.5	3.8	3.2	3.7	4.2
Cheese [7]	Pounds	17.5	24.6	26.9	29.8	31.3	31.5	32.5
American [8]	Pounds	9.6	11.1	11.7	12.7	12.9	12.6	13.1
Cheddar	Pounds	6.8	9.0	9.0	9.7	10.3	10.3	10.4
Italian [8]	Pounds	4.4	9.0	10.3	12.1	12.9	13.3	13.8
Mozzarella	Pounds	3.0	6.9	8.0	9.3	9.9	10.2	10.5
Other [8]	Pounds	3.3	4.3	5.0	4.8	5.3	4.7	5.0
Swiss	Pounds	1.3	1.4	1.1	1.0	1.2	1.3	1.3
Cream and Neufchatel	Pounds	0.9	1.6	2.2	2.3	2.3	2.4	2.5
Cottage cheese, total	Pounds	4.5	3.4	2.7	2.6	2.6	2.6	2.6
Lowfat	Pounds	0.8	1.2	1.2	1.3	1.3	1.4	1.4
Frozen dairy products	Pounds	26.4	28.5	29.0	28.0	26.4	24.9	24.8
Ice cream	Pounds	17.5	15.8	15.5	16.7	15.4	14.5	14.4
Lowfat ice cream	Pounds	7.1	7.7	7.4	7.3	7.8	6.7	6.8
Sherbet	Pounds	1.2	1.2	1.3	1.2	1.2	1.2	1.1
Frozen yogurt	Pounds	(NA)	2.8	3.4	2.0	1.8	1.3	1.4
Fats and oils:								
Total, fat content only	Pounds	56.9	62.3	64.2	82.3	87.5	85.7	84.5
Butter (product weight)	Pounds	4.5	4.4	4.4	4.5	4.6	4.5	4.7
Margarine (product weight)	Pounds	11.3	10.9	9.1	7.5	5.3	4.0	4.6
Lard (direct use)	Pounds	2.3	0.9	0.4	0.8	0.7	1.6	1.7
Edible beef tallow (direct use)	Pounds	1.1	0.6	2.7	4.0	4.0	3.8	3.9
Shortening	Pounds	18.2	22.2	22.2	31.6	32.6	29.2	24.9
Salad and cooking oils	Pounds	21.2	25.2	26.5	34.8	40.8	42.7	44.5
Other edible fats and oils	Pounds	1.5	1.2	1.6	1.5	1.5	1.6	2.1
Flour and cereal products [9]	Pounds	144.9	181.0	188.7	199.2	191.5	191.9	192.8
Wheat flour	Pounds	116.9	135.9	140.0	146.3	134.3	134.2	134.5
Rice, milled	Pounds	9.5	15.8	17.1	18.9	20.4	20.5	20.7
Corn products	Pounds	12.9	21.4	24.9	28.4	30.9	31.4	31.9
Oat products	Pounds	3.9	6.5	5.5	4.4	4.7	4.6	4.6
Caloric sweeteners, total [10]	Pounds	120.2	132.4	144.1	148.8	141.0	142.2	138.9
Sugar, refined cane and beet	Pounds	83.6	64.4	64.9	65.5	61.5	63.1	62.3
Corn sweeteners [11]	Pounds	35.3	66.8	77.9	81.8	78.1	77.6	75.0
High-fructose corn syrup	Pounds	19.0	49.6	57.6	62.6	59.2	59.1	58.2
Other:								
Cocoa beans	Pounds	3.4	5.4	4.5	5.9	6.0	6.5	6.6
Coffee (green beans)	Pounds	10.3	10.3	7.9	10.3	9.6	9.5	9.5
Peanuts (shelled)	Pounds	5.1	6.1	5.7	5.9	6.7	6.6	6.5
Tree nuts (shelled)	Pounds	1.8	2.5	1.9	2.6	3.6	2.8	3.4

NA Not available. [1] Excludes edible offals. [2] Excludes shipments to Puerto Rico and the other U.S. possessions. [3] Milk-equivalent, milk-fat basis. Includes butter. [4] Fluid milk figures are aggregates of commercial sales and milk produced and consumed on farms. [5] Includes eggnog, not shown separately. [6] Heavy cream, light cream, and half-and-half. [7] Excludes full-skim American, cottage, pot, and baker's cheese. [8] Includes other cheeses not shown separately. [9] Includes rye flour and barley products not shown separately. Excludes quantities used in alcoholic beverages. [10] Dry weight. Includes edible syrups (maple, molasses, etc.) and honey not shown separately. [11] Includes glucose and dextrose not shown separately.

Source: U.S. Department of Agriculture, Economic Research Service, *Food Consumption, Prices, and Expenditures, Food Availability (Per Capita) Data System*; <http://www.ers.usda.gov/data/foodconsumption/>.

Health and Nutrition   135

Table 210. **Per Capita Utilization of Selected Commercially Produced Fruits and Vegetables: 1980 to 2006**

[**In pounds, farm weight.** Domestic food use of fresh fruits and vegetables reflects the fresh-market share of commodity production plus imports and minus exports]

Commodity	1980	1990	1995	2000	2002	2003	2004	2005	2006
Fruits and vegetables, total [1]	**603.6**	**642.5**	**682.3**	**708.9**	**680.9**	**701.2**	**700.0**	**685.3**	**675.3**
Fruits, total	265.0	256.8	274.6	285.6	268.5	279.9	279.0	270.6	269.5
Fresh fruits	106.2	116.6	123.1	128.5	126.7	128.2	128.0	126.3	129.1
Noncitrus	80.5	95.6	99.6	105.0	103.4	104.3	105.3	104.6	107.5
Apples	19.4	19.8	18.9	17.5	16.0	16.9	18.8	16.7	17.8
Bananas	20.8	24.3	27.1	28.4	26.8	26.2	25.8	25.2	25.1
Cantaloupes	5.8	9.2	9.0	11.1	11.1	10.8	10.0	9.8	9.6
Grapes	4.0	7.9	7.5	7.4	8.4	7.7	7.8	8.6	7.7
Peaches and nectarines	7.1	5.5	5.3	5.3	5.2	5.2	5.1	4.8	4.6
Pears	2.6	3.3	3.4	3.4	3.1	3.1	3.0	2.9	3.2
Pineapples	1.5	2.0	1.9	3.2	3.8	4.4	4.4	4.9	5.2
Plums and prunes	1.5	1.5	0.9	1.2	1.3	1.2	1.1	1.1	1.0
Strawberries	2.0	3.2	4.1	4.9	4.6	5.3	5.5	5.8	6.1
Watermelons	10.7	13.3	15.2	13.8	14.0	13.5	13.0	14.0	15.9
Other [2]	5.1	5.4	6.3	8.7	9.1	10.1	10.8	10.7	11.4
Fresh citrus	26.1	21.4	23.8	23.5	23.4	23.9	22.7	21.7	21.6
Oranges	14.3	12.4	11.8	11.7	11.7	11.9	10.8	11.4	10.2
Grapefruit	7.3	4.4	6.0	5.1	4.6	4.1	4.1	2.6	2.3
Other [3]	4.5	4.6	6.0	6.7	7.0	8.0	7.8	7.6	9.0
Processed fruits	158.8	140.2	151.4	157.1	141.7	151.7	150.9	144.4	140.4
Frozen fruits [4]	3.3	4.3	5.2	4.2	4.1	5.5	4.9	5.2	5.0
Dried fruits [5]	11.2	12.1	12.6	10.4	10.4	9.8	9.2	10.0	10.0
Canned fruits [6]	24.5	20.9	17.3	17.5	16.7	17.2	16.9	16.5	15.3
Fruit juices [7]	119.0	102.7	116.0	124.6	110.3	118.9	119.4	112.2	109.4
Vegetables, total	338.6	385.7	407.7	423.4	412.4	421.3	421.0	414.7	405.8
Fresh vegetables	151.6	170.5	181.3	199.2	195.2	199.8	201.0	197.6	195.5
Asparagus (all uses)	0.3	0.6	0.6	1.0	1.0	1.0	1.1	1.1	1.1
Broccoli	1.4	3.4	4.3	5.9	5.3	5.5	5.6	5.6	6.1
Cabbage	8.0	8.3	8.1	8.9	8.3	7.6	8.3	8.1	8.2
Carrots	6.2	8.3	11.2	9.2	8.4	8.8	8.8	8.8	8.7
Cauliflower	1.1	2.2	1.6	1.7	1.4	1.6	1.6	1.5	1.7
Celery (all uses)	7.4	7.2	6.9	6.3	6.3	6.3	6.2	5.9	6.1
Corn	6.5	6.7	7.8	9.0	9.0	9.5	9.2	8.9	8.7
Cucumbers	3.9	4.7	5.6	6.4	6.6	6.2	6.5	6.3	6.3
Head lettuce	25.6	27.7	22.2	23.5	22.5	22.2	21.3	21.1	20.2
Mushrooms	1.2	2.0	2.0	2.6	2.6	2.6	2.6	2.6	2.6
Onions	11.4	15.1	17.8	18.9	19.3	19.5	21.6	21.1	19.8
Snap beans	1.3	1.1	1.6	2.0	2.1	2.0	1.9	1.8	2.1
Bell peppers (all uses)	2.9	4.5	6.2	7.0	6.7	6.9	7.0	7.1	7.0
Potatoes	51.1	46.7	49.2	47.1	44.3	46.9	45.8	42.4	37.3
Sweet potatoes (all uses)	4.4	4.4	4.2	4.2	3.8	4.7	4.6	4.5	4.6
Tomatoes	12.8	15.5	16.8	19.0	20.3	19.5	20.0	20.2	19.9
Other fresh vegetables [8]	6.0	11.8	14.7	26.7	27.3	29.2	28.9	30.5	35.0
Processed vegetables	187.0	215.2	226.4	224.1	217.2	221.5	220.1	217.0	210.2
Selected vegetables for freezing [9]	51.5	66.8	78.8	79.3	76.8	78.7	78.8	75.5	74.5
Selected vegetables for canning [10]	102.5	110.3	108.2	103.2	100.6	100.9	102.8	104.9	94.8
Vegetables for dehydrating [11]	10.5	14.6	14.5	17.3	15.8	17.3	15.2	13.7	15.0
Potatoes for chips	16.5	16.4	16.4	15.9	16.5	17.3	16.5	16.0	18.9
Pulses [12]	5.9	7.2	8.4	8.5	7.5	7.3	6.7	7.0	7.1

[1] Excludes wine grapes.   [2] Apricots, avocados, cherries, cranberries, kiwifruit, mangoes, papayas, and honeydew melons.
[3] Lemons, limes, tangerines, and tangelos.   [4] Apples, apricots, blackberries, blueberries, boysenberries, cherries, loganberries, peaches, plums, prunes, raspberries, and strawberries.   [5] Apples, apricots, dates, figs, peaches, pears, prunes, and raisins.
[6] Apples, apricots, cherries, olives, peaches, pears, pineapples, plums, and prunes.   [7] Apple, cranberry, grape, grapefruit, lemon, lime, orange, pineapple, and prunes.   [8] Artichokes, brussels sprouts, eggplant, escarole, endive, garlic, romaine, leaf lettuce, radishes, spinach, and squash. Beginning 2000, includes collard greens, kale, mustard greens, okra, pumpkin, and turnip greens.   [9] Asparagus, snap beans, lima beans, broccoli, carrots, cauliflower, sweet corn, green peas, potatoes, spinach, and miscellaneous vegetables.   [10] Asparagus, snap beans, beets, cabbage, carrots, chili peppers, sweet corn, cucumbers for pickling, green peas, lima beans, mushrooms, spinach, and tomatoes.   [11] Onions and potatoes.   [12] Dry peas, lentils, and dry edible beans.

Source: U.S. Department of Agriculture, Economic Research Service, *Food Consumption, Prices, and Expenditures, Food Availability (Per Capita) Data System;* <http://www.ers.usda.gov/data/foodconsumption/>.

Section 4
Education

This section presents data primarily concerning formal education as a whole, at various levels, and for public and private schools. Data shown relate to the school-age population and school enrollment, educational attainment, education personnel, and financial aspects of education. In addition, data are shown for charter schools, security measures used in schools, computer usage in schools, and adult education. The chief sources are the decennial census of population and the Current Population Survey (CPS), both conducted by the U.S. Census Bureau (see text, Section 1, Population); annual, biennial, and other periodic surveys conducted by the National Center for Education Statistics (NCES), a part of the U.S. Department of Education; and surveys conducted by the National Education Association.

The censuses of population have included data on school enrollment since 1840 and on educational attainment since 1940. The CPS has reported on school enrollment annually since 1945 and on educational attainment periodically since 1947.

The NCES is continuing the pattern of statistical studies and surveys conducted by the U.S. Office of Education since 1870. The annual *Digest of Education Statistics* provides summary data on pupils, staff, finances, including government expenditures, and organization at the elementary, secondary, and higher education levels. It is also a primary source for detailed information on federal funds for education, projections of enrollment, graduates, and teachers. *The Condition of Education,* issued annually, presents a summary of information on education of particular interest to policymakers. NCES also conducts special studies periodically.

The census of governments, conducted by the Census Bureau every 5 years (for the years ending in "2" and "7"), provides data on school district finances and state and local government expenditures for education. Reports published by the Bureau of Labor Statistics contain data relating civilian labor force experience to educational attainment (see also Tables 572, 599, and 607 in Section 12, Labor Force, Employment, and Earnings).

Types and sources of data—The statistics in this section are of two general types. One type, exemplified by data from the Census Bureau, is based on direct interviews with individuals to obtain information about their own and their family members' education. Data of this type relate to school enrollment and level of education attained, classified by age, sex, and other characteristics of the population. The school enrollment statistics reflect attendance or enrollment in any regular school within a given period; educational attainment statistics reflect the highest grade completed by an individual, or beginning 1992, the highest diploma or degree received.

Beginning in 2001, the CPS used Census 2000 population controls. From 1994 to 2000, the CPS used 1990 census population controls plus adjustment for undercount. Also the survey changed from paper to computer-assisted technology. For years 1981 through 1993, 1980 census population controls were used; 1971 through 1980, 1970 census population controls had been used. These changes had little impact on summary measures (e.g., medians) and proportional measures (e.g., enrollment rates); however, use of the controls may have significant impact on absolute numbers.

The second type, generally exemplified by data from the NCES and the National Education Association, is based on reports from administrators of educational institutions and of state and local agencies having jurisdiction over education. Data of this type relate to enrollment, attendance, staff, and finances for the nation, individual states, and local areas.

U.S. Census Bureau, Statistical Abstract of the United States: 2009

Unlike the NCES, the Census Bureau does not regularly include specialized vocational, trade, business, or correspondence schools in its surveys. The NCES includes nursery schools and kindergartens that are part of regular grade schools in their enrollment figures. The Census Bureau includes all nursery schools and kindergartens. At the higher education level, the statistics of both agencies are concerned with institutions granting degrees or offering work acceptable for degree-credit, such as junior colleges.

School attendance—All states require that children attend school. While state laws vary as to the ages and circumstances of compulsory attendance, generally they require that formal schooling begin by age 6 and continue to age 16.

Schools—The NCES defines a school as "a division of the school system consisting of students composing one or more grade groups or other identifiable groups, organized as one unit with one or more teachers to give instruction of a defined type, and housed in a school plant of one or more buildings. More than one school may be housed in one school plant, as is the case when the elementary and secondary programs are housed in the same school plant."

Regular schools are those which advance a person toward a diploma or degree. They include public and private nursery schools, kindergartens, graded schools, colleges, universities, and professional schools.

Public schools are schools controlled and supported by local, state, or federal governmental agencies; private schools are those controlled and supported mainly by religious organizations or by private persons or organizations.

The Census Bureau defines *elementary* schools as including grades 1 through 8; *high* schools as including grades 9 through 12; and *colleges* as including junior or community colleges, regular 4-year colleges, and universities and graduate or professional schools. Statistics reported by the NCES and the National Education Association by type of organization, such as elementary level and secondary level, may not be strictly comparable with those from the Census Bureau because the grades included at the two levels vary, depending on the level assigned to the middle or junior high school by the local school systems.

School year—Except as otherwise indicated in the tables, data refer to the school year which, for elementary and secondary schools, generally begins in September of the preceding year and ends in June of the year stated. For the most part, statistics concerning school finances are for a 12-month period, usually July 1 to June 30. Enrollment data generally refer to a specific point in time, such as fall, as indicated in the tables.

Statistical reliability—For a discussion of statistical collection, estimation, and sampling procedures and measures of statistical reliability applicable to the Census Bureau and the NCES data, see Appendix III.

U.S. Census Bureau, Statistical Abstract of the United States: 2009

Table 211. **School Enrollment: 1980 to 2017**

[In thousands (58,305 represents 58,305,000). As of fall]

Year	All levels			Pre-K through grade 8		Grades 9 through 12		College [1]	
	Total	Public	Private	Public	Private	Public	Private	Public	Private
1980	58,305	50,335	7,971	27,647	3,992	13,231	1,339	9,457	2,640
1985	57,226	48,901	8,325	27,034	4,195	12,388	1,362	9,479	2,768
1987	58,253	49,982	8,272	27,933	4,232	12,076	1,247	9,973	2,793
1988	58,485	50,349	8,136	28,501	4,036	11,687	1,206	10,161	2,894
1989	59,279	51,120	8,159	29,152	4,035	11,390	1,163	10,578	2,961
1990	60,269	52,061	8,208	29,878	4,084	11,338	1,150	10,845	2,974
1991	62,087	53,357	8,730	30,506	4,518	11,541	1,163	11,310	3,049
1992	62,987	54,208	8,779	31,088	4,528	11,735	1,148	11,385	3,102
1993	63,438	54,654	8,784	31,504	4,536	11,961	1,132	11,189	3,116
1994	64,177	55,245	8,932	31,898	4,624	12,213	1,162	11,134	3,145
1995	65,020	55,933	9,087	32,341	4,721	12,500	1,197	11,092	3,169
1996	65,913	56,733	9,180	32,764	4,720	12,847	1,213	11,121	3,247
1997	66,573	57,323	9,250	33,073	4,726	13,054	1,218	11,196	3,306
1998	67,034	57,677	9,357	33,346	4,748	13,193	1,240	11,138	3,369
1999	67,667	58,166	9,501	33,488	4,765	13,369	1,254	11,309	3,482
2000	68,685	58,956	9,729	33,688	4,878	13,515	1,292	11,753	3,560
2001	69,920	59,905	10,014	33,938	4,993	13,734	1,326	12,233	3,695
2002	71,015	60,935	10,080	34,116	4,886	14,067	1,334	12,752	3,860
2003	71,540	61,397	10,143	34,202	4,761	14,338	1,338	12,857	4,043
2004	72,200	61,775	10,379	34,178	4,731	14,617	1,356	12,980	4,292
2005	72,674	62,135	10,539	34,205	4,699	14,909	1,374	13,022	4,466
2006, proj. [2]. . .	73,318	62,644	10,674	34,422	4,711	15,041	1,384	13,180	4,579
2007, proj.	73,686	63,017	10,668	34,589	4,681	15,055	1,385	13,373	4,603
2008, proj.	74,079	63,387	10,692	34,903	4,681	14,922	1,372	13,562	4,638
2009, proj.	74,532	63,814	10,718	35,240	4,695	14,826	1,355	13,748	4,668
2010, proj.	75,012	64,243	10,769	35,653	4,721	14,700	1,326	13,890	4,722
2011, proj.	75,603	64,762	10,840	36,096	4,760	14,626	1,300	14,041	4,781
2012, proj.	76,322	65,395	10,928	36,527	4,813	14,667	1,267	14,201	4,847
2013, proj.	77,116	66,081	11,035	36,972	4,879	14,729	1,237	14,380	4,919
2014, proj.	77,979	66,831	11,147	37,403	4,933	14,881	1,228	14,547	4,986
2015, proj.	78,842	67,587	11,256	37,711	4,976	15,199	1,241	14,677	5,039
2016, proj.	79,678	68,306	11,372	38,052	5,021	15,451	1,262	14,804	5,089
2017, proj.	80,524	69,030	11,494	38,399	5,066	15,689	1,290	14,942	5,138

[1] Data beginning 1996 based on new classification system. See footnote 1, Table 269.   [2] Pre-K through 12 are projections; college data are actual.

Source: U.S. National Center for Education Statistics, *Digest of Education Statistics,* annual, and *Projections of Education Statistics,* annual.

Table 212. **School Expenditures by Type of Control and Level of Instruction in Constant (2006–2007) Dollars: 1980 to 2007**

[In millions of dollars (420,922 represents $420,922,000,000). For school years ending in year shown. Data shown reflect historical revisions. Total expenditures for public elementary and secondary schools include current expenditures, interest on school debt and capital outlay. Data deflated by the Consumer Price Index, all urban consumers, on a school-year basis (supplied by the National Center for Education Statistics). See also Appendix III. Based on survey of state education agencies; see source for details]

Year	Total	Elementary and secondary schools			Colleges and universities [2]		
		Total	Public	Private [1]	Total	Public	Private
1980	420,922	271,266	252,333	18,933	149,656	99,312	50,344
1985	461,965	288,353	264,420	23,933	173,612	112,551	61,061
1988	531,811	331,294	304,332	26,962	200,518	128,009	72,506
1989	561,325	352,679	325,055	27,624	208,646	132,977	75,667
1990	588,138	371,652	342,070	29,582	216,486	137,893	78,593
1991	602,607	379,916	349,734	30,182	222,691	141,706	80,984
1992	617,318	386,621	356,046	30,575	230,697	146,001	84,696
1993	630,033	393,358	362,278	31,081	236,674	149,775	86,899
1994	643,836	401,816	370,403	31,413	242,020	152,610	89,410
1995	658,756	410,426	378,667	31,759	248,330	156,712	91,618
1996	671,902	420,229	387,990	32,239	251,673	157,926	93,747
1997	692,228	435,427	402,283	33,143	256,801	161,835	94,966
1998	720,004	456,402	421,946	34,456	263,602	167,668	95,934
1999	749,159	477,198	441,468	35,731	271,960	174,358	97,602
2000	782,975	497,452	460,433	37,019	285,522	183,679	101,844
2001	821,972	518,601	478,961	39,640	303,371	198,603	104,768
2002	862,390	540,800	498,757	42,044	321,589	210,145	111,444
2003	891,948	552,423	509,938	42,485	339,525	220,861	118,664
2004	910,809	563,341	520,230	43,111	347,467	224,955	122,512
2005	932,310	575,560	531,472	44,088	356,751	230,024	126,726
2006	946,869	581,663	537,551	44,112	365,206	232,870	132,336
2007	972,000	599,000	553,000	46,000	373,000	239,000	134,000

[1] Estimated.   [2] Data beginning 1996 based on new classification system. See footnote 1, Table 269.

Source: U.S. National Center for Education Statistics, *Digest of Education Statistics,* annual.

Education   139

Table 213. School Enrollment, Faculty, Graduates, and Finances—Projections: 2007 to 2013

[As of fall, except as indicated (55,710 represents 55,710,000)]

Item	Unit	2007	2008	2009	2010	2011	2012	2013
ELEMENTARY AND SECONDARY SCHOOLS								
School enrollment, total	1,000 ...	55,710	55,879	56,116	56,400	56,781	57,275	57,817
Pre-kindergarten through grade 8	1,000 ...	39,271	39,585	39,935	40,374	40,855	41,341	41,851
Grades 9 through 12	1,000 ...	16,439	16,294	16,181	16,026	15,926	15,934	15,966
Public	1,000 ...	49,644	49,825	50,067	50,353	50,722	51,194	51,701
Pre-kindergarten through grade 8	1,000 ...	34,589	34,903	35,240	35,653	36,096	36,527	36,972
Grades 9 through 12	1,000 ...	15,055	14,922	14,826	14,700	14,626	14,667	14,729
Private	1,000 ...	6,066	6,054	6,049	6,047	6,059	6,081	6,116
Pre-kindergarten through grade 8	1,000 ...	4,681	4,681	4,695	4,721	4,760	4,813	4,879
Grades 9 through 12	1,000 ...	1,385	1,372	1,355	1,326	1,300	1,267	1,237
Classroom teachers, total FTE [1]	1,000 ...	3,663	3,713	3,760	3,808	3,859	3,914	3,970
Public	1,000 ...	3,204	3,246	3,286	3,326	3,369	3,417	3,465
Private	1,000 ...	459	467	474	482	489	497	505
High school graduates, total [2]	1,000 ...	3,346	3,328	3,327	3,286	3,234	3,235	3,197
Public	1,000 ...	3,026	3,011	3,005	2,973	2,925	2,933	2,903
Public schools: [2]								
Average daily attendance (ADA)	1,000 ...	46,242	46,410	46,635	46,902	47,246	47,685	48,158
Current dollars: [3]								
Current school expenditure	Bil. dol...	493	517	543	569	(NA)	(NA)	(NA)
Per pupil in fall enrollment	Dollar ...	9,929	10,384	10,844	11,296	(NA)	(NA)	(NA)
Constant (2005–2006) dollars: [3, 4]								
Current school expenditure	Bil. dol...	474	487	501	515	529	542	556
Per pupil in fall enrollment	Dollar ...	9,543	9,770	10,005	10,227	10,422	10,588	10,756
HIGHER EDUCATION								
Enrollment, total	1,000 ...	17,976	18,200	18,416	18,613	18,822	19,048	19,299
Male	1,000 ...	7,704	7,822	7,929	8,022	8,118	8,213	8,306
Full-time	1,000 ...	4,968	5,055	5,133	5,197	5,254	5,305	5,350
Part-time	1,000 ...	2,737	2,767	2,796	2,825	2,863	2,907	2,956
Female	1,000 ...	10,271	10,378	10,487	10,590	10,704	10,835	10,993
Full-time	1,000 ...	6,136	6,208	6,280	6,349	6,423	6,511	6,623
Part-time	1,000 ...	4,135	4,170	4,207	4,242	4,281	4,324	4,371
Public	1,000 ...	13,373	13,562	13,748	13,890	14,041	14,201	14,380
Four-year institutions	1,000 ...	6,981	7,092	7,204	7,290	7,379	7,473	7,575
Two-year institutions	1,000 ...	6,392	6,470	6,544	6,601	6,662	6,728	6,805
Private	1,000 ...	4,603	4,638	4,668	4,722	4,781	4,847	4,919
Four-year institutions	1,000 ...	4,299	4,330	4,356	4,407	4,464	4,526	4,595
Two-year institutions	1,000 ...	304	308	312	315	317	320	324
Undergraduate	1,000 ...	15,366	15,571	15,770	15,939	16,106	16,273	16,457
Graduate	1,000 ...	2,259	2,275	2,290	2,312	2,348	2,398	2,455
First-time professional	1,000 ...	351	354	357	361	368	377	387
Full-time equivalent	1,000 ...	13,647	13,925	14,201	14,451	14,692	14,930	15,182
Public	1,000 ...	9,792	9,988	10,182	10,354	10,518	10,677	10,847
2-year	1,000 ...	3,838	3,909	3,976	4,028	4,078	4,129	4,187
4-year	1,000 ...	5,954	6,080	6,206	6,326	6,439	6,548	6,660
Private	1,000 ...	3,855	3,937	4,019	4,097	4,175	4,253	4,335
2-year	1,000 ...	285	292	299	304	308	313	319
4-year	1,000 ...	3,570	3,645	3,720	3,794	3,866	3,940	4,016
Degrees conferred, total [2]	1,000 ...	3,063	3,136	3,189	3,215	3,240	3,268	3,300
Associate's	1,000 ...	718	731	741	743	745	747	750
Bachelor's	1,000 ...	1,563	1,603	1,634	1,653	1,667	1,681	1,692
Master's	1,000 ...	631	649	659	663	670	680	694
Doctoral	1,000 ...	59	60	60	61	62	63	65
First-professional	1,000 ...	92	93	94	95	96	97	99

NA Not available.   [1] Full-time equivalent.   [2] For school year ending in June the following year.   [3] Limited financial projections are shown due to the uncertain behavior of inflation over the long term.   [4] Based on the Consumer Price Index (CPI) for all urban consumers, U.S. Bureau of Labor Statistics. CPI adjusted to a school year basis by NCES.

Source: U.S. National Center for Education Statistics, *Projections of Education Statistics to 2017*, NCES 2008-060. See Internet site <http://www.nces.ed.gov/surveys/AnnualReports/>.

Table 214. Federal Funds for Education and Related Programs: 2005 to 2007

[In millions of dollars (145,989.2 represents $145,989,200,000), except percent. For fiscal years ending in September. Figures represent on-budget funds]

Level, agency, and program	2005	2006	2007 [1]
Total, all programs	**145,989.2**	**166,486.3**	**(NA)**
Percent of federal budget outlays	5.9	6.3	(NA)
Elementary/secondary education programs	**68,957.7**	**70,948.2**	**71,708.1**
Department of Education [2]	37,477.6	38,863.4	39,245.7
Grants for the disadvantaged	14,635.6	14,695.8	14,842.9
School improvement programs	7,918.1	7,463.5	7,697.0
Indian education	121.9	120.4	120.9
Special education	10,940.3	11,836.5	11,543.0
Vocational and adult education	1,967.1	1,987.5	2,091.6
Education reform—Goals 2000	-35.0	16.5	16.5
Department of Agriculture [2]	12,577.3	13,412.6	14,102.6
Child nutrition programs	[3] 11,901.9	[3] 12,660.8	[3] 13,345.6
Agricultural Marketing Service—commodities [4]	399.3	463.8	465.0
Special milk program	(3)	(3)	(3)
Department of Defense [2]	1,786.3	1,755.9	1,684.8
Overseas dependents schools	1,060.9	1,063.9	1,001.7
Section VI schools [5]	410.2	383.8	360.6
Department of Health and Human Services	8,003.3	8,118.9	8,057.6
Head Start	6,842.3	6,851.2	6,900.0
Social security student benefits	1,161.0	1,267.7	1,157.6
Department of Homeland Security [6]	0.5	0.5	0.6
Department of the Interior [2]	938.5	928.6	845.9
Mineral Leasing Act and other funds	140.0	133.4	109.3
Indian Education	797.5	746.8	735.7
Department of Justice	554.5	514.3	527.3
Inmate programs	554.5	513.3	525.3
Department of Labor	5,654.0	5,355.0	5,378.0
Job Corps	1,521.0	1,599.0	1,606.0
Department of Veterans Affairs	1,815.0	1,866.0	1,736.0
Vocational rehab for disabled veterans	1,815.0	1,866.0	1,736.0
Other agencies and programs	162.9	132.9	129.6
Higher education programs [2]	**38,591.1**	**57,738.3**	**36,623.3**
Department of Education [2]	31,420.0	50,624.6	28,879.0
Student financial assistance	15,209.5	14,864.1	15,723.3
Federal Family Education Loans [7]	10,777.5	26,336.7	4,851.0
Department of Agriculture	62.0	62.3	64.4
Department of Commerce	—		
Department of Defense	1,858.3	1,833.4	1,969.4
Tuition assistance for military personnel	608.1	564.0	624.3
Service academies [8]	300.8	321.9	336.6
Senior ROTC	537.5	498.2	577.9
Professional development education [1]	411.9	449.4	430.6
Department of Health and Human Services [2]	1,433.5	1,264.6	1,325.7
Health professions training programs	581.7	420.1	460.1
National Health Service Corps scholarships [9]	45.0	40.0	40.0
National Institutes of Health training grants [9]	756.0	748.6	771.6
Department of Homeland Security [6]	36.4	44.0	45.4
Department of the Interior	249.2	165.3	162.3
Shared revenues, Mineral Leasing Act and other receipts—estimated education share	146.2	59.6	53.7
Indian programs	103.0	105.7	108.6
Department of State	424.0	443.0	434.0
Department of Transportation	73.0	71.0	72.0
Department of Veterans Affairs [2]	2,478.6	2,662.1	3,103.2
Post-Vietnam veterans	1.1	1.3	1.3
All-volunteer-force educational assistance	2,071.0	2,230.0	2,632.7
Other agencies and programs [2]	556.0	567.9	567.9
National Endowment for the Humanities	29.5	34.1	32.0
National Science Foundation	490.0	496.0	497.0
Other education programs [2]	**6,908.7**	**7,074.5**	**7,584.1**
Department of Education [2]	3,538.9	3,692.9	4,171.4
Administration	548.8	557.8	537.5
Rehabilitative services and handicapped research	2,973.3	3,115.8	3,553.0
Department of Agriculture	468.6	475.4	471.3
Department of Health and Human Services [6]	313.0	312.0	315.0
Department of Homeland Security [6]	278.2	194.7	223.0
Department of Justice	26.1	26.7	28.7
Department of State	109.3	112.0	117.2
Other agencies and programs [2]	2,173.4	3,808.3	3,819.6
Agency for International Development	574.0	566.8	591.2
Library of Congress	430.0	435.0	428.0
National Endowment for the Arts	2.5	2.5	2.7
National Endowment for the Humanities and	88.0	86.3	84.0
Research programs at universities and related institutions [2]	**31,535.7**	**30,725.3**	**(NA)**
Department of Agriculture	819.9	552.3	(NA)
Department of Defense	2,880.8	2,312.7	(NA)
Department of Energy	4,216.5	4,024.4	(NA)
Department of Health and Human Services	16,121.7	16,220.1	(NA)
National Aeronautics and Space Administration	2,867.2	3,010.6	(NA)
National Science Foundation	3,521.7	3,610.9	(NA)

- Represents or rounds to zero. NA Not available. [1] Estimated except U.S. Department of Education, which are actual budget reports. [2] Includes other programs and agencies, not shown separately. [3] The Special Milk Program is included in the Child Nutrition Program. [4] Purchased under Section 32 of the Act of August 1935 for use in child nutrition programs. [5] Program provides for the education of dependents of federal employees residing on federal property where free public education is unavailable in the nearby community. [6] The U.S. Department of Homeland Security was created on January 24, 2003, under public law (107-296). [7] Includes Federal Direct Loans. [8] Instructional costs only including academics, audiovisual, academic computer center, faculty training, military training, physical education, and libraries. [9] Includes alcohol, drug abuse, and mental health training programs.

Source: U.S. National Center for Education Statistics, *Digest of Education Statistics*, annual.

U.S. Census Bureau, Statistical Abstract of the United States: 2009

Table 215. School Enrollment by Age: 1970 to 2006

[As of October (60,357 represents 60,357,000). Covers civilian noninstitutional population enrolled in nursery school and above. Based on Current Population Survey, see text, Section 1, and Appendix III]

Age	1970	1980	1985	1990	1995	2000	2003	2004	2005	2006
ENROLLMENT (1,000)										
Total, 3 to 34 years old....	**60,357**	**57,348**	**58,013**	**60,588**	**66,939**	**69,560**	**72,116**	**72,418**	**72,768**	**72,270**
3 and 4 years old	1,461	2,280	2,801	3,292	4,042	4,097	4,590	4,552	4,383	4,534
5 and 6 years old	7,000	5,853	6,697	7,207	7,901	7,648	7,309	7,561	7,486	7,628
7 to 13 years old	28,943	23,751	22,849	25,016	27,003	28,296	28,184	28,006	27,936	27,504
14 and 15 years old	7,869	7,282	7,362	6,555	7,651	7,885	8,329	8,327	8,375	8,252
16 and 17 years old	6,927	7,129	6,654	6,098	6,997	7,341	8,177	8,086	8,472	8,203
18 and 19 years old	3,322	3,788	3,716	4,044	4,274	4,926	4,856	4,961	5,109	5,306
20 and 21 years old	1,949	2,515	2,708	2,852	3,025	3,314	3,684	3,904	4,069	3,839
22 to 24 years old.	1,410	1,931	2,068	2,231	2,545	2,731	3,397	3,221	3,254	3,256
25 to 29 years old.	1,011	1,714	1,942	2,013	2,216	2,030	2,212	2,479	2,340	2,373
30 to 34 years old.	466	1,105	1,218	1,281	1,284	1,292	1,378	1,321	1,344	1,376
35 years old and over	(NA)	1,290	1,766	2,439	2,830	2,653	2,797	3,042	3,013	2,927
ENROLLMENT RATE										
Total, 3 to 34 years old....	**56.4**	**49.7**	**48.3**	**50.2**	**53.7**	**55.8**	**56.2**	**56.2**	**56.5**	**56.0**
3 and 4 years old	20.5	36.7	38.9	44.4	48.7	52.1	55.1	54.0	53.6	55.7
5 and 6 years old	89.5	95.7	96.1	96.5	96.0	95.6	94.5	95.4	95.4	94.6
7 to 13 years old	99.2	99.3	99.2	99.6	98.9	98.2	98.3	98.4	98.6	98.3
14 and 15 years old	98.1	98.2	98.1	99.0	98.9	98.7	97.5	98.5	98.0	98.3
16 and 17 years old	90.0	89.0	91.7	92.5	93.6	92.8	94.9	94.5	95.1	94.6
18 and 19 years old	47.7	46.4	51.6	57.3	59.4	61.2	64.5	64.4	67.6	65.5
20 and 21 years old	31.9	31.0	35.3	39.7	44.9	44.1	48.3	48.9	48.7	47.5
22 to 24 years old.	14.9	16.3	16.9	21.0	23.2	24.6	27.8	26.3	27.3	26.7
25 to 29 years old.	7.5	9.3	9.2	9.7	11.6	11.4	11.8	13.0	11.9	11.7
30 to 34 years old.	4.2	6.4	6.1	5.8	6.0	6.7	6.8	6.6	6.9	7.2
35 years old and over	(NA)	1.4	1.6	2.1	2.2	1.9	1.9	2.0	2.0	1.9

NA Not available.

Source: U.S. Census Bureau, Current Population Reports, PPL-148; and earlier PPL and P-20 reports; and data published on the Internet. See Internet site <http://www.census.gov/population/www/socdemo/school.html>.

Table 216. School Enrollment by Race, Hispanic Origin, and Age: 1980 to 2006

[(47,673 represents 47,673,000). See headnote, Table 215]

Age	White [1]			Black [1]			Hispanic origin [2]		
	1980	1990	2006	1980	1990	2006	1980	1990	2006
ENROLLMENT (1,000)									
Total, 3 to 34 years old....	**47,673**	**48,899**	**55,237**	**8,251**	**8,854**	**10,882**	**4,263**	**6,073**	**12,825**
3 and 4 years old	1,844	2,700	3,463	371	452	732	172	249	900
5 and 6 years old	4,781	5,750	5,851	904	1,129	1,132	491	835	1,613
7 to 13 years old	19,585	20,076	21,002	3,598	3,832	4,177	2,009	2,794	5,480
14 and 15 years old	6,038	5,265	6,294	1,088	1,023	1,325	568	739	1,452
16 and 17 years old	5,937	4,858	6,266	1,047	962	1,268	454	592	1,305
18 and 19 years old	3,199	3,271	4,103	494	596	796	226	329	751
20 and 21 years old	2,206	2,402	3,040	242	305	474	111	213	430
22 to 24 years old.	1,669	1,781	2,436	196	274	447	93	121	393
25 to 29 years old.	1,473	1,706	1,781	187	162	322	84	130	298
30 to 34 years old.	942	1,090	1,001	124	119	209	54	72	203
35 years old and over	1,104	2,096	2,182	186	238	517	(NA)	145	287
ENROLLMENT RATE									
Total, 3 to 34 years old....	**48.9**	**49.5**	**55.6**	**53.9**	**51.9**	**58.4**	**49.8**	**47.4**	**51.3**
3 and 4 years old	36.3	44.9	55.6	38.2	41.6	59.2	28.5	29.8	48.8
5 and 6 years old	95.8	96.5	95.0	95.4	96.3	92.6	94.5	94.8	93.4
7 to 13 years old	99.2	99.6	98.4	99.4	99.8	97.2	99.2	99.4	98.2
14 and 15 years old	98.3	99.1	98.4	97.9	99.2	97.5	94.3	99.0	98.4
16 and 17 years old	88.6	92.5	95.0	90.6	91.7	93.3	81.8	85.4	91.1
18 and 19 years old	46.3	57.1	64.9	45.7	55.2	64.7	37.8	44.1	53.4
20 and 21 years old	31.9	41.0	48.2	23.4	28.4	39.1	19.5	27.2	30.6
22 to 24 years old.	16.4	20.2	25.5	13.6	20.0	27.3	11.7	9.9	17.9
25 to 29 years old.	9.2	9.9	11.3	8.8	6.1	11.8	6.9	6.3	7.3
30 to 34 years old.	6.3	5.9	6.7	6.8	4.4	8.6	5.1	3.6	5.3
35 years old and over	1.3	2.1	1.7	1.8	2.1	3.1	(NA)	2.1	1.8

NA Not available. [1] 2006 for persons who selected this race group only. See footnote 2, Table 221. [2] Persons of Hispanic origin may be of any race.

Source: U.S. Census Bureau, Current Population Reports, PPL-148; and earlier PPL and P-20 reports; and data published on the Internet. See Internet site <http://www.census.gov/population/www/socdemo/school.html>.

Table 217. Enrollment in Public and Private Schools: 1970 to 2006

[In millions (52.2 represents 52,200,000), except percent. As of October. For civilian noninstitutional population. For **1970 to 1985,** persons 3 to 34 years old; **beginning 1988,** for 3 years old and over. For college enrollment 35 years old and over, see Table 215]

Year	Public Total	Public Nursery	Public Kindergarten	Public Elementary	Public High school	Public College	Private Total	Private Nursery	Private Kindergarten	Private Elementary	Private High school	Private College
1970	52.2	0.3	2.6	30.0	13.5	5.7	8.1	0.8	0.5	3.9	1.2	1.7
1975	52.8	0.6	2.9	27.2	14.5	7.7	8.2	1.2	0.5	3.3	1.2	2.0
1980	(NA)	0.6	2.7	24.4	(NA)	(NA)	(NA)	1.4	0.5	3.1	(NA)	(NA)
1985	49.0	0.9	3.2	23.8	12.8	8.4	9.0	1.6	0.6	3.1	1.2	2.5
1989 [1]	52.5	0.9	3.3	25.9	12.1	10.3	8.9	1.9	0.6	2.7	0.8	2.9
1990	53.8	1.2	3.3	26.6	11.9	10.7	9.2	2.2	0.6	2.7	0.9	2.9
1991	54.5	1.1	3.5	26.6	12.2	11.1	9.4	1.8	0.6	3.0	1.0	3.0
1992	55.0	1.1	3.5	27.1	12.3	11.1	9.4	1.8	0.6	3.1	1.0	3.0
1993	56.0	1.2	3.5	27.7	12.6	10.9	9.4	1.8	0.7	2.9	1.0	3.0
1994	58.6	1.9	3.3	28.1	13.5	11.7	10.7	2.3	0.6	3.4	1.1	3.3
1995	58.7	2.0	3.2	28.4	13.7	11.4	11.1	2.4	0.7	3.4	1.2	3.3
1996	59.5	1.9	3.4	28.1	14.1	12.0	10.8	2.3	0.7	3.4	1.2	3.2
1997	61.6	2.3	3.3	29.3	14.6	12.1	10.5	2.2	0.7	3.1	1.2	3.3
1998	60.8	2.3	3.1	29.1	14.3	12.0	11.3	2.3	0.7	3.4	1.2	3.6
1999	60.8	2.3	3.2	29.2	14.4	11.7	11.4	2.3	0.7	3.6	1.3	3.5
2000	61.2	2.2	3.2	29.4	14.4	12.0	11.0	2.2	0.7	3.5	1.3	3.3
2001	62.4	2.2	3.1	29.8	14.8	12.4	10.8	2.1	0.6	3.4	1.2	3.5
2002	62.8	2.2	3.0	29.7	15.1	12.8	11.3	2.2	0.6	3.5	1.3	3.7
2003	63.8	2.6	3.1	29.2	15.8	13.1	11.1	2.4	0.6	3.4	1.3	3.5
2004	64.3	2.5	3.4	29.2	15.5	13.7	11.3	2.3	0.6	3.4	1.3	3.7
2005	64.2	2.5	3.3	29.0	15.8	13.4	11.5	2.1	0.6	3.4	1.4	4.0
2006	64.1	2.5	3.6	29.0	15.6	13.5	11.1	2.2	0.5	3.1	1.5	3.8
Percent White:												
1970	84.5	59.5	84.4	83.1	85.6	90.7	93.4	91.1	88.2	94.1	96.1	92.8
1980	(NA)	68.2	80.7	80.9	(NA)	(NA)	(NA)	89.0	87.0	90.7	(NA)	(NA)
1990	79.8	71.7	78.3	78.9	79.2	84.1	87.4	89.6	83.2	88.2	89.4	85.0
2000	77.0	69.4	77.3	76.7	78.0	78.0	83.5	84.9	82.8	85.9	84.6	79.8
2003 [2]	75.6	74.7	76.4	75.0	75.6	77.1	82.3	84.3	80.3	83.8	86.0	79.0
2004 [2]	75.2	68.5	75.2	75.0	75.4	76.7	82.4	82.7	82.1	85.1	88.0	77.8
2005 [2]	75.7	71.3	78.0	75.2	76.0	76.7	81.4	83.6	79.0	83.0	83.6	78.4
2006 [2]	75.6	72.1	76.0	75.7	74.9	76.8	80.9	83.4	78.4	81.9	83.1	78.0

NA Not available. [1] Beginning 1989, based on a revised edit and tabulation package. [2] Beginning 2003, for persons who selected this race group only. See footnote 2, Table 221.

Source: U.S. Census Bureau, Current Population Reports, PPL-148; and earlier PPL and P-20 reports; and data published on the Internet. See Internet site <http://www.census.gov/population/www/socdemo/school.html>.

Table 218. School Enrollment by Sex and Level: 1970 to 2006

[In millions (60.4 represents 60,400,000). As of Oct. For the civilian noninstitutional population. **1970-1979,** for persons 3 to 34 years old; **beginning 1980,** 3 years old and over. Elementary includes kindergarten and grades 1–8; high school, grades 9–12; and college, 2-year and 4-year colleges, universities, and graduate and professional schools. Data for college represent degree-credit enrollment. See headnote, Table 215]

Year	All levels [1] Total	All levels Male	All levels Female	Elementary Total	Elementary Male	Elementary Female	High school Total	High school Male	High school Female	College Total	College Male	College Female
1970	60.4	31.4	28.9	37.1	19.0	18.1	14.7	7.4	7.3	7.4	4.4	3.0
1980	58.6	29.6	29.1	30.6	15.8	14.9	14.6	7.3	7.3	11.4	5.4	6.0
1985	59.8	30.0	29.7	30.7	15.7	15.0	14.1	7.2	6.9	12.5	5.9	6.6
1988 [2]	61.1	30.7	30.5	32.2	16.6	15.6	13.2	6.7	6.4	13.1	5.9	7.2
1989	61.5	30.8	30.7	32.5	16.7	15.8	12.9	6.6	6.3	13.2	6.0	7.2
1990	63.0	31.5	31.5	33.2	17.1	16.0	12.8	6.5	6.4	13.6	6.2	7.4
1991	63.9	32.1	31.8	33.8	17.3	16.4	13.1	6.8	6.4	14.1	6.4	7.6
1992	64.6	32.2	32.3	34.3	17.7	16.6	13.3	6.8	6.5	14.0	6.2	7.8
1993	65.4	32.9	32.5	34.8	17.9	16.9	13.6	7.0	6.6	13.9	6.3	7.6
1994	69.3	34.6	34.6	35.4	18.2	17.2	14.6	7.4	7.2	15.0	6.8	8.2
1995	69.8	35.0	34.8	35.7	18.3	17.4	15.0	7.7	7.3	14.7	6.7	8.0
1996	70.3	35.1	35.2	35.5	18.3	17.3	15.3	7.9	7.4	15.2	6.8	8.4
1997	72.0	35.9	36.2	36.3	18.7	17.6	15.8	8.0	7.7	15.4	6.8	8.6
1998	72.1	36.0	36.1	36.4	18.7	17.7	15.6	7.9	7.6	15.5	6.9	8.6
1999	72.4	36.3	36.1	36.7	18.8	17.9	15.9	8.2	7.7	15.2	7.0	8.2
2000	72.2	35.8	36.4	36.7	18.9	17.9	15.8	8.1	7.7	15.3	6.7	8.6
2001	73.1	36.3	36.9	36.9	19.0	17.9	16.1	8.2	7.8	15.9	6.9	9.0
2002	74.0	36.8	37.3	36.7	18.9	17.8	16.4	8.3	8.0	16.5	7.2	9.3
2003	74.9	37.3	37.6	36.3	18.7	17.6	17.1	8.6	8.4	16.6	7.3	9.3
2004	75.5	37.4	38.0	36.5	19.0	17.6	16.8	8.4	8.4	17.4	7.6	9.8
2005	75.8	37.4	38.4	36.4	18.6	17.7	17.4	8.9	8.5	17.5	7.5	9.9
2006	75.2	37.2	38.0	36.1	18.5	17.6	17.1	8.8	8.4	17.2	7.5	9.7

[1] Includes nursery schools not shown separately. [2] Data beginning 1988, based on a revised edit and tabulation package.

Source: U.S. Census Bureau, Current Population Reports, PPL-148; and earlier PPL and P-20 reports; and data published on the Internet. See Internet site <http://www.census.gov/population/www/socdemo/school.html>.

U.S. Census Bureau, Statistical Abstract of the United States: 2009

Table 219. **School Enrollment by Control and Level: 1980 to 2007**

[In thousands (58,305 represents 58,305,000). As of fall. Data below college level are for regular day schools and exclude subcollegiate departments of colleges, federal schools, and home-schooled children. College data include degree-credit and nondegree-credit enrollment. Based on survey of state education agencies; see source for details. For more projections, see Tables 211 and 213]

Control of school and level	1980	1990	1995	2000	2002	2003	2004	2005	2006, proj.	2007, proj.
Total	58,305	60,269	65,020	68,685	71,015	71,540	72,200	72,712	73,197	73,720
Public.	50,335	52,061	55,933	58,956	60,935	61,397	61,775	62,135	62,622	63,067
Private	7,971	8,208	9,087	9,729	10,080	10,143	10,425	10,577	10,575	10,653
Pre-kindergarten through 8 . .	31,639	33,962	37,062	38,566	39,002	38,964	38,951	38,941	39,166	39,376
Public	27,647	29,878	32,341	33,688	34,116	34,202	34,178	34,205	34,387	34,592
Private	3,992	4,084	4,721	4,878	4,886	4,761	4,773	4,736	4,779	4,784
Grades 9 through 12	14,570	12,488	13,697	14,807	15,402	15,676	15,977	16,285	16,358	16,386
Public	13,231	11,338	12,500	13,515	14,067	14,338	14,617	14,909	14,983	15,018
Private	1,339	1,150	1,197	1,292	1,334	1,338	1,360	1,376	1,375	1,368
College [1]	12,097	13,819	14,261	15,312	16,612	16,900	17,272	17,487	17,672	17,959
Public	9,457	10,845	11,092	11,753	12,752	12,857	12,980	13,022	13,252	13,457
Private	2,640	2,974	3,169	3,560	3,860	4,043	4,292	4,466	4,420	4,501
Not-for-profit	2,528	2,760	2,929	3,109	3,265	3,341	3,412	(NA)	(NA)	(NA)
For profit	112	214	240	450	594	703	880	(NA)	(NA)	(NA)

NA Not available.   [1] Data beginning 2000, reflects new classification system. See footnote 1, Table 269.

Source: U.S. National Center for Education Statistics, *Digest of Education Statistics,* annual, and *Projections of Education Statistics,* annual.

Table 220. **Students Who Are Foreign Born or Who Have Foreign-Born Parents: 2006**

[In thousands (49,238 represents 49,238,000), except percent. As of October. Covers civilian noninstitutional population enrolled in elementary school and above. Based on Current Population Survey, see text, Section 1 and Appendix III]

Characteristic	All students	Students with at least one foreign-born parent					
		Total		Foreign-born student		Native student	
		Number	Percent	Number	Percent	Number	Percent
ELEMENTARY AND HIGH SCHOOL							
Total [1]	49,238	11,414	23.2	2,513	5.1	8,901	18.1
White [2]	37,438	8,003	21.4	1,728	4.6	6,275	16.8
White, non-Hispanic.	28,845	2,254	7.8	443	1.5	1,811	6.3
Black [2]	7,744	1,056	13.6	256	3.3	800	10.3
Asian [2, 3]	1,897	1,773	93.5	489	25.8	1,284	67.7
Hispanic [4]	9,385	6,093	64.9	1,349	14.4	4,744	50.6
COLLEGE, 1 TO 4 YEARS							
Total [1]	13,854	3,089	22.3	1,387	10.0	1,702	12.3
White [2]	10,686	1,817	17.0	742	6.9	1,075	10.1
White, non-Hispanic.	9,150	832	9.1	322	3.5	510	5.6
Black [2]	1,960	428	21.8	210	10.7	218	11.1
Asian [2, 3]	738	677	91.7	388	52.6	289	39.2
Hispanic [4]	1,697	1,073	63.2	444	26.2	629	37.1
GRADUATE SCHOOL							
Total [1]	3,378	980	29.0	590	17.5	390	11.5
White [2]	2,587	555	21.4	288	11.1	266	10.3
White, non-Hispanic.	2,335	403	17.2	213	9.1	190	8.1
Black [2]	374	85	22.6	50	13.4	34	9.1
Asian [2, 3]	346	325	93.9	244	70.5	81	23.4
Hispanic [4]	272	154	56.6	77	28.4	77	28.2

[1] Includes other races not shown separately.   [2] For persons who selected this race group only. See footnote 2, Table 221. [3] Data are for Asians only; excludes Pacific Islanders.   [4] Persons of Hispanic origin may be of any race.

Source: U.S. Census Bureau, Current Population Survey, unpublished data. See Internet site <http://www.census.gov/population/www/socdemo/school.html>.

144   Education

Table 221. Educational Attainment by Race and Hispanic Origin: 1960 to 2007

[In percent. For persons 25 years old and over. 1960, 1970, and 1980 as of April 1 and based on sample data from the censuses of population. Other years as of March and based on the Current Population Survey; see text, Section 1, and Appendix III. See Table 222 for data by sex]

Year	Total [1]	White [2]	Black [2]	Asian and Pacific Islander [2]	Hispanic [3] Total [4]	Mexican	Puerto Rican	Cuban
HIGH SCHOOL GRADUATE OR MORE [5]								
1960	41.1	43.2	20.1	(NA)	(NA)	(NA)	(NA)	(NA)
1970	52.3	54.5	31.4	(NA)	32.1	24.2	23.4	43.9
1980	66.5	68.8	51.2	(NA)	44.0	37.6	40.1	55.3
1990	77.6	79.1	66.2	80.4	50.8	44.1	55.5	63.5
1995	81.7	83.0	73.8	(NA)	53.4	46.5	61.3	64.7
2000	84.1	84.9	78.5	85.7	57.0	51.0	64.3	73.0
2004	85.2	85.8	80.6	[6]86.8	58.4	51.9	71.8	72.1
2005	85.2	85.7	81.1	87.6	58.5	52.2	72.3	73.5
2006	85.5	86.1	80.7	87.4	59.3	53.1	72.3	74.9
2007	85.7	86.2	82.3	87.8	60.3	53.9	73.5	79.8
COLLEGE GRADUATE OR MORE [5]								
1960	7.7	8.1	3.1	(NA)	(NA)	(NA)	(NA)	(NA)
1970	10.7	11.3	4.4	(NA)	4.5	2.5	2.2	11.1
1980	16.2	17.1	8.4	(NA)	7.6	4.9	5.6	16.2
1990	21.3	22.0	11.3	39.9	9.2	5.4	9.7	20.2
1995	23.0	24.0	13.2	(NA)	9.3	6.5	10.7	19.4
2000	25.6	26.1	16.5	43.9	10.6	6.9	13.0	23.0
2004	27.7	28.2	17.6	[6]49.4	12.1	7.9	14.0	24.0
2005	27.6	28.0	17.6	50.1	12.0	8.3	13.8	24.7
2006	28.0	28.4	18.5	49.7	12.4	8.5	15.1	24.4
2007	28.7	29.1	18.5	52.1	12.7	9.0	16.4	27.2

NA Not available. [1] Includes other races not shown separately. [2] Beginning 2004, for persons who selected this race group only. The 2003 Current Population Survey (CPS) allowed respondents to choose more than one race. Beginning 2003, data represent persons who selected this race group only and exclude persons reporting more than one race. The CPS in prior years only allowed respondents to report one race group. See also comments on race in the text for Section 1. [3] Persons of Hispanic origin may be of any race. [4] Includes persons of other Hispanic origin not shown separately. [5] Through 1990, completed 4 years of high school or more and 4 years of college or more. [6] Starting in 2004, data are for Asians only, excludes Pacific Islanders.

Source: U.S. Census Bureau, U.S. Census of Population, 1960, 1970, and 1980, Vol. 1; and Current Population Reports P20-550 and earlier reports; and data published on the Internet. See Internet site <http://www.census.gov/population/www/socdemo/educ-attn.html>.

Table 222. Educational Attainment by Race, Hispanic Origin, and Sex: 1960 to 2007

[In percent. See Table 221 for headnote and totals for both sexes]

Year	All races [1] Male	Female	White [2] Male	Female	Black [2] Male	Female	Asian and Pacific Islander [2] Male	Female	Hispanic [3] Male	Female
HIGH SCHOOL GRADUATE OR MORE [4]											
1960	39.5	42.5	41.6	44.7	18.2	21.8	(NA)	(NA)	(NA)	(NA)
1970	51.9	52.8	54.0	55.0	30.1	32.5	(NA)	(NA)	37.9	34.2
1980	67.3	65.8	69.6	68.1	50.8	51.5	(NA)	(NA)	67.3	65.8
1990	77.7	77.5	79.1	79.0	65.8	66.5	84.0	77.2	50.3	51.3
1995	81.7	81.6	83.0	83.0	73.4	74.1	(NA)	(NA)	52.9	53.8
2000	84.2	84.0	84.8	85.0	78.7	78.3	88.2	83.4	56.6	57.5
2004	84.8	85.4	85.3	86.3	80.4	80.8	[5]88.7	[5]85.0	57.3	59.5
2005	84.9	85.5	85.2	86.2	81.0	81.2	90.4	85.2	57.9	59.1
2006	85.0	85.9	85.5	86.7	80.1	81.2	89.6	85.5	58.5	60.1
2007	85.0	86.4	85.3	87.1	81.9	82.6	89.8	85.9	58.2	62.5
COLLEGE GRADUATE OR MORE [4]											
1960	9.7	5.8	10.3	6.0	2.8	3.3	(NA)	(NA)	(NA)	(NA)
1970	13.5	8.1	14.4	8.4	4.2	4.6	(NA)	(NA)	7.8	4.3
1980	20.1	12.8	21.3	13.3	8.4	8.3	(NA)	(NA)	9.4	6.0
1990	24.4	18.4	25.3	19.0	11.9	10.8	44.9	35.4	9.8	8.7
1995	26.0	20.2	27.2	21.0	13.6	12.9	(NA)	(NA)	10.1	8.4
2000	27.8	23.6	28.5	23.9	16.3	16.7	47.6	40.7	10.7	10.6
2004	29.4	26.1	30.0	26.4	16.6	18.5	[5]53.7	[5]45.6	11.8	12.3
2005	28.9	26.5	29.4	26.8	16.0	18.8	54.0	46.8	11.8	12.1
2006	29.2	26.9	29.7	27.1	17.2	19.4	52.5	47.1	11.9	12.9
2007	29.5	28.0	29.9	28.3	18.0	19.0	55.2	49.3	11.8	13.7

NA Not available. [1] Includes other races not shown separately. See footnote 2, Table 221. [2] Beginning 2004, for persons who selected this race group only. See footnote 2, Table 221. [3] Persons of Hispanic origin may be of any race. [4] Through 1990, completed 4 years of high school or more and 4 years of college or more. [5] Starting in 2004, data are for Asians only, excludes Pacific Islanders.

Source: U.S. Census Bureau, U.S. Census of Population, 1960, 1970, and 1980, Vol. 1; and Current Population Reports P20-550 and earlier reports; and data published on the Internet. See Internet site <http://www.census.gov/population/www/socdemo/educ-attn.html>.

Table 223. Educational Attainment by Selected Characteristic: 2007

[For persons 25 years old and over (194,318 represents 194,318,000). As of March. Based on the Current Population Survey; see text, Section 1, and Appendix III. For composition of regions, see map inside front cover]

Characteristic	Population (1,000)	Percent of population—highest level					
		Not a high school graduate	High school graduate	Some college, but no degree	Associate's degree [1]	Bachelor's degree	Advanced degree
Total persons	**194,318**	**14.3**	**31.6**	**16.7**	**8.6**	**18.9**	**9.9**
Age:							
25 to 34 years old	39,868	12.9	28.6	18.1	9.3	22.8	8.3
35 to 44 years old	42,762	11.8	29.7	16.4	9.6	22.2	10.4
45 to 54 years old	43,461	11.2	32.1	17.1	9.8	19.3	10.5
55 to 64 years old	32,191	12.8	30.9	17.8	8.5	17.8	12.3
65 to 74 years old	18,998	20.7	36.8	15.0	6.1	12.3	9.2
75 years old or over	17,037	27.4	38.1	13.2	4.7	9.8	6.9
Sex:							
Male	93,421	15.0	31.7	16.1	7.7	18.7	10.8
Female	100,897	13.6	31.6	17.3	9.5	19.0	9.0
Race:							
White [2]	159,262	13.8	31.7	16.7	8.7	19.1	10.0
Black [2]	21,924	17.7	36.2	18.8	8.7	13.0	5.6
Other	13,132	14.2	23.8	12.9	7.6	25.6	15.7
Hispanic origin:							
Hispanic	24,551	39.7	28.4	13.0	6.2	9.4	3.3
Non-Hispanic	169,767	10.6	32.1	17.2	9.0	20.2	10.8
Region:							
Northeast	36,333	12.9	33.5	12.3	8.1	20.3	12.9
Midwest	42,949	10.8	35.4	17.6	9.4	17.9	9.0
South	70,571	16.2	32.1	16.7	8.3	17.9	8.8
West	44,465	15.6	25.9	19.5	8.9	20.1	9.9
Marital status:							
Never married	31,862	14.9	30.3	17.1	8.1	21.1	8.5
Married, spouse present	118,164	12.0	30.4	16.3	8.9	20.7	11.6
Married, spouse absent [3]	3,190	31.6	31.8	12.0	6.0	12.1	6.6
Separated	4,659	24.1	35.7	17.8	7.7	9.9	4.8
Widowed	13,886	28.3	38.9	13.7	5.6	9.0	4.5
Divorced	22,556	12.0	34.6	20.9	10.2	14.9	7.4
Civilian labor force status:							
Employed	125,537	9.5	29.3	17.2	9.9	22.1	11.9
Unemployed	4,987	21.4	36.0	18.6	7.8	11.6	4.6
Not in the labor force	63,186	23.3	36.0	15.5	6.2	12.9	6.1

[1] Includes vocational degrees.　[2] For persons who selected this race group only. See footnote 2, Table 221.　[3] Excludes those separated.

Source: U.S. Census Bureau, Current Population Survey. See Internet site <http://www.census.gov/population/www/socdemo/educ-attn.html>.

Table 224. Mean Earnings by Highest Degree Earned: 2006

[In dollars. For persons 18 years old and over with earnings. Persons as of March the following year. Based on Current Population Survey; see text, Section 1, and Appendix III. For definition of mean, see Guide to Tabular Presentation]

Characteristic	Total persons	Mean earnings by level of highest degree (dol.)							
		Not a high school graduate	High school graduate only	Some college, no degree	Associate's	Bachelor's	Master's	Professional	Doctorate
All persons [1]	**41,412**	**20,873**	**31,071**	**32,289**	**39,724**	**56,788**	**70,358**	**116,514**	**103,944**
Age:									
25 to 34 years old	36,407	21,153	28,448	31,026	35,180	48,724	55,069	78,119	62,158
35 to 44 years old	48,625	24,333	35,083	40,943	45,018	63,335	75,724	133,151	116,721
45 to 54 years old	51,120	25,438	37,173	43,027	45,600	66,061	85,166	131,011	121,238
55 to 64 years old	48,111	25,688	34,845	40,968	40,497	60,393	67,911	123,759	103,112
65 years old and over	32,705	18,740	24,072	27,630	28,184	43,805	45,271	88,361	82,623
Sex:									
Male	49,647	24,072	37,356	38,932	47,575	69,818	87,981	132,991	116,473
Female	32,015	15,352	23,236	25,649	33,052	43,302	53,209	86,010	77,968
White [2]	42,395	21,464	32,083	32,917	40,465	57,932	71,063	117,787	105,541
Male	51,013	24,579	38,833	39,924	49,061	71,735	89,837	133,988	118,003
Female	32,148	15,483	23,334	25,595	32,889	47,903	53,062	85,112	78,389
Black [2]	32,443	17,823	26,368	29,308	35,817	47,903	55,654	101,374	85,237
Male	36,045	21,294	30,122	34,033	36,534	52,569	62,396	(B)	(B)
Female	29,371	14,277	22,643	25,832	35,328	44,326	50,916	80,038	(B)
Hispanic [3]	29,155	20,581	27,508	29,442	36,106	45,371	65,240	82,627	(B)
Male	32,532	23,060	32,148	34,414	41,445	51,336	81,885	97,035	(B)
Female	24,104	15,072	20,608	23,628	31,675	38,825	51,344	(B)	(B)

B Base figure too small to meet statistical standards for reliability of a derived figure.　[1] Includes other races not shown separately.　[2] For persons who selected this race group only. See footnote 2, Table 221.　[3] Persons of Hispanic origin may be of any race.

Source: U.S. Census Bureau, Current Population Survey. See Internet site <http://www.census.gov/population/www/socdemo/educ-attn.html>.

Table 225. Educational Attainment by State: 1990 to 2006

[In percent. 1990 and 2000 as of April. 2006, represents annual averages for calendar year. For persons 25 years old and **over**. Based on the 1990 and 2000 Census of Population and the American Community Survey; see text, Section 1, and Appendix III]

State	1990			2000			2006		
	High school graduate or more	Bach-elor's degree or more	Advanced degree or more	High school graduate or more	Bach-elor's degree or more	Advanced degree or more	High school graduate or more	Bach-elor's degree or more	Advanced degree or more
United States . . .	**75.2**	**20.3**	**7.2**	**80.4**	**24.4**	**8.9**	**84.1**	**27.0**	**9.9**
Alabama	66.9	15.7	5.5	75.3	19.0	6.9	80.1	21.1	7.7
Alaska.	86.6	23.0	8.0	88.3	24.7	8.6	89.7	26.9	9.5
Arizona	78.7	20.3	7.0	81.0	23.5	8.4	83.8	25.5	9.2
Arkansas	66.3	13.3	4.5	75.3	16.7	5.7	80.5	18.2	6.2
California	76.2	23.4	8.1	76.8	26.6	9.5	80.1	29.0	10.4
Colorado	84.4	27.0	9.0	86.9	32.7	11.1	88.0	34.3	12.4
Connecticut	79.2	27.2	11.0	84.0	31.4	13.3	88.0	33.7	14.4
Delaware	77.5	21.4	7.7	82.6	25.0	9.4	85.5	27.0	10.5
District of Columbia . . .	73.1	33.3	17.2	77.8	39.1	21.0	84.3	45.9	25.4
Florida.	74.4	18.3	6.3	79.9	22.3	8.1	84.5	25.3	8.9
Georgia	70.9	19.3	6.4	78.6	24.3	8.3	82.2	26.6	9.2
Hawaii.	80.1	22.9	7.1	84.6	26.2	8.4	89.0	29.7	9.8
Idaho	79.7	17.7	5.3	84.7	21.7	6.8	87.3	23.3	7.1
Illinois	76.2	21.0	7.5	81.4	26.1	9.5	85.0	28.9	10.8
Indiana	75.6	15.6	6.4	82.1	19.4	7.2	85.2	21.7	8.0
Iowa	80.1	16.9	5.2	86.1	21.2	6.5	88.9	24.0	7.4
Kansas	81.3	21.1	7.0	86.0	25.8	8.7	88.5	28.6	9.8
Kentucky	64.6	13.6	5.5	74.1	17.1	6.9	79.6	20.0	8.2
Louisiana	68.3	16.1	5.6	74.8	18.7	6.5	79.4	20.3	6.8
Maine	78.8	18.8	6.1	85.4	22.9	7.9	88.7	25.8	8.9
Maryland	78.4	26.5	10.9	83.8	31.4	13.4	87.1	35.1	15.7
Massachusetts	80.0	27.2	10.6	84.8	33.2	13.7	87.9	37.0	15.6
Michigan	76.8	17.4	6.4	83.4	21.8	8.1	87.2	24.5	9.2
Minnesota	82.4	21.8	6.3	87.9	27.4	8.3	90.7	30.4	9.6
Mississippi	64.3	14.7	5.1	72.9	16.9	5.8	77.9	18.8	6.1
Missouri.	73.9	17.8	6.1	81.3	21.6	7.6	84.8	24.3	8.7
Montana	81.0	19.8	5.7	87.2	24.4	7.2	90.1	27.4	8.4
Nebraska.	81.8	18.9	5.9	86.6	23.7	7.3	89.5	26.9	8.4
Nevada	78.8	15.3	5.2	80.7	18.2	6.1	83.9	20.8	7.2
New Hampshire	82.2	24.4	7.9	87.4	28.7	10.0	89.9	31.9	11.2
New Jersey	76.7	24.9	8.8	82.1	29.8	11.0	86.1	33.4	12.4
New Mexico	75.1	20.4	8.3	78.9	23.5	9.8	81.5	25.3	10.9
New York.	74.8	23.1	9.9	79.1	27.4	11.8	84.1	31.2	13.3
North Carolina	70.0	17.4	5.4	78.1	22.5	7.2	82.0	24.8	8.3
North Dakota	76.7	18.1	4.5	83.9	22.0	5.5	88.1	25.6	6.5
Ohio	75.7	17.0	5.9	83.0	21.1	7.4	86.2	23.0	8.3
Oklahoma	74.6	17.8	6.0	80.6	20.3	6.8	84.3	22.1	7.2
Oregon	81.5	20.6	7.0	85.1	25.1	8.7	87.6	27.5	10.0
Pennsylvania	74.7	17.9	6.6	81.9	22.4	8.4	86.2	25.4	9.6
Rhode Island	72.0	21.3	7.8	78.0	25.6	9.7	82.4	29.6	11.3
South Carolina	68.3	16.6	5.4	76.3	20.4	6.9	81.3	22.7	7.9
South Dakota	77.1	17.2	4.9	84.6	21.5	6.0	88.3	24.8	7.2
Tennessee	67.1	16.0	5.4	75.9	19.6	6.8	80.9	21.7	7.5
Texas	72.1	20.3	6.5	75.7	23.2	7.6	78.6	24.7	8.0
Utah	85.1	22.3	6.8	87.7	26.1	8.3	90.2	28.6	9.4
Vermont	80.8	24.3	8.9	86.4	29.4	11.1	89.8	32.4	12.8
Virginia	75.2	24.5	9.1	81.5	29.5	11.6	85.4	32.7	13.2
Washington	83.8	22.9	7.0	87.1	27.7	9.3	89.0	30.5	10.7
West Virginia	66.0	12.3	4.8	75.2	14.8	5.9	81.0	16.5	6.6
Wisconsin	78.6	17.7	5.6	85.1	22.4	7.2	88.4	25.1	8.4
Wyoming	83.0	18.8	5.7	87.9	21.9	7.0	90.2	22.7	7.4

Source: U.S. Census Bureau, 1990 Census of Population, CPH-L-96; 2000 Census of Population, Table P37, Sex by Educational Attainment for the Population 25 Years and Over, using American FactFinder®; 2006 American Community Survey, Table R1501 "Percent of Persons 25 Years and Over Who Have Completed High School," Table R1502 "Percent of Persons 25 Years and Over Who Have Completed a Bachelor's Degree," and Table R1503 "Percent of Persons 25 Years and Over Who Have Completed an Advanced Degree," using American FactFinder®.

Table 226. **Children's Involvement in Home Literacy Activities: 1993 and 2005**

[In percent, except number of children (8,579 represents 8,579,000). For children 3 to 5 years old not yet enrolled in kindergarten who participated in activities with a family member. Based on the School Readiness Early Childhood Program Participation Surveys of the National Household Education Surveys Program; see source and Appendix III. See also Table 229]

Characteristic	Children (1,000)		Read to [1]		Told a story [1]		Taught letters, words, or numbers [1]		Visited a library [2]	
	1993	2005	1993	2005	1993	2005	1993	2005	1993	2005
Total.	8,579	9,066	78	86	43	54	58	77	38	42
Age:										
3 years old	3,889	4,070	79	86	46	54	57	75	34	40
4 years old	3,713	3,873	78	85	41	53	58	77	41	44
5 years old	976	1,123	76	86	36	55	58	80	38	46
Race/ethnicity:										
White, non-Hispanic	5,902	5,177	85	92	44	53	58	76	42	45
Black, non-Hispanic	1,271	1,233	66	78	39	54	63	81	29	44
Hispanic.	1,026	1,822	58	72	38	50	54	74	26	32
Other.	381	834	73	88	50	64	59	82	43	48
Mother's home language: [3]										
English	7,805	7,618	81	89	44	55	58	78	39	45
Not English.	603	1,245	42	66	36	45	52	69	26	29
Mother's highest education: [3]										
Less than high school	1,036	886	60	64	37	39	56	70	22	23
High school.	3,268	2,687	76	82	41	51	56	78	31	33
Vocational ed or some college . . .	2,624	2,461	83	88	45	57	60	79	44	45
College degree	912	1,832	90	92	48	56	56	75	55	52
Graduate/professional training or degree	569	997	90	94	50	64	60	76	59	60

[1] Three or more times in the past week.   [2] At least once in the past month.   [3] Excludes children with no mother in the household and no female guardian.

Source: U.S. National Center for Education Statistics, Statistical Brief, NCES 2000-026, November 1999; and the Early Childhood Program Participation Survey, National Household Education Surveys Program, 2005, unpublished data. See Internet site <http://nces.ed.gov/nhes>.

Table 227. **Children Who Speak a Language Other Than English at Home by Region: 2006**

[In thousands (10,862 represents 10,862,000), except percent. For children 5 to 17 years old. Based on the American Community Survey; see text Section 1, and Appendix III]

Characteristic	U.S.	Northeast	Midwest	South	West
Children who speak another language at home	10,862	1,872	1,315	3,362	4,312
Percent of children 5 to 17 years old	20.3	20.1	11.1	17.3	33.6
Speak Spanish	7,805	1,035	789	2,649	3,332
Speak English "very well"	5,728	813	564	1,907	2,444
Speak English less than "very well".	2,076	222	225	741	888
Speak other Indo-European languages	1,458	518	277	363	300
Speak English "very well"	1,169	411	215	293	249
Speak English less than "very well".	290	107	62	70	51
Speak Asian and Pacific Island languages	1,177	227	152	249	549
Speak English "very well"	856	167	107	181	401
Speak English less than "very well".	321	60	45	69	148
Speak other languages.	422	92	97	102	131
Speak English "very well"	342	71	77	84	110
Speak English less than "very well".	79	21	20	17	21
Have difficulty speaking English [1].	2,767	410	352	897	1,108
Language spoken at home in linguistically isolated [2] households	2,976	461	329	907	1,279
Speak only English	144	32	16	42	54
Speak Spanish	2,209	256	211	727	1,015
Speak other Indo-European languages	224	82	39	55	48
Speak Asian and Pacific Island languages	332	74	40	71	147
Speak other languages.	67	17	22	12	15

[1] Children ages 5 to 17 who speak English less than "very well."   [2] A household in which no person age 14 or over speaks English at least "very well."

Source: U.S. Census Bureau, 2006 American Community Survey; B16003. Age by Language Spoken at Home for the Population 5 Years and Over; and C16004. Age By Language Spoken at Home For the Population 5 Years and Over in Liguistically Isolated Households; using American Factfinder®; <http://factfinder.census.gov/>; (accessed 12 August 2008).

Table 228. **Preprimary School Enrollment—Summary: 1970 to 2006**

[As of October. Civilian noninstitutional population (10,949 represents 10,949,000). Includes public and nonpublic nursery school and kindergarten programs. Excludes 5-year-olds enrolled in elementary school. Based on Current Population Survey; see text, Section 1, and Appendix III]

Item	1970	1975	1980	1985	1990	1995	2000	2005	2006
NUMBER OF CHILDREN (1,000)									
Population, 3 to 5 years old	10,949	10,183	9,284	10,733	11,207	12,518	11,858	12,134	12,187
Total enrolled [1]	4,104	4,954	4,878	5,865	6,659	7,739	7,592	7,801	8,009
Nursery	1,094	1,745	1,981	2,477	3,378	4,331	4,326	4,529	4,636
Public	332	570	628	846	1,202	1,950	2,146	2,409	2,481
Private	762	1,174	1,353	1,631	2,177	2,381	2,180	2,120	2,156
Kindergarten	3,010	3,211	2,897	3,388	3,281	3,408	3,266	3,272	3,373
Public	2,498	2,682	2,438	2,847	2,767	2,799	2,701	2,804	2,960
Private	511	528	459	541	513	608	565	468	413
White [2]	3,443	4,105	3,994	4,757	5,389	6,144	5,861	6,025	6,145
Black [2]	586	731	725	919	964	1,236	1,265	1,148	1,225
Hispanic [3]	(NA)	(NA)	370	496	642	1,040	1,155	1,494	1,624
3 years old	454	683	857	1,035	1,205	1,489	1,540	1,715	1,716
4 years old	1,007	1,418	1,423	1,765	2,086	2,553	2,556	2,668	2,817
5 years old	2,643	2,852	2,598	3,065	3,367	3,697	3,496	3,418	3,476
ENROLLMENT RATE									
Total enrolled [1]	37.5	48.6	52.5	54.6	59.4	61.8	64.0	64.3	65.7
White [2]	37.8	48.6	52.7	54.7	59.7	63.0	63.2	65.1	66.0
Black [2]	34.9	48.1	51.8	55.8	57.8	58.9	68.5	62.0	66.7
Hispanic [3]	(NA)	(NA)	43.3	43.3	49.0	51.1	52.6	56.1	59.8
3 years old	12.9	21.5	27.3	28.8	32.6	35.9	39.2	41.3	42.4
4 years old	27.8	40.5	46.3	49.1	56.0	61.6	64.9	66.2	68.8
5 years old	69.3	81.3	84.7	86.5	88.8	87.5	87.6	86.4	85.8

NA Not available. [1] Includes races not shown separately. [2] Beginning 2003, for persons who selected this race group only. See footnote 2, Table 221. [3] Persons of Hispanic origin may be of any race. The method of identifying Hispanic children was changed in 1980 from allocation based on status of mother to status reported for each child. The number of Hispanic children using the new method is larger.

Source: U.S. Census Bureau, Current Population Reports, PPL-148; and earlier PPL and P-20 reports; and data published on the Internet. See Internet site <http://www.census.gov/population/www/socdemo/school.html>.

Table 229. **Children's School Readiness Skills: 1993 and 2005**

[In percent. For children 3 to 5 years old not yet enrolled in kindergarden. Based on the School Readiness Surveys of the National Household Education Survey Program; see source for details. See also Table 226]

Characteristic	Recognizes all letters		Counts to 20 or higher		Writes name		Reads or pretends to read storybooks		Has 3 to 4 skills	
	1993	2005	1993	2005	1993	2005	1993	2005	1993	2005
Total	21	26	52	61	50	59	72	70	35	42
Age:										
3 years old	11	16	37	46	22	32	66	67	15	24
4 years old	28	31	62	71	70	78	75	73	49	55
5 years old	36	44	78	81	84	91	81	72	65	66
Sex:										
Male	19	26	49	59	47	57	68	70	32	40
Female	23	26	56	64	53	60	76	71	39	45
Race/ethnicity:										
White, non-Hispanic	23	29	56	65	52	60	76	75	39	47
Black, non-Hispanic	18	24	53	69	45	61	63	67	31	44
Hispanic	10	16	32	42	42	51	59	55	22	26
Other	22	31	49	65	52	63	70	79	36	48
Mother's employment status [1]:										
Employed	23	28	57	65	52	62	75	72	39	46
Unemployed	17	18	41	49	46	53	67	61	29	32
Not in the labor force	18	24	49	57	47	55	68	69	32	39
Family type:										
Two parents	22	27	54	63	51	59	74	72	37	44
None or one parent	18	22	49	56	47	57	65	65	31	36
Poverty status: [2]										
Above threshold	24	29	57	64	53	61	74	75	40	47
Below threshold	12	14	41	49	41	52	64	54	23	26

[1] Excludes children with no mother in the household and no female guardian. [2] Children are considered poor if they lived in households with incomes below the poverty threshold, which is a dollar amount determined by the federal government to meet the household's need, given its size and composition.

Source: U.S. Department of Education, U.S. National Center for Education Statistics, *Home Literacy Activities and Signs of Children's Emerging Literacy,* 1993, NCES 2000-026, November 1999; and the Early Childhood Program Participation Survey, National Household Education Surveys Program, 2005, unpublished data. See Internet site <http://nces.ed.gov/nhes>.

U.S. Census Bureau, Statistical Abstract of the United States: 2009

Table 230. **Public Charter and Traditional Schools—Selected Characteristics: 2005–2006**

[**(44,259 represents 44,259,000.)** A public charter school is a public school that, in accordance with an enabling state statute, has been granted a charter exempting it from selected state and local rules and regulations. Schools open as public charter schools during 2004–05 and still open in the 2005–06 school year were surveyed]

Characteristic	All schools		Elementary		Secondary		Combined	
	Tradi-tional	Public charter	Tradi-tional	Public charter	Tradi-tional	Public charter	Tradi-tional	Public charter
Number of schools................	80,243	3,690	56,929	1,953	19,247	1,038	4,067	699
Enrollment (1,000)..............	44,259	1,013	28,300	531	14,763	220	1,195	261
PERCENT DISTRIBUTION OF STUDENTS								
Race/ethnicity..................	100.0	100.0	100.0	100.0	100.0	100.0	100.0	100.0
White, non-Hispanic..............	55.5	40.1	53.6	36.6	58.9	36.8	57.5	49.9
Black, non-Hispanic..............	17.2	31.8	17.5	36.8	16.3	27.4	20.3	25.2
Hispanic [1].....................	20.8	22.1	22.3	21.2	18.1	28.7	16.6	18.4
Asian/Pacific Islander...........	4.7	3.5	4.7	3.6	5.0	3.7	3.0	3.4
American Indian/Alaska Native......	1.1	1.4	1.1	1.0	1.2	2.2	2.2	1.5
Other..........................	0.7	1.1	0.8	0.8	0.5	1.2	0.4	1.6
PERCENT DISTRIBUTION OF SCHOOLS								
Size of enrollment...............	100.0	100.0	100.0	100.0	100.0	100.0	100.0	100.0
Less than 300 students...........	28.3	69.5	23.7	66.2	33.9	80.3	66.3	62.5
300 to 599 students.............	39.1	21.1	46.9	24.3	20.0	14.8	19.3	21.3
600 to 999 students.............	22.0	6.5	24.4	7.9	17.3	2.2	9.9	8.9
1,000 students or more...........	10.7	3.0	5.0	1.6	28.8	2.6	4.6	7.3
Percent minority enrollment.........	100.0	100.0	100.0	100.0	100.0	100.0	100.0	100.0
Less than 10.0..................	26.6	11.8	25.5	10.9	31.2	11.5	21.2	15.0
10.0 to 24.9...................	18.4	17.5	18.5	16.8	18.4	16.7	16.9	20.6
25.0 to 49.9...................	18.9	17.8	18.9	17.2	18.6	16.7	19.7	20.9
50.0 to 74.9...................	13.5	12.6	13.4	10.5	12.7	16.2	17.7	13.2
75.0 or more...................	22.7	40.3	23.7	44.5	19.2	39.0	24.5	30.3
Percent of students eligible for free or reduced-price lunch [2].............	100.0	100.0	100.0	100.0	100.0	100.0	100.0	100.0
Less than 15.0..................	19.0	29.7	17.9	24.4	21.4	34.8	24.2	37.6
15.0 to 29.9...................	17.1	10.5	15.5	10.8	22.9	10.7	11.6	9.5
30.0 to 49.9...................	23.0	14.1	22.0	15.2	27.0	14.4	19.9	10.8
50.0 to 74.9...................	22.9	19.5	24.1	19.8	19.0	20.3	24.6	17.4
75.0 or more...................	17.9	26.1	20.5	29.9	9.7	19.8	19.7	24.7

[1] Persons of Hispanic origin may be of any race.   [2] Excludes data for schools not providing information on eligibility for free or reduced-price lunch.

Source: U.S. National Center for Education Statistics, Common Core of Data, "Public Elementary/Secondary School Universe Survey," 2005–06, unpublished data.

Table 231. **Public Elementary and Secondary Schools by Type and Size of School: 2005–2006**

[**Enrollment in thousands (48,912 represents 48,912,000).** Data reported by schools, rather than school districts. Based on the Common Core of Data Survey; see source for details]

Enrollment size of school	Number of schools					Enrollment [1]				
	Total	Elemen-tary [2]	Second-ary [3]	Com-bined [4]	Other [5]	Total	Elemen-tary [2]	Second-ary [3]	Com-bined [4]	Other [5]
Total	**97,382**	**67,291**	**23,800**	**5,707**	**584**	**48,912**	**31,104**	**16,219**	**1,526**	**63**
PERCENT										
Total	**100.00**	**100.00**	**100.00**	**100.00**	**100.00**	**100.00**	**100.00**	**100.00**	**100.00**	**100.00**
Under 100 students.....	11.03	6.22	18.42	37.01	57.49	0.96	0.65	1.11	5.04	18.57
100 to 199 students	9.63	8.57	10.98	16.33	23.00	2.75	2.74	2.25	7.53	25.47
200 to 299 students	11.47	12.63	8.45	10.30	8.62	5.55	6.76	2.96	7.98	16.67
300 to 399 students	13.58	16.03	7.79	8.32	5.75	9.11	11.86	3.82	9.09	15.48
400 to 499 students	13.16	16.15	6.11	6.86	2.26	11.31	15.28	3.87	9.63	7.58
500 to 599 students	11.00	13.36	5.66	5.25	1.23	11.55	15.44	4.37	9.01	5.22
600 to 699 students	8.14	9.46	5.28	4.42	0.41	10.10	12.91	4.83	9.04	2.15
700 to 799 students	5.63	6.31	4.40	2.77	0.41	8.07	9.95	4.64	6.53	2.50
800 to 999 students	6.58	6.76	6.82	3.54	0.41	11.20	12.63	8.59	9.93	2.77
1,000 to 1,499 students ...	5.89	4.00	11.96	3.40	0.41	13.49	9.82	20.64	12.77	3.58
1,500 to 1,999 students ...	2.08	0.42	7.11	1.00	–	6.86	1.48	17.33	5.37	–
2,000 to 2,999 students ...	1.47	0.09	5.67	0.46	–	6.66	0.45	18.90	3.44	–
3,000 or more students ...	0.35	0.01	1.33	0.33	–	2.39	0.04	6.68	4.64	–
Average enrollment [1].....	521	473	709	318	128	521	473	709	318	128

– Represents zero.   [1] Exclude data for schools not reporting enrollment.   [2] Includes schools beginning with grade 6 or below and with no grade higher than 8.   [3] Includes schools with no grade lower than 7.   [4] Includes schools beginning with grade 6 or below and ending with grade 9 or above.   [5] Includes special education, alternative, and other schools not classified by grade span.

Source: U.S. National Center for Education Statistics, *Digest of Education Statistics*, annual.

Table 232. Public Elementary and Secondary Schools—Summary: 1980 to 2006

[For school year ending in year shown, except as indicated (48,041 represents 48,041,000). Data are estimates]

Item	Unit	1980	1985	1990	1995	2000	2005	2006
School districts, total	Number...	**16,044**	**15,812**	**15,552**	**14,947**	**15,403**	**15,745**	**15,728**
ENROLLMENT								
Population 5–17 years old [1]	1,000	48,041	44,787	44,949	48,855	52,811	53,158	53,132
Percent of resident population	Percent	21.4	19.0	18.2	18.6	18.8	18.1	18.0
Fall enrollment [2]	1,000	41,778	39,354	40,527	43,898	46,577	48,392	48,728
Percent of population 5–17 years old	Percent	87.0	87.9	90.2	89.9	88.2	91.0	91.7
Elementary [3]	1,000	24,397	23,830	26,253	28,148	29,243	29,626	29,707
Secondary [4]	1,000	17,381	15,524	14,274	15,750	17,334	18,766	19,021
Average daily attendance (ADA)	1,000	38,411	36,530	37,573	40,792	43,313	45,121	45,485
High school graduates	1,000	2,762	2,424	2,327	2,282	2,544	2,806	2,844
INSTRUCTIONAL STAFF								
Total [5]	1,000	**2,521**	**2,473**	**2,685**	**2,919**	**3,273**	**3,516**	**3,566**
Classroom teachers	1,000	2,211	2,175	2,362	2,565	2,891	3,077	3,122
Average salaries:								
Instructional staff	Dollar	16,715	24,666	32,638	38,349	43,837	49,425	50,924
Classroom teachers	Dollar	15,970	23,600	31,367	36,675	41,807	47,659	49,026
REVENUES								
Revenue receipts	Mil. dol.	97,635	141,013	208,656	273,255	369,754	477,526	505,490
Federal	Mil. dol.	9,020	9,533	13,184	18,764	26,346	42,909	45,455
State	Mil. dol.	47,929	69,107	100,787	129,958	183,986	225,879	238,948
Local	Mil. dol.	40,686	62,373	94,685	124,533	159,421	208,738	221,087
EXPENDITURES								
Total	Mil. dol.	**96,105**	**139,382**	**209,698**	**276,584**	**374,782**	**495,518**	**521,701**
Current expenditures (day schools)	Mil. dol.	85,661	127,230	186,583	242,995	320,954	421,834	443,415
Other current expenditures [6]	Mil. dol.	1,859	2,109	3,341	5,564	6,618	8,700	9,539
Capital outlay	Mil. dol.	6,504	7,529	16,012	21,646	37,552	48,616	52,952
Interest on school debt	Mil. dol.	2,081	2,514	3,762	6,379	9,659	16,368	15,795
In current dollars:								
Revenue receipts per pupil enrolled	Dollar	2,337	3,583	5,149	6,225	7,939	9,868	10,374
Current expenditures per pupil enrolled	Dollar	2,050	3,233	4,604	5,535	6,891	8,717	9,100
In constant (2006) dollars: [7]								
Revenue receipts per pupil enrolled	Dollar	5,508	6,722	7,848	8,223	9,253	10,121	10,374
Current expenditures per pupil enrolled	Dollar	4,832	6,065	7,018	7,313	8,032	8,940	9,100

[1] Estimated resident population as of July 1 of the previous year, except 1980, 1990, and 2000 population enumerated as of April 1. Estimates reflect revisions based on the 2000 Census of Population. [2] Fall enrollment of the previous year. [3] Kindergarten through grade 6. [4] Grades 7 through 12. [5] Full-time equivalent. [6] Current expenses for summer schools, adult education, post-high school vocational education, personnel retraining, etc., when operated by local school districts and not part of regular public elementary and secondary day-school program. [7] Compiled by U.S. Census Bureau. Deflated by the Consumer Price Index, all urban consumers (for school year July through June) supplied by U.S. National Center for Education Statistics.

Source: Except as noted, National Education Association, Washington, DC, Estimates of School Statistics Database (copyright).

Table 233. Public Elementary and Secondary School Enrollment by Grade: 1980 to 2005

[In thousands (40,877 represents 40,877,000). As of fall of year. Based on survey of state education agencies; see source for details]

Grade	1980	1985	1990	1995	1998	1999	2000	2001	2002	2003	2004	2005
Pupils enrolled [1]	**40,877**	**39,422**	**41,217**	**44,840**	**46,539**	**46,857**	**47,204**	**47,672**	**48,183**	**48,540**	**48,795**	**49,113**
Pre-kindergarten to 8 [1]	27,647	27,034	29,878	32,341	33,346	33,488	33,688	33,938	34,116	34,202	34,178	34,205
Pre-K and Kindergarten	2,689	3,192	3,610	4,173	4,172	4,148	4,158	4,244	4,349	4,453	4,534	4,656
First	2,894	3,239	3,499	3,671	3,727	3,684	3,636	3,614	3,594	3,613	3,663	3,691
Second	2,800	2,941	3,327	3,507	3,681	3,656	3,634	3,593	3,565	3,544	3,560	3,606
Third	2,893	2,895	3,297	3,445	3,696	3,691	3,676	3,653	3,623	3,611	3,580	3,586
Fourth	3,107	2,771	3,248	3,431	3,592	3,686	3,711	3,695	3,669	3,619	3,612	3,578
Fifth	3,130	2,776	3,197	3,438	3,520	3,604	3,707	3,727	3,711	3,685	3,635	3,633
Sixth	3,038	2,789	3,110	3,395	3,497	3,564	3,663	3,769	3,788	3,772	3,735	3,670
Seventh	3,085	2,938	3,067	3,422	3,530	3,541	3,629	3,720	3,821	3,841	3,818	3,777
Eighth	3,086	2,982	2,979	3,356	3,480	3,497	3,538	3,616	3,709	3,809	3,825	3,802
Grades 9 to 12 [1]	13,231	12,388	11,338	12,500	13,193	13,369	13,515	13,734	14,067	14,338	14,617	14,909
Ninth	3,377	3,439	3,169	3,704	3,856	3,935	3,963	4,012	4,105	4,190	4,281	4,287
Tenth	3,368	3,230	2,896	3,237	3,382	3,415	3,491	3,528	3,584	3,675	3,750	3,866
Eleventh	3,195	2,866	2,612	2,826	3,021	3,034	3,083	3,174	3,229	3,277	3,369	3,455
Twelfth	2,925	2,550	2,381	2,487	2,722	2,782	2,803	2,863	2,990	3,046	3,094	3,180

[1] Includes unclassified students not shown separately.

Source: U.S. National Center for Education Statistics, *Digest of Education Statistics*, annual.

U.S. Census Bureau, Statistical Abstract of the United States: 2009

Table 234. Public Elementary and Secondary Schools and Enrollment—States: 2005–2006

[**For schools with membership (48,912 represents 48,912,000).** Based on the Common Core of Data Program; see source for details]

State	Total number of schools with member-ship	Total number of students (1,000)	Type of school							
			Regular		Special education [1]		Vocational education [2]		Alternative education [3]	
			Number of schools	Percent of students	Number of schools	Percent of students	Number of schools	Percent of students	Number of schools	Percent of students
Total	**93,845**	**48,912**	**86,792**	**98.0**	**1,673**	**0.5**	**385**	**0.4**	**4,995**	**1.1**
Alabama	1,377	742	1,344	99.7	13	0.1	2	(Z)	18	0.2
Alaska.........	499	133	447	90.5	3	0.4	1	0.2	48	8.9
Arizona	2,024	1,094	1,846	93.1	8	(Z)	115	5.8	55	1.1
Arkansas	1,111	474	1,099	99.8	5	(Z)	–	–	7	0.2
California	9,553	6,312	8,224	97.0	126	0.5	–	–	1,203	2.5
Colorado	1,703	780	1,613	98.2	8	0.1	5	0.1	77	1.6
Connecticut	1,098	575	1,015	97.2	31	0.6	17	1.8	35	0.5
Delaware	200	121	173	92.8	13	1.3	5	4.8	9	1.1
District of Columbia	229	77	203	93.1	15	4.3	1	0.4	10	2.2
Florida.........	3,589	2,675	3,011	97.7	124	0.5	22	0.1	432	1.6
Georgia	2,100	1,598	2,067	99.6	8	0.1	–	–	25	0.4
Hawaii.........	284	185	280	99.8	3	0.1	–	–	1	0.1
Idaho..........	677	262	603	98.2	4	0.1	–	–	70	1.8
Illinois	4,232	2,112	3,899	98.3	218	1.3	–	–	115	0.4
Indiana	1,917	1,035	1,864	99.6	26	0.2	–	–	27	0.2
Iowa	1,504	481	1,421	99.0	9	0.2	–	–	74	0.8
Kansas	1,406	466	1,406	100.0	–	–	–	–	–	–
Kentucky	1,357	642	1,212	98.8	8	0.1	–	–	137	1.1
Louisiana	1,367	654	1,231	97.7	39	0.2	–	–	97	2.1
Maine	650	195	646	100.0	4	(Z)	–	–	–	–
Maryland	1,386	860	1,282	97.0	44	0.8	10	1.0	50	1.2
Massachusetts ...	1,875	972	1,818	96.3	1	(Z)	39	3.4	17	0.2
Michigan	3,872	1,712	3,444	97.0	157	1.2	14	0.1	257	1.7
Minnesota	2,239	839	1,631	96.4	252	1.5	1	(Z)	355	2.1
Mississippi	896	495	896	100.0	–	–	–	–	–	–
Missouri........	2,261	916	2,190	99.6	11	0.2	–	–	60	0.2
Montana	840	145	834	99.9	2	(Z)	–	–	4	0.1
Nebraska.......	1,163	287	1,131	99.4	32	0.6	–	–	–	–
Nevada	552	412	519	98.8	1	(Z)	1	(Z)	31	1.1
New Hampshire...	480	206	480	100.0	–	–	–	–	–	–
New Jersey	2,466	1,396	2,332	97.7	78	0.7	56	1.6	–	–
New Mexico	854	327	784	98.0	14	0.3	3	0.2	53	1.5
New York	4,654	2,838	4,374	96.5	151	1.7	30	1.4	99	0.4
North Carolina....	2,336	1,416	2,241	99.5	22	0.2	2	(Z)	71	0.4
North Dakota	498	98	498	100.0	–	–	–	–	–	–
Ohio	3,866	1,837	3,846	99.9	10	0.1	8	(Z)	2	(Z)
Oklahoma	1,788	635	1,788	100.0	–	–	–	–	–	–
Oregon	1,236	535	1,204	99.4	2	(Z)	–	–	30	0.6
Pennsylvania	3,184	1,828	3,141	98.2	14	0.9	19	0.9	10	(Z)
Rhode Island	328	152	310	97.3	3	0.1	4	1.2	11	1.4
South Carolina ...	1,119	702	1,091	99.2	9	0.1	7	0.4	12	0.3
South Dakota	713	122	689	99.2	3	0.1	–	–	21	0.8
Tennessee	1,676	954	1,628	99.3	16	0.2	10	0.3	22	0.2
Texas	7,997	4,524	7,036	98.4	–	–	–	–	961	1.6
Utah	922	508	773	97.9	42	0.8	3	(Z)	104	1.2
Vermont........	354	97	316	97.9	36	2.0	–	–	2	(Z)
Virginia	1,862	1,214	1,838	99.7	5	(Z)	–	–	19	0.2
Washington	2,213	1,032	1,861	96.1	92	0.4	6	0.2	254	3.3
West Virginia	747	281	713	99.5	7	0.1	2	(Z)	25	0.4
Wisconsin.......	2,218	875	2,154	99.5	4	(Z)	2	(Z)	58	0.4
Wyoming	373	84	346	98.4	–	–	–	–	27	1.6

– Represents zero.   Z Less than 0.05 percent.   [1] Focuses on special education with materials and instructional approaches adapted to meet the students' needs.   [2] Focuses on vocational, technical, or career education and provides education and training in at least one semi-skilled or technical occupation.   [3] Addresses the needs of students that typically cannot be met in the regular school setting and provides nontraditional education.

Source: U.S. National Center for Education Statistics, *Numbers and Types of Public Elementary and Secondary Schools From the Common Core of Data: School Year 2005–06,*" NCES 2007-354rev, July 2007.

Table 235. **Selected Statistics for the Largest Public School Districts: 2005–2006**

[**For the 50 largest districts by enrollment size.** Based on reports from state education agencies in the spring 2006. Data from the Common Core Data Program; see source for details. School district boundaries are not necessarily the same as city or county boundaries]

School district	City	County	Number of students [1]	Number of full-time equiv- alent (FTE) teachers	Number of 2004–05 complet- ers [2]	Number of schools
New York City Public Schools, NY	New York	New York	1,014,058	70,889	41,322	1,408
Los Angeles Unified, CA	Los Angeles	Los Angeles	727,319	34,961	29,741	808
Puerto Rico Department of Education, PR	San Juan	San Juan	563,490	42,036	30,371	1,523
City of Chicago, IL	Chicago	Cook	420,982	27,039	16,866	633
Dade County, FL	Miami	Miami-Dade	362,070	20,606	18,702	394
Clark County, NV	Las Vegas	Clark	294,131	14,862	10,314	314
Broward County, FL	Fort Lauderdale	Broward	271,630	15,717	14,436	285
Houston Independent School District, TX	Houston	Harris	210,292	12,082	8,476	312
Hillsborough County, FL	Tampa	Hillsborough	193,757	10,924	9,614	261
Philadelphia City School District, PA	Philadelphia	Philadelphia	184,560	10,060	10,819	270
Hawaii Department of Education, HI	Honolulu	Honolulu	182,818	11,226	11,014	285
Orange County, FL	Orlando	Orange	175,609	10,737	9,434	211
Palm Beach County, FL	West Palm Beach	Palm Beach	174,935	10,084	9,523	236
Fairfax County, VA	Falls Church	Fairfax	163,753	13,090	11,570	207
Dallas Independent School District, TX	Dallas	Dallas	161,244	10,324	6,832	255
Gwinnett County, GA	Lawrenceville	Gwinnett	144,598	9,801	7,045	122
Montgomery County, MD	Rockville	Montgomery	139,398	9,371	9,351	199
Prince George's County Public Schools, MD	Upper Marlboro	Prince George's	133,325	8,395	7,947	205
Detroit City, MI	Detroit	Wayne	133,255	7,187	5,673	235
San Diego Unified, CA	San Diego	San Diego	132,482	7,332	6,653	219
Duval County, FL	Jacksonville	Duval	126,662	7,526	6,276	182
Charlotte-Mecklenburg, NC	Charlotte	Mecklenburg	124,005	8,616	5,836	142
Wake County, NC	Raleigh	Wake	120,996	8,179	6,659	138
Memphis City School District, TN	Memphis	Shelby	120,275	7,085	5,946	194
Pinellas County, FL	Largo	Pinellas	112,174	6,799	5,949	173
Baltimore County, MD	Baltimore	Baltimore	107,043	7,388	7,238	168
Cobb County, GA	Marietta	Cobb	106,724	7,065	6,354	110
DeKalb County, GA	Decatur	De Kalb	102,310	6,858	5,199	148
Jefferson County, KY	Louisville	Jefferson	98,537	5,780	5,194	172
Albuquerque, NM	Albuquerque	Bernalillo	94,022	6,139	4,650	169
Long Beach Unified, CA	Long Beach	Los Angeles	93,589	4,298	4,956	90
Milwaukee, WI	Milwaukee	Milwaukee	92,395	5,420	3,915	235
Polk County, FL	Bartow	Polk	89,443	6,046	4,380	153
Baltimore City, MD	Baltimore	Baltimore City	87,643	5,666	4,145	197
Jefferson County, CO	Golden	Jefferson	86,332	4,785	5,651	162
Cypress-Fairbanks Independent School District, TX	Houston	Harris	86,256	5,521	4,622	75
Austin Independent School District, TX	Austin	Travis	81,155	5,630	3,746	124
Fulton County, GA	Atlanta	Fulton	81,100	5,634	4,291	95
Fort Worth Independent School District, TX	Fort Worth	Tarrant	80,336	4,794	3,608	147
Fresno Unified, CA	Fresno	Fresno	79,046	3,737	4,022	106
Northside Independent School District, TX	San Antonio	Bexar	78,711	4,867	4,238	95
Jordan, UT	Sandy	Salt Lake	77,110	3,120	4,922	92
Lee County School District, FL	Fort Myers	Lee	75,634	4,322	3,728	101
Brevard County, FL	Viera	Brevard	75,233	4,489	4,493	117
Mesa Unified District, AZ	Mesa	Maricopa	74,626	3,805	4,391	89
Virginia Beach City Public Schools, VA	Virginia Beach	Va. Beach City	74,303	5,647	4,778	88
Anne Arundel County, MD	Annapolis	Anne Arundel	73,565	4,754	4,861	121
Nashville-Davidson, TN	Nashville	Davidson	72,713	4,951	3,390	132
Denver County, CO	Denver	Denver	72,312	3,974	2,849	148
Guilford County Schools, NC	Greensboro	Guilford	68,951	4,621	4,087	111

[1] Number of students receiving educational services from the school district.   [2] Includes high school diploma recipients and other completers (for example certificates of attendance) but does not include high school equivalents (GEDs).

Source: U.S. Department of Education, National Center for Education Statistics, Common Core of Data (CCD), "Local Education Agency Universe Survey," 2005–06, Version 1a.

Education 153

Table 236. Public Elementary and Secondary School Enrollment by State: 1980 to 2005

[In thousands (27,647 represents 27,647,000), except rate. As of fall. Includes unclassified students. Based on survey of state education agencies; see source for details]

State	Enrollment								Enrollment rate [2]			
	Prekindergarten through grade 8 [1]				Grades 9 through 12 [1]							
	1980	1990	2000	2005, est.	1980	1990	2000	2005, est.	1980	1990	2000	2005, est.
United States. . . .	**27,647**	**29,878**	**33,688**	**34,205**	**13,231**	**11,338**	**13,515**	**14,909**	**86.2**	**91.2**	**88.8**	**92.4**
Alabama	528	527	539	529	231	195	201	212	87.6	93.2	89.6	93.5
Alaska	60	85	94	91	26	29	39	42	94.0	97.4	93.4	96.9
Arizona	357	479	641	740	157	161	237	355	88.9	93.3	88.4	97.7
Arkansas	310	314	318	336	138	123	132	138	90.3	95.8	90.2	97.1
California	2,730	3,615	4,408	4,466	1,347	1,336	1,733	1,971	87.1	92.6	90.5	91.8
Colorado	374	420	517	550	172	154	208	230	92.2	94.6	89.7	92.8
Connecticut	364	347	406	400	168	122	156	175	83.3	90.2	90.7	92.2
Delaware	62	73	81	85	37	27	34	36	79.5	87.2	80.3	86.1
District of Columbia . .	71	61	54	56	29	19	15	21	91.8	100.6	84.0	103.2
Florida	1,042	1,370	1,760	1,873	468	492	675	802	84.4	92.6	89.7	90.7
Georgia	742	849	1,060	1,145	327	303	385	453	86.8	93.7	91.4	95.7
Hawaii	110	123	132	127	55	49	52	55	83.4	87.4	84.8	87.3
Idaho	144	160	170	183	59	61	75	79	95.4	96.9	90.3	97.7
Illinois	1,335	1,310	1,474	1,480	649	512	575	631	82.6	86.9	86.4	90.1
Indiana	708	676	703	724	347	279	286	311	88.0	90.4	85.8	88.3
Iowa	351	345	334	326	183	139	161	157	88.4	92.1	91.3	98.7
Kansas	283	320	323	320	133	117	147	147	88.7	92.5	90.0	96.1
Kentucky	464	459	471	487	206	177	194	192	83.7	90.5	91.4	95.7
Louisiana	544	586	547	482	234	199	197	172	80.2	88.1	82.6	79.3
Maine	153	155	146	133	70	60	61	62	91.6	96.5	90.3	93.2
Maryland	493	527	609	589	258	188	244	271	83.9	89.1	84.9	84.2
Massachusetts	676	604	703	675	346	230	273	297	88.6	88.8	88.5	91.6
Michigan	1,227	1,145	1,222	1,191	570	440	498	551	86.9	90.3	89.5	92.9
Minnesota	482	546	578	558	272	211	277	281	87.2	91.3	89.5	93.9
Mississippi	330	372	364	358	147	131	134	137	79.6	91.3	87.5	92.2
Missouri	567	588	645	635	277	228	268	283	83.8	86.5	86.5	91.5
Montana	106	111	105	98	50	42	50	48	92.9	94.1	89.1	96.0
Nebraska	189	198	195	195	91	76	91	92	86.6	88.7	86.2	93.0
Nevada	101	150	251	296	49	51	90	116	93.4	98.6	91.8	92.2
New Hampshire	112	126	147	139	55	46	61	67	85.3	89.1	89.1	89.3
New Jersey	820	784	968	971	426	306	346	425	81.5	85.9	85.9	88.3
New Mexico	186	208	225	230	85	94	95	97	89.5	94.4	85.0	92.0
New York	1,838	1,828	2,029	1,909	1,033	770	853	906	80.8	86.6	83.6	85.4
North Carolina	786	783	945	1,003	343	304	348	413	90.1	94.8	90.4	92.3
North Dakota	77	85	72	66	40	33	37	33	85.9	92.6	90.9	98.5
Ohio	1,312	1,258	1,294	1,261	645	514	541	578	84.8	88.0	86.1	90.7
Oklahoma	399	425	445	457	179	154	178	178	92.9	95.1	95.4	104.2
Oregon	319	340	379	380	145	132	167	173	88.5	90.6	87.5	88.4
Pennsylvania	1,231	1,172	1,258	1,228	678	496	556	603	80.4	83.5	82.8	87.5
Rhode Island	98	102	114	104	51	37	44	50	80.1	87.5	85.6	84.7
South Carolina	426	452	493	498	193	170	184	204	88.1	93.9	90.9	94.1
South Dakota	86	95	88	84	42	34	41	38	87.4	89.9	85.3	89.7
Tennessee	602	598	668	677	252	226	241	277	87.8	93.5	88.8	95.1
Texas	2,049	2,511	2,943	3,268	851	872	1,117	1,257	92.4	98.4	94.9	101.6
Utah	250	325	333	358	93	122	148	151	98.2	97.8	94.5	100.2
Vermont	66	71	70	65	29	25	32	32	87.9	94.3	90.5	95.8
Virginia	703	728	816	841	307	270	329	373	90.7	94.2	89.5	92.6
Washington	515	613	694	699	242	227	310	333	91.7	94.1	89.8	94.7
West Virginia	270	224	201	197	113	98	85	84	92.6	95.7	95.6	100.1
Wisconsin	528	566	595	584	303	232	285	291	82.1	86.1	86.0	91.5
Wyoming	70	71	60	57	28	27	30	27	97.3	97.7	92.7	101.4

[1] Includes unclassified.   [2] Percent of persons 5–17 years old. Based on enumerated resident population as of April 1, 1980, and 1990, and estimated resident population as of July 1 for 2000 and 2005.

Source: U.S. National Center for Education Statistics, *Digest of Education Statistics*, annual.

U.S. Census Bureau, Statistical Abstract of the United States: 2009

Table 237. Public Schools Reporting Incidents of Crime, by Incident Type and Selected School Characteristic: 2005–06

[For school year. Includes incidents that happen in school buildings, on school grounds, on school buses, and at places that hold school-sponsored events or activities. Based on sample; see source for details]

School characteristic	Total number of schools	Percent of schools with—				Rate per 1,000 students			
		Violent incidents [1]	Serious violent incidents [2]	Theft [3]	Other incidents [4]	Violent incidents [1]	Serious violent incidents [2]	Theft [3]	Other incidents [4]
All public schools	**83,200**	**78**	**17**	**46**	**68**	**31.2**	**1.2**	**5.1**	**9.6**
Level: [5]									
Primary.	48,600	67	11	28	55	25.2	0.9	1.6	4.7
Middle.	15,500	94	25	69	88	51.6	1.9	7.8	11.9
High school	11,700	95	32	86	94	25.7	1.4	8.7	15.7
Combined	7,400	84	17	55	75	29.2	1.1	7.0	12.8
Enrollment size:									
Less than 300	20,800	64	11	30	53	34.5	2.8	(S)	12.3
300 to 499.	23,800	77	12	37	63	34.0	0.7	3.3	6.7
500 to 999.	29,300	82	19	52	74	30.9	1.1	4.5	7.7
1,000 or more	9,300	96	37	86	95	28.6	1.3	7.2	13.4
Percent minority enrollment: [6]									
Less than 5 percent	16,600	72	13	43	62	26.9	0.9	4.8	8.6
5 to 20 percent.	20,600	74	16	43	63	22.9	0.9	5.2	9.3
20 to 50 percent.	18,600	80	17	48	71	28.4	1.4	5.5	9.6
50 percent or more	25,600	83	22	48	72	39.9	1.5	4.8	10.1

S Figure does not meet publication standards. [1] Violent incidents include rape, sexual battery other than rape, physical attack or fight with or without a weapon, threat of physical attack with or without a weapon, and robbery with or without a weapon. [2] Serious violent incidents include rape, sexual battery other than rape, physical attack or fight with a weapon, threat of physical attack with a weapon, and robbery with or without a weapon. [3] Theft or larceny (taking things worth over $10 without personal confrontation). Includes pocket picking, stealing purse or backpack (if left unattended or no force was used to take from owner), theft from motor vehicles, etc. [4] Other incidents include possession of a firearm or explosive device, possession of knife or sharp object, distribution of illegal drugs, possession or use of alcohol or illegal drugs, and vandalism. [5] Primary schools are defined as schools in which the lowest grade is not higher than grade 3 and the highest grade is not higher than grade 8. Middle schools are defined as schools in which the lowest grade is not lower than grade 4 and the highest grade is not higher than grade 9. High schools are defined as schools in which the lowest grade is not lower than grade 9 and the highest grade is not higher than grade 12. Combined schools include all other combination of grades, including K–12 schools. [6] These estimates exclude data from Tennessee because schools in this state did not report estimates of student race.

Source: U.S. National Center for Education Statistics, *Crime, Violence, Discipline, and Safety in U.S. Public Schools 2005–06*, NCES 2007-361, September 2007.

Table 238. Percent of Public Schools Reporting Selected Types of Disciplinary Problems Occurring at School, by Selected School Characteristic: 2005–06

[In percent. For school year. "At school" includes activities that happen in school buildings, on school grounds, on school buses, and at places that hold school-sponsored events or activities. Based on sample; see source for details]

School characteristic	Happens daily or at least once a day						Happens at all	
	Student racial tensions	Student bullying	Student sexual harassment of other students [1]	Student verbal abuse of teachers	Wide-spread disorder in class-rooms	Student acts of disrespect for teachers	Undesirable gang activities [2]	Undesirable cult or extremist group activities [3]
All public schools.	**2.8**	**24.5**	**3.5**	**9.5**	**2.3**	**18.3**	**16.8**	**3.6**
Level: [4]								
Primary.	1.5	20.6	1.6	6.1	[5]0.8	12.1	7.6	[5]1.1
Middle	6.0	43.0	8.6	16.0	5.2	30.5	31.5	5.0
High school	5.0	22.3	6.2	17.3	4.8	30.4	38.7	11.0
Combined	(S)	14.5	(S)	[5]5.6	(S)	14.3	12.4	[5]5.8
Enrollment size:								
Less than 300	(S)	19.4	[5]2.3	5.9	[5]1.5	12.1	7.5	[5]2.4
300 to 499	2.5	21.9	2.4	8.3	[5]1.6	14.2	9.4	[5]2.3
500 to 999	3.2	28.5	4.1	9.5	2.7	20.7	18.9	2.9
1,000 or more . . . . [6]	6.4	29.9	7.4	20.4	4.9	34.8	50.9	12.1
Percent minority enrollment: [6]								
Less than 5 percent	[5]0.6	20.5	2.2	2.7	[5]0.8	11.0	7.4	[5]1.1
5 to 20 percent	1.9	23.4	4.3	6.1	0.8	12.9	7.8	2.9
20 to 50 percent.	5.1	23.3	3.1	12.0	2.1	21.4	19.6	5.9
50 percent or more	3.4	28.9	3.6	15.3	4.8	25.2	31.6	3.8

S Figure does not meet publication standards. [1] Sexual harassment includes "unsolicited, offensive behavior that inappropriately asserts sexuality over another person. This behavior may be verbal or nonverbal." [2] Gang includes an "ongoing loosely organized association of three or more persons, whether formal or informal, that has a common name, signs, symbols, or colors, whose members engage, either individually or collectively, in violent or other forms of illegal behavior." [3] Cult or extremist group includes "a group that espouses radical beliefs and practices, which may include a religious component, that are widely seen as threatening the basic values and cultural norms of society at large." [4] Primary schools are defined as schools in which the lowest grade is not higher than grade 3 and the highest grade is not higher than grade 8. Middle schools are defined as schools in which the lowest grade level is not lower than grade 4 and the highest grade is not higher than grade 9. High schools are defined as schools in which the lowest grade is not lower than grade 9 and the highest grade is not higher than grade 12. Combined schools include all other combinations of grades, including K–12 schools. [5] Intepret data with caution. [6] These estimates exclude data from Tennessee because schools in this state did not report estimates of student race.

Source: U.S. National Center for Education Statistics, *Crime, Violence, Discipline, and Safety in U.S. Public Schools 2005–06*, NCES 2007-361, September 2007.

Table 239. Students Who Reported Carrying a Weapon: 1995 to 2005

[In percent. For students in grades 9 to 12. Percentages are based on students who reported carrying a weapon at least one day during the previous thirty days. Weapons are such things as guns, knives, and clubs. Based on the Youth Risk Behavior Surveillance System. See source for details. See also <http://www.cdc.gov/HealthyYouth/yrbs/index.htm>]

Student Characteristic	Anywhere					On school property				
	1995	1999	2001	2003	2005	1995	1999	2001	2003	2005
Total.	20.0	17.3	17.4	17.1	18.5	9.8	6.9	6.4	6.1	6.5
Sex:										
Male	31.1	28.6	29.3	26.9	29.8	14.3	11.0	10.2	8.9	10.2
Female.	8.3	6.0	6.2	6.7	7.1	4.9	2.8	2.9	3.1	2.6
Race/ethnicity:										
White, non-Hispanic	18.9	16.4	17.9	16.7	18.7	9.0	6.4	6.1	5.5	6.1
Black, non-Hispanic	21.8	17.2	15.2	17.3	16.4	10.3	5.0	6.3	6.9	5.1
Hispanic [2]	24.7	18.7	16.5	16.5	19.0	14.1	7.9	6.4	6.0	8.2
Asian, non-Hispanic	[1]	13.0	10.6	11.6	7.0	[1]	6.5	7.2	[3]6.6	[3]2.8
American Indian, non-Hispanic . . .	32.0	21.8	31.2	29.3	25.6	[3]13.0	[3]11.6	16.4	12.9	7.2
Pacific Islander, non-Hispanic. . . .	[1]	25.3	17.4	[3]16.3	[3]20.0	[1]	9.3	[3]10.0	[3]4.9	[3]15.4
More than one race	[1]	22.2	25.2	29.8	26.7	[1]	11.4	13.2	[3]13.3	11.9
Grade:										
9th.	22.6	17.6	19.8	18.0	19.9	10.7	7.2	6.7	5.3	6.4
10th.	21.1	18.7	16.7	15.9	19.4	10.4	6.6	6.7	6.0	6.9
11th.	20.3	16.1	16.8	18.2	17.1	10.2	7.0	6.1	6.6	5.9
12th.	16.1	15.9	15.1	15.5	16.9	7.6	6.2	6.1	6.4	6.7

[1] The response categories for race/ethnicity changed in 1999 making comparisons of some categories with earlier years problematic.   [2] Persons of Hispanic origin may be of any race.   [3] Data should be interpreted with caution.

Source: U.S. Department of Education, National Center for Education Statistics and U.S. Department of Justice, Bureau of Justice Statistics, *Indicators of School Crime and Safety: 2006,* December 2006, NCES 2007-003. See also <http://nces.ed.gov/surveys/ssocs>.

Table 240. Public Schools Using Selected Safety and Security Measures, by School Characteristics: 2000 to 2006

[In percent. For school year ending in year shown. Based on survey of principals or persons knowledgeable about discipline issues at the school. Refers only to those times during normal school hours or when school activities or events were in session. Based on the School Survey on Crime and Safety and subject to sampling error; for details see source]

Measure	2000	2004	2006
Controlled access during school hours:			
Buildings (locked or monitored doors).	74.6	83.0	84.9
Grounds (locked or monitored gates)	33.7	36.2	41.1
Closed the campus for most students during lunch	64.6	66.0	66.1
Drug testing:			
Any students	4.1	5.3	(NA)
Athletes	(NA)	4.2	5.0
Students in extracurricular activities other than athletes . . .	(NA)	2.6	3.4
Any other students	(NA)	(NA)	3.0
Prohibited all tobacco use on school grounds.	90.1	88.8	90.3
Required to wear badges or picture IDs:			
Students.	3.9	6.4	6.1
Faculty and staff.	25.4	48.0	47.8
Metal detector checks on students:			
Random checks [1]	7.2	5.6	4.9
Require to pass through daily	0.9	1.1	1.1
Sweeps and technology:			
Random dog sniffs to check for drugs [1]	20.6	21.3	23.0
Random sweeps for contraband [1,2]	11.8	12.8	13.1
Use security cameras to monitor school [1]	19.4	36.0	42.8
Provided telephones in most classrooms.	44.6	60.8	66.8
Provided two-way radios	(NA)	71.2	70.8
Visitor requirements:			
Sign-in or check-in	96.6	98.3	97.6
Pass through metal detectors	0.9	0.9	1.0
Dress code:			
Required students to wear uniforms	11.8	13.8	13.8
Enforced a strict dress code	47.4	55.1	55.3
School supplies and equipment:			
Required clear book bags or banned book bags on school grounds.	5.9	6.2	6.4
Provided school lockers to students	46.5	49.5	50.6

NA Not available.   [1] One or more.   [2] For example, drugs or weapons. Does not include dog sniffs.

Source: U.S. Department of Education, National Center for Education Statistics and U.S. Department of Justice, Bureau of Justice Statistics, *Indicators of School Crime and Safety,* 2007, NCES 2008-021. See also <http://nces.ed.gov/surveys/ssocs>.

Table 241. School Enrollment Below Postsecondary—Summary by Sex, Race, and Hispanic Origin: 2006

[In thousands (57,965 represents 57,965,000), except percent and rate. As of October. Covers civilian noninstitutional population enrolled in nursery school through high school. Based on Current Population Survey, see text, Section 1 and Appendix III]

Characteristic	Total			Race and Hispanic origin				
				White [2]				
	Number [1]	Male	Female	Total	Non-Hispanic	Black [2]	Asian [2]	Hispanic [3]
All students	**57,965**	**29,711**	**28,254**	**44,146**	**33,901**	**9,067**	**2,203**	**11,141**
Nursery	4,688	2,422	2,266	3,624	2,769	715	143	911
Full day	2,355	1,231	1,125	1,663	1,206	529	64	484
Part day	2,333	1,191	1,142	1,961	1,562	186	79	427
Kindergarten	4,039	2,094	1,945	3084	2,288	608	162	846
Elementary	32,089	16,418	15,671	24,472	18,622	4,952	1,235	6,394
High school	17,149	8,777	8,372	12,966	10,222	2,792	663	2,990
Students in public schools	50,662	26,030	24,633	38,133	28,486	8,285	1,930	10,470
Nursery	2,519	1,300	1,219	1,815	1,152	513	65	707
Full day	1,380	716	664	920	566	380	29	373
Part day	1,139	584	555	895	587	133	36	334
Kindergarten	3,552	1,840	1,712	2,701	1,940	536	149	798
Elementary	28,975	14,896	14,079	21,923	16,322	4,608	1,105	6,109
High school	15,617	7,994	7,623	11,694	9,072	2,628	611	2,856
Population 15 to 17 years old	12,926	6,574	6,352	9,813	7,827	2,059	476	2,615
Percent below modal grade [4]	30.5	35	25.9	29.9	28.6	35.7	23.0	35.3
Students, 10th to 12th grade	11,604	5,932	5,672	8,924	7,171	1,767	445	1,923
Annual dropout rate	3.5	3.8	3.2	3.5	2.8	3.7	4.2	6.4
Population 18 to 24 years old	28,372	14,300	14,073	22,169	17,565	4,085	1,148	5,006
Percent dropouts	11.0	12.2	9.9	10.8	6.8	13.0	4.0	26.2
Percent high school graduates	82.6	80.5	84.7	83.4	88.0	77.3	91.1	65.9
Percent enrolled in college	37.3	34.1	40.6	37.4	41.0	32.3	57.6	23.6

[1] Includes other races not shown separately.   [2] For persons who selected this race group only. See footnote 2, Table 221.
[3] Persons of Hispanic origin may be of any race.   [4] The modal grade is the grade most common for a given age.

Source: U.S. Census Bureau, Current Population Survey, unpublished data. See Internet site <http://www.census.gov/population/www/socdemo/school.html>.

Table 242. Elementary and Secondary Schools—Teachers, Enrollment, and Pupil-Teacher Ratio: 1970 to 2006

[In thousands (2,292 represents 2,292,000), except ratios. As of fall. Data are for full-time equivalent teachers. Based on surveys of state education agencies and private schools; see source for details]

Year	Teachers			Enrollment			Pupil-teacher ratio		
	Total	Public	Private	Total	Public	Private	Total	Public	Private
1970	2,292	2,059	233	51,257	45,894	5,363	22.4	22.3	23.0
1975	2,453	2,198	255	49,819	44,819	5,000	20.3	20.4	19.6
1980	2,485	2,184	301	46,208	40,877	5,331	18.6	18.7	17.7
1981	2,440	2,127	313	45,544	40,044	5,500	18.7	18.8	17.6
1982	2,458	2,133	325	45,166	39,566	5,600	18.4	18.6	17.2
1983	2,476	2,139	337	44,967	39,252	5,715	18.2	18.4	17.0
1984	2,508	2,168	340	44,908	39,208	5,700	17.9	18.1	16.8
1985	2,549	2,206	343	44,979	39,422	5,557	17.6	17.9	16.2
1986	2,592	2,244	348	45,205	39,753	5,452	17.4	17.7	15.7
1987	2,631	2,279	352	45,487	40,008	5,479	17.3	17.6	15.6
1988	2,668	2,323	345	45,430	40,189	5,242	17.0	17.3	15.2
1989	2,713	2,357	356	45,741	40,543	5,198	17.0	17.2	15.7
1990	2,759	2,398	361	46,451	41,217	5,234	17.0	17.2	15.6
1991	2,797	2,432	365	47,728	42,047	5,681	17.1	17.3	15.6
1992	2,827	2,459	368	48,500	42,823	5,677	17.2	17.4	15.4
1993	2,874	2,504	370	49,133	43,465	5,668	17.1	17.4	15.3
1994	2,925	2,552	373	49,898	44,111	5,787	17.1	17.3	15.5
1995	2,974	2,598	376	50,759	44,840	5,918	17.1	17.3	15.7
1996	3,051	2,667	384	51,544	45,611	5,933	16.9	17.1	15.5
1997	3,138	2,746	391	52,071	46,127	5,944	16.6	16.8	15.2
1998	3,230	2,830	400	52,525	46,539	5,988	16.3	16.4	15.0
1999	3,319	2,911	408	52,876	46,857	6,018	15.9	16.1	14.7
2000	3,366	2,941	424	53,373	47,204	6,169	15.9	16.0	14.5
2001	3,440	3,000	441	53,992	47,672	6,320	15.7	15.9	14.3
2002	3,476	3,034	442	54,403	48,183	6,220	15.7	15.9	14.1
2003	3,490	3,049	441	54,639	48,540	6,099	15.7	15.9	13.8
2004	3,537	3,090	[1]447	54,928	48,795	[1]6,133	15.5	15.8	[1]13.7
2005	3,588	3,137	[1]451	55,224	49,113	[1]6,111	15.4	15.7	[1]13.5
2006 [1]	3,637	3,177	460	55,524	49,370	6,155	15.3	15.5	13.4

[1] Projection.

Source: U.S. National Center for Education Statistics, *Digest of Education Statistics,* annual and *Projections of Educational Statistics.*

U.S. Census Bureau, Statistical Abstract of the United States: 2009

Table 243. Public Elementary and Secondary School Teachers—Selected Characteristics: 2004—2005

[For school year (449 represents 449,000). Based on the 2004–2005 Teacher Follow-up Survey, a component of the School and Staffing Survey, and subject to sampling error; for details, see source Web site at <http://nces.ed.gov/surveys/sass/>. Excludes prekindergarten teachers. See Table 255 for similar data on private school teachers]

Characteristic	Unit	Age				Sex		Race/ethnicity		
		Under 30 years old	30–39 years old	40–49 years old	Over 50 years old	Male	Female	White [1]	Black [1]	Hispanic
Total teachers [2]	1,000 ...	**449**	**769**	**750**	**976**	**723**	**2,220**	**2,502**	**216**	**124**
Highest degree held:										
Bachelor's	Percent..	80.9	57.1	44.9	37.6	2.4	0.7	49.7	53.7	67.9
Master's	Percent..	17.7	38.8	48.8	49.4	51.8	50.9	43.2	38.7	22.1
Education specialist	Percent..	0.6	3.4	5.5	9.6	38.8	42.6	5.5	5.8	7.6
Doctorate	Percent..	(X)	0.3	0.5	1.3	6.5	5.3	0.6	1.2	0.2
Full-time teaching experience:										
Less than 3 years	Percent..	26.2	4.3	2.5	0.8	5.5	6.2	5.7	6.5	9.8
3–9 years	Percent..	73.3	56.7	19.3	8.8	35.9	33.1	31.9	47.3	40.0
10–20 years	Percent..	0.5	39.0	47.5	25.4	26.7	32.1	31.6	20.3	37.8
20 years or more	Percent..	(X)	(X)	30.7	65.0	31.9	28.6	30.9	26.0	12.4
Full-time teachers	1,000 ...	411	706	687	902	687	2,018	2,284	207	120
Earned income	Dollars..	37,510	43,288	48,392	54,577	50,823	46,328	47,710	45,981	45,941
Salary	Dollars..	37,093	42,607	47,662	53,590	49,207	45,865	46,864	45,672	45,646

X Not applicable.   [1] Non-Hispanic.   [2] Includes teachers with no degrees and associate's degrees not shown separately.

Source: U.S. National Center for Education Statistics, "Teacher Follow-up Survey, 2004–05," unpublished data.

Table 244. Public Elementary and Secondary Schools—Number and Average Salary of Classroom Teachers, 1990 to 2006, and by State, 2006

[Estimates for school year ending in June of year shown (2,362 represents 2,362,000). Schools classified by type of organization rather than by grade-group; elementary includes kindergarten]

Year and state	Teachers [1] (1,000)			Avg. salary ($1,000)			Year and state	Teachers [1] (1,000)			Avg. salary ($1,000)		
	Total	Elementary	Secondary	All teachers	Elementary	Secondary		Total	Elementary	Secondary	All teachers	Elementary	Secondary
1990	2,362	1,390	972	31.4	30.8	32.0	MD......	57.7	33.7	24.0	54.3	54.1	54.6
1995	2,565	1,517	1,048	36.7	36.1	37.5	MA......	73.6	29.4	44.2	56.4	56.4	56.4
1998	2,746	1,630	1,116	39.4	39.0	39.9	MI......	103.4	52.3	51.0	54.7	54.7	54.7
1999	2,818	1,669	1,149	40.5	40.2	41.2	MN......	51.4	26.0	25.4	48.5	48.5	48.5
2000	2,891	1,696	1,195	41.8	41.3	42.5	MS......	32.1	19.3	12.8	40.6	40.1	41.3
2001	2,947	1,735	1,213	43.4	42.9	44.1	MO......	66.1	33.9	32.2	40.5	40.5	40.4
2002	2,992	1,751	1,240	44.7	44.2	45.3	MT......	10.3	6.9	3.4	39.8	39.8	39.8
2003	3,021	1,764	1,257	45.7	45.4	46.1	NE......	20.9	13.4	7.5	40.4	40.4	40.4
2004	3,043	1,773	1,269	46.6	46.3	46.7	NV......	21.7	12.6	9.1	44.4	44.0	45.1
2005	3,077	1,790	1,286	47.7	47.2	47.9	NH......	15.5	10.6	4.9	45.3	45.3	45.3
2006, U.S. ..	**3,122**	**1,814**	**1,308**	**49.0**	**48.6**	**49.3**	NJ......	110.9	43.1	67.8	58.2	57.2	59.3
AL.....	49.7	28.3	21.4	40.3	40.0	40.8	NM......	22.0	15.5	6.5	41.6	41.2	42.8
AK.....	8.0	5.4	2.6	53.6	53.6	53.6	NY......	228.9	113.0	115.9	57.4	57.4	57.4
AZ.....	46.4	29.2	17.2	44.7	44.7	44.7	NC......	94.1	66.8	27.3	43.9	43.9	43.9
AR.....	33.5	16.3	17.1	42.8	42.8	42.8	ND......	7.6	5.1	2.5	37.8	38.1	37.1
CA.....	300.2	213.6	86.6	59.8	59.8	59.8	OH......	119.6	81.2	38.3	50.3	50.3	50.3
CO.....	45.8	22.9	22.9	44.4	44.4	44.4	OK......	41.6	20.8	20.9	38.8	38.1	39.5
CT.....	42.8	29.2	13.6	59.3	59.1	60.4	OR......	28.2	18.4	9.8	50.0	49.9	50.3
DE.....	7.7	3.9	3.9	54.3	54.1	54.4	PA......	122.4	61.2	61.2	54.0	54.0	54.0
DC.....	5.0	3.5	1.5	59.0	59.0	59.0	RI......	14.5	9.0	5.5	54.7	54.7	54.7
FL.....	162.8	82.7	80.1	43.3	43.3	43.3	SC......	47.4	33.2	14.2	44.0	40.9	41.8
GA.....	107.8	65.2	42.7	48.3	47.7	49.2	SD......	9.0	6.3	2.7	34.7	34.8	34.5
HI	11.4	6.1	5.3	49.3	49.3	49.3	TN......	60.7	42.8	17.9	42.5	42.1	43.6
ID	14.5	7.5	7.0	41.2	41.2	41.1	TX......	302.4	155.4	147.0	41.7	41.3	42.2
IL	132.1	89.1	43.0	58.7	53.2	61.2	UT......	22.8	12.3	10.5	40.0	40.0	40.0
IN	60.5	32.4	28.0	47.3	48.3	47.2	VT......	9.0	4.6	4.4	46.6	46.6	46.6
IA	35.2	23.0	12.2	41.1	41.2	40.8	VA......	91.8	54.6	37.1	43.8	43.8	43.8
KS.....	32.4	15.9	16.4	41.5	41.5	41.5	WA......	53.6	29.3	24.3	46.3	46.4	46.2
KY.....	40.5	28.8	11.7	42.6	42.4	43.2	WV	19.8	14.2	5.6	38.3	38.1	38.8
LA.....	44.2	31.2	13.0	40.0	40.0	40.0	WI	59.6	40.8	18.8	46.4	46.4	46.4
ME.....	16.0	10.8	5.1	40.7	40.8	40.6	WY	6.6	3.3	3.3	43.3	43.2	43.3

[1] Full-time equivalent.

Source: National Education Association, Washington, DC, Estimates of School Statistics Database (copyright).

Table 245. Teacher Stayers, Movers, and Leavers, by Sector: 1988–89 and 2004–05

[2,386.5 represents 2,386,500. Data compare the teaching status of teacher between one school year and the prior year. Stayers are teachers who were teaching in the same school in both years. Movers are teachers who were still teaching in the current school year but in a different school. Leavers are teachers who left the teaching profession. Based on the School and Staffing Survey; see source for details]

Characteristic	Public				Private			
	Total[1]	Stayers	Movers	Leavers	Total[1]	Stayers	Movers	Leavers
NUMBER (1,000)								
1988–89	2,386.5	2,065.8	188.4	132.3	311.9	242.5	29.7	39.7
2004–05	3,214.9	2,684.2	261.1	269.6	465.3	374.6	27.6	63.1
PERCENT DISTRIBUTION								
Total, 2004–05	100.0	83.5	8.1	8.4	100.0	80.5	5.9	13.6
Age:								
Less than 30 years old	100.0	76.3	14.7	9.0	100.0	68.1	11.8	20.1
30 to 39 years old	100.0	84.2	9.0	6.8	100.0	80.6	5.2	14.2
40 to 49 years old	100.0	87.6	7.1	5.3	100.0	84.3	5.0	10.7
50 years old or more	100.0	83.7	4.5	11.8	100.0	84.7	3.8	[2]11.5
Sex:								
Male	100.0	83.9	8.3	7.7	100.0	80.5	5.2	14.2
Female	100.0	83.4	8.1	8.6	100.0	80.5	6.1	13.4
Race/ethnicity:								
White, non-Hispanic	100.0	83.9	7.9	8.2	100.0	81.3	5.7	13.0
Black, non-Hispanic	100.0	79.3	9.7	11.0	100.0	67.8	9.2	[2]23.0
Hispanic, single or more than one race	100.0	80.6	10.1	9.3	100.0	70.3	7.6	22.1
Asian, Native Hawaiian, or Other Pacific Islander, non-Hispanic	100.0	81.8	7.9	[2]10.3	100.0	89.7	2.7	7.6
American Indian/Alaska Native, non-Hispanic	100.0	93.1	5.0	1.9	100.0	65.5	[2]18.5	[2]16.0
More than one race, non-Hispanic	100.0	88.1	6.6	[2]5.3	100.0	65.8	[2]13.4	[2]20.8
Full-time teaching experience:								
No full-time teaching experience	100.0	63.3	17.1	19.6	100.0	73.6	4.0	22.3
1 to 3 years' experience	100.0	77.1	14.8	8.1	100.0	71.0	10.1	18.9
4 to 9 years' experience	100.0	82.7	9.4	7.9	100.0	77.2	6.7	16.1
10 to 19 years' experience	100.0	88.2	6.3	5.5	100.0	88.3	3.8	7.8
20 years or more experience	100.0	84.9	3.9	11.2	100.0	89.7	3.3	7.0
Main assignment field:								
Early childhood/general elementary	100.0	84.5	7.4	8.1	100.0	81.1	6.8	12.2
Special education	100.0	78.9	11.1	10.0	100.0	72.2	[2]7.4	20.4
Arts/music	100.0	84.7	9.3	6.0	100.0	77.6	4.4	18.0
English/language arts	100.0	83.2	9.0	7.8	100.0	81.1	5.6	13.3
Mathematics	100.0	84.6	8.6	6.8	100.0	83.8	5.4	10.7
Natural sciences	100.0	88.5	5.6	5.9	100.0	84.0	5.9	10.1
Social sciences	100.0	85.6	6.0	8.4	100.0	81.8	4.8	13.4
Other	100.0	81.3	8.0	10.7	100.0	79.2	5.3	15.5

[1] Total teachers prior school year. [2] Interpret data with caution. The standard error for this estimate is equal to 50 percent.

Source: U.S. National Center for Education Statistics, *Teacher Attrition and Mobility: Results for the 2004–05 Teacher Follow-up Survey* NCES 2007-307, January 2007.

Table 246. Public and Private School Teachers Who Moved to a Different School or Left Teaching, by Reason: 2004–05

[In percent. Movers are teachers who were still teaching in the current school year but had moved to a different school after the 2003–04 school year. Leavers are teachers who left the teaching profession after the 2003–04 school year. Based on the School and Staffing Survey; see source for details]

Reason for moving	Movers		Reason for leaving	Leavers	
	Public	Private		Public	Private
New school is closer to home	26.2	22.8	Changed residence	11.2	17.4
Better safety and benefits	16.5	46.4	Pregnancy or child rearing	18.7	24.6
Higher job security	19.1	33.4	Health	11.8	13.2
Opportunity for a better teaching assignment	38.1	33.1	Retirement	31.4	10.2
Dissatisfaction with workplace conditions at previous school	32.7	21.4	School staffing action[1]	14.6	17.7
			Better salary or benefits	14.2	21.8
Dissatisfaction with support from administrators at previous school	37.2	27.0	To pursue a position other than that of a K–12 teacher	25.3	29.5
Dissatisfaction with changes in job description or responsibilities	18.3	17.5	To take courses to improve career opportunities within the field of education	8.9	9.8
Laid off or involuntarily transferred	18.7	19.2	To take courses to improve career opportunities outside the field of education	5.3	7.3
Did not have enough autonomy over classroom at previous school	10.4	7.6	Dissatisfied with teaching as a career	14.6	10.8
Dissatisfaction with opportunities for professional development at previous school	12.8	19.7	Dissatisfied with previous school or teaching assignment	16.0	18.1
Other dissatisfaction with previous school	31.2	29.7	Other family or personal reasons	20.4	30.6

[1] For example reduction in force, lay-off, school closing, school reorganization, reassignment.

Source: U.S. National Center for Education Statistics, *Teacher Attrition and Mobility: Results for the 2004–05 Teacher Follow-up Survey,* NCES 2007-307, January 2007.

U.S. Census Bureau, Statistical Abstract of the United States: 2009

Table 247. **Average Salary and Wages Paid in Public School Systems: 1985 to 2007**

[**In dollars.** For school year ending in year shown. Data reported by a stratified sample of school systems enrolling 300 or more pupils. Data represent unweighted means of average salaries paid school personnel reported by each school system]

Position	1985	1990	1995	2000	2003	2004	2005	2006	2007
ANNUAL SALARY									
Central-office administrators:									
Superintendent (contract salary)...	56,954	75,425	90,198	112,158	126,268	125,609	128,770	134,436	141,191
Deputy/assoc. superintendent....	52,877	69,623	81,266	97,251	112,104	113,790	116,186	122,078	128,307
Assistant superintendent........	48,003	62,698	75,236	88,913	98,623	100,808	103,212	106,492	111,963
Administrators for—............									
Finance and business........	40,344	52,354	61,323	73,499	81,451	82,269	83,678	86,390	91,718
Instructional services.........	43,452	56,359	66,767	79,023	84,640	84,866	88,950	91,094	95,025
Public relations/information.....	35,287	44,926	53,263	60,655	67,298	70,291	70,502	72,378	77,121
Staff personnel services.......	44,182	56,344	65,819	76,608	85,041	86,333	86,966	90,097	94,761
Technology	(X)	(X)	(X)	(X)	73,931	76,139	76,308	78,249	81,809
Subject area supervisors........	34,422	45,929	54,534	63,103	66,582	67,098	68,714	71,984	75,982
School building administrators:									
Principals:									
Elementary..............	36,452	48,431	58,589	69,407	75,291	75,144	76,182	79,496	82,414
Junior high/middle	39,650	52,163	62,311	73,877	80,708	80,060	81,514	84,685	87,866
Senior high	42,094	55,722	66,596	79,839	86,452	86,160	86,938	90,260	92,965
Assistant principals:									
Elementary..............	30,496	40,916	48,491	56,419	62,230	62,213	63,140	65,770	67,735
Junior high/middle	33,793	44,570	52,942	60,842	67,288	66,360	67,600	70,268	73,020
Senior high	35,491	46,486	55,556	64,811	70,847	70,495	71,401	73,622	75,121
Classroom teachers	23,587	31,278	37,264	42,213	45,026	45,646	45,884	48,160	49,294
Auxiliary professional personnel:									
Counselors.................	27,593	35,979	42,486	48,195	51,706	52,303	52,500	53,744	55,930
Librarians.................	24,981	33,469	40,418	46,732	49,611	50,403	50,720	53,331	54,881
School nurses..............	19,944	26,090	31,066	35,540	39,165	40,201	40,520	41,746	43,277
Secretarial/clerical personnel:									
Central office:									
Secretaries	15,343	20,238	23,935	28,405	31,295	31,830	32,716	34,132	35,629
Accounting/payroll clerks......	15,421	20,088	24,042	28,498	32,154	32,632	33,217	34,812	35,991
Typists/data entry clerks	12,481	16,125	18,674	22,853	25,793	25,318	26,214	26,899	28,940
School building level:									
Secretaries	12,504	16,184	19,170	22,630	24,853	24,964	25,381	26,396	27,398
Library clerks.............	9,911	12,152	14,381	16,509	18,170	18,427	18,443	19,125	19,806
HOURLY WAGE RATE									
Other support personnel:									
Teacher aides:									
Instructional..............	5.89	7.43	8.77	10.00	10.93	11.22	11.35	11.77	12.32
Noninstructional	5.60	7.08	8.29	9.77	10.98	11.08	11.23	11.75	12.19
Custodians...............	6.90	8.54	10.05	11.35	12.40	12.47	12.61	13.20	13.78
Cafeteria workers...........	5.42	6.77	7.89	9.02	9.98	10.18	10.33	10.70	11.16
Bus drivers...............	7.27	9.21	10.69	12.48	13.85	13.79	14.18	14.81	15.48

X Not applicable.

Table 248. **Public School Employment: 1990 and 2006**

[**In thousands (3,181 represents 3,181,000).** Covers all public elementary-secondary school districts with 100 or more full-time employees]

Occupation	1990					2006 [1]				
	Total	Male	Female	White [2]	Black [2]	Total	Male	Female	White [2]	Black [2]
All occupations	**3,181**	**914**	**2,267**	**2,502**	**463**	**4,615**	**1,179**	**3,436**	**3,476**	**606**
Officials, administrators	43	28	15	37	4	64	30	34	51	7
Principals and assistant principals.................	90	56	34	70	13	125	57	68	91	22
Classroom teachers [3]	1,746	468	1,278	1,469	192	2,534	611	1,923	2,070	239
Elementary schools	875	128	747	722	103	1,272	170	1,102	1,031	111
Secondary schools	662	304	358	570	66	957	379	578	791	91
Other professional staff	227	58	170	187	30	383	76	308	305	47
Teachers' aides [4]	324	54	270	208	69	483	60	423	313	92
Clerical, secretarial staff.......	226	5	221	181	24	300	10	290	214	35
Service workers [5]	524	245	279	348	129	726	335	391	431	164

[1] Excludes HI state. [2] Excludes individuals of Hispanic origin. [3] Includes other classroom teachers not shown separately. [4] Includes technicians. [5] Includes craftworkers and laborers.

Table 249. Finances of Public Elementary and Secondary School Systems by Enrollment-Size Group: 2005–2006

[In millions of dollars (521,116 represents $521,116,000,000). Data are based on annual survey. For details, see source. See also Appendix III]

Item	All school systems	School systems with enrollment of—						
		50,000 or more	25,000 to 49,999	15,000 to 24,999	7,500 to 14,999	5,000 to 7,499	3,000 to 4,999	Under 3,000
General revenue	521,116	108,839	64,508	48,670	72,956	47,420	60,765	117,958
From federal sources.	47,101	11,601	6,174	4,181	5,973	3,299	4,403	11,470
Through state	43,529	10,964	5,837	3,943	5,455	3,046	4,124	10,159
Child nutrition programs.	8,913	2,242	1,265	934	1,211	693	904	1,665
Direct	3,572	637	336	238	518	253	278	1,312
From state sources [1]	242,785	48,544	31,212	25,025	34,957	20,926	26,590	55,532
General formula assistance	163,966	29,831	21,158	17,510	24,352	14,299	18,046	38,771
Compensatory programs.	5,873	1,137	1,490	675	818	570	459	725
Special education	15,248	3,794	1,640	1,193	1,886	1,235	1,691	3,807
From local sources	231,230	48,694	27,122	19,464	32,027	23,196	29,773	50,955
Taxes	153,671	25,109	17,845	13,456	22,804	16,800	21,404	36,254
Contributions from parent government	39,189	16,726	3,923	2,391	4,181	3,193	4,079	4,696
From other local governments . . .	5,297	567	772	331	479	433	714	2,000
Current charges	13,737	2,171	1,601	1,292	2,037	1,272	1,648	3,717
School lunch	6,769	977	798	700	1,066	711	904	1,613
Other	19,337	4,121	2,982	1,994	2,525	1,498	1,927	4,289
General expenditure	526,649	111,992	65,993	50,060	73,612	47,654	59,912	117,426
Current spending	451,488	93,831	54,925	42,076	63,200	41,350	52,377	103,729
By function: Instruction	271,843	58,082	33,008	25,368	38,253	25,156	31,655	60,321
Support services	156,003	30,680	18,981	14,346	21,672	14,218	18,143	37,964
Other current spending	23,642	5,069	2,936	2,362	3,274	1,976	2,580	5,444
By object:								
Total salaries and wages	272,654	56,693	34,055	26,216	38,832	25,197	31,637	60,025
Total employee benefits.	88,151	17,981	10,059	8,355	12,760	8,384	10,597	20,015
Other	90,683	19,158	10,811	7,505	11,608	7,769	10,144	23,688
Capital outlay	58,809	14,736	8,919	6,548	7,967	4,690	5,648	10,301
Interest on debt	13,752	3,124	1,995	1,352	1,959	1,221	1,573	2,529
Payments to other governments . . .	2,600	301	154	85	486	393	313	867
Debt outstanding	322,725	73,690	42,808	32,278	45,929	29,413	38,048	60,559
Long-term	312,753	69,555	42,282	31,759	44,723	28,769	37,080	58,586
Short-term.	9,972	4,135	526	519	1,206	644	968	1,974
Long-term debt issued	52,171	12,900	7,024	6,045	7,307	4,792	5,500	8,604
Long-term debt retired.	27,194	4,511	3,245	2,506	4,267	2,879	3,600	6,187

[1] Includes other sources not shown separately.

Source: U.S. Census Bureau, *Public Education Finances, 2006,* April 2008. See Internet site <http://www.census.gov/govs/www /school.html>.

Table 250. Per Pupil Amounts of Finances of Public Elementary and Secondary School Systems by Enrollment-Size Group: 2005–2006

[In dollars, except as indicated (48,381 represents 48,381,000). Data are based on annual survey. For details, see source. See also Appendix III]

Item	All school systems	School systems with enrollment of—						
		50,000 or more	25,000 to 49,999	15,000 to 24,999	7,500 to 14,999	5,000 to 7,499	3,000 to 4,999	Under 3,000
Fall enrollment (1,000)	48,381	9,957	6,456	5,043	7,059	4,369	5,542	9,956
General revenue	10,771	10,931	9,992	9,650	10,335	10,855	10,965	11,848
From federal sources	974	1,165	956	829	846	755	794	1,152
From state sources [1]	5,018	4,876	4,835	4,962	4,952	4,790	4,798	5,578
General formula assistance . . .	3,389	2,996	3,277	3,472	3,450	3,273	3,257	3,894
Special education	315	381	254	237	267	283	305	382
From local sources [1]	4,779	4,891	4,201	3,859	4,537	5,310	5,373	5,118
Taxes	3,176	2,522	2,764	2,668	3,231	3,845	3,863	3,642
Contributions from parent government	810	1,680	608	474	592	731	736	472
Current charges	284	218	248	256	289	291	297	373
School lunch	140	98	124	139	151	163	164	162
General expenditure [1]	10,692	11,003	10,044	9,769	10,263	10,724	10,631	11,592
Current spending	9,138	9,179	8,329	8,186	8,788	9,281	9,271	10,217
By function: Instruction	5,543	5,726	5,041	4,987	5,360	5,667	5,631	5,994
Support services	3,225	3,081	2,940	2,845	3,070	3,254	3,274	3,813
By object:								
Total salaries and wages	5,636	5,694	5,275	5,198	5,501	5,768	5,709	6,029
Total employee benefits	1,822	1,806	1,558	1,657	1,808	1,919	1,912	2,010
Capital outlay	1,216	1,480	1,382	1,298	1,129	1,074	1,019	1,035
Interest on debt	284	314	309	268	278	279	284	254
Debt outstanding.	6,671	7,401	6,631	6,400	6,506	6,733	6,866	6,083
Long-term.	6,464	6,986	6,550	6,297	6,336	6,585	6,691	5,885

[1] Includes other sources of revenue and expenditures not shown separately.

Source: U.S. Census Bureau, *Public Education Finances, 2006,* April 2008. See Internet site <http://www.census.gov/govs/www /school.html>.

Table 251. **Public Elementary and Secondary Estimated Finances, 1980 to 2006, and by State, 2006**

[In millions of dollars (101,724 represents $101,724,000,000), except as noted. For school years **ending in June of year shown**]

Year and state	Receipts						Expenditures				
		Revenue receipts							Current expenditures		
			Source							Average per pupil in ADA[4]	
	Total	Total	Federal	State	Local	Non-revenue receipts[1]	Total[2]	Per capita[3] (dol.)	Elementary and secondary day schools	Amount (dol.)	Rank
1980	101,724	97,635	9,020	47,929	40,686	4,089	96,105	427	85,661	2,230	(X)
1985	146,976	141,013	9,533	69,107	62,373	5,963	139,382	591	127,230	3,483	(X)
1990	218,126	208,656	13,184	100,787	94,685	9,469	209,698	850	186,583	4,966	(X)
1995	288,501	273,255	18,764	129,958	124,533	15,246	276,584	1,051	242,995	5,957	(X)
1999	370,735	345,901	23,583	170,606	151,711	24,835	350,539	1,271	301,380	7,011	(X)
2000	390,861	369,754	26,346	183,986	159,421	21,106	374,782	1,343	320,954	7,410	(X)
2001	426,200	397,255	28,300	198,802	170,152	28,946	404,271	1,437	344,033	7,870	(X)
2002	449,039	416,891	32,213	206,112	178,565	32,148	427,577	1,500	363,551	8,210	(X)
2003	472,194	435,746	36,116	214,019	185,611	36,449	451,421	1,568	385,566	8,651	(X)
2004	489,161	455,063	40,623	215,763	198,677	34,097	469,404	1,616	400,657	8,917	(X)
2005	519,626	477,526	42,909	225,879	208,738	42,101	495,518	1,690	421,834	9,349	(X)
2006, total....	**548,331**	**505,490**	**45,455**	**238,948**	**221,087**	**42,841**	**521,701**	**1,763**	**443,415**	**9,749**	**(X)**
Alabama.......	7,000	6,349	751	3,569	2,029	651	6,540	1,441	5,691	8,004	43
Alaska.......	1,489	1,325	166	842	317	164	1,462	2,184	1,357	11,726	9
Arizona........	8,007	7,979	631	4,114	3,235	28	6,893	1,158	5,641	5,791	50
Arkansas.......	4,392	4,154	483	2,308	1,363	238	4,264	1,538	3,808	9,586	26
California......	73,272	64,401	6,630	39,709	18,062	8,871	68,045	1,891	53,547	8,823	32
Colorado......	8,299	7,275	549	3,100	3,626	1,024	8,341	1,785	6,918	9,555	28
Connecticut....	8,028	8,015	494	3,127	4,394	13	8,025	2,302	7,173	12,936	5
Delaware......	1,785	1,592	145	1,025	421	194	1,778	2,116	1,456	12,770	6
District of Columbia....	868	868	115	–	753	–	1,182	2,031	954	17,152	(X)
Florida	28,208	25,088	2,502	9,796	12,790	3,120	26,832	1,513	20,720	8,305	40
Georgia	16,770	16,050	1,488	6,886	7,676	720	15,563	1,709	13,641	9,176	29
Hawaii	2,740	2,704	224	2,432	48	37	2,029	1,601	1,806	10,696	15
Idaho........	2,290	1,894	203	1,063	629	396	2,043	1,433	1,844	7,475	45
Illinois........	23,688	21,218	1,636	5,831	13,752	2,470	22,590	1,776	19,966	10,477	18
Indiana........	11,996	11,211	771	5,505	4,935	785	11,315	1,808	9,242	9,696	23
Iowa.........	5,003	4,632	316	2,141	2,176	371	4,421	1,496	3,774	8,325	39
Kansas........	5,047	4,644	341	2,641	1,662	403	4,717	1,721	3,912	9,613	25
Kentucky.......	5,910	5,899	710	3,401	1,788	11	5,855	1,404	5,328	9,031	30
Louisiana	8,062	6,776	1,273	2,925	2,578	1,286	6,523	1,451	5,572	8,602	33
Maine........	2,458	2,310	222	941	1,147	148	2,458	1,873	2,247	12,223	8
Maryland.......	10,329	10,046	714	3,875	5,457	283	9,409	1,688	8,403	10,497	17
Massachusetts...	13,875	13,873	754	6,549	6,571	1	14,216	2,211	12,242	13,407	4
Michigan.......	19,597	19,245	1,703	11,903	5,638	352	18,793	1,859	17,209	10,818	14
Minnesota	10,280	9,085	645	6,529	1,910	1,195	10,191	1,993	8,084	10,361	19
Mississippi.....	4,341	4,091	857	2,109	1,126	249	3,945	1,360	3,564	7,503	44
Missouri	9,955	8,870	801	2,937	5,131	1,086	8,236	1,423	7,056	8,518	36
Montana.......	1,359	1,331	163	632	537	28	1,270	1,357	1,216	9,620	24
Nebraska......	2,548	2,527	216	922	1,389	21	2,455	1,400	2,256	8,534	35
Nevada........	4,316	2,930	208	953	1,769	1,386	3,696	1,534	2,792	7,200	48
New Hampshire ..	2,425	2,277	140	956	1,180	148	2,303	1,768	2,098	11,110	13
New Jersey	20,032	20,023	655	7,361	12,007	9	19,938	2,303	19,222	14,149	3
New Mexico.....	3,268	3,116	457	2,219	439	152	3,248	1,695	2,818	9,580	27
New York	41,800	41,346	2,844	18,861	19,641	454	42,895	2,227	38,154	14,568	2
North Carolina ...	11,602	10,597	1,181	6,761	2,655	1,005	11,858	1,366	10,564	8,163	41
North Dakota....	956	932	136	318	478	24	937	1,474	758	8,458	37
Ohio.........	24,259	20,636	1,311	9,580	9,746	3,623	21,237	1,853	18,692	11,316	12
Oklahoma......	5,210	4,865	650	2,482	1,733	345	4,854	1,373	4,406	7,449	47
Oregon.......	5,639	5,514	530	2,736	2,249	125	5,353	1,475	4,837	9,846	22
Pennsylvania....	22,979	22,678	1,840	8,029	12,810	301	22,751	1,840	19,608	11,521	11
Rhode Island	1,588	1,588	53	579	955	–	1,870	1,753	1,788	11,693	10
South Carolina ...	8,585	6,588	688	2,923	2,976	1,998	7,175	1,686	5,815	8,971	31
South Dakota....	1,189	1,102	196	365	540	87	1,088	1,395	955	8,334	38
Tennessee......	7,382	7,021	818	3,165	3,039	361	6,945	1,160	6,558	7,453	46
Texas	44,733	39,942	4,918	13,551	21,472	4,791	42,311	1,852	34,005	8,078	42
Utah.........	3,769	3,339	352	1,807	1,180	430	3,237	1,292	2,591	5,815	49
Vermont	1,353	1,331	102	1,155	74	22	1,316	2,123	1,180	14,836	1
Virginia........	13,697	12,790	925	5,065	6,800	908	14,123	1,869	11,266	10,011	21
Washington	11,166	9,601	878	5,934	2,790	1,565	10,590	1,689	8,224	8,563	34
West Virginia	3,205	2,946	371	1,744	832	259	3,253	1,802	2,766	10,103	20
Wisconsin	10,427	9,727	586	5,087	4,054	700	10,183	1,838	8,721	10,672	16
Wyoming.......	1,156	1,151	116	507	527	5	1,146	2,263	971	12,484	7

– Represents or rounds to zero. X Not applicable. [1] Amount received by local education agencies from the sales of bonds and real property and equipment, loans, and proceeds from insurance adjustments. [2] Includes interest on school debt and other current expenditures not shown separately. [3] Based on U.S. Census Bureau estimated resident population, as of July 1, the previous year, except 1980, 1990, and 2000 population enumerated as of April 1. [4] Average daily attendance.

Source: National Education Association, Washington, DC, Estimates of School Statistics Database (copyright).

Table 252. **Computers for Student Instruction in Elementary and Secondary Schools: 2005–2006**

[**(54,848 represents 54,848,000.)** Market Data Retrieval collects student use computer information in elementary and secondary schools nationwide through a comprehensive annual technology survey that utilizes mail, telephone, and Internet data methods]

Level	Total schools	Total enroll-ment (1,000)	Number of com-puters [1] (1,000)	Stu-dents per com-puter	Schools with a wireless network (per-cent)	Schools with distance learning programs for stu-dents (per-cent) [2]	Schools with lap-top com-puters (per-cent) [3]	Schools with high speed Internet access (per-cent) [4]	Schools with video-stream-ing (per-cent)
U.S. total	**114,749**	**54,848**	**14,165**	**3.9**	**54.2**	**19.1**	**59.7**	**84.3**	**43.4**
Public schools, total	91,977	49,567	12,914	3.8	54.4	20.3	60.0	85.7	45.0
Elementary	53,245	23,805	5,612	4.2	49.1	11.2	55.4	85.0	41.3
Middle/junior high	14,310	9,376	2,503	3.7	61.6	15.6	66.2	85.8	53.2
Senior high	17,282	14,028	4,067	3.4	64.0	43.8	67.9	87.5	50.4
K to 12/other	7,140	2,358	733	3.2	54.7	43.2	61.7	85.9	41.0
Catholic schools, total	7,673	2,481	554	4.5	51.0	7.1	60.3	74.0	29.7
Elementary	6,326	1,797	358	5.0	46.5	3.8	57.9	71.6	27.3
Secondary	1,179	621	179	3.5	67.7	20.8	70.0	83.8	38.8
K to 12/other	168	63	17	3.8	73.1	7.7	65.4	73.1	38.5
Other private schools, total	15,099	2,800	697	4.0	52.1	6.5	50.1	66.4	24.1
Elementary	7,426	1,171	283	4.1	52.9	2.0	51.4	67.6	26.5
Secondary	1,274	265	77	3.4	67.5	18.1	54.2	68.7	24.1
K to 12/other	6,399	1,363	338	4.0	47.1	9.5	47.4	64.2	20.8

[1] Includes estimates for schools not reporting number of computers. [2] Distance learning programs as determined by respondents. [3] For student instruction. [4] Statistics based on responses to those indicating type of Internet connection. High speed includes Internet connection types: T1, T3, and cable modem.

Source: Market Data Retrieval, Shelton, CT, unpublished data (copyright).

Table 253. **Computer and Internet Use by Children and Adolescents: 2003**

[**For persons 5 to 17 years old (53,561 represents 53,561,000). As of September.** Based on the Current Population Survey; see source and Appendix III for details]

User characteristic	Number of chil-dren (1,000)	Percent using computers at school	Percent using computers at home [1]	Home use activity (percent)				
				Word process-ing	Connect to the Internet	E-mail	Complete school assign-ments	Play games
Total	**53,561**	**84.5**	**68.6**	**33.4**	**46.6**	**32.9**	**49.2**	**56.9**
Age: 5 to 7 years old	11,785	72.2	59.3	9.6	23.3	7.7	16.6	51.7
8 to 10 years old	11,849	86.3	66.1	23.5	38.2	19.5	42.7	58.0
11 to 14 years old	17,173	89.0	72.0	42.7	54.8	40.9	61.8	61.0
15 to 17 years old	12,753	87.9	75.0	51.9	64.7	57.7	68.1	55.4
Sex: Male	27,422	84.2	68.0	31.2	45.5	30.2	47.5	57.8
Female	26,139	84.7	69.3	35.6	47.7	35.7	50.9	56.0
Race/ethnicity:								
White alone, non-Hispanic	32,279	86.6	79.6	40.1	56.9	41.1	56.6	67.3
Black alone, non-Hispanic	8,048	82.6	47.2	20.5	28.0	18.6	35.9	39.1
Hispanic	9,503	79.7	48.3	20.2	27.2	17.1	34.4	37.8
Other	3,731	82.1	71.4	35.9	46.4	32.6	50.8	54.7
Parent educational attainment:								
Less than high school credential	10,001	77.9	43.7	17.7	24.2	16.3	29.5	34.6
High school credential	15,270	84.1	61.4	26.9	39.9	28.2	43.7	50.6
Some college	14,384	86.8	75.4	35.5	51.9	35.7	54.1	63.4
Bachelor's degree	9,410	86.9	86.5	47.4	62.9	45.2	63.2	73.0
Graduate education	4,495	87.6	89.5	53.8	67.9	50.5	66.0	73.6
Household language:								
Spanish-only	2,680	75.3	33.6	12.7	14.3	9.0	24.1	26.7
Not Spanish-only	50,881	84.9	70.5	34.4	48.3	34.1	50.5	58.5
Family income:								
Under $20,000	16,459	81.3	51.7	23.1	30.7	21.7	36.2	41.2
$20,000 to $34,999	8,615	81.9	55.7	22.9	33.3	23.2	38.2	45.4
$35,000 to $49,999	6,993	85.9	72.2	33.2	46.7	32.3	50.5	60.5
$50,000 to $74,999	9,053	86.0	80.5	38.6	56.7	39.2	57.6	67.1
$75,000 or more	12,441	88.5	89.3	50.5	69.3	50.1	67.0	76.4

[1] Includes other home activities not shown separately.

Source: U.S. National Center for Education Statistics, CPS October (Education) Supplement, October 2003, special tabulation.

Education 163

Table 254. Private Schools: 2005–2006

[(5,058 represents 5,058,000.) Based on the Private School Survey, conducted every 2 years; see source for details. For composition of regions, see map, inside front cover]

Characteristic	Schools — Number	Schools — Elementary	Schools — Secondary	Schools — Combined	Students (1,000) — Total	Students (1,000) — Elementary	Students (1,000) — Secondary	Students (1,000) — Combined	Teachers (1,000)[1] — Total	Teachers (1,000)[1] — Elementary	Teachers (1,000)[1] — Secondary	Teachers (1,000)[1] — Combined
Total	**28,996**	**16,812**	**2,927**	**9,257**	**5,058**	**2,551**	**859**	**1,647**	**435**	**195**	**71**	**170**
School type:												
Catholic	7,634	6,251	1,079	305	2,246	1,549	598	100	149	97	43	10
Parochial	3,669	3,467	149	54	982	895	66	22	61	55	5	2
Diocesan	2,972	2,386	505	81	896	589	285	22	58	37	19	2
Private	993	398	425	170	368	65	247	56	30	6	18	6
Other religious	14,445	7,269	838	6,338	1,885	707	136	1,041	175	63	14	98
Conservative Christian	5,704	2,054	208	3,441	824	221	34	569	72	19	3	50
Affiliated	3,655	2,249	318	1,089	585	276	58	251	58	26	7	25
Unaffiliated	5,086	2,966	312	1,808	476	210	43	222	45	19	4	23
Nonsectarian	6,916	3,292	1,010	2,615	927	295	126	505	111	35	14	62
Regular	2,770	1,443	387	939	604	174	86	344	67	19	9	39
Special emphasis	2,626	1,643	384	599	218	110	28	80	26	14	4	9
Special education	1,521	206	239	1,077	104	10	12	82	18	2	2	14
Program emphasis:												
Regular elem/sec	23,368	14,298	2,142	6,928	4,570	2,373	789	1,408	374	173	62	138
Montessori	1,477	1,268	(B)	203	90	73	(B)	16	11	9	(B)	1
Special program emphasis	1,231	598	193	440	206	73	38	95	22	8	4	10
Special education	1,742	247	255	1,240	116	12	13	91	20	2	2	16
Vocational/tech	(B)	(B)	(B)	(B)	(B)	(B)	(B)	(B)	(B)	(B)	(B)	(B)
Alternative	1,002	267	315	420	66	14	17	36	8	2	2	4
Early childhood	158	134	(X)	(B)	7	6	(X)	(B)	1	1	(X)	(B)
Size:												
Less than 50	9,520	5,189	793	3,538	236	133	19	85	36	18	4	14
50 to 149	8,277	5,065	609	2,602	763	478	55	230	85	48	7	30
150 to 299	6,202	4,262	476	1,464	1,322	905	104	312	106	64	10	31
300 to 499	2,843	1,678	402	763	1,090	642	155	293	84	43	14	27
500 to 749	1,342	527	330	484	805	308	199	298	59	18	14	27
750 or more	812	90	315	406	842	86	328	429	66	5	21	40
Region:												
Northeast	6,548	3,870	934	1,744	1,203	623	279	301	113	48	26	38
Midwest	7,200	4,893	627	1,679	1,233	770	225	238	94	54	17	23
South	9,224	4,494	651	4,079	1,626	632	174	820	149	54	15	81
West	6,024	3,554	715	1,755	995	526	181	288	79	38	14	27

B Does not meet standard of reliability or precision.   X Not applicable.   [1] Full-time equivalents.

Source: U.S. National Center for Education Statistics, *Characteristics of Private Schools in the United States: Results from the 2005–2006 Private School Universe Survey,* NCES 2008-315, March 2008. See Internet site <http://nces.ed.gov/surveys/pss/>.

Table 255. Private Elementary and Secondary School Teachers— Selected Characteristics: 2004–2005

[For school year (63 represents 63,000). Based on the 2004–2005 Teacher Follow-up Survey, a component of the School and Staffing Survey, and subject to sampling error; for details, see source Web site at <http://nces.ed.gov/surveys/sass/>. Excludes prekindergarten teachers. See Table 243 for similar data on public school teachers]

Characteristic	Unit	Age — Under 30 years old	Age — 30 to 39 years old	Age — 40 to 49 years old	Age — 50 years old and over	Sex — Male	Sex — Female	Race/ethnicity — White[1]	Race/ethnicity — Black[1]	Race/ethnicity — Hispanic
Total teachers[2]	**1,000**	**63**	**91**	**100**	**148**	**90**	**312**	**359**	**13**	**13**
Highest degree held:										
Bachelor's	Percent	78.2	64.4	58.2	49.1	4.4	8.1	58.4	66.4	78.3
Master's	Percent	13.6	22.1	29.2	38.0	55.5	60.5	30.2	13.6	12.6
Education specialist	Percent	(X)	1.1	2.4	4.0	33.3	27.0	2.3	3.7	–
Doctorate	Percent	(X)	2.1	3.1	3.7	1.3	2.6	2.2	–	3.3
Full-time teaching experience:										
Less than 3 years	Percent	24.3	6.7	4.0	1.5	9.6	6.1	6.4	10.4	8.9
3 to 9 years	Percent	75.7	60.4	33.3	12.5	35.4	39.3	38.2	51.2	32.6
10 to 20 years	Percent	(X)	32.8	43.6	25.8	23.4	29.1	28.3	8.1	36.0
20 years or more	Percent	(X)	(X)	19.1	60.2	31.7	25.6	27.1	30.3	22.5
Full-time teachers	1,000	55	73	74	125	68	259	292	12	9
Earned income	Dol.	30,455	33,200	36,413	40,448	42,618	34,577	36,212	29,414	44,844
Salary	Dol.	29,489	32,335	35,325	39,391	40,981	33,737	35,164	28,919	43,414

– Represents or rounds to zero.   X Not applicable.   [1] Non-Hispanic.   [2] Includes teachers with no degrees and associate's degrees not shown separately.

Source: U.S. National Center for Education Statistics, "Teacher Follow-up Survey, 2004–05," unpublished data.

Table 256. Percentage of Students Participating in After-School Activities, by School Activity and Student Characteristics: 2005

[Estimates include all students in kindergarten through eighth grade, not older than 15 years, not homeschooled, participating in weekly after-school activity. Students could participate in multiple activities and are not limited to students who have activities for supervision, therefore percentages may sum to more than 100. Includes participation in school-based or center-based after-school programs and participation in after-school activities that were not part of school- or center-based programs]

Characteristic	Number of students (1,000)	After-school activities						
		Sports	Religious activities or instruction	Arts (e.g., music, dance, painting)	Scouts	Volunteer work or community service	Academic activities (e.g., tutoring, math lab)	Clubs (e.g., yearbook, debate club)
Total.	14,282	73	46	42	22	19	16	13
GRADE								
K to 2.	3,932	72	41	42	26	7	8	5
3 to 5.	5,125	73	45	43	29	16	17	12
6 to 8.	5,225	74	51	42	13	32	21	20
SEX								
Male	7,150	81	44	30	21	17	17	11
Female.	7,131	65	48	55	23	21	15	15
RACE/ETHNICITY								
White, non-Hispanic	9,927	75	47	44	25	20	14	14
Black, non-Hispanic	1,549	59	53	33	14	19	29	9
Hispanic.	1,627	77	40	36	14	15	16	10
Asian or Pacific Islander, non-Hispanic. . .	334	67	29	53	15	16	29	20
Other race, non-Hispanic [1]	844	66	45	53	25	21	15	12
HOUSEHOLD INCOME								
$25,000 or less	1,819	63	49	35	16	16	19	10
$25,001 to $50,000	2,794	62	49	37	21	21	18	13
$50,001 to $75,000	3,450	74	47	41	26	17	15	12
$75,001 to $100,000.	2,327	77	45	45	26	21	16	15
$100,001 or more.	3,892	82	43	49	21	19	14	14

[1] "Other race, non-Hispanic" includes children who were multiracial and not of Hispanic ethnicity, or who were American Indian or Alaska Native, or were not Hispanic, White, Black, Asian, or Pacific Islander.

Source: U.S. National Center for Education Statistics, After-School Programs and Activities Survey of the 2006 National Household Education Surveys Program (ASPA-NHES: 2005); <http://nces.ed.gov/pubs2006/afterschool/tables/table_13.asp?referrer=report>.

Table 257. Percentage of Students Participating in Weekly Nonparental After-School Care Arrangements, by Activities, Arrangement Type, and Student Characteristics: 2005

[Estimates include all students in kindergarten through eighth grade, not older than 15 years, not homeschooled participating in weekly after-school activity. Students could participate in multiple activities and are not limited to students who have activities for supervision, therefore percentages may sum to more than 100]

Characteristic	Number of students (1,000)	After-school activities						
		Homework, educational activities, reading, writing	Computers	Arts (perform or study music, crafts, drama)	Chores, work	Outdoor play, sports	Indoor play	Television, videos, video games, listen to music
Total.	16,005	77	18	24	9	43	30	42
ARRANGEMENT TYPE								
Relative	5,274	81	14	12	9	37	26	61
Nonrelative	1,962	71	2	16	5	52	42	37
School- or center-based	7,065	70	17	38	2	46	32	11
Self-care.	4,267	76	20	10	19	26	13	22
GRADE								
K to 2.	4,839	68	14	32	4	49	43	39
3 to 5.	5,364	83	18	25	7	48	33	37
6 to 8.	5,802	80	21	18	14	35	17	50
SEX								
Male	8,599	75	17	19	8	50	31	45
Female.	7,406	80	18	31	10	36	29	39
RACE/ETHNICITY								
White, non-Hispanic	8,130	73	17	25	8	46	32	42
Black, non-Hispanic	3,324	86	21	20	10	40	28	42
Hispanic.	3,060	81	16	25	8	43	31	43
Asian or Pacific Islander, non-Hispanic. . . .	404	80	24	35	4	40	21	30
Other race, non-Hispanic[1]	1,087	76	14	31	9	40	30	45
HOUSEHOLD INCOME								
$25,000 or less	4,246	79	20	21	9	41	29	47
$25,001 to $50,000	4,100	77	17	25	11	44	30	46
$50,001 to $75,000	3,246	76	17	23	8	44	32	38
$75,001 to $100,000.	2,023	77	17	27	7	41	31	39
$100,001 or more.	2,389	76	17	28	6	47	31	35

[1] Other race, non-Hispanic includes children who were multiracial and not of Hispanic ethnicity, or who were American Indian or Alaska Native, or were not Hispanic, White, Black, Asian, or Pacific Islander.

Source: U.S. National Center for Education Statistics, After-School Programs and Activities Survey of the 2006 National Household Education Surveys Program (ASPA-NHES: 2005); <http://nces.ed.gov/pubs2006/afterschool/tables/table_9.asp?referrer=report>.

U.S. Census Bureau, Statistical Abstract of the United States: 2009

Table 258. SAT Scores and Characteristics of College-Bound Seniors: 1970 to 2007

[**For school year ending in year shown**. Data are for the SAT I: Reasoning Tests. SAT I: Reasoning Test replaced the SAT in March 1994. Scores between the two tests have been equated to the same 200-800 scale and are thus comparable. Scores for 1995 and prior years have been recentered and revised]

Type of test and characteristic	Unit	1970	1975	1980	1985	1990	1995	2000	2005	2006	2007
AVERAGE TEST SCORES [1]											
Critical reading, total [2]	Point	537	512	502	509	500	504	505	508	503	502
Male	Point	536	515	506	514	505	505	507	513	505	504
Female	Point	538	509	498	503	496	502	504	505	502	502
Math, total [2]	Point	512	498	492	500	501	506	514	520	518	515
Male	Point	531	518	515	522	521	525	533	538	536	533
Female	Point	493	479	473	480	483	490	498	504	502	499
Writing	Point	(X)	(X)	(X)	(X)	(X)	(X)	(X)	(X)	497	494
Male	Point	(X)	(X)	(X)	(X)	(X)	(X)	(X)	(X)	491	489
Female	Point	(X)	(X)	(X)	(X)	(X)	(X)	(X)	(X)	502	500
PARTICIPANTS											
Total [3]	1,000	(NA)	996	922	977	1,026	1,068	1,260	1,476	1,466	1,495
Male	Percent	(NA)	49.9	48.2	48.3	47.8	46.4	46.2	46.5	46.4	46.4
White	Percent	(NA)	86.0	82.1	81.0	73.0	69.2	66.4	62.3	62.1	60.8
Black	Percent	(NA)	7.9	9.1	7.5	10.0	10.7	11.2	11.6	11.3	11.7
Obtaining scores [1] of—											
600 or above:											
Critical reading	Percent	(NA)	(NA)	(NA)	(NA)	20.3	21.9	21.1	22.5	21.4	21.2
Math	Percent	(NA)	(NA)	(NA)	(NA)	20.4	23.4	24.2	26.5	25.8	24.5
Writing	Percent	(X)	(X)	(X)	(X)	(X)	(X)	(X)	(X)	18.9	18.4
Below 400:											
Critical reading	Percent	(NA)	(NA)	(NA)	(NA)	17.3	16.4	15.9	15.5	16.6	16.5
Math	Percent	(NA)	(NA)	(NA)	(NA)	15.8	16.0	14.7	13.8	14.3	14.8
Writing	Percent	(X)	(X)	(X)	(X)	(X)	(X)	(X)	(X)	17.8	18.4

NA Not available. X Not applicable. [1] Minimum score 200; maximum score, 800. [2] 1967 and 1970 are estimates based on total number of persons taking SAT. For 2007, based on 1,494,531 test takers. [3] 996 represents 996,000.

Source: Data from "2007 College-Bound Seniors" Copyright © 2007 The College Board, www.collegeboard.com. Reproduced with permission.

Table 259. ACT Program Scores and Characteristics of College-Bound Students: 1970 to 2007

[**For academic year ending in year shown**. Except as indicated, test scores and characteristics of college-bound students. Through 1980, data based on 10 percent sample; thereafter, based on all ACT tested graduating seniors]

Type of test and characteristic	Unit	1970	1975	1980	1985	1990 [1]	1995 [1]	2000 [1]	2005 [1]	2006 [1]	2007 [1]
TEST SCORES [2]											
Composite	Point	19.9	18.6	18.5	18.6	20.6	20.8	21.0	20.9	21.1	21.2
Male	Point	20.3	19.5	19.3	19.4	21.0	21.0	21.2	21.1	21.2	21.2
Female	Point	19.4	17.8	17.9	17.9	20.3	20.7	20.9	20.9	21.0	21.0
English	Point	18.5	17.7	17.9	18.1	20.5	20.2	20.5	20.4	20.6	20.7
Male	Point	17.6	17.1	17.3	17.6	20.1	19.8	20.0	20.0	20.1	20.2
Female	Point	19.4	18.3	18.3	18.6	20.9	20.6	20.9	20.8	21.0	21.0
Math	Point	20.0	17.6	17.4	17.2	19.9	20.2	20.7	20.7	20.8	21.0
Male	Point	21.1	19.3	18.9	18.6	20.7	20.9	21.4	21.3	21.5	21.6
Female	Point	18.8	16.2	16.2	16.0	19.3	19.7	20.2	20.2	20.3	20.4
Reading [3]	Point	19.7	17.4	17.2	17.4	(NA)	21.3	21.4	21.3	21.4	21.5
Male	Point	20.3	18.7	18.2	18.3	(NA)	21.1	21.2	21.0	21.1	21.2
Female	Point	19.0	16.4	16.4	16.6	(NA)	21.4	21.5	21.5	21.6	21.6
Science reasoning [4]	Point	20.8	21.1	21.1	21.2	(NA)	21.0	21.0	20.9	20.9	21.0
Male	Point	21.6	22.4	22.4	22.6	(NA)	21.6	21.6	21.4	21.2	21.4
Female	Point	20.0	20.0	20.0	20.0	(NA)	20.5	20.6	20.5	21.0	20.5
PARTICIPANTS [5]											
Total [6]	1,000	788	714	822	739	817	945	1,065	1,186	1,206	1,301
Male	Percent	52	46	45	46	46	44	43	44	44	45
White	Percent	(NA)	77	83	82	79	75	76	71	70	72
Black	Percent	4	7	8	8	9	10	11	13	13	14
Obtaining composite scores of— [7]											
27 or above	Percent	14	14	13	14	12	13	14	14	14	15
18 or below	Percent	21	33	33	32	35	34	32	34	33	32

NA Not available. [1] Beginning 1990, not comparable with previous years because a new version of the ACT was introduced. Estimated average composite scores for prior years: 1989, 20.6; 1988, 1987, and 1986, 20.8. [2] Minimum score, 1; maximum score, 36. [3] Prior to 1990, social studies; data not comparable with previous years. [4] Prior to 1990, natural sciences; data not comparable with previous years. [5] Beginning 1985, data are for seniors who graduated in year shown and had taken the ACT in their junior or senior years. Data by race are for those responding to the race question. [6] 788 represents 788,000. [7] Prior to 1990, 26 or above and 15 or below.

Source: ACT, Inc., Iowa City, IA, *High School Profile Report*, annual.

Table 260. **Proficiency Levels on Selected NAEP Tests for Students in Public Schools, by State: 2007**

[Represents percent of public school students scoring at or above basic and proficient levels. Basic denotes mastery of the knowledge and skills that are fundamental for proficient work at a given grade level. Proficient represents solid academic performance. Students reaching this level demonstrated competency over challenging subject matter. For more detail see <http://www.nagb.org /pubs/pubs.html>. Based on the National Assessment of Educational Progress (NAEP) tests which are administered to a representative sample of students in public schools, private schools, and Department of Defense schools. Data shown here are for public school students only]

State	Grade 4 Math		Grade 8 Math		Grade 4 Reading		Grade 8 Reading	
	At or above basic	At or above proficient	At or above basic	At or above proficient	At or above basic	At or above proficient	At or above basic	At or above proficient
U.S. average	**81**	**39**	**70**	**31**	**66**	**32**	**73**	**29**
Alabama	70	26	55	18	62	29	62	21
Alaska	79	38	73	32	62	29	71	27
Arizona	74	31	66	26	56	24	65	24
Arkansas	81	37	65	24	64	29	70	25
California	70	30	59	24	53	23	62	21
Colorado	82	41	75	37	70	36	79	35
Connecticut	84	45	73	35	73	41	77	37
Delaware	87	40	74	31	73	34	77	31
District of Columbia	49	14	34	8	39	14	48	12
Florida	86	40	68	27	70	34	71	28
Georgia	79	32	64	25	66	28	70	26
Hawaii	77	33	59	21	59	26	62	20
Idaho	85	40	75	34	70	35	78	32
Illinois	79	36	70	31	65	32	75	30
Indiana	89	46	76	35	68	33	76	31
Iowa	87	43	77	35	74	36	80	36
Kansas	89	51	81	40	72	36	81	35
Kentucky	79	31	69	27	68	33	73	28
Louisiana	73	24	64	19	52	20	64	19
Maine	85	42	78	34	73	36	83	37
Maryland	80	40	74	37	69	36	76	33
Massachusetts	93	58	85	51	81	49	84	43
Michigan	80	37	66	29	66	32	72	28
Minnesota	87	51	81	43	73	37	80	37
Mississippi	70	21	54	14	51	19	60	17
Missouri	82	38	72	30	67	32	75	31
Montana	88	44	79	38	75	39	85	39
Nebraska	80	38	74	35	71	35	79	35
Nevada	74	30	60	23	57	24	63	22
New Hampshire	91	52	78	38	76	41	82	37
New Jersey	90	52	77	40	77	43	81	39
New Mexico	70	24	57	17	58	24	62	17
New York	85	43	70	30	69	36	75	32
North Carolina	85	41	73	34	64	29	71	28
North Dakota	91	46	86	41	75	35	84	32
Ohio	87	46	76	35	73	36	79	36
Oklahoma	82	33	66	21	65	27	72	26
Oregon	79	35	73	35	62	28	77	34
Pennsylvania	85	47	77	38	73	40	79	36
Rhode Island	80	34	65	28	65	31	69	27
South Carolina	80	36	71	32	59	26	69	25
South Dakota	86	41	81	39	71	34	83	37
Tennessee	76	29	64	23	61	27	71	26
Texas	87	40	78	35	66	30	73	28
Utah	83	39	72	32	69	34	75	30
Vermont	89	49	81	41	74	41	84	42
Virginia	87	42	77	37	74	38	79	34
Washington	84	44	75	36	70	36	77	34
West Virginia	81	33	61	19	63	28	68	23
Wisconsin	85	47	76	37	70	36	76	33
Wyoming	88	44	80	36	73	36	80	33

Source: U.S. Department of Education, National Center for Education Statistics, National Assessment of Educational Progress (NAEP), 2007 Mathematics and Reading Assessments. See Internet site <http://nces.ed.gov/nationsreportcard/> (accessed 15 March 2008).

Education 167

Table 261. **Public High School Graduates by State: 1980 to 2006**

[In thousands (2,747.7 represents 2,747,700). For school year ending in year shown]

State	1980	1990	2000	2006, proj.	State	1980	1990	2000	2006, proj.
United States . . .	**2,747.7**	**2,320.3**	**2,553.8**	**2,881.8**	Missouri.	62.3	49.0	52.8	57.9
Alabama	45.2	40.5	37.8	37.2	Montana	12.1	9.4	10.9	10.3
Alaska.	5.2	5.4	6.6	7.7	Nebraska.	22.4	17.7	20.1	20.1
Arizona	28.6	32.1	38.3	50.5	Nevada.	8.5	9.5	14.6	17.6
Arkansas	29.1	26.5	27.3	27.5	New Hampshire	11.7	10.8	11.8	13.8
California	249.2	236.3	309.9	371.9					
					New Jersey	94.6	69.8	74.4	95.0
Colorado	36.8	33.0	38.9	46.5	New Mexico	18.4	14.9	18.0	18.1
Connecticut	37.7	27.9	31.6	36.6	New York	204.1	143.3	141.7	160.9
Delaware	7.6	5.6	6.1	7.1	North Carolina	70.9	64.8	62.1	78.4
District of Columbia [1] . .	5.0	3.6	2.7	3.0	North Dakota	9.9	7.7	8.6	7.5
Florida.	87.3	88.9	106.7	148.3					
					Ohio	144.2	114.5	111.7	119.9
Georgia	61.6	56.6	62.6	73.1	Oklahoma	39.3	35.6	37.6	36.9
Hawaii.	11.5	10.3	10.4	10.5	Oregon	29.9	25.5	30.2	33.6
Idaho	13.2	12.0	16.2	16.2	Pennsylvania	146.5	110.5	114.0	126.9
Illinois	135.6	108.1	111.8	125.0	Rhode Island	10.9	7.8	8.5	10.0
Indiana	73.1	60.0	57.0	58.9					
					South Carolina	38.7	32.5	31.6	35.7
Iowa	43.4	31.8	33.9	33.9	South Dakota	10.7	7.7	9.3	8.3
Kansas	30.9	25.4	29.1	29.9	Tennessee	49.8	46.1	41.6	47.9
Kentucky	41.2	38.0	36.8	36.6	Texas	171.4	172.5	212.9	251.2
Louisiana	46.3	36.1	38.4	35.8	Utah	20.0	21.2	32.5	31.1
Maine	15.4	13.8	12.2	13.3					
					Vermont	6.7	6.1	6.7	7.2
Maryland	54.3	41.6	47.8	55.9	Virginia	66.6	60.6	65.6	76.1
Massachusetts	73.8	55.9	53.0	60.8	Washington	50.4	45.9	57.6	62.2
Michigan	124.3	93.8	97.7	100.5	West Virginia	23.4	21.9	19.4	16.8
Minnesota	64.9	49.1	57.4	59.3	Wisconsin	69.3	52.0	58.5	63.0
Mississippi	27.6	25.2	24.2	24.0	Wyoming	6.1	5.8	6.5	5.5

[1] Beginning in 1990, graduates from adult programs are excluded.

Source: U.S. National Center for Education Statistics, *Digest of Education Statistics*, annual.

Table 262. **High School Dropouts by Race and Hispanic Origin: 1975 to 2006**

[In percent. As of October]

Item	1975	1980	1985	1990 [1]	1995	2000	2001	2002	2003	2004	2005	2006
EVENT DROPOUTS [2]												
Total [3]	**5.8**	**6.0**	**5.2**	**4.5**	**5.4**	**4.5**	**4.7**	**3.3**	**3.8**	**4.4**	**3.6**	**3.5**
White [4]	5.4	5.6	4.8	3.9	5.1	4.3	4.6	3.0	3.7	4.2	3.1	3.5
Male	5.0	6.4	4.9	4.1	5.4	4.7	5.3	3.0	3.9	4.9	3.4	3.9
Female	5.8	4.9	4.7	3.8	4.8	4.0	3.8	3.0	3.4	3.5	2.7	3.1
Black [4]	8.7	8.3	7.7	7.7	6.1	5.6	5.7	4.4	4.5	5.2	6.9	3.7
Male	8.3	8.0	8.3	6.9	7.9	7.6	6.1	5.1	4.1	4.8	7.5	3.2
Female	9.0	8.5	7.2	8.6	4.4	3.8	5.4	3.8	4.9	5.7	6.2	4.3
Hispanic [5]	10.9	11.5	9.7	7.7	11.6	6.8	8.1	5.3	6.5	8.0	4.7	6.4
Male	10.1	16.9	9.3	7.6	10.9	7.1	7.6	6.2	7.7	11.5	5.6	6.3
Female	11.6	6.9	9.8	7.7	12.5	6.5	8.7	4.4	5.4	4.6	3.9	6.6
STATUS DROPOUTS [6]												
Total [3]	**15.6**	**15.6**	**13.9**	**14.4**	**13.9**	**12.4**	**13.0**	**12.3**	**11.8**	**12.1**	**11.3**	**11.0**
White [4]	13.9	14.4	13.5	14.1	13.6	12.2	13.4	12.2	11.6	11.9	11.3	10.8
Male	13.5	15.7	14.7	15.4	14.3	13.5	15.3	13.7	13.3	13.7	13.2	12.4
Female	14.2	13.2	12.3	12.8	13.0	10.9	11.4	10.6	9.8	10.0	9.4	9.2
Black [4]	27.3	23.5	17.6	16.4	14.4	15.3	13.8	14.6	14.2	15.1	12.9	13.0
Male	27.8	26.0	18.8	18.6	14.2	17.4	16.9	16.9	16.7	17.9	14.8	11.2
Female	26.9	21.5	16.6	14.5	14.6	13.5	11.0	12.5	12.0	12.7	11.2	14.7
Hispanic [5]	34.9	40.3	31.5	37.7	34.7	32.3	31.7	30.1	28.4	28.0	27.3	26.2
Male	32.6	42.6	35.8	40.3	34.2	36.8	37.1	33.8	31.7	33.5	32.1	31.0
Female	36.8	38.1	27.0	35.0	35.4	27.3	25.5	25.6	24.7	21.7	21.8	21.0

[1] Beginning 1990, reflects new editing procedures for cases with missing data on school enrollment. [2] Percent of students who drop out in a single year without completing high school. For grades 10 to 12. [3] Includes other races not shown separately. [4] Beginning 2003, for persons who selected this race group only. See footnote 2, Table 221. [5] Persons of Hispanic origin may be of any race. [6] Percent of the population who have not completed high school and are not enrolled, regardless of when they dropped out. For persons 18 to 24 years old.

Source: U.S. Census Bureau, Current Population Reports, PPL-148; and earlier PPL and P-20 reports; and data published on the Internet. See Internet site <http://www.census.gov/population/www/socdemo/school.html>.

Table 263. High School Dropouts by Age, Race, and Hispanic Origin: 1980 to 2006

[As of October (5,212 represents 5,212,000). For persons 14 to 24 years old. See Table 265 for definition of dropouts]

Age and race	Number of dropouts (1,000)					Percent of population				
	1980	1990	1995	2000	2006	1980	1990	1995	2000	2006
Total dropouts [1,2] . . .	**5,212**	**3,854**	**3,963**	**3,883**	**3,592**	**12.0**	**10.1**	**9.9**	**9.1**	**7.9**
16 to 17 years.	709	418	406	460	464	8.8	6.3	5.4	5.8	2.7
18 to 21 years.	2,578	1,921	1,980	2,005	1,695	15.8	13.4	14.2	12.9	10.5
22 to 24 years.	1,798	1,458	1,491	1,310	1,433	15.2	13.8	13.6	11.8	11.8
White [2,3]	4,169	3,127	3,098	3,065	2,735	11.3	10.1	9.7	9.1	7.8
16 to 17 years.	619	334	314	366	336	9.2	6.4	5.4	5.8	2.6
18 to 21 years.	2,032	1,516	1,530	1,558	1,305	14.7	13.1	13.8	12.6	10.3
22 to 24 years.	1,416	1,235	1,181	1,040	1,094	14.0	14.0	13.4	11.7	11.5
Black [2,3]	934	611	605	705	622	16.0	10.9	10.0	10.9	9.1
16 to 17 years.	80	73	70	84	89	6.9	6.9	5.8	7.0	3.3
18 to 21 years.	486	345	328	383	290	23.0	16.0	15.8	16.0	11.9
22 to 24 years.	346	185	194	232	242	24.0	13.5	12.5	14.3	14.7
Hispanic [2,4]	919	1,122	1,355	1,499	1,444	29.5	26.8	24.7	23.5	18.2
16 to 17 years.	92	89	94	121	131	16.6	12.9	10.7	11.0	4.5
18 to 21 years.	470	502	652	733	640	40.3	32.9	29.9	30.0	22.8
22 to 24 years.	323	523	598	602	672	40.6	42.8	37.4	35.5	30.6

[1] Includes other groups not shown separately. [2] Includes persons 14 to 15 years not shown separately. [3] For 2006, for persons who selected this race group only. See footnote 2, Table 221. [4] Persons of Hispanic origin may be of any race.
Source: U.S. Census Bureau, *Current Population Reports*, PPL-148; and earlier PPL and P-20 reports; and data published on the Internet. See Internet site <http://www.census.gov/population/www/socdemo/school.html>.

Table 264. Enrollment Status by Race, Hispanic Origin, and Sex: 1975 and 2006

[As of October (15,693 represents 15,693,000). For persons 18 to 21 years old. For the civilian noninstitutional population. Based on the Current Population Survey; see text, Section 1, and Appendix III]

Characteristic	Total persons 18 to 21 years old (1,000)		Percent distribution							
			Enrolled in high school		High school graduates				Not high school graduates	
					Total		In college			
	1975	2006	1975	2006	1975	2006	1975	2006	1975	2006
Total [1]	**15,693**	**16,176**	**5.7**	**10.5**	**78.0**	**78.9**	**33.5**	**45.9**	**16.3**	**10.5**
White [2]	13,448	12,629	4.7	9.4	80.6	80.1	34.6	47.0	14.7	10.3
Black [2]	1,997	2,442	12.5	15.6	60.4	72.1	24.9	36.0	27.0	11.9
Hispanic [3]	899	2,810	12.0	12.4	57.2	64.7	24.4	29.5	30.8	22.8
Male [1]	7,584	8,149	7.4	12.2	76.6	75.5	35.4	41.5	15.9	12.1
White [2]	6,545	6,372	6.2	10.7	79.7	76.9	36.9	42.5	14.1	12.4
Black [2]	911	1,188	15.9	20.8	55.0	67.1	23.9	29.9	29.0	11.7
Hispanic [3]	416	1,425	17.3	12.5	54.6	59.2	25.2	25.2	27.9	28.2
Female [1]	8,109	8,027	4.2	8.7	79.2	82.3	31.8	50.3	16.6	8.8
White [2]	6,903	6,257	3.2	8.0	81.4	83.5	32.4	51.6	15.3	8.3
Black [2]	1,085	1,254	9.7	10.8	65.0	76.9	25.8	41.9	25.4	12.1
Hispanic [3]	484	1,384	7.6	12.3	59.3	70.3	23.6	34.0	33.1	17.2

[1] Includes other races not shown separately. [2] For 2006, for persons who selected this race group only. See footnote 2, Table 221. [3] Persons of Hispanic origin may be of any race.
Source: U.S. Census Bureau, Current Population Reports, PPL-148; and earlier PPL and P-20 reports; and data published on the Internet. See Internet site <http://www.census.gov/population/www/socdemo/school.html>.

Table 265. Employment Status of High School Graduates and School Dropouts: 1980 to 2007

[In thousands (11,622 represents 11,622,000), except percent. As of October. For civilian noninstitutional population 16 to 24 years old. Based on Current Population Survey; see text, Section 1, and Appendix III]

Employment status, sex, and race	Graduates [1]				Dropouts [3]			
	1980	1990	2000 [2]	2007 [2]	1980	1990	2000 [2]	2007 [2]
Civilian population.	**11,622**	**8,370**	**7,351**	**7,413**	**5,254**	**3,800**	**3,776**	**3,278**
In labor force	9,795	7,107	6,195	5,915	3,549	2,506	2,612	2,185
Percent of population	84.3	84.9	84.3	79.8	67.5	66.0	69.2	66.7
Employed	8,567	6,279	5,632	5,146	2,651	1,993	2,150	1,819
Percent of labor force	87.5	88.3	90.9	87.0	74.7	79.5	82.3	83.2
Unemployed	1,228	828	563	769	898	513	463	367
Unemployment rate, total [4]	12.5	11.7	9.1	13.0	25.3	20.5	17.7	16.8
Male	13.5	11.1	9.3	13.4	23.5	18.8	16.3	15.7
Female	11.5	12.3	8.8	12.4	28.7	23.5	20.3	19.0
White [5]	10.8	9.0	7.2	(NA)	21.6	17.0	15.0	(NA)
Black [5]	26.1	26.0	18.1	(NA)	43.9	43.3	33.2	(NA)
Not in labor force	1,827	1,262	1,156	1,498	1,705	1,294	1,163	1,092
Percent of population	15.7	15.1	15.7	20.2	32.5	34.1	30.8	33.3

NA Not available. [1] For persons not enrolled in college who have completed 4 years of high school only. [2] Data not strictly comparable with data for earlier years. See text, this section, and February 2000 and 2007 issues of *Employment and Earnings*. [3] For persons not in regular school and who have not completed the 12th grade nor received a general equivalency degree. [4] Includes other races not shown separately. [5] For 2007, for persons who selected this race group only. See footnote 2, Table 221.
Source: U.S. Bureau of Labor Statistics; *News*, USDL 08-0559, 25 April 2008; and unpublished data. See Internet site <http://www.bls.gov/news.release/hsgec.toc.htm>.

U.S. Census Bureau, Statistical Abstract of the United States: 2009

Table 266. **General Educational Development (GED) Credentials Issued: 1975 to 2005**

[GEDs issued in thousands (340 represents 340,000). For the 50 states and DC]

Year	GEDs issued	Percent distribution by age of test taker				
		19 years old or under	20 to 24 years old	25 to 29 years old	30 to 34 years old	35 years old and over
1975	340	33	26	14	9	18
1980	479	37	27	13	8	15
1985	413	32	26	15	10	16
1990	410	36	25	13	10	15
1995	504	38	25	13	9	15
2000	487	45	25	11	7	13
2001	648	41	26	11	8	14
2002	330	49	25	10	6	11
2003	387	47	26	10	7	11
2004	406	46	26	11	6	10
2005	424	45	26	12	7	11

Source: U.S. National Center for Education Statistics, *Digest of Education Statistics,* annual.

Table 267. **College Enrollment of Recent High School Completers: 1970 to 2006**

[2,758 represents 2,758,000. For persons 16 to 24 years old who graduated from high school in the preceding 12 months. Includes persons receiving GEDs. Based on surveys and subject to sampling error; data will not agree with data in other tables]

Year	Number of high school completers (1,000)						Percent enrolled in college [5]					
	Total [1]	Male	Female	White [2]	Black [2,3]	His-panic [3,4]	Total [1]	Male	Female	White [2]	Black [2,3]	His-panic [3,4]
1970 . . .	2,758	1,343	1,415	2,461	(NA)	(NA)	51.7	55.2	48.5	52.0	(NA)	(NA)
1975 . . .	3,185	1,513	1,672	2,701	302	132	50.7	52.6	49.0	51.1	41.7	58.0
1980 . . .	3,088	1,498	1,589	2,554	350	130	49.3	46.7	51.8	49.8	42.7	52.3
1985 . . .	2,668	1,287	1,381	2,104	332	141	57.7	58.6	56.8	60.1	42.2	51.0
1990 . . .	2,362	1,173	1,189	1,819	331	121	60.1	58.0	62.2	63.0	46.8	42.7
1993 . . .	2,342	1,120	1,223	1,719	304	201	62.6	59.9	65.2	62.9	55.6	62.2
1994 . . .	2,517	1,244	1,273	1,915	316	178	61.9	60.6	63.2	64.5	50.8	49.1
1995 . . .	2,599	1,238	1,361	1,861	349	288	61.9	62.6	61.3	64.3	51.2	53.7
1996 . . .	2,660	1,297	1,363	1,875	406	227	65.0	60.1	69.7	67.4	56.0	50.8
1997 . . .	2,769	1,354	1,415	1,909	384	336	67.0	63.6	70.3	68.2	58.5	65.6
1998 . . .	2,810	1,452	1,358	1,980	386	314	65.6	62.4	69.1	68.5	61.9	47.4
1999 . . .	2,897	1,474	1,423	1,978	436	329	62.9	61.4	64.4	66.3	58.9	42.3
2000 . . .	2,756	1,251	1,505	1,938	393	300	63.3	59.9	66.2	65.7	54.9	52.9
2001 . . .	2,549	1,277	1,273	1,834	381	241	61.8	60.1	63.5	64.3	55.0	51.7
2002 . . .	2,796	1,412	1,384	1,903	382	344	65.2	62.1	68.4	69.1	59.4	53.6
2003 . . .	2,677	1,306	1,372	1,832	327	314	63.9	61.2	66.5	66.2	57.5	58.6
2004 . . .	2,752	1,327	1,425	1,854	398	286	66.7	61.4	71.5	68.8	62.5	61.8
2005 . . .	2,675	1,262	1,414	1,799	345	390	68.6	66.5	70.4	73.2	55.7	54.0
2006 . . .	2,692	1,328	1,363	1,805	318	382	66.0	65.8	66.1	68.5	55.5	57.9

NA Not available. [1] Includes other races not shown separately. [2] Beginning 2003, for persons of this race group only. See footnote 2, Table 221. [3] Due to small sample size, data are subject to relatively large sampling errors. [4] Persons of Hispanic origin may be of any race. [5] As of October.

Source: U.S. National Center for Education Statistics, *Digest of Education Statistics,* annual.

Table 268. **College Enrollment by Sex and Attendance Status: 1983 to 2006**

[As of fall. In thousands (12,465 represents 12,465,000)]

Sex and age	1983		1988		1993		1998 [1]		2006 [1], proj.	
	Total	Part-time	Total	Part-time	Total	Part-time	Total	Part-time	Total	Part-time
Total	**12,465**	**5,204**	**13,055**	**5,619**	**14,305**	**6,177**	**14,507**	**5,944**	**17,672**	**6,689**
Male	6,024	2,264	6,002	2,340	6,427	2,537	6,369	2,436	7,470	2,634
14 to 17 years old	102	16	55	5	83	10	45	5	80	38
18 to 19 years old	1,256	158	1,290	132	1,224	138	1,535	296	1,626	239
20 to 21 years old	1,241	205	1,243	216	1,294	209	1,374	245	1,792	319
22 to 24 years old	1,158	382	1,106	378	1,260	392	1,127	350	1,330	396
25 to 29 years old	1,115	624	875	485	950	564	908	485	989	544
30 to 34 years old	570	384	617	456	661	484	463	322	530	298
35 years old and over. . .	583	494	816	668	955	739	917	733	1,122	802
Female	6,441	2,940	7,053	3,278	7,877	3,640	8,138	3,508	10,202	4,056
14 to 17 years old	142	16	115	17	93	6	74	21	91	27
18 to 19 years old	1,496	179	1,536	195	1,416	172	1,847	292	2,084	344
20 to 21 years old	1,125	204	1,278	218	1,414	279	1,437	295	2,064	437
22 to 24 years old	884	378	932	403	1,263	493	1,250	463	1,730	566
25 to 29 years old	947	658	932	633	1,058	689	1,083	617	1,463	729
30 to 34 years old	721	553	698	499	811	575	732	506	801	489
35 years old and over. . .	1,126	953	1,563	1,313	1,824	1,427	1,715	1,315	1,970	1,462

[1] Data beginning in 1998 reflect the new classification of institutions. See footnote 1, Table 269.

Source: U.S. National Center for Education Statistics, *Digest of Education Statistics,* annual.

Table 269. Higher Education—Institutions and Enrollment 1980 to 2005

[As of fall (686 represents 686,000). Covers universities, colleges, professional schools, junior and teachers' colleges, both publicly and privately controlled, regular session. Includes estimates for institutions not reporting. See also Appendix III]

Item	Unit	1980	1990	2000	2001	2002	2003	2004	2005
ALL INSTITUTIONS									
Number of institutions [1]	Number...	3,231	3,559	4,182	4,197	4,168	4,236	4,216	4,276
4-year	Number...	1,957	2,141	2,450	2,487	2,466	2,530	2,533	2,582
2-year	Number...	1,274	1,418	1,732	1,710	1,702	1,706	1,683	1,694
Instructional staff—									
(lecturer or above) [2]	1,000...	686	817	(NA)	1,113	(NA)	1,175	(NA)	1,290
Percent full-time	Percent...	66	61	(NA)	56	(NA)	54	(NA)	52
Total enrollment [3,4]	1,000...	12,097	13,819	15,312	15,928	16,612	16,900	17,272	17,487
Male	1,000...	5,874	6,284	6,722	6,961	7,202	7,256	7,387	7,456
Female	1,000...	6,223	7,535	8,591	8,967	9,410	9,645	9,885	10,032
4-year institutions	1,000...	7,571	8,579	9,364	9,677	10,082	10,408	10,726	10,999
2-year institutions	1,000...	4,526	5,240	5,948	6,251	6,529	6,493	6,546	6,488
Full-time	1,000...	7,098	7,821	9,010	9,448	9,946	10,312	10,610	10,797
Part-time	1,000...	4,999	5,998	6,303	6,480	6,665	6,589	6,662	6,690
Public	1,000...	9,457	10,845	11,753	12,233	12,752	12,857	12,980	13,022
Private	1,000...	2,640	2,974	3,560	3,695	3,860	4,043	4,292	4,466
Not-for-profit	1,000...	2,528	2,760	3,109	3,167	3,265	3,341	3,412	3,455
For profit	1,000...	112	213	450	528	594	703	880	1,011
Undergraduate [4]	1,000...	10,475	11,959	13,155	13,716	14,257	14,474	14,781	14,964
Men	1,000...	5,000	5,380	5,778	6,004	6,192	6,224	6,340	6,409
Women	1,000...	5,475	6,579	7,377	7,711	8,065	8,250	8,441	8,555
First-time freshmen	1,000...	2,588	2,257	2,428	2,497	2,571	2,605	2,630	2,657
First professional	1,000...	278	273	307	309	319	329	335	337
Men	1,000...	199	167	164	161	163	166	168	170
Women	1,000...	78	107	143	148	156	163	166	167
Graduate [4]	1,000...	1,343	1,586	1,850	1,904	2,036	2,098	2,157	2,186
Men	1,000...	675	737	780	796	847	865	879	877
Women	1,000...	670	849	1,071	1,108	1,189	1,233	1,278	1,309
2-YEAR INSTITUTIONS									
Number of institutions [1,5]	Number...	1,274	1,418	1,732	1,710	1,702	1,706	1,683	1,694
Public	Number...	945	972	1,076	1,085	1,081	1,086	1,061	1,053
Private	Number...	329	446	656	625	621	620	622	641
Instructional staff—									
(lecturer or above) [2]	1,000...	192	(NA)	(NA)	349	(NA)	359	(NA)	373
Enrollment [3,4]	1,000...	4,526	5,240	5,948	6,251	6,529	6,494	6,546	6,488
Public	1,000...	4,329	4,996	5,697	5,997	6,270	6,209	6,244	6,184
Private	1,000...	198	244	251	254	259	285	302	304
Male	1,000...	2,047	2,233	2,559	2,675	2,753	2,690	2,698	2,680
Female	1,000...	2,479	3,007	3,390	3,575	3,776	3,804	3,848	3,808
4-YEAR INSTITUTIONS									
Number of institutions [1,5]	Number...	1,957	2,141	2,450	2,487	2,466	2,530	2,533	2,582
Public	Number...	552	595	622	628	631	634	639	640
Private	Number...	1,405	1,546	1,828	1,835	1,896	1,894	1,942	1,986
Instructional staff—									
(lecturer or above) [2]	1,000...	494	(NA)	(NA)	764	(NA)	814	(NA)	917
Enrollment [3,4]	1,000...	7,571	8,579	9,364	9,677	10,082	10,417	10,726	10,999
Public	1,000...	5,129	5,848	6,055	6,236	6,482	6,649	6,737	6,838
Private	1,000...	2,442	2,730	3,308	3,441	3,601	3,768	3,990	4,162
Male	1,000...	3,827	4,051	4,163	4,286	4,449	4,570	4,690	4,776
Female	1,000...	3,743	4,527	5,201	5,392	5,634	5,847	6,037	6,224

NA Not available. [1] Number of institutions includes count of branch campuses. Due to revised survey procedures, data beginning 1990 are not comparable with previous years. Beginning 1996 (2000 for this table), data reflect a new classification of institutions; this classification includes some additional, primarily 2-year, colleges and excludes a few institutions that did not award degrees. Includes institutions that were eligible to participate in Title IV federal financial aid programs. [2] Due to revised survey methods, data beginning 1990 not comparable with previous years. [3] Branch campuses counted according to actual status, e.g., 2-year branch in 2-year category. [4] Includes unclassified students. (Students taking courses for credit, but are not candidates for degrees.) [5] Includes schools accredited by the National Association of Trade and Technical Schools.

Source: U.S. National Center for Education Statistics, *Digest of Education Statistics,* annual; and unpublished data.

U.S. Census Bureau, Statistical Abstract of the United States: 2009

Table 270. College Enrollment by Selected Characteristics: 1990 to 2005

[In thousands (13,818.6 represents 13,818,600). **As of fall.** Nonresident alien students are not distributed among racial/ethnic groups]

Characteristic	1990	2000 [1]	2001 [1]	2002 [1]	2003 [1]	2004 [1]	2005 [1]
Total	**13,818.6**	**15,312.3**	**15,928.0**	**16,611.7**	**16,900.5**	**17,272.0**	**17,487.5**
Male	6,283.9	6,721.8	6,960.8	7,202.1	7,255.6	7,387.3	7,455.9
Female.	7,534.7	8,590.5	8,967.2	9,409.6	9,644.9	9,884.8	10,031.6
Public.	10,844.7	11,752.8	12,233.2	12,752.0	12,857.1	12,980.1	13,021.8
Private	2,973.9	3,559.5	3,694.8	3,859.7	4,043.4	4,291.9	4,465.6
2-year	5,240.1	5,948.4	6,250.6	6,529.4	6,492.9	6,545.9	6,488.1
4-year	8,578.6	9,363.9	9,677.4	10,082.3	10,407.6	10,726.2	10,999.4
Undergraduate.	11,959.2	13,155.4	13,715.6	14,257.1	14,473.9	14,780.6	14,964.0
Graduate	1,586.2	1,850.3	1,903.7	2,035.7	2,097.5	2,156.9	2,186.5
First professional	273.4	306.6	308.6	319.0	329.1	334.5	337.0
White [2]	10,722.5	10,462.1	10,774.5	11,140.2	11,275.4	11,422.8	11,495.4
Male	4,861.0	4,634.6	4,762.3	4,897.9	4,927.9	4,988.0	5,007.2
Female.	5,861.5	5,827.5	6,012.2	6,242.3	6,347.5	6,434.8	6,488.2
Public.	8,385.4	7,963.4	8,214.0	8,490.5	8,531.4	8,546.3	8,518.2
Private	2,337.0	2,498.7	2,560.5	2,649.8	2,744.1	2,876.5	2,977.3
2-year	3,954.3	3,804.1	3,955.7	4,086.5	4,076.7	4,063.8	3,998.6
4-year	6,768.1	6,658.0	6,818.8	7,053.8	7,198.7	7,359.0	7,496.9
Undergraduate.	9,272.6	8,983.5	9,278.7	9,564.9	9,662.5	9,771.3	9,828.6
Graduate	1,228.4	1,258.5	1,275.1	1,348.0	1,378.6	1,413.3	1,428.7
First professional	221.5	220.1	220.8	227.4	234.3	238.2	238.1
Black [2]	1,247.0	1,730.3	1,850.4	1,978.7	2,068.9	2,164.7	2,214.6
Male	484.7	635.3	672.4	708.6	730.6	758.4	774.1
Female.	762.3	1,095.0	1,178.0	1,270.2	1,338.2	1,406.3	1,440.4
Public.	976.4	1,319.2	1,397.1	1,487.2	1,533.5	1,574.6	1,580.4
Private	270.6	411.1	453.3	491.6	535.3	590.1	634.2
2-year	524.3	734.9	795.7	859.1	879.9	905.8	901.1
4-year	722.8	995.4	1,054.7	1,119.7	1,189.0	1,258.9	1,313.4
Undergraduate.	1,147.2	1,548.9	1,657.1	1763.8	1,838.2	1,918.5	1,955.4
Graduate	83.9	157.9	169.4	189.6	204.9	220.4	233.2
First professional	15.9	23.5	23.9	25.3	25.8	25.9	26.0
Hispanic	782.4	1,461.8	1,560.6	1,661.7	1,716.0	1,809.6	1,882.0
Male	353.9	627.1	664.2	699.0	709.1	745.1	774.6
Female.	428.5	834.7	896.4	962.7	1,006.9	1,064.5	1,107.3
Public.	671.4	1,229.3	1,308.8	1,388.7	1,414.6	1,477.4	1,525.6
Private	111.0	232.5	251.8	273.1	301.4	332.2	356.4
2-year	424.2	843.9	904.3	958.9	932.6	972.4	981.5
4-year	358.2	617.9	656.3	702.9	783.4	837.2	900.5
Undergraduate.	724.6	1,351.0	1,444.4	1,533.3	1,579.6	1,666.9	1,733.6
Graduate	47.2	95.4	100.5	112.3	119.5	125.8	130.7
First professional	10.7	15.4	15.6	16.1	16.9	17.0	17.7
American Indian/ Alaska Native	102.8	151.2	158.2	165.9	172.7	176.1	176.3
Male	43.1	61.4	63.6	65.7	67.1	68.6	68.4
Female.	59.7	89.7	94.5	100.2	105.6	107.5	107.9
Public.	90.4	127.3	133.6	140.0	144.3	144.4	143.0
Private	12.4	23.9	24.6	25.9	28.3	31.8	33.3
2-year	54.9	74.7	78.2	81.3	82.2	82.2	80.7
4-year	47.9	76.5	80.0	84.6	90.4	93.9	95.6
Undergraduate.	95.5	138.5	144.8	151.7	157.8	160.3	160.4
Graduate	6.2	10.3	11.2	11.9	12.5	13.4	13.4
First professional	1.1	2.3	2.1	2.2	2.3	2.4	2.5
Asian/ Pacific Islander	572.4	978.2	1,019.0	1,074.2	1,075.7	1,108.7	1,134.4
Male	294.9	465.9	480.8	503.9	498.1	511.6	522.0
Female.	277.5	512.3	538.3	570.2	577.6	597.1	612.4
Public.	461.0	770.5	806.1	851.6	845.2	866.1	881.9
Private	111.5	207.7	213.0	222.6	230.5	242.6	252.4
2-year	215.2	401.9	417.5	441.0	425.3	430.7	434.4
4-year	357.2	576.3	601.6	633.1	650.4	678.0	700.0
Undergraduate.	500.5	845.5	883.9	927.4	922.7	949.9	971.4
Graduate	53.2	95.8	97.4	107.1	111.7	115.9	118.4
First professional	18.7	36.8	37.7	39.6	41.3	42.9	44.6
Nonresident alien . . .	391.5	528.7	565.3	590.9	591.8	590.2	584.8
Male	246.3	297.3	317.4	327.0	322.7	315.6	309.5
Female.	145.2	231.4	247.8	263.9	269.2	274.6	275.3
Public.	260.0	343.1	373.6	394.1	388.0	371.4	372.8
Private	131.4	185.6	191.6	196.8	203.9	218.8	212.0
2-year	67.1	89.0	99.2	102.6	96.2	90.9	91.8
4-year	324.3	439.7	466.1	488.3	495.6	499.2	493.1
Undergraduate.	218.7	288.0	306.7	316.0	313.0	313.8	314.7
Graduate	167.3	232.3	250.1	266.6	270.4	268.1	262.1
First professional	5.4	8.4	8.4	8.3	8.4	8.2	8.1

[1] Data beginning 2000 reflect a new classification of institutions; see footnote 1, Table 269.   [2] Non-Hispanic.

Source: U.S. National Center for Education Statistics, *Digest of Education Statistics,* annual.

Table 271. Degree-Granting Institutions, Number and Enrollment by State: 2005

[17,487 represents 17,487,000. Number of institutions beginning in academic year. Opening fall enrollment of resident and extension students attending full-time or part-time. Excludes students taking courses for credit by mail, radio, or TV, and students in branches of U.S. institutions operated in foreign countries. See Appendix III]

State	Number of institu- tions [1]	Enrollment (1,000)							Minority enrollment			Non- resi- dent alien
		Total	Male	Female	Public	Private	Full- time	White [2]	Total [3]	Black [2]	His- panic	
United States..	**4,276**	**17,487**	**7,456**	**10,032**	**13,022**	**4,466**	**10,797**	**11,495**	**5,407**	**2,215**	**1,882**	**585**
Alabama	66	256	106	150	228	28	170	166	84	75	4	6
Alaska.	8	30	12	18	29	1	13	22	8	1	1	1
Arizona	76	546	223	322	321	225	353	347	172	49	86	26
Arkansas	48	143	58	85	128	15	94	108	33	26	3	3
California	408	2,400	1,057	1,343	2,008	392	1,222	1,034	1,291	186	632	74
Colorado	78	303	132	170	235	68	180	231	65	16	34	6
Connecticut	44	175	72	102	112	63	111	127	41	19	14	6
Delaware	10	52	20	31	39	13	33	37	14	10	2	1
District of Columbia	15	105	42	62	6	99	62	50	48	36	5	7
Florida.	169	873	359	514	649	224	495	493	348	155	160	31
Georgia	132	427	172	255	342	85	282	256	159	131	11	12
Hawaii.	23	67	28	39	50	17	40	18	44	2	2	5
Idaho	14	78	35	43	60	17	53	69	7	1	4	2
Illinois	172	833	357	476	555	278	486	543	266	119	96	24
Indiana	100	361	162	200	267	94	251	299	49	30	10	13
Iowa	65	228	98	130	149	79	149	197	24	12	6	7
Kansas	62	192	85	107	170	21	113	156	30	11	9	6
Kentucky	76	245	105	140	202	43	153	213	28	21	3	4
Louisiana	90	198	79	119	181	17	147	123	68	60	4	6
Maine	30	66	26	39	48	18	41	60	4	1	1	1
Maryland	58	314	128	187	256	58	169	181	121	87	12	12
Massachusetts . . .	121	443	188	256	188	255	305	321	96	35	27	26
Michigan	104	627	267	360	506	121	364	478	127	83	18	22
Minnesota	109	362	152	210	241	121	229	300	53	24	8	9
Mississippi	41	150	58	93	136	15	115	87	62	59	1	2
Missouri.	128	374	158	216	218	157	226	296	69	47	11	9
Montana	23	48	22	26	43	5	36	41	6	(Z)	1	1
Nebraska.	39	121	54	67	93	28	80	105	13	5	4	3
Nevada	23	111	48	62	100	11	53	70	38	9	16	3
New Hampshire . .	26	70	29	41	41	29	48	63	5	1	2	2
New Jersey	59	380	163	217	304	75	228	227	138	54	51	15
New Mexico	42	131	53	78	121	10	69	57	72	4	54	3
New York.	308	1,152	482	670	626	526	811	699	384	160	130	69
North Carolina . . .	128	484	194	291	397	88	309	326	147	117	12	12
North Dakota	22	49	24	26	43	7	37	43	5	1	(Z)	2
Ohio	200	616	265	352	453	163	417	496	102	75	12	17
Oklahoma	57	208	90	118	179	29	135	146	52	19	7	9
Oregon	60	200	89	111	164	36	121	163	32	5	11	6
Pennsylvania	259	692	300	392	380	312	502	546	123	71	21	23
Rhode Island	14	81	35	46	40	41	59	65	14	5	5	3
South Carolina . . .	64	210	82	128	175	36	142	142	65	58	3	3
South Dakota	24	49	21	28	38	11	33	43	5	1	1	1
Tennessee	98	283	117	166	200	83	204	211	67	55	5	6
Texas	213	1,241	536	705	1,081	159	695	645	547	153	325	48
Utah	31	201	102	99	149	52	122	175	20	2	10	6
Vermont	25	40	18	22	24	16	29	36	3	1	1	1
Virginia	107	439	186	253	349	90	269	300	128	85	17	11
Washington	80	348	152	196	297	52	216	264	74	15	20	10
West Virginia	44	100	43	56	85	14	74	89	8	5	1	2
Wisconsin	68	335	143	192	269	66	215	288	40	17	10	7
Wyoming	10	35	16	19	33	3	20	32	3	(Z)	2	1
U.S. military [4] . .	5	15	13	3	15	(X)	15	12	3	1	1	(Z)

X Not applicable.   Z Fewer than 500.   [1] Branch campuses counted as separate institutions.   [2] Non-Hispanic.   [3] Includes other races not shown separately.   [4] Service schools.

Source: U.S. National Center for Education Statistics, *Digest of Education Statistics,* annual.

Education   173

Table 272. College Enrollment by Sex, Age, Race, and Hispanic Origin: 1980 to 2006

[In thousands (11,387 represents 11,387,000). As of October for the civilian noninstitutional population, 14 years old and over. Based on the Current Population Survey; see text, Section 1, and Appendix III]

Characteristic	1980	1985	1990 [1]	1995	2000	2001	2002	2003	2004	2005	2006
Total [2]	11,387	12,524	13,621	14,715	15,314	15,873	16,497	16,638	17,383	17,472	17,020
Male [3]	5,430	5,906	6,192	6,703	6,682	6,875	7,240	7,318	7,575	7,539	7,427
18 to 24 years.	3,604	3,749	3,922	4,089	4,342	4,437	4,629	4,697	4,866	4,972	4,874
25 to 34 years.	1,325	1,464	1,412	1,561	1,361	1,476	1,460	1,590	1,604	1,486	1,571
35 years old and over. . .	405	561	772	985	918	908	1,071	970	1,033	1,019	982
Female [3]	5,957	6,618	7,429	8,013	8,631	8,998	9,258	9,319	9,808	9,933	9,593
18 to 24 years.	3,625	3,788	4,042	4,452	5,109	5,192	5,404	5,667	5,742	5,859	5,712
25 to 34 years.	1,378	1,599	1,749	1,788	1,846	1,946	1,941	1,904	2,091	2,115	2,087
35 years old and over. . .	802	1,100	1,546	1,684	1,589	1,776	1,797	1,660	1,850	1,838	1,793
White [3, 4]	9,925	10,781	11,488	12,021	11,999	12,208	12,781	12,870	13,381	13,467	13,112
18 to 24 years.	6,334	6,500	6,635	7,011	7,566	7,548	7,921	8,150	8,354	8,499	8,298
25 to 34 years.	2,328	2,604	2,698	2,686	2,339	2,469	2,515	2,545	2,748	2,647	2,725
35 years old and over. . .	1,051	1,448	2,023	2,208	1,978	2,103	2,236	2,075	2,143	2,206	2,090
Male	4,804	5,103	5,235	5,535	5,311	5,383	5,719	5,714	5,944	5,844	5,772
Female	5,121	5,679	6,253	6,486	6,689	6,826	7,062	7,155	7,438	7,624	7,340
Black [3, 4]	1,163	1,263	1,393	1,772	2,164	2,230	2,278	2,144	2,301	2,297	2,304
18 to 24 years.	688	734	894	988	1,216	1,206	1,227	1,225	1,238	1,229	1,321
25 to 34 years.	289	295	258	426	567	562	542	503	522	520	502
35 years old and over. . .	156	213	207	334	361	429	454	388	502	448	480
Male	476	552	587	710	815	781	802	798	776	864	886
Female	686	712	807	1,062	1,349	1,449	1,476	1,346	1,525	1,435	1,418
Hispanic origin [3, 5]	443	580	748	1,207	1,426	1,700	1,656	1,714	1,975	1,942	1,914
18 to 24 years.	315	375	435	745	899	1,035	979	1,115	1,223	1,216	1,182
25 to 34 years.	118	189	168	250	309	392	414	380	460	438	461
35 years old and over. . .	(NA)	(NA)	130	193	195	260	249	207	271	257	271
Male	222	279	364	568	619	731	705	703	852	804	789
Female	221	299	384	639	807	969	951	1,011	1,123	1,139	1,125

NA Not available. [1] Beginning 1990, based on a revised edit and tabulation package. [2] Includes other races not shown separately. [3] Includes persons 14 to 17 years old not shown separately. [4] Beginning 2003, for persons who selected this race group only. See footnote 2, Table 221. [5] Persons of Hispanic origin may be of any race.

Source: U.S. Census Bureau, *Current Population Reports*, PPL-148; and earlier PPL and P-20 reports. See Internet site <http://www.census.gov/population/www/socdemo/school.html>.

Table 273. Foreign (Nonimmigrant) Student Enrollment in College: 1980 to 2007

[In thousands (286 represents 286,000). For fall of the previous year]

Region of origin	1980	1985	1990	1995	1997	1998	1999	2000	2001	2002	2003	2004	2005	2006	2007
All regions . . .	286	342	387	453	458	481	491	515	548	583	586	573	565	565	583
Africa.	36	40	25	21	22	23	26	30	34	38	40	38	36	36	36
Nigeria	16	18	4	2	2	2	3	4	4	4	6	6	6	6	6
Asia [1, 2]	165	200	245	292	291	308	308	315	339	363	367	356	356	346	367
China [3]	1	10	33	39	43	47	51	54	60	63	65	62	63	63	68
Taiwan [3]	18	23	31	36	30	31	31	29	29	29	28	26	26	28	29
Hong Kong	10	10	11	13	11	10	9	8	8	8	8	7	7	8	8
India.	9	15	26	34	31	34	37	42	55	67	75	80	80	77	84
Indonesia	2	7	9	12	12	13	12	11	12	12	10	9	8	8	7
Iran	51	17	7	3	2	2	2	2	2	2	2	2	2	2	3
Japan.	12	13	30	45	46	47	46	47	46	47	46	41	42	39	35
Malaysia	4	22	14	14	15	15	12	9	8	7	7	6	6	6	5
Saudi Arabia	10	8	4	4	4	5	5	5	6	4	4	4	3	3	8
South Korea	5	16	22	34	37	43	39	41	46	49	52	52	53	59	62
Thailand	7	7	7	11	13	15	12	11	11	12	10	9	9	9	9
Europe [4]	23	33	46	65	68	72	74	78	81	82	78	74	72	85	83
Latin America [1, 5] . . .	42	49	48	47	50	51	55	62	64	68	69	66	68	65	65
Mexico	6	6	7	9	9	10	10	11	11	13	13	13	13	14	14
Venezuela	10	10	3	4	5	5	5	5	5	6	5	6	5	5	5
North America	16	16	19	23	24	23	23	24	26	27	27	28	29	29	29
Canada.	15	15	18	23	23	22	23	24	25	27	27	27	28	28	28
Oceania	4	4	4	4	4	4	4	5	5	5	5	5	5	5	4

[1] Includes countries not shown separately. [2] Beginning 2006, excludes Cyprus and Turkey. [3] With the establishment of diplomatic relations with China on January 1, 1979, the U.S. government recognized the People's Republic of China as the sole legal government of China and acknowledged the Chinese position that there is only one China and that Taiwan is part of China. [4] Beginning 2006, includes Cyprus and Turkey. [5] Includes Central America, Caribbean, and South America.

Source: Institute of International Education, New York, NY, *Open Doors Report on International Educational Exchange*, annual (copyright).

U.S. Census Bureau, Statistical Abstract of the United States: 2009

Table 274. College Enrollment—Summary by Sex, Race, and Hispanic Origin: 2006

[In thousands (17,232 represents 17,232,000), except percent. As of October. Covers civilian noninstitutional population 15 years old and over enrolled in colleges and graduate schools. Based on Current Population Survey, see text, Section 1, and Appendix III]

Characteristic	Total			Race and Hispanic origin				
				White [2]				
	Number [1]	Male	Female	Total	Non-Hispanic	Black [2]	Asian [2]	Hispanic [3]
Total enrollment	**17,232**	**7,506**	**9,726**	**13,273**	**11,485**	**2,334**	**1,084**	**1,968**
15 to 17 years old	212	79	133	161	114	30	8	54
18 to 19 years old	3,746	1,703	2,043	2,982	2,564	464	204	444
20 to 21 years old	3,675	1,682	1,993	2,958	2,606	416	215	386
22 to 24 years old	3,166	1,489	1,677	2,358	2,030	441	242	353
25 to 29 years old	2,312	1,033	1,278	1,740	1,494	303	187	271
30 to 34 years old	1,346	537	809	985	830	199	103	190
35 years old and over	2,775	982	1,793	2,089	1,848	481	125	270
Type of school:								
2-year	4,294	1,788	2,506	3,228	2,602	688	185	689
15 to 19 years old	1,367	650	717	1,094	864	201	36	238
20 to 24 years old	1,361	610	751	1,026	836	188	73	211
25 years old and over	1,567	529	1,039	1,108	902	300	76	241
4-year	9,560	4,346	5,213	7,457	6,546	1,271	553	1,007
15 to 19 years old	2,573	1,128	1,445	2,031	1,799	294	175	257
20 to 24 years old	4,667	2,272	2,395	3,682	3,272	574	284	448
25 years old and over	2,320	947	1,373	1,744	1,475	404	95	302
Graduate school	3,378	1,371	2,007	2,586	2,335	372	345	271
15 to 24 years old	831	293	538	623	542	94	102	82
25 to 34 years old	1,479	663	816	1,113	1,021	135	190	107
35 years old and over	1,067	414	653	850	772	143	53	83
Public	13,466	5,896	7,571	10,337	8,821	1,815	861	1,664
2-year	3,879	1,602	2,277	2,935	2,347	591	179	643
4-year	7,390	3,424	3,966	5,734	4,968	983	439	845
Graduate	2,197	870	1,328	1,668	1,506	242	244	176
Percent of students:								
Employed full-time	17.5	17.5	17.6	17.5	17.8	19.1	13.6	16.1
Employed part-time	25.2	22.6	27.5	27.2	28.6	16.8	22.3	20.0

[1] Includes other races not shown separately. [2] For persons who selected this race group only. See footnote 2, Table 221. [3] Persons of Hispanic origin may be of any race.

Source: U.S. Census Bureau, unpublished data. See Internet site <http://www.census.gov/population/www/socdemo/school.html>.

Table 275. Higher Education Enrollments in Languages Other than English: 1970 to 2006

[As of fall (1,111.5 represents 1,111,500). For credit enrollment]

Enrollment	1970	1980	1983	1986	1990	1995	1998	2002	2006
Registrations [1] (1,000)	**1,111.5**	**924.8**	**966.0**	**1,003.2**	**1,184.1**	**1,138.8**	**1,193.8**	**1,397.3**	**1,577.8**
By selected language (1,000):									
Spanish	389.2	379.4	386.2	411.3	533.9	606.3	656.6	746.3	823.0
French	359.3	248.4	270.1	275.3	272.5	205.4	199.1	202.0	206.4
German	202.6	126.9	128.2	121.0	133.3	96.3	89.0	91.1	94.3
Italian	34.2	34.8	38.7	40.9	49.7	43.8	49.3	63.9	78.4
American Sign Language	(X)	(X)	(X)	(X)	1.6	4.3	11.4	60.8	78.8
Japanese	6.6	11.5	16.1	23.5	45.7	44.7	43.1	52.2	66.6
Chinese	6.2	11.4	13.2	16.9	19.5	26.5	28.5	34.2	51.6
Latin	27.6	25.0	24.2	25.0	28.2	25.9	26.1	29.8	32.2
Russian	36.2	24.0	30.4	34.0	44.6	24.7	23.8	23.9	24.8
Hebrew	16.6	19.4	18.2	15.6	13.0	13.1	15.8	22.8	23.8
Ancient Greek	16.7	22.1	19.4	17.6	16.4	16.3	16.4	20.4	22.8
Arabic	1.3	3.5	3.4	3.4	3.5	4.4	5.5	10.6	24.0
Portuguese	5.1	4.9	4.4	5.1	6.2	6.5	6.9	8.4	10.3
Korean	0.1	0.4	0.7	0.9	2.3	3.3	4.5	5.2	7.1
Index (1965 = 100)	107.3	89.3	93.2	96.8	114.3	109.9	115.2	134.9	152.3

X Not applicable. [1] Includes other foreign languages not shown separately.

Source: Association of Departments of Foreign Languages, New York, NY, ADFL Bulletin, Vol. 39, No. 2, Winter 2008 (copyright). For 1970 to 2002, consult prior ADFL Bulletins.

U.S. Census Bureau, Statistical Abstract of the United States: 2009

Table 276. College Freshmen—Summary Characteristics: 1970 to 2007

[In percent, except as indicated (12.8 represents $12,800). As of fall for first-time full-time freshmen in 4-year colleges and universities. Based on sample survey and subject to sampling error; see source]

Characteristic	1970	1980	1985	1990	1995	2000	2005	2006	2007
Sex: Male	52.1	48.8	48.9	46.9	45.6	45.2	45.0	45.1	45.2
Female	47.9	51.2	51.1	53.1	54.4	54.8	55.0	54.9	54.8
Applied to three or more colleges	(NA)	31.5	35.4	42.9	44.4	50.5	55.4	56.5	56.5
Average grade in high school:									
A– to A+	19.6	26.6	28.7	29.4	36.1	42.9	46.6	46.0	45.9
B– to B+	62.5	58.2	57.1	57.0	54.2	50.5	48.0	49.4	49.0
C to C+	17.7	14.9	14.0	13.4	9.6	6.5	5.4	4.6	5.0
D	0.3	0.2	0.2	0.2	0.1	0.1	0.1	0.1	0.1
Political orientation:									
Liberal	35.7	21.0	22.4	24.6	22.9	24.8	27.1	28.4	29.3
Middle of the road	43.4	57.0	53.1	51.7	51.3	51.9	45.0	43.3	43.4
Conservative	17.3	19.0	21.3	20.6	21.8	18.9	22.6	23.9	23.1
Probable field of study:									
Arts and humanities	(NA)	10.5	10.1	10.5	11.2	12.1	12.8	13.1	12.8
Biological sciences	(NA)	4.5	4.5	4.9	8.3	6.6	7.6	8.3	8.6
Business	(NA)	21.2	24.6	21.1	15.4	16.7	17.4	17.9	17.7
Education	(NA)	8.4	6.9	10.3	10.1	11.0	9.9	9.5	9.2
Engineering	(NA)	11.2	11.0	9.7	8.1	8.7	8.3	8.0	7.5
Physical science	(NA)	3.2	3.2	2.8	3.1	2.6	3.1	3.1	3.2
Social science	(NA)	8.2	9.4	11.0	9.9	10.0	10.7	11.2	11.1
Professional	(NA)	15.5	13.1	13.0	16.5	11.6	14.6	13.0	14.5
Technical	(NA)	3.1	2.4	1.1	1.2	2.1	1.2	1.1	1.0
Data processing/computer programming	(NA)	1.7	1.7	0.7	0.8	1.5	0.5	0.5	0.6
Other [1]	(NA)	14.0	15.1	15.8	16.0	17.9	14.1	14.2	14.2
Communications	(NA)	2.4	2.8	2.9	1.8	2.7	2.0	2.2	1.8
Computer science	(NA)	2.6	2.4	1.7	2.2	3.7	1.1	1.1	1.1
Personal objectives—very important or essential:									
Being very well off financially	36.2	62.5	69.2	72.3	72.8	73.4	74.5	73.4	74.4
Developing a meaningful philosophy of life	79.1	62.5	46.9	45.9	45.4	42.4	45.0	46.3	49.2
Keeping up to date with political affairs	57.2	45.2	(NA)	46.6	32.3	28.1	36.4	37.2	37.2
Attitudes—agree or strongly agree:									
Capital punishment should be abolished	59.4	34.8	27.6	23.1	22.0	31.2	33.3	34.5	(NA)
Legalize marijuana	40.6	37.1	21.4	18.8	33.4	34.2	37.7	37.1	38.2
There is too much concern for the rights of criminals	50.7	65.0	(NA)	65.1	73.2	66.5	57.9	55.9	55.9
Abortion should be legalized	85.7	53.7	56.4	65.5	59.9	53.9	55.2	56.8	56.9
Median family income ($1,000)	12.8	24.5	37.3	46.6	54.8	64.4	73.2	76.2	78.2

NA Not available.   [1] Includes other fields not shown separately.

Source: The Higher Education Research Institute, University of California, Los Angeles, CA, *The American Freshman: National Norms,* annual.

Table 277. Students Reported Disability Status by Selected Characteristic: 2003–2004

[(19,054 represents 19,054,000). Disabled students reported that they had one or more of the following conditions: a specific learning disability, a visual handicap, hard of hearing, deafness, a speech disability, an orthopedic handicap, or a health impairment. Based on the 2003–2004 National Postsecondary Student-Aid Study; see source for details. Includes Puerto Rico. See also Appendix III]

Student characteristic	Undergraduate			Graduate and first-professional		
	All students	Disabled students	Nondisabled students	All students	Disabled students	Nondisabled students
Total students (1,000)	**19,054**	**2,156**	**16,897**	**2,826**	**189**	**2,637**
PERCENT DISTRIBUTION						
Total	100.0	100.0	100.0	100.0	100.0	100.0
Age:						
15 to 23 years old	56.8	45.8	58.2	11.2	8.5	11.4
24 to 29 years old	17.3	15.5	17.5	39.6	33.9	40.0
30 years or older	25.9	38.7	24.3	49.2	57.6	48.6
Sex:						
Male	42.4	42.1	42.4	41.9	38.0	42.2
Female	57.6	57.9	57.6	58.1	62.0	57.8
Race/ethnicity of student:						
White, non-Hispanic	63.1	65.1	62.9	68.3	67.0	68.4
Black, non-Hispanic	14.0	13.2	14.1	9.6	12.5	9.3
Hispanic	12.7	12.3	12.8	7.7	7.9	7.6
Asian/Pacific Islander	5.9	3.8	6.2	11.0	5.9	11.3
American Indian/Alaska Native	0.9	1.2	0.9	0.6	0.4	0.6
Other	3.3	4.4	3.2	2.9	6.3	2.7
Attendance status:						
Full-time, full-year	38.6	33.5	39.2	32.7	28.9	32.9
Part-time or part-year	61.4	66.5	60.8	67.3	71.1	67.1
Student housing status:						
On-campus	13.8	10.7	14.2	(NA)	(NA)	(NA)
Off-campus	55.2	61.5	54.4	(NA)	(NA)	(NA)
With parents or relatives	31.0	27.7	31.4	(NA)	(NA)	(NA)
Dependency status:						
Dependent	49.7	39.4	51.0	(NA)	(NA)	(NA)
Independent, unmarried	15.2	19.5	14.7	47.5	48.1	47.5
Independent, married	7.9	9.1	7.8	18.8	15.7	19.0
Independent with dependents	27.1	32.0	26.5	33.7	36.2	33.6

NA Not available.

Source: U.S. National Center for Education Statistics, *Digest of Education Statistics, 2005.*

Table 278. Percent of Undergraduates Receiving Aid and Average Total Price of Attendance of Undergraduate Education: 2003–2004

[In dollars, except percent. Excludes students attending more than one institution. Types of financial aid are grants, loans, and work study. Price of attendance includes tuition and fees, books and supplies, room and board, transportation, and personal and other expenses allowed for federal cost of attendance budgets. Based on the 2003-2004 National Postsecondary Student-Aid Study; see source for details. Includes Puerto Rico. See also Appendix III]

Student characteristic	Percent of under-gradu-ates receiv-ing aid	Average total price of attendance						
				Type of institution				
				Public 4-year		Private not-for-profit 4-year		
		All institu-tions [1]	Public 2-year	Non-doctor-ate	Doctor-ate	Non-doctor-ate	Doctor-ate	Private for-profit
Total	**63.2**	**11,300**	**6,100**	**10,800**	**13,100**	**19,400**	**26,800**	**14,900**
Age: [2]								
18 years or younger	65.5	13,500	6,900	12,300	14,800	24,900	30,800	16,500
19 to 23 years	63.9	13,200	6,600	11,700	13,900	23,500	29,300	15,200
24 to 29 years	66.8	9,500	6,100	9,400	11,200	14,900	17,200	14,700
30 to 39 years	63.3	8,600	5,900	9,100	9,800	12,900	14,000	14,600
40 years or older	53.9	7,500	5,200	8,400	8,700	11,600	13,300	14,300
Sex:								
Male	60.6	11,600	6,100	11,000	13,200	19,400	27,100	16,200
Female	65.2	11,000	6,200	10,700	13,000	19,400	26,500	14,000
Race:								
One race:								
White	61.5	11,600	6,200	10,900	13,100	20,500	27,500	15,100
Black or African American	75.8	10,500	6,300	10,200	13,400	16,700	23,500	14,100
Asian	51.6	12,500	6,600	11,200	14,500	22,800	31,300	17,400
American Indian/Alaska Native	67.4	9,100	5,800	10,300	11,000	18,600	(S)	13,600
Native Hawaiian or Other Pacific Islander	51.3	9,500	4,900	(S)	13,800	(S)	(S)	17,400
Other race	66.4	11,700	7,100	11,300	12,500	19,600	26,800	15,700
More than one race	61.9	11,400	6,100	11,100	13,300	19,500	29,600	15,800
Hispanic or Latino [3]	63.2	9,900	5,800	10,300	11,900	16,000	21,400	14,600
Attendance pattern:								
Full-time, full-year	76.2	17,200	10,500	13,700	15,900	25,400	32,300	20,300
Full-time, part-year	66.2	9,800	5,700	7,500	9,000	15,600	20,200	12,800
Part-time, full-year	60.5	8,700	6,500	9,200	11,100	14,400	18,500	13,800
Part-time, part-year	40.5	4,200	3,200	4,400	5,200	6,700	8,800	8,500
Housing:								
On campus	79.2	19,900	7,100	13,400	15,200	26,900	32,000	17,200
Off campus	62.9	10,000	6,100	10,400	12,700	15,100	21,900	14,800
With parents/other relatives	53.6	9,100	6,300	9,600	11,100	17,600	21,100	15,000

S Data do not meet publication standards.   [1] Includes public less-than-2-year and private not-for-profit less-than-4-year.   [2] As of December 31, 2003.   [3] Persons of Hispanic origin may be of any race.

Source: U.S. National Center for Education Statistics, "Student Financing of Undergraduate Education 2003-04" NCES 2006-186 (released 23 August 2006). See Internet site <http://nces.ed.gov/surveys/npsas/>.

Table 279. Higher Education Price Indexes: 1970 to 2007

[1983 = 100. For years ending June 30. Reflects prices paid by colleges and universities. Minus sign (–) indicates decrease]

Item and year	Index, total	Personnel compensation					Contracted services, supplies, and equipment		
		Faculty salaries	Adminis-trative salaries	Clerical salaries	Service employee salaries	Fringe benefits	Miscella-neous services	Supplies and materials	Utilities
INDEXES									
1970	39.5	(NA)	(NA)	(NA)	(NA)	24.7	(NA)	37.6	16.3
1980	77.5	(NA)	(NA)	(NA)	(NA)	72.6	(NA)	84.6	64.1
1990	140.8	(NA)	(NA)	(NA)	(NA)	171.4	(NA)	119.6	90.1
2000	196.9	(NA)	(NA)	(NA)	(NA)	254.8	(NA)	145.0	104.9
2001	206.5	214.5	229.2	197.7	182.6	261.7	199.8	130.4	140.7
2002	215.0	222.7	236.4	205.4	189.6	277.1	205.8	130.6	149.4
2003	221.2	229.4	255.7	211.1	193.9	292.3	209.5	129.0	127.0
2004	231.5	234.2	263.3	217.1	197.6	312.8	216.4	133.8	174.6
2005	239.8	240.7	274.0	223.4	201.4	327.2	222.7	140.2	190.1
2006	251.8	248.2	287.7	229.5	205.5	343.7	228.8	151.9	241.8
2007	260.3	257.6	299.2	237.7	213.6	360.8	238.3	162.2	223.5
ANNUAL PERCENT CHANGE [1]									
1990	6.0	(NA)	(NA)	(NA)	(NA)	7.9	(NA)	5.5	5.6
2000	4.1	(NA)	(NA)	(NA)	(NA)	6.5	(NA)	–0.1	4.4
2005	3.6	2.8	4.1	2.9	1.9	4.6	2.9	4.8	8.9
2006	5.0	3.1	5.0	2.7	2.0	5.0	2.7	8.3	27.2
2007	3.4	3.8	4.0	3.6	4.0	5.0	4.2	6.8	–7.6

NA Not available.   [1] Percent change from the immediate prior year.

Source: The Commonfund Institute, Wilton, CT, (copyright). See Internet site <http://www.commonfund.org>.

U.S. Census Bureau, Statistical Abstract of the United States: 2009

Table 280. Federal Student Financial Assistance: 1995 to 2008

[For award years July 1 of year shown to the following June 30 (35,477 represents ($35,477,000,000). Funds utilized exclude operating costs, etc., and represent funds given to students]

Type of assistance	1995	2000	2004	2005	2006	2007, est.	2008, est.
FUNDS UTILIZED (mil. dol.)							
Total.	35,477	44,007	69,053	72,634	77,191	82,934	92,484
Federal Pell Grants	5,472	7,956	13,149	12,693	12,817	12,954	15,176
Academic Competitiveness Grants	(X)	(X)	(X)	(X)	340	420	830
SMART[1] Grants	(X)	(X)	(X)	(X)	310	310	350
Federal Supplemental Educational Opportunity Grant . .	764	907	1,065	1,084	1,080	976	959
Federal Work-Study	764	939	1,082	1,050	1,042	1,171	1,171
Federal Perkins Loan	1,029	1,144	1,651	1,593	1,618	1,105	1,103
Federal Direct Student Loan (FDSL)	8,296	10,348	12,840	12,930	12,677	13,596	15,050
Federal Family Education Loans (FFEL)	19,152	22,712	39,266	43,284	47,307	52,402	57,845
NUMBER OF AWARDS (1,000)							
Total.	13,667	15,043	20,777	21,317	22,304	22,761	23,625
Federal Pell Grants	3,612	3,899	5,308	5,167	5,165	5,274	5,478
Academic Competitiveness Grants	(X)	(X)	(X)	(X)	400	497	662
SMART[1] Grants	(X)	(X)	(X)	(X)	80	82	93
Federal Supplemental Educational Opportunity Grant . .	1,083	1,175	1,408	1,419	1,417	1,277	1,255
Federal Work-Study	702	713	762	710	694	792	793
Federal Perkins Loan	688	639	748	727	725	504	503
Federal Direct Student Loan (FDSL)	2,339	2,739	3,001	2,971	2,841	2,839	2,935
Federal Family Education Loans (FFEL)	5,243	5,878	9,550	10,323	10,982	11,496	11,906
AVERAGE AWARD (dol.)							
Total.	2,596	2,925	3,324	3,407	3,461	3,644	3,915
Federal Pell Grants	1,515	2,041	2,477	2,456	2,482	2,456	2,770
Academic Competitiveness Grants/SMART [2] Grants . .	(X)	(X)	(X)	(X)	850	845	1,254
SMART[1] Grants	(X)	(X)	(X)	(X)	3,875	3,780	3,763
Federal Supplemental Educational Opportunity Grant . .	705	772	759	764	762	764	764
Federal Work-Study	1,088	1,318	1,419	1,478	1,500	1,478	1,478
Federal Perkins Loan	1,496	1,790	2,206	2,190	2,231	2,190	2,190
Federal Direct Student Loan (FDSL)	3,547	3,778	4,279	4,352	4,462	4,789	5,128
Federal Family Education Loans (FFEL)	3,653	3,864	4,112	4,193	4,308	4,558	4,858
COHORT DEFAULT RATE [2]							
Federal Perkins Loan	12.6	9.9	8.1	8.1	7.8	(NA)	(NA)

NA Not available.   X Not applicable.   [1] National Science and Mathematics Access to Retain Talent.   [2] As of June 30. Represents the percent of borrowers entering repayment status in year shown who defaulted in the following year.
Source: U.S. Dept. of Education, Office of Postsecondary Education, unpublished data.

Table 281. State and Local Financial Support for Higher Education by State: 2006–2007

[For 2006–2007 fiscal year, except as indicated (10,237.9 represents 10,237,900). Data for the 50 states]

State	FTE enrollment [1] (1,000)	Educational appropriations per FTE [2] (dol.)	Appropriations for higher ed. as a percent of state and local tax revenue 2005–2006 [3]	State	FTE enrollment [1] (1,000)	Educational appropriations per FTE [2] (dol.)	Appropriations for higher ed. as a percent of state and local tax revenue 2005–2006 [3]
Total . . .	10,237.9	6,773	6.2	MO	174.7	6,060	5.6
				MT	35.3	4,297	5.8
AL.	182.4	6,629	10.8	NE.	73.9	7,165	9.3
AK.	18.7	13,824	6.9	NV	61.3	8,589	6.2
AZ.	221.6	6,935	8.0	NH	32.1	3,370	2.5
AR.	103.4	6,167	8.8	NJ	226.1	8,076	4.5
CA.	1,686.8	7,001	7.3	NM	83.0	9,669	12.8
CO.	157.4	3,807	3.6	NY.	508.9	8,657	3.5
CT.	75.0	10,079	4.1	NC	344.1	7,909	10.0
DE.	31.3	6,970	6.0	ND	35.4	4,765	9.1
FL.	518.1	5,855	4.4	OH	383.3	4,915	5.0
GA	297.8	8,231	8.3	OK	132.1	6,691	8.1
HI	35.0	12,195	8.1	OR	125.1	4,948	5.3
ID	43.6	7,785	8.0	PA.	337.4	5,788	3.9
IL	387.8	7,230	5.9	RI	28.9	6,548	4.0
IN	223.6	5,351	5.9	SC.	145.7	5,838	8.0
IA	112.9	6,007	7.6	SD.	29.2	4,569	7.4
KS.	127.2	5,948	8.9	TN.	168.2	7,346	7.5
KY.	145.6	6,945	8.5	TX.	794.2	7,084	8.4
LA.	166.7	6,640	8.1	UT.	102.4	6,271	8.3
ME	35.5	6,406	4.2	VT.	19.5	3,030	2.6
MD	197.5	7,456	5.7	VA.	273.0	5,972	5.1
MA	139.7	8,666	4.0	WA	214.8	6,769	6.0
MI	384.2	5,825	6.7	WV	72.7	4,651	7.0
MN	191.5	5,986	5.8	WI	215.1	6,504	6.5
MS	115.7	5,926	9.9	WY	22.6	15,155	10.3

[1] Full-time equivalent. Includes degree enrollment and enrollment in public postsecondary programs resulting in a certificate or other formal recognition. Includes summer sessions. Excludes medical enrollments.   [2] State and local appropriations for general operating expenses of public postsecondary education. Includes state-funded financial aid to students attending in-state public institutions. Excludes sums for research, agricultural extension, and teaching hospitals and medical schools.   [3] Includes state and local appropriations for public and independent postsecondary education (including sums for research, agricultural extension, and teaching hospitals and medical schools).
Source: State Higher Education Executive Officers, Boulder, CO (copyright). See Internet site <http://www.sheeo.org>.

U.S. Census Bureau, Statistical Abstract of the United States: 2009

Table 282. **Institutions of Higher Education—Charges: 1985 to 2007**

[In dollars. Estimated. **For the entire academic year ending in year shown.** Figures are average charges per full-time equivalent student. Room and board are based on full-time students]

Academic control and year	Tuition and required fees [1]				Board rates [2]				Dormitory charges			
	All institutions	2-yr. colleges	4-yr. colleges	Other 4-yr. schools	All institutions	2-yr. colleges	4-yr. colleges	Other 4-yr. schools	All institutions	2-yr. colleges	4-yr. colleges	Other 4-yr. schools
Public:												
1985......	971	584	1,386	1,117	1,241	1,302	1,276	1,201	1,196	921	1,237	1,200
1990......	1,356	756	2,035	1,608	1,635	1,581	1,728	1,561	1,513	962	1,561	1,554
1995......	2,057	1,192	2,977	2,499	1,949	1,712	2,108	1,866	1,959	1,232	1,992	2,044
2000......	2,506	1,338	3,768	3,091	2,364	1,834	2,628	2,239	2,440	1,549	2,516	2,521
2003......	2,903	1,483	4,686	3,668	2,669	2,164	2,895	2,580	2,930	1,954	3,023	3,032
2004......	3,319	1,702	5,363	4,141	2,823	2,233	3,084	2,724	3,107	2,086	3,232	3,198
2005......	3,629	1,849	5,939	4,512	2,931	2,353	3,222	2,809	3,304	2,174	3,427	3,413
2006......	3,874	1,935	6,399	4,765	3,035	2,306	3,372	2,899	3,545	2,251	3,654	3,672
2007, prel. ...	4,101	2,017	6,836	5,043	3,185	2,398	3,494	3,076	3,747	2,394	3,873	3,871
Private:												
1985......	5,315	3,485	6,843	5,135	1,462	1,294	1,647	1,405	1,426	1,424	1,753	1,309
1990......	8,147	5,196	10,348	7,778	1,948	1,811	2,339	1,823	1,923	1,663	2,411	1,774
1995......	11,111	6,914	14,537	10,653	2,509	2,023	3,035	2,362	2,587	2,233	3,469	2,347
2000......	14,081	8,235	19,307	13,361	2,882	2,922	3,157	2,790	3,224	2,808	4,070	2,976
2003......	16,383	10,651	22,716	15,416	3,206	3,870	3,602	3,071	3,752	3,232	4,724	3,478
2004......	17,327	11,546	24,128	16,298	3,364	4,432	3,778	3,222	3,945	3,581	4,979	3,647
2005......	18,154	12,122	25,643	17,050	3,485	3,728	3,855	3,370	4,171	4,243	5,263	3,854
2006......	18,862	12,450	26,954	17,702	3,647	4,726	4,039	3,517	4,380	3,994	5,517	4,063
2007, prel. ...	19,991	12,620	28,524	18,826	3,787	3,307	4,175	3,675	4,607	4,240	5,700	4,302

[1] For in-state students.　[2] Beginning 1990, rates reflect 20 meals per week, rather than meals served 7 days a week.

Source: U.S. National Center for Education Statistics, *Digest of Education Statistics,* annual.

Table 283. **Voluntary Financial Support of Higher Education: 1990 to 2007**

[For school years ending in years shown (9,800 represents $9,800,000,000). Voluntary support, as defined in Gift Reporting Standards, excludes income from endowment and other invested funds as well as all support received from federal, state, and local governments and their agencies and contract research]

Item	Unit	1990	1995	2000	2003	2004	2005	2006	2007
Estimated support, total	**Mil. dol.** ...	**9,800**	**12,750**	**23,200**	**23,900**	**24,400**	**25,600**	**28,000**	**29,750**
Individuals..............	Mil. dol. ...	4,770	6,540	12,220	11,150	11,900	12,100	14,100	13,920
Alumni..............	Mil. dol. ...	2,540	3,600	6,800	6,600	6,700	7,100	8,400	8,270
Business corporations	Mil. dol. ...	2,170	2,560	4,150	4,250	4,400	4,400	4,600	4,800
Foundations.............	Mil. dol. ...	1,920	2,460	5,080	6,600	6,200	7,000	7,100	8,500
Fundraising consortia and other organizations	Mil. dol. ...	700	940	1,380	1,540	1,550	1,730	1,825	2,150
Religious organizations	Mil. dol. ...	240	250	370	360	350	370	375	380
Current operations	Mil. dol. ...	5,440	7,230	11,270	12,900	13,600	14,200	15,000	16,100
Capital purposes..........	Mil. dol. ...	4,360	5,520	11,930	11,000	10,800	11,400	13,000	13,650
Support per student........	Dollars ...	724	893	1,568	1,439	1,444	1,482	1,614	1,684
In **2007** dollars	Dollars ...	1,147	1,213	1,886	1,619	1,583	1,572	1,658	1,684
Expenditures, higher education........	Bil. dol. ...	134.66	182.97	236.78	302.76	316.75	341.40	363.50	409.36
Expenditures per student	Dollars ...	9,946	12,814	16,008	18,225	18,743	19,766	20,951	23,175
In **2007** dollars	Dollars ...	15,760	17,413	19,253	20,514	20,548	20,960	21,523	23,175
Institutions reporting support ...	Number...	1,056	1,086	945	954	971	997	1,014	1,023
Total support reported	**Mil. dol.** ...	**8,214**	**10,992**	**19,419**	**19,823**	**19,630**	**20,953**	**23,475**	**25,247**
Private 4-year institutions	Mil. dol. ...	5,072	6,500	11,047	10,318	10,695	11,011	12,857	13,675
Public 4-year institutions.	Mil. dol. ...	3,056	4,382	8,254	9,400	8,802	9,780	10,421	11,321
2-year colleges...........	Mil. dol. ...	85	110	117	105	133	163	197	251

Source: Council for Aid to Education, New York, NY, *Voluntary Support of Education,* annual.

Table 284. **Average Salaries for College Faculty Members: 2006 to 2008**

[In thousands of dollars (68.4 represents $68,400). For academic year ending in year shown. Figures are for 9 months teaching for full-time faculty members in 2-year and 4-year institutions with ranks. Fringe benefits averaged in 2006, $18,677 in public institutions and $22,170 in private institutions; and in 2007, $19,746 in public institutions and $23,040 in private institutions; and in 2008, $20,178 in public institutions and $24,193 in private institutions]

Type of control and academic rank	2006	2007	2008	Type of control and academic rank	2006	2007	2008
Public: All ranks............	68.4	71.4	73.2	Private: [1] All ranks...........	81.5	84.2	88.2
Professor	91.4	95.6	98.3	Professor	111.8	116.2	122.2
Associate professor	66.3	69.2	72.2	Associate professor	73.3	75.7	79.2
Assistant professor........	55.9	58.5	60.8	Assistant professor........	61.0	62.9	65.8
Instructor	40.1	41.8	43.3	Instructor	44.5	45.6	49.9

[1] Excludes church-related colleges and universities.

Source: American Association of University Professors, Washington, DC, *AAUP Annual Report on the Economic Status of the Profession.*

U.S. Census Bureau,　Statistical Abstract of the United States: 2009

Table 285. **Employees in Higher Education Institutions by Sex and Occupation: 1991 to 2005**

[In thousands (2,545.2 represents 2,545,200). As of fall. Based on complete census taken every other year; see source]

Year and status	Total	Professional staff Total	Executive, administrative, and managerial Male	Female	Faculty [1] Male	Female	Research/ instruction assistants Male	Female	Other Male	Female	Nonpro-fessional staff, total
1991, total	2,545.2	1,595.5	85.4	59.3	525.6	300.7	119.1	78.6	165.4	261.3	949.8
Full-time	1,812.9	1,031.8	82.9	56.2	366.2	169.4	–	–	142.2	214.8	781.1
Part-time	732.3	563.7	2.5	3.1	159.4	131.2	119.1	78.6	23.2	46.4	168.7
1997, total [2] ...	2,752.5	1,835.9	81.9	69.4	587.4	402.4	125.9	96.9	187.6	284.4	916.6
Full-time	1,828.5	1,104.8	78.9	65.6	363.9	204.8	–	–	159.3	232.3	723.7
Part-time	924.0	731.1	3.0	3.8	223.5	197.6	125.9	96.9	28.3	52.1	192.9
2005, total	3,379.1	2,459.9	95.2	101.1	714.5	576.0	167.5	149.6	262.8	393.2	919.2
Full-time	2,179.9	1,432.1	92.9	97.2	401.5	274.1	–	–	231.4	335.0	747.8
Part-time	1,199.2	1,027.8	2.4	3.9	312.9	301.9	167.5	149.6	31.4	58.2	171.4

– Represents zero. [1] Instruction and research. [2] In this table, 1997 data reflect the new classification of institutions. See footnote 1, Table 269.

Source: U.S. National Center for Education Statistics, *Digest of Education Statistics,* annual.

Table 286. **Faculty in Institutions of Higher Education: 1980 to 2005**

[In thousands (686 represents 686,000), except percent. As of fall. Based on complete census taken every other year; see source]

Year	Total	Employment status Full-time	Part-time	Control Public	Private	Level 4-Year	2-Year or less	Percent Part-time	Public	2-Year or less
1980 [1]	686	450	236	495	191	494	192	34	72	28
1985 [1]	715	459	256	503	212	504	211	36	70	30
1991 [2]	826	536	291	581	245	591	235	35	70	28
1993	915	546	370	650	265	626	290	40	71	32
1995	932	551	381	657	275	647	285	41	70	31
1997 [3]	990	569	421	695	295	683	307	43	70	31
1999 [3]	1,028	591	437	713	315	714	314	43	69	31
2001 [3]	1,113	618	495	771	342	764	349	44	69	31
2003 [3]	1,175	632	543	793	382	816	359	46	67	31
2005 [3]	1,290	676	615	841	449	917	373	48	65	29

[1] Estimated on the basis of enrollment. [2] Data beginning 1991 not comparable to prior years. [3] In this table, data beginning in 1997 reflect the new classification of institutions. See footnote 1, Table 269.

Source: U.S. National Center for Education Statistics, *Digest of Education Statistics,* annual.

Table 287. **Salary Offers to Candidates for Degrees: 2005 to 2007**

[In dollars. Data are average beginning salaries based on offers made by business, industrial, government, nonprofit, and educational employers to graduating students. Data from representative colleges throughout the United States]

Field of study	Bachelor's 2005	2006	2007	Master's [1] 2005	2006	2007	Doctoral 2005	2006	2007
Accounting...........	42,940	44,928	46,292	45,992	47,003	49,723	(NA)	(NA)	(NA)
Business administration/ management [2]	39,480	41,155	43,256	[3]50,513	[3]47,824	[3]55,222	[3]66,500	[3]81,438	[3]90,625
Marketing.............	36,409	37,191	39,269	[3]47,000	[3]38,000	(NA)	(NA)	(NA)	(NA)
Engineering:									
Civil..............	43,774	46,084	48,998	48,619	50,953	51,297	[3]59,216	[3]63,100	[3]62,275
Chemical	53,639	56,269	59,218	62,845	[3]59,008	[3]66,542	[3]73,317	75,659	[3]76,688
Computer...........	52,242	53,096	55,920	58,631	[3]66,545	[3]67,304	[3]69,625	[3]74,750	[3]95,250
Electrical	51,773	53,300	55,333	64,781	66,687	[3]68,247	[3]75,066	81,297	[3]77,860
Mechanical........	50,175	[3]51,808	54,057	60,223	61,234	63,209	69,757	[3]69,034	[3]70,928
Nuclear [4]	[3]51,225	[3]54,616	55,966	[3]59,059	[3]53,798	[3]62,848	(NA)	(NA)	(NA)
Petroleum..........	62,236	[3]67,069	[3]59,408	[3]65,000	[3]68,833	[3]57,000	(NA)	(NA)	(NA)
Engineering technology..	45,790	48,514	50,808	(NA)	(NA)	(NA)	(NA)	(NA)	(NA)
Chemistry...........	38,635	39,804	41,820	(NA)	[3]51,136	(NA)	55,874	68,458	[3]61,822
Mathematics.........	43,304	44,672	46,547	[3]34,500	[3]51,767	[3]54,688	[3]55,047	[3]63,952	[3]56,727
Physics.............	[3]44,700	[3]45,120	[3]43,886	[3]62,500	[3]52,333	[3]67,406	[3]54,897	[3]72,357	[3]50,725
Humanities..........	31,565	[3]31,183	31,345	[3]35,212	[3]40,952	[3]39,808	[3]43,728	[3]48,938	[3]44,199
Social sciences [5].	31,621	32,134	33,881	[3]40,575	[3]42,220	[3]42,930	[3]46,838	[3]48,487	[3]49,225
Computer science	50,664	50,744	53,051	64,840	71,165	65,463	[3]84,025	[3]76,630	[3]79,086

NA Not available. [1] Candidates with 1 year or less of full-time nonmilitary employment. [2] For master's degree, offers are after nontechnical undergraduate degree. [3] Fewer than 50 offers reported. [4] Includes engineering physics. [5] Excludes economics.

Source: National Association of Colleges and Employers, Bethlehem, PA (copyright). Reprinted with permission from Fall 2005, 2006, and 2007 Salary Survey. All rights reserved.

Table 288. Earned Degrees Conferred by Level and Sex: 1960 to 2006

[In thousands (477 represents 477,000), except percent. Based on survey; see Appendix III]

Year ending	All degrees Total	Percent male	Associate's Male	Female	Bachelor's Male	Female	Master's Male	Female	First professional Male	Female	Doctoral Male	Female
1960 [1]	477	65.8	(NA)	(NA)	254	138	51	24	(NA)	(NA)	9	1
1970	1,271	59.2	117	89	451	341	126	83	33	2	26	4
1975	1,666	56.0	191	169	505	418	162	131	49	7	27	7
1980	1,731	51.1	184	217	474	456	151	147	53	17	23	10
1985	1,828	49.3	203	252	483	497	143	143	50	25	22	11
1989	1,873	47.3	186	250	483	535	149	161	45	26	23	13
1990	1,940	46.6	191	264	492	560	154	171	44	27	24	14
1991	2,025	45.8	199	283	504	590	156	181	44	28	25	15
1992	2,108	45.6	207	297	521	616	162	191	45	29	26	15
1993	2,167	45.5	212	303	533	632	169	200	45	30	26	16
1994	2,206	45.1	215	315	532	637	176	211	45	31	27	17
1995 [2]	2,218	44.9	218	321	526	634	179	219	45	31	27	18
1996 [2]	2,248	44.2	220	336	522	642	179	227	45	32	27	18
1997 [2]	2,288	43.6	224	347	521	652	181	238	46	33	27	19
1998 [2]	2,298	43.2	218	341	520	664	184	246	45	34	27	19
1999 [2]	2,323	42.7	218	342	519	682	186	254	44	34	25	19
2000 [2]	2,385	42.6	225	340	530	708	192	265	44	36	25	20
2001 [2]	2,416	42.4	232	347	532	712	194	274	43	37	25	20
2002 [2]	2,494	42.2	238	357	550	742	199	283	43	38	24	20
2003 [2]	2,621	42.1	253	380	573	775	211	301	42	39	24	22
2004 [2]	2,755	41.8	260	405	595	804	230	329	42	41	25	23
2005 [2]	2,850	41.6	268	429	613	826	234	341	44	43	27	26
2006 [2]	2,936	41.3	270	443	631	855	238	356	44	44	29	27

NA Not available. [1] First-professional degrees are included with bachelor's degrees. [2] Data beginning in 1996 reflect the new classification of institutions. See footnote 1, Table 269.

Source: U.S. National Center for Education Statistics, *Digest of Education Statistics*, annual.

Table 289. Degrees Earned by Level and Race/Ethnicity: 1990 to 2006

[For school year ending in year shown. Based on survey; see Appendix III]

Level of degree and race/ethnicity	Total 1990	1995	2000 [1]	2005 [1]	2006 [1]	Percent distribution 1990	2000 [1]	2006 [1]
Associate's degrees, total	**455,102**	**539,691**	**564,933**	**696,660**	**713,066**	**100.0**	**100.0**	**100.0**
White, non-Hispanic	376,816	420,656	408,772	475,513	485,297	82.8	72.4	68.1
Black, non-Hispanic	34,326	47,067	60,221	86,402	89,784	7.5	10.7	12.6
Hispanic	21,504	35,962	51,573	78,557	80,854	4.7	9.1	11.3
Asian or Pacific Islander	13,066	20,677	27,782	33,669	35,201	2.9	4.9	4.9
American Indian/Alaska Native	3,430	5,482	6,497	8,435	8,552	0.8	1.2	1.2
Nonresident alien	5,960	9,847	10,088	14,084	13,378	1.3	1.8	1.9
Bachelor's degrees, total	**1,051,344**	**1,160,134**	**1,237,875**	**1,439,264**	**1,485,242**	**100.0**	**100.0**	**100.0**
White, non-Hispanic	887,151	914,610	929,106	1,049,141	1,075,561	84.4	75.1	72.4
Black, non-Hispanic	61,046	87,236	108,013	136,122	142,420	5.8	8.7	9.6
Hispanic	32,829	54,230	75,059	101,124	107,588	3.1	6.1	7.2
Asian or Pacific Islander	39,230	60,502	77,912	97,209	102,376	3.7	6.3	6.9
American Indian/Alaska Native	4,390	6,610	8,719	10,307	10,940	0.4	0.7	0.7
Nonresident alien	26,698	36,946	39,066	45,361	46,357	2.5	3.2	3.1
Master's degrees, total	**324,301**	**397,629**	**457,056**	**574,618**	**594,065**	**100.0**	**100.0**	**100.0**
White, non-Hispanic	254,299	293,345	320,485	379,350	393,357	78.4	70.1	66.2
Black, non-Hispanic	15,336	24,166	35,874	54,482	58,976	4.7	7.8	9.9
Hispanic	7,892	12,905	19,253	31,485	32,438	2.4	4.2	5.5
Asian or Pacific Islander	10,439	16,847	23,218	32,783	34,029	3.2	5.1	5.7
American Indian/Alaska Native	1,090	1,621	2,246	3,295	3,504	0.3	0.5	0.6
Nonresident alien	35,245	48,745	55,980	73,223	71,761	10.9	12.2	12.1
Doctor's degrees, total	**38,371**	**44,446**	**44,808**	**52,631**	**56,067**	**100.0**	**100.0**	**100.0**
White, non-Hispanic	26,221	27,846	27,843	30,261	31,601	68.3	62.1	56.4
Black, non-Hispanic	1,149	1,667	2,246	3,056	3,122	3.0	5.0	5.6
Hispanic	780	984	1,305	1,824	1,882	2.0	2.9	3.4
Asian or Pacific Islander	1,225	2,689	2,420	2,911	3,257	3.2	5.4	5.8
American Indian/Alaska Native	98	130	160	237	230	0.3	0.4	0.4
Nonresident alien	8,898	11,130	10,834	14,342	15,975	23.2	24.2	28.5
First-professional degrees, total	**70,988**	**75,800**	**80,057**	**87,289**	**87,655**	**100.0**	**100.0**	**100.0**
White, non-Hispanic	60,487	59,402	59,637	63,429	63,590	85.2	74.5	72.5
Black, non-Hispanic	3,409	4,747	5,555	6,313	6,223	4.8	6.9	7.1
Hispanic	2,425	3,231	3,865	4,445	4,446	3.4	4.8	5.1
Asian or Pacific Islander	3,362	6,396	8,584	10,501	10,645	4.7	10.7	12.1
American Indian/Alaska Native	257	413	564	564	710	0.4	0.7	0.8
Nonresident alien	1,048	1,611	1,852	2,037	2,041	1.5	2.3	2.3

[1] In this table, data beginning in 2000 reflect the new classification of institutions. See footnote 1, Table 269.

Source: U.S. National Center for Education Statistics, *Digest of Education Statistics,* annual.

U.S. Census Bureau, Statistical Abstract of the United States: 2009

Table 290. **Degrees and Awards Earned Below Bachelor's by Field: 2006**

[Covers associate's degrees and other awards based on postsecondary curriculums of less than 4 years in institutions of higher education. Based on survey; see Appendix III]

Field of study	Less than 1-year awards		1- to less than 4-year awards		Associate's degrees	
	Total	Women	Total	Women	Total	Women
Total	**228,999**	**129,055**	**183,600**	**112,611**	**713,066**	**442,971**
Agriculture and natural resources, total	3,252	911	1,886	691	6,168	2,376
Architecture and related services	161	62	173	128	656	409
Area, ethnic, cultural, and gender studies	407	322	114	95	124	87
Biological and biomedical sciences	104	82	24	13	1,827	1,201
Business, management, and marketing	29,137	19,748	16,406	12,575	96,933	66,061
Communications and communications technologies	1,118	483	1,118	483	1,118	483
Computer and information sciences	9,277	3,444	5,799	2,196	31,246	8,782
Construction trades	7,750	397	7,389	307	3,850	217
Education	3,016	2,604	2,150	1,957	14,475	12,243
Engineering and engineering technologies	6,986	1,117	6,986	1,117	6,986	1,117
English language and literature/letters	559	374	79	56	1,105	735
Family and consumer sciences	11,485	9,669	3,743	3,032	9,488	9,070
Foreign languages and literatures	835	602	455	425	1,161	945
Health professions and related sciences	89,285	72,045	81,176	70,613	134,931	115,263
Nursing	3,526	3,187	28,776	25,886	1,481	1,332
Legal professions and studies	1,653	1,453	2,466	2,139	10,509	9,416
Liberal arts and sciences, general studies, and humanities	390	287	3,490	2,211	244,689	154,734
Library science	179	158	89	82	136	121
Mathematics	60	26	12	8	753	270
Mechanics and repairers	16,252	1,195	22,960	920	14,454	741
Military technologies	62	15	–	–	610	100
Multi/interdisciplinary studies	438	239	487	368	14,473	8,249
Parks, recreation, leisure, and fitness	303	148	185	81	1,128	472
Personal and culinary services	5,991	4,491	9,743	8,037	17,162	7,898
Philosophy and religion	10	2	71	37	367	270
Physical sciences and science technologies	452	218	292	134	2,902	1,200
Precision production trades	5,028	292	4,997	277	1,977	177
Psychology	90	65	31	30	1,944	1,498
Public administration and social services	823	698	519	401	4,415	3,773
Security and protective services	19,534	4,795	5,184	1,440	26,425	11,847
Social sciences and history	381	212	233	97	6,730	4,392
Theology and religious vocations	93	50	474	221	570	322
Transportation and material moving	11,313	1,709	1,046	117	1,472	204
Visual and performing arts	2,575	1,142	4,307	2,559	21,754	12,461

– Represents zero.

Source: U.S. National Center for Education Statistics, *Digest of Education Statistics,* annual.

Table 291. **Bachelor's Degrees Earned by Field: 1980 to 2006**

[The new Classification of Instructional Programs was introduced in 2002–03. Data for previous years has been reclassified where necessary to conform to the new classifications. Based on survey; see Appendix III]

Field of study	1980	1990	2000	2004	2005	2006
Total	**929,417**	**1,051,344**	**1,237,875**	**1,399,542**	**1,439,264**	**1,485,242**
Agriculture and natural resources	22,802	12,900	24,238	22,835	23,002	23,053
Architecture and related services	9,132	9,364	8,462	8,838	9,237	9,515
Area, ethnic, cultural, and gender studies	2,840	4,447	6,212	7,181	7,569	7,879
Biological and biomedical sciences	46,190	37,204	63,005	61,509	64,611	69,178
Business	186,264	248,568	256,070	307,149	311,574	318,042
Communication, journalism, and related programs [1]	28,616	51,572	57,058	73,002	75,238	76,936
Computer and information sciences	11,154	27,347	37,788	59,488	54,111	47,480
Education	118,038	105,112	108,034	106,278	105,451	107,238
Engineering and engineering technologies	69,387	82,480	73,419	78,227	79,743	81,223
English language and literature/letters	32,187	46,803	50,106	53,984	54,379	55,096
Family and consumer sciences/human sciences	18,411	13,514	16,321	19,172	20,074	20,775
Foreign languages, literatures, and linguistics	12,480	13,133	15,886	17,754	18,386	19,410
Health professions and related clinical sciences	63,848	58,983	80,863	73,934	80,685	91,973
Legal professions and studies	683	1,632	1,969	2,841	3,161	3,302
Liberal arts and sciences, general studies, and humanities	23,196	27,985	36,104	42,106	43,751	44,898
Mathematics and statistics	11,378	14,276	11,418	13,327	14,351	14,770
Multi/interdisciplinary studies	11,457	16,557	28,561	29,162	30,243	32,012
Parks, recreation, leisure, and fitness studies	5,753	4,582	17,571	22,164	22,888	25,490
Philosophy and religious studies	7,069	7,034	8,535	11,152	11,584	11,985
Physical sciences and science technologies	23,407	16,056	18,331	17,983	18,905	20,318
Psychology	42,093	53,952	74,194	82,098	85,614	88,134
Public administration and social services	16,644	13,908	20,185	20,552	21,769	21,986
Security and protective services	15,015	15,354	24,877	28,175	30,723	35,319
Social sciences and history	103,662	118,083	127,101	150,357	156,892	161,485
Theology and religious vocations	6,170	5,185	6,789	8,126	9,284	8,548
Transportation and materials moving	213	2,387	3,395	4,824	4,904	5,349
Visual and performing arts	40,892	39,934	58,791	77,181	80,955	83,297
Other and unclassified	436	2,992	2,592	143	180	164

[1] Includes technologies.

Source: U.S. National Center for Education Statistics, *Digest of Education Statistics,* annual; and unpublished data.

Table 292. **Master's and Doctoral Degrees Earned by Field: 1980 to 2006**

[The new Classification of Instructional Programs was introduced in 2002–03. Data for previous years has been reclassified where necessary to conform to the new classifications. Based on survey; see Appendix III]

Field of study	1980	1990	2000	2004	2005	2006
MASTER'S DEGREES						
Total	**298,081**	**324,301**	**457,056**	**558,940**	**574,618**	**594,065**
Agriculture and natural resources	3,976	3,382	4,360	4,783	4,746	4,640
Architecture and related services	3,139	3,499	4,268	5,424	5,674	5,743
Area, ethnic, cultural, and gender studies	852	1,191	1,544	1,683	1,755	2,080
Biological and biomedical sciences	6,322	4,906	6,781	7,657	8,199	8,681
Business	55,008	76,676	111,532	139,347	142,617	146,406
Communication, journalism, and related programs [1]	3,082	4,353	5,525	6,900	7,195	7,745
Computer and information sciences	3,647	9,677	14,990	20,143	18,416	17,055
Education	101,819	84,890	123,045	162,345	167,490	174,620
Engineering and engineering technologies	16,765	25,294	26,726	35,197	35,133	33,530
English language and literature/letters	6,026	6,317	7,022	7,956	8,468	8,845
Family and consumer sciences/human sciences	2,690	1,679	1,882	1,794	1,827	1,983
Foreign languages, literatures, and linguistics	3,067	3,018	3,037	3,124	3,407	3,539
Health professions and related clinical sciences	15,374	20,406	42,593	44,939	46,703	51,380
Legal professions and studies	1,817	1,888	3,750	4,243	4,170	4,453
Liberal arts and sciences, general studies, and humanities	2,646	1,999	3,256	3,697	3,680	3,702
Library science	5,374	4,341	4,577	6,015	6,213	6,448
Mathematics and statistics	2,860	3,624	3,208	4,191	4,477	4,730
Multi/interdisciplinary studies	2,494	3,182	3,487	4,047	4,252	4,491
Parks, recreation, leisure, and fitness studies	647	529	2,322	3,199	3,740	3,992
Philosophy and religious studies	1,204	1,327	1,376	1,578	1,647	1,739
Physical sciences and science technologies	5,167	5,410	4,810	5,570	5,678	5,922
Psychology	9,938	10,730	15,740	17,898	18,830	19,770
Public administration and social services	17,560	17,399	25,594	28,250	29,552	30,510
Security and protective services	1,805	1,151	2,609	3,717	3,991	4,277
Social sciences and history	12,176	11,634	14,066	16,110	16,952	17,369
Theology and religious vocations	3,872	4,941	5,534	5,486	5,815	6,092
Visual and performing arts	8,708	8,481	10,918	12,906	13,183	13,530
DOCTORAL DEGREES						
Total	**32,615**	**38,371**	**44,808**	**48,378**	**52,631**	**56,067**
Agriculture and natural resources	991	1,295	1,168	1,185	1,173	1,194
Architecture and related services	79	103	129	173	179	201
Area, ethnic, cultural, and gender studies	151	125	205	209	189	226
Biological and biomedical sciences	3,527	3,837	5,180	5,242	5,578	5,775
Business	767	1,093	1,194	1,481	1,498	1,711
Communication, journalism, and related programs [1]	193	272	357	426	468	464
Computer and information sciences	240	627	779	909	1,119	1,416
Education	7,314	6,503	6,409	7,088	7,681	7,584
Engineering and engineering technologies	2,546	5,030	5,421	5,981	6,601	7471
English language and literature/letters	1,196	986	1,470	1,207	1,212	1,254
Family and consumer sciences/human sciences	192	273	327	329	331	340
Foreign languages, literatures, and linguistics	857	816	1,086	1,031	1,027	1,074
Health professions and related clinical sciences	821	1,449	2,053	4,361	5,868	7,128
Legal professions and studies	40	111	74	119	98	129
Liberal arts and sciences, general studies, and humanities	192	63	83	95	109	84
Mathematics and statistics	724	917	1,075	1,060	1,176	1,293
Multi/interdisciplinary studies	318	442	792	876	983	987
Parks, recreation, leisure, and fitness studies	21	35	134	222	207	194
Philosophy and religious studies	374	445	598	595	586	578
Physical sciences and science technologies	3,044	4,116	3,963	3,815	4,114	4,489
Psychology	3,395	3,811	4,731	4,827	5,106	4,921
Public administration and social services	342	508	537	649	673	704
Security and protective services	18	38	52	54	94	80
Social sciences and history	3,230	3,010	4,095	3,811	3,819	3,914
Theology and religious vocations	1,315	1,317	1,630	1,304	1,422	1,429
Visual and performing arts	655	849	1,127	1,282	1,278	1,383

[1] Includes technologies.

Source: U.S. National Center for Education Statistics, *Digest of Education Statistics,* annual; and unpublished data.

Table 293. First Professional Degrees Earned in Selected Professions: 1970 to 2006

[First professional degrees include degrees which require at least 6 years of college work for completion (including at least 2 years of preprofessional training). Based on survey; see Appendix III]

Type of degree and sex of recipient	1970	1975	1980	1985	1990	1995	2000	2004	2005	2006
Medicine (M.D.):										
Institutions conferring degrees.....	86	104	112	120	124	119	118	118	120	119
Degrees conferred, total.........	8,314	12,447	14,902	16,041	15,075	15,537	15,286	15,442	15,461	15,455
Percent to women	8.4	13.1	23.4	30.4	34.2	38.8	42.7	46.4	47.3	48.9
Dentistry (D.D.S. or D.M.D.):										
Institutions conferring degrees.....	48	52	58	59	57	53	54	53	53	54
Degrees conferred, total.........	3,718	4,773	5,258	5,339	4,100	3,897	4,250	4,335	4,454	4,389
Percent to women	0.9	3.1	13.3	20.7	30.9	36.4	40.1	41.6	43.8	44.5
Law (LL.B. or J.D.):										
Institutions conferring degrees.....	145	154	179	181	182	183	190	195	198	197
Degrees conferred, total.........	14,916	29,296	35,647	37,491	36,485	39,349	38,152	40,209	43,423	43,440
Percent to women	5.4	15.1	30.2	38.5	42.2	42.6	45.9	49.4	48.7	48.0
Theological (B.D., M.Div., M.H.L.):										
Institutions conferring degrees.....	(NA)	(NA)	(NA)	(NA)	(NA)	192	198	200	(NA)	(NA)
Degrees conferred, total.........	5,298	5,095	7,115	7,221	5,851	5,978	6,129	5,332	5,533	5,666
Percent to women	2.3	6.8	13.8	18.5	24.8	25.7	29.2	34.2	35.6	33.6

NA Not available.
Source: U.S. National Center for Education Statistics, *Digest of Education Statistics*, annual.

Table 294. Participation in Adult Education: 2004–2005

[In thousands (211,607 represents 211,607,000), except percent. For the civilian noninstitutional population 16 years old. Adult education includes enrollment in formal education activities in the previous 12 months. Excludes participants in only postsecondary degree, certificate, or diploma programs as full-time students. Based on the Adult Education Survey of the National Household Education Survey Program and subject to sampling error; see source and Appendix III for details. For more data on adult education, see Tables 616 and 617]

Characteristic	Adult population (1,000)	Participants in adult education				
		Number taking adult education courses [1] (1,000)	Percent of total [1]	Type of course (percent)		
				College or university degree program	Work-related course	Personal interest course
Total, 2005.............	**211,607**	**93,939**	**44**	**4**	**27**	**21**
Age:						
16 to 30 years old............	48,544	25,040	52	8	25	23
31 to 40 years old............	40,009	20,839	52	6	34	23
41 to 50 years old............	45,662	21,983	48	3	36	20
51 to 65 years old............	46,211	18,767	41	2	28	20
66 years old and over	31,181	7,310	23	–	5	19
Sex:						
Male.....................	101,596	41,724	41	4	24	18
Female	110,011	52,216	47	4	29	24
Race/ethnicity:						
White, Non-Hispanic	146,614	66,909	46	4	29	22
Black, Non-Hispanic	23,467	10,878	46	4	27	24
Hispanic	26,101	9,824	38	4	17	15
Other	15,426	6,328	41	5	24	22
Educational attainment:						
Less than high school	31,017	6,851	22	–	4	11
High school diploma or GED......	64,334	20,955	33	2	17	16
Some college..............	58,545	30,070	51	6	31	25
Bachelor's degree or higher	57,711	36,063	62	7	46	29
Marital status:						
Married...................	132,008	58,748	45	3	29	21
Living with partner, unmarried	12,498	4,879	39	4	26	16
Separated/divorced/widowed......	30,170	10,874	36	2	20	19
Never married	36,930	19,439	53	8	23	26
Employment/occupation:						
Employed	152,450	78,879	52	5	36	22
Professional or managerial	48,647	34,138	70	8	56	29
Services, sales, or support	65,289	31,609	48	5	31	22
Trades.................	38,514	13,132	34	2	19	13
Unemployed or not in labor force in past 12 months	59,157	15,060	25	1	4	20
Household income:						
$20,000 or less	34,670	9,552	28	2	11	16
$20,001 to $35,000	35,839	12,866	36	4	18	17
$35,001 to $50,000	33,376	14,122	42	2	23	22
$50,001 to $75,000	47,114	22,494	48	5	33	21
$75,001 or more............	60,607	34,904	58	5	39	27
Children under 10 in household:						
Yes	57,560	26,746	46	5	29	20
No	154,047	67,193	44	4	26	22

– Represents or rounds to zero. [1] Includes English as a second language, basic education skills, vocational or technical diploma programs, and apprenticeship programs each with a total participation rate of about 1 percent.
Source: U.S. Department of Education, National Center for Education Statistics, Adult Education Survey of the National Household Education Surveys Program 2005, unpublished data.

Section 5
Law Enforcement, Courts, and Prisons

This section presents data on crimes committed, victims of crimes, arrests, and data related to criminal violations and the criminal justice system. The major sources of these data are the Bureau of Justice Statistics (BJS), the Federal Bureau of Investigation (FBI), and the Administrative Office of the U.S. Courts. BJS issues many reports—see our Guide to Sources for a complete listing. The Federal Bureau of Investigation's major annual reports are *Crime in the United States, Law Enforcement Officers Killed and Assaulted,* annual, and *Hate Crimes,* annual, which present data on reported crimes as gathered from state and local law enforcement agencies.

Legal jurisdiction and law enforcement—Law enforcement is, for the most part, a function of state and local officers and agencies. The U.S. Constitution reserves general police powers to the states. By act of Congress, federal offenses include only offenses against the U.S. government and against or by its employees while engaged in their official duties and offenses which involve the crossing of state lines or an interference with interstate commerce. Excluding the military, there are 52 separate criminal law jurisdictions in the United States: one in each of the 50 states, one in the District of Columbia, and the federal jurisdiction. Each of these has its own criminal law and procedure and its own law enforcement agencies. While the systems of law enforcement are quite similar among the states, there are often substantial differences in the penalties for like offenses.

Law enforcement can be divided into three parts: Investigation of crimes and arrests of persons suspected of committing them; prosecution of those charged with crime; and the punishment or treatment of persons convicted of crime.

Crime—The U.S. Department of Justice administers two statistical programs to measure the magnitude, nature, and impact of crime in the nation: the Uniform Crime Reporting (UCR) Program and the National Crime Victimization Survey (NCVS). Each of these programs produces valuable information about aspects of the nation's crime problem. Because the UCR and NCVS programs are conducted for different purposes, use different methods, and focus on somewhat different aspects of crime, the information they produce together provides a more comprehensive panorama of the nation's crime problem than either could produce alone.

Uniform Crime Reports (UCR)—The FBI's UCR Program, which began in 1929, collects information on the following crimes reported to law enforcement authorities—Part 1 offenses (detail data reported): murder and nonnegligent manslaughter, forcible rape, robbery, aggravated assault, burglary, larceny-theft, motor vehicle theft, and arson. For Part 2 offenses, law enforcement agencies report only arrest data for 21 additional crime categories. For UCR definitions of criminal offenses (including those listed), please go to: <www.fbi.gov/ucr/cius2006/about/offense_definitions.html>.

The UCR Program compiles data from monthly law enforcement reports or individual crime incident records transmitted directly to the FBI or to centralized state agencies that then report to the FBI. The Program thoroughly examines each report it receives for reasonableness, accuracy, and deviations that may indicate errors. Large variations in crime levels may indicate modified records procedures, incomplete reporting, or changes in a jurisdiction's boundaries. To identify any unusual fluctuations in an agency's crime counts, the Program compares monthly reports to previous submissions of the agency and with those for similar agencies.

The UCR Program presents crime counts for the nation as a whole, as well as for regions, states, counties, cities, towns, tribal law enforcement, and colleges and

U.S. Census Bureau, Statistical Abstract of the United States: 2009

universities. This permits studies among neighboring jurisdictions and among those with similar populations and other common characteristics.

The UCR Program annually publishes its findings in a preliminary release in the spring of the following calendar year, followed by a detailed annual report, *Crime in the United States*, issued in the fall. In addition to crime counts and trends, this report includes data on crimes cleared, persons arrested (age, sex, and race), law enforcement personnel (including the number of sworn officers killed or assaulted), and the characteristics of homicides (including age, sex, and race of victims and offenders; victim-offender relationships; weapons used; and circumstances surrounding the homicides). Other periodic reports are also available from the UCR Program.

National Crime Victimization Survey (NCVS)—The 2006 national crime victimization estimates are not comparable to previous years because of changes in methodology. The methodological changes included: a new sample, a change in the method of handling first-time interviews with households, and a change in the method of interviewing. For more information on methodology, go to <http://www.ojp.usdoj.gov/bjs/abstract/cv06.htm>.

A second perspective on crime is provided by this survey of the Bureau of Justice Statistics (BJS). The NCVS is an annual data collection (interviews of persons age 12 or older), conducted by the U.S. Census Bureau for the BJS. As an ongoing survey of households, the NCVS measures crimes of violence and theft both reported and not reported to police. It produces national rates and levels of personal and property victimization. No attempt is made to validate the information against police records or any other source.

The NCVS measures rape/sexual assault, robbery, assault, pocket-picking, purse snatching, burglary, and motor vehicle theft. The NCVS includes crimes reported to the police, as well as those not reported.

Murder and kidnapping are not covered. The so-called victimless crimes, such as drunkenness, drug abuse, and prostitution, also are excluded, as are crimes for which it is difficult to identify knowledgeable respondents or to locate data records.

Crimes of which the victim may not be aware also cannot be measured effectively. Buying stolen property may fall into this category, as may some instances of embezzlement. Attempted crimes of many types probably are under recorded for this reason. Events in which the victim has shown a willingness to participate in illegal activity also are excluded.

In any encounter involving a personal crime, more than one criminal act can be committed against an individual. For example, a rape may be associated with a robbery, or a household offense, such as a burglary, can escalate into something more serious in the event of a personal confrontation. In classifying the survey-measured crimes, each criminal incident has been counted only once—by the most serious act that took place during the incident and ranked in accordance with the seriousness classification system used by the FBI. The order of seriousness for crimes against persons is as follows: rape, robbery, assault, and larceny. Personal crimes take precedence over household offenses.

A *victimization*, basic measure of the occurrence of crime, is a specific criminal act as it affects a single victim. The number of victimizations is determined by the number of victims of such acts. Victimization counts serve as key elements in computing rates of victimization. For crimes against persons, the rates are based on the total number of individuals age 12 and over or on a portion of that population sharing a particular characteristic or set of traits. As general indicators of the danger of having been victimized during the reference period, the rates are not sufficiently refined to represent true measures of risk for specific individuals or households.

An *incident* is a specific criminal act involving one or more victims; therefore the number of incidents of personal crimes is lower than that of victimizations.

Courts—Statistics on criminal offenses and the outcome of prosecutions are incomplete for the country as a whole, although data are available for many states individually.

Since 1982, through its National Judicial Reporting Program, the BJS has surveyed a nationally representative sample of 300 counties every 2 years and collected detailed information on demographic characteristics of felons, conviction offenses, type of sentences, sentence lengths, and time from arrest to conviction and sentencing.

The bulk of civil and criminal litigation in the country is commenced and determined in the various state courts. Only when the U.S. Constitution and acts of Congress specifically confer jurisdiction upon the federal courts may civil or criminal litigation be heard and decided by them. Generally, the federal courts have jurisdiction over the following types of cases: suits or proceedings by or against the United States; civil actions between private parties arising under the Constitution, laws, or treaties of the United States; civil actions between private litigants who are citizens of different states; civil cases involving admiralty, maritime, or private jurisdiction; and all matters in bankruptcy.

There are several types of courts with varying degrees of legal jurisdiction. These jurisdictions include original, appellate, general, and limited or special. A court of original jurisdiction is one having the authority initially to try a case and pass judgment on the law and the facts; a court of appellate jurisdiction is one with the legal authority to review cases and hear appeals; a court of general jurisdiction is a trial court of unlimited original jurisdiction in civil and/or criminal cases, also called a "major trial court"; a court of limited or special jurisdiction is a trial court with legal authority over only a particular class of cases, such as probate, juvenile, or traffic cases.

The 94 federal courts of original jurisdiction are known as the U.S. district courts. One or more of these courts is established in every state and one each in the District of Columbia, Puerto Rico, the Virgin Islands, the Northern Mariana Islands, and Guam. Appeals from the district courts are taken to intermediate appellate courts of which there are 13, known as U.S. courts of appeals and the United States Court of Appeals for the Federal Circuit. The Supreme Court of the United States is the final and highest appellate court in the federal system of courts.

Juvenile offenders—For statistical purposes, the FBI and most states classify as juvenile offenders persons under the age of 18 years who have committed a crime or crimes.

Delinquency cases are all cases of youths referred to a juvenile court for violation of a law or ordinance or for seriously "antisocial" conduct. Several types of facilities are available for those adjudicated delinquents, ranging from the short-term physically unrestricted environment to the long-term very restrictive atmosphere.

Prisoners and jail inmates—BJS started to collect annual data in 1979 on prisoners in federal and state prisons and reformatories. Adults convicted of criminal activity may be given a prison or jail sentence. A *prison* is a confinement facility having custodial authority over adults sentenced to confinement of more than 1 year. A *jail* is a facility, usually operated by a local law enforcement agency, holding persons detained pending adjudication and/or persons committed after adjudication to 1 year or less.

Data on inmates in local jails were collected by the BJS for the first time in 1970. Since then, BJS has conducted censuses of facilities and inmates every 5 to 6 years. In 1984, BJS initiated an annual survey of jails conducted in noncensus years.

Statistical reliability—For discussion of statistical collection, estimation and sampling procedures, and measures of statistical reliability pertaining to the National Crime Victimization Survey and Uniform Crime Reporting Program, see Appendix III.

U.S. Census Bureau, *Statistical Abstract of the United States: 2009*

Table 295. **Crimes and Crime Rates by Type of Offense: 1980 to 2006**

[**(1,345 represents 1,345,000).** Data include offenses actually reported to law enforcement and also offense estimations for nonreporting and partially reporting agencies within each state. Rates are based on Census Bureau estimated resident population as of **July 1; 1980, 1990, and 2000, enumerated as of April 1.** See source for details. For definitions of types of crimes, go to <http://www.fbi.gov/ucr/cius2006/about/offense_definitions.html/>]

Item and year	Violent crime					Property crime			
	Total	Murder [1]	Forcible rape	Robbery	Aggra-vated assault	Total	Burglary	Larceny/ theft	Motor vehicle theft
Number of offenses (1,000):									
1980	1,345	23	83	566	673	12,064	3,795	7,137	1,132
1985	1,328	19	88	498	723	11,103	3,073	6,926	1,103
1990	1,820	23	103	639	1,055	12,655	3,074	7,946	1,636
1992	1,932	24	109	672	1,127	12,506	2,980	7,915	1,611
1993	1,926	25	106	660	1,136	12,219	2,835	7,821	1,563
1994	1,858	23	102	619	1,113	12,132	2,713	7,880	1,539
1995	1,799	22	97	581	1,099	12,064	2,594	7,998	1,472
1996	1,689	20	96	536	1,037	11,805	2,506	7,905	1,394
1997	1,636	18	96	499	1,023	11,558	2,461	7,744	1,354
1998	1,534	17	93	447	977	10,952	2,333	7,376	1,243
1999	1,426	16	89	409	912	10,208	2,101	6,956	1,152
2000	1,425	16	90	408	912	10,183	2,051	6,972	1,160
2001 [2]	1,439	16	91	424	909	10,437	2,117	7,092	1,228
2002	1,424	16	95	421	891	10,455	2,151	7,057	1,247
2003	1,384	17	94	414	859	10,443	2,155	7,027	1,261
2004	1,360	16	95	401	847	10,319	2,144	6,937	1,238
2005	1,391	17	94	417	862	10,175	2,155	6,783	1,236
2006	1,418	17	92	447	861	9,984	2,184	6,607	1,193
Rate per 100,000 population:									
1980	597	10	37	251	299	5,353	1,684	3,167	502
1985	558	8	37	209	304	4,666	1,292	2,911	464
1990	730	9	41	256	423	5,073	1,232	3,185	656
1992	758	9	43	264	442	4,904	1,168	3,104	632
1993	747	10	41	256	441	4,740	1,100	3,034	606
1994	714	9	39	238	428	4,660	1,042	3,027	591
1995	685	8	37	221	418	4,591	987	3,043	560
1996	637	7	36	202	391	4,451	945	2,980	526
1997	611	7	36	186	382	4,316	919	2,892	506
1998	568	6	35	166	361	4,053	863	2,730	460
1999	523	6	33	150	334	3,744	770	2,551	423
2000	507	6	32	145	324	3,618	729	2,477	412
2001 [2]	505	6	32	149	319	3,658	742	2,486	431
2002	494	6	33	146	310	3,631	747	2,451	433
2003	476	6	32	143	295	3,591	741	2,417	434
2004	463	6	32	137	289	3,514	730	2,362	422
2005	469	6	32	141	291	3,432	727	2,288	417
2006	474	6	31	149	288	3,335	729	2,207	398

[1] Includes nonnegligent manslaughter. [2] The murder and nonnegligent homicides that occurred as a result of the events of September 11, 2001, were not included in this table.

Source: U.S. Department of Justice, Federal Bureau of Investigation. *Crime in the United States*, annual. See also <http://www.fbi.gov/ucr/cius2006/index.html>.

Table 296. **Crimes and Crime Rates by Type and Area: 2006**

[**In thousands (1,418 represents 1,418,000), except rate. Rate per 100,000 population;** based on Census Bureau estimated resident population as of **July 1.** See headnote, Table 295. For definitions of types of crimes, go to <http://www.fbi.gov/ucr/cius2006/about/offense_definitions.html/>]

Type of crime	United States		Metropolitan statistical areas [1]		Cities outside metropolitan areas		Nonmetropolitan counties	
	Total	Rate	Total	Rate	Total	Rate	Total	Rate
Violent crime	1,418	474	1,280	515	77	382	61	199
Murder and nonnegligent manslaughter	17	6	15	6	1	3	1	3
Forcible rape	92	31	77	31	8	39	7	24
Robbery	447	149	430	173	12	62	5	16
Aggravated assault	861	288	757	304	56	278	48	156
Property crime	9,984	3,335	8,707	3,500	771	3,849	506	1,654
Burglary	2,184	729	1,862	749	160	798	162	528
Larceny-theft	6,607	2,207	5,730	2,303	574	2,865	303	992
Motor vehicle theft	1,193	398	1,115	448	37	187	41	133

[1] For definition, see Appendix II.

Source: U.S. Department of Justice, Federal Bureau of Investigation. *Crime in the United States*, annual. See <http://www.fbi.gov/ucr/cius2006/index.html/>.

Table 297. Crime Rates by State, 2005 and 2006, and by Type, 2006

[**Rates per 100,000 population.** Data include offenses actually reported to law enforcement and also offense estimations for nonreporting and partially reporting agencies within each state. Based on Census Bureau estimated resident population as of **July 1.** For definitions of types of crimes, go to <http://www.fbi.gov/ucr/cius2006/about/offense_definitions.htm/>]

State	Violent crime						Property crime				
	2005, total	2006					2005, total	2006			
		Total	Mur-der [1]	Forc-ible rape	Rob-bery	Aggra-vated assault		Total	Bur-glary	Lar-ceny/ theft	Motor vehicle theft
United States . . .	**469**	**474**	**5.7**	**31**	**149**	**288**	**3,432**	**3,335**	**729**	**2,207**	**398**
Alabama.	433	425	8.3	36	154	228	3,900	3,936	969	2,644	323
Alaska	632	688	5.4	76	90	516	3,615	3,605	617	2,610	377
Arizona.	512	501	7.5	32	150	313	4,827	4,628	925	2,813	890
Arkansas	529	552	7.3	47	98	399	4,068	3,968	1,140	2,562	266
California	526	533	6.8	25	195	306	3,321	3,171	676	1,829	666
Colorado.	397	392	3.3	44	81	264	4,041	3,451	682	2,332	438
Connecticut.	273	281	3.1	18	121	139	2,579	2,504	419	1,788	296
Delaware	633	682	4.9	47	203	427	3,118	3,418	725	2,363	330
District of Columbia [2]	1,380	1,508	29.1	32	658	789	4,490	4,654	660	2,735	1,259
Florida	709	712	6.2	36	189	481	4,013	3,986	945	2,619	423
Georgia	446	471	6.4	23	166	276	4,145	3,889	909	2,519	461
Hawaii	256	281	1.6	28	89	163	4,800	4,230	678	2,949	604
Idaho	257	247	2.5	40	21	184	2,697	2,419	513	1,740	166
Illinois [3, 4]	552	542	6.1	32	185	318	3,092	3,020	602	2,124	293
Indiana.	324	315	5.8	29	115	165	3,460	3,502	731	2,425	346
Iowa	293	284	1.8	28	44	210	2,845	2,803	604	2,031	168
Kansas.	389	425	4.6	45	68	308	3,806	3,750	723	2,712	315
Kentucky	267	263	4.0	31	86	142	2,531	2,545	645	1,680	220
Louisiana	597	698	12.4	36	134	515	3,696	3,994	1,049	2,580	365
Maine.	113	116	1.7	26	29	59	2,419	2,519	513	1,904	101
Maryland	704	679	9.7	21	256	392	3,551	3,481	667	2,270	544
Massachusetts.	461	447	2.9	27	125	292	2,358	2,391	547	1,565	279
Michigan.	554	562	7.1	52	141	362	3,098	3,213	754	1,964	495
Minnesota [4].	297	312	2.4	32	105	173	3,088	3,080	584	2,237	259
Mississippi	280	299	7.7	34	107	150	3,274	3,209	936	1,986	287
Missouri	526	546	6.3	30	130	379	3,929	3,827	764	2,627	435
Montana	282	254	1.8	29	17	206	3,146	2,688	311	2,192	185
Nebraska	287	282	2.8	31	64	184	3,432	3,341	535	2,521	285
Nevada	608	742	9.0	43	282	408	4,246	4,089	995	2,014	1,080
New Hampshire	135	139	1.0	26	32	79	1,839	1,874	331	1,435	108
New Jersey.	355	352	4.9	14	153	179	2,337	2,292	452	1,557	283
New Mexico	646	643	6.8	56	108	473	4,132	3,937	1,070	2,396	472
New York	444	435	4.8	16	179	235	2,102	2,053	355	1,531	166
North Carolina.	469	476	6.1	28	152	289	4,080	4,121	1,213	2,568	340
North Dakota.	111	128	1.3	30	11	85	2,025	2,000	376	1,465	159
Ohio	350	350	4.7	40	167	139	3,668	3,679	910	2,443	326
Oklahoma.	509	497	5.8	42	88	363	4,047	3,604	961	2,271	373
Oregon.	287	280	2.3	32	73	173	4,402	3,672	645	2,636	391
Pennsylvania.	425	439	5.9	27	169	238	2,422	2,444	463	1,743	237
Rhode Island.	252	228	2.6	27	69	129	2,728	2,587	507	1,744	336
South Carolina.	767	766	8.3	41	137	580	4,370	4,242	990	2,873	380
South Dakota	179	171	1.2	43	15	112	1,767	1,620	339	1,189	92
Tennessee	757	760	6.8	36	184	534	4,300	4,128	1,041	2,713	374
Texas.	528	516	5.9	36	159	316	4,319	4,082	917	2,758	406
Utah	225	224	1.8	34	49	140	3,837	3,516	577	2,615	325
Vermont	126	137	1.9	24	18	93	2,370	2,305	529	1,682	94
Virginia.	283	282	5.2	23	101	152	2,649	2,478	418	1,867	194
Washington.	346	346	3.0	43	100	200	4,890	4,480	912	2,851	718
West Virginia	274	280	4.1	21	47	207	2,633	2,622	634	1,772	216
Wisconsin	242	284	3.0	20	100	161	2,669	2,818	486	2,080	253
Wyoming	230	240	1.7	27	14	197	3,158	2,981	451	2,379	151

[1] Includes nonnegligent manslaughter. [2] Includes offenses reported by the Zoological Police and the Metro Transit Police.
[3] Limited data for 2005 and 2006 were available for Illinois. [4] The data collection methodology for the offense of forcible rape used by the Illinois state (with the exception of Rockford, Illinois) and the Minnesota state (2006 data only) Uniform Crime Reporting (UCR) Programs do not comply with national UCR Program guidelines. Consequently, their figures for forcible rape were estimated for inclusion in this table.

Source: U.S. Department of Justice, Federal Bureau of Investigation. *Crime in the United States,* annual. See <http://www.fbi.gov/ucr/cius2006/index.html/>.

U.S. Census Bureau, Statistical Abstract of the United States: 2009

Table 298. **Crime Rates by Type—Selected Large Cities: 2006**

[**Offenses known to the police per 100,000 population.** Based on U.S. Census Bureau estimated resident population. For definitions of types of crimes, go to <http://www.fbi.gov/ucr/cius2006/about/offense_definitions.htm/>]

City ranked by population size, 2006	Violent crime					Property crime			
	Total	Murder	Forcible rape	Robbery	Aggravated assault	Total	Burglary	Larceny-theft	Motor vehicle theft
New York, NY	638	7.3	13.1	288	330	1,879	271	1,413	195
Los Angeles, CA.	787	12.4	27.3	370	377	2,718	525	1,539	654
Chicago, IL	(¹)	16.4	(¹)	555	610	4,539	845	2,930	764
Houston, TX	1,169	18.2	41.2	548	562	5,837	1,296	3,525	1,017
Phoenix, AZ.	738	15.4	36.2	288	398	5,934	1,064	3,283	1,587
Philadelphia, PA.	1,562	27.7	65.5	749	720	4,275	788	2,691	796
Las Vegas MPD, NV	983	11.6	54.6	409	508	4,667	1,134	2,038	1,496
San Antonio, TX	617	9.2	39.8	180	389	6,085	1,132	4,441	512
San Diego, CA.	504	5.4	27.5	171	301	3,569	611	1,904	1,053
Dallas, TX	1,206	15.0	53.3	554	584	6,857	1,735	4,006	1,116
San Jose, CA.	387	3.2	23.6	112	248	2,633	480	1,377	776
Honolulu, HI.	301	1.9	25.1	105	169	4,197	601	2,908	689
Detroit, MI	2,419	47.3	67.0	819	1,486	7,048	2,050	2,407	2,591
Indianapolis, IN	960	17.5	68.5	406	468	6,192	1,465	3,612	1,116
Jacksonville, FL	837	13.8	27.4	290	507	5,416	1,208	3,665	543
San Francisco, CA	876	11.5	20.6	517	326	4,958	867	3,202	889
Columbus, OH	813	14.2	80.1	498	220	7,122	2,025	4,221	875
Austin, TX.	515	2.8	44.9	191	276	5,857	1,052	4,447	358
Charlotte-Mecklenburg PD, NC . . .	1,077	11.9	49.5	459	557	6,990	1,942	4,025	1,022
Memphis, TN.	1,989	21.6	62.4	780	1,125	8,358	2,416	4,955	987
Fort Worth, TX	656	7.6	38.5	221	389	5,683	1,402	3,760	522
Baltimore, MD	1,696	43.3	21.6	663	968	5,070	1,193	2,894	982
Louisville Metro, KY	613	8.0	28.0	278	299	4,654	1,212	2,852	590
El Paso, TX ²	392	2.1	47.3	82	261	3,343	359	2,412	572
Seattle, WA	711	5.1	22.1	286	398	6,772	1,286	4,091	1,396
Washington, DC.	1,446	29.1	31.3	620	766	4,474	658	2,602	1,214
Milwaukee, WI	1,325	17.7	19.3	621	667	6,580	973	4,190	1,418
Denver, CO	761	9.0	60.2	225	467	4,621	1,151	2,353	1,117
Boston, MA	1,339	13.3	48.9	480	797	4,462	733	3,004	725
Nashville, TN	1,527	14.3	57.1	432	1,024	5,817	1,136	4,143	539
Portland, OR	714	3.7	54.0	239	417	5,901	1,012	4,064	826
Oklahoma City, OK	802	10.3	61.0	220	511	6,398	1,736	3,763	899
Tucson, AZ	856	9.5	54.9	313	478	(³)	957	(³)	1,378
Albuquerque, NM	908	6.8	57.1	234	611	6,339	1,268	3,970	1,101
Atlanta, GA	1,554	22.6	35.2	609	887	6,635	1,523	3,901	1,210
Long Beach, CA.	715	8.6	28.0	301	377	2,672	605	1,380	687
Fresno, CA	757	11.2	28.6	276	442	5,031	938	3,030	1,063
Sacramento, CA.	1,206	12.4	42.6	475	676	5,670	1,341	2,771	1,558
Mesa, AZ	436	5.7	44.2	111	275	4,634	714	3,125	795
Cleveland, OH	1,547	16.6	98.3	947	485	6,233	2,131	2,658	1,443
Kansas City, MO ²	1,444	25.0	71.6	456	891	6,939	1,651	4,057	1,230
Virginia Beach, VA	284	4.3	26.0	153	100	2,903	463	2,306	134
New Orleans, LA	523	37.6	20.2	177	289	2,825	948	1,213	664
Omaha, NE	601	7.9	44.9	203	345	5,228	761	3,640	826
Oakland, CA	1,905	36.4	76.7	886	906	6,104	1,271	2,188	2,645
Miami, FL	1,509	19.6	25.7	537	927	5,163	1,130	3,046	987
Tulsa, OK	1,248	13.7	74.9	258	901	6,223	1,637	3,764	822
Colorado Springs, CO	569	4.0	66.6	162	336	4,797	888	3,434	475
Minneapolis, MN.	(¹)	15.2	(¹)	807	756	6,011	1,552	3,493	966
Arlington, TX	731	3.8	51.5	239	437	5,271	1,083	3,727	461
Wichita, KS	929	7.3	67.2	146	709	5,474	1,063	3,858	553
Raleigh, NC.	638	5.5	27.8	224	380	3,631	855	2,488	289
St. Louis, MO	2,481	37.2	97.2	907	1,439	11,744	2,453	6,802	2,492
Santa Ana, CA	582	7.6	21.3	229	324	2,513	313	1,443	757
Anaheim, CA	455	3.0	32.0	174	246	2,634	563	1,576	494
Tampa, FL.	1,158	7.5	40.1	365	745	5,668	1,343	3,394	931
Pittsburgh, PA	1,070	17.3	31.4	530	491	4,694	1,144	2,975	575
Cincinnati, OH	1,218	28.8	94.1	757	339	7,152	1,944	4,375	833
Aurora, CO	613	5.6	71.7	198	338	4,228	816	2,738	675
Toledo, OH	1,147	11.6	56.0	414	666	7,529	2,292	4,389	848
Bakersfield, CA	528	8.0	14.4	184	322	5,337	1,251	3,227	859
Riverside, CA.	688	3.8	28.4	278	378	4,191	810	2,552	828
Corpus Christi, TX	710	7.2	57.3	161	485	6,565	1,031	5,235	299
Stockton, CA	1,481	12.8	35.2	525	908	6,811	1,325	4,215	1,271
Newark, NJ	1,011	37.4	31.0	459	484	4,079	706	1,558	1,815
Buffalo, NY	1,411	26.4	62.0	609	713	5,503	1,585	3,160	758
Anchorage, AK.	933	6.1	89.3	167	671	4,221	624	3,076	520
St. Paul, MN.	(¹)	6.1	(¹)	307	507	4,369	1,209	2,389	772
Lexington, KY ²	634	3.3	47.4	187	396	3,863	808	2,794	260
Plano, TX	289	1.6	16.3	60	211	3,351	542	2,583	226
St. Petersburg, FL	1,482	8.3	44.2	407	1,022	6,479	1,368	4,020	1,090
Mobile, AL ⁴.	467	13.6	33.2	274	146	6,336	1,464	4,340	532

¹ The data collection methodology for the offense of forcible rape used by the Illinois (with the exception of Rockford, Illinois) and the Minnesota state UCR Programs does not comply with national UCR Program guidelines. Consequently, their figures for forcible rape and violent crime (of which forcible rape is a part) are not published in this table. ² Because of changes in the state/local agency's reporting practices, figures are not comparable to previous years' data. ³ It was determined that the agency did not follow national Uniform Crime Reporting (UCR) Program guidelines for reporting an offense. Consequently, this figure is not included in this table. ⁴ The population for the city of Mobile, Alabama, includes 56,876 inhabitants from the jurisdiction of the Mobile County Sheriff's Department.

Source: U.S. Department of Justice, Federal Bureau of Investigation, *Crime in the United States,* annual. See <http://www.fbi.gov/ucr/cius2006/data/table08.html/>.

Table 299. Murder Victims—Circumstances and Weapons Used or Cause of Death: 2000 to 2006

[The Uniform Crime Reporting (UCR) Program defines murder and nonnegligent manslaughter as the willful nonnegligent killing of one human being by another. The classification of this offense is based solely on police investigation as opposed to the determination of a court, medical examiner, coroner, jury, other judicial body. For more information on murder, go to <http://www.fbi.gov/ucr/cius2006/offenses/violent_crime/murder_homicide.html/]

Characteristic	2000	2004	2005	2006	Characteristic	2000	2004	2005	2006
Murders, total. . . .	**13,230**	**14,210**	**14,965**	**14,990**	Unknown.	4,070	4,984	5,635	5,223
CIRCUMSTANCE [1]									
					TYPE OF WEAPON OR CAUSE OF DEATH [2]				
Felonies, total	2,229	2,099	2,189	2,436					
Rape.	58	37	45	32					
Robbery	1,077	993	930	1,041	Total firearms.	8,661	9,385	10,158	10,177
Burglary.	76	78	91	79	Handguns	6,778	7,286	7,565	7,795
Narcotics	589	558	597	796	Rifles	411	403	445	436
Other not specified . .	429	433	526	488	Shotguns	485	507	522	481
Suspected felony type . .	60	119	45	58	Other not specified . .	987	1189	1626	1465
Other than felony type					Knives or cutting				
total	6,871	7,008	7,096	7,273	instruments	1,782	1,866	1,920	1,822
Romantic triangle . . .	122	97	118	103	Blunt objects [3]	617	667	608	607
Brawl due to influence					Personal weapons [4] . . .	927	943	905	833
of alcohol.	188	140	123	107	Fire	134	118	125	115
Gangland killings. . . .	65	95	96	118	Strangulations	166	156	118	135
Juvenile gang killings .	653	805	756	865	Asphyxiations.	92	109	96	107
Other not specified . .	5,637	5,650	5,793	5,882	All other [5]	851	966	1,035	1,194

[1] Other types of circumstances not shown separately.   [2] Other types of weapons or causes of deaths not shown separately.   [3] Refers to club, hammer, etc.   [4] Hands, fists, feet, etc.   [5] Includes poison, drowning, explosives, narcotics, and unknown.

Source: U.S. Department of Justice, Federal Bureau of Investigation, *Crime in the United States,* annual. See also <http://www.fbi.gov/ucr/cius2006/index.html>.

Table 300. Murder Victims by Age, Sex, and Race: 2006

[See headnote, Table 299]

Age	Total	Sex			Race			
		Male	Female	Unknown	White	Black	Other	Unknown
Murders, total	**14,990**	**11,793**	**3,156**	**41**	**6,956**	**7,421**	**406**	**207**
Percent of total	100.0	78.7	21.1	0.3	46.4	49.5	2.7	1.4
Under 18 years old [1]	1,539	1,125	413	1	747	734	40	18
18 years old and over [1]	13,174	10,485	2,676	13	6,098	6,587	361	128
Infant (under 1 year old)	203	121	82	–	141	51	3	8
1 to 4 years old	299	174	125	–	141	145	9	4
5 to 8 years old	95	46	48	1	61	29	4	1
9 to 12 years old	83	55	28	–	46	31	6	–
13 to 16 years old	485	395	90	–	217	259	8	1
17 to 19 years old	1,485	1,308	175	2	563	860	50	12
20 to 24 years old	2,831	2,454	375	2	1,077	1,653	70	31
25 to 29 years old	2,273	1,916	356	1	913	1,304	41	15
30 to 34 years old	1,549	1,304	243	2	628	863	40	18
35 to 39 years old	1,250	939	310	1	615	587	36	12
40 to 44 years old	1,123	800	323	–	595	493	28	7
45 to 49 years old	985	721	261	3	540	393	40	12
50 to 54 years old	727	517	208	2	420	270	28	9
55 to 59 years old	455	325	130	–	276	157	15	7
60 to 64 years old	316	230	86	–	214	87	12	3
65 to 69 years old	147	94	53	–	94	48	4	1
70 to 74 years old	144	89	55	–	101	39	3	1
75 years old and over	263	122	141	–	203	52	4	4
Age unknown	277	183	67	27	111	100	5	61

– Represents zero.   [1] Does not include unknown ages.

Source: U.S. Department of Justice, Federal Bureau of Investigation. *Crime in the United States,* annual. See <http://www.fbi.gov/ucr/cius2006/index.html>.

U.S. Census Bureau, Statistical Abstract of the United States: 2009

Table 301. **Homicide Trends: 1980 to 2005**

[Not all agencies which report offense information to the FBI also submit supplemental data on homicides. To account for the total number of homicide victims, the data was weighted to match national and state estimates prepared by the FBI; hence, detail may not equal total. For more information on the methodology, go to <http://www.ojp.usdoj.gov/bjs/homicide/homtrnd.htm#contents>]

Year	Number of victims						Rate [1]					
	Total	Male	Female	White	Black	Other	Total	Male	Female	White	Black	Other
1980	23,040	17,788	5,232	12,275	9,767	327	10.2	16.2	4.5	6.3	37.7	5.7
1985	18,976	14,079	4,880	10,590	7,891	399	8.0	12.2	4.0	5.2	27.6	5.5
1990	23,438	18,304	5,115	11,279	11,488	400	9.4	15.0	4.0	5.4	37.6	4.2
1993	24,526	18,937	5,550	11,278	12,435	601	9.5	15.0	4.2	5.3	38.7	5.5
1994	23,326	18,294	5,007	10,773	11,856	526	9.0	14.4	3.8	5.0	36.4	4.6
1995	21,606	16,552	5,022	10,376	10,444	581	8.2	12.9	3.7	4.8	31.6	4.9
1996	19,645	15,153	4,469	9,483	9,476	512	7.4	11.7	3.3	4.3	28.3	4.1
1997	18,208	14,057	4,125	8,620	8,842	524	6.8	10.7	3.0	3.9	26.0	4.1
1998	16,974	12,753	4,139	8,389	7,931	393	6.3	9.7	3.0	3.8	23.0	2.9
1999	15,522	11,704	3,800	7,777	7,139	458	5.7	8.8	2.7	3.5	20.5	3.3
2000	15,586	11,818	3,733	7,560	7,425	399	5.5	8.6	2.6	3.3	20.5	2.7
2001	16,037	12,232	3,775	7,884	7,522	424	5.6	8.8	2.6	3.4	20.4	2.8
2002	16,204	12,410	3,764	7,784	7,758	437	5.6	8.8	2.6	3.3	20.8	2.7
2003	16,582	12,804	3,693	7,932	7,893	468	5.7	9.0	2.5	3.4	20.9	2.8
2004	16,137	12,556	3,543	7,944	7,562	417	5.5	8.7	2.4	3.3	19.7	2.4
2005	16,692	13,122	3,545	8,017	7,999	437	5.5	9.0	2.3	3.3	20.6	2.5

[1] Rate is per 100,000 inhabitants.

Source: U.S. Department of Justice, Office of Justice Programs, Bureau of Justice Statistics, *Homicide Trends in the United States, 1976–2005* See also <http://www.ojp.usdoj.gov/bjs/homicide/homtrnd.htm#contents>.

Table 302. **Homicide Victims by Race and Sex: 1980 to 2005**

[**Rates per 100,000 resident population in specified group.** Excludes deaths to nonresidents of United States. Effective with data for 1999, causes of death are classified by The Tenth Revision International Classification of Diseases (ICD-10), replacing the Ninth Revision (ICD-9) used for 1979–98 data. In ICD-9, the category Homicide also includes death as a result of legal intervention. ICD-10 has two separate categories for these two causes of death. Some caution should be used in comparing data between 1998 and 1999. see text, Section 2]

Year	Homicide victims					Homicide rate [2]				
		White		Black			White		Black	
	Total [1]	Male	Female	Male	Female	Total [1]	Male	Female	Male	Female
1980	24,278	10,381	3,177	8,385	1,898	10.7	10.9	3.2	66.6	13.5
1985	19,893	8,122	3,041	6,616	1,666	8.3	8.2	2.9	48.4	11.0
1990	24,932	9,147	3,006	9,981	2,163	10.0	9.0	2.8	69.2	13.5
1993	26,009	9,054	3,232	10,640	2,297	10.1	8.6	3.0	69.7	13.6
1994	24,926	9,055	2,921	10,083	2,124	9.6	8.5	2.6	65.1	12.4
1995	22,895	8,336	3,028	8,847	1,936	8.7	7.8	2.7	56.3	11.1
1996	20,971	7,570	2,747	8,183	1,800	7.9	7.0	2.5	51.5	10.2
1997	19,846	7,343	2,570	7,601	1,652	7.4	6.7	2.3	47.1	9.3
1998	18,272	6,707	2,534	6,873	1,547	6.8	6.1	2.2	42.1	8.6
1999	16,889	6,162	2,466	6,214	1,434	6.2	5.6	2.2	37.5	7.8
2000	16,765	5,925	2,414	6,482	1,385	6.1	5.3	2.1	38.6	7.5
2001	20,308	8,254	3,074	6,780	1,446	7.1	7.2	2.6	38.3	7.4
2002	17,638	6,282	2,403	6,896	1,391	6.1	5.4	2.0	38.4	7.0
2003	17,732	6,337	2,372	7,083	1,309	6.1	5.4	2.0	38.9	6.6
2004	17,357	6,302	2,341	6,839	1,296	5.9	5.3	1.9	37.1	6.4
2005	18,124	6,457	2,313	7,412	1,257	6.1	5.4	1.9	39.7	6.2

[1] Includes races not shown separately.   [2] Rate based on enumerated population figures as of April 1 for 1980, 1990, and 2000; estimated resident population as of July 1 for other years.

Source: U.S. National Center for Health Statistics, *Vital Statistics of the United States*, annual; and *National Vital Statistics Reports (NVSR)* (formerly *Monthly Vital Statistics Report)*; and unpublished data.

Table 303. **Forcible Rape—Number and Rate: 1980 to 2006**

[For definition of rape, go to <http://www.fbi.gov/ucr/cius2006/about/offense_definitions.html/>]

Item	1980	1990	1995	2000	2001	2002	2003	2004	2005	2006
NUMBER										
Total	82,990	102,560	97,460	90,186	90,863	95,235	93,883	95,089	94,347	92,455
By force	63,599	86,541	85,249	81,111	82,004	86,655	85,837	87,953	86,231	84,042
Attempt	19,391	16,019	12,211	9,075	8,859	8,580	8,046	7,856	7,703	8,413
RATE										
Per 100,000 population	36.8	41.1	37.1	32.0	31.8	33.1	32.3	32.4	31.8	30.9
Per 100,000 females	71.6	80.5	72.5	62.7	62.6	65.0	63.5	63.8	62.5	60.9

Source: U.S. Department of Justice, Federal Bureau of Investigation, *Population-at-Risk Rates and Selected Crime Indicators*, annual. See also <http://www.fbi.gov/ucr/cius2006/offenses/violent_crime/forcible_rape.html>.

Table 304. **Criminal Victimizations and Victimization Rates: 1995 to 2006**

[(39,926 represents 39,926,000). Based on National Crime Victimization Survey; see text, this section and Appendix III. **The 2006 national crime victimization estimates are not comparable to previous years because of changes in methodology.** For more information on these changes, go to <http://www.ojp.usdoj.gov/bjs/pub/pdf/cv06.pdf> For definitions of crimes, go to <http://www.ojp .usdoj.gov/bjs/abstract/cvus/definitions.htm>]

Type of crime	Number of victimizations (1,000)				Victimization rates [1]			
	1995	2000	2005	2006	1995	2000	2005	2006
All crimes, total	**39,926**	**25,893**	**23,441**	**25,183**	(X)	(X)	(X)	(X)
Personal crimes [2]	**10,436**	**6,597**	**5,401**	**6,268**	**46.2**	**29.1**	**22.1**	**25.4**
Crimes of violence	10,022	6,323	5,174	6,094	44.5	27.9	21.2	24.7
Completed violence	2,960	2,044	1,659	2,019	12.9	9.0	6.8	8.2
Attempted/threatened violence . . .	7,061	4,279	3,515	4,075	31.6	18.9	14.4	16.5
Rape/sexual assault	363	261	192	261	1.6	1.2	0.8	1.1
Rape/attempted rape	252	147	130	192	1.1	0.6	0.5	0.8
Rape	153	92	69	117	0.7	0.4	0.3	0.5
Attempted rape	99	55	61	76	0.4	0.2	0.2	0.3
Sexual assault	112	114	62	69	0.5	0.5	0.3	0.3
Robbery	1,171	732	625	713	5.3	3.2	2.6	2.9
Completed/property taken	753	520	415	482	3.5	2.3	1.7	2.0
With injury.	224	160	143	208	1.0	0.7	0.6	0.8
Without injury	529	360	272	274	2.4	1.6	1.1	1.1
Attempted to take property	418	212	210	230	1.8	0.9	0.9	0.9
With injury.	84	66	64	43	0.4	0.3	0.3	0.2
Without injury	335	146	145	187	1.4	0.6	0.6	0.8
Assault	8,487	5,330	4,357	5,121	37.6	23.5	17.8	20.7
Aggravated.	2,050	1,293	1,052	1,344	8.8	5.7	4.3	5.4
With injury.	533	346	331	467	2.4	1.5	1.4	1.9
Threatened with weapon	1,517	946	722	878	6.4	4.2	3.0	3.5
Simple.	6,437	4,038	3,305	3,777	28.9	17.8	13.5	15.3
With minor injury	1,426	989	795	901	6.0	4.4	3.3	3.6
Without injury	5,012	3,048	2,510	2,876	22.9	13.4	10.3	11.6
Personal theft [3]	414	274	227	173	1.7	1.2	0.9	0.7
Property crimes	**29,490**	**19,297**	**18,040**	**18,916**	**279.5**	**178.1**	**154.0**	**160.5**
Household burglary.	5,004	3,444	3,456	3,561	47.4	31.8	29.5	30.2
Completed.	4,232	2,909	2,900	2,848	40.0	26.9	24.8	24.2
Attempted forcible entry	773	534	556	713	7.4	4.9	4.7	6.0
Motor vehicle theft	1,717	937	978	992	16.2	8.6	8.4	8.4
Completed.	1,163	642	775	792	10.8	5.9	6.6	6.7
Attempted	554	295	203	200	5.5	2.7	1.7	1.7
Theft	22,769	14,916	13,606	14,363	215.9	137.7	116.2	121.9
Completed [4].	21,857	14,300	13,116	13,791	207.6	132.0	112.0	117.0
Attempted	911	616	489	572	8.4	5.7	4.2	4.8

X Not applicable. [1] Per 1,000 persons age 12 or older or per 1,000 households. [2] The victimization survey cannot measure murder because of the inability to question the victim. [3] Includes pocket picking, purse snatching, and attempted purse snatching. [4] Includes thefts in which the amount taken was not ascertained.
  Source: U.S. Department of Justice, Office of Justice Programs, Bureau of Justice Statistics, *Criminal Victimization,* annual; and series NCJ-219413, December 2007. See also <http://www.ojp.usdoj.gov/bjs/abstract/cv06.htm>.

Table 305. **Victimization Rates by Type of Crime and Characteristic of the Victim: 2006**

[**Rate per 1,000 persons age 12 years or older**. See head note, Table 304]

Characteristic of the victim	All crimes	Crimes of violence						Purse snatching/ pocket picking [1]
		Total	Rape/ sexual assault	Robbery	Assault			
					Total	Aggra-vated	Simple	
Total	**25.4**	**24.7**	**1.1**	**2.9**	**20.7**	**5.4**	**15.3**	**0.7**
Male	27.4	26.7	[2]0.2	3.9	22.6	6.3	16.3	0.7
Female.	23.4	22.7	1.8	2.0	18.9	4.6	14.3	0.7
12 to 15 years old	47.8	46.9	3.4	4.0	39.6	8.3	31.3	[2]0.8
16 to 19 years old	52.8	51.7	2.5	4.6	44.7	11.6	33.1	[2]1.1
20 to 24 years old	45.1	44.2	1.8	7.3	35.1	11.9	23.2	[2]0.9
25 to 34 years old	36.6	36.0	1.4	4.6	30.1	7.7	22.4	[2]0.6
35 to 49 years old	20.6	19.7	0.7	2.0	17.0	4.7	12.3	0.9
50 to 64 years old	13.6	13.2	[2]0.5	1.3	11.4	2.5	8.9	[2]0.4
65 years old and over . . .	3.9	3.3	[2]–	1.1	2.2	[2]0.7	1.6	[2]0.5
White.	23.9	23.3	1.1	2.8	19.5	4.6	14.9	0.6
Black.	32.9	32.1	[2]1.1	3.8	27.2	9.6	17.6	[2]0.8
Other.	20.4	18.4	[2]0.7	[2]2.7	15.0	5.9	9.1	[2]1.9
Hispanic.	28.4	27.7	[2]0.9	4.9	22.0	6.3	15.7	[2]0.6
Non-Hispanic.	24.9	24.2	1.1	2.6	20.6	5.3	15.2	0.7
Household income:								
Less than $7,500	64.6	63.5	5.1	7.2	51.2	13.3	38.0	[2]1.1
$7,500–$14,999	45.9	45.0	[2]0.5	6.5	38.1	8.3	29.7	[2]0.9
$15,000–$24,999	31.4	29.8	[2]1.2	4.2	24.4	8.3	16.2	[2]1.6
$25,000–$34,999	34.5	33.6	[2]1.6	5.3	26.6	7.6	19.0	[2]1.0
$35,000–$49,999	22.5	22.3	[2]0.5	1.5	20.2	4.8	15.5	[2]0.3
$50,000–$74,999	24.5	24.0	1.1	2.2	20.7	5.6	15.2	[2]0.4
$75,000 or more	14.6	13.9	[2]0.4	2.0	11.5	2.9	8.7	0.7

– Rounds to zero. [1] Formerly personal theft. [2] Based on 10 or fewer sample cases.
  Source: U.S. Department of Justice, Office of Justice Programs, Bureau of Justice Statistics, *Criminal Victimization,* annual; and series NCJ-219413, December 2007. See also <http://www.ojp.usdoj.gov/bjs/abstract/cv06.htm>.

Law Enforcement, Courts, and Prisons   **193**

Table 306. Victim-Offender Relationship in Crimes of Violence by Characteristics of the Criminal Incident: 2006

[In percent. Covers only crimes of violence. Based on National Crime Victimization Survey; see text, this section, and Appendix III. The 2006 national crime victimization estimates are not comparable to previous years because of changes in methodology. See head note, Table 304]

Selected characteristic of incident	Total	Rape/ sexual assault	Robbery	Assault Total	Assault Aggra- vated[1]	Assault Simple
Total.	**100**	**100**	**100**	**100**	**100**	**100**
Victim/offender relationship: [2]						
Relatives.	11.7	[3]7.7	6.3	12.7	13.7	12.4
Well-known	24.6	27.4	13.1	26.1	24.2	26.8
Casual acquaintance.	16.2	26.6	6.9	17.0	13.5	18.2
Stranger	38.0	34.0	59.2	35.2	38.8	34.0
Time of day: [4]						
6 a.m. to 6 p.m.	52.4	30.1	39.5	55.3	52.4	56.3
6 p.m. to midnight.	32.8	33.3	42.5	31.5	31.8	31.3
Midnight to 6 a.m..	10.9	34.5	14.2	9.2	11.3	8.4
Location of crime:						
At or near victim's home or lodging	37.5	45.1	40.6	36.6	41.4	34.9
Friend's/relative's/neighbor's home.	7.9	18.6	[3]5.0	7.7	7.2	7.9
Commercial places	12.5	10.9	2.8	13.8	11.1	14.7
Parking lots/garages	7.0	[3]4.8	13.2	6.2	7.7	5.7
School	11.4	[3]2.5	6.2	12.6	6.5	14.6
Streets other than near victim's home. . .	15.4	[3]7.2	23.7	14.8	19.0	13.3
Other [5]	8.5	10.8	8.4	8.3	7.1	8.8
Victim's activity: [6]						
At work or traveling to or from work	18.2	8.4	17.9	(NA)	16.3	19.6
School	11.0	4.7	6.9	(NA)	6.9	13.6
Activities at home	29.7	38.3	19.4	(NA)	35.8	28.9
Shopping/errands	4.2	[3]2.0	7.8	(NA)	4.6	3.5
Leisure activities away from home	22.5	30.9	19.5	(NA)	22.1	22.6
Traveling.	8.8	[3]7.7	22.4	(NA)	7.9	6.8
Other [7]	5.4	[3]7.9	6.1	(NA)	6.5	4.7
Distance from victim's home: [8]						
Inside home or lodging	20.3	33.2	18.2	19.9	25.3	18.0
Near victim's home	17.8	[3]12.3	18.5	17.9	19.2	17.5
1 mile or less.	19.4	[3]10.7	24.6	19.2	18.8	19.3
5 miles or less	21.1	19.6	18.6	21.5	16.3	23.2
50 miles or less	17.8	18.8	14.7	18.1	17.6	18.3
More than 50 miles	2.8	[3]2.3	[3]3.3	2.8	2.4	2.9
Weapons:						
No weapons present	67.4	71.6	40.6	70.8	8.8	91.7
Weapons present	25.0	18.1	44.5	22.8	90.0	–
Firearm	8.8	[3]12.9	21.7	6.8	27.0	–
Other type of weapon [9].	16.2	5.2	22.8	16.0	63.0	–

– Represents zero.   NA Not available.   [1] An aggravated assault is any assault in which an offender possesses or uses a weapon or inflicts serious injury.   [2] Excludes "don't know" relationships.   [3] Based on 10 or fewer sample cases.   [4] Excludes "not known and not available" time of day.   [5] Includes areas on public transportation or inside station, in apartment yard, park, field, playground, or other areas.   [6] Excludes "don't know" and "not available" victim activity.   [7] Includes sleeping.   [8] Excludes "don't know" and "not available" distance from victim's home.   [9] Includes knives, other sharp objects, blunt objects, and other types of weapons.

Source: U.S. Department of Justice, Office of Justice Programs, Bureau of Justice Statistics, *Criminal Victimization,* annual; and series NCJ-219413, December 2007. See also <http://www.ojp.usdoj.gov/bjs/abstract/cv06.htm>.

Table 307. Violence by Intimate Partners by Sex, 1995 to 2004, and by Type of Crime, 2004

[Violent acts covered include murder, rape, sexual assault, robbery, and aggravated and simple assault. Intimate partners involve current spouses, former spouses, current boy/girlfriends, and former boy/girlfriends. Based on the National Criminal Victimization Survey; see text, this section, and Appendix III. For definitions, go to <http://www.ojp.usdoj.gov/bjs/intimate/definitions.htm/>]

Year and type of crime	All persons Number	All persons Rate per 100,000[1]	Female victims Number	Female victims Rate per 100,000[1]	Male victims Number	Male victims Rate per 100,000[1]
1995	1,063,520	493.0	953,700	855.8	109,820	105.3
1996	1,008,860	462.8	879,290	781.7	129,570	122.8
1997	953,780	432.7	848,480	747.3	105,300	98.5
1998	1,054,260	475.7	896,030	780.9	158,230	146.7
1999	783,120	347.7	672,330	578.4	110,790	101.6
2000	630,530	277.2	547,310	466.5	83,220	75.5
2001	693,321	301.4	589,692	497.1	103,629	92.8
2002	568,690	245.4	495,772	214.0	72,918	31.5
2003	521,760	218.0	437,990	183.0	83,750	35.0
2004, total	**627,410**	**258.7**	**475,940**	**381.9**	**151,470**	**128.5**
Rape or sexual assault	28,900	11.9	28,900	23.2	(B)	(B)
Robbery	64,340	19.2	46,620	37.4	17,720	15.0
Aggravated assault.	97,000	30.9	74,820	60.0	22,180	18.8
Simple assault.	437,170	134.3	325,600	261.3	111,570	94.6
Murder.	1,544	0.5	1,159	0.8	385	0.3

B Base figure too small to meet statistical standards for reliability of derived figure.   [1] Rates are the number of victimizations per 100,000 persons.

Source: U.S. Department of Justice, Office of Justice Programs, Bureau of Justice Statistics, Intimate Partner Violence, Series NCJ-210675, December 2006 and unpublished data; <http://www.ojp.usdoj.gov/bjs/intimate/ipv.htm>.

Table 308. Robbery and Property Crimes by Type and Selected Characteristic: 1990 to 2006

[**(639 represents 639,000.)** For definitions of types of crimes, go to <http://www.fbi.gov/ucr/cius2006/about/offense_definitions.html>]

Characteristic of offense	Number of offenses (1,000)				Rate per 100,000 population				Average value lost (dol.)	
	1990	2000	2005	2006	1990	2000	2005	2006	2005	2006
Robbery, total [1]	**639**	**408**	**417**	**447**	**256.3**	**144.9**	**140.7**	**149.4**	**1,239**	**1,268**
Type of crime:										
Street or highway	359	188	184	199	144.2	66.7	62.1	66.5	1,020	980
Commercial house	73	57	60	61	29.5	20.1	20.1	20.4	1,662	1,589
Gas station	18	12	12	12	7.1	4.1	4.0	4.0	1,104	1,169
Convenience store	39	26	24	24	15.6	9.3	8.0	8.3	677	761
Residence	62	50	59	64	25.1	17.7	20.0	21.4	1,332	1,469
Bank	9	9	9	10	3.8	3.1	3.0	3.2	4,113	4,330
Weapon used:										
Firearm	234	161	175	157	94.1	57.0	59.0	63.0	(NA)	(NA)
Knife or cutting instrument	76	36	37	32	30.7	12.8	12.5	12.8	(NA)	(NA)
Other dangerous weapon	61	53	39	34	24.5	18.9	13.2	13.8	(NA)	(NA)
Strongarm	268	159	166	149	107.7	56.4	56.0	59.5	(NA)	(NA)
Burglary, total	**3,074**	**2,050**	**2,154**	**2,184**	**1,232.2**	**728.4**	**726.7**	**729.4**	**1,771**	**1,834**
Forcible entry	2,150	1,297	1,310	1,330	864.5	460.7	440.0	460.6	(NA)	(NA)
Unlawful entry	678	615	701	710	272.8	218.7	237.5	245.7	(NA)	(NA)
Attempted forcible entry	245	138	133	144	98.7	49.0	45.2	49.8	(NA)	(NA)
Residence	2,033	1,335	1,417	1,446	817.4	474.3	477.9	482.8	1,813	1,823
Nonresidence	1,041	715	738	738	418.5	254.1	248.8	246.6	1,687	1,855
Occurred during the night [2]	1,135	699	708	718	456.4	248.3	238.9	240.0	(NA)	(NA)
Occurred during the day	1,151	836	890	939	462.8	297.2	328.8	313.8	(NA)	(NA)
Larceny-theft, total	**7,946**	**6,972**	**6,783**	**6,607**	**3,185.1**	**2,477.3**	**2,286.3**	**2,206.8**	**857**	**855**
Pocket picking	81	36	29	29	32.4	12.7	9.8	9.6	346	443
Purse snatching	82	37	42	40	32.8	13.2	14.2	13.4	404	440
Shoplifting	1,291	959	940	873	519.1	340.7	317.0	291.5	184	194
From motor vehicles	1,744	1,754	1,752	1,752	701.3	623.3	590.6	585.3	704	734
Motor vehicle accessories	1,185	677	693	639	476.3	240.6	233.6	213.3	482	522
Bicycles	443	312	249	231	178.2	110.9	83.9	77.2	267	263
From buildings	1,118	914	852	830	449.4	324.6	287.3	277.1	1,738	1,170
From coin-operated machines	63	46	41	35	25.4	16.2	13.8	11.8	232	317
Other	1,940	2,232	2,184	2,178	780.0	793.0	736.1	727.5	1,137	1,280
Motor vehicles, total [3]	**1,636**	**1,160**	**1,236**	**1,193**	**655.8**	**412.2**	**417.4**	**398.4**	**6,204**	**6,649**
Automobiles	1,304	877	907	877	524.3	311.5	304.5	311.6	(NA)	(NA)
Trucks and buses	238	209	219	212	95.5	74.1	76.2	75.5	(NA)	(NA)

NA Not available.   [1] Includes other crimes not shown separately.   [2] Other data not shown.   [3] Includes other types of motor vehicles not shown separately.

Source: U.S. Department of Justice, Federal Bureau of Investigation, *Population-at-Risk Rates and Selected Crime Indicators,* annual. See also <http://www.fbi.gov/ucr/cius2006/index.html>.

Table 309. Property Victimization Rates by Selected Household Characteristic: 2006

[**Victimizations per 1,000 households.** Based on National Crime Victimization Survey (NCVS); see text, this section and Appendix III. The 2006 national crime victimization estimates are not comparable to previous years because of changes in methodology. See headnote, Table 304]

Characteristic	Total	Burglary	Motor vehicle theft	Theft
Total	**160.5**	**30.2**	**8.4**	**121.9**
Race:				
White	156.7	28.6	7.3	120.8
Black	185.6	42.4	14.8	128.4
Other	137.7	21.8	10.2	105.6
Ethnicity:				
Hispanic	211.7	40.2	13.5	158.0
Non-Hispanic	154.7	29.1	7.8	117.9
Household income:				
Less than $7,500	217.3	55.7	11.3	150.3
$7,500 to $14,999	195.7	45.8	8.4	141.6
$15,000 to $24,999	183.1	35.6	15.9	131.6
$25,000 to $34,999	179.4	30.3	12.9	136.2
$35,000 to $49,999	166.2	32.3	9.1	124.8
$50,000 to $74,999	166.8	28.2	7.5	131.1
$75,000 or more	162.0	22.4	6.4	133.2

Source: U.S. Department of Justice, Office of Justice Programs, Bureau of Justice Statistics, *Criminal Victimization,* annual; and series NCJ-219413, December 2007. See also <http://www.ojp.usdoj.gov/bjs/abstract/cv06.htm>.

U.S. Census Bureau, Statistical Abstract of the United States: 2009

Table 310. Hate Crimes—Number of Incidents, Offenses, Victims, and Known Offenders by Bias Motivation: 2000 to 2006

[The FBI collected statistics on hate crimes from 12,620 law enforcement agencies representing over 255 million inhabitants in 2006. Hate crime offenses cover incidents motivated by race, religion, sexual orientation, ethnicity/national origin, and disability]

Bias motivation	Incidents reported	Offenses	Victims [1]	Known offenders [2]
2000, total	8,213	9,619	10,117	7,690
2004, total	7,679	9,065	9,561	7,175
2005, total	7,163	8,380	8,804	6,804
2006, Total	**7,722**	**9,080**	**9,652**	**7,330**
Race, total	**4,000**	**4,737**	**5,020**	**3,957**
Anti-White	890	1,008	1,054	1,074
Anti-Black	2,640	3,136	3,332	2,437
Anti-American Indian/Alaska native	60	72	75	72
Anti-Asian/Pacific Islander	181	230	239	181
Anti-multiracial group	229	291	320	193
Ethnicity/national origin, total	**984**	**1,233**	**1,305**	**1,209**
Anti-Hispanic	576	770	819	802
Anti-other ethnicity/national origin	408	463	486	407
Religion, total	**1,462**	**1,597**	**1,750**	**705**
Anti-Jewish	967	1,027	1,144	362
Anti-Catholic	76	81	86	44
Anti-Protestant	59	62	65	35
Anti-Islamic	156	191	208	147
Anti-other religious group	124	140	147	63
Anti-multi-religious group	73	88	92	49
Anti-atheism/agnosticism/etc.	7	8	8	5
Sexual orientation, total	**1,195**	**1,415**	**1,472**	**1,380**
Anti-male homosexual	747	881	913	914
Anti-female homosexual	163	192	202	154
Anti-homosexual	238	293	307	268
Anti-heterosexual	26	28	29	26
Anti-bisexual	21	21	21	18
Disability, total	**79**	**94**	**95**	**73**
Anti-physical	17	20	21	17
Anti-mental	62	74	74	56
Multiple bias [3]	**2**	**4**	**10**	**6**

[1] The term "victim" may refer to a person, business, institution, or a society as a whole. [2] The term "known offender" does not imply that the identity of the suspect is known, but only that an attribute of the suspect is identified which distinguishes him/her from an unknown offender. [3] In a "multiple-bias incident" two conditions must be met: more than one offense type must occur in the incident and at least two offense types must be motivated by different biases.

Source: U.S. Department of Justice, Federal Bureau of Investigation, Uniform Crime Reports, *Hate Crime Statistics*, annual. See <http://www.fbi.gov/ucr/hc2006/>.

Table 311. Hate Crimes Reported by State: 2006

[(255,087 represents 255,087,000). See headnote, Table 310]

State	Number of participating agencies	Population covered (1,000)	Agencies submitting incidents	Incidents reported	State	Number of participating agencies	Population covered (1,000)	Agencies submitting incidents	Incidents reported
United States [1]	**12,620**	**255,087**	**2,105**	**7,722**	Montana	93	924	14	24
					Nebraska	197	1,472	10	56
Alabama	42	694	1	1	Nevada	34	2,496	11	125
Alaska	2	284	1	6	New Hampshire	134	987	20	34
Arizona	80	5,889	24	149	New Jersey	513	8,725	225	759
Arkansas	257	2,739	42	113	New Mexico	46	1,220	5	20
California	728	36,458	250	1,297					
Colorado	220	4,725	45	138	New York	277	15,094	41	522
Connecticut	99	3,504	51	131	North Carolina	434	8,381	40	100
Delaware	53	853	17	48	North Dakota	72	571	9	16
District of Columbia	2	582	2	57	Ohio	493	8,638	87	300
Florida	491	18,045	91	216	Oklahoma	294	3,568	28	51
Georgia	61	1,146	4	13	Oregon	169	3,697	32	141
Idaho	105	1,461	12	23	Pennsylvania	954	11,741	27	97
Illinois	66	5,264	49	156	Rhode Island	47	1,068	12	19
Indiana	124	2,797	15	39	South Carolina	476	4,318	56	110
Iowa	223	2,930	15	28					
Kansas	359	2,135	49	109	South Dakota	91	600	7	76
Kentucky	320	3,731	28	64	Tennessee	459	6,037	65	202
Louisiana	108	2,292	13	22	Texas	996	23,483	68	245
Maine	148	1,322	31	59	Utah	111	2,517	21	35
Maryland	153	5,616	34	212	Vermont	78	612	10	21
Massachusetts	328	6,040	85	379	Virginia	399	7,621	91	341
Michigan	598	9,981	185	653	Washington	253	6,393	56	177
Minnesota	289	4,306	53	137	West Virginia	340	1,708	18	34
Mississippi	62	830	–	–	Wisconsin	371	5,557	25	84
Missouri	309	3,532	26	78	Wyoming	62	503	4	5

– Represents zero. [1] No data available for Hawaii. Source: U.S. Department of Justice, Federal Bureau of Investigation, Uniform Crime Reports, *Hate Crime Statistics*, annual. See <http://www.fbi.gov/ucr/hc2006/>.

U.S. Census Bureau, Statistical Abstract of the United States: 2009

Table 312. **Persons Arrested by Charge and Selected Characteristics: 2006**

[**In thousands (10,472.4 represents 10,472,400).** Represents arrests (not charges) reported by approximately 11,249 agencies with a total 2006 population of almost 217 million as estimated by FBI. Age and sex data are mandatory, while race data are optional and not always reported with arrest data; hence, two different total number of arrests. See source for details. For definitions of crimes, go to <http://www.fbi.gov/ucr/cius2006/about/offense_definitions.html>]

Offense	Total arrests	Male	Female	Total arrests	White	Black	American Indian or Alaska Native	Asian or Pacific Islander
Total	**10,472.4**	**7,985.5**	**2,486.9**	**10,437.6**	**7,270.2**	**2,924.7**	**130.6**	**112.1**
Serious crimes:								
Murder and nonnegligent manslaughter	9.8	8.7	1.1	9.8	4.6	5.0	0.1	0.1
Forcible rape	17.1	16.9	0.2	17.0	11.1	5.5	0.2	0.2
Robbery	93.5	83.0	10.5	93.4	39.4	52.5	0.6	0.8
Aggravated assault	327.5	259.5	67.9	326.7	206.4	112.6	3.9	3.7
Burglary	222.2	190.1	32.1	221.7	153.0	64.7	2.1	2.0
Larceny/theft	801.6	499.3	302.4	799.0	548.1	231.0	9.4	10.6
Motor vehicle theft	100.8	82.9	17.8	100.6	63.1	35.1	1.0	1.4
Arson	12.0	10.0	2.0	12.0	9.1	2.6	0.1	0.2
Other assaults	952.7	714.1	238.6	949.9	619.8	306.1	13.1	10.9
Nonserious crimes:								
Forgery and counterfeiting	79.5	48.4	31.1	79.3	55.6	22.3	0.4	0.9
Fraud	197.7	109.7	88.0	196.9	135.3	59.1	1.2	1.3
Embezzlement	14.8	7.0	7.8	14.7	9.7	4.7	0.1	0.2
Stolen property—buying, receiving, possessing	90.1	73.1	17.0	89.9	58.1	30.3	0.7	0.8
Vandalism	220.4	183.4	37.0	219.7	165.5	48.8	3.0	2.4
Weapons; carrying, possessing, etc.	147.6	135.8	11.8	147.3	84.9	59.9	1.1	1.4
Prostitution and commercialized vice	59.7	21.4	38.4	59.6	33.8	23.6	0.6	1.6
Sex offenses (except forcible rape and prostitution)	63.2	57.7	5.5	63.0	46.2	15.5	0.6	0.7
Drug abuse violations	1,379.9	1,118.7	261.2	1,376.8	875.1	483.9	8.2	9.6
Gambling	9.0	8.1	0.9	9.0	2.4	6.5	–	0.2
Offenses against family and children	92.1	69.5	22.5	91.6	61.3	28.1	1.7	0.6
Driving under the influence	1,038.6	830.5	208.1	1,034.7	914.2	95.3	13.5	11.7
Liquor laws	469.2	342.1	127.1	466.3	398.1	50.0	12.8	5.4
Drunkenness	409.5	346.1	63.4	408.4	344.2	54.1	7.9	2.3
Disorderly conduct	519.0	383.3	135.7	517.3	326.0	179.7	7.6	3.9
Vagrancy	27.1	21.0	6.0	27.0	15.3	11.2	0.3	0.1
Suspicion	1.7	1.3	0.4	1.7	1.0	0.7	–	–
Curfew and loitering law violations	114.3	78.7	35.6	114.2	69.6	42.5	0.8	1.2
Runaways	83.9	36.4	47.5	83.7	57.4	20.9	1.5	4.0
All other offenses (except traffic)	2,917.8	2,248.6	669.2	2,906.3	1,962.0	872.6	37.9	33.8

– Rounds to zero.

Source: U.S. Department of Justice, Federal Bureau of Investigation. Crime in the United States, annual. See also <http://www.fbi.gov/ucr/cius2006/arrests/index.html> (release September 2007).

Table 313. **Juvenile Arrests for Selected Offenses: 1980 to 2006**

[**169,439 represents 169,439,000.** Juveniles are persons under 18 years of age]

Offense	1980	1990	1995	2000	2001	2002	2003	2004	2005	2006
Number of contributing agencies	8,178	10,765	10,037	9,904	10,281	10,946	11,368	11,437	11,778	11,376
Population covered (1,000)	169,439	204,543	206,762	204,965	215,380	220,157	219,562	222,147	230,176	237,345
NUMBER										
Violent crime, total	77,220	97,103	123,131	78,450	78,443	71,059	69,060	68,247	73,377	80,195
Murder	1,475	2,661	2,812	1,027	1,069	1,014	960	829	968	1,018
Forcible rape	3,668	4,971	4,556	3,402	3,504	3,553	3,195	3,186	3,088	2,783
Robbery	38,529	34,944	47,240	24,206	23,408	19,491	18,950	19,000	22,356	27,638
Aggravated assault	33,548	54,527	68,523	49,815	50,462	47,001	45,955	45,232	46,965	48,756
Weapon law violations	21,203	33,123	46,506	28,514	29,290	26,786	29,512	30,530	34,468	37,032
Drug abuse, total	86,685	66,300	149,236	146,594	146,758	133,557	134,746	135,056	137,809	145,153
Sale and manufacturing	13,004	24,575	34,077	26,432	24,649	22,086	21,987	21,136	21,607	22,466
Heroin/cocaine	1,318	17,511	19,187	11,000	10,535	8,832	7,848	7,852	7,863	8,261
Marijuana	8,876	4,372	10,682	11,792	10,552	9,962	10,463	9,743	9,845	10,333
Synthetic narcotics	465	346	701	945	911	974	1,043	1,119	1,071	1,262
Dangerous nonnarcotic drugs	2,345	2,346	3,507	2,695	2,651	2,318	2,633	2,422	2,828	2,610
Possession	73,681	41,725	115,159	120,432	122,109	111,471	112,759	113,920	116,202	122,687
Heroin/cocaine	2,614	15,194	21,253	12,586	11,734	10,969	9,932	10,805	11,131	12,024
Marijuana	64,465	20,940	82,015	95,962	97,088	85,769	87,909	87,717	88,909	95,120
Synthetic narcotics	1,524	1,155	2,047	2,052	2,237	2,805	2,872	3,279	3,235	3,337
Dangerous nonnarcotic drugs	5,078	4,436	9,844	9,832	11,050	11,928	12,046	12,119	12,927	12,206

Source: U.S. Department of Justice, Federal Bureau of Investigation, *Crime in the United States,* annual, Person arrested. See also <http://www.fbi.gov/ucr/cius2006/arrests/index.html> (released September 2007).

Law Enforcement, Courts, and Prisons   197

Table 314. Suspects Arrested for Federal Offenses and Booked by United States Marshals Service (USMS), by Offense: 1994 to 2004

[Persons suspected of violating federal law may be arrested by any one of the many federal agencies empowered to make arrests, or by state or local authorities. Regardless of which agency makes the arrest, federal suspects are typically transferred to the custody of the U.S. Marshals Service for booking, processing, and detention. See Methodology for a listing of detailed offense categories within each major offense category]

Most serious offense	1994	1995	1996	1997	1998[2]	1999[1,2]	2000[2]	2001[2]	2002[2]	2003	2004
All offenses[3]	80,730	83,324	85,195	91,747	104,119	109,340	115,589	118,896	124,074	131,064	140,755
Violent offenses[4]	3,905	3,873	4,519	4,801	4,989	4,254	4,250	4,843	4,723	4,484	4,587
Property offenses	15,540	16,245	16,191	16,288	16,786	16,569	16,842	16,824	17,268	17,258	15,609
Fraudulent[5]	11,919	12,804	12,729	12,912	13,219	13,116	13,432	13,397	13,976	14,169	12,709
Other[6]	3,621	3,441	3,462	3,376	3,567	3,453	3,410	3,427	3,292	3,089	2,900
Drug offenses	23,268	23,768	24,682	26,843	30,012	31,867	32,630	33,589	33,730	34,217	32,980
Public-order offenses	11,596	10,336	9,578	9,324	9,234	9,841	10,063	9,156	8,772	8,591	8,618
Regulatory	530	697	656	749	775	752	621	687	524	425	335
Other	11,066	9,639	8,922	8,575	8,459	9,089	9,442	8,469	8,248	8,166	8,283
Weapon offenses[7]	3,885	3,724	3,131	3,235	3,539	4,268	5,203	6,007	7,488	9,416	9,936
Immigration offenses[7]	8,777	10,600	12,026	14,994	20,942	22,849	25,205	24,794	25,270	27,620	39,135
Supervision violations	12,719	13,498	13,304	13,995	15,157	15,603	17,133	18,978	21,777	23,605	23,399
Material witness	886	1,143	1,617	2,169	3,398	4,016	4,203	3,679	3,918	4,615	5,385
Unknown or indeterminable offenses	154	137	147	163	62	73	60	1,026	1,128	1,258	1,106

[1] Starting in 1999 and through the current year of data, nonviolent sex offenses were reclassified from "Violent offenses" to "Public-order offenses."   [2] Data for 1998 through 2002 are not directly comparable to 2003 and 2004 because of changes in the data-processing methodology. See note 2 on page 24, chapter 1 of the 2004 Compendium of Federal Justice Statistics.   [3] Includes suspects whose offense category could not be determined.   [4] In this table, "Violent offenses" may include nonnegligent manslaughter.   [5] Fradulent property excludes tax fraud.   [6] Excludes fraudulent property and includes destruction of property and trespassing.   [7] Beginning in 2001, "Weapon" and "Immigration" offenses became major offense categories. Previously, these offenses were classified within "Public-order offenses."

Source: U.S. Department of Justice, Office of Justice Programs, Bureau of Justice Statistics, *Federal Criminal Justice Trends, 2003,* Series NCJ 205331, August 2006; <http://www.ojp.usdoj.gov/bjs/abstract/fcjt03.htm>. *Compendium of Federal Justice Statistics, 2004,* Series NCJ 213476, December 2006; <http://www.ojp.usdoj.gov/bjs/abstract/cfjs04.htm>.

Table 315. Suspects in Criminal Matters Investigated by U.S. Attorneys by Offense: 1994 to 2004

[The most serious offense investigated is based on the criminal lead charge as determined by the assistant U.S. attorney responsible for the criminal matter]

Most serious offense investigated	1994	1995	1996	1997	1998	1999[1]	2000	2001	2002	2003	2004
All offenses[2]	99,251	102,220	97,776	110,034	115,692	117,994	123,559	121,818	124,335	130,078	141,212
Violent offenses[3]	5,570	5,720	6,570	7,354	7,527	5,768	6,036	6,225	6,392	5,688	5,714
Property offenses	32,579	31,759	28,962	29,916	30,125	28,011	28,423	28,608	27,321	27,375	24,956
Fraudulent[4]	28,491	27,836	25,245	25,854	26,328	24,200	24,679	25,275	24,019	24,261	22,182
Other[5]	4,088	3,923	3,717	4,062	3,797	3,811	3,744	3,333	3,302	3,114	2,774
Drug offenses	29,311	31,686	30,227	34,027	36,355	37,313	38,959	37,944	38,150	37,416	37,501
Public-order offenses	19,143	19,036	18,918	22,857	21,244	22,816	24,180	23,980	23,472	23,717	21,277
Regulatory	5,059	5,371	5,154	5,423	6,541	6,332	5,737	5,411	4,738	5,366	4,959
Other	14,084	13,665	13,764	17,434	14,703	16,484	18,443	18,569	18,734	18,351	16,318
Weapon offenses[6]	5,996	5,376	4,462	4,870	4,907	6,982	8,589	8,989	11,200	14,022	14,398
Immigration offenses[6]	5,526	7,256	7,122	9,366	14,114	15,539	16,495	15,378	16,699	20,341	35,858
Unknown or indeterminable offenses	1,126	1,387	1,515	1,644	1,420	1,565	877	694	1,101	1,519	1,508

[1] Starting in 1999 and through the current year of data, nonviolent sex offenses were reclassified from "Violent offenses" to "Public-order offenses."   [2] Includes suspects whose offense category could not be determined. See Methodology for a listing of detailed offense categories within each major offense category.   [3] In this table, "Violent offenses" may include nonnegligent manslaughter; "Fraudulent property" excludes tax fraud; and "Other nonfraudulent property" excludes fraudulent property and includes destruction of property and trespassing.   [4] Fradulent property excludes tax fraud.   [5] Excludes fraudulent property and includes destruction of property and trespassing.   [6] Beginning in 2001, "Weapon" and "Immigration" offenses became major offense categories. Previously, these offenses were classified within "Public-order offenses."

Source: U.S. Department of Justice, Office of Justice Programs, Bureau of Justice Statistics, *Federal Criminal Justice Trends,* 2003. Series NCJ 205331, August 2006. See also, <http://www.ojp.usdoj.gov/bjs/abstract/fcjt03.htm>. *Compendium of Federal Justice Statistics, 2004,* Series NCJ 213476, December 2006; <http://www.ojp.usdoj.gov/bjs/abstract/cfjs04.htm>.

Table 316. Drug Arrest Rates for Drug Abuse Violations, 1990 to 2006, and by Region, 2006

[Rate per 100,000 inhabitants. Based on Census Bureau estimated resident population as of July 1, except 1990 and 2000, enumerated as of April 1. For composition of regions, see map, inside front cover]

Offense	1990	2000	2005	2006 Total	North-east	Mid-west	South	West
Drug arrest rate, total	**435.3**	**587.1**	**600.9**	**594.8**	**520.6**	**440.4**	**663.5**	**675.5**
Sale and/or manufacture	139.0	122.7	109.9	104.8	118.6	76.2	116.7	101.6
Heroin or cocaine [1]	93.7	60.8	47.8	47.8	76.3	25.1	55.4	36.8
Marijuana	26.4	34.2	29.6	29.0	28.1	29.5	29.0	27.9
Synthetic or manufactured drugs	2.7	6.4	8.6	9.0	5.1	4.6	18.5	4.4
Other dangerous nonnarcotic drugs	16.2	21.3	23.9	18.9	9.0	17.0	13.9	32.5
Possession	296.3	464.4	490.9	490.0	402.1	364.2	546.8	573.9
Heroin or cocaine [1]	144.4	138.7	131.5	134.0	124.6	71.8	162.9	153.7
Marijuana	104.9	244.4	228.9	235.5	221.0	220.9	301.6	176.9
Synthetic or manufactured drugs	6.6	12.0	21.0	20.4	10.8	13.5	29.0	21.2
Other dangerous nonnarcotic drugs	40.4	69.4	109.6	100.1	45.7	58.0	53.4	222.1

[1] Includes other derivatives such as morphine, heroin, and codeine.

Source: U.S. Department of Justice, Federal Bureau of Investigation, *Crime in the United States,* annual. See also <http://www.fbi.gov/ucr/06cius/arrests/index.html>; (as of 17 February 2007).

Table 317. Federal Drug Arrests and Seizures by Type of Drug: 1990 to 2007

[For fiscal years ending in year shown]

Drug	1990	1995	2000	2002	2003	2004	2005	2006	2007
Number of arrests, total [1,2]	**23,153**	**25,010**	**40,455**	**30,939**	**29,283**	**29,732**	**30,811**	**29,573**	**29,219**
Heroin	2,056	2,548	3,622	2,559	2,514	2,478	2,442	2,251	2,099
Cocaine	12,400	12,036	16,369	12,349	11,363	11,934	12,955	12,797	12,392
Marijuana	5,155	6,231	8,574	5,716	6,029	6,309	6,092	5,935	6,674
Methamphetamine	2,474	2,886	8,274	6,396	6,068	6,075	6,479	5,762	5,421
Seizure in pounds, total [3,4]	**738,008**	**1,574,890**	**2,888,282**	**2,650,186**	**2,959,007**	**3,043,245**	**2,808,630**	**2,653,031**	**3,694,331**
Cocaine	235,889	234,342	248,895	225,355	245,580	336,247	391,981	333,023	363,064
Heroin	1,704	2,971	3,341	6,859	5,923	4,088	4,020	4,186	5,696
Marijuana	483,353	1,305,701	2,612,059	2,417,786	2,706,131	2,702,419	2,412,216	2,305,637	3,323,008
Methamphetamine	(NA)	(NA)	7,107	6,229	8,564	8,194	10,748	9,229	8,330

NA Not available. [1] Arrests are for Drug Enforcement Administration only. [2] Includes other drug-related arrests not shown. [3] Reflects the combined drug seizure effort of the Drug Enforcement Administration, the Federal Bureau of Investigation, the U.S. Customs Services, and, beginning October 1995, the U.S. Border Patrol within the jurisdiction of the United States as well as maritime seizures by the U.S. Coast Guard. Based on reports to the federal-wide Drug Seizure System, which eliminates duplicate reporting of a seizure involving more than one federal agency. [4] Includes other drug seizures not shown.

Source: U.S. Drug Enforcement Administration, unpublished data from federal-wide Drug Seizure System. (Data are as of 15 May 2008.)

Table 318. Background Checks for Firearm Transfers: 1994 to 2007

[In thousands (87,180 represents 87,180,000), except rates]

Inquiries and rejections	Total 1994–2007 [1]	Interim period 1994–1998 [2]	Permanent Brady [3] 1998 [4]	2000	2002	2003	2004	2005	2006	2007
Applications and rejections:										
Applications received	87,180	12,740	893	7,699	7,806	7,831	8,084	8,278	8,612	8,658
Applications rejected	1,631	312	20	153	136	126	126	132	134	136
Rejection rate	1.9	2.4	2.2	2.0	1.7	1.6	1.6	1.6	1.6	1.6

[1] Number of applications and estimates of denials for firearm transfers or permits since the inception of the Brady Act, 1994–2007. [2] Background checks on applicants were conducted by state and local agencies, mainly on handgun transfers. See *"Presale Handgun Checks, the Brady Interim Period, 1994–98"* (NCJ 175034). [3] The period beginning November 30, 1998, is the effective date for the Brady Handgun Violence Prevention Act, P.L. 103-159, 1993. The National Instant Criminal Background Check System (NICS) began operations. Checks on handgun and long gun transfers are conducted by the Federal Bureau of Investigation (FBI), and by state and local agencies. Totals combine Firearm Inquiry Statistics (FIST) estimates for state and local agencies with transactions and denials reported by the FBI. [4] For the period of November 30 to December 31, 1998. Counts are from the NICS operations report and may include multiple transactions for the same application.

Source: U.S. Department of Justice, Office of Justice Programs, Bureau of Justice Statistics, Background Checks for Firearm Transfers, 2007, Series NCJ 223197, July 2008. See internet site <http://www.ojp.usdoj.gov/bjs/guns.htm>.

Table 319. Law Enforcement Officers Killed and Assaulted: 1990 to 2006

[Contains statistics on felonious and accidental deaths of duly sworn local, state, tribal, and federal law enforcement officers. For composition of regions, see map, inside front cover]

Item	1990	1995	2000	2001 [1]	2002	2003	2004	2005	2006
OFFICERS KILLED									
Total killed	**132**	**133**	**134**	**218**	**131**	**133**	**139**	**122**	**114**
Geographical region									
Northeast	13	16	13	79	10	13	18	12	12
Midwest	20	19	32	26	22	20	25	23	20
South.	68	63	67	68	64	66	66	58	48
West	23	32	19	38	28	31	24	24	31
Puerto Rico.	8	2	3	7	7	3	5	5	3
Island areas, foreign countries.	–	1	–	–	–	–	1	–	–
Total feloniously killed	65	74	51	142	56	52	57	55	48
Firearms	56	63	47	61	51	45	54	50	46
Handgun	47	44	33	46	38	34	36	42	36
Rifle	8	14	10	11	10	10	13	3	8
Shotgun.	1	5	4	4	3	1	5	5	2
Blunt instrument	–	–	–	1	–	1	–	–	–
Bomb	–	8	–	–	–	–	–	–	–
Knife/cutting instrument . . .	3	1	1	–	1	–	1	–	–
Personal weapons [2]	2	–	–	1	–	–	–	–	–
Vehicle	1	2	3	7	4	6	2	5	2
Other	3	–	–	72	–	–	–	–	–
Total accidentally killed	67	59	83	76	75	81	82	67	66
OFFICERS ASSAULTED									
Population covered(1,000) [3] . .	197,426	191,759	204,599	213,645	219,425	225,770	226,273	222,874	222,640
Number of—									
Reporting agencies	9,343	8,503	8,940	9,773	10,164	10,539	10,589	10,119	10,346
Officers employed	410,131	428,379	452,531	471,096	491,009	501,738	501,462	489,393	495,270
Total assaulted	**72,091**	**57,762**	**58,398**	**57,463**	**59,526**	**58,600**	**59,692**	**57,820**	**58,634**
Firearm	3,651	2,354	1,749	1,841	1,927	1,879	2,114	2,157	2,278
Knife/cutting instrument	1,647	1,356	1,015	1,168	1,061	1,084	1,123	1,059	1,047
Other dangerous weapon . . .	7,423	6,414	8,132	8,233	8,526	8,180	8,645	8,379	8,512
Personal weapons [2]	59,370	47,638	47,502	46,221	48,012	47,457	47,810	46,225	46,797

– Represents zero. [1] The 72 felonious deaths that resulted from the events of September 11, 2001, are included in this table. [2] Includes hands, fists, feet, etc. [3] Represents the number of persons covered by agencies shown.

Source: U.S. Department of Justice, Federal Bureau of Investigation, *Law Enforcement Officers Killed and Assaulted,* annual. <http://www.fbi.gov/ucr/killed/2006/index.html/>.

Table 320. Fraud Complaints and Identity Theft Victims by State: 2007

[Rate per 100,000 population. As of December 31. Based on Census Bureau population estimates. Federal Trade Commission (FTC) has developed and maintained a complaint data base called the Consumer Sentinel. This database collects information about consumer fraud and identity theft from the FTC and over 115 other organizations and makes the information available to law enforcement. See appendixes in the annual report for list of contributing organizations]

Consumer state	Fraud complaints		Identity theft victims		Consumer state	Fraud complaints		Identity theft victims	
	Number	Rate	Number	Rate		Number	Rate	Number	Rate
U.S. [1]	**500,770**	**166.0**	**250,687**	**83.1**	MO	12,912	219.7	3,962	67.4
					MT.	1,496	156.2	391	40.8
AL	6,451	139.4	3,221	69.6	NE	2,831	159.5	793	44.7
AK	1,432	209.5	321	47.0	NV	5,138	200.3	2,930	114.2
AZ	13,903	219.3	8,688	137.1	NH	2,702	205.3	643	48.9
AR	3,482	122.8	1,601	56.5	NJ	14,542	167.4	6,864	79.0
CA	61,409	168.0	43,892	120.1	NM	2,697	136.9	1,723	87.5
CO	11,364	233.8	4,328	89.0	NY	27,219	141.0	19,319	100.1
CT	5,264	150.3	2,409	68.8	NC	14,846	163.8	6,069	67.0
DE	1,341	155.1	603	69.7	ND	726	113.5	182	28.5
DC	1,375	233.7	784	133.2	OH	18,964	165.4	7,178	62.6
FL	33,027	181.0	19,270	105.6	OK	4,828	133.5	2,312	63.9
GA	15,936	167.0	8,744	91.6	OR	7,704	205.6	2,552	68.1
HI	2,520	196.4	589	45.9	PA	19,197	154.4	9,016	72.5
ID	2,563	170.9	737	49.2	RI	1,511	142.8	592	56.0
IL	21,602	168.1	10,304	80.2	SC	6,041	137.1	2,670	60.6
IN	10,405	164.0	4,026	63.4	SD	880	110.5	245	30.8
IA	4,014	134.3	1,063	35.6	TN	9,920	161.1	3986	64.7
KS	3,875	139.6	1,694	61.0	TX	36,367	152.1	25,796	107.9
KY	5,502	129.7	1,836	43.3	UT	5,110	193.2	1,529	57.8
LA	5,319	123.9	2,674	62.3	VT	880	141.6	237	38.1
ME	2,111	160.3	530	40.2	VA	14,733	191.0	5,319	69.0
MD	11,745	209.0	4,821	85.8	WA	14,918	230.6	4,942	76.4
MA	9,766	151.4	4,292	66.5	WV	2,654	146.5	729	40.2
MI	14,780	146.7	7,079	70.3	WI	9,852	175.9	2,450	43.7
MN	9,388	180.6	2,857	55.0	WY	884	169.1	222	42.5
MS	2,644	90.6	1,673	57.3					

[1] Data represents only fraud complaints from consumer states and identity theft victims by state listed in this table.

Source: U.S. Federal Trade Commission, *Consumer Fraud and Identity Theft Complaint Data, January—December 2007.* Issued February 2008. See also <http://www.consumer.gov/sentinel/pubs/Top10Fraud2007.pdf>.

Table 321. U.S. Supreme Court—Cases Filed and Disposition: 1980 to 2006

[Statutory term of court begins first Monday in **October**]

Action	1980	1990	1995	2000	2002	2003	2004	2005	2006
Total cases on docket.........	5,144	6,316	7,565	8,965	9,406	8,882	8,588	9,608	10,256
Appellate cases on docket............	2,749	2,351	2,456	2,305	2,190	2,058	2,041	2,025	2,069
From prior term	527	365	361	351	321	336	300	354	346
Docketed during present term........	2,222	1,986	2,095	1,954	1,869	1,722	1,741	1,671	1,723
Cases acted upon..............	2,324	2,042	2,130	2,024	1,899	1,798	1,727	1,703	1,736
Granted review	167	114	92	85	83	74	69	63	62
Denied, dismissed, or withdrawn	1,999	1,802	1,945	1,842	1,727	1,641	1,529	1,554	1,611
Summarily decided	90	81	62	63	46	37	89	46	39
Cases not acted upon	425	309	326	281	291	260	314	322	333
Pauper cases on docket	2,371	3,951	5,098	6,651	7,209	6,818	6,543	7,575	8,181
Cases acted upon [1]...........	2,027	3,436	4,514	5,736	6,488	6,036	5,815	6,533	7,186
Granted review	17	27	13	14	8	13	11	15	15
Denied, dismissed, or withdrawn	1,968	3,369	4,439	5,658	6,459	6,005	5,061	6,459	6,925
Summarily decided	32	28	55	61	17	13	737	58	239
Cases not acted upon	344	515	584	915	721	782	728	1,042	995
Original cases on docket	24	14	11	9	7	6	4	8	6
Cases disposed of during term	7	3	5	2	1	2	–	4	1
Total cases available for argument	264	201	145	138	139	140	128	122	108
Cases disposed of	162	131	93	89	87	93	87	87	80
Cases argued	154	125	90	86	84	91	87	88	78
Cases dismissed or remanded without argument	8	6	3	3	3	2	–	1	2
Cases remaining	102	70	52	49	52	47	41	31	28
Cases decided by signed opinion	144	121	87	83	79	89	85	82	74
Cases decided by per curiam opinion.....	8	4	3	4	5	2	2	5	4
Number of signed opinions............	123	112	75	77	71	73	74	69	67

– Represents zero. [1] Includes cases granted review and carried over to next term, not shown separately.

Source: Office of the Clerk, Supreme Court of the United States, unpublished data.

Table 322. U.S. District Courts—Civil Cases Commenced and Pending: 2000 to 2007

[For years ending **June 30**]

Type of case	Cases commenced				Cases pending			
	2000	2005	2006	2007	2000	2005	2006	2007
Cases total [1]	263,049	282,758	244,343	272,067	249,692	267,270	246,547	267,774
Contract actions [1]........	54,494	28,590	28,139	34,071	38,262	26,712	26,671	30,631
Recovery of overpayments [2]...	25,636	3,380	2,856	3,053	12,107	1,953	1,789	1,708
Real property actions	6,481	4,541	4,761	4,456	4,249	4,512	4,178	4,321
Tort actions................	40,877	75,273	53,809	77,257	63,116	76,821	64,701	83,046
Personal injury	36,867	52,215	49,834	73,004	59,232	72,716	60,569	78,464
Personal injury product liability [1].............	15,349	35,615	32,515	51,557	31,772	46,575	34,280	52,346
Asbestos	7,893	1,628	8,709	15,422	4,949	1,073	856	14,525
Other personal injury	21,518	16,600	17,319	21,447	27,460	26,141	26,289	26,118
Personal property damage	4,010	23,058	3,975	4,253	3,884	4,105	4,132	4,582
Actions under statutes [1]	161,187	171,922	157,536	156,152	144,053	157,357	150,891	149,622
Civil rights [1]..............	41,226	36,724	33,417	31,975	44,259	40,596	38,384	36,469
Employment.............	21,404	17,998	14,851	13,608	24,456	21,344	18,591	16,863
Bankruptcy suits	3,378	3,428	3,193	3,182	2,555	2,650	2,565	2,533
Commerce (ICC rates, etc.) ...	1,007	492	404	317	444	395	351	276
Environmental matters........	894	726	874	763	1,355	1,193	1,148	1,045
Prisoner petitions	57,706	62,698	55,775	53,222	43,560	47,870	46,655	47,172
Forfeiture and penalty	2,246	2,214	2,318	2,221	1,772	2,156	2,309	2,245
Labor laws................	14,229	18,643	16,853	18,630	11,267	15,725	14,014	15,111
Protected property rights [3]	8,745	11,809	11,745	11,132	7,858	10,507	10,274	9,827
Securities commodities and exchanges...............	2,500	2,371	1,654	1,369	3,578	5,192	4,463	4,030
Social security laws..........	14,365	16,066	14,052	12,964	13,667	15,420	14,202	13,214
Tax suits.................	938	1,348	1,498	1,485	1,068	1,222	1,331	1,376
Freedom of information	335	426	309	325	380	378	370	380

[1] Includes other types not shown separately. [2] Includes enforcement of judgments in student loan cases, and overpayments of veterans' benefits. [3] Includes copyright, patent, and trademark rights.

Source: Administrative Office of the U.S. Courts, *Statistical Tables for the Federal Judiciary,* annual; <http://www.uscourts.gov/>.

U.S. Census Bureau, Statistical Abstract of the United States: 2009

Table 323. U.S. District Courts—Offenders Convicted and Sentenced to Prison and Length of Sentence: 2000 and 2004

Selected most serious offense of conviction	Offenders convicted [1]		Offenders sentenced to prison [1,2]		Mean length of sentence for incarceration (months) [3]	
	2000	2004	2000	2004	2000	2004
Total	68,156	74,782	50,451	58,106	56.7	59.7
Violent offenses [4]	2,557	2,569	2,360	2,402	86.5	96.2
Murder [5]	283	190	249	175	94.2	111.2
Negligent manslaughter	1	1	1	1	(B)	(B)
Assault	253	465	188	384	33.0	44.8
Property offenses	12,454	12,202	7,462	7,323	24.2	27.4
Fraudulent	10,396	10,403	6,272	6,267	22.5	25.8
Embezzlement	917	646	506	302	14.8	16.0
Fraud [6]	8,177	8,677	5,008	5,278	23.5	26.6
Forgery	86	73	41	44	19.1	20.0
Counterfeiting	1,216	1,007	717	643	20.8	24.1
Other [4]	2,058	1,799	1,190	1,056	33.2	36.7
Larceny [7]	1,394	1,307	689	695	27.3	31.3
Arson	158	165	134	136	71.8	75.2
Transportation of stolen property	272	166	200	115	33.4	35.0
Drug offenses [4]	24,206	24,472	22,352	22,744	75.5	83.6
Public-order offenses [4]	4,585	4,398	2,989	3,135	45.8	43.6
Regulatory	1,376	1,106	647	580	28.4	32.3
Other	3,209	3,292	2,342	2,555	46.5	46.2
Tax law violations [8]	655	425	355	265	18.5	26.5
Escape	487	415	447	380	19.2	18.7
Racketeering and extortion	951	844	778	651	81.5	70.9
Nonviolent sex offenses	475	724	429	692	47.1	57.0
Obscene material [9]	28	32	7	25	(B)	32.7
Weapon offenses [10]	4,196	8,082	3,834	7,518	91.4	84.3
Immigration offenses [10]	11,125	14,819	10,073	13,387	29.5	26.9
Misdemeanors [11]	8,961	8,240	1,356	1,597	10.4	5.6

B Base figures too small to meet statistical standards for reliability of a derived figure.   [1] Total may not equal the sum of individual sanctions.   [2] All sentences to incarceration, including split, mixed, life, and indeterminate sentences.   [3] Excludes sentences of life, death, and indeterminate sentences.   [4] Includes offenses not shown separately.   [5] Includes nonnegligent manslaughter.   [6] Excludes tax fraud.   [7] Excludes transportation of stolen property.   [8] Includes tax fraud.   [9] Denotes the mail or transport thereof.   [10] Beginning in 2001, "Weapon and Immigration" offenses became major offense categories. Previously, these offenses were classified within "Public-order offenses."   [11] Includes misdemeanors, petty offenses, unknown offense levels, and drug possession.

Source: U.S. Department of Justice, Office of Justice Programs, Bureau of Justice Statistics, *Federal Criminal Justice Trends, 2003*, Series NCJ 205331, August 2006; <http://www.ojp.usdoj.gov/bjs/abstract/cfjs03.htm>. *Compendium of Federal Justice Statistics, 2004*, Series NCJ 213476, December 2006; <http://www.ojp.usdoj.gov/bjs/abstract/cfjs04.htm>.

Table 324. Criminal Appeals Filed, by Offense: 1994 to 2004

[Appeals were classified into the offense category that represents the offense of conviction. Offenses represent the statutory offense charged against a defendant in a criminal appeal]

Most serious offense of conviction	1994	1995	1996	1997	1998	1999 [1]	2000	2001	2002	2003	2004
All offenses [2]	10,674	10,162	10,889	10,521	10,535	10,251	9,162	11,281	11,569	11,968	12,517
Violent offenses [3]	856	700	685	739	742	559	490	591	606	601	673
Property offenses	1,949	1,767	2,093	1,972	1,947	1,739	1,482	1,681	1,726	1,842	1,873
Fraudulent [4]	1,410	1,323	1,581	1,519	1,439	1,338	1,164	1,299	1,389	1,478	1,524
Other [5]	539	444	512	453	508	401	318	382	337	364	349
Drug offenses	5,102	4,499	5,099	4,750	4,845	4,513	3,843	4,529	4,689	4,565	4,678
Public-order offenses	1,037	886	985	1,050	878	954	827	1,024	876	894	955
Regulatory	288	220	196	224	178	162	150	144	128	137	142
Other	749	666	789	826	700	792	677	880	642	757	813
Weapon offenses [6]	1,141	1,034	1,183	1,135	982	1,070	872	1,266	1,386	1,681	2,024
Immigration offenses [6]	261	277	353	417	693	934	1,179	1,654	1,679	1,821	1,856
Unknown or indeterminable offenses	328	999	491	458	448	482	469	536	607	564	458

[1] Starting in 1999 and through the current data year, nonviolent sex offenses were reclassified from "Violent offenses" to "Public-order offenses."   [2] Include suspects whose offense category could not be determined. See Methodology for a listing of detailed offense categories within each major offense category.   [3] In this table, "Violent offenses" may include nonnegligent manslaughter; "Fraudulent property" excludes tax fraud; and "Other nonfraudulent property" excludes fraudulent property and includes destruction of property and trespassing.   [4] Excludes fraudulent property excludes tax fraud.   [5] Excludes fraudulent property and includes destruction of property and trespassing.   [6] Beginning in 2001, "Weapon" and "Immigration" offenses became major offense categories. Previously, these offenses were classified within "Public-order offenses."

Source: U.S. Department of Justice, Office of Justice Programs, Bureau of Justice Statistics, *Federal Criminal Justice Trends, 2003*. Series NCJ 205331, August 2006. See also <http://www.ojp.usdoj.gov/bjs/abstract/fcjt03.htm>; *Compendium of Federal Justice Statistics, 2004*, Series NCJ 213476, December 2006; <http://www.ojp.usdoj.gov/bjs/abstract/cfjs04.htm>.

Table 325. Authorized Intercepts of Communication—Summary: 1980 to 2007

[As of December 31. Data for jurisdictions with statutes authorizing or approving interception of wire or oral communication]

Item	1980	1990	1995	2000	2002	2003	2004	2005	2006	2007
Jurisdictions: [1]										
With wiretap statutes	28	40	41	45	47	47	47	47	47	47
Reporting interceptions	22	25	19	26	20	24	20	23	24	25
Intercept applications authorized	564	872	1,156	1,266	1,358	1,442	1,710	1,773	1,839	2,208
Intercept installations [2]	524	812	1,024	1,139	1,273	1,367	1,633	1,694	1,714	2,119
Federal	79	321	527	472	490	576	723	624	461	454
State	445	491	497	667	783	791	910	1,070	1,253	1,665
Intercepted communications, average [3]	1,058	1,487	2,028	1,769	1,708	3,004	3,017	2,835	2,685	3,106
Incriminating average [3]	315	321	459	402	403	993	619	629	547	920
Persons arrested [4]	1,871	2,057	2,577	3,411	3,060	3,674	4,506	4,674	4,376	4,830
Convictions [4]	259	420	494	736	493	844	634	776	711	984
Major offense specified:										
Gambling	199	116	95	49	82	49	90	42	56	55
Drugs	282	520	732	894	1,052	1,104	1,308	1,433	1,473	1,792
Homicide and assault	13	21	30	72	58	80	48	82	119	132
Racketeering	(NA)	(NA)	98	76	72	96	138	94	90	98
Other	70	215	201	175	94	113	126	122	101	131

NA Not available   [1] Jurisdictions include federal government, 44 states and the Virgin Islands, and the District of Columbia. [2] Based on the number of orders for which intercept devices were installed as reported by the prosecuting official.   [3] Average per authorized installation.   [4] Based on information received from intercepts installed in year shown; additional arrests/convictions will occur in subsequent years but are not shown here.

Source: Administrative Office of the U.S. Courts, *Report on Applications for Orders Authorizing or Approving the Interception of Wire, Oral or Electronic Communications* (Wiretap Report), annual. See also <http://www.uscourts.gov/wiretap07/contents.html> (accessed April 2008).

Table 326. Federal Prosecutions of Public Corruption: 1980 to 2006

[As of December 31. Prosecution of persons who have corrupted public office in violation of Federal Criminal Statutes]

Prosecution status	1980	1985	1990	1995	1999	2000	2001	2002	2003	2004	2005	2006
Total: [1] Charged	727	1,157	1,176	1,051	1,134	1,000	1,087	1,136	1,150	1,213	1,163	1,150
Convicted	602	997	1,084	878	1,065	938	920	1,011	868	1,020	1,027	1,030
Awaiting trial	213	256	300	323	329	327	437	413	412	419	451	439
Federal officials: Charged . .	123	563	615	527	480	441	502	478	479	424	445	463
Convicted	131	470	583	438	460	422	414	429	421	381	390	407
Awaiting trial	16	90	103	120	101	92	131	119	129	98	118	112
State officials: Charged	72	79	96	61	115	92	95	110	94	111	96	101
Convicted	51	66	79	61	80	91	61	132	87	81	94	116
Awaiting trial	28	20	28	23	44	37	75	50	38	48	51	38
Local officials: Charged . . .	247	248	257	236	237	211	224	299	259	268	309	291
Convicted	168	221	225	191	219	183	184	262	119	252	232	241
Awaiting trial	82	49	98	89	95	89	110	118	106	105	148	141
Others involved: Charged . .	285	267	208	227	302	256	266	249	318	410	313	295
Convicted	252	240	197	188	306	242	261	188	241	306	311	266
Awaiting trial	87	97	71	91	89	109	121	126	139	168	134	148

[1] Includes individuals who are neither public officials nor employees, but were involved with public officials or employees in violating the law, not shown separately.

Source: U.S. Department of Justice, Criminal Division, *Federal Prosecutions of Corrupt Public Officials, 1970–1980* and *Report to Congress on the Activities and Operations of the Public Integrity Section,* annual; <http://www.usdoj.gov/criminal/pin/>.

U.S. Census Bureau, Statistical Abstract of the United States: 2009

Table 327. **Delinquency Cases Disposed by Juvenile Courts by Reason for Referral: 1990 to 2005**

[**In thousands (1,346 represents 1,346,000), except rate.** A delinquency offense is an act committed by a juvenile for which an adult could be prosecuted in a criminal court. Disposition of a case involves taking a definite action such as waiving the case to criminal court, dismissing the case, placing the youth on probation, placing the youth in a facility for delinquents, or such actions as fines, restitution, and community service. Data have been revised through 2004]

Reason for referral	1990	1995	1997	1998	1999	2000	2001	2002	2003	2004	2005
All delinquency offenses ...	**1,346**	**1,807**	**1,870**	**1,799**	**1,720**	**1,702**	**1,688**	**1,676**	**1,674**	**1,688**	**1,682**
Case rate [1]	52.5	63.0	63.4	60.3	56.9	55.4	54.3	53.4	53.1	53.5	53.2
Person offenses [2]	257	398	413	404	396	391	402	401	408	416	428
Criminal homicide	2	3	2	2	2	2	2	2	1	1	1
Forcible rape	4	6	5	5	4	4	5	4	5	4	4
Robbery	28	42	36	30	26	22	22	21	22	21	26
Aggravated assault	52	73	61	57	51	51	48	46	47	47	49
Property offenses [2]	786	906	861	786	709	678	641	637	624	616	591
Burglary	145	148	147	135	117	111	107	106	104	99	96
Larceny-theft	349	432	406	360	326	314	293	292	284	283	262
Motor vehicle theft	71	54	52	45	39	37	38	38	38	35	33
Arson	7	11	9	9	9	9	9	9	9	9	8
Drug law violations	71	162	189	188	188	196	203	192	191	196	194
Public-order offenses [2]	232	341	408	420	426	438	442	445	452	462	470
Obstruction of justice	89	137	192	212	209	215	217	214	217	216	225
Disorderly conduct	56	91	92	89	96	100	104	114	116	125	128
Weapons offenses	31	47	45	43	40	37	37	35	37	41	44
Liquor law violations	17	18	16	19	20	25	25	26	26	26	25
Nonviolent sex offenses	11	10	12	12	13	14	15	15	14	14	14

[1] Number of cases disposed per 1,000 youth (ages 10 to 17) at risk of referral to juvenile court.   [2] Total include other offenses not shown.

Source: National Center for Juvenile Justice, Pittsburgh, PA, *Juvenile Court Statistics,* annual. See also <http://www.ojjdp.ncjrs.org/ojstatbb/index.html>.

Table 328. **Delinquency Cases and Case Rates by Sex and Race: 1995 to 2005**

[Data have been revised. See head note, Table 327]

Sex, race, and offense	Number of cases disposed			Case rate [1]		
	1995	2000	2005	1995	2000	2005
Male, total	**1,401,800**	**1,271,100**	**1,221,600**	**95.1**	**80.6**	**75.5**
Person	299,600	281,600	301,000	20.3	17.9	18.6
Property	701,000	506,200	429,600	47.6	32.1	26.5
Drugs	138,500	162,600	155,200	9.4	10.3	9.6
Public order	262,600	320,600	335,900	17.8	20.3	20.8
Female, total	**405,500**	**431,200**	**460,300**	**29.0**	**28.8**	**29.9**
Person	98,800	109,300	126,600	7.1	7.3	8.2
Property	204,800	172,100	160,900	14.7	11.5	10.4
Drugs	23,600	33,000	39,000	1.7	2.2	2.5
Public order	78,400	116,900	133,700	5.6	7.8	8.7
White, total	**1,215,300**	**1,164,800**	**1,080,600**	**53.2**	**48.2**	**44.0**
Person	236,300	243,700	243,100	10.3	10.1	9.9
Property	647,300	474,800	397,500	28.3	19.7	16.2
Drugs	107,000	146,800	142,900	4.7	6.1	5.8
Public order	224,700	299,500	297,100	9.8	12.4	12.1
Black, total	**541,400**	**489,000**	**556,000**	**124.3**	**101.1**	**107.8**
Person	152,000	137,000	174,800	34.9	28.3	33.9
Property	230,100	179,800	174,300	52.8	37.2	33.8
Drugs	52,300	44,500	46,300	12.0	9.2	9.0
Public order	107,100	127,700	160,700	24.6	26.4	31.2
Other races, total	**568,900**	**514,700**	**578,500**	**33.8**	**27.8**	**24.5**
Person	157,200	142,400	179,700	6.8	5.8	5.3
Property	245,300	192,000	183,100	19.1	13.6	10.1
Drugs	53,800	47,000	49,200	1.9	2.5	2.7
Public order	112,600	133,300	166,600	6.2	5.9	6.4

[1] Cases per 1,000 youth (ages 10 to 17) at risk.

Source: National Center for Juvenile Justice, Pittsburgh, PA, *Juvenile Court Statistics,* annual. See also <http://www.ojjdp.ncjrs.org/ojstatbb/index.html>.

Table 329. Child Abuse and Neglect Cases Substantiated and Indicated— Victim Characteristics: 1990 to 2006

[Based on reports alleging child abuse and neglect that were referred for investigation by the respective child protective services agency in each state. The reporting period may be either calendar or fiscal year. The majority of States provided duplicated counts. Also, varying number of states reported the various characteristics presented below. A substantiated case represents a type of investigation disposition that determines that there is sufficient evidence under state law to conclude that maltreatment occurred or that the child is at risk of maltreatment. An indicated case represents a type of disposition that concludes that there was a reason to suspect maltreatment had occurred]

Item	1990		2000		2005 [1]		2006	
	Number	Percent	Number	Percent	Number	Percent	Number	Percent
TYPES OF SUBSTANTIATED MALTREATMENT [2]								
Victims, total	**690,658**	**(X)**	**864,837**	**116.5**	**900,146**	**113.1**	**885,245**	**114.08**
Neglect	338,770	49.1	517,118	59.8	565,499	62.8	567,787	64.14
Physical abuse	186,801	27.0	167,713	19.4	149,328	16.6	142,041	16.05
Sexual abuse	119,506	17.3	87,770	10.2	83,775	9.3	78,120	8.82
Emotional maltreatment	45,621	6.6	66,965	7.7	63,478	7.1	58,577	6.62
Medical neglect	(NA)	(NA)	25,498	3.0	17,633	2.0	19,180	2.17
Other and unknown	67,272	9.7	146,184	16.9	138,366	15.4	144,199	16.29
SEX OF VICTIM [3]								
Victims, total	**742,519**	**100.0**	**864,837**	**100.0**	**884,339**	**100.0**	**885,245**	**100.0**
Male	323,339	43.5	413,744	47.8	425,773	48.1	427,027	48.24
Female	369,919	49.8	446,230	51.6	455,961	51.6	455,510	51.46
AGE OF VICTIM [3]								
Victims, total	**731,282**	**100.0**	**864,837**	**100.0**	**884,339**	**100.0**	**885,245**	**100.0**
1 year and younger	97,101	13.3	133,094	15.4	155,136	17.5	160,268	18.1
2 to 5 years old	172,791	23.6	205,790	23.8	222,244	25.1	221,909	25.1
6 to 9 years old	157,681	21.6	212,186	24.5	192,962	21.8	194,233	21.9
10 to 13 years old	135,130	18.5	176,071	20.4	171,661	19.4	164,685	18.6
14 to 17 years old	103,383	14.1	126,207	14.6	138,848	15.7	140,789	15.9
18 years old and over	4,880	0.7	992	0.1	470	0.1	535	0.1

NA Not available. X Not applicable. [1] 2005 data have been revised. [2] A child may be a victim of more than one maltreatment. Therefore, the total for this item adds up to more than 100 percent. [3] The increase in unknown age, sex, and race in 2005 is due to some states reporting summary data without breakdown of corresponding fields.

Source: U.S. Department of Health and Human Services, Administration for Children and Families, Statistics and Research, *Child Maltreatment 2006,* annual; <http://www.acf.hhs.gov/programs/cb/pubs/cm06/index.htm>.

Table 330. Child Abuse and Neglect Cases Reported and Investigated by State: 2006

[See headnote, Table 329]

State and outlying area	Population under 18 years old	Number of reports [1]	Number of children subject of an investigation [2]	Number of child victims [3]	State and outlying area	Population under 18 years old	Number of reports [1]	Number of children subject of an investigation [2]	Number of child victims [3]
Total	**74,754,213**	**1,907,264**	**3,511,590**	**885,245**	MT	217,848	8,737	14,171	1,775
					NE	445,033	13,109	30,500	6,160
AL	1,114,301	18,651	27,340	9,378	NV	634,520	14,982	30,475	5,345
AK	181,434	5,755	9,500	3,481	NH	297,625	6,640	9,399	822
AZ	1,628,198	33,743	76,455	4,469	NJ	2,089,338	28,134	47,172	11,680
AR	691,186	25,524	52,206	9,180					
CA	9,532,614	225,911	427,122	89,500	NM	508,930	16,565	26,471	5,926
CO	1,169,301	30,940	48,610	10,862	NY	4,514,342	150,796	253,436	80,077
CT	818,286	28,500	42,286	10,174	NC	2,155,387	67,524	130,966	28,422
DE	203,366	5,781	13,864	1,933	ND	144,934	3,791	6,722	1,438
DC	114,881	5,077	12,315	2,759	OH	2,770,035	73,156	116,129	41,449
FL	4,021,555	151,822	340,672	134,567	OK	894,034	36,673	64,962	13,414
GA	2,455,020	60,277	142,268	39,802	OR	856,259	25,598	41,245	12,927
					PA	2,804,873	23,071	23,071	4,177
HI	298,081	2,285	4,261	2,045	RI	237,451	8,441	12,996	4,400
ID	394,280	6,662	9,924	1,651	SC	1,039,653	16,712	37,922	10,795
IL	3,215,244	66,495	145,633	27,756					
IN	1,577,629	44,051	67,511	20,925	SD	194,681	3,908	7,135	1,529
IA	710,194	25,029	38,767	14,589	TN	1,442,593	61,886	98,163	19,182
KS	695,837	15,164	22,688	2,630	TX	6,493,965	166,728	280,913	69,065
KY	999,531	48,649	77,035	19,833	UT	791,198	20,206	32,181	13,043
LA	1,090,001	25,536	41,795	12,472	VT	133,389	2,315	2,841	861
ME	280,994	5,949	9,788	3,548	VA	1,806,847	29,141	58,826	6,828
MD	1,360,531	(NA)	(NA)	(NA)	WA	1,526,267	35,698	53,576	7,294
					WV	389,071	23,210	51,674	8,345
MA	1,448,884	38,918	79,855	36,151	WI	1,312,530	29,029	41,230	8,583
MI	2,478,356	70,036	186,754	27,148	WY	121,794	2,437	4,819	786
MN	1,257,264	19,846	29,521	7,623					
MS	759,405	16,888	26,306	6,272	PR	1,018,651	13,797	31,849	15,066
MO	1,416,592	47,491	70,270	7,108					

NA Not available. [1] The number of investigations includes assessments. The number of investigations is based on the total number of investigations that received a disposition in 2006. [2] The number of "Children Subject of an Investigation" is based on the total number of children who were included in an investigation or assessment. [3] Victims are defined as children subject of a substantiated, indicated, or alternative response-victim maltreatment.

Source: U.S. Department of Health and Human Services, Administration for Children and Families, Statistics and Research, *Child Maltreatment 2006,* annual; <http://www.acf.hhs.gov/programs/cb/pubs/cm06/index.htm>.

Table 331. **State and Local Government Expenditures Per Capita by Criminal Justice Function and State: 2005**

[In dollars]

State	Total justice system	Police protec- tion	Judicial and legal	Correc- tions	State	Total justice system	Police protec- tion	Judicial and legal	Correc- tions
Total	**569**	**251**	**118**	**200**	Missouri	419	200	74	145
Alabama	387	181	74	133	Montana	471	193	110	167
Alaska	841	311	231	299	Nebraska	414	170	81	164
Arizona	603	258	130	215	Nevada	718	324	163	230
Arkansas	413	173	75	164	New Hampshire	395	193	85	117
California	815	340	203	272	New Jersey	691	325	153	213
Colorado	539	255	92	192	New Mexico	603	246	118	239
Connecticut	559	238	155	165	New York	802	383	165	253
Delaware	700	282	160	258	North Carolina	427	193	59	175
District of Columbia	1,153	753	101	299	North Dakota	352	157	90	106
Florida	640	317	113	211	Ohio	526	230	134	162
Georgia	493	190	99	204	Oklahoma	420	177	75	168
Hawaii	535	210	192	134	Oregon	572	250	93	229
Idaho	453	182	95	175	Pennsylvania	536	192	114	230
Illinois	511	281	95	135	Rhode Island	569	271	134	164
Indiana	382	168	62	152	South Carolina	369	175	58	136
Iowa	381	180	91	110	South Dakota	359	160	79	119
Kansas	443	212	98	133	Tennessee	418	197	82	139
Kentucky	409	161	88	160	Texas	467	200	80	187
Louisiana	554	234	111	209	Utah	489	208	111	170
Maine	369	164	71	134	Vermont	459	216	88	155
Maryland	642	267	114	261	Virginia	502	214	85	204
Massachusetts	539	246	132	162	Washington	525	205	105	216
Michigan	562	224	114	223	West Virginia	356	123	100	134
Minnesota	483	231	112	140	Wisconsin	558	245	95	218
Mississippi	362	176	63	123	Wyoming	906	290	150	466

Source: U.S. Department of Justice, Office of Justice Programs,Bureau of Justice Statistics, *Expenditures and Employment Statistics, Series NCJ 219370;* <http://www.ojp.usdoj.gov/bjs/eande.htm>.

Table 332. **Detainees Under the Jurisdiction of the Bureau of Immigration and Customs Enforcement (ICE): 2000 to 2006**

[Data obtained from the U.S. Immigration and Customs Enforcement agency through the Bureau of Justice Statistics' (BJS) National Prisoners Statistics program]

Type of facility, reason, and offense	2000	2001	2002	2003	2004	2005	2006
Total	[1]19,862	19,137	21,065	23,514	19,057	19,562	27,634
FACILITY							
ICE operated facilities	4,775	4,550	5,087	5,109	4,545	3,782	6,079
Private facilities under exclusive contracts to ICE	1,832	1,947	1,936	1,935	1,678	2,365	3,358
Federal Bureau of Prisons	1,417	1,276	1,100	1,338	1,214	860	574
Other federal facilities	178	162	130	88	50	46	18
Intergovernmental agreements	11,660	11,202	12,812	15,044	11,570	12,509	17,605
State prisons	383	419	453	477	178	276	96
Local jails	9,168	8,681	9,764	11,376	7,877	8,322	12,482
Other facilities	2,109	2,102	2,595	3,191	3,515	3,911	5,027
REASON HELD							
Immigration law violation	7,037	6,764	8,577	8,950	6,724	7,826	14,015
Criminal offenses	11,065	10,784	10,763	12,603	10,931	10,153	11,052
Pending charges	1,759	1,589	1,725	1,961	1,402	1,583	2,567
TYPE OF OFFENSE							
Total [2]	**12,826**	**12,373**	**12,488**	**14,564**	**12,333**	**11,736**	**13,619**
Violent offenses	4,337	4,017	3,944	4,618	3,956	3,286	3,632
Drug offenses	4,055	3,994	3,920	4,291	3,718	3,365	3,796
Property offenses	1,728	1,792	1,839	2,151	1,914	1,792	1,957
Public-order offenses	1,295	1,361	1,574	2,135	1,744	2,253	2,611
Other/unspecified offenses	1,411	1,209	1,211	1,369	1,001	1,040	1,623

[1] Excludes 2 detainees for whom facility location was not reported.   [2] Includes detainees held for criminal offenses or pending charges.

Source: U.S. Department of Justice, Office of Justice Programs, Bureau of Justice Statistics, *Prisoners in 2006*, Series NCJ 219416; and earlier reports; <http://www.ojp.usdoj.gov/bjs/abstract/p06.htm>.

Table 333. Prisoners Under Jurisdiction of Federal or State Correctional Authorities—Summary by State: 1990 to 2006

[For years ending December 31. To have jurisdiction over a prisoner, a state or the federal system must have legal authority over the prisoner. Minus sign (–) indicates decrease]

State	1990	2000	2005	2006, advance Total	2006, advance Percent change, 2005–2006	State	1990	2000	2005	2006, advance Total	2006, advance Percent change, 2005–2006
U.S. [1]	773,919	1,391,261	1,527,929	1,570,861	2.8						
Federal	65,526	145,416	187,618	193,046	2.9	MS	8,375	20,241	20,515	21,068	2.7
State	708,393	1,245,845	1,340,311	1,377,815	2.8	MO	14,943	27,543	30,823	30,167	–2.1
						MT	1,425	3,105	3,532	3,572	1.1
AL	15,665	26,332	27,888	28,241	1.3	NE	2,403	3,895	4,455	4,407	–1.1
AK [2]	2,622	4,173	4,812	5,069	5.3	NV	5,322	10,063	11,782	12,901	9.5
AZ [3]	14,261	26,510	33,565	35,892	6.9	NH	1,342	2,257	2,530	2,805	10.9
AR	7,322	11,915	13,541	13,729	1.4	NJ	21,128	29,784	27,359	27,371	–
CA	97,309	163,001	170,676	175,512	2.8	NM	3,187	5,342	6,571	6,639	1.0
CO [2]	7,671	16,833	21,456	22,481	4.8	NY	54,895	70,199	62,743	63,315	0.9
CT [2]	10,500	18,355	19,442	20,566	5.8	NC	18,411	31,266	36,365	37,460	3.0
DE [2]	3,471	6,921	6,966	7,206	3.4	ND	483	1,076	1,385	1,363	–1.6
DC [4, 5]	9,947	7,456	NA	NA	(X)	OH	31,822	45,833	45,854	49,166	7.2
FL [3]	44,387	71,319	89,768	92,969	3.6	OK	12,285	23,181	26,676	26,243	–1.6
GA [3]	22,411	44,232	48,749	52,792	8.3	OR	6,492	10,580	13,411	13,707	2.2
HI [2]	2,533	5,053	6,146	5,967	–2.9	PA	22,290	36,847	42,380	44,397	4.8
ID	1,961	5,535	6,818	7,124	4.5	RI [2]	2,392	3,286	3,654	3,996	9.4
IL	27,516	45,281	44,919	45,106	0.4	SC	17,319	21,778	23,160	23,616	2.0
IN	12,736	20,125	24,455	26,091	6.7	SD	1,341	2,616	3,463	3,359	–3.0
IA [3]	3,967	7,955	8,737	8,875	1.6	TN	10,388	22,166	26,369	25,745	–2.4
KS	5,775	8,344	9,068	8,816	–2.8	TX	50,042	166,719	169,003	172,116	1.8
KY	9,023	14,919	19,662	20,000	1.7	UT [2]	2,496	5,637	6,382	6,430	0.8
LA	18,599	35,207	36,083	37,012	2.6	VT [2]	1,049	1,697	2,078	2,215	6.6
ME	1,523	1,679	2,023	2,120	4.8	VA	17,593	30,168	35,344	36,688	3.8
MD	17,848	23,538	22,737	22,945	0.9	WA	7,995	14,915	17,382	17,561	1.0
MA	8,345	10,722	10,701	11,032	3.1	WV	1,565	3,856	5,312	5,733	7.9
MI	34,267	47,718	49,546	51,577	4.1	WI	7,465	20,754	22,697	23,431	3.2
MN	3,176	6,238	9,281	9,108	–1.9	WY	1,110	1,680	2,047	2,114	3.3

– Rounds to zero.   NA Not available.   X Not applicable.   [1] U.S. total includes federal prisoners not distributed by state. This total includes all inmates held in public and private adult correctional facilities.   [2] Data Include both total jail and prison population. Prisons and jails form one integrated system.   [3] Numbers are for custody rather than jurisdiction counts.   [4] The transfer of responsibility for sentenced felons from the District of Columbia to the federal system was completed by the year end 2001.   [5] The District of Columbia inmates sentenced to more than 1 year are now under the responsibility of the Bureau of Prisons.

Source: U.S. Department of Justice, Office of Justice Programs, Bureau of Justice Statistics, *Prisoners in 2006*, Series NCJ 219416; and earlier reports; <http://www.ojp.usdoj.gov/bjs/abstract/p06.htm/>.

Table 334. Adults on Probation or Parole, Incarcerated in Jail or Prison: 1980 to 2006

[As of December 31, except jail counts as of June 30]

Year	Total [1]	Supervision rate per 100,000 adults	Community supervision Probation	Community supervision Parole	Incarceration Jail	Incarceration Prison	Male [2]	Female [2]
1980	1,840,400	1.1	1,118,097	220,438	182,288	319,598	(NA)	(NA)
1985	3,011,500	1.7	1,968,712	300,203	254,986	487,593	2,606,000	405,500
1987	3,459,600	1.9	2,247,158	355,505	294,092	562,814	3,021,000	438,600
1988	3,714,100	2.0	2,356,483	407,977	341,893	607,766	3,223,000	491,100
1989	4,055,600	2.2	2,522,125	456,803	393,303	683,367	3,501,600	554,000
1990	4,350,343	2.3	2,670,234	531,407	405,320	743,382	3,746,300	601,700
1991	4,535,600	2.4	2,728,472	590,442	424,129	792,535	3,913,000	622,600
1992	4,762,600	2.5	2,811,611	658,601	441,781	850,566	4,050,300	712,300
1993	4,944,000	2.6	2,903,061	676,100	455,500	909,381	4,215,300	728,200
1994	5,141,300	2.7	2,981,022	690,371	479,800	990,147	4,377,400	763,900
1995	5,342,900	2.8	3,077,861	679,421	507,044	1,078,542	4,513,000	822,100
1996	5,482,700	2.8	3,164,996	679,733	510,400	1,127,528	4,629,900	852,800
1997	5,725,800	2.9	3,296,513	694,787	557,974	1,176,564	4,825,300	900,500
1998	6,126,100	3.1	3,670,441	696,385	584,372	1,224,469	(NA)	(NA)
1999	6,331,400	3.1	3,779,922	714,457	596,485	1,287,172	(NA)	(NA)
2000 [3]	6,445,100	3.1	3,826,209	723,898	621,149	1,316,333	5,376,300	1,068,800
2001 [3]	6,581,700	3.1	3,931,731	732,333	631,240	1,330,007	5,468,900	1,112,800
2002 [3]	6,758,800	3.1	4,024,067	750,934	665,475	1,367,547	5,579,500	1,179,300
2003 [3, 4]	6,924,500	3.2	4,120,012	769,925	691,301	1,390,279	5,724,200	1,200,300
2004 [3]	6,995,100	3.2	4,143,792	771,852	713,990	1,421,345	5,767,300	1,227,800
2005 [3]	7,047,800	3.1	4,166,757	780,616	747,529	1,444,321	5,819,800	1,228,000
2006, advance [3]	7,211,400	3.2	4,237,023	798,202	766,010	1,492,973	5,910,000	1,301,400

NA Not available.   [1] Totals may not add due to individuals having multiple correctional statuses.   [2] Estimated.   [3] The jail population includes juveniles held as adults.   [4] Due to changes in reporting, total probation and parole counts include estimated counts for Massachusetts, Pennsylvania, and Washington based on reporting methods comparable to 2004–2006.

Source: U.S. Department of Justice, Office of Justice Programs, Bureau of Justice Statistics, *Probation and Parole in the United States, 2006, Prisoners in 2006, and Prison and Jail Inmates at Midyear, 2006.* <http://www.ojp.usdoj.gov/bjs/correct.htm>.

U.S. Census Bureau, Statistical Abstract of the United States: 2009

Table 335. Jail Inmates by Sex, Race, and Hispanic Origin: 1990 to 2006

[As of June 30. Data based on the Annual Survey of Jails, a sample survey and subject to sampling variability]

Characteristic	1990	1995	2000	2002	2003	2004	2005	2006
Total inmates [1, 2]	405,320	507,044	621,149	665,475	691,301	713,990	747,529	766,010
Incarceration rate per 100,000 residents	163	193	220	231	238	243	252	256
Rated capacity [3, 4]	389,171	545,763	677,787	713,899	736,471	755,603	789,001	810,863
Adult	403,019	499,300	613,534	658,228	684,431	706,907	740,770	759,906
Male	365,821	448,000	543,120	581,411	602,781	619,908	646,807	661,329
Female	37,198	51,300	70,414	76,817	81,650	86,999	93,963	98,577
Juveniles [5]	2,301	7,800	7,615	7,248	6,869	7,083	6,759	6,104
White, non-Hispanic	169,600	203,300	260,500	291,800	301,200	317,400	331,000	336,600
Black, non-Hispanic	172,300	220,600	256,300	264,900	271,000	275,400	290,500	296,000
Hispanic/Latino	58,100	74,400	94,100	98,000	106,600	108,300	111,900	119,200
Other [6]	5,400	8,800	10,200	10,800	10,800	12,500	13,000	13,500

[1] Total does not include offenders who were supervised outside of jail facilities.   [2] Race/Hispanic origin data do not include the two or more race data.   [3] Beginning 1995, rated capacity subject to sampling error.   [4] Rated capacity is the number of beds or inmates assigned by a rating official to facilities within each jurisdiction.   [5] Juveniles are persons held under the age of 18. Includes juveniles who were tried or awaiting trial as adults.   [6] Includes American Indians, Alaska Natives, Asians, and Pacific Islanders.

Source: U.S. Department of Justice, Office of Justice Programs, Bureau of Justice Statistics, Jail Inmates, annual; beginning 1995, Prison and Jail Inmates at Midyear, Series NCJ 217675, annual; <http://www.ojp.usdoj.gov/bjs/jails.htm>.

Table 336. Prisoners Under State or Federal Jurisdiction, by Sex: 1980 to 2006

[Prisoners, as of December 31. Includes all persons under jurisdiction of federal and state authorities rather than those in the custody of such authorities. Represents inmates sentenced to maximum term of more than a year]

Year	Total [1]	Rate [2]	State	Male	Female	Year	Total [1]	Rate [2]	State	Male	Female
1980 . . .	315,974	139	295,363	303,643	12,331	1996 . . .	1,137,722	427	1,048,907	1,068,123	69,599
1985 . . .	480,568	202	447,873	459,223	21,345	1997 . . .	1,195,498	445	1,100,511	1,121,663	73,835
1987 . . .	560,812	231	521,289	533,990	26,822	1998 . . .	1,245,402	461	1,141,720	1,167,802	77,600
1988 . . .	603,732	247	560,994	573,587	30,145	1999 . . .	1,304,074	476	1,189,799	1,221,611	82,463
1989 . . .	680,907	276	633,739	643,643	37,264	2000 . . .	1,331,278	[3]470	1,204,323	1,246,234	85,044
1990 . . .	739,980	297	689,577	699,416	40,564	2001 . . .	1,345,217	470	1,208,708	1,260,033	85,184
1991 . . .	789,610	313	732,914	745,808	43,802	2002 . . .	1,380,516	476	1,237,476	1,291,450	89,066
1992 . . .	846,277	332	780,571	799,776	46,501	2003 . . .	1,408,361	482	1,256,442	1,315,790	92,571
1993 . . .	932,074	359	857,675	878,037	54,037	2004 . . .	1,433,728	486	1,274,591	1,337,730	95,998
1994 . . .	1,016,691	389	936,896	956,566	60,125	2005 . . .	1,527,929	491	1,340,311	1,420,303	107,626
1995 . . .	1,085,022	411	1,001,359	1,021,059	63,963	2006 . . .	1,570,861	501	1,377,815	1,458,363	112,498

[1] Includes federal.   [2] Rate per 100,000 estimated population. Based on U.S. Census Bureau estimated resident population.   [3] Decrease in incarceration rate from 1999 to 2000 due to use of new Census numbers.

Source: U.S. Department of Justice, Office of Justice Programs, Bureau of Justice Statistics, Prisoners in 2006, Series NCJ 219416, annual; <http://www.ojp.usdoj.gov/bjs/abstract/p06.htm>.

Table 337. Prisoners Under Sentence of Death by Characteristic: 1980 to 2006

[As of December 31. Excludes prisoners under sentence of death who remained within local correctional systems pending exhaustion of appellate process or who had not been committed to prison]

Characteristic	1980	1990	1995	1998	1999	2000	2001	2002	2003	2004	2005	2006
Total [1, 2]	688	2,346	3,064	3,465	3,540	3,601	3,577	3,562	3,377	3,320	3,245	3,228
White	418	1,368	1,732	1,917	1,960	1,989	1,968	1,939	1,882	1,856	1,802	1,802
Black and other	270	978	1,332	1,548	1,580	1,612	1,609	1,623	1,495	1,464	1,443	1,426
Under 20 years old	11	8	20	16	16	11	4	4	1	1	–	–
20 to 24 years old	173	168	264	273	251	237	192	153	133	95	61	51
25 to 34 years old	334	1,110	1,068	1,108	1,103	1,103	1,099	1,058	965	896	816	735
35 to 54 years old	186	1,006	1,583	1,897	1,958	2,019	2,043	2,069	1,969	1,977	2,012	2,043
55 years old and over	10	64	119	171	194	223	243	273	306	345	365	399
Years of school completed:												
7 years or less	68	178	191	208	201	214	212	215	213	207	192	186
8 years	74	186	195	218	221	233	236	234	227	221	206	195
9 to 11 years	204	775	979	1,122	1,142	1,157	1,145	1,130	1,073	1,053	1,030	1,015
12 years	162	729	995	1,128	1,157	1,184	1,183	1,173	1,108	1,091	1,105	1,098
More than 12 years	43	209	272	301	307	315	304	294	270	262	256	248
Unknown	163	279	422	488	499	490	501	511	483	480	465	486
Marital status:												
Never married	268	998	1,412	1,645	1,689	1,749	1,763	1,746	1,641	1,622	1,586	1,577
Married	229	632	718	752	731	739	716	709	684	658	649	626
Divorced [3]	217	726	924	1,068	1,107	1,105	1,102	1,102	1,049	1,034	1,019	1,025
Time elapsed since sentencing:												
Less than 12 months	185	231	287	293	259	208	151	147	137	117	122	105
12 to 47 months	389	753	784	816	800	786	734	609	495	421	399	382
48 to 71 months	102	438	423	482	499	507	476	468	451	388	299	262
72 months and over	38	934	1,560	1,874	1,969	2,092	2,220	2,333	2,291	2,388	2,434	2,479
Legal status at arrest:												
Not under sentence	384	1,345	1,764	2,036	2,088	2,202	2,189	2,165	2,048	2,026	1,979	1,952
Parole or probation [4]	115	578	866	879	886	921	918	909	845	809	792	778
Prison or escaped	45	128	110	127	125	126	135	141	137	145	144	142
Unknown	170	305	314	423	428	344	339	342	344	334	339	356

– Represents zero.   [1] Revisions to the total number of prisoners were not carried to the characteristics except for race.   [2] Includes races not shown separately.   [3] Includes persons married but separated, widows, widowers, and unknown.   [4] Includes prisoners on mandatory conditional release, work release, other leave, AWOL, or bail. Covers 28 prisoners in 1990, 33 in 1995, 26 in 1998, 21 in 1999 and 2000, and 17 in 2001, 2002, and 2003; 15 in 2004; and 14 in 2005 and 2006.

Source: U.S. Department of Justice, Office of Justice Programs, Bureau of Justice Statistics, Capital Punishment, Series NCJ 220219, annual. See also <http://www.ojp.usdoj.gov/bjs/cp.htm>.

Table 338. **Movement of Prisoners Under Sentence of Death: 1980 to 2006**

[Prisoners reported under sentence of death by civil authorities. The term "under sentence of death" begins when the court pronounces the first sentence of death for a capital offense]

Status	1980	1990	1995	1998	1999	2000	2001	2002	2003	2004	2005	2006
Under sentence of death, Jan. 1	595	2,243	2,905	3,328	3,465	3,540	3,601	3,577	3,562	3,377	3,320	3,245
Received death sentence [1]	203	244	310	285	272	214	155	159	144	125	128	115
White	125	147	168	145	157	122	89	83	92	75	70	72
Black	77	94	138	132	104	86	61	73	44	50	52	42
Dispositions other than executions . . .	101	108	105	93	112	76	109	108	267	129	134	79
Executions	–	23	56	68	98	85	66	71	65	59	60	53
Under sentence of death, Dec. 31 [1,2] .	697	2,356	3,054	3,452	3,527	3,593	3,581	3,557	3,374	3,314	3,254	3,228
White	425	1,375	1,730	1,906	1,948	1,990	1,969	1,931	1,878	1,850	1,805	1,802
Black	268	943	1,275	1,486	1,514	1,535	1,538	1,554	1,418	1,390	1,372	1,352

– Represents zero. [1] Includes races other than White or Black. [2] Revisions to total number of prisoners under death sentence not carried to this category.

Source: U.S. Department of Justice, Office of Justice Programs, Bureau of Justice Statistics, *Capital Punishment,* annual. Series NCJ 220219. See also <http://www.ojp.usdoj.gov/bjs/pub/html/cp/2006/cp06st.htm>.

Table 339. **Prisoners Executed Under Civil Authority by Sex and Race: 1930 to 2007**

[Excludes executions by military authorities. The Army (including the Air Force) carried out 160 (148 between 1942 and 1950; 3 each in 1954, 1955, and 1957; and 1 each in 1958, 1959, and 1961). Of the total, 106 were executed for murder (including 21 involving rape), 53 for rape, and 1 for desertion. The Navy carried out no executions during the period]

Year or period	Total [1]	Male	Female	White	Black	Executed for murder Total [1]	Executed for murder White	Executed for murder Black
All years, 1930–2007 . . .	**4,958**	**4,915**	**43**	**2,459**	**2,442**	**4,433**	**2,372**	**2,006**
1930 to 1939	1,667	1,656	11	827	816	1,514	803	687
1940 to 1949 [2]	1,284	1,272	12	490	781	1,064	458	595
1950 to 1959 [2]	717	709	8	336	376	601	316	280
1960 to 1967	191	190	1	98	93	155	87	68
1968 to 1976	–	–	–	–	–	–	–	–
1977 to 2007	1,099	1,088	11	708	376	1,099	708	376
1985	18	18	–	11	7	18	11	7
1990	23	23	–	16	7	23	16	7
1991	14	14	–	7	7	14	7	7
1992	31	31	–	19	11	31	19	11
1993	38	38	–	23	14	38	23	14
1994	31	31	–	20	11	31	20	11
1995	56	56	–	33	22	56	33	22
1996	45	45	–	31	14	45	31	14
1997	74	74	–	45	27	74	45	27
1998	68	66	2	48	18	68	48	18
1999	98	98	–	61	33	98	61	33
2000	85	83	2	49	35	85	49	35
2001	66	63	3	48	17	66	48	17
2002	71	69	2	53	18	71	53	18
2003	65	65	–	44	20	65	44	20
2004	59	59	–	39	19	59	39	19
2005	60	59	1	41	19	60	41	19
2006	53	53	–	32	21	53	32	21
2007	42	42	–	28	14	42	28	14

– Represents zero. [1] Includes races other than White or Black. [2] Includes 25 armed robbery, 20 kidnapping, 11 burglary, 8 espionage (6 in 1942 and 2 in 1953), and 6 aggravated assault.

Source: Through 1978, U.S. Law Enforcement Assistance Administration; thereafter, U.S. Department of Justice, Office of Justice Programs, Bureau of Justice Statistics, *Correctional Populations in the United States*, Series NCJ 220219, annual; <http://www.ojp.usdoj.gov/bjs/pub/html/cp/2006/cp06st.htm and *Capital Punishment,* annual; <http://www.ojp.usdoj.gov/bjs/abstract /cp06.htm>.

Table 340. **Prisoners Executed Under Civil Authority by State: 1977 to 2007**

[Alaska, District of Columbia, Hawaii, Iowa, Maine, Massachusetts, Michigan, Minnesota, New Jersey, North Dakota, Rhode Island, Vermont, West Virginia, and Wisconsin are jurisdictions without a death penalty]

State	1977 to 2007	2004	2005	2006	2007	State	1977 to 2007	2004	2005	2006	2007	State	1977 to 2007	2004	2005	2006	2007
U.S. .	**1,099**	**59**	**60**	**53**	**42**	IL	12	–	5	–	–	OK . . .	86	6	4	4	3
						IN	19	–	5	1	2	OR . . .	2	–	–	–	–
AL . . .	38	2	4	1	3	KY	2	–	–	–	–	PA . . .	3	–	–	–	–
AZ . . .	23	–	–	–	1	LA . . .	27	–	–	–	–	SC . . .	37	4	3	1	1
AR . . .	27	1	1	–	–	MD . . .	5	1	1	–	–	TN . . .	4	–	–	1	2
CA . . .	13	–	2	1	–	MS . . .	8	–	1	1	–	TX . . .	405	23	19	24	26
DE . . .	14	–	1	–	–	MO . . .	66	–	5	–	–	UT . . .	6	–	–	–	–
FL. . . .	64	2	1	4	–	NV . . .	12	2	–	1	–	VA . . .	98	5	–	4	–
GA . . .	40	2	3	–	1	NC . . .	43	4	5	4	–	WA . . .	4	–	–	–	–
ID	1	–	–	–	–	OH . . .	26	7	4	5	2	WY . . .	1	–	–	–	–

– Represents zero.

Source: Through 1978, U.S. Law Enforcement Assistance Administration; thereafter, U.S. Department of Justice, Office of Justice Programs, Bureau of Justice Statistics, *Capital Punishment, Series NCJ 220219,* annual; <http://www.ojp.usdoj.gov/bjs/cp.htm>.

Law Enforcement, Courts, and Prisons   **209**

Table 341. Fire Losses—Total and Per Capita: 1980 to 2006

[5,579 represents $5,579,000,000. Includes allowance for uninsured and unreported losses but excludes losses to government property and forests. Represents incurred losses]

Year	Total (mil. dol.)	Per capita [1] (dol.)	Year	Total (mil. dol.)	Per capita [1] (dol.)	Year	Total (mil. dol.)	Per capita [1] (dol.)
1980	5,579	24.56	1991	11,302	44.82	1999	12,428	45.58
1984	7,602	32.35	1992	13,588	53.28	2000	13,457	47.68
1985	7,753	32.70	1993	11,331	43.96	2001 [2]	17,118	60.04
1986	8,488	35.21	1994	12,778	49.08	2002	17,586	61.07
1987	8,504	34.96	1995	11,887	45.23	2003	21,129	72.65
1988	9,626	39.11	1996	12,544	47.29	2004	17,344	59.06
1989	9,514	38.33	1997	12,940	48.32	2005	20,427	68.89
1990	9,495	38.07	1998	11,510	45.59	2006	18,072	60.36

[1] Based on U.S. Census Bureau estimated resident population as of July 1. Enumerated population as of April 1 for 1980, 1990, and 2000. [2] Does not include insured fire losses related to terrorism.

Source: Based on data from ISO; Highline Data LLC; Insurance Information Institute, New York, NY, *The III Insurance Fact Book*, annual (copyright).

Table 342. Fires—Number and Loss by Type and Property Use: 2003 to 2006

[1,584 represents 1,584,000 and property loss of 12,367 represents $12,367,000,000. Based on annual sample survey of fire departments. No adjustments were made for unreported fires and losses]

Type and property use	Number (1,000)				Direct property loss (mil. dol.) [1]			
	2003	2004	2005	2006	2003	2004	2005	2006
Fires, total	**1,584**	**1,550**	**1,602**	**1,642**	**12,367**	**9,794**	**10,672**	**11,307**
Structure	520	526	511	524	8,678	8,314	9,193	9,636
Outside of structure [2]	66	69	78	82	162	108	93	262
Brush and rubbish	550	514	594	627	–	–	–	–
Vehicle	312	297	290	278	1,356	1,304	1,318	1,319
Other	136	144	129	131	[3]2,171	68	68	90
Structure by property use:								
Public assembly	14	13	13	13	302	316	320	444
Educational	7	7	6	6	69	68	67	105
Institutional	7	6	8	8	28	25	40	42
Stores and offices	25	24	23	20	721	586	687	691
Residential	402	411	396	413	6,074	5,948	6,875	6,990
1–2 family units [4]	297	302	287	304	5,052	4,948	5,781	5,936
Apartments	92	94	94	92	897	885	948	896
Other residential [5]	13	15	15	17	125	115	146	158
Storage [5]	32	32	30	29	675	748	590	650
Industry, utility, defense [6]	11	12	12	12	625	423	376	573
Special structures	22	21	23	23	184	200	238	141

– Represents zero. [1] Direct property damage figures do not include indirect losses, like business interruption, and adjustments for inflation. [2] Includes outside storage, crops, timber, etc. [3] Includes Southern California wildfires where there was an estimated $2.044 billion in property loss. [4] Includes mobile homes. [5] Includes hotels and motels, college dormitories, boarding houses, etc. [6] Data underreported as some incidents were handled by private fire brigades or fixed suppression systems which do not report.

Source: National Fire Protection Association, Quincy, MA, "2006 U.S. Fire Loss," *NFPA Journal*, November 2007, and prior issues (copyright 2007); <http://www.nfpa.org/index.asp>.

Table 343. Fires and Property Loss for Incendiary and Suspicious Fires and Civilian Fire Deaths and Injuries by Selected Property Type: 2003 to 2006

[520 represents 520,000. Based on sample survey of fire departments]

Characteristic	2003	2004	2005	2006	Characteristic	2003	2004	2005	2006
NUMBER (1,000)					CIVILIAN FIRE DEATHS				
					Deaths, total [2]	**3,925**	**3,900**	**3,675**	**3,245**
Structure fires, total	**520**	**526**	**511**	**524**	Residential property	3,165	3,225	3,055	2,620
					1- and 2-family dwellings	2,735	2,680	2,575	2,155
Structure fires that were intentionally set	38	37	32	31	Apartments	410	510	460	425
					Vehicles	475	550	520	490
PROPERTY LOSS [1] (mil. dol.)					CIVILIAN FIRE INJURIES				
					Injuries, total [2]	**18,125**	**17,785**	**17,925**	**16,400**
Structure fires, total	**8,678**	**8,314**	**9,193**	**9,636**	Residential property	14,075	14,175	13,825	12,925
					1- and 2-family dwellings	10,000	10,500	10,300	8,800
Structure fires that were intentionally set	692	714	664	775	Apartments	3,650	3,200	3,000	3,700
					Vehicles	1,600	1,500	1,650	1,200

[1] Direct property loss only. [2] Includes other not shown separately.

Source: National Fire Protection Association, Quincy, MA, "2006 U.S. Fire Loss," *NFPA Journal*, November 2007, and prior issues (copyright 2007); <http://www.nfpa.org/index.asp>.

Section 6
Geography and Environment

This section presents a variety of information on the physical environment of the United States, starting with basic area measurement data and ending with climatic data for selected weather stations around the country. The subjects covered between those points are mostly concerned with environmental trends but include related subjects such as land use, water consumption, air pollutant emissions, toxic releases, oil spills, hazardous waste sites, municipal waste and recycling, threatened and endangered wildlife, and the environmental industry.

The information in this section is selected from a wide range of federal agencies that compile the data for various administrative or regulatory purposes, such as the Environmental Protection Agency (EPA), U.S. Geological Survey (USGS), National Oceanic and Atmospheric Administration (NOAA), Natural Resources Conservation Service (NRCS), and National Atlas® of the United States. New information on border lengths with Canada and Mexico, coastlines, lakes, and shorelines may be found in Tables 350–352.

Area—For the 2000 census, area measurements were calculated by computer based on the information contained in a single, consistent geographic database, the Topologically Integrated Geographic Encoding & Referencing system (TIGER®) database, rather than relying on historical, local, and manually calculated information. Information from the 2000 census may be found in Table 344.

Geography—The USGS conducts investigations, surveys, and research in the fields of geography, geology, topography, geographic information systems, mineralogy, hydrology, and geothermal energy resources as well as natural hazards. The USGS provides United States cartographic data through the Earth Sciences Information Center, water resources data through the *Water Resources of the United States* at <http://water.usgs.gov/pubs/>.

In a joint project with the U.S. Census Bureau, during the 1980s, the USGS provided the basic information on geographic features for input into a national geographic and cartographic database prepared by the Census Bureau, called TIGER® database. Since then, using a variety of sources, the Census Bureau has updated these features and their related attributes (names, descriptions, etc.) and inserted current information on the boundaries, names, and codes of legal and statistical geographic entities; very few of these updates added aerial water features. Maps prepared by the Census Bureau using the TIGER® database show the names and boundaries of entities and are available on a current basis.

An inventory of the nation's land resources by type of use/cover was conducted by the National Resources Inventory Conservation Services (NRCS) every 5 years beginning in 1977 through 1997. Beginning with the release of the 2001 estimates, this program shifted to become an annual release of land use data. The most recent survey results, which were published for the year 2003, covered all nonfederal land for the contiguous 48 states. Tables 350 to 352 provide results from the survey.

Environment—The principal federal agency responsible for pollution abatement and control activities is the Environmental Protection Agency (EPA). It is responsible for establishing and monitoring national air quality standards, water quality activities, solid and hazardous waste disposal, and control of toxic substances. Many of these series now appear in the Envirofacts portion of the EPA Web site at <http://www.epa.gov/enviro/>.

The Clean Air Act, which was last amended in 1990, requires the EPA to set National Ambient Air Quality Standards (NAAQS) (CFR part 50) for pollutants considered harmful to public health and the environment. The EPA Office of Air Quality

U.S. Census Bureau, Statistical Abstract of the United States: 2009

Planning and Standards (OAQPS) has set National Ambient Air Quality Standards for six principal pollutants, which are called "criteria" pollutants. These pollutants are: Carbon Monoxide, Lead, Nitrogen Dioxide, Particulate Matter ($PM_{2.5}$ and $_{10}$), Ozone, and Sulfur Dioxide. NAAQS are periodically reviewed and revised to include any additional or new health or welfare data. Table 357 gives some of the health-related standards for the six air pollutants having NAAQS. Data gathered from state networks are periodically submitted to EPA's National Aerometric Information Retrieval System (AIRS) for summarization in annual reports on the nationwide status and trends in air quality. For details, see "Air Trends" on the EPA Web site at <http://www.epa.gov/airtrends/index.html>.

The Toxics Release Inventory (TRI), published by the EPA, is a valuable source of information on nearly 650 chemicals that are being used, manufactured, treated, transported, or released into the environment. Sections 313 of the Emergency Planning and Community Right-to-Know Act (EPCRA) and 6607 of the Pollution Prevention Act (PPA), mandate that a publicly-accessible toxic chemical database be developed and maintained by EPA. This database, known as the TRI, contains information concerning waste management activities and the release of toxic chemicals by facilities that manufacture, process, or otherwise use said materials. Data on the release of these chemicals are collected from over 23,000 facilities and facilities added in 1998 that have the equivalent of 10 or more full-time employees and meet the established thresholds for manufacturing, processing, or "other use" of listed chemicals. Facilities must report their releases and other waste management quantities. Since 1994 federal facilities have been required to report their data regardless of industry classification. In May 1997, EPA added seven new industry sectors that reported to the TRI for the first time in July 1999 for the 1998 reporting year. More current information on this program can be found at <http://www.epa.gov/tri/index.htm>.

Climate—NOAA, through the National Weather Service and the National Environmental Satellite, Data, and Information Service, is responsible for climate data. NOAA maintains about 11,600 weather stations, of which over 3,000 produce autographic precipitation records, about 600 take hourly readings of a series of weather elements, and the remainder record data once a day. These data are reported monthly in the Climatological Data and Storm Data, published monthly and annually in the Local Climatological Data (published by location for major cities).

The normal climatological temperatures, precipitation, and degree days listed in this publication are derived for comparative purposes and are averages for the 30-year period, 1971–2000. For stations that did not have continuous records for the entire 30 years from the same instrument site, the normals have been adjusted to provide representative values for the current location. The information in all other tables is based on data from the beginning of the record at that location through 2006.

U.S. Census Bureau, Statistical Abstract of the United States: 2009

Table 344. **Land and Water Area of States and Other Entities: 2000**

[One square mile = 2.59 square kilometers. Area is calculated from the specific boundary recorded for each entity in the U.S. Census Bureau's geographic TIGER® database]

State and other areas	Total area Sq. mi.	Total area Sq. km.	Land area Sq. mi.	Land area Sq. km.	Water area Total Sq. mi.	Water area Total Sq. km.	Inland (sq. mi.)	Coastal (sq. mi.)	Great Lakes (sq. mi.)	Territorial (sq. mi.)
Total	3,803,290	9,850,521	3,541,479	9,172,430	261,811	678,090	79,018	42,241	60,251	77,777
United States. .	3,794,083	9,826,675	3,537,438	9,161,966	256,645	664,710	78,797	42,225	60,251	75,372
Alabama	52,419	135,765	50,744	131,426	1,675	4,338	956	519	(X)	200
Alaska	663,267	1,717,854	571,951	1,481,347	91,316	236,507	17,243	27,049	(X)	47,024
Arizona	113,998	295,254	113,635	294,312	364	942	364	–	(X)	–
Arkansas	53,179	137,732	52,068	134,856	1,110	2,876	1,110	–	(X)	–
California	163,696	423,970	155,959	403,933	7,736	20,037	2,674	222	(X)	4,841
Colorado	104,094	269,601	103,718	268,627	376	974	376	–	(X)	–
Connecticut	5,543	14,357	4,845	12,548	699	1,809	161	538	(X)	–
Delaware	2,489	6,447	1,954	5,060	536	1,388	72	371	(X)	93
District of Columbia	68	177	61	159	7	18	7	–	(X)	–
Florida	65,755	170,304	53,927	139,670	11,828	30,634	4,672	1,311	(X)	5,845
Georgia	59,425	153,909	57,906	149,976	1,519	3,933	1,016	48	(X)	455
Hawaii	10,931	28,311	6,423	16,635	4,508	11,677	38	–	(X)	4,470
Idaho	83,570	216,446	82,747	214,314	823	2,131	823	–	(X)	–
Illinois	57,914	149,998	55,584	143,961	2,331	6,037	756	–	1,575	–
Indiana	36,418	94,321	35,867	92,895	551	1,427	316	–	235	–
Iowa	56,272	145,743	55,869	144,701	402	1,042	402	–	(X)	–
Kansas	82,277	213,096	81,815	211,900	462	1,197	462	–	(X)	–
Kentucky	40,409	104,659	39,728	102,896	681	1,763	681	–	(X)	–
Louisiana	51,840	134,264	43,562	112,825	8,278	21,440	4,154	1,935	(X)	2,189
Maine	35,385	91,646	30,862	79,931	4,523	11,715	2,264	613	(X)	1,647
Maryland	12,407	32,133	9,774	25,314	2,633	6,819	680	1,843	(X)	110
Massachusetts . . .	10,555	27,336	7,840	20,306	2,715	7,031	423	977	(X)	1,314
Michigan	96,716	250,494	56,804	147,121	39,912	103,372	1,611	–	38,301	–
Minnesota	86,939	225,171	79,610	206,189	7,329	18,982	4,783	–	2,546	–
Mississippi	48,430	125,434	46,907	121,489	1,523	3,945	785	590	(X)	148
Missouri	69,704	180,533	68,886	178,414	818	2,120	818	–	(X)	–
Montana	147,042	380,838	145,552	376,979	1,490	3,859	1,490	–	(X)	–
Nebraska	77,354	200,345	76,872	199,099	481	1,247	481	–	(X)	–
Nevada	110,561	286,351	109,826	284,448	735	1,903	735	–	(X)	–
New Hampshire . . .	9,350	24,216	8,968	23,227	382	989	314	–	(X)	68
New Jersey	8,721	22,588	7,417	19,211	1,304	3,377	396	401	(X)	507
New Mexico	121,590	314,915	121,356	314,309	234	606	234	–	(X)	–
New York	54,556	141,299	47,214	122,283	7,342	19,016	1,895	981	3,988	479
North Carolina . . .	53,819	139,389	48,711	126,161	5,108	13,229	3,960	–	(X)	1,148
North Dakota	70,700	183,112	68,976	178,647	1,724	4,465	1,724	–	(X)	–
Ohio	44,825	116,096	40,948	106,056	3,877	10,040	378	–	3,499	–
Oklahoma	69,898	181,036	68,667	177,847	1,231	3,189	1,231	–	(X)	–
Oregon	98,381	254,805	95,997	248,631	2,384	6,174	1,050	80	(X)	1,254
Pennsylvania	46,055	119,283	44,817	116,075	1,239	3,208	490	–	749	–
Rhode Island	1,545	4,002	1,045	2,706	500	1,295	178	9	(X)	314
South Carolina . . .	32,020	82,932	30,110	77,983	1,911	4,949	1,008	72	(X)	831
South Dakota	77,117	199,731	75,885	196,540	1,232	3,191	1,232	–	(X)	–
Tennessee	42,143	109,151	41,217	106,752	926	2,399	926	–	(X)	–
Texas	268,581	695,621	261,797	678,051	6,784	17,570	5,056	404	(X)	1,324
Utah	84,899	219,887	82,144	212,751	2,755	7,136	2,755	–	(X)	–
Vermont	9,614	24,901	9,250	23,956	365	945	365	–	(X)	–
Virginia	42,774	110,785	39,594	102,548	3,180	8,237	1,006	1,728	(X)	446
Washington	71,300	184,665	66,544	172,348	4,756	12,317	1,553	2,537	(X)	666
West Virginia	24,230	62,755	24,078	62,361	152	394	152	–	(X)	–
Wisconsin	65,498	169,639	54,310	140,663	11,188	28,976	1,830	–	9,358	–
Wyoming	97,814	253,336	97,100	251,489	713	1,847	713	–	(X)	–
Puerto Rico	5,325	13,790	3,425	8,870	1,900	4,921	(NA)	(NA)	(X)	(NA)
Island Areas:	3,866	10,014	600	1,554	3,266	8,460	(NA)	(NA)	(X)	(NA)
American Samoa .	584	1,511	77	200	506	1,311	(NA)	(NA)	(X)	(NA)
Guam	571	1,478	210	544	361	934	(NA)	(NA)	(X)	(NA)
No. Mariana Islands	1,975	5,114	179	464	1,796	4,651	(NA)	(NA)	(X)	(NA)
Virgin Islands of the U.S.	737	1,910	134	346	604	1,564	(NA)	(NA)	(X)	(NA)
U.S. minor outlying islands [1]	16	41	16	41	–	–	(NA)	(NA)	(X)	(NA)

– Represents or rounds to zero. NA Not available. X Not applicable. [1] Baker, Howland, and Jarvis Islands; Johnston Atoll, Kingman Reef, Midway Islands, Navassa Island, Palmyra Atoll, and Wake Island.

Source: U.S. Census Bureau, 2000 Census of Population and Housing, *Summary Population and Housing Characteristics,* Series PHC-1, PHC-3, and unpublished data from the Census TIGER® database.

U.S. Census Bureau, Statistical Abstract of the United States: 2009

Table 345. U.S.–Canada and U.S–Mexico Border Lengths

[For 2006, there were more than 67 million passenger trips between the United States and Canada, and more than 228 million between the United States and Mexico. See Table 1243 for more passenger trip detail. Only those states with international borders are included in the table below. For more information on the National Atlas of the United States, please see <http://nationalatlas.gov/partners.html>]

State	Length of international border (statute miles)[1]	State	Length of international border (statute miles)[1]
United States–Canada total	**5,525**	Ohio	146
Alaska	1,585	Pennsylvania	42
Idaho	45	Vermont	90
Maine	611	Washington	427
Michigan	721		
Minnesota	547	**United States–Mexico total**	**1,933**
Montana	545	Arizona	373
New Hampshire	58	California	140
New York	445	New Mexico	180
North Dakota	310	Texas	1,241

[1] Statute mile equals one mile.

Source: U.S. Geological Survey, The National Atlas of the United States, *Borders*; <http://nationalatlas.gov/articles/mapping/a_general.html>.

Table 346. Coastline and Shoreline of the United States by State

[**In statute miles**. Each statute mile equals one mile. The term **coastline** is used to describe the general outline of the seacoast. For the table below, United States coastline measurements were made from small-scale maps, and the coastline was generalized. The coastlines of large sounds and bays were included. Measurements were made in 1948. **Shoreline** is the term used to describe a more detailed measure of the seacoast. The tidal shoreline figures in the table below were obtained in 1939–1940 from the largest-scale charts and maps then available. Shoreline of the outer coast, offshore islands, sounds, and bays were included, as well as the tidal portion of rivers and creeks. Only states with a coastline or shoreline are included in the following table. For more information on the National Atlas of the United States, please see <http://nationalatlas.gov/partners.html>]

State	General coastline	Tidal shoreline	State	General coastline	Tidal shoreline
United States	**12,383**	**88,633**	Mississippi	44	359
Alabama	53	607	New Hampshire	13	131
Alaska	6,640	33,904	New Jersey	130	1,792
California	840	3,427	New York	127	1,850
Connecticut	–	618	North Carolina	301	3,375
Delaware	28	381	Oregon	296	1,410
Florida	1,350	8,426	Pennsylvania	–	89
Georgia	100	2,344	Rhode Island	40	384
Hawaii	750	1,052	South Carolina	187	2,876
Louisiana	397	7,721	Texas	367	3,359
Maine	228	3,478	Virginia	112	3,315
Maryland	31	3,190	Washington	157	3,026
Massachusetts	192	1,519			

– Represents zero.

Source: U.S. Geological Survey and National Oceanic Atmospheric Administration, The National Atlas of the United States, *Coastline and Shoreline*; <http://nationalatlas.gov/articles/mapping/a_general.html>.

U.S. Census Bureau, Statistical Abstract of the United States: 2009

Table 347. Largest Lakes in the United States

[The list of lakes include manmade lakes and those that are only partially within the United States. For more information on the National Atlas of the United States®, please see <http://nationalatlas.gov/partners.html>]

Lake	Location	Area in sq. miles	Lake	Location	Area in sq. miles
Lake Superior	MI-MN-WI-Ontario	31,700	Lake Pontchartrain	Louisiana	631
Lake Huron	MI-Ontario	23,000	Lake Sakakawea[1]	North Dakota	520
Lake Michigan	IL-IN-MI-WI	22,300	Lake Champlain	NY-VT-Quebec	490
Lake Erie	MI-NY-OH-PA-Ontario	9,910	Becharof Lake	Alaska	453
Lake Ontario	NY-Ontario	7,340	Lake St. Clair	MI-Ontario	430
Great Salt Lake	Utah	2,117	Red Lake	Minnesota	427
Lake of the Woods	MN-Manitoba-Ontario	1,485	Selawik Lake	Alaska	404
Iliamna Lake	Alaska	1,014	Fort Peck Lake[1]	Montana	393
Lake Oahe[1]	ND-SD	685	Salton Sea	California	347
Lake Okeechobee	Florida	662	Rainy Lake	MN-Ontario	345

[1] Manmade lakes.

Source: U.S. Geological Survey and National Oceanic Atmospheric Administration, The National Atlas of the United States of America, *Lakes*; <http://nationalatlas.gov/articles/mapping/a_general.html>.

Table 348. Flows of Largest U.S. Rivers—Length Discharge, and Drainage Area

River	Location of mouth	Source stream (name and location)	Length (miles) [1]	Average discharge at mouth (1,000 cubic ft. per second)	Drainage area (1,000 sq. mi.)
Missouri	Missouri	Red Rock Creek, MT	2,540	76.2	[2,5]529
Mississippi	Louisiana	Mississippi River, MN	[2]2,340	[4]593	[2,5]1,150
Yukon	Alaska	McNeil River, Canada	1,980	225	[2]328
St. Lawrence	Canada	North River, MN	1,900	348	[2]396
Rio Grande	Mexico-Texas	Rio Grande, CO	1,900	[7]	336
Arkansas	Arkansas	East Fork Arkansas River, CO	1,460	41	161
Colorado	Mexico	Colorado River, CO	1,450	[7]	246
Atchafalaya[6]	Louisiana	Tierra Blanca Creek, NM	1,420	58	95.1
Ohio	Illinois-Kentucky	Allegheny River, PA	1,310	281	203
Red	Louisiana	Tierra Blanca Creek, NM	1,290	56	93.2
Brazos	Texas	Blackwater Draw, NM	1,280	[7]	45.6
Columbia	Oregon-Washington	Columbia River, Canada	1,240	265	[2]258
Snake	Washington	Snake River, WY	1,040	56.9	108
Platte	Nebraska	Grizzly Creek, CO	990	[7]	84.9
Pecos	Texas	Pecos River, NM	926	[7]	44.3
Canadian	Oklahoma	Canadian River, CO	906	[7]	46.9
Tennessee	Kentucky	Courthouse Creek, NC	886	68	40.9
Colorado (of Texas)	Texas	Colorado River, TX	862	[7]	42.3
North Canadian	Oklahoma	Corrumpa Creek, NM	800	[7]	17.6
Mobile	Alabama	Tickanetley Creek, GA	774	67.2	44.6
Kansas	Kansas	Arikaree River, CO	743	[7]	59.5
Kuskokwim	Alaska	South Fork Kuskokwim River, AK	724	67	48
Yellowstone	North Dakota	North Folk Yellowstone River, WY	692	[7]	70
Tanana	Alaska	Nabesna River, AK	659	41	44.5
Gila	Arizona	Middle Fork Gila River, NM	649	[7]	58.2
Porcupine	Alaska	Porcupine River, Canada	569	23	45.1
Susquehanna	Maryland	Hayden Creek, NY	447	38.2	27.2
Stikine	Alaska	Stikine River, Canada	379	56	[2]20
Susitna	Alaska	Susitna River, AK	313	51	20
Willamette	Oregon	Middle Fork Willamette River, OR	309	37.4	11.4
Copper	Alaska	Copper River, AK	286	59	24.4
Nushagak	Alaska	Nushagak River, AK	285	36	13.4

[1] From source to mouth. [2] Drainage area includes both the United States and Canada. [3] The length from the source of the Missouri River to the Mississippi River and thence to the Gulf of Mexico is about 3,710 miles. [4] Includes about 167,000 cubic ft. per second diverted from the Mississippi into the Atchafalaya River but excludes the flow of the Red River. [5] Excludes the drainage areas of the Red and Atchafalaya Rivers. [6] In east-central Louisiana, the Red River flows into the Atchafalaya River, a distributary of the Mississippi River. Data on average discharge, length, and drainage area include the Red River, but exclude all water diverted into the Atchafalaya from the Mississippi River. [7] Less than 15,000 cubic feet per second.

Source: U.S. Geological Survey, "Largest Rivers in the United States," <http://pubs.usgs.gov/of/1987/ofr87-242/>.

Table 349. Extreme and Mean Elevations by State and Other Areas

[One foot = .305 meter. There are 2,130 square miles of the United States below sea level (Death Valley is the lowest point). There are 20,230 square miles above 10,000 feet (Mount McKinley is the highest point in the United States)]

State and other areas	Highest point Name	Elevation Feet	Elevation Meters	Lowest point Name	Elevation Feet	Elevation Meters	Approximate mean elevation Feet	Approximate mean elevation Meters
U.S.	**Mt. McKinley (AK)**	**20,320**	**6,198**	**Death Valley (CA)**. . . .	**−282**	**−86**	**2,500**	**763**
AL	Cheaha Mountain	2,407	734	Gulf of Mexico	(1)	(1)	500	153
AK	Mount McKinley	20,320	6,198	Pacific Ocean.	(1)	(1)	1,900	580
AZ	Humphreys Peak.	12,633	3,853	Colorado River	70	21	4,100	1,251
AR	Magazine Mountain	2,753	840	Ouachita River	55	17	650	198
CA	Mount Whitney	14,494	4,419	Death Valley.	−282	−86	2,900	885
CO	Mt. Elbert.	14,433	4,402	Arikaree River.	3,315	1,011	6,800	2,074
CT	Mt. Frissell on south slope . .	2,380	726	Long Island Sound . . .	(1)	(1)	500	153
DE	Ebright Road [2]	448	137	Atlantic Ocean	(1)	(1)	60	18
DC	Tenleytown at Reno Reservoir.	410	125	Potomac River	1	(Z)	150	46
FL	Britton Hill	345	105	Atlantic Ocean	(1)	(1)	100	31
GA	Brasstown Bald.	4,784	1,459	Atlantic Ocean	(1)	(1)	600	183
HI	Pu'u Wekiu, Mauna Kea. . . .	13,796	4,208	Pacific Ocean.	(1)	(1)	3,030	924
ID	Borah Peak	12,662	3,862	Snake River	710	217	5,000	1,525
IL	Charles Mound	1,235	377	Mississippi River	279	85	600	183
IN	Hoosier Hill	1,257	383	Ohio River	320	98	700	214
IA	Hawkeye Point	1,670	509	Mississippi River	480	146	1,100	336
KS	Mount Sunflower	4,039	1,232	Verdigris River	679	207	2,000	610
KY	Black Mountain.	4,145	1,264	Mississippi River	257	78	750	229
LA	Driskill Mountain	535	163	New Orleans	−8	−2	100	31
ME	Mount Katahdin	5,268	1,607	Atlantic Ocean	(1)	(1)	600	183
MD	Hoye Crest.	3,360	1,025	Atlantic Ocean	(1)	(1)	350	107
MA	Mount Greylock.	3,491	1,065	Atlantic Ocean	(1)	(1)	500	153
MI	Mount Arvon.	1,979	604	Lake Erie.	571	174	900	275
MN	Eagle Mountain	2,301	702	Lake Superior.	601	183	1,200	366
MS	Woodall Mountain	806	246	Gulf of Mexico	(1)	(1)	300	92
MO	Taum Sauk Mountain	1,772	540	St. Francis River	230	70	800	244
MT	Granite Peak	12,799	3,904	Kootenai River	1,800	549	3,400	1,037
NE	Panorama Point	5,424	1,654	Missouri River.	840	256	2,600	793
NV	Boundary Peak.	13,140	4,007	Colorado River	479	146	5,500	1,678
NH	Mount Washington.	6,288	1,918	Atlantic Ocean	(1)	(1)	1,000	305
NJ	High Point	1,803	550	Atlantic Ocean	(1)	(1)	250	76
NM	Wheeler Peak.	13,161	4,014	Red Bluff Reservoir . . .	2,842	867	5,700	1,739
NY	Mount Marcy	5,344	1,630	Atlantic Ocean	(1)	(1)	1,000	305
NC	Mount Mitchell	6,684	2,039	Atlantic Ocean	(1)	(1)	700	214
ND	White Butte	3,506	1,069	Red River of the North .	750	229	1,900	580
OH	Campbell Hill	1,550	473	Ohio River	455	139	850	259
OK	Black Mesa	4,973	1,517	Little River	289	88	1,300	397
OR	Mount Hood	11,239	3,428	Pacific Ocean.	(1)	(1)	3,300	1,007
PA	Mount Davis.	3,213	980	Delaware River	(1)	(1)	1,100	336
RI	Jerimoth Hill	812	248	Atlantic Ocean	(1)	(1)	200	61
SC	Sassafras Mountain	3,560	1,086	Atlantic Ocean	(1)	(1)	350	107
SD	Harney Peak	7,242	2,209	Big Stone Lake	966	295	2,200	671
TN	Clingmans Dome.	6,643	2,026	Mississippi River	178	54	900	275
TX	Guadalupe Peak	8,749	2,668	Gulf of Mexico	(1)	(1)	1,700	519
UT	Kings Peak	13,528	4,126	Beaverdam Wash	2,000	610	6,100	1,861
VT	Mount Mansfield	4,393	1,340	Lake Champlain	95	29	1,000	305
VA	Mount Rogers.	5,729	1,747	Atlantic Ocean	(1)	(1)	950	290
WA	Mount Rainier.	14,411	4,395	Pacific Ocean.	(1)	(1)	1,700	519
WV	Spruce Knob	4,863	1,483	Potomac River	240	73	1,500	458
WI	Timms Hill	1,951	595	Lake Michigan	579	177	1,050	320
WY	Gannett Peak	13,804	4,210	Belle Fourche River . . .	3,099	945	6,700	2,044
Puerto Rico	Cerro de Punta	4,390	1,339	Atlantic Ocean	(1)	(1)	1,800	549
American Samoa . .	Lata Mountain	3,160	964	Pacific Ocean.	(1)	(1)	1,300	397
Guam	Mount Lamlam	1,332	406	Pacific Ocean.	(1)	(1)	330	101
U.S. Virgin Islands .	Crown Mountain	1,556	475	Atlantic Ocean	(1)	(1)	750	229

Z Less than 0.5 meter. [1] Sea level. [2] At DE-PA state line.

Source: U.S. Geological Survey, for highest and lowest points, "Elevations and Distances in the United States" at <http://erg.usgs.gov/isb/pubs/booklets/elvadist/elvadist.html> (released 29 April 2005). For mean elevations see, *Elevations and Distances in the United States*, 1983 edition.

Table 350. **Land Cover/Use by Type: 1982 to 2003**

[**In millions of acres (1,937.7 represents 1,937,700,000), except percent.** Excludes Alaska, Hawaii, and District of Columbia. For inventory-specific glossary of key terms, see <http://www.nrcs.usda.gov/technical/NRI/glossaries.html>]

Year	Total surface area	Nonfederal rural land						Devel-oped land	Water areas	Fed-eral land
		Rural land, total [1]	Crop-land	Pasture land	Range-land	Forest land	Other rural land			
1982	1,937.7	1,417.2	420.4	131.4	414.5	402.6	48.3	72.8	48.6	399.1
1992	1,937.6	1,400.2	381.2	125.1	406.6	404.0	49.3	86.5	49.4	401.5
2003	1,937.7	1,377.3	367.9	117.0	405.1	405.6	50.2	108.1	50.4	401.9
Percent of total land										
1982	100.0	73.1	21.7	6.8	21.4	20.8	2.5	3.8	2.5	20.6
1992	100.0	72.3	19.7	6.5	21.0	20.9	2.5	4.5	2.5	20.7
2003	100.0	71.1	19.0	6.0	20.9	20.9	2.6	5.6	2.6	20.7

[1] Includes Conservation Reserve Program land not shown separately.

Source: U.S. Department of Agriculture, Natural Resources and Conservation Service, *2003 Annual National Resources Inventory*. See also <http://www.nrcs.usda.gov/technical/NRI/>.

Table 351. **Wetlands on Nonfederal Land and Water Areas by Land Cover/Use and Farm Production Region: 2003**

[**In thousands of acres (110,760 represents 110,760,000).** Represents palustrine and estuarine wetlands; see source]

Farm production region [1]	Total	Crop-land [2]	Forest land	Range-land	Other rural land	Developed land	Water area
Wetlands, total	**110,760**	**16,730**	**65,440**	**7,740**	**15,800**	**1,590**	**3,460**
Lake states	22,460	2,710	15,480	–	3,880	160	230
Southeast	22,360	940	16,010	970	3,460	420	560
Delta states	17,950	3,240	11,020	270	2,730	190	500
Northeast	14,150	1,250	10,890	–	1,550	240	220
Northern plains	7,640	3,020	210	2,870	1,090	80	370
Appalachian	7,460	400	6,080	–	570	110	300
Southern plains	5,590	970	2,350	970	520	230	550
Mountain	4,780	1,570	220	2,010	820	30	130
Corn belt	4,690	1,330	2,440	–	380	100	440
Pacific	3,680	1,300	740	650	800	30	160

– Represents or rounds to zero.   [1] Ten regions established by USDA, Economic Research Service, that group states according to differences in soils, slope of land, climate, distance to market, and storage and marketing facilities.   [2] Includes pastureland and Conservation Reserve Program (CRP) lands.

Source: U.S. Department of Agriculture, Natural Resources Conservation Service, *2003 Annual National Resources Inventory*. See also <http://www.nrcs.usda.gov/technical/NRI/>.

Table 352. **Land Cover/Use by State: 2003**

[**In thousands of acres (1,937,664 represents 1,937,664,000), except percent.** Excludes Alaska, District of Columbia, Hawaii, and Island Areas]

State	Total surface area	Selected nonfederal rural land, percent of total			State	Total surface area	Selected nonfederal rural land, percent of total		
		Crop-land	Range-land	Forest land			Crop-land	Range-land	Forest land
United States . . .	**1,937,664**	**19.0**	**20.9**	**20.9**	Nebraska	49,510	39.5	46.6	1.6
Alabama	33,424	7.5	0.2	64.4	Nevada	70,763	0.9	11.7	0.4
Arizona	72,964	1.3	44.2	5.7	New Hampshire . . .	5,941	2.1	–	65.6
Arkansas	34,037	22.1	0.1	44.1	New Jersey	5,216	10.1	–	30.8
California	101,510	9.3	17.5	13.7	New Mexico	77,823	2.0	51.3	7.0
Colorado	66,625	12.5	37.2	4.9	New York	31,361	17.1	–	56.1
Connecticut	3,195	5.4	–	53.4	North Carolina	33,709	16.4	–	45.9
Delaware	1,534	29.8	–	22.2	North Dakota	45,251	53.6	24.5	1.0
Florida	37,534	7.7	7.2	33.9	Ohio	26,445	42.5	–	27.3
Georgia	37,741	11.0	–	58.0	Oklahoma	44,738	20.1	31.6	16.5
Idaho	53,488	10.2	12.0	7.5	Oregon	62,161	6.0	15.1	20.5
Illinois	36,059	66.5	–	11.0	Pennsylvania	28,995	17.7	–	53.9
Indiana	23,158	57.5	–	16.5	Rhode Island	813	2.5	–	45.9
Iowa	36,017	70.8	–	6.4	South Carolina	19,939	11.9	–	56.0
Kansas	52,661	50.3	30.1	2.9	South Dakota	49,358	34.6	44.7	1.0
Kentucky	25,863	21.2	–	40.6	Tennessee	26,974	17.6	–	44.3
Louisiana	31,377	17.3	0.9	42.5	Texas	171,052	14.9	56.2	6.2
Maine	20,966	1.8	–	84.0	Utah	54,339	3.1	19.6	3.5
Maryland	7,870	19.3	–	30.1	Vermont	6,154	9.5	–	67.1
Massachusetts	5,339	4.7	–	49.9	Virginia	27,087	10.6	–	48.7
Michigan	37,349	21.7	–	44.7	Washington	44,035	14.7	13.3	28.9
Minnesota	54,010	39.1	–	30.3	West Virginia	15,508	5.3	–	68.1
Mississippi	30,527	16.3	–	54.9	Wisconsin	35,920	28.7	–	40.4
Missouri	44,614	30.7	0.2	28.1	Wyoming	62,603	3.5	44.0	1.5
Montana	94,110	15.4	39.0	5.7					

– Represents zero.

Source: U.S. Department of Agriculture, Natural Resources and Conservation Service, Summary Report, *2003 Annual National Resources Inventory*. See also <http://www.nrcs.usda.gov/technical/NRI/>.

Geography and Environment   217

Table 353. U.S. Wetland Resources and Deepwater Habitats by Type: 1998 to 2004

[In thousands of acres (148,618.8 represents 148,618,800). Wetlands and deepwater habitats are defined separately because the term wetland does not include permanent water bodies. Deepwater habitats are permanently flooded land lying below the deepwater boundary of wetlands. Deepwater habitats include environments where surface water is permanent and often deep, so that water, rather than air, is the principal medium within which the dominant organisms live, whether or not they are attached to the substrate. As in wetlands, the dominant plants are hydrophytes; however, the substrates are considered nonsoil because the water is too deep to support emergent vegetation. In general terms, wetlands are lands where saturation with water is the dominant factor determining the nature of soil development and the types of plant and animal communities living in the soil and on its surface. The single feature that most wetlands share is soil or substrate that is at least periodically saturated with or covered by water. Wetlands are lands transitional between terrestrial and aquatic systems where the water table is usually at or near the surface or the land is covered by shallow water. For more information on wetlands, see the "Classification of Wetlands and Deepwater Habitats of the United States" at <http://www.fws.gov/nwi/Pubs_Reports/Class_Manual/class_titlepg.htm>]

Wetland or deepwater category	Estimated area, 1998	Estimated area, 2004	Change, 1998 to 2004
All wetlands and deepwater habitats, total	**148,618.8**	**149,058.5**	**439.7**
All deepwater habitats, total	41,046.6	41,304.5	247.9
Lacustrine [1]	16,610.5	16,773.4	162.9
Riverine [2]	6,765.5	6,813.3	47.7
Estuarine Subtidal [3]	17,680.5	17,717.8	37.3
All wetlands, total	107,562.3	107,754.0	191.8
Intertidal wetlands [4]	5,328.7	5,300.3	−28.4
Marine intertidal	130.4	128.6	−1.9
Estuarine intertidal nonvegetated	594.1	600.0	5.9
Estuarine intertidal vegetated	4,604.2	4,571.7	−32.4
Freshwater wetlands	102,233.6	102,453.8	220.2
Freshwater nonvegetated	5,918.7	6,633.9	715.3
Freshwater vegetated	96,414.9	95,819.8	−495.1
Freshwater emergent [5]	26,289.6	26,147.0	−142.6
Freshwater forested [6]	51,483.1	52,031.4	548.2
Freshwater shrub [7]	18,542.2	17,641.4	−900.8

[1] The lacustrine system includes deepwater habitats with all of the following characteristics: (1) situated in a topographic depression or a dammed river channel; (2) lacking trees, shrubs, persistent emergents, emergent mosses or lichens with greater than 30 percent coverage; (3) total area exceeds 20 acres (8 hectares).   [2] The riverine system includes deepwater habitats contained within a channel, with the exception of habitats with water containing ocean derived salts in excess of 0.5 parts per thousand.   [3] The estuarine system consists of deepwater tidal habitats and adjacent tidal wetlands that are usually semi-enclosed by land but have open, partly obstructed, or sporadic access to the open ocean, and in which ocean water is at least occasionally diluted by freshwater runoff from the land. Subtidal is where the substrate is continuously submerged by marine or estuarine waters.   [4] Intertidal is where the substrate is exposed and flooded by tides. Intertidal includes the splash zone of coastal waters.   [5] Emergent wetlands are characterized by erect, rooted, herbaceous hydrophytes, excluding mosses and lichens. This vegetation is present for most of the growing season in most years. These wetlands are usually dominated by perennial plants. [6] Forested wetlands are characterized by woody vegetation that is 20 feet tall or taller.   [7] Shrub wetlands include areas dominated by woody vegetation less than 20 feet tall. The species include true shrubs, young trees, and trees or shrubs that are small or stunted because of environmental conditions.

Source: U.S. Fish and Wildlife Service, *Status and Trends of Wetlands in the Conterminous United States, 1998 to 2004*, December 2005. See also <http://wetlandsfws.er.usgs.gov/status_trends/national_reports/trends_2005_report.pdf>.

Table 354. U.S. Water Withdrawals Per Day by End Use: 1940 to 2000

[(140 represents 140,000,000,000). Includes the District of Columbia, Puerto Rico and U.S. Virgin Islands. Withdrawal signifies water physically withdrawn from a source. Includes fresh and saline water; excludes water used for hydroelectric power]

Year	Total (bil. gal.)	Per capita [1] (gal.)	Irrigation (bil. gal.)	Public supply (bil. gal.) [2]	Rural (bil. gal.) [3]	Industrial and misc. [4] (bil. gal.)	Steam electric utilities (bil. gal.)
1940	140	1,027	71	10	3.1	29	23
1950	180	1,185	89	14	3.6	37	40
1955	240	1,454	110	17	3.6	39	72
1960	270	1,500	110	21	3.6	38	100
1965	310	1,602	120	24	4.0	46	130
1970	370	1,815	130	27	4.5	47	170
1975	420	1,972	140	29	4.9	45	200
1980	440	1,953	150	34	5.6	45	210
1985	399	1,650	137	38	7.8	31	187
1990	408	1,620	137	41	7.9	30	195
1995	402	1,500	134	40	8.9	29	190
2000	408	1,430	137	43	9.2	23	196

[1] Based on U.S. Census Bureau resident population as of July 1.   [2] Includes commercial water withdrawals.   [3] Rural farm and nonfarm household and garden use, and water for farm stock and dairies.   [4] For 1940 to 1960, includes manufacturing and mineral industries, rural commercial industries, air-conditioning, resorts, hotels, motels, military, and other state and federal agencies, and miscellaneous; thereafter, includes manufacturing, mining and mineral processing, ordnance, construction, and miscellaneous.

Source: 1940–1960, U.S. Bureau of Domestic Business Development, based principally on committee prints, *Water Resources Activities in the United States,* for the Senate Committee on National Water Resources, U.S. Senate, thereafter, U.S. Geological Survey, *Estimated Use of Water in the United States in 2000,* circular 1268. See also <http://water.usgs.gov/pubs/circ /2004/circ1268/> (released 12 March 2004).

Table 355. Oil Spills in U.S. Water—Number and Volume: 2000 to 2004

[Based on reported discharges into U.S. navigable waters, including territorial waters (extending 3 to 12 miles from the coastline), tributaries, the contiguous zone, onto shoreline, or into other waters that threaten the marine environment. Data found in U.S. Coast Guard polluting incident database]

Spill characteristic	Number of spills				Spill volume (gallons)			
	2000	2002	2003	2004	2000	2002	2003	2004
Total	8,354	4,497	4,192	3,897	1,431,370	638,882	401,140	1,416,714
Size of spill (gallons):								
1 to 100	8,058	4,269	3,975	3,677	39,355	35,728	32,881	31,150
101 to 1,000	219	176	169	170	78,779	62,331	59,661	60,387
1,001 to 3,000	37	34	19	34	67,529	60,706	33,722	66,152
3,001 to 5,000	12	2	12	2	45,512	7,686	44,630	7,840
5,001 to 10,000	16	5	11	4	112,415	37,340	77,366	26,739
10,001 to 50,000	6	8	6	5	108,400	186,065	152,880	86,430
50,001 to 100,000.	4	2	–	1	266,380	144,126	–	58,036
100,001 to 1,000,000.	2	1	–	4	713,000	104,900	–	1,079,981
1,000,000 and over	–	–	–	–	–	–	–	–
Waterbody:								
Atlantic Ocean	150	83	39	31	135,010	7,852	2,223	332,110
Pacific Ocean	623	103	118	143	36,301	8,336	3,003	345,276
Gulf of Mexico	1,838	733	801	908	112,069	106,465	49,617	31,935
Great Lakes	96	41	37	77	4,535	505	3,339	895
Lakes	32	16	24	6	349	881	175	93
Rivers and canals	1,816	1,415	1,501	1,426	663,404	227,898	165,022	163,841
Bays and sounds	1,248	804	688	569	49,783	46,399	107,419	35,797
Harbors	801	999	714	630	273,095	153,965	19,033	504,321
Other	1,750	303	270	107	156,824	86,581	51,308	2,447
Source:								
Tankship	111	55	38	35	608,176	4,753	4,450	636,834
Tankbarge	229	126	156	143	133,540	30,219	102,874	215,822
All other vessels	5,220	1,635	1,521	1,527	291,927	212,410	103,481	453,901
Facilities	1,054	1,219	1,083	1,099	311,604	198,718	78,202	42,675
Pipelines	25	–	1	1	17,021	–	14,952	15,000
All other nonvessels	566	67	56	37	45,136	2,153	361	12,781
Unknown	1,149	1,395	1,337	1,055	23,966	190,630	96,819	39,700

– Represents zero.

Source: U.S. Coast Guard, *Pollution Incidents In and Around U.S. Waters, A Spill/Release Compendium: 1969–2004* <http://www.uscg.mil/hq/g-m/nmc/response/stats/ac.htm>.

Table 356. Hazardous Waste Generated, Shipped, and Received by State and Other Area: 2005

[**In thousands of tons (38,347.0 represents 38,347,000).** Covers hazardous wastes regulated under the Resource Conservation and Recovery Act (RCRA) of 1976 as amended. Generation quantities exclude hazardous waste received from off site for storage/bulking and subsequently transferred off site for treatment or disposal is excluded from generation quantities. For further information on coverage, see source]

State and other area	Generated	Shipped	Received	State and other area	Generated	Shipped	Received
Total	38,347.0	7,686.3	8,545.9	Montana	7.2	6.0	–
				Nebraska	30.9	33.6	36.1
United States.	38,256.6	7,622.7	8,534.2	Nevada	12.9	16.6	62.0
				New Hampshire	6.1	6.2	–
Alabama	874.7	210.0	120.9	New Jersey	993.1	322.4	166.2
Alaska	2.4	1.2	0.1	New Mexico	944.6	5.9	9.0
Arizona	24.3	26.5	35.6	New York	1,124.2	195.5	286.5
Arkansas	443.7	284.5	273.3	North Carolina	384.1	106.5	91.1
California	747.2	710.8	1,770.3	North Dakota	549.7	1.6	0.6
Colorado	95.5	53.9	23.4	Ohio	2,145.4	946.7	853.2
Connecticut	44.0	55.4	22.7	Oklahoma	211.9	38.5	48.2
Delaware	14.4	14.1	0.4	Oregon	40.3	32.1	93.9
District of Columbia . . .	0.3	0.3	–	Pennsylvania	360.8	316.8	467.2
Florida	237.1	39.0	18.0	Rhode Island	6.3	10.3	38.6
Georgia	480.3	321.4	6.9	South Carolina	177.7	219.2	177.4
Hawaii	1.5	1.4	0.4	South Dakota	1.0	1.2	0.1
Idaho	25.9	28.9	136.0	Tennessee	776.1	67.8	23.7
Illinois	1,164.1	407.7	437.5	Texas	15,224.2	886.2	600.3
Indiana	1,017.4	426.6	642.5	Utah	78.1	77.8	154.4
Iowa	52.7	52.5	0.5	Vermont	3.5	2.8	0.3
Kansas	229.2	132.2	193.9	Virginia	134.4	83.0	36.8
Kentucky	1,152.1	206.3	86.9	Washington	141.9	120.7	33.3
Louisiana	5,460.3	385.1	362.7	West Virginia	72.6	46.4	11.8
Maine	4.1	3.5	2.4	Wisconsin	108.3	111.5	53.8
Maryland	39.7	58.4	127.1	Wyoming	3.1	2.3	–
Massachusetts	372.7	70.1	28.0	Guam	0.1	0.1	0.1
Michigan	295.8	316.2	440.0	Navajo Nation	0.1	0.1	–
Minnesota	249.5	62.1	303.6	Puerto Rico	87.5	61.2	11.6
Mississippi	1,599.5	27.1	56.7	Trust Territories	–	–	–
Missouri	89.8	70.1	199.9	Virgin Islands	2.6	2.2	–

– Represents zero or rounds to zero.

Source: U.S. Environmental Protection Agency, *The National Biennial RCRA Hazardous Waste Report (Based on 2005 Data),* series EPA530-R-03-007. See also <http://www.epa.gov/epaoswer/hazwaste/data/br05/index.htm> (released December 2006).

Table 357. National Ambient Air Pollutant Concentrations by Type of Pollutant: 1990 to 2006

[Data represent annual composite averages of pollutant based on daily 24-hour averages of monitoring stations, except carbon monoxide, which is based on the second-highest, nonoverlapping, 8-hour average; ozone, the fourth-highest maximum 8-hour value; and lead, the maximum quarterly average of ambient lead levels. Based on data from the Air Quality System. $\mu g/m^3$ = micrograms of pollutant per cubic meter of air; ppm = parts per million]

Pollutant	Unit	Monitoring stations, number	Air quality standard [1]	1990	1995	2000	2003	2004	2005	2006
Carbon monoxide	ppm. . . .	243	[2]9	6.0	4.8	3.5	2.8	2.6	2.4	2.3
Ozone	ppm. . . .	588	[3]0.075	0.085	0.088	0.080	0.080	0.073	0.078	0.077
Sulfur dioxide	ppm. .	295	[4]0.03	0.0081	0.0055	0.0049	0.0043	0.0041	0.0042	0.0038
Particulates (PM-10). . .	$\mu g/m^3$. . .	391	[5]150	79.1	66.4	60.8	59.5	52.3	55.8	55.3
Fine particulates (PM-2.5).	$\mu g/m^3$.	752	[6]15	(NA)	(NA)	13.5	12.2	11.8	12.8	11.6
Nitrogen dioxide	ppm. .	170	[7]0.053	0.020	0.019	0.017	0.016	0.015	0.015	0.014
Lead	$\mu g/m^3$. . .	44	[8]1.5	0.13	0.07	0.07	0.06	0.06	0.08	0.06

NA Not available.   [1] Refers to the primary National Ambient Air Quality Standard.   [2] Based on 8-hour standard of 9 ppm.   [3] Based on annual standard of 0.03 ppm.   [4] Based on 8-hour standard of 0.075 ppm. On March 12, 2008, EPA revised the level of the primary and secondary 8-hour ozone standards to 0.075 ppm.   [5] Based on 24-hour (daily) standard of 150 mg/m³. The particulates (PM-10) standard replaced the previous standard for total suspended particulates in 1987. In 2006, EPA revoked the annual PM-10 standard.   [6] Based on annual standard of 15 mg/m³. The PM-2.5 national monitoring network was deployed in 1999. National trend data prior to that time is not available.   [7] Based on annual standard of 0.053 ppm.   [8] Based on 3-month standard of 1.5 µg/m³.

Source: U.S. Environmental Protection Agency, *Latest Findings on National Air Quality - Status and Trends through 2006;* released January 2008; <http://www.epa.gov/air/airtrends/2007/index.html>.

Table 358. Selected National Air Pollutant Emissions: 1970 to 2005

[In thousands of tons (12,184 represents 12,184,000), except as indicated. PM-10 is equal to or less than ten microns in diameter; PM-2.5 is equal to or less than 2.5 microns effective diameter. Methodologies to estimate data for 1970 to 1980 period and 1985 to present emissions differ. Beginning with 1985, the methodology for more recent years is described in the document available at <http://www.epa.gov/ttn/chief/net/2002inventory.html>]

Year	PM-10	PM-10, misc.[1]	PM-2.5	PM-2.5, misc.[1]	Sulfur dioxide	Nitrogen dioxide	Volatile organic compounds	Carbon monoxide	Lead (tons)[2]
1970	12,184	839	(NA)	(NA)	31,218	26,883	34,659	204,043	220,869
1975	6,987	569	(NA)	(NA)	28,043	26,337	30,765	188,398	159,659
1980	6,161	852	(NA)	(NA)	25,925	27,079	31,106	185,407	74,153
1985	3,588	37,736	(NA)	(NA)	23,307	25,757	27,404	176,844	22,890
1990	3,216	24,536	2,326	5,233	23,076	25,529	24,108	154,186	4,975
1995	3,054	22,765	2,203	4,726	18,619	24,956	22,041	126,777	3,929
1999	2,395	20,179	1,897	4,504	17,545	22,845	18,270	114,541	3,356
2000	2,319	20,642	1,821	4,681	16,347	22,598	17,512	114,467	(NA)
2001	2,362	20,573	1,840	4,382	15,932	21,549	17,111	106,262	(NA)
2002	2,340	16,095	1,308	4,728	14,728	21,186	20,749	114,592	1,640
2003	2,312	15,556	1,304	1,750	15,122	20,392	20,141	112,008	(NA)
2004	2,285	15,018	1,300	1,705	14,761	19,490	19,533	109,426	(NA)
2005	2,258	14,479	1,297	1,660	14,709	18,878	18,925	106,843	(NA)

NA Not available.   [1] Sources such as agricultural tilling, construction, mining and quarrying, paved roads, unpaved roads, and wind erosion.   [2] Beginning 1996, lead and lead compounds are inventoried through the hazardous air pollutants (HAPs) portion of the National Emission Inventory (NEI) every three years.

Source: U.S. Environmental Protection Agency, *National Emissions Inventory (NEI) Air Pollution Emissions Trends Data, 1970–2002.* See also <http://www.epa.gov/ttn/chief/trends/index.html#tables>; *Air and Radiation; Air Trends.* See also <http://www.epa.gov/airtrends/reports.html>.

Table 359. Selected Air Pollutant Emissions by Pollutant and Source: 2003

[In thousands of tons, except as indicated (17,868 represents 17,868,000. See headnote, Table 358]

Source	PM-10 [1]	PM-2.5	Sulfur dioxide	Nitrogen dioxide	Volatile organic compounds	Carbon monoxide
Total emissions	**17,868**	**3,054**	**15,122**	**20,392**	**20,141**	**112,008**
Fuel combustion, stationary sources	529	284	13,192	7,169	1,730	5,463
Electric utilities	222	118	10,846	4,390	50	666
Industrial	241	115	1,795	2,072	154	1,263
Other fuel combustion	66	52	551	707	1,526	3,534
Residential						
Industrial processes	1,282	595	1,099	1,045	7,236	3,889
Chemical and allied product manufacturing . . .	37	28	261	71	248	291
Metals processing	69	45	219	71	48	1,013
Petroleum and related industries	23	16	256	336	583	342
Other	854	258	332	431	437	503
Solvent utilization	8	6	–	7	4,297	5
Storage and transport	51	19	5	19	1,230	123
Waste disposal and recycling	240	224	26	110	393	1,613
Highway vehicles	198	142	240	7,750	4,458	60,744
Off highway [2]	304	283	463	4,218	3,007	24,111
Miscellaneous [3]	15,556	1,750	128	210	3,709	17,801

– Rounds to zero.   [1] Represents both PM-10 and PM-10 fugitive dust; see Table 358.   [2] Includes emissions from farm tractors and other farm machinery, construction equipment, industrial machinery, recreational marine vessels, and small general utility engines such as lawn mowers.   [3] Includes emissions such as from forest fires and other kinds of burning, various agricultural activities, fugitive dust from paved and unpaved roads, and other construction and mining activities, and natural sources.

Source: U.S. Environmental Protection Agency, *National Emissions Inventory (NEI) Air Pollution Emissions Trends Data, 1970–2002.* See also <http://www.epa.gov/ttn/chief/trends/index.html#tables>; *Air and Radiation; Air Trends.* See also <http://www.epa.gov/airtrends/reports.html>.

Table 360. **Emissions of Greenhouse Gases by Type and Source: 1990 to 2006**

[In millions of metric tons (6,146.7 represents 6,146,700,000). **Metric ton = 2,200 lbs.** Emission estimates were mandated by Congress through Section 1605(a) of the Energy Policy Act of 1992 (Title XVI). Data shown below are for gases that contain carbon and are measured in terms of their carbon dioxide equivalent]

Type and source	1990	2000	2002	2003	2004	2005	2006 [1]
CARBON DIOXIDE EQUIVALENT							
Total emissions	**6,146.7**	**6,978.4**	**6,944.9**	**7,012.4**	**7,133.5**	**7,181.4**	**7,075.6**
Carbon dioxide, total	5,017.5	5,890.5	5,875.9	5,940.4	6,019.9	6,045.0	5,934.4
Energy use by sector							
Residential	961.6	1,181.5	1,196.2	1,224.1	1,221.5	1,253.0	1,204.2
Commercial	787.5	1,015.1	1,018.1	1,027.1	1,041.6	1,065.4	1,045.2
Industrial	1,679.9	1,778.1	1,707.8	1,712.8	1,735.7	1,677.1	1,650.8
Transportation	1,582.6	1,872.6	1,890.9	1,901.4	1,958.6	1,986.2	1,990.1
Energy adjustments [2]	-82.4	-59.0	-36.4	-27.3	-42.8	-43.8	-64.8
Adjusted energy subtotal	4,929.3	5,788.3	5,776.6	5,838.2	5,914.6	5,937.8	5,825.5
Other sources	88.2	102.2	99.3	102.2	105.3	107.1	108.8
Methane	708.4	608.0	598.6	603.7	605.9	607.3	605.1
Energy sources	275.0	257.2	254.8	254.0	258.2	255.1	250.4
Agricultural sources	171.1	178.1	178.4	178.9	178.9	181.5	181.1
Waste management	259.6	169.8	162.8	168.1	166.2	168.3	171.2
Industrial processes	2.7	2.9	2.7	2.6	2.6	2.5	2.4
Nitrous oxide	333.7	341.9	332.5	331.7	358.3	368.0	378.9
Agricultural sources	249.5	252.2	247.3	248.3	273.4	279.2	289.1
Energy use	50.8	67.2	64.0	63.7	65.2	68.7	69.5
Industrial processes	28.6	16.6	15.2	13.6	13.6	13.9	13.8
Waste management	4.9	5.8	6.0	6.1	6.1	6.2	6.3
High-GWP gases [3]	87.1	138.0	137.8	136.6	149.4	161.2	157.6

[1] 2006 preliminary data. [2] CO2 emissions from U.S. Territories are added to the U.S. total, and CO2 emissions from fuels used for international transport (both ocean-going vessels and airplanes), are subtracted to derive total U.S. greenhouse emissions. [3] High-global warming potential gases (Hydrofluorocarbons, Perfluorocarbons, and Sulfur Hexafluoride).

Source: U.S. Energy Information Administration, *Emissions of Greenhouse Gases in the United States, 2006,* Series DOE/EIA-0573 (2006), annual. See also <http://www.eia.doe.gov/oiaf/1605/ggrpt/index.html>.

Table 361. **Municipal Solid Waste Generation, Materials Recovery, Combustion with Energy Recovery, and Discards in the United States: 1980 to 2006**

[In millions of tons (151.6 represents 151,600,000), except as indicated. Covers post-consumer residential and commercial solid wastes which comprise the major portion of typical municipal collections. Excludes mining, agricultural and industrial processing, demolition and construction wastes, sewage sludge, and junked autos and obsolete equipment wastes. Based on material-flows estimating procedure and wet weight as generated]

Item and material	1980	1990	2000	2003	2004	2005	2006
Waste generated	151.6	205.2	238.3	240.4	249.2	248.2	251.3
Per person per day (lb.)	3.7	4.5	4.6	4.5	4.7	4.6	4.6
Total materials recovery	14.5	33.2	69.3	74.9	77.9	79.1	81.8
Per person per day (lb.)	0.4	0.7	1.4	1.4	1.5	1.5	1.5
Combustion with energy recovery	2.7	29.7	33.7	33.7	34.4	33.4	31.4
Per person per day (lb.)	0.1	0.6	0.7	0.6	0.6	0.6	0.6
Discards to landfill, other disposal	134.4	142.3	135.3	131.9	136.9	135.6	138.2
Per person per day (lb.)	3.2	3.1	2.6	2.5	2.6	2.5	2.5
PERCENT DISTRIBUTION OF GENERATION							
Total materials in products	71.8	71.4	74.3	73.7	73.9	73.3	73.2
Paper and paperboard	36.4	35.4	36.8	34.5	35.1	34.3	33.9
Glass	10.0	6.4	5.3	5.1	5.1	5.1	5.3
Metals	10.2	8.1	7.7	7.8	7.5	7.5	7.6
Plastics	4.5	8.3	10.6	11.5	11.7	11.7	11.7
Rubber and leather	2.8	2.8	2.7	2.8	2.7	2.7	2.6
Textiles	1.7	2.8	4.0	4.4	4.4	4.5	4.7
Wood	4.6	6.0	5.5	5.7	5.5	5.6	5.5
Other	1.7	1.6	1.8	1.8	1.8	1.8	1.8
Total other waste	28.2	28.6	25.7	26.3	26.1	26.7	26.8
Food wastes	8.6	10.1	11.4	11.7	11.9	12.3	12.4
Yard wastes	18.1	17.1	12.8	13.1	12.7	12.9	12.9
Other wastes	1.5	1.4	1.5	1.5	1.5	1.5	1.5

Source: Franklin Associates, a Division of ERG, Prairie Village, KS, *Municipal Solid Waste in the United States: 2006 Facts and Figures.* See also <http://www.epa.gov/epaoswer/non-hw/muncpl/msw99.htm>.

Geography and Environment 221

Table 362. Generation and Recovery of Selected Materials in Municipal Solid Waste: 1980 to 2006

[In millions of tons (151.6 represents 151,600,000), except as indicated. Covers post-consumer residential and commercial solid wastes which comprise the major portion of typical municipal collections. Excludes mining, agricultural and industrial processing, demolition wastes, sewage sludge, and junked autos and obsolete equipment wastes. Based on material-flows and construction estimating procedure and wet weight as generated]

Item and material	1980	1990	2000	2003	2004	2005	2006
Waste generated, total [1]	**151.6**	**205.2**	**238.3**	**240.4**	**249.2**	**248.2**	**251.3**
Paper and paperboard	55.2	72.7	87.7	83.0	87.6	85.1	85.3
Glass	15.1	13.1	12.6	12.3	12.7	12.8	13.2
Metals: Ferrous	12.6	12.6	13.5	14.0	14.0	13.8	14.2
Aluminum	1.7	2.8	3.2	3.2	3.2	3.2	3.3
Other nonferrous	1.2	1.1	1.6	1.6	1.6	1.7	1.7
Plastics	6.8	17.1	25.3	27.6	29.2	29.0	29.5
Food, other	13.0	20.8	27.1	28.2	29.7	30.5	31.3
Yard trimmings	27.5	35.0	30.5	31.5	31.8	32.1	32.4
Materials recovered, total [1]	**14.5**	**33.2**	**69.3**	**74.9**	**77.9**	**79.1**	**81.8**
Paper and paperboard	11.7	20.2	37.6	40.0	40.8	42.0	44.0
Glass	0.8	2.6	2.9	2.7	2.7	2.8	2.9
Metals: Ferrous	0.4	2.2	4.6	5.1	5.1	4.9	5.1
Aluminum	0.3	1.0	0.9	0.7	0.7	0.7	0.7
Other nonferrous	0.5	0.7	1.1	1.1	1.2	1.2	1.2
Plastics	0.2	0.4	1.5	1.4	1.7	1.8	2.0
Food, other	(Z)	(Z)	0.7	0.8	0.7	0.7	0.7
Yard trimings	(Z)	4.2	15.8	18.3	19.8	19.9	20.1
Percent of generation recovered, total [1]	**9.6**	**16.2**	**29.1**	**31.1**	**31.3**	**31.9**	**32.5**
Paper and paperboard	21.3	27.8	42.8	48.2	46.6	49.4	51.6
Glass	5.0	20.1	22.8	21.5	21.6	21.6	21.8
Metals: Ferrous	2.9	17.6	34.1	36.4	36.5	35.7	35.7
Aluminum	17.9	35.9	27.3	21.6	22.3	21.6	21.2
Other nonferrous	46.6	66.4	67.9	66.7	72.6	71.9	71.5
Plastics	0.3	2.2	5.8	5.1	5.9	6.1	6.9
Food, other	(Z)	(Z)	2.5	2.7	2.2	2.3	2.2
Yard trimings	(Z)	12.0	51.7	58.2	62.4	61.9	62.0

Z Less than 5,000 tons or .05 percent.   [1] Includes products not shown separately.

Source: Franklin Associates, a Division of ERG, Prairie Village, KS, *Municipal Solid Waste in the United States: 2006 Facts and Figures*. Prepared for the U.S. Environmental Protection Agency. See also <http://www.epa.gov/epaoswer/non-hw/muncpl/msw99.htm>.

Table 363. Municipal Solid Waste—Generation, Recovery, and Discards by Selected Type of Product: 2006

[See headnote, Table 362]

Type of product	Generation (1,000 tons)	Recovery		Discards (1,000 tons)
		Products recovered (1,000 tons)	Percent of generation	
Paper and paperboard products [1]	85,280	44,020	51.6	41,260
Nondurable goods	44,840	20,160	45.0	24,680
Newsprint	8,830	7,780	88.1	1,050
Groundwood inserts	3,530	3,090	87.5	440
Magazines	2,570	1,040	40.5	1,530
Office-type papers	6,320	4,150	65.7	2,170
Standard mail	5,890	2,280	38.7	3,610
Other commercial printing	6,630	1,400	21.1	5,230
Containers and packaging	40,440	23,860	59.0	16,580
Corrugated boxes	31,430	22,630	72.0	8,800
Folding cartons	5,570	890	16.0	4,680
Glass products [1]	13,200	2,880	21.8	10,320
Containers and packaging	11,390	2,880	25.3	8,510
Beer and soft drink bottles	7,500	2,300	30.7	5,200
Wine and liquor bottles	1,670	250	15.0	1,420
Food and other bottles and jars	2,220	330	14.9	1,890
Metal products [1]	19,130	6,950	36.3	12,180
Ferrous	14,220	5,080	35.7	9,140
Aluminum	3,260	690	21.2	2,570
Other nonferrous	1,650	1,180	71.5	470
Plastics [1]	29,490	2,040	6.9	27,450
Plastics in durable goods	8,790	530	6.0	8,260
Plastics in nondurable goods	6,470	(Z)	(Z)	6,470
Plastics in containers and packaging	14,230	1,510	10.6	12,720
Rubber and leather [1]	6,540	870	13.3	5,670
Rubber in tires	2,490	870	34.9	1,620

Z Less than 5,000 tons or .05 percent.   [1] Includes products not shown separately.

Source: Franklin Associates, a Division of ERG, Prairie Village, KS, *Municipal Solid Waste in the United States: 2006 Facts and Figures*. Prepared for the U.S. Environmental Protection Agency. See also <http://www.epa.gov/epaoswer/non-hw/muncpl/msw99.htm>.

Table 364. Toxic Chemical Releases and Transfers by Media: 2001 to 2006

[In millions of pounds (5,584.8 represents 5,584,800,000), except as indicated. Based on reports filed as required by section 313 of the Emergency Planning and Community Right-to-Know Act (EPCRA, or Title III of the Superfund Amendments and Reauthorization Act of 1986), Public Law 99-499. Owners and operators of facilities that are classified within North American Industrial Classification Code groups 31 through 33, 2121, 2122, 2211, 4246, 4247 and 562; have 10 or more full-time employees, and that manufacture, process, or otherwise use any listed toxic chemical in quantities greater than the established threshold in the course of a calendar year are covered and required to report]

Media	2001	2002	2003	2004	2005	2006
Total facilities reporting	25,758	25,051	24,445	24,197	23,797	22,880
Total on- and off-site disposal or other releases	**5,584.8**	**4,750.5**	**4,442.2**	**4,238.7**	**4,353.9**	**4,248.9**
On-site releases	5,088.4	4,260.0	3,958.7	3,726.5	3,820.6	3,725.5
Air emissions [1]	1,630.2	1,613.6	1,584.0	1,540.4	1,512.6	1,408.3
Surface water discharges	243.2	242.5	229.7	245.1	250.4	243.0
Underground injection class I	193.6	206.5	207.2	210.3	211.5	199.7
Underground injection class II–V	22.0	20.5	22.0	27.7	20.2	20.1
RCRA subtitle C landfills [2]	173.5	156.0	199.8	155.5	158.5	155.3
Other landfills	311.0	267.2	265.0	257.0	255.8	250.9
Land treatment/application farming	17.2	24.3	18.2	21.5	23.7	26.8
Surface impoundments	973.8	771.6	822.6	726.8	790.9	830.8
Other land disposal	1,523.8	957.8	610.2	542.1	597.0	590.8
Off-site releases	496.4	490.5	483.5	512.2	533.4	523.3
Total transfers offsite for further waste management	**4,037.2**	**3,929.4**	**3,692.4**	**3,978.0**	**3,921.1**	**3,937.2**
Tranfers to recycling	2,028.0	2,015.6	1,898.9	2,059.7	2,074.2	2,157.0
Transfers to energy recovery	775.6	739.9	650.0	649.8	608.3	547.7
Transfers to treatment	272.3	264.0	278.9	326.1	336.2	327.4
Transfers to POTWs [3]	343.4	304.0	269.8	258.9	262.9	255.1
Transfers to POTWs metal and metal compounds [3]	2.2	2.0	1.9	1.7	1.8	2.8
Other off-site transfers	0.9	0.9	0.9	71.5	0.4	0.2
Transfers off-site for disposal or other releases [4]	614.8	603.1	592.0	610.4	637.2	647.0
Total production-related waste managed	**27,098.8**	**25,992.6**	**25,054.4**	**25,818.0**	**24,785.6**	**24,368.2**
Recycled on-site	7,512.2	7,651.9	7,143.7	7,143.8	6,603.7	6,656.5
Recycled off-site	2,066.7	2,009.9	1,901.0	2,059.3	2,078.5	2,182.0
Energy recovery on-site	2,588.9	2,789.1	2,641.7	2,596.1	2,409.9	2,604.5
Energy recovery off-site	764.7	740.6	649.7	649.0	608.2	547.0
Treated on-site	7,842.2	7,356.2	7,620.3	8,454.7	8,042.1	7,425.6
Treated off-site	611.4	552.6	518.7	564.7	573.6	548.2
Quantity disposed or otherwise release of on- and off-site	5,712.8	4,892.4	4,579.3	4,350.2	4,469.6	4,404.5
Non-production-related waste managed	42.9	18.2	24.9	18.8	23.9	18.2

[1] Air emissions include both fugitive and point source. [2] RCRA = Resource Conservation and Recovery Act. [3] POTW (Publicly Owned Treatment Work) is a wastewater treatment facility that is owned by a state or municipality. [4] Does not include off-site disposal or other releases transferred to other TRI facilities that reported the amounts as on-site disposal or other releases.
Source: U.S. Environmental Protection Agency, "Toxic Release Inventory (TRI) Program, 2006 TRI Public Data Release eReport." See also <http://www.epa.gov/tri/tridata/tri06/index.htm> (released 21 February 2008).

Table 365. Toxic Chemical Releases by Industry: 2006

[In millions of pounds (4,248.9 represents 4,248,900,000), except as indicated. See headnote, Table 364]

Industry	2002 NAICS [1] code	Total on- and off-site releases	On-site release Total	Air emissions	Other surface impound- ments	Off-site releases/ transfers to disposal [2]
Total [3]	(X)	**4,248.9**	**3,725.5**	**1,408.3**	**827.5**	**523.3**
Coal mining	2121	16.9	16.9	1.2	3.4	(Z)
Metal mining	2122	1,216.4	1,213.1	3.7	658.1	3.4
Electric utilities	2211	1,022.1	951.4	670.4	119.7	70.7
Food/beverages/tobacco	311/312	163.8	156.4	49.1	0.2	7.5
Textiles	313/314	3.7	2.8	2.4	0.2	0.9
Apparel	315	0.1	0.1	0.1	–	0.1
Leather	316	1.4	0.4	0.4	–	1.1
Wood products	321	21.7	20.7	20.0	(Z)	1.0
Paper	322	211.6	205.2	165.1	3.7	6.4
Printing and publishing	323/51	12.9	12.5	12.5	–	0.4
Petroleum	324	76.1	70.1	45.8	0.1	6.0
Chemicals	325	514.3	460.8	188.9	14.2	53.5
Plastics and rubber	326	64.0	55.7	55.1	(Z)	8.3
Stone/clay/glass	327	·34.1	28.8	25.6	0.1	5.3
Cement	32731	10.9	10.8	8.9	0.1	0.1
Primary metals	331	468.6	187.8	44.2	25.9	280.8
Fabricated metals	332	62.8	37.4	32.6	(Z)	25.4
Machinery	333	9.6	5.5	5.4	–	4.1
Computers/electronic products	334	9.2	6.4	2.0	–	2.8
Electrical equipment	335	9.4	4.7	4.5	(Z)	4.7
Transportation equipment	336	60.6	51.1	50.0	(Z)	9.5
Furniture	337	9.8	9.7	9.7	–	0.1
Chemical wholesalers	4246	1.3	1.2	1.2	–	0.1
Petroleum bulk terminals	4247	3.3	3.1	2.3	(Z)	0.2
Hazardous waste	562	204.4	177.3	0.4	0.6	27.1
No codes [3]	(X)	31.7	30.7	1.8	1.2	1.0

– Represents zero. X Not applicable. Z less than 50,000. [1] North American Industry Classification System, see text, Section 12. [2] Includes off-site disposal to underground injection for Class I wells, Class II to V wells, other surface impoundments, land releases, and other releases, not shown separately. [3] Includes industries with no specific industry identified.
Source: U.S. Environmental Protection Agency, "2006 TRI Public Data Release eReport." See also <http://www.epa.gov/tri/tridata/tri06/index.htm> (released 21 February 2008).

U.S. Census Bureau, Statistical Abstract of the United States: 2009

Table 366. Toxic Chemical Releases by State and Outlying Area: 2006

[In millions of pounds (4,248.9 represents 4,248,900,000). Based on reports filed as required by section 313 of the Emergency Planning. See headnote, Table 364]

State and outlying area	Total on-and off-site releases, total	On-site release Total[1]	Air emissions	Other surface impoundments	Off-site releases/transfers to disposal
Total	**4,248.9**	**3,725.5**	**1,408.3**	**827.5**	**523.3**
U.S. total	**4,240.1**	**3,718.0**	**1,401.1**	**827.5**	**522.0**
AL	121.1	95.8	54.8	14.2	25.3
AK	667.6	667.3	1.9	281.3	0.3
AZ	98.6	96.3	4.5	12.9	2.3
AR	50.5	39.7	20.1	1.9	10.8
CA	43.0	36.1	16.8	(Z)	6.9
CO	24.7	18.5	3.0	3.1	6.2
CT	4.9	3.5	3.0	(Z)	1.5
DE	15.8	11.1	6.3	(Z)	4.7
DC	(Z)	(Z)	(Z)	(Z)	(Z)
FL	119.4	116.3	55.8	9.1	3.1
GA	129.8	126.4	98.0	14.8	3.4
HI	3.0	2.8	2.3	–	0.2
ID	67.2	66.3	4.0	9.0	0.9
IL	112.6	87.7	40.9	8.2	24.9
IN	236.9	136.3	73.0	9.9	100.6
IA	46.8	34.0	25.7	2.2	12.8
KS	27.5	23.5	11.9	2.5	4.0
KY	97.1	89.6	64.6	8.1	7.5
LA	131.6	123.6	50.2	3.3	8.0
ME	10.6	9.2	5.0	–	1.3
MD	39.8	36.7	32.0	(Z)	3.1
MA	7.0	4.9	4.4	0.5	2.1
MI	87.2	66.5	48.5	5.4	20.7
MN	26.1	23.5	11.2	6.9	2.6
MS	60.8	58.7	24.2	11.1	2.1
MO	109.9	105.4	17.4	56.9	4.4
MT	43.3	42.2	4.0	8.2	1.2
NE	34.8	30.2	7.8	(Z)	4.6
NV	217.1	215.9	1.6	159.4	1.2
NH	4.2	4.1	4.0	(Z)	0.1
NJ	21.8	18.2	11.4	(Z)	3.6
NM	23.7	23.5	1.0	0.6	0.2
NY	35.5	29.1	16.0	0.8	6.4
NC	134.1	117.4	95.0	5.7	16.7
ND	22.3	13.6	3.6	7.4	8.7
OH	291.3	230.1	119.7	12.0	61.3
OK	29.7	25.4	15.1	0.5	4.2
OR	23.9	22.8	11.3	(Z)	1.1
PA	154.1	101.1	79.6	0.8	53.0
RI	0.5	0.3	0.3	–	0.2
SC	75.3	62.7	51.7	2.4	12.6
SD	7.2	6.6	1.8	(Z)	0.6
TN	131.4	116.9	63.4	28.8	14.6
TX	238.5	209.2	81.1	3.9	29.3
UT	148.2	145.9	9.9	117.3	2.3
VT	0.6	0.2	(Z)	–	0.4
VA	70.8	66.0	41.6	1.3	4.8
WA	29.5	27.4	9.8	13.4	2.1
WV	101.6	85.0	69.1	2.5	16.5
WI	46.0	30.4	20.6	(Z)	15.6
WY	15.4	14.2	2.4	1.1	1.2
American Samoa	(Z)	(Z)	(Z)	–	–
Guam	0.2	0.2	0.1	(Z)	(Z)
Northern Marianas	(Z)	(Z)	(Z)	(Z)	(Z)
Puerto Rico	7.7	6.4	6.4	–	1.2
U.S. Virgin Islands	0.9	0.9	0.7	–	(Z)

– Represents zero. Z Less than 50,000. [1] Includes other types of release not shown separately.

Source: U.S. Environmental Protection Agency, Toxic Release Inventory (TRI) Program, "2006 TRI Public Data Release eReport." See also <http://www.epa.gov/tri/tridata/tri06/index.htm> (released 21 February 2008).

Table 367. Hazardous Waste Sites on the National Priority List by State and Outlying Area: 2007

[As of December 31. Includes both proposed and final sites listed on the National Priorities List for the Superfund program as authorized by the Comprehensive Environmental Response, Compensation, and Liability Act (CERCLA) of 1980 and the Superfund Amendments and Reauthorization Act (SARA) of 1986. For information on CERCLA and SARA, go to <http://www.epa.gov/superfund/action/law/cercla.htm>]

State and outlying area	Total sites	Rank	Percent distribution	Federal	Non-federal
Total	**1,311**	**(X)**	**(X)**	**162**	**1,149**
United States	**1,294**	**(X)**	**(X)**	**160**	**1,134**
Alabama	15	24	1.2	3	12
Alaska	5	45	0.4	5	–
Arizona	8	43	0.6	2	6
Arkansas	10	40	0.8	–	10
California	96	2	7.7	24	72
Colorado	19	21	1.5	3	16
Connecticut	15	25	1.2	1	14
Delaware	14	27	1.1	1	13
District of Columbia	1	(X)	0.1	1	–
Florida	49	6	3.9	6	43
Georgia	16	23	1.3	2	14
Hawaii	3	46	0.2	2	1
Idaho	9	41	0.7	2	7
Illinois	49	7	3.9	5	44
Indiana	32	12	2.6	–	32
Iowa	12	33	1.0	1	11
Kansas	12	34	1.0	1	11
Kentucky	14	28	1.1	1	13
Louisiana	14	29	1.1	1	13
Maine	12	35	1.0	3	9
Maryland	18	22	1.4	9	9
Massachusetts	32	13	2.6	6	26
Michigan	67	5	5.4	1	66
Minnesota	25	18	2.0	2	23
Mississippi	6	44	0.5	–	6
Missouri	29	16	2.3	3	26
Montana	15	26	1.2	–	15
Nebraska	13	32	1.0	1	12
Nevada	1	49	0.1	–	1
New Hampshire	21	19	1.7	1	20
New Jersey	116	1	9.3	8	108
New Mexico	14	30	1.1	1	13
New York	87	4	7.0	4	83
North Carolina	31	14	2.5	2	29
North Dakota	–	50	0.0	–	–
Ohio	38	10	3.0	5	33
Oklahoma	11	39	0.9	1	10
Oregon	12	36	1.0	2	10
Pennsylvania	96	3	7.7	6	90
Rhode Island	12	37	1.0	2	10
South Carolina	25	17	2.0	2	23
South Dakota	2	47	0.2	1	1
Tennessee	14	31	1.1	4	10
Texas	47	9	3.8	4	43
Utah	19	20	1.5	4	15
Vermont	11	38	0.9	–	11
Virginia	30	15	2.4	11	19
Washington	48	8	3.8	13	35
West Virginia	9	42	0.7	2	7
Wisconsin	38	11	3.0	–	38
Wyoming	2	48	0.2	1	1
Guam	2	(X)	(X)	1	1
Puerto Rico	13	(X)	(X)	1	12
Virgin Islands	2	(X)	(X)	–	2

– Represents zero. X Not applicable.

Source: U.S. Environmental Protection Agency, Supplementary Materials: CERCLIS3/WasteLan Database; (released 7 May 2008). See also <http://www.epa.gov/superfund/about.htm>.

U.S. Census Bureau, Statistical Abstract of the United States: 2009

Table 368. Environmental Industry—Revenues and Employment, by Industry Segment: 2000 to 2007

[**218.7 represents $218,700,000,000.** Covers approximately 30,000 private and public companies engaged in revenue-generating environmental activities]

Industry segment	Revenue (bil. dol.)				Employment			
	2000	2005	2006	2007	2000	2005	2006	2007
Industry total	**218.7**	**265.6**	**282.1**	**295.1**	**1,410,500**	**1,595,100**	**1,664,800**	**1,718,000**
Analytical services [1]	1.8	1.8	1.8	1.9	20,200	20,000	20,100	20,000
Wastewater treatment works [2]	28.7	35.6	37.5	39.2	118,800	141,100	147,600	153,200
Solid waste management [3]	39.4	47.8	50.6	52.7	221,400	256,500	269,100	278,200
Hazardous waste management [4]	8.2	8.7	9.0	9.1	44,800	45,000	45,900	45,600
Remediation/industrial services	10.1	11.0	11.6	12.1	100,200	96,600	100,000	103,100
Consulting and engineering	17.4	22.4	24.0	25.4	184,000	220,800	234,900	246,400
Water equipment and chemicals	19.8	24.8	26.1	27.6	130,500	153,000	159,200	166,100
Instrument manufacturing	3.8	4.8	5.1	5.5	30,200	35,500	37,300	39,200
Air pollution control equipment [5]	19.0	18.8	18.5	18.3	129,600	123,400	121,200	118,900
Waste management equipment [6]	10.0	10.1	10.5	10.8	75,500	72,900	74,800	75,400
Process and prevention technology	1.2	1.5	1.7	1.8	29,000	28,100	30,000	30,700
Water utilities [7]	29.9	35.1	36.6	38.0	130,000	145,200	150,000	154,200
Resource recovery [8]	16.0	21.0	24.1	25.1	127,000	156,600	166,400	171,900
Clean energy systems and power [9]	13.4	22.3	24.9	27.7	69,300	100,400	108,300	115,100

[1] Covers environmental laboratory testing and services. [2] Mostly revenues collected by municipal entities for sewage or wastewater plants. [3] Covers such activities as collection, transportation, transfer stations, disposal, landfill ownership and management for solid waste and recyclables. [4] Transportation and disposal of hazardous, medical, and nuclear waste. [5] Includes stationary and mobile sources. [6] Includes vehicles, containers, liners, processing, and remediation equipment. [7] Revenues generated from the sale of water, majority in public sector. [8] Revenues generated from the sale of recovered metals, paper, plastic, etc. [9] Revenues generated from the sale of equipment & systems and electricity.

Source: Environmental Business International, Inc., San Diego, CA, *Environmental Business Journal*, monthly (copyright). See also <http://www.ebiusa.com/>.

Table 369. Threatened and Endangered Wildlife and Plant Species— Number: 2008

[**As of April.** Endangered species: One in danger of becoming extinct throughout all or a significant part of its natural range. Threatened species: One likely to become endangered in the foreseeable future]

Item	Mammals	Birds	Reptiles	Amphibians	Fishes	Snails	Clams	Crustaceans	Insects	Arachnids	Plants
Total listings	**357**	**275**	**119**	**32**	**151**	**76**	**72**	**22**	**61**	**12**	**747**
Endangered species, total	**325**	**254**	**79**	**21**	**85**	**65**	**64**	**19**	**51**	**12**	**599**
United States	69	75	13	13	74	64	62	19	47	12	598
Foreign	256	179	66	8	11	1	2	–	4	–	1
Threatened species, total	**32**	**21**	**40**	**11**	**66**	**11**	**8**	**3**	**10**	**–**	**148**
United States	12	15	24	10	65	11	8	3	10	–	146
Foreign	20	6	16	1	1	–	–	–	–	–	2

– Represents zero.

Source: U.S. Fish and Wildlife Service, *Endangered Species Bulletin,* bimonthly; and <http://ecos.fws.gov/tesspublic/Boxscore .do/> (accessed 01 May 2008).

Table 370. Tornadoes, Floods, Tropical Storms, and Lightning: 1995 to 2006

Weather type	1995	1998	1999	2000	2001	2002	2003	2004	2005	2006
Tornadoes: [1]										
Number	1,235	1,424	1,343	1,071	1,216	941	1,376	1,819	1,264	1,032
Lives lost	30	130	94	41	40	55	54	35	38	67
Injuries	650	1,868	1,842	882	743	968	1,087	396	537	990
Property loss (mil. dol.)	411	1,714	1,990	424	630	801	1,263	537	422	752
Floods and flash floods:										
Lives lost	80	136	68	38	48	49	85	82	43	76
Injuries	57	6,440	301	47	277	88	65	128	38	23
Property loss (mil. dol.)	1,251	2,325	1,421	1,255	1,220	655	2,541	1,696	1,538	3,768
North Atlantic tropical storms and hurricanes [2]	19	14	12	15	15	12	21	16	27	10
Direct deaths on U.S. mainland	17	9	19	–	24	51	14	34	1,016	–
Property loss in U.S. (bil.dol.)	5.9	3.5	4.2	8.1	5.2	1.1	1.9	18.9	93.0	2.4
Lightning:										
Deaths	85	44	46	51	44	51	44	32	38	48
Injuries	433	283	243	364	371	256	237	280	309	246

– Represents zero. [1] Source: U.S. National Weather Service, Internet site <http://www.spc.noaa.gov/climo/torn/monthlytornstats.html>. A violent, rotating column of air descending from a cumulonimbus cloud in the form of a tubular- or funnel-shaped cloud, usually characterized by movements along a narrow path and wind speeds from 100 to over 300 miles per hour. Also known as a "twister" or "waterspout." [2] Source: National Hurricane Center (NHC), Coral Gables, FL, unpublished data. For data on individual hurricanes, see the NHC Internet site at <http://www.nhc.noaa.gov/>.

Source: Except as noted, U.S. National Oceanic and Atmospheric Administration (NOAA), National Weather Service (NWS), *Office of Climate, Water, and Weather Services, Natural Hazard Statistics,* monthly. See also NOAA Web site at <http://www.nws .noaa.gov/om/hazstats.shtml>.

Table 371. Major U.S. Weather Disasters: 2001 to 2007

[5 represents $5,000,000,000. Covers only weather-related disasters costing $1 billion or more]

Event	Description	Time period	Estimated cost [1] (bil.dol.)	Deaths
Great Plains and eastern drought	Severe drought with periods of extreme heat resulting in major reductions in crop yields, along with very low stream flows, and lake levels.	Entire year 2007	5	[2]
Western wildfires	Continued drought conditions and high winds over much of the western U.S., resulting in numerous wildfires.	Summer–Fall 2007	Over 1	12
Spring freeze	Widespread severe freeze over much of the east and midwest causing losses in fruit crops, field crops, and in the ornamental industry.	Apr. 2007	2	–
Severe storms and tornadoes	Flooding, hail, tornadoes, and severe thunderstorms across numerous eastern and southern states.	Apr. 2007	1.5	9
Freeze	Widespread agricultural freeze over a good portion of California, destroying numerous agricultural crops.	Jan. 2007	1.4	1
Widespread drought	Rather severe drought affected crops in states especially during the spring–summer, centered over the Great Plains region, with other areas affected across portions of the south and far west.	Spring-Summer 2006	Over 6	[2]
Severe storms and tornadoes	Outbreak of tornadoes over portions of the midwest and south during a week-long period.	March 2006	Over 1	10+
Numerous wildfires	Wildfires mainly over the western half of the country, due to dry weather and high wind burning nearly 10 million acres (new record for period since 1960).	Entire year 2006	Over 1	28+
Hurricane Wilma	Category 3 hurricane makes landfall in southwest Florida, causing considerable damage from major flooding and strong winds in south-east Florida.	Oct. 2005	Over 10	35
Hurricane Rita	Category 3 hurricane makes landfall on the Texas-Lousiana border coastal region, causing surge/wind damage along the coast and flood damage in FL, MS, LA, AR, and TX.	Sept. 2005	Over 8	119
Hurricane Katrina	Category 3 hurricane makes landfall as a category 1 near Miami, FL, and on the LA, MS coast, causing massive damage in addition to flood and wind damage in AL, FL, TN, KY, OH, and GA.	Aug. 2005	Over 100	1,300+
Hurricane Dennis	Category 3 hurricane makes landfall in western Florida causing wind and surge damage, also causing wind and flood damage to GA, MS, and TN.	July 2005	Over 2	12+
Midwest drought	Midwest drought causing crop losses in AR, IL, IN, MO, OH, and WI.	Spring–summer 2005	Over 1.0	–
Hurricane Jeanne	Category 3 hurricane makes landfall in east-central Florida, causing considerable damage in Florida and some flood damage in GA, SC, NC, VA, MD, DE, NJ, PA, and NY.	Sept. 2004	Over 6.9	28
Hurricane Ivan	Category 3 hurricane makes landfall on Gulf coast of Alabama causing significant damage in AL and FL and wind/flood damage in GA, SC, NC, LA, MS, WV, MD, TN, KY, OH, DE, NJ, PA, and NY.	Sept. 2004	Over 14	57
Hurricane Frances	Category 2 hurricane makes landfall in east-central Florida causing significant damage in FL and considerable flood damage in GA, SC, NC, and NY.	Sept. 2004	Over 9	48
Hurricane Charley	Category 4 hurricane makes landfall in southwest FL resulting in major damage in FL and some damage in SC and NC.	Aug. 2004	15	34
Southern California wildfires	Dry weather, high winds, and resulting wildfires in southern CA burned 743,000 acres and destroyed 3,700 homes.	Oct.– Nov. 2003	2.5	22
Hurricane Isabel	Category 2 hurricane makes landfall in eastern NC, causing damage along coasts of NC, VA, and MD with wind damage and flooding in NC, VA, MD, DE, WV, NJ, NY, and PA.	Sept. 2003	5	55
Midwest severe storms and tornadoes	Numerous tornadoes over the midwest, MS River valley, and OH/TN River valleys with record 400 tornadoes in one week.	May 2003	Over 3.4	51
Storms and hail	Severe storms and large hail over southern plains, lower MS River valley, and TX.	April 2003	Over 1.6	3
Widespread drought	Moderate to extreme drought over large portions of 30 states.	Spring to fall 2002	Over 10	–
Western fire season	Major fires over 11 western states from Rockies to west coast.	Spring to fall 2002	Over 2.0	21
Tropical Storm Allison	Tropical storm produced rainfall and severe flooding in coastal portions of TX and LA and damage in MS, FL, VA, and PA.	June 2001	5.0	43
Midwest and Ohio Valley hail and tornadoes	Storms, tornadoes, and hail in TX, OK, KS, NE, IA, MO, IL, IN, WI, MI, OH, KY, and PA.	April 2001	Over 1.9	3

– Represents zero.   [1] Represents actual dollar costs at the time of event and is not adjusted for inflation.   [2] Some deaths reported due to heat but not beyond typical annual averages.

Source: U.S. National Oceanic and Atmospheric Administration, National Climatic Data Center, "Billion Dollar U.S. Weather Disasters, 1980–2007" (released 1 January 2008). See also <http://www.ncdc.noaa.gov/oa/reports/billionz.html>.

Table 372. **Highest and Lowest Temperatures by State Through 2003**

State	Highest temperature Station	Highest temperature Temperature (°F)	Highest temperature Date	Lowest temperature Station	Lowest temperature Temperature (°F)	Lowest temperature Date
U.S. . . .	**Greenland Ranch, CA. .**	**134**	**Jul. 10, 1913**	**Prospect Creek, AK . . .**	**−80**	**Jan. 23, 1971**
AL	Centerville	112	Sep. 5, 1925	New Market	−27	Jan. 30, 1966
AK	Fort Yukon	100	[1]Jun. 27, 1915	Prospect Creek Camp . .	−80	Jan. 23, 1971
AZ	Lake Havasu City	128	Jun. 29, 1994	Hawley Lake	−40	Jan. 7, 1971
AR	Ozark	120	Aug. 10, 1936	Pond	−29	Feb. 13, 1905
CA	Greenland Ranch	134	Jul. 10, 1913	Boca	−45	Jan. 20, 1937
CO	Bennett	118	Jul. 11, 1888	Maybell	−61	Feb. 1, 1985
CT	Danbury	106	Jul. 15, 1995	Coventry	−32	[2]Jan. 22, 1961
DE	Millsboro	110	Jul. 21, 1930	Millsboro	−17	Jan. 17, 1893
FL	Monticello	109	Jun. 29, 1931	Tallahassee	−2	Feb. 13, 1899
GA	Greenville	112	Aug. 20, 1983	CCC Camp F-16	−17	[1]Jan. 27, 1940
HI	Pahala	100	Apr. 27, 1931	Mauna Kea Obs. 111.2. .	12	May 17, 1979
ID	Orofino	118	Jul. 28, 1934	Island Park Dam	−60	Jan. 18, 1943
IL	East St. Louis	117	Jul. 14, 1954	Congerville	−36	Jan. 5, 1999
IN	Collegeville	116	Jul. 14, 1936	New Whiteland	−36	Jan. 19, 1994
IA	Keokuk	118	Jul. 20, 1934	Elkader	−47	[2]Feb. 3, 1996
KS	Alton (near)	121	[2]Jul. 24, 1936	Lebanon	−40	Feb. 13, 1905
KY	Greensburg	114	Jul. 28, 1930	Shelbyville	−37	Jan. 19, 1994
LA	Plain Dealing	114	Aug. 10, 1936	Minden	−16	Feb. 13, 1899
ME	North Bridgton	105	[2]Jul. 10, 1911	Van Buren	−48	Jan. 19, 1925
MD	Cumberland & Frederick.	109	[2]Jul. 10, 1936	Oakland	−40	Jan. 13, 1912
MA	New Bedford & Chester .	107	Aug. 2, 1975	Chester	−35	Jan. 12, 1981
MI	Mio	112	Jul. 13, 1936	Vanderbilt	−51	Feb. 9, 1934
MN	Moorhead	114	[2]Jul. 6, 1936	Tower	−60	Feb. 2, 1996
MS	Holly Springs	115	Jul. 29, 1930	Corinth	−19	Jan. 30, 1966
MO	Warsaw & Union	118	[2]Jul. 14, 1954	Warsaw	−40	Feb. 13, 1905
MT	Medicine Lake	117	Jul. 5, 1937	Rogers Pass	−70	Jan. 20, 1954
NE	Minden	118	[2]Jul. 24, 1936	Oshkosh	−47	[2]Dec. 22, 1989
NV	Laughlin	125	[2]Jun. 29, 1994	San Jacinto	−50	Jan. 8, 1937
NH	Nashua	106	Jul. 4, 1911	Mt. Washington	−47	Jan. 29, 1934
NJ	Runyon	110	Jul. 10, 1936	River Vale	−34	Jan. 5, 1904
NM	Waste Isolat Pilot Plt . . .	122	Jun. 27, 1994	Gavilan	−50	Feb. 1, 1951
NY	Troy	108	Jul. 22, 1926	Old Forge	−52	[2]Feb. 18, 1979
NC	Fayetteville	110	Aug. 21, 1983	Mt. Mitchell	−34	Jan. 21, 1985
ND	Steele	121	Jul. 6, 1936	Parshall	−60	Feb. 15, 1936
OH	Gallipolis (near)	113	[2]Jul. 21, 1934	Milligan	−39	Feb. 10, 1899
OK	Tipton	120	[2]Jun. 27, 1994	Watts	−27	[2]Jan. 18, 1930
OR	Pendleton	119	[2]Aug. 10, 1898	Seneca	−54	[2]Feb. 10, 1933
PA	Phoenixville	111	[2]Jul. 10, 1936	Smethport	−42	[1]Jan. 5, 1904
RI	Providence	104	Aug. 2, 1975	Greene	−25	Feb. 5, 1996
SC	Camden	111	[2]Jun. 28, 1954	Caesars Head	−19	Jan. 21, 1985
SD	Gannvalley	120	Jul. 5, 1936	McIntosh	−58	Feb. 17, 1936
TN	Perryville	113	[2]Aug. 9, 1930	Mountain City	−32	Dec. 30, 1917
TX	Monahans	120	[2]Jun. 28, 1994	Seminole	−23	[2]Feb. 8, 1933
UT	Saint George	117	Jul. 5, 1985	Peter's Sink	−69	Feb. 1, 1985
VT	Vernon	105	Jul. 4, 1911	Bloomfield	−50	Dec. 30, 1933
VA	Balcony Falls	110	Jul. 15, 1954	Mtn. Lake Bio. Stn.	−30	Jan. 22, 1985
WA	Ice Harbor Dam	118	[2]Aug. 5, 1961	Mazama & Winthrop	−48	Dec. 30, 1968
WV	Martinsburg	112	[2]Jul. 10, 1936	Lewisburg	−37	Dec. 30, 1917
WI	Wisconsin Dells	114	Jul. 13, 1936	Couderay	−55	Feb. 4, 1996
WY	Basin	115	Aug. 8, 1983	Riverside R.S.	−66	Feb. 9, 1933

[1] Estimated.   [2] Also on earlier dates at the same or other places.

Source: U.S. National Oceanic and Atmospheric Administration, National Environmental Satellite, Data, and Information Services (NESDIS), National Climatic Data Center (NCDC), Temperature Extremes and Drought; <http://www.ncdc.noaa.gov /oa/climate/severeweather/temperatures.html>.

Table 373. Normal Daily Mean, Maximum, and Minimum Temperatures—Selected Cities

[**In Fahrenheit degrees.** Airport data except as noted. Based on standard 30-year period, 1971 through 2000]

State	Station	Daily mean temperature			Daily maximum temperature			Daily minimum temperature		
		Jan.	July	Annual average	Jan.	July	Annual average	Jan.	July	Annual average
AL	Mobile	50.1	81.5	66.8	60.7	91.2	77.4	39.5	71.8	56.2
AK	Juneau	25.7	56.8	41.5	30.6	64.3	47.6	20.7	49.2	35.3
AZ	Phoenix	54.2	92.8	72.9	65.0	104.2	84.5	43.4	81.4	61.1
AR	Little Rock	40.1	82.4	62.1	49.5	92.8	72.7	30.8	72.0	51.5
CA	Los Angeles	57.1	69.3	63.3	65.6	75.3	70.6	48.6	63.3	56.1
	Sacramento	46.3	75.4	61.1	53.8	92.4	73.7	38.8	58.3	48.4
	San Diego	57.8	70.9	64.4	65.8	75.8	70.8	49.7	65.9	58.1
	San Francisco	49.4	62.8	57.3	55.9	71.1	65.1	42.9	54.5	49.6
CO	Denver	29.2	73.4	50.1	43.2	88.0	64.2	15.2	58.7	35.8
CT	Hartford	25.7	73.7	50.2	34.1	84.9	60.5	17.2	62.4	40.0
DE	Wilmington	31.5	76.6	54.4	39.3	86.0	63.6	23.7	67.3	45.1
DC	Washington	34.9	79.2	57.5	42.5	88.3	66.4	27.3	70.1	48.6
FL	Jacksonville	53.1	81.6	68.0	64.2	90.8	78.4	41.9	72.4	57.6
	Miami	68.1	83.7	76.7	76.5	90.9	84.2	59.6	76.5	69.1
GA	Atlanta	42.7	80.0	62.2	51.9	89.4	72.0	33.5	70.6	52.3
HI	Honolulu	73.0	80.8	77.5	80.4	87.8	84.7	65.7	73.8	70.2
ID	Boise	30.2	74.7	52.0	36.7	89.2	62.6	23.6	60.3	41.3
IL	Chicago	22.0	73.3	49.1	29.6	83.5	58.3	14.3	63.2	39.8
	Peoria	22.5	75.1	50.8	30.7	85.7	60.7	14.3	64.6	40.9
IN	Indianapolis	26.5	75.4	52.5	34.5	85.6	62.3	18.5	65.2	42.7
IA	Des Moines	20.4	76.1	50.0	29.1	86.0	59.8	11.7	66.1	40.2
KS	Wichita	30.2	81.0	56.4	40.1	92.9	67.4	20.3	69.1	45.2
KY	Louisville	33.0	78.4	57.0	41.0	87.0	66.0	24.9	69.8	47.9
LA	New Orleans	52.6	82.7	68.8	61.8	91.1	78.0	43.4	74.2	59.6
ME	Portland	21.7	68.7	45.8	30.9	78.8	55.2	12.5	58.6	36.3
MD	Baltimore	32.3	76.5	54.6	41.2	87.2	65.1	23.5	65.8	44.2
MA	Boston	29.3	73.9	51.6	36.5	82.2	59.3	22.1	65.5	43.9
MI	Detroit	24.5	73.5	49.8	31.1	83.4	58.4	17.8	63.6	41.0
	Sault Ste. Marie	13.2	63.9	40.1	21.5	75.7	49.6	4.9	52.0	30.5
MN	Duluth	8.4	65.5	39.1	17.9	76.3	48.7	-1.2	54.6	29.3
	Minneapolis-St. Paul. . .	13.1	73.2	45.4	21.9	83.3	54.7	4.3	63.0	35.9
MS	Jackson	45.0	81.4	64.1	55.1	91.4	75.0	35.0	71.4	53.2
MO	Kansas City	26.9	78.5	54.2	36.0	88.8	64.3	17.8	68.2	44.0
	St. Louis	29.6	80.2	56.3	37.9	89.8	65.7	21.2	70.6	46.9
MT	Great Falls	21.7	66.2	43.8	32.1	82.0	56.4	11.3	50.4	31.1
NE	Omaha	21.7	76.7	50.7	31.7	87.4	61.5	11.6	65.9	39.8
NV	Reno	33.6	71.3	51.3	45.5	91.2	67.4	21.8	51.4	35.2
NH	Concord	20.1	70.0	45.9	30.6	82.9	57.7	9.7	57.1	34.1
NJ	Atlantic City	32.1	75.3	53.5	41.4	85.1	63.6	22.8	65.4	43.3
NM	Albuquerque	35.7	78.5	56.8	47.6	92.3	70.4	23.8	64.7	43.2
NY	Albany	22.2	71.1	47.6	31.1	82.2	57.6	13.3	60.0	37.5
	Buffalo	24.5	70.8	48.0	31.1	79.6	55.9	17.8	62.1	39.9
	New York [1]	32.1	76.5	54.6	38.0	84.2	61.7	26.2	68.8	47.5
NC	Charlotte	41.7	80.3	61.4	51.3	90.1	71.7	32.1	70.6	51.0
	Raleigh	39.7	78.8	59.6	49.8	89.1	70.6	29.6	68.5	48.6
ND	Bismarck	10.2	70.4	42.3	21.1	84.5	54.5	-0.6	56.4	30.1
OH	Cincinnati	29.7	76.3	54.2	38.0	86.4	64.0	21.3	66.1	44.3
	Cleveland	25.7	71.9	49.7	32.6	81.4	58.1	18.8	62.3	41.2
	Columbus	28.3	75.1	52.9	36.2	85.3	62.6	20.3	64.9	43.2
OK	Oklahoma City	36.7	82.0	60.1	47.1	93.1	71.1	26.2	70.8	49.2
OR	Portland	39.9	68.1	53.5	45.6	79.3	62.1	34.2	56.9	44.8
PA	Philadelphia	32.3	77.6	55.3	39.0	85.5	63.2	25.5	69.7	47.4
	Pittsburgh	27.5	72.6	51.0	35.1	82.7	60.4	19.9	62.4	41.5
RI	Providence	28.7	73.3	51.1	37.1	82.6	60.2	20.3	64.1	42.0
SC	Columbia	44.6	82.0	63.6	55.1	92.1	74.8	34.0	71.8	52.5
SD	Sioux Falls	14.0	73.0	45.1	25.2	85.6	57.2	2.9	60.3	33.0
TN	Memphis	39.9	82.5	62.4	48.6	92.1	72.1	31.3	72.9	52.5
	Nashville	36.8	79.1	58.9	45.6	88.7	69.0	27.9	69.5	48.8
TX	Dallas-Fort Worth.	44.1	85.0	65.5	54.1	95.4	75.8	34.0	74.6	55.1
	El Paso	45.1	83.3	64.7	57.2	94.5	77.1	32.9	72.0	52.1
	Houston	51.8	83.6	68.8	62.3	93.6	79.4	41.2	73.5	58.2
UT	Salt Lake City	29.2	77.0	52.0	37.0	90.6	62.9	21.3	63.4	41.2
VT	Burlington	18.0	70.6	45.2	26.7	81.4	54.5	9.3	59.8	35.8
VA	Norfolk	40.1	79.1	59.6	47.8	86.8	67.8	32.3	71.4	51.4
	Richmond	36.4	77.9	57.6	45.3	87.5	67.8	27.6	68.3	47.4
WA	Seattle-Tacoma	40.9	65.3	52.3	45.8	75.3	59.8	35.9	55.3	44.8
	Spokane	27.3	68.6	47.3	32.8	82.5	57.4	21.7	54.6	37.2
WV	Charleston	33.4	73.9	54.5	42.6	84.9	65.4	24.2	62.9	43.5
WI	Milwaukee	20.7	72.0	47.5	28.0	81.1	55.9	13.4	62.9	39.2
WY	Cheyenne	25.9	67.7	45.0	37.1	81.9	57.6	14.8	53.4	32.3
PR	San Juan	76.6	82.2	79.9	82.4	87.4	85.5	70.8	76.9	74.2

[1] City office data.

Source: U.S. National Oceanic and Atmospheric Administration, National Environmental Satellite, Data, and Information Services (NESDIS), National Climatic Data Center (NCDC), Temperature Extremes and Drought. Weather/Climate events. See also <http://www.ncdc.noaa.gov/oa/climate/online/ccd/nrmmax.txt>; and <http://www.ncdc.noaa.gov/oa/climate/online/ccd/nrmmin.txt>; and <http://www.ncdc.noaa.gov/oa/climate/online/ccd/nrmavg.txt>.

228 Geography and Environment

Table 374. Highest Temperature of Record—Selected Cities

[**In Fahrenheit degrees.** Airport data, except as noted. For period of record through 2006]

State	Station	Length of record (years)	Jan.	Feb.	Mar.	Apr.	May	June	July	Aug.	Sept.	Oct.	Nov.	Dec.	Annual [1]
AL	Mobile	65	84	82	90	94	100	102	104	105	99	93	87	81	105
AK	Juneau	62	57	57	61	74	82	86	90	84	73	61	56	54	90
AZ	Phoenix	69	88	92	100	105	113	122	121	116	118	107	95	88	122
AR	Little Rock	65	83	85	91	95	98	105	112	109	106	97	86	80	112
CA	Los Angeles	71	91	92	95	102	97	104	97	98	110	106	101	94	110
	Sacramento	56	70	76	88	95	105	115	114	110	108	104	87	72	115
	San Diego	66	88	90	93	98	96	101	99	98	111	107	97	88	111
	San Francisco	79	72	78	85	92	97	106	105	100	103	99	85	75	106
CO	Denver	64	73	77	84	90	96	104	105	101	97	89	80	75	105
CT	Hartford	52	66	73	89	96	99	100	102	102	99	91	81	76	102
DE	Wilmington	59	75	78	86	94	96	100	102	101	100	91	85	75	102
DC	Washington	65	79	82	89	95	99	101	104	105	101	94	86	79	105
FL	Jacksonville	65	85	88	91	95	100	103	105	102	100	96	88	84	105
	Miami	64	88	89	93	96	96	98	98	98	97	95	91	87	98
GA	Atlanta	58	79	80	89	93	95	101	105	102	98	95	84	79	105
HI	Honolulu	37	88	88	88	91	93	92	94	93	95	94	93	89	95
ID	Boise	67	63	71	81	92	99	109	111	110	102	94	78	65	111
IL	Chicago	48	65	72	88	91	93	104	104	101	99	91	78	71	104
	Peoria	67	70	72	86	92	94	105	104	103	100	93	81	71	105
IN	Indianapolis	67	71	76	85	89	93	102	104	102	100	90	81	74	104
IA	Des Moines	67	67	73	91	93	98	103	105	108	101	95	81	69	108
KS	Wichita	54	75	87	89	96	100	110	113	110	108	97	86	83	113
KY	Louisville	59	77	77	86	91	95	102	106	101	104	92	84	76	106
LA	New Orleans	60	83	85	89	92	96	100	101	102	101	94	87	84	102
ME	Portland	66	64	64	88	85	94	98	99	103	95	88	74	71	103
MD	Baltimore	56	75	79	89	94	98	101	104	105	100	92	83	77	105
MA	Boston	55	66	70	89	94	95	100	102	102	100	90	79	76	102
MI	Detroit	48	62	70	81	89	93	104	102	100	98	91	77	69	104
	Sault Ste. Marie	66	45	49	75	85	89	93	97	98	95	81	67	62	98
MN	Duluth	65	52	55	78	88	90	94	97	97	95	86	71	55	97
	Minneapolis-St. Paul	68	58	61	83	95	97	102	105	102	98	90	77	68	105
MS	Jackson	43	83	85	89	94	99	105	106	107	104	95	88	84	107
MO	Kansas City	34	71	78	86	93	95	105	107	109	106	95	82	74	109
	St. Louis	49	76	85	89	93	94	102	107	107	104	94	85	76	107
MT	Great Falls	69	67	70	78	89	93	101	105	106	98	91	76	69	106
NE	Omaha	70	69	78	89	97	99	105	114	110	104	96	83	72	114
NV	Reno	65	71	75	83	89	97	103	108	105	101	91	77	70	108
NH	Concord	65	68	67	89	95	97	98	102	101	98	90	80	73	102
NJ	Atlantic City	63	78	75	87	94	99	106	104	103	99	90	84	77	106
NM	Albuquerque	67	69	76	85	89	98	107	105	101	100	91	77	72	107
NY	Albany	60	65	68	89	92	94	99	100	99	100	89	82	71	100
	Buffalo	63	72	71	81	94	91	96	97	99	98	87	80	74	99
	New York [2]	138	72	75	86	96	99	101	106	104	102	94	84	75	106
NC	Charlotte	67	79	81	90	93	100	103	103	103	104	98	85	78	104
	Raleigh	62	80	84	92	95	97	104	105	105	104	98	88	80	105
ND	Bismarck	67	63	69	81	93	98	111	112	109	105	95	79	65	111
OH	Cincinnati	45	69	75	84	89	93	102	103	102	98	88	81	75	103
	Cleveland	65	73	74	83	88	92	104	103	102	101	90	82	77	104
	Columbus	67	74	75	85	89	94	102	100	101	100	90	80	76	102
OK	Oklahoma City	53	80	92	93	100	104	105	110	110	108	96	87	86	110
OR	Portland	66	66	71	80	90	100	102	107	107	105	92	73	65	107
PA	Philadelphia	65	74	74	87	95	97	100	104	101	100	96	81	73	104
	Pittsburgh	54	72	76	82	89	91	98	103	100	97	87	82	74	103
RI	Providence	53	69	72	85	98	95	97	102	104	100	86	78	77	104
SC	Columbia	59	84	84	91	94	101	107	107	107	101	101	90	83	107
SD	Sioux Falls	61	66	70	87	94	100	110	108	108	104	94	81	63	110
TN	Memphis	65	79	81	85	94	99	104	108	107	103	95	86	81	108
	Nashville	67	78	84	86	91	97	106	107	104	105	94	84	79	107
TX	Dallas-Fort Worth	53	88	95	96	101	103	113	110	109	111	102	89	89	113
	El Paso	67	80	83	89	98	105	114	112	108	104	96	87	80	114
	Houston	37	84	91	91	95	99	103	104	107	109	96	89	85	109
UT	Salt Lake City	78	63	69	78	86	99	104	107	106	100	89	75	69	107
VT	Burlington	63	66	62	84	91	93	100	100	101	98	85	75	67	101
VA	Norfolk	58	80	82	88	97	100	101	103	104	99	95	86	80	104
	Richmond	77	81	83	93	96	100	104	105	102	103	99	86	81	105
WA	Seattle-Tacoma	62	64	70	78	85	93	96	100	99	98	89	74	64	100
	Spokane	59	59	63	71	90	96	101	108	108	98	86	67	56	108
WV	Charleston	59	79	79	89	94	93	98	104	101	102	92	85	80	104
WI	Milwaukee	66	62	68	82	91	93	101	103	103	98	89	77	68	103
WY	Cheyenne	71	66	71	74	83	91	100	100	96	95	83	75	69	100
PR	San Juan	52	92	96	96	97	96	97	95	97	97	98	96	94	98

[1] Represents the highest observed temperature in any month.   [2] City office data.

Source: U.S. National Oceanic and Atmospheric Administration, *Comparative Climatic Data,* annual; <http://www.ncdc.noaa.gov/oa/climate/online/ccd/hghtmp.txt>.

Geography and Environment   229

Table 375. Lowest Temperature of Record—Selected Cities

[**In Fahrenheit degrees.** Airport data, except as noted. For period of record through 2006]

State	Station	Length of record (years)	Jan.	Feb.	Mar.	Apr.	May	June	July	Aug.	Sept.	Oct.	Nov.	Dec.	Annual [1]
AL	Mobile	65	3	11	21	32	43	49	60	59	42	30	22	8	3
AK	Juneau	62	−22	−22	−15	6	25	31	36	27	23	11	−5	−21	−22
AZ	Phoenix	69	17	22	25	32	40	50	61	60	47	34	25	22	17
AR	Little Rock	65	−4	−5	11	28	40	46	54	52	37	29	17	−1	−5
CA	Los Angeles	71	23	32	34	39	43	48	49	51	47	16	34	32	16
	Sacramento	56	23	23	26	31	36	41	48	49	43	36	26	18	18
	San Diego	66	29	36	39	41	48	51	55	57	51	43	38	34	29
	San Francisco	79	24	25	30	31	36	41	43	42	38	34	25	20	20
CO	Denver	64	−25	−30	−11	−2	22	30	43	41	17	3	−8	−25	−30
CT	Hartford	52	−26	−21	−6	9	28	35	44	36	30	17	1	−14	−26
DE	Wilmington	59	−14	−6	2	18	30	41	48	43	36	24	14	−7	−14
DC	Washington	65	−5	4	11	24	34	47	54	49	39	29	16	1	−5
FL	Jacksonville	65	7	19	23	34	45	47	61	59	48	36	21	11	7
	Miami	64	30	32	32	46	53	60	69	68	68	51	39	30	30
GA	Atlanta	58	−8	5	10	26	37	46	53	55	36	28	3	–	−8
HI	Honolulu	37	53	53	55	57	60	65	66	67	66	61	57	54	53
ID	Boise	67	−17	−15	6	19	22	31	35	34	23	11	−3	−25	−25
IL	Chicago	48	−27	−19	−8	7	24	36	40	41	28	17	1	−25	−27
	Peoria	67	−25	−19	−10	14	25	39	47	41	26	19	−2	−23	−25
IN	Indianapolis	67	−27	−21	−7	16	28	37	44	41	28	17	−2	−23	−27
IA	Des Moines	67	−24	−26	−22	9	30	38	47	40	26	14	−4	−22	−26
KS	Wichita	54	−12	−21	−2	15	31	43	51	48	31	18	1	−16	−21
KY	Louisville	59	−22	−19	−1	22	31	42	50	46	33	23	−1	−15	−22
LA	New Orleans	60	14	16	25	32	41	50	60	60	42	35	24	11	11
ME	Portland	66	−26	−39	−21	8	23	33	40	33	23	15	3	−21	−39
MD	Baltimore	56	−7	−3	6	20	32	40	50	45	35	25	13	–	−7
MA	Boston	55	−12	−4	6	16	34	45	50	47	38	28	15	−7	−12
MI	Detroit	48	−21	−15	−4	10	25	36	41	38	29	17	9	−10	−21
	Sault Ste. Marie	66	−36	−35	−24	−2	18	26	36	29	25	16	−10	−31	−36
MN	Duluth	65	−39	−39	−29	−5	17	27	35	32	22	8	−23	−34	−39
	Minneapolis-St. Paul	68	−34	−32	−32	2	18	34	43	39	26	13	−17	−29	−34
MS	Jackson	43	2	10	15	27	38	47	51	54	35	26	17	4	2
MO	Kansas City	34	−17	−19	−10	12	30	42	51	43	31	17	1	−23	−23
	St. Louis	49	−18	−12	−5	22	31	43	51	47	36	23	1	−16	−18
MT	Great Falls	69	−37	−35	−29	−6	15	31	36	30	16	−11	−25	−43	−43
NE	Omaha	70	−23	−21	−16	5	27	38	44	43	25	13	−9	−23	−23
NV	Reno	65	−16	−16	−2	13	18	21	33	24	20	8	1	−16	−16
NH	Concord	65	−33	−37	−16	8	21	30	35	29	21	10	−5	−22	−37
NJ	Atlantic City	63	−10	−11	5	12	25	37	42	40	32	20	10	−7	−11
NM	Albuquerque	67	−17	−5	8	19	16	40	52	50	37	21	−7	−7	−17
NY	Albany	60	−28	−21	−21	10	26	36	40	34	24	16	5	−22	−28
	Buffalo	63	−16	−20	−7	12	26	35	43	38	32	20	9	−10	−20
	New York [2]	138	−6	−15	3	12	32	44	52	50	39	28	5	−13	−15
NC	Charlotte	67	−5	5	4	24	32	45	53	50	39	24	11	2	−5
	Raleigh	62	−9	–	11	23	31	38	48	46	37	19	11	4	−9
ND	Bismarck	67	−44	−43	−31	−12	15	30	35	33	11	−10	−30	−43	−44
OH	Cincinnati	45	−25	−11	−11	15	27	39	47	43	31	16	1	−20	−25
	Cleveland	65	−20	−15	−5	10	25	31	41	38	32	19	3	−15	−20
	Columbus	67	−22	−13	−6	14	25	35	43	39	31	20	5	−17	−22
OK	Oklahoma City	53	−4	−3	3	20	37	47	53	51	36	16	11	−8	−8
OR	Portland	66	−2	−3	19	29	29	39	43	44	34	26	13	6	−3
PA	Philadelphia	65	−7	−4	7	19	28	44	51	44	35	25	15	1	−7
	Pittsburgh	54	−22	−12	−1	14	26	34	42	39	31	16	−1	−12	−22
RI	Providence	53	−13	−7	1	14	29	41	48	40	33	20	6	−10	−13
SC	Columbia	59	−1	5	4	26	34	44	54	53	40	23	12	4	−1
SD	Sioux Falls	61	−36	−31	−23	5	17	33	38	34	22	9	−17	−28	−36
TN	Memphis	65	−4	−11	12	29	38	48	52	48	36	25	9	−13	−13
	Nashville	67	−17	−13	2	23	34	42	51	47	36	26	−1	−10	−17
TX	Dallas-Fort Worth	53	4	7	15	29	41	51	59	56	43	29	20	−1	−1
	El Paso	67	−8	8	14	23	31	46	57	56	41	25	1	5	−8
	Houston	37	12	3	22	31	44	52	62	60	48	29	19	7	3
UT	Salt Lake City	78	−22	−30	2	14	25	35	40	37	27	16	−14	−21	−30
VT	Burlington	63	−30	−30	−20	2	24	33	39	35	25	15	−2	−26	−30
VA	Norfolk	58	−3	8	18	28	36	45	54	49	45	27	20	7	−3
	Richmond	77	−12	−10	11	23	31	40	51	46	35	21	10	−1	−12
WA	Seattle-Tacoma	62	–	1	11	29	28	38	43	44	35	28	6	6	–
	Spokane	59	−22	−24	−7	17	24	33	37	35	22	7	−21	−25	−25
WV	Charleston	59	−16	−12	–	19	26	33	46	41	34	17	6	−12	−16
WI	Milwaukee	66	−26	−26	−10	12	21	33	40	44	28	18	−5	−20	−26
WY	Cheyenne	71	−29	−34	−21	−8	16	25	38	36	8	−1	−16	−28	−34
PR	San Juan	52	61	62	60	64	66	69	69	70	69	46	66	59	46

– Represents zero.   [1] Represents the lowest observed temperature in any month.   [2] City office data.

Source: U.S. National Oceanic and Atmospheric Administration, *Comparative Climatic Data,* annual. See also <http://www.ncdc.noaa.gov/oa/climate/online/ccd/lowtmp.txt>.

Table 376. **Normal Monthly and Annual Precipitation—Selected Cities**

[**In inches.** Airport data, except as noted. The table data are the 30-year average values computed from the data recorded during the period 1971–2000]

State	Station	Jan.	Feb.	Mar.	Apr.	May	June	July	Aug.	Sept.	Oct.	Nov.	Dec.	Annual
AL	Mobile	5.75	5.10	7.20	5.06	6.10	5.01	6.54	6.20	6.01	3.25	5.41	4.66	66.29
AK	Juneau	4.81	4.02	3.51	2.96	3.48	3.36	4.14	5.37	7.54	8.30	5.43	5.41	58.33
AZ	Phoenix	0.83	0.77	1.07	0.25	0.16	0.09	0.99	0.94	0.75	0.79	0.73	0.92	8.29
AR	Little Rock	3.61	3.33	4.88	5.47	5.05	3.95	3.31	2.93	3.71	4.25	5.73	4.71	50.93
CA	Los Angeles	2.98	3.11	2.40	0.63	0.24	0.08	0.03	0.14	0.26	0.36	1.13	1.79	13.15
	Sacramento	3.84	3.54	2.80	1.02	0.53	0.20	0.05	0.06	0.36	0.89	2.19	2.45	17.93
	San Diego	2.28	2.04	2.26	0.75	0.20	0.09	0.03	0.09	0.21	0.44	1.07	1.31	10.77
	San Francisco	4.45	4.01	3.26	1.17	0.38	0.11	0.03	0.07	0.20	1.04	2.49	2.89	20.11
CO	Denver	0.51	0.49	1.28	1.93	2.32	1.56	2.16	1.82	1.14	0.99	0.98	0.63	15.81
CT	Hartford	3.84	2.96	3.88	3.86	4.39	3.85	3.67	3.98	4.13	3.94	4.06	3.60	46.16
DE	Wilmington	3.43	2.81	3.97	3.39	4.15	3.59	4.28	3.51	4.01	3.08	3.19	3.40	42.81
DC	Washington	3.21	2.63	3.60	2.77	3.82	3.13	3.66	3.44	3.79	3.22	3.03	3.05	39.35
FL	Jacksonville	3.69	3.15	3.93	3.14	3.48	5.37	5.97	6.87	7.90	3.86	2.34	2.64	52.34
	Miami	1.88	2.07	2.56	3.36	5.52	8.54	5.79	8.63	8.38	6.19	3.43	2.18	58.53
GA	Atlanta	5.02	4.68	5.38	3.62	3.95	3.63	5.12	3.67	4.09	3.11	4.10	3.82	50.20
HI	Honolulu	2.73	2.35	1.89	1.11	0.78	0.43	0.50	0.46	0.74	2.18	2.26	2.85	18.29
ID	Boise	1.39	1.14	1.41	1.27	1.27	0.74	0.39	0.30	0.76	0.76	1.38	1.38	12.19
IL	Chicago	1.75	1.63	2.65	3.68	3.38	3.63	3.51	4.62	3.27	2.71	3.01	2.43	36.27
	Peoria	1.50	1.67	2.83	3.56	4.17	3.84	4.02	3.16	3.12	2.76	2.99	2.40	36.03
IN	Indianapolis	2.48	2.41	3.44	3.61	4.35	4.13	4.42	3.82	2.88	2.76	3.61	3.03	40.95
IA	Des Moines	1.03	1.19	2.21	3.58	4.25	4.57	4.18	4.51	3.15	2.62	2.10	1.33	34.72
KS	Wichita	0.84	1.02	2.71	2.57	4.16	4.25	3.31	2.94	2.96	2.45	1.82	1.35	30.38
KY	Louisville	3.28	3.25	4.41	3.91	4.88	3.76	4.30	3.41	3.05	2.79	3.80	3.69	44.54
LA	New Orleans	5.87	5.47	5.24	5.02	4.62	6.83	6.20	6.15	5.55	3.05	5.09	5.07	64.16
ME	Portland	4.09	3.14	4.14	4.26	3.82	3.28	3.32	3.05	3.37	4.40	4.72	4.24	45.83
MD	Baltimore	3.47	3.02	3.93	3.00	3.89	3.43	3.85	3.74	3.98	3.16	3.12	3.35	41.94
MA	Boston	3.92	3.30	3.85	3.60	3.24	3.22	3.06	3.37	3.47	3.79	3.98	3.73	42.53
MI	Detroit	1.91	1.88	2.52	3.05	3.05	3.55	3.16	3.10	3.27	2.23	2.66	2.51	32.89
	Sault Ste. Marie	2.64	1.60	2.41	2.57	2.50	3.00	3.14	3.47	3.71	3.32	3.40	2.91	34.67
MN	Duluth	1.12	0.83	1.69	2.09	2.95	4.25	4.20	4.22	4.13	2.46	2.12	0.94	31.00
	Minneapolis-St. Paul. . . .	1.04	0.79	1.86	2.31	3.24	4.34	4.04	4.05	2.69	2.11	1.94	1.00	29.41
MS	Jackson	5.67	4.50	5.74	5.98	4.86	3.82	4.69	3.66	3.23	3.42	5.04	5.34	55.95
MO	Kansas City	1.15	1.31	2.44	3.38	5.39	4.44	4.42	3.54	4.64	3.33	2.30	1.64	37.98
	St. Louis	2.14	2.28	3.60	3.69	4.11	3.76	3.90	2.98	2.96	2.76	3.71	2.86	38.75
MT	Great Falls	0.68	0.51	1.01	1.40	2.53	2.24	1.45	1.65	1.23	0.93	0.59	0.67	14.89
NE	Omaha	0.77	0.80	2.13	2.94	4.44	3.95	3.86	3.21	3.17	2.21	1.82	0.92	30.22
NV	Reno	1.06	1.06	0.86	0.35	0.62	0.47	0.24	0.27	0.45	0.42	0.80	0.88	7.48
NH	Concord	2.97	2.36	3.04	3.07	3.33	3.10	3.37	3.21	3.16	3.46	3.57	2.96	37.60
NJ	Atlantic City	3.60	2.85	4.06	3.45	3.38	2.66	3.86	4.32	3.14	2.86	3.26	3.15	40.59
NM	Albuquerque	0.49	0.44	0.61	0.50	0.60	0.65	1.27	1.73	1.07	1.00	0.62	0.49	9.47
NY	Albany	2.71	2.27	3.17	3.25	3.67	3.74	3.50	3.68	3.31	3.23	3.31	2.76	38.60
	Buffalo	3.16	2.42	2.99	3.04	3.35	3.82	3.14	3.87	3.84	3.19	3.92	3.80	40.54
	New York [1]	4.13	3.15	4.37	4.28	4.69	3.84	4.62	4.22	4.23	3.85	4.36	3.95	49.69
NC	Charlotte	4.00	3.55	4.39	2.95	3.66	3.42	3.79	3.72	3.83	3.66	3.36	3.18	43.51
	Raleigh	4.02	3.47	4.03	2.80	3.79	3.42	4.29	3.78	4.26	3.18	2.97	3.04	43.05
ND	Bismarck	0.45	0.51	0.85	1.46	2.22	2.59	2.58	2.15	1.61	1.28	0.70	0.44	16.84
OH	Cincinnati	2.92	2.75	3.90	3.96	4.59	4.42	3.75	3.79	2.82	2.96	3.46	3.28	42.60
	Cleveland	2.48	2.29	2.94	3.37	3.50	3.89	3.52	3.69	3.77	2.73	3.38	3.14	38.71
	Columbus	2.53	2.20	2.89	3.25	3.88	4.07	4.61	3.72	2.92	2.31	3.19	2.93	38.52
OK	Oklahoma City	1.28	1.56	2.90	3.00	5.44	4.63	2.94	2.48	3.98	3.64	2.11	1.89	35.85
OR	Portland	5.07	4.18	3.71	2.64	2.38	1.59	0.72	0.93	1.65	2.88	5.61	5.71	37.07
PA	Philadelphia	3.52	2.74	3.81	3.49	3.88	3.29	4.39	3.82	3.88	2.75	3.16	3.31	42.05
	Pittsburgh	2.70	2.37	3.17	3.01	3.80	4.12	3.96	3.38	3.21	2.25	3.02	2.86	37.85
RI	Providence	4.37	3.45	4.43	4.16	3.66	3.38	3.17	3.90	3.70	3.69	4.40	4.14	46.45
SC	Columbia	4.66	3.84	4.59	2.98	3.17	4.99	5.54	5.41	3.94	2.89	2.88	3.38	48.27
SD	Sioux Falls	0.51	0.51	1.81	2.65	3.39	3.49	2.93	3.01	2.58	1.93	1.36	0.52	24.69
TN	Memphis	4.24	4.31	5.58	5.79	5.15	4.30	4.22	3.00	3.31	3.31	5.76	5.68	54.65
	Nashville	3.97	3.69	4.87	3.93	5.07	4.08	3.77	3.28	3.59	2.87	4.45	4.54	48.11
TX	Dallas-Fort Worth	1.90	2.37	3.06	3.20	5.15	3.23	2.12	2.03	2.42	4.11	2.57	2.57	34.73
	El Paso	0.45	0.39	0.26	0.23	0.38	0.87	1.49	1.75	1.61	0.81	0.42	0.77	9.43
	Houston	3.68	2.98	3.36	3.60	5.15	5.35	3.18	3.83	4.33	4.50	4.19	3.69	47.84
UT	Salt Lake City	1.37	1.33	1.91	2.02	2.09	0.77	0.72	0.76	1.33	1.57	1.40	1.23	16.50
VT	Burlington	2.22	1.67	2.32	2.88	3.32	3.43	3.97	4.01	3.83	3.12	3.06	2.22	36.05
VA	Norfolk	3.93	3.34	4.08	3.38	3.74	3.77	5.17	4.79	4.06	3.47	2.98	3.03	45.74
	Richmond	3.55	2.98	4.09	3.18	3.95	3.54	4.67	4.18	3.98	3.60	3.06	3.12	43.91
WA	Seattle-Tacoma	5.13	4.18	3.75	2.59	1.77	1.49	0.79	1.02	1.63	3.19	5.90	5.62	37.07
	Spokane	1.82	1.51	1.53	1.28	1.60	1.18	0.76	0.68	0.76	1.06	2.24	2.25	16.67
WV	Charleston	3.25	3.19	3.90	3.25	4.30	4.09	4.86	4.11	3.45	2.67	3.66	3.32	44.05
WI	Milwaukee	1.85	1.65	2.59	3.78	3.06	3.56	3.58	4.03	3.30	2.49	2.70	2.22	34.81
WY	Cheyenne	0.45	0.44	1.05	1.55	2.48	2.12	2.26	1.82	1.43	0.75	0.64	0.46	15.45
PR	San Juan	3.02	2.30	2.14	3.71	5.29	3.52	4.16	5.22	5.60	5.06	6.17	4.57	50.76

[1] City office data.

Source: U.S. National Oceanic and Atmospheric Administration, *Comparative Climatic Data*, annual. See also <http://www.ncdc.noaa.gov/oa/climate/online/ccd/nrmpcp.txt>.

Table 377. Mean Number of Days With Precipitation of 0.01 Inch or More—Selected Cities

[0.01 is the smallest amount of precipitation numerically recorded, and includes the liquid water equivalent of frozen precipitation. Airport data, except as noted. For period of record through 2006]

State	Station	Length of record (years)	Jan.	Feb.	Mar.	Apr.	May	June	July	Aug.	Sept.	Oct.	Nov.	Dec.	Annual
AL	Mobile	65	10	9	10	7	8	11	15	13	9	5	7	9	113
AK	Juneau	62	18	16	17	16	16	15	17	17	21	23	19	21	216
AZ	Phoenix	67	3	4	3	1	–	–	4	4	2	2	2	3	28
AR	Little Rock	64	9	9	10	9	10	8	8	6	7	7	8	9	100
CA	Los Angeles	71	6	6	5	3	1	–	–	1	1	2	3	5	33
	Sacramento	67	10	8	8	5	2	1	1	1	1	3	7	9	56
	San Diego	66	6	6	6	4	2	–	1	–	1	2	4	6	38
	San Francisco	79	11	10	10	6	2	1	1	1	1	3	7	10	63
CO	Denver.	64	5	5	8	8	10	8	9	8	6	5	5	5	82
CT	Hartford	52	11	10	11	11	12	11	9	9	9	8	10	11	122
DE	Wilmington	59	10	9	10	11	11	9	9	8	8	7	9	9	110
DC	Washington	65	10	8	10	9	11	9	9	8	8	7	8	9	106
FL	Jacksonville	65	8	7	8	6	7	12	14	14	13	8	6	7	110
	Miami	64	6	6	6	6	10	15	16	17	17	13	8	6	126
GA	Atlanta.	72	11	10	11	8	8	9	10	11	9	7	6	8	10	110
HI	Honolulu	57	9	8	8	8	6	5	7	5	6	8	9	9	88
ID	Boise.	67	11	9	9	8	7	5	2	2	3	5	10	11	82
IL	Chicago.	48	10	9	12	12	11	9	9	9	9	9	10	10	119
	Peoria	67	9	8	10	11	11	9	8	8	8	8	9	9	108
IN	Indianapolis	67	11	10	12	12	12	10	9	8	7	8	10	11	120
IA	Des Moines	67	7	7	9	10	11	10	9	9	8	7	7	7	101
KS	Wichita	53	5	5	7	7	7	10	9	7	7	6	5	5	80
KY	Louisville	59	11	10	12	11	11	10	10	8	7	7	10	11	118
LA	New Orleans.	58	9	8	8	6	7	11	14	13	9	6	7	9	107
ME	Portland.	66	11	9	11	11	12	11	9	9	8	9	11	11	122
MD	Baltimore	56	10	9	10	10	11	9	9	9	7	7	8	9	108
MA	Boston.	55	11	10	11	11	11	10	9	9	8	9	10	11	120
MI	Detroit.	48	13	10	12	12	11	10	9	9	9	9	11	13	128
	Sault Ste. Marie.	65	18	14	12	11	11	11	10	10	13	14	17	19	160
MN	Duluth	65	11	9	10	10	12	12	11	11	11	9	10	11	127
	Minneapolis-St. Paul. . .	68	9	7	10	10	11	11	10	9	9	8	8	9	111
MS	Jackson.	43	10	9	10	8	9	8	10	9	7	6	8	9	103
MO	Kansas City	34	7	7	9	10	11	10	8	8	8	7	7	6	98
	St. Louis	49	8	8	10	11	11	9	8	8	7	8	9	9	106
MT	Great Falls	69	8	7	9	9	11	12	7	7	7	6	6	7	96
NE	Omaha	70	6	6	8	9	11	10	9	8	8	6	5	6	92
NV	Reno	64	6	6	6	4	4	3	2	2	2	2	4	6	47
NH	Concord.	65	10	9	11	11	12	11	10	9	9	9	11	10	122
NJ	Atlantic City	63	10	9	10	11	10	8	9	8	7	7	9	9	107
NM	Albuquerque	67	3	4	4	3	4	3	8	9	5	4	3	4	54
NY	Albany.	60	12	10	12	12	13	11	10	10	9	9	11	12	131
	Buffalo.	63	19	16	15	14	12	10	10	10	11	11	15	19	162
	New York [1]	137	11	9	11	10	11	10	10	9	8	8	9	10	116
NC	Charlotte	67	10	9	10	8	9	9	11	9	7	6	7	9	104
	Raleigh	62	10	9	10	9	10	9	11	10	7	7	8	9	109
ND	Bismarck	67	7	6	8	7	9	11	9	8	7	5	6	7	90
OH	Cincinnati.	59	12	11	12	12	12	10	10	9	7	8	10	11	124
	Cleveland.	65	16	14	15	14	13	10	10	9	9	11	14	16	151
	Columbus.	67	13	11	13	13	13	11	10	9	8	8	11	12	132
OK	Oklahoma City	67	5	6	7	7	9	8	6	6	7	6	5	5	77
OR	Portland.	66	18	15	17	14	12	9	3	4	7	12	18	18	147
PA	Philadelphia	66	10	9	10	10	11	10	9	9	8	7	9	10	112
	Pittsburgh.	54	16	13	15	13	12	11	10	9	9	10	12	15	145
RI	Providence	53	11	9	11	11	11	10	8	9	8	8	10	11	117
SC	Columbia	59	10	9	10	8	8	10	11	10	7	6	7	9	105
SD	Sioux Falls	61	6	6	8	9	10	11	9	8	8	6	6	6	93
TN	Memphis	56	10	9	10	9	9	8	8	7	7	6	8	9	100
	Nashville	65	11	10	11	10	11	9	10	8	7	7	9	10	113
TX	Dallas-Fort Worth.	53	6	6	7	7	8	6	4	4	6	6	6	6	72
	El Paso	67	3	3	2	1	2	3	7	7	5	4	2	3	42
	Houston.	37	10	8	9	6	8	9	9	9	8	7	8	9	100
UT	Salt Lake City	78	10	8	9	9	8	5	4	5	5	6	8	9	86
VT	Burlington.	63	14	11	12	12	13	12	12	12	11	11	14	14	148
VA	Norfolk.	58	10	9	10	10	10	9	11	10	8	7	8	9	111
	Richmond.	69	10	9	10	9	10	9	11	9	8	7	8	9	109
WA	Seattle-Tacoma	62	18	15	16	13	10	9	5	5	8	13	17	18	147
	Spokane	59	14	10	11	9	9	7	4	4	5	7	12	14	106
WV	Charleston	59	15	13	14	13	13	11	12	10	9	9	11	13	143
WI	Milwaukee	66	11	9	11	12	11	10	9	9	8	9	10	10	119
WY	Cheyenne	71	5	6	9	9	12	11	10	10	7	6	6	5	96
PR	San Juan	51	17	13	12	13	16	15	19	18	17	17	18	19	194

– Represents zero.   [1] City office data.

Source: U.S. National Oceanic and Atmospheric Administration, *Comparative Climatic Data,* annual. See also <http://www.ncdc.noaa.gov/oa/climate/online/ccd/prge01.txt>.

Table 378. Snow, Hail, Ice Pellets, and Sleet—Selected Cities

[**In inches.** Airport data, except as noted. For period of record through 2006. **T denotes trace.** Stations may show snowfall (hail) during the warm months]

State	Station	Length of record (years)	Jan.	Feb.	Mar.	Apr.	May	June	July	Aug.	Sept.	Oct.	Nov.	Dec.	Annual
AL	Mobile..........	64	0.1	0.1	0.1	T	T	–	T	–	–	–	T	0.1	0.4
AK	Juneau.........	62	25.9	18.4	14.5	3.3	T	T	–	–	T	1	12.5	21.3	96.2
AZ	Phoenix.........	62	T	–	T	T	T	–	–	–	–	T	–	T	–
AR	Little Rock.......	56	2.4	1.5	0.5	T	T	T	–	–	–	T	0.2	0.6	5.2
CA	Los Angeles......	62	T	T	T	–	–	–	–	–	–	–	–	T	–
	Sacramento......	50	T	T	T	–	T	–	–	–	–	–	–	T	–
	San Diego.......	60	T	–	T	T	–	–	–	–	–	–	T	T	–
	San Francisco	69	–	T	T	–	–	–	–	–	–	–	–	–	–
CO	Denver..........	62	8.0	7.4	12.4	8.8	1.6	–	T	T	1.6	3.8	9.0	7.7	60.3
CT	Hartford.........	49	13.5	12.5	10.1	1.5	–	T	–	–	–	0.1	2.1	10.5	50
DE	Wilmington.......	56	6.9	6.7	3.2	0.2	T	T	T	–	–	0.1	0.9	3.4	21.3
DC	Washington......	63	5.5	5.6	2.3	T	T	T	T	T	–	–	0.8	3.0	17.1
FL	Jacksonville......	60	T	–	–	T	–	T	T	–	–	–	–	–	–
	Miami..........	59	–	–	–	–	T	–	–	–	–	–	–	–	–
GA	Atlanta.........	67	1.0	0.5	0.4	T	–	–	T	–	–	T	T	0.2	2.1
HI	Honolulu	52	–	–	–	–	–	–	–	–	–	–	–	–	–
ID	Boise	67	6.4	3.6	1.7	0.6	0.1	T	T	T	T	0.1	2.3	5.6	20.6
IL	Chicago.........	47	11.4	7.6	6.7	1.6	0.1	T	T	T	T	0.4	2.1	8.1	38.2
	Peoria	63	6.6	5.0	4.2	0.8	T	T	T	–	T	0.1	2.1	6.2	25.1
IN	Indianapolis	75	6.9	5.5	3.5	0.5	T	T	T	–	–	0.2	1.9	5.4	24.1
IA	Des Moines	63	8.2	7.2	6.1	1.9	T	T	T	–	T	0.3	3.1	6.5	33.6
KS	Wichita	53	3.9	4.2	2.7	0.2	T	T	T	T	T	–	1.4	3.5	15.9
KY	Louisville........	59	5.2	4.2	3.1	0.1	T	T	T	T	–	0.1	1.0	2.5	16.3
LA	New Orleans	51	T	0.1	T	T	T	–	–	–	–	–	T	0.1	0.2
ME	Portland	66	19.2	16.4	13.3	2.9	0.2	–	T	–	T	0.2	3.3	14.5	70.6
MD	Baltimore........	56	6.3	7.2	3.6	0.1	T	T	T	–	–	T	1.0	3.3	21.4
MA	Boston	69	13.0	12.1	8.2	1.9	–	T	T	–	–	T	1.3	7.7	43.3
MI	Detroit..........	48	11.0	9.0	6.8	1.9	T	–	–	–	T	0.2	2.5	10.0	41.9
	Sault Ste. Marie ...	59	29.1	18.4	14.4	5.8	0.5	T	T	T	T	0.1	2.4	15.6	30.7	117.4
MN	Duluth..........	63	18.1	12.3	13.8	6.7	0.7	T	T	T	T	0.1	1.6	12.7	15.3	81.5
	Minneapolis-St. Paul.	64	10.6	8.0	10.6	2.8	0.1	T	T	T	T	0.5	7.7	9.4	49.9
MS	Jackson.........	38	0.5	0.2	0.2	T	–	–	–	T	–	–	T	0.1	1.0
MO	Kansas City	72	5.4	4.4	3.4	0.8	–	T	T	T	–	0.1	1.3	4.4	20.0
	St. Louis	70	5.3	4.5	3.7	0.5	T	T	T	–	–	T	1.4	4.0	19.5
MT	Great Falls.......	69	9.3	8.4	10.8	6.9	1.9	0.3	T	0.1	1.5	3.5	7.5	8.1	58.4
NE	Omaha	71	7.5	6.9	6.3	1.1	0.1	T	T	T	T	0.3	2.6	5.7	30.6
NV	Reno	57	6.1	5.2	4.3	1.2	0.8	–	–	–	–	0.3	2.5	4.6	25
NH	Concord	65	18.0	14.1	11.4	2.7	0.1	T	–	–	T	0.1	3.8	13.8	64.5
NJ	Atlantic City	57	5.0	5.7	2.5	0.3	T	T	T	–	–	T	0.4	2.4	16.3
NM	Albuquerque......	67	2.5	2.1	1.8	0.6	T	T	T	T	T	0.1	1.2	3.0	11.0
NY	Albany	60	17.2	13.4	11.6	2.8	0.1	T	T	T	T	0.2	4.1	14.4	64.4
	Buffalo	63	24.4	17.7	12.5	3.2	0.2	T	T	T	T	0.7	11.1	23.9	94.1
	New York [1].......	138	7.7	8.7	5.1	0.9	T	–	T	–	–	T	0.9	5.6	28.8
NC	Charlotte........	67	2.2	1.8	1.2	T	T	T	–	–	–	T	0.1	0.5	5.8
	Raleigh	62	2.8	2.6	1.3	T	T	T	T	–	–	–	0.1	0.8	7.6
ND	Bismarck........	67	7.8	6.8	8.5	3.9	0.9	T	T	T	T	0.2	1.9	6.8	7.0	43.9
OH	Cincinnati........	59	7.2	5.5	4.2	0.5	–	T	T	T	–	0.3	2.0	3.8	23.7
	Cleveland	65	14.2	12.3	10.9	2.7	0.1	T	T	–	T	0.6	5.1	12.7	59.0
	Columbus	59	8.8	6.1	4.5	1.0	T	T	T	–	T	0.1	2.2	5.4	28.4
OK	Oklahoma City	67	3.2	2.4	1.5	T	T	T	T	T	T	T	0.6	1.9	9.5
OR	Portland	55	3.2	1.1	0.4	T	T	–	T	T	–	0.4	1.4	6.5
PA	Philadelphia......	64	6.2	7.1	3.4	0.3	T	T	–	–	–	T	0.7	3.4	21.1
	Pittsburgh	54	11.9	9.2	8.3	1.8	0.1	T	T	T	T	0.4	3.4	8.4	43.8
RI	Providence.......	53	9.9	9.9	7.4	0.7	0.2	–	–	–	–	0.1	1.3	7	36.7
SC	Columbia........	58	0.6	0.8	0.2	T	T	–	T	T	–	–	T	0.3	1.9
SD	Sioux Falls.......	61	6.9	7.9	9.3	3	T	T	T	T	T	0.9	6.1	6.9	41.4
TN	Memphis	49	2.2	1.4	0.8	T	T	T	–	–	–	T	0.1	0.6	5.1
	Nashville	60	3.7	3.0	1.5	–	–	T	–	T	–	–	0.4	1.4	10.1
TX	Dallas-Fort Worth ..	48	1.1	1.0	0.2	T	T	–	–	–	–	T	0.1	0.2	2.6
	El Paso.........	57	1.3	0.8	0.4	0.3	T	T	T	–	T	–	0.9	1.6	5.3
	Houston	72	0.2	0.2	T	T	T	T	–	–	–	–	–	0.4	0.4
UT	Salt Lake City.....	78	13.4	9.9	9.1	4.9	0.6	T	T	T	T	0.1	1.3	6.9	11.9	58.1
VT	Burlington	63	19.4	16.4	13.8	4.1	0.2	–	T	T	T	0.2	6.6	18.3	79.2
VA	Norfolk	56	3.0	2.9	1.0	–	T	T	–	–	–	–	–	1.0	7.9
	Richmond	67	5.0	3.9	2.4	0.1	–	T	–	T	–	T	0.4	2.0	13.8
WA	Seattle-Tacoma....	52	4.9	1.6	1.3	0.1	T	–	T	–	T	–	1.1	2.4	11.4
	Spokane	59	15.2	7.4	3.9	0.6	0.1	T	–	–	T	0.4	6.4	14.0	48.3
WV	Charleston.......	52	10.8	8.6	5.4	0.9	–	T	T	–	T	0.2	2.4	5.2	33.9
WI	Milwaukee	66	13.9	9.2	8.3	1.9	0.1	T	T	T	T	0.2	3.0	10.4	47.1
WY	Cheyenne	71	6.1	6.5	11.9	9.3	3.4	0.2	T	T	1.1	3.9	7.2	6.5	55.9
PR	San Juan........	51	–	–	–	–	–	–	–	–	T	–	–	–	–

– Represents zero.   [1] City office data.

Source: U.S. National Oceanic and Atmospheric Administration, *Comparative Climatic Data,* annual. See also <http://www.ncdc.noaa.gov/oa/climate/online/ccd/avgsnf.txt>.

Table 379. Cloudiness, Average Wind Speed, Heating and Cooling Degree Days, and Average Relative Humidity—Selected Cities

[Airport data, except as noted. For period of record through 2006, except heating and cooling normals for period 1971–2000. M = morning. A = afternoon]

State	Station	Cloudiness—average percentage of days [1] Length of record (yr.)	An-nual	Average wind speed (m.p.h.) Length of record (yr.)	An-nual	Jan.	July	Heating degree days	Cooling degree days	Length of record (yr.)	Annual M	Annual A	Jan. M	Jan. A	July M	July A
AL	Mobile	47	72.1	58	8.8	10.1	6.9	1,667	2,548	44	87	64	82	66	89	67
AK	Juneau	47	87.9	61	8.2	8.0	7.5	8,574	–	40	80	70	78	75	79	67
AZ	Phoenix	57	42.3	61	6.2	5.3	7.1	1,040	4,355	46	49	23	63	31	42	19
AR	Little Rock	35	67.5	64	7.7	8.4	6.7	3,084	2,086	42	82	62	79	65	85	61
CA	Los Angeles	60	59.8	58	7.5	6.7	7.9	1,286	682	47	79	66	71	61	86	68
	Sacramento	49	48.5	56	7.8	6.9	8.9	2,666	1,248	20	83	46	91	70	76	29
	San Diego	55	60.0	66	7.0	6.0	7.5	1,063	866	46	77	63	72	58	82	67
	San Francisco	68	56.2	79	10.6	7.2	13.6	2,862	142	47	84	63	86	68	86	60
CO	Denver	61	68.5	50	8.7	8.7	8.3	6,128	695	38	67	40	63	48	67	33
CT	Hartford	41	77.5	52	8.4	8.9	7.3	6,104	759	47	77	53	72	57	78	51
DE	Wilmington	47	73.4	58	9.0	9.8	7.8	4,887	1,125	59	78	55	75	60	79	54
DC	Washington	48	73.8	58	9.4	10.0	8.3	3,999	1,560	46	75	54	70	55	76	53
FL	Jacksonville	47	74.2	57	7.8	8.1	7.0	1,353	2,636	70	89	56	87	57	88	58
	Miami	46	79.7	57	9.2	9.5	7.9	155	4,383	42	83	61	84	59	82	63
GA	Atlanta	61	69.9	68	9.1	10.4	7.7	2,827	1,810	46	82	56	78	58	87	59
HI	Honolulu	47	75.3	57	11.3	9.4	13.1	–	4,561	37	72	56	80	61	67	51
ID	Boise	56	67.1	67	8.7	7.9	8.4	5,809	769	67	69	43	80	70	53	21
IL	Chicago	37	77.0	48	10.3	11.6	8.4	6,493	835	48	80	64	77	70	81	61
	Peoria	52	73.9	63	9.8	10.9	7.8	6,095	998	47	82	66	79	72	85	65
IN	Indianapolis	64	76.0	58	9.6	10.9	7.5	5,521	1,042	47	84	62	81	70	86	59
IA	Des Moines	46	71.3	57	10.7	11.4	8.9	6,432	1,052	45	80	65	76	70	82	63
KS	Wichita	39	64.9	53	12.2	11.9	11.3	4,765	1,658	53	79	60	78	66	78	55
KY	Louisville	47	74.6	59	8.3	9.5	6.8	4,352	1,443	46	81	58	77	64	84	57
LA	New Orleans	47	72.3	58	8.2	9.3	6.1	1,417	2,776	58	87	67	84	69	90	69
ME	Portland	54	72.3	66	8.7	9.0	7.6	7,325	347	66	79	59	75	60	80	59
MD	Baltimore	45	71.2	56	8.8	9.3	7.6	4,634	1,220	53	78	54	72	57	80	53
MA	Boston	60	73.2	49	12.4	13.7	11.0	5,630	777	42	73	58	68	58	73	57
MI	Detroit	37	79.5	48	10.2	11.8	8.5	6,449	727	48	81	60	80	69	81	54
	Sault Ste. Marie	54	81.9	65	9.2	9.6	7.8	9,230	145	65	85	66	80	73	88	61
MN	Duluth	47	79.0	57	11.0	11.6	9.4	9,742	189	45	81	68	77	72	85	64
	Minneapolis-St. Paul	57	74.0	68	10.5	10.5	9.4	7,882	699	47	78	64	75	69	79	60
MS	Jackson	30	69.6	43	6.9	8.2	5.2	2,368	2,290	43	89	64	85	69	92	66
MO	Kansas City	23	67.1	34	10.6	11.1	9.2	5,249	1,325	34	80	66	76	68	83	66
	St. Louis	47	72.4	57	9.6	10.6	8.0	4,757	1,561	46	81	64	80	69	82	61
MT	Great Falls	57	78.4	65	12.5	14.8	10.0	7,675	326	45	68	45	66	61	67	30
NE	Omaha	49	69.6	70	10.5	10.9	8.8	6,312	1,095	42	81	65	78	69	83	64
NV	Reno	53	56.7	64	6.6	5.6	7.2	5,601	493	43	68	31	79	50	58	18
NH	Concord	54	75.3	64	6.7	7.2	5.7	7,485	442	41	81	53	76	58	83	51
NJ	Atlantic City	37	74.2	48	9.8	10.7	8.3	5,113	935	42	81	56	78	58	82	57
NM	Albuquerque	56	54.2	67	8.9	8.0	8.9	4,281	1,290	46	58	29	67	38	58	27
NY	Albany	57	81.1	68	8.9	9.8	7.5	6,861	544	41	80	58	77	63	80	55
	Buffalo	52	85.2	67	11.8	13.9	10.2	6,693	548	46	80	63	79	72	78	55
	New York [2]	42	70.8	69	9.3	10.6	7.6	4,744	1,160	72	72	56	68	59	75	55
NC	Charlotte	49	70.2	57	7.4	7.8	6.6	3,208	1,644	46	82	53	77	55	86	56
	Raleigh	47	69.7	57	7.6	8.2	6.7	3,465	1,521	42	85	54	79	54	88	57
ND	Bismarck	56	74.5	67	10.2	10.0	9.2	8,809	471	47	80	62	76	71	83	55
OH	Cincinnati	44	77.8	59	9.0	10.4	7.2	5,200	1,053	44	82	60	79	68	85	57
	Cleveland	54	81.9	65	10.5	12.2	8.6	6,097	712	46	80	62	78	70	81	57
	Columbus	46	80.3	57	8.3	9.9	6.9	5,546	925	47	81	59	77	67	83	55
OK	Oklahoma City	44	61.9	58	12.2	12.5	10.9	3,663	1,907	41	79	61	77	63	79	57
OR	Portland	47	81.3	58	7.9	9.9	7.6	4,366	398	66	85	59	85	75	81	44
PA	Philadelphia	55	74.5	66	9.5	10.3	8.2	4,759	1,235	47	76	54	73	59	78	53
	Pittsburgh	43	83.8	54	9.0	10.4	7.3	5,829	726	46	80	58	77	66	83	54
RI	Providence	42	73.2	53	10.4	10.9	9.4	5,754	714	43	75	55	71	56	77	56
SC	Columbia	48	68.5	58	6.8	7.2	6.3	2,595	2,063	40	86	51	82	53	88	53
SD	Sioux Falls	50	71.2	58	11.0	10.9	9.8	7,746	757	43	82	66	78	71	83	61
TN	Memphis	43	67.7	58	8.8	10.0	7.5	3,033	2,190	67	80	60	77	65	83	61
	Nashville	54	72.0	65	8.0	9.3	6.9	3,658	1,656	41	82	63	78	67	87	63
TX	Dallas-Fort Worth	42	63.0	53	10.7	11.0	9.8	2,370	2,571	43	80	61	78	64	77	55
	El Paso	53	47.1	64	8.8	8.3	8.3	2,604	2,165	46	56	27	64	33	60	29
	Houston	26	75.3	37	7.6	8.1	6.9	1,525	2,893	37	89	67	84	69	91	65
UT	Salt Lake City	69	65.8	77	8.8	7.5	9.5	5,607	1,089	46	67	43	79	69	51	21
VT	Burlington	52	84.1	63	9.0	9.7	8.0	7,665	489	41	77	59	73	64	78	53
VA	Norfolk	47	71.0	58	10.5	11.4	8.9	3,342	1,630	58	78	58	74	59	81	59
	Richmond	50	72.7	58	7.7	8.1	6.9	3,878	1,466	72	83	53	79	56	84	56
WA	Seattle-Tacoma	51	84.2	58	8.8	9.5	8.1	4,797	173	47	84	62	82	74	82	49
	Spokane	48	76.4	59	8.9	8.7	8.6	6,820	394	47	78	52	86	79	64	27
WV	Charleston	47	82.2	59	5.8	6.9	4.8	5,427	1,064	59	84	57	78	63	90	59
WI	Milwaukee	55	75.3	66	11.5	12.6	9.7	7,096	616	46	79	67	76	70	81	65
WY	Cheyenne	60	71.0	49	12.9	15.1	10.4	7,289	280	47	65	44	57	50	69	37
PR	San Juan	40	80.0	51	8.3	8.3	9.6	–	5,426	51	79	65	82	64	79	67

– Represents zero.   [1] Percent of days that are either partly cloudy or cloudy.   [2] Airport data for sunshine.

Source: U.S. National Oceanic and Atmospheric Administration, Comparative Climatic Data, annual. See also <http://www.ncdc.noaa.gov/oa/climate/online/ccd/clpcdy.txt>;   <http://www.ncdc.noaa.gov/oa/climate/online/ccd/wndspd.txt>; <http://www.ncdc.noaa.gov/oa/climate/online/ccd/nrmhdd.txt>; <http://www.ncdc.noaa.gov/oa/climate/online/ccd/nrmcdd.txt>; and <http://www.ncdc.noaa.gov/oa/climate/online/ccd/relhum.txt>.

Section 7
Elections

This section relates primarily to presidential, congressional, and gubernatorial elections. Also presented are summary tables on congressional legislation; state legislatures; Black, Hispanic, and female officeholders; population of voting age; voter participation; and campaign finances.

Official statistics on federal elections, collected by the Clerk of the House, are published biennially in *Statistics of the Presidential and Congressional Election* and *Statistics of the Congressional Election.* Federal and state elections data appear also in *America Votes,* a biennial volume published by CQ Press (a division of Congressional Quarterly, Inc.), Washington, DC. Federal elections data also appear in the U.S. Congress, *Congressional Directory,* and in official state documents. Data on reported registration and voting for social and economic groups are obtained by the U.S. Census Bureau as part of the Current Population Survey (CPS) and are published in Current Population Reports, Series P20 (see text, Section 1).

Almost all federal, state, and local governmental units in the United States conduct elections for political offices and other purposes. The conduct of elections is regulated by state laws or, in some cities and counties, by local charter. An exception is that the U.S. Constitution prescribes the basis of representation in Congress and the manner of electing the president and grants to Congress the right to regulate the times, places, and manner of electing federal officers. Amendments to the Constitution have prescribed national criteria for voting eligibility. The 15th Amendment, adopted in 1870, gave all citizens the right to vote regardless of race, color, or previous condition of servitude. The 19th Amendment, adopted in 1919, further extended the right to vote to all citizens regardless of sex. The payment of poll taxes as a prerequisite to voting in federal elections was banned by the 24th Amendment in 1964. In 1971, as a result of the 26th Amendment, eligibility to vote in national elections was extended to all citizens, 18 years old and over.

Presidential election—The Constitution specifies how the president and vice president are selected. Each state elects, by popular vote, a group of electors equal in number to its total of members of Congress. The 23d Amendment, adopted in 1961, grants the District of Columbia three presidential electors, a number equal to that of the least populous state. Subsequent to the election, the electors meet in their respective states to vote for president and vice president. Usually, each elector votes for the candidate receiving the most popular votes in his or her state. A majority vote of all electors is necessary to elect the president and vice president. If no candidate receives a majority, the House of Representatives, with each state having one vote, is empowered to elect the president and vice president, again, with a majority of votes required.

The 22nd Amendment to the Constitution, adopted in 1951, limits presidential tenure to two elective terms of 4 years each or to one elective term for any person who, upon succession to the presidency, has held the office or acted as President for more than 2 years.

Congressional election—The Constitution provides that representatives be apportioned among the states according to their population, that a census of population be taken every 10 years as a basis for apportionment, and that each state have at least one representative. At the time of each apportionment, Congress decides what the total number of representatives will be. Since 1912, the total has been 435, except during 1960 to 1962 when it increased to 437, adding one representative each for Alaska and Hawaii. The total reverted to 435 after

Elections   235

reapportionment following the 1960 census. Members are elected for 2-year terms, all terms covering the same period. The District of Columbia, American Samoa, Guam, and the Virgin Islands each elect one nonvoting delegate, and Puerto Rico elects a nonvoting resident commissioner.

The Senate is composed of 100 members, two from each state, who are elected to serve for a term of 6 years. One-third of the Senate is elected every 2 years. Senators were originally chosen by the state legislatures. The 17th Amendment to the Constitution, adopted in 1913, prescribed that senators be elected by popular vote.

Voter eligibility and participation— The Census Bureau publishes estimates of the population of voting age and the percent casting votes in each state for presidential and congressional election years. These voting-age estimates include a number of persons who meet the age requirement but are not eligible to vote, (e.g. aliens and some institutionalized persons). In addition, since 1964, voter participation and voter characteristics data have been collected during November of election years as part of the CPS. These survey data include noncitizens in the voting age population estimates, but exclude members of the Armed Forces and the institutional population.

Statistical reliability—For a discussion of statistical collection and estimation, sampling procedures, and measures of statistical reliability applicable to Census Bureau data, see Appendix III.

Figure 7.1
Vote Cast for President by Major Political Party: 1996 to 2004

Democratic
Republican
Other major candidates[1]

Millions of votes

[1]Candidates with 1 million or more votes: 1996—Reform, Ross Perot; 2000—Green, Ralph Nader.

Source: Chart prepared by U.S. Census Bureau. For data, see Tables 380 and 381.

U.S. Census Bureau, Statistical Abstract of the United States: 2009

Table 380. **Vote Cast for President by Major Political Party: 1948 to 2004**

[**In thousands (48,834 represents 48,834,000), except percent and electoral vote.** Prior to 1960, excludes Alaska and Hawaii; prior to 1964, excludes DC. Vote cast for major party candidates includes the votes of minor parties cast for those candidates]

Year	Candidates for President		Vote cast for President						
	Democratic	Republican	Total popular vote [1] (1,000)	Democratic			Republican		
				Popular vote		Electoral vote	Popular vote		Electoral vote
				Number (1,000)	Per-cent		Number (1,000)	Per-cent	
1948....	Truman......	Dewey.......	48,834	24,106	49.4	303	21,969	45.0	189
1952....	Stevenson....	Eisenhower...	61,552	27,315	44.4	89	33,779	54.9	442
1956....	Stevenson....	Eisenhower...	62,027	26,739	43.1	73	35,581	57.4	457
1960....	Kennedy.....	Nixon.......	68,836	34,227	49.7	303	34,108	49.5	219
1964....	Johnson.....	Goldwater....	70,098	42,825	61.1	486	27,147	38.7	52
1968....	Humphrey....	Nixon........	73,027	30,989	42.4	191	31,710	43.4	301
1972....	McGovern....	Nixon........	77,625	28,902	37.2	17	46,740	60.2	520
1976....	Carter.......	Ford........	81,603	40,826	50.0	297	39,148	48.0	240
1980....	Carter.......	Reagan.......	86,497	35,481	41.0	49	43,643	50.5	489
1984....	Mondale.....	Reagan.......	92,655	37,450	40.4	13	54,167	58.5	525
1988....	Dukakis.....	Bush........	91,587	41,717	45.5	111	48,643	53.1	426
1992....	Clinton......	Bush........	104,600	44,858	42.9	370	38,799	37.1	168
1996....	Clinton......	Dole........	96,390	47,402	49.2	379	39,198	40.7	159
2000....	Gore........	Bush........	105,594	50,996	48.3	266	50,465	47.8	271
2004....	Kerry........	Bush........	122,349	58,895	48.1	251	61,873	50.6	286

[1] Include votes for minor party candidates, independents, unpledged electors, and scattered write-in votes.

Source: U.S. House of Representatives, Office of the Clerk, *Statistics of the Presidential and Congressional Election*, biennial. See also <http://clerk.house.gov/member_info/election.html>.

Table 381. **Vote Cast for Leading Minority Party Candidates for President: 1948 to 2004**

[**In thousands (1,169 represents 1,169,000).** See headnote, Table 380. Data do not include write-ins, scatterings, or votes for candidates who ran on party tickets not shown]

Year	Candidate	Party	Popular vote (1,000)	Candidate	Party	Popular vote (1,000)
1948 ..	Strom Thurmond ...	States' Rights.......	1,169	Henry Wallace.....	Progressive.........	1,156
1952 [1]	Vincent Hallinan....	Progressive........	135	Stuart Hamblen....	Prohibition.........	73
1956 [1]	T. Coleman Andrews.	States' Rights.......	91	Eric Hass........	Socialist Labor......	41
1960 ..	Eric Hass........	Socialist Labor.....	46	Rutherford Decker ..	Prohibition.........	46
1964 ..	Eric Hass........	Socialist Labor.....	43	Clifton DeBerry....	Socialist Workers ...	22
1968 [1]	George Wallace....	American Independent.	9,446	Henning Blomen ...	Socialist Labor......	52
1972 [1]	John Schmitz.....	American..........	993	Benjamin Spock.....	People's...........	9
1976 ..	Eugene McCarthy ..	Independent........	680	Roger McBride.....	Libertarian.........	172
1980 ..	John Anderson	Independent........	5,251	Ed Clark.........	Libertarian.........	920
1984 ..	David Bergland	Libertarian.........	227	Lyndon H. LaRouche.	Independent	79
1988 ..	Ron Paul........	Libertarian.........	410	Lenora B. Fulani...	New Alliance.......	129
1992 ..	H. Ross Perot.....	Independent........	19,722	Andre Marrou	Libertarian.........	281
1996 ..	H. Ross Perot.....	Reform...........	7,137	Ralph Nader	Green...........	527
2000 ..	Ralph Nader......	Green............	2,530	Pat Buchanan	Reform...........	324
2004 ..	Ralph Nader......	Green............	116	Michael Badnarik ...	Libertarian.........	369

[1] Data include write-ins, scatterings, and/or votes for candidates who ran on party tickets not shown.

Source: U.S. House of Representatives, Office of the Clerk, *Statistics of the Presidential and Congressional Election*, biennial. See also <http://clerk.house.gov/member_info/election.html>.

Table 382. **Democratic and Republican Percentages of Two-Party Presidential Vote by Selected Characteristics of Voters: 2000 and 2004**

[**In percent.** Covers citizens of voting age living in private housing units in the contiguous United States. Percentages for Democratic Presidential vote are computed by subtracting the percentage Republican vote from 100 percent; third-party or independent votes are not included as valid data. Data are from the National Election Studies and are based on a sample and subject to sampling variability; for details, see source]

| Characteristic | 2000 | | 2004 | | Characteristic | 2000 | | 2004 | |
	Demo-cratic	Repub-lican	Demo-cratic	Repub-lican		Demo-cratic	Repub-lican	Demo-cratic	Repub-lican
Total [1]	**52**	**48**	**50**	**50**	Black	92	8	90	10
Year of birth:					Education:				
1975 or later....	63	37	66	34	Less than high				
1959 to 1974 ...	46	54	45	55	school	65	35	69	31
1943 to 1958 ...	53	47	44	56	High school				
1927 to 1942 ...	48	52	51	49	diploma/				
1911 to 1926 ...	64	36	52	48	equivalent	53	47	46	54
1895 to 1910 ...	–	100	–	–	Some college,				
Sex:					no degree	50	50	47	53
Male.........	47	53	46	54	College	50	50	50	50
Female.......	56	44	53	47	Union household ..	61	39	64	36
Race:					Nonunion house-				
White	46	54	42	58	hold	50	50	46	54

– Represents zero.   [1] Includes other characteristics, not shown separately.

Source: American National Election Studies; <http://www.electionstudies.org/>.

U.S. Census Bureau, Statistical Abstract of the United States: 2009

Table 383. **Electoral Vote Cast for President by Major Political Party—States: 1964 to 2004**

[D = Democratic, R = Republican. For composition of regions, see map, inside front cover]

State	1964	1968 [1]	1972 [2]	1976 [3]	1980	1984	1988 [4]	1992	1996	2000 [5]	2004 [6]
Democratic . . .	**486**	**191**	**17**	**297**	**49**	**13**	**111**	**370**	**379**	**266**	**251**
Republican . . .	**52**	**301**	**520**	**240**	**489**	**525**	**426**	**168**	**159**	**271**	**286**
Northeast:											
Democratic	126	102	14	86	4	–	53	106	106	102	101
Republican	–	24	108	36	118	113	60	–	–	4	–
Midwest:											
Democratic	149	31	–	58	10	10	29	100	100	68	57
Republican	–	118	145	87	135	127	108	29	29	61	66
South:											
Democratic	121	45	3	149	31	3	8	68	80	15	16
Republican	47	77	165	20	138	174	168	116	104	168	173
West:											
Democratic	90	13	–	4	4	–	21	96	93	81	77
Republican	5	82	102	97	98	111	90	23	26	38	47
AL.	R-10	(1)	R-9	D-9	R-9	R-9	R-9	R-9	R-9	R-9	R-9
AK.	D-3	R-3	R-3	R-3	R-3	R-3	R-3	R-3	R-3	R-3	R-3
AZ.	R-5	R-5	R-6	R-6	R-6	R-7	R-7	R-8	D-8	R-8	R-10
AR.	D-6	(1)	R-6	D-6	R-6	R-6	R-6	D-6	D-6	R-6	R-6
CA.	D-40	R-40	R-45	R-45	R-45	R-47	R-47	D-54	D-54	D-54	D-55
CO.	D-6	R-6	R-7	R-7	R-7	R-8	R-8	D-8	R-8	R-8	R-9
CT.	D-8	D-8	R-8	R-8	R-8	R-8	R-8	D-8	D-8	D-8	D-7
DE.	D-3	R-3	R-3	D-3	R-3	R-3	R-3	D-3	D-3	D-3	D-3
DC.	D-3	D-3	D-3	D-3	D-3	D-3	D-3	D-3	D-3	5D-2	D-3
FL.	D-14	R-14	R-17	D-17	R-17	R-21	R-21	R-25	D-25	R-25	R-27
GA.	R-12	(1)	R-12	D-12	D-12	R-12	R-12	D-13	R-13	R-13	R-15
HI	D-4	D-4	R-4	D-4	D-4	R-4	D-4	D-4	D-4	D-4	D-4
ID	D-4	R-4	R-4	R-4	R-4	R-4	R-4	R-4	R-4	R-4	R-4
IL	D-26	R-26	R-26	R-26	R-26	R-24	R-24	D-22	D-22	D-22	D-21
IN	D-13	R-13	R-13	R-13	R-13	R-12	R-12	R-12	R-12	R-12	R-11
IA	D-9	R-9	R-8	R-8	R-8	R-8	D-8	D-7	D-7	D-7	R-7
KS.	D-7	R-7	R-7	R-7	R-7	R-7	R-7	R-6	R-6	R-6	R-6
KY.	D-9	R-9	R-9	D-9	R-9	R-9	R-9	D-8	D-8	R-8	R-8
LA.	R-10	(1)	R-10	D-10	R-10	R-10	R-10	D-9	D-9	R-9	R-9
ME	D-4	D-4	R-4	R-4	R-4	R-4	R-4	D-4	D-4	D-4	D-4
MD	D-10	D-10	R-10	D-10	D-10	R-10	R-10	D-10	D-10	D-10	D-10
MA	D-14	D-14	D-14	D-14	R-14	R-13	D-13	D-12	D-12	D-12	D-12
MI	D-21	D-21	R-21	R-21	R-21	R-20	R-20	D-18	D-18	D-18	D-17
MN	D-10	D-10	R-10	D-10	D-10	D-10	D-10	D-10	D-10	D-10	6D-9
MS	R-7	(1)	R-7	D-7	R-7	R-7	R-7	R-7	R-7	R-7	R-6
MO	D-12	R-12	R-12	D-12	R-12	R-11	R-11	D-11	D-11	R-11	R-11
MT	D-4	R-4	R-4	R-4	R-4	R-4	R-4	D-3	R-3	R-3	R-3
NE.	D-5	R-5	R-5	R-5	R-5	R-5	R-5	R-5	R-5	R-5	R-5
NV.	D-3	R-3	R-3	R-3	R-3	R-4	R-4	D-4	D-4	R-4	R-5
NH	D-4	R-4	R-4	R-4	R-4	R-4	R-4	D-4	D-4	R-4	D-4
NJ	D-17	R-17	R-17	R-17	R-17	R-16	R-16	D-15	D-15	D-15	D-15
NM	D-4	R-4	R-4	R-4	R-4	R-5	R-5	D-5	D-5	D-5	R-5
NY.	D-43	D-43	R-41	D-41	R-41	R-36	D-36	D-33	D-33	D-33	D-31
NC	D-13	1R-12	R-13	D-13	R-13	R-13	R-13	R-14	R-14	R-14	R-15
ND	D-4	R-4	R-3	R-3	R-3	R-3	R-3	R-3	R-3	R-3	R-3
OH	D-26	R-26	R-25	D-25	R-25	R-23	R-23	D-21	D-21	R-21	R-20
OK	D-8	R-8	R-8	R-8	R-8	R-8	R-8	R-8	R-8	R-8	R-7
OR	D-6	R-6	R-6	R-6	R-6	R-7	D-7	D-7	D-7	D-7	D-7
PA.	D-29	D-29	R-27	D-27	R-27	R-25	R-25	D-23	D-23	D-23	D-21
RI	D-4	D-4	R-4	D-4	D-4	R-4	D-4	D-4	D-4	D-4	D-4
SC.	R-8	R-8	R-8	D-8	R-8	R-8	R-8	R-8	R-8	R-8	R-8
SD.	D-4	R-4	R-4	R-4	R-4	R-3	R-3	R-3	R-3	R-3	R-3
TN.	D-11	R-11	R-10	D-10	R-10	R-11	R-11	D-11	D-11	R-11	R-11
TX.	D-25	D-25	R-26	D-26	R-26	R-29	R-29	R-32	R-32	R-32	R-34
UT.	D-4	R-4	R-4	R-4	R-4	R-5	R-5	R-5	R-5	R-5	R-5
VT.	D-3	R-3	R-3	R-3	R-3	R-3	R-3	D-3	D-3	D-3	D-3
VA.	D-12	R-12	2R-11	R-12	R-12	R-12	R-12	R-13	R-13	R-13	R-13
WA	D-9	D-9	R-9	3R-8	R-9	R-10	D-10	D-11	D-11	D-11	D-11
WV	D-7	D-7	R-6	D-6	D-6	R-6	4D-5	D-5	D-5	R-5	R-5
WI.	D-12	R-12	R-11	D-11	R-11	R-11	D-11	D-11	D-11	D-11	D-10
WY	D-3	R-3	R-3	R-3	R-3	R-3	R-3	R-3	R-3	R-3	R-3

– Represents zero. [1] Excludes 46 electoral votes cast for American Independent George C. Wallace as follows: AL 10, AR 6, GA 12, LA 10, MS 7, and NC 1. [2] Excludes one electoral vote cast for Libertarian John Hospers in Virginia. [3] Excludes one electoral vote cast for Ronald Reagan in Washington. [4] Excludes one electoral vote cast for Lloyd Bentsen for President in West Virginia. [5] Excludes one electoral vote left blank by a Democratic elector in the District of Columbia. [6] Excludes one electoral vote cast for Democratic vice presidential nominee John Edwards in Minnesota.

Source: U.S. House of Representatives, Office of the Clerk, *Statistics of the Presidential and Congressional Election*, biennial. See also <http://clerk.house.gov/member_info/election.html>.

U.S. Census Bureau, Statistical Abstract of the United States: 2009

Table 384. Popular Vote Cast for President by Political Party—States: 2000 and 2004

[In thousands (105,594 represents 105,594,000), except percent]

State	2000			Percent of total vote		2004			Percent of total vote	
	Total [1]	Demo-cratic Party	Repub-lican Party	Demo-cratic Party	Repub-lican Party	Total [1]	Demo-cratic Party	Repub-lican Party	Demo-cratic Party	Repub-lican Party
United States..	**105,594**	**50,996**	**50,465**	**48.3**	**47.8**	**122,349**	**58,895**	**61,873**	**48.1**	**50.6**
Alabama.........	1,666	693	941	41.6	56.5	1,883	694	1,176	36.8	62.5
Alaska..........	286	79	167	27.7	58.6	313	111	191	35.5	61.1
Arizona..........	1,532	685	782	44.7	51.0	2,013	894	1,104	44.4	54.9
Arkansas	922	423	473	45.9	51.3	1,055	470	573	44.5	54.3
California	10,966	5,861	4,567	53.4	41.7	12,421	6,745	5,510	54.3	44.4
Colorado.........	1,741	738	884	42.4	50.8	2,130	1,002	1,101	47.0	51.7
Connecticut......	1,460	816	561	55.9	38.4	1,579	857	694	54.3	43.9
Delaware	328	180	137	55.0	41.9	375	200	172	53.3	45.8
District of Columbia .	202	172	18	85.2	9.0	228	203	21	89.2	9.3
Florida	5,963	2,912	2,913	48.8	48.8	7,610	3,584	3,965	47.1	52.1
Georgia	2,583	1,116	1,420	43.2	55.0	3,302	1,366	1,914	41.4	58.0
Hawaii	368	205	138	55.8	37.5	429	232	194	54.0	45.3
Idaho...........	502	139	337	27.6	67.2	598	181	409	30.3	68.4
Illinois	4,742	2,589	2,019	54.6	42.6	5,274	2,892	2,346	54.8	44.5
Indiana..........	2,199	902	1,246	41.0	56.6	2,468	969	1,479	39.3	59.9
Iowa	1,353	639	634	47.2	46.9	1,507	742	752	49.2	49.9
Kansas..........	1,072	399	622	37.2	58.0	1,188	435	736	36.6	62.0
Kentucky	1,544	639	873	41.4	56.5	1,796	713	1,069	39.7	59.5
Louisiana	1,766	792	928	44.9	52.6	1,943	820	1,102	42.2	56.7
Maine...........	652	320	287	49.1	44.0	741	397	330	53.6	44.6
Maryland	2,025	1,144	814	56.5	40.2	2,384	1,334	1,025	56.0	43.0
Massachusetts.....	2,734	1,616	879	59.1	32.1	2,927	1,804	1,071	61.6	36.6
Michigan.........	4,233	2,170	1,953	51.3	46.1	4,839	2,479	2,314	51.2	47.8
Minnesota........	2,439	1,168	1,110	47.9	45.5	2,828	1,445	1,347	51.1	47.6
Mississippi	994	405	573	40.7	57.6	1,140	458	673	40.2	59.0
Missouri	2,360	1,111	1,190	47.1	50.4	2,731	1,259	1,456	46.1	53.3
Montana.........	411	137	240	33.4	58.4	450	174	266	38.6	59.1
Nebraska	697	232	434	33.3	62.2	778	254	513	32.7	65.9
Nevada	609	280	302	45.9	49.5	830	397	419	47.9	50.5
New Hampshire....	569	266	274	46.8	48.1	678	341	331	50.2	48.8
New Jersey.......	3,187	1,789	1,284	56.1	40.3	3,612	1,911	1,670	52.9	46.2
New Mexico	599	287	286	47.9	47.8	756	371	377	49.0	49.8
New York	6,960	4,108	2,403	59.0	34.5	7,448	4,181	2,807	56.1	37.7
North Carolina.....	2,915	1,258	1,631	43.1	56.0	3,501	1,526	1,961	43.6	56.0
North Dakota......	288	95	175	33.1	60.7	313	111	197	35.5	62.9
Ohio	4,702	2,184	2,350	46.4	50.0	5,628	2,741	2,860	48.7	50.8
Oklahoma........	1,234	474	744	38.4	60.3	1,464	504	960	34.4	65.6
Oregon..........	1,534	720	714	47.0	46.5	1,837	943	867	51.3	47.2
Pennsylvania......	4,912	2,486	2,281	50.6	46.4	5,770	2,938	2,794	50.9	48.4
Rhode Island......	409	250	131	61.0	31.9	437	260	169	59.4	38.7
South Carolina.....	1,384	566	787	40.9	56.9	1,618	662	938	40.9	58.0
South Dakota	316	119	191	37.6	60.3	388	149	233	38.4	59.9
Tennessee	2,076	982	1,062	47.3	51.1	2,437	1,036	1,384	42.5	56.8
Texas...........	6,408	2,434	3,800	38.0	59.3	7,411	2,833	4,527	38.2	61.1
Utah	771	203	515	26.3	66.8	928	241	664	26.0	71.5
Vermont	294	149	120	50.6	40.7	312	184	121	58.9	38.8
Virginia..........	2,739	1,217	1,437	44.4	52.5	3,195	1,455	1,717	45.5	53.7
Washington.......	2,487	1,248	1,109	50.2	44.6	2,859	1,510	1,305	52.8	45.6
West Virginia......	648	295	336	45.6	51.9	756	327	424	43.2	56.1
Wisconsin........	2,599	1,243	1,237	47.8	47.6	2,997	1,490	1,478	49.7	49.3
Wyoming	214	60	148	28.3	69.2	244	71	168	29.0	68.7

[1] Includes other parties.

Source: U.S. House of Representatives, Office of the Clerk, *Statistics of the Presidential and Congressional Election*, biennial. See also <http://clerk.house.gov/member_info/election.html>.

U.S. Census Bureau, Statistical Abstract of the United States: 2009

Table 385. Vote Cast for United States Senators, 2004 and 2006, and Incumbent Senators, 2008—States

[1,839 represents 1,839,000. D = Democrat, R = Republican, I = Independent]

State	2004 Total (1,000)[2]	2004 Percent for leading party	2006 Total (1,000)[2]	2006 Percent for leading party	Incumbent senators and year term expires[1] Name, party, and year	Incumbent senators and year term expires[1] Name, party, and year
Alabama	1,839	R-67.5	(X)	(X)	Jeffrey Sessions (R) 2009	Richard Shelby (R) 2011
Alaska	308	R-48.6	(X)	(X)	Lisa Murkowski (R) 2011	Ted Stevens (R) 2009
Arizona	1,962	R-76.7	1,527	R-53.3	Jon Kyl (R) 2013	John McCain (R) 2011
Arkansas	1,039	D-55.9	(X)	(X)	Blanche Lincoln (D) 2011	Mark Pryor (D) 2009
California	12,053	D-57.7	8,541	D-59.4	Barbara Boxer (D) 2011	Dianne Feinstein (D) 2013
Colorado	2,107	D-51.3	(X)	(X)	Wayne Allard (R) 2009	Ken Salazar (D) 2011
Connecticut	1,425	D-66.4	1,135	D-39.7	Christopher Dodd (D) 2011	Joseph Lieberman (I) 2013
Delaware	(X)	(X)	243	D-70.2	Joseph Biden (D) 2009	Thomas Carper (D) 2013
Florida	7,430	R-49.4	4,794	D-60.3	Mel Martinez (R) 2011	Bill Nelson (D) 2013
Georgia	3,221	R-57.8	(X)	(X)	Saxby Chambliss (R) 2009	Johnny Isakson (R) 2011
Hawaii	415	D-75.5	343	D-61.3	Daniel Akaka (D) 2013	Daniel Inouye (D) 2011
Idaho	504	R-99.2	(X)	(X)	Larry Craig (R) 2009	Michael Crapo (R) 2011
Illinois	5,142	D-70.0	(X)	(X)	Richard Durbin (D) 2009	Barack Obama (D) 2011
Indiana	2,428	D-61.6	1,341	R-87.4	Evan Bayh (D) 2011	Richard Lugar (R) 2013
Iowa	1,479	R-70.2	(X)	(X)	Chuck Grassley (R) 2011	Tom Harkin (D) 2009
Kansas	1,129	R-69.2	(X)	(X)	Sam Brownback (R) 2011	Pat Roberts (R) 2009
Kentucky	1,724	R-50.7	(X)	(X)	Jim Bunning (R) 2011	Mitch McConnell (R) 2009
Louisiana[3]	1,848	R-51.0	(X)	(X)	Mary Landrieu (D) 2009	David Vitter (R) 2011
Maine	(X)	(X)	545	R-74.4	Susan Collins (R) 2009	Olympia Snowe (R) 2013
Maryland	2,322	D-64.8	62	R-68.0	Barbara Mikulski (D) 2011	Benjamin Cardin (D) 2013
Massachusetts	(X)	(X)	2,244	D-66.9	Edward Kennedy (D) 2013	John Kerry (D) 2009
Michigan	(X)	(X)	3,780	D-56.9	Carl Levin (D) 2009	Debbie Stabenow (D) 2013
Minnesota	(X)	(X)	2,203	D-58.1	Norm Coleman (R) 2009	Amy Klobuchar (D) 2013
Mississippi	(X)	(X)	611	R-63.6	Thad Cochran (R) 2009	Roger Wicker (R) 2013
Missouri	2,706	R-56.1	2,128	D-49.6	Christopher Bond (R) 2011	Claire McCaskill (D) 2013
Montana	(X)	(X)	407	D-49.2	Max Baucus (D) 2009	John Tester (D) 2013
Nebraska	(X)	(X)	592	D-63.9	Chuck Hagel (R) 2009	Ben Nelson (D) 2013
Nevada	810	D-61.1	583	R-55.4	John Ensign (R) 2013	Harry Reid (D) 2011
New Hampshire	657	R-66.2	(X)	(X)	Judd Gregg (R) 2011	John Sununu (R) 2009
New Jersey	(X)	(X)	102	D-57.2	Robert Menendez (D) 2013	Frank Lautenberg (D) 2009
New Mexico	(X)	(X)	559	D-70.6	Jeff Bingaman (D) 2013	Pete Domenici (R) 2009
New York	7,448	D-58.9	4,701	D-57.4	Hillary Clinton (D) 2013	Charles Schumer (D) 2011
North Carolina	3,472	R-51.6	(X)	(X)	Richard Burr (R) 2011	Elizabeth Dole (R) 2009
North Dakota	311	D-68.3	218	D-68.8	Kent Conrad (D) 2013	Byron Dorgan (D) 2011
Ohio	5,426	R-63.8	2,258	D-100.0	Sherrod Brown (D) 2013	George Voinovich (R) 2011
Oklahoma	1,447	R-52.8	(X)	(X)	Tom Coburn (R) 2011	James Inhofe (R) 2009
Oregon	1,781	D-63.4	(X)	(X)	Gordon Smith (R) 2009	Ron Wyden (D) 2011
Pennsylvania	5,559	R-52.6	2,393	D-100.0	Robert Casey Jr. (D) 2013	Arlen Specter (R) 2011
Rhode Island	(X)	(X)	385	D-53.5	Sheldon Whitehouse (D) 2013	Jack Reed (D) 2009
South Carolina	1,597	R-53.7	(X)	(X)	Jim DeMint (R) 2011	Lindsey Graham (R) 2009
South Dakota	391	R-50.6	(X)	(X)	Tim Johnson (D) 2009	John Thune (R) 2011
Tennessee	(X)	(X)	1,834	R-50.7	Lamar Alexander (R) 2009	Bob Corker (R) 2013
Texas	(X)	(X)	4,315	R-61.7	John Cornyn (R) 2009	Kay Hutchison (R) 2013
Utah	912	R-68.7	571	R-62.4	Robert Bennett (R) 2011	Orrin Hatch (R) 2013
Vermont	307	D-70.6	262	R-32.4	Bernard Sanders (I) 2013	Patrick Leahy (D) 2011
Virginia	(X)	(X)	2,370	D-49.6	Jim Webb (D) 2013	John Warner (R) 2009
Washington	2,819	D-55.0	2,084	D-56.9	Maria Cantwell (D) 2013	Patty Murray (D) 2011
West Virginia	(X)	(X)	207	D-77.0	Robert Byrd (D) 2013	John Rockefeller (D) 2009
Wisconsin	2,950	D-55.4	2,138	D-67.3	Russell Feingold (D) 2011	Herb Kohl (D) 2013
Wyoming	(X)	(X)	196	R-68.9	Michael Enzi (R) 2009	John Barrasso (R) 2013

X Not applicable. [1] As of March 13, 2008. [2] Includes vote cast for minor parties. [3] Louisiana holds an open-primary election with candidates from all parties running on the same ballot. Any candidate who receives a majority is elected.

Source: U.S. House of Representatives, Office of the Clerk, *Statistics of the Presidential and Congressional Election*, biennial. See also <http://clerk.house.gov/member_info/electionInfo/index.html>.

Table 386. **Vote Cast for United States Representatives by Major Political Party—States: 2002 to 2006**

[In thousands (74,707 represents 74,707,000), except percent. R = Republican, D = Democrat, and I = Independent. In each state, totals represent the sum of votes cast in each Congressional District or votes cast for Representative-at-Large in states where only one member is elected. In all years there are numerous districts within the state where either the Republican or Democratic party had no candidate. In some states the Republican and Democratic vote includes votes cast for the party candidate by endorsing parties]

State	2002				2004				2006			
	Total[1]	Democratic	Republican	Percent for leading party	Total[1]	Democratic	Republican	Percent for leading party	Total[1]	Democratic	Republican	Percent for leading party
U.S.	**74,707**	**33,642**	**37,091**	**R-49.6**	**113,192**	**52,745**	**55,713**	**R-49.2**	**80,588**	**42,082**	**35,734**	**D-52.2**
AL	1,269	507	695	R-54.7	1,793	708	1,080	R-60.2	1,199	502	686	R-57.2
AK	228	39	170	R-74.5	300	67	213	R-71.1	235	94	133	R-56.6
AZ	1,194	472	682	R-57.1	1,871	598	1,128	R-60.3	1,493	627	771	R-51.7
AR	688	392	284	D-57.0	791	426	358	D-53.9	763	457	306	D-59.8
CA	7,258	3,731	3,226	D-51.4	11,624	6,224	5,031	D-53.5	8,293	4,720	3,314	D-56.9
CO	1,397	589	753	R-53.9	2,039	995	992	D-48.8	1,539	833	624	D-54.1
CT	989	509	466	D-51.5	1,429	786	630	D-55.0	1,075	649	420	D-60.4
DE	228	61	165	R-72.1	356	106	246	R-69.1	252	98	144	R-57.2
FL [2]	3,767	1,537	2,161	R-57.4	5,627	2,212	3,319	R-59.0	3,852	1,600	2,183	R-56.7
GA	1,919	814	1,105	R-57.6	2,961	1,141	1,820	R-61.5	2,070	932	1,138	R-55.0
HI	360	232	117	D-64.5	417	262	148	D-62.9	338	220	118	D-65.0
ID	405	138	256	R-63.3	572	171	401	R-70.1	445	177	248	R-55.7
IL	3,429	1,741	1,657	D-50.8	4,989	2,675	2,272	D-53.6	3,453	1,986	1,423	D-57.5
IN	1,521	641	841	R-55.3	2,416	999	1,382	R-57.2	1,667	812	832	R-49.9
IA	1,013	454	546	R-54.0	1,458	625	823	R-56.4	1,033	493	522	R-50.6
KS	830	260	536	R-64.6	1,156	387	724	R-62.6	845	369	459	R-54.3
KY	1,094	351	694	R-63.4	1,635	602	1,017	R-62.2	1,254	602	612	R-48.8
LA	1,140	391	668	R-58.6	1,259	478	780	R-62.0	916	309	580	R-63.3
ME	495	290	206	D-58.5	710	418	283	D-58.9	536	351	163	D-65.4
MD	1,659	904	753	D-54.5	2,254	1,311	896	D-58.2	1,701	1,099	547	D-64.6
MA	2,220	1,529	290	D-68.8	2,927	2,060	435	D-70.4	2,244	1,632	199	D-72.7
MI	3,056	1,507	1,474	D-49.3	4,631	2,242	2,289	R-49.4	3,646	1,923	1,625	D-52.7
MN	2,202	1,098	1,030	D-49.9	2,722	1,400	1,236	D-51.4	2,179	1,153	925	D-52.9
MS	678	320	339	R-50.0	1,116	335	659	R-59.0	601	260	304	R-50.7
MO	1,854	829	986	R-53.2	2,667	1,193	1,430	R-53.6	2,097	992	1,049	R-50.0
MT	331	108	214	R-64.6	444	146	286	R-64.4	406	159	239	R-58.9
NE	474	47	387	R-81.6	765	231	515	R-67.3	596	262	334	R-56.1
NV	502	171	301	R-60.0	791	334	421	R-53.2	575	288	260	D-50.1
NH	443	176	255	R-57.5	652	244	396	R-60.8	403	209	190	D-52.0
NJ	2,006	1,030	934	D-51.4	3,285	1,721	1,515	D-52.4	2,137	1,208	903	D-56.5
NM	437	262	175	D-59.9	743	385	358	D-51.8	561	313	248	D-55.8
NY	4,701	1,778	1,526	D-37.8	7,448	3,457	2,209	D-46.4	4,687	2,538	1,160	D-54.1
NC	2,244	971	1,209	R-53.9	3,413	1,670	1,743	R-51.1	1,941	1,027	914	D-52.9
ND	231	121	110	D-52.4	311	185	126	D-59.6	218	143	75	D-65.7
OH	3,158	1,332	1,776	R-56.2	5,184	2,515	2,650	R-51.1	3,961	2,082	1,870	D-52.6
OK	1,002	392	547	R-54.6	1,375	389	875	R-63.7	905	373	518	R-57.2
OR	1,240	677	529	D-54.6	1,772	952	762	D-53.7	1,357	766	557	D-56.4
PA	3,310	1,349	1,859	R-56.2	5,151	2,478	2,565	R-49.8	4,011	2,229	1,732	D-55.6
RI	329	225	97	D-68.3	402	279	113	D-69.5	373	265	42	D-71.0
SC	984	345	569	R-57.8	1,439	486	913	R-63.5	1,086	473	600	R-55.2
SD	337	154	180	R-53.5	389	208	179	D-53.4	334	230	98	D-69.1
TN	1,529	708	771	R-50.4	2,219	1,032	1,161	R-52.3	1,715	861	800	D-50.2
TX	4,295	1,885	2,291	R-53.3	6,959	2,714	4,013	R-57.7	4,141	1,831	2,094	R-50.6
UT	557	221	322	R-57.8	909	362	520	R-57.3	570	244	292	R-51.3
VT	225	(X)	73	I-64.3	305	22	74	I-67.5	263	140	117	D-53.2
VA	1,516	440	956	R-63.0	3,004	1,023	1,817	R-60.5	2,297	947	1,223	R-53.2
WA	1,739	907	779	D-52.2	2,730	1,609	1,095	D-58.9	2,054	1,244	798	D-60.6
WV	400	264	136	D-66.0	722	415	303	D-57.6	455	264	191	D-58.0
WI	1,638	677	889	R-54.3	2,822	1,369	1,381	R-48.9	2,063	1,003	1,040	R-50.4
WY	182	66	110	R-60.5	239	100	132	R-55.2	196	92	93	R-47.6

X Not applicable. [1] Includes votes cast for minor parties. [2] State law does not require tabulation of votes for unopposed candidates.

Source: U.S. House of Representatives, Office of the Clerk, *Statistics of the Presidential and Congressional Election*, biennial. See also <http://clerk.house.gov/member_info/electionInfo/index.html>.

Table 387. **Vote Cast for United States Representatives by Major Political Party—Congressional Districts: 2006**

[In some states the Democratic and Republican vote includes votes cast for the party candidate by endorsing parties]

State and district	Democratic candidate Name	Percent of total	Republican candidate Name	Percent of total
AL	(X)........	(X)	(X)......	(X)
1st...	Beckerle....	31.82	Bonner.....	68.10
2d...	James	30.43	Everett.....	69.47
3d...	Pierce.....	28.34	Rogers.....	70.11
4th..	Bobo	29.71	Aderholt....	70.18
5th..	Cramer, Jr. ..	98.25	(1)......	(1)
6th..	(1)........	(1)	Bachus.....	98.32
7th..	Davis......	99.04	(1)......	(1)
AK	Benson....	40.01	Young.....	56.57
AZ	(X)........	(X)	(X)........	(X)
1st...	Simon.....	43.45	Renzi.....	51.75
2d...	Thrasher....	38.89	Franks.....	58.62
3d...	Paine......	38.23	Shadegg....	59.27
4th..	Pastor.....	72.52	Karg	23.92
5th..	Mitchell.....	50.41	Hayworth...	46.44
6th..	(1)........	(1)	Flake	74.80
7th..	Grijalva.....	61.09	Drake......	35.35
8th..	Giffords.....	54.25	Graf.......	42.09
AR	(X)........	(X)	(X)........	(X)
1st...	Berry......	69.26	Stumbaugh ..	30.74
2d...	Snyder.....	60.53	Mayberry....	39.47
3d...	Anderson ..	37.77	Boozman...	62.23
4th..	Ross......	74.73	Ross	25.27
CA	(X)........	(X)	(X)........	(X)
1st...	Thompson ..	66.23	Jones......	28.98
2d...	Sekhon	32.46	Herger.....	64.18
3d...	Durston	37.83	Lungren	59.48
4th..	Brown	45.87	Doolittle	49.05
5th..	Matsui	70.80	Yan	23.52
6th..	Woolsey....	70.22	Hooper.....	26.11
7th..	Miller	83.99	(1)......	(1)
8th..	Pelosi......	80.39	Denunzio ...	10.72
9th..	Lee	86.35	Dendulk	10.73
10th..	Tauscher...	66.43	Linn.......	33.54
11th..	McNerney...	53.27	Pombo	46.73
12th..	Lantos	76.05	Moloney	23.95
13th..	Stark	74.89	Bruno......	25.11
14th..	Eshoo	71.08	Smith......	24.22
15th..	Honda	72.33	Chukwu	27.67
16th..	Lofgren	72.71	Winston	27.29
17th..	Farr	77.07	De Maio	22.93
18th..	Cardoza ...	65.48	Kanno	34.52
19th..	Cox	39.42	Radanovich..	60.58
20th..	Costa......	100.00	(1)......	(1)
21st..	Haze	29.94	Nunes	66.74
22d...	Beery	29.30	McCarthy ...	70.70
23d...	Capps	65.17	Tognazzini ..	34.83
24th..	Martinez....	37.97	Gallegly	62.02
25th..	Rodriguez ..	35.66	McKeon	59.95
26th..	Matthews ...	37.89	Dreier......	56.95
27th..	Sherman ...	68.77	Hankwitz....	31.23
28th..	Berman	73.92	Kesselman ..	19.09
29th..	Schiff......	63.47	Bodell	27.42
30th..	Waxman....	71.45	Jones......	26.40
31st..	Becerra	100.00	(1)......	(1)
32d...	Solis	82.96	(1)......	(1)
33d...	Watson.....	100.00	(1)......	(1)
34th..	Roybal-Allard.	76.80	Miller	23.20
35th..	Waters.....	83.75	(1)......	(1)
36th..	Harman	63.39	Gibson	31.94
37th..	Millender-McDonald ..	82.40	(1)......	(1)
38th..	Napolitano ..	75.33	Street......	24.67
39th..	Sanchez...	65.87	Andion	34.13
40th..	Hoffman	30.68	Royce	66.76
41st..	Contreras ...	33.07	Lewis......	66.93
42d...	(1)......	(1)	Miller	100.00
43d...	Baca	64.49	Folkens	35.51
44th..	Vandenberg..	37.02	Calvert	59.98
45th..	Roth	39.34	Bono	60.66
46th..	Brandt	36.69	Rohrabacher .	59.56
47th..	Sanchez....	62.33	Nguyen	37.67
48th..	Young	37.23	Campbell ...	59.91
49th..	Criscenzo...	33.45	Issa.......	63.30
50th..	Busby	43.50	Bilbray	53.14
51st..	Filner......	67.43	Miles	30.15
52d...	Rinaldi	31.98	Hunter	64.64
53d...	Davis	67.56	Woodrum ...	30.00
CO	(X)........	(X)	(X)........	(X)
1st...	Degette	79.77	(1)........	(1)
2d...	Udall	68.24	Mancuso ...	28.31
3d...	Salazar.....	61.59	Tipton	36.55
4th..	Paccione ...	43.12	Musgrave ...	45.61
5th..	Fawcett	40.35	Lamborn....	59.62
6th...	Winter	39.87	Tancredo ...	58.61
7th...	Perlmutter...	54.93	O'Donnell ...	42.06
CT	(X)........	(X)	(X)........	(X)
1st...	Larson	74.44	MacLean ...	25.54
2d...	Courtney ...	50.02	Simmons ...	49.98
3d...	Delauro	76.01	Vollano	22.43
4th...	Farrell	47.58	Shays	50.96
5th...	Murphy.....	56.46	Johnson ...	43.54
DE	Spivack	38.76	Castle	57.17
FL	(X)........	(X)	(X)........	(X)
1st...	Roberts	31.46	Miller	68.54
2d...	Boyd	(2)	(1)......	(1)
3d...	Brown	(2)	(1)......	(1)
4th..	Harms	30.32	Crenshaw ..	69.67
5th..	Russell.....	40.15	Brown-Waite .	59.85
6th..	Bruderly	40.12	Stearns	59.88
7th..	Chagnon ...	36.92	Mica	63.08
8th..	Stuart......	45.73	Keller......	52.79
9th..	Busansky ...	44.08	Bilirakis	55.91
10th..	Simpson....	34.07	Young	65.93
11th..	Castor	69.65	Adams, Jr. ..	30.34
12th..	(1)........	(1)	Putnam	69.12
13th..	Jennings....	49.92	Buchanan ..	50.08
14th..	Neeld......	35.63	Mack	64.37
15th..	Bowman....	43.72	Weldon.....	56.28
16th..	Mahoney ...	49.55	Negron	47.66
17th..	Meek	99.97	(1)......	(1)
18th..	Patlak	37.85	Ros-Lehtinen .	62.15
19th..	Wexler	(2)	(1)......	(1)
20th..	Schultz.....	(2)	(1)......	(1)
21st..	Gonzalez ...	40.53	Diaz-Balart ..	59.47
22d...	Klein	50.88	Shaw, Jr. ...	47.13
23d...	Hastings ...	(2)	(1)......	(1)
24th..	Curtis......	42.06	Feeney.....	57.94
25th..	Calderin	41.53	Diaz-Balart ..	58.47
GA	(X)........	(X)	(X)........	(X)
1st...	Nelson	31.50	Kingston....	68.50
2d...	Bishop, Jr. ..	67.87	Hughes	32.13
3d...	McGraw	32.35	Westmore-land	67.65
4th..	Johnson, Jr. .	75.36	Davis	24.64
5th..	Lewis......	100.00	(1)........	(1)
6th..	Sinton	27.61	Price	72.39
7th..	Burns	29.09	Linder	70.91
8th..	Marshall ...	50.55	Collins	49.45
9th..	Bradbury ...	23.37	Deal.......	76.63
10th..	Holley	32.64	Norwood....	67.36
11th..	Pillion......	28.94	Gingrey	71.06
12th..	Barrow	50.30	Burns......	49.70
13th..	Scott	69.24	Honeycutt...	30.76
HI	(X)........	(X)	(X)........	(X)
1st...	Abercrombie .	69.35	Hough	30.65
2d...	Hirono	61.04	Hogue	38.96
ID	(X)........	(X)	(X)........	(X)
1st...	Grant	44.80	Sali	49.94
2d...	Hansen	34.43	Simpson....	62.00

See footnotes at end of table.

U.S. Census Bureau, Statistical Abstract of the United States: 2009

Table 387. **Vote Cast for United States Representatives by Major Political Party—Congressional Districts: 2006**—Con.

[See headnote, p. 242]

State and district	Democratic candidate Name	Percent of total	Republican candidate Name	Percent of total	State and district	Democratic candidate Name	Percent of total	Republican candidate Name	Percent of total
IL.....	(X)	(X)	(X)	(X)	6th..	Tierney	66.35	Barton	28.82
1st..	Rush	84.06	Tabour	15.94	7th..	Markey	76.02	[1]	[1]
2d..	Jackson, Jr.	84.84	Belin	11.82	8th..	Capuano	78.73	[1]	[1]
3d..	Lipinski	77.10	Wardingley	22.90	9th..	Lynch	72.25	Robinson	20.09
4th..	Gutierrez	85.84	Melichar	14.16	10th..	Delahunt	62.08	Beatty	28.34
5th..	Emanuel	77.99	White	22.00	MI.....	(X)	(X)	(X)	(X)
6th..	Duckworth	48.65	Roskam	51.35	1st..	Stupak	69.42	Hooper	27.99
7th..	Davis	86.70	Hutchinson	13.30	2d..	Kotos	31.57	Hoekstra	66.45
8th..	Bean	50.90	McSweeney	44.01	3d..	Rinck	34.58	Ehlers	63.10
9th..	Schakowsky	74.59	Shannon	25.41	4th..	Huckleberry	37.94	Camp	60.57
10th..	Seals	46.62	Kirk	53.38	5th..	Kildee	72.89	Klammer	25.23
11th..	Pavich	44.90	Weller	55.10	6th..	Clark	37.93	Upton	60.59
12th..	Costello	100.00	[1]	[1]	7th..	Renier	45.98	Walberg	49.93
13th..	Shannon	41.66	Biggert	58.33	8th..	Marcinkowski	42.92	Rogers	55.27
14th..	Laesch	40.21	Hastert	59.79	9th..	Skinner	46.21	Knollenberg	51.56
15th..	Gill	42.41	Johnson	57.59	10th..	Denison	31.32	Miller	66.22
16th..	Auman	32.13	Manzullo	63.55	11th..	Trupiano	42.99	McCotter	54.05
17th..	Hare	57.17	Zinga	42.83	12th..	Levin	70.78	Shafer	26.34
18th..	Waterworth	32.72	LaHood	67.28	13th..	Kilpatrick	99.99	[1]	[1]
19th..	Stover	39.29	Shimkus	60.71	14th..	Conyers, Jr.	85.30	Miles	14.70
IN....	(X)	(X)	(X)	(X)	15th..	Dingell	87.95	[1]	[1]
1st..	Visclosky	69.65	Leyva	26.83	MN....	(X)	(X)	(X)	(X)
2d..	Donnelly	53.98	Chocola	46.02	1st..	Walz	52.74	Gutknecht	47.12
3d..	Hayhurst	45.72	Souder	54.28	2d..	Rowley	40.04	Kline	56.20
4th..	Sanders	37.62	Buyer	62.38	3d..	Wilde	35.04	Ramstad	64.85
5th..	Carr	31.41	Burton	64.96	4th..	McCollum	69.54	Sium	30.23
6th..	Welsh	39.99	Pence	60.01	5th..	Ellison	55.56	Fine	21.34
7th..	Carson	53.76	Dickerson	46.24	6th..	Wetterling	42.07	Bachmann	50.05
8th..	Ellsworth	61.02	Hostettler	38.98	7th..	Peterson	69.66	Barrett	28.99
9th..	Hill	50.01	Sodrel	45.49	8th..	Oberstar	63.61	Grams	34.39
IA.....	(X)	(X)	(X)	(X)	MS....	(X)	(X)	(X)	(X)
1st..	Braley	55.10	Whalen	43.25	1st..	Hurt	34.08	Wicker	65.92
2d..	Loebsack	51.43	Leach	48.57	2d..	Thompson	64.27	Brown	35.73
3d..	Boswell	51.90	Lamberti	46.50	3d..	[1]	[1]	Pickering	77.67
4th..	Spencer	42.79	Latham	57.21	4th..	Taylor	79.79	McDonnell	20.21
5th..	Schulte	35.58	King	58.53	MO....	(X)	(X)	(X)	(X)
KS....	(X)	(X)	(X)	(X)	1st..	Clay	72.89	Byrne	24.66
1st..	Doll	19.95	Moran	78.61	2d..	Weber	36.59	Akin	61.35
2d..	Boyda	50.60	Ryun	47.14	3d..	Carnahan	65.58	Bertelsen	31.70
3d..	Moore	64.61	Ahner	33.68	4th..	Skelton	67.64	Noland	29.40
4th..	McGinn	33.93	Tiahrt	63.53	5th..	Cleaver	64.25	Turk	32.30
KY....	(X)	(X)	(X)	(X)	6th..	Shettles	35.73	Graves	61.64
1st..	Barlow	40.42	Whitfield	59.58	7th..	Truman	30.11	Blunt	66.75
2d..	Weaver	44.59	Lewis	55.41	8th..	Hambacker	26.40	Emerson	71.64
3d..	Yarmuth	50.62	Northup	48.18	9th..	Burghard	35.91	Hulshof	61.45
4th..	Lucas	43.38	Davis	51.69	MT....	Lindeen	39.13	Rehberg	58.88
5th..	Stepp	26.24	Rogers	73.76	NE....	(X)	(X)	(X)	(X)
6th..	Chandler	85.46	[1]	[1]	1st..	Moul	41.64	Fortenberry	58.36
LA [3]	(X)	(X)	(X)	(X)	2d..	Esch	45.34	Terry	54.66
1st..	Gereighty	7.37	Jindal	88.10	3d..	Kleeb	45.01	Smith	54.99
2d..	Jefferson	32.69	Lavigne	11.63	NV....	(X)	(X)	(X)	(X)
3d..	Melancon	55.03	Romero	40.31	1st..	Berkley	64.84	Wegner	31.20
4th..	Cash, Sr.	16.95	McCrery	57.40	2d..	Derby	44.94	Heller	50.35
5th..	Hearn	29.00	Alexander	68.26	3d..	Hafen	46.57	Porter	48.46
6th..	[1]	[1]	Baker	82.81	NH....	(X)	(X)	(X)	(X)
7th..	Stagg	29.30	Boustany, Jr.	70.70	1st..	Shea-Porter	51.27	Bradley	48.64
ME....	(X)	(X)	(X)	(X)	2d..	Hodes	52.71	Bass	45.61
1st..	Allen	60.84	Curley	31.32	NJ....	(X)	(X)	(X)	(X)
2d..	Michaud	70.52	D'Amboise	29.48	1st..	Andrews	100.00	[1]	[1]
MD....	(X)	(X)	(X)	(X)	2d..	Thomas-Hughes	35.60	LoBiondo	61.61
1st..	Corwin	31.11	Gilchrest	68.80	3d..	Sexton	41.04	Saxton	58.40
2d..	Ruppersberger	69.21	Mathis	30.68	4th..	Gay	33.19	Smith	65.68
3d..	Sarbanes	64.03	White	33.76	5th..	Aronsohn	43.82	Garrett	54.91
4th..	Wynn	80.67	Starkman	18.64	6th..	Pallone, Jr.	68.59	Bellew	30.28
5th..	Hoyer	82.68	[1]	[1]	7th..	Stender	47.95	Ferguson	49.43
6th..	Duck	38.43	Bartlett	58.97	8th..	Pascrell, Jr.	70.89	Sandoval	28.37
7th..	Cummings	98.06	[1]	[1]	9th..	Rothman	71.48	Micco	27.60
8th..	Hollen	76.52	Stein	21.90	10th..	Payne	100.00	[1]	[1]
MA....	(X)	(X)	(X)	(X)	11th..	Wyka	36.64	Frelinghuysen	62.09
1st..	Olver	71.87	[1]	[1]	12th..	Holt	65.70	Sinagra	34.30
2d..	Neal	76.74	[1]	[1]	13th..	Sires	77.52	Guarini	19.36
3d..	McGovern	77.63	[1]	[1]					
4th..	Frank	77.79	[1]	[1]					
5th..	Meehan	73.38	[1]	[1]					

See footnotes at end of table.

[See headnote, p. 242]

State and district	Democratic candidate Name	Percent of total	Republican candidate Name	Percent of total	State and district	Democratic candidate Name	Percent of total	Republican candidate Name	Percent of total
NM.	(X)	(X)	(X)	(X)	3d	Blumenauer	73.49	Broussard	23.47
1st	Madrid	49.80	Wilson	50.20	4th	DeFazio	62.23	Feldkamp	37.59
2d	Kissling	40.49	Pearce	59.42	5th	Hooley	53.99	Erickson	42.77
3d	Udall	74.64	Dolin	25.36	**PA.**	(X)	(X)	(X)	(X)
NY.	(X)	(X)	(X)	(X)	1st	Brady	100.00	[1]	[1]
1st	Bishop	58.26	Zanzi	35.36	2d	Fattah	88.56	Gessner	9.23
2d	Israel	64.35	Bugler	27.03	3d	Porter	42.06	English	53.63
3d	Mejias	41.39	King	52.76	4th	Altmire	51.93	Hart	48.07
4th	McCarthy	59.69	Blessinger	32.26	5th	Hilliard	39.91	Peterson	60.09
5th	Ackerman	65.12	[1]	[1]	6th	Murphy	49.34	Gerlach	50.66
6th	Meeks	70.03	[1]	[1]	7th	Sestak	56.38	Weldon	43.62
7th	Crowley	64.45	Brawley	12.31	8th	Murphy	50.30	Fitzpatrick	49.70
8th	Nadler	76.15	Friedman	12.22	9th	Barr	39.67	Shuster	60.33
9th	Weiner	66.41	[1]	[1]	10th	Carney	52.95	Sherwood	47.05
10th	Towns	70.05	Anderson	4.53	11th	Kanjorski	72.47	Leonardi	27.53
11th	Clarke	77.61	Finger	6.54	12th	Murtha	60.80	Irey	39.20
12th	Velazquez	74.51	Romaguera	8.51	13th	Schwartz	66.13	Bhakta	33.87
13th	Harrison	38.89	Fossella	51.13	14th	Doyle	90.09	[1]	[1]
14th	Maloney	77.71	Maio	14.28	15th	Dertinger	43.50	Dent	53.57
15th	Rangel	80.44	Daniels	5.10	16th	Herr	39.55	Pitts	56.57
16th	Serrano	76.50	Mohamed	3.76	17th	Holden	64.53	Wertz	35.47
17th	Engel	65.95	Faulkner	20.32	18th	Kluko	42.16	Murphy	57.84
18th	Lowey	62.35	Hoffman	25.82	19th	Avillo, Jr.	33.50	Platts	63.97
19th	Hall	47.79	Kelly	45.52	**RI.**	(X)	(X)	(X)	(X)
20th	Gillibrand	50.01	Sweeney	44.17	1st	Kennedy	69.20	Scott	23.23
21st	McNulty	72.27	Redlich	20.16	2d	Langevin	72.69	[1]	[1]
22d	Hinchey	62.20	[1]	[1]	**SC.**	(X)	(X)	(X)	(X)
23d	Johnson	33.70	McHugh	57.74	1st	Maatta	37.86	Brown, Jr.	59.87
24th	Arcuri	51.03	Meier	42.57	2d	Ellisor	37.29	Wilson	62.64
25th	Maffei	47.12	Walsh	48.62	3d	Ballenger	37.10	Barrett	62.86
26th	Davis	45.06	Reynolds	48.78	4th	Griffith	31.95	Inglis	64.22
27th	Higgins	79.27	McHale	20.73	5th	Spratt, Jr.	56.90	Norman	43.06
28th	Slaughter	66.87	Donnelly	24.52	6th	Clyburn	64.36	McLeod	34.15
29th	Massa	46.15	Kuhl, Jr.	48.93	**SD.**	Herseth	69.09	Whalen	29.34
NC.	(X)	(X)	(X)	(X)	**TN.**	(X)	(X)	(X)	(X)
1st	Butterfield	100.00	[1]	[1]	1st	Trent	36.97	Davis	61.11
2d	Etheridge	66.53	Mansell	33.47	2d	Greene	22.28	Duncan, Jr.	77.72
3d	Weber	31.36	Jones	68.64	3d	Benedict	34.31	Wamp	65.69
4th	Price	64.99	Acuff	35.01	4th	Davis	66.45	Martin	33.55
5th	Sharpe	42.84	Foxx	57.16	5th	Cooper	69.00	Kovach	27.90
6th	Blake	29.17	Coble	70.83	6th	Gordon	67.09	Davis	31.39
7th	McIntyre	72.80	Davis	27.20	7th	Morrison	31.82	Blackburn	66.05
8th	Kissell	49.86	Hayes	50.14	8th	Tanner	73.18	Farmer	26.82
9th	Glass	33.47	Myrick	66.53	9th	Cohen	59.88	White	17.96
10th	Carsner	38.20	McHenry	61.80	**TX.**	(X)	(X)	(X)	(X)
11th	Shuler	53.79	Taylor	46.21	1st	Owen	30.25	Gohmert	68.01
12th	Watt	67.01	Fisher	32.99	2d	Binderim	32.70	Poe	65.64
13th	Miller	63.71	Robinson	36.29	3d	Dodd	34.91	Johnson	62.51
ND.	Pomeroy	65.68	Mechtel	34.32	4th	Melancon	33.45	Hall	64.44
OH.	(X)	(X)	(X)	(X)	5th	Thompson	35.59	Hensarling	61.76
1st	Cranley	47.75	Chabot	52.25	6th	Harris	37.08	Barton	60.46
2d	Wulsin	49.39	Schmidt	50.45	7th	Henley	38.45	Culberson	59.19
3d	Chema	41.46	Turner	58.54	8th	Wright	32.72	Brady	67.28
4th	Siferd	40.01	Jordan	59.99	9th	Green	100.00	[1]	[1]
5th	Weirauch	43.15	Gillmor	56.85	10th	Ankrum	40.40	McCaul	55.29
6th	Wilson	62.08	Blasdel	37.92	11th	[1]	[1]	Conaway	100.00
7th	Conner	39.38	Hobson	60.62	12th	Morris	31.09	Granger	66.95
8th	Meier	36.20	Boehner	63.80	13th	Waun	23.01	Thornberry	74.35
9th	Kaptur	73.63	Leavitt	26.37	14th	Sklar	39.81	Paul	60.19
10th	Kucinich	66.41	Dovilla	33.59	15th[4]	Hinojosa	61.78	Haring	23.72
11th	Jones	83.44	String	16.56	16th	Reyes	78.67	[1]	[1]
12th	Shamansky	42.70	Tiberi	57.30	17th	Edwards	58.12	Taylor	40.31
13th	Sutton	61.22	Foltin	38.78	18th	Jackson-Lee	76.62	Hassan	19.11
14th	Katz	39.05	LaTourette	57.55	19th	Ricketts	29.77	Neugebauer	67.70
15th	Kilroy	49.72	Pryce	50.20	20th	Gonzalez	87.35	[1]	[1]
16th	Shaw	41.66	Regula	58.34	21st[4]	Courage	24.51	Smith	60.11
17th	Ryan	80.25	Manning II	19.75	22d[5,6]	Lampson	51.79	[1]	[1]
18th	Space	62.06	Padgett	37.94	23d[4,7]	Rodriguez	54.28	Bonilla	45.72
OK.	(X)	(X)	(X)	(X)	24th	Page	37.16	Marchant	59.82
1st	Gentges	30.87	Sullivan	63.64	25th[4]	Doggett	67.26	Rostig	26.30
2d	Boren	72.74	Miller	27.26	26th	Barnwell	37.24	Burgess	60.21
3d	Barton	32.54	Lucas	67.46	27th	Ortiz	56.77	Vaden	38.91
4th	Spake	35.39	Cole	64.61	28th[4]	Cuellar	76.89	[1]	[1]
5th	Hunter	37.30	Fallin	60.38	29th	Green	73.54	Story	24.43
OR.	(X)	(X)	(X)	(X)	30th	Johnson	80.19	Aurbach	17.60
1st	Wu	62.83	Kitts	33.71	31st	Harrell	38.80	Carter	58.48
2d	Voisin	30.36	Walden	66.81	32d	Pryor	41.27	Sessions	56.42

See footnotes at end of table.

U.S. Census Bureau, Statistical Abstract of the United States: 2009

Table 387. **Vote Cast for United States Representatives by Major Political Party—Congressional Districts: 2006**—Con.

[See headnote, p. 242]

State and district	Democratic candidate Name	Percent of total	Republican candidate Name	Percent of total	State and district	Democratic candidate Name	Percent of total	Republican candidate Name	Percent of total
UT	(X)........	(X)	(X).........	(X)	4th...	Wright	40.07	Hastings....	59.93
1st...	Olsen......	32.45	Bishop	63.06	5th...	Goldmark ...	43.60	McMorris ...	56.40
2d...	Matheson ...	59.00	Christensen..	37.30	6th...	Dicks	70.60	Cloud......	29.40
3d...	Burridge	32.24	Cannon	57.71	7th...	McDermott ..	79.41	Beren......	15.73
VT	Welch	53.22	Rainville	44.54	8th...	Burner	48.54	Reichert	51.46
VA	(X)........	(X)	(X)........	(X)	9th...	Smith	65.72	Cofchin.....	34.28
1st...	O'Donnell ...	35.48	Davis	62.96	**WV**	(X)........	(X)	(X)........	(X)
2d...	Kellam	48.45	Drake......	51.27	1st...	Mollohan. ..	64.29	Wakim	35.65
3d...	Scott	96.08	(¹).........	(¹)	2d...	Callaghan. ..	42.82	Capito	57.18
4th...	(¹)........	(¹)	Forbes	76.12	3d...	Rahall II	69.36	Wolfe......	30.64
5th...	Weed II	39.93	Goode, Jr...	59.11	**WI**	(X)........	(X)	(X)........	(X)
6th...	(¹)........	(¹)	Goodlatte ...	75.09	1st...	Thomas	37.17	Ryan	62.63
7th...	Nachman ...	34.40	Cantor	63.85	2d...	Baldwin	62.82	Magnum....	37.09
8th...	Moran	66.40	O'Donoghue .	30.58	3d...	Kind.......	64.79	Nelson.....	35.12
9th...	Boucher	67.76	Carrico	32.17	4th...	Moore	71.31	Rivera	28.42
10th...	Feder......	40.96	Wolf.......	57.32				Sensenbren-	
11th...	Hurst	43.57	Davis	55.45	5th...	Kennedy....	35.68	ne	61.76
WA	(X)........	(X)	(X)........	(X)	6th...	(¹)........	(¹)	Petri.......	98.92
1st...	Inslee......	67.72	Ishmael	32.28	7th...	Obey	62.17	Reid.......	34.97
2d...	Larsen	64.16	Roulstone ...	35.84	8th...	Kagen	50.90	Gard	48.76
3d...	Baird	63.12	Messmore...	36.88	**WY**	Trauner	47.05	Cubin......	47.57

X Not applicable.   ¹ No candidate.   ² According to state law, it is not required to tabulate votes for unopposed candidates. ³ Louisiana holds an open-primary election with candidates from all parties running on the same ballot. Any candidate who receives a majority is elected; if no candidate receives 50 percent, there is a run-off election in November between the top two finishers. ⁴ On June 28, 2006, the U.S. Supreme Court declared that the Texas legislature's redistricting plan violated the Voting Rights Act. As a result, on August 4, 2006, replacement district boundaries were announced for the 2006 election for the 15th, 21st, 23rd, 25th, and 28th districts. On election day in November, these five redrawn districts held a special election, pursuant to section 204.021 of the Texas Election Code. If any candidate received over 50%, they were elected. Otherwise, a run-off election in December would decide the seat.   ⁵ A special election was held to fill the unexpired term of Tom DeLay. Don Richardson (7,405 votes) and Shelley Sekula Gibbs (76,924 votes) ran as Republicans in the special election and as write-in candidates in the general election for the 22nd District. Sekula Gibbs won the special election and was sworn in November 13, 2006, representing the district for the few remaining weeks of the 109th Congress. Lampson won the general election and was sworn in on January 4, 2007.   ⁶ Reflects votes cast in the general election.   ⁷ Reflects votes cast in the run-off election held on December 12, 2006.

Source: U.S. House of Representatives, Office of the Clerk, *Statistics of the Presidential and Congressional Election*, biennial. See also <http://clerk.house.gov/member_info/election.html>.

Table 388. **Composition of Congress by Political Party: 1975 to 2008**

[D = Democratic, R = Republican. As of beginning of first session of each Congress, except as noted. Data reflect immediate result of elections. Vacancies and third party candidates are noted]

Year	Party and president	Congress	House Majority party	House Minority party	House Other	Senate Majority party	Senate Minority party	Senate Other
1975 [1]	R (Ford)	94th	D-291	R-144	–	D-61	R-37	2
1977 [2]	D (Carter)	95th	D-292	R-143	1	D-61	R-38	1
1979 [2]	D (Carter)	96th	D-277	R-158	–	D-58	R-41	1
1981 [2]	R (Reagan)	97th	D-242	R-192	1	R-53	D-46	1
1983	R (Reagan)	98th	D-269	R-166	–	R-54	D-46	–
1985	R (Reagan)	99th	D-253	R-182	–	R-53	D-47	–
1987	R (Reagan)	100th	D-258	R-177	–	D-55	R-45	–
1989 [3]	R (Bush)	101st	D-260	R-175	–	D-55	R-45	–
1991 [3]	R (Bush)	102d	D-267	R-167	1	D-56	R-44	–
1993 [3]	D (Clinton)	103d	D-258	R-176	1	D-57	R-43	–
1995 [3]	D (Clinton)	104th	R-230	D-204	1	R-52	D-48	–
1997 [4]	D (Clinton)	105th	R-226	D-207	2	R-55	D-45	–
1999 [3]	D (Clinton)	106th	R-223	D-211	1	R-55	D-45	–
2001 [4]	R (Bush)	107th	R-221	D-212	2	D-50	R-50	–
2003 [5, 6]	R (Bush)	108th	R-229	D-204	1	R-51	D-48	1
2005 [5]	R (Bush)	109th	R-232	D-202	1	R-55	D-44	1
2007 [7, 8, 9]	R (Bush)	110th	D-233	R-202	–	D-49	R-49	2
2008 ...	R (Bush)	110th	D-233	R-198	–	D-49	R-49	2

– Represents zero.   ¹ Senate had one Independent and one Conservative-Republican.   ² Senate had one Independent. ³ House had one Independent-Socialist.   ⁴ House had one Independent-Socialist and one Independent.   ⁵ House and Senate each had one Independent.   ⁶ House had one vacancy.   ⁷ Senate had two Independents.   ⁸ House had 4 vacancies.   ⁹ As of beginning of second session, 13 March 2008.

Source: U.S. House of Representatives, Office of the Clerk, *Official List of Members,* annual. See also <http://clerk.house.gov /member_info/olm_110.pdf>.

Table 389. Composition of Congress by Political Party Affiliation—States: 2003 to 2008

[Figures are for the beginning of the first session (as of January 3), except as noted. Dem. = Democratic; Rep. = Republican]

State	Representatives 108th Cong.,[1] 2003 Dem.	Rep.	109th Cong.,[1,2,3] 2005 Dem.	Rep.	110th Cong., 2007 Dem.	Rep.	110th Cong.,[4,5] 2008 Dem.	Rep.	Senators 108th Cong.,[6] 2003 Dem.	Rep.	109th Cong.,[2,6] 2005 Dem.	Rep.	110th Cong.,[7] 2007 Dem.	Rep.	110th Cong.,[4,7] 2008 Dem.	Rep.
U.S. . . .	205	229	202	231	233	202	233	198	48	51	44	55	49	49	49	49
AL	2	5	2	5	2	5	2	5	–	2	–	2	–	2	–	2
AK	–	1	–	1	–	1	–	1	–	2	–	2	–	2	–	2
AZ	2	6	2	6	4	4	4	4	–	2	–	2	–	2	–	2
AR	3	1	3	1	3	1	3	1	2	–	2	–	2	–	2	–
CA	33	20	33	20	34	19	33	19	2	–	2	–	2	–	2	–
CO	2	5	3	4	4	3	4	3	–	2	1	1	1	1	1	1
CT	2	3	2	3	4	1	4	1	2	–	2	–	1	–	1	–
DE	–	1	–	1	–	1	–	1	2	–	2	–	2	–	2	–
FL	7	18	7	18	9	16	9	16	2	–	1	1	1	1	1	1
GA	5	8	6	7	6	7	6	7	1	1	–	2	–	2	–	2
HI	2	–	2	–	2	–	2	–	2	–	2	–	2	–	2	–
ID	–	2	–	2	–	2	–	2	–	2	–	2	–	2	–	2
IL	9	10	10	9	10	9	11	8	1	1	2	–	2	–	2	–
IN	3	6	2	7	5	4	5	4	1	1	1	1	1	1	1	1
IA	1	4	1	4	3	2	3	2	1	1	1	1	1	1	1	1
KS	1	3	1	3	2	2	2	2	–	2	–	2	–	2	–	2
KY	1	5	1	5	2	4	2	4	–	2	–	2	–	2	–	2
LA	3	4	2	5	2	5	2	3	2	–	1	1	1	1	1	1
ME	2	–	2	–	2	–	2	–	–	2	–	2	–	2	–	2
MD	6	2	6	2	6	2	6	2	2	–	2	–	2	–	2	–
MA	10	–	10	–	10	–	10	–	2	–	2	–	2	–	2	–
MI	6	9	6	9	6	9	6	9	2	–	2	–	2	–	2	–
MN	4	4	4	4	5	3	5	3	1	1	1	1	1	1	1	1
MS	2	2	2	2	2	2	2	1	–	2	–	2	–	2	–	2
MO	4	5	4	5	4	5	4	5	–	2	–	2	1	1	1	1
MT	–	1	–	1	–	1	–	1	1	1	1	1	2	–	2	–
NE	–	3	–	3	–	3	–	3	1	1	1	1	1	1	1	1
NV	1	2	1	2	1	2	1	2	1	1	1	1	1	1	1	1
NH	–	2	–	2	2	–	2	–	–	2	–	2	–	2	–	2
NJ	7	6	7	6	7	6	7	6	2	–	2	–	2	–	2	–
NM	1	2	1	2	1	2	1	2	1	1	1	1	1	1	1	1
NY	19	10	20	9	23	6	23	6	2	–	2	–	2	–	2	–
NC	6	7	6	7	7	6	7	6	1	1	–	2	–	2	–	2
ND	1	–	1	–	1	–	1	–	2	–	2	–	2	–	2	–
OH	6	12	6	11	7	11	7	11	–	2	–	2	1	1	1	1
OK	1	4	1	4	1	4	1	4	–	2	–	2	–	2	–	2
OR	4	1	4	1	4	1	4	1	1	1	1	1	1	1	1	1
PA	7	12	7	12	11	8	11	8	–	2	–	2	1	1	1	1
RI	2	–	2	–	2	–	2	–	1	1	1	1	2	–	2	–
SC	2	4	2	4	2	4	2	4	1	1	–	2	–	2	–	2
SD	–	1	1	–	1	–	1	–	2	–	1	1	1	1	1	1
TN	5	4	5	4	5	4	5	4	–	2	–	2	–	2	–	2
TX	17	15	11	21	13	19	13	19	–	2	–	2	–	2	–	2
UT	1	2	1	2	1	2	1	2	–	2	–	2	–	2	–	2
VT	–	–	–	–	1	–	1	–	1	–	1	–	1	–	1	–
VA	3	8	3	8	3	8	3	8	–	2	–	2	1	1	1	1
WA	6	3	6	3	6	3	6	3	2	–	2	–	2	–	2	–
WV	2	1	2	1	2	1	2	1	2	–	2	–	2	–	2	–
WI	4	4	4	4	5	3	5	3	2	–	2	–	2	–	2	–
WY	–	1	–	1	–	1	–	1	–	2	–	2	–	2	–	2

– Represents zero. [1] Vermont had one Independent-Socialist representative. [2] Ohio had one vacancy due to the resignation of Rob Portman, 29 April 2005. [3] As of June 28, 2005. [4] As of beginning of second session, 13 March 2008. [5] 4 vacancies—one in California due to the death of Tom Lantos, 11 February 2008; two in Louisiana due to the resignations of Bobby Jindal, 14 January 2008, and Richard Baker, 2 February 2008; and one in Mississippi due to the resignation of Roger Wicker, 31 December 2007. [6] Vermont had one Independent senator. (Jeffords was reelected in Vermont in 2000 as a Republican, but subsequently switched to Independent status in June 2001.) [7] Vermont and Connecticut both had one Independent senator.

Source: U.S. Congress, Joint Committee on Printing, *Congressional Directory*, biennial through 2001; Starting in 2003, Office of the Clerk, *Official List of Members by State,* annual. See also <http://clerk.house.gov/member_info/olm_110.pdf>.

Table 390. Members of Congress—Selected Characteristics: 1993 to 2007

[As of beginning of first session of each Congress, (January 3), except as noted. Figures for Representatives exclude vacancies]

Members of Congress and year	Male	Female	Black [1]	API [2]	His-panic [3]	Under 40	40 to 49	50 to 59	60 to 69	70 and over	Less than 2 yrs.	2 to 9 yrs.	10 to 19 yrs.	20 to 29 yrs.	30 yrs. or more
						Age [4] (in years)					Seniority [5,6]				
REPRESENTATIVES															
103d Cong., 1993 [7]...	388	47	[8]38	7	17	47	151	128	89	15	118	141	132	32	12
104th Cong., 1995....	388	47	[9]40	7	17	53	155	135	79	13	92	188	110	36	9
106th Cong., 1999....	379	56	[9]39	6	19	23	116	173	87	35	41	236	104	46	7
107th Cong., 2001....	376	59	[9]39	7	19	14	97	167	117	35	44	155	158	63	14
108th Cong., 2003....	376	59	[9]39	5	22	19	86	174	121	32	54	178	140	48	13
109th Cong., 2005....	369	65	[9]42	4	23	22	96	175	113	28	37	173	158	48	18
110th Cong., 2007....	361	74	[9]42	4	23	20	91	172	118	34	62	159	160	37	17
SENATORS															
103d Cong., 1993 [7]...	93	7	1	2	–	1	16	48	22	12	15	30	39	11	5
104th Cong., 1995....	92	8	1	2	–	1	14	41	27	17	12	38	30	15	5
106th Cong., 1999....	91	9	–	2	–	–	14	38	35	13	8	39	33	14	6
107th Cong., 2001....	87	13	–	2	–	–	8	39	33	18	11	34	30	14	9
108th Cong., 2003....	86	14	–	2	–	1	12	29	34	24	9	42	29	13	7
109th Cong., 2005....	86	14	1	2	2	–	17	29	33	21	9	41	29	14	7
110th Cong., 2007....	84	16	1	2	3	–	11	31	34	24	12	42	24	13	9

– Represents zero. [1] Source: Joint Center for Political and Economic Studies, Washington, DC, *Black Elected Officials: Statistical Summary*, annual (copyright). [2] Asian and Pacific Islanders. Source: Prior to 2005, Library of Congress, Congressional Research Service, "Asian Pacific Americans in the United States Congress," Report 94-767 GOV; starting 2005, U.S. House of Representatives, "House Press Gallery," <http://www.house.gov/daily/110th%20Hispanic.htm> (as of 8 May 2008) and U.S. Senate, "Minorities in the Senate," <http://www.senate.gov/artandhistory/history/common/briefing/minority_senators.htm> (as of 8 May 2008). [3] Source: National Association of Latino Elected and Appointed Officials, Washington, DC, *National Roster of Hispanic Elected Officials*, annual. [4] Some members do not provide date of birth. [5] Represents consecutive years of service. [6] Some members do not provide years of service. [7] Includes members elected to fill vacant seats through June 14, 1993. [8] Includes District of Columbia delegate but not Virgin Islands delegate. [9] Includes District of Columbia and Virgin Islands delegate.

Source: Except as noted, compiled by U.S. Census Bureau from data published in *Congressional Directory*, biennial. See also <http://www.gpoaccess.gov/cdirectory/browse.html>.

Table 391. U.S. Congress—Measures Introduced and Enacted and Time in Session: 1991 to 2007

[Excludes simple and concurrent resolutions]

Item	102d Cong., 1991–92	103d Cong., 1993–94	104th Cong., 1995–96	105th Cong., 1997–98	106th Cong., 1999–00	107th Cong., 2001–02	108th Cong., 2003–04	109th Cong., 2005–06	110th Cong., 2007
Measures introduced	6,775	8,544	6,808	7,732	9,158	9,130	8,625	10,703	7,556
Bills	6,212	7,883	6,545	7,532	8,968	8,953	8,468	10,560	7,454
Joint resolutions	563	661	263	200	190	177	157	143	102
Measures enacted	609	473	337	404	604	337	504	418	138
Public [1]	589	465	333	394	580	331	498	417	138
Private [2]	20	8	4	10	24	6	6	1	–
HOUSE OF REPRESENTATIVES									
Number of days	280	265	290	251	272	265	243	241	164
Number of hours	1,796	1,887	2,445	2,001	2,179	1,694	1,894	1,917	1,478
Number of hours per day...	6.4	7.1	8.4	8.0	8.0	6.4	7.8	8.0	9.0
SENATE									
Number of days	287	291	343	296	303	322	300	297	190
Number of hours	2,292	2,514	2,876	2,188	2,200	2,279	2,486	2,250	1,376
Number of hours per day...	8.0	8.6	8.4	7.4	7.3	7.1	8.3	7.6	7.2

– Represents zero. [1] Laws on public matters that apply to all persons. [2] Laws designed to provide legal relief to specified persons or entities adversely affected by laws of general applicability.

Source: U.S. Congress, *Congressional Record* and *Daily Calendar*, selected issues. See also <http://www.senate.gov/pagelayout/reference/two_column_table/Resumes.htm>.

Table 392. Congressional Bills Vetoed: 1961 to 2008

Period	President	Total vetoes	Regular vetoes	Pocket vetoes	Vetoes sustained	Bills passed over veto
1961–63.............	John F. Kennedy......	21	12	9	21	–
1963–69.............	Lyndon B. Johnson....	30	16	14	30	–
1969–74.............	Richard M. Nixon.....	43	26	17	36	7
1974–77.............	Gerald R. Ford.......	66	48	18	54	12
1977–81.............	Jimmy Carter.......	31	13	18	29	2
1981–89.............	Ronald W. Reagan....	78	39	39	69	9
1989–93.............	George Bush........	44	29	15	43	1
1993–2001	William J. Clinton.....	37	36	1	34	2
2001–2008 [1]	George W. Bush......	8	8	–	7	1

– Represents zero. [1] Through 15 April 2008.

Source: U.S. Congress, Senate Library, *Presidential Vetoes ... 1789–1968*; U.S. Congress, *Calendars of the U.S. House of Representatives and History of Legislation,* annual. See also <http://clerk.house.gov/art_history/house_history/vetoes.html>.

U.S. Census Bureau, Statistical Abstract of the United States: 2009

Table 393. Number of Governors by Political Party Affiliation: 1975 to 2008

[Reflects figures after inaugurations for each year]

Year	Demo-cratic	Repub-lican	Indepen-dent/other	Year	Demo-cratic	Repub-lican	Indepen-dent/other	Year	Demo-cratic	Repub-lican	Indepen-dent/other
1975	36	13	1	1997	17	32	1	2003	23	27	–
1980	31	19	–	1998	17	32	1	2004	22	28	–
1985	34	16	–	1999	17	31	1	2005	22	28	–
1990	29	21	–	2000	18	30	2	2006	22	28	–
1995	19	30	1	2001	19	29	2	2007	28	22	–
1996 [1] . . .	18	31	1	2002	22	27	1	2008	28	22	–

– Represents zero. [1] Arkansas's Democratic governor was succeeded midyear by a Republican.
Source: National Governors Association, Washington, DC, 1970–87 and 1991–2008, *Directory of Governors of the American States, Commonwealths & Territories*, annual; and 1988–90, *Directory of Governors*, annual (copyright).

Table 394. Vote Cast for and Governor Elected by State: 2004 to 2007

[In thousands (1,250 represents 1,250,000), except percent. D = Democratic, R = Republican]

State	2004 Total vote [1]	2004 Repub-lican	2004 Demo-crat	2004 Percent leading party	2006 Total vote [1]	2006 Repub-lican	2006 Demo-crat	2006 Percent leading party	Current governor [2]
AL.	(X)	(X)	(X)	(X)	1,250	718	520	R-57.4	Bob Riley
AK.	(X)	(X)	(X)	(X)	238	115	97	R-48.1	Sarah Palin
AZ.	(X)	(X)	(X)	(X)	1,534	544	960	D-62.6	Janet Napolitano
AR.	(X)	(X)	(X)	(X)	774	315	430	D-55.5	Mike Beebe
CA.	(X)	(X)	(X)	(X)	8,679	4,850	3,377	R-55.9	Arnold Schwarzenegger
CO.	(X)	(X)	(X)	(X)	1,558	626	888	D-57.0	Bill Ritter
CT.	(X)	(X)	(X)	(X)	1,123	710	398	R-63.2	M. Jodi Rell
DE.	365	167	186	D-50.9	(X)	(X)	(X)	(X)	Ruth Ann Minner
FL.	(X)	(X)	(X)	(X)	4,829	2,520	2,178	R-52.2	Charlie Crist
GA	(X)	(X)	(X)	(X)	2,122	1,230	811	R-57.9	Sonny Perdue
HI	(X)	(X)	(X)	(X)	349	215	122	R-61.7	Linda Lingle
ID	(X)	(X)	(X)	(X)	489	276	199	R-52.7	C. L. "Butch" Otter
IL	(X)	(X)	(X)	(X)	3,586	1,369	1,736	D-48.4	Rod Blagojevich
IN	2,448	1,303	1,114	R-53.2	(X)	(X)	(X)	(X)	Mitch Daniels
IA	(X)	(X)	(X)	(X)	1,059	467	569	D-53.7	Chet Culver
KS.	(X)	(X)	(X)	(X)	850	344	492	D-57.9	Kathleen Sebelius
KY [3]	1,083	596	487	R-55.0	1,055	436	620	D-58.7	Steven Beshear
LA [3]	1,416	369	872	D-52.0	1,298	699	398	R-54.0	Bobby Jindal
ME	(X)	(X)	(X)	(X)	551	166	210	D-38.1	John Baldacci
MD	(X)	(X)	(X)	(X)	1,717	825	942	D-52.7	Martin O'Malley
MA	(X)	(X)	(X)	(X)	2,244	784	1,235	D-55.0	Deval Patrick
MI	(X)	(X)	(X)	(X)	3,801	1,608	2,143	D-56.3	Jennifer M. Granholm
MN	(X)	(X)	(X)	(X)	2,218	1,029	1,007	R-46.4	Tim Pawlenty
MS [3]	894	470	410	R-52.6	744	431	313	R-57.9	Haley Barbour
MO	2,720	1,382	1,301	R-50.8	(X)	(X)	(X)	(X)	Matt Blunt
MT	456	205	225	D-50.4	(X)	(X)	(X)	(X)	Brian Schweitzer
NE.	(X)	(X)	(X)	(X)	593	436	145	R-73.3	Dave Heineman
NV.	(X)	(X)	(X)	(X)	582	279	256	R-47.9	Jim Gibbons
NH	684	326	340	D-51.0	404	105	298	D-74.0	John Lynch
NJ [4]	2,290	985	1,225	D-53.5	(X)	(X)	(X)	(X)	Jon Corzine
NM	(X)	(X)	(X)	(X)	559	174	385	D-68.8	Bill Richardson
NY [5]	(X)	(X)	(X)	(X)	4,698	1,106	2,741	D-58.3	David Paterson
NC	3,487	1,495	1,939	D-55.6	(X)	(X)	(X)	(X)	Michael Easley
ND	310	221	85	R-71.3	(X)	(X)	(X)	(X)	John Hoeven
OH	(X)	(X)	(X)	(X)	4,184	1,471	2,428	D-58.0	Ted Strickland
OK	(X)	(X)	(X)	(X)	926	310	616	R-66.5	Brad Henry
OR	(X)	(X)	(X)	(X)	1,400	534	579	D-41.3	Ted Kulongoski
PA.	(X)	(X)	(X)	(X)	4,093	1,622	2,471	D-60.4	Edward Rendell
RI	(X)	(X)	(X)	(X)	387	197	190	R-51.0	Don Carcieri
SC.	(X)	(X)	(X)	(X)	1,092	602	489	R-55.1	Mark Sanford
SD.	(X)	(X)	(X)	(X)	356	207	121	R-61.7	Mike Rounds
TN.	(X)	(X)	(X)	(X)	1,819	541	1,247	D-68.6	Phil Bredesen
TX.	(X)	(X)	(X)	(X)	4,399	1,717	1,310	R-39.0	Rick Perry
UT.	907	525	374	R-57.8	(X)	(X)	(X)	(X)	Jon Huntsman
VT.	309	182	117	R-58.7	263	148	108	R-56.3	Jim Douglas
VA [4]	1,984	912	1,026	D-52.0	(X)	(X)	(X)	(X)	Tim Kaine
WA	2,883	1,373	1,373	D-48.8	(X)	(X)	(X)	(X)	Chris Gregoire
WV	744	253	473	D-63.5	(X)	(X)	(X)	(X)	Joe Manchin III
WI.	(X)	(X)	(X)	(X)	2,162	979	1,139	D-52.7	Jim Doyle
WY	(X)	(X)	(X)	(X)	194	58	136	D-69.8	Dave Freudenthal

X Not applicable. [1] Includes minor party and scattered votes. [2] As of 3 April 2008. Source: National Governors Association, Washington, DC. See Internet site: <http://www.nga.org/>. [3] Voting years 2003 and 2007. [4] Voting year 2005. [5] Data are for Eliot Spitzer, who served from January 2007 until his resignation 17 March 2008. Lieutenant governor, David Paterson was sworn into office on the same day.
Source: Except as noted, The Council of State Governments, Lexington, KY, *The Book of States 2008*, annual (copyright).

Table 395. Composition of State Legislatures by Political Party Affiliation: 2007 and 2008

[Data as of March and reflect February election results in year shown, except as noted. Figures reflect immediate results of elections, including holdover members in state houses which do not have all of their members running for reelection. Dem. = Democrat, Rep. = Republican, Vac. = Vacancies. In general, Lower House refers to body consisting of state representatives; Upper House, of state senators]

State	Lower House 2007 Dem.	Rep.	Other	Vac.	Lower House 2008 Dem.	Rep.	Other	Vac.	Upper House 2007 Dem.	Rep.	Other	Vac.	Upper House 2008 Dem.	Rep.	Other	Vac.
U.S.	2,971	2,422	15	3	2,985	2,403	17	7	1,010	909	3	–	1,020	898	3	1
AL [1]	62	43	–	–	62	43	–	–	23	12	–	–	23	12	–	–
AK [2]	17	23	–	–	17	23	–	–	9	11	–	–	9	11	–	–
AZ [3]	27	33	–	–	27	33	–	–	13	17	–	–	13	17	–	–
AR [2]	75	25	–	–	75	25	–	–	27	8	–	–	27	8	–	–
CA [2]	48	32	–	–	47	32	–	1	25	15	–	–	25	15	–	–
CO [2]	39	26	–	–	40	25	–	–	20	15	–	–	20	15	–	–
CT [3]	107	44	–	–	107	44	–	–	24	12	–	–	24	12	–	–
DE [2]	18	23	–	–	19	22	–	–	13	8	–	–	13	8	–	–
FL [2]	41	79	–	–	42	78	–	–	14	26	–	–	14	26	–	–
GA [3]	74	106	–	–	73	107	–	–	22	34	–	–	22	34	–	–
HI [2]	43	8	–	–	44	7	–	–	20	5	–	–	21	4	–	–
ID [3]	19	51	–	–	19	51	–	–	7	28	–	–	7	28	–	–
IL [4]	66	52	–	–	67	51	–	–	37	22	–	–	37	22	–	–
IN [2]	51	49	–	–	51	49	–	–	17	33	–	–	17	33	–	–
IA [2]	54	46	–	–	53	47	–	–	30	20	–	–	30	20	–	–
KS [2]	47	78	–	–	47	78	–	–	10	30	–	–	10	30	–	–
KY [2]	61	39	–	–	64	36	–	–	16	21	1	–	15	22	1	–
LA [1]	59	43	1	2	60	43	1	1	24	15	–	–	25	14	–	–
ME [3]	89	60	2	–	90	59	2	–	18	17	–	–	18	17	–	–
MD [1]	104	37	–	–	104	37	–	–	33	14	–	–	33	14	–	–
MA [3]	141	19	–	–	140	19	–	1	35	5	–	–	35	5	–	–
MI [2]	58	52	–	–	58	52	–	–	17	21	–	–	17	21	–	–
MN [2]	85	49	–	–	85	48	1	–	44	23	–	–	45	22	–	–
MS [1]	74	47	–	1	75	47	–	–	25	27	–	–	27	25	–	–
MO [2]	71	92	–	–	71	92	–	–	13	21	–	–	14	20	–	–
MT [2]	49	50	1	–	49	50	1	–	26	24	–	–	26	24	–	–
NE [5]	(5)	(5)	(5)	(5)	(5)	(5)	(5)	(5)	(5)	(5)	(5)	(5)	(5)	(5)	(5)	(5)
NV [2]	27	15	–	–	27	15	–	–	10	11	–	–	10	11	–	–
NH [3]	239	161	–	–	237	158	1	4	14	10	–	–	14	10	–	–
NJ [2]	49	31	–	–	48	32	–	–	22	18	–	–	23	17	–	–
NM [2]	42	28	–	–	42	28	–	–	24	18	–	–	24	18	–	–
NY [3]	105	45	–	–	108	42	–	–	29	33	–	–	29	33	–	–
NC [3]	68	52	–	–	68	52	–	–	31	19	–	–	31	19	–	–
ND [1]	33	61	–	–	33	61	–	–	21	26	–	–	21	26	–	–
OH [2]	46	53	–	–	46	53	–	–	12	21	–	–	12	21	–	–
OK [2]	44	57	–	–	44	57	–	–	24	24	–	–	24	24	–	–
OR [2]	31	29	–	–	31	29	–	–	17	11	2	–	18	10	1	1
PA [2]	102	101	–	–	102	101	–	–	21	29	–	–	21	29	–	–
RI [3]	62	13	–	–	61	13	1	–	33	5	–	–	33	5	–	–
SC [2]	51	73	–	–	51	73	–	–	20	26	–	–	19	27	–	–
SD [3]	20	50	–	–	20	50	–	–	15	20	–	–	15	20	–	–
TN [2]	53	46	–	–	53	46	–	–	16	17	–	–	16	16	1	–
TX [2]	69	81	–	–	71	79	–	–	11	20	–	–	11	20	–	–
UT [2]	20	55	–	–	20	55	–	–	8	21	–	–	8	21	–	–
VT [3]	93	49	8	–	93	49	8	–	23	7	–	–	23	7	–	–
VA [2]	40	57	3	–	44	54	2	–	17	23	–	–	21	19	–	–
WA [2]	62	36	–	–	63	35	–	–	32	17	–	–	32	17	–	–
WV [2]	72	28	–	–	72	28	–	–	23	11	–	–	23	11	–	–
WI [2]	47	52	–	–	47	52	–	–	18	15	–	–	18	15	–	–
WY [2]	17	43	–	–	17	43	–	–	7	23	–	–	7	23	–	–

– Represents zero. [1] Members of both houses serve 4-year terms. [2] Upper House members serve 4-year terms and Lower House members serve 2-year terms. [3] Members of both houses serve 2-year terms. [4] Illinois—4- and 2-year term depending on district. [5] Nebraska—4-year term and only state to have a nonpartisan legislature.

Source: The Council of State Governments, Lexington, KY, *The Book of States 2008*, annual (copyright).

U.S. Census Bureau, Statistical Abstract of the United States: 2009

Table 396. Political Party Control of State Legislatures by Party: 1983 to 2008

[As of beginning of year. Nebraska has a nonpartisan legislature]

Year	Legislatures under—			Year	Legislatures under—			Year	Legislatures under—		
	Democratic control	Split control or tie	Republican control		Democratic control	Split control or tie	Republican control		Democratic control	Split control or tie	Republican control
1983 [1] . . .	34	4	11	1994	24	17	8	2002	17	15	17
1985	27	11	11	1995	18	12	19	2003	16	12	21
1987	28	12	9	1996	16	15	18	2004	17	11	21
1989 [2] . . .	28	13	8	1997	20	11	18	2005	19	10	20
1990	29	11	9	1999	20	12	17	2006	19	10	20
1992	29	14	6	2000	16	15	18	2007	22	12	15
1993	25	16	8	2001	16	15	18	2008	23	14	12

[1] Two 1984 midterm recall elections resulted in a change in control of the Michigan State Senate. At the time of the 1984 election, therefore, Democrats controlled 33 legislatures. [2] A party change during the year by a Democratic representative broke the tie in the Indiana House of Representatives, giving the Republicans control of both chambers.

Source: National Conference of State Legislatures, Denver, CO, *State Legislatures*, periodic.

Table 397. Women Holding State Public Offices by Office and State: 2007

[As of January. For data on women in U.S. Congress, see Table 390]

State	Total	State-wide elective executive office [1]	State legislature		State	Total	State-wide elective executive office [1]	State legislature	
			Total	Percent [2]				Total	Percent [2]
U.S.	**1,808**	**76**	**1,732**	**24**	MO	41	3	38	19
					MT	38	1	37	25
AL	23	5	18	13	NE	10	1	9	(3)
AK	14	1	13	22	NV	22	3	19	30
AZ	33	3	30	33	NH	151	–	151	36
AR	29	1	28	21	NJ	26	–	26	22
CA	34	1	33	28	NM	37	3	34	30
CO	36	2	34	34	NY	51	–	51	24
CT	57	4	53	28	NC	48	4	44	26
DE	20	1	19	31	ND	27	2	25	18
FL	38	1	37	23	OH	23	2	21	16
GA	49	3	46	19	OK	22	3	19	13
HI	26	1	25	33	OR	29	1	28	31
ID	26	1	25	24	PA	39	2	37	15
IL	49	1	48	27	RI	23	1	22	19
IN	31	2	29	19	SC	15	–	15	9
IA	35	1	34	23	SD	18	–	18	17
KS	51	3	48	29	TN	22	–	22	17
KY	17	1	16	12	TX	37	2	35	19
LA	26	1	25	17	UT	18	–	18	17
ME	58	–	58	31	VT	69	1	68	38
MD	60	–	60	32	VA	24	–	24	17
MA	50	1	49	25	WA	52	2	50	34
MI	31	2	29	20	WV	20	1	19	14
MN	73	3	70	35	WI	33	3	30	23
MS	25	1	24	14	WY	22	1	21	23

– Represents zero. [1] Excludes women elected to the judiciary, women appointed to state cabinet-level positions, women elected to executive posts by the legislature, and elected members of university Board of Trustees or Board of Education. [2] Calculated by U.S. Census Bureau based on total state legislature (both upper and lower houses) data from Table 395. [3] Nebraska—4-year term and only state to have a nonpartisan legislature.

Source: Center for the American Woman and Politics, Eagleton Institute of Politics, Rutgers University, New Brunswick, NJ, information releases, (copyright).

Table 398. **Black Elected Officials by Office, 1970 to 2002, and State, 2002**

[As of January 2002, no Black elected officials had been identified in Montana or South Dakota]

State	Total	U.S. and state legislatures[1]	City and county offices[2]	Law enforcement[3]	Education[4]	State	Total	U.S. and state legislatures[1]	City and county offices[2]	Law enforcement[3]	Education[4]
1970 (Feb.)	1,469	179	715	213	362	MD	192	40	101	41	10
1980 (July)	4,890	326	2,832	526	1,206	MA	79	6	60	2	11
1990 (Jan.)	7,335	436	4,485	769	1,645	MI	353	24	153	62	114
1995 (Jan.)	8,385	604	4,954	987	1,840	MN	20	2	4	10	4
1999 (Jan.)	8,896	618	5,354	997	1,927	MS	950	46	646	121	137
2000 (Jan.)	9,001	621	5,420	1,037	1,923	MO	206	19	145	17	25
2001 (Jan.)	9,061	633	5,456	1,044	1,928	NE	9	1	5	–	3
						NV	13	5	4	2	2
2002 (Jan.)	9,430	636	5,753	1,081	1,960	NH	5	5	–	–	–
AL	757	36	569	56	96	NJ	269	18	162	–	89
AK	2	1	1	–	–	NM	4	1	–	2	1
AZ	13	1	1	6	5	NY	328	34	90	84	120
AR	535	15	374	17	129	NC	523	28	369	31	95
CA	234	10	78	76	70	ND	1	–	1	–	–
CO	17	4	5	8	–	OH	305	21	197	35	52
CT	69	14	46	3	6	OK	115	6	85	4	20
DE	29	4	18	–	7	OR	5	3	1	1	–
DC	174	5[2]	169	–	3	PA	215	19	85	75	36
FL	275	25	180	43	27	RI	8	7	1	–	–
GA	640	53	413	48	126	SC	547	32	345	12	158
HI	1	1	–	–	–	TN	195	18	118	28	31
ID	1	–	1	–	–	TX	466	19	306	47	94
IL	619	28	327	59	205	UT	5	1	3	1	–
IN	94	13	54	13	14	VT	1	1	–	–	–
IA	12	1	8	1	2	VA	248	16	132	16	84
KS	16	7	4	3	2	WA	24	2	9	11	2
KY	62	5	45	6	6	WV	19	2	13	3	1
LA	739	32	408	132	167	WI	33	8	15	5	5
ME	2	–	1	–	1	WY	1	1	–	–	–

– Represents zero. [1] Includes elected state administrators. [2] County commissioners and councilmen, mayors, vice mayors, aldermen, regional officials, and other. [3] Judges, magistrates, constables, marshals, sheriffs, justices of the peace, and other. [4] Members of state education agencies, college boards, school boards, and other. [5] Includes one shadow senator (an elected official who lobbied Congress on D.C. issues, but is not sworn in at the federal level and has no voting privileges).

Source: Joint Center for Political and Economic Studies, Washington, DC, *Black Elected Officials: A Statistical Summary*, annual (copyright) and <http://www.jointcenter.org/publications_recent_publications/black_elected_officials>.

Table 399. **Hispanic Public Elected Officials by Office, 1985 to 2007, and State, 2007**

[**As of January of year shown.** For states not shown, no Hispanic public officials had been identified]

State	Total	State executives and legislators[1]	County and municipal officials	Judicial and law enforcement	Education and school boards	State	Total	State executives and legislators[1]	County and municipal officials	Judicial and law enforcement	Education and school boards
1985	3,147	129	1,316	517	1,185	MD	10	4	5	–	1
1990	4,004	144	1,819	583	1,458	MA	19	4	10	–	5
1994	5,459	199	2,197	651	2,412	MI	16	3	3	3	7
2000	5,019	217	1,852	447	2,503	MN	5	3	1	1	–
2001	5,205	223	1,846	454	2,682	MO	2	1	1	–	–
2002	4,303	227	1,960	532	1,603	MT	2	1	–	1	–
2003	4,432	231	1,958	549	1,694	NE	2	1	–	–	1
2004	4,651	253	2,059	638	1,723	NV	10	3	4	2	1
2005	4,853	266	2,149	678	1,760	NH	3	2	1	–	–
2006	4,932	244	2,151	693	1,835	NJ	103	8	56	–	39
						NM	632	47	331	105	149
2007	4,954	270	2,152	685	1,847	NY	63	19	26	16	2
AK	1	–	1	–	–	NC	4	2	2	–	–
AZ	346	19	135	48	144	ND	1	–	1	–	–
CA	1,090	35	391	45	619	OH	5	–	4	1	–
CO	150	7	103	9	31	OK	2	–	–	–	2
CT	27	6	17	–	4	OR	12	2	5	5	–
DE	2	1	1	–	–	PA	12	1	7	2	2
FL	131	21	77	26	7	RI	7	3	4	–	–
GA	8	3	3	2	–	SC	1	1	–	–	–
HI	1	1	–	–	–	TN	2	1	1	–	–
ID	2	2	–	–	–	TX	2,118	43	866	402	807
IL	92	12	61	6	13	UT	7	2	3	2	–
IN	15	1	9	3	2	VA	3	1	1	–	1
IA	1	–	1	–	–	WA	13	3	4	–	6
KS	12	4	7	–	1	WI	11	1	4	4	2
KY	2	–	1	–	1	WY	6	2	4	–	–
LA	3	–	1	2	–						

– Represents zero. [1] Includes U.S. Senators and Representatives, not shown separately.

Source: National Association of Latino Elected and Appointed Officials (NALEO) Educational Fund, Washington, DC, *National Directory of Latino Elected Officials*, annual.

Table 400. Voting-Age Population, Percent Reporting Registered, and Voted: 1994 to 2006

[190.3 represents 190,300,000. As of November. Covers civilian noninstitutional population 18 years old and over. Includes aliens. Figures are based on Current Population Survey (see text, Section 1, Population, and Appendix III) and differ from those in Table 402 based on population estimates and official vote counts]

| Characteristic | Voting-age population (mil.) | | | | | | | Percent reporting they registered | | | | | | | Percent reporting they voted | | | | | | |
| | | | | | | | | Presidential election years | | | Congressional election years | | | | Presidential election years | | | Congressional election years | | | |
	1994	1996	1998	2000	2002	2004	2006	1996	2000	2004	1994	1998	2002	2006	1996	2000	2004	1994	1998	2002	2006
Total [1]	190.3	193.7	198.2	202.6	210.4	215.7	220.6	65.9	63.9	65.9	62.0	62.1	60.9	61.6	54.2	54.7	58.3	44.6	41.9	42.3	43.6
18 to 20 years old	10.3	10.8	11.4	11.9	11.7	11.5	11.6	45.6	40.5	50.7	37.2	32.1	32.6	37.0	31.2	28.4	41.0	16.5	13.5	15.1	17.1
21 to 24 years old	13.9	13.9	14.1	14.9	15.6	16.4	16.2	51.2	49.3	55.6	45.5	35.0	42.5	44.9	33.4	35.4	42.5	22.3	19.2	18.7	21.9
25 to 34 years old	41.1	40.1	38.6	37.3	38.5	39.0	39.4	56.9	54.7	55.6	51.5	52.4	50.2	50.3	43.1	43.7	46.9	32.2	28.0	27.1	28.3
35 to 44 years old	41.9	43.3	44.4	44.5	43.7	43.1	42.6	66.5	63.8	64.2	63.3	62.4	60.0	59.3	54.9	55.0	56.9	46.0	40.7	40.2	40.1
45 to 64 years old	50.9	53.7	57.4	61.4	66.9	71.0	75.0	73.5	71.2	72.7	71.0	71.1	69.4	69.6	64.4	64.1	66.6	56.0	53.6	53.1	54.3
65 years old and over	31.1	31.9	32.3	32.8	33.9	34.7	35.8	77.0	76.1	76.9	75.6	75.4	75.8	75.4	67.0	67.6	68.9	60.7	59.5	61.0	60.5
Male	91.0	92.6	95.2	97.1	100.9	103.8	106.5	64.4	62.2	64.0	60.8	60.6	58.9	59.5	52.8	53.1	56.3	44.4	41.4	41.4	42.4
Female	99.3	101.0	103.0	105.5	109.5	111.9	114.1	67.3	65.6	67.6	63.2	63.5	62.8	63.5	55.5	56.2	60.1	44.9	42.4	43.0	44.7
White [2]	160.3	162.8	165.8	168.7	174.1	176.6	179.9	67.7	65.6	67.9	64.2	63.9	63.1	64.0	56.0	56.4	60.3	46.9	43.3	44.1	45.8
Black [2]	21.8	22.5	23.3	24.1	24.4	24.9	25.7	63.5	63.6	64.4	58.3	60.2	58.8	57.4	50.6	53.5	56.3	37.0	39.6	39.7	38.6
Asian [2,3]	(NA)	(NA)	(NA)	8.0	9.6	9.3	9.9	(NA)	30.7	34.9	(NA)	(NA)	30.7	32.9	(NA)	25.4	29.8	(NA)	(NA)	19.4	21.8
Hispanic [4]	17.5	18.4	20.3	21.6	25.2	27.1	29.0	35.7	34.9	34.3	30.0	33.7	32.6	32.1	26.7	27.5	28.0	19.1	20.0	18.9	19.3
Region: [5]																					
Northeast	38.4	38.3	38.5	38.9	41.1	41.0	41.2	64.7	63.7	65.3	60.9	60.8	60.8	60.3	54.5	55.2	58.6	45.2	41.2	41.4	42.8
Midwest	44.5	45.2	45.9	46.4	48.8	48.4	49.1	71.6	70.2	72.8	68.7	68.2	66.5	68.3	59.3	60.9	65.0	48.8	47.3	47.1	50.7
South	66.4	68.1	70.1	71.8	74.2	77.2	80.0	65.9	64.5	65.5	60.7	62.7	61.6	62.0	52.2	53.5	56.4	40.5	38.6	41.6	40.3
West	41.0	42.1	43.7	45.5	46.3	49.1	50.4	60.8	56.9	60.1	58.1	56.0	54.0	55.4	51.8	49.9	54.4	46.4	42.3	39.0	42.4
School years completed:																					
8 years or less	14.7	14.1	13.3	12.9	12.3	12.6	12.1	40.7	36.1	32.5	40.1	40.2	32.4	29.5	28.1	26.8	23.6	23.2	24.6	19.4	17.1
High school:																					
Less than high school graduate	20.7	21.0	21.0	20.1	20.9	20.7	20.2	47.9	45.9	45.8	44.7	43.4	41.6	39.6	33.8	33.6	34.6	27.0	25.0	23.3	22.8
High school graduate or GED [6]	64.9	65.2	65.6	66.3	68.9	68.5	70.0	62.2	60.1	61.5	58.9	58.6	57.1	57.5	49.1	49.4	52.4	40.5	37.1	37.1	37.6
College:																					
Some college or associate's degree	50.4	50.9	52.9	55.3	57.3	58.9	60.2	72.9	70.0	73.7	68.4	68.3	66.7	68.3	60.5	60.3	66.1	49.1	46.2	45.8	47.3
Bachelor's or advanced degree	39.4	42.5	45.4	48.0	51.0	54.9	58.2	80.4	77.3	78.1	76.3	75.1	74.4	73.9	73.0	72.0	74.2	63.1	57.2	58.5	59.5
Employed	122.6	125.6	130.5	133.4	134.9	138.8	143.8	67.0	64.7	67.1	62.9	62.6	61.7	62.7	55.2	55.5	60.0	45.2	41.2	42.1	43.9
Unemployed	6.5	6.4	5.2	4.9	7.7	7.3	6.2	52.5	46.1	56.3	46.4	48.5	48.1	48.5	37.2	35.1	46.4	28.3	28.4	27.2	28.0
Not in labor force	61.2	61.6	62.5	64.2	67.8	69.6	70.5	65.1	63.8	64.4	61.9	62.1	60.9	60.7	54.1	54.5	56.2	45.3	44.5	44.2	44.3

NA Not available. [1] Includes other races not shown separately. [2] Beginning with the 2003 Current Population Survey (CPS), respondents could choose more than one race. 2004 and 2006 data represent persons who selected this race group only and exclude persons reporting more than one race. The CPS in prior years only allowed respondents to report one race group. See also comments on race in the text for Section 1. [3] Prior to 2004, this category was 'Asian and Pacific Islanders,' therefore rates are not comparable with prior years. [4] Hispanic persons may be any race. [5] For composition of regions, see map, inside cover. [6] The General Educational Development (GED) Test measures how well a non-high school graduate has mastered the skills and general knowledge that are acquired in a 4-year high school education. Successfully passing the exam is a credential generally considered to be equivalent to a high school diploma.

Source: U.S. Census Bureau, Current Population Reports, P20-556, and earlier reports; "Voting and Registration in the Election of November 2006" (published June 2008); <http://www.census.gov/population/www/socdemo/voting.html>; and unpublished data.

U.S. Census Bureau, Statistical Abstract of the United States: 2009

Table 401. **Persons Reported Registered and Voted by State: 2006**

[220,603 represents 220,603,000. As of November. See headnote, Table 400]

State	Voting-age population (1,000)	Percent of voting-age population Registered	Percent of voting-age population Voted	State	Voting-age population (1,000)	Percent of voting-age population Registered	Percent of voting-age population Voted
U.S..	220,603	61.6	43.6	MO	4,388	72.2	52.6
AL	3,447	72.0	48.4	MT.	735	69.7	59.2
AK	469	70.9	52.9	NE.	1,298	65.7	48.9
AZ	4,418	53.8	40.2	NV.	1,839	49.2	37.3
AR	2,076	63.4	43.9	NH.	1,015	67.7	47.0
CA	26,318	50.3	38.4	NJ	6,488	53.7	37.1
CO.	3,464	65.7	49.9	NM.	1,436	66.2	50.9
CT	2,640	62.5	46.2	NY	14,376	56.6	37.6
DE	647	63.0	42.6	NC	6,490	64.1	37.3
DC	419	65.8	44.6	ND	484	82.0	53.4
FL	13,929	56.4	38.4	OH	8,508	69.6	51.8
GA	6,630	59.6	40.3	OK	2,616	67.9	44.9
HI	967	50.9	40.1	OR	2,802	68.7	57.1
ID	1,064	62.0	49.1	PA	9,436	63.5	46.6
IL	9,392	61.5	42.2	RI	806	66.6	53.5
IN	4,629	63.6	44.3	SC	3,197	62.1	43.0
IA	2,252	73.9	52.4	SD	577	77.2	62.1
KS	2,035	62.6	44.3	TN	4,571	61.9	43.8
KY	3,142	71.3	48.0	TX	16,512	58.6	33.5
LA	3,071	71.0	39.1	UT	1,753	53.1	34.4
ME.	1,034	78.5	57.5	VT	491	70.2	55.5
MD.	4,175	65.1	51.4	VA	5,578	61.0	43.6
MA	4,864	65.4	50.0	WA	4,745	65.1	49.4
MI	7,458	70.5	54.8	WV	1,394	62.6	36.8
MN.	3,855	74.2	61.6	WI	4,202	70.2	56.0
MS	2,083	69.0	42.2	WY	388	65.3	51.4

Source: U.S. Census Bureau, *Current Population Reports*, P20-556 and earlier reports; "Voting and Registration in the Election of November 2004" (published 25 May 2005); <http://www.census.gov/population/www/socdemo/voting.html>; and unpublished data.

Table 402. **Participation in Elections for President and U.S. Representatives: 1932 to 2006**

[75,768 represents 75,768,000. As of November, except as noted. Estimated resident population 21 years old and over, 1932–70, except as noted, and 18 years old and over thereafter; includes Armed Forces stationed in the U.S. Prior to 1958, excludes Alaska and prior to 1960, excludes Hawaii. District of Columbia is included in votes cast for President beginning 1964]

Year	Resident population (incl. aliens) of voting age [1] (1,000)	For President (1,000)	Percent of voting-age population	For U.S. Representatives (1,000)	Percent of voting-age population	Year	Resident population (incl. aliens) of voting age [1] (1,000)	For President (1,000)	Percent of voting-age population	For U.S. Representatives (1,000)	Percent of voting-age population
1932 . . .	75,768	39,817	52.6	(NA)	(NA)	1970 . . .	124,498	(X)	(X)	54,259	43.6
1934 . . .	77,997	(X)	(X)	32,804	42.1	1972 . . .	140,777	77,625	55.1	71,188	50.6
1936 . . .	80,174	45,647	56.9	(NA)	(NA)	1974 . . .	146,338	(X)	(X)	52,313	35.7
1938 . . .	82,354	(X)	(X)	(NA)	(NA)	1976 . . .	152,308	81,603	53.6	74,259	48.8
1940 . . .	84,728	49,815	58.8	(NA)	(NA)	1978 . . .	158,369	(X)	(X)	54,584	34.5
1942 . . .	86,465	(X)	(X)	28,074	32.5	1980 . . .	163,945	86,497	52.8	77,874	47.5
1944 . . .	85,654	48,026	56.1	45,110	52.7	1982 . . .	169,643	(X)	(X)	63,881	37.7
1946 . . .	92,659	(X)	(X)	34,410	37.1	1984 . . .	173,995	92,655	53.3	82,422	47.4
1948 . . .	95,573	48,834	51.1	46,220	48.4	1986 . . .	177,922	(X)	(X)	59,758	33.6
1950 . . .	98,134	(X)	(X)	40,430	41.2	1988 . . .	181,956	91,587	50.3	81,682	44.9
1952 . . .	99,929	61,552	61.6	57,571	57.6	1990 . . .	185,812	(X)	(X)	62,355	33.6
1954 . . .	102,075	(X)	(X)	42,583	41.7	1992 . . .	189,493	104,600	55.2	97,198	51.3
1956 . . .	104,515	62,027	59.3	58,886	56.3	1994 . . .	193,010	(X)	(X)	70,494	36.5
1958 . . .	106,447	(X)	(X)	45,719	43.0	1996 . . .	196,789	96,390	49.0	90,233	45.9
1960 . . .	109,672	68,836	62.8	64,124	58.5	1998 . . .	201,270	(X)	(X)	66,605	33.1
1962 . . .	112,952	(X)	(X)	51,242	45.4	2000 . . .	[2]209,834	105,594	50.3	98,800	47.1
1964 . . .	114,090	70,098	61.4	65,879	57.7	2002 . . .	[2]215,026	(X)	(X)	74,707	34.7
1966 . . .	116,638	(X)	(X)	52,902	45.4	2004 . . .	[2]219,973	122,349	55.6	113,192	51.5
1968 . . .	120,285	73,027	60.7	66,109	55.0	2006 . . .	[2]225,087	(X)	(X)	80,588	35.8

NA Not available.   X Not applicable.   [1] Population 18 and over in Georgia, 1944–70, and in Kentucky, 1956–70; 20 and over in Alaska and 20 and over in Hawaii, 1960–70. Source: Through 1990, U.S. Census Bureau, "Table 4. Participation in Elections for President and U.S. Representatives: 1930 to 1992"; <http://www.census.gov/population/socdemo/voting/p25-1117/tab03-04.pdf> (released May 1994). For 1992–1998, "Estimates and Projections of the Voting-Age Population, 1992 to 2000, and Percent Casting Votes for President, by State: November 1992 and 1996" (published 31 July 2000); <http://www.census.gov /population/socdemo/voting/proj00/tab03.txt>. Starting 2000, "Annual Estimates of the Population by Selected Age Groups and Sex for the United States: April 1, 2000 to July 1, 2006," (NC-EST2006-02); <http://www.census.gov/popest/national/asrh /NC-EST2006-sa.html/> (released 17 May 2007).   [2] As of July 1.

Source: Except as noted, U.S. House of Representatives, Office of the Clerk, Statistics of the Presidential and Congressional Election, biennial. See also <http://clerk.house.gov/member_info/electionInfo/index.html>.

Elections   253

Table 403. Resident Population of Voting Age and Percent Casting Votes— States: 2000 to 2006

[**209,834 represents 209,834,000**. Estimated population, 18 years old and over. Includes Armed Forces stationed in each state, aliens, and institutional population]

State	Voting-age population (1,000) [1]			Percent casting votes for—				
				Presidential electors		U.S. Representatives		
	2000	2004	2006	2000	2004	2000	2004	2006
U.S.	209,834	219,973	225,087	50.3	55.6	47.1	51.5	35.8
AL.	3,330	3,401	3,471	50.0	55.4	43.2	52.7	34.6
AK.	437	477	494	65.3	65.6	62.8	62.9	47.5
AZ.	3,792	4,228	4,540	40.4	47.6	38.6	44.3	32.9
AR.	1,998	2,062	2,113	46.1	51.2	31.7	38.4	36.1
CA.	24,737	26,287	26,849	44.3	47.3	42.2	44.2	30.9
CO	3,222	3,461	3,592	54.0	61.5	50.4	58.9	42.8
CT.	2,570	2,641	2,669	56.8	59.8	51.1	54.1	40.3
DE.	592	628	649	55.4	59.7	52.9	56.7	38.8
DC	457	464	471	44.2	49.0	(X)	(X)	(X)
FL.	12,394	13,449	14,025	48.1	56.6	40.4	41.8	27.5
GA	6,053	6,564	6,867	42.7	50.3	39.9	45.1	30.1
HI	917	967	995	40.1	44.4	37.1	43.1	34.0
ID	930	1,010	1,065	54.0	59.2	53.0	56.7	41.8
IL	9,194	9,455	9,574	51.6	55.8	47.8	52.8	36.1
IN	4,517	4,643	4,719	48.7	53.2	47.7	52.0	35.3
IA	2,195	2,233	2,260	61.6	67.5	58.1	65.3	45.7
KS.	1,980	2,032	2,062	54.2	58.4	52.3	56.9	41.0
KY.	3,054	3,146	3,201	50.6	57.1	47.0	52.0	39.2
LA.	3,252	3,317	3,176	54.3	58.6	37.0	37.9	28.8
ME	976	1,018	1,032	66.8	72.8	65.4	69.8	52.0
MD	3,954	4,160	4,234	51.2	57.3	48.7	54.2	40.2
MA	4,862	4,956	4,988	56.2	59.1	56.2	59.1	45.0
MI	7,360	7,562	7,619	57.5	64.0	55.3	61.2	47.9
MN	3,645	3,817	3,894	66.9	74.1	64.8	71.3	56.0
MS	2,074	2,122	2,135	47.9	53.7	47.6	52.6	28.1
MO	4,178	4,326	4,413	56.5	63.1	55.7	61.7	47.5
MT	674	707	728	61.0	63.7	60.9	62.9	55.8
NE.	1,263	1,299	1,319	55.2	59.9	54.1	58.9	45.2
NV.	1,502	1,734	1,853	40.6	47.8	39.1	45.6	31.0
NH	930	987	1,009	61.2	68.8	59.8	66.0	39.9
NJ.	6,344	6,533	6,586	50.2	55.3	47.1	50.3	32.4
NM	1,313	1,396	1,445	45.6	54.2	44.7	53.2	38.8
NY.	14,313	14,691	14,815	48.6	50.7	48.5	50.7	31.6
NC	6,111	6,456	6,706	47.7	54.2	45.5	52.9	28.9
ND	481	490	494	59.9	63.8	59.4	63.4	44.1
OH	8,479	8,634	8,689	55.5	65.2	54.1	60.0	45.6
OK	2,563	2,639	2,688	48.2	55.5	42.4	52.1	33.7
OR	2,584	2,736	2,834	59.4	67.1	55.7	64.8	47.9
PA.	9,368	9,504	9,596	52.4	60.7	48.6	54.2	41.8
RI	803	828	825	51.0	52.8	47.9	48.6	45.2
SC.	3,013	3,173	3,281	45.9	51.0	43.9	45.4	33.1
SD.	553	578	592	57.2	67.1	56.9	67.3	56.3
TN.	4,304	4,484	4,612	48.2	54.4	43.1	49.5	37.2
TX.	15,045	16,217	16,918	42.6	45.7	39.8	42.9	24.5
UT.	1,523	1,677	1,783	50.6	55.3	49.8	54.2	32.0
VT.	462	480	487	63.6	65.1	61.3	63.6	54.0
VA.	5,363	5,662	5,819	51.1	56.4	45.2	53.1	39.5
WA	4,396	4,675	4,849	56.6	61.2	54.2	58.4	42.4
WV	1,406	1,414	1,420	46.1	53.4	41.2	51.0	32.0
WI.	4,005	4,170	4,246	64.9	71.9	62.6	67.7	48.6
WY	365	381	390	58.5	64.1	58.1	62.8	50.3

X Not applicable.   [1] As of July 1. Source: U.S. Census Bureau, "Annual Estimates of the Population by Selected Age Groups and Sex for the United States: April 1, 2000, to July 1, 2007," (NC-EST2007-02); <http://www.census.gov/popest/datasets.html> (released 1 May 2008).

Source: U.S. House of Representatives, Office of the Clerk, *Statistics of the Presidential and Congressional Election,* biennial. See also <http://clerk.house.gov/member_info/electionInfo/index.html>.

Table 404. Political Action Committees—Number by Committee Type: 1980 to 2007

[As of December 31]

Committee type	1980	1990	1995	2000	2003	2004	2005	2006	2007
Total	**2,551**	**4,172**	**4,016**	**3,706**	**4,023**	**4,867**	**4,343**	**4,168**	**4,234**
Corporate	1,206	1,795	1,674	1,523	1,552	1,756	1,638	1,586	1,601
Labor	297	346	334	316	308	328	296	273	273
Trade/membership/health	576	774	815	812	877	986	912	926	925
Nonconnected	374	1,062	1,020	902	1,147	1,650	1,357	1,247	1,300
Cooperative	42	59	44	39	36	38	37	37	38
Corporation without stock	56	136	129	114	103	109	103	99	97

Source: U.S. Federal Election Commission, press release of January 2008.

Table 405. Political Action Committees—Financial Activity Summary by Committee Type: 2001 to 2006

[In millions of dollars (685.3 represents $685,300,000). Covers financial activity during 2-year calendar period indicated]

Committee type	Receipts			Disbursements [1]			Contributions to candidates		
	2001–02	2003–04	2005–06	2001–02	2003–04	2005–06	2001–02	2003–04	2005–06
Total	**685.3**	**915.7**	**477.4**	**656.5**	**842.9**	**394.1**	**282.0**	**310.5**	**141.1**
Corporate	191.7	239.0	131.2	178.3	221.6	116.3	99.6	115.6	56.5
Labor	167.8	191.7	100.3	158.0	182.9	73.1	53.9	52.1	21.1
Trade/membership/health	166.7	181.8	95.4	165.7	170.1	74.6	46.3	83.2	38.0
Nonconnected	145.8	289.4	141.6	141.3	255.2	122.6	75.1	52.5	22.0
Cooperative	3.7	4.2	2.7	3.6	3.9	1.9	2.7	2.9	1.4
Corporation without stock	9.7	9.6	6.1	9.6	9.2	5.7	4.4	4.2	2.1

[1] Comprises contributions to candidates, independent expenditures, and other disbursements.

Source: U.S. Federal Election Commission, *FEC Reports on Financial Activity, Final Report, Party and Non-party Political Committees,* biennial.

Table 406. Presidential Campaign Finances—Federal Funds for General Election: 1992 to 2004

[In millions of dollars (110.4 represents $110,400,000). Based on FEC certifications, audit reports, and Dept. of Treasury reports]

1992		1996		2000		2004	
Candidate	Amount	Candidate	Amount	Candidate	Amount	Candidate	Amount
Total	**110.4**	**Total**	**152.6**	**Total**	**147.7**	**Total**	**150.1**
Bush	55.2	Clinton	61.8	Bush	67.6	Bush	74.6
Clinton	55.2	Dole	61.8	Gore	67.6	Kerry	74.6
Perot	–	Perot	29.0	Buchanan	12.6	Nader	0.9

– Represents zero.

Source: U.S. Federal Election Commission, periodic press releases.

Table 407. Presidential Campaign Finances—Primary Campaign Receipts and Disbursements: 1995 to 2004

[In millions of dollars (243.9 represents $243,900,000). Covers campaign finance activity during 2-year calendar period indicated. Covers candidates who received federal matching funds or who had significant financial activity]

Item	Total [1]			Democratic			Republican		
	1995–96	1999–00	2003–04	1995–96	1999–00	2003–04	1995–96	1999–00	2003–04
Receipts, total [2]	**243.9**	**351.6**	**673.9**	**46.2**	**96.6**	**401.8**	**187.0**	**236.7**	**269.6**
Individual contributions	126.4	238.2	611.4	31.3	66.7	351.0	93.1	159.1	258.9
Federal matching funds	56.0	61.6	28.0	14.0	29.3	27.2	41.6	26.5	–
Disbursements	**234.1**	**343.5**	**661.1**	**41.8**	**92.2**	**389.7**	**182.1**	**233.2**	**268.9**

– Represents zero. [1] Includes other parties, not shown separately. [2] Includes other types of receipts, not shown separately.

Source: U.S. Federal Election Commission, *FEC Reports on Financial Activity, Final Report, Presidential Pre-Nomination Campaigns,* quadrennial.

U.S. Census Bureau, Statistical Abstract of the United States: 2009

Table 408. Congressional Campaign Finances—Receipts and Disbursements: 2001 to 2006

[**643.3 represents $643,300,000.** Covers all campaign finance activity during 2-year calendar period indicated for primary, general, run-off, and special elections. Data have been adjusted to eliminate transfers between all committees within a campaign. For further information on legal limits of contributions, see Federal Election Campaign Act of 1971, as amended]

Item	House of Representatives						Senate					
	Amount (mil. dol.)			Percent distribution			Amount (mil. dol.)			Percent distribution		
	2001–02	2003–04	2005–06	2001–02	2003–04	2005–06	2001–02	2003–04	2005–06	2001–02	2003–04	2005–06
Total receipts [1]	**643.3**	**708.5**	**875.4**	**100**	**100**	**100**	**326.1**	**497.6**	**564.6**	**100**	**100**	**100**
Individual contributions	322.5	396.7	478.9	50	56	55	214.3	324.1	383.2	66	65	68
Other committees	214.1	225.4	279.8	33	32	32	60.2	63.7	68.9	18	13	12
Candidate loans	72.0	47.4	56.1	11	7	6	28.1	39.8	47.0	9	8	8
Candidate contributions	9.2	7.8	14.7	1	1	2	0.8	38.2	37.5	(Z)	8	7
Democrats	314.2	307.4	417.5	49	43	48	162.9	250.6	291.8	50	50	52
Republicans	326.3	399.2	453.6	51	56	52	162.7	246.1	245.8	50	49	44
Others	2.8	1.9	4.2	(Z)	(Z)	(Z)	0.6	0.9	26.9	(Z)	(Z)	5
Incumbents	369.8	452.6	532.6	57	64	61	145.0	171.7	278.4	44	35	49
Challengers	107.0	118.2	188.7	17	17	22	109.7	79.5	186.6	34	16	33
Open seats [2]	166.5	137.8	154.1	26	19	18	71.4	246.4	99.6	22	50	18
Total disbursements	**613.9**	**660.3**	**854.8**	**100**	**100**	**100**	**322.4**	**496.4**	**562.9**	**100**	**100**	**100**
Democrats	301.1	288.5	395.5	49	44	46	162.9	254.6	288.6	51	51	51
Republicans	310.0	370.0	455.2	50	56	53	158.9	241.0	249.3	49	49	44
Others	2.9	1.8	4.1	(Z)	(Z)	(Z)	0.6	0.8	25.0	(Z)	(Z)	4
Incumbents	343.9	410.1	519.2	56	62	61	145.6	171.7	274.3	45	35	49
Challengers	103.9	116.6	185.6	17	18	22	108.4	76.6	187.1	34	15	33
Open seats [2]	166.1	133.6	150.0	27	20	18	68.5	248.1	101.5	21	50	18

Z Less than $50,000 or 0.5 percent.   [1] Includes other types of receipts, not shown separately.   [2] Elections in which an incumbent did not seek reelection.

Source: U.S. Federal Election Commission, *FEC Reports on Financial Activity, Final Report, U.S. Senate and House Campaigns*, biennial.

Table 409. Contributions to Congressional Campaigns by Political Action Committees (PAC) by Type of Committee: 1995 to 2006

[**In millions of dollars (155.8 represents $155,800,000).** Covers amounts given to candidates in primary, general, run-off, and special elections during the 2-year calendar period indicated. For number of political action committees, see Table 404]

Type of committee	Total [1]	Democrats	Republicans	Incumbents	Challengers	Open seats [2]
HOUSE OF REPRESENTATIVES						
1995–96	155.8	77.3	77.7	113.9	21.4	20.5
1997–98	158.7	77.6	80.9	124.0	14.9	19.8
1999–00	193.4	98.2	94.7	150.5	19.9	23.0
2001–02	206.9	102.6	104.2	161.0	13.8	32.1
2003–04	225.4	98.6	126.6	187.3	15.6	22.5
2005–06, total [3]	**279.8**	**125.0**	**154.8**	**232.0**	**24.4**	**23.5**
Corporate	96.1	31.7	64.4	90.4	1.5	4.2
Trade association [4]	79.6	30.3	49.3	70.7	3.2	5.7
Labor	47.6	42.1	5.5	32.8	9.8	5.0
Nonconnected [5]	50.3	18.2	32.1	32.4	9.7	8.2
SENATE						
1995–96	45.6	16.6	29.0	19.4	6.9	19.3
1997–98	48.1	20.7	27.3	34.3	6.6	7.2
1999–00	51.9	18.7	33.2	33.5	7.1	11.3
2001–02	59.2	25.4	33.8	37.0	14.2	8.1
2003–04	63.7	28.4	35.3	39.3	5.6	18.8
2005–06, total [3]	**68.9**	**28.6**	**37.5**	**50.0**	**9.9**	**8.7**
Corporate	27.3	9.1	17.1	23.1	1.7	2.6
Trade association [4]	16.4	6.0	9.8	12.6	1.8	2.1
Labor	6.7	5.8	0.5	3.4	2.1	1.2
Nonconnected [5]	17.1	7.1	9.5	9.9	4.3	2.8

[1] Includes other parties, not shown separately.   [2] Elections in which an incumbent did not seek reelection.   [3] Includes other types of political action committees not shown separately.   [4] Includes membership organizations and health organizations.   [5] Represents "ideological" groups as well as other issue groups not necessarily ideological in nature.

Source: U.S. Federal Election Commission, *FEC Reports on Financial Activity, Party and Non-Party Political Committees, Final Report*, biennial.

Section 8
State and Local Government Finances and Employment

This section presents data on revenues, expenditures, debt, and employment of state and local governments. Nationwide statistics relating to state and local governments, their numbers, finances, and employment are compiled primarily by the U.S. Census Bureau through a program of censuses and surveys. Every fifth year (for years ending in "2" and "7"), the Census Bureau conducts a census of governments involving collection of data for all governmental units in the United States. In addition, the Census Bureau conducts annual surveys which cover all the state governments and a sample of local governments.

Annually, the Census Bureau releases information on the Internet which presents financial data for the federal government, nationwide totals for state and local governments, and state-local data by states. Also released annually is a series on state, city, county, and school finances and on state and local public employment. There is also a series of quarterly data releases covering tax revenue and finances of major public employee retirement systems.

Basic information for Census Bureau statistics on governments is obtained by mail canvass from state and local officials; however, financial data for each of the state governments and for many of the large local governments are compiled from their official records and reports by Census Bureau personnel. In over two-thirds of the states, all or part of local government financial data are obtained through central collection arrangements with state governments. Financial data on the federal government are primarily based on the *Budget* published by the Office of Management and Budget (see text, Section 9, Federal Government Finances and Employment).

Governmental units—The governmental structure of the United States includes, in addition to the federal government and the states, thousands of local governments—counties, municipalities, townships, school districts, and many "special districts." In 2007, 89,527 local governments were identified by the census of governments (see Tables 410–412). As defined by the census, governmental units include all agencies or bodies having an organized existence, governmental character, and substantial autonomy. While most of these governments can impose taxes, many of the special districts—such as independent public housing authorities and numerous local irrigation, power, and other types of districts—are financed from rentals, charges for services, benefit assessments, grants from other governments, and other nontax sources. The count of governments excludes semi-autonomous agencies through which states, cities, and counties sometimes provide for certain functions—for example, "dependent" school systems, state institutions of higher education, and certain other "authorities" and special agencies which are under the administrative or fiscal control of an established governmental unit.

Finances—The financial statistics relate to government fiscal years ending June 30 or at some date within the 12 previous months. The following governments are exceptions and are included as though they were part of the June 30 group; ending September 30, the state governments of Alabama and Michigan, the District of Columbia, and Alabama school districts; and ending August 31, the state governments of Nebraska, Texas, and Chicago school districts. New York State ends its fiscal year on March 31. The federal government ended the fiscal year June 30 until 1976 when its fiscal year, by an act of Congress, was revised to extend from Oct. 1 to Sept. 30. A 3-month quarter (July 1 to Sept. 30, 1976) bridged the transition.

Nationwide government finance statistics have been classified and presented in

U.S. Census Bureau, Statistical Abstract of the United States: 2009

terms of uniform concepts and categories, rather than according to the highly diverse terminology, organization, and fund structure utilized by individual governments.

Statistics on governmental finances distinguish among general government, utilities, liquor stores, and insurance trusts. *General government* comprises all activities except utilities, liquor stores, and insurance trusts. Utilities include government water supply, electric light and power, gas supply, and transit systems. Liquor stores are operated by 17 states and by local governments in 6 states. Insurance trusts relate to employee retirement, unemployment compensation, and other social insurance systems administered by the federal, state, and local governments.

Data for cities or counties relate only to municipal or county and their dependent agencies and do not include amounts for other local governments in the same geographic location. Therefore, expenditure figures for "education" do not include spending by the separate school districts which administer public schools within most municipal or county areas. Variations in the assignment of governmental responsibility for public assistance, health, hospitals, public housing, and other functions to a lesser degree also

have an important effect upon reported amounts of city or county expenditure, revenue, and debt.

Employment and payrolls—These data are based mainly on mail canvassing of state and local governments. Payroll includes all salaries, wages, and individual fee payments for the month specified, and employment relates to all persons on governmental payrolls during a pay period of the month covered—including paid officials, temporary help, and (unless otherwise specified) part-time as well as full-time personnel. Effective with the 1997 Census of Governments, the reference period for measuring government employment was changed from October of the calendar year to March of the calendar year. As a result, there was no annual survey of government employment covering the October 1996 period. The prior reference month of October was used from 1958 to 1995. Figures shown for individual governments cover major dependent agencies such as institutions of higher education, as well as the basic central departments and agencies of the government.

Statistical reliability—For a discussion of statistical collection and estimation, sampling procedures, and measures of statistical reliability applicable to Census Bureau data, see Appendix III.

U.S. Census Bureau, Statistical Abstract of the United States: 2009

Table 410. **Number of Governmental Units by Type: 1962 to 2007**

Type of government	1962	1967	1972	1977	1982	1987	1992	1997	2002	2007
Total units	91,237	81,299	78,269	79,913	81,831	83,237	85,006	87,504	87,576	89,527
U.S. government	1	1	1	1	1	1	1	1	1	1
State government.	50	50	50	50	50	50	50	50	50	50
Local governments.	91,186	81,248	78,218	79,862	81,780	83,186	84,955	87,453	87,525	89,476
County	3,043	3,049	3,044	3,042	3,041	3,042	3,043	3,043	3,034	3,033
Municipal.	18,000	18,048	18,517	18,862	19,076	19,200	19,279	19,372	19,429	19,492
Township and town . . .	17,142	17,105	16,991	16,822	16,734	16,691	16,656	16,629	16,504	16,519
School district.	34,678	21,782	15,781	15,174	14,851	14,721	14,422	13,726	13,506	13,051
Special district	18,323	21,264	23,885	25,962	28,078	29,532	31,555	34,683	35,052	37,381

Source: U.S. Census Bureau, *Census of Governments, Volume 1, Number 1, Government Organization,* Series GC07(1)-1, quinquennial; <http://www.census.gov/govs/www/cog2007.html>.

Table 411. **Number of Local Governments by Type—States: 2002**

[Governments in existence in January. Limited to governments actually in existence. Excludes, therefore, a few counties and numerous townships and "incorporated places" existing as areas for which statistics can be presented as to population and other subjects, but lacking any separate organized county, township, or municipal government. See Appendix III]

State	All govern-mental units [1]	County	Municipal	Town-ship [1]	School district	Special district [2] Total [3]	Natural resources	Fire protection	Housing & community develop-ment
United States.	87,525	3,034	19,429	16,504	13,506	35,052	6,979	5,725	3,399
Alabama	1,171	67	451	–	128	525	68	12	152
Alaska	175	12	149	–	–	14	–	–	13
Arizona.	638	15	87	–	231	305	83	151	–
Arkansas.	1,588	75	499	–	310	704	258	80	122
California.	4,409	57	475	–	1,047	2,830	484	368	71
Colorado.	1,928	62	270	–	182	1,414	178	250	91
Connecticut	580	–	30	149	17	384	1	64	93
Delaware.	339	3	57	–	19	260	239	–	3
District of Columbia. . .	2	–	1	–	–	1	–	–	–
Florida.	1,191	66	404	–	95	626	124	57	105
Georgia	1,448	156	531	–	180	581	38	2	201
Hawaii	19	3	1	–	–	15	14	–	–
Idaho	1,158	44	200	–	116	798	176	142	10
Illinois.	6,903	102	1,291	1,431	934	3,145	979	823	112
Indiana	3,085	91	567	1,008	294	1,125	141	1	63
Iowa.	1,975	99	948	–	386	542	251	67	23
Kansas	3,887	104	627	1,299	324	1,533	261	–	199
Kentucky.	1,439	119	424	–	176	720	166	163	17
Louisiana	473	60	302	–	66	45	4	–	–
Maine.	826	16	22	467	99	222	15	–	23
Maryland.	265	23	157	–	–	85	44	–	21
Massachusetts	841	5	45	306	82	403	16	16	250
Michigan	2,804	83	533	1,242	580	366	80	4	–
Minnesota	3,482	87	854	1,793	345	403	114	–	167
Mississippi.	1,000	82	296	–	164	458	242	34	57
Missouri	3,422	114	946	312	536	1,514	183	317	136
Montana	1,127	54	129	–	352	592	125	155	12
Nebraska	2,791	93	531	446	575	1,146	80	421	125
Nevada.	210	16	19	–	17	158	33	19	5
New Hampshire	559	10	13	221	167	148	10	14	21
New Jersey	1,412	21	324	242	549	276	16	196	2
New Mexico.	858	33	101	–	96	628	583	–	6
New York	3,420	57	616	929	683	1,135	3	911	–
North Carolina	960	100	541	–	–	319	155	–	91
North Dakota	2,735	53	360	1,332	226	764	79	281	39
Ohio.	3,636	88	942	1,308	667	631	98	73	77
Oklahoma	1,798	77	590	–	571	560	97	26	105
Oregon	1,439	36	240	–	236	927	179	256	20
Pennsylvania	5,031	66	1,018	1,546	516	1,885	7	–	90
Rhode Island	118	–	8	31	4	75	3	34	25
South Carolina	701	46	269	–	85	301	48	86	46
South Dakota.	1,866	66	308	940	176	376	102	72	40
Tennessee.	930	92	349	–	14	475	108	–	98
Texas	4,784	254	1,196	–	1,089	2,245	442	141	398
Utah.	605	29	236	–	40	300	81	19	16
Vermont	733	14	47	237	283	152	14	19	10
Virginia	521	95	229	–	1	196	47	–	–
Washington	1,787	39	279	–	296	1,173	170	387	41
West Virginia	686	55	234	–	55	342	15	–	39
Wisconsin	3,048	72	585	1,265	442	684	191	–	164
Wyoming	722	23	98	–	55	546	134	64	–

– Represents zero. [1] Includes "town" governments in the six New England States and in Minnesota, New York, and Wisconsin. [2] Single function districts. [3] Includes other special districts not shown separately.

Source: U.S. Census Bureau, *Census of Governments, Volume 1, Number 1, Government Organization,* Series GC02(1)-1, quinquennial; <http://www.census.gov/govs/www/cog2002.html>.

U.S. Census Bureau, Statistical Abstract of the United States: 2009

Table 412. County, Municipal, and Township Governments by Population Size: 2002

[Number of governments as of **January 2002**. Population enumerated as of **April 1, 2000. (252,051 represents 252,051,000).** Consolidated city-county governments are classified as municipal rather than county governments. Township governments include "towns" in the six New England states, Minnesota, New York, and Wisconsin. See Appendix III]

Population-size group	County governments			Municipal governments			Township governments		
	Number, 2002	Population, **2000**		Number, 2002	Population, **2000**		Number, 2002	Population, **2000**	
		Number (1,000)	Percent		Number (1,000)	Percent		Number (1,000)	Percent
Total	3,034	252,051	100	19,429	174,882	100	16,504	57,365	100
300,000 or more	161	131,575	52	58	47,768	27	3	1,527	3
200,000 to 299,999 . . .	84	20,606	8	30	7,163	4	3	728	1
100,000 to 199,999 . . .	228	31,576	13	153	21,076	12	30	3,974	7
50,000 to 99,999	383	27,160	11	364	24,960	14	97	6,588	11
25,000 to 49,999	638	22,913	9	643	22,576	13	273	9,275	16
10,000 to 24,999	869	14,488	6	1,436	22,589	13	773	12,067	21
5,000 to 9,999	385	2,911	1	1,637	11,644	7	1,085	7,560	13
2,500 to 4,999	173	643	(Z)	2,070	7,352	4	1,909	6,732	12
1,000 to 2,499	84	158	(Z)	3,677	5,951	3	3,679	5,905	10
Less than 1,000	29	21	(Z)	9,361	3,803	2	8,652	3,008	5

Z Less than 0.5 percent.

Source: U.S. Census Bureau, *Census of Governments, Volume 1, Number 1, Government Organization,* Series GC02(1)-1, quinquennial; <http://www.census.gov/govs/www/cog2002.html>.

Table 413. State and Local Government Current Receipts and Expenditures in the National Income and Product Accounts: 1990 to 2007

[**In billions of dollars (737.8 represents $737,800,000,000).** For explanation of national income, see text, Section 13. Minus sign (–) indicates net loss]

Item	1990	1995	2000	2002	2003	2004	2005	2006	2007
Current receipts	**737.8**	**990.2**	**1,319.5**	**1,410.1**	**1,494.2**	**1,594.3**	**1,706.9**	**1,797.7**	**1,886.4**
Current tax receipts	519.1	672.1	893.2	929.0	979.4	1,061.2	1,156.0	1,232.3	1,292.7
Personal current taxes	122.6	158.1	236.6	221.3	226.6	249.0	276.7	301.2	320.4
Income taxes	109.6	141.7	217.3	200.8	204.5	225.0	251.8	275.1	293.5
Other	13.0	16.4	19.4	20.5	22.2	23.9	24.9	26.1	26.9
Taxes on production and imports . . .	374.1	482.4	621.1	675.5	717.5	769.2	822.6	868.8	908.6
Sales taxes	184.3	242.7	316.6	330.2	347.7	370.0	395.3	415.4	429.1
Property taxes	161.5	202.6	254.6	290.1	307.9	327.5	346.3	367.8	389.7
Other	28.3	37.0	49.9	55.2	61.9	71.7	81.0	85.5	89.8
Taxes on corporate income	22.5	31.7	35.5	32.2	35.3	43.0	56.7	62.4	63.7
Contributions for government social insurance	10.0	13.6	11.0	15.8	19.8	23.6	25.5	26.0	25.9
Income receipts on assets	68.4	68.4	92.2	78.2	72.9	75.4	81.0	87.1	89.5
Interest receipts	64.1	62.9	84.0	69.6	62.9	64.3	69.0	73.8	75.9
Dividends	0.2	1.0	1.9	2.0	2.2	2.4	2.4	2.6	2.7
Rents and royalties	4.2	4.5	6.3	6.6	7.9	8.7	9.6	10.7	10.9
Current transfer receipts	133.5	224.1	315.4	384.7	422.7	437.2	454.8	462.9	490.4
Federal grants-in-aid	111.4	184.1	247.3	304.6	338.5	349.1	361.2	358.6	377.5
From business (net)	7.1	13.5	28.8	32.6	33.5	32.2	33.3	40.6	43.2
From persons	14.9	26.5	39.2	47.5	50.6	56.0	60.3	63.7	69.7
Current surplus of governmemt enterprises	6.7	12.0	7.7	2.5	–0.6	–3.0	–10.3	–10.7	–12.2
Current expenditures	**730.5**	**978.2**	**1,269.5**	**1,444.3**	**1,514.5**	**1,592.8**	**1,691.7**	**1,773.0**	**1,898.2**
Consumption expenditures	544.6	696.1	917.8	1,025.3	1,073.8	1,120.3	1,197.2	1,276.5	1,365.9
Government social benefit payments to persons	127.7	217.6	271.7	332.0	353.0	383.8	403.8	400.8	433.0
Interest payments	57.9	64.2	79.5	86.0	87.7	88.4	89.9	94.3	98.5
Subsidies	0.4	0.3	0.5	0.9	0.1	0.4	0.4	0.4	7.1
Net state and local government saving	**7.2**	**12.0**	**50.0**	**–34.2**	**–20.4**	**1.5**	**15.2**	**24.6**	**–11.8**
Social insurance funds	2.0	4.0	2.0	1.7	3.8	7.1	8.0	7.1	6.1
Other	5.3	8.0	47.9	–35.9	–24.1	–5.6	7.2	17.5	–17.9

– Represents or rounds to zero.

Source: U.S. Bureau of Economic Analysis, *Survey of Current Business,* April 2008. See also <http://www.bea/gov/national/nipaweb/SelectTable.asp?selected=N>.

Table 414. **Federal Grants-in-Aid to State and Local Governments: 1990 to 2008**

[135,325 represents $135,325,000,000, except as indicated. **For year ending Sept. 30.** Minus sign (−) indicates decrease]

Year	Current dollars		Grants to individuals		Grants as percent of—			Constant (2000) dollars	
	Total grants (mil. dol.)	Annual percent change [1]	Total (mil. dol.)	Percent of total grants	State/local govt. expenditures [2]	Federal outlays	Gross domestic product	Total grants (bil. dol.)	Annual percent change [1]
1990	135,325	11.0	77,264	57.1	25.2	10.8	2.4	172.1	6.3
1993	193,612	8.7	124,155	64.1	29.6	13.7	3.0	223.9	5.9
1994	210,596	8.8	134,153	63.7	30.9	14.4	3.0	238.1	6.3
1995	224,991	6.8	144,427	64.2	31.5	14.8	3.1	247.9	4.1
1996	227,811	1.3	146,493	64.3	30.8	14.6	3.0	245.5	−1.0
1997	234,160	2.8	148,236	63.3	30.2	14.6	2.9	247.7	0.9
1998	246,128	5.1	160,305	65.1	30.3	14.9	2.9	257.3	3.9
1999	267,886	8.5	172,384	64.5	31.2	15.7	2.9	275.6	7.1
2000	285,874	6.6	182,592	64.1	27.4	16.0	2.9	285.9	3.7
2001	318,542	11.4	203,920	64.0	28.3	17.1	3.2	310.7	8.7
2002	352,895	10.8	227,373	64.4	29.4	17.5	3.4	338.4	8.9
2003	388,542	10.1	246,570	63.5	31.0	18.0	3.6	363.3	7.4
2004	407,512	4.9	262,177	64.3	31.3	17.8	3.5	370.4	2.0
2005	428,018	5.0	273,898	64.0	31.0	17.3	3.5	373.6	0.9
2006	434,099	1.4	272,585	62.8	29.3	16.3	3.3	364.0	−2.6
2007	443,797	2.2	284,362	64.1	27.9	16.3	3.2	361.6	−0.7
2008, est.	466,568	5.1	300,459	64.4	(NA)	15.9	3.3	367.4	1.6

NA Not available. [1] Average annual percent change from prior year shown. For explanation, see Guide to Tabular Presentation. For 1990, change from 1989. [2] Expenditures from own sources as defined in the national income and product accounts.

Source: U.S. Office of Management and Budget, *Budget of the United States Government, Historical Tables,* annual; <http://www.whitehouse.gov/omb/budget/fy2009/pdf/hist.pdf>.

Table 415. **Total Outlays for Grants to State and Local Governments—Selected Agencies and Programs: 1990 to 2008**

[In millions of dollars (135,325 represents $135,325,000,000). **For year ending Sept 30.** Includes trust funds]

Selected programs	1990	1995	2000	2004	2005	2006	2007	2008 est.
Total outlays for grants	135,325	224,991	285,874	407,512	428,018	434,099	443,797	466,568
Energy.	461	492	433	608	636	651	667	550
Natural resources and environment	3,745	3,985	4,595	6,009	5,858	6,062	6,060	5,605
Environmental Protection Agency [1]	2,874	2,912	3,490	4,018	3,734	3,966	4,016	3,185
Agriculture	1,285	780	724	995	933	749	803	829
Transportation	19,174	25,787	32,222	41,298	43,368	46,681	47,945	52,880
Grants for airports [1]	1,220	1,859	1,624	2,958	3,530	3,841	3,874	2,970
Federal-aid highways [2]	13,854	18,945	24,711	29,791	30,915	32,703	33,222	36,796
Urban mass transportation [1]	3,728	4,353	5,262	7,777	8,114	8,484	8,984	10,626
Community and regional development	4,965	7,230	8,665	12,604	20,167	21,285	20,653	21,255
Rural community advance program	139	333	479	797	814	773	760	(NA)
Community development fund	2,818	4,333	4,955	5,388	4,985	5,012	10,867	11,458
Homeland Security	1,184	1,772	2,439	5,490	13,541	14,731	8,267	7,934
State and local programs	(NA)	(NA)	(NA)	1,535	2,116	2,601	2,385	1,601
Firefighter assistance grants	(NA)	(NA)	(NA)	508	1,185	228	499	662
Operations, planning, and support	11	79	192	387	132	(NA)	(NA)	(NA)
Mitigation grants	(NA)	(NA)	13	23	39	34	32	62
Disaster relief	1,173	1,693	2,234	3,037	10,069	11,868	5,351	5,609
Education, training, employment, social services	21,780	30,881	36,672	54,201	57,247	60,512	58,077	59,596
Education for the disadvantaged [3]	4,437	6,785	8,511	12,417	14,539	14,604	14,409	14,927
School improvement programs [3]	1,080	1,288	2,394	6,542	6,569	5,589	5,299	5,219
Special education	1,485	2,938	4,696	9,465	10,661	11,582	11,585	11,495
Social services—block grant	2,749	2,797	1,827	1,752	1,822	1,848	1,956	1,936
Children and family services programs	2,618	4,463	5,843	8,326	8,490	8,492	8,496	8,529
Training and employment services	3,042	3,620	2,957	3,883	3,372	4,566	3,006	2,975
Health	43,890	93,587	124,843	189,883	197,848	197,347	208,311	220,432
Substance abuse, and mental health services [3]	1,241	2,444	1,931	2,241	3,203	3,183	3,179	1,187
Grants to states for Medicaid [3]	41,103	89,070	117,921	176,231	181,720	180,625	190,624	203,788
State children's health insurance fund [3]	(NA)	(NA)	1,220	4,607	5,129	5,451	6,000	7,600
Income security	36,768	58,366	68,653	85,983	90,885	89,816	90,971	94,232
Food stamp program [3]	2,130	2,740	3,508	4,204	4,385	4,608	4,602	4,808
Child nutrition programs [3]	4,871	7,387	9,060	11,035	11,726	12,263	12,871	14,278
Temporary assistance for needy families [3] . . .	(NA)	(NA)	15,464	17,725	17,357	16,897	16,876	17,030
Veterans benefits and services [3]	134	253	434	493	552	625	639	677
Administration of justice	574	1,222	5,263	5,084	4,784	4,961	4,603	4,340

NA Not available. [1] Grants include trust funds. [2] Trust funds. [3] Includes grants for payments to individuals.

Source: U. S. Office of Management and Budget, *Budget of the United States Government, Historical Tables,* annual; <http://www.whitehouse.gov/omb>.

U.S. Census Bureau, Statistical Abstract of the United States: 2009

Table 416. Federal Aid to State and Local Governments—Selected Programs by State: 2005

[In millions of dollars (403,660 represents $403,660,000,000). For fiscal year ending September 30. Negative amounts (–) are refunds (from the recipients) of advances from a prior year, or represent reductions in the amount of funds originally obligated to the recipients for the particular program or program category during the fiscal year]

State and island area	Federal aid, total [1]	Department of Agriculture					Department of Education				
		Total	Food and nutrition service				Total	Office of Elementary and Secondary Education			
			Child nutrition programs	Food stamp program [2]	Special supplemental food program (WIC)	Other		Special education programs	No child left behind act	Title 1 programs	Other
United States, total .	403,660	23,996	11,681	4,256	4,985	3,074	34,139	8,693	4,888	10,500	10,058
Alabama	6,306	383	214	33	84	52	591	168	95	191	137
Alaska	2,671	144	33	9	22	80	154	1	5	–	149
Arizona	7,965	449	254	40	112	43	787	159	85	214	330
Arkansas	4,179	280	144	26	52	58	352	102	55	118	77
California	46,029	2,912	1,469	397	830	216	5,468	1,072	743	2,059	1,593
Colorado	4,538	222	109	28	47	37	494	140	62	110	181
Connecticut	4,539	163	86	20	35	22	369	118	61	106	84
Delaware	1,142	67	35	9	11	12	131	33	28	32	38
District of Columbia	3,450	56	23	14	13	6	142	14	29	47	52
Florida	19,046	1,051	661	82	237	70	1,985	571	306	564	544
Georgia	8,914	764	473	68	158	65	91	2	10	–	79
Hawaii	1,731	107	40	11	29	26	229	42	27	41	119
Idaho	1,814	134	52	11	20	51	181	51	32	42	56
Illinois	14,616	831	449	95	186	101	1,486	428	220	533	305
Indiana	6,483	351	206	38	69	38	566	226	81	162	98
Iowa	3,594	216	102	20	40	55	361	118	45	71	127
Kansas	2,872	203	115	18	38	33	136	13	11	–	112
Kentucky	5,779	378	199	35	77	67	159	12	8	–	139
Louisiana	7,148	520	281	56	100	83	37	2	4	–	31
Maine	2,623	94	39	14	13	27	181	55	34	46	46
Maryland	6,800	289	156	39	60	35	592	202	85	120	183
Massachusetts	9,989	301	180	39	61	21	819	276	112	236	195
Michigan	12,113	617	301	96	127	92	1,234	385	211	416	222
Minnesota	5,878	365	176	54	74	61	111	10	12	–	89
Mississippi	5,168	420	199	30	67	123	463	112	87	159	105
Missouri	7,407	414	218	48	71	77	103	3	14	–	86
Montana	2,021	105	34	11	13	46	205	38	33	39	95
Nebraska	2,256	152	74	20	25	33	242	87	38	33	83
Nevada	2,213	121	62	15	29	15	208	57	33	60	58
New Hampshire	1,483	58	22	6	11	19	147	46	29	29	43
New Jersey	10,479	433	230	79	93	31	976	349	119	262	245
New Mexico	4,097	234	128	25	42	39	412	69	47	111	185
New York	43,438	1,524	775	299	345	105	3,231	680	509	1,331	711
North Carolina	11,568	660	370	67	139	84	1,022	300	133	275	314
North Dakota	1,394	87	27	9	12	40	149	25	29	31	64
Ohio	13,726	751	339	171	157	84	88	6	11	–	71
Oklahoma	4,935	387	195	47	74	70	594	135	83	151	225
Oregon	4,808	437	123	65	63	185	441	122	53	123	144
Pennsylvania	18,103	735	346	154	144	91	1,328	413	192	444	280
Rhode Island	1,937	63	34	8	15	7	18	1	–	–	16
South Carolina	5,326	345	206	27	67	45	101	8	10	–	83
South Dakota	1,336	90	34	11	14	30	84	1	13	–	70
Tennessee	9,083	457	250	44	101	61	728	228	97	199	204
Texas	25,622	2,017	1,269	142	471	136	3,199	808	461	1,101	828
Utah	2,633	186	93	26	34	33	267	80	36	40	111
Vermont	1,213	67	19	14	11	23	134	30	30	27	47
Virginia	6,330	402	176	79	79	68	792	238	86	167	301
Washington	7,681	439	192	45	107	95	629	199	94	148	188
West Virginia	3,482	170	83	16	34	36	259	68	46	91	54
Wisconsin	6,563	322	156	41	67	57	680	205	91	157	227
Wyoming	2,243	40	18	5	8	9	130	27	29	30	45
Island area:											
American Samoa	120	26	13	5	6	1	26	5	1	–	20
Micronesia	106	1	–	–	–	1	7	4	–	–	3
Guam	335	17	6	2	7	2	48	16	–	–	32
Marshall Islands	62	–	–	–	–	–	3	2	–	–	1
Northern Marianas . . .	112	19	7	11	–	1	22	6	–	–	16
Palau	36	–	–	–	–	–	3	1	–	–	2
Puerto Rico	5,191	1,870	178	1,477	179	36	737	123	120	386	109
Virgin Islands	271	17	5	3	5	4	5	–	–	–	5
Undistributed amounts . .	665	33	–	–	–	33	–	–	–	–	–

See footnotes at end of table.

U.S. Census Bureau, Statistical Abstract of the United States: 2009

Table 416. Federal Aid to State and Local Governments—Selected Programs by State: 2005—Con.

[See headnote, page 262]

State and island area	FEMA total [3]	Department of Housing and Urban Development						Department of Labor			
		Total	Community development block grants	Public housing programs			Other	State unemployment insurance and employment service Total	Employment service	Workforce invest-ment	Other
				Low rent housing assistance	Housing certificate program	Capital program					
United States, total ..	**5,386**	**28,709**	**4,991**	**3,617**	**11,096**	**3,152**	**5,853**	**8,379**	**3,468**	**3,350**	**1,561**
Alabama.............	266	440	66	114	104	84	72	125	42	60	22
Alaska.............	11	194	24	8	17	2	143	53	31	15	7
Arizona.............	9	353	67	17	63	12	195	125	46	54	25
Arkansas	42	185	32	27	80	24	22	72	28	27	17
California	458	2,743	565	116	1,314	110	638	1,035	460	471	104
Colorado............	11	266	43	17	133	13	59	105	54	38	13
Connecticut.........	5	470	53	53	246	26	92	105	67	24	14
Delaware	4	84	9	9	34	6	25	25	13	7	6
District of Columbia	5	495	33	57	136	194	75	155	132	11	11
Florida	1,508	1,037	213	97	392	78	256	326	115	163	47
Georgia	46	690	109	120	230	101	129	172	79	63	29
Hawaii	8	117	30	11	40	24	12	43	17	12	14
Idaho..............	2	64	14	1	28	1	19	48	23	13	12
Illinois	17	1,665	227	247	647	240	304	371	158	154	60
Indiana.............	47	396	84	43	166	28	74	152	52	47	53
Iowa	15	166	56	6	64	6	35	67	32	16	19
Kansas.............	44	155	41	16	53	14	30	52	24	17	11
Kentucky	34	388	77	52	132	41	86	127	38	47	42
Louisiana	352	431	74	65	124	70	96	129	33	77	19
Maine..............	13	160	30	9	83	8	31	53	19	15	19
Maryland	20	645	96	74	302	44	128	140	73	34	32
Massachusetts.......	62	1,288	137	114	763	85	190	180	80	72	29
Michigan............	14	753	172	53	330	43	154	353	144	126	83
Minnesota..........	15	486	87	41	218	40	100	123	60	28	34
Mississippi	80	235	49	27	84	27	48	90	36	41	12
Missouri	12	423	92	37	156	37	101	145	60	64	21
Montana...........	22	95	18	4	20	4	49	31	15	10	7
Nebraska	11	118	28	12	38	13	27	36	21	9	7
Nevada	17	117	24	16	45	4	28	59	30	20	8
New Hampshire.......	4	101	21	7	52	5	17	27	15	8	4
New Jersey..........	13	1,075	113	171	538	92	160	243	126	87	30
New Mexico	10	124	31	9	37	10	36	49	20	23	7
New York	1,118	3,710	592	878	1,280	430	530	536	218	256	63
North Carolina.......	86	611	83	102	214	60	151	288	71	120	97
North Dakota.........	8	65	12	2	20	6	24	24	13	5	5
Ohio	90	1,167	234	166	441	100	226	331	141	139	50
Oklahoma...........	21	324	51	25	88	22	138	76	31	27	18
Oregon.............	35	245	50	16	96	14	69	146	56	61	29
Pennsylvania........	106	1,439	282	250	472	169	267	396	175	130	92
Rhode Island........	8	205	23	21	107	18	36	35	18	10	8
South Carolina.......	16	293	49	31	125	25	62	117	41	44	32
South Dakota	5	102	24	3	30	3	42	28	13	8	7
Tennessee	39	503	64	93	155	73	118	135	48	54	33
Texas..............	167	1,275	310	122	496	104	242	511	160	271	80
Utah	16	94	30	4	30	4	25	73	40	20	13
Vermont	4	60	12	3	32	2	12	19	9	5	5
Virginia............	63	587	87	65	277	44	113	174	65	41	68
Washington..........	31	487	84	37	142	38	187	236	83	93	61
West Virginia........	38	202	55	17	96	14	19	66	21	29	16
Wisconsin...........	16	380	82	19	153	26	99	180	79	52	49
Wyoming	3	27	5	1	10	1	10	21	12	5	3
Island areas:											
American Samoa	4	1	1	–	–	–	–	1	–	–	1
Micronesia..........	5	–	–	–	–	–	–	2	–	2	–
Guam.............	18	20	3	4	10	1	2	5	1	3	1
Marshall Islands	–	–	–	–	–	–	–	1	–	1	–
Northern Marianas ...	5	4	2	–	2	–	1	4	–	3	1
Palau	–	–	–	–	–	–	–	–	–	–	–
Puerto Rico	88	587	136	101	136	172	41	146	26	115	6
Virgin Islands........	–	41	3	18	11	5	4	9	4	2	3
Undistributed amounts ..	218	324	–	–13	1	336	–	–	–	–	–

See footnotes at end of table.

U.S. Census Bureau, Statistical Abstract of the United States: 2009

[See headnote, page 262]

State and island area	Department of Health and Human Services						Department of Transportation				Other federal aid [4]
		Administration for children			Centers for Medi-care and Medi-caid services						
	Total	Chil-dren & family ser-vices (Head Start)	Foster care and adop-tion assis-tance	Tem-porary assis-tance to needy families		Other	Total	High-way trust fund	Fed-eral transit admini-stration	Other	
United States, total . .	240,303	8,424	6,407	16,351	185,980	23,142	42,064	29,849	2,681	9,534	20,684
Alabama.	3,470	133	32	103	2,872	330	719	580	44	95	313
Alaska	969	51	26	45	712	134	628	395	155	77	517
Arizona.	5,255	200	107	268	4,229	452	665	492	63	110	322
Arkansas	2,646	91	44	50	2,258	203	480	407	31	42	121
California	28,232	1,063	1,608	3,571	19,452	2,538	3,821	2,089	238	1,494	1,360
Colorado.	2,246	160	94	133	1,523	336	614	373	46	195	581
Connecticut.	2,824	73	108	270	2,089	284	420	317	7	96	183
Delaware	623	20	8	30	486	79	124	103	7	14	84
District of Columbia	1,354	55	30	111	955	203	444	135	4	304	799
Florida	10,393	346	204	72	8,544	1,227	2,175	1,722	134	319	571
Georgia	5,803	212	94	406	4,493	597	1,029	791	95	144	319
Hawaii	859	37	34	71	616	100	216	155	24	37	152
Idaho	978	43	12	38	768	117	275	245	18	12	131
Illinois	8,185	322	338	573	6,034	918	1,599	939	112	547	462
Indiana.	4,085	116	97	175	3,306	392	745	631	34	81	141
Iowa	2,157	72	58	140	1,676	210	397	328	25	45	214
Kansas.	1,766	85	41	117	1,344	179	376	333	19	25	140
Kentucky	3,838	146	76	188	3,129	300	590	487	47	55	265
Louisiana	4,808	175	78	196	4,005	353	628	478	59	91	242
Maine.	1,787	43	20	84	1,539	102	209	176	19	13	127
Maryland	3,614	103	149	182	2,745	435	855	486	29	340	646
Massachusetts.	6,307	151	88	416	5,093	557	716	460	21	235	316
Michigan.	7,447	297	226	851	5,317	757	1,169	948	102	119	526
Minnesota.	3,913	119	93	212	3,071	418	627	452	50	125	238
Mississippi	3,247	190	11	76	2,740	229	463	379	31	54	171
Missouri	5,148	147	85	219	4,262	436	918	715	86	117	243
Montana.	752	49	17	33	544	108	311	272	21	19	500
Nebraska	1,248	47	24	49	962	165	292	253	21	18	157
Nevada	987	36	25	52	727	148	284	199	41	44	421
New Hampshire	831	23	22	31	666	89	174	146	16	11	139
New Jersey	5,968	154	85	618	4,451	659	1,378	678	40	661	393
New Mexico	2,308	84	33	129	1,861	200	308	240	15	53	653
New York	29,186	553	696	2,783	23,345	1,809	2,998	1,601	88	1,309	1,134
North Carolina	7,408	204	101	350	6,104	649	1,135	935	76	124	359
North Dakota.	518	35	14	24	367	79	269	233	17	19	274
Ohio	9,501	297	364	377	7,425	1,038	1,377	1,100	74	203	420
Oklahoma.	2,724	133	57	158	2,072	302	554	432	32	90	255
Oregon.	2,593	113	82	182	1,936	280	554	387	39	128	356
Pennsylvania.	11,809	289	389	942	9,148	1,041	1,836	1,210	94	532	453
Rhode Island.	1,255	31	20	86	1,023	96	244	210	9	25	110
South Carolina.	3,475	109	23	82	2,953	309	782	700	28	53	196
South Dakota	608	44	8	23	444	88	267	217	16	34	153
Tennessee	5,940	145	49	159	5,153	433	745	616	34	96	537
Texas.	13,971	631	262	539	11,087	1,452	3,686	3,098	174	415	795
Utah	1,404	58	31	78	1,056	182	361	240	30	91	232
Vermont	713	18	7	46	552	89	142	124	3	15	74
Virginia.	3,260	197	62	117	2,399	485	660	467	61	132	392
Washington.	4,361	171	109	384	3,219	478	1,063	591	125	347	434
West Virginia.	2,065	65	40	85	1,687	189	498	388	20	90	184
Wisconsin.	4,018	132	112	334	2,992	448	711	549	39	123	257
Wyoming	366	24	3	25	262	53	301	254	28	19	1,355
Island area:											
American Samoa	6	–	–	–	5	2	14	6	7	1	41
Micronesia.	–	–	–	–	–	–	–	–	–	–	91
Guam.	32	5	–	2	9	15	22	11	8	2	173
Marshall Islands	1	–	–	–	–	1	–	–	–	–	58
Northern Marianas . . .	5	–	–	–	3	2	10	1	8	1	42
Palau	–	–	–	–	–	–	–	–	–	–	32
Puerto Rico	985	310	12	64	259	339	165	63	12	90	612
Virgin Islands	42	12	–	2	8	19	18	12	3	3	139
Undistributed amounts . .	8	2	–	–	–	6	2	–	–	1	80

– Represents or rounds to zero   [1] Total includes programs not shown separately.   [2] For Puerto Rico, amount shown is for nutritional assistance grant program, all other amounts are grant payments for food stamp administration.   [3] FEMA = Federal Emergency Management Agency. FEMA is part of the U.S. Department of Homeland Security.   [4] Represents aid for other programs not shown.

Source: U.S. Census Bureau, Federal Aid to States For Fiscal Year 2005 (issued September 2007). See also <http://www.census.gov/prod/2007pubs/fas-05.pdf>.

Table 417. State and Local Governments—Summary of Finances: 1990 to 2005

[In millions of dollars (1,032,115 represents $1,032,115,000,000) except as indicated. For fiscal year ending in year shown; see text, this section. Local government amounts are estimates subject to sampling variation; see Appendix III and source. Minus sign (–) indicates net loss]

Item	1990	2000	2002	2003	2004	2005
Revenue [1]	**1,032,115**	**1,942,328**	**1,806,592**	**2,047,337**	**2,435,084**	**2,529,193**
From federal government	136,802	291,950	360,546	389,264	425,683	438,432
Public welfare	59,961	148,549	183,893	199,789	217,176	225,691
Highways	14,368	24,414	30,382	30,052	30,692	33,672
Education	23,233	45,873	55,997	61,901	71,010	74,136
Health and hospitals	5,904	15,611	19,678	21,491	23,316	22,725
Housing and community development	9,655	17,690	22,637	24,713	26,560	28,018
Other and unallocable	23,683	39,812	47,959	51,317	56,929	54,191
From state and local sources	895,313	1,650,379	1,446,045	1,658,073	2,009,401	2,090,761
General, net intergovernmental	712,700	1,249,373	1,324,333	1,373,948	1,464,058	1,588,462
Taxes	501,619	872,351	905,101	938,972	1,010,277	1,099,200
Property	155,613	249,178	279,191	296,683	318,242	335,981
Sales and gross receipts	177,885	309,290	324,123	337,787	360,629	384,383
Individual income	105,640	211,661	202,832	199,407	215,215	242,273
Corporation net income	23,566	36,059	28,152	31,369	33,716	43,138
Other	38,915	66,164	70,803	73,726	82,475	93,425
Charges and miscellaneous	211,081	377,022	419,232	434,976	453,781	489,262
Utility and liquor stores	58,642	89,546	107,417	108,388	114,054	119,843
Water supply system	17,674	30,515	33,236	34,736	36,087	37,377
Electric power system	29,268	42,436	54,404	53,938	55,980	59,157
Gas supply system	5,216	8,049	8,950	8,985	9,783	10,382
Transit system	3,043	3,954	5,762	5,391	6,506	6,937
Liquor stores	3,441	4,592	5,065	5,338	5,698	5,990
Insurance trust revenue [2]	123,970	311,460	14,295	175,737	431,289	382,456
Employee retirement	94,268	273,881	–30,920	120,157	365,265	316,576
Unemployment compensation	18,441	23,366	27,086	35,335	38,362	35,243
Direct expenditure	**972,695**	**1,742,914**	**2,047,150**	**2,159,772**	**2,260,330**	**2,368,791**
By function:						
Direct general expenditure [2]	831,573	1,502,768	1,732,478	1,817,513	1,903,194	2,012,594
Education [2]	288,148	521,612	594,694	621,335	655,361	689,057
Elementary and secondary	202,009	365,181	411,216	428,503	452,055	473,406
Higher education	73,418	134,352	156,814	164,187	173,086	182,146
Highways	61,057	101,336	115,295	117,696	118,179	124,604
Public welfare	107,287	233,350	281,176	306,463	335,257	362,932
Health	24,223	51,366	59,456	61,703	63,125	66,971
Hospitals	50,412	75,976	87,609	93,175	96,551	103,476
Police protection	30,577	56,798	64,458	67,361	69,707	74,727
Fire protection	13,186	23,102	25,998	27,854	28,330	31,439
Corrections	24,636	48,805	54,615	55,471	56,521	59,151
Natural resources	12,330	20,235	22,000	22,808	23,299	25,057
Sanitation and sewerage	28,453	45,261	50,309	51,723	55,908	58,069
Housing and community development	15,479	26,590	31,623	35,275	37,221	39,969
Parks and recreation	14,326	25,038	30,101	31,765	30,467	31,941
Financial administration	16,217	29,300	32,660	34,911	36,163	36,519
Interest on general debt [3]	49,739	69,814	75,287	77,277	81,723	81,119
Utility and liquor stores [3]	77,801	114,916	143,879	148,996	159,732	160,682
Water supply system	22,101	35,789	40,555	43,260	44,806	45,799
Electric power system	30,997	39,719	55,952	54,355	59,299	58,612
Gas supply system	2,989	3,724	5,720	5,300	6,717	7,075
Transit system	18,788	31,883	37,468	41,678	44,237	44,310
Liquor stores	2,926	3,801	4,183	4,402	4,673	4,885
Insurance trust expenditure [2]	63,321	125,230	170,792	193,263	197,405	195,516
Employee retirement	38,355	95,679	114,931	127,197	137,537	145,796
Unemployment compensation	16,499	18,648	42,196	51,547	43,278	29,776
By character and object:						
Current operation	700,131	1,288,746	1,499,243	1,579,290	1,662,510	1,764,526
Capital outlay	123,102	217,063	257,071	263,198	269,976	277,299
Construction	89,144	161,694	197,528	203,035	209,395	216,268
Equipment, land, and existing structures	33,958	55,369	59,543	60,162	60,581	61,032
Assistance and subsidies	27,227	31,375	33,110	35,080	36,922	39,469
Interest on debt (general and utility)	58,914	80,499	86,933	88,940	93,518	91,981
Insurance benefits and repayments	63,321	125,230	170,792	193,263	197,405	195,516
Expenditure for salaries and wages [4]	*340,654*	*548,796*	*609,563*	*647,211*	*666,041*	*693,146*
Debt outstanding, year end	**858,006**	**1,451,815**	**1,681,377**	**1,812,667**	**1,951,661**	**2,085,597**
Long-term	838,700	1,427,524	1,638,136	1,772,197	1,913,286	2,054,838
Short-term	19,306	24,291	43,242	40,470	38,374	30,759
Long-term debt:						
Issued	108,468	184,831	262,683	345,784	346,813	321,960
Retired	64,831	121,897	161,885	215,218	241,111	231,790

[1] Aggregates exclude duplicative transactions between state and local governments; see source. [2] Includes amounts not shown separately. [3] Interest on utility debt included in "utility and liquor stores expenditure." For total interest on debt, see "Interest on debt (general and utility)." [4] Included in items above.

Source: U.S. Census Bureau; *Federal, State and Local Governments, State Government Finances,* series GF, No. 3 thereafter; <http://www.census.gov/govs/www/estimate05.html> (September 2007).

U.S. Census Bureau, Statistical Abstract of the United States: 2009

Table 418. **State and Local Governments—Revenue and Expenditures by Function: 2004 and 2005**

[**In millions of dollars (2,435,084 represents $2,435,084,000,000) For fiscal year ending in year shown;** see text, this section. Local government amounts are estimates subject to sampling variation; see Appendix III and source]

Item	2004			2005		
	State and local	State	Local	State and local	State	Local
Revenue [1]	**2,435,084**	**1,586,665**	**1,247,463**	**2,529,193**	**1,641,957**	**1,308,507**
Intergovernmental revenue [1]	425,683	394,613	430,114	438,432	407,860	451,844
Total revenue from own sources [1]	2,009,401	1,192,052	817,349	2,090,761	1,234,097	856,663
General revenue from own sources	1,464,058	799,443	664,615	1,588,462	878,854	709,608
Taxes [2]	1,010,277	590,414	419,863	1,099,200	650,612	448,588
Property	318,242	10,714	307,528	335,981	11,342	324,639
Individual income	215,215	196,255	18,960	242,273	221,597	20,676
Corporation income	33,716	30,229	3,487	43,138	38,691	4,447
Sales and gross receipts	360,629	293,326	67,303	384,383	312,584	71,798
General sales	244,891	197,949	46,942	262,981	212,921	50,060
Selective sales [2]	115,738	95,377	20,361	121,402	99,663	21,739
Motor fuel	34,944	33,762	1,181	35,767	34,567	1,200
Alcoholic beverages	4,986	4,593	392	5,125	4,706	419
Tobacco products	12,626	12,303	323	13,337	12,917	420
Public utilities	21,427	10,709	10,717	22,390	10,909	11,480
Motor vehicle and operators' licenses	20,707	19,329	1,378	21,713	20,270	1,443
Death and gift	5,758	5,732	26	5,422	5,340	82
Charges and miscellaneous [2]	453,781	209,029	244,752	489,262	228,242	261,020
Current charges [2]	288,642	114,843	173,799	309,826	124,186	185,639
Education [2]	84,420	64,290	20,130	90,153	69,010	21,143
School lunch sales	6,326	21	6,305	6,500	22	6,479
Higher education	71,780	63,423	8,357	76,683	68,010	8,673
Natural resources	3,264	2,344	920	3,369	2,349	1,021
Hospitals	72,652	26,480	46,171	79,092	29,378	49,714
Sewerage	29,792	39	29,753	31,610	39	31,571
Solid waste management	12,083	422	11,661	12,931	473	12,458
Parks and recreation	7,982	1,328	6,653	8,024	1,360	6,663
Housing and community development	4,770	578	4,193	4,846	573	4,273
Airports	13,345	931	12,414	14,391	1,042	13,350
Sea and inland port facilities	3,107	879	2,227	3,394	987	2,407
Highways	8,991	5,533	3,458	9,845	6,028	3,817
Interest earnings	53,194	28,414	24,781	59,011	31,917	27,094
Special assessments	6,453	722	5,731	6,323	752	5,571
Sale of property	1,960	690	1,270	2,837	1,060	1,777
Utility and liquor store revenue	114,054	17,821	96,234	119,843	19,746	100,097
Insurance trust revenue	431,289	374,788	56,500	382,456	335,498	46,958
Expenditure [1]	**2,265,051**	**1,406,175**	**1,257,581**	**2,373,408**	**1,471,936**	**1,313,908**
Intergovernmental expenditure [1]	4,721	389,706	13,720	4,617	403,488	13,565
Direct expenditure [1]	2,260,330	1,016,469	1,243,861	2,368,791	1,068,449	1,300,342
General expenditure [2]	1,903,194	819,730	1,083,464	2,012,594	874,491	1,138,103
Education [2]	655,361	180,984	474,376	689,057	191,553	497,504
Elementary and secondary education	452,055	5,851	446,204	473,406	5,614	467,792
Higher education	173,086	144,913	28,173	182,146	152,434	29,712
Public welfare	335,257	291,968	43,289	362,932	318,144	44,788
Hospitals	96,551	40,011	56,541	103,476	42,676	60,801
Health	63,125	29,608	33,517	66,971	31,452	35,519
Highways	118,179	72,194	45,985	124,604	76,575	48,028
Police protection	69,707	9,471	60,236	74,727	10,011	64,716
Fire protection	28,330	–	28,330	31,439	–	31,439
Corrections	56,521	36,963	19,558	59,156	38,321	20,835
Natural resources	23,299	17,226	6,072	25,057	17,094	7,963
Sewerage	35,535	1,568	33,966	36,600	1,109	35,491
Solid waste management	20,373	2,952	17,421	21,469	3,184	18,285
Housing and community development	37,221	4,273	32,948	39,969	4,982	34,987
Governmental administration	100,741	43,453	57,289	108,874	47,710	61,163
Parks and recreation	30,467	4,571	25,896	31,941	4,482	27,459
Interest on general debt	81,723	32,953	48,770	81,119	34,315	46,804
Utility	155,059	21,676	133,382	155,797	21,824	133,973
Liquor store expenditure	4,673	3,924	749	4,885	4,082	803
Insurance trust expenditure	197,405	171,139	26,266	195,516	168,052	27,463
By character and object:						
Current operation	1,662,510	691,652	970,858	1,764,526	739,988	1,024,538
Capital outlay	269,976	90,950	179,026	277,299	94,181	183,119
Construction	209,395	73,372	136,022	216,268	77,039	139,229
Equipment, land, and existing structures	60,581	17,578	43,004	61,032	17,142	43,890
Assistance and subsidies	36,922	28,104	8,818	39,469	30,181	9,287
Interest on debt (general and utility)	93,518	34,624	58,894	91,981	36,047	55,935
Insurance benefits and repayments	197,405	171,139	26,266	195,516	168,052	27,463
Expenditure for salaries and wages [3]	*666,041*	*185,827*	*480,214*	*693,146*	*194,447*	*498,699*

– Represents or rounds to zero.   [1] Aggregates exclude duplicative transactions between levels of government; see source.
[2] Includes amounts not shown separately.   [3] Included in items shown above.

Source: U.S. Census Bureau, *Federal, State, and Local Governments, Finance, State and Local Government Finances,* 2004–05; <http://www.census.gov/govs/www/estimate05.html> (September 2007).

Table 419. State and Local Governments—Capital Outlays: 1990 to 2005

[In millions of dollars (123,102 represents $123,102,000,000), except percent. For fiscal year ending in year shown; see text, this section. Local government amounts are subject to sampling variation; see Appendix III and source. Minus sign (–) indicates net loss]

Level and function	1990	1995	2000	2001	2002	2003	2004	2005
State & local governments: Total . . .	**123,102**	**151,440**	**217,063**	**233,258**	**257,071**	**263,198**	**269,976**	**277,299**
Annual percent change [1]	9.0	10.1	9.4	7.5	10.2	2.4	2.6	2.7
By function:								
Education [2]	25,997	35,708	60,968	65,116	71,680	70,813	74,597	77,779
Elementary and secondary. . . .	18,057	24,808	45,150	48,404	53,294	51,118	52,977	54,509
Higher education	7,441	10,461	15,257	15,911	17,652	19,044	21,121	22,782
Highways.	33,867	42,561	56,439	60,108	66,017	65,523	65,964	69,644
Health and hospitals	3,848	4,883	5,502	5,630	6,126	7,158	7,241	7,711
Natural resources	2,545	2,891	4,347	4,908	4,247	4,244	4,657	4,543
Housing [3].	3,997	4,527	6,184	5,888	6,939	7,660	7,578	7,880
Air transportation.	3,434	3,802	6,717	8,420	8,551	9,066	9,731	9,326
Water transportation [4].	924	1,101	1,618	4,306	1,691	3,721	1,798	1,598
Sewerage	8,356	8,894	10,093	9,224	11,574	12,467	14,068	14,171
Parks and recreation	3,877	4,085	6,916	8,540	9,093	9,224	7,866	8,151
Utilities	16,601	19,028	24,847	24,553	30,241	34,538	37,432	34,879
Water.	6,873	7,466	10,542	10,742	11,831	13,536	13,651	14,402
Electric.	3,976	3,715	4,177	4,812	6,538	6,438	7,173	6,055
Gas.	310	340	400	453	358	422	582	544
Transit	5,443	7,507	9,728	8,545	11,514	14,142	16,026	13,879
Other	19,657	23,961	33,431	36,566	40,912	38,784	39,044	41,618
State governments: Total.	**45,524**	**57,829**	**76,233**	**81,881**	**89,767**	**91,943**	**90,950**	**94,181**
Annual percent change [1].	5.6	9.3	11.3	7.4	9.6	2.4	–1.1	3.6
By function:								
Education [2]	7,253	10,042	14,077	14,936	16,589	17,727	19,632	20,632
Highways.	24,850	31,687	41,651	44,761	49,119	48,719	48,566	51,578
Health and hospitals	1,531	2,402	2,228	2,390	2,241	2,930	2,763	3,278
Natural resources	1,593	1,956	2,758	3,105	2,766	2,788	2,957	2,670
Housing [3].	119	187	860	600	582	774	222	338
Air transportation.	339	356	561	667	525	846	795	615
Water transportation [4].	202	223	310	362	346	410	388	367
Sewerage	333	853	403	393	405	405	881	486
Parks and recreation	601	650	1,044	1,185	1,483	1,098	945	931
Utilities	2,605	2,226	4,232	3,641	5,145	7,084	5,211	4,319
Other	6,098	7,246	8,108	9,840	10,567	9,163	8,589	8,967
Local governments: Total	**77,578**	**93,611**	**140,830**	**151,377**	**167,304**	**171,255**	**179,026**	**183,119**
Annual percent change [1].	4.5	10.6	8.4	7.5	10.5	2.4	4.5	2.3
By function:								
Education [2]	18,744	29,858	46,890	50,180	55,091	53,087	54,965	57,147
Elementary and secondary. . . .	17,669	28,402	44,629	47,808	52,804	50,475	52,261	54,068
Higher education	1,076	1,456	2,261	2,372	2,286	2,612	2,704	3,079
Highways.	9,017	10,874	14,789	15,347	16,898	16,804	17,398	18,066
Health and hospitals	2,316	2,481	3,274	3,239	3,886	4,228	4,478	4,433
Natural resources	952	935	1,589	1,803	1,481	1,456	1,699	1,873
Housing [3].	3,878	4,340	5,324	5,288	6,358	6,886	7,356	7,542
Air transportation.	3,095	3,446	6,156	7,753	8,026	8,221	8,936	8,712
Water transportation [4].	722	877	1,308	3,944	1,345	3,310	1,410	1,231
Sewerage	8,023	8,040	9,690	8,831	11,169	12,062	13,186	13,685
Parks and recreation	3,276	3,435	5,872	7,355	7,611	8,126	6,921	7,221
Utilities	13,996	16,801	20,615	20,912	25,096	27,455	32,221	30,560
Other	13,559	16,715	25,323	26,726	30,345	29,621	30,454	32,650

[1] Change from immediate/prior year except 1990, change from 1989.   [2] Includes other education.   [3] Includes community development.   [4] Includes terminals.

Source: U.S. Census Bureau , *Federal, State, and Local Governments, Finance, State and Local Government Finances,* 2004–05, and unpublished data. See also <http://www.census.gov/govs/www/estimate05.html>; (accessed May 2008).

Table 420. State and Local Governments—Expenditure for Public Works: 1995 to 2005

[In millions of dollars (180,148 represents $180,148,000,000), except percent. Public works include expenditures for current operations and capital outlays on highways, airports, water transport terminals, and sewerage, solid waste management, water supply, and mass transit systems. Represents direct expenditures excluding intergovernmental grants]

Item	Total	Highways	Airport transpor- tation	Water transport and terminals	Sewer- age	Solid waste manage- ment	Water supply	Mass transit
1995, Total	180,148	77,109	8,397	2,309	23,583	14,990	28,041	25,719
State.	56,392	46,893	783	604	1,462	1,658	178	4,814
Local.	123,756	30,216	7,614	1,706	22,121	13,331	27,863	20,904
Capital expenditures (percent) . . .	40.7	55.2	45.3	47.7	37.7	13.2	26.6	29.2
2000, Total	230,569	101,336	13,160	3,141	28,052	17,208	35,789	31,883
State.	74,974	61,942	1,106	863	955	2,347	354	7,407
Local.	155,595	39,394	12,054	2,277	27,098	14,861	35,435	24,476
Capital expenditures (percent) . . .	41.9	55.7	51.0	51.5	36.0	8.9	29.5	30.5
2005, Total	294,695	124,604	17,962	3,951	36,600	21,469	45,799	44,310
State.	92,823	76,575	1,406	1,156	1,109	3,184	319	9,074
Local.	201,872	48,028	16,556	2,795	35,491	18,285	45,480	35,237
Capital expenditures (percent) . . .	42.4	55.9	51.9	40.4	38.7	9.3	31.4	31.3

Source: U.S. Census Bureau, Federal, State, and Local Governments, Finance, State and Local Government Finances, 2004–05, and unpublished data. See also <http://www.census.gov/govs/www/estimate05.html>; (accessed May 2008).

State and Local Government Finances and Employment   267

Table 421. **State and Local Governments—Indebtedness: 1990 to 2005**

[In billions of dollars (858.0 represents $858,000,000,000). For fiscal year ending in year shown; see text, this section. Local government amounts are estimates subject to sampling variation; see Appendix III and source]

Item	Debt outstanding						Long-term		
			Long-term						
	Total	Cash and security holdings	Total	Public debt for private sources	All other	Short-term	Net long-term[1]	Debt issued	Debt retired
1990: Total	**858.0**	**1,490.8**	**838.7**	**294.1**	**544.6**	**19.3**	**474.4**	**108.5**	**64.8**
State	318.3	963.3	315.5	154.4	161.1	2.8	125.5	43.5	22.9
Local	539.8	527.5	523.2	139.7	383.5	16.5	348.9	65.0	42.0
1993: Total	**1,017.7**	**1,751.0**	**995.0**	**306.0**	**689.0**	**22.7**	**617.1**	**195.6**	**147.0**
State	389.7	1,148.6	385.9	172.6	213.2	3.9	176.9	77.1	60.7
Local	628.0	602.4	609.1	133.4	475.8	18.8	440.1	118.4	86.3
1994: Total	**1,074.7**	**1,888.5**	**1,048.0**	**301.6**	**746.4**	**26.7**	**672.8**	**207.8**	**166.6**
State	411.0	1,247.7	406.1	170.2	235.9	4.9	200.8	78.5	61.3
Local	663.7	640.9	641.9	131.5	510.5	21.8	472.0	129.3	105.3
1995: Total	**1,115.4**	**2,058.5**	**1,088.3**	**300.6**	**787.7**	**27.0**	**697.3**	**129.3**	**95.1**
State	427.2	1,393.9	421.1	176.8	244.4	6.1	205.3	52.6	37.5
Local	688.1	664.6	667.2	123.9	543.3	20.9	491.9	76.8	57.6
1996: Total	**1,169.7**	**2,261.7**	**1,145.7**	**312.6**	**833.0**	**24.0**	**751.6**	**141.1**	**106.5**
State	452.4	1,562.9	446.5	186.4	260.2	5.8	220.3	60.2	42.4
Local	717.3	698.8	699.1	126.3	572.8	18.2	531.3	80.9	64.1
1997: Total	**1,224.5**	**2,546.9**	**1,207.9**	**329.0**	**878.9**	**16.6**	**797.7**	**151.3**	**109.3**
State	456.7	1,785.1	454.5	193.7	260.8	2.1	222.6	54.4	41.1
Local	767.9	761.8	753.4	135.3	618.1	14.5	575.1	96.8	68.2
1998: Total	**1,283.6**	**2,890.2**	**1,266.3**	**335.8**	**930.5**	**17.3**	**842.6**	**204.4**	**144.6**
State	483.1	2,058.6	480.9	202.3	278.7	2.2	237.2	83.4	58.1
Local	800.4	831.6	785.4	133.6	651.8	15.1	605.4	120.9	86.5
1999: Total	**1,369.3**	**3,168.5**	**1,351.4**	**351.1**	**1,000.3**	**17.8**	**907.3**	**229.4**	**153.1**
State	510.5	2,265.9	507.8	213.9	293.9	2.7	249.4	83.2	55.6
Local	858.8	902.5	843.6	137.2	706.4	15.2	657.9	146.2	97.5
2000: Total	**1,451.8**	**3,503.7**	**1,427.5**	**372.6**	**1,054.9**	**24.3**	**959.6**	**184.8**	**121.9**
State	547.9	2,518.9	541.5	227.3	314.2	6.4	266.9	75.0	44.4
Local	903.9	984.8	886.0	145.3	740.7	17.9	692.7	109.8	77.5
2001: Total	**1,554.0**	**3,592.1**	**1,531.9**	**395.1**	**1,136.8**	**22.1**	**1,038.6**	**199.6**	**130.6**
State	576.5	2,537.7	572.8	238.2	334.7	3.7	287.4	81.3	50.7
Local	977.5	1,054.3	959.1	157.0	802.1	18.5	751.2	118.3	79.9
2002: Total	**1,681.4**	**3,650.7**	**1,638.1**	**417.7**	**1,220.5**	**43.2**	**1,121.0**	**262.7**	**161.9**
State	636.8	2,555.4	618.2	258.5	359.6	18.6	311.8	104.2	64.9
Local	1,044.6	1,095.3	1,020.0	159.2	860.8	24.6	809.2	158.5	97.0
2003: Total	**1,812.7**	**3,696.1**	**1,772.2**	**431.4**	**1,340.8**	**40.5**	**1,242.7**	**345.8**	**215.2**
State	697.9	2,594.2	681.8	267.3	414.5	16.1	366.2	148.8	85.9
Local	1,114.7	1,101.9	1,090.4	164.1	926.3	24.3	876.5	196.9	129.3
2004: Total	**1,951.7**	**4,120.1**	**1,913.3**	**448.4**	**1,464.9**	**38.4**	**1,349.6**	**346.8**	**241.1**
State	754.2	2,930.1	740.4	268.4	472.0	13.7	412.2	158.4	107.1
Local	1,197.5	1,189.9	1,172.9	180.0	992.9	24.6	937.4	188.5	134.0
2005: Total	**2,085.6**	**4,439.4**	**2,054.8**	**480.6**	**1,574.2**	**30.8**	**1,441.1**	**322.0**	**231.8**
State	813.8	3,156.4	808.3	296.1	512.2	5.6	444.7	131.5	101.8
Local	1,271.8	1,283.0	1,246.5	184.5	1,062.0	25.2	996.4	190.5	130.0

[1] Net long-term debt outstanding is the amount of long-term debt held by a government for which no funds have been set aside for its repayment.

Source: U.S. Census Bureau, 1990, *Government Finances*, Series GF, No. 5, annual; thereafter, *Federal, State, and Local Governments, Finance, State and Local Government Finances*, 2004–05, and unpublished data. See also <http://www.census.gov/govs/www/estimate05.html>.

Table 422. **New Security Issues, State and Local Governments: 1990 to 2007**

[In billions of dollars, (122.9 represents 122,900,000,000)]

Type of issue, issuer, or use	1990	1995	2000	2001	2002	2003	2004	2005	2006	2007
All issues, new and refunding [1]	**122.9**	**145.7**	**180.4**	**291.9**	**363.9**	**384.3**	**357.9**	**409.6**	**389.3**	**425.5**
By type of issue:										
General obligation	39.5	57.0	64.5	118.6	145.3	144.1	130.5	145.8	115.0	131.2
Revenue	83.3	88.7	115.9	170.0	214.8	238.0	227.4	263.8	274.3	294.3
By type of issuer:										
State	15.0	14.7	19.9	30.1	33.9	49.8	47.4	31.6	28.3	35.0
Special district of statutory authority [2]	75.9	93.5	121.2	197.5	259.1	253.5	234.2	298.6	293.2	315.0
Municipality, county, or township	32.0	37.5	39.3	61.0	67.1	79.0	76.3	79.4	67.8	75.6
Issues for new capital	**97.9**	**102.4**	**154.3**	**200.3**	**242.9**	**264.7**	**228.4**	**223.8**	**263.1**	**276.1**
By use of proceeds:										
Education	17.1	24.0	38.7	50.1	57.9	70.4	65.4	71.0	70.3	70.6
Transportation	11.8	11.9	19.7	21.4	22.1	23.8	20.5	25.4	30.2	27.9
Utilities and conservation	10.0	9.6	11.9	21.9	33.4	10.3	9.2	9.9	7.8	11.4
Industrial aid	6.6	6.6	7.1	6.6	7.2	22.3	19.1	18.6	35.0	38.2
Other purposes	31.7	30.8	47.3	55.7	73.0	97.7	80.4	60.6	72.7	83.0

[1] Par amounts of long-term issues based on date of sale. [2] Includes school districts.

Source: Board of Governors of the Federal Reserve System, *Statistical Supplement to the Federal Reserve Bulletin*, monthly. Based on data from Securities Data Company <http://www.federalreserve.gov/pubs/supplement/2008/04/table1_45.htm>.

Table 423. State and Local Governments—Total Revenue and Expenditures by State: 2000 to 2005

[In millions of dollars (1,942,328 represents $1,942,328,000,000), except as indicated. For fiscal year ending in year shown; see text, this section. These data cannot be used to compute the deficit or surplus for any single government, as these are estimates for all state and local governments wtihin a state area. For further information, see the 2006 Government Finance and Employment Classification Manual at <http://www.census.gov/govs/www/class06.html/>]

State	Revenue				Expenditures			
	2000	2002	2004	2005	2000	2002	2004	2005
United States...	1,942,328	1,806,592	2,435,084	2,529,193	1,746,943	2,051,537	2,265,051	2,373,408
Alabama	25,726	24,113	32,065	33,377	25,319	28,531	31,268	33,241
Alaska	10,525	6,993	11,038	11,404	8,628	9,397	10,019	10,027
Arizona	27,778	30,083	38,388	41,103	27,293	31,863	36,072	39,300
Arkansas	13,833	13,566	18,027	18,866	12,245	14,599	16,323	17,224
California	270,380	250,725	358,673	381,910	236,645	293,328	328,029	344,704
Colorado	29,603	26,325	38,744	38,915	26,173	32,393	34,395	35,063
Connecticut	25,828	24,831	29,295	30,490	24,011	27,592	28,837	29,649
Delaware	6,224	5,813	7,102	7,637	5,153	5,946	6,922	7,595
District of Columbia	6,383	7,352	8,829	9,919	6,527	7,832	8,493	8,787
Florida	92,402	93,275	129,687	135,562	84,301	99,291	115,547	130,858
Georgia	49,310	46,166	57,902	60,297	43,517	53,610	58,435	58,905
Hawaii	8,488	7,452	9,983	11,000	8,254	9,402	9,870	10,534
Idaho	7,590	6,873	9,754	10,004	6,404	7,565	8,426	8,915
Illinois	80,695	73,670	100,247	99,826	74,727	87,401	95,421	97,745
Indiana	32,716	34,221	40,977	44,261	31,250	36,271	39,333	42,048
Iowa	17,220	17,601	22,545	23,204	17,275	19,294	20,634	21,486
Kansas	16,235	15,982	18,550	19,990	14,419	16,715	18,361	18,948
Kentucky	25,200	22,475	26,834	28,044	21,473	24,795	26,871	26,963
Louisiana	27,109	27,388	34,107	35,858	25,018	27,342	31,089	32,578
Maine	8,554	8,019	11,131	11,383	7,652	8,677	10,031	10,207
Maryland	33,949	33,468	44,288	45,075	30,598	35,727	38,540	41,373
Massachusetts	46,103	41,902	60,795	62,109	44,362	51,125	58,208	59,312
Michigan	70,112	63,401	80,185	81,055	61,506	69,687	77,621	75,980
Minnesota	38,785	35,131	42,956	45,465	35,424	40,516	42,144	42,936
Mississippi	16,672	15,905	20,670	21,113	15,379	17,285	19,450	20,041
Missouri	31,635	30,621	40,033	41,340	27,953	33,036	35,571	37,186
Montana	5,643	5,511	7,088	7,438	4,983	5,616	6,198	6,412
Nebraska	11,650	12,031	15,479	15,905	10,831	12,492	14,075	14,332
Nevada	11,885	12,809	16,888	18,953	11,230	13,971	16,182	17,405
New Hampshire	6,948	6,729	8,703	8,911	6,222	7,066	8,346	8,679
New Jersey	62,331	54,835	75,083	79,126	54,590	64,289	72,660	79,845
New Mexico	13,073	11,503	14,918	16,656	11,195	12,689	14,068	15,596
New York	188,907	170,982	224,429	234,681	171,858	198,536	219,325	226,951
North Carolina	50,542	48,597	63,458	64,813	46,135	51,839	56,543	60,747
North Dakota	4,495	4,227	6,524	5,239	4,041	4,190	4,486	4,794
Ohio	80,074	70,976	105,382	102,498	68,418	80,851	89,598	91,959
Oklahoma	18,760	19,161	23,954	24,552	15,962	20,776	20,879	22,005
Oregon	28,644	23,193	33,734	32,406	24,086	27,731	28,215	29,084
Pennsylvania	80,546	73,694	102,238	103,692	75,624	86,262	94,598	101,484
Rhode Island	7,427	6,862	9,665	9,731	6,432	7,939	8,937	9,226
South Carolina	23,467	24,985	30,547	33,278	23,436	28,104	30,451	33,011
South Dakota	4,277	3,964	5,593	5,857	3,760	4,276	4,612	4,973
Tennessee	33,625	33,483	42,125	44,863	32,010	36,638	41,760	42,708
Texas	120,666	113,817	153,761	162,748	109,634	129,636	144,880	151,927
Utah	14,954	13,789	18,917	19,183	13,044	15,523	16,707	17,269
Vermont	4,019	4,046	5,266	5,393	3,766	4,218	4,812	5,179
Virginia	44,175	38,780	54,162	56,658	38,092	43,688	47,801	51,529
Washington	46,372	42,124	54,738	57,510	41,794	50,431	54,317	55,800
West Virginia	10,760	11,375	14,117	14,576	9,990	11,958	12,201	12,120
Wisconsin	43,003	31,424	48,698	48,235	34,559	39,262	42,410	43,146
Wyoming	7,030	4,346	6,816	7,084	3,743	4,337	5,080	5,619

Source: U.S. Census Bureau, Annual Survey of State & Local Government Finances, 2000–2005, <http://www.census.gov/govs/www/estimate.html/>.

U.S. Census Bureau, Statistical Abstract of the United States: 2009

Table 424. **State and Local Governments—Revenue by State: 2005**

[**In millions of dollars (2,529,193 represents $2,529,193,000,000). For fiscal year ending in year shown;** see text, this section]

State	Total revenue	General revenue			Select taxes					
		Total	Intergovernmental from federal government	General revenue from own sources	Total [1]	Property	Sales and gross receipts	Individual income	Corporation income	Other taxes
United States....	**2,529,193**	**2,026,894**	**438,432**	**1,588,462**	**1,099,200**	**335,981**	**384,383**	**242,273**	**43,138**	**73,769**
Alabama	33,377	27,370	7,287	20,084	11,661	1,792	5,707	2,645	397	901
Alaska.	11,404	9,825	2,553	7,272	2,947	892	400	–	589	998
Arizona	41,103	33,744	8,239	25,506	18,331	5,126	8,750	2,848	702	734
Arkansas	18,866	16,023	4,339	11,684	8,040	1,159	4,315	1,875	277	289
California	381,910	271,500	54,898	216,602	146,692	34,083	49,044	42,992	8,670	9,403
Colorado	38,915	29,774	5,103	24,671	15,683	4,942	5,697	3,771	316	720
Connecticut	30,490	27,560	4,399	23,160	18,897	7,156	5,128	5,033	575	799
Delaware	7,637	6,642	1,184	5,457	3,277	486	405	932	249	1,170
District of Columbia . .	9,919	8,297	2,794	5,503	4,235	1,136	1,211	1,148	199	516
Florida.	135,562	112,273	22,146	90,126	59,867	20,392	29,786	–	1,786	6,693
Georgia	60,297	50,184	10,579	39,605	27,486	8,215	10,137	7,326	712	810
Hawaii.	11,000	9,554	1,965	7,590	5,524	818	2,895	1,381	124	118
Idaho	10,004	8,300	1,877	6,423	4,183	1,154	1,524	1,041	141	205
Illinois	99,826	80,127	15,389	64,738	48,760	18,312	16,694	7,937	2,183	2,092
Indiana	44,261	39,579	7,184	32,394	22,000	8,303	7,280	4,812	825	570
Iowa	23,204	19,376	4,380	14,996	9,705	3,302	3,155	2,313	186	350
Kansas	19,990	16,997	3,403	13,594	9,460	3,106	3,498	2,080	248	356
Kentucky	28,044	23,831	6,116	17,715	12,262	2,247	4,649	3,792	479	896
Louisiana.	35,858	29,888	7,849	22,039	14,302	2,429	7,677	2,393	352	1,336
Maine	11,383	9,985	2,647	7,337	5,364	2,152	1,468	1,299	136	210
Maryland	45,075	39,021	7,500	31,521	23,751	5,594	5,611	9,153	807	2,106
Massachusetts	62,109	49,729	9,346	40,384	28,777	10,341	5,952	9,690	1,333	1,143
Michigan	81,055	66,659	14,195	52,464	35,296	12,919	11,784	6,565	1,907	1,215
Minnesota	45,465	37,392	7,308	30,084	20,957	5,251	6,832	6,341	934	1,074
Mississippi	21,113	17,801	6,007	11,794	7,491	1,967	3,585	1,174	283	368
Missouri.	41,340	33,941	8,573	25,368	17,374	4,695	7,032	4,319	237	816
Montana	7,438	6,288	2,046	4,242	2,721	996	459	713	98	312
Nebraska.	15,905	12,284	2,670	9,615	6,579	2,095	2,314	1,394	198	462
Nevada	18,953	15,375	2,241	13,134	9,044	2,321	5,334	–	–	1,234
New Hampshire	8,911	7,700	1,625	6,075	4,308	2,650	705	68	476	321
New Jersey	79,126	67,752	10,627	57,125	43,871	19,197	10,238	9,538	2,225	2,250
New Mexico	16,656	14,015	4,258	9,757	6,076	870	2,854	1,086	242	864
New York.	234,681	194,245	45,702	148,544	112,244	34,150	29,145	34,844	6,994	6,255
North Carolina	64,813	52,884	13,067	39,817	27,307	6,450	9,423	8,428	1,272	1,242
North Dakota	5,239	4,586	1,311	3,275	2,121	620	791	242	76	341
Ohio	102,498	77,061	17,162	59,899	41,719	11,974	12,743	13,079	1,346	1,739
Oklahoma	24,552	20,422	5,179	15,242	10,073	1,719	3,891	2,469	169	1,266
Oregon	32,406	23,327	5,258	18,069	11,106	3,562	972	4,829	365	957
Pennsylvania	103,692	83,998	19,298	64,700	46,019	13,390	13,638	11,462	1,703	5,002
Rhode Island	9,731	8,149	2,108	6,041	4,500	1,819	1,387	998	113	129
South Carolina	33,278	27,623	7,102	20,522	11,801	3,739	4,231	2,691	247	732
South Dakota	5,857	4,547	1,374	3,173	2,119	736	1,131	–	49	131
Tennessee	44,863	34,844	9,072	25,772	15,993	3,895	9,381	155	806	1,370
Texas	162,748	131,986	28,842	103,144	69,153	30,289	31,117	–	–	6,156
Utah	19,183	15,010	3,194	11,817	7,321	1,792	3,017	1,927	189	299
Vermont	5,393	4,825	1,313	3,511	2,575	1,056	787	500	69	100
Virginia	56,658	47,347	6,834	40,514	27,659	8,390	7,641	8,352	606	2,173
Washington	57,510	42,195	8,337	33,858	22,969	6,632	13,825	–	–	2,125
West Virginia	14,576	12,181	3,538	8,643	5,551	1,008	2,212	1,172	463	606
Wisconsin	48,235	36,721	7,101	29,620	21,404	7,796	6,108	5,465	783	922
Wyoming	7,084	6,156	1,913	4,243	2,646	864	820	–	–	891

See footnotes at end of table.

U.S. Census Bureau, Statistical Abstract of the United States: 2009

Table 424. **State and Local Governments—Revenue by State: 2005**—Con.

[See headnote page 270]

State	General revenue from own sources								Utility and liquor stores	Insurance trust revenue
	Current charges and miscellaneous revenue									
		Current charges				Miscellaneous revenue				
	Total	Total [1]	Education	Hospitals	Sewerage	Total [1]	Interest earnings	Special assessments		
United States ..	**489,262**	**309,826**	**90,153**	**79,092**	**31,610**	**179,436**	**59,011**	**6,323**	**119,843**	**382,456**
Alabama	8,423	6,440	1,812	3,421	338	1,983	736	20	2,336	3,670
Alaska.	4,324	897	175	85	64	3,428	1,145	13	247	1,333
Arizona	7,175	4,104	1,527	467	487	3,071	850	44	3,359	4,000
Arkansas	3,644	2,552	919	838	198	1,092	407	9	731	2,112
California	69,910	47,412	8,179	12,131	4,583	22,498	7,563	1,106	22,293	88,117
Colorado	8,988	5,657	1,923	1,146	558	3,331	1,233	302	1,908	7,234
Connecticut	4,264	2,345	892	374	249	1,919	755	31	556	2,375
Delaware	2,180	1,041	426	15	126	1,139	235	294	250	745
District of Columbia . .	1,268	520	29	–	163	748	144	1	753	869
Florida.	30,260	18,887	3,384	4,467	1,995	11,373	3,490	1,112	6,647	16,642
Georgia	12,118	8,256	2,065	3,104	770	3,863	944	30	3,575	6,537
Hawaii.	2,066	1,340	255	343	155	726	174	13	218	1,227
Idaho	2,240	1,573	374	560	133	667	242	30	264	1,441
Illinois	15,978	9,367	3,530	1,201	897	6,611	2,308	300	2,954	16,744
Indiana	10,394	6,865	2,824	2,234	780	3,529	1,024	38	1,735	2,947
Iowa	5,291	3,920	1,388	1,590	280	1,371	498	39	869	2,959
Kansas	4,134	2,616	1,116	561	261	1,519	495	105	938	2,055
Kentucky	5,454	3,329	1,199	1,084	302	2,124	965	40	1,075	3,138
Louisiana	7,737	4,963	1,095	2,404	306	2,774	1,000	25	1,074	4,896
Maine	1,973	1,032	383	71	132	942	281	5	142	1,257
Maryland	7,770	4,844	2,150	135	731	2,926	836	107	812	5,242
Massachusetts	11,607	5,525	1,977	450	781	6,082	2,265	440	2,553	9,827
Michigan	17,168	11,339	4,412	2,634	1,301	5,830	1,609	172	2,619	11,776
Minnesota	9,128	5,904	2,073	1,157	536	3,224	1,042	321	1,685	6,388
Mississippi	4,303	3,426	887	1,853	161	876	283	8	814	2,498
Missouri.	7,993	5,104	2,023	1,497	493	2,889	1,189	63	1,289	6,110
Montana	1,521	852	418	49	65	669	239	60	135	1,015
Nebraska	3,036	1,692	682	473	112	1,344	325	54	2,475	1,146
Nevada	4,091	2,467	496	519	335	1,623	535	116	919	2,659
New Hampshire	1,766	1,006	489	6	82	761	365	1	482	729
New Jersey	13,254	8,222	2,784	791	1,150	5,032	1,508	25	1,524	9,850
New Mexico	3,680	1,471	475	435	122	2,210	741	53	431	2,211
New York	36,300	21,212	3,804	5,310	1,545	15,089	3,717	113	11,011	29,425
North Carolina	12,510	9,311	2,531	3,448	1,227	3,199	1,345	47	3,300	8,629
North Dakota	1,154	663	328	3	35	491	213	57	100	554
Ohio	18,179	11,804	4,852	2,498	1,505	6,375	2,128	188	2,652	22,786
Oklahoma	5,169	3,466	1,510	791	221	1,703	489	16	1,148	2,982
Oregon	6,964	4,587	1,286	880	620	2,376	630	109	1,553	7,525
Pennsylvania	18,681	11,661	4,110	1,777	1,666	7,020	3,111	89	3,704	15,991
Rhode Island	1,542	742	347	4	82	799	323	7	171	1,411
South Carolina	8,721	6,486	1,647	3,356	309	2,235	682	39	2,544	3,112
South Dakota	1,054	535	247	36	47	519	241	22	208	1,101
Tennessee	9,774	5,798	1,587	2,137	489	3,982	668	89	6,774	3,245
Texas	33,990	20,446	6,512	6,046	2,240	13,544	5,337	128	8,199	22,562
Utah	4,496	3,187	1,113	777	222	1,308	489	54	1,616	2,557
Vermont	937	542	362	–	43	395	143	3	220	348
Virginia	12,854	8,463	2,680	2,108	852	4,391	1,376	156	1,871	7,439
Washington	10,889	7,992	2,116	2,058	1,099	2,897	939	98	5,555	9,760
West Virginia	3,092	1,572	601	263	162	1,520	351	11	228	2,167
Wisconsin	8,217	5,425	1,992	894	558	2,792	1,022	114	1,148	10,367
Wyoming	1,597	966	166	612	41	631	380	6	181	747

– Represents or rounds to zero. [1] Includes items not shown separately.

Source: U.S. Census Bureau; *Federal, State and Local Governments, State Government Finances;* <http://www.census.gov/govs/www/estimate05.html> (accessed May 2008).

Table 425. **State and Local Governments—Expenditures and Debt by State: 2005**

[In millions of dollars (2,373,408 represents $2,373,408,000,000), except as indicated. For fiscal year ending in year shown; see text, this section]

State	Total expenditure	General expenditure	Direct general expenditure							
		Total [1]	Total [1]	Education	Public welfare	Health	Hospitals	Highways	Police protection	Corrections
United States..	**2,373,408**	**2,017,211**	**2,012,594**	**689,057**	**362,932**	**66,971**	**103,476**	**124,604**	**74,727**	**59,156**
Alabama	33,241	29,047	29,047	9,877	5,043	1,184	3,916	1,753	823	606
Alaska.	10,027	8,795	8,795	2,361	1,379	178	121	1,202	206	198
Arizona	39,300	32,970	32,970	10,878	5,912	1,438	813	2,070	1,533	1,318
Arkansas	17,224	15,476	15,475	5,879	3,304	361	783	1,113	481	457
California	344,704	280,585	277,137	88,631	44,246	10,780	14,788	12,205	12,481	9,846
Colorado	35,063	28,963	28,958	10,116	3,232	991	1,393	2,207	1,193	894
Connecticut	29,649	25,892	25,892	9,126	4,347	633	1,126	1,267	838	580
Delaware	7,595	6,845	6,844	2,432	1,122	311	58	611	238	218
District of Columbia	8,787	7,033	7,033	1,406	1,761	482	158	79	436	173
Florida.	130,858	113,308	113,308	32,043	17,634	3,714	5,597	7,955	5,636	3,747
Georgia	58,905	50,704	50,704	19,916	8,823	1,489	3,490	1,908	1,727	1,849
Hawaii.	10,534	9,329	9,329	2,648	1,440	457	378	467	268	170
Idaho	8,915	8,069	8,069	2,779	1,405	194	590	684	261	251
Illinois	97,745	81,993	81,993	28,578	13,148	3,037	2,292	5,275	3,569	1,728
Indiana	42,048	38,137	38,137	14,616	5,999	761	2,845	2,295	1,052	954
Iowa	21,486	19,269	19,212	7,259	3,236	387	1,836	1,792	533	327
Kansas	18,948	16,847	16,847	6,287	2,765	382	664	1,701	594	353
Kentucky	26,963	23,442	23,442	8,249	5,419	559	1,088	1,633	604	628
Louisiana.	32,578	28,537	28,537	8,981	4,492	695	3,155	1,785	1,060	946
Maine	10,207	9,510	9,497	2,866	2,334	511	114	706	216	178
Maryland	41,373	36,754	36,754	13,533	5,959	1,377	512	2,257	1,494	1,460
Massachusetts . . .	59,312	50,190	50,005	16,037	10,788	809	1,243	2,368	1,571	1,037
Michigan	75,980	66,549	66,549	27,161	10,063	3,475	2,837	3,647	2,277	2,258
Minnesota	42,936	37,399	37,399	12,197	9,106	880	1,407	2,836	1,186	718
Mississippi	20,041	17,846	17,846	5,860	4,072	355	2,127	1,308	515	358
Missouri.	37,186	32,618	32,614	11,279	6,348	1,017	2,197	2,434	1,159	841
Montana	6,412	5,751	5,751	1,988	804	318	89	646	179	156
Nebraska.	14,332	11,052	11,030	4,136	2,022	266	566	1,026	299	288
Nevada	17,405	14,935	14,933	4,485	1,637	348	723	1,556	783	556
New Hampshire . .	8,679	7,852	7,852	2,894	1,624	128	53	534	253	154
New Jersey	79,845	68,477	68,477	26,599	11,208	1,415	1,699	3,142	2,831	1,855
New Mexico	15,596	14,116	14,116	4,879	3,156	370	672	972	475	460
New York.	226,951	184,723	184,094	53,849	42,642	4,838	10,262	8,833	7,373	4,816
North Carolina . . .	60,747	52,585	52,585	18,680	9,656	2,969	4,030	3,551	1,710	1,518
North Dakota . . .	4,794	4,348	4,348	1,600	714	77	22	522	100	67
Ohio	91,959	77,964	77,961	27,509	15,303	3,781	3,251	4,409	2,632	1,862
Oklahoma	22,005	19,122	19,081	7,557	3,765	521	776	1,327	626	597
Oregon	29,084	23,726	23,726	7,880	3,806	869	1,020	1,670	910	834
Pennsylvania	101,484	87,512	87,350	30,203	20,421	3,647	2,013	6,784	2,390	2,859
Rhode Island	9,226	7,917	7,889	2,516	2,080	157	108	376	291	176
South Carolina . . .	33,011	28,002	28,002	9,763	5,203	958	3,429	1,647	746	578
South Dakota	4,973	4,466	4,466	1,520	745	123	88	636	130	103
Tennessee	42,708	33,866	33,866	10,346	8,637	1,258	2,611	1,912	1,175	830
Texas	151,927	131,197	131,197	52,825	19,387	2,346	8,576	9,892	4,584	4,191
Utah	17,269	14,522	14,522	5,522	2,226	426	699	938	525	420
Vermont	5,179	4,729	4,729	1,905	1,130	133	1	363	134	97
Virginia	51,529	46,539	46,538	17,585	6,732	1,639	2,446	2,957	1,616	1,606
Washington	55,800	43,950	43,946	14,524	6,758	2,030	2,909	2,765	1,289	1,355
West Virginia	12,120	10,973	10,962	3,919	2,340	312	285	1,041	224	243
Wisconsin	43,146	37,724	37,724	13,805	7,002	1,350	1,030	3,024	1,354	1,206
Wyoming	5,619	5,055	5,055	1,573	554	236	592	522	148	237

See footnotes at end of table.

U.S. Census Bureau, Statistical Abstract of the United States: 2009

Table 425. **State and Local Governments—Expenditures and Debt by State: 2005**—Con.

[See headnote, page 272]

State	General expenditure								Utility and liquor store expenditures	Insurance trust expenditures	Debt outstanding
	Direct general expenditure										
	Natural resources	Parks and recreation	Housing and community development	Sewerage	Solid waste management	Governmental administration	Interest on general debt	Other direct general expenditures			
United States . .	**25,057**	**31,941**	**39,969**	**36,600**	**21,469**	**108,874**	**81,119**	**182,812**	**160,682**	**195,516**	**2,085,597**
Alabama	243	461	439	490	261	1,120	883	1,855	2,332	1,862	22,532
Alaska	311	75	230	80	72	616	375	1,629	356	875	8,758
Arizona	584	875	398	548	377	2,018	1,117	2,934	3,906	2,425	32,830
Arkansas	220	200	171	206	195	870	415	911	747	1,001	11,203
California	4,740	4,897	7,959	4,833	3,373	18,652	10,457	28,572	30,749	33,370	285,986
Colorado	316	1,025	625	601	88	1,754	1,541	2,795	2,725	3,375	39,443
Connecticut	91	283	633	356	364	1,516	1,446	3,005	888	2,869	31,209
Delaware	101	85	119	156	71	556	250	602	314	435	6,237
District of Columbia	1	138	436	257	223	428	292	602	1,728	26	6,741
Florida	2,831	2,320	1,537	2,291	2,226	6,593	4,702	15,167	8,662	8,889	113,260
Georgia	498	741	869	1,082	529	2,770	1,087	3,692	4,609	3,592	38,974
Hawaii	118	225	166	199	169	593	526	1,521	419	786	9,292
Idaho	230	105	45	133	95	515	242	679	251	595	3,979
Illinois	548	2,396	1,930	1,228	484	4,336	4,605	7,833	5,445	10,308	106,714
Indiana	325	418	765	1,036	223	1,876	1,410	3,327	1,935	1,976	32,124
Iowa	258	342	158	231	162	868	452	1,478	910	1,307	11,649
Kansas	248	232	230	276	120	908	731	1,389	1,006	1,095	17,554
Kentucky	377	234	357	326	193	1,023	1,235	1,603	1,074	2,447	30,197
Louisiana	593	502	515	481	302	1,561	1,210	2,467	1,302	2,738	24,762
Maine	161	60	214	132	119	469	338	1,159	101	596	6,962
Maryland	466	663	969	564	491	2,456	1,404	3,040	1,412	3,208	29,512
Massachusetts . . .	262	306	1,494	881	413	2,358	3,626	6,217	3,983	5,139	83,013
Michigan	436	951	889	1,650	470	3,180	2,572	4,385	3,072	6,359	68,990
Minnesota	539	852	753	517	315	2,053	1,529	2,807	1,915	3,621	36,262
Mississippi	252	180	221	143	133	781	479	1,127	827	1,368	10,189
Missouri	303	458	570	628	141	1,543	1,355	2,109	1,685	2,883	31,333
Montana	237	68	106	80	58	400	199	610	136	525	5,365
Nebraska	248	194	162	164	77	510	260	948	2,797	484	8,554
Nevada	264	619	249	239	31	1,217	702	1,453	1,497	973	18,659
New Hampshire . .	67	81	216	76	95	412	428	768	434	394	9,292
New Jersey	1,613	960	1,051	1,169	1,121	3,256	2,629	8,849	3,256	8,112	72,894
New Mexico	257	293	232	141	149	827	436	892	423	1,057	10,443
New York	470	2,124	4,372	3,177	2,492	8,656	8,364	19,984	20,541	21,687	232,890
North Carolina . . .	542	780	778	840	656	2,030	1,188	3,570	4,428	3,734	40,906
North Dakota	195	96	57	34	35	219	157	625	102	345	3,314
Ohio	431	958	1,740	2,254	491	4,713	2,880	4,837	3,176	10,819	60,720
Oklahoma	222	258	206	297	139	980	561	1,161	1,117	1,766	14,413
Oregon	414	465	474	636	147	1,516	1,046	2,129	1,733	3,625	25,857
Pennsylvania	585	727	1,892	1,597	702	4,831	4,184	4,846	4,951	9,021	100,474
Rhode Island	46	60	210	122	122	503	317	628	259	1,050	8,699
South Carolina . . .	244	267	354	293	283	1,659	996	1,605	2,677	2,332	29,917
South Dakota	126	103	84	51	35	253	150	402	220	287	3,840
Tennessee	240	419	559	421	372	1,520	896	2,434	6,947	1,896	25,573
Texas	1,423	1,512	1,595	2,275	1,027	5,326	5,432	10,525	10,243	10,487	150,695
Utah	214	346	254	300	140	1,208	463	886	1,833	914	14,831
Vermont	87	35	123	58	35	228	159	293	250	199	3,629
Virginia	238	861	858	965	636	2,490	1,711	3,643	2,120	2,869	44,535
Washington	783	821	1,109	1,055	521	1,970	1,691	4,341	7,282	4,568	53,049
West Virginia	165	159	140	208	60	780	357	845	309	838	8,516
Wisconsin	693	611	441	781	384	1,646	1,556	3,074	1,408	4,014	36,925
Wyoming	200	100	16	45	52	308	77	557	188	377	1,899

[1] Includes items not shown separately.

Source: U.S. Census Bureau; *Federal, State, and Local Governments, State and Local Government Finances* <http://www.census.gov/govs/estimate05.html>; (accessed April 2008).

U.S. Census Bureau, Statistical Abstract of the United States: 2009

Table 426. State Resources, Expenditures, and Balances: 2006 and 2007

[In millions of dollars (1,340,034 represents $1,340,034,000,000). For fiscal year ending in year shown; see text; this section. **General funds** exclude special funds earmarked for particular purposes, such as highway trust funds and federal funds; they support most on-going broad-based state services and are available for appropriation to support any governmental activity.

State	Expenditures by fund source			State general fund					
	Total, 2006	2007 [1]		Resources [3, 4]		Expenditures [4]		Balance [5]	
		Total [2]	General fund	Federal fund	2006	2007 [1]	2006	2007 [1]	2006	2007 [1]
United States...	**1,340,034**	**1,461,625**	**651,591**	**405,548**	**660,496**	**706,200**	**598,987**	**654,671**	**54,827**	**44,098**
Alabama	33,673	38,734	14,859	11,725	7,894	8,568	6,962	7,971	949	611
Alaska	9,628	11,874	4,295	3,401	3,247	5,466	3,247	5,466	–	–
Arizona	25,376	27,443	10,478	9,207	9,815	10,584	8,768	10,203	1,047	380
Arkansas	15,303	18,265	4,059	6,209	3,825	4,059	3,825	4,059	–	–
California	173,181	192,522	102,137	56,376	102,408	106,381	91,592	101,656	[6]10,816	[6]4,339
Colorado	15,380	16,276	6,807	3,760	7,360	7,835	6,451	7,047	909	788
Connecticut	22,580	24,026	14,969	1,298	14,999	15,743	14,552	15,473	447	270
Delaware	5,570	5,745	3,360	1,065	3,871	3,981	3,181	3,390	[6]691	[6]591
Florida	61,597	73,637	29,135	21,132	31,004	31,633	26,014	29,382	4,990	2,252
Georgia	33,414	34,685	18,473	10,038	19,820	21,722	17,804	19,211	[6]2,017	[6]2,512
Hawaii	9,475	11,299	5,456	2,106	5,411	5,874	4,679	5,381	732	493
Idaho	5,030	5,868	2,586	1,992	2,520	2,831	2,218	2,577	302	255
Illinois	43,422	48,226	21,707	12,103	27,856	29,230	24,193	25,604	590	642
Indiana	21,831	22,464	12,248	6,987	12,553	13,115	11,954	12,247	411	537
Iowa	14,669	15,641	5,300	4,149	5,382	5,647	5,021	5,385	149	77
Kansas	11,433	12,372	5,586	3,334	5,873	6,543	5,139	5,610	734	932
Kentucky	21,027	22,903	8,671	7,175	9,294	9,655	8,436	8,787	681	579
Louisiana	21,917	31,167	7,351	15,792	8,605	10,541	7,740	8,466	827	1,076
Maine	7,100	7,437	2,994	2,548	2,984	3,174	2,872	2,978	14	18
Maryland	26,380	29,689	14,192	6,618	13,703	14,459	12,342	14,174	1,362	285
Massachusetts	39,207	39,357	22,272	6,561	27,064	29,669	25,585	28,923	[6]3,208	[6]2,901
Michigan	41,728	43,151	9,111	13,442	9,030	9,113	9,028	9,111	3	3
Minnesota	25,753	27,592	16,513	6,202	17,355	18,062	15,542	15,956	[6]1,813	[6]2,106
Mississippi	14,803	17,284	4,182	8,677	4,385	4,825	4,314	4,407	35	227
Missouri	19,661	21,990	7,938	6,138	7,821	8,616	7,125	7,863	695	753
Montana	4,455	5,074	1,715	1,758	1,989	2,260	1,567	1,701	422	552
Nebraska	7,973	9,698	3,325	2,970	3,482	3,716	2,916	3,125	566	591
Nevada	7,404	8,131	3,452	1,499	3,285	3,715	2,934	3,531	351	184
New Hampshire . . .	4,470	4,511	1,389	1,420	1,411	1,448	1,334	1,366	26	62
New Jersey	42,304	45,856	30,127	9,489	29,812	32,136	28,033	29,930	[6]1,779	[6]2,188
New Mexico	11,842	11,940	5,671	3,679	6,522	6,811	5,415	5,970	[6]798	[6]544
New York	104,342	112,764	51,591	35,453	49,752	54,636	46,495	51,591	[6]3,257	[6]3,045
North Carolina	35,205	36,677	19,088	10,496	18,353	20,209	17,065	18,662	749	1,221
North Dakota	3,295	3,684	1,032	1,410	1,162	1,420	966	1,023	196	296
Ohio	53,448	54,550	25,148	9,181	25,984	26,410	24,866	25,148	632	216
Oklahoma	16,243	19,193	5,928	5,577	6,124	5,887	5,533	5,552	134	196
Oregon	20,215	20,840	6,256	4,947	6,621	6,968	6,077	5,539	544	1,429
Pennsylvania	53,911	56,755	26,327	18,037	25,350	27,006	24,665	26,319	514	531
Rhode Island	6,716	7,123	3,211	1,998	3,129	3,232	3,073	3,219	38	8
South Carolina	17,960	19,614	6,629	7,191	6,759	7,646	5,640	6,565	[6]988	[6]1,081
South Dakota	2,979	3,173	1,055	1,055	1,057	1,092	1,056	1,091	–	–
Tennessee	23,598	25,749	10,978	9,387	10,367	11,293	9,064	10,429	744	726
Texas	70,873	75,259	38,169	24,077	40,499	44,795	32,021	36,119	7,063	6,987
Utah	8,904	10,174	4,712	2,362	4,532	4,712	4,532	4,712	–	–
Vermont	4,946	5,138	1,192	1,085	1,157	1,207	1,113	1,176	–	–
Virginia	31,882	34,834	16,835	6,244	16,609	18,260	15,232	17,934	1,377	326
Washington	27,839	32,449	14,144	6,390	14,320	14,930	13,621	14,144	699	786
West Virginia	20,403	18,660	3,684	3,460	4,076	4,222	3,562	3,701	469	432
Wisconsin	33,481	34,474	13,217	7,160	12,814	13,161	12,385	13,105	49	66
Wyoming	6,208	5,658	2,037	1,188	1,252	1,702	1,242	1,697	10	5

– Represents zero.   [1] Estimated.   [2] Includes bonds and other state funds not shown separately.   [3] Includes funds budgeted, adjustments, and balances from previous year.   [4] May or may not include budget stabilization fund transfers, depending on state accounting practices.   [5] Resources less expenditures.   [6] Ending balance includes the balance in a budget stabilization fund.

Source: National Association of State Budget Officers, Washington, DC, *2006 State Expenditure Report,* and *State General Fund from NASBO, Fiscal Survey of the States,* semi-annual (copyright); <http://www.nasbo.org/publications.php>.

U.S. Census Bureau, Statistical Abstract of the United States: 2009

Table 427. Bond Ratings for State Governments by State: 2007

[**As of fourth quarter.** Key to investment grade ratings are in declining order of quality. The ratings from AA to CCC may be modified by the addition of a (+) or (−) sign to show relative standing within the major rating categories. *S&P:* AAA, AA, A, BBB, BB, B, CCC, CC, C; *Moody's:* Aaa, Aa, A, Baa, Ba, B, Caa, Ca, C; Numerical modifiers 1, 2, and 3 are added to letter-rating. *Fitch:* AAA, AA, A, BBB, BB, B, CCC, CC, C]

State	Standard & Poor's	Moody's	Fitch	State	Standard & Poor's	Moody's	Fitch
Alabama	AA	Aa2	AA	Montana	AA−	Aa2	AA
Alaska	AA+	Aa2	(NA)	Nebraska	[1]AA+ (ICR)	(NA)	(NA)
Arizona	[1]AA (ICR)	Aa3	(NA)	Nevada	AA+	Aa1	AA+
Arkansas	AA	Aa2	(NA)	New Hampshire	AA	Aa2	AA
California	A+	A1	A+	New Jersey	AA	Aa3	AA−
Colorado	[1]AA (ICR)	(NA)	(NA)	New Mexico	AA+	Aa1	(NA)
Connecticut	AA	Aa3	AAA	New York	AA	Aa3	AA−
Delaware	AAA	Aaa	AAA	North Carolina	AAA	Aaa	AAA
Florida	AAA	Aa1	AA+	North Dakota	[1]AA (ICR)	Aa2	(NA)
Georgia	AAA	Aaa	AAA	Ohio	AA+	Aa1	AA+
Hawaii	AA	Aa2	AA	Oklahoma	AA	Aa3	AA
Idaho	[1]AA (ICR)	Aa2	(NA)	Oregon	AA	Aa2	AA−
Illinois	AA	Aa3	AA	Pennsylvania	AA	Aa2	AA
Indiana	[1]AA+ (ICR)	Aa1	(NA)	Rhode Island	AA	Aa3	AA
Iowa	[1]AA+ (ICR)	Aa1	AA+	South Carolina	AA+	Aaa	AAA
Kansas	[1]AA+ (ICR)	Aa1	(NA)	South Dakota	[1]AA (ICR)	(NA)	(NA)
Kentucky	[1]AA− (ICR)	Aa2	(NA)	Tennessee	AA+	Aa1	AA+
Louisiana	A	A2	A	Texas	AA	Aa1	AA+
Maine	AA	Aa3	AA	Utah	AAA	Aaa	AAA
Maryland	AAA	Aaa	AAA	Vermont	AA+	Aaa	AA+
Massachusetts	AA	Aa2	AA	Virginia	AAA	Aaa	AAA
Michigan	AA−	Aa3	AA−	Washington	AA+	Aa1	AA
Minnesota	AAA	Aa1	AAA	West Virginia	AA−	Aa3	AA−
Mississippi	AA	Aa3	AA	Wisconsin	AA−	Aa3	AA−
Missouri	AAA	Aaa	AAA	Wyoming	[1]AA (ICR)	(NA)	(NA)

NA Not available.   [1] Standard and Poor's Issue Credit Rating (ICR) is a current opinion of the credit worthiness of an obliger with respect to a specific financial obligation, a specific class of financial obligations, or a specific financial program.

Source: Standard & Poor's, New York, NY (copyright), <http://www2.standardandpoors.com/portal/site/sp/en/us/page.home/home/0,0,0,0,0,0,0,0,0,0,0,0,0,0,0,0,0.html/>; Moody's Investors Service, New York, NY (copyright); <http://www.moodys.com/cust/default_alt.asp>; Fitch Ratings, New York, NY (copyright), <http://www.fitchratings.com/>.

Table 428. Bond Ratings for City Governments by Largest Cities: 2007

[**As of fourth quarter.** See headnote in Table 427]

Cities ranked by **2000** population	Standard & Poor's	Moody's	Fitch	Cities ranked by **2000** population	Standard & Poor's	Moody's	Fitch
New York, NY	AA	Aa3	AA−	Oakland, CA	AA−	A1	A+
Los Angeles, CA	AA	Aa2	AA	Mesa, AZ	AA−	A1	(NA)
Chicago, IL	AA−	Aa3	AA	Tulsa, OK	AA	Aa2	(NA)
Houston, TX	AA	Aa3	AA−	Omaha, NE	AAA	Aaa	(NA)
Philadelphia, PA	BBB	Baa1	BBB+	Minneapolis, MN	AAA	Aa1	AAA
Phoenix, AZ	AA	Aa1	NA	Honolulu, HI	AA	Aa2	AA
San Diego, CA	([1])	A3	BBB+	Miami, FL	A+	A2	A
Dallas, TX	AA+	Aa1	(NA)	Colorado Springs, CO	AA	Aa3	(NA)
San Antonio, TX	AA+	Aa1	AA+	St. Louis, MO	A	A3	(NA)
Detroit, MI	BBB	Baa2	BBB	Wichita, KS	AA	Aa2	(NA)
San Jose, CA	AA+	Aa1	AA+	Santa Ana, CA	([1])	([1])	(NA)
Indianapolis, IN	AAA	Aa1	(NA)	Pittsburgh, PA	BBB	Baa2	BBB
San Francisco, CA	AA	Aa3	AA−	Arlington, TX	AA	Aa2	AA
Jacksonville, FL	([1])	Aa2	(NA)	Cincinnati, OH	AA+	Aa1	(NA)
Columbus, OH	AAA	Aaa	AAA	Anaheim, CA	AA	Aa2	(NA)
Austin, TX	AAA	Aa1	(NA)	Toledo, OH	A	A3	(NA)
Baltimore, MD	AA−	Aa3	A+	Tampa, FL	([1])	[2]Aa2	(NA)
Memphis, TN	A	A1	A+	Buffalo, NY	BBB	Baa2	(NA)
Milwaukee, WI	AA	Aa2	AA+	St. Paul, MN	AAA	Aa2	AA+
Boston, MA	AA+	Aa1	AA	Corpus Christi, TX	A+	A1	AA−
Washington, DC	A+	A1	(NA)	Aurora, CO	AA	Aa2	(NA)
El Paso, TX	AA	Aa3	AA−	Raleigh, NC	AAA	Aaa	AAA
Seattle, WA	AAA	Aaa	AAA	Newark, NJ	AA	Baa2	(NA)
Denver, CO	AA+	Aa1	AA+	Lexington-Fayette, KY	NR	Aa2	(NA)
Nashville-Davidson, TN	AA	Aa2	AA	Anchorage, AK	AA	Aa3	AA
Charlotte, NC	AAA	Aaa	AAA	Louisville, KY	([1])	Aa2	(NA)
Fort Worth, TX	AA+	Aa2	AA	Riverside, CA	AA−	([1])	AA
Portland, OR	([1])	Aaa	(NA)	St. Petersburg, FL	NR	A1	(NA)
Oklahoma City, OK	AA	Aa1	(NA)	Bakersfield, CA	NR	([1])	(NA)
Tucson, AZ	AA	Aa3	AA	Stockton CA	A+	[2]A1	(NA)
New Orleans, LA	BB	Baa3	BBB−	Birmingham, AL	AA	[2]Aa3	AA−
Las Vegas, NV	AA	Aa2	AA	Jersey City, NJ	([1])	Baa2	BBB
Cleveland, OH	A− (Lease)	A2	A+	Norfolk, VA	AA	A1	AA
Long Beach, CA	AA−	[2]Aa3	(NA)	Baton Rouge, LA	([1])	([1])	(NA)
Albuquerque, NM	AA	Aa3	(NA)	Hialeah, FL	([1])	([1])	(NA)
Kansas City, MO	AA	Aa3	AAA	Lincoln, NE	AAA	Aaa	(NA)
Fresno, CA	AA	A1	AA−	Greensboro, NC	AAA	Aaa	AAA
Virginia Beach, VA	AAA	Aa1	AA+	Plano, TX	AAA	Aaa	AAA
Atlanta, GA	AA−	Aa3	(NA)	Rochester, NY	A	A2	(NA)
Sacramento, CA	AA	Aa2	(NA)				

NA Not available.   [1] Not reviewed.   [2] Issuer Rating/No General Obligation.

Source: Standard & Poor's, New York, NY (copyright), <http://www2.standardandpoors.com/portal/site/sp/en/us/page.home/home/0,0,0,0,0,0,0,0,0,0,0,0,0,0,0,0,0.html/> Moody's Investors Service, New York, NY (copyright); <http://www.moodys.com/cust/default_alt.asp>; Fitch Ratings, New York, NY (copyright), <http://www.fitchratings.com/>.

State and Local Government Finances and Employment   275

Table 429. Estimated State and Local Taxes Paid by a Family of Three for Largest City in Selected States: 2006

[Data based on average family of three (two wage earners and one school-age child) owning their own home and living in a city where taxes apply. Comprises state and local sales, income, auto, and real estate taxes. For definition of median, see Guide to Tabular Presentation]

City	Total taxes paid by gross family income level (dollars)					Total taxes paid as percent of income				
	$25,000	$50,000	$75,000	$100,000	$150,000	$25,000	$50,000	$75,000	$100,000	$150,000
Albuquerque, NM . . .	2,457	3,742	5,828	7,564	11,255	9.8	7.5	7.8	7.6	7.5
Atlanta, GA	3,228	4,857	7,764	10,181	15,295	12.9	9.7	10.4	10.2	10.2
Baltimore, MD	2,216	5,040	7,731	10,172	15,132	8.9	10.1	10.3	10.2	10.1
Boston, MA	3,113	5,489	7,698	9,503	13,099	12.5	11.0	10.3	9.5	8.7
Charlotte, NC	3,044	4,317	7,066	9,481	14,247	12.2	8.6	9.4	9.5	9.5
Chicago, IL	3,269	5,496	7,453	8,848	11,976	13.1	11.0	9.9	8.8	8.0
Columbus, OH.	3,112	5,061	7,621	10,025	15,287	12.4	10.1	10.2	10.0	10.2
Denver, CO.	2,836	3,524	5,728	7,458	10,356	11.3	7.0	7.6	7.5	6.9
Detroit, MI.	3,443	5,639	8,140	10,242	14,820	13.8	11.3	10.9	10.2	9.9
Honolulu, HI	3,094	2,919	5,305	7,524	12,258	12.4	5.8	7.1	7.5	8.2
Houston, TX	2,465	3,204	4,608	5,329	7,027	9.9	6.4	6.1	5.3	4.7
Indianapolis, IN	3,082	5,707	7,971	10,096	14,475	12.3	11.4	10.6	10.1	9.7
Jacksonville, FL. . . .	2,439	2,308	3,419	4,091	5,668	9.8	4.6	4.6	4.1	3.8
Kansas City, MO . . .	3,174	4,270	7,003	8,868	13,711	12.7	8.5	9.3	8.9	9.1
Las Vegas, NV	2,451	3,174	4,150	4,792	6,167	9.8	6.3	5.5	4.8	4.1
Los Angeles, CA . . .	2,703	4,950	7,532	9,653	15,655	10.8	9.9	10.0	9.7	10.4
Memphis, TN.	2,705	3,012	4,344	4,924	6,495	10.8	6.0	5.8	4.9	4.3
Milwaukee, WI.	2,272	4,837	7,083	9,345	13,839	9.1	9.7	9.4	9.3	9.2
Minneapolis, MN . . .	2,843	4,495	6,813	8,900	13,713	11.4	9.0	9.1	8.9	9.1
New Orleans, LA . . .	2,769	3,540	7,673	10,580	17,910	11.1	7.1	10.2	10.6	11.9
New York City, NY . .	2,871	4,562	5,934	7,748	11,433	11.5	9.1	7.9	7.7	7.6
Oklahoma City, OK. .	3,183	3,565	6,446	8,547	12,699	12.7	7.1	8.6	8.5	8.5
Omaha, NE.	2,519	4,337	6,979	9,225	14,302	10.1	8.7	9.3	9.2	9.5
Philadelphia, PA. . . .	4,118	6,839	9,446	11,754	16,634	16.5	13.7	12.6	11.8	11.1
Phoenix, AZ	2,904	3,338	5,120	6,575	9,766	11.6	6.7	6.8	6.6	6.5
Portland, OR	3,028	4,214	6,841	9,532	14,966	12.1	8.4	9.1	9.5	10.0
Seattle, WA.	2,843	4,257	5,789	6,157	7,497	11.4	8.5	7.7	6.2	5.0
Virginia Beach, VA . .	2,794	3,834	6,269	8,149	11,873	11.2	7.7	8.4	8.1	7.9
Washington, DC. . . .	3,045	4,052	6,986	9,482	15,027	12.2	8.1	9.3	9.5	10.0
Wichita, KS.	2,549	3,335	6,031	8,358	12,751	10.2	6.7	8.0	8.4	8.5
Average [1]	2,775	4,364	6,649	8,517	12,578	11.1	8.7	8.9	8.5	8.4
Median [1]	2,794	4,214	6,841	8,868	13,103	11.2	8.4	9.1	8.9	8.7

[1] Based on selected cities and District of Columbia. For complete list of cities, see Table 430.

Source: Government of the District of Columbia, Office of the Chief Financial Officer, *Tax Rates and Revenues, Tax Burden Comparisons, Nationwide Comparison* annual; <http://www.cfo.dc.gov/cfo/site>.

Table 430. Residential Property Tax Rates for Largest City in Each State: 2006

[The real property tax is a function of housing values, real estate tax rates, assessment levels, homeowner exemptions and credits. Effective rate is the amount each jurisdiction considers based upon assessment level used. Assessment level is ratio of assessed value to assumed market value. Nominal rates represent the "announced" rates levied by the jurisdiction]

City	Effective tax rate per $100		Assessment level (percent)	Nominal rate per $100	City	Effective tax rate per $100		Assessment level (percent)	Nominal rate per $100
	Rank	Rate				Rank	Rate		
Indianapolis, IN	1	3.55	100.0	3.55	Little Rock, AR	29	1.38	20.0	6.90
Providence, RI	2	3.03	100.0	3.03	Wichita, KS	30	1.35	11.5	11.77
Bridgeport, CT	3	2.96	70.0	4.23	Boise, ID.	31	1.29	93.1	1.39
Houston, TX	4	2.87	100.0	2.87	Albuquerque, NM	32	1.27	33.3	3.81
Manchester, NH	5	2.84	100.0	2.84	Louisville, KY.	33	1.24	100.0	1.24
Burlington, VT	6	2.72	100.0	2.72	Oklahoma City, OK . . .	34	1.21	11.0	10.98
Philadelphia, PA	7	2.64	32.0	8.26	Minneapolis, MN.	36	1.21	94.3	1.28
Baltimore MD.	8	2.29	100.0	2.29	Charlotte, NC.	35	1.20	93.8	1.28
Milwaukee, WI	9	2.22	94.5	2.35	Kansas City, MO.	38	1.19	19.0	6.26
Des Moines, IA.	10	2.11	46.0	4.59	Portland, OR	37	1.17	60.4	1.94
Fargo, ND	11	2.04	4.4	46.76	Las Vegas, NV.	39	1.15	35.0	3.28
Newark, NJ	12	2.03	81.4	2.49	Los Angeles, CA.	40	1.10	100.0	1.10
Detroit, MI.	13	2.01	30.4	6.60	Boston, MA	41	1.09	100.0	1.09
Omaha, NE.	14	1.98	95.3	2.08	Phoenix, AZ.	42	1.08	10.0	10.76
Memphis, TN.	15	1.87	25.0	7.47	Seattle, WA	43	0.96	91.6	1.04
Columbia, SC.	16	1.83	4.0	45.81	Washington, DC	44	0.92	100.0	0.92
Atlanta, GA	17	1.75	40.0	4.39	Virginia Beach, VA . . .	45	0.91	74.8	1.22
New Orleans, LA	18	1.75	10.0	17.52	Charleston, WV	46	0.87	60.0	1.45
Columbus, OH	19	1.75	35.0	4.99	Cheyenne, WY	47	0.72	9.5	7.60
Jacksonville, FL	21	1.72	94.6	1.82	Birmingham, AL	48	0.70	10.0	6.95
Jackson, MS	20	1.72	10.0	17.21	New York City, NY . . .	49	0.66	4.2	15.66
Salt Lake City, UT. . . .	22	1.58	97.3	1.62	Denver, CO	50	0.56	8.0	7.02
Chicago, IL	23	1.58	20.4	7.74	Honolulu, HI.	51	0.36	100.0	0.36
Portland, ME	24	1.55	95.0	1.63					
Billings, MT	25	1.57	80.0	1.96	Unweighted Average . .	(X)	1.60	59.5	6.24
Anchorage, AK	26	1.50	100.0	1.50	Median	(X)	1.50	(X)	(X)
Wilmington, DE	27	1.44	47.2	3.05					
Sioux Falls, SD	28	1.40	85.0	1.65					

X Not Applicable.

Source: Government of the District of Columbia, Office of the Chief Financial Officer, *Tax Rates and Revenues, Tax Burden Comparisons, Nationwide Comparison* annual; <http://www.cfo.dc.gov/cfo/site>.

U.S. Census Bureau, Statistical Abstract of the United States: 2009

Table 431. Gross Revenue From Parimutuel and Amusement Taxes and Lotteries by State: 2003 to 2005

[In millions of dollars (46,673.7 represents $46,673,700,000). For **fiscal years**; see text, this section]

State	2003, Total gross revenue	2004, Total gross revenue	2005 Total gross revenue	2005 Amusement taxes [1]	2005 Parimutuel taxes	Lottery revenue Total [2]	Lottery revenue Apportionment of funds Prizes	Lottery revenue Apportionment of funds Administration	Lottery revenue Apportionment of funds Proceeds available from ticket sales
United States . . .	**46,673.7**	**50,758.5**	**72,695.9**	**5,242.0**	**309.8**	**67,144.1**	**49,448.8**	**2,091.1**	**15,604.2**
Alabama	3.5	3.3	3.2	0.1	3.1	(X)	(X)	(X)	(X)
Alaska	2.6	2.4	2.5	2.5	(X)	(X)	(X)	(X)	(X)
Arizona.	302.0	343.3	372.1	0.6	0.5	371.1	220.3	34.5	116.3
Arkansas	4.4	4.6	4.8	(X)	4.8	(X)	(X)	(X)	(X)
California	2,634.0	2,810.6	3,139.6	(X)	38.5	3,101.1	1,795.3	159.8	1,146.1
Colorado.	464.6	510.8	513.9	99.1	3.8	411.0	264.5	31.5	115.0
Connecticut.	1,302.4	1,355.3	1,307.4	416.5	9.7	881.2	573.0	34.3	273.9
Delaware	367.3	379.6	6,842.4	(X)	0.2	6,842.2	6,496.0	46.4	299.9
Florida	2,743.5	2,928.5	3,307.1	(X)	28.3	3,278.7	2,044.2	141.6	1,092.9
Georgia	2,284.1	2,376.3	2,546.6	(X)	(X)	2,546.6	1,633.3	111.0	802.3
Hawaii	(X)	(X)	(X)	(X)	(X)	(X)	(X)	(X)	(X)
Idaho	90.8	101.4	105.3	(X)	(X)	105.3	69.6	10.6	25.1
Illinois	2,152.2	2,370.4	2,521.8	826.4	11.7	1,683.8	1,042.9	59.6	581.3
Indiana.	1,281.2	1,439.4	1,486.5	793.6	4.7	688.2	455.3	47.1	185.8
Iowa	356.8	412.0	419.4	221.7	4.4	193.3	113.5	28.6	51.3
Kansas	196.7	215.7	198.4	0.6	3.2	194.6	112.6	20.6	61.5
Kentucky	650.7	695.8	676.7	0.2	14.3	662.1	457.7	43.0	161.5
Louisiana	809.9	855.6	848.0	510.1	47.8	290.1	153.3	28.8	108.0
Maine	164.3	193.5	199.1	0.4	4.2	194.4	128.9	15.1	50.4
Maryland	1,336.9	1,408.9	1,401.1	10.9	2.0	1,388.1	856.2	49.9	482.0
Massachusetts.	4,214.1	4,386.5	4,222.7	4.6	4.7	4,213.4	3,211.5	81.5	920.3
Michigan	1,666.0	1,952.7	2,035.1	145.8	10.9	1,878.3	1,179.6	61.6	637.1
Minnesota.	370.5	403.2	420.8	55.0	1.5	364.3	255.0	22.2	87.1
Mississippi	184.6	167.3	223.1	223.1	(X)	(X)	(X)	(X)	(X)
Missouri	952.6	1,049.5	1,064.5	327.4	(X)	737.1	487.9	36.9	212.3
Montana	78.6	85.2	85.1	53.1	0.1	31.9	17.8	6.8	7.2
Nebraska	88.1	99.0	100.4	5.9	0.3	94.2	58.4	12.3	23.5
Nevada	739.3	861.5	934.6	934.6	(X)	(X)	(X)	(X)	(X)
New Hampshire	217.1	232.2	220.6	0.4	3.6	216.6	132.7	15.0	69.0
New Jersey	2,307.6	2,533.7	2,623.2	475.7	(X)	2,147.6	1,266.1	80.7	800.7
New Mexico	168.8	178.2	177.5	46.4	0.9	130.2	80.9	17.0	32.3
New York	5,109.8	5,528.5	5,873.5	0.7	31.5	5,841.3	3,523.5	246.5	2,071.3
North Carolina	11.1	11.5	11.2	11.2	(X)	(X)	(X)	(X)	(X)
North Dakota	16.9	12.7	28.2	9.6	0.3	18.3	9.1	(X)	(X)
Ohio	2,093.8	2,170.6	2,039.9	(X)	14.6	2,025.3	1,280.8	83.1	661.4
Oklahoma	9.4	8.2	6.2	4.4	1.8	(X)	(X)	(X)	(X)
Oregon.	1,526.5	1,612.5	1,735.3	0.0	2.2	1,733.1	1,234.0	62.0	437.1
Pennsylvania.	1,987.6	2,189.5	2,453.4	0.5	26.0	2,426.8	1,529.4	63.4	833.9
Rhode Island.	1,124.8	1,314.0	1,460.8	(X)	4.0	1,456.9	1,143.4	6.8	306.7
South Carolina.	709.0	922.7	925.6	36.1	(X)	889.4	573.6	38.3	277.5
South Dakota	137.0	141.6	564.1	0.0	0.5	563.6	441.0	7.3	115.3
Tennessee	(X)	(X)	789.4	(X)	(X)	789.4	518.6	(X)	(X)
Texas.	3,164.3	3,522.8	3,511.1	24.5	11.6	3,475.0	2,228.0	177.8	1,069.2
Utah	(X)	(X)	(X)	(X)	(X)	(X)	(X)	(X)	(X)
Vermont	74.8	87.0	87.2	(X)	(X)	87.2	57.9	8.3	20.9
Virginia.	1,137.4	1,262.4	1,258.4	0.1	(X)	1,258.3	774.6	60.5	423.2
Washington	462.3	483.3	431.3	0.1	1.8	429.4	280.9	32.9	115.6
West Virginia.	566.8	683.3	13,094.2	(X)	10.2	13,084.0	12,485.4	27.7	570.9
Wisconsin.	406.7	451.2	422.4	0.3	1.5	420.5	262.2	28.2	130.1
Wyoming	0.2	0.2	0.4	(X)	0.4	(X)	(X)	(X)	(X)

X Not applicable. [1] Represents nonlicense taxes. [2] Excludes commissions.

Source: U.S. Census Bureau, Federal, State and Local Governments, State Government Finances, Lottery, and unpublished data, <http://ftp2.census.gov/govs/state/05lottery.pdf>.

Table 432. Lottery Sales—Type of Game and Use of Proceeds: 1980 to 2007

[In millions of dollars (2,393 represents $2,393,000,000). For fiscal years]

Game	1980	1990	1995	2000	2004	2005	2006	2007
Total ticket sales	**2,393**	**20,017**	**31,931**	**37,201**	**47,697**	**47,364**	**51,595**	**52,414**
Instant [1]	527	5,204	11,511	15,459	23,011	25,946	28,342	29,736
Three-digit [2]	1,554	4,572	5,737	5,341	5,389	5,428	5,456	5,586
Four-digit [2]	55	1,302	1,941	2,711	3,195	3,300	3,400	3,499
Lotto [3]	52	8,563	10,594	9,160	10,472	9,707	11,015	10,014
Other [4]	206	376	2,148	4,530	5,630	2,983	3,382	3,579
State proceeds (net income) [5] . . .	978	7,703	11,100	11,404	15,094	15,779	17,220	17,627

[1] Player scratches a latex section on ticket which reveals instantly whether ticket is a winner. [2] Players choose and bet on three or four digits, depending on game, with various payoffs for different straight order or mixed combination bets. [3] Players typically select six digits out of a large field of numbers. Varying prizes are offered for matching three through six numbers drawn by lottery. [4] Includes break-open tickets, spiel, keno, video lottery, etc. [5] Sales minus prizes and expenses equal net government income.

Source: TLF Publications, Inc., Boyds, MD, *2008 World Lottery Almanac* (copyright), <http://www.lafleurs.com/>.

State and Local Government Finances and Employment 277

Table 433. **State Governments—Summary of Finances: 1990 to 2005**

[In millions of dollars (673,119 represents $673,119,000,000), for fiscal year ending in year shown; see text; this section]

Item	1990	1995	2000	2001	2002	2003	2004	2005
Borrowing and revenue	**673,119**	**957,452**	**1,336,798**	**1,257,148**	**1,205,999**	**1,430,303**	**1,727,347**	**1,750,227**
Borrowing	40,948	53,697	75,968	76,843	108,170	134,644	140,682	108,270
Total Revenue	632,172	903,756	1,260,829	1,180,305	1,097,829	1,295,659	1,586,665	1,641,957
General revenue	517,429	739,016	984,783	1,049,298	1,062,305	1,112,349	1,194,056	1,286,714
Taxes	300,489	399,148	539,655	559,679	535,241	548,991	590,414	650,612
Sales and gross receipts	147,069	196,851	252,147	258,018	262,361	273,811	293,326	312,584
General	99,702	132,236	174,461	179,319	179,665	184,597	197,949	212,921
Motor fuels	19,379	25,440	29,968	31,026	31,968	32,269	33,762	34,567
Alcoholic beverages	3,191	3,597	4,104	4,167	4,249	4,399	4,593	4,706
Tobacco products	5,541	7,348	8,391	8,644	8,902	11,482	12,303	12,917
Other	19,256	28,230	35,222	34,863	37,576	41,065	44,718	47,474
Licenses	18,842	26,083	32,598	32,866	35,391	35,863	39,679	42,584
Motor vehicles	9,848	12,433	15,099	15,141	15,641	16,009	17,336	18,221
Corporations in general	3,099	5,018	6,460	6,384	5,842	6,129	6,339	7,148
Other	5,895	8,632	11,039	11,341	13,908	13,725	16,004	17,216
Individual income	96,076	125,610	194,573	208,079	185,697	181,933	196,255	221,597
Corporation net income	21,751	29,075	32,522	31,687	25,123	28,384	30,229	38,691
Property	5,848	9,518	10,996	10,430	9,702	10,471	10,714	11,342
Other	10,902	12,014	16,819	18,597	16,967	18,529	20,211	23,813
Charges and miscellaneous	90,612	124,310	170,747	183,998	191,641	201,741	209,029	228,242
Intergovernmental revenue	126,329	215,558	274,382	305,621	335,423	361,617	394,613	407,860
From federal government	118,353	202,485	259,114	288,309	317,581	343,308	374,694	386,283
Public welfare	59,397	114,945	147,150	165,800	181,517	196,954	214,528	222,909
Education	21,271	31,944	42,086	45,760	51,103	56,362	64,913	68,275
Highways	13,931	19,419	23,790	27,894	29,641	29,481	29,606	32,677
Health and hospitals	5,475	10,344	14,223	16,426	17,875	19,559	20,377	20,443
Other	18,279	25,834	31,865	32,428	37,445	40,951	45,270	41,980
From local governments	7,976	13,073	15,268	17,312	17,842	18,309	19,919	21,576
Utility revenue	3,305	3,845	4,513	6,930	11,935	12,518	12,955	14,627
Liquor store revenue	2,907	3,073	3,895	4,092	4,288	4,518	4,866	5,118
Insurance trust revenue [1]	108,530	157,821	267,639	119,985	19,301	166,274	374,788	335,498
Employee retirement	78,898	104,451	230,166	79,527	-25,244	110,839	308,896	269,617
Unemployment compensation	18,370	37,041	23,260	23,221	26,960	35,191	38,230	35,243
Expenditure and debt redemption	**592,213**	**874,365**	**1,125,828**	**1,235,568**	**1,334,969**	**1,426,715**	**1,497,114**	**1,550,551**
Total Expenditure	572,318	836,894	1,084,097	1,186,108	1,280,290	1,359,048	1,406,175	1,471,936
General expenditure	508,284	733,504	964,723	1,045,296	1,109,227	1,163,968	1,209,436	1,277,979
Education	184,935	249,670	346,465	374,444	389,390	411,094	429,341	191,553
Public welfare	104,971	194,854	238,890	262,346	287,016	314,407	339,409	370,219
Health	20,029	30,865	42,066	43,732	50,293	50,221	49,559	48,957
Hospitals	22,637	29,139	32,578	34,538	37,393	38,395	40,426	43,103
Highways	44,249	57,374	74,415	78,786	84,198	85,726	86,166	91,063
Police protection	5,166	6,451	9,788	10,145	10,706	11,144	10,766	11,426
Corrections	17,266	26,069	35,129	38,165	38,918	39,188	39,314	40,592
Natural resources	9,909	12,534	15,967	17,309	17,821	18,577	18,652	18,850
Housing and community development	2,856	3,466	4,726	5,009	5,989	8,112	7,191	7,708
Other and unallocable	96,267	123,081	164,698	180,823	187,504	187,106	188,613	454,508
Utility expenditure	7,131	7,586	10,723	18,632	20,279	22,405	21,676	21,824
Liquor store expenditure	2,452	2,522	3,195	3,347	3,498	3,697	3,924	4,082
Insurance trust expenditure [1]	54,452	93,282	105,456	118,833	147,286	168,979	171,139	168,052
Employee retirement	29,562	47,541	75,971	83,770	91,971	103,049	111,376	118,333
Unemployment compensation	16,423	35,032	18,583	22,920	42,017	51,411	43,174	29,776
By character and object:								
Intergovernmental expenditure	175,028	240,978	327,070	350,327	364,789	382,197	389,706	403,488
Direct expenditure	397,291	595,916	757,027	835,782	915,501	976,852	1,016,469	1,068,449
Current operation	258,046	396,035	523,114	580,374	620,763	656,989	691,652	739,988
Capital outlay	45,524	57,829	76,233	81,881	89,919	91,943	90,950	94,181
Construction	34,803	46,113	59,681	64,668	71,035	72,374	73,372	77,039
Land and existing structure	3,471	39	4,681	4,643	5,305	6,945	6,576	17,142
Equipment	7,250	11,676	11,871	12,570	13,579	12,623	11,002	10,883
Assistance and subsidies	16,902	23,511	22,136	23,496	24,313	25,901	28,104	30,181
Interest on debt	22,367	25,259	30,089	31,198	33,220	33,040	34,624	36,047
Insurance benefits [2]	54,452	93,282	105,456	118,833	147,286	168,979	171,139	168,052
Debt redemption	19,895	37,471	41,730	49,460	54,678	67,666	90,939	78,615
Debt outstanding, year end	**318,254**	**427,239**	**547,876**	**576,494**	**642,202**	**697,929**	**754,150**	**813,846**
Long-term [3]	315,490	421,139	541,497	572,831	623,558	681,796	740,414	808,293
Full-faith and credit	74,972	116,195	138,525	147,130	159,502	179,372	209,385	(NA)
Nonguaranteed	240,518	304,944	402,972	425,701	464,056	502,424	531,030	(NA)
Short-term	2,764	6,100	6,379	3,663	18,644	16,133	13,736	5,553
Net long-term [4]	125,524	205,348	266,870	287,450	317,829	366,207	412,194	444,685
Full-faith and credit only	63,481	106,571	128,384	137,341	149,580	170,137	200,295	(NA)

NA Not available.   [1] Includes other items not shown separately.   [2] Includes repayments.   [3] As of fiscal year 2005, the Census Bureau no longer collects government debt information by the character of long-term debt. For further information, see the 2006 Government Finance and Employment Classification Manual at <http://www.census.gov/govs/www/class06.html>.   [4] Less cash and investment assets specifically held for redemption of long-term debt.

Source: U.S. Census Bureau, *Federal, State, and Local Governments, Finance, Survey of State Government Finances*, 2005. See also <http://www.census.gov/govs/www/state05.html>.

U.S. Census Bureau, Statistical Abstract of the United States: 2009

Table 434. **State Governments—Revenue by State: 2005**

[In millions of dollars (1,641,957 represents $1,641,957,000,000), except as noted. **For fiscal year ending in year shown;** See text, this section. Includes local shares of state imposed taxes]

State	Total revenue [1,2]	General revenue							Utility and liquor store revenue	Insurance trust revenue
			Intergovernmental		General revenue from own sources					
		Total	Total	From federal govern- ment	Total	Total taxes	Current charges	Miscel- laneous		
United States...	**1,641,957**	**1,286,714**	**407,860**	**386,283**	**878,854**	**650,612**	**124,186**	**104,055**	**19,746**	**335,498**
Alabama	22,297	18,910	7,304	6,691	11,606	7,774	2,687	1,146	178	3,209
Alaska	9,185	7,881	2,317	2,313	5,563	1,858	480	3,225	17	1,288
Arizona	25,311	21,492	7,566	7,102	13,925	11,008	1,284	1,633	26	3,793
Arkansas	14,918	12,834	4,110	4,085	8,724	6,539	1,583	602	–	2,084
California	250,278	171,786	51,564	47,401	120,223	98,435	12,777	9,011	5,664	72,828
Colorado	22,453	15,843	4,536	4,470	11,307	7,648	1,941	1,718	–	6,610
Connecticut	20,457	18,563	3,963	3,951	14,600	11,585	1,480	1,536	24	1,869
Delaware	6,165	5,468	1,157	1,123	4,311	2,590	731	990	10	686
Florida	77,356	62,354	19,400	19,232	42,954	33,895	4,319	4,740	20	14,983
Georgia	36,112	30,053	9,861	9,702	20,192	15,676	2,499	2,017	2	6,057
Hawaii	9,092	7,864	1,786	1,784	6,078	4,434	1,027	617	–	1,227
Idaho	7,204	5,679	1,750	1,740	3,930	2,934	501	495	86	1,439
Illinois	58,907	46,553	12,999	12,345	33,554	26,412	3,284	3,858	–	12,355
Indiana	27,122	24,263	6,949	6,764	17,313	12,854	2,797	1,663	–	2,859
Iowa	15,631	12,527	4,104	3,949	8,423	5,751	1,826	846	150	2,955
Kansas	12,554	10,581	3,220	3,162	7,361	5,638	1,031	692	–	1,973
Kentucky	21,248	18,157	5,840	5,822	12,317	9,091	2,004	1,222	–	3,091
Louisiana	24,852	20,177	7,089	7,046	13,089	8,639	2,537	1,913	6	4,668
Maine	8,456	7,148	2,529	2,520	4,619	3,216	604	799	52	1,257
Maryland	28,648	24,431	6,664	6,463	17,767	13,367	2,487	1,912	106	4,110
Massachusetts	42,143	34,905	8,417	8,039	26,488	18,035	3,179	5,275	139	7,098
Michigan	55,398	45,632	12,993	12,398	32,639	23,525	5,444	3,669	689	9,078
Minnesota	31,724	25,790	6,575	6,437	19,215	15,881	2,040	1,294	–	5,934
Mississippi	15,518	12,817	5,769	5,614	7,048	5,432	1,208	408	203	2,498
Missouri	26,821	21,425	7,904	7,756	13,521	9,544	2,068	1,909	–	5,396
Montana	5,692	4,624	1,855	1,842	2,769	1,876	443	451	52	1,015
Nebraska	8,740	7,816	2,503	2,472	5,313	3,797	730	786	–	924
Nevada	11,535	8,773	1,901	1,744	6,873	5,670	609	594	103	2,659
New Hampshire	6,137	5,027	1,739	1,491	3,288	2,011	645	633	396	713
New Jersey	52,662	42,184	10,258	9,694	31,926	24,248	4,609	3,069	645	9,833
New Mexico	13,344	11,133	3,978	3,880	7,155	4,478	800	1,876	–	2,211
New York	143,890	114,653	47,757	40,184	66,896	51,326	7,493	8,076	6,321	22,916
North Carolina	44,892	36,303	12,842	12,119	23,461	18,640	3,039	1,782	–	8,589
North Dakota	3,877	3,343	1,205	1,170	2,138	1,403	442	293	–	534
Ohio	72,208	49,041	15,746	15,377	33,296	24,011	5,779	3,506	618	22,549
Oklahoma	17,874	14,609	4,909	4,815	9,700	6,859	1,710	1,130	374	2,891
Oregon	22,603	14,769	4,474	4,445	10,295	6,523	2,267	1,505	311	7,524
Pennsylvania	69,760	54,095	16,724	16,360	37,371	27,263	6,101	4,007	1,171	14,494
Rhode Island	7,255	5,899	2,081	1,968	3,818	2,629	487	703	28	1,328
South Carolina	22,991	18,743	7,180	6,766	11,562	7,318	2,980	1,263	1,140	3,108
South Dakota	4,059	2,995	1,236	1,218	1,759	1,110	233	416	–	1,064
Tennessee	25,847	23,278	8,661	8,459	14,617	10,007	1,698	2,912	–	2,570
Texas	95,821	75,791	26,579	25,811	49,212	32,785	7,887	8,540	–	20,030
Utah	13,119	10,411	2,936	2,861	7,475	4,703	2,046	726	151	2,557
Vermont	4,599	4,222	1,260	1,260	2,961	2,243	404	315	38	340
Virginia	37,037	30,201	6,304	5,851	23,898	15,919	5,018	2,961	439	6,396
Washington	36,802	26,950	7,398	7,040	19,552	14,840	3,116	1,596	466	9,386
West Virginia	12,008	9,804	3,339	3,276	6,465	4,301	954	1,210	62	2,142
Wisconsin	34,243	24,611	6,694	6,448	17,918	13,152	2,745	2,020	–	9,632
Wyoming	5,112	4,304	1,935	1,824	2,369	1,740	132	497	60	747

– Represents or rounds to zero. [1] Includes categories not shown separately. [2] Duplicate intergovernmental transactions are excluded.

Source: U.S. Census Bureau, *Federal, State, and Local Governments, Finance, Survey of State Government Finances,* 2005. See also <http://www.census.gov/govs/www/state05.html>.

U.S. Census Bureau, Statistical Abstract of the United States: 2009

Table 435. **State Government Tax Collections, by State: 2006**

[In millions of dollars (650,612 represents $650,612,000,000]

State	All taxes	Total property tax	Sales and gross receipts taxes		Selective sales taxes						
			Total	General sales and gross receipts	Total [1]	Alcoholic beverages	Insurance premiums	Motor fuels	Public Utilities	Tobacco products	Other
United States [2]...	650,612	11,342	312,584	212,921	99,663	4,706	14,842	34,567	10,909	12,917	16,170
Alabama	7,774	231	3,963	2,033	1,930	118	273	560	630	153	192
Alaska	1,858	43	199	–	199	35	53	40	4	56	9
Arizona	11,008	374	6,699	5,208	1,491	59	397	706	38	291	–
Arkansas	6,539	543	3,458	2,574	884	43	125	437	–	148	126
California	98,435	2,164	37,673	29,967	7,706	314	2,233	3,366	569	1,096	89
Colorado	7,648	–	3,057	2,003	1,054	32	192	589	9	130	–
Connecticut	11,585	–	5,128	3,268	1,860	44	238	477	217	273	184
Delaware	2,590	–	397	–	397	14	69	114	38	80	82
Florida	33,895	300	25,486	19,056	6,430	623	765	2,094	1,841	466	614
Georgia	15,676	67	6,967	5,310	1,657	150	332	926	–	249	–
Hawaii	4,434	–	2,749	2,137	612	44	87	86	109	85	201
Idaho	2,934	–	1,501	1,128	373	7	87	220	2	52	6
Illinois	26,412	56	13,356	7,195	6,160	147	367	1,420	1,726	656	1,005
Indiana	12,854	9	7,195	5,001	2,194	39	187	807	12	343	9
Iowa	5,751	–	2,627	1,722	906	14	131	438	–	96	–
Kansas	5,638	61	2,791	2,005	786	90	122	423	1	124	22
Kentucky	9,091	475	4,252	2,595	1,657	82	358	496	–	38	669
Louisiana	8,639	45	4,586	2,861	1,724	54	363	603	8	106	33
Maine	3,216	44	1,467	935	533	13	81	228	25	92	89
Maryland	13,367	529	5,152	2,890	2,262	27	269	753	133	276	791
Massachusetts	18,035	–	5,803	3,891	1,912	69	402	686	–	424	322
Michigan	23,525	2,152	11,534	8,074	3,460	151	250	1,076	29	1,180	618
Minnesota	15,881	619	6,641	4,204	2,437	69	311	651	–	174	1,175
Mississippi	5,432	44	3,523	2,588	935	40	164	436	9	56	8
Missouri	9,544	23	4,599	3,036	1,563	28	288	742	–	110	67
Montana	1,876	185	455	–	455	22	61	192	29	61	37
Nebraska	3,797	2	1,973	1,517	456	24	39	305	4	71	7
Nevada	5,670	149	4,597	2,915	1,682	36	216	308	9	137	42
New Hampshire	2,011	392	705	–	705	12	80	132	69	102	305
New Jersey	24,248	3	10,172	6,552	3,620	99	454	525	981	800	284
New Mexico	4,478	48	2,171	1,557	614	35	95	223	14	48	151
New York	51,326	–	17,331	11,004	6,328	185	987	769	976	2,845	
North Carolina	18,640	–	7,616	4,602	3,013	221	442	1,338	328	43	630
North Dakota	1,403	2	710	410	300	6	31	122	33	21	77
Ohio	24,011	37	11,146	8,194	2,952	90	440	1,672	156	579	–
Oklahoma	6,859	–	2,500	1,661	839	71	172	414	18	128	29
Oregon	6,523	24	699	–	699	14	55	373	11	244	–
Pennsylvania	27,263	58	13,227	8,065	5,162	237	677	1,908	1,131	1,031	152
Rhode Island	2,629	2	1,378	844	534	11	53	133	86	136	110
South Carolina	7,318	10	3,883	2,903	980	142	129	485	50	30	109
South Dakota	1,110	–	904	622	282	12	58	125	3	28	56
Tennessee	10,007	–	7,648	6,118	1,530	97	361	844	5	121	101
Texas	32,785	–	25,851	16,356	9,495	626	1,168	2,936	826	599	3,303
Utah	4,703	–	2,330	1,710	619	30	120	351	26	61	30
Vermont	2,243	745	778	311	467	18	52	86	11	48	252
Virginia	15,919	19	5,479	3,094	2,385	152	374	913	132	103	711
Washington	14,840	1,591	11,642	9,147	2,495	199	357	931	374	354	277
West Virginia	4,301	4	2,154	1,095	1,059	9	113	320	156	103	348
Wisconsin	13,152	112	5,791	4,039	1,751	49	145	957	284	310	4
Wyoming	1,740	181	642	522	119	1	20	68	3	27	–

See footnotes at end of table.

U.S. Census Bureau, Statistical Abstract of the United States: 2009

Table 435. **State Government Tax Collections, by State: 2006**—Con.

[See headnote, page 280]

| State | License taxes | | | | Income taxes | | | Other taxes | | |
| | Total [1] | Selected license taxes | | | Total | Indi-vidual | Cor-pora-tion net | Total [1] | Selected other taxes | |
		Cor-pora-tion	Motor vehicle oper-ators	Occu-pancy and busi-ness, n.e.c. [3]					Death and gift	Sever-ance
United States [2]...	**42,584**	**7,148**	**2,049**	**12,094**	**260,288**	**221,597**	**38,691**	**23,813**	**5,340**	**8,132**
Alabama	438	81	15	123	2,934	2,537	397	208	14	145
Alaska.	101	1	–	15	589	–	589	927	2	926
Arizona	326	12	17	91	3,550	2,848	702	59	33	26
Arkansas	312	21	25	107	2,152	1,875	277	73	14	19
California	6,708	64	217	3,717	51,662	42,992	8,670	227	213	14
Colorado	337	4	15	42	4,087	3,771	316	168	23	145
Connecticut	377	17	46	94	5,608	5,033	575	471	265	–
Delaware	929	569	2	250	1,131	882	249	133	6	–
Florida.	1,894	176	167	279	1,785		1,785	4,429	295	59
Georgia	528	53	52	115	8,039	7,326	712	75	43	–
Hawaii.	143	2	1	22	1,506	1,381	124	37	13	–
Idaho	238	2	7	50	1,181	1,041	141	14	9	2
Illinois	2,471	191	86	745	10,120	7,937	2,183	409	301	–
Indiana	467	5	209	40	5,038	4,213	825	145	144	1
Iowa	589	38	14	82	2,441	2,254	186	93	77	–
Kansas	291	51	19	23	2,328	2,080	248	167	50	117
Kentucky	554	199	13	107	3,515	3,036	479	295	63	229
Louisiana	520	289	11	75	2,745	2,393	352	742	30	712
Maine	203	6	7	78	1,435	1,299	136	67	32	–
Maryland	734	65	41	133	6,469	5,661	807	484	183	–
Massachusetts	686	26	92	145	11,023	9,690	1,333	523	255	–
Michigan	1,340	20	51	144	8,016	6,109	1,907	483	101	68
Minnesota	957	7	42	292	7,275	6,341	934	389	69	32
Mississippi	330	98	26	67	1,457	1,174	283	78	12	66
Missouri.	642	119	17	133	4,233	4,015	218	47	39	–
Montana	235	1	6	41	812	713	98	188	4	181
Nebraska.	203	7	8	64	1,592	1,394	198	26	14	3
Nevada	704	59	15	363	–	–	–	220	21	40
New Hampshire	193	4	13	67	544	68	476	176	11	–
New Jersey	1,289	247	37	491	11,763	9,538	2,225	1,020	521	–
New Mexico	210	3	6	25	1,328	1,086	242	722	5	713
New York.	1,244	69	156	157	30,885	28,100	2,785	1,867	898	–
North Carolina	1,109	388	80	144	9,700	8,428	1,272	216	154	2
North Dakota	110	–	4	40	318	242	76	264	2	262
Ohio	1,998	418	83	702	10,762	9,434	1,327	68	60	8
Oklahoma	850	46	15	200	2,637	2,469	169	872	76	763
Oregon	655	9	26	131	5,064	4,699	365	79	57	12
Pennsylvania	2,725	845	60	847	9,979	8,276	1,703	1,273	695	–
Rhode Island	91	4	1	29	1,111	998	113	47	32	–
South Carolina	403	68	39	124	2,938	2,691	247	85	19	–
South Dakota	150	3	2	64	49	–	49	7	4	3
Tennessee	1,090	517	43	229	961	155	806	309	86	1
Texas	4,485	2,234	112	679	–	–	–	2,449	102	2,348
Utah	182	4	19	35	2,116	1,927	189	76	3	73
Vermont	103	5	4	24	569	500	69	48	19	–
Virginia	623	49	46	147	8,958	8,352	606	840	150	2
Washington	726	21	49	188	–	–	–	880	–	43
West Virginia	184	9	–	40	1,635	1,172	463	324	5	307
Wisconsin	799	15	31	279	6,248	5,465	783	203	112	3
Wyoming	108	7	2	18	–	–	–	809	3	806

– Represents or rounds to zero.   X Not applicable.   [1] Includes other items not shown separately.   [2] Details will not add to total shown due to rounding.   [3] n.e.c. means not elsewhere classified.

Source: U.S. Census Bureau, *Federal, State, and Local Governments, Tax collections, State government tax collections,* Annual. See also <http://www.census.gov/govs/www/statetax.html>; (accessed April 2008).

U.S. Census Bureau, Statistical Abstract of the United States: 2009

Table 436. **State Governments—Expenditures and Debt by State: 2005**

[**In millions of dollars (1,471,936 represents $1,471,936,000,000) except as indicated.** For fiscal year ending in year shown; see text, this section]

State	Total expenditure	General expenditure		Direct expenditures						
		Total	Inter-govern-mental	Total	Educa-tion	Public welfare	Health	Hospi-tals	High-ways	Police protec-tion
United States ...	1,471,936	1,277,979	403,488	874,491	191,553	318,144	31,452	42,676	76,575	10,011
Alabama.	21,047	19,111	4,494	14,617	4,072	4,993	865	1,314	1,047	115
Alaska	8,056	7,115	1,145	5,970	963	1,375	124	25	1,046	69
Arizona.	23,957	21,623	8,029	13,594	3,024	5,332	1,206	62	1,141	196
Arkansas	13,636	12,668	3,904	8,764	2,034	3,286	327	573	794	99
California	210,407	177,304	80,948	96,355	19,414	30,095	2,063	5,372	6,507	1,222
Colorado.	18,734	15,647	5,188	10,460	3,116	2,682	722	339	995	106
Connecticut.	19,926	17,159	3,517	13,643	2,345	4,230	520	1,126	804	173
Delaware	5,964	5,475	984	4,491	1,011	1,122	288	58	495	84
Florida	71,155	63,004	17,476	45,528	6,319	16,659	2,926	577	5,328	472
Georgia	33,807	30,460	9,521	20,939	5,713	8,678	530	680	918	213
Hawaii	8,405	7,620	147	7,473	2,648	1,415	415	378	278	11
Idaho	6,144	5,487	1,520	3,968	887	1,371	121	41	443	41
Illinois	55,395	48,028	14,213	33,815	6,567	12,658	2,418	913	2,663	339
Indiana.	26,363	24,473	7,993	16,480	4,976	5,558	540	281	1,556	233
Iowa	13,898	12,490	3,642	8,848	2,286	3,116	91	888	987	74
Kansas.	11,765	10,708	3,281	7,427	1,917	2,698	152	113	1,055	79
Kentucky	20,090	17,674	3,915	13,759	3,295	5,376	386	737	1,266	148
Louisiana	21,411	18,819	4,589	14,230	3,109	4,453	542	1,623	1,177	196
Maine.	7,470	6,868	1,093	5,775	832	2,300	489	52	499	61
Maryland	26,763	23,586	5,680	17,906	3,731	5,821	1,085	512	1,519	315
Massachusetts.	38,315	34,291	6,498	27,793	4,983	10,723	698	426	1,641	360
Michigan.	51,480	45,736	19,308	26,429	7,852	9,266	587	1,911	1,446	291
Minnesota.	29,560	26,264	10,109	16,155	3,815	7,588	405	267	1,205	207
Mississippi	14,705	13,172	4,006	9,166	1,801	4,050	254	747	801	74
Missouri	23,151	20,680	5,489	15,191	2,732	6,215	695	1,182	1,451	155
Montana.	4,809	4,239	1,005	3,234	715	778	245	39	509	38
Nebraska	7,240	6,900	1,659	5,241	1,302	1,945	204	206	616	56
Nevada	9,158	8,076	3,273	4,803	1,194	1,396	214	174	622	91
New Hampshire	5,781	5,043	1,225	3,818	761	1,444	103	53	350	38
New Jersey.	50,964	40,561	10,642	29,918	6,642	10,280	979	1,558	1,966	473
New Mexico	12,632	11,575	3,617	7,958	1,658	3,068	323	568	667	109
New York	135,811	111,894	43,731	68,163	9,178	32,660	1,482	4,071	3,998	617
North Carolina	39,482	35,644	10,676	24,968	6,807	8,315	1,076	1,160	3,067	380
North Dakota.	3,491	3,157	701	2,456	686	674	45	22	328	22
Ohio	60,554	49,491	16,368	33,123	7,929	12,727	1,315	1,904	2,359	241
Oklahoma.	15,660	13,627	3,698	9,929	2,853	3,727	393	148	794	133
Oregon.	19,217	15,502	4,765	10,738	2,249	3,530	252	793	957	173
Pennsylvania.	63,881	54,867	13,308	41,559	8,645	17,203	822	1,987	5,465	607
Rhode Island.	6,600	5,568	908	4,660	755	2,070	149	108	283	53
South Carolina.	22,709	19,122	4,246	14,875	3,540	5,186	800	1,051	1,347	147
South Dakota	3,266	2,990	608	2,381	460	732	101	50	426	29
Tennessee	23,954	22,469	5,706	16,763	3,351	8,486	966	387	1,261	147
Texas.	81,277	71,796	17,490	54,306	13,723	19,057	734	2,940	7,123	486
Utah	11,149	10,122	2,190	7,933	2,409	2,142	261	669	647	126
Vermont	4,436	4,188	1,267	2,921	701	1,129	126	1	223	76
Virginia.	32,709	29,944	9,720	20,224	5,425	5,468	488	2,237	2,303	250
Washington.	33,048	28,204	7,443	20,760	5,479	6,667	1,215	1,439	1,627	191
West Virginia.	9,679	8,801	2,016	6,785	1,475	2,335	245	73	966	53
Wisconsin.	28,828	25,168	9,201	15,967	3,782	5,525	293	838	1,204	111
Wyoming	4,000	3,570	1,337	2,233	390	540	174	3	405	31

See footnote at end of table.

U.S. Census Bureau, Statistical Abstract of the United States: 2009

Table 436. **State Governments—Expenditures and Debt by State: 2005**—Con.

[See headnote, page 282]

State	General expenditure—Con.								Expenditures			
	Direct expenditures—Con.											
	Corrections	Parks and recreation	Housing and community development	Sewerage	Solid waste management	Governmental administration	Interest on general debt	Other	Utility and liquor store	Insurance trust	Cash and security holdings	Debt outstanding, total
United States. .	38,321	4,482	4,982	1,109	3,184	47,710	34,315	69,976	25,905	168,052	3,156,390	813,846
Alabama	416	40	6	–	6	481	303	958	183	1,753	34,273	6,262
Alaska	197	9	115	–	–	459	290	1,299	88	853	44,891	5,767
Arizona	802	214	67	–	26	513	255	755	31	2,304	41,753	8,037
Arkansas	348	83	14	–	25	571	135	475	–	969	21,346	4,298
California	5,804	363	191	145	1,224	8,002	4,222	11,732	5,893	27,210	465,078	107,373
Colorado	621	70	76	2	17	569	503	642	13	3,073	52,485	12,745
Connecticut	580	59	145	–	162	1,032	1,129	1,335	256	2,511	34,391	23,206
Delaware	218	49	52	–	56	420	170	467	88	402	11,896	4,361
Florida	2,307	147	77	–	223	2,576	1,105	6,812	66	8,084	175,621	28,255
Georgia	1,251	132	48	–	3	830	456	1,487	30	3,317	66,176	9,245
Hawaii	170	66	92	–	–	412	399	1,188	–	786	14,440	5,844
Idaho	177	24	12	1	–	293	174	382	63	594	13,100	2,386
Illinois	1,118	130	179	34	82	1,356	2,325	3,033	–	7,368	115,868	51,285
Indiana	649	70	210	13	16	656	732	990	36	1,854	43,958	14,948
Iowa	224	19	21	5	3	485	196	452	102	1,305	29,155	4,931
Kansas	253	22	54	–	4	393	239	448	–	1,057	14,979	5,118
Kentucky	412	114	124	18	50	711	374	749	–	2,416	38,095	8,564
Louisiana	476	180	28	–	22	640	625	1,160	4	2,589	46,661	11,501
Maine	124	11	119	2	12	283	236	755	6	596	14,545	4,627
Maryland	1,022	63	220	69	20	1,493	730	1,307	631	2,546	50,542	15,230
Massachusetts . . .	797	130	368	232	41	1,485	3,030	2,880	219	3,806	82,612	61,017
Michigan	1,638	82	486	–	9	981	966	914	557	5,186	85,405	26,339
Minnesota	346	150	60	–	41	893	389	788	99	3,197	53,900	7,265
Mississippi	268	37	6	–	–	286	195	646	165	1,368	24,771	4,328
Missouri	633	45	132	–	27	579	721	623	–	2,471	62,172	16,184
Montana	125	12	49	–	1	256	130	338	45	525	13,238	3,949
Nebraska	193	28	1	–	–	196	87	406	–	340	10,556	1,742
Nevada	242	22	11	–	13	324	195	304	109	973	25,156	4,076
New Hampshire . .	111	12	99	3	12	195	322	317	351	387	10,894	6,864
New Jersey	1,307	425	216	22	175	1,706	1,446	2,723	2,303	8,101	94,926	42,313
New Mexico	291	65	43	–	5	468	270	423	–	1,057	38,308	5,873
New York	2,470	438	340	29	213	4,709	3,421	4,535	9,935	13,982	276,565	102,565
North Carolina . . .	1,174	161	141	1	63	875	465	1,284	126	3,712	80,366	15,773
North Dakota	50	16	22	–	–	121	86	382	–	334	8,997	1,683
Ohio	1,382	79	236	364	29	1,767	1,227	1,563	387	10,675	173,817	23,177
Oklahoma	505	88	12	–	6	436	344	491	310	1,723	30,796	7,469
Oregon	448	67	102	–	43	769	473	881	169	3,546	62,347	10,464
Pennsylvania	1,658	127	37	–	77	2,388	1,210	1,331	1,132	7,882	113,364	27,573
Rhode Island	166	15	35	32	80	363	250	303	110	921	13,758	6,829
South Carolina . . .	398	77	116	–	4	859	498	853	1,259	2,328	37,720	13,370
South Dakota	73	29	37	–	–	135	100	210	–	276	10,598	2,573
Tennessee	460	102	27	15	55	606	177	722	5	1,480	32,362	3,574
Texas	2,905	80	32	3	153	1,525	834	4,712	16	9,465	206,403	18,153
Utah	289	40	61	9	12	705	208	355	112	914	22,400	5,267
Vermont	97	14	77	–	10	149	134	184	56	192	5,790	2,788
Virginia	1,008	74	102	67	43	827	659	1,273	407	2,358	65,501	16,901
Washington	901	64	237	–	49	681	783	1,429	416	4,428	74,261	17,023
West Virginia	200	56	19	42	7	501	196	616	70	809	12,729	5,097
Wisconsin	835	50	24	–	61	627	855	1,762	3	3,657	83,832	18,763
Wyoming	182	29	7	–	3	126	44	300	52	377	13,592	868

– Represents or rounds to zero.

Source: U.S. Census Bureau; *Federal, State, and Local Governments, Finance, Survey of State Government Finances*, 2005. See also <http://www.census.gov/govs/www/state05.html> (accessed April 2008).

State and Local Government Finances and Employment   283

Table 437. Local Governments—Revenue by State: 2005

[In millions of dollars (1,308,507 represents $1,308,507,000,000), except as noted. For fiscal year ending in year shown; see text, this section]

State		General revenue								
				General revenue from own sources						
					Taxes					
	Total revenue [1]	Total	Inter-govern-mental revenue	Total	Total	Property	Sales and gross receipt	Indi-vidual income	Corpor-ation income	Other taxes
United States....	**1,308,507**	**1,161,451**	**451,844**	**709,608**	**448,588**	**324,639**	**71,798**	**20,676**	**4,447**	**27,028**
Alabama	16,398	13,778	5,301	8,477	3,887	1,561	1,744	108	–	473
Alaska...........	3,138	2,864	1,156	1,708	1,089	849	201	–	–	38
Arizona	23,864	20,325	8,745	11,580	7,323	4,752	2,051	–	–	520
Arkansas	7,651	6,892	3,931	2,960	1,501	616	857	–	–	29
California........	213,739	181,820	85,441	96,379	48,257	31,919	11,371	–	–	4,967
Colorado	21,285	18,754	5,390	13,364	8,034	4,942	2,639	–	–	453
Connecticut	13,827	12,790	4,230	8,560	7,312	7,156	–	–	–	156
Delaware........	2,568	2,269	1,122	1,146	687	486	8	50	–	143
District of Columbia ..	9,919	8,297	2,794	5,503	4,235	1,136	1,211	1,148	199	541
Florida...........	76,346	68,059	20,888	47,172	25,972	20,092	4,299	–	–	1,580
Georgia..........	33,524	29,470	10,057	19,413	11,811	8,148	3,170	–	–	493
Hawaii...........	2,107	1,889	377	1,512	1,089	818	147	–	–	124
Idaho	4,373	4,193	1,700	2,493	1,248	1,154	23	–	–	72
Illinois..........	55,667	48,322	17,138	31,184	22,348	18,256	3,338	–	–	755
Indiana..........	25,034	23,212	8,131	15,081	9,146	8,294	85	598	–	170
Iowa............	11,179	10,456	3,883	6,573	3,954	3,302	528	59	–	65
Kansas	10,685	9,664	3,431	6,233	3,822	3,045	707	–	–	70
Kentucky	10,617	9,496	4,098	5,399	3,171	1,771	398	756	–	246
Louisiana.........	15,724	14,428	5,478	8,950	5,663	2,384	3,091	–	–	189
Maine	4,066	3,976	1,257	2,718	2,149	2,108	1	–	–	39
Maryland	22,032	20,195	6,440	13,754	10,384	5,066	459	3,492	–	1,367
Massachusetts	28,784	23,642	9,747	13,895	10,742	10,341	150	–	–	251
Michigan	43,854	39,225	19,400	19,825	11,770	10,767	250	456	–	297
Minnesota	23,139	21,000	10,131	10,869	5,076	4,632	191	–	–	252
Mississippi	9,335	8,724	3,978	4,746	2,059	1,923	61	–	–	74
Missouri..........	19,809	17,805	5,958	11,847	7,830	4,672	2,433	304	19	402
Montana	2,671	2,588	1,115	1,473	845	811	4	–	–	30
Nebraska........	8,911	6,215	1,913	4,302	2,783	2,092	341	–	–	349
Nevada	11,672	10,855	4,594	6,261	3,373	2,172	737	–	–	465
New Hampshire	4,284	4,183	1,397	2,786	2,298	2,258	–	–	–	40
New Jersey	38,303	37,407	12,207	25,200	19,623	19,193	66	–	–	364
New Mexico.......	6,638	6,208	3,606	2,602	1,598	822	684	–	–	92
New York.........	139,104	127,906	46,258	81,648	60,917	34,150	11,814	6,744	4,209	4,000
North Carolina	31,773	28,434	12,077	16,356	8,668	6,450	1,808	–	–	410
North Dakota	2,056	1,937	800	1,137	718	619	82	–	–	18
Ohio............	47,141	44,870	18,267	26,603	17,708	11,937	1,597	3,645	18	511
Oklahoma	10,263	9,398	3,855	5,543	3,214	1,719	1,392	–	–	104
Oregon	14,480	13,236	5,461	7,775	4,583	3,537	272	130	–	643
Pennsylvania	51,056	47,027	19,698	27,329	18,756	13,332	411	3,186	–	1,827
Rhode Island	3,587	3,361	1,138	2,223	1,871	1,818	9	–	–	45
South Carolina	14,721	13,314	4,355	8,959	4,482	3,729	348	–	–	405
South Dakota	2,373	2,128	714	1,414	1,009	736	228	–	–	45
Tennessee........	24,222	16,773	5,617	11,156	5,986	3,895	1,734	–	–	358
Texas	86,834	76,102	22,171	53,931	36,368	30,289	5,266	–	–	813
Utah............	8,461	6,996	2,655	4,341	2,618	1,792	688	–	–	137
Vermont	2,032	1,842	1,292	550	332	312	9	–	–	11
Virginia	29,041	26,566	9,950	16,616	11,740	8,372	2,162	–	–	1,207
Washington	29,259	23,797	9,491	14,306	8,129	5,041	2,183	–	–	905
West Virginia	4,464	4,273	2,095	2,178	1,250	1,005	58	–	–	187
Wisconsin	23,288	21,405	9,703	11,703	8,251	7,684	317	–	–	250
Wyoming	3,208	3,087	1,213	1,874	906	684	178	–	–	44

See footnotes at end of table.

U.S. Census Bureau, Statistical Abstract of the United States: 2009

Table 437. Local Governments—Revenue by State: 2005—Con.

[See headnote, page 284]

State	General revenue — Current charges and miscellaneous general revenue	General revenue from own sources — Current charges — Total [1]	Current charges — Education	Current charges — Hospital	Current charges — Sewerage	Miscellaneous general revenue — Total [1]	Miscellaneous general revenue — Interest earnings	Miscellaneous general revenue — Special assessment	Utility revenue	Liquor store revenue	Insurance trust revenue
United States ...	**261,020**	**185,639**	**21,143**	**49,714**	**31,571**	**75,381**	**27,094**	**5,571**	**99,225**	**872**	**46,958**
Alabama	4,590	3,753	317	2,463	338	837	371	20	2,159	–	461
Alaska	619	417	39	82	64	202	118	13	230	–	44
Arizona	4,258	2,820	457	467	487	1,438	547	44	3,332	–	207
Arkansas	1,459	969	151	215	198	490	238	9	731	–	28
California	48,122	34,635	2,256	8,146	4,583	13,487	4,487	1,066	16,630	–	15,288
Colorado	5,329	3,716	371	909	558	1,613	508	302	1,908	–	624
Connecticut	1,248	865	123	–	249	383	103	31	531	–	506
Delaware	459	310	17	–	126	149	58	22	240	–	58
District of Columbia	1,268	520	29	–	163	748	144	1	753	–	869
Florida	21,200	14,568	1,673	4,190	1,995	6,633	2,268	1,112	6,627	–	1,659
Georgia	7,602	5,756	505	2,726	770	1,846	701	30	3,574	–	480
Hawaii	422	314	–	–	155	109	32	11	218	–	–
Idaho	1,245	1,072	82	535	133	172	48	30	178	–	1
Illinois	8,836	6,083	1,139	799	897	2,753	898	300	2,954	–	4,390
Indiana	5,934	4,068	361	2,228	780	1,867	319	38	1,735	–	88
Iowa	2,619	2,094	421	919	279	525	176	39	719	–	4
Kansas	2,411	1,584	340	496	261	827	341	105	938	–	82
Kentucky	2,228	1,326	114	361	302	902	609	40	1,075	–	46
Louisiana	3,286	2,426	62	1,249	306	860	406	25	1,068	–	228
Maine	570	427	42	69	132	143	48	5	90	–	–
Maryland	3,370	2,357	558	–	731	1,013	306	107	527	179	1,131
Massachusetts	3,153	2,346	256	442	781	808	184	27	2,413	–	2,728
Michigan	8,055	5,894	1,009	790	1,301	2,160	602	172	1,930	–	2,699
Minnesota	5,794	3,864	394	1,003	536	1,930	729	321	1,449	236	454
Mississippi	2,687	2,218	293	1,445	161	469	181	8	611	–	–
Missouri	4,016	3,036	619	995	493	981	430	63	1,289	–	715
Montana	628	409	62	44	65	219	73	60	83	–	–
Nebraska	1,519	962	194	325	112	558	151	54	2,475	–	222
Nevada	2,888	1,858	110	504	335	1,030	295	111	817	–	–
New Hampshire	489	361	50	–	82	128	32	1	86	–	16
New Jersey	5,576	3,613	955	115	1,135	1,963	418	25	879	–	18
New Mexico	1,004	671	97	100	122	333	118	53	431	–	–
New York	20,730	13,718	1,235	2,893	1,545	7,012	1,701	113	4,690	–	6,509
North Carolina	7,689	6,272	506	2,767	1,227	1,417	524	47	2,862	438	39
North Dakota	419	221	44	–	35	198	57	57	100	–	20
Ohio	8,895	6,026	1,016	1,043	1,502	2,869	1,287	188	2,034	–	237
Oklahoma	2,329	1,755	255	635	221	573	208	16	774	–	91
Oregon	3,192	2,320	424	234	620	872	263	109	1,243	–	2
Pennsylvania	8,573	5,560	768	44	1,666	3,013	1,804	89	2,533	–	1,496
Rhode Island	352	256	28	1	81	96	25	7	143	–	83
South Carolina	4,477	3,506	226	2,298	309	971	433	39	1,403	–	4
South Dakota	405	302	59	36	47	103	38	22	190	19	37
Tennessee	5,170	4,100	413	2,071	489	1,070	461	89	6,774	–	676
Texas	17,563	12,559	1,802	3,666	2,232	5,004	2,643	128	8,199	–	2,533
Utah	1,724	1,142	69	29	222	582	205	53	1,464	–	9
Vermont	218	139	21	–	43	80	14	3	182	–	9
Virginia	4,875	3,445	328	220	852	1,430	565	156	1,432	–	1,043
Washington	6,177	4,876	297	1,288	1,099	1,301	447	98	5,089	–	374
West Virginia	928	619	33	197	152	310	147	11	165	–	25
Wisconsin	3,451	2,679	459	68	558	772	272	93	1,148	–	735
Wyoming	968	834	62	609	41	134	63	6	121	–	–

– Represents or rounds to zero.   [1] Includes items not shown separately.

Source: U.S. Census Bureau; *Federal, State, and Local Governments, State Government Finances*; <http://www.census.gov/govs/www/estimate05.html> (accessed April 2008).

U.S. Census Bureau, Statistical Abstract of the United States: 2009

Table 438. Local Governments—Expenditures and Debt by State: 2005

[**In millions of dollars, (1,313,908 represents $1,313,908,000,000), except as indicated**. For fiscal year ending in year shown; see text, this section]

State	Total expen-ditures	General expenditures							
		Total [1]	Direct expenditures						
			Total [1]	Edu-cation	Public welfare	Health	Hos-pitals	High-ways	Police protec-tion
United States ...	**1,313,908**	**1,151,668**	**1,138,103**	**497,504**	**44,788**	**35,519**	**60,801**	**48,028**	**64,716**
Alabama.........	16,698	14,440	14,430	5,805	50	320	2,602	706	708
Alaska..........	3,116	2,826	2,826	1,398	4	54	95	156	138
Arizona.........	23,678	19,681	19,375	7,854	579	231	751	929	1,336
Arkansas	7,493	6,713	6,711	3,845	18	35	210	320	382
California	212,144	181,129	180,782	69,218	14,151	8,717	9,416	5,698	11,258
Colorado........	21,524	18,510	18,498	7,000	551	269	1,054	1,212	1,087
Connecticut......	13,243	12,253	12,250	6,781	117	113	–	463	665
Delaware	2,617	2,356	2,353	1,421	–	23	–	116	154
District of Columbia .	8,787	7,033	7,033	1,406	1,761	482	158	79	436
Florida	77,442	68,042	67,780	25,724	975	788	5,020	2,627	5,164
Georgia	34,718	29,864	29,766	14,203	145	958	2,811	991	1,514
Hawaii	2,276	1,856	1,856	–	25	42	–	189	257
Idaho..........	4,294	4,104	4,101	1,892	34	74	549	241	219
Illinois	56,587	48,202	48,178	22,011	491	619	1,379	2,613	3,230
Indiana.........	23,691	21,669	21,657	9,640	441	220	2,564	739	820
Iowa	11,261	10,451	10,364	4,973	120	296	948	805	459
Kansas.........	10,475	9,430	9,420	4,371	67	230	551	646	515
Kentucky	10,791	9,686	9,682	4,955	43	172	351	367	456
Louisiana	15,768	14,320	14,307	5,872	39	153	1,532	607	864
Maine..........	3,818	3,723	3,722	2,033	33	22	62	207	155
Maryland	20,540	19,097	18,848	9,801	138	293	–	738	1,180
Massachusetts.....	27,987	22,890	22,212	11,054	65	111	817	727	1,212
Michigan........	43,898	40,211	40,121	19,309	796	2,888	926	2,201	1,986
Minnesota.......	23,596	21,356	21,245	8,381	1,518	475	1,140	1,631	979
Mississippi	9,343	8,681	8,680	4,060	21	101	1,379	507	441
Missouri	19,521	17,425	17,423	8,547	133	321	1,015	983	1,004
Montana........	2,608	2,518	2,517	1,274	27	73	50	137	142
Nebraska	8,734	5,793	5,789	2,833	77	63	360	410	243
Nevada	11,521	10,134	10,130	3,292	241	134	549	933	693
New Hampshire....	4,190	4,101	4,034	2,133	180	25	–	185	215
New Jersey.......	39,835	38,871	38,559	19,956	928	436	141	1,176	2,358
New Mexico	6,612	6,189	6,158	3,222	89	46	104	304	366
New York	142,298	123,987	115,932	44,671	9,983	3,356	6,191	4,835	6,756
North Carolina.....	32,612	28,288	27,617	11,873	1,341	1,893	2,870	484	1,331
North Dakota......	2,014	1,901	1,892	913	41	31	–	194	77
Ohio	48,068	45,136	44,838	19,579	2,577	2,466	1,346	2,050	2,390
Oklahoma........	10,002	9,152	9,152	4,704	38	128	628	533	494
Oregon.........	15,100	13,457	12,989	5,631	276	617	226	713	737
Pennsylvania.....	50,752	45,794	45,791	21,557	3,217	2,826	26	1,319	1,783
Rhode Island......	3,508	3,229	3,229	1,761	10	9	–	93	239
South Carolina.....	14,581	13,159	13,126	6,223	17	158	2,377	301	598
South Dakota	2,316	2,085	2,085	1,060	13	22	39	210	101
Tennessee	24,498	17,140	17,103	6,995	152	293	2,224	651	1,028
Texas..........	89,292	78,043	76,891	39,102	331	1,613	5,637	2,769	4,098
Utah	8,318	6,597	6,589	3,114	84	165	30	290	399
Vermont	2,010	1,808	1,808	1,204	1	7	–	141	58
Virginia.........	28,562	26,337	26,314	12,160	1,263	1,151	209	654	1,367
Washington.......	30,217	23,211	23,186	9,045	91	816	1,470	1,138	1,098
West Virginia......	4,452	4,183	4,178	2,443	5	66	212	75	171
Wisconsin........	23,546	21,783	21,756	10,023	1,477	1,057	192	1,821	1,242
Wyoming	2,958	2,822	2,821	1,184	15	62	589	117	117

See footnotes at end of table.

U.S. Census Bureau, Statistical Abstract of the United States: 2009

Table 438. **Local Governments—Expenditures and Debt by State: 2005**—Con.

[See headnote, page 286]

| State | General expenditures—Con. | | | | | | | | | | |
| | Direct expenditures—Con. | | | | | | | | | | |
	Correc-tions	Sewer-age	Solid waste	Parks and recre-ation	Hous-ing and com-munity devel-opment	Govern-mental admin-istration	Interest on general debt	Other	Utility expen-ditures	Insur-ance trust expen-ditures	Debt out-standing
United States..	**20,835**	**35,491**	**18,285**	**27,459**	**34,987**	**61,163**	**46,804**	**110,285**	**134,776**	**27,463**	**1,271,751**
Alabama	190	490	256	421	433	639	580	870	2,149	109	16,270
Alaska.	2	80	72	66	116	157	85	298	268	22	2,992
Arizona	516	548	351	661	331	1,505	862	2,154	3,876	121	24,792
Arkansas	109	206	169	117	157	299	299	392	747	32	6,904
California	4,042	4,689	2,149	4,534	7,768	10,650	6,235	16,544	24,856	6,160	178,613
Colorado	273	599	70	955	549	1,185	1,039	2,132	2,712	302	26,698
Connecticut	–	356	201	224	488	484	317	1,614	632	358	8,003
Delaware.	–	156	14	37	67	136	80	124	227	34	1,876
District of Columbia	173	257	223	138	436	428	292	602	1,728	26	6,741
Florida.	1,440	2,291	2,003	2,172	1,460	4,018	3,597	8,193	8,595	805	85,005
Georgia	597	1,082	527	609	821	1,940	632	2,176	4,579	275	29,729
Hawaii.	–	199	169	159	75	181	127	312	419	–	3,448
Idaho	74	132	95	80	34	221	68	286	188	2	1,593
Illinois	610	1,194	402	2,266	1,750	2,980	2,279	4,728	5,445	2,940	55,429
Indiana	305	1,023	207	348	555	1,220	678	2,305	1,899	122	17,176
Iowa	103	226	159	323	136	383	256	1,000	808	2	6,718
Kansas	101	276	117	211	176	515	492	925	1,006	38	12,436
Kentucky	216	308	142	120	234	312	861	817	1,074	32	21,633
Louisiana.	470	481	280	322	488	922	585	1,266	1,299	149	13,260
Maine	54	130	108	49	94	186	102	381	95	–	2,335
Maryland	438	495	471	600	748	964	674	1,676	781	661	14,282
Massachusetts . . .	239	649	372	176	1,126	873	597	3,283	3,765	1,333	21,996
Michigan	620	1,650	461	869	403	2,199	1,606	3,373	2,514	1,173	42,650
Minnesota	371	517	274	702	693	1,160	1,140	1,968	1,816	424	28,997
Mississippi	90	143	133	143	216	495	284	461	662	–	5,861
Missouri.	208	628	114	413	438	964	634	1,456	1,685	412	15,150
Montana	32	80	57	56	57	144	70	258	90	–	1,416
Nebraska.	94	164	77	165	161	314	173	528	2,797	144	6,813
Nevada	314	239	18	596	237	893	506	1,113	1,388	–	14,584
New Hampshire . .	43	73	83	70	117	217	106	440	82	7	2,428
New Jersey	548	1,147	946	535	834	1,550	1,183	6,053	953	11	30,581
New Mexico	169	141	144	227	189	359	166	448	423	–	4,571
New York.	2,346	3,148	2,278	1,686	4,032	3,947	4,942	15,242	10,606	7,705	130,325
North Carolina . . .	345	839	594	620	637	1,155	723	2,239	4,302	22	25,133
North Dakota	17	34	35	80	35	98	71	234	102	11	1,631
Ohio	480	1,890	462	879	1,504	2,946	1,653	3,232	2,788	143	37,544
Oklahoma	91	297	133	171	193	544	217	635	807	43	6,944
Oregon	386	636	104	398	372	747	573	1,219	1,565	79	15,393
Pennsylvania	1,201	1,596	625	600	1,855	2,442	2,974	3,229	3,818	1,139	72,901
Rhode Island	10	90	42	44	176	140	67	300	149	129	1,869
South Carolina . . .	181	293	279	190	238	800	498	703	1,418	4	16,547
South Dakota	29	51	35	74	48	118	50	187	220	11	1,267
Tennessee.	369	406	317	317	532	914	719	1,683	6,942	416	21,999
Texas	1,286	2,272	874	1,431	1,563	3,801	4,598	5,691	10,227	1,022	132,542
Utah	131	291	128	306	193	503	255	521	1,722	–	9,564
Vermont	–	58	25	21	46	79	25	101	194	8	840
Virginia	598	898	593	787	756	1,663	1,052	2,336	1,713	512	27,634
Washington	455	1,055	471	757	872	1,289	908	2,843	6,866	140	36,026
West Virginia	43	165	53	102	121	280	160	202	240	29	3,419
Wisconsin	371	781	323	561	417	1,019	700	1,260	1,405	357	18,162
Wyoming	55	45	49	71	9	183	33	251	135	–	1,031

– Represents or rounds to zero.   [1] Includes other items not shown separately.

Source: U.S. Census Bureau, *Federal, State, and Local Governments, State Governmental Finances*, 2005; <http://www.census.gov/govs/www/estimate05.html> (accessed April 2008).

Table 439. City Governments—Revenue for Largest Cities: 2005

[In millions of dollars (77,232 represents $77,232,000,000). For fiscal years ending in year shown; see text this section. Cities ranked by estimated resident population as of July 1. Data reflect inclusion of fiscal activity of dependent school systems where applicable. Regarding intercity comparisons, see text this section. See Appendix III]

Cities ranked by 2005 population	Total revenue [1]	General revenue — Total	Intergovernmental — Total	From federal govt	From state/local govt	From local govt	Gen. rev. from own sources — Total [1]	Taxes — Total [1]	Taxes — Property	Sales & gross receipts — Total [1]	General sales	Public utilities	Current charges — Total [1]	Parks and recreation	Sewerage [2]	Miscellaneous — Total [1]	Interest earnings	Utility revenue [3]	Insurance trust revenue
New York, NY [4]	77,232	67,309	26,128	4,549	20,633	946	41,181	31,595	11,839	5,779	4,375	464	5,880	68	1,055	3,706	761	7,180	6,509
Los Angeles, CA	12,721	7,397	895	257	638	–	6,502	3,024	1,016	1,307	525	644	2,356	86	552	1,121	400	2,844	2,481
Chicago, IL	6,676	4,925	1,246	428	817	–	3,680	1,936	387	1,273	230	515	1,008	–	145	737	191	332	1,419
Houston, TX	3,823	2,562	240	167	52	21	2,322	1,356	738	576	371	163	735	25	304	232	115	312	950
Phoenix, AZ	3,043	2,639	979	504	432	42	1,660	893	240	589	450	78	588	27	210	179	117	424	150
Philadelphia, PA [4]	6,989	5,593	2,501	743	1,628	130	3,092	2,360	393	211	120	–	608	1	223	124	64	943	454
San Antonio, TX	2,991	1,295	198	54	141	4	1,096	515	260	232	162	24	397	27	228	184	100	1,507	189
San Diego, CA	3,173	2,161	438	181	236	21	1,724	825	340	383	193	68	621	66	342	277	105	275	745
Dallas, TX	2,712	1,863	101	73	26	2	1,762	828	472	330	195	99	744	29	216	189	122	186	664
San Jose, CA	1,798	1,421	201	55	114	32	1,221	641	281	223	100	107	422	14	185	158	109	19	358
Honolulu, HI [4]	1,337	1,192	179	105	74	–	1,014	694	500	108	–	57	245	21	202	74	20	173	–
Detroit, MI	5,453	3,806	2,118	336	1,781	–	1,688	1,050	498	210	–	53	386	12	314	252	50	372	1,363
Jacksonville, FL [4]	3,141	1,817	354	75	279	–	1,462	685	344	333	184	100	333	19	153	445	221	1,089	292
Indianapolis, IN	3,470	2,802	568	46	510	11	2,234	1,629	1,480	48	–	1	468	24	77	137	62	645	44
San Francisco, CA [4]	7,655	5,553	2,304	130	1,584	591	3,249	1,853	839	543	298	86	1,033	27	149	364	101	1,005	1,728
Columbus, OH	1,156	999	194	78	110	7	805	539	40	18	–	6	209	8	164	57	13	157	–
Austin, TX	2,168	983	101	50	27	24	882	436	243	177	118	29	357	22	157	89	24	948	237
Louisville/Jefferson, KY [4]	782	678	143	26	114	4	535	320	106	60	–	3	141	11	–	73	29	103	–
Memphis, TN	3,653	1,904	1,060	57	585	418	843	557	410	135	95	10	120	9	72	166	78	1,417	349
Ft. Worth, TX	961	579	27	–	27	–	552	352	228	85	75	–	139	5	111	61	38	164	218
Baltimore, MD [4]	3,144	2,690	1,396	246	1,116	34	1,294	936	543	76	2	48	251	10	142	107	32	99	355
Charlotte, NC	1,277	1,179	332	83	101	147	847	328	263	33	–	–	296	–	163	224	56	163	34
El Paso, TX	699	489	70	53	15	2	420	251	133	110	77	30	129	3	–	39	14	85	137
Boston, MA	3,406	2,796	1,147	89	1,056	3	1,649	1,266	1,194	38	–	–	188	–	73	195	32	108	502
Seattle, WA	2,464	1,348	148	42	105	1	1,200	720	264	285	131	115	365	45	117	116	14	908	214
Washington, DC	8,512	7,973	2,497	2,497	–	–	5,477	4,235	1,136	1,211	770	221	520	24	277	721	122	102	343
Milwaukee, WI	1,504	900	422	71	301	50	479	241	229	56	–	–	189	4	165	49	25	58	546
Denver, CO [4]	2,414	2,060	296	27	264	4	1,764	778	185	496	427	24	776	43	103	210	54	142	213
Las Vegas, NV	810	810	356	26	248	81	455	212	109	56	50	–	183	9	67	60	13	36	–
Nashville-Davidson, TN [4]	2,843	1,785	669	6	431	233	1,116	734	609	55	17	8	235	7	83	147	87	901	174
Oklahoma City, OK	970	863	88	45	40	3	775	415	49	325	294	26	251	13	79	109	19	68	41
Portland, OR	954	874	167	48	66	53	707	392	241	56	–	42	258	23	185	56	25	79	1
Tucson, AZ	904	728	253	70	158	26	475	295	53	209	190	8	140	13	34	41	7	129	57
Albuquerque, NM	970	877	311	69	216	25	566	303	92	192	163	18	194	11	96	69	17	121	–
Atlanta, GA	1,568	1,227	126	33	5	89	1,101	356	188	113	–	46	643	28	164	102	49	165	176

– Represents or rounds to zero.　[1] Includes revenue sources not shown separately.　[2] Includes solid waste management.　[3] Includes water, electric, and transit.　[4] Represents, in effect, city-county consolidated government.

Source: U.S. Census Bureau, *Federal, State, and Local Governments, Government Finances, 2004–2005*. See also <http://www.census.gov/govs/www/estimate05.html>; (accessed April 2008).

Table 440. City Governments—Expenditures and Debt for Largest Cities: 2005

[In millions of dollars (76,725 represents $76,725,000,000). For fiscal year ending in year shown; see headnote, Table 439]

Cities ranked by 2005 population	Total expenditures	Total direct expenditures	General expenditures														Utility expenditures [3]	Insurance trust expenditures	Debt outstanding
			Total [1]	Education	Housing and community development	Public welfare	Health and hospitals	Police protection	Fire protection	Corrections	Highways	Parks and recreation	Sewerage	Solid waste management	Governmental administration [2]	Interest on general debt			
New York, NY [4]	76,725	71,369	60,292	15,624	3,626	10,054	6,267	3,959	1,307	1,208	1,690	666	1,973	1,096	1,102	2,747	8,729	7,705	80,931
Los Angeles, CA	11,516	11,516	6,819	-	260	-	171	1,635	519	-	515	318	487	210	721	425	3,394	1,303	14,218
Chicago, IL	7,344	7,227	5,837	1	212	139	193	1,188	409	15	599	149	100	186	166	701	276	1,231	15,344
Houston, TX	3,548	3,521	2,854	-	39	-	105	505	349	11	170	106	338	68	120	298	276	417	10,835
Phoenix, AZ	3,239	3,228	2,451	21	118	-	-	401	194	-	110	263	135	123	105	203	700	88	6,069
Philadelphia, PA [4]	6,502	6,416	4,913	23	197	587	1,157	507	173	356	89	91	149	96	339	121	994	595	5,899
San Antonio, TX	2,880	2,880	1,278	49	23	55	34	212	132	-	75	114	178	43	58	69	1,539	64	5,657
San Diego, CA	2,792	2,781	2,149	-	349	2	52	349	168	9	132	230	375	57	85	70	445	199	2,911
Dallas, TX	3,030	3,021	2,515	-	42	-	39	279	146	6	113	123	196	49	50	216	290	224	7,907
San Jose, CA	1,849	1,816	1,677	-	141	-	17	214	112	-	99	129	126	76	238	193	31	141	4,305
Honolulu, HI [4]	1,568	1,568	1,241	-	41	-	23	175	71	-	120	112	169	132	84	109	327	-	2,954
Detroit, MI	5,728	5,662	4,722	1,833	43	45	200	477	170	-	184	127	528	90	215	219	623	383	9,246
Jacksonville, FL [4]	3,540	3,405	1,966	-	42	79	80	181	82	55	207	96	334	79	84	231	1,406	168	10,244
Indianapolis, IN	3,023	3,011	2,286	-	266	-	544	186	63	74	107	70	274	40	184	168	666	70	3,786
San Francisco, CA [4]	6,594	6,594	5,150	101	178	446	1,271	294	199	173	108	172	125	-	602	533	900	545	8,194
Columbus, OH	1,026	1,016	881	-	9	10	30	195	131	11	62	63	135	37	68	83	145	106	1,566
Austin, TX	2,205	2,205	1,103	-	33	16	117	167	84	44	79	91	130	40	55	78	996	-	4,423
Louisville/Jefferson, KY [4]	766	765	723	-	103	-	34	121	53	-	45	35	-	18	69	42	44	-	2,555
Memphis, TN	3,359	3,340	1,823	974	34	-	12	197	128	-	62	58	29	39	42	51	1,359	177	2,818
Ft. Worth, TX [4]	1,483	1,483	1,216	-	12	2	8	124	76	-	77	21	81	38	29	57	189	78	1,158
Baltimore, MD [4]	2,831	2,757	2,475	920	108	-	138	335	123	-	155	68	139	66	140	73	104	252	1,903
Charlotte, NC	1,230	1,220	861	-	35	-	4	140	71	-	95	121	100	38	21	37	353	15	2,669
El Paso, TX	681	681	492	-	17	-	18	80	47	-	34	25	67	21	25	29	119	70	919
Boston, MA	3,015	2,773	2,577	879	77	92	178	266	154	102	58	30	144	57	57	56	102	336	1,575
Seattle, WA	2,621	2,507	1,438	-	41	35	16	185	131	13	93	186	198	113	66	53	1,096	87	3,595
Washington, DC	7,515	7,299	7,250	1,406	436	1,761	640	436	161	173	79	138	257	223	407	292	176	89	6,522
Milwaukee, WI	1,217	1,192	953	-	127	-	31	196	89	-	104	4	63	62	38	37	69	196	1,103
Denver, CO [4]	2,401	2,345	2,103	-	101	98	58	174	84	68	81	235	73	-	128	303	202	96	5,941
Las Vegas, NV	716	598	714	-	19	1	2	113	101	40	75	81	39	5	114	17	2	-	338
Nashville-Davidson, TN [4]	2,805	2,804	1,715	647	8	32	158	148	95	48	31	62	47	23	102	135	950	139	3,535
Oklahoma City, OK	908	908	748	-	57	-	-	116	106	-	54	54	112	7	108	37	144	16	995
Portland, OR [4]	2,389	2,389	2,214	-	57	-	-	133	73	-	131	93	245	2	51	104	97	78	2,357
Tucson, AZ	932	932	750	-	36	14	23	127	67	-	77	62	-	38	119	44	149	33	1,095
Albuquerque, NM	913	913	794	-	-	-	-	113	61	46	81	108	43	43	32	33	119	-	929
Atlanta, GA	1,854	1,798	1,401	-	5	-	-	134	60	33	24	95	178	43	59	76	347	105	6,050

- Represents or rounds to zero. [1] Includes expenditure sources not shown separately. [2] Excludes public buildings. [3] Includes water, electric, and transit. [4] Represents, in effect, city–county consolidated government.

Source: U.S. Census Bureau, Federal, State, and Local Governments, Government Finances, 2004–2005. See also <http://www.census.gov/govs/estimate05.html> (accessed April 2008).

U.S. Census Bureau, Statistical Abstract of the United States: 2009

Table 441. County Governments—Revenue for Largest Counties: 2005

[In millions of dollars (20,800 represents $20,800,000,000). For fiscal year ending in year shown; see text, this section. See Appendix III]

Counties ranked by 2005 population	Total revenue [1]	General revenue — Total	Intergovernmental — Total	From federal government — Total [1]	From federal government — Housing [2]	From state government — Total [1]	From state government — Public welfare	From state government — Health and hospitals	From local government	General revenue from own sources — Total	Taxes — Total [1]	Taxes — Property	Sales and gross receipts — Total	Sales and gross receipts — General sales	Current charges — Total [1]	Current charges — Parks and recreation	Current charges — Sewerage [3]	Current charges — Hospitals	Miscellaneous general revenue — Total [1]	Miscellaneous general revenue — Interest earnings
Los Angeles, CA	20,800	17,002	8,990	330	3	8,423	4,691	1,190	237	8,011	2,996	2,729	117	39	4,380	94	77	2,863	635	137
Cook, IL	3,515	2,762	570	52	–	516	260	–	2	2,193	1,519	839	656	347	577	45	–	330	98	37
Harris, TX	3,022	3,022	637	62	24	455	163	195	120	2,385	1,297	1,192	50	–	734	1	–	244	354	237
Maricopa, AZ	2,385	2,385	1,238	98	7	1,092	447	31	48	1,147	712	555	123	123	222	4	115	154	213	146
Orange, CA	4,183	3,289	1,865	57	9	1,733	648	190	76	1,424	580	488	46	43	606	42	28	–	238	138
San Diego, CA	4,594	3,736	2,557	135	104	2,334	1,007	458	88	1,178	642	546	27	18	325	3	471	953	212	75
Dade, FL	6,097	5,846	1,347	870	254	440	–	25	37	4,499	1,685	1,152	428	114	2,283	32	–	518	531	236
Dallas, TX	1,541	1,504	235	9	–	214	107	15	12	1,269	626	583	3	–	581	–	–	154	62	21
Riverside, CA	2,977	2,977	1,841	86	15	1,605	734	307	150	1,136	426	344	33	26	505	6	75	410	205	56
San Bernardino, CA	3,768	3,297	1,977	134	17	1,789	928	203	55	1,319	329	277	23	16	848	7	71	13	142	50
Wayne, MI	1,922	1,835	1,190	133	9	891	23	487	165	645	370	345	16	–	233	5	77	–	42	12
King, WA	2,186	2,073	559	160	20	281	–	170	118	1,514	974	450	494	398	450	5	328	–	90	38
Broward, FL	2,117	2,065	430	110	7	195	25	5	125	1,635	852	715	117	–	615	16	170	–	167	84
Clark, NV	4,397	4,000	1,163	116	19	883	843	12	165	2,837	1,280	561	488	109	1,034	65	88	450	522	136
Santa Clara, CA	3,242	3,242	1,565	34	3	1,488	8	168	43	1,677	700	511	142	140	836	4	3	646	141	26
Tarrant, TX	1,043	1,043	222	57	–	152	–	127	14	820	475	442	11	–	179	–	–	122	166	112
Bexar, TX	1,104	1,104	219	4	2	200	106	48	14	885	387	345	25	–	414	–	–	383	84	68
Suffolk, NY	2,687	2,567	593	37	6	547	293	147	9	1,974	1,653	534	1,089	1,084	185	10	22	–	136	31
Alameda, CA	3,003	2,412	1,270	18	3	1,216	642	286	36	1,143	394	343	24	14	606	–	–	318	143	60
Sacramento, CA	3,196	2,658	1,431	62	–	1,306	735	162	63	1,227	403	250	85	61	607	13	321	–	217	82
Nassau, NY	3,420	3,420	921	71	21	849	514	126	–	2,499	1,877	905	947	934	429	22	1	249	193	27
Cuyahoga, OH	2,070	2,070	920	20	20	895	478	252	5	1,150	561	337	180	165	365	–	4	324	225	161
Palm Beach, FL	1,640	1,591	215	59	9	153	5	–	3	1,376	865	606	144	–	294	11	83	–	217	65
Allegheny, PA	1,469	1,391	996	48	33	946	302	436	3	394	297	259	37	21	70	3	–	–	27	3
Oakland, MI	1,065	965	578	189	6	234	6	51	155	387	260	238	9	–	87	9	16	4	40	6
Hillsborough, FL	1,765	1,602	262	47	21	212	43	98	10	1,340	824	546	237	171	387	2	75	–	130	58
Hennepin, MN	1,808	1,808	772	219	9	542	328	236	25	1,036	447	430	–	–	495	4	79	315	94	30
Franklin, OH	1,045	1,044	408	7	3	376	48	–	–	636	383	278	99	85	110	–	3	–	142	127
Orange, FL	1,532	1,476	235	54	–	181	3	105	79	1,241	812	488	185	–	255	46	115	–	174	113
Contra Costa, CA	2,499	1,998	836	117	106	640	333	75	50	1,162	363	308	21	8	678	–	–	418	120	62
Fairfax, VA	4,810	4,006	983	105	56	828	133	6	–	3,022	2,439	1,918	295	168	394	36	221	–	189	90
St Louis, MO	657	616	52	16	12	36	–	–	12	564	485	148	324	291	64	1	5	–	15	4
Salt Lake, UT	495	495	74	14	6	49	–	–	2	420	339	205	106	77	59	7	7	–	22	3
Fulton, GA	1,109	935	86	10	4	73	34	14	–	849	737	484	209	194	62	1	50	–	50	9
Westchester, NY	2,406	2,398	535	20	–	509	266	132	5	1,863	1,009	604	398	384	781	29	29	542	72	47

– Represents or rounds to zero.   [1] Includes revenue sources not shown separately.   [2] Includes community development.   [3] Includes solid waste management.

Source: Source: U.S. Census Bureau, Survey of State & Local Government Finances, 2005; <http://www.census.gov/govs/www/estimate05.html>.

U.S. Census Bureau, Statistical Abstract of the United States: 2009

Table 442. County Governments—Expenditures and Debt for Largest Counties: 2005

[In millions of dollars (18,587 represents $18,587,000,000). For fiscal year ending in year shown; see text, this section and Appendix III]

Counties ranked by 2005 population	Total expenditures [1]	Total direct expenditures	General expenditures														Utility expenditures [3]	Employee retirement expenditures	Debt outstanding
			Total [1]	Education	Housing [2]	Public welfare	Health	Hospitals	Police protection	Correction	Highways	Parks and recreation	Natural resources	Sewerage and solid waste management	Governmental administration	Interest on general debt			
Los Angeles, CA	18,587	18,304	16,966	887	5	4,614	1,770	2,916	1,118	969	251	227	401	58	1,565	138	58	1,562	3,015
Cook, IL	3,175	3,164	2,801	–	10	11	39	897	94	389	136	112	–	–	689	129	–	374	3,286
Harris, TX	3,376	3,347	3,376	–	3	33	200	880	363	69	372	26	181	–	407	424	–	–	8,477
Maricopa, AZ	2,154	1,849	2,154	35	11	695	77	162	57	324	103	7	72	5	353	108	–	–	1,991
Orange, CA	3,475	3,421	3,237	241	15	735	322	–	270	252	36	1	129	90	430	161	–	238	3,173
San Diego, CA	4,014	3,704	3,764	376	105	1,038	500	–	216	300	121	20	19	48	514	108	548	249	1,950
Dade, FL	6,526	6,512	5,978	–	246	270	65	1,315	394	232	195	327	43	408	240	541	–	–	9,515
Dallas, TX	1,514	1,514	1,501	7	31	6	45	952	27	132	22	–	–	1	135	24	–	13	462
Riverside, CA	2,847	2,702	2,847	336	51	638	153	377	243	165	117	11	76	76	260	63	–	–	1,194
San Bernardino, CA	3,319	3,177	3,133	349	7	897	258	437	204	176	46	21	65	62	236	114	–	186	1,958
Wayne, MI	1,905	1,846	1,797	–	9	182	515	53	36	256	146	60	21	69	333	56	–	108	674
King, WA	2,562	2,520	1,675	49	24	2	322	1	116	120	119	40	46	391	209	103	887	–	3,052
Broward, FL	2,108	2,063	1,964	–	13	43	92	–	311	181	55	127	20	137	174	140	144	–	2,847
Clark, NV	4,028	3,983	3,452	–	17	165	70	487	392	163	571	251	127	80	290	232	576	–	5,498
Santa Clara, CA	3,214	2,939	3,214	214	13	763	344	747	94	229	133	33	3	2	322	50	–	–	811
Tarrant, TX	976	976	976	–	22	8	100	398	30	70	62	–	–	–	119	107	–	–	2,216
Bexar, TX	1,025	1,001	1,025	–	2	41	46	557	40	70	29	2	9	–	99	70	–	–	975
Suffolk, NY	2,709	2,379	2,518	163	6	555	308	–	434	121	44	25	19	76	111	61	192	194	1,511
Alameda, CA	2,451	2,447	2,211	39	4	546	297	376	82	223	28	–	38	–	277	47	46	166	1,223
Sacramento, CA	2,763	2,700	2,579	149	9	682	407	–	197	182	155	31	3	205	234	109	17	–	3,473
Nassau, NY	3,485	3,011	3,481	179	23	669	291	381	653	208	93	53	–	100	180	161	4	–	3,330
Cuyahoga, OH	2,054	2,034	2,054	–	23	411	320	584	25	98	52	–	–	14	233	171	–	–	3,220
Palm Beach, FL	3,150	3,084	3,057	300	36	49	50	–	192	97	101	77	61	193	135	182	93	56	1,760
Allegheny, PA	1,437	1,348	1,381	30	59	365	427	–	35	66	33	61	–	–	103	25	–	34	658
Oakland, MI	966	932	907	10	10	6	242	8	56	106	120	15	42	103	139	12	25	–	337
Hillsborough, FL	3,832	3,704	3,638	–	28	91	118	–	160	105	109	69	43	76	239	83	194	–	2,197
Hennepin, MN	1,628	1,625	1,621	–	21	460	228	395	64	81	29	8	–	57	125	24	7	–	538
Franklin, OH	1,082	1,051	1,079	–	8	281	290	–	30	57	45	18	–	5	161	121	3	–	2,025
Orange, FL	3,624	3,595	3,469	–	37	80	49	445	148	150	136	35	26	108	120	284	156	180	3,200
Contra Costa, CA	2,175	2,122	1,980	120	112	358	185	–	84	106	90	–	27	16	153	56	15	285	1,021
Fairfax, VA	4,399	4,270	3,957	1,993	114	221	164	–	211	35	22	100	4	238	137	172	157	24	3,582
St Louis, MO	688	474	662	–	13	27	47	–	76	21	71	25	–	4	67	56	2	–	346
Salt Lake, UT	520	520	520	–	1	46	25	–	36	60	25	83	5	10	87	5	–	–	334
Fulton, GA	1,099	868	952	–	9	76	45	77	60	59	15	12	1	63	228	24	95	53	788
Westchester, NY	2,536	2,209	2,498	95	–	463	215	598	43	130	31	53	1	149	100	60	38	–	1,426

– Represents or rounds to zero.   [1] Includes expenditure categories not shown separately.   [2] Includes community development.   [3] Includes solid waste management.

Source: U.S. Census Bureau, *Survey of State & Local Government Finances,* 2005; <http://www.census.gov/govs/www/estimate05.html>.

State and Local Government Finances and Employment   291

Table 443. Governmental Employment and Payrolls: 1982 to 2006

[Employees in thousands (15,841 represents 15,841,000), payroll in millions of dollars (23,173 represents $23,173,000,000). Data are for the month of October through 1992. Beginning with the 1997 survey, data are for the month of March. Covers both full-time and part-time employees. Local government data are estimates subject to sampling variation; see Appendix III and source]

Type of government	1982	1987	1992	1997	2000	2002	2003	2004	2005	2006
EMPLOYEES (1,000)										
Total	15,841	17,212	18,745	19,540	20,876	21,039	21,336	21,494	21,725	22,048
Federal (civilian) [1]	2,848	3,091	3,047	2,807	2,899	2,690	2,717	2,733	2,720	2,721
State and local	12,993	14,121	15,698	16,733	17,976	18,349	18,649	18,759	19,004	19,327
Percent of total	82	82	84	86	86	87	87	87	87	88
State	3,744	4,116	4,595	4,733	4,877	5,072	5,042	5,041	5,078	5,128
Local	9,249	10,005	11,103	12,000	13,099	13,277	13,606	13,719	13,926	14,199
Counties	1,824	1,963	2,253	2,425	(NA)	2,729	(NA)	(NA)	(NA)	(NA)
Municipalities	2,397	2,493	2,665	2,755	(NA)	2,972	(NA)	(NA)	(NA)	(NA)
School districts	4,194	4,627	5,134	5,675	(NA)	6,367	(NA)	(NA)	(NA)	(NA)
Townships	356	393	424	455	(NA)	488	(NA)	(NA)	(NA)	(NA)
Special districts	478	529	627	691	(NA)	721	(NA)	(NA)	(NA)	(NA)
PAYROLLS (mil. dol.)										
Total	23,173	32,669	43,120	49,156	58,166	63,923	67,194	68,759	71,599	74,638
Federal (civilian) [1]	5,959	7,924	9,937	9,744	11,485	11,599	12,672	12,844	13,475	13,896
State and local	17,214	24,745	33,183	39,412	46,681	52,323	54,522	55,914	58,123	60,741
Percent of total	74	76	77	80	80	82	81	81	81	81
State	5,022	7,263	9,828	11,413	13,279	14,838	15,116	15,477	16,062	16,769
Local	12,192	17,482	23,355	27,999	33,402	37,486	39,406	40,437	42,062	43,972
Counties	2,287	3,270	4,698	5,750	(NA)	7,902	(NA)	(NA)	(NA)	(NA)
Municipalities	3,428	4,770	6,207	7,146	(NA)	9,714	(NA)	(NA)	(NA)	(NA)
School districts	5,442	7,961	10,394	12,579	(NA)	16,720	(NA)	(NA)	(NA)	(NA)
Townships	370	522	685	869	(NA)	1,124	(NA)	(NA)	(NA)	(NA)
Special districts	665	959	1,370	1,654	(NA)	2,026	(NA)	(NA)	(NA)	(NA)

NA Not available.   [1] Includes employees outside the United States.

Source: U.S. Census Bureau, Federal, State, and Local Governments, "Public Employment and Payroll Data"; <http://www.census.gov/govs/www/apes.html>.

Table 444. All Governments—Employment and Payroll by Function: 2006

[Employees in thousands (22,048 represents 22,048,000); payroll in millions of dollars (74,638 represents $74,638,000,000). See headnote, Table 443]

Function	Employees (1,000)					Payrolls (mil. dol.)				
	Total	Federal (civilian) [1]	State and local			Total	Federal (civilian) [1]	State and local		
			Total	State	Local			Total	State	Local
Total	**22,048**	**2,721**	**19,327**	**5,128**	**14,199**	**74,638**	**13,896**	**60,741**	**16,769**	**43,972**
National defense [2]	698	698	(X)	(X)	(X)	2,657	2,657	(X)	(X)	(X)
Postal Service	772	772	(X)	(X)	(X)	3,584	3,584	(X)	(X)	(X)
Space research and technology	18	18	(X)	(X)	(X)	151	151	(X)	(X)	(X)
Elem. and secondary education	7,823	(X)	7,823	59	7,764	23,187	(X)	23,187	211	22,975
Higher education	2,896	(X)	2,896	2,335	561	7,718	(X)	7,718	6,396	1,321
Other education	109	10	98	98	(X)	417	64	353	353	(X)
Health	614	136	477	189	288	2,453	854	1,599	688	911
Hospitals	1,168	162	1,006	421	585	4,441	926	3,515	1,459	2,056
Public welfare	545	8	537	237	300	1,776	58	1,718	775	943
Social insurance administration	151	65	85	85	(X)	672	360	312	312	(X)
Police protection	1,154	161	993	106	887	5,081	891	4,190	482	3,708
Fire protection	463	(X)	463	(X)	463	1,648	(X)	1,648	(X)	1,648
Correction	765	36	730	472	258	2,804	180	2,624	1,692	931
Streets & highways	570	3	567	242	325	2,008	20	1,988	922	1,066
Air transportation	93	45	48	3	44	584	387	197	16	181
Water transport/terminals . . .	18	5	13	5	8	72	13	59	22	36
Solid waste management . . .	120	(X)	120	2	118	376	(X)	376	9	367
Sewerage	138	(X)	138	2	136	509	(X)	509	9	500
Parks & recreation	423	26	397	39	358	919	123	796	101	695
Natural resources	394	184	210	161	49	1,744	1,057	687	541	146
Housing & community development	138	16	122	–	122	537	102	435	–	435
Water supply	179	–	179	1	178	654	–	654	3	650
Electric power	79	–	79	4	75	418	–	418	25	393
Gas supply	13	–	13	–	13	46	–	46	–	46
Transit	235	–	235	33	202	1,035	–	1,035	168	868
Libraries	191	4	187	1	186	404	26	378	2	376
State liquor stores	9	(X)	9	9	(X)	65	(X)	65	21	(X)
Financial administration	549	112	437	174	264	2,163	666	1,497	658	839
Other government administration	507	59	448	175	274	2,301	486	1,815	784	1,031
Judicial and legal	512	24	489	60	429	1,266	152	1,113	220	894
Other & unallocable	703	177	526	214	313	2,994	1,139	1,855	900	954

– Represents or rounds to zero.   X Not applicable.   [1] Includes employees outside the United States.   [2] Includes international relations.

Source: U.S. Census Bureau, Federal, State, and Local Governments, "Public Employment and Payroll Data"; <http://www.census.gov/govs/www/apes.html>.

Table 445. State and Local Government—Employer Costs per Hour Worked: 2007

[In dollars. As of March. Based on a sample; see source for details. Collection of severance pay and supplemental unemployment plans, which comprised "other benefits" and was published in all tables, was discontinued beginning with the March 2006 estimates. For additional data, see Table 632]

Occupation and industry	Total compensation	Wages and salaries	Benefit cost					
			Total	Paid leave	Supplemental pay	Insurance	Retirement and savings	Legally required benefits
Total workers.	**38.66**	**25.90**	**12.76**	**3.01**	**0.33**	**4.36**	**2.82**	**2.24**
Occupational group:								
Management, professional, and related ...	47.31	33.23	14.08	3.29	0.20	4.81	3.21	2.58
Professional and related............	47.01	33.35	13.66	2.99	0.20	4.79	3.15	2.53
Teachers [1]........................	52.23	38.14	14.09	2.74	0.09	4.92	3.62	2.72
Primary, secondary, and special education school teachers..........	50.66	36.67	13.99	2.59	0.08	5.23	3.50	2.58
Sales and office.....................	26.27	16.27	10.00	2.50	0.18	4.05	1.66	1.61
Office and administrative support......	26.28	16.28	10.00	2.50	0.18	4.05	1.67	1.60
Service..............................	29.66	17.93	11.73	2.69	0.63	3.59	2.94	1.88
Industry group:								
Education and health services	40.92	28.64	12.28	2.80	0.19	4.40	2.66	2.23
Educational services	41.50	29.28	12.22	2.62	0.12	4.51	2.75	2.22
Elementary and secondary schools...	40.56	28.59	11.98	2.32	0.10	4.74	2.68	2.14
Junior colleges, colleges, and universities	44.92	31.77	13.15	3.68	0.20	3.77	3.01	2.50
Health care and social assistance	36.91	24.23	12.68	4.02	0.67	3.63	2.05	2.30
Hospitals	33.01	21.46	11.55	3.43	0.79	3.35	1.78	2.20
Public administration	35.43	21.90	13.53	3.33	0.52	4.33	3.20	2.14

[1] Includes postsecondary teachers; primary, secondary, and special education teachers; and other teachers and instructors.

Source: U.S. Bureau of Labor Statistics, *National Compensation Survey, Benefits, Archives, 2007 National Survey Compensation Publications List, Employer Costs for Employee Compensation News Release,* March 2008; <http://www.bls.gov/ncs/ncspubs.htm>; (accessed December 2007).

Table 446. State and Local Government—Full-Time Employment and Salary by Sex and Race/Ethnic Group: 1980 to 2005

[As of June 30. (2,350 represents 2,350,000). Excludes school systems and educational institutions. Based on reports from state governments (42 in 1980; 47 in 1983; 49 in 1981 and 1984 through 1987; and 50 in 1989 through 1991) and a sample of county, municipal, township, and special district jurisdictions employing 15 or more nonelected, nonappointed full-time employees. Beginning 1993, only for state and local governments with 100 or more employees. For definition of median, see Guide to Tabular Presentation]

Year and occupation	Employment (1,000)						Median annual salary ($1,000)					
	Male	Female	White [1]	Minority			Male	Female	White [1]	Minority		
				Total [2]	Black [1]	His-panic [3]				Total [2]	Black [1]	His-panic [3]
1980	2,350	1,637	3,146	842	619	163	15.2	11.4	13.8	11.8	11.5	12.3
1981	2,740	1,925	3,591	1,074	780	205	17.7	13.1	16.1	13.5	13.3	14.7
1983	2,674	1,818	3,423	1,069	768	219	20.1	15.3	18.5	15.9	15.6	17.3
1984	2,700	1,880	3,458	1,121	799	233	21.4	16.2	19.6	17.4	16.5	18.4
1985	2,789	1,952	3,563	1,179	835	248	22.3	17.3	20.6	18.4	17.5	19.2
1986	2,797	1,982	3,549	1,230	865	259	23.4	18.1	21.5	19.6	18.7	20.2
1987	2,818	2,031	3,600	1,249	872	268	24.2	18.9	22.4	20.9	19.3	21.1
1989	3,030	2,227	3,863	1,394	961	308	26.1	20.6	24.1	22.1	20.7	22.7
1990	3,071	2,302	3,918	1,456	994	327	27.3	21.8	25.2	23.3	22.0	23.8
1991	3,110	2,349	3,965	1,494	1,011	340	28.4	22.7	26.4	23.8	22.7	24.5
1993	2,820	2,204	3,588	1,436	948	341	30.6	24.3	28.5	25.9	24.2	26.8
1995	2,960	2,355	3,781	1,534	993	379	33.5	27.0	31.4	26.3	26.8	28.6
1997	2,898	2,307	3,676	1,529	973	392	34.6	27.9	32.2	30.2	27.4	29.5
1999	2,939	2,393	3,723	1,609	1,012	417	37.0	29.9	34.8	31.1	29.6	31.2
2001	3,080	2,554	3,888	1,746	1,077	471	39.8	32.1	37.5	34.0	31.5	33.8
2003	3,134	2,610	3,919	1,826	1,097	508	42.2	34.7	40.0	35.9	33.6	36.6
2005, total	**3,185**	**2,644**	**3,973**	**1,856**	**1,100**	**532**	**44.1**	**36.4**	**41.5**	**37.7**	**35.3**	**38.9**
Officials/ administrators	223	137	290	70	42	18	68.6	61.3	66.0	65.1	63.0	65.2
Professionals.......	650	839	1,067	422	234	100	54.4	47.0	50.5	48.9	44.8	49.0
Technicians........	272	203	335	140	74	43	44.1	36.0	41.0	38.0	35.6	39.1
Protective service...	959	220	832	347	208	115	45.3	36.6	44.4	42.2	38.5	47.4
Paraprofessionals...	101	286	223	164	112	38	32.7	29.8	31.5	29.2	27.6	31.7
Admin. support	126	796	596	326	186	106	32.3	30.4	30.5	31.0	30.1	31.4
Skilled craft.......	412	23	315	120	68	39	39.7	32.9	39.3	40.0	37.3	41.3
Service/ maintenance	442	138	314	266	177	73	32.3	24.9	31.1	30.0	29.2	30.8

[1] Non-Hispanic.   [2] Includes other minority groups not shown separately.   [3] Persons of Hispanic origin may be of any race.

Source: U.S. Equal Employment Opportunity Commission, 1980–1991, *State and Local Government Information Report,* annual; beginning 1993, biennial.

State and Local Government Finances and Employment   293

[In thousands (1,708.3 represents 1,708,300). **For March.** Local government amounts are estimates subject to sampling variation; see Appendix III and source]

State	Education Total [1] State	Total [1] Local	Elementary and secondary State	Elementary and secondary Local	Higher education State	Higher education Local	Public welfare State	Public welfare Local	Health State	Health Local	Hospitals State	Hospitals Local
United States..	**1,708.3**	**6,917.0**	**48.9**	**6,596.4**	**1,568.2**	**320.6**	**232.0**	**278.9**	**182.7**	**250.2**	**396.7**	**530.0**
Alabama	39.7	97.1	–	97.1	36.5	–	4.3	1.5	5.4	4.6	11.3	25.1
Alaska.	8.4	17.5	3.2	17.4	4.9	0.1	1.8	0.2	0.6	0.5	0.2	0.7
Arizona	29.5	121.5	–	109.2	26.4	12.3	5.8	2.2	2.5	2.7	0.7	3.3
Arkansas	24.2	68.1	–	68.1	22.7	–	3.7	0.1	4.8	0.4	5.1	1.6
California	152.1	775.0	–	703.6	147.8	71.4	3.6	65.6	11.7	42.9	39.2	61.5
Colorado	39.3	98.0	–	96.3	38.1	1.7	2.0	6.2	1.2	3.7	3.6	9.5
Connecticut	18.8	89.4	–	89.4	16.0	–	5.4	2.0	1.9	1.5	10.4	–
Delaware	8.0	17.3	–	17.3	7.7	–	1.6	–	2.1	0.3	1.8	–
District of Columbia	(X)	(X)	(X)	(X)	(X)	(X)	(X)	(X)	(X)	(X)	(X)	(X)
Florida.	61.2	348.0	–	323.1	57.5	24.9	9.7	6.7	24.2	5.9	3.8	46.0
Georgia	53.1	232.7	–	232.7	49.9	–	9.4	1.4	4.9	11.0	7.2	21.9
Hawaii.	33.4	–	24.8	–	8.5	–	1.0	0.1	2.6	0.2	4.3	–
Idaho	8.6	34.1	–	32.6	8.1	1.5	1.8	0.1	1.0	1.0	0.8	6.1
Illinois	58.9	292.3	–	270.0	56.7	22.3	9.8	5.8	2.7	7.5	11.4	12.8
Indiana	55.7	135.8	–	135.8	54.5	–	5.6	1.1	1.9	3.6	2.6	24.4
Iowa	26.5	82.0	–	75.5	25.3	6.5	3.0	1.7	0.4	2.9	7.1	10.4
Kansas	20.0	87.8	–	80.1	19.4	7.7	2.8	0.7	1.1	3.2	2.5	7.9
Kentucky	33.3	110.9	–	110.9	30.5	–	6.8	0.7	2.3	5.8	5.9	4.2
Louisiana	31.8	107.8	–	107.8	28.4	–	5.0	0.5	3.8	1.5	13.0	17.1
Maine	7.3	38.8	0.1	38.8	7.0	–	2.0	0.4	1.3	0.3	0.6	0.8
Maryland	28.6	128.6	–	118.8	26.3	9.7	6.8	2.9	6.8	4.8	5.0	–
Massachusetts . . .	26.8	149.8	–	149.7	25.7	0.1	6.8	2.6	7.2	3.0	7.4	3.9
Michigan	67.5	222.8	0.7	209.8	65.3	13.0	10.0	2.4	1.9	11.9	13.9	8.9
Minnesota	39.2	111.3	–	111.3	35.6	–	2.8	11.1	2.3	3.6	4.9	10.6
Mississippi	20.1	79.9	–	73.3	18.6	6.7	2.4	0.5	2.9	0.3	12.1	18.7
Missouri.	29.9	140.5	–	134.3	28.1	6.2	7.8	2.6	3.3	3.8	11.8	11.2
Montana	6.9	22.3	–	21.9	6.5	0.3	1.6	0.5	0.8	0.9	0.6	0.5
Nebraska.	12.9	49.5	–	46.5	12.3	3.0	2.6	0.7	0.7	0.6	4.1	4.3
Nevada	9.0	41.5	–	41.5	8.8	–	1.6	0.9	1.2	0.8	1.2	4.4
New Hampshire . .	6.7	34.6	–	34.6	6.3	–	1.5	2.5	0.9	0.2	0.8	–
New Jersey	54.8	218.8	19.5	207.9	31.9	10.9	8.1	10.7	4.6	4.3	18.8	1.9
New Mexico	18.7	49.7	–	45.9	17.5	3.8	1.6	0.8	2.4	0.4	10.6	0.9
New York.	56.3	485.5	–	463.3	51.8	22.2	6.3	48.8	9.4	18.5	43.1	45.1
North Carolina . . .	55.4	222.4	–	203.5	52.5	18.9	2.0	15.1	4.9	16.4	17.5	26.1
North Dakota	8.4	14.4	–	14.4	8.1	–	0.5	0.9	1.3	0.6	1.0	–
Ohio	70.2	260.8	–	255.3	67.6	5.5	3.0	24.2	3.6	18.3	10.9	12.2
Oklahoma	29.7	94.0	–	93.6	27.7	0.4	6.2	0.3	6.1	1.7	2.6	9.2
Oregon	19.5	70.8	–	62.6	18.6	8.2	5.5	1.0	2.6	4.4	4.7	2.3
Pennsylvania	61.1	247.3	–	237.8	56.8	9.5	12.4	20.3	1.8	5.4	12.2	–
Rhode Island	6.7	20.7	0.6	20.7	5.5	–	1.6	0.1	1.2	0.1	1.1	–
South Carolina . . .	32.1	100.0	–	100.0	29.4	–	4.1	0.3	6.4	2.1	7.7	19.2
South Dakota	5.5	21.1	–	20.7	5.1	0.4	1.1	0.3	0.7	0.4	1.0	0.5
Tennessee	35.8	129.6	–	129.6	33.6	–	6.5	2.2	3.8	4.2	7.7	22.3
Texas	107.1	681.6	–	641.6	102.3	39.9	22.2	3.2	12.7	22.4	30.6	47.3
Utah	25.5	48.7	–	48.7	24.3	–	3.3	0.5	2.1	1.3	5.7	0.5
Vermont	5.3	20.0	–	20.0	4.7	–	1.3	–	0.7	0.1	0.2	–
Virginia	54.5	193.8	–	192.5	51.6	1.4	2.4	9.4	5.4	5.9	12.9	3.4
Washington	53.7	98.8	–	98.8	51.7	–	9.4	1.9	5.2	4.6	9.7	13.2
West Virginia	12.6	40.6	–	40.6	11.2	–	3.4	–	0.8	1.4	1.7	2.3
Wisconsin	34.3	132.5	–	123.1	33.3	9.4	1.4	13.2	1.8	6.1	3.5	1.1
Wyoming	3.9	18.7	–	16.7	3.6	2.0	0.7	–	0.7	0.4	0.8	5.3

See footnotes at end of table.

U.S. Census Bureau, Statistical Abstract of the United States: 2009

Table 447. State and Local Government Full-Time Equivalent Employment, by Selected Function and State: 2006—Con.

[In thousands (238.2 represents 238,200). For March. Local government amounts are estimates subject to sampling variation; see Appendix III and source]

State	Highways		Police protection		Fire protection		Corrections		Parks and recreation		Government administration	
	State	Local	State	Local	State	Local	State	Local	State	Local	State	Local
United States ...	**238.2**	**306.9**	**104.5**	**814.8**	**(X)**	**327.7**	**467.5**	**249.6**	**33.9**	**233.2**	**394.3**	**704.6**
Alabama.........	4.4	7.0	1.4	12.3	(X)	4.9	4.9	3.1	0.6	3.3	6.6	8.2
Alaska.........	3.1	0.6	0.4	1.2	(X)	0.8	1.7	0.1	0.1	0.5	3.0	1.9
Arizona.........	2.9	5.8	2.0	18.6	(X)	7.5	9.7	5.4	0.4	7.3	6.7	20.1
Arkansas........	3.8	3.9	1.2	7.3	(X)	2.7	4.9	2.0	0.8	1.0	3.9	6.4
California........	20.3	20.9	12.6	88.4	(X)	33.4	50.5	31.9	3.3	36.0	29.9	99.0
Colorado........	3.1	6.2	1.2	12.7	(X)	5.6	6.6	3.9	0.3	5.8	6.3	12.3
Connecticut.......	3.0	3.3	2.1	8.9	(X)	4.7	7.8	–	0.2	2.4	8.3	4.3
Delaware........	1.9	0.5	1.0	1.6	(X)	0.2	2.8	–	0.3	0.3	2.7	1.3
District of Columbia.......	(X)	(X)	(X)	(X)	(X)	(X)	(X)	(X)	(X)	(X)	(X)	(X)
Florida..........	7.5	15.4	4.5	60.4	(X)	27.3	28.8	15.2	1.4	20.6	29.4	44.4
Georgia.........	5.9	7.9	2.0	23.8	(X)	10.8	19.7	9.2	2.6	6.3	8.9	22.6
Hawaii..........	0.8	0.8	–	3.7	(X)	1.8	2.3	–	0.2	2.0	3.8	2.7
Idaho..........	1.8	1.5	0.5	3.4	(X)	1.3	1.9	1.2	0.2	0.7	2.0	3.9
Illinois.........	7.4	12.1	3.9	43.9	(X)	16.4	13.6	10.4	0.6	14.6	10.9	30.9
Indiana.........	3.9	6.2	1.9	15.5	(X)	7.3	7.4	6.0	0.2	3.6	4.7	17.5
Iowa..........	2.5	6.9	0.9	6.8	(X)	1.9	3.2	1.3	0.1	2.2	4.3	6.9
Kansas.........	3.5	5.7	1.1	8.3	(X)	3.2	3.8	2.7	0.6	2.5	4.7	7.7
Kentucky........	4.9	3.5	2.4	8.9	(X)	4.3	4.1	4.3	1.6	1.7	9.1	6.5
Louisiana........	4.9	5.2	1.7	15.0	(X)	4.7	7.3	5.8	0.9	3.2	6.2	12.3
Maine..........	2.5	1.7	0.6	2.5	(X)	2.1	1.3	0.8	–	0.8	2.7	3.7
Maryland........	4.7	4.6	2.5	14.5	(X)	6.3	11.8	3.3	0.4	7.5	9.9	8.7
Massachusetts.....	3.8	6.9	5.9	18.1	(X)	13.1	6.5	2.9	0.5	2.2	16.1	10.3
Michigan........	2.9	10.1	2.8	20.8	(X)	7.6	17.3	5.6	0.3	4.9	7.7	26.6
Minnesota.......	4.6	7.4	1.0	10.0	(X)	2.5	4.0	5.3	0.6	4.5	7.0	13.5
Mississippi.......	3.3	5.0	1.2	7.7	(X)	3.4	3.5	2.0	0.4	1.2	2.2	7.0
Missouri.........	6.8	7.2	2.4	15.9	(X)	6.6	12.6	3.3	0.7	4.4	7.6	12.6
Montana........	2.2	1.3	0.4	2.1	(X)	0.6	1.2	0.6	0.1	0.4	1.8	2.6
Nebraska........	2.1	3.4	0.7	4.3	(X)	1.4	2.8	1.2	0.3	1.0	1.6	5.1
Nevada.........	1.7	1.2	0.8	6.3	(X)	2.5	3.5	2.5	0.2	3.5	3.0	6.2
New Hampshire....	1.8	1.6	0.4	3.4	(X)	1.9	1.4	0.6	0.2	0.5	2.2	2.1
New Jersey.......	7.4	11.8	4.6	32.6	(X)	8.8	10.2	6.6	2.1	5.8	23.1	22.5
New Mexico......	2.6	1.7	0.8	5.2	(X)	2.2	4.0	1.9	0.8	2.0	5.0	4.3
New York........	12.3	29.0	6.4	84.1	(X)	24.1	33.9	25.5	2.6	12.1	37.2	39.3
North Carolina.....	11.0	4.3	3.4	22.3	(X)	8.1	20.9	5.0	1.2	5.0	11.0	13.5
North Dakota......	1.1	1.1	0.2	1.2	(X)	0.3	0.7	0.3	0.1	0.7	1.4	1.4
Ohio..........	7.2	14.4	2.7	29.8	(X)	17.7	16.2	8.8	0.7	9.4	11.7	34.9
Oklahoma........	2.9	5.8	1.9	9.7	(X)	4.5	5.7	0.9	0.7	2.2	5.2	7.0
Oregon.........	3.4	4.2	1.2	7.6	(X)	3.8	5.0	3.8	0.5	2.8	8.2	7.5
Pennsylvania......	13.5	10.7	6.2	25.9	(X)	6.2	17.5	12.6	1.4	3.3	14.6	31.1
Rhode Island......	0.8	0.7	0.3	2.8	(X)	2.1	1.7	–	0.1	0.5	3.0	1.2
South Carolina.....	4.7	2.5	2.0	11.0	(X)	5.1	7.6	3.0	0.6	3.2	4.6	9.4
South Dakota	1.0	1.5	0.3	1.6	(X)	0.4	0.9	0.5	0.1	0.4	1.4	1.8
Tennessee	4.4	6.9	2.0	15.7	(X)	6.8	7.3	6.8	1.2	3.5	6.5	13.0
Texas..........	15.8	22.0	4.1	59.0	(X)	23.7	47.5	24.1	1.1	15.5	17.6	47.4
Utah	1.7	1.8	0.9	4.9	(X)	1.7	3.3	1.9	0.3	2.6	3.5	5.2
Vermont.........	1.0	1.1	0.6	0.9	(X)	0.4	1.2	–	0.1	0.2	1.9	1.4
Virginia.........	9.5	3.6	3.0	18.1	(X)	8.8	14.3	7.2	0.9	7.5	8.8	17.8
Washington.......	7.2	7.3	2.2	12.6	(X)	7.9	9.0	4.7	0.6	6.2	6.1	16.7
West Virginia......	5.0	1.0	1.0	2.7	(X)	1.0	3.2	0.3	0.6	0.8	3.5	3.8
Wisconsin........	1.7	10.0	0.9	14.8	(X)	4.6	9.6	3.6	0.2	3.0	5.6	12.9
Wyoming.........	1.8	0.8	0.3	1.7	(X)	0.4	1.0	0.6	0.1	0.7	1.3	1.7

– Represents or rounds to zero.   X Not applicable.   [1] Includes other categories not shown separately.

Source: U.S. Census Bureau; "Public Employment and Payroll Data." See also <http://www.census.gov/govs/www/apes.html>; (accessed May 2008).

U.S. Census Bureau, Statistical Abstract of the United States: 2009

Table 448. State and Local Government Employment and Average Monthly Earnings by State: 2000 to 2006

[4,083 represents 4,083,000. as of March. Full-time equivalent employment is a derived statistic that provides an estimate of a government's total full-time employment by converting part-time employees to a full-time amount]

State	Full-time equivalent employment (1,000)						Average monthly earnings [2] (dol.)					
	State			Local [1]			State			Local [1]		
	2000	2005	2006	2000	2005	2006	2000	2005	2006	2000	2005	2006
United States . . .	4,083	4,209	4,251	10,995	11,715	11,885	3,374	3,966	4,098	3,169	3,702	3,807
Alabama	80	85	85	182	188	187	2,841	3,572	3,681	2,431	2,728	2,903
Alaska	23	25	25	25	27	27	3,842	4,234	4,398	3,818	4,141	4,193
Arizona	65	69	67	182	213	218	3,055	3,541	3,788	2,942	3,684	3,835
Arkansas	49	54	58	96	106	104	2,842	3,335	3,138	2,175	2,570	2,724
California	355	387	394	1,322	1,384	1,425	4,451	5,319	5,497	4,062	4,927	5,065
Colorado	66	66	67	164	184	188	3,779	4,562	4,693	3,076	3,727	3,806
Connecticut	66	60	62	111	125	126	3,909	4,927	5,063	3,856	4,504	4,542
Delaware	24	25	26	21	23	24	3,222	3,869	3,946	3,163	3,815	4,147
District of Columbia . . .	(X)	(X)	(X)	45	46	47	(X)	(X)	(X)	3,923	4,775	4,992
Florida	185	186	191	580	657	676	3,149	3,407	3,519	2,865	3,476	3,608
Georgia	120	121	124	334	378	381	2,899	3,396	3,492	2,677	3,076	3,217
Hawaii	55	54	55	14	14	15	2,926	3,672	3,845	3,352	4,054	4,253
Idaho	23	23	22	51	54	57	3,022	3,454	3,579	2,478	2,954	2,930
Illinois	128	133	132	493	504	503	3,441	4,264	4,438	3,307	3,850	3,991
Indiana	83	93	90	232	240	243	2,990	3,512	3,632	2,711	3,209	3,326
Iowa	55	53	53	121	133	133	3,656	4,441	4,744	2,727	2,974	3,134
Kansas	43	44	44	128	137	141	3,071	3,622	3,580	2,491	2,950	3,001
Kentucky	74	79	79	149	159	165	3,051	3,421	3,529	2,339	2,786	2,789
Louisiana	95	91	83	185	192	192	2,807	3,455	3,516	2,278	2,638	2,772
Maine	21	21	22	51	55	56	2,983	3,608	3,676	2,609	2,931	3,071
Maryland	91	91	90	182	188	201	3,312	4,125	4,294	3,535	4,317	4,399
Massachusetts	96	89	91	232	234	241	3,683	4,420	4,586	3,403	4,097	4,171
Michigan	142	131	135	351	364	352	3,934	4,427	4,452	3,518	3,963	4,012
Minnesota	73	74	77	206	195	196	3,892	4,613	4,762	3,255	3,838	3,986
Mississippi	56	57	55	133	132	134	2,752	3,096	3,197	2,121	2,636	2,744
Missouri	91	92	90	208	227	230	2,678	3,087	3,137	2,678	2,971	3,060
Montana	18	20	19	34	36	35	2,931	3,309	3,496	2,546	2,821	2,912
Nebraska	30	32	33	78	79	85	2,514	3,263	3,345	2,779	3,368	3,383
Nevada	22	26	26	61	75	77	3,444	3,963	4,202	3,817	4,343	4,504
New Hampshire	19	19	19	46	50	51	3,079	3,630	3,899	2,830	3,199	3,317
New Jersey	133	154	157	316	348	355	4,075	4,855	5,048	3,967	4,640	4,703
New Mexico	48	50	51	70	78	77	2,811	3,160	3,300	2,494	2,785	2,938
New York	251	245	249	924	939	941	3,859	4,622	4,860	3,961	4,594	4,641
North Carolina	123	135	139	328	348	372	3,012	3,468	3,614	2,708	3,168	3,151
North Dakota	16	18	18	23	23	23	2,826	3,243	3,368	2,778	3,334	3,450
Ohio	136	136	137	459	484	480	3,369	3,909	4,053	3,118	3,532	3,633
Oklahoma	64	65	67	134	140	147	2,821	3,254	3,355	2,280	2,589	2,720
Oregon	53	58	57	124	124	124	3,269	3,725	3,832	3,332	3,748	3,917
Pennsylvania	150	160	161	388	417	407	3,436	3,923	3,905	3,296	3,791	3,924
Rhode Island	20	20	21	36	30	31	3,772	4,367	4,700	3,550	4,438	4,499
South Carolina	79	76	76	155	168	172	2,741	3,165	3,312	2,474	2,938	3,063
South Dakota	13	13	14	28	30	31	2,777	3,275	3,342	2,359	2,821	2,896
Tennessee	81	83	83	218	239	241	2,786	3,249	3,337	2,631	3,008	3,105
Texas	269	274	282	909	1,016	1,033	3,095	3,532	3,641	2,643	3,027	3,126
Utah	49	49	50	73	79	79	2,880	3,504	3,631	2,836	3,197	3,326
Vermont	14	14	15	23	25	26	3,153	3,896	4,053	2,534	2,976	3,071
Virginia	119	120	123	269	298	308	3,229	3,688	3,836	2,928	3,368	3,537
Washington	112	117	117	193	213	216	3,551	4,086	4,206	3,835	4,472	4,619
West Virginia	32	38	37	61	61	60	2,694	3,049	3,092	2,517	2,752	2,792
Wisconsin	64	70	68	220	224	220	3,710	4,321	4,465	3,210	3,771	3,841
Wyoming	11	12	13	29	32	33	2,589	3,389	3,481	2,660	3,182	3,279

X Not applicable. [1] Estimates subject to sampling variation; see Appendix III and source. [2] For full-time employees.

Source: U.S. Census Bureau; *2006 Annual Survey of Government Employment*; <http://www.census.gov/govs/www/apesstl .html>; (accessed May 2008).

Table 449. City Government Employment and Payroll—Largest Cities: 2000 to 2006

[In thousands, (458.1 represents 458,100), except as noted. As of March. See footnote 4, Table 439, for those areas representing city-county consolidated governments. See headnote, Table 448 for full-time equivalent employment definition]

Cities ranked by 2005 population [1]	Total employment (1,000)			Full-time equivalent employment		Payroll (mil. dol.)			Average monthly earnings for full-time employees (dol.)	
	2000	**2005**	**2006**	**2000**	**2006**	**2000**	**2005**	**2006**	**2000**	**2006**
New York, NY	458.1	443.4	446.4	429.3	416.6	1,708.8	1,958.4	2,006.9	4,150	4,957
Los Angeles, CA	49.4	53.5	53.8	48.4	52.1	230.1	303.6	319.7	4,793	6,161
Chicago, IL	41.3	42.6	42.6	40.7	42.1	171.3	171.3	178.3	4,239	4,268
Houston, TX	25.2	21.9	21.3	24.9	20.9	75.2	73.6	75.6	3,037	3,633
Philadelphia, PA	31.1	31.4	30.9	30.0	30.0	109.2	127.4	131.4	3,637	4,390
Phoenix, AZ	13.0	14.3	15.0	12.7	14.7	50.3	67.1	71.3	4,024	4,951
San Antonio, TX	16.9	17.3	17.4	15.7	16.2	48.0	61.8	61.3	3,160	3,877
San Diego, CA	12.3	11.7	11.5	11.4	10.9	46.9	57.7	56.4	4,201	5,290
Dallas, TX	15.6	14.8	14.8	15.2	14.4	50.4	61.7	62.8	3,332	4,416
San Jose, CA	7.6	9.4	7.3	6.9	6.5	36.3	52.4	44.5	5,569	7,213
Honolulu, HI	9.8	9.7	9.8	9.1	9.1	30.9	36.7	38.5	3,435	4,318
Detroit, MI	40.7	37.4	14.9	36.1	14.7	132.1	142.9	54.5	3,693	3,731
Indianapolis, IN	12.4	17.1	17.6	12.0	16.1	36.7	53.9	57.6	3,115	3,536
Jacksonville, FL	10.1	11.4	10.1	9.7	9.8	35.6	45.6	42.0	3,815	4,377
San Francisco, CA	27.7	29.2	27.7	27.7	27.7	141.6	191.3	184.4	5,112	6,659
Columbus, OH	9.1	8.4	8.5	8.8	8.2	30.1	35.1	36.3	3,478	4,479
Louisville, KY	4.6	8.4	8.3	4.3	7.7	11.8	25.9	26.7	2,844	3,476
Austin, TX	10.6	12.4	12.4	10.1	12.0	31.2	47.8	51.3	3,128	4,327
Memphis, TN	28.2	28.9	27.8	26.9	25.5	80.3	90.4	92.3	3,024	3,736
Boston, MA	23.3	22.4	23.1	22.0	21.1	80.2	97.0	100.2	3,734	4,801
Baltimore, MD	30.8	27.2	28.3	29.2	26.5	95.3	102.5	108.2	3,361	4,163
Ft. Worth, TX	6.1	6.4	6.6	5.7	6.2	18.9	24.1	26.0	3,394	4,351
Charlotte, NC	5.2	6.0	6.3	5.1	6.1	17.1	23.4	25.2	3,408	4,148
El Paso, TX	5.9	5.7	5.9	5.8	5.7	15.6	16.4	18.0	2,701	3,189
Milwaukee, WI	7.9	8.0	8.0	7.7	7.9	28.5	31.9	32.9	3,706	4,158
Nashville, TN	20.6	22.2	22.3	19.6	21.2	62.3	76.3	79.2	3,235	3,808
Seattle, WA	11.4	12.8	14.3	10.3	12.3	48.3	57.1	62.8	4,726	5,239
Denver, CO	14.5	12.4	13.4	13.7	12.7	47.3	53.0	56.8	3,534	4,474
Washington, DC	37.7	37.6	37.5	36.5	36.2	139.4	164.6	173.8	3,863	4,972
Las Vegas, NV	2.6	3.0	3.1	2.5	2.9	11.2	16.6	17.7	4,681	6,215
Portland, OR	6.2	6.2	6.3	5.4	5.4	23.4	27.5	28.5	4,416	5,367
Oklahoma City, OK	5.1	4.9	5.0	4.8	4.6	16.0	19.5	20.6	3,457	4,767
Tucson, AZ	7.1	6.8	6.6	5.8	6.1	16.0	24.1	26.0	2,787	4,559
Albuquerque, NM	7.1	6.9	7.2	6.6	6.9	18.3	21.5	24.3	2,868	3,677
Long Beach, CA	6.1	6.0	6.1	5.7	5.5	25.7	27.6	28.3	4,855	5,316
Atlanta, GA	8.8	8.0	8.0	8.6	7.8	25.6	29.1	29.6	2,974	3,823
Fresno, CA	3.2	4.0	4.1	3.1	4.0	12.7	17.5	18.9	4,073	5,016
Sacramento, CA	4.4	5.1	5.3	4.0	4.6	17.0	23.3	26.3	4,400	6,228
New Orleans, LA	10.5	10.0	9.8	10.1	9.5	24.4	25.3	26.6	2,446	2,797
Cleveland, OH	10.1	7.9	7.8	9.4	7.7	27.8	30.1	30.7	2,989	3,993
Kansas, MO	6.8	6.6	6.6	6.6	6.6	21.3	25.1	26.3	3,246	3,997
Mesa, AZ	3.5	4.3	4.6	3.3	4.3	13.4	19.8	21.2	4,072	5,085
Virginia Beach, VA	19.7	21.8	19.4	17.4	17.8	43.4	55.5	57.6	2,679	3,485
Omaha, NE	3.4	3.0	3.1	2.9	2.7	10.6	12.7	12.7	3,874	4,772
Baton Rouge, LA	7.1	7.1	7.0	6.0	6.2	14.7	18.9	19.3	2,653	3,210
Oakland, CA	4.2	5.5	5.8	4.2	5.7	24.8	41.0	44.4	5,861	7,726
Miami, FL	3.8	3.7	4.1	3.6	4.0	15.1	17.3	19.9	4,276	5,050
Tulsa, OK	4.5	4.3	4.3	4.5	4.2	13.7	14.9	15.8	3,126	3,762
Minneapolis, MN	6.3	5.9	5.9	5.8	5.5	21.3	24.0	25.3	3,866	4,675
Colorado Springs, CO	7.4	7.7	8.3	6.9	7.8	25.3	31.2	33.5	3,747	4,296
Arlington, TX	3.0	2.7	2.3	2.4	2.2	7.1	9.6	8.1	3,090	3,797
Wichita, KS	3.6	4.0	4.1	3.1	3.3	9.3	11.3	12.1	3,072	3,729
St. Louis, MO	8.0	6.9	6.7	7.6	6.5	24.1	23.7	24.0	3,176	3,717
Raleigh, NC	3.2	3.8	4.8	2.9	4.3	8.9	11.8	13.3	3,114	3,230
Santa Ana, CA	2.5	2.5	2.1	2.2	1.9	10.1	13.4	12.6	5,606	7,099
Anaheim, CA	3.2	3.5	3.6	2.5	2.5	11.5	15.7	16.8	5,267	6,996
Tampa, FL	4.3	4.7	4.7	4.2	4.6	14.1	18.1	19.1	3,370	4,183
Pittsburgh, PA	4.4	3.6	3.3	4.3	3.3	15.3	15.3	14.8	3,593	4,583
Cincinnati, OH	6.5	6.3	6.3	6.4	5.9	21.3	26.1	26.7	3,504	4,659
Toledo, OH	2.8	2.9	2.9	2.8	2.9	10.0	12.6	12.9	3,628	4,456
Aurora, CO	2.5	2.7	2.7	2.5	2.7	9.0	12.0	12.4	3,682	4,675
Bakersfield, CA	1.3	1.3	1.5	1.2	1.4	5.3	6.8	7.1	4,469	5,142
Riverside, CA	2.1	2.4	2.4	1.9	2.1	8.0	11.3	11.5	4,625	5,633
Stockton, CA	2.3	2.2	2.2	1.9	1.8	7.1	9.4	9.6	4,054	5,419
Corpus Christi, TX	3.5	3.1	3.1	3.3	3.0	8.6	10.1	10.6	2,675	3,498
Newark, NJ	5.5	6.9	7.4	5.2	6.2	22.3	30.6	32.7	4,371	5,411
Buffalo, NY	11.4	11.9	10.7	10.5	9.7	43.4	47.8	43.8	4,457	4,710
St. Paul, MN	4.2	3.2	3.2	3.2	2.9	13.3	13.5	14.8	4,189	5,194
Anchorage, AK	10.1	10.9	10.9	9.0	9.8	34.6	41.7	42.9	3,973	4,529
Lexington, KY	4.0	4.3	4.3	3.6	4.0	10.2	13.1	13.8	2,910	3,532
Plano, TX	2.0	2.4	2.4	1.8	2.2	6.4	9.0	9.5	3,702	4,556
St. Petersburg, FL	3.2	3.9	4.3	3.0	3.8	9.9	12.9	14.9	3,366	4,113
Jersey City, NJ	4.1	3.8	4.1	3.7	3.7	15.3	17.2	18.3	4,323	5,329
Glendale, AZ	1.5	2.2	2.3	1.4	2.1	4.7	8.6	9.2	3,275	4,670
Lincoln, NE	2.7	3.0	3.0	2.5	2.8	8.2	11.2	11.9	3,382	4,474
Chandler, AZ	1.4	1.7	1.7	1.2	1.5	3.9	7.0	7.6	3,204	5,069

[1] 2005 based on estimated resident population as of July 1.

Source: U.S. Census Bureau, *2006 Annual Survey of Government Employment*; see also <http://www.census.gov/govs/www /apesstl.html> (accessed March 2007).

U.S. Census Bureau, Statistical Abstract of the United States: 2009

Table 450. County Government Employment and Payroll—Largest Counties: 2000 to 2006

[In thousands, (98.8 represents 98,800). As of March. See text, this section. See headnote, Table 448, for full-time equivalent employment definition]

Counties ranked by 2005 population [1]	Total employment (1,000)			Full-time equivalent employment		Payroll (mil. dol.)			Average monthly earnings for full-time employees (dol.)	
	2000	2005	2006	2000	2006	2000	2005	2006	2000	2006
Los Angeles, CA	98.8	99.5	101.3	94.2	97.6	396.7	475.0	499.3	4,274	5,186
Cook, IL	28.9	27.8	26.4	28.9	26.4	99.3	126.3	123.9	3,445	4,697
Harris, TX	19.8	21.7	21.9	19.4	21.0	59.5	77.4	81.7	3,063	3,900
Maricopa, AZ	15.3	16.4	13.5	15.0	13.3	43.7	54.9	51.1	2,934	3,845
Orange, CA	24.3	25.0	25.6	22.5	23.8	81.4	104.9	113.1	3,623	4,745
San Diego, CA	19.5	19.7	20.6	18.2	19.3	66.3	83.9	93.0	3,651	4,843
Dade, FL	36.0	43.8	45.2	35.1	43.8	130.3	190.8	205.4	3,817	4,804
Dallas, TX	12.5	15.2	15.7	12.0	14.7	36.4	54.5	59.6	3,055	4,047
Wayne, MI	6.7	5.8	5.7	6.7	5.6	25.8	25.1	25.1	3,914	4,556
San Bernardino, CA	20.6	19.9	20.5	18.8	19.2	67.6	84.0	90.9	3,664	4,795
Riverside, CA	16.6	20.1	21.1	15.4	19.8	54.2	90.6	100.4	3,534	5,038
King, WA	15.8	14.5	14.5	14.2	13.7	52.1	64.6	68.5	3,812	5,145
Broward, FL	11.0	12.9	12.8	10.8	12.5	37.0	48.4	50.8	3,437	4,131
Clark, NV	16.6	19.1	18.8	15.2	17.1	60.3	88.4	94.2	4,169	5,557
Santa Clara, CA	14.9	18.0	18.5	14.3	17.8	65.3	100.4	110.2	4,655	6,261
Tarrant, TX	6.9	9.4	9.8	6.8	9.7	19.0	34.4	36.5	2,811	3,800
Bexar, TX	9.5	10.1	10.4	9.1	9.9	23.6	27.9	29.7	2,619	2,952
Suffolk, NY	12.9	14.2	15.4	11.3	14.0	51.9	68.2	76.0	4,686	5,479
Alameda, CA	12.1	11.3	11.6	11.1	11.0	51.1	60.9	65.7	4,619	6,037
Sacramento, CA	13.3	14.9	16.6	12.6	16.0	50.3	71.0	86.5	4,094	5,442
Cuyahoga, OH	16.1	15.7	15.8	16.1	15.3	49.2	57.1	60.1	3,065	3,850
Nassau, NY	18.9	16.8	18.3	16.9	16.1	71.3	76.6	85.8	4,295	5,508
Palm Beach, FL	8.6	10.5	10.8	8.5	10.3	27.0	40.4	43.5	3,200	4,268
Allegheny, PA	7.0	6.8	7.1	6.8	7.0	17.6	20.2	22.2	2,605	3,210
Oakland, MI	4.5	4.6	4.8	4.3	4.5	15.6	18.9	19.5	3,697	4,450
Hillsborough, FL	16.2	13.9	14.2	12.2	11.3	34.4	39.1	43.0	2,993	4,114
Hennepin, MN	13.0	11.4	11.1	11.0	10.2	41.5	49.3	46.1	3,815	4,554
Franklin, OH	6.6	6.7	6.6	6.5	6.3	19.2	21.7	21.8	2,962	3,522
Orange, FL	9.9	10.5	10.9	9.3	9.9	28.0	35.7	39.4	3,092	4,022
Contra Costa, CA	10.7	10.0	10.2	9.5	9.0	44.7	41.6	44.7	4,779	4,989
Fairfax, VA	35.3	44.7	51.4	32.3	43.5	117.5	165.4	191.5	3,746	4,451
St. Louis, MO	4.2	3.9	3.9	4.1	3.8	12.9	14.0	14.5	3,215	3,832
Salt Lake, UT	5.8	5.9	5.8	4.5	4.3	13.4	13.9	14.4	3,252	3,659
Westchester, NY	6.9	7.3	7.5	6.3	6.6	26.6	29.8	32.1	4,240	4,770
Erie, NY	10.9	11.3	11.4	9.8	10.3	33.4	37.4	38.7	3,578	3,934
Du Page, IL	3.9	3.6	3.5	3.6	3.3	11.8	14.1	14.7	3,360	4,415
Pinellas, FL	6.2	6.6	6.9	6.1	6.7	18.5	25.7	28.0	3,039	4,179
Montgomery, MD	37.4	40.6	43.3	28.8	33.9	123.1	175.3	191.7	4,619	5,750
Pima, AZ	8.0	7.2	7.4	7.2	6.9	20.0	22.5	24.8	2,859	3,726
Milwaukee, WI	8.5	9.3	7.1	8.1	6.5	26.5	35.7	25.2	3,314	3,990
Fulton, GA	7.9	7.6	7.9	7.7	7.6	25.0	29.2	31.0	3,356	4,229
Shelby, TN	13.1	14.2	14.9	12.4	14.3	35.1	45.4	49.7	2,842	3,487
Bergen, NJ	5.8	5.7	5.9	4.1	5.0	13.0	23.7	24.4	3,178	5,027
Travis, TX	3.5	4.6	4.7	3.5	4.7	10.6	15.7	17.1	3,057	3,658
Fresno, CA	8.6	9.2	9.3	8.2	8.6	26.0	32.9	33.4	3,293	3,891
Prince Georges, MD	29.4	32.2	34.2	26.3	30.0	90.8	112.1	120.6	3,564	4,297
Macomb, MI	3.0	3.2	3.3	2.8	3.1	8.9	12.0	12.5	3,333	4,192
Hamilton, OH	5.9	6.1	6.1	5.7	5.9	15.3	20.5	21.2	2,679	3,540
Mecklenburg, NC	23.8	27.1	29.2	21.1	26.0	58.2	82.1	89.4	2,834	3,512
Ventura, CA	8.6	8.6	8.8	8.3	8.4	31.5	43.2	47.3	3,829	5,731
Essex, NJ	5.6	5.0	5.2	5.0	4.7	19.3	21.0	22.2	4,048	4,875
Middlesex, NJ	4.5	4.3	4.4	4.0	3.8	14.4	16.6	16.5	3,881	4,596
Baltimore, MD	23.3	27.5	29.6	20.7	24.5	63.8	92.9	101.0	3,227	4,285
Montgomery, PA	3.5	4.1	4.1	3.4	3.7	9.2	12.4	13.0	2,783	3,420
Kern, CA	9.2	10.3	10.9	8.6	10.1	30.3	40.7	40.6	3,504	4,011
Pierce, WA	3.4	3.6	3.6	3.2	3.5	13.0	16.6	17.3	4,216	5,030
Wake, NC	17.8	21.0	23.6	15.8	20.7	44.7	65.3	69.1	2,876	3,319
Monroe, NY	7.0	6.9	6.9	5.9	6.0	20.4	22.8	23.5	3,430	4,027
Gwinnett, GA	3.8	4.5	4.7	3.5	4.5	11.4	16.7	17.8	3,243	3,989
El Paso, TX	4.0	4.7	4.6	4.0	4.4	10.4	15.3	15.6	2,685	3,577
Lake, IL	3.2	3.3	3.3	2.9	3.0	9.6	13.0	13.6	3,277	4,489
San Mateo, CA	6.2	7.2	7.3	5.8	6.9	24.6	35.5	37.3	4,415	5,951
Oklahoma City, OK	2.6	2.3	2.5	2.3	2.3	4.4	5.7	6.1	1,860	2,663
Hidalgo, TX	1.9	2.2	2.5	1.9	2.5	4.0	5.6	6.7	2,174	2,702
Dekalb, GA	6.5	7.1	7.4	6.2	7.2	19.5	25.1	27.6	3,170	3,853
Multnomah, OR	6.0	5.0	4.9	5.2	4.5	15.0	16.6	19.5	3,050	4,348
San Joaquin, CA	7.4	7.7	7.9	6.8	7.0	22.6	30.4	32.1	3,509	4,607
Cobb, GA	3.9	4.7	4.8	3.8	4.4	11.9	16.2	17.1	3,353	4,030
Jackson, MO	2.1	1.9	2.0	2.0	1.9	5.0	5.8	6.0	2,519	3,078
Collin, TX	1.1	1.4	1.7	1.1	1.7	2.8	5.0	6.2	2,557	3,674
Jefferson, AL	4.8	4.5	4.3	4.7	4.3	14.7	16.9	17.2	3,122	4,020
Snohomish, WA	2.4	3.2	2.8	2.4	2.8	9.3	13.5	13.3	3,906	4,794
Norfolk, MA	0.6	0.5	0.5	0.5	0.5	1.6	2.0	2.2	2,977	4,654

[1] 2005 based on estimated resident population as of July 1.

Source: U.S. Census Bureau, *2006 Annual Survey of Government Employment*; see also <http://www.census.gov/govs/www /apesstl.html> (accessed March 2007).

U.S. Census Bureau, Statistical Abstract of the United States: 2009

Section 9
Federal Government Finances and Employment

This section presents statistics relating to the financial structure and the civilian employment of the federal government. The fiscal data cover taxes, other receipts, outlays, and debt. The principal sources of fiscal data are the *Budget of the United States Government* and related documents, published annually by the Office of Management and Budget (OMB), and the U.S. Department of the Treasury's *United States Government Annual Report* and its *Appendix*. Detailed data on tax returns and collections are published annually by the Internal Revenue Service. The personnel data relate to staffing and payrolls. They are published by the Office of Personnel Management and the Bureau of Labor Statistics. Data on federally owned land and real property are collected by the General Services Administration and presented in its annual "Federal Real Property Report."

Budget concept—Under the unified budget concept, all federal monies are included in one comprehensive budget. These monies comprise both federal funds and trust funds. Federal funds are derived mainly from taxes and borrowing and are not restricted by law to any specific government purpose. Trust funds, such as the Unemployment Trust Fund, collect certain taxes and other receipts for use in carrying out specific purposes or programs in accordance with the terms of the trust agreement or statute. Fund balances include both cash balances with the Treasury and investments in U.S. securities. Part of the balance is obligated, part unobligated. Prior to 1985, the budget totals, under provisions of law, excluded some federal activities—including the Federal Financing Bank, the Postal Service, the Synthetic Fuels Corporation, and the lending activities of the Rural Electrification Administration. The Balanced Budget and Emergency Deficit Control Act of 1985 (P.L.99-177) repealed the off-budget status of these entities and placed social security (federal old-age and survivors insurance and the federal disability insurance trust funds) off-budget. Though social security is now off-budget and, by law, excluded from coverage of the congressional budget resolutions, it continues to be a federal program.

Receipts arising from the government's sovereign powers are reported as governmental receipts; all other receipts; i.e., from business-type or market-oriented activities, are offset against outlays. Outlays are reported on a checks-issued (net) basis (i.e., outlays are recorded at the time the checks to pay bills are issued).

Debt concept—For most of U.S. history, the total debt consisted of debt borrowed by the Treasury (i.e., public debt). The present debt series includes both public debt and agency debt. The *gross federal debt* includes money borrowed by the Treasury and by various federal agencies; it is the broadest generally used measure of the federal debt. *Total public debt* is covered by a statutory debt limitation and includes only borrowing by the Treasury.

Treasury receipts and outlays—All receipts of the government, with a few exceptions, are deposited to the credit of the U.S. Treasury regardless of ultimate disposition. Under the Constitution, no money may be withdrawn from the Treasury unless appropriated by the Congress.

The day-to-day cash operations of the federal government clearing through the accounts of the U.S. Treasury are reported in the *Daily Treasury Statement*. Extensive detail on the public debt is published in the *Monthly Statement of the Public Debt of the United States*.

Budget receipts such as taxes, customs duties, and miscellaneous receipts, which are collected by government agencies, and outlays represented by checks issued and cash payments made by disbursing officers as well as government agencies are reported in the *Daily Treasury Statement of Receipts and Outlays of the United States Government* and in the Treasury's *United States Government Annual Report* and its *Appendix*. These deposits in and payments from accounts maintained by government agencies are on the same basis as the unified budget.

The quarterly *Treasury Bulletin* contains data on fiscal operations and related Treasury activities, including financial statements of government corporations and other business-type activities.

Income tax returns and tax collections—Tax data are compiled by the Internal Revenue Service of the Treasury Department. The annual *Internal Revenue Service Data Book* gives a detailed account of tax collections by kind of tax. The agency's annual *Statistics of Income* reports present detailed data from individual income tax returns and corporation income tax returns. The quarterly *Statistics of Income Bulletin* presents data on such diverse subjects as tax-exempt organizations, unincorporated businesses, fiduciary income tax and estate tax returns, sales of capital assets by individuals, international income and taxes reported by corporations and individuals, and estate tax wealth.

Employment and payrolls—The Office of Personnel Management collects employment and payroll data from all departments and agencies of the federal government, except the Central Intelligence Agency, the National Security Agency, and the Defense Intelligence Agency. Employment figures represent the number of persons who occupied civilian positions at the end of the report month shown and who are paid for personal services rendered for the federal government, regardless of the nature of appointment or method of payment. Federal payrolls include all payments for personal services rendered during the report month and payments for accumulated annual leave of employees who separate from the service. Since most federal employees are paid on a biweekly basis, the calendar month earnings are partially estimated on the basis of the number of work days in each month where payroll periods overlap.

Federal employment and payroll figures are published by the Office of Personnel Management in its *Federal Civilian Workforce Statistics—Employment and Trends.* It also publishes biennial employment data for minority groups, data on occupations of white- and blue-collar workers, and data on employment by geographic area; reports on salary and wage distribution of federal employees are published annually. General schedule is primarily white-collar; wage system primarily blue-collar. Data on federal employment are also issued by the Bureau of Labor Statistics in its *Monthly Labor Review* and in Employment and Earnings and by the U.S. Census Bureau in its annual publication *Public Employment.*

Figure 9.1
Federal Budget Summary: 1980 to 2008

Receipts, outlays, and surplus or deficit
Trillions of constant (2000) dollars

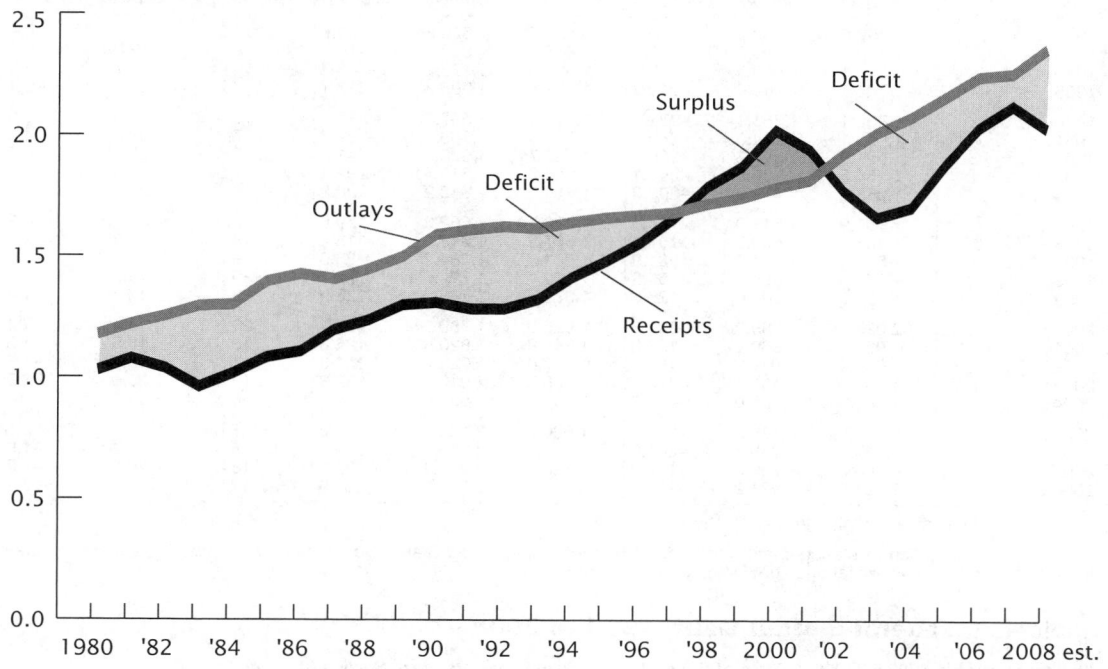

Outlays and federal debt as a percent of gross domestic product (GDP)

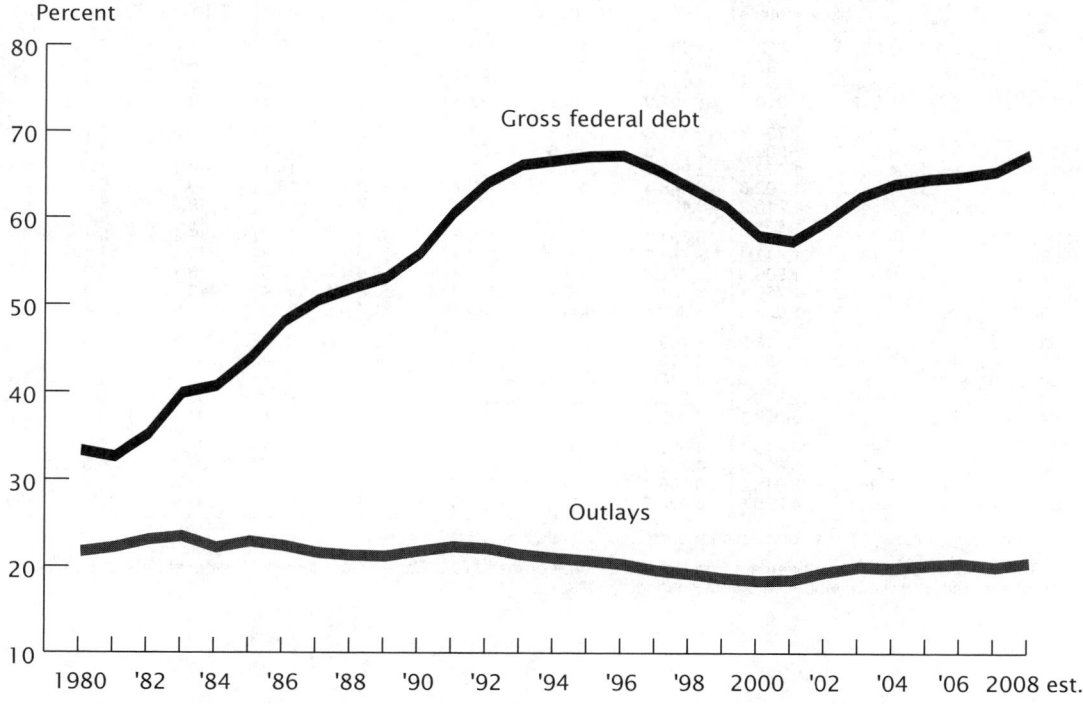

Source: Charts prepared by U.S. Census Bureau. For data, see Table 451 & 452.

Federal Government Finances and Employment   301

Table 451. Federal Budget—Receipts and Outlays: 1960 to 2008

[92.5 represents $92,500,000,000). For fiscal years ending in year shown; see text, Section 8. See also headnote, Table 453]

Fiscal year	In current dollars (bil. dol)			In constant (2000) dollars (bil. dol)			As percentage of GDP [1]		
	Receipts	Outlays	Surplus or deficit (−)	Receipts	Outlays	Surplus or deficit (−)	Receipts	Outlays	Surplus or deficit (−)
1960.........	92.5	92.2	0.3	528.5	526.8	1.7	17.9	17.8	0.1
1970.........	192.8	195.6	−2.8	815.9	828.0	−12.0	19.0	19.3	−0.3
1980.........	517.1	590.9	−73.8	1,028.3	1,175.1	−146.8	19.0	21.7	−2.7
1985.........	734.1	946.4	−212.3	1,082.6	1,395.7	−313.1	17.7	22.9	−5.1
1990.........	1,032.1	1,253.1	−221.0	1,309.4	1,589.9	−280.4	18.0	21.8	−3.9
1991.........	1,055.1	1,324.3	−269.2	1,282.6	1,609.9	−327.3	17.8	22.3	−4.5
1992.........	1,091.3	1,381.6	−290.3	1,282.7	1,623.9	−341.2	17.5	22.1	−4.7
1993.........	1,154.5	1,409.5	−255.1	1,323.2	1,615.5	−292.3	17.6	21.4	−3.9
1994.........	1,258.7	1,461.9	−203.2	1,414.0	1,642.2	−228.2	18.1	21.0	−2.9
1995.........	1,351.9	1,515.9	−164.0	1,482.4	1,662.2	−179.8	18.5	20.7	−2.2
1996.........	1,453.2	1,560.6	−107.4	1,557.9	1,673.0	−115.2	18.9	20.3	−1.4
1997.........	1,579.4	1,601.3	−21.9	1,661.2	1,684.2	−23.0	19.3	19.6	−0.3
1998.........	1,722.0	1,652.7	69.3	1,793.1	1,721.0	72.1	20.0	19.2	0.8
1999.........	1,827.6	1,702.0	125.6	1,874.9	1,746.0	128.9	20.0	18.7	1.4
2000.........	2,025.5	1,789.2	236.2	2,025.5	1,789.2	236.2	20.9	18.4	2.4
2001.........	1,991.4	1,863.2	128.2	1,945.9	1,820.6	125.3	19.8	18.5	1.3
2002.........	1,853.4	2,011.2	−157.8	1,777.8	1,929.2	−151.3	17.9	19.4	−1.5
2003.........	1,782.5	2,160.1	−377.6	1,665.5	2,018.2	−352.8	16.5	20.0	−3.5
2004.........	1,880.3	2,293.0	−412.7	1,707.2	2,081.9	−374.7	16.4	19.9	−3.6
2005.........	2,153.9	2,472.2	−318.3	1,886.2	2,165.0	−278.8	17.6	20.2	−2.6
2006.........	2,407.3	2,655.4	−248.2	2,039.0	2,249.2	−210.2	18.5	20.4	−1.9
2007.........	2,568.2	2,730.2	−162.0	2,128.8	2,263.1	−134.3	18.8	20.0	−1.2
2008 estimate...	2,521.2	2,931.2	−410.0	2,034.7	2,365.6	−330.9	17.6	20.5	−2.9

[1] Gross domestic product; see text, Section 13.

Source: U.S. Office of Management and Budget, *Budget of the United States Government, Historical Tables,* annual. See Internet site <http://www.whitehouse.gov/omb/budget/fy2009/>.

Table 452. Federal Budget Debt: 1960 to 2008

[290.5 represents $290,500,000,000. As of the end of the fiscal year. See text, Section 8]

Fiscal year	Total (bil. dol.)					As percentage of GDP [1]				
	Gross federal debt	Federal government accounts	Held by the public			Gross federal debt	Federal government accounts	Held by the public		
			Total	Federal Reserve System	Other			Total	Federal Reserve System	Other
1960.........	290.5	53.7	236.8	26.5	210.3	56.1	10.4	45.7	5.1	40.6
1970.........	380.9	97.7	283.2	57.7	225.5	37.6	9.7	28.0	5.7	22.3
1980.........	909.0	197.1	711.9	120.8	591.1	33.3	7.2	26.1	4.4	21.7
1985.........	1,817.4	310.2	1,507.3	169.8	1,337.5	43.9	7.5	36.4	4.1	32.3
1990.........	3,206.3	794.7	2,411.6	234.4	2,177.1	55.9	13.9	42.0	4.1	38.0
1991.........	3,598.2	909.2	2,689.0	258.6	2,430.4	60.6	15.3	45.3	4.4	40.9
1992.........	4,001.8	1,002.1	2,999.7	296.4	2,703.3	64.1	16.1	48.1	4.8	43.3
1993.........	4,351.0	1,102.6	3,248.4	325.7	2,922.7	66.2	16.8	49.4	5.0	44.4
1994.........	4,643.3	1,210.2	3,433.1	355.2	3,077.9	66.7	17.4	49.3	5.1	44.2
1995.........	4,920.6	1,316.2	3,604.4	374.1	3,230.3	67.2	18.0	49.2	5.1	44.1
1996.........	5,181.5	1,447.4	3,734.1	390.9	3,343.1	67.3	18.8	48.5	5.1	43.5
1997.........	5,369.2	1,596.9	3,772.3	424.5	3,347.8	65.6	19.5	46.1	5.2	40.9
1998.........	5,478.2	1,757.1	3,721.1	458.2	3,262.9	63.5	20.4	43.1	5.3	37.8
1999.........	5,605.5	1,973.2	3,632.4	496.6	3,135.7	61.4	21.6	39.8	5.4	34.4
2000.........	5,628.7	2,218.9	3,409.8	511.4	2,898.4	58.0	22.9	35.1	5.3	29.9
2001.........	5,769.9	2,450.3	3,319.6	534.1	2,785.5	57.4	24.4	33.0	5.3	27.7
2002.........	6,198.4	2,658.0	3,540.4	604.2	2,936.2	59.7	25.6	34.1	5.8	28.3
2003.........	6,760.0	2,846.6	3,913.4	656.1	3,257.3	62.5	26.3	36.2	6.1	30.1
2004.........	7,354.7	3,059.1	4,295.5	700.3	3,595.2	64.0	26.6	37.4	6.1	31.3
2005.........	7,905.3	3,313.1	4,592.2	736.4	3,855.9	64.6	27.1	37.5	6.0	31.5
2006.........	8,451.4	3,622.4	4,829.0	768.9	4,060.0	64.9	27.8	37.1	5.9	31.2
2007.........	8,950.7	3,915.6	5,035.1	779.6	4,255.5	65.5	28.6	36.8	5.7	31.1
2008 estimate...	9,654.4	4,225.8	5,428.6	(NA)	(NA)	67.5	29.5	37.9	(NA)	(NA)

NA not available. [1] Gross domestic product; see text, Section 13.

Source: U.S. Office of Management and Budget, *Budget of the United States Government, Historical Tables,* annual. See Internet site <http://www.whitehouse.gov/omb/budget/fy2009/>.

Table 453. Federal Budget Outlays by Type: 1990 to 2008

[1,253.1 represents $1,253,100,000,000. For years ending September 30. Given the inherent imprecision in deflating outlays, the data shown in constant dollars present a reasonable perspective—not precision. The deflators and the categories that are deflated are as comparable over time as feasible. Minus sign (–) indicates offset]

Type	Unit	1990	2000	2004	2005	2006	2007	2008, est.
Current dollar outlays	**Bil. dol.**	**1,253.1**	**1,789.2**	**2,293.0**	**2,472.2**	**2,655.4**	**2,730.2**	**2,931.2**
National defense [1]	Bil. dol.	299.3	294.4	455.8	495.3	521.8	552.6	607.3
Nondefense, total	Bil. dol.	953.8	1,494.8	1,837.2	1,976.9	2,133.6	2,177.7	2,324.0
Payments for individuals	Bil. dol.	585.7	1,054.5	1,397.4	1,490.0	1,591.8	1,689.3	1,796.1
Direct payments [2]	Bil. dol.	507.0	867.7	1,131.2	1,211.9	1,315.0	1,400.9	1,491.8
Grants to state and local governments	Bil. dol.	78.7	186.8	266.2	278.1	276.8	288.4	304.3
All other grants	Bil. dol.	56.4	99.1	141.3	149.9	157.3	155.4	162.2
Net Interest [2]	Bil. dol.	184.3	222.9	160.2	184.0	226.6	237.1	243.9
All other [2]	Bil. dol.	164.0	160.9	196.8	218.2	226.2	178.1	209.4
Undistributed offsetting receipts [2]	Bil. dol.	−36.6	−42.6	−58.5	−65.2	−68.3	−82.2	−87.7
Constant (2000) dollar outlays	**Bil. dol.**	**1,589.9**	**1,789.2**	**2,081.9**	**2,165.0**	**2,249.2**	**2,263.1**	**2,365.6**
National defense [1]	Bil. dol.	382.7	294.4	394.3	407.3	412.4	426.4	463.9
Nondefense, total	Bil. dol.	1,207.0	1,494.8	1,687.6	1,757.7	1,836.8	1,836.9	1,901.6
Payments for individuals	Bil. dol.	732.5	1,054.5	1,291.8	1,338.0	1,386.7	1,439.8	1,483.5
Direct payments [2]	Bil. dol.	634.0	867.7	1,045.7	1,088.5	1,145.7	1,194.3	1,232.6
Grants to state and local governments	Bil. dol.	98.4	186.8	246.0	249.6	240.9	245.5	251.0
All other grants	Bil. dol.	73.3	99.1	124.5	124.4	123.4	116.5	116.8
Net interest [2]	Bil. dol.	226.9	222.9	146.7	163.3	194.6	198.3	200.2
All other [2]	Bil. dol.	228.0	160.9	174.2	184.7	185.1	144.3	166.1
Undistributed offsetting receipts [2]	Bil. dol.	−53.5	−42.6	−49.6	−52.7	−53.0	−62.2	−65.1
Outlays as percent of GDP [3]	**Percent**	**21.8**	**18.4**	**19.9**	**20.2**	**20.4**	**20.0**	**20.5**
National defense [1]	Percent	5.2	3.0	4.0	4.0	4.0	4.0	4.2
Nondefense, total	Percent	16.6	15.4	16.0	16.2	16.4	15.9	16.2
Payments for individuals	Percent	10.2	10.9	12.2	12.2	12.2	12.4	12.6
Direct payments [2]	Percent	8.8	8.9	9.8	9.9	10.1	10.3	10.4
Grants to state and local governments	Percent	1.4	1.9	2.3	2.3	2.1	2.1	2.1
All other grants	Percent	1.0	1.0	1.2	1.2	1.2	1.1	1.1
Net interest [2]	Percent	3.2	2.3	1.4	1.5	1.7	1.7	1.7
All other [2]	Percent	2.9	1.7	1.7	1.8	1.7	1.3	1.5
Undistributed offsetting receipts [2]	Percent	−0.6	−0.4	−0.5	−0.5	−0.5	−0.6	−0.6

[1] Includes a small amount of grants to state and local governments and direct payments for individuals. [2] Includes some off-budget amounts; most of the off-budget amounts are direct payments for individuals (social security benefits). [3] Gross domestic product; see text, Section 13.

Source: U.S. Office of Management and Budget, *Budget of the United States Government, Historical Tables,* annual. See Internet site <http://www.whitehouse.gov/omb/budget/fy2009/>.

Table 454. Federal Budget Outlays by Agency: 1990 to 2008

[In billions of dollars (1,253.1 represents $1,253,100,000,000). For years ending September 30]

Department or other unit	1990	2000	2004	2005	2006	2007	2008, est.
Outlays, total [1]	**1,253.1**	**1,789.2**	**2,293.0**	**2,472.2**	**2,655.4**	**2,730.2**	**2,931.2**
Legislative Branch	2.2	2.9	3.9	4.0	4.1	4.3	4.6
The Judiciary Branch	1.6	4.1	5.4	5.5	5.8	6.0	6.2
Agriculture	45.9	75.1	71.6	85.3	93.5	84.4	94.8
Commerce	3.7	7.8	5.8	6.1	6.4	6.5	8.2
Defense—Military	289.7	281.1	437.0	474.4	499.4	529.9	583.1
Education	23.0	33.5	62.8	72.9	93.4	66.4	68.0
Energy	12.1	15.0	19.9	21.3	19.6	20.1	23.2
Health and Human Services	175.5	382.3	543.0	581.5	614.3	672.0	709.4
Homeland Security	7.2	13.2	26.6	38.7	69.1	39.2	42.3
Housing and Urban Development	20.2	30.8	45.0	42.5	42.4	45.6	52.3
Interior	5.8	8.0	8.6	9.3	9.1	10.5	11.1
Justice	5.9	16.8	29.6	22.4	23.3	23.3	25.0
Labor	26.1	31.9	56.7	46.9	43.1	47.5	49.7
State	4.8	6.7	10.9	12.7	13.0	13.7	18.9
Transportation	25.6	41.6	54.9	56.6	60.1	61.7	68.7
Treasury	253.9	390.5	375.8	410.2	464.7	490.6	520.2
Veterans Affairs	29.0	47.1	59.6	69.8	69.8	72.8	86.6
Corps of Engineers	3.3	4.2	4.7	4.7	6.9	3.9	7.2
Other Defense—Civil Programs	21.7	32.9	41.7	43.5	44.4	47.1	49.1
Environmental Protection Agency	5.1	7.2	8.3	7.9	8.3	8.3	7.5
Executive Office of the President	0.2	0.3	3.3	7.7	5.4	3.0	2.1
International Assistance Programs	10.1	12.1	13.7	15.0	13.9	12.8	15.2
National Aeronautics and Space Administration	12.4	13.4	15.2	15.6	15.1	15.9	17.3
National Science Foundation	1.8	3.5	5.1	5.4	5.5	5.5	6.3
Office of Personnel Management	31.9	48.7	56.5	59.5	62.4	58.5	64.2
Social Security Administration (on-budget)	17.3	45.1	49.0	54.6	53.3	54.9	60.0
Social Security Administration (off-budget)	245.0	396.2	481.2	506.8	532.5	566.8	596.5
Undistributed offsetting receipts	−98.9	−173.0	−212.5	−226.2	−237.5	−260.2	−285.6

[1] Includes other agencies, not shown separately.

Source: U.S. Office of Management and Budget, *Budget of the United States Government, Historical Tables,* annual. See Internet site <http://www.whitehouse.gov/omb/budget/fy2009/>.

U.S. Census Bureau, Statistical Abstract of the United States: 2009

Table 455. Federal Outlays by Detailed Function: 1990 to 2008

[In billions of dollars (1,253.1 represents $1,253,100,000,000). For years ending September 30. Minus sign (−) indicates decrease]

Superfunction and function	1990	2000	2003	2004	2005	2006	2007	2008, est.
Total outlays	**1,253.1**	**1,789.2**	**2,160.1**	**2,293.0**	**2,472.2**	**2,655.4**	**2,730.2**	**2,931.2**
National defense [1]	299.3	294.4	404.8	455.8	495.3	521.8	552.6	607.3
Department of Defense—Military	289.7	281.1	387.2	436.5	474.1	499.3	529.8	583.1
Military personnel	75.6	76.0	106.7	113.6	127.5	127.5	128.8	137.4
Operation and maintenance	88.3	105.8	151.4	174.0	188.1	203.8	216.6	225.1
Procurement	81.0	51.7	67.9	76.2	82.3	89.8	99.6	130.5
Research, development, test, and evaluation	37.5	37.6	53.1	60.8	65.7	68.6	73.1	74.7
Military construction	5.1	5.1	5.9	6.3	5.3	6.2	7.9	10.2
Atomic energy defense activities	9.0	12.1	16.0	16.6	18.0	17.5	17.1	17.8
International affairs [1]	13.8	17.2	21.2	26.9	34.6	29.5	28.5	34.8
International development and humanitarian assistance	5.5	6.5	10.3	13.8	17.7	16.7	15.5	14.3
International security assistance	8.7	6.4	8.6	8.4	7.9	7.8	8.0	9.0
Conduct of foreign affairs	3.1	4.7	6.7	7.9	9.1	8.6	8.4	12.2
General science, space, and technology	14.4	18.6	20.9	23.1	23.6	23.6	25.6	27.6
General science and basic research	2.8	6.2	8.0	8.4	8.9	9.1	10.3	10.9
Space flight, research, and supporting activities	11.6	12.4	12.9	14.6	14.8	14.5	15.3	16.7
Energy	3.3	−0.8	−0.7	−0.2	0.4	0.8	−0.9	3.0
Energy supply	2.0	−1.8	−2.1	−1.6	−0.9	0.2	−2.0	0.9
Natural resources and environment [1]	17.1	25.0	29.7	30.7	28.0	33.1	31.8	35.5
Water resources	4.4	5.1	5.5	5.6	5.7	8.0	5.1	8.7
Conservation and land management	4.0	6.8	9.7	9.8	6.2	7.8	9.6	9.7
Recreational resources	1.4	2.6	2.9	3.0	3.0	3.1	3.0	3.4
Pollution control and abatement	5.2	7.4	8.2	8.5	8.1	8.6	8.4	7.8
Agriculture	11.8	36.5	22.5	15.4	26.6	26.0	17.7	21.0
Farm income stabilization	9.7	33.4	18.3	11.2	22.0	21.4	13.1	16.3
Agricultural research and services	2.1	3.0	4.2	4.3	4.5	4.6	4.6	4.7
Commerce and housing credit [1]	67.6	3.2	0.7	5.3	7.6	6.2	0.5	7.4
Mortgage credit	3.8	−3.3	−4.6	2.7	−0.9	−0.6	−5.0	0.3
Postal service	2.1	2.1	−5.2	−4.1	−1.2	−1.0	−3.2	−4.6
Deposit insurance	57.9	−3.1	−1.4	−2.0	−1.4	−1.1	−1.5	−1.9
Transportation [1]	29.5	46.9	67.1	64.6	67.9	70.2	72.9	80.3
Ground transportation	19.0	31.7	37.5	40.7	42.3	45.2	46.8	53.1
Air transportation	7.2	10.6	23.3	16.7	18.8	18.0	18.1	18.1
Water transportation	3.2	4.4	5.9	6.9	6.4	6.7	7.7	8.5
Community and regional development [1]	8.5	10.6	18.9	15.8	26.3	54.5	29.6	27.6
Community development	3.5	5.5	6.3	6.2	5.9	5.8	11.8	12.7
Disaster relief and insurance	2.1	2.6	10.1	7.3	17.7	46.1	15.2	12.0
Education, training, employment, and social services [1]	37.2	53.8	82.6	88.0	97.6	118.6	91.7	93.4
Elementary, secondary, and vocational education	9.9	20.6	31.5	34.4	38.3	39.7	38.4	39.8
Higher education	11.1	10.1	22.7	25.3	31.4	50.5	24.6	24.5
Research and general education aids	1.6	2.6	3.0	3.0	3.1	3.1	3.2	3.2
Training and employment	5.6	6.8	8.4	7.9	6.9	7.2	7.1	7.1
Social services	8.1	12.6	15.6	15.9	16.3	16.5	16.7	17.2
Health	57.7	154.5	219.6	240.1	250.6	252.8	266.4	284.5
Health care services	47.6	136.2	192.6	210.1	219.6	220.8	233.9	251.8
Health research and training	8.6	16.0	24.0	27.1	28.1	28.8	29.3	29.5
Consumer and occupational health and safety	1.5	2.3	2.9	2.9	2.9	3.1	3.2	3.1
Medicare	98.1	197.1	249.4	269.4	298.6	329.9	375.4	396.3
Income security [1]	148.7	253.7	334.6	333.1	345.8	352.5	366.0	388.4
General retirement and disability insurance (excluding social security)	5.1	5.2	7.0	6.6	7.0	4.6	7.8	7.9
Federal employee retirement and disability	52.0	77.2	85.2	88.7	93.4	98.3	103.9	109.1
Unemployment compensation	18.9	23.0	57.1	45.0	35.4	33.8	35.1	37.3
Housing assistance	15.9	28.9	35.5	36.8	37.9	38.3	39.7	41.0
Food and nutrition assistance	24.0	32.5	42.5	46.0	50.8	53.9	54.5	60.3
Social security	248.6	409.4	474.7	495.5	523.3	548.5	586.2	615.3
Veterans benefits and services [1]	29.1	47.1	57.0	59.8	70.2	69.8	72.8	86.6
Income security for veterans	15.3	24.9	29.1	30.8	35.8	35.8	35.7	42.5
Veterans education, training, and rehabilitation	0.2	1.3	2.1	2.6	2.8	2.6	2.7	2.9
Hospital and medical care for veterans	12.1	19.5	24.1	26.9	28.8	29.9	32.3	37.8
Veterans housing	0.5	0.4	0.5	−2.0	0.9	−1.2	−0.9	−0.4
Administration of justice	10.2	28.5	35.3	45.6	40.0	41.0	41.2	46.2
Federal law enforcement activities	4.8	12.1	15.7	19.1	19.9	20.0	19.6	24.9
Federal litigative and judicial activities	3.6	7.8	9.1	9.7	9.6	10.1	11.0	11.0
Federal correctional activities	1.3	3.7	5.4	5.5	5.9	6.2	6.3	6.2
Criminal justice assistance	0.5	4.9	5.1	11.3	4.6	4.8	4.3	4.1
General government	10.5	13.0	23.2	22.3	17.0	18.2	17.5	19.8
Net interest [1]	184.3	222.9	153.1	160.2	184.0	226.6	237.1	243.9
Interest on Treasury debt securities (gross)	264.7	361.9	318.1	321.7	352.3	405.9	430.0	459.2
Interest received by on-budget trust funds	−46.3	−69.3	−72.5	−67.8	−69.2	−71.6	−72.0	−83.5
Interest received by off-budget trust funds	−16.0	−59.8	−83.5	−86.2	−91.8	−97.7	−106.0	−114.3
Allowances	−	−	−	−	−	−	−	−
Undistributed offsetting receipts	−36.6	−42.6	−54.4	−58.5	−65.2	−68.3	−82.2	−87.7

− Represents or rounds to zero.   [1] Includes functions not shown separately.

Source: U.S. Office of Management and Budget, *Budget of the United States Government, Historical Tables,* annual. See Internet site <http://www.whitehouse.gov/omb/budget/fy2009/>.

Table 456. **Outlays for Payments for Individuals by Category and Major Program: 1990 to 2008**

[In billions of dollars (585.7 represents 585,700,000,000). For fiscal years ending September 30]

Category and Program	1990	2000	2003	2004	2005	2006	2007	2008, est.
Total, payments for individuals.....	**585.7**	**1,054.5**	**1,332.2**	**1,397.8**	**1,490.7**	**1,592.7**	**1,690.3**	**1,797.1**
Social security and railroad retirement.....	250.5	410.5	476.8	496.4	523.4	554.5	586.7	615.8
Social security:								
Old age and survivors insurance.....	221.9	351.4	400.2	414.8	434.0	457.7	483.3	506.1
Disability insurance.............	24.4	54.4	70.0	76.5	84.2	91.2	97.5	103.5
Railroad retirement (excl. social security).....................	4.1	4.6	6.6	5.2	5.3	5.6	5.8	6.2
Federal employees retirement and insurance......................	64.1	100.3	112.3	117.4	126.7	132.1	137.8	149.3
Military retirement	21.5	32.8	35.6	37.0	39.0	41.1	43.5	45.5
Civil service retirement	31.0	45.1	50.2	52.1	54.7	57.8	60.9	64.0
Veterans service-connected compensation	10.7	20.8	24.7	26.3	30.9	31.0	31.1	37.3
Other...............	0.8	1.7	1.8	2.0	2.2	2.2	2.4	2.6
Unemployment assistance	17.4	21.1	55.0	43.1	33.1	31.9	33.2	35.5
Medical care................	164.3	362.7	478.5	515.4	562.5	606.0	682.5	728.1
Medicare:								
Hospital insurance	65.9	127.9	151.3	164.1	182.8	183.9	205.0	226.6
Supplementary medical insurance....	41.5	87.2	121.8	131.8	151.0	191.7	230.1	233.3
State children's health insurance	–	1.2	4.4	4.6	5.1	5.5	6.0	7.6
Medicaid	41.1	117.9	160.7	176.2	181.7	180.6	190.6	203.8
Indian health.................	1.1	2.4	2.9	3.1	3.1	3.3	3.3	3.7
Hospital and medical care for veterans.................	12.0	19.3	24.5	21.6	23.1	24.4	30.5	35.5
Health resources and services	1.4	3.9	5.3	5.5	5.9	6.1	5.9	5.7
Substance abuse and mental health services	1.2	2.5	3.0	3.1	3.2	3.2	3.2	3.3
Health care tax credit	–	–	(Z)	0.1	0.1	0.1	0.1	0.1
Uniformed Services retiree health care fund	–	–	4.3	5.2	6.3	7.1	7.6	8.3
Other..................	(Z)	0.3	0.2	0.1	0.2	0.2	0.2	0.2
Assistance to students	11.2	10.9	22.8	25.7	32.1	51.7	31.0	31.4
Veterans education benefits...........	0.8	1.6	2.0	2.4	3.2	3.3	3.4	3.7
Student assistance, Department of Education and other	10.4	9.2	20.7	23.3	28.9	48.4	27.5	27.7
Housing assistance	15.9	24.1	29.7	30.8	31.8	32.1	33.0	33.6
Food and nutrition assistance	23.9	32.4	42.4	45.9	50.7	53.8	54.3	60.1
Food stamp program (including Puerto Rico)	15.9	18.3	25.3	28.6	32.6	34.6	34.9	38.8
Child nutrition and special milk programs	5.0	9.2	10.8	11.2	11.9	12.4	13.0	14.5
Supplemental feeding programs (WIC [1] and CSFP [2])	2.1	4.0	4.5	4.9	5.0	5.1	5.3	6.0
Commodity donations and other	0.8	0.9	1.7	1.2	1.2	1.7	1.1	0.9
Public assistance and related programs....	34.9	88.3	108.9	111.5	123.3	125.1	126.3	134.3
Supplemental security income program	11.5	29.5	30.4	31.2	35.3	34.3	32.8	38.2
Family support payments to states and TANF [3]	12.2	18.4	23.1	21.5	21.3	20.9	21.1	21.3
Low income home energy assistance ...	1.3	1.5	2.0	1.9	2.1	2.6	2.5	2.5
Earned income tax credit............	4.4	26.1	32.0	33.1	34.6	36.2	38.3	39.5
Legal services	0.3	0.3	0.3	0.3	0.3	0.3	0.3	0.4
Payments to states for daycare assistance	–	3.3	5.2	4.8	4.9	5.3	5.1	5.0
Veterans non-service-connected pensions.....................	3.6	3.0	3.2	3.3	3.7	3.5	3.4	3.9
Payments to states for foster care/adoption assistance	1.6	5.5	6.1	6.3	6.4	6.4	6.6	6.7
Payment where child credit exceeds tax liability.................	–	0.8	6.4	8.9	14.6	15.5	16.2	16.3
Other public assistance.............	–	–	–	–	(Z)	0.1	0.1	0.2
All other payments for individuals........	3.5	4.3	5.8	11.5	7.1	5.6	5.6	9.0
Coal miners and black lung benefits	1.5	1.0	0.8	0.8	0.7	0.7	0.6	0.6
Veterans insurance and burial benefits...	1.4	1.4	1.3	1.4	1.4	1.4	1.3	1.4
D.C. employee retirement	–	0.4	0.5	0.5	2.2	0.5	0.5	0.5
Aging services programs...........	–	0.9	1.3	1.3	1.4	1.4	1.4	1.4
Energy employees compensation fund....	–	–	0.3	0.3	0.6	0.9	1.0	0.9
September 11th victim compensation....	–	–	0.7	6.3	(Z)	(Z)	–	–
Refugee assistance and other	0.6	0.6	0.9	0.9	0.8	0.8	0.8	4.2

– Represents zero.   Z Less than $50,000,000.   [1] WIC means Women, Infants, and Children.   [2] CSFP means Commodity Supplemental Food Program.   [3] TANF means Temporary Assistance for Needy Families.

Source: U.S. Office of Management and Budget, *Budget of the United States Government, Historical Tables,* annual. See Internet site <http://www.whitehouse.gov/omb/budget/fy2009/>.

Table 457. **Federal Budget Receipts by Source: 1990 to 2008**

[In billions of dollars (1,032.1 represents $1,032,100,000,000). **For years ending September 30.** Receipts reflect collections. Covers both federal funds and trust funds; see text, this section]

Source	1990	2000	2003	2004	2005	2006	2007	2008, est.
Total federal receipts	**1,032.1**	**2,025.5**	**1,782.5**	**1,880.3**	**2,153.9**	**2,407.3**	**2,568.2**	**2,521.2**
Individual income taxes	466.9	1,004.5	793.7	809.0	927.2	1,043.9	1,163.5	1,219.7
Corporation income taxes	93.5	207.3	131.8	189.4	278.3	353.9	370.2	345.3
Social insurance and retirement receipts	380.0	652.9	713.0	733.4	794.1	837.8	869.6	910.1
Excise taxes	35.3	68.9	67.5	69.9	73.1	74.0	65.1	68.8
Other	56.3	92.0	76.6	78.7	81.1	97.6	99.8	−22.8
Social insurance and retirement receipts	**380.0**	**652.9**	**713.0**	**733.4**	**794.1**	**837.8**	**869.6**	**910.1**
Employment and general retirement	353.9	620.5	675.0	689.4	747.7	790.0	824.3	862.0
Old-age and survivors insurance (off-budget)	255.0	411.7	447.8	457.1	493.6	520.1	542.9	566.1
Disability insurance (off-budget)	26.6	68.9	76.0	77.6	83.8	88.3	92.2	96.1
Hospital insurance	68.6	135.5	147.2	150.6	166.1	177.4	184.9	195.5
Railroad retirement/pension fund	2.3	2.7	2.3	2.3	2.3	2.3	2.3	2.4
Unemployment insurance funds	21.6	27.6	33.4	39.5	42.0	43.4	41.1	43.4
Other retirement	4.5	4.8	4.6	4.6	4.5	4.4	4.3	4.7
Federal employees retirement— employee share	4.4	4.7	4.6	4.5	4.4	4.3	4.2	4.7
Excise taxes, total	**35.3**	**68.9**	**67.5**	**69.9**	**73.1**	**74.0**	**65.1**	**68.8**
Federal funds [1]	15.6	22.7	23.8	24.6	22.5	22.5	11.1	14.8
Alcohol	5.7	8.1	7.9	8.1	8.1	8.5	8.6	8.8
Tobacco	4.1	7.2	7.9	7.9	7.9	7.7	7.6	7.6
Telephone	3.0	5.7	5.8	6.0	6.0	4.9	−2.1	0.6
Transportation fuels	–	0.8	0.9	1.4	−0.8	−2.4	−3.3	−4.3
Trust funds [1]	19.8	46.2	43.7	45.3	50.5	51.5	54.0	54.0
Highway	13.9	35.0	33.7	34.7	37.9	38.5	39.4	39.2
Airport and airway	3.7	9.7	8.7	9.2	10.3	10.4	11.5	11.9
Black lung disability	0.7	0.5	0.5	0.6	0.6	0.6	0.6	0.6
Inland waterway	0.1	0.1	0.1	0.1	0.1	0.1	0.1	0.1
Oil spill liability	0.1	0.2	–	–	–	0.1	0.5	0.3
Aquatic resources	0.2	0.3	0.4	0.4	0.4	0.5	0.6	0.6
Tobacco assessments	–	–	–	–	0.9	0.9	0.9	1.0
Vaccine injury compensation	0.2	0.1	0.1	0.1	0.1	0.2	0.2	0.2

– Represents zero.   [1] Includes other funds, not shown separately.

Source: U.S. Office of Management and Budget, *Budget of the United States Government, Historical Tables,* annual. See Internet site <http://www.whitehouse.gov/omb/budget/fy2009/>.

Table 458. **Federal Trust Fund Income, Outlays, and Balances: 2007 to 2009**

[In billions of dollars (12.2 represents $12,200,000,000). **For years ending September 30.** Receipts deposited. Outlays on a checks-issued basis less refunds collected. Balances: That which have not been spent. See text, this section, for discussion of the budget concept and trust funds]

Description	Income			Outlays			Balances [1]		
	2007	2008, est.	2009, est.	2007	2008, est.	2009, est.	2007	2008, est.	2009, est.
Airport and airway trust fund	12.2	12.5	13.0	12.2	12.4	15.0	10.1	10.2	8.2
Federal civilian employees' retirement funds	91.2	97.4	101.5	78.9	65.0	67.6	716.8	749.2	783.2
Federal employees' health benefits fund	34.6	35.9	38.1	33.6	35.4	37.6	15.8	16.3	16.8
Foreign military sales trust fund	15.8	15.5	15.0	14.2	15.5	15.0	9.5	9.5	9.5
Highway trust fund	39.4	39.5	40.2	39.3	45.5	48.3	15.4	9.4	1.2
Medicare:									
Hospital insurance (HI) trust fund	223.9	237.4	244.7	207.6	229.6	244.7	311.0	314.6	324.2
Supplemental medical insurance trust fund	239.0	246.5	259.5	233.2	236.5	251.3	47.6	61.7	69.8
Military retirement fund	53.5	78.0	83.7	43.5	45.5	47.8	216.0	248.5	284.3
Railroad retirement trust funds	9.5	8.3	6.6	6.0	6.5	6.8	30.7	32.5	32.4
Social security: Old-age, survivors and disability insurance trust funds	772.8	808.4	854.2	586.2	615.3	649.4	2,180.8	2,373.9	2,578.6
Unemployment trust funds	45.1	47.8	49.9	36.3	38.5	41.0	75.4	84.8	93.7
Veterans' life insurance trust funds	1.2	1.1	1.1	1.6	1.6	1.6	11.8	11.3	10.8
Other trust funds	23.8	24.7	28.7	20.8	22.4	25.5	45.2	47.5	50.7

[1] Balances available on a cash basis (rather than an authorization basis) at the end of the year. Balances are primarily invested in federal debt securities.

Source: U.S. Office of Management and Budget, *Budget of the United States Government, Analytical Perspectives,* annual. See Internet site <http://www.whitehouse.gov/omb/budget/fy2009/>.

Table 459. Tax Expenditures Estimates Relating to Individual and Corporate Income Taxes by Selected Function: 2007 to 2010

[In millions of dollars (3,220 represents $3,220,000,000). For years ending September 30. Tax expenditures are defined as revenue losses attributable to provisions of the federal tax laws which allow a special exclusion, exemption, or deduction from gross income or which provide a special credit, a preferential rate of tax, or a deferral of liability]

Function and provision	2007	2008	2009	2010
National Defense:				
Exclusion of benefits and allowances to armed forces personnel	3,220	3,350	3,480	3,620
International affairs:				
Exclusion of income earned abroad by U.S. citizens	2,630	2,760	2,900	3,050
Extraterritorial income exclusion	4,400	1,630	–	–
Deferral of income from controlled foreign corporations (normal tax method)	12,490	13,120	13,780	14,480
Deferred taxes for financial firms on certain income earned overseas	2,370	2,490	1,060	–
General science, space, and technology:				
Expensing of research and experimentation expenditures (normal tax method)	5,190	4,720	4,990	4,470
Credit for increasing research activities	10,320	4,660	2,100	920
Energy:				
Alternative fuel production credit	2,920	1,310	70	80
Commerce and housing:				
Financial institutions and insurance:				
Exclusion of interest on life insurance savings	19,910	21,840	23,500	25,200
Housing:				
Deductibility of mortgage interest on owner-occupied homes	84,850	94,790	100,810	107,020
Deductibility of state and local property tax on owner-occupied homes	19,120	16,360	16,640	16,820
Capital gains exclusion on home sales	31,480	33,050	34,710	36,440
Exclusion of net imputed rental income	3,890	5,440	7,550	10,478
Exception from passive loss rules for $25,000 of rental loss	7,840	8,430	8,840	9,160
Credit for low-income housing investments	5,030	5,380	5,780	6,180
Accelerated depreciation on rental housing (normal tax method)	9,860	10,780	11,760	12,720
Commerce:				
Capital gains (except agriculture, timber, iron ore, and coal)	53,230	55,540	55,940	59,170
Step-up basis of capital gains at death	32,600	35,900	36,750	37,950
Accelerated depreciation of machinery and equipment (normal tax method)	26,410	35,180	44,120	49,760
Expensing of certain small investments (normal tax method)	3,660	3,660	3,400	500
Graduated corporation income tax rate (normal tax method)	5,400	5,220	5,290	5,510
Deduction for U.S. production activities	9,800	14,020	15,330	21,110
Transportation:				
Exclusion of reimbursed employee parking expenses	2,830	2,950	3,070	3,200
Education, training, employment, and social services:				
Education:				
HOPE tax credit	3,370	3,380	3,640	3,750
Lifetime Learning tax credit	2,210	2,220	2,340	2,420
Exclusion of interest on bonds for private nonprofit educational facilities	1,750	1,870	1,930	1,980
Parental personal exemption for students age 19 years or over	2,690	1,880	1,760	1,710
Deductibility of charitable contributions (education)	4,330	4,880	5,270	5,670
Training, employment, and social services:				
Child credit	30,910	30,160	29,950	29,870
Credit for child and dependent care expenses	2,780	1,810	1,720	1,650
Deductibility of charitable contributions, other than education and health	38,200	43,370	46,980	50,550
Health:				
Exclusion of employer contributions for medical insurance premiums [1]	133,790	151,810	168,460	185,250
Self-employed medical insurance premiums	4,260	4,680	5,170	5,710
Deductibility of medical expenses	4,470	5,060	5,920	6,800
Exclusion of interest on hospital construction bonds	2,760	2,950	3,040	3,120
Deductibility of charitable contributions (health)	4,310	4,890	5,300	5,700
Income security:				
Exclusion of workers' compensation benefits	5,740	5,830	5,920	6,010
Net exclusion of pension contributions and earnings:				
Employer plans	47,060	46,120	45,670	44,370
401(k) plans	46,000	49,000	51,000	55,000
Individual Retirement Accounts	9,500	10,800	11,700	12,200
Keogh plans	11,000	12,000	13,000	14,000
Exclusion of other employee benefits:				
Premiums on group term life insurance	2,100	2,170	2,250	2,290
Earned income tax credit	4,990	5,200	5,440	5,720
Social security:				
Exclusion of social security benefits:				
Social security benefits for retired workers	17,690	18,480	18,640	19,720
Social security benefits for disabled	5,050	5,540	5,810	6,150
Social security benefits for dependents and survivors	3,270	3,320	3,240	3,340
Veterans' benefits and services:				
Exclusion of veterans' death benefits and disability compensation	3,760	3,870	3,950	4,140
General purpose fiscal assistance:				
Exclusion of interest on public purpose state and local bonds	23,540	25,140	25,900	26,670
Deductibility of nonbusiness state and local taxes other than on owner-occupied homes	37,500	32,730	33,200	34,450
Addendum: Aid to state and local governments:				
Deductibility of:				
Property taxes on owner-occupied homes	19,120	16,360	16,640	16,820
Nonbusiness state and local taxes other than on owner-occupied homes	37,500	32,730	33,200	34,450
Exclusion of interest on state and local bonds for:				
Public purposes	23,540	25,140	25,900	26,670
Private nonprofit educational facilities	1,770	1,870	1,930	1,980
Hospital construction	2,760	2,950	3,040	3,120

– Represents zero. [1] Includes medical care.

Source: U.S. Office of Management and Budget, *Budget of the United States Government, Analytical Perspectives,* annual. See Internet site <http://www.whitehouse.gov/omb/budget/fy2009/>.

U.S. Census Bureau, Statistical Abstract of the United States: 2009

Table 460. **U.S. Savings Bonds: 1990 to 2007**

[In billions of dollars (122.5 represents $122,500,000,000), except percent. As of September 30]

Item	1990	1995	1999	2000	2001	2002	2003	2004	2005	2006	2007
Amounts outstanding, total [1] . . .	122.5	181.5	166.5	177.7	179.5	185.5	192.6	194.1	189.9	189.2	181.5
Sales	7.8	7.2	6.5	5.6	8.0	12.5	13.2	10.3	6.5	8.5	3.6
Accrued discounts	8.0	9.5	8.4	6.9	8.4	7.7	7.3	6.9	6.7	7.5	7.2
Redemptions [2]	7.5	11.8	16.6	14.5	13.8	12.5	12.2	14.6	13.8	16.0	10.8
Percent of total outstanding. . .	6.1	6.5	10.0	8.2	7.7	6.7	6.3	7.5	7.3	8.5	6.0

[1] Interest-bearing debt only for amounts at end of year.   [2] Matured and unmatured bonds.

Source: U.S. Department of the Treasury, Bureau of Public Debt. See Internet site <http://www.treasurydirect.gov/govt/reports/pd/pd_sbntables_downloadable_files.htm> (accessed January 2008).

Table 461. **Federal Funds—Summary Distribution by State: 2006**

[In millions of dollars (2,448,201 represents $2,448,201,000,000), except as indicated. For year ending Sept. 30. Data for grants, salaries and wages, and direct payments to individuals are on an expenditures basis; procurement data are on an obligation basis]

State and Island area	Federal funds		Agency		Object category			
	Total	Per capita [1] (dol.)	Defense	Non-defense	Direct payments	Procure-ment	Grants	Salaries and wages
United States [2]	**2,448,201**	**8,195**	**399,899**	**2,048,302**	**1,309,002**	**408,665**	**487,057**	**243,478**
Alabama.	43,934	9,571	9,526	34,408	24,403	8,329	7,515	3,686
Alaska	9,250	13,654	3,198	6,052	1,910	2,172	3,077	2,092
Arizona.	46,358	7,519	11,897	34,461	23,036	10,625	8,782	3,914
Arkansas	21,503	7,655	1,916	19,587	13,930	1,333	4,642	1,598
California	253,972	7,006	46,236	207,736	132,307	43,271	55,013	23,382
Colorado.	34,424	7,222	7,154	27,270	16,022	7,522	6,036	4,844
Connecticut.	30,609	8,756	8,533	22,076	15,062	8,368	5,431	1,749
Delaware	5,852	6,862	543	5,308	3,704	250	1,370	528
District of Columbia	40,360	68,938	6,040	34,320	4,797	14,225	4,177	17,161
Florida	142,749	7,905	19,157	123,592	94,155	14,830	22,496	11,269
Georgia	64,558	6,910	12,201	52,357	33,375	10,103	11,809	9,271
Hawaii	13,495	10,555	5,379	8,116	5,324	2,148	2,312	3,711
Idaho	9,950	6,797	714	9,236	5,267	1,715	2,006	964
Illinois	82,194	6,433	5,810	76,384	52,277	6,805	16,043	7,068
Indiana.	43,737	6,939	5,788	37,950	27,712	5,355	8,059	2,612
Iowa	21,830	7,344	1,408	20,422	14,593	1,972	3,952	1,312
Kansas.	21,520	7,809	3,409	18,111	12,803	2,755	3,355	2,607
Kentucky	37,607	8,945	8,074	29,533	19,517	7,298	6,929	3,863
Louisiana	69,409	16,357	6,878	62,531	34,197	9,534	22,843	2,836
Maine.	10,980	8,350	1,729	9,251	6,079	1,249	2,683	969
Maryland	68,661	12,256	14,640	54,021	26,773	21,804	8,837	11,247
Massachusetts.	57,552	8,944	10,088	47,464	29,698	10,930	13,170	3,755
Michigan.	67,332	6,665	4,986	62,346	44,742	5,853	12,907	3,830
Minnesota.	31,901	6,189	2,293	29,607	19,659	2,681	7,048	2,513
Mississippi	42,253	14,574	7,336	34,917	17,179	7,020	15,989	2,066
Missouri	52,258	8,952	11,685	40,573	27,999	11,112	8,593	4,555
Montana.	8,013	8,464	664	7,350	4,481	531	2,029	973
Nebraska	13,926	7,895	1,606	12,320	8,971	1,034	2,526	1,395
Nevada	14,603	5,859	1,866	12,738	8,261	2,274	2,573	1,495
New Hampshire	8,872	6,763	1,519	7,353	5,036	1,411	1,740	686
New Jersey.	61,270	7,070	7,768	53,502	37,084	8,403	11,298	4,483
New Mexico	20,945	10,784	2,366	18,579	8,048	6,030	4,659	2,209
New York	152,948	7,932	10,600	142,347	85,976	11,872	45,290	9,810
North Carolina	62,011	6,992	9,560	52,450	36,251	4,669	13,009	8,082
North Dakota.	6,312	9,903	741	5,571	3,662	429	1,415	806
Ohio	80,750	7,044	8,696	72,054	49,617	8,875	16,495	5,764
Oklahoma.	29,085	8,130	4,841	24,245	16,901	2,876	5,606	3,703
Oregon.	23,591	6,391	1,270	22,321	14,792	1,332	5,459	2,007
Pennsylvania.	103,243	8,324	10,389	92,855	65,316	10,849	20,175	6,904
Rhode Island.	8,764	8,255	1,006	7,758	5,082	601	2,236	844
South Carolina.	33,831	7,813	5,362	28,468	19,081	4,997	6,259	3,494
South Dakota	7,991	10,135	742	7,249	5,116	623	1,483	769
Tennessee	50,600	8,329	4,282	46,317	28,575	8,851	9,559	3,614
Texas	166,647	7,119	38,102	128,544	83,975	35,618	30,511	16,543
Utah	15,710	6,090	3,689	12,021	7,085	3,150	3,175	2,301
Vermont	5,274	8,496	933	4,341	2,567	870	1,368	470
Virginia.	103,062	13,489	44,601	58,461	36,309	41,915	7,589	17,248
Washington.	48,463	7,602	9,753	38,710	24,835	8,134	8,968	6,525
West Virginia	16,216	8,966	741	15,476	10,045	1,158	3,556	1,458
Wisconsin.	34,532	6,197	2,835	31,697	22,009	3,323	7,127	2,074
Wyoming	5,170	10,082	465	4,705	2,118	431	2,069	552

[1] Based on U.S. Census Bureau estimated resident population as of July 1.   [2] Includes Island areas not shown separately.

Source: U.S. Census Bureau, Consolidated Federal Federal Funds Report, 2006 (issued April 2008). See Internet site <http://www.census.gov/govs/www/cffr.html>.

Table 462. **Internal Revenue Gross Collections by Type of Tax: 2003 to 2007**

[1,953 represents $1,953,000,000,000. **For years ending September 30.** See text, this section, for information on taxes]

Type of tax	Gross collection (bil. dol.)					Percent of total				
	2003	2004	2005	2006	2007	2003	2004	2005	2006	2007
United States, total.	1,953	2,019	2,269	2,519	2,692	100.0	100.0	100.0	100.0	100.0
Individual income taxes.	987	990	1,108	1,236	1,366	50.5	49.1	48.8	49.1	50.8
Withheld by employers.	735	747	787	849	929	37.6	37.0	34.7	33.7	34.5
Employment taxes	696	717	771	815	850	35.6	35.5	34.0	32.4	31.6
Old-age and disability insurance . . .	685	706	760	803	838	35.1	35.0	33.5	31.9	31.1
Unemployment insurance.	7	7	7	8	7	0.3	0.3	0.3	0.3	0.3
Railroad retirement	4	4	5	5	5	0.2	0.2	0.2	0.2	0.2
Corporation income taxes	194	231	307	381	396	9.9	11.4	13.5	15.1	14.7
Estate and gift taxes.	23	26	26	29	27	1.2	1.3	1.1	1.1	1.0
Excise taxes	53	55	57	58	53	2.7	2.7	2.5	2.3	2.0

Source: U.S. Internal Revenue Service, *IRS Data Book,* annual, (Publication 55B).

Table 463. **Individual Income Tax Returns Filed—Examination Coverage: 1995 to 2007**

[114,683 represents 114,683,000. See the annual *IRS Data Book* (Publication 55B) for a detailed explanation]

Year	Returns filed [1] (1,000)	Returns examined		Total recommended additional tax [3] ($1,000)	Average recommended additional tax per return (dollars) [3]
		Total [2] (1,000)	Percent coverage		
1995	114,683	1,919	1.7	7,756,954	4,041
1996	116,060	1,942	1.7	7,600,191	3,915
1997	118,363	1,519	1.3	8,363,918	5,505
1998	120,342	1,193	1.0	6,095,698	5,110
1999	122,547	1,100	0.9	4,458,474	4,052
2000	124,887	618	0.5	3,388,905	5,486
2001	127,097	732	0.6	3,301,860	4,512
2002	129,445	744	0.6	3,636,486	4,889
2003	130,341	849	0.7	4,559,902	5,369
2004	130,134	997	0.8	6,201,693	6,220
2005	130,577	1,199	0.9	13,355,087	11,138
2006	132,276	1,284	1.0	13,045,221	10,160
2007	134,543	1,385	1.0	15,705,155	11,343

[1] Returns filed in previous calendar year.   [2] Includes taxpayer examinations by correspondence.   [3] For 1995 to 1997, amount includes associated penalties.

Source: U.S. Internal Revenue Service, *IRS Data Book,* annual, Publication 55B. See Internet site <http://www.irs.gov /taxstats/article/0,,id=102174,00.html>.

Table 464. **Federal Individual Income Tax Returns—Adjusted Gross Income, Taxable Income, and Total Income Tax: 2004 and 2005**

[132,226 represents 132,226,000. **For tax years.** Based on a sample of returns, see source and Appendix III]

Item	2004		2005		Percent change in amount, 2004–05
	Number of returns (1,000)	Amount (mil. dol.)	Number of returns (1,000)	Amount (mil. dol.)	
Adjusted gross income (less deficit).	132,226	6,788,805	134,373	7,422,496	9.3
Exemptions [1].	263,896	800,690	269,043	839,904	4.9
Taxable income	102,738	4,670,166	104,331	5,137,166	10.0
Total income tax.	89,102	831,976	90,593	934,836	12.4
Alternative minimum tax.	3,096	13,029	4,005	17,421	33.7

[1] The number of returns columns represent the number of exemptions.

Source: U.S. Internal Revenue Service, *Statistics of Income Bulletin,* Fall issues.

U.S. Census Bureau, Statistical Abstract of the United States: 2009

Table 465. Federal Individual Income Tax Returns—Adjusted Gross Income (AGI) by Selected Source of Income and Income Class: 2005

[In millions of dollars (7,422,496 represents $7,422,496,000,000), except as indicated. For the tax year. Minus sign (–) indicates net loss was greater than net income. Based on sample; see Appendix III]

Item	Total [1]	Under $10,000	$10,000 to $19,999	$20,000 to $29,999	$30,000 to $39,999	$40,000 to $49,999	$50,000 to $99,999	$100,000 and over
Number of all returns (1,000)	134,373	25,352	22,762	18,522	13,940	10,619	28,801	14,376
Adjusted gross income [2]	7,422,496	35,302	339,522	459,302	483,976	475,519	2,028,146	3,600,729
Salaries and wages	5,155,407	113,394	256,306	377,503	401,927	390,239	1,619,615	1,996,423
Interest received	162,433	9,107	8,460	7,555	6,669	6,637	29,140	94,865
Dividends in AGI	166,482	5,167	5,106	4,608	4,498	4,822	24,803	117,478
Business, profession, net profit less loss	269,701	5,418	23,334	17,390	14,776	12,604	56,717	139,462
Sales of property, [3] net gain less loss	671,678	6,570	2,044	2,660	3,280	4,942	31,516	620,666
Pensions and annuities in AGI. . .	420,145	9,516	35,619	37,367	36,810	36,406	151,999	112,427
Rents and royalties, net income less loss [4]	25,203	–3,561	–187	–506	–995	–557	221	30,786

[1] Includes a small number of returns with no adjusted gross income.   [2] Includes other sources, not shown separately.
[3] Includes sales of capital assets and other property; net gain less loss.   [4] Excludes rental passive losses disallowed in the computation of AGI; net income less loss.

Source: U.S. Internal Revenue Service, *Statistics of Income Bulletin*, Fall issues.

Table 466. Federal Individual Income Tax Returns—Total and Selected Sources of Adjusted Gross Income: 2004 and 2005

[132,226 represents 132,226,000. For tax years. Based on a sample of returns, see source and Appendix III. Minus sign (–) indicates decrease]

Item	2004 Number of returns (1,000)	2004 Amount (mil. dol.)	2005 Number of returns (1,000)	2005 Amount (mil. dol.)	Change in amount, 2004–05 Net change (mil. dol.)	Change in amount, 2004–05 Percent change
Adjusted gross income (less deficit) [1]	132,226	6,788,805	134,373	7,422,496	633,691	9.3
Salaries and wages	112,370	4,921,806	114,071	5,155,407	233,601	4.7
Taxable interest	57,606	125,474	59,249	162,433	36,959	29.5
Ordinary dividends.	30,687	146,839	31,175	166,482	19,643	13.4
Qualified dividends.	24,550	110,500	25,854	118,980	8,480	7.7
Business or profession net income (less loss). . .	20,252	247,217	21,057	269,701	22,484	9.1
Net capital gain.	25,267	473,662	26,196	668,015	194,354	41.0
Capital gain distributions [2]	10,733	15,336	13,393	35,581	20,245	132.0
Sales of property other than capital assets, net gain (less loss).	1,750	2,503	1,777	3,663	1,160	46.4
Sales of property other than capital assets, net gain	858	10,473	901	12,843	2,370	22.6
Taxable social security benefits	11,692	110,462	12,661	124,829	14,367	13.0
Total rental and royalty net income (less net loss) [3]	9,751	27,384	9,949	28,237	853	3.1
Partnership and S corporation net income (less loss)	7,236	315,993	7,531	402,327	86,334	27.3
Estate and trust net income (less loss)	543	14,001	529	16,484	2,483	17.7
Farm net income (less loss)	2,005	–13,239	1,981	–12,169	1,070	8.1
Farm net income	589	7,371	611	8,484	1,113	15.1
Unemployment compensation	9,095	32,740	7,888	27,857	–4,883	–14.9
Taxable pensions and annuities	23,123	394,286	23,247	420,145	25,859	6.6
Taxable Individual Retirement Account distributions	8,914	101,672	9,387	112,277	10,605	10.4
Other net income (less loss) [4]	(NA)	23,198	(NA)	26,863	3,666	15.8
Gambling earnings	1,709	23,313	1,809	24,884	1,570	6.7

NA Not available.   [1] Includes sources of income not shown separately.   [2] Includes both Schedule D and non-Schedule D capital gain distributions.   [3] Includes farm rental net income (less loss).   [4] Other net income (less loss) represents data reported on Form 1040, line 21, except net operating loss, the foreign-earned income exclusion, and gambling earnings.

Source: U.S. Internal Revenue Service, *Statistics of Income Bulletin,* Fall issues.

Table 467. Federal Individual Income Tax Returns—Net Capital Gains and Capital Gain Distributions from Mutual Funds: 1988 to 2005

[**14,309 represents 14,309,000.** For tax years. Based on a sample of returns, see source and Appendix III. Minus sign (–) indicates decrease]

Tax year	Net capital gain (less loss)				Capital gain distributions [2]			
	Number of returns (1,000)	Current dollars (mil. dol.)	Constant (1982–1984) dollars [1]		Number of returns (1,000)	Current dollars (mil. dol.)	Constant (1982–1984) dollars [1]	
			Amount (mil. dol.)	Percent change			Amount (mil. dol.)	Percent change
1988	14,309	153,768	129,981	(X)	4,274	3,879	3,279	(X)
1989	15,060	145,631	117,444	–9.6	5,191	5,483	4,422	34.9
1990	14,288	114,231	87,400	–25.6	5,069	3,905	2,988	–32.4
1991	15,009	102,776	75,460	–13.7	5,796	4,665	3,425	14.6
1992	16,491	118,230	84,269	11.7	5,917	7,426	5,293	54.5
1993	18,409	144,172	99,773	18.4	9,998	11,995	8,301	56.8
1994	18,823	142,288	96,011	–3.8	9,803	11,322	7,640	–8.0
1995	19,963	170,415	111,821	16.5	10,744	14,391	9,443	23.6
1996	22,065	251,817	160,495	43.5	12,778	24,722	15,757	66.9
1997	24,240	356,083	221,859	38.2	14,969	45,132	28,120	78.5
1998	25,690	446,084	273,671	23.4	16,070	46,147	28,311	0.7
1999	27,701	542,758	325,785	19.0	17,012	59,473	35,698	26.1
2000	29,521	630,542	366,169	12.4	17,546	79,079	45,923	28.6
2001	25,956	326,527	184,375	–49.6	12,216	13,609	7,685	–83.3
2002	24,189	238,789	132,734	–28.0	7,567	5,343	2,970	–61.4
2003	22,985	294,354	159,975	20.5	7,265	4,695	2,552	–14.1
2004	25,267	473,662	250,747	56.7	10,733	15,336	8,119	218.1
2005	26,196	668,015	342,046	36.4	13,393	35,581	18,219	124.4

X Not applicable.   [1] Constant dollars were calculated using the U.S. Bureau of Labor Statistics consumer price index for urban consumers (CPI-U, 1982–84 = 100). See Table 703.   [2] Capital gain distributions are included in net capital gain (less loss). For 1988–1996, and 1999 and later years, capital gain distributions from mutual funds are the sum of the amounts reported on the Form 1040 and Schedule D. For 1997 and 1998, capital gain distributions were reported entirely on the Schedule D.

Source: U.S. Internal Revenue Service, *Statistics of Income Bulletin,* Fall issues.

Table 468. Alternative Minimum Tax: 1986 to 2005

[**609 represents 609,000.** For tax years. Based on a sample of returns, see source and Appendix III]

Tax year	Highest statutory alternative minimum tax rate (percent)	Alternative minimum tax		Tax year	Highest statutory alternative minimum tax rate (percent)	Alternative minimum tax	
		Number of returns (1,000)	Amount (mil. dol.)			Number of returns (1,000)	Amount (mil. dol.)
1986	20	609	6,713	1996	28	478	2,813
1987	21	140	1,675	1997	28	618	4,005
1988	21	114	1,028	1998	[1]28	853	5,015
1989	21	117	831	1999	[1]28	1,018	6,478
1990	21	132	830	2000	[1]28	1,304	9,601
1991	24	244	1,213	2001	[1]28	1,120	6,757
1992	24	287	1,357	2002	[1]28	1,911	6,854
1993	28	335	2,053	2003	[1]28	2,358	9,470
1994	28	369	2,212	2004	[1]28	3,096	13,029
1995	28	414	2,291	2005	[1]28	4,005	17,421

[1] Top rate on most long-term capital gains was 20 percent; beginning 2003, the rate was 15 percent.

Source: U.S. Internal Revenue Service, *Statistics of Income Bulletin,* Fall 2007, volume 27, no. 2. See also <http://www.irs.gov /taxstats/index.html>.

Table 469. Federal Individual Income Tax Returns—Sources of Net Losses Included in Adjusted Gross Income: 2003 to 2005

[4,973 represents 4,973,000. For tax years. Based on a sample of returns, see source and Appendix III]

Item	2003 Number of returns (1,000)	2003 Amount (mil. dol.)	2004 Number of returns (1,000)	2004 Amount (mil. dol.)	2005 Number of returns (1,000)	2005 Amount (mil. dol.)
Total net losses	(NA)	279,243	(NA)	303,458	(NA)	319,587
Business or profession net loss.	4,973	38,927	5,194	43,007	5,308	45,016
Net capital loss [1]	12,808	28,952	11,513	25,492	10,023	22,137
Net loss, sales of property other than capital assets.	955	8,469	892	7,971	877	9,180
Total rental and royalty net loss.	[2]4,242	33,453	4,380	38,466	4,554	43,988
Partnership and S corporation net loss. . . .	2,553	78,972	2,498	82,697	2,539	89,694
Estate and trust net loss	33	1,084	36	1,436	36	1,654
Farm net loss	1,405	19,844	1,416	20,610	1,371	20,653
Net operating loss [3]	712	62,825	830	75,012	863	79,452
Other net loss [4]	290	6,718	359	8,768	346	7,811

NA Not available. [1] Includes only the portion of capital losses allowable in the calculation of adjusted gross income. Only $3,000 of net capital loss per return ($1,500 for married filing separately) are allowed to be included in negative total income. Any excess is carried forward to future years. [2] Includes farm rental net loss. [3] Net operating loss is a carryover of the loss from a business when taxable income from a prior year was less than zero. [4] Other net loss represents losses reported on Form 1040, line 21, except net operating loss and the foreign-earned income exclusion.

Source: U.S. Internal Revenue Service, *Statistics of Income Bulletin,* Fall issues.

Table 470. Federal Individual Income Tax Returns—Number, Income Tax, and Average Tax by Size of Adjusted Gross Income: 2000 and 2005

[129,374 represents 129,374,000. Based on sample of returns; see Appendix III]

Size of adjusted gross income	Number of returns (1,000) 2000	Number of returns (1,000) 2005	Adjusted gross income (AGI) (bil. dol.) 2000	Adjusted gross income (AGI) (bil. dol.) 2005	Income tax total [1] (bil. dol.) 2000	Income tax total [1] (bil. dol.) 2005	Tax as percent of AGI (for taxable returns only) 2000	Tax as percent of AGI (for taxable returns only) 2005	Average tax (for taxable returns only) (dol.) 2000	Average tax (for taxable returns only) (dol.) 2005
Total	129,374	134,373	6,365	7,422	981	935	16	14	10,129	10,319
Less than $1,000 [2]	2,966	3,502	−58	−84	−	−	2	(X)	648	1,703
$1,000 to $2,999	5,385	4,846	11	10	−	−	7	4	134	77
$3,000 to $4,999	5,599	4,889	22	20	−	−	4	3	179	129
$5,000 to $6,999	5,183	4,879	31	29	1	−	5	2	297	112
$7,000 to $8,999	4,972	4,851	40	39	1	−	4	3	331	228
$9,000 to $10,999	5,089	4,745	51	47	1	1	5	2	470	241
$11,000 to $12,999.	4,859	4,743	58	57	2	1	6	3	704	390
$13,000 to $14,999	4,810	4,532	67	64	3	1	6	4	883	539
$15,000 to $16,999	4,785	4,612	76	74	3	2	7	4	1,052	715
$17,000 to $18,999	4,633	4,368	83	79	4	2	7	5	1,279	863
$19,000 to $21,999	6,502	6,289	133	129	7	4	8	5	1,565	1,080
$22,000 to $24,999	5,735	5,642	135	132	8	5	8	6	1,815	1,423
$25,000 to $29,999	8,369	8,738	229	240	16	11	8	7	2,248	1,828
$30,000 to $39,999	13,548	13,940	471	484	40	27	9	7	3,094	2,457
$40,000 to $49,999	10,412	10,619	466	476	46	33	10	8	4,462	3,526
$50,000 to $74,999	17,076	18,351	1,045	1,128	116	93	11	9	6,824	5,307
$75,000 to $99,999	8,597	10,450	738	900	100	86	14	10	11,631	8,324
$100,000 to $199,999 . . .	8,083	10,810	1,066	1,431	184	189	17	13	22,783	17,597
$200,000 to $499,999. . .	2,136	2,738	614	789	146	159	24	20	68,628	58,339
$500,000 to $999,999 . . .	396	525	269	355	76	85	28	24	192,092	161,826
$1,000,000 or more	240	304	817	1,026	226	236	28	23	945,172	777,496

− Represents or rounds to zero. (X) Not available. [1] Consists of income tax after credits (including alternative minimum tax). [2] In addition to low income taxpayers, this size class (and others) includes taxpayers with "tax preferences," not reflected in adjusted gross income or taxable income which are subject to the "alternative minimum tax" (included in total income tax).

Source: U.S. Internal Revenue Service, *Statistics of Income Bulletin,* quarterly and Fall issues.

Table 471. **Federal Individual Income Tax Returns—Selected Itemized Deductions and the Standard Deduction: 2004 and 2005**

[**46,335 represents 46,335,000.** For tax years. Based on a sample of returns, see source and Appendix III. Minus sign (–) indicates decrease]

Item	2004		2005		Percent change, 2004–05	
	Number of returns [1] (1,000)	Amount (mil. dol.)	Number of returns [1] (1,000)	Amount (mil. dol.)	Number of returns [1]	Amount
Total itemized deductions before limitation	46,335	1,035,000	47,755	1,167,135	3.1	12.8
Medical and dental expenses after 7.5 percent AGI limitation [2] . . .	9,531	61,503	9,917	67,354	4.1	9.5
Taxes paid [2] . . .	46,009	362,609	47,353	400,390	2.9	10.4
State and local income taxes	33,516	202,306	34,570	227,581	3.1	12.5
State and local general sales taxes	11,249	17,527	11,423	17,271	1.6	–1.5
Interest paid [3] . . .	38,110	356,356	39,016	405,718	2.4	13.9
Home mortgage interest.	37,692	340,476	38,575	383,733	2.3	12.7
Charitable contributions.	40,623	165,564	41,381	183,391	1.9	10.8
Other than cash contributions	25,267	43,373	25,371	48,057	0.4	10.8
Casualty and theft losses.	185	3,510	814	14,984	339.4	326.9
Miscellaneous deductions after 2 percent AGI limitation. .	12,025	68,533	12,407	76,183	3.2	11.2
Total unlimited miscellaneous deductions	1,457	16,925	1,522	19,114	4.4	12.9
Itemized deductions in excess of limitation	5,724	36,762	6,323	45,324	10.5	23.3
Total itemized deductions after limitation	46,335	998,238	47,755	1,121,811	3.1	12.4
Total standard deduction	84,017	560,933	84,841	580,748	1.0	3.5
Total deductions (after itemized deduction limitation).	130,352	1,559,171	132,597	1,702,559	1.7	9.2

[1] Returns with no adjusted gross income are excluded from the deduction counts. For this reason, the sum of the number of returns with total itemized deductions and the number of returns with total standard deduction is less than the total number of returns for all filers. [2] Includes real estate taxes, personal property taxes, and other taxes not shown separately. [3] Includes investment interest and deductible mortgage "points" not shown separately.

Source: U.S. Internal Revenue Service, *Statistics of Income Bulletin,* Fall issues.

Table 472. **Federal Individual Income Tax Returns—Statutory Adjustments: 2004 and 2005**

[**32,154 represents 32,154,000.** For tax years. Based on a sample of returns, see source and Appendix III]

Item	2004		2005		Percent change in amount, 2004–05
	Number of returns (1,000)	Amount (mil. dol.)	Number of returns [1] (1,000)	Amount (mil. dol.)	
Total statutory adjustments	32,154	98,047	33,591	109,397	11.6
Payments to an Individual Retirement Account	3,331	10,029	3,256	12,003	19.7
Educator expenses deduction.	3,402	858	3,504	878	2.3
Moving expenses adjustment	1,096	2,952	1,134	3,077	4.2
Student loan interest deduction.	7,527	4,399	8,073	5,053	14.9
Tuition and fees deduction	4,710	10,589	4,696	10,847	2.4
Self-employment tax deduction	15,920	21,109	16,695	22,734	7.7
Self-employment health insurance deduction	3,884	18,457	3,901	19,646	6.4
Payments to a self-employed retirement (Keogh) plan. . .	1,201	19,296	1,257	21,268	10.2
Forfeited interest penalty	780	210	806	266	26.7
Alimony paid	574	8,470	588	8,954	5.7
Other adjustment [1]	(NA)	1,234	(NA)	1,515	22.8

NA Not available. [1] Includes foreign housing adjustment, Medical Savings Accounts deduction, certain business expenses of reservists, performing artists, etc., and other adjustments. For 2004, other adjustments include these plus the health savings account deduction (90,857 returns totaling $190.7 million).

Source: U.S. Internal Revenue Service, *Statistics of Income Bulletin,* Fall issues.

U.S. Census Bureau, Statistical Abstract of the United States: 2009

Table 473. Federal Individual Income Tax Returns—Itemized Deductions and Statutory Adjustments by Size of Adjusted Gross Income: 2005

[47,775 represents 47,775,000. Based on a sample of returns; see Appendix III]

Item	Unit	Total	Under $10,000	$10,000 to $19,999	$20,000 to $29,999	$30,000 to $39,999	$40,000 to $49,999	$50,000 to $99,999	$100,000 and over
Returns with itemized deductions:									
Number of returns [1,2]	1,000	47,755	951	2,425	3,562	4,363	4,631	18,803	13,020
Amount [1,2]	Mil. dol.	1,121,811	13,524	33,982	50,443	63,750	71,017	354,741	534,354
Medical and dental expenses:[3]									
Returns	1,000	9,917	606	1,423	1,506	1,381	1,199	3,030	772
Amount	Mil. dol.	67,354	4,621	10,594	9,439	8,317	6,417	18,795	9,171
Taxes paid:									
Returns [2]	1,000	47,353	901	2,345	3,487	4,291	4,588	18,743	12,999
Amount, total	Mil. dol.	400,390	2,511	6,087	9,926	14,149	18,141	108,930	240,645
State and local income taxes:[4]									
Returns	1,000	45,994	790	2,160	3,315	4,123	4,447	18,329	12,831
Amount	Mil. dol.	244,852	557	1,535	3,580	5,902	8,332	57,159	167,788
Real estate taxes:									
Returns	1,000	41,311	689	1,754	2,630	3,382	3,794	16,828	12,234
Amount	Mil. dol.	144,702	1,819	4,220	5,778	7,517	8,939	47,833	68,596
Interest paid:									
Returns	1,000	39,016	589	1,464	2,438	3,283	3,675	16,199	11,367
Amount	Mil. dol.	405,718	4,750	10,905	17,890	24,619	28,513	146,289	172,751
Home mortgage interest:									
Returns	1,000	38,575	581	1,444	2,416	3,257	3,655	16,094	11,127
Amount	Mil. dol.	383,733	4,689	10,745	17,656	24,328	28,151	144,477	153,687
Charitable contributions:									
Returns	1,000	41,381	601	1,743	2,738	3,470	3,839	16,688	12,301
Amount	Mil. dol.	183,391	681	2,978	5,403	7,290	8,474	45,288	113,276
Unreimbursed employee business expenses:									
Returns	1,000	15,920	87	466	1,058	1,535	1,708	7,056	4,010
Amount	Mil. dol.	75,824	298	2,085	5,061	7,483	8,068	30,184	22,645
Returns with statutory adjustments:									
Number of returns [2]	1,000	33,591	4,277	4,200	3,550	3,202	2,924	9,367	6,071
Amount of adjustments	Mil. dol.	109,397	5,745	6,066	6,219	6,366	6,700	25,846	52,453
Payments to IRAs:[4]									
Returns	1,000	3,256	93	240	359	416	399	1,091	658
Amount	Mil. dol.	12,003	228	673	1,021	1,274	1,398	4,101	3,308
Deduction for self-employment tax:									
Returns	1,000	16,695	3,174	2,740	1,682	1,318	1,123	3,639	3,018
Amount	Mil. dol.	22,734	1,318	2,061	1,666	1,489	1,292	5,347	9,560
Self-employment health insurance:									
Returns	1,000	3,901	418	379	384	314	267	940	1,200
Amount	Mil. dol.	19,646	1,339	1,252	1,383	1,369	1,129	4,578	8,596
Payments to Keogh plans:									
Returns	1,000	1,257	25	26	36	50	57	292	770
Amount	Mil. dol.	21,268	106	152	192	310	352	2,676	17,480

[1] After limitations. [2] Includes other deductions and adjustments, not shown separately. [3] Before limitation. [4] State and local taxes include income taxes and sales taxes.

Source: U.S. Internal Revenue Service, *Statistics of Income Bulletin,* Fall issues.

Table 474. Federal Individual Income Tax Returns—Selected Tax Credits: 2003 to 2005

[41,091 represents 41,091,000. For tax years. Based on a sample of returns, see source and Appendix III]

Item	2003 Number of returns (1,000)	2003 Amount (mil. dol.)	2004 Number of returns (1,000)	2004 Amount (mil. dol.)	2005 Number of returns (1,000)	2005 Amount (mil. dol.)
Total tax credits [1]	**41,091**	**41,996**	**41,694**	**52,367**	**42,246**	**55,316**
Child care credit	6,313	3,207	6,317	3,338	6,501	3,462
Earned income credit [2]	3,606	926	2,975	768	2,896	745
Foreign tax credit	4,145	5,806	4,700	6,758	5,398	9,362
General business credit	263	613	249	635	251	878
Minimum tax credit	251	917	275	902	290	1,081
Child tax credit [3]	25,672	22,788	25,989	32,300	25,951	32,048
Education credits	7,298	5,843	7,181	6,017	7,057	6,120
Retirement savings contribution credit	5,297	1,034	5,289	1,012	5,294	945

[1] Includes credits not shown separately. [2] Represents portion of earned income credit used to offset income tax before credits. [3] Excludes refundable portion.

Source: U.S. Internal Revenue Service, *Statistics of Income Bulletin,* Fall issues.

Table 475. **Federal Individual Income Tax Returns by State: 2005**

[**135,258 represents 135,258,000. For tax year.** Data will not agree with data in other tables due to differing survey methodology used to derive state data]

State	Total number of returns (1,000)	Adjusted gross income (mil. dol.) Total [1]	Adjusted gross income (mil. dol.) Salaries and wages	Adjusted gross income (mil. dol.) Net capital gain [2]	Itemized deductions (mil. dol.) Total	Itemized deductions (mil. dol.) State and local income tax	Itemized deductions (mil. dol.) Real estate taxes	Itemized deductions (mil. dol.) Mortgage interest paid	Income tax (mil. dol.)
U.S....	135,258	7,364,640	5,161,583	625,706	1,136,072	230,092	145,630	413,969	938,184
AL.......	1,956	88,629	63,539	5,443	11,757	1,938	496	4,076	9,843
AK.......	347	16,726	12,048	815	1,562	20	257	781	2,077
AZ.......	2,474	135,510	90,065	14,784	21,333	3,156	1,650	9,244	16,445
AR.......	1,154	47,857	34,474	2,693	5,922	1,336	271	1,735	5,035
CA.......	15,573	970,449	657,968	101,693	195,483	45,920	20,710	82,532	128,916
CO.......	2,160	125,994	86,642	12,301	20,628	3,581	1,641	9,623	16,043
CT.......	1,682	132,285	90,532	13,765	20,595	5,699	3,764	6,890	21,504
DE.......	403	23,184	16,198	1,843	3,183	784	241	1,304	2,963
DC.......	282	19,713	12,991	2,238	3,639	1,140	236	1,203	2,986
FL.......	8,411	481,888	282,439	72,956	66,737	2,066	9,437	25,757	67,204
GA.......	3,918	199,215	146,048	14,743	33,878	6,856	3,044	12,637	23,638
HI.......	621	31,284	21,257	2,945	4,839	1,115	240	2,178	3,564
ID.......	614	28,226	19,048	2,758	4,453	930	410	1,613	3,056
IL.......	5,836	335,321	237,471	27,199	47,062	6,622	8,914	17,557	44,693
IN.......	2,884	134,325	100,471	6,517	16,573	3,503	1,729	6,611	14,852
IA.......	1,347	61,644	44,832	2,766	7,764	1,819	865	2,323	6,448
KS.......	1,242	60,484	43,670	3,336	7,920	1,749	877	2,402	6,978
KY.......	1,780	77,640	57,074	4,027	10,295	2,824	800	3,399	8,216
LA.......	1,770	77,629	55,831	4,432	13,599	1,541	328	2,555	8,444
ME.......	621	27,764	19,459	1,959	3,882	1,028	561	1,277	2,900
MD.......	2,674	170,125	123,428	11,532	33,514	9,131	3,435	12,308	21,782
MA.......	3,083	206,949	142,671	20,940	31,804	8,141	4,859	11,538	29,464
MI.......	4,563	226,439	166,561	10,674	33,571	5,729	5,176	13,035	26,291
MN.......	2,446	137,232	99,347	8,849	22,497	5,787	2,388	8,704	16,734
MS.......	1,170	45,340	33,583	2,116	7,929	922	313	1,617	4,348
MO.......	2,611	122,775	89,110	6,549	16,657	3,516	1,696	5,639	14,006
MT.......	448	18,315	11,861	1,698	2,589	583	259	860	1,893
NE.......	816	37,831	27,507	2,318	5,196	1,122	703	1,526	4,163
NV.......	1,150	72,209	43,902	11,417	11,291	387	920	5,220	10,105
NH.......	650	37,534	27,055	3,172	4,886	396	1,204	2,051	4,783
NJ.......	4,153	282,306	207,235	18,492	49,805	12,036	11,220	15,798	40,681
NM.......	843	35,786	25,130	2,227	4,384	853	317	1,747	3,871
NY.......	8,716	552,244	375,355	58,164	96,608	32,171	14,750	24,747	80,375
NC.......	3,880	186,048	134,484	11,503	29,906	7,452	2,532	11,057	20,701
ND.......	307	12,970	9,171	603	1,113	150	157	311	1,390
OH.......	5,460	252,435	187,390	11,446	35,828	9,987	4,581	12,063	28,271
OK.......	1,496	66,783	46,205	4,104	8,822	2,036	592	2,560	7,730
OR.......	1,645	81,024	54,996	6,379	15,027	4,136	1,677	5,542	8,945
PA.......	5,867	299,494	215,042	19,395	38,990	9,408	6,479	12,802	36,863
RI.......	502	26,529	19,055	1,751	4,216	971	723	1,485	3,243
SC.......	1,885	84,322	59,833	5,630	12,845	2,748	980	4,420	8,995
SD.......	367	16,166	10,565	1,281	1,363	36	161	455	1,878
TN.......	2,658	123,252	90,643	8,391	13,595	337	1,230	5,211	14,520
TX.......	9,728	507,165	365,232	39,790	55,603	858	10,502	19,161	67,483
UT.......	1,031	51,061	36,347	3,991	9,186	1,786	635	3,356	5,449
VT.......	310	14,704	10,032	1,370	1,860	422	362	623	1,616
VA.......	3,541	214,672	154,584	15,707	34,585	7,520	3,869	14,317	27,708
WA.......	2,932	168,673	115,630	16,080	23,524	527	3,279	11,270	21,463
WV.......	754	30,318	22,366	1,289	2,508	666	142	835	3,071
WI.......	2,656	132,137	96,572	7,635	19,994	5,096	3,606	6,309	15,028
WY.......	248	14,299	8,358	2,318	1,335	62	87	477	1,952
Other [3]	1,594	61,737	60,276	9,679	3,937	1,493	325	1,229	7,577

[1] Includes other items, not shown separately. [2] Less loss. [3] Includes returns filed from Army Post Office and Fleet Post Office addresses by members of the armed forces stationed overseas; returns by other U.S. citizens abroad; and returns filed by residents of Puerto Rico with income from sources outside of Puerto Rico or with income earned as U.S. government employees.

Source: U.S. Internal Revenue Service, *Statistics of Income Bulletin*, Spring issues.

Table 476. Federal Individual Income Tax—Tax Liability and Effective and Marginal Tax Rates for Selected Income Groups: 2000 to 2007

[Refers to income after exclusions but before deductions for itemized or standard deductions and for personal exemptions. Tax liability is after reductions for tax credits. As a result of the tax credits, tax liability can be negative, which means that the taxpayer receives a payment from the government. The effective rate represents tax liability, which may be negative as a result of the tax credits, divided by stated income. The marginal tax rate is the percentage of the first additional dollar of income which would be paid in income tax. Tax credits which increase with income can result in negative marginal tax rates. Computations assume itemized deductions (in excess of floors) of 18 percent of adjusted gross income or the standard deduction, whichever is greater. All income is assumed to be from wages and salaries. Does not include social security and Medicare taxes imposed on most wages and salaries]

Adjusted gross income	2000	2003	2004	2005	2006	2007[1]
TAX LIABILITY (dol.)						
Single person, no dependents:						
$5,000	[2]-353	[2]-382	[2]-383	[2]-383	[2]-383	[1,2]-683
$10,000	[2]391	[2]126	[2]91	[2]46	[2]-7	[1,2]-373
$20,000	1,920	1,480	1,450	1,405	1,355	[1]696
$30,000	3,270	2,883	2,868	2,845	2,818	[1]2,189
$40,000	4,988	4,248	4,163	4,075	4,048	[1]3,419
$50,000	7,284	6,298	6,213	6,115	5,983	[1]5,224
$75,000	13,024	11,423	11,338	11,240	11,108	[1]10,349
$100,000	19,233	16,852	16,719	16,571	16,368	16,119
Married couple, two dependents, with one spouse working:						
$5,000	[2]-2,000	[2]-2,000	[2]-2,000	[2]-2,000	[2]-2,000	[1,2]-3,200
$10,000	[2]-3,888	[2]-4,000	[2]-4,000	[2]-4,000	[2]-4,000	[1,2]-5,200
$20,000	[2,3]-2,349	[2,4]-4,044	[2,4]-4,643	[2,4]-4,986	[2,4]-5,169	[1,2,4]-6,604
$30,000	[2,3]475	[2,3,4]-2,158	[2,3,4]-2,359	[2,3,4]-2,810	[2,3,4]-3,108	[1,2,3,4]-4,690
$40,000	[3]2,218	[3]45	[3,4]-30	[3,4]-150	[3,4]-280	[1,3,4]-2,228
$50,000	[3]3,470	[3]1,545	[3]1,470	[3]1,350	[3]1,200	[1,3]-728
$75,000	[3]7,384	[3]4,695	[3]4,650	[3]4,575	[3]4,490	[1,3]2,603
$100,000	[3]13,124	[3]9,070	[3]8,875	[3]8,630	[3]8,315	[1,3]6,148
EFFECTIVE RATE (percent)						
Single person, no dependents:						
$5,000	[2]-7.1	[2]-7.6	[2]-7.7	[2]-7.7	[2]-7.7	[1,2]-13.7
$10,000	[2]3.9	[2]1.3	[2]0.9	[2]0.5	[2]-0.1	[1,2]-3.7
$20,000	9.6	7.4	7.3	7	6.8	[2]3.5
$30,000	10.9	9.6	9.6	9.5	9.4	[2]7.3
$40,000	12.5	10.6	10.4	10.2	10.1	[2]8.5
$50,000	14.6	12.6	12.4	12.2	12.0	[2]10.4
$75,000	17.4	15.2	15.1	15	14.8	[2]13.8
$100,000	19.2	16.9	16.7	16.6	16.4	16.1
Married couple, two dependents, with one spouse working:						
$5,000	[2]-40.0	[2]-40.0	[2]-40.0	[2]-40.0	[2]-40.0	[1,2]-64.0
$10,000	[2]-38.9	[2]-40.0	[2]-40.0	[2]-40.0	[2]-39.3	[1,2]-52.0
$20,000	[2,3]-11.7	[2,4]-20.2	[2,4]-23.2	[2,4]-24.9	[2,4]-21.2	[1,2,4]-33.0
$30,000	[2,3]1.6	[2,3,4]-7.2	[2,3,4]-7.9	[2,3,4]-9.4	[2,3,4]-4.3	[1,2,3,4]-15.6
$40,000	[3]5.5	[3]0.1	[3,4]-0.1	[3,4]-0.5	[3,4]1.6	[1,3,4]-5.6
$50,000	[3]6.9	[3]3.1	[3]2.9	[3]2.7	[3]4.2	[1,3]-1.7
$75,000	[3]9.8	[3]6.3	[3]6.2	[3]6.1	[3]6.9	[1,3]3.5
$100,000	[3]13.1	[3]9.1	[3]8.9	[3]8.6	[3]10.4	[1,3]6.1
MARGINAL TAX RATE (percent)						
Single person, no dependents:						
$5,000	–	–	[2]-7.7	[2]-7.7	[2]-7.7	[2]-7.7
$10,000	[2]22.7	[2]17.7	[2]17.7	[2]17.7	[2]17.7	[2]17.7
$20,000	15.0	15.0	15.0	15.0	15.0	15.0
$30,000	15.0	15.0	15.0	15.0	15.0	15.0
$40,000	28.0	25.0	25.0	15.0	15.0	15.0
$50,000	28.0	25.0	25.0	25.0	25.0	25.0
$75,000	28.0	25.0	25.0	25.0	25.0	[2]30.0
$100,000	31.0	28.0	28.0	28.0	28.0	28.0
Married couple, two dependents, with one spouse working:						
$5,000	[2]-40.0	[2]-40.0	[2]-40.0	[2]-40.0	[2]-40.0	[2]-40.0
$10,000	–	[2]-40.0	[2]-40.0	[2]-40.0	[2]-40.0	[2]-40.0
$20,000	[2,3]21.1	[2,4]11.1	[2,4]6.1	[2,4]6.1	[2,4]6.1	[2,4]6.1
$30,000	[2]36.1	[2,3,4]31.1	[2,3,4]31.1	[2,3,4]31.1	[2,3,4]31.1	[2,3,4]31.1
$40,000	15.0	15.0	[3,4]15.0	[3,4]15.0	[3,4]15.0	[3,4]15.0
$50,000	15.0	15.0	15.0	15.0	15.0	15.0
$75,000	28.0	15.0	15.0	15.0	15.0	15.0
$100,000	28.0	25.0	25.0	25.0	25.0	25.0

– Represents zero.   [1] Includes effect of the Recovery Rebate paid in 2008 under the Economic Stimulus Act of 2008 (P.L. 110-185).   [2] Includes effect from the refundable earned income credit.   [3] Includes effect from the child tax credit.   [4] Includes effect from the additional (refundable) child tax credit.

Source: U.S. Department of the Treasury, Office of Tax Analysis, unpublished data.

Table 477. Federal Individual Income Tax—Current Income Equivalent to 2000 Constant Income for Selected Income Groups: 2000 to 2007

[Constant 2000 incomes calculated by using the U.S. Bureau of Labor Statistics Consumer Price Index for Urban Consumers (CPI-U); see Table 703, Section 14. See also headnote, Table 476]

Adjusted gross income Constant 2000 dollars	2000	2003	2004	2005	2006	2007[1]
REAL INCOME EQUIVALENT (dol.)						
$5,000	5,000	5,340	5,480	5,670	5,850	6,020
$10,000	10,000	10,690	10,970	11,340	11,710	12,040
$20,000	20,000	21,370	21,940	22,680	23,410	24,080
$30,000	30,000	32,060	32,910	34,020	35,120	36,120
$40,000	40,000	42,740	43,880	45,370	46,830	48,160
$50,000	50,000	53,430	54,850	56,710	58,540	60,200
$75,000	75,000	80,140	82,270	85,060	87,800	90,310
$100,000	100,000	106,850	109,700	113,410	117,070	120,410
TAX LIABILITY (dol.) Single person, no dependents:						
$5,000	[2]−353	[2]−382	[2]−390	[2]−399	[2]−412	[1,2]−728
$10,000	[2]391	[2]248	[2]262	[2]283	[2]295	[1,2]−42
$20,000	1,920	1,686	1,741	1,807	1,867	[1]1,308
$30,000	3,270	3,136	3,225	3,339	3,447	[1]2,942
$40,000	4,988	4,809	4,958	5,166	5,333	[1]4,847
$50,000	7,284	7,001	7,207	7,491	7,733	[1]7,315
$75,000	13,024	12,476	12,828	13,302	13,732	14,087
$100,000	19,233	18,425	18,946	19,649	20,287	20,805
Married couple, 2 dependents with one spouse working:						
$5,000	[2]−2,000	[2]−2,136	[2]−2,192	[2]−2,268	[2]−2,340	[1,2]−3,608
$10,000	[2]−3,888	[2,4]−4,223	[2,4]−4,333	[2,4]−4,451	[2,4]−4,598	[1,2]−5,960
$20,000	[2,3]−2,349	[2,4]−3,893	[2,4]−4,525	[2,4]−4,823	[2,4]−4,963	[1,2,4]−6,357
$30,000	[2,3]475	[2,3,4]−1,518	[2,3,4]−1,456	[2,3,4]−1,561	[2,3,4]−1,518	[1,2,3,4]−3,371
$40,000	[3]2,218	[3]456	[3]552	[3]656	[3]745	[1,3,4]−1,004
$50,000	[3]3,470	[3]2,042	[3]2,172	[3]2,325	[3]2,465	[1,3]782
$75,000	[3]7,384	[3]5,327	[3]5,544	[3]5,812	[3]6,064	[1,3]4,486
$100,000	[3]13,124	[3]10,474	[3]10,864	[3]11,579	[3]12,214	[1,3]10,882
EFFECTIVE TAX RATE (percent) Single person, no dependents:						
$5,000	[2]−7.1	[2]−7.1	[2]−7.1	[2]−7.0	[2]−7.0	[1,2]−12.1
$10,000	[2]3.9	[2]2.3	[2]2.4	[2]2.5	[2]2.5	[1,2]−0.3
$20,000	9.6	7.9	7.9	8.0	8.0	[4]5.4
$30,000	10.9	9.8	9.8	9.8	9.8	[4]8.1
$40,000	12.5	11.3	11.3	11.4	11.4	[4]10.1
$50,000	14.6	13.1	13.1	13.2	13.2	[4]12.2
$75,000	17.4	15.6	15.6	15.6	15.6	15.6
$100,000	19.2	17.2	17.3	17.3	17.3	17.3
Married couple, 2 dependents with one spouse working:						
$5,000	[2]−40.0	[2]−40.0	[2]−40.0	[2]−40.0	[2]−40.0	[1,2]−59.9
$10,000	[2]−38.9	[2,4]−39.5	[2,4]−39.5	[2,4]−39.3	[2,4]−39.3	[1,2]−49.5
$20,000	[2,3]−11.7	[2,4]−18.2	[2,4]−20.6	[2,4]−21.3	[2,4]−21.2	[1,2,4]−26.4
$30,000	[2,3]1.6	[2,3,4]−4.7	[2,3,4]−4.4	[2,3,4]−4.6	[2,3,4]−4.2	[1,2,3,4]−9.3
$40,000	[3]5.5	[3]1.1	[3]1.3	[3]1.4	[3]1.6	[1,3,4]−2.1
$50,000	[3]6.9	[3]3.8	[3]4.0	[3]4.1	[3]4.2	[1,3]1.3
$75,000	[3]9.8	[3]6.6	[3]6.7	[3]6.8	[3]6.9	[1,3]5.0
$100,000	[3]13.1	[3]9.8	[3]9.9	[3]10.2	[3]10.4	[1,3]9.0
MARGINAL TAX RATE (percent) Single person, no dependents:						
$5,000	−	−	−	−	−	−
$10,000	[2]22.7	[2]17.7	[2]17.7	[2]17.7	[2]17.7	[1,2]7.7
$20,000	15.0	15.0	15.0	15.0	15.0	15.0
$30,000	15.0	15.0	15.0	15.0	15.0	15.0
$40,000	28.0	25.0	25.0	25.0	25.0	25.0
$50,000	28.0	25.0	25.0	25.0	25.0	25.0
$75,000	28.0	25.0	25.0	25.0	25.0	25.0
$100,000	31.0	28.0	28.0	28.0	28.0	28.0
Married couple, 2 dependents with one spouse working:						
$5,000	[2]−40.0	[2]−40.0	[2]−40.0	[2]−40.0	[2]−40.0	[1]−40.0
$10,000	−	[4]−10.0	[4]−15.0	[4]−15.0	[4]−15.0	[3]−15.0
$20,000	[2,3]21.1	[2,4]11.1	[2,4]6.1	[2,4]6.1	[2,4]6.1	[2,4]6.1
$30,000	[2]36.1	[2,3,4]31.1	[2,3,4]31.1	[2,3,4]31.1	[2,3,4]31.1	[1,2,3,4]31.1
$40,000	15.0	15.0	15.0	15.0	15.0	15.0
$50,000	15.0	15.0	15.0	15.0	15.0	15.0
$75,000	28.0	15.0	15.0	15.0	15.0	15.0
$100,000	28.0	25.0	25.0	[3]30.1	[3]30.1	[3]30.1

− Represents zero. [1] Includes effect of the Recovery Rebate paid in 2008 under the Economic Stimulus Act of 2008 (P.L. 110-185). [2] Includes effect from the refundable earned income credit. [3] Includes effect from the child tax credit. [4] Includes effect from the additional (refundable) child tax credit.

Source: U.S. Department of the Treasury, Office of Tax Analysis, unpublished data.

U.S. Census Bureau, Statistical Abstract of the United States: 2009

Table 478. Federal Civilian Employment and Annual Payroll by Branch: 1970 to 2007

[2,997 represents 2,997,000. For fiscal year ending in year shown. See text, Section 8. Includes employees in U.S. territories and foreign countries. Data represent employees in active-duty status, including intermittent employees. Annual employment figures are averages of monthly figures. Excludes Central Intelligence Agency, National Security Agency, and, as of November 1984, the Defense Intelligence Agency; and as of October 1996, the National Imagery and Mapping Agency]

Year	Employment						Payroll (mil. dol.)				
	Total (1,000)	Percent of U.S. em- ployed [1]	Executive (1,000)		Legis- lative (1,000)	Judicial (1,000)	Total	Executive		Legis- lative	Judicial
			Total	Defense				Total	Defense		
1970 . . .	[2]2,997	3.81	2,961	1,263	29	7	27,322	26,894	11,264	338	89
1980 . . .	[2]2,987	3.01	2,933	971	40	14	58,012	56,841	18,795	883	288
1985 . . .	3,001	2.80	2,944	1,080	39	18	80,599	78,992	28,330	1,098	509
1990 . . .	[2]3,233	2.72	3,173	1,060	38	23	99,138	97,022	31,990	1,329	787
1995 . . .	2,943	2.36	2,880	852	34	28	118,304	115,328	31,753	1,598	1,379
2000 . . .	[2]2,879	2.10	2,816	681	31	32	130,832	127,472	29,607	1,619	1,741
2001 . . .	2,704	1.97	2,641	672	30	33	131,964	128,502	28,594	1,682	1,780
2002 . . .	2,699	1.98	2,635	671	31	34	136,611	132,893	28,845	1,781	1,938
2003 . . .	2,743	1.99	2,677	669	31	34	143,380	139,506	29,029	1,908	1,966
2004 . . .	2,714	1.95	2,649	668	30	34	148,037	144,134	29,128	1,977	1,927
2005 . . .	2,709	1.91	2,645	671	30	34	152,222	148,275	29,331	2,048	1,900
2006 . . .	2,700	1.87	2,636	676	30	34	160,570	156,543	29,580	2,109	1,918
2007 . . .	2,695	1.85	2,632	674	30	34	161,394	157,010	29,025	2,119	2,265

[1] Civilian employed only. See Table 567, Section 12.   [2] Includes temporary census workers.

Source: U.S. Office of Personnel Management, *Federal Civilian Workforce Statistics—Employment and Trends*, bimonthly; and unpublished data. See internet site <http://www.opm.gov/feddata>.

Table 479. Full-Time Federal Civilian Employment—Employees and Average Pay by Pay System: 2000 to 2007

[As of March 31 (1,671 represents 1,671,000). Excludes employees of Congress and federal courts, maritime seamen of U.S. Department of Commerce, and small number for whom rates were not reported. See text, this section, for explanation of general schedule and wage system]

Pay system	Employees (1,000)				Average annual pay (dol.)			
	2000	2005	2006	2007	2000	2005	2006	2007
Total, excluding postal . . .	**1,671**	**1,754**	**1,740**	**1,845**	**50,429**	**63,058**	**65,253**	**65,825**
General Schedule	1,216	1,248	1,243	1,330	49,428	62,076	64,305	65,856
Wage system	205	186	185	200	37,082	43,907	45,522	46,317
Other	250	320	312	315	66,248	78,003	80,756	78,134
Postal pay system [1]	788	705	696	685	37,627	45,123	46,807	48,752

[1] Source: Career employees—U.S. Postal Service, *Annual Report of the Postmaster General*. See also <http://www.usps .com/financials/cspo/welcome.htm>; Average pay—U.S. Postal Service, *Comprehensive Statement of Postal Operations,* annual.

Source: Except as noted, U.S. Office of Personnel Management, "Pay Structure of the Federal Civil Service," annual (publication discontinued); and unpublished data. See Internet site <http://www.opm.gov/feddata/>.

Table 480. Paid Civilian Employment in the Federal Government by State: 2000 and 2006

[As of December 31. In thousands (2,766 represents 2,766,000). Excludes Central Intelligence Agency, Defense Intelligence Agency, seasonal and on-call employees, and National Security Agency]

State	2000	2006	State	2000	2006	State	2000	2006
U.S. [1] . . .	**2,766**	**1,793**	KY	30	22	OH	84	46
AL	48	37	LA	33	20	OK	43	35
AK	14	12	ME	13	10	OR	29	20
AZ	43	37	MD	130	112	PA	107	66
AR	20	14	MA	53	27	RI	10	6
CA	248	151	MI	58	26	SC	26	19
CO	51	36	MN	34	16	SD	9	8
CT	21	8	MS	24	19	TN	50	26
DE	5	3	MO	54	34	TX	162	122
DC	181	143	MT	11	10	UT	30	28
FL	113	79	NE	15	10	VT	6	4
GA	89	70	NV	13	10	VA	145	131
HI	23	22	NH	8	4	WA	62	50
ID	11	9	NJ	62	29	WV	18	17
IL	94	47	NM	25	24	WI	30	13
IN	37	21	NY	134	66	WY	6	5
IA	18	9	NC	57	37			
KS	25	16	ND	8	6			

[1] Includes employees outside the United States and in states not specified, not shown separately.

Source: U.S. Office of Personnel Management, "Employment by Geographic Area," biennial, (publication discontinued); and unpublished data. See Internet site: <http://www.opm.gov/feddata/>.

Table 481. **Federal Civilian Employment by Branch and Agency: 1990 to 2007**

[**For years ending September 30. Annual averages of monthly figures.** Excludes Central Intelligence Agency, National Security Agency; the Defense Intelligence Agency; and, as of October 1996, the National Imagery and Mapping Agency]

Agency	1990	1995	2000	2005	2006	2007
Total, all agencies	**3,128,267**	**2,920,277**	**2,708,101**	**2,708,753**	**2,700,007**	**2,694,929**
Legislative Branch	37,495	33,367	31,157	30,303	30,067	29,573
Judicial Branch	23,605	28,993	32,186	33,690	33,834	32,921
Executive Branch	3,067,167	2,857,917	2,644,758	2,644,764	2,636,106	2,632,435
Executive Office of the President	1,731	1,573	1,658	1,736	1,709	1,719
Executive Departments	2,065,542	1,782,834	1,592,200	1,689,914	1,689,351	1,696,893
State	25,288	24,859	27,983	33,808	33,968	34,657
Treasury	158,655	155,951	143,508	114,194	112,000	111,577
Defense	1,034,152	832,352	676,268	670,790	676,452	673,722
Justice	83,932	103,262	125,970	105,102	106,159	106,946
Interior	77,679	76,439	73,818	73,599	71,593	70,256
Agriculture [1]	122,594	113,321	104,466	104,989	101,887	99,629
Commerce [1]	69,920	36,803	47,652	38,927	40,335	40,163
Labor	17,727	16,204	16,040	15,599	15,434	15,855
Health & Human Services [2]	123,959	59,788	62,605	60,944	60,756	61,217
Housing & Urban Development	13,596	11,822	10,319	10,086	9,814	9,718
Transportation [3]	67,364	63,552	63,598	55,975	53,573	53,536
Energy	17,731	19,589	15,692	15,050	14,838	14,696
Education	4,771	4,988	4,734	4,429	4,257	4,146
Veterans Affairs	248,174	263,904	219,547	236,363	236,938	245,537
Homeland Security [3]	(X)	(X)	(X)	149,977	151,771	155,397
Independent agencies [4]	999,894	1,073,510	1,050,900	953,113	945,046	933,833
Board of Governors Federal Reserve System . .	1,525	1,704	2,372	1,851	1,869	1,874
Environmental Protection Agency	17,123	17,910	18,036	17,964	18,166	19,153
Equal Employment Opportunity Commission . . .	2,880	2,796	2,780	2,421	2,285	2,191
Federal Communications Commission	1,778	2,116	1,965	1,936	1,857	1,827
Federal Deposit Insurance Corporation	17,641	14,765	6,958	4,998	4,583	4,573
Federal Trade Commission	988	996	1,019	1,046	1,027	1,094
General Services Administration	20,277	16,500	14,334	12,685	12,460	12,099
National Archives & Records Administration . . .	3,120	2,833	2,702	3,048	3,051	2,973
National Aeronautics & Space Administration . .	24,872	21,635	18,819	19,105	18,448	19,378
National Labor Relations Board	2,263	2,050	2,054	1,822	1,832	1,772
National Science Foundation	1,318	1,292	1,247	1,325	1,325	1,356
Nuclear Regulatory Commission	3,353	3,212	2,858	3,230	3,297	3,609
Office of Personnel Management	6,636	4,354	3,780	4,333	4,954	5,291
Peace Corps	1,178	1,179	1,065	1,064	1,075	1,077
Railroad Retirement Board	1,772	1,544	1,176	1,010	1,004	990
Securities & Exchange Commission	2,302	2,852	2,955	3,933	3,760	3,534
Small Business Administration	5,128	5,085	4,150	4,288	6,148	4,234
Smithsonian Institution	5,092	5,444	5,065	4,981	4,953	5,008
Social Security Administration [2]	(X)	66,850	64,474	65,861	64,884	62,769
Tennessee Valley Authority	28,392	16,545	13,145	12,721	12,624	12,293
U.S. Information Agency	8,555	7,480	2,436	2,212	2,144	2,046
U.S. International Development Cooperation Agency	4,698	3,755	2,552	2,644	2,723	2,761
U.S. Postal Service	816,886	845,393	860,726	767,972	760,039	753,254

X Not applicable.   [1] Includes enumerators for the 1990 and 2000 census.   [2] Sizeable changes in 1995 due to the Social Security Administration which was separated from the Department of Health and Human Services to become an independent agency effective April 1995.   [3] See text, Section 10, concerning the development of the Department of Homeland Security.   [4] Includes agencies with fewer than 1,000 employees in 2005, not shown separately.

Source: U.S. Office of Personnel Management, *Federal Civilian Workforce Statistics—Employment and Trends,* bimonthly. See Internet site <http://www.opm.gov/feddata/>.

Table 482. **Federal Employees—Summary Characteristics: 1990 to 2005**

[**As of September 30. In percent, except as indicated.** For civilian employees, excluding U.S. Postal Service employees]

Characteristic	1990	1995	1999	2000	2001	2002	2003	2004	2005
Average age (years) [1]	42.3	44.3	45.9	46.3	46.5	46.5	46.7	46.8	46.9
Average length of service (years)	13.4	15.5	16.9	17.1	17.1	16.8	16.8	16.6	16.4
Retirement eligible: [2]									
Civil Service Retirement System	8	10	15	17	19	23	27	30	33
Federal Employees Retirement System. . . .	3	5	10	11	10	11	12	13	13
Bachelor's degree or higher	35	39	40	41	41	41	41	42	43
Sex: Male	57	56	55	55	55	55	55	56	56
Female	43	44	45	45	45	45	45	44	44
Race and national origin:									
Total minorities	27.4	28.9	30.0	30.4	30.6	30.8	31.1	31.4	31.7
Black	16.7	16.8	17.0	17.1	17.1	17.0	17.0	17.0	17.0
Hispanic	5.4	5.9	6.5	6.6	6.7	6.9	7.1	7.3	7.4
Asian/Pacific Islander	3.5	4.2	4.5	4.5	4.6	4.7	4.8	5.0	5.1
American Indian/Alaska Native	1.8	2.0	2.2	2.2	2.2	2.2	2.1	2.1	2.1
Disabled	7.0	7.0	7.0	7.0	7.0	7.0	7.0	7.0	7.0
Veterans preference	30.0	26.0	25.0	24.0	24.0	23.0	22.0	22.0	22.0
Vietnam era veterans	17.0	17.0	14.0	14.0	13.0	13.0	13.0	12.0	11.0
Retired military	4.9	4.2	3.9	3.9	4.2	4.4	4.6	4.9	5.4
Retired officers	0.5	0.5	0.5	0.5	0.6	0.7	0.8	0.9	1.0

[1] For full-time permanent employees.   [2] Represents full-time permanent employees under the Civil Service Retirement System (excluding hires since January 1984), and the Federal Employees Retirement System (since January 1984).

Source: U.S. Office of Personnel Management, Office of Workforce Information, *The Fact Book, Federal Civilian Workforce Statistics,* annual. See Internet site <http://www.opm.gov/feddata/>.

Table 483. Federal Executive Branch (Nonpostal) Employment by Race and National Origin: 1990 to 2006

[As of Sept. 30. Covers total employment for only Executive branch agencies participating in OPM's Central Personnel Data File (CPDF). For information on the CPDF, see <http://www.opm.gov/feddata/acpdf.pdf>]

Pay system	1990	1995	2000	2004	2005	2006
All personnel [1]	**2,150,359**	**1,960,577**	**1,755,689**	**1,851,349**	**1,856,966**	**1,848,339**
White, non-Hispanic	1,562,846	1,394,690	1,224,836	1,270,366	1,267,922	1,254,308
General schedule and related	1,218,188	1,101,108	961,261	972,737	973,767	948,740
Grades 1 to 4	132,028	79,195	55,067	48,798	46,671	43,450
Grades 5 to 8	337,453	288,755	239,128	231,765	227,387	219,168
Grades 9 to 12	510,261	465,908	404,649	405,825	408,111	399,400
Grades 13 to 15	238,446	267,250	262,417	286,349	291,598	286,722
Total executive/senior pay levels	9,337	13,307	14,332	16,337	16,409	16,118
Wage pay system	244,220	186,184	146,075	134,821	135,383	133,942
Other pay systems	91,101	94,091	103,168	146,471	142,363	155,508
Black	356,867	327,302	298,701	313,099	315,644	317,697
General schedule and related	272,657	258,586	241,135	244,736	246,691	246,248
Grades 1 to 4	65,077	41,381	26,895	20,797	19,774	18,326
Grades 5 to 8	114,993	112,962	99,937	95,798	94,655	93,717
Grades 9 to 12	74,985	79,795	82,809	88,813	90,809	91,869
Grades 13 to 15	17,602	24,448	31,494	39,328	41,453	42,336
Total executive/senior pay levels	479	942	1,180	1,238	1,270	1,218
Wage pay system	72,755	55,637	42,590	37,798	37,666	37,378
Other pay systems	10,976	12,137	13,796	29,327	30,017	32,853
Hispanic	115,170	115,964	115,247	135,533	138,507	138,596
General schedule and related	83,218	86,762	89,911	102,612	104,927	105,236
Grades 1 to 4	15,738	11,081	8,526	7,969	7,768	6,854
Grades 5 to 8	28,727	31,152	31,703	34,380	33,653	33,834
Grades 9 to 12	31,615	34,056	36,813	43,868	46,268	46,951
Grades 13 to 15	7,138	10,473	12,869	16,395	17,238	17,597
Total executive/senior pay levels	154	382	547	656	682	699
Wage pay system	26,947	22,128	16,926	15,915	15,945	15,822
Other pay systems	4,851	6,692	7,863	16,350	16,953	16,839
American Indian, Alaska Native, Asian, and Pacific Islander	115,476	122,621	116,905	132,351	134,893	136,593
General schedule and related	81,499	86,768	86,074	96,014	97,866	97,870
Grades 1 to 4	15,286	11,854	9,340	8,528	8,357	7,877
Grades 5 to 8	24,960	26,580	25,691	27,601	27,417	26,986
Grades 9 to 12	31,346	33,810	33,167	37,172	38,276	38,492
Grades 13 to 15	9,907	14,524	17,876	22,713	23,816	24,515
Total executive/senior pay levels	148	331	504	760	804	873
Wage pay system	24,927	21,553	17,613	16,760	16,938	16,728
Other pay systems	8,902	13,969	12,714	18,817	19,285	21,122

[1] Beginning 2006, includes persons classified as multiracial, not shown separately.

Source: U.S. Office of Personnel Management, Central Personnel Data File.

Table 484. Area of Federally Owned Buildings in the United States by State: 2006

[3,322.8 represents 3,322,800,000. As of September 30. For executive branch agencies]

State	Total building area (mil. sq. ft)	Owned building area (mil. sq. ft)	Leased building area (mil. sq. ft.)	State	Total building area (mil. sq. ft)	Owned building area (mil. sq. ft)	Leased building area (mil. sq. ft.)
U.S. [2]	**3,322.8**	**2,820.4**	**394.5**	MO	61.9	49.5	10.0
				MT	19.1	15.5	2.9
AL	60.2	51.3	5.5	NE	17.3	13.3	2.9
AK	57.3	51.2	5.7	NV	34.2	30.7	2.9
AZ	63.4	57.9	4.5	NH	5.8	3.7	1.3
AR	25.8	20.3	2.6	NJ	62.4	50.9	9.3
CA	385.0	351.0	30.2	NM	64.3	57.5	5.4
CO	64.3	55.3	8.5	NY	130.6	105.8	19.9
CT	21.4	17.8	1.9	NC	93.4	83.7	7.4
DE	6.8	5.6	0.5	ND	24.1	20.8	1.7
DC	98.5	74.5	23.4	OH	82.1	71.1	8.5
FL	137.4	116.8	17.4	OK	68.4	57.5	8.7
GA	121.2	106.7	12.9	OR	28.7	22.0	4.4
HI	62.2	60.3	1.3	PA	94.7	79.7	12.3
ID	23.0	19.1	3.1	RI	15.2	14.0	0.7
IL	91.3	79.1	8.7	SC	20.9	57.1	3.5
IN	50.7	36.5	11.8	SD	62.7	16.1	3.4
IA	18.7	12.8	2.9	TN	77.9	68.5	6.2
KS	39.3	33.1	4.6	TX	218.1	186.3	28.7
KY	56.1	50.1	4.2	UT	36.6	30.3	4.3
LA	54.2	41.3	6.2	VT	4.8	2.9	1.3
ME	15.0	12.7	1.4	VA	183.6	151.9	30.4
MD	136.7	111.7	22.8	WA	94.5	85.0	8.0
MA	45.4	37.5	5.4	WV	23.9	18.5	3.7
MI	41.5	29.9	7.7	WI	30.0	22.6	4.7
MN	30.0	21.9	3.6	WY	15.8	13.8	1.0
MS	46.5	37.3	3.9				

[1] Includes otherwised managed square feet, not shown separately. [2] Includes location not reported, not shown separately.

Source: U.S. General Services Administration, Federal Real Property Council, "Federal Real Property Report", July 2007 (revised since issued).

Section 10
National Security and Veterans Affairs

This section displays data for national security (national defense and homeland security) and benefits for veterans. Data are presented on national defense and its human and financial costs; active and reserve military personnel; and federally sponsored programs and benefits for veterans, and funding, budget and selected agencies for homeland security. The principal sources of these data are the annual *Selected Manpower Statistics* and the *Atlas/Data Abstract for the United States and Selected Areas* issued by the Office of the Secretary of Defense; *Annual Report of Secretary of Veterans Affairs*, U.S. Department of Veterans Affairs (VA), *Budget in Brief*, U.S. Department of Homeland Security; and *The Budget of the United States Government,* Office of Management and Budget. For more data on expenditures and personnel, see Section 30.

Department of Defense (DoD)—The U.S. Department of Defense is responsible for providing the military forces of the United States. It includes the Office of the Secretary of Defense, the Joint Chiefs of Staff, the Army, the Navy, the Air Force, and the defense agencies. The President serves as Commander-in-Chief of the Armed Forces; from him, the authority flows to the Secretary of Defense and through the Joint Chiefs of Staff to the commanders of unified and specified commands (e.g., U.S. Strategic Command).

Reserve components—The Reserve Components of the Armed Forces consist of the Army National Guard of the United States, Army Reserve, Naval Reserve, Marine Corps Reserve, Air National Guard, Air Force Reserve, and Coast Guard Reserve. They provide trained personnel and units available for active duty in the Armed Forces during times of war or national emergency, and at such other times as national security may require. The National Guard has dual federal/state responsibilities and uses jointly provided equipment, facilities, and budget support. The President is empowered to mobilize

the National Guard and to use such of the Armed Forces as he considers necessary to enforce federal authority in any state. There is in each Armed Force a ready reserve, a standby reserve, and a retired reserve. The Ready Reserve includes the Selected Reserve, which provides trained and ready units and individuals to augment the active forces during times of war or national emergency, or at other times when required; and the Individual Ready Reserve, which is a manpower pool that can be called to active duty during times of war or national emergency and would normally be used as individual fillers for active, guard, and reserve units, and as a source of combat replacements. Most of the Ready Reserve serves in an active status. See Table 499 for Standby Reserve and Retired Reserve detail.

Department of Veterans Affairs (VA)—A veteran is someone 18 years and older (there are a few 17-year-old veterans) who is not currently on active duty, but who once served on active duty in the United States Army, Navy, Air Force, Marine Corps, or Coast Guard, or who served in the Merchant Marine during World War II. There are many groups whose active service makes them veterans including: those who incurred a service-connected disability during active duty for training in the Reserves or National Guard, even though that service would not otherwise have counted for veteran status; members of a national guard or reserve component who have been ordered to active duty by order of the President or who have a full-time military job. The latter are called AGRs (Active Guard and Reserve). No one who has received a dishonorable discharge is a veteran.

The VA administers laws authorizing benefits for eligible former and present members of the Armed Forces and for the beneficiaries of deceased members. Veterans' benefits available under various acts of Congress include compensation for

U.S. Census Bureau, Statistical Abstract of the United States: 2009

service-connected disability or death; pensions for non-service-connected disability or death; vocational rehabilitation, education and training; home loan insurance; life insurance; health care; special housing and automobiles or other conveyances for certain disabled veterans; burial and plot allowances; and educational assistance to families of deceased or totally disabled veterans, servicemen missing in action, or prisoners of war. Since these benefits are legislated by Congress, the dates they were enacted and the dates they apply to veterans may be different from the actual dates the conflicts occurred. VA estimates of veterans cover all persons discharged from active U.S. military service under conditions other than dishonorable.

Homeland Security—In an effort to increase homeland security following the September 11, 2001, terrorist attacks on the United States, President George W. Bush issued the *National Strategy for Homeland Security* in July 2002 and signed legislation creating the Department of Homeland Security (DHS) in November 2002.

The *National Strategy* sets forth a plan to improve homeland security through 43 initiatives that fall within six critical mission areas. These mission areas are intelligence and warning, border and transportation security, domestic counterterrorism, protection of critical infrastructure, defense against catastrophic terrorism, and emergency preparedness and response.

The funding and activities of homeland security are not only carried out by DHS, but also by other federal agencies, state, and local entities. In addition to DHS, there are 32 other federal agencies that comprise federal homeland security funding. DHS, along with four other agencies—Department of Defense (DoD), Energy (DoE), Health and Human Services (HHS), and Justice (DoJ)—account for most of the federal spending for homeland security.

Department of Homeland Security (DHS)—The mission of DHS is to lead a unified effort to secure the United States. This effort is to prevent and deter terrorist attacks and to protect against and respond to threats and hazards to the nation. This effort is to ensure safe and secure borders, to welcome lawful immigrants and visitors, and to promote the free flow of commerce.

The creation of DHS, which began operations in March 2003, represents a fusion of 22 federal agencies (legacy agencies) to coordinate and centralize the leadership of many homeland security activities under a single department. Out of these agencies, the Secret Service and Coast Guard remain intact and report directly to the Secretary. Immigration and Naturalization Services (INS) adjudications and benefits programs report directly to the Deputy Secretary as the U.S. Citizenship and Immigration Services (USCIS).

The Customs and Border Protection (CBP) is responsible for managing, securing, and controlling U.S. borders. This includes carrying out traditional border-related responsibilities, such as stemming the tide of illegal drugs and illegal aliens; securing and facilitating legitimate global trade and travel; and protecting the food supply and agriculture industry from pests and disease. CBP is composed of the Border Patrol and Inspections (both moved from INS) along with Customs (absorbed from the U.S. Department of Treasury) and Animal and Plant Health Inspections Services (absorbed from the U.S. Department of Agriculture).

Immigration and Customs Enforcement (ICE) is the largest investigation arm of DHS. ICE is composed of four law enforcement divisions: Investigations, Intelligence, Federal Protective Service, and Apprehension, Detention, and Removal. ICE investigates a wide range of national security, financial and smuggling violations including drug smuggling, human trafficking, illegal arms exports, financial crimes, commercial fraud, human smuggling, document fraud, money laundering, child pornography/exploitation, and immigration fraud.

The Transportation Security Administration (TSA) was created as part of the Aviation and Transportation Security Act on November 19, 2001. TSA was originally part of the U.S. Department of Transportation, but was moved to DHS. TSA's mission is to provide security to our nation's transportation systems with a primary focus on aviation security.

Figure 10.1
Department of Defense Manpower: 2007
(In thousands)

Total[1] = 1,380

Air Force
333

Army
522

Marines
186

Navy
338

[1]Includes National Guard, Reserve, and retired regular personnel on extended or continuous active duty.
Excludes Coast Guard.

Source: Chart prepared by U.S. Census Bureau. For data, see Table 494.

Figure 10.2
Living Veterans by Age: 2007
(In thousands)

Total = 23,816

Under 35 years old
1,900

35–39 years old
1,259

40–44 years old
1,578

45–49 years old
1,876

50–54 years old
1,950

55–59 years old
2,718

60-64 years old
3,233

65 years old and over
9,302

Source: Chart prepared by U.S. Census Bureau. For data, see Table 503.

U.S. Census Bureau, Statistical Abstract of the United States: 2009

Table 485. National Defense Outlays and Veterans Benefits: 1960 to 2009

[In billions of dollars (53.5 represents $53,500,000,000) except percent. For fiscal year ending in year shown, see text, Section 8. Includes outlays of Department of Defense, Department of Veterans Affairs, and other agencies for activities primarily related to national defense and veterans programs. For explanation of average annual percent change, see Guide to Tabular Presentation. Minus sign (–) indicates decrease]

Year	National defense and veterans' outlays (bil. dol.)				Annual percent change [1]			Defense outlays percent of—	
		Defense outlays							
	Total outlays	Current dollars	Constant (FY2000) dollars	Veterans' outlays	Total outlays	Defense outlays	Veterans' outlays	Federal outlays	Gross domestic product [2]
1960	53.5	48.1	300.2	5.4	2.5	2.4	3.1	52.2	9.3
1970	90.4	81.7	375.1	8.7	0.3	–1.0	13.6	41.8	8.1
1980	155.1	134.0	267.1	21.1	13.9	15.2	6.3	22.7	4.9
1990	328.4	299.3	382.7	29.1	–1.6	–1.4	–3.2	23.9	5.2
1995	310.0	272.1	305.9	37.9	–2.9	–3.4	0.8	17.9	3.7
1996	302.7	265.8	289.2	37.0	–2.3	–2.3	–2.4	17.0	3.5
1997	309.8	270.5	288.4	39.3	2.3	1.8	6.3	16.9	3.3
1998	310.0	268.2	282.4	41.8	0.1	–0.8	6.3	16.2	3.1
1999	320.2	274.8	286.6	43.2	3.3	2.5	3.4	16.1	3.0
2000	341.5	294.4	294.4	47.1	6.6	7.1	9.0	16.5	3.0
2001	349.8	304.8	297.2	45.0	2.4	3.5	–4.3	16.4	3.0
2002	399.5	348.5	329.3	51.0	14.2	14.3	13.2	17.3	3.4
2003	461.8	404.8	364.4	57.0	15.6	16.2	11.8	18.7	3.7
2004	515.6	455.8	394.3	59.8	11.7	12.6	4.8	19.9	4.0
2005	565.5	495.3	407.3	70.2	9.7	8.7	17.4	20.0	4.0
2006	591.7	521.8	412.4	69.8	4.6	5.4	–0.4	19.7	4.0
2007	625.4	552.6	426.4	72.8	5.7	5.9	4.3	20.2	4.0
2008, est.	693.9	607.3	463.9	86.6	10.9	9.9	18.9	20.7	4.2
2009, est.	767.0	675.1	504.7	91.9	10.5	11.2	6.1	21.7	4.5

[1] Change from immediate prior year; for 1960, change from 1955. [2] Represents fiscal year GDP; for definition, see text, Section 13.

Source: U.S. Office of Management and Budget, *Budget of the United States Government, Historical Tables*, annual. See also <http://www.whitehouse.gov/omb>.

Table 486. National Defense Budget Authority and Outlays for Defense Functions: 1990 to 2008

[In billions of dollars (303.3 represents $303,300,000,000), except percent. For year ending September 30. Minus sign (–) indicates decrease]

Function	1990	1995	2000	2001	2002	2003	2004	2005	2006	2007	2008, est.
Total budget authority [1]	**303.3**	**266.4**	**304.0**	**334.7**	**362.0**	**456.0**	**490.6**	**505.8**	**617.2**	**625.9**	**693.2**
Department of Defense–Military . . .	293.0	255.7	290.3	318.7	344.9	437.7	470.9	483.9	593.8	603.0	670.5
Military personnel	78.9	71.6	73.8	76.9	87.0	109.1	116.1	121.3	128.5	131.8	137.1
Operation and maintenance	88.4	93.7	108.7	125.2	133.2	178.3	189.8	179.2	213.5	240.2	257.1
Procurement	81.4	43.6	55.0	62.6	62.7	78.5	83.1	96.6	105.4	133.8	170.1
Research, development, test, and evaluation	36.5	34.5	38.7	41.6	48.7	58.1	64.6	68.8	72.9	77.5	79.5
Military construction.	5.1	5.4	5.1	5.4	6.6	6.7	6.1	7.3	9.5	14.0	20.2
Family housing.	3.1	3.4	3.5	3.7	4.0	4.2	3.8	4.1	4.4	4.0	2.9
Other	–0.4	3.4	5.5	3.3	2.6	2.9	7.4	6.6	59.6	1.7	3.2
Atomic energy defense activities . . .	9.7	10.1	12.4	14.3	15.2	16.4	16.8	17.9	17.4	17.2	16.4
Defense–related activities	0.7	1.0	1.3	1.8	1.9	2.0	2.8	4.0	5.9	5.7	6.3
Total outlays [1]	**299.3**	**272.1**	**294.4**	**304.8**	**348.5**	**404.8**	**455.8**	**495.3**	**521.8**	**552.6**	**607.3**
Department of Defense–Military . . .	289.8	259.4	281.1	290.2	331.9	387.2	436.5	474.1	499.3	529.8	583.1
Military personnel	75.6	70.8	76.0	74.0	86.8	106.7	113.6	127.5	127.5	128.8	137.4
Operation and maintenance	88.3	91.0	105.8	112.0	130.0	151.4	174.0	188.1	203.8	216.6	225.1
Procurement	81.0	55.0	51.7	55.0	62.5	67.9	76.2	82.3	89.8	99.6	130.5
Research, development, test, and evaluation	37.5	34.6	37.6	40.5	44.4	53.1	60.8	65.7	68.6	73.1	74.7
Military construction.	5.1	6.8	5.1	5.0	5.1	5.9	6.3	5.3	6.2	7.9	10.2
Family housing.	3.5	3.6	3.4	3.5	3.7	3.8	3.9	3.7	3.7	3.5	4.3
Other	–1.2	–2.4	1.5	0.3	–0.6	–1.6	1.6	1.5	–0.4	0.2	0.8
Atomic energy activities.	9.0	11.8	12.1	12.9	14.8	16.0	16.6	18.0	17.5	17.1	17.8
Defense–related activities	0.6	0.9	1.2	1.6	1.8	1.6	2.8	3.2	5.1	5.7	6.4

[1] Includes defense budget authority, balances, and outlays by other departments.

Source: U.S. Office of Management and Budget, *Budget of the United States Government, Historical Tables, Budget Authority by Function and Subfunction, Outlay by Function and Subfunction*, annual. See also <http://www.whitehouse.gov/omb/budget>.

Table 487. U.S. Military Sales and Assistance to Foreign Governments: 1995 to 2006

[In millions of dollars (8,495 represents $8,495,000,000). For year ending September 30. Department of Defense (DoD) sales deliveries cover deliveries against sales orders authorized under Arms Export Control Act, as well as earlier and applicable legislation. For details regarding individual programs, see source]

Item	1995	1999	2000	2001	2002	2003	2004	2005	2006
Military sales agreements	8,495	10,947	10,703	12,561	12,102	12,577	13,311	10,240	20,805
Military construction sales agreements.	24	301	284	124	70	223	673	329	170
Military sales deliveries [1]	12,100	16,449	10,671	12,287	10,481	9,257	11,058	10,985	12,132
Military sales financing	3,712	3,370	4,333	3,535	4,032	5,955	4,584	4,956	4,450
Military assistance programs [2] . . .	117	125	5	9	39	186	45	68	11
Military assistance program delivery [3]	20	36	14	21	34	182	7	62	73
IMET program/deliveries [4]	26	49	49	51	67	76	85	85	81

[1] Includes military construction sales deliveries. [2] Also includes Military Assistance Service Funded (MASF) program data, emergency drawdowns, and grant assistance; excludes training. [3] Includes Military Assistance Service Funded (MASF) program data and Section 506(a) drawdown authority. [4] International Military Education & Training. Includes military assistance service funded and emergency draw downs.

Source: U.S. Department of Defense, Defense Security Cooperation Agency, "DSCA Data and Statistics"; See also <http://www.dsca.osd.mil/data_stats.htm>.

Table 488. U.S. Military Sales Deliveries by Selected Country: 1995 to 2006

[In millions of dollars (12,100 represents $12,100,000,000). For year ending September 30. Represents Department of Defense military sales]

Country	1995	1999	2000	2001	2002	2003	2004	2005	2006
Total [1].	12,100	16,449	10,671	12,287	10,481	9,257	11,058	10,985	12,132
Australia.	303	291	332	309	232	213	185	355	382
Bahrain	40	48	54	337	84	94	78	68	74
Belgium	8	274	58	169	68	71	42	50	56
Canada	127	96	84	110	85	155	145	153	186
Denmark.	54	157	44	109	23	14	22	40	48
Egypt.	1,479	543	1,031	872	1,875	861	1,344	1,308	1,227
France	64	248	217	142	206	168	207	70	43
Germany	257	251	131	330	221	242	264	211	154
Greece.	220	463	389	448	469	1,324	1,173	318	425
Israel	327	1,213	562	766	629	846	902	1,702	1,397
Italy	54	106	41	188	103	185	282	127	318
Japan	693	436	458	491	467	430	393	411	554
Jordan	47	49	52	80	67	69	104	141	106
Korea, South.	442	585	1,399	735	533	560	601	607	584
Kuwait	471	316	321	502	131	143	209	254	255
Netherlands	153	381	161	412	249	224	271	178	806
Norway.	25	251	64	192	88	123	80	106	107
Portugal	88	12	20	42	28	116	31	84	84
Saudi Arabia	3,567	4,318	1,975	1,891	1,308	1,011	1,223	992	999
Singapore	59	549	131	244	419	168	205	209	373
Spain.	193	331	141	467	317	159	435	127	105
Taiwan [2]	1,332	2,438	784	1,160	1,410	648	1,032	1,384	1,025
Thailand	356	134	114	119	171	153	179	92	84
Turkey	368	622	216	466	281	277	290	190	249
United Arab Emirates . . .	345	81	42	24	92	85	142	150	247
United Kingdom	419	365	347	525	386	350	453	384	297

[1] Includes countries not shown. [2] See footnote 2, Table 1288.

Source: U.S. Department of Defense, Defense Security Cooperation Agency, "DSCA Data and Statistics"; See also <http://www.dsca.osd.mil/data_stats.htm>.

U.S. Census Bureau, Statistical Abstract of the United States: 2009

Table 489. Military and Civilian Personnel and Expenditures: 1990 to 2006

[Personnel in thousands (3,693 represents 3,693,000); expenditures in millions of dollars (209,904 represents $209,904,000,000). For year ending September 30. For definitions, see headnote, Tables 490 and 492]

Item	1990	1995	2000	2003	2004	2005	2006
Personnel, total [1]	**3,693**	**3,391**	**2,791**	**2,806**	**2,764**	**2,848**	**2,840**
Active duty military (including afloat)	1,185	1,085	984	1,071	1,055	1,143	1,156
Civilian	931	768	634	631	634	639	642
Reserve and National Guard	1,577	1,538	1,173	1,105	1,074	1,065	1,042
Expenditures, total	**209,904**	**209,695**	**229,072**	**316,648**	**345,891**	**381,290**	**408,249**
Payroll outlays	88,650	98,396	103,447	122,270	139,490	141,018	146,858
Active duty military pay	33,705	35,188	36,872	46,614	50,489	50,482	55,829
Civilian pay	28,230	29,932	29,935	35,041	36,234	43,798	45,105
Reserve and National Guard pay	5,556	5,681	4,646	7,306	10,303	11,087	10,123
Retired military pay [2]	21,159	27,595	31,994	33,309	42,465	35,651	35,801
Prime contract awards [2]	121,254	109,005	123,295	191,222	203,389	236,987	257,457
Grants	6,329	7,543	2,330	3,156	3,012	3,285	3,934

[1] Members in a transient status are not included. [2] Represents contract awards over $25,000.

Source: U.S. Department of Defense, *DoD Personnel and Procurement Statistics, Personnel, Publications, Atlas/Data Abstract for the United States and Selected Areas,* annual; <http://siadapp.dmdc.osd.mil>.

Table 490. Department of Defense Payroll and Contract Awards—States: 2006

[(In millions of dollars (146,858 represents $146,858,000,000); For year ending September 30. *Payroll outlays* include the gross earnings of civilian and active duty military personnel, reserve and National Guard, and retired military for services rendered to the government and for cash allowances for benefits. Excludes employer's share of employee benefits, accrued military retirement benefits and most permanent change of station costs. *Contracts,* refer to awards made in year specified; expenditures relating to awards may extend over several years. Military awards for supplies, services, and construction. Net value of contracts of over $25,000 for work in each state and DC. Figures reflect impact of prime contracting on state distribution of defense work. Often the state in which a prime contractor is located in is not the state where the subcontracted work is done. Undistributed civilians and military personnel, their payrolls, and prime contract awards for performance in classified locations are excluded]

State	Payroll Total	Payroll Active duty military	Contract awards	Grants	State	Payroll Total	Payroll Active duty military	Contract awards	Grants
U.S.	146,858	55,829	257,457	3,934	MO	2,432	724	9,393	46
AL	3,503	569	6,954	64	MT	407	146	247	32
AK	1,640	1,111	1,656	43	NE	961	371	718	11
AZ	2,656	988	9,696	79	NV	1,146	454	750	20
AR	1,080	240	881	64	NH	324	53	1,106	32
CA	15,270	6,867	32,126	350	NJ	2,004	327	6,151	77
CO	3,210	1,386	4,127	46	NM	1,466	505	1,075	30
CT	758	333	7,781	64	NY	2,669	1,154	8,020	150
DE	420	165	125	21	NC	7,132	4,373	2,690	100
DC	2,561	1,113	4,067	38	ND	501	282	240	37
FL	8,864	2,982	10,707	131	OH	3,030	446	5,980	97
GA	7,409	3,390	5,515	54	OK	3,260	1,160	2,070	33
HI	4,064	2,303	1,963	77	OR	760	49	562	47
ID	541	184	168	37	PA	3,077	162	7,515	300
IL	2,838	1,051	3,274	107	RI	645	136	431	17
IN	1,361	51	4,627	64	SC	3,431	1,696	2,197	45
IA	445	28	944	42	SD	358	128	372	21
KS	1,827	890	1,706	46	TN	1,520	146	2,866	56
KY	2,959	1,837	5,395	18	TX	11,908	5,254	27,102	168
LA	1,734	694	5,154	311	UT	1,739	245	2,304	22
ME	827	120	1,020	19	VT	168	12	829	21
MD	5,334	1,544	10,244	215	VA	16,693	6,770	29,246	85
MA	1,098	157	9,077	155	WA	5,652	2,417	4,766	60
MI	1,307	73	3,898	98	WV	384	28	392	25
MN	762	49	1,526	70	WI	681	41	2,165	56
MS	1,702	487	5,477	126	WY	306	140	161	12

Source: U.S. Department of Defense, *DoD Personnel and Procurement Statistics, Atlas/Data Abstract for the United States and Selected Areas,* annual; <http://siadapp.dmdc.osd.mil/>.

Table 491. Expenditures and Personnel by Selected Major Locations: 2006

[In thousands of dollars (11,986,749 represents $11,986,749,000), except for personnel. For year ending September 30. See headnote, Table 490]

Major locations	Expenditures Total	Payroll outlays	Contracts/ grants	Major locations	Military and civilian personnel Total	Active duty military	Civilian
Fort Worth, TX	11,986,749	251,949	11,734,800	Norfolk, VA	58,541	56,271	2,270
St. Louis, MO	7,748,183	178,105	7,570,078	Fort Hood, TX	55,444	50,501	4,943
San Diego, CA	7,611,970	3,248,103	4,363,867	Fort Bragg, NC	49,661	43,390	6,271
Washington, DC	5,486,577	1,556,360	3,930,217	San Diego, CA	49,476	43,292	6,184
Norfolk, VA	4,972,232	3,148,167	1,824,065	Camp Pendleton, CA	39,539	37,258	2,281
Long Beach, CA	4,758,941	51,948	4,706,993	Camp Lejeune, NC	37,840	35,032	2,808
Huntsville, AL	4,735,031	243,759	4,491,272	Fort Campbell, KY	32,151	29,635	2,516
Arlington, VA	4,589,230	2,431,651	2,157,579	Fort Lewis, WA	25,277	22,817	2,460
Sunnyvale, CA	4,298,814	46,253	4,252,561	Arlington, VA	25,197	9,951	15,246
Louisville, KY	3,749,472	161,180	3,588,292	Fort Benning, GA	25,098	21,702	3,396

Source: U.S. Department of Defense, *DoD Personnel and Procurement Statistics, Personnel, Publications, Atlas/Data Abstract for the United States and Selected Areas,* annual; <http://siadapp.dmdc.osd.mil/>.

Table 492. Military and Civilian Personnel in Installations: 2006

[As of September 30. *Civilian personnel* includes United States citizens and foreign national direct-hire civilians subject to Office of Management and Budget (OMB) ceiling controls and civilian personnel involved in civil functions in the United States. Excludes indirect-hire civilians and those direct-hire civilians not subject to OMB ceiling controls. Military personnel include active duty personnel based ashore or afloat, excludes personnel temporarily shore-based in a transient status]

State	Active military personnel				Reserve and National Guard, total	Civilian personnel			
	Total [1]	Army	Navy/ Marine Corps [2]	Air Force		Total [1]	Army	Navy/ Marine Corps	Air Force
United States . . .	**1,156,308**	**423,825**	**443,658**	**288,825**	**1,041,542**	**642,214**	**232,243**	**170,667**	**157,270**
Alabama	9,742	6,022	419	3,301	30,012	22,312	18,326	43	2,344
Alaska	20,363	11,183	101	9,079	5,845	4,894	2,689	17	1,844
Arizona	21,997	5,267	5,456	11,274	18,496	9,047	3,938	528	3,620
Arkansas	4,905	88	59	4,758	17,798	3,977	2,944	5	894
California	149,481	7,004	122,707	19,770	84,352	55,709	7,966	31,079	10,173
Colorado	29,932	15,593	808	13,531	16,112	10,907	3,074	45	5,489
Connecticut	6,594	23	6,465	106	8,175	2,388	499	1,021	263
Delaware	3,297	7	24	3,266	5,390	1,564	243	2	1,253
District of Columbia . . .	12,351	4,740	4,634	2,977	8,022	14,634	4,119	8,851	929
Florida	58,100	2,419	30,569	25,112	49,726	26,072	3,281	10,920	9,367
Georgia	68,928	52,107	6,907	9,914	36,150	32,862	11,697	4,216	14,729
Hawaii	45,366	18,687	21,561	5,118	11,337	17,079	4,750	9,130	2,109
Idaho	4,042	20	41	3,981	7,095	1,522	696	49	710
Illinois	24,536	504	18,652	5,380	32,779	13,617	7,084	1,590	3,584
Indiana	805	420	275	110	22,628	9,281	1,949	3,067	1,027
Iowa	390	190	141	59	14,342	1,582	1,032	5	501
Kansas	17,645	14,725	197	2,723	15,446	6,577	5,043	1	1,103
Kentucky	38,799	38,335	266	198	15,555	9,170	7,817	193	228
Louisiana	15,069	7,999	1,303	5,767	22,081	6,212	3,511	870	1,518
Maine	2,096	224	1,853	19	5,592	6,445	326	5,301	277
Maryland	29,626	7,552	15,021	7,053	21,587	30,749	12,441	14,660	2,232
Massachusetts	2,175	208	576	1,391	18,916	6,491	2,339	218	2,986
Michigan	1,073	379	562	132	22,874	8,147	5,336	22	1,108
Minnesota	729	25	389	85	24,637	2,522	1,523	17	794
Mississippi	10,158	401	3,729	6,028	19,136	8,630	3,444	2,211	2,708
Missouri	16,241	11,053	1,537	3,651	25,726	9,483	6,421	444	1,258
Montana	3,589	15	28	3,546	5,761	1,358	560	1	745
Nebraska	6,784	136	469	6,179	8,553	3,774	1,360	12	2,082
Nevada	9,127	97	1,003	8,027	7,394	2,178	384	278	1,353
New Hampshire	912	3	861	48	4,550	1,069	542	46	329
New Jersey	6,293	888	6,964	4,741	20,060	13,959	9,773	1,907	1,545
New Mexico	10,834	444	158	10,232	7,342	6,863	2,919	44	3,431
New York	26,240	23,464	2,376	400	39,353	11,145	6,946	141	2,414
North Carolina	102,845	43,384	49,775	9,686	30,031	17,447	6,837	7,273	1,370
North Dakota	7,013	23	11	6,979	5,640	1,853	526	2	1,237
Ohio	6,745	539	608	5,698	35,074	21,789	1,455	79	12,422
Oklahoma	25,064	14,297	1,953	8,814	18,399	21,539	4,763	78	15,479
Oregon	558	190	306	62	13,421	3,241	2,411	18	787
Pennsylvania	2,979	1,075	1,655	249	43,478	25,266	9,048	6,440	1,547
Rhode Island	2,403	109	2,214	80	5,112	4,213	298	3,586	230
South Carolina	38,090	12,372	16,695	9,023	21,677	9,640	3,115	3,501	1,899
South Dakota	3,150	23	4	3,123	5,668	1,237	507	1	683
Tennessee	2,441	302	1,918	221	23,695	5,334	2,419	1,004	1,081
Texas	119,176	73,654	6,986	38,536	72,955	41,462	21,777	1,352	14,758
Utah	5,188	291	163	4,734	13,770	15,081	2,377	26	11,930
Vermont	70	16	31	23	4,130	608	312	1	263
Virginia	128,515	24,084	90,758	13,673	35,668	81,342	21,247	35,582	4,763
Washington	49,887	22,787	20,285	6,815	25,925	24,501	6,928	14,682	1,957
West Virginia	373	30	308	35	10,068	1,745	1,213	90	423
Wisconsin	449	193	176	80	20,270	2,695	1,802	18	773
Wyoming	3,043	4	1	3,038	3,739	1,002	236	–	721

– Represents zero. [1] Includes Other Defense Activities (ODA) not shown separately. [2] Navy and Marine Corps personnel who are in afloat duty status at the time of the report are included in the strength counts of their homeport locations.
Source: U.S. Department of Defense, *DoD Personnel and Procurement Statistics, Personnel, Publications, Atlas/Data Abstract for the United States and Selected Areas,* annual; <http://siadapp.dmdc.osd.mil/personnel/Pubs.htm>.

Table 493. Military Personnel on Active Duty by Location: 1980 to 2007

[In thousands (2,051 represents 2,051,000). As of September 30]

Location	1980	1990	1995	2000	2002	2003	2004	2005	2006	2007
Total	**2,051**	**2,046**	**1,518**	**1,384**	**1,412**	**1,434**	**1,427**	**1,389**	**1,385**	**1,380**
Shore-based [1]	1,840	1,794	1,351	1,237	1,262	1,287	1,291	1,262	1,263	1,264
Afloat [2]	211	252	167	147	150	148	136	127	121	115
United States [3]	1,562	1,437	1,280	1,127	1,181	1,182	1,139	1,098	1,100	1,085
Foreign countries	489	609	238	258	230	253	288	291	285	295

[1] Includes Navy personnel temporarily on shore. [2] Includes Marine Corps. [3] Includes Puerto Rico and Island areas.
Source: U.S. Department of Defense, *DoD Personnel and Procurement Statistics, Personnel, Publications, Atlas/Data Abstract for the United States and Selected Areas,* annual; <http://siadapp.dmdc.osd.mil/>.

U.S. Census Bureau, Statistical Abstract of the United States: 2009

Table 494. Department of Defense Personnel: 1960 to 2007

[In thousands (2,475 represents 2,475,000). As of end of fiscal year; see text, Section 8. Includes National Guard, Reserve, and retired regular personnel on extended or continuous active duty. Excludes Coast Guard. Other officer candidates are included under enlisted personnel]

Year	Total [1,2]	Army Total [1]	Army Male Officers	Army Male Enlisted	Army Female Officers	Army Female Enlisted	Navy [2] Total [1]	Navy Male Officers	Navy Male Enlisted	Navy Female Officers	Navy Female Enlisted	Marine Corps Total [1]	Marine Corps Male Officers	Marine Corps Male Enlisted	Marine Corps Female Officers	Marine Corps Female Enlisted	Air Force Total [1]	Air Force Male Officers	Air Force Male Enlisted	Air Force Female Officers	Air Force Female Enlisted
1960	2,475	873	97	762	4.3	8.3	617	67	540	2.7	5.4	171	16	153	0.1	1.5	815	126	677	3.7	5.7
1965	2,654	969	108	846	3.8	8.5	670	75	583	2.6	5.3	190	17	172	0.1	1.4	825	128	685	4.1	4.7
1970	3,065	1,323	162	1,142	5.2	11.5	691	78	600	2.9	5.8	260	25	233	0.3	2.1	791	125	648	4.7	9.0
1975	2,128	784	98	640	4.6	37.7	535	62	449	3.7	17.5	196	19	174	0.3	2.8	613	100	478	5.0	25.2
1979	2,027	759	90	602	6.9	55.2	523	58	432	4.4	25.0	185	18	161	0.5	5.5	560	89	413	7.3	46.4
1980	2,051	777	91	612	7.6	61.7	527	58	430	4.9	30.1	189	18	164	0.5	6.2	558	90	404	8.5	51.9
1981	2,083	781	94	610	8.3	65.3	540	60	435	5.3	34.6	191	17	165	0.5	7.1	570	90	413	9.1	54.4
1982	2,109	780	94	609	9.0	64.1	553	61	444	5.7	37.3	192	18	165	0.6	7.9	583	92	421	9.9	54.5
1983	2,123	780	97	602	9.5	66.5	558	62	444	6.3	40.8	194	19	166	0.6	8.3	592	94	428	10.6	55.3
1984	2,138	780	98	601	10.2	67.1	565	62	448	6.6	42.6	196	19	167	0.6	8.6	597	95	430	11.2	55.9
1985	2,151	781	99	599	10.8	68.4	571	64	449	6.9	45.7	198	19	169	0.7	9.0	602	96	431	11.9	58.1
1986	2,169	781	99	597	11.3	69.7	581	65	457	7.3	47.2	200	19	170	0.6	9.2	608	97	434	12.4	61.2
1987	2,174	781	96	596	11.6	71.6	587	65	462	7.2	47.7	200	19	170	0.6	9.1	607	94	432	12.6	63.2
1988	2,138	772	95	588	11.8	72.0	593	65	466	7.3	49.7	197	19	168	0.7	9.0	576	92	405	12.9	61.5
1989	2,130	770	95	584	12.2	74.3	593	65	464	7.5	52.1	197	19	168	0.7	9.0	571	91	399	13.4	63.7
1990	2,044	732	92	553	12.4	71.2	579	64	451	7.8	52.1	197	19	168	0.7	8.7	535	87	370	13.3	60.8
1991	1,986	711	91	535	12.5	67.8	570	63	444	8.0	51.4	194	19	166	0.7	8.3	510	84	350	13.3	59.1
1992	1,807	610	83	449	11.7	61.7	542	61	417	8.3	51.0	185	18	157	0.6	7.9	470	77	320	12.7	56.1
1993	1,705	572	77	420	11.1	60.2	510	58	390	8.3	49.3	178	17	153	0.6	7.2	444	72	302	12.3	54.5
1994	1,610	541	74	394	10.9	59.0	469	54	355	8.0	47.9	174	17	149	0.6	7.0	426	69	287	12.3	54.0
1995	1,518	509	72	365	10.8	57.3	435	51	324	7.9	47.9	175	17	150	0.7	7.4	400	66	266	12.1	52.1
1996	1,472	491	70	347	10.6	59.0	417	50	308	7.8	46.9	175	17	149	0.8	7.8	389	64	256	12.0	52.8
1997	1,439	492	69	346	10.4	62.4	396	48	290	7.8	44.8	174	17	148	0.8	8.5	377	62	246	12.0	53.8
1998	1,407	484	68	340	10.4	61.4	382	47	280	7.8	42.9	173	17	146	0.9	8.9	368	60	237	12.0	54.2
1999	1,386	479	67	337	10.5	61.5	373	46	271	7.7	43.9	173	17	145	0.9	9.3	361	58	232	11.8	54.6
2000	1,384	482	66	339	10.8	62.9	373	46	272	7.8	43.8	173	17	146	0.9	9.5	356	57	227	11.8	55.0
2001	1,385	481	65	337	11.0	63.4	378	46	273	8.0	46.6	173	17	145	1.0	9.6	354	57	224	12.0	55.6
2002	1,414	487	66	341	11.5	63.2	385	47	279	8.2	47.3	174	17	146	1.0	9.5	368	59	233	12.9	58.6
2003	1,434	499	68	352	12.0	63.5	382	47	276	8.2	47.3	178	18	149	1.1	9.6	375	61	237	13.5	60.0
2004	1,427	500	69	358	12.3	61.0	373	46	273	8.1	46.1	178	18	149	1.1	9.7	377	61	242	13.6	60.2
2005	1,389	493	69	353	12.4	57.9	363	45	266	7.8	44.5	180	18	151	1.0	9.8	354	60	225	13.4	55.6
2006	1,385	505	69	365	12.5	58.5	350	44	255	7.6	43.2	180	18	151	1.1	10.0	349	58	223	12.8	55.8
2007	1,380	522	71	379	13.0	58.8	338	44	244	7.6	42.2	186	18	156	1.1	10.5	333	54	214	11.8	53.4

[1] Includes cadets, midshipmen, and others not shown separately. [2] Beginning 1980, excludes Navy Reserve personnel on active duty for Training and Administration of Reserves (TARS).

Source: U.S. Dept. of Defense, *Selected Manpower Statistics*, annual. See also <http://siadapp.dmdc.osd.mil.html>.

Table 495. U.S. Military Personnel on Active Duty in Selected Foreign Countries: 1995 to 2007

[As of September 30]

Country	1995	2000	2002	2003	2004	2005	2006	2007
In foreign countries [1] ...	**238,064**	**257,817**	**230,484**	**252,764**	**287,802**	**290,997**	**284,967**	**295,003**
Ashore	208,836	212,858	208,479	226,570	265,594	268,214	262,586	272,124
Afloat	29,228	44,959	22,005	26,194	20,208	22,783	22,381	22,879
Australia	314	175	171	574	196	196	347	140
Bahrain	618	949	1,560	1,514	1,712	1,641	1,357	1,495
Belgium	1,689	1,554	1,458	1,526	1,474	1,366	1,361	1,328
Bosnia and Herzegovina	1	5,708	3,082	3,041	951	263	232	209
Canada	214	156	148	141	156	150	133	141
Colombia	44	224	39	54	55	52	104	123
Cuba (Guantanamo)	5,129	688	549	697	682	950	953	932
Diego Garcia [2]	897	625	548	528	816	683	157	260
Djibouti	7	2	2	498	412	622	1,375	2,100
Egypt	1,123	499	433	385	348	410	360	250
Germany	73,280	69,203	68,701	74,796	76,058	66,418	64,319	57,080
Greece	489	678	593	583	473	428	395	363
Greenland	131	125	88	139	133	146	137	126
Honduras	193	351	402	414	448	438	414	403
Italy	12,007	11,190	12,466	13,152	12,606	11,841	10,449	9,855
Japan	39,134	40,159	41,848	40,519	36,365	35,571	33,453	32,803
Korea, South	36,016	36,565	37,743	41,145	40,840	30,983	29,086	27,014
Kuwait	771	4,602	567	([4])	([4])	([4])	([4])	([4])
Netherlands	687	659	629	703	701	583	591	579
Portugal	1,066	1,005	992	1,094	1,006	970	922	826
Qatar	2	52	71	2,997	273	463	446	411
Saudi Arabia	1,077	7,053	776	953	235	258	282	243
Senegal	13	10	8	8	9	42	7	1,361
Singapore	166	411	167	171	237	169	164	125
Spain	2,799	2,007	2,621	1,893	2,012	1,660	1,521	1,286
Turkey	3,111	2,006	1,587	2,021	1,762	1,780	1,810	1,594
United Kingdom	12,131	11,207	10,258	11,616	11,469	10,752	10,331	9,825
DEPLOYMENTS								
Operation Enduring Freedom (OEF)[3]	(X)	(X)	(X)	(NA)	(NA)	19,500	21,500	25,240
Operation Iraqi Freedom (OIF)[4]	(X)	(X)	(X)	183,002	170,647	192,600	185,500	218,500

X Not applicable.   NA Not available.   [1] Includes areas not shown separately.   [2] British Indian Ocean Territory.   [3] Total (in/around Afghanistan as of September 30)—includes deployed Reserve/National Guard.   [4] Total (in/around Iraq as of September 30)—includes deployed Reserve/National Guard.

Source: U.S. Department of Defense, *DoD Personnel and Procurement Statistics, Selected Manpower Statistics, Table 2-4, Deployments*. See also <http://siadapp.dmdc.osd.mil/personnel/>.

Table 496. Military Personnel on Active Duty by Rank or Grade: 1990 to 2007

[In thousands (2,043.7 represents 2,043,700). As of Sept. 30]

Rank/grade	1990	2000	2003	2004	2005	2006	2007
Total	**2,043.7**	**1,384.3**	**1,434.4**	**1,426.8**	**1,389.4**	**1,385.0**	**1,379.6**
Total Officers	**296.6**	**217.2**	**227.9**	**226.7**	**226.6**	**223.2**	**221.3**
General-Admiral	(Z)	(Z)	(Z)	(Z)	(Z)	(Z)	(Z)
Lieutenant General-Vice Admiral	0.1	0.1	0.1	0.1	0.1	0.1	0.1
Major General-Rear Admiral (U)	0.4	0.3	0.3	0.3	0.3	0.3	0.3
Brigadier General-Rear Admiral (L)	0.5	0.4	0.4	0.4	0.4	0.5	0.4
Colonel-Captain	14.0	11.3	11.6	11.5	11.4	11.3	11.3
Lieutenant Colonel-Commander	32.3	27.5	28.5	28.4	28.1	27.5	27.7
Major-LT Commander	53.2	43.2	44.1	44.0	44.4	45.1	44.2
Captain-Lieutenant	106.6	68.1	68.1	69.5	72.5	71.9	70.6
1st Lieutenant-Lieutenant (JG)	37.9	24.7	29.9	31.1	27.5	24.9	23.4
2nd Lieutenant-Ensign	31.9	26.4	29.1	26.9	25.9	25.2	26.0
Chief Warrant Officer W-5	(Z)	0.1	0.1	0.1	0.5	0.6	0.6
Chief Warrant Officer W-4	3.0	2.0	2.1	1.9	2.2	2.4	2.9
Chief Warrant Officer W-3	5.0	3.8	4.6	4.1	4.6	4.6	4.6
Chief Warrant Officer W-2	8.4	6.7	6.2	6.0	6.2	6.0	5.7
Warrant Officer W-1	3.2	2.1	2.4	3.1	2.5	2.9	3.4
Total Enlisted	**1,733.8**	**1,154.6**	**1,193.9**	**1,172.0**	**1,149.9**	**1,148.6**	**1,145.0**
E-9	15.3	10.2	10.8	10.7	10.5	10.4	10.6
E-8	38.0	26.0	27.7	27.1	27.1	26.7	27.4
E-7	134.1	97.7	101.4	99.6	97.8	99.3	97.1
E-6	239.1	164.9	172.4	173.1	172.4	170.3	168.4
E-5	361.5	229.5	250.7	251.1	248.5	248.8	247.4
E-4	427.8	251.0	264.5	264.1	261.7	261.4	260.1
E-3	280.1	196.3	222.1	220.1	201.7	185.4	192.5
E-2	140.3	99.0	85.1	84.3	70.8	83.5	79.9
E-1	97.6	80.0	59.2	55.8	59.5	62.8	61.7
Cadets and Midshipmen	**13.3**	**12.5**	**12.6**	**12.6**	**12.9**	**13.2**	**13.2**

Z Fewer than 50.

Source: U.S. Department of Defense, DoD Personnel and Procurement Statistics, Personnel, Military, *Military Personnel Statistics*, annual; <http://siadapp.dmdc.osd.mil/>.

U.S. Census Bureau, Statistical Abstract of the United States: 2009

Table 497. **Military Retirement System: 2007**

[Payment in millions of dollars (3,430 represents $3,430,000,000). As of September 30. The data published in this report are produced from the files maintained by the Defense Manpower Data Center (DMDC). This report compiles data primarily from the "Retiree Pay and Survivor Pay" files. Any grouping of members by address reflects mailing, not necessarily residence address. Only those members in plans administered by the Department of Defense (DoD) are included in this table. The data are preliminary because of reporting delays due to the information about many members who retired or died within one month of the September 30 reporting date. These data were not processed in time to be included in this report. For more information, please see *Introduction and Overview* at <http://www.defenselink.mil/actuary/statbook2007.pdf>]

State or other area	Retired military personnel [1]			Monthly payment	State or other area	Retired military personnel [1]			Monthly payment
	Total	Disabled [2]	Non-disabled			Total	Disabled [2]	Non-disabled	
Total [3] ..	1,983,467	179,236	1,804,231	3,430	MT........	8,326	779	7,547	13
U.S.	1,943,765	176,035	1,767,730	3,367	NE........	13,547	1,012	12,535	24
					NV........	27,196	1,825	25,371	48
AL.........	53,982	4,370	49,612	91	NH........	9,433	794	8,639	16
AK.........	9,261	575	8,686	15	NJ........	20,419	2,658	17,761	29
AZ.........	53,497	4,559	48,938	96	NM........	21,274	1,679	19,595	39
AR.........	25,381	2,367	23,014	39	NY........	36,884	5,764	31,120	47
CA.........	170,320	15,987	154,333	301	NC........	82,050	7,087	74,963	142
CO.........	47,699	3,713	43,986	95	ND........	4,634	360	4,274	7
CT.........	10,660	1,318	9,342	16	OH........	43,479	5,596	37,883	66
DE.........	7,986	549	7,437	13	OK........	34,082	2,803	31,279	53
DC.........	3,060	461	2,599	5	OR........	21,321	2,509	18,812	34
FL.........	186,102	15,451	170,651	344	PA	48,053	5,913	42,140	72
GA.........	86,998	7,265	79,733	148	RI	5,538	547	4,991	9
HI.........	15,701	1,038	14,663	29	SC........	53,592	4,124	49,468	91
ID.........	12,455	1,037	11,418	20	SD........	6,811	559	6,252	11
IL.........	34,779	4,452	30,327	55	TN	49,597	4,496	45,101	80
IN.........	23,354	2,956	20,398	33	TX........	183,005	15,020	167,985	334
IA.........	11,393	1,273	10,120	16	UT........	14,250	1,071	13,179	24
KS.........	20,281	1,589	18,692	35	VT........	3,603	336	3,267	5
KY.........	25,945	2,728	23,217	40	VA........	141,295	7,875	133,420	326
LA.........	25,524	2,694	22,830	40	WA........	69,839	5,163	64,676	123
ME.........	11,982	1,123	10,859	18	WV........	10,553	1,308	9,245	15
MD.........	49,878	3,790	46,088	94	WI	18,944	2,338	16,606	26
MA.........	19,164	2,564	16,600	27	WY	4,833	390	4,443	8
MI.........	27,234	4,131	23,103	37	GU	1,846	107	1,739	3
MN.........	16,972	2,031	14,941	23	PR	9,638	1,543	8,095	9
MS.........	25,574	2,235	23,339	39	VI.......	364	42	322	1
MO	36,025	3,773	32,252	55	Other	27,854	1,509	26,345	51

[1] Represents military personnel (officers and enlisted) receiving and not receiving pay from DoD.   [2] A disabled military member is entitled to disability retired pay if the member has at least 20 years of service or the disability is at least 30 percent (under a standard schedule of rating disabilities by the Veterans Administration) and either (a) the member has at least eight years of service; (b) the disability results from active duty; or (c) the disability occurred in the line of duty during a time of war or national emergency or certain other time periods. Please see report for more details.   [3] Includes states, U.S. territories, and retirees living in foreign countries.

Source: U.S. Department of Defense, Office of the Actuary, "Statistical Report, Fiscal Year 2007"; issued May 2008; <http://www.defenselink.mil/actuary/>.

Table 498. **U.S. Active Duty Military Deaths by Manner of Death: 1980 to 2007**

[As of December 31. 2007 data are preliminary]

Manner of death	1980–2007	1980	1990	1995	2000	2001	2002	2003	2004	2005	2006	2007
Deaths, total.	42,312	2,392	1,507	1,040	758	891	999	1,410	1,873	1,941	1,882	1,950
Accident	23,014	1,556	880	538	397	434	543	576	605	649	559	544
Hostile action	2,841	–	–	–	–	3	18	344	739	739	769	846
Homicide	2,104	174	74	67	34	49	54	43	45	52	46	42
Illness.............	7,537	419	277	174	139	187	195	234	272	289	252	227
Pending............	34	–	–	–	–	–	–	1	3	5	25	70
Self-inflicted	5,822	231	232	250	151	141	163	187	201	181	210	204
Terrorist attack	428	1	1	7	17	55	–	–	–	–	–	–
Undetermined........	532	11	43	4	20	22	26	25	8	26	21	17
Deaths per 100,000 of personnel strength....	(X)	110.7	66.8	62.5	49.5	57.4	61.4	81.4	109.4	116.7	116.8	111.3
Accident	(X)	72.0	39.0	32.4	25.9	28.0	33.4	33.2	35.3	39.0	34.7	33.8
Hostile action	(X)	–	–	–	–	0.2	1.1	19.9	43.2	44.4	47.7	52.6
Homicide	(X)	8.1	3.3	4.0	2.2	3.2	3.3	2.5	2.6	3.1	2.9	2.6
Illness.............	(X)	19.4	12.3	10.5	9.1	12.0	12.0	13.5	15.9	17.4	15.6	14.1
Pending............	(X)	–	–	–	–	–	–	0.1	0.2	0.3	1.6	4.4
Self-inflicted	(X)	10.7	10.3	15.0	9.9	9.1	10.0	10.8	11.7	10.9	13.0	12.7
Terrorist attack	(X)	–	–	0.4	1.1	3.5	–	–	–	–	–	–
Undetermined........	(X)	0.5	1.9	0.2	1.3	1.4	1.6	1.4	0.5	1.6	1.3	1.1

– Represents zero.   X Not applicable.

U.S. Department of Defense, "Military Casualty Information"; <http://siadapp.dmdc.osd.mil/personnel/CASUALTY/castop.htm>.

Table 499. **Military Reserve Personnel: 1995 to 2007**

[**As of September 30.** The Ready Reserve (Coast Guard Reserve data are included) includes the Selected Reserve which is scheduled to augment active forces during times of war or national emergency, and the Individual Ready Reserve, which, during times of war or national emergency, would be used to fill out Active, Guard, and Reserve units, and which would also be a source for casualty replacements; Ready Reservists serve in an active status (except for the Inactive National Guard—a very small pool within the Army National Guard). The Standby Reserve cannot be called to active duty, other than for training, unless authorized by Congress under "full mobilization," and a determination is made that there are not enough qualified members in the Ready Reserve in the required categories who are readily available. The Retired Reserve represents a lower potential for involuntary mobilization]

Reserve status and branch of service	1995	2000	2003	2004	2005	2006	2007
Total reserves [1] . . .	1,674,164	1,276,843	1,188,851	1,166,937	1,136,200	1,119,902	1,109,805
Ready reserve	1,648,388	1,251,452	1,167,101	1,145,035	1,113,427	1,101,565	1,088,587
Army [2]	999,462	725,771	682,522	663,209	636,355	631,856	621,422
Navy	267,356	184,080	152,855	148,643	140,821	131,802	128,421
Marine Corps.	103,668	99,855	98,868	101,443	99,820	100,522	100,787
Air Force [3]	263,011	229,009	219,895	219,159	223,551	224,637	226,806
Coast Guard	14,891	12,737	12,961	12,581	12,880	12,748	11,151
Standby reserve	25,776	25,391	21,750	21,902	22,773	18,337	21,218
Army	1,128	701	744	715	1,668	1,586	5,294
Navy	12,707	7,213	2,520	2,502	4,038	4,514	3,046
Marine Corps.	216	895	685	992	1,129	1,210	1,372
Air Force.	11,453	16,429	17,578	17,340	15,897	10,932	10,154
Coast Guard	272	153	223	353	41	95	1,352
Retired reserve . . .	505,905	573,305	601,611	614,904	627,424	637,262	648,346
Army	259,553	296,004	308,820	315,477	321,312	325,288	330,121
Navy	97,532	109,531	113,485	115,210	117,093	118,803	120,859
Marine Corps.	11,319	12,937	13,926	14,319	14,693	15,000	15,264
Air Force.	137,501	154,833	165,380	169,898	174,326	178,171	182,102

[1] Less retired reserves.   [2] Includes Army National Guard.   [3] Includes Air National Guard.

Source: U.S. Department of Defense, DoD Personnel and Procurement Statistics, Personnel, Publications, Atlas/Data Abstract for the United States and Selected Areas, *Selected Manpower Statistics,* annual. See also <http://siadapp.dmdc.osd.mil>.

Table 500. **Ready Reserve Personnel by Race, Hispanic Origin, and Sex: 1990 to 2007**

[**In thousands (1,658.7 represents 1,658,700). As of September 30**]

Year	Total [1]	Race					Sex			
							Officer		Enlisted	
		White	Black	Asian	American Indian	Hispanic [2]	Male	Female	Male	Female
1990. . .	1,658.7	1,304.6	272.3	14.9	7.8	83.1	226.8	40.5	1,204.7	186.7
1995. . .	1,648.4	1,267.7	274.5	22.0	8.8	96.2	209.9	44.7	1,196.8	196.9
1996. . .	1,536.6	1,179.0	249.8	21.5	8.6	93.1	196.9	43.6	1,108.8	187.4
1997. . .	1,451.0	1,113.7	230.6	21.7	8.4	91.5	188.7	43.2	1,037.6	181.5
1998. . .	1,353.4	1,033.9	210.4	21.7	7.8	88.2	175.9	40.3	964.1	173.1
1999. . .	1,288.8	980.0	202.6	22.6	7.6	88.9	166.2	38.4	911.2	173.1
2000. . .	1,251.5	942.2	199.6	26.7	8.4	91.8	159.4	36.9	879.9	175.3
2001. . .	1,224.1	912.7	198.4	27.9	8.5	94.3	158.0	36.6	852.2	177.3
2002. . .	1,199.3	891.3	193.2	27.9	8.8	96.0	152.1	35.6	835.2	176.4
2003. . .	1,167.1	865.7	187.5	25.4	8.5	98.0	145.1	34.0	813.7	174.3
2004. . .	1,145.0	845.3	181.3	26.2	9.1	100.2	141.9	33.6	799.7	169.8
2005. . .	1,113.4	825.4	169.9	26.9	9.5	99.8	139.2	33.3	778.0	162.9
2006. . .	1,101.6	822.4	163.5	27.7	10.1	101.1	136.7	33.1	769.4	162.3
2007. . .	1,088.6	818.1	156.6	28.1	10.8	102.7	130.0	31.8	766.5	160.2

[1] Includes other races not shown separately.   [2] Persons of Hispanic origin may be any race.

Source: U.S. Department of Defense, DoD Personnel and Procurement Statistics, Personnel, Publications, Atlas/Data Abstract for the United States and Selected Areas, annual; <http://siadapp.dmdc.osd.mil>.

Table 501. **National Guard by Sex and Race: 1995 to 2007**

[**In thousands (375 represents 375,000). As of September 30**]

Year	Army National Guard					Air National Guard				
	Total	Male[1]	Female	White	Black	Total	Male[1]	Female	White	Black
1995	375	344	31	299	59	110	94	16	96	9
2000	353	313	40	278	55	106	88	18	90	10
2001	352	309	42	276	55	108	90	19	91	10
2002	351	308	43	277	54	112	93	19	94	10
2003	351	307	44	277	52	108	89	19	91	10
2004	343	299	44	271	50	107	88	19	89	10
2005	333	290	43	264	46	106	87	19	89	9
2006	346	300	47	276	47	106	87	19	88	9
2007	353	304	49	283	47	106	87	19	88	9

[1] Male population includes unknown sex.

Source: U.S. Department of Defense, DoD Personnel and Procurement Statistics, Personnel, Publications, Atlas/Data Abstract for the United States and Selected Areas, *Selected Manpower Statistics,* annual. See also <http://siadapp.dmdc.osd.mil>.

Table 502. Veterans by Sex, Period of Service, and State: 2007

[In thousands (23,579 represents 23,579,000). As of September 30. VetPop2007 is the Department of Veterans Affairs (VA) latest official estimate and projection of the veteran population. It is based on detailed tabulations of Census 2000 data (prepared for the VA Office of the Actuary by the Census Bureau) and on recent American Community Survey data. VetPop2007 also uses administrative data and projections of service member separations from active duty provided by the Department of Defense (the Defense Manpower Data Center and the Office of the Actuary), as well as VA administrative data on veterans' benefits]

State	Total veterans [1]			Gulf War [2]	Vietnam era	Korean conflict	World War II	Peace-time
	Total	Male	Female					
United States	**23,579**	**21,815**	**1,763**	**4,921**	**7,810**	**2,922**	**2,886**	**6,013**
Alabama	417	384	33	99	142	51	42	106
Alaska	75	67	8	24	27	4	3	19
Arizona	568	522	45	117	181	81	78	140
Arkansas	262	244	19	56	90	32	30	67
California	2,132	1,965	167	440	697	277	278	537
Colorado	428	391	37	103	155	46	40	106
Connecticut	254	238	15	36	84	35	39	67
Delaware	81	74	6	17	26	11	10	21
District of Columbia	39	35	4	9	12	5	5	10
Florida	1,747	1,609	137	346	527	259	279	436
Georgia	765	694	72	211	260	72	59	199
Hawaii	119	108	11	31	37	14	13	30
Idaho	137	127	10	31	47	17	16	32
Illinois	842	786	55	162	270	104	109	216
Indiana	518	486	32	97	173	61	59	141
Iowa	251	237	14	44	84	35	34	61
Kansas	237	219	17	54	78	28	29	57
Kentucky	347	324	23	76	118	40	37	89
Louisiana	326	300	26	80	104	38	38	79
Maine	144	134	10	26	51	18	16	38
Maryland	484	437	47	121	155	50	48	132
Massachusetts	441	414	27	62	140	65	72	115
Michigan	761	716	45	123	264	94	97	200
Minnesota	408	386	23	61	147	54	50	107
Mississippi	216	199	17	54	70	27	24	53
Missouri	531	495	36	103	178	67	63	138
Montana	104	97	8	21	37	13	12	26
Nebraska	153	142	11	32	53	21	18	35
Nevada	246	225	20	53	87	29	24	65
New Hampshire	132	124	9	22	47	17	15	36
New Jersey	507	478	29	70	155	76	85	133
New Mexico	179	164	16	43	59	22	20	45
New York	1,066	1,000	66	158	333	151	165	281
North Carolina	774	708	65	193	255	86	77	199
North Dakota	58	54	4	14	19	7	6	14
Ohio	958	898	60	170	320	116	123	253
Oklahoma	338	313	25	80	115	41	39	80
Oregon	352	327	25	62	125	44	46	89
Pennsylvania	1,057	994	63	159	342	145	165	276
Rhode Island	80	74	5	13	26	11	13	20
South Carolina	410	377	33	101	141	48	41	103
South Dakota	74	69	6	16	24	10	8	18
Tennessee	512	475	37	111	181	59	51	133
Texas	1,707	1,562	145	444	580	183	170	417
Utah	157	147	10	34	52	21	21	37
Vermont	55	52	4	8	20	7	7	16
Virginia	807	721	86	261	262	76	65	198
Washington	643	590	53	151	229	70	66	161
West Virginia	178	166	11	34	60	23	22	45
Wisconsin	446	419	27	76	149	56	55	121
Wyoming	56	52	4	13	21	6	5	13

[1] Veterans serving in more than one period of service are counted only once in the total.   [2] Service from August 2, 1990, to the present.

Source: U.S. Dept. of Veterans Affairs, Veteran Data and Information, Veteran Demographics. <http://www1.va.gov/vetdata/page.cfm?pg=15>.

Table 503. Veterans Living by Age and Period of Service: 2007

[In thousands (23,816 represents 23,816,000). As of September 30. Includes those living outside U.S. See headnote, Table 502]

Age	Total veterans	Wartime veterans					Peacetime veterans
		Total [1]	Gulf War [2]	Vietnam era	Korean conflict	World War II	
Total	**23,816**	**17,739**	**4,966**	**7,884**	**2,961**	**2,912**	**6,077**
Under 35 years old	1,900	1,894	1,894	–	–	–	6
35 to 39 years old	1,259	1,064	1,064	–	–	–	196
40 to 44 years old	1,578	727	727	–	–	–	851
45 to 49 years old	1,876	556	535	23	–	–	1,320
50 to 54 years old	1,950	1,155	364	883	–	–	796
55 to 59 years old	2,718	2,540	237	2,453	–	–	179
60 to 64 years old	3,233	3,003	105	2,981	–	–	230
65 years old and over	9,302	6,802	41	1,545	2,961	2,912	2,500
Female, total	**1,780**	**1,226**	**795**	**258**	**71**	**137**	**555**

– Represents or rounds to zero.   [1] Veterans who served in more than one wartime period are counted only once in the total.   [2] Service from August 2, 1990 to the present.

Source: U.S. Dept. of Veterans Affairs, VetPop 2007, VA Office of the Actuary. <http://www1.va.gov/vetdata/page.cfm?pg=15>.

Table 504. Veterans by Sex, Race, and Hispanic or Latino Origin: 2006

[Data are based on the American Community Survey (ACS). The survey universe includes the household population and the population living in institutions, college dormitories, and other group quarters. Based on a sample and subject to sampling variability; see text of this section and Appendix III]

Characteristics	Total number	18 to 64 years	65 years and over
Total	**23,425,051**	**14,311,643**	**9,113,408**
Male	21,784,067	13,003,880	8,780,187
Female	1,640,984	1,307,763	333,221
White alone	19,831,560	11,503,156	8,328,404
Male	18,595,823	10,574,857	8,020,966
Female	1,235,737	928,299	307,438
Black or African American alone	2,430,525	1,908,960	521,565
Male	2,142,976	1,637,382	505,594
Female	287,549	271,578	15,971
American Indian/Alaska Native alone	168,985	129,243	39,742
Male	151,958	113,486	38,472
Female	17,027	15,757	1,270
Asian alone	292,095	199,177	92,918
Male	263,548	174,139	89,409
Female	28,547	25,038	3,509
Native Hawaiian and Other Pacific Islander alone	27,692	22,967	4,725
Male	24,026	19,558	4,468
Female	3,666	3,409	257
Some other race alone	378,779	317,492	61,287
Male	345,567	286,248	59,319
Female	33,212	31,244	1,968
Hispanic or Latino origin [1]	1,112,454	858,799	253,655
Male	1,017,602	771,589	246,013
Female	94,852	87,210	7,642

[1] Persons of Hispanic or Latino origin may be any race.

Source: U.S. Census Bureau, 2006 American Community Survey; using American FactFinder®, tables B21001, B21001A, B21001B, B21001C, B21001D, B21001E, B21001F, and B21001I; <http://factfinder.census.gov/>.

Table 505. Veterans Benefits—Expenditures by Program and Compensation for Service-Connected Disabilities: 1990 to 2007

[In millions of dollars (28,998 represents $28,998,000,000). For years ending September 30. Minus sign (–) indicates decrease]

Program	1990	1995	2000	2003	2004	2005	2006	2007
Total expenditures	**28,998**	**37,775**	**47,086**	**56,892**	**59,555**	**69,564**	**69,950**	**72,805**
Medical programs	11,582	16,255	19,637	25,188	28,158	29,191	31,308	33,705
Construction	661	641	466	411	318	480	497	704
General operating expenses	811	954	1,016	1,399	1,252	1,285	1,545	1,476
Compensation and pension	14,674	17,765	22,012	27,995	29,937	32,131	34,681	34,600
Vocational rehabilitation and education	452	1,317	1,610	2,565	2,827	3,033	3,163	3,180
All other [1]	818	844	2,345	–666	–2,937	3,445	–1,244	–860
Compensation for service-connected disabilities [2]	**9,284**	**11,644**	**15,511**	**20,855**	**22,387**	**24,515**	**26,551**	**28,200**

[1] Includes insurance, indemnities, and miscellaneous funds and expenditures and offsets from public receipts. (Excludes expenditures from personal funds of patients.) [2] Represents veterans receiving compensation for service-connected disabilities.

Source: U.S. Department of Veterans Affairs, *Expenditures and Workload*, annual. <http://www1.va.gov/vetdata/page.cfm?pg=3>.

Table 506. Veterans Compensation and Pension Benefits—Number on Rolls by Period of Service and Status: 1990 to 2006

[In thousands (3,548 represents 3,548,000), except as indicated. As of September 30. Living refers to veterans receiving compensation for disability incurred or aggravated while on active duty and low-income war veterans receiving pension who have permanent and total mostly nonservice-connected disabilities or are age 65 or older. Deceased refers to deceased veterans whose dependents were receiving pensions and compensation benefits]

Period of service and veteran status	1990	1995	2000	2002	2003	2004	2005	2006
Total	**3,584**	**3,330**	**3,236**	**3,285**	**3,369**	**3,432**	**3,503**	**3,582**
Living veterans	2,746	2,669	2,672	2,745	2,832	2,899	2,973	3,056
Service-connected	2,184	2,236	2,308	2,398	2,485	2,556	2,637	2,726
Nonservice-connected	562	433	364	347	347	343	336	330
Deceased veterans	838	662	564	540	538	533	530	527
Service-connected	320	307	307	310	314	318	323	326
Nonservice-connected	518	355	257	230	224	215	207	201
Prior to World War I	4	2	1	1	1	(Z)	(Z)	(Z)
Living	(Z)	(Z)	(Z)	(Z)	(Z)	(Z)	(Z)	(Z)
World War I	198	89	34	23	19	16	13	11
Living	18	3	(Z)	(Z)	(Z)	(Z)	(Z)	(Z)
World War II	1,723	1,307	968	856	813	766	718	674
Living	1,294	961	676	583	546	506	466	430
Korean conflict [1]	390	368	323	308	306	302	295	290
Living	305	290	255	243	241	237	231	226
Vietnam era [2]	774	868	969	1,052	1,120	1,172	1,218	1,260
Living	685	766	848	922	983	1,028	1,068	1,104
Gulf War [3]	(X)	138	334	431	490	552	630	716
Living	(X)	134	326	421	479	540	617	701
Peacetime	495	559	607	613	620	624	627	631
Living	444	514	567	575	583	587	591	596

X Not applicable.   Z Fewer than 500.   [1] Service during period June 27, 1950, to January 31, 1955.   [2] Service from August 5, 1964, to May 7, 1975.   [3] Service from August 2, 1990 to the present.

Source: U.S. Department of Veterans Affairs, 1990 to 1995, *Annual Report of the Secretary of Veterans Affairs*; beginning 2000, *Annual Accountability Report* and unpublished data; <http://www1.va.gov/vetdata/>.

Table 507. **Homeland Security Funding by Agency: 2006 to 2008**

[In millions of dollars (54,639.4 represents $54,639,400,000). For year ending September 30. A total of 32 agencies comprise federal homeland security funding for 2008. U.S. Department of Homeland Security (DHS) is the designated department to coordinate and centralize the leadership of many homeland security activities under a single department. In addition to DHS, the U.S. Departments of Defense (DoD), Energy (DoE), Health and Human Services (HHS), Justice (DoJ), and State Department account for most of the total government-wide homeland security funding]

Agency	2006 [1]	2007	2008
Total budget authority, excluding BioShield [2, 3]	**54,639.4**	**56,925.9**	**61,808.4**
U.S. Department of Agriculture	597.4	540.5	570.0
U.S. Department of Commerce	181.1	205.0	206.9
U.S. Department of Defense	16,479.3	16,538.3	17,374.4
U.S. Department of Education	24.7	26.2	27.1
U.S. Department of Energy	1,702.1	1,719.2	1,828.7
U.S. Department of Health and Human Services	4,351.8	4,327.0	4,300.6
U.S. Department of Homeland Security [4]	25,154.9	26,857.9	30,100.6
U.S. Department of Housing and Urban Development	1.9	1.9	1.9
U.S. Department of the Interior	59.5	47.8	49.6
U.S. Department of Justice	2,995.4	3,306.4	3,273.5
U.S. Department of Labor	48.3	49.4	47.5
U.S. Department of State	1,107.9	1,241.6	1,961.5
U.S. Department of Transportation	181.0	205.7	205.3
U.S. Department of the Treasury	113.5	126.8	116.0
U.S. Department of Veterans Affairs	297.8	259.8	271.7
Corps of Engineers	72.0	42.0	42.0
Environmental Protection Agency	129.4	166.7	138.1
Executive Office of the President	20.8	20.8	21.2
General Services Administration	98.6	168.2	143.0
National Aeronautics and Space Administration	212.6	199.2	205.2
National Science Foundation	344.2	385.4	373.9
Office of Personnel Management	2.7	2.8	2.3
Social Security Administration	176.4	194.0	212.6
District of Columbia	13.5	8.5	3.4
Federal Communications Commission	2.3	2.3	2.3
Intelligence Community Management Account	56.0	56.0	122.0
National Archives and Records Administration	18.2	17.9	17.7
Nuclear Regulatory Commission	79.3	72.2	72.1
Securities and Exchange Commission	5.0	14.3	16.4
Smithsonian Institution	83.7	80.7	93.1
United States Holocaust Memorial Museum	7.8	7.8	8.0
Corporation for National and Community Service	20.4	33.6	(NA)

NA Not available. [1] FY 06 reflects the adjustments made for the Coast Guard (DHS) and reestimates for DoD. [2] The federal spending estimates are for the Executive Branch's homeland security efforts. These estimates do not include the efforts of the Legislative or Judicial Branches. [3] The U.S. Department of Homeland Security Appropriations Act, 2004, provided $5.6 billion for Project BioShield, to remain available through 2013. Including this uneven funding stream can distort year-over-year comparisons. [4] Not all actitivies carried out by DHS constitute homeland security funding (e.g. response to natural disasters and Coast Guard search and rescue activities), DHS estimates in this table do not represent the entire DHS budget.

Source: U.S. Office of Management and Budget, Budget of the United States Government Fiscal Year 2009, The Budget Documents, *Analytical Perspectives, Budget of the United States Government Fiscal Year 2009, Crosscutting Programs, Homeland Security Funding Analysis*; <http://www.whitehouse.gov/omb/budget/fy2009/>.

Table 508. **Homeland Security Funding by National Strategy Mission Area: 2006 to 2008**

[In millions of dollars (54,639.4 represents $54,639,400,000). For Homeland Security funding analysis by OMB, agencies categorize their funding data based on the critical mission areas defined in the *National Strategy*]

Agency	2006 [1]	2007	2008
Total budget authority excluding BioShield [2, 3]	**54,639.4**	**56,925.9**	**61,808.4**
Intelligence and warning	443.0	670.8	682.7
Border and transportation security	18,042.3	19,365.3	22,286.8
Domestic counterterrorism	4,535.6	5,026.6	4,896.8
Protecting critical infrastructure and key assets	17,933.2	18,388.2	19,926.1
Defending against catastrophic threats	8,573.7	8,595.9	8,278.1
Emergency preparedness and response	4,992.3	4,822.2	5,551.4
Other	119.3	56.9	186.5

[1] FY 06 reflects the adjustments made for the Coast Guard and reestimates for DoD. See source for further details. [2] Enacted budgets. [3] See footnote 3 in Table 507.

Source: U.S. Office of Management and Budget, Budget of the United States Government Fiscal Year 2009, The Budget Documents, *Analytical Perspectives, Budget of the United States Government Fiscal Year 2009, Crosscutting Programs, Homeland Security Funding Analysis*; <http://www.whitehouse.gov/omb/budget/fy2009/>.

Table 509. Department of Homeland Security Total Budget Authority and Personnel by Organization: 2007 and 2008

[**Expenditures in thousands of dollars (43,304,935 represents $43,304,935,000). For the fiscal year ending September 30.** Not all activities carried out by DHS constitute homeland security funding (e.g., Coast Guard search and rescue activities)]

Organization	Expenditures 2007	Expenditures 2008	Full-time employees 2007	Full-time employees 2008
Total [1]	43,304,935	47,285,102	185,570	195,865
Departmental operations	603,525	571,791	950	1,119
Analysis and operations	299,663	306,000	475	518
Office of the Inspector General	98,685	108,711	545	551
U.S. Customs & Border Protection	7,746,259	9,306,725	44,414	50,417
U.S. Immigration & Customs Enforcement	4,696,641	5,054,317	16,854	17,938
Transportation Security Administration	6,329,291	6,819,859	49,195	50,871
U.S. Coast Guard	8,554,067	8,741,053	47,798	48,558
U.S. Secret Service	1,485,617	1,595,496	6,649	6,700
National Protection and Program Directorate	942,436	902,076	602	664
Office of Health Affairs	9,917	116,500	15	49
Federal Emergency Management Agency (FEMA)	4,571,716	5,522,178	6,409	6,689
FEMA Grants [2]	4,048,500	4,117,800	([3])	([3])
U.S. Citizenship & Immigration Services	2,216,240	2,539,845	10,122	10,264
Federal Law Enforcement Training Center	253,279	267,666	1,047	1,056
Science & Technology Directorate (S&T)	968,131	830,335	383	350
Domestic Nuclear Detection Office	480,968	484,750	112	121

[1] Departmental operations is comprised of the Office of the Secretary & Executive Management, the Office of the Federal Coordinator for Gulf Coast Rebuilding, the Office of the Undersecretary for Management, the Office of the Chief Financial Officer, and the Office of the Chief Information Officer. [2] Includes the following FEMA appropriations: State and Local Programs & Emergency Management Perf. Grants, and Assistance to Firefighters Grants. [3] Employee data are included in the FEMA full-time employees.

Source: U.S. Department of Homeland Security, Budget-in-Brief, Fiscal Year 2009; <http://www.dhs.gov/xabout/budget/>; (accessed 26 March 2008).

Table 510. Homeland Security Grants by State/Territories: 2006 and 2007

[**In thousands of dollars (1,677,922 represents $1,677,922,000). For years ending September 30.** Grants consist of the following programs: Citizen Corps Program (CCP), Law Enforcement Terrorism Prevention Program (LETPP), State Homeland Security Program (SHSP), Metropolitan Medical Response System (MMRS), and Urban Areas Security Initiative (UASI)]

State/Territory	2006	2007	State/Territory	2006	2007	State/Territory	2006	2007
Total ...	1,677,922	1,666,460	KY	24,119	11,757	PA	49,335	61,306
			LA	30,437	21,873	RI	7,838	12,119
U.S.	1,650,306	1,650,810	ME	7,785	6,697	SC	14,679	11,001
			MD	24,291	32,670	SD	7,734	6,682
AL	15,578	11,574	MA	41,246	35,509	TN	13,762	20,045
AK	8,294	7,195	MI	46,899	39,237	TX	89,880	121,629
AZ	20,171	33,774	MN	13,395	20,504	UT	8,271	6,989
AR	8,343	7,238	MS	8,528	7,002	VT	10,908	6,677
CA	231,951	242,245	MO	42,861	31,244	VA	16,888	33,278
CO	21,080	19,899	MT	7,930	6,686	WA	32,222	28,926
CT	13,521	10,479	NE	21,746	7,226	WV	13,294	6,712
DE	10,296	6,684	NV	20,509	19,357	WI	24,431	17,796
DC	54,015	71,985	NH	7,887	6,955	WY	7,674	6,674
FL	100,122	84,743	NJ	51,983	61,109	AS	4,695	2,218
GA	44,406	39,959	NM	8,270	6,973	GU	2,734	2,221
HI	12,935	12,114	NY	183,674	208,039	NM	2,721	2,218
ID	11,759	6,701	NC	30,484	25,256	MH	–	–
IL	90,405	86,248	ND	10,788	6,678	FM	–	–
IN	21,129	23,397	OH	41,347	46,321			
IA	13,480	7,043	OK	19,497	14,198	PR [1]	7,724	6,773
KS	14,274	8,375	OR	17,956	16,033	VI	2,742	2,220

– Represents zero. [1] PR—Puerto Rico, VI—Virgin Islands, AS—America Samoa, GU—Guam, NM—Northern Mariana Islands, MH—Marshall Islands, and FM—Micronesia.

Source: U.S. Department of Homeland Security, Prevention and Protection, Grants, Homeland Security Grants; <http://www.dhs.gov/xgovt/grants/index.shtm>.

Table 511. Coast Guard Migrant Interdictions by Nationality of Alien: 2000 to 2007

[For the year ending September 30]

Year	Total	Haiti	Dominican Republic	China [1]	Cuba	Mexico	Ecuador	Other
2000	4,210	1,113	499	261	1,000	49	1,244	44
2002	4,104	1,486	177	80	666	32	1,608	55
2003	6,068	2,013	1,748	15	1,555	–	703	34
2004	10,899	3,229	5,014	68	1,225	86	1,189	88
2005	9,455	1,850	3,612	32	2,712	55	1,149	45
2006	7,886	1,198	3,011	31	2,810	52	693	167
2007	6,338	1,610	1,469	73	2,868	26	125	46

– Represents zero. [1] See footnote 2, Table 1288.

Source: U.S. Department of Homeland Security, United States Coast Guard, Fact File, *Migrant Statistics*. <http://www.uscg.mil/hq /g-cp/comrel/factfile/>; (accessed 22 March 2008).

Table 512. Deportable Aliens Located by Program and Border Patrol Sector: 2000 to 2006

[**As of the end of September.** For purposes of statistical reporting there is no difference between the terms "apprehension" and "deportable alien located." For definitions for Immigration statistics, go to <http://www.dhs.gov/ximgtn/statistics/stdfdef.shtm>]

Program and sector	2000	2002	2003	2004	2005	2006
Total	**1,814,729**	**1,062,270**	**1,046,422**	**1,264,232**	**1,291,142**	**1,206,457**
Investigations [1]	138,291	106,960	114,865	103,837	102,034	101,854
Detention and Removal Operations [2]	(X)	(X)	(X)	(X)	(X)	15,467
Border Patrol	1,676,438	955,310	931,557	1,160,395	1,189,108	1,089,136
All southwest sectors	**1,643,679**	**929,809**	**905,065**	**1,139,282**	**1,171,428**	**1,072,018**
San Diego, CA	151,681	100,681	111,515	138,608	126,909	142,122
El Centro, CA	238,126	108,273	92,099	74,467	55,726	61,469
Yuma, AZ	108,747	42,654	56,638	98,060	138,438	118,537
Tucson, AZ	616,346	333,648	347,263	491,771	439,090	392,104
El Paso, TX	115,696	94,154	88,816	104,399	122,689	122,261
Marfa, TX	13,689	11,392	10,319	10,530	10,536	7,517
Del Rio, TX	157,178	66,985	50,145	53,794	68,510	42,634
Laredo, TX	108,973	82,095	70,521	74,706	75,342	74,843
Rio Grande Valley, TX	133,243	89,927	77,749	92,947	134,188	110,531
All other sectors	**32,759**	**25,501**	**26,492**	**21,113**	**17,680**	**17,118**
Blaine, WA	2,581	1,732	1,380	1,354	1,001	809
Buffalo, NY	1,570	1,102	564	671	400	1,517
Detroit, MI	2,057	1,511	2,345	1,912	1,792	1,282
Grand Forks, ND	562	1,369	1,223	1,225	754	517
Havre, MT	1,568	1,463	1,406	986	949	567
Houlton, ME	489	432	292	263	233	175
Livermore, CA [3]	6,205	4,371	3,565	1,850	117	–
Miami, FL	6,237	5,143	5,931	4,602	7,243	6,032
New Orleans, LA	6,478	4,665	5,151	2,889	1,358	3,054
Ramey, PR	1,731	835	1,688	1,813	1,619	1,436
Spokane, WA	1,324	1,142	992	847	279	185
Swanton, VT	1,957	1,736	1,955	2,701	1,935	1,544

– Represents zero. X Not applicable. [1] The Immigration and Customs Enforcement (ICE) Office of Investigations that focus on the enforcement of a wide variety of laws that include immigration and customs statutes. [2] Include arrests of fugitive and nonfugitive aliens under the Office of Detention and Removal Operations (DRO) National Fugitive Operations Program. [3] Livermore sector closed July 30, 2004.

Source: U.S. Department of Homeland Security, Office of Immigration Statistics, *Yearbook of Immigration Statistics, 2006*. See also <http://www.dhs.gov/ximgtn/statistics/publications/yearbook.shtm>.

Table 513. Deportable Aliens Located: 1925 to 2006

[See headnote, Table 512]

Year	Number	Year	Number	Year	Number	Year	Number
1925	22,199	1946	99,591	1967	161,608	1988	1,008,145
1926	12,735	1947	193,657	1968	212,057	1989	954,243
1927	16,393	1948	192,779	1969	283,557	1990	1,169,939
1928	23,566	1949	288,253	1970	345,353	1991	1,197,875
1929	32,711	1950	468,339	1971	420,126	1992	1,258,481
1930	20,880	1951	509,040	1972	505,949	1993	1,327,261
1931	22,276	1952	543,535	1973	655,968	1994	1,094,719
1932	22,735	1953	885,587	1974	788,145	1995	1,394,554
1933	20,949	1954	1,089,583	1975	766,600	1996	1,649,986
1934	10,319	1955	254,096	1976 [1]	1,097,739	1997	1,536,520
1935	11,016	1956	87,696	1977	1,042,215	1998	1,679,439
1936	11,728	1957	59,918	1978	1,057,977	1999	1,714,035
1937	13,054	1958	53,474	1979	1,076,418	2000	1,814,729
1938	12,851	1959	45,336	1980	910,361	2001	1,387,486
1939	12,037	1960	70,684	1981	975,780	2002	1,062,279
1940	10,492	1961	88,823	1982	970,246	2003	1,046,422
1941	11,294	1962	92,758	1983	1,251,357	2004	1,264,232
1942	11,784	1963	88,712	1984	1,246,981	2005	1,291,142
1943	11,175	1964	86,597	1985	1,348,749	2006 [2]	1,206,457
1944	31,174	1965	110,371	1986	1,767,40		
1945	69,164	1966	138,520	1987	1,190,488		

[1] Includes the 15 months from July 1, 1975, to September 30, 1976, because the end date of fiscal years was changed from June 30 to September 30. [2] Detention and Removal Operations (DRO) data are included beginning in Fiscal Year 2006.

Source: U.S. Department of Homeland Security, Office of Immigration Statistics, *Yearbook of Immigration Statistics, 2006*. See also <http://www.dhs.gov/ximgtn/statistics/publications/yearbook.shtm>.

Table 514. **Principal Immigration-Related Activities of Immigration and Customs Enforcement (ICE) Investigations: 2006**

[Data refer to criminal cases only; administrative cases are not included due to changes in reporting]

Activities	Criminal arrests	Criminal indict-ments	Criminal convictions	Number of seizures	Value of seizures (dollars)
Total, all immigration-related categories	**8,778**	**6,514**	**6,872**	**3,755**	**33,861,911**
Financial investigations [1]	27	16	14	60	3,996,732
Human smuggling and trafficking investigations [2]	2,154	1,585	1,596	1,609	11,046,622
General and criminal alien investigations [3]	4,589	3,434	3,689	532	4,804,781
Identity and benefit fraud (IBF) investigations [4]	1,272	1,032	1,073	1,281	12,230,727
Compliance and worksite enforcement [5]	20	6	7	12	602
Worksite enforcement [6]	716	441	493	261	1,782,447

[1] Financial investigations refer to cases developed to counteract organizations involved in money laundering and related financial crimes. [2] Human smuggling and trafficking investigations refer to cases targeted against persons or organizations that bring, transport, harbor, or smuggle illegal aliens into or within the United States. [3] General investigations refer to general investigative activities, including those targeting aliens who attempt illegal reentry, have absconded, or commit other crimes in the United States. Criminal alien investigations focus on large-scale organizations engaged in ongoing criminal activity. [4] Identity and benefit fraud investigations seek to penetrate fraud schemes that are used to violate immigration and related laws, or used to shield the true status of illegal aliens in order to obtain entitlement benefits from federal, state, or local agencies. [5] The compliance enforcement program focuses on preventing foreign nationals from exploiting the nation's immigration system by developing cases for investigation from Department of Homeland Security systems containing information on the status of students and other nonimmigrants. [6] The worksite enforcement program focuses on monitoring and inspecting work sites to apprehend unauthorized alien workers and to provide for penalties and fines against employers who knowingly hire, recruit, or refer aliens for employment for a fee.

Source: U.S. Department of Homeland Security, Office of Immigration Statistics, *2006 Yearbook of Immigration Statistics*. See also <http://uscis.gov/graphics/shared/statistics/yearbook/index.htm> (accessed 10 June 2008).

Table 515. **Aliens Returned or Removed by Crime Categories and Country of Nationality: 2002 to 2006**

[**As of the end of September.** For definitions of immigration enforcement terms, see "Immigration Enforcement Actions, 2006 Yearbook of Immigration Statistics." "Crime categories" and "Countries of nationality" ranked by latest data year]

Violations	2002	2003	2004	2005	2006
Total Aliens Returned or Removed:	**1,174,981**	**1,152,725**	**1,403,508**	**1,338,698**	**1,315,770**
Returns [1]	1,012,116	945,294	1,166,576	1,096,920	1,043,381
Removals [2]	162,865	207,431	236,932	241,778	272,389
Noncriminal	90,309	125,097	146,029	150,879	176,637
Criminal [3]	72,556	82,334	90,903	90,899	95,752
Leading crime categories					
Dangerous drugs.	29,614	32,441	34,071	33,979	33,046
Immigration	11,278	11,790	15,174	16,909	22,697
Assault	7,486	8,878	9,654	9,492	9,373
Burglary.	2,881	3,324	3,406	3,342	3,454
Robbery.	2,690	2,887	2,924	2,993	2,861
Larceny	2,089	2,606	2,830	2,714	2,713
Sexual assault	1,810	2,316	2,777	2,635	2,485
Family offenses.	1,857	2,277	2,478	2,160	2,232
Stolen vehicles	1,331	1,577	1,797	1,788	1,918
Sex offenses.	1,170	1,631	1,984	1,910	1,859
Other	10,350	12,607	13,808	12,977	13,114
Leading country of nationality					
Mexico	56,960	64,641	70,113	69,704	70,951
Honduras.	1,481	1,996	2,483	2,588	5,591
El Salvador	1,756	2,066	2,768	2,767	3,688
Guatemala	1,240	1,565	1,937	1,895	3,608
Dominican Republic.	2,016	2,194	2,556	2,350	2,250
Colombia.	1,497	1,380	1,493	1,379	1,313
Jamaica.	1,550	1,522	1,670	1,499	1,250
Nicaragua	250	323	407	357	588
Brazil.	134	220	763	1,428	560
Canada	578	474	565	525	479
Other	5,094	5,953	6,148	6,407	5,474

[1] Returns are the confirmed movement of an inadmissible or deportable alien out of the United States not based on an order of removal. Most of the voluntary departures are of Mexican nationals who have been apprehended by the U.S. Border Patrol and are returned to Mexico. [2] Removals are the compulsory and confirmed movement of an inadmissible or deportable alien out of the United States based on an order of removal. An alien who is removed has administrative or criminal consequences placed on subsequent reentry owing to the fact of the removal. [3] Refers to persons removed based on a criminal charge or those with a criminal conviction.

Source: U.S. Department of Homeland Security, Office of Immigration Statistics, *2006 Yearbook of Immigration Statistics* and unpublished data. See also <http://www.dhs.gov/ximgtn/statistics/publications/yearbook.shtm> (accessed 9 June 2008).

U.S. Census Bureau, Statistical Abstract of the United States: 2009

Table 516. Customs and Border Protection (CBP)—Processed and Cleared Passengers, Planes, Vehicles, and Containers: 2000 to 2007

[In thousands (80,519 represents 80,519,000). For year ending September 30]

Characteristic	2000	2003	2004	2005	2006	2007
Air						
Passengers.............	80,519	72,959	80,866	86,123	87,906	91,574
Commercial planes [1].........	829	790	824	866	881	916
Private planes..............	146	132	140	135	139	139
Land						
Passengers [2, 3].............	397,312	329,998	326,693	317,765	289,048	299,004
Autos [2].................	127,095	120,376	121,419	121,654	119,372	112,428
Rail containers.............	2,157	2,472	2,588	2,655	2,735	2,737
Truck containers [4]..........	10,397	11,163	11,252	11,308	11,489	11,459
Sea						
Passengers [5]...............	10,990	15,127	22,234	26,228	26,223	27,059
Vessels [6]..............	211	204	142	113	168	170
Vessel containers [7]..........	5,813	9,092	9,796	11,341	11,622	11,703

[1] A commercial aircraft is any aircraft transporting passengers and/or cargo for some payment or other consideration, including money or services rendered. [2] See Table 1231 for more details. [3] Includes pedestrians. [4] Truck containers—number of trucks entering the U.S. [5] Does not include passengers on ferries. [6] Number of vessels. Includes every description of water craft or other contrivance used or capable of being used as a means of transportation on water, does not include aircraft. [7] Number of vessel containers.

Source: U.S. Department of Homeland Security, Customs and Border Protection, *About CBP, Statistics and Accomplishments, National Workload Statistics, 2000–2005* and unpublished data. See also <http://www.cbp.gov/xp/cgov/about/accomplish/national_workload_stats.xml>

Table 517. Prohibited Items Intercepted at U.S. Airport Screening Checkpoints: 2003 to 2007

[**Passengers boarding aircraft in thousands (646,275 represents 646,275,000). For the calendar year.** Transportation Security Administration (TSA) assumed responsibility for airport security on February 17, 2002, and by November 19, 2002, TSA assumed control over all passenger screenings from private contractors]

Year	2003	2004	2005	2006	2007
Passengers boarding aircraft total [1]..........	**646,275**	**702,921**	**738,327**	**744,242**	**769,186**
Domestic.................	592,412	640,698	670,418	671,796	693,190
International...............	53,863	62,222	67,908	72,445	75,996
Total prohibited items................	**6,167,497**	**7,103,560**	**15,886,014**	**13,709,065**	**6,515,995**
Knife [2].................	1,969,003	2,055,306	1,822,846	1,607,014	1,056,662
Other cutting items [3]...........	3,029,318	3,409,724	3,276,936	163,419	(X)
Club [4].................	25,578	28,998	20,531	12,295	9,443
Box cutter................	21,396	22,428	21,319	15,999	11,908
Firearm [5].................	638	254	850	820	769
Flammables and irritants [6].......	485,792	697,242	371,711	94,096	73,165
Lighters [7].................	(X)	(X)	9,420,653	11,616,217	5,124,344
Other [8].................	635,772	889,608	952,018	200,025	240,473

X Not applicable. [1] Data comes from the Air Transport Association. Data are for U.S. passenger and cargo airlines only. [2] Knife includes any length and type except round-bladed, butter, and plastic cutlery. [3] Other cutting instruments refer to, e.g., scissors, screwdrivers, swords, sabers, and ice picks. [4] Club refers to baseball bats, night sticks, billy clubs, bludgeons; etc. [5] Firearm refers to items like pistols, revolvers, rifles, automatic weapons, shotguns, parts of guns and firearms. [6] Incendiaries refer to categories of ammunition and gunpowder, flammables/irritants, and explosives. [7] As of April 14, 2005, passengers are prohibited from carrying all lighters on their person or in carry-on luggage or onboard an airplane. [8] Beginning December 22, scissors with a cutting edge of 4 inches or less and tools such as screwdrivers, wrenches, and pliers smaller than 7 inches will be permitted on board. Scissors longer than 4 inches and tools such as crowbars, drills, hammers, and saws will continue to be prohibited from carry-on bags.

Source: U.S. Department of Homeland Security, Transportation Security Administration, unpublished data; 13 May 2008; <http://www.tsa.gov>. Air Transport Association of America, Washington, DC. Annual Traffic and Operations: U.S. Airlines; <http://www.airlines.org/home/default.aspx>.

Table 518. Seizure Statistics for Intellectual Property Rights (IPR): 2003 to 2007

[**In thousands of dollars (94,019 represents $94,019,000, except as indicated).** Customs and Border Protection (CBP) is dedicated to protecting against the importation of goods which infringe/violate Intellectual Property Rights (IPR) by devoting substantial resources toward identifying and seizing shipments of infringing articles]

Item	2003	2004	2005	2006	2007
Number of IPR Seizures	6,500	7,255	8,022	14,675	13,657
Total domestic value of IPR seizures ($1,000) [1]........	94,019	138,768	93,235	155,369	196,754
Selected IPR commodities seized by value:					
Footwear.......................	2,555	2,049	8,941	63,446	77,781
Wearing apparel...................	13,889	51,737	16,100	24,321	27,006
Handbags/wallets/backpacks.............	11,458	23,190	14,955	14,750	14,214
Computers/hardware	(NA)	1,684	4,799	14,288	9,337
Consumer electronics [2]	3,780	8,880	8,794	7,057	16,042
Watches/parts....................	3,384	2,543	3,071	2,832	13,356
Media [3]	7,358	5,050	(NA)	6,965	7,884
All others	51,595	43,636	36,576	21,710	31,134

NA Not available. [1] Domestic value is the cost of the seized goods, plus the costs of shipping and importing the goods into the U.S. and an amount for profit. [2] Consumer electronics includes cell phones and accessories, radios, power strips, electrical tools, and appliances. [3] Includes motion pictures on tape, laser disc, and DVD; interactive and computer software on CD-ROM and floppy discs; and music on CD or tape.

Source: U.S. Department of Homeland Security, Customs and Border Protection, "Import, Commercial Enforcement, Intellectual Property Rights, Seizure Statistics"; <http://www.cbp.gov/xp/cgov/trade/priority_trade/ipr/seizure/trading>.

Section 11
Social Insurance and Human Services

This section presents data related to governmental expenditures for social insurance and human services; governmental programs for old-age, survivors, disability, and health insurance (OASDHI); governmental employee retirement; private pension plans; government unemployment and temporary disability insurance; federal supplemental security income payments and aid to the needy; child and other welfare services; and federal food programs. Also included here are selected data on workers' compensation and vocational rehabilitation, child support, child care, charity contributions, and philanthropic trusts and foundations.

The principal source for these data is the Social Security Administration's *Annual Statistical Supplement to the Social Security Bulletin* which presents current data on many of the programs.

Social insurance under the Social Security Act—Programs established by the Social Security Act provide protection against wage loss resulting from retirement, prolonged disability, death, or unemployment, and protection against the cost of medical care during old age and disability. The federal OASDI program provides monthly benefits to retired or disabled insured workers and their dependents and to survivors of insured workers. To be eligible, a worker must have had a specified period of employment in which OASDI taxes were paid. The age of eligibility for full retirement benefits had been 65 years old for many years. However, for persons born in 1938 or later that age gradually increases until it reaches age 67 for those born after 1959. Reduced benefits may be obtained as early as age 62. The worker's spouse is under the same limitations. Survivor benefits are payable to dependents of deceased insured workers. Disability benefits are payable to an insured worker under full retirement age with a prolonged disability and to the disabled worker's dependents on the same basis as

dependents of retired workers. Disability benefits are provided at age 50 to the disabled widow or widower of a deceased worker who was fully insured at the time of death. Disabled children, aged 18 or older, of retired, disabled, or deceased workers are also eligible for benefits. A lump-sum benefit is generally payable on the death of an insured worker to a spouse or minor children. For information on the Medicare program, see Section 3, Health and Nutrition.

Retirement, survivors, disability, and hospital insurance benefits are funded by a payroll tax on annual earnings (up to a maximum of earnings set by law) of workers, employers, and the self-employed. The maximum taxable earnings are adjusted annually to reflect increasing wage levels (see Table 525). Effective January 1994, there is no dollar limit on wages and self-employment income subject to the hospital insurance tax. Tax receipts and benefit payments are administered through federal trust funds. Special benefits for uninsured persons; hospital benefits for persons aged 65 and over with specified amounts of social security coverage less than that required for cash benefit eligibility; and that part of the cost of supplementary medical insurance not financed by contributions from participants are financed from federal general revenues.

Unemployment insurance is presently administered by the U.S. Employment and Training Administration and each state's employment security agency. By agreement with the U.S. Secretary of Labor, state agencies also administer unemployment compensation for eligible ex-military personnel and federal employees. Under state unemployment insurance laws, benefits related to the individual's past earnings are paid to unemployed eligible workers. State laws vary concerning the length of time benefits are paid and their amount. In most states, benefits are payable for 26 weeks and, during periods

Social Insurance and Human Services   339

of high unemployment, extended benefits are payable under a federal-state program to those who have exhausted their regular state benefits. Some states also supplement the basic benefit with allowances for dependents.

Unemployment insurance is funded by a federal unemployment tax levied on the taxable payrolls of most employers. Taxable payroll under the federal act and 12 state laws is the first $7,000 in wages paid each worker during a year. Forty-one states have taxable payrolls above $7,000. Employers are allowed a percentage credit of taxable payroll for contributions paid to states under state unemployment insurance laws. The remaining percent of the federal tax finances administrative costs, the federal share of extended benefits, and advances to states. About 97 percent of wage and salary workers are covered by unemployment insurance.

Retirement programs for government employees—The Civil Service Retirement System (CSRS) and the Federal Employees' Retirement System (FERS) are the two major programs providing age and service, disability, and survivor annuities for federal civilian employees. In general, employees hired after December 31, 1983, are covered under FERS and the social security program (OASDHI), and employees on staff prior to that date are members of CSRS and are covered under Medicare. CSRS employees were offered the option of transferring to FERS during 1987 and 1998. There are separate retirement systems for the uniformed services (supplementing OASDHI) and for certain special groups of federal employees. State and local government employees are covered for the most part by state and local retirement systems similar to the federal programs. In many jurisdictions these benefits supplement OASDHI coverage.

Workers' compensation—All states provide protection against work-connected injuries and deaths, although some states exclude certain workers (e.g., domestic workers). Federal laws cover federal employees, private employees in the District of Columbia, and longshoremen and harbor workers. In addition, the Department of Labor administers "black lung"

benefits programs for coal miners disabled by pneumoconiosis and for specified dependents and survivors. Specified occupational diseases are compensable to some extent. In most states, benefits are related to the worker's salary. The benefits may or may not be augmented by dependents' allowances or automatically adjusted to prevailing wage levels.

Income support—Income support programs are designed to provide benefits for persons with limited income and resources. The Supplemental Security Income (SSI) program and Temporary Assistance for Needy Families (TANF) program are the major programs providing monthly payments. In addition, a number of programs provide money payments or in-kind benefits for special needs or purposes. Several programs offer food and nutritional services. Also, various federal-state programs provide energy assistance, public housing, and subsidized housing to individuals and families with low incomes. General assistance may also be available at the state or local level.

The SSI program, administered by the Social Security Administration, provides income support to persons aged 65 or older and blind or disabled adults and children. Eligibility requirements and federal payment standards are nationally uniform. Most states supplement the basic SSI payment for all or selected categories of persons.

The Personal Responsibility and Work Opportunity Reconciliation Act of 1996 contained provisions that replaced the Aid to Families With Dependent Children (AFDC), Job Opportunities and Basic Skills (JOBS), and Emergency Assistance programs with the Temporary Assistance for Needy Families block grant program. This law contains strong work requirements, comprehensive child support enforcement, support for families moving from welfare to work, and other features. The TANF became effective as soon as each state submitted a complete plan implementing TANF, but no later than July 1, 1997. The AFDC program provided cash assistance based on need, income, resources, and family size.

U.S. Census Bureau, Statistical Abstract of the United States: 2009

Federal food stamp program—Under the food stamp program, single persons and those living in households meeting nationwide standards for income and assets may receive coupons redeemable for food at most retail food stores or provides benefits through electronic benefit transfer. The monthly amount of benefits or allotments a unit receives is determined by household size and income. Households without income receive the determined monthly cost of a nutritionally adequate diet for their household size. This amount is updated to account for food price increases. Households with income receive the difference between the amount of a nutritionally adequate diet and 30 percent of their income, after certain allowable deductions.

To qualify for the program, a household must have less than $2,000 in disposable assets ($3,000 if one member is aged 60 or older), gross income below 130 percent of the official poverty guidelines for the household size, and net income below 100 percent of the poverty guidelines. Households with a person aged 60 or older or a disabled person receiving SSI, social security, state general assistance, or veterans' disability benefits may have gross income exceeding 130 percent of the poverty guidelines. All households in which all members receive TANF or SSI are categorically eligible for food stamps without meeting these income or resource criteria. Households are certified for varying lengths of time, depending on their income sources and individual circumstances.

Health and welfare services— Programs providing health and welfare services are aided through federal grants to states for child welfare services, vocational rehabilitation, activities for the aged, maternal and child health services, maternity and infant care projects, comprehensive health services, and a variety of public health activities. For information about the Medicaid program, see Section 3, Health and Nutrition.

Noncash benefits—The U.S. Census Bureau annually collects data on the characteristics of recipients of noncash (in-kind) benefits to supplement the collection of annual money income data in the Current Population Survey (see text, Section 1, Population, and Section 13, Income, Expenditures, Poverty, and Wealth). Noncash benefits are those benefits received in a form other than money which serve to enhance or improve the economic well-being of the recipient. As for money income, the data for noncash benefits are for the calendar year prior to the date of the interview. The major categories of noncash benefits covered are public transfers (e.g., food stamps, school lunch, public housing, and Medicaid) and employer or union-provided benefits to employees.

Statistical reliability—For discussion of statistical collection, estimation, and sampling procedures and measures of statistical reliability applicable to HHS and Census Bureau data, see Appendix III.

U.S. Census Bureau, Statistical Abstract of the United States: 2009

Table 519. Selected Payments to Individuals by Function: 1960 to 2006

[In billions of dollars (35 represents $35,000,000,000)]

Source and sector	1960	1970	1980	1990	1995	1998	1999	2000	2001	2002	2003	2004	2005	2006
All benefits	35	108	422	1,027	1,492	1,696	1,786	1,908	2,067	2,244	2,383	2,532	2,667	2,841
Retirement income benefits	15	51	202	482	661	775	813	863	918	974	1,020	1,068	1,103	1,167
Social Security Old-Age, Survivors, and Disability Insurance	10	31	119	244	328	369	380	401	425	447	463	485	513	544
Private employer pension and profit sharing	2	7	35	136	191	236	253	270	289	309	320	332	322	332
Public employer retirement plans	4	12	48	102	142	169	180	192	204	219	236	251	269	291
Federal civilian employee retirement [1]	1	3	16	32	40	46	47	50	52	53	55	58	62	67
State and local government retirement	1	4	15	41	66	84	92	100	110	121	132	141	151	165
Military retirement [2]	1	3	13	22	28	32	32	33	35	36	41	43	46	49
Railroad retirement	1	2	5	7	8	8	8	8	8	9	9	9	9	10
Health benefits	4	22	99	300	454	517	545	597	645	702	761	832	903	1,015
Medicare hospital insurance and supplementary medical insurance	–	7	36	108	179	206	209	220	244	261	278	303	333	402
Group health insurance	4	15	62	191	274	310	335	376	400	439	481	527	568	610
Military health insurance [3]	–	–	–	2	2	1	1	1	1	2	2	2	2	3
Other employee benefits [4]	9	17	51	88	103	106	112	113	130	157	161	147	147	150
Unemployment insurance [5]	3	4	16	18	22	20	21	20	32	54	53	36	32	30
Workers' compensation [5]	2	3	13	38	43	44	46	48	52	54	55	56	56	57
Group life insurance	1	3	7	12	16	18	20	17	17	18	19	18	20	20
Miscellaneous disability [6]	–	1	3	4	3	3	3	4	4	4	4	5	5	5
Veterans' benefits [7]	4	7	13	16	19	21	22	23	25	28	30	32	35	38
Public assistance [8]	4	18	70	157	275	299	318	336	374	412	441	485	514	510

– Represents or rounds to zero. [1] Consists of civil service, foreign service, Public Health Service officers, Tennessee Valley Authority, and several small retirement programs. [2] Includes the U.S. Coast Guard. [3] Consists of payments for medical services for dependents of active duty military personnel at nonmilitary facilities. [4] Consists of state, railroad employee, and federal employee unemployment benefits; special unemployment benefits; and supplemental unemployment benefits. [5] Includes payments from private, federal, and state and local workers' compensation funds. [6] Includes federal black-lung payments and payments from state and local temporary disability insurance. [7] Consists of pension and disability, readjustment, and other veterans' benefits. [8] Consists of federal benefits (food stamp benefits, Supplemental Security Income, direct relief, earned income credit, payments to nonprofit institutions, aid to students, and payments for medical services for retired military personnel and their dependents at nonmilitary facilities) and state benefits (medical care, Aid to Families with Dependent Children, Supplemental Security Income, general assistance, emergency assistance, and medical insurance premium payments on behalf of indigents). Financed from state and federal general revenues.

Source: Employee Benefit Research Institute, Washington, DC, *EBRI Databook on Employee Benefits, Twelfth Edition,* and unpublished data (copyright). EBRI tabulations based on U.S. Department of Commerce, Bureau of Economic Analysis. See also <http://www.ebri.org/publications/books/index.cfm?fa=databook>.

Table 520. **Government Transfer Payments to Individuals—Summary: 1980 to 2006**

[In billions of dollars (263.4 represents $263,400,000,000)]

Year	Total	Retirement & disability insurance benefits	Medical payments	Income maintenance benefits	Unemployment insurance benefits	Veterans benefits	Federal education & training assistance payments [1]	Other [2]
1980	263.4	128.8	62.6	34.3	18.7	14.7	4.1	0.2
1990	561.5	264.2	188.8	63.5	18.2	17.7	7.3	1.8
1995	840.0	350.3	336.5	100.4	21.8	20.5	9.0	1.4
1996	883.1	364.9	361.7	102.6	22.4	21.4	8.6	1.6
1997	912.8	379.3	377.3	100.5	20.3	22.2	11.5	1.6
1998	932.6	391.8	383.7	101.1	19.9	23.2	11.2	1.8
1999	966.5	402.5	401.1	104.8	20.8	24.1	11.4	1.9
2000	1,018.1	424.8	427.7	106.6	20.7	24.9	11.0	2.4
2001	1,117.2	450.4	482.5	109.4	32.2	26.5	13.1	3.1
2002	1,220.0	474.9	525.4	119.7	53.7	29.3	14.5	2.4
2003	1,286.0	493.8	556.8	133.2	53.6	31.6	13.9	3.0
2004	1,363.0	516.8	608.7	143.6	37.1	34.1	15.0	7.6
2005	1,448.2	545.7	654.6	158.1	32.3	36.5	16.0	5.0
2006	1,548.1	578.7	719.6	160.8	30.9	39.1	15.9	3.2

[1] See footnote 9, Table 521.   [2] See footnote 10, Table 521.

Source: U.S. Bureau of Economic Analysis, "Regional Accounts Data, Annual State Personal Income"; <http://www.bea.gov/bea/regional/spi/>; (accessed March 2008).

Table 521. **Government Transfer Payments to Individuals by Type: 1990 to 2006**

[In millions of dollars (561,484 represents $561,484,000,000)

Item	1990	1995	2000	2003	2004	2005	2006
Total	561,484	840,034	1,018,106	1,286,001	1,362,992	1,448,181	1,548,090
Retirement & disability insurance benefit payments	264,230	350,310	424,810	493,780	516,830	545,732	578,681
Old age, survivors, & disability insurance . . .	244,135	327,667	401,218	463,406	485,244	512,551	544,118
Railroad retirement and disability	7,221	8,028	8,265	8,855	9,009	9,194	9,518
Workers' compensation payments (federal & state)	8,618	10,530	10,845	14,547	15,240	15,952	16,755
Other government disability insurance & retirement [1]	4,256	4,085	4,482	6,972	7,337	8,035	8,290
Medical payments	188,808	336,506	427,689	556,843	608,682	654,612	719,561
Medicare	107,638	179,147	219,612	277,932	302,804	332,757	402,276
Public assistance medical care [2]	78,176	155,007	205,021	273,916	300,074	315,618	310,445
Military medical insurance [3]	2,994	2,352	3,056	4,995	5,804	6,237	6,840
Income maintenance benefit payments	63,481	100,443	106,616	133,199	143,631	158,139	160,773
Supplemental Security Income (SSI)	16,670	27,726	31,675	35,703	37,299	38,779	40,414
Family assistance [4]	19,187	22,637	18,440	18,367	18,371	18,216	18,249
Food stamps	14,741	22,447	14,896	22,127	25,631	29,528	29,399
Other income maintenance [5]	12,883	27,633	41,605	57,002	62,330	71,616	72,711
Unemployment insurance benefit payments . . .	18,208	21,838	20,680	53,581	37,081	32,285	30,898
State unemployment insurance compensation	17,644	20,937	19,913	52,364	35,595	31,010	29,607
Unemployment compensation for federal civilian employees	215	339	226	333	281	224	218
Unemployment compensation for railroad employees	89	62	81	94	79	72	78
Unemployment compensation for veterans . . .	144	320	182	365	431	446	447
Other unemployment compensation [6]	116	180	278	425	695	533	548
Veterans benefit payments	17,687	20,546	24,935	31,610	34,076	36,484	39,065
Veterans pension and disability	15,550	17,565	21,895	27,955	30,224	32,618	35,204
Veterans readjustment [7]	257	1,086	1,323	1,936	2,158	2,256	2,292
Veterans life insurance benefits	1,868	1,884	1,707	1,707	1,682	1,596	1,554
Other assistance to veterans [8]	12	11	10	12	12	14	15
Federal education & training assistance payments [9]	7,300	9,007	10,985	13,946	15,045	15,968	15,909
Other payments to individuals [10]	1,770	1,384	2,391	3,042	7,647	4,961	3,203

[1] Consists largely of temporary disability payments, pension benefit guaranty payments, and black lung payments.
[2] Consists of medicaid and other medical vendor payments.   [3] Consists of payments made under the TriCare Management Program (formerly called CHAMPUS) for the medical care of dependents of active duty military personnel and of retired military personnel and their dependents at nonmilitary medical facilities.   [4] Through 1995, consists of emergency assistance and aid to families with dependent children. Beginning with 1998, consists of benefits—generally known as temporary assistance for needy families—provided under the Personal Responsibility and Work Opportunity Reconciliation Act of 1996.   [5] Consists largely of general assistance expenditures for food under the supplemental program for women, infants, and children; refugee assistance; foster home care and adoption assistance; earned income tax credits; and energy assistance.   [6] Consists of trade readjustment allowance payments, Redwood Park benefit payments, public service employment benefit payments, and transitional benefit payments.   [7] Consists largely of veterans' readjustment benefit payments, educational assistance to spouses and children of disabled or deceased veterans, payments to paraplegics, and payments for autos and conveyances for disabled veterans.
[8] Consists largely of state and local government payments to veterans.   [9] Excludes veterans. Consists largely of federal fellowship payments (National Science Foundation fellowships and traineeships, subsistence payments to state maritime academy cadets, and other federal fellowships), interest subsidy on higher education loans, basic educational opportunity grants, and Job Corps payments.   [10] Consists largely of Bureau of Indian Affairs payments, education exchange payments, Alaska Permanent Fund dividend payments, compensation of survivors of public safety officers, compensation of victims of crime, disaster relief payments, compensation for Japanese internment, and other special payments to individuals.

Source: U.S. Bureau of Economic Analysis, "Regional Accounts Data, Annual State Personal Income"; <http://www.bea.gov/bea/regional/spi/> (accessed March 2008).

Social Insurance and Human Services   343

Table 522. **Government Transfer Payments to Individuals by State: 2000 to 2006**

[In millions of dollars (1,018,106 represents $1,018,106,000,000)]

State	2000, total	2005, total	2006							
			Total	Retirement & disability insurance benefits	Medical payments	Income maintenance benefits	Unemployment insurance benefits	Veterans' benefits	Federal education & training assistance payments [1]	Other [2]
U.S. . . .	1,018,106	1,448,181	1,548,090	578,681	719,561	160,773	30,898	39,065	15,909	3,203
AL.	16,643	23,817	25,726	10,163	11,038	2,957	233	948	320	67
AK.	2,966	3,423	3,689	724	1,455	381	96	134	17	881
AZ.	15,959	26,638	29,156	11,475	13,397	2,535	252	932	470	95
AR.	10,006	14,701	16,057	6,155	7,086	1,718	280	621	183	13
CA.	114,559	162,941	175,738	59,517	82,306	24,179	4,360	3,312	1,938	128
CO	11,169	16,464	17,748	7,410	7,551	1,541	298	703	223	23
CT	14,086	18,291	19,757	7,427	9,995	1,392	542	280	114	6
DE.	2,857	4,233	4,685	1,896	2,173	380	102	101	31	3
DC	2,709	3,632	3,743	748	2,273	521	63	66	62	9
FL.	64,208	93,464	100,804	40,589	46,797	8,507	842	3,130	895	44
GA	23,696	36,187	38,788	14,309	16,880	5,106	612	1,383	441	58
HI	3,844	5,414	5,679	2,342	2,285	695	100	209	46	2
ID	3,804	5,758	6,280	2,798	2,533	500	122	225	96	6
IL	41,726	58,885	60,157	23,483	26,475	6,944	1,669	894	652	41
IN	20,081	28,638	31,103	13,088	13,525	2,754	779	568	378	12
IA	10,046	13,520	15,010	6,471	6,596	1,092	324	310	207	10
KS.	8,908	12,164	13,291	5,535	5,861	1,148	238	337	163	8
KY.	15,778	21,743	23,577	9,131	10,317	2,735	435	669	282	8
LA.	16,582	26,608	25,133	7,603	12,324	3,174	322	693	310	707
ME	5,307	7,860	8,007	2,915	3,864	697	117	351	61	3
MD	16,981	24,687	26,219	9,758	12,931	2,203	452	637	224	15
MA	26,471	38,137	39,802	12,578	20,542	4,358	1,304	722	286	12
MI	36,675	50,000	53,762	21,616	23,445	5,300	1,971	893	516	21
MN	15,748	22,419	24,648	9,469	11,819	1,798	670	633	245	15
MS	10,803	16,772	16,965	5,840	7,742	2,216	187	450	245	285
MO	20,904	29,850	31,772	12,455	14,900	2,871	433	783	312	19
MT	3,127	4,260	4,651	2,095	1,846	378	69	195	59	9
NE.	5,694	7,766	8,470	3,503	3,772	710	95	289	97	4
NV.	5,588	8,804	9,669	4,279	3,918	785	256	362	56	13
NH	3,918	5,507	5,923	2,679	2,551	368	88	191	45	2
NJ.	33,092	44,745	48,904	18,666	24,661	2,809	1,733	672	338	24
NM	6,014	9,219	9,930	3,416	4,561	1,144	113	484	131	81
NY.	95,735	127,322	135,368	39,211	75,850	15,224	2,259	1,525	1,254	45
NC	28,108	41,729	45,311	17,399	20,023	4,995	833	1,572	461	27
ND	2,322	3,008	3,274	1,457	1,381	227	45	101	46	17
OH	43,149	59,188	62,877	25,648	28,408	5,905	1,142	1,166	582	25
OK	11,999	17,436	19,174	7,484	8,363	1,945	158	963	243	18
OR	12,243	16,959	18,257	8,173	7,101	1,596	514	664	193	17
PA.	54,928	75,254	79,220	30,188	38,666	6,287	2,134	1,341	577	28
RI	4,748	6,585	6,801	2,482	3,313	587	201	144	70	3
SC.	14,340	21,254	22,927	9,117	9,707	2,660	379	812	235	16
SD.	2,490	3,439	3,787	1,541	1,675	304	26	151	54	34
TN.	21,864	31,106	32,379	12,540	14,400	3,725	455	931	300	28
TX.	59,911	91,277	98,206	34,242	45,010	12,661	1,247	3,556	1,253	235
UT.	4,962	7,270	7,934	3,496	3,231	690	102	207	195	13
VT.	2,245	3,242	3,582	1,277	1,784	311	85	93	30	2
VA.	19,916	29,473	32,319	13,428	13,365	3,487	381	1,328	314	15
WA	20,817	28,339	30,528	13,123	12,444	2,707	771	1,170	281	33
WV	8,894	11,635	12,524	5,181	5,434	1,180	164	438	121	5
WI	17,902	24,838	26,286	11,407	10,952	2,223	811	645	230	17
WY	1,583	2,280	2,495	1,154	1,035	161	32	82	28	3

[1] Excludes veterans. Consists largely of federal fellowship payments (National Science Foundation, fellowships and traineeships, subsistence payments to state maritime academy cadets, and other federal fellowships), interest subsidy on higher education loans, basic educational opportunity grants, and Job Corps payments. [2] Consists largely of Bureau of Indian Affairs payments, education exchange payments, Alaska Permanent Fund dividend payments, compensation of survivors of public safety officers, compensation of victims of crime, disaster relief payments, compensation for Japanese internment, and other special payments to individuals.

Source: U.S. Bureau of Economic Analysis, "Regional Accounts Data, Annual State Personal Income"; <http://www.bea.gov/bea/regional/spi/>; (accessed March 2008).

Table 523. Number of Persons With Income by Specified Sources of Income: 2006

[In thousands (208,491 represents 208,491,000). Persons 15 years old and over as of March of the following year. Based on Current Population Survey; see text, Sections 1 and 13, and Appendix III]

Source of income	Total persons with income	Under 65 years old	65 years old and over	White [1]	Black [2]	Hispanic origin [3]
Total..................	208,491	173,670	34,821	171,629	23,274	25,448
Earnings......................	157,611	150,860	6,751	129,265	17,538	21,521
Wages and salary............	147,971	142,361	5,610	120,890	16,946	20,426
Nonfarm self-employment........	13,099	11,980	1,120	11,335	895	1,385
Farm self-employment..........	2,327	2,065	262	2,089	143	136
Unemployment compensation.......	5,230	5,074	156	4,211	732	589
State or local only...........	5,005	4,858	146	4,043	685	561
Combinations...............	225	216	10	168	46	28
Workers' compensation...........	1,710	1,534	175	1,423	190	220
State payments.............	619	559	60	516	58	106
Employment insurance..........	668	625	43	553	80	73
Own insurance..............	27	27	–	20	5	2
Other...................	558	475	83	485	52	82
Social security, railroad retirement....	41,191	10,065	31,126	35,559	3,981	2,612
Supplemental Security Income (SSI)...	4,992	3,966	1,026	3,340	1,236	827
Public assistance..............	1,857	1,804	53	1,074	638	351
TANF/Welfare (AFDC) only [4]......	1,238	1,213	25	691	446	233
Other assistance only..........	564	536	28	359	163	102
Both..................	55	55	–	24	28	16
Veterans payments..............	2,416	1,443	973	2,039	282	105
Disability only..............	1,414	969	445	1,206	151	66
Survivors only..............	213	62	151	169	33	4
Pension only...............	596	260	336	502	78	22
Education only.............	51	51	–	43	6	5
Other only................	88	56	32	74	9	3
Combinations..............	55	46	9	46	6	5
Means-tested..............	453	269	184	370	62	33
Nonmeans-tested.............	1,963	1,174	790	1,669	220	72
Survivors benefits..............	2,812	893	1,919	2,535	183	123
Company or union............	1,195	251	943	1,075	79	63
Federal government...........	304	78	226	260	33	9
Military retirement...........	197	39	158	169	16	2
State or local government........	266	76	190	249	10	9
Disability benefits..............	1,793	1,606	187	1,415	274	187
Workers' compensation.........	233	220	13	211	12	52
Company or union............	417	376	41	312	69	25
Federal government...........	137	117	20	105	24	7
Military retirement...........	57	42	14	44	9	7
State or local government........	309	284	26	220	73	33
Pensions...................	16,060	5,213	10,847	14,265	1,284	568
Company or union............	11,251	3,251	8,001	10,036	854	397
Federal government...........	1,611	572	1,040	1,313	221	70
Military retirement...........	1,283	730	553	1,124	114	59
State or local government........	4,245	1,766	2,479	3,736	376	171
Property income [5].............	98,117	78,853	19,264	86,262	5,856	5,564
Interest.................	92,575	74,348	18,227	81,462	5,479	5,144
Dividends................	33,269	26,376	6,894	30,250	1,162	1,016
Rents, royalties, estates, or trusts...	10,517	7,906	2,612	9,340	594	626
Education..................	7,007	6,994	14	5,334	1,051	652
Pell grant only..............	1,613	1,612	–	1,067	422	213
Other government only..........	1,068	1,061	7	848	151	110
Scholarships only............	2,203	2,201	2	1,760	203	171
Child support................	5,132	5,116	17	3,988	908	587
Alimony...................	395	345	50	352	28	27
Financial assistance from outside the household.................	2,161	2,009	152	1,654	271	206
Other income................	812	719	93	621	91	62
Combinations of income types:						
Government transfer payments.....	58,223	25,860	32,363	48,363	7,126	4,690
Public assistance or SSI..........	6,637	5,571	1,066	4,297	1,798	1,146

– Represents or rounds to zero. [1] Beginning with the 2003 CPS, respondents could choose one or more races. For example, "White" refers to people who reported White and did not report any other race category. The use of this single-race population does not imply that it is the preferred method of presenting or analyzing data. Information on people who reported more than one race, such as "Asian and Black or African American," is available from Census 2000 through American FactFinder®. [2] "Black" refers to people who reported Black and did not report any other race category. [3] Persons of Hispanic origin may be of any race. [4] TANF—Temporary Assistance for Needy Families program; AFDC—Aid to Families with Dependent Children program. [5] Includes estates and trusts reported as survivor benefits.

Source: U.S. Census Bureau, "Table PINC-09. Source of Income in 2006—Number With Income and Mean Income of Specified Type in 2006 of People 15 Years Old and Over, by Race, Hispanic Origin and Sex." See also <http://pubdb3.census.gov/macro/032007/perinc/new09_000.htm>.

U.S. Census Bureau, Statistical Abstract of the United States: 2009

Table 524. Persons Living in Households Receiving Selected Noncash Benefits: 2006

[In thousands (296,450 represents 296,450,000), except percent. Persons, as of March 2007, who lived with someone (a nonrelative or a relative) who received aid. Not every person tallied here received the aid themselves. Persons living in households receiving more than one type of aid are counted only once. Excludes members of the Armed Forces except those living off post or with their families on post. Population controls for 2007 based on Census 2000 and an expanded sample of households. Based on Current Population Survey; see text, Section 1 and Appendix III]

Age, sex, and race	Total	In household that received means-tested assistance [1]		In household that received means-tested cash assistance		In household that received food stamps		In household in which one or more persons were covered by Medicaid		Lived in public or authorized housing	
		Number	Percent	Number	Percent	Number	Percent	Number	Percent	Number	Percent
Total	296,450	77,058	26.0	17,056	5.8	21,780	7.3	60,453	20.4	10,250	3.5
Under 18 years	73,727	28,988	39.3	5,111	6.9	9,421	12.8	22,638	30.7	3,773	5.1
18 to 24 years	28,405	7,706	27.1	1,605	5.7	2,275	8.0	6,331	22.3	1,095	3.9
25 to 34 years	39,868	10,948	27.5	1,977	5.0	3,186	8.0	8,778	22.0	1,283	3.2
35 to 44 years	42,762	10,149	23.7	2,093	4.9	2,502	5.9	7,663	17.9	1,000	2.3
45 to 54 years	43,461	8,000	18.4	2,342	5.4	1,879	4.3	6,311	14.5	931	2.1
55 to 59 years	18,221	2,812	15.4	1,074	5.9	711	3.9	2,222	12.2	353	1.9
60 to 64 years	13,970	2,235	16.0	907	6.5	566	4.1	1,814	13.0	370	2.7
65 years and over	36,035	6,221	17.3	1,947	5.4	1,241	3.4	4,696	13.0	1,444	4.0
65 to 74 years	18,998	3,253	17.1	1,033	5.4	684	3.6	2,551	13.4	644	3.4
75 years and over. . .	17,037	2,968	17.4	914	5.4	557	3.3	2,145	12.6	800	4.7
Male	145,486	35,475	24.4	7,535	5.2	9,347	6.4	27,888	19.2	4,053	2.8
Female.	150,964	41,582	27.5	9,521	6.3	12,433	8.2	32,566	21.6	6,197	4.1
White alone [2]	237,619	54,388	22.9	10,773	4.5	13,312	5.6	43,043	18.1	5,120	2.2
Black alone [2].	37,306	16,257	43.6	4,658	12.5	6,794	18.2	12,248	32.8	4,218	11.3
Asian alone [2].	13,177	3,075	23.3	729	5.5	416	3.2	2,526	19.2	368	2.8
Hispanic [3]	44,784	21,145	47.2	3,239	7.2	4,824	10.8	16,390	36.6	1,943	4.3
White alone, Non-Hispanic [2].	196,049	34,926	17.8	7,957	4.1	9,080	4.6	28,047	14.3	3,543	1.8

[1] Means-tested assistance includes means-tested cash assistance, food stamps, Medicaid, and public or authorized housing.　[2] Refers to people who reported specific race and did not report any other race category.　[3] People of Hispanic origin may be of any race.

Source: U.S. Census Bureau, *Current Population Reports*, P60-231. See also <http://pubdb3.census.gov/macro/032007/pov/new26_001.htm>.

Table 525. Social Security—Covered Employment, Earnings, and Contribution Rates: 1990 to 2007

[164.7 represents 164,700,000. Includes Puerto Rico, Virgin Islands, American Samoa, and Guam. Represents all reported employment. Data are estimated. OASDHI = Old-age, survivors, disability, and health insurance; SMI = Supplementary medical insurance]

Item	Unit	1990	1995	2000	2001	2002	2003	2004	2005	2006	2007
Workers with insured status [1]	Million . . .	164.7	173.6	185.8	188.2	190.3	192.0	193.7	196.2	198.5	200.8
Male	Million . . .	86.8	90.6	96.0	97.0	97.9	98.5	99.3	100.4	101.5	102.6
Female.	Million . . .	77.9	83.1	89.9	91.2	92.4	93.4	94.4	95.7	96.9	98.2
Under 25 years	Million . . .	21.2	18.8	20.8	21.2	21.1	20.6	20.2	20.2	20.2	20.2
25 to 34 years	Million . . .	41.6	39.5	36.6	36.4	36.5	36.4	36.4	36.5	36.6	37.0
35 to 44 years	Million . . .	36.5	40.7	42.6	42.4	42.1	41.8	41.4	41.1	40.7	40.1
45 to 54 years	Million . . .	23.0	29.7	36.1	36.9	37.8	38.6	39.5	40.4	41.2	41.9
55 to 59 years	Million . . .	8.9	9.9	12.3	13.2	14.0	14.7	15.4	16.3	16.8	17.1
60 to 64 years	Million . . .	8.8	8.6	9.6	10.0	10.5	11.1	11.4	11.9	12.5	13.4
65 to 69 years	Million . . .	8.1	8.0	7.9	8.0	8.2	8.5	8.7	8.9	9.2	9.7
70 years and over	Million . . .	16.5	18.5	19.8	20.0	20.2	20.4	20.6	20.9	21.2	21.4
Workers reported with—											
Taxable earnings [2]	Million . . .	133	141	155	155	154	155	156	159	161	163
Maximum earnings [2]	Million . . .	8	8	10	9	8	8	9	10	10	10
Earnings in covered employment [2]	Bil. dol. . .	2,716	3,407	4,840	4,940	4,954	5,091	5,389	5,700	6,062	6,405
Reported taxable [2]	Bil. dol. . .	2,359	2,920	4,009	4,171	4,250	4,355	4,553	4,766	5,048	5,300
Percent of total.	Percent . .	86.8	85.7	82.8	84.4	85.8	85.5	84.5	83.6	83.3	82.8
Average per worker:											
Total earnings [2]	Dollars . .	20,385	24,157	31,303	31,909	32,105	32,934	34,487	35,868	37,601	39,250
Taxable earnings [2]	Dollars . .	17,703	20,702	25,926	26,939	27,539	28,174	29,142	29,991	31,313	32,480
Annual maximum taxable earnings [3]	Dollars . .	51,300	61,200	76,200	80,400	84,900	87,000	87,900	90,000	94,200	97,500
Contribution rates for OASDHI: [4]											
Each employer and employee. . .	Percent . .	7.65	7.65	7.65	7.65	7.65	7.65	7.65	7.65	7.65	7.65
Self-employed [5]	Percent . .	15.30	15.30	15.30	15.30	15.30	15.30	15.30	15.30	15.30	15.30
SMI, monthly premium [6]	Dollars . .	28.60	46.10	45.50	50.00	54.00	58.70	66.60	78.20	88.50	93.50

[1] Estimated number fully insured for retirement and/or survivor benefits as of end of year.　[2] Includes self-employment. Averages per worker computed with unrounded earnings and worker amounts, thus may not agree with rounded table amounts.　[3] Beginning 1995, upper limit on earnings subject to HI taxes was repealed.　[4] As of January 1, 2006, each employee and employer pays 7.65 percent and the self-employed pay 15.3 percent.　[5] Self-employed pays 15.3 percent, and half of the tax is deductible for income tax purposes and for computing self-employment income subject to social security tax.　[6] As of January 1.

Source: U.S. Social Security Administration, *Annual Statistical Supplement* to the *Social Security Bulletin;* and unpublished data. See also <http://www.ssa.gov/policy/docs/statcomps/supplement/2007/>.

Table 526. Social Security (OASDI)—Benefits by Type of Beneficiary: 1990 to 2006

[**39,832 represents 39,832,000.** A person eligible to receive more than one type of benefit is generally classified or counted only once as a retired-worker beneficiary. OASDI = Old-age, survivors, and disability insurance. See also headnote, Table 527, and Appendix III]

Type of beneficiary	1990	1995	1999	2000	2001	2002	2003	2004	2005	2006
Number of benefits [1] (1,000)	**39,832**	**43,387**	**44,596**	**45,415**	**45,878**	**46,444**	**47,038**	**47,688**	**48,434**	**49,123**
Retired workers [2] (1,000)	24,838	26,673	27,775	28,499	28,837	29,190	29,532	29,953	30,461	30,971
Disabled workers [3] (1,000)	3,011	4,185	4,879	5,042	5,274	5,544	5,874	6,198	6,519	6,812
Wives and husbands [2,4] (1,000)	3,367	3,290	2,987	2,963	2,899	2,833	2,773	2,722	2,680	2,632
Children (1,000)	3,187	3,734	3,795	3,803	3,839	3,910	3,961	3,986	4,025	4,041
Under age 18	2,497	2,956	2,970	2,976	2,994	3,043	3,080	3,097	3,130	3,133
Disabled children [5]	600	686	721	729	737	745	753	759	769	777
Students [6]	89	92	104	98	109	123	128	130	127	131
Of retired workers	422	442	442	459	467	477	480	483	488	490
Of deceased workers	1,776	1,884	1,885	1,878	1,890	1,908	1,910	1,905	1,903	1,899
Of disabled workers	989	1,409	1,468	1,466	1,482	1,526	1,571	1,599	1,633	1,652
Widowed mothers [7] (1,000)	304	275	212	203	197	194	190	184	178	171
Widows and widowers [2,8] (1,000)	5,111	5,226	4,944	4,901	4,828	4,771	4,707	4,643	4,569	4,494
Parents [2] (1,000)	6	4	3	3	3	2	2	2	2	2
Special benefits [9] (1,000)	7	1	(Z)	(Z)	(Z)	(Z)	(Z)	(Z)	(Z)	(Z)
AVERAGE MONTHLY BENEFIT, CURRENT DOLLARS										
Retired workers [2]	603	720	804	844	874	895	922	955	1,002	1,044
Retired worker and wife [2]	1,027	1,221	1,357	1,420	1,466	1,494	1,535	1,586	1,660	1,726
Disabled workers [3]	587	682	754	786	814	834	862	894	938	978
Wives and husbands [2,4]	298	354	398	416	430	439	450	464	485	502
Children of retired workers	259	322	373	395	413	426	444	465	493	518
Children of deceased workers	406	469	526	550	571	585	603	625	656	684
Children of disabled workers	164	183	216	228	238	245	254	265	279	290
Widowed mothers [7]	409	478	566	595	621	640	664	689	725	757
Widows and widowers, nondisabled [2]	556	680	775	810	841	861	888	920	967	1,007
Parents [2]	482	591	674	704	729	753	779	810	851	892
Special benefits [9]	167	192	209	217	224	227	232	238	247	256
AVERAGE MONTHLY BENEFIT, CONSTANT (2006) DOLLARS [10]										
Retired workers [2]	909	947	964	979	999	998	1,010	1,013	1,027	1,044
Retired worker and wife [2]	1,549	1,605	1,627	1,647	1,674	1,667	1,681	1,682	1,702	1,726
Disabled workers [3]	885	897	904	912	930	930	943	948	962	978
Wives and husbands [2,4]	449	465	477	482	491	490	493	492	497	502
Children of deceased workers	612	617	631	638	652	653	660	663	673	684
Widowed mothers [7]	617	628	679	690	709	714	727	731	743	757
Widows and widowers, nondisabled [2]	839	894	929	939	960	960	972	976	991	1,007
Number of benefits awarded (1,000)	**3,717**	**3,882**	**3,917**	**4,290**	**4,162**	**4,336**	**4,322**	**4,459**	**4,672**	**4,621**
Retired workers [2]	1,665	1,609	1,690	1,961	1,779	1,813	1,791	1,883	2,000	1,999
Disabled workers [3]	468	646	620	622	691	750	777	796	830	799
Wives and husbands [2,4]	379	322	322	385	358	363	353	367	379	378
Children [7]	695	809	773	777	796	846	852	859	908	897
Widowed mothers [7]	58	52	42	40	41	41	39	40	38	36
Widows and widowers [2,8]	452	445	470	505	496	523	508	514	517	512
Parents [2]	(Z)	(Z)	(Z)	(Z)	(Z)	(Z)	(Z)	(Z)	(Z)	(Z)
Special benefits [9]	(Z)	(Z)	(Z)	(Z)	(Z)	(Z)	(Z)	(Z)	(Z)	(Z)
BENEFIT PAYMENTS DURING YEAR (bil. dol.)										
Total [11]	**247.8**	**332.6**	**385.8**	**407.6**	**431.9**	**453.8**	**470.8**	**493.3**	**520.8**	**552.8**
Monthly benefits [12]	247.6	332.4	385.6	407.4	431.7	453.6	470.6	493.1	520.6	552.6
Retired workers [2]	156.8	205.3	238.5	253.5	269.0	281.6	291.5	304.3	321.7	342.9
Disabled workers [3]	22.1	36.6	46.5	49.8	54.2	59.9	64.8	71.7	78.4	85.0
Wives and husbands [2,4]	14.5	17.9	18.8	19.4	19.9	20.3	20.4	20.6	20.5	21.5
Children	12.0	16.1	18.6	19.3	20.4	21.5	22.3	23.3	24.5	25.8
Under age 18	9.0	11.9	13.6	14.1	14.8	15.7	16.2	17.0	17.9	18.8
Disabled children [5]	2.5	3.6	4.4	4.6	4.8	5.1	5.2	5.5	5.8	6.1
Students [6]	0.5	0.6	0.7	0.7	0.7	0.8	0.8	0.9	0.8	1.0
Of retired workers	1.3	1.7	2.0	2.1	2.3	2.5	2.6	2.7	2.9	3.1
Of deceased workers	8.6	10.7	12.1	12.5	13.1	13.7	14.1	14.5	15.1	15.8
Of disabled workers	2.2	3.7	4.4	4.7	4.9	5.3	5.7	6.1	6.5	6.9
Widowed mothers [7]	1.4	1.6	1.4	1.4	1.4	1.5	1.5	1.5	1.5	1.6
Widows and widowers [2,8]	40.7	54.8	61.8	63.9	66.8	68.8	70.1	71.7	73.4	75.9
Parents [2]	(Z)	(Z)	(Z)	(Z)	(Z)	(Z)	(Z)	(Z)	(Z)	(Z)
Special benefits [9]	(Z)	(Z)	(Z)	(Z)	(Z)	(Z)	(Z)	(Z)	(Z)	(Z)
Lump sum	0.2	0.2	0.2	0.2	0.2	0.2	0.2	0.2	0.2	0.2

Z Fewer than 500 or less than $50 million. [1] Number of benefit payments in current-payment status, i.e., actually being made at a specified time with no deductions or with deductions amounting to less than a month's benefit. [2] 62 years and over. [3] Disabled workers under age 65. [4] Includes wife beneficiaries with entitled children in their care and entitled divorced wives. [5] 18 years old and over. Disability began before age 18. [6] Full-time students aged 18 and 19. [7] Includes surviving divorced mothers with entitled children in their care and widowed fathers with entitled children in their care. [8] Includes widows aged 60–61, surviving divorced wives aged 60 and over, disabled widows and widowers aged 50 and over; and widowers aged 60–61. [9] Benefits for persons aged 72 and over not insured under regular or transitional provisions of Social Security Act. [10] Constant dollar figures are based on the consumer price index (CPI-U) for December as published by the U.S. Bureau of Labor Statistics. [11] Represents total disbursements of benefit checks by the U.S. Department of the Treasury during the years specified. [12] Distribution by type estimated.

Source: U.S. Social Security Administration, *Annual Statistical Supplement* to the *Social Security Bulletin;* and unpublished data. See also <http://www.ssa.gov/policy/>.

Social Insurance and Human Services 347

Table 527. Social Security—Beneficiaries, Annual Payments, and Average Monthly Benefit, 1990 to 2006, and by State and Other Areas, 2006

[Number of beneficiaries in current-payment status (**39,832 represents 39,832,000**) and average monthly benefit as of **December**. Data based on 10-percent sample of administrative records. See also headnote, Table 526, and Appendix III]

Year, state, and other area	Number of beneficiaries (1,000)				Annual payments [2] (mil. dol.)				Average monthly benefit (dol.)		
	Total	Retired workers and dependents [1]	Survivors	Disabled workers and dependents	Total	Retired workers and dependents [1]	Survivors	Disabled workers and dependents	Retired workers [3]	Disabled workers	Widows and widowers [4]
1990	39,832	28,369	7,197	4,266	247,796	172,042	50,951	24,803	603	587	557
1995	43,380	30,139	7,379	5,862	332,581	224,381	67,302	40,898	720	682	680
2000	45,417	31,761	6,981	6,675	407,431	274,645	77,848	54,938	845	787	810
2003	46,448	32,360	6,870	7,220	470,546	314,024	85,621	70,899	922	862	888
2004	47,707	33,025	6,730	7,952	493,078	327,139	87,737	78,202	955	894	920
2005	48,446	33,488	6,650	8,307	520,561	345,094	90,073	85,394	1,002	938	967
2006, total [5]	**49,123**	**33,945**	**6,566**	**8,612**	**552,636**	**366,952**	**93,300**	**92,384**	**1,044**	**978**	**1,007**
United States	**47,894**	**33,148**	**6,347**	**8,400**	**543,728**	**361,957**	**91,251**	**90,520**	**(NA)**	**(NA)**	**(NA)**
Alabama	921	553	139	229	9,913	5,743	1,804	2,366	1,005	951	937
Alaska	67	44	10	13	715	454	125	136	999	968	958
Arizona	940	671	110	158	10,774	7,428	1,584	1,762	978	1,011	917
Arkansas	577	58	80	139	6,053	3,627	1,015	1,411	1,066	930	1,044
California	4,505	3,229	564	711	50,790	34,700	8,220	7,870	1,044	996	1,033
Colorado	600	431	76	94	6,685	4,562	1,107	1,016	1,027	974	1,023
Connecticut	587	436	66	85	7,266	5,249	1,064	952	1,142	1,017	1,127
Delaware	154	108	18	27	1,830	1,246	276	308	1,104	1,027	1,083
District of Columbia . . .	71	49	11	12	709	469	121	120	909	871	839
Florida	3,445	2,545	393	507	38,876	27,627	5,717	5,532	1,040	980	1,033
Georgia	1,270	827	184	259	13,872	8,741	2,398	2,733	1,020	964	955
Hawaii	204	158	22	24	2,277	1,699	310	268	1,033	1,007	979
Idaho	234	165	29	40	2,563	1,737	413	412	1,021	955	1,030
Illinois	1,906	1,349	265	293	22,453	15,211	4,014	3,228	1,083	1,002	1,076
Indiana	1,081	743	148	189	12,752	8,501	2,226	2,024	1,099	980	1,075
Iowa	556	405	74	77	6,298	4,381	1,115	801	1,042	938	1,040
Kansas	455	325	60	70	5,261	3,621	906	733	1,069	952	1,066
Kentucky	813	474	123	215	8,654	4,807	1,612	2,235	990	957	923
Louisiana	723	430	140	153	7,618	4,247	1,805	1,566	976	974	926
Maine	275	182	32	61	2,879	1,829	445	604	967	902	969
Maryland	779	556	106	116	9,016	6,158	1,540	1,318	1,059	1,007	1,030
Massachusetts	1,072	747	122	203	12,239	8,247	1,851	2,141	1,052	965	1,049
Michigan	1,776	1,213	243	319	21,475	14,129	3,739	3,606	1,127	1,036	1,089
Minnesota	801	585	98	118	9,125	6,382	1,477	1,266	1,051	968	1,032
Mississippi	554	324	86	144	5,701	3,247	1,033	1,422	965	921	885
Missouri	1,077	720	144	213	11,973	7,723	2,025	2,225	1,029	954	1,012
Montana	173	123	23	27	1,871	1,266	326	279	995	945	1,009
Nebraska	294	212	39	43	3,277	2,270	571	435	1,028	926	1,035
Nevada	354	258	39	58	4,068	2,833	566	669	1,051	1,038	1,046
New Hampshire	226	158	23	45	2,647	1,800	365	482	1,077	991	1,073
New Jersey	1,381	1,016	165	201	17,267	12,277	2,619	2,371	1,152	1,069	1,106
New Mexico	320	215	44	61	3,332	2,146	564	622	977	938	933
New York	3,075	2,173	370	533	36,528	24,943	5,574	6,011	1,102	1,028	1,060
North Carolina	1,550	1,036	190	324	17,101	11,134	2,510	3,457	1,028	960	951
North Dakota	115	83	18	14	1,232	824	263	144	973	905	968
Ohio	1,976	1,360	302	315	22,638	14,802	4,501	3,335	1,056	957	1,040
Oklahoma	647	433	93	121	7,036	4,496	1,272	1,268	1,003	955	977
Oregon	631	461	74	95	7,231	5,045	1,125	1,062	1,053	984	1,058
Pennsylvania	2,438	1,712	333	394	28,490	19,183	5,061	4,247	1,075	990	1,057
Rhode Island	193	136	20	37	2,188	1,500	299	390	1,045	945	1,041
South Carolina	801	525	106	170	8,834	5,626	1,372	1,836	1,028	973	946
South Dakota	143	104	20	19	1,494	1,035	274	186	966	898	950
Tennessee	1,116	719	158	239	12,173	7,612	2,082	2,480	1,021	943	958
Texas	3,029	2,029	473	527	32,986	21,043	6,444	5,499	1,016	968	978
Utah	282	203	37	42	3,160	2,200	527	433	1,052	970	1,069
Vermont	115	80	13	21	1,274	865	195	213	1,040	920	1,010
Virginia	1,161	788	153	220	12,980	8,467	2,130	2,382	1,034	985	977
Washington	962	690	113	159	11,257	7,754	1,730	1,773	1,086	992	1,078
West Virginia	419	244	69	107	4,695	2,552	954	1,189	1,032	1,025	971
Wisconsin	967	702	119	146	11,237	7,853	1,820	1,564	1,072	975	1,063
Wyoming	83	60	11	12	939	649	157	133	1,041	973	1,044
Puerto Rico	723	415	118	190	5,544	2,845	1,042	1,657	698	836	616
Guam	12	8	2	1	93	55	22	15	701	850	695
American Samoa . . .	6	2	1	2	37	14	11	12	671	750	607
Virgin Islands	17	12	2	2	159	113	24	23	906	984	788
Northern Mariana Islands	2	1	1	(Z)	14	7	5	2	599	652	443
Abroad	468	357	94	17	3,061	1,961	945	155	585	866	649

NA Not available.   Z Less than 500.   [1] Includes special benefits for persons aged 72 years and over not insured under regular or transitional provisions of Social Security Act.   [2] Unnegotiated checks not deducted. 1990 and 1995 include lump-sum payments to survivors of deceased workers.   [3] Excludes persons with special benefits.   [4] Nondisabled only.   [5] Includes those with state or area unknown.

Source: U.S. Social Security Administration, *Annual Statistical Supplement to the Social Security Bulletin.* See also <http://www.ssa.gov/policy/docs/statcomps/supplement/2007/supplement07.pdf>.

Table 528. **Social Security Trust Funds: 1990 to 2007**

[In billions of dollars (272.4 represents $272,400,000,000)]

Type of trust fund	1990	1995	2000	2002	2003	2004	2005	2006	2007
Old-age and survivors insurance (OASI):									
Net contribution income [1]	272.4	310.1	433.0	468.1	468.6	487.4	520.7	534.8	560.9
Interest received [2]	16.4	32.8	57.5	71.2	75.2	79.0	84.0	91.8	97.0
Benefit payments [3]	223.0	291.6	352.7	388.1	399.8	415.0	435.4	454.5	489.1
Assets, end of year	214.2	458.5	931.0	1,217.5	1,355.3	1,500.6	1,663.0	1,844.3	2,023.6
Disability insurance (DI):									
Net contribution income [1]	28.7	54.7	71.8	78.2	78.4	81.4	87.2	90.8	109.9
Interest received [2]	0.9	2.2	6.9	9.2	9.7	10.0	10.3	10.6	13.2
Benefit payments [3]	24.8	40.9	55.0	65.7	70.9	78.2	85.4	91.7	95.9
Assets, end of year	11.1	37.6	118.5	160.5	175.4	186.2	195.6	203.8	214.9

[1] Includes deposits by states and deductions for refund of estimated employee-tax overpayment. Includes government contributions on deemed wage credits for military service 1957–2001. Includes taxation of benefits. [2] In 1990, includes interest on advance tax transfers. Includes interest on reimbursement for unnegotiated checks. [3] Includes payments for vocational rehabilitation services furnished to disabled persons receiving benefits because of their disabilities. Amounts reflect deductions for unnegotiated benefit checks.

Source: U.S. Social Security Administration, *Annual Report of Board of Trustees, OASI, DI, HI, and SMI Trust Funds*; <http://www.ssa.gov/OACT/TR/TR08/>. Also published in *Social Security Bulletin*, quarterly.

Table 529. **Public Employee Retirement Systems—Participants and Finances: 1980 to 2006**

[4,629 represents 4,629,000. For fiscal year of retirement system, except data for the Thrift Savings Plan are for calendar year. For a definition of defined benefit, see headnote, Table 533]

Retirement plan	Unit	1980	1990	1995	2000	2002	2003	2004	2005	2006, proj.
TOTAL PARTICIPANTS [1]										
Federal retirement systems:										
Defined benefit:										
Civil Service Retirement System	1,000	4,629	4,167	3,731	3,256	3,201	3,133	3,035	2,958	2,878
Federal Employees Retirement System [2]	1,000	(X)	1,180	1,512	1,935	2,019	2,140	2,104	2,196	2,290
Military Service Retirement System [3]	1,000	3,380	3,763	3,387	3,397	3,453	3,457	3,545	3,536	3,560
Thrift Savings Plan [4]	1,000	(X)	1,625	2,195	2,500	3,000	3,200	3,400	3,600	3,700
State and local retirement systems [5, 6]	1,000	(NA)	16,858	14,734	16,834	17,264	17,650	17,890	17,932	18,484
ACTIVE PARTICIPANTS										
Federal retirement systems:										
Defined benefit:										
Civil Service Retirement System	1,000	2,700	1,826	1,525	978	906	854	788	722	650
Federal Employees Retirement System [2]	1,000	(X)	1,136	1,318	1,668	1,717	1,808	1,882	1,952	2,014
Military Service Retirement System [3]	1,000	2,050	2,130	1,572	1,437	1,465	1,468	1,480	1,445	1,443
Thrift Savings Plan [4]	1,000	(X)	1,419	1,930	1,900	2,300	2,400	2,500	2,800	2,600
State and local retirement systems [5, 6]	1,000	(NA)	11,345	12,524	13,917	14,123	14,249	14,181	14,116	14,529
ASSETS										
Total	Bil. dol.	258	1,047	1,655	2,950	3,016	3,092	3,472	3,697	4,023
Federal retirement systems	Bil. dol.	73	326	537	782	858	920	977	1,039	1,111
Defined benefit	Bil. dol.	73	318	502	684	756	791	825	866	904
Civil Service Retirement System	Bil. dol.	73	220	311	395	417	425	433	440	442
Federal Employees Retirement System [2]	Bil. dol.	(X)	18	60	126	162	183	204	228	254
Military Service Retirement System [3]	Bil. dol.	([7])	80	131	163	177	183	188	198	208
Thrift Savings Plan [4]	Bil. dol.	(X)	8	35	98	102	129	152	173	207
State and local retirement systems [5]	Bil. dol.	185	721	1,118	2,168	2,158	2,172	2,495	2,658	2,912
CONTRIBUTIONS										
Total	Bil. dol.	83	103	127	143	151	161	187	189	205
Federal retirement systems	Bil. dol.	19	61	67	78	85	86	95	98	108
Defined benefit	Bil. dol.	19	59	61	69	73	72	79	82	88
Civil Service Retirement System	Bil. dol.	19	28	31	33	34	29	34	33	34
Federal Employees Retirement System [2]	Bil. dol.	(X)	4	6	8	10	11	13	13	15
Military Service Retirement System [3]	Bil. dol.	([7])	27	24	28	30	32	32	38	39
Thrift Savings Plan [4]	Bil. dol.	(X)	2	6	9	12	14	16	16	20
State and local retirement systems [5]	Bil. dol.	64	42	60	65	66	75	92	91	97
BENEFITS										
Total	Bil. dol.	39	89	125	172	196	211	226	240	257
Federal retirement systems	Bil. dol.	27	53	66	81	86	89	93	99	105
Defined benefit	Bil. dol.	27	53	65	78	84	86	89	94	98
Civil Service Retirement System	Bil. dol.	15	31	37	44	47	48	50	52	54
Federal Employees Retirement System [2]	Bil. dol.	(X)	(Z)	1	1	2	2	2	3	3
Military Service Retirement System [3]	Bil. dol.	12	22	28	33	35	36	37	39	41
Thrift Savings Plan [4]	Bil. dol.	(X)	(Z)	1	3	2	3	4	5	7
State and local retirement systems [5]	Bil. dol.	12	36	59	91	110	122	133	141	152

NA Not available.   X Not applicable.   Z Less than $500 million.   [1] Includes active, separated vested, retired employees and survivors.   [2] The Federal Employees Retirement System was established June 6, 1986.   [3] Includes nondisability and disability retirees, surviving families, and all active personnel with the exception of active reserves.   [4] The Thrift Savings Plan (a defined contribution plan) was established April 1, 1987.   [5] Excludes state and local plans that are fully supported by employee contributions.   [6] Not adjusted for double counting of individuals participating in more than one plan.   [7] The Military Retirement System was unfunded until October 1, 1984.

Source: Employee Benefit Research Institute, Washington, DC, *EBRI Databook on Employee Benefits, Twelfth Edition*, and unpublished data (copyright). See also <http://www.ebri.org/>.

Table 530. Federal Civil Service Retirement: 1980 to 2007

[As of September 30 or for year ending September 30 (2,720 represents 2,720,000). Covers both Civil Service Retirement System and Federal Employees Retirement System]

Item	Unit	1980	1990	1995	2000	2003	2004	2005	2006	2007
Employees covered [1]	1,000....	2,720	2,945	2,668	2,764	2,662	2,670	2,674	2,611	2,618
Annuitants, total	**1,000....**	**1,675**	**2,143**	**2,311**	**2,376**	**2,389**	**2,404**	**2,433**	**2,449**	**2,463**
Age and service	1,000....	905	1,288	1,441	1,501	1,523	1,544	1,568	1,602	1,625
Disability	1,000....	343	297	263	242	234	231	229	226	222
Survivors	1,000....	427	558	607	633	632	629	636	621	616
Receipts, total [2]	**Mil. dol...**	**24,389**	**52,689**	**65,684**	**75,967**	**78,366**	**82,412**	**83,691**	**87,164**	**89,860**
Employee contributions	Mil. dol...	3,686	4,501	4,498	4,637	4,522	4,483	4,353	4,304	4,205
Federal government contributions	Mil. dol...	15,562	27,368	33,130	37,722	36,583	42,240	43,093	46,427	48,397
Disbursements, total [3]	**Mil. dol...**	**14,977**	**31,416**	**38,435**	**45,194**	**50,368**	**52,277**	**54,790**	**57,983**	**78,146**
Age and service annuitants [4]	Mil. dol...	12,639	26,495	32,070	37,546	42,018	43,727	46,029	48,895	68,776
Survivors	Mil. dol...	1,912	4,366	5,864	7,210	7,951	8,127	8,338	8,642	8,905
Average monthly benefit:										
Age and service	Dollars...	992	1,369	1,643	1,885	2,085	2,154	2,240	2,363	2,473
Disability	Dollars...	723	1,008	1,164	1,240	1,291	1,305	1,327	1,366	1,394
Survivors	Dollars...	392	653	819	952	1,044	1,073	1,106	1,157	1,200
Cash and security holdings	Bil. dol...	73.7	238.0	366.2	508.1	601.7	631.8	660.8	690.0	701.7

[1] Excludes employees in leave-without-pay status. [2] Includes interest on investments. [3] Includes refunds, death claims, and administration. [4] Includes disability annuitants.

Source: U.S. Office of Personnel Management, *Civil Service Retirement and Disability Trust Fund Annual Report.*

Table 531. State and Local Government Retirement Systems—Beneficiaries and Finances: 1990 to 2006

[In billions of dollars (111.3 represents 111,300,000,000), except as indicated. For fiscal years closed during the 12 months ending June 30]

Year and level of government	Number of beneficiaries (1,000)	Receipts					Benefits and withdrawals			Cash and security holdings
		Total	Employee contributions	Government contributions		Earnings on investments	Total	Benefits	Withdrawals	
				State	Local					
1990: All systems	4,026	111.3	13.9	14.0	18.6	64.9	38.4	36.0	2.4	721
State-administered	3,232	89.2	11.6	14.0	11.5	52.0	29.6	27.6	2.0	575
Locally administered	794	22.2	2.2	(Z)	7.0	12.9	8.8	8.4	0.4	145
1995: All systems	4,979	148.8	18.6	16.6	24.4	89.2	61.5	58.8	2.7	1,118
State-administered	4,025	123.3	15.7	16.2	15.4	76.0	48.0	45.8	2.2	914
Locally administered	954	25.5	2.9	0.4	9.0	13.3	13.5	13.0	0.5	204
2000: All systems	6,292	297.0	25.0	17.5	22.6	231.9	95.7	91.3	4.4	2,169
State-administered	4,786	247.4	20.7	17.2	16.7	192.8	76.0	72.2	3.8	1,798
Locally administered	1,506	49.7	4.3	0.4	5.9	39.1	19.8	19.1	0.7	371
2005: All systems	6,946	353.5	31.5	24.0	35.7	262.2	156.0	142.1	3.7	2,672
State-administered	5,846	293.4	26.8	23.6	22.1	220.9	126.8	115.2	3.1	2,226
Locally administered	1,100	60.1	4.8	0.4	13.6	41.3	29.3	26.9	0.5	445
2006: All systems	7,301	392.8	32.7	26.4	38.1	295.6	166.3	152.1	4.1	2,912
State-administered	6,184	326.2	27.7	25.9	23.7	248.9	135.6	124.1	3.4	2,424
Locally administered	1,117	66.5	5.0	0.5	14.3	46.7	30.7	28.0	0.7	488

Z Less than $50 million.

Source: U.S. Census Bureau, through 1995, *Finances of Employee-Retirement Systems of State and Local Governments*, Series GF, No. 2, annual; beginning 2000, "Federal, State, and Local Governments, State and Local Government Public Employee Retirement Systems"; <http://www.census.gov/govs/www/retire.html>.

Table 532. Percent of Workers Participating in Retirement Benefits by Worker Characteristics: 2004 to 2007

[Based on National Compensation Survey, a sample survey of 10,370 private industry establishments of all sizes, representing over 105 million workers; see Appendix III. Survey covers all 50 states and the District of Columbia. For a definition of defined benefit and defined contribution, see headnote, Table 533. See also Table 634]

Characteristic	Total [1]				Defined benefit				Defined contribution			
	2004	2005	2006	2007	2004	2005	2006	2007	2004	2005	2006	2007
Total	**50**	**50**	**51**	**51**	**21**	**21**	**20**	**20**	**42**	**42**	**43**	**43**
White-collar occupations	61	61	60	69	24	24	22	28	53	53	53	60
Blue-collar occupations	50	51	52	51	25	26	25	25	38	38	40	40
Service occupations	22	22	24	25	6	7	7	7	18	18	20	20
Full-time	60	60	60	60	24	25	23	23	50	50	51	50
Part-time	20	19	21	23	9	9	8	9	14	14	16	18
Union	81	85	80	81	69	72	68	67	42	43	44	41
Nonunion	47	46	47	47	15	15	14	15	42	41	43	43

[1] Total is less than the sum of the individual retirement items because many employees participated in both types of plans.

Source: U.S. Bureau of Labor Statistics, *Employee Benefits in Private Industry in the United States, March 2007*, Summary 07-05, March 2007. See also <http://www.bls.gov/ncs/ebs/sp/ebsm0006.pdf>.

Table 533. **Private Pension Plans—Summary by Type of Plan: 1990 to 2005**

[712.3 represents 712,300. "**Pension plan**" is defined by the Employee Retirement Income Security Act (ERISA) as "any plan, fund, or program which was heretofore or is hereafter established or maintained by an employer or an employee organization, or by both, to the extent that such plan (a) provides retirement income to employees, or (b) results in a deferral of income by employees for periods extending to the termination of covered employment or beyond, regardless of the method of calculating the contributions made to the plan, the method of calculating the benefits under the plan, or the method of distributing benefits from the plan." A **defined benefit** plan provides a definite benefit formula for calculating benefit amounts—such as a flat amount per year of service or a percentage of salary times years of service. A **defined contribution** plan is a pension plan in which the contributions are made to an individual account for each employee. The retirement benefit is dependent upon the account balance at retirement. The balance depends upon amounts contributed, investment experience, and, in the case of profit sharing plans, amounts which may be allocated to the account due to forfeitures by terminating employees. Employee Stock Ownership Plans (ESOP) and 401(k) plans are included among defined contribution plans. Data are based on Form 5500 series reports filed with the U.S. Department of Labor]

Item	Unit	Total				Defined contribution plan				Defined benefit plan			
		1990	1995	2000	2005	1990	1995	2000	2005	1990	1995	2000	2005
Number of plans [1]	1,000 . . .	712.3	693.4	736.0	679.1	599.2	623.9	686.9	631.4	113.1	69.5	48.7	47.6
Total participants [2]	Million . . .	76.9	87.5	103.3	117.4	38.1	47.7	61.7	75.5	38.8	39.7	41.6	41.9
Active participants [3] . . .	Million . . .	61.8	66.2	73.1	82.7	35.5	42.7	50.9	62.4	26.3	23.5	22.2	20.3
Assets [4]	Bil. dol. . .	1,674	2,724	4,203	5,062	712	1,322	2,216	2,808	962	1,402	1,986	2,254
Contributions [5]	Bil. dol. . .	98.8	158.8	231.9	341.4	75.8	117.4	198.5	248.8	23.0	41.4	33.4	92.7
Benefits [6]	Bil. dol. . .	129.4	183.0	341.0	354.5	63.0	97.9	213.5	218.0	66.4	85.1	127.5	136.6

[1] Excludes all plans covering only one participant.   [2] Includes active, retired, and separated vested participants not yet in pay status. Also includes double counting of workers in more than one plan.   [3] Includes any workers currently in employment covered by a plan and who are earning or retaining credited service under a plan. Includes individuals who are eligible to elect to have the employer make payments to a Code section 401(k) plan. Also includes any nonvested former employees who have not yet incurred breaks in service.   [4] Asset amounts shown exclude funds held by life insurance companies under allocated group insurance contracts for payment of retirement benefits. These excluded funds make up roughly 10 to 15 percent of total private fund assets.   [5] Includes both employer and employee contributions.   [6] Includes benefits paid directly from trust and premium payments made from plans to insurance carriers. Excludes benefits paid directly by insurance carriers.

Source: U.S. Department of Labor, Employee Benefits Security Administration, *Private Pension Plan Bulletin* (released February 2008). See also <http://www.dol.gov/ebsa/pdf/privatepensionplanbulletinhistoricaltables.pdf>.

Table. 534. **Defined Benefit Retirement Plans—Selected Features: 2006**

[In percent. Covers full-time employees in private industry. Based on National Compensation Survey, a sample survey of 3,227 private industry establishments of all sizes, representing over 102 million workers; see Appendix III. For definition of defined benefit, see headnote, Table 533. See also Table 634]

Feature	All workers	White collar	Blue collar	Ser-vice	Goods pro-ducing	Ser-vice pro-ducing	1–99 workers	100 workers or more	Union	Non-union
Plan provisions:										
Benefits based on earnings	53	56	43	73	39	59	48	54	37	61
Early retirement benefits available . . .	82	82	89	94	90	79	76	84	87	80
Availability of lump sum benefits at retirement	52	64	34	57	40	59	49	54	40	59
Benefit formula:										
Percent of terminal earnings.	39	46	10	41	32	42	27	42	21	48
Percent of career earnings.	14	10	16	32	7	17	21	12	15	13
Dollar amount formula	18	6	37	12	42	6	16	19	15	13
Percent of contribution formula	4	3	7	(Z)	7	3	9	3	10	1
Cash balance	23	33	12	14	10	30	25	23	12	29
Pension equity.	2	2	1	1	2	2	1	2	(Z)	3
Requirements for normal retirement [1]:										
No age requirement	11	15	7	3	6	13	20	8	8	12
Less than 30 years of service	9	13	4	3	4	11	14	7	5	11
30 years of service	2	2	3	–	3	2	6	1	3	2
At age 55	1	1	2	(Z)	2	1	1	1	2	1
At age 60	9	8	10	16	7	10	8	10	14	7
At age 62	15	11	23	7	24	11	15	15	21	12
At age 65	59	63	48	74	55	60	47	62	43	67
Sum of age plus service [2]	1	1	1	–	2	(Z)	1	1	1	1

– Represents or rounds to zero.   Z Less than 0.5 percent.   [1] Normal retirement is defined as the point at which the participant could retire and immediately receive all accrued benefits by virtue of service and earnings, without reduction due to age. If a plan had alternative age and service requirements, the earliest age and associated service were tabulated; if one alternative did not specify an age, it was the requirement tabulated. Some age and service requirements are not shown separately.   [2] In some plans, participants must also satisfy a minimum age or service requirement.

Source: U.S. Bureau of Labor Statistics, *National Compensation Survey: Employee Benefits in Private Industry in the United States, 2006*; and unpublished data.

Social Insurance and Human Services   351

Table 535. **Percent of U.S. Households Owning IRAs: 2000 to 2007**

[Incidence of IRA ownership is based on an annual tracking survey of 3,000 randomly selected, representative U.S. households; see source for details]

Year and characteristic	Any type of IRA[1]	Tradi-tional IRA	Roth IRA	Employer-spon-sored IRA[2]	Year and characteristic	Any type of IRA[1]	Tradi-tional IRA	Roth IRA	Employer-spon-sored IRA[2]
2000	35.7	28.7	9.2	6.8	**Total, 2007**	**39.8**	**32.5**	**14.9**	**7.9**
2001	36.2	28.9	9.8	8.0					
2002	34.8	28.2	10.8	7.7	Under 35 years . . .	35.0	17.0	12.0	6.0
2003	36.7	29.6	12.5	7.5	35 to 44 years	57.0	29.0	19.0	9.0
2004	36.5	29.6	11.6	8.0	45 to 54 years	65.0	37.0	16.0	12.0
2005	37.9	30.0	12.8	7.4	55 to 64 years	74.0	46.0	19.0	9.0
2006	38.3	31.7	13.4	7.7	65 years and over. .	51.0	38.0	9.0	4.0

[1] Excludes ownership of Coverdell Education Savings Accounts, which were referred to as Education IRAs before July 2001. [2] Employer-sponsored Individual Retirement Accounts (IRAs) include SIMPLE IRAs, Simplified Employee Pension IRAs (SEP-IRAs), and SAR-SEP IRAs (SEP IRAs with salary reduction plans included).

Source: Investment Company Institute, Washington, DC, *Research Fundamentals*, "Appendix: Additional Data on IRA Ownership in 2007"; Vol 17, No. 1A, January 2008 (copyright). See also <http://www.ici.org/statements/fundamentals/fm-v17n1appendix.pdf>.

Table 536. **Characteristics of U.S. Households Owning IRAs: 2007**

[See headnote, Table 535]

Characteristic	Households owning IRAs			Households not owning IRAs[2]
	Total[1]	Traditional IRA	Roth IRA	
MEDIAN PER HOUSEHOLD				
Age of household sole or co-decision-maker for investing.	54	56	50	46
Household income	80,000	78,000	87,500	34,000
Household financial assets[3]	250,000	300,000	300,000	40,000
Household financial assets in all types of IRAs.	50,000	50,700	50,100	(X)
Share of household financial assets in type of IRA indicated. . .	27	27	6	(X)
PERCENT OF HOUSEHOLDS				
Household has defined contribution account or				
Defined benefit plan coverage (total)[4]	80	79	87	51
Defined contribution retirement plan account	70	69	80	42
Defined benefit plan coverage	47	47	50	22
Types of IRAs owned: [4,5]				
Traditional IRA	87	100	68	(X)
Roth IRA	40	31	100	(X)
Employer-sponsored IRA[6]	15	15	16	(X)

X Not applicable. [1] Households owning IRAs include households that own Traditional or Roth IRAs. Households owning only employer-sponsored IRAs are not included. [2] Households not owning IRAs exclude households with traditional, Roth, or employer-sponsored IRAs. [3] Household financial assets include assets in employer-sponsored defined contribution retirement plans but exclude primary residence. [4] Multiple responses are included. [5] Data are from ICI's 2007 Mutual Fund Shareholder Tracking Survey. [6] Employer-sponsored IRAs include SEP IRAs, SAR-SEP IRAs, and SIMPLE IRAs. Among households owning employer-sponsored IRAs, 63 percent have traditional IRAs and 31 percent have Roth IRAs.

Source: Investment Company Institute, Washington, DC, *Research Fundamentals*, "Appendix: Additional Data on IRA Ownership in 2007"; Vol 17, No. 1A, January 2008 (copyright). See also <http://www.ici.org/statements/fundamentals/>.

Table 537. **Percent Distribution of Assets in IRAs, by Type of IRA: 2007**

[See headnote, Table 535]

Assets category	Unit	Total assets in IRAs	Type of IRA owned	
			Traditional IRAs	Roth IRAs
PERCENT DISTRIBUTION OF ASSETS IN IRAS				
Less than $10,000	Percent . . .	17	17	38
$10,000 to $24,999	Percent . . .	16	18	27
$25,000 to $49,999	Percent . . .	16	18	16
$50,000 to $99,999	Percent . . .	16	15	11
$100,000 to $249,999	Percent . . .	18	16	5
$250,000 or more.	Percent . . .	17	16	3
TOTAL ASSETS IN IRA				
Mean	Dollars . . .	134,600	124,600	41,400
Median	Dollars . . .	50,000	42,500	14,500

Source: Investment Company Institute, Washington, DC, *Research Fundamentals* , "Appendix: Additional Data on IRA Ownership in 2007"; Vol. 17, No. 1A, January 2008 (copyright). See also <http://www.ici.org/statements/fundamentals/>.

Table 538. **401(k) Plans—Selected Features: 2006**

[**In percent.** Covers full-time employees in private industry. Based on National Compensation Survey, a sample survey of 3,227 private industry establishments of all sizes, representing 102 million workers; see Appendix III. See also Table 634]

Feature	All employees	White Collar	Blue Collar	Service
MAXIMUM PRETAX EMPLOYEE CONTRIBUTIONS [1]				
Percent of employee earnings	53	51	56	55
Specified dollar amount	(Z)	(Z)	(S)	(Z)
Up to the Internal Revenue code limit	46	47	44	39
Average maximum pretax contribution [2]	18.3	18.6	17.8	17.5
INVESTMENT CHOICES				
Employee permitted to choose investments [3]	91	91	92	91
Employee not permitted to choose investments	1	1	(Z)	3

S Indicates no employees in this category, or data do not meet publication criteria.   Z Less than 0.5 percent.   [1] Includes contributions that are not matched by the employer. If maximum contributions vary, such as by length of service, the highest possible contribution was tabulated.   [2] The average is presented for all covered workers; averages exclude workers without the plan provision.   [3] Sums of individual items exceed totals because multiple choices are available to many employees.

Source: U.S. Bureau of Labor Statistics, *National Compensation Survey: Employee Benefits in Private Industry in the United States, 2006,* and unpublished data

Table 539. **State Unemployment Insurance—Summary: 1990 to 2007**

[**2,522 represents 2,522,000.** Includes unemployment compensation for state and local government employees where covered by state law]

Item	Unit	1990	1995	2000	2002	2003	2004	2005	2006	2007
Insured unemployment, average weekly	1,000	2,522	2,572	2,110	3,585	3,531	2,950	2,661	2,475	2,571
Percent of covered employment [1]	Percent . . .	2.4	2.3	1.7	2.8	2.8	2.3	2.1	1.9	2.0
Percent of civilian unemployed	Percent . . .	35.8	34.7	37.6	43.2	40.7	36.8	35.7	35.3	36.3
Unemployment benefits, average weekly	Dollars . . .	161	187	221	257	262	263	267	277	288
Percent of weekly wage	Percent . . .	36.0	35.5	32.9	36.8	36.5	35.2	34.6	34.3	35.1
Weeks compensated.	Million	116.2	118.3	96.0	166.3	163.2	135.1	121.2	112.2	116.3
Beneficiaries, first payments	1,000	8,629	8,035	7,033	10,088	9,935	8,369	7,922	7,350	7,641
Average duration of benefits [2] . . .	Weeks. . . .	13.4	14.7	13.7	16.5	16.4	16.1	15.3	15.2	15.3
Claimants exhausting benefits . . .	1,000	2,323	2,662	2,144	4,416	4,417	3,532	2,856	2,676	2,670
Percent of first payment [3]	Percent . . .	29.4	34.3	31.8	42.5	43.4	39.0	35.9	35.4	35.3
Contributions collected [4]	Bil. dol. . . .	15.2	22.0	19.9	19.7	25.3	31.2	34.8	34.1	34.5
Benefits paid	Bil. dol. . . .	18.1	21.2	20.5	42.0	41.4	34.4	31.2	29.8	30.1
Funds available for benefits [5] . . .	Bil. dol. . . .	37.9	35.4	53.4	35.2	23.4	23.0	29.0	35.8	32.5
Average employer contribution rate [6]	Percent . . .	1.95	2.44	1.75	1.80	2.20	2.68	2.86	2.68	2.61

[1] Insured unemployment as percent of average covered employment in preceding year.   [2] Weeks compensated divided by first payment.   [3] Based on first payments for 12-month period ending June 30.   [4] Contributions from employers; also employees in states which tax workers.   [5] End of year. Sum of balances in state clearing accounts, benefit-payment accounts, and state accounts in federal unemployment trust funds.   [6] As percent of taxable wages.

Source: U.S. Department of Labor, Employment and Training Administration, *Unemployment Insurance Financial Data Handbook.* See also <http://www.ows.doleta.gov/unemploy/hb394.asp>.

Table 540. **State Unemployment Insurance by State and Other Area: 2007**

[7,642 represents 7,642,000. See headnote, Table 539. For state data on insured unemployment, see Table 609]

State or other area	Beneficiaries, first payments (1,000)	Benefits paid (mil. dol.)	Avg. weekly unemployment benefits (dol.)	State or other area	Beneficiaries, first payments (1,000)	Benefits paid (mil. dol.)	Avg. weekly unemployment benefits (dol.)
Total . . .	**7,642**	**32,247**	**288**	MT	21	70	228
AL	102	219	188	NE	32	93	234
AK	38	102	200	NV	81	339	284
AZ	84	278	202	NH	26	89	264
AR	83	284	257	NJ.	312	1,925	359
CA	1,018	5,157	298	NM	30	130	256
CO	71	301	327	NY	458	2,274	295
CT	121	575	310	NC	243	718	276
DE	24	109	256	ND	13	45	268
DC	17	90	286	OH	278	1,151	290
FL.	330	1,123	237	OK	42	156	251
GA	212	583	263	OR	138	524	286
HI	23	115	384	PA	462	2,149	323
ID	45	122	255	RI	41	229	359
IL	353	1,850	305	SC	114	354	230
IN	187	725	290	SD	8	22	227
IA	91	330	293	TN	143	441	222
KS	58	224	302	TX	280	1,110	287
KY	115	412	284	UT	26	99	294
LA	55	176	204	VT	23	91	287
ME	33	115	254	VA	112	380	267
MD	106	447	282	WA	169	711	335
MA	219	1,357	379	WV	43	148	240
MI.	436	1,853	293	WI.	280	877	267
MN	142	746	341	WY	10	36	278
MS	54	143	177	PR	99	204	111
MO	139	438	225	VI	2	9	319

Source: U.S. Employment and Training Administration, *Unemployment Insurance Financial Data Handbook*. See also <http://www.ows.doleta.gov/unemploy/hb394.asp>.

Table 541. **Persons With Work Disability by Selected Characteristics: 2007**

[**In thousands, except percent (19,963 represents 19,963,000). As of March.** Covers civilian noninstitutional population and members of Armed Forces living off post or with their families on post. Persons are classified as having a work disability if they (1) have a health problem or disability which prevents them from working or which limits the kind or amount of work they can do; (2) have a service-connected disability or ever retired or left a job for health reasons; (3) did not work in survey reference week or previous year because of long-term illness or disability; or (4) are under age 65, and are covered by medicare or receive supplemental security income. Based on Current Population Survey; see text, Section 1, and Appendix III]

Age and participation status in assistance programs	Total [1]	Male	Female	White alone [2]	Black alone [3]	Hispanic [4]
Persons with work disability	**19,963**	**9,626**	**10,337**	**15,097**	**3,695**	**2,247**
16 to 24 years old.	1,499	788	711	1,038	373	218
25 to 34 years old.	2,272	1,061	1,211	1,666	465	318
35 to 44 years old.	3,431	1,593	1,838	2,536	708	462
45 to 54 years old.	5,748	2,768	2,981	4,372	1,028	593
55 to 64 years old.	7,012	3,416	3,596	5,485	1121	656
Percent work disabled of total population . . .	10.2	10.0	10.5	9.7	15.2	7.9
16 to 24 years old.	4.0	4.2	3.9	3.6	6.8	3.3
25 to 34 years old.	5.7	5.4	6.1	5.4	9.0	3.9
35 to 44 years old.	8.1	7.6	8.5	7.5	13.4	6.9
45 to 54 years old.	13.3	13.0	13.5	12.3	20.3	12.8
55 to 64 years old.	21.8	22.1	21.5	20.2	34.9	24.9
Percent of work disabled—						
Receiving social security income	33.7	33.7	33.7	34.9	30.9	24.8
Receiving food stamps	19.1	15.5	22.5	15.9	31.2	23.8
Covered by Medicaid.	65.4	68.4	62.6	68.2	54.7	54.3
Residing in public housing	6.8	5.7	7.8	5.1	13.3	7.7
Residing in subsidized housing	3.6	2.6	4.5	2.6	6.9	5.0

[1] Includes other races not shown separately. [2] Beginning with the 2003 Current Population Survey, respondents were asked to choose one or more races. White alone refers to people who reported White and did not report any other race category. The use of this single-race population does not imply that it is the preferred method of presenting or analyzing data. The Census Bureau uses a variety of approaches. Information on people who reported more than one race, such as "White and American Indian and Alaska Native" or "Asian and Black or African American," is available from Census 2000 through American FactFinder®. About 2.6 percent of people reported more than one race in 2000. [3] Black alone refers to people who reported Black and did not report any other race category. [4] Hispanic persons may be of any race.
Source: U.S. Census Bureau, unpublished data.

Table 542. **Workers' Compensation Payments: 1990 to 2005**

[In billions of dollars, except as indicated (53.1 represents $53,100,000,000). See headnote, Table 543]

Item	1990	1995	1998	1999	2000	2001	2002	2003	2004	2005
Workers covered (mil.)	106	113	122	124	127	127	126	125	126	128
Premium amounts paid [1]	**53.1**	**57.1**	**53.4**	**55.8**	**60.1**	**66.6**	**73.4**	**82.0**	**86.8**	**88.8**
Private carriers [1]	35.1	31.6	30.4	33.4	35.7	37.8	41.4	45.3	48.0	50.9
State funds	8.0	10.5	7.9	7.5	8.8	11.5	14.6	17.8	19.1	18.2
Federal programs [2]	2.2	2.6	3.5	3.5	3.6	3.8	3.9	4.0	4.1	4.1
Self-insurers	7.9	12.5	11.7	11.4	11.9	13.6	13.6	14.9	15.8	15.7
Annual benefits paid [1]	**38.2**	**42.1**	**44.0**	**46.3**	**47.7**	**50.8**	**52.4**	**55.1**	**56.1**	**55.3**
By private carriers [1]	22.2	20.1	23.6	26.4	26.9	27.9	28.2	28.6	28.1	28.1
From state funds [3]	8.8	10.8	10.1	9.9	10.3	11.1	12.5	13.7	14.4	14.0
Employers' self-insurance [4]	7.2	11.2	10.4	10.0	10.5	11.8	11.8	12.8	13.6	13.2
Type of benefit:										
Medical/hospitalization	15.2	16.7	18.6	20.1	20.9	23.1	24.3	25.8	26.4	26.2
Compensation payments	23.1	25.4	25.4	26.3	26.8	27.7	28.1	29.2	29.7	29.1
Percent of covered payroll: [1]										
Workers' compensation costs [5, 6] . . .	2.18	1.82	1.38	1.35	1.34	1.45	1.59	1.74	1.75	1.70
Benefits [6]	1.53	1.34	1.13	1.12	1.06	1.10	1.14	1.17	1.13	1.06

[1] Premium and benefit amounts include estimated payments under insurance policy deductible provisions. Deductible benefits are allocated to private carriers and state funds.   [2] Years 1990–1995 includes federal employer compensation program and that portion of federal black lung benefits program financed from employer contributions. Years 1997–2002 includes federal employer compensation program only due to changes in reporting methods.   [3] Net cash and medical benefits paid by competitive and exclusive state funds and by federal workers' compensation programs.   [4] Cash and medical benefits paid by self-insurers, plus value of medical benefits paid by employers carrying workers' compensation policies that exclude standard medical coverage.   [5] Premiums written by private carriers and state funds, and benefits paid by self-insurers increased by 5–10 prior to 1995 and by 11 percent for 1995–2002 for administrative costs. Also includes benefits paid and administrative costs of federal system for government employees.   [6] Excludes programs financed from general revenue—black lung benefits and supplemental pensions in some states.

Source: National Academy of Social Insurance, Washington, DC, *Workers' Compensation: Benefits, Coverage, and Costs*, annual. See also <http://www.nasi.org/>.

Table 543. **Workers' Compensation Payments by State: 2000 to 2005**

[In millions of dollars (47,699 represents $47,699,000,000). Calendar-year data. Payments represent compensation and medical benefits and include insurance losses paid by private insurance carriers (compiled from state workers' compensation agencies and A.M. Best Co.); disbursements of state funds (compiled from the A.M. Best Co. and state workers' compensation agencies); and self-insurance payments (compiled from state workers' compensation agencies and authors' estimates)]

State	2000	2002	2003	2004	2005	State	2000	2002	2003	2004	2005
Total	**47,699**	**52,416**	**55,066**	**56,074**	**55,307**	Montana.	155	196	217	223	239
						Nebraska	230	266	267	283	298
Alabama.	529	565	580	576	609	Nevada	347	316	329	359	394
Alaska.	139	179	182	187	189	New Hampshire. . . .	177	213	221	212	217
Arizona.	498	478	515	548	536	New Jersey.	1,378	1,382	1,660	1,479	1,608
Arkansas	214	217	224	227	208	New Mexico	144	176	189	196	231
California	9,449	10,974	12,410	12,460	10,938	New York	2,761	2,976	3,143	3,279	2,895
Colorado.	810	761	753	843	896	North Carolina	865	994	1,077	1,160	1,398
Connecticut.	638	676	677	711	713	North Dakota.	70	74	78	83	82
Delaware	118	137	156	157	168	Ohio	2,099	2,388	2,442	2,435	2,447
District of Columbia .	78	89	84	96	91	Oklahoma.	485	509	555	580	588
Florida	2,577	2,623	2,806	2,710	2,899						
Georgia	965	917	981	1,114	1,198	Oregon.	425	504	498	534	551
Hawaii	231	268	275	271	251	Pennsylvania.	2,379	2,479	2,565	2,594	2,678
Idaho	114	202	214	236	243	Rhode Island.	127	144	134	148	142
Illinois	1,944	2,149	2,147	2,246	2,404	South Carolina	515	593	657	688	770
Indiana.	545	547	564	595	610	South Dakota	63	73	74	77	86
Iowa	343	402	427	447	474	Tennessee	774	722	783	819	880
Kansas	323	342	296	371	383	Texas	2,160	2,371	1,968	1,641	1,555
Kentucky	584	692	717	720	706	Utah	172	213	187	217	241
						Vermont	101	119	120	124	122
Louisiana	547	621	669	726	667	Virginia.	597	630	706	753	854
Maine.	245	260	233	268	269	Washington.	1,527	1,716	1,801	1,836	1,864
Maryland	641	664	723	787	770	West Virginia	661	792	823	797	696
Massachusetts.	801	887	1,059	968	904	Wisconsin	765	900	844	1,039	1,188
Michigan.	1,474	1,512	1,477	1,517	1,474	Wyoming	89	107	114	120	117
Minnesota.	798	921	885	931	946						
Mississippi	293	290	291	310	312	Federal total [1]	2,957	3,154	3,185	3,256	3,258
Missouri	780	1,033	1,081	1,120	1,051	Federal employees . .	2,119	2,317	2,368	2,445	2,462

[1] Federal benefits include: those paid under the Federal Employees Compensation Act for civilian employees; the portion of the Black Lung benefit program that is financed by employers; and a portion of benefits under the Longshore and Harbor Workers Compensation Act that are not reflected in state data, namely, benefits paid by self-insured employers and by special funds under the LHWCA. See Appendix H of source for more information about federal programs.

Source: National Academy of Social Insurance, Washington, DC, *Workers' Compensation: Benefits, Coverage, and Costs*, annual. See also <http://www.nasi.org/>.

U.S. Census Bureau, Statistical Abstract of the United States: 2009

Table 544. Supplemental Security Income—Recipients and Payments: 1990 to 2006

[**In thousands (4,817 represents 4,817,000), except as noted**. Recipients and monthly payment as of December. Payments for calendar year. Persons with a federal SSI payment and/or federally administered state supplementation. See also Appendix III]

Program	Unit	1990	1995	2000	2002	2003	2004	2005	2006
Recipients, total	1,000.	4,817	6,514	6,602	6,788	6,902	6,988	7,114	7,236
Aged	1,000.	1,454	1,446	1,289	1,252	1,233	1,211	1,214	1,212
Blind	1,000.	84	84	79	78	77	76	75	73
Disabled.	1,000.	3,279	4,984	5,234	5,459	5,593	5,701	5,825	5,951
Payments, total [1]	Mil. dol. . . .	16,133	27,037	30,672	33,719	34,693	36,065	37,236	38,889
Aged	Mil. dol. . . .	3,559	4,239	4,540	4,803	4,857	4,894	4,965	5,116
Blind	Mil. dol. . . .	329	367	386	416	409	412	414	409
Disabled.	Mil. dol. . . .	12,245	22,431	25,746	28,500	29,429	30,745	31,857	33,364
Average monthly payment, total	Dollars . . .	276	335	379	407	417	428	439	455
Aged	Dollars. . . .	208	250	300	330	342	351	360	373
Blind	Dollars. . . .	319	355	413	445	455	463	475	488
Disabled.	Dollars. . . .	303	358	398	425	433	444	455	471

[1] Includes payments not distributed by reason for eligibility.

Source: U.S. Social Security Administration, *Social Security Bulletin*, quarterly and *Annual Statistical Supplement to the Social Security Bulletin*. See also <http://www.ssa.gov/policy/docs/statcomps/supplement/>.

Table 545. Supplemental Security Income (SSI)—Recipients and Payments by State and Other Area: 2000 to 2006

[**Recipients as of December; payments for calendar year (6,602 represents 6,602,000)**. Data cover federal SSI payments and/or federally administered state supplementation. For explanation of methodology, see Appendix III]

State and other area	Recipients (1,000)		Payments for year (mil. dol.)			State and other area	Recipients (1,000)		Payments for year (mil. dol.)		
	2000	2006	2000	2005	2006		2000	2006	2000	2005	2006
Total . . .	6,602	7,236	30,672	37,236	38,889	MO.	112	120	471	573	598
U.S	6,601	7,235	30,669	37,232	38,885	MT.	14	15	57	70	74
AL	159	165	659	776	805	NE	21	23	85	103	108
AK	9	11	37	53	56	NV	25	34	108	163	171
AZ	81	99	355	482	506	NH	12	14	49	67	72
AR	85	93	333	407	433	NJ	146	154	672	763	800
CA	1,088	1,227	6,386	8,146	8,300	NM	47	55	193	248	263
CO	54	57	228	264	279	NY	617	642	3,197	3,561	3,714
CT	49	53	216	260	272	NC	191	203	732	894	945
DE	12	14	50	66	69	ND	8	8	30	33	35
DC	20	22	93	113	119	OH	240	254	1,114	1,295	1,347
FL	377	428	1,621	2,031	2,128	OK	72	82	302	381	406
GA	197	206	785	944	986	OR	52	62	228	298	314
HI.	21	23	104	119	125	PA	284	326	1,367	1,659	1,757
ID.	18	23	76	106	114	RI.	28	31	130	161	166
IL.	249	261	1,174	1,337	1,395	SC	107	105	429	488	503
IN.	88	101	382	488	519	SD	13	13	48	55	57
IA.	40	44	158	193	203	TN	164	163	664	752	784
KS	36	40	151	187	194	TX	409	524	1,575	2,191	2,417
KY	174	182	741	862	902	UT	20	24	87	110	117
LA	166	157	715	771	760	VT	13	13	51	63	67
ME.	30	33	116	146	153	VA	132	139	535	632	667
MD.	88	96	400	481	506	WA	101	119	484	616	656
MA.	168	175	807	902	953	WV	71	78	318	376	396
MI	210	225	988	1,157	1,206	WI	85	94	357	437	466
MN	64	76	272	355	383	WY	6	6	23	26	28
MS	129	124	512	572	589	N. Mariana . . .	1	1	3	4	4

Source: U.S. Social Security Administration, *Annual Statistical Supplement* to the *Social Security Bulletin*. See also <http://www.ssa.gov/policy/docs/statcomps/supplement/>.

Table 546. Temporary Assistance for Needy Families (TANF)—Families and Recipients: 1980 to 2006

[**In thousands (3,712 represents 3,712,000). Average monthly families and recipients for calendar year**. Prior to TANF, the cash assistance program to families was called Aid to Families with Dependent Children (1980–1996). Under the new welfare law (Personal Responsibility and Work Opportunity Reconciliation Act of 1996), the program became TANF. See text, this section. Includes Puerto Rico, Guam, and Virgin Islands]

Year	Families	Recipients	Year	Families	Recipients	Year	Families	Recipients
1980	3,712	10,774	1991	4,497	12,930	1999	2,554	6,824
1984	3,714	10,831	1992	4,829	13,773	2000	2,265	5,943
1985	3,701	10,855	1993	5,012	14,205	2001	2,117	5,423
1986	3,763	11,038	1994	5,033	14,161	2002	2,065	5,148
1987	3,776	11,027	1995	4,791	13,418	2003	2,032	4,967
1988	3,749	10,915	1996	4,434	12,321	2004	1,987	4,784
1989	3,799	10,993	1997	3,740	10,376	2005	1,921	4,549
1990	4,057	11,695	1998	3,050	8,347	2006	1,807	4,230

Source: U.S. Department of Health and Human Services, Administration for Children and Families, unpublished data.

Table 547. Temporary Assistance for Needy Families (TANF)—Recipients by State and Other Areas: 2000 to 2006

[In thousands (2,265 represents 2,265,000). Average monthly families and recipients for calendar year. See headnote, Table 546]

State or other area	Families 2000	Families 2005	Families 2006	Recipients 2000	Recipients 2005	Recipients 2006	State or other area	Families 2000	Families 2005	Families 2006	Recipients 2000	Recipients 2005	Recipients 2006
Total...	2,265	1,921	1,807	5,943	4,549	4,230	MT	5	5	4	13	12	10
U.S.	2,229	1,902	1,790	5,838	4,495	4,179	NE	10	10	10	24	25	24
AL	19	20	19	46	47	45	NV	6	7	5	16	16	12
AK	7	4	4	22	12	10	NH	6	6	6	14	14	14
AZ	34	44	40	87	99	87	NJ	52	43	41	130	105	101
AR	12	9	8	29	19	18	NM	24	18	17	72	45	43
CA	498	464	450	1,299	1,088	1,049	NY	259	142	135	724	323	308
CO	11	15	14	29	38	37	NC	46	34	30	100	68	59
CT	28	20	18	66	40	37	ND	3	3	3	8	7	7
DE	6	6	6	13	13	12	OH	98	83	79	245	179	170
DC	17	17	16	47	42	39	OK	14	12	10	35	28	23
FL	67	60	52	151	107	86	OR	17	19	19	39	44	42
GA	53	42	32	129	90	63	PA	90	97	95	250	253	245
HI	14	8	7	47	20	17	RI	16	11	10	45	27	24
ID	1	2	2	2	3	3	SC	18	16	16	41	36	36
IL	84	38	36	254	96	90	SD	3	3	3	7	6	6
IN	36	44	43	99	125	119	TN	56	71	68	145	186	180
IA	20	18	17	53	43	40	TX	128	87	71	342	201	161
KS	13	18	17	32	46	45	UT	8	9	7	22	23	18
KY	39	35	33	89	75	70	VT	6	5	4	16	11	11
LA	28	16	12	75	37	27	VA	32	10	9	73	28	26
ME	11	10	9	28	26	25	WA	57	57	54	153	137	128
MD	29	23	20	72	55	47	WV	12	12	11	32	27	24
MA	44	49	47	101	104	93	WI	17	20	18	38	47	40
MI	74	81	83	207	215	220	WY	1	1	1	1	1	1
MN	39	29	27	116	73	67	PR	32	15	14	92	42	39
MS	15	16	13	34	35	28	GU	3	3	3	10	11	11
MO	47	40	39	125	97	94	VI	1	–	–	3	1	1

– Represents or rounds to zero.

Source: U.S. Department of Health and Human Services, Administration for Children and Families, unpublished data.

Table 548. Temporary Assistance for Needy Families (TANF)—Expenditures by State: 2000 to 2006

[In millions of dollars (24,781 represents $24,781,000,000). Represents federal and state funds expended in fiscal year]

State	2000, total	2005, total	2006 Total [1]	2006 Expenditures on assistance	State	2000, total	2005, total	2006 Total [1]	2006 Expenditures on assistance
U.S.	24,781	25,444	25,594	11,287	MO	321	299	323	122
AL	96	123	107	38	MT	44	44	43	21
AK	93	74	70	43	NE	79	78	92	63
AZ	261	299	309	144	NV	69	70	68	41
AR	139	67	74	15	NH	73	63	70	42
CA	6,481	5,882	6,280	3,979	NJ	321	858	586	104
CO	205	214	209	67	NM	149	127	109	77
CT	436	459	469	132	NY	3,512	3,970	4,241	2,029
DE	55	61	77	41	NC	440	448	250	93
DC	157	156	193	62	ND	33	34	32	20
FL	781	868	808	200	OH	995	990	1,120	341
GA	386	520	582	131	OK	130	174	151	98
HI	162	128	156	85	OR	169	269	251	115
ID	43	40	39	7	PA	1,327	1,190	994	427
IL	879	998	982	128	RI	172	168	144	68
IN	342	307	316	111	SC	245	230	145	39
IA	163	162	166	77	SD	21	30	30	21
KS	151	154	152	85	TN	293	233	266	122
KY	203	216	190	118	TX	727	851	731	191
LA	118	186	183	46	UT	100	108	96	41
ME	108	127	108	79	VT	62	68	64	41
MD	336	349	357	107	VA	418	290	291	143
MA	690	689	794	336	WA	535	525	633	284
MI	1,264	1,175	1,187	377	WV	134	124	115	58
MN	381	392	404	129	WI	382	446	440	111
MS	62	79	74	24	WY	34	32	23	14

[1] Includes other items not shown separately.

Source: U.S. Administration for Children and Families, *Temporary Assistance for Needy Families (TANF) Program, Annual Report to Congress.*

Table 549. Child Support—Award and Recipiency Status of Custodial Parent: 2005

[In thousands except as noted (13,605 represents 13,605,000). Custodial parents 15 years and older with own children under 21 years of age present from absent parents as of spring 2006. Covers civilian noninstitutional population. Based on Current Population Survey; see text, Section 1 and Appendix III. For definition of mean, see Guide to Tabular Presentation]

Award and recipiency status	All custodial parents				Custodial parents below the poverty level			
	Total		Mothers	Fathers	Total		Mothers	Fathers
	Number	Percent distribution			Number	Percent distribution		
Total	**13,605**	(X)	**11,406**	**2,199**	**3,406**	(X)	**3,160**	**245**
With child support agreement or award [1]	7,802	(X)	7,002	800	1,796	(X)	1,710	85
Supposed to receive payments in 2005	6,809	100.0	6,131	678	1,502	100.0	1,427	75
Actually received payments in 2005	5,259	77.2	4,754	505	1,090	72.6	1,036	53
Received full amount	3,192	46.9	2,900	292	595	39.6	566	29
Received partial payments	2,068	30.4	1,855	213	495	33.0	470	24
Did not receive payments in 2005	1,550	22.8	1,377	174	412	27.4	390	22
Child support not awarded	5,803	(X)	4,404	1,399	1,610	(X)	1,450	160
MEAN INCOME AND CHILD SUPPORT								
Received child support payments in 2005:								
Mean total money income (dol.)	29,454	(X)	28,018	42,977	7,799	(X)	7,773	8,295
Mean child support received (dol.)	4,717	(X)	4,719	4,691	3,372	(X)	3,369	3,428
Received the full amount due:								
Mean total money income (dol.)	31,934	(X)	30,403	47,134	7,766	(X)	7,698	9,112
Mean child support received (dol.)	6,002	(X)	5,981	6,210	4,683	(X)	4,686	4,615
Received partial payments:								
Mean total money income (dol.)	25,626	(X)	24,288	37,278	7,838	(X)	7,864	7,328
Mean child support received (dol.)	2,733	(X)	2,747	2,608	1,796	(X)	1,784	2,022
Received no payments in 2005:								
Mean total money income (dol.)	25,961	(X)	24,475	37,751	7,706	(X)	7,559	10,315
Without child support agreement or award:								
Mean total money income (dol.)	29,787	(X)	23,127	50,756	6,488	(X)	6,217	8,952

X Not applicable.   [1] As of April 2006.

Source: U.S. Census Bureau, unpublished data.

Table 550. Child Support Enforcement Program—Caseload and Collections: 1990 to 2007

[For years ending Sept. 30 (12,796 represents 12,796,000). Includes Puerto Rico, Guam, and the Virgin Islands. The child support enforcement program locates absent parents, establishes paternity of children born out of wedlock, and establishes and enforces support orders. By law, these services are available to all families that need them. The program is operated at the state and local government level, but 66 percent of administrative costs are paid by the federal government. Child support collected for families not receiving Temporary Assistance for Needy Families (TANF) goes to the family to help it remain self-sufficient. Most of the child support collected on behalf of TANF families goes to federal and state governments to offset TANF payments. Some states pass-through a portion of the CS collections to help families become self-sufficient. Based on data reported by state agencies. Minus sign (–) indicates net outlay]

Item	Unit	1990	1995	2000	2003	2004	2005	2006	2007, prel.
Total cases [1]	1,000	**12,796**	**19,162**	**17,334**	**15,923**	**15,854**	**15,861**	**15,844**	**15,755**
Paternities established, total [2]	1,000	393	659	867	663	692	690	675	640
Support orders established, total [3]	1,000	1,022	1,051	1,175	1,161	1,181	1,180	1,159	1,178
FINANCES									
Collections, total	Mil. dol.	**6,010**	**10,827**	**17,854**	**21,176**	**21,861**	**23,006**	**23,933**	**24,855**
TANF/FC collections [4]	Mil. dol.	1,750	2,689	2,593	2,972	2,221	2,191	2,112	2,050
State share	Mil. dol.	620	939	1,080	947	927	911	875	852
Estimated incentive payments to states	Mil. dol.	264	400	353	356	361	365	402	431
Federal share [5]	Mil. dol.	533	822	968	1,167	1,147	1,129	1,086	1,054
Current Assistance Medical Support Collections	Mil. dol.	(NA)	(NA)	27	20	12	11	12	11
Current Assistance Payments to Families or Foster Care	Mil. dol.	(NA)	(NA)	165	837	136	140	139	133
Non-TANF collections	Mil. dol.	4,260	8,138	15,261	18,204	19,641	20,815	21,822	22,804
Administrative expenditures, total	Mil. dol.	1,606	3,012	4,526	5,216	5,322	5,353	5,561	5,594
State share	Mil. dol.	545	918	1,519	1,765	1,803	1,813	1,884	1,902
Federal share	Mil. dol.	1,061	2,095	3,006	3,450	3,519	3,540	3,677	3,692
Program savings, total	Mil. dol.	–190	–852	–2,125	–3,098	–3,249	–3,312	–3,600	–3,687
State share	Mil. dol.	338	421	–87	–461	–515	–537	–607	–619
Federal share	Mil. dol.	–528	–1,273	–2,038	–2,637	–2,734	–2,776	–2,993	–3,068

NA Not Available.   [1] Passage of the Personal Responsibility and Work Opportunity Reconciliation Act of 1996 (PRWORA) mandated new categories in 1999 and cases were no longer double counted resulting in a 2 million case reduction.   [2] Does not include in-hospital paternities.   [3] Includes modifications to orders.   [4] Collections for current assistance cases where the children are: (1) recipients of TANF under title IV-A of the Social Security Act or (2) entitled to Foster Care (FC) maintenance under title IV-E of the Social Security Act plus collections distributed as assistance reimbursements. Includes assistance reimbursements, which are collections that will be divided between the state and federal governments to reimburse their respective shares of either Title IV-A assistance payments or Title IV-E Foster Care maintenance payments.   [5] Prior to fiscal year 2002, incentives were paid out of the federal share of collections and the net federal share was reported.

Source: U.S. Department of Health and Human Services, Office of Child Support Enforcement, *Annual Report to Congress*.

Table 551. **Federal Food Programs: 1990 to 2007**

[20.0 represents 20,000,000, except as noted. For years ending September 30. Program data include Puerto Rico, Virgin Islands, Guam, American Samoa, Northern Marianas, and the former Trust Territory when a federal food program was operated in these areas. Participation data are average monthly figures except as noted. Participants are not reported for the commodity distribution programs. Cost data are direct federal benefits to recipients; they exclude federal administrative payments and applicable state and local contributions. Federal costs for commodities and cash in-lieu of commodities are shown separately from direct cash benefits for those programs receiving both]

Program	Unit	1990	1995	2000	2003	2004	2005	2006	2007
Food Stamp:									
Participants	Million. . .	20.0	26.6	17.2	21.3	23.9	25.7	26.7	26.5
Federal cost	Mil. dol. . .	14,143	22,764	14,983	21,404	24,619	28,568	30,187	30,373
Monthly average coupon value per recipient	Dollars . .	58.78	71.27	72.62	83.90	85.99	92.57	94.32	95.63
Nutrition assistance program for Puerto Rico:									
Federal cost	Mil. dol. . .	937	1,131	1,268	1,395	1,413	1,495	1,518	1,551
National school lunch program (NSLP):									
Free lunches served	Million. . .	1,662	2,090	2,205	2,335	2,397	2,477	2,496	2,506
Reduced-price lunches served	Million. . .	273	308	409	453	462	479	488	501
Children participating [1]	Million. . .	24.1	25.7	27.3	28.4	29.0	29.6	30.1	30.5
Federal cost	Mil. dol. . .	3,214	4,466	5,493	6,341	6,663	7,055	7,390	7,706
School breakfast (SB):									
Children participating [1]	Million. . .	4.1	6.3	7.6	8.4	8.9	9.4	9.8	10.1
Federal cost	Mil. dol. . .	596	1,048	1,393	1,652	1,776	1,927	2,043	2,164
Special supplemental food program (WIC): [2]									
Participants	Million. . .	4.5	6.9	7.2	7.6	7.9	8.0	8.1	8.3
Federal cost	Mil. dol. . .	1,637	2,512	2,853	3,230	3,562	3,603	3,598	3,887
Child and adult care (CAC): [3]									
Participants [4]	Million. . .	1.5	2.3	2.7	2.9	3.0	3.1	3.1	3.2
Federal cost . . . . [5]	Mil. dol. . .	719	1,296	1,500	1,726	1,812	1,904	1,944	2,024
Federal cost of commodities donated to— [5]									
Child nutrition (NSLP, CACFP, SFS, and SBP)	Mil. dol. . .	644	733	704	909	1,031	1,047	877	1,115
Emergency feeding [6]	Mil. dol. . .	282	100	182	396	361	314	243	191

[1] Average monthly participation (excluding summer months of June through August). Includes children in public and private elementary and secondary schools and in residential child care institutes. [2] WIC serves pregnant and postpartum women, infants, and children up to age 5. [3] CACFP provides year-round subsidies to feed preschool children in child care centers and family day care homes. Certain care centers serving disabled or elderly adults also receive meal subsidies. [4] Average quarterly daily attendance at participating institutions. [5] Includes the federal cost of commodity entitlements, cash in-lieu of commodities, and bonus foods. [6] Provides free commodities to needy persons for home consumption through food banks, hunger centers, soup kitchens, and similar nonprofit agencies. Includes the Emergency Food Assistance Program, the commodity purchases for soup kitchens/food banks program (FY 1989–96), and commodity disaster relief.

Source: U.S. Department of Agriculture, Food and Nutrition Service, "Food and Nutrition Service, Program Data"; <http://www.fns.usda.gov/pd/>; updated monthly.

Table 552. **Federal Food Stamp Program by State: 2000 to 2007**

[Participation data are average monthly numbers (17,194 represents 17,194,000). For years ending September 30. Food stamp costs are for benefits only and exclude administrative expenditures]

State	Persons (1,000)			Benefits (mil. dol.)			State	Persons (1,000)			Benefits (mil. dol.)		
	2000	2006	2007	2000	2006	2007		2000	2006	2007	2000	2006	2007
Total [1] .	17,194	26,672	26,469	14,983	30,174	30,373	MO	423	796	824	358	740	745
U.S.	17,156	26,631	26,427	14,927	30,099	30,295	MT	59	82	80	51	90	90
AL.	396	547	546	344	594	601	NE.	82	120	121	61	124	126
AK.	38	57	56	46	86	86	NV.	61	118	122	57	124	134
AZ.	259	541	545	240	626	647	NH	36	56	59	28	58	62
AR.	247	385	380	206	414	412							
CA.	1,831	2,000	2,048	1,639	2,363	2,570	NJ.	345	406	415	304	456	483
CO	156	251	251	127	321	311	NM	169	245	234	140	253	249
CT.	165	210	213	138	239	253	NY.	1,439	1,786	1,802	1,361	2,240	2,324
DE.	32	66	67	31	70	75	NC	488	854	883	403	921	972
DC	81	89	87	77	104	104	ND	32	45	45	25	46	52
FL.	882	1,418	1,233	771	1,684	1,400	OH	610	1,064	1,077	520	1,266	1,293
							OK	253	436	421	208	467	459
GA	559	947	950	489	1,098	1,126	OR	234	434	438	198	463	477
HI	118	88	90	166	148	157	PA	777	1,092	1,135	656	1,182	1,259
ID	58	91	87	46	100	96	RI	74	73	76	59	81	89
IL	817	1,225	1,246	777	1,503	1,565							
IN	300	575	587	268	648	677							
IA	123	226	238	100	244	265	SC.	295	534	545	249	589	618
KS.	117	183	182	83	188	193	SD.	43	58	60	37	66	71
KY.	403	589	602	337	645	674	TN.	496	870	865	415	976	1,004
LA.	500	830	650	448	1,032	746	TX.	1,333	2,623	2,422	1,215	2,939	2,718
ME	102	160	163	81	169	171	UT.	82	132	123	68	140	133
							VT.	41	47	53	32	50	56
MD	219	305	318	199	336	357	VA.	336	507	515	263	526	551
MA	232	432	456	182	422	472	WA	295	536	536	241	595	601
MI.	603	1,134	1,204	457	1,239	1,368	WV	227	268	269	185	266	275
MN	196	264	276	165	282	296	WI	193	368	383	129	347	363
MS	276	448	426	226	507	444	WY	22	24	23	19	26	25

[1] Includes Guam and the Virgin Islands. Several outlying areas receive nutrition assistance grants in lieu of food stamps (Puerto Rico, American Samoa, and the Northern Marianas).

Source: U.S. Department of Agriculture, Food and Nutrition Service. "Food and Nutrition Service, Program Data"; <http://www.fns.usda.gov/pd/>; updated monthly.

Table 553. Selected Characteristics of Food Stamp Households and Participants: 1990 to 2006

[7,796 represents 7,796,000. For years ending September 30. Data for 1990 exclude Guam and the Virgin Islands. Based on a sample of households from the Food Stamp Quality Control System]

Year	Households				Participants		
		Percent of total				Percent of total	
	Total [1] (1,000)	With children	With elderly [2]	With disabled [3]	Total [1] (1,000)	Children	Elderly [2]
1990	7,796	60.3	18.1	8.9	20,049	49.6	7.7
1995	10,879	59.7	16.0	18.9	26,619	51.5	7.1
2000	7,325	53.9	21.0	27.5	17,139	51.3	10.0
2002	8,193	54.1	18.7	27.0	19,098	51.0	8.9
2003	9,154	54.7	18.0	23.3	21,260	50.8	8.5
2004	10,279	54.3	17.3	22.9	23,858	50.2	8.2
2005	11,184	53.8	17.1	23.1	25,683	50.0	8.2
2006	11,315	52.2	17.9	23.1	25,595	49.2	8.7

[1] Total does not include those who are ineligible or those receiving disaster benefits. [2] Persons 60 years old and over. [3] The substantial increase in 1995 and decrease in 2003 are due in part to the changes in definition of a diasbled household. Prior to 1995, disabled households were defined as households with SSI income but no members over age 59. In 1995, that definition changed to households with at least one member under 65 who received SSI, or at least one member age 18–61 who received social security, veterans' benefits, or other government benefits as a result of a disability. Because of changes to the QC data in 2003, the definition of a disabled household changed to households either SSI income or a medical expense deduction and without an elderly person, and households containing a nonelderly adult who does not appear to be working and who is receiving social security, veterans' benefits, or workers' compensation.

Source: U.S. Department of Agriculture, Food and Nutrition Service, Totals obtained from the National Data Bank. Percentages obtained from *Characteristics of Food Stamp Households: Fiscal Year 2006*, September 2007. See also <http://www.fns.usda .gov/oane/menu/Published/FSP/FSPPartHH.htm>.

Table 554. Food Stamp Households and Participants—Summary: 2006

[11,315 represents 11,315,000. For year ending September 30. Based on a sample of households from the Food Stamp Quality Control System. Figures are lower than official participation counts because they do not include ineligible participants or those receiving disaster food stamp assistance]

Household type and income source	Households		Age, sex, race, and Hispanic origin	Participants	
	Number (1,000)	Percent		Number (1,000)	Percent
Total	**11,315**	**100.0**	Total.	**25,595**	**100.0**
With children	5,906	52.2	Children	12,603	49.2
Single-parent households	3,717	32.9	Under 5 years old.	4,243	16.6
Married-couple households	1,009	8.9	5 to 17 years old	8,631	32.7
Other	1,180	10.4	Adults	12,992	50.8
With elderly	2,024	17.9	18 to 35 years old	5,560	21.7
Living alone	1,613	14.3	36 to 59 years old	5,203	20.3
Not living alone.	411	3.6	60 years old and over	2,229	8.7
Disabled.	2,619	23.1			
Living alone	1,484	13.1	Male	10,580	41.3
Not living alone.	1,134	10.0	Female	15,014	58.7
Earned income.	3,364	29.7	White, non-Hispanic	10,966	42.8
Wages and salaries.	3,010	26.6	Black, non-Hispanic	8,468	33.1
Unearned income.	7,666	67.8	Hispanic.	5,006	19.6
TANF [1]	1,462	13.0	Asian.	611	2.4
Supplemental security income	3,029	26.8	Native American	426	1.7
Social security	2,733	24.2	Other.	118	0.1
No income	1,581	14.0			

[1] Temporary Assistance for Needy Families (TANF) program.

Source: U.S. Department of Agriculture, Food and Nutrition Service, *Characteristics of Food Stamp Households: Fiscal Year 2006*, September 2007. See also <http://www.fns.usda.gov/oane/menu/Published/FSP/FSPPartHH.htm>.

Table 555. Head Start—Summary: 1980 to 2007

[For years ending September 30 (376 represents 376,000)]

Year	Enrollment (1,000)	Appropriation (mil. dol.)	Age and race	Enrollment, 2007 (percent)	Item	Number
1980 ...	376	735	Under 3 years old	10	Average cost per child:	
1990 ...	541	1,552	3 years old.	36	1995	$4,534
1995 ...	751	3,534	4 years old.	51	2000	$5,951
1998 ...	822	4,347	5 years old and over ...	3	2007	$7,326
1999 ...	826	4,658				
2000 ...	858	5,267	White	40	Paid staff (1,000):	
2001 ...	905	6,200	Black	30	1995	147
2002 ...	912	6,537	Hispanic	35	2000	180
2003 ...	910	6,668	American Indian/		2007	220
2004 ...	906	6,775	Alaska Native	4	Volunteers (1,000):	
2005 ...	907	6,843	Asian	2	1995	1,235
2006 ...	909	6,872	Hawaiian/		2000	1,252
2007 ...	908	6,888	Pacific Islander	1	2007	1,384

Source: U.S. Department of Health and Services, Administration for Children and Families, "Head Start Statistical Fact Sheet"; <http://www.acf.hhs.gov/programs/ohs/about/>.

Table 556. Number of Emergency and Transitional Beds in Homeless Assistance Systems Nationwide: 2006

[Data include beds located in Puerto Rico, Guam, and the Virgin Islands. Data are based on a nationally representative sample of 80 jurisdictions that collect data from emergency shelters and transitional providers. The data estimate homeless persons who used emergency shelters or transitional housing from January 1 through June 30, 2006. As a compliment to the survey, a "Continuum of Care" community was derived from each jurisdiction in order to estimate the number of unsheltered homeless persons and the number of emergency shelter and transitional housing beds available on a single night in January 2006. The data do not include homeless individuals living outside a sampled jurisdiction or homeless individuals not using an emergency shelter or a transitional housing program. For more information on data collection and methodology, see Appendix B of source]

Homeless programs	Year-round units/beds [1]			Total year-round beds	Other beds	
	Family units	Family beds	Individual beds		Seasonal beds [2]	Overflow/ voucher [3]
Emergency Shelters	28,745	95,301	111,576	206,877	21,769	55,047
Transitional Housing	32,802	103,743	95,966	199,709	(NA)	(NA)
Total Inventory	61,547	199,044	207,542	406,586	21,769	55,047
Permanent Supportive Housing.	29,935	87,275	109,351	196,626	(NA)	(NA)

NA Not available.   [1] Year-round beds are available for use throughout the year and are considered part of the stable inventory of beds for homeless persons.   [2] Seasonal beds are typically available during particularly high-demand seasons of the year (e.g. winter months in the North or summer months in the South) to accommodate increased need for emergency shelters to prevent illness or death due to the weather.   [3] Overflow beds are typically used during unanticipated emergencies (e.g., precipitous temperature drops or a natural disaster that displaces residents). Voucher beds are made available in a hotel or motel, and often function like overflow beds.

Source: U.S. Department of Housing and Urban Development, *The Second Annual Homeless Assessment Report to Congress* (released March 2008). See also <http://www.hudhre.info/documents/2ndHomelessAssessmentReport.pdf>.

Table 557. Social Assistance Services—Revenue for Employer Firms: 2000 to 2006

[In millions of dollars (77,032 represents $77,032,000,000). Based on the North American Industry Classification System, 2002, (NAICS), see text, Section 15. See Appendix III]

Kind of business	NAICS code	2000, total	2005, total	2006		
				Total	Taxable firms	Tax-exempt firms
Social assistance, total.	**624**	**77,032**	**111,125**	**117,066**	**27,266**	**89,800**
Individual and family services	6241	37,311	53,047	57,766	8,818	48,948
Child and youth services	62411	7,517	10,405	11,078	1,141	9,937
Services for elderly and disabled persons	62412	12,804	19,160	21,436	4,112	17,324
Other individual and family services	62419	16,990	23,482	25,252	3,565	21,687
Community, emergency and other relief services . . .	6242	12,281	18,983	18,887	(S)	18,679
Community food services	62421	2,835	3,784	3,980	28	3,952
Community housing services.	62422	4,888	6,621	6,886	85	6,801
Emergency and other relief services.	62423	4,558	8,578	8,021	(S)	7,926
Vocational rehabilitation services.	6243	9,458	13,937	13,916	2,756	11,160
Child day care services	6244	17,982	25,158	26,497	15,484	11,013

S Figure does not meet publication standards.

Source: U.S. Census Bureau, *Service Annual Survey*, 2006. See also <http://www.census.gov/svsd/www/services/sas /sas_data/sas62.htm>.

Table 558. Social Assistance—Nonemployer Establishments and Receipts: 1997 to 2005

[Receipts in millions of dollars (5,451 represents $5,451,000,000). Includes only firms subject to federal income tax. Nonemployers are businesses with no paid employees. Based on the North American Industry Classification System 2002 (NAICS), see text, Section 15]

Kind of business	NAICS code	Establishments			Receipts		
		1997	2000	2005	1997	2000	2005
Social assistance, total.	**624**	**526,512**	**642,946**	**807,729**	**5,451**	**7,539**	**10,265**
Individual & family services	6241	33,227	72,433	112,909	592	1,106	1,920
Community, emergency and other relief services . . .	6242	1,338	3,560	5,533	24	54	81
Vocational rehabilitation services.	6243	3,213	7,314	11,022	82	151	245
Child day care services	6244	488,734	559,639	678,265	4,754	6,228	8,018

Source: U.S. Census Bureau, "Nonemployer Statistics"; <http://www.census.gov/epcd/nonemployer/index.html> (released June 2007).

Table 559. Child Care Arrangements of Preschool Children by Type of Arrangement: 1991 to 2005

[In percent, except as indicated (8,428 represents 8,428,000). Estimates are based on children 3 to 5 years old who have not entered kindergarten. Based on interviews from a sample survey of the civilian, noninstitutional population in households with telephones; see source for details. See also Appendix III]

Characteristic	Children		Type of nonparental arrangement [1]			
	Number (1,000)	Percent distribution	In relative care	In nonrelative care	In center-based program [2]	With parental care only
1991, total	8,428	100.0	16.9	14.8	52.8	31.0
1995, total	9,232	100.0	19.4	16.9	55.1	25.9
2005, total	**9,066**	**100.0**	**22.6**	**11.6**	**57.2**	**26.3**
Age:						
3 years old	4,070	44.9	24.0	14.4	42.5	33.4
4 years old	3,873	42.7	20.8	9.2	69.2	20.6
5 years old	1,123	12.4	23.8	9.9	68.7	20.4
Race-ethnicity:						
White, non-Hispanic	5,177	57.1	21.4	15.0	59.1	24.1
Black, non-Hispanic	1,233	13.6	25.0	5.2	66.5	19.5
Hispanic	1,822	20.1	22.7	8.1	43.4	38.0
Other	834	9.2	26.4	8.1	61.5	24.7
Household income:						
Less than $10,001	795	8.8	25.1	8.6	53.4	33.4
$10,001 to $20,000	978	10.8	26.0	7.8	49.2	27.2
$20,001 to $30,000	1,183	13.1	25.4	6.3	43.9	38.5
$30,001 to $40,000	1,124	12.4	23.8	6.9	48.7	33.4
$40,001 to $50,000	808	8.9	21.8	11.6	50.0	35.4
$50,001 to $75,000	1,849	20.4	21.1	13.3	57.1	25.5
$75,001 or more	2,329	25.7	19.8	18.0	75.1	11.4

[1] Columns do not add to 100.0 because some children participated in more than one type of nonparental arrangement. [2] Center-based programs include day care centers, Head Start programs, preschools, prekindergarten, and nursery schools.

Source: U.S. Department of Education, National Center for Education Statistics, Early Childhood Program Participation Survey of the National Household Education Surveys Program (NHES), 2005.

Table 560. Children in Foster Care and Awaiting Adoption: 2000 and 2006

[Data are preliminary and cover the period from October 1 of prior year through September 30 of year shown]

Characteristic	In foster care		Entered foster care		Exited foster care		Waiting to be adopted		Adopted from foster care	
	2000	2006	2000	2006	2000	2006	2000	2006	2000	2006
Total	**552,000**	**510,000**	**293,000**	**303,000**	**272,000**	**289,000**	**131,000**	**129,000**	**51,000**	**51,000**
AGE										
Under 1 year	22,839	30,418	37,996	47,536	11,025	13,948	3,957	5,102	939	1,099
1 to 5 years	134,378	139,082	72,365	84,103	70,667	87,865	44,126	47,108	23,135	26,529
6 to 10 years	136,003	100,580	63,346	57,673	63,228	58,082	44,980	33,396	17,831	13,871
11 to 15 years	160,077	135,921	86,555	78,880	65,550	60,851	33,143	33,698	7,946	7,863
16 to 20 years [1]	98,701	104,003	32,737	34,809	61,531	68,251	4,793	9,696	1,149	1,637
RACE										
White [2]	207,970	205,662	136,214	136,354	121,322	130,945	44,898	49,637	19,462	22,979
Black [2]	217,615	162,722	84,460	80,212	84,065	77,720	57,345	41,591	19,566	13,783
Asian [2]	4,370	2,978	3,565	2,420	3,307	2,384	664	651	290	289
Hispanic [3]	81,823	96,967	42,769	57,444	39,909	51,711	17,050	25,481	7,430	9,569
SEX										
Male	289,187	267,027	(NA)	(NA)	(NA)	(NA)	68,620	68,006	25,472	25,994
Female	262,813	242,973	(NA)	(NA)	(NA)	(NA)	62,380	60,994	25,528	25,006

NA Not available. [1] For children waiting to be adopted, includes ages 16 to 17 years only. [2] Beginning with the 2000 census, respondents could choose more than one race. Data represent persons who selected this race group only and exclude persons reporting more than one race. The census in prior years only allowed respondents to report one race group. See also comments on race in text, Section 1. [3] Hispanic persons may be any race.

Source: U.S. Department of Health and Human Services, Administration for Children and Families, Adoption and Foster Care Analysis and Reporting System Reports, annual. See also <http://www.acf.hhs.gov/programs/cb/stats_research/index.htm#afcars>.

Table 561. **Private Philanthropy Funds by Source and Allocation: 1990 to 2006**

[In billions of dollars (101.4 represents $101,400,000,000). Estimates for sources of funds based on U.S. Internal Revenue Service reports of individual charitable deductions and household surveys of giving by Independent Sector and the Center on Philanthropy at Indiana University. For corporate giving, data are corporate charitable deductions from the U.S. Internal Revenue Service and the contributions made by corporate foundations as reported by the Foundation Center. Data about foundation donations are based upon surveys of foundations and data provided by the Foundation Center. Estimates of the allocation of funds were derived from surveys of nonprofits conducted by various sources]

Source and allocation	1990	1995	1997	1998	1999	2000	2001	2002	2003	2004	2005	2006
Total funds	101.4	123.7	163.0	176.8	202.7	229.7	231.1	231.5	236.3	259.0	283.1	295.0
Individuals.	81.0	95.4	124.2	138.4	154.6	174.5	172.4	172.8	180.2	200.8	213.5	222.9
Foundations [1]	7.2	10.6	13.9	17.0	20.5	24.6	27.2	27.0	26.8	32.4	32.4	36.5
Corporations	5.5	7.4	8.6	8.5	10.2	10.7	11.6	10.8	11.1	13.8	13.8	12.7
Charitable bequests	7.6	10.4	16.3	13.0	17.4	19.9	19.8	20.9	18.2	18.5	23.4	22.9
Allocation:												
Religion.	49.8	58.1	64.7	68.3	71.3	77.0	79.9	82.9	84.6	88.0	92.7	96.8
Health.	9.9	13.9	12.8	13.2	15.2	16.4	18.3	17.8	17.8	20.2	20.7	20.2
Education	12.4	15.6	20.4	23.8	27.2	29.7	32.7	30.0	30.0	33.8	37.3	41.0
Human service	11.8	9.7	12.6	15.6	17.9	20.0	21.8	24.4	24.4	24.4	32.6	29.6
Arts, culture, and humanities. . .	7.9	5.7	7.3	9.9	9.2	10.5	11.4	10.8	10.8	11.8	11.4	12.5
Public/societal benefit	4.9	11.3	12.9	14.0	13.0	15.4	16.5	18.0	16.4	18.8	20.3	21.4
Environment/wildlife.	2.5	2.3	3.1	3.5	4.2	4.8	5.3	5.3	5.4	5.5	6.5	6.6
International.	1.3	3.0	4.2	5.1	6.6	7.2	8.3	8.7	9.8	11.6	12.5	11.3
Gifts to foundations [1]	3.8	8.5	14.0	19.9	28.8	24.7	25.7	19.2	21.6	20.3	27.5	29.5
Unallocated [2]	−3.0	−4.4	11.0	3.6	9.4	24.2	11.3	14.6	13.8	24.8	21.7	26.1

[1] Data are from the Foundation Center through 2001. [2] Money deducted as a charitable contribution by donors but not allocated to sources. May include gifts to governmental entities, in-kind giving, gifts to new charities.

Source: Giving USA Foundation, Glenview, IL, researched and written by the Center on Philanthropy at Indiana University, *Giving USA*, annual (copyright).

Table 562. **Foundations—Number and Finances by Asset Size: 1990 to 2006**

[Figures are for latest year reported by foundations (142,500 represents $142,500,000,000). Covers nongovernmental nonprofit organizations with funds and programs managed by their own trustees or directors, whose goals were to maintain or aid social, educational, religious, or other activities deemed to serve the common good. Excludes organizations that make general appeals to the public for funds, act as trade associations for industrial or other special groups, or do not currently award grants]

Asset size	Number	Assets (mil. dol.)	Gifts received (mil. dol.)	Total giving [1] (mil. dol.)
1990	32,401	142,500	5,000	8,700
1995	40,140	226,700	10,300	12,300
2000	56,582	486,100	27,600	27,600
2005	71,095	550,600	31,500	36,400
2006, total	**72,477**	**614,656**	**36,569**	**40,287**
Under $50,000	11,990	178	2,580	2,734
$50,000–$99,999	4,664	344	213	249
$100,000–$249,999.	9,236	1,551	382	441
$250,000–$499,999.	8,700	3,171	432	487
$500,000–$999,999.	10,007	7,243	749	868
$1,000,000–$4,999,999	17,483	39,491	4,365	4,372
$5,000,000–$9,999,999	4,250	29,694	2,115	2,078
$10,000,000–$49,999,999.	4,632	98,623	7,951	7,067
$50,000,000–$99,999,999. . . .	752	52,398	3,778	3,303
$100,000,000–$249,999,999 . . .	493	74,311	4,877	4,232
$250,000,000 or more	270	307,654	9,127	14,457

[1] Includes grants, scholarships, and employee matching gifts; excludes set-asides, loans, program-related investments (PRIs), and program expenses.

Source: The Foundation Center, New York, NY, *Foundation Yearbook*, annual (copyright).

Table 563. **Domestic Private Foundations—Information Returns: 1990 to 2004**

[Money amounts in billions of dollars (122.4 represents $122,400,000,000). Minus sign (–) indicates loss]

Item	1990	1995	1997	1998	1999	2000	2001	2002	2003	2004
Number of returns.	40,105	47,917	55,113	56,658	62,694	66,738	70,787	73,255	76,348	76,897
Nonoperating foundations [1] . . .	36,880	43,966	50,541	52,460	58,840	61,501	63,650	67,101	70,004	70,613
Operating foundations [2]	3,226	3,951	4,572	4,198	3,854	5,238	7,137	6,154	6,344	6,284
Total assets, book value.	122.4	195.6	280.9	325.7	384.6	409.5	413.6	383.5	418.5	455.5
Total assets, fair market value. . .	151.0	242.9	342.7	397.1	466.9	471.6	455.4	413.0	475.0	509.9
Investments in securities.	115.0	190.7	272.4	317.9	363.4	361.4	329.4	294.4	344.3	361.2
Total revenue	19.0	30.8	55.5	59.7	83.3	72.8	45.3	27.8	48.4	58.7
Total expenses	11.3	17.2	22.4	25.9	33.9	37.4	36.7	34.4	35.1	36.6
Contributions, gifts, and grants paid	8.6	12.3	16.4	19.4	22.8	27.6	27.4	26.3	26.7	27.6
Excess of revenue over expenses (net)	7.7	13.6	33.0	33.8	49.4	35.3	8.6	−6.6	13.3	22.1
Net investment income [3]	11.9	20.4	34.8	39.3	57.1	48.8	25.7	17.6	25.2	34.0

[1] Generally provide charitable support through grants and other financial means to charitable organizations; the majority of foundations are nonoperating. [2] Generally conduct their own charitable activities, e.g., museums. [3] Represents income not considered related to a foundation's charitable purpose, e.g., interest, dividends, and capital gains. Foundations could be subject to an excise tax on such income.

Source: Internal Revenue Service, Statistics of Income, SOI Tax Stats—Charities & Other Tax-Exempt Organizations; <http://www.irs.gov/taxstats/charitablestats/article/0,,id=97176,00.html#2> (accessed 18 January 2008).

Social Insurance and Human Services **363**

Table 564. Nonprofit Charitable Organizations—Information Returns: 2000 to 2004

[In billions of dollars (1,562.5 represents $1,562,500,000,000), except as indicated. Categories based on The National Taxonomy of Exempt Entities (NTEE), a classification system that uses 26 major field areas that are aggregated into 10 categories. Includes data reported by organizations described in Internal Revenue Code section 501(3), excluding private foundations and most religious organizations. Organizations with receipts under $25,000 were not required to file]

Year and category	Number of returns (1,000)	Total assets	Total fund balance or net worth	Revenue Total	Revenue Program service revenue [1]	Revenue Contributions, gifts, and grants	Total expenses	Excess of revenue over expenses (net)
2000	230.2	1,562.5	1,023.2	866.2	579.1	199.1	796.4	69.8
2004, total	**276.2**	**2,058.6**	**1,276.1**	**1,153.0**	**801.2**	**248.6**	**1,058.5**	**94.5**
Arts, culture, and humanities. . .	28.6	81.1	66.0	25.5	6.3	14.2	22.1	3.4
Education	48.9	677.1	486.7	220.1	116.6	64.5	185.1	35.0
Environment, animals	11.6	30.5	25.1	11.1	2.5	6.8	9.5	1.7
Health.	36.4	801.8	424.6	655.1	575.5	46.6	619.0	36.0
Human services	104.8	236.3	114.7	157.7	81.8	62.9	151.5	6.1
International, foreign affairs. . . .	3.5	15.1	11.0	17.1	1.1	15.4	15.9	1.1
Mutual, membership benefit . . .	0.7	13.3	9.7	2.6	1.7	0.2	2.1	0.7
Public, societal benefit	24.1	184.8	123.3	55.2	14.3	32.4	45.9	9.2
Religion related	17.4	18.6	15.0	8.4	1.3	5.8	7.2	1.2

[1] Represents fees collected by organizations in support of their tax-exempt purposes, and income such as tuition and fees at educational institutions, hospital patient charges, and admission and activity fees collected by museums and other nonprofit organizations or institutions.

Source: Internal Revenue Service, Statistics of Income, SOI Tax Stats—Charities & Other Tax-Exempt Organizations Statistics. See also <http://www.irs.gov/taxstats/charitablestats/article/0,,id=97176,00.html>; (accessed 17 January 2008).

Table 565. Individual Charitable Contributions by State: 2005

[In millions of dollars (181,644 represents 181,644,000,000, except as indicated. For tax year. Data will not agree with data in other tables due to differing survey methodology used to derive state data]

State	Charitable contribution Number of returns (1,000)	Charitable contribution Amount (mil. dol.)	State	Charitable contribution Number of returns (1,000)	Charitable contribution Amount (mil. dol.)	State	Charitable contribution Number of returns (1,000)	Charitable contribution Amount (mil. dol.)	State	Charitable contribution Number of returns (1,000)	Charitable contribution Amount (mil. dol.)
U.S.[1] .	**41,395**	**181,644**	ID	182	872	MO	706	2,968	PA	1,674	6,259
AL	541	2,786	IL	1,867	7,617	MT	115	394	RI	172	447
AK	71	276	IN	745	2,965	NE	223	980	SC	551	2,549
AZ	826	3,374	IA	370	1,284	NV	361	1,750	SD	58	359
AR	244	1,595	KS	335	1,513	NH	202	637	TN	587	3,545
CA	5,336	24,450	KY	473	1,795	NJ	1,698	5,823	TX	2,096	11,901
CO	774	3,153	LA	369	1,657	NM	186	685	UT	376	2,601
CT	678	2,928	ME	166	482	NY	3,071	15,734	VT	76	248
DE	132	534	MD	1,193	5,154	NC	1,247	5,465	VA	1,264	5,316
DC	105	748	MA	1,150	4,365	ND	49	196	WA	912	3,722
FL	2,322	11,346	MI	1,490	5,417	OH	1,565	5,234	WV	108	431
GA	1,365	6,529	MN	914	3,376	OK	391	2,432	WI	877	2,689
HI	181	600	MS	262	1,380	OR	572	2,014	WY	43	436

[1] The sum for the states does not add to the total because other components are not shown in this table.

Source: Internal Revenue Service, Statistics of Income Bulletin, Spring issue. See also <http://www.irs.gov/taxstats/article/0,,id=171535,00.html>.

Table 566. Volunteers by Selected Characteristics and Type of Main Organization: 2007

[In percent, except as noted. Data on volunteers relate to persons who performed unpaid volunteer activities for an organization at any point from September 1, 2006, through September 2007. Data represent the percent of the population involved in the activity]

Total and type of main organization [1]	Total, both sexes	Sex Men	Sex Women	Educational attainment [2] Less than a high school diploma	Educational attainment [2] High school graduate, no college [3]	Educational attainment [2] Less than a bachelor's degree [4]	Educational attainment [2] College graduates
Total volunteers (1,000)	**60,838**	**25,727**	**35,114**	**2,394**	**11,379**	**15,468**	**23,799**
Percent of population	26.2	22.9	29.3	9.0	18.6	30.7	41.8
Median annual hours [5]	52	52	52	50	52	52	60
Civic and political [6]	5.1	6.5	4.1	3.3	4.2	5.4	6.0
Educational or youth service.	26.2	24.3	27.5	22.0	22.3	25.3	27.5
Environmental or animal care	1.9	2.0	1.9	0.8	1.4	1.7	2.3
Hospital or other health	7.8	5.7	9.4	5.0	6.9	8.4	8.1
Public safety	1.3	2.3	0.6	0.8	1.9	1.6	0.9
Religious	35.6	35.0	36.0	48.3	41.4	36.1	33.1
Social or community service	13.1	13.9	12.4	13.4	13.3	13.2	12.6
Sport and hobby [7]	3.5	4.2	3.1	2.0	3.3	3.4	4.1

[1] Main organization is defined as the organization for which the volunteer worked the most hours during the year. See headnote for more details.   [2] Data refer to persons 25 years and over.   [3] Includes high school diploma or equivalent.   [4] Includes the categories, some college, no degree; and associate's degree.   [5] For those reporting annual hours.   [6] Includes professional and/or international.   [7] Includes cultural and/or arts.

Source: U.S. Bureau of Labor Statistics, News, USDL 08-0090, 23 January 2008. See also <http://www.bls.gov/news.release/pdf/volun.pdf>.

Section 12
Labor Force, Employment, and Earnings

This section presents statistics on the labor force; its distribution by occupation and industry affiliation; and the supply of, demand for, and conditions of labor. The chief source of these data is the Current Population Survey (CPS) conducted by the U.S. Census Bureau for the Bureau of Labor Statistics (BLS). Comprehensive historical and current data are available from the BLS Internet site <http://www.bls.gov/cps/>. These data are published on a current basis in the BLS monthly publication *Employment and Earnings.* Detailed data on the labor force are also available from the Census Bureau's decennial census of population.

Types of data—Most statistics in this section are obtained by two methods: household interviews or questionnaires and reports of establishment payroll records. Each method provides data that the other cannot suitably supply. Population characteristics, for example, are readily obtainable only from the household survey, while detailed industrial classifications can be readily derived only from establishment records.

Household data are obtained from a monthly sample survey of the population. The CPS is used to gather data for the calendar week including the 12th of the month and provides current comprehensive data on the labor force (see text, Section 1, Population). The CPS provides information on the work status of the population without duplication since each person is classified as employed, unemployed, or not in the labor force. Employed persons holding more than one job are counted only once, according to the job at which they worked the most hours during the survey week.

Monthly, quarterly, and annual data from the CPS are published by BLS in *Employment and Earnings*. Data presented include national totals of the number of persons in the civilian labor force by sex, race, Hispanic or Latino origin, and age; the number employed; hours of work; industry and occupational groups; and the number unemployed, reasons for, and duration of unemployment. Annual data shown in this section are averages of monthly figures for each calendar year, unless otherwise specified. Historical national CPS data are available on the Web site <http://www.bls.gov/cps/>.

The CPS also produces annual estimates of employment and unemployment for each state, 50 large metropolitan statistical areas, and selected cities. These estimates are published by BLS in its annual *Geographic Profile of Employment and Unemployment* available at <http://www.bls.gov/gps/>. More detailed geographic data (e.g., for counties and cities) are provided by the decennial population censuses.

Data based on establishment records are compiled by BLS and cooperating state agencies as part of an ongoing Current Employment Statistics program. Survey data, gathered monthly from a sample of employers through electronic interviewing (including electronic data interchange, touchtone data entry, and computer-assisted telephone interviewing) or by mail, fax, on magnetic tape or computer diskette, are supplemented by data from other government agencies and adjusted at intervals to data from government social insurance program reports. The estimates exclude self-employed persons, private household workers, unpaid family workers, agricultural workers, and the Armed Forces. In March 2007, reporting establishments employed 3.5 million manufacturing workers (25 percent of the total manufacturing employment at the time), 20.1 million workers in private nonmanufacturing industries (26.1 percent of the total in private nonmanufacturing), and 15.3 million federal, state, and local government employees (68 percent of total government).

U.S. Census Bureau, Statistical Abstract of the United States: 2009

The establishment survey counts workers each time they appear on a payroll during the reference period (the payroll period that includes the 12th of the month). Thus, unlike the CPS, a person with two jobs is counted twice. The establishment survey is designed to provide detailed industry information for the nation, states, and metropolitan areas on non-farm wage and salary employment, average weekly hours, and average hourly and weekly earnings. Establishment survey data also are published in *Employment and Earnings*. Historical national data are available on the Web site <http://www.bls.gov/ces/>. Historical data for states and metropolitan areas are available on the Web site <http://www.bls.gov/sae/>.

In June 2003, BLS completed a comprehensive sample redesign of the establishment survey begun in June 2000, changing from a quota-based sample to a probability-based sample. Also in June 2003, all establishment survey employment, hours, and earnings series were converted from being classified by the 1987 Standard Industrial Classification (SIC) system to being classified by the 2002 North American Industry Classification System (NAICS). The NAICS conversion resulted in major definitional changes to many of the previously published SIC-based series. All establishment survey historical time series were reconstructed as part of the NAICS conversion process and all published series have a NAICS-based history extending back to at least 1990. For total nonfarm industries and other high-level aggregates, NAICS history was reconstructed back to the previously existing start date for the series, 1939 in most cases. More information on the sample redesign, the conversion to NAICS, and other changes to the establishment survey implemented in June 2003 appears in "Revisions to the Current Employment Statistics National Estimates Effective May 2003" in the June 2003 issue of *Employment and Earnings,* as well as the Establishment Data portion of the Explanatory Notes and Estimates of Error section of *Employment and Earnings.*

The completion of the sample redesign and the conversion to NAICS for state and metropolitan area establishment survey data were implemented in March 2003 with the release of January 2003 estimates. For a discussion of the changes to the state and area establishment survey data, see "Revisions to the Current Employment Statistics State and Area Estimates Effective January 2003" in the March 2003 issue of *Employment and Earnings.*

Labor force—According to the CPS definitions, the civilian labor force comprises all civilians in the noninstitutionalized population 16 years and over classified as "employed" or "unemployed" according to the following criteria: Employed civilians comprise (a) all civilians, who, during the reference week, did any work for pay or profit (minimum of an hour's work) or worked 15 hours or more as unpaid workers in a family enterprise and (b) all civilians who were not working but who had jobs or businesses from which they were temporarily absent for noneconomic reasons (illness, weather conditions, vacation, labor-management dispute, etc.) whether they were paid for the time off or were seeking other jobs. Unemployed persons comprise all civilians who had no employment during the reference week, who made specific efforts to find a job within the previous 4 weeks (such as applying directly to an employer or to a public employment service or checking with friends) and who were available for work during that week, except for temporary illness. Persons on layoff from a job and expecting recall also are classified as unemployed. All other civilian persons, 16 years old and over, are classified as "not in the labor force."

Various breaks in the CPS data series have occurred over time due to the introduction of population adjustments and other changes. For details on these breaks in series and the effect that they had on the CPS data, see the section on noncomparability of labor force levels in the Household Data portion of the Explanatory Notes and Estimates of Error section of *Employment and Earnings* available on the site <http://www.bls.gov/cps/eetech_methods.pdf>.

Beginning in January 2006, the CPS data reflect the introduction of revised population controls. The effect of the revised population controls on the monthly CPS estimates was to decrease the December 2005 employment level by 123,000 and the civilian noninstitutional population by 67,000. The updated controls had little or no effect on unemployment rates and other ratios. For additional information on the effects of the revised population controls on estimates from the CPS, see "Adjustments to Household Survey Population Estimates in January 2006" in the February 2006 issue of *Employment and Earnings*, available on the Internet at <http://www.bls.gov/cps/cps06adj.pdf>.

Hours and earnings—Average hourly earnings, based on establishment data, are gross earnings (i.e., earnings before payroll deductions) and include overtime premiums; they exclude irregular bonuses and value of payments in kind. Hours are those for which pay was received. Wages and salaries from the CPS consist of total monies received for work performed by an employee during the income year. It includes wages, salaries, commissions, tips, piece-rate payments, and cash bonuses earned before deductions were made for taxes, bonds, union dues, etc. Persons who worked 35 hours or more are classified as working full-time.

Industry and occupational groups— Industry data derived from the CPS for 1983–91 utilize the 1980 census industrial classification developed from the 1972 SIC. CPS data from 1971 to 1982 were based on the 1970 census classification system, which was developed from the 1967 SIC. Most of the industry categories were not affected by the change in classification.

The occupational classification system used in the 1980 census and in the CPS for 1983–91, evolved from the 1980 Standard Occupational Classification (SOC) system, first introduced in 1977. Occupational categories used in the 1980 census classification system are so radically different from the 1970 census system used in the CPS through 1982, that their implementation represented a break in historical data series.

Beginning in January 1992, the occupational and industrial classification systems used in the 1990 census were introduced into the CPS. (These systems were largely based on the 1980 SOC and the 1987 SIC systems, respectively.)

Beginning in 2003, the 2002 Census Bureau occupational and industrial classification systems were introduced into the CPS. These systems were derived from the 2000 SOC and the 2002 NAICS. The composition of detailed occupational and industrial classifications in the new classification systems was substantially changed from the previous systems in use, as was the structure for aggregating them into broad groups. Consequently, the use of the new classification systems created breaks in existing data series at all levels of aggregation. CPS data using the new classification systems are available beginning 2000. Additional information on the 2002 Census Bureau occupational and industrial classifications systems appears in "Revisions to the Current Population Survey Effective in January 2003" in the February 2003 issue of *Employment and Earnings*, available on the BLS Web site <http://www.bls.gov /cps/rvcps03.pdf>.

For details on the changes over time in the industrial and occupational classification systems used in the CPS, see the section on changes in the occupational and industrial classification systems in the Household Data portion of the Explanatory Notes and Estimates of Error section of *Employment and Earnings* available on the site <http://www.bls.gov/cps/eetech _methods.pdf>.

Establishments responding to the establishment survey are classified according to the 2002 NAICS. Previously they were classified according to the SIC manual. See text, Section 15, Business Enterprise, for information about the SIC manual and NAICS.

Productivity—BLS publishes data on productivity as measured by output per hour (labor productivity), output per combined unit of labor and capital input (multifactor productivity), and, for industry groups and industries, output per combined unit of capital, labor, energy, materials, and purchased service inputs. Labor productivity and related indexes are published for the business sector as a whole and its major subsectors: nonfarm business, manufacturing, and nonfinancial corporations, and for over 200 detailed industries. Productivity indexes that take into

Labor Force, Employment, and Earnings   367

account capital, labor, energy, materials, and service inputs are published for 18 major manufacturing industry groups, 86 detailed manufacturing industries, utility services, and air and railroad transportation. The major sector data are published in the BLS quarterly news release *Productivity and Costs* and in the annual *Multifactor Productivity Trends* release. Industry productivity measures are updated and published annually in the news releases *Productivity and Costs by Industry* and *Multifactor Productivity Trends by Industry*. The latest data are available at the Labor Productivity and Costs Web site <http://www.bls.gov/lpc/> and the Multifactor Productivity Web site <http://www.bls.gov/mfp>. Detailed information on methods, limitations, and data sources appears in the BLS *Handbook of Methods*, BLS Bulletin 2490 (1997), Chapters 10 and 11 <http://www.bls.gov/opub/hom/home.htm>.

Unions—As defined here, unions include traditional labor unions and employee associations similar to labor unions. Data on union membership status provided by BLS are for employed wage and salary workers and relate to their principal job. Earnings by union membership status are usual weekly earnings of full-time wage and salary workers. The information is collected through the Current Population Survey.

Work stoppages—Work stoppages include all strikes and lockouts known to BLS that last for at least 1 full day or shift and involve 1,000 or more workers. All stoppages, whether or not authorized by a union, legal or illegal, are counted. Excluded are work slowdowns and instances where employees report to work late or leave early to attend mass meetings or mass rallies.

Seasonal adjustment—Many economic statistics reflect a regularly recurring seasonal movement that can be estimated on the basis of past experience. By eliminating that part of the change which can be ascribed to usual seasonal variation (e.g., climate or school openings and closings), it is possible to observe the cyclical and other nonseasonal movements in the series. However, in evaluating deviations from the seasonal pattern—that is, changes in a seasonally adjusted series—it is important to note that seasonal adjustment is merely an approximation based on past experience. Seasonally adjusted estimates have a broader margin of possible error than the original data on which they are based, since they are subject not only to sampling and other errors, but also are affected by the uncertainties of the adjustment process itself. Consistent with BLS practices, annual estimates will be published only for not-seasonally-adjusted data.

Statistical reliability—For discussion of statistical collection, estimation, sampling procedures, and measures of statistical reliability applicable to Census Bureau and BLS data, see Appendix III.

Table 567. Civilian Population—Employment Status: 1970 to 2007

[In thousands (137,085 represents 137,085,000), except as indicated. Annual averages of monthly figures. Civilian noninstitutional population 16 years old and over. Based on Current Population Survey; see text, Section 1, and Appendix III]

Year	Civilian noninsti- tutional population	Civilian labor force						Not in labor force	
		Total	Percent of population	Employed	Employ- ment/ population ratio[1]	Unemployed			
						Number	Percent of labor force	Number	Percent of population
1970	137,085	82,771	60.4	78,678	57.4	4,093	4.9	54,315	39.6
1980	167,745	106,940	63.8	99,303	59.2	7,637	7.1	60,806	36.2
1985	178,206	115,461	64.8	107,150	60.1	8,312	7.2	62,744	35.2
1990 [2]	189,164	125,840	66.5	118,793	62.8	7,047	5.6	63,324	33.5
1991	190,925	126,346	66.2	117,718	61.7	8,628	6.8	64,578	33.8
1992	192,805	128,105	66.4	118,492	61.5	9,613	7.5	64,700	33.6
1993	194,838	129,200	66.3	120,259	61.7	8,940	6.9	65,638	33.7
1994 [2]	196,814	131,056	66.6	123,060	62.5	7,996	6.1	65,758	33.4
1995	198,584	132,304	66.6	124,900	62.9	7,404	5.6	66,280	33.4
1996 [2]	200,591	133,943	66.8	126,708	63.2	7,236	5.4	66,647	33.2
1997 [2]	203,133	136,297	67.1	129,558	63.8	6,739	4.9	66,837	32.9
1998 [2]	205,220	137,673	67.1	131,463	64.1	6,210	4.5	67,547	32.9
1999 [2]	207,753	139,368	67.1	133,488	64.3	5,880	4.2	68,385	32.9
2000 [2]	212,577	142,583	67.1	136,891	64.4	5,692	4.0	69,994	32.9
2001	215,092	143,734	66.8	136,933	63.7	6,801	4.7	71,359	33.2
2002 [2]	217,570	144,863	66.6	136,485	62.7	8,378	5.8	72,707	33.4
2003 [2]	221,168	146,510	66.2	137,736	62.3	8,774	6.0	74,658	33.8
2004 [2]	223,357	147,401	66.0	139,252	62.3	8,149	5.5	75,956	34.0
2005 [2]	226,082	149,320	66.0	141,730	62.7	7,591	5.1	76,762	34.0
2006 [2]	228,815	151,428	66.2	144,427	63.1	7,001	4.6	77,387	33.8
2007 [2]	231,867	153,124	66.0	146,047	63.0	7,078	4.6	78,743	34.0

[1] Civilian employed as a percent of the civilian noninstitutional population.   [2] Data not strictly comparable with data for earlier years. See text, this section, and February 1994, March 1996, February 1997–99, and February 2003–08 issues of *Employment and Earnings.*

Source: U.S. Bureau of Labor Statistics, "Employment and Earnings Online" January 2008 issue. See Internet site <http://www.bls.gov/opub/ee/home.htm> and <http://www.bls.gov/cps/home.htm>.

Table 568. Civilian Labor Force and Participation Rates With Projections: 1980 to 2016

[106.9 represents 106,900,000. Civilian noninstitutional population 16 years old and over. Annual averages of monthly figures. Rates are based on annual average civilian noninstitutional population of each specified group and represent proportion of each specified group in the civilian labor force. Based on Current Population Survey; see text, Section 1, and Appendix III]

Race, Hispanic origin, sex, and age	Civilian labor force (millions)						Participation rate (percent)					
	1980	1990 [1]	2000 [1]	2005 [1]	2007 [1]	2016, proj.	1980	1990 [1]	2000 [1]	2005 [1]	2007 [1]	2016, proj.
Total [2]	**106.9**	**125.8**	**142.6**	**149.3**	**153.1**	**164.2**	**63.8**	**66.5**	**67.1**	**66.0**	**66.0**	**65.5**
White [3]	93.6	107.4	118.5	122.3	124.9	130.7	64.1	66.9	67.3	66.3	66.4	65.5
Male	54.5	59.6	64.5	66.7	68.2	71.3	78.2	77.1	75.5	74.1	74.0	72.9
Female	39.1	47.8	54.1	55.6	56.8	59.4	51.2	57.4	59.5	58.9	59.0	58.4
Black [3]	10.9	13.7	16.4	17.0	17.5	20.1	61.0	64.0	65.8	64.2	63.7	64.9
Male	5.6	6.8	7.7	8.0	8.3	9.4	70.3	71.0	69.2	67.3	66.8	67.1
Female	5.3	6.9	8.7	9.0	9.2	10.7	53.1	58.3	63.1	61.6	61.1	63.1
Asian [3, 4]	(NA)	(NA)	6.3	6.5	7.1	8.7	(NA)	(NA)	67.2	66.1	66.5	65.9
Male	(NA)	(NA)	3.4	3.5	3.8	4.6	(NA)	(NA)	76.1	74.8	75.1	74.1
Female	(NA)	(NA)	2.9	3.0	3.3	4.1	(NA)	(NA)	59.2	58.2	58.6	67.1
Hispanic [5]	6.1	10.7	16.7	19.8	21.6	26.9	64.0	67.4	69.7	68.0	68.8	68.6
Male	3.8	6.5	9.9	12.0	13.0	15.8	81.4	81.4	81.5	80.1	80.5	79.0
Female	2.3	4.2	6.8	7.8	8.6	11.1	47.4	53.1	57.5	55.3	56.5	57.8
Male	61.5	69.0	76.3	80.0	82.1	87.8	77.4	76.4	74.8	73.3	73.2	72.3
16 to 19 years	5.0	4.1	4.3	3.6	3.5	2.9	60.5	55.7	52.8	43.2	41.4	36.8
20 to 24 years	8.6	7.9	7.5	8.1	8.1	8.0	85.9	84.4	82.6	79.1	78.7	76.4
25 to 34 years	17.0	19.9	17.8	17.8	18.3	20.9	95.2	94.1	93.4	91.7	92.2	95.7
35 to 44 years	11.8	17.5	20.1	19.5	19.3	18.4	95.5	94.3	92.7	92.1	92.3	91.7
45 to 54 years	9.9	11.1	16.3	18.1	18.8	18.2	91.2	90.7	88.6	87.7	88.2	86.6
55 to 64 years	7.2	6.6	7.8	10.0	10.9	13.9	72.1	67.8	67.3	69.3	69.6	70.1
65 years and over . . .	1.9	2.0	2.5	3.0	3.2	5.5	19.0	16.3	17.7	19.8	20.5	27.1
Female	45.5	56.8	66.3	69.3	71.0	76.5	51.5	57.5	59.9	59.3	59.3	59.2
16 to 19 years	4.4	3.7	4.0	3.6	3.5	3.0	52.9	51.6	51.2	44.2	41.5	38.3
20 to 24 years	7.3	6.8	6.7	7.1	7.1	7.0	68.9	71.3	73.1	70.1	70.1	67.2
25 to 34 years	12.3	16.1	14.9	14.5	14.8	16.4	65.5	73.5	76.1	73.9	74.5	75.0
35 to 44 years	8.6	14.7	17.5	16.5	16.2	15.3	65.5	76.4	77.2	75.8	75.5	75.1
45 to 54 years	7.0	9.1	14.8	16.3	16.9	16.9	59.9	71.2	76.8	76.0	76.0	77.8
55 to 64 years	4.7	4.9	6.6	8.9	9.8	13.4	41.3	45.2	51.9	57.0	58.3	63.5
65 years and over . . .	1.2	1.5	1.8	2.3	2.6	4.6	8.1	8.6	9.4	11.5	12.6	17.5

NA Not available.   [1] See footnote 2, Table 567.   [2] Includes other races not shown separately.   [3] The 2003 Current Population Survey (CPS) allowed respondents to choose more than one race. Beginning 2005, data represent persons who selected this race group only and exclude persons reporting more than one race. The CPS prior to 2003 only allowed respondents to report one race group. See also comments on race in the text for Section 1.   [4] Prior to 2005, includes Pacific Islanders.   [5] Persons of Hispanic or Latino origin may be any race.

Source: U.S. Bureau of Labor Statistics, "Employment and Earnings Online," January 2008 issue See <http://www.bls.gov/opub/ee /home.htm/>; *Monthly Labor Review*, November 2007; and <http://www.bls.gov/emp/emplab1.htm>.

Table 569. Civilian Population—Employment Status by Sex, Race, and Ethnicity: 1970 to 2007

[**In thousands (64,304 represents 64,304,000), except as indicated**. Annual averages of monthly figures. See Table 567 for U.S. totals and coverage]

Year, sex, race, and Hispanic origin	Civilian noninstitutional population	Civilian labor force						Not in labor force	
		Total	Percent of population	Employed	Employ-ment/popu-lation ratio [1]	Unemployed			
						Number	Percent of labor force	Number	Percent of population
Male: 1970	64,304	51,228	79.7	48,990	76.2	2,238	4.4	13,076	20.3
1980	79,398	61,453	77.4	57,186	72.0	4,267	6.9	17,945	22.6
1990 [2]	90,377	69,011	76.4	65,104	72.0	3,906	5.7	21,367	23.6
1995	95,178	71,360	75.0	67,377	70.8	3,983	5.6	23,818	25.0
2000 [2]	101,964	76,280	74.8	73,305	71.9	2,975	3.9	25,684	25.2
2005 [2]	109,151	80,033	73.3	75,973	69.6	4,059	5.1	29,119	26.7
2006 [2]	110,605	81,255	73.5	77,502	70.1	3,753	4.6	29,350	26.5
2007 [2]	112,173	82,136	73.2	78,254	69.8	3,882	4.7	30,036	26.8
Female:									
1970	72,782	31,543	43.3	29,688	40.8	1,855	5.9	41,239	56.7
1980	88,348	45,487	51.5	42,117	47.7	3,370	7.4	42,861	48.5
1990 [2]	98,787	56,829	57.5	53,689	54.3	3,140	5.5	41,957	42.5
1995	103,406	60,944	58.9	57,523	55.6	3,421	5.6	42,462	41.1
2000 [2]	110,613	66,303	59.9	63,586	57.5	2,717	4.1	44,310	40.1
2005 [2]	116,931	69,288	59.3	65,757	56.2	3,531	5.1	47,643	40.7
2006 [2]	118,210	70,173	59.4	66,925	56.6	3,247	4.6	48,037	40.6
2007 [2]	119,694	70,988	59.3	67,792	56.6	3,196	4.5	48,707	40.7
White: [3]									
1980	146,122	93,600	64.1	87,715	60.0	5,884	6.3	52,523	35.9
1990 [2]	160,625	107,447	66.9	102,261	63.7	5,186	4.8	53,178	33.1
1995	166,914	111,950	67.1	106,490	63.8	5,459	4.9	54,965	32.9
2000 [2]	176,220	118,545	67.3	114,424	64.9	4,121	3.5	57,675	32.7
2005 [2]	184,446	122,299	66.3	116,949	63.4	5,350	4.4	62,148	33.7
2006 [2]	186,264	123,834	66.5	118,833	63.8	5,002	4.0	62,429	33.5
2007 [2]	188,253	124,935	66.4	119,792	63.6	5,143	4.1	63,319	33.6
Black: [3]									
1980	17,824	10,865	61.0	9,313	52.2	1,553	14.3	6,959	39.0
1990 [2]	21,477	13,740	64.0	12,175	56.7	1,565	11.4	7,737	36.0
1995	23,246	14,817	63.7	13,279	57.1	1,538	10.4	8,429	36.3
2000 [2]	24,902	16,397	65.8	15,156	60.9	1,241	7.6	8,505	34.2
2005 [2]	26,517	17,013	64.2	15,313	57.7	1,700	10.0	9,504	35.8
2006 [2]	27,007	17,314	64.1	15,765	58.4	1,549	8.9	9,693	35.9
2007 [2]	27,485	17,496	63.7	16,051	58.4	1,445	8.3	9,989	36.3
Asian: [3][4]									
2000 [2]	9,330	6,270	67.2	6,043	64.8	227	3.6	3,060	32.8
2005 [2]	9,842	6,503	66.1	6,244	63.4	259	4.0	3,339	33.9
2006 [2]	10,155	6,727	66.2	6,522	64.2	205	3.0	3,427	33.7
2007 [2]	10,633	7,067	66.5	6,839	64.3	229	3.2	3,566	33.5
Hispanic: [5]									
1980	9,598	6,146	64.0	5,527	57.6	620	10.1	3,451	36.0
1990 [2]	15,904	10,720	67.4	9,845	61.9	876	8.2	5,184	32.6
1995	18,629	12,267	65.8	11,127	59.7	1,140	9.3	6,362	34.2
2000 [2]	23,938	16,689	69.7	15,735	65.7	954	5.7	7,249	30.3
2005 [2]	29,133	19,824	68.0	18,632	64.0	1,191	6.0	9,310	32.0
2006 [2]	30,103	20,694	68.7	19,613	65.2	1,081	5.2	9,409	31.3
2007 [2]	31,383	21,602	68.8	20,382	64.9	1,220	5.6	9,781	31.2
Mexican:									
1990 [2]	9,752	6,707	68.8	6,146	63.0	561	8.4	3,045	31.2
1995	11,609	7,765	66.9	7,016	60.4	750	9.7	3,844	33.1
2000 [2]	15,333	10,783	70.3	10,144	66.2	639	5.9	4,550	29.7
2005 [2]	18,523	12,671	68.4	11,887	64.2	784	6.2	5,851	31.6
2006 [2]	19,036	13,158	69.1	12,477	65.5	681	5.2	5,877	30.9
2007 [2]	19,770	13,672	69.2	12,908	65.3	764	5.6	6,098	30.8
Puerto Rican:									
1990 [2]	1,718	960	55.9	870	50.6	91	9.5	758	44.1
1995	1,896	1,098	57.9	974	51.4	123	11.2	798	42.1
2000 [2]	2,193	1,411	64.3	1,318	60.1	92	6.6	783	35.7
2005 [2]	2,654	1,619	61.0	1,492	56.2	126	7.8	1,035	39.0
2006 [2]	2,600	1,599	61.5	1,484	57.1	115	7.2	1,001	38.5
2007 [2]	2,711	1,684	62.1	1,551	57.2	133	7.9	1,027	37.9
Cuban:									
1990 [2]	918	603	65.7	559	60.9	44	7.2	315	34.3
1995	1,019	613	60.2	568	55.7	45	7.4	406	39.8
2000 [2]	1,174	740	63.1	707	60.3	33	4.5	434	37.0
2005 [2]	1,259	755	60.0	730	58.0	25	3.3	503	40.0
2006 [2]	1,326	807	60.9	778	58.7	29	3.6	519	39.1
2007 [2]	1,421	898	63.2	862	60.7	36	4.0	523	36.8

[1] Civilian employed as a percent of the civilian noninstitutional population. [2] See footnote 2, Table 567. [3] Beginning 2005, for persons in this race group only. See footnote 3, Table 568. [4] Prior to 2005, includes Pacific Islanders. [5] Persons of Hispanic or Latino ethnicity may be any race. Includes persons of other Hispanic or Latino ethnicity, not shown separately.

Source: U.S. Bureau of Labor Statistics, "Employment and Earnings Online," January 2008 issue. See Internet site <http://www.bls.gov/opub/ee/home.htm> and <http://www.bls.gov/cps/home.htm>.

Table 570. Foreign-born and Native-born Populations—Employment Status by Selected Characteristics: 2007

[231,867 represents 231,867,000. For civilian noninstitutional population 16 years old and over, except as indicated. Annual averages of monthly figures. Based on Current Population Survey; see text, Section 1, and Appendix III]

Characteristic	Civilian noninstitutional population (1,000)	Civilian labor force			Unemployed (1,000)	
		Total (1,000)	Partici- pation rate [1]	Employed (1,000)	Number (1,000)	Unemploy- ment rate
Total	**231,867**	**153,124**	**66.0**	**146,047**	**7,078**	**4.6**
Male	112,173	82,136	73.2	78,254	3,882	4.7
Female	119,694	70,988	59.3	67,792	3,196	4.5
FOREIGN BORN						
Total [2]	**35,017**	**23,994**	**68.5**	**22,967**	**1027**	**4.3**
Sex:						
Male	17,670	14,470	81.9	13,883	588	4.1
Female	17,347	9,524	54.9	9,085	439	4.6
Age:						
16 to 24 years old	4,205	2,454	58.4	2,266	188	7.7
25 to 34 years old	8,243	6,421	77.9	6,147	274	4.3
35 to 44 years old	8,322	6,782	81.5	6,546	236	3.5
45 to 54 years old	6,278	5,126	81.7	4,930	196	3.8
55 to 64 years old	3,850	2,531	65.7	2,424	107	4.2
65 years old and over	4,119	680	16.5	655	25	3.7
Race and Hispanic ethnicity:						
White non-Hispanic	7492	4,599	61.4	4428	171	3.7
Black non-Hispanic	2,610	1,901	72.8	1,795	106	5.6
Asian non-Hispanic	7,762	5,264	67.8	5,106	158	3.0
Hispanic [3]	16,817	11,987	71.3	11,405	582	4.9
Educational attainment:						
Total 25 years old and over	30,812	21,540	69.9	20,701	839	3.9
Less than a high school diploma	9,456	5,893	62.3	5,585	308	5.2
High school graduates, no college [4]	7,863	5,400	68.7	5,188	212	3.9
Some college or associate's degree	4,780	3,538	74.0	3,387	151	4.3
Bachelor's degree and higher [5]	8,713	6,709	77.0	6,541	168	2.5
NATIVE BORN						
Total [2]	**196,850**	**129,130**	**65.6**	**123,079**	**6,051**	**4.7**
Sex:						
Male	94,503	67,666	71.6	64,372	3,294	4.9
Female	102,347	61,464	60.1	58,707	2,757	4.5
Age:						
16 to 24 years old	33,204	19,763	59.5	17,608	2,155	10.9
25 to 34 years old	31,509	26,708	84.8	25,439	1,270	4.8
35 to 44 years old	34,079	28,745	84.3	27,756	989	3.4
45 to 54 years old	37,266	30,571	82.0	29,633	938	3.1
55 to 64 years old	28,683	18,219	63.5	17,684	535	2.9
65 years old and over	32,109	5,124	16.0	4,959	165	3.2
Race and Hispanic ethnicity:						
White non-Hispanic	151,596	100,279	66.1	96,411	3,868	3.9
Black non-Hispanic	23,921	14,961	62.5	13,671	1,290	8.6
Asian non-Hispanic	2,708	1,683	62.2	1,620	63	3.7
Hispanic [3]	14,566	9,615	66.0	8,977	638	6.6
Educational attainment:						
Total, 25 years and over	163,645	109,367	66.8	105,471	3,896	3.6
Less than a high school diploma	17,177	6,514	37.9	5,936	578	8.9
High school graduates, no college [4]	53,510	33,139	61.9	31,670	1,470	4.4
Some college or associate's degree	45,051	32,349	71.8	31,225	1,124	3.5
Bachelor's degree and higher [5]	47,908	37,365	78.0	36,640	725	1.9

[1] Civilian labor force as a percent of the civilian noninstitutional population.   [2] Includes other races not shown separately.
[3] Persons of Hispanic origin may be any race.   [4] Includes persons with a high school diploma or equivalent.   [5] Includes persons with bachelor's, master's, professional, and doctoral degrees.

Source: U.S. Bureau of Labor Statistics, *Foreign-Born Workers: Labor Force Characteristics in 2007*, News, USDL 08-0409, March 26, 2008. See Internet site <http://bls.gov/bls/newsrels.htm#OEUS>.

Table 571. Civilian Labor Force—Percent Distribution by Sex and Age: 1980 to 2007

[**106,940 represents 106,940,000.** Civilian noninstitutional population 16 years old and over. Annual averages of monthly figures. Based on Current Population Survey; see text, Section 1, and Appendix III]

Year and sex	Civilian labor force (1,000)	Percent distribution						
		16 to 19 years	20 to 24 years	25 to 34 years	35 to 44 years	45 to 54 years	55 to 64 years	65 yrs. and over
Total: 1980	106,940	8.8	14.9	27.3	19.1	15.8	11.2	2.9
1990 [1]	125,840	6.2	11.7	28.6	25.5	16.1	9.2	2.7
2000 [1]	142,583	5.8	10.0	23.0	26.3	21.8	10.1	3.0
2005 [1]	149,320	4.8	10.1	21.7	24.1	23.0	12.7	3.5
2007 [1]	153,124	4.6	9.9	21.6	23.2	23.3	13.6	3.8
Male: 1980	61,453	8.1	14.0	27.6	19.3	16.1	11.8	3.1
1990 [1]	69,011	5.9	11.4	28.8	25.3	16.1	9.6	2.9
2000 [1]	76,280	5.6	9.9	23.4	26.3	21.3	10.2	3.3
2005 [1]	80,033	4.5	10.1	22.3	24.4	22.6	12.6	3.7
2007 [1]	82,136	4.3	9.9	22.3	23.5	22.9	13.3	3.9
Female: 1980	45,487	9.6	16.1	26.9	19.0	15.4	10.4	2.6
1990 [1]	56,829	6.5	12.0	28.3	25.8	16.1	8.7	2.6
2000 [1]	66,303	6.0	10.2	22.5	26.4	22.3	9.9	2.7
2005 [1]	69,288	5.2	10.2	20.9	23.9	23.6	12.9	3.3
2007 [1]	70,988	4.9	10.0	20.9	22.9	23.8	13.9	3.7

[1] See footnote 2, Table 567.

Source: U.S. Bureau of Labor Statistics, "Employment and Earnings Online," January 2008 issue. See Internet site <http://www.bls.gov/opub/ee/home.htm> and <http://www.bls.gov/cps/home.htm>.

Table 572. Civilian Labor Force and Participation Rates by Educational Attainment, Sex, Race, and Hispanic Origin: 1995 to 2007

[**110,851 represents 110,851,000.** Civilian noninstitutional population 25 years old and over. Annual averages of monthly figures. See Table 607 for unemployment data. Based on Current Population Survey; see text, Section 1, and Appendix III]

Year, sex, and race	Civilian labor force					Participation rate [1]				
		Percent distribution								
	Total (1,000)	Less than high school diploma	High school graduate, no degree	Less than a bachelor's degree	College graduate	Total	Less than high school diploma	High school graduate, no degree	Less than a bachelor's degree	College graduate
Total: [2]										
1995	110,851	10.8	33.1	27.9	28.1	66.7	39.9	65.4	74.5	81.0
2000 [3]	120,061	10.4	31.4	27.7	30.5	67.3	43.5	64.4	73.9	79.4
2005 [3]	127,030	10.0	30.1	27.5	32.4	67.1	45.5	63.2	72.5	77.9
2007 [3]	130,908	9.5	29.4	27.4	33.7	67.3	46.6	62.8	72.0	77.8
Male:										
1995 . .	59,986	12.2	32.3	26.1	29.4	76.0	52.1	76.5	82.1	85.8
2000 [3] . .	64,490	11.8	31.1	25.9	31.2	76.1	56.0	75.1	80.9	84.4
2005 [3] . .	68,389	11.7	30.9	25.4	32.1	75.4	58.6	73.6	79.3	82.9
2007 [3] . .	70,501	11.3	30.3	25.3	33.0	75.6	60.2	73.2	78.7	82.9
Female:										
1995 . .	50,865	9.2	34.2	30.0	26.6	58.3	29.2	56.4	68.1	75.4
2000 [3] . .	55,572	8.8	31.8	29.7	29.7	59.4	32.3	55.5	68.0	74.0
2005 [3] . .	58,641	8.0	29.2	30.0	32.8	59.4	32.9	53.8	66.8	72.9
2007 [3] . .	60,406	7.3	28.4	29.9	34.4	59.7	33.1	53.4	66.4	72.9
White: [4]										
1995 . .	94,139	10.1	33.0	27.8	29.1	66.7	40.0	64.8	73.8	80.6
2000 [3] . .	99,964	10.1	31.4	27.5	31.0	67.0	44.1	63.6	73.1	79.0
2005 [3] . .	104,240	9.8	29.9	27.6	32.7	66.9	46.4	62.5	72.0	77.5
2007 [3] . .	106,962	9.4	29.3	27.4	33.9	67.2	47.9	62.3	71.4	77.4
Black: [4]										
1995 . .	12,152	13.9	37.1	30.7	18.3	66.0	36.2	69.7	79.8	85.6
2000 [3] . .	13,582	12.4	36.0	31.2	20.5	68.2	39.3	69.9	79.3	84.4
2005 [3] . .	14,252	11.2	36.4	30.2	22.2	67.2	39.8	67.9	75.6	82.0
2007 [3] . .	14,720	10.0	35.0	30.9	24.0	67.0	39.1	65.4	75.3	83.0
Asian: [4, 5]										
2000 [3] . .	5,402	9.1	20.7	20.2	50.1	70.9	46.0	65.6	76.4	79.1
2005 [3] . .	5,805	8.0	17.7	17.3	57.0	69.4	45.3	61.8	71.6	77.5
2007 [3] . .	6,378	6.9	18.4	17.1	57.7	70.0	43.8	63.2	72.5	77.5
Hispanic: [6]										
1995 . .	9,599	37.2	29.3	21.7	11.7	67.5	55.3	74.3	79.7	83.1
2000 [3] . .	12,975	36.7	29.3	20.6	13.4	71.5	61.9	75.0	80.8	83.5
2005 [3] . .	16,135	35.5	29.4	20.9	14.2	70.8	61.4	74.3	78.8	81.7
2007 [3] . .	17,783	34.0	30.1	20.8	15.2	71.7	62.6	74.3	79.1	82.2

[1] See headnote, Table 568. [2] Includes other races not shown separately. [3] See footnote 2, Table 567. [4] Beginning 2005, for persons in this race group only. See footnote 3, Table 568. [5] 2000 data include Pacific Islanders. [6] Persons of Hispanic or Latino origin may be any race.

Source: U.S. Bureau of Labor Statistics, "Employment and Earnings Online," January 2008 issue. See Internet site <http://www.bls.gov/opub/ee/home.htm> and <http://www.bls.gov/cps/home.htm>.

Table 573. **Characteristics of the Civilian Labor Force by State: 2007**

[**In thousands (153,124 represents 153,124,000), except ratio and rate.** Civilian noninstitutional population, 16 years old and over. Annual averages of monthly figures. Because of separate processing and weighting procedures, the totals for the United States may differ from results obtained by aggregating totals for states]

State	Total		Employed		Employed population ratio [1]	Unemployed					Participation rate [3]	
						Total		Rate [2]				
	Number	Female	Total	Female		Number	Female	Total	Male	Female	Male	Female
United States	**153,124**	**70,988**	**146,047**	**67,792**	**63.0**	**7,078**	**3,196**	**4.6**	**4.7**	**4.5**	**73.2**	**59.3**
Alabama	2,201	1,037	2,113	999	58.9	88	38	4.0	4.3	3.7	68.4	55.0
Alaska	347	162	326	154	66.1	21	9	6.2	7.0	5.2	75.0	65.8
Arizona	3,048	1,344	2,930	1,290	61.4	118	54	3.9	3.8	4.0	72.6	55.5
Arkansas	1,376	641	1,299	605	59.7	77	36	5.6	5.6	5.6	70.2	56.8
California	18,207	8,073	17,234	7,654	62.1	973	418	5.3	5.5	5.2	74.3	57.2
Colorado	2,678	1,209	2,580	1,162	69.6	98	47	3.7	3.5	3.9	80.2	64.5
Connecticut	1,890	888	1,804	849	65.7	86	39	4.5	4.6	4.4	76.1	62.1
Delaware	445	215	430	207	64.2	16	8	3.5	3.5	3.5	72.5	61.1
District of Columbia	318	164	300	154	64.3	18	10	5.5	5.0	6.0	72.0	64.7
Florida	9,235	4,313	8,861	4,149	61.2	374	163	4.1	4.3	3.8	70.6	57.6
Georgia	4,870	2,285	4,659	2,178	65.3	211	107	4.3	4.0	4.7	75.5	61.6
Hawaii	647	305	628	296	63.7	19	9	2.9	2.7	3.0	72.2	59.6
Idaho	765	341	742	331	66.2	23	10	3.0	2.9	3.1	76.0	60.5
Illinois	6,721	3,114	6,378	2,972	64.5	342	142	5.1	5.6	4.5	75.2	61.2
Indiana	3,207	1,475	3,059	1,413	62.7	148	62	4.6	5.0	4.2	73.0	58.9
Iowa	1,673	794	1,611	764	69.3	62	30	3.7	3.6	3.8	77.2	66.9
Kansas	1,495	699	1,434	671	68.1	61	29	4.1	4.0	4.1	77.3	64.9
Kentucky	2,041	948	1,932	899	59.1	110	49	5.4	5.5	5.2	69.6	55.8
Louisiana	2,003	960	1,917	917	58.9	85	42	4.3	4.1	4.4	67.8	56.0
Maine	706	338	673	323	63.1	33	15	4.7	4.9	4.4	71.4	61.3
Maryland	2,978	1,452	2,871	1,396	65.9	107	56	3.6	3.3	3.9	74.3	63.0
Massachusetts	3,410	1,592	3,253	1,528	63.8	156	65	4.6	5.0	4.1	74.5	59.9
Michigan	5,021	2,389	4,667	2,218	59.6	354	171	7.1	7.0	7.1	69.4	59.2
Minnesota	2,906	1,382	2,772	1,326	68.7	134	57	4.6	5.1	4.1	76.5	67.6
Mississippi	1,320	628	1,239	587	56.3	81	41	6.1	5.8	6.5	66.9	53.9
Missouri	3,063	1,466	2,910	1,395	64.2	153	71	5.0	5.1	4.9	73.3	62.2
Montana	510	244	492	236	65.7	18	8	3.6	3.7	3.4	71.9	64.5
Nebraska	988	463	958	449	70.7	31	14	3.1	3.2	2.9	79.1	67.1
Nevada	1,346	599	1284	573	65.6	62	26	4.6	4.9	4.3	75.7	61.7
New Hampshire	746	349	719	337	68.2	27	12	3.6	3.9	3.3	76.9	64.9
New Jersey	4,516	2,073	4,325	1,992	63.5	191	81	4.2	4.5	3.9	74.5	58.6
New Mexico	951	447	916	430	61.0	35	16	3.7	3.7	3.7	69.5	57.5
New York	9,456	4,458	9,020	4,275	59.7	436	183	4.6	5.1	4.1	69.5	56.3
North Carolina	4,494	2,133	4,290	2,029	62.5	203	104	4.5	4.2	4.9	72.2	59.3
North Dakota	368	173	356	168	71.9	12	5	3.2	3.6	2.8	79.4	69.3
Ohio	6,035	2,854	5,699	2,709	64.0	335	145	5.6	6.0	5.1	74.4	61.7
Oklahoma	1,730	802	1,653	765	60.6	77	37	4.4	4.3	4.7	70.8	56.6
Oregon	1,943	893	1,843	846	62.4	100	47	5.2	5.1	5.2	72.3	59.5
Pennsylvania	6,337	2,977	6,065	2,866	61.7	273	111	4.3	4.8	3.7	71.4	58.1
Rhode Island	579	278	551	265	65.5	28	13	4.9	5.0	4.8	75.0	63.2
South Carolina	2,150	1021	2,029	959	60.2	121	61	5.6	5.3	6.0	70.7	57.6
South Dakota	442	209	429	203	71.5	13	6	2.9	3.0	2.8	78.8	68.7
Tennessee	3,061	1,416	2,921	1,349	61.7	141	68	4.6	4.4	4.8	72.4	57.5
Texas	11,540	5,123	11,047	4,877	62.9	493	246	4.3	3.8	4.8	75.0	56.8
Utah	1,344	591	1,309	573	70.3	35	17	2.6	2.4	2.9	81.3	63.2
Vermont	355	171	341	164	67.3	14	6	4.0	4.3	3.7	74.6	65.9
Virginia	4,041	1,923	3,916	1,867	66.6	125	56	3.1	3.2	2.9	75.7	62.4
Washington	3,429	1,604	3,270	1,533	65.0	159	70	4.6	4.8	4.4	74.0	62.5
West Virginia	820	376	782	361	53.8	38	15	4.6	5.0	4.1	63.0	50.1
Wisconsin	3,085	1,471	2,930	1,404	67.1	155	67	5.0	5.4	4.6	75.2	66.3
Wyoming	288	129	280	125	69.1	8	4	2.9	2.8	3.1	78.3	63.9

[1] Civilian employment as a percent of civilian noninstitutional population.   [2] Percent unemployed of the civilian labor force.
[3] Percent of civilian noninstitutional population of each specified group in the civilian labor force.

Source: U.S. Bureau of Labor Statistics, Local Area Unemployment Statistics, *Geographic Profile of Employment and Unemployment, 2007 Annual Averages.* See Internet site <http://www.bls.gov/gps/> (accessed 26 July 2008).

U.S. Census Bureau, Statistical Abstract of the United States: 2009

Table 574. **Civilian Labor Force by Selected Metropolitan Area: 2007**

[**153,124 represents 153,124,000.** Civilian noninstitutional population 16 years old and over. Annual averages of monthly figures. Data are derived from the Local Area Unemployment Statistics Program. For metro areas with a 2000 Census population of one million or more. For definition of metropolitan areas, see Appendix II. Metropolitan areas defined as of December 2005]

Metropolitan areas ranked by population, **2000**	Civilian labor force (1,000)	Unem- ploy- ment rate [1]	Metropolitan areas ranked by population, **2000**	Civilian labor force (1,000)	Unem- ploy- ment rate [1]
United States	**153,124**	**4.6**	Cleveland-Elyria-Mentor, OH	1,095	5.9
New York-Northern New Jersey- Long Island, NY-NJ-PA . .	9,320	4.4	Orlando-Kissimmee, FL	1,094	3.8
Los Angeles-Long Beach- Santa Ana, CA	6,554	4.7	Sacramento–Arden-Arcade– Roseville, CA	1,056	5.4
Chicago-Naperville-Joliet, IL-IN-WI	4,902	4.9	Kansas City, MO-KS	1,041	5.0
Dallas-Fort Worth-Arlington, TX . .	3,099	4.3	Columbus, OH	958	4.7
Washington-Arlington-Alexandria, DC-VA-MD-WV	2,982	3.0	Las Vegas-Paradise, NV	954	4.8
Philadelphia-Camden-Wilmington, PA-NJ-DE-MD	2,948	4.3	San Antonio, TX	925	4.1
Miami-Fort Lauderdale-Miami Beach, FL .	2,825	3.8	Indianapolis-Carmel, IN	896	4.0
Houston-Sugar Land-Baytown, TX	2,733	4.3	San Jose-Sunnyvale-Santa Clara, CA. . .	880	4.8
Atlanta-Sandy Springs-Marietta, GA	2,730	4.3	Austin-Round Rock, TX	848	3.6
Boston-Cambridge-Quincy, MA-NH NECTA	2,483	4.1	Charlotte-Gastonia-Concord, NC-SC . . .	837	4.7
San Francisco-Oakland-Fremont, CA . . .	2,230	4.4	Virginia Beach-Norfolk-Newport News, VA-NC	815	3.2
Detroit-Warren-Livonia, MI	2,141	7.7	Milwaukee-Waukesha-West Allis, WI . . .	800	5.1
Phoenix-Mesa-Scottsdale, AZ	2,052	3.3	Nashville-Davidson—Murfreesboro,TN . .	790	3.9
Minneapolis-St. Paul-Bloomington, MN-WI	1,848	4.3	Providence-Fall River-Warwick, RI-MA NECTA	712	5.2
Seattle-Tacoma-Bellevue, WA	1,825	4.0	Jacksonville, FL	668	3.9
Riverside-San Bernardino-Ontario, CA . .	1,795	5.9	Richmond, VA	642	3.1
San Diego-Carlsbad-San Marcos, CA. . .	1,542	4.6	Louisville-Jefferson County, KY-IN	630	5.1
St. Louis, MO-IL	1,449	5.3	Memphis, TN-MS-AR.	620	5.2
Baltimore-Towson, MD.	1,398	3.7	Hartford-West Hartford-East Hartford, CT NECTA	586	4.7
Denver-Aurora, CO	1,379	3.9	Buffalo-Niagara Falls, NY	577	4.8
Tampa-St. Petersburg-Clearwater, FL. . .	1,342	4.2	Oklahoma City, OK	571	4.3
Pittsburgh, PA	1,197	4.3	Birmingham-Hoover, AL	537	3.2
Portland-Vancouver-Beaverton, OR-WA . .	1,148	4.9	Rochester, NY	530	4.4
Cincinnati-Middletown, OH-KY-IN.	1,120	5.0	New Orleans-Metairie-Kenner, LA	507	3.5

[1] Percent unemployed of the civilian labor force.

Source: U.S. Bureau of Labor Statistics, Local Area Unemployment Statistics program. See Internet site <http://www.bls.gov/lau/>.

Table 575. **School Enrollment and Labor Force Status: 2007**

[**In thousands (37,480 represents 37,480,000), except percent. As of October.** Civilian noninstitutional population. Based on Current Population Survey; see text, Section 1, and Appendix III]

Characteristic	Population	Civilian labor force	Employed	Unemployed Total	Rate [1]	Not in labor force
Total, 16 to 24 years [2]	**37,480**	**22,243**	**19,921**	**2,637**	**10.4**	**15,237**
Enrolled in school [2]	21,061	8,979	8,181	798	8.9	12,083
Enrolled in high school.	9,724	2,855	2,421	434	15.2	6,869
Male	5,118	1,431	1,203	227	15.9	3,687
Female	4,607	1,425	1,218	206	14.5	3,182
Enrolled in college.	11,337	6,124	5,760	364	5.9	5,213
Enrolled in 2-year college . . .	3,217	2,066	1,946	121	5.8	1,151
Enrolled in 4-year college . . .	8,120	4,057	3,814	243	6.0	4,063
Race/ethnicity:						
White [3]						
Enrolled in high school . . .	7,370	2,371	2,053	318	13.4	4,999
Enrolled in college	8,912	5,008	4,759	249	5.0	3,904
Black [3]						
Enrolled in high school . . .	1,590	294	222	72	24.6	1,296
Enrolled in college	1,423	674	607	67	9.9	749
Asian [3]						
Enrolled in high school . . .	352	72	58	14	([4])	281
Enrolled in college	668	240	223	17	7.0	428
Hispanic or Latino ethnicity						
Enrolled in high school . . .	1,659	368	302	66	17.9	1,291
Enrolled in college	1,414	836	800	36	4.3	578
Not enrolled [2]	16,419	13,264	11,740	1,524	11.5	3,155
White [3]	12,740	10,441	9,441	1,000	9.6	2,299
Black [3]	2,542	1,938	1,521	417	21.5	604
Asian [3]	462	379	342	37	9.9	83
Hispanic or Latino ethnicity	3,559	2,655	2,349	305	11.5	904

[1] Percent unemployed of civilian labor force in each category.   [2] Includes other races not shown separately.   [3] Data for persons in this race group only. See footnote 3, Table 570.   [4] Data not shown where base is less than 75,000.

Source: U.S. Bureau of Labor Statistics; *College Enrollment and Work Activity of High School Graduates, News,* USDL 08-0559, April 25, 2008. See Internet site <http://www.bls.gov/news.release/pdf/hsgec.pdf>.

Table 576. **Labor Force Participation Rates by Marital Status, Sex, and Age: 1970 to 2007**

[**For the civilian noninstitutional population 16 years old and over. Annual averages of monthly figures.** See Table 573 for definition of participation rate. Based on Current Population Survey; see text, Section 1 and Appendix III]

Marital status and year	Male participation rate							Female participation rate						
	Total	16–19 years	20–24 years	25–34 years	35–44 years	45–64 years	65 years and over	Total	16–19 years	20–24 years	25–34 years	35–44 years	45–64 years	65 years and over
Single:														
1970	65.5	54.6	73.8	87.9	86.2	75.7	25.2	56.8	44.7	73.0	81.4	78.6	73.0	19.7
1980	72.6	59.9	81.3	89.2	82.2	66.9	16.8	64.4	53.6	75.2	83.3	76.9	65.6	13.9
1985	73.8	56.3	81.5	89.4	84.6	65.5	15.6	66.6	52.3	76.3	82.4	80.8	67.9	9.8
1990 [1]	74.8	55.1	81.6	89.9	84.5	67.3	15.7	66.7	51.7	74.5	80.9	80.8	66.2	12.1
1995	73.7	54.4	80.3	88.7	81.4	67.0	17.9	66.8	52.2	72.9	80.2	79.5	67.3	11.6
2000 [1]	73.6	52.5	80.5	89.4	82.9	69.7	17.3	68.9	51.1	76.1	83.9	80.9	69.9	10.8
2001	72.7	50.0	79.6	89.0	83.2	69.8	15.4	68.1	49.1	75.3	83.2	81.3	69.9	12.1
2002	71.7	47.2	78.7	88.7	83.1	69.6	16.9	67.4	47.3	74.5	83.3	79.9	69.6	14.3
2003 [1]	70.4	44.0	77.9	87.7	82.9	67.6	19.4	66.2	44.8	72.9	82.2	79.8	69.9	15.2
2004 [1]	70.2	43.6	77.7	87.9	82.7	67.8	20.3	65.9	43.8	73.1	81.8	80.5	70.9	14.7
2005 [1]	70.1	42.9	77.0	87.9	82.9	68.6	18.8	66.0	44.2	72.6	81.4	80.7	70.9	15.5
2006 [1]	70.7	43.4	77.8	87.7	83.5	69.9	19.3	65.7	43.7	71.8	81.4	79.8	70.5	15.0
2007 [1]	70.1	40.8	76.9	88.5	84.0	70.3	22.6	65.3	41.4	72.6	82.1	78.0	70.4	18.4
Married: [2]														
1970	86.1	92.3	94.7	98.0	98.1	91.2	29.9	40.5	37.8	47.9	38.8	46.8	44.0	7.3
1980	80.9	91.3	96.9	97.5	97.2	84.3	20.5	49.8	49.3	61.4	58.8	61.8	46.9	7.3
1985	78.7	91.0	95.6	97.4	96.8	81.7	16.8	53.8	49.6	65.7	65.8	68.1	49.4	6.6
1990 [1]	78.6	92.1	95.6	96.9	96.7	82.6	17.5	58.4	49.5	66.1	69.6	74.0	56.5	8.5
1995	77.5	89.2	94.9	96.3	95.4	82.4	18.0	61.0	51.6	64.7	72.0	75.7	62.7	9.1
2000 [1]	77.3	79.5	94.1	96.7	95.8	83.0	19.2	61.1	53.2	63.8	70.3	74.8	65.4	10.1
2001	77.4	77.7	94.2	95.9	95.6	83.7	19.1	61.2	45.1	63.9	69.9	74.5	66.1	10.3
2002	77.4	81.1	93.3	95.7	95.1	83.8	19.4	61.0	49.6	63.4	69.3	73.8	66.5	10.7
2003 [1]	77.3	76.6	93.2	95.3	95.1	83.5	19.9	61.0	46.7	62.6	68.5	73.3	67.4	11.3
2004 [1]	77.1	77.4	92.4	95.6	95.1	83.1	20.4	60.5	41.1	60.9	67.6	72.7	67.0	11.6
2005 [1]	77.2	71.4	93.4	95.3	95.2	83.6	21.4	60.7	44.1	61.1	68.4	73.0	67.0	12.5
2006 [1]	77.1	79.2	93.3	95.5	95.2	83.6	21.8	61.0	39.6	59.8	69.0	73.3	67.8	12.4
2007 [1]	76.9	86.9	92.9	95.7	95.3	83.6	21.8	61.0	43.3	61.7	68.6	73.1	67.7	13.6
Other: [3]														
1970	60.7	(B)	90.4	93.7	91.1	78.5	19.3	40.3	48.6	60.3	64.6	68.8	61.9	10.0
1980	67.5	(B)	92.6	94.1	91.9	73.3	13.7	43.6	50.0	68.4	76.5	77.1	60.2	8.2
1985	68.7	(B)	95.1	93.7	91.8	72.8	11.4	45.1	51.9	66.2	76.9	81.6	61.0	7.5
1990 [1]	68.9	(B)	93.1	93.0	90.7	74.9	12.0	47.2	53.9	65.4	77.0	82.1	65.0	8.4
1995	66.2	(B)	92.7	90.9	88.2	72.4	12.1	47.4	55.8	67.2	77.1	80.7	67.2	8.4
2000 [1]	66.8	60.5	88.1	93.2	89.9	73.9	12.9	49.0	46.0	74.0	83.1	82.9	69.8	8.7
2001	66.0	57.3	85.4	92.4	89.4	73.5	13.9	49.0	47.2	75.5	81.6	82.6	69.3	8.9
2002	65.5	57.5	87.4	91.2	89.6	74.1	13.2	49.2	46.2	74.7	80.7	82.7	69.7	8.9
2003 [1]	65.0	45.6	88.0	91.4	89.3	72.4	14.3	49.6	44.1	71.4	79.1	81.9	70.7	9.8
2004 [1]	64.9	53.1	87.2	90.6	88.6	72.8	14.3	49.6	48.7	70.0	79.4	81.7	69.8	10.4
2005 [1]	64.9	54.9	86.4	90.4	89.4	72.7	15.1	49.4	46.8	67.4	78.1	80.9	69.4	10.5
2006 [1]	65.6	47.8	86.0	91.5	88.9	73.8	16.3	49.6	45.3	71.5	78.2	80.9	69.3	10.9
2007 [1]	65.6	43.4	82.5	92.1	89.4	73.7	16.1	49.5	44.6	63.8	78.4	81.4	69.3	11.4

B Percentage not shown where base is less than 35,000. [1] See footnote 2, Table 567. [2] Spouse present. [3] Widowed, divorced, and married (spouse absent).

Source: U.S. Bureau of Labor Statistics, Bulletin 2217; and unpublished data.

Table 577. **Marital Status of Women in the Civilian Labor Force: 1970 to 2007**

[**31,543 represents 31,543,000.** For civilian noninstitutional population 16 years and over. Annual averages of monthly figures. Based on the Current Population Survey; see text, Section 1, and Appendix III]

Year	Female civilian labor force (1,000)				Female participation rate [3]			
	Total	Never married	Married [1]	Other [2]	Total	Never married	Married [1]	Other [2]
1970	31,543	7,265	18,475	5,804	43.3	56.8	40.5	40.3
1975	37,475	9,125	21,484	6,866	46.3	59.8	44.3	40.1
1980	45,487	11,865	24,980	8,643	51.5	64.4	49.8	43.6
1985	51,050	13,163	27,894	9,993	54.5	66.6	53.8	45.1
1990 [4]	56,829	14,612	30,901	11,315	57.5	66.7	58.4	47.2
1995	60,944	15,467	33,359	12,118	58.9	66.8	61.0	47.4
2000 [4]	66,303	17,849	35,146	13,308	59.9	68.9	61.1	49.0
2001	66,848	18,021	35,236	13,592	59.8	68.1	61.2	49.0
2002	67,363	18,203	35,477	13,683	59.6	67.4	61.0	49.2
2003 [4]	68,272	18,397	36,046	13,828	59.5	66.2	61.0	49.6
2004 [4]	68,421	18,616	35,845	13,961	59.2	65.9	60.5	49.6
2005 [4]	69,288	19,183	35,941	14,163	59.3	66.0	60.7	49.4
2006 [4]	70,173	19,474	36,314	14,385	59.4	65.7	61.0	49.6
2007 [4]	70,988	19,745	36,881	14,362	59.3	65.3	61.0	49.5

[1] Husband present. [2] Widowed, divorced, or separated. [3] See footnote 3, Table 573 for definition of participation rate. [4] See footnote 2, Table 567.

Source: U.S. Bureau of Labor Statistics, *Women in the Labor Force: A Databook,* September 2007, and unpublished data. See Internet site <http://www.bls.gov/cps/wlf-databook2007.htm>.

Labor Force, Employment, and Earnings 375

Table 578. **Employment Status of Women by Marital Status and Presence and Age of Children: 1970 to 2007**

[**As of March (7.0 represents 7,000,000).** Civilian noninstitutional persons 16 years old and over. Based on the Current Population Survey; see text, Section 1, and Appendix III]

Item	Total			With any children								
				Total			Children 6 to 17 yrs. only			Children under 6 yrs.		
	Single	Married[1]	Other[2]	Single	Married[1]	Other[2]	Single	Married[1]	Other[2]	Single	Married[1]	Other[2]
IN LABOR FORCE (mil.)												
1970	7.0	18.4	5.9	(NA)	10.2	1.9	(NA)	6.3	1.3	(NA)	3.9	0.6
1980	11.2	24.9	8.8	0.6	13.7	3.6	0.2	8.4	2.6	0.3	5.2	1.0
1990	14.0	31.0	11.2	1.5	16.5	4.2	0.6	9.3	3.0	0.9	7.2	1.2
1995	15.0	33.6	12.0	2.1	18.0	4.6	0.8	10.2	3.3	1.3	7.8	1.3
2000	17.8	35.0	13.2	3.1	18.2	4.5	1.2	10.8	3.4	1.8	7.3	1.1
2005[3]	18.6	35.7	14.3	3.4	18.0	4.6	1.4	10.8	3.4	1.9	7.2	1.2
2006[3]	19.0	36.2	14.2	3.3	18.1	4.6	1.4	10.7	3.5	1.9	7.4	1.1
2007[3]	19.2	37.3	14.3	3.5	18.6	4.8	1.4	10.9	3.6	2.1	7.7	1.2
PARTICIPATION RATE[4]												
1970	53.0	40.8	39.1	(NA)	39.7	60.7	(NA)	49.2	66.9	(NA)	30.3	52.2
1980	61.5	50.1	44.0	52.0	54.1	69.4	67.6	61.7	74.6	44.1	45.1	60.3
1990	66.4	58.2	46.8	55.2	66.3	74.2	69.7	73.6	79.7	48.7	58.9	63.6
1995	65.5	61.1	47.3	57.5	70.2	75.3	67.0	76.2	79.5	53.0	63.5	66.3
2000	68.6	62.0	50.2	73.9	70.6	82.7	79.7	77.2	85.0	70.5	62.8	76.6
2005[3]	65.1	60.2	49.8	72.9	68.1	79.8	79.7	75.0	82.2	68.5	59.8	73.5
2006[3]	64.7	60.9	49.1	71.5	68.4	80.4	76.2	75.3	82.5	68.6	60.3	74.3
2007[3]	64.7	61.6	49.5	71.4	69.3	80.0	78.0	76.2	82.9	67.4	61.5	72.2
EMPLOYMENT (mil.)												
1970	6.5	17.5	5.6	(NA)	9.6	1.8	(NA)	6.0	1.2	(NA)	3.6	0.6
1980	10.1	23.6	8.2	0.4	12.8	3.3	0.2	8.1	2.4	0.2	4.8	0.9
1990	12.9	29.9	10.5	1.2	15.8	3.8	0.5	8.9	2.7	0.7	6.9	1.1
1995	13.7	32.3	11.3	1.8	17.2	4.2	0.7	9.8	3.1	1.1	7.3	1.2
2000	16.4	34.0	12.7	2.7	17.6	4.3	1.1	10.6	3.2	1.6	7.1	1.1
2005[3]	17.0	34.6	13.5	2.9	17.4	4.3	1.3	10.4	3.2	1.6	7.0	1.1
2006[3]	17.4	35.2	13.5	2.9	17.5	4.3	1.2	10.4	3.3	1.7	7.1	1.0
2007[3]	17.9	36.4	13.6	3.1	18.0	4.5	1.3	10.6	3.4	1.8	7.4	1.1
UNEMPLOYMENT RATE[5]												
1970	7.1	4.8	4.8	(NA)	6.0	7.2	(NA)	4.8	5.9	(NA)	7.9	9.8
1980	10.3	5.3	6.4	23.2	5.9	9.2	15.6	4.4	7.9	29.2	8.3	12.8
1990	8.2	3.5	5.7	18.4	4.2	8.5	14.5	3.8	7.7	20.8	4.8	10.2
1995	8.7	3.9	5.8	16.6	4.3	8.1	11.8	3.6	7.1	19.5	5.3	10.8
2000	7.3	2.7	4.3	11.0	2.9	5.1	8.7	2.6	4.8	12.6	3.5	5.9
2005[3]	8.9	3.0	5.3	15.1	3.1	6.9	10.9	2.9	5.8	18.2	3.4	9.8
2006[3]	8.1	2.8	4.8	12.7	3.2	6.2	10.4	2.8	5.4	14.2	3.7	8.9
2007[3]	6.7	2.6	4.9	10.8	2.8	6.0	9.8	2.5	5.3	11.6	3.4	8.1

NA Not available.　[1] Husband present.　[2] Widowed, divorced, or separated.　[3] See footnote 2, Table 567.　[4] Percent of women in each specific category in the labor force.　[5] Unemployed as a percent of civilian labor force in specified group.

Source: U.S. Bureau of Labor Statistics, Bulletin 2307; and unpublished data.

Table 579. **Labor Force Participation Rates for Wives, Husband Present by Age of Own Youngest Child: 1975 to 2007** [3]

[**As of March.** Civilian noninstitutional population, 16 years old and over. For definition of participation rate, see Table 573, footnote 3. Based on Current Population Survey; see text, Section 1, and Appendix III]

Presence and age of child	1975, total	1990, total	2000[1], total	2005[1], total	2007[1]				
					Total	White[2]	Black[2]	Asian[2,3]	Hispanic[4]
Wives, total	**44.4**	**58.2**	**62.0**	**60.4**	**61.8**	**61.3**	**68.3**	**60.2**	**55.4**
No children under 18 years	43.8	51.1	54.7	54.1	55.7	55.5	58.3	56.4	52.1
With children under 18 years	44.9	66.3	70.6	68.1	69.3	68.9	78.8	63.4	57.1
Under 6 years, total	36.7	58.9	62.8	59.8	61.5	60.9	72.2	55.4	48.4
Under 3 years	32.7	55.5	59.0	57.3	58.9	58.3	68.8	51.4	44.2
1 year or under	30.8	53.9	58.3	55.8	57.8	57.6	65.8	48.9	42.8
2 years	37.1	60.9	61.9	60.8	61.4	60.0	75.7	57.9	47.1
3 to 5 years	42.2	64.1	68.4	64.8	65.6	64.7	76.6	60.1	54.2
3 years	41.2	63.1	66.0	62.7	64.4	64.5	78.4	47.4	52.9
4 years	41.2	65.1	69.7	64.9	63.4	62.0	71.5	67.8	55.9
5 years	44.4	64.5	70.6	67.5	69.4	68.0	79.8	72.4	54.2
6 to 13 years	51.8	73.0	75.8	73.2	74.5	73.9	84.7	69.6	65.8
14 to 17 years	53.5	75.1	80.6	79.6	79.8	80.0	81.5	75.1	71.1

[1] See footnote 2, Table 567.　[2] For persons in this race group only. See footnote 3, Table 568.　[3] Excludes Pacific Islanders.　[4] Persons of Hispanic or Latino origin may be any race.

Source: U.S. Bureau of Labor Statistics, Bulletin 2340; and unpublished data.

Table 580. Married Couple Households by Labor Force Status of Spouse: 1990 to 2007

[**52,317 represents 52,317,000.** Data represent married couple households. Based on the Current Population Survey and subject to sampling error; for details see source and Appendix III]

Year	All married couples	Number (1,000) In labor force Husband and wife	Number (1,000) In labor force Husband only	Number (1,000) In labor force Wife only	Husband and wife not in labor force	Percent distribution In labor force Husband and wife	Percent distribution In labor force Husband only	Percent distribution In labor force Wife only	Husband and wife not in labor force
TOTAL									
1990	52,317	28,056	13,013	2,453	8,794	53.6	24.9	4.7	16.8
1995	53,858	29,999	11,777	3,043	9,039	55.7	21.9	5.7	16.8
2000	55,311	31,095	11,815	3,301	9,098	56.2	21.4	6.0	16.4
2001	56,592	31,794	12,213	3,274	9,311	56.2	21.6	5.8	16.5
2002	56,747	31,637	12,327	3,388	9,395	55.8	21.7	6.0	16.6
2003	57,320	31,951	12,443	3,553	9,373	55.7	21.7	6.2	16.4
2004	57,719	31,536	12,980	3,684	9,519	54.6	22.5	6.4	16.5
2005	57,975	31,398	13,385	3,641	9,551	54.2	23.1	6.3	16.5
2006	58,179	31,783	12,990	3,754	9,652	54.6	22.3	6.5	16.6
2007	60,676	33,337	13,351	4,031	9,958	54.9	22.0	6.6	16.4
WITH CHILDREN UNDER 18									
1990	24,537	15,768	7,667	558	544	64.3	31.2	2.3	2.2
1995	25,241	17,024	6,863	756	598	67.4	27.2	3.0	2.4
2000	25,248	17,116	6,950	795	387	67.8	27.5	3.1	1.5
2001	25,980	17,563	7,210	784	422	67.6	27.8	3.0	1.6
2002	25,792	17,233	7,301	777	482	66.8	28.3	3.0	1.9
2003	25,914	17,065	7,499	893	457	65.9	28.9	3.4	1.8
2004	25,793	16,691	7,715	952	433	64.7	29.9	3.7	1.7
2005	25,919	16,789	7,806	925	400	64.8	30.1	3.6	1.5
2006	25,982	16,909	7,754	900	420	65.1	29.9	3.5	1.6
2007	26,802	17,670	7,743	920	469	65.9	28.9	3.4	1.7
WITH CHILDREN UNDER 6									
1990	12,051	6,932	4,692	192	235	57.5	38.9	1.6	2.0
1995	11,951	7,406	4,059	233	253	62.0	34.0	1.9	2.1
2000	11,393	6,984	4,077	211	121	61.3	35.8	1.9	1.1
2001	11,732	7,054	4,296	247	134	60.1	36.6	2.1	1.1
2002	11,531	6,796	4,311	250	175	58.9	37.4	2.2	1.5
2003	11,743	6,747	4,507	298	191	57.5	38.4	2.5	1.6
2004	11,711	6,657	4,579	317	158	56.8	39.1	2.7	1.3
2005	11,802	6,813	4,553	299	137	57.7	38.6	2.5	1.2
2006	11,984	6,939	4,572	324	149	57.9	38.2	2.7	1.2
2007	12,468	7,337	4,633	331	167	58.8	37.2	2.7	1.3

Source: U.S. Bureau of the Census, Table MC-1, Married Couples by Labor Force Status of Spouses: 1986 to Present; released 28 July 2008. See Internet site <http://www.census.gov/population/www/socdemo/hh-fam.html>.

Table 581. Employed Civilians and Weekly Hours: 1980 to 2007

[**In thousands (99,303 represents 99,303.000), except as indicated.** Annual averages of monthly figures. Civilian noninstitutional population 16 years old and over. Based on Current Population Survey; see text, Section 1 and Appendix III]

Item	1980	1990 [1]	1995	2000 [1]	2005 [1]	2006 [1]	2007 [1]
Total employed	**99,303**	**118,793**	**124,900**	**136,891**	**141,730**	**144,427**	**146,047**
Age:							
16 to 19 years old	7,710	6,581	6,419	7,189	5,978	6,162	5,911
20 to 24 years old	14,087	13,401	12,443	13,229	13,792	13,878	13,964
25 to 34 years old	27,204	33,935	32,356	31,549	30,680	31,051	31,586
35 to 44 years old	19,523	30,817	34,202	36,433	34,630	34,569	34,302
45 to 54 years old	16,234	19,525	24,378	30,310	33,207	34,052	34,562
55 to 64 years old	11,586	11,189	11,435	14,002	18,349	19,389	20,108
65 years old and over	2,960	3,346	3,666	4,179	5,094	5,325	5,613
Class of worker:							
Nonagricultural industries	95,938	115,570	121,460	134,427	139,532	142,221	143,952
Wage and salary worker [2]	88,525	106,598	112,448	125,114	129,931	132,449	134,283
Self-employed	7,000	8,719	8,902	9,205	9,509	9,685	9,557
Unpaid family workers	413	253	110	108	93	87	112
Agriculture and related industries	3,364	3,223	3,440	2,464	2,197	2,206	2,095
Wage and salary worker [2]	1,425	1,740	1,814	1,421	1,212	1,287	1,220
Self-employed	1,642	1,378	1,580	1,010	955	901	856
Unpaid family workers	297	105	45	33	30	18	19
Weekly hours:							
Nonagricultural industries:							
Wage and salary workers [2]	38.1	39.2	39.2	39.6	39.1	(NA)	39.1
Self-employed	41.2	40.8	39.4	39.7	38.4	(NA)	(NA)
Unpaid family workers	34.7	34.0	33.5	32.5	32.2	(NA)	(NA)
Agriculture and related industries:							
Wage and salary workers [2]	41.6	41.2	41.1	43.2	43.7	(NA)	43.2
Self-employed	49.3	46.8	43.5	45.3	43.6	(NA)	(NA)
Unpaid family workers	38.6	38.5	42.0	38.3	44.0	(NA)	(NA)

NA Not available.   [1] See footnote 2, Table 567.   [2] Includes the incorporated self-employed.

Source: U.S. Bureau of Labor Statistics, "Employment and Earnings Online," January 2008 issue. See Internet site <http://www.bls.gov/opub/ee/home.htm> and <http://www.bls.gov/cps/home.htm>.

Labor Force, Employment, and Earnings   377

Table 582. **Persons at Work by Hours Worked: 2007**

[In thousands (140,328 represents 140,328,000), except as indicated. Annual averages of monthly figures. Civilian noninstitutional population 16 years old and over. Based on Current Population Survey; see text, Section 1, and Appendix III. See headnote, Table 585, regarding industries]

Hours of work	Persons at work (1,000)			Percent distribution		
	Total	Agriculture and related industries	Non-agricultural industries	Total	Agriculture and related industries	Non-agricultural industries
Total	**140,328**	**2,007**	**138,321**	**100.0**	**100.0**	**100.0**
1 to 34 hours	32,435	534	31,902	23.1	26.6	23.1
1 to 4 hours	1,395	38	1,357	1.0	1.9	1.0
5 to 14 hours	5,093	127	4,965	3.6	6.4	3.6
15 to 29 hours	16,094	254	15,840	11.5	12.7	11.5
30 to 34 hours	9,854	114	9,740	7.0	5.7	7.0
35 hours and over	107,892	1,473	106,419	76.9	73.4	76.9
35 to 39 hours	9,368	90	9,278	6.7	4.5	6.7
40 hours	59,973	542	59,431	42.7	27.0	43.0
41 hours and over	38,552	841	37,710	27.5	41.9	27.3
41 to 48 hours	13,612	131	13,481	9.7	6.5	9.7
49 to 59 hours	14,522	250	14,273	10.3	12.4	10.3
60 hours and over	10,417	460	9,956	7.4	22.9	7.2
Average weekly hours: Persons at work	39.2	43.2	39.1	(X)	(X)	(X)
Persons usually working full-time	42.8	49.1	42.7	(X)	(X)	(X)

X Not applicable.

Source: U.S. Bureau of Labor Statistics, "Employment and Earnings Online," January 2008 issue. See Internet site <http://www.bls.gov/opub/ee/home.htm> and <http://www.bls.gov/cps/home.htm>.

Table 583. **Persons With a Job, But Not at Work: 1980 to 2007**

[In thousands (5,881 represents 5,881,000), except percent. For civilian noninstitutional population 16 years old and over. Annual averages of monthly figures. Based on Current Population Survey; see text, Section 1 and Appendix III]

Reason for not working	1980	1990 [1]	1995	2000 [1]	2001	2002	2003 [1]	2004 [1]	2005 [1]	2006 [1]	2007 [1]
All industries, number	**5,881**	**6,160**	**5,582**	**5,681**	**5,631**	**5,394**	**5,469**	**5,482**	**5,511**	**5,746**	**5,719**
Percent of employed	5.9	5.2	4.5	4.2	4.1	4.0	4.0	3.9	3.9	4.0	3.9
Reason for not working:											
Vacation	3,320	3,529	2,982	3,109	3,039	2,929	2,922	2,923	2,892	3,101	3,056
Illness	1,426	1,341	1,084	1,156	1,095	1,072	1,090	1,058	1,088	1,096	1,064
Bad weather	155	90	122	89	100	97	123	133	145	117	140
Industrial dispute	105	24	21	14	9	7	18	10	6	7	10
All other	876	1,177	1,373	1,313	1,388	1,289	1,316	1,358	1,381	1,425	1,449

[1] See footnote 2, Table 567.

Source: U.S. Bureau of Labor Statistics, Current Population Survey, unpublished data. See Internet site <http://www.bls.gov/cps/home.htm>.

Table 584. **Class of Worker by Sex and Selected Characteristic: 2007**

[In percent, except as indicated (10,413 represents 10,413,000). Civilian noninstitutional population 16 years old and over. Annual averages of monthly figures. Based on Current Population Survey; see text Section 1, and Appendix III]

Characteristic	Unincorporated self-employed			Incorporated self-employed			Wage and salary workers[1]		
	Total	Male	Female	Total	Male	Female	Total	Male	Female
Total (1,000)	**10,413**	**6,543**	**3,870**	**5,736**	**4,202**	**1,533**	**129,767**	**67,468**	**62,300**
PERCENT DISTRIBUTION	100.0	100.0	100.0	100.0	100.0	100.0	100.0	100.0	100.0
Age: 16 to 19 years old	0.8	0.8	0.7	0.2	0.2	0.3	4.5	4.2	4.7
20 to 24 years old	2.8	3.1	2.3	1.2	1.2	1.2	10.5	10.5	10.4
25 to 34 years old	14.4	14.7	13.9	11.5	11.7	11.0	22.7	23.7	21.5
35 to 44 years old	23.5	22.9	24.5	26.7	26.0	28.4	23.3	23.8	22.8
45 to 54 years old	28.5	28.0	29.4	31.9	31.7	32.5	22.9	22.3	23.6
55 to 64 years old	20.5	20.9	19.9	20.9	21.3	19.8	12.9	12.3	13.6
65 years old and over	9.5	9.6	9.4	7.6	7.9	6.7	3.2	3.1	3.3
Race/ethnicity: White[2]	87.3	87.6	86.9	88.6	89.8	85.4	81.3	82.6	79.9
Black[2]	6.0	5.9	6.3	4.3	4.0	5.0	11.7	10.3	13.2
Asian[2]	4.6	4.5	4.7	5.7	4.7	8.3	4.6	4.7	4.6
Hispanic[3]	11.8	13.1	9.7	6.9	6.8	7.4	14.4	16.5	12.2
Country of birth: U.S. born	83.4	82.3	85.1	(NA)	(NA)	(NA)	(NA)	(NA)	(NA)
Foreign born	16.6	17.7	14.8	(NA)	(NA)	(NA)	(NA)	(NA)	(NA)

[1] Excludes the incorporated self-employed.   [2] For persons in this race group only.   [3] Persons of Hispanic or Latino origin may be of any race.

Source: U.S. Bureau of Labor Statistics, Current Population Survey, unpublished data.

Table 585. **Self-Employed Workers by Industry and Occupation: 2000 to 2007**

[In thousands (10,214 represents 10,214,000). Civilian noninstitutional population 16 years old and over. Annual averages of monthly figures. Data represent the unincorporated self-employed; the incorporated self-employed are considered wage and salary workers. Based on the occupational and industrial classification derived from those used in the 2000 census. See text, this section. Based on the Current Population Survey; see text, Section 1, and Appendix III]

Item	2000	2003	2004 [1]	2005 [1]	2006 [1]	2007 [1]
Total self-employed	**10,214**	**10,295**	**10,431**	**10,464**	**10,586**	**10,413**
Industry:						
Agriculture and related industries	1,010	951	964	955	901	856
Mining	12	9	13	11	10	19
Construction	1,728	1,717	1,848	1,830	1,910	1,890
Manufacturing	334	325	316	327	326	348
Wholesale and retail trade	1,221	1,247	1,153	1,251	1,139	1,116
Transportation and utilities	348	357	410	442	428	405
Information	139	152	146	126	120	135
Financial activities [2]	735	736	792	785	841	829
Professional and business services [2]	1,927	1,908	1,993	1,957	1,992	2,009
Education and health services [2]	1,107	1,138	1,105	1,071	1,158	1,102
Leisure and hospitality [2]	660	686	660	674	685	679
Other services [3]	993	1,071	1,031	1,036	1,076	1,026
Occupation:						
Management, professional, and related occupations	4,169	4,176	4,179	4,085	(NA)	(NA)
Service occupations	1,775	1,690	1,757	1,774	(NA)	(NA)
Sales and office occupations	1,982	1,945	1,909	1,986	(NA)	(NA)
Natural resources, construction, and maintenance occupations	1,591	1,795	1,847	1,864	(NA)	(NA)
Production, transportation, and material-moving occupations	698	689	739	756	(NA)	(NA)

NA Not available. [1] See footnote 2, Table 567. [2] For composition of industries, see Table 605. [3] Includes private households.

Source: U.S. Bureau of Labor Statistics, "Employment and Earnings Online," January 2008 issue. See Internet site <http://www.bls.gov/opub/ee/home.htm> and <http://www.bls.gov/cps/home.htm>.

Table 586. **Persons Doing Job-Related Work at Home: 2004**

[136,602 represents 136,602,000. As of May. For persons at work 16 years and over in nonagricultural industries doing job-related work at home at least once a week as part of their primary job. Based on the Current Population Survey; see text, Section 1, and Appendix III. Industry and occupational classifications are those based on the 2000 census. See text, this section]

Characteristic	Total employed [1] (1,000)	Persons who usually worked at home [2]				
		Total (1,000)	Percent of employed	Percent distribution by class of worker		
					Wage and salary workers	
				Total [3]	Paid work at home	Unpaid work at home	Self employed [4]

Characteristic	Total employed [1] (1,000)	Total (1,000)	Percent of employed	Total [3]	Paid work at home	Unpaid work at home	Self employed [4]
Total [5]	**136,602**	**20,673**	**15.1**	**100.0**	**16.2**	**49.3**	**33.7**
SEX							
Male	72,417	10,780	14.9	100.0	14.7	47.3	37.6
Female	64,185	9,893	15.4	100.0	17.8	51.4	29.4
RACE AND HISPANIC ORIGIN							
White [6]	111,756	18,255	16.3	100.0	16.4	49.0	33.8
Black [6]	15,800	1,245	7.9	100.0	14.2	53.0	31.0
Asian [6]	5,630	718	12.7	100.0	14.2	52.1	33.7
Hispanic origin [7]	17,577	1,255	7.1	100.0	19.1	45.0	34.4
OCCUPATION							
Management, professional, and related occupations	47,829	13,445	28.1	100.0	13.9	59.9	25.7
Management, business, and financial operations occupations	19,205	5,602	29.2	100.0	16.2	46.6	36.9
Professional and related occupations	28,623	7,842	27.4	100.0	12.2	69.5	17.7
Service occupations	22,752	1,414	6.2	100.0	20.6	20.9	54.8
Sales and office occupations	35,133	4,291	12.2	100.0	24.1	36.1	38.6
Sales and related occupations	15,886	3,137	19.7	100.0	21.8	35.4	42.2
Office and administrative support occupations	19,247	1,154	6.0	100.0	30.5	38.0	28.9
Natural resources, construction, and maintenance occupations	13,111	1,036	7.9	100.0	10.2	15.1	73.8
Farming, fishing, and forestry occupations	195	3	1.5	100.0	(B)	(B)	(B)
Construction and extraction occupations	7,927	705	8.9	100.0	6.1	13.3	80.6
Installation, maintenance, and repair occupations	4,989	329	6.6	100.0	18.4	19.1	59.6
Production, transportation, and material-moving occupations	17,777	488	2.7	100.0	10.6	26.6	62.8
Production occupations	9,240	276	3.0	100.0	12.8	22.1	65.0
Transportation and material-moving occupations	8,538	212	2.5	100.0	7.7	32.5	59.8

B Data not shown where the base is less than 75,000. [1] Includes persons who did not report information on work at home. [2] Persons who worked at home at least once per week as part of their primary job. [3] Unpaid family workers and wage and salary workers who did not report pay status are included in the total but not shown separately. [4] Includes the incorporated and unincorporated self-employed. [5] Includes other races not shown separately. [6] For persons in this race group only. See footnote 2, Table 568. [7] Persons of Hispanic origin may be of any race.

Source: U.S. Bureau of Labor Statistics, *Work at Home in 2004, News,* USDL 05-1768, September 22, 2005. See Internet site <http://www.bls.gov/bls/newsrels.htm#OEUS>.

Labor Force, Employment, and Earnings 379

Table 587. **Persons on Flexible Schedules: 2004**

[**In thousands, except percent. (99,778 represents 99,778,000.) As of May.** For employed full-time wage and salary workers 16 years old and over. Excludes all self-employed persons, regardless of whether or not their businesses were incorporated. Data related to the primary job. Based on the Current Population Survey; see text, Section 1, and Appendix III]

Item	Total	Total With flexible schedules		Male	Male With flexible schedules		Female	Female With flexible schedules	
	Total [1]	Number	Percent	Total [1]	Number	Percent	Total [1]	Number	Percent
Total.	**99,778**	**27,411**	**27.5**	**56,412**	**15,853**	**28.1**	**43,366**	**11,558**	**26.7**
AGE									
16 to 19 years old	1,427	336	23.6	903	185	20.5	524	151	28.9
20 years and over	98,351	27,075	27.5	55,509	15,668	28.2	42,842	11,406	26.6
20 to 24 years old	9,004	2,058	22.9	5,147	1,065	20.7	3,856	993	25.8
25 to 34 years old	24,640	6,902	28.0	14,358	4,051	28.2	10,283	2,851	27.7
35 to 44 years old	26,766	7,807	29.2	15,424	4,605	29.9	11,342	3,202	28.2
45 to 54 years old	24,855	6,651	26.8	13,440	3,769	28.0	11,415	2,882	25.2
55 to 64 years old	11,745	3,181	27.1	6,383	1,865	29.2	5,361	1,316	24.5
65 years old and over	1,341	475	35.4	757	314	41.4	585	161	27.6
RACE AND HISPANIC ORIGIN									
White [2]	80,498	23,121	28.7	46,222	13,582	29.4	34,276	9,539	27.8
Black [2]	12,578	2,476	19.7	6,447	1,193	18.5	6,131	1,283	20.9
Asian [2]	4,136	1,132	27.4	2,300	720	31.3	1,836	412	22.4
Hispanic origin [3]	14,110	2,596	18.4	8,621	1,430	16.6	5,489	1,166	21.2
MARITAL STATUS									
Married, spouse present	57,630	16,270	28.2	34,926	10,382	29.7	22,704	5,888	25.9
Not married	42,148	11,141	26.4	21,486	5,471	25.5	20,662	5,670	27.4
Never married	25,144	6,693	26.6	14,469	3,605	24.9	10,676	3,088	28.9
Other marital status	17,004	4,448	26.2	7,018	1,866	26.6	9,986	2,582	25.9
PRESENCE AND AGE OF CHILDREN									
Without own children under 18	61,761	16,759	27.1	34,680	9,410	27.1	27,081	7,349	27.1
With own children under 18.	38,018	10,652	28.0	21,733	6,443	29.6	16,285	4,209	25.8
With youngest child 6 to 17.	21,739	5,960	27.4	11,477	3,341	29.1	10,262	2,619	25.5
With youngest child under 6.	16,279	4,692	28.8	10,256	3,102	30.2	6,023	1,590	26.4

[1] Includes persons who did not provide information on flexible schedules. [2] For persons in the race group only. See footnote 3, Table 568. [3] Persons of Hispanic origin may be of any race.

Source: U.S. Bureau of Labor Statistics, *Workers on Flexible and Shift Schedules in May 2004, News,* USDL 05-1198, July 1, 2005. See Internet site <http://www.bls.gov/bls/newsrels.htm#OEUS>.

Table 588. **Employed Workers With Alternative and Traditional Work Arrangements: 2005**

[**In thousands (138,952 represents 138,952,000). As of February.** For employed workers 16 years old and over. Based on the Current Population Survey; see text, Section 1, Population, and Appendix III]

Characteristic	Total employed [1]	Workers with alternative arrangements Independent contractors	Workers with alternative arrangements On-call workers	Workers with alternative arrangements Temporary help agency workers	Workers with alternative arrangements Workers provided by contract firms	Workers with traditional arrangements
Total employed.	**138,952**	**10,342**	**2,454**	**1,217**	**813**	**123,843**
16 to 19 years old	5,510	89	133	33	7	5,194
20 to 24 years old	13,114	356	355	202	87	12,055
25 to 34 years old	30,103	1,520	535	362	205	27,427
35 to 44 years old	34,481	2,754	571	253	196	30,646
45 to 54 years old	32,947	2,799	417	200	186	29,324
55 to 64 years old	17,980	1,943	267	135	114	15,496
65 years old and over	4,817	881	175	33	18	3,701
Male.	73,946	6,696	1,241	574	561	64,673
16 to 19 years old	2,579	32	82	24	7	2,389
20 to 24 years old	6,928	194	200	107	61	6,331
25 to 34 years old	16,624	1,006	299	185	138	14,950
35 to 44 years old	18,523	1,824	252	120	140	16,130
45 to 54 years old	17,193	1,764	209	71	143	15,003
55 to 64 years old	9,485	1,287	108	52	70	7,954
65 years old and over	2,615	589	91	16	3	1,917
Female.	65,006	3,647	1,212	643	252	59,170
16 to 19 years old	2,931	57	52	9	–	2,805
20 to 24 years old	6,186	162	155	95	27	5,724
25 to 34 years old	13,480	514	236	177	67	12,477
35 to 44 years old	15,958	930	319	133	57	14,516
45 to 54 years old	15,754	1,035	208	129	43	14,322
55 to 64 years old	8,495	656	158	83	44	7,542
65 years old and over	2,202	292	84	17	15	1,785
Full-time workers	113,798	7,732	1,370	979	695	102,889
Part-time workers	25,154	2,611	1,084	238	119	20,954

– Represents zero. [1] Includes day laborers (an alternative arrangement) and a small number of workers who were both "on call" and "provided by contract firms," not shown separately.

Source: U.S. Bureau of Labor Statistics, *Contingent and Alternative Employment Arrangements, February 2005, News,* USDL 05-1443, July 27, 2005. See Internet site <http://www.bls.gov/bls/newsrels.htm#OEUS>.

Table 589. Multiple Jobholders: 2007

[**Annual average of monthly figures (7,655 represents 7,655,000).** Civilian noninstitutional population 16 years old and over. Multiple jobholders are employed persons who, either 1) had jobs as wage or salary workers with two employers or more; 2) were self-employed and also held a wage and salary job; or 3) were unpaid family workers on their primary jobs but also held a wage and salary job. Based on the Current Population Survey; see text, Section 1, Population, and Appendix III]

Characteristic	Total		Male		Female	
	Number (1,000)	Percent of employed	Number (1,000)	Percent of employed	Number (1,000)	Percent of employed
Total [1]	**7,655**	**5.2**	**3,833**	**4.9**	**3,822**	**5.6**
Age:						
16 to 19 years old.	249	4.2	96	3.3	153	5.1
20 to 24 years old.	738	5.3	309	4.2	429	6.5
25 to 54 years old.	5,432	5.4	2,783	5.1	2,649	5.7
55 to 64 years old.	1,022	5.1	522	4.9	501	5.2
65 years old and over	214	3.8	123	4.0	91	3.6
Race and Hispanic ethnicity:						
White [2]	6,467	5.4	3,250	5.0	3,217	5.9
Black [2]	753	4.7	375	5.0	379	4.4
Asian [2]	249	3.6	119	3.2	130	4.1
Hispanic [3]	638	3.1	353	2.9	284	3.5
Marital status:						
Married, spouse present.	4,215	5.1	2,435	5.3	1,780	5.0
Widowed, divorced, or separated.	1,339	5.7	446	4.6	893	6.5
Single, never married.	2,101	5.2	952	4.3	1,149	6.3
Full- or part-time status:						
Primary job full-time, secondary job part-time. . . .	4,174	(X)	2,320	(X)	1,854	(X)
Both jobs part-time.	1,764	(X)	531	(X)	1,233	(X)
Both jobs full-time.	288	(X)	193	(X)	95	(X)
Hours vary on primary or secondary job	1,383	(X)	765	(X)	618	(X)

X Not applicable. [1] Includes a small number of persons who work part-time on their primary job and full-time on their secondary job(s), not shown separately. Includes other races not shown separately. [2] For persons who selected this race group only. See footnote 3, Table 568. [3] Persons of Hispanic or Latino ethnicity may be any race.

Source: U.S. Bureau of Labor Statistics, "Employment and Earnings Online," January 2008 issue. See Internet site <http://www.bls.gov/opub/ee/home.htm> and <http://www.bls.gov/cps/home.htm>.

Table 590. Average Number of Jobs Held From Ages 18 to 42: 1978 to 2006

[**For persons aged 41 to 50 in 2006–07.** A job is an uninterrupted period of work with a particular employer. Educational attainment as of 2006–07. Based on the National Longitudinal Survey of Youth 1979; see source for details]

Sex and educational attainment	Total [1]	Number of jobs held by age				
		18 to 22 years old	23 to 27 years old	28 to 32 years old	33 to 37 years old	38 to 42 years old
Total [2]	**10.8**	**4.4**	**3.3**	**2.6**	**2.2**	**1.9**
Less than a high school diploma	10.9	3.9	3.2	2.6	2.2	1.9
High school graduate, no college.	10.5	4.2	3.1	2.6	2.2	1.9
Some college or associate's degree	11.1	4.5	3.4	2.7	2.3	2.0
Bachelor's degree or more	11.1	5.0	3.6	2.6	2.1	1.9
Male.	11.0	4.6	3.5	2.8	2.3	2.0
Less than a high school diploma.	12.5	4.6	3.8	3.0	2.4	2.0
High school graduate, no college.	10.7	4.5	3.4	2.8	2.2	1.9
Some college or associate's degree	11.1	4.5	3.5	2.8	2.4	2.0
Bachelor's degree or more.	10.7	4.6	3.4	2.6	2.2	1.9
Female	10.6	4.3	3.1	2.4	2.1	1.9
Less than a high school diploma.	8.7	2.9	2.3	2.1	1.9	1.6
High school graduate, no college	10.2	3.9	2.7	2.3	2.2	1.9
Some college or associate's degree	11.0	4.5	3.3	2.5	2.2	1.9
Bachelor's degree or more.	11.5	5.3	3.7	2.6	2.0	1.8
White, non-Hispanic.	10.9	4.6	3.3	2.6	2.2	1.9
Less than a high school diploma.	11.5	4.2	3.3	2.7	2.3	1.9
High school graduate, no college	10.4	4.4	3.1	2.6	2.2	1.9
Some college or associate's degree	11.3	4.7	3.4	2.7	2.3	1.9
Bachelor's degree or more.	11.1	5.1	3.6	2.6	2.1	1.8
Black, non-Hispanic.	10.4	3.6	3.1	2.6	2.3	2.0
Less than a high school diploma.	9.8	2.9	2.9	2.6	2.0	1.8
High school graduate, no college	10.6	3.5	3.0	2.6	2.3	2.0
Some college or associate's degree	10.4	3.8	3.1	2.7	2.4	2.1
Bachelor's degree or more.	10.9	4.2	3.6	2.8	2.4	2.2
Hispanic or Latino [3]	10.5	4.1	3.0	2.5	2.2	1.9
Less than a high school diploma.	10.4	4.0	2.8	2.4	2.0	1.7
High school graduate, no college	10.6	4.0	3.0	2.5	2.2	1.9
Some college or associate's degree	10.3	4.2	3.0	2.5	2.2	2.1
Bachelor's degree or more.	10.7	4.4	3.3	2.7	2.3	1.9

[1] Jobs held in more than one age category were counted in each category, but only once in the total. [2] Includes other races not shown separately. [3] Persons of Hispanic or Latino origin may be any race.

Source: U.S. Bureau of Labor Statistics, Number of Jobs Held, Labor Market Activity, and *Earnings Growth Among Youngest Baby Boomers: Results from a Longitudinal Survey, News* USDL 08-0860, June 27, 2008. See Internet site <http://www.bls.gov/nls/home.htm>.

Table 591. **Distribution of Workers by Tenure With Current Employer: 2006**

[125,668 represents 125,668,000. As of January. For employed wage and salary workers 16 years old and over. Data exclude the incorporated and unincorporated self-employed. Based on the Current Population Survey and subject to sampling error; see source and Appendix III]

Characteristic	Number employed (1,000)	Percent distribution by tenure with current employer								Median years [1]
		12 months or less	13 to 23 months	2 years	3 to 4 years	5 to 9 years	10 to 14 years	15 to 19 years	20 years or more	
Total [2].............	125,668	24.4	7.0	5.2	16.9	20.9	9.5	6.7	9.4	4.0
AGE AND SEX										
16 to 19 years old	5,563	75.1	10.5	7.2	6.8	0.4	–	–	–	(NA)
20 to 24 years old	13,083	50.4	12.5	10.2	19.4	7.5	(Z)	–	–	1.3
25 to 34 years old	28,392	28.8	9.3	6.8	23.4	25.3	5.6	0.8	(Z)	2.9
35 to 44 years old	30,466	18.6	6.2	4.6	17.2	26.1	13.7	9.3	4.4	4.9
45 to 54 years old	28,845	13.5	4.6	3.2	14.0	21.7	12.7	11.1	19.2	7.3
55 to 64 years old	15,619	11.4	3.9	2.6	12.9	19.7	12.7	11.3	25.5	9.3
65 years old and over.......	3,699	10.4	3.1	2.8	12.6	22.6	12.8	10.3	25.4	8.8
Male	65,212	23.9	6.8	5.3	16.7	20.7	9.6	6.6	10.3	4.1
16 to 19 years old.......	2,696	74.1	9.9	8.3	7.2	0.4	–	–	–	(NA)
20 to 24 years old.......	6,840	49.7	12.0	10.2	20.8	7.3	0.1	–	–	1.4
25 to 34 years old.......	15,477	28.0	9.1	7.2	22.8	25.9	6.0	1.0	(Z)	2.9
35 to 44 years old.......	16,184	17.9	5.8	4.5	16.5	25.5	14.9	9.8	5.1	5.1
45 to 54 years old.......	14,392	13.0	4.3	3.1	13.0	20.6	12.5	11.3	22.2	8.1
55 to 64 years old.......	7,750	11.6	4.1	3.0	12.8	18.5	11.7	9.5	28.8	9.5
65 years old and over	1,873	10.7	3.4	3.0	12.4	23.3	12.4	8.9	25.9	8.3
Female.................	60,456	24.9	7.2	5.0	17.2	21.2	9.3	6.8	8.4	3.9
16 to 19 years old.......	2,867	76.0	11.1	6.2	6.4	0.3	–	–	–	(NA)
20 to 24 years old.......	6,243	51.2	13.0	10.2	17.8	7.7	–	–	–	1.2
25 to 34 years old.......	12,915	29.8	9.5	6.5	24.0	24.6	5.2	0.5	–	2.8
35 to 44 years old.......	14,282	19.3	6.8	4.7	17.9	26.7	12.3	8.8	3.6	4.6
45 to 54 years old.......	14,453	14.0	4.9	3.4	14.9	22.8	13.0	10.8	16.2	6.7
55 to 64 years old.......	7,870	11.1	3.6	2.3	13.1	20.9	13.6	13.2	22.2	9.2
65 years old and over	1,826	10.0	2.7	2.6	12.8	22.0	13.2	11.7	25.0	9.5
RACE AND HISPANIC ORIGIN										
White [3]................	102,900	24.0	6.9	5.1	16.8	20.9	9.7	6.9	9.8	(NA)
Male.................	54,241	23.4	6.7	5.1	16.6	20.7	9.9	6.9	10.8	(NA)
Female...............	48,659	24.6	7.2	5.0	17.0	21.1	9.4	6.9	8.7	(NA)
Black [3]................	14,265	26.2	6.6	5.7	17.2	21.1	8.4	6.5	8.2	(NA)
Male.................	6,501	26.4	6.7	6.4	17.8	19.8	8.6	5.5	8.9	(NA)
Female...............	7,764	26.1	6.6	5.1	16.7	22.2	8.2	7.5	7.7	(NA)
Asian [3]................	5,463	23.7	8.3	5.8	19.0	22.5	9.9	4.3	6.4	(NA)
Male.................	2,941	23.1	9.0	6.2	17.5	24.9	9.3	3.5	6.5	(NA)
Female...............	2,522	24.5	7.4	5.3	20.7	19.8	10.7	5.2	6.4	(NA)
Hispanic origin [4]........	17,741	30.1	6.5	7.3	20.2	20.3	7.2	4.6	3.7	(NA)
Male.................	10,550	29.7	6.0	7.7	20.5	20.5	7.4	4.7	3.5	(NA)
Female...............	7,191	30.6	7.3	6.8	19.7	20.1	7.0	4.4	4.1	(NA)

– Represents zero.   NA Not available.   Z Less than .05 percent.   [1] For definition of median, see Guide to Tabular Presentation.   [2] Includes other races not shown separately.   [3] For persons in this race group only. See footnote 3, Table 568.   [4] Persons of Hispanic or Latino origin may be any race.

Source: U. S. Bureau of Labor Statistics, News, *Employee Tenure in 2006, News*, USDL 06-1563, September 8, 2006. See Internet site <http://www.bls.gov/bls/newsrels.htm#OEUS>.

Table 592. **Part-Time Workers by Reason: 2007**

[In thousands (32,435 represents 32,435,000), except hours. For persons working 1 to 34 hours per week. For civilian noninstitutional population 16 years old and over. Annual average of monthly figures. Based on the Current Population Survey and subject to sampling error; see text, Section 1, and Appendix III]

Reason	All industries			Nonagriculture industries		
		Usually work—			Usually work—	
	Total	Full-time	Part-time	Total	Full-time	Part-time
Total working fewer than 35 hours	**32,435**	**9,976**	**22,460**	**31,902**	**9,813**	**22,089**
Economic reasons	4,401	1,697	2,704	4,317	1,647	2,670
Slack work or business conditions	2,877	1,436	1,441	2,827	1,403	1,423
Could find only part-time work	1,210	(S)	1,210	1,199	(S)	1,199
Seasonal work	175	122	53	154	106	48
Job started or ended during the week	139	139	(S)	137	137	(S)
Noneconomic reasons	28,034	8,278	19,756	27,585	8,166	19,419
Child-care problems.................	728	72	656	723	72	651
Other family or personal obligations	5,739	799	4,940	5,657	787	4,870
Health or medical limitations	853	(S)	853	830	(S)	830
In school or training.................	6,239	89	6,150	6,165	87	6,079
Retired or social security limit on earnings	2,200	(S)	2,200	2,106	(S)	2,106
Vacation or personal day	3,579	3,579	(S)	3,539	3,539	(S)
Holiday, legal or religious	582	582	(S)	579	579	(S)
Weather-related curtailment.............	669	669	(S)	645	645	(S)
Other	7,443	2,488	4,956	7,340	2,457	4,883
Average hours per week:						
Economic reasons.................	23.1	23.8	22.6	23.1	23.8	22.7
Noneconomic reasons	21.3	25.0	19.8	21.4	25.0	19.8

S No data or data do not meet publication standards.

Source: U.S. Bureau of Labor Statistics, "Employment and Earnings Online," January 2008. See Internet site <http://www.bls.gov/opub/ee/home.htm> and <http://www.bls.gov/cps/home.htm>.

Table 593. **Displaced Workers by Selected Characteristics: 2007**

[In percent, except total (3,641 represents 3,641,000). As of January. For persons 20 years old and over with tenure of 3 years or more who lost or left a job between January 2005 and December 2007 because of plant closings or moves, slack work, or the abolishment of their positions. Based on Current Population Survey and subject to sampling error; see source and Appendix III]

Characteristic	Total (1,000)	Employment status			Reason for job loss		
		Employed	Unem-ployed	Not in the labor force	Plant or company closed down or moved	Slack/ insufficient work	Position or shift abolished
Total [1]	3,641	67.1	18.0	15.0	45.3	23.9	30.8
20 to 24 years old	127	67.5	22.8	9.7	42.4	39.8	17.7
25 to 54 years old	2,602	72.6	17.4	10.0	44.8	25.2	30.0
55 to 64 years old	708	60.8	20.7	18.5	45.7	17.6	36.7
65 years old and over . . .	204	18.4	12.6	69.0	52.2	19.2	28.5
Males	2,024	69.9	18.8	11.2	43.6	27.9	28.5
20 to 24 years old	75	66.4	22.5	11.1	34.2	52.6	13.2
25 to 54 years old	1,490	74.4	19.1	6.5	42.0	29.1	28.9
55 to 64 years old	356	68.0	17.9	14.0	49.7	18.7	31.6
65 years old and over . . .	103	14.4	15.4	70.2	52.3	24.3	23.4
Females	1,617	63.5	16.9	19.6	47.4	19.0	33.6
20 to 24 years old	53	(2)	(2)	(2)	(2)	(2)	(2)
25 to 54 years old	1,112	70.1	15.1	14.8	48.5	20.1	31.4
55 to 64 years old	352	53.4	23.6	23.0	41.6	16.5	41.9
65 years old and over . . .	101	22.4	9.8	67.8	52.2	14.1	33.8
White [3]	3,032	67.9	16.8	15.3	45.4	23.5	31.1
Black [3]	408	58.6	28.2	13.3	46.6	26.9	26.4
Asian [3]	122	67.3	11.7	21.0	44.7	15.7	39.5
Hispanic origin [4]	423	68.4	17.4	14.1	43.5	39.5	17.0

[1] Includes other races not shown separately. [2] Data not shown where base is less than 75,000. [3] For persons in this race group only. See footnote 3, Table 568. [4] Persons of Hispanic or Latino origin may be of any race.

Source: U.S. Bureau of Labor Statistics, *Worker Displacement, 2005–2007*, News, USDL 08-1183, August 20, 2008. See Internet site <http://www.bls.gov/bls/newsrels.htm#OEUS>.

Table 594. **Labor Force Status of Persons With a Work Disability by Age: 2006**

[In percent, except as indicated (24,461 represents 24,461,000). As of March. For civilians 16 to 74 who have a condition which prevents them from working or limits the amount of work they can do. Data from the Current Population Survey and subject to sampling error; see text, Section 1, and Appendix III]

Labor force status	Total	Age						
		16 to 24 years old	25 to 34 years old	35 to 44 years old	45 to 54 years old	55 to 64 years old	65 to 69 years old	70 to 74 years old
Number (1,000)	24,461	1,566	2,376	3,683	5,610	6,741	2,390	2,094
In labor force	22.6	31.0	37.5	29.6	26.4	18.0	9.8	6.5
Employed	19.7	23.2	30.6	26.5	23.2	16.5	9.2	5.8
Full-time.	11.8	9.9	20.6	17.1	15.0	10.0	3.2	1.5
Not in labor force	77.4	69.0	62.5	70.4	73.6	82.0	90.2	93.5
Unemployment rate	12.8	25.1	18.3	10.4	12.0	8.3	6.5	11.8

Source: U.S. Census Bureau, Disability Data from the March Current Population Survey; <http://www.census.gov/hhes/www/disability/disabcps.html>; (accessed 11 July 2008).

Table 595. **Persons Not in the Labor Force: 2007**

[In thousands (78,743 represents 78,743,000). Annual average of monthly figures. Civilian noninstitutional population 16 years old and over. Based on the Current Population Survey; see text, Section 1, and Appendix III]

Status and reason	Total	Age			Sex	
		16 to 24 years old	25 to 54 years old	55 years old and over	Male	Female
Total not in the labor force.	78,743	15,192	21,343	42,207	30,036	48,707
Do not want a job now [1]	74,040	13,510	19,256	41,275	27,914	46,126
Want a job now	4,703	1,683	2,088	933	2,122	2,581
In the previous year—						
Did not search for a job.	2,748	931	1,148	668	1,173	1,575
Did search for a job [2]	1,955	751	939	265	950	1,005
Not available for work now	560	272	234	53	223	336
Available for work now, not looking for work. . .	1,395	479	705	211	726	669
Reason for not currently looking for work:						
Discouraged over job prospects [3]	369	110	199	61	226	143
Family responsibilities	160	31	109	21	37	123
In school or training	180	149	27	3	102	78
Ill health or disability.	114	11	66	37	57	58
Other [4].	572	178	304	90	305	267

[1] Includes some persons who are not asked if they want a job. [2] Persons who had a job in the prior 12 months must have searched since the end of that job. [3] Includes such things as believes no work available, could not find work, lacks necessary schooling or training, employer thinks too young or old, and other types of discrimination. [4] Includes such things as child care and transportation problems.

Source: U.S. Bureau of Labor Statistics, "Employment and Earnings Online," January 2008 issue. See Internet site <http://www.bls.gov/opub/ee/home.htm> and <http://www.bls.gov/cps/home.htm>.

U.S. Census Bureau, Statistical Abstract of the United States: 2009

Table 596. Employed Civilians by Occupation, Sex, Race, and Hispanic Origin: 2007

[146,047 represents 146,047,000. Civilian noninstitutional population 16 years old and over. Annual average of monthly figures. Based on Current Population Survey; see text, Section 1, and Appendix III. Occupational classifications are those used in the 2000 census and are not comparable to those used in the 1990 census]

Occupation	Total employed (1,000)	Percent of total			
		Female	Black [1]	Asian [1]	Hispanic [2]
Total, 16 years and over	**146,047**	**46.4**	**11.0**	**4.7**	**14.0**
Management, professional and related occupations	**51,788**	**50.6**	**8.4**	**6.4**	**7.0**
Management, business, and financial operations occupations	21,577	42.7	7.5	5.0	7.3
Management occupations [3]	15,486	37.5	6.3	4.5	7.4
Chief executives	1,649	25.6	3.5	4.3	5.0
General and operations managers.	971	27.5	4.6	3.6	7.9
Advertising and promotions managers	77	56.2	5.6	3.0	3.1
Marketing and sales managers	848	38.8	5.1	3.5	5.8
Administrative services managers	98	32.7	8.6	4.2	2.9
Computer and information systems managers	467	27.8	7.7	8.5	3.4
Financial managers	1,181	54.6	7.1	6.7	8.0
Human resources managers	253	70.3	11.6	3.3	7.1
Industrial production managers	264	16.7	4.7	3.7	9.8
Purchasing managers	168	40.3	8.5	4.8	6.4
Transportation, storage, and distribution managers	260	17.2	10.0	1.8	13.6
Farm, ranch, and other agricultural managers	204	22.5	0.6	1.1	5.3
Farmers and ranchers.	742	25.5	1.1	0.5	2.3
Construction managers	1,176	8.1	2.6	1.5	9.2
Education administrators	810	64.1	12.6	1.0	7.4
Engineering managers	114	8.0	2.8	8.1	1.5
Food service managers	1,002	44.3	7.2	9.9	14.3
Lodging managers	151	50.6	7.4	13.4	7.7
Medical and health services managers.	536	69.9	11.3	5.1	7.4
Property, real estate, and community association managers.	594	50.5	7.1	4.7	9.5
Social and community service managers	331	65.8	13.5	4.0	8.6
Business and financial operations occupations [3]	6,091	55.9	10.5	6.4	7.2
Wholesale and retail buyers, except farm products	200	51.5	7.2	5.1	7.9
Purchasing agents, except wholesale, retail, and farm products . . .	280	55.5	8.2	3.9	6.9
Claims adjusters, appraisers, examiners, and investigators	289	61.8	17.3	3.1	7.8
Compliance officers, except agriculture, construction, health and safety, and transportation	139	50.6	8.9	4.5	8.0
Cost estimators	115	15.4	0.2	4.6	5.1
Human resources, training, and labor relations specialists	793	71.1	14.2	3.6	7.5
Management analysts	627	44.3	5.4	6.5	6.4
Accountants and auditors	1,806	61.9	10.5	9.1	5.9
Appraisers and assessors of real estate	118	25.8	4.9	5.1	5.4
Financial analysts.	109	34.3	4.0	14.7	5.8
Personal financial advisors.	373	31.7	7.6	6.0	6.5
Insurance underwriters	94	71.2	14.3	6.1	2.5
Loan counselors and officers	467	52.7	14.4	4.2	13.1
Tax preparers	104	62.2	13.6	5.8	10.1
Professional and related occupations	30,210	56.2	9.0	7.3	6.8
Computer and mathematical occupations [3]	3,441	25.6	7.2	17.8	5.2
Computer scientists and systems analysts	825	27.1	8.8	15.5	5.6
Computer programmers.	526	24.7	5.2	19.6	6.2
Computer software engineers.	907	20.8	4.9	29.4	2.8
Computer support specialists	332	30.0	11.2	8.8	6.0
Database administrators	104	35.9	5.8	16.2	3.8
Network and computer systems administrators	214	14.7	7.9	10.1	7.8
Network systems and data communications analysts	383	26.3	7.4	9.1	6.9
Operations research analysts	87	47.5	13.1	5.3	7.8
Architecture and engineering occupations [3]	2,932	14.4	5.3	9.7	6.4
Architects, except naval.	240	24.7	4.4	8.6	7.0
Aerospace engineers	123	10.5	6.6	13.4	3.1
Civil engineers.	382	11.5	2.9	8.8	6.1
Computer hardware engineers	79	9.6	5.6	22.8	4.9
Electrical and electronics engineers.	347	8.6	6.9	13.5	4.1
Industrial engineers, including health and safety	161	17.5	4.4	8.0	3.0
Mechanical engineers	296	7.3	4.2	12.1	3.8
Drafters	187	20.6	5.3	4.1	8.8
Engineering technicians, except drafters.	420	22.4	8.3	5.9	11.2
Surveying and mapping technicians	92	10.5	5.0	1.2	5.8
Life, physical, and social science occupations [3]	1,382	42.7	5.8	12.9	4.6
Biological scientists.	92	42.6	2.0	13.5	1.7
Medical scientists.	152	49.1	7.4	31.9	2.8
Chemists and materials scientists	118	40.8	6.8	18.3	5.1
Environmental scientists and geoscientists	98	29.9	5.4	3.9	0.3
Market and survey researchers.	159	56.8	5.2	9.9	5.1
Psychologists	185	64.4	7.0	4.6	3.5
Chemical technicians	62	32.4	7.4	6.0	14.5
Community and social services occupations [3]	2,265	60.7	18.4	3.2	9.5
Counselors	686	65.9	18.6	2.9	8.3
Social workers.	673	82.0	22.9	3.2	11.9
Miscellaneous community and social service specialists	317	63.2	23.8	3.0	14.6
Clergy	422	15.1	11.1	3.5	5.0

See footnotes at end of table.

U.S. Census Bureau, Statistical Abstract of the United States: 2009

Table 596. **Employed Civilians by Occupation, Sex, Race, and Hispanic Origin: 2007**—Con.

[**146,047 represents 146,047,000.** Civilian noninstitutional population 16 years old and over. Annual average of monthly figures. Based on Current Population Survey; see text, Section 1, and Appendix III. Occupational classifications are those used in the 2000 census and are not comparable to those used in the 1990 census]

Occupation	Total employed (1,000)	Percent of total			
		Female	Black [1]	Asian [1]	Hispanic [2]
Legal occupations	1,668	51.5	6.7	2.8	6.0
Lawyers	1,001	32.6	4.9	2.6	4.3
Paralegals and legal assistants	347	88.4	9.7	3.4	9.0
Miscellaneous legal support workers	253	77.5	8.7	3.6	8.1
Education, training, and library occupations [3]	8,485	73.3	9.6	3.7	7.6
Postsecondary teachers	1,261	46.2	5.6	11.7	4.2
Preschool and kindergarten teachers	667	97.3	14.3	3.0	10.4
Elementary and middle school teachers	2,943	80.9	10.3	1.6	6.9
Secondary school teachers	1,158	56.9	7.1	1.4	7.0
Special education teachers	363	81.5	8.7	1.4	4.5
Other teachers and instructors	732	63.8	10.4	5.6	6.7
Librarians	215	83.2	6.0	2.0	4.1
Teacher assistants	974	91.5	12.8	2.2	15.8
Arts, design, entertainment, sports, and media occupations [3]	2,789	47.1	5.7	3.9	8.7
Artists and related workers	227	52.9	2.6	3.9	5.2
Designers	852	54.7	4.0	5.6	8.5
Producers and directors	149	30.5	4.7	1.9	7.4
Athletes, coaches, umpires, and related workers	253	36.3	8.2	1.4	7.6
Musicians, singers, and related workers	170	31.5	9.5	2.0	13.2
News analysts, reporters and correspondents	84	42.1	6.4	2.7	6.8
Public relations specialists	132	63.3	5.5	4.3	7.2
Editors	163	49.5	5.8	3.7	6.3
Writers and authors	179	59.5	2.6	4.1	3.2
Broadcast and sound engineering technicians and radio operators	89	11.6	9.1	4.3	9.3
Photographers	173	47.5	5.7	1.9	10.3
Healthcare practitioner and technical occupations [3]	7,248	73.6	10.2	8.2	5.6
Dentists	184	28.2	5.4	10.9	3.4
Dietitians and nutritionists	100	87.6	15.8	9.3	5.3
Pharmacists	247	53.3	5.9	16.6	2.5
Physicians and surgeons	888	30.0	5.6	16.9	5.2
Physician assistants	87	70.1	7.2	5.6	8.2
Registered nurses	2,629	91.7	9.9	7.9	4.6
Occupational therapists	79	85.6	1.4	3.4	6.7
Physical therapists	212	68.2	3.5	12.0	5.3
Respiratory therapists	97	66.9	11.0	3.2	8.9
Speech-language pathologists	122	98.0	6.3	1.8	4.5
Clinical laboratory technologists and technicians	332	75.9	18.3	10.4	5.0
Dental hygienists	156	99.2	1.4	3.8	5.4
Diagnostic-related technologists and technicians	287	69.2	8.0	3.3	8.4
Emergency medical technicians and paramedics	162	26.5	8.6	0.7	7.0
Health diagnosing and treating practitioner support technicians	462	78.0	14.0	6.0	8.8
Licensed practical and licensed vocational nurses	533	93.2	22.4	3.9	5.8
Medical records and health information technicians	83	93.0	17.9	3.7	15.8
Service occupations	**24,137**	**57.2**	**15.5**	**4.5**	**20.3**
Healthcare support occupations [3]	3,138	89.2	24.0	3.9	14.0
Nursing, psychiatric, and home health aides	1,879	88.3	33.6	4.2	13.8
Massage therapists	134	89.1	2.7	5.1	6.9
Dental assistants	275	96.3	6.8	1.2	16.7
Protective service occupations [3]	3,071	22.5	18.9	2.1	10.0
First-line supervisors/managers of police and detectives	116	14.5	11.2	0.8	10.6
Firefighters	288	5.3	10.0	0.9	6.2
Bailiffs, correctional officers, and jailers	444	29.5	23.9	0.4	7.3
Detectives and criminal investigators	135	23.2	14.9	3.0	11.2
Police and sheriff's patrol officers	669	13.7	12.7	2.6	9.1
Private detectives and investigators	86	31.1	7.9	2.8	9.7
Security guards and gaming surveillance officers	891	23.2	28.3	3.3	12.4
Food preparation and serving related occupations	7,699	56.4	11.5	5.5	21.2
Chefs and head cooks	345	20.6	12.2	13.6	19.5
First-line supervisors/managers of food preparation and serving workers	610	57.3	13.9	2.9	16.3
Cooks	1,939	40.1	15.4	6.0	31.0
Food preparation workers	681	61.2	12.2	5.3	23.4
Bartenders	375	54.0	3.3	3.1	10.9
Combined food preparation and serving workers, including fast food	302	70.1	12.4	4.2	12.6
Counter attendants, cafeteria, food concession, and coffee shop	323	64.5	10.6	3.7	14.7
Waiters and waitresses	1,978	74.0	7.7	5.6	15.3
Food servers, nonrestaurant	182	73.4	20.9	6.4	16.9
Dining room and cafeteria attendants and bartender helpers	392	48.9	10.9	5.5	27.9
Dishwashers	281	24.8	11.8	4.4	36.6
Hosts and hostesses, restaurant, lounge, and coffee shop	284	85.8	9.8	5.7	11.9
Building and grounds cleaning and maintenance occupations	5,469	40.0	15.2	2.8	34.3
First-line supervisors/managers of housekeeping and janitorial workers	319	34.1	19.2	2.6	21.2
First-line supervisors/managers of landscaping, lawn service, and groundskeeping workers	234	5.9	4.3	2.0	19.3
Janitors and building cleaners	2,080	34.2	19.2	3.2	28.0
Maids and housekeeping cleaners	1,427	89.2	17.6	3.3	40.4
Pest control workers	77	4.0	12.9	5.3	14.2
Grounds maintenance workers	1,332	5.9	7.5	1.7	44.4

See footnotes at end of table.

U.S. Census Bureau, Statistical Abstract of the United States: 2009

Table 596. Employed Civilians by Occupation, Sex, Race, and Hispanic Origin: 2007—Con.

[**146,047 represents 146,047,000.** Civilian noninstitutional population 16 years old and over. Annual average of monthly figures. Based on Current Population Survey; see text, Section 1, and Appendix III. Occupational classifications are those used in the 2000 census and are not comparable to those used in the 1990 census]

Occupation	Total employed (1,000)	Percent of total			
		Female	Black [1]	Asian [1]	Hispanic [2]
Personal care and service occupations [3]	4,760	79.3	14.3	6.9	13.6
First-line supervisors/managers of gaming workers	139	43.2	10.0	3.9	6.2
First-line supervisors/managers of personal service workers	157	71.3	9.3	11.7	5.5
Nonfarm animal caretakers	140	78.0	1.7	1.0	13.4
Gaming services workers	111	50.3	9.8	23.8	7.8
Barbers	102	26.1	27.3	2.4	22.6
Hairdressers, hairstylists, and cosmetologists	778	92.9	11.1	5.5	12.5
Miscellaneous personal appearance workers	223	84.9	5.9	49.1	6.8
Baggage porters, bellhops, and concierges	60	16.7	20.3	10.0	26.7
Transportation attendants	148	75.9	18.5	7.7	9.8
Child care workers	1,341	94.6	16.0	2.7	16.8
Personal and home care aides	766	88.2	22.5	6.2	18.8
Recreation and fitness workers	331	61.7	7.8	1.8	6.9
Sales and office occupations	**36,212**	**63.4**	**11.6**	**4.1**	**11.9**
Sales and related occupations [3]	16,698	49.6	9.9	4.7	11.3
First-line supervisors/managers of retail sales workers	3,445	42.6	8.0	5.3	9.6
First-line supervisors/managers of nonretail sales workers	1,333	28.2	7.2	5.8	8.8
Cashiers	3,022	75.6	17.4	5.8	17.0
Counter and rental clerks	158	53.4	15.9	3.1	11.0
Parts salespersons	132	17.4	7.9	0.3	11.9
Retail salespersons	3,492	51.5	10.9	4.1	12.2
Advertising sales agents	219	57.5	7.2	1.4	7.7
Insurance sales agents	538	45.4	7.7	3.1	8.2
Securities, commodities, and financial services sales agents	398	31.2	7.4	7.3	8.3
Travel agents	111	75.3	7.7	9.6	9.1
Sales representatives, services, all other	590	36.2	8.5	3.3	8.4
Sales representatives, wholesale and manufacturing	1,442	27.1	4.2	3.4	8.4
Models, demonstrators, and product promoters	75	83.4	2.1	3.7	8.1
Real estate brokers and sales agents	1,050	55.4	5.3	5.0	10.1
Telemarketers	160	60.2	19.5	1.2	13.4
Door-to-door sales workers, news and street vendors, and related workers	265	66.7	10.5	3.9	17.5
Office and administrative support occupations [3]	19,513	75.2	13.0	3.7	12.4
First-line supervisors/managers of office and administrative support workers	1,629	73.4	9.5	3.9	11.3
Bill and account collectors	216	63.2	24.3	2.1	14.4
Billing and posting clerks and machine operators	442	89.5	14.9	4.4	11.6
Bookkeeping, accounting, and auditing clerks	1,490	90.3	7.3	3.8	9.5
Payroll and timekeeping clerks	181	89.1	8.8	4.7	12.2
Tellers	472	87.5	10.5	4.9	13.3
Court, municipal, and license clerks	99	80.7	11.7	5.3	11.1
Customer service representatives	1,917	68.5	18.0	3.6	14.1
File clerks	403	82.0	17.9	3.8	13.1
Hotel, motel, and resort desk clerks	118	68.1	13.7	3.6	16.2
Interviewers, except eligibility and loan	141	81.5	17.6	3.6	13.3
Library assistants, clerical	113	84.2	8.7	10.4	12.6
Loan interviewers and clerks	155	80.4	7.7	4.1	14.6
Order clerks	102	70.1	14.9	4.1	12.5
Receptionists and information clerks	1,441	93.0	11.3	2.7	14.3
Reservation and transportation ticket agents and travel clerks	144	59.1	15.3	3.3	15.3
Couriers and messengers	254	15.1	15.9	4.7	11.1
Dispatchers	286	55.1	11.6	1.0	12.0
Postal service clerks	172	53.0	24.8	9.1	10.4
Postal service mail carriers	364	36.9	15.9	6.1	7.5
Postal service mail sorters, processors, and processing machine operators	84	43.3	37.0	12.2	6.5
Production, planning, and expediting clerks	258	54.3	6.5	2.6	10.2
Shipping, receiving, and traffic clerks	539	33.4	11.6	2.8	23.0
Stock clerks and order fillers	1,512	35.5	17.4	3.6	17.3
Weighers, measurers, checkers, and samplers, recordkeeping	68	48.7	14.0	0.9	19.9
Secretaries and administrative assistants	3,401	96.7	9.0	2.2	9.3
Computer operators	160	51.1	15.0	4.8	11.3
Data entry keyers	449	78.6	16.5	7.3	10.7
Word processors and typists	214	89.6	19.6	3.0	11.8
Insurance claims and policy processing clerks	283	87.0	15.4	1.7	13.8
Mail clerks and mail machine operators, except postal service	123	48.6	25.7	5.2	11.6
Office clerks, general	1,097	85.3	14.0	5.5	13.8
Natural resources, construction, and maintenance occupations	**15,740**	**4.2**	**7.1**	**1.9**	**25.2**
Farming, fishing, and forestry occupations [3]	960	20.9	4.9	1.7	40.4
Logging workers	88	1.5	7.7	0.2	15.1
Construction and extraction occupations [3]	9,535	2.7	6.7	1.2	29.9
First-line supervisors/managers of construction trades and extraction workers	918	3.2	3.8	0.7	15.9
Brickmasons, blockmasons, and stonemasons	233	1.2	9.1	0.7	37.2
Carpenters	1,824	1.9	5.6	1.8	26.9

See footnotes at end of table.

U.S. Census Bureau, Statistical Abstract of the United States: 2009

[**146,047 represents 146,047,000.** Civilian noninstitutional population 16 years old and over. Annual average of monthly figures. Based on Current Population Survey; see text, Section 1, and Appendix III. Occupational classifications are those used in the 2000 census and are not comparable to those used in the 1990 census]

Occupation	Total employed (1,000)	Percent of total			
		Female	Black [1]	Asian [1]	Hispanic [2]
Carpet, floor, and tile installers and finishers	258	2.1	5.1	1.1	43.3
Cement masons, concrete finishers, and terrazzo workers	112	2.2	12.9	0.4	52.1
Construction laborers	1,771	2.7	8.6	1.7	44.6
Operating engineers and other construction equipment operators	411	2.7	7.4	0.4	15.1
Drywall installers, ceiling tile installers, and tapers	232	3.6	3.5	0.2	53.6
Electricians	912	1.7	5.9	1.2	14.3
Painters, construction and maintenance	714	6.9	5.6	1.5	41.0
Pipelayers, plumbers, pipefitters, and steamfitters	697	1.5	8.3	1.0	23.0
Roofers	269	0.9	4.9	0.1	45.1
Sheet metal workers	143	3.7	4.8	2.2	15.9
Helpers, construction trades	117	4.2	14.0	0.4	39.2
Construction and building inspectors	107	10.0	7.8	4.1	8.0
Highway maintenance workers	109	0.5	14.4	(S)	19.5
Installation, maintenance, and repair occupations [3]	5,245	3.9	8.3	3.1	13.8
First-line supervisors/managers of mechanics, installers, and repairers	330	5.4	6.4	1.5	11.4
Computer, automated teller, and office machine repairers	318	10.6	12.8	9.8	10.2
Radio and telecommunications equipment installers and repairers	203	14.8	12.2	3.9	10.9
Aircraft mechanics and service technicians	126	2.1	7.8	2.8	11.7
Automotive body and related repairers	155	1.6	5.0	4.4	24.9
Automotive service technicians and mechanics	879	0.7	7.9	3.6	17.7
Bus and truck mechanics and diesel engine specialists	365	1.1	7.6	1.7	12.7
Heavy vehicle and mobile equipment service technicians and mechanics	226	1.3	5.6	1.2	12.2
Heating, air conditioning, and refrigeration mechanics and installers	403	0.9	6.3	2.2	13.7
Industrial and refractory machinery mechanics	426	3.2	8.3	2.6	11.4
Maintenance and repair workers, general	488	3.1	10.5	3.6	14.6
Electrical power-line installers and repairers	103	1.4	6.0	0.3	6.3
Telecommunications line installers and repairers	227	7.5	13.5	1.1	14.9
Production, transportation, and material occupations	**18,171**	**23.0**	**14.6**	**3.6**	**19.7**
Production occupations [3]	9,395	30.1	12.6	4.8	20.4
First-line supervisors/managers of production and operating workers	941	19.4	11.6	4.8	10.2
Electrical, electronics, and electromechanical assemblers	205	57.9	13.1	16.7	20.0
Bakers	192	54.1	6.8	5.7	24.5
Butchers and other meat, poultry, and fish processing workers	281	26.8	13.1	4.0	41.1
Food batchmakers	92	58.0	12.5	2.2	32.4
Cutting, punching, and press machine setters, operators, and tenders, metal and plastic	118	21.6	9.4	0.8	22.0
Machinists	422	5.2	5.0	5.2	13.9
Tool and die makers	80	2.0	(S)	1.3	5.7
Welding, soldering, and brazing workers	577	5.6	7.3	2.8	20.3
Printing machine operators	222	17.2	11.7	4.6	16.2
Laundry and dry-cleaning workers	229	56.4	21.0	7.6	30.9
Sewing machine operators	265	81.6	12.8	14.4	35.5
Tailors, dressmakers, and sewers	90	75.3	5.9	18.5	29.0
Cabinetmakers and bench carpenters	91	6.5	4.4	3.6	19.3
Stationary engineers and boiler operators	95	1.3	15.5	1.8	9.2
Water and liquid waste treatment plant and system operators	72	6.2	16.4	(S)	6.6
Crushing, grinding, polishing, mixing, and blending workers	118	12.5	15.7	4.8	19.4
Cutting workers	94	24.4	10.1	3.0	26.9
Inspectors, testers, sorters, samplers, and weighers	737	39.5	13.5	5.0	14.7
Medical, dental, and ophthalmic laboratory technicians	107	44.0	7.7	7.1	13.9
Packaging and filling machine operators and tenders	279	57.1	22.2	3.9	36.7
Painting workers	193	11.0	9.3	0.6	29.0
Transportation and material-moving occupations [3]	8,776	15.4	16.8	2.3	19.0
Supervisors, transportation and material-moving workers	225	20.3	15.1	2.7	10.3
Aircraft pilots and flight engineers	123	4.2	0.5	3.0	2.0
Bus drivers	578	51.6	26.8	1.1	11.3
Driver/sales workers and truck drivers	3,460	5.3	13.8	1.4	17.5
Taxi drivers and chauffeurs	333	15.4	24.3	12.8	18.8
Service station attendants	90	7.0	8.2	8.7	15.8
Industrial truck and tractor operators	571	5.9	23.0	1.5	23.8
Cleaners of vehicles and equipment	326	13.0	19.1	1.3	30.0
Laborers and freight, stock, and material movers, hand	1,877	18.6	17.9	1.9	20.1
Packers and packagers, hand	406	64.4	15.6	4.7	41.2
Refuse and recyclable material collectors	79	6.4	23.8	0.7	24.1

S Data does not meet publication standards   [1] The Current Population Survey (CPS) allows respondents to choose more than one race. Data represent persons who selected this race group only and exclude persons reporting more than one race. See also comments on race in the text for Section 1.   [2] Persons of Hispanic or Latino ethnicity may be any race.   [3] Includes other occupations not shown separately.

Source: U.S. Bureau of Labor Statistics, "Employment and Earnings Online," January 2008 issue. See Internet site <http://www.bls.gov/opub/ee/home.htm> and <http://www.bls.gov/cps/home.htm>.

Table 597. Employed Civilians by Occupation—States: 2007

[In thousands (146,047 represents 146,047,000). Occupation classifications are those used in the 2000 Census and are not comparable to those in other tables using 1990 Census classifications. Based on the Current Population Survey and subject to sampling error; see text, Section 1, and Appendix III]

State		Management, professional, and related occupations			Sales and office occupations		Natural resources, construction, and maintenance occupations			Production, transportation, and material-moving occupations	
	Total	Management, business, and financial operations	Professional and related occupations	Service occupations	Sales and related occupations	Office and administrative support occupations	Farming, fishing, and forestry occupations	Construction and extraction occupations	Installation, maintenance, and repair occupations	Production occupations	Transportation and material-moving occupations
Total...	146,047	21,577	30,210	24,137	16,698	19,513	960	9,535	5,245	9,395	8,776
AL......	2,113	266	378	352	235	272	14	150	92	230	125
AK......	326	47	68	54	32	49	4	25	14	11	22
AZ......	2,930	458	545	474	383	437	15	253	107	120	137
AR......	1,299	163	243	195	143	170	20	90	54	119	101
CA......	17,234	2,695	3,608	2,817	2,084	2,223	215	1,174	547	919	952
CO......	2,580	462	571	367	327	326	15	191	81	121	120
CT......	1,804	305	430	312	192	220	3	97	50	114	80
DE......	430	62	90	74	50	63	2	26	18	21	22
DC......	300	65	106	49	22	36	(Z)	8	3	3	9
FL......	8,861	1,303	1,642	1,613	1,168	1,226	33	679	337	348	510
GA......	4,659	680	932	696	575	623	16	309	200	311	319
HI......	628	84	114	150	76	79	7	43	23	18	35
ID......	742	112	141	116	82	94	18	60	27	43	48
IL......	6,378	961	1,283	1,023	731	894	15	335	222	486	429
IN......	3,059	409	575	478	309	401	14	186	131	333	224
IA......	1,611	224	312	259	175	218	17	86	57	140	125
KS......	1,434	227	297	232	155	194	8	82	53	111	76
KY......	1,932	229	385	303	211	264	18	116	84	167	155
LA......	1,917	251	396	323	216	270	7	150	59	119	127
ME......	673	84	135	119	74	92	13	46	27	45	39
MD......	2,871	542	743	429	270	387	8	168	99	98	127
MA......	3,253	545	907	510	366	376	8	165	81	145	151
MI......	4,667	664	979	796	515	640	15	209	177	419	252
MN......	2,772	473	611	438	314	358	15	150	77	206	132
MS......	1,239	146	218	190	113	166	14	115	50	132	94
MO.....	2,910	405	535	472	344	427	16	160	121	219	210
MT......	492	80	94	79	56	69	6	43	17	20	27
NE......	958	161	190	137	114	137	12	48	30	70	59
NV......	1,284	176	186	305	162	178	3	111	46	42	77
NH......	719	124	169	99	83	90	3	48	25	42	34
NJ......	4,325	739	1000	716	496	604	6	208	140	182	233
NM......	916	129	203	163	98	127	7	69	35	32	54
NY......	9,020	1,244	2,067	1,761	1,010	1,178	12	547	276	408	515
NC......	4,290	611	917	675	500	517	28	307	167	324	243
ND......	356	58	68	61	39	45	10	23	11	20	22
OH......	5,700	784	1,144	977	574	754	24	294	195	548	405
OK......	1,653	250	309	273	177	232	11	108	76	108	108
OR......	1,843	293	381	307	195	228	37	113	50	131	106
PA......	6,065	819	1,346	1,000	636	849	32	318	240	417	406
RI......	550	74	127	102	60	74	2	29	15	42	25
SC......	2,029	236	379	352	248	257	22	130	91	191	123
SD......	429	77	76	66	45	61	9	24	14	32	25
TN......	2,921	379	518	465	327	388	15	238	109	276	203
TX......	11,047	1,521	2,086	1,816	1,281	1,536	72	922	434	662	715
UT......	1,309	182	251	166	167	206	5	116	50	89	76
VT......	341	50	87	55	33	42	3	24	11	21	15
VA......	3,916	714	873	582	426	485	22	284	130	185	215
WA.....	3,270	502	731	497	358	415	53	191	133	195	195
WV.....	782	79	159	132	92	100	3	79	31	43	64
WI.....	2,930	395	555	463	335	403	27	153	113	301	185
WY.....	280	39	50	44	25	33	5	32	15	15	23

Z Less than 500.

Source: U.S. Bureau of Labor Statistics, Local Area Unemployment Statistics, *Geographic Profile of Employment and Unemployment, 2007*. See Internet site <http://www.bls.gov/gps/>.

Table 598. Employment Projections by Occupation: 2006 and 2016

[In thousands (262 represents 262,000), except percent and rank. Estimates based on the Current Employment Statistics Program; the Occupational Employment Statistics Survey; and the Current Population Survey. See source for methodological assumptions. Occupations based on the 2000 Standard Occupational Classification system]

Occupation	Employment (1,000)		Change 2006–2016		Quartile rank by 2006 median annual earnngs [1]	Most significant source of postsecondary education or training
	2006	2016	Number (1,000)	Percent		
FASTEST GROWING						
Network systems and data communications analysts	262	402	140	53.4	VH	Bachelor's degree
Personal and home care aides	767	1,156	389	50.6	VL	Short-term on-the-job training
Home health aides	787	1,171	384	48.7	VL	Short-term on-the-job training
Computer software engineers, applications	507	733	226	44.6	VH	Bachelor's degree
Veterinary technologists and technicians	71	100	29	41.0	L	Associate's degree
Personal financial advisors	176	248	72	41.0	VH	Bachelor's degree
Makeup artists, theatrical and performance	2	3	1	39.8	H	Postsecondary
Medical assistants	417	565	148	35.4	L	Moderate-term on-the-job training
Veterinarians	62	84	22	35.0	VH	First professional degree
Substance abuse and behavioral disorder counselors	83	112	29	34.3	H	Bachelor's degree
Skin care specialists	38	51	13	34.3	L	Postsecondary vocational award
Financial analysts	221	295	75	33.8	VH	Bachelor's degree
Social and human service assistants	339	453	114	33.6	L	Moderate-term on-the-job training
Gaming surveillance officers and gaming investigators	9	12	3	33.6	L	Moderate-term on-the-job training
Physical therapist assistants	60	80	20	32.4	H	Associate's degree
Pharmacy technicians	285	376	91	32.0	L	Moderate-term on-the-job training
Forensic science technicians	13	17	4	30.7	H	Bachelor's degree
Dental hygienists	167	217	50	30.1	VH	Associate's degree
Mental health counselors	100	130	30	30.0	H	Master's degree
Mental health and substance abuse social workers	122	159	37	29.9	H	Master's degree
Marriage and family therapists	25	32	7	29.8	H	Master's degree
Dental assistants	280	362	82	29.2	L	Moderate-term on-the-job training
Computer systems analysts	504	650	146	29.0	VH	Bachelor's degree
Database administrators	119	154	34	28.6	VH	Bachelor's degree
Computer software engineers, systems software	350	449	99	28.2	VH	Bachelor's degree
Gaming and sports book writers and runners	18	24	5	28.0	VL	Short-term on-the-job training
Environmental science and protection technicians, including health	36	47	10	28.0	H	Associate's degree
Manicurists and pedicurists	78	100	22	27.6	VL	Postsecondary vocational award
Physical therapists	173	220	47	27.1	VH	Master's degree
Physician assistants	66	83	18	27.0	VH	Master's degree
LARGEST JOB GROWTH						
Registered nurses	2,505	3,092	587	23.5	VH	Associate's degree
Retail salespersons	4,477	5,034	557	12.4	VL	Short-term on-the-job training
Customer service representatives	2,202	2,747	545	24.8	L	Moderate-term on-the-job training
Combined food preparation and serving workers, including fast food	2,503	2,955	452	18.1	VL	Short-term on-the-job training
Office clerks, general	3,200	3,604	404	12.6	L	Short-term on-the-job training
Personal and home care aides	767	1,156	389	50.6	VL	Short-term on-the-job training
Home health aides	787	1,171	384	48.7	VL	Short-term on-the-job training
Postsecondary teachers	1,672	2,054	382	22.9	VH	Doctoral degree
Janitors and cleaners, except maids and housekeeping cleaners	2,387	2,732	345	14.5	VL	Short-term on-the-job training
Nursing aides, orderlies, and attendants	1,447	1,711	264	18.2	L	Postsecondary vocational award
Bookkeeping, accounting, and auditing clerks	2,114	2,377	264	12.5	L	Moderate-term on-the-job training
Waiters and waitresses	2,361	2,615	255	10.8	VL	Short-term on-the-job training
Child care workers	1,388	1,636	248	17.8	VL	Short-term on-the-job training
Executive secretaries and administrative assistants	1,618	1,857	239	14.8	H	Work experience in a related occupation
Computer software engineers, applications	507	733	226	44.6	VH	Bachelor's degree
Accountants and auditors	1,274	1,500	226	17.7	VH	Bachelor's degree
Landscaping and groundskeeping workers	1,220	1,441	221	18.1	L	Short-term on-the-job training
Elementary school teachers except special education	1,540	1,749	209	13.6	H	Bachelor's degree
Receptionsts and information clerks	1,173	1,375	202	17.2	L	Short-term on-the-job training
Truck drivers, heavy and tractor-trailer	1,860	2,053	193	10.4	H	Moderate-term on-the-job training
Maids and housekeeping cleaners	1,470	1,656	186	12.7	VL	Short-term on-the-job training
Security guards	1,040	1,216	175	16.9	L	Short-term on-the-job training
Carpenters	1,462	1,612	150	10.3	H	Long-term on-the-job training
Management analysts	678	827	149	21.9	VH	Bachelor's or higher degree, plus work experience
Medical assistants	417	565	148	35.4	L	Moderate-term on-the-job training
Computer systems analysts	504	650	146	29.0	VH	Bachelor's degree
Maintenance and repair workers, general	1,391	1,531	140	10.1	H	Moderate-term on-the-job training
Network systems and data communications analysts	262	402	140	53.4	VH	Bachelor's degree
Food preparation worker	902	1,040	138	15.3	VL	Short-term on-the-job training
Teacher assistants	1,312	1,449	137	10.4	VL	Short-term on-the-job training

[1] Quartile ranks based on the Occupational Employment Statistics annual earnings. VH = very high ($46,360 and over), H = high ($30,630 to $46,300), L = low ($21,260 to $30,560), and VL = very low (up to $21,220). The rankings were based on quartiles using one-fourth of total employment to define each quartile. Earnings are for wage and salary workers.

Source: U.S. Bureau of Labor Statistics "Occupational employment projections to 2016", *Monthly Labor Review,* November 2007. See Internet site <http://www.bls.gov/emp/home.htm>.

U.S. Census Bureau, Statistical Abstract of the United States: 2009

Table 599. Occupations of the Employed by Selected Characteristic: 2007

[In thousands (126,172 represents 126,172,000). **Annual averages of monthly figures.** Civilian noninstitutional population 25 years old and over. Based on Current Population Survey; see text, Section 1, and Appendix III. See headnote Table, 585, regarding occupations]

Sex, race, and educational attainment	Total employed	Managerial, professional, and related	Service	Sales and office	Natural resources, construction, and maintenance	Production, transportation, and material moving
Total [1]	**126,172**	**48,666**	**18,353**	**29,704**	**13,544**	**15,905**
Less than a high school diploma	11,521	734	3,376	1,504	2,892	3,015
High school graduates, no college	36,857	5,704	7,277	10,178	5,918	7,781
Less than a bachelor's degree	34,612	11,126	5,314	10,670	3,701	3,801
College graduates	43,182	31,103	2,385	7,352	1,033	1,308
White [2]	103,477	40,630	13,805	24,542	11,897	12,604
Less than a high school diploma	9,446	614	2,543	1,218	2,596	2,476
High school graduates, no college	30,140	4,921	5,298	8,545	5,235	6,141
Less than a bachelor's degree	28,355	9,362	4,082	8,756	3,185	2,970
College graduates	35,535	25,733	1,882	6,022	881	1,016
Black [2]	13,811	4,089	3,110	3,267	1,008	2,338
Less than a high school diploma	1,293	66	542	172	172	341
High school graduates, no college	4,783	533	1,439	1,143	451	1,216
Less than a bachelor's degree	4,300	1,187	869	1,316	309	619
College graduates	3,435	2,302	260	635	76	161
Asian [2]	6,200	3,121	935	1,269	270	606
Less than a high school diploma	425	36	176	54	37	121
High school graduates, no college	1,136	141	352	309	76	257
Less than a bachelor's degree	1,048	320	208	312	98	110
College graduates	3,592	2,624	199	593	58	117
Hispanic [3]	16,973	3,294	3,978	3,254	3,318	3,129
Less than a high school diploma	5,677	181	1,763	534	1,727	1,473
High school graduates, no college	5,110	561	1,272	1,172	1,015	1,091
Less than a bachelor's degree	3,542	938	651	1,085	437	431
College graduates	2,644	1,614	293	463	139	135

[1] Includes other races not shown separately.　　[2] For persons in this race group only. See footnote 3, Table 568.　　[3] Persons of Hispanic or Latino ethnicity may be any race.

Source: U.S. Bureau of Labor Statistics, unpublished data.

Table 600. Employment by Industry: 2000 to 2007

[In thousands (136,891 represents 136,891,000), except percent. See headnote, Table 585]

Industry	2000	2005 [1]	2006 [1]	2007 [1]	2007, percent [1] Female	Black [2]	Asian [2]	Hispanic [3]
Total employed	**136,891**	**141,730**	**144,427**	**146,047**	**46.4**	**11.0**	**4.7**	**14.0**
Agriculture and related industries	2,464	2,197	2,206	2,095	23.4	2.5	1.4	20.3
Mining	475	624	687	736	13.8	4.3	1.9	13.4
Construction	9,931	11,197	11,749	11,856	9.4	5.7	1.5	25.3
Manufacturing	19,644	16,253	16,377	16,302	30.0	9.7	5.2	14.5
Durable goods	12,519	10,333	10,499	10,363	26.0	8.4	5.5	12.4
Nondurable goods	7,125	5,919	5,877	5,938	36.9	11.9	4.8	18.1
Wholesale trade	4,216	4,579	4,561	4,367	29.2	8.1	4.4	14.4
Retail trade	15,763	16,825	16,767	16,570	49.1	10.4	4.4	13.2
Transportation and utilities	7,380	7,360	7,455	7,650	24.6	17.3	3.8	13.5
Transportation and warehousing	6,096	6,184	6,269	6,457	25.1	18.4	4.0	14.4
Utilities	1,284	1,176	1,186	1,193	21.6	11.7	2.7	8.8
Information	4,059	3,402	3,573	3,566	42.1	11.9	5.0	9.5
Financial activities	9,374	10,203	10,490	10,488	55.4	10.1	5.4	10.4
Finance and insurance	6,641	7,035	7,254	7,306	58.5	10.6	5.8	9.3
Real estate and rental and leasing	2,734	3,168	3,237	3,182	48.1	9.0	4.4	13.0
Professional and business services	13,649	14,294	14,868	15,621	42.6	9.4	6.1	13.8
Professional and technical services	8,266	8,584	8,776	9,208	43.9	5.9	8.0	6.8
Management, administrative, and waste services	5,383	5,709	6,092	6,412	40.8	14.3	3.3	23.8
Education and health services	26,188	29,174	29,938	30,662	74.7	13.9	4.8	9.6
Educational services	11,255	12,264	12,522	12,828	69.1	10.6	3.8	8.7
Health care and social assistance	14,933	16,910	17,416	17,834	78.7	16.2	5.6	10.2
Hospitals	5,202	5,719	5,712	5,955	75.4	15.5	7.2	7.7
Health services, except hospitals	7,009	8,332	8,639	8,733	78.8	15.6	5.3	10.5
Social assistance	2,722	2,860	3,065	3,147	84.8	19.1	3.4	14.2
Leisure and hospitality	11,186	12,071	12,145	12,415	51.4	10.6	5.9	19.4
Arts, entertainment, and recreation	2,539	2,765	2,671	2,833	46.6	8.8	4.0	11.7
Accommodation and food services	8,647	9,306	9,474	9,582	52.8	11.2	6.5	21.7
Other services	6,450	7,020	7,088	6,972	52.0	10.4	5.8	16.2
Other services, except private households	5,731	6,208	6,285	6,159	47.0	10.2	6.1	13.7
Private households	718	812	803	813	90.7	11.9	3.3	34.8
Government workers	6,113	6,530	6,524	6,746	44.9	15.8	3.6	8.7

[1] See footnote 2, Table 567.　　[2] Persons in this race group only. See footnote 3, Table 568.　　[3] Persons of Hispanic or Latino origin may be any race.

Source: U.S. Bureau of Labor Statistics, "Employment and Earnings Online," January 2008 issue. See Internet site <http://www.bls.gov/opub/ee/home.htm> and <http://www.bls.gov/cps/home.htm>.

Table 601. **Employment Projections by Industry: 2006 to 2016**

[**9,382.9 represents 9,382,900**. Estimates based on the Current Employment Statistics program. See source for methodological assumptions. Minus sign (−) indicates decline]

Industry	2002 NAICS code [1]	Employment (1,000) 2006	Employment (1,000) 2016	Change, 2006–2016 (1,000)	Average annual rate of change 2006–2016
LARGEST GROWTH					
Food service and drinking places.	722	9,382.9	10,406.5	1,023.6	1.0
Offices of health practitioners	6211–6213	3,508.3	4,365.4	857.1	2.2
Construction	23	7,688.9	8,469.6	780.7	1.0
Management, scientific, and technical consulting services	5416	920.9	1,638.7	717.8	5.9
Individual and family services	6241	973.6	1,687.0	713.4	5.7
Hospitals, private	622	4,427.1	5,118.9	691.8	1.5
Employment services.	5613	3,656.6	4,348.1	691.5	1.7
Retail trade	44, 45	15,319.4	16,006.4	687.0	0.4
Residential care facilities	6232, 6233, 6239	1,316.7	1,829.2	512.5	3.3
Local government educational services.	(X)	7,938.5	8,450.1	511.6	0.6
Computer systems design and related services	5415	1,278.2	1,767.6	489.4	3.3
Home health care services	6216	867.1	1,347.6	480.5	4.5
Amusement, gambling, and recreation industries	713	1,404.4	1,876.8	472.4	2.9
Wholesale trade	42	5,897.7	6,326.2	428.5	0.7
Securities, commodity contracts, and other financial investments and related activities.	523	816.3	1,192.4	376.1	3.9
Services to buildings and dwellings	5617	1,797.0	2,160.8	363.8	1.9
Architectural, engineering, and related services	5413	1,385.6	1,731.0	345.4	2.3
MOST RAPID GROWTH					
Management, scientific, and technical consulting services	5416	920.9	1,638.7	717.8	5.9
Individual and family services	6241	973.6	1,687.0	713.4	5.7
Home health care services	6216	867.1	1,347.6	480.5	4.5
Securities, commodity contracts, and other financial investment and related activities	523	816.3	1,192.4	376.1	3.9
Facilities support services.	5612	122.8	179.1	56.3	3.8
Residential care facilities	6232, 6233, 6239	1,316.7	1,829.2	512.5	3.3
Independent artists, writers, and performers.	7115	46.8	64.8	18.0	3.3
Computer systems design and related services	5415	1,278.2	1,767.6	489.4	3.3
Museums, historical sites, and similar institutions	712	123.9	167.4	43.5	3.1
Child day care services	6244	806.7	1,078.4	271.7	2.9
Amusement, gambling, and recreation industries	713	1,404.4	1,876.8	472.4	2.9
Specialized design services	5414	135.8	179.3	43.5	2.8
Software publishers.	5112	243.4	321.3	77.9	2.8
Funds, trusts, and other financial vehicles	525	93.1	122.4	29.3	2.8
Other educational services	6114, 6117	534.2	702.5	168.3	2.8
Promoters of events, and agents and managers.	7114	100.0	131.3	31.3	2.8
Local government excluding enterprises, educational services, and hospitals	(X)	1,027.1	1,347.0	319.9	2.7
Other support services.	5619	305.4	399.0	93.6	2.7
Scenic and sightseeing transportation.	487	27.0	34.7	7.7	2.5
Lessors of nonfinancial intangible assets (except copyrighted works)	533	28.9	36.6	7.7	2.4
MOST RAPID DECLINE					
Cut-and-sew apparel manufacturing	3152	185.5	77.2	−108.3	−8.4
Footwear manufacturing.	3162	17.4	8.1	−9.3	−7.3
Federal enterprises except the postal service and electric utilities	(X)	45.1	26.5	−18.6	−5.2
Apparel knitting mills	3151	34.0	20.1	−13.9	−5.1
Textile and fabric finishing and fabric coating mills . . .	3133	57.6	34.4	−23.2	−5.0
Leather and hide tanning and finishing, and other leather and allied product manufacturing	3169	20.0	12.1	−7.9	−4.9
Apparel accessories and other apparel manufacturing	3159	18.9	12.4	−6.5	−4.1
Tobacco manufacturing	3122	23.4	15.5	−7.9	−4.0
Computer and peripheral equipment manufacturing. . .	3341	198.8	132.3	−66.5	−4.0
Iron and steel mills and ferroalloy manufacturing	3311	94.4	63.7	−30.7	−3.9
Pipeline transportation	486	39.0	26.4	−12.6	−3.8
Fabric mills	3132	89.9	61.2	−28.7	−3.8
Nonferrous metal (except aluminum) production and processing	3314	73.0	50.3	−22.7	−3.7
Pulp, paper, and paperboard mills	3221	136.0	93.8	−42.2	−3.6
Hardware manufacturing	3325	34.0	23.5	−10.5	−3.6
Alumina and aluminum production and processing . . .	3313	72.7	50.3	−22.4	−3.6
Rubber product manufacturing	3262	159.3	113.8	−45.5	−3.3
Electric lighting equipment manufacturing	3351	58.9	42.5	−16.4	−3.2
Spring and wire product manufacturing.	3326	58.2	42.1	−16.1	−3.2
Cutlery and handtool manufacturing	3322	54.1	39.7	−14.4	−3.0
Foundries	3315	162.1	119.8	−42.3	−3.0

X Not applicable.　　[1] Based on the North American Industry Classification System, 2002; see text, this section.

Source: U.S. Bureau of Labor Statistics, "Industry output and employment projections to 2016," *Monthly Labor Review*, November 2007. See Internet site <http://www.bls.gov/emp/home.htm>.

Table 602. **Unemployed Workers—Summary: 1980 to 2007**

[In thousands (7,637 represents 7,637,000), except as indicated. For civilian noninstitutional population 16 years old and over. Annual averages of monthly figures. Based on the Current Population Survey; see text Section 1, and Appendix III. For data on unemployment insurance, see Table 539]

Age, sex, race, Hispanic origin	1980	1990 [1]	1995	2000 [1]	2004 [1]	2005 [1]	2006 [1]	2007 [1]
UNEMPLOYED								
Total [2]	**7,637**	**7,047**	**7,404**	**5,692**	**8,149**	**7,591**	**7,001**	**7,078**
16 to 19 years old	1,669	1,212	1,346	1,081	1,208	1,186	1,119	1,101
20 to 24 years old	1,835	1,299	1,244	1,022	1,431	1,335	1,234	1,241
25 to 44 years old	2,964	3,323	3,390	2,340	3,362	3,061	2,800	2,769
45 to 64 years old	1,075	1,109	1,269	1,117	1,970	1,825	1,689	1,777
65 years and over	94	105	153	132	179	184	159	190
Male	4,267	3,906	3,983	2,975	4,456	4,059	3,753	3,882
16 to 19 years old	913	667	744	599	664	667	622	623
20 to 24 years old	1,076	715	673	547	811	775	705	721
25 to 44 years old	1,619	1,803	1,776	1,159	1,819	1,559	1,452	1,490
45 to 64 years old	600	662	697	587	1,057	955	887	940
65 years and over	58	59	94	83	104	102	88	108
Female	3,370	3,140	3,421	2,717	3,694	3,531	3,247	3,196
16 to 19 years old	755	544	602	483	543	519	496	478
20 to 24 years old	760	584	571	475	619	560	530	520
25 to 44 years old	1,345	1,519	1,615	1,181	1,543	1,502	1,348	1,279
45 to 64 years old	473	447	574	529	914	870	801	837
65 years and over	36	46	60	50	75	82	71	81
White [3]	5,884	5,186	5,459	4,121	5,847	5,350	5,002	5,143
16 to 19 years old	1,291	903	952	795	890	845	794	805
20 to 24 years old	1,364	899	866	682	959	878	832	851
Black [3]	1,553	1,565	1,538	1,241	1,729	1,700	1,549	1,445
16 to 19 years old	343	268	325	230	241	267	253	235
20 to 24 years old	426	349	311	281	353	358	318	300
Asian [3, 4]	(NA)	(NA)	(NA)	227	277	259	205	229
16 to 19 years old	(NA)	(NA)	(NA)	40	20	20	22	20
20 to 24 years old	(NA)	(NA)	(NA)	41	46	35	28	30
Hispanic [5]	620	876	1,140	954	1,342	1,191	1,081	1,220
16 to 19 years old	145	161	205	194	203	191	170	197
20 to 24 years old	138	167	209	190	255	227	194	213
Full-time workers	6,269	5,677	5,909	4,538	6,762	6,175	5,675	5,789
Part-time workers	1,369	1,369	1,495	1,154	1,388	1,415	1,326	1,289
UNEMPLOYMENT RATE (percent) [6]								
Total [2]	**7.1**	**5.6**	**5.6**	**4.0**	**5.5**	**5.1**	**4.6**	**4.6**
16 to 19 years old	17.8	15.5	17.3	13.1	17.0	16.6	15.4	15.7
20 to 24 years old	11.5	8.8	9.1	7.2	9.4	8.8	8.2	8.2
25 to 44 years old	6.0	4.9	4.8	3.3	4.9	4.5	4.1	4.0
45 to 64 years old	3.7	3.5	3.4	2.5	3.8	3.4	3.1	3.1
65 years and over	3.1	3.0	4.0	3.1	3.6	3.5	2.9	3.3
Male	6.9	5.7	5.6	3.9	5.6	5.1	4.6	4.7
16 to 19 years old	18.3	16.3	18.4	14.0	18.4	18.6	16.9	17.6
20 to 24 years old	12.5	9.1	9.2	7.3	10.1	9.6	8.7	8.9
25 to 44 years old	5.6	4.8	4.7	3.1	4.9	4.2	3.9	4.0
45 to 64 years old	3.5	3.7	3.5	2.4	3.9	3.4	3.1	3.2
65 years and over	3.1	3.0	4.3	3.3	3.7	3.4	2.8	3.4
Female	7.4	5.5	5.6	4.1	5.4	5.1	4.6	4.5
16 to 19 years old	17.2	14.7	16.1	12.1	15.5	14.5	13.8	13.8
20 to 24 years old	10.4	8.5	9.0	7.1	8.7	7.9	7.6	7.3
25 to 44 years old	6.4	4.9	5.0	3.6	5.0	4.8	4.3	4.1
45 to 64 years old	4.0	3.2	3.3	2.5	3.7	3.4	3.1	3.1
65 years and over	3.1	3.1	3.7	2.7	3.4	3.5	3.0	3.1
White [3]	6.3	4.8	4.9	3.5	4.8	4.4	4.0	4.1
16 to 19 years old	15.5	13.5	14.5	11.4	15.0	14.2	13.2	13.9
20 to 24 years old	9.9	7.3	7.7	5.9	7.9	7.2	6.9	7.0
Black [3]	14.3	11.4	10.4	7.6	10.4	10.0	8.9	8.3
16 to 19 years old	38.5	30.9	35.7	24.5	31.7	33.3	29.1	29.4
20 to 24 years old	23.6	19.9	17.7	15.0	18.4	18.3	16.2	15.2
Asian [3, 4]	(NA)	(NA)	(NA)	3.6	4.4	4.0	3.0	3.2
16 to 19 years old	(NA)	(NA)	(NA)	14.2	11.5	12.4	14.0	12.7
20 to 24 years old	(NA)	(NA)	(NA)	6.9	8.6	6.5	5.6	5.6
Hispanic [5]	10.1	8.2	9.3	5.7	7.0	6.0	5.2	5.6
16 to 19 years old	22.5	19.5	24.1	16.6	20.4	18.4	15.9	18.1
20 to 24 years old	12.1	9.1	11.5	7.5	9.3	8.6	7.2	7.8
Experienced workers [7]	6.9	5.3	5.4	3.8	5.3	4.8	(NA)	(NA)
Women maintaining families	9.2	8.3	8.0	5.9	8.0	7.8	(NA)	(NA)
Married men, wife present	4.2	3.4	3.3	2.0	3.1	2.8	2.4	2.5
Percent without work for—								
Fewer than 5 weeks	43.2	46.3	36.5	44.9	33.1	35.1	37.3	35.9
5 to 10 weeks	23.4	23.5	22.0	23.0	19.6	20.7	20.9	21.6
11 to 14 weeks	9.0	8.5	9.6	8.9	9.7	9.7	9.4	9.9
15 to 26 weeks	13.8	11.7	14.6	11.8	15.9	14.9	14.7	15.0
27 weeks and over	10.7	10.0	17.3	11.4	21.8	19.6	17.6	17.6
Unemployment duration, average (weeks)	11.9	12.0	16.6	12.6	19.6	18.4	16.8	16.8

NA Not available. [1] See footnote 2, Table 567. [2] Includes other races not shown separately. [3] Includes other ages not shown separately. Also beginning 2003, for this race group only. See footnote 3, Table 568. [4] Prior to 2004, includes Pacific Islanders. [5] Persons of Hispanic or Latino origin may be any race. Also includes ages not shown separately. [6] Unemployed as percent of civilian labor force in specified group. [7] Wage and salary workers.
Source: U.S. Bureau of Labor Statistics, "Employment and Earnings Online," January 2008 issue. See Internet site <http://www.bls.gov/opub/ee/home.htm> and <http://www.bls.gov/cps/home.htm/.

Table 603. **Unemployed Jobseekers' Job Search Activities: 2007**

[7,078 represents 7,078,000. For the civilian noninstitutional population 16 years old and over. Annual average of monthly data. Based on the Current Population Survey; see text, Section 1 and Appendix III]

Characteristic	Population (1,000)		Jobseekers' job search methods (percent)						Average number of methods used
	Total unem- ployed	Total job- seekers [1]	Employer directly	Sent out a resume or filled out appli- cations	Placed or answered ads	Friends or rela- tives	Public employ- ment agency	Private employ- ment agency	
Total, 16 years and over [2] . . .	7,078	6,102	57.4	50.7	16.0	21.7	17.7	7.6	1.84
16 to 19 years old.	1,101	1,039	55.5	55.6	9.7	14.6	8.1	2.6	1.54
20 to 24 years old.	1,241	1,136	59.3	52.5	15.1	20.1	15.4	6.1	1.80
25 to 34 years old.	1,544	1,329	57.6	50.3	17.5	23.4	19.4	7.8	1.91
35 to 44 years old.	1,225	1,019	59.3	48.9	18.3	25.3	22.4	11.0	2.00
45 to 54 years old.	1,135	934	58.1	49.1	18.3	23.5	22.5	10.1	1.98
55 to 64 years old.	642	512	52.9	47.3	18.1	23.8	20.8	9.5	1.89
65 years old and over	190	134	50.3	39.5	13.3	28.1	12.7	5.6	1.64
Male.	3,882	3,266	58.3	48.5	15.7	23.2	17.8	7.8	1.85
16 to 19 years old	623	588	55.3	54.9	9.9	15.0	8.0	2.7	1.54
20 to 24 years old	721	649	59.3	49.9	15.4	21.6	15.3	5.9	1.79
25 to 34 years old	856	701	59.2	45.8	15.9	25.9	19.5	8.0	1.89
35 to 44 years old	634	502	61.1	47.4	18.0	28.2	23.3	12.8	2.06
45 to 54 years old	591	470	59.3	46.8	20.0	25.3	24.1	10.5	2.04
55 to 64 years old	349	276	55.3	45.6	18.1	23.2	20.6	9.2	1.91
65 years old and over . . .	108	80	50.7	39.2	11.7	29.5	13.7	5.7	1.66
Female	3,196	2,836	56.3	53.3	16.2	20.0	17.6	7.4	1.84
16 to 19 years old	478	451	55.7	56.5	9.6	14.0	8.4	2.5	1.55
20 to 24 years old	520	486	59.3	56.0	14.8	18.1	15.6	6.4	1.82
25 to 34 years old	688	628	55.9	55.3	19.3	20.5	19.3	7.6	1.93
35 to 44 years old	591	517	57.6	50.4	18.5	22.5	21.6	9.2	1.94
45 to 54 years old	544	464	56.9	51.3	16.6	21.7	20.9	9.7	1.92
55 to 64 years old	293	236	50.0	49.4	18.1	24.5	21.1	9.8	1.88
65 years old and over . . .	81	54	49.6	39.8	15.7	26.0	11.3	5.4	1.61
White [3]	5,143	4,337	57.5	51.1	16.5	21.8	16.5	7.3	1.85
Male	2,869	2,353	58.5	48.7	16.0	23.3	16.6	7.6	1.85
Female	2,274	1,985	56.2	53.9	17.1	20.2	16.4	7.0	1.84
Black [3]	1,445	1,323	58.1	49.7	15.0	20.7	22.3	8.2	1.85
Male	752	683	57.9	48.0	15.2	21.9	22.6	8.3	1.84
Female	693	641	58.3	51.6	14.7	19.5	22.0	8.1	1.86
Asian [3]	229	212	56.5	45.5	13.2	27.5	13.2	9.3	1.84
Male	119	111	58.3	44.5	13.4	29.6	14.5	10.3	1.91
Female	110	101	54.4	46.6	12.9	25.2	11.8	8.2	1.76
Hispanic [4]	1,220	1,035	56.8	42.7	12.9	30.2	16.5	6.8	1.78
Male	695	567	58.7	39.7	12.1	32.4	16.2	6.9	1.77
Female	525	469	54.4	46.4	14.0	27.7	16.9	6.6	1.78

[1] Excludes persons on temporary layoff. [2] Includes other races not shown separately. [3] Data for this race group only. See footnote 3, Table 568. [4] Persons of Hispanic or Latino origin may be any race.

Source: U.S. Bureau of Labor Statistics, "Employment and Earnings Online," January 2008 issue. See Internet site <http://www.bls.gov/opub/ee/home.htm> and <http://www.bls.gov/cps/home.htm>.

Table 604. **Unemployed Persons by Sex and Reason: 1980 to 2007**

[In thousands (4,267 represents 4,267,000). For civilian noninstitutional population 16 years old and over. Annual averages of monthly figures. Based on Current Population Survey; see text, Section 1, and Appendix III]

Sex and reason	1980	1985	1990 [1]	1995	2000 [1]	2001	2002	2003 [1]	2004 [1]	2005 [1]	2006 [1]	2007 [1]
Male, total	4,267	4,521	3,906	3,983	2,975	3,690	4,597	4,906	4,456	4,059	3,753	3,882
Job losers [2]	2,649	2,749	2,257	2,190	1,516	2,119	2,820	3,024	2,603	2,188	2,021	2,175
Job leavers	438	409	528	407	387	422	434	422	437	445	406	408
Reentrants.	776	876	806	1,113	854	925	1,068	1,141	1,070	1,067	1,015	956
New entrants	405	487	315	273	217	223	274	320	346	359	312	343
Female, total. . .	3,370	3,791	3,140	3,421	2,717	3,111	3,781	3,868	3,694	3,531	3,247	3,196
Job losers [2]	1,297	1,390	1,130	1,286	1,001	1,356	1,787	1,814	1,595	1,479	1,300	1,340
Job leavers	453	468	513	417	393	413	432	397	421	427	421	385
Reentrants.	1,152	1,380	1,124	1,412	1,107	1,105	1,300	1,336	1,338	1,319	1,223	1,186
New entrants	468	552	373	306	217	237	262	321	340	306	304	285

[1] See footnote 2, Table 567. [2] Beginning 1995, persons who completed temporary jobs are identified separately and are included as job losers.

Source: U.S. Bureau of Labor Statistics, "Employment and Earnings Online," January 2008 issue. See Internet site <http://www.bls.gov/opub/ee/home.htm> and <http://www.bls.gov/cps/home.htm>.

Labor Force, Employment, and Earnings   393

Table 605. Unemployment Rates by Industry, 2000 to 2007, and by Sex, 2000 and 2007

[In percent. Civilian noninstitutional population 16 years old and over. Annual averages of monthly figures. Rate represents unemployment as a percent of labor force in each specified group. Based on Current Population Survey; see text, Section 1 and Appendix III. See headnote, Table 585, regarding industries]

Industry	2000	2005 [1]	2006 [1]	2007 [1]	Male 2000	Male 2007 [1]	Female 2000	Female 2007 [1]
All unemployed [2]	**4.0**	**5.1**	**4.6**	**4.6**	**3.9**	**4.7**	**4.1**	**4.5**
Wage and salary workers:								
Agriculture and related industries	9.0	8.3	7.2	6.3	8.3	5.4	11.5	9.4
Mining	4.4	3.1	3.2	3.4	4.6	3.3	2.8	4.1
Construction	6.2	7.4	6.7	7.4	6.4	7.5	5.1	6.6
Manufacturing	3.5	4.9	4.2	4.3	3.0	3.8	4.5	5.4
Wholesale trade	3.3	4.0	3.2	3.3	2.8	2.6	4.4	4.9
Retail trade	4.6	5.7	5.4	5.1	4.0	4.8	5.1	5.4
Transportation and utilities	3.4	4.1	4.0	3.9	3.2	3.8	4.2	4.5
Transportation and warehousing	3.8	4.5	4.3	4.3	1.9	4.2	4.6	4.8
Utilities	1.9	1.9	2.0	1.5	2.8	1.4	2.1	2.0
Information	3.2	5.0	3.7	3.6	2.7	3.4	3.7	3.9
Telecommunications	2.3	5.2	3.6	3.1	1.5	3.1	3.3	3.3
Financial activities	2.4	2.9	2.7	3.0	2.1	2.9	2.6	3.1
Finance and insurance	2.2	2.7	2.6	2.7	1.7	2.5	2.5	2.8
Real estate and rental and leasing	3.1	3.3	3.2	3.7	2.9	3.6	3.2	3.8
Professional and business services	4.8	6.2	5.6	5.3	4.4	5.2	5.2	5.5
Professional and technical services	2.5	3.5	3.0	3.0	2.2	2.7	2.9	3.4
Management, administrative, and waste services	8.1	10.2	9.3	8.5	7.6	8.5	8.8	8.5
Education and health services	2.5	3.4	3.0	3.0	2.2	3.0	2.5	3.0
Educational services	2.4	3.7	3.1	3.8	2.1	4.3	2.5	3.5
Health care and social assistance	2.5	3.3	3.0	2.8	2.3	2.5	2.5	2.9
Leisure and hospitality	6.6	7.8	7.3	7.4	6.2	7.2	7.0	7.5
Arts, entertainment, and recreation	5.9	6.9	7.2	7.3	6.1	8.2	5.7	6.2
Accommodation and food services	6.8	8.0	7.3	7.4	6.2	7.0	7.3	7.7
Other services [3]	3.9	4.8	4.7	3.9	3.7	3.6	4.0	4.2
Government workers	2.1	2.6	2.3	2.3	2.1	2.3	2.2	2.4

[1] See footnote 2, Table 567.   [2] Includes the self-employed, unpaid family workers, and persons with no previous work experience not shown separately.   [3] Includes private household workers.

Source: U.S. Bureau of Labor Statistics, "Employment and Earnings Online," January 2008 issue. See Internet site <http://www.bls.gov/opub/ee/home.htm> and <http://www.bls.gov/cps/home.htm>.

Table 606. Unemployment by Occupation, 2000 to 2007, and by Sex, 2007

[5,692 represents 5,692,000. Civilian noninstitutional population 16 years old and over. Annual averages of monthly data. Rate represents unemployment as a percent of the labor force for each specified group. Based on Current Population Survey; see text, Section 1 and Appendix III. See also headnote, Table 585, regarding occupations]

Occupation	Number (1,000) 2000	Number (1,000) 2005 [1]	Number (1,000) 2007 [1]	Unemployment rate 2000	Unemployment rate 2005 [1]	2007 [1] Total	2007 [1] Male	2007 [1] Female
Total [2]	**5,692**	**7,591**	**7,078**	**4.0**	**5.1**	**4.6**	**4.7**	**4.5**
Management, professional, and related occupations	827	1,172	1,090	1.8	2.3	2.1	2.0	2.2
Management, business, and financial operations	320	464	429	1.6	2.2	1.9	1.7	2.2
Management	214	322	278	1.5	2.1	1.8	1.7	1.9
Business and financial operations	106	142	151	2.0	2.4	2.4	2.1	2.7
Professional and related occupations	507	708	662	1.9	2.4	2.1	2.1	2.1
Computer and mathematical	74	96	76	2.2	2.9	2.1	2.1	2.3
Architecture and engineering	51	60	47	1.7	2.1	1.6	1.5	1.9
Life, physical, and social science	18	39	28	1.4	2.7	2.0	1.7	2.4
Community and social services	40	52	53	2.0	2.4	2.3	1.9	2.6
Legal	18	27	40	1.2	1.6	2.3	1.4	3.2
Education, training, and library	136	210	198	1.8	2.5	2.3	2.3	2.3
Arts, design, entertainment, sports, and media	97	135	127	3.5	4.7	4.4	5.0	3.7
Healthcare practitioner and technical	73	90	93	1.2	1.3	1.3	1.3	1.3
Service occupations	1,132	1,587	1,521	5.2	6.4	5.9	6.0	5.9
Healthcare support	101	154	147	4.0	4.7	4.5	4.1	4.5
Protective service	70	121	118	2.7	4.0	3.7	3.0	6.0
Food preparation and serving-related	469	615	626	6.6	7.7	7.5	7.9	7.2
Building and grounds cleaning and maintenance	301	429	392	5.8	7.6	6.7	6.6	6.8
Personal care and service	190	268	238	4.4	5.6	4.8	4.9	4.7
Sales and office occupations	1,446	1,820	1,638	3.8	4.8	4.3	4.2	4.4
Sales and related	673	874	835	4.1	5.0	4.8	3.8	5.7
Office and administrative support	773	946	804	3.6	4.6	4.0	4.9	3.7
Natural resources, construction, and maintenance	758	1,069	1,052	5.3	6.5	6.3	6.1	10.4
Farming, fishing, and forestry	133	103	89	10.2	9.6	8.5	7.0	13.8
Construction and extraction	507	751	781	6.2	7.6	7.6	7.5	11.2
Installation, maintenance, and repair	119	214	182	2.4	3.9	3.4	3.3	5.6
Production, transportation, and material moving	1,081	1,245	1,128	5.1	6.5	5.8	5.4	7.3
Production	575	677	564	4.8	6.7	5.7	5.0	7.2
Transportation and material moving	505	568	564	5.6	6.2	6.0	5.7	7.7

[1] See footnote 2, Table 567.   [2] Includes persons with no previous work experience and those whose last job was in the Armed Forces.

Source: U.S. Bureau of Labor Statistics, "Employment and Earnings Online," January 2008 issue. See Internet site <http://www.bls.gov/opub/ee/home.htm> and <http://www.bls.gov/cps/home.htm>.

U.S. Census Bureau, Statistical Abstract of the United States: 2009

Table 607. Unemployed and Unemployment Rates by Educational Attainment, Sex, Race, and Hispanic Origin: 1992 to 2007

[6,543 represents 6,543,000. **Annual averages of monthly figures.** Civilian noninstitutional population 25 years old and over. See Table 572 for civilian labor force and participation rate data. Based on Current Population Survey; see text, Section 1 and Appendix III]

Year, sex, and race	Unemployed (1,000)					Unemployment rate [1]				
	Total	Less than high school diploma	High school graduates, no college	Some college or associate's degree	Bachelor's degree or more	Total	Less than high school diploma	High school graduates, no college	Some college or associate's degree	Bachelor's degree or more
Total: [2]										
1992 . . .	6,543	1,533	2,590	1,527	893	6.1	11.5	6.8	5.6	3.2
2000 [3] . . .	3,589	791	1,298	890	610	3.0	6.3	3.4	2.7	1.7
2007 [3] . . .	4,735	886	1,682	1,275	892	3.6	7.1	4.4	3.6	2.0
Male:										
1992	3,767	942	1,462	829	533	6.4	11.4	7.4	5.9	3.3
2000 [3]	1,829	411	682	427	309	2.8	5.4	3.4	2.6	1.5
2007 [3]	2,538	523	951	610	454	3.6	6.6	4.4	3.4	1.9
Female:										
1992	2,776	591	1,128	697	361	5.8	11.5	6.3	5.4	3.0
2000 [3]	1,760	380	616	463	301	3.2	7.8	3.5	2.8	1.8
2007 [3]	2,198	363	731	666	438	3.6	8.2	4.3	3.7	2.1
White: [4]										
1992	4,978	1,145	1,928	1,162	743	5.5	10.7	6.0	5.0	3.0
2000 [3]	2,644	564	924	667	489	2.6	5.6	2.9	2.4	1.6
2007 [3]	3,487	660	1,214	932	681	3.3	6.5	3.9	3.2	1.9
Black: [4]										
1992	1,269	322	565	301	81	11.0	15.3	12.3	9.8	4.4
2000 [3]	731	179	315	169	68	5.4	10.7	6.4	4.0	2.5
2007 [3]	910	177	375	252	106	6.2	12.0	7.3	5.5	3.0
Asian: [4, 5]										
2000 [3]	146	28	34	35	49	2.7	5.7	3.0	3.2	1.8
2007 [3]	180	13	38	41	88	2.8	2.9	3.2	3.7	2.4
Hispanic: [6]										
1992	853	434	235	134	50	9.8	12.8	9.1	7.7	5.0
2000 [3]	569	297	150	85	38	4.4	6.2	3.9	3.2	2.2
2007 [3]	810	363	234	150	63	4.6	6.0	4.4	4.1	2.3

[1] Percent unemployed of the civilian labor force. [2] Includes other races not shown separately. [3] See footnote 2, Table 567. [4] 2007 data are for persons in this race group only. See footnote 3, Table 568. [5] 2000 data include Pacific Islanders. [6] Persons of Hispanic or Latino origin may be any race.

Source: U.S. Bureau of Labor Statistics, "Employment and Earnings Online," January 2008 issue. See Internet site <http://www.bls.gov/opub/ee/home.htm> and <http://www.bls.gov/cps/home.htm>.

Table 608. Unemployed Persons by Reason of Unemployment: 2007

[7,078 represents 7,078,000. **Annual averages of monthly data.** Based on Current Population Survey; see text, Section 1, and Appendix III]

Age, sex, and reason	Total unemployed (1,000)	Percent distribution by duration				
		Less than 5 weeks	5 to 14 weeks	15 weeks and over		
				Total	15 to 26 weeks	27 weeks or longer
Total 16 years old and over	**7,078**	**35.9**	**31.5**	**32.5**	**15.0**	**17.6**
16 to 19 years old	1,101	46.2	32.2	21.5	11.9	9.6
Total 20 years old and over	**5,977**	**34.0**	**31.4**	**34.6**	**15.6**	**19.0**
Males	**3,259**	**33.2**	**31.6**	**35.2**	**15.6**	**19.6**
Job losers and persons who completed temporary jobs	2,064	35.1	33.1	31.8	15.6	16.2
On temporary layoff	580	52.8	33.4	13.8	10.7	3.1
Not on temporary layoff	1,483	28.1	33.0	38.8	17.5	21.3
Permanent job losers	1,013	25.0	32.6	42.4	19.5	22.9
Persons who completed temporary jobs	470	35.0	34.0	31.0	13.3	17.8
Job leavers	371	37.4	30.6	32.0	15.9	16.1
Reentrants	723	27.2	28.6	44.2	15.9	28.3
New entrants	101	23.3	24.7	52.0	11.9	40.1
Females	**2,718**	**35.0**	**31.2**	**33.8**	**15.5**	**18.3**
Job losers and persons who completed temporary jobs	1,276	36.6	32.0	31.5	16.0	15.5
On temporary layoff	333	56.7	33.3	10.0	7.3	2.7
Not on temporary layoff	943	29.4	31.5	39.0	19.0	20.0
Permanent job losers	696	27.1	30.7	42.2	20.1	22.1
Persons who completed temporary jobs	247	35.9	33.9	30.2	16.0	14.2
Job leavers	351	37.3	34.4	28.3	14.2	14.1
Reentrants	984	32.1	29.2	38.8	15.5	23.3
New entrants	107	35.5	29.4	35.2	14.6	20.5

Source: U.S. Bureau of Labor Statistics, "Employment and Earnings Online," January 2008 issue. See Internet site <http://www.bls.gov/opub/ee/home.htm> and <http://www.bls.gov/cps/home.htm>.

U.S. Census Bureau, Statistical Abstract of the United States: 2009

Table 609. **Total Unemployed and Insured Unemployed by State: 2000 to 2007**

[5,692 represents 5,692,000. Civilian noninstitutional population 16 years old and over. Annual averages of monthly figures. Total unemployment estimates based on the Current Population Survey; see text, Section 1, and Appendix III.

State	Total unemployed								Insured unemployed [3]			
	Number (1,000)				Percent [1]				Number (1,000)		Percent [4]	
	2000	2005 [2]	2006 [2]	2007 [2]	2000	2005 [2]	2006 [2]	2007 [2]	2000	2007	2000	2007
United States. . . .	5,692	7,591	7,001	7,078	4.0	5.1	4.6	4.6	[5]2658.5	[5]2550.05	[5]2.1	1.9
Alabama	87	82	76	77	4.1	3.9	3.5	3.5	28.2	27.4	1.6	1.5
Alaska	20	24	23	22	6.2	6.9	6.5	6.2	12.5	10.4	4.5	3.6
Arizona	100	133	121	115	4.0	4.6	4.1	3.8	29.6	30.2	1.3	1.2
Arkansas.	53	69	72	74	4.2	5.1	5.3	5.4	27.9	29.6	2.5	2.6
California.	833	961	877	979	4.9	5.4	4.9	5.4	348.9	364.9	2.4	2.4
Colorado	65	133	115	104	2.7	5.1	4.3	3.8	25.4	22.9	1.2	1.1
Connecticut	39	88	80	85	2.3	4.9	4.4	4.6	40.9	39.5	2.5	2.4
Delaware.	14	17	16	15	3.3	4.0	3.5	3.4	8.2	8.4	2.0	2.0
District of Columbia. .	18	21	19	19	5.7	6.6	5.9	5.7	4.2	4.1	0.9	0.9
Florida	300	334	305	368	3.8	3.9	3.4	4.0	88.6	110.2	1.2	1.4
Georgia	148	239	216	212	3.5	5.2	4.6	4.4	54.0	56.0	1.4	1.4
Hawaii	24	17	16	17	4.0	2.7	2.5	2.6	6.3	6.8	1.1	1.2
Idaho	31	28	23	20	4.6	3.9	3.2	2.7	13.3	12.1	2.3	1.9
Illinois.	291	371	301	336	4.5	5.8	4.6	5.0	137.1	129.4	2.4	2.3
Indiana	92	172	160	146	2.9	5.4	4.9	4.5	54.4	55.2	1.9	1.9
Iowa.	45	71	63	63	2.8	4.3	3.8	3.8	24.4	23.5	1.7	1.6
Kansas.	53	75	64	60	3.8	5.1	4.3	4.1	20.5	17.4	1.6	1.3
Kentucky.	83	121	118	112	4.2	6.0	5.8	5.5	30.5	30.9	1.8	1.8
Louisiana	101	139	78	77	5.0	6.7	3.9	3.8	66.7	20.7	3.6	1.2
Maine.	22	34	32	33	3.3	4.8	4.6	4.7	10.7	10.3	1.8	1.8
Maryland.	100	121	112	107	3.6	4.1	3.8	3.6	36.0	36.1	1.6	1.5
Massachusetts	92	164	164	153	2.7	4.9	4.8	4.5	82.5	81.3	2.7	2.6
Michigan	190	348	351	360	3.7	6.9	6.9	7.2	140.4	140.1	3.3	3.3
Minnesota	87	120	118	134	3.1	4.2	4.0	4.6	47.2	50.5	1.8	1.9
Mississippi.	74	103	88	83	5.7	7.8	6.7	6.3	28.9	19.5	2.7	1.8
Missouri	98	160	145	153	3.3	5.4	4.8	5.0	52.1	48.4	2.0	1.8
Montana	22	18	16	16	4.8	3.8	3.3	3.1	7.8	7.4	2.0	1.8
Nebraska	27	38	30	30	2.8	3.9	3.0	3.0	12.1	9.7	1.4	1.1
Nevada.	48	52	54	64	4.5	4.2	4.2	4.8	18.5	24.6	1.7	2.0
New Hampshire	19	26	26	26	2.7	3.6	3.5	3.6	6.7	7.5	1.1	1.2
New Jersey	157	199	209	190	3.7	4.5	4.7	4.2	113.2	111.8	3.0	2.9
New Mexico.	42	48	40	33	5.0	5.2	4.3	3.5	11.8	11.6	1.6	1.5
New York	416	473	435	432	4.5	5.0	4.6	4.5	191.8	173.8	2.4	2.1
North Carolina	155	229	211	211	3.7	5.3	4.7	4.7	77.4	76.8	2.1	2.0
North Dakota	10	12	12	12	2.9	3.4	3.2	3.2	3.5	3.4	1.1	1.1
Ohio.	234	345	322	336	4.0	5.9	5.4	5.6	100.2	98.2	1.9	1.9
Oklahoma	52	77	71	75	3.1	4.5	4.1	4.3	16.8	14.3	1.2	1.0
Oregon	93	116	102	101	5.1	6.2	5.4	5.2	45.8	43.0	2.9	2.6
Pennsylvania	255	311	287	274	4.2	5.0	4.6	4.4	168.6	163.2	3.1	3.0
Rhode Island	23	29	29	29	4.2	5.1	5.1	5.0	12.6	13.4	2.7	2.9
South Carolina	71	140	135	125	3.6	6.7	6.4	5.9	39.3	38.7	2.2	2.1
South Dakota	11	16	13	13	2.7	3.6	3.1	3.0	2.7	2.2	0.8	0.6
Tennessee.	115	163	154	143	4.0	5.6	5.1	4.7	44.2	41.2	1.7	1.5
Texas	452	604	562	500	4.4	5.4	4.9	4.3	128.6	96.8	1.4	1.0
Utah.	38	53	39	36	3.4	4.2	3.0	2.7	10.7	8.6	1.0	0.8
Vermont	9	12	13	14	2.7	3.5	3.7	3.9	6.3	6.6	2.2	2.2
Virginia	82	138	121	123	2.3	3.5	3.0	3.0	31.5	31.9	0.9	0.9
Washington	151	180	163	155	5.0	5.5	4.9	4.5	59.0	48.8	2.3	1.8
West Virginia	44	39	38	37	5.5	5.0	4.7	4.6	14.0	13.4	2.1	2.0
Wisconsin	101	146	145	151	3.4	4.8	4.7	4.9	73.4	74.3	2.7	2.7
Wyoming.	10	10	9	9	3.8	3.7	3.3	3.0	2.8	2.4	1.2	0.9

[1] Total unemployment as percent of civilian labor force.   [2] See footnote 2, Table 567.   [3] Source: U.S. Employment and Training Administration, *Unemployment Insurance, Financial Handbook,* annual updates.   [4] Insured unemployment as percent of average covered employment in the previous year.   [5] Includes 55,600 in Puerto Rico and the Virgin Islands in 2000; and 40,700 in 2007.

Source: Except as noted, U.S. Bureau of Labor Statistics, *Geographic Profile of Employment and Unemployment,* annual. See Internet site <http://www.bls.gov/gps/>.

Table 610. Nonfarm Establishments—Employees, Hours, and Earnings by Industry: 1990 to 2007

[Annual averages of monthly data. (109,487 represents 109,487,000). Based on data from establishment reports. Includes all full- and part-time employees who worked during, or received pay for, any part of the pay period reported. Excludes proprietors, the self-employed, farm workers, unpaid family workers, private household workers, and Armed Forces. Establishment data shown here conform to industry definitions in the 2007 North American Industry Classification System (NAICS) and are adjusted to March 2007 employment benchmarks. Based on the Current Employment Statistics Program; see source and Appendix III]

Item and year	Total nonfarm	Private industry																Government
		Total [1]	Construction	Manufacturing	Wholesale trade	Retail trade	Transportation and warehousing	Utilities	Information	Finance and insurance	Real estate and rental and leasing	Professional and technical services	Administrative and waste services	Educational services	Health care and social assistance	Arts, entertainment, and recreation	Accommodations and food services	
EMPLOYEES (1,000)																		
1990	109,487	91,072	5,263	17,695	5,268	13,182	3,476	740	2,688	4,976	1,637	4,538	4,643	1,688	9,296	1,132	8,156	18,415
2000	131,785	110,995	6,787	17,263	5,933	15,280	4,410	601	3,630	5,677	2,011	6,702	8,168	2,390	12,718	1,788	10,074	20,790
2002	130,341	108,828	6,716	15,259	5,652	15,025	4,224	596	3,395	5,814	2,033	6,649	7,622	2,643	13,556	1,783	10,203	21,513
2004	131,435	109,814	6,976	14,315	5,663	15,058	4,249	564	3,118	5,945	2,086	6,747	7,923	2,763	14,190	1,850	10,643	21,621
2005	133,703	111,899	7,336	14,226	5,764	15,280	4,361	554	3,061	6,019	2,134	7,025	8,170	2,836	14,536	1,892	10,923	21,804
2006	136,086	114,113	7,691	14,155	5,905	15,353	4,470	549	3,038	6,156	2,173	7,357	8,398	2,901	14,925	1,929	11,181	21,974
2007	137,623	115,420	7,614	13,884	6,028	15,491	4,536	553	3,029	6,147	2,162	7,662	8,454	2,949	15,378	1,978	11,496	22,203
WEEKLY EARNINGS [2] (dol.)																		
1990	(NA)	349.75	513.43	436.16	444.48	235.62	471.72	670.40	479.50	378.21	286.96	504.83	273.60	(NA)	319.80	219.02	147.89	(NA)
2000	(NA)	481.01	685.78	590.77	631.40	333.38	562.31	955.66	700.86	589.64	396.38	745.77	387.49	(NA)	449.27	273.79	207.44	(NA)
2002	(NA)	506.75	711.82	618.75	644.38	360.81	579.75	979.09	737.77	632.34	420.30	784.03	418.68	(NA)	495.17	301.84	214.60	(NA)
2004	(NA)	529.09	735.55	658.49	667.09	371.13	614.82	1,048.44	777.25	683.78	455.44	828.25	425.64	(NA)	537.87	313.01	221.68	(NA)
2005	(NA)	544.33	750.22	673.33	685.00	377.58	618.58	1,095.90	805.08	703.51	487.99	862.79	431.92	(NA)	560.43	330.19	226.48	(NA)
2006	(NA)	567.87	781.21	691.02	718.63	383.02	636.97	1,135.34	850.42	738.17	496.59	907.74	464.97	(NA)	581.55	332.66	236.70	(NA)
2007	(NA)	589.72	816.06	711.36	748.90	385.20	654.83	1,182.17	873.63	774.52	518.30	954.03	485.85	(NA)	606.90	349.34	251.24	(NA)
WEEKLY HOURS [2]																		
1990	(NA)	34.3	38.3	40.5	38.4	30.6	37.7	41.5	35.8	36.4	33.1	36.1	32.3	(NA)	31.8	26.1	25.9	(NA)
2000	(NA)	34.3	39.2	41.3	38.8	30.7	37.4	42.0	36.8	37.1	32.6	36.2	33.1	(NA)	32.1	25.6	26.2	(NA)
2002	(NA)	33.9	38.4	40.5	38.0	30.9	36.8	40.9	36.5	36.6	32.8	35.6	33.0	(NA)	32.3	25.7	25.8	(NA)
2004	(NA)	33.7	38.3	40.8	37.8	30.7	37.2	40.9	36.3	36.6	32.8	35.6	32.9	(NA)	32.7	25.7	25.6	(NA)
2005	(NA)	33.8	38.6	40.7	37.7	30.6	37.0	41.1	36.5	36.8	33.5	35.7	32.8	(NA)	32.9	25.7	25.7	(NA)
2006	(NA)	33.9	39.0	41.1	38.0	30.5	36.9	41.4	36.6	36.8	32.9	35.9	33.4	(NA)	32.8	25.2	25.8	(NA)
2007	(NA)	33.8	39.0	41.2	38.2	30.2	36.9	42.4	36.5	37.0	32.9	35.9	33.5	(NA)	32.8	24.8	25.6	(NA)
HOURLY EARNINGS [2] (dol.)																		
1990	(NA)	10.20	13.42	10.78	11.58	7.71	12.50	16.14	13.40	10.40	8.66	13.99	8.48	(NA)	10.05	8.41	5.70	(NA)
2000	(NA)	14.02	17.48	14.32	16.28	10.86	15.05	22.75	19.07	15.90	12.15	20.61	11.69	(NA)	13.98	10.68	7.92	(NA)
2002	(NA)	14.97	18.52	15.29	16.98	11.67	15.76	23.96	20.20	17.28	12.81	22.01	12.69	(NA)	15.32	11.75	8.31	(NA)
2004	(NA)	15.69	19.23	16.14	17.65	12.08	16.52	25.61	21.40	18.70	13.89	23.23	12.94	(NA)	16.45	12.17	8.65	(NA)
2005	(NA)	16.13	19.46	16.56	18.16	12.36	16.70	26.68	22.06	19.09	14.57	24.15	13.16	(NA)	17.05	12.85	8.80	(NA)
2006	(NA)	16.76	20.02	16.81	18.91	12.57	17.28	27.40	23.23	20.05	15.08	25.27	13.93	(NA)	17.75	13.21	9.19	(NA)
2007	(NA)	17.42	20.95	17.26	19.59	12.76	17.73	27.87	23.94	20.92	15.76	26.54	14.49	(NA)	18.48	14.11	9.81	(NA)

NA Not available.   [1] Includes other industries not shown separately.   [2] Average hours and earnings of production workers for natural resources and mining, manufacturing, and construction; average hours and earnings of nonsupervisory workers for the service-providing industries.

Source: U.S. Bureau of Labor Statistics, Employment, Hours, and Earnings from Current Employment Statistics survey (National); <http://www.bls.gov/ces/home.htm>.

Labor Force, Employment, and Earnings   397

Table 611. Employees in Nonfarm Establishments—States: 2007

[In thousands (137,331 represents 137,331,000). For coverage, see headnote, Table 610. National totals differ from the sum of the state figures because of differing benchmarks among states and differing industrial and geographic stratification. Based on North American Industry Classification System, 2007; see text, this section]

State	Total [1]	Construction	Manufacturing	Trade, transportation, and utilities	Information	Financial activities [2]	Professional and business services [3]	Education and health services [4]	Leisure and hospitality [5]	Other services [6]	Government
U.S. . . .	**137,623**	**7,614**	**13,884**	**26,608**	**3,029**	**8,308**	**17,962**	**18,327**	**13,474**	**5,491**	**22,203**
AL.	2,006	113	297	396	28	100	221	209	174	81	376
AK.	318	18	13	64	7	15	25	37	32	12	82
AZ.	2,666	224	182	525	43	184	402	304	273	97	423
AR.	1,204	56	189	250	20	53	117	154	99	45	210
CA.	15,163	892	1,463	2,911	473	907	2,263	1,664	1,553	514	2,497
CO	2,330	167	146	430	76	160	348	240	270	93	375
CT.	1,698	69	191	311	39	145	206	288	136	64	249
DE.	437	[7]28	33	83	7	45	60	58	41	20	61
DC	695	[7]13	2	28	22	29	154	98	55	63	232
FL.	8,041	598	389	1,611	161	542	1,329	1,007	929	344	1,124
GA	4,147	222	431	888	115	231	560	456	397	161	676
HI	624	[7]39	15	121	11	30	76	73	110	27	122
ID	656	53	66	132	11	33	83	74	63	19	118
IL	5,981	271	676	1,212	116	405	869	779	531	262	851
IN	2,988	151	550	588	40	139	290	396	284	112	432
IA	1,517	73	230	309	34	103	121	203	137	58	250
KS.	1,379	65	186	264	41	74	144	171	116	52	258
KY.	1,869	85	256	387	30	93	182	241	173	76	325
LA.	1,921	134	158	383	28	97	201	247	194	69	359
ME	617	31	59	126	11	33	54	116	60	20	104
MD	2,610	[7]191	132	477	51	158	397	374	235	118	479
MA	3,277	137	295	571	88	225	482	624	302	120	433
MI	4,262	166	617	788	66	211	573	595	405	177	657
MN	2,771	121	341	530	58	179	329	428	248	117	415
MS	1,152	58	170	227	13	47	95	126	126	37	244
MO	2,796	148	300	549	63	167	338	384	281	121	440
MT	443	33	20	92	8	22	41	59	58	17	85
NE.	963	[7]51	101	205	19	69	104	132	82	35	164
NV.	1,292	134	51	232	16	65	158	92	339	37	157
NH	649	28	78	142	12	39	66	103	64	22	94
NJ.	4,074	172	313	876	98	275	608	580	340	164	648
NM	843	59	37	144	16	35	109	111	88	30	195
NY.	8,738	351	554	1,526	265	731	1,137	1,602	699	363	1,504
NC	4,146	255	539	778	73	211	500	514	394	180	695
ND	358	19	26	76	8	20	30	51	33	15	76
OH	5,424	225	773	1,051	88	301	666	790	500	222	798
OK	1,566	71	150	288	29	84	181	193	140	63	321
OR	1,732	104	204	340	36	107	198	212	172	60	290
PA.	5,796	263	658	1,135	107	332	704	1,074	500	257	744
RI	493	22	51	80	11	35	56	99	51	23	65
SC.	1,950	128	250	377	28	106	227	201	218	74	338
SD.	406	[7]23	42	82	7	31	28	60	43	16	76
TN.	2,797	[7]138	381	611	50	144	322	350	276	103	421
TX.	10,359	642	935	2,104	221	644	1,291	1,255	980	354	1,728
UT.	1,252	104	128	246	32	75	161	140	113	36	207
VT.	308	17	36	59	6	13	22	57	33	10	54
VA.	3,761	241	279	668	91	194	644	417	346	185	686
WA	2,932	208	293	553	103	155	345	348	281	105	533
WV	757	39	59	143	11	30	61	114	71	56	145
WI	2,882	126	501	547	50	163	277	399	262	138	416
WY	288	26	10	55	4	11	18	23	34	12	67

[1] Includes natural resources and mining, not shown separately. [2] Finance and insurance; real estate and rental and leasing. [3] Professional, scientific, and technical services; management of companies and enterprises; administrative and support and waste management and remediation services. [4] Education services; health care and social assistance. [5] Arts, entertainment, and recreation; accommodations and food services. [6] Includes repair and maintenance; personal and laundry services; and membership associations and organizations. [7] Natural resources and mining included with construction.

Source: U.S. Bureau of Labor Statistics, the Current Employment Statistics program Internet site <http://www.bls.gov/sae/home.htm>. Compiled from data supplied by cooperating state agencies.

Table 612. Nonfarm Industries—Employees and Earnings: 1990 to 2007

[**Annual averages of monthly figures (109,487 represents 109,487,000)**. Covers all full- and part-time employees who worked during, or received pay for, any part of the pay period including the 12th of the month. See also headnote, Table 610]

Industry	2007 NAICS [1] code	All employees (1,000)					Average hourly earnings [2] (dol.)		
		1990	2000	2005	2006	2007	2000	2005	2007
Total nonfarm	(X)	**109,487**	**131,785**	**133,703**	**136,086**	**137,623**	**(NA)**	**(NA)**	**(NA)**
Goods-producing [3]	(X)	23,723	24,649	22,190	22,531	22,221	15.27	17.60	18.67
Service-providing [4]	(X)	85,764	107,136	111,513	113,556	115,402	(NA)	(NA)	(NA)
Total private	(X)	**91,072**	**110,995**	**111,899**	**114,113**	**115,420**	**14.02**	**16.13**	**17.42**
Natural resources and mining	(X)	**765**	**599**	**628**	**684**	**723**	**16.55**	**18.72**	**20.96**
Mining	21	**680**	**520**	**562**	**620**	**662**	**16.94**	**19.04**	**21.43**
Oil and gas extraction	211	190	125	126	135	146	19.43	19.34	24.20
Mining, except oil and gas	212	302	225	213	220	225	18.07	20.18	20.77
Support activities for mining	213	188	171	224	265	292	14.55	17.89	21.06
Construction	23	**5,263**	**6,787**	**7,336**	**7,691**	**7,614**	**17.48**	**19.46**	**20.95**
Construction of buildings	236	1,413	1,633	1,712	1,805	1,761	16.74	19.05	20.61
Residential building	2361	673	823	960	1,009	951	15.18	17.72	19.10
Nonresidential building	2362	741	809	752	796	810	18.18	20.55	22.13
Heavy and civil engineering construction . . .	237	813	937	951	985	1,001	16.80	19.60	21.05
Highway, street, and bridge construction. .	2373	289	340	351	348	345	18.17	20.12	21.45
Specialty trade contractors [5]	238	3,037	4,217	4,673	4,901	4,852	17.91	19.55	21.03
Building foundation and exterior contractors	2381	703	919	1,083	1,133	1,076	16.93	18.44	19.96
Building equipment contractors	2382	1,282	1,897	1,918	2,013	2,053	19.52	21.01	22.59
Building finishing contractors	2383	665	857	992	1,030	1,010	16.44	18.82	20.02
Manufacturing	31–33	**17,695**	**17,263**	**14,226**	**14,155**	**13,884**	**14.32**	**16.56**	**17.26**
Durable goods	(X)	**10,737**	**10,877**	**8,956**	**8,981**	**8,816**	**14.92**	**17.33**	**18.19**
Wood products	321	541	613	559	559	520	11.63	13.16	13.67
Nonmetallic mineral products	327	528	554	505	510	503	14.53	16.61	16.93
Cement and concrete products	3273	195	234	240	248	243	14.64	16.68	17.23
Primary metals	331	689	622	466	464	456	16.64	18.94	19.66
Foundries	3315	214	217	164	161	155	14.72	17.50	18.38
Fabricated metal products [5]	332	1,610	1,753	1,522	1,553	1,563	13.77	15.80	16.53
Architectural and structural metals	3323	357	428	398	412	416	13.43	15.10	15.94
Machine shops and threaded products . . .	3327	309	365	345	352	361	14.53	16.43	17.40
Machinery [5]	333	1,410	1,457	1,166	1,183	1,188	15.21	17.02	17.72
Agricultural, construction, and mining machinery	3331	229	222	208	220	230	14.21	15.91	17.06
HVAC and commercial refrigeration equip.	3334	165	194	154	157	154	13.10	14.60	14.71
Metalworking machinery	3335	267	274	202	200	193	16.66	17.86	18.69
Computer and electronic products [5]	334	1,903	1,820	1,316	1,308	1,272	14.73	18.39	19.95
Computer and peripheral equipment	3341	367	302	205	196	187	18.39	22.75	21.86
Communications equipment	3342	223	239	141	136	129	14.39	18.05	19.81
Semiconductors and electronic components	3344	574	676	452	458	445	13.46	17.03	18.29
Electronic instruments	3345	635	488	441	445	444	15.80	17.71	21.10
Electrical equipment and appliances	335	633	591	434	433	427	13.23	15.24	15.94
Electrical equipment	3353	244	210	152	155	155	13.28	15.31	16.10
Transportation equipment [5]	336	2,135	2,057	1,772	1,769	1,711	18.89	22.09	23.02
Motor vehicles	3361	271	291	248	237	223	24.45	29.01	29.23
Motor vehicle parts	3363	653	840	678	655	609	17.95	21.10	20.80
Aerospace products and parts	3364	841	517	455	474	487	20.52	24.82	28.39
Furniture and related products	337	604	683	568	560	535	11.73	13.45	14.32
Household and institutional furniture	3371	401	443	383	374	350	11.39	13.15	13.98
Miscellaneous manufacturing	339	686	728	647	644	641	11.93	14.07	14.66
Medical equipment and supplies	3391	283	305	300	303	306	12.70	14.71	15.06
Nondurable goods	(X)	**6,958**	**6,386**	**5,271**	**5,174**	**5,068**	**13.31**	**15.27**	**15.67**
Food manufacturing [5]	311	1,507	1,553	1,478	1,479	1,481	11.77	13.04	13.54
Fruit and vegetable preserving and specialty	3114	218	197	174	176	173	11.90	12.81	14.00
Animal slaughtering and processing	3116	427	507	504	506	507	10.27	11.47	11.81
Bakeries and tortilla manufacturing	3118	292	306	280	280	278	11.45	12.57	12.99
Beverages and tobacco products	312	218	207	192	194	196	17.40	18.76	18.49
Beverages	3121	173	175	167	171	174	17.19	18.28	17.54
Textile mills	313	492	378	218	195	170	11.23	12.38	13.00
Textile product mills	314	236	230	176	167	158	10.43	11.61	11.78
Apparel	315	903	484	251	232	213	8.60	10.26	11.05
Cut and sew apparel	3152	750	380	193	178	164	8.40	10.05	10.95
Leather and allied products	316	133	69	40	37	34	10.35	11.50	12.04
Paper and paper products	322	647	605	484	471	461	15.91	17.99	18.43
Pulp, paper, and paperboard mills	3221	238	191	142	136	132	20.62	22.99	24.03
Converted paper products	3222	409	413	343	334	329	13.58	15.71	15.97
Printing and related support activities	323	809	807	646	634	624	14.09	15.74	16.15
Petroleum and coal products	324	153	123	112	113	113	22.80	24.47	25.26
Chemicals [5]	325	1,036	980	872	866	863	17.09	19.67	19.56
Basic chemicals	3251	249	188	150	147	150	21.06	23.80	23.24
Pharmaceuticals and medicines	3254	207	274	288	292	297	17.27	21.31	20.35
Plastics and rubber products	326	825	951	802	786	754	12.70	14.80	15.38
Plastics products	3261	618	737	634	630	606	12.04	14.01	14.67
Rubber products	3262	207	214	168	156	148	14.83	17.58	18.13

See footnotes at end of table.

U.S. Census Bureau, Statistical Abstract of the United States: 2009

Table 612. **Nonfarm Industries—Employees and Earnings: 1990 to 2007**—Con.

[Annual averages of monthly figures (109,487 represents 109,487,000). Covers all full- and part-time employees who worked during, or received pay for, any part of the pay period including the 12th of the month. See also headnote, Table 610]

Industry	2007 NAICS [1] code	All employees (1,000)					Average hourly earnings [2] (dol.)		
		1990	2000	2005	2006	2007	2000	2005	2007
Trade, transportation, and utilities	(X)	**22,666**	**26,225**	**25,959**	**26,276**	**26,608**	**13.31**	**14.92**	**15.79**
Wholesale trade.	**42**	**5,268**	**5,933**	**5,764**	**5,905**	**6,028**	**16.28**	**18.16**	**19.59**
Durable goods [5]	423	2,834	3,251	2,999	3,075	3,131	16.71	18.88	19.88
Motor vehicles and parts	4231	309	356	344	348	350	14.27	16.18	16.52
Lumber and construction supplies	4233	181	227	254	264	260	13.61	16.78	17.65
Commercial equipment	4234	597	722	639	651	665	20.29	23.67	24.24
Electric goods	4236	357	425	342	346	355	19.43	21.78	23.05
Hardware and plumbing	4237	216	247	245	254	258	15.07	16.47	18.53
Machinery and supplies	4238	690	725	659	677	694	16.47	18.71	19.60
Nondurable goods [5]	424	1,900	2,065	2,022	2,041	2,069	14.33	16.15	17.63
Paper and paper products	4241	162	177	152	150	144	15.65	17.23	18.32
Druggists' goods.	4242	136	192	213	211	214	18.98	19.20	21.32
Grocery and related products	4244	623	689	699	709	724	13.57	15.38	17.01
Electronic markets and agents and brokers.	425	535	618	743	789	828	20.79	20.71	23.60
Retail trade	**44,45**	**13,182**	**15,280**	**15,280**	**15,353**	**15,491**	**10.86**	**12.36**	**12.76**
Motor vehicle and parts dealers [5] . . .	441	1,494	1,847	1,919	1,910	1,913	14.94	16.33	16.45
Automobile dealers	4411	983	1,217	1,261	1,247	1,245	16.95	17.85	17.61
Auto parts, accessories, and tire stores	4413	418	499	491	494	497	11.04	12.74	13.34
Furniture and home furnishings stores . . .	442	432	544	576	587	581	12.33	14.23	15.23
Furniture stores	4421	244	289	298	299	290	13.37	14.87	15.28
Home furnishings stores	4422	188	254	278	288	291	11.06	13.46	15.17
Electronics and appliance stores.	443	382	564	536	541	544	13.67	17.73	18.39
Building material and garden supply stores.	444	891	1,142	1,276	1,324	1,305	11.25	13.14	13.59
Building material and supplies dealers .	4441	753	982	1,134	1,179	1,163	11.30	13.24	13.64
Food and beverage stores	445	2,779	2,993	2,818	2,821	2,849	9.76	10.85	11.32
Grocery stores	4451	2,406	2,582	2,446	2,457	2,485	9.71	10.80	11.28
Specialty food stores.	4452	232	270	236	229	226	9.97	11.04	11.32
Beer, wine, and liquor stores.	4453	141	141	136	136	138	10.40	11.48	12.16
Health and personal care stores	446	792	928	954	961	989	11.68	14.03	15.10
Gasoline stations	447	910	936	871	864	861	8.05	8.92	9.20
Clothing & clothing accessories stores . . .	448	1,313	1,322	1,415	1,451	1,500	9.96	11.07	11.45
Clothing stores.	4481	930	954	1,066	1,101	1,148	9.88	10.63	10.71
Shoe stores	4482	216	193	180	183	188	8.96	10.05	11.14
Jewelry, luggage, and leather goods stores	4483	167	175	169	166	164	11.48	14.10	15.30
Sporting goods, hobby, book, and music stores.	451	532	686	647	646	658	9.33	10.35	11.27
Sporting goods and musical instrument stores	4511	352	437	447	458	472	9.55	10.68	11.49
Book, periodical, and music stores. . . .	4512	180	249	200	187	186	8.91	9.59	10.74
General merchandise stores	452	2,500	2,820	2,934	2,935	2,985	9.22	10.53	10.61
Department stores	4521	1,494	1,755	1,595	1,557	1,577	(NA)	(NA)	(NA)
Miscellaneous store retailers [5]	453	738	1,007	900	881	869	10.20	11.22	11.70
Florists	4531	121	130	101	95	93	8.95	9.88	10.12
Office supplies, stationery, and gift stores	4532	358	471	391	374	364	10.46	11.65	12.60
Nonstore retailers.	454	419	492	435	433	438	13.22	14.56	15.45
Electronic shopping and mail-order houses	4541	157	257	240	241	247	13.38	14.52	15.29
Transportation and warehousing.	**48,49**	**3,476**	**4,410**	**4,361**	**4,470**	**4,536**	**15.05**	**16.70**	**17.73**
Air transportation	481	529	614	501	487	493	(NA)	(NA)	(NA)
Scheduled air transportation	4811	503	570	456	442	447	(NA)	(NA)	(NA)
Rail transportation	482	272	232	228	228	234	(NA)	(NA)	(NA)
Water transportation	483	57	56	61	63	64	(NA)	(NA)	(NA)
Truck transportation	484	1,122	1,406	1,398	1,436	1,441	15.86	16.74	17.60
General freight trucking	4841	807	1,013	981	1,005	1,006	16.37	17.20	17.66
Specialized freight trucking	4842	315	393	417	431	435	14.51	15.60	17.45
Transit and ground passenger transportation [5]	485	274	372	389	399	410	11.88	13.00	13.58
Urban transit systems	4851	21	35	40	40	40	14.99	17.18	16.18
Taxi and limousine service	4853	57	72	66	69	72	(NA)	(NA)	(NA)
School and employee bus transportation.	4854	114	152	169	172	177	11.42	12.74	13.49
Pipeline transportation	486	60	46	38	39	40	19.86	24.33	24.60
Scenic and sightseeing transportation . . .	487	16	28	29	28	29	12.49	13.75	15.16
Support activities for transportation [5] . . .	488	364	537	552	571	583	14.57	17.66	18.57
Support activities for air transportation .	4881	96	141	148	157	164	13.42	15.07	16.57
Support activities for water transportation.	4883	91	97	94	99	100	19.57	27.08	29.16
Support activities for road transportation.	4884	35	66	79	81	83	13.98	15.41	14.34
Freight transportation arrangement . . .	4885	111	178	177	180	183	13.46	16.94	17.59
Couriers and messengers	492	375	605	571	582	583	13.51	15.33	15.78
Couriers and express delivery services .	4921	340	546	522	533	533	13.92	15.76	16.23
Warehousing and storage	493	407	514	595	638	659	14.46	15.06	15.11
Utilities.	**22**	**740**	**601**	**554**	**549**	**553**	**22.75**	**26.68**	**27.87**
Power generation and supply	2211	550	434	401	396	398	23.13	27.63	29.25
Natural gas distribution	2212	155	121	107	106	107	23.41	26.86	26.76
Water, sewage and other systems	2213	35	46	45	46	49	16.93	17.70	19.01

See footnotes at end of table.

Table 612. **Nonfarm Industries—Employees and Earnings: 1990 to 2007**—Con.

[**Annual averages of monthly figures (109,487 represents 109,487,000).** Covers all full- and part-time employees who worked during, or received pay for, any part of the pay period including the 12th of the month. See also headnote, Table 610]

Industry	2007 NAICS [1] code	All employees (1,000)					Average hourly earnings [2] (dol.)		
		1990	2000	2005	2006	2007	2000	2005	2007
Information.	**51**	**2,688**	**3,630**	**3,061**	**3,038**	**3,029**	**19.07**	**22.06**	**23.94**
Publishing industries, except Internet	511	871	1,035	904	902	898	20.18	24.20	25.35
Newspaper, book, and directory publishers	5111	773	774	666	658	646	15.06	18.57	19.68
Software publishers	5112	98	261	238	244	252	28.48	38.11	38.43
Motion picture and sound recording industries	512	255	383	378	376	380	21.25	18.75	20.49
Motion picture and video industries	5121	232	352	357	354	357	21.33	18.88	20.78
Broadcasting, except Internet	515	284	344	328	328	326	16.74	21.22	23.66
Radio and television broadcasting	5151	232	253	239	238	235	17.13	22.15	23.37
Cable and other subscription programming	5152	52	91	89	90	91	(NA)	(NA)	(NA)
Telecommunications [5]	517	980	1,397	1,071	1,048	1,028	18.59	22.13	24.57
Wired telecommunications carriers	5171	673	922	690	669	655	18.62	22.46	23.67
Wireless telecommunications carriers (except satellite)	5172	36	186	191	200	209	14.40	20.40	27.93
Data processing, hosting and related services	518	211	316	263	263	271	16.97	19.97	21.38
Other information services	519	30	157	118	121	126	21.84	21.79	22.70
Financial activities	**(X)**	**6,614**	**7,687**	**8,153**	**8,328**	**8,308**	**14.98**	**17.94**	**19.64**
Finance and insurance [5]	52	4,979	5,680	6,023	6,156	6,147	15.90	19.09	20.92
Credit intermediation and related activities	522	2,425	2,548	2,869	2,925	2,882	13.14	15.85	17.29
Depository credit intermediation	5221	1,909	1,681	1,769	1,802	1,823	11.97	14.13	16.02
Commercial banking	52211	1,362	1,251	1,296	1,323	1,346	11.83	13.79	15.66
Nondepository credit intermediation	5222	398	644	770	776	724	15.30	19.24	19.85
Activities related to credit intermediation	5223	119	222	330	347	335	15.39	16.48	18.22
Securities, commodity contracts, investments	523	458	805	786	818	848	20.20	26.59	29.95
Securities and commodity contracts brokerage and exchanges	5232	338	566	499	511	519	20.07	27.68	30.12
Other financial investment activities	5239	120	239	287	308	329	20.48	24.69	29.69
Insurance carriers and related activities	524	2,016	2,221	2,259	2,304	2,308	17.37	20.66	22.09
Insurance carriers	5241	1,338	1,433	1,386	1,413	1,399	17.92	21.67	23.11
Insurance agencies, brokerages, and related services	5242	678	788	874	891	910	16.28	18.88	20.42
Funds, trusts, and other financial vehicles	525	56	85	88	88	88	17.66	21.12	22.15
Real estate and rental and leasing [5]	**53**	**1,637**	**2,011**	**2,134**	**2,173**	**2,162**	**12.14**	**14.55**	**15.76**
Real estate	531	1,107	1,312	1,457	1,499	1,492	12.24	14.67	15.87
Lessors of real estate	5311	564	607	600	602	595	11.16	13.75	15.41
Offices of real estate agents and brokers	5312	217	281	356	375	366	12.57	14.90	16.30
Activities related to real estate	5313	327	424	502	522	531	13.60	15.64	16.09
Rental and leasing services [5]	532	514	667	646	646	640	11.69	14.05	15.11
Automotive equipment rental and leasing	5321	163	208	199	199	195	10.70	13.64	14.25
Consumer goods rental	5322	220	292	275	268	262	9.53	12.39	12.75
Professional and business services	**(X)**	**10,848**	**16,666**	**16,954**	**17,566**	**17,962**	**15.52**	**18.08**	**20.13**
Professional and technical services [5]	54	4,557	6,734	7,053	7,357	7,662	20.61	24.15	26.54
Legal services	5411	944	1,066	1,168	1,173	1,176	21.38	23.96	26.67
Accounting and bookkeeping services	5412	664	866	849	889	947	14.42	17.45	19.17
Architectural and engineering services	5413	942	1,238	1,311	1,386	1,436	20.49	23.96	26.29
Computer systems design and related services	5415	410	1,254	1,195	1,285	1,360	27.13	31.64	34.97
Management and technical consulting services	5416	305	673	824	886	953	20.83	23.97	25.58
Scientific research and development services	5417	494	515	577	592	601	21.39	28.33	31.20
Advertising and related services	5418	382	497	446	459	469	16.99	19.49	21.16
Other professional and technical services	5419	317	462	524	549	577	13.55	15.53	16.82
Management of companies and enterprises	**55**	**1,667**	**1,796**	**1,759**	**1,811**	**1,846**	**15.28**	**18.08**	**20.75**
Administrative and waste services [5]	**56**	**4,624**	**8,136**	**8,142**	**8,398**	**8,454**	**11.69**	**13.16**	**14.49**
Administrative and support services [5]	561	4,395	7,823	7,804	8,050	8,097	11.53	12.93	14.27
Office administrative services	5611	211	264	345	365	390	14.68	17.82	20.22
Employment services	5613	1,494	3,817	3,578	3,681	3,601	11.89	13.04	14.45
Temporary help services	56132	1,156	2,636	2,549	2,637	2,605	11.79	12.00	13.38
Business support services	5614	505	787	766	793	806	11.08	13.14	13.59
Travel arrangement and reservation services	5615	250	299	224	226	227	12.72	14.55	15.77
Investigation and security services	5616	507	689	737	758	777	9.78	11.64	13.04
Services to buildings and dwellings	5617	1,175	1,571	1,738	1,801	1,851	10.02	11.44	12.25
Waste management and remediation services	562	229	313	338	348	357	15.29	17.69	18.63

See footnotes at end of table.

Labor Force, Employment, and Earnings 401

Table 612. **Nonfarm Industries—Employees and Earnings: 1990 to 2007**—Con.

[**Annual averages of monthly figures (109,487 represents 109,487,000).** Covers all full- and part-time employees who worked during, or received pay for, any part of the pay period including the 12th of the month. See also headnote, Table 610]

Industry	2007 NAICS [1] code	All employees (1,000)					Average hourly earnings [2] (dol.)		
		1990	2000	2005	2006	2007	2000	2005	2007
Education and health services	(X)	**10,984**	**15,109**	**17,372**	**17,826**	**18,327**	**13.95**	**16.71**	**18.11**
Educational services	61	**1,688**	**2,390**	**2,836**	**2,901**	**2,949**	**(NA)**	**(NA)**	**(NA)**
Elementary and secondary schools	6111	461	716	837	835	827	(NA)	(NA)	(NA)
Junior colleges	6112	44	79	100	88	76	(NA)	(NA)	(NA)
Colleges and universities	6113	939	1,196	1,393	1,446	1,487	(NA)	(NA)	(NA)
Business, computer, and management training	6114	60	86	77	75	78	(NA)	(NA)	(NA)
Technical and trade schools	6115	72	91	102	107	110	(NA)	(NA)	(NA)
Other schools and instruction	6116	96	184	250	268	283	(NA)	(NA)	(NA)
Educational support services	6117	17	39	78	83	89	(NA)	(NA)	(NA)
Health care and social assistance	62	**9,296**	**12,718**	**14,536**	**14,925**	**15,378**	**13.98**	**17.05**	**18.48**
Ambulatory health care services [5]	621	2,842	4,320	5,114	5,286	5,477	14.99	17.86	19.68
Offices of physicians	6211	1,278	1,840	2,094	2,148	2,204	15.65	18.95	21.32
Offices of dentists	6212	513	688	774	786	812	15.96	19.40	21.52
Offices of other health practitioners . . .	6213	276	438	549	573	599	14.24	16.70	18.22
Outpatient care centers	6214	261	386	473	493	507	15.29	18.96	19.91
Medical and diagnostic laboratories . . .	6215	129	162	198	204	212	15.74	18.67	21.60
Home health care services	6216	288	633	821	866	913	12.86	14.42	15.40
Hospitals [5]	622	3,513	3,954	4,345	4,423	4,517	16.71	21.30	22.94
General medical and surgical hospitals .	6221	3,305	3,745	4,096	4,163	4,245	16.75	21.40	23.06
Psychiatric and substance abuse hospitals	6222	113	86	93	98	100	14.97	17.79	18.72
Nursing and residential care facilities [5] . . .	623	1,856	2,583	2,855	2,893	2,952	10.67	12.37	13.26
Nursing care facilities	6231	1,170	1,514	1,577	1,581	1,601	11.08	13.08	13.85
Residential mental health facilities	6232	269	437	497	510	527	9.96	11.30	12.55
Community care facilities for the elderly	6233	330	478	615	638	661	9.83	11.33	12.32
Social assistance	624	1,085	1,860	2,222	2,324	2,431	9.78	11.35	12.15
Individual and family services	6241	389	678	921	980	1,048	10.57	12.44	13.00
Emergency and other relief services . . .	6242	67	117	129	131	135	10.95	13.48	14.84
Vocational rehabilitation services	6243	242	370	383	394	399	9.57	10.67	11.83
Child day care services	6244	388	696	790	818	849	8.88	10.14	10.90
Leisure and hospitality	(X)	**9,288**	**11,862**	**12,816**	**13,110**	**13,474**	**8.32**	**9.38**	**10.41**
Arts, entertainment, and recreation	71	**1,132**	**1,788**	**1,892**	**1,929**	**1,978**	**10.68**	**12.85**	**14.11**
Performing arts and spectator sports	711	273	382	376	399	412	13.11	18.67	19.56
Museums, historical sites, zoos, and parks	712	68	110	121	124	130	12.21	13.67	14.57
Amusements, gambling, and recreation . .	713	791	1,296	1,395	1,406	1,435	9.86	11.08	12.38
Accommodations and food services	72	**8,156**	**10,074**	**10,923**	**11,181**	**11,496**	**7.92**	**8.80**	**9.81**
Accommodations	721	1,616	1,884	1,819	1,832	1,856	9.48	10.75	12.21
Traveler and other longer-term accommodations	7211	1,582	1,837	1,765	1,778	1,802	9.49	10.78	12.26
RV parks and recreational camps	7212	34	47	53	54	54	9.03	9.78	10.17
Food services and drinking places	722	6,540	8,189	9,104	9,349	9,640	7.49	8.34	9.24
Full-service restaurants	7221	3,070	3,845	4,316	4,435	4,587	7.78	8.84	9.83
Limited-service eating places	7222	2,765	3,462	3,889	4,004	4,136	6.87	7.49	8.28
Special food services	7223	392	491	538	551	554	9.45	10.48	11.33
Drinking places, alcoholic beverages . .	7224	312	391	361	360	363	7.24	7.89	9.07
Other services	81	**4,261**	**5,168**	**5,395**	**5,438**	**5,491**	**12.73**	**14.34**	**15.42**
Repair and maintenance	811	1,009	1,242	1,236	1,249	1,257	13.28	14.82	15.69
Automotive repair and maintenance	8111	659	888	886	887	888	12.45	14.11	14.71
Personal and laundry services	812	1,120	1,243	1,277	1,288	1,305	10.18	11.81	12.46
Personal care services	8121	430	490	577	590	610	10.18	12.44	13.20
Death care services	8122	123	136	137	135	132	13.04	15.34	16.30
Dry-cleaning and laundry services	8123	371	388	347	343	335	9.17	10.18	10.96
Dry-cleaning and laundry services, except coin-operated	81232	215	211	180	177	169	8.14	9.14	9.56
Other personal services	8129	196	229	216	221	228	10.52	11.29	11.32
Pet care services, except veterinary . . .	81291	23	31	44	48	52	(NA)	(NA)	(NA)
Parking lots and garages	81293	68	93	103	108	110	8.81	9.89	10.08
Membership associations & organizations [5] .	813	2,132	2,683	2,882	2,901	2,929	13.66	15.20	16.60
Social advocacy organizations	8133	126	143	174	180	191	12.08	13.89	14.86
Civic and social organizations.	8134	377	404	409	411	416	9.85	11.16	11.96
Professional and similar organizations . . .	8139	379	473	492	503	510	15.98	18.60	20.64
Government	92	**18,415**	**20,790**	**21,804**	**21,974**	**22,203**	**(NA)**	**(NA)**	**(NA)**
Federal	(X)	3,196	2,865	2,732	2,732	2,727	(NA)	(NA)	(NA)
State	(X)	4,305	4,786	5,032	5,075	5,125	(NA)	(NA)	(NA)
Local	(X)	10,914	13,139	14,041	14,167	14,351	(NA)	(NA)	(NA)

NA Not available. X Not applicable. [1] Based on the North American Industry Classification System, 2007. See text, this section. [2] Production workers in the goods-producing industries and nonsupervisory workers in service-producing industries. See footnotes 3 and 4. [3] Natural resources and mining, construction, and manufacturing. [4] Trade, transportation and utilities, information, financial activities, professional and business services, education and health services, leisure and hospitality, other services, and government. [5] Includes other industries not shown separately.

Source: U.S. Bureau of Labor Statistics, Employment, Hours, and Earnings from Current Employment Statistics survey (National); <http://www.bls.gov/ces/home.htm>.

Table 613. **Private Sector Job Gains and Losses: 1999 to 2007**

[In thousands (353 represents 353,000). For the three months ending in month shown. Data are for establishments and are seasonally adjusted. Based on the Quarterly Census of Employment and Wages; for details see source. Minus sign (–) indicates loss]

Year and month ending	Net change [1]	Gross job gains			Gross job losses		
		Total	Expanding establishments	Opening establishments	Total	Contracting establishments	Closing establishments
1999:							
March	353	8,585	6,626	1,959	8,232	6,395	1,837
June	644	8,539	6,661	1,878	7,895	6,210	1,685
September	588	8,571	6,734	1,837	7,983	6,250	1,733
December	1,005	8,749	6,956	1,793	7,744	6,076	1,668
2000:							
March	789	8,792	6,924	1,868	8,003	6,341	1,662
June	492	8,499	6,814	1,685	8,007	6,387	1,620
September	296	8,506	6,728	1,778	8,210	6,483	1,727
December	295	8,400	6,702	1,698	8,105	6,433	1,672
2001:							
March	–156	8,436	6,694	1,742	8,592	6,717	1,875
June	–792	8,009	6,319	1,690	8,801	7,050	1,751
September	–1,184	7,608	5,917	1,691	8,792	6,991	1,801
December	–960	7,591	5,932	1,659	8,551	6,858	1,693
2002:							
March	–39	8,049	6,259	1,790	8,088	6,424	1,664
June	–38	7,890	6,164	1,726	7,928	6,290	1,638
September	–171	7,608	6,015	1,593	7,779	6,248	1,531
December	–198	7,522	5,960	1,562	7,720	6,171	1,549
2003:							
March	–420	7,423	5,901	1,522	7,843	6,306	1,537
June	–96	7,415	5,944	1,471	7,511	6,040	1,471
September	180	7,369	5,898	1,471	7,189	5,828	1,361
December	332	7,560	6,027	1,533	7,228	5,792	1,436
2004:							
March	439	7,669	6,174	1,495	7,230	5,796	1,434
June	636	7,771	6,251	1,520	7,135	5,651	1,484
September	182	7,612	6,036	1,576	7,430	5,889	1,541
December	797	7,883	6,268	1,615	7,086	5,655	1,431
2005:							
March	352	7,578	6,107	1,471	7,226	5,800	1,426
June	590	7,796	6,248	1,548	7,206	5,789	1,417
September	651	7,943	6,362	1,581	7,292	5,846	1,446
December	539	7,846	6,278	1,568	7,307	5,936	1,371
2006:							
March	774	7,679	6,261	1,418	6,905	5,633	1,272
June	416	7,811	6,292	1,519	7,395	6,015	1,380
September	11	7,473	6,032	1,441	7,462	6,110	1,352
December	512	7,809	6,271	1,538	7,297	5,943	1,354
2007:							
March	438	7,509	6,158	1,351	7,071	5,796	1,275
June	241	7,644	6,257	1,387	7,403	6,008	1,395
September	–235	7,249	5,821	1,428	7,484	6,134	1,350
December	317	7,650	6,213	1,437	7,333	5,985	1,348

[1] Difference between the total gross job gains and total gross job losses.

Source: U.S. Bureau of Labor Statistics, *Business Employment Dynamics: Fourth Quarter* 2007, USDL 08-1141, August 12, 2008. See Internet site: <http://www.bls.gov/bdm/home.htm>.

Table 614. **Average Percent Share of Private Sector Gross Job Gains and Losses, by Firm Size: 1992 through 2007**

[In percent. Covers third quarter 1992 through fourth quarter 2007. Data are for firms (legal businesses, either corporate or otherwise, which may consist of several establishments). Based on the Quarterly Census of Employment and Wages; for details see source]

Item	1 to 4 employ-ees	5 to 9 employ-ees	10 to 19 employ-ees	20 to 49 employ-ees	50 to 99 employ-ees	100 to 249 employ-ees	250 to 499 employ-ees	500 to 999 employ-ees	1,000 or more
Gross job gains	15.5	11.4	11.7	13.8	8.8	9.3	5.6	4.6	19.3
Expanding firms . . .	7.2	10.7	11.9	14.9	9.8	10.8	6.6	5.3	22.8
Opening firms.	61.8	15.5	10.1	7.7	2.8	1.4	0.3	0.2	0.2
Gross job losses	16.1	12.3	12.4	14.5	9.0	9.1	5.4	4.5	16.7
Contracting firms. . .	8.0	11.6	12.7	15.7	10.1	10.5	6.3	5.3	19.8
Closing firms	59.8	16.4	10.8	8.0	3.0	1.6	0.4	–	–

– Represents or rounds to zero.

Source: U.S. Bureau of Labor Statistics, *Business Employment Dynamics, Fourth Quarter 2007 News*, USDL 08-1141, August 12, 2008. See Internet site <http://www.bls.gov/bdm/home.htm>.

Labor Force, Employment, and Earnings   403

Table 615. **Hires and Separations Affecting Establishment Payrolls: 2004 to 2007**

[**54,721 represents 54,721,000.** Hires represent any additions to payrolls, including new and rehired employees, full- and part-time workers, short-term and seasonal workers, etc. Separations represent terminations of employment, including quits, layoffs, and discharges etc. Based on a monthly survey of private nonfarm establishments and governmental entities]

Industry	Annual hires (1,000)				Annual separations (1,000)			
	2004	2005	2006	2007	2004	2005	2006	2007
Total.	**54,721**	**57,491**	**59,158**	**57,778**	**51,779**	**54,609**	**55,199**	**54,641**
Private industry	50,858	53,416	54,612	53,158	48,479	51,286	51,492	50,925
Natural resources and mining	229	257	242	287	216	206	219	275
Construction	4,677	5,150	4,530	4,151	4,638	4,847	4,657	4,285
Manufacturing	4,316	4,112	4,282	4,274	4,255	4,469	4,442	4,612
Durable goods	2,718	2,592	2,545	2,437	2,661	2,829	2,546	2,734
Nondurable goods	1,598	1,521	1,742	1,836	1,591	1,640	1,894	1,880
Trade, transportation, and utilities	11,988	12,289	12,669	11,843	11,704	11,983	12,031	11,859
Wholesale trade	1,702	1,720	1,618	1,955	1,720	1,602	1,732	1,885
Retail trade	8,392	8,530	8,964	8,219	8,177	8,424	8,559	8,301
Transportation, warehousing, and utilities. .	1,893	2,039	2,087	1,669	1,810	1,955	1,739	1,672
Information	792	881	965	807	927	893	945	824
Financial activities.	2,292	2,281	2,505	2,634	2,161	2,134	2,545	2,603
Finance and insurance	1,354	1,436	1,597	1,804	1,339	1,367	1,613	1,746
Real estate and rental and leasing	939	845	909	831	824	769	931	858
Professional and business services	9,416	10,554	10,989	10,379	8,568	9,816	9,824	9,709
Education and health services.	5,253	5,619	5,888	6,009	4,710	4,969	5,078	5,131
Educational services	713	721	842	882	594	638	677	714
Health care and social assistance.	4,541	4,898	5,042	5,127	4,118	4,331	4,403	4,417
Leisure and hospitality	9,670	9,893	10,388	10,661	9,012	9,674	9,762	9,643
Arts, entertainment, and recreation	1,495	1,503	1,545	1,631	1,493	1,409	1,386	1,419
Accommodation and food services	8,173	8,391	8,843	9,030	7,520	8,266	8,379	8,223
Other services	2,223	2,384	2,152	2,114	2,285	2,300	1,988	1,988
Government workers.	3,863	4,075	4,546	4,621	3,298	3,325	3,707	3,715
Federal.	464	492	680	873	414	446	656	739
State and local	3,399	3,586	3,866	3,749	2,888	2,880	3,051	2,978

Source: U.S. Bureau of Labor Statistics, *Job Openings and Labor Turnover*, monthly, January 2008 release, News, USDL 08-0332, March 12, 2008. See Internet site <http://www.bls.gov/jlt/home.htm>.

Table 616. **Employed Adults in Selected Work-Related Formal Learning Activities by Form of Employer Support: 2004–2005**

[(**47,760 represents 47,760,000).** Civilian noninstitutional population 16 years old and over not enrolled in elementary or secondary school. Based on the Adult Education Survey of the National Household Education Survey Program and subject to sampling error; see source and Appendix III for details]

Characteristic	Employed adults enrolled in work-related formal learning activities (1,000)	Form of employer support (percent)				
		Any employer support	Financial support (tuition, books, materials)	Program offered at workplace	Program taken during regular work hours	Salary paid during time of training
Total	**47,760**	**91**	**83**	**56**	**75**	**77**
Age:						
16 to 24 years old	4,275	75	60	32	55	43
25 to 34 years old	10,970	88	80	52	73	74
35 to 44 years old	12,434	95	90	58	74	79
45 to 54 years old	13,028	95	87	65	82	85
55 to 64 years old	6,167	94	86	56	80	84
65 years old and over.	886	91	73	63	77	83
Sex:						
Male	20,488	92	86	56	80	79
Female	27,272	90	81	56	72	75
Race/ethnicity:						
White, non-Hispanic.	36,010	92	84	57	76	76
Black, non-Hispanic	5,133	89	81	60	75	78
Asian or Pacific Islander, non-Hispanic. . . .	1,376	95	91	54	72	84
Other, non-Hispanic	1,716	80	66	45	66	72
Hispanic [1].	3,525	92	89	48	71	78
Educational attainment:						
Less than high school.	939	83	64	30	68	60
High school diploma or equivalent.	8,755	93	83	58	76	79
Some college	15,532	89	82	55	74	76
BA degree	14,131	92	87	55	76	78
Graduate degree or higher	8,404	93	82	60	75	76
Household income:						
$20,000 or less	2,670	79	68	41	54	62
$20,001 to $35,000	4,981	88	81	54	67	70
$35,001 to $50,000	6,630	93	84	61	75	74
$50,001 to $75,000	13,443	92	84	53	74	76
$75,001 or more	20,037	93	86	58	81	82

[1] Persons of Hispanic origin may be any race.

Source: U.S. National Center for Education Statistics, Adult Education Survey of the National Household Education Surveys Program 2005. See also<http://nces.ed.gov/pubs2006/adulted/index.asp>.

Table 617. Adults in Selected Work-Related Formal Learning Activities by Type of Educational Activity: 2004–2005

[(211,607 represents 211,607,000). Civilian noninstitutional population 16 years old and over not enrolled in elementary or secondary school. Based on the Adult Education Survey of the National Household Education Survey Program and subject to sampling error; see source and Appendix III for details]

Characteristic	Total adults (1,000)	Adults participating in work-related formal learning activities (percent)				
		Any activities	College degree program	Vocational degree/ diploma program	Apprenticeship	Work-related courses
Total	**211,607**	**33**	**7**	**1**	**1**	**27**
Age:						
16 to 24 years old	25,104	46	28	3	3	21
25 to 44 years old	81,674	39	7	2	2	33
45 to 64 years old	70,908	34	2	1	–	33
65 years old and over	33,922	5	–	–	–	5
Sex:						
Male	101,596	31	6	2	2	24
Female	110,011	35	8	1	1	29
Race/ethnicity:						
White, non-Hispanic	146,614	34	7	1	1	29
Black, non-Hispanic	23,467	34	6	2	2	27
Asian or Pacific Islander, non-Hispanic	7,080	35	12	1	1	24
Other, non-Hispanic	8,346	34	11	2	2	23
Hispanic [1]	26,101	23	4	2	2	17
Educational attainment:						
Less than high school	38,538	8	1	1	2	6
High school diploma or equivalent	63,701	23	2	2	1	18
Some college	51,657	43	14	2	2	32
BA degree	37,244	49	9	1	–	44
Graduate degree or higher	20,466	55	8	1	1	51

– Represents or rounds to zero.   [1] Persons of Hispanic origin may be of any race.

Source: U.S. National Center for Education Statistics, Adult Education Survey of the National Household Education Surveys Program 2005, unpublished data.

Table 618. Average Hours Worked Per Day by Employed Persons: 2007

[(155,502 represents 155,502,000). Civilian noninstitutional population 15 years old and over, except as indicated. Includes work at main and any other job(s). Excludes travel related to work. Based on the American Time Use Survey, a survey conducted continuously throughout the year, and subject to sampling error; see source for details]

Characteristic	Total employed (1,000)	Employed persons who worked on their diary day						
		Number (1,000)	Percent of employed	Hours of work	Worked at workplace		Worked at home [1]	
					Percent of employed [2]	Hours of work	Percent of employed [2]	Hours of work
Total	**155,502**	**108,042**	**69.5**	**7.57**	**86.5**	**7.86**	**19.9**	**2.82**
Work status:								
Full-time workers [3]	121,444	89,049	73.3	8.05	88.1	8.24	19.2	2.92
Part-time workers [3]	34,058	18,993	55.8	5.36	78.8	5.88	22.8	2.40
Male	83,012	59,279	71.4	7.89	87.2	8.11	19.9	2.83
Full-time workers [3]	71,243	52,917	74.3	8.21	88.5	8.35	19.6	2.90
Part-time workers [3]	11,770	6,362	54.1	5.19	76.8	5.79	21.8	2.27
Female	72,490	48,763	67.3	7.20	85.6	7.55	19.9	2.80
Full-time workers [3]	50,201	36,133	72.0	7.81	87.6	8.07	18.6	2.96
Part-time workers [3]	22,288	12,631	56.7	5.44	79.9	5.93	23.3	2.46
Job-holding status:								
Single job-holders	140,447	95,901	68.3	7.47	86.8	7.77	18.4	2.85
Multiple job-holders	15,055	12,141	80.6	8.43	84	8.56	31.3	2.66
Educational attainment: [4]								
Less than high school	11,503	8,073	70.2	7.88	92.6	7.92	6.2	(B)
High school diploma [5]	38,947	26,457	67.9	7.87	90.6	8.01	12.8	2.91
Some college	34,697	23,596	68.0	7.67	86.6	7.97	19.7	2.78
BA degree or higher	45,418	33,834	74.5	7.47	78.8	7.94	34.5	2.77

B Percent not shown where base is less than 800,000.   [1] Represents doing activities that were "part of one's job."
[2] Percent of employed who worked on their diary day.   [3] Full-time workers usually worked 35 or more hours per week at all jobs combined; part-time workers fewer than 35 hours per week.   [4] For those 25 years old and over.   [5] Or equivalent.

Source: U.S. Bureau of Labor Statistics, *American Time Use Survey—2007 Results Announced by BLS, News,* USDL 08-0859, June 25, 2008. See Internet site <http://www.bls.gov/tus/home.htm>.

U.S. Census Bureau, Statistical Abstract of the United States: 2009

Table 619. Annual Indexes of Output Per Hour for Selected NAICS Industries: 1987 to 2006

[For a discussion of productivity measures, see text, this section. Minus sign (–) indicates decrease]

Industry	2002 NAICS code [1]	Indexes (1997 = 100)						Average annual percent change [2]
		1987	1990	1995	2000	2005	2006	
Mining	21	85.5	85.1	101.7	111.0	96.0	87.2	0.1
Oil and gas extraction	211	80.1	75.7	95.3	119.4	107.8	100.3	1.2
Mining, except oil and gas	212	69.8	79.3	94.0	106.3	114.0	110.6	2.5
Utilities:								
Power generation and supply	2211	65.6	71.1	88.5	107.0	114.3	115.4	3.0
Natural gas distribution	2212	67.8	71.4	89.0	113.2	122.2	119.0	3.0
Manufacturing:								
Fruit and vegetable preserving and specialty	3114	92.4	87.6	98.3	111.8	132.0	126.9	1.7
Dairy products	3115	82.7	91.1	97.6	95.9	109.6	110.2	1.5
Animal slaughtering and processing	3116	97.4	94.3	99.0	102.6	117.4	116.9	1.0
Bakeries and tortilla manufacturing	3118	100.9	94.5	100.7	108.3	115.4	110.5	0.5
Other food products	3119	97.5	92.5	104.1	112.6	116.2	116.3	0.9
Beverages	3121	77.1	87.6	103.2	90.8	120.3	112.0	2.0
Fabric mills	3132	68.0	75.3	95.5	110.1	164.1	170.5	5.0
Cut-and-sew apparel	3152	69.8	70.1	85.2	119.8	113.5	117.6	2.8
Sawmills and wood preservation	3211	77.6	79.4	90.4	105.4	127.3	129.7	2.7
Plywood and engineered wood products	3212	99.7	102.8	101.4	98.8	110.2	117.4	0.9
Other wood products	3219	103.0	105.3	99.8	103.0	126.3	125.3	1.0
Pulp, paper, and paperboard mills	3221	81.7	84.0	98.4	116.3	147.7	151.1	3.3
Converted paper products	3222	89.0	90.1	97.2	101.1	114.8	116.6	1.4
Printing and related support activities	3231	97.6	97.5	98.9	104.6	119.5	121.1	1.1
Petroleum and coal products	3241	71.1	75.4	89.9	113.5	123.8	122.8	2.9
Basic chemicals	3251	94.6	93.4	91.3	117.5	165.2	169.3	3.1
Resin, rubber, and artificial fibers	3252	77.4	76.4	95.4	109.8	130.5	134.9	3.0
Pharmaceuticals and medicines	3254	87.3	91.3	95.9	95.6	110.0	115.0	1.5
Plastics products	3261	83.1	85.2	94.5	112.3	135.6	133.8	2.5
Rubber products	3262	75.5	83.5	92.9	101.7	118.7	124.9	2.7
Glass and glass products	3272	82.4	79.1	87.5	108.1	123.1	132.9	2.5
Cement and concrete products	3273	93.6	96.6	99.7	101.6	106.5	103.1	0.5
Foundries	3315	81.4	86.5	93.1	103.6	128.6	131.8	2.6
Forging and stamping	3321	85.4	89.0	93.9	121.1	147.6	152.7	3.1
Architectural and structural metals	3323	88.7	87.9	93.3	100.6	109.2	113.5	1.3
Machine shops and threaded products	3327	76.9	79.2	98.3	108.2	116.3	117.1	2.2
Coating, engraving, and heat treating metals	3328	75.5	81.3	102.2	105.5	136.5	135.5	3.1
Other fabricated metal products	3329	91.0	86.5	96.3	99.9	112.5	117.7	1.4
Agriculture, construction, and mining machinery	3331	74.6	83.3	95.4	100.3	129.4	129.1	2.9
Industrial machinery	3332	75.1	81.6	97.1	130.0	122.4	135.3	3.1
HVAC and commercial refrigeration equipment	3334	84.0	90.6	96.4	107.9	137.1	133.4	2.5
Metalworking machinery	3335	85.1	86.5	99.2	106.1	127.3	128.3	2.2
Other general purpose machinery	3339	83.5	86.8	94.0	113.7	138.4	143.8	2.9
Computer and peripheral equipment	3341	11.9	14.7	49.8	235.0	543.3	715.7	24.1
Communications equipment	3342	39.8	48.4	74.4	164.1	143.7	178.2	8.2
Semiconductors and electronic components	3344	19.8	21.9	63.8	232.2	381.6	380.4	16.8
Electronic instruments	3345	70.2	78.5	97.9	116.7	146.6	150.6	4.1
Electrical equipment	3353	68.7	73.6	98.0	99.4	118.5	118.1	2.9
Other electrical equipment and components	3359	78.8	76.1	92.0	119.7	121.6	115.7	2.0
Motor vehicles	3361	75.4	85.6	88.5	109.7	148.4	163.8	4.2
Motor vehicle bodies and trailers	3362	85.0	75.9	97.4	98.8	114.2	110.9	1.4
Motor vehicle parts	3363	78.7	76.0	92.2	112.3	144.1	143.7	3.2
Aerospace products and parts	3364	87.2	89.1	95.7	103.4	125.0	117.9	1.6
Ship and boat building	3366	95.5	99.6	93.1	121.9	131.7	127.3	1.5
Household and institutional furniture	3371	85.2	88.2	97.2	101.9	120.8	124.0	2.0
Office furniture and fixtures	3372	85.8	82.2	84.9	100.2	134.9	134.4	2.4
Medical equipment and supplies	3391	76.3	82.9	96.6	115.5	148.5	152.8	3.7
Other miscellaneous manufacturing	3399	85.4	90.5	95.9	113.6	137.8	143.2	2.8
Wholesale trade	42	73.2	79.9	94.0	116.6	135.2	141.1	3.5
Durable goods	423	62.3	67.5	90.1	125.1	167.3	175.8	5.6
Nondurable goods	424	91.0	98.9	98.5	105.1	114.3	117.4	1.3
Electronic markets and agents and brokers	425	64.3	74.3	95.4	120.1	87.3	93.6	2.0
Retail trade	44–45	79.1	81.4	94.0	116.1	141.5	148.5	3.4
Motor vehicle and parts dealers	441	78.3	82.7	95.5	114.3	127.0	129.8	2.7
Automobile dealers	4411	79.2	84.1	95.8	113.7	123.8	126.8	2.5
Other motor vehicle dealers	4412	70.6	69.7	88.3	115.3	135.1	136.3	3.5
Auto parts, accessories, and tire stores	4413	71.8	79.0	95.2	108.4	115.9	115.8	2.5
Furniture and home furnishings stores	442	75.1	79.0	93.7	115.9	151.4	162.6	4.2
Furniture stores	4421	77.3	84.8	93.6	112.0	143.4	155.5	3.7
Home furnishings stores	4422	71.3	71.0	93.3	121.0	161.9	172.6	4.8
Electronics and appliance stores	443	38.0	47.7	87.8	173.7	369.6	416.2	13.4
Building material and garden supply stores	444	75.8	79.5	91.9	113.3	134.9	143.6	3.4
Building material and supplies dealers	4441	77.6	81.6	93.4	115.1	134.9	142.9	3.3
Lawn and garden equipment and supplies stores	4442	66.9	69.0	83.9	103.1	135.6	150.1	4.3
Food and beverage stores	445	110.8	107.4	102.3	101.0	118.3	122.1	0.5
Grocery stores	4451	111.1	106.9	102.7	101.1	117.1	119.2	0.4
Specialty food stores	4452	138.5	127.2	102.9	98.5	127.7	153.3	0.5
Beer, wine, and liquor stores	4453	93.6	97.6	94.2	105.7	141.8	148.8	2.5
Health and personal care stores	446	84.0	91.0	91.4	112.2	133.2	139.7	2.7
Gasoline stations	447	83.9	84.2	99.4	107.7	124.6	121.8	2.0

See footnotes at end of table.

Table 619. **Annual Indexes of Output Per Hour for Selected NAICS Industries: 1987 to 2006**—Con.

[For a discussion of productivity measures, see text, this section. Minus sign (–) indicates decrease]

Industry	2002 NAICS code [1]	Indexes (1997 = 100)						Average annual percent change [2]
		1987	1990	1995	2000	2005	2006	
Retail Trade—Con.								
Clothing and clothing accessories stores	448	66.3	69.8	92.7	123.5	147.8	163.3	4.9
Clothing stores	4481	67.1	70.0	91.7	125.0	153.1	169.9	5.0
Shoe stores	4482	65.3	70.8	96.4	110.0	132.9	149.3	4.4
Jewelry, luggage, and leather goods stores.	4483	64.5	68.1	94.1	130.5	139.0	148.8	4.5
Sporting goods, hobby, book, and music stores. . . .	451	74.9	82.3	95.0	121.1	164.8	175.3	4.6
Sporting goods and musical instrument stores. . .	4511	73.2	82.2	95.5	129.4	181.7	203.1	5.5
Book, periodical, and music stores	4512	78.9	82.3	93.9	105.8	133.7	124.9	2.4
General merchandise stores	452	73.5	75.1	92.0	120.2	145.0	152.3	3.9
Department stores	4521	87.2	83.9	94.6	106.2	109.9	113.1	1.4
Other general merchandise stores.	4529	54.8	61.2	87.2	147.3	199.7	210.4	7.3
Miscellaneous store retailers	453	65.1	69.5	88.8	114.1	142.0	159.3	4.8
Florists.	4531	77.6	73.3	82.4	115.2	120.6	125.3	2.6
Office supplies, stationery, and gift stores	4532	61.4	66.4	91.7	127.3	187.9	215.5	6.8
Used merchandise stores	4533	64.5	70.4	85.9	116.5	159.5	166.6	5.1
Other miscellaneous store retailers	4539	68.3	75.0	88.9	104.4	103.5	118.5	2.9
Nonstore retailers	454	50.7	54.7	79.8	152.2	218.4	256.3	8.9
Electronic shopping and mail-order houses.	4541	39.4	43.4	72.5	160.2	285.2	337.1	12.0
Vending machine operators	4542	95.5	95.1	86.4	111.1	105.1	110.7	0.8
Direct selling establishments	4543	70.8	74.1	93.2	122.5	121.5	135.6	3.5
Transportation and warehousing:								
Air transportation.	481	81.1	77.5	95.3	98.1	135.5	142.5	3.0
Line-haul railroads.	482111	58.9	69.8	92.0	114.3	138.4	142.8	4.8
General freight trucking, long-distance.	48412	85.7	89.2	95.8	101.9	113.2	112.3	1.4
Used household and office goods moving	48421	106.7	112.6	101.4	94.8	88.3	87.0	–1.1
Postal service.	491	90.9	94.2	97.7	105.5	111.2	111.3	1.1
Couriers and messengers	492	148.3	138.5	101.5	121.9	125.1	128.6	–0.7
Warehousing and storage	493	(NA)	(NA)	89.5	109.3	124.9	122.3	2.9
General warehousing and storage.	49311	(NA)	(NA)	85.4	115.8	132.2	127.9	3.7
Refrigerated warehousing and storage	49312	(NA)	(NA)	99.1	95.4	97.5	88.5	–1.0
Information:								
Newspaper, book, and directory publishers	5111	105.0	95.5	91.9	107.7	107.6	110.8	0.3
Software publishers	5112	10.2	28.5	73.4	119.2	173.7	177.0	16.2
Motion picture and video exhibition	51213	90.7	109.2	99.4	106.5	102.4	105.7	0.8
Broadcasting, except Internet	515	99.5	98.2	102.5	103.6	117.7	125.5	1.2
Radio and television broadcasting	5151	98.1	97.7	104.8	92.1	100.9	109.5	0.6
Cable and other subscription programming	5152	105.6	100.3	92.8	141.2	164.6	169.9	2.5
Wired telecommunications carriers	5171	56.9	66.0	87.6	122.7	138.2	146.2	5.1
Wireless telecommunications carriers	5172	75.6	70.4	90.0	152.8	381.9	435.9	9.7
Cable and other program distribution.	5175	105.2	100.0	92.6	91.6	110.6	110.6	0.3
Finance and insurance:								
Commercial banking	52211	72.8	80.7	95.6	102.7	108.5	114.2	2.4
Real estate and rental and leasing:								
Passenger car rental	532111	92.7	90.8	100.7	112.3	110.2	111.8	1.0
Truck, trailer, and RV rental and leasing	53212	60.3	68.5	88.9	121.7	145.1	162.2	5.3
Video tape and disc rental.	53223	77.0	97.1	119.5	134.9	144.2	176.4	4.5
Professional and technical services:								
Tax preparation services.	541213	82.9	76.2	90.6	100.9	103.6	99.7	1.0
Architectural services	54131	90.0	93.8	106.5	107.6	120.8	119.1	1.5
Engineering services	54133	90.2	99.4	94.4	102.0	115.4	116.2	1.3
Advertising agencies	54181	95.9	107.9	102.5	107.5	131.5	132.8	1.7
Photography studios, portrait	541921	98.1	95.9	107.3	108.9	93.5	95.3	–0.2
Administrative and waste services:								
Employment placement agencies	56131	(NA)	(NA)	86.6	89.8	115.9	122.9	3.2
Travel agencies	56151	89.3	94.6	93.0	119.4	182.4	189.9	4.1
Janitorial services	56172	75.1	94.3	90.4	101.0	121.5	115.6	2.3
Health care and social assistance:								
Medical and diagnostic laboratories	6215	(NA)	(NA)	90.9	131.9	137.9	140.1	4.0
Medical laboratories	621511	(NA)	(NA)	91.3	127.4	126.0	128.2	3.1
Diagnostic imaging centers	621512	(NA)	(NA)	90.0	139.9	154.0	156.3	5.1
Arts, entertainment, and recreation:								
Amusement and theme parks	71311	112.0	112.5	96.3	106.0	109.9	97.7	–0.7
Bowling centers.	71395	106.0	94.0	92.1	93.4	106.1	110.6	0.2
Accommodation and food services:								
Traveler accommodations	7211	85.1	81.9	97.6	111.8	115.0	111.8	1.4
Food services and drinking places	722	96.0	102.4	100.3	103.5	108.2	110.9	0.8
Full-service restaurants	7221	92.1	99.4	96.2	103.0	105.6	108.6	0.9
Limited-service eating places	7222	96.5	103.6	104.1	102.0	107.8	111.2	0.8
Special food services	7223	89.9	99.8	100.8	115.0	119.2	116.4	1.4
Drinking places, alcoholic beverages	7224	136.7	123.3	104.6	100.6	121.1	124.2	–0.5
Other services:								
Automotive repair and maintenance	8111	85.9	89.9	103.2	109.4	111.9	112.8	1.4
Hair, nail, and skin care services	81211	83.5	82.1	93.4	108.2	129.9	122.3	2.0
Funeral homes and funeral services	81221	103.7	98.4	102.4	94.8	93.2	99.7	–0.2
Drycleaning and laundry services	8123	97.1	94.8	99.2	107.6	120.5	119.6	1.1
Photofinishing.	81292	95.8	107.7	108.0	73.8	112.4	114.4	0.9

NA Not available. [1] North American Industry Classification System, 2002 (NAICS); see text, this section. [2] Average annual percent change, 1987 to 2004, based on compound rate formula. For NAICS industries 56131, 6215, 621511, and 621512 annual percent changes are for 1995–2005. The rates of change are calculated using index numbers to three decimal places.
Source: U.S. Bureau of Labor Statistics. Latest data available at: <http://www.bls.gov/lpc/home.htm> (accessed May 2008).

Labor Force, Employment, and Earnings **407**

Table 620. Productivity and Related Measures: 1990 to 2007

[See text, Section 12. Minus sign (−) indicates decrease]

Item	1990	1995	2000	2002	2003	2004	2005	2006	2007
INDEXES (1992 = 100)									
Output per hour, business sector	94.4	101.5	116.1	123.9	128.7	132.4	135.0	136.4	139.0
Nonfarm business	94.5	102.0	115.7	123.5	128.0	131.6	134.1	135.4	137.9
Manufacturing	93.9	111.0	139.1	151.0	160.4	163.9	171.9	173.8	179.7
Output,[1] business sector	96.9	111.4	140.5	143.1	147.5	153.3	159.3	164.3	168.1
Nonfarm business	97.1	111.8	140.8	143.4	147.8	153.9	159.5	164.5	168.4
Manufacturing	98.5	115.9	144.2	136.0	137.3	139.7	144.8	147.5	149.9
Hours,[2] business sector	102.7	109.7	121.0	115.4	114.6	116.1	118.0	120.5	121.0
Nonfarm business	102.7	109.6	121.7	116.1	115.4	117.0	118.9	121.5	122.1
Manufacturing	104.9	104.4	103.7	90.1	85.6	85.2	84.3	84.9	83.4
Compensation per hour,[3] business sector	90.6	105.8	134.7	145.3	151.2	156.9	163.2	169.6	178.1
Nonfarm business	90.4	105.9	134.2	144.6	150.4	155.9	162.1	168.5	176.9
Manufacturing	90.5	107.3	134.7	147.8	158.2	161.5	168.3	173.0	182.3
Real hourly compensation,[3] business sector	96.2	98.7	112.0	115.7	117.7	119.0	119.7	120.5	123.0
Nonfarm business	96.0	98.8	111.6	115.1	117.1	118.2	118.9	119.7	122.2
Manufacturing	96.1	100.1	112.0	117.7	123.2	122.4	123.5	122.8	125.9
Unit labor costs,[4] business sector	96.0	104.2	116.0	117.3	117.5	118.5	120.9	124.4	128.2
Nonfarm business	95.7	103.8	116.0	117.1	117.5	118.5	120.9	124.5	128.3
Manufacturing	96.4	96.7	96.9	97.9	98.7	98.5	97.9	99.5	101.4
ANNUAL PERCENT CHANGE [5]									
Output per hour, business sector	2.1	0.1	2.9	4.1	3.8	2.9	2.0	1.0	1.9
Nonfarm business	1.9	0.5	2.8	4.1	3.7	2.8	1.9	1.0	1.8
Manufacturing	2.2	4.5	4.1	6.9	6.2	2.2	4.9	1.1	3.4
Output,[1] business sector	1.5	2.9	3.9	1.5	3.1	4.2	3.6	3.1	2.3
Nonfarm business	1.5	3.2	3.8	1.5	3.1	4.1	3.6	3.2	2.3
Manufacturing	−0.3	5.3	2.7	−0.7	1.0	1.7	3.7	1.8	1.6
Hours,[2] business sector	−0.6	2.8	1.0	−2.5	−0.7	1.3	1.6	2.1	0.4
Nonfarm business	−0.4	2.8	1.0	−2.6	−0.6	1.3	1.7	2.2	0.5
Manufacturing	−2.5	0.7	−1.3	−7.1	−4.9	−0.5	−1.2	0.8	−1.7
Compensation per hour,[3] business sector	6.3	2.1	7.1	3.5	4.1	3.8	4.0	4.0	5.0
Nonfarm business	6.1	2.1	7.2	3.6	4.0	3.6	4.0	3.9	4.9
Manufacturing	4.4	1.9	9.1	7.2	7.0	2.1	4.2	2.8	5.4
Real hourly compensation,[3] business sector	1.3	−0.3	3.6	1.9	1.8	1.0	0.6	0.7	2.1
Nonfarm business	1.0	−0.3	3.7	2.0	1.8	0.9	0.6	0.6	2.1
Manufacturing	−0.5	−0.5	5.6	5.5	4.7	−0.6	0.9	−0.5	2.5
Unit labor costs,[4] business sector	4.1	1.9	4.1	−0.5	0.2	0.9	2.0	2.9	3.1
Nonfarm business	4.1	1.6	4.2	−0.5	0.3	0.9	2.1	2.9	3.1
Manufacturing	2.2	−2.6	4.9	0.3	0.8	−0.2	−0.6	1.7	1.9

[1] Refers to gross sectoral product, annual weighted. [2] Hours at work of all persons engaged in the business and nonfarm business sectors (employees, proprietors, and unpaid family workers); employees' and proprietors' hours in manufacturing. [3] Wages and salaries of employees plus employers' contributions for social insurance and private benefit plans. Also includes an estimate of same for self-employed. Real compensation deflated by the consumer price index for all urban consumers, see text, Section 14. [4] Hourly compensation divided by output per hour. [5] All changes are from the immediate prior year.

Source: U.S. Bureau of Labor Statistics, *Productivity and Costs*, News USDL 08-0618, May 7, 2008; and Internet site <http://www.bls.gov/lpc/home.htm>.

Table 621. Annual Total Compensation and Wages and Salary Accruals Per Full-Time Equivalent Employee by Industry: 2000 to 2006

[In dollars. Wage and salary accruals include executives' compensation, bonuses, tips, and payments-in-kind; total compensation includes in addition to wages and salaries, employer contributions for social insurance, employer contributions to private and welfare funds, director's fees, jury and witness fees, etc. Based on the 1997 North American Industry Classification System (NAICS); see text, this section]

Industry	Annual total compensation				Annual wages and salary			
	2000	2002	2004	2006	2000	2002	2004	2006
Domestic industries	46,407	49,229	53,541	57,784	38,762	40,263	43,280	46,758
Private industries	45,240	47,658	51,495	55,470	38,446	39,610	42,505	45,995
Agriculture, forestry, fishing, and hunting	29,332	26,956	29,673	32,712	25,847	23,700	26,022	28,768
Mining	70,413	74,873	85,236	96,422	58,291	61,069	67,649	79,162
Utilities	78,147	87,398	102,588	111,495	64,271	68,268	72,718	79,001
Construction	44,764	49,330	50,886	55,995	37,196	40,394	41,493	46,263
Manufacturing	54,219	58,071	63,944	68,860	44,216	44,864	48,659	52,307
Wholesale trade	56,264	61,167	65,641	71,207	48,017	51,506	55,212	60,021
Retail trade	30,225	31,275	33,116	34,568	26,307	26,675	28,181	29,390
Transportation and warehousing	48,336	50,505	54,765	57,202	39,463	40,116	42,526	44,536
Information	74,196	71,761	80,034	86,596	63,217	59,681	65,733	70,846
Finance and insurance	74,821	79,542	87,893	99,184	64,049	65,721	72,500	82,770
Real estate and rental and leasing	41,906	43,801	48,017	53,609	36,178	37,389	41,128	46,095
Professional, scientific, and technical services	68,436	73,007	77,648	84,016	58,886	62,038	66,539	72,413
Management of companies and enterprises [1]	89,496	86,677	97,383	108,158	75,984	72,971	80,935	90,682
Administrative and waste management services	28,540	31,901	33,780	37,045	25,181	27,654	28,933	31,911
Educational services	32,736	35,658	38,362	40,743	28,974	31,259	33,288	35,399
Health care and social assistance	40,897	43,830	47,564	50,357	35,127	37,374	40,232	42,746
Arts, entertainment, and recreation	35,898	37,340	41,545	43,623	31,259	32,154	35,282	37,043
Accommodation and food services	19,092	21,279	23,492	24,170	16,830	18,419	20,189	20,811
Other services, except government	28,630	30,637	33,236	35,538	25,495	27,062	29,063	30,993
Government	52,845	57,475	64,274	70,358	40,501	43,694	47,345	50,899

[1] Consists of offices of bank and other holding companies and of corporate, subsidiary, and regional managing offices.

Source: U.S. Bureau of Economic Analysis, *Survey of Current Business*, April 2008; and Internet site <http://www.bea.gov/bea/dn/nipaweb/SelectTable.asp?Selected=N> (accessed 15 May 2008).

408   Labor Force, Employment, and Earnings

Table 622. Average Hourly Earnings by Private Industry Group: 1990 to 2007

[**In dollars.** Average earnings include overtime. Data are for production workers in natural resources and mining, manufacturing, and construction, and nonsupervisory employees in the service-providing industries. See headnote, Table 610]

Private industry group	Current dollars					Constant (**1982**) dollars [1]				
	1990	2000	2005	2006	2007	1990	2000	2005	2006	2007
AVERAGE HOURLY EARNINGS										
Total private	**10.20**	**14.02**	**16.13**	**16.76**	**17.42**	**7.66**	**8.04**	**8.18**	**8.24**	**8.32**
Natural resources and mining	13.40	16.55	18.72	19.90	20.96	10.07	9.50	9.50	9.78	10.02
Construction	13.42	17.48	19.46	20.02	20.95	10.08	10.03	9.87	9.84	10.01
Manufacturing	10.78	14.32	16.56	16.81	17.26	8.10	8.22	8.40	8.26	8.25
Trade, transportation, and utilities	9.83	13.31	14.92	15.39	15.79	7.39	7.64	7.57	7.57	7.55
Information	13.40	19.07	22.06	23.23	23.94	10.07	10.94	11.19	11.42	11.44
Financial activities [2]	9.99	14.98	17.95	18.80	19.64	7.51	8.59	9.11	9.24	9.39
Professional and business services [2]	11.14	15.52	18.08	19.13	20.13	8.37	8.90	9.17	9.41	9.62
Education and health services [2]	10.00	13.95	16.71	17.38	18.11	7.51	8.00	8.48	8.54	8.65
Leisure and hospitality [2]	6.02	8.32	9.38	9.75	10.41	4.52	4.77	4.76	4.79	4.97
Other services	9.08	12.73	14.34	14.77	15.42	6.82	7.30	7.28	7.26	7.37
AVERAGE WEEKLY EARNINGS										
Total private	**350**	**481**	**544**	**568**	**590**	**263**	**276**	**276**	**279**	**282**
Natural resources and mining	603	735	854	908	962	453	422	433	446	460
Construction	513	686	750	781	816	386	393	381	384	390
Manufacturing	436	591	673	691	711	328	339	342	340	340
Trade, transportation, and utilities	332	450	498	514	526	249	258	253	253	252
Information	480	701	805	850	874	360	402	408	418	418
Financial activities [2]	355	537	645	672	705	266	308	327	330	337
Professional and business services [2]	381	535	619	662	700	286	307	314	326	335
Education and health services [2]	319	449	545	565	590	240	258	276	278	282
Leisure and hospitality [2]	156	217	241	250	265	117	125	122	123	127
Other services	298	413	443	457	477	224	237	225	224	228

[1] Earnings in current dollars divided by the Consumer Price Index (CPI-W) on a 1982 base; see text, Section 14, Prices.
[2] For composition of industries, see Table 605.
Source: U.S. Bureau of Labor Statistics, the Current Employment Statistics program Internet site <http://www.bls.gov/ces/home.htm>.

Table 623. Mean Hourly Earnings and Weekly Hours by Selected Characteristics: 2006

[Covers civilian workers in private industry establishments and state and local governments in the 50 states and DC. Excludes private households, federal government and agriculture. Based on survey of 36,433 establishments representing over 128 million workers; see source and Appendix III for details about the National Compensation Survey]

Item	Mean hourly earnings (dol.) [1]			Mean weekly hours		
	Total	Private industry	State and local govern-ment	Total	Private industry	State and local govern-ment
Total	**19.29**	**18.56**	**23.99**	**35.6**	**35.4**	**36.6**
WORKER CHARACTERISTIC						
Management, professional and related	31.45	31.66	30.79	37.1	37.5	35.9
Management, business and financial	34.89	35.17	33.03	39.8	40.0	38.4
Professional and related	29.76	29.54	30.30	35.9	36.2	35.4
Service	11.31	9.72	18.51	31.5	30.5	37.1
Sales and office	15.46	15.42	15.86	34.9	34.7	37.2
Sales and related	16.57	16.57	15.10	32.6	32.6	33.0
Office and administrative support	14.86	14.71	15.87	36.3	36.2	37.3
Natural resources, construction, and maintenance	19.49	19.46	19.84	39.4	39.4	39.3
Construction and extraction	19.46	19.46	19.52	39.4	39.4	39.5
Installation, maintenance, and repair	19.70	19.64	20.39	39.6	39.6	39.4
Production, transportation, and material moving	14.78	14.64	18.33	37.3	37.3	35.4
Production	15.11	15.02	20.75	38.9	38.9	39.3
Transportation and material moving	14.42	14.22	17.60	35.6	35.7	34.4
Full-time [2]	20.44	19.76	24.46	39.6	39.7	38.9
Part-time [2]	11.00	10.61	16.57	20.6	20.7	18.8
Union [3]	23.33	21.41	26.01	36.6	36.4	36.8
Nonunion	18.53	18.21	22.07	35.4	35.3	36.4
Time [4]	18.97	18.13	23.98	35.5	35.3	36.6
Incentive [4]	24.88	24.86	(NA)	38.0	38.0	(NA)
ESTABLISHMENT CHARACTERISTIC						
Goods producing [5]	(X)	20.06	(X)	(X)	39.5	(X)
Service producing [5]	(X)	18.09	(X)	(X)	34.4	(X)
1 to 49 workers	16.19	16.18	17.50	34.2	34.2	36.8
50 to 99 workers	17.45	17.36	19.81	35.0	35.0	35.3
100 to 499 workers	18.81	18.47	22.00	36.2	36.2	35.8
500 workers or more	23.93	23.50	24.69	37.0	37.2	36.8

NA Not available.   X Not applicable.   [1] Earnings are straight time hourly wages or salary, including incentive pay, cost-of-living adjustments, and hazard pay. Excludes premium pay for overtime, vacations and holidays, nonproduction bonuses and tips.   [2] Based on definition used by each establishment.   [3] Workers whose wages are determined through collective bargaining.   [4] Time worker wages are based solely on an hourly rate or salary. Incentive workers wages are based at least in part on productivity payments such as piece rates or commissions.   [5] For private industry only. See footnotes 3 and 4, Table 612, for composition of goods and service producing industries.
Source: U.S. Bureau of Labor Statistics, *National Compensation Survey: Occupational Wages in the United States,* Summary 07-03, June 2007. See Internet site <http://www.bls.gov/ncs/home.htm>.

Table 624. Employment and Wages: 1995 to 2006

[(115,488 represents 115,488,000). See headnote, Table 625]

Employment and wages	Unit	1995	2000	2002	2003	2004	2005	2006
Average annual employment:								
Total	1,000	115,488	129,877	128,234	127,796	129,278	131,572	133,834
Excluding federal	1,000	112,540	127,006	125,475	125,032	126,539	128,838	131,105
Private	1,000	96,895	110,015	107,577	107,066	108,490	110,611	112,719
State government	1,000	4,202	4,370	4,485	4,482	4,485	4,528	4,566
Local governments	1,000	11,442	12,620	13,413	13,484	13,564	13,699	13,820
Federal government	1,000	2,948	2,871	2,759	2,764	2,740	2,734	2,729
Annual wages:								
Total	Bil. dol. ...	3,216	4,588	4,714	4,826	5,088	5,352	5,693
Excluding federal	Bil. dol. ...	3,102	4,455	4,571	4,676	4,929	5,188	5,523
Private	Bil. dol. ...	2,659	3,888	3,931	4,016	4,246	4,480	4,781
State government	Bil. dol. ...	128	159	176	180	184	191	200
Local governments	Bil. dol. ...	315	409	464	481	499	517	541
Federal government	Bil. dol. ...	114	133	144	150	158	164	170
Average wage per employee:								
Total	Dol.	27,846	35,323	36,764	37,765	39,354	40,677	42,535
Excluding federal	Dol.	27,567	35,077	36,428	37,401	38,955	40,270	42,124
Private	Dol.	27,441	35,337	36,539	37,508	39,134	40,505	42,414
State government	Dol.	30,497	36,296	39,212	40,057	41,118	42,249	43,875
Local governments	Dol.	27,552	32,387	34,605	35,669	36,805	37,718	39,179
Federal government	Dol.	38,523	46,228	52,050	54,239	57,782	59,864	62,274
Average weekly wage per employee:								
Total	Dol.	536	679	707	726	757	782	818
Excluding federal	Dol.	530	675	701	719	749	774	810
Private	Dol.	528	680	703	721	753	779	816
State government	Dol.	586	698	754	770	791	812	844
Local governments	Dol.	530	623	665	686	708	725	753
Federal government	Dol.	741	889	1,001	1,043	1,111	1,151	1,198

Source: U.S. Bureau of Labor Statistics. "Employment and Wages, Annual Averages," 2005 and 2006. See Internet site <http://www.bls.gov/cew/home.htm>.

Table 625. Average Annual Wage by State: 2005 and 2006

[In dollars, except percent change. For workers covered by state unemployment insurance laws and for federal civilian workers covered by unemployment compensation for federal employees, approximately 97 percent of employees on nonfarm payrolls in 2006. Excludes most agricultural workers on small farms, all Armed Forces, elected officials in most states, railroad employees, most domestic workers, most student workers at school, value of meals and lodging, and tips and other gratuities]

State	Average wage per employee 2005	Average wage per employee 2006	Percent change, 2005–06	State	Average wage per employee 2005	Average wage per employee 2006	Percent change, 2005–06
United States	**40,677**	**42,535**	**4.6**	Missouri	35,951	37,143	3.3
Alabama	34,598	36,204	4.6	Montana	29,150	30,596	5.0
Alaska	40,216	41,750	3.8	Nebraska	32,422	33,814	4.3
Arizona	38,154	40,019	4.9	Nevada	38,763	40,070	3.4
Arkansas	31,266	32,389	3.6	New Hampshire	40,551	42,447	4.7
California	46,211	48,345	4.6	New Jersey	49,471	51,645	4.4
Colorado	41,601	43,506	4.6	New Mexico	32,605	34,567	6.0
Connecticut	52,954	54,814	3.5	New York	51,937	55,479	6.8
Delaware	44,622	46,285	3.7	North Carolina	35,912	37,439	4.3
District of Columbia	66,696	70,151	5.2	North Dakota	29,956	31,316	4.5
Florida	36,800	38,485	4.6	Ohio	37,333	38,568	3.3
Georgia	39,096	40,370	3.3	Oklahoma	31,721	34,022	7.3
Hawaii	36,353	37,799	4.0	Oregon	36,588	38,077	4.1
Idaho	30,777	32,580	5.9	Pennsylvania	39,661	41,349	4.3
Illinois	43,744	45,650	4.4	Rhode Island	38,751	40,454	4.4
Indiana	35,431	36,553	3.2	South Carolina	32,927	34,281	4.1
Iowa	33,070	34,320	3.8	South Dakota	29,149	30,291	3.9
Kansas	33,864	35,696	5.4	Tennessee	35,879	37,564	4.7
Kentucky	33,965	35,201	3.6	Texas	40,150	42,458	5.7
Louisiana	33,566	36,604	9.1	Utah	33,328	35,130	5.4
Maine	32,701	33,794	3.3	Vermont	34,197	35,542	3.9
Maryland	44,368	46,162	4.0	Virginia	42,287	44,051	4.2
Massachusetts	50,095	52,435	4.7	Washington	40,721	42,897	5.3
Michigan	41,214	42,157	2.3	West Virginia	31,347	32,728	4.4
Minnesota	40,800	42,185	3.4	Wisconsin	35,471	36,821	3.8
Mississippi	29,763	31,194	4.8	Wyoming	33,251	36,662	10.3

Source: U.S. Bureau of Labor Statistics. "Employment and Wages, Annual Averages", 2005 and 2006; and computed by U.S. Census Bureau. See Internet site <http://www.bls.gov/cew/home.htm>.

Table 626. Full-Time Wage and Salary Workers—Number and Earnings: 2000 to 2007

[In current dollars of usual weekly earnings. **Data represent annual averages (101,210 represents 101,210,000).** Occupational classifications are those used in the 2000 census; see text this section. Based on the Current Population Survey; see text, Section 1, and Appendix III. For definition of median, see Guide to Tabular Presentation]

Characteristic	Number of workers (1,000)			Median weekly earnings (dol.)		
	2000	2005 [1]	2007 [1]	2000	2005 [1]	2007 [1]
All workers [2]	**101,210**	**103,560**	**107,339**	**576**	**651**	**695**
SEX						
Male	57,107	58,406	60,298	641	722	766
16 to 24 years old	6,770	6,396	6,458	375	409	443
25 years old and over	50,337	52,010	53,840	693	771	823
Female	44,103	45,154	47,041	493	585	614
16 to 24 years old	5,094	4,711	4,792	344	381	409
25 years old and over	39,009	40,443	42,249	516	612	646
RACE/ETHNICITY						
White [3]	83,228	84,110	86,653	590	672	716
Male	48,085	48,572	49,889	662	743	788
Female	35,143	35,538	36,764	502	596	626
Black [3]	12,410	12,388	13,061	474	520	569
Male	5,911	5,916	6,186	510	559	600
Female	6,500	6,472	6,874	429	499	533
Asian [3, 4]	4,598	4,651	5,155	615	753	830
Male	2,538	2,597	2,858	685	825	936
Female	2,060	2,054	2,297	547	665	731
Hispanic origin [5]	12,761	14,673	16,201	399	471	503
Male	8,077	9,433	10,248	417	489	520
Female	4,684	5,241	5,953	366	429	473
OCCUPATION						
Management, professional and related occupations	34,831	36,908	39,147	810	937	996
Management, business, and financial operations	14,240	14,977	15,977	877	997	1,080
Management occupations	9,952	10,340	11,009	937	1,083	1,161
Business and financial operations occupations	4,288	4,637	4,968	760	871	941
Professional and related occupations	20,590	21,931	23,170	770	902	951
Computer and mathematical occupations	3,051	2,924	3,117	938	1,132	1,229
Architecture and engineering occupations	2,781	2,509	2,633	949	1,105	1,213
Life, physical, and social science occupations	989	1,164	1,152	811	965	1,053
Community and social services occupations	1,641	1,797	1,893	629	725	755
Legal occupations	1,039	1,162	1,167	919	1,052	1,148
Education, training, and library occupations	5,467	6,066	6,500	704	798	841
Arts, design, entertainment, sports, and media	1,488	1,488	1,568	724	819	829
Healthcare practitioner and technical occupations	4,134	4,821	5,140	727	878	920
Service occupations	12,595	14,123	14,716	365	413	454
Healthcare support occupations	1,731	2,085	2,187	358	410	454
Protective service occupations	2,281	2,549	2,736	591	678	719
Food preparation and serving-related occupations	3,483	4,007	4,107	317	356	385
Building and grounds cleaning and maintenance	3,354	3,425	3,520	351	394	422
Personal care and service occupations	1,746	2,057	2,166	351	409	434
Sales and office occupations	25,606	25,193	25,702	492	575	598
Sales and related occupations	9,650	10,031	10,448	525	622	643
Office and administrative support occupations	15,956	15,161	15,253	480	550	581
Natural resources, construction, and maintenance occupations	10,958	12,086	12,486	582	623	670
Farming, fishing, and forestry occupations	842	755	739	310	372	372
Construction and extraction occupations	5,852	6,826	7,227	580	604	646
Installation, maintenance, and repair occupations	4,263	4,504	4,520	628	705	749
Production, transportation, and material-moving occupations	17,221	15,251	15,289	475	540	577
Production occupations	10,378	8,403	8,389	471	538	581
Transportation and material-moving occupations	6,843	6,848	6,900	481	543	570

[1] See footnote 2, Table 567.   [2] Includes other races, not shown separately.   [3] Beginning 2005, for persons in this race group only. See footnote 3, table 568.   [4] 2000, includes Pacific Islanders.   [5] Persons of Hispanic or Latino origin may be any race.

Source: U.S. Bureau of Labor Statistics, "Employment and Earnings Online," January 2008 issue. See Internet site <http://www.bls.gov/opub/ee/home.htm> and <http://www.bls.gov/cps/home.htm>.

Table. 627. Workers With Earnings by Occupation of Longest Held Job and Sex: 2006

[**Covers persons 15 years old and over as of March 2007. (73,683, represents 73,683,000).** Based on Current Population Survey; see text, Section 1, and Appendix III. For definition of median, see Guide to Tabular Presentation. Occupational classifications are those used in the 2000 census and are not comparable to those used in the 1990 census]

Major occupation of longest job held in **2006**	All workers				Full-time, year-round			
	Women		Men		Women		Men	
	Number (1,000)	Median earnings (dol.)	Number (1,000)	Median earnings (dol.)	Number (1,000)	Median earnings (dol.)	Number (1,000)	Median earnings (dol.)
Total	**73,683**	**24,466**	**83,928**	**35,879**	**44,663**	**32,515**	**63,055**	**42,261**
Management, business, and financial occupations	9,654	45,531	12,431	61,212	7,707	50,278	10,826	65,777
Professional and related occupations	17,796	36,140	13,670	56,161	11,173	43,005	10,952	61,950
Service occupations	15,500	13,414	11,351	20,627	7,171	21,202	7,041	29,452
Sales and office occupations	25,032	22,254	14,440	32,188	15,123	30,365	10,500	41,244
Natural resources, construction, and maintenance	752	19,191	16,409	31,111	421	27,362	12,074	36,249
Production, transportation, and material-moving occupations	4,887	19,276	15,041	30,111	3,019	23,253	11,135	33,815
Armed Forces	62	(B)	586	39,063	48	(B)	528	40,697

B Data not shown where base is less than 75,000.

Source: U.S. Census Bureau Internet site <http://pubdb3.census.gov/macro/032007/perinc/toc.htm>, Table PINC-07, "Occupation of Longest Job in 2005—People 15 years Old and Over, by Total Money Earnings in 2006, Work Experience in 2006 Race, Hispanic Origin, and Sex" (accessed 17 June 2008).

Table. 628. Employment Cost Index (ECI), Total Compensation by Occupation and Industry: 2002 to 2007

[**As of December.** The ECI is a measure of the rate of change in employee compensation (wages, salaries, and employer costs for employee benefits). Data are not seasonally adjusted: Survey; beginning in 2006, based on North American Industry Classification (NAICS)] Beginning in 2006, based on the 2007 North American Industry Classification (NAICS) for classifying by industry and based on the 2000 Standard Occupational Classification (SOC) for classifying by occupation

Item	Indexes (**December 2005 = 100**)					Percent change for 12 months ending Dec.—					
	2002	2003	2004	2006	2007	2002	2003	2004	2005	2006	2007
Civilian workers [1]	**90.0**	**93.5**	**97.0**	**103.3**	**106.7**	**3.3**	**3.9**	**3.7**	**3.1**	**3.3**	**3.3**
State and local government	**89.7**	**92.8**	**96.1**	**104.1**	**108.4**	**4.1**	**3.5**	**3.6**	**4.1**	**4.1**	**4.1**
Workers, by occupational group:											
Management, professional, and related occupations	90.3	93.1	96.2	104.0	108.3	4.0	3.1	3.3	4.0	4.0	4.1
Sales and office occupations	89.1	92.8	96.5	104.1	108.6	4.6	4.2	4.0	3.6	4.1	4.3
Service occupations	88.0	91.6	95.5	104.5	109.1	3.9	4.1	4.3	4.7	4.5	4.4
Workers, by industry division:											
Service-providing industries:											
Education and health services	90.4	93.2	96.1	104.3	108.2	3.8	3.1	3.1	4.1	4.3	3.7
Schools	90.4	93.1	96.1	104.1	108.0	3.7	3.0	3.2	4.1	4.1	3.7
Elementary and secondary	89.9	92.7	96.0	104.2	108.0	3.7	3.1	3.6	4.2	4.2	3.6
Health care and social assistance	90.6	93.5	96.5	105.7	109.3	4.4	3.2	3.2	3.6	5.7	3.4
Hospitals	90.6	93.4	96.7	104.3	108.2	4.6	3.1	3.5	3.4	4.3	3.7
Public administration [2]	88.3	92.0	95.8	103.8	109.1	4.5	4.2	4.1	4.4	3.8	5.1
Private industry workers [3]	**90.0**	**93.6**	**97.2**	**103.2**	**106.3**	**3.1**	**4.0**	**3.8**	**2.9**	**3.2**	**3.0**
Workers, by occupational group:											
Management, professional, and related occupations	89.7	93.8	97.1	103.5	106.8	2.6	4.6	3.5	3.0	3.5	3.2
Sales and office occupations	89.8	93.1	96.8	102.9	106.1	3.3	3.7	4.0	3.3	2.9	3.1
Natural resources, construction, and maintenance occupations	89.7	93.3	97.1	103.6	106.7	3.6	4.0	4.1	3.0	3.6	3.0
Production, transportation, and material-moving occupations	90.3	93.6	97.8	102.3	104.5	3.3	3.7	4.5	2.2	2.3	2.2
Service occupations	92.0	95.0	97.7	103.1	107.0	2.9	3.3	2.8	2.4	3.1	3.8
Workers, by industry division:											
Goods-producing industries [4]	89.0	92.6	96.9	102.5	105.0	3.5	4.0	4.6	3.2	2.5	2.4
Manufacturing											
Service-providing industries [5]	90.4	94.0	97.3	103.4	106.7	3.0	4.0	3.5	2.8	3.4	3.2
Trade, transportation, and utilities	90.9	94.0	97.0	103.0	105.5	3.1	3.4	3.2	3.1	3.0	2.4
Professional and business services	91.0	94.7	98.5	103.5	107.5	1.1	4.1	4.0	1.5	3.5	3.9
Education and health services	89.6	93.0	96.7	104.1	107.7	3.7	3.8	4.0	3.4	4.1	3.5
Leisure and hospitality	94.4	96.3	97.7	103.7	108.1	2.4	2.0	1.5	2.4	3.7	4.2
Bargaining status											
Union	88.2	92.3	97.3	103.0	105.1	4.0	4.6	5.4	2.8	3.0	2.0
Nonunion	90.3	93.9	97.2	103.2	106.5	2.8	4.0	3.5	2.9	3.2	3.2

[1] Includes private industry and state and local government workers and excludes farm, household, and federal government workers. [2] Consists of executive, legislative, judicial, administrative, and regulatory activities. [3] Excludes farm and household workers. [4] Includes the following NAICS industries: construction and manufacturing. [5] Includes all other NAICS industries, except government. For a description of NAICS industries, see text this section and Table 607.

Source: U.S. Bureau of Labor Statistics, "Employment Cost Index Historical Listing Current-dollar"; <http://www.bls.gov/ncs/ect/home.htm>. See also *Monthly Labor Review,* April 2006, volume 129 number 4.

Table 629. Federal Minimum Wage Rates: 1940 to 2009

Year	Current dollars	Year	Current dollars
1940	0.30	1995	4.25
1945	0.40	1996	4.75
1950	0.75	1997	5.15
1955	0.75	1998	5.15
1960	1.00	1999	5.15
1965	1.25	2000	5.15
1970	1.60	2001	5.15
1975	2.10	2002	5.15
1980	3.10	2003	5.15
1985	3.35	2004	5.15
1990	3.80	2005	5.15
1991	4.25	2006	5.15
1992	4.25	2007	5.85
1993	4.25	2008	6.55
1994	4.25	2009	7.25

Source: U.S. Employment Standards Administration, Internet site: <http://www.dol.gov/esa/whd/flsa/>.

Table 630. Labor Force Violations: 2003 to 2007

[In thousands except as indicated]

Labor violation	2003	2004	2005	2006	2007
BACK WAGES					
Back wages collected (in dollars)	212,538	196,664	166,005	171,956	220,614
Employees receiving back wages	342.4	288.3	241.4	246.9	341.6
CHILD LABOR					
Cases with child labor violations	1.6	1.6	1.1	1.1	1.2
Minors employed in violation	7.2	5.8	3.7	3.7	4.7
FAMILY AND MEDICAL LEAVE ACT (FMLA)					
Complaint cases	3.6	3.4	2.8	2.2	2.0
Violation cases	1.7	1.5	1.4	1.1	1.1
No violation cases	1.9	1.8	1.4	1.1	0.9

Source: U.S. Employment Standards Administration, "2007 Statistics Fact Sheet," December 2007 <http://www.dol.gov/esa/whd/>.

Table 631. Workers Paid Hourly Rates by Selected Characteristics: 2007

[**Data are annual averages (75,873 represents 75,873,000).** For employed wage and salary workers, excluding the incorporated self-employed. Based on the Current Population Survey; see text, Section 1, and Appendix III]

Characteristic	Number of workers paid hourly rates (1,000)			Number of workers at or below prevailing federal minimum wage	
	Total	Below (federal minimum wage)	At (federal minimum wage)	Number (1,000)	Percent of hourly paid workers
Total, 16 years old and over [1]	**75,873**	**1,462**	**267**	**1,729**	**2.3**
16 to 24 years old	16,275	669	145	814	5.0
25 years old and over	59,597	793	122	915	1.5
Male, 16 years old and over	37,790	460	86	546	1.4
16 to 24 years old	8,314	190	52	242	2.9
25 years old and over	29,476	270	34	304	1.0
Female, 16 years old and over	38,082	1,002	181	1,183	3.1
16 to 24 years old	7,961	479	93	572	7.2
25 years old and over	30,121	523	88	611	2.0
White [2]	61,061	1,216	204	1,420	2.3
Black [2]	9,965	150	55	205	2.1
Asian [2]	2,730	50	1	50	1.8
Hispanic origin [3]	13,168	205	41	246	1.9
Full-time workers [4]	57,745	658	94	751	1.3
Part-time workers [4]	17,997	799	172	971	5.4
Private sector industries	66,432	1,386	232	1,618	2.4
Public sector industries	9,441	76	35	111	1.2

[1] Includes races not shown separately. Also includes a small number of multiple jobholders whose full- or part-time status can not be determined for their principal job. [2] For persons in this race group only. See footnote 3, Table 568. [3] Persons of Hispanic or Latino origin may be any race. [4] Working fewer than 35 hours per week.

Source: U.S. Bureau of Labor Statistics, "Employment and Earnings Online"; <http://www.bls.gov/cps/home.htm>.

U.S. Census Bureau, Statistical Abstract of the United States: 2009

Table 632. Employer Costs for Employee Compensation Per Hour Worked: 2007

[In dollars. As of December, for civilian workers. Based on a sample of establishments from the National Compensation Survey; see source for details. See also Appendix III]

Compensation component	Total civilian workers	State and local government workers	Private industry workers						
			Total	Goods produc-ing[1]	Service provid-ing[2]	Union workers	Non-union workers	Full-time workers	Part-time workers
Total compensation	**28.11**	**37.73**	**26.42**	**30.94**	**25.30**	**36.09**	**25.29**	**29.99**	**14.67**
Wages and salaries	19.62	25.04	18.67	20.62	18.18	22.34	18.24	20.86	11.45
Total benefits	8.49	12.69	7.75	10.32	7.12	13.75	7.05	9.13	3.21
Paid leave.	1.96	2.97	1.79	1.97	1.74	2.78	1.67	2.18	0.48
Vacation	0.95	1.12	0.91	1.05	0.88	1.43	0.85	(NA)	(NA)
Holiday	0.63	0.89	0.59	0.71	0.56	0.84	0.56	(NA)	(NA)
Sick	0.30	0.73	0.22	0.17	0.23	0.36	0.20	(NA)	(NA)
Other	0.09	0.22	0.06	0.05	0.07	0.14	0.05	(NA)	(NA)
Supplemental pay.	0.72	0.34	0.79	1.27	0.67	1.19	0.74	0.95	0.23
Insurance	2.34	4.25	2.01	2.83	1.81	4.17	1.76	2.40	0.72
Health insurance.	2.21	4.11	1.87	2.62	1.69	3.90	1.63	(NA)	(NA)
Retirement and savings. . . .	1.24	2.86	0.95	1.43	0.84	2.47	0.78	1.17	0.24
Defined benefit.	0.75	2.54	0.43	0.82	0.34	1.78	0.28	(NA)	(NA)
Defined contributions. . . .	0.49	0.32	0.52	0.61	0.50	0.69	0.50	(NA)	(NA)
Legally required	2.23	2.27	2.22	2.83	2.07	3.14	2.11	2.42	1.55
Social security and Medicare	1.59	1.77	1.56	1.76	1.51	1.96	1.51	(NA)	(NA)
Social security.	1.27	1.37	1.25	1.42	1.21	1.58	1.21	(NA)	(NA)
Medicare	0.32	0.40	0.31	0.34	0.30	0.38	0.30	(NA)	(NA)
Federal unemployment. . .	0.03	–	0.03	0.03	0.03	0.03	0.03	(NA)	(NA)
State unemployment	0.14	0.06	0.16	0.20	0.14	0.22	0.15	(NA)	(NA)
Workers' compensation . .	0.47	0.43	0.47	0.84	0.38	0.92	0.42	(NA)	(NA)

– Represents or rounds to zero.   NA Not available.   [1] Based on the North American Industry Classification System, 2002 (NAICS). See text, this section. Includes mining, construction, and manufacturing. The agriculture, forestry, farming, and hunting sector is excluded.   [2] Based on the 2002 NAICS. Includes utilities; wholesale and retail trade; transportation and warehousing; information; finance and insurance; real estate and rental and leasing; professional and technical services; management of companies and enterprises; administrative and waste services; education services; health care and social assistance; arts, entertainment, and recreation; accommodations and food services; and other services, except public administration.

Source: U.S. Bureau of Labor Statistics, *Employer Costs for Employee Compensation, News,* USDL 07-0453, March 12, 2008. See Internet site <http://www.bls.gov/ncs/ect/home.htm>.

Table 633. Percent of Workers in Private Industry With Access to Retirement and Health Care Benefits by Selected Characteristics: 2007

[As of March. Based on National Compensation Survey. The NCS benefits survey obtained data from 12,821 private industry establishments of all sizes, representing over 108 million workers; see Appendix III. See also Tables 149 and 150. For explanation of benefits, see source]

Characteristic	Retirement benefits			Healthcare benefits			
	All plans[1]	Defined benefit	Defined contri-bution	Medical care	Dental care	Vision care	Outpatient prescrip-tion drug coverage
Total.	**61**	**21**	**55**	**71**	**46**	**29**	**68**
WORKER CHARACTERISTIC							
Management, professional, and related occupations.	76	29	71	85	62	39	82
Service occupations	36	8	32	46	28	20	44
Sales and office occupations	64	19	60	71	47	27	67
Natural resources, construction, and maintenance occupations.	61	26	51	76	43	31	72
Production, transportation, and material moving occupations	65	26	56	78	49	30	75
Full-time[2].	70	24	64	85	56	35	81
Part-time[2]	31	10	27	24	16	11	23
Union[3].	84	69	49	88	68	53	85
Nonunion[3]	58	15	56	69	44	26	66
Average wage less than $15 per hour	47	11	44	57	34	20	54
Average wage $15 per hour or more	76	33	69	87	61	39	84
ESTABLISHMENT CHARACTERISTIC							
1 to 99 workers	45	9	42	59	30	19	55
100 or more workers.	78	34	70	84	64	40	81
Goods producing[4].	70	29	62	85	54	33	81
Service producing[4]	58	19	53	67	44	28	64

[1] Employees may have access to both defined benefit and defined contribution plans. Total excludes duplication. [2] Employees are classified as working either a full-time or part-time schedule based on the definition used by each establishment.   [3] Union workers are those whose wages are determined through collective bargaining.   [4] See footnotes 3 and 4, Table 612, for composition of goods and service producing industries.

Source: U.S. Bureau of Labor Statistics, *Employee Benefits in Private Industry in the United States, March 2007,* Summary 07-05, August 2007. See Internet site <http://www.bls.gov/ncs/ebs/home.htm>.

Table 634. Percent of Workers in Private Industry With Access to Selected Employee Benefits: 2007

[As of March. Based on National Compensation Survey. The NCS benefits survey obtained data from 12,821 private industry establishments of all sizes, representing over 108 million workers; see Appendix III. See also Tables 149 and 150. For explanation of benefits, see source]

Characteristic	Paid holidays	Paid sick leave	Paid vacation	Paid personal leave	Paid military leave	Family leave — Paid	Family leave — Unpaid	Employer assistance for child care — Total[1]	Employer assistance for child care — On-site and off-site child care	Employer assistance for child care — Child care resource and referral services	Long-term care insurance	Flexible work place[2]	Subsidized commuting[3]
Total	77	57	77	38	49	8	83	15	5	11	12	5	5
WORKER CHARACTERISTIC													
Management, professional, and related occupations	89	80	87	57	67	14	90	27	11	20	22	11	11
Service occupations	51	39	59	26	34	5	79	10	5	5	5	1	2
Sales and office occupations	81	63	80	40	50	9	84	14	3	11	15	5	6
Natural resources, construction, and maintenance occupations	75	44	75	27	38	6	75	6	2	5	7	1	4
Production, transportation, and material moving occupations	84	47	83	33	47	4	84	10	2	8	9	2	2
Full-time[4]	88	68	90	44	54	9	86	16	6	12	15	5	6
Part-time[4]	39	23	38	21	30	5	73	9	4	6	6	2	2
Union[5]	84	61	84	48	55	7	90	21	6	18	17	2	6
Nonunion[5]	76	57	77	37	48	8	83	14	5	10	12	5	5
Average wage, less than $15 per hour	67	44	69	30	39	5	80	9	3	5	7	2	2
Average wage, $15 per hour or more	88	72	88	48	59	11	88	22	7	17	19	8	9
ESTABLISHMENT CHARACTERISTIC													
Goods producing[6]	85	47	85	33	50	6	84	12	3	10	8	3	3
Service producing[6]	74	60	76	40	48	9	83	15	6	11	14	5	6
1 to 99 workers	69	48	71	27	36	6	75	5	2	3	4	3	3
100 or more workers	85	67	85	51	62	10	93	25	9	19	21	6	8
GEOGRAPHIC AREA[7]													
New England	78	65	75	43	52	9	88	17	8	13	14	6	9
Middle Atlantic	80	64	80	48	53	8	84	15	7	11	13	7	6
East North Central	76	53	76	42	50	8	81	18	6	13	13	5	3
West North Central	73	54	75	31	47	6	82	14	5	9	12	5	5
South Atlantic	76	54	79	34	50	9	84	12	4	8	13	5	3
East South Central	81	54	80	38	43	6	89	8	3	5	9	3	2
West South Central	79	56	79	36	47	8	81	16	5	10	11	4	3
Mountain	74	56	75	37	46	6	80	15	3	12	11	5	9
Pacific	74	59	76	35	44	10	84	15	4	12	12	3	10

[1] Includes employer-provided funds not shown separately. [2] Arrangements permitting employees to work at home several days of the work week. [3] Employers subsidize employees' cost of commuting to and from work via public transportation, company-sponsored van pool, discounted subway fares, etc. [4] Employees are classified as working either a full-time or part-time schedule based on the definition used by each establishment. [5] Union workers are those whose wages are determined through collective bargaining. [6] See footnotes 3 and 4, Table 612, for composition of goods and service producing industries. [7] For composition of divisions, see map, inside front cover.

Source: U.S. Bureau of Labor Statistics, *Employee Benefits in Private Industry in the United States, March 2007*, Summary 07-05, August 2007. See Internet site <http://www.bls.gov/ncs/ebs/home.htm>.

Table 635. **Workers Killed or Disabled on the Job: 1970 to 2006**

[Data for 2006 are preliminary estimates (1.7 represents 1,700). Excludes homicides and suicides. Estimates based on data from the U.S. National Center for Health Statistics, state vital statistics departments, state industrial commissions and beginning 1995, Bureau of Labor Statistics, Census of Occupational Fatalities. Numbers of workers based on data from the U.S. Bureau of Labor Statistics]

Year	Deaths				Dis-abling injuries [2] (mil.)	Year and industry group	Deaths, 2006		Dis-abling injuries 2006 [2] (1,000)
	Manufacturing		Non-manufacturing				Number	Rate [1]	
	Number (1,000)	Rate [1]	Number (1,000)	Rate [1]					
1970 . . .	1.7	9	12.1	21	2.2	Total, 2006 [3]	4,988	3.4	3,700
1980 . . .	1.7	8	11.5	15	2.2	Agriculture [4]	626	28.7	80
1985 . . .	1.2	6	10.3	12	2.0	Mining [5]	188	27.5	20
1990 . . .	1.0	5	9.1	9	3.9	Construction	1,187	10.5	480
1995 . . .	0.6	3	4.4	4	3.6	Manufacturing	417	2.6	450
1996 . . .	0.7	3	4.4	4	3.9	Wholesale trade	206	4.5	120
1997 . . .	0.7	3	4.5	4	3.8	Retail trade	186	1.1	460
1998 . . .	0.6	3	4.5	4	3.8	Transportation and warehousing	781	15.3	270
1999 . . .	0.6	3	4.6	4	3.8	Utilities	51	6.0	20
2000 . . .	0.6	3	4.4	4	3.9	Information	59	1.7	50
2001 . . .	0.5	3	4.5	4	3.9	Financial activities [6]	80	0.8	100
2002 . . .	0.5	3	4.2	3	3.7	Professional & business services [6] . . .	400	2.8	200
2003 . . .	0.4	2	4.3	4	3.4	Educational & health services	137	0.7	530
2004 . . .	0.4	3	4.6	4	3.7	Leisure & hospitality [6]	128	1.1	250
2005 . . .	0.4	2	4.6	4	3.7	Other services [7]	138	2.0	120
2006 . . .	0.4	3	4.7	4	3.7	Government	396	1.8	550

[1] Per 100,000 workers. [2] Disabling injury defined as one which results in death, some degree of physical impairment, or renders the person unable to perform regular activities for a full day beyond the day of the injury. Due to change in methodology, data beginning 1990 not comparable with prior years. [3] Includes deaths where industry is not known. [4] Includes forestry, fishing, and hunting. [5] Includes oil and gas extraction. [6] For composition of industry, see Table 611. [7] Excludes public service administration.

Source: National Safety Council, Itasca, IL, *Accident Facts,* annual through 1998 edition; thereafter, *Injury Facts,* annual (copyright).

Table 636. **Worker Deaths, Injuries, and Production Time Lost: 2000 to 2006**

[47.0 represents 47,000. Data may not agree with Table 638 because data here are not revised]

Item	Deaths (1,000)			Disabling injuries [1] (mil.)			Production time lost (mil. days)					
							In current year			In future years [2]		
	2000	2005	2006	2000	2005	2006	2000	2005	2006	2000	2005	2006
All accidents	**47.0**	**54.3**	**58.2**	**10.5**	**11.9**	**13.1**	**240**	**275**	**305**	**460**	**535**	**580**
On the job	5.2	5.0	5.0	3.9	3.7	3.7	80	80	80	60	65	65
Off the job	41.8	49.3	53.2	6.6	8.2	9.4	160	195	225	400	470	515
Motor vehicle	22.8	24.1	24.0	1.2	1.3	1.3	(NA)	(NA)	(NA)	(NA)	(NA)	(NA)
Public nonmotor vehicle . .	8.3	10.0	11.0	2.8	3.3	3.7	(NA)	(NA)	(NA)	(NA)	(NA)	(NA)
Home	10.7	15.2	18.2	2.6	3.6	4.4	(NA)	(NA)	(NA)	(NA)	(NA)	(NA)

NA Not available. [1] See footnote 2, Table 635, for a definition of disabling injuries. [2] Based on an average of 5,850 days lost in future years per fatality and 565 days lost in future years per permanent injury.

Source: National Safety Council, Itasca, IL, *Injury Facts,* annual (copyright).

Table 637. **Industries With the Highest Total Case Incidence Rates for Nonfatal Injuries and Illnesses: 2006**

[Rates refer to any Occupational Safety and Health Administration (OSHA)-recordable occupational injury or illness, whether or not it resulted in days away from work, job transfer, or restriction. Incidence rates were calculated as: Number of injuries and illnesses divided by total hours worked by all employees during the year multiplied by 200,000 as base for 100 full-time equivalent workers working 40 hours per week, 50 weeks per year]

Industry	2002 NAICS [1] code	Rate	Industry	2002 NAICS [1] code	Rate
Private industry [2]	(X)	4.4	Aluminum foundries (except die-casting) . .	331524	12.1
Nonclay refractory manufacturing	327125	16.9	Metal tank (heavy gauge) manufacturing . .	33242	11.9
Motor home manufacturing	336213	16.8	Motor vehicle body manufacturing	336211	11.8
Iron foundries	331511	15.1	Beet sugar manufacturing	311313	11.7
Light truck and utility vehicle manufacturing	336112	14.6	Amusement and theme parks	71311	11.7
Prefabricated wood building manufacturing	321992	14.3	Couriers	4291	11.0
Truck trailer manufacturing	336212	13.9	Ambulance services	62191	11.0
Manufactured (mobile) home manufacturing	321991	13.2	Iron and steel forging	332111	10.9
Skiing facilities	71392	13.2	Heavy duty truck manufacturing	33612	10.9
Travel trailer and camper manufacturing . . .	336214	13.1	Scheduled passenger air transportation . . .	481111	10.8
Sports teams and clubs	711211	12.8	Ship building and repairing	336611	10.7
Animal slaughtering	311611	12.5	Soft drink manufacturing	312111	10.6
Steel foundries (except investment)	331513	12.1	Household furniture (except wood and metal) manufacturing	337125	10.6

X Not applicable. [1] Based on the North American Industry Classification System, 2002 (NAICS). See text, this section. [2] Excludes farms with fewer than 11 employees.

Source: U.S. Bureau of Labor Statistics, *Workplace Injuries and Illnesses in 2006.* See Internet site <http://www.bls.gov/iif/>.

Table 638. **Nonfatal Occupational Injury and Illness Incidence Rates: 2006**

[Rates per 100 full-time employees. Except as noted, data refer to any Occupational Safety and Health Administration (OSHA) recordable occupational injury or illness, whether or not it resulted in days away from work, job transfer, or restriction. Incidence rates were calculated as: Number of injuries and illnesses divided by total hours worked by all employees during the year multiplied by 200,000 as base for 100 full-time equivalent workers (working 40 hours, per week, 50 weeks per year)]

Industry	2002 NAICS code [1]	Rate	Industry	2002 NAICS code [1]	Rate
Private industry [2]	(X)	4.4	Truck transportation	484	5.8
Agriculture, forestry, fishing, hunting [2]	11	6.0	Support activities for transportation	488	4.5
Crop production [2]	111	5.8	Couriers and messengers	492	10.5
Mining [3]	21	3.5	Warehousing and storage	493	8.0
Construction	23	5.9	Utilities	22	4.1
Construction of buildings	236	5.1	Information	51	1.9
Heavy and civil engineering construction	237	5.3	Telecommunications	517	2.2
Specialty trade contractors	238	6.3	Finance and insurance [4]	52	0.9
Manufacturing [4]	31–33	6.0	Credit intermediation and related		
Food manufacturing	311	7.4	activities	522	1.0
Wood product manufacturing	321	8.5	Insurance carriers and related activities	524	1.0
Paper manufacturing	322	4.3	Real estate and rental and leasing	53	3.3
Printing and related support activities	323	4.2	Real estate	531	2.9
Chemical manufacturing	325	2.9	Rental and leasing services	532	4.2
Plastics and rubber products mfg	326	6.8	Professional, scientific, and technical		
Nonmetallic mineral product mfg	327	7.1	services	54	1.2
Primary metal manufacturing	331	8.6	Management of companies and		
Fabricated metal product mfg	332	7.6	enterprises	55	2.1
Machinery manufacturing	333	6.2	Administrative and support and waste		
Computer and electronic product mfg	334	2.0	management and remediation services	56	3.4
Electrical equipment, appliance, and			Administrative and support services	561	3.1
component manufacturing	335	5.1	Waste management and remediation		
Transportation equipment manufacturing	336	8.0	services	562	6.5
Furniture and related product mfg	337	7.5	Educational services	61	2.3
Miscellaneous manufacturing	339	4.2	Health care and social assistance	62	5.8
Wholesale trade [4]	42	4.1	Ambulatory health care services	621	3.1
Merchant wholesalers, durable goods	423	3.9	Hospitals	622	8.1
Merchant wholesalers, nondurable goods	424	5.4	Nursing and residential care facilities	623	8.9
Retail trade [4]	44–45	4.9	Social assistance	624	3.9
Motor vehicle and parts dealers	441	4.4	Arts, entertainment, and recreation	71	5.3
Furniture and home furnishings stores	442	4.7	Amusement, gambling, and recreation		
Building material and garden equipment			industries	713	5.1
and supplies dealers	444	7.4	Accommodation and food services	72	4.5
Food and beverage stores	445	5.9	Accommodation	721	5.8
Gasoline stations	447	3.6	Food services and drinking places	722	4.2
Clothing and clothing accessories stores	448	2.7	Other services, except public admin	81	2.9
General merchandise stores	452	6.7	Repair and maintenance	811	3.5
Miscellaneous store retailers	453	3.9	Personal and laundry services	812	2.6
Transportation and warehousing [4, 5]	48–49	6.5	Religious, grantmaking, civic,		
Air transportation	481	9.9	professional, and similar organizations	813	2.7

X Not applicable. [1] North American Industry Classification System, 2002; see text, this section. [2] Excludes farms with fewer than 11 employees. [3] Data for mining operators in coal, metal, and nonmetal mining are provided to BLS by the Mine Safety and Health Administration (MHSA), U.S. Department of Labor. Independent mining contractors are excluded. Data provided by MSHA do not reflect 2002 OSHA recordkeeping requirements; therefore, estimates for these industries are not comparable with estimates for other industries. [4] Includes other industries, not shown separately. [5] Data for employers in railroad transportation are provided to BLS by the Federal Railroad Administration, U.S. Department of Transportation.

Source: U.S. Bureau of Labor Statistics, *Workplace Injuries and Illnesses in 2006*. See Internet site <http://www.bls.gov/iif/>.

Table 639. **Fatal Work Injuries by Event or Exposure: 2006**

[For the 50 states and DC. Based on the Census of Fatal Occupational Injuries. For details, see source. Due to methodological differences, data differ from National Safety Council data]

Cause	Number of fatalities	Percent distribution	Cause	Number of fatalities	Percent distribution
Total	**5,840**	**100**	Struck by object [1]	589	10
Transportation accidents [1]	2,459	42	Struck by falling objects	382	7
Highway accidents [1]	1,356	23	Struck by flying object	70	1
Collision between vehicles,			Caught in or compressed by—		
mobile equipment	657	11	equipment or objects	283	5
Noncollision accidents	303	5	Caught in or crushed in		
Nonhighway accident (farm,			collapsing materials	108	2
industrial premises)	345	6	Falls	827	14
Aircraft accidents	217	4			
Workers struck by a vehicle	379	6	Exposure to harmful substances or		
Water vehicle accidents	96	2	environments [1]	547	9
Railway accidents	65	1	Contact with electric current	250	4
Assaults and violent acts [1]	788	13	Exposure to caustic, noxious		
Homicides [1]	540	9	or allergenic substances	165	3
Shooting	436	7	Oxygen deficiency	68	1
Stabbing	39	1	Drowning, submersion	53	1
Self-inflicted injury	208	4	Fires and explosions	202	3
Contacts with objects and equipment [1]	993	17	Other events and exposures	24	(Z)

Z Less than 0.5 percent. [1] Includes other causes, not shown separately.

Source: U.S. Bureau of Labor Statistics, "Census of Fatal Occupational Injuries (CFOI)—Current and Revised Data." See Internet site <http://www.bls.gov/iif/oshcfoi1.htm>.

Labor Force, Employment, and Earnings **417**

Table 640. Workplace Violence Incidence and Security Measures: 2005

[In percent. **Covers period September 2004 to June 2005.** Based on establishment survey and subject to sampling error; see source for details]

Incident or security measure	All estab-lish-ments	Industry			Employment size class				
		Private industry [1]	State govern-ment	Local govern-ment	1 to 10 employ-ees	11 to 49 employ-ees	50 to 249 employ-ees	250 to 999 employ-ees	1,000 or more employ-ees
Any workplace violence incidents	5.3	4.8	32.2	14.7	2.4	9.1	16.0	28.8	49.9
Criminal	2.2	2.1	8.7	3.7	1.4	3.5	4.7	6.8	17.2
Customer or client.	2.2	1.9	15.4	10.3	1.0	3.9	6.4	12.2	28.3
Co-worker	2.3	2.1	17.7	4.3	0.6	4.6	8.1	16.8	34.1
Domestic violence	0.9	0.8	5.5	2.1	0.1	2.0	2.9	9.0	24.1
No incident	92.1	92.5	65.3	85.1	95.6	87.8	77.8	63.9	43.8
Selected types of security provided:									
Intruder/burglar systems. . . .	41.8	42.1	29.1	35.5	35.7	53.9	57.5	54.2	61.0
Surveillance cameras.	22.6	22.2	45.2	32.7	17.0	29.2	47.9	69.1	77.9
Motion detectors	26.9	27.1	14.8	21.3	24.0	32.9	33.7	28.3	36.4
Metal detectors.	0.9	0.7	16.0	4.3	0.5	1.1	2.5	7.2	15.7
Electronic badges [2]	6.3	6.0	35.6	9.0	3.9	7.2	20.8	45.1	60.1
Security guards	9.5	9.1	48.6	10.5	6.4	11.7	24.8	53.9	65.3
Limited access [3]	30.7	30.0	58.0	50.7	26.0	35.9	52.5	68.3	83.2
Physical barriers [4]	13.4	13.1	27.2	23.6	10.2	18.2	24.5	33.5	46.5
Lighting of work areas	39.1	38.7	55.8	48.5	32.2	50.0	62.1	71.9	80.4
Workplace violence training provided:									
Any training	20.8	20.2	58.0	32.3	14.6	29.1	45.7	64.2	67.8
No training.	78.4	78.9	42.0	67.6	84.3	70.5	54.0	35.6	32.0

[1] Excludes farms with fewer than 11 employees. [2] Or ID scanner at entry or exit. [3] Secured entry/locked doors. [4] Between work areas and the public.

Source: U.S. Bureau of Labor Statistics, *Survey of Workplace Violence and Prevention, 2005 News,* USDL 06-1860, October, 27, 2006. See Internet site <http://www.bls.gov/iif/home.htm>.

Table 641. Work Stoppages: 1960 to 2007

[**896 represents 896,000.** Excludes work stoppages involving fewer than 1,000 workers and lasting less than 1 day. Information is based on reports of labor disputes appearing in daily newspapers, trade journals, and other public sources. The parties to the disputes are contacted by telephone, when necessary, to clarify details of the stoppages]

Year	Number of stop-pages [1]	Workers involved [2] (1,000)	Days idle		Year	Number of stop-pages [1]	Workers involved [2] (1,000)	Days idle	
			Number [3] (1,000)	Percent estimated working time [4]				Number [3] (1,000)	Percent estimated working time [4]
1960	222	896	13,260	0.09	1990	44	185	5,926	0.02
1965	268	999	15,140	0.10	1991	40	392	4,584	0.02
1970	381	2,468	52,761	0.29	1992	35	364	3,989	0.01
1975	235	965	17,563	0.09	1993	35	182	3,981	0.01
1976	231	1,519	23,962	0.12	1994	45	322	5,021	0.02
1977	298	1,212	21,258	0.10	1995	31	192	5,771	0.02
1978	219	1,006	23,774	0.11	1996	37	273	4,889	0.02
1979	235	1,021	20,409	0.09	1997	29	339	4,497	0.01
1980	187	795	20,844	0.09	1998	34	387	5,116	0.02
1981	145	729	16,908	0.07	1999	17	73	1,996	0.01
1982	96	656	9,061	0.04	2000	39	394	20,419	0.06
1983	81	909	17,461	0.08	2001	29	99	1,151	(Z)
1984	62	376	8,499	0.04	2002	19	46	660	(Z)
1985	54	324	7,079	0.03	2003	14	129	4,091	0.01
1986	69	533	11,861	0.05	2004	17	171	3,344	0.01
1987	46	174	[5]4,481	0.02	2005	22	100	1,736	0.01
1988	40	118	[5]4,381	0.02	2006	20	70	2,688	0.01
1989	51	452	16,996	0.07	2007	21	189	1,265	(Z)

Z Less than 0.005 percent. [1] Beginning in year indicated. [2] Workers counted more than once if involved in more than one stoppage during the year. [3] Resulting from all stoppages in effect in a year, including those that began in an earlier year. [4] Agricultural and government employees are included in the total working time; private household and forestry and fishery employees are excluded. [5] Revised since originally published.

Source: U.S. Bureau of Labor Statistics, *Major Work Stoppages in 2007, News,* USDL 08-0202, February 13, 2008. See Internet site <http://www.bls.gov/wsp/>.

Table 642. Labor Union Membership by Sector: 1985 to 2007

[See headnote, Table 644. **(16,996 represents 16,996,000)**]

Sector	1985	1990	1995	2000	2003	2004	2005	2006	2007
TOTAL (1,000)									
Wage and salary workers:									
Union members	16,996	16,740	16,360	16,258	15,776	15,472	15,685	15,359	15,670
Covered by unions	19,358	19,058	18,346	17,944	17,448	17,087	17,223	16,860	17,243
Public sector workers:									
Union members.	5,743	6,485	6,927	7,111	7,324	7,267	7,430	7,378	7,557
Covered by unions. . . .	6,921	7,691	7,987	7,976	8,185	8,131	8,262	8,172	8,373
Private sector workers:									
Union members.	11,253	10,255	9,432	9,148	8,452	8,205	8,255	7,981	8,114
Covered by unions. . . .	12,438	11,366	10,360	9,969	9,264	8,956	8,962	8,688	8,870
PERCENT									
Wage and salary workers:									
Union members	18.0	16.1	14.9	13.5	12.9	12.5	12.5	12.0	12.1
Covered by unions	20.5	18.3	16.7	14.9	14.3	13.8	13.7	13.1	13.3
Public sector workers:									
Union members.	35.7	36.5	37.7	37.5	37.2	36.4	36.5	36.2	35.9
Covered by unions. . . .	43.1	43.3	43.5	42.0	41.5	40.7	40.5	40.1	39.8
Private sector workers:									
Union members.	14.3	11.9	10.3	9.0	8.2	7.9	7.8	7.4	7.5
Covered by unions. . . .	15.9	13.2	11.3	9.8	9.0	8.6	8.5	8.1	8.2

Source: The Bureau of National Affairs, Inc., Washington, DC, *Union Membership and Earnings Data Book: Compilations from the Current Population Survey (2008 edition),* (copyright by BNA PLUS); authored by Barry Hirsch of Georgia State University and David Macpherson of Florida State University. Internet sites <http://plusdocs.bna.com/LaborReports.aspx> and <http://www.unionstats.com>.

Table 643. Union Members by Selected Characteristics: 2007

[**Annual averages of monthly data (129,767 represents 129,767,000).** Covers employed wage and salary workers 16 years old and over. Excludes self-employed workers whose businesses are incorporated although they technically qualify as wage and salary workers. Based on Current Population Survey, see text, Section 1, and Appendix III]

Characteristic	Employed wage and salary workers			Median usual weekly earnings [3] (dol.)			
		Percent					
	Total (1,000)	Union members [1]	Repre-sented by unions [2]	Total	Union members [1]	Repre-sented by unions [2]	Not repre-sented by unions
Total [4]	**129,767**	**12.1**	**13.3**	**695**	**863**	**857**	**663**
16 to 24 years old	19,395	4.8	5.5	424	566	551	418
25 to 34 years old	29,409	10.4	11.4	643	789	781	622
35 to 44 years old	30,296	13.1	14.4	769	910	907	745
45 to 54 years old	29,731	15.7	17.1	790	900	899	763
55 to 64 years old	16,752	16.1	17.7	803	925	921	766
65 years and over	4,183	8.5	9.6	605	634	682	597
Men.	67,468	13.0	14.1	766	913	910	738
Women	62,299	11.1	12.4	614	790	784	592
White [5]	**105,515**	**11.8**	**13.0**	**716**	**889**	**884**	**684**
Men.	55,771	12.8	13.8	788	937	934	757
Women	49,743	10.8	12.1	626	814	807	603
Black [5]	**15,177**	**14.3**	**15.8**	**569**	**732**	**727**	**533**
Men.	6,945	15.8	17.3	600	768	763	573
Women	8,232	13.0	14.6	533	697	691	513
Asian [5]	**6,016**	**10.9**	**12.0**	**830**	**853**	**881**	**823**
Men.	3,168	10.2	11.0	936	867	898	940
Women	2,849	11.6	13.1	731	842	871	712
Hispanic [6]	**18,778**	**9.8**	**10.8**	**503**	**736**	**729**	**487**
Men.	11,163	9.9	10.8	520	793	782	505
Women	7,615	9.6	10.7	473	675	672	446
Private sector industry.	108,714	7.5	8.2	666	818	813	651
Agriculture and related industries	1,046	1.5	1.8	412	(B)	(B)	411
Mining.	705	9.3	10.2	969	960	950	975
Construction	8,561	13.9	14.4	673	1,000	993	624
Manufacturing	15,341	11.3	12.0	719	783	779	708
Wholesale and retail trade	18,896	5.2	5.7	587	639	632	584
Transportation and utilities	5,488	22.1	23.4	738	902	894	695
Information	3,211	12.1	13.1	891	1,000	994	867
Financial activities [7]	8,858	2.0	2.4	782	728	738	784
Professional and business services [7] . . .	12,022	2.4	3.0	783	800	822	782
Education and health services [7]	18,120	8.8	10.0	671	779	781	657
Leisure and hospitality [7]	10,956	2.8	3.2	440	580	572	431
Other services	5,510	2.9	3.3	581	803	789	574
Public sector	21,053	35.9	39.8	816	901	896	749

B Data not shown where base is less than 50,000.   [1] Members of a labor union or an employee association similar to a labor union.   [2] Members of a labor union or an employee association similar to a union as well as workers who report no union affiliation but whose jobs are covered by a union or an employee association contract.   [3] For full-time employed wage and salary workers.   [4] Includes races not shown separately. Also includes a small number of multiple jobholders whose full- and part-time status cannot be determined for their principal job.   [5] For persons in this race group only. See footnote 3, Table 568.   [6] Persons of Hispanic or Latino ethnicity may be any race.   [7] For composition of industries, see Table 605.

Source: U.S. Bureau of Labor Statistics, *Employment and Earnings,* January 2008. News,USDL-08-0092, January 25, 2008. See Internet site <http://www.bls.gov/cps/home.htm>.

Labor Force, Employment, and Earnings   419

Table 644. **Labor Union Membership by State: 1983 and 2007**

[**Annual averages of monthly figures (17,717.4 represents 17,717,400).** For wage and salary workers in agriculture and non-agriculture. Data represent union members by place of residence. Based on the Current Population Survey and subject to sampling error. For methodological details, see source]

| State | Union members (1,000) | | Workers covered by unions (1,000) | | Percent of workers | | | | | |
| | | | | | Union members | | Covered by unions | | Private sector union members | |
	1983	2007	1983	2007	1983	2007	1983	2007	1983	2007
United States . . .	**17,717.4**	**15,670.3**	**20,532.1**	**17,243.3**	**20.1**	**12.1**	**23.3**	**13.3**	**16.5**	**7.5**
Alabama [1]	228.2	180.4	268.2	201.4	16.9	9.5	19.8	10.6	15.3	4.9
Alaska.	41.7	67.5	49.2	70.0	24.9	23.8	29.3	24.7	17.3	13.0
Arizona [1]	125.0	229.6	156.4	254.9	11.4	8.8	14.3	9.7	8.6	6.5
Arkansas [1]	82.2	61.9	103.2	75.2	11.0	5.4	13.8	6.5	10.2	3.4
California.	2,118.9	2,473.9	2,505.2	2,650.4	21.9	16.7	25.9	17.8	17.7	9.6
Colorado	177.9	190.8	209.6	202.3	13.6	8.7	16.0	9.2	11.2	5.6
Connecticut	314.0	253.1	345.1	268.8	22.7	15.6	25.0	16.6	16.7	7.6
Delaware	49.2	47.4	54.1	50.5	20.1	12.0	22.1	12.8	15.9	7.2
District of Columbia . . .	52.4	28.7	69.4	37.7	19.5	10.3	25.9	13.6	15.2	7.4
Florida [1]	393.7	454.8	532.9	562.4	10.2	5.9	13.8	7.3	7.1	2.5
Georgia [1]	267.0	185.6	345.1	225.8	11.9	4.4	15.3	5.4	11.1	2.8
Hawaii.	112.6	130.3	124.9	134.8	29.2	23.4	32.4	24.2	21.9	15.2
Idaho [1]	41.3	33.4	53.7	40.8	12.5	5.3	16.2	6.4	10.3	3.4
Illinois	1,063.8	842.2	1,205.1	884.1	24.2	14.5	27.4	15.2	21.5	9.7
Indiana	503.3	333.2	544.5	359.1	24.9	12.0	27.0	12.9	25.0	9.8
Iowa [1]	185.9	148.7	231.3	185.0	17.2	10.5	21.5	13.1	14.6	6.2
Kansas [1]	125.2	89.2	170.4	110.2	13.7	7.0	18.7	8.7	12.2	4.8
Kentucky	223.7	157.4	259.8	191.7	17.9	9.1	20.8	11.1	18.2	7.5
Louisiana [1]	204.2	93.8	267.8	108.4	13.8	5.6	18.1	6.5	11.0	4.0
Maine	88.0	67.2	100.4	79.4	21.0	11.7	24.0	13.8	14.2	5.1
Maryland	346.5	335.3	423.1	375.7	18.5	12.9	22.6	14.5	14.4	7.2
Massachusetts	603.2	379.5	661.4	402.2	23.7	13.2	26.0	14.0	17.6	7.6
Michigan	1,005.4	818.6	1,084.6	865.2	30.4	19.5	32.8	20.6	25.3	13.9
Minnesota	393.9	400.4	439.4	419.4	23.2	16.3	25.9	17.0	17.1	9.6
Mississippi [1]	79.4	71.8	99.7	95.2	9.9	6.7	12.5	8.9	9.0	5.4
Missouri.	374.4	275.4	416.7	307.5	20.8	10.7	23.2	11.9	21.5	8.7
Montana	49.5	54.0	55.5	62.4	18.3	13.5	20.5	15.6	14.8	6.0
Nebraska [1]	80.6	64.8	94.8	81.0	13.6	7.8	16.0	9.7	9.7	3.9
Nevada [1]	90.0	181.6	106.7	208.1	22.4	15.4	26.6	17.7	19.6	12.8
New Hampshire	48.5	61.0	60.8	70.4	11.5	9.7	14.4	11.2	7.5	3.8
New Jersey	822.1	747.5	918.2	802.4	26.9	19.2	30.0	20.6	21.1	10.1
New Mexico	52.6	61.7	70.6	91.3	11.8	7.7	15.8	11.4	10.1	3.8
New York.	2,155.6	2,054.9	2,385.9	2,146.2	32.5	25.2	36.0	26.3	24.0	15.8
North Carolina [1]	178.7	113.6	238.1	146.9	7.6	3.0	10.2	3.9	5.4	2.0
North Dakota [1]	28.4	19.4	35.1	23.2	13.2	6.4	16.3	7.6	9.5	4.0
Ohio	1,011.0	730.3	1,125.0	796.6	25.1	14.1	27.9	15.4	22.5	9.0
Oklahoma [2]	131.5	103.3	168.2	124.4	11.5	7.1	14.7	8.5	9.1	3.5
Oregon	222.9	226.6	261.9	243.4	22.3	14.3	26.2	15.4	16.4	7.7
Pennsylvania	1,195.7	829.8	1,350.0	909.6	27.5	15.1	31.1	16.6	23.2	9.7
Rhode Island	85.8	74.5	93.7	78.4	21.5	15.0	23.5	15.8	13.7	7.5
South Carolina [1]	69.6	77.5	100.6	111.0	5.9	4.1	8.6	5.9	3.9	2.7
South Dakota [1]	26.8	22.8	34.8	27.3	11.5	6.5	14.9	7.7	8.0	3.4
Tennessee [1]	252.4	137.8	300.9	166.3	15.1	5.3	18.0	6.4	12.4	3.1
Texas [1]	583.7	462.7	712.8	566.4	9.7	4.7	11.9	5.7	8.1	2.7
Utah [1]	81.6	67.4	100.9	78.3	15.2	5.8	18.9	6.8	11.3	3.3
Vermont	25.9	29.8	31.5	35.0	12.6	10.4	15.3	12.2	6.7	4.5
Virginia [1]	268.3	128.7	346.1	166.9	11.7	3.7	15.1	4.8	10.2	2.5
Washington	419.9	579.3	499.7	616.0	27.1	20.2	32.3	21.4	22.0	13.1
West Virginia	142.7	96.6	160.6	106.8	25.3	13.3	28.5	14.7	26.1	10.8
Wisconsin	465.5	375.7	526.7	404.9	23.8	14.3	26.9	15.4	19.8	8.3
Wyoming [1]	27.1	18.9	31.8	22.4	13.9	7.9	16.2	9.4	10.4	5.6

[1] Right to work state.   [2] Passed right to work law in 2001.

Source: The Bureau of National Affairs (BNA), Inc., Washington, DC, *Union Membership and Earnings Data Book: Compilations from the Current Population Survey (2008 edition),* (copyright by BNA PLUS); authored by Barry Hirsch of Georgia State University and David Macpherson of Florida State University. Internet sites <http://plusdocs.bna.com/LaborReports.aspx> and <http://www.unionstats.com>.

Section 13
Income, Expenditures, Poverty, and Wealth

This section presents data on gross domestic product (GDP), gross national product (GNP), national and personal income, saving and investment, money income, poverty, and national and personal wealth. The data on income and expenditures measure two aspects of the U.S. economy. One aspect relates to the National Income and Product Accounts (NIPA), a summation reflecting the entire complex of the nation's economic income and output and the interaction of its major components; the other relates to the distribution of money income to families and individuals or consumer income.

The primary source for data on GDP, GNP, national and personal income, gross saving and investment, and fixed assets and consumer durables is the *Survey of Current Business*, published monthly by the Bureau of Economic Analysis (BEA). A comprehensive revision to the NIPA was released beginning in December 2003. Discussions of the revision appeared in the January, June, August, September, and December 2003 issues of the *Survey of Current Business*. Summary historical estimates appeared in the August 2007 issue of the *Survey of Current Business*. Detailed historical data can be found on BEA's Web site at <http://www.bea.gov/>.

Sources of income distribution data are the decennial censuses of population, the Current Population Survey (CPS), and the American Community Survey, all products of the U.S. Census Bureau (see text, Section 1 and Section 4). Annual data on income of families, individuals, and households are presented in *Current Population Reports, Consumer Income*, P60 Series, in print. Many data series are also found on the Census Web site at <http://www.census.gov/hhes/www /income/income.html>. Data on the household sector's saving and assets are published by the Board of Governors of the Federal Reserve System in the quarterly statistical release *Flow of Funds Accounts*. The Federal Reserve Board also periodically conducts the *Survey of Consumer Finances*, which presents financial information on family assets and net worth. Detailed information on personal wealth is published periodically by the Internal Revenue Service (IRS) in *SOI Bulletin*.

National income and product—Gross domestic product is the total output of goods and services produced by labor and property located in the United States, valued at market prices. GDP can be viewed in terms of the expenditure categories that comprise its major components: purchases of goods and services by consumers and government, gross private domestic investment, and net exports of goods and services. The goods and services included are largely those bought for final use (excluding illegal transactions) in the market economy. A number of inclusions, however, represent imputed values, the most important of which is the rental value of owner-occupied housing. GDP, in this broad context, measures the output attributable to the factors of production located in the United States. Gross domestic product by state is the gross market value of the goods and services attributable to labor and property located in a state. It is the state counterpart of the nation's gross domestic product.

The featured measure of real GDP is an index based on chain-type annual weights. Changes in this measure of real output and prices are calculated as the average of changes based on weights for the current and preceding years. (Components of real output are weighted by price, and components of prices are weighted by output.) These annual changes are "chained" (multiplied) together to form a time series that allows for the effects of changes in relative prices and changes in the composition of output over time. Quarterly and monthly changes are based on quarterly and monthly weights, respectively. The new

Income, Expenditures, Poverty, and Wealth   421

output indexes are expressed as 2000 = 100, and for recent years, in 2000 dollars; the price indexes are also based to 2000 = 100. For more information on chained-dollar indexes, see the article on this subject in the November 2003 issue of the *Survey of Current Business.*

Chained (2000) dollar estimates of most components of GDP are not published for periods prior to 1990, because during periods far from the base period, the levels of the components may provide misleading information about their contributions to an aggregate. Values are published in index form (2000 = 100) for 1929 to the present to allow users to calculate the percent changes for all components, which are accurate for all periods. In addition, BEA publishes estimates of contributions of major components to the percent change in GDP for all periods.

Gross national product measures the output attributable to all labor and property supplied by United States residents. GNP differs from "national income" mainly in that GNP includes allowances for depreciation—that is, consumption of fixed capital.

National Income includes all net incomes net of consumption of fixed capital (CFC), earned in production. National income is the sum of compensation of employees, proprietors' income with inventory valuation adjustment (IVA) and capital consumption adjustment (CCAdj), rental income of persons with CCAdj, corporate profits with IVA and CCAdj, net interest and miscellaneous payments, taxes on production and imports, business current transfer payments (net), current surplus of government enterprises, less subsidies.

Capital consumption adjustment for corporations and for nonfarm sole proprietorships and partnerships is the difference between capital consumption based on income tax returns and capital consumption measured using empirical evidence on prices of used equipment and structures in resale markets, which have shown that depreciation for most types of assets approximates a geometric pattern. The tax return data are valued at historical costs and reflect changes over time in service lives and depreciation patterns as

permitted by tax regulations. *Inventory valuation adjustment* represents the difference between the book value of inventories used up in production and the cost of replacing them.

Personal income is the current income received by persons from all sources minus their personal contributions for government social insurance. Classified as "persons" are individuals (including owners of unincorporated firms), non-profit institutions that primarily serve individuals, private trust funds, and private noninsured welfare funds. Personal income includes personal current transfer receipts (payments not resulting from current production) from government and business such as social security benefits, public assistance, etc., but excludes transfers among persons. Also included are certain nonmonetary types of income chiefly, estimated net rental value to owner-occupants of their homes and the value of services furnished without payment by financial intermediaries. Capital gains (and losses) are excluded.

Disposable personal income is personal income less personal current taxes. It is the income available to persons for spending or saving. Personal current taxes are tax payments (net of refunds) by persons (except personal contributions for government social insurance) that are not chargeable to business expense. Personal taxes include income taxes, personal property taxes, motor vehicle licenses, and other miscellaneous taxes.

Gross domestic product by industry—The BEA also prepares estimates of value added by industry. *Value added* is a measure of the contribution of each private industry and of government to the nation's GDP. It is defined as an industry's gross output (which consists of sales or receipts and other operating income, commodity taxes, and inventory change) minus its intermediate inputs (which consists of energy, raw materials, semi-finished goods, and services that are purchased from domestic industries or from foreign sources). These estimates of value added are produced for 61 private industries and for 4 government

U.S. Census Bureau, Statistical Abstract of the United States: 2009

classifications—federal general government and government enterprises and state and local general government and government enterprises.

The estimates by industry are available in current dollars and are derived from the estimates of gross domestic income, which consists of three components—the compensation of employees, gross operating surplus, and taxes on production and imports, less subsidies. Real, or inflation-adjusted, estimates are also prepared.

Regional Economic Accounts—These accounts consist of estimates of state and local area personal income and of gross domestic product by state and are consistent with estimates of personal income and gross domestic product in the Bureau's national economic accounts. BEA's estimates of state and local area personal income provide a framework for analyzing individual state and local economies, and they show how the economies compare with each other. The *personal income* of a state and/or local area is the income received by, or on behalf of, the residents of that state or area. Estimates of labor and proprietors' earnings by place of work indicate the economic activity of business and government within that area, and estimates of personal income by place of residence indicate the income within the area that is available for spending. BEA prepares estimates for states, counties, metropolitan areas, and BEA economic areas.

Gross domestic product by state estimates measure the value added to the nation's production by the labor and property in each state. GDP by state is often considered the state counterpart of the nation's GDP. The GDP by state estimates provide the basis for analyzing the regional impacts of national economic trends. GDP by state is measured as the sum of the distributions by industry and state of the components of gross domestic income; that is, the sum of the costs incurred and incomes earned in the production of GDP by state. The GDP estimates are presented in current dollars and in real (chained dollars) for 63 industries.

Consumer Expenditure Survey—The Consumer Expenditure Survey program was begun in 1980. The principal objective of the survey is to collect current consumer expenditure data, which provide a continuous flow of data on the buying habits of American consumers. The data are necessary for future revisions of the Consumer Price Index.

The survey conducted by the Census Bureau for the Bureau of Labor Statistics consists of two components: (1) an interview panel survey in which the expenditures of consumer units are obtained in five interviews conducted every 3 months, and (2) a diary or recordkeeping survey completed by participating households for two consecutive 1-week periods.

Each component of the survey queries an independent sample of consumer units representative of the U.S. total population. Over 52 weeks of the year, 7,500 consumer units are sampled for the diary survey. Each consumer unit keeps a diary for two 1-week periods yielding approximately 15,000 diaries a year. The interview sample is selected on a rotating panel basis, targeted at 7,500 consumer units per quarter. Data are collected in 102 areas of the country that are representative of the U.S. total population. The survey includes students in student housing. Data from the two surveys are combined; integration is necessary to permit analysis of total family expenditures because neither the diary nor quarterly interview survey was designed to collect a complete account of consumer spending.

Distribution of money income to families and individuals—Money income statistics are based on data collected in various field surveys of income conducted since 1936. Since 1947, the Census Bureau has collected the data on an annual basis and published them in *Current Population Reports*, P60 Series. In each of the surveys, field representatives interview samples of the population with respect to income received during the previous year. *Money income* as defined by the Census Bureau differs from the BEA concept of "personal income." Data on consumer income collected in the CPS by

Income, Expenditures, Poverty, and Wealth   423

the Census Bureau cover money income received (exclusive of certain money receipts such as capital gains) before payments for personal income taxes, social security, union dues, medicare deductions, etc. Therefore, money income does not reflect the fact that some families receive part of their income in the form of noncash benefits (see Section 11) such as food stamps, health benefits, and subsidized housing; that some farm families receive noncash benefits in the form of rent-free housing and goods produced and consumed on the farm; or that noncash benefits are also received by some nonfarm residents which often take the form of the use of business transportation and facilities, full or partial payments by business for retirement programs, medical and educational expenses, etc. These elements should be considered when comparing income levels. None of the aggregate income concepts (GDP, national income, or personal income) is exactly comparable with money income, although personal income is the closest.

Poverty—Families and unrelated individuals are classified as being above or below poverty following the Office of Management and Budget's Statistical Policy Directive 14. The Census Bureau uses a set of thresholds that vary by family size and composition.

The poverty calculation is based solely on money income and does not reflect the fact that many low-income persons receive noncash benefits such as food stamps, medicaid, and public housing. The original thresholds were based on the U.S. Department of Agriculture's 1961 Economy Food Plan and reflected the different consumption requirements of families. The poverty thresholds are updated every year to reflect changes in the Consumer Price Index. The following technical changes to the thresholds were made in 1981: (1) distinctions based on sex of householder were eliminated, (2) separate thresholds for farm families were dropped, and (3) the matrix was expanded to families of nine or more persons from the old cutoff of seven or more persons. These changes were incorporated in the calculation of poverty data beginning with 1981. Besides the Census Bureau Web site at <http://www.census.gov/hhes/www/poverty/poverty.html>, information on poverty guidelines and research may be found at the U.S. Department of Human Services Web site at <http://aspe.hhs.gov/poverty/index.shtml>.

In the recent past, the Census Bureau has published a number of technical papers and reports that presented experimental poverty estimates based on income definitions that counted the value of selected government noncash benefits. The Census Bureau has also published reports on aftertax income.

Statistical reliability—For a discussion of statistical collection and estimation, sampling procedures, and measures of statistical reliability pertaining to Census Bureau data, see Appendix III.

Table 645. Gross Domestic Product in Current and Real (2000) Dollars: 1960 to 2007

[In billions of dollars (526 represents $526,000,000,000). For explanation of gross domestic product and chained dollars, see text, this section. Minus sign (−) indicates net imports]

Item	1960	1970	1980	1990	1995	1996	1997	1998	1999	2000	2001	2002	2003	2004	2005	2006	2007
CURRENT DOLLARS																	
Gross domestic product	**526**	**1,039**	**2,790**	**5,803**	**7,398**	**7,817**	**8,304**	**8,747**	**9,268**	**9,817**	**10,128**	**10,470**	**10,961**	**11,686**	**12,434**	**13,195**	**13,841**
Personal consumption expenditures	332	649	1,757	3,840	4,976	5,257	5,547	5,880	6,283	6,739	7,055	7,351	7,704	8,196	8,708	9,225	9,734
Durable goods	43	85	214	474	612	653	693	750	818	863	884	924	943	984	1,024	1,049	1,078
Nondurable goods	153	272	696	1,250	1,485	1,556	1,619	1,684	1,805	1,947	2,017	2,080	2,190	2,344	2,516	2,688	2,833
Services	136	292	847	2,116	2,879	3,049	3,236	3,446	3,660	3,929	4,154	4,347	4,571	4,868	5,168	5,488	5,823
Gross private domestic investment	79	152	479	861	1,144	1,240	1,390	1,509	1,626	1,736	1,614	1,582	1,664	1,889	2,077	2,209	2,125
Fixed investment	76	150	486	846	1,113	1,210	1,318	1,438	1,559	1,679	1,646	1,570	1,650	1,830	2,040	2,163	2,122
Change in private inventories	3	2	−6	15	31	−96	72	71	67	57	−32	12	14	59	37	47	3
Net exports of goods and services	4	4	−13	−78	−91	−96	−102	−160	−261	−380	−367	−424	−499	−615	−715	−762	−708
Exports	27	60	281	552	812	869	955	956	991	1,096	1,033	1,006	1,041	1,182	1,309	1,468	1,643
Imports	23	56	294	630	904	965	1,057	1,116	1,252	1,476	1,400	1,430	1,540	1,798	2,024	2,230	2,351
Government consumption expenditures and gross investment	112	234	566	1,180	1,369	1,416	1,469	1,518	1,621	1,722	1,826	1,961	2,093	2,217	2,363	2,523	2,690
Federal	64	114	244	508	519	527	531	530	556	579	613	680	756	826	878	933	976
National defense	53	88	168	374	349	355	350	346	361	370	393	437	497	551	589	624	660
Nondefense	11	26	76	134	171	173	181	185	195	209	220	243	259	275	290	308	316
State and local	48	120	322	672	850	889	938	988	1,065	1,143	1,213	1,282	1,336	1,391	1,485	1,591	1,714
CHAINED (2000) DOLLARS																	
Gross domestic product	**2,502**	**3,772**	**5,162**	**7,113**	**8,032**	**8,329**	**8,704**	**9,067**	**9,470**	**9,817**	**9,891**	**10,049**	**10,301**	**10,676**	**11,003**	**11,319**	**11,567**
Personal consumption expenditures	1,597	2,452	3,374	4,770	5,434	5,619	5,832	6,126	6,439	6,739	6,910	7,099	7,295	7,561	7,804	8,044	8,278
Durable goods	(NA)	(NA)	(NA)	454	553	596	647	720	805	863	901	965	1,021	1,085	1,137	1,181	1,235
Nondurable goods	(NA)	(NA)	(NA)	1,484	1,639	1,680	1,725	1,794	1,877	1,947	1,987	2,037	2,103	2,178	2,255	2,338	2,393
Services	(NA)	(NA)	(NA)	2,852	3,260	3,356	3,468	3,615	3,758	3,929	4,023	4,100	4,179	4,311	4,427	4,546	4,675
Gross private domestic investment	267	427	645	895	1,134	1,234	1,388	1,524	1,643	1,736	1,598	1,557	1,613	1,770	1,869	1,920	1,826
Fixed investment	(NA)	(NA)	(NA)	887	1,110	1,209	1,321	1,455	1,576	1,679	1,629	1,545	1,597	1,713	1,831	1,875	1,820
Change in private inventories	(NA)	(NA)	(NA)	15	30	29	71	73	69	57	−32	13	14	54	33	40	5
Net exports of goods and services	(NA)	(NA)	(NA)	−55	−71	−80	−105	−204	−296	−380	−399	−471	−519	−594	−618	−625	−556
Exports	91	161	324	553	778	843	944	967	1,008	1,096	1,037	1,013	1,026	1,126	1,203	1,304	1,410
Imports	103	213	311	607	849	923	1,048	1,170	1,304	1,476	1,436	1,485	1,545	1,720	1,822	1,929	1,965
Government consumption expenditures and gross investment	715	1,013	1,115	1,530	1,550	1,565	1,594	1,624	1,687	1,722	1,780	1,859	1,905	1,932	1,946	1,981	2,022
Federal	(NA)	(NA)	(NA)	659	580	574	568	561	574	579	601	643	687	716	727	742	755
National defense	(NA)	(NA)	(NA)	479	389	384	373	365	372	370	385	413	449	475	482	492	505
Nondefense	(NA)	(NA)	(NA)	179	191	190	195	196	202	209	217	230	238	241	244	251	250
State and local	(NA)	(NA)	(NA)	868	968	991	1,026	1,063	1,113	1,143	1,179	1,215	1,218	1,216	1,220	1,239	1,266
Residual	−65	−68	14	−91	−51	−39	−24	−15	−6	–	2	3	3	–	−12	−28	−45

− Represents or rounds to zero.   NA Not available.

Source: U.S. Bureau of Economic Analysis, *Survey of Current Business*, April 2008. See also <http://www.bea.gov/national/nipaweb/SelectTable.asp?Selected=N>.

Income, Expenditures, Poverty, and Wealth   425

Table 646. GDP Components in Real (2000) Dollars—Annual Percent Change: 1990 to 2007

[Change from immediate previous year; for example, 1990, change from 1989. Minus sign (–) indicates decrease]

Component	1990	1995	2000	2001	2002	2003	2004	2005	2006	2007
Gross domestic product (GDP)...	**1.9**	**2.5**	**3.7**	**0.8**	**1.6**	**2.5**	**3.6**	**3.1**	**2.9**	**2.2**
Personal consumption expenditures	2.0	2.7	4.7	2.5	2.7	2.8	3.6	3.2	3.1	2.9
Durable goods.................	–0.3	4.4	7.3	4.3	7.1	5.8	6.3	4.9	3.8	4.7
Nondurable goods..............	1.6	2.2	3.8	2.0	2.5	3.2	3.5	3.6	3.6	2.4
Services.....................	2.9	2.6	4.5	2.4	1.9	1.9	3.2	2.7	2.7	2.8
Gross private domestic investment.....	–3.4	3.1	5.7	–7.9	–2.6	3.6	9.7	5.6	2.7	–4.9
Fixed investment.............	–2.1	6.5	6.5	–3.0	–5.2	3.4	7.3	6.9	2.4	–2.9
Nonresidential.............	0.5	10.5	8.7	–4.2	–9.2	1.0	5.8	7.1	6.6	4.7
Structures	1.5	6.4	6.8	–2.3	–17.1	–4.1	1.3	0.5	8.4	12.9
Equipment and software......	–	12.0	9.4	–4.9	–6.2	2.8	7.4	9.6	5.9	1.3
Residential	–8.6	–3.2	0.8	0.4	4.8	8.4	10.0	6.6	–4.6	–17.0
Exports.....................	9.0	10.1	8.7	–5.4	–2.3	1.3	9.7	6.9	8.4	8.1
Goods...................	8.4	11.7	11.2	–6.1	–4.0	1.8	9.0	7.5	9.9	7.9
Services..................	10.5	6.3	2.9	–3.7	1.9	–	11.5	5.4	4.8	8.5
Imports.....................	3.6	8.0	13.1	–2.7	3.4	4.1	11.3	5.9	5.9	1.9
Goods...................	3.0	9.0	13.5	–3.2	3.7	4.9	11.3	6.6	6.0	1.6
Services..................	6.5	3.3	11.1	–0.3	2.1	–	11.5	2.3	5.2	3.5
Government consumption expenditures and gross investment.............	3.2	0.5	2.1	3.4	4.4	2.5	1.4	0.7	1.8	2.0
Federal....................	2.0	–2.7	0.9	3.9	7.0	6.8	4.2	1.5	2.2	1.7
National defense	–	–3.8	–0.5	3.9	7.4	8.7	5.8	1.5	1.9	2.8
Nondefense................	8.3	–0.4	3.5	3.9	6.3	3.4	1.1	1.3	2.8	–0.4
State and local	4.1	2.6	2.7	3.2	3.1	0.2	–0.2	0.3	1.6	2.2

– Represents or rounds to zero.

Source: U.S. Bureau of Economic Analysis, *Survey of Current Business,* April 2008. See also <http://www.bea.gov/national /nipaweb/SelectTable.asp?Selected=N>.

Table 647. Gross Domestic Product in Current and Real (2000) Dollars by Type of Product and Sector: 1990 to 2007

[**In billions of dollars (5,803 represents $5,803,000,000,000).** For explanation of chained dollars, see text, this section]

Type of product and sector	1990	1995	2000	2002	2003	2004	2005	2006	2007
CURRENT DOLLARS									
Gross domestic product	**5,803**	**7,398**	**9,817**	**10,470**	**10,961**	**11,686**	**12,434**	**13,195**	**13,841**
PRODUCT									
Goods.......................	2,156	2,661	3,449	3,442	3,524	3,707	3,874	4,092	4,266
Durable goods	958	1,236	1,689	1,575	1,585	1,651	1,754	1,819	1,872
Nondurable goods	1,198	1,425	1,760	1,867	1,939	2,056	2,120	2,274	2,395
Services [1]	3,114	4,098	5,426	6,031	6,367	6,778	7,214	7,665	8,163
Structures	534	638	942	996	1,069	1,201	1,346	1,438	1,412
SECTOR									
Business	4,463	5,701	7,667	8,041	8,412	8,988	9,603	10,193	10,655
Nonfarm....................	4,386	5,632	7,595	7,970	8,323	8,873	9,502	10,097	10,525
Farm......................	77	69	72	71	88	115	101	96	130
Households and institutions	619	816	1,081	1,227	1,269	1,350	1,405	1,500	1,602
General government	722	882	1,070	1,202	1,280	1,348	1,426	1,502	1,585
Federal	259	285	315	353	384	413	439	459	477
State and local	463	597	754	849	896	936	987	1,043	1,108
CHAINED (2000) DOLLARS									
Gross domestic product	**7,113**	**8,032**	**9,817**	**10,049**	**10,301**	**10,676**	**11,003**	**11,319**	**11,567**
PRODUCT									
Goods.......................	2,253	2,639	3,449	3,433	3,538	3,705	3,866	4,058	4,191
Durable goods	877	1,125	1,689	1,627	1,682	1,782	1,900	1,980	2,065
Nondurable goods	1,407	1,532	1,760	1,805	1,856	1,925	1,973	2,083	2,136
Services [1]	4,170	4,655	5,426	5,693	5,811	5,973	6,112	6,255	6,436
Structures	718	754	942	922	952	1,001	1,035	1,034	985
SECTOR									
Business	5,287	6,077	7,667	7,807	8,050	8,387	8,692	8,966	9,171
Nonfarm....................	5,238	6,030	7,595	7,737	7,974	8,304	8,604	8,878	9,083
Farm......................	49	50	72	70	76	82	87	88	87
Households and institutions	841	945	1,081	1,131	1,129	1,166	1,183	1,222	1,252
General government	1,004	1,021	1,070	1,110	1,124	1,129	1,139	1,147	1,160
Federal	372	334	315	323	332	335	337	337	339
State and local	634	687	754	787	792	794	802	810	821

[1] Includes government consumption expenditures, which are for services (such as education and national defense) produced by government. In current dollars, these services are valued at their cost of production.

Source: U.S. Bureau of Economic Analysis, *Survey of Current Business,* April 2008. See also <http://www.bea.gov/national /nipaweb/SelectTable.asp?Selected=N>.

Table 648. Gross Domestic Product in Current and Real (2000) Dollars by Industry: 2000 to 2007

[In billions of dollars (9,817 represents $9,817,000,000,000). Data are based on the 1997 North American Industry Classification System (NAICS); see text, Section 15. Data include nonfactor charges (capital consumption allowances, indirect business taxes, etc.) as well as factor charges against gross product; corporate profits and capital consumption allowances have been shifted from a company to an establishment basis]

Industry	Current dollars				Chained (2000) dollars			
	2000	2005	2006	2007	2000	2005	2006	2007
Gross domestic product [1]	**9,817**	**12,434**	**13,195**	**13,841**	**9,817**	**11,003**	**11,319**	**11,567**
Private industries	8,614	10,861	11,556	12,104	8,614	9,726	10,063	10,276
Agriculture, forestry, and fishing	98	129	125	161	98	117	118	119
Farms	72	101	96	(NA)	72	87	88	(NA)
Agricultural services	27	28	30	(NA)	27	29	29	(NA)
Mining	121	226	262	276	121	105	112	112
Oil and gas extraction	81	150	159	(NA)	81	69	72	(NA)
Mining, except oil and gas	27	38	43	(NA)	27	26	27	(NA)
Mining support activities	13	38	59	(NA)	13	11	13	(NA)
Utilities	189	249	273	296	189	207	203	213
Construction	436	608	630	563	436	432	406	357
Manufacturing	1,426	1,484	1,550	1,616	1,426	1,493	1,537	1,572
Durable goods	865	841	883	927	865	943	1,000	1,049
Wood products	31	37	37	(NA)	31	31	33	(NA)
Nonmetallic mineral products	46	51	55	(NA)	46	46	44	(NA)
Primary metals	48	58	63	(NA)	48	45	41	(NA)
Fabricated metal products	122	123	131	(NA)	122	113	119	(NA)
Machinery	109	115	123	(NA)	109	113	120	(NA)
Computer and electronic products	186	133	140	(NA)	186	301	366	(NA)
Electrical equipment, appliances, and components	51	44	45	(NA)	51	44	42	(NA)
Motor vehicles, bodies & trailers, & parts	118	99	97	(NA)	118	130	144	(NA)
Other transportation equipment	64	82	90	(NA)	64	69	74	(NA)
Furniture and related products	33	31	31	(NA)	33	29	29	(NA)
Miscellaneous manufacturing	58	69	70	(NA)	58	66	68	(NA)
Nondurable goods	561	643	667	689	561	558	552	546
Food & beverage & tobacco	155	164	161	(NA)	155	150	153	(NA)
Textile mills and textile product mills	27	21	19	(NA)	27	22	19	(NA)
Apparel and leather and allied products	25	17	16	(NA)	25	17	17	(NA)
Paper products	56	53	52	(NA)	56	56	52	(NA)
Printing and related support activities	49	45	46	(NA)	49	44	45	(NA)
Petroleum and coal products	26	78	86	(NA)	26	34	32	(NA)
Chemical products	157	200	214	(NA)	157	171	173	(NA)
Plastics and rubber products	67	66	71	(NA)	67	66	64	(NA)
Wholesale trade	592	724	762	799	592	678	690	696
Retail trade	662	813	848	887	662	819	860	902
Transportation and warehousing	302	359	385	403	302	348	366	378
Air transportation	58	45	50	(NA)	58	80	83	(NA)
Rail transportation	26	33	37	(NA)	26	26	33	(NA)
Water transportation	7	9	10	(NA)	7	6	7	(NA)
Truck transportation	93	119	125	(NA)	93	101	103	(NA)
Transit & ground passenger transport	15	17	18	(NA)	15	15	15	(NA)
Pipeline transportation	9	9	11	(NA)	9	11	11	(NA)
Other transportation & support	70	91	97	(NA)	70	80	84	(NA)
Warehousing and storage	25	35	37	(NA)	25	32	33	(NA)
Information	458	571	599	645	458	624	669	729
Publishing industries (includes software)	117	142	150	(NA)	117	149	155	(NA)
Motion picture and sound recording	33	42	43	(NA)	33	37	38	(NA)
Broadcasting and telecommunications	271	324	337	(NA)	271	377	405	(NA)
Information and data processing services	38	62	68	(NA)	38	62	72	(NA)
Finance and insurance	741	982	1,094	1,114	741	878	964	961
Real estate and rental and leasing	1,191	1,566	1,663	1,747	1,191	1,358	1,404	1,434
Professional, scientific, and technical services	675	852	925	1,003	675	783	830	875
Legal services	136	176	187	(NA)	136	137	137	(NA)
Computer systems design, related services	126	133	146	(NA)	126	140	151	(NA)
Miscellaneous services	413	543	592	(NA)	413	508	546	(NA)
Management of companies & enterprises	183	235	242	262	183	182	178	179
Admin./support waste management/ remediation services	282	366	393	419	282	315	324	340
Educational services	79	114	121	129	79	85	86	89
Health care and social assistance	599	848	901	961	599	716	744	769
Ambulatory health care services	308	434	465	(NA)	308	387	410	(NA)
Hospitals, nursing, residential care	239	340	358	(NA)	239	261	264	(NA)
Social assistance	53	74	79	(NA)	53	70	73	(NA)
Arts, entertainment, and recreation	89	117	126	131	89	99	103	104
Performing arts, spectator sports, museums, and related activities	40	55	60	(NA)	40	45	47	(NA)
Amusements, gambling, & recreation	49	62	66	(NA)	49	55	56	(NA)
Accommodation and food services	261	331	354	375	261	284	292	299
Accommodation	91	105	112	(NA)	91	91	95	(NA)
Food services and drinking places	171	226	241	(NA)	171	193	197	(NA)
Other services, except government	229	288	301	317	229	230	229	234
Government	1,203	1,569	1,649	1,741	1,203	1,263	1,268	1,283
Federal	379	503	526	547	379	394	393	395
State and local	824	1,066	1,123	1,194	824	869	875	888

NA Not available. [1] Beginning 2005, the sum of value added for all industries differs from GDP because estimates in these years are based in part on data from the Census Bureau's accelerated November 2007 release of the Annual Survey of Manufactures. These data were not available for the July 2007 release of the national income and product accounts.

Source: U.S. Bureau of Economic Analysis, *Survey of Current Business,* May 2008. See also <http://www.bea.gov /newsreleases/industry/gdpindustry/gdpindnewsrelease.htm>(released 29 April 2008).

Income, Expenditures, Poverty, and Wealth **427**

Table 649. Gross Domestic Product by State in Current and Real (2000) Dollars by State: 2000 to 2007

[In billions of dollars (9,749.1 represents $9,749,100,000,000). For definition of gross domestic product or chained dollars, see text, this section]

State	Current dollars					Chained (2000) dollars				
	2000	2004	2005	2006	2007, prel.	2000	2004	2005	2006	2007, prel.
United States [1] . . .	9,749.1	11,607.0	12,346.9	13,119.9	13,743.0	9,749.1	10,580.2	10,899.7	11,240.1	11,467.5
Alabama.	114.6	141.5	150.5	158.6	165.8	114.6	127.8	131.9	134.6	137.0
Alaska	27.0	35.1	39.3	43.1	44.5	27.0	28.9	29.3	30.5	30.6
Arizona.	158.5	193.4	215.8	237.4	247.0	158.5	180.5	196.4	209.6	213.3
Arkansas	66.8	82.1	86.1	90.9	95.4	66.8	74.2	75.9	77.6	78.8
California	1,287.1	1,519.4	1,632.8	1,742.2	1,813.0	1,287.1	1,406.8	1,470.4	1,526.2	1,549.0
Colorado.	171.9	197.3	213.3	226.3	236.3	171.9	180.6	188.7	194.4	198.4
Connecticut.	160.4	182.1	193.3	205.0	216.3	160.4	165.8	171.1	176.9	181.8
Delaware	41.5	52.3	57.3	59.6	60.1	41.5	46.7	49.4	49.7	48.9
District of Columbia	58.7	77.9	83.0	88.2	93.8	58.7	67.5	69.4	71.3	74.4
Florida	471.3	607.3	670.2	716.5	734.5	471.3	548.6	588.8	609.8	609.9
Georgia	290.9	338.5	359.7	376.4	396.5	290.9	310.7	322.1	327.3	336.6
Hawaii	40.2	50.4	54.9	58.7	61.5	40.2	44.6	46.9	48.4	49.9
Idaho	35.0	42.6	46.4	48.4	51.1	35.0	39.6	42.6	43.7	44.7
Illinois	464.2	534.4	554.1	584.0	609.6	464.2	487.6	490.2	501.1	508.6
Indiana.	194.4	228.3	232.8	238.7	246.4	194.4	209.5	207.7	207.0	207.6
Iowa	90.2	111.9	115.6	121.9	129.0	90.2	100.9	102.3	105.3	107.0
Kansas.	82.8	98.4	103.3	110.6	117.3	82.8	88.3	90.1	93.8	96.5
Kentucky	111.9	131.7	138.5	146.4	154.2	111.9	119.9	122.8	125.9	128.8
Louisiana	131.5	163.4	184.0	203.2	216.1	131.5	139.3	141.2	147.2	151.0
Maine.	35.5	43.2	44.4	46.3	48.1	35.5	38.9	38.9	39.4	39.9
Maryland	180.4	228.2	243.9	257.6	268.7	180.4	205.5	213.2	218.2	222.5
Massachusetts.	274.9	306.8	317.6	335.3	351.5	274.9	286.5	289.4	298.0	305.4
Michigan.	337.2	363.1	372.2	375.8	382.0	337.2	337.9	339.3	334.7	330.8
Minnesota.	185.1	223.5	232.0	242.1	255.0	185.1	205.1	207.2	210.4	214.9
Mississippi	64.3	76.5	79.5	84.6	88.5	64.3	67.9	68.2	70.2	71.4
Missouri	176.7	204.9	213.0	220.1	229.5	176.7	186.4	188.4	189.1	191.6
Montana.	21.4	27.5	30.0	32.0	34.3	21.4	24.0	25.3	26.1	27.0
Nebraska	55.5	68.4	71.2	75.3	80.1	55.5	60.9	62.1	64.4	65.8
Nevada	73.7	100.2	112.5	123.1	127.2	73.7	89.9	97.3	102.5	103.2
New Hampshire	43.5	51.4	53.5	56.1	57.3	43.5	47.7	48.4	49.2	49.2
New Jersey	344.8	410.1	425.5	448.4	465.5	344.8	375.8	378.4	386.9	391.3
New Mexico	50.7	63.5	68.2	72.2	76.2	50.7	56.9	57.7	59.3	61.0
New York	777.2	896.4	953.6	1,028.3	1,103.0	777.2	829.9	861.5	906.6	946.3
North Carolina	273.7	324.4	349.2	380.9	399.4	273.7	295.6	309.7	328.4	335.7
North Dakota.	17.8	22.7	24.6	25.9	27.7	17.8	20.0	21.1	21.5	22.2
Ohio	372.0	423.7	439.3	451.6	466.3	372.0	387.4	390.0	388.9	390.3
Oklahoma.	89.8	111.5	120.8	130.1	139.3	89.8	97.3	99.2	102.5	106.6
Oregon.	112.4	132.8	138.1	151.0	158.2	112.4	125.9	129.2	139.2	143.7
Pennsylvania.	389.6	459.9	482.4	508.8	531.1	389.6	416.2	422.0	430.4	437.1
Rhode Island.	33.6	42.1	43.1	45.7	46.9	33.6	37.8	37.6	38.6	38.7
South Carolina.	112.5	131.9	138.6	146.2	152.8	112.5	119.9	122.5	124.9	127.4
South Dakota	23.1	29.5	30.5	32.0	33.9	23.1	26.6	27.1	27.7	28.3
Tennessee	174.9	214.8	224.2	235.8	243.9	174.9	197.2	200.9	206.0	207.7
Texas.	727.2	901.7	979.3	1,068.1	1,142.0	727.2	806.0	825.2	867.8	903.4
Utah	67.6	80.9	88.9	98.0	105.7	67.6	73.0	77.5	82.3	86.7
Vermont	17.8	21.8	22.7	23.6	24.5	17.8	20.3	20.7	20.9	21.2
Virginia.	260.7	324.9	350.3	368.6	383.0	260.7	294.2	308.1	314.9	321.0
Washington.	222.0	253.2	273.3	291.3	311.3	222.0	230.0	241.8	250.4	261.1
West Virginia.	41.5	49.7	53.0	56.0	57.7	41.5	43.8	44.7	45.1	45.2
Wisconsin.	175.7	205.9	214.1	223.4	232.3	175.7	188.0	190.6	193.4	195.4
Wyoming	17.3	23.4	26.6	29.9	31.5	17.3	19.0	19.4	20.7	21.1

[1] For chained (2000) dollar estimates, states will not add to U.S. total.

Source: U.S. Bureau of Economic Analysis, *Survey of Current Business,* July 2008; and "Gross Domestic Product by State"; published 5 June 2008; <http://www.bea.gov/regional/gsp/>.

Table 650. **Gross Domestic Product by Selected Industries and State: 2007**

[**In billions of dollars (13,743.0 represents $13,743,000,000,000)**. Preliminary data. For definition of gross domestic product by state, see text, this section. Industries based on 1997 North American Industry Classification System; see text, Section 15]

State	Total [1]	Manu-facturing	Whole-sale trade	Retail trade	Infor-mation	Finance and insur-ance	Real estate, rental, and leasing	Profes-sional and tech-nical ser-vices	Health care and social assis-tance	Govern-ment [2]
United States.	13,743.0	1,615.8	799.1	886.5	645.3	1,113.6	1,747.1	1,003.1	961.3	1,639.2
Alabama.	165.8	28.6	9.6	13.3	4.9	9.0	15.2	9.8	11.8	25.7
Alaska	44.5	1.0	0.9	1.9	1.1	1.2	3.3	1.6	2.3	7.8
Arizona.	247.0	19.6	14.2	20.0	7.2	20.8	37.7	15.3	17.9	29.9
Arkansas	95.4	16.9	6.2	7.1	3.9	3.8	8.5	3.7	7.3	12.9
California	1,813.0	179.0	104.1	125.7	112.6	120.5	301.2	159.1	108.8	205.2
Colorado.	236.3	15.2	13.2	14.3	21.4	13.9	30.2	22.5	13.8	28.0
Connecticut.	216.3	27.4	11.2	11.8	9.0	35.6	29.0	16.1	16.1	19.4
Delaware	60.1	4.4	2.0	2.6	1.3	19.5	7.3	3.8	3.4	5.3
District of Columbia	93.8	0.2	0.9	1.2	5.9	4.7	9.8	19.3	4.1	30.5
Florida	734.5	36.6	47.3	56.7	30.9	51.9	125.9	48.1	54.6	85.6
Georgia	396.5	43.6	30.7	26.2	25.9	25.9	46.6	26.6	23.9	52.1
Hawaii	61.5	1.1	2.0	4.4	1.6	2.5	10.9	2.8	4.1	14.1
Idaho	51.1	5.3	2.8	4.4	1.3	2.4	6.4	3.9	3.6	6.9
Illinois	609.6	76.6	42.6	35.1	24.1	57.7	76.4	53.2	40.8	58.7
Indiana.	246.4	62.7	14.0	15.8	6.0	13.2	24.0	10.3	18.8	24.3
Iowa	129.0	26.1	7.3	7.7	4.0	13.8	10.7	4.2	8.7	14.9
Kansas.	117.3	17.7	7.1	7.8	7.8	6.5	10.1	6.2	8.2	16.8
Kentucky	154.2	29.1	9.4	10.4	4.4	7.3	13.4	6.2	12.3	23.2
Louisiana	216.1	49.7	9.1	13.0	4.7	6.7	15.9	8.5	11.8	22.3
Maine.	48.1	5.3	2.5	4.4	1.4	3.2	6.4	2.3	5.3	6.9
Maryland	268.7	14.5	13.3	16.4	10.5	15.4	45.1	28.0	20.0	46.9
Massachusetts.	351.5	34.7	20.2	17.8	18.2	37.2	48.8	39.6	32.3	30.9
Michigan.	382.0	64.5	23.1	25.6	11.7	23.4	44.7	31.0	31.1	43.3
Minnesota.	255.0	33.9	17.3	15.2	9.7	24.0	30.6	16.1	21.4	26.3
Mississippi	88.5	13.8	4.5	7.6	2.2	3.7	7.6	3.1	6.4	15.3
Missouri	229.5	30.6	14.9	15.8	11.4	13.6	22.9	14.9	17.9	27.7
Montana.	34.3	1.5	1.8	2.4	1.0	1.7	3.6	1.7	3.0	5.3
Nebraska	80.1	9.0	4.5	4.7	2.7	6.8	7.0	3.6	5.8	11.0
Nevada	127.2	5.6	5.2	9.8	2.6	9.3	19.5	6.5	6.3	12.8
New Hampshire	57.3	6.3	3.7	4.7	2.2	4.6	7.9	4.0	5.2	5.4
New Jersey	465.5	40.8	36.4	29.4	24.1	38.5	77.5	42.0	33.6	47.8
New Mexico	76.2	5.6	2.6	5.1	2.0	2.4	7.9	6.2	5.0	12.9
New York	1,103.0	66.4	52.3	55.8	83.3	197.4	158.0	93.1	79.3	110.1
North Carolina	399.4	74.3	21.2	25.0	12.7	50.8	37.7	19.7	24.7	51.5
North Dakota.	27.7	2.6	2.0	1.9	1.1	1.6	2.3	0.9	2.4	4.2
Ohio	466.3	85.1	28.5	30.3	13.2	37.9	49.3	26.9	38.1	51.7
Oklahoma.	139.3	15.5	6.5	9.4	4.7	5.9	11.8	5.9	9.3	21.8
Oregon.	158.2	30.2	10.4	8.9	5.7	8.2	20.5	8.0	12.1	19.4
Pennsylvania.	531.1	75.2	32.1	33.0	21.1	39.6	59.3	40.6	50.8	52.1
Rhode Island	46.9	4.5	2.4	2.9	1.8	5.7	7.1	2.5	4.4	5.8
South Carolina.	152.8	24.5	9.0	12.4	4.5	7.6	16.7	7.6	9.2	25.4
South Dakota	33.9	3.3	1.9	2.4	1.1	6.7	2.4	0.9	3.0	4.2
Tennessee	243.9	39.4	16.4	20.9	8.5	14.3	23.6	13.6	21.6	26.9
Texas.	1,142.0	153.2	73.3	69.4	48.1	64.8	102.4	75.1	65.0	121.9
Utah	105.7	12.0	5.3	8.1	4.0	10.0	12.0	6.6	5.8	13.8
Vermont	24.5	2.8	1.2	2.0	1.0	1.4	3.0	1.4	2.4	3.4
Virginia.	383.0	33.9	16.4	22.4	19.5	25.0	50.1	45.8	20.9	68.8
Washington.	311.3	31.1	18.5	22.5	28.0	17.0	44.0	20.8	20.6	42.8
West Virginia	57.7	6.4	2.7	4.5	1.6	2.3	5.2	2.3	5.5	10.1
Wisconsin	232.3	47.7	13.2	14.6	7.6	16.1	27.5	10.5	19.6	25.3
Wyoming	31.5	1.0	1.2	1.8	0.5	0.7	2.4	0.9	1.3	4.2

[1] Includes industries not shown separately. [2] Includes federal civilian and military and state and local government.

Source: U.S. Bureau of Economic Analysis, *Survey of Current Business,* July 2008; and "Gross Domestic Product by State"; published 5 June 2008; <http://www.bea.gov/regional/gsp/>.

Income, Expenditures, Poverty, and Wealth   429

Table 651. Relation of GDP, GNP, Net National Product, National Income, Personal Income, Disposable Personal Income, and Personal Saving: 1990 to 2007

[In billions of dollars (5,803 represents $5,803,000,000,000). For definitions, see text, this section. Minus sign (–) indicates deficit or net disbursement]

Item	1990	1995	2000	2003	2004	2005	2006	2007
Gross domestic product (GDP)	**5,803**	**7,398**	**9,817**	**10,961**	**11,686**	**12,434**	**13,195**	**13,841**
Plus: Income receipts from the rest of the world.	189	234	383	337	438	544	691	818
Less: Income payments to the rest of the world.	154	198	344	280	361	476	633	722
Equals: Gross national product (GNP) . . .	**5,838**	**7,433**	**9,856**	**11,018**	**11,762**	**12,502**	**13,253**	**13,937**
Less: Consumption of fixed capital	683	878	1,188	1,337	1,436	1,610	1,615	1,687
Equals: Net national product	**5,155**	**6,555**	**8,668**	**9,681**	**10,326**	**10,893**	**11,638**	**12,251**
Less: Statistical discrepancy	*66*	*101*	*–127*	*49*	*19*	*5*	*–18*	*29*
Equals: National income	**5,089**	**6,454**	**8,795**	**9,632**	**10,307**	**10,888**	**11,656**	**12,221**
Less: Corporate profits [1]	438	697	818	993	1,231	1,373	1,554	1,595
Taxes on production and imports less subsidies	399	524	665	759	819	863	918	961
Contributions for government social insurance	410	533	703	779	829	875	928	979
Net interest and miscellaneous payments on assets	442	367	559	525	491	558	599	603
Business current transfer payments (net)	39	47	87	84	83	67	90	94
Current surplus of government enterprises	2	11	5	2	–4	–15	–14	–15
Wage accruals less disbursements	–	16	–	15	–15	5	8	23
Plus: Personal income receipts on assets	924	1,016	1,387	1,337	1,432	1,618	1,797	1,947
Personal current transfer receipts	595	877	1,084	1,351	1,423	1,521	1,613	1,732
Equals: Personal income	**4,879**	**6,152**	**8,430**	**9,164**	**9,727**	**10,301**	**10,983**	**11,660**
Less: Personal current taxes	593	744	1,236	1,001	1,046	1,209	1,354	1,483
Equals: Disposable personal income	**4,286**	**5,408**	**7,194**	**8,163**	**8,681**	**9,092**	**9,629**	**10,177**
Less: Personal outlays	3,986	5,157	7,026	7,988	8,499	9,047	9,590	10,134
Equals: Personal saving	**299**	**251**	**169**	**175**	**182**	**45**	**39**	**43**

– Represents or rounds to zero.   [1] Corporate profits with inventory valuation and capital consumption adjustments.

Source: U.S. Bureau of Economic Analysis, *Survey of Current Business,* April 2008. See also <http://www.bea.gov /national/nipaweb/SelectTable.asp?Selected=N>.

Table 652. Gross Saving and Investment: 1990 to 2007

[In billions of dollars (940 represents $940,000,000,000)]

Item	1990	1995	2000	2003	2004	2005	2006	2007
Gross saving	**940**	**1,185**	**1,771**	**1,459**	**1,618**	**1,735**	**1,867**	**1,853**
Net saving.	258	306	583	123	182	125	252	167
Net private saving	423	491	343	515	551	428	447	399
Personal saving.	299	251	169	175	182	45	39	43
Undistributed corporate profits with IVA and CCA [1]	123	224	175	325	384	379	401	334
Wage accruals less disbursements	–	16	–	15	–15	5	8	23
Net government saving.	–165	–185	239	–393	–369	–303	–195	–232
Federal	–172	–197	190	–372	–371	–318	–220	–221
State and local	7	12	50	–20	2	15	25	–12
Consumption of fixed capital	683	878	1,188	1,337	1,436	1,610	1,615	1,687
Private	552	713	991	1,118	1,206	1,357	1,348	1,399
Domestic business.	466	600	836	917	970	1,060	1,081	1,119
Households and institutions	85	113	155	202	236	297	266	280
Government.	131	165	197	218	230	252	268	288
Federal	68	82	87	90	94	99	105	110
State and local	63	83	110	128	136	153	162	178
Gross domestic investment, capital acct. transactions, and net lending. . .	**1,007**	**1,286**	**1,643**	**1,508**	**1,637**	**1,740**	**1,849**	**1,883**
Gross domestic investment.	1,077	1,377	2,040	2,020	2,261	2,475	2,643	2,593
Gross private domestic investment	861	1,144	1,736	1,664	1,889	2,077	2,209	2,125
Gross government investment	216	233	305	356	373	398	434	468
Capital account transactions (net)	7	1	1	3	2	4	4	2
Net lending or net borrowing	–77	–92	–397	–516	–627	–739	–798	–712
Statistical discrepancy.	66	101	–127	49	19	5	–18	29
Addenda:								
Gross private saving	974	1,205	1,334	1,633	1,757	1,785	1,795	1,798
Gross government saving	–34	–20	436	–174	–139	–51	72	56
Federal	–104	–115	277	–282	–277	–219	–115	–110
State and local	70	95	160	107	138	169	187	166
Net domestic investment.	394	498	852	684	825	866	1,028	907
Gross saving as a percentage of gross national income	16.3	16.2	17.7	13.3	13.8	13.9	14.1	13.3
Net saving as a percentage of gross national income.	4.5	4.2	5.8	1.1	1.5	1.0	1.9	1.2

– Represents or rounds to zero.   [1] IVA and CCA = Inventory valuation adjustment and capital consumption adjustment.

Source: U.S. Bureau of Economic Analysis, *Survey of Current Business,* April 2008. See also <http://www.bea.gov /national/nipaweb/SelectTable.asp?Selected=N>.

Table 653. Flow of Funds Accounts—Composition of Individuals' Savings: 1990 to 2007

[In billions of dollars (518.5 represents $518,500,000,000). Combined statement for households, farm business, and nonfarm noncorporate business. Minus sign (–) indicates decrease]

Composition of savings	1990	1995	2000	2003	2004	2005	2006	2007
Net acquisition of financial assets	**518.5**	**534.2**	**363.3**	**980.8**	**1,338.1**	**908.9**	**969.0**	**1,092.1**
Foreign deposits	1.4	4.6	7.6	2.2	5.4	4.1	5.9	19.0
Checkable deposits and currency	–9.5	–43.3	–78.6	–41.1	52.0	–73.2	–17.9	–23.3
Time and savings deposits	33.8	143.4	352.6	341.2	443.3	503.7	552.1	510.0
Money market fund shares	30.6	101.2	152.4	–109.2	–50.6	50.0	174.6	243.7
Securities	211.1	26.6	–647.8	302.0	211.0	–162.4	–352.1	–339.9
Open market paper	5.8	2.0	12.4	–4.5	30.2	28.1	23.4	–28.0
U.S. savings bonds	8.5	5.1	–1.7	8.9	0.6	0.7	–2.7	–6.0
Other Treasury securities	89.3	–17.6	–209.0	22.4	51.2	–90.5	–58.7	–169.4
Agency and GSE-backed securities [1]	36.3	28.2	38.6	153.4	97.7	84.3	–28.8	428.3
Municipal securities	34.7	–59.9	4.6	24.8	40.3	78.8	45.2	50.7
Corporate and foreign bonds	52.5	91.1	78.2	–91.4	43.9	–24.9	193.9	66.0
Corporate equities [2]	–47.6	–69.0	–637.7	–86.0	–269.3	–467.4	–761.0	–988.6
Mutual fund shares	31.5	46.7	66.7	274.4	216.4	228.5	236.7	307.1
Life insurance reserves	26.5	45.8	50.2	66.8	33.1	16.1	65.6	27.4
Pension fund reserves	191.0	176.8	271.6	258.5	288.4	238.3	198.2	124.4
Miscellaneous and other assets	33.5	79.1	255.4	160.4	355.5	332.3	342.5	530.7
Gross investment in tangible assets	**808.0**	**1,012.4**	**1,487.2**	**1,680.7**	**1,818.8**	**1,961.7**	**2,009.7**	**1,945.8**
Minus: Consumption of fixed capital	*558.8*	*712.1*	*940.9*	*1,057.6*	*1,141.7*	*1,274.1*	*1,258.7*	*1,289.2*
Equals: Net investment in tangible assets	**249.2**	**300.3**	**546.3**	**623.2**	**677.1**	**687.6**	**751.0**	**656.6**
Net increase in liabilities	**229.1**	**409.7**	**932.5**	**1,107.4**	**1,515.1**	**1,702.4**	**1,699.2**	**1,418.9**
Mortgage debt on nonfarm homes	205.5	167.8	425.0	796.4	1,023.2	1,096.1	1,061.5	689.7
Other mortgage debt [3]	–1.9	6.1	109.5	130.0	153.9	134.7	229.0	265.8
Consumer credit	15.1	147.0	176.5	104.4	115.0	94.5	104.4	132.3
Policy loans	4.1	10.5	2.8	–0.7	1.6	0.8	3.3	4.9
Security credit	–3.7	3.5	7.2	34.3	81.5	–31.6	59.7	32.8
Other liabilities [3]	10.0	74.8	211.4	43.0	139.9	408.0	241.4	293.4
Personal saving with consumer durables [4]	553.7	445.6	13.6	511.3	516.1	–89.7	39.2	333.3
Personal saving without consumer durables [4]	477.7	349.9	–192.4	305.6	309.5	–291.4	–151.9	122.2
Personal saving (NIPA, excludes consumer durables) [5]	299.4	250.9	168.5	174.9	181.7	44.6	38.8	42.7

[1] GSE = government-sponsored enterprises. [2] Only directly held and those in closed-end and exchange-traded funds. Other equities are included in mutual funds and life insurance and pension reserves. [3] Includes corporate farms. [4] Flow of Funds measure. [5] National Income and Product Accounts measure.

Source: Board of Governors of the Federal Reserve System, "Federal Reserve Statistical Release, Z.1, Flow of Funds Accounts of the United States"; published: 6 March 2008; <http://www.federalreserve.gov/releases/z1/20080306/>.

Table 654. Government Consumption Expenditures and Gross Investment in Current and Real (2000) Dollars by Level of Government and Type: 2000 to 2007

[In billions of dollars (1,721.6 represents $1,721,600,000,000). Government consumption expenditures are services (such as education and national defense) produced by government that are valued at their cost of production. Excludes government sales to other sectors and government own-account investment (construction and software). Gross government investment consists of general government and government enterprise expenditures for fixed assets; inventory investment is included in government consumption expenditures. For explanation of national income and chained dollars, see text, Section 13]

Item	Current dollars				Chained (2000) dollars			
	2000	2005	2006	2007	2000	2005	2006	2007
Government consumption expenditures and gross investment, total	**1,721.6**	**2,363.4**	**2,523.0**	**2,689.8**	**1,721.6**	**1,946.3**	**1,981.4**	**2,021.6**
Consumption expenditures	1,417.1	1,965.7	2,089.3	2,221.9	1,417.1	1,598.0	1,620.7	1,652.2
Gross investment	304.5	397.8	433.8	467.9	304.5	348.1	361.1	369.8
Structures	189.3	252.0	277.2	308.9	189.3	199.9	203.8	209.9
Equipment and software	115.2	145.8	156.5	159.0	115.2	151.2	161.6	163.7
Federal	**578.8**	**878.4**	**932.5**	**976.0**	**578.8**	**726.5**	**742.3**	**755.0**
Consumption expenditures	499.3	768.5	812.8	856.0	499.3	619.9	629.3	642.5
Gross investment	79.5	109.9	119.7	120.0	79.5	107.8	115.1	114.0
Structures	13.3	15.3	16.8	17.8	13.3	12.2	12.5	12.6
Equipment and software	66.2	94.6	102.9	102.2	66.2	96.4	103.6	102.3
National defense	**370.3**	**588.7**	**624.3**	**660.1**	**370.3**	**482.4**	**491.5**	**505.1**
Consumption expenditures	321.5	515.8	544.8	578.9	321.5	411.7	416.6	429.3
Gross investment	48.8	72.9	79.5	81.2	48.8	71.7	76.6	77.3
Structures	5.0	5.9	6.3	7.4	5.0	4.7	4.6	5.2
Equipment and software	43.8	67.0	73.2	73.9	43.8	67.2	72.4	72.3
Nondefense	**208.5**	**289.8**	**308.2**	**315.9**	**208.5**	**243.9**	**250.7**	**249.6**
Consumption expenditures	177.8	252.7	268.0	277.2	177.8	207.9	212.6	213.0
Gross investment	30.7	37.0	40.2	38.7	30.7	36.2	38.5	36.8
Structures	8.3	9.4	10.5	10.4	8.3	7.5	7.9	7.5
Equipment and software	22.3	27.7	29.7	28.3	22.3	29.1	31.3	30.0
State and local	**1,142.8**	**1,485.0**	**1,590.5**	**1,713.8**	**1,142.8**	**1,219.6**	**1,239.0**	**1,266.4**
Consumption expenditures	917.8	1,197.2	1,276.5	1,365.9	917.8	977.7	990.9	1,009.2
Gross investment	225.0	287.8	314.0	347.9	225.0	241.8	248.0	257.0
Structures	176.0	236.7	260.5	291.1	176.0	187.7	191.3	197.3
Equipment and software	49.0	51.1	53.6	56.9	49.0	54.6	57.7	61.3

Source: U.S. Bureau of Economic Analysis, *Survey of Current Business,* April 2008. See also <http://www.bea.gov/national/nipaweb/SelectTable.asp?Selected=N>.

Income, Expenditures, Poverty, and Wealth 431

Table 655. Personal Consumption Expenditures in Current and Real (2000) Dollars by Type: 2000 to 2006

[In billions of dollars (6,739.4 represents $6,739,400,000,000). For definition of "chained" dollars, see text, this section]

Expenditure	Current dollars 2000	2004	2005	2006	Chained (2000) dollars 2000	2004	2005	2006
Total expenditures [1]	**6,739.4**	**8,195.9**	**8,707.8**	**9,224.5**	**6,739.4**	**7,561.4**	**7,803.6**	**8,044.1**
Food and tobacco [1]	1,003.7	1,200.6	1,273.5	1,351.6	1,003.7	1,080.7	1,118.8	1,159.9
Food purchased for off-premise consumption...	566.7	677.2	721.2	762.6	566.7	618.4	647.6	673.0
Purchased meals and beverages [2]	348.8	424.5	450.2	482.4	348.8	380.7	391.6	406.7
Tobacco products	78.5	87.5	89.7	92.4	78.5	72.3	70.5	70.2
Clothing, accessories, and jewelry [1]	397.0	441.5	464.1	491.1	397.0	463.2	488.7	514.1
Shoes	47.0	51.9	55.1	58.2	47.0	53.9	55.6	58.3
Clothing	250.4	272.7	286.3	298.7	250.4	296.5	316.8	332.7
Jewelry and watches	50.6	56.3	58.4	62.2	50.6	59.5	62.7	65.2
Personal care	93.4	106.7	111.9	115.7	93.4	102.0	105.4	107.1
Toilet articles and preparations	55.0	58.3	61.1	63.8	55.0	58.3	61.1	63.2
Barbershops, beauty parlors, and health clubs...	38.4	48.4	50.8	51.9	38.4	43.6	44.4	44.1
Housing [1]	1,006.5	1,226.8	1,298.7	1,381.3	1,006.5	1,083.8	1,118.3	1,148.3
Owner-occupied nonfarm dwellings—space rent	712.2	898.0	952.6	1,014.5	712.2	793.9	822.9	846.9
Tenant-occupied nonfarm dwellings—space rent	227.5	251.8	262.7	277.0	227.5	220.6	223.4	227.6
Household operation [1]	719.3	822.4	878.1	923.4	719.3	800.3	826.8	845.4
Furniture [3]	67.6	75.3	79.9	84.5	67.6	79.5	85.2	89.4
Semidurable house furnishings [4]	36.5	41.1	43.2	45.4	36.5	49.1	52.9	59.6
Cleaning and polishing preparations	61.6	72.8	77.1	81.3	61.6	70.5	73.2	74.1
Household utilities [1]	209.9	254.3	283.2	297.8	209.9	215.5	217.7	211.4
Electricity	102.3	120.1	133.4	146.3	102.3	108.0	113.0	110.6
Gas	41.0	55.3	65.3	63.5	41.0	41.3	40.8	38.8
Water and other sanitary services	50.8	60.6	63.3	66.4	50.8	51.8	51.4	51.4
Telephone and telegraph	125.1	133.0	134.3	137.6	125.1	139.7	142.3	144.7
Medical care [1]	1,218.3	1,670.2	1,782.1	1,899.8	1,218.3	1,457.0	1,504.6	1,556.1
Drug preparations and sundries [5]	169.4	251.4	265.2	286.0	169.4	218.3	223.8	232.2
Physicians	236.8	322.0	344.6	366.3	236.8	302.2	317.7	334.7
Dentists	61.8	80.2	85.2	90.3	61.8	67.5	68.0	68.5
Other professional services [6]	161.6	217.1	230.9	246.1	161.6	196.6	204.4	213.7
Hospitals and nursing homes [7]	482.6	646.8	690.7	735.8	482.6	549.8	564.5	578.3
Health insurance	84.0	129.5	141.3	149.2	84.0	101.9	105.8	108.4
Medical care [8]	68.4	109.9	117.8	125.9	68.4	81.8	84.7	87.9
Personal business [1]	539.1	610.9	651.5	691.9	539.1	558.1	579.9	600.2
Brokerage charges and investment counseling	100.6	86.4	92.7	104.2	100.6	93.9	99.5	108.5
Bank service charges, trust services, and safe deposit box rental	64.2	88.5	99.2	108.0	64.2	79.2	88.0	93.2
Expense of handling life insurance [9]	96.1	99.4	108.9	114.9	96.1	85.5	90.7	92.5
Legal services	63.9	82.0	86.0	91.8	63.9	67.1	67.6	69.8
Transportation [1]	853.4	976.5	1,049.9	1,093.4	853.4	921.5	924.4	916.9
User-operated transportation [1]	793.8	917.5	988.3	1,028.2	793.8	859.0	861.2	853.4
New autos	103.6	97.7	104.0	107.1	103.6	101.9	107.5	109.7
Net purchases of used autos	60.7	54.3	57.6	58.0	60.7	56.1	57.0	56.5
Other motor vehicles	173.2	230.5	225.4	209.3	173.2	241.8	233.3	217.7
Tires, tubes, accessories, etc.	49.0	54.4	57.9	59.8	49.0	51.4	53.6	53.2
Repair, greasing, washing, parking, storage, rental, and leasing	183.5	189.5	198.4	208.4	183.5	173.1	175.9	178.6
Gasoline and oil	175.7	231.4	280.7	318.6	175.7	186.7	186.1	186.8
Insurance	43.0	53.7	57.8	60.1	43.0	44.5	44.2	44.3
Purchased intercity transportation	47.4	45.2	46.9	49.5	47.4	51.5	52.2	52.2
Recreation [1, 10]	585.7	707.8	746.9	791.1	585.7	743.7	792.9	847.8
Nondurable toys and sport supplies	56.6	63.3	66.5	71.4	56.6	76.8	85.1	94.8
Wheel goods, sports and photographic equipment, boats, and pleasure aircraft	57.6	71.3	76.2	78.9	57.6	75.0	80.5	83.6
Video and audio goods, including musical instruments	72.8	81.7	85.8	90.1	72.8	104.5	117.9	134.5
Computers, peripherals, and software	43.8	51.6	56.5	61.4	(NA)	(NA)	(NA)	(NA)
Commercial participant amusements	75.8	100.9	106.8	115.3	75.8	91.0	93.5	97.7
Education and research	163.8	212.8	225.9	239.6	163.8	173.9	175.1	176.9
Higher education	86.4	118.9	126.4	134.1	86.4	95.3	95.7	96.3
Religious and welfare activities	172.3	219.0	225.1	241.3	172.3	194.4	193.7	199.4
Foreign travel and other, net [1]	−13.0	0.8	0.1	4.1	−13.0	−7.9	−9.7	−4.8
Foreign travel by U.S. residents	84.4	92.5	100.0	108.7	84.4	77.8	79.6	84.8
Less: Expenditures in the United States by nonresidents	100.7	96.8	104.9	109.9	100.7	88.9	92.2	92.3

NA Not available. [1] Includes other expenditures not shown separately. [2] Consists of purchases (including tips) of meals and beverages from retail, service, and amusement establishments; hotels; dining and buffet cars; schools; school fraternities; institutions; clubs; and industrial lunch rooms. Includes meals and beverages consumed both on- and off-premise. [3] Includes mattresses and bedsprings. [4] Consists largely of textile house furnishings including piece goods allocated to house furnishing use. Also includes lamp shades, brooms, and brushes. [5] Excludes drug preparations and related products dispensed by physicians, hospitals, and other medical services. [6] Consists of osteopathic physicians, chiropractors, private duty nurses, chiropodists, podiatrists, and others providing health and allied services, not elsewhere classified. [7] Consists of (1) current expenditures (including consumption of fixed capital) of nonprofit hospitals and nursing homes and (2) payments by patients to proprietary and government hospitals and nursing homes. [8] Consists of (1) premiums, less benefits and dividends, for health hospitalization and accidental death and dismemberment insurance provided by commercial insurance carriers and (2) administrative expenses (including consumption of fixed capital) of Blue Cross and Blue Shield plans and of other independent prepaid and self-insured health plans. [9] Consists of (1) operating expenses of life insurance carriers and private noninsured pension plans and (2) premiums less benefits and dividends of fraternal benefit societies. Excludes expenses allocated by commercial carriers to accident and health insurance. [10] For additional details, see Table 1199.

Source: U.S. Bureau of Economic Analysis, *Survey of Current Business,* April 2008. See also <http://www.bea.gov/national/nipaweb/SelectTable.asp?Selected=N>.

Table 656. Personal Income and Its Disposition: 1990 to 2007

[**In billions of dollars (4,879 represents $4,879,000,000,000), except as indicated.** For definition of personal income and chained dollars, see text, this section]

Item	1990	1995	2000	2003	2004	2005	2006	2007
Personal income.	**4,879**	**6,152**	**8,430**	**9,164**	**9,727**	**10,301**	**10,983**	**11,660**
Compensation of employees, received . .	3,338	4,177	5,783	6,310	6,671	7,025	7,441	7,852
Wage and salary disbursements.	2,754	3,419	4,829	5,113	5,395	5,668	6,018	6,360
Supplements to wages and salaries . .	584	758	953	1,198	1,277	1,357	1,423	1,492
Proprietors' income [1]	381	492	728	811	912	970	1,007	1,043
Farm	32	23	23	29	37	31	19	36
Nonfarm	349	470	706	782	874	939	987	1,006
Rental income of persons [1]	51	122	150	133	118	43	55	65
Personal income receipts on assets	924	1,016	1,387	1,337	1,432	1,618	1,797	1,947
Personal interest income.	755	763	1,011	914	895	1,019	1,100	1,155
Personal dividend income	169	253	376	423	537	599	696	793
Personal current transfer receipts.	595	877	1,084	1,351	1,423	1,521	1,613	1,732
Government social benefits to persons	573	858	1,042	1,317	1,396	1,483	1,585	1,704
Old-age, survivors, disability, and health insurance benefits	352	507	621	741	788	845	946	1,023
Other current transfer receipts, from business (net)	22	19	42	34	26	38	27	28
Less: Contributions for government social insurance	410	533	703	779	829	875	928	979
Less: Personal current taxes	*593*	*744*	*1,236*	*1,001*	*1,046*	*1,209*	*1,354*	*1,483*
Equals: Disposable personal income . . .	**4,286**	**5,408**	**7,194**	**8,163**	**8,681**	**9,092**	**9,629**	**10,177**
Less: Personal outlays	*3,986*	*5,157*	*7,026*	*7,988*	*8,499*	*9,047*	*9,590*	*10,134*
Personal consumption expenditures	3,840	4,976	6,739	7,704	8,196	8,708	9,225	9,734
Personal interest payments.	116	133	205	183	191	218	238	263
Personal current transfer payments	30	49	82	102	112	122	128	137
Equals: Personal saving	**299**	**251**	**169**	**175**	**182**	**45**	**39**	**43**
Personal saving as a percentage of disposable personal income	7.0	4.6	2.3	2.1	2.1	0.5	0.4	0.4
Addenda:								
Disposable personal income:								
Total, billions of chained (**2000**) dollars . .	5,324	5,906	7,194	7,730	8,009	8,148	8,397	8,654
Per capita:								
Current dollars	17,131	20,287	25,472	28,053	29,563	30,677	32,183	33,689
Chained (**2000**) dollars	21,281	22,153	25,472	26,566	27,274	27,492	28,064	28,649

[1] With inventory valuation adjustments and capital consumption adjustment.

Source: U.S. Bureau of Economic Analysis, *Survey of Current Business,* April 2008. See also <http://www.bea.gov/national/nipaweb/SelectTable.asp?Selected=N>.

Table 657. Selected Per Capita Income and Product Measures in Current and Real (2000) Dollars: 1960 to 2007

[**In dollars.** Based on U.S. Census Bureau estimated population including Armed Forces abroad; based on quarterly averages. For explanation of chained dollars, see text, this section]

Year	Current dollars					Chained (**2000**) dollars				
	Gross domestic product	Gross national product	Personal income	Disposable personal income	Personal consumption expenditures	Gross domestic product	Gross national product	Disposable personal income	Personal consumption expenditures
1960	2,912	2,929	2,277	2,022	1,835	13,840	13,938	9,735	8,837
1965	3,700	3,727	2,860	2,563	2,283	16,420	16,554	11,594	10,331
1970	5,064	5,095	4,090	3,587	3,162	18,391	18,520	13,563	11,955
1975	7,586	7,646	6,181	5,498	4,789	19,961	20,133	15,291	13,320
1980	12,249	12,400	10,134	8,822	7,716	22,666	22,956	16,940	14,816
1985	17,695	17,806	14,787	13,037	11,406	25,382	25,548	19,476	17,040
1990	23,195	23,335	19,500	17,131	15,349	28,429	28,600	21,281	19,067
1991	23,650	23,770	19,923	17,609	15,722	28,007	28,150	21,109	18,848
1992	24,668	24,783	20,870	18,494	16,485	28,556	28,693	21,548	19,208
1993	25,578	25,700	21,356	18,872	17,204	28,940	29,079	21,493	19,593
1994	26,844	26,944	22,176	19,555	18,004	29,741	29,850	21,812	20,082
1995	27,749	27,884	23,078	20,287	18,665	30,128	30,271	22,153	20,382
1996	28,982	29,112	24,176	21,091	19,490	30,881	31,015	22,546	20,835
1997	30,424	30,544	25,334	21,940	20,323	31,886	32,010	23,065	21,365
1998	31,674	31,752	26,880	23,161	21,291	32,833	32,912	24,131	22,183
1999	33,181	33,302	27,933	23,968	22,491	33,904	34,027	24,564	23,050
2000	34,759	34,896	29,847	25,472	23,862	34,759	34,896	25,472	23,862
2001	35,490	35,643	30,571	26,235	24,722	34,659	34,809	25,697	24,215
2002	36,326	36,432	30,817	27,167	25,504	34,866	34,971	26,238	24,632
2003	37,671	37,866	31,494	28,053	26,476	35,403	35,590	26,566	25,073
2004	39,796	40,056	33,126	29,563	27,911	36,356	36,595	27,274	25,750
2005	41,954	42,185	34,757	30,677	29,381	37,127	37,334	27,492	26,330
2006	44,100	44,294	36,709	32,183	30,831	37,832	38,002	28,064	26,885
2007	45,819	46,136	38,597	33,689	32,223	38,290	38,557	28,649	27,402

Source: U.S. Bureau of Economic Analysis, *Survey of Current Business,* April 2008. See also <http://www.bea.gov/national/nipaweb/SelectTable.asp?Selected=N>.

U.S. Census Bureau, Statistical Abstract of the United States: 2009

Table 658. Personal Income in Current and Constant (2000) Dollars by State: 2000 to 2007

[In billions of dollars (8,422.1 represents $8,422,100,000,000). Represents a measure of income received from all sources during the calendar year by residents of each state. Data exclude federal employees overseas and U.S. residents employed by private U.S. firms on temporary foreign assignment. Totals may differ from those in Tables 651, 656, and 657]

State	Current dollars					Constant (2000) dollars [1]				
	2000	2004	2005	2006	2007, prel.	2000	2004	2005	2006	2007, prel.
United States	8,422.1	9,711.4	10,284.4	10,968.4	11,645.9	8,422.1	8,959.5	9,216.4	9,564.8	9,903.7
Alabama	105.8	126.3	133.0	141.8	150.0	105.8	116.5	119.2	123.7	127.5
Alaska.	18.7	22.4	24.3	25.8	27.6	18.7	20.7	21.8	22.5	23.5
Arizona	132.6	164.9	180.9	196.9	209.4	132.6	152.2	162.1	171.7	178.0
Arkansas	58.7	70.7	74.8	80.0	85.2	58.7	65.2	67.0	69.7	72.5
California	1,103.8	1,266.0	1,348.3	1,436.4	1,519.5	1,103.8	1,168.0	1,208.2	1,252.6	1,292.2
Colorado	144.4	163.7	175.7	188.2	199.5	144.4	151.1	157.5	164.1	169.7
Connecticut	141.6	159.3	167.2	177.5	189.5	141.6	147.0	149.8	154.7	161.2
Delaware	24.3	29.3	31.2	33.4	35.1	24.3	27.1	27.9	29.1	29.9
District of Columbia . . .	23.1	29.2	31.6	33.8	35.9	23.1	26.9	28.4	29.5	30.6
Florida.	457.5	565.7	617.2	663.1	701.6	457.5	521.9	553.1	578.2	596.7
Georgia	230.4	264.9	284.1	299.8	319.3	230.4	244.3	254.6	261.5	271.6
Hawaii.	34.5	41.0	44.3	47.3	50.4	34.5	37.9	39.7	41.3	42.8
Idaho	31.3	38.1	40.4	43.8	46.8	31.3	35.1	36.2	38.2	39.8
Illinois	400.4	445.2	464.1	490.8	518.2	400.4	410.7	415.9	428.0	440.7
Indiana	165.3	186.2	193.3	203.5	213.3	165.3	171.8	173.3	177.5	181.4
Iowa	77.8	90.4	93.2	98.2	104.7	77.8	83.4	83.5	85.6	89.0
Kansas	74.6	84.6	89.7	95.9	102.1	74.6	78.1	80.4	83.6	86.8
Kentucky	98.8	111.8	118.4	125.0	132.0	98.8	103.2	106.1	109.0	112.2
Louisiana.	103.2	122.3	111.9	135.0	149.2	103.2	112.9	100.3	117.7	126.9
Maine	33.2	39.5	40.6	42.2	44.4	33.2	36.4	36.4	36.8	37.8
Maryland	182.0	220.1	232.2	245.3	258.6	182.0	203.1	208.1	213.9	219.9
Massachusetts	240.2	266.6	280.4	297.9	316.6	240.2	246.0	251.3	259.8	269.2
Michigan	294.2	318.7	330.5	341.3	353.4	294.2	294.1	296.2	297.7	300.5
Minnesota	158.0	183.8	190.5	200.3	213.3	158.0	169.6	170.7	174.7	181.4
Mississippi	59.8	69.7	73.9	78.4	84.2	59.8	64.3	66.3	68.3	71.6
Missouri.	152.7	173.9	181.9	191.4	202.2	152.7	160.4	163.0	166.9	171.9
Montana	20.7	25.8	27.3	29.2	31.1	20.7	23.8	24.5	25.4	26.4
Nebraska.	47.3	55.4	57.7	60.7	64.7	47.3	51.1	51.7	53.0	55.0
Nevada	61.4	80.2	90.2	97.2	103.8	61.4	74.0	80.8	84.8	88.3
New Hampshire	41.4	47.2	48.9	52.1	54.6	41.4	43.5	43.9	45.5	46.5
New Jersey	323.6	361.8	377.4	405.3	427.3	323.6	333.8	338.3	353.4	363.4
New Mexico	40.3	49.8	54.0	58.1	62.0	40.3	46.0	48.4	50.7	52.7
New York.	663.0	740.0	790.1	848.9	914.4	663.0	682.7	708.0	740.3	777.6
North Carolina	218.7	250.9	266.6	286.0	304.8	218.7	231.5	238.9	249.4	259.2
North Dakota	16.1	18.6	20.3	20.9	22.3	16.1	17.2	18.2	18.2	19.0
Ohio	320.5	352.1	366.0	382.0	399.9	320.5	324.8	328.0	333.1	340.1
Oklahoma	84.3	100.0	106.5	115.9	123.5	84.3	92.3	95.4	101.1	105.1
Oregon	96.4	109.7	114.7	122.9	130.4	96.4	101.2	102.8	107.2	110.9
Pennsylvania	364.8	413.9	432.0	456.7	482.2	364.8	381.8	387.1	398.3	410.1
Rhode Island	30.7	36.8	38.4	39.8	41.7	30.7	34.0	34.4	34.7	35.5
South Carolina	98.3	113.6	121.1	128.9	136.7	98.3	104.8	108.5	112.4	116.2
South Dakota	19.4	23.9	24.6	25.3	27.0	19.4	22.0	22.1	22.0	23.0
Tennessee	148.8	174.6	184.6	195.4	204.9	148.8	161.1	165.5	170.4	174.2
Texas	593.1	694.9	759.6	823.2	888.9	593.1	641.1	680.7	717.8	755.9
Utah	53.6	63.6	70.1	75.9	82.5	53.6	58.6	62.8	66.1	70.2
Vermont	16.9	19.8	20.3	21.6	22.8	16.9	18.2	18.2	18.9	19.4
Virginia	220.8	267.5	286.9	302.1	318.9	220.8	246.8	257.1	263.4	271.2
Washington	187.9	218.4	224.7	243.6	261.4	187.9	201.5	201.4	212.4	222.3
West Virginia	39.6	45.7	47.9	51.0	53.5	39.6	42.1	42.9	44.5	45.5
Wisconsin	153.5	174.7	181.9	191.7	201.9	153.5	161.1	163.0	167.2	171.7
Wyoming	14.1	17.8	18.9	20.8	22.6	14.1	16.4	16.9	18.2	19.2

[1] Constant dollar estimates are computed by the U.S. Census Bureau using the national implicit price deflator for personal consumption expenditures from the Bureau of Economic Analysis. Any regional differences in the rate of inflation are not reflected in these constant dollar estimates.

Except as noted, U.S. Bureau of Economic Analysis, *Survey of Current Business*, April 2008, and unpublished data. See also <http://www.bea.gov/regional/spi>.

Table 659. Personal Income Per Capita in Current and Constant (2000) Dollars by State: 2000 to 2007

[In dollars, except as indicated. 2007 preliminary. See headnote, Table 658]

State	Current dollars				Constant (2000) dollars [1]				Income rank	
	2000	2005	2006	2007	2000	2005	2006	2007	2000	2007
United States.....	29,845	34,757	36,714	38,611	29,845	31,148	32,016	32,835	(X)	(X)
Alabama..........	23,767	29,306	30,894	32,404	23,767	26,263	26,940	27,557	44	42
Alaska..........	29,869	36,261	38,138	40,352	29,869	32,495	33,257	34,316	15	15
Arizona..........	25,653	30,386	31,936	33,029	25,653	27,231	27,849	28,088	37	40
Arkansas..........	21,926	26,989	28,473	30,060	21,926	24,186	24,829	25,563	48	48
California..........	32,462	37,462	39,626	41,571	32,462	33,572	34,555	35,352	8	7
Colorado..........	33,361	37,600	39,491	41,042	33,361	33,695	34,437	34,902	7	10
Connecticut........	41,492	47,943	50,762	54,117	41,492	42,964	44,266	46,021	1	1
Delaware..........	30,869	37,083	39,131	40,608	30,869	33,232	34,123	34,533	13	12
District of Columbia...	40,403	54,371	57,746	61,092	40,403	48,725	50,356	51,953	(X)	(X)
Florida...........	28,508	34,798	36,720	38,444	28,508	31,184	32,021	32,693	20	20
Georgia	27,987	31,193	32,095	33,457	27,987	27,954	27,988	28,452	26	38
Hawaii	28,435	34,935	37,023	39,239	28,435	31,307	32,285	33,369	22	18
Idaho...........	24,077	28,301	29,920	31,197	24,077	25,362	26,091	26,530	42	44
Illinois...........	32,186	36,489	38,409	40,322	32,186	32,700	33,494	34,290	9	16
Indiana..........	27,133	30,900	32,288	33,616	27,133	27,691	28,156	28,587	31	37
Iowa............	26,556	31,535	33,038	35,023	26,556	28,260	28,810	29,784	33	27
Kansas..........	27,691	32,709	34,799	36,768	27,691	29,312	30,346	31,268	27	22
Kentucky..........	24,412	28,387	29,729	31,111	24,412	25,439	25,925	26,457	40	46
Louisiana	23,081	24,901	31,821	34,756	23,081	22,315	27,749	29,557	45	31
Maine...........	25,973	30,952	32,095	33,722	25,973	27,738	27,988	28,677	35	35
Maryland..........	34,261	41,657	43,788	46,021	34,261	37,331	38,184	39,136	5	5
Massachusetts......	37,750	43,612	46,299	49,082	37,750	39,083	40,374	41,740	3	3
Michigan..........	29,554	32,694	33,788	35,086	29,554	29,299	29,464	29,837	17	26
Minnesota........	32,014	37,256	38,859	41,034	32,014	33,387	33,886	34,896	10	11
Mississippi.........	21,007	25,490	27,028	28,845	21,007	22,843	23,569	24,530	50	50
Missouri..........	27,242	31,426	32,789	34,389	27,242	28,163	28,593	29,245	30	32
Montana..........	22,933	29,183	30,790	32,458	22,933	26,152	26,850	27,602	46	41
Nebraska	27,624	32,882	34,440	36,471	27,624	29,467	30,033	31,015	29	24
Nevada..........	30,433	37,450	38,994	40,480	30,433	33,561	34,004	34,424	14	13
New Hampshire	33,399	37,557	39,753	41,512	33,399	33,657	34,666	35,302	6	8
New Jersey........	38,372	43,598	46,763	49,194	38,372	39,071	40,779	41,835	2	2
New Mexico........	22,143	28,175	29,929	31,474	22,143	25,249	26,099	26,766	47	43
New York	34,901	41,016	44,027	47,385	34,901	36,757	38,393	40,296	4	4
North Carolina......	27,064	30,713	32,247	33,636	27,064	27,524	28,120	28,604	32	36
North Dakota.......	25,103	31,871	32,763	34,846	25,103	28,561	28,570	29,633	38	29
Ohio............	28,206	31,939	33,320	34,874	28,206	28,622	29,056	29,657	24	28
Oklahoma.........	24,409	30,107	32,391	34,153	24,409	26,980	28,246	29,044	41	33
Oregon...........	28,096	31,599	33,299	34,784	28,096	28,318	29,038	29,580	25	30
Pennsylvania.......	29,696	34,927	36,825	38,788	29,696	31,300	32,112	32,986	16	19
Rhode Island.......	29,213	35,987	37,523	39,463	29,213	32,250	32,721	33,560	18	17
South Carolina......	24,423	28,460	29,767	31,013	24,423	25,505	25,958	26,374	39	47
South Dakota.......	25,721	31,557	32,030	33,905	25,721	28,280	27,931	28,833	36	34
Tennessee.........	26,095	30,827	32,172	33,280	26,095	27,626	28,055	28,301	34	39
Texas............	28,314	33,253	35,166	37,187	28,314	29,800	30,666	31,624	23	21
Utah............	23,864	27,992	29,406	31,189	23,864	25,085	25,643	26,523	43	45
Vermont	27,681	32,833	34,871	36,670	27,681	29,423	30,409	31,184	28	23
Virginia..........	31,083	37,968	39,540	41,347	31,083	34,025	34,480	35,162	12	9
Washington........	31,777	35,838	38,212	40,414	31,777	32,116	33,322	34,368	11	14
West Virginia.......	21,904	26,523	28,206	29,537	21,904	23,769	24,596	25,118	49	49
Wisconsin	28,570	32,829	34,405	36,047	28,570	29,420	30,002	30,655	19	25
Wyoming..........	28,469	37,316	40,655	43,226	28,469	33,441	35,452	36,760	21	6

X Not applicable. [1] Constant dollar estimates are computed by the U.S. Census Bureau using the national implicit price deflator for personal consumption expenditures from the Bureau of Economic Analysis. Any regional differences in the rate of inflation are not reflected in these constant dollar estimates.

Source: Except as noted, U.S. Bureau of Economic Analysis, *Survey of Current Business,* April 2008. See also <http://www.bea.gov/bea/regional/spi>.

Income, Expenditures, Poverty, and Wealth 435

Table 660. Disposable Personal Income Per Capita in Current and Constant (2000) Dollars by State: 2000 to 2007

[In dollars, except percent. 2007 preliminary. Disposable personal income is the income available to persons for spending or saving; it is calculated as personal income less personal tax and nontax payments. See headnote, Table 658]

State	Current dollars				Constant (2000) dollars [1]				Percent of U.S. average	
	2000	2005	2006	2007	2000	2005	2006	2007	2000	2007
United States.....	25,470	30,675	32,185	33,697	25,470	27,490	28,066	28,656	100.0	100.0
Alabama.........	21,048	26,523	27,811	29,077	21,048	23,769	24,252	24,727	82.6	86.3
Alaska...........	26,427	33,060	34,576	36,483	26,427	29,627	30,151	31,025	103.8	108.3
Arizona..........	22,321	27,034	28,190	29,056	22,321	24,227	24,583	24,709	87.6	86.2
Arkansas........	19,376	24,420	25,670	27,040	19,376	21,884	22,385	22,995	76.1	80.2
California........	26,715	32,523	34,037	35,588	26,715	29,146	29,681	30,264	104.9	105.6
Colorado........	28,227	33,211	34,627	35,760	28,227	29,762	30,196	30,410	110.8	106.1
Connecticut......	33,385	40,092	41,967	44,354	33,385	35,929	36,596	37,719	131.1	131.6
Delaware........	26,277	32,329	33,913	35,179	26,277	28,972	29,573	29,916	103.2	104.4
District of Columbia...	33,364	47,070	49,739	52,450	33,364	42,182	43,374	44,604	131.0	155.7
Florida..........	24,809	30,919	32,391	33,802	24,809	27,708	28,246	28,745	97.4	100.3
Georgia..........	24,051	27,701	28,304	29,349	24,051	24,824	24,682	24,959	94.4	87.1
Hawaii...........	24,853	30,894	32,551	34,444	24,853	27,686	28,385	29,291	97.6	102.2
Idaho...........	20,960	25,299	26,525	27,513	20,960	22,672	23,131	23,397	82.3	81.6
Illinois..........	27,413	32,232	33,689	35,196	27,413	28,885	29,378	29,931	107.6	104.4
Indiana..........	23,648	27,692	28,816	29,913	23,648	24,816	25,128	25,438	92.8	88.8
Iowa............	23,391	28,468	29,658	31,378	23,391	25,512	25,863	26,684	91.8	93.1
Kansas..........	24,045	29,281	30,900	32,495	24,045	26,240	26,946	27,634	94.4	96.4
Kentucky.........	21,344	25,395	26,580	27,715	21,344	22,758	23,179	23,569	83.8	82.2
Louisiana........	20,576	22,608	29,066	31,728	20,576	20,260	25,346	26,982	80.8	94.2
Maine..........	22,492	27,625	28,499	29,830	22,492	24,756	24,852	25,368	88.3	88.5
Maryland.........	28,803	35,922	37,493	39,153	28,803	32,192	32,695	33,296	113.1	116.2
Massachusetts......	30,305	37,369	39,357	41,446	30,305	33,488	34,320	35,246	119.0	123.0
Michigan.........	25,437	29,347	30,239	31,294	25,437	26,299	26,369	26,613	99.9	92.9
Minnesota........	27,184	32,568	33,767	35,528	27,184	29,186	29,446	30,213	106.7	105.4
Mississippi.......	18,937	23,619	24,940	26,564	18,937	21,166	21,748	22,590	74.4	78.8
Missouri.........	23,677	28,131	29,174	30,485	23,677	25,210	25,441	25,925	93.0	90.5
Montana.........	20,237	26,226	27,526	28,939	20,237	23,503	24,003	24,610	79.5	85.9
Nebraska........	24,088	29,551	30,750	32,507	24,088	26,482	26,815	27,644	94.6	96.5
Nevada..........	26,318	33,074	34,151	35,300	26,318	29,639	29,781	30,019	103.3	104.8
New Hampshire.....	28,569	33,706	35,465	36,838	28,569	30,206	30,927	31,327	112.2	109.3
New Jersey.......	32,016	37,705	40,248	42,070	32,016	33,789	35,097	35,777	125.7	124.8
New Mexico.......	19,585	25,593	27,031	28,374	19,585	22,935	23,572	24,129	76.9	84.2
New York.........	28,884	34,844	37,095	39,621	28,884	31,226	32,348	33,694	113.4	117.6
North Carolina.....	23,392	27,217	28,408	29,469	23,392	24,391	24,773	25,061	91.8	87.5
North Dakota......	22,592	29,204	29,751	31,519	22,592	26,171	25,944	26,804	88.7	93.5
Ohio............	24,263	28,225	29,342	30,616	24,263	25,294	25,587	26,036	95.3	90.9
Oklahoma........	21,519	27,071	28,995	30,497	21,519	24,260	25,284	25,935	84.5	90.5
Oregon..........	23,905	27,664	28,975	30,223	23,905	24,791	25,267	25,702	93.9	89.7
Pennsylvania......	25,575	30,901	32,377	33,948	25,575	27,692	28,234	28,870	100.4	100.7
Rhode Island......	25,057	31,905	33,013	34,630	25,057	28,592	28,788	29,450	98.4	102.8
South Carolina.....	21,500	25,531	26,601	27,570	21,500	22,880	23,197	23,446	84.4	81.8
South Dakota......	23,163	29,054	29,253	30,863	23,163	26,037	25,509	26,246	90.9	91.6
Tennessee........	23,407	28,330	29,402	30,299	23,407	25,388	25,639	25,766	91.9	89.9
Texas...........	24,965	30,241	31,765	33,424	24,965	27,101	27,700	28,424	98.0	99.2
Utah............	20,790	24,928	25,961	27,390	20,790	22,339	22,639	23,293	81.6	81.3
Vermont.........	24,011	29,302	30,995	32,524	24,011	26,259	27,029	27,659	94.3	96.5
Virginia..........	26,211	33,032	34,099	35,490	26,211	29,602	29,735	30,181	102.9	105.3
Washington.......	27,307	32,312	34,228	36,008	27,307	28,957	29,848	30,621	107.2	106.9
West Virginia......	19,539	24,085	25,511	26,611	19,539	21,584	22,246	22,630	76.7	79.0
Wisconsin........	24,498	29,014	30,261	31,554	24,498	26,001	26,388	26,834	96.2	93.6
Wyoming.........	24,504	33,237	35,970	37,969	24,504	29,785	31,367	32,289	96.2	112.7

[1] Constant dollar estimates are computed by the Census Bureau using the national implicit price deflator for personal consumption expenditures from the Bureau of Economic Analysis. Any regional differences in the rate of inflation are not reflected in these constant dollar estimates.

Source: Except as noted, U.S. Bureau of Economic Analysis, *Survey of Current Business,* April 2008. See also <http://www.bea.gov/bea/regional/spi>.

Table 661. Personal Income by Selected Large Metropolitan Area: 2000 to 2006

[8,422,074 represents $8,422,074,000,000. Metropolitan areas as defined December 2007. MSA = Metropolitan Statistical Area. See Appendix II]

Metropolitan area ranked by 2006 population	Personal income				Per capita personal income			
	2000 (mil. dol.)	2005 (mil. dol.)	2006 (mil. dol.)	Annual percent change, 2005–2006	2000 (dol.)	2005 (dol.)	2006 (dol.)	Percent of national average, 2006
United States..................	8,422,074	10,284,356	10,968,393	6.7	29,845	34,757	36,714	100.0
New York-Northern New Jersey-Long Island, NY-NJ-PA MSA	732,799	866,981	935,178	7.9	39,920	46,221	49,789	135.6
Los Angeles-Long Beach-Santa Ana, CA MSA..	385,053	482,011	513,123	6.5	31,044	37,441	39,880	108.6
Chicago-Naperville-Joliet, IL-IN-WI MSA......	318,439	371,160	393,382	6.0	34,920	39,454	41,591	113.3
Dallas-Fort Worth-Arlington, TX MSA	176,530	221,192	238,858	8.0	33,967	38,089	39,924	108.7
Philadelphia-Camden-Wilmington, PA-NJ-DE-MD MSA	193,919	237,201	251,979	6.2	34,061	40,948	43,364	118.1
Houston-Sugar Land-Baytown, TX MSA	161,398	216,765	237,784	9.7	34,047	40,734	43,174	117.6
Miami-Fort Lauderdale-Pompano Beach, FL MSA.	157,015	206,523	220,610	6.8	31,230	38,342	40,737	111.0
Washington-Arlington-Alexandria, DC-VA-MD-WV MSA......	196,093	258,222	272,861	5.7	40,667	49,442	51,868	141.3
Atlanta-Sandy Springs-Marietta, GA MSA	141,817	174,810	184,911	5.8	33,116	35,262	36,060	98.2
Detroit-Warren-Livonia, MI MSA	151,793	167,565	171,339	2.3	34,051	37,204	38,119	103.8
Boston-Cambridge-Quincy, MA-NH MSA	182,380	211,565	225,705	6.7	41,425	47,491	50,542	137.7
San Francisco-Oakland-Fremont, CA MSA	199,989	224,702	240,484	7.0	48,330	54,191	57,747	157.3
Phoenix-Mesa-Scottsdale, AZ MSA	92,975	126,848	138,465	9.2	28,353	32,660	34,215	93.2
Riverside-San Bernardino-Ontario, CA MSA ...	74,781	104,067	111,596	7.2	22,813	26,818	27,936	76.1
Seattle-Tacoma-Bellevue, WA MSA	115,203	135,770	148,015	9.0	37,737	42,356	45,369	123.6
Minneapolis-St. Paul-Bloomington, MN-WI MSA	109,818	133,237	140,320	5.3	36,830	42,457	44,237	120.5
San Diego-Carlsbad-San Marcos, CA MSA	92,654	118,793	126,194	6.2	32,789	40,383	42,801	116.6
St. Louis, MO-IL MSA	84,222	99,882	105,191	5.3	31,174	35,991	37,652	102.6
Tampa-St. Petersburg-Clearwater, FL MSA	68,891	89,013	95,750	7.6	28,651	33,678	35,541	96.8
Baltimore-Towson, MD MSA	85,144	108,479	114,592	5.6	33,294	40,933	43,026	117.2
Denver-Aurora, CO MSA.............	82,196	100,447	107,788	7.3	37,838	42,476	44,691	121.7
Pittsburgh, PA MSA	74,361	85,876	91,101	6.1	30,613	36,159	38,550	105.0
Portland-Vancouver-Beaverton, OR-WA MSA ..	62,190	73,087	78,618	7.6	32,118	34,921	36,845	100.4
Cincinnati-Middletown, OH-KY-IN MSA.......	61,393	74,295	77,740	4.6	30,472	35,326	36,650	99.8
Cleveland-Elyria-Mentor, OH MSA.........	67,935	75,337	78,752	4.5	31,627	35,555	37,406	101.9
Sacramento-Arden-Arcade-Roseville, CA MSA..	54,236	71,974	76,481	6.3	29,986	35,318	37,078	101.0
Orlando-Kissimmee, FL MSA	44,751	61,757	66,129	7.1	27,008	31,828	33,092	90.1
Kansas City, MO-KS MSA	58,247	69,531	73,692	6.0	31,606	35,839	37,566	102.3
San Antonio, TX MSA	45,997	58,722	63,546	8.2	26,751	31,189	32,810	89.4
Las Vegas-Paradise, NV MSA	41,239	63,041	68,032	7.9	29,595	36,893	38,281	104.3
San Jose-Sunnyvale-Santa Clara, CA MSA....	92,947	89,926	97,685	8.6	53,404	51,277	55,020	149.9
Columbus, OH MSA	49,770	59,651	62,635	5.0	30,730	34,777	36,110	98.4
Indianapolis-Carmel, IN MSA	48,862	59,477	63,030	6.0	31,911	36,160	37,735	102.8
Virginia Beach-Norfolk-Newport News, VA-NC MSA	41,659	54,862	57,899	5.5	26,360	33,259	34,858	94.9
Providence-New Bedford-Fall River, RI-MA MSA	45,976	57,029	59,425	4.2	28,972	35,412	37,040	100.9
Charlotte-Gastonia-Concord, NC-SC MSA	43,120	55,683	60,483	8.6	32,174	36,580	38,164	103.9
Milwaukee-Waukesha-West Allis, WI MSA	49,151	57,351	60,906	6.2	32,717	37,361	39,536	107.7
Austin-Round Rock, TX MSA	41,157	50,988	55,665	9.2	32,514	34,701	36,328	98.9
Nashville-Davidson-Murfreesboro-Franklin, TN MSA.	40,309	52,295	56,135	7.3	30,593	36,056	37,758	102.8
Jacksonville, FL MSA	33,151	44,281	47,972	8.3	29,435	35,439	37,519	102.2
Memphis, TN-MS-AR MSA.............	34,459	42,718	45,108	5.6	28,519	34,052	35,470	96.6
Louisville/Jefferson County, KY-IN MSA	34,250	41,296	43,935	6.4	29,396	34,162	36,000	98.1
Richmond, VA MSA	33,603	43,550	45,699	4.9	30,543	37,082	38,233	104.1
Hartford-West Hartford-East Hartford, CT MSA .	42,568	50,523	53,147	5.2	36,984	42,782	44,835	122.1
Oklahoma City, OK MSA	29,092	38,449	41,907	9.0	26,498	33,243	35,637	97.1
Buffalo-Niagara Falls, NY MSA	31,806	36,323	38,311	5.5	27,211	31,825	33,803	92.1
Birmingham-Hoover, AL MSA	29,898	38,575	41,067	6.5	28,382	35,448	37,331	101.7
Salt Lake City, UT MSA	27,081	35,098	37,883	7.9	27,840	33,469	35,145	95.7
Rochester, NY MSA	30,455	35,424	37,300	5.3	29,329	34,294	36,179	98.5
Raleigh-Cary, NC MSA	27,062	34,010	37,242	9.5	33,638	35,585	37,221	101.4
New Orleans-Metairie-Kenner, LA MSA	34,606	26,102	39,829	52.6	26,304	19,926	40,211	109.5
Tucson, AZ MSA	20,514	27,496	29,807	8.4	24,171	29,658	31,418	85.6
Honolulu, HI MSA..................	26,605	33,684	35,954	6.7	30,401	37,343	39,653	108.0
Bridgeport-Stamford-Norwalk, CT MSA......	52,190	61,623	66,407	7.8	58,997	68,840	74,281	202.3
Tulsa, OK MSA	24,984	31,043	34,131	9.9	29,005	35,180	38,219	104.1
Fresno, CA MSA	17,628	22,752	23,980	5.4	21,974	26,052	27,081	73.8
Albany-Schenectady-Troy, NY MSA.......	25,168	30,582	32,527	6.4	30,442	36,107	38,213	104.1
New Haven-Milford, CT MSA	28,379	33,127	34,964	5.5	34,398	39,354	41,454	112.9
Dayton, OH MSA..................	24,210	26,685	27,823	4.3	28,547	31,739	33,195	90.4
Omaha-Council Bluffs, NE-IA MSA	24,230	30,732	32,917	7.1	31,504	37,869	40,106	109.2
Albuquerque, NM MSA	18,910	24,804	26,764	7.9	25,844	31,061	32,727	89.1
Allentown-Bethlehem-Easton, PA-NJ MSA	22,220	26,461	28,129	6.3	29,949	33,677	35,369	96.3
Oxnard-Thousand Oaks-Ventura, CA MSA	25,364	32,303	33,940	5.1	33,528	40,845	42,746	116.4
Worcester, MA MSA	24,539	28,498	30,206	6.0	32,601	36,666	38,748	105.5
Grand Rapids-Wyoming, MI MSA	20,818	24,593	25,635	4.2	28,018	31,966	33,172	90.4
Bakersfield, CA MSA...............	13,891	18,804	20,042	6.6	20,934	25,050	25,938	70.6
Baton Rouge, LA MSA	17,206	22,016	24,038	9.2	24,329	30,154	31,443	85.6
El Paso, TX MSA	12,650	17,156	18,123	5.6	18,572	24,081	24,977	68.0
Columbia, SC MSA.................	17,429	21,441	22,953	7.1	26,848	31,001	32,614	88.8
Akron, OH MSA..................	20,593	23,649	24,635	4.2	29,588	33,739	35,188	95.8

Source: U.S. Bureau of Economic Analysis, *Survey of Current Business*, May 2008. See also <http://www.bea.gov/regional/reis>.

Income, Expenditures, Poverty, and Wealth   437

Table 662. Average Annual Expenditures of All Consumer Units by Selected Major Types of Expenditure: 1990 to 2006

[In dollars, except as indicated (96,968 represents $96,968,000). Based on Consumer Expenditure Survey. Data are averages for the noninstitutional population. Expenditures reported here are out-of-pocket]

Type	1990	1995	2000	2002	2003	2004	2005	2006
Number of consumer units (1,000)	96,968	103,123	109,367	112,108	115,356	116,282	117,356	118,843
Expenditures, total [1]	**$28,381**	**$32,264**	**$38,045**	**$40,677**	**$40,817**	**$43,395**	**$46,409**	**$48,398**
Food	4,296	4,505	5,158	5,375	5,340	5,781	5,931	6,111
Food at home [1]	2,485	2,803	3,021	3,099	3,129	3,347	3,297	3,417
Meats, poultry, fish, and eggs	668	752	795	798	825	880	764	797
Dairy products	295	297	325	328	328	371	378	368
Fruits and vegetables	408	457	521	552	535	561	552	592
Other food at home	746	856	927	970	999	1,075	1,158	1,212
Food away from home.	1,811	1,702	2,137	2,276	2,211	2,434	2,634	2,694
Alcoholic beverages	293	277	372	376	391	459	426	497
Housing [1]	8,703	10,458	12,319	13,283	13,432	13,918	15,167	16,366
Shelter	4,836	5,928	7,114	7,829	7,887	7,998	8,805	9,673
Utilities, fuels, and public services . . .	1,890	2,191	2,489	2,684	2,811	2,927	3,183	3,397
Apparel and services	1,618	1,704	1,856	1,749	1,640	1,816	1,886	1,874
Transportation [1]	5,120	6,014	7,417	7,759	7,781	7,801	8,344	8,508
Vehicle purchases	2,129	2,638	3,418	3,665	3,732	3,397	3,544	3,421
Gasoline and motor oil	1,047	1,006	1,291	1,235	1,333	1,598	2,013	2,227
Other vehicle expenses	1,642	2,015	2,281	2,471	2,331	2,365	2,339	2,355
Health care.	1,480	1,732	2,066	2,350	2,416	2,574	2,664	2,766
Entertainment	1,422	1,612	1,863	2,079	2,060	2,218	2,388	2,376
Reading.	153	162	146	139	127	130	126	117
Tobacco products, smoking supplies . . .	274	269	319	320	290	288	319	327
Personal insurance and pensions	2,592	2,964	3,365	3,899	4,055	4,823	5,204	5,270
Life and other personal insurance . . .	345	373	399	406	397	390	381	322
Pensions and social security.	2,248	2,591	2,966	3,493	3,658	4,433	4,823	4,948

[1] Includes expenditures not shown separately.

Source: U.S. Bureau of Labor Statistics, *Consumer Expenditures in 2006*; <http://stats.bls.gov/cex/home.htm>.

Table 663. Average Annual Expenditures of All Consumer Units by Metropolitan Area: 2005–2006

[In dollars. Covers 2-year period, 2005–2006. Metropolitan areas defined June 30, 1983, CMSA = Consolidated Metropolitan Statistical Area; MSA = Metropolitan Statistical Area; PMSA = Primary Metropolitan Statistical Area. See text, Section 1 and Appendix II. See headnote, Table 662]

Metropolitan area	Total expenditures [1]	Food	Housing Total [1]	Housing Shelter	Housing Utility fuels [2]	Transportation Total [1]	Transportation Vehicle purchases	Transportation Gasoline and motor oil	Health care
Atlanta, GA MSA	43,727	5,289	16,158	9,539	3,773	7,599	3,146	2,124	2,017
Baltimore, MD MSA	47,494	4,921	17,063	10,813	3,424	7,554	2,929	2,073	2,551
Boston-Lawrence-Salem, MA-NH CMSA	53,691	6,865	18,922	12,256	3,590	9,170	4,011	1,958	2,794
Chicago-Gary-Lake County, IL-IN-WI CMSA	54,757	6,902	19,059	11,755	3,620	8,453	3,352	2,092	2,878
Cleveland-Akron-Lorain, OH CMSA. . .	43,611	5,043	14,654	8,546	3,624	7,596	2,965	1,825	3,035
Dallas-Fort Worth, TX CMSA	53,294	6,537	17,854	9,883	4,424	9,662	3,919	2,410	3,075
Detroit-Ann Arbor, MI CMSA	50,345	6,614	16,831	9,899	3,794	8,652	2,252	2,405	2,349
Houston-Galveston-Brazoria, TX CMSA	56,260	6,063	17,198	9,427	4,179	11,636	5,305	2,743	3,259
Los Angeles-Long Beach, CA PMSA . .	58,404	7,222	21,190	14,312	2,996	10,716	4,443	2,566	2,316
Miami-Fort Lauderdale, FL CMSA. . . .	42,379	5,637	15,928	10,053	3,421	8,186	3,199	2,069	2,190
Minneapolis-St. Paul, MN-WI MSA . . .	61,428	6,393	20,380	11,650	3,245	8,915	3,593	2,031	3,322
New York-Northern New Jersey-Long Island, NY-NJ-CT CMSA	55,137	7,101	20,865	13,848	3,709	7,792	2,416	1,798	2,607
Philadelphia-Wilmington-Trenton, PA-NJ-DE-MD CMSA	45,922	6,031	16,417	9,722	3,771	7,092	2,661	1,783	2,188
Phoenix-Mesa, AZ MSA	53,570	7,187	16,469	9,279	3,348	10,964	5,422	2,217	3,134
San Diego, CA MSA.	62,321	6,238	23,034	15,654	3,001	11,115	4,959	2,542	3,421
San Francisco-Oakland-San Jose, CA CMSA	66,344	7,942	26,382	18,845	2,925	10,080	3,492	2,309	2,820
Seattle-Tacoma, WA CMSA	55,544	6,887	19,142	12,279	3,046	10,127	4,145	2,221	2,889
Washington, DC-MD-VA MSA.	58,236	6,357	24,059	15,976	3,827	7,341	2,133	1,958	2,505

[1] Includes expenditures not shown separately.   [2] Includes public services.

Source: U.S. Bureau of Labor Statistics, *Consumer Expenditures in 2006*; <http://stats.bls.gov/cex/home.htm>.

Table 664. Average Annual Expenditures of All Consumer Units by Race, Hispanic Origin, and Age of Householder: 2006

[**In dollars.** Based on Consumer Expenditure Survey. Data are averages for the noninstitutional population. Expenditures reported here are out-of-pocket]

Type	All consumer units [1]	White and all other races	Asian	Black or African American	Hispanic or Latino	Age of householder Under 25 years	Age of householder 65 years and over
Expenditures, total	**48,398**	**49,994**	**57,544**	**34,583**	**43,053**	**28,181**	**35,058**
Food	6,111	6,289	7,411	4,530	6,170	3,919	4,319
Food at home	3,417	3,486	3,947	2,796	3,719	1,946	2,659
Cereals and bakery products	446	455	524	366	427	240	370
Cereals and cereal products	143	141	216	133	164	94	102
Bakery products	304	314	308	232	263	146	268
Meats, poultry, fish, and eggs [2]	797	782	1,022	845	999	434	611
Beef	236	239	256	213	310	129	176
Pork	157	153	172	186	197	89	127
Poultry	141	134	173	179	185	80	96
Fish and seafood	122	113	285	141	146	53	101
Dairy products	368	390	298	237	384	219	293
Fresh milk and cream	140	146	131	101	176	92	113
Other dairy products	228	244	167	135	208	127	181
Fruits and vegetables [2]	592	605	884	432	735	319	507
Fresh fruits	195	202	291	123	258	99	172
Fresh vegetables	193	198	348	120	250	99	162
Processed fruits [2]	109	109	142	102	123	68	94
Other food at home [2]	1,212	1,254	1,219	916	1,173	734	878
Sugar and other sweets	125	130	114	90	101	69	118
Nonalcoholic beverages	332	340	332	278	365	200	222
Food away from home	2,694	2,802	3,463	1,735	2,451	1,973	1,659
Alcoholic beverages	497	545	302	210	326	473	263
Housing	16,366	16,676	21,332	12,754	15,412	9,355	11,787
Shelter	9,673	9,791	14,782	7,378	9,639	5,923	6,281
Owned dwellings	6,516	6,781	10,168	3,600	5,355	1,405	4,210
Mortgage interest and charges	3,753	3,832	6,589	2,378	3,459	910	1,303
Property taxes	1,649	1,744	2,422	753	1,181	358	1,573
Maintenance, repair, insurance, other expenses	1,115	1,205	1,157	469	715	137	1,334
Rented dwellings	2,590	2,409	3,655	3,555	4,031	4,315	1,630
Other lodging	567	600	958	223	253	203	441
Utilities, fuels, and public services	3,397	3,395	3,221	3,461	3,224	1,781	3,008
Natural gas	509	498	475	593	377	186	507
Electricity	1,266	1,265	1,063	1,333	1,203	693	1,154
Fuel oil and other fuels	138	156	54	39	40	30	176
Telephone	1,087	1,074	1,176	1,154	1,202	722	770
Water and other public services	397	403	453	342	403	150	400
Household operations	948	1,003	1,005	545	661	374	720
Personal services	393	407	474	269	330	213	105
Other household expenses	555	596	530	276	331	161	615
Housekeeping supplies [2]	640	665	557	482	529	295	554
Laundry and cleaning supplies	151	147	117	188	176	83	112
Postage and stationery	159	171	144	76	73	64	153
Household furnishings and equipment [2]	1,708	1,822	1,767	888	1,359	982	1,224
Household textiles	154	160	249	87	154	56	163
Furniture	463	483	552	300	424	350	274
Major appliances	241	258	261	119	205	104	208
Miscellaneous household equipment	693	750	596	319	465	396	454
Apparel and services [2]	1,874	1,881	2,117	1,762	2,278	1,464	930
Men and boys	444	449	514	385	603	294	207
Women and girls	751	765	814	636	844	554	416
Footwear	304	289	380	391	427	251	133
Other apparel products and services	280	283	329	241	262	234	154
Transportation	8,508	8,796	9,722	6,130	8,286	5,667	5,658
Vehicle purchases (net outlay) [2]	3,421	3,555	3,823	2,362	3,400	2,396	2,301
Cars and trucks, new	1,798	1,869	2,672	1,046	1,661	943	1,384
Cars and trucks, used	1,568	1,626	1,151	1,280	1,690	1,406	917
Gasoline and motor oil	2,227	2,298	2,191	1,740	2,319	1,637	1,359
Other vehicle expenses	2,355	2,435	2,519	1,742	2,152	1,413	1,584
Vehicle finance charges	298	308	220	246	326	199	123
Maintenance and repair	688	722	678	456	610	400	508
Vehicle insurance	886	905	1,037	710	814	548	689
Vehicle rental, leases, licenses, other charges	482	500	584	330	402	266	264
Public transportation	505	508	1,189	286	414	221	414
Health care [3]	2,766	2,967	2,262	1,497	1,659	706	4,331
Entertainment [4]	2,376	2,564	1,941	1,172	1,568	1,348	1,584
Personal care products and services	585	587	772	519	537	348	475
Reading	117	128	100	46	43	46	136
Education	888	885	2,332	495	633	1,259	219
Tobacco products and smoking supplies	327	353	181	187	150	286	171
Miscellaneous	846	896	670	544	575	388	762
Cash contributions	1,869	1,950	1,568	1,384	1,343	632	2,579
Personal insurance and pensions	5,270	5,478	6,837	3,354	4,074	2,291	1,844
Life and other personal insurance	322	330	410	245	151	42	299
Pensions and social security	4,948	5,148	6,428	3,109	3,923	2,249	1,545
Personal taxes	**2,432**	**2,656**	**3,223**	**626**	**1,034**	**522**	**1,230**

[1] Includes other householders not shown separately. [2] Includes other types not shown separately. [3] For additional health care expenditures, see Table 133. [4] For additional recreation expenditures, see Section 26.

Source: U.S. Bureau of Labor Statistics, *Consumer Expenditures in 2006.* See also <http://www.bls.gov/cex/2006/Standard/race.pdf> and <http://www.bls.gov/cex/2006/Standard/hispanic.pdf> and <http://www.bls.gov/cex/2006/Standard/age.pdf> (released October 2007).

Income, Expenditures, Poverty, and Wealth 439

Table 665. Average Annual Expenditures of All Consumer Units by Region and Size of Unit: 2006

[In dollars. For composition of regions, see map, inside front cover. See headnote, Table 662]

Type	Region				Size of consumer unit				
	North-east	Mid-west	South	West	One person	Two persons	Three persons	Four persons	Five or more
Expenditures, total	**49,164**	**45,085**	**44,501**	**57,486**	**29,374**	**50,652**	**56,382**	**63,897**	**64,654**
Food	6,220	5,763	5,649	7,158	3,249	6,203	7,195	8,543	9,334
Food at home	3,463	3,260	3,134	4,018	1,728	3,328	4,010	4,833	5,880
Cereals and bakery products	477	433	407	499	224	430	504	654	790
Cereals and cereal products	154	134	130	162	65	130	158	223	279
Bakery products	323	299	277	337	159	299	345	431	511
Meats, poultry, fish, and eggs [1]	818	738	764	899	367	768	941	1,120	1,508
Beef	218	224	231	274	102	232	278	321	469
Pork	141	155	163	163	71	148	191	219	309
Poultry	167	115	137	150	65	131	158	216	265
Fish and seafood	135	102	109	153	60	123	149	159	208
Dairy products	380	365	328	429	188	358	429	537	615
Fresh milk and cream	141	133	136	155	69	123	166	216	267
Other dairy products	239	232	193	274	119	235	264	321	348
Fruits and vegetables [1]	635	530	512	758	307	593	689	818	982
Fresh fruits	208	180	157	265	107	193	227	263	325
Fresh vegetables	211	163	172	245	98	195	227	272	312
Processed fruits	123	101	90	139	58	108	127	149	185
Other food at home [1]	1,153	1,193	1,123	1,433	643	1,179	1,447	1,703	1,985
Sugar and other sweets	125	132	114	134	74	125	138	174	186
Nonalcoholic beverages	318	317	326	372	175	325	413	475	509
Food away from home	2,757	2,503	2,515	3,140	1,521	2,875	3,185	3,710	3,454
Alcoholic beverages	519	523	366	667	428	586	537	483	367
Housing	17,682	14,660	14,457	20,061	11,067	16,507	18,751	21,311	21,361
Shelter	11,035	8,220	7,876	12,885	7,187	9,569	10,767	12,148	12,441
Owned dwellings	7,291	5,868	5,347	8,395	3,651	6,732	7,645	9,375	8,765
Mortgage interest and charges	3,609	3,109	3,088	5,607	1,888	3,461	4,658	6,057	5,744
Property taxes	2,520	1,709	1,189	1,575	998	1,852	1,756	2,237	1,973
Maintenance, repair, insurance, other expenses	1,162	1,050	1,070	1,213	765	1,420	1,231	1,081	1,048
Rented dwellings	3,042	1,812	2,143	3,719	3,235	2,058	2,465	2,180	3,163
Other lodging	701	540	387	770	300	778	656	593	513
Utilities, fuels, and public services	3,584	3,283	3,554	3,101	2,153	3,501	3,990	4,347	4,602
Natural gas	658	775	312	423	361	506	560	644	701
Electricity	1,175	1,057	1,588	1,042	771	1,335	1,503	1,586	1,733
Fuel oil and other fuels	404	108	56	71	93	167	155	147	143
Telephone	1,051	998	1,167	1,081	684	1,081	1,333	1,439	1,459
Water and other public services	296	345	431	485	244	411	439	532	568
Household operations	932	926	863	1,120	430	780	1,328	1,777	1,293
Personal services	407	469	337	390	42	93	764	1,150	782
Other household expenses	525	457	525	730	389	687	564	627	511
Housekeeping supplies [1]	583	606	660	691	330	708	698	842	961
Laundry and cleaning supplies	125	132	168	166	66	160	177	222	236
Postage and stationery	155	152	135	209	101	202	163	177	152
Household furnishings and equipment [1]	1,548	1,624	1,504	2,264	967	1,949	1,968	2,197	2,064
Household textiles	125	150	135	213	81	191	184	175	172
Furniture	347	415	419	684	281	495	550	594	597
Major appliances	229	197	223	328	120	261	303	356	289
Miscellaneous household equipment	678	727	582	853	387	821	785	898	765
Apparel and services [1]	2,057	1,700	1,737	2,126	950	1,877	2,319	2,710	2,796
Men and boys	479	394	429	490	212	420	556	683	712
Women and girls	812	726	690	827	360	784	936	1,108	1,032
Footwear	358	256	279	349	146	290	394	443	490
Other apparel products and services	316	227	250	350	210	327	285	293	310
Transportation	7,819	7,502	8,497	10,156	4,433	8,805	10,471	11,836	12,239
Vehicle purchases (net outlay) [1]	2,894	2,730	3,643	4,230	1,558	3,409	4,424	5,024	5,335
Cars and trucks, new	1,617	1,317	1,889	2,303	826	1,944	2,028	2,613	2,803
Cars and trucks, used	1,239	1,369	1,716	1,821	726	1,397	2,302	2,360	2,431
Gasoline and motor oil	1,910	2,142	2,356	2,382	1,188	2,263	2,707	3,146	3,253
Other vehicle expenses	2,386	2,225	2,182	2,741	1,324	2,531	2,813	3,147	3,093
Vehicle finance charges	237	250	338	335	117	300	395	455	470
Maintenance and repair	651	625	650	847	419	740	804	906	852
Vehicle insurance	860	824	874	994	508	938	1,090	1,152	1,181
Vehicle rental, leases, licenses, other charges	638	526	320	565	281	553	524	633	588
Public transportation	629	405	316	804	363	603	528	520	558
Health care [2]	2,591	2,816	2,775	2,853	1,827	3,641	2,868	2,824	2,516
Entertainment [3]	2,346	2,261	2,096	2,970	1,464	2,576	2,580	3,232	2,965
Personal care products and services	557	537	571	681	361	619	703	750	735
Reading	132	129	85	144	91	145	111	127	97
Education	1,080	951	707	948	477	632	1,260	1,453	1,602
Tobacco products and smoking supplies	331	355	336	279	227	360	394	347	392
Miscellaneous	883	805	727	1,051	662	887	990	921	935
Cash contributions	1,470	1,902	1,762	2,350	1,611	2,211	1,693	1,725	2,032
Personal insurance and pensions	5,477	5,179	4,736	6,042	2,528	5,602	6,509	7,634	7,283
Life and other personal insurance	334	344	313	304	136	386	395	446	392
Pensions and social security	5,144	4,835	4,423	5,738	2,391	5,216	6,114	7,188	6,891
Personal taxes	**2,466**	**2,078**	**2,051**	**3,381**	**1,602**	**3,146**	**2,553**	**2,586**	**2,214**

[1] Includes other types not shown separately. [2] For additional health care expenditures, see Table 133. [3] For additional recreation expenditures, see Section 26.

Source: U.S. Bureau of Labor Statistics, *Consumer Expenditures in 2006.* See also <http://www.bls.gov/cex/2006/Standard/cusize.pdf> and <http://www.bls.gov/cex/2006/Standard/region.pdf> (released October 2007).

Table 666. **Average Annual Expenditures of All Consumer Units by Income Level: 2006**

[**In dollars.** Based on Consumer Expenditure Survey. Data are averages for the noninstitutional population. Expenditures reported here are out-of-pocket]

Income level	Total expenditures [1]	Food	Housing			Transportation			Health care	Pensions and social security
			Total [1]	Shelter	Utility fuels [2]	Total [1]	Vehicle purchases	Gasoline and motor oil		
All consumer units . .	**48,398**	**6,111**	**16,366**	**9,673**	**3,397**	**8,508**	**3,421**	**2,227**	**2,766**	**4,948**
Consumer units with complete reporting:										
Less than $70,000	33,490	4,660	11,927	6,976	2,881	5,891	2,151	1,751	2,318	2,303
$70,000 to $79,999	57,352	7,094	18,832	11,260	3,921	10,921	4,322	2,909	3,216	6,537
$80,000 to $99,999	65,810	8,491	21,242	12,565	4,088	12,206	5,155	3,138	3,345	8,256
$100,000 and over	100,386	10,547	32,157	19,323	5,087	17,059	7,706	3,568	4,244	14,138
$100,000 to $119,999 . . .	78,129	9,310	24,337	14,564	4,525	13,601	5,502	3,318	3,699	10,332
$120,000 to $149,999 . . .	88,647	10,159	28,672	17,280	4,865	15,661	6,805	3,598	3,889	12,819
$150,000 and over	128,681	12,029	41,579	24,963	5,738	21,097	10,284	3,763	4,984	18,415

[1] Includes expenditures not shown separately.   [2] Includes public service.

Source: U.S. Bureau of Labor Statistics, *Consumer Expenditures in 2006.* See also <http://www.bls.gov/cex/2006/share/higherincome.pdf> (released October 2007).

Table 667. **Annual Expenditure Per Child by Husband-Wife Families by Family Income and Expenditure Type: 2007**

[**In dollars.** Data are for a child in a two-child family. Excludes expenses for college. Expenditures based on data from the 1990–92 Consumer Expenditure Survey updated to 2007 dollars using the Consumer Price Index. For more on the methodology, see report cited below and notes sheet]

Family income and age of child	Total	Expenditure type						
		Housing	Food	Transportation	Clothing	Health care	Child care and education	Miscellaneous [1]
INCOME: LESS THAN $45,800								
Less than 2 years old	7,830	2,970	1,070	930	340	600	1,220	700
3 to 5 years old	8,020	2,930	1,190	900	340	570	1,370	720
6 to 8 years old	8,000	2,830	1,530	1,050	370	650	810	760
9 to 11 years old	7,950	2,560	1,830	1,140	420	710	490	800
12 to 14 years old	8,830	2,850	1,930	1,290	700	720	340	1,000
15 to 17 years old	8,810	2,300	2,080	1,730	620	770	580	730
INCOME: $45,800 TO $77,100								
Less than 2 years old	10,960	4,010	1,280	1,390	410	780	2,000	1,090
3 to 5 years old	11,280	3,980	1,470	1,360	400	750	2,210	1,110
6 to 8 years old	11,130	3,880	1,880	1,510	440	850	1,420	1,150
9 to 11 years old	10,930	3,600	2,210	1,600	480	920	930	1,190
12 to 14 years old	11,690	3,900	2,230	1,740	820	930	680	1,390
15 to 17 years old	12,030	3,350	2,480	2,200	730	980	1,170	1,120
INCOME: MORE THAN $77,100								
Less than 2 years old	16,290	6,380	1,690	1,950	530	900	3,020	1,820
3 to 5 years old	16,670	6,340	1,910	1,910	520	860	3,290	1,840
6 to 8 years old	16,310	6,240	2,310	2,060	570	990	2,260	1,880
9 to 11 years old	15,980	5,970	2,680	2,150	620	1,060	1,580	1,920
12 to 14 years old	16,810	6,260	2,820	2,300	1,030	1,070	1,210	2,120
15 to 17 years old	17,500	5,710	2,970	2,780	940	1,120	2,120	1,860

[1] Expenses include personal care items, entertainment, and reading materials.

Source: U.S. Department of Agriculture, Center for Nutrition Policy and Promotion, *Expenditures on Children by Families, 2007 Annual Report.* See also <http://www.cnpp.usda.gov/Publications/CRC/crc2007.pdf> (released March 2008).

U.S. Census Bureau, Statistical Abstract of the United States: 2009

Table 668. Money Income of Households—Percent Distribution by Income Level, Race, and Hispanic Origin, in Constant (2006) Dollars: 1980 to 2006

[Constant dollars based on CPI-U-RS deflator. Households as of March of following year. (82,368 represents 82,368,000). Based on Current Population Survey, Annual Social and Economic Supplement (ASEC); see text, Sections 1 and 13, and Appendix III. For data collection changes over time, see <http://www.census.gov/hhes/www/income/histinc/hstchg.html>. For definition of median, see Guide to Tabular Presentation]

Year	Number of house-holds (1,000)	Percent distribution							Median income (dollars)
		Under $15,000	$15,000– $24,999	$25,000– $34,999	$35,000– $49,999	$50,000– $74,999	$75,000– $99,999	$100,000 and over	
ALL HOUSEHOLDS [1]									
1980	82,368	16.6	13.6	12.6	17.0	21.2	10.3	8.6	41,258
1990 [2]	94,312	15.3	12.3	12.0	16.2	19.9	11.3	13.0	44,778
2000 [2]	108,209	13.1	11.7	10.9	15.1	18.6	12.3	18.3	49,163
2005	114,384	14.2	12.1	11.1	14.8	18.3	11.4	18.2	47,845
2006	116,011	13.4	11.8	11.5	14.6	18.2	11.3	19.1	48,201
WHITE									
1980	71,872	14.7	13.0	12.6	17.3	22.1	10.9	9.3	43,527
1990 [2]	80,968	13.2	12.1	12.0	16.5	20.5	12.0	13.8	46,705
2000 [2]	90,030	11.8	11.3	10.8	15.1	18.9	12.9	19.4	51,418
2005 [3, 4]	93,588	12.5	11.7	11.1	14.8	18.7	11.9	19.3	50,146
2006 [3, 4]	94,705	11.8	11.5	11.3	14.6	18.8	11.8	20.2	50,673
BLACK									
1980	8,847	32.3	18.4	13.3	14.5	13.5	5.2	2.7	25,076
1990 [2]	10,671	31.7	14.8	12.6	14.3	15.0	6.0	5.7	27,929
2000 [2]	13,174	22.3	15.2	12.8	16.0	16.6	8.2	8.8	34,735
2005 [3, 5]	14,002	25.4	16.0	12.3	15.1	15.3	7.3	8.5	31,870
2006 [3, 5]	14,354	24.4	15.2	13.5	14.8	15.2	7.7	9.1	31,969
ASIAN AND PACIFIC ISLANDER									
1990 [2]	1,958	11.8	9.4	8.2	13.5	22.1	13.3	21.7	57,500
2000 [2]	3,963	9.9	7.8	8.4	13.1	17.7	14.9	28.2	65,281
2005 [3, 6]	4,273	12.3	8.1	7.1	11.3	19.4	13.0	28.9	63,097
2006 [3, 6]	4,454	10.4	7.7	8.5	12.8	17.0	12.8	30.8	64,238
HISPANIC [7]									
1980	3,906	21.5	18.3	15.5	17.4	16.8	6.7	3.9	31,802
1990 [2]	6,220	21.9	16.2	14.1	17.6	17.2	6.8	6.2	33,394
2000 [2]	10,034	15.7	15.6	13.4	18.0	18.3	9.9	9.1	38,834
2005	12,519	17.0	15.9	14.6	17.1	17.5	8.5	9.4	37,146
2006	12,973	16.3	15.5	14.0	17.5	17.3	8.9	10.5	37,781

[1] Includes other races not shown separately.   [2] Data reflect implementation of Census 2000-based population controls and a 28,000 household sample expansion to 78,000 households.   [3] Beginning with the 2003 Current Population Survey (CPS), the questionnaire allowed respondents to choose more than one race. For 2002 and later, data represent persons who selected this race group only and exclude persons reporting more than one race. The CPS in prior years allowed respondents to report only one race group. See also comments on race in the text for Section 1.   [4] Data represent White alone, which refers to people who reported White and did not report any other race category.   [5] Data represent Black alone, which refers to people who reported Black and did not report any other race category.   [6] Data represent Asian alone, which refers to people who reported Asian and did not report any other race category.   [7] People of Hispanic origin may be of any race.

Source: U.S. Census Bureau, *Current Population Reports,* P60-233; and Internet sites <http://www.census.gov/prod/2007pubs /p60-233.pdf> (released August 2007) and <http://www.census.gov/hhes/www/income/histinc/h17.html>.

Table 669. Money Income of Households—Median Income by Race and Hispanic Origin, in Current and Constant (2006) Dollars: 1980 to 2006

[In dollars. See headnote, Table 668]

Year	Median income in current dollars					Median income in constant (2006) dollars				
	All house-holds [1]	White [2]	Black [3]	Asian, Pacific Islander [4]	His-panic [5]	All house-holds [1]	White [2]	Black [3]	Asian, Pacific Islander [4]	His-panic [5]
1980	17,710	18,684	10,764	(NA)	13,651	41,258	43,527	25,076	(NA)	31,802
1990	29,943	31,231	18,676	38,450	22,330	44,778	46,705	27,929	57,500	33,394
1995 [6]	34,076	35,766	22,393	40,614	22,860	44,764	46,985	29,417	53,353	30,030
1998	38,885	40,912	25,351	46,637	28,330	48,034	50,538	31,316	57,610	34,996
1999 [7]	40,696	42,325	27,910	50,960	30,746	49,244	51,215	33,773	61,664	37,204
2000 [8]	41,990	43,916	29,667	55,757	33,168	49,163	51,418	34,735	65,281	38,834
2001	42,228	44,517	29,470	53,635	33,565	48,091	50,698	33,562	61,082	38,225
2002 [9]	42,409	45,086	29,026	52,626	33,103	47,530	50,530	32,531	58,980	37,100
2003	43,318	45,631	29,645	55,699	32,997	47,488	50,023	32,499	61,061	36,173
2004 [10]	44,334	46,658	30,095	57,504	34,271	47,323	49,803	32,124	61,380	36,581
2005	46,326	48,554	30,858	61,094	35,967	47,845	50,146	31,870	63,097	37,146
2006	48,201	50,673	31,969	64,238	37,781	48,201	50,673	31,969	64,238	37,781

NA Not available.   [1] Includes other races not shown separately.   [2] Beginning with 2002, data represent White alone, which refers to people who reported White and did not report any other race category.   [3] Beginning with 2002, data represent Black alone, which refers to people who reported Black and did not report any other race category.   [4] Beginning with 2002, data represent Asian alone, which refers to people who reported Asian and did not report any other race category.   [5] People of Hispanic origin may be of any race.   [6] Data reflect full implementation of the 1990 census-based sample design and metropolitan definitions, 7,000 household sample reduction, and revised race edits.   [7] Implementation of Census 2000-based population controls.   [8] Implementation of a 28,000 household sample expansion.   [9] See footnote 3, Table 668. See also comments on race in the text for Section 1.   [10] Data have been revised to reflect a correction to the weights in the 2005 ASEC.

Source: U.S. Census Bureau, *Current Population Reports,* P60-233; and Internet sites <http://www.census.gov/prod/2007pubs /p60-233.pdf> (released August 2007) and <http://www.census.gov/hhes/www/income/histinc/h05.html>.

Table 670. Money Income of Households—Distribution by Income Level and Selected Characteristics: 2006

[116,011 represents 116,011,000. Households as of **March of the following year**. Based on Current Population Survey; see text, Sections 1 and 13, and Appendix III. For definition of median, see Guide to Tabular Presentation]

Characteristic	Number of households (1,000)								Median income (dollars)
	Total	Under $15,000	$15,000–$24,999	$25,000–$34,999	$35,000–$49,999	$50,000–$74,999	$75,000–$99,999	$100,000 and over	
Total	**116,011**	**15,569**	**13,737**	**13,353**	**16,926**	**21,150**	**13,124**	**22,151**	**48,201**
Age of householder:									
15 to 24 years old	6,662	1,568	1,135	1,026	1,186	1,003	358	385	30,937
25 to 34 years old	19,435	2,039	2,061	2,389	3,367	4,291	2,474	2,814	49,164
35 to 44 years old	22,779	1,897	1,823	2,237	3,280	4,700	3,252	5,588	60,405
45 to 54 years old	24,140	2,195	1,746	2,032	3,085	4,776	3,456	6,852	64,874
55 to 64 years old	19,266	2,350	1,846	1,918	2,636	3,652	2,304	4,565	54,592
65 years old and over	23,729	5,520	5,122	3,751	3,373	2,730	1,284	1,948	27,798
Region: [1]									
Northeast	21,261	2,900	2,283	2,220	2,752	3,734	2,482	4,892	52,057
Midwest	26,508	3,458	3,190	2,997	4,088	5,101	3,176	4,499	47,836
South	42,587	6,279	5,397	5,387	6,461	7,549	4,459	7,056	43,884
West	25,656	2,931	2,866	2,749	3,627	4,770	3,008	5,704	52,249
Size of household:									
One person	31,132	9,176	6,107	4,611	4,441	3,805	1,412	1,583	25,504
Two people	38,580	3,324	4,351	4,846	6,107	7,786	4,727	7,442	51,536
Three people	18,808	1,528	1,544	1,743	2,760	3,797	2,720	4,714	61,436
Four people	16,172	881	941	1,122	2,008	3,359	2,647	5,214	72,870
Five people	7,202	372	504	653	985	1,512	1,064	2,114	66,823
Six people	2,702	196	186	252	404	560	384	721	61,859
Seven or more people	1,415	93	105	127	222	330	176	363	60,864
Type of household:									
Family household	78,425	5,899	6,973	8,025	11,471	15,857	10,849	19,350	59,894
Married-couple	58,945	2,221	3,981	5,171	8,194	12,450	9,264	17,665	69,716
Male householder, wife absent	5,063	473	562	694	935	1,119	587	692	47,078
Female householder, husband absent	14,416	3,204	2,429	2,161	2,342	2,291	998	993	31,818
Nonfamily household	37,587	9,670	6,765	5,330	5,453	5,292	2,278	2,801	29,083
Male householder	17,338	3,366	2,602	2,539	2,901	2,896	1,356	1,677	35,614
Female householder	20,249	6,302	4,164	2,790	2,552	2,397	919	1,124	23,876
Educational attainment of householder: [2]									
Total	**109,349**	**14,000**	**12,601**	**12,327**	**15,740**	**20,147**	**12,766**	**21,766**	**50,004**
Less than 9th grade	5,701	1,998	1,261	754	807	526	185	170	20,901
9th to 12th grade (no diploma) .	9,127	2,597	1,828	1,346	1,439	1,133	401	383	25,912
High school graduate	32,851	4,965	4,988	4,708	5,481	6,187	3,211	3,312	39,426
Some college, no degree	19,321	2,128	2,079	2,396	3,113	3,934	2,547	3,126	49,691
Associate's degree	9,723	852	910	1,044	1,470	2,115	1,388	1,943	56,017
Bachelor's degree or more	32,626	1,462	1,534	2,079	3,432	6,249	5,035	12,833	81,723
Bachelor's degree	21,082	1,068	1,105	1,563	2,421	4,238	3,346	7,341	75,861
Master's degree	8,128	275	294	399	765	1,583	1,328	3,484	88,422
Professional degree	1,860	72	79	64	114	220	197	1,114	100,000
Doctoral degree	1,556	46	55	52	133	211	165	894	100,000
Number of earners:									
No earners	24,305	10,228	5,579	3,322	2,433	1,547	504	690	17,865
One earner	42,906	4,789	6,617	7,291	8,314	7,905	3,346	4,643	39,309
Two earners and more	48,800	553	1,540	2,739	6,177	11,696	9,276	16,817	78,994
Two earners	38,987	514	1,448	2,462	5,456	9,755	7,281	12,073	74,513
Three earners	7,349	35	85	250	620	1,604	1,537	3,217	91,500
Four earners or more	2,464	4	7	29	102	337	460	1,528	100,000
Work experience of householder:									
Total	**116,011**	**15,569**	**13,737**	**13,353**	**16,926**	**21,150**	**13,124**	**22,151**	**48,201**
Worked	80,490	4,590	6,869	8,483	12,315	17,214	11,459	19,561	60,613
Worked at full-time jobs . . .	68,612	2,639	5,184	7,071	10,594	15,278	10,249	17,599	62,983
50 weeks or more	59,302	1,330	3,988	5,909	9,108	13,495	9,232	16,238	66,210
27 to 49 weeks	6,064	541	709	753	1,031	1,292	734	1,004	49,977
26 weeks or less	3,245	768	486	408	455	490	280	357	33,616
Worked at part-time jobs . . .	11,879	1,950	1,686	1,413	1,720	1,935	1,212	1,962	42,009
50 weeks or more	6,613	788	923	774	1,014	1,126	731	1,256	46,654
27 to 49 weeks	2,526	428	366	297	359	410	273	390	41,819
26 weeks or less	2,740	734	398	340	348	398	207	316	32,964
Did not work	35,521	10,981	6,869	4,869	4,610	3,936	1,666	2,590	24,840
Tenure:									
Owner-occupied	79,266	6,664	7,458	7,931	10,928	15,802	10,782	19,699	59,688
Renter-occupied	35,129	8,420	5,941	5,187	5,779	5,150	2,269	2,383	30,801
Occupier paid no cash rent . .	1,617	482	339	234	217	200	73	69	24,223

[1] For composition of regions, see map, inside front cover. [2] People 25 years old and over.

Source: U.S. Census Bureau, Current Population Reports, P60-233; and Internet site <http://pubdb3.census.gov/macro/032007/hhinc/toc.htm> (released 28 August 2007).

Table 671. Money Income of Households—Number and Distribution by Race and Hispanic Origin: 2006

[Households as of **March of the following year. (116,011 represents 116,011,000).** Based on Current Population Survey (CPS); see text, Sections 1 and 13, and Appendix III. The 2007 CPS allowed respondents to choose more than one race. Data represent persons who selected this race group only and excludes persons reporting more than one race. See also comments on race in the text for Section 1]

Income interval	Number (1,000)					Percent distribution				
	All races	White alone	Black alone	Asian alone	Hispanic [1]	All races	White alone	Black alone	Asian alone	Hispanic [1]
All households.....	**116,011**	**94,705**	**14,354**	**4,454**	**12,973**	**100.0**	**100.0**	**100.0**	**100.0**	**100.0**
Under $10,000.........	8,689	5,871	2,271	291	1,195	7.5	6.2	15.8	6.5	9.2
$10,000 to $14,999......	6,880	5,298	1,238	174	924	5.9	5.6	8.6	3.9	7.1
$15,000 to $19,999......	6,846	5,397	1,113	166	972	5.9	5.7	7.8	3.7	7.5
$20,000 to $24,999......	6,891	5,469	1,071	176	1,034	5.9	5.8	7.5	4.0	8.0
$25,000 to $29,999......	6,630	5,323	937	218	850	5.7	5.6	6.5	4.9	6.6
$30,000 to $34,999......	6,723	5,411	996	162	965	5.8	5.7	6.9	3.6	7.4
$35,000 to $39,999......	5,975	4,849	808	177	793	5.2	5.1	5.6	4.0	6.1
$40,000 to $44,999......	5,877	4,784	755	190	797	5.1	5.1	5.3	4.3	6.1
$45,000 to $49,999......	5,074	4,202	563	202	681	4.4	4.4	3.9	4.5	5.2
$50,000 to $59,999......	9,530	7,943	1,074	300	1,059	8.2	8.4	7.5	6.7	8.2
$60,000 to $74,999......	11,620	9,846	1,111	456	1,183	10.0	10.4	7.7	10.2	9.1
$75,000 to $84,999......	6,180	5,252	547	259	593	5.3	5.5	3.8	5.8	4.6
$85,000 to $99,999......	6,944	5,947	557	314	562	6.0	6.3	3.9	7.0	4.3
$100,000 to $149,999....	13,385	11,451	917	786	928	11.5	12.1	6.4	17.6	7.2
$150,000 to $199,999....	4,751	4,114	245	304	288	4.1	4.3	1.7	6.8	2.2
$200,000 to $249,999....	1,776	1,566	80	117	61	1.5	1.7	0.6	2.6	0.5
$250,000 and above.....	2,240	1,984	70	165	88	1.9	2.1	0.5	3.7	0.7

[1] Persons of Hispanic origin may be of any race.

Source: U.S. Census Bureau, *Current Population Reports*, P60-233; and Internet site <http://pubdb3.census.gov/macro/032007/hhinc/new06_000.htm> (released 28 August 2007).

Table 672. Money Income of Families—Number and Distribution by Race and Hispanic Origin: 2006

[Families as of **March of the following year. (78,454 represents 78,454,000).** Based on Current Population Survey (CPS); see text, Sections 1 and 13, and Appendix III. The 2007 CPS allowed respondents to choose more than one race. Data represent persons who selected this race group only and excludes persons reporting more than one race. See also comments on race in the text for Section 1]

Income interval	Number (1,000)					Percent distribution				
	All races	White alone	Black alone	Asian alone	Hispanic [1]	All races	White alone	Black alone	Asian alone	Hispanic [1]
All families [1]	**78,454**	**64,120**	**9,274**	**3,346**	**10,155**	**100.0**	**100.0**	**100.0**	**100.0**	**100.0**
Under $10,000.........	3,832	2,467	1,104	129	726	4.9	3.8	11.9	3.9	7.1
$10,000 to $14,999......	2,714	1,891	635	87	651	3.5	2.9	6.8	2.6	6.4
$15,000 to $19,999......	3,411	2,550	645	114	770	4.3	4.0	7.0	3.4	7.6
$20,000 to $24,999......	3,805	2,976	627	100	796	4.8	4.6	6.8	3.0	7.8
$25,000 to $29,999......	3,982	3,094	624	158	694	5.1	4.8	6.7	4.7	6.8
$30,000 to $34,999......	4,226	3,392	620	110	792	5.4	5.3	6.7	3.3	7.8
$35,000 to $39,999......	3,893	3,175	523	108	646	5.0	5.0	5.6	3.2	6.4
$40,000 to $44,999......	3,950	3,189	522	143	628	5.0	5.0	5.6	4.3	6.2
$45,000 to $49,999......	3,508	2,913	381	147	549	4.5	4.5	4.1	4.4	5.4
$50,000 to $59,999......	6,767	5,623	743	233	872	8.6	8.8	8.0	7.0	8.6
$60,000 to $74,999......	8,763	7,379	870	351	933	11.2	11.5	9.4	10.5	9.2
$75,000 to $84,999......	4,892	4,147	423	219	493	6.2	6.5	4.6	6.5	4.9
$85,000 to $99,999......	5,709	4,936	440	238	453	7.3	7.7	4.7	7.1	4.5
$100,000 to $149,999....	11,332	9,704	763	671	778	14.4	15.1	8.2	20.1	7.7
$150,000 to $199,999....	4,114	3,557	216	277	250	5.2	5.5	2.3	8.3	2.5
$200,000 to $249,999....	1,562	1,371	69	109	52	2.0	2.1	0.7	3.3	0.5
$250,000 and above.....	1,993	1,756	67	151	70	2.5	2.7	0.7	4.5	0.7

[1] Persons of Hispanic origin may be of any race.

Source: U.S. Census Bureau, Current Population Report, P60-233; and Internet site <http://pubdb3.census.gov/macro/032007/faminc/new07_000.htm> (released 28 August 2007).

Table 673. **Money Income of Families—Percent Distribution by Income Level in Constant (2006) Dollars: 1980 to 2006**

[Constant dollars based on CPI-U-RS deflator. Families as of March of following year (60,309 represents 60,309,000). Based on Current Population Survey, Annual Social and Economic Supplement (ASEC); see text, Sections 1 and 13, and Appendix III. For data collection changes over time, see <http://www.census.gov/hhes/www/income/histinc/hstchg.html>. For definition of median, see Guide to Tabular Presentation]

Year	Number of families (1,000)	Percent distribution							Median income (dollars)
		Under $15,000	$15,000–$24,999	$25,000–$34,999	$35,000–$49,999	$50,000–$74,999	$75,000–$99,999	$100,000 and over	
ALL FAMILIES [1]									
1980	60,309	9.7	11.6	12.2	18.1	24.9	12.7	10.8	48,976
1990 [2]	66,322	9.7	10.1	11.0	16.3	22.7	13.7	16.4	52,869
2000 [2]	73,778	7.7	9.4	10.0	15.0	20.4	14.8	22.9	59,398
2005	77,418	8.7	9.7	10.3	14.4	20.1	13.7	23.0	58,036
2006	78,454	8.4	9.2	10.5	14.5	19.8	13.5	24.2	58,407
WHITE									
1980	52,710	7.9	10.7	12.0	18.4	26.0	13.5	11.6	51,029
1990 [2]	56,803	7.4	9.6	10.8	16.6	23.4	14.6	17.5	55,205
2000 [2]	61,330	6.3	8.7	9.6	14.9	20.8	15.5	24.3	62,087
2005 [3,4]	63,414	7.0	8.9	10.1	14.5	20.7	14.4	24.4	61,262
2006 [3,4]	64,120	6.8	8.6	10.1	14.5	20.3	14.2	25.6	61,280
BLACK									
1980	6,317	24.8	19.0	13.9	15.7	16.3	6.8	3.5	29,526
1990 [2]	7,471	26.3	14.6	13.0	14.6	17.2	7.1	7.2	32,037
2000 [2]	8,731	17.0	14.6	13.2	16.4	18.2	9.7	10.9	39,428
2005 [3,5]	9,051	19.9	15.5	12.8	14.9	16.7	8.9	11.2	36,627
2006 [3,5]	9,274	18.8	13.7	13.4	15.4	17.4	9.3	12.0	38,269
ASIAN AND PACIFIC ISLANDER									
1990 [2]	1,536	8.5	8.5	8.0	12.7	22.3	15.1	24.8	63,177
2000 [2]	2,982	6.6	6.6	7.3	12.5	18.4	15.9	32.6	73,313
2005 [3,6]	3,208	7.7	7.4	6.9	10.6	19.8	14.5	33.1	71,218
2006 [3,6]	3,346	6.4	6.4	8.0	11.9	17.5	13.7	36.1	74,612
HISPANIC ORIGIN [7]									
1980	3,235	17.5	18.2	16.0	18.5	18.4	7.2	4.2	34,283
1990 [2]	4,981	19.2	16.3	14.5	17.4	18.3	7.3	6.9	35,040
2000 [2]	8,017	13.7	15.4	13.5	18.6	18.9	10.1	9.7	40,325
2005	9,868	14.3	16.0	14.8	17.4	18.4	9.1	10.1	39,109
2006	10,155	13.6	15.4	14.6	17.9	17.8	9.3	11.3	40,000

[1] Includes other races not shown separately. [2] Data reflect implementation of Census 2000-based population controls and a 28,000 household sample expansion to 78,000 households. [3] Beginning with the 2003 Current Population Survey (CPS), the questionnaire allowed respondents to choose more than one race. For 2002 and later, data represent persons who selected this race group only and excludes persons reporting more than one race. The CPS in prior years allowed respondents to report only one race group. See also comments on race in the text for Section 1. [4] Data represent White alone, which refers to people who reported White and did not report any other race category. [5] Data represent Black alone, which refers to people who reported Black and did not report any other race category. [6] Data represent Asian alone, which refers to people who reported Asian and did not report any other race category. [7] People of Hispanic origin may be of any race.

Source: U.S. Census Bureau, *Current Population Reports*, P60-233, and Internet sites <http://www.census.gov/prod/2007pubs/p60-233.pdf> (released August 2007) and <http://www.census.gov/hhes/www/income/histinc/f23.html>.

Table 674. **Money Income of Families—Median Income by Race and Hispanic Origin in Current and Constant (2006) Dollars: 1990 to 2006**

[See headnote, Table 673]

Year	Median income in current dollars					Median income in constant (2006) dollars				
	All families [1]	White [2]	Black [3]	Asian, Pacific Islander [4]	Hispanic [5]	All families [1]	White [2]	Black [3]	Asian, Pacific Islander [4]	Hispanic [5]
1990 [6]	35,353	36,915	21,423	42,246	23,431	52,869	55,205	32,037	63,177	35,040
1995 [6]	40,611	42,646	25,970	46,356	24,570	53,349	56,023	34,116	60,896	32,277
2000 [7,8]	50,732	53,029	33,676	62,617	34,442	59,398	62,087	39,428	73,313	40,325
2001	51,407	54,067	33,598	60,158	34,490	58,545	61,574	38,263	68,511	39,279
2002 [9]	51,680	54,633	33,525	60,984	34,185	57,920	61,229	37,573	68,347	38,313
2003	52,680	55,768	34,369	63,251	34,272	57,751	61,136	37,677	69,340	37,571
2004 [10]	54,061	56,723	35,148	65,420	35,440	57,705	60,547	37,517	69,830	37,829
2005	56,194	59,317	35,464	68,957	37,867	58,036	61,262	36,627	71,218	39,109
2006	58,407	61,280	38,269	74,612	40,000	58,407	61,280	38,269	74,612	40,000

NA Not available. [1] Includes other races not shown separately. [2] Beginning with 2002, data represent White alone, which refers to people who reported White and did not report any other race category. [3] Beginning with 2002, data represent Black alone, which refers to people who reported Black and did not report any other race category. [4] Beginning with 2002, data represent Asian alone, which refers to people who reported Asian and did not report any other race category. [5] People of Hispanic origin may be of any race. [6] Data reflect full implementation of the 1990 census-based sample design and metropolitan definitions, 7,000 household sample reduction, and revised race edits. [7] Implementation of Census 2000-based population controls. [8] Implementation of a 28,000 household sample expansion. [9] See footnote 3, Table 673. See also comments on race in the text for Section 1. [10] Data have been revised to reflect a correction to the weights in the 2005 ASEC.

Source: U.S. Census Bureau, *Current Population Reports,* P60-233; and Internet sites <http://www.census.gov/prod/2007pubs/p60-233.pdf> (released August 2007) and <http://www.census.gov/hhes/www/income/histinc/f05.html>.

U.S. Census Bureau, Statistical Abstract of the United States: 2009

Table 675. **Share of Aggregate Income Received by Each Fifth and Top 5 Percent of Households: 1990 to 2006**

[**Households as of March of the following year (94,312 represents 94,312,000).** Income in constant **2006** CPI-U-RS-adjusted dollars. Based on the Current Population Survey; see text, Sections 1 and 13, and Appendix III. For data collection changes over time, see <http://www.census.gov/hhes/www/income/histinc/hstchg.html>]

Year	Number of households (1,000)	Income at selected positions (dollars)					Percent distribution of aggregate income					
		Upper limit of each fifth				Top 5 percent	Lowest 5th	Second 5th	Third 5th	Fourth 5th	Highest 5th	Top 5 percent
		Lowest	Second	Third	Fourth							
1990	94,312	18,693	35,385	54,135	82,557	141,691	3.8	9.6	15.9	24.0	46.6	18.5
1995[1]	99,627	18,917	35,356	55,177	85,551	148,444	3.7	9.1	15.2	23.3	48.7	21.0
2000 [2, 3] . . .	108,209	20,981	38,637	61,086	95,733	170,026	3.6	8.9	14.8	23.0	49.8	22.1
2001	109,297	20,465	37,940	60,359	95,094	171,395	3.5	8.7	14.6	23.0	50.1	22.4
2002	111,278	20,079	37,407	59,581	94,160	168,114	3.5	8.8	14.8	23.3	49.7	21.7
2003	112,000	19,715	37,273	59,695	95,229	168,956	3.4	8.7	14.8	23.4	49.8	21.4
2004 [4] . . .	113,343	19,732	37,013	58,953	93,934	167,746	3.4	8.7	14.7	23.2	50.1	21.8
2005	114,384	19,807	37,180	59,550	94,712	171,443	3.4	8.6	14.6	23.0	50.4	22.2
2006	116,011	20,035	37,774	60,000	97,032	174,012	3.4	8.6	14.5	22.9	50.5	22.3

[1] Data reflect full implementation of the 1990 census-based sample design and metropolitan definitions, 7,000 household sample reduction, and revised race edits. [2] Implementation of Census 2000-based population controls. [3] Implementation of a 28,000 household sample expansion. [4] Data have been revised to reflect a correction to the weights in the 2005 ASEC.

Source: U.S. Census Bureau, *Current Population Reports*, P60-233; and Internet sites <http://www.census.gov/prod/2007pubs/p60-233.pdf> (released August 2007), <http://www.census.gov/hhes/www/income/histinc/h01ar.html>, and <http://www.census.gov/hhes /www/income/histinc/h02ar.html>.

Table 676. **Money Income of Families—Distribution by Family Characteristics and Income Level: 2006**

[**78,454 represents 78,454,000.** See headnote, Table 673. For composition of regions, see map inside front cover]

Characteristic	Number of families (1,000)								Median income (dollars)
	Total	Under $15,000	$15,000 to $24,999	$25,000 to $34,999	$35,000 to $49,999	$50,000 to $74,999	$75,000 to $99,999	$100,000 and over	
All families	**78,454**	**6,546**	**7,216**	**8,208**	**11,351**	**15,530**	**10,601**	**19,000**	**58,407**
Age of householder:									
15 to 24 years old	3,534	903	545	479	599	587	204	214	31,471
25 to 34 years old	13,678	1,635	1,420	1,550	2,212	2,929	1,833	2,100	50,122
35 to 44 years old	18,055	1,336	1,325	1,623	2,406	3,650	2,700	5,016	65,282
45 to 54 years old	17,816	909	976	1,230	2,051	3,640	2,903	6,105	75,692
55 to 64 years old	12,981	780	880	1,069	1,671	2,687	1,901	3,989	68,747
65 years old and over	12,389	982	2,070	2,255	2,409	2,036	1,060	1,577	39,649
Region:									
Northeast	14,197	1,109	1,125	1,335	1,816	2,648	1,972	4,190	65,487
Midwest	17,706	1,328	1,450	1,776	2,640	3,810	2,714	3,986	59,886
South	29,142	2,873	3,043	3,351	4,462	5,601	3,597	6,214	52,436
West	17,409	1,233	1,598	1,746	2,434	3,470	2,317	4,610	61,166
Type of family:									
Married-couple families	58,964	2,235	4,010	5,226	8,195	12,464	9,238	17,597	69,404
Male householder, no spouse present	5,067	609	637	793	902	1,047	491	588	41,844
Female householder, no spouse present	14,424	3,703	2,568	2,189	2,255	2,022	874	815	28,829
Unrelated subfamilies	567	219	133	74	71	48	12	7	20,111
Educational attainment of householder:									
Persons 25 years old and over, total	**74,920**	**5,644**	**6,671**	**7,729**	**10,753**	**14,943**	**10,394**	**18,787**	**60,275**
Less than 9th grade	3,640	703	861	624	703	450	162	137	28,884
9th to 12th grade (no diploma) . . .	6,068	1,151	1,116	1,009	1,184	931	347	331	32,090
High school graduate (includes equivalency)	22,282	2,013	2,581	3,045	3,956	4,968	2,775	2,945	47,784
Some college, no degree	13,288	898	1,036	1,452	2,124	2,965	2,117	2,695	58,710
Associate's degree	6,851	351	443	625	990	1,612	1,175	1,655	65,523
Bachelor's degree or more	22,792	529	633	973	1,794	4,017	3,817	11,024	97,102
Bachelor's degree	14,579	369	475	688	1,305	2,824	2,566	6,354	90,056
Master's degree	5,709	121	105	204	363	930	990	2,995	100,000
Professional degree	1,377	20	35	51	71	143	141	918	100,000
Doctoral degree	1,127	20	20	29	56	122	121	758	100,000
Number of earners:									
No earners	11,185	3,350	2,344	2,010	1,634	1,021	373	452	24,564
One earner	25,013	2,769	3,708	4,025	4,662	4,562	2,050	3,239	40,717
Two earners or more	42,256	427	1,162	2,172	5,057	9,948	8,178	15,309	81,413

Source: U.S. Census Bureau, *Current Population Reports*, P60-233; and Internet site <http://pubdb3.census.gov/macro/032007 /faminc/new01_000.htm> (released 28 August 2007).

Table 677. Median Income of Families by Type of Family in Current and Constant (2006) Dollars: 1990 to 2006

[**In dollars.** See headnote, Table 673. For definition of median, see Guide to Tabular Presentation]

Year	Current dollars						Constant (2006) dollars					
		Married-couple families			Male house-holder, no spouse present	Female house-holder, no spouse present		Married-couple families			Male house-holder, no spouse present	Female house-holder, no spouse present
	Total	Total	Wife in paid labor force	Wife not in paid labor force			Total	Total	Wife in paid labor force	Wife not in paid labor force		
1990	35,353	39,895	46,777	30,265	29,046	16,932	52,869	59,661	69,953	45,260	43,437	25,321
1995 [1] . . .	40,611	47,062	55,823	32,375	30,358	19,691	53,349	61,824	73,333	42,530	39,880	25,867
2000 [2,3] . .	50,732	59,099	69,235	39,982	37,727	25,716	59,398	69,194	81,062	46,812	44,171	30,109
2001	51,407	60,335	70,834	40,782	36,590	25,745	58,545	68,712	80,669	46,444	41,670	29,320
2002	51,680	61,130	72,806	40,102	37,739	26,423	57,920	68,511	81,597	44,944	42,296	29,613
2003	52,680	62,281	75,170	41,122	38,032	26,550	57,751	68,276	82,406	45,080	41,693	29,106
2004 [4] . . .	54,061	63,626	76,854	42,215	40,361	26,969	57,705	67,915	82,035	45,061	43,082	28,787
2005	56,194	65,906	78,755	44,457	41,111	27,244	58,036	68,067	81,337	45,915	42,459	28,137
2006	58,407	69,404	82,788	45,757	41,844	28,829	58,407	69,404	82,788	45,757	41,844	28,829

[1] Data reflect full implementation of the 1990 census-based sample design and metropolitan definitions, 7,000 household sample reduction, and revised race edits. [2] Implementation of Census 2000-based population controls. [3] Implementation of a 28,000 household sample expansion. [4] Data have been revised to reflect a correction to the weights in the 2005 ASEC.

Source: U.S. Census Bureau, *Current Population Reports*, P60-233, and Internet sites <http://www.census.gov/prod/2007pubs /p60-233.pdf> (released August 2007) and <http://www.census.gov/hhes/www/income/histinc/f07ar.html>.

Table 678. Married-Couple Families—Number and Median Income by Work Experience of Husbands and Wives and Presence of Children: 2006

[**58,964 represents 58,964,000.** See headnote, Table 673. For definition of median, see Guide to Tabular Presentaton]

Work experience of husband or wife	Number (1,000)					Median income (dollars)				
	All married-couple families	No related chil-dren	One or more related children under 18 years old			All married-couple families	No related chil-dren	One or more related children under 18 years old		
			Total	One child	Two or more			Total	One child	Two or more
All married-couple families . . .	**58,964**	**31,647**	**27,317**	**10,604**	**16,713**	**69,404**	**64,362**	**74,049**	**76,152**	**72,307**
Husband worked	46,265	20,605	25,661	9,766	15,894	79,791	83,553	76,425	79,238	74,795
Wife worked.	33,914	15,472	18,442	7,624	10,818	86,773	91,290	83,411	85,556	81,903
Wife did not work	12,351	5,133	7,219	2,143	5,076	56,815	59,557	55,028	52,306	55,684
Husband year-round, full-time worker. .	38,970	16,345	22,625	8,545	14,079	82,838	88,218	79,630	81,542	77,522
Wife worked.	28,732	12,564	16,169	6,649	9,520	90,253	95,149	86,338	87,937	85,387
Wife did not work	10,237	3,781	6,456	1,896	4,560	60,621	63,775	57,452	56,846	57,948
Husband did not work	12,699	11,043	1,656	837	819	35,722	35,842	34,589	36,622	32,831
Wife worked.	3,879	2,866	1,012	497	516	47,846	49,674	42,263	43,695	41,488
Wife did not work	8,820	8,176	644	341	303	31,125	31,535	21,339	24,291	18,615

Source: U.S. Census Bureau, *Current Population Reports*, P60-233; and Internet site <http://pubdb3.census.gov/macro/032007 /faminc/new04_000.htm> (released 28 August 2007).

Table 679. Median Income of People With Income in Constant (2006) Dollars by Sex, Race, and Hispanic Origin: 1990 to 2006

[**In dollars. People as of March of following year.** People 15 years old and over. Constant dollars based on CPI-U-RS deflator. Based on the Current Population Survey; see text, Sections 1 and 13, and Appendix III. For data collection changes over time, see <http://www.census.gov/hhes/www/income/histinc/hstchg.html>]

Race and Hispanic origin	Male					Female				
	1990	2000 [1]	2004 [2,3]	2005	2006	1990	2000 [1]	2004 [2,3]	2005	2006
All races [4]	**30,347**	**33,185**	**32,573**	**32,300**	**32,265**	**15,059**	**18,807**	**18,858**	**19,185**	**20,014**
White [5]	31,659	34,887	33,458	33,234	33,843	15,429	18,826	18,892	19,281	20,082
Black [6]	19,244	24,989	24,220	23,396	25,064	12,454	18,594	18,529	18,209	19,103
Asian [7]	(NA)	(NA)	35,245	35,337	37,417	(NA)	(NA)	21,905	22,351	22,201
Hispanic [8]	20,144	22,829	23,009	22,813	23,452	11,264	14,340	15,426	15,529	15,758
White non-Hispanic.	32,837	36,890	35,948	36,504	36,564	15,823	19,512	19,678	20,089	20,727

NA Not available. [1] Implementation of Census 2000-based population controls and sample expanded by 28,000 households. [2] Beginning with the 2003 Current Population Survey (CPS), the questionnaire allowed respondents to choose more than one race. For 2002 and later, data represent persons who selected this race group only and excludes persons reporting more than one race. The CPS in prior years allowed respondents to report only one race group. See also comments on race in the text for Section 1. [3] Data have been revised to reflect a correction to the weights in the 2005 Annual Social and Economic Supplement (ASEC). [4] Includes other races not shown separately. [5] Beginning with 2002, data represent White alone, which refers to people who reported White and did not report any other race category. [6] Beginning with 2002, data represent Black alone, which refers to people who reported Black and did not report any other race category. [7] Beginning with 2002, data represent Asian alone, which refers to people who reported Asian and did not report any other race category. [8] People of Hispanic origin may be of any race.

Source: U.S. Census Bureau, *Current Population Reports*, P60-233; and Internet sites <http://www.census.gov/prod/2007pubs /p60-233.pdf> (released August 2007) and <http://www.census.gov/hhes/www/income/histinc/p02.html>.

[**People as of March 2007 (114,576 represents 114,576,000).** Covers people 15 years old and over. Median income in constant dollars based on CPI-U-RS deflator. For definition of median, see Guide to Tabular Presentation. For composition of regions, see map, inside front cover. Based on the Current Population Survey (CPS), see Appendix III]

Characteristic	All persons (1,000)	Total (1,000)	Under $5,000 [1]	$5,000 to $9,999	$10,000 to $14,999	$15,000 to $24,999	$25,000 to $34,999	$35,000 to $49,999	$50,000 to $74,999	$75,000 and over	Median income (dollars)
MALE											
Total	**114,576**	**103,909**	**6,743**	**7,016**	**8,690**	**17,283**	**15,073**	**16,571**	**16,257**	**16,273**	**32,265**
15 to 24 years old	21,156	14,093	4,206	2,344	1,915	2,797	1,462	853	359	158	10,964
25 to 34 years old	20,024	19,045	663	981	1,334	3,573	3,762	3,904	3,071	1,757	32,131
35 to 44 years old	21,181	20,374	479	814	884	2,700	2,875	3,925	4,165	4,532	42,637
45 to 54 years old	21,296	20,427	526	884	1,070	2,369	2,652	3,570	4,363	4,994	45,693
55 to 64 years old	15,478	14,905	509	788	1,052	1,832	1,977	2,482	2,928	3,338	41,477
65 years old and over	15,443	15,064	359	1,206	2,434	4,013	2,345	1,837	1,371	1,498	23,500
Region:											
Northeast	21,099	19,123	1,362	1,255	1,441	2,887	2,554	3,009	3,056	3,561	35,220
Midwest	25,449	23,408	1,660	1,534	1,760	3,763	3,500	3,958	3,967	3,269	32,863
South	41,131	37,141	2,193	2,697	3,401	6,530	5,693	5,908	5,400	5,318	31,150
West	26,898	24,236	1,529	1,529	2,087	4,104	3,326	3,698	3,834	4,128	32,786
Educational attainment of householder: [2]											
Total	**93,421**	**89,816**	**2,536**	**4,673**	**6,774**	**14,486**	**13,611**	**15,719**	**15,899**	**16,116**	**36,847**
Less than 9th grade	5,708	5,283	244	855	1,081	1,605	771	465	179	83	17,169
9th to 12th grade [3]	8,294	7,684	325	930	1,169	2,109	1,405	961	543	239	21,184
High school graduate [4]	29,604	28,253	830	1,615	2,468	5,782	5,468	5,530	4,474	2,088	31,009
Some college, no degree	15,063	14,526	438	573	951	2,206	2,402	3,143	2,822	1,992	37,271
Associate's degree	7,156	6,973	183	218	345	827	1,108	1,477	1,686	1,130	41,807
Bachelor's degree or more	27,597	27,097	517	481	761	1,956	2,455	4,143	6,197	10,588	61,168
Bachelor's degree	17,487	17,129	361	353	547	1,347	1,845	2,949	4,119	5,610	54,403
Master's degree	6,416	6,350	113	79	145	413	439	840	1,517	2,804	67,425
Professional degree	2,015	1,969	22	19	48	123	94	189	301	1,173	96,926
Doctoral degree	1,678	1,649	22	29	21	72	75	166	262	1,000	90,511
Tenure:											
Owner-occupied	82,488	75,560	4,841	4,242	5,465	10,666	10,175	12,363	13,363	14,443	37,057
Renter-occupied	30,608	27,050	1,782	2,604	3,078	6,298	4,723	4,033	2,758	1,777	24,455
Occupier paid no cash rent	1,481	1,298	118	171	148	320	176	176	137	52	21,538
FEMALE											
Total	**121,443**	**104,582**	**13,549**	**14,515**	**13,457**	**19,963**	**14,225**	**13,000**	**9,740**	**6,129**	**20,014**
15 to 24 years old	20,546	13,267	4,610	2,595	1,916	2,358	963	611	174	42	8,653
25 to 34 years old	19,843	17,151	2,048	1,505	1,770	3,461	3,116	2,752	1,708	791	24,179
35 to 44 years old	21,582	19,199	2,292	1,577	1,752	3,441	2,943	3,222	2,288	1,682	26,368
45 to 54 years old	22,166	20,135	1,883	1,634	1,894	3,553	3,145	3,261	2,928	1,839	27,844
55 to 64 years old	16,713	15,073	1,523	1,910	1,564	2,700	2,185	2,059	1,881	1,252	24,186
65 years old and over	20,593	19,757	1,194	5,294	4,559	4,453	1,872	1,097	763	527	13,603
Region:											
Northeast	22,782	19,956	2,557	2,771	2,549	3,645	2,458	2,388	2,123	1,463	20,284
Midwest	26,773	23,872	3,093	3,176	3,081	4,784	3,577	3,039	2,090	1,030	20,145
South	44,446	37,636	4,851	5,596	4,831	7,277	5,337	4,671	3,186	1,889	19,284
West	27,443	23,118	3,048	2,974	2,996	4,256	2,855	2,904	2,341	1,746	20,575
Educational attainment of householder: [2]											
Total	**100,897**	**91,315**	**8,940**	**11,921**	**11,541**	**17,605**	**13,260**	**12,390**	**9,569**	**6,089**	**21,900**
Less than 9th grade	5,584	4,257	531	1,484	1,040	829	257	62	36	18	10,451
9th to 12th grade [3]	8,157	6,750	889	1,841	1,482	1,613	508	265	109	45	11,914
High school graduate [4]	31,887	28,538	2,780	4,579	4,630	7,145	4,527	2,970	1,358	550	17,546
Some college, no degree	17,410	16,099	1,571	1,797	1,932	3,356	2,874	2,407	1,464	699	22,709
Associate's degree	9,614	9,043	775	811	874	1,768	1,689	1,510	1,148	470	26,295
Bachelor's degree or more	28,245	26,626	2,394	1,409	1,584	2,895	3,407	5,174	5,453	4,311	39,450
Bachelor's degree	19,171	17,931	1,814	1,086	1,238	2,203	2,593	3,440	3,269	2,287	35,094
Master's degree	7,191	6,876	473	252	298	582	703	1,478	1,791	1,300	46,250
Professional degree	1,075	1,037	71	41	27	62	68	147	193	425	60,463
Doctoral degree	808	782	34	30	21	48	44	107	199	301	61,091
Tenure:											
Owner-occupied	87,310	76,349	9,950	9,606	9,098	13,698	10,384	10,143	8,156	5,314	21,410
Renter-occupied	32,705	27,051	3,372	4,663	4,185	5,988	3,694	2,802	1,542	803	16,568
Occupier paid no cash rent	1,428	1,182	227	247	174	277	146	55	43	12	12,847

[1] Includes persons with income deficit.   [2] Persons 25 years and over.   [3] No diploma attained.   [4] Includes high school equivalency.

Source: U.S. Census Bureau, *Current Population Reports*, series P60-233; and Internet site <http://pubdb3.census.gov /macro/032007/perinc/new01_000.htm> (released 28 August 2007).

Table 681. Average Earnings of Year-Round, Full-Time Workers by Educational Attainment: 2006

[In dollars. For people 18 years old and over as of March 2007. See headnote, Table 679]

| Sex and Age | All workers | Less than 9th grade | High school | | College | | |
			9th to 12th grade (no diploma)	High school graduate [1]	Some college, no degree	Associate's degree	Bachelor's degree or more
Male, total	**57,791**	**26,789**	**31,434**	**42,466**	**48,431**	**51,485**	**88,843**
18 to 24 years old	26,170	19,361	20,918	24,974	26,957	29,698	38,275
25 to 34 years old	46,181	23,453	29,347	37,181	41,073	42,357	67,195
35 to 44 years old	63,247	29,302	31,018	45,316	53,080	58,759	95,002
45 to 54 years old	67,635	28,988	35,615	49,199	56,320	57,363	101,763
55 to 64 years old	65,956	29,913	41,136	47,741	56,120	51,978	92,223
65 years old and over	58,565	26,062	32,810	42,766	51,091	48,347	85,106
Female, total	**41,518**	**20,499**	**23,351**	**29,410**	**35,916**	**40,463**	**59,052**
18 to 24 years old	23,462	(B)	17,514	20,427	21,822	26,638	32,865
25 to 34 years old	38,581	18,180	21,955	26,299	32,853	38,857	50,341
35 to 44 years old	44,183	21,152	24,637	30,769	37,323	41,892	63,427
45 to 54 years old	45,332	21,633	24,304	31,984	39,785	44,191	65,001
55 to 64 years old	43,870	19,681	25,078	31,015	40,749	39,477	64,054
65 years old and over	38,629	(B)	27,948	29,170	43,082	37,079	58,288

B Base figure too small to meet statistical standards for reliability of derived figure. [1] Includes equivalency.

Source: U.S. Census Bureau, *Current Population Reports*, series P60-233; and Internet site <http://pubdb3.census.gov/macro/032007/perinc/new04_000.htm> (released 28 August 2007).

Table 682. Per Capita Money Income in Current and Constant (2006) Dollars by Race and Hispanic Origin: 1990 to 2006

[In dollars. Constant dollars based on CPI-U-RS deflator. People as of March of following year. Based on the Current Population Survey, Annual Social and Economic Supplement (ASEC); see text, Sections 1 and 13, and Appendix III. For data collection changes over time, see <http://www.census.gov/hhes/www/income/histinc/hstchg.html>]

| Year | Current dollars | | | | | Constant (2006) dollars | | | | |
	All races [1]	White [2]	Black [3]	Asian, Pacific Islander [4]	His-panic [5]	All races [1]	White [2]	Black [3]	Asian, Pacific Islander [4]	His-panic [5]
1990	14,387	15,265	9,017	(NA)	8,424	21,515	22,828	13,485	(NA)	12,598
1995 [6]	17,227	18,304	10,982	16,567	9,300	22,631	24,045	14,427	21,763	12,217
2000 [7, 8]	22,346	23,582	14,796	23,350	12,651	26,163	27,610	17,323	27,339	14,812
2001	22,851	24,127	14,953	24,277	13,003	26,024	27,477	17,029	27,648	14,808
2002 [9]	22,794	24,142	15,441	24,131	13,487	25,546	27,057	17,305	27,045	15,115
2003	23,276	24,626	15,775	24,604	13,492	25,517	26,997	17,294	26,972	14,791
2004 [10]	23,857	25,223	16,025	26,165	14,105	25,465	26,923	17,105	27,929	15,056
2005	25,036	26,496	16,874	27,331	14,483	25,857	27,365	17,427	28,227	14,958
2006	26,352	27,821	17,902	30,474	15,421	26,352	27,821	17,902	30,474	15,421

NA Not available. [1] Includes other races not shown separately. [2] Beginning with 2002, data represents White alone, which refers to people who reported White and did not report any other race category. [3] Beginning with 2002, data represents Black alone, which refers to people who reported Black and did not report any other race category. [4] Beginning with 2002, data represents Asian alone, which refers to people who reported Asian and did not report any other race category. [5] People of Hispanic origin may be of any race. [6] Data reflect full implementation of the 1990 census-based sample design and metropolitan definitions, 7,000 household sample reduction, and revised race edits. [7] Implementation of Census 2000-based population controls. [8] Implementation of a 28,000 household sample expansion. [9] See footnote 3, Table 673. See also comments on race in the text for Section 1. [10] Data have been revised to reflect a correction to the weights in the 2005 ASEC.

Source: U.S. Census Bureau, *Current Population Reports*, P60-233; and Internet sites <http://www.census.gov/prod/2007pubs/p60-233.pdf> (released August 2007) and <http://www.census.gov/hhes/www/income/histinc/incpertoc.html>.

Table 683. Money Income of People—Number by Income Level and by Sex, Race, and Hispanic Origin: 2006

[In thousands (114,576 represents 114,576,000). People as of March of the following year. Based on Current Population Survey (CPS); see text, Sections 1 and 13, and Appendix III]

| Income interval | Male | | | | | Female | | | | |
	All races [1]	White [2]	Black [3]	Asian [4]	His-panic [5]	All races [1]	White [2]	Black [3]	Asian [4]	His-panic [5]
All households [1]	**114,576**	**94,029**	**12,716**	**5,088**	**16,444**	**121,443**	**97,550**	**15,413**	**5,591**	**15,449**
Under $10,000 [6]	24,426	17,922	4,346	1,287	4,164	44,926	35,200	6,109	2,305	7,858
$10,000 to $19,999	17,394	14,109	2,155	618	3,596	24,194	19,721	3,085	835	3,138
$20,000 to $29,999	15,871	13,113	1,820	540	3,139	16,820	13,569	2,206	653	1,908
$30,000 to $39,999	13,851	11,559	1,524	484	2,095	11,911	9,605	1,607	453	1,013
$40,000 to $49,999	10,501	8,950	946	389	1,295	7,720	6,306	912	370	601
$50,000 to $59,999	8,078	6,969	646	337	678	5,081	4,243	523	238	338
$60,000 to $74,999	8,179	7,088	540	425	613	4,659	3,810	481	295	276
$75,000 to $84,999	3,737	3,228	211	238	279	1,705	1,390	167	127	97
$85,000 to $99,999	3,241	2,788	231	172	161	1,333	1,101	112	92	85
$100,000 to $149,999	5,584	4,952	200	369	282	2,085	1,756	147	147	101
$150,000 to $199,999	1,858	1,664	57	114	76	516	443	23	40	17
$200,000 to $249,999	670	625	10	33	21	239	201	20	17	7
$250,000 and above	1,182	1,064	32	80	45	251	206	23	21	11

[1] Includes races not shown separately. [2] White alone refers to people who reported White and did not report any other race category. [3] Black alone refers to people who reported Black and did not report any other race category. [4] Asian alone refers to people who reported Asian and did not report any other race category. [5] Persons of Hispanic origin may be of any race. [6] Includes persons without income.

Source: U.S. Census Bureau, Current Population Reports, P60-233; and Internet site <http://pubdb3.census.gov/macro/032007/perinc/new11_000.htm> (released 28 August 2007).

Income, Expenditures, Poverty, and Wealth   449

Table 684. Household Income—Distribution by Income Level and State: 2006

[In thousands (111,617 represents 111,617,000), except as indicated. The American Community Survey universe includes the household population and the population living in institutions, college dormitories, and other group quarters. Based on a sample and subject to sampling variability; see Appendix III. For definition of median, see Guide to Tabular Presentation]

State	Number of households (1,000)								Median income (dollars)
	Total	Under $25,000	$25,000–$49,999	$50,000–$74,999	$75,000–$99,999	$100,000–$149,999	$150,000–$199,999	$200,000 and over	
United States . .	**111,617**	**28,260**	**28,958**	**21,222**	**13,215**	**12,164**	**3,981**	**3,817**	**48,451**
Alabama	1,796	602	485	317	177	139	38	37	38,783
Alaska.	230	42	54	47	35	33	12	7	59,393
Arizona	2,225	539	625	430	254	235	75	66	47,265
Arkansas	1,103	380	329	193	100	68	18	16	36,599
California	12,151	2,589	2,804	2,223	1,541	1,697	650	648	56,645
Colorado	1,847	408	475	352	237	228	77	70	52,015
Connecticut	1,325	244	279	247	187	203	77	89	63,422
Delaware	320	68	83	64	43	41	11	10	52,833
District of Columbia . .	250	67	53	40	26	29	14	21	51,847
Florida.	7,106	1,849	2,007	1,360	776	680	205	228	45,495
Georgia	3,377	882	899	642	388	348	115	102	46,832
Hawaii.	433	81	94	86	62	67	22	20	61,160
Idaho	549	145	168	116	58	42	11	9	42,865
Illinois	4,724	1,107	1,150	933	594	570	190	180	52,006
Indiana	2,435	636	690	507	292	212	55	43	45,394
Iowa	1,209	312	363	251	139	99	24	22	44,491
Kansas	1,088	282	311	213	129	101	27	24	45,478
Kentucky	1,652	549	455	299	162	128	32	27	39,372
Louisiana	1,565	525	414	274	158	126	36	33	39,337
Maine	548	154	156	111	62	44	12	9	43,439
Maryland	2,089	336	448	409	301	347	132	115	65,144
Massachusetts	2,446	531	499	452	329	375	133	127	59,963
Michigan	3,869	991	1,037	766	460	405	118	91	47,182
Minnesota	2,042	421	513	431	288	250	74	66	54,023
Mississippi	1,076	408	293	175	97	71	17	15	34,473
Missouri.	2,305	651	663	446	247	196	56	47	42,841
Montana	372	112	111	75	37	26	7	4	40,627
Nebraska	701	184	200	144	81	65	14	13	45,474
Nevada	937	189	246	203	130	106	35	28	52,998
New Hampshire	505	94	115	106	77	72	24	17	59,683
New Jersey	3,135	580	637	565	438	499	211	206	64,470
New Mexico	726	226	203	132	74	61	17	13	40,629
New York.	7,088	1,782	1,659	1,272	848	859	316	352	51,384
North Carolina	3,454	997	973	652	367	296	86	83	42,625
North Dakota	272	79	80	56	29	19	4	4	41,919
Ohio	4,500	1,235	1,246	876	515	416	113	99	44,532
Oklahoma	1,385	446	406	251	133	97	26	27	38,770
Oregon	1,450	371	406	288	169	139	39	37	46,230
Pennsylvania	4,846	1,299	1,282	933	565	484	148	134	46,259
Rhode Island	406	99	96	76	57	52	14	12	51,814
South Carolina	1,657	500	480	304	176	129	34	34	41,100
South Dakota	312	88	91	65	35	22	5	6	42,791
Tennessee	2,375	741	677	434	233	181	55	54	40,315
Texas	8,109	2,240	2,184	1,455	890	820	260	261	44,922
Utah	814	164	230	184	107	86	24	18	51,309
Vermont	254	62	70	52	31	27	6	5	47,665
Virginia	2,905	588	698	563	371	387	153	145	56,277
Washington	2,472	539	628	500	326	304	93	82	52,583
West Virginia	743	270	219	126	67	44	9	9	35,059
Wisconsin	2,230	525	613	484	288	219	52	48	48,772
Wyoming	207	48	59	44	26	21	5	4	47,423

Source: U.S. Census Bureau, *Income, Earnings, and Poverty From the 2006 American Community Survey,* series ACS-01; and 2006 American Community Survey; B19001. Household Income in the Past 12 Months; B19013. Median Household Income in the Past 12 Months (In 2006 Inflation-Adjusted Dollars); using American FactFinder®; <http://factfinder.census.gov/>; (accessed 10 January 2008).

Table 685. Family Income—Distribution by Income Level and State: 2006

[In thousands (74,564 represents 74,564,000), except as indicated. The American Community Survey universe includes the household population and the population living in institutions, college dormitories, and other group quarters. Based on a sample and subject to sampling variability; see Appendix III. For definition of median, see Guide to Tabular Presentation]

State	Number of families (1,000)								Median income (dollars)
	Total	Under $25,000	$25,000– $49,999	$50,000– $74,999	$75,000– $99,999	$100,000– $149,999	$150,000– $199,999	$200,000 and over	
United States . .	**74,564**	**13,037**	**18,381**	**15,594**	**10,640**	**10,195**	**3,415**	**3,303**	**58,526**
Alabama	1,223	282	338	255	155	126	35	32	49,207
Alaska.	158	20	33	32	28	27	10	6	69,872
Arizona	1,476	260	400	303	201	193	63	57	55,709
Arkansas	758	186	234	158	88	61	17	15	45,093
California	8,304	1,355	1,831	1,555	1,152	1,341	529	540	64,563
Colorado	1,196	174	273	244	187	190	68	60	64,614
Connecticut	894	97	161	168	149	172	67	80	78,154
Delaware	214	29	52	45	34	35	9	9	62,623
District of Columbia . .	109	25	21	15	11	14	9	14	61,105
Florida.	4,633	839	1,269	996	613	555	170	191	54,445
Georgia	2,297	448	572	475	316	294	100	91	56,112
Hawaii.	301	38	62	61	49	56	18	17	70,277
Idaho	383	70	114	94	49	38	9	8	51,640
Illinois	3,146	493	709	666	478	477	166	158	63,121
Indiana	1,645	277	448	394	249	189	50	38	55,781
Iowa	797	124	225	196	123	88	21	21	55,735
Kansas	725	117	194	164	112	91	24	22	56,857
Kentucky	1,106	263	304	235	140	111	29	24	48,726
Louisiana.	1,073	267	286	215	133	111	32	29	48,261
Maine	358	64	102	86	50	37	11	8	52,793
Maryland	1,406	143	264	270	226	283	116	104	77,839
Massachusetts	1,566	202	286	301	249	305	113	110	74,463
Michigan	2,579	434	650	570	379	358	106	82	57,996
Minnesota	1,330	162	286	311	233	215	65	59	66,809
Mississippi	742	218	206	141	84	64	16	13	42,805
Missouri.	1,519	281	425	343	207	171	49	42	53,026
Montana	240	44	73	58	33	23	6	4	51,006
Nebraska.	462	71	126	114	70	56	13	12	56,940
Nevada	612	86	153	139	100	84	28	22	61,466
New Hampshire	336	34	67	77	62	61	20	15	71,176
New Jersey	2,180	255	388	404	343	418	187	185	77,875
New Mexico	477	111	135	94	62	51	15	11	48,199
New York.	4,574	805	1,019	883	640	683	257	287	62,138
North Carolina	2,310	465	630	502	308	258	74	73	52,336
North Dakota	169	26	48	44	26	17	4	4	55,385
Ohio	2,953	519	777	662	438	366	102	89	56,148
Oklahoma	927	213	268	198	115	85	23	24	47,955
Oregon	927	157	248	209	133	115	33	32	55,923
Pennsylvania	3,174	512	812	704	473	423	130	120	58,148
Rhode Island	262	39	56	56	44	44	12	11	64,733
South Carolina	1,123	244	314	242	150	113	30	31	50,334
South Dakota	206	35	57	54	30	20	4	5	53,806
Tennessee	1,597	357	445	337	201	160	49	49	49,804
Texas	5,687	1,235	1,471	1,090	729	701	229	230	52,355
Utah	615	88	166	151	95	76	21	17	58,141
Vermont	163	24	42	39	26	23	5	4	58,163
Virginia	1,940	259	427	395	285	313	134	128	66,886
Washington	1,595	229	366	349	255	251	77	68	63,705
West Virginia	502	129	154	105	60	39	8	7	44,012
Wisconsin	1,456	206	359	365	246	193	46	43	60,634
Wyoming	137	21	36	32	22	18	4	3	57,505

Source: U.S. Census Bureau, *Income, Earnings, and Poverty From the 2006 American Community Survey,* series ACS-01; and 2006 American Community Survey; B19101. Family Income in the Past 12 Months; B19113. Median Family Income in the Past 12 Months (In 2006 Inflation-Adjusted Dollars); using American FactFinder®; <http://factfinder.census.gov/>; (accessed 10 January 2008).

U.S. Census Bureau, Statistical Abstract of the United States: 2009

Table 686. **Household Income, Family Income, and Per Capita Income and Individual and Family Below Poverty Level by City: 2006**

[For number and percent below poverty, see headnote, Table 687. The American Community Survey universe includes the household population and the population living in institutions, college dormitories, and other group quarters. Based on a sample and subject to sampling variability; see Appendix III. For definition of median, see Guide to Tabular Presentation]

City	Median household income (dol.)	Median family income (dol.)	Per capita income (dol.)	Number below poverty level [1]		Percent below poverty level [1]	
				Individuals	Families	Individuals	Families
Albuquerque, NM	43,021	55,295	24,497	70,938	12,884	14.6	10.8
Anaheim, CA	55,720	60,730	22,320	42,009	7,429	12.3	10.1
Anchorage municipality, AK	63,656	77,028	31,072	26,186	5,207	9.6	7.5
Arlington, TX	50,582	60,364	23,650	45,371	8,146	12.8	9.5
Atlanta, GA	41,612	52,357	31,627	97,003	14,083	23.2	19.2
Aurora, CO	47,471	55,555	23,087	42,698	8,916	14.4	12.1
Austin, TX	47,212	58,241	28,250	124,517	19,331	17.7	12.7
Bakersfield, CA	51,421	59,130	23,413	49,296	9,936	16.4	13.4
Baltimore, MD	36,031	43,889	20,791	118,798	19,981	19.5	15.8
Boston, MA	47,974	52,817	29,243	108,617	16,983	19.8	15.6
Buffalo, NY	27,850	37,240	17,411	74,741	13,862	29.9	23.8
Charlotte, NC	48,670	59,452	29,825	78,818	15,110	12.4	9.3
Chicago, IL	43,223	49,113	24,219	571,313	100,688	21.2	17.2
Cincinnati, OH	31,103	41,832	22,167	79,900	15,042	27.8	23.4
Cleveland, OH	26,535	33,477	15,635	107,033	20,329	27.0	22.2
Colorado Springs, CO	50,892	64,231	26,416	37,663	6,403	9.6	6.3
Columbus, OH	40,074	49,622	21,894	144,832	24,611	20.7	14.7
Corpus Christi, TX	36,245	45,649	19,554	61,389	13,184	21.9	18.2
Dallas, TX	38,276	41,281	24,691	259,235	49,894	22.1	19.1
Denver, CO	40,900	50,167	26,548	112,155	18,819	20.0	15.2
Detroit, MI	28,364	33,067	13,977	265,600	48,579	32.5	27.0
El Paso, TX	33,103	36,268	15,756	156,097	34,359	26.4	23.6
Fort Wayne, IN	40,439	50,912	21,841	35,571	7,623	14.5	12.0
Fort Worth, TX	45,276	51,538	22,526	102,846	19,562	16.6	13.3
Fresno, CA	40,328	43,946	18,697	107,076	19,685	22.8	18.6
Honolulu, HI [2]	54,720	69,530	30,292	41,021	6,800	11.5	8.1
Houston, TX	39,682	42,925	23,041	434,683	78,444	21.3	17.0
Indianapolis, IN [3]	41,520	49,924	22,811	125,684	24,699	16.3	12.9
Jacksonville, FL	45,285	56,805	23,646	109,541	20,402	14.0	10.3
Kansas City, MO	40,920	51,873	24,180	78,705	15,477	18.5	14.8
Las Vegas, NV	53,000	61,038	26,773	62,704	11,724	11.2	8.4
Lexington-Fayette, KY	44,211	64,243	27,304	42,206	6,548	16.2	10.0
Long Beach, CA	45,906	49,569	22,908	91,219	16,085	19.8	16.4
Los Angeles, CA	44,445	48,741	24,349	705,154	121,684	19.0	15.6
Memphis, TN	32,594	37,676	19,252	146,173	27,793	23.5	18.8
Mesa, AZ	47,810	56,019	22,571	53,609	8,880	11.0	8.0
Miami, FL	27,088	31,195	17,911	94,530	18,150	26.9	22.8
Milwaukee, WI	33,990	38,840	18,129	142,944	27,369	26.2	21.6
Minneapolis, MN	43,369	55,361	27,487	80,207	12,560	22.7	17.8
Nashville-Davidson, TN [3]	41,194	52,911	24,920	88,868	17,061	16.7	13.0
New Orleans, LA	35,859	47,754	23,809	47,211	6,406	22.2	16.0
New York, NY	46,480	51,830	27,420	1,547,152	297,032	19.2	16.3
Newark, NJ	34,521	40,958	16,077	61,803	11,344	24.2	19.6
Oakland, CA	45,552	51,727	26,473	70,294	12,581	18.8	16.6
Oklahoma City, OK	39,024	50,218	22,665	91,188	16,413	17.1	12.3
Omaha, NE	42,321	55,953	23,759	55,373	9,263	14.8	10.1
Philadelphia, PA	33,229	43,049	18,924	354,135	59,192	25.1	19.6
Phoenix, AZ	46,645	54,438	23,076	242,347	39,596	17.2	12.7
Pittsburgh, PA	31,779	44,027	21,606	61,746	9,196	22.2	14.9
Plano, TX	77,038	96,867	38,534	13,441	2,359	5.1	3.5
Portland, OR	44,273	57,952	27,429	85,193	13,948	16.2	11.6
Raleigh, NC	51,123	71,009	27,919	44,595	5,412	13.8	7.4
Riverside, CA	52,023	58,101	21,531	41,576	6,141	13.7	9.2
Sacramento, CA	46,055	52,341	23,886	66,282	11,749	15.4	12.1
San Antonio, TX	40,650	47,306	19,884	224,665	45,165	18.1	15.1
San Diego, CA	58,815	71,026	29,846	162,352	24,726	13.4	9.0
San Francisco, CA	65,497	79,423	41,734	88,676	9,811	12.1	6.8
San Jose, CA	73,804	83,089	30,794	93,080	16,142	10.3	7.7
Santa Ana, CA	54,050	52,480	15,799	49,257	7,515	14.3	12.0
Seattle, WA	58,311	82,867	38,648	67,483	8,287	12.5	7.1
St. Louis, MO	30,936	37,635	18,720	90,379	16,558	26.8	22.8
St. Paul, MN	43,654	54,537	23,675	54,674	8,209	20.9	14.7
St. Petersburg, FL	41,639	53,331	24,778	34,900	5,195	13.6	8.7
Stockton, CA	45,615	52,141	19,495	43,260	7,715	15.5	11.8
Tampa, FL	39,602	45,823	28,257	63,136	12,365	20.1	16.4
Toledo, OH	33,691	43,553	18,326	64,341	12,429	22.7	17.6
Tucson, AZ	36,095	44,217	19,250	100,850	15,290	19.9	13.3
Tulsa, OK	36,137	47,124	24,227	75,070	15,784	20.3	16.8
Virginia Beach, VA	61,333	69,468	28,477	30,312	6,098	7.2	5.4
Washington, DC	51,847	61,105	37,043	108,100	17,690	19.6	16.3
Wichita, KS	41,089	52,090	22,734	53,831	11,503	15.3	12.6

[1] See headnote, Table 687.   [2] Data shown for census designated place (CDP).   [3] Represents the portion of a consolidated city that is not within one or more separately incorporated places.

Source: U.S. Census Bureau, *Income, Earnings, and Poverty From the 2006 American Community Survey,* series ACS-01; and 2006 American Community Survey; B19013, B19113, B19301, B17001, and B17010; using American FactFinder®; <http://factfinder.census.gov/>; (accessed 10 January 2008).

Table 687. Individuals and Families Below Poverty Level—Number and Rate by State: 2000 and 2006

[In thousands (33,311 represents 33,311,000), except as indicated. Represents number and percent below poverty in the past 12 months. The American Community Survey universe includes the household population and the population living in institutions, college dormitories, and other group quarters. Poverty status was determined for all people except institutionalized people, people in military group quarters, people in college dormitories, and unrelated individuals under 15 years old. These groups were excluded from the numerator and denominator when calculating poverty rates. Based on a sample and subject to sampling variability; see Appendix III]

State	Number below poverty level (1,000)				Percent below poverty level			
	Individuals		Families		Individuals		Families	
	2000	2006	2000	2006	2000	2006	2000	2006
United States........	33,311	38,757	6,615	7,283	12.2	13.3	9.3	9.8
Alabama.............	672	742	146	154	15.6	16.6	12.4	12.6
Alaska..............	55	71	11	13	9.1	10.9	6.8	8.2
Arizona.............	780	857	150	148	15.6	14.2	11.6	10.1
Arkansas............	439	471	96	99	17.0	17.3	13.0	13.1
California...........	4,520	4,690	832	809	13.7	13.1	10.7	9.7
Colorado............	363	556	64	101	8.7	12.0	5.7	8.4
Connecticut..........	254	280	51	52	7.7	8.3	5.8	5.9
Delaware............	70	92	14	16	9.3	11.1	6.7	7.6
District of Columbia	94	108	17	18	17.5	19.6	15.4	16.3
Florida.............	1,987	2,227	387	417	12.8	12.6	9.3	9.0
Georgia............	999	1,334	206	254	12.6	14.7	10.0	11.1
Hawaii.............	103	116	19	21	8.8	9.3	6.8	7.1
Idaho..............	144	180	26	36	11.4	12.6	7.7	9.3
Illinois.............	1,335	1,539	262	286	11.1	12.3	8.6	9.1
Indiana.............	592	778	113	149	10.1	12.7	7.1	9.0
Iowa...............	281	316	53	58	10.0	11.0	7.0	7.3
Kansas.............	247	331	43	62	9.5	12.4	6.2	8.6
Kentucky............	640	693	148	145	16.4	17.0	13.5	13.1
Louisiana...........	862	793	182	155	20.0	19.0	16.0	14.4
Maine..............	124	166	22	31	10.1	12.9	6.6	8.7
Maryland............	477	428	89	74	9.3	7.8	6.6	5.3
Massachusetts........	586	620	110	109	9.6	9.9	7.1	7.0
Michigan............	975	1,332	196	248	10.1	13.5	7.7	9.6
Minnesota...........	328	492	66	86	6.9	9.8	5.1	6.5
Mississippi..........	498	593	104	125	18.2	21.1	14.2	16.8
Missouri............	606	770	118	151	11.2	13.6	7.7	10.0
Montana............	117	126	23	21	13.4	13.6	9.5	8.6
Nebraska...........	158	197	28	36	9.6	11.5	6.5	7.8
Nevada	194	254	34	46	9.9	10.3	6.9	7.6
New Hampshire..........	63	102	11	17	5.3	8.0	3.5	4.9
New Jersey..........	651	742	126	141	7.9	8.7	6.0	6.4
New Mexico	320	354	64	66	18.0	18.5	14.2	13.8
New York	2,391	2,662	491	497	13.1	14.2	10.7	10.9
North Carolina........	1,018	1,261	203	248	13.1	14.7	9.6	10.7
North Dakota.........	71	69	14	12	11.6	11.4	8.1	7.0
Ohio..............	1,216	1,486	246	290	11.1	13.3	8.4	9.8
Oklahoma...........	459	588	100	118	13.8	17.0	11.0	12.8
Oregon.............	439	481	84	86	13.2	13.3	9.5	9.2
Pennsylvania.........	1,240	1,448	247	262	10.5	12.1	7.8	8.2
Rhode Island.........	108	114	23	20	10.7	11.1	8.5	7.8
South Carolina........	557	656	123	134	14.4	15.7	11.7	11.9
South Dakota	83	102	16	17	11.5	13.6	8.4	8.4
Tennessee	745	952	158	198	13.5	16.2	10.5	12.4
Texas..............	3,056	3,869	639	759	15.1	16.9	12.3	13.3
Utah	192	265	40	48	8.8	10.6	7.2	7.8
Vermont	63	62	12	11	10.7	10.3	7.5	6.7
Virginia.............	630	709	124	132	9.2	9.6	6.8	6.8
Washington..........	667	737	127	128	11.6	11.8	8.6	8.0
West Virginia.........	327	307	72	64	18.6	17.3	14.7	12.7
Wisconsin...........	461	592	75	107	8.9	11.0	5.6	7.3
Wyoming	55	47	10	9	11.4	9.4	7.9	6.3

Source: U.S. Census Bureau, 2006 American Community Survey; B17001. Poverty Status in the Past 12 Months by Sex and Age, and B17010. Poverty Status in the Past 12 Months of Familes by Family Type by Presence of Related Children under 18 Years by Age of Related Children; using American FactFinder®; <http://factfinder.census.gov/>; (accessed 18 January 2008).

Income, Expenditures, Poverty, and Wealth   453

Table 688. **Weighted Average Poverty Thresholds by Size of Unit: 1980 to 2006**

[**In dollars.** For information on the official poverty thresholds; see text, this section. For data collection changes over time, see <http://www.census.gov/hhes/www/income/histinc/hstchg.html>]

Size of family unit	1980	1990	1995	2000 [1]	2002	2003	2004 [2]	2005	2006
One person (unrelated individual)	4,190	6,652	7,763	8,791	9,183	9,393	9,646	9,973	10,294
Under 65 years old	4,290	6,800	7,929	8,959	9,359	9,573	9,827	10,160	10,488
65 years old and over	3,949	6,268	7,309	8,259	8,628	8,825	9,060	9,367	9,669
Two persons	5,363	8,509	9,933	11,235	11,756	12,015	12,335	12,755	13,167
Householder under 65 years old	5,537	8,794	10,259	11,589	12,110	12,384	12,714	13,145	13,569
Householder 65 years old and over . .	4,983	7,905	9,219	10,418	10,885	11,133	11,430	11,815	12,201
Three persons	6,565	10,419	12,158	13,740	14,348	14,680	15,066	15,577	16,079
Four persons	8,414	13,359	15,569	17,604	18,392	18,810	19,307	19,971	20,614
Five persons	9,966	15,792	18,408	20,815	21,744	22,245	22,830	23,613	24,382
Six persons	11,269	17,839	20,804	23,533	24,576	25,122	25,787	26,683	27,560
Seven persons	12,761	20,241	23,552	26,750	28,001	28,544	29,233	30,249	31,205
Eight persons	14,199	22,582	26,237	29,701	30,907	31,589	32,641	33,610	34,774
Nine or more persons	16,896	26,848	31,280	35,150	37,062	37,656	39,062	40,288	41,499

[1] Implementation of Census 2000-based population controls and sample expanded by 28,000 households.   [2] The 2004 data have been revised to reflect a correction to the weights in the 2005 Annual Social and Economic Supplement (ASEC).

Source: U.S. Census Bureau, *Current Population Reports*, P60-233; and Internet sites <http://www.census.gov/prod/2007pubs/p60-233.pdf> (released August 2007) and <http://www.census.gov/hhes/www/poverty/histpov/hstpov1.html>.

Table 689. **People Below Poverty Level and Below 125 Percent of Poverty Level by Race and Hispanic Origin: 1980 to 2006**

[**(29,272 represents 29,272,000.) People as of March of the following year**. Based on Current Population Survey, Annual Social and Economic Supplement (ASEC); See text, Section 1, and Appendix III. For data collection changes over time, see <http://www.census.gov/hhes/www/income/histinc/hstchg.html>]

Year	Number below poverty level (1,000)					Percent below poverty level					Below 125 percent of poverty level	
	All races [1]	White [2]	Black [3]	Asian and Pacific Islander [4]	His-panic [5]	All races [1]	White [2]	Black [3]	Asian and Pacific Islander [4]	His-panic [5]	Num-ber (1,000)	Percent of total popu-lation
1980	29,272	19,699	8,579	(NA)	3,491	13.0	10.2	32.5	(NA)	25.7	40,658	18.1
1985	33,064	22,860	8,926	(NA)	5,236	14.0	11.4	31.3	(NA)	29.0	44,166	18.7
1986	32,370	22,183	8,983	(NA)	5,117	13.6	11.0	31.1	(NA)	27.3	43,486	18.2
1987 [6] . .	32,221	21,195	9,520	1,021	5,422	13.4	10.4	32.4	16.1	28.0	43,032	17.9
1988	31,745	20,715	9,356	1,117	5,357	13.0	10.1	31.3	17.3	26.7	42,551	17.5
1989	31,528	20,785	9,302	939	5,430	12.8	10.0	30.7	14.1	26.2	42,653	17.3
1990	33,585	22,326	9,837	858	6,006	13.5	10.7	31.9	12.2	28.1	44,837	18.0
1991	35,708	23,747	10,242	996	6,339	14.2	11.3	32.7	13.8	28.7	47,527	18.9
1992 [7] . .	38,014	25,259	10,827	985	7,592	14.8	11.9	33.4	12.7	29.6	50,592	19.7
1993 [8] . .	39,265	26,226	10,877	1,134	8,126	15.1	12.2	33.1	15.3	30.6	51,801	20.0
1994	38,059	25,379	10,196	974	8,416	14.5	11.7	30.6	14.6	30.7	50,401	19.3
1995	36,425	24,423	9,872	1,411	8,574	13.8	11.2	29.3	14.6	30.3	48,761	18.5
1996	36,529	24,650	9,694	1,454	8,697	13.7	11.2	28.4	14.5	29.4	49,310	18.5
1997	35,574	24,396	9,116	1,468	8,308	13.3	11.0	26.5	14.0	27.1	47,853	17.8
1998	34,476	23,454	9,091	1,360	8,070	12.7	10.5	26.1	12.5	25.6	46,036	17.0
1999 [9] . .	32,791	22,169	8,441	1,285	7,876	11.9	9.8	23.6	10.7	22.7	45,030	16.3
2000 [10] .	31,581	21,645	7,982	1,258	7,747	11.3	9.5	22.5	9.9	21.5	43,612	15.6
2001	32,907	22,739	8,136	1,275	7,997	11.7	9.9	22.7	10.2	21.4	45,320	16.1
2002 [11] .	34,570	23,466	8,602	1,161	8,555	12.1	10.2	24.1	10.1	21.8	47,084	16.5
2003	35,861	24,272	8,781	1,401	9,051	12.5	10.5	24.4	11.8	22.5	48,687	16.9
2004 [12] .	37,040	25,327	9,014	1,201	9,122	12.7	10.8	24.7	9.8	21.9	49,693	17.1
2005	36,950	24,872	9,168	1,402	9,368	12.6	10.6	24.9	11.1	21.8	49,327	16.8
2006	36,460	24,416	9,048	1,353	9,243	12.3	10.3	24.3	10.3	20.6	49,688	16.8

NA Not available.   [1] Includes other races not shown separately.   [2] Beginning 2002, data represent White alone, which refers to people who reported White and did not report any other race category.   [3] Beginning 2002, data represent Black alone, which refers to people who reported Black and did not report any other race category.   [4] Beginning 2002, data represent Asian alone, which refers to people who reported Asian and did not report any other race category.   [5] People of Hispanic origin may be of any race.   [6] Implementation of a new March CPS processing system.   [7] Implementation of 1990 census population controls.   [8] The March 1994 income supplement was revised to allow for the coding of different income amounts on selected questionnaire items. Limits either increased or decreased in the following categories: earnings increased to $999,999; social security increased to $49,999; supplemental security income and public assistance increased to $24,999; veterans' benefits increased to $99,999; child support and alimony decreased to $49,999.   [9] Implementation of Census 2000-based population controls.   [10] Implementation of sample expansion by 28,000 households.   [11] Beginning with the 2003 Current Population Survey (CPS), the questionnaire allowed respondents to choose more than one race. For 2002 and later, data represent persons who selected this race group only and exclude persons reporting more than one race. The CPS in prior years allowed respondents to report only one race group. See also comments on race in the text for Section 1, Population.   [12] Data have been revised to reflect a correction to the weights in the 2005 ASEC.

Source: U.S. Census Bureau, *Current Population Reports*, P60-233; and Internet sites <http://www.census.gov/prod/2007pubs/p60-233.pdf> (released August 2007) and <http://www.census.gov/hhes/www/poverty/histpov/perindex.html>.

Table 690. **Children Below Poverty Level by Race and Hispanic Origin: 1980 to 2006**

[11,114 represents 11,114,000. Persons as of March of the following year. Covers only related children in families under 18 years old. Based on Current Population Survey; see text, this section and Section 1, and Appendix III. For data collection changes over time, see <http://www.census.gov/hhes/www/income/histinc/hstchg.html>]

Year	Number below poverty level (1,000)					Percent below poverty level				
	All races [1]	White [2]	Black [3]	Asian and Pacific Islander [4]	His-panic [5]	All races [1]	White [2]	Black [3]	Asian and Pacific Islander [4]	His-panic [5]
1980	11,114	6,817	3,906	(NA)	1,718	17.9	13.4	42.1	(NA)	33.0
1985	12,483	7,838	4,057	(NA)	2,512	20.1	15.6	43.1	(NA)	39.6
1987 [6]	12,275	7,398	4,234	432	2,606	19.7	14.7	44.4	22.7	38.9
1988	11,935	7,095	4,148	458	2,576	19.0	14.0	42.8	23.5	37.3
1989	12,001	7,164	4,257	368	2,496	19.0	14.1	43.2	18.9	35.5
1990	12,715	7,696	4,412	356	2,750	19.9	15.1	44.2	17.0	37.7
1991 [7]	13,658	8,316	4,637	348	2,977	21.1	16.1	45.6	17.1	39.8
1992 [7]	14,521	8,752	5,015	352	3,440	21.6	16.5	46.3	16.0	39.0
1993 [8]	14,961	9,123	5,030	358	3,666	22.0	17.0	45.9	17.6	39.9
1994	14,610	8,826	4,787	308	3,956	21.2	16.3	43.3	17.9	41.1
1995	13,999	8,474	4,644	532	3,938	20.2	15.5	41.5	18.6	39.3
1996	13,764	8,488	4,411	553	4,090	19.8	15.5	39.5	19.1	39.9
1997	13,422	8,441	4,116	608	3,865	19.2	15.4	36.8	19.9	36.4
1998 [9]	12,845	7,935	4,073	542	3,670	18.3	14.4	36.4	17.5	33.6
1999 [9]	11,678	7,194	3,698	367	3,561	16.6	13.1	32.8	11.5	29.9
2000 [10] . . .	11,005	6,834	3,495	407	3,342	15.6	12.4	30.9	12.5	27.6
2001 [11]	11,175	7,086	3,423	353	3,433	15.8	12.8	30.0	11.1	27.4
2002 [11]	11,646	7,203	3,570	302	3,653	16.3	13.1	32.1	11.4	28.2
2003 [12] . . .	12,340	7,624	3,750	331	3,982	17.2	13.9	33.6	12.1	29.5
2004 [12] . . .	12,473	7,876	3,702	265	3,985	17.3	14.3	33.4	9.4	28.6
2005	12,335	7,652	3,743	312	3,977	17.1	13.9	34.2	11.0	27.7
2006	12,299	7,522	3,690	351	3,959	16.9	13.6	33.0	12.0	26.6

NA Not available. [1] Includes other races not shown separately. [2] Beginning 2002, data represent White alone, which refers to people who reported White and did not report any other race category. [3] Beginning 2002, data represent Black alone, which refers to people who reported Black and did not report any other race category. [4] Beginning 2002, data represent Asian alone, which refers to people who reported Asian and did not report any other race category. [5] People of Hispanic origin may be of any race. [6] Implementation of a new March CPS processing system. [7] Implementation of 1990 census population controls. [8] The March 1994 income supplement was revised to allow for the coding of different income amounts on selected questionnaire items. Limits either increased or decreased in the following categories: earnings increased to $999,999; social security increased to $49,999; supplemental security income and public assistance increased to $24,999; veterans' benefits increased to $99,999; child support and alimony decreased to $49,999. [9] Implementation of Census 2000-based population controls. [10] Implementation of sample expansion to 28,000 households. [11] Beginning with the 2003 Current Population Survey (CPS), the questionnaire allowed respondents to choose more than one race. For 2002 and later, data represent persons who selected this race group only and excludes persons reporting more than one race. The CPS in prior years allowed respondents to report only one race group. See also comments on race in the text for Section 1. [12] Data have been revised to reflect a correction to the weights in the 2005 Annual Social and Economic Supplement (ASEC).

Source: U.S. Census Bureau, *Current Population Reports*, P60-233; and Internet sites <http://www.census.gov/prod/2007pubs/p60-233.pdf> (released August 2007) and <http://www.census.gov/hhes/www/poverty/histpov/hstpov3.html>.

Table 691. **Persons Below Poverty Level by Selected Characteristics: 2006**

[36,460 represents 36,460,000. People as of March 2007. Based on Current Population Survey (CPS); see text, this section and Section 1, and Appendix III. The 2007 CPS allowed respondents to choose more than one race. For 2006, data represent persons who selected this race group only and exclude persons reporting more than one race. The CPS in prior years allowed respondents to report only one race group. See also comments on race in the text for Section 1. For composition of regions, see map, inside front cover]

Characteristic	Number below poverty level (1,000)					Percent below poverty level				
	All races [1]	White alone	Black alone	Asian alone	His-panic [2]	All races [1]	White alone	Black alone	Asian alone	His-panic [2]
Total	**36,460**	**24,416**	**9,048**	**1,353**	**9,243**	**12.3**	**10.3**	**24.3**	**10.3**	**20.6**
Male	16,000	10,746	3,823	663	4,333	11.0	9.1	22.0	10.4	18.8
Female.	20,460	13,670	5,225	690	4,910	13.6	11.4	26.2	10.1	22.6
Under 18 years old.	12,827	7,908	3,777	360	4,072	17.4	14.1	33.4	12.2	26.9
18 to 24 years old	5,047	3,514	1,120	203	1,068	17.8	15.9	27.5	16.6	21.0
25 to 34 years old	4,920	3,338	1,208	203	1,453	12.3	10.7	23.1	8.7	17.9
35 to 44 years old	4,049	2,833	864	182	1,133	9.5	8.3	16.3	7.7	16.8
45 to 54 years old	3,399	2,293	819	157	601	7.8	6.4	16.1	8.3	12.9
55 to 59 years old	1,468	1,054	297	60	244	8.1	6.9	15.6	8.1	16.1
60 to 64 years old	1,357	1,002	261	45	200	9.7	8.4	20.0	8.9	17.8
65 years old and over . . .	3,394	2,473	701	142	472	9.4	7.9	22.7	12.0	19.4
65 to 74 years old. . . .	1,636	1,134	390	60	271	8.6	7.0	21.2	9.2	18.8
75 years old and over .	1,757	1,339	311	82	201	10.3	8.9	24.9	15.3	20.4
Northeast	6,222	4,144	1,589	376	1,491	11.5	9.5	24.0	12.1	24.4
Midwest	7,324	4,908	1,950	174	760	11.2	8.8	29.4	10.7	19.5
South.	14,882	9,289	4,772	237	3,459	13.8	11.3	23.1	9.2	21.7
West	8,032	6,075	737	566	3,532	11.6	10.8	21.8	9.6	18.8
Native	30,790	20,396	8,430	462	5,609	11.9	9.6	24.8	9.7	20.9
Foreign born	5,670	4,019	618	891	3,633	15.2	16.2	18.8	10.6	20.2
Naturalized citizen. . . .	1,345	807	213	277	562	9.3	9.5	14.5	6.5	12.3
Not a citizen.	4,324	3,212	404	614	3,071	19.0	19.8	22.3	14.8	22.9

[1] Includes other races not shown separately. [2] Persons of Hispanic origin may be any race.

Source: U.S. Census Bureau, *Current Population Reports*, P60-233; and Internet site <http://pubdb3.census.gov/macro/032007/pov/toc.htm> (released 28 August 2007).

Income, Expenditures, Poverty, and Wealth 455

Table 692. Work Experience During 2006 by Poverty Status, Sex, and Age: 2006

[107,734 represents 107,734,000. Covers only persons 16 years old and over. Based on Current Population Survey; see text, this section, Section 1, and Appendix III]

Sex and age	Worked full-time year-round			Did not work full-time year-round			Did not work		
	Number (1,000)	Below poverty level		Number (1,000)	Below poverty level		Number (1,000)	Below poverty level	
		Number (1,000)	Percent		Number (1,000)	Percent		Number (1,000)	Percent
BOTH SEXES									
Total	107,734	2,906	2.7	49,618	6,275	12.6	74,448	15,715	21.1
16 to 17 years old	100	3	2.5	2,701	192	7.1	6,277	1,069	17.0
18 to 64 years old	104,626	2,871	2.7	43,163	5,984	13.9	38,899	11,385	29.3
18 to 24 years old. . . .	8,186	439	5.4	12,200	2,124	17.4	8,018	2,484	31.0
25 to 34 years old. . . .	24,530	967	3.9	9,118	1,655	18.2	6,220	2,298	36.9
35 to 54 years old. . . .	56,270	1,295	2.3	15,770	1,801	11.4	14,184	4,352	30.7
55 to 64 years old. . . .	15,640	169	1.1	6,075	404	6.7	10,476	2,252	21.5
65 years old and over . . .	3,008	33	1.1	3,755	100	2.7	29,272	3,261	11.1
MALE									
Total	63,058	1,637	2.6	20,709	2,556	12.3	28,671	5,962	20.8
16 to 17 years old	70	–	(B)	1,347	92	6.9	3,178	555	17.5
18 to 64 years old	61,158	1,616	2.6	17,470	2,418	13.8	13,772	4,454	32.3
18 to 24 years old. . . .	4,870	248	5.1	5,794	845	14.6	3,758	1,058	28.2
25 to 34 years old. . . .	14,610	550	3.8	3,785	654	17.3	1,629	747	45.9
35 to 54 years old. . . .	32,836	721	2.2	5,350	742	13.9	4,290	1,714	39.9
55 to 64 years old. . . .	8,842	98	1.1	2,541	176	6.9	4,094	936	22.9
65 years old and over . . .	1,831	21	1.1	1,891	46	2.4	11,721	953	8.1
FEMALE									
Total	44,676	1,269	2.8	28,910	3,719	12.9	45,776	9,753	21.3
16 to 17 years old	30	3	(B)	1,353	99	7.4	3,099	514	16.6
18 to 64 years old	43,468	1,255	2.9	25,692	3,566	13.9	25,126	6,930	27.6
18 to 24 years old. . . .	3,316	192	5.8	6,407	1,278	20.0	4,260	1,426	33.5
25 to 34 years old. . . .	9,920	417	4.2	5,333	1,001	18.8	4,591	1,550	33.8
35 to 54 years old. . . .	23,434	575	2.5	10,419	1,058	10.2	9,894	2,638	26.7
55 to 64 years old. . . .	6,798	71	1.0	3,534	228	6.5	6,381	1,316	20.6
65 years old and over . . .	1,177	12	1.0	1,864	53	2.9	17,551	2,308	13.2

– Represents zero.   B Base figure too small to meet statistical standards for reliability of a derived figure.

Source: U.S. Census Bureau, *Current Population Reports*, series P60-233; and Internet site <http://pubdb3.census.gov/macro/032007/pov/new22_100_01.htm> (released 28 August 2007).

Table 693. Families Below Poverty Level and Below 125 Percent of Poverty by Race and Hispanic Origin: 1980 to 2006

[6,217 represents 6,217,000. **Families as of March of the following year** . Based on Current Population Survey. See text, this section, Section 1, and Appendix III. For data collection changes over time, see <http://www.census.gov/hhes/www/income/histinc/hstchg.html>]

Year	Number below poverty level (1,000)					Percent below poverty level					Below 125 percent of poverty level	
	All races [1]	White [2]	Black [3]	Asian and Pacific Islander [4]	His-panic [5]	All races [1]	White [2]	Black [3]	Asian and Pacific Islander [4]	His-panic [5]	Num-ber (1,000)	Percent
1980 . . .	6,217	4,195	1,826	(NA)	751	10.3	8.0	28.9	(NA)	23.2	8,764	14.5
1985 . . .	7,223	4,983	1,983	(NA)	1,074	11.4	9.1	28.7	(NA)	25.5	9,753	15.3
1990 . . .	7,098	4,622	2,193	169	1,244	10.7	8.1	29.3	11.0	25.0	9,564	14.4
1995 . . .	7,532	4,994	2,127	264	1,695	10.8	8.5	26.4	12.4	27.0	10,223	14.7
1997 . . .	7,324	4,990	1,985	244	1,721	10.3	8.4	23.6	10.2	24.7	10,032	14.2
1998 . . .	7,186	4,829	1,981	270	1,648	10.0	8.0	23.4	11.0	22.7	9,714	13.6
1999 [6] . .	6,792	4,447	1,887	258	1,593	9.3	7.3	21.8	10.3	20.5	9,320	12.9
2000 [7] . .	6,400	4,333	1,686	233	1,540	8.7	7.1	19.3	7.8	19.2	9,032	12.2
2001 . . .	6,813	4,579	1,829	234	1,649	9.2	7.4	20.7	7.8	19.4	9,525	12.8
2002 [8] . .	7,229	4,862	1,923	210	1,792	9.6	7.8	21.5	7.4	19.7	9,998	13.2
2003 . . .	7,607	5,058	1,986	311	1,925	10.0	8.1	22.3	10.2	20.8	10,360	13.6
2004 [9] . .	7,835	5,293	2,035	232	1,953	10.2	8.4	22.8	7.4	20.5	10,499	13.7
2005 . . .	7,657	5,068	1,997	289	1,948	9.9	8.0	22.1	9.0	19.7	10,442	13.7
2006 . . .	7,668	5,118	2,007	260	1,922	9.8	8.0	21.6	7.8	18.9	10,531	13.4

NA Not available.   [1] Includes other races not shown separately.   [2] Beginning 2002, data represent White alone, which refers to people who reported White and did not report any other race category.   [3] Beginning 2002, data represent Black alone, which refers to people who reported Black and did not report any other race category.   [4] Beginning 2002, data represent Asian alone, which refers to people who reported Asian and did not report any other race category.   [5] People of Hispanic origin may be of any race.   [6] Implementation of Census-2000-based population controls.   [7] Implementation of a 28,000 household sample expansion.   [8] Beginning with the 2003 Current Population Survey (CPS), the questionnaire allowed respondents to choose more than one race. For 2002 and later, data represent persons who selected this race group only and excludes persons reporting more than one race. The CPS in prior years allowed respondents to report only one race group. See also comments on race in the text for Section 1, Population.   [9] Data have been revised to reflect a correction to the weights in the 2005 Annual Social and Economic Supplement (ASEC).

Source: U.S. Census Bureau, *Current Population Reports*, P60-233; and Internet sites <http://www.census.gov/prod/2007pubs/p60-233.pdf> (released August 2007) and <http://www.census.gov/hhes/www/poverty/histpov/hstpov4.html>.

Table 694. **Families Below Poverty Level by Selected Characteristics: 2006**

[7,668 represents 7,668,000. **Families as of March 2007.** Based on Current Population Survey (CPS); see text, this section, Section 1, and Appendix III. The 2007 CPS allowed respondents to choose more than one race. For 2006, data represent persons who selected this race group only and exclude persons reporting more than one race. See also comments on race in the text for Section 1. For composition of regions, see map, inside front cover]

Characteristic	Number below poverty level (1,000)					Percent below poverty level				
	All races [1]	White alone	Black alone	Asian alone	His-panic [2]	All races [1]	White alone	Black alone	Asian alone	His-panic [2]
Total families	**7,668**	**5,118**	**2,007**	**260**	**1,922**	**9.8**	**8.0**	**21.6**	**7.8**	**18.9**
Age of householder:										
15 to 24 years old	963	641	281	15	196	29.1	25.9	44.7	14.8	26.4
25 to 34 years old	2,155	1,383	657	43	637	15.8	12.9	33.2	6.9	22.5
35 to 44 years old	1,829	1,254	427	70	554	10.1	8.7	18.5	7.2	19.6
45 to 54 years old	1,108	706	306	55	232	6.2	4.8	14.5	7.5	12.3
55 to 64 years old	818	587	159	32	156	6.3	5.3	13.3	6.0	15.1
65 years old and over	752	518	167	43	129	6.1	4.8	16.3	11.8	16.9
Region:										
Northeast	1,274	831	347	79	332	9.0	7.1	21.3	9.9	22.9
Midwest	1,536	1,017	447	30	145	8.7	6.6	26.3	7.5	17.1
South	3,278	2,078	1,054	39	739	11.2	9.1	20.5	6.0	19.9
West	1,579	1,192	160	113	706	9.1	8.3	19.9	7.5	17.1
Type of family:										
Married couple	2,910	2,278	346	178	903	4.9	4.5	7.9	6.5	13.3
Male householder, no spouse present	671	440	177	26	139	13.2	11.5	20.4	11.6	14.7
Female householder, no spouse present	4,087	2,400	1,484	57	881	28.3	25.1	36.6	15.4	36.0

[1] Includes other races not shown separately.   [2] Hispanic persons may be of any race.

Source: U.S. Census Bureau, *Current Population Reports*, P60-233; and Internet site <http://pubdb3.census.gov/macro/032007/pov/toc.htm> (released 28 August 2007).

Table 695. **People and Families With Alternative Definitions of Income Below Poverty: 2006**

[296,450 represents 296,450,000. **People and families as of March 2007**]

Race and Hispanic origin	Number (1,000)	Alternative definitions of income, percent below poverty			
		Money income [1]	Market income [2]	Post-social insurance income [3]	Disposable income [4]
PEOPLE					
Total [5]	**296,450**	**12.2**	**18.5**	**12.5**	**10.2**
White alone or in combination	242,306	10.3	16.6	10.5	8.7
White alone [6]	237,619	10.2	16.5	10.3	8.6
White alone, not Hispanic	196,049	8.1	14.7	8.0	6.9
Black alone or in combination	39,013	23.8	31.3	25.3	19.1
Black alone [7]	37,306	23.9	31.4	25.3	19.2
Asian alone or in combination	14,331	10.3	12.8	10.5	8.9
Asian alone [8]	13,177	10.5	13.2	10.7	9.1
Hispanic [9]	44,784	20.4	25.4	21.9	17.2
FAMILIES					
Total [5]	**78,454**	**10.2**	**16.5**	**10.4**	**8.2**
White alone or in combination	64,963	8.4	14.8	8.5	6.8
White alone [6]	64,120	8.4	14.7	8.4	6.8
White alone, not Hispanic	54,657	6.5	13.0	6.4	5.3
Black alone or in combination	9,504	21.9	29.3	23.4	17.1
Black alone [7]	9,274	22.1	29.5	23.5	17.3
Asian alone or in combination	3,489	8.3	11.1	8.6	7.0
Asian alone [8]	3,346	8.3	11.2	8.5	7.0
Hispanic [9]	10,155	19.6	25.1	21.1	16.2

[1] Money income concept includes all money income received by individuals who are 15 years or older. It consists of income before deductions for taxes and other expenses and does not include lump-sum payments or capital gains. It also does not include the value of noncash benefits such as food stamps. This income concept is the basis for the official U.S. poverty measure.   [2] Market income concept includes money income except government cash transfers; includes imputed realized capital gains and losses; includes imputed rate of return on home equity; and subtracts imputed work expenses.   [3] Post-Social insurance income concept includes money income except government means-tested cash transfers; includes imputed realized capital gains and losses; includes imputed rate of return on home equity; and subtracts imputed work expenses.   [4] Disposable income concept includes money income; includes the value of noncash transfers (food stamps, public or subsidized housing, and free or reduced-price school lunches); includes imputed realized capital gains and losses; includes imputed rate of return on home equity; and subtracts imputed work expenses, federal payroll taxes, federal and state income taxes, and property taxes on owner-occupied homes.   [5] Data for American Indians and Alaska Natives, Asian, and Native Hawaiian and Other Pacific Islanders are not shown separately.   [6] White alone refers to people who reported White and did not report any other race category.   [7] Black alone refers to people who reported Black and did not report any other race category.   [8] Asian alone refers to people who reported Asian and did not report any other race category.   [9] Persons of Hispanic origin may be of any race.

Source: U.S. Census Bureau, *The Effects of Government Taxes and Transfers on Income and Poverty: 2006.* See also <http://pubdb3.census.gov/macro/032007/alttoc/toc.htm> (released 31 December 2007).

Table 696. Top Wealth Holders With Gross Assets of $1.5 Million or More by Type of Property, Sex, and Size of Net Worth: 2004

[2,728 represents 2,728,000. Net worth is defined as assets minus liabilities. Figures are estimates based on a sample of federal estate tax returns (Form 706). Based on the estate multiplier technique; for more information on this methodology, see source]

Sex and net worth	Number of top wealth holders (1,000)	Assets (mil. dol.)				
		Total [1]	Personal residences	Other real estate	Closely held stock	Publicly traded stock
Both sexes, total	**2,728**	**11,076,759**	**1,185,941**	**1,402,029**	**1,127,194**	**2,247,269**
Size of net worth:						
Under $1.5 million [2]	531	736,039	176,105	134,674	42,431	63,062
$1.5 million under $2.0 million	746	1,386,077	229,369	206,626	69,066	219,818
$2.0 million under $3.5 million	846	2,316,701	342,206	329,893	141,272	415,249
$3.5 million under $5.0 million	247	1,082,889	127,444	152,634	95,958	209,459
$5.0 million under $10.0 million	231	1,668,002	148,543	230,146	165,781	373,575
$10.0 million under $20.0 million	79	1,155,326	76,472	137,770	136,144	246,824
$20.0 million or more	47	2,731,726	85,802	210,286	476,542	719,282
Males, total	**1,555**	**6,471,540**	**597,971**	**828,055**	**833,929**	**1,140,665**
Size of net worth:						
Under $1.5 million [2]	389	528,017	117,554	96,796	36,177	42,494
$1.5 million under $2.0 million	359	675,321	97,605	105,224	44,376	94,788
$2.0 million under $3.5 million	465	1,289,522	163,984	179,481	102,116	199,844
$3.5 million under $5.0 million	131	578,304	60,123	80,919	63,006	95,417
$5.0 million under $10.0 million	135	989,077	68,653	151,731	110,961	200,003
$10.0 million under $20.0 million	47	679,613	38,710	75,459	97,601	135,157
$20.0 million or more	30	1,731,686	51,342	138,446	379,692	372,962
Females, total	**1,173**	**4,605,219**	**587,970**	**573,974**	**293,264**	**1,106,604**
Size of net worth:						
Under $1.5 million [2]	143	208,021	58,550	37,879	6,255	20,568
$1.5 million under $2.0 million	387	710,757	131,764	101,402	24,690	125,030
$2.0 million under $3.5 million	380	1,027,179	178,222	150,412	39,155	215,405
$3.5 million under $5.0 million	116	504,585	67,321	71,714	32,953	114,042
$5.0 million under $10.0 million	96	678,924	79,890	78,416	54,820	173,572
$10.0 million under $20.0 million	33	475,713	37,762	62,312	38,543	111,667
$20.0 million or more	18	1,000,040	34,461	71,840	96,849	346,320

[1] Includes other types of assets not shown separately. [2] Includes individuals with zero net worth.

Source: U.S. Internal Revenue Service, Statistics of Income Division, July 2008, unpublished data. See also <http://www.irs.gov/taxstats/indtaxstats/article/0,,id=96426,00.html>.

Table 697. Top Wealth Holders With Net Worth of $1.5 Million or More—Number and Net Worth by State: 2004

[2,196 represents 2,196,000. Estimates based on a sample of federal estate tax returns (Form 706). Estimates of wealth by state can be subject to significant year-to-year fluctuations and this is especially true for individuals at the extreme tail of the net worth distribution and for states with relatively small decedent populations. Based on the estate mulitiplier technique; for more information on this methodology, see source]

State	Number of top wealth holders (1,000)	Net worth (mil. dol.)	State	Number of top wealth holders (1,000)	Net worth (mil. dol.)
Total	**2,196**	**9,721,133**	Montana	7	23,966
Alabama	18	79,123	Nebraska	13	83,265
Alaska	1	4,776	Nevada	15	80,768
Arizona	36	139,861	New Hampshire	7	27,342
Arkansas	11	94,704	New Jersey	79	324,712
California	428	1,793,642	New Mexico	9	28,107
Colorado	32	163,324	New York	168	942,812
Connecticut	47	197,801	North Carolina	59	223,408
Delaware	8	30,923	North Dakota	1	3,988
District of Columbia	7	27,850	Ohio	61	228,532
Florida	199	904,014	Oklahoma	17	58,554
Georgia	56	270,677	Oregon	15	61,328
Hawaii	7	22,552	Pennsylvania	86	399,312
Idaho	5	23,982	Rhode Island	8	30,782
Illinois	101	476,354	South Carolina	14	67,856
Indiana	32	112,272	South Dakota	6	18,850
Iowa	18	55,332	Tennessee	25	100,778
Kansas	21	65,084	Texas	108	492,663
Kentucky	18	65,404	Utah	8	52,674
Louisiana	22	92,315	Vermont	4	20,584
Maine	8	35,173	Virginia	59	223,984
Maryland	50	191,279	Washington	50	180,008
Massachusetts	83	335,482	West Virginia	12	28,415
Michigan	47	261,085	Wisconsin	26	127,515
Minnesota	33	135,682	Wyoming	5	106,698
Mississippi	8	61,786			
Missouri	33	115,716	Other areas [1]	5	28,042

[1] Includes U.S. territories and possessions.

Source: U.S. Internal Revenue Service, Statistics of Income Division, July 2008, unpublished data. See also <http://www.irs.gov/taxstats/indtaxstats/article/0,,id=96426,00.html>.

Table 698. **Nonfinancial Assets Held by Families by Type of Asset: 2004**

[**172.9 represents $172,900.** Families include one-person units and, as used in this table, are comparable to the U.S. Census Bureau household concept. For definition of family, see text, Section 1. Based on Survey of Consumer Finance; see Appendix III. For data on financial assets, see Table 1133. For definition of median, see Guide to Tabular Presentation]

Family characteristic	Any financial or non-financial asset	Any non-financial asset	Vehicles	Primary residence	Other residential property	Equity in nonresidential property	Business equity	Other
PERCENT OF FAMILIES HOLDING ASSET								
All families, total	**97.9**	**92.5**	**86.3**	**69.1**	**12.5**	**8.3**	**11.5**	**7.8**
Age of family head:								
Under 35 years old	96.5	88.6	82.9	41.6	5.1	3.3	6.9	5.5
35 to 44 years old	97.7	93.0	89.4	68.3	9.4	6.4	13.9	6.0
45 to 54 years old	98.3	94.7	88.8	77.3	16.3	11.4	15.7	9.7
55 to 64 years old	97.5	92.6	88.6	79.1	19.5	12.8	15.8	9.2
65 to 74 years old	99.5	95.6	89.1	81.3	19.9	10.6	8.0	9.0
75 years old and over	99.6	92.5	76.9	85.2	9.7	7.7	5.3	8.5
Race or ethnicity of respondent:								
White non-Hispanic	99.3	95.8	90.3	76.1	14.0	9.2	13.6	9.3
Non-White or Hispanic	94.4	84.0	76.1	50.8	8.9	5.8	5.9	3.8
Tenure:								
Owner-occupied	100.0	100.0	92.3	100.0	15.7	11.0	14.7	9.2
Renter-occupied or other	93.3	75.9	73.0	(X)	5.4	2.4	4.3	4.6
MEDIAN VALUE [1] **($1,000)**								
All families, total	**172.9**	**147.8**	**14.2**	**160.0**	**100.0**	**60.0**	**100.0**	**15.0**
Age of family head:								
Under 35 years old	39.2	32.3	11.3	135.0	82.5	55.0	50.0	5.0
35 to 44 years old	173.4	151.3	15.6	160.0	80.0	42.2	100.0	10.0
45 to 54 years old	234.9	184.5	18.8	170.0	90.0	43.0	144.0	20.0
55 to 64 years old	351.2	226.3	18.6	200.0	135.0	75.0	190.9	25.0
65 to 74 years old	233.2	161.1	12.4	150.0	80.0	78.0	100.0	30.0
75 years old and over	185.2	137.1	8.4	125.0	150.0	85.8	80.3	11.0
Race or ethnicity of respondent:								
White non-Hispanic	224.5	164.8	15.7	165.0	105.0	66.0	135.0	16.5
Non-White or Hispanic	59.6	64.1	9.8	130.0	80.0	30.0	66.7	10.0
Tenure:								
Owner-occupied	289.9	201.6	17.5	160.0	100.0	62.0	122.8	17.5
Renter-occupied or other	12.2	8.4	7.2	(X)	80.0	56.0	50.0	8.0

X Not applicable.   [1] Median value of asset for families holding such assets.

Source: Board of Governors of the Federal Reserve System, "2004 Survey of Consumer Finances"; published 28 February 2006; <http://www.federalreserve.gov/pubs/oss/oss2/2004/scf2004home.html>.

Table 699. **Family Net Worth—Mean and Median Net Worth in Constant (2004) Dollars by Selected Family Characteristics: 1995 to 2004**

[**Net worth in thousands of constant (2004) dollars (260.8 represents $260,800).** Constant dollar figures are based on consumer price index for all urban consumers published by U.S. Bureau of Labor Statistics. Families include one-person units and as used in this table are comparable to the U.S. Census Bureau household concept. Based on Survey of Consumer Finance; see Appendix III. For definition of mean and median, see Guide to Tabular Presentation]

Family characteristic	1995 Mean	1995 Median	1998 Mean	1998 Median	2001 Mean	2001 Median	2004 Mean	2004 Median
All families	**260.8**	**70.8**	**327.5**	**83.1**	**422.9**	**92.2**	**448.2**	**93.1**
Age of family head:								
Under 35 years old	53.2	14.8	74.0	10.6	96.6	12.5	73.5	14.2
35 to 44 years old	176.8	64.2	227.6	73.5	276.6	82.6	299.2	69.4
45 to 54 years old	364.8	116.8	420.2	122.3	517.6	141.6	542.7	144.7
55 to 64 years old	471.1	141.9	617.0	148.2	779.5	197.4	843.8	248.7
65 to 74 years old	429.3	136.6	541.1	169.8	722.6	189.4	690.9	190.1
75 years old and over	317.9	114.5	360.3	145.6	499.6	165.4	528.1	163.1
Race or ethnicity of respondent:								
White non-Hispanic	308.7	94.3	391.1	111.0	520.2	130.2	561.8	140.7
Non-White or Hispanic	94.9	19.5	116.5	19.3	125.1	19.1	153.1	24.8
Tenure:								
Owner-occupied	373.7	128.1	468.7	153.2	596.9	183.8	624.9	184.4
Renter-occupied or other	53.8	6.0	50.4	4.9	58.6	5.1	54.1	4.0

Source: Board of Governors of the Federal Reserve System, "2004 Survey of Consumer Finances"; published 28 February 2006; <http://www.federalreserve.gov/pubs/oss/oss2/2004/scf2004home.html>.

U.S. Census Bureau, Statistical Abstract of the United States: 2009

Table 700. Household and Nonprofit Organization Sector Balance Sheet: 1990 to 2007

[In billions of dollars (23,968 represents $23,968,000,000,000). As of December 31. For details of financial assets and liabilities, see Table 1132]

Item	1990	1995	2000	2002	2003	2004	2005	2006	2007
Assets	**23,968**	**32,792**	**49,055**	**47,901**	**53,962**	**59,128**	**63,971**	**69,255**	**72,093**
Tangible assets [1]	9,355	11,234	15,770	18,336	19,914	22,032	24,427	26,037	26,760
Real estate	7,381	8,758	12,610	14,895	16,350	18,268	20,486	21,932	22,483
Households [2]	6,580	7,975	11,374	13,585	14,937	16,702	18,695	19,887	20,155
Consumer durable goods	1,899	2,371	3,015	3,273	3,380	3,565	3,727	3,875	4,035
Financial assets [1]	14,613	21,558	33,285	29,564	34,048	37,096	39,544	43,218	45,333
Deposits [1]	3,300	3,327	4,350	5,129	5,328	5,706	6,088	6,733	7,389
Time and savings deposits	2,485	2,306	3,062	3,656	3,986	4,451	4,921	5,428	5,880
Money market fund shares	391	472	960	1,072	960	904	949	1,114	1,344
Credit market instruments [1]	1,768	2,297	2,556	2,646	2,930	3,213	3,450	3,667	3,977
Agency and GSE-backed securities [3]	114	218	604	298	432	398	496	518	947
Municipal securities	648	533	531	679	704	743	821	866	916
Corporate and foreign bonds	245	508	618	1,137	1,108	1,255	1,286	1,469	1,505
Corporate equities	1,961	4,434	8,199	4,623	5,767	5,938	5,875	6,178	5,447
Mutual fund shares	512	1,253	2,704	2,218	2,904	3,417	3,840	4,536	5,082
Security credit	62	128	412	413	475	578	575	656	853
Life insurance reserves	392	566	819	921	1,013	1,060	1,083	1,164	1,205
Pension fund reserves	3,330	5,737	9,188	8,220	9,744	10,655	11,391	12,324	12,780
Equity in noncorporate business	3,033	3,487	4,677	4,959	5,397	5,986	6,651	7,330	7,892
Liabilities [1]	**3,718**	**5,059**	**7,398**	**8,834**	**9,857**	**11,035**	**12,191**	**13,454**	**14,375**
Credit market instruments [1]	3,596	4,862	7,009	8,514	9,497	10,575	11,754	12,948	13,825
Home mortgages	2,504	3,333	4,818	6,034	6,882	7,838	8,866	9,854	10,509
Consumer credit	824	1,168	1,741	2,000	2,104	2,219	2,314	2,418	2,551
Net worth	**20,250**	**27,732**	**41,656**	**39,066**	**44,105**	**48,093**	**51,780**	**55,800**	**57,718**
Replacement cost value of structures:									
Residential [1]	4,624	6,105	8,468	9,766	10,657	11,998	13,219	13,956	14,327
Households	4,367	5,817	8,106	9,369	10,239	11,545	12,737	13,462	13,832
Nonresidential (nonprofits)	472	591	813	907	958	1,062	1,172	1,285	1,324
Owners' equity in household real estate	4,077	4,643	6,556	7,551	8,055	8,864	9,829	10,033	9,646
Owners' equity as percentage of household real estate	62.0	58.2	57.6	55.6	53.9	53.1	52.6	50.5	47.9

[1] Includes types of assets and/or liabilities not shown separately. [2] At market value. All types of owner-occupied housing including farm houses and mobile homes, as well as second homes that are not rented, vacant homes for sale, and vacant land. [3] GSE = Government-sponsored enterprises.

Source: Board of Governors of the Federal Reserve System, "Federal Reserve Statistical Release, Z.1, Flow of Funds Accounts of the United States"; published: 6 March 2008; <http://www.federalreserve.gov/releases/z1/20080306/>.

Table 701. Net Stock of Fixed Reproducible Tangible Wealth in Current and Real (2000) Dollars: 1990 to 2006

[In billions of dollars (18,111 represents $18,111,000,000,000). As of December 31. For explanation of chained dollars, see text, this section]

Item	1990	1995	2000	2001	2002	2003	2004	2005	2006
CURRENT DOLLARS									
Net stock, total	**18,111**	**22,670**	**29,917**	**31,609**	**33,061**	**34,805**	**38,202**	**41,584**	**44,432**
Fixed assets	16,212	20,299	26,902	28,465	29,788	31,424	34,637	37,857	40,557
Private	12,611	15,794	21,190	22,485	23,523	24,917	27,423	29,937	31,819
Nonresidential	6,500	7,954	10,514	11,020	11,330	11,692	12,620	13,691	14,715
Equipment and software	2,469	3,067	4,077	4,203	4,271	4,381	4,549	4,750	5,028
Information processing equipment and software	622	811	1,238	1,294	1,319	1,350	1,390	1,455	1,543
Structures	4,031	4,887	6,437	6,817	7,059	7,311	8,071	8,942	9,687
Residential	6,111	7,840	10,676	11,465	12,193	13,225	14,803	16,245	17,104
Housing units	4,955	6,354	8,663	9,320	9,922	10,771	12,079	13,260	13,939
Government	3,601	4,505	5,713	5,980	6,266	6,508	7,214	7,920	8,739
Nonresidential	3,452	4,317	5,481	5,733	6,002	6,228	6,918	7,588	8,397
Equipment and software	551	675	703	711	723	738	784	817	857
Structures	2,900	3,642	4,778	5,022	5,279	5,490	6,134	6,772	7,541
Residential	149	188	232	247	264	280	296	332	341
Federal	1,079	1,291	1,425	1,447	1,470	1,499	1,591	1,694	1,829
Defense	735	865.3	896	904	914	928	983	1,041	1,120
State and local	2,522	3,213	4,288	4,533	4,796	5,009	5,623	6,227	6,909
Consumer durable goods	1,899	2,371	3,015	3,144	3,273	3,380	3,565	3,727	3,875
Motor vehicles and parts	670	842	1,092	1,156	1,214	1,256	1,326	1,372	1,381
Furniture and household equipment	814	1,011	1,260	1,292	1,335	1,366	1,439	1,507	1,585
Other	415	518	662	696	725	759	800	848	909
CHAINED (2000) DOLLARS									
Net stock, total	**22,580**	**25,156**	**29,528**	**30,393**	**31,189**	**32,004**	**32,865**	**33,721**	**34,654**
Fixed assets	20,726	22,939	26,498	27,170	27,759	28,368	29,025	29,688	30,438
Private	16,029	17,804	20,880	21,438	21,901	22,384	22,915	23,464	24,087
Nonresidential	7,809	8,638	10,392	10,669	10,841	10,986	11,147	11,337	11,581
Equipment and software	2,532	2,972	4,091	4,249	4,343	4,422	4,523	4,670	4,842
Structures	5,347	5,702	6,302	6,422	6,499	6,568	6,632	6,688	6,777
Residential	8,223	9,174	10,488	10,769	11,068	11,401	11,763	12,115	12,489
Government	4,700	5,137	5,618	5,731	5,857	5,984	6,110	6,222	6,347
Nonresidential	4,507	4,926	5,390	5,501	5,623	5,747	5,869	5,978	6,101
Equipment and software	631	686	706	714	727	739	757	778	802
Structures	3,872	4,237	4,684	4,786	4,896	5,007	5,112	5,201	5,302
Residential	201	220	227	231	234	238	241	244	246
Consumer durable goods	1,903	2,242	3,030	3,228	3,441	3,662	3,886	4,107	4,319

Source: U.S. Bureau of Economic Analysis, *Survey of Current Business,* September 2007, and <http://www.bea.gov/bea/dn/FA2004/SelectTable.asp> (released 8 August 2007).

Section 14
Prices

This section presents indexes of producer and consumer prices, actual prices for selected commodities, and energy prices. The primary sources of these data are monthly publications of the U.S. Department of Labor, Bureau of Labor Statistics (BLS), which include *Monthly Labor Review, Consumer Price Index, Detailed Report, Producer Price Indexes,* and *U.S. Import and Export Price Indexes.* The U.S. Department of Commerce, Bureau of Economic Analysis is the source for gross domestic product measures. Cost of living data for many urban and metropolitan areas are provided by the ACCRA, a private organization in Alexandria, VA. Table 707 on housing price indexes appears in this edition from the Office of Federal Housing Enterprise Oversight, *Housing Price Index.* Other commodity, housing, and energy prices may be found in the Energy and Utilities, Natural Resources, and Construction and Housing sections.

Consumer price indexes (CPI)—The CPI is a measure of the average change in prices over time in a "market basket" of goods and services purchased either by urban wage earners and clerical workers or by all urban consumers. In 1919, BLS began to publish complete indexes at semiannual intervals, using a weighting structure based on data collected in the expenditure survey of wage-earner and clerical-worker families in 1917–19 (BLS Bulletin 357, 1924). The first major revision of the CPI occurred in 1940, with subsequent revisions in 1953, 1964, 1978, 1987, and 1998.

Beginning with the release of data for January 1988 in February 1988, most consumer price indexes shifted to a new reference base year. All indexes previously expressed on a base of 1967 = 100, or any other base through December 1981, have been rebased to 1982–84 = 100. The expenditure weights are based upon data tabulated from the Consumer Expenditure Surveys.

BLS publishes CPIs for two population groups: (1) a CPI for all urban consumers (CPI-U), which covers approximately 80 percent of the total population; and (2) a CPI for urban wage earners and clerical workers (CPI-W), which covers 32 percent of the total population. The CPI-U includes, in addition to wage earners and clerical workers, groups which historically have been excluded from CPI coverage, such as professional, managerial, and technical workers; the self-employed; short-term workers; the unemployed; and retirees and others not in the labor force.

The current CPI is based on prices of food, clothing, shelter, fuels, transportation fares, charges for doctors' and dentists' services, drugs, etc. purchased for day-to-day living. Prices are collected in 87 areas across the country from over 50,000 housing units and 23,000 establishments. Area selection was based on the 1990 census. All taxes directly associated with the purchase and use of items are included in the index. Prices of food, fuels, and a few other items are obtained every month in all 87 locations. Prices of most other commodities and services are collected monthly in the three largest geographic areas and every other month in other areas.

In calculating the index, each item is assigned a weight to account for its relative importance in consumers' budgets. Price changes for the various items in each location are then averaged. Local data are then combined to obtain a U.S. city average. Separate indexes are also published for regions, area size-classes, cross-classifications of regions and size-classes, and for 26 local areas, usually consisting of the Metropolitan Statistical Area (MSA); see Appendix II. Area definitions are those established by the Office of Management and Budget in 1983. Definitions do not include revisions made since 1992. Area indexes do not measure differences in the level of prices among cities; they only measure the average

U.S. Census Bureau, Statistical Abstract of the United States: 2009

change in prices for each area since the base period. For further detail regarding the CPI, see the BLS *Handbook of Methods,* Bulletin 2490 (June 2008), Chapter 17; the *Consumer Price Index,* and the CPI home page: <http://www.bls.gov/cpi/>. In January 1983, the method of measuring homeownership costs in the CPI-U was changed to a rental equivalence approach. This treatment calculates homeowner costs of shelter based on the implicit rent owners would pay to rent the homes they own. The rental equivalence approach was introduced into the CPI-W in 1985. The CPI-U was used to prepare the consumer price tables in this section.

Producer price index (PPI)—This index, dating from 1890, is the oldest continuous statistical series published by BLS. It is designed to measure average changes in prices received by domestic producers of all commodities, at various stages of processing.

The index has undergone several revisions (see *Monthly Labor Review,* February 1962, April 1978, and August 1988). It is now based on approximately 10,000 individual products and groups of products along with about 100,000 quotations per month. Indexes for the net output of manufacturing and mining industries have been added in recent years. Prices used in constructing the index are collected from sellers and generally apply to the first significant large-volume commercial transaction for each commodity—i.e., the manufacturer's or other producer's selling price or the selling price on an organized exchange or at a central market.

The weights used in the index represent the total net selling value of commodities produced or processed in this country. Values are f.o.b. (free on board) production point and are exclusive of excise taxes. Effective with the release of data for January 1988, many important producer price indexes were changed to a new reference base year, 1982 = 100, from 1967 = 100. The reference year of the PPI shipment weights has been taken primarily from the 2002 Census of Manufactures. For further detail regarding the PPI, see the BLS *Handbook of Methods,* Bulletin 2490 (June 2008), Chapter 14. The PPI Web page is <http://www.bls.gov/ppi/>.

BEA price indexes—Chain-weighted price indexes, produced by the Bureau of Economic Analysis (BEA), are weighted averages of the detailed price indexes used in the deflation of the goods and services that make up the gross domestic product (GDP) and its major components. Growth rates are constructed for years and quarters using quantity weights for the current and preceding year or quarter; these growth rates are used to move the index for the preceding period forward a year or quarter at a time. All chain-weighted price indexes are expressed in terms of the reference year value 2000 = 100.

Personal consumption expenditures (PCE) price and quantity indexes are based on market transactions for which there are corresponding price measures. The price index provides a measure of the prices paid by persons for domestic purchases of goods and services, which may be a useful measure of consumer prices for some analytical purposes. PCEs are defined as market value of spending by individuals and not-for-profit institutions on all goods and services. Personal consumption expenditures also include the value of certain imputed goods and services—such as the rental value of owner-occupied homes and compensation paid in kind—such as employer-paid health and life insurance premiums. More information on this index may be found at <http://www.bea.gov/bea/mp_National.htm>.

Measures of inflation—Inflation is defined as a time of generally rising prices for goods and factors of production. The BLS samples prices of items in a representative market basket and publishes the result as the CPI. The media invariably announce the inflation rate as the percent change in the CPI from month to month. A much more meaningful indicator of inflation is the percent change from the same month of the prior year. The PPI measures prices at the producer level only. The PPI shows the same general pattern of inflation as does the CPI but is more volatile. The PPI can be

462   Prices

roughly viewed as a leading indicator. It often tends to foreshadow trends that later occur in the CPI.

Other measures of inflation include the gross domestic purchases chain-weighted price index, the index of industrial materials prices; the Futures Price and Spot Market prices from the Commodity Research Bureau; the Employment Cost Index, the Hourly Compensation Index, or the Unit Labor Cost Index found in Section 12 on Labor Force, Employment, and Earnings, as a measure of the change in cost of the labor factor of production; and changes in long-term interest rates that are often used to measure changes in the cost of the capital factor of production.

International price indexes—The BLS International Price Program produces export and import price indexes for non-military goods traded between the United States and the rest of the world.

The export price index provides a measure of price change for all products sold by U.S. residents to foreign buyers. The

import price index provides a measure of price change for goods purchased from other countries by U.S. residents. The reference period for the indexes is 2000 = 100, unless otherwise indicated. The product universe for both the import and export indexes includes raw materials, agricultural products, semifinished manufactures, and finished manufactures, including both capital and consumer goods. Price data for these items are collected primarily by mail questionnaire. In nearly all cases, the data are collected directly from the exporter or importer, although in a few cases, prices are obtained from other sources.

To the extent possible, the data gathered refer to prices at the U.S. border for exports and at either the foreign border or the U.S. border for imports. For nearly all products, the prices refer to transactions completed during the first week of the month. Survey respondents are asked to indicate all discounts, allowances, and rebates applicable to the reported prices, so that the price used in the calculation of the indexes is the actual price for which the product was bought or sold.

Table 702. **Purchasing Power of the Dollar: 1950 to 2007**

[Indexes: PPI, 1982 = $1.00; CPI, 1982–84 = $1.00. Producer prices prior to 1961, and consumer prices prior to 1964, exclude Alaska and Hawaii. Producer prices based on finished goods index. Obtained by dividing the average price index for the 1982 = 100, PPI; 1982–84 = 100, CPI base periods (100.0) by the price index for a given period and expressing the result in dollars and cents. Annual figures are based on average of monthly data]

Year	Annual average as measured by—		Year	Annual average as measured by—	
	Producer prices	Consumer prices		Producer prices	Consumer prices
1950	3.546	4.151	1979	1.289	1.380
1951	3.247	3.846	1980	1.136	1.215
1952	3.268	3.765	1981	1.041	1.098
1953	3.300	3.735	1982	1.000	1.035
1954	3.289	3.717	1983	0.984	1.003
			1984	0.964	0.961
1955	3.279	3.732			
1956	3.195	3.678	1985	0.955	0.928
1957	3.077	3.549	1986	0.969	0.913
1958	3.012	3.457	1987	0.949	0.880
1959	3.021	3.427	1988	0.926	0.846
			1989	0.880	0.807
1960	2.994	3.373			
1961	2.994	3.340	1990	0.839	0.766
1962	2.985	3.304	1991	0.822	0.734
1963	2.994	3.265	1992	0.812	0.713
1964	2.985	3.220	1993	0.802	0.692
			1994	0.797	0.675
1965	2.933	3.166			
1966	2.841	3.080	1995	0.782	0.656
1967	2.809	2.993	1996	0.762	0.638
1968	2.732	2.873	1997	0.759	0.623
1969	2.632	2.726	1998	0.765	0.613
			1999	0.752	0.600
1970	2.545	2.574			
1971	2.469	2.466	2000	0.725	0.581
1972	2.392	2.391	2001	0.711	0.565
1973	2.193	2.251	2002	0.720	0.556
1974	1.901	2.029	2003	0.698	0.543
			2004	0.673	0.529
1975	1.718	1.859			
1976	1.645	1.757	2005	0.642	0.512
1977	1.546	1.649	2006	0.623	0.496
1978	1.433	1.532	2007 [1]	0.600	0.482

[1] PPI data are preliminary.

Source: U.S. Bureau of Labor Statistics. *CPI Detailed Report*, monthly, and at <http://www.bls.gov/cpi/cpi_dr.htm>. See also *Monthly Labor Review* at <http://www.bls.gov/opub/mlr/welcome.htm> and *Producer Price Indexes*, monthly and annual.

U.S. Census Bureau, Statistical Abstract of the United States: 2009

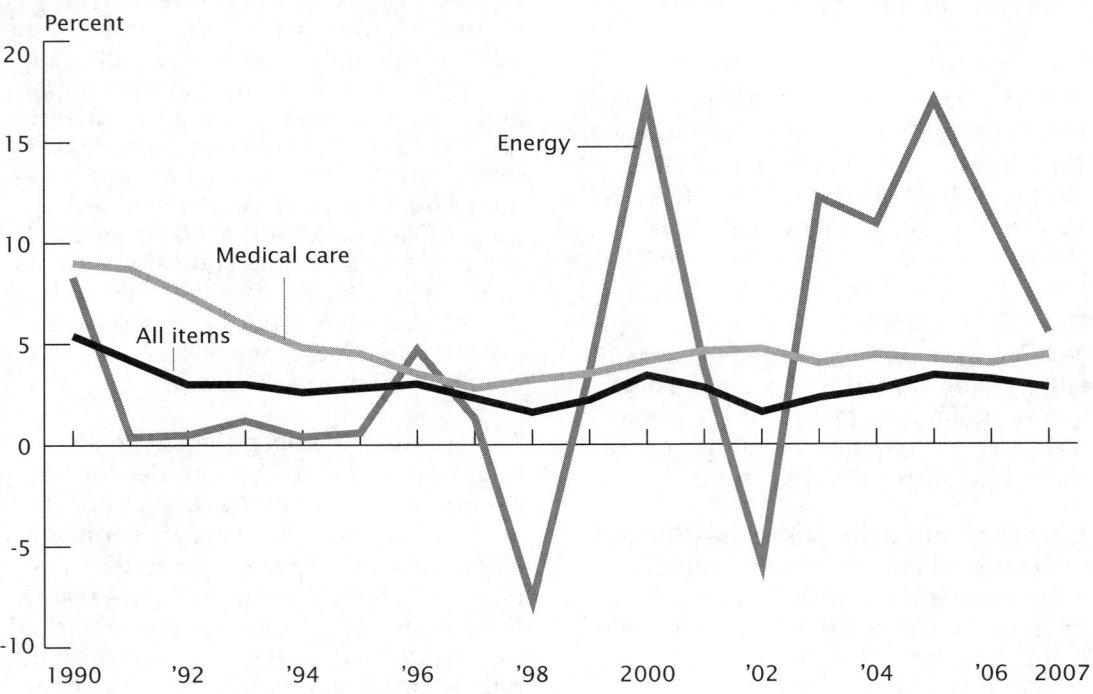

Figure 14.1
Annual Percent Change in Consumer Price Indexes: 1990 to 2007

Percent

Energy

Medical care

All items

Source: Chart prepared by U.S. Census Bureau. For data, see Table 703.

Figure 14.2
Percent Change[1] in Single-Family Housing Price Indexes: 2006 to 2007

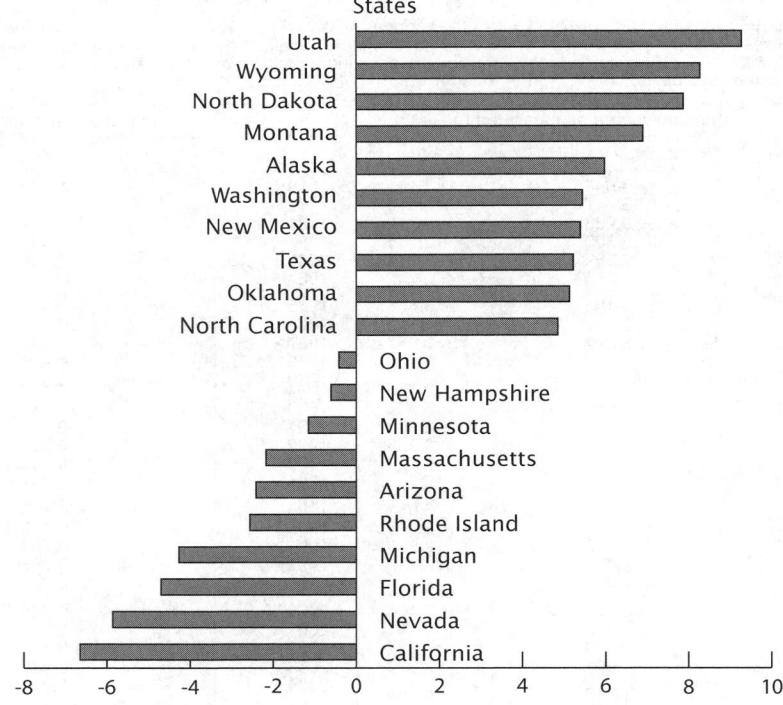

States

[1]Based on fourth quarter home values in 2006 and 2007.

Source: Chart prepared by U.S. Census Bureau. For data, see Table 707.

Table 703. Consumer Price Indexes (CPI-U) by Major Groups: 1990 to 2007

[1982–84 = 100, except as indicated. Represents annual averages of monthly figures. Reflects buying patterns of all urban consumers. Minus sign (–) indicates decrease. See text, this section]

Year	All items	Commodities	Services	Food	Energy	All items less food and energy	Food and beverages	Housing	Apparel	Transportation	Medical care	Education and communication [1]
1990	130.7	122.8	139.2	132.4	102.1	135.5	132.1	128.5	124.1	120.5	162.8	(NA)
1993	144.5	131.5	157.9	140.9	104.2	152.2	141.6	141.2	133.7	130.4	201.4	85.5
1994	148.2	133.8	163.1	144.3	104.6	156.5	144.9	144.8	133.4	134.3	211.0	88.8
1995	152.4	136.4	168.7	148.4	105.2	161.2	148.9	148.5	132.0	139.1	220.5	92.2
1996	156.9	139.9	174.1	153.3	110.1	165.6	153.7	152.8	131.7	143.0	228.2	95.3
1997	160.5	141.8	179.4	157.3	111.5	169.5	157.7	156.8	132.9	144.3	234.6	98.4
1998	163.0	141.9	184.2	160.7	102.9	173.4	161.1	160.4	133.0	141.6	242.1	100.3
1999	166.6	144.4	188.8	164.1	106.6	177.0	164.6	163.9	131.3	144.4	250.6	101.2
2000	172.2	149.2	195.3	167.8	124.6	181.3	168.4	169.6	129.6	153.3	260.8	102.5
2001	177.1	150.7	203.4	173.1	129.3	186.1	173.6	176.4	127.3	154.3	272.8	105.2
2002	179.9	149.7	209.8	176.2	121.7	190.5	176.8	180.3	124.0	152.9	285.6	107.9
2003	184.0	151.2	216.5	180.0	136.5	193.2	180.5	184.8	120.9	157.6	297.1	109.8
2004	188.9	154.7	222.8	186.2	151.4	196.6	186.6	189.5	120.4	163.1	310.1	111.6
2005	195.3	160.2	230.1	190.7	177.1	200.9	191.2	195.7	119.5	173.9	323.2	113.7
2006	201.6	164.0	238.9	195.2	196.9	205.9	195.7	203.2	119.5	180.9	336.2	116.8
2007	207.3	167.5	246.8	202.9	207.7	210.7	203.3	209.6	119.0	184.7	351.1	119.6
PERCENT CHANGE [2]												
1990	5.4	5.2	5.5	5.8	8.3	5.0	5.8	4.5	4.6	5.6	9.0	(NA)
1993	3.0	1.9	3.9	2.2	1.2	3.3	2.1	2.7	1.4	3.1	5.9	(NA)
1994	2.6	1.7	3.3	2.4	0.4	2.8	2.3	2.5	–0.2	3.0	4.8	3.9
1995	2.8	1.9	3.4	2.8	0.6	3.0	2.8	2.6	–1.0	3.6	4.5	3.8
1996	3.0	2.6	3.2	3.3	4.7	2.7	3.2	2.9	–0.2	2.8	3.5	3.4
1997	2.3	1.4	3.0	2.6	1.3	2.4	2.6	2.6	0.9	0.9	2.8	3.3
1998	1.6	0.1	2.7	2.2	–7.7	2.3	2.2	2.3	0.1	–1.9	3.2	1.9
1999	2.2	1.8	2.5	2.1	3.6	2.1	2.2	2.2	–1.3	2.0	3.5	0.9
2000	3.4	3.3	3.4	2.3	16.9	2.4	2.3	3.5	–1.3	6.2	4.1	1.3
2001	2.8	1.0	4.1	3.2	3.8	2.6	3.1	4.0	–1.8	0.7	4.6	2.6
2002	1.6	–0.7	3.1	1.8	–5.9	2.4	1.8	2.2	–2.6	–0.9	4.7	2.6
2003	2.3	1.0	3.2	2.2	12.2	1.4	2.1	2.5	–2.5	3.1	4.0	1.8
2004	2.7	2.3	2.9	3.4	10.9	1.8	3.4	2.5	–0.4	3.5	4.4	1.6
2005	3.4	3.6	3.3	2.4	17.0	2.2	2.5	3.3	–0.7	6.6	4.2	1.9
2006	3.2	2.4	3.8	2.4	11.2	2.5	2.4	3.8	–	4.0	4.0	2.7
2007	2.8	2.1	3.3	4.0	5.5	2.3	3.9	3.1	–0.4	2.1	4.4	2.4

– Represents zero.   NA Not available.   [1] Dec. 1997 = 100.   [2] Change from immediate prior year. 1990 change from 1989.
Source: U.S. Bureau of Labor Statistics, *CPI Detailed Report,* monthly, and at <http://www.bls.gov/cpi/cpi_dr.htm>. See also *Monthly Labor Review* at <http://www.bls.gov/opub/mlr/welcome.htm>.

Table 704. Annual Percent Changes From Prior Year in Consumer Price Indexes (CPI-U)—Selected Areas: 2007

[Percent changes computed from annual averages of monthly figures published by source. Local area CPI indexes are by-products of the national CPI program. Each local index has a smaller sample size than the national index and is therefore subject to substantially more sampling and other measurement error. As a result, local area indexes show greater volatility than the national index, although their long-term trends are similar. Area definitions are those established by the Office of Management and Budget in 1983. For further detail, see the U.S. Bureau of Labor Statistics Handbook of Methods, Bulletin 2285, Chapter 19, the Consumer Price Index, and Report 736, the CPI: 1987 Revision. Minus sign (–) indicates decrease. See also text, this section and Appendix III]

Area	All items	Food and beverages	Food	Housing	Apparel	Transportation	Medical care	Fuel and other utilities
U.S. city average	**2.8**	**3.9**	**4.0**	**3.1**	**–0.4**	**2.1**	**4.4**	**3.0**
Anchorage, AK MSA	2.2	4.6	4.8	2.7	–2.8	1.2	3.0	12.7
Atlanta, GA MSA	3.2	2.8	3.0	4.2	8.9	2.9	–3.2	3.2
Boston, MA MSA	1.9	3.6	3.5	1.5	2.0	0.7	5.4	0.2
Chicago-Gary, IL-IN CMSA	3.3	3.2	3.3	4.2	–2.1	3.4	3.9	14.2
Cincinnati-Hamilton, OH-KY-IN CMSA	2.8	3.6	3.0	2.1	2.2	3.2	4.9	4.3
Cleveland-Akron-Lorain, OH CMSA	2.5	3.2	3.3	1.6	–1.5	3.7	7.4	–1.6
Dallas-Fort Worth, TX CMSA	1.7	4.3	4.4	0.8	–3.2	1.3	3.1	–0.7
Denver-Boulder-Greely, CO CMSA	2.2	4.1	4.3	0.9	–3.3	2.8	6.5	–5.1
Detroit-Ann Arbor-Flint, MI CMSA	1.8	3.1	3.2	0.7	–1.9	3.1	7.1	–1.7
Honolulu, HI MSA.	4.8	5.5	5.6	7.2	–0.2	1.4	(NA)	5.3
Houston-Galveston-Brazoria, TX CMSA	1.8	3.6	3.5	0.5	–1.2	0.6	7.5	–3.9
Kansas City, MO-KS CMSA	2.3	3.3	3.5	2.5	1.5	2.8	1.4	5.5
Los Angeles-Anaheim-Riverside, CA CMSA . . .	3.3	3.7	3.7	5.1	–1.5	0.9	3.6	0.8
Miami-Fort Lauderdale, FL CMSA	4.2	3.6	3.7	5.9	0.8	2.3	1.6	–2.0
Milwaukee, WI PMSA	2.2	3.5	3.5	1.5	2.9	3.5	3.0	1.0
Minneapolis-St. Paul, MN-WI MSA	2.6	3.6	3.6	1.9	3.2	2.0	7.4	1.5
New York-Northern New Jersey-Long Island, NY-NJ-CT CMSA	2.8	3.9	4.0	3.5	–1.9	1.2	5.5	5.4
Philadelphia-Wilmington-Trenton, PA-NJ-DE-MD CMSA. . .	2.2	3.3	3.5	2.7	–1.7	0.4	3.3	4.0
Pittsburgh, PA MSA	3.0	5.3	5.8	2.7	5.2	2.7	3.6	4.8
Portland, OR MSA	3.7	3.4	3.4	3.2	0.1	5.0	12.7	6.3
San Diego, CA MSA	2.3	4.1	4.1	2.6	–3.1	1.5	(NA)	0.6
San Francisco-Oakland-San Jose, CA CMSA . .	3.3	4.1	4.1	3.3	–1.7	3.2	6.8	3.9
Seattle-Tacoma, WA CMSA	4.4	4.2	4.2	4.8	6.1	1.6	4.9	5.7
St. Louis-East St. Louis, MO-IL CMSA	2.0	3.3	3.4	0.8	6.0	1.8	2.2	0.1
Tampa-St. Petersburg-Clearwater, FL MSA . . .	5.2	4.9	5.2	5.9	0.6	3.9	14.7	2.8
Washington-Baltimore, DC-MD-VA-WV CMSA	3.6	3.5	3.6	4.8	1.1	2.0	3.4	12.7

NA Not available.
Source: U.S. Bureau of Labor Statistics, *CPI Detailed Report,* monthly, and at <http://www.bls.gov/cpi/cpi_dr.htm>. See also *Monthly Labor Review* at <http://www.bls.gov/opub/mlr/welcome.htm>.

Table 705. Consumer Price Indexes for All Urban Consumers (CPI-U) for Selected Items and Groups: 2000 to 2007

[1982–84 = 100, except as noted. Annual averages of monthly figures. Minus sign (–) indicates a decrease. See headnote, Table 703]

Item	2000	2002	2003	2004	2005	2006	2007	Annual percentage change, 2006–2007
All items	**172.2**	**179.9**	**184.0**	**188.9**	**195.3**	**201.6**	**207.3**	**2.8**
Food and beverages	168.4	176.8	180.5	186.6	191.2	195.7	203.3	3.9
Food	167.8	176.2	180.0	186.2	190.7	195.2	202.9	4.0
Food at home	167.9	175.6	179.4	186.2	189.8	193.1	201.2	4.2
Cereals and bakery products	188.3	198.0	202.8	206.0	209.0	212.8	222.1	4.4
Cereals and cereal products	175.9	181.8	185.2	186.2	186.7	187.3	194.7	3.9
Bakery products	194.1	206.1	211.7	216.2	220.5	226.4	236.6	4.5
Bread [1]	107.4	115.4	118.5	121.1	126.2	130.4	140.1	7.4
Cakes, cupcakes, and cookies	187.9	196.7	202.8	206.4	209.8	214.2	221.7	3.5
Other bakery products	191.5	203.0	207.3	211.8	211.4	215.5	220.5	2.3
Meats, poultry, fish, and eggs	154.5	162.1	169.3	181.7	184.7	186.6	195.6	4.8
Meats, poultry, and fish	155.5	163.2	169.7	182.3	186.7	188.2	195.4	3.8
Meats	150.7	160.3	169.0	183.2	187.5	188.8	195.0	3.3
Beef and veal	148.1	160.6	175.1	195.3	200.4	202.1	211.1	4.4
Uncooked ground beef	125.2	138.1	149.2	166.3	175.1	176.3	184.3	4.5
Uncooked beef steaks [1]	109.1	116.6	127.6	144.7	145.1	146.1	151.8	3.9
Pork	156.5	161.8	164.9	174.2	177.7	177.3	180.9	2.0
Other meats	152.0	161.9	166.0	173.4	177.5	180.7	184.8	2.3
Poultry	159.8	167.0	169.1	181.7	185.3	182.0	191.4	5.1
Chicken [1]	102.5	107.6	108.9	118.2	120.6	117.6	124.4	5.8
Fish and seafood	190.4	188.1	190.0	194.3	200.1	209.5	219.1	4.6
Dairy products	160.7	168.1	167.9	180.2	182.4	181.4	194.8	7.4
Milk [1]	107.8	110.6	111.5	125.0	127.0	125.5	140.1	11.6
Cheese and related products	162.8	170.0	169.4	180.8	183.3	180.8	191.5	5.9
Fruits and vegetables	204.6	220.9	225.9	232.7	241.4	252.9	262.6	3.8
Fresh fruits and vegetables	238.8	258.4	265.3	274.7	285.3	300.4	312.1	3.9
Fresh fruits	258.3	270.2	279.1	286.8	297.4	315.2	329.5	4.5
Fresh vegetables	219.4	245.4	250.5	261.2	271.7	284.3	293.5	3.2
Processed fruits and vegetables [1]	105.6	113.1	114.1	115.5	119.3	122.8	127.2	3.6
Nonalcoholic beverages and beverage materials	137.8	139.2	139.8	140.4	144.4	147.4	153.4	4.1
Juices and nonalcoholic drinks [1]	105.6	107.8	108.0	108.5	110.6	113.2	117.9	4.1
Carbonated drinks	123.4	125.6	125.6	127.9	131.9	134.2	140.1	4.4
Nonfrozen noncarbonated juices and drinks [1]	104.2	106.4	106.5	105.7	106.5	109.5	112.9	3.1
Beverage materials including coffee and tea [1]	97.9	96.3	97.4	97.6	102.4	104.1	108.2	4.0
Other food at home	155.6	160.8	162.6	164.9	167.0	169.6	173.3	2.2
Sugar and sweets	154.0	159.0	162.0	163.2	165.2	171.5	176.8	3.1
Candy and chewing gum [1]	103.8	106.2	107.8	108.4	109.5	112.2	116.1	3.5
Fats and oils	147.4	155.4	157.4	167.8	167.7	168.0	172.9	2.9
Other food	172.2	177.1	178.8	179.7	182.5	185.0	188.2	1.8
Frozen and freeze dried prepared food	148.5	152.6	150.6	152.5	153.2	153.7	156.7	2.0
Snacks	166.3	168.7	173.1	173.7	178.5	181.2	184.9	2.1
Spices, seasonings, condiments, sauces	175.6	184.6	185.5	185.3	188.0	190.3	195.5	2.7
Other miscellaneous food [1]	107.5	109.2	110.3	110.4	111.3	113.9	115.1	1.1
Food away from home	169.0	178.3	182.1	187.5	193.4	199.4	206.7	3.6
Full service meals and snacks [1]	106.8	113.0	115.3	118.4	121.9	125.7	130.2	3.6
Limited service meals and snacks [1]	106.3	112.7	114.9	118.6	122.4	126.0	130.6	3.6
Food at employee sites and schools [1]	104.4	108.2	112.4	115.5	118.6	122.6	126.8	3.4
Other food away from home [1]	109.0	117.7	121.3	125.3	131.3	136.6	144.1	5.5
Alcoholic beverages	174.7	183.6	187.2	192.1	195.9	200.7	207.0	3.2
Alcoholic beverages at home	158.1	164.0	166.5	170.2	172.3	174.9	179.1	2.4
Beer, ale, and other malt beverages at home	156.8	164.7	168.5	174.6	176.4	178.1	184.1	3.4
Wine at home	151.6	152.3	153.1	153.8	156.2	159.8	162.9	1.9
Alcoholic beverages away from home	207.1	222.5	228.6	236.6	244.5	254.6	266.0	4.5
Housing	169.6	180.3	184.8	189.5	195.7	203.2	209.6	3.1
Shelter	193.4	208.1	213.1	218.8	224.4	232.1	240.6	3.7
Rent of primary residence	183.9	199.7	205.5	211.0	217.3	225.1	234.7	4.3
Lodging away from home [1]	117.5	118.3	119.3	125.9	130.3	136.0	142.8	5.0
Other lodging away from home including hotels and motels	252.4	251.4	252.2	265.3	274.2	285.6	299.9	5.0
Owners' equivalent rent of primary residence [2]	198.7	214.7	219.9	224.9	230.2	238.2	246.2	3.4
Tenants' and household insurance [1]	103.7	108.7	114.8	116.2	117.6	116.5	117.0	0.4
Fuels and utilities	137.9	143.6	154.5	161.9	179.0	194.7	200.6	3.0
Household energy	122.8	127.2	138.2	144.4	161.6	177.1	181.7	2.6
Fuel oil and other fuels	129.7	115.5	139.5	160.5	208.6	234.9	251.5	7.0
Fuel oil	130.3	111.5	136.6	160.0	216.4	244.6	262.6	7.4
Propane, kerosene, and firewood [3]	155.5	154.8	181.9	202.1	240.6	268.8	286.0	6.4

See footnotes at end of table.

Table 705. Consumer Price Indexes for All Urban Consumers (CPI-U) for Selected Items and Groups: 2000 to 2007—Con.

[1982–84 = 100, except as noted. Annual averages of monthly figures. See headnote, Table 703]

Item	2000	2002	2003	2004	2005	2006	2007	Annual percentage change, 2006–2007
Gas (piped) and electricity	128.0	134.4	145.0	150.6	166.5	182.1	186.3	2.3
Electricity	128.5	136.2	139.5	142.1	150.8	169.2	175.8	3.9
Utility (piped) gas service	132.0	135.3	166.3	180.1	215.4	220.8	217.7	−1.4
Water and sewer and trash collection services [1]	106.5	113.0	117.2	124.0	130.3	136.8	143.7	5.0
Water and sewerage maintenance	227.5	242.5	251.7	268.1	283.4	297.2	312.6	5.2
Garbage and trash collection [4]	269.8	283.0	291.9	303.3	314.0	330.1	345.6	4.7
Household furnishings and operations	128.2	128.3	126.1	125.5	126.1	127.0	126.9	−0.1
Window and floor coverings and other linens [1]	100.9	96.2	91.5	88.8	87.4	84.2	80.7	−4.1
Furniture and bedding	134.4	129.4	127.7	127.3	125.9	127.0	125.8	−0.9
Bedroom furniture	138.4	135.3	133.9	137.3	142.7	145.4	144.7	−0.5
Living room, kitchen, and dining room furniture [1]	102.4	98.6	97.2	95.9	92.7	92.8	91.6	−1.3
Appliances [1]	96.3	92.7	89.5	85.9	86.9	88.1	89.8	1.9
Other household equipment and furnishings [1]	98.0	93.8	89.3	87.4	85.5	80.4	76.9	−4.3
Clocks, lamps, and decorator items	111.7	103.3	96.2	91.4	88.0	79.6	73.6	−7.5
Tools, hardware, outdoor equipment, and supplies [1]	97.0	95.7	94.0	93.5	94.4	94.6	94.6	−
Tools, hardware, and supplies [1]	97.3	95.5	93.3	94.8	98.1	99.4	99.7	0.3
Outdoor equipment and supplies [1]	96.8	95.7	94.2	92.6	92.4	92.1	92.0	−0.1
Housekeeping supplies	153.4	159.8	157.5	157.4	159.9	166.6	169.4	1.7
Household cleaning products [1]	105.1	109.9	108.2	107.0	107.9	111.6	112.3	0.6
Household paper products [1]	113.8	119.2	117.2	120.8	125.4	132.0	135.6	2.7
Miscellaneous household products [1]	104.3	107.4	106.1	105.3	106.4	111.0	113.6	2.3
Household operations [1]	110.5	119.0	121.8	125.0	130.3	136.6	140.6	2.9
Domestic services [1]	109.7	118.3	121.3	123.8	128.3	133.1	138.1	3.7
Gardening and lawncare services [1]	111.4	118.3	120.2	122.9	127.9	136.6	140.5	2.9
Apparel	129.6	124.0	120.9	120.4	119.5	119.5	119.0	−0.4
Men's and boys' apparel	129.7	121.7	118.0	117.5	116.1	114.1	112.4	−1.5
Men's apparel	133.1	125.7	122.1	121.4	121.4	119.8	118.2	−1.4
Men's shirts and sweaters [1]	98.3	88.8	85.2	85.3	84.2	84.7	82.5	−2.6
Women's and girls' apparel	121.5	115.8	113.1	113.0	110.8	110.7	110.3	−0.4
Women's apparel	121.9	116.1	113.1	113.3	111.8	112.5	112.1	−0.4
Women's suits and separates [1]	98.2	91.4	88.1	89.8	87.3	88.2	88.9	0.8
Women's underwear, nightwear, sportswear, and accessories [1]	101.8	97.1	95.9	94.2	95.4	94.4	91.8	−2.7
Footwear	123.8	121.4	119.6	119.3	122.6	123.5	122.4	−0.9
Men's footwear	129.5	125.9	120.7	119.7	121.3	123.5	120.9	−2.1
Women's footwear	119.6	119.0	118.4	118.4	121.9	122.8	122.5	−0.3
Jewelry and watches [3]	137.0	133.2	128.7	129.5	127.6	130.7	137.1	4.9
Jewelry [3]	141.2	138.1	133.2	133.6	131.3	134.8	142.4	5.7
Transportation	153.3	152.9	157.6	163.1	173.9	180.9	184.7	2.1
Private transportation	149.1	148.8	153.6	159.4	170.2	177.0	180.8	2.1
New and used motor vehicles [1]	100.8	99.2	96.5	94.2	95.6	95.6	94.3	−1.4
New vehicles	142.8	140.0	137.9	137.1	137.9	137.6	136.3	−1.0
Used cars and trucks	155.8	152.0	142.9	133.3	139.4	140.0	135.7	−3.0
Leased cars and trucks [5]	(NA)	99.0	96.8	93.6	92.7	93.1	92.6	−0.5
Motor fuel	129.3	116.6	135.8	160.4	195.7	221.0	239.1	8.2
Gasoline (all types)	128.6	116.0	135.1	159.7	194.7	219.9	238.0	8.2
Motor vehicle parts and equipment	101.5	106.9	107.8	108.7	111.9	117.3	121.6	3.7
Motor vehicle maintenance and repair	177.3	190.2	195.6	200.2	206.9	215.6	223.0	3.4
Motor vehicle maintenance and servicing	162.7	175.0	179.5	182.8	189.2	195.7	202.1	3.3
Motor vehicle repair [1]	108.2	116.0	119.6	122.7	126.7	132.7	137.4	3.5
Motor vehicle insurance	256.7	291.6	314.4	323.2	329.9	331.8	333.1	0.4
Motor vehicle fees [1]	107.3	112.5	116.5	131.0	134.7	138.8	141.2	1.7
State and local registration and license [1]	105.1	108.5	112.7	131.3	133.2	137.3	138.8	1.1
Public transportation	209.6	207.4	209.3	209.1	217.3	226.6	230.0	1.5
Airline fare	239.4	231.6	231.3	227.2	236.6	247.3	251.7	1.8
Medical care	260.8	285.6	297.1	310.1	323.2	336.2	351.1	4.4
Medical care commodities	238.1	256.4	262.8	269.3	276.0	285.9	290.0	1.4
Prescription drugs	285.4	316.5	326.3	337.1	349.0	363.9	369.2	1.4
Nonprescription drugs and medical supplies [3]	149.5	150.4	152.0	152.3	151.7	154.6	156.8	1.4
Internal and respiratory over-the-counter drugs	176.9	178.8	181.2	180.9	179.7	183.4	186.4	1.6
Medical care services	266.0	292.9	306.0	321.3	336.7	350.6	369.3	5.3
Professional medical services	237.7	253.9	261.2	271.5	281.7	289.3	300.8	4.0
Physicians' services	244.7	260.6	267.7	278.3	287.5	291.9	303.2	3.9
Dental services	258.5	281.0	292.5	306.9	324.0	340.9	358.4	5.1
Services by other medical professionals [3]	161.9	171.8	177.1	181.9	186.8	192.2	197.4	2.7
Hospital and related services	317.3	367.8	394.8	417.9	439.9	468.1	498.9	6.6
Hospital services [6]	115.9	134.7	144.7	153.4	161.6	172.1	183.6	6.7

See footnotes at end of table.

U.S. Census Bureau, Statistical Abstract of the United States: 2009

Table 705. Consumer Price Indexes for All Urban Consumers (CPI-U) for Selected Items and Groups: 2000 to 2007—Con.

[1982–84 = 100, except as noted. Annual averages of monthly figures. See headnote, Table 703]

Item	2000	2002	2003	2004	2005	2006	2007	Annual percentage change, 2006–2007
Recreation [1]	103.3	106.2	107.5	108.6	109.4	110.9	111.4	0.5
Video and audio [1]	101.0	102.8	103.6	104.2	104.2	104.6	102.9	−1.6
Cable and satellite television and radio service [4]	266.8	295.0	309.5	322.4	331.9	344.9	351.5	1.9
Pets, pet products, and services [1]	106.1	113.2	115.7	120.1	123.6	128.4	133.8	4.2
Pets and pet products	144.3	149.7	150.3	154.5	155.8	161.7	166.6	3.0
Pet services including veterinary [1]	114.6	128.2	134.9	142.3	150.3	156.5	165.7	5.9
Sporting goods	119.0	116.4	115.3	115.0	115.5	117.1	116.4	−0.6
Sports vehicles, including bicycles	130.9	131.8	130.3	130.8	133.2	138.0	137.9	−0.1
Other recreational goods [1]	87.8	80.5	76.1	73.3	69.5	67.2	64.3	−4.3
Recreation services [1]	111.7	119.6	124.5	127.5	130.5	135.1	139.4	3.2
Club membership dues and fees for participant sports [1]	108.9	112.9	116.1	116.7	117.4	121.9	123.7	1.5
Admissions	230.5	251.4	263.2	272.9	282.3	291.9	303.8	4.1
Education and communication [1]	102.5	107.9	109.8	111.6	113.7	116.8	119.6	2.4
Education [1]	112.5	126.0	134.4	143.7	152.7	162.1	171.4	5.7
Tuition/child care fees and other school fees	324.0	362.1	386.7	414.3	440.9	468.1	494.1	5.5
College tuition and fees	331.9	372.6	403.9	442.1	475.1	507.0	538.7	6.2
Elementary and high school tuition and fees	349.9	398.4	424.9	453.5	483.2	511.2	539.4	5.5
Child care and nursery school [7]	156.3	172.5	180.3	187.1	195.4	206.0	214.9	4.3
Communication [1]	93.6	92.3	89.7	86.7	84.7	84.1	83.4	−0.9
Information and information processing [1]	92.8	90.8	87.8	84.6	82.6	81.7	80.7	−1.2
Telephone services [1]	98.5	99.7	98.3	95.8	94.9	95.8	98.2	2.6
Land-line telephone services, local charges	175.6	193.2	201.1	204.1	209.6	213.9	222.1	3.8
Land-line telephone services, long distance charges [1]	91.8	84.9	77.8	70.9	67.5	68.3	71.5	4.6
Wireless telephone services [1]	76.0	67.4	66.8	66.2	65.0	64.6	64.4	−0.3
Information technology, hardware, and services [8]	25.9	18.3	16.1	14.8	13.6	12.5	10.6	−15.2
Other goods and services	271.1	293.2	298.7	304.7	313.4	321.7	333.3	3.6
Tobacco and smoking products	394.9	461.5	469.0	478.0	502.8	519.9	554.2	6.6
Cigarettes [1]	159.9	187.7	190.4	193.5	203.5	210.4	224.8	6.8
Personal care	165.6	174.7	178.0	181.7	185.6	190.2	195.6	2.9
Personal care products	153.7	154.7	153.5	153.9	154.4	155.8	158.3	1.6
Hair, dental, shaving, and miscellaneous personal care products [1]	103.3	104.4	102.5	102.1	101.8	102.6	103.6	1.0
Cosmetics, perfume, bath, nail preparations, and implements	166.8	167.2	168.0	169.5	171.3	173.1	177.0	2.3
Personal care services	178.1	188.4	193.2	197.6	203.9	209.7	216.6	3.3
Haircuts and other personal care services [1]	108.7	114.9	117.9	120.6	124.4	127.9	132.1	3.3
Miscellaneous personal services	252.3	274.4	283.5	293.9	303.0	313.6	325.0	3.6
Legal services [3]	189.3	211.1	221.7	232.3	241.8	250.0	260.3	4.1
Funeral expenses [3]	187.8	204.1	212.1	221.3	228.8	240.6	252.6	5.0
SPECIAL AGGREGATE INDEXES								
Commodities	149.2	149.7	151.2	154.7	160.2	164.0	167.5	2.1
Commodities less food and beverages	137.7	134.2	134.5	136.7	142.5	145.9	147.5	1.1
Nondurables less food and beverages	147.4	145.1	149.7	157.2	168.4	176.7	182.5	3.3
Nondurables less food, beverages, and apparel	162.5	162.2	171.5	183.9	202.6	216.3	226.2	4.6
Durables	125.4	121.4	117.5	114.8	115.3	114.5	112.5	−1.8
Services	195.3	209.8	216.5	222.8	230.1	238.9	246.8	3.3
Rent of shelter [2]	201.3	216.7	221.9	227.9	233.7	241.9	250.8	3.7
Transportation services	196.1	209.1	216.3	220.6	225.7	230.8	233.7	1.3
Other services	229.9	246.4	254.4	261.3	268.4	277.5	285.6	2.9
All items less food	173.0	180.5	184.7	189.4	196.0	202.7	208.1	2.7
All items less shelter	165.7	170.8	174.6	179.3	186.1	191.9	196.6	2.5
All items less medical care	167.3	174.3	178.1	182.7	188.7	194.7	200.1	2.8
Commodities less food	139.2	136.0	136.5	138.8	144.5	148.0	149.7	1.2
Nondurables less food	149.1	147.4	151.9	159.3	170.1	178.2	184.0	3.3
Nondurables less food and apparel	162.9	163.3	172.1	183.8	201.2	213.9	223.4	4.4
Nondurables	158.2	161.1	165.3	172.2	180.2	186.7	193.5	3.6
Apparel less footwear	126.2	120.1	116.8	116.3	114.4	114.1	113.8	−0.2
Services less rent of shelter [2]	202.9	217.5	226.4	233.5	243.2	253.3	260.8	2.9
Services less medical care services	188.9	202.5	208.7	214.5	221.2	229.6	236.8	3.2
Energy	124.6	121.7	136.5	151.4	177.1	196.9	207.7	5.5
All items less energy	178.6	187.7	190.6	194.4	198.7	203.7	208.9	2.6
All items less food and energy	181.3	190.5	193.2	196.6	200.9	205.9	210.7	2.3
Commodities less food and energy commodities	144.9	143.7	140.9	139.6	140.3	140.6	140.1	−0.4
Energy commodities	129.5	117.1	136.7	161.2	197.4	223.0	241.0	8.1
Services less energy services	202.1	217.5	223.8	230.2	236.6	244.7	253.1	3.4
Domestically produced farm food	170.1	179.2	183.7	191.7	195.0	198.1	206.5	4.2
Utilities and public transportation	152.6	158.4	164.3	167.5	176.6	186.7	191.3	2.5

– Represents zero. NA Not available. [1] December 1997 = 100. [2] December 1982 = 100. [3] December 1986 = 100. [4] December 1983 = 100. [5] December 2001 = 100. [6] December 1996 = 100. [7] December 1990 = 100. [8] December 1988 = 100.
Source: U.S. Bureau of Labor Statistics, *CPI Detailed Report,* monthly; <http://www.bls.gov/cpi/cpi_dr.htm>. See also *Monthly Labor Review,* <http://www.bls.gov/opub/mlr/welcome.htm>.

Table 706. Cost of Living Index—Selected Urban Areas: Annual Average 2007

[Measures relative price levels for consumer goods and services in participating areas for a mid-management standard of living. **The nationwide average equals 100 and each index is read as a percent of the national average.** The index does not measure inflation, but compares prices at a single point in time. Excludes taxes. For definition of urban areas, see source. For international comparisons, see Table 1313, Section 30]

Urban areas	Composite index (100%)	Grocery items (13%)	Housing (29%)	Utilities (10%)	Transportation (10%)	Health care (4%)	Misc. goods and services (35%)
Akron, OH.	93.6	98.7	80.8	99.6	101.8	92.4	98.1
Albuquerque, NM	98.3	100.3	102.8	86.7	99.0	98.9	96.9
Amarillo, TX	87.4	89.8	79.8	86.8	98.2	93.9	88.9
Anchorage, AK	126.0	129.8	137.9	106.1	103.5	132.5	126.6
Asheville, NC.	99.6	101.3	104.6	92.7	95.2	103.2	97.9
Atlanta, GA	96.1	98.7	91.8	84.9	103.5	103.4	98.7
Austin, TX.	94.5	89.8	80.8	94.7	99.2	98.1	105.3
Baltimore, MD	118.0	106.7	151.2	116.4	108.3	104.1	100.6
Baton Rouge, LA	91.2	95.4	83.0	89.3	92.4	99.9	95.5
Bergen-Passaic, NJ	128.8	112.2	173.9	107.1	103.0	106.5	115.0
Bethesda-Gaithersburg-Frederick, MD	132.1	107.1	188.2	127.9	114.5	109.5	105.4
Birmingham, AL	92.1	96.6	77.6	98.8	96.1	99.4	98.0
Boston, MA.	134.7	120.0	164.0	129.2	104.7	136.0	126.8
Bradenton, FL	99.6	97.1	107.9	96.3	98.4	104.4	94.6
Brownsville, TX	85.9	86.4	71.4	104.7	98.4	95.9	87.2
Burlington-Chittenden Co, VT	116.3	110.4	130.7	124.5	106.2	104.8	108.7
Camden, SC	93.1	98.0	83.7	94.4	86.6	91.5	100.5
Cedar Rapids, IA	91.1	87.4	77.9	95.5	99.1	108.8	97.3
Champaign-Urbana, IL	98.2	95.9	89.0	111.5	99.0	101.3	102.0
Charleston, WV	90.8	87.1	84.8	97.4	96.1	94.3	93.2
Charleston-North Charleston, SC	97.8	100.5	90.3	102.0	97.8	110.3	100.1
Charlotte, NC	89.7	99.1	75.6	83.2	92.3	104.3	96.8
Cheyenne, WY	99.2	105.9	102.0	96.2	95.5	96.3	96.8
Chicago, IL	110.3	108.3	125.0	107.8	113.1	104.3	99.9
Cincinnati, OH	90.4	89.2	80.4	99.3	98.8	91.9	93.9
Cleveland, OH.	98.9	106.5	89.3	112.9	101.6	102.4	98.6
Colorado Springs, CO	93.8	94.7	89.3	87.7	104.2	104.5	94.6
Columbia, SC	89.2	98.4	77.2	95.2	84.7	102.1	93.5
Columbus, OH	97.4	96.3	95.9	102.3	103.5	104.1	94.9
Conroe, TX	87.0	86.3	74.5	94.7	91.7	97.6	92.6
Corpus Christi, TX	88.2	82.0	79.9	98.2	93.3	87.4	92.8
Covington, KY	90.6	86.7	78.8	92.5	102.6	93.6	97.2
Dallas, TX.	91.2	99.0	71.5	98.6	103.4	101.6	97.4
Davenport-Moline-Rock Island, IA-IL	94.9	97.1	86.6	94.6	104.8	92.0	98.4
Dayton, OH.	93.5	91.9	80.4	100.8	103.4	93.8	99.7
Denver, CO	103.4	102.9	109.3	102.4	95.4	108.5	100.8
Des Moines, IA	90.3	87.0	86.2	96.4	94.1	89.9	91.9
Dover, DE.	102.7	110.6	93.0	132.9	101.1	104.7	99.3
Durham, NC	89.8	96.6	79.8	90.5	93.4	96.3	93.4
El Paso, TX.	93.0	112.1	78.5	95.6	99.2	100.3	94.3
Erie, PA	97.3	97.6	87.1	129.0	97.5	95.1	96.6
Fargo-Moorhead, ND-MN.	95.4	97.4	82.0	122.5	101.8	97.8	95.5
Fayetteville, AR	90.8	91.4	77.4	105.1	98.7	92.2	94.8
Fort Lauderdale, FL	121.0	102.6	167.6	102.8	104.8	107.2	102.0
Fort Myers-Cape Coral, FL.	102.6	98.2	109.1	98.4	99.6	101.2	101.3
Fort Smith, AR	89.0	94.6	68.5	98.4	88.4	91.0	100.5
Fort Wayne-Allen County, IN	88.7	90.3	81.5	94.1	103.2	90.5	87.9
Fort Worth, TX	88.2	95.3	74.0	97.9	97.7	90.1	91.1
Framingham-Natick, MA	131.0	116.6	164.3	141.6	105.9	114.2	115.8
Fresno, CA	119.8	115.1	148.6	107.3	112.0	108.9	105.6
Gastonia, NC.	88.2	96.6	73.5	87.9	93.6	98.0	94.1
Grand Rapids, MI.	102.5	105.5	100.4	120.9	99.1	90.9	100.0
Greeley, CO	98.3	102.9	92.0	97.2	97.1	104.0	101.6
Green Bay, WI.	93.3	91.5	84.2	106.7	102.2	97.0	94.6
Greenville, NC.	97.4	110.9	78.3	106.3	97.2	113.9	103.3
Hampton Roads-South East Virginia, VA	106.8	100.9	126.4	105.9	103.4	98.5	95.6
Harlingen, TX	83.5	78.9	69.7	100.1	92.6	96.3	87.3
Hickory, NC.	94.9	99.8	91.9	90.7	90.6	99.2	97.5
Honolulu, HI	163.1	159.1	246.5	139.7	117.5	110.3	123.7
Houston, TX	87.7	83.1	73.5	100.6	96.2	101.2	93.0

See footnotes at end of table.

U.S. Census Bureau, Statistical Abstract of the United States: 2009

Table 706. Cost of Living Index—Selected Urban Areas: Annual Average 2007—Con.

[Measures relative price levels for consumer goods and services in participating areas for a mid-management standard of living. **The nationwide average equals 100 and each index is read as a percent of the national average.** The index does not measure inflation, but compares prices at a single point in time. Excludes taxes. For definition of urban areas, see source. For international comparisons, see Table 1313, Section 30]

Urban areas	Composite index (100%)	Grocery items (13%)	Housing (29%)	Utilities (10%)	Transportation (10%)	Health care (4%)	Misc. goods and services (35%)
Huntsville, AL	92.5	93.6	78.9	84.1	96.9	95.0	103.8
Indianapolis, IN	94.7	92.3	98.4	95.6	98.6	92.3	91.6
Jackson, MS	93.5	90.8	84.9	103.3	93.6	104.5	97.3
Jacksonville, FL	98.7	99.0	95.4	88.0	106.7	96.0	102.2
Joliet-Will County, IL	99.1	107.2	93.6	90.3	105.8	102.7	100.8
Kalamazoo, MI	96.2	105.3	87.6	95.5	102.5	98.0	97.7
Kansas City, MO-KS	95.7	91.4	87.2	103.9	100.1	98.0	100.3
Knoxville, TN	87.0	89.5	75.2	89.8	87.2	89.3	94.5
Lafayette, LA	97.7	95.4	104.5	87.5	101.7	89.8	95.7
Lancaster, PA	106.4	98.7	119.5	104.4	100.3	97.7	102.1
Las Vegas, NV	109.8	100.8	133.6	106.2	104.4	107.0	96.9
Lawrence, KS	92.3	86.5	90.1	91.8	96.5	93.6	95.0
Little Rock-North Little Rock, AR	95.8	100.4	78.1	108.8	95.9	95.1	104.6
Los Angeles-Long Beach, CA	144.6	111.8	251.2	78.6	113.5	103.8	103.8
Louisville, KY	97.5	89.6	89.6	109.1	110.2	97.3	99.8
Loveland, CO	93.9	99.2	79.2	94.8	100.6	99.4	100.9
Lubbock, TX	86.4	91.3	71.1	83.7	102.8	98.7	91.5
McAllen, TX	84.1	79.5	72.6	77.9	97.9	95.7	91.4
Memphis, TN	89.3	90.4	76.5	83.8	92.2	97.1	99.0
Miami-Dade County, FL	115.4	103.3	138.2	106.6	109.6	105.6	106.9
Middlesex-Monmouth, NJ	126.9	113.1	167.2	106.9	103.6	110.6	114.0
Missoula, MT	101.2	113.5	96.2	101.8	98.6	99.8	101.4
Mobile, AL	93.2	101.3	77.2	102.5	92.4	86.0	101.4
Montgomery, AL	95.5	98.7	93.1	100.0	94.7	85.7	96.3
Murfreesboro-Smyrna, TN	95.1	100.4	75.7	97.5	106.7	102.4	103.8
Myrtle Beach, SC	93.8	105.1	80.1	86.2	97.2	101.3	100.8
Nassau County, NY	153.1	125.7	238.8	139.7	110.1	117.4	114.8
New Haven, CT	117.9	121.5	129.4	130.7	99.8	113.4	109.4
New York (Manhattan), NY	212.8	158.1	396.1	152.0	122.5	128.4	139.4
New York (Queens), NY	148.6	130.9	217.1	128.7	110.3	112.8	121.0
Newark-Elizabeth, NJ	126.4	111.1	164.0	107.5	104.1	107.0	116.1
Oakland, CA	146.6	138.3	211.0	87.7	118.2	121.3	125.8
Oklahoma City, OK	90.0	86.3	78.7	83.7	100.3	103.9	97.7
Olympia, WA	104.8	108.9	98.9	91.1	111.4	121.8	108.2
Omaha, NE	88.5	87.2	78.4	88.0	100.9	94.7	93.1
Orlando, FL	103.4	98.2	99.2	109.6	105.9	98.2	106.7
Palm Springs, CA	125.4	110.3	165.8	103.8	117.6	102.5	109.6
Peoria, IL	97.7	100.2	88.4	104.1	103.7	98.0	100.7
Philadelphia, PA	123.5	124.4	144.4	116.1	105.8	111.0	115.2
Phoenix, AZ	100.6	100.5	100.9	93.6	100.7	101.0	102.4
Pittsburgh, PA	98.9	98.3	92.6	108.2	105.7	87.3	101.0
Plano, TX	97.6	102.8	82.0	99.7	101.4	104.3	105.6
Portland, OR	120.8	124.3	134.3	103.6	111.0	107.9	118.0
Providence, RI	120.6	116.5	134.7	119.0	101.1	115.8	117.3
Raleigh, NC	99.3	102.1	96.7	91.3	95.6	103.7	103.1
Reno-Sparks, NV	107.8	104.3	113.9	86.5	111.2	109.0	109.3
Richland-Kennewick-Pasco, WA	93.8	94.1	84.4	89.4	106.4	116.4	96.4
Richmond, VA	106.4	94.7	111.4	112.3	108.0	102.1	105.2
Riverside City, CA	117.5	106.7	154.5	88.4	112.7	106.6	103.0
Roanoke, VA	91.6	90.0	87.8	88.7	89.9	94.9	96.1
Rochester, MN	99.9	88.6	93.5	108.2	100.7	104.0	106.3
Round Rock, TX	92.1	85.0	75.5	108.3	95.2	106.3	100.8
Sacramento, CA	124.7	130.6	153.6	101.8	104.8	114.2	112.9
Salt Lake City, UT	100.7	102.3	98.0	87.4	103.5	99.3	105.4
San Antonio, TX	94.1	83.7	84.1	83.5	100.1	102.5	106.4
San Diego, CA	139.5	111.9	218.1	104.7	111.2	116.3	107.5
San Francisco, CA	168.5	139.5	275.2	87.8	123.1	123.5	135.0
San Jose, CA	154.2	143.8	251.5	99.0	113.1	122.7	111.3
Sarasota, FL	109.3	102.0	130.2	100.6	103.3	105.8	99.8
Seattle, WA	121.0	113.0	153.2	94.6	106.1	124.0	109.6

See footnotes at end of table.

U.S. Census Bureau, Statistical Abstract of the United States: 2009

Table 706. **Cost of Living Index—Selected Urban Areas:**
Annual Average 2007—Con.

[Measures relative price levels for consumer goods and services in participating areas for a mid-management standard of living.
The nationwide average equals 100 and each index is read as a percent of the national average. The index does not measure inflation, but compares prices at a single point in time. Excludes taxes. For definitions of urban areas, see source. For international comparisons, see Table 1313, Section 30]

Urban areas	Com-posite index (100%)	Grocery items (13%)	Housing (29%)	Utilities (10%)	Transpor-tation (10%)	Health care (4%)	Misc. goods and services (35%)
Shreveport-Bossier City, LA	92.7	91.9	87.5	93.3	91.9	93.1	97.3
Slidell-St. Tammany Parish, LA	99.6	108.5	98.3	89.9	99.8	96.4	100.3
South Bend, IN	90.5	93.5	80.8	91.5	96.6	94.6	94.7
Spokane, WA	95.8	98.2	84.1	86.4	108.0	108.3	101.9
Springfield, IL	92.9	94.5	84.5	97.4	107.3	112.0	91.5
Springfield, MO	89.1	95.7	73.4	91.2	100.0	92.7	95.0
St. Cloud, MN	99.4	95.2	89.6	105.6	102.7	98.2	106.3
St. Louis, MO-IL.	91.5	106.1	77.9	90.9	96.0	97.2	95.0
St. Petersburg-Clearwater, FL.	100.6	104.0	99.9	114.9	101.6	93.6	96.3
Syracuse, NY	98.7	99.5	81.5	121.0	101.8	94.0	105.5
Tacoma, WA	110.1	123.8	112.0	99.3	110.4	121.3	105.3
Tampa, FL	98.6	97.6	95.8	98.6	102.7	94.1	100.5
Temple, TX	88.7	80.6	74.8	107.6	97.2	90.9	94.7
Tucson, AZ	100.3	105.4	95.9	96.3	100.5	102.3	102.7
Tulsa, OK	91.6	92.1	75.1	91.6	107.2	102.8	98.8
Waco, TX	89.3	81.4	78.3	99.2	94.8	97.2	95.7
Washington-Arlington-Alexandria, DC-VA . .	136.4	106.6	210.6	111.4	109.8	110.0	106.0
Wilmington, DE	107.1	119.1	97.8	122.7	103.0	113.2	106.2
Wilmington, NC	100.2	106.7	98.5	93.2	102.9	113.0	98.9
Winston-Salem, NC	89.8	97.7	75.4	85.1	88.5	101.9	98.8
York County, PA.	99.9	92.4	106.0	101.6	94.6	90.1	99.9

Source: C2ER, P.O.Box 100127, Arlington, VA 22210, *ACCRA Cost of Living Index,* Annual Average 2007 (copyright).

Table 707. **Single-Family Housing Price Indexes by State: 2000 to 2007**

[**Index 1980, 1st quarter = 100.** The index reflects average price changes in repeat sales or refinancings on the same properties.
Since the data are for the fourth quarter, the index represents the annual percentage change in home values in the fourth quarter
of the year shown relative to the fourth quarter of the previous year. The information is obtained by reviewing repeat mortgage
transactions on single-family properties whose mortages have been purchased or securitized by either Fannie Mae or Freddie
Mac; for more information on methodology, see Appendix III. Minus sign (–) indicates decrease]

State	2000	2005	2006	2007	Per-cent change 2006–2007	State	2000	2005	2006	2007	Per-cent change 2006–2007
U.S. . . .	**241**	**366**	**387**	**390**	**0.84**						
AL	204	262	284	297	4.45	MT	218	333	369	395	6.90
AK	170	257	269	285	5.97	NE	205	249	255	261	2.45
AZ	207	394	431	420	–2.41	NV	194	396	411	387	–5.86
AR	184	240	255	264	3.63	NH	296	493	502	499	–0.61
CA	285	617	644	602	–6.65	NJ	295	547	579	577	–0.27
CO	280	355	365	370	1.37	NM	203	290	328	346	5.39
CT	276	457	473	477	0.81	NY	361	627	660	664	0.66
DE	279	475	512	522	1.95	NC	243	307	332	348	4.85
DC	267	614	657	670	1.87	ND	167	229	242	261	7.87
FL	214	445	486	464	–4.70	OH	223	268	271	270	–0.42
GA	250	322	339	348	2.55	OK	150	190	200	210	5.13
HI	238	501	538	549	2.01	OR	256	400	455	472	3.85
ID	201	299	342	358	4.56	PA	244	376	402	413	2.83
IL	252	358	378	385	1.95	RI	296	586	601	585	–2.56
IN	211	251	256	260	1.47	SC	220	287	311	322	3.73
IA	192	241	248	255	2.73						
KS	186	231	242	248	2.54	SD	203	269	284	298	4.83
KY	221	274	285	295	3.51	TN	221	279	301	314	4.14
LA	164	219	243	253	4.14	TX	166	204	218	229	5.22
ME	295	489	511	521	1.91	UT	242	306	360	394	9.27
MD	248	493	538	542	0.80	VT	263	432	464	475	2.41
MA	440	725	723	708	–2.17	VA	243	441	475	478	0.81
MI	264	321	318	305	–4.27	WA	279	429	487	514	5.44
MN	239	362	372	368	–1.15	WV	161	217	229	236	3.04
MS	186	233	255	266	4.12	WI	231	316	328	334	1.94
MO	215	288	300	308	2.46	WY	157	235	267	290	8.27

Source: Office of Federal Housing Enterprise Oversight, *Housing Price Index, 4th quarter 2007,* at <http://www.ofheo.gov/media
/pdf/4q07hpi.pdf> (released 26 February 2008). For most recent release, see <http://www.ofheo.gov/hpi.aspx?Nav=62>.

Table 708. **Weekly Food Cost of a Nutritious Diet by Type of Family and Individual: 2007**

[**In dollars**. Assumes that food for all meals and snacks is purchased at the store and prepared at home. See source for details on estimation procedures]

Family type	December 2007			
	Thrifty plan	Low-cost plan	Moderate-cost plan	Liberal plan
FAMILIES				
Family of two:				
19 to 50 years old	77.50	98.60	121.20	152.00
51 to 70 years old	73.40	94.40	116.40	140.60
Family of four:				
Couple, 19 to 50 years old and children—				
2 to 3 and 4 to 5 years old	112.60	143.10	175.50	217.60
6 to 8 and 9 to 11 years old	129.60	167.70	208.60	254.10
INDIVIDUALS [1]				
Child:				
1 year old	19.50	25.90	29.80	36.30
2 to 3 years old	20.60	26.10	31.60	38.30
4 to 5 years old	21.60	27.40	33.80	41.10
6 to 8 years old	27.40	36.70	45.40	53.60
9 to 11 years old	31.80	41.40	53.10	62.30
Male:				
12 to 13 years old	33.30	46.50	57.60	68.50
14 to 18 years old	34.40	47.90	59.30	69.60
19 to 50 years old	37.10	47.80	59.20	72.40
51 to 70 years old	33.90	45.40	55.60	67.40
71 and over	34.00	45.20	56.20	67.60
Female:				
12 to 13 years old	33.30	40.60	49.30	59.30
14 to 18 years old	33.20	40.80	48.90	59.60
19 to 50 years old	33.30	41.80	51.00	65.80
51 to 70 years old	32.80	40.40	50.30	60.40
71 years old and over	32.60	40.40	50.60	60.80

[1] The costs given are for individuals in 4-person families. For individuals in other size families, the following adjustments are suggested: 1-person, add 20 percent; 2-person, add 10 percent; 3-person, add 5 percent; 5- or 6-person, subtract 5 percent; 7- (or more) person, subtract 10 percent.

Source: U.S. Department of Agriculture, *Official USDA Food Plans: Cost of Food at Home at Four Levels,* monthly. See also <http://www.cnpp.usda.gov/Publications/FoodPlans/2007/CostofFoodDec07.pdf> (released January 2008).

Table 709. **Food—Retail Prices of Selected Items: 2000 to 2007**

[**In dollars per pound, except as indicated. As of December.** See Appendix III]

Food	2000	2006	2007	Food	2000	2006	2007
Cereals and bakery products:				Fresh fruits and vegetables:			
Flour, white, all purpose	0.28	0.32	0.40	Apples, Red Delicious	0.82	1.03	1.12
Rice, white, lg. grain, raw	(NA)	0.56	0.55	Bananas	0.49	0.50	0.53
Spaghetti and macaroni	0.88	0.89	0.85	Oranges, navel	0.62	0.96	0.91
Bread, white, pan	0.99	1.14	1.28	Grapefruit	0.58	0.97	0.91
Bread, whole wheat	1.36	1.62	1.81	Grapes, Thompson seedless	2.36	2.89	2.72
Beef:				Lemons	1.11	1.66	2.05
Ground beef, 100% beef	1.63	2.26	2.23	Pears, Anjou	(NA)	1.24	1.27
Ground chuck, 100% beef	1.98	2.61	2.70	Potatoes, white	0.35	0.52	0.52
Ground beef, lean and extra lean	2.33	2.95	3.07	Lettuce, iceberg	0.85	0.90	0.95
Round steak, USDA Choice	3.28	3.99	4.04	Tomatoes, field grown	1.57	1.64	2.15
Sirloin steak, boneless	4.81	5.79	5.91	Processed fruits and vegetables:			
Pork:				Orange juice, frozen concentrate,			
Bacon, sliced	3.03	3.46	3.69	12 oz. can, per 16 oz.	1.88	2.23	2.53
Chops, center cut, bone-in	3.46	3.15	3.38	Sugar and sweets:			
Ham, boneless, excluding canned	2.75	3.09	3.04	Sugar, white, all sizes	0.41	0.51	0.50
Poultry, fish, and eggs:				Sugar, white, 33–80 oz. pkg.	0.40	0.48	0.48
Chicken, fresh, whole	1.08	1.06	1.17	Fats and oils:			
Chicken legs, bone-in	1.26	1.23	1.36	Margarine, stick	(NA)	0.88	1.01
Turkey, frozen, whole	0.99	0.99	1.01	Margarine, tubs, soft	0.84	1.14	1.24
Eggs, Grade A, large, (dozen)	0.96	1.54	2.10	Peanut butter, creamy, all sizes	1.96	1.72	1.88
Dairy products:				Nonalcoholic beverages:			
Milk, fresh, whole, fortified (per gal.)	2.79	3.00	3.87	Coffee, 100% ground roast, all sizes	3.21	3.11	3.69
Butter, salted, grade AA, stick	2.80	2.89	2.98	Other prepared foods:			
American processed cheese	3.69	3.61	3.91	Potato chips, per 16 oz.	3.44	3.41	3.65
Cheddar cheese, natural	3.76	4.02	4.45				
Ice cream, prepack., bulk, reg. (1/2 gal.)	3.66	3.90	4.08				

NA Not available.

Source: U.S. Bureau of Labor Statistics, *CPI Detailed Report,* monthly, and <http://www.bls.gov/cpi/cpi_dr.htm>. See also *Monthly Labor Review,* <http://www.bls.gov/opub/mlr/welcome.htm>.

Table 710. Average Prices of Selected Fuels and Electricity: 1990 to 2007

[In dollars per unit, except electricity, in cents per kWh. Represents price to end-users, except as noted]

Type	Unit [1]	1990	1995	2000	2001	2002	2003	2004	2005	2006	2007
Crude oil, composite [2]	Barrel	22.22	17.23	28.26	22.95	24.10	28.53	36.98	50.24	60.24	67.93
Motor gasoline: [3]											
Unleaded regular	Gallon	1.16	1.15	1.51	1.46	1.36	1.59	1.88	2.30	2.59	2.80
Unleaded premium	Gallon	1.35	1.34	1.69	1.66	1.56	1.78	2.07	2.49	2.81	3.03
No. 2 heating oil	Gallon	0.73	0.56	0.93	0.83	0.74	0.93	1.17	1.71	1.98	2.24
No. 2 diesel fuel	Gallon	0.73	0.56	0.94	0.84	0.76	0.94	1.24	1.79	2.10	2.27
Propane, consumer grade	Gallon	0.75	0.49	0.60	0.51	0.42	0.58	0.84	1.09	1.36	1.49
Residual fuel oil	Gallon	0.44	0.39	0.60	0.53	0.57	0.70	0.74	1.05	1.22	1.37
Natural gas, residential	1,000 cu/ft.	5.80	6.06	7.76	9.63	7.89	9.63	10.75	12.70	13.75	13.01
Electricity, residential	kWh	7.83	8.40	8.24	8.58	8.44	8.72	8.95	9.45	10.40	10.64

[1] See headnote.   [2] Refiner acquisition cost.   [3] Average, all service.

Source: U.S. Energy Information Administration, *Monthly Energy Review*. For most current issue, see <http://www.eia.doe.gov/emeu/mer/contents.html>.

Table 711. Retail Gasoline Prices—Selected Areas: 2005 to 2007

[In cents per gallon. Prices are annual averages]

Area	Regular			Midgrade			Premium		
	2005	2006	2007	2005	2006	2007	2005	2006	2007
Boston, MA	225.7	256.3	271.0	236.3	268.2	283.6	246.4	278.7	294.2
Chicago, IL	231.8	266.3	294.1	241.9	276.6	305.1	251.9	286.8	315.4
Cleveland, OH	222.0	249.4	275.9	232.2	259.7	286.4	243.0	270.6	297.2
Denver, CO	223.9	253.1	276.8	235.4	264.7	289.0	245.4	274.5	299.7
Houston, TX	216.8	246.6	260.6	226.8	256.7	272.1	236.5	266.6	283.1
Los Angeles, CA	249.0	283.3	304.7	258.6	293.4	315.5	268.1	303.3	325.7
Miami, FL	238.9	267.1	286.0	249.3	277.9	299.1	258.5	286.9	309.8
New York, NY	230.0	263.1	278.9	241.5	275.8	293.3	251.3	286.4	304.4
San Francisco, CA	248.1	279.1	317.1	259.4	291.0	329.7	269.4	301.1	340.0
Seattle, WA	236.3	268.3	294.7	247.3	278.9	305.1	257.6	289.1	315.4

Source: U.S. Energy Information Administration, *Weekly U.S. Retail Gasoline Prices,* Gasoline Historical Data. See also <http://www.eia.doe.gov/oil_gas/petroleum/data_publications/wrgp/mogas_history.html>.

Table 712. Producer Price Indexes by Stage of Processing: 1990 to 2007

[1982 = 100, except as indicated. See Appendix III. Minus sign (−) indicates decrease]

Year	Crude materials			Inter-mediate materials, supplies, and com-ponents	Finished goods		Finished consumer foods		Finished consumer goods excl. food
	Total	Food-stuffs and feed-stuffs	Fuel	Crude nonfood materials except fuel		Con-sumer goods	Capital equip-ment	Crude	Pro-cessed	
1990	108.9	113.1	84.8	107.3	114.5	118.2	122.9	123.0	124.4	115.3
1994	101.8	106.5	82.4	97.0	118.5	123.3	134.1	111.3	127.9	121.6
1995	102.7	105.8	72.1	105.8	124.9	125.6	136.7	118.8	129.8	124.0
1996	113.8	121.5	92.6	105.7	125.7	129.5	138.3	129.2	133.8	127.6
1997	111.1	112.2	101.3	103.5	125.6	130.2	138.2	126.6	135.1	128.2
1998	96.8	103.9	86.7	84.5	123.0	128.9	137.6	127.2	134.8	126.4
1999	98.2	98.7	91.2	91.1	123.2	132.0	137.6	125.5	135.9	130.5
2000	120.6	100.2	136.9	118.0	129.2	138.2	138.8	123.5	138.3	138.4
2001	121.0	106.1	151.4	101.5	129.7	141.5	139.7	127.7	142.4	141.4
2002	108.1	99.5	117.3	101.0	127.8	139.4	139.1	128.5	141.0	138.8
2003	135.3	113.5	185.7	116.9	133.7	145.3	139.5	130.0	147.2	144.7
2004	159.0	127.0	211.4	149.2	142.6	151.7	141.4	138.2	153.9	150.9
2005	182.2	122.7	279.7	176.7	154.0	160.4	144.6	140.2	156.9	161.9
2006	184.8	119.3	241.5	210.0	164.0	166.0	146.9	151.3	157.1	169.2
2007 [1]	207.3	146.7	237.5	238.8	170.6	173.5	149.5	169.6	166.7	175.6
PERCENT CHANGE [2]										
1990	5.6	1.7	−0.6	12.0	2.2	5.4	3.5	2.8	4.9	5.9
1994	−0.6	−1.8	−5.4	3.1	2.0	0.2	2.1	−2.7	1.1	−0.1
1995	0.9	−0.7	−12.5	9.1	5.4	1.9	1.9	6.7	1.5	2.0
1996	10.8	14.8	28.4	−0.1	0.6	3.1	1.2	8.8	3.1	2.9
1997	−2.4	−7.7	9.4	−2.1	−0.1	0.5	−0.1	−2.0	1.0	0.5
1998	−12.9	−7.4	−14.4	−18.4	−2.1	−1.0	−0.4	0.5	−0.2	−1.4
1999	1.4	−5.0	5.2	7.8	0.2	2.4	0.0	−1.3	0.8	3.2
2000	22.8	1.5	50.1	29.5	4.9	4.7	0.9	−1.6	1.8	6.1
2001	0.3	5.9	10.6	−14.0	0.4	2.4	0.6	3.4	3.0	2.2
2002	−10.7	−6.2	−22.5	−0.5	−1.5	−1.5	−0.4	0.6	−1.0	−1.8
2003	25.2	14.1	58.3	15.7	4.6	4.2	0.3	1.2	4.4	4.3
2004	17.5	11.9	13.8	27.6	6.7	4.4	1.4	6.3	4.6	4.3
2005	14.6	−3.4	32.3	18.4	8.0	5.7	2.3	1.4	1.9	7.3
2006	1.4	−2.8	−13.7	18.8	6.5	3.5	1.6	7.9	0.1	4.5
2007 [1]	12.2	23.0	−1.7	13.7	4.0	4.5	1.8	12.1	6.1	3.8

[1] Preliminary.   [2] Change from immediate prior year. 1990, change from 1989.

Source: U.S. Bureau of Labor Statistics, *Producer Price Indexes,* monthly and annual. See also *Monthly Labor Review* at <http://www.bls.gov/opub/mlr/welcome.htm>.

Prices   473

Table 713. Producer Price Indexes by Stage of Processing and Commodity: 1990 to 2007

[1982 = 100, except as indicated. See Appendix III]

Stage of processing	1990	1995	2000	2003	2004	2005	2006	2007 [1]
Finished goods	**119.2**	**127.9**	**138.0**	**143.3**	**148.5**	**155.7**	**160.4**	**166.6**
Finished consumer goods	**118.2**	**125.6**	**138.2**	**145.3**	**151.7**	**160.4**	**166.0**	**173.5**
Finished consumer foods	**124.4**	**129.0**	**137.2**	**145.9**	**152.7**	**155.7**	**156.7**	**166.9**
Fresh fruits and melons	118.1	85.8	91.4	84.1	104.9	102.8	111.0	122.2
Fresh and dry vegetables	118.1	144.4	126.7	135.7	129.4	142.6	153.3	165.5
Eggs for fresh use (Dec. 1991 = 100)	(NA)	86.3	84.9	106.6	100.0	79.6	90.0	132.6
Bakery products	141.0	164.3	182.3	195.0	196.3	201.1	207.7	216.7
Milled rice	102.5	113.1	101.2	102.5	135.5	120.1	136.1	155.2
Pasta products (June 1985 = 100)	114.1	125.0	121.6	126.4	127.3	127.9	128.3	136.0
Beef and veal	116.0	100.9	113.7	137.9	141.2	147.4	142.3	146.1
Pork	119.8	101.5	113.4	115.7	132.7	131.9	128.0	133.2
Processed young chickens	111.0	113.5	110.4	119.7	138.9	136.2	118.1	139.4
Processed turkeys	107.6	104.9	98.7	92.5	107.8	105.1	103.6	110.6
Finfish and shellfish	147.2	170.8	198.1	195.3	206.3	222.6	237.4	242.5
Dairy products	117.2	119.7	133.7	139.4	155.9	154.5	147.5	175.7
Processed fruits and vegetables	124.7	122.4	128.6	133.8	135.2	140.4	148.9	157.4
Soft drinks	122.3	133.1	144.1	153.0	156.5	159.1	162.8	166.7
Roasted coffee	113.0	146.5	133.5	127.3	130.1	151.1	153.6	163.7
Shortening and cooking oils	123.2	142.5	132.4	160.8	193.7	176.7	183.7	214.7
Finished consumer goods excluding foods	**115.3**	**124.0**	**138.4**	**144.7**	**150.9**	**161.9**	**169.2**	**175.6**
Alcoholic beverages	117.2	128.5	140.6	148.9	152.8	158.5	160.1	160.1
Apparel	117.5	124.2	127.4	125.7	125.6	125.6	125.9	127.0
Women's/girls'/infants' cut & sew apparel (Dec. 2003 = 100)	(NA)	(NA)	(NA)	(NA)	100.2	100.3	100.3	101.1
Men's and boys' cut & sew apparel (Dec. 2003 = 100)	(NA)	(NA)	(NA)	(NA)	99.9	98.7	98.0	98.6
Textile house furnishings	109.5	119.5	122.0	122.4	123.4	122.9	123.2	125.3
Footwear	125.6	139.2	144.9	147.1	146.2	148.1	149.3	151.5
Residential electric power (Dec. 1990 = 100)	(NA)	111.8	110.8	118.8	121.4	126.4	134.8	139.2
Residential gas (Dec. 1990 = 100)	(NA)	104.4	135.5	167.6	183.2	216.8	226.7	224.8
Gasoline	78.7	63.7	94.6	102.7	128.1	168.6	197.2	222.1
Fuel oil No. 2	73.3	56.6	93.5	95.3	120.7	178.4	207.4	223.7
Soaps and synthetic detergents	117.7	122.9	128.2	130.9	132.9	134.6	142.7	144.9
Cosmetics and other toilet preparations	121.6	129.0	137.4	140.4	140.6	143.0	145.2	147.8
Tires, tubes, and tread	96.8	100.2	93.0	97.9	102.5	108.1	114.7	118.6
Sanitary papers and health products	135.3	144.4	146.7	150.5	148.5	154.6	160.1	161.8
Book publishing	153.4	185.0	218.2	243.1	253.1	264.0	275.2	284.9
Household furniture	125.1	141.8	152.7	158.2	160.5	166.5	172.3	174.6
Floor coverings	119.0	123.7	129.6	133.6	136.7	146.4	154.5	156.5
Household appliances	110.8	112.4	107.3	102.4	101.5	103.3	104.1	105.2
Home electronic equipment	82.7	78.9	71.8	67.7	65.2	62.6	60.3	58.2
Household glassware	132.5	153.2	166.0	168.9	171.4	174.7	172.3	176.7
Household flatware	122.1	138.3	142.6	145.2	145.4	147.7	152.7	(NA)
Lawn and garden equipment, except tractors	123.0	130.4	132.0	133.5	134.5	134.5	134.9	136.5
Passenger cars	118.3	134.1	132.8	129.5	131.7	131.8	128.0	126.2
Toys, games, and children's vehicles	118.1	124.3	121.9	124.9	124.9	127.0	128.5	131.0
Sporting and athletic goods	112.6	122.0	126.1	124.0	123.4	124.6	126.1	129.8
Tobacco products	221.4	231.3	397.2	431.6	434.0	457.8	460.0	489.6
Mobile homes	117.5	145.6	161.3	169.6	186.6	200.8	208.8	211.2
Jewelry, platinum, and karat gold	122.8	127.8	127.2	132.4	135.3	138.6	148.6	153.7
Costume jewelry and novelties	125.3	135.1	141.6	144.9	147.9	153.5	154.2	156.6
Capital equipment	**122.9**	**136.7**	**138.8**	**139.5**	**141.4**	**144.6**	**146.9**	**149.5**
Agricultural machinery and equipment	121.7	142.9	153.7	160.9	165.9	174.7	178.9	183.9
Construction machinery and equipment	121.6	136.7	148.6	153.2	158.5	168.3	175.4	179.6
Metal cutting machine tools	129.8	148.0	161.9	150.6	151.4	155.1	163.4	165.5
Metal forming machine tools	128.7	145.7	161.8	167.6	171.6	178.9	183.3	184.4
Pumps, compressors, and equipment	119.2	139.4	154.1	162.9	167.5	178.5	186.0	195.0
Electronic computers (Dec. 2004 = 100)	(NA)	850.1	261.6	122.3	107.3	85.5	66.5	51.5
Textile machinery	128.8	146.7	156.2	157.6	158.1	160.5	161.7	162.3
Paper industries machinery (June 1982 = 100)	134.8	151.0	164.7	170.3	173.7	178.1	180.6	183.8
Printing trades machinery	124.9	133.6	142.1	143.1	143.4	144.3	146.5	150.5
Transformers and power regulators	120.9	128.9	135.8	131.9	135.7	150.3	172.5	194.8
Communication/related equip.(Dec. 1985 = 100)	106.1	112.1	110.6	105.5	103.3	102.5	102.4	103.1
X-ray and electromedical equipment	109.8	111.8	101.5	100.5	97.5	95.7	94.9	92.8
Mining machinery and equipment	121.0	135.6	146.1	155.2	163.4	175.9	183.9	191.0
Office and store machines and equipment	109.5	111.5	112.7	112.3	113.2	115.1	114.7	114.8
Commercial furniture	133.4	148.2	158.4	162.3	165.6	172.7	177.0	181.3
Light motor trucks	130.0	159.0	157.6	150.2	151.3	148.4	143.3	145.2
Heavy motor trucks	120.3	144.1	148.0	154.2	155.7	162.4	169.1	177.2
Truck trailers	110.8	131.7	139.4	139.4	148.1	157.1	164.5	169.5
Civilian aircraft (Dec. 1985 = 100)	115.3	141.8	159.6	179.9	190.5	202.2	212.4	219.5
Ships (Dec. 1985 = 100)	110.1	132.8	146.9	159.4	171.4	176.6	183.2	192.3
Railroad equipment	118.6	134.8	135.7	136.3	143.9	160.4	169.4	176.5
Intermediate materials, supplies, and components	**114.5**	**124.9**	**129.2**	**133.7**	**142.6**	**154.0**	**164.0**	**170.6**
Intermediate foods and feeds	**113.3**	**114.8**	**111.7**	**125.9**	**137.1**	**133.8**	**135.2**	**154.4**
Flour	103.6	123.0	103.8	123.6	129.0	133.6	145.8	179.8
Refined sugar	122.7	119.3	110.6	121.8	120.7	124.9	149.9	131.7
Soft drink beverage bases (December 1985 = 100)	126.2	148.3	167.1	174.3	176.2	180.4	188.4	196.1
Prepared animal feeds	107.4	109.1	102.9	112.8	124.8	115.6	118.7	142.7

See footnotes at end of table.

474 Prices

Table 713. Producer Price Indexes by Stage of Processing and Commodity: 1990 to 2007—Con.

[1982 = 100, except as indicated. See Appendix III]

Stage of processing	1990	1995	2000	2003	2004	2005	2006	2007 [1]
Intermediate materials less foods and feeds.	**114.5**	**125.5**	**130.1**	**134.2**	**143.0**	**155.1**	**165.4**	**171.5**
Synthetic fibers	106.7	109.4	107.2	106.4	106.6	112.3	115.0	114.3
Processed yarns and threads	112.6	112.8	107.9	103.6	108.7	111.7	114.0	117.0
Leather	177.5	191.4	182.2	214.0	220.6	219.6	223.7	230.3
Liquefied petroleum gas	77.4	65.1	127.1	150.9	193.3	244.7	268.5	314.6
Commercial electric power	115.3	131.7	131.5	140.9	142.8	149.8	161.3	165.6
Industrial electric power	119.6	130.8	131.5	145.8	147.2	156.2	172.8	180.5
Commercial natural gas (Dec. 1990 = 100)	(NA)	96.5	134.7	173.6	194.9	232.5	239.9	235.4
Industrial natural gas (Dec. 1990 = 100)	(NA)	90.9	139.0	180.5	201.7	249.4	246.2	242.0
Natural gas to electric utilities (Dec. 1990 = 100)	(NA)	87.7	120.7	158.2	171.6	204.0	191.4	187.8
Jet fuels	76.0	55.0	88.5	86.3	112.6	169.6	199.1	209.7
No. 2 diesel fuel	74.1	57.0	93.3	100.5	128.2	189.1	216.9	235.5
Residual fuel	57.7	52.6	84.7	101.2	100.2	148.9	161.1	174.2
Industrial chemicals	113.2	128.4	129.1	141.7	162.8	188.5	212.4	225.9
Prepared paint	124.8	142.1	160.8	170.8	175.7	187.9	201.3	208.8
Fats and oils, inedible	88.1	126.9	70.1	123.4	153.6	146.9	147.9	189.7
Mixed fertilizers	103.3	111.1	112.4	119.1	127.8	138.9	144.9	162.3
Plastic resins and materials	124.1	143.5	141.6	146.1	163.1	193.0	198.4	196.2
Synthetic rubber	111.9	126.3	119.1	125.7	132.4	151.3	162.0	169.3
Plastic construction products	117.2	133.8	135.8	138.6	144.6	158.8	181.8	179.1
Unsupported plastic film, sheet, and shapes	119.0	135.6	133.2	142.8	149.1	164.8	175.1	176.0
Plastic parts and components for manufacturing	112.9	115.9	117.3	116.3	116.5	119.8	130.3	130.0
Softwood lumber	123.8	178.5	178.6	170.8	209.8	203.6	189.4	170.7
Hardwood lumber	131.0	167.0	185.9	188.8	199.3	196.6	195.3	192.2
Plywood	114.2	165.3	157.6	167.0	198.5	186.8	172.7	176.0
Paper	128.8	159.0	149.8	146.1	149.4	159.6	167.4	169.1
Paperboard	135.7	183.1	176.7	162.7	170.2	175.5	192.0	201.7
Paper boxes and containers	129.9	163.8	172.6	172.9	177.6	183.7	192.5	197.7
Building paper and board	112.2	144.9	138.8	159.9	192.4	184.9	173.0	155.0
Commercial printing (June 1982 = 100)	128.0	144.5	155.2	158.3	159.4	161.6	165.0	166.0
Foundry and forge shop products	117.2	129.3	136.5	137.4	144.0	156.2	163.0	170.9
Primary nonferrous metals	133.4	146.8	113.6	104.8	133.6	158.2	236.0	269.8
Nonferrous wire and cable	142.6	151.5	143.7	134.5	152.5	169.4	226.9	238.5
Metal containers	114.0	117.2	106.8	109.2	116.2	123.9	126.9	133.3
Hardware	125.9	141.1	151.2	156.5	161.6	168.0	174.0	179.6
Plumbing fixtures and brass fittings	144.3	166.0	180.4	183.4	188.3	197.6	207.2	220.8
Heating equipment	131.6	147.5	155.6	163.2	169.5	179.9	185.7	195.3
Fabricated ferrous wire products (June 1982 = 100)	114.6	125.7	130.0	131.3	149.3	157.1	162.6	166.5
Mechanical power transmission equipment	125.3	146.9	163.9	171.7	179.3	189.5	197.0	204.8
Air conditioning and refrigeration equipment	122.1	130.2	135.3	137.2	139.4	146.2	150.1	157.2
Ball and roller bearings	130.6	152.0	168.8	171.3	177.1	187.1	193.1	200.1
Wiring devices	132.2	147.2	152.9	152.9	169.0	176.6	188.2	194.4
Motors, generators, motor generator sets	132.9	143.9	146.2	147.4	149.8	157.8	165.0	172.9
Switchgear and switchboard equipment	124.4	140.3	153.0	159.9	163.8	170.2	178.6	188.5
Electronic components and accessories	118.4	113.6	97.1	90.8	88.8	87.0	88.5	82.5
Internal combustion engines	120.2	135.6	143.8	144.6	145.8	147.7	152.5	154.8
Flat glass	107.5	113.2	109.7	111.0	108.6	111.0	113.5	114.2
Cement	103.7	128.1	150.1	152.0	156.8	176.4	199.3	208.9
Concrete products	113.5	129.4	147.8	153.6	161.2	177.2	195.1	203.3
Asphalt felts and coatings	97.1	100.0	104.1	116.4	117.7	130.8	144.5	144.9
Gypsum products	105.2	154.5	201.4	171.5	198.8	229.6	274.9	233.7
Glass containers	120.4	130.5	127.4	140.2	144.4	146.4	152.8	162.2
Motor vehicle parts	111.2	116.0	113.6	111.8	112.0	113.1	116.3	117.9
Aircraft engines and engine parts (Dec. 1985 = 100)	113.5	132.8	141.0	153.8	163.0	165.9	172.4	178.8
Photographic supplies	127.6	126.8	125.2	117.5	115.1	120.1	121.6	122.8
Medical/surgical/personal aid devices	127.3	141.3	146.0	154.7	157.8	159.2	161.4	163.1
Crude materials for further processing	**108.9**	**102.7**	**120.6**	**135.3**	**159.0**	**182.2**	**184.8**	**207.3**
Crude foodstuffs and feedstuffs	113.1	105.8	100.2	113.5	127.0	122.7	119.3	146.7
Wheat	87.6	118.6	80.3	98.5	106.0	102.7	116.9	172.8
Corn	100.9	109.0	76.4	93.8	97.5	75.9	95.6	141.5
Slaughter cattle	122.5	99.5	104.1	124.3	126.2	131.5	126.2	136.1
Slaughter hogs	94.1	70.2	72.7	66.1	87.8	82.7	77.2	76.1
Slaughter broilers/fryers	119.5	129.1	127.6	149.3	188.5	181.0	156.1	199.9
Slaughter turkeys	116.9	120.3	120.7	102.8	122.0	131.1	140.5	153.3
Fluid milk	100.8	93.6	92.0	93.8	120.1	113.5	96.7	143.2
Soybeans	100.8	102.2	83.4	108.8	130.0	102.6	96.8	137.9
Crude nonfood materials	101.5	96.8	130.4	148.2	179.2	223.4	230.6	246.7
Raw cotton	118.2	156.2	95.2	92.9	85.6	78.9	79.7	82.1
Coal	97.5	95.0	87.9	99.9	109.2	116.8	126.6	130.7
Natural gas	80.4	66.6	155.5	214.5	245.9	335.4	280.3	274.7
Crude petroleum	71.0	51.1	85.2	83.0	108.2	150.1	176.0	192.3
Logs and timber	142.8	220.4	196.4	181.8	193.3	197.4	201.2	216.8
Wastepaper	138.9	371.1	282.5	197.3	231.4	230.9	234.8	370.2
Iron ore	83.3	91.8	94.8	95.9	98.2	116.9	132.5	128.8
Iron and steel scrap	166.0	202.7	142.1	182.6	323.7	289.8	335.2	407.9
Nonferrous metal ores (Dec. 1983 = 100)	98.3	101.6	68.0	78.5	113.7	150.0	215.9	245.9
Copper base scrap	181.3	193.5	123.7	128.4	186.5	258.6	436.8	484.2
Aluminum base scrap	172.6	209.4	177.0	168.7	194.1	210.1	275.7	274.8
Construction sand, gravel, and crushed stone	125.4	142.3	163.1	177.1	183.3	195.8	213.9	232.2
Industrial sand	117.6	132.5	146.0	160.4	165.3	174.4	183.2	191.6

NA Not available.   [1] Preliminary data.

Source: U.S. Bureau of Labor Statistics, *Producer Price Indexes,* monthly and annual. See also *Monthly Labor Review* at <http://www.bls.gov/opub/mlr/welcome.htm>.

U.S. Census Bureau, Statistical Abstract of the United States: 2009

Table 714. **Producer Price Indexes for the Net Output of Selected Industries: 2003 to 2007**

[Indexes are based on selling prices reported by establishments of all sizes by probability sampling. Manufacturing industries selected by shipment value. N.e.c.= not elsewhere classified. See text, Section 22. See Appendix III]

Industry	NAICS code [1]	Index base [2]	2003	2004	2005	2006	2007 [3]
Logging industries.	**113310**	**12/81**	**168.8**	**175.3**	**179.2**	**176.7**	**174.9**
Total mining industries.	**21**	**12/84**	**131.3**	**153.4**	**201.0**	**208.7**	**220.2**
Crude petroleum and natural gas extraction	211111	06/02	152.3	183.4	253.5	252.3	261.7
Natural gas liquid extraction	211112	06/02	181.2	216.5	285.4	258.1	286.1
Bituminous coal and lignite surface mining	212111	12/01	101.5	107.1	111.9	117.1	121.0
Anthracite mining.	212113	12/79	168.4	180.9	205.4	234.9	240.7
Iron ore mining	212210	12/84	95.0	97.2	115.7	131.2	127.5
Gold ore mining	212221	06/85	107.6	121.6	131.7	177.5	203.9
Copper ore and nickel ore mining	212234	06/88	90.1	150.1	200.8	360.4	399.8
Crushed and broken limestone mining and quarrying . . .	212312	12/83	159.2	165.4	174.3	189.5	204.7
Crushed and broken granite mining and quarrying	212313	12/83	197.5	203.7	217.3	242.5	277.8
Construction sand and gravel mining	212321	06/82	188.9	195.0	209.9	229.1	247.1
Clay and ceramic and refractory minerals mining	212325	06/84	142.5	144.4	148.3	156.9	163.2
Drilling oil and gas wells	213111	12/85	153.5	168.0	258.8	377.7	362.5
Nonmetallic minerals support activity (except fuels)	213115	06/85	114.6	119.6	127.5	137.2	140.2
Total manufacturing industries	**31–33**	**12/84**	**137.1**	**142.9**	**150.8**	**156.9**	**162.9**
Dog and cat food manufacturing	311111	12/85	136.2	144.0	145.8	147.8	155.7
Flour milling	311211	06/83	113.7	117.4	117.5	127.4	154.7
Rice milling	311212	06/84	87.6	113.1	102.1	114.5	129.3
Soybean processing	311222	12/79	87.1	102.3	91.5	93.1	115.0
Fats and oils refining and blending	311225	12/81	158.1	186.8	171.7	177.2	207.6
Chocolate and confectionery mfg. from cacao beans . . .	311320	06/83	156.2	155.0	157.5	161.0	165.9
Frozen fruit, juice, and vegetable manufacturing	311411	06/81	147.8	149.3	156.0	171.1	175.4
Frozen specialty food manufacturing	311412	12/82	139.2	142.1	143.6	144.4	145.5
Fruit and vegetable canning.	311421	06/81	144.8	146.5	151.4	155.9	165.2
Fluid milk	311511	12/82	147.7	162.5	165.2	163.2	193.7
Ice cream and frozen dessert manufacturing	311520	06/83	160.4	166.0	168.2	171.8	177.7
Animal (except poultry) slaughtering	311611	12/80	130.1	137.8	141.0	136.4	142.6
Meat processed from carcasses	311612	12/82	129.7	132.9	136.6	137.1	139.6
Poultry processing	311615	12/81	121.9	137.5	135.3	124.1	139.7
Seafood canning	311711	12/84	110.2	114.5	114.0	118.2	123.4
Fresh and frozen seafood processing	311712	12/82	161.5	164.1	171.1	171.7	181.6
Cookie and cracker manufacturing.	311821	06/83	181.6	183.4	184.4	187.8	193.0
Flour mixes and dough mfg. from purchased flour	311822	06/85	131.9	134.0	135.9	139.3	146.2
Dry pasta manufacturing	311823	06/85	126.3	127.1	127.8	127.7	135.2
Coffee and tea manufacturing.	311920	06/81	139.4	142.2	161.0	164.1	173.9
Spice and extracts manufacturing	311942	12/03	(NA)	100.3	99.1	99.8	102.4
Soft drinks manufacturing	312111	06/81	161.5	165.3	168.6	173.0	177.4
Bottled water manufacturing	312112	12/03	(NA)	100.7	101.5	101.8	99.4
Breweries.	312120	06/82	145.8	151.9	158.4	158.4	156.0
Wineries.	312130	12/83	140.8	140.0	144.8	152.7	155.3
Distilleries	312140	06/83	165.1	164.7	165.5	167.8	175.5
Tobacco stemming and redrying	312210	06/84	117.5	119.4	119.9	109.4	112.6
Cigarettes.	312221	12/82	411.7	412.6	437.0	440.1	470.6
Men's/boys' cut & sew trouser/slack/jean mfg.	315224	12/81	128.4	126.6	123.2	121.5	122.3
Women's/girls' cut & sew dress manufacturing.	315233	12/80	122.8	124.9	123.7	123.4	120.8
Sawmills.	321113	12/80	141.1	163.4	162.0	158.3	152.2
Wood preservation	321114	06/85	154.0	167.7	175.7	169.4	163.9
Hardwood veneer and plywood manufacturing.	321211	06/85	138.6	143.6	146.2	149.8	151.0
Softwood veneer or plywood manufacturing	321212	12/80	154.4	189.0	172.7	151.1	154.8
Wood window and door manufacturing	321911	12/03	(NA)	101.9	103.1	106.6	107.2
Manufactured homes (mobile homes) manufacturing. . . .	321991	06/81	175.8	190.0	204.4	212.4	214.9
Pulp mills	322110	12/82	120.9	131.3	137.4	144.8	163.1
Paper (except newsprint) mills	322121	12/03	(NA)	102.4	108.4	112.7	116.0
Newsprint mills	322122	12/03	(NA)	104.0	115.7	123.9	107.0
Paperboard mills	322130	12/82	180.4	190.1	196.2	213.0	225.3
Book printing	323117	12/83	150.2	151.5	154.9	158.2	158.7
Petroleum refineries	324110	06/85	121.2	151.5	205.3	241.0	266.9
Petroleum lubricating oils and greases	324191	12/80	191.5	199.4	231.2	284.5	304.7
Industrial gas manufacturing.	325120	12/03	(NA)	108.3	118.3	123.0	123.4
Plastics material and resins manufacturing	325211	12/80	167.8	192.0	228.5	235.5	232.5
Synthetic rubber manufacturing.	325212	06/81	125.2	131.6	150.6	161.9	170.3
Nitrogenous fertilizer manufacturing	325311	12/79	177.0	203.9	236.9	245.6	278.0
Phosphatic fertilizer manufacturing	325312	12/79	145.4	161.3	173.3	183.7	265.0
Pharmaceutical preparation manufacturing	325412	06/81	343.3	360.1	378.7	397.9	413.8
Plastics pipe and pipe fitting manufacturing.	326122	06/93	124.7	140.8	171.9	214.1	197.2
Cement manufacturing	327310	06/82	150.5	155.4	175.2	197.7	207.6
Lime	327410	12/85	128.1	133.1	144.6	156.6	166.2
Steel investment foundries	331512	06/81	199.8	197.7	204.8	216.0	236.0
Steel foundries (except investment)	331513	06/81	137.5	146.2	160.1	170.5	183.9
Aluminum die-casting foundries.	331521	06/91	111.5	114.1	116.4	125.1	126.2
Iron and steel forging	332111	12/83	112.8	117.5	128.1	133.9	140.4
Hand and edge tools, except machine tools and handsaws	332212	06/83	165.1	168.8	177.0	183.7	188.9
Saw blade and handsaw manufacturing	332213	06/83	142.9	142.9	146.0	150.2	152.3
Metal window and door manufacturing	332321	06/83	161.0	166.5	175.2	183.5	188.1
Sheetmetal work manufacturing	332322	12/82	144.4	159.4	165.6	171.6	176.9
Heating equipment (except warm air furnaces) mfg.	333414	06/80	199.8	206.2	215.4	222.3	231.1
Laboratory apparatus and furniture	339111	12/91	137.3	141.2	148.1	152.5	158.7
Surgical and medical instrument manufacturing	339112	06/82	133.1	134.6	135.2	134.0	134.5
Services industries							
New car dealers.	441110	12/99	111.5	113.5	116.3	122.3	124.7
Automotive parts and accessories stores	441310	12/03	(NA)	106.8	110.9	119.7	125.8

See footnotes at end of table.

U.S. Census Bureau, Statistical Abstract of the United States: 2009

Table 714. **Producer Price Indexes for the Net Output of Selected Industries: 2003 to 2007**—Con.

[See headnote, page 476]

Industry	NAICS code [1]	Index base [2]	2003	2004	2005	2006	2007 [3]
Household appliance stores	443111	06/03	(NA)	93.3	100.5	104.2	102.6
Hardware stores	444130	06/03	(NA)	103.5	108.6	112.8	114.9
Nursery, garden, and farm supply stores	444220	12/02	102.1	112.4	117.2	118.5	113.4
Grocery (except convenience) stores	445110	12/99	117.9	123.6	132.1	136.0	140.2
Beer, wine, and liquor stores	445310	06/00	106.9	110.7	111.0	111.3	113.1
Food (health) supplement stores	446191	12/99	139.1	144.9	149.2	164.6	162.6
Gasoline stations with convenience stores.	447110	12/03	(NA)	102.5	104.3	110.1	122.8
Men's clothing stores.	448110	06/02	102.2	103.8	105.8	102.5	103.4
Women's clothing stores	448120	06/03	(NA)	105.1	105.6	110.9	114.9
Family clothing stores	448140	06/03	(NA)	103.7	108.3	110.6	110.3
Sporting goods stores	451110	06/00	104.4	99.1	100.3	103.5	117.7
Book stores.	451211	06/00	113.7	118.2	114.5	117.2	121.0
Department stores, except discount	452111	12/03	(NA)	104.5	103.1	103.5	110.4
Discount department stores	452112	12/03	(NA)	106.1	106.7	107.2	112.4
Office supplies and stationery stores	453210	06/00	124.3	127.1	130.2	135.6	144.0
Manufactured (mobile) home dealers	453930	12/02	103.6	113.8	123.3	130.2	124.9
Scheduled passenger air transportation	481111	12/89	205.7	205.8	217.1	229.6	234.0
Scheduled freight air transportation	481112	12/03	(NA)	100.2	104.9	108.4	108.9
Line-haul railroads	482111	12/84	121.4	126.5	139.6	151.6	156.8
General freight trucking, local	484110	12/03	(NA)	105.2	111.5	115.3	119.9
General freight trucking, long-distance	484121	12/03	(NA)	102.7	108.6	112.0	113.5
Pipeline transportation of crude oil	486110	06/86	111.1	115.2	125.5	135.3	138.2
Pipeline transportation of refined petroleum products. . .	486910	06/86	112.7	116.0	120.3	123.8	131.2
Marine cargo handling.	488320	12/91	111.5	113.2	115.1	118.4	123.1
United States Postal Service.	491110	06/89	155.0	155.0	155.0	164.7	171.9
Couriers	492110	12/03	(NA)	106.6	115.0	123.2	133.6
Newspaper publishers	511110	12/79	395.6	409.7	426.2	439.1	450.7
Periodical publishers	511120	12/79	332.3	339.1	347.6	354.4	369.7
Commercial banking	522110	12/03	(NA)	102.8	106.1	113.0	113.8
Savings institutions	522120	12/03	(NA)	100.9	98.8	101.2	105.6
Direct life insurance carriers	524113	12/98	103.4	105.2	106.4	107.0	107.2
Direct health and medical insurance carriers	524114	12/02	106.2	111.8	116.8	121.5	124.9
Direct property and casualty insurance carriers	524126	06/98	115.1	118.8	121.1	121.8	122.1
General medical and surgical hospitals.	622110	12/92	135.3	141.9	147.3	153.5	158.6
Nursing care facilities	623110	12/94	149.4	155.6	161.4	166.2	173.5
Hotels (except casino hotels) and motels	721110	12/03	(NA)	103.5	110.0	114.1	119.4
Casino hotels.	721120	12/03	(NA)	105.0	107.5	110.8	113.3

NA Not available.   [1] North American Industry Classification System, 1997.   [2] Index base year equals 100.   [3] Preliminary data.

Source: U.S. Bureau of Labor Statistics, *Producer Price Indexes,* monthly and annual. See also *Monthly Labor Review* at <http://www.bls.gov/opub/mlr/welcome.htm>.

Table 715. **Commodity Research Bureau Futures Price Index: 1990 to 2007**

[**1967 = 100**. Index computed daily. Represents unweighted geometric average of commodity futures prices (through 6 months forward) of 17 major commodity futures markets. Represents end of year index]

Item	1990	1995	1998	1999	2000	2001	2002	2003	2004	2005	2006	2007
All commodities	**222.6**	**243.2**	**191.2**	**205.1**	**227.8**	**190.6**	**234.5**	**255.3**	**283.9**	**347.9**	**394.9**	**476.1**
Softs [1]	276.0	354.4	344.8	280.9	254.4	252.8	303.7	250.5	343.5	420.5	475.9	467.5
Industrials	245.5	272.5	185.3	192.9	211.0	141.8	176.6	256.6	232.1	302.5	368.8	418.3
Grains and oilseeds [2]	171.2	218.6	172.8	156.6	174.9	159.0	188.2	225.8	177.0	193.8	279.1	427.0
Energy	246.0	180.0	135.0	221.0	355.8	204.9	320.7	358.7	457.3	705.3	591.6	825.1
Oilseeds [3]	223.6	277.5	(3)	(3)	(3)	(3)	(3)	(3)	(3)	(3)	(3)	(3)
Livestock and meats	226.2	192.4	186.7	239.6	253.6	247.4	251.0	237.8	303.6	300.3	294.6	297.7
Metals (precious)	257.8	276.0	234.3	253.4	265.7	246.8	289.1	364.1	396.6	478.1	611.9	773.6

[1] Prior to 1997, reported as imported. Softs include commodities that are grown and not mined such as coffee, cocoa, lumber, cotton, and sugar.   [2] Prior to 1997, reported as grains.   [3] Incorporated into grains and oilseeds beginning 1997.

Source: Commodity Research Bureau (CRB), Chicago, IL, *CRB Commodity Index Report,* weekly (copyright).

Table 716. **Indexes of Spot Primary Market Prices: 1990 to 2007**

[**1967 = 100.** Computed daily Represents unweighted geometric average of price quotations of 23 commodities; much more sensitive to changes in market conditions than is a monthly producer price index]

Items and number of commodities	1990	1995	1998	1999	2000	2001	2002	2003	2004	2005	2006	2007
All commodities (23).	**258.1**	**289.1**	**235.2**	**227.3**	**224.0**	**212.1**	**244.3**	**283.6**	**293.0**	**303.3**	**368.2**	**426.7**
Foodstuffs (10)	206.4	236.4	197.5	178.1	184.7	201.6	238.1	250.2	256.0	241.7	276.0	335.9
Raw industrials (13).	301.2	332.2	265.3	268.9	255.8	217.3	248.6	309.1	321.5	354.7	449.3	503.2
Livestock and products (5) . . .	292.7	307.4	232.3	265.7	265.5	257.2	317.8	365.9	365.0	326.6	378.6	402.6
Metals (5)	283.2	300.6	218.5	214.0	214.0	172.5	184.5	276.7	357.7	440.9	744.7	933.0
Textiles and fibers (4).	257.6	274.3	237.5	223.8	245.7	217.4	230.2	255.2	237.9	252.5	254.4	267.5
Fats and oils (4)	188.7	226.7	236.0	174.8	163.6	175.8	234.0	297.2	262.6	223.4	273.9	363.4

Source: Commodity Research Bureau, Chicago, IL, *CRB Commodity Index Report,* weekly (copyright).

U.S. Census Bureau, Statistical Abstract of the United States: 2009

Table 717. Chain-Type Price Indexes For Personal Consumption Expenditures by Type of Expenditure: 1990 to 2006

[2000 = 100. For explanation of "chain-type," see text, Section 13. See also Table 655]

Type of expenditure	1990	1995	2000	2003	2004	2005	2006
Total expenditures [1]	**80.5**	**91.6**	**100.0**	**105.6**	**108.4**	**111.6**	**114.7**
Food and tobacco [1]	78.2	86.8	100.0	107.9	111.1	113.8	116.5
Food purchased for off-premise consumption	82.7	90.4	100.0	106.2	109.5	111.4	113.3
Purchased meals and beverages [2]	78.6	88.2	100.0	108.2	111.5	115.0	118.6
Tobacco products	46.7	57.6	100.0	118.8	121.0	127.3	131.6
Clothing, accessories, and jewelry [1]	105.6	105.7	100.0	95.1	95.3	95.0	95.5
Shoes	103.7	106.2	100.0	96.6	96.3	99.0	99.8
Clothing	109.4	106.3	100.0	92.3	92.0	90.4	89.8
Jewelry and watches	114.4	117.9	100.0	93.9	94.5	93.1	95.4
Personal care	83.1	91.8	100.0	103.4	104.6	106.1	108.0
Housing [1]	74.5	86.1	100.0	110.4	113.2	116.1	120.3
Owner-occupied nonfarm dwellings—space rent	74.8	86.2	100.0	110.7	113.2	115.7	119.8
Tenant-occupied nonfarm dwellings—space rent	75.4	86.2	100.0	111.3	114.1	117.6	121.7
Household operation [1]	89.3	96.6	100.0	102.0	102.8	106.2	109.2
Furniture [3]	91.9	99.6	100.0	95.0	94.7	93.7	94.5
Semidurable house furnishings [4]	112.0	111.0	100.0	87.7	83.9	81.7	76.1
Cleaning and polishing preparations	84.2	89.5	100.0	102.8	103.2	105.3	109.7
Household utilities	80.9	90.3	100.0	112.3	118.1	130.1	140.9
Electricity	91.5	100.9	100.0	109.3	111.4	118.1	132.4
Gas	73.2	77.3	100.0	123.8	134.3	160.0	163.8
Water and other sanitary services	66.1	87.1	100.0	110.2	116.7	123.1	129.1
Fuel oil and coal	76.9	69.9	100.0	109.7	125.4	159.6	180.3
Telephone and telegraph	103.8	107.0	100.0	97.2	95.2	94.4	95.1
Medical care [1]	70.1	88.0	100.0	110.3	114.6	118.4	122.1
Drug preparations and sundries [5]	72.7	87.2	100.0	112.0	115.1	118.5	123.2
Physicians	71.2	92.3	100.0	104.3	106.5	108.5	109.4
Dentists	60.6	80.1	100.0	113.2	118.7	125.3	131.8
Hospitals and nursing homes [6]	70.1	87.7	100.0	112.8	117.6	122.4	127.2
Health insurance	62.0	82.4	100.0	114.2	126.8	133.5	137.5
Medical care [7]	60.3	84.2	100.0	120.0	134.4	139.1	143.2
Personal business [1]	76.0	90.3	100.0	105.9	109.2	112.3	115.3
Expense of handling life insurance [8]	61.7	75.2	100.0	110.4	116.6	120.0	124.3
Legal services	65.7	80.5	100.0	116.5	122.0	127.1	131.5
Funeral and burial expenses	63.7	82.1	100.0	113.0	117.8	121.8	128.1
Transportation	79.9	90.8	100.0	101.8	106.1	113.6	119.2
User-operated transportation [1]	79.5	90.8	100.0	102.4	107.0	114.8	120.5
New autos	87.5	99.9	100.0	96.6	96.0	96.7	97.6
Net purchases of used autos	69.1	95.6	100.0	97.4	98.0	101.0	102.7
Tires, tubes, accessories, etc.	102.2	101.8	100.0	105.2	105.7	108.2	112.6
Repair, greasing, washing, parking, storage, rental, and leasing	77.6	90.4	100.0	108.0	109.6	112.8	116.7
Gasoline and oil	78.4	77.8	100.0	105.2	123.9	150.8	170.5
Purchased local transportation	77.0	90.2	100.0	112.8	119.5	125.0	129.2
Mass transit systems	77.9	90.9	100.0	112.8	119.5	125.0	129.2
Taxicab	75.0	88.7	100.0	112.8	119.5	125.0	129.2
Purchased intercity transportation [1]	87.9	91.4	100.0	88.9	87.8	89.8	94.8
Railway (commutation)	76.2	85.7	100.0	107.6	98.4	99.2	107.8
Bus	86.8	86.6	100.0	110.5	114.8	118.9	127.5
Airline	91.5	93.0	100.0	84.8	83.3	84.9	89.7
Recreation [1]	104.9	109.0	100.0	95.8	95.2	94.2	93.3
Magazines, newspapers, and sheet music	73.9	89.4	100.0	105.9	109.0	111.8	113.6
Nondurable toys and sport supplies	115.9	118.4	100.0	85.8	82.4	78.2	75.3
Video and audio products, including musical instruments and computer goods	284.8	205.9	100.0	68.7	62.9	56.8	51.1
Computers, peripherals, and software	1,516.2	516.5	100.0	49.2	43.6	37.6	32.6
Education and research	66.6	82.6	100.0	115.4	122.2	129.0	135.5
Higher education	62.9	82.8	100.0	117.0	124.7	132.0	139.3
Religious and welfare activities	73.1	84.5	100.0	109.3	112.6	116.2	121.0
Foreign travel and other, net:							
Foreign travel by U.S. residents	80.1	95.1	100.0	111.6	117.1	125.6	128.1
Expenditures abroad by U.S. residents	102.0	124.1	100.0	124.3	137.8	145.4	153.9
Less: Expenditures in the United States by nonresidents	76.9	87.3	100.0	104.5	109.0	113.8	119.0
Less: Personal remittances in kind to nonresidents	87.8	93.8	100.0	101.3	103.7	107.4	109.9

[1] Includes other types not shown separately. [2] Consists of purchases (including tips) of meals and beverages from retail, service, and amusement establishments; hotels; dining and buffet cars; schools; school fraternities; institutions; clubs; and industrial lunch rooms. Includes meals and beverages consumed both on- and off-premise. [3] Includes mattresses and bedsprings. [4] Consists largely of textile house furnishings including piece goods allocated to house furnishing use. Also includes lamp shades, brooms, and brushes. [5] Excludes drug preparations and related products dispensed by physicians, hospitals, and other medical services. [6] Consists of (1) current expenditures (including consumption of fixed capital) of nonprofit hospitals and nursing homes and (2) payments by patients to proprietary and government hospitals and nursing homes. [7] Consists of (1) premiums, less benefits and dividends, for health hospitalization and accidental death and dismemberment insurance provided by commercial insurance carriers and (2) administrative expenses (including consumption of fixed capital) of Blue Cross and Blue Shield plans and of other independent prepaid and self-insured health plans. [8] Consists of (1) operating expenses of life insurance carriers and private noninsured pension plans and (2) premiums less benefits and dividends of fraternal benefit societies. Excludes expenses allocated by commercial carriers to accident and health insurance.

Source: U.S. Bureau of Economic Analysis, *Survey of Current Business*, April 2008. See also <http://www.bea.doc.gov/bea/dn/nipaweb/SelectTable.asp?Selected=N> (released April 2008).

Table 718. Chain-Type Price Indexes for Gross Domestic Product: 1990 to 2007

[**2000 = 100.** For explanation of "chain-type," see text, Section 13]

Component	1990	1995	2000	2003	2004	2005	2006	2007
Gross domestic product	**81.6**	**92.1**	**100.0**	**106.4**	**109.5**	**113.0**	**116.6**	**119.7**
Personal consumption expenditures.	**80.5**	**91.6**	**100.0**	**105.6**	**108.4**	**111.6**	**114.7**	**117.6**
Durable goods	104.6	110.7	100.0	92.4	90.7	90.0	88.9	87.3
Nondurable goods.	84.2	90.6	100.0	104.1	107.6	111.6	115.0	118.4
Services	74.2	88.3	100.0	109.4	112.9	116.7	120.7	124.6
Gross private domestic investment	**96.4**	**100.9**	**100.0**	**103.2**	**106.7**	**111.2**	**115.1**	**116.5**
Fixed investment	95.5	100.3	100.0	103.3	106.8	111.4	115.4	116.7
Nonresidential.	104.7	106.2	100.0	99.6	100.9	103.8	107.0	108.3
Structures.	74.0	83.9	100.0	113.9	120.9	135.0	150.8	155.8
Equipment and software	118.2	115.2	100.0	94.9	94.6	94.5	94.5	94.9
Residential	74.9	85.8	100.0	112.4	120.6	128.7	134.3	135.5
Net exports of goods and services:								
Exports	100.0	104.4	100.0	101.4	105.0	108.8	112.5	116.5
Goods	108.0	109.2	100.0	100.6	104.3	107.5	111.1	115.2
Services	82.5	93.1	100.0	103.3	106.6	111.8	115.9	119.7
Imports	103.8	106.4	100.0	99.7	104.5	111.1	115.6	119.6
Goods	108.2	108.6	100.0	98.1	102.9	109.6	114.2	118.3
Services	85.7	96.1	100.0	108.3	113.0	119.3	123.0	126.5
Government consumption expenditures and gross investment	**77.1**	**88.4**	**100.0**	**109.8**	**114.8**	**121.4**	**127.3**	**133.1**
Federal	77.1	89.5	100.0	110.1	115.3	120.9	125.6	129.3
National defense	78.0	89.6	100.0	110.8	115.9	122.0	127.0	130.7
Nondefense	75.3	89.4	100.0	108.9	114.2	118.8	123.0	126.5
State and local	77.4	87.8	100.0	109.7	114.4	121.8	128.4	135.3

Source: U.S. Bureau of Economic Analysis, *Survey of Current Business,* April 2008. See also <http://www.bea.gov/bea/dn/nipaweb/SelectTable.asp?Selected=N> (released April 2008).

Table 719. Import and Export Price Indexes by End-Use Category: 1990 to 2007

[**As of June.** Import indexes are weighted by the 2000 Tariff Schedule of the United States Annotated, a scheme for describing and reporting product composition and value of U.S. imports. Import prices are based on U.S. dollar prices paid by importer. Export indexes are weighted by 2000 export values according to the Schedule B classification system of the U.S. Census Bureau. Prices used in these indexes were collected from a sample of U.S. manufacturers of exports and are factory transaction prices, except as noted. Minus sign (–) indicates decrease]

Year	Index (2000 = 100)						Percent change					
	Imports			Exports			Imports			Exports		
	Total	Petroleum imports	Non-petroleum imports	Total	Agricultural exports	Non-agricultural exports	Total	Petroleum imports	Non-petroleum imports	Total	Agricultural exports	Non-agricultural exports
1990	90.8	55.4	96.4	95.1	107.7	93.5	−0.8	−13.4	0.5	−0.1	−4.0	0.5
1995	101.4	62.9	107.6	104.5	117.0	103.3	5.3	9.2	4.9	6.1	7.0	5.9
2000	100.2	101.9	99.9	100.1	100.5	100.0	7.9	87.0	1.1	1.9	−0.6	2.1
2001	97.6	89.4	98.9	99.4	100.9	99.3	−2.6	−12.3	−1.0	−0.7	0.4	−0.7
2002	94.1	85.3	96.2	98.0	100.7	97.8	−3.6	−4.6	−2.7	−1.4	−0.2	−1.5
2003	96.2	96.4	97.3	99.5	110.0	98.7	2.2	13.0	1.1	1.5	9.2	0.9
2004	101.7	129.7	99.7	103.4	127.4	101.5	5.7	34.5	2.5	3.9	15.8	2.8
2005	109.2	181.5	102.0	106.7	123.9	105.4	7.4	39.9	2.3	3.2	−2.7	3.8
2006	117.3	242.6	104.2	111.2	124.1	110.3	7.4	33.7	2.2	4.2	0.2	4.6
2007	120.0	245.6	107.1	116.0	146.7	113.8	2.3	1.2	2.8	4.3	18.2	3.2

Source: U.S. Bureau of Labor Statistics, *U.S. Import and Export Price Indexes,* monthly. See also <http://www.bls.gov/web/ximpim.supp.toc.htm#long_tables>.

U.S. Census Bureau, Statistical Abstract of the United States: 2009

Table 720. Export Price Indexes—Selected Commodities: 1995 to 2007

[2000 = 100. As of June. Indexes are weighted by 2000 export values according to the Schedule B classification system of the U.S. Census Bureau. Prices used in these indexes were collected from a sample of U.S. manufacturers of exports and are factory transaction prices, except as noted]

Commodities	1995	2000 [1]	2002	2003	2004	2005	2006	2007
All commodities	**104.5**	**100.1**	**98.0**	**99.5**	**103.4**	**106.7**	**111.2**	**116.0**
Animal products	104.2	102.2	94.3	104.5	121.5	130.9	125.1	153.2
Fish	108.2	99.1	98.4	109.6	105.2	114.2	122.8	124.3
Vegetable products	122.2	100.0	105.0	115.0	140.3	130.3	131.0	159.3
Fruit and nuts	112.1	94.8	97.6	97.3	109.2	126.5	114.5	117.5
Cereals	137.6	100.0	106.6	119.3	143.3	118.1	136.9	179.2
Wheat	132.8	99.4	113.4	121.4	136.2	130.0	154.3	180.4
Corn (maize)	144.6	101.0	104.8	121.3	146.9	111.8	127.1	189.8
Oilseeds	109.4	102.8	104.7	121.5	161.0	136.2	121.5	157.4
Beverages and tobacco	101.0	100.0	99.3	102.8	110.7	110.3	112.5	120.5
Mineral products	78.1	97.8	92.8	106.4	129.7	182.3	238.4	243.4
Fuels	71.4	97.4	92.1	106.2	127.9	172.8	219.6	230.5
Chemicals and related products	107.5	100.3	96.7	102.4	107.7	115.3	122.8	130.1
Plastics and rubber products	107.9	101.5	97.2	102.6	105.7	118.4	128.7	131.3
Hides, skins, and leather products	107.8	95.7	102.6	104.3	108.6	113.0	116.8	122.6
Wood products	114.7	100.0	89.9	93.0	103.8	104.3	107.8	113.5
Woodpulp and paper products	120.1	101.6	92.7	95.1	98.1	101.9	105.5	110.6
Textiles	120.6	100.2	95.0	97.7	98.8	100.8	101.9	101.9
Stone and glass products	96.3	100.7	100.7	100.2	99.0	103.5	104.1	110.1
Gems and precious metals	92.0	98.1	89.7	92.1	101.6	106.5	141.8	162.7
Base metals	105.6	100.5	98.4	100.2	119.6	131.8	151.9	169.3
Iron and steel	123.4	101.7	96.8	102.7	152.9	164.0	173.7	209.2
Articles of iron and steel	90.6	100.2	102.0	104.7	115.3	124.8	134.6	148.5
Copper	137.4	98.7	92.7	93.4	122.7	143.1	230.6	243.9
Aluminum	113.8	98.4	94.3	94.6	107.3	113.2	146.0	149.5
Machinery	109.9	99.9	97.2	95.4	94.9	94.9	93.8	94.3
Nonelectrical machinery	106.7	100.0	98.9	99.1	99.9	100.5	101.5	102.7
Electrical machinery	114.1	99.8	95.1	91.2	89.4	88.6	85.3	85.2
Transportation equipment	92.1	100.0	102.9	104.5	106.5	108.8	111.5	113.8
Motor vehicles	96.1	100.0	100.3	101.1	102.4	103.2	104.6	105.6
Instruments	96.4	100.0	100.6	101.2	101.2	101.3	102.4	103.3
Miscellaneous manufactured articles	98.0	100.4	101.5	100.5	99.2	100.6	101.1	104.7

[1] June 2000 may not equal 100 because indexes were reweighted to an "average" trade value in 2000.

Source: U.S. Bureau of Labor Statistics, *U.S. Import and Export Price Indexes,* monthly. See also <http://stats.bls.gov/news.release/ximpim.toc.htm>.

Table 721. Import Price Indexes—Selected Commodities: 1995 to 2007

[2000 = 100. As of June. Indexes are weighted by the 2000 Tariff Schedule of the United States Annotated, a scheme for describing and reporting product composition and value of U.S. imports. Import prices are based on U.S. dollar prices paid by importer]

Commodity	1995	2000 [1]	2002	2003	2004	2005	2006	2007
All commodities	**101.4**	**100.2**	**94.1**	**96.2**	**101.7**	**109.2**	**117.1**	**120.0**
Animal products	93.6	99.9	88.2	95.1	107.8	112.7	118.2	127.4
Meat	96.4	100.5	104.1	104.1	130.8	138.7	137.2	146.8
Fish	88.6	100.2	79.8	81.9	83.4	88.3	96.6	100.2
Vegetable products	121.6	97.1	94.7	102.7	103.0	116.9	108.6	129.3
Vegetables	84.6	93.9	106.7	122.7	113.8	136.8	143.6	175.3
Fruit and nuts	99.6	96.9	97.5	96.5	96.3	89.7	81.7	90.9
Beverages and tobacco	104.3	100.0	101.8	105.4	108.9	114.0	119.8	124.3
Mineral products	63.7	101.3	85.5	100.6	130.9	178.1	229.2	234.0
Fuels	62.4	101.3	84.4	99.5	130.0	177.5	229.0	233.7
Chemicals and related products	102.8	99.8	96.3	99.1	103.6	111.3	114.5	123.8
Organic chemicals	102.3	100.6	95.7	97.0	100.1	109.6	118.0	120.5
Pharmaceutical products	93.9	99.8	98.8	101.8	106.9	111.0	106.5	107.6
Plastics and rubber products	116.2	99.9	98.6	103.9	105.9	113.5	120.1	121.7
Hides, skins, and leather products	100.1	100.2	97.9	99.9	101.5	104.0	105.2	107.0
Wood products	92.9	100.5	99.8	96.1	129.5	124.2	120.7	113.5
Woodpulp and paper products	114.5	100.0	91.3	95.2	98.2	102.3	107.9	108.0
Textiles	100.6	99.7	98.5	99.8	100.3	100.4	100.7	102.1
Footwear and clothing accessories	98.9	99.6	99.1	99.4	99.8	99.9	100.6	101.5
Footwear	99.4	99.6	99.2	100.0	100.2	100.3	101.0	101.3
Stone and glass products	100.7	99.5	101.0	102.4	103.8	105.4	108.6	110.4
Gems and precious metals	87.0	99.3	87.5	87.8	93.5	98.3	125.1	132.8
Gold	(NA)	98.3	112.3	127.0	137.1	150.7	241.2	238.2
Platinum	(NA)	(NA)	111.2	89.9	116.2	125.7	230.1	257.2
Base metals	109.6	101.5	93.4	96.5	118.9	132.1	157.9	176.7
Iron and steel	106.4	104.1	94.3	103.3	155.1	170.6	173.8	206.2
Articles of iron and steel	108.6	100.6	95.6	96.8	109.0	122.7	125.1	129.0
Copper	134.0	97.2	93.0	94.3	119.0	142.7	291.6	307.5
Aluminum	113.4	97.9	97.5	96.8	110.5	113.2	150.0	146.8
Machinery	124.6	100.2	95.0	92.8	90.7	89.7	88.1	87.8
Nonelectrical machinery	125.8	99.8	94.7	92.9	90.9	90.1	88.3	88.2
Electrical machinery	123.5	100.5	95.4	92.8	90.5	89.4	87.9	87.5
Transportation equipment	97.2	100.0	100.4	101.0	102.8	104.4	104.9	105.9
Motor vehicles	97.5	100.1	100.2	100.7	102.3	103.8	104.3	105.1
Instruments	111.0	99.8	97.9	99.6	99.1	100.1	99.6	99.4
Miscellaneous manufactured articles	104.5	99.7	97.2	97.5	97.4	99.4	99.5	101.1
Furniture	103.6	99.5	97.7	98.3	99.7	103.4	103.3	104.6

NA Not available. [1] June 2000 may not equal 100 because indexes were reweighted to an "average" trade value in 2000.

Source: U.S. Bureau of Labor Statistics, *U.S. Import and Export Price Indexes,* monthly. See also <http://stats.bls.gov/news.release/ximpim.toc.htm>.

Section 15
Business Enterprise

This section relates to the place and behavior of the business firm and to business initiative in the American economy. It includes data on the number, type, and size of businesses; financial data of domestic and multinational U.S. corporations; business investments, expenditures, and profits; and sales and inventories.

The principal sources of these data are the *Survey of Current Business*, published by the Bureau of Economic Analysis (BEA), the *Statistical Supplement to the Federal Reserve Bulletin*, issued by the Board of Governors of the Federal Reserve System, the annual *Statistics of Income (SOI)* reports of the Internal Revenue Service (IRS), and the Census Bureau's Economic Census, *County Business Patterns, Quarterly Financial Report for Manufacturing, Mining, and Trade Corporations (QFR), Survey of Business Owners*, and *Annual Capital Expenditures Survey*.

Business firms—A firm is generally defined as a business organization under a single management and may include one or more establishments. The terms firm, business, company, and enterprise are used interchangeably throughout this section. A firm doing business in more than one industry is classified by industry according to the major activity of the firm as a whole.

The IRS concept of a business firm relates primarily to the legal entity used for tax reporting purposes. A sole proprietorship is an unincorporated business owned by one person and may include large enterprises with many employees and hired managers and part-time operators. A partnership is an unincorporated business owned by two or more persons, each of whom has a financial interest in the business. A corporation is a business that is legally incorporated under state laws. While many corporations file consolidated tax returns, most corporate tax returns represent individual corporations, some

of which are affiliated through common ownership or control with other corporations filing separate returns.

Economic census—The economic census is the major source of facts about the structure and functioning of the nation's economy. It provides essential information for government, business, industry, and the general public. It furnishes an important part of the framework for such composite measures as the gross domestic product estimates, input/output measures, production and price indexes, and other statistical series that measure short-term changes in economic conditions. The Census Bureau takes the economic census every 5 years, covering years ending in "2" and "7."

The economic census is collected on an establishment basis. A company operating at more than one location is required to file a separate report for each store, factory, shop, or other location. Each establishment is assigned a separate industry classification based on its primary activity and not that of its parent company. Establishments responding to the establishment survey are classified into industries on the basis of their principal product or activity (determined by annual sales volume). The statistics issued by industry in the 2002 Economic Census are classified primarily on the 2002 North American Industry Classification System (NAICS), and, to a lesser extent, on the 1997 NAICS used in the previous census (see below).

More detailed information about the scope, coverage, methodology, classification system, data items, and publications for each of the economic censuses and related surveys is published in the *Guide to the 2002 Economic Census* at <http://www.census.gov/econ/census02/guide/>.

Data from the 2002 Economic Census were released through the Census Bureau's American FactFinder® service, on

U.S. Census Bureau, Statistical Abstract of the United States: 2009

DVD-ROM, in Adobe Acrobat PDF reports and in hypertext "drill-down" tables available on the Census Bureau Web site. For more information on these various media of release, see the following page on the Census Bureau Web site <http://www.census.gov/econ/census02/>.

Survey of Business Owners—The Survey of Business Owners (SBO), formerly known as the Surveys of Minority- and Women-Owned Business Enterprises (SMOBE/SWOBE), provides statistics that describe the composition of U.S. businesses by gender, Hispanic or Latino origin, and race. Data from SBO are published in a series of reports: *American Indian- and Alaska Native-Owned Firms, Asian-Owned Firms, Black-Owned Firms, Hispanic-Owned Firms, Native Hawaiian- and Other Pacific Islander-Owned Firms, Women-Owned Firms,* and *Company Summary*. Data are presented by industry classifications and/or geographic area and size of firm (employment and receipts). The reports include totals for all U.S. businesses based on the 2002 Economic Census and estimates of business ownership by gender, Hispanic or Latino origin, and race based on the 2002 SBO. Each owner had the option of selecting more than one race and therefore is included in each race selected. For information on confidentiality protection and survey methodology, see Appendix III and the SBO Web site <http://www.census.gov/csd/sbo/>.

North American Industry Classification System (NAICS)—NAICS has replaced the previous Standard Industrial Classification (SIC) system.

NAICS 2002 is the same as NAICS 1997 for 14 of the 20 sectors. Construction and wholesale trade are substantially changed, but the revisions also modify a number of retail classifications and the organization of the information sector. Very minor boundary adjustments affect administrative and support services and mining. A key feature of NAICS is the revision for the Information sector. A few of the new and important industries created in this section include: Internet service providers and Web search portals, and Internet publishing and broadcasting. Included in the Retail Trade sector is electronic shopping and electronic auctions.

Quarterly Financial Report—The Quarterly Financial Report (QFR) program publishes quarterly aggregate statistics on the financial conditions of U.S. corporations. The QFR requests companies to report estimates from their statements of income and retained earnings, and balance sheets. The statistical data are classified and aggregated by type of industry and asset size. The QFR sample includes manufacturing companies with assets of $250 thousand and above, and mining, wholesale, and retail companies with assets of $50 million and above. The data are available quarterly in the *Quarterly Financial Report for Manufacturing, Mining, and Trade Corporations* on the Internet at <http://www.census.gov/csd/qfr/>.

Multinational Companies—BEA collects financial and operating data on U.S. multinational companies. These data provide a picture of the overall activities of foreign affiliates and U.S. parent companies, using a variety of indicators of their financial structure and operations. The data on foreign affiliates cover the entire operations of the affiliate, irrespective of the percentage of U.S. ownership. These data cover items that are needed in analyzing the characteristics, performance, and economic impact of multinational companies, such as sales, value added, employment and compensation of employees, capital expenditures, exports and imports, and research and development expenditures. Separate tabulations are available for all affiliates and for affiliates that are majority-owned by their U.S. parent(s). More information is available at <http://www.bea.gov/international/index.htm#omc>.

Statistical reliability—For a discussion of statistical collection, estimation, and sampling procedures and measures of reliability applicable to data from the Census Bureau and the Internal Revenue Service, see Appendix III.

Table 722. **Number of Tax Returns, Receipts, and Net Income by Type of Business: 1990 to 2005**

[**14,783 represents 14,783,000.** Covers active enterprises only. Figures are estimates based on sample of unaudited tax returns; see Appendix III]

Item	Number of returns (1,000)			Business receipts [1] (bil. dol.)			Net income (less loss) [2] (bil. dol.)		
	Nonfarm propri-etor-ships	Partner-ships	Corpora-tions	Nonfarm propri-etor-ships	Partner-ships	Corpora-tions	Nonfarm propri-etor-ships	Partner-ships	Corpora-tions
1990	14,783	1,554	3,717	731	541	10,914	141	17	371
1991	15,181	1,515	3,803	713	539	10,963	142	21	345
1992	15,495	1,485	3,869	737	571	11,272	154	43	402
1993	15,848	1,468	3,965	757	627	11,814	156	67	498
1994	16,154	1,494	4,342	791	732	12,858	167	82	577
1995	16,424	1,581	4,474	807	854	13,969	169	107	714
1996	16,955	1,654	4,631	843	1,042	14,890	177	145	806
1997	17,176	1,759	4,710	870	1,297	15,890	187	168	915
1998	17,409	1,855	4,849	918	1,534	16,543	202	187	838
1999	17,576	1,937	4,936	969	1,829	18,009	208	228	929
2000	17,905	2,058	5,045	1,021	2,316	19,593	215	269	928
2001	18,338	2,132	5,136	1,017	2,569	19,308	217	276	604
2002	18,926	2,242	5,267	1,030	2,669	18,849	221	271	564
2003	19,710	2,375	5,401	1,050	2,818	19,755	230	301	780
2004	20,591	2,547	5,558	1,140	3,142	21,717	248	385	1,112
2005	21,468	2,764	5,671	1,223	3,719	24,060	270	546	1,949

[1] Excludes investment income except for partnerships and corporations in finance, insurance, and real estate before 1998. Beginning 1998, finance and insurance, real estate, and management of companies included investment income for partnerships and corporations. Excludes investment income for S corporations; for definition, see footnote 1, Table 731. [2] Net income (less loss) is defined differently by form of organization, basically as follows: (a) Proprietorships: Total taxable receipts less total business deductions, including cost of sales and operations, depletion, and certain capital expensing, excluding charitable contributions and owners' salaries; (b) Partnerships: Total taxable receipts (including investment income except capital gains) less deductions, including cost of sales and operations and certain payments to partners, excluding charitable contributions, oil and gas depletion, and certain capital expensing; (c) Corporations: Total taxable receipts (including investment income, capital gains, and income from foreign subsidiaries deemed received for tax purposes, except for S corporations) less business deductions, including cost of sales and operations, depletion, certain capital expensing, and officers' compensation excluding S corporation charitable contributions and investment expenses; net income is before income tax.

Source: U.S. Internal Revenue Service, *Statistics of Income,* various publications.

Table 723. **Number of Tax Returns and Business Receipts by Size of Receipts: 2000 to 2005**

[**5,045 represents 5,045,000.** Covers active enterprises only. Figures are estimates based on sample of unaudited tax returns; see Appendix III]

Size-class of receipts	Returns (1,000)					Business receipts [1] (bil. dol.)				
	2000	2002	2003	2004	2005	2000	2002	2003	2004	2005
Corporations	**5,045**	**5,267**	**5,401**	**5,558**	**5,671**	**19,593**	**18,849**	**19,755**	**21,717**	**24,060**
Under $25,000 [2]	1,220	1,283	1,280	1,317	1,300	4	4	3	4	4
$25,000 to $49,999	302	314	346	334	340	10	12	13	12	12
$50,000 to $99,999	477	514	522	545	544	35	38	39	40	40
$100,000 to $499,999	1,515	1,583	1,649	1,703	1,755	397	395	412	424	437
$500,000 to $999,999	582	611	623	635	644	407	434	441	448	458
$1,000,000 or more	946	962	981	1,023	1,088	18,738	17,967	18,848	20,788	23,108
Partnerships.	**2,058**	**2,242**	**2,375**	**2,547**	**2,764**	**2,316**	**2,669**	**2,818**	**3,142**	**3,719**
Under $25,000 [2]	1,105	1,204	1,284	1,373	1,465	5	5	5	5	5
$25,000 to $49,999	183	185	192	193	218	7	7	7	7	8
$50,000 to $99,999	187	195	206	226	233	13	14	15	16	17
$100,000 to $499,999	353	394	410	436	489	82	92	95	102	114
$500,000 to $999,999	92	105	111	121	131	66	74	78	86	92
$1,000,000 or more	137	159	172	198	227	2,143	2,478	2,619	2,925	3,482
Nonfarm proprietorships	**17,905**	**18,926**	**19,710**	**20,591**	**21,468**	**1,021**	**1,030**	**1,050**	**1,140**	**1,223**
Under $25,000 [2]	11,997	12,716	13,308	13,916	14,456	82	87	93	97	100
$25,000 to $49,999	2,247	2,358	2,450	2,536	2,587	80	83	87	90	92
$50,000 to $99,999	1,645	1,752	1,805	1,792	1,981	117	124	128	128	140
$100,000 to $499,999	1,733	1,803	1,851	2,020	2,091	355	362	373	405	425
$500,000 to $999,999	190	203	200	218	235	126	138	135	147	160
$1,000,000 or more	92	93	96	109	117	261	234	235	273	306

[1] Finance and insurance, real estate, and management of companies included investment income for partnerships and corporations. [2] Includes firms with no receipts.

Source: U.S. Internal Revenue Service, *Statistics of Income Bulletin;* and unpublished data.

Business Enterprise   483

Table 724. Number of Tax Returns, Receipts, and Net Income by Type of Business and Industry: 2005

[**21,468 represents 21,468,000**. Covers active enterprises only. Figures are estimates based on sample of unaudited tax returns; see Appendix III. Based on the North American Industry Classification System (NAICS), 2002; see text, this section]

Industry	2002 NAICS code	Number of returns (1,000)			Business receipts [1] (bil. dol.)			Net income (less loss) (bil. dol.)		
		Non-farm proprietor-ships	Partner-ships	Corpo-rations	Non-farm proprietor-ships	Partner-ships	Corpo-rations	Non-farm proprietor-ships	Partner-ships	Corpo-rations
Total	(X)	**21,468**	**2,764**	**5,671**	**1,223**	**3,719**	**24,060**	**270**	**546**	**1,949**
Agriculture, forestry, fishing, and hunting [2]	11	268	128	142	16	23	126	1	2	5
Mining	21	121	28	33	11	84	280	2	34	47
Utilities	22	11	3	8	(Z)	162	604	(Z)	3	21
Construction	23	2,821	182	752	222	276	1,427	35	27	74
Special trade contractors	238	2,235	66	454	149	48	575	26	3	22
Manufacturing	31–33	340	45	278	25	705	6,506	3	50	680
Wholesale and retail trade [3]	(X)	(NA)	190	993	(NA)	753	6,652	(NA)	17	215
Wholesale trade	42	348	48	374	46	437	3,289	5	13	106
Retail trade [4]	44–45	2,474	142	616	197	316	3,362	9	4	109
Motor vehicle and parts dealers	441	159	19	94	41	107	836	1	1	11
Food and beverage stores	445	108	17	97	29	55	498	1	3	13
Gasoline stations	447	20	7	39	26	53	241	(Z)	1	2
Transportation and warehousing [4]	48–49	1,043	42	187	73	93	659	10	6	19
Information [4]	51	335	37	123	9	200	887	2	26	75
Broadcasting (except Internet)	515	[5]51	2	6	[5]2	35	107	[5](Z)	3	5
Telecommunications	517	(5)	4	18	(5)	118	389	(5)	16	26
Finance and insurance	52	706	288	243	72	447	3,302	19	198	501
Real estate and rental and leasing	53	1,350	1,296	642	83	285	268	33	72	30
Professional, scientific, and technical services [4]	54	2,883	170	786	145	267	814	61	67	31
Legal services	5411	338	27	104	38	115	83	16	42	8
Accounting, tax preparation, bookkeeping, and payroll services	5412	356	20	67	12	43	35	5	9	3
Management, scientific, and technical consulting services	5416	763	43	226	35	36	164	18	7	12
Management of companies and enterprises	55	(NA)	25	51	(NA)	46	895	(NA)	16	161
Administrative and support and waste management and remediation services	56	1,916	48	258	52	61	431	14	5	23
Educational services	61	552	11	45	7	4	33	2	(Z)	3
Health care and social assistance	62	1,769	60	381	107	131	515	43	19	27
Arts, entertainment, and recreation	71	1,157	49	116	27	39	80	6	(Z)	4
Accommodation and food services	72	392	96	287	43	124	396	1	3	28
Accommodation	721	56	32	34	6	55	82	(Z)	2	9
Food services and drinking places	722	336	64	254	38	68	314	1	2	19
Other services [4]	81	2,559	62	345	82	20	184	20	1	6
Auto repair and maintenance	8111	338	19	106	23	7	64	3	(Z)	2
Personal and laundry services	812	1,488	32	140	38	9	75	11	(Z)	2
Religious, grantmaking, civic, professional, and similar organizations	813	244	1	40	4	(Z)	10	2	(Z)	(Z)
Unclassified	(X)	423	4	3	4	(Z)	(Z)	2	(Z)	(Z)

NA Not available.   X Not applicable.   Z Less than $500 million.   [1] Includes investment income for partnerships and corporations in finance and insurance, real estate, and management of companies' industries.   Excludes investment income for S corporations; for definition, see footnote 1, Table 731.   [2] For corporations, represents agricultural services only.   [3] For corporations, includes trade business not identified as wholesale or retail.   [4] Includes other industries not shown separately.   [5] Broadcasting includes telecommunications.

Source: U.S. Internal Revenue Service, *Statistics of Income,* various publications.

Table 725. Nonfarm Sole Proprietorships—Selected Income and Deduction Items: 1990 to 2005

[**In billions of dollars (731 represents $731,000,000,000) except as indicated**. All figures are estimates based on samples. Tax law changes have affected the comparability of the data over time; see *Statistics of Income* reports for a description. See Appendix III]

Item	1990	1995	1999	2000	2001	2002	2003	2004	2005
Number of returns (1,000)	14,783	16,424	17,576	17,905	18,338	18,926	19,710	20,591	21,468
Returns with net income (1,000)	11,222	12,213	13,159	13,308	13,604	13,751	14,448	15,053	15,750
Business receipts	731	807	969	1,021	1,017	1,030	1,050	1,140	1,223
Income from sales and operations	719	797	955	1,008	1,002	1,015	1,034	1,122	1,205
Business deductions [1]	589	638	761	806	800	809	820	892	953
Cost of goods sold/operations [1]	291	307	370	387	363	352	338	371	397
Purchases	210	219	256	269	247	227	218	239	253
Labor costs	23	24	29	29	28	30	28	32	32
Materials and supplies	30	34	42	43	44	46	47	53	56
Advertising	(NA)	(NA)	9	10	11	11	12	13	14
Car and truck expenses	22	33	41	46	47	50	53	59	71
Commissions	9	10	11	12	12	14	14	13	15
Contract labor	(NA)	(NA)	(NA)	(NA)	(NA)	(NA)	(NA)	25	28
Depreciation	24	27	31	32	33	37	42	43	39
Insurance	13	13	13	14	14	16	17	19	19
Interest paid [2]	13	10	11	12	13	11	11	11	12
Office expenses	(NA)	(NA)	10	10	11	11	12	12	13
Rent paid [3]	23	28	31	33	34	35	36	37	39
Repairs	9	10	12	12	12	13	13	15	15
Salaries and wages (net)	47	54	61	63	64	66	68	71	75
Supplies	(NA)	(NA)	22	22	23	25	26	27	29
Taxes paid	10	13	14	14	14	15	15	16	17
Utilities	14	17	18	19	20	21	22	21	23
Net income (less loss) [4]	141	169	208	215	217	221	230	248	270
Net income [4]	162	192	233	245	250	257	269	291	315
Constant (2000) Dollars [5]									
Business receipts	896	877	991	1,021	993	991	991	1,045	1,085
Business deductions	722	693	778	806	781	778	774	818	846
Net income (less loss)	173	184	213	215	212	213	217	227	239
Net income	198	208	239	245	244	248	254	266	279

NA Not available. [1] Includes other amounts not shown separately. [2] Interest paid includes "mortgage interest" and "other interest paid on business indebtedness." [3] Rent paid includes "Rent on machinery and equipment" and "Rent on other business property." [4] After adjustment for the passive loss carryover from prior years. Therefore, "business receipts" minus "total deductions" do not equal "net income." [5] Based on the overall implicit price deflator for gross domestic product.

Source: U.S. Internal Revenue Service, *Statistics of Income Bulletin.*

Table 726. Partnerships—Selected Income and Balance Sheet Items: 1990 to 2005

[**In billions of dollars (1,735 represents $1,735,000,000,000), except as indicated.** Covers active partnerships only. All figures are estimates based on samples. See Appendix III]

Item	1990	1995	1999	2000	2001	2002	2003	2004	2005
Number of returns (1,000)	1,554	1,581	1,937	2,058	2,132	2,242	2,375	2,547	2,764
Returns with net income (1,000)	854	955	1,226	1,261	1,301	1,325	1,357	1,441	1,580
Number of partners (1,000)	17,095	15,606	15,924	13,660	14,232	14,328	14,108	15,557	16,212
Assets [1, 2]	1,735	2,719	5,999	6,694	8,428	8,867	9,675	11,608	13,734
Depreciable assets (net)	681	767	1,314	1,487	1,646	1,792	1,846	1,988	2,176
Inventories, end of year	57	88	174	150	208	203	214	276	315
Land	215	221	326	359	392	423	455	509	607
Liabilities [1, 2]	1,415	1,886	3,453	3,696	4,835	4,972	5,303	6,248	7,483
Accounts payable	67	91	244	230	362	346	276	336	400
Short-term debt [3]	88	124	232	252	289	283	274	296	373
Long-term debt [4]	498	544	989	1,132	1,286	1,375	1,389	1,546	1,772
Nonrecourse loans	470	466	582	639	700	770	800	854	914
Partners' capital accounts [2]	320	832	2,546	2,999	3,593	3,895	4,372	5,360	6,251
Receipts [1]	566	890	1,907	2,405	2,665	2,773	2,923	3,260	3,863
Business receipts [5]	483	854	1,829	2,316	2,569	2,669	2,818	3,142	3,719
Interest received	21	31	62	82	85	70	71	88	134
Deductions [1]	550	784	1,679	2,136	2,389	2,502	2,621	2,876	3,317
Cost of goods sold/operations	243	395	902	1,226	1,338	1,430	1,523	1,666	1,976
Salaries and wages	56	80	170	201	231	238	245	269	293
Taxes paid	9	13	27	31	35	36	39	42	47
Interest paid	30	43	74	93	97	68	65	64	103
Depreciation	60	23	52	59	72	83	84	90	71
Net income (less loss)	17	107	228	269	276	271	301	385	546
Net income	116	179	348	410	446	440	469	566	724

[1] Includes items not shown separately. [2] Assets, liabilities, and partners' capital accounts are understated because not all partnerships file complete balance sheets. [3] Mortgages, notes, and bonds payable in less than 1 year. [4] Mortgages, notes, and bonds payable in 1 year or more. [5] Excludes investment income except for partnerships in finance, insurance, and real estate in 1995. Beginning 1999, finance and insurance, real estate, and management of companies included investment income for partnerships.

Source: U.S. Internal Revenue Service, *Statistics of Income,* various issues.

Table 727. **Partnerships—Selected Items by Industry: 2005**

[In billions of dollars (13,734 represents $13,734,000,000,000), except as indicated. Covers active partnerships only. Figures are estimates based on samples. Based on the North American Industry Classification System (NAICS), 2002; see text, this section. See Appendix III]

Industry	2002 NAICS code	Number of partnerships (1,000) Total	With net income	With net loss	Total assets [1]	Business receipts [2]	Total deductions	Net income less loss	Net income	Net loss
Total [3]	(X)	**2,764**	**1,580**	**1,183**	**13,734**	**3,719**	**3,317**	**546.2**	**723.6**	**177.4**
Agriculture, forestry, fishing, and hunting	11	128	74	53	111	23	29	1.7	7.3	5.6
Mining	21	28	19	9	173	84	60	34.1	38.8	4.7
Utilities	22	3	1	2	219	162	164	3.5	9.4	6.0
Construction	23	182	109	73	270	276	256	27.3	33.5	6.2
Manufacturing	31–33	45	21	24	422	705	678	49.5	61.7	12.2
Wholesale trade	42	48	23	26	123	437	431	13.1	16.0	3.0
Retail trade	44–45	142	66	76	108	316	320	3.9	8.7	4.9
Transportation and warehousing	48–49	42	22	20	132	93	92	5.5	8.9	3.3
Information	51	37	14	23	544	200	197	25.8	37.1	11.3
Finance and insurance	52	288	213	75	7,659	447	249	197.9	215.6	17.7
Real estate and rental and leasing	53	1,296	709	587	3,101	285	223	72.1	144.5	72.4
Professional, scientific, and technical services	54	170	111	59	131	267	216	66.5	72.2	5.6
Management of companies and enterprises	55	25	15	10	373	46	30	16.4	22.3	6.0
Admin/support waste mgt/ remediation services	56	48	32	16	36	61	59	5.1	6.5	1.5
Educational services	61	11	5	6	3	4	4	0.2	0.6	0.3
Health care and social assistance	62	60	39	21	79	131	120	19.1	22.8	3.6
Arts, entertainment, and recreation	71	49	18	31	66	39	44	0.3	5.4	5.1
Accommodation and food services	72	96	53	43	170	124	126	3.1	10.2	7.1
Other services	81	62	37	25	15	20	20	1.1	2.2	1.1

X Not applicable.   [1] Total assets are understated because not all partnerships file complete balance sheets.   [2] Finance and insurance, real estate, and management of companies includes investment income for partnerships.   [3] Includes businesses not allocable to individual industries.

Source: U.S. Internal Revenue Service, *Statistics of Income*, various issues.

Table 728. **Nonfarm Noncorporate Business-Sector Balance Sheet: 1990 to 2007**

[In billions of dollars (3,707 represents $3,707,000,000,000), except as noted. Represents year-end outstandings]

Item	1990	1995	2000	2002	2003	2004	2005	2006	2007
Assets	**3,707**	**4,109**	**6,368**	**6,983**	**7,431**	**8,186**	**9,224**	**10,142**	**10,989**
Tangible assets	3,351	3,561	4,945	5,326	5,679	6,137	6,791	7,407	7,910
Real estate [1]	3,040	3,210	4,508	4,867	5,203	5,633	6,254	6,832	7,301
Residential	2,121	2,365	3,320	3,674	3,966	4,325	4,802	5,199	5,450
Nonresidential	919	845	1,187	1,193	1,237	1,308	1,453	1,633	1,851
Equipment and software [2]	263	294	367	390	405	426	453	486	515
Residential [3]	32	36	39	40	40	42	45	49	50
Nonresidential	232	259	329	350	365	384	408	438	465
Inventories [2]	47	56	70	69	71	78	84	88	94
Financial assets	356	548	1,423	1,657	1,752	2,049	2,433	2,735	3,079
Checkable deposits and currency . . .	71	105	164	167	173	259	323	344	363
Time and savings deposits	51	71	248	269	314	318	352	396	455
Money market fund shares	7	17	49	61	64	69	74	83	98
Treasury securities	13	24	40	43	45	50	56	63	69
Municipal securities	–	2	2	3	3	4	4	5	6
Mortgages	31	22	23	26	26	31	36	41	46
Trade receivables	98	140	342	363	338	364	431	486	551
Miscellaneous assets	86	167	554	724	791	953	1,156	1,316	1,491
Insurance receivables	39	44	46	52	57	60	65	67	69
Equity investment in GSEs [4]	1	1	2	2	2	2	2	2	2
Other	47	122	506	670	732	891	1,089	1,248	1,420
Liabilities	**1,349**	**1,396**	**2,674**	**3,084**	**3,173**	**3,517**	**4,052**	**4,474**	**4,958**
Credit market instruments	1,093	1,062	1,796	2,107	2,199	2,443	2,775	3,122	3,525
Bank loans n.e.c. [5]	136	165	361	430	442	466	624	691	818
Other loans and advances	94	92	128	127	132	133	135	149	159
Mortgages	863	805	1,308	1,550	1,625	1,844	2,016	2,282	2,547
Trade payables	60	86	260	281	255	277	329	360	395
Taxes payable	32	33	65	70	70	78	87	92	99
Miscellaneous liabilities	164	215	553	626	649	718	860	900	939
Net worth	**2,358**	**2,712**	**3,695**	**3,899**	**4,259**	**4,670**	**5,172**	**5,668**	**6,030**
Debt/net worth (percent)	46.4	39.2	48.6	54.0	51.6	52.3	53.7	55.1	58.5

– Represents or rounds to zero.   [1] At market value.   [2] At replacement (current) cost.   [3] Durable goods in rental properties.   [4] GSEs = government-sponsored enterprises. Equity in the Farm Credit System.   [5] Not elsewhere classified.

Source: Board of Governors of the Federal Reserve System, "Federal Reserve Statistical Release, Z.1, Flow of Funds Accounts of the United States"; published 6 March 2008; <http://www.federalreserve.gov/releases/z1/20080306/>.

Table 729. Nonfinancial Corporate Business-Sector Balance Sheet: 1990 to 2007

[In billions of dollars (9,683 represents $9,683,000,000,000). Represents year-end outstandings]

Item	1990	1995	2000	2002	2003	2004	2005	2006	2007
Assets	**9,683**	**11,461**	**19,017**	**19,473**	**20,063**	**21,660**	**23,706**	**25,400**	**27,428**
Tangible assets	6,108	6,502	9,245	9,531	9,954	10,728	11,797	13,053	14,526
Real estate [1]	3,388	3,146	4,844	5,035	5,358	5,896	6,707	7,672	8,856
Equipment and software [2]	1,819	2,287	3,067	3,193	3,250	3,351	3,496	3,700	3,883
Inventories [2]	901	1,070	1,334	1,303	1,345	1,480	1,594	1,681	1,788
Financial assets [3]	3,575	4,959	9,772	9,942	10,109	10,932	11,909	12,347	12,902
Checkable deposits and currency	166	205	246	141	191	178	252	173	161
Time and savings deposits	75	100	272	291	363	400	450	445	392
Money market fund shares	20	60	191	336	299	324	366	431	592
Commercial paper	14	20	58	65	76	95	111	127	95
Mortgages	53	58	44	50	52	67	68	70	72
Consumer credit	67	85	81	75	58	59	59	57	55
Trade receivables	967	1,185	1,939	1,720	1,702	1,831	2,109	2,215	2,321
Mutual fund shares [1]	10	46	122	96	126	140	156	207	250
Liabilities [3]	**4,729**	**6,010**	**9,611**	**9,923**	**9,867**	**10,349**	**11,145**	**11,133**	**11,346**
Credit market instruments	2,536	2,924	4,555	4,750	4,863	5,030	5,273	5,696	6,330
Commercial paper	117	157	278	120	85	102	94	117	128
Municipal securities [4]	115	135	154	161	164	169	177	182	189
Corporate bonds [5]	1,008	1,357	2,254	2,720	2,870	2,945	2,998	3,212	3,526
Bank loans n.e.c. [6]	545	602	853	636	548	550	515	570	675
Other loans and advances	473	454	649	665	667	684	723	742	840
Mortgages	277	220	366	449	529	581	767	874	972
Trade payables	626	878	1,541	1,457	1,403	1,500	1,699	1,775	1,848
Taxes payable	38	40	78	93	81	88	93	92	93
Net worth (market value)	**4,954**	**5,451**	**9,406**	**9,550**	**10,195**	**11,310**	**12,560**	**14,266**	**16,082**
Debt/net worth (percent)	51.2	53.6	48.4	49.7	47.7	44.5	42.0	39.9	39.4

[1] At market value. [2] At replacement (current) cost. [3] Includes items not shown separately. [4] Industrial revenue bonds. Issued by state and local governments to finance private investment and secured in interest and principal by the industrial user of the funds. [5] Through 1992, corporate bonds include net issues by Netherlands Antillean financial subsidiaries. [6] Not elsewhere classified.

Source: Board of Governors of the Federal Reserve System, "Federal Reserve Statistical Release, Z.1, Flow of Funds Accounts of the United States"; published 6 March 2008; <http://www.federalreserve.gov/releases/z1/20080306/>.

Table 730. Corporate Funds—Sources and Uses: 1990 to 2007

[In billions of dollars (238 represents $238,000,000,000). Covers nonfarm nonfinancial corporate business]

Item	1990	1995	2000	2002	2003	2004	2005	2006	2007
Profits before tax (book)	238	419	422	336	424	660	936	1,041	1,037
− Taxes on corporate income	98	141	170	97	135	190	263	287	311
− Net dividends	117	177	250	253	291	364	196	445	491
+ Capital consumption allowance [1]	365	463	629	734	733	745	585	575	585
= U.S. internal funds, book	388	564	632	721	732	851	1,061	883	820
+ Foreign earnings retained abroad	45	53	100	93	113	121	−30	147	154
+ Inventory valuation adjustment (IVA)	−13	−18	−14	−2	−14	−43	−36	−36	−38
= Internal funds + IVA	420	598	718	811	831	928	995	994	936
Gross investment	369	653	900	782	819	1,000	912	1,216	1,152
Capital expenditures	429	618	929	737	750	826	915	1,033	1,036
Fixed investment [2]	422	577	882	734	748	788	890	985	1,045
Inventory change + IVA	12	40	55	14	13	48	36	45	2
Nonproduced nonfinancial assets	−5	1	−9	−11	−11	−11	−10	2	−11
Net financial investment	−59	36	−28	45	69	174	−3	183	116
Net acquisition of financial assets [3]	124	426	1,209	130	83	783	958	375	533
Checkable deposits and currency	6	4	15	−41	50	−13	74	−79	−12
Time and savings deposits	−6	3	35	10	71	38	50	−5	−53
Money market fund shares	9	23	37	34	−37	25	42	65	161
Commercial paper	(Z)	1	10	5	11	19	16	16	−31
Trade receivables	29	78	282	−98	−17	129	278	106	106
Mutual fund shares	−1	5	4	1	11	1	7	33	33
Miscellaneous assets [3]	114	320	819	191	−10	555	450	236	332
U.S. direct investment abroad [4]	36	90	128	130	123	242	−16	212	191
Insurance receivables	13	8	–	17	18	19	21	7	10
Net increase in liabilities [3]	184	391	1,237	85	13	609	961	192	417
Net funds raised in markets	73	182	218	−33	40	41	−120	−188	−209
Net new equity issues	−63	−58	−118	−42	−42	−127	−363	−614	−837
Credit market instruments [3]	136	240	337	9	82	167	243	426	627
Commercial paper	10	18	48	−58	−35	17	−8	23	11
Corporate bonds [4]	47	104	157	129	150	74	54	213	314
Bank loans n.e.c [5]	3	75	44	−108	−99	2	−36	55	99
Other loans and advances [3]	56	32	64	12	2	17	39	22	98
Finance companies	16	24	55	3	−2	9	25	17	19
Rest of the world	50	(Z)	−2	10	−1	6	28	(Z)	85
Asset-backed securities' issuers	4	6	7	−3	−1	1	−17	2	−10
Mortgages	22	8	22	31	61	52	187	107	98
Trade payables	28	81	313	20	−55	97	199	73	73
Miscellaneous liabilities [3]	82	128	699	86	40	464	877	308	552
Foreign direct investment in U.S.	59	54	192	28	24	29	43	105	155

− Represents or rounds to zero. Z Less than $500 million. [1] Consumption of fixed capital plus capital consumption adjustment. [2] Nonresidential fixed investment plus residential fixed investment. [3] Includes other items not shown separately. [4] 1990, corporate bonds include net issues by Netherlands Antillean financial subsidiaries, and U.S. direct investment abroad excludes net inflows from those bond issues. [5] Not elsewhere classified.

Source: Board of Governors of the Federal Reserve System, "Federal Reserve Statistical Release, Z.1, Flow of Funds Accounts of the United States"; published 6 March 2008; <http://www.federalreserve.gov/releases/z1/20080306/>.

U.S. Census Bureau, Statistical Abstract of the United States: 2009

Table 731. Corporations—Selected Financial Items: 1990 to 2005

[In billions of dollars (18,190 represents $18,190,000,000,000), except as noted. Covers active corporations only. All corporations are required to file returns except those specifically exempt. See source for changes in law affecting comparability of historical data. Based on samples; see Appendix III]

Item	1990	1995	1999	2000	2001	2002	2003	2004	2005
Number of returns (1,000)	3,717	4,474	4,936	5,045	5,136	5,267	5,401	5,558	5,671
Number with net income (1,000) . . .	1,911	2,455	2,812	2,819	2,822	2,801	2,932	3,116	3,324
S Corporation returns [1] (1,000)	1,575	2,153	2,726	2,860	2,986	3,154	3,342	3,518	3,684
Assets [2]	18,190	26,014	41,464	47,027	49,154	50,414	53,645	60,118	66,445
Cash	771	962	1,597	1,820	1,926	1,923	2,120	2,730	2,823
Notes and accounts receivable	4,198	5,307	7,745	8,754	8,756	8,886	8,995	10,691	11,962
Inventories.	894	1,045	1,198	1,272	1,208	1,221	1,267	1,386	1,505
Investments in government obligations	921	1,363	1,340	1,236	1,392	1,527	1,656	1,571	1,613
Mortgage and real estate	1,538	1,713	2,555	2,822	3,229	3,687	4,073	4,627	4,777
Other investments	4,137	7,429	15,799	17,874	18,344	18,728	20,536	22,657	25,162
Depreciable assets	4,318	5,571	6,936	7,292	7,614	7,678	7,805	7,974	8,416
Depletable assets	129	154	184	191	199	226	237	270	310
Land.	210	242	286	303	320	326	342	363	407
Liabilities [2]	18,190	26,014	41,464	47,027	49,154	50,414	53,645	60,118	66,445
Accounts payable	1,094	1,750	2,792	3,758	3,927	4,074	4,338	5,645	6,029
Short-term debt [3]	1,803	2,034	3,658	4,020	4,132	3,814	4,002	4,399	4,192
Long-term debt [4]	2,665	3,335	5,448	6,184	6,782	7,185	7,384	8,154	8,332
Net worth	4,739	8,132	15,363	17,349	17,615	17,545	18,819	20,814	23,525
Capital stock.	1,585	2,194	3,522	3,966	4,253	4,000	3,151	2,308	2,482
Paid-in or capital surplus.	2,814	5,446	10,186	12,265	13,920	15,287	15,258	16,160	17,828
Retained earnings [5]	1,410	2,191	3,970	3,627	2,132	1,111	2,282	3,278	4,331
Receipts [2, 6]	11,410	14,539	18,892	20,606	20,273	19,749	20,690	22,712	25,505
Business receipts [6, 7]	9,860	12,786	16,314	17,637	17,504	17,297	18,264	19,976	21,800
Interest [8]	977	1,039	1,354	1,628	1,549	1,282	1,182	1,368	1,773
Rents and royalties	133	145	223	254	251	252	270	274	290
Deductions [2, 6]	11,033	13,821	17,967	19,692	19,683	19,199	19,941	21,636	23,613
Cost of sales and operations [7]	6,611	8,206	10,284	11,135	11,042	10,607	11,319	12,498	13,816
Compensation of officers	205	304	374	401	383	381	389	417	445
Rent paid on business property	185	232	347	380	398	411	407	420	439
Taxes paid.	251	326	371	390	392	397	417	447	473
Interest paid.	825	744	1,019	1,272	1,203	913	818	939	1,287
Depreciation	333	437	584	614	650	711	692	691	531
Advertising	126	163	216	234	220	218	225	239	253
Net income (less loss) [6, 9]	371	714	929	928	604	564	780	1,112	1,949
Net income	553	881	1,229	1,337	1,112	1,053	1,176	1,456	2,235
Deficit.	182	166	300	409	509	489	396	344	286
Income subject to tax	366	565	694	760	635	601	699	857	1,201
Income tax before credits [10]	119	194	242	266	221	210	244	300	419
Tax credits	32	42	49	62	54	56	66	75	107
Foreign tax credit.	25	30	38	49	41	42	50	57	82
Income tax after credits [11]	96	156	193	204	167	154	178	224	312

[1] Represents certain small corporations with up to 75 shareholders (35 for 1990 and 1995), mostly individuals, electing to be taxed at the shareholder level.   [2] Includes items not shown separately.   [3] Payable in less than 1 year.   [4] Payable in 1 year or more.   [5] Appropriated and unappropriated and "adjustments to shareholders' equity."   [6] Receipts, deductions, and net income of S corporations are limited to those from trade or business. Those from investments are excluded.   [7] Includes gross sales and cost of sales of securities, commodities, and real estate by exchanges, brokers, or dealers selling on their own accounts. Excludes investment income.   [8] Includes tax-exempt interest in state and local government obligations.   [9] Excludes regulated investment companies.   [10] Consists of regular (and alternative tax) only.   [11] Includes minimum tax, alternative minimum tax, adjustments for prior year credits, and other income-related taxes.

Source: U.S. Internal Revenue Service, *Statistics of Income, Corporation Income Tax Returns*, annual.

Table 732. **Corporations by Receipt-Size Class and Industry: 2005**

[Number of returns in thousands (5,671 represents 5,671,000); receipts and net income in billions of dollars (24,060 represents $24,060,000,000,000). Covers active enterprises only. Figures are estimates based on a sample of unaudited tax returns; see Appendix III. Numbers in parentheses represent North American Industry Classification System 2002 codes, see text, this section]

Industry	Total	Under $1 mil. [1]	$1 mil.– $4.9 mil.	$5 mil.– $9.9 mil.	$10 mil.– $49.9 mil.	$50 mil. or more
Total: [2]						
Number of returns..............	5,671	4,583	807	130	120	32
Business receipts [3]...........	24,060	952	1,730	905	2,447	18,026
Net income (less loss)...........	1,949	35	72	37	127	1,679
Agriculture, forestry, fishing, and hunting (11):						
Number.......................	142	124	15	1	1	(Z)
Business receipts [3]...........	126	18	30	10	23	44
Mining (21):						
Number.......................	33	25	6	1	1	(Z)
Business receipts [3]...........	280	4	12	8	22	234
Utilities (22):						
Number.......................	8	7	1	(Z)	(Z)	(Z)
Business receipts [3]...........	604	1	1	1	2	599
Construction (23):						
Number.......................	752	573	137	21	18	3
Business receipts [3]...........	1,427	145	299	150	345	488
Manufacturing (31–33):						
Number.......................	278	165	70	18	18	7
Business receipts [3]...........	6,506	45	161	128	373	5,798
Wholesale and retail trade (42,44–45):						
Number.......................	993	671	219	44	46	12
Business receipts [3]...........	6,652	176	500	306	982	4,688
Transportation and warehousing (48–49):						
Number.......................	187	149	27	6	4	1
Business receipts [3]...........	659	28	60	40	81	450
Information (51):						
Number.......................	123	103	14	2	2	1
Business receipts [3]...........	887	15	30	15	47	780
Finance and insurance (52):						
Number.......................	243	197	29	6	7	3
Business receipts [3]...........	3,302	38	63	42	152	3,007
Real estate and rental and leasing (53):						
Number.......................	642	609	28	3	2	(Z)
Business receipts [3]...........	268	61	58	18	37	94
Professional, scientific, and technical services (54):						
Number.......................	786	688	81	9	7	2
Business receipts [3]...........	814	123	159	66	135	332
Management of companies and enterprises (55):						
Number.......................	51	44	2	1	2	1
Business receipts [3]...........	895	1	7	10	41	836
Administrative and support and waste management and remediation services (56):						
Number.......................	258	216	33	5	3	1
Business receipts [3]...........	431	45	68	34	49	236
Educational services (61):						
Number.......................	45	42	3	(Z)	(Z)	(Z)
Business receipts [3]...........	33	7	6	1	3	16
Health care and social assistance (62):						
Number.......................	381	308	62	5	5	1
Business receipts [3]...........	515	92	123	31	88	181
Arts, entertainment, and recreation (71):						
Number.......................	116	106	9	1	1	(Z)
Business receipts [3]...........	80	17	18	6	11	28
Accommodation and food services (72):						
Number.......................	287	238	43	4	2	(Z)
Business receipts [3]...........	396	70	83	26	33	185
Other services (81):						
Number.......................	345	314	28	2	1	(Z)
Business receipts [3]...........	184	68	52	12	22	29

Z Less than 500 returns.   [1] Includes businesses without receipts.   [2] Includes businesses not allocable to individual industries.   [3] Includes investment income for corporations in finance and insurance and management of companies' industries. Excludes investment income for S corporations (certain small corporations with up to 75 shareholders, mostly individuals, electing to be taxed at the shareholder level).

Source: U.S. Internal Revenue Service, *Statistics of Income, Corporation Income Tax Returns*, annual.

U.S. Census Bureau, Statistical Abstract of the United States: 2009

Table 733. **Corporations by Asset-Size Class and Industry: 2005**

[**In billions of dollars (141 represents $141,000,000,000), except number of returns.** Covers active corporations only. Excludes corporations not allocable by industry. Numbers in parentheses represent North American Industry Classification System 2002 codes, see text, this section]

Industry	Total	Asset-size class					
		Under $10 mil. [1]	$10–$24.9 mil.	$25–$49.9 mil.	$50–$99.9 mil.	$100–$249.9 mil.	$250 mil. and over
Agriculture, forestry, fishing, and hunting (11):							
Returns	142,439	141,428	652	180	102	53	25
Total receipts	141	84	13	6	9	11	17
Mining (21):							
Returns	32,589	31,125	668	317	147	132	200
Total receipts	314	37	10	7	8	13	238
Utilities (22):							
Returns	7,536	7,126	115	61	35	43	155
Total receipts	653	5	2	2	4	8	632
Construction (23):							
Returns	751,521	743,480	5,633	1,370	595	287	157
Total receipts	1,453	840	158	86	67	66	236
Manufacturing (31–33):							
Returns	277,618	262,211	7,533	3,159	1,699	1,343	1,673
Total receipts	7,280	557	219	181	174	283	5,866
Wholesale and retail trade (42, 44–45):							
Returns	992,818	974,511	11,699	3,495	1,383	903	827
Total receipts	6,818	1,989	596	369	257	351	3,257
Transportation and warehousing (48–49):							
Returns	187,051	185,090	1,164	311	188	144	154
Total receipts	687	201	35	21	21	30	379
Information (51):							
Returns	122,825	120,081	1,147	561	351	273	411
Total receipts	1,053	87	20	20	19	30	879
Finance and insurance (52):							
Returns	242,686	223,283	3,593	2,446	2,714	3,544	7,107
Total receipts	3,302	253	30	23	33	64	2,898
Real estate and rental and leasing (53):							
Returns	641,947	635,301	4,473	1,204	517	268	185
Total receipts	317	167	20	14	10	14	92
Professional, scientific, and technical services (54):							
Returns	786,275	782,488	2,130	702	382	294	278
Total receipts	856	490	48	32	28	45	213
Management of companies and enterprises (55):							
Returns	50,921	44,179	1,157	1,034	1,260	1,635	1,655
Total receipts	895	12	2	3	6	17	856
Administrative and support and waste management and remediation services (56):							
Returns	257,623	256,400	656	223	131	97	116
Total receipts	455	214	24	15	19	25	158
Educational services (61):							
Returns	44,885	44,716	83	24	25	25	13
Total receipts	34	15	2	1	2	4	10
Health care and social assistance (62):							
Returns	380,940	379,949	457	230	118	103	83
Total receipts	532	349	17	16	13	23	115
Arts, entertainment, and recreation (71):							
Returns	116,451	115,688	436	168	66	52	41
Total receipts	88	49	5	4	3	7	20
Accommodation and food services (72):							
Returns	287,490	286,130	766	260	115	93	126
Total receipts	439	203	16	11	13	17	179
Other services (81):							
Returns	344,877	344,338	373	63	57	27	20
Total receipts	189	152	7	3	6	6	15

[1] Includes returns with zero assets.

Source: U.S. Internal Revenue Service, *Statistics of Income, Corporation Income Tax Returns*, annual.

Table 734. **Economic Census Summary (NAICS 1997 Basis): 1997 and 2002**

[**25 represents 25,000**. Covers establishments with payroll. Data are based on the 1997 and 2002 economic censuses which are subject to nonsampling error. Data for the construction sector are also subject to sampling errors. For details on survey methodology and nonsampling and sampling errors, see Appendix III]

Kind of business	1997 NAICS code [1]	Establishments (1,000)		Sales, receipts or shipments (bil. dol.)		Annual payroll (bil. dol.)		Paid employees [2] (1,000)	
		1997	2002	1997	2002	1997	2002	1997	2002
Mining.	21	25	24	174	184	20.8	21.6	509	488
Oil & gas extraction	211	8	8	103	113	5.5	5.3	111	99
Mining (except oil & gas)	212	7	7	51	47	9.4	8.9	229	195
Mining support activities.	213	9	9	20	24	5.9	7.3	169	194
Utilities.	22	16	17	412	399	36.6	42.4	703	663
Construction	23	656	709	859	1,207	174.2	253.6	5,665	7,174
Manufacturing	31-33	363	351	3,835	3,915	569.8	575.2	16,805	14,664
Wholesale trade	42	453	439	4,060	4,637	214.9	260.2	5,797	5,903
Wholesale trade, durable goods	421	291	286	2,180	2,460	133.2	164.1	3,398	3,530
Wholesale trade, nondurable goods. .	422	163	153	1,880	2,178	81.7	96.1	2,398	2,373
Retail trade.	44-45	1,118	1,111	2,461	3,054	237.2	301.5	13,991	14,623
Motor vehicle & parts dealers	441	123	121	645	799	50.2	64.0	1,719	1,821
Furniture & home furnishings stores. .	442	65	65	72	92	10.0	12.8	483	535
Electronics & appliance stores	443	43	47	69	82	7.1	9.3	345	391
Bldg. material & garden equipment & supplies dealers	444	(NA)	88	(NA)	247	(NA)	30.1	(NA)	1,160
Food & beverage stores	445	149	149	402	457	40.6	48.7	2,893	2,839
Health & personal care stores.	446	83	82	118	178	15.2	20.3	904	1,024
Gasoline stations	447	127	121	198	249	11.5	13.7	922	927
Clothing & clothing accessories stores.	448	157	150	136	168	16.6	21.4	1,280	1,427
Sporting goods, hobby, book, & music stores	451	69	62	62	73	7.1	8.7	561	611
General merchandise stores.	452	36	41	330	445	30.9	42.6	2,508	2,525
Miscellaneous store retailers.	453	130	129	78	91	10.2	12.8	753	792
Nonstore retailers.	454	44	55	113	173	12.3	17.1	506	571
Transportation & warehousing [3]	48-49	178	200	318	382	82.3	116.0	2,921	3,651
Information [3]	51	114	138	623	898	129.5	195.4	3,066	3,749
Publishing industries	511	34	33	179	247	43.4	67.2	1,006	1,114
Motion picture & sound recording industries	512	22	22	56	78	9.4	12.7	276	304
Broadcasting & telecommunications. .	513	43	59	346	490	63.5	86.9	1,434	1,737
Information & data processing services [3]	514	15	23	42	83	13.3	28.6	350	594
Finance & insurance [4]	52	395	440	2,198	2,804	264.6	377.8	5,835	6,579
Real estate & rental & leasing [4]	53	288	323	241	336	41.6	60.2	1,702	1,949
Professional, scientific, & technical services [3]	54	621	740	595	868	231.4	369.6	5,361	6,978
Management of companies & enterprises	55	47	49	92	108	154.2	179.2	2,618	2,608
Admin/support waste management/ remediation services [3]	56	276	273	296	397	137.3	194.9	7,347	8,261
Administrative & support services [3] . .	561	260	255	257	346	128.4	182.6	7,067	7,929
Waste management & remediation services [3]	562	16	19	39	51	8.9	12.2	281	332
Educational services [3]	61	41	49	20	31	6.4	10.2	321	430
Health care and social assistance. . . .	62	646	709	885	1,211	378.2	497.4	13,562	15,144
Ambulatory health care services	621	455	489	355	489	155.9	203.4	4,414	4,925
Hospitals.	622	7	6	379	500	155.8	197.2	4,933	5,174
Nursing & residential care facilities . .	623	57	69	93	127	42.2	59.0	2,471	2,831
Social assistance	624	126	144	57	95	24.4	37.9	1,744	2,213
Arts, entertainment, & recreation.	71	99	110	105	142	32.8	45.2	1,588	1,849
Performance arts, spectator sports, & related industries	711	31	38	38	58	14.5	21.2	327	423
Museums, historical sites, & like institutions.	712	6	7	7	9	1.8	2.9	92	123
Amusement, gambling, & recreation industries	713	63	66	58	75	20.8	21.0	1,146	1,303
Accommodation & food services.	72	545	566	350	449	97.0	127.6	9,451	10,121
Accommodation	721	58	61	98	128	26.7	35.0	1,697	1,813
Food services & drinking places	722	487	505	252	321	70.3	92.6	7,755	8,308
Other services (except public administration) [3]	81	520	525	266	302	65.5	81.0	3,256	3,352
Repair & maintenance [3]	811	235	231	105	118	29.9	35.1	1,276	1,286
Personal and laundry services [3]	812	185	193	58	71	18.6	22.4	1,217	1,263
Religious/grantmaking/prof/like organizations	813	99	101	103	113	17.1	23.4	763	803

NA Not available.   [1] Based on North American Industry Classification System, 1997; see text this section.   [2] For pay period including March 12.   [3] Enterprise support establishments are included in the 2002 data but not in the 1997 data affecting comparability for this industry.   [4] For detailed industries, see Table 1126.

Source: U.S. Census Bureau, "2002 Economic Census, Comparative Statistics for United States, Summary Statistics by 1997 NAICS"; published 31 July 2006; <http://www.census.gov/econ/census02/data/comparative/USCS.HTM>.

U.S. Census Bureau, Statistical Abstract of the United States: 2009

Table 735. **Nonemployer Establishments and Receipts by Industry: 2000 to 2005**

[**Establishments: 16,530 represents 16,530,000.** Includes only firms subject to federal income tax. Nonemployers are businesses with no paid employees. Data originate chiefly from administrative records of the Internal Revenue Service; see Appendix III. Data for 2000 based on the North American Industry Classification System (NAICS), 1997; 2004 and 2005 based on NAICS 2002, see text, this section]

Kind of business	NAICS code	Establishments (1,000)			Receipts (mil. dol.)		
		2000	2004	2005	2000	2004	2005
All industries	(X)	**16,530**	**19,524**	**20,392**	**709,379**	**887,002**	**951,206**
Forestry, fishing & hunting, & agricultural support services.	113–115	223	231	231	9,196	10,180	10,567
Mining	21	86	91	100	5,227	7,025	8,739
Utilities	22	14	16	15	504	653	671
Construction	23	2,014	2,392	2,531	107,538	140,052	153,760
Manufacturing	31–33	285	303	298	13,022	14,748	15,064
Wholesale trade.	42	388	384	381	31,684	33,227	34,091
Retail trade	44–45	1,743	1,893	1,881	73,810	82,916	83,599
Transportation & warehousing	48–49	747	916	962	37,824	51,537	58,650
Information	51	238	283	291	7,620	9,470	10,158
Finance & insurance.	52	692	718	742	49,058	44,032	47,244
Real estate & rental & leasing	53	1,696	2,218	2,442	133,398	189,905	207,688
Professional, scientific, & technical services . . .	54	2,420	2,725	2,854	90,272	110,596	118,575
Admin/support waste mgt/ remediation services	56	1,032	1,337	1,417	23,754	30,932	33,028
Educational services	61	283	410	454	3,736	5,588	6,028
Health care & social assistance	62	1,317	1,609	1,669	36,550	47,883	50,307
Arts, entertainment, & recreation.	71	782	923	972	17,713	22,448	23,704
Accommodation & food services	72	218	275	279	13,418	15,510	15,307
Other services (except public administration). . .	81	2,350	2,800	2,873	55,056	70,299	74,025

X Not applicable.

Source: U.S. Census Bureau, "Nonemployer Statistics"; <http://www.census.gov/epcd/nonemployer/>.

Table 736. **Establishments, Employees, and Payroll by Employment-Size Class: 1990 to 2005**

[**6,176 represents 6,176,000.** Excludes most government employees, railroad employees, self-employed persons. Employees are for the week including March 12. Covers establishments with payroll. An *establishment* is a single physical location where business is conducted or where services or industrial operations are performed. For statement on methodology, see Appendix III]

Employment-size class	Unit	1990	1995	2000	2001	2002	2003	2004	2005
Establishments, total	1,000	**6,176**	**6,613**	**7,070**	**7,095**	**7,201**	**7,255**	**7,388**	**7,500**
Under 20 employees.	1,000	5,354	5,733	6,069	6,083	6,199	6,240	6,359	6,468
20 to 99 employees	1,000	684	730	826	836	835	845	856	856
100 to 499 employees.	1,000	122	135	157	157	149	151	154	157
500 to 999 employees.	1,000	10	10	12	12	11	11	12	12
1,000 or more employees . . .	1,000	6	6	7	7	7	7	7	7
Employees, total	1,000	**93,476**	**100,335**	**114,065**	**115,061**	**112,401**	**113,398**	**115,075**	**116,317**
Under 20 employees.	1,000	24,373	25,785	27,569	27,681	28,116	28,313	28,701	28,874
20 to 99 employees	1,000	27,414	29,202	33,147	33,555	33,335	33,760	34,288	34,302
100 to 499 employees.	1,000	22,926	25,364	29,736	29,692	28,101	28,549	28,976	29,591
500 to 999 employees.	1,000	6,551	7,021	8,291	8,357	7,743	7,638	7,815	8,053
1,000 or more employees . . .	1,000	12,212	12,962	15,322	15,776	15,105	15,138	15,295	15,497
Annual payroll, total	Bil. dol. . . .	**2,104**	**2,666**	**3,879**	**3,989**	**3,943**	**4,041**	**4,254**	**4,483**
Under 20 employees.	Bil. dol. . . .	485	608	818	839	866	885	926	970
20 to 99 employees	Bil. dol. . . .	547	696	1,006	1,037	1,041	1,068	1,124	1,177
100 to 499 employees.	Bil. dol. . . .	518	675	1,031	1,052	1,021	1,054	1,106	1,176
500 to 999 employees.	Bil. dol. . . .	174	219	336	342	329	334	355	376
1,000 or more employees . . .	Bil. dol. . . .	381	467	690	719	685	700	743	784

Source: U.S. Census Bureau, "County Business Patterns." See <http://www.census.gov/epcd/cbp/view/cbpview.html>.

Table 737. Establishments, Employees, and Payroll by Employment-Size Class and Industry: 2000 to 2005

[Establishments and employees in thousands (7,070.0 represents 7,070,000); payroll in billions of dollars. See headnote, Table 736. Data for 2000 based on the North American Industry Classification System (NAICS), 1997; 2004 and 2005 data based on NAICS 2002. See text, this section]

Industry	NAICS code	2000, total	2004, total	2005					
				Total	Under 20 employ-ees	20 to 99 employ-ees	100 to 499 employ-ees	500 to 999 employ-ees	1,000 or more employ-ees
Establishments, total [1]	(X)	7,070.0	7,387.7	7,499.7	6,468.2	855.9	156.9	11.8	6.9
Agriculture, forestry, fishing & hunting. . .	11	26.1	25.5	24.1	22.6	1.3	0.2	(Z)	(Z)
Mining	21	23.7	23.8	24.7	20.0	3.9	0.7	0.1	(Z)
Utilities	22	17.3	17.7	17.3	12.2	3.8	1.2	0.1	0.1
Construction	23	709.6	760.4	787.7	719.9	59.8	7.5	0.4	0.1
Manufacturing	31–33	354.5	339.1	333.5	228.7	75.6	25.7	2.4	1.1
Wholesale trade	42	446.2	429.5	429.8	367.6	53.8	7.7	0.5	0.2
Retail trade	44–45	1,113.6	1,119.8	1,123.2	968.7	128.1	25.7	0.6	(Z)
Transportation and warehousing	48–49	190.0	206.9	211.2	176.3	28.0	6.0	0.6	0.3
Information	51	133.6	139.7	141.3	114.3	20.9	5.3	0.6	0.3
Finance and insurance	52	423.7	470.6	476.8	430.5	38.1	6.8	0.9	0.6
Real estate and rental and leasing. . . .	53	300.2	348.7	370.7	354.5	14.3	1.7	0.1	(Z)
Professional, scientific, and technical services.	54	722.7	804.6	826.1	764.0	52.5	8.5	0.7	0.4
Management of companies and enterprises.	55	47.4	46.3	47.6	31.4	10.9	4.2	0.7	0.4
Admin/support waste mgt/remediation services.	56	351.5	358.9	369.5	308.8	43.5	15.0	1.3	0.8
Educational services	61	68.0	78.8	80.5	61.7	15.0	3.0	0.4	0.4
Health care and social assistance	62	658.6	731.9	746.6	634.6	87.6	20.8	1.7	1.9
Arts, entertainment, and recreation	71	103.8	118.8	121.8	102.7	16.0	2.8	0.2	0.1
Accommodation and food services.	72	542.4	591.0	603.4	434.3	158.4	10.2	0.4	0.2
Other services [2]	81	723.3	734.5	740.0	691.5	44.6	3.8	0.1	0.1
Unclassified establishments	99	99.0	41.2	24.0	23.9	0.1	(Z)	–	–
Employees, total [1]	(X)	114,065	115,075	116,317	28,874	34,302	29,591	8,053	15,497
Agriculture, forestry, fishing & hunting. . .	11	184	182	169	80	(NA)	(NA)	7	6
Mining	21	456	470	497	94	155	145	46	58
Utilities	22	655	635	633	65	170	230	84	83
Construction	23	6,573	6,648	6,781	2,660	2,297	1,366	248	210
Manufacturing	31–33	16,474	13,822	13,667	1,326	3,319	5,161	1,641	2,221
Wholesale trade	42	6,112	5,907	5,969	1,763	2,099	1,443	324	341
Retail trade	44–45	14,841	15,351	15,339	5,119	5,172	4,621	341	86
Transportation and warehousing	48–49	3,790	4,099	4,168	717	1,154	1,151	412	734
Information	51	3,546	3,472	3,403	506	884	1,055	398	559
Finance and insurance	52	5,963	6,481	6,432	1,890	1,475	1,366	627	1,074
Real estate and rental and leasing.	53	1,942	2,086	2,144	1,155	538	312	87	53
Professional, scientific, and technical services.	54	6,816	7,570	7,689	2,577	2,037	1,651	456	969
Management of companies and enterprises.	55	2,874	2,825	2,856	172	487	890	474	834
Admin/support waste mgt/remediation services.	56	9,138	8,708	9,280	1,177	1,923	2,980	903	2,297
Educational services	61	2,532	2,893	2,879	293	628	585	285	1,087
Health care and social assistance	62	14,109	15,815	16,025	3,316	3,514	3,863	1,226	4,106
Arts, entertainment, and recreation	71	1,741	1,889	1,936	385	667	517	120	247
Accommodation and food services.	72	9,881	10,750	11,026	2,643	6,102	1,586	279	415
Other services [2]	81	5,293	5,416	5,391	2,906	1,628	643	96	117
Unclassified establishments	99	144	55	31	28	(NA)	(NA)	–	–
Annual payroll, total [1]	(X)	3,879	4,254	4,483	970	1,177	1,176	376	784
Agriculture, forestry, fishing & hunting. . .	11	5	5	5	2	(D)	(D)	(Z)	(Z)
Mining	21	22	27	31	5	9	10	3	4
Utilities	22	41	45	46	4	11	17	7	7
Construction	23	240	268	293	98	104	68	12	10
Manufacturing	31–33	644	593	601	46	129	218	78	129
Wholesale trade	42	270	291	309	82	104	76	21	26
Retail trade	44–45	303	334	348	110	121	106	8	4
Transportation and warehousing	48–49	126	148	154	25	41	42	15	31
Information	51	209	200	203	27	47	66	24	40
Finance and insurance	52	347	422	447	95	104	106	46	96
Real estate and rental and leasing.	53	59	74	82	40	22	13	4	2
Professional, scientific, and technical services.	54	362	427	456	127	129	113	30	57
Management of companies and enterprises.	55	211	222	243	16	39	74	40	74
Admin/support waste mgt/remediation services.	56	210	236	255	40	57	73	22	63
Educational services	61	62	80	83	7	16	17	6	37
Health care and social assistance	62	431	560	590	132	117	113	47	181
Arts, entertainment, and recreation	71	43	51	53	13	13	17	3	6
Accommodation and food services.	72	126	147	156	37	75	26	6	12
Other services [2]	81	110	123	127	64	39	19	3	4
Unclassified establishments	99	4	1	1	1	(D)	(D)	–	–

– Represents zero.   D Data withheld to avoid disclosure.   NA Not available.   X Not applicable.   Z Less than 50 establishments or 500 million dollars.   [1] Totals for 2000 include auxiliaries. Beginning 2004, cases previously classified under NAICS code 95 (auxiliaries) are coded in the operating NAICS sector of the establishment.   [2] Except public administration.

Source: U.S. Census Bureau, "County Business Patterns"; see <http://www.census.gov/epcd/cbp/view/cbpview.html>.

Business Enterprise   **493**

Table 738. **Employer Firms, Establishments, Employment, and Annual Payroll by Enterprise Size: 1990 to 2005**

[In thousands except as noted (5,074 represents 5,074,000). Firms are an aggregation of all establishments owned by a parent company with some annual payroll. Establishments are locations with active payroll in any quarter. This table illustrates the changing importance of enterprise sizes over time, not job growth, as enterprises can grow or decline and change enterprise size cells over time]

Item	Total	All industries—employment size of enterprise						
		0 to 4 [1]	5 to 9	10 to 19	20 to 99	100 to 499	Less than 500	500 or more
Firms:								
1990	5,074	3,021	952	563	454	70	5,060	14
1995	5,369	3,250	981	577	470	76	5,354	15
2000	5,653	3,397	1,021	617	516	84	5,635	17
2001	5,658	3,402	1,019	616	518	85	5,640	17
2002	5,698	3,466	1,011	614	508	82	5,681	17
2003	5,767	3,504	1,025	620	515	85	5,750	17
2004	5,886	3,580	1,043	633	526	87	5,869	17
2005	5,984	3,678	1,050	630	521	87	5,966	17
Establishments:								
1990	6,176	3,032	971	600	590	255	5,448	728
1995	6,613	3,260	998	618	639	284	5,799	814
2000	7,070	3,406	1,035	652	674	312	6,080	990
2001	7,095	3,410	1,034	650	670	316	6,080	1,015
2002	7,201	3,471	1,024	653	693	333	6,173	1,028
2003	7,255	3,510	1,038	655	687	331	6,222	1,033
2004	7,388	3,586	1,056	667	693	330	6,331	1,056
2005	7,500	3,684	1,063	662	679	332	6,421	1,079
Employment:								
1990	93,469	5,117	6,252	7,543	17,710	13,545	50,167	43,302
1995	100,315	5,395	6,440	7,734	18,422	14,660	52,653	47,662
2000	114,065	5,593	6,709	8,286	20,277	16,260	57,124	56,941
2001	115,061	5,630	6,698	8,275	20,370	16,410	57,383	57,678
2002	112,401	5,698	6,640	8,246	19,874	15,909	56,366	56,034
2003	113,398	5,768	6,732	8,330	20,187	16,430	57,448	55,950
2004	115,075	5,845	6,853	8,500	20,643	16,758	58,597	56,477
2005	116,317	5,937	6,898	8,454	20,444	16,911	58,645	57,672
Annual payroll (bil. dol.):								
1990	2,104	117	114	144	352	279	1,007	1,097
1995	2,666	142	137	175	437	361	1,252	1,414
2000	3,879	186	174	231	608	528	1,727	2,152
2001	3,989	188	179	237	624	539	1,768	2,222
2002	3,943	194	182	241	624	536	1,777	2,166
2003	4,041	197	187	247	635	552	1,818	2,222
2004	4,254	206	196	258	670	588	1,917	2,337
2005	4,483	220	206	269	700	617	2,013	2,470

[1] Employment is measured in March, thus some firms (start-ups after March, closures before March, and seasonal firms) will have zero employment and some annual payroll.

Source: U.S. Small Business Administration, Office of Advocacy, "Statistics of U.S. Businesses"; <http://www.sba.gov/advo/research/data.html>; accessed 28 January 2008.

Table 739. **Firm Births and Deaths by Employment Size of Enterprise: 1990 to 2005**

[In thousands (541.1 represents 541,100). Data represent activity from March of the beginning year to March of the ending year. Establishments with no employment in the first quarter of the beginning year were excluded. This table provides the number of births and deaths of initial establishments (based on Census ID) as an approximation of firm births and deaths]

Item	Births (initial locations)				Deaths (initial locations)			
	Total	Less than 20 employees	Less than 500 employees	500 employees or more	Total	Less than 20 employees	Less than 500 employees	500 employees or more
Firms:								
1990 to 1991	541.1	515.9	540.9	0.3	546.5	517.0	546.1	0.4
1995 to 1996	597.8	572.4	597.5	0.3	512.4	485.5	512.0	0.4
1999 to 2000	574.3	548.0	574.0	0.3	542.8	514.2	542.4	0.5
2000 to 2001	585.1	558.0	584.8	0.3	553.3	524.0	552.8	0.5
2001 to 2002 [1]	569.8	541.5	568.3	1.5	586.9	557.1	586.5	0.4
2002 to 2003	612.3	585.6	612.0	0.3	540.7	514.6	540.3	0.3
2003 to 2004	628.9	601.9	628.7	0.3	541.0	515.0	540.7	0.3
2004 to 2005	644.1	616.0	643.9	0.3	565.7	539.1	565.5	0.3
Employment:								
1990 to 1991	3,105	1,713	2,907	198	3,208	1,723	3,044	164
1995 to 1996	3,256	1,845	3,056	200	3,100	1,560	2,808	291
1999 to 2000	3,229	1,793	3,031	198	3,177	1,654	2,946	230
2000 to 2001	3,418	1,821	3,109	310	3,262	1,701	3,050	212
2001 to 2002 [1]	3,370	1,748	3,034	336	3,660	1,755	3,257	403
2002 to 2003	3,667	1,856	3,174	493	3,324	1,608	2,880	445
2003 to 2004	3,575	1,889	3,241	334	3,221	1,615	2,868	353
2004 to 2005	3,609	1,931	3,279	330	3,307	1,685	2,981	326

[1] A change in methodology ("based on Census ID" rather than "plant number") has affected the allocation of firms by employment size.

Source: U.S. Small Business Administration, Office of Advocacy, "Firm Size Data, Statistics of U.S. Businesses and Nonemployer Statistics"; <http://www.sba.gov/advo/research/data.html>.

Table 740. **Employer Firms, Employment, and Annual Payroll by Enterprise Size and Industry: 2005**

[**5,984 represents 5,984,000**. A firm is an aggregation of all establishments owned by a parent company (within a geographic location and/or industry) with some annual payroll. A firm may be a single location or it can include multiple locations. Employment is measured in March and payroll is annual leading to some firms with zero employment. Numbers in parentheses represent North American Industry Classification System codes, 2002; see text this section]

Industry and data type	Unit	Total	All industries—employment size of enterprise						
			0 to 4	5 to 9	10 to 19	20 to 99	100 to 499	Less than 500	500 or more
Total [1]:									
Firms	1,000 . . .	5,984	3,678	1,050	630	521	87	5,966	17
Employment	1,000 . . .	116,317	5,937	6,898	8,454	20,444	16,911	58,645	57,672
Annual payroll	Bil. dol. . .	4,483	220	206	269	700	617	2,013	2,470
Construction (23):									
Firms	1,000 . . .	778	511	129	74	56	7	777	1
Employment	1,000 . . .	6,781	778	845	993	2,092	1,133	5,842	940
Annual payroll	Bil. dol. . .	293	30	28	38	91	54	241	51
Manufacturing (31–33):									
Firms	1,000 . . .	289	114	54	46	57	14	285	4
Employment	1,000 . . .	13,667	211	360	623	2,331	2,514	6,039	7,629
Annual payroll	Bil. dol. . .	601	8	11	21	87	100	227	373
Wholesale trade (42):									
Firms	1,000 . . .	337	191	59	40	37	8	334	3
Employment	1,000 . . .	5,969	322	385	531	1,375	1,024	3,637	2,332
Annual payroll	Bil. dol. . .	309	15	16	23	64	49	167	142
Retail trade (44–45):									
Firms	1,000 . . .	737	435	151	82	58	9	735	2
Employment	1,000 . . .	15,339	777	988	1,085	2,171	1,288	6,308	9,031
Annual payroll	Bil. dol. . .	348	18	20	25	62	40	165	183
Transportation & warehousing (48–49):									
Firms	1,000 . . .	169	108	24	16	15	4	167	2
Employment	1,000 . . .	4,168	157	158	214	565	492	1,587	2,582
Annual payroll	Bil. dol. . .	154	5	5	7	19	17	52	102
Information (51):									
Firms	1,000 . . .	75	45	11	8	8	2	74	1
Employment	1,000 . . .	3,403	65	75	108	321	321	890	2,512
Annual payroll	Bil. dol. . .	203	4	3	5	16	18	47	157
Finance & insurance (52):									
Firms	1,000 . . .	260	184	37	17	16	4	258	2
Employment	1,000 . . .	6,432	308	239	225	637	720	2,129	4,303
Annual payroll	Bil. dol. . .	447	14	12	14	41	45	124	322
Professional, scientific & technical services (54):									
Firms	1,000 . . .	757	549	104	56	39	7	754	3
Employment	1,000 . . .	7,689	802	675	744	1,444	1,076	4,741	2,948
Annual payroll	Bil. dol. . .	456	40	30	38	87	68	263	194
Management of companies & enterprises (55):									
Firms	1,000 . . .	27	4	1	1	5	8	20	7
Employment	1,000 . . .	2,856	5	4	7	67	255	338	2,518
Annual payroll	Bil. dol. . .	243	(Z)	(Z)	(Z)	4	16	21	222
Admin/support waste mgt/ remediation services (56):									
Firms	1,000 . . .	320	204	48	29	28	8	317	3
Employment	1,000 . . .	9,280	294	312	390	1,111	1,512	3,620	5,661
Annual payroll	Bil. dol. . .	255	11	9	11	33	37	101	154
Educational services (61):									
Firms	1,000 . . .	72	36	11	9	13	3	71	1
Employment	1,000 . . .	2,879	53	73	125	523	520	1,294	1,585
Annual payroll	Bil. dol. . .	83	2	1	3	13	15	33	50
Health care and social assistance (62):									
Firms	1,000 . . .	599	307	139	77	57	16	596	4
Employment	1,000 . . .	16,025	563	917	1,023	2,252	2,994	7,749	8,276
Annual payroll	Bil. dol. . .	590	27	35	41	81	86	269	320
Accommodation & food services (72):									
Firms	1,000 . . .	463	204	88	80	81	9	461	2
Employment	1,000 . . .	11,026	323	593	1,093	3,040	1,564	6,612	4,414
Annual payroll	Bil. dol. . .	156	7	7	12	38	21	85	71
Other services (except public administration) (81):									
Firms	1,000 . . .	676	428	136	66	41	4	675	1
Employment	1,000 . . .	5,391	790	885	864	1,454	619	4,613	778
Annual payroll	Bil. dol. . .	127	17	18	19	33	17	105	23

Z Less than $500 million.   [1] Includes other industries not shown separately.

Source: U.S. Small Business Administration, Office of Advocacy, "Statistics of U.S. Businesses"; <http://www.sba.gov/advo/research/data.html>; accessed 28 January 2008.

Table 741. Employer Firms, Employment, and Payroll by Employment Size of Enterprise and State: 2000 and 2005

[5,652.5 represents 5,652,500. A firm is an aggregation of all establishments owned by a parent company (within a state) with some annual payroll. A firm may be a single location or it can include multiple locations. Employment is measured in March and payroll is annual leading to some firms with zero employment]

| State | Employer firms (1,000) | | | | | Employment, 2005 (mil.) | | | Annual payroll, 2005 (bil. dol.) | | |
| | 2000 | | 2005 | | | | | | | | |
	Total	Less than 20 employees	Total	Less than 20 employees	Less than 500 employees	Total	Less than 20 employees	Less than 500 employees	Total	Less than 20 employees	Less than 500 employees
U.S....	5,652.5	5,035.0	5,983.5	5,357.9	5,966.1	116.3	21.3	58.6	4,482.7	695.6	2,012.6
AL	79.9	68.2	80.2	68.3	77.9	1.7	0.3	0.8	53.4	8.1	23.9
AK	15.9	14.0	16.8	14.8	16.3	0.2	0.1	0.1	9.8	2.2	5.1
AZ	93.0	79.3	106.1	90.9	103.3	2.2	0.4	1.0	76.3	11.7	33.9
AR	52.4	45.4	53.6	46.4	52.1	1.0	0.2	0.5	30.2	4.8	12.8
CA	664.6	581.1	712.7	629.7	707.1	13.4	2.5	6.9	588.5	93.7	269.9
CO	116.2	101.5	127.6	112.9	124.8	1.9	0.4	1.0	75.5	13.4	34.6
CT	78.5	67.2	78.5	67.4	76.6	1.5	0.3	0.8	75.6	11.3	32.9
DE	20.2	16.6	21.1	17.1	19.7	0.4	0.1	0.2	16.9	2.2	6.5
DC	16.3	12.4	16.8	12.7	15.7	0.4	0.1	0.2	25.2	3.0	11.2
FL.....	354.0	319.3	421.9	384.2	417.7	7.1	1.3	3.2	239.2	42.6	105.5
GA	160.4	138.3	177.6	154.4	173.8	3.5	0.6	1.6	128.8	18.9	54.0
HI.....	24.3	20.8	26.3	22.4	25.5	0.5	0.1	0.3	16.2	3.1	8.6
ID.....	32.2	28.0	37.6	33.0	36.5	0.5	0.1	0.3	15.4	3.3	8.0
IL.....	254.1	218.1	262.3	227.7	258.1	5.2	0.9	2.6	217.2	32.0	97.3
IN.....	116.3	98.1	117.9	100.2	115.1	2.6	0.4	1.3	88.1	11.9	38.5
IA.....	65.6	56.2	66.2	57.0	64.6	1.3	0.2	0.7	39.4	5.9	18.3
KS	61.6	52.4	62.1	53.0	60.2	1.1	0.2	0.6	36.6	5.8	17.6
KY	72.3	61.0	73.1	61.8	70.9	1.5	0.3	0.8	48.0	7.1	21.4
LA	81.7	69.5	82.7	70.3	80.7	1.6	0.3	0.9	50.7	8.1	24.5
ME	34.1	30.1	35.9	31.7	35.0	0.5	0.1	0.3	15.9	3.4	9.0
MD	106.0	90.4	114.4	98.1	111.8	2.2	0.4	1.2	89.0	14.4	43.3
MA	148.2	127.8	145.4	125.7	142.5	3.0	0.5	1.5	140.6	20.2	61.4
MI.....	193.9	167.2	193.3	168.5	190.3	3.8	0.7	2.0	148.5	22.4	66.9
MN	116.2	99.4	124.6	107.6	122.1	2.4	0.4	1.3	97.0	13.3	42.1
MS	48.3	41.5	48.2	41.3	46.7	0.9	0.2	0.5	25.8	4.2	11.8
MO	118.1	101.1	125.3	108.1	122.6	2.4	0.4	1.2	82.3	12.0	36.5
MT	28.0	25.0	31.5	28.3	30.8	0.3	0.1	0.2	9.0	2.5	5.8
NE	41.4	35.5	42.6	36.6	41.3	0.8	0.1	0.4	24.2	3.7	11.2
NV	40.3	33.4	48.8	40.7	46.9	1.1	0.2	0.5	39.3	5.8	16.8
NH	32.1	27.3	33.3	28.3	32.2	0.6	0.1	0.3	21.0	4.1	11.2
NJ.....	202.2	178.4	209.2	185.3	206.1	3.6	0.7	1.8	166.0	27.3	74.0
NM	35.5	30.1	37.2	31.5	35.9	0.6	0.1	0.3	18.2	3.5	9.5
NY	424.8	379.2	445.9	400.8	441.8	7.4	1.4	3.9	370.8	56.0	161.7
NC	163.6	142.0	173.9	151.3	170.5	3.4	0.6	1.7	115.7	18.0	49.8
ND	17.2	14.7	17.8	15.1	17.1	0.3	0.1	0.2	7.8	1.5	4.5
OH	212.5	180.5	210.6	180.0	207.0	4.8	0.8	2.3	168.4	23.4	73.9
OK	70.2	61.0	72.4	62.9	70.5	1.2	0.3	0.7	37.6	6.7	18.5
OR	85.1	74.2	91.4	80.2	89.4	1.4	0.3	0.8	50.0	9.0	25.0
PA	237.5	204.6	242.7	209.8	238.8	5.1	0.9	2.6	189.7	27.2	83.8
RI.....	25.2	21.5	26.8	22.9	25.9	0.4	0.1	0.3	15.8	2.9	8.3
SC	78.4	67.2	82.9	71.5	80.7	1.6	0.3	0.8	49.5	8.1	21.9
SD	20.6	17.7	21.8	18.8	21.1	0.3	0.1	0.2	8.9	1.8	5.1
TN	102.4	86.7	102.8	87.0	99.8	2.4	0.4	1.1	81.0	11.2	34.2
TX	369.0	321.3	385.9	336.7	381.0	8.3	1.4	3.9	315.8	45.8	130.7
UT	46.2	39.3	55.9	48.3	54.2	1.0	0.2	0.5	31.0	5.1	14.8
VT	19.1	16.7	19.6	17.1	19.0	0.3	0.1	0.2	8.3	1.9	4.9
VA	139.7	120.3	154.2	133.4	151.1	3.1	0.5	1.5	121.8	18.1	54.3
WA	138.2	120.9	147.4	130.0	144.9	2.3	0.5	1.3	94.9	15.9	45.3
WV	33.5	28.8	32.7	28.0	31.6	0.6	0.1	0.3	16.3	2.8	7.8
WI.....	115.6	98.2	118.5	101.0	116.1	2.4	0.4	1.3	85.8	12.7	40.4
WY	15.9	13.9	17.3	15.1	16.8	0.2	0.1	0.1	6.2	1.6	3.7

Source: U.S. Small Business Administration, Office of Advocacy, "Statistics of U.S. Businesses"; <http://www.sba.gov/advo/research/data.html>; accessed 28 January 2008.

Table 742. Employer Firm Births and Deaths and Business Bankruptcies by State: 2005 to 2007

[Births represent an employing unit which is determined, for the first time, as meeting the definition of "employer" in the state unemployment compensation law or a previously terminated employing unit, which again is determined as meeting the definition of employer]

State	Births			Deaths			Business bankruptcies		
	2005	2006	2007	2005	2006	2007	2005	2006	2007
United States [1]. . . .	**938,927**	**933,982**	**923,932**	**935,736**	**933,019**	**926,283**	**39,201**	**19,695**	**23,889**
Alabama	10,575	10,096	9,813	10,168	11,128	10,710	331	219	285
Alaska.	1,982	1,904	1,777	2,294	2,239	3,615	83	45	63
Arizona	21,339	21,555	18,208	18,249	13,508	16,019	525	261	332
Arkansas	7,591	9,551	8,157	7,021	7,289	7,596	426	276	63
California	121,482	115,684	113,829	151,944	149,212	143,591	4,236	2,098	2,697
Colorado	26,610	22,708	23,035	14,035	24,158	23,080	1,120	435	536
Connecticut	9,220	9,516	9,265	11,131	11,214	11,052	156	219	250
Delaware	3,299	3,153	2,921	3,355	3,295	2,775	218	244	243
District of Columbia . . .	4,316	4,232	4,302	3,952	3,111	3,378	46	27	35
Florida.	84,890	79,870	75,533	58,737	64,423	60,724	1,622	991	1,455
Georgia	29,804	31,677	30,062	29,315	29,787	29,517	2,232	1,148	1,316
Hawaii.	3,763	3,813	3,611	3,794	3,789	4,185	81	25	43
Idaho	9,312	9,159	8,065	6,334	6,713	6,995	141	56	79
Illinois	30,445	30,230	30,013	32,846	33,426	33,213	1,042	669	868
Indiana	14,545	14,653	13,863	16,504	13,851	12,826	758	376	484
Iowa	6,004	5,877	5,903	6,802	7,248	7,601	455	208	227
Kansas	7,095	6,973	7,799	7,330	7,000	8,376	410	158	196
Kentucky	9,617	8,973	8,816	8,515	10,230	8,320	409	200	258
Louisiana	9,393	11,034	10,356	9,123	8,972	8,334	718	476	451
Maine	4,251	4,497	4,243	4,711	4,769	4,565	144	85	118
Maryland	22,083	21,535	20,168	21,769	20,745	20,835	760	333	406
Massachusetts	19,723	17,800	18,427	18,878	22,376	21,695	406	253	297
Michigan	24,642	23,508	23,166	26,971	21,268	20,359	1,071	753	1,019
Minnesota	12,555	13,739	12,313	15,302	14,403	12,004	1,721	381	473
Mississippi	6,071	6,862	6,871	6,823	7,898	7,550	200	187	234
Missouri.	17,239	15,805	15,510	20,109	18,124	19,422	438	284	316
Montana	4,768	4,727	4,751	4,394	4,469	4,476	129	39	47
Nebraska.	5,127	4,820	4,752	4,982	5,117	5,092	296	182	202
Nevada	11,299	10,743	11,057	8,485	8,423	9,222	333	178	234
New Hampshire	4,758	4,703	4,588	5,406	5,481	5,523	586	218	306
New Jersey	33,022	36,258	36,381	32,751	32,959	34,183	765	493	705
New Mexico	5,272	5,536	6,158	5,670	5,274	6,003	828	95	102
New York.	62,045	61,718	67,577	62,667	61,190	65,500	2,112	1,201	1,235
North Carolina	25,906	26,729	29,042	22,867	23,165	23,570	612	403	473
North Dakota	1,893	1,821	1,812	2,512	2,181	2,192	95	32	57
Ohio	22,542	22,213	21,900	23,429	25,412	23,434	2,099	957	1,172
Oklahoma	8,609	9,962	8,961	7,231	7,829	7,777	944	236	315
Oregon	14,445	15,085	14,333	14,804	14,039	13,479	1,160	301	298
Pennsylvania	36,609	34,928	34,558	36,989	35,805	34,528	1,356	742	889
Rhode Island	3,677	3,739	3,460	4,164	4,572	4,536	136	48	65
South Carolina	12,341	12,373	12,554	10,681	11,661	11,603	176	82	118
South Dakota	2,102	2,258	2,124	2,354	2,449	2,442	196	47	74
Tennessee	17,484	17,207	17,619	17,135	16,395	17,602	574	397	483
Texas	55,858	58,943	55,865	55,039	54,479	55,269	3,590	2,081	2,241
Utah	11,536	13,379	13,403	11,871	11,190	11,419	449	148	139
Vermont	1,911	1,957	2,228	2,346	2,365	2,374	78	36	56
Virginia	25,061	23,686	28,174	21,359	20,972	21,726	476	283	436
Washington	30,353	32,726	33,191	40,944	36,331	35,077	786	401	439
West Virginia	3,493	3,823	3,434	4,869	4,854	4,824	282	114	117
Wisconsin	13,656	13,371	12,663	13,397	13,060	12,920	820	307	363
Wyoming	2,632	2,570	2,707	2,689	2,773	2,903	84	40	35

[1] Includes Puerto Rico and Virgin Islands, not shown separately. Bankruptcy data also includes Guam and Northern Mariana Islands.

Source: U.S. Employment and Training Administration, unpublished data, and Administrative Office of the U.S. Courts, "Bankruptcy Statistics"; <http://www.uscourts.gov/bnkrpctystats/statistics.htm>.

Table 743. Small Business Administration Loans to Minority-Owned Small Businesses: 2000 to 2007

[**3,634 represents $3,634,000,000. For year ending September 30**. A small business must be independently owned and operated, must not be dominant in its particular industry, and must meet standards set by the Small Business Administration as to its annual receipts or number of employees]

Minority group	Number of loans					Amount (mil. dol.)				
	2000	2004	2005	2006	2007	2000	2004	2005	2006	2007
Total minority loans	**11,999**	**25,413**	**29,722**	**33,780**	**36,320**	**3,634**	**5,144**	**6,132**	**6,607**	**6,852**
Percent of all loans	24.8	28.4	28.3	31.5	32.9	29.4	29.3	30.2	32.6	33.3
African American	2,120	4,827	6,635	7,238	8,914	388	481	627	694	919
Asian American	5,838	12,100	13,456	14,446	15,429	2,383	3,400	4,056	4,238	4,324
Hispanic American	3,500	7,686	8,796	11,215	11,049	761	1,151	1,325	1,561	1,482
Native American	541	800	835	881	928	101	113	123	114	127

Source: U.S. Small Business Administration, Management Information Summary, unpublished data.

U.S. Census Bureau, Statistical Abstract of the United States: 2009

Table 744. U.S. Firms—Ownership by Women, Race, and Hispanic or Latino Origin: 2002

[22,975 represents 22,975,000. A Hispanic firm may be of any race and, therefore may be included in more than one race group. See text, this section and Appendix III]

Group	All firms [1]		Firms with paid employees			
	Firms (1,000)	Sales and receipts (bil. dol.)	Firms (1,000)	Sales and receipts (bil. dol.)	Employees (1,000)	Annual payroll (bil. dol.)
All firms [2]	**22,975**	**22,604**	**5,525**	**21,836**	**110,767**	**3,812**
Female-owned......................	6,489	940	917	803	7,141	174
Male-owned	13,184	7,061	3,525	6,564	42,429	1,320
Equally male-/female-owned...........	2,693	732	718	627	5,665	130
Publicly held and other firms [3]	494	13,820	353	13,797	55,398	2,186
Hispanic or Latino origin	1,573	222	200	180	1,537	37
Black.........................	1,198	89	95	66	754	18
American Indian and Alaska Native	201	27	24	22	191	5
Asian.........................	1,104	327	319	291	2,214	56
Native Hawaiian and Other Pacific Islander...	29	4	4	4	29	1

[1] Both firms with paid employees and firms with no paid employees. [2] U.S. totals are based on the 2002 Economic Census, whereas the gender, Hispanic or Latino origin, and race estimates are based on the 2002 Survey of Business Owners. [3] Publicly held and other firms not classifiable by gender, Hispanic or Latino origin, and race.

Source: U.S. Census Bureau, *2002 Economic Census, Survey of Business Owners, Women-Owned Firms: 2002* (SB02-00CS-WMN)(RV); *Hispanic-Owned Firms: 2002* (SB02-00CS-HISP)(RV); *Black-Owned Firms: 2002* (SB02-00CS-BLK)(RV); *American Indian- and Alaska Native-Owned Firms: 2002* (SB02-00CS-AIAN)(RV); *Asian-Owned Firms: 2002* (SB02-00CS-ASIAN)(RV); and *Native Hawaiian- and Other Pacific Islander-Owned Firms: 2002* (SB02-00CS-NHPI)(RV).

Table 745. Women-Owned and Minority-Owned Firms With Paid Employees by Employment Size: 2002

[917 represents 917,000. Employment reflects number of paid employees during the March 12 pay period. Based on the 2002 Survey of Business Owners; see text, this section and Appendix III]

Item	Unit	Total	Number of employees							
			None [1]	1 to 4	5 to 9	10 to 19	20 to 49	50 to 99	100 to 499	500 or more
WOMEN-OWNED										
Firms.....................	1,000...	917	161	462	149	83	43	11	7	1
Sales and receipts...........	Mil. dol. .	802,851	23,539	113,447	96,282	103,160	117,875	74,053	114,484	160,012
Employees...............	1,000...	7,141	–	939	971	1,105	1,269	750	1,194	913
Annual payroll..............	Mil. dol. .	173,529	3,953	20,483	21,360	25,946	31,578	19,316	30,015	20,877
HISPANIC-OWNED										
Firms.....................	1,000...	200	37	100	31	18	9	3	1	(Z)
Sales and receipts...........	Mil. dol. .	179,508	6,703	28,292	26,627	26,945	29,496	19,447	27,206	14,792
Employees...............	1,000...	1,537	–	202	205	248	267	185	244	186
Annual payroll..............	Mil. dol. .	36,712	1,153	4,568	4,958	5,705	6,393	4,817	5,900	3,217
BLACK-OWNED										
Firms.....................	1,000...	95	19	47	14	7	4	1	1	(Z)
Sales and receipts...........	Mil. dol. .	65,799	2,986	10,679	7,773	7,769	10,912	9,697	11,193	4,790
Employees...............	1,000...	754	–	96	92	100	133	87	162	82
Annual payroll..............	Mil. dol. .	17,550	541	2,251	2,133	2,279	3,034	2,154	3,623	1,535
AMERICAN INDIAN- AND ALASKA NATIVE-OWNED										
Firms.....................	1,000...	24	5	12	4	2	1	(Z)	(Z)	(Z)
Sales and receipts...........	Mil. dol. .	21,987	1,021	3,378	2,411	2,996	3,814	3,092	2,842	2,433
Employees...............	1,000...	191	–	26	23	28	36	23	26	29
Annual payroll..............	Mil. dol. .	5,135	137	578	528	706	945	675	773	793
ASIAN-OWNED										
Firms.....................	1,000...	319	54	161	55	30	15	3	2	(Z)
Sales and receipts...........	Mil. dol. .	291,163	10,287	56,967	46,155	44,109	50,950	30,759	32,955	18,980
Employees...............	1,000...	2,214	–	347	353	393	437	226	302	155
Annual payroll..............	Mil. dol. .	56,045	1,616	7,946	7,992	9,130	10,947	6,048	8,211	4,154
NATIVE HAWAIIAN- AND OTHER PACIFIC ISLANDER-OWNED										
Firms.....................	1,000...	4	1	2	1	(Z)	(Z)	(Z)	(Z)	–
Sales and receipts...........	Mil. dol. .	3,502	73	520	413	574	805	420	698	–
Employees...............	1,000...	29	–	4	4	5	7	4	5	–
Annual payroll..............	Mil. dol. .	826	12	133	99	123	228	100	132	–

– Represents zero. Z Less than 500. [1] Firms reported annual payroll, but did not report any employees on their payroll during specified period in 2002.

Source: U.S. Census Bureau, *2002 Economic Census, Survey of Business Owners, Women-Owned Firms: 2002* (SB02-00CS-WMN)(RV). *Hispanic-Owned Firms: 2002* (SB02-00CS-HISP)(RV); *Black-Owned Firms: 2002* (SB02-00CS-BLK)(RV); *American Indian- and Alaska Native-Owned Firms: 2002* (SB02-00CS-AIAN)(RV); *Asian-Owned Firms: 2002* (SB02-00CS-ASIAN)(RV); and *Native Hawaiian- and Other Pacific Islander-Owned Firms: 2002* (SB02-00CS-NHPI)(RV).

Table 746. Bankruptcy Petitions Filed and Pending by Type and Chapter: 1990 to 2007

[For years ending June 30. Covers only bankruptcy cases filed under the Bankruptcy Reform Act of 1978. *Bankruptcy:* legal recognition that a company or individual is insolvent and must restructure or liquidate. Petitions "filed" means the commencement of a proceeding through the presentation of a petition to the clerk of the court; "pending" is a proceeding in which the administration has not been completed]

Item	1990	1995	2000	2002	2003	2004	2005	2006	2007
Total filed.	725,484	858,104	1,276,922	1,505,306	1,650,279	1,635,725	1,637,254	1,484,570	751,056
Business [1]	64,688	51,288	36,910	39,201	37,182	35,739	32,406	31,562	23,889
Nonbusiness [2]	660,796	806,816	1,240,012	1,466,105	1,613,097	1,599,986	1,604,848	1,453,008	727,167
Chapter 7 [3]	468,171	552,244	864,183	1,030,372	1,144,658	1,146,761	1,174,681	1,142,958	435,064
Chapter 11 [4]	2,116	1,755	722	894	966	935	847	749	540
Chapter 13 [5]	190,509	252,817	375,107	434,835	467,466	452,286	429,315	309,298	291,560
Voluntary.	723,886	856,991	1,276,146	1,504,500	1,649,543	1,635,099	1,636,678	1,484,085	750,577
Involuntary	1,598	1,113	776	806	736	626	576	485	479
Chapter 7 [3]	505,337	581,390	885,447	1,053,230	1,165,993	1,167,101	1,196,212	1,164,815	450,332
Chapter 9 [6]	7	12	8	8	7	7	6	10	7
Chapter 11 [4]	19,591	13,221	9,947	11,401	10,602	11,048	6,703	6,224	5,586
Chapter 12 [7]	1,351	904	732	367	775	302	290	360	386
Chapter 13 [5]	199,186	262,551	380,770	440,231	472,811	457,171	433,945	313,085	294,693
Section 304 [8]	12	26	18	69	91	96	98	[9]36	(X)
Chapter 15 [9]	(X)	(X)	(X)	(X)	(X)	(X)	(X)	40	52
Total pending. . .	961,919	1,090,446	1,400,416	1,613,742	1,729,139	1,697,267	1,750,562	1,411,212	1,312,016

X Not applicable.   [1] Business bankruptcies include those filed under chapters 7, 9, 11, or 12.   [2] Includes other petitions not shown separately.   [3] Chapter 7, liquidation of nonexempt assets of businesses or individuals.   [4] Chapter 11, individual or business reorganization.   [5] Chapter 13, adjustment of debts of an individual with regular income.   [6] Chapter 9, adjustment of debts of a municipality.   [7] Chapter 12, adjustment of debts of a family farmer with regular income, effective November 26, 1986.   [8] Chapter 11, U.S.C., Section 304, cases ancillary to foreign proceedings.   [9] Chapter 15 was added and Section 304 was terminated by changes in the Bankruptcy Laws effective October 17, 2005.

Source: Administrative Office of the U.S. Courts, *Statistical Tables for the Federal Judiciary* and "Bankruptcy Statistics"; <http://www.uscourts.gov/bnkrpctystats/statistics.htm>.

Table 747. Bankruptcy Cases Filed by State: 2000 to 2007

[In thousands (1,276.9 represents 1,276,900). For years ending June 30. Covers only bankruptcy cases filed under the Bankruptcy Reform Act of 1978. *Bankruptcy:* legal recognition that a company or individual is insolvent and must restructure or liquidate. Petitions "filed" means the commencement of a proceeding through the presentation of a petition to the clerk of the court]

State	2000	2005	2006	2007	State	2000	2005	2006	2007
Total [1]	1,276.9	1,637.3	1,484.6	751.1	Missouri	26.3	39.2	38.6	19.0
					Montana	3.3	4.4	4.3	2.0
Alabama	31.4	42.6	34.8	22.5	Nebraska	5.6	9.6	8.7	5.0
Alaska	1.4	1.6	1.7	0.7	Nevada	14.3	16.3	17.2	8.1
Arizona	21.7	32.4	26.7	8.8	New Hampshire	3.9	4.9	4.2	2.6
Arkansas	16.3	25.5	21.5	11.1					
California	160.6	122.6	117.6	55.1	New Jersey	38.7	40.7	34.2	17.3
					New Mexico	7.1	10.1	8.2	3.0
Colorado	15.6	30.2	31.1	13.0	New York	61.7	81.7	77.4	37.0
Connecticut	11.4	11.8	11.5	5.2	North Carolina	25.8	37.5	31.6	18.9
Delaware	4.9	3.6	3.3	1.8	North Dakota	2.0	2.5	2.5	1.0
District of Columbia . . .	2.6	1.9	1.7	0.6					
Florida	74.0	85.8	73.5	32.7	Ohio	53.6	95.8	98.8	45.5
					Oklahoma	19.3	28.2	27.7	8.7
Georgia	57.9	77.3	61.3	45.7	Oregon	18.1	25.3	22.9	8.6
Hawaii	5.0	3.2	3.2	1.2	Pennsylvania	43.8	62.3	56.4	28.1
Idaho	7.3	9.7	8.2	3.5	Rhode Island	4.8	4.4	4.0	2.2
Illinois	62.3	83.6	76.6	36.8					
Indiana	37.5	55.9	60.0	27.7	South Carolina	11.7	15.2	10.9	6.9
					South Dakota	2.1	2.9	3.0	1.2
Iowa	8.2	14.3	12.8	6.2	Tennessee	47.1	60.8	49.2	36.2
Kansas	11.4	17.3	16.3	7.5	Texas	62.9	97.5	86.8	41.4
Kentucky	20.8	29.2	30.0	15.5	Utah	14.4	20.5	14.0	6.0
Louisiana	23.1	31.1	25.3	13.1					
Maine	4.1	4.7	4.6	1.9	Vermont	1.6	1.7	2.0	0.8
					Virginia	37.1	38.8	30.9	16.5
Maryland	31.1	28.5	24.6	11.2	Washington	31.2	37.7	32.3	13.9
Massachusetts	16.7	19.6	19.6	11.7	West Virginia	8.2	12.6	12.1	4.0
Michigan	36.4	68.5	67.2	41.1	Wisconsin	18.0	29.0	27.2	13.9
Minnesota	15.4	19.4	18.5	10.4	Wyoming	2.0	2.5	2.2	0.8
Mississippi	17.9	21.8	16.2	10.5					

[1] Includes island areas not shown separately.

Source: Administrative Office of the U.S. Courts, *Statistical Tables for the Federal Judiciary* and "Bankruptcy Statistics"; <http://www.uscourts.gov/bnkrpctystats/statistics.htm>.

U.S. Census Bureau, Statistical Abstract of the United States: 2009

Table 748. **Patents and Trademarks: 1990 to 2007**

[In thousands (99.2 represents 99,200). Calendar year data. Covers U.S. patents issued to citizens of the United States and residents of foreign countries. For data on foreign countries, see Table 1346]

Type	1990	1995	2000	2002	2003	2004	2005	2006	2007
Patents issued	**99.2**	**113.8**	**176.0**	**184.4**	**187.0**	**181.3**	**157.7**	**196.4**	**182.9**
Inventions	90.4	101.4	157.5	167.3	169.0	164.3	143.8	173.8	157.3
Individuals	17.3	17.4	22.4	20.5	19.6	17.6	14.7	16.6	14.0
Corporations:									
United States	36.1	44.0	70.9	74.2	75.3	73.0	65.2	78.9	70.5
Foreign [1]	36.0	39.1	63.3	71.8	73.2	72.9	63.2	77.4	72.0
U.S. government	1.0	1.0	0.9	0.9	0.9	0.8	0.7	0.8	0.7
Designs	8.0	11.7	17.4	15.5	16.6	15.7	13.0	21.0	24.1
Botanical plants	0.3	0.4	0.5	1.1	1.0	1.0	0.7	1.1	1.0
Reissues	0.4	0.3	0.5	0.5	0.4	0.3	0.2	0.5	0.5
U.S. residents	52.8	64.4	96.9	97.1	98.6	94.1	82.6	102.2	93.7
Foreign country residents	46.2	49.4	79.1	87.3	88.5	87.2	75.2	94.2	89.2
Percent of total	46.7	43.4	44.9	47.3	47.3	48.1	47.6	48.0	48.8
Trademarks:									
Applications filed	127.3	181.0	361.8	264.1	271.7	304.5	334.7	362.3	401.0
Issued	60.8	92.5	115.2	176.0	166.6	146.0	154.8	193.7	218.8
Trademarks	53.6	85.6	106.4	146.9	130.9	113.7	121.6	153.3	170.8
Trademark renewals	7.2	6.9	8.8	29.2	35.6	32.3	33.3	40.4	48.1

[1] Includes patents to foreign governments.

Source: U.S. Patent and Trademark Office, "Statistical Reports Available For Viewing, Calendar Year Patent Statistics"; <http://www.uspto.gov/web/offices/ac/ido/oeip/taf/reports.htm> and unpublished data.

Table 749. **Patents by State and Island Areas: 2007**

[Includes only U.S. patents granted to residents of the United States and territories]

State	Total	Inventions	Designs	Botanical plants	Reissues	State	Total	Inventions	Designs	Botanical plants	Reissues
Total	**93,665**	**79,527**	**13,494**	**364**	**280**	Missouri	861	702	151	6	2
Alabama	358	300	55	2	1	Montana	131	110	21	–	–
Alaska	24	18	6	–	–	Nebraska	254	203	49	1	1
Arizona	1,826	1,571	249	–	6	Nevada	468	367	97	–	4
Arkansas	169	113	53	2	1	New Hampshire . . .	618	542	74	–	2
California	22,594	19,600	2799	127	68	New Jersey	3,152	2,693	442	7	10
Colorado	1,983	1,745	232	1	5	New Mexico	304	286	15	–	3
Connecticut	1,611	1,384	220	1	6	New York	6,025	5,007	983	21	14
Delaware	359	330	28	–	1	North Carolina	2,007	1,745	253	6	3
District of						North Dakota	92	82	10	–	–
Columbia	71	63	8	–	–	Ohio	3,058	2,255	785	–	18
Florida	3,092	2,358	642	83	9	Oklahoma	526	470	55	–	1
Georgia	1,580	1,310	244	19	7	Oregon	2,282	1,877	369	31	5
Hawaii	82	64	16	–	2	Pennsylvania	2,986	2,500	473	3	10
Idaho	1,388	1,350	34	–	4	Rhode Island	380	263	116	–	1
Illinois	3,711	2,894	802	6	9	South Carolina	542	411	130	1	–
Indiana	1,381	1,137	238	3	3	South Dakota	66	60	6	–	–
Iowa	664	601	59	1	3	Tennessee	793	618	170	3	2
Kansas	523	424	97	1	1	Texas	6,228	5,733	467	8	20
Kentucky	505	429	75	–	1	Utah	766	638	126	–	2
Louisiana	294	262	31	1	–	Vermont	546	472	74	–	–
Maine	126	110	16	–	–	Virginia	1,162	1,004	149	1	8
Maryland	1,408	1,246	156	–	6	Washington	3,894	3,228	655	5	6
Massachusetts	3,835	3,510	313	6	6	West Virginia	116	106	10	–	–
Michigan	3,695	3,141	528	8	18	Wisconsin	1,927	1,412	504	4	7
Minnesota	2,920	2,554	357	5	4	Wyoming	62	54	8	–	–
Mississippi	184	142	41	1	–	Island areas	36	33	3	–	–

– Represents zero.

Source: U.S. Patent and Trademark Office, "Statistical Reports Available For Viewing, Calendar Year Patent Statistics"; <http://www.uspto.gov/web/offices/ac/ido/oeip/taf/reports.htm>.

Table 750. **Copyright Registration by Subject Matter: 2000 to 2007**

[In thousands (497.6 represents 497,600). For years ending September 30. Comprises claims to copyrights registered for both U.S. and foreign works. Semiconductor chips and renewals are not considered copyright registration claims]

Subject matter	2000	2005	2006	2007	Subject matter	2000	2005	2006	2007
Total copyright claims . . .	**497.6**	**515.2**	**509.7**	**524.7**	Works of the visual arts [3]	85.8	82.5	90.7	89.2
Monographs [1]	169.7	191.4	182.7	198.6					
Serials	69.0	57.7	61.1	52.6	Semiconductor chip				
Sound recordings	34.2	49.9	50.8	53.7	products	0.7	0.5	0.3	0.3
Musical works [2]	138.9	133.7	124.4	130.6	Renewals	16.8	15.8	10.7	1.3

[1] Includes computer software and machine readable works. [2] Includes dramatic works, accompanying music, choreography, pantomimes, motion pictures, and filmstrips. [3] Two-dimensional works of fine and graphic art, including prints and art reproductions; sculptural works; technical drawings and models; photographs; commercial prints and labels; works of applied arts, cartographic works, and multimedia works.

Source: The Library of Congress, Copyright Office, *Annual Report*.

Table 751. **Net Stock of Private Fixed Assets by Industry: 2000 to 2006**

[In billions of dollars (21,190 represents $21,190,000,000,000). **Estimates as of Dec. 31**. Net stock estimates are presented in terms of current cost and cover equipment, software, and structures]

Industry	1997 NAICS code [1]	2000	2004	2005	2006
Private fixed assets	(X)	**21,190**	**27,423**	**29,937**	**31,819**
Agriculture, forestry, fishing, and hunting	11	406	485	518	543
Farms [2]	111, 112	379	454	484	506
Forestry, fishing, and related activities	113-115	27	31	34	37
Mining	21	580	788	1,017	1,159
Oil and gas extraction	211	442	631	837	959
Mining, except oil and gas	212	92	105	117	129
Mining support activities	213	46	53	63	70
Utilities	22	1,039	1,299	1,377	1,467
Construction	23	173	205	220	239
Manufacturing	31-33	1,759	1,877	1,957	2,037
Durable goods	(X)	996	1,065	1,111	1,155
Wood products	321	31	33	35	36
Nonmetallic mineral products	327	55	61	64	67
Primary metals	331	124	123	126	129
Fabricated metal products	332	112	119	123	127
Machinery	333	140	156	165	173
Computer and electronic products	334	245	257	268	280
Electrical equipment, appliances, and components	335	45	48	49	50
Motor vehicles, bodies and trailers, and parts	3361-3363	105	114	118	121
Other transportation equipment	3364, 3365, 3369	79	87	93	98
Furniture and related products	337	16	18	19	20
Miscellaneous manufacturing	339	43	48	51	54
Nondurable goods	(X)	763	813	847	882
Food and beverage and tobacco products	311, 312	182	195	204	212
Textile mills and textile product mills	313, 314	44	41	42	42
Apparel and leather and allied products	315, 316	17	17	17	18
Paper products	322	100	99	100	101
Printing and related support activities	323	41	45	47	50
Petroleum and coal products	324	92	104	113	121
Chemical products	325	220	240	250	261
Plastics and rubber products	326	67	72	75	77
Wholesale trade	42	348	397	430	469
Retail trade	44-45	641	804	874	937
Transportation and warehousing	48-49	805	907	943	985
Air transportation	481	196	236	238	242
Railroad transportation	482	267	284	292	301
Water transportation	483	39	47	49	52
Truck transportation	484	68	69	78	89
Transit and ground passenger transportation	485	34	38	39	42
Pipeline transportation	486	74	102	111	120
Other transportation and support activites [3]	487, 488, 492	105	105	107	109
Warehousing and storage	493	22	27	29	31
Information	51	817	908	977	1,055
Publishing industries (includes software)	511	50	53	54	56
Motion picture and sound recording industries	512	32	34	35	37
Broadcasting and telecommunications	513	716	794	858	930
Information and data processing services	514	19	28	30	33
Finance and insurance	52	822	985	1,063	1,147
Federal Reserve banks	521	11	14	15	16
Credit intermediation and related activities	522	465	549	587	630
Securities, commodity contracts, and investments	523	86	101	108	116
Insurance carriers and related activities	524	165	190	201	212
Funds, trusts, and other financial vehicles	525	95	130	151	174
Real estate and rental and leasing	53	11,476	15,769	17,287	18,224
Real estate	531	11,233	15,466	16,963	17,870
Rental and leasing services and lessors of intangible assets [4]	532, 533	243	304	324	353
Professional, scientific, and technical services	54	205	276	306	338
Legal services	5411	20	23	25	27
Computer systems design and related services	5415	50	64	68	72
Miscellaneous professional, scientific, and technical services [5]	(⁵)	135	188	213	239
Management of companies and enterprises [6]	551111, 551112	269	334	363	390
Admin/support waste mgt/remediation services	56	153	191	204	220
Administrative and support services	561	84	114	123	134
Waste management and remediation services	562	68	77	81	87
Educational services	61	213	300	331	375
Health care and social assistance	62	693	914	1,004	1,092
Ambulatory health care services	621	190	242	265	287
Hospitals	622	449	603	664	724
Nursing and residential care facilities	623	29	38	42	46
Social assistance	624	24	30	33	36
Arts, entertainment, and recreation	71	128	174	192	209
Performing arts, spectator sports, museums, & related activities	711, 712	48	68	75	83
Amusements, gambling, and recreation industries	713	80	106	116	126
Accommodation and food services	72	336	403	437	471
Accommodation	721	177	203	217	231
Food services and drinking places	722	160	201	220	240
Other services, except public administration	81	329	405	437	464

X Not applicable.   [1] Based on North American Industry Classification System, 1997; see text this section.   [2] NAICS crop and animal production.   [3] Consists of scenic and sightseeing transportation; transportation support activities; and couriers and messengers.   [4] Intangible assets include patents, trademarks, and franchise agreements, but not copyrights.   [5] Consists of accounting, tax preparation, bookkeeping, and payroll services (NAICS code 5412); architectural, engineering, and related services (5413); specialized design services (5414); management, scientific, and technical consulting services (5416); scientific research and development services (5417); advertising and related services (5418); and other professional, scientific, and technical services (5419).   [6] Consists of bank and other holding companies.

Source: U.S. Bureau of Economic Analysis, "Table 3.1ES. Current-Cost Net Stock of Private Fixed Assets by Industry"; published 8 August 2007; <http://www.bea.gov/bea/dn/FA2004/SelectTable.asp#S3>.

Business Enterprise   **501**

Table 752. Private Domestic Investment in Current and Real (2000) Dollars: 1990 to 2006

[In billions of dollars (861 represents $861,000,000,000). Covers equipment, software, and structures. For explanation of chained dollars, see text, Section 13]

Item	1990	1995	2000	2002	2003	2004	2005	2006
CURRENT DOLLARS								
Gross private domestic investment . . .	861	1,144	1,736	1,582	1,664	1,889	2,077	2,209
Less: Consumption of fixed capital	552	713	991	1,080	1,118	1,206	1,357	1,348
Equals: Net private domestic investment	309	431	745	502	546	683	720	862
Fixed investment	846	1,113	1,679	1,570	1,650	1,830	2,040	2,163
Less: Consumption of fixed capital. . . .	552	713	991	1,080	1,118	1,206	1,357	1,348
Equals: Net fixed investment	295	400	688	490	532	624	683	815
Nonresidential	622	810	1,232	1,066	1,077	1,155	1,272	1,398
Residential.	224	303	447	504	572	676	768	765
Change in private inventories	15	31	57	12	14	59	37	47
CHAINED (2000) DOLLARS								
Gross private domestic investment . . .	895	1,134	1,736	1,557	1,613	1,770	1,869	1,920
Less: Consumption of fixed capital	572	707	991	1,080	1,108	1,167	1,268	1,217
Equals: Net private domestic investment	323	427	745	477	505	603	602	702
Fixed investment	887	1,110	1,679	1,545	1,597	1,713	1,831	1,875
Nonresidential	595	763	1,232	1,072	1,082	1,144	1,226	1,307
Residential.	299	353	447	470	509	560	597	570
Change in private inventories	15	30	57	13	14	54	33	40

Source: U.S. Bureau of Economic Analysis, "Table 5.2.5. Gross and Net Domestic Investment by Major Type" and "Table 5.2.6. Real Gross and Net Domestic Investment by Major Type, Chained Dollars"; published 1 August 2007; <http://www.bea.gov/national/nipaweb/SelectTable.asp?Selected=N>.

Table 753. Information and Communications Technology (ICT) Equipment and Computer Software Expenditures: 2005 and 2006

[In millions of dollars (91,591 represents $91,591,000,000). Covers only companies with employees. The Information and Communication Technology Survey collects noncapitalized and capitalized data on information and communication technology equipment, including computer software. This survey is sent to a sample of approximately 46,000 private nonfarm employer businesses operating in the United States]

Type of expenditure and industry	2002 NAICS code [1]	Noncapitalized expenditures [2]		Capitalized expenditures [3]	
		2005	2006	2005	2006
Total expenditures for ICT equipment and computer software	(X)	91,591	90,768	144,239	159,925
Total equipment expenditures	(X)	37,453	36,764	(NA)	(NA)
Purchases	(X)	18,310	18,612	94,140	100,585
Computer and peripheral equipment	(X)	12,204	12,990	54,172	56,733
Information and communication technology equipment	(X)	5,822	5,334	34,894	39,237
Electromedical and electrotherapeutic apparatus	(X)	284	288	5,074	4,615
Operating leases and rental payments	(X)	19,143	18,152	(NA)	(NA)
Computer and peripheral equipment	(X)	12,753	11,805	(NA)	(NA)
Information and communication technology equipment	(X)	5,397	5,308	(NA)	(NA)
Electromedical and electrotherapeutic apparatus	(X)	993	1,038	(NA)	(NA)
Total computer software expenditures	(X)	54,138	54,004	(NA)	(NA)
Purchases and payroll for developing software	(X)	31,377	30,677	50,099	59,339
Software licensing and service/maintenance agreements	(X)	22,761	23,327	(NA)	(NA)
Forestry, fishing, and agricultural services.	113–115	70	51	85	46
Mining	21	699	685	919	1,248
Utilities.	22	1,323	1,469	2,541	2,365
Construction	23	863	999	1,591	1,521
Manufacturing	31-33	16,643	16,910	16,403	17,999
Durable goods industries	321,327,33	11,266	11,303	9,792	10,400
Nondurable goods industries.	31,322–326	5,377	5,607	6,611	7,599
Wholesale trade.	42	2,958	2,703	4,901	5,308
Retail trade	44-45	4,099	3,838	10,371	10,929
Transportation and warehousing	48-49	1,625	1,576	3,286	3,416
Information	51	15,715	13,999	39,405	48,680
Finance and insurance	52	19,989	20,781	24,334	27,512
Real estate and rental and leasing	53	1,064	1,241	2,088	2,006
Professional, scientific, and technical services	54	13,454	12,212	13,024	13,646
Management of companies and enterprises	55	469	662	758	774
Admin/support and waste management/remediation services	56	2,143	2,226	3,527	4,305
Educational services.	61	1,634	1,637	1,850	1,880
Health care and social assistance	62	5,873	6,006	14,011	13,032
Arts, entertainment, and recreation	71	527	532	858	885
Accommodation and food services	72	794	934	1,979	1,702
Other services (except public administration).	81	1,322	1,954	1,941	2,306
Equipment expenditures serving multiple industry codes . . .	(X)	326	356	367	367

NA Not available.   X Not applicable.   [1] Based on North American Industry Classification System, 2002; see text, this section.   [2] Expenses for ICT equipment including computer software not charged to asset accounts for which depreciation or amortization accounts are ordinarily maintained.   [3] Expenses for ICT equipment including computer software chargeable to asset accounts for which depreciation or amortization accounts are ordinarily maintained.

Source: U.S. Census Bureau, "2006 Information and Communication Technology Survey"; published 6 March 2008; <http://www.census.gov/csd/ict/xls/2006/Full%20Report.htm>.

Table 754. **Capital Expenditures: 2000 to 2006**

[**In billions of dollars (1,161 represents $1,161,000,000,000)**. Based on a sample survey and subject to sampling error; see source for details]

Item	All companies				Companies with employees				Companies without employees			
	2000	2004	2005	2006	2000	2004	2005	2006	2000	2004	2005	2006
Capital expenditures, total	1,161	1,042	1,145	1,309	1,090	953	1,063	1,217	71	89	82	93
Structures	364	369	402	490	338	335	369	456	26	33	33	35
New	329	325	366	451	309	300	341	422	20	24	25	29
Used	35	44	36	39	29	35	28	33	6	9	8	6
Equipment and software	797	673	743	819	752	618	694	761	45	56	49	58
New	751	628	701	775	718	588	665	732	32	41	37	43
Used	46	45	42	44	34	30	29	29	12	15	13	15
Capital leases	20	18	18	24	19	18	18	24	(Z)	(Z)	(Z)	1

Z Less than $500 million.

Source: U.S. Census Bureau, "2006 Annual Capital Expenditures Survey"; published 24 January 2008; <http://www.census.gov /csd/ace/xls/2006/Full%20Report.htm> and earlier reports.

Table 755. **Capital Expenditures by Industry: 2000 and 2006**

[**In billions of dollars (1,090 represents $1,090,000,000,000)**. Covers only companies with employees. Based on the North American Industry Classification System (NAICS), 2002; see text this section. Based on a sample survey and subject to sampling error; see source for details]

Industry	2002 NAICS code	2000	2006	Industry	2002 NAICS code	2000	2006
Total expenditures	**(X)**	**1,090**	**1,217**	Professional, scientific, and technical services	54	34	30
Forestry, fishing, and agricultural services	113–115	1	3	Management of companies and enterprises	55	5	3
Mining	21	43	98	Admin/support waste mgt/ remediation services	56	18	19
Utilities	22	61	70	Educational services	61	18	23
Construction	23	25	30	Health care and social assistance	62	52	75
Manufacturing	31–33	215	191	Arts, entertainment, and recreation	71	19	17
Durable goods	321, 327, 33	134	105	Accommodation and food services	72	26	36
Nondurable goods	31, 322–326	81	86	Other services (except public administration)	81	21	26
Wholesale trade	42	34	43	Structure and equipment expenditures serving multiple industry categories. . . .	(X)	2	2
Retail trade	44–45	70	87				
Transportation and warehousing	48–49	60	67				
Information	51	160	105				
Finance and insurance	52	134	169				
Real estate and rental and leasing	53	92	122				

X Not applicable.

Source: U.S. Census Bureau, "2006 Annual Capital Expenditures Survey"; published 24 January 2008; <http://www.census.gov /csd/ace/xls/2006/Full%20Report.htm> and earlier reports.

Table 756. **Business Cycle Expansions and Contractions—Months of Duration: 1945 to 2001**

[A trough is the low point of a business cycle; a peak is the high point. Contraction, or recession, is the period from peak to subsequent trough; expansion is the period from trough to subsequent peak. Business cycle reference dates are determined by the National Bureau of Economic Research, Inc.]

Business cycle reference date				Contraction (peak to trough)	Expansion (previous trough to this peak)	Length of cycle	
Peak		Trough				Trough from previous trough	Peak from previous peak
Month	Year	Month	Year				
February	1945	October	1945	8	[1]80	[1]88	[2]93
November	1948	October	1949	11	37	48	45
July	1953	May.	1954	10	45	55	56
August	1957	April	1958	8	39	47	49
April	1960	February	1961	10	24	34	32
December	1969	November	1970	11	106	117	116
November	1973	March	1975	16	36	52	47
January	1980	July.	1980	6	58	64	74
July	1981	November	1982	16	12	28	18
July	1990	March	1991	8	92	100	108
March	2001	November	2001	8	120	128	128
Average, all cycles: 1945 to 2001 (10 cycles) . . .				10	57	67	67
Average, peacetime cycles: 1945 to 2001 (8 cycles) . . .				10	52	63	63

[1] Previous trough: June 1938.   [2] Previous peak: May 1937.

Source: National Bureau of Economic Research, Inc., Cambridge, MA, "Business Cycle Expansions and Contractions"; <http://www.nber.org/cycles.html>; (accessed 17 April 2008).

U.S. Census Bureau, Statistical Abstract of the United States: 2009

Table 757. Composite Indexes of Leading, Coincident, and Lagging Economic Indicators: 2000 to 2007

[299.4 represents 299,400]

Item	Unit	2000	2003	2004	2005	2006	2007
Leading index, composite	2004 = 100. . . .	**86.3**	**93.4**	**100.0**	**102.7**	**104.0**	**103.7**
Average weekly hours, manufacturing . . .	Hours	41.2	40.4	40.8	40.6	41.1	41.2
Average weekly initial claims for unemployment insurance	1,000.	299.4	401.8	342.6	331.2	313.1	322.3
Manufacturers' new orders, consumer goods, and materials (1982 dol.)	Mil. dol.	152,044	144,855	145,359	149,852	147,325	142,764
Vendor performance, slower deliveries diffusion index [1]	Percent	53.3	53.1	62.6	54.1	54.3	51.2
Manufacturers' new orders, nondefense capital goods (1982 dol.)	Mil. dol.	49,807	37,902	39,514	45,262	49,299	50,121
Building permits, new private housing units	1,000.	1,598	1,888	2,058	2,160	1,842	1,371
Stock prices, 500 common stocks [1]	1941–43 = 10 . .	1,426.8	963.7	1,130.6	1,207.1	1,310.0	1,476.7
Money supply, M2 (chain 2000 dol.)	Bil. dol.	4,785	5,666	5,781	5,865	5,981	6,176
Interest rate spread, 10-year Treasury bonds less federal funds	Percent	−0.21	2.89	2.93	1.08	−0.17	−0.39
Index of consumer expectations [1]	1966:1 = 100 . .	102.7	81.4	88.5	77.4	75.9	75.6
Coincident index, composite	2004 = 100. . . .	**98.8**	**98.0**	**100.0**	**102.5**	**105.0**	**106.7**
Employees on nonagricultural payrolls. . .	1,000.	131,794	129,996	131,419	133,695	136,092	137,618
Personal income less transfer payments (chain 2000 dol.)	Bil. dol.	7,345	7,412	7,647	7,872	8,178	8,461
Industrial production.	2002 = 100. . . .	103.7	101.2	103.8	107.2	109.6	111.4
Manufacturing and trade sales (chain 2000 dol.)	Mil. dol.	844,794	855,746	888,784	927,514	956,254	969,587
Lagging index, composite	2004 = 100. . . .	**99.6**	**99.5**	**100.0**	**103.1**	**106.4**	**109.4**
Average duration of unemployment.	Weeks.	12.7	19.2	19.6	18.4	16.9	16.9
Inventories to sales ratio, manufacturing and trade (chain 2000 dol.)	Ratio	1.38	1.37	1.35	1.33	1.33	1.32
Change in labor cost per unit of output, manufacturing.	Percent	2.3	1.2	−0.8	−1.4	1.2	1.0
Average prime rate	Percent	9.2	4.1	4.3	6.2	8.0	8.1
Commercial and industrial loans outstanding (chain 2000 dol.)	Mil. dol.	1,033,254	641,988	587,269	621,168	655,668	728,473
Consumer installment credit to personal income ratio	Percent	19.2	22.2	22.0	21.8	21.3	21.1
Change in consumer price index for services	Percent	3.8	3.1	3.0	3.5	3.7	3.3

[1] Data are from private sources and provided through the courtesy of the compilers and are subject to their copyrights: stock prices, Standard & Poor's Corporation; index of consumer expectations, University of Michigan's Survey Research Center; vendor performance, Institute for Supply Management.

Source: The Conference Board, New York, NY 10022-6601, *Business Cycle Indicators*, monthly, <http://www.conference -board.org/economics/bci/> (copyright).

Table 758. Manufacturing and Trade—Sales and Inventories: 1992 to 2007

[In billions of dollars (541 represents $541,000,000,000), except ratios. Based on North American Industry Classification System (NAICS) 2002; see text, this section]

Year	Sales, average monthly [1]				Inventories [2]				Inventory-sales ratios [3]			
	Total	Manu-fac-turing	Retail trade	Mer-chant whole-salers	Total	Manu-fac-turing	Retail trade	Mer-chant whole-salers	Total	Manu-fac-turing	Retail trade	Mer-chant whole-salers
1992	541	242	151	147	837	379	261	197	1.53	1.57	1.67	1.31
1993	568	252	162	154	864	380	280	205	1.50	1.50	1.68	1.30
1994	610	270	176	165	927	400	305	222	1.46	1.44	1.66	1.29
1995	655	290	185	180	986	425	323	238	1.48	1.44	1.72	1.29
1996	687	300	197	190	1,005	430	334	241	1.46	1.43	1.67	1.27
1997	724	320	206	198	1,047	444	345	259	1.42	1.37	1.64	1.26
1998	743	325	216	202	1,079	449	357	272	1.43	1.39	1.62	1.31
1999	787	336	234	217	1,139	464	385	290	1.40	1.35	1.59	1.30
2000	834	351	249	235	1,198	482	407	309	1.41	1.35	1.59	1.29
2001	819	331	256	232	1,120	428	395	297	1.42	1.38	1.58	1.32
2002	824	326	261	236	1,140	423	416	301	1.36	1.28	1.55	1.25
2003	854	335	272	247	1,147	408	432	306	1.34	1.24	1.56	1.22
2004	923	359	290	275	1,238	441	461	336	1.30	1.19	1.56	1.17
2005	1,001	395	307	299	1,305	473	472	360	1.27	1.17	1.51	1.17
2006	1,068	418	324	326	1,390	511	489	390	1.27	1.19	1.49	1.16
2007	1,114	423	337	354	1,444	531	501	412	1.27	1.23	1.47	1.13

[1] Averages of monthly not-seasonally-adjusted figures. [2] Seasonally adjusted end-of-year data. [3] Averages of seasonally adjusted monthly ratios.

Source: U.S. Council of Economic Advisors, *Economic Indicators*, May 2008.

Table 759. **Industrial Production Indexes by Industry: 1990 to 2007**

[**2002 = 100**. Except as noted, based on the North American Industry Classification System (NAICS); 2002; see text this section]

Industry	2002 NAICS code	1990	2000	2001	2003	2004	2005	2006	2007
Total index	(X)	**68.7**	**103.6**	**100.1**	**101.2**	**103.8**	**107.2**	**109.6**	**111.4**
Manufacturing (SIC) [1]	(X)	**65.9**	**104.3**	**100.1**	**101.3**	**104.2**	**108.4**	**111.1**	**112.9**
Manufacturing (NAICS)	31–33	64.5	104.0	99.8	101.5	104.6	109.0	112.1	114.1
Durable goods	(X)	51.4	105.4	100.5	102.7	106.9	112.7	117.9	121.0
Wood products	321	84.4	104.2	97.1	100.7	104.4	110.4	110.0	99.3
Nonmetallic mineral products	327	83.8	104.2	99.8	100.5	103.6	108.1	109.8	108.2
Primary metals	331	96.2	110.3	99.4	99.1	110.0	108.0	112.4	110.4
Fabricated metal products	332	80.7	111.2	102.6	98.7	98.9	103.5	109.1	112.0
Machinery	333	86.8	117.7	104.2	99.7	103.8	110.2	115.5	116.1
Computers and electronic products	334	11.9	101.8	103.6	113.8	129.0	143.5	164.6	183.0
Electrical equipment, appliances, and components . . .	335	88.4	122.9	109.2	97.3	99.0	100.6	101.3	104.9
Motor vehicles and parts	3361–3	55.5	99.5	91.4	103.5	103.7	103.9	100.2	97.2
Aerospace and other misc. transportation equipment	3364–9	123.0	99.5	105.9	95.8	94.3	105.1	110.9	122.4
Furniture and related products . . .	337	74.6	102.3	96.7	98.2	100.9	104.6	104.2	101.9
Miscellaneous products.	339	66.8	96.5	95.5	103.1	103.2	109.8	113.2	115.9
Nondurable goods.	(X)	87.7	102.3	98.9	100.1	102.0	104.8	105.6	106.6
Food, beverage, and tobacco products.	311,2	90.0	101.2	100.9	102.0	102.5	106.2	106.7	110.1
Textile and product mills	313,4	99.7	112.7	100.3	96.0	94.6	96.7	88.0	80.5
Apparel and leather	315,6	172.8	151.2	128.2	93.3	82.0	80.4	79.2	78.5
Paper	322	97.2	105.0	99.3	96.8	97.6	97.5	97.5	95.9
Printing and related support.	323	102.1	113.1	106.3	96.2	96.9	99.0	99.5	99.8
Petroleum and coal products	324	86.9	96.9	96.4	97.9	106.0	110.1	109.7	108.7
Chemical	325	78.3	95.0	93.3	101.3	105.6	109.3	112.6	114.2
Plastics and rubber products	326	67.7	103.5	96.9	100.3	101.5	102.3	102.8	103.4
Other manufacturing (non-NAICS) [2] . . .	1133, 5111	96.7	109.6	105.7	97.1	97.9	98.5	94.3	92.9
Mining.	21	**106.9**	**103.5**	**104.8**	**99.9**	**99.6**	**98.3**	**101.4**	**101.5**
Utilities	2211,2	**77.9**	**97.4**	**97.0**	**101.9**	**103.3**	**105.5**	**104.8**	**108.2**
Electric power generation, transmission, and distribution	2211	76.7	97.2	96.9	102.1	104.2	107.2	107.8	110.4
Natural gas distribution	2212	85.6	98.6	97.2	100.9	98.2	98.8	91.3	98.1

X Not applicable.   [1] Standard Industrial Classification (SIC); see text this section.   [2] Those industries—logging and newspaper, periodical, book, and directory publishing—that have traditionally been considered to be manufacturing.

Source: Board of Governors of the Federal Reserve System, *Statistical Supplement to the Federal Reserve Bulletin,* monthly; and *Industrial Production and Capacity Utilization,* Statistical Release G.17, monthly. See also <http://www.federalreserve.gov/releases/g17/>.

Table 760. **Index of Industrial Capacity: 1990 to 2007**

[**2002 output = 100**. Annual figures are averages of monthly data. Capacity represents estimated quantity of output relative to output in 2002 which the current stock of plant and equipment was capable of producing]

Year	Index of capacity		Relation of output to capacity (percent)				
	Total industry	Manufacturing	Total industry	Crude [1]	Primary and semifinished [2]	Finished [3]	Manufacturing
1990	83.4	80.7	82.4	88.2	82.7	80.3	81.6
1995	95.0	93.6	84.0	88.6	86.8	79.5	83.1
1998	114.3	115.5	82.8	87.3	84.0	80.5	81.7
1999	120.9	123.1	81.9	86.6	84.1	78.5	80.8
2000	126.9	130.3	81.7	88.2	84.3	77.0	80.1
2001	131.4	135.4	76.1	85.3	77.6	72.4	73.9
2002	133.7	137.4	74.8	82.8	77.1	70.5	72.8
2003	133.2	136.9	76.0	84.6	78.4	71.4	74.0
2004	133.1	136.6	78.0	86.4	80.4	72.9	76.3
2005	133.7	137.9	80.2	86.7	82.5	75.3	78.6
2006	135.4	140.0	80.9	88.8	82.4	76.4	79.4
2007	137.5	142.3	81.0	88.5	81.7	77.4	79.4

[1] Crude processing, covers a relatively small portion of total industrial capacity and consists of logging (NAICS 1133), much of mining (excluding stone, sand, and gravel mining, and oil and gas drilling, which are NAICS 21231, 21221–2, and 213111) and some basic manufacturing industries, including basic chemicals (NAICS 3251); fertilizers, pesticides, and other agricultural chemicals (NAICS 32531,2); pulp, paper, and paperboard mills (NAICS 3221); and alumina, aluminum, and other nonferrous production and processing mills (NAICS 3313,4).   [2] Primary and semifinished processing loosely corresponds to the previously published aggregate, primary processing. Includes utilities and portions of several 2-digit SIC industries included in the former advanced processing group. These include printing and related support activities (NAICS 3231); paints and adhesives (NAICS 3255); and newspaper, periodical, book, and directory publishers (NAICS 5111).   [3] Finished processing generally corresponds to the previously published aggregate, advanced processing. Includes oil and gas well drilling and carpet and rug mills.

Source: Board of Governors of the Federal Reserve System, *Industrial Production and Capacity Utilization,* Statistical Release G.17, monthly. (Based on data from Federal Reserve Board, U.S. Dept. of Commerce, U.S. Bureau of Labor Statistics, and McGraw-Hill Information Systems Company, New York, NY; and other sources.)

Table 761. Corporate Profits, Taxes, and Dividends: 1990 to 2007

[**In billions of dollars (438 represents $438,000,000,000).** Covers corporations organized for profit and other entities treated as corporations. Represents profits to U.S. residents, without deduction of depletion charges and exclusive of capital gains and losses; intercorporate dividends from profits of domestic corporations are eliminated; net receipts of dividends, reinvested earnings of incorporated foreign affiliates, and earnings of unincorporated foreign affiliates are added. CCA = capital consumption adjustment]

Item	1990	2000	2003	2004	2005	2006	2007
Corporate profits with IVA and CCA	438	818	993	1,231	1,373	1,554	1,595
Taxes on corporate income	145	265	243	307	393	454	467
Profits after tax with IVA and CCA	292	553	750	924	980	1,100	1,129
Net dividends	169	378	425	540	601	699	795
Undistributed profits with IVA and CCA . . .	123	175	325	384	379	401	334
Cash flow:							
Net cash flow with IVA and CCA	491	865	1,085	1,182	1,235	1,291	1,255
Undistributed profits with IVA and CCA . . .	123	175	325	384	379	401	334
Consumption of fixed capital	368	690	760	797	857	890	922
Less: Inventory valuation adjustment (IVA). . .	−13	−14	−14	−43	−36	−36	−46
Equals: Net cash flow	504	879	1,099	1,225	1,272	1,327	1,301

Source: U.S. Bureau of Economic Analysis, *Survey of Current Business,* monthly. See also <http://www.bea.gov/national /nipaweb/Index.asp>.

Table 762. Corporate Profits With Inventory Valuation and Capital Consumption Adjustments—Financial and Nonfinancial Industries: 2000 to 2007

[**In billions of dollars (818 represents $818,000,000,000).** Based on the North American Industry Classification System 1997; see text, this section. Minus sign (−) indicates loss. See headnote, Table 761]

Item	2000	2003	2004	2005	2006	2007
Corporate profits with IVA/CCA [1] . . .	**818**	**993**	**1,231**	**1,373**	**1,554**	**1,595**
Domestic industries	672	828	1,038	1,155	1,296	1,258
Rest of the world	146	166	193	218	257	338
Corporate profits with IVA [1]	**759**	**895**	**1,162**	**1,543**	**1,770**	**1,831**
Domestic industries	614	729	968	1,325	1,512	1,493
Financial [2]	200	317	349	424	505	499
Nonfinancial.	413	412	619	902	1,007	995
Utilities	24	12	19	28	36	44
Manufacturing.	144	76	153	251	293	306
Wholesale trade	60	55	79	95	97	99
Retail trade	60	87	91	114	125	138
Transportation and warehousing.	15	7	14	28	42	47
Information.	−18	3	44	75	85	103
Other nonfinancial [3]	128	172	220	310	329	258
Rest of the world	146	166	193	218	257	338

[1] Inventory valuation adjustment and capital consumption adjustment. [2] Consists of finance and insurance and bank and other holding companies. [3] Consists of agriculture, forestry, fishing, and hunting; mining; construction; real estate and rental and leasing; professional, scientific, and technical services; administrative and waste management services; educational services; health care and social assistance; arts, entertainment, and recreation; accommodation and food services; and other services, except government.

Source: U.S. Bureau of Economic Analysis, *Survey of Current Business,* April 2008. See also <http://www.bea.gov/national /nipaweb/Index.asp>.

Table 763. Corporate Profits Before Taxes by Industry: 2000 to 2006

[**In billions of dollars (773 represents $773,000,000,000).** Profits are without inventory valuation and capital consumption adjustments. Minus sign (−) indicates loss. See headnote, Table 761]

Industry	1997 NAICS code [1]	2000	2003	2004	2005	2006
Corporate profits before tax	(X)	**773**	**908**	**1,205**	**1,580**	**1,806**
Domestic industries	(X)	628	743	1,011	1,361	1,549
Agriculture, forestry, fishing, and hunting	11	2	2	3	5	5
Mining.	21	15	16	24	45	57
Utilities	221	25	12	19	29	35
Construction	23	42	39	56	82	64
Manufacturing	31–33	153	83	175	269	313
Wholesale trade	42	62	60	89	102	108
Retail trade	44–45	61	88	98	120	129
Transportation and warehousing	48–49	15	7	14	29	42
Information	51	−18	3	43	75	86
Finance and insurance.	52	113	196	210	273	341
Real estate and rental and leasing	53	9	10	13	26	28
Professional, scientific, and technical services . . .	54	1	26	35	37	41
Management of companies and enterprises [2]. . . .	551111, 551112	87	121	139	151	164
Admin/support waste mgt/remediation services. . .	56	9	14	15	23	27
Educational services	61	2	3	4	5	5
Health care and social assistance	62	25	40	43	52	58
Arts, entertainment, and recreation.	71	2	3	5	6	9
Accommodation and food services	72	14	12	16	21	24
Other services, except public administration.	81	8	8	8	12	13
Rest of the world [3]	(X)	146	165	193	218	257

X Not applicable. [1] Based on North American Industry Classification System, 1997; see text, this section. [2] Consists of bank and other holding companies. [3] Consists of receipts by all U.S. residents, including both corporations and persons, of dividends from foreign corporations, and, for U.S. corporations, their share of reinvested earnings of their incorporated foreign affiliates, and earnings of unincorporated foreign affiliates, net of corresponding payments.

Source: U.S. Bureau of Economic Analysis, *Survey of Current Business*, August 2007. See also <http://www.bea.gov/national /nipaweb/Index.asp>.

Table 764. **Manufacturing, Mining, and Trade Corporations—Profits and Stockholders' Equity by Industry: 2006 and 2007**

[Averages of quarterly figures at annual rates. Manufacturing data exclude estimates for corporations with less than $250,000 in assets at time of sample selection. Based on sample; see source for discussion of methodology. Based on North American Industry Classification System (NAICS), 2002; see text, this section. Minus sign (–) indicates loss]

Industry	2002 NAICS code	Ratio of profits after taxes to stockholders' equity (percent)		Profits after taxes per dollar of sales (cents)		Ratio of stockholders' equity to debt	
		2006	2007	2006	2007	2006	2007
Manufacturing	31–33	**17.6**	**15.4**	**8.1**	**7.3**	**2.0**	**2.0**
Nondurable manufacturing	(X)	21.4	19.4	9.7	9.0	1.8	1.8
Food	311	19.0	16.7	5.2	5.4	1.2	1.4
Beverage and tobacco products	312	20.1	30.4	16.9	19.5	1.5	1.2
Textile mills and textile product mills	313, 314	7.8	7.3	2.9	2.8	1.8	1.9
Apparel and leather products	315, 316	19.7	17.6	7.4	7.0	2.4	2.1
Paper	322	11.3	5.6	4.2	2.1	1.0	1.1
Printing and related support activities	323	18.5	14.7	4.0	3.3	0.7	0.7
Petroleum and coal products	324	28.8	25.5	10.6	9.6	3.0	3.0
Chemicals	325	18.3	16.5	13.7	12.4	2.0	1.9
Plastics and rubber products	326	13.4	15.1	3.1	4.1	0.8	0.9
Durable manufacturing	(X)	13.9	11.6	6.6	5.7	2.3	2.2
Wood products	321	15.6	7.3	4.4	2.0	1.4	1.2
Nonmetallic mineral products	327	22.8	13.7	7.6	6.5	1.1	1.3
Primary metals	331	23.8	17.5	8.5	7.9	1.9	2.4
Fabricated metal products	332	24.4	23.0	7.5	7.5	1.6	1.6
Machinery	333	17.8	18.4	7.6	8.2	2.0	2.0
Computer and electronic products	334	12.4	10.2	11.2	9.6	4.3	4.2
Electrical equipment, appliances, & components	335	18.1	18.3	14.7	14.4	4.1	3.7
Transportation equipment	336	2.3	–9.3	0.6	–1.8	1.2	1.0
Furniture and related products	337	17.6	13.9	5.1	4.2	1.2	1.2
Miscellaneous manufacturing	339	11.3	14.6	8.3	10.6	2.6	2.4
All mining	21	**23.9**	**15.1**	**31.7**	**21.6**	**2.3**	**2.1**
All wholesale trade	42	**15.1**	**14.2**	**2.1**	**2.0**	**1.6**	**1.5**
Durable goods	421	14.0	12.2	2.6	2.4	1.8	1.7
Nondurable goods	422	17.2	17.9	1.7	1.7	1.4	1.2
All retail trade	44–45	**16.2**	**14.9**	**3.2**	**3.0**	**1.8**	**1.7**
Food and beverage stores	445	13.0	19.8	1.6	2.4	1.1	1.1
Clothing and general merchandise stores	448, 452	16.3	15.6	4.0	3.8	2.2	1.8
All other retail trade	(X)	16.9	13.1	3.1	2.6	1.8	1.7

X Not applicable.

Source: U.S. Census Bureau, *Quarterly Financial Report for Manufacturing, Mining, and Trade Corporations.*

Table 765. **Value Added, Employment, and Capital Expenditures of Nonbank U.S. Multinational Companies: 1999 to 2005**

[Value added and capital expenditures in billions of dollars (2,481 represents $2,481,000,000,000); employees in thousands. See headnote, Table 766. MNC = Multinational company. MOFA = Majority-owned foreign affiliate. Minus sign (–) indicates decrease]

Item	1999	2000	2001	2002	2003	2004	2005	Percent change at annual rates	
								1999–2004	2004–2005
VALUE ADDED									
MNCs worldwide:									
Parents and all affiliates	(NA)	(NA)	(NA)	(NA)	(NA)	(NA)	(NA)	(NA)	(NA)
Parents and MOFAs	2,481	2,748	2,478	2,460	2,656	2,992	3,185	3.8	6.5
Parents	1,914	2,141	1,892	1,859	1,958	2,173	2,303	2.6	6.0
Affiliates, total	(NA)	(NA)	(NA)	(NA)	(NA)	(NA)	(NA)	(NA)	(NA)
MOFAs	566	607	586	602	698	818	882	7.6	7.8
Other	(NA)	(NA)	(NA)	(NA)	(NA)	(NA)	(NA)	(NA)	(NA)
EMPLOYEES									
MNCs worldwide:									
Parents and all affiliates	32,227	33,598	32,539	31,894	30,762	31,245	32,102	–0.6	2.7
Parents and MOFAs	30,773	32,057	30,929	30,373	29,347	29,843	30,724	–0.6	3.0
Parents	23,007	23,885	22,735	22,118	21,105	21,177	21,769	–1.6	2.8
Affiliates, total	9,220	9,713	9,804	9,776	9,658	10,068	10,333	1.8	2.6
MOFAs	7,766	8,171	8,194	8,256	8,242	8,667	8,956	2.2	3.3
Other	1,454	1,542	1,610	1,520	1,415	1,402	1,378	–0.7	–1.7
CAPITAL EXPENDITURES									
MNCs worldwide:									
Parents and all affiliates	514	(NA)	(NA)	(NA)	(NA)	457	(NA)	–2.3	(NA)
Parents and MOFAs	483	507	524	443	425	434	451	–2.1	3.9
Parents	370	396	413	333	315	310	324	–3.4	4.4
Affiliates, total	144	(NA)	(NA)	(NA)	(NA)	147	(NA)	0.4	(NA)
MOFAs	113	111	111	110	110	123	127	1.7	2.8
Other	31	(NA)	(NA)	(NA)	(NA)	24	(NA)	–5.3	(NA)

NA Not available.

Source: U.S. Bureau of Economic Analysis, *Survey of Current Business*, November 2007.

Table 766. U.S. Multinational Companies—Selected Characteristics: 2005

[**Preliminary. In billions of dollars (16,787 represents $16,787,000,000,000), except as indicated.** Consists of nonbank U.S. parent companies and their nonbank foreign affiliates. U.S. parent comprises the domestic operations of a multinational and is a U.S. person that owns or controls, directly or indirectly, 10 percent or more of the voting securities of an incorporated foreign business enterprise, or an equivalent interest in an unincorporated foreign business enterprise. A U.S. person can be an incorporated business enterprise. A majority-owned foreign affiliate (MOFA) is a foreign business enterprise in which a U.S. parent company owns or controls more than 50 percent of the voting securities]

| Industry [1] | 2002 NAICS code | U.S. parents | | | | MOFAs | | |
		Total assets	Capital expenditures	Value added	Employment (1,000)	Capital expenditures	Value added	Employment (1,000)
All industries	(X)	**16,787**	**323.9**	**2,303**	**21,769**	**126.9**	**882**	**8,956**
Mining	21	260	18.5	52	168	31.9	110	171
Utilities	22	594	25.4	76	267	2.8	11	50
Manufacturing [2]	31–33	5,014	122.8	1,053	8,022	50.6	429	4,397
Petroleum and coal products	324	533	14.9	148	223	4.0	76	37
Chemicals	325	891	20.4	188	958	9.1	84	574
Computers and electronic products	334	484	13.0	105	868	6.7	41	655
Transportation equipment	336	1,607	37.0	195	1,875	12.1	57	937
Wholesale trade	42	691	21.6	130	1,003	7.0	119	731
Information [2]	51	1,430	49.2	266	1,869	4.2	38	323
Broadcasting (except Internet) and telecommunications	515,517	1,132	43.1	183	1,217	2.6	9	71
Finance (except depository institutions) and insurance	52 exc. 521, 522	7,221	18.0	156	1,088	7.1	32	271
Professional, scientific, and technical services	54	320	6.9	122	1,042	3.4	53	544
Other industries [2]	(X)	1,258	61.4	448	8,311	19.9	90	2,470
Retail trade	44–45	435	24.8	202	4,176	6.3	37	810

X Not applicable.   [1] Represents North American Industry Classification System 2002-based industry of U.S. parent or industry of foreign affiliate.   [2] Includes other industries not shown separately.

Source: U.S. Bureau of Economic Analysis, *Survey of Current Business*, November 2007 and unpublished data.

Table 767. U.S. Multinational Companies—Value Added: 2000 and 2005

[**In billions of dollars (2,748 represents $2,748,000,000,000).** See headnote, Table 766. Data are by industry of U.S. parent. Based on the North American Industry Classification System, 2002 (NAICS); see text this section]

| Industry | 2002 NAICS code | U.S. multinationals | | U.S. parents | | Majority-owned foreign affiliates | |
		2000	2005	2000	2005	2000	2005
All industries	(X)	**2,748**	**3,185**	**2,141**	**2,303**	**607**	**882**
Mining	21	39	84	28	52	11	32
Utilities	22	86	83	81	76	5	8
Manufacturing [1]	31–33	1,410	1,645	995	1,053	415	592
Petroleum and coal products	324	232	332	112	148	120	184
Chemicals	325	212	287	141	188	71	99
Computers and electronic products	334	188	156	142	105	46	52
Transportation equipment	336	271	275	209	195	62	80
Wholesale trade	42	133	162	99	130	34	31
Information [1]	51	325	309	302	266	22	43
Broadcasting (except Internet) and telecommunications	515,517	(NA)	196	(NA)	183	(NA)	13
Finance (except depository institutions) and insurance	52 exc. 521, 522	181	193	157	156	24	37
Professional, scientific, and technical services	54	141	177	101	122	41	55
Other industries [1]	(X)	433	532	379	448	54	84
Retail trade	44–45	166	231	149	202	18	29

NA Not available.   X Not applicable.   [1] Includes other industries not shown separately.

Source: U.S. Bureau of Economic Analysis, *Survey of Current Business*, November 2003 and November 2007.

Table 768. U.S. Majority-Owned Foreign Affiliates—Value Added by Industry of Affiliate and Country: 2005

[**In millions of dollars (882,099 represents $882,099,000,000.** See headnote, Table 766. Numbers in parentheses represent North American Industry Classification System 2002 codes; see text, this section]

| Country | All industries [1] | Mining (21) | Manufacturing (31–33) | | | Wholesale trade (42) | Professional, scientific, and technical services (54) |
			Total [1]	Chemicals (325)	Transportation equipment (336)		
All countries [2]	**882,099**	**109,525**	**429,254**	**84,382**	**57,071**	**119,251**	**52,959**
United Kingdom	136,274	12,315	55,736	8,491	5,895	15,633	14,005
Canada	106,248	21,073	48,332	4,174	11,750	7,920	4,632
Germany	75,662	1,574	51,688	5,695	10,710	10,321	3,550
France	49,280	102	27,433	6,560	3,071	7,284	2,368
Japan	47,855	4	21,272	4,391	613	7,891	6,130
Ireland	37,431	62	24,485	13,358	56	3,254	1,266
Australia	31,743	4,772	11,390	1,600	1,754	5,519	2,956
Italy	28,383	26	19,598	3,484	1,052	3,727	1,540
Netherlands	26,588	1,016	17,325	5,172	1,622	3,649	1,976
Mexico	24,969	1,436	15,654	3,450	(D)	1,334	493

D Data withheld to avoid disclosure.   [1] Includes other industries not shown separately.   [2] Includes other countries not shown separately.

Source: U.S. Bureau of Economic Analysis, *Survey of Current Business*, November 2007.

Section 16
Science and Technology

This section presents statistics on scientific, engineering, and technological resources, with emphasis on patterns of research and development (R&D) funding and on scientific, engineering, and technical personnel; education; and employment. Also included are statistics on space program outlays. Principal sources of these data are the National Science Foundation (NSF) and the National Aeronautics and Space Administration (NASA).

NSF gathers data chiefly through recurring surveys. Current NSF publications containing data on funds for research and development and on scientific and engineering personnel include detailed statistical tables; info briefs; and annual, biennial, and special reports <http://www.nsf.gov/statistics>. Titles or the areas of coverage of these reports include the following: *Science and Engineering Indicators; National Patterns of R&D Resources; Women, Minorities, and Persons with Disabilities in Science and Engineering, Federal Funds for Research and Development*; Federal R&D Funding by Budget Function; Federal Support to Universities, Colleges, and Selected Nonprofit Institutions; *Research and Development in Industry*; R&D expenditures and graduate enrollment and support in academic science and engineering; and characteristics of doctoral scientists and engineers and of recent graduates in the United States. Statistical surveys in these areas pose problems of concept and definition and the data should therefore be regarded as broad estimates rather than precise, quantitative statements. See sources for methodological and technical details.

The National Science Board's biennial *Science and Engineering Indicators* <http://www.nsf.gov/statistics/indicators/> contains data and analysis of international and domestic science and technology, including measures of inputs and outputs. The *Budget of the United States Government,* published by the U.S. Office of Management and Budget, contains summary financial data on federal R&D programs.

Research and development outlays—NSF defines research as "systematic study directed toward fuller scientific knowledge of the subject studied" and development as "the systematic use of scientific knowledge directed toward the production of useful materials, devices, systems, or methods, including design and development of prototypes and processes."

National coverage of R&D expenditures is developed primarily from periodic surveys in four principal economic sectors: (1) *Government,* made up primarily of federal executive agencies; (2) *industry,* consisting of manufacturing and nonmanufacturing firms and the federally funded research and development centers (FFRDCs) they administer; (3) *universities and colleges,* composed of universities, colleges, and their affiliated institutions, agricultural experiment stations, and associated schools of agriculture and of medicine, and FFRDCs administered by educational institutions; and (4) *other nonprofit institutions,* consisting of such organizations as private philanthropic foundations, nonprofit research institutes, voluntary health agencies, and FFRDCs administered by nonprofit organizations.

The R&D funds reported consist of current operating costs, including planning and administration costs, except as otherwise noted. They exclude funds for routine testing, mapping and surveying, collection of general-purpose data, dissemination of scientific information, and training of scientific personnel.

Scientists, engineers, and technicians—Scientists and engineers are defined as persons engaged in scientific and engineering work at a level requiring a knowledge of sciences equivalent at least to that acquired through completion of a 4-year college course. Technicians are defined as persons engaged in technical work at a level requiring knowledge acquired through a technical institute,

U.S. Census Bureau, Statistical Abstract of the United States: 2009

junior college, or other type of training less extensive than 4-year college

training. Craftsmen and skilled workers are excluded.

Table 769. Research and Development (R&D) Expenditures by Source and Objective: 1970 to 2007

[In millions of dollars (26,272 represents $26,272,000,000), except as indicated. For calendar years]

Year	Total	Sources of funds					Objective (percent of total)			Character of work		
		Federal government	Indus-try	Univer-sities/col-leges	Non-profit	Non-federal govern-ment [1]	Defense related [2]	Space related [3]	Other	Basic research	Applied research	Devel-opment
1970....	26,272	14,984	10,449	259	343	237	33	10	56	3,594	5,752	16,925
1971....	26,952	15,210	10,824	290	366	262	33	10	58	3,720	5,833	17,399
1972....	28,741	16,039	11,715	312	393	282	33	8	59	3,850	6,147	18,743
1973....	30,953	16,587	13,299	343	422	302	32	7	61	4,099	6,655	20,197
1974....	33,359	17,287	14,885	393	474	320	29	7	64	4,511	7,344	21,504
1975....	35,671	18,533	15,824	432	534	348	28	8	65	4,875	8,091	22,706
1976....	39,435	20,292	17,702	480	592	369	27	8	65	5,373	8,976	25,085
1977....	43,338	22,071	19,642	569	662	394	27	7	66	6,008	9,662	27,667
1978....	48,720	24,414	22,457	679	727	443	26	6	68	6,959	10,704	31,056
1979....	55,380	27,225	26,097	785	791	482	25	6	70	7,836	12,097	35,445
1980....	63,225	29,986	30,929	920	871	519	24	5	70	8,745	13,714	40,765
1981....	72,293	33,739	35,948	1,058	967	581	24	5	70	9,658	16,329	46,305
1982....	80,748	37,133	40,692	1,207	1,095	621	26	5	69	10,651	18,218	51,879
1983....	89,950	41,451	45,264	1,357	1,220	658	28	4	68	11,880	20,298	57,771
1984....	102,243	46,470	52,187	1,514	1,351	721	29	3	68	13,332	22,451	66,461
1985....	114,671	52,641	57,962	1,743	1,491	834	30	3	67	14,748	25,401	74,522
1986....	120,248	54,622	60,991	2,019	1,647	969	31	3	66	17,154	27,240	75,855
1987....	126,361	58,609	62,576	2,262	1,849	1,065	32	3	65	18,481	27,951	79,929
1988....	133,880	60,130	67,977	2,527	2,081	1,165	30	4	66	19,786	29,528	84,566
1989....	141,889	60,464	74,966	2,852	2,333	1,274	28	4	69	21,889	32,277	87,723
1990....	151,990	61,607	83,208	3,187	2,589	1,399	25	4	71	23,028	34,896	94,067
1991....	160,872	60,780	92,300	3,457	2,852	1,483	22	5	73	27,139	38,629	95,104
1992....	165,347	60,912	96,229	3,568	3,113	1,525	22	4	74	27,604	37,933	99,810
1993....	165,727	60,524	96,549	3,709	3,388	1,557	21	4	74	28,743	37,280	99,704
1994....	169,202	60,773	99,203	3,938	3,665	1,623	20	5	76	29,651	36,615	102,936
1995....	183,620	62,964	110,870	4,110	3,925	1,751	19	5	77	29,610	40,933	113,077
1996....	197,340	63,389	123,416	4,435	4,239	1,861	18	4	78	32,799	43,165	121,375
1997....	212,144	64,568	136,227	4,837	4,590	1,922	17	4	79	36,917	46,551	128,676
1998....	226,457	66,376	147,845	5,162	5,102	1,972	16	4	80	35,333	46,388	144,735
1999....	245,041	67,046	164,660	5,618	5,619	2,098	15	3	82	38,875	52,097	154,069
2000....	267,562	66,406	186,136	6,231	6,542	2,247	13	2	84	42,767	56,932	167,863
2001....	277,746	72,826	188,440	6,826	7,257	2,397	14	2	84	47,792	64,708	165,245
2002....	276,602	77,699	180,711	7,343	8,292	2,557	15	2	82	51,410	51,035	174,157
2003....	289,039	83,606	186,174	7,649	8,868	2,742	16	2	82	54,839	61,690	172,509
2004....	299,905	88,749	191,377	7,933	8,962	2,884	17	2	81	56,378	70,172	173,354
2005....	323,005	93,734	207,841	8,575	9,905	2,950	17	2	81	60,003	70,355	192,647
2006 [4]....	347,872	97,701	227,276	9,282	10,542	3,071	17	2	81	61,721	76,788	209,362
2007 [4]...	368,097	98,331	245,027	9,866	11,647	3,226	16	2	82	64,417	81,211	222,470

[1] Nonfederal R&D expenditures to university and college performers. [2] R&D spending by the Department of Defense, including space activities, and a portion of the Department of Energy funds. [3] For the National Aeronautics and Space Administration only. [4] Preliminary.

Source: U.S. National Science Foundation, *National Patterns of R&D Resources*, annual. See also <http://www.nsf.gov/statistics/>.

Table 770. Performance Sector of Research and Development (R&D) Expenditures: 2000 to 2007

[In millions of dollars (267,562 represents $267,562,000,000). For calendar year. FFRDCs are federally funded research and development centers]

Year	Total	Federal govern-ment	Industry: Total	Industry: Federal govern-ment	Industry: Industry[1]	Industry: Industry FFRDCs	Univ: Total	Univ: Federal govern-ment	Univ: Non-federal govern-ment[2]	Univ: Industry	Univ: Universities & colleges	Univ: Non-profits	Univ: University & college FFRDCs[3]	Other nonprofit: Total	Other nonprofit: Federal govern-ment	Other nonprofit: Industry	Other nonprofit: Non-profits
RESEARCH AND DEVELOPMENT TOTAL																	
2000	267,562	17,917	199,961	17,117	182,844	2,001	30,693	17,717	2,247	2,174	6,231	2,325	5,742	9,782	4,447	1,118	4,217
2003	289,038	22,752	200,724	17,798	182,926	2,458	40,470	25,116	2,742	2,129	7,649	2,833	7,301	12,839	5,686	1,118	6,035
2004	299,905	22,844	208,301	20,266	188,035	2,485	43,111	27,157	2,884	2,191	7,933	2,946	7,658	12,862	5,695	1,151	6,016
2005	323,005	24,459	226,159	21,909	204,250	2,601	45,191	28,203	2,950	2,338	8,575	3,126	7,812	13,954	5,922	1,253	6,779
2006 [4]	347,871	25,327	247,669	24,304	223,365	2,562	46,987	28,784	3,071	2,536	9,282	3,314	7,866	14,507	5,905	1,374	7,228
2007	368,098	24,744	265,193	24,450	240,743	2,539	48,913	29,468	3,226	2,799	9,866	3,553	8,126	15,346	5,767	1,485	8,094
BASIC RESEARCH																	
2000	42,767	3,765	7,040	925	6,115	547	22,864	13,915	1,549	1,499	4,297	1,603	2,874	5,062	2,099	621	2,341
2003	54,839	4,664	8,330	1,386	6,944	299	30,084	19,600	1,872	1,454	5,223	1,935	3,747	6,686	2,714	621	3,351
2004	56,378	4,697	7,835	1,072	6,763	175	32,105	21,143	1,981	1,506	5,450	2,024	3,729	6,768	2,788	639	3,341
2005	60,003	4,826	8,667	1,108	7,559	136	34,009	22,159	2,057	1,631	5,982	2,180	3,814	7,370	2,910	696	3,764
2006 [4]	61,721	4,952	8,384	1,444	6,940	131	35,413	22,661	2,151	1,777	6,502	2,322	3,907	7,680	2,904	763	4,013
2007	64,417	4,869	8,933	1,453	7,480	130	36,801	23,199	2,257	1,958	6,901	2,485	4,047	8,260	2,941	824	4,494
APPLIED RESEARCH																	
2000	56,932	6,105	39,176	2,682	36,494	269	6,653	3,350	572	553	1,586	592	1,329	3,183	1,831	283	1,069
2003	61,690	7,672	37,334	4,473	32,861	1,434	8,832	4,838	713	554	1,989	737	1,756	4,300	2,487	283	1,529
2004	70,172	7,455	45,432	4,775	40,657	1,509	9,230	5,136	740	562	2,035	756	1,920	4,264	2,448	292	1,525
2005	70,355	7,594	45,284	5,289	39,995	1,487	9,284	5,070	732	580	2,126	775	1,858	4,439	2,403	318	1,718
2006 [4]	76,788	7,692	51,173	6,140	45,033	1,446	9,623	5,153	754	623	2,279	814	1,779	4,635	2,455	348	1,832
2007	81,211	7,839	54,713	6,177	48,537	1,414	10,102	5,310	795	690	2,431	875	1,844	4,844	2,417	376	2,051
DEVELOPMENT																	
2000	167,863	8,047	153,745	13,510	140,235	1,185	1,177	452	126	121	348	130	1,539	1,537	517	214	807
2003	172,509	10,416	155,060	11,939	143,121	725	1,555	678	157	122	437	162	1,798	1,853	485	214	1,155
2004	173,354	10,692	155,034	14,419	140,615	801	1,776	878	163	123	447	166	2,008	1,830	459	220	1,151
2005	192,647	12,039	172,208	15,512	156,696	979	1,899	974	161	127	467	170	2,140	2,145	609	240	1,297
2006 [4]	209,362	12,682	188,112	16,720	171,392	985	1,951	970	166	137	500	179	2,180	2,192	546	263	1,383
2007	222,470	12,037	201,547	16,820	184,726	995	2,010	958	175	151	534	192	2,236	2,242	409	284	1,549

[1] Includes all nonfederal sources of industry R&D expenditures. [2] Includes all nonfederal sources. [3] Includes all R&D expenditures of FFRDCs administered by academic institutions and funded by the federal government. [4] Preliminary.

Source: National Science Foundation. Data derived from: *Research and Development in Industry,* annual; *Academic Research and Development Expenditures,* annual; and *Federal Funds For Research and Development,* annual. See also <http://www.nsf.gov/statistics/>.

Table 771. National Research and Development (R&D) Expenditures as a Percent of Gross Domestic Product by Country: 1990 to 2006

Year	Total R&D						Nondefense R&D [1]		
	United States	Japan [2]	Unified Germany [3]	France	United Kingdom	Italy	Canada	Russia	Total OECD [4]
1990	2.62	2.81	2.61	2.33	2.15	1.25	1.51	2.03	2.26
1995	2.48	2.71	2.19	2.29	1.95	0.97	1.70	0.85	2.07
2000	2.73	3.05	2.45	2.15	1.86	1.05	1.92	1.05	2.23
2002	2.64	3.18	2.49	2.23	1.83	1.13	2.04	1.25	2.24
2003	2.63	3.20	2.52	2.17	1.79	1.11	2.01	1.28	2.25
2004	2.56	3.18	2.50	2.14	1.73	1.10	2.01	1.16	2.25
2005	2.59	(NA)	2.51	2.13	(NA)	(NA)	1.98	1.07	(NA)
2006	2.60	(NA)	(NA)	(NA)	(NA)	(NA)	1.95	(NA)	(NA)

NA Not available. [1] Estimated. [2] Data on Japanese research and development in 2000 and later years may not be consistent with data in earlier years because of changes in methodology. [3] Data for 1990 are for West Germany only. [4] Organization for Economic Cooperation and Development.

Source: National Science Foundation, *National Patterns of R&D Resources,* annual; and Organization for Economic Cooperation and Development.

Table 772. Federal Obligations for Research in Current and Constant (2000) Dollars by Field of Science: 1980 to 2007

[In millions of dollars (11,597 represents $11,597,000,000). For fiscal years ending in year shown; see text, Section 8. Excludes R&D plant]

Field of science	1980	1990	2000	2002	2003	2004	2005	2006, prel.	2007, prel.
CURRENT DOLLARS									
Research, total	**11,597**	**21,622**	**38,471**	**48,007**	**51,072**	**54,450**	**53,738**	**54,964**	**55,089**
Basic	4,674	11,286	19,570	23,668	24,751	26,121	27,140	27,680	28,264
Applied	6,923	10,337	18,901	24,338	26,320	27,237	26,598	27,284	26,825
Life sciences	4,192	8,830	17,965	25,477	27,772	27,729	28,543	28,207	27,811
Psychology	199	449	1,627	906	1,104	1,855	1,916	1,934	1,912
Physical sciences	2,001	3,809	4,788	4,983	5,022	5,211	5,473	5,394	5,648
Environmental sciences	1,261	2,174	3,329	3,418	3,741	3,742	3,876	3,754	3,636
Mathematics and computer sciences . . .	241	841	2,206	2,631	2,672	2,949	3,115	3,081	3,182
Engineering	2,830	4,227	6,346	8,275	8,405	8,866	9,481	9,397	9,487
Social sciences	524	630	1,050	983	1,026	1,090	1,132	1,178	1,215
Other sciences, n.e.c. [1]	350	664	1,160	1,334	1,329	1,916	2,010	2,034	2,199
CONSTANT (2000) DOLLARS [2]									
Research, total	**21,848**	**26,622**	**38,471**	**46,272**	**48,236**	**50,179**	**48,032**	**47,658**	**46,080**
Basic	8,806	13,896	19,570	22,686	23,271	24,072	24,258	24,001	23,642
Applied	13,043	12,727	18,901	23,328	24,747	25,101	23,774	23,657	22,438
Life sciences	7,898	10,872	17,965	24,419	26,112	25,458	25,510	24,584	23,263
Psychology	375	553	1,627	868	1,038	1,703	1,712	1,686	1,599
Physical sciences	3,770	4,690	4,788	4,776	4,721	4,784	4,892	4,701	4,724
Environmental sciences	2,376	2,677	3,329	3,276	3,517	3,435	3,464	3,272	3,041
Mathematics and computer sciences . . .	454	1,035	2,206	2,521	2,513	2,708	2,784	2,685	2,662
Engineering	5,332	5,204	6,346	7,931	7,903	8,140	8,473	8,190	7,936
Social sciences	987	776	1,050	942	964	1,000	1,011	1,026	1,016
Other sciences, n.e.c. [1]	659	818	1,160	1,279	1,250	1,759	1,797	1,773	1,839

[1] Not elsewhere classified. [2] Based on gross domestic product implicit price deflator.

Source: U.S. National Science Foundation, *Federal Funds for Research and Development,* annual. See also <http://www.nsf.gov/statistics/>.

Table 773. Federal Budget Authority for Research and Development (R&D) in Current and Constant (2000) Dollars by Selected Budget Functions: 2005 to 2008

[In millions of dollars (126,601 represents $126,601,000,000). For year ending September 30. Excludes R&D plant. Represents budget authority. Functions shown are those for which $1 billion or more was authorized since 2001]

Function	Current dollars				Constant (2000) dollars [1]			
	2005	2006	2007, prel.	2008, prel.	2005	2006	2007, prel.	2008, prel.
Total [2]	**126,601**	**131,624**	**137,026**	**138,332**	**112,335**	**113,050**	**114,618**	**113,517**
National defense	74,047	78,037	81,667	82,383	65,703	67,025	68,312	67,605
Health	28,824	28,797	29,481	29,242	25,576	24,733	24,660	23,996
Space research and technology	7,300	8,204	8,933	9,506	6,477	7,046	7,472	7,801
Energy	1,296	1,195	1,581	1,468	1,150	1,026	1,322	1,205
General science	6,570	6,691	7,185	7,752	5,830	5,747	6,010	6,361
Natural resources and environment . . .	2,168	2,120	1,932	1,944	1,924	1,821	1,616	1,595
Transportation	1,847	1,711	1,490	1,368	1,639	1,470	1,246	1,123
Agriculture	1,820	1,869	1,824	1,629	1,615	1,605	1,526	1,337

[1] Based on gross domestic product implicit price deflator. [2] Includes other functions, not shown separately.

Source: U.S. National Science Foundation, *Federal R&D Funding by Budget Function,* annual. See also <http://www.nsf.gov/statistics/fedfunds/>.

Table 774. Research and Development (R&D) Funds in R&D-Performing Manufacturing and Nonmanufacturing Companies by Industry: 2004 to 2006

Industry	NAICS [1] code	Total R&D funds as a percent of net sales			Company R&D funds as a percent of net sales		
		2004	2005	2006	2004	2005	2006
All industries, total	(X)	**3.7**	**3.7**	**3.7**	**3.4**	**3.3**	**3.4**
All manufacturing industries, total	(X)	**3.8**	**4.0**	**4.0**	**3.4**	**3.6**	**3.6**
Food	311	0.6	0.7	0.7	0.6	0.7	0.7
Paper, printing, and support activities	322, 326	(D)	(D)	(D)	1.5	1.5	1.2
Petroleum and coal products	324	0.4	(D)	0.3	0.4	0.4	0.3
Chemicals	325	(D)	6.9	7.6	6.6	6.9	7.5
Plastic and rubber products	326	(D)	2.0	2.0	1.6	1.9	1.9
Nonmetallic mineral products	327	1.8	1.8	2.1	1.8	1.8	1.9
Primary metals	331	0.7	0.6	0.5	0.7	0.5	0.5
Fabricated metal products	332	1.5	0.8	1.4	1.4	0.8	1.4
Machinery	333	3.7	3.7	3.6	3.6	3.6	3.6
Navigational, measuring, electromedical, and control instruments	3345	13.8	12.8	13.1	7.1	7.0	7.5
Electrical equipment, appliances, and components	335	2.8	2.4	2.6	2.7	2.3	2.5
Motor vehicles, trailers, and parts	3361–3363	2.4	(D)	(D)	2.4	2.5	2.4
Aerospace products and parts	3364	5.7	6.6	6.7	4.0	4.8	4.9
All nonmanufacturing industries, total	(X)	**3.5**	**3.2**	**3.2**	**3.2**	**2.9**	**2.9**
Transportation and warehousing services	48, 49	(D)	(D)	(D)	0.5	0.4	0.3
Software publishing	5112	(D)	21.9	(D)	23.3	21.9	19.9
Architectural, engineering, and related services	5413	12.2	9.4	14.4	6.6	4.9	10.7
Computer systems design and related services	5415	12.1	10.0	5.3	11.7	9.6	4.9
Scientific R&D services	5417	35.8	35.6	35.1	29.6	27.4	24.2

D Figure withheld to avoid disclosure of information pertaining to a specific organization or individual.   NA Not applicable.
X Not applicable.   [1] North American Industry Classification System 1997 (NAICS); see text, Section 15.

Source: U.S. National Science Foundation, *Research and Development in Industry,* annual. See also <http://www.nsf.gov /statistics/pubseri.cfm?TopID=2&SubID=5&SeriID=26>.

Table 775. Funds for Performance of Industrial Research and Development (R&D) by Source of Funds and Selected Industries: 2003 to 2006

[In millions of dollars (200,724 represents $200,724,000,000). For calendar years. Covers basic research, applied research, and development. Based on the Survey of Industry Research and Development]

Industry	NAICS [1] code	2003	2004	2005	2006
CURRENT DOLLARS					
Total funds [2]	(X)	**200,724**	**208,301**	**226,159**	**247,669**
Company and other funds	(X)	**182,926**	**188,035**	**204,250**	**223,365**
Federal funds	(X)	**17,798**	**20,266**	**21,909**	**24,304**
Petroleum and coal products	324	(D)	1,603	(D)	1,432
Chemicals and allied products	325	23,001	(D)	42,995	46,329
Pharmaceuticals and medicines	3254	(D)	31,477	34,839	38,901
Machinery	333	6,304	6,579	8,531	9,848
Computer and electronic products	334	39,001	48,296	(D)	56,773
Navigational, measuring, electromedical, and control instruments	3345	14,014	15,214	15,204	18,300
Electrical equipment, appliances, and components	335	2,073	2,664	2,424	2,281
Motor vehicles, trailers, and parts	3361–3363	(D)	15,677	(D)	(D)
Aerospace products and parts	3364	13,205	13,086	15,055	16,367
Information	51	(D)	22,593	23,836	26,883
Professional, scientific, and technical services	54	27,967	28,709	32,021	38,049
Computer systems design and related services	5415	9,032	11,575	13,592	14,841
Scientific R&D services	5417	12,460	11,355	12,299	14,525
CONSTANT (2000) DOLLARS [3]					
Total funds [2]	(X)	**188,650**	**190,351**	**200,602**	**213,342**
Company and other funds	(X)	**171,923**	**171,831**	**181,169**	**192,407**
Federal funds	(X)	**19,454**	**18,520**	**19,433**	**20,935**
Petroleum and coal products	324	(D)	1,465	(D)	1,234
Chemicals	325	21,617	(D)	38,136	39,908
Pharmaceuticals and medicines	3254	(D)	28,765	30,902	33,509
Machinery	333	5,925	6,012	7,567	8,483
Computer and electronic products	334	36,655	44,134	(D)	48,904
Navigational, measuring, electromedical, and control instruments	3345	13,171	13,903	13,486	15,764
Electrical equipment, appliances, and components	335	1,948	2,434	2,150	1,965
Motor vehicles, trailers, and parts	3361–3363	(D)	14,326	(D)	(D)
Aerospace products and parts	3364	12,411	11,958	13,354	14,099
Information	51	(D)	20,646	21,142	23,157
Professional, scientific, and technical services	54	26,285	26,235	28,403	32,775
Computer systems design and related services	5415	8,489	10,578	12,056	12,784
Scientific R&D services	5417	11,711	10,376	10,909	12,512

D Figure withheld to avoid disclosure of information pertaining to a specific organization or individual.   X Not applicable.
[1] North American Industry Classification System, 1997; see text, Section 15.   [2] Includes other industries not shown separately.
[3] Based on gross domestic product implicit price deflator.

Source: U.S. National Science Foundation, *Research and Development in Industry,* annual. See also <http://www.nsf.gov /statistics/pubseri.cfm?TopID=2&SubID=5&SeriID=26>.

Science and Technology   513

[44,945,923 represents $44,945,923,000. For definition of research and development (R&D), see text this section]

State	Academic R&D ($1,000)	Academic R&D per $1,000 of GDP	Industry-performed R&D (mil. dol)	Industry-performed R&D per private-industry output (percent)[1]	State	Academic R&D ($1,000)	Academic R&D per $1,000 of GDP	Industry-performed R&D (mil. dol)	Industry-performed R&D per private-industry output (percent)[1]
U.S. ...	44,945,923	3.63	222,427	2.04	MT	170,791	5.71	[3]77	[3]0.31
AL	589,860	3.90	1,417	1.10	NE	360,148	4.99	407	0.65
AK	153,721	3.90	32	[2]0.10	NV	178,492	1.62	382	0.39
AZ	720,184	3.39	[2]2,980	1.60	NH	287,472	5.31	1,435	2.92
AR	209,518	2.41	[3]271	[3]0.36	NJ	867,121	2.03	13,214	3.45
CA	6,272,890	3.88	50,683	3.53	NM	345,844	4.96	405	0.71
CO	825,984	3.85	4,299	2.28	NY	3,604,414	3.75	9,474	1.10
CT	669,199	3.46	7,885	4.47	NC	1,652,049	4.71	5,158	1.69
DE	115,751	2.04	1,511	2.90	ND	149,994	6.02	104	0.49
DC	302,921	3.67	166	0.30	OH	1,530,915	3.46	5,900	1.50
FL	1,448,634	2.17	4,164	0.71	OK	291,697	2.40	422	0.41
GA	1,274,410	3.56	2,282	0.73	OR	536,228	3.78	3,252	2.66
HI	240,247	4.39	168	0.40	PA	2,353,640	4.84	8,846	2.02
ID	119,871	2.61	642	1.62	RI	199,709	4.58	[3]1,387	[3]3.63
IL	1,770,938	3.19	9,712	1.94	SC	486,399	3.47	1,402	1.19
IN	759,419	3.21	[3]4,610	[3]2.17	SD	67,012	2.19	68	0.26
IA	548,237	4.66	1,039	1.00	TN	726,078	3.23	1,246	0.62
KS	348,751	3.31	[3]1,993	[3]2.23	TX	3,073,724	3.11	12,438	1.41
KY	452,265	3.26	660	0.56	UT	400,276	4.53	1,234	1.63
LA	579,734	3.21	300	0.19	VT	117,442	5.09	360	1.80
ME	81,624	1.82	350	0.91	VA	914,166	2.61	4,379	1.51
MD	[4]1,678,649	[4]6.87	3,706	1.82	WA	901,102	3.32	9,736	4.17
MA	2,079,463	6.50	13,342	4.57	WV	145,150	2.73	242	0.55
MI	1,455,849	3.91	16,752	5.04	WI	998,449	4.60	2,729	1.42
MN	559,585	2.42	6,340	3.06	WY	83,449	3.06	30	0.13
MS	353,445	4.43	194	0.29					
MO	893,013	4.15	2,602	1.37					

[1] Gross Domestic Product (GDP) by state for private industries.   [2]More than 50 percent of industrial R&D value imputed because of raking of state data for Alaska.   [3]More than 50 percent of industrial R&D value imputed.   [4] For Maryland, academic R&D excludes R&D performed by Applied Physics Laboratory (APL) at Johns Hopkins University. APL employs more than 3,000 people and supports government agencies rather than focusing on academic research.

Source: National Science Foundation, Division of Science Resources Statistics, *Science and Engineering Indicators, 2008* (biennial) January 2008. For more information, see <http://www.nsf.gov/statistics/seind08/start.htm>.

Table 777. **Research and Development (R&D) Expenditures in Science and Engineering at Universities and Colleges in Current and Constant (2000) Dollars: 1990 to 2006**

[In millions of dollars (16,286 represents $16,286,000,000)]

Characteristic	Current dollars				Constant (2000) dollars[1]			
	1990	2000	2005	2006	1990	2000	2005	2006
Total ...	16,286	30,073	45,777	47,760	20,044	30,073	40,618	41,020
Basic research[2]	10,643	22,456	34,348	36,044	13,099	22,456	30,477	30,958
Applied R&D[2]	5,643	7,617	11,429	11,717	6,945	7,617	10,141	10,064
Source of funds:								
Federal government	9,638	17,538	29,191	30,033	11,862	17,538	25,902	25,795
State and local government	1,324	2,200	2,942	3,016	1,630	2,200	2,610	2,590
Institutions' own funds	3,006	5,924	8,258	9,062	3,700	5,924	7,327	7,783
Industry	1,127	2,156	2,294	2,428	1,387	2,156	2,035	2,085
Other	1,191	2,254	3,093	3,221	1,466	2,254	2,744	2,766
Fields:								
Physical sciences	1,807	2,712	3,704	3,823	2,224	2,712	3,287	3,284
Environmental sciences	1,069	1,765	2,551	2,602	1,316	1,765	2,264	2,235
Mathematical sciences	222	342	495	530	273	342	439	455
Computer sciences	515	876	1,406	1,438	634	876	1,248	1,235
Life sciences	8,726	17,471	27,604	28,831	10,740	17,471	24,493	24,763
Psychology	253	517	826	875	311	517	733	752
Social sciences	703	1,299	1,685	1,703	865	1,299	1,495	1,463
Other sciences	336	535	769	882	414	535	682	758
Engineering	2,656	4,555	6,738	7,076	3,269	4,555	5,979	6,077

[1] Based on gross domestic product implicit price deflator.   [2] Basic research and applied R&D statistics were reestimated for FY 2001 and forward. These data are not directly comparable to those from earlier years.

Source: U.S. National Science Foundation, *Survey of Research and Development Expenditures at Universities and Colleges,* annual. See also <http://www.nsf.gov/statistics/showsrvy.cfm?srvyCatID=4&srvySeri=12>.

Table 778. Federal Research and Development (R&D) Obligations to Selected Universities and Colleges: 2004 and 2005

[In millions of dollars (23,811.0 represents $23,811,000,000). For years ending September 30. For the top 40 institutions receiving federal R&D funds in 2005. Awards to the administrative offices of university systems are excluded from totals for individual institutions because that allocation of funds is unknown, but those awards are included in "total all institutions"]

Major institution ranked by total 2005 federal R&D obligations	2004	2005	Major institution ranked by total 2005 federal R&D obligations	2004	2005
Total, all institutions [1]	**23,811.0**	**25,010.7**	University Southern California	288.3	314.8
Johns Hopkins University	1,034.9	1,045.4	Case Western Reserve University	241.5	287.7
University of Washington	589.6	601.1	Vanderbilt University	259.5	279.2
University of Pennsylvania	494.2	519.6	Pennsylvania State University	316.2	270.2
University of California—Los Angeles	470.3	494.0	Baylor College of Medicine	252.6	250.9
University of Michigan	477.3	472.7	University of Rochester	236.3	248.5
Stanford University	472.3	460.9	University of California—Berkeley	246.9	245.5
University of California—San Francisco	395.5	447.2	The Scripps Research Institute	229.1	241.2
Duke University	392.6	432.0	University of Alabama—Birmingham	211.6	232.9
Columbia University—City of NY	369.5	411.0	University of Chicago	209.5	227.1
Harvard University	379.1	405.5	Emory University	214.0	223.5
University of Pittsburgh	371.9	405.4	Ohio State University	202.9	219.1
Washington University	386.4	403.2	University of California—Davis	205.1	217.3
University of California—San Diego	420.3	401.4	Northwestern University	208.5	216.0
University of Wisconsin—Madison	364.0	374.7	University of Arizona	206.9	201.4
Yale University	343.0	356.3	Boston University	208.7	200.4
Massachusetts Institute of Technology	340.2	342.8	University of Florida	179.0	197.0
University of Colorado	336.7	336.2	University of Illinois—Urbana Champaign	198.2	188.3
University of Minnesota	328.7	329.0	University of Virginia	188.8	185.6
Cornell University	328.6	323.3	University of Iowa	178.1	182.2
University of North Carolina at Chapel Hill	305.7	323.0			

[1] Includes other institutions, not shown separately.

Source: U.S. National Science Foundation, *Federal S&E Support to Universities and Colleges and Nonprofit Institutions*, annual.

Table 779. Graduate Science/Engineering Students in Doctorate-Granting Colleges by Characteristic and Field: 1990 to 2006

[In thousands (409.4 represents 409,400). As of fall. Includes outlying areas]

Field of science or engineering	Total			Female			Foreign		Part-time		
	1990	2000	2006	1990	2000	2006	2000	2006	1990	2000	2006
Total, all surveyed fields	**409.4**	**443.5**	**542.1**	**155.5**	**201.8**	**263.6**	**123.3**	**144.5**	**130.8**	**123.6**	**148.9**
Science/engineering	360.6	374.8	445.0	117.9	150.3	188.9	118.0	136.6	107.5	99.3	113.7
Engineering, total	101.0	98.8	116.6	13.8	19.7	26.3	46.3	52.9	36.7	28.2	31.5
Sciences, total	259.6	275.9	328.4	104.2	130.7	162.6	71.7	83.7	70.8	71.1	82.2
Physical sciences	32.9	29.6	35.9	7.7	8.8	11.6	11.5	14.5	3.9	3.5	3.6
Environmental	13.1	13.0	14.0	3.8	5.3	6.5	2.6	2.7	3.2	2.8	2.9
Mathematical sciences	18.1	14.4	19.0	5.6	5.2	6.8	5.9	7.4	4.7	3.0	4.0
Computer sciences	29.2	40.3	43.0	6.8	11.7	10.8	19.7	19.1	14.1	16.7	16.1
Agricultural sciences	11.0	11.3	12.1	3.2	4.8	5.8	2.4	2.6	2.0	2.4	3.2
Biological sciences	46.7	53.1	65.9	21.4	27.8	36.9	11.6	16.6	7.2	7.6	8.8
Psychology	38.5	40.3	47.2	25.5	29.0	35.5	2.1	2.6	12.0	10.8	14.3
Social sciences	70.0	73.9	91.2	30.1	38.1	48.6	15.8	18.1	23.8	24.3	29.3
Health fields, total	48.8	68.8	97.0	37.6	51.5	74.7	5.4	7.9	23.3	24.3	35.3

Source: U.S. National Science Foundation, *Survey of Graduate Science Engineering Students and Postdoctorates*, annual. See also <http://www.nsf.gov/statistics/gradpostdoc/>.

Table 780. Non-U.S. Citizens Awarded Doctorates in Science and Engineering by Visa Type and Country of Citizenship: 1997 to 2006

[For description of science and engineering fields, see Table 785]

Visa and country/economy	1997	1998	1999	2000	2001	2002	2003	2004	2005	2006
All non-U.S. citizens	**9,788**	**9,736**	**8,894**	**9,070**	**9,217**	**8,867**	**9,483**	**10,158**	**11,519**	**12,775**
Canada	263	286	289	294	306	316	324	380	368	363
Mexico	148	176	172	208	206	182	218	181	206	183
Brazil	151	164	164	131	142	126	108	136	156	139
United Kingdom	92	124	142	100	138	134	109	109	108	100
Germany	181	210	183	229	220	197	192	185	182	176
China	2,395	2,503	2,234	2,379	2,407	2,402	2,503	2,878	3,482	4,280
Japan	155	155	158	201	149	157	201	186	211	222
Korea	901	822	760	754	865	856	958	1,057	1,179	1,219
Taiwan	1,093	910	746	676	539	469	440	394	444	431
Thailand	97	122	134	153	237	264	314	272	252	199
India	1,281	1,134	915	834	818	681	773	864	1,110	1,524
Iran	113	93	92	80	100	59	68	60	136	148
Turkey	170	172	192	275	307	345	374	344	342	357
Science	6,440	6,678	6,299	6,269	6,129	5,945	6,305	6,605	7,481	8,203
Engineering	3,148	3,058	2,595	2,801	3,088	2,922	3,178	3,553	4,038	4,572
Permanent visa	2,281	1,991	1,654	1,409	1,271	1,173	1,099	1,003	1,113	1,253
Temporary visa	7,507	7,745	7,240	7,661	7,946	7,694	8,384	9,155	10,406	11,522

Source: U.S. National Science Foundation, *Science and Engineering Doctorate Awards*, annual. See also <http://www.nsf.gov/statistics/nsf07305/> (released December 2007).

Science and Technology **515**

Table 781. Science and Engineering (S&E) Degrees Awarded, by Degree Level and Sex of Recipient: 1980 to 2006

[For a description of science and engineering degree categories, see Appendix B of source <http://www.nsf.gov/statistics/nsf07307/content.cfm?pubid=3634&id=4>]

Academic year ending	Bachelor's degree				Master's degree				Doctoral degree			
	Total S&E	Men	Women	Percent women	Total S&E	Men	Women	Percent women	Total S&E	Men	Women	Percent women
1980	304,695	191,215	113,480	37.2	64,089	46,004	18,085	28.2	17,775	13,814	3,961	22.3
1990	329,094	189,082	140,012	42.5	77,788	51,230	26,558	34.1	22,867	16,498	6,369	27.9
2000	398,622	197,669	200,953	50.4	95,683	54,213	41,470	43.3	25,912	16,519	9,393	36.2
2004	455,848	225,909	229,939	50.4	118,470	66,798	51,672	43.6	26,274	16,418	9,856	37.4
2005	466,003	230,806	235,197	50.5	120,025	66,974	53,051	44.2	27,946	17,407	10,539	37.7
2006	473,533	234,260	239,273	50.5	120,337	66,262	54,075	44.9	29,810	18,341	11,469	38.5

Source: U.S. National Science Foundation, *Science and Engineering Degrees: 1966–2006*, January, 2008. See also <http://www.nsf.gov/statistics/degrees/>.

Table 782. Doctorates Conferred by Characteristics of Recipients: 2000 and 2006

[**In percent, except as indicated**. Based on the Survey of Earned Doctorate Awards; for description of methodology, see source]

Characteristic	2000, total	2006									
		All fields [1]	Engineer-ing	Physical sci-ences [2]	Earth sci-ences	Mathe-matics	Computer sci-ences	Biological sci-ences [3]	Agricul-tural	Social sci-ences [4]	Psychol-ogy
Total conferred (number).	**41,365**	**45,596**	**7,191**	**3,925**	**757**	**1,327**	**1,452**	**6,631**	**1,033**	**4,275**	**3,623**
Male.	56.0	55.0	79.8	72.2	64.7	70.4	78.7	50.8	60.2	54.3	28.7
Female.	43.8	45.0	20.2	27.8	35.3	29.6	21.3	49.2	39.8	45.7	71.3
CITIZENSHIP [5]											
Total conferred (number).	**39,596**	**42,864**	**6,757**	**3,717**	**713**	**1,283**	**1,374**	**6,313**	**974**	**4,062**	**3,041**
U.S. citizen	70.7	62.8	32.3	49.4	62.4	42.8	35.2	66.0	56.1	62.2	89.5
Foreign citizen	29.3	37.2	67.7	50.6	37.6	57.2	64.8	34.0	43.9	37.8	10.5
RACE/ETHNICITY [6]											
Total conferred (number).	**29,936**	**28,746**	**2,485**	**1,993**	**473**	**615**	**579**	**4,467**	**577**	**2,725**	**2,798**
White [7].	79.2	76.4	69.3	81.3	85.8	77.2	70.3	76.1	83.0	74.9	75.7
Black [7].	5.8	6.2	4.1	2.4	1.1	3.3	2.6	3.3	4.2	7.4	6.3
Asian/Pacific [7]. . . .	7.6	8.3	17.6	9.2	5.1	11.4	21.8	12.1	5.0	6.8	6.1
Indian/Alaskan [7]. . . .	0.6	0.4	(D)	(D)	(D)	(D)	(D)	0.1	D	0.5	0.5
Hispanic.	4.4	5.3	4.5	4.0	4.4	4.1	1.2	5.0	4.7	6.1	7.5
Other/unknown [8] . . .	2.4	3.5	(D)	(D)	(D)	(D)	(D)	(D)	(D)	4.3	3.8

[1] Includes other fields, not shown separately. [2] Astronomy, physics, and chemistry. [3] Biochemistry, botany, microbiology, physiology, zoology, and related fields. [4] Anthropology, sociology, political science, economics, international relations and related fields. [5] For those with known citizenship. Includes those with temporary visas. [6] Excludes those with temporary visas. [7] Non-Hispanic. [8] 2006 data includes Native Hawaiians and Other Pacific Islanders, respondents choosing multiple races (excluding those selecting an Hispanic ethnicity), and respondents with unknown race/ethnicity.

Source: U.S. National Science Foundation, *Science and Engineering Doctorate Awards,* annual. See also <http://www.nsf.gov/statistics/nsf07305/> (released December 2007).

Table 783. Science and Engineering (S&E) Doctorates by State: 2005 and 2006

[**Per 1,000 population**. Data on U.S. S&E doctorate holders classified by employer location. Population of doctorate holders consisted of all individuals under 76 years of age who received a research doctorate in S&E from a U.S. institution and were residing in the United States. Excludes medical doctorates]

State	S&E doctorates conferred 2005	Doctorate holders 2006 [1]	Doctorate holders per capita 2006 [1]	State	S&E doctorates conferred 2005	Doctorate holders 2006 [1]	Doctorate holders per capita 2006 [1]	State	S&E doctorates conferred 2005	Doctorate holders 2006 [1]	Doctorate holders per capita 2006 [1]
U.S. . .	**27,930**	**708,080**	**2.4**	KS	246	4,830	1.8	ND [2] . . .	45	1,550	2.4
				KY	242	5,760	1.4	OH	1,041	23,630	2.1
AL [2]	338	7,090	1.5	LA [2]	338	6,290	1.5	OK	232	5,290	1.5
AK [2]	25	1,330	2.0	ME [2]	24	2,930	2.2	OR	260	10,900	3.0
AZ	473	10,050	1.6	MD	744	29,870	5.3	PA	1,397	32,780	2.6
AR	116	3,250	1.2	MA	1,632	35,440	5.5	RI	175	3,290	3.1
CA	3,600	99,110	2.7	MI	1,075	19,790	2.0	SC	227	6,920	1.6
CO	522	16,080	3.4	MN	504	13,220	2.6	SD [2]	38	1,220	1.5
CT	428	11,830	3.4	MS	168	3,910	1.3	TN	377	11,380	1.9
DE	128	3,880	4.6	MO	489	10,340	1.8	TX	1,781	41,420	1.8
DC	307	13,750	23.5	MT	59	2,480	2.6	UT [2]	290	6,730	2.6
FL	977	22,020	1.2	NE	166	3,320	1.9	VT [2]	37	2,070	3.3
GA	742	14,890	1.6	NV	90	2,940	1.2	VA	695	22,800	3.0
HI	99	3,230	2.5	NH	117	2,760	2.1	WA [2]	495	19,900	3.1
ID	56	3,190	2.2	NJ	628	23,610	2.7	WV [2]	108	2,510	1.4
IL	1,332	26,800	2.1	NM	176	9,960	5.1	WI	532	11,200	2.0
IN	686	11,380	1.8	NY	2,419	50,760	2.6	WY [2]	36	990	1.9
IA	355	5,740	1.9	NC	863	21,670	2.4				

[1] Data for 2006 S&E doctorate holders are preliminary. [2] Estimates for S&E doctorate holders may vary between 10 percent and 25 percent because geography is not part of sample design.

Source: National Science Foundation, *Science and Engineering Indicators, 2008*, (biennial), published January 2008. See <http://nsf.gov/statistics/seind08/>.

Table 784. Scientists and Engineers by Selected Demographic Characteristics: 2006

[In thousands (22,630 represents 22,630,000). Scientists and engineers refer to all persons who have received a bachelor's degree or higher in science and engineering (S&E), or S&E related field, plus persons holding a non–S&E degree or higher, employed in S&E or S&E related field]

Characteristic	Both sexes	Female	Male	Characteristic	Both sexes	Female	Male
All scientists and engineers. .	**22,630**	**10,230**	**12,400**	Highest degree attained			
Age:				Bachelor's	13,228	6,223	7,005
Under 30 years	2,732	1,542	1,190	Master's	6,411	3,039	3,373
30–39 years	5,302	2,596	2,705	Doctorate	1,018	308	710
40–49 years	5,849	2,699	3,150	Professional	1,973	660	1,312
50–59 years	5,400	2,303	3,097				
60–69 years	2,497	835	1,662	Citizenship status			
70 years or older	851	254	596	U.S. citizen, native	19,131	8,743	10,387
				U.S. citizen, naturalized.	2,373	1,062	1,311
Race/ethnicity:				Non–U.S. citizen, permanent			
American Indian/Alaska Native . .	102	51	50	resident	835	330	505
Asian.	2,255	994	1,261	Non–U.S. citizen, temporary			
Black	1,258	738	520	resident	291	95	196
Native Hawaiian/Other Pacific							
Islander	85	33	53	Marital status			
White.	17,420	7,670	9,751	Married	16,100	6,655	9,445
Multiple race.	316	156	159	Living in marriage–like			
Hispanic, any race	1,193	588	605	relationship	892	482	410
				Widowed	356	245	111
Children in the home?				Separated	243	131	111
Yes	10,966	5,015	5,951	Divorced.	1,518	887	631
No	11,664	5,215	6,449	Never married	3,521	1,829	1,692

Source: National Science Foundation/Division of Science Resource Statistics, Scientists and Engineers Statistical Data System (SESTAT) March 2008; see <http://www.nsf.gov/statistics/sestat/>.

Table 785. Doctorates Awarded by Field of Study and Year of Doctorate: 2000 to 2006

Field of study	2000	2001	2002	2003	2004	2005	2006
Total, all fields	**41,365**	**40,737**	**40,025**	**40,757**	**42,123**	**43,385**	**45,596**
Science and engineering, total.	25,966	25,528	24,608	25,281	26,275	27,989	29,854
Engineering, total	5,323	5,511	5,079	5,280	5,777	6,425	7,191
Aeronautical/astronautical	214	203	209	200	201	219	238
Chemical	726	730	705	649	726	875	893
Civil	556	595	627	673	673	758	803
Electrical	1,543	1,579	1,394	1,465	1,651	1,851	2,133
Industrial/manufacturing	176	206	230	214	217	221	235
Materials/metallurgical	451	497	396	474	511	540	624
Mechanical.	864	953	827	814	852	978	1,148
Other	793	748	691	791	946	983	1,117
Science, total.	20,643	20,017	19,529	20,001	20,498	21,564	22,663
Biological/agricultural sciences	6,890	6,672	6,703	6,755	6,985	7,406	7,664
Agricultural sciences	1,037	975	1,009	1,060	1,045	1,038	1,033
Biological sciences	5,853	5,697	5,694	5,695	5,940	6,368	6,631
Earth, atmospheric, and ocean							
sciences.	694	660	689	683	686	714	757
Atmospheric	143	116	117	139	126	145	147
Earth	387	393	426	374	420	420	469
Ocean sciences	164	151	146	170	140	149	141
Mathematical/computer sciences, total. . . .	1,910	1,840	1,730	1,859	2,024	2,335	2,779
Computer sciences.	860	830	810	866	948	1,130	1,452
Mathematics	1,050	1,010	920	993	1,076	1,205	1,327
Physical sciences, total.	3,378	3,364	3,186	3,289	3,338	3,645	3,925
Astronomy	185	186	141	167	165	186	197
Chemistry	1,989	1,981	1,922	2,041	1,987	2,126	2,363
Physics	1,204	1,197	1,123	1,081	1,186	1,333	1,365
Psychology.	3,616	3,399	3,207	3,276	3,327	3,323	3,263
Social sciences, total	4,155	4,082	4,014	4,139	4,138	4,141	4,275
Economics	1,086	1,081	1,027	1,050	1,069	1,183	1,142
Political science	986	984	939	1,025	946	990	998
Sociology	637	579	567	612	599	556	602
Other social sciences	1,446	1,438	1,481	1,452	1,524	1,412	1,533
Nonscience and engineering, total	15,399	15,209	15,417	15,476	15,848	15,396	15,742
Education	6,436	6,349	6,503	6,643	6,635	6,226	6,123
Health.	1,591	1,541	1,654	1,633	1,720	1,785	1,906
Humanities	5,213	5,178	5,051	5,020	5,013	4,949	5,122
Professional/other/unknown	2,159	2,141	2,209	2,180	2,480	2,436	2,591

Source: U.S. National Science Foundation, *Science and Engineering Doctorate Awards*, annual. See also <http://www.nsf.gov/statistics/nsf07305/> (released December 2007).

Table 786. Civilian Employment of Scientists, Engineers, and Related Occupations by Occupation and Industry: 2006

[In thousands (263.7 represents 263,700). Based on sample and subject to sampling error. For details, see source]

Occupation	Total employment, all workers[1]	Wage and salary workers						Self employ-ed[3]
		Mining (NAICS 21)[2]	Con-struc-tion (NAICS 23)	Manu-factur-ing (NAICS 31–33)	Infor-mation (NAICS 51)	Profes-sional, scientific and tech-nical services (NAICS 54)	Govern-ment (NAICS 99)	
Computer and information systems managers....................	263.7	0.5	0.7	24.7	31.0	65.3	18.1	3.6
Engineering managers.............	187.1	2.1	5.4	80.9	5.2	55.9	16.5	0.1
Natural science managers...........	40.7	0.3	(NA)	5.5	0.2	14.6	14.3	0.2
Computer and mathematical scientists...	3,313.2	8.4	7.7	268.3	413.2	1,004.6	240.5	130.9
Computer specialists.............	3,199.6	0.4	7.5	262.4	406.2	978.8	221.5	129.5
Mathematical science occupations	113.6	(NA)	0.2	5.9	7.1	25.7	19.0	1.5
Surveyors, cartographers,and photogrammetrists.............	72.2	0.8	4.1	(NA)	(NA)	52.2	9.5	2.6
Engineers[4].....................	1,511.5	21.0	40.3	563.7	41.3	430.6	180.0	45.7
Aerospace engineers	89.8	(NA)	(NA)	58.4	(NA)	15.9	9.1	1.3
Civil engineers.................	256.3	0.5	24.3	2.7	1.1	130.9	69.1	12.5
Computer and hardware engineers	78.5	(NA)	(NA)	33.8	(NA)	23.3	4.5	2.8
Electrical and electronics engineers...	291.2	0.2	4.9	103.2	30.6	70.8	26.1	6.3
Industrial engineers[5]...........	226.7	2.3	5.9	149.5	3.0	29.2	5.2	2.1
Mechanical engineers...........	225.8	0.8	2.9	120.6	0.3	63.2	11.9	5.1
Drafters, engineering, and mapping technicians[6]...................	839.8	4.9	25.2	240.4	24.2	309.3	107.6	20.9
Engineering technicians...........	511.0	3.6	4.8	178.0	21.8	126.5	90.7	4.4
Surveying and mapping technicians...	75.6	0.6	0.9	0.2	0.4	54.2	11.6	3.2
Life, physical, and social science occupations	1,406.9	18.3	3.6	151.1	30.0	346.1	302.4	97.4
Life scientists.................	258.5	(NA)	(NA)	31.1	(NA)	60.8	66.9	11.5
Physical scientists.............	266.8	8.7	0.4	42.4	1.9	98.4	73.9	4.7
Social scientists and related occupations	530.2	(NA)	2.9	24.2	27.4	100.0	75.4	77.7
Life, physical, and social science technicians	351.4	9.2	0.4	53.5	(NA)	86.9	86.2	3.5

NA Not available. [1] Standard Occupational Classification system categorizes workers in 1 of 801 detailed occupations. For a list of occupations, see <http://bls.gov/oes/current/oes_stru.htm/>. [2] Includes oil and gas extraction. [3] Includes secondary jobs and unpaid private household employment. [4] Includes kinds of engineers not shown separately. [5] Includes health and safety engineers. [6] Includes other drafters, technicians, and mapping technicians.

Source: U.S. Bureau of Labor Statistics, *National Employment Matrix*, February 2008. (Data collected biennially.) For more information, see <http://www.bls.gov/emp/empoils.htm>.

Table 787. Employment and Earnings in Science & Engineering (S&E) Occupations by Industry: 2006

[As of May 2006. Industries ordered by Science and Engineering share of total employment. See headnote, Table 788]

Industry	2002 NAICS code	Workers employed (number)		S&E workers as percent of all employed	Mean earnings in S&E occupations (dollars)
		All occupations	S&E occupations		
Computer systems design and related services	5415	1,254,320	609,590	48.6	75,040
Software publishers.......................	5112	240,130	116,260	48.4	79,120
Scientific research and development services	5417	586,220	247,310	42.2	81,220
Computer and peripheral equipment manufacturing...	3341	199,370	79,040	39.6	90,710
Internet service providers and Web search portals	5181	119,560	46,120	38.6	69,720
Data processing, hosting, and related services......	5182	264,320	83,470	31.6	70,460
Internet publishing and broadcasting	5161	33,220	9,810	29.5	69,800
Architectural, engineering, and related services	5413	1,361,280	397,910	29.2	74,570
Communications equipment manufacturing	3342	144,200	39,270	27.2	83,400
Navigational, measuring, electromedical, and control instruments manufacturing	3345	435,510	117,950	27.1	82,190
Aerospace product and parts manufacturing	3364	464,990	114,620	24.6	80,410
Securities and commodity exchanges............	5232	8,850	1,930	21.8	74,000
Semiconductor and other electronic component manufacturing.....................	3344	452,060	93,940	20.8	83,490
Pharmaceutical and medicine manufacturing	3254	288,270	55,640	19.3	73,710
Other telecommunications	5179	5,300	980	18.5	73,820

Source: National Science Foundation, *Science and Engineering Indicators 2008*, January 2008. (biennial). For more information, see <http://www.bls.gov/oes/home.htm>.

Table 788. Individuals Employed in Science and Engineering (S&E) Occupations as Share of Workforce by State and Other Areas: 2007

[In thousands (7,449.0 represents 7,449,000), except as noted. As of May 2007. The Occupational Employment Statistics Survey (OES) collects data in six semiannual panels over a 3-year period on occupational employment and wages of wage and salary workers in nonfarm establishments in the United States, Guam, Puerto Rico, and the Virgin Islands. The OES survey uses the Standard Occupational Classification (SOC) system to categorize workers in 1 of 801 detailed occupations. For a list of occupations see <http://bls.gov/oes/current/oes/nat.htm>. For more information about methodology, see <http://bls.gov/oes_nat.htm/>]

State	S&E occupations [1]	Employed workforce	Work-force in S&E occupations [1] (percent)	State	S&E occupations [1]	Employed workforce	Work-force in S&E occupations [1] (percent)
United States.....	**7,449.0**	**135,474.0**	**5.5**	Nebraska.........	41.7	914.7	4.6
Alabama..........	91.3	1,932.0	4.7	Nevada...........	39.5	1,285.5	3.1
Alaska...........	17.9	301.9	5.9	New Hampshire.....	36.7	632.6	5.8
Arizona..........	145.5	2,648.0	5.5	New Jersey........	249.6	3,980.1	6.3
Arkansas.........	40.9	1,172.8	3.5	New Mexico.......	47.0	798.6	5.9
California.........	975.0	15,202.5	6.4	New York.........	436.8	8,516.0	5.1
Colorado.........	176.6	2,258.2	7.8	North Carolina......	191.6	4,013.5	4.8
Connecticut.......	107.9	1,682.2	6.4	North Dakota.......	12.8	342.0	3.7
Delaware.........	29.7	426.0	7.0	Ohio............	256.0	5,341.4	4.8
District of Columbia...	73.7	621.0	11.9	Oklahoma.........	68.0	1,528.9	4.4
Florida..........	336.7	7,963.0	4.2	Oregon..........	95.6	1,682.2	5.7
Georgia.........	184.0	4,058.4	4.5	Pennsylvania.......	285.6	5,663.1	5.0
Hawaii..........	24.7	610.3	4.0	Rhode Island.......	22.8	485.9	4.7
Idaho...........	37.7	642.0	5.9	South Carolina......	76.8	1,878.0	4.1
Illinois..........	294.5	5,894.7	5.0	South Dakota......	14.3	389.4	3.7
Indiana..........	113.8	2,928.8	3.9	Tennessee........	97.3	2,739.2	3.6
Iowa...........	61.3	1,488.4	4.1	Texas...........	599.6	10,061.8	6.0
Kansas..........	65.7	1,347.7	4.9	Utah............	71.8	1,206.2	6.0
Kentucky.........	64.2	1,801.8	3.6	Vermont.........	16.1	301.1	5.3
Louisiana........	61.8	1,847.2	3.3	Virginia..........	312.4	3,645.3	8.6
Maine...........	23.2	600.0	3.9	Washington........	236.3	2,811.7	8.4
Maryland.........	204.9	2,551.9	8.0	West Virginia.......	23.7	713.2	3.3
Massachusetts.....	260.2	3,207.8	8.1	Wisconsin........	136.1	2,768.8	4.9
Michigan.........	276.8	4,210.6	6.6	Wyoming.........	11.6	273.2	4.2
Minnesota........	173.1	2,687.7	6.4				
Mississippi........	37.0	1,129.0	3.3	Guam...........	1.8	57.9	3.2
Missouri.........	132.5	2,732.9	4.8	Puerto Rico........	35.0	1,015.0	3.4
Montana.........	20.9	435.5	4.8	Virgin Islands......	1.0	46.9	2.2

[1] Science and Engineering includes those occupations listed under SOC11-3021, SOC11-9041, SOC11-9121, SOC15-0000, SOC 17-0000, and SOC 19-0000.

Source: U.S. Bureau of Labor Statistics, *May 2007 National Occupational Employment and Wage Estimates*;

Table 789. Research and Development (R&D) Scientists and Engineers— Employment and Cost by Industry: 2004 to 2006

[1,133.7 represents 1,133,700]

Industry	NAICS [1] code	Employed scientists and engineers [2] (1,000)			Cost per scientist or engineer, constant (**2000**) dollars [3,4] ($1,000)		
		2004	**2005**	**2006**	**2004**	**2005**	**2006**
All industries [5].....................	(X)	**1,133.7**	**1,104.5**	**1,116.6**	**180.7**	**192.9**	**202.6**
Chemicals.................................	325	105.0	118.3	123.2	301.4	329.4	331.8
Machinery.................................	333	59.0	61.1	62.3	109.4	125.6	141.9
Electrical equipment, appliances, and components....	335	17.9	18.7	16.9	(D)	(D)	(D)
Motor vehicles, trailers, and parts................	3361–3363	(NA)	42.0	42.0	(D)	(D)	(D)
Aerospace products and parts..................	3364	39.3	39.7	39.5	319.3	336.3	361.3
Software publishing..........................	5112	100.1	93.4	46.5	168.2	163.0	174.9
Architectural, engineering, and related services.......	5413	39.9	35.8	41.2	111.3	129.7	147.1
Computer systems design and related services.......	5415	69.7	82.4	93.1	163.3	158.9	158.0
Scientific R&D services.......................	5417	45.8	43.7	44.3	292.2	264.7	299.7

D Withheld to avoid disclosure. NA Not available. X Not applicable. [1] North American Industry Classification System 1997 (NAICS); see text, Section 15. [2] The mean number of full-time equivalent R&D scientists and engineers employed in January of the year shown and the following January. [3] Based on gross domestic product implicit price deflator. [4] Represents the arithmetic mean of the numbers of R&D scientists and engineers reported in each industry for January in 2 consecutive years divided into total R&D expenditures in each industry. [5] Includes other industries not shown separately.

Source: U.S. National Science Foundation, *Research and Development in Industry*, annual. See also <http://www.nsf.gov /statistics/showpub.cfm?TopID=5&SubID=36>.

Science and Technology 519

Table 790. Federal Outlays for General Science, Space, and Other Technology, 1970 to 2007, and Projections, 2008 and 2009

[In billions of dollars (4.5 represents $4,500,000,000). For fiscal years ending in year shown; see text Section 8]

Year	Current dollars			Constant (2000) dollars		
	Total	General science/basic research	Space and other technologies	Total	General science/basic research	Space and other technologies
1970	4.5	0.9	3.6	19.3	4.0	15.2
1980	5.8	1.4	4.5	12.0	2.8	9.1
1985	8.6	2.0	6.6	13.7	3.2	10.5
1990	14.4	2.8	11.6	20.0	3.9	16.1
1995 [1]	16.7	4.1	12.6	18.7	4.6	14.1
2000	18.6	6.2	12.4	18.6	6.2	12.4
2001	19.7	6.5	13.2	19.3	6.4	12.9
2002	20.7	7.2	13.5	19.7	6.9	12.8
2003	20.8	7.9	12.9	19.2	7.3	11.9
2004	23.0	8.3	14.6	20.3	7.4	13.0
2005	23.6	8.8	14.8	20.0	7.4	12.5
2006	23.5	9.0	14.5	19.2	7.4	11.9
2007	25.5	10.2	15.3	20.7	8.3	12.4
2008, proj.	27.4	10.7	16.7	21.8	8.5	13.3
2009, proj.	29.0	11.5	17.6	22.5	8.9	13.6

[1] Due to the effects of the Credit Reform Act of 1990 on the measurement and classification of federal credit activities, the discretionary outlays for years prior to 1995 are not strictly comparable to those for 1995 and after. However, the discretionary outlays shown for 1995 are no more than $1 billion higher than they would have been if measured on the same (pre-credit reform) basis as the 1990 outlays.

Source: U.S. Office of Management and Budget, *Budget of the United States, Historical Tables, Fiscal Year 2009,* annual. See also <http://www.gpoaccess.gov/usbudget/fy08/hist.html>.

Table 791. U.S. and Worldwide Commercial Space Industry Revenue by Type: 2000 to 2006

[In billions of dollars (19.3 represents $19,300,000,000). For calendar years]

Industry	U.S.				World			
	2000	2004	2005	2006	2000	2004	2005	2006
Revenue, total	**19.3**	**26.5**	**30.8**	**(NA)**	**64.2**	**82.7**	**88.8**	**106.1**
Satellite manufacturing [1]	6.0	3.9	3.2	5.0	11.5	10.2	7.8	12.0
Launch industry	2.7	1.5	1.5	1.0	5.3	2.8	3.0	2.7
Satellite services [2].	10.6	21.1	26.1	(NA)	28.9	46.9	52.8	62.6
Ground equipment manufacturing [3]	(NA)	(NA)	(NA)	(NA)	18.5	22.8	25.2	28.8

NA Not available.   [1] Includes revenues from the construction and sale of satellites to both commercial and government.   [2] Includes revenues derived from transponder leasing and subscription/retail services such as direct-to-home television, satellite radio, remote sensing, and satellite mobile and data communications.   [3] Includes revenues from the manufacture of gateways and satellite control stations, satellite news-gathering trucks, very small aperture terminals, direct-to-home television equipment and mobile satellite phones.

Source: Satellite Industry Association/Futron Corporation, Bethesda, MD, *2006-2007 Satellite Industry Indicators Survey* (copyright). See also <http://www.sia.org/>.

Table 792. National Aeronautics and Space Administration— Budget Appropriations, 2008, and Projections, 2009 to 2013

[In millions of dollars (17,309.4 represents $17,309,400,000)]

Item	2008	2009	2010	2011	2012	2013
Appropriations, total	**17,309.4**	**17,614.2**	**18,026.3**	**18,460.4**	**18,905.0**	**19,358.8**
Science	4,706.2	4,441.5	4,482.0	4,534.9	4,643.4	4,761.6
Earth science	1,280.3	1,367.5	1,350.7	1,250.9	1,264.4	1,290.3
Heliophysics.	840.9	[1]577.3	598.9	689.4	741.2	746.6
Planetary science	1,247.5	1,334.2	1,410.1	1,537.5	1,570.0	1,608.7
Astrophysics	1,337.5	1,162.5	1,122.4	1,057.1	1,067.7	1,116.0
Exploration systems	3,143.1	3,500.5	3,737.7	7,048.2	7,116.8	7,666.8
Constellation systems	2,471.9	3,048.2	3,252.8	6,479.5	6,521.4	7,080.5
Advanced capabilities	671.1	452.3	484.9	568.7	595.5	586.3
Aeronautics.	511.7	446.5	447.5	452.4	456.7	467.7
Cross-agency support programs	3,242.9	3,299.9	3,323.9	3,363.7	3,436.1	3,511.3
Center management	2,013.0	2,045.6	2,046.7	2,088.0	2,155.3	2,211.6
Agency management.	830.2	945.6	945.5	939.8	950.5	961.3
Institutional investments	319.7	308.7	331.7	335.9	330.4	338.3
Congressionally directed items	80.0	–	–	–	–	–
Education	146.8	115.6	126.1	123.8	123.8	123.8
Space operations	5,526.2	5,774.7	5,872.8	2,900.1	3,089.9	2,788.5
Space shuttle.	3,266.7	2,981.7	2,983.7	95.7	–	–
International space station	1,813.2	2,060.2	2,277.0	2,176.4	2,448.2	2,143.1
Space and flight support	446.3	[1]732.8	612.1	628.0	641.7	645.4
Inspector General.	32.6	35.5	36.4	37.3	38.3	39.2

– Represents zero.   [1] Deep Space and Near Earth Networks transfers $256 million to Space and Flight Support in FY 2009.
Source: U.S. National Aeronautics and Space Administration, *Fiscal Year 2009 Budget* <http://www.nasa.gov/about/budget /index.html> (accessed 11 February 2008).

520   Science and Technology

Agriculture

This section presents statistics on farms and farm operators; land use; farm income, expenditures, and debt; farm output, productivity, and marketings; foreign trade in agricultural products; specific crops; and livestock, poultry, and their products.

The principal sources are the reports issued by the National Agricultural Statistics Service (NASS) and the Economic Research Service (ERS) of the U.S. Department of Agriculture (USDA). The information from the 2002 Census of Agriculture is available in printed form in the Volume 1, Geographic Area Series; in electronic format on CD-ROM; and on the Internet site <http://www.agcensus.usda.gov /Publications/2002/index.asp>. The Department of Agriculture publishes annually *Agricultural Statistics,* a general reference book on agricultural production, supplies, consumption, facilities, costs, and returns. The ERS publishes data on farm assets, debt, and income on the Internet site <http://www.ers.usda .gov/briefing/farmincome/>. Sources of current data on agricultural exports and imports include *Outlook for U.S. Agricultural Trade,* published by the ERS; the ERS Internet site <http://www.ers.usda.gov /briefing/AgTrade/>; and the foreign trade section of the U.S. Census Bureau Web site <http://www.census.gov /foreign-trade/statistics/index.html>.

The field offices of the NASS collect data on crops, livestock and products, agricultural prices, farm employment, and other related subjects mainly through sample surveys. Information is obtained on crops and livestock items as well as scores of items pertaining to agricultural production and marketing. State estimates and supporting information are sent to the Agricultural Statistics Board of NASS, which reviews the estimates and issues reports containing state and national data. Among these reports are annual summaries such as *Crop Production, Crop Values, Agricultural Prices,* and *Livestock*

Production, Disposition and Income. For more information about concepts and methods underlying USDA's statistical series, see *Major Statistical Series of the U.S. Department of Agriculture* (Agricultural Handbook No. 671), a 12-volume set of publications.

Farms and farmland—The definitions of a farm have varied through time. Since 1850, when minimum criteria defining a farm for census purposes first were established, the farm definition has changed nine times. The current definition, first used for the 1974 census, is any place from which $1,000 or more of agricultural products were produced and sold, or normally would have been sold, during the census year.

Acreage designated as "land in farms" consists primarily of agricultural land used for crops, pasture, or grazing. It also includes woodland and wasteland not actually under cultivation or used for pasture or grazing, provided it was part of the farm operator's total operation. Land in farms includes acres set aside under annual commodity acreage programs as well as acres in the Conservation Reserve and Wetlands Reserve Programs for places meeting the farm definition. Land in farms is an operating unit concept and includes land owned and operated as well as land rented from others. All grazing land, except land used under government permits on a per-head basis, was included as "land in farms" provided it was part of a farm or ranch.

An evaluation of coverage has been conducted for each census of agriculture since 1945 to provide estimates of the completeness of census farm counts. The 2002 coverage evaluation shows the census covered 96 percent of the farms with $50,000 or more in sales, but only 78 percent of farms with less than $50,000 in sales. The overall coverage of all farms was 82 percent. The census covered nearly 98 percent of all land in farms and

Agriculture   521

97 percent of the market value of agricultural products sold. In 2002, census farm counts and totals were statistically adjusted for coverage and reported at the county level. The size of the adjustments varies considerably by state. In general, farms not on the census mail list tended to be small in acreage, production, and sales of farm products. For more explanation about census mail list compilation, collection methods, coverage measurement, and adjustments, see Appendixes A and C, 2002 Census of Agriculture, Volume 1 reports.

Farm income—The final agricultural sector output comprises cash receipts from farm marketings of crops and livestock, federal government payments made directly to farmers for farm-related activities, rental value of farm homes, value of farm products consumed in farm homes, and other farm-related income such as machine hire and custom work. Farm marketings represent quantities of agricultural products sold by farmers multiplied by prices received per unit of production at the local market. Information on prices received for farm products is generally obtained by the NASS Agricultural Statistics Board from surveys of firms (such as grain elevators, packers, and processors) purchasing agricultural commodities directly from producers. In some cases, the price information is obtained directly from the producers.

Crops—Estimates of crop acreage and production by the NASS are based on current sample survey data obtained from individual producers and objective yield counts, reports of carlot shipments, market records, personal field observations by field statisticians, and reports from other sources. Prices received by farmers are marketing year averages. These averages are based on U.S. monthly prices weighted by monthly marketings during specific periods. U.S. monthly prices are state average prices weighted by marketings during the month. Marketing year average prices do not include allowances for outstanding loans, government purchases, deficiency payments or disaster payments.

All state prices are based on individual state marketing years, while U.S. marketing year averages are based on standard marketing years for each crop. For a listing of the crop marketing years and the participating states in the monthly program, see *Crop Values*. Value of production is computed by multiplying state prices by each state's production. The U.S. value of production is the sum of state values for all states. Value of production figures shown in Tables 818–822 and 824 should not be confused with cash receipts from farm marketings which relate to sales during a calendar year, irrespective of the year of production.

Livestock—Annual inventory numbers of livestock and estimates of livestock, dairy, and poultry production prepared by the Department of Agriculture are based on information from farmers and ranchers obtained by probability survey sampling methods.

Statistical reliability—For a discussion of statistical collection and estimation, sampling procedures, and measures of statistical reliability pertaining to Department of Agriculture data, see Appendix III.

Table 793. **Farms by Size and Type of Organization: 1974 to 2002**

[**2,314 represents 2,314,000**. For comments on adjustment, see text this section]

Size and type of organization	Unit	Not adjusted for coverage						1997 [1]	2002 [1]
		1974	1978	1982	1987	1992	1997		
Farms.	1,000	2,314	2,258	2,241	2,088	1,925	1,912	2,216	2,129
Land in farms.	Mil. acres. . .	1,017	1,015	987	964	946	932	955	938
Average size of farm	Acres	440	449	440	462	491	487	431	441
Farms by size:									
Under 10 acres.	1,000	128	151	188	183	166	154	205	179
10 to 49 acres	1,000	380	392	449	412	388	411	531	564
50 to 179 acres.	1,000	828	759	712	645	584	593	694	659
180 to 499 acres.	1,000	616	582	527	478	428	403	428	389
500 to 999 acres.	1,000	207	213	204	200	186	176	179	162
1,000 to 1,999 acres	1,000	93	98	97	102	102	101	103	99
2,000 acres or more	1,000	62	63	65	67	71	75	74	78
Farms by type of organization:									
Family or individual	1,000	(NA)	1,966	1,946	1,809	1,653	1,643	1,923	1,910
Partnership	1,000	(NA)	233	223	200	187	169	186	130
Corporation	1,000	(NA)	50	60	67	73	84	90	74
Other [2]	1,000	(NA)	9	12	12	12	15	17	16

NA Not available.   [1] Data have been adjusted for coverage; see text this section.   [2] Cooperative, estate or trust, institutional, etc.

Source: U.S. Department of Agriculture, National Agricultural Statistics Service, *2002 Census of Agriculture*, Vol. 1.

Table 794. **Farms—Number and Acreage by Size of Farm: 1997 and 2002**

[**2,216 represents 2,216,000**. Data have been adjusted for coverage; see text this section]

Size of farm	Number of farms (1,000)		Land in farms (mil. acres)		Cropland harvested (mil. acres)		Percent distribution, 2002		
	1997	2002	1997	2002	1997	2002	Number of farms	All land in farms	Cropland harvested
Total	2,216	2,129	954.8	938.3	318.9	302.7	100.0	100.0	100.0
Under 10 acres	205	179	0.9	0.8	0.3	0.2	8.4	0.1	0.1
10 to 49 acres	531	564	14.0	14.7	4.3	4.1	26.5	1.6	1.4
50 to 69 acres	154	152	9.0	8.8	2.7	2.5	7.1	0.9	0.8
70 to 99 acres	200	191	16.5	15.7	5.2	4.7	9.0	1.7	1.5
100 to 139 acres	187	175	21.7	20.2	7.0	6.1	8.2	2.2	2.0
140 to 179 acres	153	142	24.1	22.3	8.4	7.3	6.7	2.4	2.4
180 to 219 acres	100	91	19.8	18.0	7.2	6.2	4.3	1.9	2.1
220 to 259 acres	79	72	18.8	17.1	7.5	6.5	3.4	1.8	2.1
260 to 499 acres	249	226	89.2	80.6	40.1	34.1	10.6	8.6	11.3
500 to 999 acres	179	162	124.6	112.4	66.5	56.7	7.6	12.0	18.7
1,000 to 1,999 acres. . .	103	99	140.7	135.7	75.9	72.8	4.7	14.5	24.0
2,000 acres or more . . .	74	78	475.6	491.9	94.1	101.6	3.7	52.4	33.6

Source: U.S. Department of Agriculture, National Agricultural Statistics Service, *2002 Census of Agriculture*, Vol. 1.

Table 795. **Farms—Number, Acreage, and Value by Tenure of Principal Operator and Type of Organization: 1997 and 2002**

[**2,216 represents 2,216,000**. Full owners own all the land they operate. Part owners own a part and rent from others the rest of the land they operate. A principal operator is the person primarily responsible for the on-site, day-to-day operation of the farm or ranch business. Data have been adjusted for coverage; see text this section]

Item and year	Unit	Total [1]	Tenure of operator			Type of organization		
			Full owner	Part owner	Tenant	Family or individual	Partnership	Corporation
NUMBER OF FARMS								
1997.	1,000	2,216	1,385	616	215	1,923	186	90
2002, total	1,000	2,129	1,428	551	150	1,910	130	74
Under 50 acres	1,000	743	639	64	41	697	24	18
50 to 179 acres	1,000	659	487	131	41	611	31	12
180 to 499 acres	1,000	389	203	153	33	344	29	12
500 to 999 acres	1,000	162	54	91	17	133	17	10
1,000 acres or more.	1,000	177	46	112	18	125	29	21
LAND IN FARMS								
1997.	Mil. acres. . .	955	332	512	111	605	151	133
2002.	Mil. acres. . .	938	357	495	87	622	146	108
Value of land and buildings, **2002** [2] . . .	Bil. dol.	1,145	495	551	99	836	158	129
Value of farm products sold, **2002**	Bil. dol.	201	88	91	22	104	37	57

[1] Includes other types, not shown separately.   [2] Based on a sample of farms.

Source: U.S. Department of Agriculture, National Agricultural Statistics Service, *2002 Census of Agriculture*, Vol. 1.

Table 796. Farms—Number and Acreage: 1990 to 2007

[As of June 1 (2,146 represents 2,146,000). Based on 1974 census definition; for definition of farms and farmland, see text of this section. Activities included as agriculture have undergone changes in recent years. Data for period 1995 to 2007 are not directly comparable with data for 1990. Data for 2002 have been adjusted for underenumeration. Minus sign (–) indicates decrease]

Item	Unit	1990	1995	2000	2002	2003	2004	2005	2006	2007
Number of farms	1,000.	2,146	2,196	2,167	2,135	2,127	2,113	2,099	2,089	2,076
Annual change [1] . . .	1,000.	–29	–1	–21	–13	–9	–14	–14	–10	–13
Land in farms	Mil. acres . . .	987	963	945	940	939	936	933	932	931
Average per farm . . .	Acres.	460	438	436	440	441	443	445	446	449

[1] Annual change from immediate preceding year.

Source: U.S. Dept. of Agriculture, National Agricultural Statistics Service, *Farms and Land in Farms, Final Estimates, 1988–1992; Farms and Land in Farms, Final Estimates, 1993–1997; Farm Numbers and Land in Farms, Final Estimates, 1998–2002*; and *Farms, Land in Farms, and Livestock Operations*, annual.

Table 797. Farms—Number and Acreage by State: 2000 and 2007

[2,167 represents 2,167,000. See headnote, Table 796]

State	Farms (1,000) 2000	Farms (1,000) 2007	Acreage (mil.) 2000	Acreage (mil.) 2007	Acreage per farm 2000	Acreage per farm 2007	State	Farms (1,000) 2000	Farms (1,000) 2007	Acreage (mil.) 2000	Acreage (mil.) 2007	Acreage per farm 2000	Acreage per farm 2007
U.S	2,167	2,076	945	931	436	449	Montana	28	28	59	60	2,133	2,120
Alabama	47	43	9	9	191	200	Nebraska	52	47	46	46	887	964
Alaska	1	1	1	1	1,569	1,364	Nevada	3	3	6	6	2,065	2,100
Arizona	11	10	27	26	2,514	2,600	New Hampshire . .	3	3	(Z)	(Z)	133	132
Arkansas	48	47	15	14	304	308	New Jersey	10	10	1	1	86	81
California	83	75	28	26	337	349	New Mexico	18	18	45	45	2,494	2,500
Colorado	30	31	32	31	1,053	990	New York	38	34	8	8	205	219
Connecticut	4	4	(Z)	(Z)	86	86	North Carolina . . .	56	48	9	9	166	183
Delaware	3	2	1	1	215	234	North Dakota	31	30	39	39	1,279	1,309
Florida	44	40	10	10	236	250	Ohio	79	76	15	14	187	188
Georgia	49	48	11	10	222	211	Oklahoma	85	83	34	34	400	408
Hawaii	6	6	1	1	251	236	Oregon	40	38	17	17	433	444
Idaho	25	25	12	12	486	478	Pennsylvania	59	58	8	8	130	132
Illinois	77	73	28	27	357	377	Rhode Island	1	1	(Z)	(Z)	75	71
Indiana	63	59	15	15	240	255	South Carolina . . .	24	25	5	5	203	196
Iowa	94	88	33	32	346	356	South Dakota . . .	32	31	44	44	1,358	1,396
Kansas	65	64	48	47	736	740	Tennessee	88	79	12	11	134	144
Kentucky	90	83	14	14	152	165	Texas	228	229	131	130	573	566
Louisiana	29	27	8	8	277	291	Utah	16	15	12	12	748	773
Maine	7	7	1	1	190	192	Vermont	7	6	1	1	192	197
Maryland	12	12	2	2	172	170	Virginia	49	47	9	9	180	181
Massachusetts . . .	6	6	1	1	89	85	Washington	37	33	16	15	420	458
Michigan	53	53	10	10	192	189	West Virginia	21	21	4	4	173	168
Minnesota	81	79	28	27	344	347	Wisconsin	78	76	16	15	206	200
Mississippi	42	42	11	11	266	264	Wyoming	9	9	35	34	3,750	3,909
Missouri	109	105	30	30	277	287							

Z Less than 500,000 acres.

Source: U.S. Department of Agriculture, National Agricultural Statistics Service, *Farm Numbers and Land in Farms, Final Estimates, 1998–2002* and *Farms, Land in Farms, and Livestock Operations*, annual.

Table 798. Certified Organic Farmland Acreage and Livestock: 2000 to 2005

["Certified organic" means that agricultural products have been grown and processed according to USDA's national organic standards and certified by USDA-accredited state and private certification organizations]

Item	Unit	2000	2004	2005	Crop	Certified organic acreage (1,000) 2000	Certified organic acreage (1,000) 2005
Certified growers	Number . . .	6,592	8,021	8,493	Corn	78	131
					Wheat	181	277
Certified organic acreage,					Oats	30	46
total	1,000	1,776	3,045	4,054	Barley	42	39
Pastureland and rangeland . . .	1,000	557	1,593	2,331	Rice	27	26
Cropland	1,000	1,219	1,452	1,723	Millet	15	14
					Soybeans	136	122
Certified animals:					Dry beans	14	11
Beef cows	1,000	13.8	36.7	36.1	Dry peas and lentils	10	18
Milk cows	1,000	38.2	74.8	87.1	Flax	25	31
Other cows	1,000	(NA)	36.6	58.8	Lettuce	11	12
Hogs and pigs	1,000	1.7	4.9	10.0	Tree nuts	4	16
Sheep and lambs	1,000	2.3	4.3	4.5	Apples	9	13
Layer hens	1,000	1,114	1,788	2,415	Grapes	13	23
Broilers	1,000	1,925	4,769	10,406	Peanuts	2	12
Turkeys	1,000	9	164	144	Trees for maple syrup . . .	12	12

NA Not available.

Source: U.S. Department of Agriculture, Economic Research Service, "Organic Production"; <http://www.ers.usda.gov/data/organic>.

Table 799. **Balance Sheet of the Farming Sector: 1990 to 2006**

[In billions of dollars, except as indicated (841 represents $841,000,000,000). As of December 31]

Item	1990	1995	1998	1999	2000	2001	2002	2003	2004	2005	2006
Assets	**841**	**966**	**1,083**	**1,139**	**1,203**	**1,256**	**1,304**	**1,379**	**1,585**	**1,769**	**1,979**
Real estate	619	740	840	887	946	996	1,046	1,112	1,308	1,485	1,682
Livestock and poultry [1]	71	58	63	73	77	79	76	79	79	81	81
Machinery, motor vehicles [2]	86	88	90	90	90	93	94	96	102	105	113
Crops [3]	23	27	30	28	28	25	23	24	24	24	23
Purchased inputs	3	3	5	4	5	4	6	6	6	6	6
Financial assets	38	49	55	57	57	59	60	62	66	67	74
Claims	841	966	1,083	1,139	1,203	1,256	1,304	1,379	1,585	1,769	1,979
Debt [4]	131	143	165	168	164	171	177	175	183	193	207
Real estate debt	68	72	83	87	85	89	95	94	97	102	109
Nonreal estate debt	63	71	82	80	79	82	82	81	86	92	98
Equity	**709**	**823**	**919**	**971**	**1,039**	**1,085**	**1,127**	**1,204**	**1,402**	**1,576**	**1,772**
FINANCIAL RATIOS (percent)											
Farm debt/equity ratio	18.5	17.4	17.9	17.3	15.9	15.8	15.8	14.6	13.1	12.3	11.7
Farm debt/asset ratio	15.6	14.8	15.2	14.7	13.7	13.7	13.6	12.7	11.5	10.9	10.5
Rate of return on assets from:											
Total	3.5	4.3	5.1	5.3	7.9	6.9	4.8	8.1	20.2	15.7	14.1
Current income [5]	4.1	2.2	2.4	1.8	2.2	2.6	1.0	2.3	4.2	3.7	1.9
Real capital gains [6]	−0.7	2.1	2.7	3.4	5.7	4.4	3.8	5.7	16.0	12.0	12.2
Rate of return on equity from:											
Total	3.0	3.9	4.8	5.1	7.9	6.8	4.7	8.3	22.2	16.9	14.9
Current income [7]	3.0	1.1	1.4	0.7	1.2	1.8	0.1	1.7	4.0	3.4	1.2
Real capital gains [8]	0.1	2.8	3.4	4.3	6.7	5.1	4.6	6.6	18.2	13.5	13.7

[1] Excludes horses, mules, and broilers. [2] Includes only farm share value for trucks and autos. [3] All non-CCC crops held on farms plus the value above loan rate for crops held under Commodity Credit Corporation. [4] Excludes debt for nonfarm purposes. [5] Returns to farm assets from current income/farm business assets. Measures how efficiently the farm business uses its assets; the per dollar return on farm assets from current income only. [6] Real capital gains on farm business assets/farm business assets. The per dollar return on farm assets from real capital gains. [7] Returns to farm assets from current income minus interest/farm business equity. Measures the returns to equity capital employed in farm business from current income less interest. [8] Real capital gains on farm business assets/farm business equity. The per dollar return on farm equity from real capital gains.

Source: U.S. Department of Agriculture, Economic Research Service, "Farm Balance Sheet"; <http://www.ers.usda.gov/Data/FarmBalanceSheet/FBSDMU.HTM>; accessed 26 February 2008.

Table 800. **Farm Sector Output and Value Added: 1990 to 2006**

[In billions of dollars (180.1 represents $180,100,000,000). For definition of value added, see text, Section 13. Minus sign (−) indicates decrease]

Item	1990	1995	1998	1999	2000	2001	2002	2003	2004	2005	2006
CURRENT DOLLARS											
Farm output, total	**180.1**	**192.0**	**208.9**	**198.5**	**203.6**	**210.8**	**202.1**	**227.7**	**260.5**	**253.3**	**254.8**
Cash receipts from farm marketings	172.1	194.3	199.0	190.2	196.6	200.1	194.6	214.8	238.0	239.6	238.6
Farm products consumed on farms	0.7	0.5	0.5	0.5	0.6	0.5	0.5	0.5	0.5	0.5	0.5
Other farm income	4.9	6.3	8.5	9.4	8.4	9.5	10.6	11.8	13.8	13.9	17.0
Change in farm finished goods inventories	2.4	−9.2	0.8	−1.6	−2.0	0.6	−3.7	0.7	8.2	−0.8	−1.3
Less: Intermediate goods and services consumed [1]	103.5	123.5	130.0	129.8	132.1	137.7	131.2	139.5	145.8	152.4	159.1
Equals: **Gross farm value added**	**76.6**	**68.5**	**78.9**	**68.8**	**71.5**	**73.1**	**70.8**	**88.3**	**114.7**	**100.9**	**95.7**
Less: Consumption of fixed capital	18.6	19.6	20.9	21.2	21.3	27.4	27.0	27.7	29.6	31.4	33.1
Equals: Net farm value added	58.0	48.9	58.0	47.6	50.2	45.7	43.9	60.6	85.1	69.4	62.6
Compensation of employees	13.4	15.4	18.2	18.9	19.7	20.9	20.8	20.0	22.0	22.1	22.7
Taxes on production and imports	3.8	4.2	4.3	4.9	4.7	4.8	5.0	4.9	5.0	5.7	6.7
Less: Subsidies to operators	7.6	6.1	10.5	18.6	19.6	18.3	9.6	14.9	11.8	21.6	13.7
Net operating surplus	48.5	35.4	46.0	42.4	45.4	38.3	27.7	50.6	69.9	63.1	47.0
CHAINED (**2000**) DOLLARS [2]											
Farm output, total	**164.5**	**179.6**	**198.4**	**200.5**	**203.6**	**200.7**	**201.4**	**207.9**	**211.5**	**215.3**	**215.0**
Cash receipts from farm marketings	159.0	183.5	189.2	192.0	196.6	190.1	194.1	195.5	191.9	202.0	200.2
Farm products consumed on farms	0.7	0.5	0.6	0.6	0.6	0.5	0.5	0.4	0.4	0.4	0.4
Other farm income	4.8	5.8	7.9	9.5	8.4	9.4	10.1	10.7	11.8	12.5	14.2
Change in farm finished goods inventories	2.1	−8.8	0.9	−1.8	−2.0	0.6	−3.6	0.6	6.0	−0.7	−1.1
Less: Intermediate goods and services consumed [1]	117.5	134.4	137.5	138.1	132.1	135.3	131.3	131.7	128.4	127.0	126.3
Equals: **Gross farm value added**	**49.3**	**49.6**	**61.6**	**62.9**	**71.5**	**65.6**	**70.1**	**76.0**	**82.1**	**87.0**	**87.5**
Less: Consumption of fixed capital	23.0	21.3	21.6	21.6	21.3	27.0	26.2	26.5	27.3	27.9	28.4
Equals: Net farm value added	29.4	30.4	40.2	41.5	50.2	39.0	44.2	49.7	54.8	58.9	58.9

[1] Includes rent paid to nonoperator landlords. [2] See text, Section 13.

Source: U.S. Bureau of Economic Analysis, *Survey of Current Business*, August 2007. See also <http://www.bea.gov/national/nipaweb/SelectTable.asp?Selected=N>.

Agriculture 525

Table 801. Value Added to Economy by Agricultural Sector: 1990 to 2006

[In billions of dollars (188.5 represents $188,500,000,000). Data are consistent with the net farm income accounts and include income and expenses related to the farm operator dwellings. The concept presented is consistent with that employed by the Organization for Economic Cooperation and Development. Minus sign (–) indicates decrease]

Item	1990	1995	1998	1999	2000	2001	2002	2003	2004	2005	2006
Value of agricultural sector production	**188.5**	**203.6**	**220.2**	**213.4**	**220.5**	**229.4**	**220.4**	**243.5**	**283.0**	**275.2**	**275.7**
Value of crop production	83.2	95.9	102.1	92.8	94.9	95.1	98.4	108.5	124.5	113.6	118.0
Food grains	7.5	10.4	8.8	6.9	6.5	6.4	6.8	8.0	8.9	8.6	9.1
Feed crops	18.7	24.5	22.6	19.5	20.5	21.5	24.0	24.7	27.4	24.6	28.0
Cotton	5.5	6.9	6.1	4.6	2.9	3.6	3.4	6.4	4.8	6.3	6.2
Oil crops	12.3	15.5	17.4	13.4	13.5	13.3	15.0	18.0	17.9	18.4	18.2
Tobacco	2.7	2.5	2.8	2.3	2.3	1.9	1.7	1.6	1.6	1.1	1.2
Fruits and tree nuts	9.4	11.0	12.0	12.0	12.4	12.0	12.6	13.5	15.5	17.7	17.0
Vegetables	11.3	15.0	15.0	15.0	15.5	15.4	17.2	16.9	16.2	16.9	17.9
All other crops	12.9	15.2	17.6	18.4	18.7	19.3	20.2	20.8	21.5	22.3	22.4
Home consumption	0.1	0.2	0.2	0.2	0.2	0.2	0.2	0.1	0.1	0.1	0.1
Value of inventory adjustment	2.8	-5.3	-0.3	0.5	2.2	1.5	-2.9	-1.6	10.7	-2.4	-2.0
Value of livestock production	90.0	87.8	94.2	95.2	99.1	106.4	93.5	105.0	124.4	126.4	120.1
Meat animals	51.1	44.9	43.4	45.7	53.0	53.3	48.1	56.2	62.4	64.8	63.7
Dairy products	20.2	19.9	24.1	23.2	20.6	24.7	20.6	21.2	27.4	26.7	23.4
Poultry and eggs	15.3	19.1	23.0	22.9	21.9	24.6	21.1	24.0	29.5	28.9	27.5
Miscellaneous livestock	2.5	3.4	3.8	3.9	4.2	4.1	4.1	4.2	4.4	4.5	4.7
Home consumption	0.5	0.3	0.2	0.1	0.1	0.1	0.1	0.1	0.2	0.3	0.3
Value of inventory adjustment	0.4	0.2	-0.3	-0.7	-0.6	-0.4	-0.6	-0.8	0.6	1.3	0.5
Services and forestry	15.3	19.9	23.9	25.4	26.5	28.0	28.5	30.0	34.1	35.2	37.6
Machine hire and customwork	1.8	1.9	2.2	2.0	2.2	2.1	2.2	3.0	3.4	2.8	2.7
Forest products sold	1.8	2.8	3.0	2.7	2.8	2.6	2.5	2.2	2.4	2.5	2.5
Other farm income	4.5	5.8	8.7	10.1	8.7	10.1	10.2	10.5	11.3	10.9	12.3
Gross imputed rental value of farm dwellings	7.2	9.4	10.0	10.6	12.7	13.1	13.6	14.3	17.0	19.0	20.1
Less: Purchased inputs	92.2	108.8	117.7	118.7	121.8	125.7	123.0	131.1	137.5	144.6	151.4
Farm origin	39.5	41.8	44.8	45.5	47.9	48.2	48.3	53.7	57.5	56.9	59.8
Feed purchased	20.4	23.8	25.0	24.5	24.5	24.8	24.9	27.5	29.7	28.0	30.5
Livestock and poultry purchased	14.6	12.5	12.6	13.8	15.9	15.2	14.4	16.7	18.2	18.4	18.2
Seed purchased	4.5	5.5	7.2	7.2	7.5	8.2	8.9	9.4	9.6	10.4	11.0
Manufactured inputs	22.0	26.1	28.1	27.1	28.7	29.4	28.5	28.7	31.6	35.4	37.0
Fertilizers and lime	8.2	10.0	10.6	9.9	10.0	10.3	9.6	10.0	11.4	12.8	13.3
Pesticides	5.4	7.7	9.0	8.6	8.5	8.6	8.3	8.4	8.6	8.8	8.8
Petroleum fuel and oils	5.8	5.4	5.6	5.6	7.2	6.9	6.6	6.8	8.2	10.3	11.1
Electricity	2.6	3.0	2.9	3.0	3.0	3.6	3.9	3.5	3.4	3.5	3.7
Other purchased inputs	30.7	40.9	44.8	46.1	45.2	48.1	46.3	48.7	48.3	52.3	54.7
Repair and maintenance of capital items	8.6	9.6	10.5	10.7	10.9	11.2	10.3	10.7	11.9	11.9	12.4
Machine hire and custom work	3.0	3.9	4.6	4.4	4.1	4.0	4.0	3.5	3.6	3.5	3.5
Marketing, storage, and transportation expenses	4.2	7.2	6.9	7.3	7.5	7.8	7.5	7.3	7.2	8.8	9.0
Contract labor	1.6	2.0	2.4	2.5	2.7	3.1	2.7	3.3	3.1	3.1	3.1
Miscellaneous expenses	13.4	18.2	20.4	21.3	19.9	21.9	21.7	23.9	22.4	25.1	26.8
Plus: Net government transactions [1]	3.1	0.4	5.3	14.3	15.8	15.0	5.2	9.2	5.4	15.8	6.2
Direct government payments	9.3	7.3	12.4	21.5	23.2	22.4	12.4	16.5	13.0	24.4	15.8
Motor vehicle registration and licensing fees	0.4	0.4	0.5	0.4	0.5	0.5	0.4	0.5	0.5	0.6	0.5
Property taxes	5.8	6.4	6.6	6.8	6.9	6.9	6.8	6.8	7.0	8.0	9.0
Equals: Gross value added	**99.3**	**95.1**	**107.8**	**109.0**	**114.5**	**118.8**	**102.5**	**121.5**	**151.0**	**146.4**	**130.5**
Less: Capital consumption	18.1	18.9	19.6	19.8	20.1	20.6	21.0	21.5	23.1	25.0	26.1
Equals: Net value added	**81.2**	**76.2**	**88.2**	**89.2**	**94.4**	**98.2**	**81.6**	**100.0**	**127.8**	**121.4**	**104.4**
Less: Employee compensation	12.4	14.3	16.8	17.4	17.9	18.8	19.1	18.7	20.4	20.7	21.3
Less: Net rent received by nonoperator landlords	9.0	9.6	10.9	10.4	11.2	11.2	9.6	10.2	10.0	10.6	9.3
Less: Real estate and nonreal estate interest	13.5	12.6	13.5	13.8	14.6	13.3	12.7	11.5	11.4	13.0	14.7
Equals: Net farm income	**46.3**	**39.8**	**47.1**	**47.7**	**50.7**	**55.0**	**40.1**	**59.7**	**85.9**	**77.1**	**59.0**

[1] Direct government payments minus motor vehicle registration and licensing fees and property taxes.

Source: U.S. Dept. of Agriculture, Economic Research Service, "United States and State Farm Income Data"; <http://www.ers.usda.gov/Data/farmincome/finfidmu.htm>; accessed 19 November 2007.

Table 802. Cash Receipts for Selected Commodities—Leading States: 2006

[In millions of dollars (49,148 represents $49,148,000,000). See headnote, Table 803]

State	Value	State	Value	State	Value	State	Value
Cattle and calves	**49,148**	**Dairy products**	**23,422**	**Corn**	**21,716**	**Broilers**	**18,852**
Texas	7,441	California	4,492	Iowa	4,206	Georgia	2,731
Nebraska	6,629	Wisconsin	3,075	Illinois	3,594	Arkansas	2,325
Kansas	6,247	New York	1,610	Nebraska	2,403	Alabama	2,162
Colorado	3,271	Pennsylvania	1,561	Minnesota	2,029	North Carolina	2,088
Oklahoma	2,751	Idaho	1,282	Indiana	1,851	Mississippi	1,772

Source: U.S. Department of Agriculture, Economic Research Service, "Farm Income"; published 30 August 2007; <http://www.ers.usda.gov/Data/FarmIncome/firkdmuXls.htm>.

Table 803. Farm Income—Cash Receipts From Farm Marketings: 2000 to 2006

[In millions of dollars (192,066 represents $192,066,000,000). Represents gross receipts from commercial market sales as well as net Commodity Credit Corporation loans. The source estimates and publishes individual cash receipt values only for major commodities and major producing states. The U.S. receipts for individual commodities, computed as the sum of the reported states, may understate the value of sales for some commodities. The degree of underestimation in some of the minor commodities can be substantial]

Commodity	2000	2004	2005	2006	Commodity	2000	2004	2005	2006
Total.	192,066	237,350	240,729	239,272	Lettuce [1]	1,863	1,928	1,940	2,008
Livestock and					Head	1,202	1,116	1,017	977
products [1]	99,635	123,602	124,863	119,320	Leaf	356	459	534	603
Cattle and calves	40,783	47,507	49,295	49,148	Onions	713	738	791	859
Hogs.	11,758	14,333	14,992	14,085	Peppers, green	531	517	535	586
Sheep and lambs	470	512	560	473	Tomatoes	1,845	2,150	2,237	2,281
Dairy products	20,587	27,387	26,698	23,422	Fresh	1,195	1,431	1,616	1,603
Broilers	13,989	20,446	20,878	18,852	Processing	650	720	621	678
Chicken eggs	4,289	5,239	4,007	4,340					
Turkeys	2,771	2,996	3,108	3,483	Fruits/nuts	12,435	15,536	17,710	17,011
Horses/mules	1,239	1,161	1,228	1,313	Lemons	267	310	324	438
Aquaculture [1,2]	798	895	887	937	Oranges	1,775	1,708	1,921	1,759
Catfish	501	480	482	481	Apples	1,466	1,756	1,722	2,100
					Cherries	327	507	548	523
Crops [1]	92,431	113,748	115,867	119,951	Grapes [1]	3,100	3,011	3,635	3,332
Rice	837	1,768	1,591	1,773	Wine	1,909	1,605	2,215	1,848
Wheat.	5,672	7,120	6,994	7,318	Table	437	536	533	656
Barley	556	601	533	469	Raisins	487	625	595	528
Corn	15,162	21,200	18,480	21,716	Peaches.	470	462	512	513
Hay	3,855	4,681	4,712	4,912	Strawberries	1,045	1,296	1,396	1,515
Sorghum grain	864	818	693	725	Blueberries	223	297	382	558
Cotton	2,950	4,784	6,320	6,173	Almonds.	666	2,189	2,526	2,040
Tobacco	2,316	1,578	1,097	1,156	Walnuts	296	452	557	554
Peanuts	897	814	843	602	Pistachios.	245	465	580	455
Soybeans	12,047	16,441	16,906	16,921	Sugar beets	1,113	1,109	1,193	1,193
Vegetables [1]	15,530	16,205	16,938	17,935	Cane for sugar	881	926	812	744
Potatoes	2,375	2,374	2,487	2,930	Greenhouse/nursery [1]	13,710	16,120	16,840	16,892
Beans, snap	393	394	416	448	Floriculture	4,576	5,285	5,435	3,996
Broccoli	622	638	570	653	Christmas trees	502	494	512	512
Carrots.	390	573	597	577	Mushrooms	867	916	890	865
Corn, sweet	709	751	814	825	Other forest products . .	2,849	2,450	2,494	2,498

[1] Includes other commodities not shown separately.   [2] See also Table 857.

Source: U.S. Department of Agriculture, Economic Research Service, "United States and State Farm Income Data"; <http://www.ers.usda.gov/Data/farmincome/finfidmu.htm>; accessed: 19 November 2007.

Table 804. Farm Output, Income, and Government Payments by State: 2005 and 2006

[In millions of dollars (275,202 represents $275,202,000,000). Farm income data are after inventory adjustment and include income and expenses related to the farm operator's dwelling]

State	Final agricultural sector output		Net farm income		Govern-ment pay-ments,	State	Final agricultural sector output		Net farm income		Govern-ment pay-ments,
	2005	2006	2005	2006	2006		2005	2006	2005	2006	2006
U.S. . . .	275,202	275,700	77,128	59,005	15,789	MT.	2,987	2,792	818	257	275
AL	4,888	4,656	2,063	1,580	219	NE.	12,735	13,191	2,847	2,297	812
AK	59	73	12	20	3	NV.	578	566	138	85	9
AZ	3,670	3,457	1,249	774	109	NH.	207	201	54	43	8
AR	6,833	6,981	2,042	1,951	516	NJ.	1,010	1,062	285	305	18
CA.	35,024	34,139	10,112	5,906	530	NM.	2,911	2,735	817	423	83
CO.	6,340	6,418	1,305	734	245	NY.	4,002	3,922	1,112	869	128
CT.	621	623	198	183	9	NC.	9,950	10,226	3,756	3,702	738
DE	1,095	1,122	406	388	22	ND.	4,501	4,373	1,244	606	453
FL.	8,298	7,710	3,303	2,340	141	OH.	6,443	6,829	1,452	1,614	442
GA.	7,263	7,302	2,869	2,388	483	OK.	6,218	5,665	1,663	877	243
HI	652	626	141	106	4	OR.	4,593	4,812	969	876	118
ID	4,981	5,014	1,151	758	141	PA.	5,432	5,608	1,635	1,516	134
IL.	9,047	10,154	1,372	1,511	1,045	RI	80	81	29	26	3
IN	6,408	6,899	1,531	1,545	541	SC.	2,087	2,293	717	722	184
IA	15,994	16,410	3,889	3,275	1,252	SD.	5,426	4,893	1,807	742	412
KS.	11,259	11,138	2,459	1,614	648	TN.	3,345	3,451	943	722	326
KY.	5,124	5,214	2,117	1,742	495	TX.	19,867	19,052	6,477	4,866	1,508
LA	2,447	2,567	738	766	341	UT.	1,660	1,642	422	264	40
ME.	591	670	163	217	15	VT.	635	553	205	103	20
MD.	2,091	2,007	702	595	67	VA.	3,462	3,413	967	678	172
MA.	535	552	121	115	13	WA	6,549	6,933	979	958	196
MI	5,114	5,389	1,269	1,321	248	WV	634	648	81	50	16
MN.	10,915	11,044	2,972	2,494	768	WI	8,198	8,078	1,626	1,091	414
MS.	4,696	4,385	1,965	1,230	633	WY	1,287	1,233	301	65	37
MO	6,462	6,895	1,637	1,697	510						

Source: U.S. Department of Agriculture, Economic Research Service, "Farm Income Summary Totals for 50 States"; published 25 July 2007; <http://www.ers.usda.gov/Data/FarmIncome/FinfidmuXls.htm>.

Table 805. **Farm Income—Farm Marketings, 2005 and 2006, and Principal Commodities, 2006, by State**

[In millions of dollars (240,729 represents $240,729,000,000). Cattle include calves; and greenhouse includes nursery]

State	2005			2006			
	Total	Crops	Live-stock	Total	Crops	Live-stock	State rank for total farm marketings and four principal commodities in order of marketing receipts
U.S. . . .	**240,729**	**115,867**	**124,863**	**239,272**	**119,951**	**119,320**	**Cattle, dairy products, corn, broilers**
AL	4,174	799	3,375	3,739	696	3,043	27-Broilers, cattle, greenhouse, chicken eggs
AK	50	26	24	64	25	39	50-Greenhouse, hay, dairy products, potatoes
AZ	3,074	1,661	1,412	2,879	1,558	1,321	29-Cattle, dairy products, lettuce, cotton
AR	6,474	2,257	4,217	6,164	2,397	3,767	11-Broilers, rice, cotton, soybeans
CA	32,766	24,340	8,426	31,403	23,788	7,615	1-Dairy products, greenhouse, grapes, almonds
CO	5,395	1,440	3,954	5,614	1,553	4,062	16-Cattle, dairy products, greenhouse, corn
CT	524	363	161	524	372	151	43-Greenhouse, dairy products, chicken eggs, aquaculture
DE	965	174	791	969	183	786	39-Broilers, corn, greenhouse, soybeans
FL	7,702	6,296	1,407	6,974	5,669	1,305	9-Greenhouse, oranges, tomatoes, cattle
GA	6,212	2,200	4,012	6,005	2,240	3,765	13-Broilers, cotton, greenhouse, chicken eggs
HI	576	487	89	555	467	88	42-Greenhouse, pineapples, sugar cane, macadamia nuts
ID	4,455	1,863	2,592	4,416	2,000	2,416	22-Dairy products, cattle, potatoes, wheat
IL	8,844	6,849	1,995	8,636	6,841	1,795	7-Corn, soybeans, hogs, cattle
IN	5,429	3,383	2,045	5,973	3,919	2,054	14-Corn, soybeans, hogs, dairy products
IA	14,523	6,618	7,905	15,108	7,229	7,879	3-Corn, hogs, soybeans, cattle
KS	10,103	3,237	6,866	10,336	3,365	6,971	5-Cattle, wheat, corn, soybeans
KY	3,982	1,274	2,708	4,007	1,299	2,708	23-Horses/mules, cattle, broilers, corn
LA	2,171	1,254	917	2,186	1,322	864	34-Cotton, sugar cane, rice, cattle
ME	544	250	295	592	303	289	41-Potatoes, dairy products, blueberries, chicken eggs
MD	1,704	704	1,001	1,598	726	872	36-Broilers, greenhouse, dairy products, corn
MA	409	317	92	433	344	89	47-Greenhouse, cranberries, dairy products, sweet corn
MI	4,224	2,496	1,728	4,488	2,833	1,654	21-Dairy products, greenhouse, corn, soybeans
MN	9,307	4,345	4,962	9,770	5,128	4,642	6-Corn, hogs, soybeans, dairy products
MS	4,172	1,268	2,903	3,789	1,245	2,544	26-Broilers, cotton, soybeans, aquaculture
MO	5,653	2,544	3,109	5,621	2,628	2,994	15-Cattle, soybeans, corn, hogs
MT	2,304	1,026	1,279	2,349	1,070	1,279	33-Cattle, wheat, barley, hay
NE	11,482	3,935	7,546	12,042	4,359	7,683	4-Cattle, corn, soybeans, hogs
NV	465	157	308	447	166	280	46-Cattle, hay, dairy products, onions
NH	163	93	70	162	98	64	48-Greenhouse, dairy products, cattle, apples
NJ	874	691	182	924	763	161	40-Greenhouse, horses/mules, blueberries, peaches
NM	2,612	622	1,990	2,464	602	1,861	32-Dairy products, cattle, hay, pecans
NY	3,661	1,333	2,327	3,509	1,527	1,982	28-Dairy products, greenhouse, apples, cattle
NC	8,264	2,668	5,596	8,199	2,925	5,274	8-Broilers, hogs, greenhouse, turkeys
ND	3,847	2,859	988	3,981	3,088	892	25-Wheat, cattle, soybeans, corn
OH	5,154	3,105	2,049	5,480	3,448	2,031	17-Soybeans, corn, dairy products, greenhouse
OK	5,390	1,170	4,220	5,094	974	4,120	18-Cattle, hogs, broilers, wheat
OR	3,681	2,642	1,039	3,991	2,961	1,030	24-Greenhouse, cattle, dairy products, hay
PA	4,732	1,516	3,216	4,692	1,723	2,968	20-Dairy products, cattle, greenhouse, mushrooms
RI	64	54	10	66	56	10	49-Greenhouse, dairy products, sweet corn, aquaculture
SC	1,827	737	1,090	1,891	788	1,103	35-Broilers, greenhouse, turkeys, cattle
SD	4,837	2,237	2,600	4,716	2,065	2,652	19-Cattle, corn, soybeans, hogs
TN	2,565	1,298	1,267	2,565	1,373	1,192	31-Cattle, broilers, cotton, greenhouse
TX	16,593	5,950	10,643	16,027	5,703	10,324	2-Cattle, cotton, greenhouse, broilers
UT	1,354	307	1,047	1,244	313	931	37-Cattle, dairy products, hogs, hay
VT	567	83	484	501	86	415	44-Dairy products, cattle, greenhouse, hay
VA	2,705	824	1,881	2,689	834	1,855	30-Broilers, cattle, dairy products, turkeys
WA	5,913	4,084	1,829	6,139	4,524	1,615	12-Apples, dairy products, cattle, wheat
WV	456	76	380	450	80	370	45-Broilers, cattle, turkeys, chicken eggs
WI	6,814	1,802	5,012	6,791	2,135	4,656	10-Dairy products, cattle, corn, soybeans
WY	976	152	824	1,021	162	859	38-Cattle, hay, sugar beets, hogs

Source: U.S. Department of Agriculture, Economic Research Service, "Farm Income: Cash Receipts"; published 30 August 2007; <http://www.ers.usda.gov/Data/FarmIncome/firkdmuXls.htm>.

Table 806. **Indexes of Prices Received and Paid by Farmers: 2000 to 2007**

[1990–1992 = 100, except as noted]

Item	2000	2005	2006	2007	Item	2000	2005	2006	2007
Prices received,					**Prices paid, total** [2] **. . . . .**	**118**	**142**	**151**	**162**
all products	**96**	**115**	**116**	**137**	Production	116	140	148	160
					Feed	102	117	124	151
Crops	96	111	120	142	Livestock and poultry	110	138	134	130
Food grains	85	111	134	186	Seed	124	168	182	205
Feed grains and hay	86	95	109	153	Fertilizer	110	164	176	208
Cotton	82	70	78	81	Agricultural chemicals	120	123	128	131
Tobacco	107	94	91	77	Fuels	134	216	239	263
Oil-bearing crops	85	106	100	137	Supplies and repairs	124	140	145	150
Fruits and nuts	98	131	155	155	Autos and trucks	119	114	112	111
Commercial vegetables [1] . . .	121	130	136	158	Farm machinery	139	173	182	189
Potatoes and dry beans . . .	93	109	125	128	Building materials	121	142	152	155
All other crops	110	113	116	118	Farm services	119	134	140	146
					Rent	110	129	141	151
Livestock and products	97	120	112	132	Interest	113	114	139	154
Meat animals	94	120	116	118	Taxes	123	154	174	188
Dairy products	94	116	99	147	Wage rates	140	165	171	171
Poultry and eggs	106	124	117	148	Parity ratio (1910–14 = 100) [3] . . .	38	39	37	41

[1] Excludes potatoes and dry beans.   [2] Includes production items, interest, taxes, wage rates, and a family living component. The family living component is the Consumer Price Index for all urban consumers from the Bureau of Labor Statistics. See text Section 14 and Table 703.   [3] Ratio of prices received by farmers to prices paid.

Source: U.S. Department of Agriculture, National Agricultural Statistics Service, *Agricultural Prices: Annual Summary.*

Table 807. **Civilian Consumer Expenditures for Farm Foods: 1990 to 2006**

[In billions of dollars, except percent (449.8 represents $449,800,000,000). Excludes imported and nonfarm foods, such as coffee and seafood, as well as food consumed by the military, or exported]

Item	1990	1995	1998	1999	2000	2001	2002	2003	2004	2005	2006
Consumer expenditures, total. . .	**449.8**	**529.5**	**585.0**	**625.3**	**661.1**	**687.5**	**709.4**	**744.2**	**788.9**	**830.7**	**880.7**
Farm value, total	106.2	113.8	119.6	122.2	123.3	130.0	132.5	140.2	155.5	157.8	163.2
Marketing bill, total [1]	343.6	415.7	465.4	503.1	537.8	557.5	576.9	604.0	633.4	672.9	717.5
Percent of total consumer expenditures	76.4	78.5	79.6	80.5	81.3	81.1	81.3	81.2	80.3	81.0	81.5
At-home expenditures [2]	276.2	316.9	346.8	370.7	390.2	403.9	416.8	437.2	463.5	488.1	517.5
Farm value	80.2	76.1	77.0	78.7	79.6	83.9	85.7	91.4	98.5	99.3	103.2
Marketing bill [1]	196.0	240.8	269.8	292.0	310.6	320.0	331.1	345.8	365.0	388.8	414.3
Away-from-home expenditures	173.6	212.6	238.2	254.6	270.9	283.6	292.6	307.0	325.4	342.6	363.2
Farm value	26.0	37.7	42.6	43.5	43.7	46.1	46.8	48.8	57.0	58.5	60.0
Marketing bill [1]	147.6	174.9	195.6	211.1	227.2	237.5	245.8	258.2	268.4	284.1	303.2
Marketing bill cost components:											
Labor cost	154.0	196.6	229.9	241.5	252.9	263.8	273.1	285.9	303.7	319.8	341.0
Packaging materials	36.5	48.2	50.4	50.9	53.5	55.0	56.8	59.5	63.1	66.5	70.5
Rail and truck transport	19.8	22.3	24.4	25.2	26.4	27.5	28.4	29.7	31.6	33.2	35.2
Corporate profits before taxes	13.2	19.5	25.5	29.2	31.1	32.0	33.0	34.6	35.5	37.4	39.7
Fuels and electricity.	15.2	18.6	20.7	22.0	23.1	24.1	24.9	26.1	27.6	31.6	33.5
Advertising	17.1	19.8	23.4	24.8	26.1	27.5	28.1	29.4	30.8	32.7	34.9
Depreciation	16.3	18.9	21.6	23.0	24.2	24.5	25.3	26.5	27.8	29.5	31.5
Net interest	13.5	11.6	12.9	14.4	16.9	18.6	19.2	20.1	21.1	22.4	23.9
Net rent	13.9	19.8	23.7	25.3	26.7	29.4	30.3	31.7	33.2	35.3	37.6
Repairs	6.2	7.9	9.0	9.6	10.1	10.6	10.9	11.4	12.0	12.7	13.5
Taxes	15.7	19.1	20.9	22.2	23.5	24.1	24.9	26.1	27.4	29.1	31.0
Other	22.2	13.4	3.0	15.0	23.3	20.4	22.0	23.0	19.6	22.7	25.2

[1] The difference between expenditures for domestic farm-originated food products and the farm value or payment farmers received for the equivalent farm products.   [2] Food primarily purchased from retail food stores for use at home.

Source: U.S. Department of Agriculture, Economic Research Service, *Food Cost Review, 1950–97*, ERS Agricultural Economic Report No. AER780, June 1999; and "ERS/USDA Briefing Room—Food marketing and price spreads: USDA marketing bill"; <http://www.ers.usda.gov/Briefing/FoodPriceSpreads/bill/>.

Table 808. **Agricultural Exports and Imports—Volume by Principal Commodities: 1990 to 2007**

[In thousands of metric tons (7,703 represents 7,703,000), except fruit juices, wine and malt beverages in thousands of hectoliters (1,000 hectoliters equals 264.18 gallons). Includes Puerto Rico, U.S. territories, and shipments under foreign aid programs. Excludes fish, forest products, distilled liquors, manufactured tobacco, and products made from cotton; but includes raw tobacco, raw cotton, rubber, beer and wine, and processed agricultural products]

Commodity	1990	1995	2000	2004	2005	2006	2007
EXPORTS							
Fruit juices and wine	7,703	10,688	14,356	15,383	13,982	14,438	14,452
Beef, pork, lamb, and poultry meats [1] . . .	1,451	3,723	4,935	4,033	4,620	4,919	5,421
Wheat, unmilled	27,384	32,317	27,568	31,044	27,040	23,206	32,888
Wheat products	863	1,142	844	381	313	281	468
Rice, paddy, milled	2,534	3,275	3,241	3,518	4,388	3,779	3,491
Feed grains	61,066	66,795	54,946	53,324	50,865	62,555	63,219
Feed grain products	1,430	2,018	2,062	4,342	5,368	5,987	6,086
Feeds and fodders [2]	10,974	13,338	13,065	11,393	11,422	11,372	11,813
Fresh fruits and nuts	2,648	3,323	3,450	3,501	3,675	3,569	3,578
Fruit products.	390	462	471	531	483	505	546
Vegetables, fresh	1,297	1,708	2,029	2,034	2,077	1,983	1,934
Vegetables, frozen and canned	529	892	1,112	1,046	1,086	1,149	1,262
Oilcake and meal	5,079	6,404	6,462	5,526	6,905	7,943	8,229
Oilseeds	15,820	23,596	28,017	26,091	26,462	29,373	31,111
Vegetable oils	1,226	2,532	2,043	1,939	1,937	2,222	2,546
Tobacco, unmanufactured	223	209	180	164	154	180	187
Cotton, excluding linters.	1,696	2,039	1,485	2,885	3,405	3,507	3,258
IMPORTS							
Fruit juices.	33,116	21,922	31,154	33,670	43,077	39,002	49,748
Wine	2,510	2,781	4,584	6,549	7,262	7,950	8,618
Malt beverages	10,382	13,251	23,464	27,946	29,947	34,356	34,751
Coffee, including products	1,214	989	1,370	1,323	1,307	1,359	1,393
Rubber and allied gums, crude	840	1,044	1,232	1,158	1,169	1,012	1,028
Beef, pork, lamb, and poultry meats [1] . . .	1,169	1,050	1,579	1,876	1,804	1,631	1,631
Grains [3]	2,071	4,553	4,622	3,701	3,726	4,718	5,576
Biscuits, pasta, and noodles	300	489	711	934	1,001	1,033	1,084
Feeds and fodders [2]	959	1,247	1,224	1,063	963	1,022	1,236
Fruits, nuts, and preparations [4]	5,401	6,530	8,354	9,122	9,570	9,897	10,711
Vegetables, fresh or frozen.	1,898	2,777	3,763	5,061	5,183	5,404	5,965
Tobacco, unmanufactured	173	190	216	254	233	249	245
Oilseeds and oilnuts	509	713	1,056	800	818	1,091	1,276
Vegetable oils and waxes.	1,204	1,509	1,846	2,274	2,386	2,897	3,117
Oilcake and meal	316	805	1,254	1,779	1,541	1,663	1,716

[1] Includes variety meats.   [2] Excluding oil meal.   [3] Includes wheat, corn, oats, barley, and rice.   [4] Includes bananas and plantains.

Source: U.S. Department of Agriculture, Economic Research Service, "Foreign Agricultural Trade of the United States (FATUS)"; <http://www.ers.usda.gov/data/fatus/> and "U.S. Trade Internet System"; <http://www.fas.usda.gov/ustrade>.

Table 809. **Agricultural Exports and Imports—Value: 1990 to 2007**

[In billions of dollars, except percent (16.6 represents $16,600,000,000). Includes Puerto Rico, U.S. territories, and shipments under foreign aid programs. Excludes fish, forest products, distilled liquors, manufactured tobacco, and products made from cotton; but includes raw tobacco, raw cotton, rubber, beer and wine, and processed agricultural products]

Year	Trade balance	Exports, domestic products	Percent of all exports	Imports for con- sumption	Percent of all imports	Year	Trade balance	Exports, domestic products	Percent of all exports	Imports for con- sumption	Percent of all imports
1990...	16.6	39.5	11	22.9	5	2001...	14.3	53.7	8	39.4	3
1995...	26.0	56.3	10	30.3	4	2002...	11.2	53.1	8	41.9	4
1996...	26.8	60.3	10	33.5	4	2003...	12.0	59.4	9	47.4	4
1997...	21.0	57.2	9	36.1	4	2004...	7.4	61.4	8	54.0	4
1998...	14.9	51.8	8	36.9	4	2005...	3.9	63.2	8	59.3	4
1999...	10.7	48.4	8	37.7	4	2006...	5.6	70.9	8	65.3	4
2000...	12.3	51.3	7	39.0	3	2007...	18.0	89.9	9	71.9	4

Source: U.S. Department of Agriculture, Economic Research Service, "Foreign Agricultural Trade of the United States (FATUS)"; <http://www.ers.usda.gov/data/fatus/> and U.S. Department of Agriculture, Foreign Agricultural Service, "U.S. Trade Internet System"; <http://www.fas.usda.gov/ustrade>.

Table 810. **Agricultural Imports—Value by Selected Commodity: 1990 to 2007**

[22,918 represents $22,918,000,000. See headnote, Table 809]

Commodity	Value (mil. dol.)							Percent distribution		
	1990	2000	2003	2004	2005	2006	2007	1990	2000	2007
Total [1]	22,918	38,974	47,376	53,977	59,317	65,326	71,937	100.0	100.0	100.0
Cattle, live............	978	1,152	867	543	1,039	1,546	1,878	4.3	3.0	2.6
Beef and veal	1,872	2,399	2,623	3,626	3,651	3,221	3,285	8.2	6.2	4.6
Pork.................	938	997	1,190	1,367	1,281	1,197	1,163	4.1	2.6	1.6
Dairy products	891	1,671	1,978	2,424	2,686	2,711	2,880	3.9	4.3	4.0
Grains and feeds	1,188	3,075	3,910	4,291	4,527	5,321	6,422	5.2	7.9	8.9
Fruits and preparations ...	2,167	3,846	4,722	5,079	5,842	6,517	7,445	9.5	9.9	10.3
Vegetables and preparations [2]........	1,979	3,958	5,349	6,077	6,410	7,008	7,714	8.6	10.2	10.7
Sugar and related products	1,213	1,555	2,129	2,107	2,494	3,046	2,595	5.3	4.0	3.6
Wine	917	2,207	3,268	3,416	3,762	4,155	4,641	4.0	5.7	6.5
Malt beverages	923	2,179	2,681	2,767	3,096	3,583	3,625	4.0	5.6	5.0
Oilseeds and products....	952	1,847	2,013	2,944	2,998	3,505	4,329	4.2	4.7	6.0
Coffee and products	1,915	2,700	1,958	2,263	2,976	3,313	3,770	8.4	6.9	5.2
Cocoa and products	1,072	1,404	2,439	2,484	2,751	2,659	2,662	4.7	3.6	3.7
Rubber, crude natural	707	842	1,047	1,466	1,552	2,029	2,119	3.1	2.2	2.9

[1] Includes other commodities not shown separately.   [2] Includes pulses.

Source: U.S. Department of Agriculture, Economic Research Service, "Foreign Agricultural Trade of the United States (FATUS)"; <http://www.ers.usda.gov/data/fatus/> and U.S. Department of Agriculture, Foreign Agricultural Service, "U.S. Trade Internet System"; <http://www.fas.usda.gov/ustrade>.

Table 811. **Agricultural Imports—Value by Selected Countries of Origin: 1990 to 2007**

[22,918 represents $22,918,000,000. See headnote, Table 809]

Country	Value (mil. dol.)							Percent distribution		
	1990	2000	2003	2004	2005	2006	2007	1990	2000	2007
Total [1]	22,918	38,974	47,376	53,977	59,317	65,326	71,937	100.0	100.0	100.0
European Union [2]	5,016	8,303	11,005	12,402	13,413	14,465	15,287	21.9	21.3	21.3
Canada.............	3,171	8,661	10,286	11,453	12,270	13,432	15,245	13.8	22.2	21.2
Mexico.............	2,614	5,077	6,301	7,262	8,331	9,391	10,169	11.4	13.0	14.1
China [3].............	273	812	1,288	1,615	1,872	2,265	2,918	1.2	2.1	4.1
Brazil..............	1,563	1,144	1,550	1,662	1,975	2,231	2,644	6.8	2.9	3.7
Australia............	1,174	1,592	2,120	2,486	2,421	2,487	2,632	5.1	4.1	3.7
Indonesia	683	998	1,227	1,490	1,702	2,042	2,081	3.0	2.6	2.9
Chile	481	1,026	1,216	1,342	1,521	1,777	1,841	2.1	2.6	2.6
New Zealand.........	855	1,132	1,318	1,598	1,712	1,669	1,734	3.7	2.9	2.4
Colombia............	790	1,123	1,031	1,162	1,437	1,480	1,540	3.4	2.9	2.1
Thailand............	470	779	926	1,083	1,094	1,330	1,507	2.0	2.0	2.1
Costa Rica	400	812	869	899	916	1,163	1,237	1.7	2.1	1.7
India...............	285	826	687	858	923	1,042	1,164	1.2	2.1	1.6
Malaysia	308	353	446	577	666	829	1,139	1.3	0.9	1.6
Argentina	389	672	572	616	831	992	1,084	1.7	1.7	1.5
Guatemala	497	710	764	784	920	924	1,067	2.2	1.8	1.5
Philippines...........	418	468	492	553	568	640	704	1.8	1.2	1.0
Ecuador	482	451	559	581	596	669	691	2.1	1.2	1.0
Peru...............	90	196	277	348	448	602	683	0.4	0.5	0.9
Vietnam	(NA)	200	249	376	422	495	663	(NA)	0.5	0.9

NA Not available.   [1] Includes other countries not shown separately.   [2] For consistency, data for all years are shown on the basis of 27 countries in the European Union; see footnote 3, Table 1330.   [3] See footnote 2, Table 1288.

Source: U.S. Department of Agriculture, Foreign Agricultural Service, "U.S. Trade Internet System"; <http://www.fas.usda.gov /ustrade>; (accessed: 14 May 2008).

530   Agriculture

Table 812. **Selected Farm Products—United States and World Production and Exports: 2000 to 2007**

[In metric tons, except as indicated (61 represents 61,000,000). Metric ton = 1.102 short tons or .984 long tons]

Commodity	Unit	Amount						United States as percent of world		
		United States			World					
		2000	2005	2007	2000	2005	2007	2000	2005	2007
PRODUCTION [1]										
Wheat	Million	61	57	56	581	621	606	10.4	9.2	9.3
Corn for grain	Million	252	282	332	590	699	780	42.7	40.4	42.6
Soybeans	Million	75	83	70	176	221	220	42.6	37.8	32.0
Rice, milled	Million	5.9	7.1	6.3	398	418	427	1.5	1.7	1.5
Cotton [2]	Million bales [3] . . .	17.0	23.3	21.6	87.7	121.4	122.1	19.3	19.2	17.7
EXPORTS [4]										
Wheat [5]	Million	28.0	27.4	35.5	104.0	113.5	110.5	26.9	24.2	32.1
Corn	Million	48.3	56.1	63.0	76.4	82.6	97.7	63.3	67.9	64.5
Soybeans	Million	27.1	25.6	29.7	53.9	63.9	75.3	50.3	40.0	39.4
Rice, milled basis	Million	2.8	3.9	3.0	22.8	29.2	31.3	12.5	13.2	9.7
Cotton [2]	Million bales [3] . . .	6.8	14.4	13.0	27.1	35.0	37.3	24.9	41.2	34.9

[1] Production years vary by commodity. In most cases, includes harvests from July 1 of the year shown through June 30 of the following year.   [2] For production and trade years ending in year shown.   [3] Bales of 480 lb. net weight.   [4] Trade years may vary by commodity. Wheat, corn, and soybean data are for trade year beginning in year shown. Rice data are for calendar year.   [5] Includes wheat flour on a grain equivalent.

Source: U.S. Department of Agriculture, Foreign Agricultural Service, *Foreign Agricultural Commodity Circular Series*, periodic; <http://www.fas.usda.gov/commodities.asp>.

Table 813. **Percent of U.S. Agricultural Commodity Output Exported: 1990 to 2006**

[All export shares are estimated from export and production weights]

Commodity group	1990–94, average	1995–99, average	2000–04, average	2000	2003	2004	2005	2006
Total agriculture	21.9	22.1	21.7	22.0	21.6	21.2	21.6	22.1
Livestock [1]	4.1	4.6	4.7	4.7	4.9	4.2	4.4	4.6
Red meat	4.1	7.1	8.0	8.1	9.0	5.8	7.3	8.7
Poultry meat	7.4	15.5	14.6	15.1	14.2	13.4	14.3	14.1
Dairy products	3.4	1.4	1.0	1.0	1.1	1.0	0.7	0.8
Crops [2]	25.1	25.4	24.9	25.2	24.9	24.3	24.8	25.5
Wheat and rice [3]	50.8	47.5	47.8	45.9	50.6	49.3	48.8	47.1
Coarse grains [4]	24.7	24.9	19.3	21.0	19.4	17.8	19.7	19.6
Oilseeds/meal/oil [5]	22.2	23.4	22.8	23.1	20.3	22.5	20.8	23.8
Fruits and nuts [6]	18.1	19.2	20.1	18.3	20.0	21.1	22.0	23.2
Vegetables [7]	9.9	12.1	9.2	8.7	9.3	9.2	9.7	10.5
Cotton and tobacco	40.7	38.1	58.5	43.8	66.1	65.9	75.9	70.0

[1] Includes live animals, eggs, fats and oils, wool, and fresh bovine hides.   [2] Includes sugar, honey, maple syrup. Excludes beer and confections.   [3] Includes wheat flour and other wheat products.   [4] Includes corn, barley, sorghum, oats, rye, and their products.   [5] The oilseed equivalent weights of oilmeals and vegetable oils are used.   [6] Includes fruit juices and wine, whose volume measures are converted to farm weight.   [7] Includes pulses (legumes) and hops. Frozen and canned exports are in farm-weight equivalent.

Source: U.S. Department of Agriculture, Economic Research Service, USDA's commodity yearbooks, "Foreign Agricultural Trade of the U.S."; <http://www.ers.usda.gov/data/fatus/> and "Production, Supply, and Distribution database"; <http://www.fas.usda.gov/psd/>.

Table 814. **Top 10 U.S. Export Markets for Selected Commodities: 2007**

[In thousands of metric tons (56,795 represents 56,795,000)]

Corn		Wheat [1]		Soybeans		Cotton [2]	
Country	Amount	Country	Amount	Country	Amount	Country	Amount
World, total	56,795	World, total . . .	32,888	World, total . . .	29,820	World, total . . .	3,258
Japan	14,952	Japan	3,278	China [3]	11,771	China [3]	1,046
Mexico	8,204	Egypt	3,120	Mexico	3,696	Turkey	575
Korea, South	4,568	Nigeria	2,665	Japan	3,293	Mexico	310
Taiwan [3]	4,170	Mexico	2,519	Taiwan [3]	2,095	Indonesia	242
Egypt	3,744	Iraq	1,553	Indonesia	1,257	Pakistan	169
Colombia	3,105	Philippines	1,482	Netherlands	1,136	Thailand	133
Canada	2,505	Taiwan [3]	1,292	Germany	865	Taiwan [3]	97
Syria	1,654	Korea, South	1,283	Egypt	543	Korea, South	83
Algeria	1,235	Yemen	1,087	Korea, South	489	Japan	71
Dominican Republic . .	1,145	Indonesia	1,042	Turkey	396	Vietnam	67
Rest of world	11,513	Rest of world	13,567	Rest of world . . .	4,279	Rest of world	466

[1] Unmilled.   [2] Excluding linters.   [3] See footnote 2, Table 1288.

Source: U.S. Department of Agriculture, Foreign Agricultural Service, "FAS Online, U.S. Trade Exports—FATUS Commodity Aggregations"; <http://www.fas.usda.gov/ustrade/USTExFatus.asp>; (accessed: 15 May 2008).

U.S. Census Bureau, Statistical Abstract of the United States: 2009

Table 815. **Agricultural Exports—Value by Principal Commodities: 1990 to 2007**

[**(39,495 represents $39,495,000,000)**. See headnote, Table 809]

Commodity	Value (mil. dol.)							Percent distribution		
	1990	2000	2003	2004	2005	2006	2007	1990	2000	2007
Total agricultural exports . . .	**39,495**	**51,265**	**59,392**	**61,426**	**63,182**	**70,948**	**89,907**	**100.0**	**100.0**	**100.0**
Animals and animal products [1]	6,636	11,600	12,161	10,369	12,226	13,497	17,163	16.8	22.6	19.1
Meat and meat products	2,558	5,276	5,741	3,240	4,299	5,185	6,108	6.5	10.3	6.8
Poultry and poultry products	910	2,235	2,287	2,577	3,138	2,932	4,095	2.3	4.4	4.6
Grains and feeds [1]	14,386	13,620	15,054	17,636	16,364	19,142	27,871	36.4	26.6	31.0
Wheat and products	4,035	3,578	4,099	5,273	4,520	4,359	8,588	10.2	7.0	9.6
Corn	6,037	4,469	4,724	5,875	4,789	6,992	9,755	15.3	8.7	10.8
Fruits and preparations	2,007	2,743	2,973	3,162	3,468	3,760	4,152	5.1	5.4	4.6
Fresh fruits	1,486	2,080	2,273	2,394	2,697	2,871	3,134	3.8	4.1	3.5
Nuts and preparations	978	1,322	1,762	2,276	2,992	3,153	3,385	2.5	2.6	3.8
Vegetables and preparations [2]	1,836	3,112	3,056	3,258	3,571	3,913	4,305	4.6	6.1	4.8
Oilseeds and products	5,725	8,584	11,652	10,439	10,229	11,307	15,599	14.5	16.7	17.3
Soybeans	3,550	5,258	7,960	6,668	6,274	6,936	10,004	9.0	10.3	11.1
Tobacco, unmanufactured	1,441	1,204	1,038	1,044	990	1,141	1,208	3.6	2.3	1.3
Cotton, excluding linters	2,783	1,873	3,361	4,226	3,921	4,502	4,578	7.0	3.7	5.1
Other.	3,702	7,207	8,336	9,016	9,421	10,533	11,646	9.4	14.1	13.0

[1] Includes commodities not shown separately.　　[2] Includes pulses.

Source: U.S. Department of Agriculture, Economic Research Service, "Foreign Agricultural Trade of the United States (FATUS)"; <http://www.ers.usda.gov/data/fatus/> and U.S. Department of Agriculture, Foreign Agricultural Service, "U.S. Trade Internet System"; <http://www.fas.usda.gov/ustrade>.

Table 816. **Agricultural Exports—Value by Selected Countries of Destination: 1990 to 2007**

[**(39,495 represents $39,495,000,000)**. See headnote, Table 809]

Country	Value (mil. dol.)							Percent distribution		
	1990	2000	2003	2004	2005	2006	2007	1990	2000	2007
Total agricultural exports [1] . . .	**39,495**	**51,265**	**59,392**	**61,426**	**63,182**	**70,948**	**89,907**	**100.0**	**100.0**	**100.0**
Canada	4,214	7,643	9,315	9,742	10,618	11,951	14,004	10.7	14.9	15.6
Mexico	2,560	6,410	7,891	8,510	9,429	10,881	12,704	6.5	12.5	14.1
Caribbean.	1,015	1,408	1,590	1,850	1,913	2,114	2,588	2.6	2.7	2.9
Central America	483	1,121	1,338	1,429	1,589	1,832	2,373	1.2	2.2	2.6
South America.	1,063	1,704	1,912	1,955	1,943	2,364	3,508	2.7	3.3	3.9
Asia, excluding Middle East [2]	15,857	19,877	23,688	23,009	22,543	25,743	32,354	40.1	38.8	36.0
Japan	8,142	9,292	8,906	8,147	7,931	8,390	10,104	20.6	18.1	11.2
Korea, South	2,650	2,546	2,886	2,489	2,233	2,851	3,518	6.7	5.0	3.9
Taiwan [3]	1,663	1,996	2,025	2,065	2,301	2,477	3,112	4.2	3.9	3.5
China [3, 4]	818	1,716	5,017	5,542	5,233	6,711	8,314	2.1	3.3	9.2
Indonesia	275	668	996	925	958	1,102	1,542	0.7	1.3	1.7
Europe/Eurasia [2]	10,162	7,676	7,815	8,319	8,569	8,761	10,827	25.7	15.0	12.0
European Union [5]	7,474	6,515	6,736	6,953	7,052	7,408	8,770	18.9	12.7	9.8
Middle East [2]	1,728	2,323	2,549	2,833	2,844	3,332	4,960	4.4	4.5	5.5
Turkey	226	658	921	944	1,062	1,030	1,489	0.6	1.3	1.7
Africa [2]	1,848	2,308	2,489	2,953	2,773	3,087	5,197	4.7	4.5	5.8
Egypt	687	1,050	967	935	819	1,022	1,801	1.7	2.0	2.0
Oceania	343	490	621	601	742	760	964	0.9	1.0	1.1

X Not applicable.　[1] Totals include transshipments through Canada, but transshipments are not distributed by country after 1998.　[2] Includes areas not shown separately.　[3] See footnote 2, Table 1288.　[4] China includes Macao. However Hong Kong remains separate economically until 2050 and is not included.　[5] For consistency, data for all years are shown on the basis of 27 countries in the European Union; see footnote 3, Table 1330.

Source: U.S. Department of Agriculture, Economic Research Service, "Foreign Agricultural Trade of the United States (FATUS)"; <http://www.ers.usda.gov/data/fatus/> and U.S. Department of Agriculture, Foreign Agricultural Service, "U.S. Trade Internet System"; <http://www.fas.usda.gov/ustrade>.

Table 817. **Cropland Used for Crops and Acreages of Crops Harvested: 1990 to 2007**

[In millions of acres, except as indicated (341 represents 341,000,000)]

Item	1990	1995	2000	2001	2002	2003	2004	2005	2006	2007
Cropland used for crops	**341**	**332**	**345**	**340**	**340**	**342**	**336**	**337**	**330**	**336**
Index (**1977 = 100**)	90	88	91	90	90	90	89	89	87	89
Cropland harvested [1]	310	302	314	311	307	316	312	314	304	312
Crop failure	6	8	11	10	17	10	9	6	11	7
Cultivated summer fallow	25	22	20	19	16	16	15	16	15	16
Cropland idled by all federal programs	62	55	31	34	34	34	35	35	37	37
Acres of crops harvested [2] . . .	**322**	**314**	**325**	**321**	**316**	**324**	**321**	**321**	**312**	**321**

[1] Land supporting one or more harvested crops.　[2] Area in principal crops harvested as reported by Crop Reporting Board plus acreages in fruits, vegetables for sale, tree nuts, and other minor crops.

Source: U.S. Department of Agriculture, Economic Research Service, *Major Uses of Land in the United States, 2002*, 2006; Also in *Agricultural Statistics*, annual. Beginning 1995, *Agricultural Resources and Environmental Indicators*, periodic, and *AREI Updates: Cropland Use.* See also ERS Briefing Room at <http://www.ers.usda.gov/Briefing/LandUse/majorlandusechapter.htm#trends>.

Table 818. **Principal Crops—Production, Supply, and Disappearance: 1990 to 2007**

[**67.0 represents 67,000,000.** Marketing year beginning January 1 for potatoes, May 1 for hay, June 1 for wheat, August 1 for cotton, September 1 for soybeans and corn. Acreage, production, and yield of all crops periodically revised on basis of census data]

Item	Unit	1990	2000	2003	2004	2005	2006	2007
CORN FOR GRAIN								
Acreage harvested	Million	67.0	72.4	70.9	73.6	75.1	70.6	86.5
Yield per acre	Bushel	119	137	142	160	148	149	151
Production	Mil. bu.	7,934	9,915	10,089	11,807	11,114	10,535	13,074
Farm price [1]	Dol./bu.	2.28	1.85	2.42	2.06	2.00	3.04	4.00
Farm value	Mil. dol.	18,192	18,499	24,477	24,381	22,198	32,095	52,090
Total supply [2]	Mil. bu.	9,282	11,639	11,190	12,776	13,237	12,514	14,393
Total disappearance [3]	Mil. bu.	7,761	9,740	10,232	10,662	11,270	11,210	12,955
Ethanol	Mil. bu.	(NA)	(NA)	1,168	1,323	1,603	2,117	3,200
Exports	Mil. bu.	1,725	1,941	1,900	1,818	2,134	2,125	2,450
Ending stocks	Mil. bu.	1,521	1,899	958	2,114	1,967	1,304	1,438
SOYBEANS								
Acreage harvested	Million	56.5	72.4	72.5	74.0	71.3	74.6	62.8
Yield per acre	Bushel	34.1	38.1	33.9	42.2	43.0	42.7	41.0
Production	Mil. bu.	1,926	2,758	2,454	3,124	3,063	3,188	2,585
Farm price [1]	Dol./bu.	5.74	4.54	7.34	5.74	5.66	6.43	10.40
Farm value	Mil. dol.	11,042	12,467	18,014	17,895	17,269	20,416	26,752
Total supply [2]	Mil. bu.	2,169	3,052	2,638	3,242	3,322	3,647	3,165
Total disappearance [3]	Mil. bu.	1,840	2,804	2,525	2,986	2,873	3,073	3,005
Exports	Mil. bu.	557	996	887	1,097	940	1,118	1,005
Ending stocks	Mil. bu.	329	248	112	256	449	574	160
HAY								
Acreage harvested	Million	61.0	59.9	63.4	62.0	61.7	60.9	61.6
Yield per acre	Sh. tons	2.40	2.54	2.49	2.55	2.45	2.34	2.44
Production	Mil. sh. tons	146	152	158	158	151	142	150
Farm price [4, 5]	Dol./ton	80.60	84.60	85.50	92.00	98.20	110.00	133.00
Farm value	Mil. dol.	10,462	11,417	12,007	12,212	12,585	13,791	16,961
WHEAT								
Acreage harvested	Million	69.1	53.1	53.1	50.0	50.1	46.8	51.0
Yield per acre	Bushel	39.5	42.0	44.2	43.2	42.0	38.7	40.5
Production	Mil. bu.	2,730	2,228	2,345	2,158	2,105	1,812	2,067
Farm price [1]	Dol./bu.	2.61	2.62	3.40	3.40	3.42	4.26	6.65
Farm value	Mil. dol.	7,184	5,782	7,929	7,283	7,171	7,710	13,669
Total supply [2]	Mil. bu.	3,303	3,268	2,899	2,775	2,726	2,505	2,613
Total disappearance [3]	Mil. bu.	2,435	2,392	2,353	2,235	2,155	2,049	2,341
Exports	Mil. bu.	1,069	1,062	1,158	1,066	1,003	909	1,200
Ending stocks	Mil. bu.	868	876	546	540	571	456	272
COTTON								
Acreage harvested	Million	11.7	13.1	12.0	13.1	13.8	12.7	10.5
Yield per acre	Pounds	634	632	730	855	831	814	871
Production [6]	Mil. bales [7]	15.5	17.2	18.3	23.3	23.9	21.6	19.0
Farm price [1]	Cents/lb.	68.2	51.6	63.0	43.5	49.7	48.4	56.9
Farm value	Mil. dol.	5,076	4,260	5,517	4,854	5,695	5,013	5,197
Total supply [2]	Mil. bales [7]	18.5	21.1	23.7	26.7	29.4	27.7	28.5
Total disappearance [3]	Mil. bales [7]	16.5	15.6	20.0	21.1	23.4	18.0	20.3
Exports	Mil. bales [7]	7.8	6.7	13.8	14.4	17.6	13.0	15.7
Ending stocks [8]	Mil. bales [7]	2.3	6.0	3.5	5.5	6.1	9.5	8.2
POTATOES								
Acreage harvested	Million	1.4	1.3	1.2	1.2	1.1	1.1	1.1
Yield per acre	Cwt. [9]	293	381	367	391	390	393	398
Production	Mil. cwt. [9]	402	514	458	456	424	441	449
Farm price [1]	Dol./cwt. [9]	6.08	5.08	5.89	5.66	7.06	7.33	7.12
Farm value	Mil. dol.	2,431	2,591	2,686	2,575	2,991	3,226	3,198

NA Not available. [1] Marketing year average price. U.S. prices are computed by weighting U.S. monthly prices by estimated monthly marketings and do not include an allowance for outstanding loans and government purchases and payments. [2] Comprises production, imports, and beginning stocks. [3] Includes feed, residual, and other domestic uses not shown separately. [4] Prices are for hay sold baled. [5] Season average prices received by farmers. U.S. prices are computed by weighting state prices by estimated sales. [6] State production figures, which conform with annual ginning enumeration with allowance for cross-state ginnings, rounded to thousands and added for U.S. totals. [7] Bales of 480 pounds, net weight. [8] Stock estimates based on Census Bureau data which results in an unaccounted difference between supply and use estimates and changes in ending stocks. [9] Cwt = hundredweight (100 pounds).

Source: Production—U.S. Department of Agriculture, National Agricultural Statistics Service, *Crop Production*, annual; and *Crop Values*, annual. Supply and disappearance—U.S. Department of Agriculture, Economic Research Service, *Feed Situation*, quarterly; *Fats and Oils Situation*, quarterly; *Wheat Situation*, quarterly; *Cotton and Wool Outlook Statistics*, periodic; and *Agricultural Supply and Demand Estimates*, periodic. Data are also in *Agricultural Statistics*, annual; and "Agricultural Outlook: Statistical Indicators"; <http://www.ers.usda.gov/publications/agoutlook/aotables/>.

Agriculture 533

Table 819. Corn—Acreage, Production, and Value by Leading States: 2005 to 2007

[75,117 represents 75,117,000. One bushel of corn = 56 pounds]

State	Acreage harvested (1,000 acres) 2005	2006	2007	Yield per acre (bu.) 2005	2006	2007	Production (mil. bu.) 2005	2006	2007	Price ($/bu.) 2005	2006	2007	Farm value (mil. dol.) 2005	2006	2007
U.S.[1]..	75,117	70,648	86,542	148	149	151	11,114	10,535	13,074	2.00	3.04	4.00	22,198	32,095	52,090
IA	12,500	12,350	13,850	173	166	171	2,163	2,050	2,368	1.94	3.03	4.00	4,195	6,212	9,473
IL	11,950	11,150	13,050	143	163	175	1,709	1,817	2,284	2.08	3.07	4.05	3,554	5,580	9,249
NE	8,250	7,750	9,200	154	152	160	1,271	1,178	1,472	1.92	3.00	4.00	2,439	3,534	5,888
MN	6,850	6,850	7,800	174	161	146	1,192	1,103	1,139	1.86	2.89	3.85	2,217	3,187	4,384
IN	5,770	5,380	6,370	154	157	155	889	845	987	2.00	3.17	4.05	1,777	2,678	3,999
SD	3,950	3,220	4,500	119	97	121	470	312	545	1.79	2.88	3.85	841	900	2,096
OH	3,250	2,960	3,610	143	159	150	465	471	542	1.98	3.08	3.95	920	1,450	2,139
KS	3,450	3,000	3,700	135	115	140	466	345	518	2.07	3.08	4.00	964	1,063	2,072
MO	2,970	2,630	3,250	111	138	142	330	363	462	2.03	3.06	3.95	669	1,111	1,823
WI	2,900	2,800	3,280	148	143	135	429	400	443	1.94	3.04	3.90	833	1,217	1,727
TX	1,850	1,450	2,000	114	121	148	211	175	296	2.47	3.20	4.15	521	561	1,228
MI	2,010	1,960	2,350	143	147	124	287	288	291	1.88	3.10	3.95	540	893	1,151
ND	1,200	1,400	2,350	129	111	116	155	155	273	1.80	2.77	3.75	279	430	1,022
KY	1,180	1,040	1,360	132	146	129	156	152	175	2.21	3.18	4.10	344	483	719
CO	950	860	1,060	148	156	142	141	134	151	2.23	3.02	4.00	314	405	602
MS	365	325	940	129	110	150	47	36	141	2.22	2.84	3.70	105	102	522
PA	960	960	980	122	122	128	117	117	125	2.30	3.54	4.35	269	415	546
LA	330	290	730	136	140	165	45	41	120	2.25	2.80	3.80	101	114	458
NC	700	740	1,020	120	132	100	84	98	102	2.33	3.03	3.85	196	296	393
AR	230	180	590	131	146	168	30	26	99	2.15	2.73	3.75	65	72	372
TN	595	500	785	130	125	106	77	63	83	2.07	2.93	3.70	160	183	308

[1] Includes other states, not shown separately.

Source: U.S. Department of Agriculture, National Agricultural Statistics Service, *Crop Production*, annual; and *Crop Values*, annual.

Table 820. Soybeans—Acreage, Production, and Value by Leading States: 2005 to 2007

[71,251 represents 71,251,000. One bushel of soybeans = 60 pounds]

State	Acreage harvested (1,000 acres) 2005	2006	2007	Yield per acre (bu.) 2005	2006	2007	Production (mil. bu.) 2005	2006	2007	Price ($/bu.) 2005	2006	2007	Farm value (mil. dol.) 2005	2006	2007
U.S.[1]..	71,251	74,602	62,820	43	43	41	3,063	3,188	2,585	5.66	6.43	10.40	17,269	20,416	26,752
IA	10,000	10,100	8,520	53	51	52	525	510	439	5.54	6.58	10.90	2,909	3,356	4,783
IL	9,450	10,050	8,150	47	48	43	439	482	350	5.76	6.68	11.00	2,531	3,222	3,855
MN	6,800	7,250	6,150	45	44	41	306	319	252	5.53	6.26	10.10	1,692	1,997	2,547
IN	5,380	5,680	4,680	49	50	45	264	284	211	5.78	6.53	10.50	1,524	1,855	2,211
OH	4,480	4,620	4,130	45	47	47	202	217	194	5.74	6.46	10.10	1,157	1,403	1,961
NE	4,660	5,010	3,770	51	50	51	235	251	190	5.55	6.05	9.95	1,306	1,516	1,894
MO	4,910	5,110	4,550	37	38	37	182	194	168	5.67	6.47	10.50	1,030	1,256	1,768
SD	3,850	3,850	3,180	35	34	42	135	131	134	5.39	6.03	9.80	726	789	1,309
ND	2,900	3,870	2,990	36	31	35	104	120	105	5.37	5.98	9.80	561	717	1,026
AR	3,000	3,070	2,790	34	35	36	102	107	100	5.92	6.41	9.80	604	689	984
KS	2,850	3,080	2,550	37	32	33	105	99	84	5.45	6.37	10.60	575	628	892
MI	1,990	1,990	1,740	39	45	39	77	90	68	5.73	6.27	9.85	439	561	668
MS	1,590	1,650	1,420	37	26	40	58	43	57	5.92	6.23	9.25	344	267	525
WI	1,580	1,640	1,330	44	44	39	70	72	52	5.64	6.04	9.70	392	436	503

[1] Includes other states, not shown separately.

Source: U.S. Department of Agriculture, National Agricultural Statistics Service, *Crop Production*, annual; and *Crop Values*, annual.

Table 821. Wheat—Acreage, Production, and Value by Leading States: 2005 to 2007

[50,119 represents 50,119,000. One bushel of wheat = 60 pounds]

State	Acreage harvested (1,000 acres) 2005	2006	2007	Yield per acre (bu.) 2005	2006	2007	Production (mil. bu.) 2005	2006	2007	Price ($/bu.) 2005	2006	2007	Farm value (mil. dol.) 2005	2006	2007
U.S.[1]..	50,119	46,810	51,011	42.0	38.7	40.5	2,105	1,812	2,067	3.42	4.26	6.65	7,171	7,710	13,669
ND	8,835	8,290	8,405	34.4	30.4	35.7	304	252	300	3.55	4.50	7.70	1,077	1,130	2,332
KS	9,500	9,100	8,600	40.0	32.0	33.0	380	291	284	3.31	4.56	6.20	1,258	1,328	1,760
MT	5,235	5,215	5,065	36.8	29.4	29.6	192	153	150	3.63	4.54	7.60	698	694	1,138
SD	3,193	2,576	3,328	41.8	32.6	44.3	133	84	148	3.65	4.44	6.55	485	374	961
TX	3,000	1,400	3,800	32.0	24.0	37.0	96	34	141	3.44	4.47	6.30	330	150	886
WA	2,225	2,225	2,137	62.6	62.9	60.2	139	140	129	3.32	4.49	7.60	456	626	978
OK	4,000	3,400	3,500	32.0	24.0	28.0	128	82	98	3.39	4.70	6.30	434	384	617
CO	2,219	1,919	2,369	24.4	21.6	40.3	54	42	96	3.43	4.54	6.35	186	189	608

[1] Includes other states, not shown separately.

Source: U.S. Department of Agriculture, National Agricultural Statistics Service, *Crop Production*, annual; and *Crop Values*, annual.

Table 822. Commercial Vegetable and Other Specified Crops—Area, Production, and Value, 2005 to 2007, and Leading Producing States, 2007

[303 represents 303,000. Except as noted, relates to commercial production for fresh market and processing combined. Includes market garden areas but excludes minor producing acreage in minor producing states. Excludes production for home use in farm and nonfarm gardens. Value is for season or crop year and should not be confused with calendar-year income]

Crop	Area [1] (1,000 acres)			Production [2] (1,000 short tons)			Value [3] (mil. dol.)			Leading states in order of production, 2007
	2005	2006	2007	2005	2006	2007	2005	2006	2007	
Beans, snap	303	300	301	1,096	1,104	1,091	415	445	521	WI, OR, MI [4]
Beans, dry edible	1,534	1,538	1,479	1,339	1,212	1,269	516	556	677	ND, MI
Broccoli	135	139	138	997	1,010	1,018	570	674	737	CA, AZ
Cabbage [5]	74	74	74	1,214	1,241	1,291	326	343	413	CA, NY, GA
Cantaloupes [5]	90	86	86	1,056	1,023	1,060	336	352	313	CA, AZ, GA
Carrots	99	97	99	1,805	1,693	1,703	597	565	639	CA [5]
Cauliflower	42	40	39	364	351	350	222	221	238	CA
Celery	27	28	28	934	962	1,014	259	350	413	CA, MI
Corn, sweet	642	613	602	4,526	4,421	4,309	814	817	863	(NA)
Fresh market	238	228	234	1,351	1,335	1,412	597	611	626	FL, CA, GA
Processed	404	385	368	3,175	3,086	2,897	217	206	237	WA, MN
Cucumbers	166	158	149	1,025	990	976	362	395	396	FL, GA [4]
Garlic	30	30	30	239	241	245	208	153	219	CA, OR
Lettuce, head [5]	177	180	183	3,287	3,150	3,156	1,019	1,062	1,387	CA, AZ
Lettuce, leaf [5]	65	92	93	794	1,121	1,096	531	794	656	CA, AZ
Lettuce, Romaine [5] . . .	60	86	85	997	1,325	1,377	386	594	708	CA, AZ
Mushrooms [6]	29	28	28	419	417	407	862	849	915	PA, CA
Onions	165	165	159	3,675	3,659	3,971	849	1,057	840	CA, WA
Peppers, bell	57	55	54	802	762	734	535	512	468	CA, FL, GA
Potatoes	1,087	1,122	1,129	21,196	22,067	22,458	2,991	3,226	3,198	ID, WA
Squash	55	57	54	417	461	394	214	223	228	MI, CA, GA
Sweet potatoes	88	87	98	787	812	923	284	295	374	NC, CA, MS
Tomatoes	408	422	433	12,107	12,452	14,512	2,220	2,324	2,180	(NA)
Fresh market	126	123	119	1,913	1,840	1,852	1,599	1,619	1,278	FL, CA, GA
Processed	282	299	314	10,193	10,612	12,660	621	705	902	CA
Watermelons	138	141	151	1,920	2,112	2,143	446	437	476	GA, FL, CA

NA Not available.   [1] Area of crops for harvest for fresh market, including any partially harvested or not harvested because of low prices or other factors, plus area harvested for processing.   [2] Excludes some quantities not marketed.   [3] Fresh market vegetables valued at f.o.b. shipping point. Processing vegetables are equivalent returns at packinghouse door.   [4] Processed only.   [5] Fresh market only.   [6] Area is shown in million square feet. All data are for marketing year ending June 30.

Source: U.S. Department of Agriculture, National Agricultural Statistics Service, *Vegetables, 2007 Summary*, January 2008. Also in *Agricultural Statistics*, annual.

Table 823. Fresh Fruits and Vegetables—Supply and Use: 2000 to 2007

[In millions of pounds, except per capita in pounds (8,355 represents 8,355,000,000)]

Year	Utilized production [1]	Imports [2]	Supply, [1] total	Exports [2]	Consumption	
					Total	Per capita [3]
FRUITS						
Citrus:						
2000	8,355	720	9,075	2,445	6,630	23.5
2002	8,256	707	8,962	2,245	6,718	23.4
2003	8,442	969	9,411	2,456	6,955	23.9
2004	8,156	993	9,149	2,495	6,654	22.7
2005	7,320	1,123	8,443	2,035	6,408	21.6
2006	7,306	1,163	8,469	2,021	6,447	21.5
Noncitrus: [4]						
2000	13,850	11,225	25,074	3,389	21,685	76.6
2002	12,833	11,552	24,385	2,902	21,483	74.4
2003	13,386	12,164	25,550	2,835	22,716	77.9
2004	14,335	12,325	26,660	3,079	23,581	80.1
2005	14,389	12,460	26,849	3,479	23,370	78.6
2006	13,955	13,109	27,064	3,055	24,009	80.0
VEGETABLES AND MELONS						
2000	46,922	6,719	54,986	4,200	48,563	172.0
2002	46,724	7,697	55,762	4,265	49,388	171.4
2003	46,901	8,076	56,227	4,251	49,944	171.6
2004	48,247	8,193	57,693	4,363	50,700	172.7
2005	47,536	8,932	57,959	4,264	51,658	174.3
2006	48,732	9,522	59,534	3,953	53,590	179.1
2007	50,009	10,208	61,379	3,815	55,220	182.8
POTATOES						
2000	13,185	806	13,990	677	13,313	47.1
2002	12,567	883	13,450	693	12,757	44.3
2003	13,349	872	14,221	590	13,631	46.8
2004	13,181	755	13,936	479	13,457	45.8
2005	12,428	788	13,216	639	12,577	42.4
2006	12,410	817	13,227	626	12,601	42.0
2007	12,825	940	13,765	565	13,200	43.6

[1] Crop-year basis for fruits. Supply data for vegetables include ending stocks of previous year.   [2] Fiscal year for fruits; calendar year for vegetables and potatoes.   [3] Based on Census Bureau estimated total population.   [4] Includes bananas.

Source: U.S. Department of Agriculture, Economic Research Service, *Fruit and Tree Nuts Situation and Outlook Yearbook*, and *Vegetables and Melons Situation and Outlook Yearbook*.

Table 824. Fruits and Nuts—Utilized Production and Value, 2005 to 2007, and Leading Producing States, 2007

[4,801 represents 4,801,000]

Fruit or nut	Unit	Utilized production [1]			Farm value (mil. dol.)			Leading states in order of production, 2007
		2005	2006	2007	2005	2006	2007	
Apples [2]	1,000 tons	4,801	4,878	4,650	1,675	2,238	2,398	WA, NY, MI
Apricots	1,000 tons	77	45	88	40	30	43	CA, WA
Avocados	1,000 tons	312	146	(NA)	354	264	(NA)	CA, FL
Blackberries, cultivated (OR)	1,000 tons	24	21	29	37	36	28	OR
Blueberries	1,000 tons	149	178	180	381	558	589	MI, ME, NJ
Cherries, sweet	1,000 tons	244	288	319	484	465	584	WA, CA, OR
Cherries, tart	1,000 tons	134	125	125	64	54	67	MI, UT, NY
Cranberries	1,000 tons	312	340	320	222	262	280	WI, MA, NJ
Dates (California)	1,000 tons	17	19	18	25	25	32	CA
Grapefruit	1,000 tons	1,018	1,232	1,577	383	345	283	FL, TX, CA
Grapes (13 states)	1,000 tons	7,811	6,366	6,729	3,494	3,304	3,381	CA, WA, NY
Lemons	1,000 tons	870	980	703	306	410	403	CA
Nectarines	1,000 tons	251	232	252	127	121	86	CA, WA
Olives (California)	1,000 tons	142	24	133	80	18	87	CA
Oranges [3]	1,000 tons	9,252	9,021	7,589	1,475	1,830	2,111	FL, CA
Peaches	1,000 tons	1,145	987	1,101	512	513	499	CA, NJ, MI
Pears	1,000 tons	822	831	880	294	330	346	WA, CA, OR
Pineapples	1,000 tons	212	188	(NA)	79	76	(NA)	HI
Plums (CA)	1,000 tons	171	158	142	92	109	94	CA
Prunes (dried basis) (CA)	1,000 tons	94	189	77	138	263	112	CA
Raspberries	1,000 tons	91	92	82	256	285	328	CA
Strawberries	1,000 tons	1,161	1,202	1,250	1,396	1,520	1,746	CA, FL
Tangerines	1,000 tons	335	417	339	127	138	141	FL, CA
Almonds (shelled basis) (CA)	Mil. lb.	915	1,120	1,360	2,526	2,259	2,325	CA
Hazelnuts (in the shell)	1,000 tons	28	43	36	62	46	66	OR
Macadamia nuts	1,000 tons	27	29	18	44	39	22	HI
Pecans (in the shell) (11 states)	1,000 tons	140	103	175	407	321	376	GA, NM, TX
Pistachios	1,000 tons	142	119	205	580	450	549	CA
Walnuts, English (in the shell)	1,000 tons	355	346	320	557	564	(NA)	CA

NA Not available. [1] Excludes quantities not harvested or not marketed. [2] Production in commercial orchards with 100 or more bearing age trees. [3] Temples included in early, midseason, and Navel varieties beginning with the 2006–2007 season.

Source: U.S. Department of Agriculture, National Agricultural Statistics Service, *Noncitrus Fruits and Nuts, 2007 Preliminary Summary*, January 2008; and *Citrus Fruits, 2007 Summary*, September 2007.

Table 825. Nuts—Supply and Use: 2000 to 2006

[In millions of pounds (shelled) (331 represents 331,000,000). For marketing season beginning in year shown]

Year	Beginning stocks	Marketable production [1]	Imports	Supply, total	Consumption	Exports	Ending stocks
2000	331	1,117	293	1,741	723	781	237
2001	237	1,335	339	1,911	810	849	252
2002	252	1,562	363	2,177	926	928	323
2003	323	1,504	431	2,258	998	963	297
2004	299	1,546	504	2,348	1,000	1,040	308
2005	308	1,499	433	2,241	822	1,126	293
2006, total [2]	**293**	**1,652**	**470**	**2,415**	**1,011**	**1,116**	**287**
Almonds	112	1,083	10	1,206	304	768	134
Pecans	69	91	86	246	149	37	60
Pistachios	56	119	1	176	48	72	57
Hazelnuts	1	36	14	51	23	26	2
Walnuts	55	296	2	353	160	158	35

[1] Utilized production minus inedibles and noncommercial usage. [2] Includes macadamia nuts, Brazil nuts, cashew nuts, pine nuts, chestnuts, and mixed nuts not shown separately.

Source: U.S. Department of Agriculture, Economic Research Service, *Fruit and Tree Nuts Situation and Outlook Yearbook*.

Table 826. Meat Supply and Use: 1990 to 2007

[**In millions of pounds** (carcass weight equivalent) (**62,255 represents 62,255,000,000**). 2007 data are forecasts. Carcass weight equivalent is the weight of the animal minus entrails, head, hide, and internal organs; includes fat and bone. Covers federal and state inspected, and farm slaughter]

Year and type of meat	Production	Imports	Supply [1]	Exports	Consumption [2]	Ending stocks
RED MEAT AND POULTRY						
1990	62,255	3,295	66,673	2,472	62,937	1,263
2000	82,372	4,136	88,480	9,344	77,068	2,069
2004	85,140	4,993	92,157	8,089	81,877	2,192
2005	86,783	4,845	93,819	9,274	82,333	2,212
2006	89,164	4,326	95,702	10,069	83,499	2,135
2007	90,736	4,301	97,172	11,154	83,844	2,174
ALL RED MEATS						
1990	38,787	3,295	42,742	1,250	40,784	707
2000	46,299	4,127	51,340	3,760	46,559	1,021
2004	45,555	4,960	51,574	2,649	47,737	1,187
2005	45,848	4,803	51,838	3,373	47,385	1,080
2006	47,679	4,265	53,024	4,158	47,700	1,166
2007	48,815	4,227	54,208	4,621	48,395	1,192
Beef:						
1990	22,743	2,356	25,434	1,006	24,031	397
2000	26,888	3,032	30,332	2,468	27,338	525
2004	24,650	3,679	28,847	460	27,750	637
2005	24,787	3,599	29,023	697	27,754	571
2006	26,258	3,085	29,914	1,145	28,139	630
2007	26,520	3,048	30,198	1,431	28,137	631
Pork:						
1990	15,354	898	16,565	238	16,031	296
2000	18,952	965	20,406	1,287	18,642	478
2004	20,529	1,099	22,160	2,181	19,437	543
2005	20,705	1,024	22,272	2,666	19,112	494
2006	21,075	990	22,559	2,995	19,050	514
2007	21,962	986	23,462	3,179	19,742	541
Veal:						
1990	327	(NA)	331	(NA)	325	6
2000	225	(NA)	230	(NA)	225	5
2004	176	(NA)	181	(NA)	177	4
2005	165	(NA)	169	(NA)	164	5
2006	156	(NA)	161	(NA)	155	6
2007	146	(NA)	152	(NA)	145	7
Lamb and mutton:						
1990	363	41	412	6	397	8
2000	234	130	372	5	354	13
2004	200	181	385	8	373	3
2005	191	180	375	9	355	10
2006	190	190	390	18	356	16
2007	187	192	395	11	372	13
POULTRY, TOTAL						
1990	23,468	–	23,931	1,222	22,153	556
2000	36,073	9	37,140	5,584	30,508	1,048
2004	39,585	33	40,584	5,439	34,140	1,005
2005	40,935	42	41,981	5,901	34,948	1,132
2006	41,485	61	42,678	5,911	35,799	969
2007	41,921	74	42,963	6,533	35,449	982
Broilers:						
1990	18,430	–	18,651	1,143	17,266	242
2000	30,209	6	31,011	4,918	25,295	798
2004	33,699	27	34,334	4,783	28,837	713
2005	34,986	34	35,733	5,203	29,607	924
2006	35,369	47	36,340	5,205	30,389	745
2007	35,564	61	36,370	5,801	29,827	741
Mature chicken:						
1990	523	–	530	25	496	9
2000	531	2	540	220	311	9
2004	504	2	509	213	293	3
2005	516	1	520	129	388	2
2006	504	3	509	159	345	5
2007	498	3	506	169	335	2
Turkeys:						
1990	4,514	–	4,750	54	4,390	306
2000	5,333	1	5,589	445	4,902	241
2004	5,383	5	5,741	442	5,010	288
2005	5,432	8	5,728	570	4,952	206
2006	5,612	12	5,829	547	5,065	218
2007	5,859	10	6,088	562	5,286	239

– Represents zero.   NA Not available.   [1] Total supply equals production plus imports plus ending stocks of previous year.
[2] Includes shipments to territories.

Source: U.S. Department of Agriculture, Economic Research Service, *Food Consumption, Prices, and Expenditures, 1970–1997*; and "Agricultural Outlook: Statistical Indicators"; <http://www.ers.usda.gov/publications/agoutlook/aotables/>.

Agriculture   537

Table 827. Livestock Inventory and Production: 1990 to 2008

[95.8 represents 95,800,000. **Production in live weight**; includes animals-for-slaughter market, younger animals shipped to other states for feeding or breeding purposes, farm slaughter and custom slaughter consumed on farms where produced, minus livestock shipped into states for feeding or breeding with an adjustment for changes in inventory]

Type of livestock	Unit	1990	1995	2000	2002	2003	2004	2005	2006	2007	2008
ALL CATTLE [1]											
Inventory: [2] Number on farms	Mil.	95.8	102.8	98.2	96.7	96.1	94.9	95.4	96.7	97.0	96.7
Total value.	Bil. dol. . .	59.0	63.2	67.1	72.3	69.9	77.6	87.4	97.6	89.4	95.4
Value per head.	Dol.	616	615	683	747	728	818	916	1,009	922	987
Production: Quantity	Bil. lb. . . .	39.2	42.5	43.0	42.4	42.2	41.5	41.4	41.9	41.5	(NA)
Beef, price per 100 lb. . .	Dol.	74.60	61.80	68.60	66.50	79.70	85.80	89.70	87.20	89.90	(NA)
Calves, price per 100 lb. . .	Dol.	95.60	73.10	104.00	96.40	102.00	119.00	135.00	133.00	119.00	(NA)
Value of production	Bil. dol. . .	29.3	24.7	28.5	27.1	32.1	34.8	36.6	35.6	36.1	(NA)
HOGS AND PIGS											
Inventory: [3] Number on farms	Mil.	53.8	59.7	59.3	59.7	59.6	60.4	61.0	61.4	62.5	65.1
Total value.	Bil. dol. . .	4.3	3.2	4.3	4.6	4.2	4.0	6.3	5.8	5.6	4.7
Value per head.	Dol.	79	53	72	77	71	67	103	95	89	73
Production: Quantity	Bil. lb. . . .	21.3	24.4	25.7	26.3	26.3	26.7	27.4	28.1	29.6	(NA)
Price per 100 lb.	Dol.	53.70	40.50	42.30	33.40	37.20	49.30	50.20	46.00	46.60	(NA)
Value of production	Bil. dol. . .	11.3	9.8	10.8	8.7	9.7	13.1	13.6	12.7	13.5	(NA)
SHEEP AND LAMBS											
Inventory: [2] Number on farms	Mil.	11.4	9.0	7.0	6.6	6.3	6.1	6.1	6.2	6.2	6.1
Total value.	Mil. dol. . . .	901	663	670	614	657	724	799	875	824	836
Value per head.	Dol.	79	75	95	92	104	119	130	141	134	138
Production: Quantity	Mil. lb. . . .	781	602	512	485	470	464	473	473	461	(NA)
Sheep, price per 100 lb. . . .	Dol.	23.20	28.00	34.30	28.20	34.90	38.80	45.10	35.20	31.00	(NA)
Lambs, price per 100 lb. . . .	Dol.	55.50	78.20	79.80	74.10	94.40	101.00	110.00	95.50	98.50	(NA)
Value of production	Mil. dol. . .	374	414	365	314	392	411	453	380	384	(NA)

NA Not available.   [1] Includes milk cows.   [2] As of January 1.   [3] As of December 1 of preceding year.

Source: U.S. Department of Agriculture, National Agricultural Statistics Service, *Meat Animals—Production, Disposition, and Income Final Estimates 1998–2002*, May 2004; *Meat Animals Production, Disposition, and Income*, annual; and annual livestock summaries. Also in *Agricultural Statistics*, annual.

Table 828. Livestock Operations by Size of Herd: 2000 to 2007

[**In thousands (1,076 represents 1,076,000)**. An operation is any place having one or more head on hand at any time during the year]

Size of herd	2000	2005	2006	2007	Size of herd	2000	2005	2006	2007
CATTLE [1]					MILK COWS [2]				
Total operations	**1,076**	**983**	**971**	**967**	**Total operations . . . . . .**	**105**	**78**	**75**	**72**
1 to 49 head.	671	612	605	601	1 to 49 head.	53	37	35	33
50 to 99 head.	186	164	160	161	50 to 99 head.	31	23	22	21
100 to 499 head	192	178	176	176	100 head or more	21	18	17	17
500 to 999 head	19	19	19	19					
1,000 head or more	10	10	10	11	HOGS AND PIGS				
					Total operations	**87**	**67**	**67**	**65**
BEEF COWS [2]					1 to 99 head	50	41	40	40
Total operations	**831**	**770**	**763**	**758**	100 to 499 head	17	10	10	9
1 to 49 head.	655	597	591	585	500 to 999 head	8	5	4	4
50 to 99 head.	100	95	94	94	1,000 to 1,999 head.	6	4	4	4
100 to 499 head	71	73	73	73	2,000 to 4,999 head.	5	5	5	5
500 head or more	6	5	6	6	5,000 head or more	2	2	2	3

[1] Includes calves.   [2] Included in operations with cattle.

Source: U.S. Department of Agriculture, National Agricultural Statistics Service, *Livestock Operations Final Estimates 1998–2002*, April 2004; *Farms, Land in Farms, and Livestock Operations 2006 Summary*, February 2008; and *Agricultural Statistics*, annual.

Table 829. Hogs and Pigs—Number, Production, and Value by State: 2005 to 2007

[**61,449 represents 61,449,000.** See headnote, Table 827]

State	Number on farms [1] (1,000)			Quantity produced (mil. lb.)			Value of production (mil. dol.)			Commercial slaughter [2] (mil. lb.)	
	2005	2006	2007	2005	2006	2007	2005	2006	2007	2006	2007
U.S. [3] **. . . .**	**61,449**	**62,490**	**65,110**	**27,416**	**28,149**	**29,567**	**13,607**	**12,702**	**13,468**	**28,143**	**29,314**
IA.	16,600	17,300	18,200	7,788	8,025	8,500	3,636	3,421	3,662	8,023	8,074
NC	9,800	9,500	9,900	3,840	3,779	3,807	2,089	1,890	1,940	2,891	2,926
MN	6,600	6,900	7,200	3,238	3,329	3,543	1,570	1,502	1,647	2,452	2,492
MO	2,700	2,800	3,050	1,115	1,464	1,798	537	589	713	([4])	1,906
IN.	3,250	3,350	3,500	1,487	1,484	1,588	704	643	704	1,947	2,034
NE	2,850	3,050	3,150	1,368	1,417	1,441	730	702	729	1,943	1,995
IL	4,000	4,200	4,150	1,614	1,467	1,440	902	755	752	2,648	2,798

[1] As of December 1.   [2] Includes slaughter in federally inspected and other slaughter plants; excludes animals slaughtered on farms.   [3] Includes other states not shown separately.   [4] Included in U.S. total. Not printed to avoid disclosing individual operation.

Source: U.S. Department of Agriculture, National Agricultural Statistics Service, *Meat Animals—Production, Disposition and Income*, annual; and *Livestock Slaughter*, annual.

Table 830. Cattle and Calves—Number, Production, and Value by State: 2005 to 2008

[96,702 represents 96,702,000. Includes milk cows. See headnote, Table 827]

State	Number on farms [1] (1,000)			Quantity produced (mil. lb.)			Value of production (mil. dol.)			Commercial slaughter [2] (mil. lb.)	
	2006	2007	2008	2005	2006	2007	2005	2006	2007	2006	2007
U.S. [3]	96,702	97,003	96,669	41,448	41,906	41,496	36,629	35,555	36,067	42,820	43,483
TX........	14,100	14,000	13,800	7,304	6,792	6,820	6,437	5,800	6,106	7,817	7,446
NE........	6,500	6,650	6,550	4,499	4,798	4,657	3,831	4,043	4,211	9,288	9,262
KS........	6,650	6,400	6,700	3,993	4,132	4,090	2,973	2,971	3,347	9,509	9,700
OK........	5,450	5,250	5,400	2,064	2,134	2,001	2,187	2,111	2,022	31	24
CA........	5,450	5,500	5,450	1,929	1,997	1,977	1,214	1,177	1,289	2,016	2,054
CO........	2,650	2,700	2,750	1,797	1,921	1,898	1,813	1,914	1,915	2,753	2,862
IA........	3,800	3,950	4,000	1,730	1,814	1,819	1,410	1,462	1,526	(⁴)	(⁴)
SD........	3,750	3,700	3,700	1,501	1,539	1,496	1,528	1,498	1,432	(⁴)	(⁴)
WI	3,400	3,400	3,400	1,075	1,160	1,175	858	867	874	2,117	2,265
MT........	2,400	2,400	2,600	956	919	1,149	1,018	881	1,063	23	23
ID	2,110	2,180	2,230	1,032	1,065	1,103	868	858	920	(⁴)	277

[1] As of January 1.   [2] Data cover cattle only. Includes slaughter in federally inspected and other slaughter plants; excludes animals slaughtered on farms.   [3] Includes other states not shown separately.   [4] Included in U.S. total. Not printed to avoid disclosing individual operation.

Source: U.S. Department of Agriculture, National Agricultural Statistics Service, *Meat Animals—Production, Disposition and Income*, annual; and *Livestock Slaughter*, annual.

Table 831. Milk Cows—Number, Production, and Value by State: 2005 to 2007

[9,043 represents 9,043,000]

State	Number on farms [1] (1,000)			Milk produced on farms (mil. lb.)			Value of production [2] (mil. dol.)		
	2005	2006	2007	2005	2006	2007	2005	2006	2007
United States [3] ...	9,043	9,112	9,158	176,929	181,796	185,602	26,874	23,558	35,653
California.........	1,755	1,780	1,813	37,564	38,830	40,683	5,229	4,497	7,335
Wisconsin........	1,236	1,243	1,247	22,866	23,398	24,080	3,567	3,112	4,647
New York.........	648	638	627	12,078	12,045	12,103	1,920	1,614	2,384
Idaho	455	488	513	10,161	10,905	11,549	1,423	1,287	2,056
Pennsylvania	561	554	550	10,503	10,742	10,682	1,775	1,568	2,233
Minnesota	453	450	460	8,195	8,370	8,656	1,262	1,088	1,714
Michigan	312	320	335	6,750	7,115	7,598	1,040	946	1,497
Texas	320	335	349	6,442	7,145	7,379	986	950	1,454
New Mexico.......	328	355	342	6,951	7,630	7,306	994	923	1,374

[1] Average number during year. Represents cows and heifers that have calved, kept for milk; excluding heifers not yet fresh.   [2] Valued at average returns per 100 pounds of milk in combined marketings of milk and cream. Includes value of milk fed to calves.   [3] Includes other states not shown separately.

Source: U.S. Department of Agriculture, National Agricultural Statistics Service, *Dairy Products*, annual; and *Milk: Production, Disposition, and Income*, annual.

Table 832. Milk Production and Manufactured Dairy Products: 1990 to 2007

[193 represents 193,000]

Item	Unit	1990	1995	2000	2002	2003	2004	2005	2006	2007
Number of farms with milk cows	1,000	193	140	105	91	86	82	78	75	72
Cows and heifers that have calved, kept for milk	Mil. head ..	10.0	9.5	9.2	9.1	9.1	9.0	9.0	9.1	9.2
Milk produced on farms.............	Bil. lb.....	148	155	167	170	170	171	177	182	186
Production per cow	1,000 lb. ...	14.8	16.4	18.2	18.6	18.8	19.0	19.6	20.0	20.3
Milk marketed by producers [1]	Bil. lb.....	146	154	166	169	169	170	176	181	184
Value of milk produced	Bil. dol. ...	20.4	20.1	20.8	20.7	21.4	27.6	26.9	23.6	35.7
Cash receipts from marketing of milk and cream [1]	Bil. dol. ...	20.1	19.9	20.6	20.6	21.2	27.4	26.7	23.4	35.4
Number of dairy manufacturing plants	Number...	1,723	1,495	1,164	1,149	1,119	1,093	1,088	1,094	1,109
Manufactured dairy products:										
Butter (incl. whey butter)	Mil. lb.....	1,302	1,264	1,256	1,355	1,242	1,247	1,347	1,448	1,533
Cheese, total [2].................	Mil. lb.....	6,059	6,917	8,258	8,547	8,557	8,873	9,149	9,525	9,700
American (excl. full-skim American) ...	Mil. lb.....	2,894	3,131	3,642	3,691	3,622	3,739	3,808	3,913	3,878
Cream and Neufchatel	Mil. lb.....	431	544	687	686	677	699	715	756	773
All Italian varieties.............	Mil. lb.....	2,207	2,674	3,289	3,470	3,524	3,662	3,803	3,973	4,134
Cottage cheese: Creamed [3]	Mil. lb.....	832	711	735	748	769	788	784	778	782
Condensed bulk milk...............	Mil. lb.....	1,426	1,372	1,202	1,191	1,047	1,021	1,182	1,427	1,852
Evaporated and condensed canned milk..	Mil. lb.....	615	503	465	593	595	549	548	507	516
Nonfat dry milk [4]	Mil. lb.....	902	1,243	1,457	1,596	1,589	1,412	1,210	1,244	1,298
Dry whey [5]	Mil. lb.....	1,143	1,147	1,188	1,115	1,085	1,035	1,041	1,110	1,134
Yogurt, plain and fruit-flavored	Mil. lb.....	(NA)	1,646	1,837	2,311	2,507	2,707	3,058	3,301	3,478
Ice cream, regular	Mil. gal....	824	862	980	1,005	993	920	960	982	951
Ice cream, lowfat [6]	Mil. gal....	352	357	373	339	398	387	360	377	383

NA Not available.   [1] Comprises sales to plants and dealers, and retail sales by farmers direct to consumers.   [2] Includes varieties not shown separately.   [3] Includes partially creamed (low fat).   [4] Includes dry skim milk for animal feed through 2000.   [5] Includes animal but excludes modified whey production.   [6] Includes freezer-made milkshake in most states.

Source: U.S. Department of Agriculture, National Agricultural Statistics Service, *Dairy Products*, annual; and *Milk: Production, Disposition, and Income*, annual.

Agriculture   539

Table 833. **Milk Production and Commercial Use: 1990 to 2007**

[In billions of pounds milkfat basis (147.7 represents 147,700,000,000) except as noted]

Year	Produc-tion	Farm use	Commercial Farm market-ings	Commercial Begin-ning stock	Imports	Commer-cial supply, total	CCC net remov-als [1]	Commercial Ending stock	Commercial Disap-pearance	Milk price per 100 lb. [2] (dol.)
1990 . . .	147.7	2.0	145.7	4.1	2.7	152.5	8.5	5.1	138.8	13.68
1995 . . .	155.3	1.6	153.7	4.3	2.9	160.9	2.1	4.1	154.7	12.78
2000 . . .	167.4	1.3	166.1	6.1	4.4	176.7	0.8	6.8	169.0	12.40
2003 . . .	170.4	1.1	169.3	9.9	5.0	184.2	1.2	8.3	174.7	12.52
2004 . . .	170.9	1.1	169.8	8.3	5.3	183.4	−0.1	7.2	176.4	16.05
2005 . . .	176.9	1.1	175.8	7.2	5.0	188.0	–	8.0	180.0	15.13
2006 . . .	181.8	1.1	180.7	8.0	5.0	193.6	–	9.5	184.1	12.90
2007 . . .	185.6	1.1	184.5	9.5	4.6	198.6	–	10.4	188.3	19.13

– Represents zero.   [1] Removals from commercial supply by Commodity Credit Corporation (CCC).   [2] Wholesale price received by farmers for all milk delivered to plants and dealers.

Source: U.S. Department of Agriculture, Economic Research Service, "Agricultural Outlook: Statistical Indicators"; <http://www.ers.usda.gov/publications/agoutlook/aotables/>.

Table 834. **Broiler, Turkey, and Egg Production: 1990 to 2007**

[For year ending November 30 (353 represents 353,000,000)]

Item	Unit	1990	1995	2000	2001	2002	2003	2004	2005	2006	2007
Chickens:[1]											
Number [2]	Million	353	388	437	444	444	450	454	453	454	455
Value per head [2]. . . .	Dollars . . .	2.29	2.41	2.44	2.41	2.38	2.48	2.48	2.52	2.61	2.95
Value, total [2]	Mil. dol. . . .	808	935	1,064	1,069	1,055	1,116	1,123	1,141	1,185	1,344
Number sold	Million	208	180	218	202	200	190	192	193	173	167
Price per lb..	Cents	9.6	6.5	5.7	4.5	4.8	4.9	5.8	6.5	5.8	5.6
Value of sales	Mil. dol. . . .	94	60	64	47	50	48	58	65	54	51
PRODUCTION											
Broilers: [3]											
Number.	Million	5,864	7,326	8,284	8,390	8,591	8,493	8,741	8,872	8,868	8,898
Weight	Bil. lb.. . . .	25.6	34.2	41.6	42.5	44.1	44.0	45.8	47.9	48.8	49.2
Price per lb..	Cents	32.6	34.4	33.6	39.3	30.5	34.6	44.6	43.6	36.3	43.6
Production value. . . .	Mil. dol. . . .	8,366	11,762	13,989	16,696	13,437	15,215	20,446	20,878	17,739	21,460
Turkeys:											
Number.	Million	282	292	270	273	275	274	264	252	262	272
Weight	Bil. lb.. . . .	6.0	6.8	7.0	7.2	7.5	7.5	7.3	7.1	7.5	7.9
Price per lb..	Cents	39.6	41.0	40.6	39.0	36.5	36.1	42.0	44.9	47.9	47.2
Production value. . . .	Mil. dol. . . .	2,393	2,769	2,828	2,797	2,732	2,700	3,065	3,183	3,574	3,711
Eggs:											
Number.	Billion	68.1	74.8	84.7	86.1	87.3	87.5	89.1	90.0	91.3	90.6
Price per dozen	Cents	70.8	62.5	61.6	62.0	58.9	73.2	71.4	54.0	58.2	88.5
Production value. . . .	Mil. dol. . . .	4,021	3,893	4,346	4,446	4,281	5,333	5,299	4,049	4,432	6,678

[1] Excludes commercial broilers.   [2] As of December 1.   [3] Young chickens of the heavy breeds and other meat-type birds, to be marketed at 2–5 lbs. live weight and from which no pullets are kept for egg production.

Source: U.S. Department of Agriculture, National Agricultural Statistics Service, *Poultry Production and Value Final Estimates 1998–2002*, April 2004; *Turkeys Final Estimates 1998–2002*, April 2004; *Chickens and Eggs Final Estimates 1998–2002*, April 2004; *Poultry—Production and Value*, annual; *Turkeys*, annual; and *Chickens and Eggs*, annual.

Table 835. **Broiler and Turkey Production by State: 2005 to 2007**

[In millions of pounds, live weight production (47,856 represents 47,856,000,000)]

State	Broilers 2005	Broilers 2006	Broilers 2007	Turkeys 2005	Turkeys 2006	Turkeys 2007	State	Broilers 2005	Broilers 2006	Broilers 2007	Turkeys 2005	Turkeys 2006	Turkeys 2007
U.S. [1]. . .	47,856	48,830	49,208	7,096	7,464	7,869	MS	4,775	4,662	4,614	(NA)	(NA)	(NA)
AL	5,604	5,688	5,582	(NA)	(NA)	(NA)	MO	(NA)	(NA)	(NA)	628	634	630
AR	6,314	6,283	6,213	566	585	601	NC	4,852	5,099	5,390	1,054	1,125	1,193
CA	(NA)	(NA)	(NA)	396	428	445	ND	(NA)	(NA)	(NA)	30	48	51
DE	1,612	1,614	1,598	(NA)	(NA)	(NA)	OH	228	242	274	224	191	194
FL.	458	443	425	(NA)	(NA)	(NA)	OK	1,325	1,352	1,287	(NA)	(NA)	(NA)
GA	6,752	7,066	7,414	(NA)	(NA)	(NA)	PA	800	829	832	207	195	200
IL	(NA)	(NA)	(NA)	93	91	87	SC	1,280	1,408	1,481	310	386	419
IN	(NA)	(NA)	(NA)	429	462	543	SD	(NA)	(NA)	(NA)	138	158	169
IA	(NA)	(NA)	(NA)	306	274	281	TN	1,003	1,089	1,056	(NA)	(NA)	(NA)
KY	1,638	1,590	1,678	(NA)	(NA)	(NA)	TX	3,265	3,330	3,266	(NA)	(NA)	(NA)
MD	1,390	1,607	1,592	15	26	26	VA	1,328	1,332	1,301	502	555	574
MI	(NA)	(NA)	(NA)	169	175	182	WV	363	359	356	68	93	99
MN	230	230	242	1,202	1,211	1,291	WI	160	169	193	(NA)	(NA)	(NA)

NA Not available.   [1] Includes other states not shown separately.

Source: U.S. Department of Agriculture, National Agricultural Statistics Service, *Poultry—Production and Value*, annual.

Section 18
Natural Resources

This section presents data on the area, ownership, production, trade, reserves, and disposition of natural resources. Natural resources is defined here as including forestry, fisheries, and mining and mineral products.

Forestry—Presents data on the area, ownership, and timber resource of commercial timberland; forestry statistics covering the National Forests and Forest Service cooperative programs; product data for lumber, pulpwood, woodpulp, paper and paperboard, and similar data.

The principal sources of data relating to forests and forest products are *Forest Resources of the United States, 2002; Timber Demand and Technology Assessment; U.S. Timber Production, Trade, Consumption, and Price Statistics, 1965–2002; Land Areas of the National Forest System,* issued annually by the Forest Service of the U.S. Department of Agriculture; *Agricultural Statistics* issued by the Department of Agriculture; and reports of the annual survey of manufactures, and the annual *Current Industrial Reports,* issued by the U.S. Census Bureau on the Internet and in print in the annual *Manufacturing Profiles.* Additional information is published in the monthly *Survey of Current Business* of the Bureau of Economic Analysis, and the annual *Wood Pulp* and *Fiber Statistics* and *The Annual Statistics of Paper, Paperboard, and Wood Pulp* of the American Forest and Paper Association, Washington, DC.

The completeness and reliability of statistics on forests and forest products vary considerably. The data for forest land area and stand volumes are much more reliable for areas that have been recently surveyed than for those for which only estimates are available. In general, more data are available for lumber and other manufactured products such as particle board and softwood panels, etc., than for the primary forest products such as poles and piling and fuelwood.

Fisheries—The principal source of data relating to fisheries is *Fisheries of the United States,* issued annually by the National Marine Fisheries Service (NMFS), National Oceanic and Atmospheric Administration (NOAA). The NMFS collects and disseminates data on commercial landings of fish and shellfish. Annual reports include quantity and value of commercial landings of fish and shellfish disposition of landings and number and kinds of fishing vessels and fishing gear. Reports for the fish-processing industry include annual output for the wholesaling and fish processing establishments, annual and seasonal employment. The principal source for these data is the annual *Fisheries of the United States.* Aquaculture farming and sales data come primarily from the Census of Aquaculture, conducted roughly every 7 years by the U.S. Department of Agriculture's National Agricultural Statistics Service.

Mining and mineral products—
Presents data relating to mineral industries and their products, general summary measures of production and employment, and more detailed data on production, prices, imports and exports, consumption, and distribution for specific industries and products. Data on mining and mineral products may also be found in Sections 19, 21, and 28 of this *Abstract;* data on mining employment may be found in Section 12.

Mining comprises the extraction of minerals occurring naturally (coal, ores, crude petroleum, natural gas) and quarrying, well operation, milling, refining and processing, and other preparation customarily done at the mine or well site or as a part of extraction activity. (Mineral preparation plants are usually operated together with mines or quarries.) Exploration for minerals is included as is the development of mineral properties.

The principal governmental sources of these data are the *Minerals Yearbook* and *Mineral Commodity Summaries,* published

U.S. Census Bureau, Statistical Abstract of the United States: 2009

by the U.S. Geological Survey, U.S. Department of the Interior, and various monthly and annual publications of the Energy Information Administration, U.S. Department of Energy. See text, Section 19, for a list of Department of Energy publications. In addition, the Census Bureau conducts a census of mineral industries every 5 years.

Nongovernment sources include the *Annual Statistical Report* of the American Iron and Steel Institute, Washington, DC; *Metals Week* and the monthly *Engineering and Mining Journal,* issued by the McGraw-Hill Publishing Co., New York, NY; *The Iron Age,* issued weekly by the Chilton Co., Philadelphia, PA; and the *Joint Association Survey of the U.S. Oil and Gas Industry,* conducted jointly by the American Petroleum Institute, Independent Petroleum Association of America, and Mid-Continent Oil and Gas Association.

Mineral statistics, with principal emphasis on commodity detail, have been collected by the U.S. Geological Survey and the former Bureau of Mines since 1880. Current data in U.S. Geological Survey publications include quantity and value of nonfuel minerals produced, sold, or used by producers, or shipped; quantity of minerals stocked; crude materials treated and prepared minerals recovered; and consumption of mineral raw materials.

Censuses of mineral industries have been conducted by the Census Bureau at various intervals since 1840. Beginning with the 1967 census, legislation provides for a census to be conducted every 5 years for years ending in "2" and "7." The most recent results, published for 2002, are based on the North American Industry Classification System (NAICS). The censuses provide, for the various types of mineral establishments, information on operating costs, capital expenditures, labor, equipment, and energy requirements in relation to their value of shipments and other receipts. Commodity statistics on many manufactured mineral products are also collected by the Census Bureau at monthly, quarterly, or annual intervals and issued in its *Current Industrial Reports* series.

In general, figures shown in the individual commodity tables include data for outlying areas and may therefore not agree with summary tables. Except for crude petroleum and refined products, the export and import figures include foreign trade passing through the customs districts of United States and Puerto Rico but exclude shipments between U.S. territories and the customs districts.

Table 836. **Gross Domestic Product of Natural Resource-Related Industries in Current and Real (2000) Dollars by Industry: 2000 to 2007**

[In billions of dollars (9,817.0 represents $9,817,000,000,000). Data are based on the 2002 North American Industry Classification System (NAICS); see text, Section 15. Data include nonfactor charges (capital consumption allowances, indirect business taxes, etc.) as well as factor charges against gross product; corporate profits and capital consumption allowances have been shifted from a company to an establishment basis]

Industry	Current dollars				Chained (2000) dollars			
	2000	2005	2006	2007	2000	2005	2006	2007
All industries, total [1]	9,817.0	12,433.9	13,194.7	13,841.3	9,817.0	11,003.4	11,319.4	11,566.8
Industries covered	306.3	444.0	477.7	(NA)	306.3	308.0	314.3	(NA)
Percent of all industries	3.1	3.6	3.6	(NA)	3.1	2.8	2.8	(NA)
Agriculture, forestry, fishing, and hunting	98.0	128.8	125.4	161.4	98.0	116.5	117.6	119.2
Farms	71.5	100.9	95.7	(NA)	71.5	87.0	87.5	(NA)
Forestry, fishing, and related activities	26.5	27.9	29.7	(NA)	26.5	28.8	29.3	(NA)
Mining	121.3	225.7	262.4	275.8	121.3	105.1	111.6	111.6
Oil and gas extraction	81.0	149.6	159.4	(NA)	81.0	69.3	71.5	(NA)
Mining, except oil and gas	27.0	37.7	43.5	(NA)	27.0	26.1	26.6	(NA)
Support activities for mining	13.4	38.4	59.5	(NA)	13.4	10.9	13.1	(NA)
Timber-related manufacturing	87.0	89.6	89.9	(NA)	87.0	86.4	85.2	(NA)
Wood products	31.4	37.1	37.4	(NA)	31.4	30.9	32.8	(NA)
Paper products	55.6	52.5	52.5	(NA)	55.6	55.5	52.4	(NA)

NA Not available.   [1] Includes industries not shown separately.

Source: U.S. Bureau of Economic Analysis, *Survey of Current Business,* May 2008. See also <http://www.bea.gov/industry/gdpbyind_data.htm> (released 26 April 2008).

Table 837. Natural Resource-Related Industries—Establishments, Sales, Payroll, and Employees by Industry: 1997 and 2002

[174 represents $174,000,000,000. Includes only establishments of firms with payroll. Data are based on the 1997 and 2002 economic censuses, which are subject to nonsampling error. For details on methodology and nonsampling and sampling errors, see Appendix III]

Industry	1997 NAICS code [1]	Establishments (number)		Value of shipments (bil. dol.)		Annual payroll (bil. dol.)		Paid employees [2] (1,000)	
		1997	2002	1997	2002	1997	2002	1997	2002
Mining	21	25,000	24,284	174	184	21	22	509	488
Oil & gas extraction	211	8,312	7,722	103	113	6	5	111	99
Mining (except oil & gas)	212	7,348	7,196	51	47	9	9	229	195
Mining support activities	213	9,340	9,366	20	24	6	7	169	194
Manufacturing [3]	31–33	362,829	350,728	3,835	3,915	570	575	16,805	14,664
Wood product mfg	321	17,367	17,255	88	89	14	16	570	543
Paper mfg	322	5,868	5,495	150	153	22	21	574	489
Petroleum & coal products manufacturing	324	2,146	2,268	177	216	6	6	108	104

[1] North American Industry Classification System, 1997. [2] For pay period including March 12. [3] Includes other industries not shown separately.

Source: U.S. Census Bureau, 2002 Economic Census, *Comparative Statistics*, issued July 2006; <http://www.census.gov/econ/census02>.

Table 838. Natural Resource-Related Industries—Establishments, Employees, and Annual Payroll, by Industry: 2000 and 2005

[1,791.3 represents 1,791,300. Excludes government employees, railroad employees, self-employed persons, etc. See "General Explanation" in source for definitions and statement on reliability of data. An establishment is a single physical location where business is conducted or where services or industrial operations are performed]

Industry	2002 NAICS code [1]	Establishments (number)		Number of employees [2] (1,000)		Annual payroll (bil. dol.)	
		2000	2005	2000	2005	2000	2005
Natural resource-related industries, total	(X)	**72,932**	**70,778**	**1,791.3**	**1,675.9**	**66.58**	**75.71**
Forestry, fishing, hunting, and agriculture support	11	26,076	24,102	183.6	168.7	4.68	5.10
Forestry and logging	113	13,347	11,048	83.1	69.5	2.26	2.27
Timber tract operations	1131	469	472	3.3	4.5	0.13	0.19
Forest nurseries and gathering forest products	1132	258	219	1.7	1.8	0.07	0.06
Logging	1133	12,620	10,357	78.1	63.2	2.06	2.01
Fishing, hunting and trapping	114	2,671	2,415	10.0	7.2	0.34	0.31
Fishing	1141	2,308	2,047	7.5	5.5	0.27	0.26
Hunting and trapping	1142	363	368	2.5	1.7	0.08	0.05
Agriculture and forestry support activities	115	10,058	10,639	90.4	92.0	2.08	2.52
Crop production support activities	1151	5,061	4,665	57.6	58.9	1.35	1.62
Animal production support activities	1152	3,450	4,273	18.2	18.8	0.38	0.48
Forestry support activities	1153	1,547	1,701	14.7	14.3	0.35	0.42
Mining	21	23,738	24,696	456.1	497.3	22.09	30.82
Oil and gas extraction	211	7,740	7,390	83.0	85.6	5.39	7.74
Mining (except oil and gas)	212	7,231	7,130	204.3	196.9	9.34	10.89
Coal mining	2121	1,253	1,132	70.7	74.3	3.54	4.56
Metal ore mining	2122	522	301	34.8	26.4	1.72	1.65
Nonmetallic mineral mining and quarrying	2123	5,456	5,697	98.8	96.3	4.08	4.69
Mining support activities	213	8,767	10,176	168.8	214.8	7.35	12.19
Timber-related manufacturing	(X)	23,118	21,980	1,151.6	1,009.9	39.80	39.79
Wood product manufacturing	321	17,328	16,707	597.7	555.9	16.51	18.23
Sawmills and wood preservation	3211	4,695	4,271	131.4	117.3	3.78	4.04
Veneer, plywood, and engineered wood product manufacturing	3212	1,904	1,903	120.6	116.4	3.75	4.16
Other wood product manufacturing	3219	10,729	10,533	345.8	322.2	8.95	10.03
Paper manufacturing	322	5,790	5,273	553.9	454.0	23.29	21.56
Pulp, paper, and paperboard mills	3221	597	621	177.1	146.9	9.48	8.83
Converted paper product manufacturing	3222	5,193	4,652	376.8	307.0	13.82	12.73

X Not applicable. [1] North American Industry Classification System, 2002. [2] Covers full- and part-time employees who are on the payroll in the pay period including March 12.

Source: U.S. Census Bureau, County Business Patterns; annual. See also <http://www.census.gov/epcd/cbp/view/cbpview.html>.

Natural Resources 543

Table 839. Timber-Based Manufacturing Industries—Establishments, Shipments, Payroll, and Employees: 2002

[89,085,026 represents $89,085,026,000. Includes only establishments or firms with payroll. Data based on the 2002 Economic Census. See Appendix III]

Industry	2002 NAICS code [1]	Estab-lishments	Value of shipments ($1,000)	Annual payroll ($1,000)	Paid employees
Wood product manufacturing	**321**	**17,202**	**89,085,026**	**16,054,554**	**540,565**
Sawmills and wood preservation	3211	4,318	25,922,616	3,496,055	108,045
Saw mills	321113	3,805	21,388,581	3,123,879	95,724
Wood preservation	321114	513	4,534,035	372,176	12,321
Veneer, plywood, and engineered wood product manufacturing	3212	1,925	20,201,016	3,681,187	114,300
Other wood product manufacturing.	3219	10,959	42,961,394	8,877,312	318,220
Millwork	32191	4,725	22,557,817	4,415,940	151,245
Wood container and pallet manufacturing.	32192	2,948	5,055,879	1,154,283	51,003
All other wood product manufacturing	32199	3,286	15,347,698	3,307,089	115,972
Paper manufacturing.	**322**	**5,520**	**153,766,022**	**21,497,243**	**491,436**
Pulp, paper, and paperboard mills	3221	561	70,031,347	8,854,439	158,619
Pulp mills	32211	31	3,650,916	487,324	8,043
Paper mills	32212	327	45,163,754	5,700,302	102,571
Paperboard mills	32213	203	21,216,677	2,666,813	48,005
Converted paper product manufacturing	3222	4,959	83,734,675	12,642,804	332,817
Paperboard container manufacturing	32221	2,669	43,494,303	7,091,160	184,884
Paper bag and coated and treated paper manufacturing	32222	929	18,242,228	2,640,583	66,296
Stationery product manufacturing	32223	636	7,977,966	1,300,452	38,595
Other converted paper product manufacturing	32229	725	14,020,178	1,610,609	43,042

[1] North American Industry Classification System, 2002.

Source: U.S. Census Bureau, 2002 Economic Census, *Manufacturing, General Summary*, issued October 2005. See also <http://www.census.gov/econ/census02>.

Table 840. Timber-Based Manufacturing Industries—Employees, Payroll, and Shipments: 2006

[In thousands (12,990 represents 12,990,000). Based on the Annual Survey of Manufactures; see Appendix III]

Selected industry	2002 NAICS code [1]	All employees			Produc-tion workers, total (1,000)	Value added by manufactures		Value of ship-ments (mil. dol.)
		Number (1,000)	Payroll			Total (mil. dol.)	Per produc-tion worker (dol.)	
			Total (mil. dol.)	Per employee (dol.)				
Manufacturing, all industries [2]	31–33	12,990	592,342	45,599	9,179	2,305,589	251,179	5,019,963
Timber-based manufacturing, total	321–322	950	38,781	40,816	754	125,032	165,826	282,765
Percent of total manufacturing. . .	(X)	7.31	6.55	(X)	8.21	5.42	(X)	5.63
Wood product manufacturing	321	536	18,141	33,839	432	44,432	102,776	112,404
Sawmills and wood preservation	3211	104	3,863	37,146	87	9,854	112,833	32,163
Veneer, plywood, and engineered wood product	3212	115	4,171	36,360	92	10,475	113,662	25,746
Other wood product	3219	317	10,107	31,844	253	24,103	95,334	54,496
Millwork	32191	160	5,355	33,524	127	12,781	100,684	30,436
Wood container and pallet	32192	52	1,398	27,064	43	3,016	69,885	6,542
All other wood products.	32199	106	3,354	31,640	83	8,306	100,402	17,518
Paper manufacturing	322	414	20,640	49,849	322	80,601	250,558	170,361
Pulp, paper, and paperboard mills . . .	3221	128	8,015	62,687	102	42,047	414,237	79,961
Pulp mills	32211	7	486	72,161	5	1,767	331,685	4,257
Paper mills	32212	85	5,227	61,430	68	28,494	420,245	52,485
Paperboard mills	32213	36	2,302	63,884	28	11,787	415,361	23,219
Converted paper product	3222	286	12,625	44,114	220	38,554	175,101	90,400
Paperboard container	32221	162	7,226	44,655	124	18,631	149,807	48,733
Paper bag and coated and treated paper.	32222	56	2,618	46,338	42	9,033	216,072	19,858
Stationery product	32223	32	1,230	39,005	25	3,470	140,136	8,360
Other converted paper products . . .	32229	36	1,551	42,683	29	7,419	253,696	13,448

X Not applicable.   [1] North American Industry Classification System, 2002; see text, Section 15.   [2] Includes other industries not shown separately.

Source: U.S. Census Bureau, "Annual Survey of Manufactures, 2006"; <http://www.census.gov/mcd/asm-as1.html> (released 31 December 2006).

Table 841. Forest Land and Timberland by Type of Owner and Region: 2002

[In thousands of acres (748,923 represents 748,923,000). As of January 1. Forest land is land at least 10 percent stocked by forest trees of any size, including land that formerly had such tree cover and that will be naturally or artificially regenerated. The minimum area for classification of forest land is 1 acre or strips of timber with a crown width of at least 120 feet wide. Timberland is forest land that is producing, or is capable of producing, crops of industrial wood and that is not withdrawn from timber utilization by statute or administrative regulation]

Region	Forest land, total	Timberland Total	Federal Total	Federal National forest	Federal Other	State, county, and municipal	Private Total	Private National forest	Private Farmer and other private[1]
Total	748,923	541,098	147,278	96,644	50,634	37,559	356,261	65,595	290,666
North	169,684	179,998	32,547	9,840	22,707	21,285	126,166	14,648	111,518
Northeast	85,031	85,834	10,085	2,164	7,921	7,464	68,285	10,855	57,430
North Central	84,653	94,164	22,462	7,676	14,786	13,821	57,881	3,793	54,088
South	214,605	208,051	21,227	11,246	9,981	5,378	181,446	35,915	145,531
Southeast	88,561	87,429	9,609	4,710	4,899	2,655	75,165	14,180	60,985
South Central	126,044	120,622	11,618	6,536	5,082	2,723	106,281	21,735	84,546
Rocky Mountains	144,343	73,467	50,268	43,959	6,309	2,839	20,360	2,926	17,434
Great Plains	4,783	4,521	1,277	1,020	257	180	3,064	–	3,064
Intermountain	139,560	68,946	48,991	42,939	6,052	2,659	17,296	2,926	14,370
Pacific Coast	220,291	79,582	43,236	31,599	11,637	8,057	28,289	12,106	16,183
Alaska	126,869	16,209	9,094	3,772	5,322	4,344	2,771	–	2,771
Pacific Northwest[2]	51,441	44,386	23,505	17,911	5,594	3,207	17,674	9,174	8,500
Pacific Southwest[2]	41,981	18,987	10,637	9,916	721	506	7,844	2,932	4,912

– Represents or rounds to zero.   [1] Includes Indian lands.   [2] Includes Hawaii.

Source: U.S. Department of Agriculture, National Agricultural Statistics Service, *Agricultural Statistics, 2007*. See also <http://www.nass.usda.gov/Publications/Ag_Statistics/index.asp>.

Table 842. Timber Volume, Growth, and Removal on Timberland by Species, Group, and Region: 2002

[856,061 represents 856,061,000,000]

Region	Net volume[1] Growing stock[2] (mil. cu. ft.) All species	Soft-woods	Hard-woods	Sawtimber[3] (bil. board ft.) All species	Soft woods	Hard woods	Timber growth[4] (mil. cu. ft.) All species	Soft woods	Hard woods	Timber removals[5] (mil. cu. ft.) All species	Soft woods	Hard woods
Total	856,061	491,803	364,258	3,317	2,270	1,047	23,689	13,651	9,971	16,012	10,064	5,948
North	217,624	49,878	167,746	598	149	449	5,418	1,167	4,184	2,865	680	2,185
Northeast	123,667	31,476	92,191	334	94	239	2,833	658	2,175	1,275	414	861
North Central	93,957	18,402	75,555	264	55	209	2,585	525	2,061	1,590	266	1,324
South	267,965	108,018	159,947	895	400	495	11,522	6,467	5,055	10,126	6,506	3,620
Southeast	124,002	52,758	71,244	396	177	219	5,157	3,097	2,059	4,363	2,881	1,482
South Central	143,963	55,260	88,703	499	223	276	6,365	3,370	2,995	5,763	3,625	2,138
Rocky Mountains	131,659	120,837	10,822	516	492	24	2,062	1,858	204	532	502	30
Great Plains	4,260	1,880	2,380	15	7	8	87	42	45	37	21	16
Intermountain	127,399	118,957	8,442	501	485	16	1,975	1,816	159	495	481	14
Pacific Coast	238,813	213,070	25,743	1,308	1,229	79	4,687	4,159	528	2,489	2,376	113
Alaska	31,997	29,124	2,873	146	142	5	207	122	85	140	137	3
Pacific Northwest	148,635	135,591	13,044	843	795	47	3,154	2,841	313	1,721	1,621	99
Pacific Southwest[6]	58,181	48,355	9,826	319	292	28	1,326	1,196	131	628	618	10

[1] As of January 1.   [2] Live trees of commercial species meeting specified standards of quality or vigor. Cull trees are excluded. Includes only trees 5.0-inches in diameter or larger at 4-1/2 feet above ground.   [3] Live trees of commercial species containing at least one 12-foot sawlog or two noncontiguous 8-foot logs, and meeting regional specifications for freedom from defect. Softwood trees must be at least 9.0 inches in diameter and hardwood trees must be at least 11.0 inches in diameter at 4-1/2 feet above ground.   [4] The net increase in the volume of trees during a specified year. Components include the increment in net volume of trees at the beginning of the specific year surviving to its end, plus the net volume of trees reaching the minimum size class during the year, minus the volume of trees that died during the year, and minus the net volume of trees that became cull trees during the year.   [5] The net volume of trees removed from the inventory during a specified year by harvesting, cultural operations such as timber stand improvement, or land clearing.   [6] Includes Hawaii.

Source: U.S. Department of Agriculture, National Agricultural Statistics Service, *Agricultural Statistics, 2007*. See also <http://www.nass.usda.gov/Publications/Ag_Statistics/index.asp>.

U.S. Census Bureau, Statistical Abstract of the United States: 2009

Table 843. **Timber Removals—Roundwood Product Output by Source and Species Group: 2002**

[In million cubic feet (16,001 represents 16,001,000,000)]

Source and species group	Total	Sawlogs	Pulpwood	Veneer logs	Other products [1]	Fuelwood [2]
Total	**16,001**	**7,237**	**4,977**	**1,353**	**814**	**1,621**
Softwoods	10,107	5,218	2,865	1,183	444	397
Hardwoods	5,894	2,019	2,112	170	370	1,224
Growing stock [3]	13,750	6,793	4,352	1,285	728	592
Softwoods	9,167	4,962	2,528	1,124	396	156
Hardwoods	4,583	1,831	1,824	160	331	436
Other sources [4]	2,251	444	625	68	86	1,029
Softwoods	941	256	337	58	48	241
Hardwoods	1,310	187	288	9	38	788

[1] Includes such items as cooperage, pilings, poles, posts, shakes, shingles, board mills, charcoal, and export logs. [2] Downed and dead wood volume left on the ground after trees have been cut on timberland. [3] Includes live trees of commercial species meeting specified standards of quality or vigor. Cull trees are excluded. Includes only trees 5.0 inches in diameter or larger at 4-1/2 feet above the ground. [4] Includes salvable dead trees, rough and rotten trees, trees of noncommercial species, trees less than 5.0 inches in diameter at 4-1/2 feet above the ground, tops, and roundwood harvested from nonforest land (for example, fence rows).

Source: U.S. Department of Agriculture, National Agricultural Statistics Service, *Agricultural Statistics, 2007*. See also <http://www.nass.usda.gov/Publications/Ag_Statistics/index.asp>.

Table 844. **Total Wildland Fires and Acres: 1970 to 2007**

[Includes only nonstructure fires that occur in the wildland. Data do not include prescribed fires, which are ignited by management action under certain predetermined conditions to meet specific objectives related to hazardous fuels or habitat improvement]

Year	Fires	Acres (1,000)	Year	Fires	Acres (1,000)	Year	Fires	Acres (1,000)	Year	Fires	Acres (1,000)
1970	121,736	3,279	1992	87,394	2,070	1998	81,043	1,330	2004 [1]	65,461	8,098
1975	134,872	1,791	1993	58,810	1,798	1999	92,487	5,626	2005	66,753	8,689
1980	234,892	5,261	1994	79,107	4,074	2000	92,250	7,393	2006	96,385	9,874
1985	82,591	2,896	1995	82,234	1,841	2001	84,079	3,571	2007	85,705	9,328
1990	66,481	4,622	1996	96,363	6,066	2002	73,457	7,185			
1991	75,754	2,954	1997	66,196	2,857	2003	63,629	3,961			

[1] 2004 fires and acres do not include state lands for North Carolina.

Source: National Interagency Coordination Center, "Wildland Fires and Acres (1960–2007)"; <http://www.nifc.gov/fire_info/fires_acres.htm> (accessed 23 April 2008).

Table 845. **Timber Products—Production, Foreign Trade, and Consumption by Type of Product: 1990 to 2006**

[In millions of cubic feet, roundwood equivalent (15,577 represents 15,577,000,000)]

Type of product	1990	1995	1998	1999	2000	2001	2002	2003	2004	2005	2006
Industrial roundwood:											
Domestic production	15,577	15,537	15,620	15,632	15,436	14,634	14,902	14,571	15,139	15,465	14,891
Softwoods	10,968	10,191	10,097	10,381	10,201	9,859	10,124	10,290	10,710	11,002	10,514
Hardwoods	4,609	5,347	5,523	5,251	5,235	4,775	4,778	4,282	4,428	4,463	4,377
Imports	3,091	3,907	4,157	4,370	4,529	4,605	4,505	5,096	5,805	5,802	5,396
Exports	2,307	2,282	1,951	1,964	1,996	1,759	1,769	1,535	1,604	1,646	1,446
Consumption	16,361	17,161	17,827	18,038	17,969	17,481	17,637	18,132	19,339	19,622	18,841
Softwoods	11,779	11,961	12,339	12,754	12,659	12,552	12,790	13,398	14,357	14,652	13,985
Hardwoods	4,582	5,200	5,488	5,284	5,310	4,929	4,847	4,734	4,983	4,970	4,856
Lumber:											
Domestic production	7,317	6,815	7,093	7,379	7,199	6,820	7,060	7,131	7,510	7,889	7,552
Imports	1,909	2,522	2,721	2,807	2,845	2,903	3,036	3,193	3,704	3,737	3,439
Exports	589	460	350	404	428	354	353	347	348	389	390
Consumption	8,637	8,877	9,463	9,782	9,616	9,369	9,744	9,977	10,866	11,237	10,602
Plywood and veneer:											
Domestic production	1,423	1,303	1,201	1,208	1,187	1,067	1,074	1,054	1,086	1,068	1,003
Imports	97	107	131	160	155	173	205	240	354	373	369
Exports	109	89	55	45	42	32	31	35	43	37	35
Consumption	1,410	1,321	1,277	1,323	1,300	1,208	1,249	1,259	1,397	1,403	1,337
Pulp products:											
Domestic production	5,313	6,079	6,114	5,813	5,881	5,691	5,708	5,557	5,692	5,679	5,679
Imports	1,038	1,248	1,269	1,355	1,459	1,458	1,180	1,579	1,669	1,570	1,490
Exports	646	905	818	768	842	801	810	643	680	708	683
Consumption	5,704	6,422	6,565	6,400	6,498	6,348	6,078	6,493	6,680	6,541	6,486
Logs:											
Imports	4	13	30	47	68	70	81	80	73	114	94
Exports	674	451	316	326	331	307	309	356	366	345	339
Pulpwood chips, exports	288	377	412	422	353	265	265	155	168	166	–
Fuelwood consumption	3,019	2,937	2,523	2,542	2,561	2,571	2,581	1,515	1,540	1,550	1,550

– Represents zero.

Source: U.S. Forest Service, *U.S. Timber Production, Trade, Consumption, and Price Statistics, 1965–1999*, Research Paper FPL-RP-595; and unpublished data. See also <http://www.fpl.fs.fed.us/documnts/fplrp/fplrp595.pdf>.

Table 846. **Selected Timber Products—Imports and Exports: 1990 to 2007**

[In million board feet (13,063 represents 13,063,000,000) except as indicated]

Product	Unit	1990	1995	2000	2002	2003	2004	2005	2006	2007
IMPORTS [1]										
Lumber, total [2]	Mil. bd. ft.	13,063	17,524	19,906	21,434	21,981	25,493	25,738	23,695	18,442
From Canada	Percent	91	97	92	90	90	83	85	86	85
Logs, total	Mil. bd. ft. [3]	23	80	435	525	497	454	710	585	418
From Canada	Percent	84	70	96	97	98	97	85	85	89
Paper and board [4]	1,000 tons	12,195	14,292	17,555	19,433	20,034	21,146	20,438	20,293	18,634
Woodpulp	1,000 tons [5]	4,893	5,969	7,227	7,247	6,691	6,726	6,762	6,939	6,793
Plywood	Mil. sq. ft. [5]	1,687	1,951	2,917	3,868	4,489	5,896	6,325	6,324	(NA)
EXPORTS										
Lumber, total [2]	Mil. bd. ft.	4,623	2,958	2,700	2,186	2,193	3,842	2,682	2,651	2,119
To: Canada	Percent	14	22	26	27	29	12	28	28	25
Japan	Percent	28	33	12	7	7	11	3	4	6
Europe	Percent	15	17	19	16	16	9	15	16	(NA)
Logs, total	Mil. bd. ft. [3]	4,213	2,820	2,068	1,934	2,224	2,287	2,157	2,120	2,189
To: Canada	Percent	9	25	41	50	54	49	54	52	43
Japan	Percent	62	61	45	34	29	28	27	26	26
China	Percent	9	1	–	2	2	3	4	5	7
Paper and board [4]	1,000 tons	5,163	7,621	10,003	11,564	11,868	12,566	13,434	13,349	14,582
Woodpulp	1,000 tons [5]	5,905	8,261	6,409	6,254	5,847	6,225	6,413	6,606	(NA)
Plywood	Mil. sq. ft. [5]	1,766	1,517	754	563	640	783	568	749	(NA)

– Represents zero.   NA Not available.   [1] Customs value of imports; see text, Section 28.   [2] Includes railroad ties.   [3] Log scale.   [4] Includes paper and board products. Excludes hardboard.   [5] 3/8 inch basis.

Source: U.S. Forest Service, *U.S. Timber Production, Trade, Consumption, and Price Statistics, 1965–1999,* Research Paper FPL-RP-595; and unpublished data. See also <http://www.fpl.fs.fed.us/documnts/fplrp/fplrp595.pdf>.

Table 847. **Lumber Consumption by Species Group and End Use: 1995 to 2007**

[In billion board feet (59.3 represents 59,300,000,000), except per capita in board feet. Per capita consumption based on estimated resident population as of **July 1**]

Item	1995	1998	1999	2000	2001	2002	2003	2004	2005	2006	2007
Consumption, total	**59.3**	**65.1**	**68.3**	**66.1**	**64.6**	**67.5**	**67.0**	**73.1**	**75.6**	**71.3**	**60.8**
Per capita	225	241	250	240	227	235	230	249	255	238	201
SPECIES GROUP											
Softwoods	47.6	52.1	54.5	54.0	53.7	56.4	56.5	62.0	64.4	60.4	50.5
Hardwoods	11.7	13.0	13.8	12.2	11.0	11.1	10.5	11.1	11.2	10.9	10.3
END USE											
New housing	15.9	20.6	22.1	20.6	20.1	23.4	24.0	26.1	28.6	27.1	26.2
Residential upkeep and improvements	14.3	14.7	15.1	16.4	17.0	17.8	18.3	20.0	20.6	20.8	20.9
New nonresidential construction [1]	5.8	7.8	7.6	5.1	5.6	4.5	4.4	4.4	4.3	4.1	3.9
Manufacturing	5.5	8.4	(NA)	(NA)	(NA)	(NA)	8.1	7.9	7.7	7.5	7.3
Shipping	8.5	7.2	7.4	7.7	8.1	8.0	7.5	7.8	7.6	7.6	7.7
Other [2]	9.3	(NA)	16.1	16.3	13.8	13.8	4.7	6.9	7.0	7.0	(NA)

NA Not available.   [1] In addition to new construction, includes railroad ties laid as replacements in existing track and lumber used by railroads for railcar repair.   [2] Includes upkeep and improvement of nonresidential buildings and structures; made-at-home projects, such as furniture, boats, and picnic tables; made-on-the-job items such as advertising and display structures; and miscellaneous products and uses.

Source: U.S. Forest Service, *U.S. Timber Production, Trade, Consumption, and Price Statistics, 1965–1999,* Research Paper FPL-RP-595; and unpublished data. See also <http://www.fpl.fs.fed.us/documnts/fplrp/fplrp595.pdf>.

Table 848. **Selected Species—Stumpage Prices in Current and Constant (1996) Dollars: 2000 to 2007**

[In dollars per 1,000 board feet. Stumpage prices are based on sales of sawtimber from national forests]

Species	Current dollars				Constant (1996) dollars [1]			
	2000	2005	2006	2007	2000	2005	2006	2007
Softwoods:								
Douglas fir [2]	433	321	68	103	397	260	54	76
Southern pine [3]	258	193	113	175	237	157	87	129
Sugar pine [4]	187	114	38	81	172	93	30	60
Ponderosa pine [4, 5]	155	103	39	61	142	84	30	45
Western hemlock [6]	46	70	101	21	42	57	78	15
Hardwoods:								
All eastern hardwoods [7]	341	415	275	(NA)	313	337	213	(NA)
Oak, white, red, and black [7]	258	329	180	(NA)	237	267	140	(NA)
Maple, sugar [8]	314	648	533	362	288	526	413	267

NA Not available.   [1] Deflated by the producer price index, all commodities.   [2] Western Washington and western Oregon.   [3] Southern region.   [4] Pacific Southwest region (formerly California region).   [5] Includes Jeffrey pine.   [6] Pacific Northwest region.   [7] Eastern and Southern regions.   [8] Eastern region.

Source: U.S. Forest Service, *Timber Demand and Technology Assessment,* RWU-4851. Also in *Agricultural Statistics,* annual.

Table 849. **Selected Timber Products—Producer Price Indexes: 1990 to 2007**

[**1982 = 100.** For information about producer prices, see text, Section 14]

Product	1990	1995	2000	2002	2003	2004	2005	2006	2007
Lumber and wood products [1]	**129.7**	**178.1**	**178.2**	**173.3**	**177.4**	**195.6**	**196.5**	**194.4**	**192.4**
Lumber	124.6	173.4	178.8	170.6	174.3	203.6	198.6	188.6	174.7
Softwood lumber	123.8	178.5	178.6	170.8	170.8	209.8	203.6	189.4	170.7
Hardwood lumber	131.0	167.0	185.9	178.3	188.8	199.3	196.6	195.3	192.2
Millwork [1]	130.4	163.8	176.4	179.8	181.8	191.9	197.2	201.8	201.3
General millwork	132.0	165.4	178.0	183.3	185.4	193.1	196.1	201.3	203.8
Prefabricated structural members	122.3	163.5	175.1	168.5	171.0	193.7	206.9	206.6	189.3
Plywood	114.2	165.3	157.6	151.7	167.0	198.5	186.8	172.7	176.0
Softwood plywood	119.6	188.1	173.3	164.1	195.9	250.9	223.5	190.5	197.7
Hardwood plywood and related products	102.7	122.2	130.2	131.5	129.0	134.4	138.1	(NA)	(NA)
Other wood products [1]	114.7	143.7	130.5	127.2	129.9	134.3	139.2	142.8	142.0
Boxes	119.1	145.0	155.2	154.3	157.6	163.1	164.9	167.2	170.1
Pulp, paper, and allied products [1]	**141.2**	**172.2**	**183.7**	**185.9**	**190.0**	**195.7**	**202.6**	**209.8**	**216.8**
Pulp, paper, and prod., excl. bldg. paper [1]	132.9	163.4	161.4	155.3	157.1	162.1	169.8	178.4	186.7
Woodpulp	151.3	183.2	145.3	116.2	121.4	132.2	138.0	144.1	161.5
Wastepaper	138.9	371.1	282.5	173.1	197.3	231.4	230.9	234.8	370.2
Paper [1]	128.8	159.0	149.8	144.7	146.1	149.4	159.6	167.4	169.1
Writing and printing papers	129.1	158.4	146.6	143.8	144.7	146.0	156.1	162.8	166.5
Newsprint	119.6	161.8	127.5	105.7	112.1	124.5	138.5	151.8	131.7
Paperboard	135.7	183.1	176.7	164.3	162.7	170.2	175.5	192.0	201.7
Converted paper and paperboard products [1]	135.2	157.0	162.7	163.8	165.3	168.3	176.1	184.1	187.8
Office supplies and accessories	121.4	134.9	133.8	135.7	137.4	137.6	143.1	146.2	151.0
Building paper & building board mill prods	112.2	144.9	138.8	129.3	159.9	192.4	184.9	173.0	155.0

NA Not available.   [1] Includes other products not shown separately.

Source: U.S. Bureau of Labor Statistics, *Producer Price Indexes,* monthly.

Table 850. **Pulpwood Consumption, Woodpulp Production, and Paper and Board Production and Consumption: 1995 to 2005**

[Revised to match data from American Forest and Paper Association and American Pulpwood Association]

Item	Unit	1995	1998	1999	2000	2001	2002	2003	2004	2005
Pulpwood consumption [1]	1,000 cords [2]	97,052	96,305	94,265	95,904	92,181	90,500	85,436	87,110	88,595
Woodpulp production [3]	1,000 tons	67,103	65,163	62,914	62,758	58,198	58,069	53,197	54,301	60,267
Paper and board [4]:										
Production	1,000 tons	89,509	94,510	97,020	94,491	88,913	89,636	80,712	83,612	91,031
Consumption or new supply [5]	1,000 tons	96,126	100,978	104,873	103,147	97,303	97,227	94,422	95,068	101,864
Per capita	Pounds	731	747	768	731	683	676	629	627	687

[1] Includes changes in stocks.   [2] One cord equals 128 cubic feet.   [3] Excludes defibrated and exploded woodpulp used for hard pressed board.   [4] Excludes hardboards.   [5] Production plus imports, minus exports (excludes products); changes in inventories not taken into account.

Source: U.S. Department of Agriculture, National Agricultural Statistics Service, *Agricultural Statistics, 2007.* See also <http://www.nass.usda.gov/Publications/Ag_Statistics/index.asp>.

Table 851. **Paper and Paperboard—Production and New Supply: 1990 to 2006**

[In millions of short tons (80.45 represents 80,450,000). 1 short ton = 2,000 lbs.]

Item	1990	1995	2000	2001	2002	2003	2004	2005	2006
Production, total	**80.45**	**91.33**	**96.05**	**90.38**	**91.11**	**89.81**	**93.41**	**92.61**	**93.72**
Paper, total	39.36	42.87	45.52	42.10	41.56	40.37	41.82	41.40	41.81
Paperboard, total	39.32	46.64	48.97	46.81	48.13	48.02	50.08	49.71	50.41
Unbleached kraft	20.36	22.70	21.80	20.44	21.09	21.73	22.67	22.58	23.41
Semichemical	5.64	5.66	5.95	5.58	5.84	6.10	6.53	6.41	6.22
Bleached kraft	4.40	5.30	5.44	5.30	5.30	5.36	5.65	5.66	5.70
Recycled	8.92	12.98	15.79	15.50	15.91	14.83	15.24	15.05	15.07
Wet machine board	0.15	0.15	0.06	0.05	0.05	0.05	0.05	0.05	0.05
Building paper	0.81	0.81	0.64	0.58	0.55	0.55	0.58	0.57	0.56
Insulating board	0.86	0.86	0.86	0.85	0.83	0.83	0.88	0.88	0.88
New supply, all grades, excluding products	**87.68**	**98.16**	**105.02**	**83.58**	**100.57**	**99.76**	**103.74**	**101.81**	**102.28**
Paper, total	49.49	52.77	57.13	37.69	53.66	53.22	54.88	53.69	53.56
Newsprint	13.41	12.76	12.92	–	11.18	11.05	10.84	10.12	9.50
Printing/writing papers	25.46	29.55	32.99	30.62	31.09	31.03	32.68	31.99	32.36
Packaging and ind. conv. papers	4.72	4.24	4.27	–	4.20	3.96	4.14	4.05	4.10
Tissue	5.90	6.22	6.95	7.07	7.20	7.18	7.22	7.53	7.60
Paperboard, total	36.30	43.45	46.02	44.09	45.29	44.95	47.20	46.51	47.11
Construction and other	1.90	1.95	1.88	1.80	1.62	1.59	1.66	1.61	1.62

– Represents or rounds to zero.

Source: American Forest and Paper Association, Washington, DC, *Monthly Statistical Summary of Paper, Paperboard and Woodpulp.*

Table 852. **Fishery Products—Domestic Catch, Imports, and Disposition: 1990 to 2006**

[**Live weight, in millions of pounds (16,349 represents 16,349,000,000).** For data on commercial catch for selected countries, see Table 1328, Section 30]

Item	1990	1995	2000	2001	2002	2003	2004	2005	2006
Total	**16,349**	**16,484**	**17,340**	**18,119**	**19,028**	**19,850**	**20,412**	**20,612**	**20,966**
For human food	12,662	13,584	14,738	15,303	16,007	17,187	17,648	18,147	18,560
For industrial use	3,687	2,900	2,599	2,812	3,021	2,663	2,765	2,382	2,406
Domestic catch.	**9,404**	**9,788**	**9,069**	**9,492**	**9,397**	**9,507**	**9,683**	**9,707**	**9,489**
For human food	7,041	7,667	6,912	7,314	7,205	7,521	7,794	7,997	7,808
For industrial use.	2,363	2,121	2,157	2,178	2,192	1,986	1,889	1,710	1,681
Imports [1]	**6,945**	**6,696**	**8,271**	**8,627**	**9,631**	**10,343**	**10,729**	**10,905**	**11,477**
For human food	5,621	5,917	7,828	7,992	8,802	9,666	9,854	10,158	10,752
For industrial use [2]	1,324	779	443	635	829	677	875	747	725
Exports [1]	**4,627**	**5,166**	**5,758**	**7,107**	**6,979**	**6,756**	**8,203**	**8,420**	**7,710**
For human food	3,832	4,175	4,587	5,774	5,587	5,392	6,462	6,385	6,251
For industrial use [2]	795	991	1,171	1,333	1,392	1,364	1,741	2,035	1,459
Disposition of domestic catch	**9,404**	**9,788**	**9,069**	**9,489**	**9,397**	**9,507**	**9,683**	**9,707**	**9,489**
Fresh and frozen	6,501	7,099	6,657	7,082	6,826	7,266	7,488	7,776	7,752
Canned.	751	769	530	536	652	498	552	563	463
Cured.	126	90	119	123	117	119	137	160	108
Reduced to meal, oil, etc.. . .	2,026	1,830	1,763	1,748	1,802	1,624	1,506	1,208	1,166

[1] Excludes imports of edible fishery products consumed in Puerto Rico; includes landings of tuna caught by foreign vessels in American Samoa. [2] Fish meal and sea herring.

Source: U.S. National Oceanic and Atmospheric Administration, National Marine Fisheries Service, *Fisheries of the United States,* annual. See also <http://www.st.nmfs.noaa.gov/st1/fus/fus06/index.html> (released July 2007).

Table 853. **Fisheries—Quantity and Value of Domestic Catch: 1980 to 2006**

[**In millions of pounds (6,482 represents 6,482,000,000), except as noted**]

Year	Quantity (mil. lb. [1])			Value (mil. dol.)	Average price per lb. (cents)	Year	Quantity (mil. lb. [1])			Value (mil. dol.)	Average price per lb. (cents)
	Total	For human food	For industrial products [2]				Total	For human food	For industrial products [2]		
1980 . . .	6,482	3,654	2,828	2,237	34.5	1999 . . .	9,339	6,832	2,507	3,467	37.1
1985 . . .	6,258	3,294	2,964	2,326	37.2	2000 . . .	9,069	6,912	2,157	3,550	39.1
1990 . . .	9,404	7,041	2,363	3,522	37.5	2001 . . .	9,489	7,311	2,178	3,218	33.9
1994 . . .	10,461	7,936	2,525	3,807	36.4	2002 . . .	9,397	7,205	2,192	3,092	32.9
1995 . . .	9,788	7,667	2,121	3,770	38.5	2003 . . .	9,507	7,521	1,986	3,347	35.2
1996 . . .	9,565	7,474	2,091	3,487	36.5	2004 . . .	9,683	7,794	1,889	3,756	38.8
1997 . . .	9,842	7,244	2,598	3,448	35.0	2005 . . .	9,707	7,997	1,710	3,942	40.6
1998 . . .	9,194	7,173	2,021	3,126	34.0	2006 . . .	9,489	7,809	1,680	3,993	42.1

[1] Live weight. [2] Meal, oil, fish solubles, homogenized condensed fish, shell products, bait, and animal food.

Source: U.S. National Oceanic and Atmospheric Administration, National Marine Fisheries Service, *Fisheries of the United States,* annual. See also <http://www.st.nmfs.noaa.gov/st1/fus/fus06/index.html> (released July 2007).

Table 854. **Domestic Fish and Shellfish Catch and Value by Major Species Caught: 2000 to 2006**

[**In thousands (9,068,985 represents 9,068,985,000)**]

Species	Quantity (1,000 lb.)				Value ($1,000)			
	2000	2004	2005	2006	2000	2004	2005	2006
Total	**9,068,985**	**9,682,981**	**9,707,275**	**9,489,031**	**3,549,481**	**3,755,778**	**3,942,376**	**3,993,370**
Fish, total [1]	**7,689,661**	**8,415,959**	**8,462,473**	**8,349,316**	**1,594,815**	**1,748,308**	**1,836,448**	**1,932,418**
Cod: Atlantic	25,060	16,069	13,920	12,588	26,384	21,691	20,828	20,453
Pacific	530,505	590,650	548,746	518,733	142,330	148,982	150,738	197,243
Flounder	412,723	359,781	419,430	445,787	109,910	123,956	135,176	150,834
Halibut	75,190	80,056	76,263	71,847	143,826	176,405	177,593	200,490
Herring, Atlantic	160,269	189,281	215,565	282,947	9,972	15,084	20,467	25,095
Herring, Pacific.	74,835	75,330	87,295	81,932	12,043	15,246	13,799	8,039
Menhaden	1,760,498	1,497,617	1,243,723	1,304,208	112,403	72,447	62,465	66,235
Pollock, Alaska.	2,606,802	3,353,374	3,411,307	3,400,812	160,525	271,630	306,972	329,879
Salmon.	628,638	738,726	899,457	663,044	270,213	302,641	330,699	310,486
Tuna	50,779	56,541	44,316	49,345	95,176	91,138	85,922	86,194
Whiting (Atlantic, silver) . . .	26,855	18,965	16,561	12,281	11,370	9,918	8,284	6,687
Whiting (Pacific, hake)	452,718	474,528	569,381	570,489	18,809	21,823	29,145	35,234
Shellfish, total [1]	**1,379,324**	**1,267,022**	**1,075,840**	**1,107,996**	**1,954,666**	**2,007,470**	**2,084,060**	**2,042,939**
Clams.	118,482	119,411	105,640	108,456	153,973	166,407	173,655	165,627
Crabs.	299,006	315,643	299,137	322,498	405,006	449,821	415,057	428,799
Lobsters: American	83,180	88,386	88,032	92,515	301,300	366,006	416,597	394,711
Oysters.	41,146	38,654	33,963	27,344	90,667	112,122	110,679	121,720
Scallops, sea	32,747	64,580	56,702	59,006	164,609	321,377	433,512	385,971
Shrimp	332,486	309,295	260,884	292,236	690,453	427,619	406,344	419,280
Squid, Pacific.	259,508	89,580	126,107	113,312	27,077	19,831	31,601	27,202

[1] Includes other types of fish and shellfish not shown separately.

Source: U.S. National Oceanic and Atmospheric Administration, National Marine Fisheries Service, *Fisheries of the United States,* annual. See also <http://www.st.nmfs.noaa.gov/st1/fus/fus06/index.html> (released July 2007).

Table 855. **Marketable Aquaculture Sales by Species: 2005**

[**6,258 represents 6,258,000, except as noted.** Includes foodsize aquaculture only (grown aquaculture products ready for market). Does not include stockers, fingerlings, fry, broodstock, or eggs (aquaculture used for reproduction or not yet fully grown)]

Species	Farms	Number sold (1,000)	Live weight (pounds) Average	Live weight (pounds) Total ($1,000)	Sales Average price per pound (dollars)	Sales Total ($1,000)
FOOD FISH	1,847	(X)	(X)	(X)	(X)	672,377
Bass, hybrid striped	67	6,258	1.8	10,970	2.52	27,655
Carp, grass	25	115	3.5	406	1.59	643
Catfish	1,017	396,554	1.5	607,933	0.71	429,245
Perch, yellow	40	210	0.5	110	3.08	338
Salmon	9	2,408	8.6	20,726	1.81	37,439
Sturgeon	10	103	(D)	(D)	(D)	(D)
Tilapia	128	13,272	1.3	17,203	1.72	29,620
Trout	336	56,355	1.1	60,636	1.08	65,469
SPORT FISH	303	(X)	(X)	(X)	(X)	18,126
Bass, largemouth	58	1,667	2.5	4,185	1.99	8,334
Crappie	12	17	1.0	16	3.25	53
Northern Pike	5	1	2.1	3	4.07	12
Sunfish	54	660	1.6	1,024	0.93	950
Walleye	6	(D)	(D)	6	(D)	(D)
CRUSTACEANS	925	(X)	(X)	(X)	(X)	53,381
Crabs, softshell[1]	154	337,912	(X)	(X)	16.54	5,588
Crawfish	647	(X)	(X)	35,933	0.59	21,143
Lobster	1	(D)	(D)	(D)	(D)	(D)
Prawns, freshwater	76	19,553	41	482	5.56	2,680
Shrimp, saltwater	34	175,494	22	8,037	2.32	18,684
MOLLUSKS	980	(X)	(X)	(X)	(X)	203,183
Clams, hard	406	412,876	5	85,175	0.66	56,130
Clams, Manila	103	159,886	18	8,673	1.92	16,653
Mussels	28	83,494	15	5,639	0.88	4,990
Oysters, eastern	386	256,537	2	121,668	0.33	39,892
Oysters, Pacific	187	238,560	5	47,009	1.12	52,710

D Withheld to avoid disclosing data for individual farms.   X Not applicable.   [1] Number sold is dozen sold. Average price is price per dozen.

Source: U.S. Department of Agriculture, National Agricultural Statistics Service, Census of Aquaculture: 2005, Volume 3, Special Studies Part 2, issued October 2006. See also <http://www.agcensus.usda.gov/Publications/2002/Aquaculture/AQUACEN.pdf>.

Table 856. **Sales of Aquaculture Products by Type, by State: 2005**

[Includes all sizes of aquaculture products (foodsize, stockers, fingerlings, fry, broodstock, and eggs)]

State	Total sales[1] ($1,000)	Food fish[2] ($1,000)	Sport fish[3] ($1,000)	State	Total sales[1] ($1,000)	Food fish[2] ($1,000)	Sport fish[3] ($1,000)
U.S.. . .	**4,309**	**1,847**	**303**	MO	35	29	5
AL	215	201	20	MT	8	8	1
AK	26	1	–	NE	26	21	10
AZ	11	7	–	NV	–	–	–
AR	211	152	14	NH	10	6	1
CA	118	69	11	NJ	87	6	3
CO	15	13	1	NM	3	2	–
CT	30	3	1	NY	54	29	11
DE	3	2	1	NC	186	118	5
DC	(NA)	(NA)	(NA)	ND	1	1	1
FL	359	49	8	OH	55	36	27
GA	79	66	11	OK	20	14	6
HI	59	31	–	OR	47	18	3
ID	35	34	3	PA	56	46	8
IL	47	37	12	RI	12	–	–
IN	18	9	3	SC	85	24	12
IA	21	13	10	SD	7	5	4
KS	12	10	6	TN	45	31	4
KY	65	38	6	TX	95	63	8
LA	873	35	4	UT	11	9	1
ME	50	14	–	VT	9	8	–
MD	86	5	1	VA	147	22	–
MA	157	12	3	WA	194	18	–
MI	34	25	9	WV	21	19	2
MN	77	20	27	WI	84	70	33
MS	403	393	8	WY	7	5	–

– Represents zero.   NA Not available.   [1] Total includes food fish, sport fish, baitfish, ornamental fish, crustaceans, mollusks, and other miscellaneous aquaculture not listed in footnotes 2 and 3.   [2] Food fish includes arctic char, hybrid striped bass, carp, catfish, Pacific threadfin, yellow perch, red drum, salmon, sturgeon, tilapia, trout, and other food fish.   [3] Sport fish includes largemouth and smallmouth bass, crappie, muskie, northern pike, sunfish, walleye, and other sport fish.

Source: U.S. Department of Agriculture, National Agricultural Statistics Service, Census of Aquaculture: 2005, Volume 3, Special Studies Part 2, issued October 2006. See also <http://www.agcensus.usda.gov/Publications/2002/Aquaculture/AQUACEN.pdf>.

Table 857. U.S. Private Aquaculture—Trout and Catfish Production and Value: 1990 to 2007

[67.8 represents 67,800,000. Data are for calendar year and foodsize fish (those over 12 inches long)]

Item	Unit	1990	1995	2000	2003	2004	2005	2006	2007
TROUT FOODSIZE									
Number sold.	Mil.	67.8	60.2	58.4	46.1	49.6	55.5	52.5	59.7
Total weight	Mil. lb.	56.8	55.6	59.0	50.8	57.6	59.7	65.3	69.3
Total value of sales	Mil. dol. . . .	64.6	60.8	63.3	52.9	59.4	62.7	72.7	80.0
Avg. price received by processors. . .	Dol./lb.	1.14	1.09	1.07	1.04	1.03	1.05	1.11	1.15
Percent sold to processors	Percent . . .	58	68	70	68	73	66	69	67
CATFISH FOODSIZE									
Number sold.	Mil.	272.9	321.8	420.1	381.7	389.3	405.4	370.9	352.7
Total weight	Mil. lb.	392.4	481.5	633.8	699.3	682.2	638.9	587.0	548.4
Total value of sales	Mil. dol. . . .	305.1	378.1	468.8	397.1	450.9	450.2	455.1	408.8
Avg. price received by processors. . .	Dol./lb.	0.78	0.79	0.74	0.57	0.66	0.70	0.78	0.75
Fish sold to processors.	Mil. lb.	360.4	446.9	593.6	661.5	630.5	600.7	566.1	496.2
Avg. price paid by processors	Cents/lb. . . .	75.8	78.6	75.1	58.1	69.7	72.5	79.5	76.7
Processor sales.	Mil. lb.	183.1	227.0	297.2	319.3	306.8	300.0	284.0	252.5
Avg. price received by processors. . .	Dol./lb.	2.24	2.40	2.36	2.05	2.23	2.29	2.46	2.44
Inventory (Jan. 1)	Mil. lb.	9.4	10.9	13.6	13.6	15.2	13.7	18.2	15.1

Source: U.S. Department of Agriculture, National Agricultural Statistics Service, *Trout Production,* released February; *Catfish Production,* released January; and *Catfish Processing,* released May. Also in *Agricultural Statistics,* annual.

Table 858. Supply of Selected Fishery Items: 1990 to 2006

[In millions of pounds (734 represents 734,000,000). Totals available for U.S. consumption are supply minus exports plus imports. Round weight is the complete or full weight as caught]

Species	Unit	1990	1995	2000	2001	2002	2003	2004	2005	2006
Shrimp	Heads-off weight. . .	734	832	1,172	1,312	1,430	1,608	1,670	1,559	1,862
Tuna, canned	Canned weight	856	875	980	796	922	982	874	895	858
Snow crab	Round weight	37	42	122	171	172	198	168	171	187
Clams	Meat weight	152	144	133	139	144	143	132	120	122
Salmon, canned	Canned weight	148	147	95	81	135	111	98	123	56
American lobster.	Round weight	95	94	124	125	135	128	138	144	150
Spiny lobster	Round weight	89	89	99	79	87	93	93	83	77
Scallops	Meat weight	74	62	78	76	91	94	94	86	94
Sardines, canned	Canned weight	61	44	(NA)	(NA)	(NA)	(NA)	(NA)	(NA)	(NA)
Oysters	Meat weight	56	63	71	58	62	69	53	47	42
King crab.	Round weight	19	21	41	38	47	47	52	78	110
Crab meat, canned . . .	Canned weight	9	12	29	35	44	47	56	59	58

NA Not available.

Source: U.S. National Oceanic and Atmospheric Administration, National Marine Fisheries Service, *Fisheries of the United States,* annual. See also <http://www.st.nmfs.noaa.gov/st1/fus/fus06/index.html> (released July 2007).

Table 859. Canned, Fresh, and Frozen Fishery Products—Production and Value: 1990 to 2006

[In millions of pounds (1,178 represents 1,178,000,000). Fresh fishery products exclude Alaska and Hawaii. Canned fishery products data are for natural pack only]

Product	Production (mil. lb.)					Value (mil. dol.)				
	1990	1995	2000	2005	2006	1990	1995	2000	2005	2006
Canned, total [1]	**1,178**	**1,927**	**1,747**	**1,082**	**1,081**	**1,562**	**1,887**	**1,626**	**1,211**	**1,330**
Tuna	581	667	671	446	445	902	939	856	628	705
Salmon	196	244	171	219	152	366	419	288	301	250
Clam products.	110	129	127	123	112	76	110	120	127	122
Sardines, Maine	13	14	(Z)	(NA)	(NA)	17	24	(Z)	(NA)	(NA)
Shrimp.	1	1	2	1	(Z)	3	7	11	3	1
Crabs	1	(Z)	(Z)	(Z)	(Z)	4	(Z)	(Z)	(Z)	(Z)
Oysters [2]	1	(Z)	(Z)	(Z)	(Z)	1	(Z)	1	(Z)	(Z)
Fish fillets and steaks [3] . . .	**441**	**385**	**368**	**615**	**630**	**843**	**841**	**823**	**1,136**	**1,293**
Cod.	65	65	56	47	41	132	152	167	116	119
Flounder	54	35	27	20	19	154	86	71	65	74
Haddock	7	3	6	24	16	24	11	24	89	69
Ocean perch, Atlantic	1	(Z)	(Z)	1	1	1	1	1	4	3
Rockfish.	33	25	11	3	2	53	38	25	8	5
Pollock, Atlantic.	12	4	2	3	2	21	10	4	6	4
Pollock, Alaska	164	135	160	383	398	174	184	178	404	488
Other.	105	118	106	134	151	284	359	353	444	532

NA Not available.   Z Less than 500,000 pounds or $500,000.   [1] Includes other products not shown separately.
[2] Includes oyster specialties.   [3] Fresh and frozen.

Source: U.S. National Oceanic and Atmospheric Administration, National Marine Fisheries Service, *Fisheries of the United States,* annual. See also <http://www.st.nmfs.gov/st1/fus/fus06/index.html> (released July 2007).

U.S. Census Bureau, Statistical Abstract of the United States: 2009

Table 860. Mineral Industries—Employment, Hours, and Earnings: 1990 to 2007

[**In thousands (680 represents 680,000), except as noted.** Based on the Current Employment Statistics Program, see Appendix III]

Industry and item	Unit	1990	1995	2000	2003	2004	2005	2006	2007
All mining:									
All employees.	1,000	680	558	520	503	523	562	620	662
Production workers	1,000	469	391	383	364	384	419	466	495
Avg. weekly hours	Number. . .	46.1	46.8	45.5	44.4	45.4	46.4	46.3	46.2
Avg. weekly earnings . . .	Dollars . . .	630	711	771	796	837	884	938	989
Coal mining:									
All employees.	1,000	136	97	72	70	71	74	78	78
Production workers	1,000	110	78	59	59	59	61	67	69
Avg. weekly hours	Number. . .	44.7	45.7	45.6	46.2	47.7	48.5	49.5	47.8
Avg. weekly earnings . . .	Dollars . . .	822	929	945	963	1,029	1,071	1,093	1,050
Oil and gas extraction:									
All employees.	1,000	190	152	125	120	123	126	135	146
Production workers	1,000	84	73	67	67	70	72	78	83
Avg. weekly hours	Number. . .	44.4	43.6	41.3	41.1	43.5	44.3	43.0	41.9
Avg. weekly earnings . . .	Dollars . . .	591	677	802	778	808	856	921	1,015
Metal ore mining:									
All employees.	1,000	53	48	38	27	28	29	32	37
Production workers	1,000	43	39	29	20	20	22	25	28
Avg. weekly hours	Number. . .	42.5	43.4	43.4	43.7	45.2	44.2	43.5	45.8
Avg. weekly earnings . . .	Dollars . . .	646	788	871	957	1,035	1,001	974	1,077
Nonmetallic minerals mining, and quarrying:									
All employees.	1,000	113	108	115	106	107	110	110	110
Production workers	1,000	85	81	87	78	81	84	82	82
Avg. weekly hours	Number. . .	45.0	46.3	46.1	45.1	44.6	45.9	46.1	46.4
Avg. weekly earnings . . .	Dollars . . .	532	632	722	773	791	830	863	872

Source: U.S. Bureau of Labor Statistics, the Current Employment Statistics program Internet site <http://www.bls.gov/ces/home.htm>.

Table 861. Mine Safety: 2000 to 2007

[Reported injury rates per 200,000 employee hours]

Item	All mines			Coal			Metal and nonmetal		
	2000	2006	2007	2000	2006	2007	2000	2006	2007
Number of mines.	14,413	14,885	14,786	2,124	2,113	2,013	12,289	12,772	12,773
Number of miners	348,548	363,497	376,386	108,098	122,975	122,328	240,450	240,522	254,058
Fatalities	85	73	64	38	47	33	47	26	31
Fatal injury rate.	0.03	0.02	0.02	0.04	0.40	0.29	0.02	0.01	0.01
All injury rate	5.13	3.64	3.42	6.64	4.46	4.19	4.45	3.19	3.01
Coal production (mil. tons)	1,078	1,163	1,141	1,078	1,163	1,141	(X)	(X)	(X)
Total mining area inspection hours/mine.	57	43	44	178	161	169	28	19	19
Citations and orders.	120,269	140,268	145,050	58,394	77,732	84,722	61,875	62,536	60,328
S&S [1] citations and orders (percent). . .	36	33	31	42	40	38	31	24	23
Amount assessed [2] (mil. dol.)	24.7	35.1	74.5	12.0	22.5	63.5	12.7	12.7	21.0

X Not applicable.   [1] A violation that "significantly and substantially" contributes to the cause and effect of a coal or other mine safety or health hazard.   [2] Government penalties or fines.

Source: U.S. Mine Safety and Health Administration, Office of Program Education and Outreach Services, "Mine Safety and Health At a Glance" (released 6 February 2008); <http://www.msha.gov/MSHAINFO/FactSheets/MSHAFCT10.HTM>.

Table 862. Mining and Primary Metal Production Indexes: 1990 to 2007

[Index 2002 = 100]

Industry group	NAICS code [1]	1990	1995	2000	2002	2003	2004	2005	2006	2007
Mining [2]	**21**	**106.9**	**104.4**	**103.5**	**100.0**	**100.2**	**99.6**	**98.3**	**101.4**	**101.5**
Oil and gas extraction [2]	211	107.3	104.0	101.0	100.0	99.0	96.0	92.0	93.4	94.9
Crude oil and natural gas	211111	109.2	104.8	100.9	100.0	99.7	95.9	92.1	93.4	94.9
Coal mining	2121	98.3	96.8	99.2	100.0	97.5	100.8	102.5	105.2	103.7
Metal ore mining	2122	112.1	122.6	120.2	100.0	95.4	98.2	106.1	109.9	109.6
Iron ore	21221	109.8	121.8	122.2	100.0	94.1	106.0	105.2	102.3	101.7
Gold ore and silver ore	21222	99.6	106.6	118.8	100.0	92.9	86.8	86.1	84.5	81.7
Copper, nickel, lead, and zinc. . .	21223	120.2	137.7	121.8	100.0	98.5	100.6	99.2	103.4	103.6
Oil and gas drilling.	213111	102.3	89.5	114.4	100.0	116.2	126.9	142.5	164.4	170.3
Primary metal manufacturing [2]	**331**	**96.2**	**105.4**	**110.3**	**100.0**	**99.1**	**110.0**	**108.0**	**112.4**	**110.4**
Iron and steel	3311	95.1	105.6	110.9	100.0	101.2	118.2	110.1	119.5	115.8
Aluminum.	3313	102.4	98.0	103.4	100.0	95.8	96.4	102.5	104.8	104.3
Nonferrous metals [2].	3314	109.2	120.7	109.0	100.0	100.3	103.7	103.3	98.4	100.7
Copper.	33142	142.5	263.1	133.9	100.0	86.9	90.7	81.7	67.6	71.1

[1] Based on the 2002 North American Industry Classification System (NAICS).   [2] Includes other industries not shown separately.

Source: Board of Governors of the Federal Reserve System, *The Statistical Supplement to the Federal Reserve Bulletin*, monthly; and *Industrial Production and Capacity Utilization*, Statistical Release G.17, monthly.

Table 863. **Mineral Production: 1990 to 2007**

[**1,029.1 represents 1,029,100,000.** Data represent production as measured by mine shipments, mine sales, or marketable production; see Appendix IV]

Minerals and Metals	Unit	1990	2000	2005	2006	2007, est.
FUEL MINERALS						
Coal, total	Mil. sh. tons	1,029.1	1,073.6	1,131.5	1,162.7	1,145.6
Bituminous	Mil. sh. tons	693.2	574.3	571.2	561.6	534.9
Subbituminous	Mil. sh. tons	244.3	409.2	474.7	515.3	530.6
Lignite	Mil. sh. tons	88.1	85.6	83.9	84.2	78.5
Anthracite	Mil. sh. tons	3.5	4.6	1.7	1.5	1.6
Natural gas (marketed production)	Tril. cu. ft.	18.59	20.20	18.93	19.38	20.15
Petroleum (crude)	Mil. bbl. [1]	2,685	2,131	1,890	1,862	1,862
Uranium (recoverable content)	Mil. lb.	8.9	4.0	2.7	4.1	4.5
NONFUEL MINERALS						
Asbestos (sales)	1,000 metric tons	(D)	5	–	–	–
Barite, primary, sold/used by producers	1,000 metric tons	430	392	489	589	540
Boron minerals, sold or used by producers	1,000 metric tons	1,090	1,070	1,150	(D)	(D)
Bromine, sold or used by producers	1,000 metric tons	177	228	226	243	235
Cement:						
Portland [2]	Mil. metric tons	67	84	94	93	90
Masonry [3]	Mil. metric tons	3	4	5	5	4
Clays	1,000 metric tons	42,900	40,800	41,200	41,200	40,600
Diatomite	1,000 metric tons	631	677	653	799	830
Feldspar [4]	1,000 metric tons	630	790	750	760	760
Fluorspar, finished shipments	1,000 metric tons	64	–	–	–	–
Garnet (industrial)	1,000 metric tons	47	60	40	34	34
Gypsum, crude	Mil. metric tons	15	20	21	21	22
Helium [5]	Mil. cu. meters	65	98	76	79	80
Lime, sold or used by producers	Mil. metric tons	16	20	20	21	20
Mica, scrap & flake, sold/used by producers	1,000 metric tons	109	101	78	110	72
Peat, sales by producers	1,000 metric tons	721	847	751	734	747
Perlite, processed, sold or used	1,000 metric tons	576	672	508	454	444
Phosphate rock (marketable)	Mil. metric tons	46	39	36	30	30
Potash (K_2O equivalent) sales	1,000 metric tons	1,710	1,300	1,200	1,100	1,200
Pumice & pumicite, producer sales	1,000 metric tons	443	1,050	1,270	1,540	1,410
Salt, common, sold/used by producers	Mil. metric tons	37	46	45	44	44
Sand & gravel, sold/used by producer	Mil. metric tons	855	1,148	1,301	1,352	1,205
Construction	Mil. metric tons	829	1,120	1,270	1,320	1,170
Industrial	Mil. metric tons	26	28	31	32	35
Sodium carbonate (natural) (soda ash)	1,000 metric tons	9,100	10,200	11,000	11,000	11,100
Sodium sulfate (natural)	1,000 metric tons	349	(NA)	309	290	300
Stone [6]	Mil. metric tons	1,110	2,810	3,060	3,050	2,940
Crushed and broken	Mil. metric tons	1,110	1,560	1,700	1,720	1,440
Dimension [7]	1,000 metric tons	1,120	1,250	1,360	1,330	1,500
Sulfur: Total shipments	1,000 metric tons	11,500	10,700	9,480	8,960	8,860
Sulfur: Frasch mines (shipments)	1,000 metric tons	3,680	900	–	–	–
Talc and pyrophyllite, crude	1,000 metric tons	1,270	851	856	895	839
Vermiculite concentrate	1,000 metric tons	209	150	100	100	100
METALS						
Antimony ore and concentrate	Metric tons	(D)	(D)	–	–	–
Aluminum	1,000 metric tons	4,048	3,668	2,481	2,284	2,550
Bauxite (dried)	1,000 metric tons	(D)	(NA)	(NA)	(NA)	(NA)
Copper (recoverable content)	1,000 metric tons	1,590	1,450	1,140	1,200	1,180
Gold (recoverable content)	Metric tons	294	353	256	252	240
Iron ore (gross weight) [8]	Mil. metric tons	57	61	53	53	49
Lead (recoverable content)	1,000 metric tons	484	449	426	419	420
Magnesium metal	1,000 metric tons	139	(D)	(D)	(D)	(D)
Manganiferous ore (gross weight) [9]	1,000 metric ton	(D)	–	(NA)	(NA)	(NA)
Mercury [10]	Metric tons	(NA)	(NA)	(NA)	(NA)	(NA)
Molybdenum (concentrate)	1,000 metric tons	62	41	58	60	59
Nickel ore (recovered Ni content)	1,000 metric tons	330	–	–	–	–
Palladium metal	Kilograms	5,930	10,300	13,300	14,400	13,500
Platinum metal	Kilograms	1,810	3,110	3,920	4,290	3,400
Silicon (Si content)	1,000 metric tons	418	367	270	146	156
Silver (recoverable content)	Metric tons	2,120	1,860	1,230	1,140	1,220
Titanium concentrate (TiO_2 content)	1,000 metric tons	(D)	300	300	300	300
Tungsten ore and concentrate [11]	Metric tons	(D)	–	–	–	(D)
Zinc (recoverable content)	1,000 metric tons	515	805	748	727	740

– Represents zero.   D Withheld to avoid disclosing individual company data.   NA Not available.   [1] 42 gal. bbl.   [2] Data for 1990 includes Puerto Rico.   [3] Excludes Puerto Rico for 2000–2006.   [4] Beginning 2000, includes aplite.   [5] Refined.   [6] Excludes abrasive stone, bituminous limestone and sandstone, and ground soapstone, all included elsewhere in table; includes calcareous marl and slate.   [7] Includes Puerto Rico in 1990.   [8] Represents shipments; includes by-product ores.   [9] 5- to 35-percent manganiferous ore.   [10] Covers mercury recovered as a by-product of gold ores only.   [11] Content of ore and concentrate.

Source: Nonfuels, 1990 only, U.S. Bureau of Mines, thereafter, U.S. Geological Survey, *Minerals Yearbook* and *Mineral Commodities Summaries,* annual. See also <http://minerals.er.usgs.gov/minerals/pubs/mcs/>. Fuels, U.S. Energy Information Administration, *Annual Energy Review,* 2007; most recent year from "Monthly Energy Review" and "Annual Coal Report"; <http://www.eia.doe.gov>.

U.S. Census Bureau, Statistical Abstract of the United States: 2009

Table 864. **Nonfuel Mineral Commodities—Summary: 2007**

[**2,550 represents 2,550,000.** Preliminary estimates. Average price in dollars per metric tons except as noted]

Mineral	Unit	Mineral disposition				Average price per unit (dollars)	Employment (number)
		Production	Exports	Net import reliance [1] (percent)	Consumption, apparent		
Aluminum	1,000 metric tons	2,550	2,800	30	5,500	[2]1.11	60,000
Antimony (contained)	Metric tons	[3]–	3,060	86	22,900	[2]2.59	10
Asbestos	1,000 metric tons	–	1	100	2	(NA)	–
Barite	1,000 metric tons	540	20	83	3,260	[4]40.00	330
Bauxite and alumina (metal equivalent)	1,000 metric tons	(NA)	590	100	3,490	[4]30.00	(NA)
Beryllium (contained)	Metric tons	100	90	[5]	91	(NA)	(NA)
Bismuth (contained)	Metric tons	–	670	95	2,130	[2]13.75	(NA)
Boron (B$_2$O$_3$ content)	1,000 metric tons	(D)	200	[5]	(D)	[4,6](NA)	1,300
Bromine (contained)	1,000 metric tons	235	10	13	270	[7,8]200	1,000
Cadmium (contained)	Metric tons	[3](D)	304	[5]	441	[2,9]3.72	(NA)
Cement	1,000 metric tons	94,000	[10]1,850	17	115,000	[4]102	16,000
Chromium	1,000 metric tons	[11](D)	210	62	630	(NA)	(NA)
Clays	1,000 metric tons	40,600	6,050	[5]	34,800	(NA)	1,220
Cobalt (contained)	Metric tons	[11]2,000	3,100	78	9,200	[2]30.20	(NA)
Copper (mine, recoverable)	1,000 metric tons	1,180	935	37	2,300	328	7.3
Diamond (industrial)	Million carats	295	104	52	617	[12]0.19	(NA)
Diatomite	1,000 metric tons	830	175	[5]	659	[4]220	1,020
Feldspar	1,000 metric tons	760	11	[5]	753	[4]59.00	400
Fluorspar	1,000 metric tons	–	13	100	601	(NA)	–
Garnet (industrial)	Metric tons	34,000	12,500	56	77,600	[4]50–2,000	160
Gemstones	Million dollars	64	11,400	99	8,260	(NA)	1,200
Germanium (contained)	Kilograms	4,600	14,500	(NA)	(NA)	[7]1,240	65
Gold (contained)	Metric tons	240	580	[5]	(NA)	[13]675	8,700
Graphite (crude)	1,000 metric tons	–	23	100	32	[4,14]598	(NA)
Gypsum (crude)	1,000 metric tons	22,000	150	26	42,400	[4]7.50	6,000
Iodine	Metric tons	(D)	2,970	(D)	(D)	[7,15]20.63	30
Iron ore (usable)	Million metric tons	[16]49.0	9.0	–	52.0	[4]63.00	4,470
Iron and steel scrap (metal)	Million metric tons	71	15	[5]	(NA)	[4,17]249	30,000
Iron and steel slag (metal)	1,000 metric tons	[18]20,000	1,000	7	19,900	[4]20.00	2,500
Lead (contained)	1,000 metric tons	420	300	[5]	1,630	[2]1.23	2,940
Lime	1,000 metric tons	20,200	200	1	20,400	[19]84.00	5,300
Magnesium compounds	1,000 metric tons	266	27	57	619	(NA)	370
Magnesium metal	1,000 metric tons	(D)	13	47	110	[2]2.00	400
Manganese (gross weight)	1,000 metric tons	–	2	100	910	[20]3.32	(NA)
Mercury	Metric tons	[11](NA)	300	[5]	(NA)	[21]550	(NA)
Mica, scrap and flake	1,000 metric tons	72	8	32	106	[4]112	(NA)
Molybdenum (contained)	Metric tons	59,400	35,200	[5]	44,000	[7]64.68	940
Nickel (contained)	Metric tons	–	116,000	[22]17	112,000	[23]37,216	–
Niobium (contained)	Metric tons	–	600	100	10,000	(NA)	(NA)
Nitrogen (fixed)-ammonia	1,000 metric tons	8,300	100	44	14,700	[24]300	1,050
Peat	1,000 metric tons	615	55	60	1,540	[4]25.57	625
Perlite	1,000 metric tons	444	30	30	634	[4]51.61	101
Phosphate rock	1,000 metric tons	29,700	–	14	(NA)	[4]39.30	2,350
Platinum-group metals	Kilograms	16,900	81,000	94	(NA)	[13,25]1,260	1,700
Potash (K$_2$O equivalent)	1,000 metric tons	1,200	300	81	6,200	[4,26]390	1,130
Pumice and pumicite	1,000 metric tons	1,410	22	20	1,760	[4]30.33	115
Salt	1,000 metric tons	43,800	1,000	18	49,900	[4,27]150.00	4,100
Silicon (contained)	1,000 metric tons	[28](D)	27	[29]	[30]354	[31]73	(NA)
Silver (contained)	Metric tons	1,220	1,000	55	7,980	[13]13.40	900
Sodium carbonate (soda ash)	1,000 metric tons	11,100	5,100	[5]	6,000	[32]170	2,500
Sodium sulfate	1,000 metric tons	300	80	[5]	250	[33]134	225
Stone (crushed)	Million metric tons	1,440	1	1	1,460	[4]8.75	82,600
Sulfur (all forms)	1,000 metric tons	8,860	910	24	11,600	[4,34]40.00	2,700
Talc	1,000 metric tons	839	220	[5]	829	[4]108	430
Thallium (contained)	Kilograms	–	2,070	100	(NA)	[7]4,560	(NA)
Tin (contained)	Metric tons	[11]2,800	5,100	79	58,600	[2]8.42	–
Titanium dioxide	1,000 metric tons	1,450	600	[5]	1,110	[2,35](NA)	4,300
Tungsten (contained)	Metric tons	[11]4,400	6,040	70	14,400	[36]190	(NA)
Vermiculite	1,000 metric tons	100	5	40	170	[4]140	95
Zinc (contained)	1,000 metric tons	740	789	73	936	[2,37]1.51	1,470
Zirconium (ZrO$_2$)	Metric tons	(D)	48,100	[5]	(D)	[4,38]840	(NA)

– Represents zero. D Withheld to avoid disclosure. NA Not available. [1] Calculated as a percent of apparent consumption. [2] Dollars per pound. [3] Refinery production. [4] Dollars per metric ton. [5] Net exporter. [6] Granulated pentahydrate borax in bulk, f.o.b mine. [7] Dollars per kilogram. [8] Bulk, purified bromine. [9] 1- to 5-short ton lots. [10] Excludes Puerto Rico. [11] Secondary production. [12] Value of imports, dollars per carat. [13] Dollars per troy ounce. [14] Price of flake imports. [15] C.i.f. value, crude, per kilogram. [16] Shipments of usable ore. [17] Delivered, No. 1 Heavy Melting composite price. [18] Sales of processed slag. [19] Quick lime only. [20] 46–48 percent Mn metallurgical ore, per unit contained Mn, c.i.f. U.S. ports. [21] Dollars per 76-pound flask. [22] Exports include both primary and secondary materials. [23] London Metal Exchange cash price. [24] F.o.b. Gulf Coast. [25] Dealer price of platinum. [26] Price of K$_2$O, muriate. [27] Vacuum and open pan, bulk, pellets and packaged, f.o.b. mine and plant. [28] Silicon metal only. [29] Value less than or equal to 50,000 metric tons. Ferrosilicon statistics include: production (156,001 tons), exports (6,000 tons), and net import reliance (56%). [30] Ferrosilicon only. [31] Ferrosilicon, 50 percent. [32] Quoted year-end price, dense, bulk, f.o.b. Green River, WY, dollars per short ton. [33] Quoted price, bulk, f.o.b. works, East, dollars per short ton. [34] Elemental sulfur, f.o.b. mine and/or plant. [35] Rutile, list, year-end. [36] Dollars per metric ton unit WO$_3$ (7.93 kilograms of contained tungsten per metric ton unit). [37] London Metal Exchange cash price for Special High Grade zinc. [38] Price for imported zircon, f.o.b. U.S. East Coast.

Source: U.S. Geological Survey, *Mineral Commodity Summaries,* annual. See also <http://minerals.er.usgs.gov/minerals/pubs /mcs/2008/mcs2008.pdf> (released 30 January 2008).

Table 865. **Selected Mineral Products—Average Prices: 1990 to 2007**

[Excludes Alaska and Hawaii, except as noted]

Year	Nonfuels								Fuels		
	Copper, cathode [1] (cents per lb.)	Plati-num [2] (dol./ troy oz.)	Gold (dol./ troy oz.[3])	Silver (dol./ troy oz.[3])	Lead [4] (cents per lb.)	Tin (New York) [5] (cents per lb.)	Zinc [6] (cents per lb.)	Sulfur, crude [7] (dol./ metric ton)	Bitumi-nous coal [8] (dol./ short ton)	Crude petro-leum [8] (dol./ bbl.)	Natural gas [8] (dol./ 1,000 cu. ft.)
1990	123	455	385	4.82	46	386	75	80.14	27.43	20.03	1.71
1994	111	411	385	5.29	37	369	49	30.08	25.68	13.19	1.85
1995	138	425	386	5.15	42	416	56	44.46	25.56	14.62	1.55
1996	109	398	389	5.19	49	412	51	34.11	25.17	18.46	2.17
1997	107	397	332	4.89	47	381	65	36.06	24.64	17.23	2.32
1998	79	375	295	5.54	45	373	51	29.14	24.87	10.87	1.96
1999	76	379	280	5.25	44	366	53	37.81	23.92	15.56	2.19
2000	88	549	280	5.00	44	370	56	24.73	24.15	26.72	3.68
2001	77	533	272	4.39	44	315	44	10.01	25.36	21.84	4.00
2002	76	543	311	4.62	44	292	39	11.84	26.57	22.51	2.95
2003	85	694	365	4.91	44	340	41	28.70	26.73	27.56	4.88
2004	134	849	411	6.69	51	547	53	32.62	30.56	36.77	5.46
2005	174	900	446	7.34	61	483	67	30.88	36.80	50.28	7.33
2006	315	1,144	606	11.61	77	565	159	32.85	39.32	59.69	6.40
2007	328	1,260	675	13.40	123	842	159	40.00	40.83	66.52	6.39

[1] U.S. producer price. [2] Average annual dealer prices. [3] 99.95 percent purity. [4] Nationwide delivered basis. [5] Composite price. [6] Platt's Metals Week price for North American Special High Grade zinc. Average prices for 1990 are for U.S. High Grade Zinc. [7] F.o.b. (Free on Board) works. [8] Average value at the point of production or domestic first purchase price.

Source: Nonfuels, through 1994, U.S. Bureau of Mines, thereafter, U.S. Geological Survey, *Minerals Yearbook* and *Mineral Commodities Summaries*, annual. See also <http://minerals.er.usgs.gov/minerals/pubs/mcs/>. Fuels, U.S. Energy Information Administration, *Annual Energy Review* and most recent year from Monthly Energy Review; <http://www.eia.doe.gov>.

Table 866. **Value of Domestic Nonfuel Mineral Production by State: 2000 to 2007**

[**In millions of dollars (39,400 represents $39,400,000,000).** For similar data on fuels, see Table 871]

State	2000	2006	2007 [1]	State	2000	2006	2007 [1]
United States . .	[2]**39,400**	**66,500**	**68,000**				
				Montana	596	1,070	1,290
Alabama	930	1,360	1,340	Nebraska	[3]84	129	214
Alaska	1,140	3,010	3,430	Nevada	2,980	5,140	5,210
Arizona	2,510	6,740	7,380	New Hampshire.	[3]57	112	115
Arkansas	484	789	913	New Jersey	[3]291	547	582
California	3,270	4,590	4,390				
				New Mexico	786	1,470	1,520
Colorado	592	1,680	1,940	New York.	1,020	1,330	1,330
Connecticut	[3]112	168	181	North Carolina.	744	1,020	986
Delaware	[3]14	22	34	North Dakota	35	44	56
Florida.	1,820	3,220	3,190	Ohio	999	1,270	1,240
Georgia	1,620	2,080	2,110				
				Oklahoma	473	684	678
Hawaii	[3]92	145	150	Oregon	299	509	505
Idaho.	358	797	817	Pennsylvania	[3]1,250	1,710	1,760
Illinois	913	1,220	1,220	Rhode Island	[3]20	44	44
Indiana	695	982	997	South Carolina	[3]551	735	562
Iowa	503	696	674				
				South Dakota	233	223	227
Kansas	629	973	967	Tennessee	737	856	842
Kentucky	501	806	913	Texas	1,950	2,980	2,900
Louisiana	325	481	385	Utah	1,430	3,960	3,940
Maine	96	158	156	Vermont	[3]67	84	93
Maryland	[3]358	653	725				
				Virginia	710	1,270	1,100
Massachusetts	[3]200	294	433	Washington	607	718	680
Michigan	1,640	1,910	1,910	West Virginia	172	230	207
Minnesota	1,460	2,540	2,550	Wisconsin.	[3]372	566	552
Mississippi	149	270	257	Wyoming	978	1,590	1,670
Missouri	1,370	2,070	2,210				

[1] Preliminary. [2] Includes undistributed not shown separately. [3] Partial data only; excludes values withheld to avoid disclosing individual company data.

Source: U.S. Geological Survey, *Minerals Yearbook,* annual, and *Mineral Commodities Summaries,* annual. See also <http://minerals.er.usgs.gov/minerals/pubs/mcs/2008/mcs2008.pdf> (released 30 January 2008).

U.S. Census Bureau, Statistical Abstract of the United States: 2009

Table 867. Principal Fuels, Nonmetals, and Metals—World Production and the U.S. Share: 1990 to 2007

[In millions of short tons (5,354 represents 5,354,000,000), except as indicated; see Appendix IV]

Mineral	Unit	World production				Percent U.S. of world			
		1990	2000	2005	2007	1990	2000	2005	2007
Fuels: [1]									
Coal	Mil. sh. tons	5,354	4,949	6,490	(NA)	19	22	17	(NA)
Petroleum (crude)	Bil. bbl.	22.1	25.0	26.9	(NA)	12	8	7	(NA)
Natural gas (dry, marketable)	Tril. cu. ft.	73.6	88.3	101.5	(NA)	24	22	18	(NA)
Natural gas plant liquids	Bil. bbl.	1.7	2.4	2.8	(NA)	34	30	22	(NA)
Nonmetals:									
Asbestos	1,000 metric tons	4,010	2,110	2,320	2,290	(D)	–	–	–
Barite	1,000 metric tons	5,770	6,470	8,110	8,000	7	6	6	7
Feldspar	1,000 metric tons	5,990	9,580	15,100	16,500	11	8	5	5
Fluorspar	1,000 metric tons	5,120	4,470	5,280	5,310	1	–	–	–
Gypsum	Mil. metric tons	104	106	122	127	15	19	21	22
Mica (incl. scrap)	1,000 metric tons	217	328	294	360	50	31	27	20
Nitrogen (N content)	Mil. metric tons	98	108	122	125	13	11	7	7
Phosphate rock (gross wt.)	Mil. metric tons	162	132	147	147	29	30	25	20
Potash (K$_2$O equivalent)	Mil. metric tons	28	27	31	33	6	4	4	4
Sulfur, elemental basis	Mil. metric tons	58	58	66	66	20	19	14	13
Metals, mine basis:									
Bauxite	Mil. metric tons	113	136	172	190	(D)	(NA)	(NA)	NA
Copper	1,000 metric tons	8,950	13,200	15,000	15,600	18	11	8	8
Gold	Metric tons	2,180	2,590	2,470	2,500	14	14	10	10
Iron ore (gross wt.)	Mil. metric tons	983	1,070	1,540	1,900	6	6	4	3
Lead [2]	1,000 metric tons	3,370	3,184	3,450	3,550	15	15	13	12
Mercury	Metric tons	4,520	1,350	1,680	1,500	12	(NA)	(D)	(D)
Molybdenum	1,000 metric tons	111	133	185	187	55	31	31	32
Nickel [2]	1,000 metric tons	974	1,270	1,480	1,660	(Z)	(Z)	–	–
Silver	1,000 metric tons	16	18	19	21	13	11	6	6
Tantalum concentrates (Ta content)	Metric tons	344	1,040	1,260	1,400	–	–	–	–
Titanium mineral concentrates (titanium content) [3]	1,000 metric tons	3,600	(NA)	5,200	6,100	(D)	(NA)	6	5
Tungsten [2]	1,000 metric tons	52	44	88	90	(D)	(NA)	–	(D)
Vanadium [2]	1,000 metric tons	33	56	58	59	6	–	–	–
Zinc [2]	1,000 metric tons	7,150	8,788	9,930	10,500	8	10	8	7
Metals, smelter basis:									
Aluminum	1,000 metric tons	19,300	24,400	31,900	38,000	21	15	8	7
Cadmium	1,000 metric tons	20	20	20	20	8	10	7	(D)
Copper	1,000 metric tons	9,470	11,000	13,600	14,200	15	9	4	4
Iron, pig	Mil. metric tons	539	573	825	940	9	8	4	4
Lead [4]	1,000 metric tons	5,950	6,580	7,700	8,030	22	22	17	16
Magnesium [5]	1,000 metric tons	354	428	622	670	39	(D)	(D)	(D)
Raw Steel	Mil. metric tons	777	845	1,130	1,320	12	12	8	7
Tin [6]	1,000 metric tons	220	271	290	300	–	2	–	–
Zinc	1,000 metric tons	7,180	9,137	10,400	10,600	5	4	3	3

– Represents or rounds to zero. D Withheld to avoid disclosing company data. NA Not available. Z Less than half the unit of measure. [1] Source: Energy Information Administration, *International Energy Annual.* [2] Content of ore and concentrate. [3] Before 2005, excludes U.S. production. [4] Refinery production. [5] Primary production; no smelter processing necessary. [6] Production from primary sources only.

Source: Nonfuels, through 1990, U.S. Bureau of Mines, thereafter, U.S. Geological Survey, *Minerals Yearbook,* annual, and *Mineral Commodities Summaries,* annual; fuels, U.S. Energy Information Administration, "International Energy Annual"; <http://minerals.er.usgs.gov/minerals/pubs/mcs/2008/mcs2008.pdf> (released 30 January 2008).

Table 868. Net U.S. Imports of Selected Minerals and Metals as Percent of Apparent Consumption: 1980 to 2007

[In percent. Based on net imports which equal the difference between imports and exports plus or minus government stockpile and industry stock changes]

Minerals and metals	1980	1990	1995	2000	2003	2004	2005	2006	2007 [1]
Bauxite [2]	(NA)	98	99	100	100	100	100	100	100
Fluorspar	87	91	92	100	100	100	100	100	100
Manganese	98	100	100	100	100	100	100	100	100
Mica (sheet)	100	100	100	100	100	100	100	100	100
Strontium	100	100	100	100	100	100	100	100	100
Tantalum	90	86	80	80	100	100	100	100	100
Vanadium	35	(D)	84	100	100	100	100	100	100
Platinum	(NA)	(NA)	(NA)	78	91	92	93	90	94
Barite	44	71	65	84	77	78	84	81	83
Titanium	(NA)	(NA)	70	79	68	58	71	71	82
Potash	65	68	75	80	80	80	80	79	81
Tin	79	71	84	88	89	92	78	79	79
Cobalt	93	84	79	78	79	77	83	82	78
Zinc	60	64	71	72	70	72	68	78	73
Tungsten	53	81	90	66	63	73	68	68	70
Chromium	67	80	75	77	57	64	59	64	62
Silver	7	(NA)	(NA)	43	65	54	54	38	55
Nickel	76	64	60	55	45	49	48	49	17
Iron and steel	13	13	21	18	10	14	15	17	12
Iron ore	25	21	14	10	12	6	4	8	–

– Represents or rounds to zero. D Withheld to avoid disclosure. NA Not available. [1] Preliminary. [2] Includes alumina.

Source: Through 1990, U.S. Bureau of Mines; thereafter, U.S. Geological Survey, *Mineral Commodity Summaries and Minerals Yearbook,* annual and *Historical Statistics for Mineral and Material Commodities in the United States*; import and export data from U.S. Census Bureau.

556   Natural Resources

Table 869. **Petroleum Industry—Summary: 1990 to 2007**

[602 represents 602,000. Includes all costs incurred for drilling and equipping wells to point of completion as productive wells or abandonment after drilling becomes unproductive. Based on sample of operators of different size drilling establishments]

Item	Unit	1990	1995	2000	2002	2003	2004	2005	2006	2007 [1]
Crude oil producing wells (Dec. 31). .	1,000 . . .	602	574	534	529	513	510	498	497	500
Daily output per well [2]	Bbl.	12.2	11.4	10.9	10.9	11.1	10.7	10.4	10.3	10.2
Completed wells drilled, total	1,000 . . .	26.92	18.19	25.64	24.34	28.24	30.21	37.41	45.50	49.15
Crude oil.	1,000 . . .	11.78	7.28	7.32	5.99	7.14	7.44	9.22	11.76	13.84
Gas	1,000 . . .	10.43	7.87	15.63	16.03	18.67	20.49	25.48	30.03	31.25
Dry	1,000 . . .	4.70	3.04	2.70	2.33	2.42	2.27	2.71	3.71	4.05
Average depth per well	Feet	4,653	5,523	4,723	5,125	5,408	5,482	5,511	5,695	6,379
Average cost per well	$1,000 . .	384	513	755	1,054	1,200	1,673	1,721	2,102	(NA)
Average cost per foot	Dollars . .	76.07	87.22	142.16	195.31	216.27	292.57	306.50	378.03	(NA)
Crude oil production, total	Mil. bbl. .	2,685	2,394	2,131	2,097	2,073	1,983	1,890	1,862	1,862
Value at wells [3, 4]	Bil. dol. . .	53.77	35.00	56.93	47.21	57.14	72.93	95.03	111.16	123.89
Average price per barrel	Dollars . .	20.03	14.62	26.72	22.51	27.56	36.77	50.28	59.69	66.52
Lower 48 states [5]	Mil. bbl. .	2,037	1,853	1,776	1,738	1,718	1,651	1,575	1,592	1,600
Alaska	Mil. bbl. .	647	542	355	359	356	332	315	270	262
Onshore	Mil. bbl. .	2,290	1,838	1,482	1,366	1,339	1,294	1,265	1,241	1,233
Offshore	Mil. bbl. .	395	557	649	731	735	689	625	621	629
Imports: Crude oil [4, 6]	Mil. bbl. .	2,151	2,639	3,320	3,336	3,528	3,692	3,696	3,693	3,656
Refined petroleum products	Mil. bbl. .	775	586	874	872	949	1,119	1,310	1,310	1,249
Exports: Crude oil	Mil. bbl. .	39.7	34.5	18.4	3.3	4.5	9.8	11.6	9.0	10.0
Proved reserves	Bil. bbl. . .	26.3	22.4	22.0	22.7	21.9	21.4	21.8	21.0	(NA)
Operable refineries.	Number. .	205	175	158	153	149	149	148	149	149
Capacity (Jan. 1)	Mil. bbl. .	5,684	5,633	6,027	6,127	6,116	6,166	6,251	6,329	6,367
Refinery input, total.	Mil. bbl. .	5,325	5,555	5,964	5,955	6,027	6,135	6,136	6,198	6,189
Crude oil [4]	Mil. bbl. .	4,894	5,100	5,514	5,456	5,586	5,664	5,555	5,563	5,529
Natural gas plant liquids	Mil. bbl. .	171	172	139	156	153	154	161	183	181
Other liquids	Mil. bbl. .	260	283	311	344	289	317	420	452	479
Refinery output, total [7]	Mil. bbl. .	5,574	5,838	6,311	6,305	6,383	6,520	6,497	6,561	6,556
Motor gasoline	Mil. bbl. .	2,540	2,722	2,910	2,987	2,991	3,025	3,036	3,053	3,045
Jet fuel	Mil. bbl. .	543	517	588	553	543	566	564	541	529
Distillate fuel oil	Mil. bbl. .	1,067	1,152	1,310	1,311	1,353	1,396	1,443	1,475	1,508
Residual fuel oil	Mil. bbl. .	347	288	255	219	241	240	229	232	244
Liquefied petroleum gases	Mil. bbl. .	182	239	258	245	240	236	209	229	236
Utilization rate	Percent. .	87.1	92.0	92.6	90.7	92.6	93.0	90.6	89.7	88.5

NA Not available. [1] Preliminary. [2] Based on number of wells producing at end of year. [3] Values based on domestic first purchase price. [4] Includes lease condensate. [5] Excluding Alaska and Hawaii. [6] Includes imports for the Strategic Petroleum Reserve. [7] Includes other products not shown separately.

Source: U.S. Energy Information Administration, *Annual Energy Review 2007*. See also <http://www.eia.doe.gov/emeu/aer/contents.html>.

Table 870. **Supply, Disposition, and Ending Stocks of Crude Oil and Petroleum Products: 2006**

[In millions of barrels (1,862.3 represents 1,862,300,000). Minus sign (–) indicates decrease]

Commodity	Supply				Disposition				Ending stocks
	Field production	Refinery and blender net production	Imports	Adjustments[1]	Stock change	Refinery and blender net inputs	Exports	Products supplied[2]	
Crude oil.	1,862.3	(NA)	3,693.1	9.6	–7.4	5,563.4	9.0	–	1,000.9
Commercial	1,862.3	(NA)	3,690.0	9.6	–11.4	(NA)	9.0	(NA)	312.3
Alaskan	270.5	(NA)	(NA)	(NA)	(NA)	(NA)	(NA)	(NA)	(NA)
Lower 48 states	1,591.8	(NA)	(NA)	(NA)	(NA)	(NA)	(NA)	(NA)	(NA)
SPR.	(NA)	(NA)	3.1	(NA)	4.1	(NA)	(NA)	(NA)	688.6
Imports by SPR.	(NA)	(NA)	–	(NA)	(NA)	(NA)	(NA)	(NA)	(NA)
Imports into SPR by others	(NA)	(NA)	3.1	(NA)	(NA)	(NA)	(NA)	(NA)	(NA)
Natural gas liquids and LRGs. . .	634.7	229.0	131.2	(NA)	7.7	182.9	24.8	779.5	125.1
Pentanes plus	95.8	(NA)	9.9	(NA)	4.0	67.3	4.2	30.3	12.0
Liquefied petroleum gases . . .	538.8	229.0	121.3	(NA)	3.7	115.6	20.6	749.1	113.1
Ethane/ethylene	246.8	6.8	0.2	(NA)	–4.4	–	–	258.1	20.3
Propane/propylene	183.0	198.2	83.1	(NA)	4.4	–	16.5	443.4	61.6
Normal butane/butylene . . .	49.6	24.6	25.6	(NA)	4.0	49.2	4.1	42.2	24.8
Isobutane/isobutylene.	59.4	–0.3	12.5	(NA)	–0.2	66.4	–	5.4	6.4
Finished motor gasoline.	(NA)	3,052.8	173.4	183.0	–19.7	(NA)	51.8	3,377.2	116.1
Kerosene-type jet fuel	(NA)	540.6	67.7	(NA)	–2.6	(NA)	14.9	596.0	39.1
Distillate fuel oil[3]	(NA)	1,471.7	133.1	–	7.6	(NA)	78.5	1,521.7	143.7

– Represents zero. NA Not available. [1] Includes an adjustment for crude oil, previously referred to as "Unaccounted For Crude Oil." Also included is an adjustment for motor gasoline blending components, fuel ethanol, and distillate fuel oil. See Appendix B of source for more details. [2] Products supplied is equal to field production, plus refinery and blender net production, plus imports, plus adjustments, minus stock change, minus refinery and blender net imputs, minus exports. [3] Distillate stocks located in the "Northeast Heating Oil Reserve" are not included. For details, see Appendix C of source.

Source: U.S. Energy Information Administration, "Petroleum Supply Annual, Volume 1"; <http://www.eia.doe.gov/pub/oilgas/petroleum/datapublications/petroleumsupplyannual/psavolume1/current/pdf/table01.pdf>.

Natural Resources 557

Table 871. Crude Petroleum and Natural Gas—Production and Value by Major Producing States: 2004 to 2006

[1,983 represents 1,983,000,000 barrels]

State	Crude petroleum						Natural gas marketed production [1]					
	Quantity (mil. bbl.)			Value (mil. dol.)			Quantity (bil. cu. ft.)			Value (mil. dol.)		
	2004	2005	2006	2004	2005	2006	2004	2005	2006	2004	2005	2006
Total [2]	1,983	1,890	1,862	72,926	95,035	111,158	19,517	18,927	19,382	106,522	138,751	123,993
AL	7	8	8	289	419	476	316	297	286	2,103	2,751	2,168
AK	332	315	270	23,868	31,933	15,380	472	487	445	1,612	2,313	2,576
AR	7	6	6	247	323	358	187	191	193	1,063	1,383	1,244
CA	240	230	223	8,280	10,842	12,813	320	318	315	1,808	2,365	2,039
CO	22	23	23	892	1,263	1,492	1,079	1,133	1,203	5,622	8,418	7,362
FL	3	3	2	(NA)	(NA)	(NA)	3	3	3	(NA)	(NA)	(NA)
IL	11	10	10	426	523	616	(Z)	(Z)	(Z)	(NA)	(NA)	(NA)
IN.	2	2	2	67	88	103	3	3	3	21	29	18
KS	34	34	36	1,327	1,806	2,165	397	377	371	1,961	2,456	2,082
KY	3	3	2	94	125	136	94	93	95	495	634	842
LA	83	75	74	3,376	4,080	4,745	1,353	1,296	1,361	8,071	11,305	9,429
MI	6	6	5	251	298	310	260	261	365	1,000	1,383	(NA)
MS	17	18	17	635	877	1,030	63	53	61	369	452	414
MT	25	33	36	953	1,730	2,056	97	108	113	437	709	624
NE	3	2	2	96	126	134	1	1	1	5	5	(NA)
NM	64	61	60	2,521	3,205	3,693	1,633	1,645	1,609	8,119	11,369	9,947
NY	(Z)	(Z)	(Z)	(NA)	(NA)	(NA)	46	55	56	321	429	399
ND	31	36	40	1,224	1,868	2,263	55	53	55	315	441	361
OH	6	6	5	221	302	341	90	84	86	602	754	669
OK	63	62	63	2,497	3,384	3,966	1,656	1,639	1,689	9,146	11,821	10,671
PA	3	4	4	100	215	232	197	169	158	(NA)	(NA)	(NA)
TX	393	388	397	15,239	20,396	24,354	5,067	5,276	5,513	29,561	39,813	36,365
UT	15	17	18	576	899	1,069	278	301	348	1,458	2,157	1,984
WV	1	2	2	51	84	110	197	221	226	(NA)	(NA)	(NA)
WY	52	52	53	1,812	2,356	2,817	1,592	1,639	1,816	7,893	11,245	10,627
Federal offshore ..	130	131	121	40,652	80,118	93,384	(NA)	(NA)	(NA)	(NA)	(NA)	(NA)
Lower 48 states ..	1,651	1,575	1,592	49,058	63,101	95,778	19,046	18,440	18,937	104,910	136,437	121,417

NA Not available.   Z Less than 500,000 barrels or 500 million cubic feet.   [1] Excludes nonhydrocarbon gases.   [2] Includes other states not shown separately. State production does not include state offshore production. U.S. level totals shown in Tables 869 and 875 may contain revisions not carried to state level.

Source: U.S. Energy Information Administration, "Petroleum Supply Annual, Vol. 1"; "Petroleum Marketing Annual"; "Natural Gas Annual"; and "Natural Gas Monthly."

Table 872. Crude Oil, Natural Gas, and Natural Gas Liquids—Reserves by State: 2004 to 2006

[21,371 mil. bbl. represents 21,371,000,000 bbl. As of December 31. Proved reserves are estimated quantities of the mineral, which geological and engineering data demonstrate with reasonable certainty, to be recoverable in future years from known reservoirs under existing economic and operating conditions. Based on a sample of operators of oil and gas wells]

Area	2004			2005			2006		
	Crude oil proved reserves (mil. bbl.)	Natural gas (bil. cu. ft.)	Natural gas liquids (mil. bbl.)	Crude oil proved reserves (mil. bbl.)	Natural gas (bil. cu. ft.)	Natural gas liquids (mil. bbl.)	Crude oil proved reserves (mil. bbl.)	Natural gas (bil. cu. ft.)	Natural gas liquids (mil. bbl.)
United States [1] ...	21,371	192,513	7,928	21,757	204,385	8,165	20,972	211,085	8,472
Alabama	53	4,120	50	55	3,965	61	45	3,911	56
Alaska	4,327	8,407	369	4,171	8,171	352	3,879	10,245	338
Arkansas	51	1,835	3	40	1,964	3	37	2,269	4
California	3,376	2,634	122	3,435	3,228	137	3,389	2,794	132
Colorado	225	14,743	465	250	16,596	484	274	17,149	478
Florida	65	78	12	59	77	7	38	45	3
Illinois	92	(NA)	(NA)	95	(NA)	(NA)	89	(NA)	(NA)
Indiana	11	(NA)	(NA)	16	(NA)	(NA)	12	(NA)	(NA)
Kansas	245	4,652	271	281	4,314	224	263	3,931	209
Kentucky	27	1,880	72	23	2,151	70	25	2,227	105
Louisiana	427	9,588	263	432	10,447	292	428	10,474	280
Michigan	53	3,091	48	62	2,910	39	63	3,065	42
Mississippi	178	691	6	189	755	7	186	813	8
Montana	364	995	6	427	986	9	419	1,057	10
Nebraska	15	(NA)	(NA)	16	(NA)	(NA)	14	(NA)	(NA)
New Mexico	669	18,512	864	690	18,201	840	705	17,934	861
New York	(NA)	324	(NA)	(NA)	349	(NA)	(NA)	363	(NA)
North Dakota	389	417	43	418	453	49	412	479	55
Ohio	49	974	(NA)	46	898	(NA)	49	975	(NA)
Oklahoma	570	16,238	790	630	17,123	839	569	17,464	892
Pennsylvania	12	2,361	(NA)	14	2,782	(NA)	20	3,050	(NA)
Texas	4,613	49,955	2,801	4,919	56,507	3,080	4,871	61,836	3,335
Utah	215	3,866	([2])	256	4,295	([2])	334	5,146	([2])
Virginia	(NA)	1,742	(NA)	(NA)	2,018	(NA)	(NA)	2,302	(NA)
West Virginia	11	3,397	85	21	4,459	85	23	4,509	110
Wyoming	628	22,632	[3]927	704	23,774	[3]879	706	23,549	[3]887
Federal offshore	4,691	19,271	721	4,483	17,831	696	4,096	15,360	653
Lower 48 states.....	17,044	184,106	7,559	17,586	196,214	7,813	17,093	200,840	8,134

NA Not available.   [1] Includes states not shown separately.   [2] Included with Wyoming.   [3] Includes Utah.

Source: Energy Information Administration, "U.S. Crude Oil, Natural Gas, and Natural Gas Liquids Reserves, 2006 Annual Report"; <http://www.eia.doe.gov/oil_gas/natural_gas/data_publications/crude_oil_natural_gas_reserves/cr.html> (released 31 December 2007).

558 Natural Resources

Table 873. Federal Offshore Leasing, Exploration, Production, and Revenue: 1990 to 2007

[In millions (56.79 represents 56,790,000), except as indicated. **Data presented by fiscal year.** See source for explanation of terms and for reliability statement]

Item	Unit	1990	1995	2000	2003	2004	2005	2006	2007
Tracts offered	Number	10,459	10,995	7,992	12,147	9,123	11,447	7,905	4,992
Tracts leased	Number	825	835	553	957	888	989	763	360
Acres offered	Millions	56.79	59.70	42.89	64.77	48.35	61.08	42.24	26.63
Acres leased	Millions	4.30	4.34	2.92	5.03	4.69	5.24	4.12	2.01
Bonus paid for leased tracts	Bil. dol	0.6	0.4	0.3	0.4	0.6	0.7	0.9	0.3
New wells being drilled:									
Active	Number	120	124	224	135	156	242	209	164
Suspended	Number	266	247	146	48	56	67	61	76
Cumulative wells (since 1953):									
Wells completed	Number	13,167	13,475	13,718	18,424	18,260	18,001	17,801	17,429
Wells plugged and abandoned	Number	14,677	18,008	22,814	32,251	33,746	34,878	36,407	38,351
Revenue, total [1]	Bil. dol	3.4	2.7	5.2	5.9	5.3	6.3	7.6	7.0
Bonuses	Bil. dol	0.8	0.4	0.4	1.1	0.5	0.6	0.9	0.4
Oil and gas royalties [1]	Bil. dol	2.6	2.1	4.1	4.5	4.6	5.5	6.5	6.4
Rentals	Bil. dol	0.09	0.09	0.21	0.25	0.21	0.22	0.22	0.20
Sales value [2]	Bil. dol	17.0	13.8	27.4	29.0	30.6	37.2	45.6	45.5
Oil	Bil. dol	7.0	6.3	11.5	8.3	8.4	15.4	24.2	27.8
Natural gas	Bil. dol	9.5	7.5	15.9	20.7	22.2	21.8	21.4	17.7
Sales volume: [3]									
Oil	Mil. bbls	324	409	566	310	248	332	391	471
Natural gas	Bil. cu. ft	5,093	4,692	4,723	3,501	3,941	3,504	2,581	2,547

[1] Includes condensate royalties. [2] Production value is value at time of production, not current value. [3] Excludes sales volumes for gas lost, gas plant products, or sulfur.

Source: U.S. Dept. of the Interior, Minerals Management Service, *Federal Offshore Statistics,* annual; for revenue, sales value, and sales volume data after 2000, Minerals Revenue Management, Annual Reported Royalty Revenue Statistical Information; <http://www.mrm.mms.gov/MRMWebStats/Home.aspx>.

Table 874. Oil and Gas Extraction Industry—Establishments, Employees, and Payroll by State: 2005

[6,612,547 represents 6,612,547,000. Excludes government employees, railroad employees, self-employed persons, etc. See "General Explanation" in source for definitions and statement on reliability of data. An establishment is a single physical location where business is conducted or where services or industrial operations are performed. See Appendix III]

State	Crude petroleum and natural gas extraction (211111) [1]			State	Natural gas liquid extraction (211112) [1]		
	Establishments	Number of employees [2]	Annual payroll ($1,000)		Establishments	Number of employees [2]	Annual payroll ($1,000)
United States	6,948	72,350	6,612,547	United States	442	13,212	1,130,942
Colorado	346	3,474	405,001	Colorado	23	586	83,372
Florida	26	75	4,967	Florida	11	72	4,606
Kansas	372	2,429	124,673	Kansas	17	232	14,638
Louisiana	350	7,341	683,139	Louisiana	47	2,939	189,268
Michigan	91	774	50,642	Michigan	10	256	12,518
New Mexico	157	1,899	143,765	New Mexico	25	625	43,002
Ohio	205	1,347	64,956	Ohio	4	8	318
Oklahoma	1,043	9,407	772,208	Oklahoma	33	471	26,739
Texas	2,841	28,888	3,064,619	Texas	117	5,236	547,013
Utah	46	913	58,334	Utah	10	114	7,656
Wyoming	174	2,003	137,921	Wyoming	31	660	48,195

[1] Based on North American Industry Classification System, 2005. [2] Covers full- and part-time employees who are on the payroll in the pay period including March 12.

Source: U.S. Census Bureau, County Business Patterns; annual. See also <http://www.census.gov/epcd/cbp/view/cbpview.html>.

U.S. Census Bureau, Statistical Abstract of the United States: 2009

Table 875. Natural Gas—Supply, Consumption, Reserves, and Marketed Production: 1990 to 2007

[269 represents 269,000)]

Item	Unit	1990	1995	2000	2002	2003	2004	2005	2006	2007
Producing wells (year-end)	1,000	269	299	342	388	393	406	426	449	427
Production value at wells	Bil. of dol. . .	31.8	30.2	74.3	58.7	97.5	106.6	138.7	124.0	128.8
Avg. per 1,000 cu. ft.	Dollars	1.71	1.55	3.68	2.95	4.88	5.46	7.33	6.40	6.39
Proved reserves [1]	Tril. cu. ft. . .	169	165	177	187	189	193	204	211	(NA)
Marketed production [2]	**Bil. cu. ft.** . .	**18,594**	**19,506**	**20,198**	**19,885**	**19,974**	**19,517**	**18,927**	**19,382**	**20,151**
Minus: Extraction losses [3]	Bil. cu. ft. . .	784	908	1,016	957	876	927	876	906	874
Equals: Dry production.	Bil. cu. ft. . .	17,810	18,599	19,182	18,928	19,099	18,591	18,051	18,476	19,278
Plus: Supplemental gas supplies . .	Bil. cu. ft. . .	123	110	90	68	68	60	64	66	61
Equals: Dry production with supplemental gas	Bil. cu. ft. . .	17,932	18,709	19,272	18,996	19,166	18,651	18,114	18,542	19,338
Plus: Withdrawals from storage . . .	Bil. cu. ft. . .	1,986	3,025	3,550	3,180	3,161	3,088	3,107	2,527	3,321
Plus: Imports	Bil. cu. ft. . .	1,532	2,841	3,782	4,015	3,944	4,259	4,341	4,186	4,602
Plus: Balancing item [4]	Bil. cu. ft. . .	307	396	-306	45	44	448	232	85	-253
Equals: Total supply	Bil. cu. ft. . .	21,758	24,971	26,298	26,237	26,314	26,445	25,794	25,340	27,007
Minus: Exports	Bil. cu. ft. . .	86	154	244	516	680	854	729	724	809
Minus: Additions to storage [5]	Bil. cu. ft. . .	2,499	2,610	2,721	2,713	3,358	3,202	3,055	2,963	3,144
Equals: Consumption, total	**Bil. cu. ft.** . .	**19,174**	**22,207**	**23,333**	**23,007**	**22,277**	**22,389**	**22,011**	**21,653**	**23,055**
Lease and plant fuel	Bil. cu. ft. . .	1,236	1,220	1,151	1,113	1,122	1,098	1,112	1,124	1,168
Pipeline fuel	Bil. cu. ft. . .	660	700	642	667	591	566	584	584	622
Residential	Bil. cu. ft. . .	4,391	4,850	4,996	4,889	5,079	4,869	4,827	4,368	4,724
Commercial [6]	Bil. cu. ft. . .	2,623	3,031	3,182	3,144	3,179	3,129	2,999	2,835	3,008
Industrial	Bil. cu. ft. . .	8,255	9,384	9,293	8,620	8,273	8,341	7,709	7,618	7,800
Vehicle fuel	Bil. cu. ft. . .	(Z)	5	13	15	18	21	23	25	26
Electric power sector	Bil. cu. ft. . .	3,245	4,237	5,206	5,672	5,135	5,464	5,869	6,222	6,874
World production (dry)	Tril. cu. ft. . .	73.6	78.0	88.3	92.2	95.4	98.5	101.5	(NA)	(NA)
U.S. production (dry)	Tril. cu. ft. . .	17.8	18.6	19.2	18.9	19.1	18.6	18.1	(NA)	(NA)
Percent U.S. of world	Percent . . .	24.2	23.9	21.7	20.5	20.0	18.9	17.8	(NA)	(NA)

Z Less than 500 million cubic feet. NA Not available. [1] Estimated, end of year. Source: U.S. Energy Information Administration, *U.S. Crude Oil, Natural Gas, and Natural Gas Liquids Reserves,* annual. [2] Marketed production includes gross withdrawals from reservoirs less quantities used for reservoir repressuring and quantities vented or flared. Excludes nonhydrocarbon gases subsequently removed. [3] Volumetric reduction in natural gas resulting from the removal of natural gas plant liquids, which are transferred to petroleum supply. [4] Quantities lost and imbalances in data due to differences among data sources. Since 1980, excludes intransit shipments that cross U.S.-Canada border (i.e., natural gas delivered to its destination via the other country). [5] Underground storage. Through 2004, includes liquefied natural gas (LNG) storage in above-ground tanks. [6] Includes deliveries to municipalities and public authorities for institutional heating and other purposes.

Source: Except as noted, U.S. Energy Information Administration, *Annual Energy Review;* "International Energy Annual"; "U.S. Crude Oil, Natural Gas, and Natural Gas Liquids Reserves"; and "Natural Gas Annual"; <http://www.eia.doe.gov>.

Table 876. Natural Gas Plant Liquids—Production and Value: 1990 to 2006

[Barrels of 42 gallons (566 represents 566,000,000)]

Item	Unit	1990	1995	2000	2001	2002	2003	2004	2005	2006
Field production [1]	Mil. bbl.	566	643	699	682	686	686	662	627	635
Pentanes plus	Mil. bbl.	112	122	112	112	109	109	101	97	96
Liquefied petroleum gases . . .	Mil. bbl.	454	521	587	570	577	577	561	529	539
Natural gas processed	Tril. cu. ft. . . .	15	17	17	17	16	15	15	15	15

[1] Includes other finished petroleum products, not shown separately.

Source: U.S. Energy Information Administration, "Petroleum Supply Annual" and "Natural Gas Annual"; <http://www.eia.doe.gov>.

Table 877. Coal Supply, Disposition, and Prices: 2000 to 2007

[In millions of short tons (1,073.6 represents 1,073,600,000). 1 short ton = 2,000 lbs.]

Item	2000	2002	2003	2004	2005	2006	2007
United States, total supply	**1,073.6**	**1,094.3**	**1,071.8**	**1,112.1**	**1,131.5**	**1,162.7**	**1,145.6**
Consumption by sector:							
Total	1,084.1	1,066.4	1,094.9	1,107.3	1,126.0	1,112.3	1,128.8
Electric power	985.8	977.5	1,005.1	1,016.3	1,037.5	1,026.5	1,046.4
Coke plants	28.9	23.7	24.2	23.7	23.4	23.0	22.7
Other industrial plants	65.2	60.7	61.3	62.2	60.3	59.5	56.5
Combined heat and power (CHP)	(NA)	26.2	24.8	26.6	25.9	25.3	24.1
Noncombined heat and power	(NA)	34.5	36.4	35.6	34.5	34.2	32.4
Residential/commercial users	4.1	4.4	4.2	5.1	4.7	3.2	3.2
Year-end coal stocks:							
Total	140.0	192.1	165.5	154.0	144.3	86.9	189.4
Electric power	102.0	141.7	121.6	106.7	101.1	141.0	151.1
Coke plants	1.5	1.4	0.9	1.3	2.6	2.9	1.9
Other industrial plants	4.6	5.8	4.7	4.8	5.6	6.5	5.6
Producers/distributors	31.9	43.3	38.3	41.2	35.0	36.5	30.8
U.S. coal trade:							
Net exports	46.0	22.7	18.0	20.7	19.5	13.4	22.8
Exports	58.5	39.6	43.0	48.0	49.9	49.6	59.2
Steam coal	25.7	18.1	20.9	21.2	21.3	22.1	27.0
Metallurgical coal	32.8	21.5	22.1	26.8	28.7	27.5	32.2
Imports	12.5	16.9	25.0	27.3	30.5	36.2	36.3
Average delivered price (dollars per short ton):							
Electric utilities [1]	24.28	24.74	25.82	27.30	31.22	34.26	36.08
Independent power producers [1]	(NA)	27.96	26.2	27.27	30.39	3.04	33.47
Coke plants	44.38	50.67	50.63	61.50	83.79	92.87	94.97
Other industrial plants	31.46	35.49	34.70	39.30	47.63	51.67	54.42
Average free alongside ship (f.a.s.):							
Exports	34.90	40.44	35.98	54.11	67.10	70.93	70.25
Steam coal	29.67	34.51	26.94	42.03	47.64	46.25	47.90
Metallurgical coal	38.99	45.41	44.55	63.63	81.56	90.81	88.99
Imports	30.10	35.51	31.45	37.52	46.71	49.10	47.64

NA Not available. [1] Average delivered price is through November 2007.

Source: U.S. Energy Information Administration, "U.S. Coal Supply and Demand: 2007 Review," annual; <http://www.eia.doe.gov/cneaf/coal/page/special/feature.html> (released 16 April 2008).

Table 878. Coal and Coke—Summary: 1990 to 2007

[In millions of short tons (1,029 represents 1,029,000,000), except as indicated. Includes coal consumed at mines. Recoverability varies between 40 and 90 percent for individual deposits; 50 percent or more of overall U.S. coal reserve base is believed to be recoverable]

Item	Unit	1990	1995	2000	2003	2004	2005	2006	2007
COAL									
Coal production, total [1], [2]	**Mil. sh. tons**	**1,029**	**1,033**	**1,074**	**1,072**	**1,112**	**1,131**	**1,163**	**1,146**
Value [3]	Bil. dol.	22.39	19.45	18.02	19.13	22.16	26.69	29.25	29.10
Anthracite production [2]	Mil. sh. tons	3.5	4.7	4.6	1.3	1.7	1.7	1.5	1.6
Bituminous coal and lignite [4]	Mil. sh. tons	1,026	1,028	1,069	1,070	1,110	1,130	1,161	1,144
Underground	Mil. sh. tons	425	396	374	353	368	369	359	351
Surface [2]	Mil. sh. tons	605	637	700	719	745	763	804	794
Exports	Mil. sh. tons	106	89	58	43	48	50	50	59
Imports	Mil. sh. tons	3	9	13	25	27	30	36	36
Consumption [5]	Mil. sh. tons	904	962	1,084	1,095	1,107	1,126	1,112	1,129
Electric power sector	Mil. sh. tons	783	850	986	1,005	1,016	1,037	1,027	1,046
Industrial	Mil. sh. tons	115	106	94	86	86	84	82	79
Number of mines	Number	3,243	2,104	1,453	1,316	1,379	1,415	1,438	(NA)
Daily employment	1,000	131	90	72	71	74	79	83	(NA)
Production, by state:									
Alabama	Mil. sh. tons	29	25	19	20	22	21	19	(NA)
Illinois	Mil. sh. tons	60	48	33	32	32	32	33	(NA)
Indiana	Mil. sh. tons	36	26	28	35	35	34	35	(NA)
Kentucky	Mil. sh. tons	173	154	131	113	114	120	121	(NA)
Montana	Mil. sh. tons	38	39	38	37	40	40	42	(NA)
Ohio	Mil. sh. tons	35	26	22	22	23	25	23	(NA)
Pennsylvania	Mil. sh. tons	71	62	75	64	66	67	66	(NA)
Virginia	Mil. sh. tons	47	34	33	32	31	28	30	(NA)
West Virginia	Mil. sh. tons	169	163	158	140	148	154	152	(NA)
Wyoming	Mil. sh. tons	184	264	339	376	396	404	447	(NA)
Other states	Mil. sh. tons	187	192	197	202	204	206	196	1,146
World production	Mil. sh. tons	5,354	5,105	4,949	5,657	6,097	6,490	(NA)	(NA)
Percent U.S. of world	Percent	19.2	20.2	21.7	18.9	18.2	17.4	(NA)	(NA)
COKE									
Production	Mil. sh. tons	27.6	23.7	20.8	17.2	16.9	16.7	16.4	16.2
Imports	Mil. sh. tons	0.8	3.8	3.8	2.8	6.9	3.5	4.1	2.5
Exports	Mil. sh. tons	0.6	1.4	1.1	0.7	1.3	1.7	1.6	1.4
Consumption [6]	Mil. sh. tons	27.8	25.8	23.2	19.4	22.5	18.2	18.8	17.3

NA Not available. [1] Includes bituminous coal, subbituminous coal, lignite, and anthracite. [2] Beginning 2002, includes a small amount of refuse recovery. [3] Coal values are based on free-on-board rail/barge prices, which are the free-on-board prices of coal at the point of first sale, excluding freight or shipping and insurance costs. [4] Includes subbituminous. [5] Includes some categories not shown separately. [6] Consumption is calculated as the sum of production and imports minus exports and stock change.

Source: U.S. Energy Information Administration, *Annual Energy Review*, "International Energy Annual", and "Annual Coal Report"; <http://www.eia.doe.gov>.

U.S. Census Bureau, Statistical Abstract of the United States: 2009

Table 879. Demonstrated Coal Reserves by Major Producing State: 2005 and 2006

[In millions of short tons (492,935 represents 492,935,000,000). As of January 1. The demonstrated reserve base represents the sum of coal in both measured and indicated resource categories of reliability. Measured resources of coal are estimates that have a high degree of geologic assurance from sample analyses and measurements from closely spaced and geological well-known sample sites. Indicated resources are estimates based partly from sample and analyses and measurements and partly from reasonable geologic projections]

State	2005			2006		
		Method of mining			Method of mining	
	Total reserves	Under-ground	Surface	Total reserves	Under-ground	Surface
United States [1]	**492,935**	**334,876**	**158,059**	**491,076**	**333,991**	**157,085**
Alabama.	4,205	1,007	3,198	4,174	986	3,188
Alaska.	6,110	5,423	687	6,108	5,423	685
Arkansas	417	272	144	417	272	144
Colorado.	16,223	11,461	4,762	16,158	11,397	4,761
Illinois	104,469	87,919	16,550	104,408	87,865	16,543
Indiana.	9,483	8,741	742	9,431	8,720	711
Iowa	2,189	1,732	457	2,189	1,732	457
Kansas.	972	–	972	972	–	972
Kentucky	30,020	17,055	12,965	29,814	16,909	12,906
Kentucky, Eastern.	10,516	1,178	9,337	10,362	1,080	9,282
Kentucky, Western	19,504	15,877	3,628	19,452	15,829	3,624
Maryland	643	578	65	634	572	62
Missouri	5,989	1,479	4,510	5,989	1,479	4,510
Montana.	119,230	70,958	48,272	119,177	70,957	48,220
New Mexico	12,131	6,156	5,975	12,093	6,142	5,951
North Dakota.	9,053	–	9,053	9,015	–	9,015
Ohio	23,300	17,546	5,754	23,260	17,515	5,745
Oklahoma.	1,554	1,231	323	1,551	1,230	321
Pennsylvania.	27,472	23,221	4,251	27,349	23,113	4,236
Anthracite	7,198	3,844	3,355	7,196	3,843	3,353
Bituminous	20,274	19,377	896	20,153	19,270	883
Tennessee	774	510	264	770	508	262
Texas.	12,385	–	12,385	12,328	–	12,328
Utah	5,396	5,128	268	5,344	5,076	268
Virginia.	1,693	1,130	562	1,642	1,093	548
Washington.	1,340	1,332	8	1,340	1,332	8
West Virginia.	32,960	29,184	3,775	32,706	29,015	3,691
Wyoming	63,819	42,500	21,319	63,261	42,499	20,762

– Represents or rounds to zero.   [1] Includes other states not shown separately.

Source: U.S. Energy Information Administration, *Annual Coal Report*, 2006. See also <http://www.eia.doe.gov/cneaf/coal/page/acr/acr_sum.html>.

Table 880. Uranium Concentrate (U_3O_8) Industry—Summary: 1990 to 2007

[In millions of feet (1.7 represents 1,700,000), except as indicated. See also Table 902 in Section 19]

Item	Unit	1990	1995	2000	2002	2003	2004	2005	2006	2007 [1]
Exploration and development, surface drilling.	Mil. ft.	1.7	1.3	1.0	(D)	(D)	1.2	1.7	2.7	5.1
Expenditures	Mil. dol.	(NA)	2.6	5.6	(D)	(D)	10.6	18.1	40.1	67.5
Number of mines operated.	Number.	39	12	10	6	4	6	10	11	12
Underground	Number.	27	–	1	–	1	2	4	5	6
Openpit.	Number.	2	–	–	–	–	–	–	–	–
In situ leaching	Number.	7	5	4	3	2	3	4	5	5
Other sources	Number.	3	7	5	3	1	1	2	1	1
Mine production	1,000 pounds . .	5,876	3,528	3,123	2,405	2,200	2,452	3,045	4,692	4,541
Underground	1,000 pounds . .	(D)	–	(D)	(D)	(D)	(D)	(D)	(D)	(D)
Openpit.	1,000 pounds . .	1,881	–	–	–	–	–	–	–	–
In situ leaching	1,000 pounds . .	(D)	3,372	2,995	(D)	(D)	(D)	2,681	4,259	(D)
Other sources	1,000 pounds . .	3,995	156	128	(D)	(D)	(D)	(D)	(D)	(D)
Uranium concentrate production . .	1,000 pounds . .	8,886	6,043	3,958	2,344	2,000	2,282	2,689	4,106	4,534
Concentrate shipments from mills and plants	1,000 pounds . .	12,957	5,500	3,187	3,810	1,600	2,280	2,702	3,838	4,050
Employment	Person-years . .	1,335	1,107	627	426	321	420	648	755	1,231

– Represents zero.   D Data withheld to avoid disclosing figures for individual companies.   NA Not available.   [1] Preliminary.

Source: U.S. Department of Energy, through 2002, *Uranium Industry*, annual. Thereafter, *Domestic Uranium Production Report*, annual. See also <http://www.eia.doe.gov/cneaf/nuclear/dupr/dupr.html>.

Section 19
Energy and Utilities

This section presents statistics on fuel resources, energy production and consumption, electric energy, hydroelectric power, nuclear power, solar energy, wood energy, and the electric and gas utility industries. The principal sources are the U.S. Department of Energy's Energy Information Administration (EIA), the Edison Electric Institute, Washington, DC, and the American Gas Association, Arlington, VA. The Department of Energy was created in October 1977 and assumed and centralized the responsibilities of all or part of several agencies including the Federal Power Commission (FPC), the U.S. Bureau of Mines, the Federal Energy Administration, and the U.S. Energy Research and Development Administration. For additional data on transportation, see Section 23; on fuels, see Section 18; and on energy-related housing characteristics, see Section 20.

The EIA, in its *Annual Energy Review,* provides statistics and trend data on energy supply, demand, and prices. Information is included on petroleum and natural gas, coal, electricity, hydroelectric power, nuclear power, solar, wood, and geothermal energy. Among its annual reports are *Annual Energy Review; Electric Power Annual; Natural Gas Annual; Petroleum Supply Annual; State Energy Consumption, Price, and Expenditure Data; U.S. Crude Oil, Natural Gas, and Natural Gas Liquids Reserves; Electric Sales and Revenue; Annual Energy Outlook;* and *International Energy Annual.* These various publications contain state, national, and international data on production of electricity, net summer capability of generating plants, fuels used in energy production, energy sales and consumption, and hydroelectric power. The EIA also issues the *Monthly Energy Review,* which presents current supply, disposition, and price data and monthly publications on petroleum, coal, natural gas, and electric power. Data on residential energy consumption, expenditures, and conservation activities are available from EIA's Residential Energy Consumption Survey and are published every 4 years.

The Edison Electric Institute's monthly bulletin and annual *Statistical Year Book of the Electric Utility Industry for the Year* contain data on the distribution of electric energy by public utilities; information on the electric power supply, expansion of electric generating facilities, and the manufacture of heavy electric power equipment is presented in the annual *Year-End Summary of the Electric Power Situation in the United States.* The American Gas Association, in its monthly and quarterly bulletins and its yearbook, *Gas Facts,* presents data on gas utilities and financial and operating statistics.

Btu conversion factors—Various energy sources are converted from original units to the thermal equivalent using British thermal units (Btu). A Btu is the amount of energy required to raise the temperature of 1 pound of water 1 degree Fahrenheit (F) at or near 39.2 degrees F. Factors are calculated annually from the latest final annual data available; some are revised as a result. The following list provides conversion factors used in 2007 for production and consumption, in that order, for various fuels: Petroleum, 5.800 and 5.347 mil. Btu per barrel; total coal, 20.341 and 20.169 mil. Btu per short ton; and natural gas (dry), 1,028 Btu per cubic foot for both. The factors for the production of nuclear power and geothermal power were 10,434 and 21,017 Btu per kilowatt-hour, respectively. The fossil fuel steam-electric power plant generation factor of 9,919 Btu per kilowatt-hour was used for hydroelectric power generation and for wood and waste, wind, photovoltaic, and solar thermal energy consumed at electric utilities.

U.S. Census Bureau, Statistical Abstract of the United States: 2009

In the past few years, EIA has restructured the industry categories it once used to gather and report electricity statistics. The electric power industry, previously divided into electric utilities and non-utilities, now consists of the Electric Power Sector, the Commercial Sector, and the Industrial Sector.

The Electric Power Sector is composed of electricity-only and combined-heat-and-power plants (CHPs) whose primary business is to sell electricity, or electricity and heat, to the public.

Electricity-only plants are composed of traditional electric utilities, and nontraditional participants, including energy service providers, power marketers, independent power producers (IPPs), and the portion of CHPs that produce only electricity.

A utility is defined as a corporation, person, agency, authority, or other legal entity or instrumentality aligned with distribution facilities for delivery of electric energy for use primarily by the public. Electric utilities include investor-owned electric utilities, municipal and state utilities, federal electric utilities, and rural electric cooperatives. In total, there are more than 3,100 electric utilities in the United States.

An independent power producer is an entity defined as a corporation, person, agency, authority, or other legal entity or instrumentality that owns or operates facilities whose primary business is to produce electricity for use by the public. They are not generally aligned with distribution facilities and are not considered electric utilities.

Combined-heat-and-power producers are plants designed to produce both heat and electricity from a single heat source. These types of electricity producers can be independent power producers or industrial or commercial establishments. As some independent power producers are CHPs, their information is included in the data for the combined-heat-and-power sector. There are approximately 2,800 unregulated independent power producers and CHPs in the United States.

The Commercial Sector consists of commercial CHPs and commercial electricity-only plants. Industrial CHPs and industrial electricity-only plants make up the Industrial Sector. For more information, please refer to the *Electric Power Annual 2006* Web site located at <http://www.eia.doe.gov/cneaf/electricity/epa/epa_sum.html>.

U.S. Census Bureau, Statistical Abstract of the United States: 2009

Table 881. Utilities—Establishments, Revenue, Payroll, and Employees by Kind of Business: 2002

[**398,907 represents $398,907,000,000.** Includes only establishments or firms with payroll. Data based on the 2002 Economic Census. See headnote, Table 734 and Appendix III]

Kind of business	2002 NAICS code [1]	Establish-ments (number)	Revenue		Annual payroll		Paid employ-ees for pay period including March 12 (number)
			Total (mil. dol.)	Per paid employee (dol.)	Total (mil. dol.)	Per paid employee (dol.)	
Utilities.	**22**	**17,103**	**398,907**	**601,630**	**42,418**	**63,974**	**663,044**
Electric power generation, transmission, & distribution.	2211	9,394	325,028	606,764	35,560	66,383	535,675
Electric power generation	22111	1,997	79,432	646,917	9,062	73,801	122,785
Hydroelectric power generation.	221111	371	2,729	429,013	369	58,008	6,360
Fossil fuel electric power generation. . .	221112	1,245	56,048	776,734	5,233	72,524	72,159
Nuclear electric power generation	221113	73	12,032	383,845	2,493	79,513	31,347
Other electric power generation.	221119	308	8,622	667,421	967	74,853	12,919
Electric power transmission, control & distribution	22112	7,397	245,597	594,824	26,498	64,178	412,890
Electric bulk power transmission & control	221121	72	1,588	552,587	195	67,710	2,874
Electric power distribution.	221122	7,325	244,009	595,120	26,304	64,153	410,016
Natural gas distribution.	2212	2,376	66,515	778,438	5,370	62,844	85,447
Water, sewage, & other systems	2213	5,333	7,363	175,647	1,488	35,496	41,922
Water supply & irrigation systems	22131	4,603	5,886	169,722	1,220	35,184	34,682
Sewage treatment facilities	22132	667	832	147,425	181	32,099	5,643
Steam & air-conditioning supply	22133	63	645	404,050	87	54,272	1,597

[1] North American Industry Classification System, 2002; see text, Section 15.

Source: U.S. Census Bureau, *2002 Economic Census*, Series EC02-22A-1US, issued August 2005. See also <http://www.census.gov/econ/census02/>.

Table 882. Utilities—Employees, Annual Payroll, and Establishments by Industry: 2005

[**46,293 represents $46,293,000,000.** Excludes government employees, railroad employees, self-employed persons, etc. An establishment is a single physical location where business is conducted or where services or industrial operations are performed. See Appendix III]

Year and industry	2002 NAICS code [1]	Number of employ-ees [2]	Annual payroll (mil. dol.)	Aver-age payroll per em-ployee (dol.)	Establishments by employment size-class				
					Total	Under 20 em-ployees	20 to 99 em-ployees	100 to 499 employ-ees	500 and over employ-ees
Utilities, total	**22**	**633,106**	**46,293**	**73,120**	**17,326**	**12,200**	**3,787**	**1,163**	**176**
Electric power generation, transmission, and distribution	2211	512,847	39,027	76,098	9,537	5,497	2,934	945	161
Electric power generation	22111	120,766	9,715	80,442	2,102	1,268	570	219	45
Hydroelectric power generation. . . .	221111	5,784	393	67,874	386	318	58	10	–
Fossil fuel electric power generation.	221112	74,703	5,853	78,351	1,285	684	406	183	12
Nuclear electric power generation . .	221113	28,287	2,553	90,266	68	16	15	8	29
Other electric power generation . . .	221119	11,992	916	76,362	363	250	91	18	4
Electric power transmission, control & distribution	22112	392,081	29,312	74,760	7,435	4,229	2,364	726	116
Electric bulk power transmission & control.	221121	5,613	454	80,877	102	64	23	12	3
Electric power distribution	221122	386,468	28,858	74,671	7,333	4,165	2,341	714	113
Natural gas distribution	2212	78,273	5,543	70,815	2,477	1,739	550	174	14
Water, sewage, & other systems	2213	41,986	1,723	41,042	5,312	4,964	303	44	1
Water supply & irrigation systems. . . .	22131	34,403	1,403	40,772	4,473	4,213	219	41	–
Sewage treatment facilities	22132	6,062	231	38,098	750	686	60	3	1
Steam & air-conditioning supply	22133	1,521	90	58,877	89	65	24	–	–

– Represents zero. [1] North American Industry Classification System, 2002; see text, Section 15. [2] Covers full- and part-time employees who are on the payroll in the pay period including March 12.

Source: U.S. Census Bureau, "County Business Patterns"; <http://www.census.gov/epcd/cbp/view/cbpview.html> (accessed January 2008).

Table 883. Energy Supply and Disposition by Type of Fuel: 1960 to 2007

[In quadrillion British thermal units (Btu) (42.80 represents 42,800,000,000,000,000). For definition of Btu, see source and text, this section]

Year	Production										Consumption					
	Total[1]	Crude oil[2]	Natural gas	Coal	Nuclear power	Renewable energy[3] Total[1]	Hydro-electric power	Biofuel[4]	Solar energy	Net imports, total[5]	Total[1]	Petro-leum[6,7]	Natural gas[8]	Coal	Nuclear power	Renewable energy[3] total
1960	42.80	14.93	12.66	10.82	0.01	2.93	1.61	1.32	(NA)	2.71	45.09	19.92	12.39	9.84	0.01	2.93
1970	63.50	20.40	21.67	14.61	0.24	4.08	2.63	1.43	(NA)	5.71	67.84	29.52	21.79	12.26	0.24	4.08
1975	61.36	17.73	19.64	14.99	1.90	4.72	3.15	1.50	(NA)	11.71	72.00	32.73	19.95	12.66	1.90	4.72
1978	63.14	18.43	19.49	14.91	3.02	5.04	2.94	2.04	(NA)	17.19	79.99	37.97	20.00	13.77	3.02	5.04
1979	65.95	18.10	20.08	17.54	2.78	5.17	2.93	2.15	(NA)	16.60	80.90	37.12	20.67	15.04	2.78	5.17
1980	67.23	18.25	19.91	18.60	2.74	5.49	2.90	2.48	(NA)	12.10	78.12	34.20	20.24	15.42	2.74	5.49
1981	67.01	18.15	19.70	18.38	3.01	5.48	2.76	2.60	(NA)	9.41	76.17	31.93	19.75	15.91	3.01	5.48
1982	66.62	18.31	18.32	18.64	3.13	6.03	3.27	2.66	(NA)	7.25	73.15	30.23	18.36	15.32	3.13	6.03
1983	64.18	18.39	16.59	17.25	3.20	6.56	3.53	2.90	(NA)	8.06	73.04	30.05	17.22	15.89	3.20	6.56
1984	68.92	18.85	18.01	19.72	3.55	6.52	3.39	2.97	(Z)	8.68	76.71	31.05	18.39	17.07	3.55	6.52
1985	67.80	18.99	16.98	19.33	4.08	6.18	2.97	3.02	(Z)	7.58	76.49	30.92	17.70	17.48	4.08	6.18
1986	67.18	18.38	16.54	19.51	4.38	6.22	3.07	2.93	(Z)	10.13	76.76	32.20	16.59	17.26	4.38	6.22
1987	67.66	17.67	17.14	20.14	4.75	5.74	2.63	2.87	(Z)	11.59	79.17	32.87	17.64	18.01	4.75	5.74
1988	69.03	17.28	17.60	20.74	5.59	5.57	2.33	3.02	(Z)	12.93	82.82	34.22	18.45	18.85	5.59	5.57
1989[9]	69.48	16.12	17.85	21.36	5.60	6.39	2.84	3.16	0.06	14.11	84.94	34.21	19.60	19.07	5.60	6.39
1990	70.87	15.57	18.33	22.49	6.10	6.21	3.05	2.74	0.06	14.06	84.65	33.55	19.60	19.17	6.10	6.21
1991	70.53	15.70	18.23	21.64	6.42	6.24	3.02	2.78	0.06	13.19	84.61	32.85	20.03	18.99	6.42	6.24
1992	70.13	15.22	18.38	21.69	6.48	5.99	2.62	2.93	0.06	14.44	85.96	33.53	20.71	19.12	6.48	5.99
1993	68.50	14.49	18.58	20.34	6.41	6.26	2.89	2.91	0.07	17.01	87.60	33.74	21.23	19.84	6.41	6.26
1994	70.89	14.10	19.35	22.20	6.69	6.16	2.68	3.03	0.07	18.33	89.26	34.56	21.73	19.91	6.69	6.16
1995	71.32	13.89	19.08	22.13	7.08	6.70	3.21	3.10	0.07	17.75	91.17	34.44	22.67	20.09	7.08	6.71
1996	72.64	13.72	19.34	22.79	7.09	7.17	3.59	3.16	0.07	19.07	94.17	35.67	23.08	21.00	7.09	7.17
1997	72.63	13.66	19.39	23.31	6.60	7.18	3.64	3.11	0.07	20.70	94.77	36.16	23.22	21.45	6.60	7.18
1998	73.04	13.24	19.61	24.05	7.07	6.66	3.30	2.93	0.07	22.28	95.18	36.82	22.83	21.66	7.07	6.66
1999	71.91	12.45	19.34	23.30	7.61	6.68	3.27	2.97	0.07	23.54	96.82	37.84	22.91	21.62	7.61	6.68
2000	71.49	12.36	19.66	22.74	7.86	6.26	2.81	3.01	0.07	24.97	98.98	38.26	23.82	22.58	7.86	6.26
2001	71.89	12.28	20.17	23.55	8.03	5.32	2.24	2.63	0.07	26.39	96.33	38.19	22.77	21.91	8.03	5.32
2002	70.94	12.16	19.44	22.73	8.14	5.90	2.69	2.71	0.06	25.74	97.86	38.23	23.56	21.90	8.14	5.89
2003	70.26	12.03	19.69	22.09	7.96	6.15	2.82	2.82	0.06	27.01	98.21	38.81	22.90	22.32	7.96	6.15
2004	70.38	11.50	19.09	22.85	8.22	6.25	2.69	3.01	0.06	29.11	100.35	40.29	22.93	22.47	8.22	6.26
2005	69.65	10.96	18.57	23.19	8.16	6.43	2.70	3.14	0.07	30.15	100.51	40.39	22.58	22.80	8.16	6.44
2006	71.02	10.80	18.99	23.79	8.21	6.87	2.87	3.32	0.07	29.81	99.86	39.96	22.19	22.45	8.21	6.92
2007[10]	71.71	10.80	19.82	23.48	8.41	6.80	2.46	3.58	0.08	29.24	101.60	39.82	23.64	22.77	8.41	6.83

NA Not available.   Z Less than 5 trillion.   [1] Includes types of fuel not shown separately.   [2] Includes lease condensate.   [3] Electricity net generation from conventional hydroelectric power, geothermal, solar, and wind; consumption of wood, waste, and alcohol fuels; geothermal heat pump and direct use energy; and solar thermal direct use energy.   [4] Wood, waste, and alcohol (ethanol blended into motor gasoline).   [5] Imports minus exports.   [6] Beginning in 1993, ethanol blended into motor gasoline is included in petroleum.   [7] Petroleum products supplied, including natural gas plant liquids and crude oil burned as fuel.   [8] Includes supplemental gaseous fuels.   [9] There is a discontinuity in this time series between 1989 and 1990.   [10] Preliminary.

Source: U.S. Energy Information Administration, *Annual Energy Review*, 2007. See also <http://www.eia.doe.gov/emeu/aer/overview.html> (released 23 June 2008).

Table 884. Energy Supply and Disposition by Type of Fuel—Estimates, 2005 and 2006, and Projections, 2007 to 2020

[Quadrillion Btu (69.80 represents 69,800,000,000,000,000) per year. Btu = British thermal unit. For definition of Btu, see source and text, this section. Mcf = 1,000 cubic feet. Projections are "reference" or mid-level forecasts. See report for methodology and assumptions used in generating projections]

Type of fuel	2005	2006	Projections 2007	Projections 2010	Projections 2015	Projections 2020
Production, total	**69.80**	**71.41**	**72.87**	**76.17**	**78.96**	**82.21**
Crude oil and lease condensate	10.99	10.80	10.98	12.76	13.25	13.40
Natural gas plant liquids	2.33	2.36	2.38	2.27	2.29	2.31
Natural gas, dry	18.60	19.04	19.55	19.85	20.08	20.24
Coal	23.19	23.79	23.76	23.97	24.48	25.20
Nuclear power	8.16	8.21	8.34	8.31	8.41	9.05
Renewable energy [1]	6.16	6.71	6.98	8.47	9.86	11.42
Other [2]	0.36	0.50	0.88	0.54	0.58	0.58
Imports, total	**34.62**	**34.57**	**34.25**	**32.49**	**33.31**	**33.62**
Crude oil [3]	22.09	22.08	21.79	21.14	21.80	21.58
Petroleum products [4]	7.23	7.21	6.87	5.61	5.34	5.43
Natural gas	4.45	4.29	4.66	4.80	5.12	4.68
Other imports [5]	0.85	0.98	0.93	0.95	1.04	1.93
Exports, total	**4.32**	**4.59**	**4.93**	**5.45**	**5.03**	**4.87**
Petroleum [6]	2.32	2.60	2.74	2.82	2.91	2.98
Natural gas	0.74	0.73	0.75	0.84	0.97	1.02
Coal	1.27	1.26	1.44	1.79	1.14	0.87
Consumption, total	**100.08**	**99.52**	**101.40**	**103.34**	**107.26**	**110.85**
Petroleum products [7]	40.47	40.06	40.19	40.46	41.80	42.24
Natural gas	22.65	22.30	23.58	23.93	24.35	24.01
Coal	22.78	22.50	22.70	23.03	24.19	25.87
Nuclear power	8.16	8.21	8.34	8.31	8.41	9.05
Renewable energy [1], other [8]	5.82	6.27	6.38	7.43	8.34	9.50
Other	0.21	0.19	0.22	0.18	0.17	0.17
Net imports of petroleum	**27.00**	**26.70**	**25.92**	**23.93**	**24.23**	**24.03**
Prices (2006 dollars per unit):						
Imported crude oil price [9]	50.40	59.05	62.10	65.18	52.03	51.55
Gas wellhead price (dol. per 1,000 cu. ft.) [10]	7.85	6.42	6.21	6.33	5.36	5.44
Coal minemouth price (dol. per ton)	24.08	24.63	25.45	26.16	23.38	22.51
Average electric price (cents per kWh)	8.38	8.91	8.90	9.18	8.53	8.61

[1] Includes grid-connected electricity from conventional hydroelectric; wood and wood waste; landfill gas; municipal solid waste; other biomass; wind; photovoltaic and solar thermal sources; nonelectric energy from renewable sources, such as active and passive solar systems, and wood. Excludes electricity imports using renewable sources and nonmarketed renewable energy. [2] Includes nonbiogenic municipal solid waste, liquid hydrogen, methanol, and some domestic inputs to refineries. [3] Includes imports of crude oil for the Strategic Petroleum Reserve. [4] Includes imports of finished petroleum products, imports of unfinished oils, alcohols, ethers, blending components, and renewable fuels such as ethanol. [5] Includes coal, coal coke (net), and electricity (net). [6] Includes crude oil and petroleum products. [7] Includes petroleum-derived fuels and non-petroleum-derived fuels, such as ethanol, biodiesel, and coal-based synthetic liquids. Petroleum coke, which is a solid, is included. Also included are natural gas plant liquids, crude oil consumed as a fuel, and liquid hydrogen. [8] Includes net electricity imports and natural gas losses. [9] Weighted average price delivered to U.S. refiners. [10] Represents lower 48 onshore and offshore supplies.

Source: U.S. Energy Information Administration, *Annual Energy Outlook 2008.* See also <http://www.eia.doe.gov/oiaf/aeo/excel/aeotab_1.xls> (released June 2008).

Table 885. Energy Consumption by End-Use Sector: 1970 to 2007

[67.84 represents 67,840,000,000,000,000 Btu. Btu = British thermal units. For definition of Btu, see source and text, this section. See Appendix III]

Year	Total (quad. Btu)	Residential and commercial [1] (quad. Btu)	Industrial [2] (quad. Btu)	Trans-portation (quad. Btu)	Percent of total Residential and commercial [1]	Percent of total Industrial [2]	Percent of total Trans-portation
1970	67.84	22.11	29.64	16.10	32.6	43.7	23.7
1975	72.00	24.31	29.45	18.24	33.8	40.9	25.3
1980	78.12	26.35	32.08	19.70	33.7	41.1	25.2
1985	76.49	27.53	28.88	20.09	36.0	37.7	26.3
1990	84.65	30.35	31.89	22.42	35.8	37.7	26.5
1995	91.17	33.28	34.05	23.85	36.5	37.3	26.2
1999	96.82	36.00	34.86	25.95	37.2	36.0	26.8
2000	98.98	37.66	34.76	26.55	38.1	35.1	26.8
2001	96.33	37.25	32.81	26.28	38.7	34.1	27.3
2002	97.86	38.24	32.76	26.85	39.1	33.5	27.4
2003	98.21	38.56	32.65	27.00	39.3	33.2	27.5
2004	100.35	38.84	33.61	27.90	38.7	33.5	27.8
2005	100.51	39.59	32.55	28.36	39.4	32.4	28.2
2006	99.86	38.59	32.40	28.86	38.6	32.5	28.9
2007 [3]	101.60	40.18	32.32	29.10	39.6	31.8	28.6

[1] Commercial sector fuel use, including that at commercial combined-heat-and-power (CHP) and industrial electricity-only plants. [2] Industrial sector fuel use, including that at industrial combined-heat-and-power (CHP) and industrial electricity-only plants. [3] Preliminary.

Source: U.S. Energy Information Administration, *Annual Energy Review 2007.* See also <http://www.eia.doe.gov/emeu/aer/pdf/pages/sec2_4.pdf> (released 23 June 2008).

Table 886. Energy Consumption—End-Use Sector and Selected Source, by State: 2005

[In trillions of Btu (100,369 represents 100,369,000,000,000,000), **except as indicated**. For definition of Btu, see source and text, this section. Data are preliminary]

State	Total [1]	Per capita [2] (mil. Btu)	End-use sector [3] Residential	Commercial	Industrial [1]	Transportation	Source Petroleum	Natural gas (dry) [4]	Coal	Hydro electric power [5,6]	Nuclear electric power [6]
U.S....	**100,369**	**339**	**21,743**	**17,950**	**32,323**	**28,352**	**40,733**	**22,645**	**22,795**	**2,670**	**8,149**
AL	2,119	467	398	268	961	491	627	364	890	101	330
AK	799	1,194	56	62	417	264	333	434	14	15	–
AZ	1,480	249	382	336	227	534	591	328	428	64	269
AR	1,135	409	229	162	454	289	384	216	247	31	143
CA	8,360	232	1,516	1,551	2,001	3,291	3,870	2,298	67	396	377
CO	1,426	305	325	290	386	424	494	483	387	14	–
CT	900	258	298	213	125	264	453	172	42	5	162
DE	313	372	71	58	110	73	148	49	57	–	–
DC	190	327	39	125	4	23	29	34	1	–	–
FL	4,563	257	1,333	1,068	566	1,596	2,163	814	672	3	300
GA	3,173	348	727	552	925	969	1,159	426	901	40	329
HI	333	263	37	45	72	179	295	3	18	1	–
ID	503	353	113	79	187	124	161	78	11	85	–
IL	4,122	324	1,011	765	1,234	1,111	1,486	984	1,048	1	972
IN	2,905	464	550	365	1,344	646	880	541	1,594	4	–
IA	1,228	415	239	185	502	302	446	243	430	10	47
KS	1,032	376	225	192	356	259	359	259	380	(Z)	92
KY	1,970	472	370	260	864	477	725	241	986	30	–
LA	3,613	804	364	273	2,259	718	1,587	1,367	254	8	163
ME	482	368	119	77	156	131	264	61	7	35	–
MD	1,555	279	442	286	369	459	604	212	329	17	153
MA	1,562	243	474	396	205	487	754	385	119	10	57
MI	3,166	313	838	640	882	806	1,033	928	799	14	343
MN	1,852	362	407	352	560	534	722	372	379	6	134
MS	1,182	408	231	164	429	358	463	311	176	–	105
MO	1,915	331	513	399	410	593	747	273	836	12	84
MT	419	448	76	68	158	118	193	71	199	96	–
NE	655	373	150	128	204	173	232	120	229	9	92
NV	728	302	166	126	197	239	280	237	198	17	–
NH	335	257	98	79	53	104	192	73	44	18	99
NJ	2,729	315	636	637	479	977	1,332	626	125	(Z)	327
NM	675	352	108	122	225	220	259	227	318	2	–
NY	4,180	217	1,266	1,317	525	1,071	1,849	1,108	257	257	442
NC	2,732	315	715	563	703	751	999	238	812	47	417
ND	412	648	64	61	195	92	138	55	431	13	–
OH	4,082	356	981	710	1,375	1,015	1,366	862	1,481	5	154
OK	1,551	439	305	236	571	440	567	605	397	26	–
OR	1,096	302	266	204	294	331	393	241	36	309	–
PA	4,050	327	999	717	1,298	1,036	1,535	719	1,491	22	795
RI	228	213	80	59	27	62	98	84	(Z)	(Z)	–
SC	1,694	398	360	255	651	428	572	179	431	29	554
SD	274	351	63	56	66	88	120	43	37	31	–
TN	2,339	390	536	383	773	647	826	238	658	85	290
TX	11,558	506	1,618	1,399	5,812	2,729	5,671	3,625	1,628	13	398
UT	757	302	150	143	226	237	291	169	406	8	–
VT	167	269	50	32	30	54	91	8	(Z)	12	42
VA	2,610	345	639	593	593	784	1,037	312	458	15	291
WA	2,059	328	480	371	593	614	855	273	112	720	86
WV	794	440	165	113	335	181	273	125	960	9	–
WI	1,862	336	426	356	643	437	625	416	523	15	103
WY	462	912	42	55	245	119	161	113	491	8	–

– Represents zero. Z Less than 50 billion Btu. [1] U.S. total energy and U.S. industrial sector include 50.5 trillion Btu of net imports of coal coke that is not allocated to the states. [2] Based on estimated resident population as of July 1. [3] End-use sector data include electricity sales and associated electrical system energy losses. [4] Includes supplemental gaseous fuels. [5] Conventional hydroelectric power. Does not include pumped-storage hydroelectricity. [6] Total consumed by the electric power sector only.

Source: U.S. Energy Information Administration, "State Energy Data, 2005"; <http://www.eia.doe.gov/emeu/states/_seds.html> (released 29 February 2008).

Table 887. Commercial Buildings—Energy Consumption and Expenditures: 2003

[4,645 represents 4,645,000. Covers buildings using one or more major fuel. Excludes industrial buildings, predominantly residential buildings, and buildings of less than 1,000 sq. ft. Based on a sample survey of building representatives and energy suppliers; therefore, subject to sampling variability. For characteristics of commercial buildings, see Table 963 in Section 20. For composition of regions, see inside front cover]

Building characteristic	All buildings using any major fuel		Consumption (tril. Btu)			Expenditures (mil. dol.)		
	Number (1,000)	Square feet (mil.)	Major fuel, total [1]	Electricity	Natural gas	Major fuel, total [1]	Electricity	Natural gas
All buildings	**4,645**	**64,783**	**5,820**	**3,037**	**1,928**	**92,577**	**69,032**	**14,525**
Region:								
Northeast	726	12,905	1,271	503	428	21,344	14,262	3,553
Midwest	1,266	17,080	1,690	737	705	21,521	14,172	4,844
South	1,775	23,489	1,948	1,278	474	31,595	25,540	3,866
West	878	11,310	911	519	320	18,118	15,057	2,261
Year constructed:								
1919 or before	330	3,769	302	90	143	4,131	2,319	1,134
1920 to 1945	527	6,871	620	208	229	8,670	5,123	1,708
1946 to 1959	562	7,045	565	231	216	8,540	5,729	1,610
1960 to 1969	579	8,101	737	327	255	11,378	7,714	1,872
1970 to 1979	731	10,772	1,023	572	351	16,129	12,637	2,466
1980 to 1989	707	10,332	1,034	627	291	17,346	13,902	2,270
1990 to 1999	876	12,360	1,098	690	314	18,761	15,236	2,452
Principal activity within building:								
Education	386	9,874	820	371	268	12,008	8,111	1,889
Food sales	226	1,255	251	208	39	4,990	4,627	332
Food service	297	1,654	427	217	203	6,865	5,176	1,615
Health care	129	3,163	594	248	243	7,440	4,882	1,538
Inpatient	8	1,905	475	178	204	5,329	3,198	1,241
Outpatient	121	1,258	119	69	38	2,111	1,684	297
Lodging	142	5,096	510	235	215	7,445	5,288	1,581
Retail (other than mall)	443	4,317	319	211	91	5,980	5,132	719
Office	824	12,208	1,134	719	269	20,841	17,050	2,201
Public assembly	277	3,939	370	167	102	5,790	3,943	775
Public order and safety	71	1,090	126	57	29	1,917	1,216	234
Religious worship	370	3,754	163	62	82	2,457	1,628	664
Service	622	4,050	312	149	139	4,779	3,485	1,096
Warehouse and storage	597	10,078	456	244	132	6,894	5,034	976
Other	79	1,738	286	133	87	4,420	3,049	684
Vacant	182	2,567	54	15	28	751	412	220
Square footage:								
1,001 to 5,000	2,552	6,789	672	386	250	12,812	10,348	2,155
5,001 to 10,000	889	6,585	516	262	209	9,398	7,296	1,689
10,001 to 25,000	738	11,535	776	407	309	13,140	10,001	2,524
25,001 to 50,000	241	8,668	673	350	258	10,392	7,871	1,865
50,001 to 100,000	129	9,057	759	405	244	11,897	8,717	1,868
100,001 to 200,000	65	9,064	934	483	249	13,391	9,500	1,737
200,001 to 500,000	25	7,176	725	361	205	10,347	7,323	1,343
500,001 and over	7	5,908	766	383	204	11,201	7,977	1,344

[1] Includes fuel oil, propane, and purchased steam not shown separately.

Source: U.S. Energy Information Administration, "Commercial Buildings Energy Survey: Consumption and Expenditures, 2003"; <http://www.eia.doe.gov/emeu/cbecs/cbecs2003/detailed_tables_2003/detailed_tables_2003.html> (released December 2006).

Table 888. Fossil Fuel Prices by Type of Fuel: 1990 to 2007

[In dollars per million British thermal units (Btu), except as indicated. For definition of Btu and mineral fuel conversions, see source and text, this section. All fuel prices taken as close to the point of production as possible]

Fuel	Current dollars					Constant (2000) dollars				
	1990	1995	2000	2006	2007 [1]	1990	1995	2000	2006	2007 [1]
Composite [2]	**1.84**	**1.47**	**2.60**	**4.73**	**4.99**	**2.26**	**1.60**	**2.60**	**4.06**	**4.17**
Crude oil [3]	3.45	2.52	4.61	10.29	11.47	4.23	2.74	4.61	8.83	9.58
Natural gas [4]	1.55	1.40	3.32	5.80	5.79	1.90	1.52	3.32	4.98	4.84
Coal [5]	1.00	0.88	0.80	1.24	1.25	1.22	0.96	0.80	1.06	1.04

[1] Preliminary. [2] Derived by multiplying the price per Btu of each fossil fuel by the total Btu content of the production of each fossil fuel and dividing this accumulated value of total fossil fuel production by the accumulated Btu content of total fossil fuel production. [3] Domestic first purchase prices. [4] Wellhead prices. [5] Free-on-board (f.o.b.) rail/barge prices, which are the f.o.b. prices of coal at the point of first sale, excluding freight or shipping and insurance costs. Includes bituminous coal, subbituminous coal, and lignite.

Source: U.S. Energy Information Administration, Annual Energy Review 2007. See also <http://www.eia.doe.gov/emeu/aer/pdf/pages/sec3_3.pdf> (released 23 June 2008).

U.S. Census Bureau, Statistical Abstract of the United States: 2009

Table 889. Energy Expenditures—End-Use Sector and Selected Source, by State: 2005

[In millions of dollars (1,042,934 represents $1,042,934,000,000). **Data are preliminary.** End-use sector and electric utilities exclude expenditures on energy sources such as hydroelectric, photovoltaic, solar thermal, wind, and geothermal. Also excludes expenditures for reported amounts of energy consumed by the energy industry for production, transportation, and processing operations]

State	Total [1]	End-use sector				Source			
		Residential	Commercial	Industrial	Transportation	Petroleum products	Natural gas	Coal	Electricity sales
U.S.	**1,042,934**	**216,046**	**154,576**	**205,975**	**466,337**	**595,594**	**200,303**	**36,933**	**295,789**
AL	17,946	3,328	2,047	4,448	8,123	9,695	3,251	1,681	5,628
AK	5,226	551	517	336	3,822	4,327	368	28	687
AZ	16,599	3,286	2,404	1,625	9,282	10,179	2,750	610	5,404
AR	10,608	1,948	1,112	2,656	4,893	6,187	1,927	370	2,841
CA	103,604	17,359	16,834	14,737	54,674	58,815	20,772	129	29,303
CO	14,661	3,020	2,198	2,350	7,093	8,110	3,543	414	3,660
CT	12,449	4,134	2,397	1,267	4,652	7,189	2,023	115	3,992
DE	3,079	728	469	659	1,222	1,792	538	119	932
DC	2,035	445	1,141	53	396	514	467	2	1,085
FL.	49,756	11,887	8,438	3,826	25,605	30,380	7,208	1,567	19,713
GA	32,367	6,932	4,324	5,576	15,535	17,775	5,255	1,990	9,830
HI	4,997	717	749	667	2,865	3,793	69	27	1,898
ID	4,464	818	479	1,001	2,166	2,747	628	20	1,120
IL	42,103	9,473	6,293	7,970	18,367	22,087	10,328	1,296	10,013
IN	25,287	4,716	2,621	7,193	10,757	12,937	5,463	2,753	6,200
IA	12,456	2,349	1,419	3,618	5,070	7,263	2,404	469	2,859
KS	9,559	1,981	1,346	2,127	4,105	5,242	1,935	429	2,539
KY	17,032	2,731	1,709	4,565	8,027	10,212	2,391	1,596	4,432
LA	29,766	3,186	2,283	14,024	10,273	16,982	9,351	402	6,062
ME	5,455	1,663	805	716	2,271	3,998	593	21	1,307
MD	17,571	4,304	2,633	2,521	8,112	9,815	2,611	644	5,559
MA	21,704	6,533	4,642	2,145	8,384	11,858	4,769	368	6,971
MI	32,404	7,992	5,049	5,765	13,598	17,088	7,868	1,360	7,935
MN	18,261	3,749	2,587	3,244	8,680	10,669	3,417	446	4,334
MS	11,280	2,054	1,382	2,257	5,587	6,611	2,588	397	3,391
MO	19,827	4,118	2,590	2,970	10,149	12,019	3,054	867	4,960
MT	4,030	688	514	825	2,004	2,600	521	143	894
NE	6,414	1,180	828	1,476	2,931	3,807	1,074	167	1,584
NV	8,486	1,668	1,137	1,486	4,195	4,736	1,957	307	2,877
NH	4,582	1,338	886	520	1,838	2,903	762	108	1,408
NJ.	32,213	6,963	6,438	3,907	14,905	18,406	6,186	273	8,862
NM	6,462	1,071	957	793	3,641	4,240	1,024	480	1,520
NY	56,690	18,035	16,391	4,340	17,923	26,804	13,007	552	20,941
NC	28,152	6,528	4,061	4,498	13,064	16,207	2,844	1,953	9,224
ND	3,296	535	393	988	1,380	2,066	324	542	637
OH	41,895	9,497	5,891	9,034	17,473	21,092	9,519	2,412	11,248
OK	14,211	2,522	1,712	3,280	6,698	8,109	4,398	412	3,658
OR	10,726	2,031	1,359	1,643	5,693	6,357	1,931	46	2,948
PA	42,786	11,098	6,431	7,883	17,375	23,030	8,052	2,674	12,119
RI	3,109	1,069	656	272	1,112	1,642	922	(Z)	963
SC	15,815	3,153	1,903	3,583	7,176	8,734	1,946	960	5,462
SD	2,894	543	381	521	1,449	1,908	359	55	648
TN	21,833	4,020	2,872	4,149	10,792	12,621	2,525	1,076	6,507
TX	114,410	16,912	11,825	43,413	42,261	71,673	24,495	2,190	29,987
UT	6,978	1,209	900	989	3,880	4,435	1,101	482	1,464
VT	2,264	689	359	255	961	1,531	83	(Z)	644
VA	26,208	5,895	3,812	3,565	12,935	16,097	3,518	1,084	7,223
WA	18,550	3,433	2,440	2,379	10,298	11,534	2,446	163	4,842
WV	6,948	1,213	759	2,037	2,939	4,260	1,019	1,535	1,534
WI.	19,190	4,392	2,840	4,102	7,856	10,132	4,192	720	5,225
WY	3,662	359	364	1,089	1,851	2,384	529	477	713

Z Less than $500,000. [1] Includes sources not shown separately, such as electricity imports and exports and coal coke net imports, which are not allocated to the states. Total expenditures are the sum of purchases for each source (including electricity sales) less electric utility purchases of fuel.

Source: U.S. Energy Information Administration, "State Energy Data, 2005"; <http://www.eia.doe.gov/emeu/states/_seds.html> (released 29 February 2008).

U.S. Census Bureau, Statistical Abstract of the United States: 2009

Table 890. **Energy Expenditures and Average Fuel Prices by Source and Sector: 1970 to 2005**

[In millions of dollars (82,911 represents $82,911,000,000), except as indicated. For definition of Btu, see text, this section. End-use sector and electric utilities exclude expenditures and prices on energy sources such as hydropower, solar, wind, and geothermal. Also excludes expenditures for reported amounts of energy consumed by the energy industry for production, transportation, and processing operations]

Source and sector	1970	1980	1985	1990	1995	2000	2002	2003	2004	2005
EXPENDITURES (mil. dol.)										
Total [1]	82,911	374,346	438,184	[5]472,539	514,049	689,338	660,894	754,131	868,773	1,042,934
Natural gas	10,891	51,061	72,938	65,278	75,020	119,094	111,368	144,489	162,702	200,303
Petroleum products	47,955	237,676	223,928	235,368	236,905	360,889	319,884	378,967	468,400	595,594
Motor gasoline	31,596	124,408	118,048	126,558	136,647	193,947	179,511	209,592	253,228	311,035
Coal	4,630	22,607	29,678	28,602	27,431	28,080	28,511	29,402	31,765	36,933
Electricity sales	23,345	98,095	149,233	176,691	205,876	231,577	247,598	257,995	268,136	295,789
Residential sector [2]	20,213	69,418	99,772	111,097	128,388	156,089	161,205	179,287	190,174	216,046
Commercial sector [3]	10,628	46,932	70,396	79,284	91,788	112,870	119,719	129,456	137,920	154,576
Industrial sector [4]	16,691	94,316	106,518	[5]102,402	107,060	141,533	128,386	150,205	176,229	205,975
Transportation sector	35,379	163,680	161,498	179,757	186,813	278,846	251,585	295,183	364,450	466,337
Motor gasoline	30,525	121,809	115,205	123,845	134,641	191,620	175,729	204,878	247,191	303,886
Electric utilities [4]	4,357	38,027	43,970	40,626	39,073	60,054	54,067	64,600	71,716	95,704
AVERAGE FUEL PRICES (dol. per mil. Btu)										
All sectors	1.65	6.89	8.37	[5]8.25	8.28	10.34	10.05	11.41	12.90	15.66
Residential sector [2]	2.10	7.46	10.91	11.88	12.63	14.27	14.72	15.85	17.12	19.21
Commercial sector [3]	1.98	7.85	11.65	11.89	12.64	13.93	14.68	15.61	16.58	18.57
Industrial sector [4]	0.84	4.71	6.03	[5]5.23	4.97	6.49	6.26	7.46	8.53	10.64
Transportation sector	2.31	8.61	8.27	8.28	8.09	10.79	9.63	11.21	13.37	16.84
Electric utilities [4]	0.32	1.77	1.91	1.48	1.29	1.71	1.53	1.83	1.99	2.60

[1] Includes other sources not shown separately. [2] There are no direct fuel costs for geothermal, photovoltaic, or solar thermal energy. [3] There are no direct fuel costs for hydroelectric, geothermal, photovoltaic, or solar thermal energy. [4] There are no direct fuel costs for hydroelectric, geothermal, wind, photovoltaic, or solar thermal energy. [5] There is a discontinuity in the total time series and the industrial time series between 1985 and 1990 due to the expanded coverage of nonelectric utility use of wood and waste beginning in 1989.

Source: U.S. Energy Information Administration, "State Energy Data: Prices and Expenditures," annual; <http://www.eia.doe.gov/emeu/states/state.html?q_state_a=us&q_state=UNITED%20STATES> (published 29 February 2008).

Table 891. **Renewable Energy Consumption Estimates by Source: 1995 to 2007**

[In quadrillion Btu (6.71 represents 6,710,000,000,000,000) For definition of Btu, see source and text, this section. Renewable energy is obtained from sources that are essentially inexhaustible, unlike fossil fuels of which there is a finite supply]

Source and sector	1995	2000	2003	2004	2005	2006	2007 [1]
Consumption, total	6.71	6.26	6.15	6.26	6.44	6.92	6.83
Conventional hydroelectric power [2]	3.21	2.81	2.82	2.69	2.70	2.87	2.46
Geothermal energy [3]	0.29	0.32	0.33	0.34	0.34	0.34	0.35
Biomass [4]	3.10	3.01	2.82	3.02	3.15	3.37	3.61
Solar energy [5]	0.07	0.07	0.06	0.06	0.07	0.72	0.08
Wind energy [6]	0.03	0.06	0.11	0.14	0.18	0.26	0.32
Residential [7]	0.59	0.49	0.47	0.48	0.53	0.50	0.56
Biomass [4]	0.52	0.42	0.40	0.41	0.45	0.41	0.46
Geothermal [3]	0.01	0.01	0.01	0.01	0.02	0.02	0.02
Solar [5,8]	0.06	0.06	0.06	0.06	0.06	0.07	0.07
Commercial [9]	0.12	0.13	0.11	0.12	0.12	0.12	0.12
Biomass [4]	0.11	0.12	0.10	0.11	0.10	0.10	0.10
Geothermal [3]	(Z)	0.01	0.01	0.01	0.01	0.01	0.01
Hydroelectric [2]	(Z)	(Z)	(Z)	(Z)	(Z)	(Z)	(Z)
Industrial [10]	1.99	1.93	1.73	1.86	1.88	2.00	2.03
Biomass [4]	1.93	1.88	1.68	1.82	1.85	1.97	2.00
Geothermal [3]	(Z)	(Z)	(Z)	(Z)	(Z)	(Z)	(Z)
Hydroelectric [2]	0.05	0.04	0.04	0.03	0.03	0.03	0.02
Transportation:	0.11	0.14	0.23	0.30	0.35	0.48	0.63
Alcohol fuels [11]	0.11	0.14	0.23	0.29	0.33	0.45	0.56
Electric power [12]	3.89	3.58	3.60	3.50	3.57	3.83	3.50
Biomass [4]	0.42	0.45	0.40	0.39	0.41	0.41	0.43
Geothermal [3]	0.28	0.30	0.30	0.31	0.31	0.31	0.31
Hydroelectric [2]	3.15	2.77	2.78	2.66	2.67	2.84	2.44
Solar [5]	0.01	0.01	0.01	0.01	0.01	0.01	0.01

Z Less than 5 trillion Btu. [1] Preliminary. [2] Power produced from natural stream flow as regulated by available storage. [3] As used at electric power plants, hot water or steam extracted from geothermal reservoirs in the Earth's crust that is supplied to steam turbines at electric power plants that drive generators to produce electricity. [4] Wood and wood-derived fuels, biomass waste, fuel ethanol, and biodiesel. [5] Solar thermal and photovoltaic electricity net generation and solar thermal direct use energy. [6] Energy present in wind motion that can be converted to mechanical energy for driving pumps, mills, and electric power generators. Wind pushes against sails, vanes, or blades radiating from a central rotating shaft. [7] Consists of living quarters for private households, but excludes institutional living quarters. [8] The radiant energy of the sun, which can be converted into other forms of energy, such as heat or electricity. [9] Consists of service-providing facilities and equipment of businesses, governments, and other private and public organizations. Includes institutional living quarters and sewage treatment facilities. Includes commercial combined-heat-and-power and commercial electricity-only plants. [10] Consists of all facilities and equipment used for producing, processing, or assembling goods. Includes industrial combined-heat-and-power and industrial electricity-only plants. [11] Ethanol primarily derived from corn. [12] Consists of electricity only and combined-heat-and-power plants who sell electricity and heat to the public.

Source: U.S. Energy Information Administration, *Annual Energy Review*, 2007. See also <http://www.eia.doe.gov/emeu/aer/renew.html> (released 23 June 2008).

Table 892. Renewable Energy, Consumption by Sector and Source—Estimates, 2005 and 2006, and Projections, 2010 to 2030

[In quadrillions of Btu per year. For definition of Btu, see source and text, this section. Data represent actual heat rates used to determine fuel consumption for all renewable fuels except hydropower, solar, and wind. Consumption at hydroelectric, solar, and wind facilities determined by using the fossil fuel equivalent of 10,280 Btu per kilowatt hour]

Sector and source	2005	2006	Projections				
			2010	2015	2020	2025	2030
MARKETED RENEWABLE ENERGY [1]							
Total marketed renewable energy	**6.30**	**6.77**	**8.56**	**10.00**	**11.74**	**13.44**	**13.73**
Residential (wood)	0.45	0.41	0.44	0.42	0.40	0.39	0.38
Commercial (biomass)	0.13	0.13	0.13	0.13	0.13	0.13	0.13
Industrial [2]	1.88	1.99	2.34	2.75	3.32	4.21	4.33
Conventional hydroelectric	0.03	0.03	0.03	0.03	0.03	0.03	0.03
Municipal waste [3]	0.16	0.15	0.15	0.15	0.15	0.15	0.15
Biomass	1.45	1.51	1.48	1.57	1.65	1.75	1.83
Biofuels heat and coproducts	0.24	0.30	0.67	1.00	1.49	2.28	2.31
Transportation	0.35	0.50	1.13	1.66	2.24	2.77	2.77
Ethanol used in E85 [4]	–	–	–	0.12	0.64	0.93	0.88
Ethanol used in gasoline blending	0.34	0.47	1.05	1.22	1.18	1.13	1.13
Biodiesel used in distillate blending	0.01	0.03	0.08	0.17	0.13	0.14	0.16
Liquids from biomass	–	–	–	0.15	0.29	0.56	0.60
Electric power [5]	3.49	3.74	4.53	5.05	5.64	5.94	6.13
Conventional hydroelectric	2.67	2.86	2.89	2.96	2.97	2.97	2.97
Geothermal	0.31	0.31	0.37	0.48	0.58	0.70	0.80
Municipal waste [6]	0.20	0.15	0.23	0.23	0.23	0.23	0.23
Biomass	0.18	0.16	0.28	0.48	0.82	0.87	0.86
Dedicated plants	0.14	0.12	0.12	0.16	0.27	0.30	0.36
Cofiring	0.04	0.03	0.16	0.33	0.55	0.57	0.49
Solar thermal	0.01	–	0.01	0.02	0.02	0.02	0.02
Solar photovoltaic	–	–	–	–	0.01	0.01	0.01
Wind	0.12	0.26	0.74	0.87	1.02	1.13	1.24
Ethanol, total	**0.34**	**0.47**	**1.05**	**1.34**	**1.82**	**2.06**	**2.01**
Sources:							
Corn	0.33	0.41	0.95	1.18	1.26	1.26	1.26
Cellulose	–	–	0.01	0.03	0.23	0.58	0.58
Other feedstocks	–	–	–	–	0.01	0.02	0.01
Net imports	0.01	0.06	0.09	0.14	0.31	0.19	0.15
NONMARKETED RENEWABLE ENERGY							
Selected consumption [7]:							
Residential	**0.01**	**0.02**	**0.02**	**0.03**	**0.04**	**0.05**	**0.07**
Solar hot water heating	0.01	0.01	0.02	0.02	0.03	0.04	0.05
Geothermal heat pumps	–	–	–	0.01	0.01	0.01	0.01
Solar photovoltaic	–	–	–	–	–	–	0.01
Wind	–	–	–	–	–	–	–
Commercial	0.03	0.03	0.03	0.03	0.03	0.04	0.04
Solar thermal	0.02	0.02	0.03	0.03	0.03	0.03	0.03
Solar photovoltaic	–	–	–	–	–	0.01	0.01
Wind	–	–	–	–	–	–	–

– Represents or rounds to zero.   [1] Includes nonelectric renewable energy groups for which the energy source is bought and sold in the marketplace, although all transactions may not necessarily be marketed, and marketed renewable energy inputs for electricity entering the marketplace on the electric power grid. Excludes electricity imports.   [2] Includes all electricity production by industrial and other combined heat and power for the grid and for own use.   [3] Includes municipal solid waste, landfill gas, and municipal sewage sludge. All municipal solid waste is included, although a portion of the municipal solid waste stream contains petroleum-derived plastics and other nonrenewable sources. For municipal waste used to produce electric power, incremental growth is assumed to be for landfill gas facilities.   [4] Excludes motor gasoline component of E85.   [5] Includes consumption of energy by electricity-only and combined heat and power plants whose primary business is to sell electricity, or electricity and heat, to the public. Includes small power producers and exempt wholesale generators.   [6] Includes biogenic municipal waste, landfill gas, and municipal sewage sludge. Incremental growth is assumed to be for landfill gas facilities. Only biogenic municipal waste is included.   [7] Includes selected renewable energy consumption data for which the energy is not bought or sold, either directly or indirectly as an input to marketed energy.

Source: U.S. Energy Information Administration, Annual Energy Outlook 2008. See also <http://www.eia.doe.gov/oiaf/aeo/aeoref_tab.html> (released June 2008).

Table 893. Energy Imports and Exports by Type of Fuel: 1980 to 2007

[In quadrillion of Btu. (12.10 represents 12,100,000,000,000,000 Btu). For definition of Btu, see source and text, this section]

Type of fuel	1980	1985	1990	1995	2000	2002	2003	2004	2005	2006	2007 [1]
Net imports, total [2]	**12.10**	**7.58**	**14.06**	**17.75**	**24.97**	**25.74**	**27.01**	**29.11**	**30.15**	**29.81**	**29.24**
Coal............	-2.39	-2.39	-2.70	-2.08	-1.21	-0.61	-0.49	-0.57	-0.51	-0.36	-0.60
Natural gas (dry).....	0.96	0.90	1.46	2.74	3.62	3.58	3.36	3.50	3.71	3.56	3.90
Petroleum [3]........	13.50	8.95	15.29	16.89	22.38	22.63	24.07	25.99	26.81	26.42	25.77
Other [4]..........	0.04	0.13	0.01	0.19	0.18	0.13	0.07	0.18	0.13	0.12	0.13
Imports, total........	15.80	11.78	18.82	22.26	28.97	29.41	31.06	33.54	34.71	34.67	34.60
Coal.............	0.03	0.05	0.07	0.24	0.31	0.42	0.63	0.68	0.76	0.91	0.91
Natural gas (dry).....	1.01	0.95	1.55	2.90	3.87	4.10	4.04	4.37	4.45	4.29	4.72
Petroleum [3]........	14.66	10.61	17.12	18.88	24.53	24.67	26.22	28.20	29.25	29.17	28.70
Other [4]..........	0.10	0.17	0.08	0.24	0.26	0.21	0.17	0.29	0.24	0.25	0.24
Exports, total........	3.69	4.20	4.75	4.51	4.01	3.67	4.05	4.43	4.56	4.87	5.36
Coal.............	2.42	2.44	2.77	2.32	1.53	1.03	1.12	1.25	1.27	1.26	1.51
Natural gas (dry).....	0.05	0.06	0.09	0.16	0.25	0.52	0.69	0.86	0.74	0.73	0.82
Petroleum..........	1.16	1.66	1.82	1.99	2.15	2.04	2.15	2.21	2.44	2.75	2.93
Other [4]..........	0.07	0.04	0.07	0.05	0.08	0.07	0.10	0.11	0.11	0.12	0.10

[1] Preliminary.   [2] Net imports equals imports minus exports. Minus sign (–) denotes an excess of exports over imports.
[3] Includes imports into the Strategic Petroleum Reserve.   [4] Coal coke and small amounts of electricity transmitted across U.S. borders with Canada and Mexico.

Source: U.S. Energy Information Administration, *Annual Energy Review, 2007.* See also <http://www.eia.doe.gov/emeu/aer/pdf/pages/sec1_11.pdf> (released 23 June 2008).

Table 894. U.S. Foreign Trade in Selected Mineral Fuels: 1980 to 2007

[985 represents 985,000,000,000 cu. ft. Minus sign (–) indicates an excess of imports over exports]

Mineral fuel	Unit	1980	1985	1990	1995	2000	2004	2005	2006	2007 [1]
Natural gas:										
Imports.........	Bil. cu. ft......	985	950	1,532	2,841	3,782	4,259	4,341	4,186	4,602
Exports	Bil. cu. ft......	49	55	86	154	244	854	729	724	809
Net trade	Bil. cu. ft......	-936	-894	-1,447	-2,687	-3,538	-3,404	-3,612	-3,462	-3,793
Crude oil:										
Imports [2]	Mil. bbl.......	1,926	1,168	2,151	2,639	3,320	3,692	3,696	3,693	3,657
Exports	Mil. bbl.......	105	75	40	35	18	10	12	9	10
Net trade	Mil. bbl.......	-1,821	-1,094	-2,112	-2,604	-3,301	-3,682	-3,684	-3,684	-3,647
Petroleum products:										
Imports	Mil. bbl.......	603	681	775	586	874	1,119	1,310	1,310	1,249
Exports	Mil. bbl.......	94	211	273	312	362	374	414	472	501
Net trade	Mil. bbl.......	-508	-471	-502	-274	-512	-745	-896	-838	-749
Coal:										
Imports	Mil. sh. tons ...	1.2	2.0	2.7	9.5	12.5	27.3	30.5	36.2	36.3
Exports	Mil. sh. tons ...	91.7	92.7	105.8	88.5	58.5	48.0	49.9	49.6	59.2
Net trade	Mil. sh. tons ...	90.5	90.7	103.1	79.1	46.0	20.7	19.5	13.4	22.8

[1] Preliminary.   [2] Includes strategic petroleum reserve imports.

Source: U.S. Energy Information Administration, *Annual Energy Review 2007.* See also <http://www.eia.doe.gov/emeu/aer/contents.html> (released 23 June 2008).

Table 895. Crude Oil Imports Into the U.S. by Country of Origin: 1980 to 2007

[In millions of barrels (1,921 represents 1,921,000,000). Barrels contain 42 gallons. Crude oil imports are reported by the Petroleum Administration for Defense (PAD) District in which they are to be processed. A PAD District is a geographic aggregation of the 50 states and DC into 5 districts. Includes crude oil imported for storage in the Strategic Petroleum Reserve (SPR). Total OPEC excludes, and Non-OPEC includes, petroleum imported into the United States indirectly from members of OPEC, primarily from Carribean and West European areas, as petroleum products that were refined from crude oil produced by OPEC]

Country of origin	1980	1985	1990	1995	2000	2002	2003	2004	2005	2006	2007
Total imports ...	**1,921**	**1,168**	**2,151**	**2,639**	**3,311**	**3,336**	**3,521**	**3,674**	**3,670**	**3,685**	**3,656**
OPEC, [1, 2, 3, 4] total.....	1,410	479	1,283	1,219	1,659	1,490	1,671	1,948	1,738	1,745	1,969
Algeria [2]	166	31	23	10	(Z)	11	41	79	83	130	162
Angola [2]	(NA)	(NA)	86	131	108	117	132	112	164	187	181
Iraq	10	17	188	–	226	168	171	238	190	202	177
Kuwait [5]	10	1	29	78	96	79	75	88	79	65	64
Libya	200	–	–	–	–	–	–	7	16	24	31
Saudi Arabia [5]	456	48	436	460	556	554	629	547	525	519	530
Nigeria	307	102	286	227	319	215	306	389	387	381	395
Venezuela	57	112	243	420	446	438	436	473	449	416	420
Non-OPEC, total [2, 3, 4, 6] .	511	689	869	1,419	1,652	1,846	1,850	1,838	1,932	1,940	1,687
Brazil	(NA)	(NA)	–	–	2	21	17	19	34	49	61
Canada...........	73	171	235	380	492	527	565	590	600	651	681
Colombia..........	(NA)	(NA)	51	76	116	86	59	51	57	52	50
Ecuador [3]	6	20	(NA)	35	46	37	50	83	101	99	72
Mexico	185	261	251	375	479	548	580	584	566	575	514
Russia	(NA)	(NA)	(Z)	5	3	31	54	55	70	39	41
United Kingdom	63	101	57	124	106	148	127	86	80	47	37

– Represents zero.   NA Not available.   Z Represents less than 500,000 barrels.   [1] OPEC (Organization of Petroleum Exporting Countries) includes the nations shown, as well as Iran, Qatar, United Arab Emirates, and Indonesia.   [2] Angola joined OPEC at the beginning of 2007. Prior to 2007, it is included in the non-OPEC total.   [3] Ecuador withdrew from OPEC on Dec. 31, 1992; therefore, it is included under OPEC prior to 1995. Beginning 1995, it is included in the Non-OPEC total.   [4] Gabon withdrew from OPEC on Dec. 31, 1994; therefore, it is included under OPEC prior to 1995. Beginning 1995, it is included in the Non-OPEC total.   [5] Imports from the Neutral Zone between Kuwait and Saudi Arabia are included in Saudi Arabia.   [6] Non-OPEC total includes nations not shown.

Source: U.S. Energy Information Administration, "Petroleum Supply Monthly," February 2008; <http://www.eia.doe.gov/pub/oil_gas/petroleum/data_publications/petroleum_supply_monthly/current/pdf/table38.pdf>.

Table 896. **Crude Oil and Refined Products—Summary: 1980 to 2007**

[**13,481 represents 13,481,000 bbl.** Barrels (bbl.) of 42 gallons. Data are averages]

Year	Crude oil [1] (1,000 bbl. per day)					Refined oil products (1,000 bbl. per day)			Total oil imports [4] (1,000 bbl. per day)	Crude oil stocks [1,5] (mil. bbl.)	
	Input to refineries	Domestic production	Imports		Exports	Domestic demand	Imports	Exports		Total	Strategic reserve [6]
			Total [2]	Strategic reserve [3]							
1980 . . .	13,481	8,597	5,263	44	287	17,056	1,646	258	6,909	[7]466	108
1985 . . .	12,002	8,971	3,201	118	204	15,726	1,866	577	5,067	814	493
1990 . . .	13,409	7,355	5,894	27	109	16,988	2,123	748	8,018	908	586
1995 . . .	13,973	6,560	7,230	–	95	17,725	1,605	855	8,835	895	592
2000 . . .	15,067	5,822	9,071	8	50	19,701	2,389	990	11,459	826	541
2001 . . .	15,128	5,801	9,328	11	20	19,649	2,543	951	11,871	862	550
2002 . . .	14,947	5,746	9,140	16	9	19,761	2,390	975	11,530	877	599
2003 . . .	15,304	5,681	9,665	–	12	20,034	2,599	1,014	12,264	907	638
2004 . . .	15,475	5,419	10,088	77	27	20,731	3,057	1,021	13,145	961	676
2005 . . .	15,220	5,178	10,126	52	32	20,802	3,588	1,133	13,714	1,008	685
2006 . . .	15,240	5,136	10,095	6	25	20,588	3,517	1,309	13,612	998	689
2007 . . .	15,148	5,103	10,017	6	27	20,698	(NA)	(NA)	13,439	1,015	691

– Represents zero. NA Not available. [1] Includes lease condensate. [2] Includes Strategic Petroleum Reserve. [3] SPR is the Strategic Petroleum Reserve. Through 2003, includes imports by SPR only; beginning in 2004, includes imports by SPR, and imports into SPR by others. [4] Crude oil (including Strategic Petroleum Reserve imports) plus refined products. [5] Crude oil at end of period. Includes commercial and Strategic Petroleum Reserve stocks. [6] Crude oil stocks in the Strategic Petroleum Reserve include non-U.S. stocks held under foreign or commercial storage agreements. [7] Stocks of Alaskan crude oil in transit are included from January 1985 forward.

Source: U.S. Energy Information Administration, *Monthly Energy Review,* May 2008 issue.

Table 897. **Petroleum and Coal Products Corporations—Sales, Net Profit, and Profit Per Dollar of Sales: 1990 to 2007**

[**318.5 represents $318,500,000,000.** Represents SIC group 29 (NAICS group 324). Through 2000, based on Standard Industrial Classification (SIC) code; beginning 2001, based on North American Industry Classification System, 1997 (NAICS). Profit rates are averages of quarterly figures at annual rates. Beginning 1990, excludes estimates for corporations with less than $250,000 in assets]

Item	Unit	1990	1995	1999	2000	2001	2002	2003	2004	2005	2006	2007
Sales.	Bil. dol. . .	318.5	283.1	277.0	455.2	472.5	474.9	597.8	767.7	956.0	1,037.8	1,110.6
Net profit:												
Before income taxes	Bil. dol. . .	23.1	16.5	20.3	55.5	47.2	22.4	52.8	89.7	120.2	139.8	127.0
After income taxes	Bil. dol. . .	17.8	13.9	17.2	42.6	35.8	19.5	43.6	71.8	96.3	111.0	105.4
Depreciation[1]	Bil. dol. . .	18.7	16.7	13.5	15.5	17.2	17.8	19.4	18.5	18.6	20.0	22.5
Profits per dollar of sales:												
Before income taxes	Cents . . .	7.3	5.8	7.1	12.2	9.7	4.6	10.4	15.5	17.9	17.9	15.1
After income taxes	Cents . . .	5.6	4.9	6.0	9.4	7.4	4.2	8.6	12.4	14.3	14.2	12.5
Profits on stockholders' equity:												
Before income taxes	Percent. .	16.4	12.6	13.0	29.4	21.8	9.7	20.8	32.9	38.0	36.3	30.7
After income taxes	Percent. .	12.7	10.6	11.0	22.6	16.5	8.4	17.1	26.3	30.4	28.8	25.5

[1] Includes depletion and accelerated amortization of emergency facilities.

Source: U.S. Census Bureau, *Quarterly Financial Report for Manufacturing, Mining and Trade Corporations.*

Table 898. **Major Petroleum Companies—Financial Summary: 1980 to 2007**

[**32.9 represents $32,900,000,000.** Data represent a composite of approximately 42 major worldwide petroleum companies aggregated on a consolidated total company basis. Minus sign (–) indicates deficit]

Item	1980	1990	1995	2000	2002	2003	2004	2005	2006	2007
FINANCIAL DATA (bil. dol.)										
Net income.	32.9	26.8	24.3	76.4	44.3	85.5	120.5	170.6	187.6	237.6
Depreciation, depletion, etc.	32.5	38.7	43.1	53.3	61.2	68.0	76.9	76.5	85.8	114.3
Cash flow [1]	65.4	65.5	67.4	129.7	118.0	157.7	205.1	239.9	261.2	327.1
Dividends paid.	9.3	15.9	17.6	23.0	27.3	27.5	33.5	37.5	39.2	62.2
Net internal funds available for investment or debt repayment [2]	56.1	49.6	49.8	106.7	90.7	130.3	171.5	202.4	221.7	264.9
Capital and exploratory expenditures	62.1	59.6	59.8	72.8	88.7	90.7	112.4	140.4	193.1	221.7
Long-term capitalization.	211.4	300.0	304.3	516.9	548.1	606.1	700.1	800.4	910.6	1,211.8
Long-term debt.	49.8	90.4	85.4	112.8	153.5	142.1	161.0	165.2	177.4	240.1
Preferred stock.	2.0	5.2	5.7	5.4	2.5	2.2	1.3	3.5	3.4	1.9
Common stock and retained earnings [3]. .	159.6	204.4	213.2	398.7	392.1	461.8	537.8	631.7	729.8	969.8
Excess of expenditures over cash income [4]	6.0	10.0	10.0	–33.9	–2.0	–39.5	–59.2	–62.0	–28.9	–43.2
RATIOS [5] (percent)										
Long-term debt to long-term capitalization. .	23.6	30.1	28.1	21.8	28.3	26.5	24.1	23.5	19.9	19.1
Net income to total average capital	17.0	9.1	8.1	15.7	8.7	15.2	18.9	23.0	22.3	21.2
Net income to average common equity. . . .	22.5	13.5	11.6	20.5	11.5	20.1	24.2	30.1	27.8	26.3

[1] Generally represents internally generated funds from operations. Sum of net income and noncash charges such as depreciation, depletion, and amortization. [2] Cash flow minus dividends paid. [3] Includes common stock, capital surplus, and earned surplus accounts after adjustments. [4] Capital and exploratory expenditures plus dividends paid minus cash flow. [5] Represents approximate year-to-year comparisons because of changes in the makeup of the group due to mergers and other corporate changes.

Source: Carl H. Pforzheimer & Co., New York, NY, *Comparative Oil Company Statements,* annual.

Table 899. Nuclear Power Plants—Number, Capacity, and Generation: 1980 to 2007

[51.8 represents 51,800,000 kW]

Item	1980	1985	1990	1995	2000	2001	2002	2003	2004	2005	2006	2007
Operable generating units [1, 2]	71	96	112	109	104	104	104	104	104	104	104	104
Net summer capacity [2, 3] (mil. kW)	51.8	79.4	99.6	99.5	97.9	98.2	98.7	99.2	99.6	100.0	100.0	100.0
Net generation (bil. kWh)	251.1	383.7	576.9	673.4	753.9	768.8	780.1	763.7	788.5	782.0	787.2	806.5
Percent of total electricity net generation	11.0	15.5	19.0	20.1	19.8	20.6	20.2	19.7	19.9	19.3	19.4	19.4
Capacity factor [4] (percent)	56.3	58.0	66.0	77.4	88.1	89.4	90.3	87.9	90.1	89.3	89.6	91.8

[1] Total of nuclear generating units holding full-power licenses, or equivalent permission to operate, at the end of the year. Although Browns Ferry 1 was shut down in 1985, the unit has remained fully licensed and thus has continued to be counted as operable during the shutdown. [2] As of year-end. [3] Net summer capacity is the peak steady hourly output that generating equipment is expected to supply to system load, exclusive of auxiliary and other power plant, as demonstrated by test at the time of summer peak demand. [4] Weighted average of monthly capacity factors. Monthly factors are derived by dividing actual monthly generation by the maximum possible generation for the month (number of hours in the month multiplied by the net summer capacity at the end of the month).

Source: U.S. Energy Information Administration, "Monthly Energy Review," May 2008; <http://www.eia.doe.gov/emeu/mer /nuclear.html> (accessed 24 June 2008).

Table 900. Nuclear Power Plants—Number of Units, Net Generation, and Net Summer Capacity by State: 2006

[787,219 represents 787,219,000,000 kWh]

State	Number of units	Net generation Total (mil. kWh)	Net generation Percent of total [1]	Net summer capacity Total (mil. kW)	Net summer capacity Percent of total [1]	State	Number of units	Net generation Total (mil. kWh)	Net generation Percent of total [1]	Net summer capacity Total (mil. kW)	Net summer capacity Percent of total [1]
U.S.	104	787,219	19.4	100.33	10.2	MS	1	10,419	22.5	1.27	7.6
AL	5	31,911	22.6	5.01	16.3	MO	1	10,117	11.0	1.19	5.8
AZ	3	24,012	23.0	3.87	15.1	NE	2	9,003	28.4	1.24	17.5
AR	2	15,233	29.2	1.82	12.6	NH	1	9,398	42.6	1.24	28.7
CA	4	31,959	14.7	4.39	6.9	NJ	1	32,568	53.7	3.98	21.0
CT	2	16,589	47.8	2.04	25.8	NY	6	42,224	29.7	5.16	13.0
FL	5	31,426	14.0	3.90	7.3	NC	5	39,963	31.9	4.98	18.4
GA	4	32,006	23.2	4.06	11.1	OH	3	16,847	10.8	2.12	6.3
IL	11	94,154	48.9	11.38	26.9	PA	9	75,298	34.4	9.23	20.5
IA	1	5,095	11.2	0.58	5.2	SC	7	50,797	51.2	6.47	28.4
KS	1	9,350	20.5	1.17	10.5	TN	3	24,679	26.3	3.40	16.3
LA	2	16,735	18.4	2.12	7.9	TX	4	41,264	10.3	4.86	4.8
MD	2	13,830	28.3	1.74	13.9	VT	1	5,107	72.1	0.62	55.5
MA	1	5,830	12.8	0.69	4.9	VA	4	27,594	37.8	3.43	15.2
MI	3	29,066	25.8	4.01	13.3	WA	1	9,328	8.6	1.13	4.0
MN	3	13,183	24.8	1.67	13.2	WI	3	12,234	19.8	1.58	9.6

[1] For total generation and capacity, see Table 906.
Source: U.S. Energy Information Administration, "Electric Power Annual 2006"; <http://www.eia.doe.gov/cneaf/electricity /epa/epasprdshts.html> (released 22 October 2007).

Table 901. Solar Collector Shipments by Type, End Use, and Market Sector: 1980 to 2006

[Shipments in thousands of square feet (19,398 represents 19,398,000). Solar collector is a device for intercepting sunlight, converting the light to heat, and carrying the heat to where it will be either used or stored. 1985 data are not available. Based on the Annual Solar Thermal Collector Manufacturers Survey]

Year	Number of manu-facturers	Total shipments [1, 2, 3]	Collector type Low tempera-ture [1, 2]	Collector type Medium tempera-ture, special, other [2]	End use Pool heating	End use Hot water	End use Space heating	Market sector Resi-dential	Market sector Com-mercial	Market sector Indus-trial
1980	233	19,398	12,233	7,165	12,029	4,790	1,688	16,077	2,417	488
1986 [4]	98	9,360	3,751	1,111	3,494	1,181	127	4,131	703	13
1990 [4]	51	11,409	3,645	2,527	5,016	1,091	2	5,835	294	22
1995	36	7,666	6,813	840	6,763	755	132	6,966	604	82
2000	26	8,354	7,948	400	7,863	367	99	7,473	810	57
2004	24	14,114	13,608	506	13,634	452	13	12,864	1,178	70
2005	25	16,041	15,224	702	15,041	640	228	14,681	1,160	31
2006 [5]	44	20,744	15,546	1,346	15,362	1,136	330	15,123	1,626	42

[1] Includes shipments of high temperature collectors to the government, including some military, but excluding space applications. Also includes end uses such as process heating, utility, and other market sectors not shown separately. [2] Includes imputation of shipment data to account for nonrespondents. [3] Total shipments include all domestic and export shipments and may include imported collectors that subsequently were shipped to domestic or foreign customers. [4] Declines between 1986 and 1990 are primarily due to the expiration of the federal energy tax credit and industry consolidation. [5] Preliminary.

Source: U.S. Energy Information Administration, 1980–1990, "Solar Collector Manufacturing Activity", annual reports; 1995–2002, "Renewable Energy Annual"; thereafter, "Solar Thermal and Photovoltaic Collector Manufacturing Activities 2006"; <http://www.eia.doe.gov/cneaf/solar.renewables/page/solarreport/solar.html> (released October 2007).

Table 902. **Uranium Concentrate—Supply, Inventories, and Average Prices: 1980 to 2007**

[**43.70 represents 43,700,000 pounds (lbs.). Years ending Dec. 31**. For additional data on uranium, see Section 18]

Item	Unit	1980	1990	1995	2000	2003	2004	2005	2006	2007
Production [1]	Mil. lb.	43.70	8.89	6.04	3.96	2.00	2.28	2.69	4.11	4.53
Exports [2]	Mil. lb.	5.8	2.0	9.8	13.6	13.2	13.2	20.5	18.7	14.8
Imports [2]	Mil. lb.	3.6	23.7	41.3	44.9	53.0	66.1	65.5	64.8	54.1
Electric plant purchases from domestic suppliers	Mil. lb.	(NA)	20.5	22.3	24.3	21.7	28.2	27.3	27.9	18.5
Loaded into U.S. nuclear reactors [3]	Mil. lb.	(NA)	(NA)	51.1	51.5	62.3	50.1	58.3	51.7	47.2
Inventories, total	Mil. lb.	(NA)	129.1	72.5	111.3	85.5	95.2	93.8	106.6	111.6
At domestic suppliers	Mil. lb.	(NA)	26.4	13.7	56.5	39.9	37.5	29.1	29.1	30.8
At electric plants	Mil. lb.	(NA)	102.7	58.7	54.8	45.6	57.7	64.7	77.5	80.8
Average price per pound:										
Purchased imports	Dollars	(NA)	12.55	10.20	9.84	10.59	12.25	14.83	19.31	34.18
Domestic purchases	Dollars	(NA)	15.70	11.11	11.45	10.84	11.91	13.98	18.54	33.13

NA Not available. [1] Data are for uranium concentrate, a yellow or brown powder obtained by the milling of uranium ore, processing of in situ leach mining solutions, or as a by-product of phosphoric acid production. [2] Trade data prior to 1990 were for transactions conducted by uranium suppliers only. For 1990 forward, transactions by uranium buyers (consumers) have been included. Buyer imports and exports prior to 1990 are believed to be small. [3] Does not include any fuel rods removed from reactors and later reloaded into the reactor.

Source: U.S. Energy Information Administration, *Annual Energy Review 2007*. Also see <http://www.eia.doe.gov/emeu/aer/pdf/pages/sec9_7.pdf> (released 23 June 2008).

Table 903. **Electricity Net Generation by Sector and Fuel Type: 1990 to 2007**

[**3,038.0 represents 3,038,000,000,000 kWh.** Data are for fuels consumed to produce electricity. Also includes fuels consumed to produce useful thermal output at a small number of electric utility combined-heat-and-power (CHP) plants]

Source and sector	Unit	1990	1995	2000	2004	2005	2006	2007 [1]
Net generation, total	Bil. kWh.	3,038.0	3,353.5	3,802.1	3,970.6	4,055.4	4,064.7	4,159.5
Electric power sector, total	Bil. kWh.	2,901.3	3,194.2	3,637.5	3,808.4	3,902.2	3,908.1	4,006.5
Electricity-only plants [2]	Bil. kWh.	2,840.0	3,052.8	3,472.9	3,624.1	3,721.8	3,742.7	3,827.5
Combined-heat-and-power plants [3]	Bil. kWh.	61.3	141.5	164.6	184.3	180.4	165.4	179.0
Commercial sector [4]	Bil. kWh.	5.8	8.2	7.9	8.3	8.5	8.4	8.5
Industrial sector [5]	Bil. kWh.	130.8	151.0	156.7	153.9	144.7	148.3	144.5
Net generation by source, all sectors:								
Fossil fuels, total	Bil. kWh.	2,103.8	2,293.9	2,692.5	2,825.0	2,910.0	2,884.4	2,994.9
Coal [6]	Bil. kWh.	1,594.0	1,709.4	1,966.3	1,978.6	2,013.2	1,990.9	2,020.6
Petroleum [7]	Bil. kWh.	126.6	74.6	111.2	120.8	122.5	64.4	65.7
Natural gas [8]	Bil. kWh.	372.8	496.1	601.0	708.9	758.0	813.0	893.2
Other gases [9]	Bil. kWh.	10.4	13.9	14.0	16.8	16.3	16.1	15.4
Nuclear electric power	Bil. kWh.	576.9	673.4	753.9	788.5	782.0	787.2	806.5
Hydroelectric pumped storage [10]	Bil. kWh.	-3.5	-2.7	-5.5	-8.5	-6.6	-6.6	-7.0
Renewable energy, total	Bil. kWh.	357.2	384.8	356.5	351.0	357.5	385.7	351.3
Conventional hydroelectric power	Bil. kWh.	292.9	310.8	275.6	268.4	270.3	289.2	248.3
Biomass, total	Bil. kWh.	45.8	56.9	60.7	53.1	54.2	54.8	55.4
Wood [11]	Bil. kWh.	32.5	36.5	37.6	37.6	38.7	38.6	38.5
Waste [12]	Bil. kWh.	13.3	20.4	23.1	15.5	15.5	16.1	16.9
Geothermal	Bil. kWh.	15.4	13.4	14.1	14.8	14.7	14.6	14.8
Solar [13]	Bil. kWh.	0.4	0.5	0.5	0.6	0.6	0.5	0.6
Wind	Bil. kWh.	2.8	3.2	5.6	14.1	17.8	26.6	32.1
Other [14]	Bil. kWh.	3.6	4.1	4.8	14.5	12.5	14.0	13.8
Consumption of fuels for electricity generation:								
Coal [6]	Mil. sh. tons	792.5	860.6	994.9	1,026.0	1,045.9	1,035.3	1,053.3
Petroleum, total	Mil. bbl.	219.0	132.6	195.2	209.5	211.3	115.4	118.1
Distilate fuel oil [15]	Mil. bbl.	18.1	19.6	31.7	20.7	21.2	13.4	16.6
Residual fuel oil [16]	Mil. bbl.	190.8	95.5	143.4	145.2	144.2	61.0	66.7
Other liquids [17]	Mil. bbl.	0.4	0.7	1.4	4.0	3.3	2.6	3.7
Petroleum coke	Mil. sh. tons [18]	1.9	3.4	3.7	7.9	8.5	7.7	6.2
Natural gas [8]	Bil. cu. ft.	3,691.6	4,737.9	5,691.5	6,116.6	6,486.8	6,869.6	7,507.4
Other gases [9]	Tril. Btu.	111.8	132.5	126.0	186.8	176.9	181.1	166.3
Biomass	Tril. Btu.	653.5	795.6	825.9	787.1	733.4	784.9	824.2
Wood [11]	Tril. Btu.	442.3	479.9	495.8	533.5	481.9	522.8	548.4
Waste [12]	Tril. Btu.	211.2	315.7	330.1	253.6	251.6	262.1	275.8
Other [14]	Tril. Btu.	36.0	42.0	46.2	176.0	161.4	155.1	168.5

[1] Preliminary. [2] Electricity-only plants within the NAICS 22 category whose primary business is to sell electricity to the public. Data also include a small number of electric utility combined-heat-and-power plants (CHP). [3] Combined-heat-and-power plants within the NAICS 22 category whose primary business is to sell electricity and heat to the public. Data do not include electric utility CHP plants—these are included under electricity-only plants. [4] Commercial combined-heat-and-power (CHP) and commercial electricity-only plants. [5] Industrial combined-heat-and-power (HCP) and industrial electricity-only plants. Through 1988, data are for industrial hydroelectric power only. [6] Anthracite, bituminous coal, subbituminous coal, lignite, waste coal, and coal synfuel. [7] Distillate fuel oil, residual fuel oil, petroleum coke, jet fuel, kerosene, other petroleum, and waste oil. [8] Includes a small amount of supplemental gaseous fuels that cannot be identified separately. [9] Blast furnace gas, propane gas, and other manufactured and waste gases derived from fossil fuels. [10] Pumped storage facility production minus energy used for pumping. [11] Wood and wood-derived fuels. [12] Municipal solid waste from biogenic sources, landfill gas, sludge waste, tires, agricultural by-products, and other biomass. Through 2000, also includes nonrenewable waste (municipal solid waste from nonbiogenic sources, and tire-derived fuels). [13] Solar thermal and photovoltaic energy. [14] Batteries, chemicals, hydrogen, pitch, purchased steam, sulfur, miscellaneous technologies, and beginning 2001, nonrenewable waste (municipal solid waste from nonbiogenic sources, and tire-derived fuels). [15] Fuel oil numbers 1, 2, and 4. Prior to 2001, electric utility data also include small amounts of kerosene and jet fuel. [16] Fuel oil numbers 5 and 6. Prior to 2001, electric utility data also include a small amount of fuel oil number 4. [17] Jet fuel, kerosene, other petroleum liquids, and waste oil. [18] Short tons.

Source: U.S. Energy Information Administration, *Annual Energy Review 2007*. See also <http://www.eia.doe.gov/emeu/aer/contents.html> (released 23 June 2008).

Table 904. **Total Electric Net Summer Capacity, All Sectors: 1990 to 2007**

[**In million kilowatts (734.1 represents 734,100,000).** Data are at end of year. For plants that use multiple sources of energy, capacity is assigned to the predominant energy source]

Source	1990	1995	2000	2002	2003	2004	2005	2006	2007 [1]
Net summer capacity, total	**734.1**	**769.5**	**811.7**	**905.3**	**948.4**	**962.9**	**978.0**	**986.2**	**998.8**
Fossil fuels, total	527.8	554.2	598.9	689.5	731.2	745.4	757.1	761.6	769.0
Coal [2]	307.4	311.4	315.1	315.4	313.0	313.0	313.4	313.0	313.6
Petroleum [3]	49.4	44.7	61.8	59.7	60.7	59.1	58.5	58.1	58.3
Natural gas [4]	169.3	196.4	219.6	312.5	355.4	371.0	383.1	388.3	394.9
Dual fired [5]	113.6	122.0	149.8	162.3	171.3	172.2	174.7	(NA)	(NA)
Other gases [6]	1.6	1.7	2.3	2.0	2.0	2.3	2.1	2.3	2.3
Nuclear electric power	99.6	99.5	97.9	98.7	99.2	99.6	100.0	100.3	100.6
Hydroelectric pumped storage	19.5	21.4	19.5	30.4	20.5	20.8	21.3	21.5	21.8
Renewable energy, total	86.8	93.9	94.9	96.1	96.8	96.4	98.7	101.9	106.6
Conventional hydroelectric power . . .	73.9	78.6	79.4	79.4	78.7	77.6	77.5	77.8	77.8
Biomass, total	8.1	10.3	10.0	9.6	9.6	9.7	9.8	10.1	10.4
Wood [7]	5.5	6.7	6.1	5.8	5.9	6.2	6.2	6.4	6.4
Waste [8]	2.5	3.5	3.9	3.8	3.8	3.5	3.6	3.7	3.9
Geothermal	2.7	3.0	2.8	2.3	2.1	2.2	2.3	2.3	2.3
Solar [9]	0.3	0.3	0.4	0.4	0.4	0.4	0.4	0.4	0.5
Wind	1.8	1.7	2.4	4.4	6.0	6.5	8.7	11.3	15.6
Other [10]	0.5	0.5	0.5	0.7	0.7	0.7	0.9	0.9	0.8

[1] Preliminary. [2] Anthracite, bituminous coal, subbituminous coal, lignite, waste coal, and coal synfuel. [3] Distillate fuel oil, residual fuel oil, petroleum coke, jet fuel, kerosene, other petroleum, and waste oil. [4] Includes a small amount of supplemental gaseous fuels that cannot be identified separately. [5] Petroleum and natural gas. [6] Blast furnace gas, propane gas, and other manufactured and waste gases derived from fossil fuels. [7] Wood and wood-derived fuels. [8] Municipal solid waste from biogenic sources, landfill gas, sludge waste, tires, agricultural byproducts, and other biomass. Also includes nonrenewable waste (municipal solid waste from nonbiogenic sources, and tire-derived fuels). [9] Solar thermal and photovoltaic energy. [10] Batteries, chemicals, hydrogen, pitch, purchased steam, sulfur, and miscellaneous technologies.

Source: U.S. Energy Information Administration, *Annual Energy Review 2007*. See also <http://www.eia.doe.gov/emeu/aer /elect.html> (released 23 June 2008).

Table 905. **Electricity—End Use and Average Retail Prices: 1980 to 2007**

[Beginning 2003, the category "other" has been replaced by "transportation," and the categories "commercial" and "industrial" have been redefined. Data represent revenue from electricity retail sales divided by the amount of retail electricity sold (in kilowatt-hours). Prices include state and local taxes, energy or demand charges, customer service charges, environmental surcharges, franchise fees, fuel adjustments, and other miscellaneous charges applied to end-use customers during normal billing operations. Prices do not include deferred charges, credits, or other adjustments, such as fuel or revenue from purchased power, from previous reporting periods. Data are for a census of electric utilities. Beginning in 1999, data also include energy service providers selling to retail customers]

Item	1990	1995	2000	2002	2003	2004	2005	2006	2007 [1]
END USE (Billion kilowatt-hours)									
Total end use [2]	**2,837.1**	**3,164.0**	**3,592.4**	**3,631.7**	**3,662.0**	**3,715.9**	**3,811.0**	**3,816.8**	**3,891.7**
Direct use [3]	124.5	150.7	170.9	166.2	168.3	168.5	150.0	146.9	143.6
Retail sales, total [4]	**2,712.6**	**3,013.3**	**3,421.4**	**3,465.5**	**3,493.7**	**3,547.5**	**3,661.0**	**3,669.9**	**3,748.1**
Residential.	924.0	1,042.5	1,192.4	1,265.2	1,275.8	1,292.0	1,359.2	1,351.5	1,391.9
Commercial [5]	838.3	953.1	1,159.3	1,204.5	1,198.7	1,230.4	1,275.1	1,299.7	1,342.7
Industrial [6]	945.5	1,012.7	1,064.2	990.2	1,012.4	1,017.8	1,019.2	1,011.3	1,005.8
Transportation [7]	4.8	5.0	5.4	5.5	6.8	7.2	7.5	7.4	7.7
AVERAGE RETAIL PRICES (Cents per kilowatt-hour)									
Total									
Nominal	6.57	6.89	6.81	7.20	7.44	7.61	8.14	8.90	9.14
Real	8.05	7.48	6.81	6.91	6.99	6.95	7.20	7.64	7.64
Residential									
Nominal	7.83	8.40	8.24	8.44	8.72	8.95	9.45	10.40	10.64
Real	9.60	9.12	8.24	8.10	8.20	8.18	8.36	8.92	8.89
Commercial [8]									
Nominal	7.34	7.69	7.43	7.89	8.03	8.17	8.67	9.46	9.67
Real	9.00	8.35	7.43	7.57	7.55	7.46	7.67	8.12	8.08
Industrial [6]									
Nominal	4.74	4.66	4.64	4.88	5.11	5.25	5.73	6.16	6.36
Real	5.81	5.06	4.64	4.68	4.80	4.80	5.07	5.28	5.31
Transportation [7]									
Nominal	(NA)	(NA)	(NA)	(NA)	7.54	7.18	8.57	9.54	10.40
Real	(NA)	(NA)	(NA)	(NA)	7.09	6.56	7.58	8.18	8.69
Other [9]									
Nominal	6.40	6.88	6.56	6.75	(X)	(X)	(X)	(X)	(X)
Real	7.84	7.47	6.56	6.48	(X)	(X)	(X)	(X)	(X)

NA Not available. X Not applicable. [1] Preliminary. [2] The sum of "total retail sales" and "direct use." [3] Use of electricity that is 1) self-generated, 2) produced by either the same entity that consumes the power or an affiliate, and 3) used in direct support of a service or industrial process located within the same facility or group of facilities that house the generating equipment. Direct use is exclusive of station use. [4] Electricity retail sales to ultimate customers reported by electric utilities and, beginning in 1996, other energy service providers. [5] Includes public street and highway lighting, interdepartmental sales, and other sales to public authorities. [6] Beginning 2003, includes agriculture and irrigation. [7] Includes sales to railroads and railways. [8] Beginning 2003, includes public street and highway lighting, interdepartmental sales, and other sales to public authorities. [9] Public street and highway lighting, interdepartmental sales, other sales to public authorities, agriculture and irrigation, and transportation including railroads and railways.

Source: U.S. Energy Information Administration, *Annual Energy Review 2007*. See also <http://www.eia.doe.gov/emeu /aer/elect.html> (released 23 June 2008).

Energy and Utilities   577

Table 906. Electric Power Industry—Net Generation and Net Summer Capacity by State: 2000 to 2006

[Capacity as of December 31. (3,802.1 represents 3,802,100,000,000). Covers utilities for public use]

State	Net generation (bil. kWh) 2000	Net generation (bil. kWh) 2005	2006 Net generation (bil. kWh)	2006 Percent from— Petroleum	Natural gas	Hydro-electric	Nuclear	Coal	Net summer capacity (mil. kW) 2000	Net summer capacity (mil. kW) 2006
U.S. . . .	3,802.1	4,055.4	4,064.7	1.6	20.0	7.1	19.4	49.0	811.7	986.2
AL	124.4	137.9	140.9	0.1	13.8	5.1	22.6	55.4	23.5	30.7
AK	6.2	6.6	6.7	11.5	60.8	18.3	–	9.2	2.1	1.9
AZ	88.9	101.5	104.4	0.1	31.5	6.5	23.0	38.7	15.3	25.6
AR	43.9	47.8	52.2	0.3	17.8	3.0	29.2	46.4	9.7	14.5
CA	208.1	200.3	216.8	1.1	48.8	22.2	14.7	1.0	51.9	63.2
CO	44.2	49.6	50.7	(Z)	23.4	3.5	–	71.5	8.4	11.2
CT	33.0	33.5	34.7	3.7	30.2	1.6	47.8	12.3	6.4	7.9
DE	6.0	8.1	7.2	1.8	16.3	–	–	69.2	2.1	3.4
DC	0.1	0.2	0.1	100.0	–	–	–	–	0.8	0.8
FL	191.8	220.3	223.8	10.3	42.9	0.1	14.0	29.2	41.5	53.2
GA	123.9	136.7	138.0	0.6	9.4	1.9	23.2	62.7	27.8	36.5
HI	10.6	11.5	11.6	78.4	–	1.0	–	13.4	2.4	2.4
ID	11.9	10.8	13.4	(Z)	9.6	84.0	–	0.6	3.0	3.2
IL	178.5	194.1	192.4	0.1	2.8	0.1	48.9	47.6	36.3	42.3
IN	127.8	130.4	130.5	0.1	2.0	0.4	–	94.8	23.3	27.0
IA	41.5	44.2	45.5	0.5	5.3	2.0	11.2	75.6	9.1	11.1
KS	44.8	45.9	45.5	0.1	4.0	(Z)	20.5	73.1	10.1	11.1
KY	93.0	97.8	98.8	3.4	1.2	2.6	–	92.3	16.8	20.0
LA	92.9	92.6	90.9	2.0	44.5	0.8	18.4	26.8	21.0	26.8
ME	14.0	18.8	16.8	3.5	43.4	25.4	–	1.9	4.2	4.2
MD	51.1	52.7	49.0	1.2	3.6	4.3	28.3	60.1	10.4	12.5
MA	38.7	47.5	45.6	5.2	51.0	3.3	12.8	24.4	12.4	13.9
MI	104.2	121.6	112.6	0.4	10.0	1.4	25.8	60.2	25.8	30.2
MN	51.4	53.0	53.2	0.9	4.8	1.1	24.8	62.1	10.3	12.7
MS	37.6	45.1	46.2	0.9	34.0	–	22.5	39.2	9.0	16.6
MO	76.6	90.8	91.7	0.1	4.1	0.2	11.0	84.5	17.3	20.6
MT	26.5	27.9	28.2	1.5	0.3	35.9	–	60.5	5.2	5.4
NE	29.1	31.5	31.7	0.1	2.4	2.8	28.4	65.3	6.0	7.1
NV	35.5	40.2	31.9	0.1	66.5	6.5	–	22.8	6.7	9.6
NH	15.0	24.5	22.1	2.0	27.2	6.9	42.6	17.6	2.9	4.3
NJ	58.1	60.5	60.7	0.5	25.8	0.1	53.7	17.9	16.5	19.0
NM	34.0	35.1	37.3	0.1	15.8	0.5	–	80.1	5.6	7.1
NY	138.1	146.9	142.3	4.8	29.6	19.2	29.7	14.7	35.6	39.6
NC	122.3	129.7	125.2	0.3	2.5	3.1	31.9	60.3	24.5	27.1
ND	31.3	31.9	30.9	0.1	(Z)	4.9	–	93.5	4.7	4.8
OH	149.1	157.0	155.4	0.9	1.5	0.4	10.8	85.9	28.4	33.9
OK	55.6	68.6	70.6	0.1	46.6	0.9	–	49.7	14.1	20.1
OR	51.8	49.3	53.3	(Z)	21.0	71.0	–	4.4	11.3	12.3
PA	201.7	218.1	218.8	0.7	6.2	1.3	34.4	56.0	36.7	45.0
RI	6.0	6.1	6.0	0.5	96.9	0.1	–	–	1.2	1.8
SC	93.3	102.5	99.3	0.3	6.1	1.8	51.2	39.8	18.7	22.8
SD	9.7	6.5	7.1	0.1	3.7	47.6	–	46.5	2.8	2.9
TN	95.8	97.1	93.9	0.2	0.7	8.3	26.3	64.8	19.5	20.9
TX	377.7	396.7	400.6	0.4	49.0	0.2	10.3	36.5	81.7	100.8
UT	36.6	38.2	41.3	0.2	8.2	1.8	–	89.3	5.2	6.7
VT	6.3	5.7	7.1	0.1	(Z)	21.4	72.1	–	1.0	1.1
VA	77.2	78.9	73.1	1.1	9.9	1.8	37.8	46.9	19.4	22.6
WA	108.2	102.0	108.2	(Z)	6.9	75.8	8.6	5.9	26.1	28.2
WV	92.9	93.6	93.8	0.2	0.4	1.7	–	97.5	15.0	16.4
WI	59.6	61.8	61.6	1.4	8.7	2.7	19.8	65.0	13.6	16.4
WY	45.5	45.6	45.4	0.1	1.1	1.9	–	94.5	6.2	6.7

– Represents zero.   Z Represents less than 50 million kWh or 50,000 kW.

Source: U.S. Energy Information Administration, "Electric Power Annual 2006"; <http://www.eia.doe.gov/cneaf/electricity/epa/epa_sprdshts.html> (released October 2008).

U.S. Census Bureau, Statistical Abstract of the United States: 2009

Table 907. Electric Power Industry—Capability, Peak Load, and Capacity Margin:1980 to 2007

[558,237 represents 558,237,000 kW. Excludes Alaska and Hawaii. Capability represents the maximum kilowatt output with all power sources available and with hydraulic equipment under actual water conditions, allowing for maintenance, emergency outages, and system operating requirements. Capacity margin is the difference between capability and peak load. Minus sign (–) indicates decrease]

| Year | Capability at the time of— | | | | Noncoincident peak load | | Capacity margin | | | |
| | Summer peak load (1,000 kW) | | Winter peak load (1,000 kW) | | | | Summer | | Winter | |
	Amount	Change from prior year	Amount	Change from prior year	Summer (1,000 kW)	Winter (1,000 kW)	Amount (1,000 kW)	Percent of capability	Amount (1,000 kW)	Percent of capability
1980....	558,237	13,731	572,195	17,670	427,058	384,567	131,179	23.5	187,628	32.8
1985....	621,597	17,357	636,475	14,350	460,503	423,660	161,094	25.9	212,815	33.4
1988....	661,580	13,462	676,940	13,963	529,460	466,533	132,120	20.0	210,407	31.1
1989....	673,316	11,736	685,249	8,309	524,110	496,378	149,206	22.2	188,871	27.6
1990....	685,091	11,775	696,757	11,508	546,331	484,231	138,760	20.3	212,526	30.5
1991....	690,915	5,824	703,212	6,455	551,418	485,761	139,497	20.2	217,451	30.9
1992....	695,436	4,521	707,752	4,540	548,707	492,983	146,729	21.1	214,769	30.3
1993....	694,250	−1,186	711,957	4,205	575,356	521,733	118,894	17.1	190,224	26.7
1994....	702,985	8,735	715,090	3,133	585,320	518,253	117,665	16.7	196,837	27.5
1995....	714,222	11,237	727,679	12,589	620,249	544,684	93,973	13.2	182,995	25.1
1996....	724,728	10,506	737,637	9,958	616,790	554,081	107,938	14.9	183,556	24.9
1997....	725,829	1,101	736,666	−971	637,677	529,874	88,152	12.1	206,792	28.1
1998....	724,193	−1,636	735,090	−1,576	660,293	567,558	63,900	8.8	167,532	22.8
1999....	733,481	9,288	748,271	13,181	682,122	570,915	51,359	7.0	177,356	23.7
2000....	750,771	17,290	767,505	19,234	678,413	588,426	72,358	9.6	179,079	23.3
2001....	783,737	32,966	806,598	39,093	687,812	576,312	95,925	12.2	230,286	28.6
2002....	825,145	41,408	850,984	44,386	714,565	604,986	110,580	13.4	245,998	28.9
2003....	853,649	28,504	882,120	31,136	709,375	593,874	144,274	16.9	288,246	32.7
2004....	878,830	25,181	864,849	−17,271	704,459	618,701	174,371	19.8	246,148	28.5
2005....	865,095	−13,735	878,110	13,261	758,876	626,365	106,219	12.3	251,745	28.7
2006....	872,307	7,212	899,551	21,441	789,475	640,981	82,832	9.5	258,570	28.7
2007 [1]...	883,507	11,200	914,433	14,882	785,930	651,386	97,577	11.0	263,047	28.8

[1] Preliminary.

Source: Edison Electric Institute, Washington, DC, *Statistical Yearbook of the Electric Power Industry,* annual.

Table 908. Electric Energy Retail Sales by Class of Service and State: 2006

[In billions of kilowatt-hours (3,669.9 represents 1,669,900,000,000)]

State	Total [1]	Resi-dential	Com-mercial	Indus-trial	State	Total [1]	Resi-dential	Com-mercial	Indus-trial
United States.....	3,669.9	1,351.5	1,299.7	1,011.3	Missouri..........	82.0	33.9	29.8	18.3
Alabama..........	90.7	32.3	22.1	36.3	Montana..........	13.8	4.4	4.7	4.7
Alaska...........	6.2	2.1	2.8	1.2	Nebraska..........	27.3	9.3	9.0	9.0
Arizona..........	73.3	32.4	28.6	12.3	Nevada...........	34.6	12.0	9.0	13.6
Arkansas.........	46.6	17.1	11.6	18.0	New Hampshire.....	11.1	4.4	4.6	2.1
California..........	263.0	89.8	121.3	51.0					
					New Jersey........	79.7	28.6	39.4	11.3
Colorado..........	49.7	17.0	20.2	12.6	New Mexico........	21.4	6.0	8.6	6.8
Connecticut.......	31.7	13.0	13.6	4.9	New York.........	142.2	48.4	76.0	15.0
Delaware.........	11.6	4.3	4.2	3.1	North Carolina......	126.7	52.9	44.6	29.3
District of Columbia...	11.4	1.8	9.0	0.2	North Dakota.......	11.2	3.9	4.1	3.3
Florida............	228.2	117.1	91.3	19.8					
					Ohio.............	153.4	51.4	46.1	55.9
Georgia..........	134.8	54.5	45.5	34.6	Oklahoma..........	54.9	21.7	18.2	15.0
Hawaii...........	10.6	3.2	3.5	3.9	Oregon...........	48.1	19.0	16.1	13.0
Idaho...........	22.8	8.1	5.8	8.9	Pennsylvania.......	146.2	51.8	45.6	47.9
Illinois............	142.4	46.4	50.6	44.9	Rhode Island.......	7.8	3.0	3.6	1.2
Indiana..........	105.7	32.3	23.8	49.5					
					South Carolina......	80.9	28.5	20.9	31.4
Iowa............	43.3	13.3	11.7	18.3	South Dakota.......	10.1	4.1	4.1	2.0
Kansas..........	39.8	13.5	14.8	11.5	Tennessee.........	103.9	40.8	29.0	34.1
Kentucky..........	88.7	25.9	18.9	43.9	Texas............	342.7	126.8	111.1	104.7
Louisiana........	77.5	28.1	22.0	27.4	Utah.............	26.4	8.2	9.7	8.4
Maine...........	12.3	4.4	4.1	3.8					
					Vermont..........	5.8	2.1	2.0	1.6
Maryland..........	63.2	26.9	29.7	6.1	Virginia...........	106.7	42.9	44.7	19.0
Massachusetts......	55.9	19.6	26.2	9.6	Washington........	85.0	34.4	28.6	22.0
Michigan..........	108.0	34.6	39.3	34.1	West Virginia.......	32.3	11.0	7.4	13.9
Minnesota........	66.8	21.9	22.2	22.7	Wisconsin.........	69.8	21.8	22.8	25.3
Mississippi..........	46.9	18.3	12.9	15.7	Wyoming..........	14.9	2.5	4.1	8.4

[1] Includes transportation, not shown separately.

Source: U.S. Energy Information Administration, "Electric Sales and Revenue 2006"; <http://www.eia.doe.gov/cneaf/electricity/esr/table2.xls> (released November 2007).

Table 909. Electric Energy Price by Class of Service and State: 2006

[**Revenue (in cents) per kilowatt-hour (kWh)**. Data include both bundled and unbundled consumers]

State	Total [1]	Resi-dential	Com-mercial	Indus-trial	State	Total [1]	Resi-dential	Com-mercial	Indus-trial
United States . . .	**8.90**	**10.40**	**9.46**	**6.16**					
					Missouri	6.30	7.44	6.08	4.58
Alabama	7.07	8.75	8.18	4.90	Montana	6.91	8.28	7.44	5.12
Alaska	12.84	14.83	11.93	11.54	Nebraska	6.07	7.41	6.19	4.56
Arizona	8.24	9.40	8.02	5.69	Nevada	9.63	11.08	10.12	8.03
Arkansas	6.99	8.85	6.96	5.24	New Hampshire	13.84	14.68	14.07	11.62
California	12.82	14.33	12.90	10.09					
					New Jersey	11.88	12.84	11.62	10.42
Colorado	7.61	9.02	7.50	5.88	New Mexico	7.37	9.06	7.61	5.57
Connecticut	14.83	16.86	14.03	11.71	New York	15.27	16.89	15.51	9.39
Delaware	10.13	11.85	10.21	7.67	North Carolina	7.53	9.12	7.17	5.23
District of Columbia . . .	11.08	9.88	11.17	17.43	North Dakota	6.21	7.14	6.30	5.00
Florida	10.45	11.33	9.91	7.71					
					Ohio	7.71	9.34	8.44	5.61
Georgia	7.63	8.91	7.81	5.38	Oklahoma	7.30	8.55	7.34	5.46
Hawaii	20.72	23.35	21.42	17.96	Oregon	6.53	7.48	6.77	4.85
Idaho	4.92	6.21	5.16	3.61	Pennsylvania	8.68	10.35	8.94	6.63
Illinois	7.07	8.42	7.95	4.69	Rhode Island	13.98	15.12	13.51	12.51
Indiana	6.46	8.22	7.21	4.95					
					South Carolina	6.98	9.03	7.60	4.71
Iowa	7.01	9.63	7.29	4.92	South Dakota	6.70	7.83	6.47	4.84
Kansas	6.89	8.25	6.96	5.20	Tennessee	6.97	7.75	8.00	5.17
Kentucky	5.43	7.02	6.44	4.05	Texas	10.34	12.86	9.85	7.82
Louisiana	8.30	9.14	9.03	6.87	Utah	5.99	7.59	6.15	4.21
Maine	11.80	13.80	12.42	8.83					
					Vermont	11.37	13.39	11.67	8.33
Maryland	9.95	9.71	10.56	8.14	Virginia	6.86	8.49	6.21	4.69
Massachusetts	15.45	16.60	15.54	13.04	Washington	6.14	6.82	6.63	4.44
Michigan	8.14	9.77	8.51	6.05	West Virginia	5.04	6.35	5.59	3.71
Minnesota	6.98	8.70	7.02	5.29	Wisconsin	8.13	10.51	8.37	5.85
Mississippi	8.33	9.66	9.37	5.94	Wyoming	5.27	7.75	6.28	4.04

[1] Includes transportation, not shown separately.

Source: U.S. Energy Information Administration, "Electric Sales and Revenue 2006"; <http://www.eia.doe.gov/cneaf/electricity/esr/esr_sum.html> (released November 2007).

Table 910. Total Electric Power Industry—Generation, Sales, Revenue, and Customers: 1990 to 2007

[**2,808 represents 2,808,000,000,000 kWh**. Sales and revenue are to and from ultimate customers. Commercial and Industrial are not wholly comparable on a year-to-year basis due to changes from one classification to another. For the 2003 period forward, the Energy Information Administration replaced the "Other" sector with the Transportation sector. The Transportation sector consists entirely of electrified rail and urban transit systems. Data previously reported in "Other" have been relocated to the Commercial sector, except for Agriculture (i.e., irrigation load), which have been relocated to the Industrial sector]

Class	Unit	1990	1995	2000	2002	2003	2004	2005	2006	2007 [1]
Generation [2]	Bil. kWh . .	2,808	3,353	3,802	3,858	3,883	3,971	4,055	4,065	4,160
Sales [3]	**Bil. kWh .**	**2,713**	**3,013**	**3,421**	**3,466**	**3,489**	**3,548**	**3,661**	**3,670**	**3,748**
Residential or domestic . .	Bil. kWh . .	924	1,043	1,192	1,265	1,274	1,294	1,359	1,352	1,392
Percent of total	Percent . .	34.1	34.6	34.9	36.5	36.5	36.5	37.1	36.8	37.1
Commercial [4]	Bil. kWh . .	751	863	1,055	1,105	1,197	1,229	1,275	1,300	1,343
Industrial [5]	Bil. kWh . .	946	1,013	1,064	990	1,012	1,019	1,019	1,011	1,006
Revenue [3]	**Bil. dol . . .**	**178.2**	**207.7**	**233.2**	**250.2**	**258.9**	**270.5**	**298.0**	**326.5**	**342.6**
Residential or domestic . .	Bil. dol. . .	72.4	87.6	98.2	107.1	110.8	116.0	128.4	140.6	148.0
Percent of total	Percent . .	40.6	42.2	42.1	42.8	42.8	42.9	43.1	43.1	43.2
Commercial [4]	Bil. dol. . .	55.1	66.4	78.4	87.3	95.8	100.3	110.5	122.9	129.8
Industrial [5]	Bil. dol. . .	44.9	47.2	49.4	48.6	51.8	53.7	58.4	62.3	64.0
Ultimate customers, Dec. 31 [3]	**Million . . .**	**110.6**	**118.3**	**127.6**	**133.6**	**134.5**	**136.1**	**138.4**	**140.4**	**142.4**
Residential or domestic . .	Million . . .	97.1	103.9	111.7	116.6	117.3	118.8	120.8	122.5	124.3
Commercial [4]	Million . . .	12.1	12.9	14.3	15.3	16.5	16.6	16.9	17.2	17.4
Industrial [5]	Million . . .	0.5	0.6	0.5	0.6	0.7	0.7	0.7	0.8	0.8
Avg. kWh used per customer	**1,000. . . .**	**24.5**	**25.5**	**26.8**	**25.9**	**25.9**	**26.1**	**26.5**	**26.1**	**26.3**
Residential	1,000. . . .	9.5	10.0	10.7	10.9	10.9	10.9	11.3	11.0	11.2
Commercial [4]	1,000. . . .	62.2	66.6	73.5	72.0	72.3	74.0	75.6	75.7	77.2
Avg. annual bill per customer	**Dollar . . .**	**1,612**	**1,756**	**1,828**	**1,872**	**1,924**	**1,987**	**2,154**	**2,325**	**2,405**
Residential	Dollar . . .	745	843	879	918	945	977	1,063	1,148	1,191
Commercial [4]	Dollar . . .	4,562	5,124	5,464	5,693	5,786	6,037	6,551	7,158	7,464
Avg. revenue per kWh sold	**Cents . . .**	**6.57**	**6.89**	**6.81**	**7.22**	**7.42**	**7.62**	**8.14**	**8.90**	**9.14**
Residential	Cents . . .	7.83	8.40	8.24	8.46	8.70	8.97	9.45	10.40	10.63
Commercial [4]	Cents . . .	7.34	7.69	7.43	7.90	8.00	8.16	8.67	9.46	9.66
Industrial [5]	Cents . . .	4.74	4.66	4.64	4.91	5.12	5.27	5.73	6.16	6.36

[1] Preliminary.   [2] "Generation" includes batteries, chemicals, hydrogen, pitch, sulfur, purchased steam, and miscellaneous technologies, which are not separately displayed.   [3] Includes other types not shown separately. Data for 1990 are as of December 31, data for following years are average yearly customers.   [4] Small light and power.   [5] Large light and power.

Source: Edison Electric Institute, Washington, DC, *Statistical Yearbook of the Electric Power Industry*, annual.

Table 911. Revenue and Expense Statistics for Major U.S. Investor-Owned Electric Utilities: 1995 to 2006

[In millions of nominal dollars (199,967 represents $199,967,000,000). Covers approximately 180 investor-owned electric utilities that during each of the last 3 years met any one or more of the following conditions—1 mil. megawatt-hours of total sales; 100 megawatt-hours of sales for resale, 500 megawatt-hours of gross interchange out, and 500 megawatt-hours of wheeling for other]

Item	1995	2000	2002	2003	2004	2005	2006
Utility operating revenues	**199,967**	**235,336**	**219,389**	**226,227**	**240,318**	**267,534**	**277,142**
Electric utility	183,655	214,707	200,135	202,369	213,539	235,570	247,503
Other utility	16,312	20,630	19,254	23,858	26,779	31,964	29,639
Utility operating expenses. . . .	**165,321**	**210,324**	**188,745**	**197,459**	**207,161**	**238,590**	**247,170**
Electric utility	150,599	191,329	171,291	175,473	182,337	208,461	219,171
Operation.	91,881	132,662	116,374	122,723	131,962	151,150	159,472
Production	68,983	107,352	90,649	96,181	104,287	121,058	128,016
Cost of fuel	29,122	32,555	24,132	26,476	28,678	36,161	38,158
Purchased power	29,981	61,969	58,828	62,173	67,354	78,279	79,485
Other	9,880	12,828	7,688	7,532	8,256	6,638	10,399
Transmission.	1,425	2,699	3,494	3,585	4,519	5,687	6,185
Distribution	2,561	3,115	3,113	3,185	3,301	3,517	3,658
Customer accounts.	3,613	4,246	4,165	4,180	4,087	4,243	4,424
Customer service	1,922	1,839	1,821	1,893	2,012	2,289	2,533
Sales	348	403	261	234	238	219	241
Administrative and general	13,028	13,009	12,872	13,466	13,519	14,113	14,618
Maintenance.	11,767	12,185	10,843	11,141	11,774	12,058	12,879
Depreciation	19,885	22,761	17,319	16,962	16,373	17,177	17,438
Taxes and other	27,065	23,721	26,755	24,648	22,228	26,848	28,187
Other utility	14,722	18,995	17,454	21,986	24,823	30,129	27,999
Net utility operating income. . .	**34,646**	**25,012**	**30,644**	**28,768**	**33,158**	**28,944**	**29,972**

Source: U.S. Energy Information Administration, "Electric Power Annual 2006"; <http://www.eia.doe.gov/cneaf/electricity/epa/epat8p1.html> (released 22 October 2007).

Table 912. Total Renewable Energy Net Generation of Electricity by Source and State: 2005

[In millions of kilowatt-hours (357,534 represents 357,534,000,000). MSW = municipal solid waste]

State	Total [1]	Hydro-electric	MSW/landfill gas [2]	Other bio-mass [3]	Wood/wood waste [4]	State	Total [1]	Hydro-electric	MSW/landfill gas [2]	Other bio-mass [3]	Wood/wood waste [4]
U.S.	**357,534**	**270,321**	**13,470**	**2,009**	**38,681**	MO	1,169	1,159	(NA)	9	(NA)
AL	13,904	10,145	3	17	3,738	MT.	9,653	9,587	(NA)	(NA)	65
AK	1,470	1,464	(NA)	5	(Z)	NE.	1,011	871	25	18	(NA)
AZ	6,484	6,410	45	4	12	NV	2,965	1,702	(NA)	(NA)	(NA)
AR	4,817	3,083	(NA)	28	1,707	NH	2,741	1,799	156	(NA)	786
CA	63,280	39,632	1,587	629	3,610	NJ	906	31	872	2	(NA)
CO	2,226	1,415	(NA)	34	(Z)	NM.	964	165	(NA)	5	(NA)
CT	1,232	478	746	(NA)	7	NY	27,781	25,783	1,344	14	538
DE	(NA)	(NA)	(NA)	(NA)	(NA)	NC.	7,235	5,397	87	12	1,740
DC	(NA)	(NA)	(NA)	(NA)	(NA)	ND.	1,572	1,342	(NA)	10	(NA)
FL	4,630	266	1,775	583	2,006	OH.	915	516	23	4	359
GA.	7,258	4,032	29	49	3,149	OK.	3,767	2,630	(NA)	(NA)	289
HI	635	96	163	148	(NA)	OR.	32,590	30,948	71	27	809
ID	9,119	8,542	(NA)	(NA)	577	PA	4,562	2,232	1,352	6	687
IL.	912	129	593	48	(NA)	RI	7	7	(NA)	(NA)	(NA)
IN	506	438	68	(NA)	(NA)	SC.	4,723	2,938	88	(NA)	1,697
IA	2,724	960	82	35	(NA)	SD.	3,233	3,075	(NA)	(NA)	(NA)
KS	437	11	(NA)	(NA)	(NA)	TN	9,868	9,310	27	(NA)	528
KY	3,384	2,961	62	1	359	TX	6,667	1,333	207	47	844
LA	3,535	811	(NA)	81	2,644	UT	973	784	4	(NA)	(NA)
ME.	8,166	4,091	234	55	3,787	VT	1,633	1,211	(NA)	(NA)	410
MD.	2,317	1,704	417	(NA)	195	VA	3,982	1,484	677	21	1,800
MA.	2,300	1,042	1,114	25	120	WA	74,191	72,075	171	27	1,419
MI	3,982	1,462	714	3	1,801	WV	1,602	1,448	(NA)	(Z)	(Z)
MN.	3,422	775	409	6	649	WI	3,035	1,740	325	52	825
MS.	1,525	(NA)	(NA)	5	1,520	WY	1,526	808	(NA)	(NA)	(NA)

NA Not available.   Z Less than 500,000 million kilowatt-hours.   [1] Includes types not shown separately.   [2] Includes landfill gas and municipal solid waste biogenic (paper and paper board, wood, food, leather, textiles, and yard trimmings).   [3] Agriculture by-products/crops, sludge waste, tires, and other biomass solids, liquids, and gases.   [4] Black liquor and wood/woodwaste solids and liquids.

Source: Energy Information Administration, "Renewable Energy Trends 2006"; <http://www.eia.doe.gov/cneaf/solar.renewables/page/trends/table17.pdf> (released April 2008).

Table 913. Carbon Dioxide Emissions by Sector and Source—1980 to 2006, and Projections, 2010 to 2020

[In million metric tons (4,769.6 represents 4,769.600,000), except as noted]

Sector	1980	1990	1995	2000	2005	2006 [1]	Projections 2010	Projections 2015	Projections 2020
Total [2]	**4,769.6**	**5,011.6**	**5,300.6**	**5,847.2**	**5,981.6**	**5,890.3**	**6,010.6**	**6,226.2**	**6,384.1**
Petroleum [3]	2,058.2	2,070.2	2,138.8	2,360.1	2,513.5	2,526.7	2,512.1	2,592.6	2,605.2
Natural gas [4]	869.7	855.8	962.4	957.0	872.3	823.6	890.4	921.2	939.4
Coal	301.4	265.0	238.7	223.3	194.7	190.6	195.3	193.9	212.2
Electricity [5]	1,543.4	1,820.2	1,954.9	2,300.6	2,397.1	2,343.8	2,412.8	2,518.6	2,627.3
Residential	916.5	961.6	1,039.2	1,181.5	1,253.0	1,204.2	1,258.6	1,280.4	1,323.7
Petroleum	124.3	98.9	96.7	108.1	100.5	100.3	91.1	92.3	92.1
Natural gas	257.6	239.8	264.4	270.6	261.6	237.3	262.6	274.0	281.4
Coal	5.8	2.9	1.7	1.0	0.9	0.6	0.8	0.8	0.8
Electricity [5]	528.8	620.0	676.3	801.8	890.0	866.0	904.1	913.2	949.4
Commercial	658.1	787.5	848.4	1,015.1	1,065.4	1,045.2	1,079.2	1,175.5	1,265.3
Petroleum	96.5	70.1	53.5	54.6	52.5	52.6	45.7	48.3	49.1
Natural gas	141.4	143.1	165.4	172.7	168.8	154.6	161.5	174.8	184.0
Coal	8.3	11.8	11.1	8.2	9.2	6.2	7.9	7.9	7.9
Electricity [5]	411.8	562.5	618.4	779.6	834.9	831.9	864.1	944.5	1,024.3
Industrial [6]	1,795.0	1,679.9	1,730.9	1,778.1	1,677.1	1,650.8	1,692.7	1,717.9	1,718.1
Petroleum	474.2	358.0	348.2	364.1	412.4	421.4	435.4	442.0	432.2
Natural gas [4]	436.2	436.7	494.0	478.1	408.7	399.2	430.4	434.5	433.6
Coal	287.3	250.3	225.9	214.1	184.6	183.8	186.5	185.1	203.5
Electricity [5]	600.5	634.5	657.0	715.6	667.3	640.7	640.4	656.3	648.8
Transportation	1,400.0	1,582.6	1,682.2	1,872.6	1,986.2	1,990.1	1,980.0	2,052.4	2,077.0
Petroleum [3]	1,363.2	1,543.2	1,640.4	1,833.3	1,948.1	1,952.4	1,939.9	2,010.0	2,031.8
Natural gas [7]	34.5	36.2	38.6	35.6	33.2	32.5	35.9	37.9	40.4
Electricity [5]	2.3	3.2	3.2	3.6	4.9	5.2	4.3	4.5	4.8
Electric power sector [8]	1,543.4	1,820.2	1,955.0	2,300.7	2,397.1	2,343.9	2,412.8	2,518.6	2,627.3
Petroleum	204.9	101.9	60.7	91.8	101.3	54.5	42.8	43.7	45.1
Natural gas	201.8	177.7	230.6	282.8	320.5	339.5	365.4	357.9	323.0
Coal	1,136.6	1,534.2	1,653.2	1,915.5	1,963.7	1,937.9	1,992.6	2,104.9	2,247.0

[1] Preliminary. [2] Includes other items not shown separately. [3] This includes carbon dioxide from international bunker fuels, both civilian and military, which are excluded from the accounting of carbon dioxide emissions under the United Nations convention. [4] Includes lease and plant fuel. [5] Emissions from the electric power sector are distributed to the end-use sectors. [6] Fuel consumption includes energy for combined-heat-and-power plants (CHP), except those plants whose primary business is to sell electricity, or electricity and heat, to the public. [7] Includes pipeline fuel natural gas and compressed natural gas used as vehicle fuel. [8] Includes electricity-only and combined heat and power plants whose primary business is to sell electricity, or electricity and heat, to the public. Beginning 2005, also includes emissions from municipal solid waste and geothermal electricity generation. Emissions from the electric power sector are apportioned to each end-use sector according to their share of electricity sales.

Source: U.S. Energy Information Administration, 1980, "State Energy Data Report"; 1990 to 2000, "Emissions of Greenhouse Gases in the U.S. 2006"; and 2005 and after, *Annual Energy Outlook 2008.* See also <http://www.eia.doe.gov>.

Table 914. Privately Owned Gas Utility Industry—Balance Sheet and Income Account: 1990 to 2006

[In millions of dollars (121,686 represents $121,686,000,000). The gas utility industry consists of pipeline and distribution companies. Excludes operations of companies distributing gas in bottles or tanks]

Item	1990	1995	2000	2001	2002	2003	2004	2005	2006
COMPOSITE BALANCE SHEET									
Assets, total	**121,686**	**141,965**	**165,709**	**171,681**	**185,064**	**174,756**	**168,306**	**196,215**	**203,108**
Total utility plant	112,863	143,636	162,206	175,530	197,717	188,807	180,884	207,976	212,473
Depreciation and amortization	*49,483*	*62,723*	*69,366*	*73,753*	*85,038*	*76,642*	*79,889*	*91,794*	*91,804*
Utility plant (net)	63,380	80,912	92,839	101,777	112,679	112,165	100,996	116,183	120,669
Investment and fund accounts	23,872	26,489	10,846	10,237	13,000	13,430	12,716	16,331	17,309
Current and accrued assets	23,268	18,564	35,691	29,345	25,786	22,905	22,107	32,325	26,955
Deferred debits [1]	9,576	13,923	24,279	28,553	31,928	24,663	31,033	29,574	36,278
Liabilities, total	**121,686**	**141,965**	**165,709**	**171,681**	**185,064**	**174,756**	**168,306**	**196,215**	**203,108**
Capitalization, total	74,958	90,581	96,079	107,310	117,362	112,089	105,799	120,949	126,833
Capital stock	43,810	54,402	47,051	56,870	58,067	57,605	54,252	62,470	66,144
Long-term debts	31,148	35,548	48,267	49,739	58,962	54,179	51,327	58,264	60,632
Current and accrued liabilities	29,550	28,272	42,312	34,962	30,856	28,599	25,515	34,936	32,417
Deferred income taxes [2]	11,360	14,393	17,157	20,445	24,612	23,888	23,944	24,937	27,454
Other liabilities and credits	5,818	8,715	10,161	8,964	12,235	10,179	13,048	15,393	16,404
COMPOSITE INCOME ACCOUNT									
Operating revenues, total	**66,027**	**58,390**	**72,042**	**79,276**	**68,352**	**75,527**	**80,194**	**102,018**	**97,156**
Minus: Operating expenses [3]	*60,137*	*50,760*	*64,988*	*71,209*	*60,041*	*66,677*	*71,719*	*89,385*	*87,013*
Operation and maintenance	51,627	37,966	54,602	58,873	48,521	55,036	59,920	77,673	73,459
Federal, state, and local taxes	4,957	6,182	6,163	7,394	6,249	6,581	6,472	7,513	7,350
Equals: Operating income	5,890	7,630	7,053	8,068	8,310	8,852	8,475	12,632	10,144
Utility operating income	6,077	7,848	7,166	8,192	8,564	9,198	8,619	12,812	10,185
Income before interest charges	8,081	9,484	7,589	8,266	9,305	10,053	9,609	13,972	11,586
Net income	4,410	5,139	4,245	4,038	4,792	6,198	5,942	9,777	6,931
Dividends	3,191	4,037	3,239	3,560	3,887	3,765	2,111	2,419	2,304

[1] Includes capital stock discount and expense and reacquired securities. [2] Includes reserves for deferred income taxes. [3] Includes expenses not shown separately.

Source: American Gas Association, Arlington, VA, *Gas Facts,* annual (copyright).

582   Energy and Utilities

Table 915. Gas Utility Industry—Summary: 1990 to 2006

[54,261 represents 54,261,000. Covers natural, manufactured, mixed, and liquid petroleum gas. Based on a questionnaire mailed to all privately and municipally owned gas utilities in the United States, except those with annual revenues less than $25,000]

Item	Unit	1990	1995	2000	2002	2003	2004	2005	2006
End users [1]	1,000	54,261	58,728	61,262	62,034	62,610	63,297	64,395	65,020
Residential	1,000	49,802	53,955	56,494	57,293	57,802	58,501	59,569	60,147
Commercial	1,000	4,246	4,530	4,610	4,590	4,661	4,641	4,678	4,734
Industrial and other	1,000	166	181	157	149	145	152	145	138
Sales [2]	Tril. Btu [3]	9,842	9,221	9,232	8,864	8,927	8,766	8,848	8,222
Residential	Tril. Btu	4,468	4,803	4,741	4,589	4,722	4,566	4,516	4,117
Percent of total	Percent	45	52	51	52	53	52	51	50
Commercial	Tril. Btu	2,192	2,281	2,077	2,055	2,125	2,075	2,056	1,861
Industrial	Tril. Btu	3,010	1,919	1,698	1,748	1,672	1,763	1,654	1,576
Other	Tril. Btu	171	218	715	472	408	363	622	668
Revenues [2]	Mil. dol.	45,153	46,436	59,243	57,112	72,606	79,929	96,909	91,928
Residential	Mil. dol.	25,000	28,742	35,828	35,062	43,664	47,275	55,680	53,961
Percent of total	Percent	55	62	60	61	60	59	57	59
Commercial	Mil. dol.	10,604	11,573	13,339	13,512	17,349	18,689	22,653	21,557
Industrial	Mil. dol.	8,996	5,571	7,432	6,841	9,478	11,230	13,751	12,006
Other	Mil. dol.	553	549	2,645	1,698	2,115	2,735	4,825	4,405
Prices per mil. Btu [3]	Dollars	4.59	5.05	6.42	6.44	8.13	9.13	10.95	11.18
Residential	Dollars	5.60	6.00	7.56	7.64	9.25	10.37	12.33	13.11
Commercial	Dollars	4.84	5.07	6.42	6.57	8.17	9.01	11.02	11.58
Industrial	Dollars	2.99	2.98	4.38	3.84	5.67	6.37	8.31	7.62
Gas mains mileage	1,000	1,189	1,278	1,369	1,411	1,424	1,462	1,438	1,534
Field and gathering	1,000	32	31	27	22	22	24	23	20
Transmission	1,000	292	297	297	310	304	299	297	300
Distribution	1,000	865	950	1,046	1,080	1,098	1,140	1,118	1,214
Construction expenditures [4]	Mil. dol.	7,899	10,760	8,624	11,552	13,034	16,567	10,089	10,218
Transmission	Mil. dol.	2,886	3,380	1,590	5,184	7,317	3,205	3,368	3,316
Distribution	Mil. dol.	3,714	5,394	5,437	4,890	3,870	11,636	5,129	5,165
Production and storage	Mil. dol.	309	367	138	73	258	181	179	240
General	Mil. dol.	770	1,441	1,273	1,156	1,350	1,271	1,070	1,119
Underground storage	Mil. dol.	219	177	185	249	239	274	343	379

[1] Annual average. [2] Excludes sales for resale. [3] For definition of Btu, see text, this section. [4] Includes general.

Source: American Gas Association, Arlington, VA, *Gas Facts,* annual (copyright).

Table 916. Gas Utility Industry—Customers, Sales, and Revenues by State: 2006

[65,020 represents 65,020,000. See headnote, Table 915. For definition of Btu, see text, this section]

State	Customers [1] (1,000) Total	Resi-dential	Sales [2] (tril. Btu) Total	Resi-dential	Revenues [2] (mil. dol.) Total	Resi-dential	State	Customers [1] (1,000) Total	Resi-dential	Sales [2] (tril. Btu) Total	Resi-dential	Revenues [2] (mil. dol.) Total	Resi-dential
U.S.	65,020	60,147	8,222	4,117	91,928	53,961							
AL	897	829	97	39	1,364	716	MO	1,499	1,354	154	98	2,038	1,359
AK	125	112	83	21	396	141	MT	278	245	31	20	334	219
AZ	1,146	1,089	86	37	1,097	589	NE	467	427	59	32	590	348
AR	626	556	60	33	726	446	NV	765	727	85	39	1,027	543
CA	10,763	10,300	740	506	7,900	5,779	NH	110	95	14	7	217	110
							NJ	2,754	2,541	305	201	4,110	2,894
CO	1,699	1,559	189	123	1,840	1,246	NM	580	534	50	31	567	385
CT	530	478	79	40	1,140	681	NY	4,279	3,950	509	317	6,702	4,628
DE	154	141	17	9	269	154	NC	1,135	1,022	118	58	1,704	957
DC	135	128	13	9	204	148	ND	134	117	25	10	228	104
FL	701	659	42	16	696	329	OH	2,138	1,982	228	165	3,106	2,306
GA	363	329	54	17	644	257	OK	958	880	88	54	1,025	707
HI	29	26	3	1	80	18	OR	723	648	90	42	1,122	596
ID	351	317	36	23	414	275	PA	2,629	2,416	287	195	4,457	3,115
IL	3,878	3,620	469	366	5,024	3,967	RI	247	225	26	17	424	297
IN	1,757	1,612	205	127	2,436	1,606	SC	614	555	105	26	1,234	433
IA	957	859	108	64	1,194	768	SD	182	160	24	12	235	128
KS	946	862	86	59	1,034	753	TN	1,192	1,063	149	63	1,883	900
KY	826	743	92	47	1,159	644	TX	4,403	4,068	1,473	172	11,044	2,179
LA	925	867	316	34	2,611	490	UT	811	755	99	62	994	661
ME	26	19	4	1	56	18	VT	39	34	8	3	87	41
MD	981	924	82	61	1,242	947	VA	1,112	1,028	115	67	1,619	1,045
MA	1,472	1,348	161	107	2,641	1,833	WA	1,095	998	143	78	1,715	1,009
MI	3,312	3,067	429	307	4,870	3,559	WV	388	353	46	27	649	410
MN	1,531	1,401	248	121	2,535	1,367	WI	1,776	1,612	221	124	2,389	1,468
MS	493	437	61	22	721	314	WY	87	78	13	7	136	75

[1] Averages for the year. [2] Excludes sales for resale.

Source: American Gas Association, Arlington, VA, *Gas Facts,* annual (copyright).

Table 917. Public Drinking Water Systems by Size of Community Served and Source of Water: 2006

[As of **September**. Covers systems that provide water for human consumption through pipes and other constructed conveyances to a least 15 service connections or serve an average of at least 25 persons for at least 60 days a year. Based on reported data in the Safe Drinking Water Information System maintained by the Environmental Protection Agency]

Type of system	Total	Size of community served					Water source	
		500 or fewer persons	501 to 3,300 persons	3,301 to 10,000 persons	10,001 to 100,000	100,001 persons or more	Ground water	Surface water
Total systems	**156,644**	**128,094**	**19,502**	**4,960**	**3,695**	**393**	**142,100**	**14,544**
COMMUNITY WATER SYSTEMS [1]								
Number of systems	52,339	29,448	14,098	4,745	3,659	389	40,315	12,024
Percent of systems	100	56	27	9	7	1	77	23
Population served (1,000)	281,700	4,896	20,017	27,473	103,301	126,013	85,035	196,665
Percent of population	100	2	7	10	37	45	30	70
NONTRANSIENT NONCOMMUNITY WATER SYSTEM [2]								
Number of systems	19,045	16,259	2,659	108	19	–	18,429	616
Percent of systems	100	85	14	1	–	–	97	3
Population served (1,000)	6,008	2,261	2,668	586	494	–	5,407	602
Percent of population	100	38	44	10	8	–	90	10
TRANSIENT NONCOMMUNITY WATER SYSTEM [3]								
Number of systems	85,260	82,387	2,745	107	17	4	83,356	1,904
Percent of systems	100	97	3	–	–	–	98	2
Population served (1,000)	13,981	7,261	2,691	580	454	2,994	11,281	2,699
Percent of population	100	52	19	4	3	21	81	19

– Represents zero.   [1] A public water system that supplies water to the same population year-round.   [2] A public water system that regularly supplies water to at least 25 of the same people at least 6 months per year, but not year-round. Some examples are schools, factories, and office buildings which have their own water systems.   [3] A public water system that provides water in a place such as a gas station or campground where people do not remain for long periods of time.

Source: U.S. Environmental Protection Agency, *Factoids: Drinking Water and Ground Water Statistics for 2006*, annual reports. See also <http://www.epa.gov/safewater/data/getdata.html> (published March 2008).

Table 918. Sewage Treatment Facilities: 2005

[Based on the North American Industry Classification System (NAICS), 2002; see text, Section 15]

State	Sewage treatment facilities (NAICS 22132)		State	Sewage treatment facilities (NAICS 22132)	
	Number of establishments	Paid employees		Number of establishments	Paid employees
U.S.	**750**	**6,062**	MO	21	(1)
AL	8	(1)	MT	9	(2)
AK	3	(2)	NE	3	(2)
AZ	10	24	NV	2	(2)
AR	6	35	NH	2	(2)
CA	30	(3)	NJ	13	(3)
CO	10	36	NM	6	23
CT	7	57	NY	35	294
DE	1	(2)	NC	22	(1)
DC	(NA)	(NA)	ND	(NA)	(NA)
FL	67	(4)	OH	16	(1)
GA	8	(3)	OK	10	(1)
HI	14	(1)	OR	6	(2)
ID	7	(1)	PA	96	567
IL	38	(5)	RI	3	(1)
IN	43	199	SC	11	47
IA	4	(1)	SD	2	(2)
KS	5	(1)	TN	10	84
KY	9	87	TX	66	1,344
LA	24	(3)	UT	2	(2)
ME	3	(2)	VT	2	(2)
MD	6	(2)	VA	9	(3)
MA	12	(3)	WA	6	(2)
MI	25	(1)	WV	16	83
MN	6	(1)	WI	12	(1)
MS	21	121	WY	3	36

NA Not available.   [1] 20–99 employees.   [2] 0–19 employees.   [3] 100–249 employees.   [4] 500 to 999 employees.   [5] 250–499 employees.

Source: U.S. Census Bureau, "County Business Patterns"; <http://www.census.gov/epcd/cbp/view/cbpview.html>.

Section 20
Construction and Housing

This section presents data on the construction industry and on various indicators of its activity and costs; on housing units and their characteristics and occupants; and on the characteristics and vacancy rates for commercial buildings. This edition contains data from the 2005 American Housing Survey.

The principal source of these data is the U.S. Census Bureau, which issues a variety of current publications, as well as data from the decennial census. Current construction statistics compiled by the Census Bureau appear in its *New Residential Construction* and *New Residential Sales* press releases and Web site <http://www.census.gov/const/www/>. Statistics on expenditures by owners of residential properties are issued quarterly and annually in *Expenditures for Residential Improvements and Repairs. Value of New Construction Put in Place* presents data on all types of construction. Reports of the censuses of construction industries (see below) are also issued on various topics.

Other Census Bureau publications include the *Current Housing Reports* series, which comprise the quarterly *Housing Vacancies,* the quarterly *Market Absorption of Apartments,* the biennial *American Housing Survey* (formerly *Annual Housing Survey),* and reports of the censuses of housing and of construction industries.

Other sources include the monthly *Dodge Construction Potentials* of McGraw-Hill Construction, New York, NY, which present national and state data on construction contracts; the National Association of Home Builders with state-level data on housing starts; the NATIONAL ASSOCIATION OF REALTORS®, which presents data on existing home sales; the Bureau of Economic Analysis, which presents data on residential capital and gross housing product; and the U.S. Energy Information Administration, which provides data on commercial buildings through its periodic sample surveys.

Censuses and surveys—Censuses of the construction industry were first conducted by the Census Bureau for 1929, 1935, and 1939; beginning in 1967, a census has been taken every 5 years (through 2002, for years ending in "2" and "7"). The latest reports are part of the 2002 Economic Census. See text, Section 15, Business Enterprise.

The construction sector of the economic census, covers all employer establishments primarily engaged in (1) building construction by general contractors or operative builders; (2) heavy (nonbuilding) construction by general contractors; and (3) construction by special trade contractors. This sector includes construction management and land subdividers and developers. The 2002 census was conducted in accordance with the 2002 North American Industrial Classification System (NAICS). See text, Section 15, Business Enterprise.

From 1850 through 1930, the Census Bureau collected some housing data as part of its censuses of population and agriculture. Beginning in 1940, separate censuses of housing have been taken at 10-year intervals. For the 1970 and 1980 censuses, data on year-round housing units were collected and issued on occupancy and structural characteristics, plumbing facilities, value, and rent; for 1990 such characteristics were presented for all housing units.

The American Housing Survey (*Current Housing Reports* Series H-150 and H-170), which began in 1973, provided an annual and ongoing series of data on selected housing and demographic characteristics until 1983. In 1984, the name of the survey was changed from the Annual Housing Survey. Currently, national data are collected every other year, and data for

U.S. Census Bureau, Statistical Abstract of the United States: 2009

selected metropolitan areas are collected on a rotating basis. All samples represent a cross section of the housing stock in their respective areas. Estimates are subject to both sampling and nonsampling errors; caution should therefore be used in making comparisons between years.

Data on residential mortgages were collected continuously from 1890 to 1970, except 1930, as part of the decennial census by the Census Bureau. Since 1973, mortgage status data, limited to single family homes on less than 10 acres with no business on the property, have been presented in the American Housing Survey. Data on mortgage activity are covered in Section 25, Banking and Finance.

Housing units—In general, a housing unit is a house, an apartment, a group of rooms or a single room occupied or intended for occupancy as separate living quarters; that is, the occupants live separately from any other individual in the building, and there is direct access from the outside or through a common hall. Transient accommodations, barracks for workers, and institutional-type quarters are not counted as housing units.

Statistical reliability—For a discussion of statistical collection and estimation, sampling procedures, and measures of statistical reliability applicable to Census Bureau data, see Appendix III.

U.S. Census Bureau, Statistical Abstract of the United States: 2009

Table 919. Construction—Establishments, Employees, and Payroll by Kind of Business (NAICS Basis): 2004 and 2005

[6,648 represents 6,648,000. Covers establishments with payroll. Excludes most government employees, railroad employees, and self-employed persons. Kind-of-business classification based on North American Industry Classification System (NAICS) 2002. For statement on methodology, see Appendix III]

Industry	2002 NAICS code [1]	Establishments		Paid employees [2] (1,000)		Annual payroll (mil. dol.)	
		2004	2005	2004	2005	2004	2005
Construction	**23**	**760,372**	**787,672**	**6,648**	**6,781**	**268,268**	**292,519**
Construction of buildings	236	233,617	243,567	1,579	1,613	68,877	76,180
Residential building construction	2361	190,924	200,826	873	919	35,236	40,451
New single-family housing construction (except operative builders).	236115	113,948	111,872	444	464	15,883	18,173
New multifamily housing construction (except operative builders).	236116	4,955	4,621	47	46	2,116	2,230
New housing operative builders	236117	10,774	13,213	158	166	9,944	11,756
Residential remodelers	236118	61,247	71,120	224	242	7,293	8,293
Nonresidential building construction	2362	42,693	42,741	706	694	33,641	35,728
Industrial building construction	23621	1,884	2,085	73	76	3,192	3,457
Commercial and institutional building construction	23622	40,809	40,656	633	618	30,448	32,272
Heavy and civil engineering construction	237	50,146	50,827	908	908	43,423	47,153
Utility system construction	2371	20,843	20,945	452	446	19,938	21,558
Water and sewer line and related structures . . .	23711	13,810	13,701	192	193	8,409	9,072
Oil and gas pipeline and related structures. . . .	23712	1,702	1,717	84	86	3,741	4,171
Power and communication line and related structures.	23713	5,331	5,527	176	167	7,789	8,315
Land subdivision.	2372	11,915	12,448	64	69	3,203	3,792
Highway, street, and bridge construction	2373	12,030	11,940	313	311	16,496	17,517
Other heavy and civil engineering construction. . .	2379	5,358	5,494	80	82	3,786	4,286
Specialty trade contractors.	238	476,609	493,278	4,161	4,260	155,968	169,187
Foundation, structure, and building exterior contractors	2381	113,498	115,719	1,044	1,065	35,089	38,122
Poured concrete foundation and structures contractors	23811	26,534	26,646	277	283	9,933	10,850
Structural steel and precast concrete contractors.	23812	3,500	3,524	64	65	2,596	2,815
Framing contractors	23813	18,127	18,732	162	169	4,804	5,305
Masonry contractors.	23814	26,470	26,997	225	229	7,200	7,792
Glass and glazing contractors	23815	5,292	5,328	48	48	1,779	1,905
Roofing contractors	23816	19,170	19,344	181	185	5,935	6,488
Siding contractors	23817	10,091	10,425	51	49	1,531	1,596
Other foundation, structure, and building exterior contractors	23819	4,314	4,723	36	37	1,311	1,370
Building equipment contractors	2382	171,809	177,316	1,785	1,806	73,626	78,955
Electrical contractors	23821	72,817	75,325	744	760	30,917	33,126
Plumbing, heating, and air-conditioning contractors	23822	92,898	95,478	933	936	37,416	40,073
Other building equipment contractors	23829	6,094	6,513	108	110	5,293	5,756
Building finishing contractors.	2383	123,276	129,107	863	894	28,764	31,247
Drywall and insulation contractors.	23831	20,406	21,368	294	304	10,333	11,040
Painting and wall covering contractors.	23832	39,495	41,172	217	225	6,512	7,144
Flooring contractors	23833	15,707	16,354	82	85	2,907	3,136
Tile and terrazzo contractors	23834	10,226	10,971	63	66	2,076	2,275
Finish carpentry contractors.	23835	31,501	32,921	150	156	4,871	5,403
Other building finishing contractors	23839	5,941	6,321	58	59	2,065	2,249
Other specialty trade contractors	2389	68,026	71,136	469	495	18,488	20,863
Site preparation contractors.	23891	35,622	37,749	269	289	11,017	12,590
All other specialty trade contractors.	23899	32,404	33,387	200	206	7,471	8,273

[1] North American Industry Classification System code, 2002; see text, Section 15. [2] Employees on the payroll for the pay period including March 12.

Source: U.S. Census Bureau, "County Business Patterns"; annual. See <http://www.census.gov/epcd/cbp/view/cbpview.html>.

U.S. Census Bureau, Statistical Abstract of the United States: 2009

Table 920. Construction Materials—Producer Price Indexes: 1990 to 2007

[1982 = 100, except as noted. Data for 2007 are preliminary. For discussion of producer price indexes, see text, Section 14. This index, more formally known as the special commodity grouping index for construction materials, covers materials incorporated as integral part of a building or normally installed during construction and not readily removable. Excludes consumer durables such as kitchen ranges, refrigerators, etc. This index is not the same as the stage-of-processing index of intermediate materials and components for construction]

Commodity	1990	1995	2000	2002	2003	2004	2005	2006	2007
Construction materials	**119.6**	**138.8**	**144.1**	**144.0**	**147.1**	**161.5**	**169.6**	**180.2**	**183.1**
Interior solvent-based paint	133.0	164.5	191.1	190.5	198.0	(NA)	(NA)	(NA)	(NA)
Architectural coatings	132.7	152.3	168.7	175.2	180.6	187.4	203.3	220.2	230.5
Construction products from plastics	117.2	133.8	135.8	136.1	138.6	144.6	158.8	181.8	179.1
Douglas fir, dressed	138.4	198.8	185.2	178.5	176.7	(NA)	(NA)	(NA)	(NA)
Southern pine, dressed	111.2	166.9	161.0	145.2	145.4	(NA)	(NA)	(NA)	(NA)
Softwood lumber	123.8	178.5	178.6	170.8	170.8	209.8	203.6	189.4	170.7
Millwork	130.4	163.8	176.4	179.8	181.8	191.9	197.2	201.8	201.3
Softwood plywood	119.6	188.1	173.3	164.1	195.9	250.9	223.5	190.5	197.7
Hardwood plywood and related products	102.7	122.2	130.2	131.5	129.0	134.4	138.1	(NA)	(NA)
Hardwood veneer and plywood [1]	(NA)	(NA)	(NA)	(NA)	(NA)	(NA)	(NA)	101.4	102.4
Softwood plywood veneer, excluding reinforced/backed	142.3	203.5	182.2	172.8	184.1	209.5	206.2	(NA)	(NA)
Building paper and building board mill products	112.2	144.9	138.8	129.3	159.9	192.4	184.9	173.0	155.0
Steel pipe and tubes [2]	102.6	104.4	106.6	106.7	113.3	166.3	193.3	200.8	201.9
Builders' hardware	133.0	153.2	163.8	169.3	170.3	172.9	179.2	187.8	197.8
Plumbing fixtures and brass fittings	144.3	166.0	180.4	181.9	183.4	188.3	197.6	207.2	220.8
Heating equipment	131.6	147.5	155.6	157.9	163.2	169.5	179.9	185.7	195.3
Metal doors, sash, and trim	131.4	156.5	165.1	168.0	169.9	175.8	184.9	192.9	197.3
Siding, aluminum [3]	(NA)	132.4	142.2	141.0	152.6	(NA)	(NA)	(NA)	(NA)
Sheet metal products	129.2	138.9	144.0	145.2	146.6	162.6	169.4	176.1	181.1
Outdoor lighting equipment, including parts [4]	113.0	120.8	124.7	126.2	126.9	129.4	131.8	137.7	139.8
Commercial fluorescent fixtures [5]	113.0	121.0	117.7	114.0	115.2	113.6	(NA)	(NA)	(NA)
Commercial and industrial lighting fixtures	127.5	138.9	140.3	139.5	141.9	142.3	147.0	151.9	158.3
Architectural and ornamental metalwork [6]	118.7	128.0	139.8	144.2	147.2	172.5	185.4	191.5	200.5
Fabricated ferrous wire products [2]	114.6	125.7	130.0	129.7	131.3	149.3	157.1	162.6	166.5
Elevators, escalators, and other lifts	110.1	113.0	118.7	120.0	118.7	120.5	123.5	126.0	129.4
Stamped metal switch and receptacle box	158.0	183.5	183.0	195.4	196.1	205.2	(NA)	(NA)	(NA)
Electrical conduit and conduit fittings [7]	(NA)	(NA)	(NA)	(NA)	(NA)	(NA)	106.6	116.6	111.9
Other noncurrent-carrying wiring devices [7]	(NA)	(NA)	(NA)	(NA)	(NA)	(NA)	102.3	108.0	114.1
Concrete ingredients and related products	115.3	134.7	155.6	162.6	164.8	170.4	185.3	204.9	219.8
Concrete products	113.5	129.4	147.8	152.7	153.6	161.2	177.2	195.1	203.3
Clay construction products excluding refractories	129.9	141.3	152.8	152.8	154.2	156.6	165.4	176.8	178.7
Prep asphalt and tar roofing and siding products	95.8	97.8	100.0	106.6	110.6	111.3	125.0	137.0	138.7
Gypsum products	105.2	154.5	201.4	168.9	171.5	198.8	229.6	274.9	233.7
Insulation materials	108.4	118.8	128.6	128.3	128.8	137.2	142.2	149.9	145.4
Paving mixtures and blocks	101.2	105.8	130.4	136.2	142.6	144.9	156.9	200.5	218.9

NA Not available. [1] December 2005 = 100. [2] June 1982 = 100. [3] December 1982 = 100. [4] June 1985 = 100. [5] Recessed nonair. [6] December 1983 = 100. [7] December 2004 = 100

Source: U.S. Bureau of Labor Statistics, *Producer Price Indexes,* monthly and annual. See <http://www.bls.gov/ppi/home.htm>.

Table 921. Value of New Construction Put in Place: 1980 to 2007

[In millions of dollars (273,936 represents $273,936,000,000). Represents value of construction put in place during year; differs from building permit and construction contract data in timing and coverage. Includes installed cost of normal building service equipment and selected types of industrial production equipment (largely site fabricated). Excludes cost of shipbuilding, land, and most types of machinery and equipment. For methodology, see Appendix III. For details, see Tables 922 and 923]

Year	Total	Private			Public		
		Total	Residential buildings	Non-residential	Total	Federal	State and local
1980	273,936	210,290	100,381	109,909	63,646	9,642	54,004
1985	403,416	325,601	160,520	165,081	77,815	12,004	65,811
1990	476,778	369,300	191,103	178,197	107,478	12,099	95,379
1991	432,592	322,483	166,251	156,232	110,109	12,845	97,264
1992	463,661	347,814	199,393	148,421	115,847	14,376	101,471
1993	502,435	375,073	225,067	150,006	127,362	14,424	112,938
1994	549,420	418,999	258,561	160,438	130,421	14,440	115,981
1995	567,896	427,885	247,351	180,534	140,011	15,751	124,260
1996	623,313	476,638	281,115	195,523	146,675	15,325	131,350
1997	656,171	502,734	289,014	213,720	153,437	14,087	139,350
1998	706,779	552,001	314,607	237,394	154,778	14,318	140,460
1999	768,811	599,729	350,562	249,167	169,082	14,025	155,057
2000	831,075	649,750	374,457	275,293	181,325	14,166	167,157
2001	864,159	662,247	388,324	273,922	201,912	15,081	186,830
2002	873,090	659,651	421,912	237,739	213,438	16,578	196,860
2003	921,403	705,276	475,941	229,335	216,127	17,913	198,214
2004	1,023,487	803,305	564,827	238,478	220,183	18,342	201,841
2005	1,132,149	897,989	641,345	256,644	234,160	17,300	216,860
2006	1,192,238	937,047	641,332	295,715	255,191	17,603	237,588
2007	1,161,742	875,010	525,443	349,566	286,733	19,336	267,397

Source: U.S. Census Bureau, "Construction Spending"; <http://www.census.gov/const/www/c30index.html>.

Table 922. **Value of Private Construction Put in Place: 1995 to 2007**

[**In millions of dollars (427,885 represents $427,885,000,000).** Represents value of construction put in place during year; differs from building permit and construction contract data in timing and coverage. See Appendix III and Tables 921 and 923]

Type of construction	1995	2000	2001	2002	2003	2004	2005	2006	2007
Total construction [1]	**427,885**	**649,750**	**662,247**	**659,651**	**705,276**	**803,305**	**897,989**	**937,047**	**875,010**
Residential	247,351	374,457	388,324	421,912	475,941	564,827	641,345	641,332	525,443
New single family	153,515	236,788	249,086	265,889	310,575	377,557	433,510	415,997	303,447
New multifamily	17,889	28,259	30,305	32,952	35,116	39,944	47,297	53,020	49,149
Improvements	75,947	109,410	108,933	123,071	130,250	147,326	160,538	172,315	172,848
Nonresidential	180,534	275,293	273,922	237,739	229,335	238,478	256,644	295,715	349,566
Lodging	7,131	16,304	14,519	10,467	9,930	11,982	12,666	17,687	28,604
Office [1]	22,996	52,407	49,745	35,296	30,579	32,879	37,276	46,194	55,195
General	20,569	49,637	47,136	32,356	27,380	28,679	32,962	41,390	49,785
Financial	2,339	2,689	2,586	2,857	3,174	4,186	4,285	4,742	5,281
Commercial [1]	44,096	64,055	63,606	59,008	57,505	63,195	66,584	72,148	81,745
Automotive [1]	4,191	5,967	5,650	5,807	5,039	5,235	5,614	5,463	6,353
Sales	883	1,629	2,014	2,235	2,099	2,443	2,834	2,306	2,564
Service/parts	2,448	3,009	2,394	2,308	1,866	1,978	1,805	2,089	2,394
Parking	860	1,330	1,242	1,265	1,074	814	975	1,068	1,395
Food/beverage [1]	7,169	8,786	8,765	7,914	8,369	8,232	7,795	7,417	7,761
Food	3,062	4,792	4,300	4,207	4,234	3,590	3,128	2,773	2,849
Dining/drinking	3,408	2,935	3,441	2,916	3,321	3,937	4,078	3,735	3,799
Fast food	699	1,058	1,024	792	813	705	590	908	1,113
Multiretail [1]	11,976	14,911	16,373	15,581	15,400	18,828	22,750	29,126	33,207
General merchandise	5,339	5,100	5,066	6,009	5,341	6,416	6,740	5,849	7,471
Shopping center	4,086	6,803	7,769	6,605	6,867	9,256	12,462	18,446	20,649
Shopping mall	2,175	2,523	2,701	2,108	2,231	2,138	2,631	3,320	4,064
Other commercial [1]	8,432	13,537	11,945	12,083	11,249	13,341	11,744	10,574	12,823
Drug store	536	1,682	1,185	1,644	1,790	1,427	1,315	1,301	1,479
Building supply store	1,372	2,592	3,016	2,471	2,268	2,521	2,416	2,628	3,618
Other stores	5,653	8,136	6,995	7,145	6,214	8,229	7,075	5,707	6,914
Warehouse	9,299	14,822	15,691	11,908	12,345	12,074	12,827	14,292	15,790
General commercial	8,944	13,511	14,440	10,934	11,004	10,830	11,468	13,298	14,552
Farm	3,014	5,988	5,135	5,611	5,103	5,485	5,854	5,277	5,812
Health care	15,259	19,455	19,506	22,438	24,217	26,272	28,495	33,183	36,780
Hospital	8,807	10,183	11,313	13,925	15,234	16,147	18,250	22,860	25,915
Medical building	4,064	5,066	4,638	4,924	6,068	7,615	8,031	7,292	7,631
Special care	2,388	4,206	3,555	3,538	2,915	2,510	2,213	3,032	3,234
Educational [1]	5,699	11,683	12,846	13,109	13,424	12,701	12,788	13,745	16,572
Preschool	326	770	874	593	711	674	516	489	703
Primary/secondary	1,245	2,948	3,536	3,605	3,204	3,202	2,718	3,205	3,845
Higher education [1]	3,055	6,333	6,597	6,875	7,259	6,496	6,946	7,561	9,420
Instructional	1,712	3,058	3,210	3,619	3,701	3,200	3,556	3,454	4,052
Dormitory	483	1,356	1,555	1,528	1,761	1,669	1,537	2,085	2,947
Sports/recreation	192	645	755	772	677	739	821	854	870
Other educational	817	1,318	1,421	1,651	1,785	1,998	2,294	2,067	2,235
Gallery/museum	571	920	990	1,312	1,371	1,335	1,745	1,675	1,993
Religious	4,348	8,030	8,393	8,335	8,559	8,153	7,715	7,690	7,464
House of worship	2,951	5,656	6,040	6,021	6,238	6,015	5,992	6,231	6,309
Other religious	1,389	2,347	2,330	2,312	2,322	2,138	1,723	1,459	1,155
Auxiliary building	619	1,280	1,247	1,358	1,296	1,258	1,251	1,190	1,014
Public safety	185	423	274	217	185	289	408	448	500
Amusement and recreation [1]	5,886	8,768	7,828	7,478	7,781	8,432	7,507	9,041	9,350
Theme/amusement park	563	747	462	230	270	198	200	386	486
Sports	910	1,068	1,067	1,427	1,306	900	807	839	1,682
Fitness	637	1,152	1,294	1,286	1,262	1,141	1,425	1,999	1,770
Performance/meeting center	365	732	977	900	844	1,054	1,072	783	834
Social center	1,558	2,368	2,337	2,285	1,996	2,594	1,626	1,478	1,482
Movie theater/studio	848	1,461	792	568	855	1,218	1,248	1,214	1,085
Transportation [1]	4,759	6,879	7,058	6,773	6,568	6,841	7,124	7,937	8,775
Air	666	1,804	1,993	1,281	1,012	869	748	715	613
Land	4,008	4,907	4,883	5,325	5,462	5,800	6,214	7,049	7,818
Railroad	3,509	4,263	4,456	4,584	4,851	5,392	5,816	6,589	7,212
Communication	11,112	18,799	19,596	18,384	14,456	15,468	18,846	21,621	26,194
Power [1]	22,006	29,344	31,499	32,608	33,619	27,360	26,304	30,481	39,465
Electricity	14,274	23,374	25,270	24,998	25,592	20,431	19,192	21,660	27,843
Gas	6,279	4,891	5,078	6,080	6,358	5,096	5,239	5,741	7,409
Oil	929	1,003	943	1,193	1,068	1,579	1,293	1,876	2,617
Sewage and waste disposal	576	508	402	246	278	331	240	284	328
Water supply	670	714	563	397	393	405	326	445	431
Manufacturing [1]	35,364	37,583	37,815	22,744	21,434	23,667	29,886	34,278	37,599
Food/beverage/tobacco	4,525	3,985	4,088	2,817	2,695	3,157	4,677	4,892	3,985
Textile/apparel/leather & allied	824	413	307	284	218	188	415	146	26
Wood	616	483	343	477	376	485	982	1,505	680
Paper	1,448	479	1,265	584	818	548	467	562	489
Print/publishing	1,197	848	1,232	666	630	654	777	748	240
Petroleum/coal	4,741	1,255	1,171	887	717	1,204	771	1,666	2,490
Chemical	5,531	3,798	4,896	5,625	5,368	5,507	6,588	9,239	12,981
Plastic/rubber	1,475	1,645	1,379	776	659	936	877	839	804
Nonmetallic mineral	856	1,898	2,216	536	865	896	1,163	1,961	3,806
Primary metal	2,533	1,976	773	241	436	312	836	1,489	1,378
Fabricated metal	808	2,148	1,447	833	662	595	699	568	509
Machinery	1,275	864	863	797	707	645	917	924	558
Computer/electronic/electrical	6,332	6,392	6,029	1,918	1,444	2,835	4,247	4,324	2,726
Transportation equipment	2,382	6,318	6,901	3,832	3,314	2,610	3,702	2,557	3,458
Furniture	213	148	232	148	278	217	96	131	173

[1] Includes other types of construction not shown separately.

Source: U.S. Census Bureau, "Construction Spending"; <http://www.census.gov/const/www/c30index.html>.

Table 923. Value of State and Local Government Construction Put in Place: 1995 to 2007

[In millions of dollars (124,260 represents $124,260,000,000). See Tables 921 and 922]

Type of construction	1995	2000	2001	2002	2003	2004	2005	2006	2007
Total construction [1]	124,260	167,157	186,830	196,860	198,214	201,841	216,860	237,588	267,397
Residential	4,483	2,962	3,493	3,754	3,724	4,110	4,047	4,340	5,073
Multifamily	4,410	2,945	3,440	3,671	3,593	3,956	3,740	4,027	4,485
Nonresidential	119,778	164,196	183,337	193,106	194,490	197,731	212,813	233,248	262,325
Office	3,275	4,494	5,557	6,274	6,116	6,024	5,211	5,478	6,174
Commercial [1]	1,117	1,820	2,462	2,422	2,207	1,979	1,882	1,580	1,614
Automotive	808	1,233	1,927	1,714	1,599	1,501	1,490	1,199	1,023
Parking	664	1,143	1,913	1,693	1,562	1,356	1,357	1,054	954
Warehouse	199	330	301	293	318	276	218	189	379
Health care	2,648	2,829	2,942	3,490	4,005	5,025	5,059	5,514	6,996
Hospital	1,644	1,949	2,124	2,539	2,685	3,324	3,429	4,014	5,242
Medical building	673	490	487	509	876	1,211	1,168	904	961
Special care	331	390	331	442	444	490	463	597	794
Educational [1]	27,458	46,818	52,813	59,463	59,340	59,741	65,750	70,931	80,030
Primary/secondary [1]	18,708	33,764	36,670	41,972	40,316	40,990	44,184	48,691	56,111
Elementary	5,598	12,272	14,105	15,154	13,430	14,308	14,251	14,194	17,357
Middle/junior high	3,999	5,820	6,923	8,410	7,921	8,132	9,069	10,948	11,992
High	5,144	13,326	14,072	17,142	18,561	17,950	19,892	22,952	26,057
Higher education [1]	7,354	10,749	13,365	14,280	15,451	15,864	18,033	19,102	21,002
Instructional	4,566	6,317	7,874	7,982	9,042	8,699	9,275	9,496	11,611
Parking	169	514	561	432	508	765	1,013	913	840
Administration	136	294	199	456	236	303	387	654	502
Dormitory	348	1,078	1,429	1,620	2,074	2,673	2,918	3,414	2,685
Library	321	308	374	440	544	524	588	492	758
Student union/cafeteria	254	322	618	1,031	702	632	880	996	1,409
Sports/recreation	667	966	1,287	1,546	1,329	1,370	1,769	1,783	1,713
Infrastructure	844	835	835	545	613	867	1,138	1,249	1,324
Other educational	1,185	1,645	2,164	2,629	2,687	2,357	2,735	2,335	1,955
Library/archive	752	976	1,675	2,118	1,815	1,501	2,098	1,870	1,367
Public safety [1]	4,956	5,854	6,056	5,960	5,844	5,477	6,013	6,618	8,621
Correctional	4,056	4,754	4,894	4,554	4,204	3,771	3,958	4,609	5,505
Detention	3,383	3,907	3,838	3,418	3,148	2,787	2,936	3,302	4,137
Police/sheriff	673	848	1,057	1,135	1,056	985	1,022	1,307	1,367
Other public safety	858	1,100	1,161	1,406	1,640	1,705	2,055	2,009	3,117
Fire/rescue	546	994	991	1,227	1,359	1,441	1,675	1,626	2,466
Amusement and recreation [1]	5,140	7,583	9,143	9,215	8,354	7,794	7,340	8,943	10,819
Sports	1,369	2,289	2,709	2,569	2,065	1,746	1,587	1,864	2,014
Performance/meeting center	1,466	2,075	2,915	2,915	2,260	2,061	1,921	2,043	1,812
Convention center	1,025	1,397	2,268	2,130	1,545	1,350	1,350	1,409	1,109
Social center	648	1,152	1,432	1,446	1,606	1,476	1,006	1,251	1,323
Neighborhood center	487	886	1,065	934	1,221	1,312	866	1,060	1,018
Park/camp	1,418	1,930	1,846	1,928	1,999	2,303	2,728	3,657	5,350
Transportation	9,559	13,000	15,868	17,312	16,483	16,440	16,256	17,447	20,910
Air [1]	4,104	6,700	7,849	8,123	8,146	8,715	8,993	9,651	11,457
Passenger terminal	1,289	2,930	2,770	3,040	3,778	3,972	3,310	3,728	5,151
Runway	2,313	3,196	4,354	4,305	3,793	4,049	4,861	4,915	5,326
Land [1]	4,278	5,165	6,253	7,291	7,207	6,415	5,936	6,518	7,419
Passenger terminal	1,224	1,253	1,557	1,860	2,099	1,368	907	981	1,191
Mass transit	1,851	1,484	2,492	3,375	3,160	3,067	3,208	3,152	3,593
Railroad	492	1,471	1,095	674	449	349	552	307	490
Water [1]	1,177	1,136	1,766	1,899	1,130	1,309	1,327	1,278	2,034
Dock/marina	737	863	1,258	1,203	894	1,028	930	916	1,481
Dry dock/marine terminal	217	236	483	695	235	281	397	362	553
Power	5,686	5,501	5,267	3,771	6,785	7,044	8,320	7,804	9,782
Electrical	4,087	5,257	4,963	3,244	6,041	5,851	7,091	7,143	8,712
Distribution	1,323	2,087	1,397	1,158	2,144	1,856	1,786	2,213	2,346
Highway and street [1]	38,553	51,574	56,428	56,660	56,251	57,351	63,157	70,946	75,754
Pavement	29,883	37,929	41,125	40,962	39,294	40,274	45,177	46,018	47,818
Lighting	676	856	1,228	888	1,156	1,146	1,232	1,059	1,675
Retaining wall	192	1,099	624	742	565	552	675	1,542	1,045
Tunnel	354	894	1,069	657	619	521	373	199	231
Bridge	6,788	9,302	10,910	11,741	12,980	13,150	14,244	19,905	22,918
Toll/weigh	156	325	104	217	180	233	320	660	420
Maintenance building	54	293	407	297	244	170	96	213	104
Rest facility/streetscape	172	878	961	1,155	1,213	1,306	1,042	1,351	1,524
Sewage and waste disposal [1]	12,976	14,000	14,157	15,334	15,625	17,084	18,336	21,292	23,071
Sewage/dry waste [1]	7,452	9,338	9,038	9,956	9,812	10,836	11,717	13,244	13,818
Plant	2,527	2,765	2,404	2,680	2,735	3,095	3,369	3,355	3,691
Line/pump station	4,581	6,326	6,375	7,082	6,934	7,574	8,243	9,718	9,800
Waste water	5,413	4,663	5,120	5,378	5,813	6,248	6,620	8,048	9,253
Plant	3,777	3,229	3,818	4,227	4,403	4,658	5,231	6,019	7,319
Line/drain	1,636	1,434	1,302	1,151	1,410	1,591	1,389	2,029	1,934
Water supply [1]	7,270	9,528	11,447	11,674	11,711	11,977	13,483	14,227	14,896
Plant	1,846	3,067	4,070	3,824	4,309	4,418	4,943	5,010	5,548
Well	331	378	394	555	365	318	360	622	655
Line	3,889	4,644	5,300	5,195	4,944	5,307	6,234	5,840	6,086
Pump station	444	625	684	852	767	705	776	1,293	1,179
Reservoir	320	266	410	463	450	503	502	695	576
Tank/tower	376	548	588	785	876	727	668	767	834
Conservation and development [1]	1,068	933	1,077	1,012	1,020	1,466	1,752	2,021	2,328
Dam/levee	275	303	242	279	231	297	405	603	673
Breakwater/jetty	300	270	490	397	514	654	726	811	658

[1] Includes other types of construction, not shown separately.

Source: U.S. Census Bureau, "Construction Spending"; <http://www.census.gov/const/www/c30index.html>.

590   Construction and Housing

Table 924. Construction Contracts—Value of Construction and Floor Space of Buildings by Class of Construction: 1980 to 2007

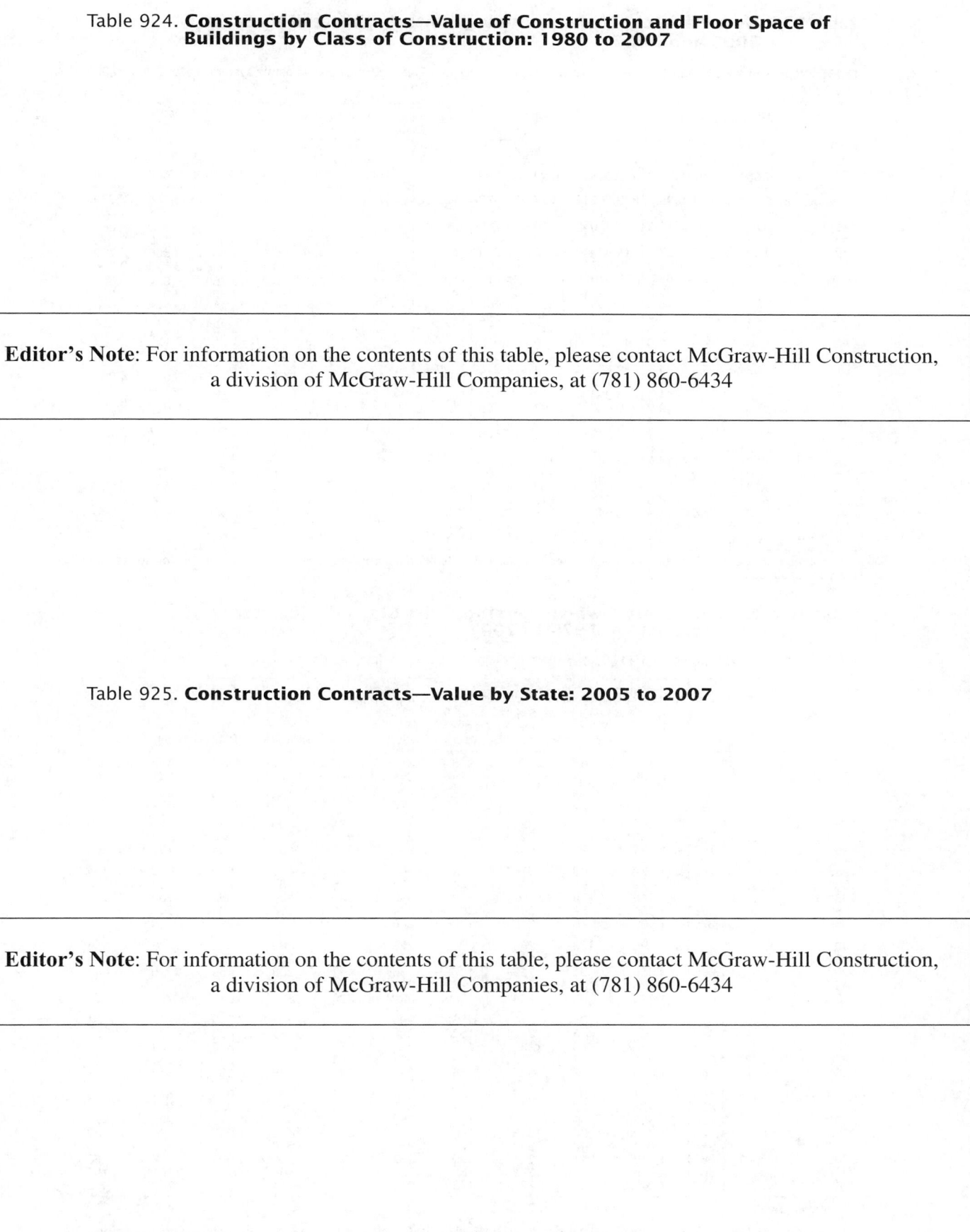

Editor's Note: For information on the contents of this table, please contact McGraw-Hill Construction, a division of McGraw-Hill Companies, at (781) 860-6434

Table 925. Construction Contracts—Value by State: 2005 to 2007

Editor's Note: For information on the contents of this table, please contact McGraw-Hill Construction, a division of McGraw-Hill Companies, at (781) 860-6434

Construction and Housing   591

Table 926. New Privately Owned Housing Units Authorized by State: 2005 and 2007

[**2,155.3 represents 2,155,300.** Based on about 20,000 places in United States having building permit systems in 2005 and 20,000 in 2007]

State	Housing units (1,000) 2005	2007 Total	2007 1 unit	Valuation (mil. dol.) 2005	2007 Total	2007 1 unit	State	Housing units (1,000) 2005	2007 Total	2007 1 unit	Valuation (mil. dol.) 2005	2007 Total	2007 1 unit
U.S..	2,155.3	1,398.4	979.9	329,255	225,237	183,679	MO . . .	33.1	21.5	14.9	4,702	3,128	2,679
							MT . . .	4.8	4.2	3.0	691	624	509
AL . . .	30.6	25.8	18.9	4,110	3,200	2,750	NE . . .	9.9	7.6	6.0	1,277	970	861
AK . . .	2.9	1.7	1.0	525	329	227	NV . . .	47.7	27.2	16.3	6,547	4,150	2,276
AZ . . .	90.9	49.6	37.7	14,487	8,213	7,019	NH . . .	7.6	4.6	3.8	1,352	856	778
AR . . .	17.9	11.0	8.0	2,257	1,437	1,200	NJ. . . .	38.6	25.4	13.1	4,993	3,675	2,604
CA . . .	205.0	110.1	68.3	38,370	21,335	15,896	NM . . .	14.2	9.2	8.2	2,169	1,694	1,607
CO . . .	45.9	29.5	20.5	8,803	6,131	5,035	NY . . .	61.9	54.1	17.1	7,828	7,091	3,688
CT . . .	11.9	7.7	5.3	2,201	1,736	1,440	NC . . .	97.9	85.8	70.3	14,814	14,298	12,956
DE . . .	8.2	5.3	4.4	988	636	562	ND . . .	4.0	3.4	2.2	458	446	354
DC . . .	2.9	1.9	0.6	228	217	79	OH . . .	47.7	27.1	20.5	7,870	4,704	4,235
FL. . . .	287.3	102.6	70.0	46,803	17,999	13,972	OK . . .	18.4	14.7	12.1	2,490	2,137	2,001
GA . . .	109.3	73.2	55.2	14,074	10,439	8,846	OR . . .	31.0	21.1	15.3	5,483	4,000	3,406
HI. . . .	9.8	7.0	4.5	2,050	1,724	1,313	PA . . .	44.5	33.7	27.5	6,776	5,362	4,861
ID. . . .	21.6	12.1	9.6	3,512	2,111	1,836	RI. . . .	2.8	1.9	1.4	384	329	292
IL. . . .	66.9	43.0	24.5	10,964	6,936	5,261	SC . . .	54.2	40.6	32.8	7,761	6,319	5,627
IN. . . .	38.5	23.8	19.2	5,807	3,893	3,508	SD . . .	5.7	5.1	3.6	693	638	524
IA. . . .	16.8	11.2	8.7	2,383	1,746	1,519	TN . . .	46.6	37.4	29.5	6,601	5,337	4,708
KS . . .	14.0	11.5	8.1	2,043	1,741	1,506	TX . . .	210.6	177.0	118.5	26,830	24,778	20,021
KY . . .	21.2	14.9	11.6	2,629	1,984	1,754	UT . . .	27.8	20.3	16.5	4,553	3,966	3,502
LA . . .	22.8	23.4	16.6	2,744	3,154	2,552	VT . . .	2.9	2.1	1.6	441	350	301
ME . . .	9.0	5.9	5.1	1,362	934	863	VA . . .	61.5	38.4	30.9	8,989	6,357	5,623
MD . . .	30.2	18.6	13.2	4,688	3,769	3,147	WA . . .	53.0	47.4	30.4	8,742	8,130	6,223
MA . . .	24.5	15.4	8.9	4,050	2,913	2,135	WV . . .	6.1	4.8	3.9	996	720	676
MI. . . .	45.3	17.8	15.2	6,642	2,908	2,673	WI. . . .	35.3	21.8	16.3	5,554	3,624	3,062
MN . . .	36.5	17.9	14.5	6,291	3,375	2,993	WY . . .	4.0	4.6	3.7	657	812	765
MS . . .	13.4	16.8	10.9	1,594	1,885	1,457							

Source: U.S. Census Bureau, Construction Reports, "New Residential Construction." See <http://www.census.gov/const/www/newresconstindex.html>.

Table 927. New Privately Owned Housing Units Started—Selected Characteristics: 1970 to 2007

[**In thousands (1,434 represents 1,434,000).** For composition of regions, see map inside front cover]

Year	Total units	Structures with— 1 unit	2 to 4 units	5 or more units	Region North-east	Mid-west	South	West	Units for sale Total	Single-family	Multi-family
1970	1,434	813	85	536	218	294	612	311	(NA)	(NA)	(NA)
1975	1,160	892	64	204	149	294	442	275	576	531	45
1980	1,292	852	110	331	125	218	643	306	689	526	163
1981	1,084	705	91	288	117	165	562	240	584	426	158
1982	1,062	663	80	320	117	149	591	205	549	409	140
1983	1,703	1,068	113	522	168	218	935	382	923	713	210
1984	1,750	1,084	121	544	204	243	866	436	934	728	206
1985	1,742	1,072	93	576	252	240	782	468	867	713	154
1986	1,805	1,179	84	542	294	296	733	483	925	782	143
1987	1,621	1,146	65	409	269	298	634	420	862	732	130
1988	1,488	1,081	59	348	235	274	575	404	808	709	99
1989	1,376	1,003	55	318	179	266	536	396	735	648	87
1990	1,193	895	38	260	131	253	479	329	585	529	56
1991	1,014	840	36	138	113	233	414	254	531	490	41
1992	1,200	1,030	31	139	127	288	497	288	659	618	41
1993	1,288	1,126	29	133	127	298	562	302	760	716	44
1994	1,457	1,198	35	224	138	329	639	351	815	763	52
1995	1,354	1,076	34	244	118	290	615	331	763	712	51
1996	1,477	1,161	45	271	132	322	662	361	833	774	59
1997	1,474	1,134	45	296	137	304	670	363	843	784	59
1998	1,617	1,271	43	303	149	331	743	395	941	882	59
1999	1,641	1,302	32	307	156	347	746	392	981	912	69
2000	1,569	1,231	39	299	155	318	714	383	946	871	75
2001	1,603	1,273	37	293	149	330	732	391	990	919	71
2002	1,705	1,359	39	308	158	350	782	416	1,070	999	71
2003	1,848	1,499	34	315	163	374	839	472	1,207	1,120	87
2004	1,956	1,611	42	303	175	356	909	516	1,360	1,240	120
2005	2,068	1,716	41	311	190	357	996	525	1,508	1,358	150
2006	1,801	1,465	43	293	167	280	910	444	1,272	1,121	151
2007	1,355	1,046	32	277	143	210	681	321	875	760	115

NA Not available.

Source: U.S. Census Bureau, Construction Reports, "New Residential Construction." See <http://www.census.gov/const/www/newresconstindex.html>.

592   Construction and Housing

Table 928. **New Privately Owned Housing Units Started by State: 2000 to 2006**

[In thousands of units (1,573 represents 1,573,000)]

State	2000	2004, est.	2005, est.	2006, est. Total units	2006, est. Single-family units	State	2000	2004, est.	2005, est.	2006, est. Total units	2006, est. Single-family units
U.S. . . .	**1,573**	**1,724**	**1,658**	**1,614**	**1,319**	MO	27.4	27.7	27.5	27.5	24.3
AL.	21.2	20.8	20.9	21.1	18.2	MT.	2.4	2.9	2.9	2.8	2.0
AK.	2.0	2.3	2.3	2.3	1.6	NE.	9.2	10.5	10.0	9.7	8.5
AZ.	59.4	64.4	61.9	60.1	53.2	NV.	31.0	37.8	36.1	35.0	27.9
AR.	12.5	13.8	13.6	13.6	10.4	NH.	6.4	7.4	7.0	6.6	5.6
CA.	137.1	177.7	165.0	154.2	120.3	NJ.	31.4	27.2	26.5	26.1	20.7
CO.	52.5	35.9	36.8	37.7	31.7	NM.	7.3	10.6	10.3	10.1	8.9
CT.	8.9	8.6	8.5	8.5	7.7	NY.	41.1	41.0	38.8	37.5	22.0
DE.	4.4	6.2	5.9	5.7	5.4	NC.	76.1	72.8	71.1	70.2	59.3
DC.	0.4	0.4	0.4	0.4	0.1	ND.	2.4	3.6	3.4	3.3	2.3
FL.	147.9	185.7	173.6	165.4	123.7	OH.	47.8	51.2	49.7	48.8	41.7
GA.	90.4	89.3	86.1	84.1	71.0	OK.	14.1	14.6	14.3	14.2	12.6
HI	4.7	6.8	6.5	6.2	5.1	OR.	18.8	19.2	19.6	20.0	15.6
ID	11.3	13.5	13.1	12.8	11.1	PA.	39.2	40.4	39.4	39.0	34.6
IL.	51.3	61.5	58.5	56.6	45.2	RI	2.6	2.4	2.4	2.4	2.0
IN	38.2	40.4	39.4	38.8	33.5	SC.	31.6	35.1	33.4	32.3	27.2
IA	12.8	15.3	14.6	14.1	11.5	SD.	4.4	5.2	4.9	4.8	4.0
KS.	13.4	14.0	13.8	13.8	11.7	TN.	34.6	34.3	34.2	34.3	30.4
KY.	21.8	20.4	20.4	20.5	17.9	TX.	145.0	163.3	154.9	149.1	117.8
LA.	15.5	18.7	18.0	17.7	15.2	UT.	18.1	20.2	19.9	19.8	16.7
ME.	6.3	7.3	6.8	6.5	6.0	VT.	2.6	2.8	2.7	2.6	2.4
MD.	28.7	27.4	27.1	27.0	22.5	VA.	47.5	53.4	51.8	50.6	43.2
MA.	17.1	16.2	16.0	16.0	12.8	WA	36.9	38.8	38.3	38.2	29.9
MI	50.4	53.4	51.7	50.7	45.2	WV	5.3	5.4	5.4	5.4	5.1
MN.	32.9	41.7	39.0	37.1	31.9	WI	32.6	38.1	36.7	35.8	27.9
MS.	14.1	12.8	12.8	12.9	11.1	WY	1.9	2.2	2.2	2.3	2.1

Source: National Association of Home Builders, Economics Division, Washington, DC. Data provided by the Econometric Forecasting Service.

Table 929. **Characteristics of New Privately Owned One-Family Houses Completed: 1990 to 2007**

[**Percent distribution, except total houses. (966 represents 966,000).** Data are percent distribution of characteristics for all houses completed (includes new houses completed, houses built for sale completed, contractor-built and owner-built houses completed, and houses completed for rent). Percents exclude houses for which characteristics specified were not reported]

Characteristic	1990	2000	2005	2007	Characteristic	1990	2000	2005	2007
Total houses (1,000)	966	1,242	1,636	1,218	**Bedrooms . . . .**	100	100	100	100
					2 or less	15	11	12	12
Construction type	100	100	100	100	3	57	54	49	50
Site built	(NA)	94	96	96	4 or more	29	35	39	38
Modular	(NA)	3	3	3					
Other	(NA)	3	2	2	**Bathrooms . . . .**	100	100	100	100
					1-1/2 or less	13	7	4	5
Exterior wall material	100	100	100	100	2	42	39	36	36
Brick	18	20	20	23	2-1/2 or more	45	54	59	59
Wood	39	14	7	8					
Stucco	18	17	22	23	**Heating fuel. . . . .**	100	100	100	100
Vinyl siding [1]	(NA)	39	34	30	Gas	59	70	66	60
Aluminum siding	5	1	1	(Z)	Electricity	33	27	31	38
Other [1]	20	7	16	16	Oil	5	3	2	1
					Other	3	1	1	1
Floor area	100	100	100	100					
Under 1,200 sq. ft	11	6	4	4	**Heating system . . . .**	100	100	100	100
1,200 to 1,599 sq. ft	22	18	16	14	Warm air furnace	65	71	67	62
1,600 to 1,999 sq. ft	22	23	20	20	Electric heat pump	23	23	29	34
2,000 to 2,399 sq. ft	17	18	18	17	Other	12	6	4	4
2,400 sq. ft. and over	29	35	42	45					
Average (sq. ft.)	2,080	2,266	2,434	2,521	**Central air-conditioning . . .**	100	100	100	100
Median (sq. ft.)	1,905	2,057	2,227	2,277	With	76	85	89	90
					Without	24	15	11	10
Number of stories	100	100	100	100					
1	46	47	44	43	**Fireplaces . . . .**	100	100	100	100
2 or more	49	52	55	56	No fireplace	34	40	45	48
Split level	4	1	(Z)	(Z)	1 or more	66	60	55	51
Foundation	100	100	100	100	**Parking facilities . . . .**	100	100	100	100
Full or partial basement. . .	38	37	31	28	Garage	82	89	91	89
Slab.	40	46	53	54	Carport.	2	1	1	1
Crawl space	21	17	16	19	No garage or carport	16	11	8	9

NA Not available.   Z Less than 0.5 percent.   [1] Prior to 2000, "other" includes vinyl siding.

Source: U.S. Census Bureau, "Characteristics of New Housing"; <http://www.census.gov/const/www/charindex.html>.

U.S. Census Bureau, Statistical Abstract of the United States: 2009

Table 930. Housing Starts and Average Length of Time from Start to Completion of New Privately Owned One-Unit Residential Buildings: 1980 to 2007

[**852 represents 852,000.** For buildings started in permit-issuing places]

Year	Total [1]	Purpose of construction			Region [2]			
		Built for sale	Contractor built	Owner built	North-east	Midwest	South	West
STARTS (1,000)								
1980	852	526	149	164	87	142	428	196
1985	1,072	713	177	157	182	148	504	239
1990	895	529	196	147	104	193	371	226
1995	1,076	712	199	133	102	234	485	256
1997	1,134	784	189	131	111	238	507	278
1998	1,271	882	209	144	122	273	574	303
1999	1,302	912	208	142	126	289	580	308
2000	1,231	871	195	128	118	260	556	297
2001	1,273	919	186	129	111	269	590	303
2002	1,359	999	198	125	118	277	628	336
2003	1,499	1,120	205	127	116	309	686	388
2004	1,611	1,240	198	130	128	306	743	433
2005	1,716	1,358	197	129	138	306	831	441
2006	1,465	1,121	189	119	118	235	757	356
2007	1,046	760	151	104	93	171	540	242
COMPLETION (months)								
1980	6.9	6.2	5.5	10.1	7.7	8.0	6.1	7.4
1985	6.2	5.4	4.9	10.6	7.2	6.0	5.7	6.7
1990	6.4	5.9	5.3	10.3	9.3	5.6	5.7	6.9
1995	5.9	5.2	5.8	9.5	7.4	6.0	5.4	6.0
1997	6.0	5.2	5.9	9.8	7.3	6.2	5.6	5.8
1998	6.0	5.4	6.0	9.5	7.1	6.2	5.5	6.1
1999	6.1	5.5	6.4	9.2	7.0	6.4	5.7	6.3
2000	6.2	5.6	6.5	9.2	7.5	6.4	5.9	6.0
2001	6.2	5.6	7.0	9.2	7.6	6.5	5.8	6.3
2002	6.1	5.5	6.6	9.6	7.3	6.4	5.6	6.2
2003	6.2	5.5	6.8	9.9	7.5	6.7	5.7	6.2
2004	6.2	5.7	7.0	9.1	7.3	6.7	5.8	6.3
2005	6.4	5.9	7.6	9.8	7.7	6.6	6.0	6.8
2006	6.9	6.3	7.8	10.7	8.3	7.1	6.3	7.4
2007	7.1	6.5	7.9	10.2	8.5	7.4	6.5	8.0

[1] Includes units built for rent not shown separately. [2] For composition of regions, see map inside front cover.

Source: U.S. Census Bureau, "New Residential Construction." See <http://www.census.gov/const/www/newresconstindex.html>.

Table 931. Price Indexes of New One-Family Houses Sold, by Region: 1980 to 2007

[**1996 = 100.** Based on kinds of homes sold in 1996. Includes value of the lot. For composition of regions, see map, inside front cover]

Year	Total	Northeast	Midwest	South	West
1980	38.9	30.2	41.2	44.4	31.9
1982	43.0	34.0	46.4	49.8	34.3
1983	43.9	36.1	46.2	51.2	34.9
1984	45.7	39.2	49.0	52.8	36.2
1985	46.2	43.1	48.2	53.9	36.4
1986	48.0	49.5	51.0	55.5	37.3
1987	50.6	56.2	54.4	57.6	39.3
1988	52.5	57.6	56.8	58.8	41.4
1989	54.6	59.2	58.1	60.5	44.0
1990	55.7	58.0	58.6	60.6	46.2
1991	56.4	56.2	60.1	61.8	46.4
1992	57.2	60.5	61.2	62.4	46.7
1993	59.4	57.4	65.2	65.5	47.8
1994	62.9	62.0	69.4	68.1	51.9
1995	64.3	62.3	70.9	70.1	52.7
1996	66.0	63.2	72.5	71.2	55.3
1997	67.5	65.9	74.3	72.7	56.5
1998	69.2	66.1	76.0	74.4	58.4
1999	72.8	69.1	79.5	78.1	62.0
2000	75.6	73.0	83.5	80.6	64.4
2001	77.9	76.7	84.4	82.8	67.1
2002	81.4	80.2	86.1	86.3	71.5
2003	86.0	84.3	90.6	89.4	78.2
2004	92.8	91.6	96.7	94.4	88.2
2005	100.0	100.0	100.0	100.0	100.0
2006	104.7	102.6	102.9	105.4	105.2
2007	104.9	101.5	102.8	107.4	102.6

Source: U.S. Census Bureau, "Construction Price Indexes." See <http://www.census.gov/const/www/constpriceindex.html>.

Table 932. New Privately Owned One-Family Houses Sold by Region and Type of Financing, 1980 to 2007, and by Sales-Price Group, 2007

[In thousands (545 represents 545,000). Based on a national probability sample of monthly interviews with builders or owners of one-family houses for which building permits have been issued or, for nonpermit areas on which construction has started. For details, see source and Appendix III. For composition of regions, see map inside front cover]

Year and sales-price group	Total sales	Region				Financing type			
		Northeast	Midwest	South	West	Conventional [1]	FHA and VA	Rural Housing Service [2]	Cash
1980	545	50	81	267	145	302	196	14	32
1985	688	112	82	323	170	403	208	11	64
1990	534	71	89	225	149	337	138	10	50
1995	667	55	125	300	187	490	129	9	39
2000	877	71	155	406	244	695	138	4	40
2001	908	66	164	439	239	726	141	2	39
2002	973	65	185	450	273	788	140	4	42
2003	1,086	79	189	511	307	911	130	4	41
2004	1,203	83	210	562	348	1,047	105	6	46
2005	1,283	81	205	638	358	1,150	79	1	52
2006	1,051	63	161	559	267	948	63	1	38
2007	**776**	**65**	**118**	**411**	**181**	**693**	**52**	**2**	**30**
Under $200,000	268	13	55	179	22	(NA)	(NA)	(NA)	(NA)
$200,000 to $299,999 . . .	227	16	37	120	54	(NA)	(NA)	(NA)	(NA)
$300,000 to $499,999 . . .	186	21	18	83	64	(NA)	(NA)	(NA)	(NA)
$500,000 and over	94	15	8	30	41	(NA)	(NA)	(NA)	(NA)

NA Not available.   [1] Includes houses reporting other types of financing   [2] Prior to 2000, the Farmers Home Administration.

Source: U.S. Census Bureau and U.S. Department of Housing and Urban Development, Current Construction Reports, Series C25, *Characteristics of New Housing,* annual; and *New One-Family Houses Sold,* monthly; publications discontinued in 2001. See "New Residential Sales" at <http://www.census.gov/const/www/newressalesindex.html>.

Table 933. Median Sales Price of New Privately Owned One-Family Houses Sold by Region: 1980 to 2007

[In dollars. For definition of median, see Guide to Tabular Presentation. For composition of regions, see map inside front cover. See Appendix III. See also headnote, Table 932]

Year	U.S.	Northeast	Midwest	South	West	Year	U.S.	Northeast	Midwest	South	West
1980	64,600	69,500	63,400	59,600	72,300	2002	187,600	264,300	178,000	163,400	238,500
1985	84,300	103,300	80,300	75,000	92,600	2003	195,000	264,500	184,300	168,100	260,900
1990	122,900	159,000	107,900	99,000	147,500	2004	221,000	315,800	205,000	181,100	283,100
1995	133,900	180,000	134,000	124,500	141,400	2005	240,900	343,800	216,900	197,300	332,600
2000	169,000	227,400	169,700	148,000	196,400	2006	246,500	346,000	213,500	208,200	337,700
2001	175,200	246,400	172,600	155,400	213,600	2007	247,900	320,200	208,600	217,700	330,900

Source: U.S. Census Bureau and U.S. Department of Housing and Urban Development, Current Construction Reports, Series C25, *Characteristics of New Housing,* annual; and *New One-Family Houses Sold,* monthly; publications discontinued in 2001. See New Residential Sales at <http://www.census.gov/const/www/newressalesindex.html>.

Table 934. New Manufactured (Mobile) Homes Placed for Residential Use and Average Sales Price by Region: 1980 to 2007

[233.7 represents 233,700. A mobile home is a moveable dwelling, 8 feet or more wide and 40 feet or more long, designed to be towed on its own chassis, with transportation gear integral to the unit when it leaves the factory, and without need of permanent foundation. Excluded are travel trailers, motor homes, and modular housing. Data are based on a probability sample and subject to sampling variability; see source. For composition of regions, see map inside front cover]

Year	Units placed (1,000)					Average sales price (dol.)				
	Total	Northeast	Midwest	South	West	U.S.	Northeast	Midwest	South	West
1980	233.7	12.3	32.3	140.3	48.7	19,800	18,500	18,600	18,200	25,400
1985	283.4	20.2	38.6	187.6	36.9	21,800	22,700	21,500	20,400	28,700
1990	195.4	18.8	37.7	108.4	30.6	27,800	30,000	27,000	24,500	39,300
1995	319.4	15.0	57.5	203.2	43.7	35,300	35,800	35,700	33,300	44,100
1997	336.3	14.3	55.3	219.4	47.3	39,800	41,300	40,300	38,000	47,300
1998	373.7	14.7	58.3	250.3	50.4	41,600	42,200	42,400	40,100	48,400
1999	338.3	14.1	53.6	227.2	43.5	43,300	44,000	44,400	41,900	49,600
2000	280.9	14.9	48.7	178.7	38.6	46,400	47,000	47,900	44,300	54,100
2002	174.3	11.8	34.2	101.0	27.2	51,300	53,200	51,700	48,000	62,600
2003	139.8	11.2	25.2	77.2	26.1	54,900	57,300	55,100	50,500	67,700
2004	124.4	11.0	20.6	67.4	25.5	58,200	60,200	58,800	52,300	73,200
2005	122.9	9.2	17.1	68.1	28.5	62,600	67,000	60,600	55,700	79,900
2006	112.4	7.9	14.5	66.1	23.9	64,300	65,300	59,100	58,900	83,400
2007	94.8	7.1	10.5	59.2	18.0	65,100	64,100	64,600	59,900	84,300

Source: U.S. Census Bureau, "Manufactured Housing"; <http://www.census.gov/const/www/mhsindex.html>.

U.S. Census Bureau, Statistical Abstract of the United States: 2009

Table 935. **Existing One-Family Homes Sold and Price by Region: 1990 to 2007**

[**2,914 represents 2,914,000.** Includes existing detached single-family homes and townhomes; excludes condos and co-ops. Based on data (adjusted and aggregated to regional and national totals) reported by participating real estate multiple listing services. For definition of median, see Guide to Tabular Presentation. See Table 938 for data on condos and co-ops. For composition of regions, see map inside front cover]

Year	Homes sold (1,000)					Median sales price (dol.)				
	Total	North-east	Mid-west	South	West	Total	North-east	Mid-west	South	West
1990	2,914	510	806	1,010	587	97,300	146,200	76,700	86,300	141,200
1991	2,885	515	808	992	569	102,700	149,300	81,000	89,800	147,400
1992	3,150	578	906	1,049	618	105,500	149,000	84,600	92,900	143,300
1993	3,427	611	961	1,173	681	109,100	149,300	87,600	95,800	144,400
1994	3,544	615	963	1,220	746	113,500	149,300	90,900	97,200	151,900
1995	3,519	609	944	1,219	747	117,000	146,500	96,500	99,200	153,600
1996	3,797	652	988	1,289	868	122,600	147,800	102,800	105,000	160,200
1997	3,964	678	1,009	1,363	914	129,000	152,400	108,900	111,300	169,000
1998	4,495	741	1,136	1,598	1,020	136,000	157,100	116,300	118,000	179,500
1999	4,649	728	1,144	1,705	1,072	141,200	160,700	121,600	122,100	189,400
2000	4,603	714	1,116	1,706	1,066	147,300	161,200	125,600	130,300	199,200
2001	4,734	709	1,155	1,793	1,076	156,600	169,400	132,300	139,600	211,700
2002	4,975	731	1,217	1,871	1,155	167,600	190,100	138,300	149,700	234,300
2003	5,443	769	1,322	2,072	1,280	180,200	220,300	143,700	159,700	254,700
2004	5,958	821	1,389	2,310	1,438	195,200	254,400	151,500	171,800	289,100
2005	6,180	838	1,411	2,457	1,474	219,000	281,600	168,300	181,100	340,300
2006	5,677	787	1,314	2,352	1,224	221,900	280,300	164,800	183,700	350,500
2007	4,939	723	1,181	2,053	982	217,900	288,100	161,400	178,800	342,500

Source: NATIONAL ASSOCIATION OF REALTORS, Washington, DC, *Real Estate Outlook; Market Trends & Insights*, monthly, (copyright). See <http://www.realtor.org/research>.

Table 936. **Median Sales Price of Existing One-Family Homes by Selected Metropolitan Area: 2005 and 2007**

[**In thousands of dollars (219.0 represents $219,000).** Includes existing detached single-family homes and townhouses. Areas are metropolitan statistical areas defined by Office of Management and Budget as of 2004, except as noted]

Metropolitan area	2005	2007	Metropolitan area	2005	2007
United States, total	**219.0**	**217.8**	New York-Wayne-White Plains, NY-NJ. .	495.2	540.3
Allentown-Bethlehem-Easton, PA-NJ	243.4	260.5	NY: Edison, NJ	375.5	380.3
Anaheim-Santa Ana-Irvine, CA [1]	691.9	699.6	NY: Nassau-Suffolk, NY	465.2	477.2
Atlantic City, NJ	256.1	269.7	NY: Newark-Union, NJ-PA.	416.8	443.7
Baltimore-Towson, MD.	265.3	286.1	Norwich-New London, CT.	255.9	267.7
Barnstable Town, MA.	398.3	384.7	Orlando, FL.	243.6	261.3
Boston-Cambridge-Quincy, MA-NH [2]	413.2	395.6	Palm Bay-Melbourne-Titusville, FL	209.7	183.6
Boulder, CO.	348.4	376.2	Philadelphia-Camden-Wilmington,		
Bridgeport-Stamford-Norwalk, CT.	482.4	486.6	PA-NJ-DE-MD	215.3	234.6
Cape Coral-Fort Myers, FL.	269.2	252.1	Phoenix-Mesa-Scottsdale, AZ	247.4	257.4
Charleston-North Charleston, SC.	197.0	215.4	Pittsfield, MA	207.3	217.4
Chicago-Naperville-Joliet, IL	264.2	276.6	Portland-South Portland-Biddeford, ME. . .	246.6	242.7
Colorado Springs, CO	205.9	217.5	Portland-Vancouver-Beaverton, OR-WA . .	244.9	295.2
Deltona-Daytona Beach-			Providence-New Bedford-		
Ormond Beach, FL	192.5	192.3	Fall River, RI-MA.	293.4	286.6
Denver-Aurora, CO	247.1	245.4	Raleigh-Cary, NC	194.9	224.2
Dover, DE	180.4	207.5	Reno-Sparks, NV	349.9	321.4
Eugene-Springfield, OR	197.6	239.6	Richmond, VA	201.9	233.7
Gainesville, FL.	184.0	211.1	Riverside-San Bernardino-Ontario, CA [1] . .	374.2	381.4
Hagerstown-Martinsburg, MD-WV	208.7	208.5	Sacramento-Arden-Arcade-		
Hartford-West Hartford-			Roseville, CA [1]	375.9	342.7
East Hartford, CT	253.3	263.2	Salem, OR	177.7	228.3
Honolulu, HI.	590.0	643.5	San Diego-Carlsbad-San Marcos, CA [1] . . .	604.3	588.7
Kingston, NY	251.0	258.4	San Francisco-Oakland-Fremont, CA [1] . . .	715.7	805.4
Las Vegas-Paradise, NV	304.7	297.7	San Jose-Sunnyvale-Santa Clara, CA [1] . .	744.5	836.8
Los Angeles-Long Beach-			Sarasota-Bradenton-Venice, FL.	354.2	310.9
Santa Ana, CA [1]	529.0	589.2	Seattle-Tacoma-Bellevue, WA	316.8	386.9
Madison, WI	218.3	226.5	Springfield, MA.	201.8	211.9
Miami-Fort Lauderdale-			Tampa-St.Petersburg-Clearwater, FL	205.3	214.9
Miami Beach, FL.	370.1	365.5	Trenton-Ewing, NJ	261.1	307.1
Milwaukee-Waukesha-West Allis, WI	215.7	223.4	Tucson, AZ	231.6	244.8
Minneapolis-St. Paul-			Virginia Beach-Norfolk-		
Bloomington, MN-WI	234.8	225.2	Newport News, VA-NC.	197.2	245.0
New Haven-Milford, CT	279.1	286.5	Washington-Arlington-		
New York-Northern New Jersey-			Alexandria, DC-VA-MD-WV.	425.8	430.8
Long Island, NY-NJ-PA.	445.2	469.7	Worcester, MA	290.7	274.6

[1] California data supplied by the California Association of REALTORS.   [2] Excludes areas in New Hampshire.

Source: NATIONAL ASSOCIATION OF REALTORS, Washington, DC, *Real Estate Outlook: Market Trends & Insights*, monthly, (copyright). See <http://www.realtor.org/research>.

Table 937. **Existing Home Sales by State: 2000 to 2007**

[In thousands (5,174 represents 5,174,000). Includes condos and co-ops as well as single-family homes. Data shown here reflect revisions from prior estimates]

State	2000	2005	2006	2007	State	2000	2005	2006	2007
United States . . .	**5,174**	**7,076**	**6,478**	**5,652**	Missouri	110.2	142.9	135.3	123.7
Alabama	67.0	128.0	125.8	118.0	Montana	17.4	25.4	26.8	24.1
Alaska	14.3	24.6	30.7	26.4	Nebraska	32.3	41.2	38.7	36.8
Arizona	104.8	199.2	142.9	105.5	Nevada	44.6	98.0	70.2	45.3
Arkansas	45.0	75.3	82.6	78.6	New Hampshire	26.7	(NA)	(NA)	(NA)
California	573.5	601.1	459.9	355.0	New Jersey	161.1	184.4	154.1	139.7
Colorado	111.5	130.4	123.7	118.2	New Mexico	29.9	57.5	58.2	44.5
Connecticut	61.5	78.0	70.8	62.6	New York	273.3	319.8	303.4	295.9
Delaware	12.9	19.3	17.8	15.7	North Carolina	134.2	215.7	234.8	214.0
District of Columbia . . .	10.6	12.1	10.1	9.6	North Dakota	10.8	15.8	14.1	14.4
Florida	393.6	547.1	395.3	286.4	Ohio	216.4	286.9	275.4	250.8
Georgia	143.6	242.1	248.8	209.9	Oklahoma	67.3	104.6	106.0	102.0
Hawaii	22.1	36.8	31.5	27.8	Oregon	62.6	100.5	85.8	74.3
Idaho	24.1	49.8	(NA)	36.3	Pennsylvania	195.9	255.2	234.5	214.0
Illinois	246.8	315.3	289.0	239.7	Rhode Island	17.0	19.8	17.4	16.4
Indiana	111.0	138.3	147.4	148.3	South Carolina	64.3	114.6	115.2	105.0
Iowa	53.3	74.9	74.6	70.5	South Dakota	12.6	18.3	18.3	18.5
Kansas	52.6	77.9	76.1	70.5	Tennessee	100.4	170.9	173.6	145.7
Kentucky	66.0	96.2	96.9	91.8	Texas	381.8	532.5	578.6	557.8
Louisiana	66.8	87.7	92.3	75.9	Utah	35.5	51.7	51.7	41.9
Maine	27.6	33.3	30.7	25.5	Vermont	12.1	15.3	15.0	14.4
Maryland	100.5	135.5	113.2	86.4	Virginia	130.0	182.5	140.1	116.5
Massachusetts	112.3	148.6	128.1	122.4	Washington	112.4	167.8	154.2	133.5
Michigan	185.0	208.6	182.4	172.4	West Virginia	22.9	38.6	32.6	29.0
Minnesota	96.3	134.9	115.4	99.8	Wisconsin	91.6	122.8	117.3	104.6
Mississippi	38.7	61.2	63.8	59.7	Wyoming	9.6	14.3	13.6	12.9

NA Not available.

Source: NATIONAL ASSOCIATION OF REALTORS, Washington, DC, *Real Estate Outlook: Market Trends & Insights,* monthly (copyright). See <http://www.realtor.org/research>.

Table 938. **Existing Apartment Condos and Co-ops—Units Sold and Median Sales Price by Region: 1990 to 2007**

[272 represents 272,000. Data shown here reflect revisions from prior estimates. For definition of median, see Guide to Tabular Presentation. For composition of regions, see map inside front cover]

Year	Units sold (1,000)					Median sales price (dol.)				
	U.S.	North-east	Mid-west	South	West	U.S.	North-east	Mid-west	South	West
1990	272	73	55	80	64	86,900	107,500	70,200	64,200	114,600
1995	333	108	66	96	63	89,000	92,500	90,700	67,800	114,800
1998	471	157	92	126	95	102,500	100,900	106,400	76,800	137,700
1999	534	182	102	145	105	110,100	109,800	114,600	80,700	143,900
2000	571	197	106	160	108	114,000	108,500	121,700	84,200	149,100
2001	601	203	116	174	108	125,600	121,200	134,800	93,200	160,400
2002	657	221	129	193	114	144,900	143,500	148,600	109,900	187,000
2003	732	250	146	211	125	168,500	178,100	162,600	126,900	222,400
2004	820	292	161	230	137	197,100	214,100	181,000	156,600	258,000
2005	896	331	177	245	143	223,900	245,100	189,100	187,300	283,800
2006	801	299	169	211	122	221,900	249,700	190,900	184,000	264,700
2007	713	283	146	182	102	226,300	256,100	195,200	185,100	263,300

Source: NATIONAL ASSOCIATION OF REALTORS, Washington, DC, *Real Estate Outlook: Market Trends & Insights,* monthly (copyright). See <http://www.realtor.org/research>.

Table 939. **New Unfurnished Apartments Completed and Rented in 3 Months by Region: 2000 to 2007**

[226.2 represents 226,200. Structures with five or more units, privately financed, nonsubsidized, unfurnished rental apartments. Based on sample and subject to sampling variability; see source for details. For composition of regions, see map, inside front cover]

Year and rent	Number (1,000)					Percent rented in 3 months				
	U.S.	North-east	Mid-west	South	West	U.S.	North-east	Mid-west	South	West
2000	226.2	14.8	39.5	125.9	45.9	72	85	76	67	77
2004	153.8	13.1	31.7	72.7	36.3	62	75	59	60	65
2005	113.0	4.7	20.5	57.8	30.0	64	75	64	62	64
2006	117.2	6.0	12.6	69.9	28.6	55	41	58	60	56
2007, prel.	**103.7**	**5.6**	**9.4**	**61.4**	**27.3**	**55**	**66**	**58**	**52**	**58**
Less than $750	17.7	0.7	4.4	11.8	0.8	55	42	61	54	44
$750 to $849	13.2	0.2	1.6	9.4	1.9	64	35	71	62	74
$850 to $949	13.5	(Z)	1.3	9.0	3.2	54	33	47	52	63
$950 to $1,049	11.1	0.5	0.7	7.6	2.4	52	92	64	46	61
$1,050 to $1,149	8.6	0.4	0.4	5.3	2.5	57	92	50	56	54
$1,150 or more	39.7	3.8	1.1	18.2	16.6	53	65	39	47	56
Median monthly asking rent (dollars) . . .	1,017	(¹)	771	955	(¹)	(X)	(X)	(X)	(X)	(X)

X Not applicable.   Z Fewer than 50 units or less than one-half of 1 percent.   ¹ Over $1,150.

Source: U.S. Census Bureau, *Current Housing Reports,* Series H130, *Market Absorption of Apartments,* and unpublished data. See <http://www.census.gov/prod/www/abs/apart.html>.

Table 940. Total Housing Inventory for the United States: 1980 to 2007

[In thousands (87,739 represents 87,739,000), except percent. Based on the Current Population Survey and the Housing Vacancy Survey and subject to sampling error; see source and Appendix III for details]

Item	1980	1990	1995	2000	2002 [1]	2003	2004	2005	2006	2007
All housing units	**87,739**	**106,283**	**112,655**	**119,628**	**119,297**	**120,834**	**122,187**	**123,925**	**126,012**	**127,958**
Vacant	8,101	12,059	12,669	13,908	14,332	15,274	15,599	15,694	16,437	17,652
Year-round vacant	5,996	9,128	9,570	10,439	10,771	11,631	11,884	11,916	12,459	13,276
For rent	1,575	2,662	2,946	3,024	3,347	3,676	3,802	3,721	3,737	3,848
For sale only	734	1,064	1,022	1,148	1,220	1,308	1,307	1,451	1,836	2,117
Rented or sold	623	660	810	856	842	976	991	1,060	1,108	1,130
Held off market	3,064	4,742	4,793	5,411	5,362	5,671	5,784	5,684	5,778	6,181
Occasional use	814	1,485	1,667	1,892	1,819	1,989	1,967	1,884	1,858	1,993
Usual residence elsewhere	568	1,068	801	1,037	995	994	1,068	1,128	1,198	1,139
Other	1,683	2,189	2,325	2,482	2,548	2,688	2,749	2,672	2,722	3,049
Seasonal [2]	2,106	2,931	3,099	3,469	3,561	3,643	3,715	3,778	3,978	4,376
Total occupied	79,638	94,224	99,985	105,720	104,965	105,560	106,588	108,231	109,575	110,306
Owner	52,223	60,248	64,739	71,250	71,278	72,054	73,575	74,553	75,380	75,159
Renter	27,415	33,976	35,246	34,470	33,687	33,506	33,013	33,678	34,195	35,147
PERCENT DISTRIBUTION										
All housing units	100.0	100.0	100.0	100.0	100.0	100.0	100.0	100.0	100.0	100.0
Vacant	9.2	11.3	11.2	11.6	12.0	12.6	12.8	12.7	13.0	13.8
Total occupied	90.8	88.7	88.8	88.4	88.0	87.4	87.2	87.3	87.0	86.2
Owner	59.5	56.7	57.5	59.6	59.7	59.6	60.2	60.2	60.3	58.7
Renter	31.2	32.0	31.3	28.8	28.2	27.7	27.0	27.2	27.5	27.5

[1] Revised. Based on 2000 census controls.   [2] Beginning 1990, includes vacant seasonal mobile homes. For years shown, seasonal vacant housing units were underreported prior to 1990.

Source: U.S. Census Bureau, "Housing Vacancies and Home Ownership"; <http://www.census.gov/hhes/www/housing/hvs/hvs.html>.

Table 941. Occupied Housing Inventory by Age of Householder: 1990 to 2007

[In thousands (94,224 represents 94,224,000). Based on the Current Population Survey/Housing Vacancy Survey; See source for details]

Age of householder	1990	1995	2000	2001	2002 [1]	2003	2004	2005	2006	2007
Total	**94,224**	**99,986**	**105,719**	**107,009**	**104,965**	**105,560**	**106,588**	**108,231**	**109,576**	**110,306**
Under 25 years old	5,143	5,502	6,221	6,460	6,372	6,441	6,538	6,536	6,578	6,494
25 to 29 years old	9,508	8,662	8,482	8,358	8,231	8,213	8,491	8,790	8,975	9,170
30 to 34 years old	11,213	11,206	10,219	10,301	10,176	10,084	9,865	9,583	9,423	9,349
35 to 39 years old	10,914	11,993	11,834	11,587	10,924	10,777	10,438	10,526	10,520	10,499
40 to 44 years old	9,893	11,151	12,377	12,504	11,839	11,748	11,768	11,722	11,484	11,125
45 to 49 years old	8,038	10,080	11,164	11,529	11,204	11,341	11,583	11,780	11,988	12,007
50 to 54 years old	6,532	7,882	9,834	10,288	10,123	10,194	10,316	10,595	10,896	11,082
55 to 59 years old	6,182	6,355	7,602	7,827	8,261	8,550	8,928	9,504	9,919	10,013
60 to 64 years old	6,446	5,860	6,215	6,345	6,422	6,776	7,112	7,336	7,604	8,108
65 to 69 years old	6,407	6,088	5,816	5,749	5,644	5,570	5,656	5,900	6,074	6,330
70 to 74 years old	5,397	5,693	5,567	5,496	5,137	5,163	5,065	5,016	5,057	5,063
75 years old and over	8,546	9,514	10,388	10,565	10,632	10,703	10,827	10,943	11,058	11,065

[1] Revised. Based on 2000 census controls.

Source: U.S. Census Bureau, "Housing Vacancies and Home Ownership"; <http://www.census.gov/hhes/www/housing/hvs/hvs.html>.

Table 942. Vacancy Rates for Housing Units—Characteristics: 2000 to 2007

[In percent. Rate is relationship between vacant housing for rent or for sale and the total rental and homeowner supply, which comprises occupied units, units rented or sold and awaiting occupancy, and vacant units available for rent or sale. Based on the Current Population/Housing Vacancy Survey; see source for details. For composition of regions, see map, inside front cover]

Characteristic	Rental units				Homeowner units			
	2000	2005	2006	2007	2000	2005	2006	2007
Total units	**8.0**	**9.8**	**9.7**	**9.7**	**1.6**	**1.9**	**2.4**	**2.7**
Northeast	5.6	6.5	7.1	7.0	1.2	1.5	1.7	2.0
Midwest	8.8	12.6	12.4	11.5	1.3	2.2	2.6	2.8
South	10.5	11.8	11.6	12.3	1.9	2.1	2.7	3.1
West	5.8	7.3	6.8	6.7	1.5	1.4	2.1	2.5
Units in structure:								
1 unit	7.0	9.9	10.0	9.6	1.5	1.7	2.1	2.4
2 units or more	8.7	10.0	9.8	10.0	4.7	6.2	7.9	8.3
5 units or more	9.2	10.4	9.9	10.3	5.8	6.6	8.5	8.5
Units with—								
3 rooms or less	10.3	12.1	11.8	11.9	10.4	12.0	13.1	14.9
4 rooms	8.2	9.6	10.0	10.0	2.9	3.3	4.6	4.9
5 rooms	6.9	9.3	8.8	8.6	2.0	2.2	2.6	3.0
6 rooms or more	5.2	8.1	7.8	7.9	1.1	1.4	1.7	2.0

Source: U.S. Census Bureau, "Housing Vacancies and Home Ownership"; <http://www.census.gov/hhes/www/housing/hvs/hvs.html>.

Table 943. **Housing Units and Tenure—States: 2006**

[**126,312 represents 126,312,000.** The American Community Survey universe includes the household population and the population living in institutions, college dormitories, and other group quarters. Based on a sample and subject to sampling variability; see Appendix III]

State	Housing units						Housing tenure			
	Total (1,000)	Occupied (1,000)	Vacant (1,000)		Vacancy rate		Owner-occupied units		Renter-occupied units	
			Total	For seasonal use [1]	Home-owner [2]	Renter [3]	Total (1,000)	Average house-hold size	Total (1,000)	Average house-hold size
United States . . .	**126,312**	**111,617**	**14,694**	**4,214**	**2.3**	**8.0**	**75,086**	**2.66**	**36,531**	**2.31**
Alabama	2,110	1,796	314	66	2.2	8.9	1,289	2.57	507	2.31
Alaska	277	230	47	23	1.6	7.6	148	2.93	82	2.60
Arizona	2,605	2,225	380	161	3.0	8.4	1,523	2.75	702	2.67
Arkansas	1,273	1,103	170	39	2.7	8.1	753	2.54	350	2.33
California	13,175	12,151	1,024	276	1.9	4.7	7,102	3.02	5,049	2.80
Colorado	2,095	1,847	248	96	2.7	8.5	1,269	2.62	578	2.30
Connecticut	1,432	1,325	107	22	1.2	6.2	921	2.71	404	2.21
Delaware	383	320	63	31	2.9	10.2	238	2.65	82	2.42
District of Columbia . . .	283	250	32	1	2.6	6.1	115	2.27	136	2.11
Florida	8,532	7,106	1,426	656	3.7	8.5	4,994	2.52	2,112	2.42
Georgia	3,873	3,377	497	76	3.1	10.5	2,285	2.75	1,092	2.58
Hawaii	500	433	67	33	1.1	6.1	258	3.04	175	2.65
Idaho	616	549	67	32	1.7	5.3	391	2.68	158	2.44
Illinois	5,200	4,724	475	36	2.3	8.8	3,301	2.77	1,423	2.36
Indiana	2,757	2,435	321	38	3.3	11.4	1,756	2.62	679	2.25
Iowa	1,320	1,209	111	18	2.0	6.4	886	2.50	323	2.05
Kansas	1,207	1,088	119	12	2.2	7.3	761	2.56	327	2.23
Kentucky	1,888	1,652	236	31	2.3	9.9	1,167	2.57	485	2.25
Louisiana	1,830	1,565	265	42	1.6	6.5	1,072	2.74	493	2.50
Maine	691	548	143	99	2.4	6.0	399	2.46	149	2.04
Maryland	2,301	2,089	212	50	1.4	7.7	1,450	2.74	639	2.34
Massachusetts	2,709	2,446	263	104	1.5	5.6	1,588	2.75	858	2.16
Michigan	4,514	3,869	644	247	3.1	10.6	2,908	2.65	961	2.22
Minnesota	2,283	2,042	241	110	1.7	8.2	1,558	2.59	484	2.03
Mississippi	1,241	1,076	166	29	1.8	9.5	760	2.67	315	2.50
Missouri	2,623	2,305	318	70	2.3	8.6	1,629	2.58	676	2.18
Montana	432	372	60	28	1.4	6.3	260	2.55	112	2.28
Nebraska	775	701	74	15	2.2	7.7	476	2.60	225	2.13
Nevada	1,065	937	128	31	3.3	9.2	581	2.69	356	2.53
New Hampshire	590	505	85	57	1.7	5.3	364	2.69	141	2.12
New Jersey	3,473	3,135	337	120	1.7	6.5	2,110	2.86	1,025	2.43
New Mexico	850	726	124	42	1.5	8.6	506	2.74	220	2.40
New York	7,908	7,088	819	256	1.7	5.0	3,941	2.81	3,147	2.42
North Carolina	4,027	3,454	572	167	2.3	10.1	2,351	2.54	1,103	2.36
North Dakota	307	272	35	12	1.3	5.9	182	2.44	91	1.81
Ohio	5,045	4,500	546	47	2.7	10.9	3,150	2.61	1,349	2.19
Oklahoma	1,607	1,385	222	34	2.2	10.3	950	2.56	435	2.37
Oregon	1,587	1,450	137	48	1.6	5.7	939	2.60	511	2.31
Pennsylvania	5,454	4,846	608	161	1.9	8.2	3,475	2.62	1,370	2.11
Rhode Island	450	406	44	15	1.3	7.3	255	2.72	150	2.20
South Carolina	1,976	1,657	319	93	2.7	11.6	1,165	2.57	492	2.40
South Dakota	352	312	40	12	0.9	7.4	216	2.54	96	2.10
Tennessee	2,681	2,375	306	53	2.2	9.8	1,660	2.55	715	2.31
Texas	9,225	8,109	1,116	194	2.3	10.4	5,291	2.95	2,818	2.58
Utah	901	814	87	37	1.4	6.3	586	3.21	228	2.74
Vermont	310	254	56	44	1.1	4.1	182	2.53	71	1.98
Virginia	3,231	2,905	326	74	2.0	7.1	2,030	2.63	875	2.35
Washington	2,700	2,472	228	68	1.6	6.2	1,620	2.66	852	2.28
West Virginia	878	743	135	42	2.2	6.3	555	2.46	188	2.16
Wisconsin	2,533	2,230	303	152	1.7	7.4	1,571	2.57	659	2.06
Wyoming	239	207	32	14	1.5	6.2	144	2.50	63	2.22

[1] For seasonal, recreational, or occasional use.   [2] Proportion of the homeowner housing inventory which is vacant for sale.
[3] Proportion of the rental inventory which is vacant for rent.

Source: U.S. Census Bureau, 2006 American Community Survey Tables B25002. Occupancy Status; B25003. Tenure; B25004. Vacancy Status; and B25010. Average Household Size of Units by Tenure; using American FactFinder®. See <http://factfinder.census.gov/>; (accessed March 2008).

U.S. Census Bureau, Statistical Abstract of the United States: 2009

Table 944. Homeownership and Rental Vacancy Rates by State: 2007

[The American Community Survey universe is limited to the household population and excludes the population living in institutions, college dormitories, and other group quarters. Based on a sample and subject to sampling variability; see Appendix III. FIPS means Federal Information Processing Standards]

State	Home-owner-ship vacancy rate	Rental vacancy rate	State	Home-owner-ship vacancy rate	Rental vacancy rate	State	Home-owner-ship vacancy rate	Rental vacancy rate
U.S.	2.7	9.7	KS	1.9	11.1	ND	1.1	7.6
			KY	2.8	10.4	OH	3.2	11.9
AL	2.9	15.3	LA	2.5	8.8	OK	2.4	9.8
AK	2.6	7.7	ME	2.5	6.4	OR	2.1	5.9
AZ	3.8	9.6	MD	2.7	11.4	PA	2.1	10.0
AR	2.2	11.8	MA	1.7	5.7	RI	1.5	9.5
CA	2.3	6.1	MI	3.8	17.0	SC	3.1	10.6
CO	3.1	10.1	MN	2.8	7.6	SD	1.7	8.9
CT	2.3	8.0	MS	1.5	9.4	TN	2.1	9.2
DE	2.8	15.0	MO	2.1	11.7	TX	2.5	13.8
DC	3.2	9.6	MT	1.4	6.0	UT	2.0	5.5
FL	5.1	13.7	NE	2.5	10.2	VT	1.0	4.9
GA	3.8	13.1	NV	4.6	9.8	VA	2.6	9.7
HI	1.7	6.3	NH	1.9	5.7	WA	1.5	4.5
ID	2.9	8.1	NJ	1.6	6.8	WV	1.5	9.6
IL	2.6	10.4	NM	2.8	9.3	WI	1.7	7.9
IN	3.2	13.3	NY	2.2	6.1	WY	1.7	5.4
IA	2.9	10.9	NC	2.4	12.4			

Source: U.S. Census Bureau, "Housing Vacancies and Home Ownership"; <http://www.census.gov/hhes/www/housing/hvs/annual07/ann07ind.html>.

Table 945. Homeownership and Rental Vacancy Rates by Metropolitan Area: 2007

[Based on the Current Population Survey and the Housing Vacancy Survey and subject to sampling error; see source and Appendix III for details]

Metropolitan area	Home-owner-ship vacancy rates	Rental vacancy rates	Metropolitan area	Home-owner-ship vacancy rates	Rental vacancy rates
Inside Metropolitan Areas	**2.8**	**9.8**	Milwaukee-Waukesha-West Allis, WI	1.4	8.3
			Minneapolis-St. Paul-Bloomington, MN-WI.	3.2	6.9
Akron, OH.	4.5	8.4	Nashville-Davidson–Murfreesboro, TN . . .	2.4	7.6
Albany-Schenectady-Troy, NY	2.1	4.9	New Haven-Milford, CT	2.2	8.6
Albuquerque, NM	2.6	8.8	New Orleans-Metairie-Kenner, LA	4.0	9.1
Allentown-Bethleham-Easton, PA-NJ	1.2	8.1	New York-Northern New Jersey-Long		
Atlanta-Sandy Springs-Marietta, GA	4.7	14.7	Island, NY	2.1	5.7
Austin-Round Rock, TX	1.5	6.8	Oklahoma City, OK	2.5	7.4
Bakersfield, CA	1.3	11.2	Omaha-Council Bluffs, NE-IA	2.5	11.9
Baltimore-Towson, MD.	2.7	11.3	Orlando, FL	7.4	11.3
Baton Rouge, LA	1.6	4.4	Oxnard-Thousand Oaks-Ventura, CA	1.9	5.4
Birmingham-Hoover, AL	2.5	17.5	Philadelphia-Camden-Wilmington, PA. . . .	1.9	12.6
Boston-Cambridge-Quincy, MA-NH	1.9	5.0	Phoenix-Mesa-Scottsdale, AZ	3.7	9.2
Bridgeport-Stamford-Norwalk, CT.	4.3	6.7	Pittsburgh, PA	3.0	9.3
Buffalo-Cheektowaga-Tonawanda, NY . . .	1.4	8.6	Portland-Vancouver-Beaverton, OR-WA . .	2.3	4.8
Charlotte-Gastonia-Concord, NC-SC	3.1	11.0	Poughkeepsie-Newburg-Middletown, NJ . .	0.1	9.8
Chicago-Naperville-Joliet, IL	2.7	11.0	Providence-New Bedford-Fall River		
Cincinnati-Middletown, OH-KY-IN.	4.0	12.0	RI-MA.	1.6	9.2
Cleveland-Elyria-Mentor, OH.	4.5	13.9	Raleigh-Cary, NC	1.6	11.2
Columbia, SC.	2.1	8.3	Richmond, VA	2.9	16.3
Columbus, OH	2.8	13.3	Riverside-San Bernardino-Ontario, CA . . .	3.8	8.9
Dallas-Ft. Worth-Arlington, TX.	2.5	11.0	Rochester, NY	1.4	6.4
Dayton, OH	1.2	16.6	Sacramento–Arden-Arade–Roseville, CA . .	4.2	9.5
Denver-Aurora, CO	3.0	10.1	St. Louis, MO-IL.	1.7	10.7
Detroit-Warren-Livonia, MI	4.1	19.4	Salt Lake City, UT.	2.2	5.3
El Paso, TX	2.2	6.3	San Antonio, TX	2.4	16.3
Fresno, CA	0.3	5.6	San Diego-Carlsbad-San Marcos, CA	3.0	7.1
Grand Rapids-Wyoming, MI	1.7	12.7	San Francisco-Oakland-Freemont, CA . . .	1.3	6.2
Greensboro-High Point, NC	2.4	8.2	San Jose-Sunnyvale-Santa Clara, CA. . . .	0.8	3.8
Hartford-West Hartford-East Hartford, CT .	0.8	7.4	Seattle-Bellevue-Everett, WA	1.8	4.9
Honolulu, HI.	1.2	5.1	Springfield, MA.	1.4	6.7
Houston-Baytown-Sugar Land, TX	3.1	17.3	Syracuse, NY.	3.1	13.6
Indianapolis, IN	4.3	14.9	Tampa-St. Petersburg-Clearwater, FL	5.1	12.8
Jacksonville, FL	4.6	14.5	Toledo, OH	2.4	8.5
Kansas City, MO-KS	2.5	15.8	Tucson, AZ	2.2	7.9
Las Vegas-Paradise, NV	4.9	10.9	Tulsa, OK	3.3	13.5
Los Angeles-Long Beach-Santa Ana, CA .	1.6	4.7	Virginia Beach-Norfolk-Newport News, VA.	3.5	7.7
Louisville, KY-IN	3.8	11.7	Washington-Arlington-Alexandria,		
Memphis, TN-AR-MS.	2.8	12.8	DC-VA-MD-WV	2.4	10.4
Miami-Fort Lauderdale-Miami Beach, FL. .	4.4	10.4	Worchester, MA	0.5	7.0

Source: U.S. Census Bureau, "Housing Vacancies and Home Ownership"; <http://www.census.gov/hhes/www/housing/hvs/annual07/ann07ind.html>.

Table 946. **Housing Units—Characteristics by Tenure and Region: 2005**

[In thousands of units (124,377 represents 124,377,000), except as indicated. As of fall. Based on the American Housing Survey; see Appendix III. For composition of regions, see map, inside front cover]

Characteristic	Total housing units	Sea-sonal	Year-round units							Vacant
			Occupied							
			Total	Owner	Renter	North-east	Mid-west	South	West	
Total units	**124,377**	**3,845**	**108,871**	**74,931**	**33,940**	**20,337**	**24,955**	**39,722**	**23,858**	**11,660**
Percent distribution	100.0	3.1	87.5	68.8	31.2	18.7	22.9	36.5	21.9	9.4
Units in structure:										
Single family detached	77,703	2,287	69,996	61,699	8,297	11,044	17,707	26,254	14,992	5,420
Single family attached.	7,046	197	6,158	3,976	2,182	1,825	1,042	2,035	1,256	691
2 to 4 units	10,071	188	8,379	1,550	6,829	2,604	1,863	2,073	1,840	1,504
5 to 9 units	6,073	125	5,109	502	4,607	917	1,004	1,824	1,364	840
10 to 19 units	5,696	94	4,739	563	4,175	817	902	1,830	1,190	863
20 to 49 units	4,402	125	3,639	436	3,203	1,041	601	964	1,033	638
50 or more units	4,757	186	3,912	689	3,222	1,589	682	809	831	659
Manufactured/mobile home [1]	8,630	644	6,940	5,516	1,424	500	1,155	3,932	1,352	1,047
Single-wide	5,584	457	4,257	3,093	1,164	371	843	2,443	600	869
Double-wide	2,897	174	2,558	2,302	255	126	312	1,435	685	165
Triple-wide or larger	118	7	107	103	4	–	–	44	64	4
Year structure built:										
Median year	1973	1972	1973	1974	1970	1956	1968	1978	1976	1971
1980 or later	42,502	1,284	37,543	28,249	9,293	3,866	7,096	17,426	9,154	3,672
1970 to 1979	25,091	831	21,858	13,860	7,998	2,907	4,854	8,695	5,403	2,401
1960 to 1969	15,192	486	13,499	9,217	4,282	2,467	3,019	4,876	3,136	1,207
1950 to 1959	13,003	366	11,555	8,469	3,086	2,527	3,025	3,490	2,513	1,082
1940 to 1949	7,904	279	6,821	4,458	2,363	1,654	1,497	2,156	1,513	805
1939 and earlier	20,686	598	17,595	10,677	6,919	6,915	5,463	3,079	2,139	2,493
Stories in structure: [2]										
1 story	39,963	1,553	34,814	26,278	8,537	1,139	4,031	19,192	10,453	3,596
2 stories	41,189	984	36,283	24,026	12,257	6,187	10,111	11,154	8,832	3,922
3 stories	26,287	393	23,714	16,375	7,340	8,482	8,342	4,353	2,537	2,180
4 to 6 stories	5,819	137	5,128	2,248	2,880	2,932	999	719	478	554
7 or more stories	2,488	135	1,992	488	1,504	1,097	317	372	206	362
Foundation: [3]										
Full basement	26,882	350	24,984	22,612	2,372	8,586	10,745	3,793	1,860	1,547
Partial building.	9,431	153	8,735	7,840	894	2,378	3,626	1,590	1,140	544
Crawlspace.	22,292	1,151	19,038	15,646	3,392	732	2,575	10,037	5,694	2,103
Concrete slab	25,514	660	23,012	19,317	3,695	1,129	1,720	12,675	7,488	1,843
Other.	629	169	384	259	125	44	82	192	66	75
Equipment:										
Lacking complete facilities	5,345	462	1,695	257	1,438	298	345	536	515	3,188
With complete facilities	119,032	3,384	107,177	74,674	32,502	20,038	24,610	39,186	23,343	8,472
Kitchen sink	123,262	3,644	108,656	74,889	33,767	20,296	24,923	39,663	23,775	10,962
Refrigerator.	121,035	3,466	108,673	74,856	33,818	20,311	24,909	39,640	23,814	8,895
Cooking stove or range	121,208	3,475	108,140	74,718	33,422	20,179	24,812	39,506	23,642	9,593
Burners only, no stove or range	189	32	131	60	71	31	19	37	43	26
Microwave oven only	481	23	397	106	291	104	68	98	126	61
Dishwasher.	75,239	1,677	68,508	54,060	14,448	11,132	14,491	26,271	16,614	5,055
Washing machine	95,272	1,979	89,287	71,997	17,290	15,039	20,969	34,138	19,141	4,006
Clothes dryer	92,179	1,949	86,169	70,348	15,821	13,976	20,765	32,893	18,534	4,062
Disposal in kitchen sink.	58,906	1,217	53,299	38,595	14,704	5,107	12,423	18,584	17,185	4,390
Trash compactor	4,513	125	4,077	3,343	734	601	659	1,638	1,179	311
Main heating equipment:										
Warm-air furnace	76,665	1,727	68,275	50,459	17,817	8,546	20,331	23,735	15,664	6,662
Steam or hot water system	14,074	176	12,880	7,719	5,161	9,496	1,996	588	800	1,018
Electric heat pump	14,551	605	12,484	9,074	3,411	344	664	9,993	1,483	1,462
Built-in electric units	5,607	310	4,699	2,116	2,583	1,065	1,116	918	1,600	598
Floor, wall, or pipeless furnace	5,916	149	5,102	2,172	2,930	443	399	1,300	2,961	664
Room heaters with flue	1,615	111	1,294	752	542	165	172	646	310	211
Room heaters without flue	1,627	76	1,327	881	447	18	42	1,222	45	224
Portable electric heaters	1,127	73	907	441	467	29	20	642	216	146
Stoves	1,171	183	896	742	155	150	143	304	299	93
Fireplaces [4]	251	47	190	166	24	24	22	69	74	15
Other.	505	65	298	167	131	18	31	159	90	142
Cooking stoves	148	–	120	50	70	34	–	50	36	28
None	1,120	324	399	194	205	4	20	96	279	397
Air conditioning: central	80,511	1,662	72,629	55,849	16,780	6,535	17,401	36,249	12,443	6,220
One or more room units	27,124	579	24,863	14,326	10,537	10,132	5,707	5,697	3,326	1,681
Source of water:										
Public system or private company . . .	108,210	2,638	95,313	62,991	32,322	17,168	20,874	34,871	22,401	10,260
Well serving 1 to 5 units	15,372	1,014	13,132	11,607	1,525	3,079	4,008	4,648	1,396	1,227
Other.	795	194	427	334	93	90	73	203	61	174
Means of sewage disposal:										
Public sewer.	98,013	1,976	86,850	55,496	31,355	16,107	20,053	29,617	21,073	9,187
Septic tank, cesspool, chemical toilet	25,976	1,685	21,967	19,403	2,564	4,229	4,888	10,067	2,783	2,323
Other.	388	184	54	32	22	–	13	38	2	151

– Represents or rounds to zero.   [1] Includes trailers. Includes width not reported, not shown separately.   [2] Excludes mobile homes; includes basements and finished attics.   [3] Limited to single-family units.   [4] With and without inserts.

Source: U.S. Census Bureau, Current Housing Reports, Series H150/05, *American Housing Survey for the United States.* See <http://www.census.gov/hhes/www/housing/ahs/nationaldata.html>.

Construction and Housing   601

Table 947. Housing Units by Units in Structure and State: 2006

[In percent, except as indicated (126,312 represents 126,312,000). The American Community Survey universe includes the household population and the population living in institutions, college dormitories, and other group quarters. Based on a sample and subject to sampling variability; see Appendix III]

State	Total housing units (1,000)	Percent of units by units in structure—								
		1-unit detached	1-unit attached	2 units	3 or 4 units	5 to 9 units	10 to 19 units	20 or more units	Mobile homes	Boat, RV, van, etc.
U.S.	126,312	61.4	5.7	4.0	4.6	4.9	4.5	7.9	6.9	0.1
AL	2,110	67.6	2.0	2.3	3.0	4.2	2.9	2.9	15.0	(Z)
AK	277	59.6	7.9	5.2	7.7	5.3	3.3	5.0	5.9	0.1
AZ	2,605	62.2	5.2	1.6	3.4	4.4	4.9	6.4	11.5	0.5
AR	1,273	70.3	1.8	3.1	3.1	3.1	3.1	2.1	13.4	(Z)
CA	13,175	58.1	7.0	2.6	5.7	6.3	5.2	10.9	4.1	0.1
CO	2,095	63.5	6.8	2.0	3.3	4.4	6.2	9.0	4.6	(Z)
CT	1,432	59.4	5.1	8.3	9.3	5.2	3.6	8.1	1.0	(Z)
DE	383	57.1	13.4	1.7	2.9	4.0	5.8	3.9	11.2	(Z)
DC	283	13.8	26.5	3.0	7.4	6.3	11.1	31.9	(Z)	0.1
FL.	8,532	53.8	5.9	2.3	3.9	5.2	6.1	12.4	10.4	0.1
GA	3,873	66.0	3.4	2.4	3.2	5.6	4.6	4.3	10.4	(Z)
HI	500	53.7	6.8	2.9	5.2	6.4	4.9	19.9	0.2	(Z)
ID.	616	72.3	2.9	2.8	4.8	2.6	1.9	2.4	10.1	(Z)
IL.	5,200	58.4	5.6	6.2	7.0	6.3	4.2	9.5	2.8	(Z)
IN	2,757	71.8	3.6	3.0	3.6	4.9	3.6	3.7	5.8	(Z)
IA	1,320	73.9	3.3	2.8	3.9	3.7	3.5	4.5	4.4	(Z)
KS	1,207	73.2	4.1	2.6	3.6	3.4	3.4	4.0	5.6	(Z)
KY	1,888	67.3	2.1	3.3	4.0	4.4	3.2	3.0	12.6	(Z)
LA	1,830	65.9	2.7	3.2	3.8	3.3	2.5	3.9	14.4	(Z)
ME	691	68.2	2.2	5.5	5.9	4.5	1.9	2.5	9.3	(Z)
MD	2,301	51.8	21.1	1.8	2.5	5.6	8.2	7.3	1.7	(Z)
MA	2,709	52.8	4.8	11.0	11.0	6.0	4.0	9.6	0.9	(Z)
MI.	4,514	71.2	4.6	2.9	2.9	4.1	3.6	4.8	6.0	(Z)
MN	2,283	68.3	7.0	2.3	2.1	2.4	3.4	10.6	3.9	(Z)
MS	1,241	69.2	1.4	2.2	3.1	4.2	2.1	1.7	15.7	0.5
MO	2,623	70.1	3.1	3.8	4.6	4.0	3.3	3.8	7.3	(Z)
MT	432	69.0	2.4	3.6	3.9	3.0	2.2	3.3	12.4	0.1
NE	775	72.9	3.5	2.0	2.8	3.8	4.8	6.1	4.1	(Z)
NV	1,065	58.6	5.1	1.6	6.6	9.3	6.0	5.9	6.7	0.2
NH	590	62.8	4.8	6.1	6.2	5.1	3.2	5.9	5.8	(Z)
NJ.	3,473	54.0	9.2	9.5	6.6	5.1	5.1	9.5	1.0	(Z)
NM	850	63.6	4.0	1.8	3.9	2.8	2.3	4.2	17.2	0.2
NY	7,908	41.7	4.9	11.3	7.2	5.3	4.1	22.9	2.5	(Z)
NC	4,027	64.9	3.3	2.4	3.2	4.4	4.0	2.9	14.9	(Z)
ND	307	63.4	4.1	2.2	4.9	3.7	5.1	8.8	7.9	(Z)
OH	5,045	68.2	4.4	5.0	4.6	4.8	4.0	4.9	4.1	(Z)
OK	1,607	72.8	2.2	2.0	2.6	4.0	3.5	3.3	9.4	(Z)
OR	1,587	63.3	4.1	2.9	4.4	4.8	3.7	7.3	9.0	0.4
PA	5,454	56.6	18.4	5.1	4.5	3.3	2.5	5.1	4.5	(Z)
RI.	450	55.5	3.5	11.8	13.0	4.4	3.7	6.8	1.2	(Z)
SC	1,976	62.0	2.3	2.1	3.1	5.0	3.0	3.2	19.1	(Z)
SD	352	68.6	2.5	2.4	3.0	4.2	3.3	6.6	9.5	0.1
TN	2,681	68.0	2.9	3.2	2.9	4.5	4.0	3.6	10.7	(Z)
TX	9,225	65.0	2.6	2.2	3.4	5.1	6.5	7.0	8.1	0.2
UT	901	68.3	5.1	3.5	4.8	3.5	4.4	5.9	4.4	0.1
VT	310	66.9	3.5	5.8	6.5	5.3	1.9	3.1	6.9	(Z)
VA	3,231	62.9	10.1	1.8	2.6	4.9	6.0	5.8	5.9	(Z)
WA	2,700	62.7	3.4	2.8	3.8	4.9	5.9	8.7	7.7	0.2
WV	878	71.3	1.7	2.4	3.2	2.6	1.8	2.1	14.8	(Z)
WI.	2,533	66.5	4.2	7.4	3.6	4.8	3.2	6.3	4.0	(Z)
WY	239	66.2	3.4	3.1	5.0	3.5	1.6	2.8	14.2	0.2

Z Less than .05 percent.

Source: U.S. Census Bureau, 2006 American Community Survey Table B25024. Units in Structure; using American FactFinder®. See <http://factfinder.census.gov/>; (accessed March 2008).

Table 948. Housing Units—Size of Units and Lot: 2005

[In thousands (124,377 represents 124,377,000), except as indicated. As of fall. Based on the American Housing Survey; see Appendix III. For composition of regions, see map inside front cover]

Item	Total housing units	Sea-sonal	Year-round units Occupied Total	Owner	Renter	North-east	Mid-west	South	West	Vacant
Total units	**124,377**	**3,845**	**108,871**	**74,931**	**33,940**	**20,337**	**24,955**	**39,722**	**23,858**	**11,660**
Rooms:										
1 room	637	80	379	9	370	128	50	40	160	177
2 rooms	1,399	106	989	46	943	338	141	185	325	303
3 rooms	10,941	622	8,692	1,043	7,649	2,173	1,815	2,489	2,215	1,627
4 rooms	22,774	1,175	18,141	6,829	11,312	3,316	3,964	6,571	4,290	3,458
5 rooms	28,619	932	24,763	16,949	7,814	3,713	5,831	10,007	5,211	2,924
6 rooms	25,325	516	23,096	19,493	3,603	4,343	5,103	8,822	4,828	1,714
7 rooms	15,284	226	14,332	13,086	1,247	2,677	3,468	5,268	2,920	725
8 rooms or more	19,399	187	18,480	17,477	1,003	3,649	4,582	6,340	3,908	732
Complete bathrooms:										
No bathrooms	2,115	497	554	224	330	157	89	198	110	1,063
1 bathroom	47,221	1,591	39,920	16,983	22,937	9,754	9,992	12,253	7,922	5,710
1 and one-half bathrooms	17,205	346	15,876	12,362	3,514	3,871	5,129	4,256	2,621	982
2 or more bathrooms	57,837	1,412	52,520	45,361	7,159	6,555	9,745	23,015	13,205	3,905
Square footage of unit:										
Single detached and mobile homes	86,333	2,931	76,936	67,215	9,720	11,544	18,862	30,186	16,344	6,467
Less than 500	1,037	215	622	395	227	104	112	248	158	200
500 to 749	2,652	454	1,775	1,092	683	235	373	822	345	423
750 to 999	6,211	463	4,959	3,597	1,362	579	1,358	2,020	1,002	789
1,000 to 1,499	20,301	610	18,135	15,144	2,991	2,035	4,284	7,588	4,228	1,556
1,500 to 1,999	19,546	375	18,035	16,161	1,875	2,415	4,190	7,056	4,374	1,135
2,000 to 2,499	13,465	240	12,559	11,732	827	2,096	3,234	4,624	2,605	666
2,500 to 2,999	6,964	95	6,565	6,255	310	1,187	1,600	2,496	1,281	304
3,000 to 3,999	6,446	112	5,932	5,745	187	1,119	1,631	2,024	1,157	403
4,000 or more	3,952	58	3,662	3,468	193	817	901	1,313	631	232
Other [1]	5,759	308	4,691	3,626	1,066	957	1,179	1,992	563	759
Median square footage	1,758	1,146	1,795	1,858	1,344	1,985	1,824	1,742	1,747	1,463
Lot size:										
Single detached and attached units and mobile homes	90,932	2,913	81,115	69,484	11,631	12,959	19,456	31,669	17,032	6,903
Less than one-eighth acre	12,409	555	10,402	8,139	2,263	2,005	2,429	2,849	3,119	1,451
One-eighth to one-quarter acre	25,467	747	22,916	18,910	4,005	2,916	5,686	7,473	6,840	1,804
One-quarter to one-half acre	17,808	432	16,203	14,359	1,844	2,464	3,929	6,461	3,349	1,172
One-half up to one acre	11,757	307	10,650	9,492	1,159	1,983	2,183	5,164	1,319	800
1 up to 5 acres	16,318	481	14,809	13,037	1,772	2,662	3,216	7,299	1,631	1,029
5 up to 10 acres	2,628	94	2,367	2,204	163	326	685	982	374	167
10 acres or more	4,545	297	3,767	3,343	424	602	1,328	1,440	398	480
Median acreage	0.36	0.34	0.36	0.38	0.24	0.41	0.35	0.46	0.22	0.29

[1] Represents units not reported or size unknown.

Source: U.S. Census Bureau, Current Housing Reports, Series H150/05, *American Housing Survey for the United States.* See <http://www.census.gov/hhes/www/housing/ahs/nationaldata.html>.

Table 949. Occupied Housing Units—Tenure by Race of Householder: 1991 to 2005

[In thousands (93,147 represents 93,147,000), except percent. As of fall. Based on the American Housing Survey; see Appendix III]

Race of householder and tenure	1991	1993	1995	1997	1999	2001	2003 [1]	2005
ALL RACES [2]								
Occupied units, total	**93,147**	**94,724**	**97,693**	**99,487**	**102,803**	**106,261**	**105,842**	**108,871**
Owner-occupied	59,796	61,252	63,544	65,487	68,796	72,265	72,238	74,931
Percent of occupied	64.2	64.7	65.0	65.8	66.9	68.0	68.3	68.8
Renter-occupied	33,351	33,472	34,150	34,000	34,007	33,996	33,604	33,940
WHITE [3]								
Occupied units, total	**79,140**	**80,029**	**81,611**	**82,154**	**83,624**	**85,292**	**87,483**	**89,449**
Owner-occupied	53,749	54,878	56,507	57,781	60,041	62,465	63,126	65,023
Percent of occupied	67.9	68.6	69.2	70.3	71.8	73.2	72.2	72.7
Renter-occupied	25,391	25,151	25,104	24,372	23,583	22,826	24,357	24,426
BLACK [3]								
Occupied units, total	**10,832**	**11,128**	**11,773**	**12,085**	**12,936**	**13,292**	**13,004**	**13,447**
Owner-occupied	4,635	4,788	5,137	5,457	6,013	6,318	6,193	6,471
Percent of occupied	42.8	43.0	43.6	45.2	46.5	47.5	47.6	48.1
Renter-occupied	6,197	6,340	6,637	6,628	6,923	6,974	6,811	6,975
HISPANIC ORIGIN [4]								
Occupied units, total	**6,239**	**6,614**	**7,757**	**8,513**	**9,041**	**9,814**	**11,038**	**11,651**
Owner-occupied	2,423	2,788	3,245	3,646	4,087	4,731	5,106	5,752
Percent of occupied	38.8	42.2	41.8	42.8	45.2	48.2	46.3	49.4
Renter-occupied	3,816	3,826	4,512	4,867	4,955	5,083	5,931	5,899

[1] Based on 2000 census controls. [2] Includes other races not shown separately. [3] The 2003 American Housing Survey (AHS) allowed respondents to choose more than one race. Beginning in 2003, data represent householders who selected this race group only and exclude householders reporting more than one race. The AHS in prior years only allowed respondents to report one race group. See also comments on race in the text for Section 1 and the below cited source. [4] Persons of Hispanic origin may be of any race.

Source: U.S. Census Bureau, Current Housing Reports, Series H150/91, H150/93, H150/95RV, H150/97, H150/99, H150/01, H150/03, and H150/05, *American Housing Survey for the United States.* See <http://www.census.gov/hhes/www/housing/ahs/nationaldata.html>.

Construction and Housing **603**

Table 950. Homeownership Rates by Age of Householder and Household Type: 1990 to 2007

[**In percent**. Represents the proportion of owner households to the total number of occupied households. Based on the Current Population Survey/Housing Vacancy Survey; see source and Appendix III for details]

Age of householder and household type	1990	1995	2000	2001	2002	2003	2004	2005	2006	2007
United States	**63.9**	**64.7**	**67.4**	**67.8**	**67.9**	**68.3**	**69.0**	**68.9**	**68.8**	**68.1**
AGE OF HOUSEHOLDER										
Less than 25 years old	15.7	15.9	21.7	22.5	22.9	22.8	25.2	25.7	24.8	24.8
25 to 29 years old	35.2	34.4	38.1	38.9	38.8	39.8	40.2	40.9	41.8	40.6
30 to 34 years old	51.8	53.1	54.6	54.8	54.9	56.5	57.4	56.8	55.9	54.4
35 to 39 years old	63.0	62.1	65.0	65.5	65.2	65.1	66.2	66.6	66.4	65.0
40 to 44 years old	69.8	68.6	70.6	70.8	71.7	71.3	71.9	71.7	71.2	70.4
45 to 49 years old	73.9	73.7	74.7	75.4	74.8	75.4	76.3	75.0	74.9	74.0
50 to 54 years old	76.8	77.0	78.5	78.2	77.9	77.9	78.2	78.3	77.7	76.9
55 to 59 years old	78.8	78.8	80.4	81.0	80.8	80.9	81.2	80.6	80.4	79.9
60 to 64 years old	79.8	80.3	80.3	81.8	81.6	81.9	82.4	81.9	81.5	81.5
65 to 69 years old	80.0	81.0	83.0	82.4	82.9	82.5	83.2	82.8	82.4	81.7
70 to 74 years old	78.4	80.9	82.6	82.5	82.5	82.0	84.4	82.9	83.0	82.4
75 years old and over	72.3	74.6	77.7	78.1	78.4	78.7	78.8	78.4	79.1	78.7
Less than 35 years old	38.5	38.6	40.8	41.2	41.3	42.2	43.1	43.0	42.6	41.7
35 to 44 years old	66.3	65.2	67.9	68.2	68.6	68.3	69.2	69.3	68.9	67.8
45 to 54 years old	75.2	75.2	76.5	76.7	76.3	76.6	77.2	76.6	76.2	75.4
55 to 64 years old	79.3	79.5	80.3	81.3	81.1	81.4	81.9	81.2	80.9	80.6
65 years and over	76.3	78.1	80.4	80.3	80.6	80.5	81.1	80.6	80.9	80.4
TYPE OF HOUSEHOLD										
Family households:										
Married-couple families	78.1	79.6	82.4	82.9	82.9	83.3	84.0	84.2	84.1	83.8
Male householder, no spouse present	55.2	55.3	57.5	57.9	57.3	57.9	59.6	59.1	58.9	57.4
Female householder, no spouse present	44.0	45.1	49.1	49.9	49.2	49.6	50.9	51.0	51.3	49.9
Nonfamily households:										
One-person	49.0	50.5	53.6	54.4	54.9	55.2	55.8	55.6	55.7	55.2
Male householder	42.4	43.8	47.4	48.2	48.6	50.0	50.5	50.3	50.5	50.2
Female householder	53.6	55.4	58.1	59.0	59.6	59.1	59.9	59.6	59.8	59.1
Other:										
Male householder	31.7	34.2	38.0	38.6	38.7	40.0	41.7	41.7	40.8	40.0
Female householder	32.5	33.0	40.6	41.0	41.9	43.1	43.5	44.8	45.5	42.9

Source: U.S. Census Bureau, "Housing Vacancies and Home Ownership." See <http://www.census.gov/hhes/www/hvs.html>.

Table 951. Homeownership Rates by State: 1990 to 2007

[**In percent**. See headnote, Table 950]

State	1990	1995	2000	2005	2006	2007	State	1990	1995	2000	2005	2006	2007
United States	**63.9**	**64.7**	**67.4**	**68.9**	**68.8**	**68.1**	Missouri	64.0	69.4	74.2	72.3	71.9	70.4
Alabama	68.4	70.1	73.2	76.6	74.2	73.3	Montana	69.1	68.7	70.2	70.4	69.5	67.3
Alaska	58.4	60.9	66.4	66.0	67.2	66.6	Nebraska	67.3	67.1	70.2	70.2	67.6	68.2
Arizona	64.5	62.9	68.0	71.1	71.6	70.4	Nevada	55.8	58.6	64.0	63.4	65.7	63.3
Arkansas	67.8	67.2	68.9	69.2	70.8	69.5	New Hampshire	65.0	66.0	69.2	74.0	74.2	73.8
California	53.8	55.4	57.1	59.7	60.2	58.3	New Jersey	65.0	64.9	66.2	70.1	69.0	68.3
Colorado	59.0	64.6	68.3	71.0	70.1	70.2	New Mexico	68.6	67.0	73.7	71.4	72.0	71.5
Connecticut	67.9	68.2	70.0	70.5	71.1	70.3	New York	53.3	52.7	53.4	55.9	55.7	55.9
Delaware	67.7	71.7	72.0	75.8	76.8	76.8	North Carolina	69.0	70.1	71.1	70.9	70.2	70.3
Dist. of Columbia	36.4	39.2	41.9	45.8	45.9	47.2	North Dakota	67.2	67.3	70.7	68.5	68.3	66.0
Florida	65.1	66.6	68.4	72.4	72.4	71.8	Ohio	68.7	67.9	71.3	73.3	72.1	71.4
Georgia	64.3	66.6	69.8	67.9	68.5	67.6	Oklahoma	70.3	69.8	72.7	72.9	71.6	70.3
Hawaii	55.5	50.2	55.2	59.8	59.9	60.1	Oregon	64.4	63.2	65.3	68.2	68.1	65.7
Idaho	69.4	72.0	70.5	74.2	75.1	74.5	Pennsylvania	73.8	71.5	74.7	73.3	73.2	72.9
Illinois	63.0	66.4	67.9	70.9	70.4	69.4	Rhode Island	58.5	57.9	61.5	63.1	64.6	64.9
Indiana	67.0	71.0	74.9	75.0	74.2	73.8	South Carolina	71.4	71.3	76.5	73.9	74.2	74.1
Iowa	70.7	71.4	75.2	73.9	74.0	73.7	South Dakota	66.2	67.5	71.2	68.4	70.6	70.4
Kansas	69.0	67.5	69.3	69.5	70.0	69.4	Tennessee	68.3	67.0	70.9	70.9	71.3	70.2
Kentucky	65.8	71.2	73.4	71.6	71.7	72.9	Texas	59.7	61.4	63.8	65.9	66.0	66.0
Louisiana	67.8	65.3	68.1	72.5	71.3	71.5	Utah	70.1	71.5	72.7	73.9	73.5	74.9
Maine	74.2	76.7	76.5	73.9	75.3	74.3	Vermont	72.6	70.4	68.7	74.2	74.0	73.7
Maryland	64.9	65.8	69.9	71.2	72.6	71.7	Virginia	69.8	68.1	73.9	71.2	71.1	71.5
Massachusetts	58.6	60.2	59.9	63.4	65.2	64.3	Washington	61.8	61.6	63.6	67.6	66.7	66.8
Michigan	72.3	72.2	77.2	76.4	77.4	76.4	West Virginia	72.0	73.1	75.9	81.3	78.4	77.6
Minnesota	68.0	73.3	76.1	76.5	75.6	73.5	Wisconsin	68.3	67.5	71.8	71.1	70.2	70.5
Mississippi	69.4	71.1	75.2	78.8	76.2	74.0	Wyoming	68.9	69.0	71.0	72.8	73.7	73.2

Source: U.S. Census Bureau, "Housing Vacancies and Home Ownership." See <http://www.census.gov/hhes/www/hvs.html>.

Table 952. Occupied Housing Units—Costs by Region: 2005

[74,931 represents 74,931,000. As of fall. See headnote, Table 953, for an explanation of housing costs. Based on the American Housing Survey; see Appendix III. For composition of regions, see map inside front cover]

Category	Number (1,000)					Percent distribution				
	Total units	North-east	Mid-west	South	West	Total units	North-east	Mid-west	South	West
OWNER-OCCUPIED UNITS										
Total	74,931	13,217	18,360	28,003	15,350	100.0	100.0	100.0	100.0	100.0
Monthly housing costs:										
Less than $300	12,426	1,027	2,652	6,942	1,804	16.6	7.8	14.4	24.8	11.8
$300 to $399	6,763	997	2,008	2,538	1,220	9.0	7.5	10.9	9.1	7.9
$400 to $499	5,096	977	1,456	1,844	819	6.8	7.4	7.9	6.6	5.3
$500 to $599	4,704	1,059	1,235	1,756	654	6.3	8.0	6.7	6.3	4.3
$600 to $699	4,192	847	1,118	1,636	591	5.6	6.4	6.1	5.8	3.9
$700 to $799	3,933	763	1,105	1,436	629	5.2	5.8	6.0	5.1	4.1
$800 to $999	7,632	1,336	2,089	2,885	1,322	10.2	10.1	11.4	10.3	8.6
$1,000 to $1,249	8,031	1,249	2,272	2,821	1,689	10.7	9.4	12.4	10.1	11.0
$1,250 to $1,499	6,184	1,213	1,595	1,884	1,492	8.3	9.2	8.7	6.7	9.7
$1,500 or more	15,971	3,749	2,830	4,261	5,130	21.3	28.4	15.4	15.2	33.4
Median (dol.) [1]	809	941	764	656	1,094	(X)	(X)	(X)	(X)	(X)
RENTER-OCCUPIED UNITS										
Total	33,940	7,120	6,595	11,719	8,507	100.0	100.0	100.0	100.0	100.0
Monthly housing costs:										
Less than $300	2,922	736	637	1,036	514	8.6	10.3	9.7	8.8	6.0
$300 to $399	1,859	316	493	765	285	5.5	4.4	7.5	6.5	3.4
$400 to $499	3,353	515	890	1,380	568	9.9	7.2	13.5	11.8	6.7
$500 to $599	3,897	625	927	1,648	698	11.5	8.8	14.1	14.1	8.2
$600 to $699	4,099	723	952	1,488	936	12.1	10.2	14.4	12.7	11.0
$700 to $799	3,694	703	721	1,317	953	10.9	9.9	10.9	11.2	11.2
$800 to $999	5,273	1,274	817	1,643	1,540	15.5	17.9	12.4	14.0	18.1
$1,000 to $1,249	3,178	816	360	847	1,154	9.4	11.5	5.5	7.2	13.6
$1,250 to $1,499	1,644	421	146	343	733	4.8	5.9	2.2	2.9	8.6
$1,500 or more	1,886	576	201	350	760	5.6	8.1	3.0	3.0	8.9
No cash rent	2,134	415	449	904	366	6.3	5.8	6.8	7.7	4.3
Median (dol.) [1]	694	762	613	639	915	(X)	(X)	(X)	(X)	(X)

X Not applicable.   [1] For explanation of median, see Guide to Tabular Presentation.

Source: U.S. Census Bureau, Current Housing Reports, Series H150/05, *American Housing Survey for the United States.* See <http://www.census.gov/hhes/www/housing/ahs/nationaldata.html>.

Table 953. Occupied Housing Units—Financial Summary by Selected Characteristics of the Householder: 2005

[In thousands of units (108,871 represents 108,871,000), except as indicated. As of fall. Housing costs include real estate taxes, property insurance, utilities, fuel, water, garbage collection, homeowner association fees, mobile home fees, and mortgage. Based on the American Housing Survey; see Appendix III]

Characteristic	Total occu-pied units	Tenure		Black [1]		Hispanic origin [2]		Elderly [3]		Households below poverty level	
		Owner	Renter	Owner	Renter	Owner	Renter	Owner	Renter	Owner	Renter
Total units [4]	108,871	74,931	33,940	6,471	6,975	5,752	5,899	17,818	4,379	6,450	8,674
Monthly housing costs:											
Less than $300	15,348	12,426	2,922	1,272	879	861	343	5,695	818	2,412	1,844
$300 to $399	8,622	6,763	1,859	613	426	399	225	3,008	366	850	736
$400 to $499	8,449	5,096	3,353	466	760	292	509	1,963	427	614	1,037
$500 to $599	8,601	4,704	3,897	474	880	284	735	1,562	386	480	1,052
$600 to $699	8,291	4,192	4,099	402	768	306	797	1,069	400	367	864
$700 to $799	7,627	3,933	3,694	404	899	309	687	735	340	282	708
$800 to $999	12,905	7,632	5,273	733	1,067	674	1,115	1,125	498	414	802
$1,000 or more	36,893	30,186	6,708	2,107	916	2,627	1,271	2,661	666	1,032	828
Median amount (dol.) [5]	753	809	694	702	646	926	734	409	588	395	530
Monthly housing costs as percent of income: [6]											
Less than 5 percent	4,304	4,051	253	300	42	217	35	732	10	20	12
5 to 9 percent	11,687	10,761	925	790	178	626	87	2,858	57	69	48
10 to 14 percent	13,771	11,412	2,359	873	373	625	338	2,989	140	172	68
15 to 19 percent	14,960	11,499	3,462	898	620	716	507	2,294	172	243	140
20 to 24 percent	12,605	8,947	3,658	746	725	627	565	1,693	297	269	215
25 to 29 percent	10,394	6,788	3,607	586	678	570	692	1,265	459	267	453
30 to 34 percent	7,652	4,658	2,994	367	613	484	659	922	355	238	449
35 to 39 percent	5,561	3,344	2,217	334	495	376	368	773	266	355	312
40 percent or more	23,967	12,628	11,339	1,469	2,617	1,463	2,288	4,182	2,062	4,041	5,278
Median amount (percent) [5] . . .	23	20	32	22	35	25	34	20	44	75	77

[1] For persons who selected this race group only. See footnote 3, Table 949.   [2] Persons of Hispanic origin may be of any race.   [3] Householders 65 years old and over.   [4] Includes units with no cash rent not shown separately.   [5] For explanation of median, see Guide to Tabular Presentation.   [6] Money income before taxes.

Source: U.S. Census Bureau, Current Housing Reports, Series H150/05, *American Housing Survey for the United States.* See <http://www.census.gov/hhes/www/housing/ahs/nationaldata.html>.

Table 954. Owner-Occupied Housing Units—Value and Costs by State: 2006

[In percent, except as indicated (75,086 represents 75,086,000). The American Community Survey universe includes the household population and the population living in institutions, college dormitories, and other group quarters. Based on a sample and subject to sampling variability; see Appendix III. For definition of median, see Guide to Tabular Presentation]

State	Total (1,000)	Percent of units with value of—			Median value (dol.)	Median selected monthly owner costs [1] (dol.)	Selected monthly owner costs as a percent of household income in the past 12 months [1]			
		$99,999 or less	$100,000 to $199,999	$200,000 or more			Less than 15 percent	15.0 to 24.9 percent	25.0 to 29.9 percent	30 percent or more
U.S. . . .	75,086	24.1	29.4	46.5	185,200	1,040	16.8	33.3	12.6	36.9
AL.	1,289	47.0	33.4	19.7	107,000	685	24.2	35.6	10.8	28.8
AK.	148	14.3	30.9	54.8	213,200	1,233	19.1	33.5	13.1	34.2
AZ.	1,523	15.1	23.4	61.5	236,500	1,062	16.8	32.0	13.2	37.4
AR.	753	53.4	32.0	14.6	93,900	611	26.2	36.4	10.1	26.9
CA.	7,102	4.9	4.7	90.3	535,700	1,737	11.0	24.7	12.0	51.8
CO	1,269	8.6	28.7	62.7	232,900	1,317	14.5	33.1	13.6	38.5
CT.	921	3.4	20.4	76.3	298,900	1,527	14.3	32.1	13.8	39.6
DE.	238	13.0	27.7	59.3	227,100	1,003	19.8	36.5	12.3	31.3
DC	115	1.9	8.1	90.1	437,700	1,558	17.5	32.0	11.8	37.8
FL.	4,994	15.0	26.2	58.8	230,600	1,045	13.5	28.6	12.4	44.9
GA	2,285	24.9	41.3	33.7	156,800	1,033	18.9	34.5	12.4	33.6
HI	258	2.4	5.8	91.8	529,700	1,465	13.9	26.9	13.1	45.7
ID	391	22.1	41.8	36.1	163,900	870	17.1	36.1	12.7	33.9
IL	3,301	21.1	28.9	50.1	200,200	1,184	15.1	32.7	13.2	38.7
IN	1,756	37.7	44.7	17.6	120,700	874	21.3	39.8	11.9	26.7
IA	886	43.1	40.1	16.7	112,600	780	21.5	40.7	12.6	25.1
KS.	761	43.6	36.6	19.8	114,400	827	21.0	40.8	12.2	25.8
KY.	1,167	44.5	37.2	18.3	111,000	692	23.2	38.1	10.7	27.7
LA.	1,072	43.8	35.7	20.5	114,700	648	25.8	34.6	10.4	28.7
ME	399	24.5	35.3	40.1	170,500	852	18.0	36.3	12.2	33.4
MD	1,450	7.6	15.3	77.1	334,700	1,446	17.1	34.2	13.3	35.0
MA	1,588	2.3	10.8	86.9	370,400	1,546	13.7	30.5	13.7	41.8
MI	2,908	24.4	44.3	31.2	153,300	1,010	16.2	34.9	13.2	35.2
MN	1,558	14.2	32.6	53.2	208,200	1,139	16.3	35.6	14.0	33.9
MS	760	56.1	30.1	13.9	88,600	615	21.1	34.7	10.5	33.1
MO	1,629	34.6	40.7	24.7	131,900	816	21.2	37.5	12.3	28.7
MT.	260	28.8	37.2	34.0	155,500	746	18.7	34.1	12.3	34.7
NE.	476	38.4	43.7	17.9	119,200	862	19.9	39.9	12.4	27.5
NV.	581	7.4	12.8	79.8	315,200	1,377	12.1	28.6	13.4	45.4
NH	364	8.4	21.4	70.2	253,200	1,369	12.7	33.8	14.3	39.0
NJ.	2,110	4.4	12.9	82.7	366,600	1,695	12.9	28.9	13.3	44.7
NM.	506	34.3	34.5	31.3	141,200	736	20.7	36.4	11.5	31.0
NY.	3,941	20.3	19.2	60.5	303,400	1,257	16.4	29.9	12.5	40.9
NC	2,351	32.1	40.3	27.6	137,200	866	19.8	36.3	12.2	31.3
ND	182	50.2	37.4	12.4	99,700	652	24.2	39.7	12.8	23.0
OH	3,150	30.2	46.5	23.3	135,200	956	17.5	37.3	13.0	31.8
OK	950	53.8	33.4	12.7	94,500	673	24.6	36.9	11.1	26.8
OR	939	10.7	26.5	62.8	236,600	1,121	14.7	32.1	13.8	39.1
PA.	3,475	32.4	34.5	33.1	145,200	892	18.6	35.8	12.7	32.6
RI	255	2.2	13.3	84.5	295,700	1,391	13.3	29.6	13.3	43.5
SC.	1,165	39.6	35.9	24.5	122,400	772	21.0	35.4	11.2	31.8
SD.	216	43.2	39.2	17.6	112,600	708	19.6	41.3	12.0	26.8
TN.	1,660	38.3	39.4	22.3	123,100	773	19.4	36.7	11.8	31.5
TX.	5,291	43.0	37.5	19.5	114,000	956	17.4	36.2	12.7	33.3
UT.	586	10.3	44.5	45.2	188,500	1,093	16.1	36.6	13.9	33.1
VT.	182	14.9	37.6	47.5	193,000	1,055	13.6	35.0	14.7	36.5
VA.	2,030	16.4	24.4	59.3	244,200	1,175	17.8	35.0	12.5	34.2
WA	1,620	9.4	22.6	68.0	267,600	1,277	13.7	32.0	14.2	39.8
WV	555	56.8	28.3	15.0	89,700	462	28.3	36.5	10.3	24.5
WI.	1,571	19.3	45.9	34.8	163,500	1,052	14.2	37.0	15.0	33.4
WY	144	26.7	44.1	29.2	148,900	749	22.4	38.0	12.5	26.9

[1] For homes with a mortgage. Includes all forms of debt where the property is pledged as security for repayment of the debt, including deeds of trust, land contracts, home equity loans. Also includes cost of property insurance, utilities, real estate taxes, etc.

Source: U.S. Census Bureau, 2006 American Community Survey Tables B25075. Value for Owner-Occupied Housing Units; B25077. Median Value for Owner-Occupied Housing Units; B25088. Median Selected Monthly Owner Costs by Mortgage Status; B25091. Mortgage Status by Selected Monthly Owner Cost as a Percentage of Household Income; using American FactFinder®. See <http://factfinder.census.gov/>; (accessed May 17, 2008).

Table 955. **Renter-Occupied Housing Units—Gross Rent by State: 2006**

[In percent, except as indicated (36,531 represents 36,531,000. The American Community Survey universe includes the household population and the population living in institutions, college dormitories, and other group quarters. Based on a sample and subject to sampling variability; see Appendix III]

State	Total [1] (1,000)	Percent of units with gross rent of—					Median gross rent (dol.)	Gross rent as a percent of household income in the past 12 months			
		$299 or less	$300 to $499	$500 to $749	$750 to $999	$1,000 or more		Less than 15 percent	15.0 to 24.9 percent	25.0 to 29.9 percent	30 percent or more
U.S.	**36,531**	**6.4**	**12.2**	**27.1**	**22.4**	**25.9**	**763**	**11.9**	**23.7**	**10.8**	**46.0**
AL	507	10.0	21.7	34.1	14.4	6.7	573	13.3	22.1	8.9	41.0
AK	82	2.2	7.6	18.2	28.3	30.4	883	13.6	23.9	10.8	37.8
AZ	702	3.8	10.5	31.3	23.7	25.1	762	11.9	25.1	10.8	45.2
AR	350	9.3	23.6	34.7	14.0	6.5	566	13.0	22.1	9.1	42.3
CA	5,049	3.1	4.8	14.8	23.2	50.4	1,029	9.4	22.6	11.2	51.9
CO	578	4.7	9.8	30.0	24.7	26.3	780	9.7	25.1	11.5	47.1
CT	404	7.2	6.4	19.6	26.7	36.3	886	12.4	22.7	12.4	47.6
DE	82	6.0	7.4	21.4	34.0	26.6	830	13.0	25.4	9.5	46.0
DC	136	10.8	6.2	18.3	21.2	41.0	914	13.4	24.0	12.2	45.3
FL	2,112	4.1	6.7	21.8	28.8	33.4	872	8.2	21.6	10.8	52.0
GA	1,092	6.3	12.6	29.4	27.2	17.9	738	12.1	22.9	10.6	45.6
HI	175	5.0	4.6	10.0	18.5	52.2	1,116	10.5	21.5	10.8	45.7
ID	158	6.2	21.3	34.9	19.3	10.0	623	12.5	28.2	10.9	38.7
IL	1,423	6.7	11.6	28.0	26.0	23.2	761	12.6	24.3	10.3	46.0
IN	679	6.5	17.9	40.2	20.0	9.3	638	12.8	24.8	10.3	44.5
IA	323	9.0	23.4	37.2	15.7	7.0	584	15.2	25.6	9.9	40.3
KS	327	7.4	21.2	35.7	17.6	10.6	609	14.2	26.3	10.2	40.8
KY	485	11.9	24.9	33.6	13.2	5.3	548	14.5	23.9	9.0	40.0
LA	493	8.5	17.4	33.0	17.1	9.9	618	12.8	20.1	8.3	42.5
ME	149	12.0	17.5	31.9	18.6	12.0	636	12.4	24.0	12.5	42.2
MD	639	5.7	5.4	15.2	26.1	42.7	953	12.4	25.9	12.1	43.7
MA	858	10.0	8.5	14.7	20.4	42.8	933	11.2	22.9	12.1	48.6
MI	961	7.6	14.7	35.1	22.2	14.7	675	11.5	22.7	10.2	47.8
MN	484	9.6	12.6	32.1	22.7	18.1	701	11.3	26.1	12.2	44.6
MS	315	9.5	19.8	31.9	15.4	6.0	584	10.7	18.0	8.7	42.7
MO	676	9.0	21.1	35.6	17.8	9.0	607	13.5	24.2	11.1	42.3
MT	112	9.9	24.4	31.0	13.0	9.3	571	14.3	21.8	10.5	40.0
NE	225	8.6	22.5	35.5	16.5	9.5	593	15.4	26.6	10.6	39.0
NV	356	2.6	4.4	21.7	30.0	38.4	917	10.1	26.6	10.9	48.1
NH	141	7.6	6.5	19.6	28.5	32.3	861	10.2	27.0	9.9	46.4
NJ	1,025	6.0	4.5	12.5	28.4	45.0	974	11.6	24.7	11.3	47.3
NM	220	7.3	21.3	33.1	15.7	11.9	617	13.9	21.7	10.0	41.9
NY	3,147	7.1	9.2	20.6	21.9	37.4	875	13.3	22.4	10.7	48.1
NC	1,103	6.4	16.5	36.8	20.8	10.9	656	13.3	23.6	10.3	42.7
ND	91	10.8	34.6	30.1	9.5	4.5	497	17.1	25.9	9.9	36.0
OH	1,349	7.9	18.8	37.6	20.2	10.0	627	12.6	24.3	10.9	44.9
OK	435	8.1	23.5	36.1	15.5	7.3	580	13.0	23.6	10.7	41.4
OR	511	5.1	11.5	36.9	23.8	18.6	714	10.9	25.2	11.5	47.0
PA	1,370	8.2	17.2	31.4	21.2	15.3	664	13.5	24.4	10.9	43.0
RI	150	11.5	7.6	18.1	31.1	28.3	840	11.6	25.2	13.7	44.9
SC	492	7.4	16.7	35.4	18.7	10.0	640	12.5	23.0	10.3	40.3
SD	96	15.8	25.2	31.9	9.9	5.9	522	16.6	28.1	9.2	34.0
TN	715	9.5	18.6	36.7	18.1	8.1	613	12.1	23.6	10.9	42.3
TX	2,818	4.6	12.6	34.8	24.0	17.3	711	12.2	24.4	10.5	44.4
UT	228	4.4	13.1	38.1	22.7	16.6	697	12.9	27.0	11.9	42.1
VT	71	9.9	9.2	31.4	24.8	17.3	716	11.3	22.6	11.0	47.1
VA	875	5.6	10.4	21.8	21.6	34.1	846	12.6	25.9	11.7	42.1
WA	852	5.6	9.6	28.7	26.0	25.7	779	12.2	25.9	11.5	44.9
WV	188	14.7	27.3	29.7	8.3	3.6	499	13.0	20.8	9.2	39.3
WI	659	6.7	16.0	38.2	22.9	11.1	658	12.4	26.9	11.2	43.3
WY	63	6.2	23.8	35.2	12.7	10.0	601	20.9	22.7	13.4	30.0

[1] Includes units with no cash rent.

Source: U.S. Census Bureau, 2006 American Community Survey Tables B25063. Gross Rent; B25064. Median Gross Rent; B25070. Gross Rent as a Percentage of Household Income; using American FactFinder®. See <http://factfinder.census.gov/>; (accessed 17 May 2008).

Table 956. Mortgage Characteristics—Owner-Occupied Units: 2005

[In thousands (74,931 represents 74,931,000). As of fall. Based on the American Housing Survey; see Appendix III]

Mortgage characteristic	Total owner-occu-pied units	Housing unit characteristics — New con-struc-tion [1]	Housing unit characteristics — Mobile homes	Household characteristics — Black [2]	Household characteristics — His-panic [3]	Household characteristics — Elderly [4]	Household characteristics — Moved in past year	Household characteristics — Below poverty level
ALL OWNERS								
Total	**74,931**	**4,919**	**5,516**	**6,471**	**5,752**	**17,818**	**6,591**	**6,450**
Mortgages currently on property:								
None, owned free and clear	24,776	839	3,066	2,078	1,539	12,139	1,258	3,690
Regular and home equity mortgages	48,394	3,987	2,352	4,190	4,098	5,224	5,192	2,512
Regular mortgage	44,652	3,843	2,233	3,971	3,964	4,115	5,064	2,338
Home equity lump sum mortage	4,385	269	87	264	253	527	269	164
Home equity line of credit	10,044	712	132	438	476	1,320	652	297
Not reported	1,694	87	96	201	115	391	139	243
Number of regular and home equity mortgages: [5]								
1 mortgage	33,409	2,815	2,053	3,208	3,085	3,878	3,634	1,824
2 mortgages	10,877	921	108	558	719	688	1,149	259
3 mortgages or more	1,164	100	5	56	90	77	146	40
Type of mortgage:								
Regular and home equity lump sum [5]	2,958	224	15	157	183	162	208	96
With home equity line of credit	587	38	–	23	44	45	54	27
No home equity line of credit	2,348	183	15	131	137	115	151	69
Regular no home equity lump sum [5]	41,694	3,619	2,218	3,814	3,781	3,953	4,855	2,242
With home equity line of credit	6,835	572	70	290	366	455	509	144
No home equity line of credit	31,992	2,899	1,962	3,162	3,223	2,936	4,089	1,714
Home equity lump sum no regular [5]	1,427	45	73	107	70	365	61	68
With home equity line of credit	307	3	15	14	3	76	22	19
No home equity line of credit	1,099	42	57	91	66	280	40	46
No regular or home equity lump sum [5]	28,851	1,031	3,210	2,393	1,718	13,338	1,466	4,045
With home equity line of credit	2,315	99	46	112	64	744	67	107
No home equity line of credit	24,842	845	3,068	2,081	1,539	12,203	1,260	3,695
OWNERS WITH ONE OR MORE REGULAR OR LUMP SUM HOME EQUITY MORTGAGES								
Total [5]	**46,079**	**3,888**	**2,306**	**4,078**	**4,034**	**4,480**	**5,125**	**2,405**
Type of primary mortgage:								
FHA	4,689	450	111	820	615	298	551	238
VA	1,809	160	37	231	115	150	203	66
RHS/RD [6]	364	41	41	44	31	23	50	29
Other types	35,908	3,087	1,894	2,561	3,049	3,332	4,059	1,621
Mortgage origination:								
Placed new mortgage(s)	45,798	3,879	2,264	4,032	3,977	4,448	5,077	2,371
Primary obtained when property acquired	27,592	3,401	1,872	2,844	2,771	2,304	4,940	1,718
Obtained later	18,206	478	392	1,188	1,206	2,144	138	653
Assumed	231	3	40	41	47	27	43	32
Wrap-around	11	6	2	–	3	3	5	–
Combination of the above	40	–	–	5	8	2	–	2
Payment plan of primary mortgage:								
Fixed payment, self amortizing	37,392	3,187	1,853	3,227	3,284	3,297	3,955	1,677
Adjustable rate mortgage	2,441	235	92	194	253	178	404	98
Adjustable term mortgage	160	–	15	13	7	43	7	14
Graduated payment mortgage	517	71	19	49	47	36	133	26
Balloon	518	76	45	22	51	37	102	32
Combination of the above	474	67	5	26	28	59	91	14
Payment plan of secondary mortgage:								
Units with two or more mortgages [5]	5,286	494	27	339	478	260	834	143
Fixed payment, self amortizing	3,897	334	25	287	344	171	571	108
Adjustable rate mortgage	460	67	–	11	37	21	110	3
Adjustable term mortgage	156	13	–	3	27	29	13	5
Graduated payment mortgage	70	13	–	5	16	–	35	2
Balloon	106	11	3	5	11	3	15	5
Other	5	–	–	–	–	–	–	–
Combination of the above	174	31	–	2	5	4	29	4
Reason primary refinanced:								
Units with a refinanced primary mortgage [7]	17,685	535	302	1,102	1,192	1,502	133	513
To get a lower interest rate	15,322	453	195	851	978	1,186	80	369
To increase payment period	568	10	13	31	57	45	10	12
To reduce payment period	2,007	29	13	68	126	111	2	128
To renew or extend a loan that has fallen due	178	–	3	20	12	17	–	12
To receive cash	2,375	60	36	169	230	261	25	70
Other reason	1,646	42	95	137	116	185	23	67
Cash received in primary mortgage refinance:								
Units receiving refinance cash	2,375	60	36	169	230	261	25	70
Median amount received (dol.)	28,084	(NA)	(NA)	19,690	31,701	33,553	(NA)	21,390

– Represents or rounds to zero.   NA Not available.   [1] Constructed in the past 4 years.   [2] For persons who selected this race group only. See footnite 3, Table 949.   [3] Persons of Hispanic origin may be of any race.   [4] 65 years old and over.   [5] Includes "don't know" and "not reported."   [6] Rural Housing Service/Rural Development Mortgage, formerly Farmers Home Administration.   [7] Persons reporting more than one reason are counted once in the total.

Source: U.S. Census Bureau, Current Housing Reports, Series H150/05, *American Housing Survey for the United States.* See <http://www.census.gov/hhes/www/housing/ahs/nationaldata.html> and <http://www.census.gov/hhes/www/housing/ahs/nationaldata.html>.

Table 957. **Occupied Housing Units—Neighborhood Indicators by Selected Characteristics of the Householder: 2005**

[In thousands (108,871 represents 108,871,000). **As of fall.** Based on the American Housing Survey; see Appendix III]

Characteristic	Total occupied units	Tenure Owner	Tenure Renter	Black [1] Owner	Black [1] Renter	Hispanic origin [2] Owner	Hispanic origin [2] Renter	Elderly [3] Owner	Elderly [3] Renter	Households below poverty level Owner	Households below poverty level Renter
Total units.	**108,871**	**74,931**	**33,940**	**6,471**	**6,975**	**5,752**	**5,899**	**17,818**	**4,379**	**6,450**	**8,674**
Street noise or traffic present [4] . . .	28,436	16,918	11,519	1,797	2,565	1,363	1,757	4,188	1,221	1,609	2,978
Condition not bothersome.	16,866	9,988	6,878	1,078	1,510	731	973	2,869	880	942	1,720
Condition bothersome	11,522	6,906	4,616	719	1,048	633	782	1,314	340	664	1,252
So bothersome they want to move	4,370	2,314	2,056	274	596	230	365	311	126	241	658
Neighborhood crime present [4] . . .	16,419	9,203	7,215	1,340	1,968	885	1,351	1,825	566	920	2,115
Condition not bothersome.	6,944	4,025	2,920	587	777	339	439	936	312	359	808
Condition bothersome	9,447	5,166	4,280	748	1,179	546	912	881	255	558	1,302
So bothersome they want to move	4,003	1,646	2,357	288	724	253	562	216	80	191	806
Odors present [4]	5,991	3,445	2,546	362	685	330	495	644	207	366	797
Condition not bothersome.	2,279	1,397	882	160	211	113	119	293	76	131	246
Condition bothersome	3,708	2,048	1,660	202	474	217	374	351	129	235	550
So bothersome they want to move	1,415	617	799	87	283	72	196	95	49	69	312
Other problems:											
Noise	2,552	1,458	1,094	155	260	137	224	314	91	144	318
Litter or housing deterioration . .	1,918	1,226	691	168	237	130	138	289	37	80	209
Poor city or county services . . .	844	513	330	102	128	84	59	106	18	41	85
People	4,057	2,530	1,527	283	381	249	272	456	67	247	505
With public transportation [4]	58,623	35,092	23,531	3,888	5,455	3,584	4,542	8,315	3,063	2,768	6,000
Household uses it at least weekly	11,219	4,148	7,071	902	2,218	616	1,838	771	859	454	2,285
Household uses it less than weekly	8,641	5,095	3,545	592	803	430	642	1,007	483	321	999
Household does not use	37,978	25,425	12,553	2,329	2,362	2,498	2,019	6,440	1,679	1,958	2,627
No public transportation.	46,499	37,361	9,138	2,392	1,268	1,958	1,196	8,956	1,188	3,422	2,393
Not reported	3,750	2,478	1,271	192	251	210	161	548	128	261	280
Police protection:											
Satisfactory	96,834	66,895	29,939	5,543	5,923	4,948	5,149	16,024	4,000	5,449	7,390
Unsatisfacory	8,391	5,714	2,676	693	781	633	572	1,195	183	726	923
Secured communities [5]:											
Community access secured with walls or fences	6,925	3,150	3,775	223	846	357	893	974	543	221	844
Community access not secured	101,136	71,201	29,935	6,163	6,069	5,353	4,977	16,690	3,803	6,137	7,754
Secured multiunits: [5]											
Multiunit access secured	5,841	1,061	4,781	81	1,029	99	694	389	1,306	154	1,308
Multiunit access not secured. . .	19,792	2,645	17,147	269	3,824	277	3,339	774	1,926	252	4,416
Senior citizen communities:											
Households with persons 55 years old and over	42,934	34,557	8,377	2,865	1,533	1,945	1,086	17,818	4,379	3,902	2,537
Community age restricted [6] . .	2,834	1,435	1,399	47	198	45	106	1,118	1,228	222	536
Access to structure:											
Enter building from outside [4,7] .	25,778	3,740	22,038	349	4,882	380	4,053	1,179	3,248	411	5,757
Use of steps not required . . .	10,049	1,498	8,550	97	1,738	165	1,634	556	1,777	165	2,517
Use of steps required	15,692	2,229	13,463	252	3,139	214	2,412	621	1,460	241	3,238
Enter home from outside [4,8] . . .	83,093	71,191	11,903	6,122	2,093	5,372	1,845	16,639	1,131	6,039	2,916
Use of steps not required . . .	39,953	34,712	5,241	2,869	903	3,197	945	8,271	527	2,689	1,228
Use of steps required	43,043	36,393	6,650	3,247	1,187	2,167	900	8,340	604	3,341	1,688
Community quality:											
Some or all activities present . .	38,786	25,667	13,119	2,219	2,632	1,783	1,836	6,522	2,210	1,815	3,281
Community center or clubhouse.	23,287	14,379	8,908	1,243	1,782	961	1,172	4,111	1,696	982	2,094
Golf in the community.	6,236	4,678	1,558	306	200	233	184	1,159	209	255	338
Trails in the community.	18,641	13,581	5,061	1,012	733	801	630	2,955	767	738	1,091
Shuttle bus.	9,565	5,831	3,734	429	542	411	500	2,084	1,142	474	1,145
Daycare.	14,531	9,883	4,648	1,111	1,209	691	722	2,212	533	736	1,319
Private or restricted beach, park, or shoreline	6,556	4,937	1,620	244	278	267	194	1,190	193	316	368
Trash, litter, or junk on street: [9]											
None	96,984	68,345	28,639	5,503	5,451	5,077	4,824	16,494	4,011	5,601	6,969
Minor accumulation	6,578	3,273	3,305	479	889	373	637	617	225	406	1,036
Major accumulation	2,757	1,450	1,308	216	414	148	322	336	70	198	467

[1] For persons who selected this race group only. See footnote 3, Table 949. [2] Persons of Hispanic origin may be of any race. [3] Householders 65 years old and over. [4] Includes those not reporting. [5] Public access is restricted (walls, gates, private security). Includes high rise apartments, retirement communities, resorts, etc. [6] At least one family member must be aged 55 years old or older. [7] Restricted to multiunits. [8] Restricted to single units. [9] Or on any properties within 300 feet.

Source: U.S. Census Bureau, Current Housing Reports, Series H150/05, *American Housing Survey for the United States.* See <http://www.census.gov/hhes/www/housing/ahs/nationaldata.html>.

Table 958. **Heating Equipment and Fuels for Occupied Units: 1995 to 2005**

[97,693 represents 97,693,000. **As of fall.** Based on American Housing Survey. See Appendix III]

Type of equipment or fuel	Number (1,000)					Percent distribution	
	1995	1999	2001	2003 [1]	2005	1995	2005
Occupied units, total.	**97,693**	**102,803**	**106,261**	**105,842**	**108,871**	**100.0**	**100.0**
Heating equipment:							
Warm air furnace.	53,165	62,018	65,262	65,380	68,275	54.4	62.7
Steam or hot water	13,669	13,153	13,441	13,257	12,880	14.0	11.8
Heat pumps	9,406	10,992	11,080	11,347	12,484	9.6	11.5
Built-in electric units.	7,035	4,939	5,063	4,760	4,699	7.2	4.3
Floor, wall, or pipeless furnace. . .	4,963	5,310	5,343	5,322	5,102	5.1	4.7
Room heaters with flue.	1,620	1,624	1,542	1,432	1,294	1.7	1.2
Room heaters without flue.	1,642	1,790	1,558	1,509	1,327	1.7	1.2
Fireplaces, stoves, portable							
heaters or other.	5,150	2,434	2,571	2,396	2,411	5.3	2.2
None.	1,044	544	401	439	399	1.1	0.4
House main heating fuel:							
Electricity.	26,771	31,142	32,590	32,341	34,263	27.4	31.5
Utility gas.	49,203	52,366	54,689	54,928	56,317	50.4	51.7
Bottled, tank, or LP gas	4,251	5,905	6,079	6,134	6,228	4.4	5.7
Fuel oil, kerosene, etc..	12,029	10,750	10,473	10,136	9,929	12.3	9.1
Coal or coke.	210	168	128	126	95	0.2	0.1
Wood and other fuel	4,186	1,927	1,902	1,735	1,640	4.3	1.5
None.	1,042	545	400	441	398	1.1	0.4
Cooking fuel:							
Electricity.	57,621	61,315	63,685	62,859	65,297	59.0	60.0
Gas [2].	39,218	41,051	42,161	42,612	43,316	40.1	39.8
Other fuel	566	69	66	62	51	0.6	(Z)
None.	287	368	349	309	206	0.3	0.2

Z Less than 0.05 percent.   [1] Based on 2000 census controls.   [2] Includes utility, bottled, tank, and LP gas.

Source: U.S. Census Bureau, Current Housing Reports, Series H150/95RV, H150/99, H150/01, H150/03, and H150/05, *American Housing Survey for the United States.* See <http://www.census.gov/hhes/www/housing/ahs/nationaldata.html>.

Table 959. **Occupied Housing Units—Housing Indicators by Selected Characteristics of the Householder: 2005**

[**In thousands of units (108,871 represents 108,871,000). As of fall.** Based on the American Housing Survey; see Appendix III]

Characteristic	Total occu-pied units	Tenure		Black [1]		Hispanic origin [2]		Elderly [3]		Households below poverty level	
		Owner	Renter	Owner	Renter	Owner	Renter	Owner	Renter	Owner	Renter
Total units	**108,871**	**74,931**	**33,940**	**6,471**	**6,975**	**5,752**	**5,899**	**17,818**	**4,379**	**6,450**	**8,674**
Amenities:											
Porch, deck, balcony,											
or patio	92,659	68,940	23,719	5,633	4,651	5,118	3,932	16,276	2,605	5,661	5,586
Telephone available	105,741	73,152	32,589	6,265	6,671	5,599	5,672	17,486	4,209	6,218	8,232
Usable fireplace	37,804	33,757	4,047	2,123	559	1,900	567	6,879	304	1,736	571
Separate dining room.	52,782	43,119	9,663	3,833	2,197	3,074	1,574	9,842	929	3,176	2,122
With 2 or more living											
rooms or rec. rooms.	32,544	30,183	2,360	2,128	327	1,572	203	6,431	204	1,468	371
Garage or carport with											
home.	68,238	57,322	10,917	3,785	1,364	4,266	1,969	13,917	1,238	3,895	1,873
Cars and trucks available:											
No cars, trucks, or vans . . .	9,227	2,462	6,765	526	2,186	158	1,224	1,528	1,938	794	3,232
Other households without											
cars	13,794	9,614	4,180	625	556	881	864	1,760	269	904	921
1 car with or without trucks											
or vans	51,687	34,948	16,740	3,090	3,328	2,449	2,687	10,216	1,945	3,379	3,774
2 cars	26,066	20,773	5,294	1,685	791	1,653	944	3,695	199	1,082	645
3 or more cars	8,097	7,134	962	544	113	612	180	621	28	290	102
Selected deficiencies:											
Signs of rats in last											
3 months	880	464	416	48	131	102	156	57	25	50	154
Signs of mice in last											
3 months	6,140	3,917	2,223	366	669	233	520	737	180	420	669
Holes in floors.	981	489	492	46	139	47	115	77	20	119	184
Open cracks or holes.	5,241	2,797	2,445	279	620	259	415	448	143	404	737
Broken plaster or peeling											
paint (interior of unit)	2,218	1,059	1,159	147	320	118	216	215	87	174	359
No electrical wiring	50	40	10	–	–	3	–	10	2	15	2
Exposed wiring	700	459	240	55	46	32	29	100	30	71	90
Rooms without electric											
outlet.	1,543	898	645	113	160	88	119	196	60	161	180
Water leakage from											
inside structure [4]	9,049	5,210	3,840	494	876	422	665	825	286	422	1,003
Water leakage from											
outside structure [4]	11,701	8,391	3,310	784	719	498	493	1,562	244	668	853

– Represents or rounds to zero.   [1] For persons who selected this race group only. See footnote 3, Table 949.   [2] Persons of Hispanic origin may be of any race.   [3] Householders 65 years old and over.   [4] During the 12 months prior to the survey.

Source: U.S. Census Bureau, Current Housing Reports, Series H150/05, *American Housing Survey for the United States.* See <http://www.census.gov/hhes/www/housing/ahs/nationaldata.html>.

Table 960. **Net Stock of Residential Fixed Assets: 1990 to 2006**

[In billions of dollars (6,260 represents $6,260,000,000,000). End of year estimates]

Item	1990	1995	2000	2001	2002	2003	2004	2005	2006
Total residential fixed assets. . .	6,260	8,028	10,907	11,712	12,457	13,504	15,098	16,577	17,445
By type of owner and legal form of organization:									
Private	6,111	7,840	10,676	11,465	12,193	13,225	14,803	16,245	17,104
Corporate.	66	77	100	105	110	116	127	139	146
Noncorporate	6,045	7,763	10,576	11,360	12,083	13,109	14,676	16,106	16,958
Government.	149	188	232	247	264	280	296	332	341
Federal	52	62	75	79	83	88	94	100	104
State and local	97	127	156	168	181	192	202	232	237
By industry:									
Private	6,111	7,840	10,676	11,465	12,193	13,225	14,803	16,245	17,104
Farm.	49	51	72	77	81	86	91	96	98
Nonfarm	6,062	7,789	10,603	11,388	12,113	13,139	14,712	16,149	17,005
By tenure group: [1]									
Owner-occupied	4,516	5,988	8,329	8,996	9,614	10,499	11,826	13,035	13,766
Farm.	49	51	72	77	81	86	91	96	98
Nonfarm	4,467	5,937	8,256	8,919	9,534	10,413	11,735	12,939	13,668
Tenant-occupied	1,719	2,011	2,543	2,677	2,802	2,962	3,224	3,491	3,626

[1] Excludes stocks of other nonfarm residential assets, which consists primarily of dormitories, and of fraternity and sorority houses.

Source: U.S. Bureau of Economic Analysis, "Table 5.1 Current-Cost Net Stock of Residential Fixed Assets by Type of Owner, Legal Form of Organization, Industry, and Tenure Group"; published 8 August 2007; <http://www.bea.gov/national/FA2004/SelectTable.asp#S5>.

Table 961. **Home Remodeling—Number of Households with Work Done by Amount Spent: 2007**

[In thousands, except percent (3,335 represents 3,335,000). As of fall 2007. For work done in the prior 12 months. Based on household survey and subject to sampling error; see source]

Remodeling project	Total households with work done [1]		Households with work done by outside contractor	Number of households by amount spent (dol.)		
	Number	Percent of all households		Under $1,000	$1,000 to $2,999	Over $3,000
Conversion of garage/attic/basement into living space	3,335	1.5	867	776	599	1,482
Remodel bathroom	15,354	7.0	4,001	6,168	2,971	3,024
Remodel kitchen.	11,066	5.0	3,773	2,921	1,698	4,166
Remodel bedroom.	8,360	3.8	1,120	4,420	965	756
Remodel/convert room to home office . . .	3,502	1.6	310	1,974	387	154
Remodel other rooms.	8,079	3.7	1,296	3,201	1,486	1,313
Add bathroom.	1,911	0.9	489	291	462	661
Add/extend garage	959	0.4	366	140	103	564
Add other rooms—exterior addition.	1,652	0.8	552	245	104	969
Add deck/porch/patio	6,310	2.9	1,946	1,585	1,462	2,011
Roofing	9,513	4.3	5,593	1,685	1,870	4,199
Siding—vinyl/metal	2,810	1.3	1,425	492	485	1,202
Aluminum windows	1,409	0.6	639	361	218	346
Clad-wood/wood windows.	1,012	0.5	374	256	216	320
Vinyl windows.	5,288	2.4	2,504	987	1,273	1,854
Ceramic tile floors	7,024	3.2	2,393	3,432	1,242	974
Hardwood floors	5,931	2.7	2,052	1,578	1,380	1,685
Laminate flooring.	5,133	2.3	1,292	2,212	1,299	508
Vinyl flooring	3,267	1.5	1,078	1,883	478	116
Carpeting.	9,518	4.3	5,896	3,406	2,784	1,488
Kitchen cabinets	5,278	2.4	2,014	1,043	1,010	1,783
Kitchen counter tops	6,520	3.0	3,228	1,836	1,205	2,029
Skylights	1,246	0.6	594	410	251	172
Exterior doors.	6,793	3.1	2,618	3,708	1,112	501
Interior doors	4,723	2.1	1,241	2,850	383	237
Garage doors	3,117	1.4	1,823	1,251	991	119
Concrete or masonry work	4,734	2.1	2,196	1,591	983	1,101
Swimming pool—inground.	556	0.3	287	87	29	237
Wall paneling	1,425	0.7	105	623	152	52
Ceramic wall tile	2,623	1.2	724	1,392	321	199

[1] Includes no response and amount unknown.

Source: Mediamark Research Inc., New York, NY, *Top-Line Reports,* (copyright). See <http://www.mediamark.com/>.

Table 962. **Expenditures by Residential Property Owners for Improvements and Maintenance and Repairs by Type of Payment and Year Structure Built: 1995 to 2007**

[In millions of dollars (124,971 represents $124,971,000,000). Based on personal interviews and mail surveys; see source for details]

Type of expenditure	All residential properties	Owner-occupied one-unit properties							
		Total [1]	Payments to contractors	Materials purchased by owners			Year structure built		
				Total	For jobs done by owners	For jobs done under contract	Before 1960	1960 to 1979	1980 to 2003
Total:									
1995	124,971	79,003	63,017	15,987	12,305	3,682	30,080	28,157	14,718
2000	152,975	100,161	84,778	15,382	11,682	3,700	30,451	27,872	32,717
2003	176,899	115,876	101,207	14,669	11,750	2,920	40,497	29,498	45,881
2004	198,556	136,080	114,197	21,883	17,213	4,670	39,452	36,035	60,594
2005	215,030	159,458	133,684	25,774	20,365	5,409	40,821	45,505	73,132
2006	228,208	167,154	141,439	25,715	21,615	4,100	43,582	39,196	84,376
2007	226,359	168,428	141,571	26,857	22,445	4,412	44,001	49,831	74,597
Maintenance and repairs:									
1995	47,032	25,460	19,487	5,973	5,498	476	9,979	8,388	5,511
2000	42,236	22,411	18,260	4,151	3,384	767	8,074	5,226	6,788
2003	44,094	18,381	15,714	2,667	2,387	279	5,583	4,545	8,253
2004	50,611	26,575	20,655	5,920	5,356	564	8,197	6,401	11,977
2005	53,293	32,888	24,574	8,314	7,869	444	9,315	8,022	15,551
2006	53,389	31,078	23,299	7,778	7,133	645	8,633	8,405	14,040
2007	54,738	33,567	24,480	9,087	8,491	597	10,353	9,089	14,126
Improvements:									
1995	77,940	53,543	43,530	10,013	6,807	3,206	20,101	19,768	9,208
2000	110,739	77,750	66,517	11,232	8,298	2,934	22,377	22,646	25,929
2003	132,805	97,495	85,494	12,003	9,362	2,640	34,914	24,953	37,628
2004	147,945	109,506	93,542	15,962	11,857	4,106	31,254	29,634	48,617
2005	161,737	126,570	109,110	17,460	12,496	4,964	31,507	37,483	57,581
2006	174,819	136,076	118,140	17,936	14,481	3,455	34,950	30,790	70,336
2007	171,621	134,861	117,091	17,769	13,954	3,816	33,648	40,744	60,470

[1] Includes year built not reported, not shown separately.

Source: U.S. Census Bureau, "Residential Improvement and Repair Statistics." See <http://www.census.gov/const/www/c50index.html>.

Table 963. **Commercial Buildings—Summary: 2003**

[4,645 represents 4,645,000. Excludes mall buildings. Building type based on predominant activity in which the occupants were engaged. Based on a sample survey of building representatives conducted in 2003, therefore subject to sampling variability. For commercial building energy expenditures, see Table 887, Section 19]

Characteristic	All buildings (1,000)	Total floor-space (mil. sq. ft.)	Total workers in all buildings (1,000)	Mean square foot per building [1] (1,000)	Mean square foot per worker [1]	Mean operating hours per week [1]
All buildings	**4,645**	**64,783**	**72,807**	**13.9**	**890**	**61**
Building floorspace (sq. ft.):						
1,001 to 5,000	2,552	6,789	9,936	2.7	683	57
5,001 to 10,000	889	6,585	7,512	7.4	877	61
10,001 to 25,000	738	11,535	10,787	15.6	1,069	67
25,001 to 50,000	241	8,668	8,881	35.9	976	72
50,001 to 100,000.	129	9,057	8,432	70.4	1,074	80
100,001 to 200,000.	65	9,064	11,632	138.8	779	89
200,001 to 500,000.	25	7,176	6,883	289.0	1,043	100
Over 500,000.	7	5,908	8,744	896.1	676	115
Principal activity within building:						
Education	386	9,874	12,489	25.6	791	50
Food sales	226	1,255	1,430	5.6	877	107
Food service	297	1,654	3,129	5.6	528	86
Health care	129	3,163	6,317	24.6	501	59
Inpatient	8	1,905	3,716	241.4	513	168
Outpatient	121	1,258	2,600	10.4	484	52
Lodging.	142	5,096	2,457	35.8	2,074	167
Retail (other than mall).	443	4,317	3,463	9.7	1,246	59
Office	824	12,208	28,154	14.8	434	55
Public assembly	277	3,939	2,395	14.2	1,645	50
Public order and safety	71	1,090	1,347	15.5	809	103
Religious worship	370	3,754	1,706	10.1	2,200	32
Service	622	4,050	3,667	6.5	1,105	55
Warehouse and storage	597	10,078	4,369	16.9	2,306	66
Other	79	1,738	1,819	21.9	956	63
Vacant	182	2,567	(NA)	14.1	(NA)	(NA)
Energy sources: [2]						
Electricity.	4,404	63,307	72,708	14.4	871	62
Natural gas	2,391	43,468	51,956	18.2	837	65
Fuel oil	451	15,157	19,625	33.6	772	68
District heat	67	5,443	10,190	81.4	534	79
District chilled water	33	2,853	7,189	86.7	397	79
Propane	502	7,076	5,858	14.1	1,208	60
Wood	62	289	262	4.6	1,105	46

NA Not available.   [1] For explanation of mean, see Guide to Tabular Presentation.   [2] More than one type may apply.

Source: U.S. Energy Information Administration, "2003 Commercial Buildings Energy Consumption Buildings (CBECS) Detailed Tables"; Table B1. See <http://www.eia.doe.gov/emeu/cbecs/cbecs2003/detailed_tables_2003/detailed_tables_2003.html>; (accessed 11 July 2007).

612   Construction and Housing

This section presents summary data for manufacturing as a whole and more detailed information for major industry groups and selected products. The types of measures shown at the different levels include data for establishments, employment and payroll, value and quantity of production and shipments, value added by manufacture, inventories, and various indicators of financial status.

The principal sources of these data are U.S. Census Bureau reports of the censuses of manufactures conducted every 5 years, the *Annual Survey of Manufactures,* and *Current Industrial Reports.* Reports on current activities of industries or current movements of individual commodities are compiled by such government agencies as the Bureau of Economic Analysis; Bureau of Labor Statistics; the Economic Research Service of the U.S. Department of Agriculture; the International Trade Administration; and by private research or trade associations.

Data on financial aspects of manufacturing industries are collected by the Census Bureau (see especially Tables 978–980) as part of the Quarterly Financial Report. Industry aggregates in the form of balance sheets, profit and loss statements, analyses of sales and expenses, lists of subsidiaries, and types and amounts of security issues are published for leading manufacturing corporations registered with the Securities and Exchange Commission. The BEA issues data on capital in manufacturing industries and capacity utilization rates in manufacturing. See also Section 15, Business Enterprise.

Several private trade associations provide industry coverage for certain sections of the economy. They include the Aluminum Association (Table 987), American Iron and Steel Institute (Tables 993 and 994), Consumer Electronics Association (Table 995), and the Aerospace Industries Association (Tables 1000 and 1002). Machine tool consumption data (Table 991) is produced jointly by the Association for Manufacturing Technology and American Machine Tool Distributors Association.

Censuses and annual surveys—The first census of manufactures covered the year 1809. Between 1809 and 1963, a census was conducted at periodic intervals. Since 1967, it has been taken every 5 years (for years ending in "2" and "7"). Results from the 2002 census are presented in this section utilizing the North American Industry Classification System (NAICS). For additional information see text, Section 15, Business Enterprise, and the Census Bureau Web site at <http://www.census.gov/econ/census02/>. Census data, either directly reported or estimated from administrative records, are obtained for every manufacturing plant with one or more paid employees.

The *Annual Survey of Manufactures* (ASM), conducted for the first time in 1949, collects data for the years between censuses for the more general measure of manufacturing activity covered in detail by the censuses. The annual survey data are estimates derived from a scientifically selected sample of establishments. The 2004 annual survey is based on a sample of about 50,000 from a universe of 346,000 establishments. These establishments represent all manufacturing establishments of multiunit companies and all single-establishment manufacturing companies mailed schedules in the 2002 Census of Manufactures. For the current panel of the ASM sample, all establishments of companies with 2002 shipments in manufacturing in excess of $500 million were included in the survey with certainty. For the remaining portion of the mail survey, the establishment was defined as the sampling unit. For this portion, all establishments with 500 employees or more and establishments with a very large value of shipments also were included. Therefore, of the 50,000 establishments included in the ASM panel, approximately 24,000 are selected with certainty. Smaller establishments in the remaining portion of the mail survey were selected by sample.

Manufactures 613

Establishments and classification— Each of the establishments covered in the 2002 Economic Census—Manufacturing was classified in 1 of 480 industries (473 manufacturing industries and 7 former manufacturing industries) in accordance with the industry definitions in the 2002 NAICS manual. In the NAICS system, an industry is generally defined as a group of establishments that have similar production processes. To the extent practical, the system uses supply-based or production-oriented concepts in defining industries. The resulting group of establishments must be significant in terms of number, value added by manufacture, value of shipments, and number of employees.

Establishments frequently make products classified both in their industry (primary products) and other industries (secondary products). Industry statistics (employment, payroll, value added by manufacture, value of shipments, etc.) reflect the activities of the establishments, which may make both primary and secondary products. Product statistics, however, represent the output of all establishments without regard for the classification of the producing establishment. For this reason, when relating the industry statistics, especially the value of shipments, to the product statistics, the composition of the industry's output should be considered.

Establishment— Establishment signifies a single physical plant site or factory. It is not necessarily identical to the business unit or company, which may consist of one or more establishments. A company operating establishments at more than one location is required to submit a separate report for each location and include establishments with payroll at any time during the year. An establishment engaged in distinctly different lines of activity and maintaining separate payroll and inventory records is also required to submit separate reports.

Durable goods— Items with a normal life expectancy of 3 years or more. Automobiles, furniture, household appliances, and mobile homes are common examples.

Nondurable goods— Items which generally last for only a short time (3 years or less). Food, beverages, clothing, shoes, and gasoline are common examples.

Statistical reliability— For a discussion of statistical collection and estimation, sampling procedures, and measures of statistical reliability applicable to Census Bureau data, see Appendix III.

U.S. Census Bureau, Statistical Abstract of the United States: 2009

Table 964. Gross Domestic Product in Current and Real (2000) Dollars by Industry: 2000 to 2007

[In billions of dollars (9,817.0 represents $9,817,000,000,000). Data include nonfactor charges (capital consumption allowances, indirect business taxes, etc.) as well as factor charges against gross product; corporate profits and capital consumption allowances have been shifted from a company to an establishment basis]

Industry	2002 NAICS code [1]	2000	2003	2004	2005	2006	2007
CURRENT DOLLARS							
Gross domestic product, total [2]	(X)	**9,817.0**	**10,960.8**	**11,685.9**	**12,433.9**	**13,194.7**	**13,841.3**
Private industries	(X)	8,614.3	9,542.3	10,194.3	10,861.5	11,556.0	12,103.8
Manufacturing	31–33	1,426.2	1,359.3	1,427.9	1,483.9	1,549.7	1,615.8
Durable goods	(X)	865.3	771.8	807.5	840.9	882.8	926.7
Wood products	321	31.4	32.1	37.5	37.1	37.4	(NA)
Nonmetallic mineral products	327	45.7	45.1	49.3	50.7	54.7	(NA)
Primary metals	331	48.2	38.4	54.5	57.8	63.4	(NA)
Fabricated metal products	332	121.7	106.3	115.2	123.3	131.1	(NA)
Machinery	333	109.3	94.3	103.4	114.8	123.2	(NA)
Computer and electronic products	334	185.6	124.0	125.5	132.7	139.7	(NA)
Electrical equipment, appliances, and components	335	50.6	48.8	45.7	44.0	45.0	(NA)
Motor vehicles, bodies and trailers, and parts	3361–63	118.1	124.1	106.9	99.1	96.9	(NA)
Other transportation equipment	3364, 66, 69	64.4	62.4	70.9	82.0	90.4	(NA)
Furniture and related products	337	32.7	33.4	31.2	30.8	31.4	(NA)
Miscellaneous manufacturing	339	57.5	62.9	67.4	68.6	69.7	(NA)
Nondurable goods	(X)	561.0	587.5	620.4	643.0	666.9	689.1
Food and beverage and tobacco products	311, 312	154.8	167.9	161.0	163.7	160.7	(NA)
Textile mills and textile product mills	313, 314	26.5	23.1	23.1	21.2	19.5	(NA)
Apparel and leather and allied products	315, 316	25.1	18.3	17.3	16.5	16.4	(NA)
Paper products	322	55.6	50.3	50.7	52.5	52.5	(NA)
Printing and related support activities	323	49.0	45.2	45.6	45.2	46.2	(NA)
Petroleum and coal products	324	26.2	39.1	56.6	77.8	86.3	(NA)
Chemical products	325	157.1	179.5	198.7	199.8	214.0	(NA)
Plastics and rubber products	326	66.7	64.0	67.3	66.3	71.4	(NA)
CHAINED (2000) DOLLARS							
Gross domestic product, total [2]	(X)	**9,817.0**	**10,301.0**	**10,675.8**	**11,003.4**	**11,319.4**	**11,566.8**
Private industries	(X)	8,614.3	9,050.9	9,406.7	9,726.4	10,063.1	10,276.0
Manufacturing	31–33	1,426.2	1,400.1	1,478.3	1,493.0	1,536.6	1,571.7
Durable goods	(X)	865.3	849.4	898.8	942.9	999.8	1,048.6
Wood products	321	31.4	30.4	30.7	30.9	32.8	(NA)
Nonmetallic mineral products	327	45.7	45.2	48.2	46.1	44.1	(NA)
Primary metals	331	48.2	42.3	48.8	45.2	41.2	(NA)
Fabricated metal products	332	121.7	104.6	110.4	112.6	119.0	(NA)
Machinery	333	109.3	91.6	103.7	112.5	119.7	(NA)
Computer and electronic products	334	185.6	214.6	248.9	301.3	366.0	(NA)
Electrical equipment, appliances, and components	335	50.6	50.1	46.6	43.8	42.1	(NA)
Motor vehicles, bodies and trailers, and parts	3361–63	118.1	137.0	125.4	129.8	144.0	(NA)
Other transportation equipment	3364, 66, 69	64.4	55.5	61.3	68.8	73.5	(NA)
Furniture and related products	337	32.7	31.4	30.5	29.1	28.9	(NA)
Miscellaneous manufacturing	339	57.5	59.1	64.6	66.4	68.0	(NA)
Nondurable goods	(X)	561.0	551.2	580.4	557.7	551.8	545.9
Food and beverage and tobacco products	311, 312	154.8	151.4	149.4	149.8	153.1	(NA)
Textile mills and textile product mills	313, 314	26.5	23.6	23.2	21.6	19.0	(NA)
Apparel and leather and allied products	315, 316	25.1	18.5	17.8	17.3	17.2	(NA)
Paper products	322	55.6	52.1	54.0	55.5	52.4	(NA)
Printing and related support activities	323	49.0	43.5	44.5	44.4	44.8	(NA)
Petroleum and coal products	324	26.2	30.7	39.7	34.0	31.9	(NA)
Chemical products	325	157.1	169.6	182.6	170.8	173.0	(NA)
Plastics and rubber products	326	66.7	63.0	68.3	66.1	63.6	(NA)

NA Not available.   X Not applicable.   [1] North American Industry Classification System, 2002; see text Section 15.
[2] Includes industries, not shown separately. For additional industries, see Table 648.

Source: U.S. Bureau of Economic Analysis, *Survey of Current Business*, May 2008. See also <http://www.bea.gov/newsreleases/industry/gdpindustry/gdpindnewsrelease.htm>; (released 29 April 2008).

Manufactures   615

Table 965. Manufacturing—Establishments, Employees, and Annual Payroll by Industry: 2004 and 2005

[(115,075 represents 115,075,000). Excludes government employees, railroad employees, self-employed persons, etc. An *establishment* is a single physical location where business is conducted or where services or industrial operations are performed. See "General Explanation" in source for definitions and statement on reliability of data. See Appendix III]

Kind of business	2002 NAICS code [1]	Establishments (number)		Employees [2] (1,000)		Payroll (mil. dol.)	
		2004	2005	2004	2005	2004	2005
All industries, total	(X)	**7,387,724**	**7,499,702**	**115,075**	**116,317**	**4,253,996**	**4,482,722**
Manufacturing, total	**31–33**	**339,083**	**333,460**	**13,822**	**13,667**	**592,830**	**600,696**
Percent of all industries	(X)	4.6	4.5	12.0	11.9	13.9	14.1
Food manufacturing	311	26,767	25,785	1,482	1,470	47,540	48,474
Beverage & tobacco products	312	3,359	3,516	155	154	7,211	7,263
Textile mills	313	3,638	3,411	224	209	6,875	6,518
Textile product mills	314	7,117	6,891	171	164	4,905	4,649
Apparel manufacturing	315	12,314	11,165	280	243	6,804	5,607
Leather & allied products	316	1,475	1,414	43	41	1,307	1,254
Wood products	321	16,783	16,707	535	556	17,194	18,232
Paper	322	5,422	5,273	465	454	21,590	21,560
Printing & related support activities	323	35,321	34,385	673	658	24,997	25,060
Petroleum & coal products	324	2,457	2,362	104	102	7,776	8,201
Chemical	325	13,364	13,220	823	810	48,816	49,210
Plastics & rubber products	326	14,886	14,707	908	902	33,160	33,391
Nonmetallic mineral products	327	16,714	16,908	472	469	18,963	19,691
Primary metal	331	5,426	5,362	451	451	21,486	22,108
Fabricated metal products	332	59,373	59,053	1,515	1,520	58,581	60,693
Machinery	333	27,037	26,723	1,088	1,107	50,459	52,653
Computer & electronic products	334	15,097	14,741	1,108	1,059	66,318	65,601
Electrical equip., appliance, & component	335	6,294	6,201	439	427	17,797	17,885
Transportation equipment	336	12,705	12,694	1,626	1,636	85,128	86,006
Furniture & related products	337	21,735	21,563	555	548	17,221	17,560
Miscellaneous	339	31,799	31,379	703	688	28,702	29,078

X Not applicable. [1] North American Industry Classification System, 2002; see text, Section 15. [2] Covers full- and part-time employees who are on the payroll in the pay period including March 12.

Source: U.S. Census Bureau, "County Business Patterns." See <http://www.census.gov/epcd/cbp/view/cbpview.html>.

Table 966. Manufacturing Establishments, Employees, and Annual Payroll by State: 2005

[(13,677 represents 13,677,000). Data are for North American Industry Classification System (NAICS) 2002 codes 31–33. See headnote, Table 965]

State	Establishments (number)	Employees (1,000)	Payroll (mil. dol.)	State	Establishments (number)	Employees (1,000)	Payroll (mil. dol.)
United States	**333,460**	**13,667**	**600,696**	Missouri	6,935	298	11,640
				Montana	1,283	19	740
Alabama	4,953	282	10,526	Nebraska	1,985	102	3,663
Alaska	514	10	403	Nevada	1,863	45	1,897
Arizona	4,858	168	7,828	New Hampshire	2,155	76	3,550
Arkansas	3,105	198	6,577	New Jersey	9,575	305	15,353
California	44,825	1,450	71,776	New Mexico	1,531	35	1,392
Colorado	5,189	136	6,279	New York	19,349	572	24,908
Connecticut	5,037	185	9,767	North Carolina	10,138	554	20,682
Delaware	652	36	1,661	North Dakota	748	25	827
District of Columbia	142	2	75	Ohio	16,617	793	35,677
Florida	14,286	371	14,907	Oklahoma	3,865	140	5,557
Georgia	8,623	428	16,219	Oregon	5,559	185	7,988
Hawaii	946	15	479	Pennsylvania	15,624	664	28,644
Idaho	1,849	61	2,393	Rhode Island	1,956	59	2,367
Illinois	16,073	676	30,078	South Carolina	4,289	271	10,959
Indiana	8,970	554	24,192	South Dakota	964	39	1,314
Iowa	3,800	226	9,026	Tennessee	6,671	396	15,565
Kansas	3,128	177	7,222	Texas	20,552	816	38,225
Kentucky	4,152	254	10,626	Utah	3,165	116	4,624
Louisiana	3,377	145	7,074	Vermont	1,126	37	1,655
Maine	1,850	61	2,497	Virginia	5,798	290	11,987
Maryland	3,742	135	6,717	Washington	7,404	257	12,548
Massachusetts	7,915	286	15,570	West Virginia	1,406	63	2,574
Michigan	14,033	635	31,631	Wisconsin	9,754	494	21,148
Minnesota	7,957	336	15,435	Wyoming	543	10	463
Mississippi	2,629	177	5,793				

[1] Covers full- and part-time employees who are on the payroll in the pay period including March 12.

Source: U.S. Census Bureau, "County Business Patterns." See <http://www.census.gov/epcd/cbp/view/cbpview.html>.

616 Manufactures

Table 967. **Manufactures—Summary by Selected Industry: 2006**

[**12,990.3 represents 12,990,300.** Based on the Annual Survey of Manufactures; see Appendix III]

Industry based on shipments	2002 NAICS code [1]	All employees [2]			Produc-tion workers [2] (1,000)	Value added by manufac-tures [3] (mil.dol.)	Value of ship-ments [4] (mil. dol.)
		Number (1,000)	Payroll				
			Total (mil. dol.)	Per employee (dol.)			
Manufacturing, total	31–33	12,990.3	592,342	45,599	9,179.1	2,305,589	5,019,963
Food [5]	311	1,417.3	48,853	34,470	1,090.1	233,741	537,787
Grain and oilseed milling	3112	52.9	2,664	50,361	39.9	20,191	57,667
Sugar and confectionery products	3113	65.2	2,724	41,742	50.9	15,748	28,225
Fruit and vegetable preserving and specialty foods	3114	161.0	5,774	35,858	133.5	27,781	56,279
Dairy products	3115	121.3	5,260	43,356	85.5	24,291	75,428
Animal slaughtering and processing	3116	488.5	13,563	27,765	421.9	52,793	149,577
Bakeries and tortillas	3118	273.6	9,153	33,455	173.5	34,348	54,173
Beverage and tobacco products	312	144.5	7,217	49,942	84.1	79,595	124,693
Beverage	3121	124.9	5,961	47,730	69.6	43,324	83,096
Tobacco	3122	19.6	1,256	64,022	14.5	36,272	41,597
Textile mills	313	173.7	5,772	33,221	144.9	17,220	38,795
Textile product mills	314	145.2	4,399	30,286	114.0	15,115	33,220
Apparel	315	202.1	5,070	25,092	156.9	15,909	30,462
Cut and sew apparel	3152	157.1	3,917	24,937	120.7	12,605	23,664
Leather and allied products	316	36.6	1,086	29,706	28.2	3,061	6,019
Wood products [5]	321	536.1	18,141	33,839	432.3	44,432	112,404
Sawmills and wood preservation	3211	104.0	3,863	37,146	87.3	9,854	32,163
Veneer, plywood, and engineered wood products	3212	114.7	4,171	36,360	92.2	10,475	25,746
Paper	322	414.0	20,640	49,849	321.7	80,601	170,361
Pulp, paper, and paperboard mills	3221	127.9	8,015	62,687	101.5	42,047	79,961
Converted paper products	3222	286.2	12,625	44,114	220.2	38,554	90,400
Printing and related support activities	323	620.3	25,151	40,547	443.8	60,380	99,688
Petroleum and coal products	324	101.4	8,106	79,952	66.1	133,994	548,955
Chemical [5]	325	747.1	45,765	61,254	430.9	350,786	657,748
Basic chemical	3251	153.0	10,400	67,978	91.7	83,979	191,269
Resin, syn. rubber, and artificial and syn. fibers and filaments	3252	78.6	4,969	63,252	55.1	36,300	94,373
Pharmaceutical and medicine	3254	233.5	16,108	68,999	114.0	137,928	184,636
Plastics and rubber products	326	868.1	33,334	38,399	676.4	99,528	211,345
Plastics products	3261	715.9	26,743	37,358	557.6	82,878	174,263
Nonmetallic mineral products	327	473.9	20,237	42,704	368.5	72,024	126,015
Cement and concrete products	3273	231.1	9,887	42,780	178.6	35,259	64,285
Primary metal [5]	331	422.2	21,900	51,868	336.7	83,542	232,558
Iron and steel mills and ferroalloy	3311	101.6	7,011	69,002	81.9	34,407	93,328
Foundries	3315	162.9	7,078	43,437	133.2	17,637	33,457
Fabricated metal products [5]	332	1,492.6	63,204	42,344	1,111.4	169,381	317,223
Architectural and structural metals	3323	370.9	15,112	40,742	267.1	40,144	83,535
Machine shops, turned product and screw, nut, and bolt	3327	377.8	16,134	42,703	286.6	34,723	56,169
Coating, engraving, heat treating, and allied activities	3328	128.2	5,008	39,067	99.3	13,947	24,344
Machinery [5]	333	1,070.5	52,615	49,148	693.5	154,369	326,430
Agriculture, construction, and mining machinery	3331	181.2	8,355	46,104	124.7	32,454	77,268
Metalworking machinery	3335	164.0	8,308	50,665	115.4	16,584	28,146
Computer and electronic products [5]	334	1,001.3	61,804	61,726	467.9	230,262	390,776
Computer and peripheral equipment	3341	96.1	5,803	60,365	35.1	34,947	67,325
Communications equipment	3342	127.1	8,332	65,531	51.4	36,888	70,174
Semiconductor and other electronic components	3344	345.8	18,704	54,088	200.6	76,035	117,663
Navigational, measuring, medical, control instruments	3345	385.2	26,815	69,621	150.2	75,838	119,036
Electrical equipment, appliance, and component	335	411.6	17,825	43,301	293.9	57,758	120,038
Electrical equipment	3353	142.8	6,340	44,401	96.1	18,432	36,916
Transportation equipment [5]	336	1,525.1	83,828	54,967	1,093.3	260,380	698,349
Motor vehicles	3361	205.8	14,015	68,114	179.0	66,035	261,842
Motor vehicle bodies and trailers	3362	150.3	5,576	37,103	120.5	13,483	36,011
Motor vehicle parts	3363	577.7	28,699	49,676	450.7	80,497	202,285
Aerospace products and parts	3364	381.6	26,396	69,177	191.9	75,387	142,387
Ship and boat building	3366	139.1	5,885	42,304	101.2	14,072	26,481
Furniture and related products [5]	337	520.1	17,728	34,083	404.7	47,104	86,749
Household and institutional furniture and kitchen cabinets	3371	342.6	10,799	31,523	272.5	26,191	48,915
Miscellaneous manufacturing	339	666.5	29,669	44,511	419.9	96,410	150,349
Medical equipment and supplies	3391	304.6	15,394	50,543	180.3	55,858	78,372

[1] North American Industry Classification System, 2002; see text, Section 15.   [2] Includes employment and payroll at administrative offices and auxiliary units. All employees represents the average of production workers plus all other employees for the payroll period ended nearest the 12th of March. Production workers represent the average of the employment for the payroll periods ended nearest the 12th of March, May, August, and November.   [3] Adjusted value added; takes into account (a) value added by merchandising operations (that is, difference between the sales value and cost of merchandise sold without further manufacture, processing, or assembly), plus (b) net change in finished goods and work-in-process inventories between beginning and end of year.   [4] Includes extensive and unmeasurable duplication from shipments between establishments in the same industry classification.   [5] Includes industries not shown separately.

Source: U.S. Census Bureau, *Annual Survey of Manufactures, Statistics for Industry Groups and Industries: 2006* using American FactFinder®. See <http://factfinder.census.gov/home/saff/main.html?_lang=en>.

Table 968. Manufactures—Summary by State: 2006

[**12,990.3 represents 12,990,300.** Data are for North American Industry Classification System (NAICS) 2002 codes 31–33. Sum of state totals may not add to U.S. total because U.S. and state figures were independently derived. See Appendix III]

State	All employees [1] Number (1,000)	Payroll Total (mil. dol.)	Payroll Per employee (dol.)	Production workers [1] Total (1,000)	Wages (mil. dol.)	Value added by manufactures [2] Total (mil. dol.)	Per production worker (dol.)	Value of shipments [3] (mil. dol.)
United States.....	12,990.3	592,342	45,599	9,179.1	344,285	2,305,589	251,179	5,019,963
Alabama	265.1	10,561	39,835	206.2	7,189	40,334	195,581	101,862
Alaska.	11.0	401	36,614	9.1	284	1,659	181,384	7,082
Arizona	161.2	8,158	50,601	100.7	3,791	27,172	269,908	50,007
Arkansas	188.8	6,586	34,885	153.3	4,706	27,574	179,922	60,674
California	1,386.7	67,796	48,890	885.9	31,747	238,084	268,749	466,573
Colorado	128.1	6,146	47,997	86.5	3,297	20,825	240,628	40,430
Connecticut	175.2	9,396	53,627	106.8	4,528	32,159	301,166	51,871
Delaware	33.5	1,667	49,803	24.2	993	8,862	366,196	24,424
District of Columbia . . .	1.7	72	41,722	1.0	40	172	170,408	273
Florida.	341.0	14,685	43,068	224.8	7,475	50,945	226,663	97,848
Georgia	408.2	16,135	39,532	314.3	10,587	61,916	196,978	140,892
Hawaii.	13.9	504	36,156	9.0	299	2,049	228,537	7,301
Idaho	55.4	2,399	43,283	37.4	1,351	7,045	188,467	14,904
Illinois	639.4	29,906	46,770	445.6	17,178	107,548	241,362	242,525
Indiana	527.4	24,433	46,324	401.4	16,432	90,192	224,696	207,504
Iowa	224.7	9,288	41,343	165.3	5,988	41,011	248,160	91,484
Kansas	173.3	7,555	43,599	125.2	4,663	25,332	202,321	68,258
Kentucky	243.2	10,620	43,664	185.8	7,227	43,009	231,433	112,695
Louisiana.	139.9	7,050	50,376	102.7	4,580	77,850	758,171	183,498
Maine	54.4	2,321	42,643	40.5	1,517	7,795	192,689	15,231
Maryland	132.2	6,704	50,722	82.3	3,228	22,812	277,021	42,126
Massachusetts	283.1	15,022	53,056	172.5	6,790	48,519	281,298	84,219
Michigan	577.5	29,854	51,690	424.6	19,646	89,022	209,639	215,504
Minnesota	326.1	15,179	46,549	220.5	8,131	49,430	224,186	101,945
Mississippi	159.9	5,607	35,057	128.4	3,881	20,690	161,190	56,300
Missouri.	285.0	12,573	44,119	214.6	8,294	45,141	210,313	103,909
Montana	17.0	729	42,877	12.5	473	3,476	277,658	9,555
Nebraska.	100.7	3,755	37,294	77.6	2,560	15,641	201,572	40,632
Nevada	44.3	2,052	46,326	29.9	1,077	7,462	249,267	12,845
New Hampshire	74.7	3,843	51,420	46.7	1,727	9,203	196,956	16,992
New Jersey	290.5	15,302	52,672	190.2	7,504	51,693	271,832	107,349
New Mexico	32.4	1,419	43,852	23.0	845	9,070	394,961	16,477
New York.	526.3	24,090	45,769	346.2	12,861	93,103	268,923	162,412
North Carolina	501.5	19,224	38,329	382.1	12,417	106,988	279,982	200,822
North Dakota	23.0	900	39,047	17.6	604	3,877	220,811	9,789
Ohio	755.7	35,133	46,490	552.8	22,701	124,949	226,037	283,939
Oklahoma	134.6	5,685	42,239	100.2	3,580	24,025	239,884	55,791
Oregon	172.4	7,775	45,092	124.8	4,645	39,502	316,541	65,536
Pennsylvania	643.5	28,999	45,065	456.2	17,104	112,486	246,549	231,725
Rhode Island	53.2	2,414	45,355	33.1	1,151	7,824	236,199	14,175
South Carolina	248.3	10,540	42,450	188.1	6,783	37,953	201,753	90,419
South Dakota	38.2	1,390	36,370	28.8	910	5,381	186,752	11,206
Tennessee	373.9	15,312	40,950	277.7	9,805	62,045	223,439	141,286
Texas	809.3	38,222	47,231	561.1	21,193	196,580	350,345	527,622
Utah	112.0	4,816	43,003	76.1	2,690	16,801	220,684	36,440
Vermont	34.4	1,607	46,692	22.0	852	5,089	231,091	10,712
Virginia	272.3	11,665	42,841	202.0	7,407	50,506	250,048	93,671
Washington	254.4	12,974	50,992	165.4	6,656	48,877	295,480	105,658
West Virginia	59.5	2,595	43,623	45.3	1,739	10,476	231,295	23,919
Wisconsin	471.7	20,794	44,079	343.3	12,824	72,015	209,802	154,050
Wyoming	10.3	488	47,467	7.8	335	3,418	437,608	7,598

[1] Includes employment and payroll at administrative offices and auxiliary units. All employees represents the average of production workers plus all other employees for the payroll period ended nearest the 12th of March. Production workers represent the average of the employment for the payroll periods ended nearest the 12th of March, May, August, and November.   [2] Adjusted value added; takes into account (a) value added by merchandising operations (that is, difference between the sales value and cost of merchandise sold without further manufacture, processing, or assembly), plus (b) net change in finished goods and work-in-process inventories between beginning and end of year.   [3] Includes extensive and unmeasurable duplication from shipments between establishments in the same industry classification.

Source: U.S. Census Bureau, *Annual Survey of Manufactures, Geographic Area Statistics: 2006* using American FactFinder®. See <http://factfinder.census.gov/home/saff/main.html?_lang=en>.

Table 969. Manufacturers' E-Commerce Shipments by Industry: 2005 and 2006

[(4,742,076 represents $4,742,076,000,000). Based on the Annual Survey of Manufactures; subject to sampling variability. For businesses with paid employees. E-commerce is the value of goods and services sold over computer-mediated networks (open or proprietary)]

Industry	2002 NAICS code [1]	2005				2006			
			E-commerce				E-commerce		
		Shipments, total (mil. dol).	Shipments, total (mil.dol.)	Percent of total shipments	Percent distribution	Shipments, total (mil. dol).	Shipments, total (mil.dol.)	Percent of total shipments	Percent distribution
Manufacturing, total . . .	31–33	**4,742,076**	**1,343,852**	**28.3**	**100.0**	**5,019,964**	**1,568,371**	**31.2**	**100.0**
Food products	311	532,402	99,090	18.6	7.4	537,787	154,083	28.7	9.8
Beverage and tobacco	312	124,086	60,651	48.9	4.5	124,693	68,177	54.7	4.3
Textile mills	313	42,328	7,512	17.8	0.6	38,795	12,377	31.9	0.8
Textile product mills	314	35,022	7,189	20.5	0.5	33,220	11,588	34.9	0.7
Apparel	315	31,401	8,908	28.4	0.7	30,462	9,307	30.6	0.6
Leather and allied products . . .	316	6,181	826	13.4	0.1	6,019	926	15.4	0.1
Wood products	321	112,095	12,248	10.9	0.9	112,404	14,952	13.3	1.0
Paper	322	161,928	30,579	18.9	2.3	170,361	40,781	23.9	2.6
Printing and related support activities	323	96,922	15,592	16.1	1.2	99,688	19,004	19.1	1.2
Petroleum and coal products . .	324	475,787	130,869	27.5	9.7	548,955	160,177	29.2	10.2
Chemicals	325	610,873	173,747	28.4	12.9	657,748	205,299	31.2	13.1
Plastics and rubber products . .	326	200,304	43,123	21.5	3.2	211,345	48,656	23.0	3.1
Nonmetallic mineral products . .	327	114,849	16,469	14.3	1.2	126,015	20,648	16.4	1.3
Primary metals	331	203,263	47,608	23.4	3.5	232,558	59,376	25.5	3.8
Fabricated metal products	332	289,432	50,661	17.5	3.8	317,223	63,942	20.2	4.1
Machinery	333	302,650	72,390	23.9	5.4	326,430	93,428	28.6	6.0
Computer and electronic products	334	372,882	113,704	30.5	8.5	390,776	120,931	31.0	7.7
Electrical equipment, appliances, and components	335	111,977	30,602	27.3	2.3	120,038	34,327	28.6	2.2
Transportation equipment	336	690,743	381,600	55.2	28.4	698,349	383,463	54.9	24.4
Furniture and related products	337	84,181	16,233	19.3	1.2	86,749	18,187	21.0	1.2
Miscellaneous	339	142,770	24,251	17.0	1.8	150,349	28,742	19.1	1.8

[1] North American Industry Classification System, 2002; see text, Section 15.

Source: U.S. Census Bureau, "E-Stats"; released 16 May 2008. See <http://www.census.gov/eos/www/ebusiness614.htm>.

Table 970. Manufacturing Employer Costs for Employee Compensation Per Hour Worked: 2000 to 2008

[As of March, for private industry workers. Based on a sample of establishments in the National Compensation Survey; see Appendix III and source for details. See also Table 632, Section 12]

Compensation component	Cost (dol.)					Percent distribution				
	2000	2005	2006	2007	2008	2000	2005	2006	2007	2008
Total compensation	**23.41**	**28.48**	**29.40**	**30.37**	**31.42**	**100.0**	**100.0**	**100.0**	**100.0**	**100.0**
Wages and salaries	16.01	18.26	19.18	20.00	20.66	68.4	64.1	65.2	65.8	65.7
Total benefits	7.40	10.21	10.22	10.38	10.76	31.6	35.9	34.8	34.2	34.3
Paid leave	1.74	2.07	2.26	2.37	2.38	7.4	7.3	7.7	7.8	7.6
Vacation	0.86	1.04	1.16	1.23	1.25	3.7	3.7	3.9	4.0	4.0
Holiday	0.65	0.76	0.81	0.85	0.86	2.8	2.7	2.8	2.8	2.7
Sick	0.13	0.16	0.20	0.21	0.21	0.6	0.6	0.7	0.7	0.7
Other	0.10	0.10	0.09	0.09	0.05	0.4	0.3	0.3	0.3	0.2
Supplemental pay	1.04	1.25	1.15	1.23	1.35	4.4	4.4	3.9	4.1	4.3
Overtime and premium pay . . .	0.58	0.61	0.54	0.52	0.54	2.5	2.1	1.8	1.7	1.7
Shift differentials	0.10	0.12	0.13	0.14	0.14	0.4	0.4	0.5	0.5	0.4
Nonproduction bonuses	0.36	0.53	0.47	0.57	0.68	1.5	1.8	1.6	1.9	2.10
Insurance	1.85	2.68	2.87	2.97	3.13	7.9	9.4	9.8	9.8	10.0
Health insurance	1.69	2.48	2.67	2.76	2.91	7.2	8.7	9.1	9.1	9.3
Retirement and savings	0.75	1.64	1.44	1.24	1.32	3.2	5.8	4.9	4.1	4.2
Defined benefit	0.34	1.13	0.90	0.67	0.68	1.5	4.0	3.1	2.2	2.1
Defined contributions	0.41	0.51	0.53	0.57	0.65	1.8	1.8	1.8	1.9	2.1
Legally required benefits	1.92	2.45	2.51	2.56	2.58	8.2	8.6	8.5	8.4	8.2
Social security	1.38	1.60	1.67	1.74	1.79	5.9	5.6	5.7	5.7	5.7
Federal unemployment	0.03	0.03	0.03	0.03	0.03	0.1	0.1	0.1	0.1	0.1
State unemployment	0.11	0.19	0.20	0.19	0.18	0.5	0.7	0.7	0.6	0.6
Workers compensation	0.40	0.64	0.61	0.60	0.58	1.7	2.2	2.1	2.0	1.8
Other benefits [1]	0.09	0.12	(NA)	(NA)	(NA)	0.4	0.4	(NA)	(NA)	(NA)

NA Not available. [1] Includes severance pay and supplemental unemployment benefits.

Source: U.S. Bureau of Labor Statistics, Economic News Release, *Employer Costs for Employee Compensation* (Released 11 June 2008). See <http://www.bls.gov/ncs/ect/home.htm>.

Table 971. **Manufacturing Industries—Employment by Industry: 1990 to 2007**

[**Annual averages of monthly figures (109,487 represents 109,487,000).** Covers all full- and part-time employees who worked during, or received pay for, any part of the pay period including the 12th of the month. Minus sign (−) indicates decrease. See also headnote, Table 612]

Industry	2002 NAICS code[1]	All employees (1,000)						Percent change	
		1990	2000	2004	2005	2006	2007	1990–2000	2000–2007
All industries	(X)	109,487	131,785	131,435	133,703	136,086	137,623	20.4	4.4
Manufacturing.	**31–33**	**17,695**	**17,263**	**14,315**	**14,226**	**14,155**	**13,884**	**−2.4**	**−19.6**
Percent of all industries.	(X)	16.2	13.1	10.9	10.6	10.4	10.1	(X)	(X)
Durable goods	(X)	10,736	10,876	8,924	8,955	8,981	8,816	1.3	−18.9
Wood products	321	541	613	550	559	559	520	13.4	−15.2
Sawmills & wood preservation	3211	148	134	119	119	118	111	−9.6	−17.1
Plywood & engineered wood products . .	3212	96	122	118	123	120	109	28.2	−11.4
Other wood products	3219	297	357	313	317	321	300	20.1	−15.8
Nonmetallic mineral products.	327	528	554	506	505	510	503	4.9	−9.2
Clay products & refractories.	3271	84	82	65	62	61	58	−1.9	−29.6
Glass & glass products	3272	152	141	113	108	102	101	−7.6	−28.6
Cement & concrete products	3273	195	234	235	240	248	243	20.1	4.0
Lime, gypsum, & other nonmetallic mineral products	3279	98	97	94	96	99	102	−0.3	4.7
Primary metals	331	689	622	467	466	464	456	−9.7	−26.7
Iron & steel mills & ferroalloy production	3311	187	135	95	96	97	100	−27.7	−25.9
Steel products from purchased steel . . .	3312	70	73	61	61	61	60	4.0	−17.8
Alumina & aluminum production	3313	108	101	74	73	73	72	−7.3	−28.6
Other nonferrous metal production	3314	109	96	71	72	73	69	−11.7	−28.6
Foundries	3315	214	217	165	164	161	155	1.4	−28.4
Fabricated metal products.	332	1,610	1,753	1,497	1,522	1,553	1,563	8.9	−10.8
Forging & stamping	3321	128	138	110	111	113	111	7.9	−19.9
Cutlery & hand tools.	3322	79	79	59	56	54	51	0.3	−34.9
Architectural & structural metals	3323	357	428	389	398	412	416	20.0	−2.8
Boilers, tanks, & shipping containers . . .	3324	117	107	92	91	94	96	−9.1	−9.7
Hardware	3325	57	50	38	36	34	33	−12.8	−33.7
Spring & wire products	3326	78	81	62	59	58	57	4.3	−30.1
Machine shops & threaded products . . .	3327	309	365	327	345	352	361	18.4	−1.2
Coating, engraving, & heat treating metals	3328	143	175	143	145	149	148	22.7	−15.6
Other fabricated metal products	3329	344	330	278	282	287	291	−4.0	−11.8
Machinery	333	1,408	1,455	1,143	1,163	1,183	1,188	3.3	−18.3
Agricultural, construction, & mining machinery	3331	229	222	195	208	220	230	−2.8	3.5
Industrial machinery	3332	152	164	121	124	124	126	8.0	−23.4
Commercial & service industry machinery	3333	147	147	115	111	109	108	0.3	−26.9
HVAC & commercial refrigeration equipment.	3334	165	194	153	153	157	154	17.9	−20.7
Metalworking machinery	3335	267	274	202	202	200	193	2.5	−29.5
Turbine & power transmission equipment.	3336	114	111	93	98	100	103	−2.4	−7.7
Other general purpose machinery	3339	335	344	265	268	273	275	2.7	−20.0
Computer & electronic products	334	1,903	1,820	1,323	1,316	1,308	1,272	−4.3	−30.1
Computer & peripheral equipment.	3341	367	302	210	205	196	187	−17.8	−38.1
Communications equipment	3342	232	239	148	147	136	129	3.1	−46.1
Audio & video equipment.	3343	60	52	33	32	31	31	−13.3	−41.5
Semiconductors & electronic components	3344	574	676	454	452	458	445	17.8	−34.3
Electronic instruments	3345	626	488	431	436	445	444	−22.1	−9.0
Magnetic media manufacturing & reproduction	3346	43	63	46	45	42	37	46.4	−41.0
Electrical equipment & appliances	335	633	591	445	434	433	427	−6.7	−27.7
Electric lighting equipment	3351	81	85	65	61	59	58	5.0	−31.4
Household appliances.	3352	114	106	90	85	80	75	−7.0	−29.1
Electrical equipment	3353	244	210	154	152	155	155	−13.9	−26.1
Other electrical equipment & components	3359	195	191	137	136	139	139	−2.3	−26.9
Transportation equipment [2]	336	2,133	2,057	1,766	1,771	1,769	1,711	−3.6	−16.8
Motor vehicles	3361	271	291	256	248	237	223	7.4	−23.5
Motor vehicle bodies & trailers	3362	130	183	165	171	179	165	40.8	−9.7
Motor vehicle parts.	3363	653	840	692	678	655	609	28.6	−27.5
Aerospace products & parts.	3364	841	517	442	455	474	487	−38.5	−5.7
Ship & boat building	3366	173	154	148	153	157	161	−10.7	4.4
Other transportation equipment	3369	35	40	38	39	40	40	14.0	−0.3

See footnotes at end of table.

U.S. Census Bureau, Statistical Abstract of the United States: 2009

[**Annual averages of monthly figures (109,487 represents 109,487,000).** Covers all full- and part-time employees who worked during, or received pay for, any part of the pay period including the 12th of the month. Minus sign (–) indicates decrease. See also headnote, Table 612]

Industry	2002 NAICS code[1]	All employees (1,000)						Percent change	
		1990	2000	2004	2005	2006	2007	1990–2000	2000–2007
Furniture & related products	337	601	683	573	565	560	535	13.5	–17.9
Household & institutional furniture	3371	398	443	385	380	374	350	11.3	–15.7
Office furniture & fixtures	3372	156	181	135	133	136	136	16.0	–27.0
Other furniture-related products	3379	47	58	53	52	51	49	23.1	–13.1
Miscellaneous manufacturing	339	690	728	656	652	644	641	5.4	–10.5
Medical equipment & supplies	3391	288	305	301	305	303	306	5.9	1.3
Other miscellaneous manufacturing	3399	403	403	354	347	341	335	0.0	–14.9
Nondurable goods	(X)	6,959	6,386	5,391	5,272	5,174	5,068	–8.2	–20.6
Food manufacturing	311	1,507	1,553	1,494	1,478	1,479	1,481	3.0	–4.6
Animal food	3111	57	55	50	49	49	51	–4.2	–6.8
Grain & oilseed milling	3112	71	65	60	61	61	61	–9.1	–5.9
Sugar & confectionery products	3113	99	92	83	79	75	74	–7.3	–19.5
Fruit & vegetable preserving & specialty	3114	218	197	181	174	176	173	–9.5	–12.5
Dairy products	3115	145	136	131	132	131	129	–5.9	–4.9
Animal slaughtering & processing	3116	427	507	505	504	506	507	18.6	0.1
Seafood product preparation & packaging	3117	54	45	42	41	41	44	–17.2	–2.9
Bakeries & tortilla manufacturing	3118	292	306	285	280	280	278	4.9	–9.3
Other food products	3119	143	150	156	159	160	165	5.0	9.6
Beverages & tobacco products	312	218	207	195	192	194	196	–4.9	–5.5
Beverages	3121	173	175	166	167	171	174	1.2	–0.3
Textile mills	313	492	378	237	218	195	170	–23.1	–55.1
Fiber, yarn, & thread mills	3131	102	81	54	50	48	42	–20.5	–48.2
Fabric mills	3132	270	192	115	104	90	76	–29.0	–60.4
Textile & fabric finishing mills	3133	120	105	68	63	58	52	–12.1	–50.6
Textile product mills	314	209	230	176	170	167	158	9.7	–31.0
Textile furnishings mills	3141	127	129	101	96	90	84	1.3	–34.7
Other textile product mills	3149	82	101	75	74	77	74	22.6	–26.3
Apparel	315	929	484	286	257	232	213	–48.0	–55.9
Apparel knitting mills	3151	112	69	42	37	35	30	–38.4	–56.2
Cut & sew apparel	3152	776	380	221	200	178	164	–51.0	–56.8
Accessories & other apparel	3159	41	34	23	21	20	19	–16.9	–45.6
Leather & allied products	316	133	69	42	40	37	34	–48.3	–50.7
Footwear	3162	83	31	19	18	17	16	–62.8	–47.2
Leather & hide tanning & finishing & other leather products	3169	51	38	23	22	19	18	–25.0	–53.2
Paper & paper products	322	647	605	496	484	471	461	–6.6	–23.8
Pulp, paper, & paperboard mills	3221	238	191	146	142	136	132	–19.7	–31.0
Converted paper products	3222	409	413	350	343	334	329	1.1	–20.5
Printing & related support activities	323	809	807	663	646	634	624	–0.2	–22.6
Petroleum & coal products	324	153	123	112	112	113	113	–19.4	–8.0
Chemicals	325	1,036	980	887	872	866	863	–5.3	–12.0
Basic chemicals	3251	249	188	156	150	147	150	–24.4	–20.4
Resin, rubber, & artificial fibers	3252	158	136	110	108	105	105	–14.2	–22.4
Agricultural chemicals	3253	52	48	42	40	38	37	–8.8	–23.0
Pharmaceuticals & medicines	3254	207	274	290	288	292	297	32.4	8.1
Paints, coatings, & adhesives	3255	85	79	68	68	67	65	–6.6	–17.5
Soaps, cleaning compounds, and toiletries	3256	132	129	115	114	111	109	–2.4	–15.1
Other chemical products and preparations	3259	153	127	107	104	105	100	–17.1	–21.1
Plastics & rubber products	326	826	951	806	803	786	754	15.1	–20.7
Plastics products	3261	619	737	633	635	630	606	19.1	–17.7
Rubber products	3262	207	214	172	168	156	148	3.3	–31.0

X Not applicable.   [1] Based on the North American Industry Classification System, 2002 (NAICS); see text, this section and Section 15.   [2] Includes railroad rolling stock manufacturing not shown separately.

Source: U.S. Bureau of Labor Statistics, the Current Employment Statistics program. See <http://www.bls.gov/ces/home.htm>.

Table 972. Average Hourly Earnings of Production Workers in Manufacturing Industries by State: 2004 to 2007

[**In dollars.** Data are based on the North American Industry Classification System (NAICS) 2002. Based on the Current Employment Statistics Program; see headnote Table 612 and Appendix III]

State	2004	2005	2006	2007	State	2004	2005	2006	2007
United States	**16.35**	**16.69**	**16.99**	**17.41**	Missouri	17.92	17.42	17.16	17.00
					Montana	14.87	15.62	15.90	15.88
Alabama	14.33	14.93	15.56	15.75	Nebraska	15.19	15.44	15.04	15.19
Alaska	12.01	14.22	14.31	15.77	Nevada	14.60	14.98	15.46	15.54
Arizona	14.20	14.55	14.88	15.61	New Hampshire	15.48	15.87	16.57	17.10
Arkansas	13.49	13.71	13.35	14.06	New Jersey	15.89	16.33	16.56	17.21
California	15.36	15.70	15.77	16.22	New Mexico	13.13	13.66	14.06	14.40
Colorado	16.46	15.91	16.59	17.76	New York	17.29	17.77	18.29	18.49
Connecticut	18.35	18.96	19.78	20.62	North Carolina	14.25	14.38	14.57	15.08
Delaware	17.66	17.74	18.11	17.83	North Dakota	14.35	15.29	14.98	14.70
District of Columbia [1] . . .	16.73	16.80	17.30	(NA)	Ohio	18.47	19.07	19.17	19.34
Florida	13.84	13.89	14.75	16.12	Oklahoma	14.24	14.56	14.77	14.56
Georgia	14.54	14.56	14.74	14.88	Oregon	15.34	15.49	15.57	16.45
Hawaii	13.50	14.34	15.89	17.06					
					Pennsylvania	15.16	15.26	15.38	15.48
Idaho	14.15	14.96	16.89	19.02	Rhode Island	13.03	13.12	13.42	13.78
Illinois	15.61	15.84	16.03	16.47	South Carolina	14.73	15.23	15.03	15.71
Indiana	17.92	18.14	18.57	18.70	South Dakota	13.37	13.47	13.75	14.27
Iowa	16.17	16.25	16.40	16.84	Tennessee	13.84	14.02	14.04	14.39
Kansas	16.57	17.14	17.69	18.07	Texas	13.98	14.03	14.00	14.07
Kentucky	16.50	16.65	16.92	16.92	Utah	15.38	14.73	15.25	16.71
Louisiana	16.40	17.30	17.94	19.33	Vermont	14.60	15.06	15.79	16.49
Maine	16.97	17.28	18.58	19.19	Virginia	16.11	16.40	16.75	17.61
Maryland	16.47	16.98	17.88	17.65	Washington	18.28	18.83	19.91	20.51
Massachusetts	16.89	17.66	18.26	19.26	West Virginia	16.57	17.14	17.89	18.71
Michigan	21.51	21.50	21.84	22.07	Wisconsin	16.19	16.29	16.54	17.37
Minnesota	16.04	16.63	17.24	17.40	Wyoming	16.58	17.08	17.44	(NA)
Mississippi	13.12	13.53	13.78	13.79					

NA Not available.   [1] Represents the Washington-Arlington-Alexandria Metropolitan Area.

Source: U.S. Bureau of Labor Statistics, the Current Employment Statistics program. See <http://www.bls.gov/ces/home.htm>.

Table 973. Manufacturing Full-Time Equivalent Employees and Wages by Industry: 2000 to 2006

[**124,707 represents 124,707,000.** Full-time equivalent employees equals the number of employees on full-time schedules plus the number of employees for part-time schedules converted to full-time basis]

Industry	2002 NAICS code [1]	Full-time equivalent (FTE) employees (1,000)				Wage and salary accruals per FTE worker (dol.)			
		2000	2004	2005	2006	2000	2004	2005	2006
All domestic industries, total. .	(X)	**124,707**	**124,422**	**126,865**	**129,011**	**38,762**	**43,280**	**44,764**	**46,758**
Manufacturing	31–33	**16,947**	**14,117**	**14,044**	**13,974**	**44,216**	**48,659**	**50,137**	**52,307**
Percent of all industries	(X)	13.6	11.3	11.1	10.8	114.1	112.4	112.0	111.9
Durable goods	(X)	10,713	8,809	8,864	8,877	47,007	51,096	52,416	54,961
Wood products	321	606	556	564	565	30,360	33,866	35,132	35,376
Nonmetallic mineral products.	327	545	495	496	506	38,879	42,935	44,814	46,103
Primary metals	331	611	458	459	455	45,745	51,715	52,682	55,522
Fabricated metal products	332	1,738	1,469	1,504	1,525	37,688	41,918	42,977	45,051
Machinery	333	1,420	1,125	1,148	1,166	46,882	51,593	52,997	55,213
Computer and electronic products	334	1,813	1,300	1,296	1,289	71,372	74,417	78,050	83,109
Electrical equipment, appliances, and components	335	568	440	429	429	42,732	46,935	48,175	50,443
Motor vehicles, bodies and trailers, and parts	3361–3363	1,283	1,106	1,093	1,057	49,727	54,649	54,236	56,591
Other transportation equipment . . .	3364–3365	736	648	669	687	52,612	62,606	64,231	68,571
Furniture and related products	337	664	561	556	549	29,660	33,062	33,950	35,165
Miscellaneous manufacturing	339	728	650	651	649	38,504	45,696	46,140	48,143
Nondurable goods	(X)	6,235	5,309	5,180	5,097	39,420	44,611	46,234	47,685
Food and beverage and tobacco products	311–312	1,719	1,648	1,627	1,631	34,110	37,622	38,681	39,624
Textile mills and textile product mills	313–314	584	405	376	346	29,018	32,673	33,407	34,604
Apparel and leather and allied products	315	538	333	301	279	24,769	29,516	31,140	32,797
Paper products	322	596	485	469	459	45,578	51,338	52,937	54,232
Printing and related support activities	323	767	663	644	635	38,966	40,537	41,856	43,031
Petroleum and coal products	324	120	109	109	109	62,310	75,222	82,368	87,074
Chemical products	325	968	872	862	853	60,928	69,092	71,931	73,955
Plastics and rubber products	326	942	793	791	786	35,375	39,764	40,206	41,433

X Not applicable   [1] North American Industry Classification System, 2002; see text, this section.

Source: U.S. Bureau of Economic Analysis, *Survey of Current Business,* monthly. See also <http://www.bea.gov/bea /dn/nipaweb/SelectTable.asp?Selected=N>; (released 01 August 2007).

Table 974. Manufacturers' Shipments, Inventories, and New Orders: 1992 to 2007

[In billions of dollars (2,904 represents $2,904,000,000,000), except ratio. Based on a sample survey; for methodology, see source]

Year	Shipments	Inventories (Dec. 31) [1]	Ratio of inventories to shipments [2]	New orders	Unfilled orders (Dec. 31)
1992	2,904	370	1.57	(NA)	448
1994	3,238	391	1.48	3,200	431
1995	3,480	415	1.47	3,427	443
1996	3,597	421	1.44	3,567	485
1997	3,835	433	1.39	3,780	508
1998	3,900	439	1.38	3,808	492
1999	4,032	453	1.38	3,957	501
2000	4,209	470	1.37	4,161	545
2001	3,970	417	1.29	3,872	510
2002	3,915	412	1.30	3,802	458
2003	4,015	398	1.22	3,964	474
2004	4,309	428	1.22	4,255	492
2005	4,742	460	1.20	4,745	570
2006	5,020	497	1.22	5,038	658
2007	5,081	516	1.25	5,131	772

NA Not available.   [1] Inventories are stated at current cost.   [2] Ratio based on December seasonally adjusted data.

Source: U.S. Census Bureau, *Current Industrial Reports, Benchmark Report for Manufacturers' Shipments, Inventories, and Orders: January 2004 through December 2007*, Series M3-3 (07); (released May 2008). See <http://www.census.gov/indicator/www/m3/>.

Table 975. Ratios of Manufacturers' Inventories to Shipments and Unfilled Orders to Shipments by Industry Group: 2000 to 2007

[Based on a sample survey; for methodology, see source]

Industry	2002 NAICS code [1]	2000	2002	2003	2004	2005	2006	2007
INVENTORIES-TO-SHIPMENTS RATIO								
All manufacturing industries.	(X)	**1.37**	**1.30**	**1.22**	**1.22**	**1.21**	**1.22**	**1.25**
Durable goods.	(X)	1.55	1.47	1.38	1.41	1.42	1.45	1.50
Wood products.	321	1.32	1.29	1.26	1.26	1.28	1.27	1.31
Nonmetallic mineral products	327	1.23	1.15	1.17	1.16	1.09	1.11	1.19
Primary metals.	331	1.69	1.68	1.61	1.62	1.57	1.60	1.52
Fabricated metals.	332	1.56	1.53	1.46	1.56	1.55	1.56	1.55
Machinery.	333	2.08	1.98	1.81	1.82	1.81	1.82	1.89
Computers and electronic products . . .	334	1.54	1.55	1.40	1.41	1.29	1.39	1.40
Electrical equipment, appliances, and components.	335	1.44	1.47	1.42	1.41	1.38	1.44	1.40
Transportation equipment.	336	1.35	1.20	1.14	1.14	1.26	1.27	1.41
Furniture and related products	337	1.35	1.25	1.19	1.25	1.22	1.16	1.17
Miscellaneous products	339	1.90	1.72	1.68	1.72	1.74	1.76	1.80
Nondurable goods	(X)	1.14	1.09	1.03	1.02	1.00	0.98	1.00
Food products	311	0.88	0.82	0.77	0.74	0.75	0.78	0.77
Beverages and tobacco products.	312	1.51	1.67	1.61	1.60	1.41	1.42	1.36
Textile mills	313	1.49	1.30	1.24	1.25	1.25	1.25	1.24
Textile product mills.	314	1.75	1.32	1.28	1.20	1.20	1.26	1.32
Apparel.	315	1.89	1.63	1.45	1.65	1.61	1.61	1.76
Leather and allied products	316	2.10	1.74	1.65	1.65	1.77	2.11	1.95
Paper products.	322	1.11	1.13	1.08	1.11	1.10	1.06	1.09
Printing.	323	0.79	0.78	0.76	0.79	0.81	0.81	0.84
Petroleum and coal products	324	0.71	0.86	0.83	0.77	0.76	0.70	0.76
Basic chemicals	325	1.40	1.28	1.21	1.20	1.19	1.18	1.19
Plastics and rubber products.	326	1.21	1.10	1.08	1.15	1.17	1.17	1.24
UNFILLED ORDERS-TO-SHIPMENTS RATIO								
All manufacturing industries.	(X)	**1.57**	**1.41**	**1.43**	**1.38**	**1.44**	**1.58**	**1.83**
Durable goods.	(X)	2.78	2.61	2.67	2.63	2.83	3.09	3.62
Primary metals.	331	1.45	1.36	1.58	1.48	1.59	1.42	1.38
Fabricated metals.	332	2.02	1.74	1.80	1.92	2.07	2.16	2.25
Machinery.	333	2.51	2.21	2.40	2.35	2.52	2.92	3.31
Computers and electronic products . . .	334	3.08	3.20	3.30	3.31	3.14	3.54	3.79
Electrical equipment, appliances, and components.	335	1.77	1.72	1.70	1.79	1.95	2.26	2.26
Transportation equipment.	336	4.91	4.56	4.52	4.50	5.27	5.94	7.50
Furniture and related products	337	1.14	1.01	1.06	1.12	1.08	0.98	1.05
Miscellaneous products	339	0.62	0.45	0.54	0.54	0.41	0.45	0.50

X Not applicable.   [1] Based on the North American Industry Classification System, 2002; see text, this section and Section 15.

Source: U.S. Census Bureau, *Current Industrial Reports, Benchmark Report for Manufacturers' Shipments, Inventories, and Orders: January 2004 through December 2007*, Series M3-3 (07); (released May 2008). See <http://www.census.gov/indicator/www/m3/>.

Manufactures   623

Table 976. Value of Manufacturers' Shipments, Inventories, and New Orders by Industry: 2000 to 2007

[In millions of dollars (4,208,584 represents $4,208,584,000,000). Based on a sample survey; for methodology, see source]

Industry	2002 NAICS code [1]	2000	2003	2004	2005	2006	2007
SHIPMENTS							
All manufacturing industries	(X)	4,208,584	4,015,388	4,308,970	4,742,077	5,019,962	5,081,075
Durable goods	(X)	2,373,688	2,142,589	2,264,667	2,424,844	2,560,891	2,562,863
Wood products	321	93,669	92,069	104,135	112,095	112,404	101,967
Nonmetallic mineral products.	327	97,329	96,945	102,880	114,849	126,015	119,189
Primary metals	331	156,598	138,270	181,602	203,261	232,558	241,511
Fabricated metals	332	268,213	245,340	261,101	289,433	317,224	326,685
Machinery	333	291,548	257,429	272,123	302,650	326,430	331,451
Computers and electronic products. . .	334	510,639	352,273	365,545	372,882	390,776	386,897
Electrical equipment, appliances, and components	335	125,443	99,906	105,084	111,977	120,040	126,995
Transportation equipment	336	639,861	655,871	662,000	690,743	698,348	693,036
Furniture and related products	337	75,107	75,275	78,280	84,181	86,748	82,266
Miscellaneous products	339	115,281	129,211	131,917	142,770	150,348	152,866
Nondurable goods	(X)	1,834,896	1,872,799	2,044,303	2,317,233	2,459,071	2,518,212
Food products	311	435,229	488,518	512,339	532,403	537,788	573,563
Beverages and tobacco products	312	111,692	109,080	113,737	124,085	124,693	132,251
Textile mills	313	52,112	42,653	40,898	42,328	38,795	36,587
Textile product mills	314	33,654	31,256	33,636	35,022	33,220	30,487
Apparel	315	60,339	38,645	32,873	31,401	30,462	29,814
Leather and allied products	316	9,647	5,807	5,812	6,181	6,019	6,299
Paper products	322	165,298	151,098	155,380	161,928	170,360	168,500
Printing	323	104,396	92,553	93,595	96,922	99,688	101,806
Petroleum and coal products	324	235,134	247,119	330,439	475,787	548,954	564,114
Basic chemicals	325	449,159	487,742	540,884	610,873	657,747	664,057
Plastics and rubber products	326	178,236	178,328	184,710	200,303	211,345	210,734
INVENTORIES (Dec. 31)							
All manufacturing industries	(X)	470,084	397,631	428,321	459,893	497,426	515,952
Durable goods	(X)	298,232	239,946	258,736	275,650	301,180	311,601
Wood products	321	10,329	9,605	10,836	11,534	11,813	11,106
Nonmetallic mineral products.	327	9,799	9,171	9,726	10,134	11,376	11,582
Primary metals	331	22,199	18,566	24,563	25,944	30,947	30,577
Fabricated metals	332	34,085	29,189	33,090	36,077	40,445	41,384
Machinery	333	49,151	37,653	40,071	43,393	47,922	50,487
Computers and electronic products. . .	334	63,024	39,779	41,597	43,655	44,092	43,788
Electrical equipment, appliances, and components	335	14,505	11,359	11,897	12,330	13,944	14,391
Transportation equipment	336	69,199	59,783	60,745	64,798	71,018	78,177
Furniture and related products	337	8,261	7,298	7,912	8,123	8,214	7,847
Miscellaneous products	339	17,680	17,543	18,299	19,662	21,409	22,262
Nondurable goods	(X)	171,852	157,685	169,585	184,243	196,246	204,351
Food products	311	31,882	31,465	31,776	33,007	34,881	36,436
Beverages and tobacco products	312	14,331	14,717	15,234	14,481	14,714	14,899
Textile mills	313	6,243	4,261	4,139	4,066	3,960	3,729
Textile product mills	314	4,698	3,229	3,256	3,302	3,378	3,239
Apparel	315	9,170	4,474	4,333	3,864	3,935	4,220
Leather and allied products	316	1,634	773	777	867	1,024	992
Paper products	322	15,205	13,444	14,237	14,219	14,906	15,221
Printing	323	6,445	5,500	5,781	5,957	6,312	6,631
Petroleum and coal products	324	12,840	15,786	19,431	27,433	29,481	33,008
Basic chemicals	325	51,623	48,295	53,210	58,189	63,357	64,505
Plastics and rubber products	326	17,781	15,741	17,411	18,858	20,298	21,471
NEW ORDERS							
All manufacturing industries	(X)	4,161,472	3,964,423	4,255,188	4,744,813	5,037,520	5,131,164
Durable goods	(X)	2,326,576	2,091,624	2,210,885	2,427,580	2,578,449	2,612,952
Wood products	321	93,669	92,069	104,135	112,095	112,404	101,967
Nonmetallic mineral products.	327	97,329	96,945	102,880	114,849	126,015	119,189
Primary metals	331	153,625	140,637	185,893	207,707	233,056	241,829
Fabricated metals	332	270,021	246,219	265,864	297,252	324,084	330,855
Machinery	333	294,608	261,968	273,909	312,885	341,606	343,454
Computers and electronic products. . .	334	436,415	287,319	297,237	296,761	336,962	330,062
Electrical equipment, appliances, and components	335	126,196	99,345	106,517	114,590	124,051	128,209
Transportation equipment	336	663,326	661,282	663,460	745,402	742,903	781,392
Furniture and related products	337	74,532	75,525	78,879	84,402	86,273	82,363
Miscellaneous products	339	116,855	130,315	132,111	141,637	151,095	153,632
Nondurable goods	(X)	1,834,896	1,872,799	2,044,303	2,317,233	2,459,071	2,518,212

X Not applicable.   [1] Based on the North American Industry Classification System, 2002; see text, this section and Section 15.

Source: U.S. Census Bureau, *Current Industrial Reports, Benchmark Report for Manufacturers' Shipments, Inventories, and Orders: January 2004 through December 2007*, Series M3-3 (07); (released May 2008). See <http://www.census.gov/indicator/www/m3/>.

Table 977. Value of Manufacturers' Shipments, Inventories, and New Orders by Market Grouping: 2000 to 2007

[In millions of dollars (4,028,584 represents $4,028,584,000,000). Based on a sample survey; for methodology, see source]

Market grouping	2000	2002	2003	2004	2005	2006	2007
SHIPMENTS							
All manufacturing industries	4,208,584	3,914,723	4,015,388	4,308,970	4,742,077	5,019,962	5,081,075
Consumer goods	1,500,532	1,494,575	1,584,329	1,700,835	1,895,119	1,988,697	2,037,553
Consumer durable goods	391,463	395,953	418,821	419,182	422,555	421,854	418,456
Consumer nondurable goods.	1,109,069	1,098,622	1,165,508	1,281,653	1,472,564	1,566,843	1,619,097
Aircraft and parts	111,658	108,639	102,931	105,850	114,061	124,375	140,827
Defense aircraft and parts.	24,560	34,136	39,096	41,515	37,952	38,812	39,700
Nondefense aircraft and parts	87,098	74,503	63,835	64,335	76,109	85,563	101,127
Construction materials and supplies	444,812	424,008	429,183	463,148	509,865	545,973	533,380
Motor vehicles and parts	471,180	469,561	491,713	494,567	501,486	500,137	479,703
Computers and related products	110,242	73,807	69,073	63,270	65,005	67,325	65,627
Information technology industries.	399,751	284,799	274,829	287,837	295,447	320,307	322,058
Nondefense capital goods	808,345	652,500	633,878	661,217	729,862	795,525	796,439
Excluding aircraft.	757,617	609,654	600,699	629,207	686,827	745,209	739,632
Defense capital goods	67,051	76,085	85,724	91,688	92,044	90,001	93,160
Durables excluding capital goods.	1,498,292	1,395,036	1,422,987	1,511,762	1,602,938	1,675,365	1,673,264
INVENTORIES (Dec. 31)							
All manufacturing industries	470,084	412,328	397,631	428,321	459,893	497,426	515,952
Consumer goods	128,148	121,561	121,435	128,535	139,501	147,293	152,757
Consumer durable goods	26,108	24,513	23,831	25,215	26,782	27,785	28,034
Consumer nondurable goods.	102,040	97,048	97,604	103,320	112,719	119,508	124,723
Aircraft and parts	36,091	33,282	31,792	31,107	33,449	36,992	44,367
Defense aircraft and parts.	9,423	8,970	10,233	10,840	11,788	11,854	13,213
Nondefense aircraft and parts	26,668	24,312	21,559	20,267	21,661	25,138	31,154
Construction materials and supplies	49,389	45,347	44,073	49,202	53,021	58,212	57,949
Motor vehicles and parts	22,283	20,890	20,795	21,991	23,084	24,580	23,357
Computers and related products	8,350	5,275	4,112	3,955	4,470	4,621	4,706
Information technology industries.	50,795	37,700	34,097	35,853	38,082	38,758	39,288
Nondefense capital goods	127,162	104,643	96,430	99,245	107,740	117,027	124,001
Excluding aircraft.	106,669	85,830	79,592	84,158	90,612	97,535	100,652
Defense capital goods	17,153	14,025	15,150	15,361	15,979	16,567	18,486
Durables excluding capital goods.	153,917	134,530	128,366	144,130	151,931	167,586	169,114
NEW ORDERS							
All manufacturing industries	4,161,472	3,801,734	3,964,423	4,255,188	4,744,813	5,037,520	5,131,164
Consumer goods	1,501,810	1,494,722	1,585,292	1,701,298	1,893,962	1,988,746	2,037,940
Consumer durable goods	392,741	396,100	419,784	419,645	421,398	421,903	418,843
Consumer nondurable goods.	1,109,069	1,098,622	1,165,508	1,281,653	1,472,564	1,566,843	1,619,097
Aircraft and parts	130,575	102,930	99,843	104,962	148,643	166,046	225,339
Defense aircraft and parts.	31,326	39,161	44,552	31,758	29,893	38,173	40,855
Nondefense aircraft and parts	99,249	63,769	55,291	73,204	118,750	127,873	184,484
Construction materials and supplies	446,792	422,093	429,281	466,301	517,655	549,140	540,104
Motor vehicles and parts	468,470	470,049	493,589	495,286	504,251	502,736	477,835
Computers and related products	107,656	74,089	68,048	61,678	63,652	67,435	65,859
Information technology industries.	409,500	265,375	276,841	293,619	296,540	337,686	327,798
Nondefense capital goods	831,335	621,802	634,697	672,945	789,245	860,705	891,459
Excluding aircraft.	767,754	582,751	609,117	630,331	702,052	775,897	755,397
Defense capital goods	79,598	70,927	96,858	92,191	92,913	88,168	97,225
Durables excluding capital goods.	1,415,643	1,317,903	1,360,069	1,445,749	1,545,422	1,629,576	1,624,268

Source: U.S. Census Bureau, *Current Industrial Reports, Benchmark Report for Manufacturers' Shipments, Inventories, and Orders: January 2004 through December 2007*, Series M3-3 (07); (released May 2008). See <http://www.census.gov/indicator /www/m3/>.

Table 978. Finances and Profits of Manufacturing Corporations: 1990 to 2007

[In billions of dollars (2,811 represents $2,811,000,000,000). Data exclude estimates for corporations with less than $250,000 in assets at time of sample selection. See Table 764 for individual industry data]

Item	1990 [1]	2000 [1]	2001 [1]	2001 [2]	2002 [2]	2003 [2]	2004 [2]	2005 [2]	2006 [2]	2007 [2]
Net sales.	2,811	4,548	4,308	4,295	4,217	4,397	4,934	5,411	5,783	6,089
Net operating profit	173	348	185	186	225	237	320	359	405	412
Net profit:										
Before taxes	160	381	82	83	196	306	447	524	605	610
After taxes	112	275	36	36	135	237	348	401	470	445
Cash dividends.	62	132	102	103	106	115	143	179	178	179
Net income retained in business . .	49	143	-67	-66	28	122	205	222	292	266

[1] Based on the Standard Industrial Classification system.   [2] Based on the North American Industry Classification System, 2002; see Text, Section 15.

Source: U.S. Census Bureau, *Quarterly Financial Report for Manufacturing, Mining, and Trade Corporations*. See also 2007 4th quarter press release issued April 2008 at <http://www.census.gov/csd/qfr/>.

U.S. Census Bureau, Statistical Abstract of the United States: 2009

Table 979. Manufacturing Corporations—Assets and Profits by Asset Size: 1990 to 2007

[In millions of dollars (2,629,458 represents $2,629,458,000,000). Corporations and assets as of end of 4th quarter; profits for entire the year. Through 2000, based on Standard Industrial Classification code; beginning 2001, based on the North American Industry Classification System; see text, Section 15. For corporations above a certain asset value based on complete canvass. The asset value for complete canvass was raised in 1995 to $250 million. Asset sizes less than these values are sampled, except as noted. For details regarding Survey description, data analysis and methodology, see source fourth quarter report. Minus sign (–) indicates loss]

Year	Total [1]	Asset-size class						
		Under $10 mil. [1]	$10–$25 mil.	$25–$50 mil.	$50–$100 mil.	$100–$250 mil.	$250–$1 bil.	$1 bil. and over
Assets:								
1990.	2,629,458	142,498	74,477	55,914	72,554	123,967	287,512	1,872,536
1993.	2,904,869	149,763	72,854	61,243	81,389	134,388	317,774	2,087,457
1994.	3,080,231	148,751	81,505	66,405	82,116	138,950	358,100	2,204,404
1995.	3,345,229	155,618	87,011	68,538	87,262	159,133	370,263	2,417,403
1996.	3,574,407	163,928	87,096	69,722	93,205	156,702	398,651	2,605,102
1997.	3,746,797	167,921	87,398	76,034	85,186	157,130	397,559	2,775,570
1998.	3,967,309	170,068	87,937	69,627	86,816	148,060	419,153	2,985,647
1999.	4,382,814	170,058	85,200	67,352	97,810	138,143	398,881	3,425,370
2000.[2]. . . .	4,852,106	171,666	85,482	72,122	90,866	149,714	389,537	3,892,720
2001 [2].	4,747,789	169,701	84,664	67,493	88,088	131,617	393,752	3,812,474
2002.	4,823,219	166,191	82,369	62,654	81,667	134,821	407,423	3,888,095
2003.	5,162,852	161,462	80,681	62,592	77,205	126,826	392,192	4,261,894
2004.	5,538,113	163,072	80,085	71,674	81,741	126,950	414,144	4,600,447
2005.	5,828,716	165,195	85,785	68,731	87,818	142,900	423,917	4,854,370
2006.	6,179,142	168,537	93,786	72,494	91,877	146,651	418,501	5,187,295
2007.	6,805,420	183,958	102,410	82,571	96,023	150,535	437,337	5,752,588
Net profit: [3]								
1990.	110,128	8,527	5,160	2,769	2,661	3,525	7,110	80,377
1993.	83,156	11,195	5,415	3,439	3,218	3,584	4,555	51,750
1994.	174,874	14,131	7,057	4,072	4,996	6,745	14,626	123,250
1995.	198,151	13,224	5,668	3,767	5,771	7,000	16,549	146,172
1996.	224,869	15,802	6,872	4,266	5,664	7,935	16,059	168,271
1997.	244,505	17,948	8,383	4,153	4,675	7,074	18,433	183,836
1998.	234,386	18,350	6,421	3,790	4,681	5,610	14,364	181,170
1999.	257,805	17,398	7,618	3,504	4,798	4,795	12,756	206,934
2000.[2]. . . .	275,313	16,578	6,820	3,403	2,742	3,510	15,121	227,136
2001 [2]. . . .	36,168	8,387	3,366	–408	403	–543	–6,782	31,746
2002.	134,686	10,003	2,784	807	1,699	3,356	–1,227	117,262
2003.	237,041	9,821	3,374	2,005	2,256	2,973	4,115	212,497
2004.	348,151	14,970	5,745	3,858	3,080	5,140	12,787	302,571
2005.	401,344	17,357	6,057	4,066	3,781	7,678	15,967	346,438
2006.	470,282	22,301	8,685	5,260	4,601	8,901	21,405	399,131
2007.	445,228	22,888	9,055	4,448	6,730	8,558	17,951	375,600

[1] Excludes estimates for corporations with less than $250,000 in assets at time of sample selection.   [2] Beginning 2001, data reported on a NAICS basis.   [3] After taxes.

Source: U.S. Census Bureau, *Quarterly Financial Report for Manufacturing, Mining, and Trade Corporations.* See also 2007 4th quarter press release issued 31 March 2008 at <http://www.census.gov/csd/qfr/>.

Table 980. Manufacturing Corporations—Selected Finances: 1990 to 2007

[In billions of dollars (2,811 represents $2,811,000,000,000). Data are not necessarily comparable from year to year due to changes in accounting procedures, industry classifications, sampling procedures, etc.; for detail, see source. Through 2000, based on Standard Industrial Classification code; beginning 2001, based on North American Industry Classification System; see text, Section 15. Minus sign (–) indicates loss]

Year	All manufacturing corps.			Durable goods industries			Nondurable goods industries		
		Profits [1]			Profits [1]			Profits [1]	
	Sales	Before taxes	After taxes	Sales	Before taxes	After taxes	Sales	Before taxes	After taxes
1990	2,811	158	110	1,357	57	41	1,454	101	69
1993 [2]	3,015	118	83	1,490	39	27	1,525	79	56
1994	3,256	244	175	1,658	121	87	1,598	123	88
1995	3,528	275	198	1,808	131	94	1,721	144	104
1996	3,758	307	225	1,942	147	106	1,816	160	119
1997	3,922	331	244	2,076	167	121	1,847	164	123
1998	3,949	315	234	2,169	175	128	1,781	140	107
1999	4,149	355	258	2,314	199	140	1,835	157	117
2000 [3]	4,548	381	275	2,457	191	132	2,091	190	144
2001 [3]	4,295	83	36	2,321	–69	–76	1,974	152	112
2002	4,217	196	135	2,261	45	21	1,955	149	113
2003	4,397	306	237	2,283	118	88	2,114	188	149
2004	4,934	447	348	2,537	200	157	2,397	248	192
2005	5,411	524	401	2,731	211	161	2,681	313	240
2006	5,783	605	470	2,910	249	193	2,873	356	278
2007	6,089	610	445	3,009	262	171	3,080	348	275

[1] Beginning 1998, profits before and after income taxes reflect inclusion of minority stockholders' interest in net income before and after income taxes.   [2] Data for 1993 first quarter, reflect the adoption of Financial Accounting Standards Board Statement 106 (Employer's Accounting for Post-Retirement Benefits Other Than Pensions). Corporations must show the cumulative effect of a change in accounting principle in the first quarter of the year in which the change is adopted.   [3] Beginning 2001, data reported on a NAICS basis.

Source: U.S. Census Bureau, *Quarterly Financial Report for Manufacturing, Mining, and Trade Corporations.* See also 2007 4th quarter press release issued 31 March 2008 at <http://www.census.gov/csd/qfr/>.

626 Manufactures

Table 981. Tobacco Products—Summary: 1990 to 2006

[**710 represents 710,000,000,000.** Production data are for calendar years. Excludes cigars produced in customs bonded manufacturing warehouses. 2006 data are preliminary]

Item	Unit	1990	1995	2000	2001	2002	2003	2004	2005	2006
PRODUCTION										
Cigarettes, total.	Billions	710	747	565	562	532	499	494	489	484
Nonfilter tip.	Billions	23	15	7	6	5	6	5	4	(NA)
Filter tip	Billions	687	732	558	556	527	494	488	486	(NA)
Cigars.	Billions	1.9	2.1	2.8	3.7	3.8	4.0	4.4	3.7	4.1
Tobacco [1]	Mil. lb.	142	131	133	130	133	137	135	143	141
Smoking.	Mil. lb.	16	12	14	13	16	18	16	17	17
Chewing tobacco	Mil. lb.	73	63	49	47	45	43	39	39	38
Snuff	Mil. lb.	53	60	70	70	73	76	79	87	86
EXPORTS										
Cigarettes	Bil. cigarettes. . .	164.3	231.1	147.9	133.9	127.4	121.5	118.7	113.3	109.9
Cigars.	Bil. cigars	72.0	94.0	113.0	124.0	122.7	130.2	171.0	301.0	180.0
Smoking tobacco	Bil. lb.	0.8	0.3	0.5	11.0	7.9	0.7	0.2	0.2	0.4
IMPORTS										
Cigarettes	Bil. cigarettes. . .	1.4	3.0	11.3	14.7	20.8	23.1	22.7	18.1	16.2
Cigars.	Bil. cigars	111.0	195.0	497.0	543.4	413.5	508.0	616.0	445.0	340.0
Smoking tobacco	Bil. lb.	2.9	4.2	4.2	1.9	2.1	2.1	1.5	3.0	3.1
CONSUMPTION										
Tobacco products per person [2] . . .	Lb. [3]	5.6	4.8	4.1	4.3	4.2	4.0	3.3	3.7	3.5
Cigarettes per person [2]	1,000	2.8	2.5	2.1	2.1	2.0	1.9	1.8	1.7	1.7
EXPENDITURES										
Consumer expenditures, total. . .	Bil. dol.	43.8	48.7	77.5	82.9	88.2	86.8	86.3	88.7	(NA)
Cigarettes	Bil. dol.	41.6	45.8	72.9	77.8	82.8	81.1	79.9	82.0	(NA)
Cigars.	Bil. dol.	0.7	1.0	1.8	2.1	2.2	2.5	2.9	3.1	(NA)
Other	Bil. dol.	1.5	2.5	2.7	3.0	3.1	3.2	3.4	3.7	(NA)

NA Not available.   [1] Smoking and chewing tobaccos and snuff output.   [2] Based on estimated population, 18 years old and over, as of July 1, including Armed Forces abroad.   [3] Unstemmed processing weight equivalent.

Source: U.S. Dept. of Agriculture, Economic Research Service, *Tobacco Situation and Outlook,* quarterly. See also <http://usda.mannlib.cornell.edu/usda/ers/TBS2000s/2007/TBS-04-24-2007.pdf>; (released 24 April 2007).

Table 982. Cotton, Wool, and Manmade Fibers—Consumption by End-Use: 2002 to 2006

[**15,682 represents 15,682,000,000.** Represents products manufactured by U.S. mills. Excludes glass fiber]

Year	Total (mil. lb.)	Cotton Total (mil. lb.)	Cotton Percent of end-use	Wool Total (mil. lb.)	Wool Percent of end-use	Manufactured fibers Total (mil. lb.)	Manufactured fibers Percent of end-use	Cellulosic Total (mil. lb.)	Cellulosic Percent of end-use	Synthetic Total (mil. lb.)	Synthetic Percent of end-use
Total:											
2002.	15,682	4,044	25.8	109	0.7	11,529	73.5	250	1.6	11,314	72.1
2003.	14,741	3,465	23.5	112	0.8	11,163	75.7	227	1.5	10,964	74.4
2004.	13,974	2,743	19.6	107	0.8	11,125	79.6	218	1.6	10,911	78.1
2005.	13,552	2,533	18.7	95	0.7	10,924	80.6	210	1.6	10,697	78.9
2006.	12,591	2,437	19.4	97	0.8	10,057	79.9	189	1.5	9,869	78.4
Apparel:											
2002.	4,777	2,297	48.1	64	1.3	2,416	50.6	113	2.4	2,303	48.2
2003.	4,145	1,902	45.9	65	1.6	2,178	52.5	93	2.2	2,085	50.3
2004.	3,457	1,438	41.6	60	1.7	1,959	56.7	76	2.2	1,883	54.5
2005.	3,232	1,392	43.1	51	1.6	1,789	55.4	62	1.9	1,727	53.4
2006.	2,943	1,369	46.5	51	1.7	1,523	51.7	40	1.3	1,484	50.4
Home textiles:											
2002.	2,380	1,370	57.6	10	0.4	999	42.0	48	2.0	951	39.9
2003.	2,069	1,180	57.0	12	0.6	877	42.4	43	2.1	834	40.3
2004.	1,745	940	53.9	10	0.6	794	45.5	40	2.3	753	43.2
2005.	1,498	797	53.2	9	0.6	691	46.1	31	2.1	660	44.1
2006.	1,272	707	55.6	12	0.9	554	43.6	23	1.8	531	41.8
Floor coverings:											
2002.	4,365	30	0.7	25	0.6	4,310	98.7	–	–	4,310	98.7
2003.	4,409	32	0.7	28	0.6	4,349	98.6	–	–	4,349	98.6
2004.	4,489	32	0.7	29	0.6	4,429	98.7	–	–	4,429	98.7
2005.	4,555	32	0.7	29	0.6	4,494	98.7	–	–	4,494	98.7
2006.	4,230	30	0.7	29	0.7	4,171	98.6	–	–	4,171	98.6
Industrial: [1]											
2002.	4,160	346	8.3	10	0.2	3,804	91.4	88	2.1	3,716	89.3
2003.	4,118	351	8.5	8	0.2	3,759	91.3	91	2.2	3,668	89.1
2004.	4,284	333	7.8	8	0.2	3,943	92.0	102	2.4	3,841	89.7
2005.	4,267	312	7.3	5	0.1	3,949	92.5	112	2.6	3,837	89.9
2006.	4,146	331	8.0	6	0.1	3,809	91.9	126	3.0	3,683	88.8

– Represents or rounds to zero.   [1] Includes consumer-type products.

Source: Fiber Economics Bureau, Inc., Arlington, VA, *Fiber Organon,* monthly (copyright).

U.S. Census Bureau, Statistical Abstract of the United States: 2009

Table 983. **Textiles—Production and Foreign Trade: 2007**

[1,500,934 represents 1,500,934,000. Fabric blends as shown in the report are reported based on the chief weight of the fiber; whereas, fabric blends as shown for imports are based on the chief value of the fiber]

Product description	Unit	Quantity (1,000)			Percent		Value ($1,000)	
		Manu-facturers' pro-duction	Imports for consump-tion	Exports of domestic mer-chandise	Imports to manu-facturers' production (quantity)	Exports to manu-facturers' production (quantity)	Imports for consump-tion [1]	Exports of domestic mer-chandise
YARN								
Spun yarn	kilograms . .	1,500,934	168,215	(S)	11.2	(S)	622,852	(S)
Textured, crimped, twisted, or bulked filament yarn	kilograms . .	1,335,568	108,853	69,755	8.2	5.2	380,449	285,034
BROADWOVEN FABRICS [2]								
Spun yarn fabrics	sq. meters . .	1,761,973	1,269,809	271,259	72.1	15.4	1,791,589	543,895
85 percent or more filament yarn fabrics, manmade	sq. meters . .	2,133,115	1,004,116	(NA)	47.1	(NA)	747,224	(NA)
Spun/filament combinations (except blue denim and other yarn dyed)	sq. meters . .	231,767	158,101	41,537	68.2	17.9	266,309	97,488
Silk fabrics	sq. meters . .	(D)	32,693	5,120	(D)	(D)	285,833	28,189
KNIT FABRICS								
Pile fabrics	kilograms . .	39,096	140,608	34,396	359.7	88.0	205,688	194,934
Elastic fabric	kilograms . .	21,704	25,035	(S)	115.3	(S)	259,059	(S)
Other warp knit fabrics	kilograms . .	43,387	27,176	14,447	62.6	33.3	168,402	137,934
Other weft knit fabrics	kilograms . .	169,825	65,470	(S)	38.6	(S)	362,900	(S)
Other narrow knit fabrics	kilograms . .	2,111	1,028	(S)	48.7	(S)	10,766	(S)
SHEETS, PILLOWCASES, AND TOWELS								
Sheets and pillowcases	dozens	3,630	53,635	2,590	1,477.6	71.3	2,199,902	46,806
Finished towels	dozens	8,059	145,369	3,902	1,803.8	48.4	1,611,910	51,618

D Withheld to avoid disclosing data for individual companies.   NA Not available.   S Does not meet publication standards.
[1] Dollar value represents the c.i.f. (cost, insurance, and freight) at the first port of entry in the United States plus calculated import duty.   [2] Represents production of gray broadwoven fabrics; import and export data represent gray as well as finished broadwoven fabrics.

Source: U.S. Census Bureau, *Current Industrial Reports, Textiles*, Series MQ313A. See <http://www.census.gov/cir/www/index.html>.

Table 984. **Footwear—Consumption, Production, and Imports: 1990 to 2006**

[In millions of pairs of shoes (1,305.2 represents 1,305,200,000), except as indicated]

Item	1990	2000	2005	2006	Item	1990	2000	2005	2006
CONSUMPTION					Other	(NA)	2.0	0.2	0.1
Consumption, total .	**1,305.2**	**1,851.5**	**2,286.5**	**2,403.1**	Rubber or fabric	(NA)	20.6	10.2	9.7
Production	184.6	86.6	34.0	31.9	Plastic or protective	(NA)	7.2	6.7	6.6
Imports	1,120.7	1,764.9	2,252.5	2,371.2					
Percent of consumption	85.9	95.3	98.5	98.7	IMPORTS				
					Men's	102.1	200.5	255.6	235.9
PRODUCTION					Men's work	13.2	24.1	31.5	33.9
					Women's	415.2	587.2	879.9	944.6
Men's	(NA)	24.0	11.5	10.9	Juveniles'	132.8	228.3	291.3	316.7
Men's work	(NA)	9.2	8.8	8.7	Athletic	212.3	288.1	374.1	371.6
Women's	(NA)	9.8	4.2	3.8	Slippers	17.9	76.3	120.8	130.5
Juveniles'	(NA)	1.4	0.2	0.2	Other	3.9	9.9	14.0	23.9
Athletic	(NA)	0.3	0.1	0.1	Rubber or fabric	199.2	317.3	315.3	169.9
Slippers	(NA)	31.2	1.0	0.5	Plastic or protective	23.9	10.4	21.5	18.9

NA Not available.

Source: American Apparel and Footwear Association, Arlington, VA, *Shoe Stats*, annual. See also <http://www.apparelandfootwear.org/>.

Table 985. **Pharmaceutical Preparations—Value of Shipments: 2000 to 2006**

[In millions of dollars (79,262 represents 79,262,000,000]

Product description	Product code	2000	2002	2003	2004	2005	2006
Pharmaceutical preparations, except biologicals	(X)	**79,262**	**100,741**	**107,561**	**109,852**	**118,647**	**127,142**
Affecting neoplasms, endocrine systems, and metabolic disease	3254121100	9,784	17,499	20,065	20,789	23,779	25,577
Acting on the central nervous system and sense organs	3254124100	18,508	24,345	24,759	25,001	25,627	29,858
Acting on the cardiovascular system	3254127100	8,993	10,339	9,671	10,224	10,232	10,901
Acting on the respiratory system	325412A100	10,179	12,504	13,758	15,148	16,367	18,516
Acting on the digestive system	325412D100	10,046	13,373	15,052	15,252	16,829	15,354
Acting on the skin	325412G100	2,941	2,844	3,083	3,283	3,657	3,719
Vitamin, nutrient, and hematinic preps.	325412L100	5,676	6,029	6,877	6,683	7,556	7,755
Affecting parasitic and infective disease	325412P100	11,037	11,337	11,848	10,819	11,228	11,654
Pharmaceutical preps. for veterinary use . . .	325412T100	2,096	2,471	2,449	2,653	3,371	3,807

X Not applicable.

Source: U.S. Census Bureau, *Current Industrial Reports, Pharmaceutical Preparations, Except Biologicals* Series MA325G. See <http://www.census.gov/mcd/index.html>.

Table 986. Inorganic Chemicals and Fertilizers—Production: 2000 to 2006

[(15,809 represents 15,809,000)]

Product description	Product code	2000	2003	2004	2005	2006
INORGANIC FERTILIZERS 1,000 short tons (2,000 lbs.)						
Ammonia, synthetic anhydrous	3253111120	15,809	11,330	12,058	11,181	10,981
Ammonium nitrate, original solution	3253111201	7,979	6,328	7,229	7,212	7,068
Ammonium sulfate	3253111240	2,808	2,871	3,005	2,906	2,870
Urea (100%)	3253114100	7,682	6,375	6,344	5,807	5,934
Nitric acid (100%).	3253111111	8,708	7,189	7,129	7,398	7,245
Phosphoric acid (100% P2O5)	3253121100	12,492	12,537	12,693	12,621	11,797
Sulfuric acid, gross (100%)	3251881100	43,643	41,144	41,934	40,996	39,578
Superphosphates and other fertilizer materials (100% P2O5)	3253124100	8,899	8,837	8,737	8,141	7,184
INORGANIC CHEMICALS 1,000 metric tons (2,205 lbs.)						
Chlorine gas	3251811111	14,000	10,361	12,329	10,272	12,443
Sodium hydroxide, total liquid	3251814111	11,523	8,796	9,620	8,517	9,735
Potassium hydroxide liquid.	3251817111	539	471	525	527	610
Finished sodium bicarbonate	3251817131	536	540	579	581	644
Hydrochloric acid	3251884131	4,717	(S)	5,302	4,619	4,740
Aluminum oxide	3313110100	(D)	(D)	(D)	(D)	(D)
Aluminum sulfate (commercial)	3251887151	1,076	965	972	967	1,022
Sodium chlorate	325188A141	940	669	556	523	615
Sodium phosphate tripoly	325188A174	(D)	(D)	(D)	(D)	(D)
Sodium silicates [1]	325188A181	1,136	1,074	1,112	1,309	1,161
Sodium metasilicates	325188A187	72	61	58	59	29
Sodium sulfate.	325188A1A7	509	89	86	93	101
Carbon activated [2]	325998H1E7	166	112	(D)	(D)	65
Hydrogen peroxide	325188G181	1,083	340	357	365	387
Phosphorous, oxychloride, and trichlorde	325188G1F1	(D)	(D)	(D)	(D)	(D)

D Withheld to avoid disclosing data for individual companies. S Does not meet publication standards. [1] Other than metasilicates. [2] Granular and pulverized.

Source: U.S. Census Bureau, *Current Industrial Reports, Inorganic Chemicals,* Series MQ325A and *Fertilizers and Related Chemicals,* Series MQ325B. See <http://www.census.gov/cir/www/index.html>.

Table 987. Aluminum—Supply, Shipments, and Foreign Trade: 1990 to 2007

[In millions of pounds (17,334 represents 17,334,000,000)]

Item	1990	1995	2000	2003	2004	2005	2006	2007, prel.
SUPPLY								
Aluminum supply, total.	**17,334**	**20,425**	**23,586**	**21,145**	**22,281**	**23,571**	**23,909**	**23,873**
Primary production	8,925	7,441	8,087	5,962	5,549	5,468	5,029	5,643
Recovery from scrap.	5,276	7,030	7,606	6,215	6,669	6,592	7,732	8,571
Imports of ingot and mill products	3,133	5,956	7,893	8,968	10,063	11,510	11,149	9,659
Aluminum net shipments, total	**17,188**	**21,019**	**24,496**	**23,392**	**24,950**	**25,541**	**25,996**	**24,344**
PRODUCT [1]								
Mill products, total	13,013	15,716	17,676	15,693	17,122	17,734	17,950	16,413
Sheet, plate, and foil	9,297	11,168	12,116	10,562	11,463	11,810	11,794	11,000
Rod, bar, and wire.	370	534	690	576	631	660	712	702
Electrical conductor	542	566	681	694	763	794	850	785
Extruded shapes and tube	2,546	3,102	3,792	3,468	3,821	4,018	4,137	3,485
Powder and paste.	106	108	142	146	155	144	140	151
Forgings and impacts	152	238	255	247	289	308	317	290
Ingot for castings and other [2]	4,175	5,303	6,820	7,699	7,828	7,807	8,046	7,931
MARKET [1]								
Domestic, total.	14,637	18,152	21,680	21,403	22,901	23,060	23,162	21,415
Building and construction	2,663	2,679	3,204	3,432	3,692	3,683	3,624	3,100
Transportation	3,205	5,749	7,947	7,804	8,509	8,683	8,669	7,885
Consumer durables.	1,122	1,369	1,692	1,498	1,585	1,561	1,644	1,474
Electrical	1,309	1,395	1,704	1,433	1,580	1,644	1,705	1,646
Machinery and equipment	992	1,257	1,496	1,452	1,610	1,634	1,680	1,623
Containers and packaging	4,772	5,088	4,992	4,941	5,098	5,115	5,113	4,895
Other	574	615	645	843	827	740	727	792
Exports	2,551	2,867	2,816	1,988	2,049	2,481	2,834	2,929
FOREIGN TRADE [3]								
Exports	3,753	3,846	4,100	3,662	4,416	5,629	6,592	6,700
Imports.	3,718	6,899	9,358	9,884	11,221	12,607	12,322	10,748

[1] Statistics on shipments and markets for 1990 to 2000 represent total U.S. producer's shipments plus imports by consumers. Beginning 2003, figures include Canada. [2] Net ingot for foundry castings, export, and destructive uses. [3] U.S. imports and exports of aluminum ingot, mill products, and scrap.

Source: The Aluminum Association, Inc., Washington, DC, *Aluminum Statistical Review,* annual.

U.S. Census Bureau, Statistical Abstract of the United States: 2009

Table 988. **Iron and Steel Industry—Summary: 1990 to 2007**

Editor's Note: For information on the contents of this table, please contact
American Iron and Steel Institute at (202) 452-7203

Table 989. **Steel Products—Net Shipments by Market Classes: 1990 to 2007**

Editor's Note: For information on the contents of this table, please contact
American Iron and Steel Institute at (202) 452-7203

Table 990. **Metalworking Machinery—Value of Shipments: 2006**
[In thousands of dollars (3,094,478 represents $3,094,478,000)]

Product description	Product code	2006
Metalworking machinery	(X)	**3,094,478**
Metal cutting type [1, 2, 3]	(X)	2,293,813
Boring and drilling machines	333512A1	178,487
Gear cutting machines [1]	33351211	(D)
Grinding and polishing machines	33351221	259,063
Lathes [2, 3, 4]	33351231	295,651
Milling machines [2, 5]	33351241	56,082
Machining centers	33351271	703,045
Station type machines	33351281	79,153
Other metal cutting machine tools	33351291	464,779
Remanufactured metal cutting machine tools	3335126111	90,172
Metal forming type [6]	(X)	800,665
Punching and shearing machines	33351311 part	130,126
Bending and forming machines	33351311 part	273,235
Presses, except forging [6]	33351331	128,599
Other metal forming type machines [6]	33351351	228,880
Remanufactured metal forming machine tools	3335137121	15,081

D Withheld to avoid disclosing data for individual companies.   X Not applicable.   [1] Data for "Gear cutting machines" are included in total "Metal cutting type."   [2] Data for "All lathes (turning machines) valued under $3,025 each" and "All Milling machines valued under $3,025 each" are included in total "Metal cutting type."   [3] Data for product code 3335123126, "Vertical NC turning machines," are included in total "Metal cutting type," but excluded from product code 33351231   [4] For 2006, Product class 33351231, "Lathes," excludes the values for product code 3335123131, "All lathes (turning machines) valued under $3,025 each."   [5] Product class 33351241, "Milling machines," excludes the value for product code 3335124101, "All milling machines valued under $3,025 each."   [6] Data for product codes 3335133101, "All presses valued under $3,025 each" and 3335135101, "All other metal forming type machine tools valued under $3,025 each," are included in total "Metal forming type," but excluded from product codes 33351331 and 33351351 respectively.

Source: U.S. Census Bureau, *Current Industrial Reports, Metalworking Machinery,* Series MQ333W. See <http://www.census.gov/cir/www/index.html>.

Table 991. U.S. Machine Tool Consumption—Gross New Orders and Exports: 2006 and 2007

[Value in millions of dollars (4,435 represents $4,435,000,000)]

Item	2006				2007			
	Total	Metal cutting machines	Metal forming machines	Other manu-facturing tech-nology	Total	Metal cutting machines	Metal forming machines	Other manu-facturing tech-nology
New order units, total . . .	**27,651**	**24,027**	**1,188**	**2,436**	**28,484**	**24,220**	**1,310**	**2,954**
Northeast [1]	4,616	4,044	185	387	4,891	4,309	195	387
South [2]	4,247	3,497	255	495	4,449	3,483	240	726
Midwest [3]	7,564	6,391	295	878	8,101	6,634	400	1,067
Central [4]	6,640	5,903	309	428	6,844	5,981	323	540
West [5]	4,584	4,192	144	248	4,199	3,813	152	234
New order value, total. . .	**4,435**	**3,762**	**182**	**491**	**4,902**	**4,021**	**240**	**641**
Northeast [1]	647	565	24	58	707	620	31	56
South [2]	596	467	38	91	639	500	44	95
Midwest [3]	1,403	1,180	53	170	1,700	1,332	90	277
Central [4]	1,129	971	48	111	1,226	1,023	52	150
West [5]	660	580	20	60	631	545	24	62
Export order units [6]	1,941	1,449	178	314	2,514	1,759	292	463
Export order value [6]	582	431	37	114	751	517	75	159

[1] Covers Maine, New Hampshire, Vermont, New York, Massachusetts, Connecticut, Rhode Island, New Jersey, and Pennsylvania. [2] Covers Delaware, Maryland, Virginia, West Virginia, Kentucky, North Carolina, South Carolina, Tennessee, Mississippi, Alabama, Georgia, and Florida. [3] Covers Wisconsin, Michigan, Ohio, Illinois, and Indiana. [4] Covers Minnesota, North Dakota, South Dakota, Montana, Wyoming, Idaho, Iowa, Nebraska, Kansas, Missouri, Oklahoma, Arkansas, Louisiana, Texas, New Mexico, Colorado, and Utah. [5] Covers Washington, Oregon, California, Nevada, and Arizona. [6] Represents orders placed with U.S. builders.

Source: The Association for Manufacturing Technology, McLean, VA, (copyright); and American Machine Tool Distributors Association, Rockville, MD, *U.S. Machine Tool Consumption Report*, monthly.

Table 992. Semiconductors, Electronic Components, and Semiconductor Manufacturing Equipment—Value of Shipments: 2000 to 2006

[In millions of dollars (703 represents $703,000,000)]

Product description	Product code	2000	2002	2003	2004	2005	2006
Semiconductor machinery	3332950	(NA)	(NA)	(NA)	(NA)	9,728	12,388
Transmittal, industrial, and special-purpose electron tubes (except x-ray)	3344111	703	584	629	641	652	690
Receiving type electron tubes and cathode ray picture tubes	3344114	3,458	2,486	1,508	1,049	621	216
Electron tube parts	3344117	144	91	63	78	72	49
Bare printed circuit boards	3344120	11,892	5,764	4,871	4,709	4,856	5,003
Integrated microcircuits (semiconductor networks)	3344131	73,664	49,726	54,830	60,097	61,631	54,730
Transistors	3344134	1,569	818	608	656	603	672
Diodes and rectifiers	3344137	621	370	391	305	372	457
Other semiconductor devices	334413A	9,757	6,632	6,519	7,247	8,330	10,051
Capacitors for electronic circuitry	3344140	2,786	1,338	1,192	1,184	1,113	1,064
Resistors for electronic circuitry	3344150	982	653	636	744	653	620
Electronic coil, transformer, and other indicator manufacturing	3344160	1,719	1,154	957	1,116	1,216	1,310
Coaxial connectors	3344171	805	464	402	403	410	407
Cylindrical connectors	3344174	725	528	563	631	738	824
Rack and panel connectors	3344177	532	264	268	291	297	332
Printed circuit connectors	334417A	1,811	776	834	1,013	937	1,101
Other connectors including parts	334417D	2,059	1,436	1,418	1,079	1,207	1,303
Printed circuit assemblies, loaded boards, and modules	334418B	37,273	23,171	19,715	19,566	20,106	20,663
Crystals, filters (except microwave) and piezoelectric devices	3344191	1,168	726	601	654	779	739
All other miscellaneous transducers	3344194	1,519	1,203	1,219	1,495	1,401	1,487
Switches, mechanical types for electronic circuitry	3344197	903	836	739	716	794	773
Microwave components and devices	334419A	2,435	1,511	1,415	1,326	1,306	1,420
All other electronic components	334419E	8,332	4,366	4,060	4,158	4,040	4,336

NA Not available.

Source: U.S. Census Bureau, *Current Industrial Reports, Semiconductors, Electronic Components, and Semiconductor Manufacturing Equipment,* Series MA334Q. See <http://www.census.gov/cir/www/index.html>.

Table 993. **Computers and Peripheral Equipment—Value of Shipments: 2000 to 2006**

[In millions of dollars (62,857 represents $62,857,000,000)]

Product	Product code	2000	2002	2003	2004	2005	2006
Electronic computers [1]	334111	62,857	40,448	38,271	37,895	38,386	37,657
Host computers (multiusers)	3341111	22,877	13,053	12,237	10,993	11,759	(D)
Single-user computers	3341117	38,981	26,586	25,164	26,309	25,906	(D)
Other computers	334111D	998	809	870	593	721	(D)
Computer storage devices (except parts, attachments, and accessories)	3341121	8,995	5,027	5,101	5,034	6,100	6,956
Parts, attachments, and accessories for computer storage devices	3341124	1,692	1,578	1,130	1,039	1,441	1,929
Computer terminals [1]	3341131	415	266	258	274	245	268
Parts, attachments, and accessories for computer terminals [1]	3341134	(D)	(D)	1	2	(D)	(D)
All other miscellaneous computer peripheral equipment	3341191	(S)	(S)	(S)	4,705	4,425	4,517
Parts, subassemblies, and accessories for computer peripheral equipment	3341194	2,766	1,905	1,849	2,257	2,743	2,720
Point-of-sale terminals and funds-transfer devices	3341197	852	632	732	513	497	621
Parts and attachments for point-of-sale terminals and funds-transfer devices	334119D	(NA)	(NA)	(NA)	(D)	(D)	35
Magnetic and optical recording media	3346130	3,206	2,207	2,271	1,586	1,303	1,364

D Withheld to avoid disclosing data for individual companies.   NA Not available.   S Does not meet publication standards.
[1] Excludes point-of-sale and funds transfer devices.

Source: U.S. Census Bureau, *Current Industrial Reports, Computers and Peripheral Equipment,* Series MA334R (beginning with 2006, MQ334R). See <http://www.census.gov/cir/www/index.html>.

Table 994. **Computers and Peripheral Equipment—Shipments: 2005 and 2006**

[24,947 represents 24,947,000]

Product	Product code	Number of companies, 2006	Quantity (1,000) 2005	Quantity (1,000) 2006	Value (mil. dol.) 2005	Value (mil. dol.) 2006
Electronic computers [1]	**334111**	**93**	**24,947**	**26,926**	**38,385**	**37,657**
Host computers, multiusers	3341111	39	(D)	(D)	11,759	(D)
Single-user computers, microprocessor-based, capable of supporting attached peripherals [1]	3341117	54	22,878	(D)	25,906	(D)
Personal computers	3341117107	23	(D)	(D)	(D)	(D)
Workstations	3341117109	27	(D)	(D)	(D)	(D)
Other computers (array, analog, hybrid, and special-use computers)	334111D	26	(D)	(D)	721	(D)
Computer storage devices (except parts, attachments, and accessories)	3341121	38	(X)	(X)	6,100	6,956
Disk subsystem and disk arrays for multiuser computer systems	3341121109	13	225	(D)	2,008	(D)
Disk drives (all sizes)	3341121112	13	(X)	(X)	11	(D)
Storage Area Networks(SANs)	3341121123	7	391	(D)	10	(D)
Tape drives (all sizes)	3341121138	9	(X)	(X)	289	285
USB flash memory (thumb drives)	3341121141	1	–	(D)	–	(D)
Other computer storage devices	3341121145	14	1,162	1,134	3,781	3,795
Parts, attachments, and accessories for computer storage devices	3341124	13	(X)	(X)	1,441	1,929
Computer terminals (except point-of-sale and funds-transfer devices, parts, attachments, and accessories)	3341131	16	(X)	(X)	245	268
Parts, attachments, and accessories for computer terminals (except point-of-sale and funds-transfer devices)	3341134	4	(X)	(X)	(D)	(D)
All other miscellaneous computer peripheral (input/output) equipment (except parts, attachments, and accessories)	3341191	115	(X)	(X)	4,425	4,517
Parts, subassemblies, and accessories for computer peripheral equipment	3341194	30	(X)	(X)	2,743	2,719
Point-of-sale terminals and funds-transfer devices	3341197	14	292	378	497	621
Magnetic and optical recording media	3346130	21	(X)	(X)	1,303	1,364

– Represents zero.   D Withheld to avoid disclosing data for individual companies.   NA Not available.   X Not applicable.
[1] Includes other products, not shown separately.

Source: U.S. Census Bureau, *Current Industrial Reports, Computers and Peripheral Equipment,* Series MA334R (beginning with 2006, MQ334R). See <http://www.census.gov/cir/www/index.html>.

U.S. Census Bureau, Statistical Abstract of the United States: 2009

Table 995. U.S. Consumer Electronics Sales and Forecasts by Product Category: 2003 to 2007 and Projections, 2008

[In millions of dollars (107,432 represents $107,432,000,000). Factory sales include imports]

Product category	2003	2004	2005	2006	2007	2008, proj.
Total	**107,432**	**118,071**	**130,346**	**149,145**	**161,655**	**171,583**
In-home technologies, total	**58,133**	**63,099**	**66,324**	**72,715**	**76,287**	**80,619**
TV sets and displays	14,528	16,783	19,022	24,726	26,007	29,171
Digital TV sets and displays [1]	8,692	12,300	15,563	23,380	25,865	29,171
Digital direct-view TV receivers	673	728	821	1,594	508	282
Digital rear projection TV	3,678	5,543	4,441	4,427	2,316	1,604
LCD flat panel	664	1,579	3,258	8,430	14,532	18,785
Plasma flat panel	1,590	2,347	3,609	5,302	4,848	4,777
Front projection	2,087	2,103	2,914	2,943	2,996	2,983
Digital combinations	(X)	(X)	520	684	665	740
High-definition TV	*6,253*	*9,212*	*11,547*	*18,410*	*19,439*	*22,489*
Analog displays	5,836	4,483	3,459	1,346	142	(X)
Video components [1]	5,440	4,658	4,206	4,611	4,779	5,384
Component DVD players/recorders	2,698	2,183	2,053	2,228	1,729	1,444
Next generation DVD players	(X)	(X)	(X)	65	403	856
Set-top boxes	2,335	2,345	2,074	2,273	2,644	3,084
Digital video recorders (DVRs)	*848*	*635*	*532*	*975*	*1,580*	*2,687*
Audio separates/systems	3,000	3,390	2,862	2,794	2,963	2,925
Audio separates components	981	1,325	1,318	1,361	1,478	1,507
Home information technologies and security [1]	32,169	35,282	37,318	37,883	40,307	41,153
Personal computers	15,584	18,233	19,400	19,553	20,672	20,321
Other computer peripherals	1,297	1,413	1,583	1,762	1,893	2,106
Personal computer software	5,211	5,748	6,173	6,655	7,121	7,619
Home security systems	2,055	2,150	2,322	2,786	3,204	3,558
Communications	2,996	2,986	2,915	2,700	2,231	1,986
In-vehicle technologies, total	**6,388**	**7,062**	**7,860**	**9,357**	**11,371**	**12,834**
Entertainment devices [1]	5,842	6,426	7,140	8,003	8,580	9,628
Aftermarket autosound equipment	2,180	2,336	2,270	2,654	2,877	3,087
Factory-installed autosound	3,245	3,569	4,318	4,719	4,979	5,788
Information and security	546	636	720	1,354	2,791	3,206
Portable and transportable navigation	163	261	349	988	2,422	2,834
Anywhere technologies, total	**28,841**	**31,317**	**38,341**	**47,893**	**53,894**	**57,139**
Digital imaging	5,923	6,390	7,315	9,827	10,496	10,461
Digital cameras	3,921	4,739	5,611	7,819	8,396	8,219
All camcorders	2,002	1,651	1,704	1,828	1,856	1,932
Digital photo frames	(X)	(X)	(X)	180	244	310
Portable entertainment	1,779	2,281	5,003	6,722	6,913	7,113
Portable Media/MP3 players	424	1,289	4,229	5,559	5,564	5,642
Electronic gaming	10,253	10,512	11,070	12,875	15,758	17,872
Electronic gaming hardware	3,188	3,162	3,029	4,425	6,636	6,367
Electronic gaming software	7,065	7,350	8,041	8,450	9,122	11,505
Portable communication	10,886	12,134	14,953	18,469	20,727	21,693
Wireless communication technologies	9,922	11,258	14,265	17,934	20,319	21,418
Consumer electronic enhancements	**14,070**	**16,593**	**17,821**	**19,181**	**20,103**	**20,991**
Accessories	10,320	11,135	12,117	13,614	14,784	15,694
Accessory products	4,914	5,405	6,215	7,459	8,363	8,999
Primary batteries	5,406	5,730	5,902	6,155	6,421	6,695
Blank media [1]	3,750	5,458	5,704	5,567	5,319	5,297
Blank computer media	1,800	1,841	2,189	1,856	1,631	1,364
Flash media	1,346	3,102	3,087	3,374	3,441	3,752

X Not applicable.　[1] Includes categories, not shown separately.

Source: Consumer Electronics Association, Washington, DC, *U.S. Consumer Electronics Sales and Forecasts, 2003–2008* (copyright).

Table 996. Telecommunication Equipment—Value of Shipments: 2000 to 2006

[In millions of dollars (15,174 represents $15,174,000,000]

Product description	Product code	2000	2002	2003	2004	2005	2006
Telephone switching and switchboard equipment	3342101	15,174	7,437	4,900	3,294	1,576	1,812
Carrier line equipment and nonconsumer modems	3342104	13,112	4,488	3,045	3,598	2,824	2,912
Wireline voice and data network equipment	3342107	28,971	13,886	12,272	12,052	12,289	18,563
Communication systems and equipment [1]	3342201	36,357	25,104	25,805	31,230	30,272	32,436
Broadcast, studio, and related electronic equipment	3342202	4,029	3,304	2,932	2,763	3,289	3,653
Alarm systems [2]	3342901	2,755	2,440	2,258	2,014	1,910	1,526
Vehicular and pedestrian traffic control equipment [3]	3342902	838	928	945	898	1,020	1,048
Intercommunications systems [4]	3342903	447	385	428	455	416	433
Modems, consumer type	3344184	95	112	75	100	98	79

[1] Includes microwave and space satellites.　[2] Includes electric sirens and horns.　[3] Includes electrical railway signals and attachments.　[4] Includes inductive paging systems (selective calling).

Source: U.S. Census Bureau, *Current Industrial Reports, Telecommunications,* Series MA334P. See <http://www.census.gov/cir/www/index.html>.

U.S. Census Bureau, Statistical Abstract of the United States: 2009

Table 997. **Motor Vehicle Manufactures—Summary by Selected Industry: 2006**

[48,290 represents $48,290,000,000. Based on the Annual Survey of Manufactures; see Appendix III]

Industry	2002 NAICS code [1]	All employees [2]			Production workers [2]	Value of shipments [3] (mil. dol.)
		Number	Payroll			
			Total (mil. dol.)	Per employee (dol.)		
Motor vehicle manufacturing, total	**3361–3363**	**933,768**	**48,290**	**51,715**	**750,171**	**500,138**
Motor vehicle, total	3361	205,756	14,015	68,114	178,992	261,842
Automobile & light duty motor vehicle	33611	173,571	12,519	72,128	152,456	232,453
Automobile	336111	74,335	5,352	71,999	64,049	94,229
Light truck & utility vehicle	336112	99,236	7,167	72,224	88,407	138,223
Heavy duty truck	33612	32,185	1,496	46,468	26,536	29,389
Motor vehicle body & trailer	3362	150,284	5,576	37,103	120,454	36,011
Motor vehicle body	336211	50,702	1,933	38,129	38,302	11,739
Truck trailer	336212	30,849	1,065	34,518	25,977	8,277
Motor home	336213	18,932	729	38,510	15,425	5,519
Travel trailer & camper	336214	49,801	1,849	37,125	40,751	10,477
Motor vehicle parts	3363	577,728	28,699	49,676	450,725	202,285
Motor vehicle gasoline engine & engine parts	33631	69,087	3,927	56,841	53,249	32,835
Motor vehicle electrical and electronic equipment	33632	72,620	3,350	46,128	52,684	21,531
Motor vehicle steering and suspension	33633	35,341	1,785	50,506	27,974	10,490
Motor vehicle brake system	33634	32,923	1,356	41,178	25,318	12,781
Motor vehicle transmission & power train parts	33635	76,874	5,193	67,553	62,719	34,974
Motor vehicle seating & interior trim	33636	47,321	1,943	41,067	33,539	18,866
Motor vehicle metal stamping	33637	95,398	5,117	53,633	77,737	25,978
Other motor vehicle parts	33639	148,164	6,029	40,689	117,504	44,831

[1] North American Industry Classification System, 2002; see text, Section 15. [2] Production workers represent average number of production workers for March 12, June 12, September 12, and December 12 pay periods. All employees include production workers and other employees for the pay period that includes the 12th of March. [3] Includes extensive and unmeasurable duplication from shipments between establishments in the same industry classification.

Source: U.S. Census Bureau, "Annual Survey of Manufactures, Statistics for Industry Groups and Industries: 2006"; using American FactFinder®. See <http://factfinder.census.gov/home/saff/main.html?_lang=en>.

Table 998. **Motor Vehicle Manufactures—Employees, Payroll, and Shipments by Major State: 2006**

[14,015 represents $14,015,000,000. Industry based on the North American Industry Classification System (NAICS), 2002; see text, Section 15. See footnote 3, Table 997 for information regarding shipments. Based on the Annual Survey of Manufactures; see Apppendix III]

Major state based on employment	Motor vehicle manufacturing (NAICS 3361)			Motor vehicle parts manufacturing (NAICS 3363)		
	Employees	Payroll (mil. dol.)	Shipments (mil. dol.)	Employees	Payroll (mil. dol.)	Shipments (mil. dol.)
United States [1]	**205,756**	**14,015**	**261,842**	**577,728**	**28,699**	**202,285**
Alabama	11,050	718	14,235	15,844	667	5,735
Arkansas	(2)	(D)	(D)	5,366	172	1,156
California	6,538	(2)	7,500	21,161	875	6,362
Florida	–	–	–	3,736	147	979
Georgia	5,435	324	5,703	8,903	350	3,016
Illinois	7,068	494	7,774	24,454	1,046	6,929
Indiana	13,855	887	18,088	71,743	3,745	23,125
Iowa	–	–	–	6,413	270	1,773
Kentucky	17,778	1,313	24,492	28,631	1,180	9,851
Michigan	36,796	2,937	49,878	122,262	7,355	47,695
Mississippi	(3)	(D)	(D)	5,525	195	1,814
Missouri	13,682	1,063	17,457	13,136	521	3,940
New York	–	–	–	19,906	1,329	7,556
North Carolina	(4)	(D)	(D)	17,422	666	7,450
Ohio	24,664	1,762	37,119	82,351	4,561	27,868
Oklahoma	1,852	101	1,775	3,840	154	997
Pennsylvania	(2)	(D)	(D)	11,510	470	2,924
South Carolina	(4)	(D)	(D)	14,278	679	6,559
Tennessee	12,764	801	13,236	34,982	1,457	16,294
Texas	6,831	462	13,010	12,603	505	3,594
Utah	–	–	–	4,386	179	1,759
Virginia	5,113	274	6,295	6,751	289	1,982
Washington	(2)	(D)	(D)	2,132	94	513
West Virginia	–	–	–	1,913	102	1,940
Wisconsin	(4)	(D)	(D)	13,359	604	4,360

– Represents zero. D Withheld to avoid disclosing data on individual companies. separately. [1] Includes states not shown [2] Employee class size of 1,000 to 2,499. [3] Employee class size of 2,500 to 4,999. [4] Employee class size of 5,000 to 9,999.

Source: U.S. Census Bureau, "Annual Survey of Manufactures, Statistics for Industry Groups and Industries: 2006"; using American FactFinder®. See <http://factfinder.census.gov/home/saff/main.html?_lang=en>.

Table 999. **Aerospace—Sales, New Orders, and Backlog: 2000 to 2006**

[**In billions of dollars (109.3 represents $109,300,000,000), except as indicated.** Reported by establishments in which the principal business is the development and/or production of aerospace products]

Item	2000	2001	2002	2003	2004	2005	2006
Net sales	**109.3**	**117.1**	**115.2**	**116.4**	**124.3**	**124.2**	**141.0**
Percent U.S. government	37.5	38.6	46.1	52.9	51.7	50.6	46.7
Complete aircraft and parts [1]	57.2	58.7	53.9	49.6	49.6	49.9	(D)
Aircraft engines and parts	12.5	15.9	14.8	13.8	16.1	18.5	19.9
Missiles and space vehicles, parts	15.6	15.5	15.6	15.6	14.2	(S)	(D)
Other products, services	24.0	26.9	30.9	37.4	44.4	45.8	(D)
Net, new orders	**140.1**	**122.3**	**114.8**	**117.7**	**131.7**	**186.4**	**208.6**
Backlog, December 31	215.0	220.1	222.5	226.9	234.3	290.0	356.9

D Withheld to avoid disclosing data on individual companies.   S Does not meet publication standards.   [1] Except engines sold separately.

Source: U.S. Census Bureau, *Current Industrial Reports, Civil Aircraft and Aircraft Engines; and Aerospace Industry,* Series MA336G. See <http://www.census.gov/cir/www/index.html>.

Table 1000. **Net Orders for U.S. Civil Jet Transport Aircraft: 1990 to 2007**

[1990 data are net new firm orders; beginning 1995, net announced orders. Minus sign (–) indicates net cancellations. In 1997, Boeing acquired McDonnell Douglas]

Type of aircraft and customer	1990	1995	2000	2003	2004	2005	2006	2007
Total number [1]	**670**	**421**	**585**	**237**	**267**	**1,004**	**1,058**	**1,417**
U.S. customers	259	138	412	84	23	220	321	281
Foreign customers	411	283	193	185	204	811	737	1,136
Boeing 737, total	189	189	378	204	142	571	739	846
U.S. customers	38	85	302	74	16	152	242	164
Foreign customers	151	104	86	145	92	439	497	682
Boeing 747, total	153	35	24	4	10	43	72	25
U.S. customers	24	2	1	–	1	13	18	–
Foreign customers	129	33	18	9	10	30	54	25
Boeing 757, total	66	–7	43	–1	–	–	–	–
U.S. customers	33	–6	38	–7	–	–	–	–
Foreign customers	33	–1	14	6	–	–	–	–
Boeing 767, total	60	26	6	10	9	15	10	36
U.S. customers	23	4	–2	–	–	–	–	27
Foreign customers	37	22	14	15	1	20	10	9
Boeing 777, total	34	83	113	12	42	154	76	141
U.S. customers	34	–	60	11	–	10	35	23
Foreign customers	–	83	53	8	43	146	41	118
Boeing 787, total	–	–	–	–	56	235	161	369
U.S. customers	–	–	–	–	–	45	26	67
Foreign customers	–	–	–	–	56	190	135	302
McDonnell Douglas MD-11, total	52	–6	–	–	–	–	–	–
U.S. customers	16	3	–	–	–	–	–	–
Foreign customers	36	–9	–	–	–	–	–	–
McDonnell Douglas MD-80/90, total	116	51	–	–	–	–	–	–
U.S. customers	91	–	–	–	–	–	–	–
Foreign customers	25	51	–	–	–	–	–	–
McDonnell Douglas MD-95, total	–	50	21	8	8	–	–	–
U.S. customers	–	50	13	6	6	–	–	–
Foreign customers	–	–	8	2	2	–	–	–

– Represents zero.   [1] Beginning 2000, includes unidentified customers.

Source: Aerospace Industries Association of America, Washington, DC, Research Center, Statistical Series 22. See <http://www.aia-aerospace.org/stats/aero_stats/aero_stats.cfm>.

Table 1001. **U.S. Aircraft Shipments, 1990 to 2006, and Projections, 2007**

[**Value in millions of dollars (64,567 represents $64,567,000,000)**]

Year	Total		Civil								Military	
			Large transports		General aviation [1]		Rotocraft					
	Units	Value	Units	Value	Units	Value	Units	Value			Units	Value
1990	3,321	64,567	521	22,215	1,144	2,007	603	254			1,053	40,091
1993	2,585	59,103	408	24,133	964	2,144	258	113			955	32,713
1994	2,309	52,718	309	18,124	928	2,357	308	185			764	32,052
1995	2,436	49,381	256	15,263	1,077	2,842	292	194			811	31,082
1996	2,220	55,583	269	18,915	1,115	3,048	278	193			558	33,427
1997	2,757	65,129	374	26,929	1,549	4,593	346	231			488	33,376
1998	3,533	75,724	559	35,663	2,193	5,534	363	252			418	34,275
1999	3,799	80,974	620	38,171	2,475	6,803	345	200			359	35,800
2000	4,113	72,669	485	30,327	2,802	8,040	493	270			333	34,032
2001	3,902	77,608	526	34,155	2,616	7,991	415	247			345	35,215
2002	3,251	73,112	379	27,547	2,196	7,261	318	157			358	38,147
2003	3,221	68,006	281	21,033	2,080	6,205	517	366			343	40,402
2004	3,804	74,526	283	20,484	2,296	6,918	805	515			420	46,609
2005	4,649	81,515	290	22,116	2,853	8,632	947	815			559	49,952
2006	5,126	86,014	398	25,875	3,134	9,550	1,019	832			575	49,757
2007, proj.	5,378	101,419	441	33,386	3,271	12,048	1,066	1,136			600	54,849

[1] Excludes off-the-shelf military aircraft.

Source: U.S. Department of Commerce, International Trade Administration. See <http://www.ita.doc.gov/td/aerospace/aerospace_statistics.htm>.

Table 1002. Aerospace Industry Sales by Product Group and Customer: 1990 to 2008

[In billions of dollars (134.4 represents $134,400,000,000). Due to reporting practices and tabulating methods, figures may differ from those in Table 999]

Group	1990	1995	2000	2003	2004	2005	2006	2007 [1]	2008 [2]
CURRENT DOLLARS									
Total sales	**134.4**	**107.8**	**144.7**	**146.6**	**155.7**	**170.1**	**183.3**	**198.8**	**210.6**
Product group:									
Aircraft, total	71.4	55.0	81.6	72.8	79.1	89.1	95.8	108.2	112.6
Civil [4]	31.3	24.0	47.6	32.4	32.5	39.2	46.0	53.3	60.4
Military	40.1	31.1	34.0	40.4	46.6	50.0	49.8	54.8	52.2
Missiles	14.2	7.4	9.3	13.5	14.7	15.3	17.0	17.7	18.7
Space	26.4	27.4	29.7	35.9	35.9	37.3	38.6	39.2	41.2
Related products and services [5]	22.4	18.0	24.1	24.4	26.0	28.3	31.9	33.8	38.2
Customer group:									
Aerospace products & services, total	112.0	89.8	120.6	122.2	129.8	141.7	151.4	165.0	172.4
DoD [6]	60.5	42.4	47.5	64.0	70.1	74.3	77.2	83.1	82.0
NASA [7] and other agencies	11.1	11.4	13.4	15.5	16.0	17.4	17.1	17.3	18.2
Other customers [8]	40.4	36.0	59.7	42.7	43.8	50.1	57.1	64.6	72.2
Related products and services [5]	22.4	18.0	24.1	24.4	26.0	28.3	31.9	33.8	38.2
CONSTANT (1987) DOLLARS [3]									
Total sales	**123.5**	**86.1**	**108.2**	**102.3**	**105.1**	**110.4**	**114.1**	**120.3**	**123.2**
Product group:									
Aircraft, total	65.6	44.0	61.0	50.8	53.4	57.8	59.6	65.5	65.9
Civil [4]	28.7	19.1	35.6	22.6	22.0	25.4	28.7	32.3	35.3
Military	36.8	24.8	25.4	28.2	31.5	32.4	31.0	33.2	30.5
Missiles	13.0	5.9	6.9	9.4	9.9	9.9	10.6	10.7	10.9
Space	24.3	21.9	22.2	25.0	24.3	24.2	24.0	23.7	24.1
Related products and services [5]	20.6	14.3	18.0	17.1	17.5	18.4	19.8	20.4	22.4
Customer group:									
Aerospace products & services, total	102.9	71.7	90.1	85.3	87.6	92.0	94.3	99.9	100.8
DoD [6]	55.6	33.9	35.5	44.7	47.3	48.2	48.1	50.3	47.9
NASA [7] and other agencies	10.2	9.1	10.0	10.8	10.8	11.3	10.6	10.5	10.7
Other customers [8]	37.1	28.8	44.6	29.8	29.5	32.5	35.6	39.1	42.2
Related products and services [5]	20.6	14.3	18.0	17.1	17.5	18.4	19.8	20.4	22.4

[1] Preliminary. [2] Estimate. [3] Based on AIA's aerospace composite price deflator. [4] All civil sales of aircraft (domestic and export sales of jet transports, commuters, business, and personal aircraft and helicopters). [5] Electronics, software, and ground support equipment, plus sales of nonaerospace products which are produced by aerospace-manufacturing use technology, processes, and materials derived from aerospace products. [6] Department of Defense. [7] National Aeronautics and Space Administration. [8] Includes civil aircraft sales (see footnote 4), commercial space sales, all exports of military aircraft and missiles, and related propulsion and parts.

Source: Aerospace Industries Association of America, Inc., Washington, DC, *2007 Year-end Review and Forecast*. See <http://www.aia-aerospace.org>.

Table 1003. Major Household Appliances—Value of Shipments: 2000 to 2007

[In millions of dollars (2,170 represents $2,170,000,000)]

Product description	Product code	2000	2003	2004	2005	2006	2007
Electric household ranges, ovens and surface cooking units, equipment and parts	3352211	2,170	2,176	2,285	2,577	2,541	2,833
Gas household ranges, ovens, and surface cooking units, equipment, and parts	3352213	779	1,018	1,120	1,392	1,363	1,710
Other household ranges, cooking equipment, and outdoor cooking equipment [1]	3352215	1,251	967	914	965	784	492
Household refrigerators, including combination refrigerator-freezers	3352221	5,396	4,993	5,002	5,405	5,427	6,523
Household laundry machines and parts	3352240	4,047	4,770	5,130	5,236	5,184	6,513
Water heaters, electric	3352281	573	570	545	638	652	623
Water heaters, except electric	3352283	844	986	884	970	903	863
Household appliances, n.e.c. [2]	3352285	2,066	2,056	2,297	2,433	2,413	2,823

[1] Includes parts and accessories. [2] n.e.c. means not elsewhere classified.

Source: U.S. Census Bureau, *Current Industrial Reports, Major Household Appliances MA335F*. See also <http://www.census.gov/cir/www/index.html>.

Wholesale and Retail Trade

This section presents statistics relating to the distributive trades, specifically wholesale trade and retail trade. Data shown for the trades are classified by kind of business and cover sales, establishments, employees, payrolls, and other items. The principal sources of these data are from the Census Bureau and include the *2002 Economic Census*, annual and monthly surveys, and the *County Business Patterns* program. These data are supplemented by several tables from trade associations, such as the National Automobile Dealers Association (Table 1018). Several notable research groups are also represented, such as Claritas, Inc. (Table 1020), Jupiter Research, Inc. (Table 1016), and Forrester Research, Inc. (Table 1015).

Data on wholesale and retail trade also appear in several other sections. For instance, labor force employment and earnings data appear in Section 12, Labor Force, Employment, and Earnings; gross domestic product of the industry (Table 646) appears in Section 13, Income, Expenditures, Poverty, and Wealth; financial data (several tables) from the quarterly *Statistics of Income Bulletin,* published by the Internal Revenue Service, appear in Section 15, Business Enterprise.

Censuses—Censuses of wholesale trade and retail trade have been taken at various intervals since 1929. Beginning with the 1967 census, legislation provides for a census of each area to be conducted every 5 years (for years ending in "2" and "7"). For more information on the most recent census, see the *Guide to the 2002 Economic Census* found at <http://www.census.gov/econ/census02/guide/>. The industries covered in the censuses and surveys of business are defined in the *North American Industry Classification System*, (NAICS). *Retail trade* refers to places of business primarily engaged in retailing merchandise to the general public; and *wholesale trade,* to establishments primarily engaged in selling goods to other businesses and normally operating from a warehouse or office that have little or no display of merchandise. Most Census Bureau tables in this section utilize the 2002 NAICS codes, which replaced the Standard Industrial Classification (SIC) system. NAICS made substantial structural improvements and identifies over 350 new industries. At the same time, it causes breaks in time series far more profound than any prior revision of the previously used SIC system. For information on this system and how it affects the comparability of wholesale and retail statistics historically, see text, Section 15, Business Enterprise, and especially the Census Bureau Web site at <http://www.census.gov/epcd/www/naics.html>. In general, the 2002 Economic Census has three series of publications for these two sectors: 1) subject series with reports such as product lines and establishment and firm sizes, 2) geographic reports with individual reports for each state, and 3) industry series with individual reports for industry groups. For information on these series, see the Census Bureau Web site at <http://www.census.gov/econ/census02/>.

Current surveys—Current sample surveys conducted by the Census Bureau cover various aspects of wholesale and retail trade. Its *Monthly Retail Trade and Food Services* release <http://www.census.gov/mrts/www/mrts.html> contains monthly estimates of sales, inventories, and inventory/sales ratios for the United States, by kind of business. Annual figures on retail sales, year-end inventories, purchases, accounts receivable, and gross margins by kind of business are located on the Census Bureau Web site at <http://www.census.gov/svsd/www/artstbl.html>. Additionally, annual data for accommodation and food services are located at the same site.

Statistics from the Bureau's monthly wholesale trade survey include national estimates of sales, inventories, and inventory/sales ratios for merchant wholesalers excluding manufacturers' sales branches and offices. Data are presented by major summary groups "durable and nondurable," and 4-digit NAICS industry groups. Merchant wholesalers excluding manufacturers' sales branches and offices are those wholesalers who take title to the goods they sell (e.g., jobbers, exporters, importers, industrial distributors). These data, based on reports submitted by a sample of firms, appear in the *Monthly Wholesale Trade Report* <http://www.census.gov /Wholesale/index.htm>. This report, along with monthly sales, inventories, and inventories/sales ratios, also provides data on annual sales, inventories, and year-end inventories/sales ratios. The Annual Wholesale Trade Survey provides data on merchant wholesalers excluding manufacturer sales branches and offices as well as summary data for all merchant wholesalers. This report also provides separate data for manufacturer sales branches and offices, and electronic markets, agents, brokers, and commission merchants. This report provides data on annual sales, year-end inventories, inventories/sales ratios, operating expenses, purchases, and gross margins. Data are presented by major summary groups "durable and nondurable" and 4-digit NAICS industry groups for sales, end-of-year inventories, and operating expenses. The reports are available as documents on the Census Bureau Web site at <http://www.census.gov/econ/www /retmenu.html>.

E-commerce—Electronic commerce (or e-commerce) is sales of goods and services over the Internet and extranet, electronic data interchange (EDI), or other online systems. Payment may or may not be made online. This edition has several tables on e-commerce sales, such as Tables 1013 to 1016 in this section, 969 in Section 21, Manufactures, and 1238 in Section 27, Accommodation, Food Services, and Other Services. Also, there are several private sources for similar data such as Forrester Research Inc., Cambridge MA; and Jupiter Research, Inc., New York, NY. These sources show estimated and projected online retail sales by key categories from business to consumers or to other businesses. Their methods of collecting the data vary widely between the sources and consequently these estimates of this activity vary also. Users of these estimates may want to contact the sources for descriptions of their methodology. Methodology for Census Bureau estimates can be found at <www.census.gov/eos/www /ebusiness614.htm>.

Statistical reliability—For a discussion of statistical collection and estimation, sampling procedures, and measures of statistical reliability applicable to Census Bureau data, see Appendix III.

Figure 22.1
E-Commerce Retail Sales by Kind of Business: 2006
(millions of dollars)

Total = $106,583

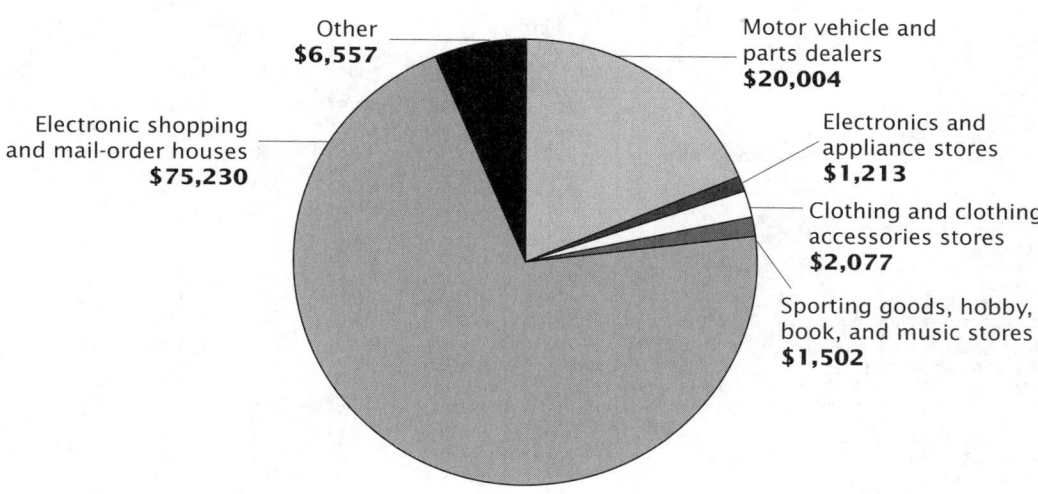

Other
$6,557

Electronic shopping
and mail-order houses
$75,230

Motor vehicle and
parts dealers
$20,004

Electronics and
appliance stores
$1,213

Clothing and clothing
accessories stores
$2,077

Sporting goods, hobby,
book, and music stores
$1,502

Source: Chart prepared by U.S. Census Bureau. For data, see Table 1013.

Figure 22.2
Merchant Wholesale Trade[1] E-Commerce Sales: 1998 to 2006

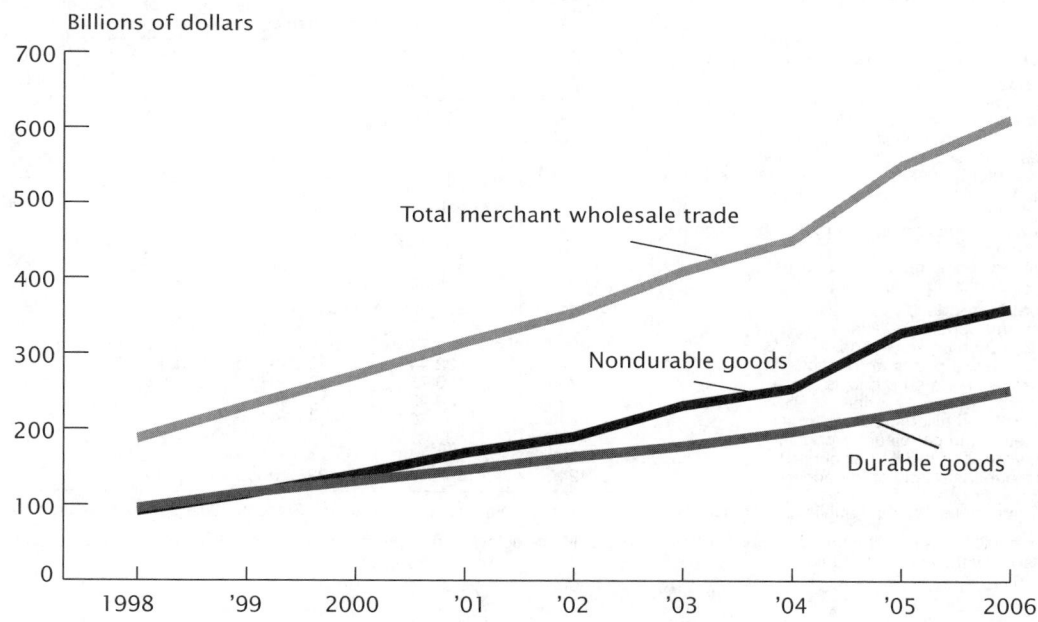

Billions of dollars

Total merchant wholesale trade

Nondurable goods

Durable goods

[1]Excludes manufacturers' sales branches and offices.

Source: Chart prepared by U.S. Census Bureau. For data, see Table 1005.

Wholesale and Retail Trade   639

Table 1004. Wholesale Trade—Establishments, Employees, and Payroll: 2004 and 2005

[**429.5 represents 429,500**. Covers establishments with payroll. Employees are for the week including March 12. Excludes most government employees, railroad employees, and self-employed persons. Kind-of-business classification based on North American Industry Classification System (NAICS), 2002; see text, Section 15, Business Enterprise. For statement on methodology, see Appendix III]

Kind of business	2002 NAICS code	Establishments (1,000)		Employees (1,000)		Payroll (bil. dol.)	
		2004	2005	2004	2005	2004	2005
Wholesale trade	42	**429.5**	**429.8**	**5,907**	**5,969**	**290.6**	**308.9**
Merchant wholesalers, durable goods	423	248.5	245.9	3,319	3,365	173.4	185.3
Motor vehicles and motor vehicle parts & supplies	4231	25.1	24.8	358	366	14.6	15.7
Furniture & home furnishing	4232	13.2	12.8	157	155	6.7	6.9
Lumber & other construction materials	4233	18.1	18.5	248	263	11.1	12.3
Professional & commercial equipment & supplies	4234	37.4	37.0	718	724	45.8	48.7
Metal & mineral (except petroleum)	4235	10.5	10.3	146	151	7.6	8.3
Electrical goods	4236	30.0	29.5	461	466	31.6	33.4
Hardware, & plumbing & heating equipment & supplies	4237	19.0	19.1	217	222	9.9	10.7
Machinery, equipment, & supplies	4238	60.4	59.4	688	689	32.7	34.9
Miscellaneous durable goods	4239	34.8	34.6	326	330	13.4	14.4
Merchant wholesalers, nondurable goods	424	134.6	132.9	2,294	2,289	104.8	109.5
Paper & paper product	4241	12.5	12.2	201	201	9.5	9.8
Drugs & druggists' sundries	4242	7.7	7.7	268	263	18.1	19.0
Apparel, piece goods & notions	4243	16.4	16.0	190	200	9.3	10.0
Grocery & related product	4244	34.3	33.9	764	764	31.0	32.2
Farm product raw material	4245	7.0	6.8	64	64	2.3	2.3
Chemical & allied products	4246	12.7	12.6	141	143	7.6	8.1
Petroleum & petroleum products	4247	7.4	7.3	105	103	5.0	5.3
Beer, wine, and distilled alcoholic beverages	4248	4.2	4.2	170	172	8.1	8.3
Miscellaneous nondurable goods	4249	32.3	32.3	389	380	14.0	14.4
Wholesale electronic markets and agents and brokers	425	46.5	51.0	294	314	12.4	14.1

Source: U.S. Census Bureau, "County Business Patterns." See <http://www.census.gov/epcd/cbp/view/cbpview.html>.

Table 1005. Merchant Wholesale Trade Sales—Total and E-Commerce: 2006

[**3,908,987 represents $3,908,987,000,000**. Covers only businesses with paid employees. Excludes manufacturers' sales branches and offices. Based on the Annual Trade Survey, see Appendix III]

Kind of business	2002 NAICS code [1]	Value of sales (mil. dol.)		E-commerce as percent of total sales	Percent distribution of e-commerce sales
		Total	E-commerce		
Merchant wholesalers, total	42	**3,908,987**	**613,245**	**15.7**	**100.0**
Durable goods	423	**1,932,088**	**252,804**	**13.1**	**41.2**
Motor vehicles and motor vehicle parts and supplies	4231	319,455	97,596	30.6	15.9
Furniture and home furnishings	4232	65,765	6,757	10.3	1.1
Lumber and other construction materials	4233	145,693	5,753	3.9	0.9
Professional & commercial equipment & supplies	4234	323,555	64,076	19.8	10.4
Computer, peripheral equipment, and software	42343	163,094	39,222	24.0	6.4
Metal and mineral (except petroleum)	4235	157,749	2,277	1.4	0.4
Electrical goods	4236	298,647	34,167	11.1	5.6
Hardware, and plumbing and heating equipment and supplies	4237	91,724	(S)	(S)	(S)
Machinery, equipment and supplies	4238	313,878	12,261	3.9	2.0
Miscellaneous durable goods	4239	215,622	18,218	8.4	3.0
Nondurable goods	424	**1,976,899**	**360,441**	**18.2**	**58.8**
Paper and paper products	4241	92,399	12,727	13.8	2.1
Drugs and druggists' sundries	4242	349,973	235,070	67.2	38.3
Apparel, piece goods and notions	4243	122,449	26,749	21.8	4.4
Grocery and related products	4244	450,754	40,435	9.0	6.6
Farm product raw materials	4245	130,482	4,987	3.8	0.8
Chemical and allied products	4246	92,760	4,479	4.8	0.7
Petroleum and petroleum products	4247	436,216	9,840	2.3	1.6
Beer, wine, and distilled alcoholic beverages	4248	96,403	4,108	4.3	0.7
Miscellaneous nondurable goods	4249	205,463	22,046	10.7	3.6

S Figure does not meet publication standards.   [1] North American Industry Classification System, 2002; see text, Section 15.

Source: U.S. Census Bureau, "E-Stats, 2006 E-commerce Multi-sector Report"; published 16 May 2008. See <http://www.census.gov/eos/www/ebusiness614.htm>.

Table 1006. Merchant Wholesalers—Summary: 2000 to 2007

[In billions of dollars (2,814.6 represents $2,814,600,000,000), except ratios. Inventories and inventories/sales ratios, as of December, seasonally adjusted. Excludes manufacturers' sales branches and offices. Data reflect latest revision. Based on data from the Annual Wholesale Trade Survey and the Monthly Wholesale Trade Survey; see Appendix III]

Kind of business	2002 NAICS code [1]	2000	2002	2003	2004	2005	2006	2007
SALES								
Merchant wholesalers	42	**2,814.6**	**2,835.5**	**2,962.3**	**3,296.5**	**3,585.6**	**3,909.0**	**4,244.0**
Durable goods	423	**1,486.7**	**1,421.5**	**1,448.9**	**1,654.6**	**1,775.6**	**1,932.1**	**2,029.5**
Motor vehicles, parts and supplies	4231	222.2	251.9	257.3	277.8	293.1	319.5	324.1
Furniture and home furnishings	4232	52.7	53.5	54.8	58.3	60.9	65.8	69.3
Lumber and construction materials	4233	87.2	95.1	105.7	128.6	140.9	145.7	127.0
Professional and commercial equipment	4234	282.2	272.5	272.6	296.3	309.6	323.6	349.6
Computer, peripheral equipment and software	42343	174.8	150.6	144.3	157.5	163.0	163.1	179.9
Metal and mineral (except petroleum)	4235	93.8	81.7	81.4	121.2	136.9	157.7	164.7
Electrical and electronic goods	4236	260.0	223.0	227.1	253.8	267.2	298.6	323.3
Hardware, plumbing and heating equipment	4237	72.1	70.4	71.2	77.5	83.7	91.7	95.0
Machinery, equipment and supplies	4238	256.1	227.8	230.8	260.2	288.6	313.9	338.3
Miscellaneous durable goods	4239	160.3	145.6	148.0	181.0	194.7	215.6	238.4
Nondurable goods	424	**1,327.9**	**1,414.0**	**1,513.3**	**1,641.9**	**1,810.0**	**1,976.9**	**2,214.5**
Paper and paper products	4241	77.8	72.6	73.9	81.6	87.5	92.4	93.5
Drugs and druggists' sundries	4242	176.0	245.6	273.5	296.6	329.0	350.0	362.8
Apparel, piece goods, and notions	4243	96.5	105.8	104.4	108.4	112.8	122.4	128.3
Grocery and related products	4244	374.7	385.9	405.3	409.7	428.6	450.8	510.3
Farm-product raw materials	4245	102.7	103.4	115.1	123.0	118.3	130.5	182.8
Chemical and allied products	4246	62.3	67.7	69.7	76.4	88.2	92.8	100.0
Petroleum and petroleum products	4247	195.8	192.7	225.7	274.9	357.2	436.2	509.8
Beer, wine, and distilled beverages	4248	71.3	79.2	82.2	85.6	90.4	96.4	104.0
Miscellaneous nondurable goods	4249	170.9	161.1	163.4	185.7	198.1	205.5	222.9
INVENTORIES								
Merchant wholesalers	42	**309.6**	**302.2**	**308.0**	**337.5**	**362.2**	**392.8**	**416.1**
Durable goods	423	**199.2**	**183.3**	**186.1**	**211.4**	**227.5**	**247.5**	**250.5**
Motor vehicles, parts and supplies	4231	28.8	29.9	31.3	33.0	36.4	38.3	39.7
Furniture and home furnishings	4232	6.3	6.2	6.6	6.8	7.3	7.8	7.8
Lumber and construction materials	4233	8.3	8.7	10.2	13.1	14.1	14.6	13.9
Professional and commercial equipment	4234	27.7	24.6	24.6	26.5	27.4	29.6	30.2
Computer, peripheral equipment and software	42343	12.1	9.0	9.5	10.2	10.3	10.6	10.6
Metal and mineral (except petroleum)	4235	13.5	12.3	12.5	19.6	20.1	25.4	23.1
Electrical and electronic goods	4236	31.1	25.2	24.5	26.8	28.3	31.7	32.7
Hardware, plumbing and heating equipment	4237	11.6	11.3	11.4	12.7	13.6	14.7	15.3
Machinery, equipment and supplies	4238	51.5	47.2	45.6	51.1	56.8	62.0	65.3
Miscellaneous durable goods	4239	20.3	18.0	19.4	21.8	23.6	23.4	22.6
Nondurable goods	424	**110.4**	**118.8**	**121.9**	**126.1**	**134.7**	**145.2**	**165.5**
Paper and paper products	4241	6.6	5.3	5.3	6.0	6.5	6.7	6.9
Drugs and druggists' sundries	4242	23.7	31.6	31.7	31.3	30.5	31.4	32.2
Apparel, piece goods, and notions	4243	13.9	14.5	13.8	14.1	14.6	15.9	16.0
Grocery and related products	4244	20.4	20.3	20.2	20.9	22.8	24.6	27.1
Farm-product raw materials	4245	11.8	12.2	15.1	11.9	13.3	18.6	27.7
Chemical and allied products	4246	6.1	6.8	6.8	7.5	8.3	8.5	9.4
Petroleum and petroleum products	4247	5.2	6.1	6.6	9.5	11.9	12.5	15.9
Beer, wine, and distilled beverages	4248	6.5	7.0	7.2	7.6	8.2	8.7	9.6
Miscellaneous nondurable goods	4249	16.2	15.1	15.2	17.3	18.5	18.3	20.9
INVENTORIES/SALES RATIO								
Merchant wholesalers	42	**1.32**	**1.28**	**1.25**	**1.23**	**1.21**	**1.21**	**1.18**
Durable goods	423	**1.61**	**1.55**	**1.54**	**1.53**	**1.54**	**1.54**	**1.48**
Motor vehicles, parts and supplies	4231	1.55	1.42	1.46	1.43	1.49	1.44	1.47
Furniture and home furnishings	4232	1.44	1.40	1.44	1.41	1.44	1.41	1.35
Lumber and construction materials	4233	1.15	1.10	1.16	1.22	1.20	1.20	1.31
Professional and commercial equipment	4234	1.18	1.08	1.08	1.07	1.06	1.10	1.04
Computer, peripheral equipment and software	42343	0.83	0.72	0.79	0.78	0.76	0.78	0.71
Metal and mineral (except petroleum)	4235	1.73	1.81	1.84	1.94	1.76	1.94	1.68
Electrical and electronic goods	4236	1.44	1.35	1.29	1.27	1.27	1.28	1.21
Hardware, plumbing and heating equipment	4237	1.93	1.92	1.92	1.97	1.95	1.93	1.93
Machinery, equipment and supplies	4238	2.41	2.48	2.37	2.36	2.36	2.37	2.32
Miscellaneous durable goods	4239	1.52	1.48	1.58	1.45	1.46	1.30	1.14
Nondurable goods	424	**1.00**	**1.01**	**0.97**	**0.92**	**0.89**	**0.88**	**0.90**
Paper and paper products	4241	1.01	0.87	0.85	0.88	0.88	0.87	0.89
Drugs and druggists' sundries	4242	1.62	1.54	1.39	1.27	1.11	1.08	1.07
Apparel, piece goods, and notions	4243	1.73	1.64	1.58	1.56	1.56	1.56	1.50
Grocery and related products	4244	0.65	0.63	0.60	0.61	0.64	0.66	0.64
Farm-product raw materials	4245	1.37	1.42	1.58	1.16	1.35	1.71	1.82
Chemical and allied products	4246	1.18	1.21	1.17	1.18	1.13	1.10	1.13
Petroleum and petroleum products	4247	0.32	0.38	0.35	0.41	0.40	0.34	0.37
Beer, wine, and distilled beverages	4248	1.09	1.05	1.05	1.07	1.09	1.08	1.11
Miscellaneous nondurable goods	4249	1.13	1.13	1.11	1.12	1.12	1.07	1.13

[1] North American Industry Classification System, 2002; see text, Section 15.

Source: U.S. Census Bureau, "Annual Revision of Monthly Wholesale Distributors: Sales and Inventories: January 1992 Through January 2008" published 21 February 2008. See <http://www.census.gov/mwts/www/mwtshist.html>.

Wholesale and Retail Trade 641

Table 1007. Wholesale and Retail Trade—Establishments, Employees, and Payroll by State: 2000 and 2005

[6,112 represents 6,112,000. Covers establishments with payroll. Employees are for the week including March 12. Excludes most government employees, railroad employees, and self-employed persons. Kind-of-business classification for 2000 based on North American Industry Classification System (NAICS) 1997; data for 2005 based on NAICS 2002. See text, Section 15. For statement on methodology, see Appendix III]

State	Wholesale trade (NAICS 42)						Retail trade (NAICS 44, 45)					
	Number of establishments		Number of employees (1,000)		Annual payroll (mil. dol.)		Number of establishments		Number of employees (1,000)		Annual payroll (mil. dol.)	
	2000	2005	2000	2005	2000	2005	2000	2005	2000	2005	2000	2005
U.S.	446,237	429,823	6,112	5,969	270,122	308,918	1,113,573	1,123,207	14,841	15,339	302,553	348,047
AL.	6,132	5,533	82	78	2,892	3,259	19,723	19,451	230	238	4,074	4,846
AK.	752	736	7	8	281	386	2,733	2,675	33	35	790	912
AZ.	6,731	6,646	86	95	3,627	4,437	16,911	18,228	255	306	5,694	7,312
AR.	3,505	3,473	45	49	1,402	1,905	12,211	11,880	135	140	2,268	2,725
CA.	58,326	59,252	808	816	40,011	47,832	107,987	112,382	1,491	1,652	36,073	43,416
CO	7,452	7,269	97	99	4,906	5,635	18,748	19,208	252	249	5,883	6,047
CT.	5,076	4,671	77	80	4,481	4,874	14,111	13,928	191	198	4,540	5,084
DE.	1,009	999	19	20	1,117	1,399	3,742	3,842	52	55	1,048	1,298
DC	372	448	5	6	282	358	1,945	1,913	19	20	431	482
FL.	30,671	31,709	315	311	12,536	13,996	67,396	72,469	903	987	18,044	23,452
GA	13,892	13,973	199	201	9,064	10,511	33,788	35,023	464	474	9,365	10,226
HI	1,809	1,861	19	20	627	764	4,924	4,924	63	69	1,313	1,646
ID	2,012	1,983	24	24	845	908	5,871	6,064	70	76	1,347	1,673
IL	21,509	20,001	344	322	16,683	17,771	43,800	43,169	637	629	12,992	14,365
IN	8,642	8,153	120	117	4,607	5,206	24,261	23,494	354	346	6,332	6,912
IA	5,155	4,815	65	63	2,173	2,559	14,382	13,643	184	178	3,169	3,494
KS.	4,876	4,541	62	54	2,333	2,346	12,261	11,562	153	149	2,747	2,952
KY.	4,939	4,560	74	70	2,536	2,993	16,988	16,566	221	224	3,804	4,341
LA.	6,192	5,604	79	73	2,723	2,990	17,755	17,426	232	228	4,032	4,572
ME	1,740	1,669	22	19	744	810	7,015	6,980	77	85	1,436	1,850
MD	6,098	6,043	95	97	4,526	5,216	19,539	19,561	285	300	6,062	7,226
MA	9,735	8,818	156	149	9,114	9,592	25,813	25,839	353	369	7,729	8,909
MI	13,576	11,981	191	173	8,887	9,278	38,862	38,675	545	499	10,667	10,365
MN	9,294	8,743	137	141	6,399	8,263	20,862	20,950	304	308	5,980	7,064
MS	3,116	2,853	40	35	1,222	1,308	12,794	12,429	141	140	2,384	2,693
MO	9,072	8,276	146	130	5,458	5,291	23,911	23,507	318	322	6,258	6,781
MT	1,537	1,491	15	14	433	488	5,101	5,192	52	56	920	1,165
NE.	3,061	2,905	41	38	1,346	1,626	8,248	8,080	110	107	1,895	2,134
NV.	2,556	2,812	31	36	1,238	1,727	6,940	8,006	108	136	2,533	3,583
NH	2,105	2,018	25	25	1,184	1,383	6,545	6,687	93	100	1,930	2,359
NJ.	17,157	16,347	279	274	14,724	17,376	34,841	35,263	439	455	9,897	11,303
NM.	2,162	1,960	22	21	753	824	7,249	7,232	91	95	1,745	2,132
NY.	36,606	35,437	422	409	20,941	22,825	75,500	78,134	844	878	18,116	21,140
NC	12,364	11,866	173	164	7,153	7,795	35,785	35,875	450	450	8,739	9,707
ND	1,543	1,452	18	17	532	668	3,435	3,435	42	44	719	854
OH	16,646	15,545	261	238	10,437	11,276	42,708	40,949	644	621	11,903	12,466
OK	5,005	4,616	62	56	2,126	2,312	14,147	13,727	168	169	2,913	3,350
OR	5,836	5,637	79	76	3,266	3,630	14,256	14,488	193	199	4,126	4,709
PA.	16,796	15,890	243	239	10,287	11,945	48,518	47,223	668	669	12,556	14,205
RI	1,530	1,419	21	18	768	857	4,342	4,201	53	55	1,149	1,284
SC.	5,091	4,795	65	64	2,353	2,823	18,619	18,590	224	221	4,083	4,511
SD.	1,390	1,278	16	14	472	521	4,181	4,282	50	50	879	982
TN.	8,006	7,336	127	116	4,848	5,574	24,624	23,798	311	320	5,908	6,875
TX.	32,631	31,133	458	450	20,176	23,894	74,758	76,335	1,021	1,081	21,846	24,318
UT.	3,294	3,434	44	46	1,583	2,010	7,952	8,454	124	130	2,455	2,840
VT.	889	875	11	10	401	445	3,974	3,905	38	41	750	930
VA.	7,893	7,790	110	111	4,651	5,583	28,794	29,335	399	424	7,949	9,552
WA	9,869	9,494	125	128	5,412	6,385	22,700	22,791	313	321	7,181	8,064
WV	1,869	1,641	22	21	698	786	7,788	7,243	92	92	1,493	1,659
WI.	7,928	7,272	119	124	4,636	5,991	21,354	21,219	322	317	5,891	6,626
WY	790	770	7	7	229	289	2,881	2,975	28	30	515	655

Source: U.S. Census Bureau, "County Business Patterns." See <http://www.census.gov/epcd/cbp/view/cbpview.html>.

U.S. Census Bureau, Statistical Abstract of the United States: 2009

Table 1008. Retail Trade—Establishments, Employees, and Payroll: 2000 and 2005

[**1,113.6 represents 1,113,600.** Covers establishments with payroll. Employees are for the week including March 12. Most government employees are excluded. For statement on methodology, see Appendix III]

Kind of business	NAICS code [1]	Establishments (1,000) 2000	Establishments (1,000) 2005	Employees (1,000) 2000	Employees (1,000) 2005	Payroll (bil. dol.) 2000	Payroll (bil. dol.) 2005
Retail trade, total	**44–45**	**1,113.6**	**1,123.2**	**14,841**	**15,339**	**302.6**	**348.0**
Motor vehicle & parts dealers	441	124.5	128.6	1,866	1,948	63.9	73.3
Automobile dealers	4411	50.9	52.4	1,222	1,290	47.8	54.7
New car dealers	44111	26.2	26.2	1,112	1,167	44.8	50.8
Used car dealers	44112	24.7	26.2	110	123	3.1	3.9
Other motor vehicle dealers	4412	14.5	16.8	127	164	3.8	5.7
Automotive parts, accessories, & tire stores	4413	59.1	59.4	517	494	12.2	13.0
Furniture & home furnishings stores	442	64.8	66.4	549	576	13.4	15.3
Furniture stores	4421	29.7	29.3	284	280	7.5	8.3
Home furnishings stores	4422	35.1	37.1	265	296	5.9	7.0
Floor covering stores	44221	15.8	14.9	103	98	3.2	3.4
Electronics & appliance stores [2]	443	45.6	50.2	407	469	11.2	12.1
Appliance, TV, & other electronics stores	44311	29.6	36.8	279	362	6.6	9.2
Household appliance stores	443111	9.8	9.5	62	69	1.5	2.0
Radio, television, and other electronics stores	443112	19.8	27.2	217	293	5.1	7.2
Computer & software stores	44312	12.9	11.0	106	91	4.2	2.6
Bldg. material & garden equip. & supp. dealers	444	91.9	87.1	1,235	1,263	32.5	35.8
Building material & supplies dealers [2]	4441	70.9	66.4	1,055	1,089	28.4	31.4
Home centers	44411	4.4	5.9	351	492	7.6	11.1
Hardware stores	44413	15.0	14.3	146	142	2.5	2.9
Lawn & garden equip. & supplies stores	4442	21.0	20.7	180	173	4.0	4.3
Nursery and garden centers	44422	16.5	16.5	152	147	3.4	3.6
Food & beverage stores	445	154.5	153.4	3,004	2,938	48.4	53.0
Grocery stores	4451	98.3	95.9	2,717	2,643	44.0	47.9
Supermarkets & other grocery (except convenience) stores	44511	68.8	67.3	2,544	2,495	41.8	45.7
Convenience stores	44512	29.5	28.7	173	147	2.2	2.1
Specialty food stores	4452	27.8	27.5	154	158	2.4	2.6
Beer, wine, & liquor stores [3]	4453	28.5	29.9	134	138	2.1	2.5
Health & personal care stores [2]	446	81.2	84.9	914	1,037	19.3	25.5
Pharmacies & drug stores	44611	40.6	40.5	680	777	14.5	19.4
Cosmetics, beauty supplies, & perfume stores	44612	9.6	12.9	61	89	0.8	1.4
Optical goods stores	44613	14.3	12.2	74	64	1.7	1.6
Gasoline stations	447	119.6	117.2	937	909	13.3	14.6
Gasoline stations with convenience stores	44711	80.5	92.5	653	717	8.9	10.9
Other gasoline stations	44719	39.1	24.7	284	191	4.4	3.7
Clothing & clothing accessories stores	448	150.9	150.6	1,369	1,556	20.2	25.0
Clothing stores [2]	4481	90.0	93.1	1,015	1,201	13.7	17.5
Men's clothing stores	44811	10.7	8.7	85	65	1.6	1.4
Women's clothing stores	44812	35.6	33.7	302	328	3.9	4.7
Children's & infants' clothing stores	44813	5.6	6.3	59	73	0.7	0.9
Family clothing stores	44814	20.6	24.7	453	612	5.9	8.5
Shoe stores	4482	29.7	26.4	185	184	2.6	3.1
Jewelry, luggage, & leather goods stores	4483	31.3	31.1	168	171	3.9	4.4
Jewelry stores	44831	29.3	29.6	156	163	3.6	4.1
Sporting goods, hobby, book, & music stores	451	65.0	61.4	616	631	8.8	9.7
Sporting goods/hobby/musical instrument stores [2]	4511	43.6	43.1	389	429	6.0	7.1
Sporting goods stores	45111	22.6	23.2	185	210	2.9	3.8
Hobby, toy, and game stores	45112	10.9	9.6	131	133	1.8	2.0
Book, periodical, & music stores [2]	4512	21.4	18.2	228	202	2.8	2.6
Book stores	451211	11.7	11.1	142	136	1.7	1.8
Prerecorded tape, CD, & record stores	45122	7.7	5.5	76	57	0.9	0.7
General merchandise stores	452	39.6	45.9	2,526	2,671	39.8	50.2
Department stores	4521	10.4	9.6	1,766	1,444	27.2	26.4
Other general merchandise stores	4529	29.2	36.3	760	1,227	12.6	23.8
Warehouse clubs & superstores	45291	2.0	3.1	478	925	8.7	19.6
All other general merchandise stores	45299	27.2	33.2	283	302	3.8	4.2
Miscellaneous store retailers [2]	453	131.0	128.0	850	820	13.8	14.6
Florists	4531	24.2	21.1	122	102	1.6	1.5
Office supplies, stationery, and gift stores	4532	43.0	42.7	350	323	5.2	5.3
Office supplies and stationery stores	45321	8.6	9.5	135	123	2.7	2.7
Gift, novelty, and souvenir stores	45322	34.4	33.2	215	201	2.5	2.6
Used merchandise stores	4533	17.5	18.1	114	128	1.6	2.0
Other miscellaneous store retailers	4539	46.4	46.0	264	266	5.4	5.9
Pet and pet supplies stores	45391	8.1	8.3	68	90	0.9	1.3
Nonstore retailers [2]	454	44.8	49.7	567	521	18.1	18.9
Electronic shopping & mail-order houses	4541	11.8	15.9	277	254	10.4	10.4
Direct selling establishments	4543	26.8	28.3	223	214	6.1	7.1
Fuel dealers	45431	11.8	10.6	106	99	3.1	3.4

[1] Data for 2000 based on North American Industry Classification System 1997; 2005 data based on NAICS 2002. See text, Section 15. [2] Includes other kinds of business not shown separately. [3] Includes government employees.

Source: U.S. Census Bureau, "County Business Patterns." See <http://www.census.gov/epcd/cbp/view/cbpview.html>.

U.S. Census Bureau, Statistical Abstract of the United States: 2009

Table 1009. **Retail Trade and Food Services—Sales by Kind of Business: 2000 to 2007**

[In billions of dollars (3,294.2 represents $3,294,200,000,000)]

Kind of business	2002 NAICS code [1]	2000	2001	2002	2003	2004	2005	2006	2007
Retail & food services sales, total . . .	44, 45, 722	**3,294.2**	**3,385.6**	**3,466.1**	**3,615.2**	**3,846.3**	**4,081.7**	**4,307.7**	**4,482.7**
Retail sales, total	44, 45	**2,988.8**	**3,067.7**	**3,134.3**	**3,265.5**	**3,474.3**	**3,688.1**	**3,887.4**	**4,040.4**
GAFO, total [2]		863.9	883.9	913.9	948.2	1,007.2	1,062.4	1,120.1	1,162.7
Motor vehicle and parts dealers.	441	797.6	816.9	820.3	841.2	864.5	886.0	898.6	919.3
Automobile and other motor vehicle dealers	4411, 4412	733.9	755.6	757.4	776.6	797.3	814.8	824.5	843.2
Automobile dealers.	4411	688.7	708.6	707.7	721.0	734.7	748.1	755.7	771.3
New car dealers.	44111	630.1	649.4	645.8	656.9	665.9	675.4	675.4	681.5
Used car dealers	44112	58.6	59.2	61.9	64.1	68.8	72.7	80.2	89.8
Automotive parts, accessories, and tire stores	4413	63.7	61.3	62.9	64.6	67.2	71.2	74.1	76.1
Furniture, home furnishings, electronics and appliance stores	442, 443	173.7	172.0	178.5	184.5	200.1	213.4	226.0	230.0
Furniture and home furnishings stores. . . .	442	91.3	91.6	94.6	97.5	105.3	111.8	117.7	118.7
Furniture stores	4421	50.7	50.6	51.3	52.1	56.5	59.8	61.9	62.7
Home furnishings stores . . . . . . ; . . .	4422	40.6	41.0	43.3	45.5	48.8	51.9	55.7	55.9
Electronics and appliance stores [3]	443	82.4	80.4	83.9	87.0	94.8	101.6	108.4	111.4
Appliance, television, and other electronics stores	44311	58.3	60.2	63.3	66.1	72.2	77.6	83.1	85.4
Household appliance stores	443111	12.6	13.5	14.2	14.5	15.7	17.0	18.1	18.1
Radio, television, and other electronics stores	443112	45.6	46.8	49.1	51.6	56.5	60.5	65.1	67.3
Computer and software stores	44312	20.7	16.9	17.3	17.5	19.1	20.5	21.7	22.4
Building materials, garden equipment & supply stores.	444	229.3	239.7	248.9	265.1	298.8	327.2	344.7	337.2
Building materials & supply dealers.	4441	197.9	207.3	217.4	232.0	263.6	290.4	306.9	295.8
Hardware stores	44413	16.2	16.6	17.0	17.6	18.1	18.6	19.4	20.9
Food and beverage stores [3]	445	445.7	463.3	465.8	477.1	495.0	515.0	533.8	560.6
Grocery stores	4451	403.0	418.6	420.3	430.0	444.6	462.6	477.7	501.1
Beer, wine, and liquor stores	4453	28.7	29.8	30.1	30.7	32.4	33.9	36.7	39.6
Health and personal care stores	446	155.4	166.7	180.1	192.2	198.9	209.0	224.8	237.4
Pharmacies and drug stores	44611	130.9	141.8	153.9	164.6	167.2	175.8	189.1	198.4
Gasoline stations	447	250.0	251.5	250.8	273.6	320.4	373.9	416.2	445.2
Clothing and clothing accessories stores [3]. . .	448	168.0	167.6	172.6	178.8	190.1	201.5	214.9	224.7
Clothing stores [3]	4481	118.2	119.3	123.0	128.3	137.1	146.1	156.2	165.1
Women's clothing stores	44812	31.5	31.5	31.3	32.5	34.7	36.8	39.1	40.4
Family clothing stores	44814	58.9	60.2	64.3	67.3	72.0	77.4	82.0	85.3
Shoe stores	4482	22.9	22.9	23.2	23.2	23.7	25.3	26.7	26.5
Jewelry stores.	44831	25.0	23.7	24.8	25.5	27.5	28.2	29.9	30.7
Sporting goods, hobby, book, & music stores [3]	451	76.1	77.1	77.0	77.3	80.1	81.8	84.8	87.3
Sporting goods stores	45111	25.4	26.3	26.3	27.2	28.9	30.9	34.3	37.1
Book stores	451211	14.9	15.1	15.5	16.2	16.8	16.9	16.7	17.0
General merchandise stores	452	404.3	427.6	446.6	468.7	497.2	525.2	552.1	576.4
Department stores (excl. L.D.) [4]	4521	232.5	228.4	220.7	214.4	215.7	214.3	212.7	209.9
Department stores (incl. L.D.) [4]	4521	239.9	235.6	227.8	221.0	222.0	220.7	219.0	215.7
Other general merchandise stores	4529	171.9	199.2	225.9	254.3	281.5	310.9	339.4	366.5
Warehouse clubs and superstores. . . .	45291	139.6	164.7	191.3	216.3	242.4	270.2	296.7	323.3
Miscellaneous store retailers.	453	108.1	104.4	104.2	103.1	105.3	108.4	115.8	118.8
Nonstore retailers [3]	454	180.7	180.8	189.5	203.9	224.0	246.7	275.7	303.4
Electronic shopping & mail order houses . .	4541	113.9	114.8	122.3	131.2	147.2	164.3	190.9	210.4
Fuel dealers.	45431	26.7	26.1	24.0	29.0	31.9	37.0	39.3	46.2
Food services and drinking places [5] . . .	722	**305.5**	**317.9**	**331.8**	**349.7**	**372.0**	**393.6**	**420.4**	**442.3**

[1] North American Industry Classification System, 2002; see text, Section 15.   [2] GAFO (General Merchandise, Apparel, Furniture, and Office Supplies) represents stores classified in the following NAICS codes: 442, 443, 448, 451, 452, and 4532.   [3] Includes other kinds of business not shown separately.   [4] L.D. represents leased departments.   [5] See also Table 1241.

Source: U.S. Census Bureau, *Current Business Reports, Annual Revision of Monthly Retail and Food Services: Sales and Inventories—January 1992 Through March 2008*, Series BR/06-A.

Table 1010. **Retail Trade Corporations—Sales, Net Profit, and Profit Per Dollar of Sales: 2006 and 2007**

[Represents North American Industry Classification System, 2007 (NAICS) groups 44 and 45. Profit rates are averages of quarterly figures at annual rates. Covers corporations with assets of $50,000,000 or more]

Item	Unit	Total retail trade		Food & beverage stores (NAICS 445)		Clothing & general merchandise stores (NAICS 448 and 452)		All other retail stores	
		2006	2007	2006	2007	2006	2007	2006	2007
Sales	Bil. dol. . .	1,972	2,059	373	380	711	740	887	939
Net profit:									
Before income taxes.	Bil. dol. . .	93.7	93.0	8.9	12.4	44.3	43.4	40.5	37.1
After income taxes	Bil. dol. . .	62.9	61.6	6.0	9.2	29.3	28.2	27.6	24.2
Profits per dollar of sales:									
Before income taxes.	Cents . . .	10.2	9.5	6.3	9.1	11.3	10.5	10.6	8.6
After income taxes	Cents . . .	6.8	6.3	4.3	6.7	7.4	6.8	7.2	5.6
Profits on stockholders' equity:									
Before income taxes.	Percent. .	24.1	22.5	19.3	26.8	24.7	24.0	24.8	20.0
After income taxes	Percent. .	16.2	14.9	13.0	19.8	16.3	15.6	16.9	13.1

Source: U.S. Census Bureau, *Quarterly Financial Report for Manufacturing, Mining and Trade Corporations*, annual. See <http://www.census.gov/csd/qfr/>.

644   Wholesale and Retail Trade

Table 1011. Retail Trade and Food Services—Estimated Per Capita Sales by Selected Kinds of Business: 2000 to 2007

[In dollars. As of Dec. 31. Based on estimated resident population estimates as of July. For statement on methodology, see Appendix III]

Kind of business	2002 NAICS code [1]	2000	2001	2002	2003	2004	2005	2006	2007
Retail and food service sales	44–45,722	**11,674**	**11,875**	**12,040**	**12,447**	**13,119**	**13,794**	**14,419**	**14,862**
Retail sales, total	44–45	**10,591**	**10,760**	**10,887**	**11,243**	**11,850**	**12,464**	**13,012**	**13,396**
Total (excluding motor vehicle and parts dealers)	*44–45, ex 441*	*7,765*	*7,894*	*8,038*	*8,347*	*8,901*	*9,470*	*10,004*	*10,348*
Motor vehicle and parts dealers	441	2,826	2,865	2,849	2,896	2,949	2,994	3,008	3,048
Furniture and home furnishings stores	442	324	321	329	336	359	378	394	393
Electronics and appliance stores	443	292	282	291	299	323	343	363	369
Building material and garden equipment and supplies dealers	444	813	841	865	913	1,019	1,106	1,154	1,118
Food and beverage stores	445	1,579	1,625	1,618	1,643	1,688	1,740	1,787	1,859
Health and personal care stores	446	551	585	626	662	679	706	752	787
Gasoline stations	447	886	882	871	942	1,093	1,263	1,393	1,476
Clothing and clothing accessories stores . .	448	595	588	600	616	648	681	719	745
Sporting goods, hobby, book, and music stores.	451	270	271	267	266	273	276	284	290
General merchandise stores	452	1,433	1,500	1,551	1,614	1,696	1,775	1,848	1,911
Miscellaneous store retailers	453	383	366	362	355	359	366	388	394
Nonstore retailers.	454	640	634	658	702	764	834	923	1,006
Food services and drinking places . . .	722	**1,082**	**1,115**	**1,153**	**1,204**	**1,269**	**1,330**	**1,407**	**1,466**

[1] North American Industry Classification System, 2002; see text, Section 15.

Source: U.S. Census Bureau, unpublished data.

Table 1012. Retail Trade—Merchandise Inventories and Inventory/Sales Ratio by Kind of Business: 2000 to 2007

[Inventories in billions of dollars (401.3 represents $401,300,000,000). As of Dec. 31. Estimates exclude food services. Includes warehouses. Adjusted for seasonal variations. Sales data also adjusted for holiday and trading-day differences. Based on data from the Monthly Retail Trade Survey, Annual Retail Trade Survey, and administrative records; see Appendix III. Data have been adjusted using results of the 2002 Economic Census]

Kind of business	2002 NAICS code [1]	Inventories				Inventory/sales ratio			
		2000	2005	2006	2007	2000	2005	2006	2007
Total [2]	44–45	**401.3**	**465.9**	**482.2**	**501.2**	**1.62**	**1.51**	**1.49**	**1.47**
Excluding motor vehicle and parts dealers	*44–45, ex 441*	*269.7*	*310.4*	*325.7*	*343.6*	*1.49*	*1.33*	*1.33*	*1.30*
Motor vehicle and parts dealers.	441	131.7	155.5	156.5	157.6	2.01	2.08	2.00	2.09
Furniture, home furnishings, electronics, and appliance stores	442,443	25.4	30.8	31.6	33.1	1.85	1.72	1.67	1.75
Building material and garden equipment and supplies dealers.	444	33.4	44.6	46.3	49.4	1.76	1.65	1.71	1.82
Food and beverage stores	445	32.9	34.9	35.8	36.6	0.85	0.78	0.77	0.76
Clothing and clothing accessories stores	448	34.0	40.1	44.3	47.3	2.61	2.52	2.58	2.56
General merchandise stores	452	60.4	69.6	72.0	76.2	1.87	1.64	1.61	1.57
Department stores.	4521	39.5	35.0	35.1	37.0	2.17	2.11	2.11	2.14

[1] North American Industry Classification System, 2002; see text, Section 15. [2] Includes kind of business not shown separately.

Source: U.S. Census Bureau, "Annual Revision of Monthly Retail and Food Services: Sales and Inventories—January 1992 Through March 2008"; published 30 April 2008. See <http://www.census.gov/mrts/www/annrev08.html>.

Table 1013. Retail Trade Sales—Total and E-Commerce by Kind of Business: 2006

[3,887,363 represents $3,887,363,000,000. Covers retailers with and without payroll. Based on the Annual Retail Trade Survey; see Appendix III]

Kind of business	2002 NAICS code [1]	Value of sales (mil. dol.)		E-commerce as percent of total sales	Percent distribution of E-commerce sales
		Total	E-commerce		
Retail trade, total [2]	44–45	**3,887,363**	**106,583**	**2.7**	**100.0**
Motor vehicle and parts dealers	441	898,624	20,004	2.2	18.8
Furniture and home furnishings stores	442	117,659	642	0.5	0.6
Electronics and appliance stores.	443	108,362	1,213	1.1	1.1
Food and beverage stores	445	533,779	752	0.1	0.7
Clothing and clothing accessories stores	448	214,876	2,077	1.0	1.9
Sporting goods, hobby, book, and music stores . . .	451	84,772	1,502	1.8	1.4
Miscellaneous store retailers	453	115,802	1,691	1.5	1.6
Nonstore retailers.	454	275,654	77,641	28.2	72.8
Electronic shopping and mail-order houses	45411	190,865	75,230	39.4	70.6

[1] North American Industry Classification System, 2002; see text, Section 15. [2] Includes other kinds of business not shown separately.

Source: U.S. Census Bureau, "E-Stats, 2006 E-commerce Multi-sector Report"; published 16 May 2008. See <http://www.census.gov /eos/www/ebusiness614.htm>.

U.S. Census Bureau, Statistical Abstract of the United States: 2009

Table 1014. **Electronic Shopping and Mail-Order Houses—Total and E-Commerce Sales by Merchandise Line: 2005 and 2006**

[**164,345 represents $164,345,000,000**. Represents NAICS code 454110, which comprises establishments primarily engaged in retailing all types of merchandise using nonstore means, such as catalogs, toll-free telephone numbers, or electronic media, such as interactive television or computer. Covers businesses with and without paid employees. Based on the Annual Retail Survey; see Appendix III]

Merchandise line	Value of sales, total, 2005 (mil. dol.)	2006					
		Value of sales (mil. dol.)		E-commerce as percent of total sales	Percent distribution		
		Total	E-commerce		Total	E-commerce	
Total..................	**164,345**	**190,865**	**75,230**	**39.4**	**100.0**	**100.0**	
Books and magazines............	5,729	6,306	(S)	(S)	3.3	(S)	
Clothing and clothing accessories (includes footwear).............	17,109	19,290	11,752	60.9	10.1	15.6	
Computer hardware.............	19,998	20,664	8,915	43.1	10.8	11.9	
Computer software.............	3,931	4,265	2,218	52.0	2.2	2.9	
Drugs, health aids, beauty aids......	45,734	59,641	4,238	7.1	31.2	5.6	
Electronics and appliances.........	8,749	10,074	6,987	69.4	5.3	9.3	
Food, beer, and wine............	2,944	3,448	1,729	50.1	1.8	2.3	
Furniture and home furnishings......	9,838	11,407	7,028	61.6	6.0	9.3	
Music and videos.............	3,824	4,436	3,141	70.8	2.3	4.2	
Office equipment and supplies......	6,858	7,860	4,869	61.9	4.1	6.5	
Sporting goods...............	3,872	4,201	2,422	57.7	2.2	3.2	
Toys, hobby goods, and games.....	3,724	3,697	1,891	51.1	1.9	2.5	
Other merchandise [1]............	24,451	26,476	11,123	42.0	13.9	14.8	
Nonmerchandise receipts [2]........	7,584	9,100	5,392	59.3	4.8	7.2	

S Figure does not meet publication standards. [1] Includes other merchandise such as jewelry, collectibles, souvenirs, auto parts and accessories, hardware, and lawn and garden equipment and supplies. [2] Includes nonmerchandise receipts such as auction commissions, shipping and handling, customer training, customer support, and advertising.

Source: U.S. Census Bureau, "E-Stats, 2006 E-commerce Multi-sector Report"; published 16 May 2008. See <http://www.census.gov/eos/www/ebusiness614.htm>.

Table 1015. **Projected Online Retail Sales: 2007 to 2012**

[**In billions of dollars (174.5 represents $174,500,000,000)**]

Online product or service	2007	2008	2009	2010	2011	2012
Retail trade, total [1].................	**174.5**	**204.0**	**235.4**	**267.8**	**301.0**	**334.7**
Apparel/accessories/footwear................	22.7	26.6	30.5	34.4	38.2	41.8
Appliances/tools......................	7.5	9.0	10.7	12.6	14.6	16.9
Auto/auto parts......................	16.8	19.3	21.9	24.8	27.8	30.9
Computer hardware/software...............	20.7	23.9	27.1	30.4	33.7	37.1
Consumer electronics...................	13.5	16.3	19.4	22.6	26.0	29.5
Food/beverages/groceries................	6.2	7.3	8.7	10.2	11.9	13.7
Home furnishings.....................	12.3	14.8	17.6	20.5	23.6	26.7
Music/videos........................	8.2	8.9	9.8	10.5	11.1	11.7

[1] Excludes travel. Includes other products/services not shown separately.

Source: Forrester Research, Inc., Cambridge, MA, *US eCommerce Forecast: 2008 To 2012*, January 18, 2008 (copyright).

Table 1016. **Online Retail Spending, 2001 to 2007, and Projections, 2008**

[**31.0 represents $31,000,000,000**]

Category	Online retail spending (bil. dol.)					Percentage of total retail spending by category				
	2001	2005	2006	2007	2008, proj.	2001	2005	2006	2007	2008, proj.
Total................	**31.0**	**83.6**	**108.1**	**128.1**	**147.6**	**(NA)**	**(NA)**	**(NA)**	**(NA)**	**(NA)**
Computer hardware and software..	11.0	18.1	21.2	24.1	26.7	26.4	36.1	40.0	43.2	45.8
Consumer electronics..........	1.5	4.7	6.8	8.4	10.0	3.3	7.8	10.0	11.3	12.8
Books, music, and videos........	3.8	7.5	9.0	9.8	11.1	7.7	13.3	15.3	16.3	17.8
Tickets...................	1.8	4.6	5.5	6.3	6.8	6.9	15.4	17.5	19.1	19.6
Consumer health............	0.4	2.6	3.4	4.2	5.3	0.5	2.4	3.1	3.8	4.5
Apparel, accessories, footwear and jewelry...............	4.7	14.0	19.1	23.2	27.1	1.6	4.2	5.4	6.3	7.1
Grocery and pet food..........	0.8	4.1	5.6	7.4	9.1	0.1	0.6	0.8	1.1	1.2
Toys and video games.........	1.0	2.9	4.1	5.2	5.9	3.2	8.4	11.1	12.7	14.5
Sporting goods.............	0.7	2.0	2.3	2.5	2.8	2.9	7.9	9.0	9.5	10.2
Flowers and specialty gifts.......	1.2	3.1	3.9	4.3	4.9	2.3	5.6	6.8	7.5	8.3
Home...................	1.8	10.0	15.0	18.8	22.7	0.5	2.0	2.9	3.6	4.1
Office products.............	0.6	3.2	4.1	4.7	5.1	2.0	9.0	10.8	11.7	12.8
Other..................	1.8	6.7	8.1	9.1	10.1	(NA)	(NA)	(NA)	(NA)	(NA)

NA Not available.

Source: Jupiter Research, Inc., New York, NY, unpublished data (copyright).

Table 1017. Retail Trade—Nonemployer Establishments and Receipts by Kind of Business: 2000 to 2005

[1,743 represents 1,743,000. Includes only firms subject to federal income tax. Nonemployers are businesses with no paid employees. Data for 2000 based on the North American Industry Classification System (NAICS), 1997; beginning 2004, based on NAICS 2002, see text, Section 15]

Kind of business	NAICS code	Establishments (1,000)			Receipts (mil. dol.)		
		2000	2004	2005	2000	2004	2005
Retail trade, total [1]	44–45	**1,743**	**1,893**	**1,881**	**73,810**	**82,916**	**83,599**
Motor vehicle & parts dealers [1]	441	122	145	147	17,355	20,097	20,072
Used car dealers	44112	74	85	85	13,255	14,739	14,574
Motorcycle & boat & other MV dealers	44122	21	28	28	1,969	2,644	2,691
Automotive parts, accessories, & tire stores	4413	25	29	30	1,872	2,353	2,402
Furniture & home furnishings stores	442	37	43	41	2,574	3,049	3,088
Bldg. material & garden equip. & supp. dealers	444	28	32	31	2,182	2,603	2,710
Building material & supplies dealers	4441	20	24	23	1,677	2,044	2,141
Food & beverage stores [1]	445	82	89	89	8,493	8,951	9,027
Grocery stores	4451	39	40	39	4,609	4,567	4,518
Specialty food stores	4452	33	39	39	2,135	2,522	2,584
Health & personal care stores	446	92	118	114	1,915	2,487	2,510
Clothing & clothing accessories stores	448	89	106	109	4,464	5,023	5,231
Clothing stores	4481	60	70	73	2,718	3,067	3,239
Sporting goods, hobby, book, & music stores	451	96	95	93	3,761	3,873	3,882
Miscellaneous store retailers	453	339	325	313	12,963	13,719	13,625
Gift, novelty, & souvenir stores	45322	73	72	68	2,104	2,172	2,095
Nonstore retailers [1]	454	792	867	873	15,401	18,218	18,608
Electronic shopping & mail-order houses	4541	49	67	73	1,391	2,310	2,587
Direct selling establishments	4543	708	769	771	13,047	15,002	15,144

[1] Includes other kinds of business not shown separately.

Source: U.S. Census Bureau, "Nonemployer Statistics." See <http://www.census.gov/epcd/nonemployer/>.

Table 1018. Franchised New Car Dealerships—Summary: 1990 to 2007

[316 represents $316,000,000,000]

Item	Unit	1990	1995	2000	2001	2002	2003	2004	2005	2006	2007
Dealerships [1]	Number	24,825	22,800	22,250	21,800	21,725	21,650	21,640	21,495	21,200	20,770
Sales	Bil. dol.	316	456	650	690	680	699	714	699	675	693
New cars sold [2]	Millions	9.3	8.6	8.8	8.4	8.1	7.6	7.5	7.7	7.8	7.6
Used vehicles sold	Millions	14.2	18.5	20.5	21.4	19.4	19.5	19.7	19.7	19.2	18.5
Employment	1,000	924	996	1,114	1,130	1,130	1,130	1,130	1,138	1,120	1,115
Dealer pretax profits as a percentage of sales	Percent	1.0	1.4	1.6	2.0	1.9	1.7	1.7	1.6	1.5	1.5
Inventory: [3]											
Domestic: [4]											
Total	1,000	2,537	2,974	3,183	2,824	2,727	3,085	3,267	2,991	2,943	2,712
Days' supply	Days	73	71	68	63	63	63	75	70	71	67
Imported: [4]											
Total	1,000	707	445	468	508	521	618	646	566	605	619
Days' supply	Days	72	72	50	51	49	49	59	52	51	51

[1] At beginning of year. [2] Data provided by "Ward's Automotive Reports." [3] Annual average. Includes light trucks. [4] Classification based on where automobiles are produced (i.e., automobiles manufactured by foreign companies but produced in the U.S. are classified as domestic).

Source: National Automobile Dealers Association, McLean, VA, *NADA Data*, annual. See <http://www.nada.org/Publications/NADADATA/>.

Table 1019. Retail Sales and Leases of New and Used Vehicles: 1990 to 2007

[In thousands, except as noted (51,390 represents 51,390,000)]

Item	1990	2000	2001	2002	2003	2004	2005	2006	2007
Vehicle sales and leases, total	**51,390**	**58,964**	**59,742**	**59,835**	**60,215**	**59,411**	**61,086**	**59,070**	**58,547**
New vehicle sales and leases	13,860	17,344	17,118	16,810	16,643	16,866	16,948	16,504	17,129
New vehicle sales [1]	13,285	13,181	13,510	13,639	13,594	13,609	13,551	13,271	13,671
Passenger cars	8,766	6,580	6,407	6,370	5,932	5,737	5,806	6,088	6,342
Light trucks	4,519	6,601	7,103	7,269	7,663	7,872	7,745	7,184	7,329
New vehicle leases [2]	575	4,163	3,608	3,171	3,049	3,257	3,397	3,233	3,458
Passenger cars	534	2,272	2,015	1,732	1,683	1,768	1,861	1,693	1,743
Light trucks	41	1,891	1,593	1,439	1,366	1,489	1,536	1,540	1,715
Used vehicle sales [3]	37,530	41,620	42,624	43,025	43,572	42,545	44,138	42,566	41,418
New and used vehicle sales, total value (bil. dol.) [4]	**446**	**737**	**737**	**721**	**738**	**765**	**776**	**786**	**774**
New vehicle sales (bil. dol.)	227	380	369	371	382	407	421	445	435
Used vehicle sales (bil. dol.)	219	356	367	350	356	358	355	341	339

[1] New vehicle sales data is calculated by subtracting CNW Marketing's vehicle leasing data from Bureau of Economic Analysis' data which combines sales and leases. [2] Consumer leases only. [3] Used car sales include sales from franchised dealers, independent dealers, and casual sales. [4] Includes leased vehicles.

Source: U.S. Bureau of Transportation Statistics, *National Transportation Statistics*, annual. See <http://www.bts.gov/publications/national_transportation_statistics/>. Data supplied by following sources: New vehicle sales and leases—U.S. Department of Commerce, Bureau of Economic Analysis; New vehicle leases—<http://bea.doc.gov/>; CNW Marketing/Research, personal communication, Mar. 18, 2007; Used vehicle sales and value: Manheim, Used Car Market Report, Atlanta, GA.

Wholesale and Retail Trade 647

Table 1020. **Retail Trade and Food Services—Sales by Type of Store and State: 2007**

[**In millions of dollars (4,506,804 represents $4,506,804,000,000).** Kind-of-business classification based on North American Industry Classification System (NAICS), 1997; see text, Section 15. Data are estimates]

State	Total retail sales plus food services and drinking places (NAICS 44–45, 722)	All retail stores [1] (NAICS 44–45)	Motor vehicle and parts dealers (NAICS 441)	Furniture and home furnishings (NAICS 442)	Electronics and appliances (NAICS 443)	Building material & garden equip. & supplies dealers (NAICS 444)	Food and beverage stores (NAICS 445)	Health and personal care (NAICS 446)
U.S....	4,506,804	4,980,407	946,504	124,956	115,531	540,746	604,554	249,860
AL	70,748	76,624	15,502	1,871	1,056	9,528	7,521	4,285
AK	11,329	12,645	2,110	262	225	1,259	1,873	202
AZ	109,696	119,671	23,769	4,025	3,364	11,957	13,000	4,567
AR	40,461	43,821	9,002	830	559	5,888	3,625	2,036
CA	546,260	606,946	122,764	16,892	20,434	63,533	80,414	25,963
CO	76,404	84,923	16,063	2,480	2,413	9,538	12,723	2,525
CT	54,381	59,842	10,565	1,573	1,272	6,512	8,156	3,348
DE	17,194	18,743	3,671	765	489	2,545	2,418	973
DC	4,490	7,047	87	229	100	281	1,228	826
FL.....	333,077	367,518	83,851	11,689	8,500	40,167	41,440	19,375
GA	137,519	152,968	30,217	4,043	3,149	17,207	16,907	7,374
HI.....	20,984	24,817	3,799	561	420	1,799	3,446	1,378
ID.....	25,662	27,557	6,262	854	486	4,179	2,859	754
IL.....	176,456	198,095	33,906	4,772	4,423	19,815	22,789	8,996
IN.....	88,559	97,570	18,246	2,029	2,146	10,973	9,408	4,855
IA	40,406	43,915	7,984	920	737	5,433	5,166	1,913
KS	34,890	38,424	7,246	750	783	4,133	4,442	1,656
KY	56,296	62,067	10,296	1,395	932	7,326	6,922	3,678
LA	60,341	66,779	13,836	1,450	1,432	7,327	6,378	3,495
ME	22,419	24,298	3,856	405	288	2,914	3,291	783
MD	88,120	97,410	19,447	2,732	2,304	11,995	13,280	4,137
MA	101,919	114,094	19,798	3,202	2,815	13,210	17,576	7,812
MI.....	134,774	147,456	28,785	3,026	3,616	17,769	15,960	9,338
MN	77,411	85,292	14,140	1,683	2,055	9,980	10,751	3,690
MS	41,287	44,814	8,222	839	697	5,406	3,781	2,595
MO	87,936	96,816	17,609	1,985	2,033	10,163	8,457	4,939
MT	16,031	17,642	3,005	526	359	2,525	1,860	444
NE	28,302	30,733	5,270	745	610	3,757	2,673	1,201
NV	51,104	57,426	11,120	1,626	1,613	4,839	5,516	1,917
NH	30,785	32,925	5,974	584	1,034	4,490	4,894	1,114
NJ.....	137,366	151,409	27,630	4,198	3,274	15,772	27,514	9,401
NM	28,046	31,042	6,011	577	529	2,961	2,558	1,111
NY	264,959	296,085	42,654	6,988	7,931	28,424	44,931	25,886
NC	133,867	147,298	29,725	4,582	2,185	18,327	15,273	8,973
ND	11,801	12,617	2,395	248	275	1,772	1,226	571
OH	144,877	161,451	29,778	3,115	3,170	16,019	22,471	7,541
OK	45,138	49,806	10,488	932	656	5,485	3,890	2,244
OR	57,778	64,230	13,003	1,702	1,555	6,674	8,506	2,215
PA	181,216	197,695	34,753	3,954	3,659	19,922	24,697	12,473
RI.....	14,432	16,340	2,980	385	328	1,721	2,244	1,653
SC	61,219	67,974	12,058	1,669	1,193	8,149	7,978	4,094
SD	14,578	15,654	2,659	295	299	2,103	1,314	522
TN	97,759	107,244	20,429	2,426	1,842	12,999	10,523	7,902
TX	330,570	367,021	75,511	8,500	8,587	33,474	40,489	12,209
UT	39,668	42,905	9,043	1,314	813	4,965	4,484	878
VT	11,419	12,269	2,070	245	201	1,730	1,819	622
VA	129,841	142,899	26,546	4,010	3,677	17,427	17,334	5,824
WA	104,264	114,121	20,387	2,687	2,650	11,730	15,385	3,615
WV	24,260	26,495	4,456	423	390	3,033	2,654	1,827
WI.....	79,097	86,668	15,438	1,800	1,844	10,560	9,595	3,940
WY	9,410	10,306	2,087	160	128	1,049	918	191

See footnotes at end of table.

U.S. Census Bureau, Statistical Abstract of the United States: 2009

Table 1020. **Retail Trade and Food Services—Sales by Type of Store and State: 2007**—Con.

[See headnote, page 648]

State	Gasoline stations (NAICS 447)	Clothing and clothing accessories (NAICS 448)	Sporting goods, hobby, book & music stores (NAICS 451)	General merchandise (NAICS 452)	Miscellaneous stores (NAICS 453)	Nonstore retailers (NAICS 454)	Food services & drinking places (NAICS 722)
U.S....	**545,781**	**235,056**	**92,116**	**602,516**	**126,231**	**322,953**	**473,603**
AL	10,129	3,003	975	11,789	1,724	3,363	5,876
AK	1,258	439	339	2,387	438	536	1,316
AZ	13,350	4,146	2,326	16,133	2,720	10,338	9,975
AR	6,234	1,324	584	8,176	1,160	1,044	3,360
CA	49,634	32,322	11,887	72,051	14,443	35,922	60,686
CO	7,241	3,477	2,446	11,539	2,339	3,620	8,519
CT	5,090	3,632	1,262	5,510	1,365	6,095	5,461
DE	1,541	817	370	2,101	826	677	1,549
DC	320	587	216	298	106	210	2,558
FL......	32,250	18,336	5,104	41,626	9,221	21,517	34,441
GA	22,550	7,245	2,123	18,464	3,254	4,987	15,449
HI......	1,684	2,873	482	3,277	873	394	3,833
ID......	3,404	636	580	3,622	950	1,077	1,895
IL......	17,847	9,918	3,881	24,697	4,241	21,170	21,639
IN......	14,206	3,765	1,589	13,129	2,637	5,576	9,010
IA	6,966	1,238	730	5,936	821	2,562	3,508
KS	5,294	1,323	686	5,798	919	1,859	3,535
KY	9,172	1,990	980	9,821	2,016	1,768	5,771
LA	9,086	2,643	1,059	10,358	1,944	1,333	6,438
ME	3,312	937	340	2,649	586	3,060	1,878
MD	7,906	5,907	2,089	10,700	1,964	5,661	9,290
MA	8,805	6,543	2,487	8,384	2,544	8,744	12,175
MI......	15,909	6,381	2,781	19,456	4,736	7,016	12,682
MN	9,897	3,292	1,964	11,319	1,804	6,836	7,881
MS	7,515	1,740	602	7,982	1,142	766	3,527
MO	14,397	3,412	1,466	13,066	2,213	8,196	8,880
MT	3,124	432	464	2,319	548	425	1,610
NE	4,270	914	618	3,816	527	3,900	2,431
NV	5,792	4,236	791	6,355	1,670	5,629	6,322
NH	3,002	1,348	637	3,381	824	3,503	2,140
NJ......	11,307	8,801	3,046	11,480	3,131	11,812	14,043
NM	5,245	1,106	473	4,769	997	1,709	2,996
NY	20,882	24,298	6,534	23,701	10,838	21,892	31,126
NC	18,853	5,654	2,046	18,194	3,490	6,564	13,431
ND	2,369	328	205	1,363	271	777	816
OH	19,512	6,066	2,705	17,551	3,698	13,251	16,575
OK	8,142	1,607	875	8,339	1,665	814	4,668
OR	5,624	2,648	1,485	8,708	1,934	3,725	6,452
PA	22,370	8,014	3,489	20,767	5,197	21,921	16,479
RI......	1,624	752	240	1,088	387	1,032	1,908
SC	10,111	3,276	1,113	8,625	1,703	1,250	6,755
SD	2,353	327	254	1,946	289	2,218	1,076
TN	13,589	4,671	1,774	13,955	2,712	4,937	9,486
TX	48,776	15,255	7,220	49,971	8,438	22,142	36,451
UT	4,878	1,368	1,056	5,601	882	4,386	3,237
VT	1,760	421	308	592	434	1,216	851
VA	18,486	6,706	2,870	18,189	3,256	5,515	13,058
WA	9,710	5,243	2,323	15,281	3,543	11,708	9,857
WV	4,424	714	325	4,144	680	1,189	2,235
WI......	12,259	2,745	1,740	10,781	1,822	6,573	7,572
WY	2,319	199	180	1,331	311	536	896

[1] Includes other types of stores, not shown separately.

Source: Market Statistics, a division of Claritas Inc., Arlington, VA, *The 2008 Survey of Buying Power* (copyright). See <http://claritas.com>.

U.S. Census Bureau, Statistical Abstract of the United States: 2009

Table 1021. **New Motor Vehicle Sales and Car Production: 1990 to 2007**

[In thousands (14,137 represents 14,137,000). Includes leases]

Type of vehicle	1990	2000	2002	2003	2004	2005	2006	2007
New motor vehicle sales . . .	**14,137**	**17,806**	**17,137**	**16,971**	**17,297**	**17,445**	**17,048**	**16,462**
New-car sales and leases	9,300	8,852	8,102	7,615	7,505	7,667	7,781	7,588
Domestic	6,897	6,833	5,871	5,527	5,350	5,480	5,436	5,221
Import	2,403	2,019	2,231	2,087	2,155	2,187	2,345	2,367
New-truck sales and leases	4,838	8,954	9,035	9,356	9,792	9,777	9,268	8,874
Light	4,560	8,492	8,713	9,028	9,361	9,281	8,723	8,501
Domestic	3,957	7,651	7,647	7,801	8,115	8,065	7,377	7,113
Import	603	841	1,066	1,227	1,246	1,216	1,347	1,389
Other	278	462	322	328	432	497	544	373
Domestic-car production.	6,231	5,542	5,019	4,510	4,230	4,321	4,367	3,925

Source: U.S. Bureau of Economic Analysis, "Auto and Truck Seasonal Adjustment." See <http://www.bea.gov/national/xls/gaphist.xls>; accessed May 2008. Data are mainly from "Ward's Automotive Reports" published by Ward's Communications, Southfield, MI.

Table 1022. **Retail Foodstores—Number and Sales by Type: 2000 to 2006**

[119.6 represents 119,600. Based on North American Industry Classification System (NAICS), 2002; see text, Section 15]

Type of foodstore	Number [1] (1,000)				Sales [2]						
					Amount (bil.dol.)				Percent distribution		
	2000	2004	2005	2006	2000	2004	2005	2006	2000	2005	2006
Total	**119.6**	**120.5**	**(NA)**	**(NA)**	**417.3**	**463.1**	**484.3**	**504.0**	**100.0**	**100.0**	**100.0**
Grocery stores	95.9	95.1	(NA)	(NA)	403.1	445.1	463.6	482.8	96.6	95.7	95.8
Supermarkets [3]	21.9	21.0	20.2	18.6	310.3	318.0	321.8	317.8	74.4	66.4	63.1
Conventional	7.2	3.6	3.0	(NA)	58.3	70.5	67.0	(NA)	14.0	13.8	(NA)
Superstore [4]	7.9	8.2	8.0	(NA)	131.0	126.0	130.9	(NA)	31.4	27.0	(NA)
Warehouse [5]	2.4	3.2	2.7	(NA)	20.2	10.4	12.3	(NA)	4.8	2.5	(NA)
Combination food and drug [6]. . .	3.7	5.2	5.6	(NA)	75.3	88.3	89.1	(NA)	18.0	18.4	(NA)
Super warehouse [7]	0.5	0.5	0.5	(NA)	16.0	10.9	11.5	(NA)	3.8	2.4	(NA)
Hypermarket [8]	0.2	0.3	0.3	(NA)	9.5	11.9	10.9	(NA)	2.3	2.3	(NA)
Convenience stores [9]	28.2	30.4	26.1	(NA)	19.2	22.6	19.9	20.5	4.6	4.1	4.1
Superette [10]	45.8	43.8	(NA)	(NA)	73.6	104.5	121.9	144.5	17.6	25.2	28.7
Specialized food stores [11]	23.7	25.4	(NA)	(NA)	14.2	18.0	20.4	21.2	3.4	4.2	4.2

NA Not available. [1] Estimated. [2] Includes nonfood items. [3] A grocery store, primarily self-service in operation, providing a full range of departments, and having at least $2.5 million in annual sales in 1985 dollars. [4] Contains greater variety of products than conventional supermarkets, including specialty and service departments, and considerable nonfood (general merchandise) products. [5] Contains limited product variety and fewer services provided, incorporating case lot stocking and shelving practices. [6] Contains a pharmacy, a nonprescription drug department, and a greater variety of health and beauty aids than that carried by conventional supermarkets. [7] A larger warehouse store that offers expanded product variety and often service meat, deli, or seafood departments. [8] A very large store offering a greater variety of general merchandise—like clothes, hardware, and seasonal goods—and personal care products than other grocery stores. [9] A small grocery store selling a limited variety of food and nonfood products, typically open extended hours. [10] A grocery store, primarily self-service in operation, selling a wide variety of food and nonfood products with annual sales below $2.5 million (1985 dollars). [11] Primarily engaged in the retail sale of a single food category such as meat and seafood stores and retail bakeries.

Source: U.S. Department of Agriculture, Economic Research Service, *The U.S. Food Marketing System, 2002*, Agricultural Economic Report 811, August 2002; and unpublished data.

Table 1023. **Food and Alcoholic Beverage Sales by Sales Outlet: 1990 to 2006**

[In billions of dollars (552.7 represents $552,700,000,000)]

Sales outlet	1990	1995	2000	2001	2002	2003	2004	2005	2006
Food sales, total [1]	**552.7**	**652.8**	**814.0**	**848.8**	**878.1**	**917.0**	**961.3**	**1,015.1**	**1082.5**
Food at home	304.5	349.2	422.5	444.1	456.6	475.4	494.6	521.6	553.4
Food stores [2]	256.4	275.3	303.5	313.1	312.0	323.9	335.2	349.4	364.4
Other stores [3]	32.3	54.7	89.4	103.0	116.4	122.6	129.4	142.4	157.1
Home-delivered, mail order.	5.3	8.6	19.2	18.0	17.9	18.2	18.8	19.2	21.0
Farmers, manufacturers, wholesalers . . .	2.8	3.5	3.9	3.8	3.7	3.9	4.0	4.2	4.4
Home production and donations	7.7	7.0	6.5	6.2	6.6	6.8	7.2	6.5	6.5
Food away from home [4]	248.1	303.6	391.4	404.7	421.5	441.6	466.7	493.5	529.1
Alcoholic beverage sales, total	**72.6**	**80.3**	**111.6**	**119.7**	**128.0**	**126.2**	**137.0**	**142.9**	**154.8**
Packaged alcoholic beverages	38.0	41.5	52.7	55.1	57.0	57.5	59.8	62.2	69.4
Liquor stores	18.6	19.0	24.5	25.3	25.5	26.0	27.7	29.4	32.2
Food stores	10.8	12.3	15.9	16.9	17.4	17.8	18.5	19.4	20.2
All other	8.6	10.3	12.9	12.9	14.2	13.7	13.5	13.5	17.1
Alcoholic drinks	34.5	38.8	58.9	64.7	70.9	68.7	77.2	80.6	85.3
Eating and drinking places [5]	26.5	30.3	41.6	44.3	47.3	44.6	52.5	55.3	59.6
Hotels and motels [5]	3.8	3.9	11.3	14.4	17.5	17.7	18.0	18.3	18.5
All other	4.2	4.6	6.0	6.0	6.2	6.4	6.7	7.0	7.3

[1] Includes taxes and tips. [2] Excludes sales to restaurants and institutions. [3] Includes eating and drinking establishments, trailer parks, commissary stores, and military exchanges. [4] Includes food furnished and donations. [5] Includes tips.

Source: U.S. Department of Agriculture, Economic Research Service, "Food CPI, Prices, and Expenditures: Food Expenditure Tables"; published 2 July 2007. See <http://www.ers.usda.gov/briefing/CPIFoodAndExpenditures/Data/>.

Transportation

This section presents data on civil air transportation, both passenger and cargo, and on water transportation, including inland waterways, oceanborne commerce, the merchant marine, cargo, and vessel tonnages.

This section also presents statistics on revenues, passenger and freight traffic volume, and employment in various revenue-producing modes of the transportation industry, including motor vehicles, trains, and pipelines. Data are also presented on highway mileage and finances, motor vehicle travel, accidents, and registrations; and characteristics of public transit, railroads, and pipelines.

Principal sources of air and water transportation data are the annual *National Transportation Statistics,* issued by the U.S. Bureau of Transportation Statistics; the *Annual Report* issued by the Air Transport Association of America, Washington, DC; and the annual *Waterborne Commerce of the United States* issued by the Corps of Engineers of the Department of the Army. In addition, the U.S. Census Bureau in its commodity flow survey (part of the census of transportation, taken every 5 years through 2002, for years ending in "2" and "7") provides data on the type, weight, and value of commodities shipped by manufacturing establishments in the United States, by means of transportation, origin, and destination. The latest reports for 2002 are part of the 2002 Economic Census. This census was conducted in accordance with the 2002 North American Industry Classification System (NAICS). See text, Section 15, Business Enterprise, for a discussion of the 2002 Economic Census and NAICS.

The principal compiler of data on public roads and on operation of motor vehicles is the U.S. Department of Transportation's (DOT) Federal Highway Administration (FHWA). These data appear in FHWA's annual *Highway Statistics* and other publications.

The U.S. National Highway Traffic Safety Administration issues data on traffic accident deaths and death rates in two annual reports: the *Fact Book* and the *Fatal Accident Reporting System Annual Report.* DOT's Federal Railroad Administration presents data on accidents involving railroads in its annual *Accident/Incident Bulletin,* and the *Rail-Highway Crossing Accident/Incident and Inventory Bulletin.*

Data are also presented in many nongovernment publications. Among them are the weekly and annual *Cars of Revenue Freight Loaded* and the annual *Yearbook of Railroad Facts,* both published by the Association of American Railroads, Washington, DC; *Transit Fact Book,* containing electric railway and motorbus statistics, published annually by the American Public Transit Association, Washington, DC; and *Injury Facts,* issued by the National Safety Council, Chicago, IL.

Civil aviation—Federal promotion and regulation of civil aviation have been carried out by the Federal Aviation Administration (FAA) and the Civil Aeronautics Board (CAB). The CAB promoted and regulated the civil air transportation industry within the United States and between the United States and foreign countries. The Board granted licenses to provide air transportation service, approved or disapproved proposed rates and fares, and approved or disapproved proposed agreements and corporate relationships involving air carriers. In December 1984, the CAB ceased to exist as an agency. Some of its functions were transferred to the DOT, as outlined below. The responsibility for investigation of aviation accidents resides with the National Transportation Safety Board.

The Office of the Secretary, DOT aviation activities include: negotiation of international air transportation rights, selection of U.S. air carriers to serve capacity-controlled international markets, oversight of international rates and fares, maintenance of essential air service to small communities, and consumer affairs. DOT's Bureau of Transportation Statistics (BTS) handles aviation information functions formerly assigned to CAB. Prior to BTS, the Research and Special Programs Administration handled these functions.

The principal activities of the FAA include: the promotion of air safety; controlling the use of navigable airspace; prescribing regulations dealing with the competency of airmen, airworthiness of aircraft and air traffic control; operation of air route traffic control centers, airport traffic control towers, and flight service stations; the design, construction, maintenance, and inspection of navigation, traffic control, and communications equipment; and the development of general aviation.

The CAB published monthly and quarterly financial and traffic statistical data for the certificated route air carriers. BTS continues these publications, including both certificated and noncertificated (commuter) air carriers. The FAA annually publishes data on the use of airway facilities; data related to the location of airmen, aircraft, and airports; the volume of activity in the field of nonair carrier (general aviation) flying; and aircraft production and registration.

General aviation comprises all civil flying (including such commercial operations as small demand air taxis, agriculture application, powerline patrol, etc.) but excludes certificated route air carriers, supplemental operators, large-aircraft commercial operators, and commuter airlines.

Air carriers and service—The CAB previously issued "certificates of public convenience and necessity" under Section 401 of the Federal Aviation Act of 1958 for scheduled and nonscheduled (charter) passenger services and cargo services. It also issued certificates under Section 418 of the Act to cargo air carriers for domestic all-cargo service only. The DOT Office of the Secretary now issues the certificates under a "fit, willing, and able" test of air carrier operations. Carriers operating only a 60-seat-or-less aircraft are given exemption authority to carry passengers, cargo, and mail in scheduled and

nonscheduled service under Part 298 of the DOT (formerly CAB) regulations. Exemption authority carriers who offer scheduled passenger service to an essential air service point must meet the "fit, willing, and able" test.

Vessel shipments, entrances, and clearances—Shipments by dry cargo vessels comprise shipments on all types of watercraft, except tanker vessels; shipments by tanker vessels comprise all types of cargo, liquid and dry, carried by tanker vessels.

A vessel is reported as entered only at the first port which it enters in the United States, whether or not cargo is unloaded at that port. A vessel is reported as cleared only at the last port at which clearance is made to a foreign port, whether or not it takes on cargo. Army and Navy vessels entering or clearing without commercial cargo are not included in the figures.

Units of measurement—Cargo (or freight) tonnage and shipping weight both represent the gross weight of the cargo including the weight of containers, wrappings, crates, etc. However, shipping weight excludes lift and cargo vans and similar substantial outer containers. Other tonnage figures generally refer to stowing capacity of vessels, 100 cubic feet being called 1 ton. Gross tonnage comprises the space within the frames and the ceiling of the hull, together with those closed-in spaces above deck available for cargo, stores, passengers, or crew, with certain minor exceptions. Net or registered tonnage is the gross tonnage less the spaces occupied by the propelling machinery, fuel, crew quarters, master's cabin, and navigation spaces. Substantially, it represents space available for cargo and passengers. The net tonnage capacity of a ship may bear little relation to weight of cargo. Deadweight tonnage is the weight in long tons required to depress a vessel from light water line (that is, with only the machinery and equipment on board) to load line. It is, therefore, the weight of the cargo, fuel, etc., which a vessel is designed to carry with safety.

Federal-aid highway systems—The Intermodal Surface Transportation Efficiency Act (ISTEA) of 1991 eliminated the historical Federal-Aid Highway Systems and created the National Highway System (NHS) and other federal-aid highway categories. The final NHS was approved by Congress in December of 1995 under the National Highway System Designation Act.

Functional systems—Roads and streets are assigned to groups according to the character of service intended. The functional systems are (1) arterial highways that generally handle the long trips, (2) collector facilities that collect and disperse traffic between the arterials and the lower systems, and (3) local roads and streets that primarily serve direct access to residential areas, farms, and other local areas.

Regulatory bodies—The Interstate Commerce Commission (ICC), created by the U.S. Congress to regulate transportation in interstate commerce, has jurisdiction over railroads, trucking companies, bus lines, freight forwarders, water carriers, coal slurry pipelines, and transportation brokers. The Federal Energy Regulatory Commission is responsible for setting rates and charges for transportation and sale of natural gas and for establishing rates or charges for transportation.

Motor carriers—For 1960–73, Class I for-hire motor carriers of freight were classified by the ICC as those with $1 million or more of gross annual operating revenue; 1974–79, the class minimum was $3 million. Effective January 1, 1980, Class I carriers are those with $5 million or more in revenue. For 1960–68, Class I motor carriers of passengers were classified by the ICC as those with $200,000 or more of gross annual operating revenue; for 1969–76, as those with revenues of $1 million or more; and since 1977, as those with $3 million or more. Effective January 1, 1988, Class I motor carriers of passengers are those with $5 million or more in operating revenues; Class II less than $5 million in operating revenues.

Railroads—Railroad companies reporting to the ICC are divided into specific groups as follows: (1) regular line-haul (interstate) railroads (and their nonoperating subsidiaries), (2) switching and terminal railroads, (3) private railroads prior to 1964 (identified by ICC as "circular" because they reported on brief circulars), and (4) unofficial railroads, so designated when their reports are received too late for tabulation. For the most part, the last three groups are not included in the statistics shown here.

For years prior to 1978, Class I railroads were those with annual revenues of $1 million or more for 1950–55; $3 million or more for 1956–64; $5 million or more for 1965–75; and $10 million or more for 1976–77. In 1978, the classification became Class I, those having more than $50 million gross annual operating revenue; Class II, from $10 million to $50 million; and Class III, less than $10 million. Effective January 1, 1982, the ICC adopted a procedure to adjust the threshold for inflation by restating current revenues in constant 1978 dollars. In 1988, the criteria for Class I and Class II railroads were $92.0 million and $18.4 million, respectively. Also effective January 1, 1982, the ICC adopted a Carrier Classification Index Survey Form for carriers not filing annual report Form R-1 with the commission. Class II and Class III railroads are currently exempted from filing any financial report with the Commission. The form is used for reclassifying carriers.

The Surface Transportation Board (STB) was established pursuant to the ICC Termination Act of 1995, Pub. L. No. 104-88, 109 Stat. 803 (1995) (ICCTA), to assume certain of the regulatory functions that had been administered by the ICC. The Board has broad economic regulatory oversight of railroads, addressing such matters as rate reasonableness, car service and interchange, mergers and line acquisitions, line construction, and line abandonments (49 U.S.C. 10101-11908). Other ICC regulatory functions were either eliminated or transferred to the Federal Highway Administration or the Bureau of Transportation Statistics within DOT.

Class I Railroads are regulated by the STB and subject to the Uniform System of Accounts and required to file annual and periodic reports. Railroads are classified based on their annual operating revenues. The class to which a carrier belongs is determined by comparing its adjusted

U.S. Census Bureau, Statistical Abstract of the United States: 2009

operating revenues for 3 consecutive years to the following scale: Class I, $250 million or more; Class II, $20 million to $250 million; and Class III, $0 to $20 million.

Postal Service—The U.S. Postal Service provides mail processing and delivery services within the United States. The Postal Reorganization Act of 1970 created the Postal Service, effective July 1971, as an independent establishment of the Federal Executive Branch.

Revenue and cost analysis describes the Postal Service's system of attributing revenues and costs to classes of mail and service. This system draws primarily upon probability sampling techniques to develop estimates of revenues, volumes, and weights, as well as costs by class of mail and special service. The costs attributed to classes of mail and special services are primarily incremental costs which vary in response to changes in volume; they account for roughly 60 percent of the total costs of the Postal Service. The balance represents "institutional costs." Statistics on revenues, volume of mail, and distribution of expenditures are presented in the Postal Service's annual report, *Cost and Revenue Analysis,* and its *Annual Report of the Postmaster General* and its annual *Comprehensive Statement on Postal Operations.*

Statistical reliability—For a discussion of statistical collection and estimation, sampling procedures, and measures of statistical reliability applicable to Census Bureau data, see Appendix III.

Table 1024. **Transportation-Related Components of U.S. Gross Domestic Product: 2000 to 2006**

[In billions of dollars (1,089.5 represents $1,089,500,000,000), except percent]

Item	2000	2002	2003	2004	2005	2006
CURRENT DOLLARS						
Total transportation-related final demand [1]	**1,089.5**	**1,106.4**	**1,138.0**	**1,212.5**	**1,322.6**	**1,401.6**
Total gross domestic product (GDP)	9,817.0	10,649.6	10,960.8	11,685.9	12,433.9	13,194.7
Transportation as a percent of GDP	11.1	10.4	10.4	10.4	10.6	10.6
Personal consumption of transportation	853.5	882.2	921.7	976.4	1,048.8	1,093.4
Motor vehicles and parts	386.5	429.3	431.7	436.8	444.9	434.2
Gasoline and oil	175.7	164.5	192.7	231.4	280.7	318.6
Transportation services	291.3	288.4	297.3	308.2	324.2	340.6
Gross private domestic investment	167.4	132.8	124.4	149.6	166.5	179.7
Transportation structures	6.6	6.5	6.1	6.7	7.0	7.8
Transportation equipment	160.8	126.3	118.3	142.9	159.5	171.9
Net exports of transportation-related goods and service [2]	−109.0	−112.1	−125.4	−136.3	−131.6	−127.0
Exports (+)	179.0	175.5	174.5	195.1	221.7	250.9
Civilian aircraft, engines, and parts	48.1	50.4	46.7	50.0	60.8	75.2
Automotive vehicles, engines, and parts	80.4	78.9	80.6	89.2	98.6	107.2
Passenger fares	20.7	17.0	15.7	18.9	21.0	22.2
Other transportation	29.8	29.2	31.5	37.0	41.3	46.3
Imports (−)	288.0	287.6	299.9	331.4	353.3	377.9
Civilian aircraft, engines, and parts	26.4	25.5	24.1	24.3	25.8	28.4
Automotive vehicles, engines, and parts	195.9	203.7	210.1	228.2	239.5	256.7
Passenger fares	24.3	20.0	21.0	24.7	26.1	27.5
Other transportation	41.4	38.4	44.7	54.2	61.9	65.3
Government transportation-related purchases	177.6	203.5	217.3	222.8	237.9	255.5
Federal purchases [3]	19.2	26.4	29.6	29.1	30.3	31.8
State and local purchases [3]	149.4	166.6	171.5	177.0	191.3	208.9
Defense-related purchases [4]	9.0	10.5	16.2	16.7	16.3	14.8
CHAINED (2000) DOLLARS						
Total transportation-related final demand [1]	**1,089.5**	**1,100.7**	**1,098.8**	**1,120.2**	**1,137.0**	**1,136.7**
Total gross domestic product (GDP)	9,817.0	10,048.8	10,301.0	10,675.8	11,003.4	11,319.4
Transportation as a percent of GDP	11.1	11.0	10.7	10.5	10.3	10.0
Personal consumption of transportation	853.5	891.1	905.9	922.1	925.2	915.3
Motor vehicles and parts	386.5	429.0	442.1	450.8	451.3	437.3
Gasoline and oil	175.7	181.9	183.2	186.7	186.1	186.8
Transportation services	291.3	280.2	280.6	284.6	287.8	291.2
Gross private domestic investment	167.4	132.1	119.4	136.5	151.1	161.7
Transportation structures	6.6	6.1	5.6	5.9	6.0	6.5
Transportation equipment	160.8	126.0	113.8	130.6	145.1	155.2
Net exports of transportation-related goods and service [2]	−109.0	−114.5	−126.1	−133.5	−130.8	−131.4
Exports (+)	179.0	170.7	164.6	178.8	193.6	212.6
Civilian aircraft, engines, and parts	48.1	46.5	41.5	43.0	50.1	59.5
Automotive vehicles, engines, and parts	80.4	78.3	79.4	87.2	95.2	102.3
Passenger fares	20.7	16.5	13.6	14.8	15.2	16.0
Other transportation	29.8	29.4	30.1	33.8	33.1	34.8
Imports (−)	288.0	285.2	290.7	312.3	324.4	344.0
Civilian aircraft, engines, and parts	26.4	24.2	22.8	22.3	22.9	24.3
Automotive vehicles, engines, and parts	195.9	203.3	208.5	222.6	231.2	246.9
Passenger fares	24.3	17.4	17.9	21.4	21.8	21.7
Other transportation	41.4	40.3	41.5	46.0	48.5	51.1
Government transportation-related purchases	177.6	192.0	199.6	195.1	191.5	191.1
Federal purchases [3]	19.2	25.0	27.1	25.4	25.4	25.6
State and local purchases [3]	149.4	157.3	158.5	155.7	152.9	153.9
Defense-related purchases [4]	9.0	9.7	14.0	14.0	13.2	11.6

[1] Sum of total personal consumption of transportation, total gross private domestic investment, net exports of transportation-related goods and services, and total government transportation-related purchases. [2] Sum of exports and imports. [3] Federal purchases and state and local purchases are the sum of consumption expenditures and gross investment. [4] Defense-related purchases are the sum of transportation of material and travel.

Source: U.S. Bureau of Transportation Statistics, *National Transportation Statistics,* annual. See Internet site <http://www.bts.gov/publications/national_transportation_statistics/>.

Table 1025. **Employment in Transportation and Warehousing: 1990 to 2007**

[In thousands (3,476 represents 3,476,000). Annual average of monthly figures. Based on Current Employment Statistics program; see Appendix III]

Industry	2007 NAICS code [1]	1990	1995	2000	2004	2005	2006	2007
Transportation and warehousing	48, 49	**3,476**	**3,838**	**4,410**	**4,249**	**4,361**	**4,470**	**4,536**
Air transportation	481	529	511	614	515	501	487	493
Rail transportation	482	272	233	232	226	228	228	234
Water transportation	483	57	51	56	56	61	63	64
Truck transportation	484	1,122	1,249	1,406	1,352	1,398	1,436	1,441
Transit and ground	485	274	328	372	385	389	399	410
Pipeline transportation	486	60	54	46	38	38	39	40
Scenic and sightseeing	487	16	22	28	27	29	28	29
Support activities	488	364	430	537	535	552	571	583
Couriers and messengers	492	375	517	605	557	571	582	583
Warehousing and storage	493	407	444	514	558	595	638	659

[1] North American Industry Classification System 2007, see text, Sections 12 and 15.

Source: U.S. Bureau of Labor Statistics, "Employment, Hours, and Earnings from the Current Employment Statistics survey (National)." See <http://stats.bls.gov/ces/home.htm>.

Transportation   655

Table 1026. Transportation System Mileage Within the U.S.: 1980 to 2006

[3,860 represents 3,860,000]

System	1980	1985	1990	1995	2000	2003	2004	2005	2006
Highway (1,000).	3,860	3,864	3,867	3,912	3,936	3,974	3,982	3,996	4,017
Class 1 rail	164,822	145,764	119,758	108,264	99,250	99,126	97,662	95,830	94,942
Amtrak	24,000	24,000	24,000	24,000	23,000	22,675	22,256	22,007	21,708
Transit:									
Commuter rail [1]	(NA)	3,574	4,132	4,160	5,209	6,809	6,875	7,118	8,076
Heavy rail [2]	(NA)	1,293	1,351	1,458	1,558	1,597	1,596	1,622	1,601
Light rail [3]	(NA)	384	483	568	834	996	1,187	1,188	1,188
Navigable channels	26,000	26,000	26,000	26,000	26,000	26,000	26,000	26,000	26,000
Oil pipeline [4]	218,393	213,605	208,752	181,912	176,996	159,889	159,889	159,512	169,346
Gas pipeline [5] (1,000) . . .	1,052	1,119	1,189	1,278	1,369	1,424	1,462	1,438	(NA)

NA Not available. [1] Also called metropolitan rail or regional rail. [2] Also called metro, subway, rapid transit, or rapid rail. [3] Also called streetcar, tramway, or trolley. [4] Includes trunk and gathering lines for crude-oil pipeline. [5] Excludes service pipelines.

Source: U.S. Bureau of Transportation Statistics, *National Transportation Statistics,* annual. See Internet site <http://www.bts .gov/publications/national_transportation_statistics>.

Table 1027. U.S. Aircraft, Vehicles, and Other Conveyances: 1980 to 2006

[121,601 represents 121,601,000]

System	1980	1990	1995	2000	2002	2004	2005	2006
Air:								
Air carrier [1]	3,808	6,083	7,411	8,055	8,194	8,186	8,225	(NA)
General aviation [2] (active fleet)	211,045	198,000	188,089	217,533	211,244	219,426	224,352	221,943
Highway, registered vehicles (1,000):								
Passenger car	121,601	133,700	128,387	133,621	135,921	136,431	136,568	135,400
Motorcycle	5,694	4,259	3,897	4,346	5,004	5,768	6,227	6,686
Van, pick-up, SUV	27,876	48,275	65,738	79,085	85,011	91,845	95,337	99,125
Truck	5,791	6,196	6,719	8,023	7,927	8,171	8,482	8,819
Bus.	529	627	686	746	761	795	807	822
Transit: [3]								
Motor bus	59,411	58,714	67,107	75,013	76,190	81,033	82,027	83,080
Light rail cars [4]	1,013	913	999	1,577	1,445	1,622	1,645	1,801
Heavy rail cars [5]	9,641	10,419	10,157	10,591	10,718	10,858	11,110	11,052
Trolley bus	823	832	885	951	600	597	615	609
Commuter rail cars and locomotives . . .	4,500	4,415	4,565	5,073	5,300	6,228	6,392	6,403
Demand response	(X)	16,471	29,352	33,080	34,699	37,078	41,958	43,509
Other [6]	(NA)	1,197	2,809	5,208	6,330	6,566	7,251	8,741
Rail:								
Class I, freight cars (1,000)	1,168	659	583	560	478	474	475	475
Class I, locomotive	28,094	18,835	18,812	20,028	20,506	22,015	22,779	23,732
Nonclass I freight cars	102,161	103,527	84,724	132,448	130,590	120,169	120,195	120,688
Car companies' and shippers'								
freight cars	440,552	449,832	550,717	688,194	691,329	693,978	717,211	750,404
Amtrak, passenger train car.	2,128	1,863	1,722	1,894	2,896	1,211	1,186	1,191
Amtrak, locomotive	419	318	313	378	372	276	258	319
Water:								
Non-self-propelled vessels [7]	31,662	31,209	31,360	33,152	32,381	31,296	32,052	(NA)
Self-propelled vessels [8]	7,126	8,236	8,281	8,202	8,621	8,994	8,976	(NA)
Ocean-going steam and motor ships								
(1,000 gross tons and over).	849	635	512	461	443	412	357	(NA)
Recreational boats (1,000)	8,578	10,997	11,735	12,782	12,854	12,781	12,942	12,746

NA Not available. X Not applicable. [1] Air carrier aircraft are those carrying passengers or cargo for hire under 14 CFR 121 and 14 CFR 135. [2] Includes air taxi aircraft. [3] 2006 data are preliminary. [4] Fixed rail streetcar or trolley, for example. [5] Metro, subway, or rapid transit, for example. [6] Includes aerial tramway, automated guideway transit, cablecar, ferry boat, inclined plane, monorail, and vanpool. [7] Includes dry-cargo barges, tank barges, and railroad-car floats. [8] Includes dry-cargo and/or passenger, offshore supply vessels, railroad-car ferries, tankers, and towboats.

Source: U.S. Bureau of Transportation Statistics, *National Transportation Statistics,* annual. See <http://www.bts.gov/publications /national_transportation_statistics/>.

656 Transportation

Table 1028. U.S. Freight Gateways—Value of Shipments: 2006

[In billions of dollars, except as indicated (2,892.3 represents $2,892,300,000,000). For the top 50 gateways ranked by value of shipments. Excludes imports of less than $1,250, exports less than $2,500, and intransit shipments]

Port	Mode	Rank	Total trade	Exports	Imports	Exports as a percent of total
Total U.S. merchandise trade	(X)	(X)	**2,892.3**	**1037.1**	**1,855.1**	**35.9**
Top 50 gateways	(X)	(X)	2,271.9	811.9	1,460.0	35.7
As a percent of total	(X)	(X)	78.6	78.3	78.7	(X)
Port of Los Angeles, CA	Water	1	170.0	26.3	143.7	15.5
Port of New York, NY and NJ	Water	2	149.3	33.2	116.1	22.3
JFK International Airport, NY	Air	3	147.8	68.4	79.4	46.3
Port of Detroit, MI	Land	4	137.2	72.8	64.5	53.0
Port of Long Beach, CA	Water	5	134.7	21.4	113.3	15.9
Port of Laredo, TX	Land	6	104.0	45.8	58.2	44.0
Port of Houston, TX	Water	7	102.9	41.9	60.9	40.8
Los Angeles International Airport, CA	Air	8	79.1	41.0	38.0	51.9
Chicago, IL	Air	9	78.1	31.3	46.7	40.1
Port of Buffalo-Niagara Falls, NY	Land	10	75.5	35.5	40.0	47.0
Port of Huron, MI	Land	11	70.3	25.5	44.9	36.2
San Francisco International Airport, CA	Air	12	63.8	29.5	34.3	46.2
Port of Charleston, SC	Water	13	55.1	16.1	39.1	29.1
Port of El Paso, TX	Land	14	46.7	21.0	25.7	44.9
Anchorage, AK	Air	15	44.6	11.5	33.2	25.7
Port of Norfolk Harbor, VA	Water	16	44.5	17.4	27.1	39.0
Dallas-Fort Worth, TX	Air	17	41.6	17.5	24.1	42.1
Port of Savannah, GA	Water	18	39.7	13.6	26.1	34.2
Port of Baltimore, MD	Water	19	36.6	9.6	27.0	26.3
Port of Seattle, WA	Water	20	34.6	8.6	26.0	24.8
Port of South Louisiana, LA	Air	21	34.1	14.2	20.0	41.5
Port of Oakland, CA	Water	22	33.3	9.8	23.6	29.3
Atlanta, GA	Air	23	33.2	12.4	20.9	37.2
Port of Tacoma, WA	Water	24	32.6	4.9	27.7	15.1
Miami International Airport, FL	Air	25	30.3	20.7	9.6	68.2
Port of Otay Mesa Station, CA	Land	26	28.6	9.9	18.7	34.8
Port of Oakland, CA	Water	27	26.0	11.5	14.5	44.4
Port of New Orleans, LA	Air	28	25.8	16.1	9.7	62.4
Cleveland, OH	Water	29	25.6	0.1	25.4	0.5
Port of Morgan City, LA	Water	30	22.0	1.9	20.2	8.5
Port of Beaumont, TX	Water	31	21.2	8.7	12.5	41.1
Port of Jacksonville, FL	Water	32	20.7	1.7	19.0	8.2
Port of Philadelphia, PA	Water	33	20.3	8.9	11.4	43.8
Port of Miami, FL	Land	34	20.0	8.3	11.8	41.2
Port of Hidalgo, TX	Land	35	19.9	7.2	12.8	36.1
Port of Champlain-Rouses Pt., NY	Water	36	19.0	3.3	15.7	17.4
Port of Corpus Christi, TX	Land	37	18.9	6.3	12.5	33.6
Port of Nogales, AZ	Water	38	18.6	8.0	10.5	43.4
Port of Blaine, WA	Land	39	17.1	8.8	8.4	51.1
Port of Pembina, ND	Land	40	15.4	8.5	6.9	55.1
Port of Newark Liberty International, NJ	Air	41	15.2	3.1	12.1	20.3
Port of Dulles International, DC	Air	42	15.1	5.1	10.0	33.7
Port of Portland, OR	Water	43	14.1	2.6	11.5	18.3
Port of Texas City, TX	Water	44	13.7	1.6	12.0	11.9
Port of General Edward Lawrence Logan International, MA	Air	45	13.6	8.3	5.3	61.0
Port of Luis Munoz Marin International, PR	Air	46	12.6	7.6	5.0	60.5
Port of Brownsville-Cameron, TX	Land	47	12.4	6.8	5.6	54.9
Port of Sweetgrass, MT	Land	48	12.2	6.3	6.0	51.1
Port of Alexandria Bay, NY	Land	49	12.2	4.7	7.5	38.9
Port of Portal, ND	Land	50	11.9	6.8	5.1	57.2

X Not applicable.

Source: U.S. Bureau of Transportation Statistics, *National Transportation Statistics,* annual. See <http://www.bts.gov/publications /national_transportation_statistics/>.

U.S. Census Bureau, Statistical Abstract of the United States: 2009

Table 1029. Transportation and Warehousing—Establishments, Revenue, Payroll, and Employees by Industry: 2002

[**382,152 represents $382,152,000,000.** For establishments with payroll. Based on the 2002 Economic Censuses; See Appendix III]

Kind of business	2002 NAICS code [1]	Number of establishments	Revenue (mil. dol.)	Annual payroll (mil. dol.)	Paid employees (1,000)
Transportation and warehousing	48-49	199,618	382,152	115,989	3,650.9
Air transportation [2]	481	3,847	19,735	3,805	99.1
Scheduled air transportation [2]	4811	1,665	12,157	2,281	67.1
Nonscheduled air transportation	4812	2,182	7,578	1,524	32.0
Water transportation	483	1,890	23,331	3,194	66.2
Deep sea, coastal, and Great Lakes water transportation	4831	1,314	19,788	2,329	47.9
Truck transportation	484	112,642	164,219	47,750	1,435.2
General freight trucking	4841	59,011	110,239	34,121	989.2
Specialized freight trucking	4842	53,631	53,980	13,630	446.0
Transit and ground passenger transportation [3]	485	17,260	18,850	7,675	398.4
Urban transit systems	4851	1,025	2,808	1,694	53.6
Taxi and limousine service	4853	6,988	4,248	1,185	66.1
School and employee bus transportation	4854	4,515	5,928	2,610	174.7
Charter bus industry	4855	1,249	1,762	565	29.3
Pipeline transportation [3]	486	2,188	22,031	2,477	36.8
Pipeline transportation of crude oil	4861	252	3,402	485	6.5
Pipeline transportation of natural gas	4862	1,431	14,797	1,575	23.7
Scenic and sightseeing transportation	487	2,523	1,859	526	22.5
Support activities for transportation [3]	488	33,942	57,414	16,202	465.6
Support activities for air transportation	4881	4,976	12,181	3,746	129.6
Support activities for water transportation	4883	2,366	8,812	2,604	64.0
Support activities for road transportation	4884	7,927	4,003	1,356	56.0
Freight transportation arrangement	4885	16,504	27,656	6,868	168.6
Couriers and messengers	492	12,655	58,165	17,175	561.5
Couriers	4921	7,382	54,821	16,180	514.9
Local messengers and local delivery	4922	5,273	3,344	995	46.6
Warehousing and storage	493	12,671	16,548	17,183	565.5

[1] North American Industry Classification System, 2002; see text Section 15.   [2] Excludes large certificated passenger carriers that do not report to the Office of Airline Information, U.S. Department of Transportation.   [3] Includes other industries not shown separately.

Source: U.S. Census Bureau, "2002 Economic Census, Geographic Area Series Reports, Transportation and Warehousing," Series EC02-48A-US; issued August 2005. See <http://www.census.gov/econ/census02/guide/geosumm.htm>.

Table 1030. U.S. Scheduled Airline Industry—Summary: 1995 to 2007

[**For calendar years or Dec. 31 (547.8 represents 547,800,000).** For domestic and international operations. Covers carriers certificated under Section 401 of the Federal Aviation Act. Minus sign (–) indicates loss]

Item	Unit	1995	2000	2002 [1]	2003 [2]	2004	2005	2006	2007
SCHEDULED SERVICE									
Revenue passengers enplaned . . .	Mil.	547.8	666.2	612.9	646.3	702.9	738.6	744.2	769.2
Revenue passenger miles	Bil.	540.7	692.8	641.1	656.9	733.6	779.0	796.8	829.0
Available seat miles	Bil.	807.1	957.0	892.6	893.8	971.4	1,003.3	1,005.5	1,037.1
Revenue passenger load factor . .	Percent . . .	67.0	72.4	71.8	73.5	75.5	77.6	79.2	79.9
Mean passenger trip length [3]	Miles.	987	1,040	1,046	1,016	1,044	1,055	1,071	1,078
Cargo ton miles	Mil.	16,921	23,888	24,591	26,735	27,978	28,036	29,339	29,524
Aircraft departures	1,000	8,062	9,035	9,187	10,839	11,398	11,562	11,264	11,365
FINANCES [4]									
Total operating revenue [5]	**Mil. dol. . .**	**95,117**	**130,839**	**106,985**	**117,920**	**134,300**	**151,255**	**164,912**	**173,104**
Passenger revenue	Mil. dol. . . .	69,835	93,622	73,577	77,379	85,669	93,500	101,419	107,011
Cargo revenue.	Mil. dol. . . .	9,882	14,456	13,525	15,003	17,146	20,704	22,848	24,531
Charter revenue.	Mil. dol. . . .	3,742	4,913	4,225	5,589	5,503	6,074	6,026	4,911
Total operating expense	Mil. dol. . . .	89,266	123,840	115,552	120,028	135,782	150,828	157,398	163,894
Operating profit (or loss)	Mil. dol. . . .	5,852	6,999	–8,566	–2,108	–1,491	427	7,514	9,210
Interest income (or expense)	Mil. dol. . . .	–2,426	–2,193	–3,263	–3,442	–3,715	–4,209	–4,150	–3,837
Net profit (or loss)	Mil. dol. . . .	2,283	2,486	–11,008	–2,371	–7,643	–5,782	3,123	4,998
Revenue per passenger mile	Cents	12.9	13.5	11.5	11.8	11.7	12.0	12.7	12.9
Operating profit margin	Percent . . .	6.2	5.3	–8.0	–1.8	–1.1	0.3	4.6	5.3
Net profit margin	Percent . . .	2.4	1.9	–10.3	–2.0	–5.7	–3.8	1.9	2.9
EMPLOYEES [6]									
Total	1,000	547.0	680.0	601.4	569.8	569.5	562.5	545.7	561.0
Pilots and copilots.	1,000	55.4	72.4	68.8	67.8	82.0	74.5	71.1	69.4

[1] Includes cash compensation remitted to carriers under the Air Transportation Safety and System Stabilization Act (P.L. 107-42).   [2] Includes security costs reimbursements remitted to carriers under the Emergency Wartime Supplemental Appropriations Act (P.L. 108-11).   [3] For definition of mean, see Guide to Tabular Presentation.   [4] 2007 data are preliminary.   [5] Includes other types of revenues not shown separately.   [6] Average full-time equivalents.

Source: Air Transport Association of America, Washington, DC, *Air Transport Annual Report*.

Table 1031. Transportation and Warehousing—Establishments, Employees, and Payroll by Kind of Business (NAICS Basis): 2000 and 2005

[3,790.0 represents 3,790,000. Covers establishments with payroll. Employees are for the week including March 12. Excludes most government employees, railroad employees, and self-employed persons. For statement on methodology, see Appendix III. County Business Patterns excludes rail transportation (NAICS 482) and the National Postal Service (NAICS 491)]

Industry	2002 NAICS code [1]	Establishments		Paid employees [2] (1,000)		Annual payroll (mil. dol.)	
		2000	2005	2000	2005	2000	2005
Transportation & warehousing	**48–49**	**190,044**	**211,150**	**3,790.0**	**4,168.0**	**125,592.4**	**154,375.9**
Air transportation	481	5,429	5,715	615.6	486.4	26,569.3	24,222.7
Scheduled air transportation	4811	3,324	3,213	570.9	446.6	24,484.5	22,066.7
Scheduled passenger air transportation . . .	481111	2,740	2,759	536.2	424.7	23,470.7	21,279.8
Scheduled freight air transportation	481112	584	454	34.7	21.9	1,013.8	786.9
Nonscheduled air transportation	4812	2,105	2,502	44.7	39.8	2,084.8	2,156.0
Water transportation	483	1,900	1,946	67.6	65.5	3,003.2	3,731.9
Deep sea, coastal, & Great Lakes water transportation	4831	1,254	1,299	47.8	46.0	2,214.2	2,767.1
Inland water transportation	4832	646	647	19.7	19.5	789.0	964.8
Inland water freight transportation	483211	402	384	16.3	19.5	673.9	964.8
Inland water passenger transportation	483212	244	263	3.5	15.6	115.1	822.2
Truck transportation	484	110,416	117,224	1,415.8	1,478.3	46,451.5	54,774.5
General freight trucking	4841	55,874	64,877	922.7	1,013.7	31,614.0	38,280.1
General freight trucking, local.	48411	20,329	26,454	153.3	191.1	4,529.8	6,745.5
General freight trucking, long distance. . . .	48412	35,545	38,423	769.5	822.6	27,084.2	31,534.6
Specialized freight trucking	4842	54,542	52,347	493.1	464.6	14,837.5	16,494.4
Used household & office goods moving . . .	48421	9,147	8,711	128.9	110.7	3,661.4	3,453.0
Specialized freight (except used goods) trucking, local	48422	32,493	31,948	200.4	205.2	5,692.4	7,295.6
Specialized freight (except used goods) trucking, long-distance	48423	12,902	11,688	163.7	148.7	5,483.7	5,745.8
Transit & ground passenger transportation	485	16,383	17,266	386.9	406.7	7,214.7	8,520.8
Urban transit systems	4851	705	926	43.1	51.8	1,295.8	1,650.6
Mixed mode systems	485111	152	60	6.2	1.5	146.9	43.2
Commuter rail	485112	15	18	(D)	0.5	(D)	15.9
Bus and other motor vehicle mode systems	485113	505	807	31.4	46.8	925.1	1,450.7
Other	485119	33	41	(D)	2.9	(D)	140.7
Interurban & rural bus transportation	4852	444	491	26.8	16.8	709.7	470.5
Taxi & limousine service	4853	6,806	7,082	67.8	65.3	1,244.3	1,405.1
Taxi service	48531	3,116	3,009	30.4	29.0	485.2	563.1
Limousine service	48532	3,690	4,073	37.5	36.3	759.1	842.0
School & employee bus transportation	4854	4,217	4,325	162.9	186.8	2,322.6	3,118.4
Charter bus industry	4855	1,451	1,234	34.1	26.8	668.7	603.4
Other transit & ground passenger transportation	4859	2,760	3,208	52.2	59.2	973.6	1,272.8
Special needs transportation	485991	1,914	2,117	34.8	44.9	648.9	983.1
Pipeline transportation.	486	2,802	2,681	53.0	38.1	3,828.6	2,901.8
Pipeline transportation of crude oil	4861	307	409	6.7	6.0	425.6	505.3
Pipeline transportation of natural gas	4862	1,938	1,546	39.2	24.1	2,961.1	1,809.9
Other pipeline transportation	4869	557	726	7.0	7.9	441.9	586.6
Scenic & sightseeing transportation	487	2,254	2,752	23.6	24.2	583.5	717.1
Scenic & sightseeing transportation, land . . .	4871	454	650	8.7	9.0	192.8	224.6
Scenic & sightseeing transportation, water . . .	4872	1,642	1,928	13.0	12.9	331.2	407.6
Scenic & sightseeing transportation, other . . .	4879	158	174	2.0	2.2	59.5	84.9
Support activities for transportation	488	31,440	36,221	472.4	543.7	16,507.0	21,831.3
Support activities for air transportation	4881	4,368	5,066	126.7	146.1	3,634.0	4,891.1
Airport operations	48811	1,834	1,589	67.9	67.1	1,569.5	1,652.8
Air traffic control	488111	137	152	0.8	1.5	29.9	65.7
Other support activities for air transportation	48819	2,534	3,477	58.8	79.0	2,064.6	3,238.3
Support activities for rail transportation	4882	821	974	21.4	27.0	714.4	1,017.7
Support activities for water transportation . . .	4883	2,543	2,359	81.6	89.0	3,250.7	4,445.7
Port and harbor operations	48831	196	244	7.4	7.5	265.8	319.3
Marine cargo handling	48832	607	549	53.5	59.7	2,194.7	3,034.7
Navigational services to shipping	48833	863	803	11.8	10.8	478.7	584.7
Other	48839	877	763	8.9	11.0	311.5	507.0
Support activities for road transportation	4884	7,010	9,352	56.2	70.1	1,308.6	1,998.0
Motor vehicle towing	48841	6,078	7,686	41.8	50.2	961.7	1,443.8
Freight transportation arrangement.	4885	15,177	16,868	161.7	182.0	6,620.3	8,320.3
Other support activities for transportation . . .	4889	1,521	1,602	24.7	29.6	978.6	1,158.5
Couriers & messengers	492	12,297	13,862	619.3	547.3	17,399.4	17,531.7
Couriers	4921	6,667	8,703	548.9	499.7	15,890.5	16,429.7
Local messengers & local delivery	4922	5,630	5,159	70.5	47.5	1,508.9	1,102.0
Warehousing & storage	493	7,123	13,483	135.9	578.0	4,035.3	20,144.1

D Figure withheld to avoid disclosure pertaining to individual companies.   [1] Based on the North American Industry Classification System (NAICS), 2002; see text, Section 15.   [2] For employees on the payroll for the pay period including March 12.

Source: U.S. Census Bureau, "County Business Patterns." See <http://www.census.gov/epcd/cbp/view/cbpview.html>.

U.S. Census Bureau, Statistical Abstract of the United States: 2009

Table 1032. Transportation Accidents, Deaths, and Injuries: 1990 to 2006

[6,471 represents 6,471,000]

Mode	Accidents					Deaths					Injuries				
	1990	1995	2000	2005	2006	1990	1995	2000	2005	2006	1990	1995	2000	2005	2006
Transit type:															
Land:															
Highway crashes (1,000) [1]	6,471	6,699	6,394	6,159	5,973	44.6	41.8	41.9	43.5	42.6	3,231	3,465	3,189	2,699	2,575
Passenger car occupants	5,561	5,594	4,926	4,499	4,342	24.1	22.4	20.7	18.5	17.8	2,376	2,469	2,052	1,573	1,475
Motorcyclists	103	66	69	101	101	3.2	2.2	2.9	4.6	4.8	84	57	58	87	88
Light truck occupants	2,152	2,750	3,208	3,382	3,355	8.6	9.6	11.5	13.0	12.7	505	722	887	872	857
Large truck occupants	372	363	438	423	368	0.7	0.6	0.8	0.8	0.8	42	30	31	27	23
Bus occupants	60	59	56	50	52	(Z)	(Z)	(Z)	0.1	(Z)	33	19	18	11	10
Pedestrians	(NA)	(NA)	(NA)	(NA)	(NA)	6.5	5.6	4.8	4.9	4.8	105	86	78	64	61
Pedacyclists	(NA)	(NA)	(NA)	(NA)	(NA)	0.9	0.8	0.7	0.8	0.8	75	67	51	45	44
Other	(NA)	(NA)	(NA)	(NA)	(NA)	0.6	0.5	0.6	0.8	0.9	11	14	15	18	18
Railroad [2]	8,594	7,092	6,485	6,299	5,823	1,297	1,146	937	887	911	25,143	14,440	11,643	9,402	8,189
Highway-rail grade crossing	5,715	4,633	3,502	3,053	2,920	698	579	425	358	368	2,407	1,894	1,219	1,020	1,021
Railroad [9]	2,879	2,459	2,983	3,246	2,903	599	567	512	529	543	22,736	12,546	10,424	8,382	7,168
Rapid rail transit	12,178	14,327	12,782	(NA)	(NA)	117	79	80	(NA)	(NA)	10,036	11,238	10,848	(NA)	(NA)
Air:															
Air carrier [3]	24	36	56	40	31	39	168	92	22	50	29	25	29	13	9
Commuter [4]	15	12	12	6	3	6	9	5	–	2	11	17	7	–	1
On-demand [5]	107	75	80	66	54	51	52	71	18	16	36	14	12	20	16
General aviation	2,242	2,056	1,837	1,669	1,515	770	735	596	563	698	409	396	309	269	261
Water:															
Recreational [6]	6,411	8,019	7,740	4,969	4,967	865	829	701	697	710	3,822	4,141	4,355	3,451	4,474
Waterborne (vessel related) [7]	3,613	5,349	5,403	4,977	5,400	85	53	53	45	48	175	154	150	140	177
Pipeline: [8]															
Gas	198	161	234	351	276	6	18	37	14	19	69	53	77	45	30
Hazard liquid	180	188	146	138	110	3	3	1	2	–	7	11	4	2	2
Other transit [9]	77,985	48,144	47,116	(NA)	(NA)	222	195	215	(NA)	(NA)	44,520	45,958	45,849	(NA)	(NA)
Hazardous materials [10]	8,879	14,853	17,557	(NA)	(NA)	8	7	16	(NA)	(NA)	423	400	251	(NA)	(NA)

– Represents or rounds to zero.   NA Not available.   Z Less than 50.   [1] Data on deaths are from U.S. National Highway Traffic Safety Administration and are based on deaths within 30 days of the accident. Includes only police reported crashes. For more details, see Table 1071.   [2] Accidents which result in damages to railroad property. Grade crossing accidents are also included when classified as a train accident. Deaths exclude fatalities in railroad-highway grade crossing accidents.   [3] See footnote 1, Table 1037. Injuries classified as serious.   [4] See footnote 2, Table 1037. Injuries classified as serious.   [5] See footnote 3, Table 1037. Injuries classified as serious.   [6] Accidents resulting in death, injury, or requiring medical treatment beyond first aid; damages exceeding $500; or a person's disappearance.   [7] Covers accidents involving commercial vessels which must be reported to U.S. Coast Guard if there is property damage exceeding $25,000; material damage affecting the seaworthiness or efficiency of a vessel; stranding or grounding; loss of life; or injury causing a person's incapacity for more than 3 days.   [8] Beginning 1990, pipeline accidents/incidents are credited to year of occurrence; prior data are credited to the year filed.   [9] Other transit includes bus, light rail, commuter rail, demand response, van pool, and automated guideway. Excludes cable car, inclined plane, jitney, and ferry boat.   [10] Incidents, deaths, and injuries involving hazardous materials cover all types of transport, excludes pipelines and bulk, nonpackaged water incidents.

Source: U.S. Bureau of Transportation Statistics, National Transportation Statistics, annual. See <http://www.bts.gov/publications/national_transportation_statistics/>.

Table 1033. **Airline Cost Indexes: 1980 to 2007**

[2000 = 100. Data prior to 1990 excludes passenger airlines with annual revenue less than $100 million]

Index	1980	1990	1995	2000	2001	2002	2003	2004	2005	2006	2007
Composite index [1]	**81.5**	**104.5**	**99.8**	**100.0**	**106.6**	**110.9**	**116.6**	**133.7**	**166.0**	**184.3**	**189.1**
Labor costs.	84.7	72.7	91.0	100.0	110.0	118.2	122.2	122.1	116.2	117.8	116.7
Fuel.	123.4	101.9	71.1	100.0	91.9	93.9	113.7	151.1	215.0	261.4	276.1
Aircraft ownership [2]	25.8	57.4	72.8	100.0	99.1	90.6	86.9	91.5	85.9	84.0	81.7
Nonaircraft ownership	37.8	88.8	104.0	100.0	140.0	112.0	112.9	105.0	102.3	100.4	99.8
Professional services	28.8	68.3	86.9	100.0	103.2	96.4	96.5	97.1	105.4	110.9	114.4
Food and beverage	91.4	125.9	107.6	100.0	92.2	86.8	72.7	67.3	62.6	58.8	57.5
Landing fees	55.6	83.2	97.7	100.0	111.7	117.1	108.7	118.6	126.1	133.2	129.4
Maintenance material	65.1	136.7	93.1	100.0	95.3	74.0	62.8	61.6	52.7	54.8	60.4
Aircraft insurance	221.8	117.1	264.7	100.0	117.0	218.3	151.2	149.0	125.0	143.8	128.2
Nonaircraft insurance	71.1	70.4	229.4	100.0	169.8	540.0	423.9	352.2	307.4	245.8	205.0
Passenger commissions	121.8	237.0	184.8	100.0	86.1	57.3	41.8	37.3	32.5	29.9	29.8
Communication	53.3	86.9	88.2	100.0	110.9	101.4	85.1	77.3	74.4	69.7	70.7
Advertising and promotion . . .	117.4	165.8	108.5	100.0	85.4	74.3	68.2	77.1	75.5	81.2	66.2
Utilities and office supplies. . .	65.8	94.2	84.6	100.0	108.0	90.1	79.7	80.0	84.1	91.3	96.5
Transportation-related expenses	(NA)	45.4	47.8	100.0	111.5	107.0	202.2	285.4	379.5	408.3	408.4
Other operating expenses . . .	85.5	101.9	93.9	100.0	99.9	112.9	91.6	96.1	111.6	102.1	107.2
Interest [3]	153.1	170.6	165.3	100.0	96.8	87.9	91.6	91.5	124.8	123.6	114.8

NA Not available.   [1] Weighted average of all components, including interest.   [2] Includes lease, aircraft and engine rentals, depreciation, and amortization.   [3] Interest on long-term debt and capital and other interest expense.

Source: Air Transport Association of America, Washington, DC, *U.S. Passenger Airline Cost Index, Major and National Carriers.* See <http://www.airlines.org/economics/> (accessed 17 July 2008).

Table 1034. **Top 40 Airports in 2006—Passengers Enplaned: 1996 and 2006**

[In thousands (558,559 represents 558,559,000), except rank. For calendar year. Airports ranked by total passengers enplaned by large certificated air carriers on scheduled and nonscheduled operations, 2006]

Airport	1996 Total	1996 Rank	2006 Total	2006 Rank	Airport	1996 Total	1996 Rank	2006 Total	2006 Rank
All airports	**558,559**	**(X)**	**691,171**	**(X)**	Baltimore, MD (BWI Intl) . . .	5,907	29	10,020	22
Total, top 40	424,361	(X)	532,456	(X)	Washington, DC (Dulles Intl) .	4,758	35	9,553	23
Atlanta, GA (Hartsfield Intl) . .	30,407	2	40,561	1	Fort Lauderdale Intl, FL	4,848	32	9,425	24
Chicago, IL (O'Hare Intl)	30,526	1	34,539	2	Chicago, IL (Midway)	4,436	38	8,913	25
Dallas/Ft. Worth Intl, TX	26,639	3	28,333	3	Tampa, FL (Tampa Intl)	5,721	30	8,847	26
Los Angeles Intl, CA	22,799	4	23,121	4	Washington, DC (Ronald Reagan Washington Natl) . .	6,772	26	8,839	27
Denver Intl, CO.	15,246	6	22,240	5	San Diego Intl, CA	6,549	27	8,612	28
Las Vegas, NV (McCarran Intl).	14,116	9	21,147	6	Honolulu Intl, HI	9,036	23	8,305	29
Phoenix Sky Harbor Intl, AZ .	14,808	7	20,331	7	Cincinnati, OH (Cincinnati/ Northern Kentucky Intl)	7,302	25	7,939	30
Houston Intercontinental, TX .	11,622	14	19,613	8	Oakland, CA (Oakland Intl) . .	4,684	36	6,990	31
Detroit, MI (Wayne County) . .	14,117	8	17,281	9	St. Louis, MO (Lambert-St. Louis)	13,547	10	6,937	32
Minneapolis-St. Paul Intl, MN.	12,616	12	17,135	10	Portland, OR (Portland Intl) . .	6,126	28	6,812	33
Newark Intl, NJ	12,952	11	16,272	11	Memphis, TN (Memphis Intl) .	3,944	41	5,508	34
Orlando Intl, FL.	10,847	16	15,378	12	Kansas City Intl, MO	4,820	34	5,418	35
Philadelphia Intl, PA	9,704	19	14,965	13	Cleveland, OH (Cleveland-Hopkins Intl)	5,287	31	5,289	36
New York, NY (JFK Intl)	8,572	24	14,438	14	San Jose Intl, CA	4,826	33	5,197	37
Seattle, WA (Seattle-Tacoma Intl)	11,487	15	14,291	15	Sacramento Intl, CA	3,321	45	5,125	38
Charlotte-Douglas Intl, NC . .	10,008	18	14,108	16	San Juan, PR (Luis Munoz Marin Intl)	4,550	37	5,070	39
San Francisco Intl, CA	16,308	5	13,907	17	Santa Ana, CA (John Wayne-Orange County) . . .	3,533	43	4,776	40
Miami Intl, FL	11,908	13	12,781	18					
Boston, MA (Logan Intl)	10,654	17	12,093	19					
New York, NY (LaGuardia) . .	9,594	20	12,071	20					
Salt Lake City Intl, UT	9,463	21	10,278	21					

X Not applicable.

Source: U.S. Bureau of Transportation Statisics, Office of Airline Information, BTS Form 41, Schedule T-3, unpublished data.

Table 1035. **Domestic Airline Markets: 2007**

[In thousands (3,532 represents 3,532,000). For calendar year. Data are for the 25 top markets and include all commercial airports in each metro area. Data represent origin and final destination of travel]

Market	Passengers	Market	Passengers
New York-Chicago	3,532	Dallas/Fort Worth-Houston	1,567
New York-Fort Lauderdale	3,487	Washington, DC-New York	1,520
New York-Orlando.	3,229	Washington, DC-Chicago	1,512
New York- Los Angeles	2,756	Dallas/Fort Worth-New York	1,460
New York- Atlanta	2,568	Chicago-Los Angeles.	1,451
New York- San Francisco	2,123	Chicago-Orlando.	1,437
Honolulu-Kahului	1,942	Chicago-Phoenix	1,368
New York-Las Vegas	1,765	Orlando-Philadelphia	1,352
New York-West Palm Beach	1,725	Honolulu-Lihue	1,348
New York-Miami	1,683	San Juan-New York	1,322
New York-Boston	1,661	Los Angeles-San Francisco	1,307
New York-Tampa	1,641	Los Angeles-Las Vegas	1,295
Chicago-Las Vegas	1,600		

Source: Air Transport Association of America, Washington, DC, *Annual Report.*

Transportation   661

Table 1036. **Worldwide Airline Fatalities: 1988 to 2007**

[For scheduled air transport operations. Excludes accidents due to acts of unlawful interference]

Year	Fatal accidents	Passenger deaths	Death rate [1]	Year	Fatal accidents	Passenger deaths	Death rate [1]
1988	29	742	0.07	1998	20	904	0.05
1989	29	879	0.08	1999	21	499	0.03
1990	27	544	0.05	2000	18	757	0.04
1991	29	638	0.06	2001	13	577	0.03
1992	28	1,070	0.09	2002	14	791	0.04
1993	33	864	0.07	2003	7	466	0.02
1994	27	1,170	0.09	2004	9	203	0.01
1995	25	711	0.05	2005	17	712	0.03
1996	24	1,146	0.07	2006	23	755	0.02
1997	25	921	0.06	2007	11	587	0.01

[1] Rate per 100 million passenger kilometers flown.

Source: International Civil Aviation Organization, Montreal, Canada, *Civil Aviation Statistics of the World,* annual.

Table 1037. **Aircraft Accidents: 1990 to 2007**

[For years ending December 31]

Item	Unit	1990	1995	2000	2004	2005	2006	2007, prel.
Air carrier accidents, all services [1]	Number. . .	24	36	56	30	40	33	26
Fatal accidents	Number. . .	6	3	3	2	3	2	1
Fatalities	Number. . .	39	168	92	14	22	50	1
Aboard	Number. . .	12	162	92	14	20	49	1
Rates per 100,000 flight hours:								
Accidents	Rate	0.198	0.267	0.306	0.159	0.206	0.171	0.135
Fatal accidents	Rate	0.049	0.022	0.016	0.011	0.015	0.010	0.005
Commuter air carrier accidents [2]	Number. . .	15	12	12	4	6	3	3
Fatal accidents	Number. . .	3	2	1	–	–	1	–
Fatalities	Number. . .	6	9	5	–	–	2	–
Aboard	Number. . .	4	9	5	–	–	2	–
Rates per 100,000 flight hours:								
Accidents	Rate	0.641	0.457	3.247	1.324	2.002	0.995	0.993
Fatal accidents	Rate	0.128	0.076	0.271	–	–	0.332	–
On-demand air taxi accidents [3]	Number. . .	107	75	80	66	65	53	62
Fatal accidents	Number. . .	29	24	22	23	11	10	14
Fatalities	Number. . .	51	52	71	64	18	16	43
Aboard	Number. . .	49	52	68	63	16	16	43
Rates per 100,000 flight hours:								
Accidents	Rate	4.76	3.02	2.04	2.04	1.70	1.42	1.69
Fatal accidents	Rate	1.29	0.97	0.56	0.71	0.29	0.27	0.38
General aviation accidents [4]	Number. . .	2,242	2,056	1,837	1,617	1,670	1,518	1,631
Fatal accidents	Number. . .	444	413	345	314	321	306	284
Fatalities	Number. . .	770	735	596	559	563	703	491
Aboard	Number. . .	765	728	585	559	558	543	486
Rates per 100,000 flight hours:								
Accidents	Rate	7.85	8.21	6.57	6.49	7.20	6.33	6.84
Fatal accidents	Rate	1.55	1.63	1.21	1.26	1.38	1.27	1.19

– Represents zero. [1] U.S. air carriers operating under 14 CFR 121. Beginning 2000, includes aircraft with 10 or more seats, previously operating under 14 CFR 135. [2] All scheduled service of U.S. air carriers operating under 14 CFR 135. Beginning 2000, only aircraft with fewer than 10 seats. [3] All nonscheduled service of U.S. air carriers operating under 14 CFR 135. [4] U.S. civil registered aircraft not operated under 14 CFR 121 or 135. Data from 2006 include 154 deaths aboard a foreign registed aircraft when it collided with a business general aviation aircraft over the Brazilian Amazon jungle. There were no fatalities in the general aviation aircraft.

Source: U.S. National Transportation Safety Board, "Aviation Accident Statistics." See <http://www.ntsb.gov/aviation/stats.htm>; (accessed 16 April 2008).

Table 1038. **U.S. Carrier Delays, Cancellations, and Diversions: 1995 to 2006**

[In thousands (5,327.4 represents 5,327,400). For calendar year. See headnote, table 1039]

Item	1995	1998	1999	2000	2001	2002	2003	2004	2005	2006
Total operations. . .	5,327.4	5,384.7	5,527.9	5,683.0	5,967.8	5,271.4	6,488.5	7,129.3	7,140.6	7,141.9
Delays:										
Late departures [1]	827.9	870.4	937.3	1,131.7	953.8	717.4	834.4	1,187.6	1,279.4	1,424.8
Late arrivals [2]	1,039.3	1,070.1	1,152.7	1,356.0	1,104.4	868.2	1,057.8	1,421.4	1,466.1	1,615.5
Cancellations [3]	91.9	144.5	154.3	187.5	231.2	65.1	101.5	127.8	133.7	121.9
Diversions [4]	10.5	13.2	13.6	14.3	12.9	8.4	11.4	13.8	14.0	16.2

[1] Late departures comprise flights departing 15 minutes or more after the scheduled departure time. [2] Late arrivals comprise flights arriving 15 minutes or more after the scheduled arrival time. [3] A cancelled flight is one that was not operated, but was listed in a carrier's computer reservation system within seven days of the scheduled departure. [4] A diverted flight is one that left from the scheduled departure airport but flew to a destination point other than the scheduled destination point.

Source: U.S. Bureau of Transportation Statistics, *National Transportation Statistics,* annual. See also <http://www.bts.gov /programs/airline_information/annual_airline_on_time_performance>.

Table 1039. On-Time Flight Arrivals and Departures at Major U.S. Airports: 2007

[In percent. Quarterly, based on gate arrival and departure times for domestic scheduled operations of U.S. major airlines. All U.S. airlines with 1 percent or more of total U.S. domestic scheduled airline passenger revenues are required to report on-time data. A flight is considered on time if it operated less than 15 minutes after the scheduled time shown in the carrier's computerized reservation system. See source for data on individual airlines]

Airport	On-time arrivals				On-time departures			
	1st qtr.	2d qtr.	3d qtr.	4th qtr.	1st qtr.	2d qtr.	3d qtr.	4th qtr.
Total major airports	**70.8**	**73.2**	**73.9**	**73.4**	**72.9**	**75.4**	**75.2**	**76.4**
Atlanta, Hartsfield.	76.6	77.0	70.1	74.5	73.2	73.5	66.3	74.9
Boston, Logan International	68.7	65.9	71.5	73.2	72.9	73.7	77.2	77.5
Baltimore/Washington International	77.9	76.4	75.5	80.5	78.1	75.0	74.3	79.6
Charlotte, Douglas	65.3	67.3	75.2	77.0	66.2	66.9	75.2	78.7
Cincinnati, Greater Cincinnati	73.0	78.5	77.2	77.9	72.8	80.6	78.6	78.7
Washington, Reagan National.	69.3	69.4	71.7	76.6	74.0	75.2	77.6	81.8
Denver International	72.3	77.0	78.5	75.2	73.0	77.4	78.0	76.7
Dallas-Fort Worth International	71.6	68.0	73.3	75.1	70.2	68.1	71.3	73.2
Detroit, Metro Wayne County	68.4	74.7	76.9	75.1	72.0	77.9	79.2	78.8
Newark International	55.0	57.1	66.7	59.0	65.4	66.4	71.0	68.4
Fort Lauderdale-Hollywood International. . .	70.2	73.2	74.3	76.5	74.6	77.6	81.3	81.0
Washington/Dulles	70.2	71.6	74.3	74.1	71.1	74.8	76.4	75.5
Houston, George Bush	78.1	76.4	80.6	79.8	80.0	76.6	80.0	82.4
New York, JFK International	60.0	59.0	63.5	68.8	64.3	67.4	69.0	75.3
Las Vegas, McCarran International	76.1	77.7	77.4	76.1	75.5	77.0	75.5	77.0
Los Angeles International.	76.1	79.2	76.9	73.4	79.2	82.3	80.6	78.8
New York, La Guardia.	58.1	58.6	62.9	54.4	70.1	72.5	74.1	69.6
Orlando International	74.0	76.8	76.3	78.8	76.3	79.6	78.7	82.4
Chicago, Midway	76.3	79.1	79.1	79.2	71.6	74.1	72.6	74.5
Miami International	71.3	70.2	70.5	71.9	74.6	72.6	71.5	74.1
Minneapolis-St. Paul International	70.9	77.4	69.9	72.0	74.5	81.7	75.9	77.5
Oakland International	79.9	80.9	79.9	78.1	80.0	81.2	78.9	78.9
Chicago, O'Hare	58.5	68.0	70.8	66.0	59.4	69.6	70.4	66.4
Portland International	74.8	78.2	78.8	72.8	82.8	84.9	84.8	81.7
Philadelphia International.	64.9	64.2	67.7	69.5	67.2	67.4	69.9	73.9
Phoenix, Sky Harbor International	75.9	78.7	78.6	78.5	75.8	77.7	77.4	79.4
San Diego, Lindbergh Field	77.6	79.9	79.3	76.8	82.3	84.1	83.0	80.7
Seattle-Tacoma International	70.9	73.3	72.1	69.2	76.4	79.0	74.7	76.1
San Francisco International	72.0	72.2	69.1	66.1	77.1	77.2	75.5	73.1
Salt Lake City International	75.1	85.0	80.7	79.2	79.2	87.7	84.1	84.5
St. Louis, Lambert	73.8	74.7	74.7	76.3	77.3	77.2	77.8	79.2
Tampa, Tampa International	74.4	76.5	76.7	78.4	80.1	81.0	80.7	82.9

Source: U.S. Department of Transportation, Aviation Consumer Protection Division, *Air Travel Consumer Report*, monthly. See <http://airconsumer.ost.dot.gov>.

Table 1040. Consumer Complaints Against U.S. Airlines: 1990 to 2007

[Calendar year data. Represents complaints filed by consumers to the U.S. Department of Transportation, Aviation Consumer Protection Division, regarding service problems with air carrier personnel. See source for data on individual airlines]

Complaint category	1990	2000	2001	2002	2003	2004	2005	2006	2007
Total	**7,703**	**20,564**	**14,076**	**7,697**	**4,601**	**5,839**	**6,900**	**6,452**	**10,960**
Flight problems [1]	3,034	8,698	5,048	1,808	1,049	1,462	1,942	1,845	4,097
Customer service [2]	758	4,074	2,531	1,478	584	742	800	870	1,214
Baggage.	1,329	2,753	1,965	1,082	802	1,085	1,586	1,400	2,154
Ticketing/boarding [3]	624	1,405	1,310	898	643	637	679	708	1,136
Refunds	701	803	942	737	428	376	530	485	745
Fares [4]	312	708	568	436	243	180	219	173	315
Disability [5]	(NA)	612	457	420	325	467	430	368	428
Oversales [6]	399	759	539	364	223	263	284	275	420
Discrimination [7]	(NA)	(NA)	164	176	71	96	100	90	82
Advertising	96	42	42	43	13	41	45	30	34
Tours	29	25	11	(8)	(8)	(8)	(8)	(8)	(8)
Animals	(NA)	1	6	–	2	3	3	3	7
Smoking	74	(9)	(9)	(9)	(9)	(9)	(9)	(9)	(9)
Credit.	5	(9)	(9)	(9)	(9)	(9)	(9)	(9)	(9)
Other.	342	684	493	255	218	487	282	205	328

– Represents zero. NA Not available. [1] Cancellations, delays, etc. from schedule. [2] Unhelpful employees, inadequate meals or cabin service, treatment of delayed passengers. [3] Errors in reservations and ticketing; problems in making reservations and obtaining tickets. [4] Incorrect or incomplete information about fares, discount fare conditions, and availability, etc. [5] Prior to 2000, included in ticketing/boarding. [6] All bumping problems, whether or not airline complied with DOT regulations. [7] Allegations of discrimination by airlines due to factors other than disability, such as race, religion, national origin, or sex. [8] Included in "Other" beginning 2002. [9] Included in "Other" beginning 2000.

Source: U.S. Department of Transportation, Aviation Consumer Protection Division, *Air Travel Consumer Report*, monthly. See <http://airconsumer.ost.dot.gov>.

Transportation 663

Table 1041. **Commuter/Regional Airline Operations Summary: 2003 to 2007**

[**Calendar year data (112.6 represents 112,600,000).** Commuter/regional airlines operate primarily aircraft of predominately 75 passengers or less and 18,000 pounds of payload capacity serving short haul and small community markets. Represents operations within all North America by U.S. Regional Carriers. Averages are means. For definition of mean, see Guide to Tabular Presentation]

Item	Unit	2003	2004	2005	2006	2007
Passenger carriers operating	Number . . .	73	75	75	71	72
Passengers enplaned	Millions . . .	112.6	134.1	154.2	153.9	159.0
Average passengers enplaned per carrier	1,000	1,542.5	1,787.7	2,055.6	2,168.0	2,208.5
Revenue passenger miles (RPM)	Billions	47.7	62.6	73.8	70.8	73.8
Average RPMs per carrier	Millions . . .	652.8	835.1	983.7	997.2	1,024.7
Available seat miles	Billions	72.2	91.6	104.8	94.8	99.0
Average load factor	Percent . . .	66.0	68.4	70.4	74.7	74.6
Departures completed	Millions . . .	4.6	5.0	5.3	5.0	5.0
Airports served	Number . . .	823	846	846	688	666
Average trip length	Miles . . .	423.2	467.1	478.5	460.0	464.0
Average seating capacity (seats)	Number . . .	48.9	52.4	54.4	51.0	52.4
Fleet flying hours	1,000	5,940.3	6,595.5	7,333.0	7,133.1	7,306.7

Source: Compiled by the Regional Airline Association and BACK Aviation from DOT Form 41 data, *Annual Report of the Regional Airline Industry* (copyright). See also <http://www.raa.org/>.

Table 1042. **Airports, Aircraft, and Airmen: 1980 to 2006**

[**As of December 31 or for years ending December 31**]

Item	1980	1990	1995	2000	2003	2004	2005	2006
Airports, total [1]	15,161	17,490	18,224	19,281	19,581	19,820	19,854	19,990
Public	4,814	5,589	5,415	5,317	5,286	5,288	5,270	5,233
Percent—with lighted runways . . .	66.2	71.4	74.3	75.9	76.2	76.3	76.8	77.2
With paved runways	72.3	70.7	74.3	74.3	74.5	74.5	74.8	75.3
Private	10,347	11,901	12,809	13,964	14,295	14,532	14,584	14,757
Percent—with lighted runways . . .	15.2	7.0	6.4	7.2	8.6	9.0	9.2	9.5
With paved runways	13.3	31.5	33.0	32.0	32.7	32.8	33.2	33.3
Certificated [2]	730	680	667	651	628	599	575	604
Civil	(X)	(X)	572	563	555	542	(NA)	(NA)
Civil military	(X)	(X)	95	88	73	57	(NA)	(NA)
General aviation	14,431	16,810	17,557	18,630	18,953	19,221	19,279	19,379
Active air carrier fleet [3]	3,805	6,083	7,411	8,055	8,176	8,186	8,225	(NA)
Fixed wing	3,803	6,072	7,293	8,016	8,144	8,150	8,182	(NA)
Helicopter	2	11	118	39	32	36	43	(NA)
General aviation fleet [4]	211,043	198,000	188,089	217,533	209,708	219,426	224,352	221,943
Fixed-wing	200,094	184,500	162,342	183,276	176,624	182,867	185,373	182,186
Turbojet	2,992	4,100	4,559	7,001	7,997	9,298	9,823	10,379
Turboprop	4,089	5,300	4,995	5,762	7,689	8,379	7,942	8,063
Piston	193,013	175,200	152,788	170,513	160,938	165,189	167,608	163,743
Rotorcraft	6,001	6,900	5,830	7,150	6,525	7,821	8,728	9,159
Other	4,945	6,600	4,741	6,700	6,008	5,939	6,454	6,277
Gliders	(X)	(X)	2,182	2,041	2,002	2,116	2,074	1,975
Lighter than air	(X)	(X)	2,559	4,660	4,006	3,823	4,380	4,303
Experimental	(X)	(X)	15,176	20,407	20,550	22,800	23,627	23,047
Airman certificates held: [5]								
Pilot, total	827,071	702,659	639,184	625,581	625,011	618,633	609,737	597,109
Women	52,902	40,515	38,032	36,757	37,694	37,243	36,584	36,101
Student	199,833	128,663	101,279	93,064	87,296	87,910	87,213	84,866
Recreational	(X)	87	232	340	310	291	278	239
Airplane:								
Private	357,479	299,111	261,399	251,561	241,045	235,994	228,619	219,233
Commercial	183,442	149,666	133,980	121,858	123,990	122,592	120,614	117,610
Air transport	69,569	107,732	123,877	141,596	143,504	142,160	141,992	141,935
Rotorcraft only [6]	6,030	9,567	7,183	7,775	7,916	8,586	9,518	10,690
Glider only	7,039	7,833	11,234	9,387	20,950	21,100	21,369	21,597
Flight instructor certificates	60,440	63,775	77,613	80,931	87,816	89,596	90,555	91,343
Instrument ratings	260,462	297,073	298,798	311,944	315,413	313,546	311,828	309,333
Nonpilot [7]	368,356	492,237	651,341	547,453	509,835	515,293	644,016	656,227
Mechanic	250,157	344,282	405,294	344,434	313,032	317,111	320,293	323,097
Repairmen	(X)	(X)	61,233	38,208	37,248	39,231	40,030	40,329
Parachute rigger	9,547	10,094	11,824	10,477	7,883	8,011	8,150	8,252
Ground instructor	61,550	66,882	96,165	72,326	72,692	73,735	74,378	74,849
Dispatcher	6,799	11,002	15,642	16,340	16,955	17,493	18,079	18,610
Flight navigator	1,936	1,290	916	570	382	336	298	264
Flight engineer	38,367	58,687	60,267	65,098	61,643	59,376	57,756	55,952

NA Not available.   X Not applicable.   [1] Existing airports, heliports, seaplane bases, etc. recorded with FAA. Includes military airports with joint civil and military use. Includes U.S. outlying areas. Airport-type definitions: Public—publicly owned and under control of a public agency; private—owned by a private individual or corporation. May or may not be open for public use.   [2] Certificated airports serve air-carriers with aircraft seating more than 30 passengers.   [3] Air-carrier aircraft are aircraft carrying passengers or cargo for hire under 14 CFR 121 (large aircraft—more than 30 seats) and 14 CFR 135 (small aircraft— 30 seats or fewer).   [4] Beginning 1995, excludes commuters.   [5] Source: U.S. Federal Aviation Administration. See Internet site <http://www.faa.gov/data_statistics/>. Prior years in the *Statistical Handbook of Aviation,* annual.   [6] Data for 1980 are for helicopters only.   [7] All certificates on record. No medical examination required.

Source: Except as noted, U.S. Bureau of Transportation Statistics, *National Transportation Statistics, annual.* See <http://www.bts.gov/publications/national_transportation_statistics/>.

Table 1043. **Freight Carried on Major U.S. Waterways: 1980 to 2006**

[In millions of tons (4.0 represents 4,000,000)]

Item	1980	1990	1995	2000	2002	2003	2004	2005	2006
Atlantic intracoastal waterway	4.0	4.2	3.5	3.1	1.9	1.9	2.3	2.7	2.6
Great Lakes.	183.5	167.1	177.8	187.5	167.2	156.5	178.4	169.4	173.0
Gulf intracoastal waterway	94.5	115.4	118.0	113.8	107.7	117.8	123.3	116.1	122.6
Mississippi River system [1]	584.2	659.1	707.2	715.5	712.8	676.8	699.8	678.0	702.1
Mississippi River mainstem	441.5	475.3	520.3	515.6	501.7	478.0	496.9	464.6	497.7
Ohio River system [2]	179.3	260.0	267.6	274.4	280.9	261.3	271.5	280.1	270.7
Columbia River.	49.2	51.4	57.1	55.2	45.0	47.2	53.5	51.5	52.3
Snake River.	5.1	4.8	6.8	6.7	4.3	5.3	5.7	5.3	5.2

[1] Main channels and all tributaries of the Mississippi, Illinois, Missouri, and Ohio Rivers.   [2] Main channels and all navigable tributaries and embayments of the Ohio, Tennessee, and Cumberland Rivers.

Source: U.S. Army Corps of Engineers, *Waterborne Commerce of the United States,* annual. See <http://www.iwr.usace .army.mil/ndc/wcsc/wcsc.htm>.

Table 1044. **Waterborne Commerce by Type of Commodity: 1995 to 2006**

[In millions of short tons (2,240.4 represents 2,240,400,000). One short ton equals 2,000 pounds. Domestic trade includes all commercial movements between United States ports and on inland rivers, Great Lakes, canals, and connecting channels of the United States, Puerto Rico, and Virgin Islands]

Commodity	1995	2000	2005	2006 Total	Domestic	Foreign imports	Foreign exports
Total.	2,240.4	2,424.6	2,527.6	2,588.4	1,023.5	1,130.9	434.0
Coal.	324.5	297.0	316.6	318.1	229.8	39.6	48.7
Petroleum and petroleum products	907.1	1,044.0	1,111.4	1,122.2	359.8	686.1	76.3
Crude petroleum	504.6	571.4	602.7	595.0	70.4	524.7	–
Petroleum products [1]	402.5	472.4	508.8	527.1	289.4	161.4	76.3
Gasoline.	114.4	125.2	156.1	154.6	79.7	64.3	10.7
Distillate fuel oil	76.7	91.7	141.1	162.3	82.4	53.7	26.2
Residual fuel oil	111.9	131.6	96.1	89.9	77.7	9.7	2.5
Chemicals and related products.	153.7	172.4	174.9	176.1	69.4	48.0	58.7
Fertilizers	35.7	35.1	34.5	31.9	11.8	7.9	12.2
Other chemicals and related products	118.0	137.3	140.4	144.3	57.6	40.1	46.5
Crude material, inedible	381.7	380.3	386.0	384.0	215.7	113.0	55.2
Forest products, wood and chips	47.2	33.1	29.4	26.3	7.5	10.2	8.7
Pulp and waste paper.	14.9	13.6	18.7	19.5	0.1	2.3	17.0
Soil, sand, gravel, rock, and stone [1]	152.5	165.0	177.9	181.1	130.4	46.3	4.5
Limestone.	54.0	67.4	73.5	74.9	53.4	18.3	3.2
Phosphate rock	10.7	3.4	6.0	5.1	2.5	2.6	–
Sand & gravel	77.0	79.0	80.2	82.3	70.4	11.0	1.0
Iron ore and scrap	104.9	97.9	85.7	90.4	58.5	16.2	15.7
Marine shells	0.5	0.3	–	0.1	(Z)	(Z)	(Z)
Nonferrous ores and scrap	27.9	29.2	29.2	26.4	5.8	17.3	3.3
Sulphur, clay, and salt.	23.4	11.3	8.7	8.3	0.9	2.4	5.0
Slag	1.9	4.0	6.0	5.9	2.6	3.2	0.1
Other nonmetal minerals	8.4	25.9	30.4	26.0	9.9	15.2	1.0
Primary manufactured goods.	106.3	153.0	166.4	189.2	47.0	123.2	19.1
Papers products	13.1	12.1	13.7	14.2	0.2	7.3	6.7
Lime, cement, and glass	33.9	55.9	62.4	65.9	20.2	44.3	1.5
Primary iron and steel products	44.1	57.1	52.1	67.8	17.1	49.2	1.5
Primary nonferrous metal products	12.3	25.5	33.5	37.0	9.4	18.4	9.2
Primary wood products	2.9	2.5	4.8	4.4	0.1	4.0	0.3
Food and farm products	303.2	283.3	251.3	271.3	79.6	36.7	154.9
Fish	3.6	2.4	3.0	3.3	0.1	2.0	1.2
Grain [1]	167.9	145.2	124.0	137.1	47.0	1.1	89.1
Wheat	48.5	43.4	36.4	32.7	8.9	0.2	23.6
Corn	105.0	88.2	75.2	93.1	34.8	0.1	58.2
Oilseeds	46.1	57.6	47.2	51.6	19.2	0.3	32.1
Soybeans	42.0	47.3	40.8	44.3	16.4	0.1	27.8
Vegetables products.	9.0	8.9	8.3	9.5	1.1	4.5	3.8
Processed grain and animal feed	33.0	23.1	18.4	18.2	5.8	0.8	11.6
Other agricultural products	43.5	46.1	50.5	51.6	6.3	28.1	17.1
All manufactured equip, machinery and products	57.0	83.6	110.3	117.0	19.9	78.5	18.6
Waste and scrap, n.e.c. [2]	5.4	4.3	2.0	2.3	2.3	–	–
Unknown or not elsewhere classified	1.6	6.8	8.7	8.2	(Z)	5.7	2.4

– Represents or rounds to zero.   [1] Includes commodities not shown separately.   [2] Not elsewhere classified.

Source: U.S. Army Corps of Engineers, *Waterborne Commerce of the United States,* annual. See <http://www.iwr.usace.army.mil/ndc /wcsc/wcsc.htm>.

U.S. Census Bureau, Statistical Abstract of the United States: 2009

Table 1045. **Selected U.S. Ports by Tons of Traffic: 2006**

[In thousands of short tons (42,439 represents 42,439,000), except rank. One short ton equals 2,000 lbs. For calendar year for the top 30 ports. Represents tons of cargo shipped from or received by the specified port. Excludes cargo carried on general ferries; coal and petroleum products loaded from shore facilities directly onto bunkers of vessels for fuel; and amounts of less than 100 tons of government-owned equipment in support of Corps of Engineers projects]

| Port name | Rank | Total | Foreign | | | Domestic |
			Total	Inbound	Outbound	
Baltimore, MD	17	42,439	28,014	19,831	8,183	14,425
Baton Rouge, LA	12	56,343	19,254	14,677	4,577	37,090
Beaumont, TX	5	79,486	57,316	51,829	5,487	22,170
Charleston, SC	30	26,425	23,375	17,081	6,293	3,051
Corpus Christi, TX	6	77,557	53,758	45,328	8,430	23,800
Duluth-Superior, MN and WI	15	46,974	14,463	526	13,936	32,511
Freeport, TX	25	32,147	27,166	24,119	3,047	4,981
Houston, TX	2	222,147	152,877	106,905	45,972	69,269
Huntington - Tristate	7	77,158	–	–	–	77,158
Lake Charles, LA	11	58,410	34,272	29,425	4,847	24,137
Long Beach, CA	4	84,394	71,559	52,620	18,939	12,835
Los Angeles, CA	9	65,978	57,032	40,880	16,152	8,946
Mobile, AL	10	59,832	34,337	24,469	9,868	25,495
New Orleans, LA	8	76,901	38,831	22,442	16,389	38,070
New York, NY and NJ	3	157,630	91,352	77,142	14,210	66,278
Norfolk Harbor, VA	23	34,249	25,876	9,061	16,815	8,373
Pascagoula, MS	21	37,652	26,654	20,948	5,707	10,997
Paulsboro, NJ	19	39,244	25,535	24,434	1,101	13,709
Port Arthur, TX	28	28,403	18,886	13,015	5,870	9,517
Philadelphia, PA	20	38,597	24,787	24,472	315	13,810
Pittsburgh, PA	18	41,982	–	–	–	41,982
Plaquemines, LA, Port of	13	55,890	20,856	8,377	12,480	35,034
Portland, OR	27	28,472	16,279	5,142	11,137	12,194
Savannah, GA	24	33,971	32,283	21,865	10,418	1,688
Seattle, WA	29	27,974	22,031	10,069	11,962	5,942
South Louisiana, LA, Port of	1	225,489	106,712	46,543	60,169	118,778
St. Louis, MO and IL	26	31,317	–	–	–	31,317
Tampa, FL	16	46,231	18,556	11,106	7,450	27,675
Texas City, TX	14	48,875	35,788	32,534	3,254	13,087
Valdez, AK	22	36,153	–	–	–	36,153

– Represents zero.

Source: U.S. Army Corps of Engineers, "Waterborne Commerce of the United States, 2006." See <http://www.iwr.usace.army.mil/ndc/wcsc/wcsc.htm>; (accessed 18 June 2008).

Table 1046. **Selected U.S. Ports/Waterways by Container Traffic: 2006**

[In thousands of twenty-foot equivalent units (TEUS). 31,319.6 represents 31,319,600. For calendar year. For the 30 leading ports/waterways in total TEUS. A TEUS is a measure of containerized cargo capacity equal to 1 standard 20-foot length by 8-foot width by 8-foot 6-inch height container]

| Port/waterway name | Rank | Total loaded | Domestic | | | Foreign loaded | |
			Total [1]	Inbound loaded	Outbound loaded	Total	Inbound
Total [2]	(X)	31,319.6	5,076.6	2,053.4	2,053.4	27,212.8	18,360.3
Anchorage, AK	17	277.1	278.5	227.1	47.6	2.3	–
Baltimore, MD	16	482.7	99.1	40.6	39.6	402.5	253.3
Boston, MA	22	158.4	33.1	12.9	7.7	137.8	78.2
Charleston, SC	7	1,482.7	–	–	–	1,482.7	870.8
Chester, PA	26	102.7	–	–	–	102.7	51.4
Freeport, TX	30	53.9	–	–	–	53.9	26.1
Gulfport, MS	21	161.4	–	–	–	161.4	97.1
Honolulu, HI	11	890.0	1,154.6	549.8	304.1	36.0	23.2
Houston, TX	10	1,316.5	66.3	24.3	34.0	1,258.2	653.0
Jacksonville, FL	15	511.7	376.4	60.6	315.8	135.4	44.4
Kahului, Maui, HI	27	94.4	133.1	72.9	21.5	–	–
Kawaihae Harbor, HI	29	64.1	95.9	51.5	12.6	–	–
Long Beach, CA	2	5,043.1	379.7	44.5	267.3	4,731.4	3,713.6
Los Angeles, CA	1	5,572.2	1.5	0.4	0.7	5,571.1	4,330.7
Miami, FL	12	740.1	–	–	–	740.1	426.1
New Orleans, LA	18	184.9	22.8	8.4	9.4	167.1	67.7
New York (NY and NJ)	3	3,811.7	241.3	75.6	112.3	3,623.9	2,576.8
Newport News, VA	28	73.8	–	–	–	73.8	43.4
Norfolk Harbor, VA	6	1,492.4	111.9	48.2	43.3	1,400.8	824.7
Oakland, CA	4	1,579.1	283.2	35.9	169.0	1,374.2	809.1
Palm Beach, FL	25	123.7	–	–	–	123.7	28.1
Philadelphia, PA	23	148.3	–	–	–	148.3	127.7
Port Everglades, FL	14	633.1	13.2	–	13.2	620.0	294.3
Portland, OR	19	183.5	30.6	19.1	0.4	164.0	85.8
San Juan, PR	13	689.9	493.7	410.1	83.6	196.2	149.7
Savannah, GA	5	1,574.4	–	–	–	1,574.4	857.5
Seattle, WA	8	1,380.4	321.3	51.4	156.6	1,172.5	742.4
Tacoma, WA	9	1,379.7	293.0	50.6	241.7	1,087.3	745.1
Wilmington, DE	20	170.4	–	–	–	170.4	126.5
Wilmington, NC	24	125.7	–	–	–	125.7	78.3

– Represents zero. [1] Includes empty TEUS. [2] Includes other ports/waterways not shown separately.

Source: U.S. Army Corps of Engineers, "U.S. Waterborne Container Traffic for U.S. Port/Waterway in 2006." See <http://www.iwr.usace.army.mil/ndc/wcsc/wcsc.htm>, (accessed 24 June 2008).

Table 1047. Highway Mileage—Urban and Rural by Ownership: 1980 to 2006

[In thousands (3,955 represents 3,955,000). As of Dec. 31. Includes Puerto Rico beginning 2000]

Type and control	1980	1990	1995	2000	2002	2003	2004	2005	2006
Total mileage [1,2]	[3]3,955	3,880	3,912	3,951	3,982	3,991	3,997	4,012	4,033
Urban mileage [1]	624	757	819	859	902	954	994	1,023	1,043
Under state control	79	96	112	112	112	127	130	144	148
Under local control	543	661	706	746	787	828	862	874	890
Rural mileage	[3]3,331	3,123	3,093	3,092	3,080	3,036	3,003	2,989	2,990
Under state control	702	703	691	664	665	653	650	637	635
Under local control	2,270	2,242	2,231	2,311	2,297	2,263	2,236	2,228	2,231
Under federal control.....	262	178	170	117	118	120	118	123	123

[1] Includes state park, state toll, other state agency, other local agency, and other roadways not identified by ownership.
[2] Roadways in federal parks, forests, and reservations that are not part of the state and local highway system. [3] Includes 98,000 miles of nonpublic road mileage previously contained in other rural categories.

Source: U.S. Federal Highway Administration, *Highway Statistics,* annual. See Internet site <http://www.fhwa.dot.gov/policy/ohpi/hss/hsspubs.htm>.

Table 1048. Hazardous Shipments—Value, Tons, and Ton-Miles: 2002

[660,181 represents $660,181,000,000. For business establishments in mining, manufacturing, wholesale trade, and selected retail industries. 2002 classified by the 1997 North American Industry Classification System (NAICS). Selected auxiliary establishments are also included. Based on the 2002 Economic Census; see Appendix III]

Mode of transportation	Value (mil. dol.) Total	Value (mil. dol.) Percent	Tons (1,000) Total	Tons (1,000) Percent	Ton-miles (mil.) Total	Ton-miles (mil.) Percent	Average miles per shipment
All modes	660,181	100.0	2,191,519	100.0	326,727	100.0	136
Single modes	644,489	97.6	2,158,533	98.5	311,897	95.5	105
Truck [1]	419,630	63.6	1,159,514	52.9	110,163	33.7	86
For-hire truck	189,803	28.8	449,503	20.5	65,112	19.9	285
Private truck.................	226,660	34.3	702,186	32.0	44,087	13.5	38
Rail	31,339	4.7	109,369	5.0	72,087	22.1	695
Water.......................	46,856	7.1	228,197	10.4	70,649	21.6	(S)
Air (includes truck and air)	1,643	0.2	64	–	85	–	2,080
Pipeline [2]	145,021	22.0	661,390	30.2	(S)	(S)	(S)
Multiple modes	9,631	1.5	18,745	0.9	12,488	3.8	849
Parcel, U.S. Postal Service or courier...	4,268	0.6	245	–	119	–	837
Other multiple modes	5,363	0.8	18,500	0.8	12,369	3.8	1,371
Other and unknown modes.......	6,061	0.9	14,241	0.6	2,342	0.7	57
Class of material................	660,181	100.0	2,191,519	100.0	326,727	100.0	136
Class 1, explosives	7,901	1.2	5,000	0.2	1,568	0.5	651
Class 2, gasses	73,932	11.2	213,358	9.7	37,262	11.4	95
Class 3, flammable liquids.........	490,238	74.3	1,788,986	81.6	218,574	66.9	106
Class 4, flammable solids	6,566	1.0	11,300	0.5	4,391	1.3	158
Class 5, oxidizers and organic peroxides.....................	5,471	0.8	12,670	0.6	4,221	1.3	407
Class 6, toxic (poison)	8,275	1.3	8,459	0.4	4,254	1.3	626
Class 7, radioactive materials	5,850	0.9	57	–	44	–	(S)
Class 8, corrosive materials........	38,324	5.8	90,671	4.1	36,260	11.1	301
Class 9, miscellaneous dangerous goods	23,625	3.6	61,018	2.8	20,153	6.2	368

– Rounds to zero.   S Data do not meet publication standards due to high sampling variability or other reasons.   [1] Truck as a single mode includes shipments that went by private truck only, for-hire truck only, or a combination of private truck and for-hire truck.   [2] Commodity Flow Survey data exclude shipments of crude oil.

Source: U.S. Bureau of Transportation Statistics and U.S. Census Bureau, 2002 Economic Census, Transportation, "2002 Commodity Flow Survey, Hazardous Shipments" Series EC02TCF-US(HM), issued December 2004. See <http://www.census.gov/svsd/www/cfsmain.html>.

Transportation 667

Table 1049. **Highway Mileage by State—Functional Systems and Urban/Rural: 2006**

[As of Dec. 31. Excludes Puerto Rico. For definition of functional systems see text, this section]

State		Functional systems					Urban	Rural
	Total	Interstate	Other free-ways and express-ways	Arterial	Collector	Local		
U.S.	4,016,741	46,630	10,748	396,128	790,791	2,772,444	1,029,366	2,987,375
AL.	96,521	908	32	9,237	20,530	65,814	21,846	74,675
AK.	14,787	1,081	–	1,516	2,829	9,361	2,370	12,417
AZ.	60,376	1,169	168	5,719	8,121	45,199	22,560	37,816
AR.	99,005	655	100	6,878	20,325	71,047	11,272	87,733
CA.	170,290	2,460	1,542	26,958	31,992	107,338	86,565	83,725
CO	88,021	954	317	8,926	16,253	61,571	19,066	68,955
CT.	21,249	346	237	2,758	3,200	14,708	15,081	6,168
DE.	6,179	41	24	644	1,052	4,418	2,920	3,259
DC	1,500	13	20	266	156	1,045	1,500	–
FL.	121,995	1,471	578	12,860	14,287	92,799	81,789	40,206
GA	118,199	1,244	116	14,011	22,651	80,177	37,325	80,874
HI	4,330	55	34	753	829	2,659	2,290	2,040
ID	47,105	612	–	4,041	10,311	32,141	4,755	42,350
IL [1]	138,997	2,169	100	14,489	21,724	100,515	40,403	98,594
IN [1]	96,250	1,169	136	7,964	22,684	64,297	21,780	74,470
IA	114,084	781	–	9,710	31,548	72,045	11,197	102,887
KS.	140,381	874	190	9,516	33,524	96,277	12,790	127,591
KY.	78,231	762	66	5,865	16,084	55,454	12,325	65,906
LA.	60,925	903	50	5,537	10,048	44,387	15,932	44,993
ME	22,783	367	20	2,173	5,985	14,238	2,972	19,811
MD	31,099	481	294	3,783	5,044	21,497	17,099	14,000
MA	35,938	573	312	6,176	4,826	24,051	27,977	7,961
MI	121,722	1,241	329	14,587	24,503	81,062	35,619	86,103
MN [2]	132,309	913	174	13,479	29,759	87,984	16,756	115,553
MS	74,408	685	71	7,429	15,488	50,735	10,681	63,727
MO	127,205	1,181	343	10,195	24,903	90,583	19,244	107,961
MT	73,148	1,192	–	6,037	16,221	49,698	2,973	70,175
NE.	93,379	482	21	8,076	20,730	64,070	6,191	87,188
NV.	33,703	571	71	3,079	4,994	24,988	7,143	26,560
NH	15,647	225	53	1,537	2,754	11,078	4,733	10,914
NJ.	38,561	431	404	5,760	4,150	27,816	31,252	7,309
NM	63,796	1,000	5	5,101	8511	49,179	7,996	55,800
NY.	113,617	1,697	791	13,821	20,664	76,644	47,744	65,873
NC	103,500	1,082	388	9,572	17,467	74,991	32,310	71,190
ND	86,839	571	–	5,912	11,778	68,578	1,870	84,969
OH	125,107	1,574	484	10,915	22,589	89,545	44,594	80,513
OK	113,085	933	191	8,195	25,260	78,506	15,640	97,445
OR	64,358	728	56	7,021	17,614	38,939	12,698	51,660
PA.	121,292	1,758	546	13,273	19,791	85,924	44,923	76,369
RI	6,528	71	87	831	884	4,655	5,261	1,267
SC.	66,242	843	92	7,184	15,081	43,042	16,444	49,798
SD.	84,229	679	12	6,389	19,127	58,022	2,828	81,401
TN.	91,416	1,104	135	9,060	17,851	63,266	21,639	69,777
TX.	305,270	3,233	1,216	28,853	63,477	208,491	83,683	221,587
UT.	43,769	936	13	3,464	7,737	31,619	10,610	33,159
VT.	14,406	320	20	1,302	3,131	9,633	1,421	12,985
VA.	72,331	1,117	240	8,316	14,090	48,568	21,700	50,631
WA	83,256	764	372	7,652	16,680	57,788	22,469	60,787
WV	37,054	555	9	3,321	8,730	24,439	4,514	32,540
WI	114,485	743	286	12,397	21,677	79,382	21,998	92,487
WY	27,834	913	3	3,590	11,147	12,181	2,618	25,216

– Represents zero.   [1] Excludes 788 miles of federal agency owned roads.   [2] Includes 274 miles of miscoded noninterstate functional system length or rural/urban categorization or both.

Source: U.S. Federal Highway Administration, *Highway Statistics,* annual. See <http://www.fhwa.dot.gov/policy/ohpi/hss/hsspubs.htm>.

Table 1050. Bridge Inventory—Total and Deficient, 1996 to 2007, and by State, 2007

[Based on the National Bridge Inventory program; for details, see source]

| State and year | Number of bridges | Deficient and obsolete | | Structurally deficient [1] | | Functionally obsolete [2] | |
		Total number	Percent	Number	Percent	Number	Percent
1996, total	581,862	182,726	31.4	101,518	17.4	81,208	14.0
1997, total	582,751	175,885	30.2	98,475	16.9	77,410	13.3
1998, total	582,984	172,582	29.6	93,076	16.0	79,506	13.6
1999, total	585,542	170,050	29.0	88,150	15.1	81,900	14.0
2000, total	587,755	167,993	28.6	87,106	14.8	80,887	13.8
2001, total	590,066	165,099	28.0	83,630	14.2	81,469	13.8
2002, total	591,220	163,010	27.6	81,437	13.8	81,573	13.8
2003, total	592,246	160,819	27.2	79,811	13.5	81,008	13.7
2004, total	593,885	158,318	26.7	77,758	13.1	80,560	13.6
2005, total	594,616	156,177	26.3	75,871	12.8	80,306	13.5
2006, total	596,842	153,990	25.8	73,764	12.4	80,226	13.4
U.S. total, 2007	**599,766**	**152,316**	**25.4**	**72,524**	**12.1**	**79,792**	**13.3**
Alabama	15,881	4,057	25.5	1,899	12.0	2,158	13.6
Alaska	1,229	334	27.2	155	12.6	179	14.6
Arizona	7,348	781	10.6	181	2.5	600	8.2
Arkansas	12,531	2,905	23.2	997	8.0	1,908	15.2
California	24,184	6,977	28.8	3,140	13.0	3,837	15.9
Colorado	8,366	1,404	16.8	580	6.9	824	9.8
Connecticut	4,175	1,400	33.5	358	8.6	1,042	25.0
Delaware	857	132	15.4	20	2.3	112	13.1
District of Columbia	245	152	62.0	24	9.8	128	52.2
Florida	11,663	1,994	17.1	302	2.6	1,692	14.5
Georgia	14,563	2,916	20.0	1,028	7.1	1,888	13.0
Hawaii	1,115	500	44.8	142	12.7	358	32.1
Idaho	4,104	801	19.5	349	8.5	452	11.0
Illinois	25,998	4,341	16.7	2,501	9.6	1,840	7.1
Indiana	18,494	4,034	21.8	2,030	11.0	2,004	10.8
Iowa	24,776	6,608	26.7	5,153	20.8	1,455	5.9
Kansas	25,461	5,363	21.1	2,991	11.7	2,372	9.3
Kentucky	13,637	4,290	31.5	1,362	10.0	2,928	21.5
Louisiana	13,342	3,960	29.7	1,780	13.3	2,180	16.3
Maine	2,387	817	34.2	349	14.6	468	19.6
Maryland	5,127	1,368	26.7	388	7.6	980	19.1
Massachusetts	5,018	2,572	51.3	585	11.7	1,987	39.6
Michigan	10,923	2,888	26.4	1,584	14.5	1,304	11.9
Minnesota	13,067	1,579	12.1	1,156	8.8	423	3.2
Mississippi	17,007	4,317	25.4	3,002	17.7	1,315	7.7
Missouri	24,071	7,541	31.3	4,433	18.4	3,108	12.9
Montana	4,980	1,014	20.4	473	9.5	541	10.9
Nebraska	15,475	3,623	23.4	2,382	15.4	1,241	8.0
Nevada	1,705	203	11.9	47	2.8	156	9.1
New Hampshire	2,364	741	31.3	383	16.2	358	15.1
New Jersey	6,448	2,251	34.9	750	11.6	1,501	23.3
New Mexico	3,850	698	18.1	404	10.5	294	7.6
New York	17,361	6,646	38.3	2,128	12.3	4,518	26.0
North Carolina	17,783	5,059	28.4	2,272	12.8	2,787	15.7
North Dakota	4,458	992	22.3	743	16.7	249	5.6
Ohio	27,998	6,863	24.5	2,862	10.2	4,001	14.3
Oklahoma	23,524	7,407	31.5	5,793	24.6	1,614	6.9
Oregon	7,318	1,669	22.8	514	7.0	1,155	15.8
Pennsylvania	22,325	9,736	43.6	5,802	26.0	3,934	17.6
Rhode Island	748	396	52.9	164	21.9	232	31.0
South Carolina	9,221	2,068	22.4	1,260	13.7	808	8.8
South Dakota	5,924	1,477	24.9	1,216	20.5	261	4.4
Tennessee	19,838	4,101	20.7	1,325	6.7	2,776	14.0
Texas	50,271	10,037	20.0	2,186	4.3	7,851	15.6
Utah	2,851	487	17.1	233	8.2	254	8.9
Vermont	2,712	967	35.7	500	18.4	467	17.2
Virginia	13,417	3,442	25.7	1,208	9.0	2,234	16.7
Washington	7,651	2,061	26.9	400	5.2	1,661	21.7
West Virginia	7,001	2,573	36.8	1,058	15.1	1,515	21.6
Wisconsin	13,798	2,091	15.2	1,302	9.4	789	5.7
Wyoming	3,030	620	20.5	389	12.8	231	7.6
Puerto Rico	2,146	1,063	49.5	246	11.5	799	37.2

[1] Bridges are structurally deficient if they have been restricted to light vehicles, require immediate rehabilitation to remain open, or are closed. [2] Bridges are functionally obsolete if they have deck geometry, load carrying capacity, clearance or approach roadway alignment that no longer meet the criteria for the system of which the bridge is carrying a part.

Source: U.S. Federal Highway Administration, Office of Bridge Technology. See <http://www.fhwa.dot.gov/bridge/nbi.htm>.

U.S. Census Bureau, Statistical Abstract of the United States: 2009

Table 1051. **Funding for Highways and Disposition of Highway-User Revenue: 1990 to 2006**

[In millions of dollars (75,444 represents $75,444,000,000). Data compiled from reports of state and local authorities]

Type	1990	1995	2000	2001	2002	2003	2004	2005	2006
Total receipts	**75,444**	**96,269**	**131,115**	**132,324**	**138,878**	**139,246**	**145,315**	**154,690**	**165,443**
Current income	69,880	87,620	119,815	119,659	123,802	124,593	129,521	137,668	147,615
Highway-user revenues	44,346	59,331	81,335	77,719	79,487	79,280	83,006	90,343	93,648
Other taxes and fees	19,827	21,732	31,137	34,190	36,168	37,783	38,956	39,214	44,455
Investment income, other receipts	5,707	6,557	7,342	7,749	8,147	7,530	7,560	8,111	9,512
Bond issue proceeds [1]	5,564	8,649	11,301	12,665	15,076	14,654	15,794	17,022	17,828
Funds drawn from or placed in reserves [2]	–36	–2,791	–8,418	–2,423	–239	4,359	2,174	–1,990	–4,382
Total funds available	75,408	93,478	122,697	129,900	138,639	143,605	147,489	152,700	161,061
Total disbursements	**75,408**	**93,478**	**122,697**	**129,900**	**138,639**	**143,605**	**147,489**	**152,700**	**161,061**
Current disbursements	72,457	88,994	117,592	124,815	131,694	136,213	139,478	144,629	153,413
Capital outlay	35,151	44,228	61,323	65,968	68,794	70,004	70,274	75,162	78,676
Maintenance and traffic services	20,365	24,319	30,636	31,677	33,893	35,011	36,327	37,882	40,426
Administration and research	6,501	8,419	10,020	10,423	10,934	11,986	12,737	11,126	13,189
Highway law enforcement and safety	7,235	8,218	11,031	11,977	12,548	13,501	14,322	14,066	14,482
Interest on debt	3,205	3,810	4,583	4,770	5,526	5,711	5,819	6,392	6,639
Bond retirement [1]	2,951	4,484	5,105	5,086	6,945	7,393	8,011	8,071	7,648

[1] Proceeds and redemptions of short-term notes and refunding issues are excluded. [2] Negative numbers indicate that funds were placed in reserves.
Source: U.S. Federal Highway Administration, *Highway Statistics,* annual. See <http://www.fhwa.dot.gov/policy/ohpi/hss/hsspubs.htm>.

Table 1052. **Federal Aid to State and Local Governments for Highway Trust Fund and Federal Transit Administration (FTA) by State: 2006**

[Year ending Sept. 30. (33,681 represents $33,681,000,000)]

State	Highway trust fund Total (mil. dol.)	Highway trust fund Per capita (dol.)[1]	FTA Total (mil. dol.)	FTA Per capita (dol.)[1]	State	Highway trust fund Total (mil. dol.)	Highway trust fund Per capita (dol.)[1]	FTA Total (mil. dol.)	FTA Per capita (dol.)[1]	State	Highway trust fund Total (mil. dol.)	Highway trust fund Per capita (dol.)[1]	FTA Total (mil. dol.)	FTA Per capita (dol.)[1]
U.S. [2]	**33,681**	**111**	**8,754**	**29**	KS	298	108	23	8	ND	238	374	10	16
U.S. [3]	**33,126**	**111**	**8,678**	**29**	KY	572	136	41	10	OH	1,302	114	139	12
AL	772	168	73	16	LA	668	158	91	22	OK	520	145	33	9
AK	381	563	64	95	ME	175	133	21	16	OR	336	91	133	36
AZ	430	70	250	41	MD	724	129	94	17	PA	1,427	115	678	55
AR	430	153	25	9	MA	446	69	209	32	RI	252	238	26	24
CA	2,750	76	1,404	39	MI	999	99	117	12	SC	733	169	24	6
CO	464	97	172	36	MN	532	103	91	18	SD	243	308	9	11
CT	438	125	98	28	MS	852	294	21	7	TN	670	110	76	12
DE	109	128	9	10	MO	747	128	78	13	TX	2,892	124	387	17
DC	114	194	299	511	MT	72	76	8	8	UT	272	105	61	24
FL	1,895	105	238	13	NE	255	145	14	8	VT	150	242	13	21
GA	923	99	131	14	NV	273	110	45	18	VA	551	72	116	15
HI	130	101	53	41	NH	165	126	12	9	WA	569	89	197	31
ID	260	177	11	7	NJ	747	86	508	59	WV	405	224	19	10
IL	986	77	679	53	NM	235	121	22	12	WI	575	103	58	10
IN	631	100	70	11	NY	1,496	78	1,459	76	WY	193	376	6	13
IA	368	124	34	11	NC	908	102	94	11					

[1] Based on estimated population as of July 1. [2] Includes outlying areas and undistributed funds, not shown separately.
[3] For the 50 states and D.C.
Source: U.S. Census Bureau, *Federal Aid to States for Fiscal Year, 2006;* (issued April 2008). See <http://www.census.gov/prod/www/abs/fas.html>.

Table 1053. **State Motor Fuel Tax Receipts, 2005 and 2006, and Gasoline Tax Rates, 2006**

[616 represents $616,000,000]

State	Net receipts (mil. dol.) 2005	Net receipts (mil. dol.) 2006	Tax rate,[1] 2006	State	Net receipts (mil. dol.) 2005	Net receipts (mil. dol.) 2006	Tax rate,[1] 2006	State	Net receipts (mil. dol.) 2005	Net receipts (mil. dol.) 2006	Tax rate,[1] 2006
AL	616	680	18.00	KY	470	528	19.70	ND	108	136	23.00
AK	31	29	8.00	LA	582	603	20.00	OH	1,771	1,873	28.00
AZ	678	705	18.00	ME	217	227	26.80	OK	435	441	17.00
AR	444	436	21.70	MD	754	746	23.50	OR	392	400	24.00
CA	3,302	3,303	18.00	MA	686	671	21.00	PA	1,913	2,092	30.00
CO	519	603	22.00	MI	1,049	1,037	19.00	RI	149	144	30.00
CT	474	581	25.00	MN	640	659	20.00	SC	515	504	16.00
DE	113	118	23.00	MS	396	423	18.40	SD	129	129	22.00
DC	26	25	20.00	MO	711	708	17.00	TN	828	832	21.40
FL	2,040	2,183	15.30	MT	172	196	27.75	TX	2,924	2,998	20.00
GA	503	811	7.50	NE	303	310	27.10	UT	335	342	24.50
HI	79	81	16.00	NV	454	481	24.80	VT	86	92	20.00
ID	215	221	25.00	NH	155	151	19.50	VA	920	907	17.50
IL	1,302	1,313	19.00	NJ	565	579	10.50	WA	912	1,004	34.00
IN	888	879	18.00	NM	249	283	18.88	WV	288	298	32.00
IA	424	430	21.00	NY	1,571	1,595	24.65	WI	937	944	30.90
KS	434	429	24.00	NC	1,385	1,532	30.15	WY	97	97	14.00

[1] State gasoline tax rates in cents per gallon. In effect December 31.
Source: U.S. Federal Highway Administration, *Highway Statistics,* annual. See <http://www.fhwa.dot.gov/policy/ohpi/hss/hsspubs.htm>.

670 Transportation

Table 1054. Public Obligations for Highways—Changes in Indebtedness During the Year: 1995 to 2006

[In millions of dollars (37,449 represents $37,449,000,000). Table summarizes state indebtedness from all state bond issues, including the toll facility issues and the state issues for local roads. This table is compiled from reports of state authorities. Table also summarizes the change in status of the highway obligations of local governments including toll authorities]

Item	1995	2000	2001	2002	2003	2004	2005	2006
STATE GOVERNMENT								
Obligations outstanding, beginning of year .	37,449	56,264	59,903	67,564	72,175	80,513	82,476	86,642
Obligations issued	4,718	9,067	11,012	13,250	16,571	13,344	19,784	11,486
Obligations retired	2,940	3,897	4,660	9,988	11,541	8,291	14,072	8,780
Obligations outstanding, end of year	39,228	61,434	66,256	70,826	77,205	85,565	88,187	96,513
LOCAL GOVERNMENT [1, 2]								
Obligations outstanding, beginning of year .	26,393	34,904	35,579	38,896	40,901	42,733	44,406	(NA)
Bonds outstanding, beginning of year . . .	25,613	34,229	34,971	38,110	40,091	41,979	43,403	(NA)
Bonds outstanding, end of year	29,505	34,949	37,086	40,400	41,979	44,368	46,168	(NA)
Obligations outstanding, end of year	30,295	35,557	37,879	41,210	42,734	45,331	47,170	(NA)

NA Not available. [1] Short-term notes data not shown. The data are included in beginning and ending year obligations. [2] The number of local government data estimated varied year to year.

Source: U.S. Federal Highway Administration, *Highway Statistics,* annual. See <http://www.fhwa.dot.gov/policy/ohpi/hss /hsspubs.htm>.

Table 1055. State Disbursements for Highways by State: 1995 to 2006

[In millions of dollars (67,615 represents $67,615,000,000). Comprises disbursements from current revenues or loans for construction, maintenance, interest and principal payments on highway bonds, transfers to local units, and miscellaneous. Includes transactions by state toll authorities. Excludes amounts allocated for collection expenses and nonhighway purposes, and mass transit]

State	1995	2000	2001	2002	2003	2004	2005	2006
United States.	**67,615**	**89,832**	**94,513**	**104,977**	**109,403**	**104,677**	**116,517**	**117,048**
Alabama.	1,002	1,246	1,433	1,575	1,572	1,562	1,519	1,684
Alaska	438	501	482	541	618	623	643	654
Arizona.	1,199	2,040	2,149	2,445	2,453	2,569	2,458	2,662
Arkansas	666	817	976	1,161	1,176	1,219	1,078	1,134
California	5,966	6,750	6,795	8,570	9,349	7,967	8,308	10,571
Colorado.	922	1,392	1,616	2,195	1,788	1,870	1,652	1,490
Connecticut.	1,153	1,304	1,236	1,848	1,743	1,677	1,434	1,223
Delaware	441	595	647	738	929	798	1,104	804
District of Columbia	140	244	406	336	368	369	327	287
Florida	3,421	4,208	4,348	4,985	6,664	5,804	7,369	7,725
Georgia	1,437	1,567	1,748	1,945	1,756	1,935	2,070	2,655
Hawaii	360	272	263	275	375	314	506	323
Idaho	350	492	480	508	547	568	608	622
Illinois	3,006	3,447	3,788	4,286	4,595	4,289	4,201	4,974
Indiana.	1,433	1,932	3,202	1,975	2,445	2,578	2,235	2,416
Iowa	1,078	1,494	1,388	1,405	1,419	1,401	1,392	1,515
Kansas.	1,019	1,206	1,271	1,951	1,891	1,387	1,394	1,521
Kentucky	1,397	1,651	1,612	1,776	2,152	1,907	1,723	1,635
Louisiana	1,198	1,301	1,154	1,287	1,498	1,576	1,387	1,866
Maine.	379	488	505	744	579	702	616	628
Maryland	1,289	1,599	1,673	1,803	1,885	1,831	2,049	2,304
Massachusetts.	2,501	3,524	3,965	3,783	3,547	3,612	3,196	2,723
Michigan.	1,974	2,748	2,920	2,859	2,799	2,930	3,561	3,263
Minnesota.	1,210	1,692	1,683	1,866	1,969	1,995	2,131	2,143
Mississippi	662	1,039	911	1,040	1,014	1,087	1,081	1,272
Missouri	1,313	1,818	2,044	2,110	2,120	2,135	2,069	2,430
Montana.	388	474	469	535	578	657	664	696
Nebraska	578	745	661	867	839	859	876	882
Nevada	484	651	668	631	807	1,045	865	1,144
New Hampshire	328	387	445	522	453	389	389	524
New Jersey.	2,102	4,503	4,276	4,863	6,364	3,849	7,119	5,561
New Mexico	535	1,162	1,119	983	862	1,164	911	942
New York	4,584	5,307	5,301	7,161	6,592	6,094	9,638	5,659
North Carolina	1,871	2,621	2,868	3,001	3,013	3,557	3,698	3,330
North Dakota.	270	385	358	385	379	388	456	506
Ohio	2,637	3,351	3,493	3,580	3,660	3,657	4,040	4,251
Oklahoma.	828	1,417	1,443	1,839	1,379	1,175	1,163	2,001
Oregon.	888	1,010	984	1,029	1,183	1,000	1,628	1,254
Pennsylvania.	3,153	4,517	4,875	5,365	5,258	4,283	4,567	5,537
Rhode Island.	290	256	380	380	299	373	407	488
South Carolina.	668	970	1,104	1,201	1,191	1,254	1,360	1,476
South Dakota	286	466	463	437	441	455	466	491
Tennessee	1,230	1,440	1,563	1,622	1,661	1,549	1,718	1,658
Texas.	3,593	5,665	5,716	6,019	6,758	7,134	8,918	9,101
Utah	431	1,072	941	956	879	1,871	986	1,128
Vermont	194	287	297	265	312	297	310	335
Virginia.	2,107	2,678	2,909	3,185	3,419	3,002	3,384	3,195
Washington.	1,909	1,871	2,042	2,276	2,288	2,469	2,625	2,656
West Virginia	781	1,170	1,289	1,210	1,169	1,056	1,425	1,117
Wisconsin	1,252	1,663	1,793	2,204	1,904	1,942	2,363	2,161
Wyoming	272	396	360	460	468	458	429	434

Source: U.S. Federal Highway Administration, *Highway Statistics,* annual. See <http://www.fhwa.dot.gov/policy/ohpi/hss /hsspubs.htm>.

Table 1056. **State Motor Vehicle Registrations: 1990 to 2006**

[In thousands (188,798 represents 188,798,000). Compiled principally from information obtained from state authorities, but it was necessary to draw on other sources and to make numerous estimates in order to complete series. Excludes motorcycles; see Table 1058]

Item	1990	1995	2000	2003	2004	2005	2006
All motor vehicles	**188,798**	**201,530**	**221,475**	**231,390**	**237,243**	**241,194**	**244,166**
Private and commercial	185,541	197,941	217,567	227,476	233,266	237,140	240,059
Publicly owned	3,257	3,589	3,908	3,914	3,977	4,054	4,106
Automobiles [1]	133,700	128,387	133,621	135,670	136,431	136,568	135,400
Private and commercial	132,164	126,900	132,247	134,337	135,077	135,192	134,012
Publicly owned	1,536	1,487	1,374	1,333	1,354	1,376	1,388
Buses	627	686	746	777	795	807	822
Private and commercial	275	288	314	325	330	331	339
Publicly owned	351	398	432	452	465	476	483
Trucks [1]	54,470	72,458	87,108	94,943	100,017	103,819	107,944
Private and commercial	53,101	70,754	85,005	92,814	97,860	101,616	105,708
Publicly owned	1,369	1,704	2,103	2,129	2,157	2,203	2,235

[1] Trucks include pickups, panels, and delivery vans. Personal passenger vans, passenger minivans, and utility-type vehicles are included in trucks.

Source: U.S. Federal Highway Administration, *Highway Statistics,* annual. See <http://www.fhwa.dot.gov/policy/ohpi/hss/hsspubs.htm>.

Table 1057. **Alternative Fueled Vehicles and Estimated Consumption of Vehicle Fuels by Fuel Type: 2003 to 2006**

[In thousands,(402,941 represents 402,941,000). Vehicles in use do not include concept and demonstration vehicles that are not ready for delivery to end users. Vehicles in use represent accumulated acquisitions, less retirements, as of the end of each calendar year]

Vehicles and fuel consumption	Unit	2003	2004	2005	2006
ALTERNATIVE FUELED VEHICLES IN USE					
Total.	Number	533,999	565,492	592,125	634,562
Compressed Natural Gas (CNG)	Number	114,406	118,532	117,699	116,131
Electric [1]	Number	47,485	49,536	51,398	53,526
Ethanol, 85 percent (E85) [2,3]	Number	179,090	211,800	246,363	297,099
Hydrogen.	Number	9	43	119	159
Liquefied Natural Gas (LNG)	Number	2,640	2,717	2,748	2,798
Liquefied Petroleum Gas (LPG)	Number	190,369	182,864	173,795	164,846
Other fuels [4].	Number	–	–	3	3
FUEL CONSUMPTION					
Alternative fuels	1,000 gal.(g-e-g)[6]	402,941	428,532	420,778	417,803
Compressed Natural Gas (CNG)	1,000 gal.(g-e-g)[6]	133,222	158,903	166,878	172,011
Electric [1]	1,000 gal.(g-e-g)[6]	5,141	5,269	5,219	5,104
Ethanol, 85 percent (E85) [2,5]	1,000 gal.(g-e-g)[6]	26,376	31,581	38,074	44,041
Hydrogen.	1,000 gal.(g-e-g)[6]	2	8	25	41
Liquefied Natural Gas (LNG)	1,000 gal.(g-e-g)[6]	13,503	20,888	22,409	23,474
Liquefied Petroleum Gas (LPG)	1,000 gal.(g-e-g)[6]	224,697	211,883	188,171	173,130
Other fuels [4].	1,000 gal.(g-e-g)[6]	–	–	2	2
Biodiesel.	1,000 gal.(g-e-g)[6]	18,220	28,244	91,649	260,606
Oxygenates: Methyl Tertiary Butyl Ether (MTBE). . . .	1,000 gal.(g-e-g)[6]	2,368,400	1,877,300	1,654,500	435,000
Ethanol in gasohol.	1,000 gal.(g-e-g)[6]	1,919,572	2,414,167	2,756,663	3,729,168
Total alternative and replacement fuels	1,000 gal.(g-e-g)[6]	4,709,133	4,748,243	4,923,590	4,842,577
FUEL CONSUMPTION (NATIVE UNITS)					
Alternative fuels:					
Compressed Natural Gas (CNG)	million cubic feet	16,051	19,145	20,106	20,724
Electric [1]	1,000 kwh	171,367	175,633	173,967	170,133
Ethanol, 85 percent (E85) [2,5]	1,000 gallons	36,633	43,862	52,881	61,168
Hydrogen.	1,000 kilograms	2	7	23	37
Liquefied Natural Gas (LNG)	1,000 gallons	20,459	31,648	33,953	35,567
Liquefied Petroleum Gas (LPG)	1,000 gallons	303,645	286,328	254,285	233,959
Biodiesel.	1,000 gallons	18,050	27,980	90,790	250,426
Oxygenates: Methyl Tertiary Butyl Ether (MTBE). . . .	1,000 gallons	2,912,700	2,309,160	2,035,320	534,912
Ethanol in gasohol.	1,000 gallons	2,794,874	3,514,909	4,013,679	5,429,217
Total alternative and replacement fuels	(X)	(X)	(X)	(X)	(X)

– Represents zero.   X Not applicable.   [1] Excludes gasoline-electric and diesel-electric hybrids because the input fuel is gasoline or diesel rather than an alternative transportation fuel.   [2] The remaining portion of 85 percent ethanol is gasoline. [3] For 2006, the EIA estimates that the number of E-85 vehicles that are capable of operating on E85, gasoline, or both, is about 6 million. Many of these alternative-fueled vehicles (AFVs) are sold and used as traditional gasoline-powered vehicles. In this table, AFVs in use include only those E-85 vehicles believed to be used as AFVs. These are primarily fleet-operated vehicles.   [4] May include P-Series fuel or any other fuel designated by the Secretary of Energy as an alternative fuel in accordance with the Energy Policy Act of 1995.   [5] Data shown are for AFVs in use to include only those E-85 vehicles to be used as AFVs.   [6] Gasoline equivalent gallons.

Source: U.S. Energy Information Administration, *Renewable and Alternative Fuels.* See <http://www.eia.doe.gov/fuelrenewable.html>.

Table 1058. **State Motor Vehicle Registrations, 1990 to 2006, and Licensed Drivers and Motorcycle Registrations by State: 2006**

[**In thousands (188,798 represents 188,798,000).** Motor vehicle registrations cover publicly, privately, and commercially owned vehicles. For uniformity, data have been adjusted to a calendar-year basis as registration years in states differ; figures represent net numbers where possible, excluding reregistrations and nonresident registrations. See also Table 1056]

| State | Motor vehicle registrations [1] | | | | | | 2006 | | Motor-cycle registra-tions [2] 2006 | Licensed drivers, 2006 |
	1990	1995	2000	2003	2004	2005	Total	Auto-mobiles (incl. taxis)		
U.S.	188,798	201,530	221,475	231,390	237,243	241,194	244,166	134,012	6,643	202,810
AL.	3,744	3,553	3,960	4,329	4,508	4,545	4,630	1,779	104	3,665
AK.	477	542	594	637	660	673	675	240	24	489
AZ.	2,825	2,873	3,795	3,574	3,776	3,972	4,182	2,172	114	4,033
AR.	1,448	1,613	1,840	1,889	1,918	1,940	1,994	949	59	2,035
CA.	21,926	22,432	27,698	30,248	31,400	32,487	33,182	19,632	710	23,021
CO	3,155	2,812	3,626	2,027	2,023	1,808	1,808	849	117	3,341
CT.	2,623	2,622	2,853	2,964	3,042	3,059	3,052	1,988	65	2,805
DE.	526	592	630	687	711	737	813	426	23	620
DC	262	243	242	228	239	237	219	165	1	358
FL.	10,950	10,369	11,781	14,526	15,057	15,691	16,374	7,313	583	13,989
GA	5,489	6,120	7,155	7,730	7,882	8,063	8,286	4,112	141	5,907
HI	771	802	738	903	947	948	1,009	530	31	867
ID	1,054	1,043	1,178	1,301	1,344	1,374	1,275	535	50	1,008
IL	7,873	8,973	8,973	9,250	9,232	9,458	9,876	5,874	293	8,071
IN	4,366	5,072	5,571	5,739	5,525	4,955	4,955	2,670	147	4,246
IA	2,632	2,814	3,106	3,369	3,369	3,398	3,346	1,734	161	2,041
KS.	2,012	2,085	2,296	2,314	2,347	2,368	2,389	865	72	2,003
KY.	2,909	2,631	2,826	3,389	3,319	3,428	3,558	1,943	59	2,896
LA.	2,995	3,286	3,557	3,714	3,767	3,819	3,873	1,898	61	3,014
ME	977	967	1,024	1,052	1,068	1,075	1,072	576	45	1,005
MD	3,607	3,654	3,848	3,877	4,120	4,322	4,488	2,643	73	3,694
MA	3,726	4,502	5,265	5,479	5,456	5,420	5,385	3,290	144	4,712
MI	7,209	7,674	8,436	8,540	8,399	8,247	8,154	4,716	247	7,113
MN	3,508	3,882	4,630	4,525	4,593	4,647	4,705	2,500	215	3,087
MS	1,875	2,144	2,289	1,951	1,964	1,978	1,998	1,108	28	1,930
MO	3,905	4,255	4,580	4,460	4,812	4,589	4,957	2,707	85	4,140
MT	783	968	1,026	1,010	1,009	1,009	1,067	441	86	724
NE.	1,384	1,467	1,619	1,677	1,689	1,703	1,733	818	37	1,328
NV.	853	1,047	1,220	1,222	1,281	1,349	1,367	670	56	1,626
NH	946	1,122	1,052	1,145	1,178	1,174	1,060	581	71	1,028
NJ.	5,652	5,906	6,390	6,712	6,224	6,262	5,958	3,652	163	5,834
NM.	1,301	1,484	1,529	1,509	1,543	1,548	1,581	684	43	1,338
NY.	10,196	10,274	10,235	10,802	11,099	11,863	11,284	8,447	203	11,146
NC	5,162	5,682	6,223	6,119	6,198	6,148	6,301	3,628	110	6,316
ND	630	695	694	694	701	695	712	341	25	469
OH	8,410	9,810	10,467	10,536	10,636	10,634	10,829	6,377	331	7,739
OK	2,649	2,856	3,014	3,074	3,151	3,725	3,202	1,593	94	2,264
OR	2,445	2,785	3,022	3,061	3,003	2,897	2,981	1,399	83	2,767
PA.	7,971	8,481	9,260	9,724	9,821	9,864	9,894	5,794	330	8,526
RI	672	699	760	806	808	812	806	503	31	742
SC.	2,521	2,833	3,095	3,162	3,257	3,339	3,454	1,954	88	3,068
SD.	704	709	793	827	841	854	844	372	53	583
TN.	4,444	5,400	4,820	4,796	5,035	4,980	5,091	2,854	134	4,388
TX.	12,800	13,682	14,070	14,889	16,907	17,470	17,538	8,689	352	14,907
UT.	1,206	1,447	1,628	2,006	2,084	2,210	2,236	1,068	51	1,619
VT.	462	492	515	516	523	508	588	307	33	532
VA.	4,938	5,613	6,046	6,346	6,497	6,591	6,636	3,996	81	5,211
WA	4,257	4,503	5,116	5,379	5,535	5,598	5,689	3,066	193	4,791
WV	1,225	1,425	1,442	1,409	1,396	1,352	1,441	721	40	1,335
WI.	3,815	3,993	4,366	4,647	4,705	4,725	4,971	2,623	270	4,049
WY	528	601	586	620	641	646	645	222	36	391

[1] Automobiles, trucks, and buses (excludes motorcycles). Excludes vehicles owned by military services. [2] Private and commercial.

Source: U.S. Federal Highway Administration, *Highway Statistics,* annual. See <http://www.fhwa.dot.gov/policy/ohpi/hss/hsspubs.htm>.

U.S. Census Bureau, Statistical Abstract of the United States: 2009

Table 1059. Roadway Congestion by Urbanized Area: 2005

[16,881 represents 16,881,000. Various federal, state, and local information sources were used to develop the database with the primary source being the Federal Highway Administration's Highway Performance Monitoring System]

Urbanized area	Freeway daily vehicle miles of travel		Annual person hours of delay		Annual congestion cost [1]		
	Total miles (1,000)	Per lane-mile of freeway	Total hours (1,000)	Per person [2]	Per person (dol.)	Delay and fuel cost (mil. dol.)	Fuel wasted (gal. per person)
Total, average	**16,881**	**16,446**	**42,323**	**23**	**441**	**796**	**16**
Akron, OH	5,555	12,916	3,293	5	100	62	4
Albany-Schenectady, NY	6,210	11,291	4,574	9	163	86	5
Albuquerque, NM	4,665	14,136	10,407	18	348	200	12
Allentown-Bethlehem, PA-NJ	5,085	12,253	7,483	12	222	137	8
Atlanta, GA	49,200	19,332	132,296	32	619	2,581	23
Austin, TX	9,390	16,051	22,580	26	494	422	18
Baltimore, MD.	26,455	17,179	56,769	25	486	1,126	18
Beaumont, TX	2,320	11,317	1,377	6	110	25	4
Birmingham, AL	9,550	14,044	12,416	18	339	234	12
Boston, MA-NH-RI.	40,875	16,029	93,374	23	447	1,820	15
Bridgeport-Stamford, CT-NY	10,380	17,157	14,510	17	322	280	13
Buffalo, NY	6,720	10,500	5,852	5	99	112	3
Cape Coral, FL	1,940	14,923	5,322	13	239	98	7
Charleston-North, Charleston, SC. . .	3,475	12,636	8,041	17	312	148	10
Charlotte, NC-SC	10,985	15,048	21,204	25	475	409	17
Chicago, IL-IN	55,050	20,239	202,835	25	487	3,968	17
Cincinnati, OH-KY-IN	18,560	15,467	24,378	15	283	459	11
Cleveland, OH	18,150	12,918	13,162	7	132	236	5
Colorado Springs, CO	4,125	12,692	7,332	15	268	131	9
Columbus, OH	14,960	15,665	21,958	18	342	409	13
Dallas-Fort, Worth-Arlington, TX. . . .	57,300	18,190	152,129	34	618	2,747	24
Dayton, OH	7,485	13,366	6,863	9	170	127	6
Denver-Aurora, CO	19,900	15,920	64,997	31	563	1,176	20
Detroit, MI	33,045	17,256	115,547	28	536	2,174	19
El Paso, TX-NM	4,555	16,268	8,675	13	235	159	9
Fresno, CA	3,865	13,328	6,625	11	207	127	7
Grand Rapids, MI	4,885	10,978	7,593	13	232	138	7
Hartford, CT	10,590	13,405	9,252	10	187	166	7
Honolulu, HI	6,015	14,494	9,342	13	236	166	9
Houston, TX	46,350	18,690	124,131	33	587	2,225	24
Indianapolis, IN	11,050	15,137	24,318	23	462	478	16
Jacksonville, FL	11,190	14,439	20,779	21	380	376	14
Kansas City, MO-KS	20,675	11,056	13,737	9	171	256	6
Las Vegas, NV	9,200	18,400	29,493	22	398	543	15
Los Angeles-Long Beach-Santa Ana, CA	140,000	23,850	490,552	39	744	9,325	31
Louisville, KY-IN	11,585	16,090	20,558	23	437	395	16
Memphis, TN-MS-AR	8,800	13,858	17,129	17	311	317	9
Miami, FL	39,470	19,254	150,146	28	512	2,730	20
Milwaukee, WI	10,750	14,828	15,402	11	193	282	7
Minneapolis-St. Paul, MN	28,140	17,264	59,746	24	436	1,099	17
Nashville-Davidson, TN	13,300	13,641	21,707	22	408	404	14
New Haven, CT	7,465	14,356	5,706	10	186	104	8
New Orleans, LA.	5,700	13,735	10,837	10	190	207	6
New York-Newark, NY-NJ-CT	117,500	16,319	384,046	22	415	7,383	14
Oklahoma City, OK	9,245	12,327	9,468	11	202	171	7
Omaha, NE-IA	3,590	11,967	8,784	14	240	154	8
Orlando, FL	12,470	13,933	40,595	30	542	738	19
Oxnard-Ventura, CA	6,700	18,873	12,184	21	395	229	14
Pensacola, FL-AL	1,400	10,000	4,773	14	242	84	8
Philadelphia, PA-NJ-DE-MD	35,325	15,325	111,704	21	392	2,076	13
Phoenix, AZ	28,370	20,192	81,727	25	516	1,687	18
Pittsburgh, PA.	12,330	9,786	16,159	9	159	285	5
Portland, OR-WA	13,620	17,804	33,712	19	362	626	14
Providence, RI-MA	11,505	12,643	19,482	16	276	343	9
Raleigh-Durham, NC	9,450	14,000	18,234	19	364	346	12
Richmond, VA.	11,680	11,177	10,081	11	197	181	7
Riverside-San Bernardino, CA	24,020	21,351	48,266	27	530	955	22
Sacramento, CA	15,415	19,637	39,577	23	417	729	17
Salem, OR.	1,490	11,920	1,773	8	140	31	5
Salt Lake City, UT	7,570	14,019	14,236	15	258	250	10
San Antonio, TX	17,065	15,656	29,380	22	390	530	15
San Diego, CA	39,395	20,048	90,711	31	588	1,708	24
San Francisco-Oakland, CA	50,000	20,202	129,919	31	583	2,414	24
San Jose, CA.	16,820	18,484	50,038	30	537	899	21
Sarasota-Bradenton, FL	2,510	15,212	8,840	14	244	156	8
Seattle, WA	30,800	17,017	75,056	25	476	1,431	18
St. Louis, MO-IL	27,200	12,710	37,772	18	338	711	11
Tampa-St. Petersburg, FL.	13,050	15,353	56,203	25	446	1,005	16
Toledo, OH-MI	4,090	12,394	4,170	8	151	78	5
Tucson, AZ	3,540	13,615	17,011	23	451	338	14
Tulsa, OK	6,960	9,342	8,453	10	184	149	6
Virginia Beach, VA.	13,105	13,868	25,602	17	303	467	11
Washington, DC-VA-MD	38,580	18,820	127,394	30	545	2,331	21

[1] Value of extra time (delay) and the extra fuel consumed by vehicles traveling at slower speeds. Fuel cost per gallon is the average price for each state. [2] The hours of extra travel time divided by the number of urban area peak period travelers. This is an annual measure indicating the sum of all extra travel time that would occur during the year for the average traveler.

Source: Texas Transportation Institute, College Station, Texas; *2007 Urban Mobility Study*; (issued September 2007) (copyright). See <http://mobility.tamu.edu/ums/>.

674 Transportation

Table 1060. Commuting to Work by State: 2006

[In percent, except as indicated (138,266 represents 138,266,000). For workers 16 years old and over. The American Community Survey universe includes the household population and the population living in institutions, college dormitories, and other group quarters. Based on a sample and subject to sampling variability; see Appendix III]

State	Total workers (1,000)	Commuted by car, truck, or van		Used public transpor- tation [1]	Walked	Used other means [2]	Worked at home	Mean travel time to work (min.)
		Drove alone	Car- pooled	Percent of workers who—				
U.S.	**138,266**	**76.0**	**10.7**	**4.8**	**2.9**	**1.7**	**3.9**	**25.0**
AL.	1,964	83.6	11.3	0.5	1.1	1.1	2.5	23.6
AK.	317	67.7	12.7	1.1	9.1	4.3	5.1	17.7
AZ.	2,732	74.6	13.9	2.1	2.3	2.5	4.5	25.0
AR.	1,224	80.2	12.9	0.4	1.8	1.4	3.3	20.7
CA.	16,336	73.0	12.4	5.0	2.7	2.1	4.8	26.8
CO	2,393	75.1	10.6	3.2	3.1	2.3	5.7	23.9
CT.	1,715	79.7	8.4	4.1	3.0	1.4	3.5	24.1
DE.	398	80.8	9.4	2.8	2.7	1.6	2.6	23.6
DC	284	35.4	6.3	39.0	11.8	3.4	4.0	29.2
FL.	8,143	79.3	10.9	2.0	1.7	2.2	4.0	25.9
GA	4,295	78.2	11.5	2.4	1.7	1.9	4.2	27.3
HI	629	67.0	16.0	5.4	4.8	2.4	4.3	25.5
ID	675	77.2	11.7	0.8	3.4	1.9	5.0	20.1
IL	5,991	74.3	9.3	8.4	2.9	1.5	3.6	27.9
IN	2,951	82.4	9.9	1.0	2.2	1.3	3.2	22.3
IA	1,505	78.5	10.8	1.0	3.7	1.3	4.7	18.2
KS.	1,377	81.8	9.2	0.6	2.6	1.5	4.3	18.5
KY.	1,837	81.5	11.3	1.0	2.0	0.9	3.2	22.4
LA.	1,808	81.6	11.6	1.1	1.8	1.7	2.2	25.1
ME	649	77.6	11.0	0.7	4.2	1.6	4.9	22.3
MD	2,813	72.8	10.7	8.8	2.6	1.4	3.6	30.6
MA	3,173	73.7	8.5	8.6	4.2	1.4	3.6	26.6
MI	4,433	82.9	9.1	1.2	2.2	1.1	3.4	23.4
MN	2,671	78.1	9.3	3.0	3.1	1.5	4.9	22.0
MS	1,178	82.2	12.1	0.4	1.8	1.4	2.1	24.0
MO	2,741	80.8	10.4	1.4	2.1	1.1	4.1	22.9
MT	460	72.7	12.0	0.9	5.3	2.4	6.7	17.6
NE.	910	79.1	10.4	0.5	3.5	1.4	5.0	17.7
NV.	1,202	76.7	12.3	3.6	2.1	2.2	3.1	24.2
NH	685	81.7	8.6	0.7	3.4	1.2	4.3	24.6
NJ.	4,129	71.9	9.3	10.3	3.4	1.9	3.2	29.1
NM	858	78.2	12.5	0.9	2.2	1.5	4.6	20.9
NY.	8,740	54.4	7.6	26.1	6.3	1.9	3.8	30.9
NC	4,104	79.8	12.5	1.0	1.8	1.3	3.6	23.4
ND	332	79.3	9.2	0.4	4.1	1.2	5.8	15.5
OH	5,326	83.1	8.3	2.0	2.5	1.1	3.1	22.1
OK	1,599	80.4	11.6	0.5	2.1	1.7	3.7	20.0
OR	1,742	71.4	11.7	4.4	3.9	2.5	6.0	21.8
PA	5,720	76.4	9.9	5.2	4.1	1.2	3.2	25.0
RI	515	81.1	8.9	2.6	3.0	1.8	2.7	22.3
SC.	1,938	81.1	11.3	0.6	1.8	1.7	3.4	22.9
SD.	398	77.5	9.6	0.4	4.3	1.5	6.6	15.9
TN.	2,698	83.3	10.2	0.7	1.4	1.1	3.2	23.5
TX.	10,515	78.5	12.7	1.7	1.9	1.8	3.5	24.6
UT.	1,190	75.2	13.1	2.6	2.8	1.8	4.6	20.8
VT.	323	75.1	11.2	0.8	6.1	1.4	5.4	21.2
VA.	3,788	77.0	11.4	4.1	2.3	1.3	3.9	26.9
WA	3,030	72.8	11.8	5.2	3.3	1.9	5.1	25.2
WV	740	80.0	12.1	1.0	3.1	1.4	2.4	25.6
WI	2,821	79.9	9.2	1.9	3.5	1.6	3.9	20.8
WY	268	76.0	12.5	1.3	3.1	2.0	5.2	17.9

[1] Excluding taxicabs. [2] Includes taxicabs, motorcycles, bicycles, and other means.

Source: U.S. Census Bureau; 2006 American Community Survey; B08006. Sex of Worker by Means of Transportation to Work; and R0801. Mean Travel Time to Work of Workers 16 Years Old and Over Who Did Not Work At Home (minutes); using American FactFinder®. See <http://factfinder.census.gov/>; (accessed 16 January 2008).

U.S. Census Bureau, Statistical Abstract of the United States: 2009

Table 1061. Motor Vehicle Distance Traveled by Type of Vehicle: 1970 to 2006

[1,110 represents 1,110,000,000,000. The travel data by vehicle type and stratification of trucks are estimated by the Federal Highway Administration (FHWA)]

Year	Vehicle-miles of travel (bil.)					Average miles traveled per vehicle (1,000)				
	Total [1]	Cars [1]	Buses [2]	Vans, pickups, SUVs [3]	Trucks [4]	Total [1]	Cars [1]	Buses [2]	Vans, pickups, SUVs [3]	Trucks [4]
1970 . . .	1,110	920	4.5	123	62	10.0	10.0	12.0	8.7	13.6
1980 . . .	1,527	1,122	6.1	291	108	9.5	8.8	11.5	10.4	18.7
1985 . . .	1,775	1,256	4.5	391	124	10.0	9.4	7.5	10.5	20.6
1986 . . .	1,835	1,280	4.7	424	127	10.1	9.5	7.9	10.8	22.1
1987 . . .	1,921	1,325	5.3	457	134	10.5	9.7	8.9	11.1	23.3
1988 . . .	2,026	1,380	5.5	502	138	10.7	10.0	8.9	11.5	22.5
1989 . . .	2,096	1,412	5.7	536	143	10.9	10.2	9.1	11.7	22.9
1990 . . .	2,144	1,418	5.7	575	146	11.1	10.3	9.1	11.9	23.6
1991 . . .	2,172	1,367	5.8	649	150	11.3	10.3	9.1	12.2	24.2
1992 . . .	2,247	1,381	5.8	707	153	11.6	10.6	9.0	12.4	25.4
1993 . . .	2,296	1,385	6.1	746	160	11.6	10.5	9.4	12.4	26.3
1994 . . .	2,358	1,416	6.4	765	170	11.7	10.8	9.6	12.2	25.8
1995 . . .	2,423	1,438	6.4	790	178	11.8	11.2	9.4	12.0	26.5
1996 . . .	2,486	1,470	6.6	817	183	11.8	11.3	9.4	11.8	26.1
1997 . . .	2,562	1,503	6.8	851	191	12.1	11.6	9.8	12.1	27.0
1998 . . .	2,632	1,550	7.0	868	196	12.2	11.8	9.8	12.2	25.4
1999 . . .	2,691	1,569	7.7	901	203	12.2	11.9	10.5	12.0	26.0
2000 . . .	2,747	1,600	7.6	923	206	12.2	11.9	10.2	11.7	25.7
2001 . . .	2,797	1,628	7.1	943	209	11.9	11.8	9.4	11.2	26.6
2002 . . .	2,856	1,658	6.8	966	215	12.2	12.2	9.0	11.4	27.1
2003 . . .	2,890	1,672	6.8	984	218	12.2	12.3	8.7	11.3	28.1
2004 . . .	2,965	1,700	6.8	1,027	221	12.2	12.5	8.5	11.2	27.0
2005 . . .	2,989	1,708	7.0	1,041	223	12.1	12.5	8.6	10.9	26.2
2006 . . .	3,014	1,683	7.0	1,089	223	12.4	12.4	8.5	11.0	27.3

[1] Motorcycles included with cars through 1994; thereafter in total, not shown separately.   [2] Includes school buses.   [3] SUV = Sport utility vehicles.   [4] Includes combinations.

Source: U.S. Federal Highway Administration, *Highway Statistics,* annual. See <http://www.fhwa.dot.gov/policy/ohpi/hss/hsspubs.htm>.

Table 1062. Domestic Motor Fuel Consumption by Type of Vehicle: 1970 to 2006

[92.3 represents 92,300,000,000. Comprises all fuel types used for propulsion of vehicles under state motor fuels laws. Excludes federal purchases for military use. Minus sign (–) indicates decrease]

Year	Annual fuel consumption (bil. gal.)						Average miles per gallon				
	All vehicles [1]	Annual percent change [2]	Cars [1]	Buses [3]	Vans, pickups, SUVs [4]	Trucks [5]	All vehicles [1]	Cars [1]	Buses [3]	Vans, pickups, SUVs [4]	Trucks [5]
1970 . . .	92.3	4.8	67.8	0.8	12.3	11.3	12.0	13.5	5.5	10.0	5.5
1980 . . .	115.0	–5.9	70.2	1.0	23.8	20.0	13.3	16.0	6.0	12.2	5.4
1985 . . .	121.3	2.2	71.7	0.8	27.4	21.4	14.6	17.5	5.4	14.3	5.8
1986 . . .	125.2	3.2	73.4	0.9	29.1	21.9	14.7	17.4	5.3	14.6	5.8
1987 . . .	127.5	1.8	73.5	0.9	30.6	22.5	15.1	18.0	5.8	14.9	5.9
1988 . . .	130.1	2.0	73.5	0.9	32.7	22.9	15.6	18.8	5.8	15.4	6.0
1989 . . .	131.9	1.4	74.1	0.9	33.3	23.5	15.9	18.0	6.0	16.1	6.1
1990 . . .	130.8	–0.8	69.8	0.9	35.6	24.5	16.4	20.3	6.4	16.1	6.0
1991 . . .	128.6	–1.7	64.5	0.9	38.2	25.0	16.9	21.2	6.7	17.0	6.0
1992 . . .	132.9	3.3	65.6	0.9	40.9	25.5	16.9	21.0	6.6	17.3	6.0
1993 . . .	137.3	3.3	67.2	0.9	42.9	26.2	16.7	20.6	6.6	17.4	6.1
1994 . . .	140.8	2.5	68.1	1.0	44.1	27.7	16.7	20.8	6.6	17.3	6.1
1995 . . .	143.8	2.1	68.1	1.0	45.6	29.0	16.8	21.1	6.6	17.3	6.1
1996 . . .	147.4	2.5	69.2	1.0	47.4	29.6	16.9	21.2	6.6	17.2	6.2
1997 . . .	150.4	2.0	69.9	1.0	49.4	29.9	17.0	21.5	6.7	17.2	6.4
1998 . . .	155.4	3.3	71.7	1.1	50.5	32.0	16.9	21.6	6.7	17.2	6.1
1999 . . .	161.4	3.9	73.2	1.1	52.8	33.9	16.7	21.4	6.7	17.0	6.0
2000 . . .	162.5	0.7	73.1	1.1	52.9	35.2	16.9	21.9	6.8	17.4	5.8
2001 . . .	163.5	0.6	73.6	1.0	53.5	35.2	17.1	22.1	6.9	17.6	5.9
2002 . . .	168.7	3.2	75.5	1.0	55.2	36.8	16.9	22.0	6.8	17.5	5.8
2003 . . .	170.0	0.8	75.5	1.0	60.7	32.7	17.0	22.2	7.0	16.2	6.7
2004 . . .	173.5	2.1	75.4	1.3	63.4	33.1	17.1	22.5	5.0	16.2	6.7
2005 . . .	174.8	0.7	77.4	1.1	58.9	37.2	17.2	22.1	6.2	17.7	6.0
2006 . . .	174.9	0.1	75.0	1.1	60.7	37.9	17.1	22.4	6.1	18.0	5.9

[1] Motorcycles included with cars through 1994; thereafter in total, not shown separately.   [2] Change from immediate prior year.   [3] Includes school buses.   [4] SUV = Sport utility vehicles.   [5] Includes combinations.

Source: U.S. Federal Highway Administration, *Highway Statistics,* annual. See <http://www.fhwa.dot.gov/policy/ohpi/hss/hsspubs.htm>.

Table 1063. Motor Vehicle Accidents—Number and Deaths: 1980 to 2006

[17.9 represents 17,900,000]

Item	Unit	1980	1990	1995	2000	2002	2003	2004	2005	2006
ACCIDENTS										
Motor vehicle accidents [1]	Million...	17.9	11.5	10.7	13.4	18.3	11.8	10.9	10.7	10.4
DEATHS										
Motor vehicle deaths within 1 yr. [2]	1,000...	53.2	46.8	43.4	43.4	45.4	44.1	44.9	45.5	44.7
Noncollision accidents	1,000...	(NA)	4.9	4.4	4.8	5.3	5.1	5.1	5.3	5.3
Collision accidents:										
With other motor vehicles	1,000...	23.0	19.9	19.0	19.1	19.2	19.8	19.6	19.4	18.5
With pedestrians	1,000...	9.7	7.3	6.4	5.9	6.1	5.7	6.0	6.2	6.1
With fixed objects	1,000...	(NA)	13.1	12.1	12.3	13.6	12.4	13.0	13.3	13.4
Deaths within 30 days [3]	1,000...	51.1	44.6	41.8	41.9	43.0	42.9	42.8	43.5	42.6
Occupants	1,000...	36.8	33.9	33.1	33.5	34.1	33.6	33.3	33.1	32.1
Passenger cars	1,000...	27.4	24.1	22.4	20.7	20.6	19.7	19.2	18.5	17.8
Light trucks [4]	1,000...	7.5	8.6	9.6	11.5	12.3	12.5	12.7	13.0	12.7
Large trucks [4]	1,000...	1.3	0.7	0.6	0.8	0.7	0.7	0.8	0.8	0.8
Buses	1,000...	(Z)	(Z)	(Z)	(Z)	(Z)	(Z)	0.0	0.1	(Z)
Other/unknown	1,000...	0.5	0.5	0.4	0.5	0.5	0.6	0.6	0.7	0.7
Motorcycle riders [5]	1,000...	5.1	3.2	2.2	2.9	3.3	3.7	4.0	4.6	4.8
Nonoccupants	1,000...	9.2	7.5	6.5	5.6	5.6	5.5	5.5	5.9	5.7
Pedestrians	1,000...	8.1	6.5	5.6	4.8	4.9	4.8	4.7	4.9	4.8
Pedalcyclist	1,000...	1.0	0.9	0.8	0.7	0.7	0.6	0.7	0.8	0.8
Other/unknown	1,000...	0.1	0.1	0.1	0.1	0.1	0.1	0.1	0.2	0.2
Traffic death rates: [3, 6]										
Per 100 million vehicle miles	Rate....	3.3	2.1	1.7	1.5	1.5	1.5	1.4	1.5	1.4
Per 100,000 licensed drivers	Rate....	35.2	26.7	23.7	22.0	22.1	21.9	21.5	21.7	21.0
Per 100,000 registered vehicles	Rate....	34.8	24.2	21.2	19.3	19.1	18.6	18.0	17.7	17.0
Per 100,000 resident population	Rate....	22.5	17.9	15.9	14.9	14.9	14.8	14.6	14.7	14.2

NA Not available.   Z Fewer than 50.   [1] Covers only accidents occurring on the road. Data are estimated. Year-to-year comparisons should be made with caution.   [2] Deaths that occur within 1 year of accident. Includes collision categories not shown separately.   [3] Within 30 days of accident. Source: U.S. National Highway Traffic Safety Administration, *Traffic Safety Facts*, annual; and unpublished data. See Internet site <http://www-nrd.nhtsa.dot.gov/CATS/Index.aspx>.   [4] See footnotes 2 and 3 in Table 1067.   [5] Includes motorized cycles.   [6] Based on 30-day definition of traffic deaths.

Source: Except as noted, National Safety Council, Itasca, IL, *Injury Facts*, annual (copyright). See <http://www.nsc.org/>.

Table 1064. Traffic Fatalities by State: 1990 to 2006

[For deaths within 30 days of the accident]

State	1990	2000	2005	2006	Fatality rate[1] 1990	Fatality rate[1] 2006	State	1990	2000	2005	2006	Fatality rate[1] 1990	Fatality rate[1] 2006
U.S...	**44,599**	**41,945**	**43,510**	**42,642**	**2.1**	**1.4**	MO....	1,097	1,157	1,257	1,096	2.2	1.6
AL....	1,121	996	1,148	1,208	2.6	2.0	MT....	212	237	251	263	2.5	2.3
AK....	98	106	73	74	2.5	1.5	NE....	262	276	276	269	1.9	1.4
AZ....	869	1,036	1,179	1,288	2.5	2.1	NV....	343	323	427	432	3.4	2.0
AR....	604	652	654	665	2.9	2.0	NH....	158	126	166	127	1.6	0.9
CA....	5,192	3,753	4,333	4,236	2.0	1.3	NJ....	886	731	747	772	1.5	1.0
CO....	544	681	606	535	2.0	1.1	NM....	499	432	488	484	3.1	1.9
CT....	385	341	278	301	1.5	1.0	NY....	2,217	1,460	1,434	1,456	2.1	1.0
DE....	138	123	133	148	2.1	1.6	NC....	1,385	1,557	1,547	1,559	2.2	1.5
DC....	48	48	48	37	1.4	1.0	ND....	112	86	123	111	1.9	1.4
FL.....	2,891	2,999	3,518	3,374	2.6	1.7	OH....	1,638	1,366	1,321	1,238	1.8	1.1
GA....	1,562	1,541	1,729	1,693	2.2	1.5	OK....	641	650	803	765	1.9	1.6
HI....	177	132	140	161	2.2	1.6	OR....	579	451	487	477	2.2	1.3
ID....	244	276	275	267	2.5	1.8	PA....	1,646	1,520	1,616	1,525	1.9	1.4
IL.....	1,589	1,418	1,363	1,254	1.9	1.2	RI.....	84	80	87	81	1.1	1.0
IN.....	1,049	886	938	899	2.0	1.3	SC....	979	1,065	1,094	1,037	2.8	2.1
IA....	465	445	450	439	2.0	1.4	SD....	153	173	186	191	2.2	2.1
KS....	444	461	428	468	1.9	1.6	TN....	1,177	1,307	1,270	1,287	2.5	1.8
KY....	849	820	985	913	2.5	1.9	TX....	3,250	3,779	3,536	3,475	2.1	1.5
LA....	959	938	963	982	2.5	2.2	UT....	272	373	282	287	1.9	1.1
ME....	213	169	169	188	1.8	1.3	VT....	90	76	73	87	1.5	1.1
MD....	707	588	614	651	1.7	1.2	VA....	1,079	929	947	963	1.8	1.2
MA....	605	433	441	430	1.3	0.8	WA....	825	631	649	630	1.8	1.1
MI....	1,571	1,382	1,129	1,085	1.9	1.0	WV....	481	411	374	410	3.1	2.0
MN....	566	625	559	494	1.5	0.9	WI....	769	799	815	724	1.7	1.2
MS....	750	949	931	911	3.1	2.2	WY....	125	152	170	195	2.1	2.1

[1] Deaths per 100 million vehicle miles traveled.

Source: U.S. National Highway Traffic Safety Administration, *Traffic Safety Facts*, annual. See <http://www-nrd.nhtsa.dot.gov/CATS/Index.aspx>.

U.S. Census Bureau, Statistical Abstract of the United States: 2009

Table 1065. **Fatal Motor Vehicle Accidents—National Summary: 1990 to 2006**

[Based on data from the Fatality Analysis Reporting System (FARS). FARS gathers data on accidents that result in loss of human life. FARS is operated and maintained by National Highway Traffic Safety Administration's (NHTSA) National Center for Statistics and Analysis (NCSA). FARS data are gathered on motor vehicle accidents that occurred on a roadway customarily open to the public, resulting in the death of a person within 30 days of the accident. Collection of these data depend on the use of police, hospital, medical examiner/coroner, and Emergency Medical Services reports; state vehicle registration, driver licensing, and highway department files; and vital statistics documents and death certificates. See source for further detail]

Item	1990	1995	2000	2002	2003	2004	2005	2006
Fatal crashes, total	**39,836**	**37,241**	**37,526**	**38,491**	**38,477**	**38,444**	**39,252**	**38,588**
One vehicle involved	23,445	21,250	21,117	22,164	21,775	21,836	22,678	22,711
Two or more vehicles involved.	16,391	15,991	16,409	16,327	16,702	16,608	16,574	15,877
Persons killed in fatal crashes [1]	**44,599**	**41,817**	**41,945**	**43,005**	**42,884**	**42,836**	**43,510**	**42,642**
Occupants.	37,134	35,291	36,348	37,375	37,341	37,304	37,646	36,902
Drivers.	25,750	24,390	25,567	26,659	26,779	26,871	27,491	27,323
Passengers	11,276	10,782	10,695	10,604	10,458	10,355	10,069	9,473
Other	108	119	86	112	104	78	86	106
Nonoccupants	7,465	6,526	5,597	5,630	5,543	5,532	5,864	5,740
Pedestrians	6,482	5,584	4,763	4,851	4,774	4,675	4,892	4,784
Pedalcyclists.	859	833	693	665	629	727	786	773
Other	124	109	141	114	140	130	186	183
Occupants killed by vehicle type:								
Passenger cars	24,092	22,423	20,699	20,569	19,725	19,192	18,512	17,800
Mini–compact (95 inches)	3,556	2,207	1,113	813	636	599	452	414
Subcompact (95 to 99 inches)	4,753	4,584	3,660	3,435	3,081	2,718	2,536	2,216
Compact (100 to 104 inches).	5,310	6,899	7,022	7,061	6,769	6,650	6,288	6,044
Intermediate (105 to 109) inches	4,849	4,666	5,204	5,514	5,583	5,667	5,571	5,420
Full-size (110 to 114) inches	2,386	2,116	2,287	2,434	2,451	2,354	2,491	2,508
Largest (115 inches and over)	2,249	1,297	897	828	782	807	796	769
Unknown	989	654	516	484	423	397	378	429
Motorcycles	3,129	2,114	2,783	3,150	3,583	3,827	4,418	4,654
Other motorized cycles	115	113	114	120	131	201	158	156
Light trucks [2]	8,601	9,568	11,526	12,274	12,546	12,674	13,037	12,721
Pickup	5,979	5,938	6,003	6,100	5,957	5,838	6,067	5,984
Utility.	1,214	1,935	3,358	4,031	4,483	4,760	4,831	4,910
Van	1,154	1,639	2,129	2,109	2,080	2,046	2,112	1,802
Other	254	56	36	34	26	30	27	25
Large trucks [3]	705	648	754	689	726	766	804	805
Medium trucks	134	96	106	87	82	99	118	107
Heavy trucks	571	552	648	602	644	667	686	698
Buses.	32	33	22	45	41	42	58	27
Other vehicles	296	307	401	424	477	512	492	499
Unknown.	164	85	49	104	112	90	167	240
Persons involved in fatal crashes.	**107,777**	**102,102**	**100,716**	**101,784**	**101,862**	**100,760**	**101,262**	**98,040**
Occupants.	99,297	94,621	94,325	95,403	95,470	94,579	94,614	91,557
Drivers.	58,893	56,164	57,280	58,113	58,517	58,395	59,220	57,695
Passengers	40,229	38,252	36,889	37,080	36,743	35,992	35,231	33,665
Other	175	205	156	210	210	192	163	197
Nonoccupants	8,480	7,481	6,391	6,381	6,392	6,181	6,648	6,483
Vehicle miles traveled (VMT) (bil.)	2,144	2,423	2,747	2,856	2,890	2,965	2,989	3,014
Licensed drivers (1,000)	167,015	176,628	190,625	194,602	196,166	198,889	200,549	202,810
Registered vehicles (1,000)	184,275	197,065	217,028	225,685	230,788	237,949	245,628	251,423
Percent distribution of fatal accidents by the highest blood alcohol concentration (BAC) in accident:								
0.00 percent	49.5	57.7	58.7	59.2	60.2	60.5	59.5	58.7
0.01 to 0.07 percent	6.5	5.7	5.9	5.6	5.6	5.4	5.6	5.8
0.08 percent and over	44.0	36.7	35.4	35.3	34.3	34.2	34.9	35.6
Fatalities per 100,000 resident population:								
Under 5 years old	4.9	4.3	3.7	3.1	3.1	3.2	2.9	2.8
5 to 15 years old	6.4	6.0	4.7	4.3	4.4	4.4	3.9	3.6
16 to 24 years old.	35.2	30.7	28.5	29.3	28.1	27.7	27.5	27.2
25 to 44 years old.	19.7	17.2	16.1	16.2	16.0	15.8	16.3	16.1
45 to 64 years old.	14.9	13.6	13.8	13.8	14.0	13.9	14.3	13.9
65 to 79 years old.	18.8	18.5	17.1	17.0	16.3	16.3	16.3	14.8
80 years old and over	26.8	28.0	25.0	23.3	24.5	22.4	21.4	19.5
Fatalities per 100 million VMT [4]	2.1	1.7	1.5	1.5	1.5	1.4	1.5	1.4
Fatalities per 100,000 licensed drivers	26.7	23.7	22.0	22.1	21.9	21.5	21.7	21.0
Licensed driver per person.	0.7	0.7	0.7	0.7	0.7	0.7	0.7	0.7
VMT [4] per registered vehicle	11,637	12,294	12,657	12,653	12,522	12,461	12,168	11,988
Fatalities per 100,000 registered vehicles . .	24.2	21.2	19.3	19.1	18.6	18.0	17.7	17.0
Fatal crashes per 100 million VMT [4]	1.9	1.5	1.4	1.3	1.3	1.3	1.3	1.3
Involved vehicles per fatal crash	1.5	1.5	1.5	1.5	1.5	1.4	1.5	1.5
Fatalities per fatal crash	1.1	1.1	1.1	1.1	1.1	1.1	1.1	1.1
Fatalities per 100,000 resident population. .	17.9	15.9	14.9	14.9	14.8	14.6	14.7	14.2

[1] Deaths within 30 days of the accident.   [2] Trucks with a gross vehicle weight rating of 10,000 pounds or less, including pickups, vans, truck-based station wagons, and utility vehicles.   [3] Trucks with a gross vehicle weight rating of over 10,000 pounds.   [4] VMT = vehicle miles of travel.

Source: U.S. National Highway Traffic Safety Administration, *Fatality Analysis Reporting System,* annual. See <http://www-nrd .nhtsa.dot.gov/CATS/Index.aspx>.

Table 1066. Motor Vehicle Occupants and Nonoccupants Killed and Injured: 1980 to 2006

[For deaths within 30 days of the accident. (3,231 represents 3,231,000)]

Year	Total	Occupants Total	Passenger cars	Light trucks [1]	Large trucks [1]	Buses	Other/ unknown [3]	Motor-cycle riders [2]	Nonoccupants Total	Pedes-trian	Pedal-cyclist	Other/ unknown [3]
KILLED												
1980	51,091	36,783	27,449	7,486	1,262	46	540	5,144	9,164	8,070	965	129
1985	43,825	31,479	23,212	6,689	977	57	544	4,564	7,782	6,808	890	84
1990	44,599	33,890	24,092	8,601	705	32	460	3,244	7,465	6,482	859	124
1995	41,817	33,064	22,423	9,568	648	33	392	2,227	6,526	5,584	833	109
1996 [4]	42,065	33,534	22,505	9,932	621	21	455	2,161	6,368	5,449	765	154
1997	42,013	33,609	22,199	10,249	723	18	420	2,116	6,288	5,321	814	153
1998	41,501	33,088	21,194	10,705	742	38	409	2,294	6,119	5,228	760	131
1999	41,717	33,392	20,862	11,265	759	59	447	2,483	5,842	4,939	754	149
2000	41,945	33,451	20,699	11,526	754	22	450	2,897	5,597	4,763	693	141
2001	42,196	33,243	20,320	11,723	708	34	458	3,197	5,756	4,901	732	123
2002	43,005	34,105	20,569	12,274	689	45	528	3,270	5,630	4,851	665	114
2003	42,884	33,627	19,725	12,546	726	41	589	3,714	5,543	4,774	629	140
2004	42,836	33,276	19,192	12,674	766	42	602	4,028	5,532	4,675	727	130
2005	43,510	33,070	18,512	13,037	804	58	659	4,576	5,864	4,892	786	186
2006	42,642	32,092	17,800	12,721	805	27	739	4,810	5,740	4,784	773	183
INJURED (1,000)												
1990	3,231	2,960	2,376	505	42	33	4	84	187	105	75	7
1995	3,465	3,246	2,469	722	30	19	4	57	162	86	67	10
1996	3,483	3,277	2,458	761	33	20	4	55	151	82	58	11
1997	3,348	3,149	2,341	755	31	17	6	53	146	77	58	11
1998	3,192	3,012	2,201	763	29	16	4	49	131	69	53	8
1999	3,236	3,047	2,138	847	33	22	7	50	140	85	51	3
2000	3,189	2,997	2,052	887	31	18	10	58	134	78	51	5
2001	3,033	2,841	1,927	861	29	15	9	60	131	78	45	8
2002	2,926	2,735	1,805	879	26	19	6	65	126	71	48	7
2003	2,889	2,697	1,756	889	27	18	7	67	124	70	46	8
2004	2,788	2,594	1,643	900	27	16	7	76	118	68	41	9
2005	2,699	2,494	1,573	872	27	11	10	87	118	64	45	8
2006	2,575	2,375	1,475	857	23	10	11	88	112	61	44	7

[1] See footnotes 2 and 3 in table 1067.   [2] Includes motorized cycles.   [3] Includes combination trucks.   [4] Total includes two fatalities of unknown person type, not specified in distribution.

Source: U.S. National Highway Traffic Safety Administration, *Traffic Safety Facts,* annual; and unpublished data. See <http://www-nrd.nhtsa.dot.gov/CATS/index.aspx>.

Table 1067. Vehicles Involved in Crashes by Vehicle Type, Rollover Occurrence, and Crash Severity: 2006

[10,480.5 represents 10,480,500. Excludes motorcycles]

Vehicle type	Total Number (1,000)	Total Percent	Rollover occurrence Yes Number (1,000)	Yes Percent	No Number (1,000)	No Percent
Vehicles involved in all crashes [1]	**10,480.5**	**100.0**	**274.4**	**2.6**	**10,206.1**	**97.4**
Passenger cars.	5,864.1	100.0	101.8	1.7	5,762.3	98.3
Light trucks: [2]						
Pickup.	1,587.8	100.0	56.4	3.6	1,531.4	96.4
Utility.	1,695.5	100.0	80.2	4.7	1,615.3	95.3
Van.	764.3	100.0	13.6	1.8	750.7	98.2
Other.	108.7	100.0	2.4	2.2	106.3	97.8
Large truck [3]	384.8	100.0	15.5	4.0	369.3	96.0
Bus.	51.6	100.0	0.1	0.1	51.5	99.9
Other/unknown	23.8	100.0	4.6	16.9	19.2	80.7
Fatal crashes.	53.0	100.0	11.4	21.5	41.6	78.5
Passenger cars.	24.1	100.0	4.1	17.0	20.0	83.0
Light trucks: [2]						
Pickup.	10.5	100.0	2.9	27.8	7.6	72.2
Utility.	8.3	100.0	2.9	35.1	5.4	64.9
Van.	3.4	100.0	0.6	19.9	2.8	83.1
Other.	0.1	100.0	(Z)	16.1	0.1	83.9
Large truck [3]	4.7	100.0	0.7	14.7	4.0	85.3
Bus.	0.3	100.0	(Z)	3.0	0.3	97.0
Other/unknown	1.6	100.0	0.2	15.6	1.4	84.4

Z Less than 50.   [1] Includes injury and property-only crashes, not shown separately.   [2] Trucks of 10,000 pounds gross vehicle weight rating or less, including pickups, vans, truck-based station wagons and utility vehicles.   [3] Trucks over 10,000 pounds gross vehicle weight rating.

Source: U.S. National Highway Traffic Safety Administration, *Traffic Safety Facts,* annual. See <http://www-nrd.nhtsa.dot.gov/CATS/index.aspx>.

Transportation   679

Table 1068. Speeding-Related Traffic Fatalities by State, Road Type, and Speed Limit: 2006

[Speeding consists of exceeding the posted speed limit or driving too fast for the road conditions or any speed-related violation charged (racing, driving above speed limit, speed greater than reasonable, exceeding special speed limit)]

State	Traffic fatalities, total	Total [1]	Interstate Over 55 mph	Interstate At or under 55 mph	Noninterstate 55 mph	50 mph	45 mph	40 mph	35 mph	Under 35 mph
United States	42,642	13,543	1,373	371	3,410	510	1,873	884	1,593	1,492
Alabama	1,208	567	65	8	122	13	196	29	67	37
Alaska	74	30	3	1	8	1	2	3	3	5
Arizona	1,288	578	104	14	41	38	92	80	51	38
Arkansas	665	96	11	–	29	5	12	6	17	10
California	4,236	1,403	241	20	304	63	147	111	169	151
Colorado	535	182	14	11	24	11	25	16	28	29
Connecticut	301	92	4	7	8	–	12	5	13	38
Delaware	148	34	1	4	4	13	2	1	8	1
District of Columbia	37	3	–	–	–	–	–	–	–	3
Florida	3,374	714	65	20	96	27	180	47	91	82
Georgia	1,693	407	30	13	107	10	79	16	67	27'
Hawaii	161	77	1	7	8	–	9	–	25	25
Idaho	267	83	6	3	8	8	14	1	12	5
Illinois	1,254	555	43	34	212	10	40	39	73	95
Indiana	899	194	7	18	59	7	25	17	19	34
Iowa	439	31	–	–	12	3	1	–	5	9
Kansas	468	128	12	2	41	1	10	9	14	21
Kentucky	913	160	9	3	100	–	15	–	25	4
Louisiana	982	257	31	2	84	12	47	7	36	24
Maine	188	72	5	2	6	14	18	4	11	6
Maryland	651	237	10	15	25	36	10	37	37	56
Massachusetts	430	148	23	11	3	1	9	25	23	45
Michigan	1,085	219	27	7	117	8	7	1	23	17
Minnesota	494	128	9	5	66	4	7	4	2	26
Mississippi	911	365	41	4	134	13	74	13	34	24
Missouri	1,096	470	46	9	169	11	33	18	64	39
Montana	263	112	9	–	4	3	9	–	13	5
Nebraska	269	64	13	–	9	10	5	–	4	9
Nevada	432	159	23	7	7	3	34	2	31	13
New Hampshire	127	42	3	–	3	3	–	4	15	13
New Jersey	772	56	4	2	2	8	6	5	9	13
New Mexico	484	173	24	5	27	9	17	5	13	17
New York	1,456	448	16	16	146	9	20	35	20	63
North Carolina	1,559	539	29	3	286	5	142	6	43	11
North Dakota	111	40	2	–	20	–	–	2	–	1
Ohio	1,238	253	20	5	116	3	22	14	32	31
Oklahoma	765	269	24	13	32	6	57	18	9	17
Oregon	477	145	7	2	80	–	11	2	14	5
Pennsylvania	1,525	675	28	22	157	12	142	97	130	59
Rhode Island	81	42	1	3	3	2	2	1	8	22
South Carolina	1,037	412	54	4	110	8	74	31	41	22
South Dakota	191	48	6	2	16	2	3	3	2	6
Tennessee	1,287	296	9	8	64	7	41	29	33	34
Texas	3,475	1,474	174	41	208	56	127	92	116	148
Utah	287	61	14	1	8	4	5	2	10	8
Vermont	87	33	7	–	–	16	–	3	5	2
Virginia	963	296	37	10	128	1	39	13	29	24
Washington	630	253	23	4	25	31	18	18	67	53
West Virginia	410	75	8	1	24	3	7	6	7	7
Wisconsin	724	283	7	2	145	–	22	5	24	53
Wyoming	195	65	23	–	3	–	4	2	1	5

– Represents zero. [1] Includes fatalities that occurred on roads for which the speed limit was unknown.

Source: U.S. National Highway Traffic Safety Administration, *Traffic Safety Facts, Speeding,* annual. See <http://www-nrd.nhtsa.dot.gov/CATS/index.aspx>.

U.S. Census Bureau, Statistical Abstract of the United States: 2009

Table 1069. Fatalities by Highest Blood Alcohol Concentration (BAC) in the Crash: 1990 to 2006

[g/dl means grams per deciliter. BAC means blood alcohol concentration. A motor vehicle crash is considered to be alcohol-related if at least one driver or nonoccupant (such as a pedestrian or pedalcyclist) involved in the crash is determined to have had a BAC of .01 or higher. Thus, any fatality that occurs in an alcohol-related crash is considered an alcohol-related fatality. The term alcohol-related does not indicate that a crash or fatality was caused by the presence of alcohol. A person is considered to be legally impaired with a BAC of .08 g/dl or more]

Item	1990	1995	2000	2002	2003	2004	2005	2006
Total fatalities	44,599	41,817	41,945	43,005	42,884	42,836	43,510	42,642
Fatalities in alcohol-related crashes . . .	22,587	17,732	17,380	17,524	17,105	16,919	17,590	17,602
Percent	50.6	42.4	41.4	40.7	40.0	39.5	40.4	41.3
BAC = 0.01-0.07 g/dl:								
Number	2,980	2,490	2,511	2,432	2,427	2,325	2,489	2,480
Percent	6.7	6.0	6.0	5.7	6.0	5.4	5.7	5.8
BAC = 0.08 g/dl or more:								
Number	19,607	15,242	14,870	15,093	14,678	14,593	15,102	15,121
Percent	44.0	36.5	35.5	35.1	34.0	34.1	34.7	35.5
Fatalities non alcohol-related crashes (BAC = 0.00 g/dl):								
Number.	22,012	24,085	24,565	25,481	25,779	25,918	25,920	25,040
Percent	49.4	57.6	58.6	59.3	60.0	60.5	59.6	58.7

Source: U.S. National Highway Traffic Safety Administration, *Traffic Safety Facts,* annual. See <http://www-nrd.nhtsa.dot.gov/CATS/index.aspx>.

Table 1070. Traffic Fatalities by State and Highest Blood Alcohol Concentration (BAC) in the Crash: 2006

[See headnote, Table 1069]

State	Traffic fatalities, total	No alcohol (BAC = 0.00 g/dl)		Any alcohol (BAC = 0.01 g/dl or more)		Low alcohol (BAC = 0.01-0.07 g/dl)		High alcohol (BAC = 0.08 g/dl or more)	
		Number	Percent	Number	Percent	Number	Percent	Number	Percent
United States . . .	42,642	25,043	59.6	17,590	40.4	2,489	5.7	15,102	34.7
Alabama	1,208	733	60.7	475	39.3	60	4.9	416	34.4
Alaska.	74	51	69.1	23	30.9	3	3.5	20	27.4
Arizona	1,288	704	54.6	585	45.4	101	7.8	484	37.5
Arkansas	665	411	61.9	254	38.1	50	7.6	203	30.6
California	4,236	2,457	58.0	1,779	42.0	274	6.5	1,506	35.5
Colorado	535	309	57.7	226	42.3	34	6.4	192	35.9
Connecticut	301	172	57.1	129	42.9	13	4.2	117	38.8
Delaware	148	91	61.3	57	38.7	7	4.4	51	34.3
District of Columbia . . .	37	19	52.4	18	47.6	2	4.3	16	43.2
Florida.	3,374	1,998	59.2	1,376	40.8	162	4.8	1,215	36.0
Georgia	1,693	1,089	64.3	604	35.7	80	4.7	524	31.0
Hawaii.	161	77	47.8	84	52.2	13	8.3	71	43.9
Idaho	267	161	60.3	106	39.7	18	6.6	88	33.0
Illinois	1,254	660	52.7	594	47.3	102	8.1	492	39.2
Indiana	899	580	64.5	319	35.5	45	5.0	275	30.5
Iowa	439	292	66.4	148	33.6	19	4.4	128	29.2
Kansas	468	298	63.7	170	36.3	27	5.8	143	30.6
Kentucky	913	641	70.2	272	29.8	37	4.0	236	25.8
Louisiana	982	507	51.6	475	48.4	60	6.2	415	42.2
Maine	188	115	60.9	74	39.1	19	10.0	55	29.1
Maryland	651	383	58.9	268	41.1	45	6.9	223	34.2
Massachusetts	430	256	59.5	174	40.5	21	5.0	153	35.5
Michigan	1,085	645	59.5	440	40.5	58	5.3	382	35.2
Minnesota	494	311	62.9	183	37.1	24	4.8	159	32.3
Mississippi	911	536	58.8	375	41.2	38	4.1	337	37.0
Missouri.	1,096	596	54.4	500	45.6	91	8.3	409	37.3
Montana	263	137	52.0	126	48.0	12	4.5	114	43.5
Nebraska.	269	180	67.0	89	33.0	15	5.6	74	27.4
Nevada	432	246	56.9	186	43.1	26	6.0	160	37.0
New Hampshire	127	75	59.1	52	40.9	4	3.2	48	37.6
New Jersey	772	432	55.9	341	44.1	70	9.1	270	35.0
New Mexico	484	298	61.6	186	38.4	21	4.3	165	34.1
New York.	1,456	898	61.7	558	38.3	95	6.5	463	31.8
North Carolina	1,559	1,005	64.4	554	35.6	73	4.7	482	30.9
North Dakota	111	61	55.3	50	44.7	6	5.2	44	39.5
Ohio	1,238	750	60.6	488	39.4	79	6.4	409	33.0
Oklahoma	765	502	65.6	263	34.4	43	5.6	221	28.8
Oregon	477	281	58.9	196	41.1	34	7.1	163	34.1
Pennsylvania	1,525	925	60.6	600	39.4	70	4.6	530	34.8
Rhode Island	81	39	48.6	42	51.4	8	10.1	33	41.2
South Carolina	1,037	514	49.6	523	50.4	60	5.8	463	44.6
South Dakota	191	111	58.3	80	41.7	9	4.9	70	36.9
Tennessee	1,287	778	60.4	509	39.6	71	5.5	439	34.1
Texas	3,475	1,798	51.7	1,677	48.3	190	5.5	1,487	42.8
Utah	287	218	76.0	69	24.0	10	3.4	59	20.6
Vermont	87	58	67.0	29	33.0	3	2.9	26	30.1
Virginia	963	584	60.7	379	39.3	52	5.4	327	34.0
Washington	630	336	53.3	294	46.7	48	7.6	247	39.1
West Virginia	410	250	60.9	161	39.1	27	6.6	133	32.5
Wisconsin	724	360	49.7	364	50.3	45	6.2	319	44.0
Wyoming	195	115	58.8	80	41.2	11	5.7	69	35.5

Source: U.S. National Highway Traffic Safety Administration, *Traffic Safety Facts,* annual. See <http://www-nrd.nhtsa.dot.gov/CATS/index.aspx>.

Transportation 681

Table 1071. Crashes by Crash Severity: 1990 to 2006

[6,471 represents 6,471,000. A crash is a police-reported event that produces injury and/or property damage, involves a vehicle in transport and occurs on a trafficway or while the vehicle is in motion after running off the trafficway]

Item	1990	1995	2000	2001	2002	2003	2004	2005	2006
Crashes (1,000)	**6,471**	**6,699**	**6,394**	**6,323**	**6,316**	**6,328**	**6,181**	**6,159**	**5,973**
Fatal.	39.8	37.2	37.5	37.9	38.5	38.5	38.4	39.2	38.6
Nonfatal injury	2,122	2,217	2,070	2,003	1,929	1,925	1,862	1,816	1,746
Property damage only	4,309	4,446	4,286	4,282	4,348	4,365	4,281	4,304	4,189
Percent of total crashes:									
Fatal.	0.6	0.6	0.6	0.6	0.6	0.6	0.6	0.6	0.6
Nonfatal injury	32.8	33.1	32.4	31.7	30.5	30.4	30.1	29.5	29.2
Property damage only	66.6	66.4	67.0	67.7	68.8	69.0	69.3	69.9	70.1

Source: U.S. National Highway Safety Traffic Administration, *Traffic Safety Facts, annual.* See <http://www-nrd.nhtsa.dot.gov/CATS/index.aspx>.

Table 1072. Alcohol Involvement for Drivers in Fatal Crashes: 1995 and 2005

[BAC = blood alcohol concentration]

Age, sex, and vehicle type	1995		2005 [1]	
	Number of drivers	Percentage with BAC of .08% or greater	Number of drivers	Percentage with BAC of .08% or greater
Total drivers involved in fatal crashes [2]	**56,164**	**22.0**	**59,220**	**21.2**
Drivers by age group:				
Under 16 years old	410	9.3	304	10.5
16 to 20 years old.	7,725	15.6	7,334	17.3
21 to 24 years old.	6,263	31.8	6,585	33.0
25 to 34 years old.	13,048	30.3	11,467	28.6
35 to 44 years old.	10,677	26.1	10,793	24.2
45 to 54 years old.	6,815	17.7	9,434	19.2
55 to 64 years old.	4,079	13.6	6,075	12.6
65 to 74 years old.	3,251	7.6	3,217	7.0
75 years old and over	2,989	4.0	3,016	4.0
Drivers by sex:				
Male.	41,235	25.0	43,282	23.9
Female	14,184	12.9	15,059	13.2
Drivers by vehicle type:				
Passenger cars	30,773	22.6	25,046	23.5
Light trucks [3]	17,483	24.6	22,879	21.6
Large trucks [3]	4,410	2.3	4,900	1.4
Motorcycles	2,262	33.0	4,679	27.0
Buses.	269	0.8	278	1.3

[1] Data have been revised.   [2] Includes age and sex unknown, and other and unknown types of vehicles.   [3] See footnotes 2 and 3 in Table 1067.

Source: U.S. National Highway Traffic Safety Administration, *Traffic Safety Facts,* annual. See <http://www-nrd.nhtsa.dot.gov/CATS/index.aspx>.

Table 1073. Licensed Drivers and Number in Accidents by Age: 2006

[202,700 represents 202,700,000]

Age group	Licensed drivers		Drivers in accidents				Accident rates per number of drivers	
			Fatal		All			
	Number (1,000)	Percent	Number	Percent	Number (1,000)	Percent	Fatal [1]	All [2]
Total	**202,700**	**100.0**	**60,600**	**100.0**	**18,000**	**100.0**	**30**	**9**
19 years old and under	10,719	5.3	6,100	10.1	2,420	13.4	57	23
Under 16 years old	37	(Z)	300	0.5	260	1.4	(3)	(3)
16 years old.	1,830	0.9	800	1.3	380	2.1	44	21
17 years old.	2,578	1.3	1,300	2.1	550	3.1	50	21
18 years old.	3,009	1.5	1,800	3.0	620	3.4	60	21
19 years old.	3,265	1.6	1,900	3.1	610	3.4	58	19
20 to 24 years old	16,837	8.3	9,000	14.9	2,490	13.8	53	15
20 years old.	3,340	1.6	1,800	3.0	570	3.2	54	17
21 years old.	3,266	1.6	2,000	3.3	510	2.8	61	16
22 years old.	3,267	1.6	1,800	3.0	470	2.6	55	14
23 years old.	3,394	1.7	1,800	3.0	470	2.6	53	14
24 years old.	3,570	1.8	1,600	2.6	470	2.6	45	13
25 to 34 years old	40,776	20.1	11,200	18.5	3,620	20.1	27	9
35 to 44 years old	45,587	22.5	10,000	16.5	3,350	18.6	22	7
45 to 54 years old	36,699	18.1	9,500	15.7	3,080	17.1	26	8
55 to 64 years old	23,322	11.5	6,400	10.6	1,680	9.3	27	7
65 to 74 years old	17,277	8.5	3,800	6.3	800	4.4	22	5
75 years old and over	11,483	5.7	4,600	7.6	560	3.1	40	5

Z Less than 0.05.   [1] Per 100,000 licensed drivers.   [2] Per 100 licensed drivers.   [3] Rates for drivers under age 16 are substantially overstated due to the high proportion of unlicensed drivers involved.

Source: National Safety Council, Itasca, IL, *Injury Facts, 2007,* (copyright). See <http://www.nsc.org/>.

Table 1074. Passenger Transit Industry—Summary: 1980 to 2006

[6,510 represents $6,510,000,000. Includes Puerto Rico. Includes aggregate information for all transit systems in the United States. Excludes nontransit services such as taxicab, school bus, unregulated jitney, sightseeing bus, intercity bus, and special application mass transportation systems (e.g., amusement parks, airports, island, and urban park ferries). Includes active vehicles only]

Item	Unit	1980	1990	1995	2000	2004	2005	2006
Operating systems	Number	1,044	5,078	5,973	6,000	6,429	6,429	6,435
Motor bus systems	Number	1,040	2,688	2,250	2,262	1,500	1,500	1,500
Revenue vehicles, active	Number	75,388	93,553	116,473	131,918	143,822	150,827	155,195
Motor bus	Number	59,411	58,714	67,107	75,013	81,033	82,027	83,080
Commuter rail	Number	4,500	5,007	5,164	5,498	6,228	6,392	6,403
Demand response	Number	(NA)	16,471	29,352	33,080	37,078	41,958	43,509
Heavy rail	Number	9,641	10,419	10,157	10,591	10,858	11,110	11,052
Light rail	Number	1,013	913	999	1,577	1,622	1,645	1,801
Trolley bus	Number	823	832	885	951	597	615	609
Other	Number	(NA)	1,197	2,809	5,208	6,406	7,080	8,741
Operating funding, total	Mil. dol.	6,510	16,053	18,241	24,243	29,718	31,708	33,713
Agency funds	Mil. dol.	2,805	6,786	8,069	11,004	12,147	12,559	13,545
Passenger funding	Mil. dol.	2,557	5,891	6,801	8,746	9,775	10,269	11,195
Other	Mil. dol.	248	895	1,268	2,258	2,373	2,290	2,350
Government funds [1]	Mil. dol.	3,705	9,267	10,172	13,239	17,571	19,149	20,168
Directly generated [2]	Mil. dol.	([3])	([3])	1,544	1,959	2,588	2,694	2,797
Local [4]	Mil. dol.	2,611	5,327	3,981	5,319	6,184	6,658	7,105
State [4]	Mil. dol.	(NA)	2,970	3,830	4,967	6,713	7,495	7,674
Federal	Mil. dol.	1,094	970	817	994	2,086	2,303	2,592
Operating expense	Mil. dol.	6,247	15,742	17,849	22,646	28,506	30,295	32,037
Vehicle operations	Mil. dol.	3,248	6,654	8,282	10,111	12,866	13,793	14,743
Maintenance	Mil. dol.	1,774	4,631	5,047	6,445	7,833	8,259	8,690
General administration	Mil. dol.	1,224	3,450	2,590	3,329	3,974	4,075	4,301
Purchased transportation	Mil. dol.	(NA)	1,008	1,930	2,761	3,833	4,168	4,304
Capital expenditures	Mil. dol.	(NA)	(NA)	7,230	9,587	13,246	12,383	13,340
Vehicle-miles operated	Million	2,287	3,242	3,550	4,081	4,471	4,601	4,684
Motor bus	Million	1,677	2,130	2,184	2,315	2,471	2,485	2,495
Trolley bus	Million	13	14	14	14	13	13	12
Heavy rail	Million	385	537	537	595	642	646	652
Light rail	Million	18	24	35	53	67	69	74
Commuter rail	Million	179	213	238	271	295	303	315
Demand response	Million	(NA)	306	507	759	890	978	1,013
Other	Million	15	18	37	74	92	107	123
Trips taken	Million	8,567	8,799	7,763	9,363	9,575	9,815	10,017
Motor bus	Million	5,837	5,677	4,848	5,678	5,731	5,855	5,894
Trolley bus	Million	142	126	119	122	106	107	100
Heavy rail	Million	2,108	2,346	2,033	2,632	2,748	2,808	2,927
Light rail	Million	133	175	251	320	350	381	407
Commuter rail	Million	280	328	344	413	414	423	441
Demand response	Million	(NA)	68	88	105	114	125	126
Other	Million	67	79	80	93	112	117	121
Avg. fare per trip	Cents	30	67	88	93	102	102	112
Employees, number (avg.) [5]	1,000	187	273	311	360	359	367	369
Payroll, employee	Mil. dol.	3,281	7,226	8,213	10,400	12,487	12,177	12,764
Fringe benefits, employee	Mil. dol.	1,353	3,986	4,484	5,413	8,172	8,093	8,424

NA Not available. [1] Represents the sum of federal, state, and local assistance. and that portion of directly generated funds that accrue from tax collections, toll transfers from other sectors of operations, and bond proceeds. [2] These are any funds generated from taxes controlled by the transit agency. [3] Funds data are included in local government data through 1993. [4] Through 1985, data for state and local are combined. [5] Through 1990, represents employee equivalents of 2,080 hours = one employee; beginning 1995, equals actual employees.

Source: American Public Transportation Association, Washington, DC, *Public Transportation Fact Book,* annual. See <http://www.apta.com/>.

Table 1075. Transit Buses Equipped for Disabilities: 1995 to 2006

[Represents ADA (Americans with Disabilities Act of 1992) lift- or ramp-equipped buses. Includes buses of transit agencies receiving federal funding for bus purchases and buses of agencies not receiving federal funds that voluntarily report data to the Federal Transit Administration]

Item	1995	2000	2001	2002	2003	2004	2005	2006
Transit buses, total	**57,322**	**65,324**	**67,379**	**68,418**	**68,596**	**68,789**	**69,504**	**70,217**
Percent ADA equipped	61.7	83.6	87.2	94.1	95.3	98.1	96.5	98.5
Small buses, total [1]	5,372	8,850	9,622	9,822	10,084	10,248	11,118	11,537
Percent ADA equipped	84.5	94.5	95.4	99.2	99.2	98.5	97.6	98.6
Medium buses, total [1]	3,879	7,455	7,830	8,693	9,346	10,031	10,631	10,983
Percent ADA equipped	66.0	92.9	93.7	98.4	97.7	100.0	98.8	100.0
Large buses, total [1]	46,355	47,017	47,925	47,764	46,608	45,919	45,524	45,403
Percent ADA equipped	59.2	79.9	84.5	92.2	93.9	97.4	95.5	98.1
Articulated buses, total [1]	1,716	2,002	2,002	2,139	2,558	2,591	2,231	2,294
Percent ADA equipped	50.2	85.5	88.5	97.2	96.4	99.8	99.7	99.8

[1] Small buses have fewer than 25 seats; medium buses have 25 to 35 seats; large ones have more than 35 seats; articulated buses are extra long and measure between 54 and 60 feet.

Source: U.S. Bureau of Transportation Statistics, *National Transportation Statistics*, annual. See <http://www.bts.gov/publications/national_transportation_statistics>.

Table 1076. **Characteristics of Rail Transit by Transit Authority: 2006**

Mode and transit agency	Primary city served	States served	Directional route-miles [1,2]	Number of highway-rail crossings [1]	Number of stations	Number of ADA-accessible stations [3]
Total [4]	34	28	9,875.3	5,502	2,917	1,753
Heavy rail	11	13	1,623.4	27	1,024	450
Chicago Transit Authority	Chicago	IL	207.8	25	144	75
Greater Cleveland Regional Transit Authority	Cleveland	OH	38.1	–	18	12
L.A. County Metropolitan Transportation Authority	Los Angeles	CA	31.9	–	16	16
Maryland Transit Administration	Baltimore	MD	29.4	–	14	14
Massachusetts Bay Transportation Authority	Boston	MA	76.3	–	53	42
Metropolitan Atlanta Rapid Transit Authority	Atlanta	GA	96.1	–	38	38
MTA New York City Transit	New York	NY	493.8	–	468	69
MTA Staten Island Railway	New York	NY	28.6	–	23	5
Miami-Dade Transit Agency	Miami	FL	45.0	–	20	20
Port Authority Trans-Hudson Corporation	New York	NY, NJ	28.6	2	13	7
Port Authority Transit Corporation	Philadelphia	PA, NJ	31.5	–	13	5
San Francisco Bay Area Rapid Transit District	San Francisco	CA	209.0	–	43	43
Southeastern Pennsylvania Transportation Authority	Philadelphia	PA	74.9	–	75	18
Washington Metropolitan Area Transit Authority	Washington	DC, MD, VA	211.8	–	86	86
Commuter rail [5]	14	18	6,971.8	2,947	1,155	698
Altamont Commuter Express Authority	San Jose	CA	172.0	127	10	10
Central Puget Sound Regional Transit Authority	Seattle	WA	146.9	45	9	9
Connecticut Department of Transportation	New Haven	CT	101.2	3	8	8
Dallas Area Rapid Transit	Dallas	TX	29.0	15	4	4
Fort Worth Transportation Authority	Dallas	TX	40.5	19	5	5
Maryland Transit Administration	Baltimore	MD, DC, WV	400.4	40	42	22
Massachusetts Bay Transportation Authority	Boston	MA, RI	702.1	233	126	84
MTA Long Island Rail Road	New York	NY	638.2	395	124	99
MTA Metro-North Railroad	New York	NY, NJ, CT	545.7	160	109	38
NE Illinois Regional Commuter Rail Corporation	Chicago	IL, WI	980.4	532	238	159
New Jersey Transit Corporation	New York	NY, NJ, PA	996.8	316	162	67
North San Diego County Transit Development Board	San Diego	CA	82.2	34	8	8
Northern Indiana Commuter Transportation District	Chicago	IL, IN	179.8	117	20	13
Peninsula Corridor Joint Powers Board	San Francisco	CA	153.7	49	32	23
Pennsylvania Department of Transportation	Philadelphia	PA	144.4	7	12	4
South Florida Regional Transportation Authority	Miami	FL	142.2	73	18	18
Southeastern Pennsylvania Transportation Authority	Philadelphia	PA	446.9	283	156	55
Southern California Regional Rail Authority	Los Angeles	CA	778.0	443	54	54
Virginia Railway Express	Washington	DC, VA	161.5	20	18	18

– Represents zero. [1] Vehicles operated in maximum service include directly operated (DO) and purchase transportation (PT) by mode. [2] The mileage in each direction over which public transportation vehicles travel while in revenue service. The mileage is computed without regard to the number of traffic lanes or rail tracks existing in the right-of-way. [3] Number of stations that comply with the American with Disabilities Act of 1992 (ADA). Additional stations may be wheelchair accessible but not comply with other provisions of the ADA. [4] Includes light rail, not shown separately. [5] Excludes commuter-type services operated independently by AMTRAK.

Source: U.S. Bureau of Transportation Statistics, *State Transportation Statistics, 2006.* See Internet site <http://www.bts.gov /publications/state_transportation_statistics/>. National Transit database; Access NTD data; RY 2006 data tables. See <http://www .ntdprogram.gov/ntdprogram/data.htm>.

Table 1077. Transit Ridership in Selected Urbanized Areas: 2005

Urbanized area	Annual unlinked passenger trips [1] (1,000)	Area rank based on trips per capita [2]	Unlinked passenger trips per capita	Percent distribution				
				Motor bus	Heavy rail [3]	Light rail [4]	Commuter rail [5]	Other [6]
U.S. urbanized areas	**9,094,071**	**(X)**	**(X)**	**57.1**	**30.9**	**4.2**	**4.7**	**3.2**
Atlanta, GA	150,252	14	42.9	52.3	47.2	–	–	0.4
Austin, TX	33,195	20	36.8	97.8	–	–	–	2.2
Baltimore, MD	105,151	11	50.6	75.7	12.2	4.9	6.5	0.6
Boston, MA-NH-RI	401,542	4	99.6	35.0	35.4	18.4	9.4	1.8
Bridgeport-Stamford, CT-NY	9,845	70	11.0	96.7	–	–	–	3.3
Buffalo, NY	23,505	30	24.1	76.8	–	22.9	–	0.3
Charlotte, NC-SC	17,842	33	23.5	95.2	–	1.8	–	3.0
Chicago, IL-IN	603,966	6	72.7	56.2	30.9	–	12.0	0.9
Cincinnati, OH-KY-IN	30,022	40	20.0	98.6	–	–	–	1.4
Cleveland, OH	66,610	18	37.3	82.9	11.2	4.6	–	1.2
Columbus, OH	14,790	56	13.1	98.9	–	–	–	1.1
Dallas-Fort Worth-Arlington, TX	82,020	41	19.8	73.6	–	21.3	2.6	2.5
Denver-Aurora, CO	86,261	12	43.5	86.6	–	12.1	–	1.3
Detroit, MI	47,559	61	12.2	95.2	–	–	–	4.8
Hartford, CT	15,097	45	17.7	86.4	–	–	2.7	10.9
Houston, TX	94,555	28	24.7	86.2	–	10.8	–	2.9
Indianapolis, IN	8,810	80	7.2	96.3	–	–	–	3.7
Jacksonville, FL	11,087	58	12.6	88.1	–	–	–	11.9
Kansas City, MO-KS	14,506	71	10.7	96.0	–	–	–	4.0
Las Vegas, NV	53,571	15	40.8	98.6	–	–	–	1.4
Los Angeles-Long Beach-Santa Ana, CA	666,052	10	56.5	86.2	5.4	5.7	1.6	1.0
Louisville, KY-IN	15,383	44	17.8	97.8	–	–	–	2.2
Memphis, TN-MS-AR	12,145	59	12.5	89.6	–	8.4	–	2.0
Miami, FL	158,502	24	32.3	79.0	10.7	–	1.8	8.5
Milwaukee, WI	53,096	16	40.6	97.7	–	–	–	2.3
Minneapolis-St. Paul, MN	81,022	22	33.9	87.8	–	9.8	–	2.5
Nashville-Davidson, TN	7,543	73	10.1	97.7	–	–	–	2.3
New Orleans, LA [7]	6,260	86	6.2	48.9	–	–	–	51.1
New York-Newark, NY-NJ-CT	3,453,093	1	195.4	37.4	54.3	0.4	7.0	0.8
Oklahoma City, OK	2,673	96	3.6	97.6	–	–	–	2.4
Orlando, FL	24,808	36	21.4	97.0	–	–	–	3.0
Philadelphia, PA-NJ-DE-MD	352,923	8	68.5	55.5	27.6	7.1	9.0	0.7
Phoenix-Mesa, AZ	60,477	38	20.8	97.0	–	–	–	3.0
Pittsburgh, PA	70,269	17	40.1	85.4	–	10.0	–	4.6
Portland, OR-WA	110,634	7	69.9	67.5	–	31.4	–	1.1
Providence, RI-MA	20,175	47	17.4	95.7	–	–	–	4.3
Richmond, VA	13,236	51	16.2	97.3	–	–	–	2.7
Riverside-San Bernardino, CA	23,322	52	15.5	95.8	–	–	–	4.2
Sacramento, CA	32,863	31	24.0	62.4	–	36.5	–	1.1
Salt Lake City, UT	38,234	13	43.1	58.5	–	37.5	–	4.0
San Antonio, TX	40,697	25	30.7	97.5	–	–	–	2.5
San Diego, CA	89,924	23	33.6	63.5	–	32.6	1.6	2.3
San Francisco-Oakland, CA	418,384	2	129.6	42.4	23.7	11.2	1.9	20.7
San Jose, CA	38,477	27	25.0	80.0	–	17.6	–	2.4
Seattle, WA	159,699	9	58.9	64.4	–	0.8	0.8	34.0
St. Louis, MO-IL	48,902	32	23.5	65.4	–	32.0	–	2.6
Tampa-St. Petersburg, FL	22,993	69	11.1	95.6	–	2.5	–	1.9
Tucson, AZ	16,621	34	23.1	97.7	–	–	–	2.3
Virginia Beach, VA	24,242	49	17.4	96.9	–	–	–	3.1
Washington, DC-VA-MD	461,503	3	117.3	42.6	56.2	–	0.8	0.4

– Represents zero. X Not applicable. [1] The number of times passengers board public transportation vehicles. A passenger is counted each time he or she boards a vehicle even if the boarding is part of the same journey from origin to destination. [2] As of April 1. Based on the 2000 decennial census. [3] Also called metro, subway, rapid transit, or rapid rail. [4] Also called streetcar, tramway, or trolley. [5] Also called metropolitan rail or regional rail. [6] Includes such modes as trolley bus, ferry, cable car, vanpool, and demand response. [7] The New Orleans Regional Transit Authority (NORTA) did not report data for 2005. Of the agencies in the New Orleans area that were required to report in 2004, NORTA accounted for approximately 86 percent of unlinked passenger trips.

Source: U.S. Bureau of Transportation Statistics, *State Transportation Statistics, 2006.* See <http://www.bts.gov /publications/state_transportation_statistics/>. National Transit database; Access NTD data; *Top transit cities.* See <http://www .ntdprogram.gov/ntdprogram/data.htm>.

U.S. Census Bureau, Statistical Abstract of the United States: 2009

Table 1078. Truck Transportation, Couriers and Messengers, and Warehousing and Storage—Estimated Revenue: 2000 to 2006

[In millions of dollars (237,812 represents $237,812,000,000). For taxable and tax-exempt employer firms. Estimates have been adjusted to the results of the 2002 Economic Census. Based on the North American Industry Classification System, 2002; see text, Section 15]

Kind of business	2002 NAICS code [1]	2000	2005	2006
Selected transportation and warehousing industries	48, 49	**237,812**	**292,756**	**312,445**
Truck transportation	484	165,421	206,550	219,539
General freight trucking	4841	108,051	138,867	146,580
General freight trucking, local	48411	17,254	22,275	25,025
General freight trucking, long-distance	48412	90,797	116,592	121,555
General freight trucking, long-distance, truckload	484121	61,562	84,567	88,854
General freight trucking, long-distance, less than truckload	484122	29,235	32,025	32,701
Specialized freight trucking	4842	57,370	67,683	72,959
Used household and office goods moving	48421	14,484	15,101	15,166
Specialized freight (except used goods) trucking, local	48422	21,912	28,347	31,428
Specialized freight (except used goods) trucking, long-distance. . .	48423	20,974	24,235	26,365
Couriers and messengers	492	57,776	67,024	71,777
Couriers	4921	54,114	63,685	68,342
Local messengers and local delivery	4922	3,662	3,339	3,435
Warehousing and storage	493	14,615	19,182	21,129
General warehousing and storage	49311	8,967	11,668	12,742
Refrigerated warehousing and storage	49312	2,859	3,314	3,361
Farm product warehousing and storage	49313	776	772	759
Other warehousing and storage	49319	2,013	3,428	4,267

[1] Based on the 2002 North American Industry Classification System; see text Section 15.

Source: U.S. Census Bureau, "2006 Service Annual Survey, Truck Transportation, Messenger Services and Warehousing."
See <http://www.census.gov/econ/www/servmenu.html>; (released December 2007).

Table 1079. Truck Transportation—Summary: 2000 to 2006

[In millions of dollars (165,421 represents $165,421,000,000). For taxable and tax-exempt employer firms. Covers NAICS 484. Estimates have been adjusted to the results of the 2002 Economic Census. Based on the North American Industry Classification System, 2002; see text, Section 15]

Item	2000	2004	2005	2006
Total operating revenue	**165,421**	**185,945**	**206,550**	**219,539**
Total motor carrier revenue	152,810	173,354	192,106	204,423
Local trucking [1]	48,837	56,666	63,271	67,943
Long-distance trucking [1]	103,973	116,688	128,835	136,480
Size of shipments:				
Less-than-truckload	36,453	40,218	42,014	50,463
Truckload	116,357	133,136	150,092	153,960
Commodities handled:				
Agricultural and fish products	13,666	15,650	17,320	18,418
Grains, alcohol, and tobacco products	4,912	6,274	7,028	8,459
Stone, nonmetallic minerals, and metallic ores	8,703	11,572	13,078	14,877
Coal and petroleum products	5,812	6,839	7,833	8,496
Pharmaceutical and chemical products	9,929	9,544	10,241	10,759
Wood products, textiles, and leathers	14,281	16,420	17,222	17,196
Base metal and machinery	12,239	15,029	16,021	17,982
Electronic, motorized vehicles, and precision instruments . . .	11,939	13,665	14,762	15,320
Used household and office goods	11,078	10,823	12,063	12,323
New furniture and miscellaneous manufactured products . . .	17,244	19,522	21,887	22,290
Other goods	43,007	48,016	54,651	58,303
Origin and destination of shipments:				
U.S. to U.S.	145,985	167,338	184,877	196,244
U.S. to Canada	1,390	1,375	1,541	1,806
U.S. to Mexico	1,434	1,257	1,545	1,650
Canada to U.S.	1,184	1,131	1,340	1,348
Mexico to U.S.	1,283	1,004	1,294	1,741
All other destinations	1,534	1,249	1,509	1,634
Inventory of revenue-generating equipment (1,000):				
Trucks	201	212	217	247
Owned and/or leased with drivers	168	189	192	218
Leased without drivers	33	24	25	28
Truck-tractors	916	838	867	895
Owned and/or leased with drivers	772	711	732	745
Leased without drivers	144	128	135	149
Trailers	1,893	1,855	1,923	1,950
Owned and/or leased with drivers	1,572	1,524	1,577	1,618
Leased without drivers	321	331	347	332
Highway miles traveled (mil.):				
Total	84,910	85,753	90,170	91,078
By loaded or partially loaded vehicles	67,558	69,661	72,854	73,444
By empty vehicles	17,352	16,093	17,315	17,634

[1] Local trucking is the carrying of goods within a single metro area and its adjacent nonurban areas; long-distance trucking is the carrying of goods between metro areas.

Source: U.S. Census Bureau, "2006 Service Annual Survey, Truck Transportation, Messenger Services, and Warehousing."
See <http://www.census.gov/econ/www/servmenu.html>; (released December 2007).

Table 1080. Railroads, Class I—Summary: 1990 to 2006

[As of Dec. 31, or calendar year data, except as noted (216 represents 216,000). Compiled from annual reports of class I railroads only, except where noted. Minus sign (–) indicates deficit]

Item	Unit	1990	2000	2001	2002	2003	2004	2005	2006
Class I line-hauling companies [1]	Number..	14	8	8	7	7	7	7	7
Employees [2]	1,000 ...	216	168	162	157	155	158	162	168
Compensation	Mil. dol..	8,654	9,623	9,430	9,387	9,576	10,337	10,879	11,419
Average per hour	Dollars ..	15.8	21.5	22.1	22.7	23.4	24.2	25.7	26.0
Average per year	Dollars ..	39,987	57,157	58,153	59,650	61,920	65,550	66,975	68,141
Mileage:									
Railroad line owned [3]	1,000 ...	146	121	119	118	117	123	121	120
Railroad track owned [4]	1,000 ...	244	205	204	200	200	211	208	206
Equipment:									
Locomotives in service	Number..	18,835	20,028	19,745	20,506	20,774	22,015	22,779	23,730
Average horsepower	1,000 lb..	2,665	3,261	3,275	3,378	3,415	3,458	3,467	3,485
Cars in service:									
Freight train [5]	1,000 ...	1,212	1,381	1,314	1,300	1,279	1,288	1,312	1,347
Freight cars [6]	1,000 ...	659	560	500	478	467	474	475	475
Average capacity	Tons....	87.5	92.3	92.7	93.1	93.7	94.3	97.2	98.8
Income and expenses:									
Operating revenues	Mil. dol..	28,370	34,102	34,576	35,327	36,639	40,517	46,118	52,152
Operating expenses	Mil. dol..	24,652	29,040	29,164	29,592	31,440	35,107	37,843	40,980
Net revenue from operations	*Mil. dol..*	*3,718*	*5,062*	*5,412*	*5,735*	*5,199*	*5,410*	*8,275*	*11,172*
Income before fixed charges	Mil. dol..	4,627	5,361	5,517	6,179	5,220	5,523	8,361	11,276
Provision for taxes [7]	Mil. dol..	1,088	1,430	1,614	1,823	1,494	1,543	2,224	3,643
Ordinary income	Mil. dol..	1,961	2,501	2,740	3,201	2,683	2,867	4,917	6,482
Net income	Mil. dol..	1,977	2,500	2,740	3,201	2,687	2,867	4,917	6,482
Net railway operating income	Mil. dol..	2,648	3,924	4,111	4,248	4,078	4,147	6,075	7,560
Total taxes [8]	Mil. dol..	3,780	4,379	4,673	4,724	4,316	4,480	5,176	6,830
Indus. return on net investment	Percent .	8.1	6.5	6.9	7.0	6.3	6.1	8.5	10.2
Gross capital expenditures	Mil. dol..	3,591	5,290	5,113	5,605	5,989	6,345	7,068	8,159
Equipment	Mil. dol..	996	1,508	1,013	1,021	1,300	1,301	1,026	1,470
Roadway and structures	Mil. dol..	2,644	4,549	4,421	4,645	4,561	4,941	5,364	6,982
Other	Mil. dol..	–49	–767	–321	–61	128	102	678	–293
Balance sheet:									
Total property investment	Mil. dol..	70,348	106,136	108,588	117,770	122,902	135,941	141,400	148,320
Accrued depreciation and amortization	Mil. dol..	22,222	23,989	24,635	26,649	29,215	29,771	32,508	37,563
Net investment	Mil. dol..	48,126	82,147	83,953	91,121	93,686	106,170	108,892	112,556
Shareholder's equity	Mil. dol..	23,662	32,401	34,822	39,675	41,151	51,955	55,828	58,901
Net working capital	Mil. dol..	–3,505	–5,783	–6,282	–6,037	–6,750	–5,171	–4,729	–4,461
Cash dividends	Mil. dol..	2,074	819	2,120	870	1,406	1,888	1,267	1,089
Amtrak passenger traffic:									
Passenger revenue	Mil. dol..	941.9	1,201.6	1,299.9	1,304.3	1,421.1	1,432.6	1,461.7	1,606.0
Revenue passengers carried	1,000 ...	22,382	22,985	23,444	23,269	24,595	25,215	25,076	24,549
Revenue passenger miles	Million...	6,125	5,574	5,571	5,314	5,680	5,511	5,381	5,410
Averages:									
Revenue per passenger	Dollars ..	42.1	52.3	55.4	56.1	57.8	56.8	58.3	65.4
Revenue per passenger mile	Cents ...	15.4	21.6	23.3	24.5	25.0	26.0	27.2	27.2
Freight service:									
Freight revenue	Mil. dol..	24,471	33,083	33,533	34,110	35,413	39,131	44,457	50,315
Per ton-mile	Cents ...	2.7	2.3	2.2	2.3	2.3	2.4	2.6	2.8
Per ton originated	Dollar ..	19.3	19.0	19.3	19.3	19.7	21.2	23.4	25.7
Revenue-tons originated	Million...	1,425	1,738	1,742	1,767	1,799	1,844	1,899	1,957
Revenue-tons carried	Million...	2,024	2,179	2,187	2,207	2,240	2,398	2,448	2,517
Tons carried one mile	Billion...	1,034	1,466	1,495	1,507	1,551	1,663	1,696	1,772
Average miles of road operated	1,000 ...	133	121	121	123	122	121	121	120
Revenue ton-miles per mile of road	1,000 ...	7,763	12,156	12,358	12,245	12,686	13,695	14,071	14,805
Revenue per ton-mile	Cents ...	3	2	2	2	2	2	3	3
Train miles	Million...	380	504	500	500	516	535	548	563
Net ton-miles per train-mile [9]	Number..	2,755	2,923	3,005	3,030	3,024	3,126	3,115	3,163
Net ton-miles per loaded car-mile [9]	Number..	69.1	73.1	72.4	71.5	71.4	78.5	79.0	82
Train-miles per train-hour	Miles ...	24	21	21	21	20	19	19	18
Haul per ton, U.S. as a system	Miles ...	726	843	858	853	862	902	893	906
Accidents/incidents: [10]									
Casualties—all railroads:									
Persons killed	Number..	1,297	937	971	951	868	895	888	910
Persons injured	Number..	25,143	11,643	10,985	11,103	9,251	9,178	9,463	8,432
Class I railroads: [11]									
Persons killed	Number..	1,166	778	805	796	749	782	738	787
Persons injured	Number..	19,284	7,655	7,232	7,722	6,161	6,186	6,238	5,442

[1] See text, this section, for definition of Class I.   [2] Average midmonth count.   [3] Represents the aggregate length of roadway of all line-haul railroads. Excludes yard tracks, sidings, and parallel lines. (Includes estimate for Class II and III railroads).   [4] Includes multiple main tracks, yard tracks, and sidings owned by both line-haul and switching and terminal. (Includes estimate for Class II and III railroads).   [5] Includes cars owned by all railroads, private car companies, and shippers.   [6] Class I railroads only.   [7] Includes state income taxes.   [8] Includes payroll, income, and other taxes.   [9] Revenue and nonrevenue freight.   [10] Source: Federal Railroad Admin., *Railroad Safety Statistics*, annual.   [11] Includes Amtrack data. Includes highway grade crossing casualties. See <http://www.fra.dot.gov/>; (accessed 29 April 2008).

Source: Except as noted, Association of American Railroads, Washington, DC, *Industry Information, Industry Statistics, Railroad Statistics*. See <http://www.aar.org/IndustryInformation/IndustryStatistics/RailCostIndexes.aspx>.

Table 1081. Railroads, Class-I Line-Haul-Revenue Freight Originated by Commodity Group: 1990 to 2007

[21,401 represents 21,401,000]

Commodity group	1990	1995	2000	2002	2003	2004	2005	2006	2007
Carloads (1,000) [1]	**21,401**	**23,726**	**27,763**	**27,901**	**28,870**	**30,095**	**31,142**	**32,114**	**31,459**
Farm products	1,689	1,692	1,437	1,471	1,519	1,519	1,510	1,590	1,681
Metallic ores	508	463	322	328	331	339	662	674	662
Coal	5,912	6,095	6,954	7,088	7,037	7,102	7,202	7,574	7,480
Nonmetallic minerals	1,202	1,159	1,309	1,310	1,370	1,430	1,488	1,470	1,398
Food and kindred products	1,307	1,377	1,377	1,472	1,478	1,461	1,448	1,487	1,493
Lumber and wood products	780	719	648	619	612	616	611	548	456
Pulp, paper, allied products	611	628	633	646	667	669	679	671	652
Chemicals, allied products	1,531	1,642	1,820	1,866	1,913	1,981	1,937	1,943	2,050
Petroleum and coal products	573	596	565	533	606	651	689	689	691
Stone, clay, and glass products	539	516	541	559	581	594	603	570	513
Primary metal products	477	575	723	656	648	701	680	728	666
Fabricated metal products	31	32	30	38	36	39	36	50	55
Machinery, exc. electrical	39	41	35	38	38	45	42	43	40
Transportation equipment	1,091	1,473	1,984	1,831	1,811	1,849	1,923	1,871	1,810
Waste and scrap materials	439	623	619	617	651	725	706	701	726
Tons (mil.) [1]	**1,425**	**1,550**	**1,738**	**1,767**	**1,799**	**1,844**	**1,899**	**1,957**	**1,940**
Farm products	147	154	136	138	141	142	140	149	152
Metallic ores	47	44	32	31	33	33	60	61	59
Coal	579	627	758	785	784	792	804	852	850
Nonmetallic minerals	109	110	126	126	133	140	146	141	138
Food and kindred products	81	91	94	102	102	100	102	105	105
Lumber and wood products	53	51	49	48	47	47	48	43	36
Pulp, paper, allied products	33	36	36	37	39	38	38	37	35
Chemicals, allied products	126	138	155	157	162	167	165	167	176
Petroleum and coal products	40	43	42	42	49	54	57	57	57
Stone, clay, and glass products	44	43	48	49	51	53	55	52	48
Primary metal products	38	47	60	55	54	59	57	61	56
Fabricated metal products	1	1	1	1	1	1	1	1	1
Machinery, exc. electrical	1	1	1	1	1	1	1	1	1
Transportation equipment	23	30	42	38	36	37	38	36	34
Waste and scrap materials	28	38	40	39	41	46	47	48	48
Gross revenue (mil. dol.) [1]	**29,775**	**33,782**	**36,331**	**36,742**	**38,434**	**41,622**	**46,743**	**52,639**	**54,637**
Farm products	2,422	3,020	2,673	2,711	2,870	3,176	3,628	4,205	4,529
Metallic ores	408	394	338	285	289	317	485	529	542
Coal	6,954	7,356	7,794	7,797	7,890	8,418	9,393	10,821	11,471
Nonmetallic minerals	885	875	969	967	1,041	1,131	1,293	1,462	1,527
Food and kindred products	2,188	2,464	2,424	2,657	2,760	2,892	3,253	3,730	4,041
Lumber and wood products	1,390	1,385	1,524	1,628	1,745	1,924	2,278	2,335	1,987
Pulp, paper, allied products	1,486	1,543	1,526	1,567	1,646	1,730	1,953	2,124	2,100
Chemicals, allied products	3,933	4,553	4,636	4,658	4,779	5,100	5,432	6,049	6,830
Petroleum and coal products	918	997	1,010	1,026	1,123	1,268	1,500	1,722	1,853
Stone, clay, and glass products	931	1,044	1,113	1,149	1,211	1,323	1,505	1,664	1,607
Primary metal products	979	1,199	1,371	1,288	1,349	1,518	1,734	2,157	2,267
Fabricated metal products	42	44	48	61	47	50	55	79	86
Machinery, exc. electrical	67	69	61	61	60	72	91	109	126
Transportation equipment	3,100	3,269	3,843	3,731	3,707	3,746	3,960	4,228	4,292
Waste and scrap materials	504	685	706	717	799	956	1,070	1,190	1,276

[1] Includes commodity groups and small packaged freight shipments not shown separately.

Source: Association of American Railroads, Washington, DC, *Freight Commodity Statistics,* annual. See <http://www.aar.org/IndustryInformation/IndustryStatistics/RailCostIndexes.aspx>.

Table 1082. Railroads, Class-I Cars of Revenue Freight Loaded, 1990 to 2007, and by Commodity Group, 2006 and 2007

[In thousands (16,177 represents 16,177,000). Figures are 52-week totals]

Year	Car-loads [1]	Commodity group	Carloads 2006 [2]	Carloads 2007 [2,3]	Commodity group	Carloads 2006 [2]	Carloads 2007 [2,3]
1990	16,177	Coal	7,232	7,163	Metals and products	674	616
2000 [2]	16,354	Metallic ores	253	240	Stone, clay, and glass products	497	454
2001 [2]	16,286	Chemicals, allied products	1,482	1,538	Crushed stone, gravel, sand	1,027	961
2002 [2]	16,101	Grain	1,177	1,178	Nonmetallic minerals	316	312
2003 [2]	16,159	Motor vehicles and equipment	1,087	1,029	Waste and scrap materials	500	501
2004 [2]	16,600	Pulp, paper, allied products	425	392	Lumber, wood products	280	227
2005 [2]	16,691	Primary forest products	139	122	Coke	287	276
2006 [2]	16,936	Food and kindred products	451	449	Petroleum products	319	334
2007 [2,3]	16,562	Grain mill products	479	466	All other carloads	314	302

[1] Excludes intermodal. [2] Excludes 3 Class I railroads. [3] 2007 data preliminary.

Source: Association of American Railroads, Washington, DC, *Weekly Railroad Traffic,* annual. See <http://www.aar.org/Pressroom/WeeklyTrafficReport.aspx>.

Table 1083. Petroleum Pipeline Companies—Characteristics: 1980 to 2006

[**173 represents 173,000.** Covers pipeline companies operating in interstate commerce and subject to jurisdiction of the Federal Energy Regulatory Commission]

Item	Unit	1980	1990	1995	2000	2002	2003	2004	2005	2006
Miles of pipeline, total	1,000	173	168	177	152	150	140	142	131	140
Gathering lines	1,000	36	32	35	18	16	14	15	14	12
Trunk lines	1,000	136	136	142	134	133	126	127	118	129
Total deliveries	Mil. Bbl.	10,600	11,378	12,862	14,450	13,343	13,236	13,394	12,732	12,768
Crude oil	Mil. Bbl.	6,405	6,563	6,952	6,923	7,019	6,941	6,612	6,675	6,668
Products	Mil. Bbl.	4,195	4,816	5,910	7,527	6,324	6,295	6,782	6,057	6,101
Total trunk line traffic	Bil. Bbl.-miles	3,405	3,500	3,619	3,508	3,563	3,591	3,652	3,485	3,536
Crude oil	Bil. Bbl.-miles	1,948	1,891	1,899	1,602	1,620	1,609	1,604	1,571	1,578
Products	Bil. Bbl.-miles	1,458	1,609	1,720	1,906	1,943	1,982	2,049	1,914	1,958
Carrier property value	Mil. dol.	19,752	25,828	27,460	29,648	32,605	32,018	29,552	29,526	32,686
Operating revenues	Mil. dol.	6,356	7,149	7,711	7,483	7,812	7,704	8,020	7,917	8,517
Net income	Mil. dol.	1,912	2,340	2,670	2,705	3,409	3,470	3,323	3,076	3,743

Source: PennWell Publishing Co., Houston, Texas, *Oil & Gas Journal,* annual (copyright).

Table 1084. U.S. Postal Service Rates for Letters and Postcards: 1991 to 2008

[**In dollars.** International rates exclude Canada and Mexico]

Domestic mail date of rate change	Letters First ounce	Letters Each added ounce	Postcards	Express mail— first 1/2 pound	International air mail date of rate change	Letters [1]	Post-cards	Aero-grammes
1991 (Feb. 3)	0.29	0.23	0.19	9.95	**First 1/2 ounce**			
1995 (Jan. 1)	0.32	0.23	0.20	10.75	1991 (Feb. 3)	0.50	0.40	0.45
1999 (Jan. 10)	0.33	0.22	0.20	11.75	1995 (July 9)	0.60	0.40	0.45
2001 (Jan. 7)	0.34	0.21	0.20	12.25	1999 (Jan. 10)	0.60	0.50	0.50
2001 (July 1)	0.34	0.23	0.21	12.45	**First ounce** [1]			
2002 (June 30)	0.37	0.23	0.23	13.65	2001 (Jan. 7)	0.80	0.70	0.70
2006 (Jan. 8)	0.39	0.24	0.24	14.40	2006 (Jan. 8)	0.84	0.75	0.75
2007 (May 14)	0.41	0.17	0.26	16.25	2007 (May 14)	0.90	0.90	(²)
2008 (May 12)	0.42	0.17	0.27	³12.60	2008 (May 12)	0.94	0.94	(²)

[1] The rates after the first ounce depend on the country grouping to which the mail piece's country of destination has been assigned. [2] Aerogrammes were discontinued on May 14, 2007. [3] On May 12, 2008, the Postal Service initiated a zoned pricing structure for Express Mail. Prices for a mail piece weighing up to a half-pound range from $12.60 if it destinates in zones 1 and 2 to $19.50 if it destinates in zone 8.

Source: U.S. Postal Service, *"United States Domestic Postage Rate: Recent History";* and unpublished data. See <http://www.usps.com/rates/welcome.htm>.

U.S. Census Bureau, Statistical Abstract of the United States: 2009

Table 1085. U.S. Postal Service—Summary: 1990 to 2007

[166,301 represents 166,301,000,000. **For years ending September 30.** Includes Puerto Rico and all outlying areas. See text, this section]

Item	1990	1995	2000	2004	2005	2006	2007
Offices, stations, and branches	**40,067**	**39,149**	**38,060**	**37,159**	**37,142**	**36,826**	**36,721**
Number of post offices	28,959	28,392	27,876	27,505	27,385	27,318	27,276
Number of stations and branches	11,108	10,757	10,184	9,654	9,757	9,508	9,445
Delivery Points (mil.)	(NA)	(NA)	135.9	142.3	144.3	146.2	148.0
Residential	(NA)	(NA)	123.9	129.6	131.3	133.0	134.6
City	(NA)	(NA)	76.1	78.0	78.5	78.9	79.5
P.O. Box	(NA)	(NA)	15.9	15.6	15.6	15.6	15.6
Rural/highway contract	(NA)	(NA)	31.9	36.0	37.2	38.4	39.5
Business	(NA)	(NA)	12.1	12.7	13.0	13.2	13.4
Pieces of mail handled (mil.)	**166,301**	**180,734**	**207,882**	**206,106**	**211,743**	**213,138**	**212,234**
Domestic [1]	165,503	179,933	206,782	205,262	210,891	212,345	211,401
First class mail [2]	89,270	96,296	103,526	97,926	98,071	97,618	95,898
Express Mail	59	57	71	54	56	56	55
Priority Mail	518	869	1,223	849	888	924	897
Periodicals (formerly 2d class)	10,680	10,194	10,365	9,135	9,070	9,023	8,796
Standard Mail (formerly Standard A)	63,725	71,112	90,057	95,564	100,942	102,460	103,516
Package Services (formerly Standard B)	663	936	1,128	1,132	1,166	1,175	1,163
Mailgram	14	5	4	2	2	–	–
U.S. Postal Service	538	412	363	529	621	1,016	1,008
Free for the blind	35	52	47	71	76	75	69
International economy mail (surface)	166	106	79	26	23	155	189
International airmail	632	696	1,021	818	829	638	644
Employees, total (1,000)	**843**	**875**	**901**	**808**	**803**	**796**	**786**
Career	761	753	788	707	705	696	685
Headquarters	2	2	2	3	3	3	3
Headquarters support	6	4	6	3	4	4	5
Inspection Service	4	4	4	4	3	3	3
Inspector General	(X)	(X)	1	1	1	1	1
Field Career	749	743	775	697	693	685	673
Postmasters	27	27	26	26	25	25	25
Supervisors/managers	43	35	39	34	33	33	33
Professional, administrative, and technical	10	11	10	9	9	9	8
Clerks	290	274	282	226	222	214	204
Mail handlers	51	57	61	55	56	57	58
City carriers	236	240	241	228	228	224	222
Motor vehicle operators	7	8	9	9	9	9	9
Rural carriers	42	46	57	63	64	66	68
Special delivery messengers	2	2	(X)	(X)	(X)	(X)	(X)
Building and equipment maintenance	33	38	42	40	40	40	40
Vehicle maintenance	5	5	6	6	5	6	5
Other [3]	1	2	2	2	2	2	1
Noncareer	83	122	114	100	98	100	101
Casuals	27	26	30	21	19	23	22
Transitional	(X)	32	13	10	8	5	5
Rural substitutes	43	50	58	56	57	59	60
Relief/Leave replacements	12	13	12	12	12	12	12
Nonbargaining temporary	(Z)	1	1	1	1	1	1
Compensation and employee benefits (mil. dol.)	34,214	41,931	49,532	52,134	53,932	56,302	64,270
Average salary per employee (dol.) [4]	37,570	45,001	50,103	60,261	62,635	64,992	65,905
Pieces of mail per employee, (1,000)	197	207	231	255	264	268	270
Total revenue (mil. dol.) [5]	**40,074**	**54,509**	**64,540**	**69,029**	**69,993**	**72,817**	**74,973**
Operating postal revenue	39,201	54,176	64,476	68,960	69,798	72,551	74,715
Mail revenue [6]	37,892	52,490	62,284	65,869	66,649	69,144	71,057
First class mail	24,023	31,955	35,516	36,377	36,062	37,039	37,564
Priority Mail [7]	1,555	3,075	4,837	4,421	4,634	5,043	5,233
Express Mail [8]	630	711	996	853	872	918	951
Mailgram	8	2	2	1	1	(X)	(X)
Periodicals (formerly 2d class)	1,509	1,972	2,171	2,192	2,161	2,215	2,188
Standard Mail (formerly Standard A)	8,082	11,792	15,193	18,123	18,954	19,877	20,779
Package Services (formerly Standard B)	919	1,525	1,912	2,207	2,201	2,259	2,306
International economy mail (surface)	222	205	180	145	134	118	147
International airmail	941	1,254	1,477	1,551	1,631	1,678	1,889
Service revenue	1,310	1,687	2,191	3,091	3,150	3,407	3,658
Registry [9]	174	118	98	75	77	73	68
Certified [9]	310	560	385	630	601	632	698
Insurance [9]	47	52	109	128	132	137	164
Collect-on-delivery	26	21	22	11	9	10	10
Money orders	155	196	235	231	208	193	212
Other [9]	592	737	1,342	2,017	2,122	2,363	2,506
Operating expenses (mil. dol.) [10]	40,490	50,730	62,992	65,851	68,283	71,681	80,105

– Represents or rounds to zero. NA Not available. X Not applicable. Z Fewer than 500. [1] Data for 1980 includes penalty and franked mail, not shown separately. [2] Items mailed at 1st class rates and weighing 11 ounces or less. [3] Includes discontinued operations, area offices, and nurses. [4] For career bargaining unit employees. Includes fringe benefits. [5] Net revenues after refunds of postage. Includes operating reimbursements, stamped envelope purchases, indemnity claims, and miscellaneous revenue and expenditure offsets. Shown in year which gave rise to the earnings. [6] For 1980, includes penalty and franked mail, not shown separately. Later years have that mail distributed into the appropriate class. [7] Provides 2 to 3 day delivery service. [8] Overnight delivery of packages weighing up to 70 pounds. [9] Beginning 2000, return receipt revenue broken out from registry, certified, and insurance and included in "other." [10] Shown in year in which obligation was incurred.

Source: U.S. Postal Service, *Annual Report of the Postmaster General* and *Comprehensive Statement on Postal Operations,* annual; and unpublished data.

Section 24
Information and Communications

This section presents statistics on the various information and communications media: publishing, including newspapers, periodicals, books, and software; motion pictures, sound recordings, broadcasting, and telecommunications; and information services, such as libraries. Statistics on computer use and Internet access are also included. Data on the usage, finances, and operations of the U.S. Postal Service previously shown in this section are now presented in Section 23, Transportation.

Information industry—The U.S. Census Bureau's *Service Annual Survey, Information Services Sector,* provides estimates of operating revenue of taxable firms and revenues and expenses of firms exempt from federal taxes for industries in the information sector of the economy. Similar estimates were previously issued in the *Annual Survey of Communications Services.* Data are based on the North American Industry Classification System (NAICS), and the information sector is a newly created economic sector. It comprises establishments engaged in the following processes: (a) producing and distributing information and cultural products, (b) providing the means to transmit or distribute these products as well as data or communications, and (c) processing data. It includes establishments previously classified in the Standard Industrial Classification (SIC) in manufacturing (publishing); transportation, communications, and utilities (telecommunications and broadcasting); and services (software publishing, motion picture production, data processing, online information services, and libraries).

This new sector is comprised of industries which existed previously, were revised from previous industry definitions, or are completely new industries. Among those which existed previously are newspaper publishers, motion picture and video production, and online information services. Revised industries include book publishers, libraries, and archives. Newly created industries include database and directory publishers, record production, music publishers, sound recording studios, cable networks, wired telecommunications carriers, paging, and satellite telecommunications.

Data from 1998 to 2003 are based on the 1997 NAICS; beginning 2004, data are based on the 2002 NAICS. Major revisions in many communications industries affect the comparability of these data. The following URL contains detailed information about NAICS <http://www.census.gov/epcd/www/naics.html>. See also the text in Section 15, Business Enterprise.

Beginning 2001, the Service Annual Survey estimates reflect the introduction of the provisional North American Product Classification System (NAPCS) for the information sector. Data for prior years are not comparable. See <http://www.census.gov/eos/www/napcs/napcs.htm>.

The 1997 Economic Census was the first economic census to cover the new information sector of the economy. The census, conducted every 5 years, for the years ending "2" and "7," provides information on the number of establishments, receipts, payroll, and paid employees for the United States and various geographic levels. The most recent reports are from the 2002 Economic Census. This census was conducted in accordance with the 2002 NAICS.

The Federal Communications Commission (FCC), established in 1934, regulates wire and radio communications. Only the largest carriers and holding companies file annual financial reports which are publically available. The FCC has jurisdiction over interstate and foreign communication services but not over intrastate or local services. The gross operating revenues of the telephone carriers reporting publically available data annually to the FCC, however, are estimated to cover

U.S. Census Bureau, Statistical Abstract of the United States: 2009

about 90 percent of the revenues of all U.S. telephone companies. Data are not comparable with Census Bureau *Annual Survey* because of coverage and different accounting practices for those telephone companies which report to the FCC.

Reports filed by the broadcasting industry cover all radio and television stations operating in the United States. The private radio services represent the largest and most diverse group of licensees regulated by the FCC. These services provide voice, data communications, point-to-point, and point-to-multipoint radio communications for fixed and mobile communicators. Major users of these services are small businesses, the aviation industry, the maritime trades, the land transportation industry, the manufacturing industry, state and local public safety and governmental authorities, emergency medical service providers, amateur radio operators, and personal radio operations (CB and the General Mobile Radio Service). The FCC also licenses entities as private and common carriers. Private and common carriers provide fixed and land mobile communications service on a for-profit basis. Principal sources of wire, radio, and television data are the FCC's *Annual Report* and its annual *Statistics of Communications Common Carriers* <http://fcc.gov/wcb/iatd/stats.html/>.

Statistics on publishing are available from the Census Bureau, as well as from various private agencies. Editor & Publisher Co., New York, NY, presents annual data on the number and circulation of daily and Sunday newspapers in its *International Year Book*. The Book Industry Study Group, New York, NY, collects data on books sold and domestic consumer expenditures. Data on academic and public libraries are collected by the U.S. National Center for Education Statistics. Data on Internet use by adults are collected by the Pew Internet and American Life Project, Washington, DC, and Mediamark Research, Inc., New York, NY.

Advertising—Data on advertising previously shown in this section are now presented in Section 27, Accommodation, Food Services, and Other Services.

Statistical reliability—For a discussion of statistical collection and estimation, sampling procedures, and measures of statistical reliability applicable to Census Bureau data, see Appendix III.

U.S. Census Bureau, Statistical Abstract of the United States: 2009

Table 1086. Information Industries—Establishments, Employees, and Payroll: 2004 and 2005

[For establishments with payroll (3,472.4 represents 3,472,400). Excludes most government employees, railroad employees, and self-employed persons. For statement on methodology, see Appendix III]

Industry	2002 NAICS code [1]	Establishments (number)		Paid employees [2] (1,000)		Annual payroll (mil. dol.)	
		2004	2005	2004	2005	2004	2005
Information industries	**51**	**139,681**	**141,290**	**3,472.4**	**3,402.6**	**200,447**	**203,130**
Publishing industries	511	31,528	31,538	1,033.5	1,032.3	66,887	67,094
Newspaper, periodical, book, and database publishers	5111	22,443	22,745	704.9	704.6	32,020	33,111
Newspaper publishers	51111	8,435	8,395	383.1	380.1	14,009	14,376
Periodical publishers	51112	7,602	7,846	154.4	158.8	9,418	9,940
Book publishers	51113	3,377	3,359	85.0	83.6	4,622	4,656
Database and directory publishers	51114	1,740	1,824	56.3	57.0	2,871	3,030
Other publishers	51119	1,289	1,321	26.1	25.0	1,099	1,109
Greeting card publishers	511191	120	120	13.1	12.5	583	580
All other publishers	511199	1,169	1,201	13.0	12.6	517	529
Software publishers	5112	9,085	8,793	328.6	327.6	34,866	33,983
Motion picture and sound recording industries	512	22,753	23,579	307.8	314.4	13,286	14,040
Motion picture and video industries	5121	19,348	20,131	282.7	292.1	11,321	12,404
Motion picture and video production	51211	11,751	12,419	122.2	131.6	8,264	9,301
Motion picture and video distribution	51212	452	457	3.4	4.3	214	257
Motion picture and video exhibition	51213	5,029	5,129	134.9	134.0	1,327	1,288
Motion picture theaters (except drive-ins)	512131	4,756	4,854	133.5	132.2	1,301	1,260
Drive-in motion picture theaters	512132	273	275	1.4	1.7	26	27
Post production and other motion picture and video industries	51219	2,116	2,126	22.1	22.3	1,516	1,559
Teleproduction and other post-production services	512191	1,784	1,804	17.4	17.5	1,194	1,201
Other motion picture and video industries	512199	332	322	4.7	4.7	323	358
Sound recording industries	5122	3,405	3,448	25.1	22.3	1,965	1,636
Record production	51221	353	349	1.4	1.5	74	72
Integrated record production/distribution	51222	415	402	9.7	7.8	1,196	891
Music publishers	51223	606	645	4.7	4.6	329	337
Sound recording studios	51224	1,513	1,561	5.4	4.9	205	204
Other sound recording industries	51229	518	491	3.8	3.4	162	132
Broadcasting (except Internet)	515	10,099	10,342	288.0	287.0	16,198	17,354
Radio and television broadcasting	5151	9,466	9,685	247.7	248.3	12,521	13,200
Radio broadcasting	51511	7,492	7,697	127.0	124.1	5,514	6,136
Radio networks	515111	729	743	11.9	11.9	728	797
Radio stations	515112	6,763	6,954	115.1	112.2	4,786	5,339
Television broadcasting	51512	1,974	1,988	120.6	124.2	7,006	7,064
Cable and other subscription programming	5152	633	657	40.4	38.8	3,677	4,154
Internet publishing and broadcasting	516	2,133	2,343	37.0	36.1	2,546	2,687
Telecommunications	517	49,786	49,431	1,327.4	1,226.5	72,683	69,687
Wired telecommunications carriers	5171	27,596	26,744	781.4	693.7	45,280	41,799
Wireless telecommunications carriers (except satellite)	5172	13,183	14,173	262.1	250.0	13,971	14,035
Paging	517211	1,224	788	11.5	7.6	503	359
Cellular and other wireless telecommunications	517212	11,959	13,385	250.6	242.3	13,468	13,676
Telecommunications resellers	5173	2,886	2,778	46.6	33.7	2,211	1,762
Satellite telecommunications	5174	649	605	18.4	15.4	1,201	992
Cable and other program distribution	5175	4,844	4,561	210.7	224.6	9,437	10,512
Other telecommunications	5179	628	570	8.3	9.2	583	587
Internet service providers, Web search portals, and data processing service	518	19,489	20,142	426.4	452.2	27,002	30,292
Internet service providers and Web search portals	5181	5,422	5,579	60.4	72.7	5,234	7,588
Internet service providers	518111	4,851	4,948	49.2	57.6	3,083	3,701
Web search portals	518112	571	631	11.2	15.1	2,151	3,887
Data processing, hosting, and related services	5182	14,067	14,563	365.9	379.4	21,767	22,704
Other information services	519	3,893	3,915	52.2	54.1	1,846	1,975
News syndicates	51911	559	606	11.2	11.8	677	705
Libraries and archives	51912	2,677	2,593	31.7	30.5	735	720
All other information services	51919	657	716	9.3	11.7	434	550

[1] North American Industry Classification System, 2002; see text, this section and Section 15.   [2] For employees on the payroll for the pay period including March 12.

Source: U.S. Census Bureau, "County Business Patterns." See <http://www.census.gov/epcd/cbp/view/cbpview.html>.

U.S. Census Bureau, Statistical Abstract of the United States: 2009

Table 1087. Information Sector Services—Estimated Revenue and Expenses: 2004 to 2006

[In millions of dollars (955,083 represents $955,083,000,000). For taxable and tax-exempt employer firms. Estimates have been adjusted to the results of the 2002 Economic Census. Based on the Service Annual Survey; see Appendix III.]

Industry	2002 NAICS code [1]	Operating revenue			Operating expenses		
		2004	2005	2006	2004	2005	2006
Information industries	**51**	**955,083**	**1,003,010**	**1,056,045**	**787,213**	**813,385**	**836,044**
Publishing industries (except Internet)	511	256,301	269,283	279,415	195,174	199,167	200,797
Newspaper, periodical, book, and directory publishers	5111	144,040	147,974	148,688	105,444	111,000	110,214
Newspaper publishers	51111	48,336	49,723	48,861	39,998	41,093	42,269
Periodical publishers	51112	42,290	44,051	46,287	34,614	37,695	36,105
Book publishers	51113	27,904	27,994	28,192	15,999	16,754	16,268
Directory and mailing list publishers	51114	18,040	19,413	18,929	10,487	11,052	10,997
Other publishers	51119	7,470	6,793	6,419	4,419	4,403	4,575
Greeting card publishers	511191	5,075	4,552	4,122	2,829	2,740	2,803
All other publishers	511199	2,395	2,241	2,297	1,590	1,663	1,772
Software publishers	5112	112,261	121,309	130,727	89,665	88,168	90,583
Motion picture and sound recording industries . . .	512	88,269	92,231	94,400	73,470	77,757	79,102
Motion picture and video industries	5121	71,774	73,503	73,241	60,624	61,238	61,110
Motion picture and video production and distribution	51211,12	56,605	58,487	57,770	48,277	48,952	49,152
Motion picture and video exhibition	51213	11,180	10,789	11,080	8,633	8,501	8,047
Motion picture theaters (except drive-ins)	512131	11,069	10,669	10,869	8,559	8,422	7,936
Drive-in motion picture theaters	512132	111	120	(S)	(S)	79	(S)
Postproduction services and other motion picture and video industries	51219	3,989	4,227	4,391	3,714	3,785	3,911
Teleproduction and other postproduction services	512191	3,193	3,366	3,480	3,018	3,015	3,091
Other motion picture and video industries	512199	796	861	911	696	770	820
Sound recording industries	5122	16,495	18,728	21,159	12,846	16,519	17,992
Record production	51221	352	338	317	279	262	301
Integrated record production/distribution. . .	51222	11,021	12,866	14,237	8,918	12,443	13,480
Music publishers	51223	3,885	4,175	5,093	2,474	2,562	2,788
Sound recording studios	51224	724	767	869	635	672	775
Other sound recording industries	51229	513	582	643	540	580	648
Broadcasting (except Internet)	515	83,466	88,911	94,872	63,130	67,145	72,127
Radio and television broadcasting	5151	52,093	53,308	56,435	41,689	43,539	46,898
Radio broadcasting	51511	16,494	17,011	18,107	13,697	14,734	17,006
Radio networks	515111	2,677	3,298	4,411	3,783	4,584	6,809
Radio stations	515112	13,817	13,713	13,696	9,914	10,150	10,197
Television broadcasting.	51512	35,599	36,297	38,328	27,992	28,805	29,892
Cable and other subscription programming . . .	5152	31,373	35,603	38,437	21,441	23,606	25,229
Internet publishing and broadcasting	516	8,695	10,603	12,448	7,011	8,197	8,342
Telecommunications	517	429,430	446,325	469,585	371,847	382,559	389,552
Wired telecommunications carriers	5171	211,176	206,778	199,933	187,541	176,525	168,661
Wireless telecommunications carriers (except satellite)	5172	127,602	140,096	160,159	106,587	124,049	134,802
Paging.	517211	1,909	2,014	1,643	1,546	1,747	1,295
Cellular and other wireless telecommunications	517212	125,693	138,082	158,516	105,041	122,302	133,507
Telecommunications resellers	5173	9,849	11,237	12,788	5,983	6,868	6,908
Satellite telecommunications	5174	6,030	5,676	4,802	5,613	4,618	3,489
Cable and other program distribution	5175	73,317	80,493	88,724	64,865	69,031	74,538
Other telecommunications	5179	1,456	2,045	1,904	1,166	1,474	1,154
Internet service providers, Web search portals, and data processing services	518	82,491	88,814	97,838	71,438	72,821	80,523
Internet service providers and Web search portals.	5181	25,161	25,863	27,775	18,729	17,465	20,391
Internet service providers	518111	20,201	18,910	18,576	16,251	14,209	15,713
Web search portals	518112	4,960	6,953	9,199	2,478	3,256	4,678
Data processing, hosting, and related services.	5182	57,330	62,951	70,063	52,772	55,739	60,132
Other information services	519	6,431	6,843	7,487	5,171	5,346	5,601
News syndicates	51911	1,972	2,089	2,241	1,868	1,827	1,871
Libraries and archives	51912	1,879	2,033	2,117	1,621	1,727	1,786
Other information services.	51919	(S)	2,721	3,129	1,682	1,792	1,944

S Data do not meet publication standards.   [1] North American Industry Classification System (NAICS), 2002; see text this section and Section 15.

Source: U.S. Census Bureau, "2006 Service Annual Survey, Information Sector Services." See <http://www.census.gov/econ/www/servmenu.html>; (released March 2008).

Table 1088. Information Industries—Establishments, Revenue, Payroll and Employees by Kind of Business: 2002

[For establishments with payroll. (891,846 represents $891,846,000,000). Based on the 2002 Economic Census; see Appendix III]

Kind of business	2002 NAICS code [1]	Number of establishments	Receipts (mil. dol.)	Annual payroll (mil. dol.)	Paid employees (1,000)
Information industries.	51	137,678	891,846	194,670	3,736.1
Publishing industries (except Internet)	511	32,287	242,216	65,681	1,089.6
Motion picture & sound recording industries	512	22,458	78,250	12,599	303.1
Motion picture & video industries	5121	19,074	62,927	10,353	271.2
Sound recording industries	5122	3,384	15,324	2,246	31.9
Broadcasting (except Internet)	515	9,540	73,962	14,439	291.4
Radio & television broadcasting	5151	8,851	48,589	11,591	252.2
Cable & other subscription programming	5152	689	25,373	2,848	39.1
Internet publishing & broadcasting	516	2,057	6,363	2,346	40.0
Telecommunications	517	49,275	411,645	72,182	1,440.1
Wired telecommunications carriers	5171	27,955	237,697	47,496	842.4
Wireless telecommunications carriers (except satellite) . . .	5172	11,155	99,193	13,207	281.4
Telecommunications resellers	5173	2,525	9,717	1,397	34.5
Satellite telecommunications	5174	646	5,748	915	14.4
Cable & other program distribution	5175	6,288	57,709	8,553	256.0
Other telecommunications	5179	706	1,581	614	11.4
Internet service providers, Web search portals, & data processing.	518	18,589	74,508	25,719	514.0
Internet service providers & Web search portals	5181	4,820	21,419	4,451	79.8
Data processing, hosting, & related services	5182	13,769	53,089	21,267	434.3
Other information services	519	3,472	4,901	1,705	57.8

[1] North American Industry Classification System, 2002; see text, this section and Section 15, Business Enterprise.

Source: U.S. Census Bureau, "2002 Economic Census, Geographic Area Series Reports, Information." See <http://www.census.gov/econ/census02/guide/geosumm.htm>; (accessed January 2008).

Table 1089. Media Usage and Consumer Spending: 2001 to 2011

[Estimates for time spent were derived using rating data for broadcast television and cable and satellite television, survey research for radio, mobile, out-of-home media and yellow pages, and consumer purchase data (units, admissions, access) for books, home video, Internet, newspapers, consumer books, consumer magazines, recorded music, videogames, and box office. Adults 18 and older were the basis for estimates for newspapers, consumer books, consumer magazines, out-of-home media, yellow pages, and home video. Persons 12 and older were the basis for the estimates for broadcast television, cable & satellite television, radio, recorded music, box office, videogames, Internet, and mobile content]

Item	2001	2003	2005	2006, proj.	2007, proj.	2008, proj.	2009, proj.	2010, proj.	2011, proj.
HOURS PER PERSON PER YEAR [1]									
Total [2]	3,388	3,505	3,548	3,530	3,532	3,559	3,569	3,596	3,624
Television.	1,553	1,615	1,659	1,673	1,686	1,704	1,714	1,728	1,742
Broadcast Television [3]	777	729	679	676	676	678	673	673	669
Network stations.	680	629	582	599	603	604	598	598	593
Independent stations [4]	97	100	97	77	73	74	75	75	76
Cable & satellite television [3]	776	886	980	997	1,010	1,027	1,041	1,055	1,073
Basic cable and satellite television.	638	728	807	835	849	865	877	891	913
Premium cable and satellite television [4]	133	157	173	161	161	162	164	164	159
Broadcast and satellite radio [3]	792	834	805	778	769	768	760	758	751
Recorded music [3]	226	187	196	186	171	165	168	174	185
Newspapers [3]	199	195	187	178	172	168	162	158	154
Pure-play Internet services [3]	125	153	169	177	181	183	184	184	183
Out-of-home media	119	122	130	133	137	141	145	149	154
Consumer magazines [3]	127	122	124	121	119	117	114	112	110
Consumer books [3]	105	108	107	108	108	108	109	109	110
Videogames [3]	66	76	73	76	82	90	91	94	100
Home video [5]	47	60	63	62	64	66	68	70	70
CONSUMER SPENDING PER PERSON PER YEAR (dol.)									
Total [2]	637.65	720.37	766.57	798.07	837.99	884.19	929.04	969.36	1,010.90
Television.	192.33	234.17	280.92	308.60	333.79	357.70	380.34	400.76	419.84
Cable and satellite television [3]	192.32	234.14	280.52	307.62	331.74	354.24	375.22	393.82	410.89
Broadcast television [3]	0.01	0.03	0.40	0.98	2.05	3.46	5.12	6.94	8.95
Home video [5]	92.44	122.26	115.24	114.60	118.35	123.74	128.55	131.71	132.20
Consumer books [3]	86.09	91.89	95.76	97.57	101.23	103.04	105.83	108.17	111.17
Pure-play Internet services [3]	56.22	59.51	56.74	52.78	51.28	54.78	58.90	62.79	66.17
Recorded music [3]	57.69	49.36	50.71	48.91	46.03	45.00	44.92	45.41	46.29
Newspapers [3]	52.48	53.62	50.56	49.54	48.60	47.92	47.33	46.80	46.44
Consumer magazines [3]	47.07	46.56	47.64	46.83	46.43	46.16	45.93	45.78	45.67
Box office [3]	35.50	39.11	36.41	38.30	40.92	41.63	44.27	45.17	48.03
Videogames [3]	29.36	32.98	32.23	34.03	37.84	43.34	44.64	46.91	51.89

[1] Can include concurrent use of media, such as watching television and reading e-mail simultaneously. Does not include media use at work. [2] Includes other media not shown separately. [3] Online and mobile use and spending on traditional media platforms, such as downloaded music, newspaper Web sites, e-books, cable modems, online video of television programs and Internet radio were included in the traditional media segment, not in pure-play Internet services or pure-play mobile content. Pure-play Internet services and pure-play mobile content included telecommunications access, such as DSL, Internet-only Web sites such as Yahoo!, GameSpy, eHarmony, and mobile-only services, such as MobiTV or text messaging services from telecommunication providers. [4] Telemundo and Univision affiliates included in independent and public stations. Pay-per-view, interactive channels, home shopping, and audio-only feeds included in premium cable and satellite services. [5] Playback of prerecorded VHS cassettes and DVDs only.

Source: Veronis Suhler Stevenson, New York, NY, *Communications Industry Forecast & Report,* annual (copyright).

Information and Communications **695**

Table 1090. Utilization of Selected Media: 1980 to 2006

[78.6 represents 78,600,000]

Item	Unit	1980	1990	1995	2000	2001	2002	2003	2004	2005	2006
Households with—											
Telephone service [1]	Percent..	93.0	93.3	93.9	94.6	94.6	95.5	95.5	94.2	92.5	92.9
Radio [2]	Millions..	78.6	94.4	98.0	100.5	101.9	105.1	106.7	108.3	109.9	110.5
Percent of total households...	Percent..	99.0	99.0	99.0	99.0	99.0	99.0	99.0	99.0	99.0	99.0
Average number of sets.....	Number..	5.5	5.6	5.6	5.6	5.6	5.6	8.0	8.0	8.0	8.0
Television [3]	Millions..	76	92	96	101	102	106	107	109	110	110
Percent of total households...	Percent..	97.9	98.2	98.3	98.2	98.2	98.2	98.2	98.2	98.2	98.2
Television sets in homes.	Millions..	128	193	217	245	248	254	260	268	287	301
Average number of sets per home	Number..	1.7	2.0	2.3	2.4	2.4	2.4	2.4	2.5	2.6	2.7
Color set households	Millions..	63	90	94	101	102	105	107	108	109	(NA)
Wired cable television [4]	Millions..	15.2	51.9	60.5	68.6	69.5	73.2	74.4	73.8	73.9	62.1
Percent of TV households....	Percent..	19.9	56.4	63.4	68.0	68.0	69.4	69.8	68.1	67.5	72.4
Alternative delivery system (ADS) households [4]	Millions..	(NA)	(NA)	4.0	11.7	14.7	17.4	19.7	21.2	23.3	24.5
Percent of TV households....	Percent..	(NA)	(NA)	4.2	11.4	14.1	16.3	18.2	19.3	20.8	28.5
VCRs [4]	Millions..	1	63	77	86	88	96	98	98	99	98
Percent of TV households....	Percent..	1.1	68.6	81.0	85.1	86.2	91.2	91.5	90.8	90.2	88.6
Computers [5]	Percent..	(NA)	22.0	36.0	58.0	59.0	61.0	64.0	68.0	73.0	78.0
Commercial radio stations: [2]											
AM	Number..	4,589	4,987	4,909	4,685	4,727	4,804	4,802	4,770	4,758	4,751
FM	Number..	3,282	4,392	5,296	5,892	6,051	6,161	6,207	6,217	6,215	6,252
Television stations: [6] Total	Number..	1,011	1,442	1,532	1,663	1,686	1,714	1,730	1,748	1,749	1,754
Commercial	Number..	734	1,092	1,161	1,288	1,309	1,333	1,349	1,366	1,370	1,373
VHF	Number..	516	547	562	567	572	581	587	589	589	786
UHF	Number..	218	545	599	721	737	752	762	777	781	587
Cable television systems [7]	Number..	4,225	9,575	11,218	10,400	10,300	9,900	9,400	8,875	7,926	7,090
Daily newspaper circulation [8]	Millions..	62.2	62.3	58.2	55.8	55.6	55.2	55.2	54.6	53.3	52.3

NA Not available. [1] For occupied housing units. 1980 as of April 1; all other years as of March. Source: U.S. Census Bureau, *1980 Census of Housing,* vol. 1; thereafter, Federal Communications Commission, *Trends in Telephone Service,* annual. [2] 1980–1995 as of December 31. Source: M Street Corp. as reported by Radio Advertising Bureau New York, NY; through 1990, Radio Facts, annual (copyright); beginning 1995, Radio Marketing Guide and Fact Book for Advertisers, annual (copyright). Number of stations on the air compiled from Federal Communications Commission reports. Beginning 2000, Federal Communications Commission, unpublished data as of Sept. 30. See Internet site <http://www.fcc.gov/mb/audio/totals>. [3] As of January of year shown. Excludes Alaska and Hawaii. Source: Television Bureau of Advertising, Inc., *Trends in Television,* annual (copyright). [4] Wired cable and VCR as of February; ADS for fourth quarter. Excludes Alaska and Hawaii. Source: See footnote 3. [5] Computer totals include notebooks and desktops sold through consumer channels. Source: Television Advertising Bureau, TV Basics, March 2008. [6] Source: Beginning 2000, Federal Communications Commission, unpublished data. See Internet site <http://www.fcc.gov/mb/audio/totals>. Beginning 2000, as of September. For prior years data, see footnote 3. [7] As of January 1. Source: Warren Communications News, Washington DC, *Television and Cable Factbook* (copyright). [8] As of September 30. Source: Editor & Publisher, Co., New York, NY, *Editor & Publisher International Year Book,* annual (copyright).

Source: Compiled from sources mentioned in footnotes.

Table 1091. Multimedia Audiences—Summary: 2007

[In percent, except total (220,847 represents 220,847,000). As of fall. For persons 18 years old and over. Represents the percent of persons participating during the prior week, except as indicated. Based on sample and subject to sampling error; see source for details]

Item	Total population (1,000)	Television viewing	Television prime time viewing	Cable viewing [1]	Radio listening	Newspaper reading	Accessed Internet [2]
Total..............	220,847	94.2	83.6	79.8	82.9	73.9	67.4
18 to 24 years old........	28,105	91.3	75.3	73.8	88.7	65.0	80.5
25 to 34 years old........	39,660	92.5	81.0	76.6	88.4	70.7	79.4
35 to 44 years old........	43,314	93.2	83.2	80.8	88.8	74.4	77.6
45 to 54 years old........	42,978	94.6	85.4	82.2	86.6	75.9	70.7
55 to 64 years old........	31,107	96.4	88.5	84.0	81.4	77.3	63.9
65 years old and over......	35,684	97.1	87.2	80.2	62.2	78.8	30.2
Male................	106,534	94.3	83.4	79.7	84.6	73.8	67.1
Female..............	114,313	94.1	83.8	79.9	81.4	74.1	67.6
Not high school graduate....	34,042	91.9	80.6	65.5	73.3	58.7	27.5
High school graduate......	69,734	95.5	85.7	80.2	81.7	72.6	54.9
Attended college........	60,792	94.8	83.1	82.3	85.9	77.4	81.2
College graduate.........	56,279	93.3	83.5	85.2	87.0	81.1	92.1
Household income:							
Less than $10,000......	12,633	92.3	78.5	57.3	76.1	63.2	35.5
$10,000 to $19,999......	21,042	93.4	82.6	63.3	73.2	64.7	33.3
$20,000 to $29,999......	22,916	93.5	82.9	70.7	75.0	70.5	43.7
$30,000 to $34,999......	11,481	94.3	82.5	75.2	78.3	71.9	55.1
$35,000 to $39,999......	10,910	95.1	84.0	80.8	80.7	73.5	57.9
$40,000 to $49,999......	21,185	94.4	83.5	78.1	82.8	72.4	64.1
$50,000 to $74,999......	43,816	94.5	84.6	83.7	85.9	74.9	75.4
$75,000 to $99,999......	29,142	94.8	85.2	87.0	88.4	78.5	84.7
$100,000 or more.......	47,723	94.4	84.1	91.0	88.4	80.2	90.8

[1] In the past 7 days. [2] In the last 30 days.

Source: Mediamark Research Inc., New York, NY, *Multimedia Audiences,* fall 2007 (copyright).

Table 1092. **Newspaper Publishers—Estimated Revenue, Expenses, and Inventories: 2004 to 2006**

[**In millions of dollars (48,366 represents $48,366,000,000).** For taxable and tax-exempt employer firms. Covers NAICS 51111. Estimates have been adjusted to the results of the 2002 Economic Census. Based on the North American Industry Classification System (NAICS), 2002. See text, this section and Section 15. See also Appendix III]

Item	2004	2005	2006
Operating revenue [1]................................	**48,366**	**49,723**	**48,861**
Breakdown of revenue by type of media:			
Print..	40,705	41,550	40,979
Online..	1,869	2,135	2,128
Other media	406	381	423
Operating expenses............................	**39,998**	**41,093**	**42,269**
Personnel costs.....................................	19,451	19,870	19,570
Gross annual payroll...........................	15,433	15,756	15,273
Employer's cost for fringe benefits............	3,766	3,884	4,056
Temporary staff and leased employee expense	251	230	241
Expensed materials, parts and supplies (not for resale)............	4,396	4,373	3,969
Expensed equipment...........................	83	72	75
Expensed purchase of other materials, parts and supplies	4,313	4,301	3,894
Expensed purchased services	3,104	3,313	3,587
Expensed software............................	79	88	96
Purchased electricity and fuels (except motor fuel)	298	340	355
Lease and rental payments.....................	545	573	587
Purchased repair and maintenance	369	368	359
Purchased advertising and promotional services.....	616	670	675
Purchased printing services	1,198	1,274	1,515
Other operating expenses............................	13,047	13,537	15,142
Depreciation and amortization charges.............	1,849	1,868	2,004
Government taxes and license fees	378	386	414
All other operating expenses.....................	10,820	11,284	12,724
Inventories at end of year........................	**683**	**703**	**687**
Finished good...................................	(S)	32	(D)
Work-in-process................................	(S)	(S)	(D)
Materials, fuels, supplies etc............................	626	641	607

S Data do not meet publication standards.   D Figure withheld to avoid disclosure pertaining to a specific organization or individual.   [1] Includes other types of revenue (e.g., printing services) not shown separately.

Source: U.S. Census Bureau, *"2006 Service Annual Survey, Information Sector Services."* See <http://www.census.gov/econ/www/servmenu.html>; (released March 2008).

Table 1093. **Daily and Sunday Newspapers—Number and Circulation: 1970 to 2007**

[**Number of newspapers as of February 1 the following year. Circulation figures as of September 30 of year shown (62.1 represents 62,100,000).** For English language newspapers only]

Type	1970	1980	1985	1990	1995	2000	2002	2003	2004	2005	2006	2007
NUMBER												
Daily: Total [1]	1,748	1,745	1,676	1,611	1,533	1,480	1,457	1,456	1,457	1,452	1,437	1,422
Morning	334	387	482	559	656	766	777	787	814	817	833	867
Evening	1,429	1,388	1,220	1,084	891	727	692	680	653	645	614	565
Sunday	586	736	798	863	888	917	913	917	915	914	907	907
NET PAID CIRCULATION (mil.)												
Daily: Total [1]	62.1	62.2	62.8	62.3	58.2	55.8	55.2	55.2	54.6	53.3	52.3	50.7
Morning	25.9	29.4	36.4	41.3	44.3	46.8	46.6	46.9	46.9	46.1	45.4	44.5
Evening	36.2	32.8	26.4	21.0	13.9	9.0	8.6	8.3	7.7	7.2	6.9	6.2
Sunday	49.2	54.7	58.8	62.6	61.5	59.4	58.8	58.5	57.8	55.3	53.2	51.2
PER CAPITA CIRCULATION [2]												
Daily: Total [1]	0.30	0.27	0.26	0.25	0.22	0.20	0.19	0.19	0.19	0.18	0.18	0.17
Morning	0.13	0.13	0.15	0.17	0.17	0.17	0.16	0.16	0.16	0.16	0.15	0.15
Evening	0.18	0.14	0.11	0.08	0.05	0.03	0.03	0.03	0.03	0.02	0.02	0.02
Sunday	0.24	0.24	0.25	0.25	0.23	0.21	0.20	0.20	0.20	0.19	0.18	0.17

[1] All-day newspapers are counted in both morning and evening columns but only once in total. Circulation is divided equally between morning and evening.   [2] Based on U.S. Census Bureau estimated resident population as of July 1.

Source: Editor & Publisher Co., New York, NY, *Editor & Publisher International Year Book,* annual (copyright).

Table 1094. Daily Newspapers—Number and Circulation by Size of City: 1980 to 2007

[Number of newspapers as of February 1 the following year. Circulation as of September 30 (29,413 represents 29,413,000). For English language newspapers only. See Table 27 for number of cities by population size. All-day newspapers are counted in both morning and evening columns; circulation is divided equally between morning and evening]

Type of daily and population-size class	Number					Net paid circulation (1,000)				
	1980	1990	2000	2005	2007	1980	1990	2000	2005	2007
Morning dailies, total...	**387**	**559**	**766**	**817**	**867**	**29,413**	**41,311**	**46,772**	**46,123**	**44,548**
In cities of—										
1,000,001 or more	20	18	26	32	30	8,795	6,508	10,820	10,791	10,159
500,001 to 1,000,000	27	22	25	33	36	5,705	4,804	5,412	6,253	6,376
100,001 to 500,000	99	138	163	166	165	8,996	20,051	17,469	16,510	15,458
50,001 to 100,000	75	100	162	160	166	2,973	4,373	5,887	5,439	5,407
25,001 to 50,000	64	102	141	157	165	1,701	3,209	3,899	3,737	3,615
Less than 25,000	102	179	249	269	305	1,243	2,365	3,285	3,392	3,533
Evening dailies, total...	**1,388**	**1,084**	**727**	**645**	**565**	**32,788**	**21,017**	**9,000**	**7,222**	**6,194**
In cities of—										
1,000,001 or more	11	7	1	1	1	2,984	1,423	1	1	1
500,001 to 1,000,000	23	12	3	5	4	4,101	1,350	519	583	371
100,001 to 500,000	123	71	32	23	21	8,178	4,687	1,603	1,138	1,030
50,001 to 100,000	156	94	54	37	37	4,896	2,941	1,332	916	815
25,001 to 50,000	246	204	124	110	93	5,106	4,278	1,898	1,517	1,274
Less than 25,000	829	696	513	469	409	7,523	6,338	3,648	3,067	2,703

Source: Editor & Publisher Co., New York, NY, *Editor & Publisher International Year Book,* annual (copyright).

Table 1095. Daily and Sunday Newspapers—Number and Circulation, 1991 to 2006 and by State, 2007

[Number of newspapers as of February 1 the following year. Circulation as of September 30 (60,687 represents 60,687,000). For English language newspapers only. California, New York, Massachusetts, and Virginia Sunday newspapers include national circulation]

State	Daily			Sunday		State	Daily			Sunday	
		Circulation [1]			Net paid circula-tion (1,000)			Circulation [1]			Net paid circula-tion (1,000)
	Number	Net paid (1,000)	Per capita [2]	Num-ber			Number	Net paid (1,000)	Per capita [2]	Num-ber	
Total, 1991 . .	1,586	60,687	0.24	875	62,068	KS	39	376	0.14	13	328
Total, 1992 . .	1,570	60,164	0.23	891	62,160	KY	23	550	0.13	14	580
Total, 1993 . .	1,556	59,812	0.23	884	62,566	LA	24	588	0.14	18	644
Total, 1994 . .	1,548	59,305	0.23	886	62,294	ME	7	214	0.16	4	176
Total, 1995 . .	1,533	58,193	0.22	888	61,529	MD	10	448	0.08	8	588
Total, 1996 . .	1,520	56,983	0.21	890	60,798	MA	32	1,290	0.20	16	1,232
Total, 1997 . .	1,509	56,728	0.21	903	60,484	MI	48	1,504	0.15	27	1,699
Total, 1998 . .	1,489	56,182	0.20	898	60,066	MN	25	797	0.15	15	1,027
Total, 1999 . .	1,483	55,979	0.20	905	59,894	MS	23	339	0.12	19	339
Total, 2000 . .	1,480	55,773	0.20	917	59,421	MO	42	863	0.15	21	1,055
Total, 2001 . .	1,468	55,578	0.19	913	59,090	MT	11	183	0.19	7	183
Total, 2002 . .	1,457	55,186	0.19	913	58,780	NE	16	382	0.22	6	365
Total, 2003 . .	1,456	55,185	0.19	917	58,495	NV	7	257	0.10	5	298
Total, 2004 . .	1,457	54,626	0.19	915	57,753	NH	11	185	0.14	8	199
Total, 2005 . .	1,452	53,345	0.18	914	55,270	NJ	18	1,123	0.13	15	1,375
Total, 2006 . .	1,437	52,329	0.18	907	53,175	NM	17	260	0.13	12	268
						NY	60	6,631	0.34	38	4,756
						NC	47	1,209	0.13	39	1,342
Total, 2007 .	**1,422**	**50,742**	**0.17**	**907**	**51,246**	ND	10	147	0.23	7	152
AL	25	593	0.13	22	651	OH	83	2,066	0.18	41	2,308
AK	7	101	0.15	5	111	OK	38	554	0.15	31	669
AZ	16	698	0.11	11	790	OR	19	626	0.17	12	648
AR	27	458	0.16	16	528	PA	80	2,449	0.20	42	2,796
CA	83	5,066	0.14	58	5,166	RI	6	186	0.18	3	223
CO	30	921	0.19	16	987	SC	16	579	0.13	14	661
CT	17	609	0.17	13	675	SD	11	147	0.18	4	125
DE	2	125	0.14	2	150	TN	26	804	0.13	19	936
DC	3	991	1.68	2	933	TX	82	2,569	0.11	77	3,232
FL	39	2,814	0.15	37	3,499	UT	6	326	0.12	6	363
GA	34	920	0.10	29	1,144	VT	8	106	0.17	3	78
HI	6	263	0.20	6	288	VA	23	3,147	0.41	17	905
ID	12	208	0.14	7	221	WA	22	940	0.15	16	1,065
IL	64	2,086	0.16	32	2,305	WV	20	363	0.20	14	377
IN	67	1,217	0.19	25	1,149	WI	34	811	0.14	17	982
IA	37	565	0.19	13	602	WY	9	86	0.16	5	71

[1] Circulation figures based on the principal community served by a newspaper which is not necessarily the same location as the publisher's office. [2] Per capita based on estimated resident population as of July 1, except 2000, enumerated resident population as of April 1.

Source: Editor & Publisher Co., New York, NY, *Editor & Publisher International Year Book,* annual (copyright).

Table 1096. Periodical Publishers—Estimated Revenue, Expenses, and Inventories: 2004 to 2006

[In millions of dollars (42,290 represents $42,290,000,000). For taxable and tax-exempt employer firms. Covers NAICS 51112. Estimates have been adjusted to the results of the 2002 Economic Census. Based on the North American Industry Classification System (NAICS), 2002. See text, this section, and Section 15. See also Appendix III]

Item	2004	2005	2006
Operating revenue [1]	**42,290**	**44,051**	**46,287**
Sources of revenue:			
General interest periodicals	23,519	24,117	25,902
Subscription and sales	8,267	8,092	8,479
Advertising space	15,252	16,025	17,423
Professional and academic periodicals	7,658	7,882	7,926
Subscription and sales	4,229	4,423	4,464
Advertising space	3,429	3,459	3,462
Other periodicals	4,254	4,680	4,732
Subscription and sales	2,156	2,336	2,355
Advertising space	2,098	2,344	2,377
Other operating revenue	6,859	7,373	7,727
Printing services for others	982	904	858
Licensing of rights to content	235	294	418
All other	5,642	6,176	6,451
Breakdown of revenue by media type:			
Print	32,909	33,834	34,841
Online	2,052	2,299	3,061
Other media	470	545	658
Operating expenses	**34,614**	**37,695**	**36,105**
Personnel costs	13,274	14,668	14,342
Expensed materials, parts and supplies (not for resale)	1,435	1,535	1,368
Expensed purchased services	6,936	7,537	7,725
Other operating expenses	12,969	13,955	12,669
Inventories at end of year	**1,639**	**1,913**	**1,804**
Finished goods	1,100	1,270	1,225
Work-in-process	128	154	150
Materials, fuels, supplies, etc.	411	489	429

[1] Includes other types of revenue (i.e., printing services) not shown elsewhere.

Source: U.S. Census Bureau, "2006 Service Annual Survey, Information Sector Services." See <http://www.census.gov/econ/www/servmenu.html>; (released March 2008).

Table 1097. Quantity of Books Sold and Value of Consumer Domestic Expenditures: 2007 to 2011

[(3,127 represents 3,127,000,000). Represents net publishers' shipments after returns. Includes all titles released by publishers in the United States and imports which appear under the imprints of American publishers. Multivolume sets, such as encyclopedias, are counted as one unit. Due to changes in methodology and scope, these data are not comparable to those previously published]

Type of publication	Net publishers' shipments (mil.)					Domestic U.S. consumer expenditures (mil. dol.)				
	2007	2008, proj.	2009, proj.	2010, proj.	2011, proj.	2007	2008, proj.	2009, proj.	2010, proj.	2011, proj.
Total	**3,127**	**3,106**	**3,107**	**3,116**	**3,132**	**56,625**	**58,129**	**59,739**	**61,575**	**63,525**
Trade	2,282	2,245	2,233	2,224	2,221	26,392	26,646	27,194	27,781	28,391
Adult	839	836	840	842	844	16,843	17,140	17,561	17,989	18,417
Hardback	421	419	418	418	418	10,193	10,371	10,585	10,818	11,049
Paperback	418	417	421	423	427	6,650	6,770	6,976	7,171	7,368
Juvenile	901	888	887	887	888	6,424	6,437	6,585	6,737	6,893
Hardback	302	290	293	296	297	3,152	3,099	3,196	3,290	3,382
Paperback	599	598	594	592	591	3,271	3,338	3,389	3,447	3,511
Mass market paperbacks	542	521	507	495	489	3,125	3,069	3,048	3,055	3,082
Religious	275	284	293	303	312	4,982	5,255	5,538	5,838	6,154
Hardback	98	100	103	107	110	2,961	3,108	3,275	3,452	3,639
Paperback	177	184	190	196	202	2,021	2,148	2,263	2,386	2,515
Professional	286	287	287	288	289	12,104	12,594	12,883	13,189	13,540
Hardback	102	106	106	106	107	7,205	7,623	7,799	7,987	8,206
Paperback	184	181	181	182	182	3,767	3,814	3,902	3,996	4,103
Subscription reference	(X)	(X)	(X)	(X)	(X)	1,132	1,157	1,181	1,206	1,230
University press	29	29	28	28	28	684	704	725	746	766
Hardback	10	10	10	10	10	341	351	361	372	382
Paperback	19	19	18	18	18	343	353	363	374	385
Elementary/high school text	178	182	185	192	200	5,713	5,942	6,168	6,544	6,949
Hardback	70	71	72	75	78	2,956	3,068	3,179	3,366	3,581
Paperback	108	111	113	118	122	2,757	2,874	2,989	3,179	3,368
College text	78	79	80	81	82	6,751	6,987	7,231	7,477	7,724
Hardback	34	35	35	36	36	4,498	4,654	4,816	4,982	5,146
Paperback	44	44	45	45	46	2,253	2,415	2,415	2,495	2,578

X Not applicable.

Source: Book Industry Study Group, Inc., New York, NY, *Book Industry Trends, 2008,* annual (copyright).

Table 1098. Book Publishers—Estimated Revenue and Inventories: 2004 to 2006

[In millions of dollars (27,853 represents $27,853,000,000). For taxable and tax-exempt employer firms. Covers NAICS 51113. Estimates have been adjusted to the results of the 2002 Economic Census. Based on the North American Industry Classification System (NAICS), 2002. See text, this section and Section 15. See also Appendix III]

Item	2004	2005	2006
Operating revenue, total	**27,853**	**28,027**	**28,192**
Sources of revenue:			
Books, print	24,398	24,239	24,272
Textbooks	9,657	9,919	10,139
Children's books	3,162	3,073	3,094
General reference books	1,520	1,144	1,136
Professional, technical, and scholarly books	3,799	3,274	3,363
Adult trade	6,260	6,829	6,540
All other operating revenue	3,455	3,788	3,919
Breakdown of revenue by media type:			
Print books	23,063	22,883	22,764
Online books	659	666	714
Other media books	675	690	795
Operating expenses	**15,999**	**16,754**	**16,268**
Personnel	6,581	6,634	6,703
Expensed materials, parts and supplies (not for resale)	560	487	465
Expensed purchased services	3,019	3,244	3,353
Other operating expenses	5,839	6,389	5,748
Inventories at end of year	4,457	4,538	4,336
Finished goods	3,748	3,791	3,657
Work-in-process	531	574	511
Materials, supplies, fuel, etc.	178	173	169

Source: U.S. Census Bureau, "2006 Service Annual Survey, Information Sector Services." See <http://www.census.gov/econ/www/servmenu.html>; (released March 2008).

Table 1099. Directory and Mailing List Publishers—Estimated Revenue, Expenses, and Inventories: 2004 to 2006

[In millions of dollars (18,040 represents $18,040,000,000). For taxable and tax-exempt employer firms. Covers NAICS 51114. Estimates have been adjusted to the results of the 2002 Economic Census. Based on the North American Industry Classification System (NAICS), 2002. See text, this section and Section 15. See also Appendix III]

Item	2004	2005	2006
Operating revenue	**18,040**	**19,458**	**18,929**
Source of revenue:			
Directories	13,581	14,300	14,039
Subscription and sales	375	411	358
Advertising space	13,206	13,889	13,681
Database and other collections	2,494	2,933	2,788
Subscription and sales	2,276	2,638	2,516
Advertising space	218	295	272
Other operating revenue	1,966	2,225	2,102
Rental or sale of mailing lists	496	584	558
All other	1,470	1,641	1,544
Breakdown of revenue by media type:			
Print directories, databases, and other collections of information	13,032	13,534	13,644
Online directories, databases, and other collections of information	2,619	3,439	2,941
Other directories, databases, and other collections of information	424	260	242
Operating expenses	**10,487**	**11,052**	**10,997**
Personnel costs	3,956	4,415	4,384
Expensed materials, parts and supplies (not for resale)	718	733	856
Expensed purchased services	1,500	1,591	1,456
Other operating expenses	4,313	4,313	4,301
Inventories at end of year	**388**	**408**	**326**
Finished goods	158	182	137
Work-in-process	29	28	(S)
Materials, fuels, supplies, etc.	202	198	268

S Data do not meet publication standards.

Source: U.S. Census Bureau, "2006 Service Annual Survey, Information Sector Services." See <http://www.census.gov/econ/www/servmenu.html>; (released March 2008).

Table 1100. Software Publishers—Estimated Revenue, Expenses, and Inventories: 2004 to 2006

[In millions of dollars (112,261 represents $112,261,000,000). For taxable and tax-exempt employer firms. Covers NAICS 5112. Estimates have been adjusted to the results of the 2002 Economic Census. Based on the North American Industry Classification System, System (NAICS), 2002. See text, this section and Section 15]

Item	2004	2005	2006
Operating revenue	**112,261**	**121,309**	**130,727**
Source of revenue:			
System software publishing [1]	45,555	48,727	50,289
Operating system software	18,742	19,118	18,904
Network software	11,021	12,733	13,239
Database management software	6,751	7,074	8,197
Development tools and programming languages software	3,761	3,706	3,541
Application software publishing [1]	41,893	45,889	48,068
General business productivity and home use applications	18,412	21,159	21,467
Cross-industry application software	12,820	13,327	14,748
Vertical market application software	7,092	7,528	7,113
Utilities software	944	1,015	1,273
Other services [1]	24,813	26,693	32,369
Customization and integration of packaged software	4,699	5,287	6,678
Information technology technical consulting services	4,208	4,638	4,123
Application service provisioning	(S)	(S)	(S)
Resale of computer hardware and software	2,793	2,425	(S)
Information technology-related training services	1,575	1,646	1,903
Breakdown of revenue by software sales type:			
System software [1]	45,555	48,727	50,289
Personal computer software	16,419	16,675	(S)
Enterprise or network software	15,718	18,049	(S)
Mainframe computer software	10,241	10,145	9,319
Application software [1]	41,893	45,889	48,068
Personal computer software	18,448	21,558	(S)
Enterprise or network software	15,571	16,847	17,225
Mainframe computer software	2,798	2,943	3,037
Operating expenses	**89,665**	**88,168**	**90,583**
Personnel costs	51,005	50,564	52,248
Expensed materials, parts and supplies (not for resale)	3,326	2,352	2,062
Expensed purchased services	9,488	10,041	10,827
Other operating expenses	25,845	25,211	25,446
Inventories at end of year	**1,438**	**1,551**	**1,516**
Finished goods	835	1,079	1,196
Works-in-process	58	54	26
Materials, supplies, fuel, etc.	545	418	294

S Data do not meet publication standards.   [1] Includes other sources of revenue and other expenses, not shown separately.

Source: U.S. Census Bureau, "2006 Service Annual Survey, Information Sector Services." See <http://www.census.gov/econ/www/servmenu.html>; (released March 2008).

Table 1101. Motion Picture and Video Exhibition—Estimated Revenue and Expenses: 2004 to 2006

[In millions of dollars (11,180 represents $11,180,000,000). For taxable and tax-exempt employer firms. For NAICS 51213. Estimates have been adjusted to the results of the 2002 Economic Census. Based on the North American Industry Classification System (NAICS), 2002. See text, this section, Section 15, and Appendix III]

Item	2004	2005	2006
Operating revenue, total	**11,180**	**10,789**	**11,080**
Sources of revenue:			
Feature film exhibition revenue	7,522	7,178	7,280
Admission to domestic films	7,358	6,996	7,063
Admission to foreign films	165	182	216
Other revenue [1]	3,657	3,611	3,800
Food and beverage sales	3,124	3,049	3,201
Advertising services	222	217	260
Coin operated games and rides	43	41	49
Operating expenses	**8,633**	**8,501**	**8,047**
Personnel costs	1,697	1,663	1,663
Gross annual payroll	1,495	1,461	1,495
Employer's cost for fringe benefits	162	163	137
Temporary staff and leased employee expense	40	39	31
Expensed materials, parts and supplies (not for resale)	191	177	185
Expensed purchased services [1]	1,971	2,057	2,159
Purchased electricity and fuels (except motor fuel)	299	314	343
Lease and rental payments	1,248	1,310	1,391
Purchased repair and maintenance	223	228	246
Purchased advertising and promotional services	197	201	172
Other operating expenses	4,773	4,603	4,040

[1] Includes other sources of revenue and other expenses, not shown separately.

Source: U.S. Census Bureau, "2006 Service Annual Survey, Information Sector Services." See <http://www.census.gov/econ/www/servmenu.html>; (released March 2008).

Table 1102. **Recording Media—Manufacturers' Shipments and Value: 2000 to 2007**

[1,079.2 represents 1,079,200,000. Based on reports of RIAA member companies who distributed about 84 percent of the pre-recorded music in 2007. These data are supplemented by other sources]

Medium	2000	2001	2002	2003	2004	2005	2006	2007
UNIT SHIPMENTS (mil.)								
Total [1]	**1,079.2**	**968.5**	**859.7**	**798.4**	**958.0**	**1,301.8**	**1,588.5**	**1,773.3**
Physical:								
Compact disks [2]	942.5	881.9	803.3	746.0	767.0	705.4	619.7	511.1
Music video [3]	18.2	17.7	14.7	19.9	32.8	33.8	23.2	27.5
Other albums [4]	78.2	47.6	33.3	3.2	2.5	2.0	1.3	1.7
Other singles [5]	40.3	21.3	8.4	12.1	6.6	5.1	3.2	3.2
Digital:								
Download single	(X)	(X)	(X)	(X)	139.4	366.9	586.4	809.9
Downnload album	(X)	(X)	(X)	(X)	4.6	13.6	27.6	42.5
Kiosk [6]	(X)	(X)	(X)	(X)	(X)	0.7	1.4	1.8
Music video	(X)	(X)	(X)	(X)	(X)	1.9	9.9	14.2
Mobile [7]	(X)	(X)	(X)	(X)	(X)	170.0	315.3	361.0
Subscription [8]	(X)	(X)	(X)	(X)	(X)	1.3	1.7	1.8
VALUE (mil. dol.)								
Total [1]	**14,323.7**	**13,740.9**	**12,614.2**	**11,854.4**	**12,345.0**	**12,296.9**	**11,758.2**	**10,370.0**
Physical:								
Compact disks [2]	13,214.5	12,909.4	12,044.1	11,232.9	11,446.5	10,520.2	9,372.6	7,452.3
Music video [3]	281.9	329.2	288.4	399.9	607.2	602.2	451.1	484.9
Other albums [4]	653.7	396.8	238.8	164.2	66.1	48.5	22.1	29.3
Other singles [5]	173.6	105.5	42.9	57.5	34.9	24.1	17.6	16.2
Digital:								
Download single	(X)	(X)	(X)	(X)	138.0	363.3	580.6	801.8
Downnload album	(X)	(X)	(X)	(X)	45.5	135.7	275.9	424.9
Kiosk [6]	(X)	(X)	(X)	(X)	(X)	1.0	1.9	2.6
Music video	(X)	(X)	(X)	(X)	(X)	3.7	19.7	28.2
Mobile [7]	(X)	(X)	(X)	(X)	(X)	421.6	774.5	878.9
Subscription [8]	(X)	(X)	(X)	(X)	(X)	149.2	206.2	200.9

X Not applicable. [1] Net, after returns. [2] Includes DualDisc. [3] Includes DVD video. [4] Includes cassette, LP/EP, DVD audio, and SACD. [5] Includes CD single, cassette single, and vinyl single. [6] Includes singles and albums. [7] Includes Master Ringtunes, Ringbacks, full length downloads and other mobile. [8] Weighted annual average. Number of units not included in total.

Source: Recording Industry Association of America, Washington, DC, *2007 Year-end Statistics* and earlier issues (copyright). See <http://www.riaa.com>; (accessed 15 May 2008).

Table 1103. **Profile of Consumer Expenditures for Sound Recordings—Percent Distribution: 1990 to 2007**

[In percent. Based on monthly telephone surveys of the population 10 years old and over]

Item	1990	2000	2002	2003	2004	2005	2006	2007
Total [1]	**100.0**	**100.0**	**100.0**	**100.0**	**100.0**	**100.0**	**100.0**	**100.0**
Age: 10 to 14 years	7.6	8.9	8.9	8.6	9.4	8.6	7.6	11.5
15 to 19 years	18.3	12.9	13.3	11.4	11.9	11.9	12.8	12.3
20 to 24 years	16.5	12.5	11.5	10.0	9.2	12.7	9.8	11.3
25 to 29 years	14.6	10.6	9.4	10.9	10.0	12.1	12.7	9.2
30 to 34 years	13.2	9.8	10.8	10.1	10.4	11.3	10.2	11.3
35 to 39 years	10.2	10.6	9.8	11.2	10.7	8.8	10.6	11.9
40 to 44 years	7.8	9.6	9.9	10.0	10.9	9.2	9.0	7.9
45 years and over	11.1	23.8	25.5	26.6	26.4	25.5	26.1	24.8
Sex: Male	54.4	50.6	49.4	49.1	49.5	51.8	50.4	49.2
Female	45.6	49.4	50.6	50.9	50.5	48.2	49.6	50.8
Sales outlet:								
Record store	69.8	42.4	36.8	33.2	32.5	39.4	35.4	31.1
Other store	18.5	40.8	50.7	52.8	53.8	32.0	32.7	29.7
Tape/record club	8.9	7.6	4.0	4.1	4.4	8.5	10.5	12.6
Ad or 800 number	2.5	2.4	2.0	1.5	1.7	2.4	2.4	1.7
Internet [2]	(NA)	3.2	3.4	5.0	5.9	8.2	9.1	10.9
Digital download	(NA)	(NA)	(NA)	(NA)	(NA)	6.0	6.8	12.0
Music type: [3]								
Rock	36.1	24.8	24.7	25.2	23.9	31.5	34.0	32.4
Country	9.6	10.7	10.7	10.4	13.0	12.5	13.0	11.5
Rap/Hip Hop.	8.5	12.9	13.8	13.3	12.1	13.3	11.4	10.8
R&B/Urban.	11.6	9.7	11.2	10.6	11.3	10.2	11.0	11.8
Pop	13.7	11.0	9.0	8.9	10.0	8.1	7.1	10.7
Religious	2.5	4.8	6.7	5.8	6.0	5.3	5.5	3.9
Classical	3.1	2.7	3.1	3.0	2.0	2.4	1.9	2.3
Jazz	4.8	2.9	3.2	2.9	2.7	1.8	2.0	2.6

NA Not available. [1] Percent distributions exclude nonresponses and responses of "Don't know." Some types of music and sales outlets are not shown separately. [2] Excludes record club purchases over the Internet or digital downloads. [3] As classified by respondent.

Source: Recording Industry Association of America, Washington, DC, *2007 Consumer Profile* and earlier issues (copyright). See <http://www.riaa.com>; (accessed 15 May 2008).

Table 1104. **Radio and Television Broadcasting—Estimated Revenue and Expenses: 2005 and 2006**

[**In millions of dollars (3,298 represents $3,298,000,000).** For taxable and tax-exempt employer firms. Estimates have been adjusted to the results of the 2002 Economic Census. Based on the North American Industry Classification System (NAICS), 2002. See text, this section, and Section 15]

Item	Radio networks (NAICS 515111)		Radio stations (NAICS 515112)		TV broadcasting (NAICS 51512)	
	2005	2006	2005	2006	2005	2006
Operating revenue	**3,298**	**4,411**	**13,713**	**13,696**	**36,297**	**38,328**
Air time	1,096	1,121	12,086	12,110	25,971	26,859
National/regional air time	582	571	2,723	2,936	16,211	16,456
Local air time	514	550	9,363	9,174	9,760	10,403
Other operating revenue	2,202	3,290	1,626	1,585	10,326	(S)
Network compensation	117	135	223	218	6,321	(S)
Public and noncommercial programming services	341	397	(S)	(S)	1,337	1,550
All other operating revenue	1,744	2,758	835	851	2,668	3,193
Operating expenses	**4,584**	**6,809**	**10,150**	**10,197**	**28,805**	**29,892**
Personnel costs	959	1,520	5,117	5,047	7,570	7,884
Gross annual payroll	819	1,150	4,255	4170	6,438	6,575
Employer's cost for fringe benefits	100	230	611	636	1,008	1,152
Temporary staff and leased employee expense	40	139	251	(S)	124	157
Expensed materials, parts and supplies (not for resale)	34	31	123	117	223	219
Expensed equipment	8	9	41	36	57	58
Expensed purchase of other materials, parts and supplies	26	23	82	81	166	161
Expensed purchased services	575	515	1,045	1,069	2,003	2,149
Expensed purchases of software	19	17	(S)	(S)	39	47
Purchased electricity and fuels (except motor fuel)	12	22	144	163	343	421
Lease and rental payments	62	79	342	325	426	490
Purchased repair and maintenance	17	26	85	80	250	(S)
Purchased advertising and promotional services	465	371	429	448	945	888
Other operating expenses	3,017	4,743	3,866	3,965	19,009	19,640
Broadcast rights and music license fees	382	552	586	611	12,036	12,802
Network compensation fees	130	198	(S)	(S)	695	609
Depreciation and amortization fees	382	428	491	490	1,385	1,458
Government taxes and license fees	16	26	489	424	150	144
All other operating expenses	2,107	3,540	2,218	2,393	4,743	4,627

S Data do not meet publication standards.

Source: U.S. Census Bureau, "2006 Service Annual Survey, Information Sector Services." See <http://www.census.gov/econ/www /servmenu.html>; (released March 2008).

Table 1105. **Cable and Premium TV—Summary: 1975 to 2007**

[**9,800 represents 9,800,000.** Cable TV for calendar year. Premium TV as of December 31 of year shown]

Year	Cable TV				Premium TV					
	Avg. basic sub-scribers (1,000)	Avg. monthly basic rate (dol.)	Revenue [1] (mil. dol.)		Units [2] (1,000)			Monthly rate (dol.)		
			Total	Basic	Total premium [3]	Premium cable	Noncable delivered premium	All premium weighted average [3]	Premium cable	Noncable delivered premium
1975	9,800	6.50	804	764	194	194	(NA)	(NA)	7.85	(NA)
1980	17,500	7.69	2,609	1,615	8,581	7,336	(NA)	8.91	8.62	(NA)
1985	35,440	9.73	8,831	4,138	29,885	29,418	(NA)	10.29	10.25	(NA)
1995	60,550	23.07	24,137	16,763	55,723	46,798	8,925	8.29	8.54	6.99
1996	62,300	24.41	26,195	18,249	63,705	49,728	13,977	7.98	8.12	7.50
1997	63,600	26.48	28,931	20,213	72,785	51,933	20,852	8.31	8.43	8.00
1998	64,650	27.81	31,191	21,574	80,605	55,280	25,325	8.58	8.74	8.22
1999	65,500	28.92	34,095	22,732	88,455	59,005	29,450	8.74	8.85	8.50
2000	66,250	30.37	36,756	24,142	102,590	65,918	36,672	8.69	8.81	8.48
2001	66,732	32.87	42,238	26,324	115,325	75,433	39,892	8.95	9.10	8.66
2002	66,472	34.71	48,623	27,690	125,662	81,128	44,534	9.19	9.29	9.00
2003	66,050	36.59	53,991	29,000	127,377	83,421	43,956	9.37	9.45	9.23
2004	65,727	38.14	59,428	30,080	140,060	90,843	49,217	10.03	10.11	9.88
2005	65,337	39.63	65,041	31,075	149,067	96,910	52,157	10.08	10.16	9.93
2006	65,319	41.17	71,841	32,274	158,069	101,464	56,605	10.26	10.26	10.02
2007	65,141	42.72	78,886	33,393	171,043	109,960	61,083	10.28	10.35	10.10

NA Not available. [1] Includes installation revenue, subscriber revenue, and nonsubscriber revenue; excludes telephony and high-speed access. [2] Individual program services sold to subscribers. [3] Includes multipoint distribution service (MDS), satellite TV (STV), multipoint multichannel distribution service (MMDS), satellite master antenna TV (SMATV), C-band satellite, and DBS satellite and Telco Video. Includes average pay unit price based on data for major premium pay movie services.

Source: SNL Kagan, a division of SNL Financial LC. From the *Broadband Cable Financial Databook* 2004, 2005, 2006, 2007 (copyright); the Cable *Cable Program Investor and Cable TV Investor: Deals & Finance* newsletters (monthly); and various other SNL Kagan publications.

U.S. Census Bureau, Statistical Abstract of the United States: 2009

Table 1106. Cable and Other Subscription Programming—Estimated Revenue and Expenses: 2004 to 2006

[In millions of dollars (31,373 represents $31,373,000,000).For taxable and tax-exempt employer firms. Covers NAICS 51521. This industry comprises establishments engaged in operating studios and facilities for the broadcasting of programs on a subscription or fee basis. Estimates have been adjusted to the results of the 2002 Economic Census. Based on the North American Industry Classification System (NAICS), 2002. See text, this section and Section 15]

Item	2004	2005	2006
Operating revenue................................	31,373	35,603	38,437
Source of revenue:			
Licensing of rights to broadcast specialty programming [1].........	15,395	16,788	18,266
Air time..	12,877	14,574	15,185
All other operating services revenue........................	3,100	4,242	4,985
Operating expenses...............................	21,441	23,606	25,229
Personnel costs.....................................	3,986	4,604	4,599
Gross annual payroll................................	3,159	3,653	3,512
Employer's cost for fringe benefits......................	544	623	653
Temporary staff and leased employee expense	283	328	434
Expensed materials, parts and supplies (not for resale)...........	267	276	318
Expensed equipment..............................	60	55	50
Expensed purchase of other materials, parts and supplies	207	222	268
Expensed purchased services	1,977	2,299	2,593
Expensed purchases of software......................	39	46	54
Purchased electricity and fuels (except motor fuel)	52	50	52
Lease and rental payments	448	515	463
Purchased repair and maintenance	(S)	101	96
Purchased advertising and promotional services.............	1,329	1,588	1,928
Other operating expenses..............................	15,210	16,426	17,719
Program and production costs........................	11,625	12,051	12,964
Depreciation and amortization charges...................	1,369	1,399	1,382
Government taxes and license fees	124	136	107
All other operating expenses..........................	2,093	2,840	3,267

S Data do not meet publication standards.   [1] Protected by copyright.

Source: U.S. Census Bureau, "2006 Service Annual Survey, Information Sector Services." See <http://www.census.gov/econ /www/servmenu.html>; (released March 2008).

Table 1107. Internet Publishing and Broadcasting—Estimated Revenue and Expenses: 2004 to 2006

[In millions of dollars (8,671 represents $8,671,000,000). For taxable and tax-exempt employer firms. Covers NAICS 516. Establishments engaged in publishing and/or broadcasting on the Internet exclusively. Estimates have been adjusted to the results of the 2002 Economic Census. Based on the North American Industry Classification System (NAICS), 2002. See text, this section and Section 15]

Item	2004	2005	2006
Operating revenue................................	8,671	10,348	10,612
Source of revenue:			
Publishing and broadcasting of content on the Internet	4,416	5,307	5,889
Online advertising space	1,594	1,979	2,221
Licensing of rights to use intellectual property	393	422	506
All other operating revenue...........................	2,268	2,640	1,997
Breakdown of revenue by type of customer:			
Government......................................	341	(S)	(S)
Business firms and not-for-profit organizations	6,236	7,367	7,185
Household consumers and individual users	2,094	2,491	2,783
Operating expenses...............................	7,011	8,197	8,342
Personnel..	3,320	3,899	3,782
Gross annual payroll................................	2,696	3,244	3,095
Employer's cost for fringe benefits......................	434	462	473
Temporary staff and leased employee expense	190	193	214
Expensed materials, parts and supplies (not for resale)...........	211	249	247
Expensed equipment..............................	90	93	94
Expensed purchase of other materials, parts and supplies	121	156	152
Expensed purchased services	1,298	1,603	1,678
Expensed purchases of software......................	80	144	216
Purchased electricity and fuels (except motor fuel)	15	16	18
Lease and rental payments	278	276	271
Purchased repair and maintenance	96	89	87
Purchased advertising and promotional services.............	829	1,078	1,086
Other operating expenses..............................	2,181	2,446	2,636
Depreciation and amortization charges...................	694	643	682
Government taxes and license fees	48	57	60
All other operating expenses..........................	1,439	1,747	1,894

S Data do not meet publication standards.

Source: U.S. Census Bureau, "2006 Service Annual Survey, Information Sector Services." See <http://www.census.gov/econ /www/servmenu.html>; (released March 2008).

Table 1108. Telecommunications Industry—Carriers, 1995 to 2004, and Revenue: 1995 to 2005

[Revenue in millions of dollars (190,076 represents $190,076,000,000). Data based on carrier filings to the FCC. Because of reporting changes, data beginning 2000 are not strictly comparable with previous years; see source for details]

Category	Carriers					Telecommunications revenue				
	1995	2000	2002 [1]	2003	2004	1995	2000	2003	2004	2005
Total [2]	**3,058**	**4,879**	**4,390**	**4,636**	**5,031**	**190,076**	**292,762**	**291,123**	**291,734**	**297,921**
Local service providers	1,675	2,641	2,531	2,681	2,864	103,792	128,075	126,860	123,067	122,609
Incumbent local exchange carriers (ILECs)	1,347	1,335	1,310	1,303	1,304	102,820	116,158	109,480	105,496	103,561
Pay telephone providers	271	699	606	605	642	349	972	523	445	481
Competitors of ILECs	57	607	615	773	918	623	10,945	16,857	17,126	18,568
CAPs and CLECs [3]	57	479	451	601	690	623	9,814	15,509	15,112	16,930
Local resellers	(4)	105	100	100	136	(4)	879	721	1,215	630
Other local exchange carriers	(4)	23	64	72	92	(4)	11	338	245	216
Private carriers	(4)	(4)	(4)	(4)	(4)	(4)	39	267	532	770
Shared tenant service providers	(4)	(4)	(4)	(4)	(4)	(4)	202	22	22	22
Wireless service providers [5]	930	1,430	927	939	963	18,627	63,280	89,342	99,465	108,809
Telephony [6]	792	783	422	413	396	17,208	59,823	88,168	98,329	107,834
Paging service providers	138	425	346	347	360	(4)	3,102	1,007	872	579
Toll service providers	453	808	932	1,026	1,204	76,447	101,407	74,920	69,204	66,503
Interexchange carriers	130	212	229	232	257	70,938	87,311	61,246	51,589	46,856
Operator service providers	25	20	18	17	19	500	635	567	523	548
Prepaid service providers	8	23	27	50	67	16	727	812	1,635	1,828
Satellite service carriers	(4)	25	33	40	40	(4)	336	663	721	714
Toll resellers	260	493	574	642	751	4,220	10,641	9,294	12,192	13,362
Other toll carriers	30	35	51	45	70	773	1,758	2,339	2,543	3,195

[1] Counts dropped in 2002 because many affiliated filers were allowed to file consolidated reports. [2] Revenue data include adjustments, not shown separately. For 1995, revenue data include some nontelecommunications revenue, formerly reported as local exchange wireless revenue. [3] Competitive access providers (CAPs) and competitive local exchange carriers (CLECs). [4] Data not available separately. [5] Beginning 2000, includes specialized mobile radio services and other services, not shown separately. [6] Cellular service, personal communications service, and specialized mobile radio.

Source: U.S. Federal Communications Commission, Telecommunications Industry Revenue. See <http://www.fcc.gov/wcb/iatd/stats.html/>.

Table 1109. Wired Telecommunications—Estimated Revenue and Expenses: 2004 to 2006

[In millions of dollars (211,176 represents $211,176,000,000). For taxable and tax-exempt employer firms. Covers NAICS 5171. Estimates have been adjusted to the results of the 2002 Economic Census. Based on the North American Industry Classification System NAICS), 2002. See text, this section]

Item	2004	2005	2006
Operating revenue	**211,176**	**206,778**	**199,933**
Fixed total [1]	101,692	94,779	90,098
Fixed local	61,634	59,445	58,039
Fixed long-distance	38,368	33,851	31,385
Fixed all distance	1,691	1,483	674
Other telecommunication services	94,803	96,431	94,537
Carrier services	38,423	38,026	33,663
Private network services	26,083	26,643	25,037
Subscriber line charges	8,546	8,223	7,769
Internet access services	11,924	13,561	15,066
Intrernet telephony	884	1,058	1,639
Telecommunications network installation services	(S)	(S)	8,270
Reselling services for telecommunications equipment, retail	2,505	2,213	(S)
Rental of telecommunications equipment	292	269	242
Repair and maintenance services for telecommunications equipment	871	825	792
All other	14,681	15,569	15,298
Operating expenses	**187,541**	**176,525**	**168,661**
Personnel costs	60,402	59,480	60,138
Gross annual payroll	39,798	40,117	42,894
Employer's cost for fringe benefits	17,168	16,533	15,540
Temporary staff and leased employee expense	3,437	2,829	1,705
Expensed materials, parts and supplies (not for resale)	6,395	6,319	6,439
Expensed equipment	451	404	317
Expensed purchase of other materials, parts, and supplies	5,944	(S)	6,121
Expensed purchased services	12,240	11,534	11,314
Expensed purchases of software	1,613	1,558	1,619
Purchased electricity and fuels (except motor fuel)	1,675	1,704	1,717
Lease and rental payments	4,025	3,848	3,801
Purchased repair and maintenance	2,145	2,031	1,360
Purchased advertising and promotional services	2,782	2,393	2,816
Other operating expenses	108,503	99,192	90,770
Access charges	33,714	31,755	23,862
Universal service contributions (USC) and other similar charges	3,386	4,267	2,885
Depreciation and amortization charges	38,371	35,556	35,464
Government taxes and license fees	5,179	5,006	5,397
All other operating expenses	27,853	22,609	23,164

S Estimate does not meet publication standard. [1] No distinction between local or long distance.

Source: U.S. Census Bureau, "2006 Service Annual Survey, Information Sector Services." See <http://www.census.gov/econ/www/servmenu.html>; (released March 2008).

Table 1110. Telephone Systems—Summary: 1985 to 2004

[112 represents 112,000,000. Covers principal carriers filing annual reports with Federal Communications Commission]

Item	Unit	1985	1990	1995	1999	2000	2001[1]	2002[1]	2003[1]	2004[1]
LOCAL EXCHANGE CARRIERS[2]										
Carriers[3]	Number	55	51	53	52	52	30	29	28	28
Access lines	Millions	112	130	166	228	245	253	262	268	270
Business access lines	Millions	31	36	46	57	58	54	54	49	46
Residential access lines	Millions	79	89	101	115	115	112	103	99	100
Other access lines (public, mobile, special)	Millions	2	6	19	55	72	87	105	120	124
Number of local calls (originating)	Billions	365	402	484	554	537	515	459	425	420
Number of toll calls (originating)	Billions	(NA)	63	94	102	106	98	90	81	92
Employees	1,000	(NA)	569	447	436	434	386	333	303	(NA)
Compensation of employees	Bil. dol.	(NA)	23	21	24	24	23	23	23	23
Average monthly residential local telephone rate[4]	Dollars	(NA)	19.24	20.01	19.93	20.78	22.62	23.38	24.31	24.52
Average monthly single-line business telephone rate[4]	Dollars	(NA)	41.21	41.80	41.21	41.80	42.43	43.59	43.75	43.49
LONG DISTANCE CARRIERS										
Total toll service revenues[5]	Bil. dol.	55	67	90	108	110	99	84	77	71
Interstate switched access minutes	Bil. min.	167	307	432	553	567	538	486	444	423
INTERNATIONAL TELEPHONE SERVICE[6]										
Number of U.S. billed calls	Millions	425	984	2,830	5,305	5,742	6,265	5,926	7,350	10,890
Number of U.S. billed minutes	Millions	3,446	8,030	15,889	28,515	30,135	35,063	42,664	63,553	
U.S. billed revenues	Mil. dol.	3,487	8,059	14,335	14,980	14,909	11,380	9,773	8,944	9,178
U.S. carrier revenue net of settlements with foreign carriers	Mil. dol.	2,332	5,188	9,397	10,379	10,982	8,034	6,931	5,964	5,546
Revenue from private-line service	Mil. dol.	172	201	514	1,216	1,480	1,467	988	620	458
Revenue from resale service	Mil. dol.	(NA)	167	1,756	4,528	7,600	5,341	4,871	5,420	5,248

NA Not available. [1] Beginning 2001, detailed financial data only filed by regional Bell-operating companies. Access lines and calls reported by 50 reporting companies. [2] Gross operating revenues, gross plant, and total assets of reporting carriers estimated at more than 90 percent of total industry. New accounting rules became effective in 1990; prior years may not be directly comparable on a one-to-one basis. Includes Virgin Islands, and prior to 1995, Puerto Rico. [3] The reporting threshold for carriers is $100 million in annual operating revenue. [4] Based on surveys conducted by FCC. [5] Series revised to include all toll revenues: toll, wireless, ILECs, carriers (ILECs) and competitive local exchange carriers (CLECs). [6] Beginning 1995, data are for all U.S. points, and include calls to and from Alaska, Hawaii, Puerto Rico, Guam, the U.S. Virgin Islands, and offshore U.S. points. Beginning 1995, carriers first started reporting traffic to and from Canada and Mexico. Data for Canada and Mexico in prior years are staff estimates.

Source: U.S. Federal Communications Commission, *Statistics of Communications Common Carriers,* annual; *Trends in Telephone Service,* annual; and *Trends in the International Telecommunications Industry.* See <http://www.fcc.gov/wcb/iatd/stats.html/>.

Table 1111. Average Annual Telephone Service Expenditures by All Consumer Units: 2001 to 2006

[Based on Consumer Expenditure Survey. A consumer unit is defined as members of a household related by blood, marriage, adoption, or some other legal arrangement; a single person living alone or sharing a household with others, but who is financially independent; or two or more persons living together who share responsibility for at least two out of the three major types of expenses: food, housing, and other expenses]

Year	Average annual expenditure (dollars)				Percent distribution			
	Total telephone services	Residential telephone/ pay phone	Cellular phone service	Other services[1]	Total telephone services	Residential telephone/ pay phone	Cellular phone service	Other services[1]
2001	914	686	210	19	100.0	75.0	23.0	2.0
2002	957	641	294	22	100.0	67.0	30.7	2.3
2003	956	620	316	20	100.0	64.8	33.1	2.1
2004	990	592	378	20	100.0	59.8	38.2	2.0
2005	1,048	570	455	23	100.0	54.4	43.4	2.2
2006	1,087	542	524	21	100.0	49.9	48.2	2.0

[1] Phone cards and pager services.

Source: Bureau of Labor Statistics, *"Consumer Expenditures in 2006,"* published October 26, 2007. See <http://www.bls.gov/cex/cellphones.htm>.

Table 1112. Cellular Telecommunications Industry: 1990 to 2007

[**Calendar year data, except as noted (5,283 represents 5,283,000).** Based on a survey sent to all facilities-based cellular, personal communications services, and enhanced special mobile radio (ESMR) systems. The number of operational systems beginning 2000 differs from that reported for previous periods as a result of the consolidated operation of ESMR systems in a broader service area instead of by a city-to-city basis]

Item	Unit	1990	2000	2002	2003	2004	2005	2006	2007
Subscribers	1,000	5,283	109,478	140,766	158,722	182,140	207,896	233,041	255,396
Employees	Number	21,382	184,449	192,410	205,629	226,016	233,067	253,793	266,782
Service revenue	Mil. dol.	4,548	52,466	76,508	87,624	102,121	113,538	125,457	138,869
Roamer revenue[1]	Mil. dol.	456	3,883	3,896	3,766	4,210	3,786	3,494	3,742
Capital investment[2]	Mil. dol.	6,282	89,624	126,922	145,867	173,794	199,025	223,449	244,591
Average monthly bill[3]	Dollars	80.90	45.27	48.40	49.91	50.64	49.98	50.56	49.79
Average length of call[3]	Minutes	2.20	2.56	2.73	2.87	3.05	3.00	3.03	(NA)

NA Not available. [1] Service revenue generated by subscribers' calls outside of their system areas. [2] Beginning 2005, cumulative capital investment figure reached by summing the incremental capital investment in year shown with cumulative capital investment of prior year. [3] As of December 31.

Source: CTIA-The Wireless Association, Washington, DC, *Semi-annual Wireless Survey* (copyright).

Table 1113. Cellular and Other Wireless (except Paging) Telecommunications— Estimated Revenue and Expenses: 2004 to 2006

[In millions of dollars (125,693 represents $125,693,000,000). For taxable and tax-exempt employer firms. Covers NAICS 517212. Estimates have been adjusted to the results of the 2002 Economic Census. Based on the North American Industry Classification System (NAICS), 2002. See text, this section and Section 15]

Item	2004	2005	2006
Operating revenue	**125,693**	**138,082**	**158,516**
Mobile services	101,195	113,058	(S)
Mobile telephony	54,781	57,803	55,734
Mobile long-distance	3,308	4,454	4,987
Mobile all-distance	36,236	42,827	(S)
Other mobile services	6,871	7,975	(S)
Other telecommunications services	6,774	7,929	10,401
Internet access services	667	1,139	(D)
Installation services for telecommunications networks	(S)	(S)	148
Reselling services for telecommunications equipment, retail	5,479	5,771	(S)
Rental of telecommunications equipment	75	(S)	(D)
Repair and maintenance services for telecommunications equipment	437	741	(S)
All other operating revenue	17,723	17,094	20,470
Operating expenses	**105,041**	**122,302**	**133,507**
Personnel costs	19,905	23,610	23,299
Gross annual payroll	14,408	17,011	16,490
Employer's cost for fringe benefits	3,682	3,709	4,158
Temporary staff and leased employee expense	1,816	2,890	2,651
Expensed materials, parts and supplies (not for resale)	9,996	10,240	12,166
Expensed equipment	930	794	850
Expensed purchase of other materials, parts and supplies	9,066	9,445	11,316
Expensed purchased services	15,764	16,630	17,536
Expensed purchases of software	929	1,111	1,225
Purchased electricity and fuels (except motor fuel)	718	872	1,005
Lease and rental payments	4,834	5,550	5,606
Purchased repair and maintenance	(S)	1,144	1,273
Purchased advertising and promotional services	7,892	7,953	8,427
Other operating expenses	59,377	71,823	80,506
Access charges	5,598	6,309	5,595
Universal service contributions (USC) and other similar charges	1,867	2,551	2,998
Depreciation and amortization charges	17,125	22,636	26,455
Government taxes and license fees	1,214	1,369	1,454
All other operating expenses	33,573	38,958	44,004

S Data do not meet publication standards.   D Figure withheld to avoid disclosure pertaining to a specific organization or individual.

Source: U.S. Census Bureau, "2006 Service Annual Survey, Information Sector Services." See <http://www.census.gov/econ/www/servmenu.html>; (released March 2008).

Table 1114. Cable and Other Programming Distribution—Estimated Revenue and Expenses: 2004 to 2006

[In millions of dollars (73,317 represents $73,317,000,000). For taxable and tax-exempt employer firms. Covers NAICS 5175. Estimates have been adjusted to the results of the 2002 Economic Census. Based on the North American Industry Classification System (NAICS), 2002; See text, this section, and Section 15]

Item	2004	2005	2006
Operating revenue	**73,317**	**80,493**	**88,724**
Multichannel programming distribution services	48,495	52,338	56,241
Basic programming package	36,848	40,031	42,918
Premium programming package	8,605	8,943	10,250
Pay-per-view	3,042	3,363	3,072
Other revenue	24,822	28,155	32,483
Air time	3,935	4,146	4,566
Rental and reselling services for program distribution equipment	2,364	2,568	3,141
Installation services for connections to program distribution networks	617	662	729
Internet access services	9,476	11,149	13,156
Internet telephony	1,045	(S)	1,420
Fixed local telephony	1,492	1,546	1,929
Fixed long-distance telephony	531	648	418
All other operating revenue	5,363	6,744	7,124
Operating expenses	**64,865**	**69,031**	**74,538**
Personnel costs	11,872	13,398	15,445
Gross annual payroll	8,761	10,220	11,954
Employer's cost for fringe benefits	2,374	2,429	2,635
Temporary staff and leased employee expense	736	748	856
Expensed materials, parts and supplies (not for resale)	1,324	1,585	747
Expensed equipment	858	1,033	(S)
Expensed purchase of other materials, parts and supplies	467	552	660
Expensed purchased services	4,308	4,239	4,548
Expensed purchases of software	231	264	244
Purchased electricity and fuels (except motor fuel)	659	518	586
Lease and rental payments	851	800	830
Purchased repair and maintenance	907	707	699
Purchased advertising and promotional services	1,661	1,951	2,189
Other operating expenses	47,361	49,810	53,798
Program and production costs	20,331	22,164	24,499
Depreciation and amortization charges	13,932	14,363	14,918
Government taxes and license fees	2,009	1,866	1,923
All other operating expenses	11,090	11,417	12,458

S Data do not meet publication standards.

Source: U.S. Census Bureau, "2006 Service Annual Survey, Information Sector Services." See <http://www.census.gov/econ/www/servmenu.html>; (released March 2008).

Table 1115. Internet Service Providers and Data Processing, Hosting, and Related Services—Estimated Revenue and Expenses: 2004 to 2006

[In millions of dollars (20,201 represents $20,201,000,000). For taxable and tax-exempt employer firms. Estimates have been adjusted to the results of the 2002 Economic Census. Based on the North American Industry Classification System (NAICS), 2002. See text, this section, and Section 15]

Item	Internet service provider (NAICS 518111) 2004	2005	2006	Data processing, hosting, and related services (NAICS 5182) 2004	2005	2006
Operating revenue, (NAICS 518111) [1]	**20,201**	**18,910**	**18,576**	**(X)**	**(X)**	**(X)**
Internet access service	14,244	12,525	10,983	(X)	(X)	(X)
Online advertising space	3,068	3,637	(S)	(X)	(X)	(X)
Internet backbone services	378	393	387	(X)	(X)	(X)
Internet telephony	(S)	(S)	(S)	(X)	(X)	(X)
Web site hosting services	548	530	886	(S)	(S)	1,898
Operating revenue, (NAICS 5182)	**(X)**	**(X)**	**(X)**	**57,330**	**62,951**	**70,063**
Data processing IT infrastructure provisioning, and hosting services [1]	(X)	(X)	(X)	28,414	31,227	35,529
Business processing management services	(X)	(X)	(X)	17,426	18,829	21,760
Data management services	(X)	(X)	(X)	5,275	5,601	5,797
Application service provisioning	(X)	(X)	(X)	3,800	4,380	5,267
Collocation services	(X)	(X)	(X)	(S)	(S)	(S)
Other operating revenue [1]	(X)	(X)	(X)	28,916	31,724	34,534
IT design and development services	(S)	(S)	(S)	(S)	6,446	6,210
IT technical support services	(X)	(X)	(X)	1,167	1,365	1,169
IT technical consulting services	(X)	(X)	(X)	1,124	1,106	1,562
Information and document transformation services	(X)	(X)	(X)	2,810	2,963	3,477
Software publishing	(X)	(X)	(X)	1,299	1,768	1,849
Reselling services for computer hardware and software, retail	(X)	(X)	(X)	1,211	1,279	2,030
Operating expenses	**16,251**	**14,209**	**15,713**	**52,772**	**55,739**	**60,132**
Personnel costs	5,280	5,167	6,427	25,454	27,304	29,630
Gross annual payroll	3,858	4,001	5,340	19,693	20,928	22,680
Employer's cost for fringe benefits	(S)	641	640	3,678	3,926	3,994
Temporary staff and leased employee expense	(S)	525	446	2,083	2,449	2,956
Expensed materials, parts and supplies (not for resale)	(S)	(S)	(S)	1,891	2,414	2,669
Expensed equipment	(S)	88	111	766	804	946
Expensed purchase of other materials, parts and supplies	(S)	(S)	(S)	1,126	1,610	1,723
Expensed purchased services	(S)	3,179	2,620	6,944	7,689	7,366
Expensed purchases of software	49	61	61	1,210	1,707	1,329
Purchased electricity and fuels (except motor fuels)	(S)	86	77	276	309	403
Lease and rental payments	466	443	415	2,678	2,932	2,859
Purchased repair and maintenance	87	79	84	1,400	1,460	1,494
Purchased advertising and promotional services	(S)	2,511	1,983	1,381	1,280	1,280
Other operating expenses	(S)	5,467	6,121	18,483	18,332	20,467
Depreciation and amortization charges	(S)	1,168	1,201	3,923	4,029	4,059
Government taxes and license fees	(S)	80	43	322	367	384
All other operating expenses	(S)	4,219	4,877	14,237	13,936	16,023

S Data do not meet publication standards.   X Not applicable.   [1] Includes other sources of revenue, not shown separately.

Source: U.S. Census Bureau, "2006 Service Annual Survey, Information Sector Services." See <http://www.census.gov/econ /www/servmenu.html>; (released March 2008).

Table 1116. Public Libraries by Selected Characteristics: 2005

[9,703 represents $9,703,000,000. Based on survey of public libraries. Data are for public libraries in the 50 states and the District of Columbia. The response rates for these items are between 98 and 100 percent]

Population of service area	Number of— Public libraries	Stationary outlets [1]	Operating income— Total (mil. dol.) [2]	Source (percent) State government	Local government	Paid staff [3] Total	Librarians with ALA-MLS [4]	Public use Internet terminals, average per stationary outlet
Total	**9,198**	**16,543**	**9,703**	**9.6**	**81.4**	**137,855**	**30,873**	**11.2**
1,000,000 or more	24	1,018	1,460	6.6	79.1	16,597	4,515	20.1
500,000 to 999,000	59	1,189	1,546	9.8	83.2	19,821	4,930	19.1
250,000 to 499,999	98	1,102	1,126	12.8	80.5	15,494	3,812	15.6
100,000 to 249,999	331	1,996	1,548	9.5	83.3	22,444	4,886	14.4
50,000 to 99,999	551	1,633	1,230	11.3	81.6	18,280	4,060	14.2
25,000 to 49,999	941	1,700	1,189	9.3	82.9	17,421	4,072	12.4
10,000 to 24,999	1,762	2,257	985	9.1	81.7	15,622	3,251	10.2
5,000 to 9,999	1,483	1,641	359	10.3	77.8	6,571	951	7.4
2,500 to 4,999	1,335	1,372	149	7.3	76.4	3,013	267	5.3
1,000 to 2,499	1,612	1,630	88	5.1	73.5	1,970	111	3.9
Fewer than 1,000	1,002	1,005	22	9.0	69.5	621	19	2.9

[1] The sum of central and branch libraries. The total number of central libraries was 9,040; the total of branch libraries was 7,503.   [2] Includes income from the federal government (0.5%) and other sources (8.4%), not shown separately.   [3] Full-time equivalents.   [4] Librarians with master's degrees from a graduate library education program accredited by the American Library Association (ALA). Total librarians, including those without ALA-MLS, were 45,354.

Source: U.S. National Center for Education Statistics, *Public Libraries in the United States: 2005,* NCES 2008-301, November 2007.

Table 1117. **Public Library Use of the Internet: 2008**

[In percent, **except number of outlets. As of spring**. Based on sample survey; see source for details]

Item	Total	Metropolitan status [1]			Poverty status [2]		
		Urban	Sub-urban	Rural	Less than 20 percent	20 to 40 percent	More than 40 percent
All libraries' outlets [3]	**16,548**	**2,921**	**5,402**	**8,225**	**13,882**	**2,481**	**185**
Connected with public access	98.9	99.4	99.4	98.4	99.1	99.7	100.0
Average number of workstations	12.0	21.0	13.9	7.5	11.0	16.2	27.2
Speed of access:							
128kbps or less	2.6	([4])	1.3	4.3	2.6	3.2	([4])
129kbps to 768kbps	5.1	([4])	3.7	7.8	5.3	3.9	2.2
257kbps to 768kbps	8.8	3.3	6.1	12.5	9.5	5.7	([4])
769kbps to 1.4mbps	8.5	3.8	8.7	10.0	8.8	7.3	1.7
1.5Mbps	38.9	51.6	42.1	32.1	37.1	48.3	48.9
1.6mbps to 5mbps	11.1	11.5	13.1	9.6	11.4	9.9	8.4
6.0mbps to 10mbps	6.0	10.1	6.3	4.3	5.8	6.5	13.4
Greater than 10mbps	8.6	17.0	8.7	5.5	8.4	9.4	16.9
Don't Know	10.0	2.1	9.6	13.2	10.8	5.7	8.4
Public library availability of wireless Internet access:							
Currently available	65.9	80.7	72.1	56.6	66.4	62.1	73.1
Plan to make available within the next year . . .	11.6	8.5	12.3	12.3	11.6	12.0	13.2

[1] Urban = inside central city; Suburban = In metro area, outside of a central city; Rural = outside a metro area. [2] Determined by the 2000 poverty status of the service area of the outlet. [3] Central libraries and branches; excludes bookmobiles. [4] Less than 1 percent.

Source: Information Use Management and Policy Institute, College of Information, Florida State University, Tallahassee, FL, *Public Libraries and the Internet 2008: Survey Results and Findings,* by John Carlo Bertot, et al., Florida State University, Tallahassee, FL. Study funded by the American Library Association.

Table 1118. **Household Internet Usage In and Outside of the Home, by Selected Characteristics: 2007**

[As of October. Based on the Current Population Survey and subject to sampling error. See Appendix III]

Characteristics	Total house-holds	In the home			Anywhere		No internet use	
		Percent						
		All house-holds	Dial-up	Broad-band	Total house-holds	Percent of total	Total house-holds	Percent of total
All households	117,840	61.7	10.7	50.8	83,708	71.0	34,132	29.0
Age of householder								
Under 25 years old	7,028	57.7	5.6	51.9	5,238	74.5	1,791	25.5
25 to 34 years old	19,718	65.6	7.0	58.3	15,566	78.9	4,152	21.1
35 to 44 years old	22,854	71.8	10.1	61.4	18,862	82.5	3,992	17.5
45 to 54 years old	24,773	70.7	12.4	58.0	19,763	79.8	5,010	20.2
55 years and older	43,467	50.2	12.4	37.5	24,280	55.9	19,188	44.1
Sex of householder								
Male	59,871	65.3	10.6	54.4	43,985	73.5	15,887	26.5
Female	57,969	58.0	10.8	47.0	39,723	68.5	18,245	31.5
Race and ethnicity of householder [1]								
White	83,294	67.0	11.8	54.9	62,593	75.2	20,701	24.9
Black	14,303	44.9	8.4	36.4	8,433	59.0	5,870	41.0
American Indian/Alaskan Native	643	41.5	11.2	29.8	385	59.9	258	40.1
Asian	4,477	75.5	6.1	69.1	3,672	82.0	805	18.0
Hispanic	13,619	43.4	8.0	35.2	7,463	54.8	6,156	45.2
Educational attainment of householder								
Elementary	5,812	18.5	5.4	13.1	1,490	25.6	4,322	74.4
Some high school	9,264	28.2	7.4	20.5	3,542	38.2	5,721	61.8
High school diploma/GED	35,295	49.1	12.1	36.8	20,973	59.4	14,322	40.6
Some college	33,078	68.9	12.1	56.5	26,498	80.1	6,580	19.9
Bachelors degree or more	34,392	84.1	9.7	74.2	31,205	90.7	3,187	9.3
Family Income of householder [1]								
Less than $15,000	13,939	82.7	18.5	63.9	5,433	120.9	8,506	179.1
$15,000 to $24,999	10,848	76.2	20.2	55.7	5,468	100.3	5,382	99.7
$25,000 to $34,999	11,650	50.9	11.2	39.7	7,565	64.9	4,085	35.1
$35,000 to $49,999	13,718	65.7	14.4	51.0	10,723	78.2	2,995	21.8
$50,000 to $74,999	17,101	80.2	13.8	66.0	15,151	88.6	1,949	11.4
$75,000 to $99,999	9,872	88.6	11.4	76.8	9,326	94.5	546	5.5
$100,000 to $149,000	8,481	92.1	8.0	83.7	8,118	95.7	363	4.3
$150,000 and over	5,570	95.5	5.0	90.3	5,450	97.9	120	2.2

[1] Includes other groups not shown seperately.

Source: U.S. Department of Commerce, National Telecommunications and Information Administration, *Networked Nation: Broadband in America 2007, January 2008.* See also <http://www.ntia.doc.gov/reports/2008/NetworkedNation.html>.

U.S. Census Bureau, Statistical Abstract of the United States: 2009

Table 1119. Household Internet Usage by Type of Internet Connection and State: 2007

[**In percent. As of October.** Based on the Current Population Survey and subject to sampling error. See Appendix III]

State	Any-where	In the home			No Internet use	State	Any-where	In the home			No Internet use
		Total	Broad-band	Dial-up				Total	Broad-band	Dial-up	
U.S. . . .	**71.0**	**61.7**	**50.8**	**10.7**	**29.0**	ME.	74.5	65.1	48.4	16.5	25.5
AL	60.6	49.8	37.4	12.4	39.4	MD.	76.8	66.4	56.1	9.9	23.2
AK	84.3	73.4	62.5	10.4	15.8	MA.	72.9	66.4	61.1	5.2	27.1
AZ	71.7	62.5	53.9	8.2	28.3	MI	70.7	58.5	45.9	12.5	29.3
AR	62.0	51.2	38.2	11.9	38.0	MN.	78.6	66.6	53.0	13.4	21.4
CA	73.6	66.1	56.4	9.4	26.4	MS.	59.7	46.0	33.2	12.5	40.3
CO	78.9	69.1	58.0	10.8	21.1	MO	67.3	56.1	45.3	10.6	32.7
CT	73.4	66.3	59.7	6.4	26.6	MT	68.6	56.9	40.2	16.7	31.4
DE	72.8	65.7	50.4	14.9	27.3	NE	73.9	63.8	54.1	9.6	26.2
DC	74.7	58.9	52.0	6.6	25.3	SC	66.8	54.7	39.1	39.1	33.3
FL	69.7	64.8	53.2	11.0	30.3	SD	73.6	60.8	47.5	47.5	26.4
GA	72.0	61.7	53.9	7.7	28.1	TN	65.9	53.5	41.6	41.6	34.2
HI	72.5	64.1	57.6	5.9	27.5	TX	68.1	57.3	47.6	47.6	31.9
ID	69.9	57.9	45.6	12.0	30.1	UT	82.0	69.5	59.3	59.3	18.0
IL	73.4	63.0	51.6	11.0	26.6	VT	79.4	70.2	46.8	46.8	20.6
IN	68.0	58.1	42.3	15.6	32.0	VA	75.0	68.0	53.3	53.3	25.0
IA	73.6	62.4	46.8	15.5	26.4	WA	81.7	71.6	58.4	58.4	18.3
KS	76.7	62.8	55.2	7.2	23.3	WV	58.2	49.1	32.7	32.7	41.8
KY	66.7	54.9	40.0	14.4	33.3	WI	76.6	65.0	52.6	52.6	23.4
LA	63.2	53.9	42.9	11.0	36.9	WY	76.4	61.4	50.4	50.4	23.6

Source: U.S. Department of Commerce, *National Telecommunications and Information Administration, Networked Nation: Broadband in America 2007*, January 2008. See also <http://www.ntia.doc.gov/reports/2008/NetworkedNation.html>.

Table 1120. Internet Access and Usage: 2007

[**For persons 18 years old and over (220,847 represents 220,847,000). As of fall.** Based on sample and subject to sampling error; see source for details]

Item	Total adults	Have Internet access			Used the Internet in the last 30 days		
		Home or work or other	Home	Work	Home or work or other	Home	Work
Total adults [1] (1,000)	**220,847**	**183,851**	**148,590**	**83,727**	**148,763**	**128,923**	**70,784**
PERCENT DISTRIBUTION							
Total	100.0	100.0	100.0	100.0	100.0	100.0	100.0
Age:							
18 to 34 years old	30.7	33.1	31.6	33.2	36.4	34.0	33.3
35 to 54 years old	39.1	41.4	43.7	50.9	43.0	44.4	51.6
55 years old and over	30.2	25.5	24.7	16.0	20.6	21.6	15.1
Census region: [2]							
Northeast	18.8	19.5	20.4	19.5	19.5	20.3	19.4
Midwest	22.4	23.2	22.5	22.3	23.1	22.9	22.2
South	36.4	34.8	33.6	34.4	33.8	32.7	33.8
West	22.4	22.5	23.5	23.9	23.6	24.1	24.6
Marital status:							
Single	25.2	26.0	23.3	24.0	27.0	24.6	23.7
Married.	55.9	58.2	63.3	62.7	59.3	62.6	63.3
Other	22.4	19.4	16.5	16.5	17.2	16.0	16.3
Educational attainment:							
Graduated college plus	25.5	29.8	34.4	44.7	34.8	37.6	48.1
Attended college	27.5	30.4	31.5	32.0	33.2	32.9	31.9
Did not attend college	47.0	39.8	34.1	23.3	32.0	29.5	20.0
Employed full-time	53.7	58.6	61.0	86.8	63.5	63.0	88.4
Employed part-time	11.6	12.5	12.7	12.7	13.1	13.3	11.1
Household income:							
Less than $50,000	45.4	38.1	30.4	21.0	32.1	28.3	19.1
$50,000 to $74,999.	19.8	21.5	22.5	22.3	22.2	22.3	21.5
$75,000 to $149,999.	26.1	30.2	34.8	40.8	33.8	36.3	42.1
$150,000 or more.	8.7	10.3	12.3	16.0	11.9	13.1	17.3

[1] Includes other labor force status, not shown separately.　　[2] For composition of regions, see map inside front cover.

Source: Mediamark Research Inc., New York, NY, *CyberStats,* fall 2007 (copyright). See <http://www.mriplus.com/pocketpiece.html>.

Table 1121. **Adult Computer and Adult Internet Users, by Selected Characteristics: 1995 to 2008**

[Percent of persons 18 years old and over. Represents persons who use a computer or the Internet at a workplace, school, home, or anywhere else, on at least an occasional basis. Based on telephone surveys of persons with land-line telephones. In 2008, 2,251 persons were interviewed. The response rate was 25 percent. For 1995, Internet users include those who ever use a home, work, or school computer and modem to connect to information services, bulletin boards, or other computers over the Internet. For 2000 and 2004, Internet users include persons who ever go online to access the Internet or World Wide Web or to send and receive e-mail. For 2008, Internet users include those who at least occasionally use the Internet or send and receive e-mail]

Characteristic	Adult computer users				Adult Internet users				All adults, by type of home connection, **2008**	
	1995	2000	2004	2008	1995	2000	2004	2008	Broad-band	Dial-up
Total adults.	**54**	**65**	**68**	**74**	**14**	**53**	**59**	**73**	**55**	**10**
Age:										
18 to 29 years old	70	82	80	90	21	72	72	90	70	11
30 to 49 years old	66	76	79	86	18	62	69	85	69	9
50 to 64 years old	46	61	69	70	9	48	59	70	50	11
65 years old and over	12	21	29	35	2	15	24	35	19	10
Sex:										
Male	58	66	68	74	18	56	61	73	58	8
Female.	51	64	68	74	10	51	58	73	53	12
Race/ethnicity:										
White, non-Hispanic	54	66	69	75	14	55	62	75	57	11
Black, non-Hispanic	50	59	58	65	11	42	45	59	43	8
English-speaking Hispanic . . .	64	64	67	77	21	48	52	80	56	15
Educational attainment:										
Less than high school	17	28	28	46	2	19	22	44	28	6
High school graduate [1]	46	56	59	65	8	41	48	63	40	13
Some college	72	80	82	83	20	69	75	84	66	13
College graduate or higher. . .	82	88	89	92	29	79	82	91	79	7
Annual household income:										
Less than $30,000	37	48	51	55	8	35	43	53	32	12
$30,000 to $49,999.	61	74	72	78	15	61	65	76	54	14
$50,000 to $74,999.	(NA)	85	87	84	23	74	80	85	67	11
$75,000 or more	(NA)	90	92	95	32	81	84	95	84	7

NA Not available.   [1] Includes those with a GED certificate.

Source: 1995 data based on the Times Mirror Center for the People & the Press survey from May and June of 1995; thereafter, Pew Internet & American Life Project Surveys from September–December 2000; November and December of 2004; and April and May 2008. See <http://www.pewinternet.org/index.asp>.

Table 1122. **Internet Activities of Adults, by Type of Home Internet Connection: 2007 and 2008**

[In percent. For Internet users 18 years old and over. For persons who have ever performed the activity. Based on telephone surveys of persons with land-line telephones. In September 2007, 2,400 persons were interviewed, including 129 cell phone users. The response rate was 20 percent. In May 2008, 2,251 persons were interviewed. The response rate was 25 percent]

Activity	Survey date (month,year)	American adults performing activity	Internet users performing activity	Home dial-up users performing activity	Home broadband users performing activity
Send or read e-mail	Sept., 2007	66	90	86	94
Use a search engine to find information	May, 2008	65	89	80	94
Check weather reports and forecasts online	May, 2008	58	80	75	84
Get news online.	May, 2008	54	73	61	80
Buy a product online.	Sept., 2007	48	66	59	74
Visit a local, state, or federal government Web site.	May, 2008	49	66	55	72
Buy or make a reservation for travel	Sept., 2007	47	64	51	72
Look for news or information about politics	May, 2008	40	55	37	62
Do any banking online.	Sept., 2007	39	53	44	61
Watch a video on a video-sharing site	May, 2008	38	52	29	60
Look online for info about a job.	May, 2008	35	47	36	50
Send instant messages	May, 2008	30	40	38	44
Get financial information online	Sept., 2007	26	36	32	40
Use online classified ads or sites like Craig's List.	Sept., 2007	24	32	24	38
Rate a product, service, or person.	Sept., 2007	24	32	28	36
Use a social networking site.	May, 2008	21	29	21	33
Participate in an online auction	Sept., 2007	19	26	16	32
Make a donation to a charity online	May, 2008	14	20	9	23
Download a podcast so you can listen to it or view it later . . .	May, 2008	14	19	8	22
Create or work on your own online journal or blog	May, 2008	9	12	8	15

Source: Pew Internet & American Life Project Surveys. See <http://www.pewinternet.org/index.asp>.

U.S. Census Bureau, Statistical Abstract of the United States: 2009

Table 1123. **Typical Daily Internet Activities of Adult Internet Users: 2007 and 2008**

[Percent of Internet users 18 years old and over. Represents persons who reported doing the activity "yesterday." Based on telephone surveys of persons with land-line telephones unless otherwise noted. In September 2007, 2,400 persons were interviewed, including 129 cell phone users. The response rate was 20 percent. In May 2008, 2,251 persons were interviewed. The response rate was 25 percent]

Activity	Survey date (month-year)	Total Internet users	Age				Sex	
			18 to 29 years old	30 to 49 years old	50 to 64 years old	65 years old and over	Male	Female
Send or read e-mail	Sept., 07	56	57	58	58	41	57	56
Use a search engine to find information	May, 08	49	55	54	40	27	53	45
Get news online	May, 08	39	41	44	35	25	48	31
Check weather reports and forecasts online	May, 08	30	25	37	28	22	35	26
Look for news or information about politics . .	May, 08	23	22	26	21	21	30	17
Do any banking online	Sept., 07	21	21	23	21	11	21	21
Watch a video on a video-sharing site	May, 08	16	30	15	7	6	21	11
Use a social networking site	May, 08	13	38	9	2	1	13	13
Send instant messages.	May, 08	13	26	12	6	4	16	10
Visit a local, state, or federal government Web site.	May, 08	13	15	14	13	4	16	10
Get financial information online.	Sept., 07	10	6	10	11	12	13	7
Buy a product online	Sept., 07	6	9	5	6	3	6	7
Look online for information about a job	May, 08	6	9	6	4	(Z)	5	7
Use online classified ads or sites like Craig's List	Sept., 07	6	10	6	5	1	7	6
Create or work on your own online journal or blog	May, 08	5	10	4	3	1	5	4
Buy or make a reservation for travel	Sept., 07	4	5	5	4	1	4	4
Rate a product, service, or person	Sept., 07	4	5	3	2	4	4	3
Participate in an online auction.	Sept., 07	3	2	3	3	1	3	2
Download a podcast so you can listen to it or view it later	May, 08	3	6	3	2	1	3	3
Make a donation to a charity online.	May, 08	1	2	1	1	1	1	1

Z Less than .05 percent.

Source: Pew Internet & American Life Project Surveys. See <http://www.pewinternet.org/index.asp>.

Table 1124. **Online News Consumption, by Selected Characteristics: 2000 to 2008**

[Percent of Internet users 18 years old and over. Represents persons who report getting news online "ever" or "yesterday." Based on telephone surveys of persons with land-line telephones. In 2008, 2,251 persons were interviewed. The response rate was 25 percent]

Characteristic	"Ever" get news online			Got news online "yesterday"		
	2000	**2004**	**2008**	**2000**	**2004**	**2008**
Total adult Internet users . . .	**60**	**72**	**73**	**22**	**27**	**39**
Age:						
18 to 29 years old	56	71	73	16	21	41
30 to 49 years old	63	74	77	25	32	44
50 to 64 years old	57	72	72	25	27	35
65 years old and over.	53	61	61	28	22	25
Sex:						
Male	66	77	75	29	34	48
Female	53	66	72	16	21	31
Race/ethnicity:						
White, non-Hispanic	60	72	73	23	28	41
Black, non-Hispanic	63	71	69	13	17	37
English-speaking Hispanic.	57	75	69	23	30	31
Annual household income:						
Less than $30,000	55	67	63	21	18	21
$30,000 to $49,999	57	73	73	20	28	33
$50,000 to $74,999	63	76	78	22	30	46
$75,000 or more	69	74	79	31	36	53
Frequency of internet use:						
Daily	66	78	83	33	39	52
Several times per week.	59	66	59	17	9	15
Less Often	51	50	38	12	1	3

Source: Pew Internet & American Life Project Surveys from March 2000; May–June of 2004; and April–May 2008. See <http://www.pewinternet.org/index.asp>.

Section 25
Banking, Finance, and Insurance

This section presents data on the nation's finances, various types of financial institutions, money and credit, securities, insurance, and real estate. The primary sources of these data are publications of several departments of the federal government, especially the U.S. Treasury Department, and independent agencies such as the Federal Deposit Insurance Corporation, the Board of Governors of the Federal Reserve System, and the Securities and Exchange Commission. National data on insurance are available primarily from private organizations, such as the American Council of Life Insurers and the Insurance Information Institute.

Flow of funds—The flow of funds accounts of the Federal Reserve Board bring together statistics on all of the major forms of financial instruments to present an economy-wide view of asset and liability relationships. In flow form, the accounts relate borrowing and lending to one another and to the nonfinancial activities that generate income and production. Each claim outstanding is included simultaneously as an asset of the lender and as a liability of the debtor. The accounts also indicate the balance between asset totals and liability totals over the economy as a whole. Several publications of the Federal Reserve Board contain information on the flow of funds accounts: Summary data on flows and outstandings, in the *Statistical Supplement to the Federal Reserve Bulletin, Flow of Funds Accounts of the United States* (quarterly); and concepts and organization of the accounts in *Guide to the Flow of Funds Accounts* (2000). Data are also available on the Federal Reserve Board's Web site <http://www .federalreserve .gov/>.

Survey of Consumer Finances (SCF)—The Federal Reserve Board, in cooperation with the Treasury Department, sponsors this survey, which is conducted every 3 years to provide detailed information on the finances of U.S. families. Among the topics covered are the balance sheet, pension, income, and other demographic characteristics of U.S. families. The survey also gathers information on the use of financial institutions. Since 1992, data for the SCF have been collected by the National Organization for Social Science and Survey Research at the University of Chicago. Data and information on the survey are available on the Web site of the Federal Reserve Board: <http://www .federalreserve.gov/pubs /oss/oss2/scfindex.html>.

Banking system—Banks in this country are organized under the laws of both the states and the federal government and are regulated by several bank supervisory agencies. National banks are supervised by the Comptroller of the Currency. *Reports of Condition* have been collected from national banks since 1863. Summaries of these reports are published in the Comptroller's *Annual Report,* which also presents data on the structure of the national banking system.

The Federal Reserve System was established in 1913 to exercise central banking functions, some of which are shared with the U.S. Treasury. It includes national banks and such state banks that voluntarily join the system. Statements of state bank members are consolidated by the Federal Reserve Board with data for national banks collected by the Comptroller of the Currency into totals for all member banks of the system. Balance sheet data for member banks and other commercial banks are published quarterly in the *Statistical Supplement to the Federal Reserve Bulletin* (also available on the Web at <http://www.federalreserve.gov>.

The Federal Deposit Insurance Corporation (FDIC), established in 1933, insures each depositor up to $100,000. Major item balance sheet and income data for all insured financial institutions are published in the *FDIC Quarterly Banking Profile.* This publication is also available on the Internet at the following address: <http://www.fdic.gov>. Quarterly financial information for individual institutions

Banking, Finance, and Insurance   713

is available through the FDIC and Federal Financial Institutions Examination Council Web sites at <http://www.fdic.gov> and <http://www.ffiec.gov>.

Credit unions—Federally chartered credit unions are under the supervision of the National Credit Union Administration. State-chartered credit unions are supervised by the respective state supervisory authorities. The administration publishes comprehensive program and statistical information on all federal and federally insured state credit unions in the *Annual Report of the National Credit Union Administration.*

Other credit agencies—Insurance companies, finance companies dealing primarily in installment sales financing, and personal loan companies represent important sources of funds for the credit market. Statistics on loans, investments, cash, etc., of life insurance companies are published principally by the American Council of Life Insurers in its *Life Insurers Fact Book.* Consumer credit data are published currently in the *Statistical Supplement to the Federal Reserve Bulletin.*

Government corporations and credit agencies make available credit of specified types or to specified groups of private borrowers, either by lending directly or by insuring or guaranteeing loans made by private lending institutions. Data on operations of government credit agencies, along with other government corporations, are available in reports of individual agencies; data on their debt outstanding are published in the *Statistical Supplement to the Federal Reserve Bulletin.*

Securities—The Securities and Exchange Commission (SEC) was established in 1934 to protect the interests of the public and investors against malpractices in the securities and financial markets and to provide the fullest possible disclosure of information regarding securities to the investing public.

Data on the securities industry and securities transactions are also available from a number of private sources. The Securities Industry and Financial Markets Association, New York, NY, <http://www.sifma .org/>, publishes the *Securities Industry Fact Book* and *Securities Industry Yearbook.* The Investment Company Institute, Washington, DC, <http://www.ici.org/>, publishes a reference book, research newsletters, and a variety of research reports that examine the industry, its shareholders, or industry issues. The annual *Mutual Fund Fact Book* is a guide to trends and statistics observed in the investment company industry. *Fundamentals* is a newsletter summarizing the findings of major Institute research projects. Institute research reports provide a detailed examination of shareholder demographics and other aspects of fund ownership.

Among the many sources of data on stock and bond prices and sales are the New York Stock Exchange, New York, NY, <http://www.nyse.com/>; NASDAQ, Washington, DC, <http://www.nasdaq .com/>; Global Financial Data, Los Angeles, CA, <http://www.globalfindata .com/>; and Dow-Jones & Company, Inc., New York, NY, <http://www.djindexes .com>.

Insurance—Insuring companies, which are regulated by the various states or the District of Columbia, are classified as either life or property. Both life and property insurance companies may underwrite health insurance. Insuring companies, other than those classified as life, are permitted to underwrite one or more property lines provided they are so licensed and have the necessary capital or surplus.

There are a number of published sources for statistics on the various classes of insurance—life, health, fire, marine, and casualty. Organizations representing certain classes of insurers publish reports for these classes. The American Council of Life Insurers publishes statistics on life insurance purchases, ownership, benefit payments, and assets in its *Life Insurers Fact Book.*

Statistical reliability—For a discussion of statistical collection, estimation, and sampling procedures and measures of reliability applicable to data from the Census Bureau and the Federal Reserve Board's Survey of Consumer Finances, see Appendix III.

Table 1125. Gross Domestic Product in Finance, Insurance, Real Estate, Rental, and Leasing in Current and Real (2000) Dollars: 2000 to 2007

[In billions of dollars, except percent (741 represents $741,000,000,000). Represents value added by industry. For definition of gross domestic product and explanation of chained dollars, see text, Section 13]

Industry	1997 NAICS code [1]	Current dollars				Chained (2000) dollars			
		2000	2005	2006	2007	2000	2005	2006	2007
Finance & insurance, total	**52**	**741**	**982**	**1,094**	**1,114**	**741**	**878**	**964**	**961**
Percent of gross domestic product . . .		7.5	8.1	8.1	8.1	7.5	8.0	8.5	8.3
Monetary authorities—central bank, credit intermediation & related activities.	521,522	319	506	570	(NA)	319	432	467	(NA)
Security, commodity contracts, & like activity	523	168	184	218	(NA)	168	225	277	(NA)
Insurance carriers & related activities. . . .	524	238	264	281	(NA)	238	209	220	(NA)
Funds, trusts, & other financial vehicles (part)	525	16	28	25	(NA)	16	20	20	(NA)
Real estate & rental & leasing, total . .	**53**	**1,191**	**1,566**	**1,663**	**1,747**	**1,191**	**1,358**	**1,404**	**1,434**
Percent of gross domestic product . . .		12.1	12.6	12.6	12.6	12.1	12.3	12.4	12.4
Real estate	531	1,082	1,461	1,557	(NA)	1,082	1,263	1,310	(NA)
Rental & leasing services [2]	532,533	108	105	106	(NA)	108	94	92	(NA)

NA Not available. [1] See footnote 1, Table 1126. [2] Includes lessors of other nonfinancial intangible assets.

Source: U.S. Bureau of Economic Analysis, *Survey of Current Business*, May 2008.

Table 1126. Finance and Insurance/Real Estate and Rental and Leasing—Establishments, Revenue, Payroll, and Employees by Kind of Business (1997 NAICS Basis): 1997 and 2002

[2,198 represents $2,198,000,000,000. For establishments with payroll. Based on the 1997 and 2002 Economic Censuses; see Appendix III]

Kind of business	1997 NAICS code [1]	Number of establishments		Revenue (bil. dol.)		Annual payroll (bil. dol.)		Paid employees (1,000)	
		1997	2002	1997	2002	1997	2002	1997	2002
Finance & insurance	**52**	**395,203**	**440,268**	**2,198**	**2,804**	**264.6**	**377.8**	**5,835**	**6,579**
Monetary authorities—central bank	521	42	47	25	29	0.9	1.2	22	22
Credit intermediation & related activities	522	166,882	196,451	809	1,056	98.7	151.2	2,745	3,300
Security, commodity contracts, & like activity	523	54,491	72,338	275	316	71.3	103.4	706	832
Insurance carriers & related activities. . .	524	172,299	169,520	1,073	1,380	92.2	120.6	2,327	2,406
Funds, trusts, and other financial vehicles (part)	525	1,489	1,912	17	23	1.4	1.3	35	19
Real estate & rental & leasing	**53**	**288,273**	**322,805**	**241**	**336**	**41.6**	**60.2**	**1,702**	**1,949**
Real estate	531	221,650	256,086	153	224	27.9	41.7	1,117	1,305
Rental & leasing services.	532	64,472	64,334	76	95	12.6	16.9	559	617
Lessors of other nonfinancial intangible assets	533	2,151	2,385	11	17	1.1	1.7	26	27

[1] 1997 North American Industry Classification System; see text, Section 15.

Source: U.S. Census Bureau, "2002 Economic Census; Comparative Statistics for United States Summary Statistics by 1997 NAICS"; published 31 July 2006; <http://www.census.gov/econ/census02/data/comparative/USCS.HTM>.

Table 1127. Finance and Insurance—Nonemployer Establishments and Receipts by Kind of Business: 2000 to 2005

[691.8 represents 691,800. Includes only firms subject to federal income tax. Nonemployers are businesses with no paid employees. Data originate chiefly from administrative records of the Internal Revenue Service; see Appendix III. Data for 2000 based on the 1997 North American Industry Classification System (NAICS); beginning 2004, based on 2002 NAICS. See text, Section 15]

Kind of business	NAICS code	Establishments (1,000)			Receipts (mil. dol.)		
		2000	2004	2005	2000	2004	2005
Finance and insurance	**52**	**691.8**	**717.5**	**741.9**	**49,058**	**44,032**	**47,244**
Credit intermediation & related activities	522	165.3	81.4	82.5	4,848	4,652	5,046
Depository credit intermediation.	5221	6.5	7.7	7.3	197	248	240
Nondepository credit intermediation	5222	134.1	28.3	29.4	3,624	2,295	2,541
Activities related to credit intermediation	5223	24.7	45.4	45.8	1,028	2,108	2,265
Security, commodity contracts, & like activity.	523	181.5	259.5	276.2	29,379	21,316	23,405
Security & commodity contracts interm & brokerage . .	5231	29.6	33.2	33.4	6,395	4,657	5,017
Investment banking and securities dealing	52311	5.6	7.8	8.0	2,043	1,324	1,499
Securities brokerage	52312	19.5	20.6	20.5	3,712	2,621	2,872
Commodity contracts dealing.	52313	1.0	1.2	1.2	238	236	211
Commodity contracts brokerage	52314	3.6	3.7	3.7	402	476	435
Securities & commodity exchanges	5232	1.6	1.9	2.0	1,495	867	571
Other financial investment activities	5239	150.2	224.4	240.7	21,488	15,793	17,817
Insurance carriers & related activities.	524	345.0	376.6	383.3	14,831	18,064	18,793
Insurance carriers	5241	1.0	0.6	0.5	98	42	37
Agencies & other insurance-related activities	5242	344.0	376.0	382.7	14,733	18,022	18,756
Insurance agencies & brokerages.	52421	245.5	255.2	256.5	11,570	13,560	13,933
Other insurance related activities	52429	98.5	120.8	126.2	3,163	4,462	4,824

Source: U.S. Census Bureau, "Nonemployer Statistics"; <http://www.census.gov/epcd/nonemployer/>.

U.S. Census Bureau, Statistical Abstract of the United States: 2009

Table 1128. Finance and Insurance—Establishments, Employees, and Payroll: 2000 and 2005

[423.7 represents 423,700. Covers establishments with payroll. Kind-of-business classification for 2000 based on North American Industry Classification System (NAICS) 1997; data for 2005 based on NAICS 2002. See text, Section 15. Employees are for the week including March 12. Most government employees are excluded. For statement on methodology, see Appendix III]

Kind of business	NAICS code	Establishments (1,000)		Employees (1,000)		Payroll (bil. dol.)	
		2000	2005	2000	2005	2000	2005
Finance & insurance, total	**52**	**423.7**	**476.8**	**5,963**	**6,432**	**346.8**	**446.7**
Monetary authorities—central bank	521	0.1	0.1	22	20	1.1	1.2
Credit intermediation & related activities	522	176.3	214.1	2,753	3,202	116.1	172.5
Depository credit intermediation [1]	5221	105.6	114.2	1,935	2,082	78.5	104.8
Commercial banking	52211	73.9	81.8	1,493	1,591	63.6	83.5
Savings institutions	52212	15.9	16.3	244	248	9.2	12.2
Credit unions	52213	15.6	16.0	192	236	5.4	8.4
Nondepository credit intermediation [1]	5222	49.3	56.9	621	763	29.6	50.1
Real estate credit	522292	19.8	28.0	238	383	10.8	26.7
Activities related to credit intermediation	5223	21.4	42.9	198	356	7.9	17.6
Security & commodity contracts & like activity	523	72.9	82.1	866	860	119.5	132.0
Security & commodity contracts intermediate & brokerage [1]	5231	38.1	37.2	539	485	80.2	80.8
Investment banking & securities dealing	52311	6.3	5.6	138	137	31.2	34.5
Securities brokerage	52312	29.5	29.1	378	326	47.0	44.0
Securities & commodity exchanges	5232	(Z)	0.1	7	7	0.5	0.8
Other financial investment activities [1]	5239	34.8	44.8	320	368	38.8	50.3
Portfolio management	52392	11.6	13.9	156	176	24.9	31.3
Insurance carriers & related activities	524	172.2	177.2	2,290	2,323	108.1	138.4
Insurance carriers [1]	5241	37.4	33.8	1,489	1,406	74.7	92.2
Direct life/health/medical insurance carriers . . .	52411	13.9	12.7	813	767	40.0	51.2
Direct life insurance carriers	524113	10.7	8.7	491	356	25.7	25.3
Direct health & medical insurance carriers . .	524114	3.1	4.0	322	411	14.3	25.9
Other direct insurance carriers [1]	52412	23.0	20.5	660	621	33.5	39.0
Direct property & casualty insurance carriers	524126	19.8	13.5	609	534	31.1	33.4
Agencies & other insurance-related activities [1] . .	5242	134.8	143.4	801	917	33.3	46.2
Insurance agencies & brokerages	52421	121.5	130.7	596	705	24.7	35.5
Funds, trusts, & other financial vehicles (part)	525	2.3	3.3	32	27	2.1	2.7

Z Less than 50.   [1] Includes industries not shown separately.
Source: U.S. Census Bureau, "County Business Patterns"; <http://www.census.gov/epcd/cbp/view/cbpview.html>.

Table 1129. Flow of Funds Accounts—Financial Assets of Financial and Nonfinancial Institutions by Holder Sector: 1990 to 2007

[In billions of dollars (35,920 represents $35,920,000,000,000). As of Dec. 31]

Sector	1990	1995	2000	2001	2002	2003	2004	2005	2006	2007
All sectors	**35,920**	**53,513**	**89,528**	**90,605**	**89,569**	**99,937**	**109,737**	**119,696**	**131,992**	**141,921**
Households [1]	14,613	21,558	33,285	31,755	29,564	34,048	37,096	39,544	43,218	45,333
Nonfinancial business	3,970	5,556	11,252	11,537	11,659	11,924	13,046	14,409	15,155	16,059
Farm business	38	49	57	59	60	62	66	67	74	79
Nonfarm noncorporate	356	548	1,423	1,579	1,657	1,752	2,049	2,433	2,735	3,079
Nonfinancial corporations	3,575	4,959	9,772	9,899	9,942	10,109	10,932	11,909	12,347	12,902
State and local government	1,020	1,122	1,662	1,748	1,800	1,908	2,030	2,220	2,385	2,527
U.S. government	442	441	506	607	599	641	602	593	599	635
Monetary authorities	342	472	636	683	754	797	841	879	908	951
Commercial banking	3,337	4,494	6,469	6,829	7,329	7,825	8,560	9,320	10,203	11,195
U.S.-chartered commercial banks	2,644	3,322	4,774	5,015	5,427	5,838	6,399	6,906	7,614	8,268
Foreign banking offices in U.S.	367	666	789	792	801	750	633	782	785	1,004
Bank-holding companies	298	467	842	942	1,026	1,153	1,429	1,524	1,695	1,813
Banks in U.S.-affiliated areas	28	39	63	80	75	84	100	109	108	109
Savings institutions	1,323	1,013	1,218	1,291	1,349	1,466	1,650	1,789	1,715	1,815
Credit unions	217	311	441	506	564	617	655	686	716	759
Life insurance companies	1,351	2,064	3,136	3,225	3,335	3,773	4,130	4,351	4,685	4,984
Property-casualty insurance companies . .	533	740	862	860	940	1,060	1,162	1,244	1,329	1,381
Private pension funds	1,651	2,921	4,490	4,070	3,699	4,542	4,937	5,318	5,701	5,842
Defined benefit plans	918	1,485	1,998	1,829	1,658	2,013	2,151	2,300	2,388	2,353
Defined contribution plans	733	1,436	2,492	2,241	2,041	2,529	2,787	3,018	3,313	3,489
State and local government employee retirement funds	730	1,327	2,293	2,207	1,930	2,349	2,578	2,721	3,050	3,152
Federal government retirement funds . . .	340	541	797	860	894	958	1,023	1,072	1,141	1,197
Money market mutual funds	493	741	1,812	2,241	2,224	2,016	1,880	2,007	2,312	3,053
Mutual funds	608	1,853	4,433	4,135	3,638	4,654	5,436	6,049	7,068	7,798
Closed-end funds	53	136	142	140	151	206	246	271	294	319
Exchange-traded funds	–	1	66	83	102	151	227	301	423	607
Government-sponsored enterprises (GSE)	478	897	1,965	2,309	2,549	2,794	2,883	2,819	2,873	3,183
Agency- and GSE-backed mortgage pools	1,020	1,571	2,493	2,832	3,159	3,327	3,375	3,542	3,837	4,443
Asset-backed securities issuers	268	663	1,483	1,731	1,945	2,174	2,600	3,271	4,044	4,221
Finance companies	596	705	1,213	1,304	1,446	1,679	1,858	1,857	1,891	1,911
Real estate investment trusts	28	33	66	76	102	136	253	330	404	338
Security brokers and dealers	262	568	1,221	1,466	1,335	1,613	1,845	2,127	2,742	3,095
Funding corporations	251	383	1,167	1,165	1,086	1,076	1,103	1,343	1,447	1,696
Rest of the world	1,991	3,403	6,421	6,946	7,414	8,202	9,720	11,635	13,851	15,424

– Represents zero.   [1] Includes nonprofit organizations.
Source: Board of Governors of the Federal Reserve System, "Federal Reserve Statistical Release, Z.1, Flow of Funds Accounts of the United States"; published: 6 March 2008; <http://www.federalreserve.gov/releases/z1/20080306/>.

Table 1130. Flow of Funds Accounts—Credit Market Debt Outstanding: 1990 to 2007

[In billions of dollars (13,767 represents $13,767,000,000,000). As of December 31. Represents credit market debt owed by sectors shown]

Item	1990	1995	2000	2001	2002	2003	2004	2005	2006	2007
Credit market debt	**13,767**	**18,465**	**27,044**	**29,216**	**31,694**	**34,466**	**37,611**	**40,951**	**44,810**	**48,808**
Domestic nonfinancial	10,835	13,664	18,099	19,226	20,625	22,327	24,301	26,546	28,862	31,212
Households [1]	3,596	4,862	7,009	7,680	8,514	9,497	10,575	11,754	12,948	13,825
Corporations	2,536	2,924	4,555	4,741	4,750	4,863	5,030	5,273	5,696	6,330
Nonfarm noncorporate business	1,093	1,062	1,796	1,959	2,107	2,199	2,443	2,775	3,122	3,525
Farm business	124	132	156	163	170	168	174	187	205	220
State and local government	987	1,047	1,198	1,303	1,447	1,568	1,683	1,854	2,006	2,190
U.S. government	2,498	3,637	3,385	3,379	3,637	4,033	4,395	4,702	4,885	5,122
Rest of the world	318	568	815	863	1,072	1,250	1,431	1,515	1,767	1,845
Financial sectors	2,614	4,233	8,130	9,128	9,997	10,889	11,879	12,890	14,181	15,751
Commercial banking	198	251	509	562	612	660	739	824	998	1,257
Savings institutions	140	115	288	286	262	297	386	410	298	401
Credit unions	–	–	3	5	7	9	11	15	19	32
Life insurance companies	–	1	2	3	5	8	11	11	14	29
Government-sponsored enterprises (GSE)	399	807	1,826	2,131	2,350	2,601	2,676	2,592	2,628	2,910
Agency- and GSE-backed mortgage pools	1,020	1,571	2,493	2,832	3,159	3,327	3,375	3,542	3,837	4,443
Asset-backed securities issuers	269	666	1,489	1,738	1,951	2,179	2,605	3,275	4,047	4,224
Finance companies	398	500	807	818	884	995	1,130	1,109	1,144	1,174
Real estate investment trusts	28	45	168	171	198	230	343	403	444	440
Security brokers and dealers	15	29	41	42	41	47	62	62	69	65
Funding corporations	147	249	503	540	528	535	541	648	683	776

– Represents or rounds to zero.   [1] Includes nonprofit organizations.

Source: Board of Governors of the Federal Reserve System, "Federal Reserve Statistical Release, Z.1, Flow of Funds Accounts of the United States"; published 6 March 2008; <http://www.federalreserve.gov/releases/z1/20080306/>.

Table 1131. Flow of Funds Accounts—Financial Assets and Liabilities of Foreign Sector: 1990 to 2007

[In billions of dollars (1,991 represents $1,991,000,000,000). As of December 31]

Type of instrument	1990	1995	2000	2001	2002	2003	2004	2005	2006	2007
Total financial assets [1]	**1,991**	**3,403**	**6,421**	**6,946**	**7,414**	**8,202**	**9,720**	**11,635**	**13,851**	**15,424**
U.S. checkable deposits and currency	108	194	287	306	327	322	346	371	393	409
U.S. time deposits	49	50	109	121	152	131	170	175	188	221
Money market fund shares	1	5	11	15	16	19	23	23	26	33
Security RPs [2]	20	68	91	151	190	460	665	713	1,029	1,100
Credit market instruments	882	1,465	2,451	2,850	3,303	3,836	4,635	5,188	6,033	6,855
Open market paper	11	43	114	108	127	193	230	240	288	292
Treasury securities	438	817	1,021	1,095	1,285	1,514	1,814	1,984	2,115	2,324
Official	286	490	640	720	812	986	1,252	1,341	1,521	1,570
Private	152	327	382	375	474	527	562	644	594	754
Agency- and GSE-backed securities [3]	49	123	348	504	630	655	875	1,012	1,189	1,378
Official	5	18	116	172	214	263	373	487	669	889
Private	44	106	232	332	416	392	502	525	520	489
Municipal securities	2	4	8	8	12	20	26	29	31	33
U.S. corporate bonds [4]	209	355	842	1,019	1,124	1,331	1,559	1,764	2,251	2,583
Loans to U.S. corporate business	172	122	117	116	126	125	131	160	159	244
U.S. corporate equities	243	485	1,483	1,441	1,222	1,675	1,905	2,039	2,455	2,806
Mutual fund shares	–	60	149	117	98	146	196	242	296	326
Trade receivables	46	49	49	46	49	50	49	57	63	80
Miscellaneous assets	590	798	1,629	1,784	1,938	1,453	1,614	2,720	3,272	3,606
Foreign direct investment in U.S. [5]	505	680	1,421	1,518	1,500	1,581	1,742	1,868	2,099	2,335
Other	85	118	208	266	438	-128	-129	852	1,172	1,272
Total liabilities	**1,375**	**2,020**	**3,330**	**3,415**	**3,867**	**4,117**	**5,004**	**5,163**	**6,104**	**6,670**
U.S. official foreign exchange and net IMF [6] position	61	64	46	47	56	62	62	46	46	74
U.S. private deposits	298	419	803	810	831	867	957	1,025	1,124	1,389
Credit market instruments [1]	318	568	815	863	1,072	1,250	1,431	1,515	1,767	1,845
Commercial paper	75	56	121	196	254	267	330	368	461	395
Bonds	145	413	573	557	705	874	993	1,028	1,181	1,323
Bank loans n.e.c. [7]	19	35	71	63	69	66	70	84	98	103
U.S. government loans	63	55	47	46	44	42	38	34	26	24
Trade payables	29	47	51	44	39	45	48	54	61	73
Miscellaneous liabilities [1]	669	923	1,615	1,651	1,869	1,893	2,506	2,523	3,107	3,289
U.S. direct investment abroad [4, 5]	630	886	1,532	1,693	1,867	2,054	2,464	2,535	2,856	3,136

– Represents zero.   [1] Includes other items not shown separately.   [2] Repurchase agreements.   [3] GSE = Government-sponsored enterprises.   [4] Through 1992, corporate bonds include net issues by Netherlands Antillean financial subsidiaries; U.S. direct investment abroad excludes net inflows from those bond issues.   [5] Direct investment is valued on a current-cost basis.   [6] IMF = International Monetary Fund.   [7] Not elsewhere classified.

Source: Board of Governors of the Federal Reserve System, "Federal Reserve Statistical Release, Z.1, Flow of Funds Accounts of the United States"; published 6 March 2008; <http://www.federalreserve.gov/releases/z1/20080306/>.

U.S. Census Bureau, Statistical Abstract of the United States: 2009

Table 1132. Flow of Funds Accounts—Assets and Liabilities of Households: 1990 to 2007

[As of December 31 (14,613 represents $14,613,000,000,000). Includes nonprofit organizations. See also Table 700]

Type of instrument	Total (bil. dol.)							Percent distribution		
	1990	2000	2003	2004	2005	2006	2007	1990	2000	2007
Total financial assets	14,613	33,285	34,048	37,096	39,544	43,218	45,333	100.0	100.0	100.0
Deposits.	3,300	4,350	5,328	5,706	6,088	6,733	7,389	22.6	13.1	16.3
Foreign deposits	13	48	52	57	62	67	86	0.1	0.1	0.2
Checkable deposits and currency	411	279	329	294	156	122	78	2.8	0.8	0.2
Time and savings deposits	2,485	3,062	3,986	4,451	4,921	5,428	5,880	17.0	9.2	13.0
Money market fund shares	391	960	960	904	949	1,114	1,344	2.7	2.9	3.0
Credit market instruments	1,768	2,556	2,930	3,213	3,450	3,667	3,977	12.1	7.7	8.8
Open-market paper	94	97	106	136	164	188	160	0.6	0.3	0.4
Treasury securities	529	605	462	555	550	490	309	3.6	1.8	0.7
Agency and GSE-backed securities [1] . .	114	604	432	398	496	518	947	0.8	1.8	2.1
Municipal securities	648	531	704	743	821	866	916	4.4	1.6	2.0
Corporate and foreign bonds.	245	618	1,108	1,255	1,286	1,469	1,505	1.7	1.9	3.3
Mortgages	139	100	118	126	132	135	141	0.9	0.3	0.3
Corporate equities [2]	1,961	8,199	5,767	5,938	5,875	6,178	5,447	13.4	24.6	12.0
Mutual fund shares.	512	2,704	2,904	3,417	3,840	4,536	5,082	3.5	8.1	11.2
Security credit	62	412	475	578	575	656	853	0.4	1.2	1.9
Life insurance reserves	392	819	1,013	1,060	1,083	1,164	1,205	2.7	2.5	2.7
Pension fund reserves [3]	3,330	9,188	9,744	10,655	11,391	12,324	12,780	22.8	27.6	28.2
Equity in noncorporate business	3,033	4,677	5,397	5,986	6,651	7,330	7,892	20.8	14.1	17.4
Miscellaneous assets	254	379	489	542	591	631	709	1.7	1.1	1.6
Total liabilities.	3,718	7,398	9,857	11,035	12,191	13,454	14,375	100.0	100.0	100.0
Credit market instruments	3,596	7,009	9,497	10,575	11,754	12,948	13,825	96.7	94.7	96.2
Home mortgages [4]	2,504	4,818	6,882	7,838	8,866	9,854	10,509	67.3	65.1	73.1
Consumer credit.	824	1,741	2,104	2,219	2,314	2,418	2,551	22.2	23.5	17.7
Municipal securities.	86	138	178	189	205	227	250	2.3	1.9	1.7
Bank loans, n.e.c.	18	65	53	35	48	96	131	0.5	0.9	0.9
Other loans	82	120	119	119	119	123	128	2.2	1.6	0.9
Commercial mortgages	83	127	160	175	201	230	257	2.2	1.7	1.8
Security credit	39	235	183	264	232	292	325	1.0	3.2	2.3
Trade payables	67	135	157	173	182	191	200	1.8	1.8	1.4
Unpaid life insurance premiums [5]	16	20	21	22	22	23	24	0.4	0.3	0.2

[1] GSE = government-sponsored enterprises. [2] Only those directly held and those in closed-end and exchange-traded funds. Other equities are included in mutual funds and life insurance and pension reserves. [3] See also Table 1177. [4] Includes loans made under home equity lines of credit and home equity loans secured by junior liens. [5] Includes deferred premiums.

Source: Board of Governors of the Federal Reserve System, "Federal Reserve Statistical Release, Z.1, Flow of Funds Accounts of the United States"; published 6 March 2008; <http://www.federalreserve.gov/releases/z1/20080306/>.

Table 1133. Percent of Families Owning Financial Assets by Type of Asset: 2001 and 2004

[All dollar figures are adjusted to 2004 dollars using the "current methods" version of the consumer price index for all urban consumers published by U.S. Bureau of Labor Statistics. Families include one-person units; for definition of family, see text, Section 1. Based on Survey of Consumer Finances; see Appendix III]

Age of family head and family income	Any financial asset [1]	Trans-action accounts [2]	Certifi-cates of deposit	Savings bonds	Stocks [3]	Pooled invest-ment funds [4]	Retire-ment accounts [5]	Life insur-ance	Other man-aged [6]
2001, total.	93.4	91.4	15.7	16.7	21.3	17.7	52.2	28.0	6.6
2004, total	**93.8**	**91.3**	**12.7**	**17.6**	**20.7**	**15.0**	**49.7**	**24.2**	**7.3**
Under 35 years old	90.1	86.4	5.6	15.3	13.3	8.3	40.2	11.0	2.9
35 to 44 years old	93.6	90.8	6.7	23.3	18.5	12.3	55.9	20.1	3.7
45 to 54 years old	93.6	91.8	11.9	21.0	23.2	18.2	57.7	26.0	6.2
55 to 64 years old	95.2	93.2	18.1	15.2	29.1	20.6	62.9	32.1	9.4
65 to 74 years old	96.5	93.9	19.9	14.9	25.4	18.6	43.2	34.8	12.8
75 years old and over. . . .	97.6	96.4	25.7	11.0	18.4	16.6	29.2	34.0	16.7
Percentiles of income: [7]									
Less than 20	80.1	75.5	5.0	6.2	5.1	3.6	10.1	14.0	3.1
20 to 39.9	91.5	87.3	12.7	8.8	8.2	7.6	30.0	19.2	4.9
40 to 59.9	98.5	95.9	11.8	15.4	16.3	12.7	53.4	24.2	7.9
60 to 79.9	99.1	98.4	14.9	26.6	28.2	18.6	69.7	29.8	7.8
80 to 89.9	99.8	99.1	16.3	32.3	35.8	26.2	81.9	29.5	12.1
90 to 100	100.0	100.0	21.5	29.9	55.0	39.1	88.5	38.1	13.0

[1] Includes other types of financial assets, not shown separately. [2] Checking, savings, and money market deposit accounts, money market mutual funds, and call accounts at brokerages. [3] Covers only those stocks that are directly held by families outside mutual funds, retirement accounts, and other managed assets. [4] Excludes money market mutual funds and indirectly held mutual funds and includes all other types of directly held pooled investment funds, such as traditional open-ended and closed-end mutual funds, real estate investment trusts, and hedge funds. [5] The tax-deferred retirement accounts consist of IRAs, Keogh accounts, and certain employer-sponsored accounts. Employer-sponsored accounts include 401(k), 403(b), and thrift saving accounts from current or past jobs; other current job plans from which loans or withdrawals can be made; and accounts from past jobs from which the family expects to receive the account balance in the future. [6] Includes personal annuities and trusts with an equity interest and managed investment accounts. [7] Percentiles of income distribution in 2004 dollars: 20th: $18,900; 40th: $33,900; 60th: $53,600; 80th: $89,300; 90th: $129,400. Percentile: A value on a scale of zero to 100 that indicates the percent of a distribution that is equal to or below it. For example, a family with income in the 80th percentile has income equal to or better than 80 percent of all other families.

Source: Board of Governors of the Federal Reserve System, "2004 Survey of Consumer Finances"; published 28 February 2006; <http://www.federalreserve.gov/pubs/oss/oss2/2004/scf2004home.html>.

Table 1134. **Percent of Families Holding Financial Debt by Type of Debt: 2001 and 2004**

[See headnote, Table 1133]

Age of family head and family income	Any debt	Secured by residential property		Lines of credit not secured by residential property	Installment loans	Credit card balances [2]	Other [3]
		Primary residence [1]	Other				
2001, total	75.1	44.6	4.6	1.5	45.2	44.4	7.2
2004, total	**76.4**	**47.9**	**4.0**	**1.6**	**46.0**	**46.2**	**7.6**
Under 35 years old	79.8	37.7	2.1	2.2	59.4	47.5	6.2
35 to 44 years old	88.6	62.8	4.0	1.5	55.7	58.8	11.3
45 to 54 years old	88.4	64.6	6.3	2.9	50.2	54.0	9.4
55 to 64 years old	76.3	51.0	5.9	0.7	42.8	42.1	8.4
65 to 74 years old	58.8	32.1	3.2	0.4	27.5	31.9	4.0
75 years old and over	40.3	18.7	1.5	(B)	13.9	23.6	2.5
Percentiles of income: [4]							
Less than 20	52.6	15.9	(B)	(B)	26.9	28.8	4.6
20 to 39.9	69.8	29.5	1.5	1.5	39.9	42.9	5.8
40 to 59.9	84.0	51.7	2.6	1.8	52.4	55.1	8.0
60 to 79.9	86.6	65.8	4.1	1.8	57.8	56.0	8.3
80 to 89.9	92.0	76.8	7.5	2.6	60.0	57.6	12.3
90 to 100	86.3	76.2	15.4	2.5	45.7	38.5	10.6

B Base figure too small. [1] First and second mortgages and home equity loans and lines of credit secured by the primary residence. [2] Families that had an outstanding balance on any of their credit cards after paying their most recent bills. [3] Includes loans on insurance policies, loans against pension accounts, borrowing on margin accounts and unclassified loans. [4] See footnote 7, Table 1133.

Source: Board of Governors of the Federal Reserve System, "2004 Survey of Consumer Finances"; published 28 February 2006; <http://www.federalreserve.gov/pubs/oss/oss2/2004/scf2004home.html>.

Table 1135. **Household Debt-Service Payments and Financial Obligations as a Percentage of Disposable Personal Income: 1990 to 2007**

[**As of end of year, seasonally adjusted.** Household debt service ratio is an estimate of the ratio of debt payments to disposable personal income. Debt payments consist of the estimated required payments on outstanding mortgage and consumer debt. The financial obligations ratio adds automobile lease payments, rental payments on tenant-occupied property, homeowners' insurance, and property tax payments to the debt service ratio]

Year	Household debt service ratio	Financial obligations ratio			Year	Household debt service ratio	Financial obligations ratio		
		Total	Home-owner	Renter			Total	Home-owner	Renter
1990 . . .	11.97	17.35	24.71	15.48	2003 . . .	13.50	18.53	26.79	16.85
1995 . . .	11.84	17.45	26.89	15.17	2004 . . .	13.56	18.51	26.21	16.99
2000 . . .	12.88	18.24	30.55	15.76	2005 . . .	14.03	19.00	26.07	17.62
2001 . . .	13.38	18.85	31.32	16.32	2006 . . .	14.35	19.33	25.97	18.04
2002 . . .	13.56	18.83	29.10	16.73	2007 . . .	14.31	19.31	25.95	18.02

Source: Board of Governors of the Federal Reserve System, "Household Debt Service and Financial Obligations Ratios"; <http://www.federalreserve.gov/releases/housedebt/default.htm>.

Table 1136. **Selected Financial Institutions— Number and Assets by Asset Size: 2007**

[**As of December. 11,176.5 represents $11,176,500,000,000**. FDIC = Federal Deposit Insurance Corporation]

Asset size	Number of institutions			Assets (bil. dol.)		
	F.D.I.C.-insured		Credit unions [1]	F.D.I.C.-insured		Credit unions [1]
	Commercial banks	Savings institutions		Commercial banks [2]	Savings institutions	
Total	**7,282**	**1,251**	**8,101**	**11,176.5**	**1,862.6**	**753.4**
Less than $25.0 million	474	74	5,120	8.1	1.0	38.1
$25.0 million to $49.9 million	978	120	1,008	36.5	4.5	35.8
$50.0 million to $99.9 million	1,610	180	754	118.0	13.3	53.0
$100.0 million to $499.9 million . . .	3,194	566	915	707.8	136.2	197.9
$500.0 million to $999.9 million . . .	514	154	178	353.6	111.8	122.1
$1.0 billion to $2.9 billion	308	93	104	507.5	147.8	161.8
$3.0 billion or more	204	64	22	9,445.0	1,448.0	144.8
	Percent distribution					
Total	**100.0**	**100.0**	**100.0**	**100.0**	**100.0**	**100.0**
Less than $25.0 million	6.5	5.9	63.2	0.1	0.1	5.1
$25.0 million to $49.9 million	13.4	9.6	12.4	0.3	0.2	4.7
$50.0 million to $99.9 million	22.1	14.4	9.3	1.1	0.7	7.0
$100.0 million to $499.9 million . . .	43.9	45.2	11.3	6.3	7.3	26.3
$500.0 million to $999.9 million . . .	7.1	12.3	2.2	3.2	6.0	16.2
$1.0 billion to $2.9 billion	4.2	7.4	1.3	4.5	7.9	21.5
$3.0 billion or more	2.8	5.1	0.3	84.5	77.7	19.2

[1] Source: National Credit Union Administration, *National Credit Union Administration Year-end Statistics 2007*. Excludes nonfederally insured state chartered credit unions and federally insured corporate credit unions. [2] Includes foreign branches of U.S. banks.

Source: Except as noted, U.S. Federal Deposit Insurance Corporation, *Statistics on Banking, 2007*.

Table 1137. FDIC-Insured Financial Institutions—Number, Assets, and Liabilities: 1990 to 2007

[In billions of dollars, except as indicated (4,649 represents $4,649,000,000,000). As of Dec. 31. 2007 data preliminary. Includes island areas. Except as noted, includes foreign branches of U.S. banks]

Item	1990	1995	2000	2002	2003	2004	2005	2006	2007
Commercial bank offices, total [1]	**63,205**	**66,799**	**73,174**	**74,790**	**75,985**	**78,473**	**80,967**	**83,860**	**86,150**
Number of main offices	12,347	9,943	8,315	7,888	7,770	7,631	7,526	7,401	7,283
Number of branches	50,858	56,856	64,859	66,902	68,215	70,842	73,441	76,459	78,867
Savings institutions, total	**2,815**	**2,030**	**1,589**	**1,466**	**1,411**	**1,345**	**1,307**	**1,279**	**1,251**
Number of financial institutions reporting	15,158	11,970	9,905	9,354	9,181	8,976	8,833	8,680	8,533
Assets, total [2]	**4,649**	**5,338**	**7,462**	**8,436**	**9,075**	**10,106**	**10,878**	**11,860**	**13,039**
Net loans and leases	2,867	3,198	4,576	4,968	5,349	6,037	6,640	7,156	7,805
Real estate loans	1,586	1,690	2,396	2,850	3,144	3,680	4,141	4,508	4,781
1–4 family residential mortgages . .	859	1,006	1,340	1,513	1,611	1,833	2,042	2,176	2,245
Commercial real estate.	328	349	525	628	682	752	826	904	968
Construction and development. . . .	171	90	197	245	272	338	450	565	629
Home equity loans [3].	86	98	151	256	346	491	534	559	607
Commercial and industrial loans	646	674	1,086	953	922	968	1,086	1,215	1,440
Loans to individuals.	451	576	672	772	848	930	949	955	1,059
Credit cards and related plans	142	224	266	292	339	399	396	385	422
Farm loans	33	40	49	47	47	49	52	54	57
Other loans and leases	245	294	448	435	478	496	494	504	572
Less: Reserve for losses	65	60	71	85	86	82	77	78	102
Less: Unearned income	29	15	3	4	3	3	3	2	2
Securities	890	1,099	1,361	1,633	1,771	1,860	1,893	1,980	1,954
Domestic office assets	4,259	4,753	6,702	7,684	8,251	9,160	9,824	10,557	11,480
Foreign office assets.	390	585	760	752	824	945	1,054	1,303	1,559
Liabilities and capital, total	**4,649**	**5,338**	**7,462**	**8,436**	**9,075**	**10,106**	**10,878**	**11,860**	**13,039**
Noninterest-bearing deposits	511	641	802	1,002	1,028	1,173	1,267	1,270	1,256
Interest-bearing deposits	3,127	3,129	4,113	4,566	4,926	5,412	5,874	6,555	7,159
Other borrowed funds	569	849	1,467	1,571	1,735	1,905	2,063	2,121	2,517
Subordinated debt	28	46	90	99	107	119	131	161	185
Other liabilities.	128	238	356	422	450	459	424	505	569
Equity capital.	286	436	634	776	831	1,039	1,119	1,248	1,352
Domestic office deposits	3,344	3,315	4,208	4,911	5,213	5,719	6,221	6,631	6,912
Foreign office deposits	293	454	707	658	741	866	921	1,194	1,503
Estimated insured deposits [4]	2,629	2,662	3,054	3,382	3,452	3,621	3,890	4,147	4,287

[1] Includes insured branches of foreign banks that file a Call Report. [2] Includes other items not shown separately. [3] For one- to four-family residential properties. [4] Excludes foreign office deposits which are uninsured.

Source: U.S. Federal Deposit Insurance Corporation, *The FDIC Quarterly Banking Profile, Historical Statistics on Banking*, annual; *Statistics on Banking*, annual; and *FDIC Quarterly Banking Profile Graph Book*.

Table 1138. FDIC-Insured Financial Institutions—Income and Selected Measures of Financial Condition: 1990 to 2007

[In billions of dollars, except as indicated (437.7 represents $437,700,000,000). 2007 data preliminary. Includes island areas. Includes foreign branches of U.S. banks]

Item	1990	1995	2000	2002	2003	2004	2005	2006	2007
Interest income	437.7	373.4	512.2	429.5	404.6	418.4	522.0	643.5	725.2
Interest expense	295.9	190.7	276.5	152.9	122.6	123.3	205.0	313.4	372.3
Net interest income	141.8	182.7	235.7	276.6	281.9	295.2	317.0	330.1	352.8
Provisions for loan losses	41.4	14.7	32.0	51.5	37.3	29.0	29.7	29.5	68.2
Noninterest income.	62.2	89.5	164.8	183.5	202.7	202.6	223.4	240.4	233.4
Percent of net operating revenue [1]	30.5	32.9	41.1	39.9	41.8	40.7	41.3	42.1	39.8
Noninterest expense.	144.2	171.6	241.6	263.7	279.7	295.5	317.4	332.3	362.5
Income taxes.	9.1	30.3	43.7	51.9	58.9	58.6	64.6	68.1	47.0
Net income	11.3	56.4	81.7	105.0	120.5	122.3	133.9	145.2	105.5
PERFORMANCE RATIOS									
Return on assets [2] (percent)	0.24	1.10	1.14	1.30	1.38	1.28	1.28	1.28	0.86
Return on equity [3] (percent).	3.95	13.63	13.55	14.12	15.04	13.20	12.43	12.30	8.17
Net interest margin [4] (percent)	3.47	4.05	3.78	3.96	3.73	3.54	3.47	3.31	3.29
Net charge-offs [5]	34.8	14.4	26.3	47.0	40.8	32.0	31.6	27.0	43.9
Net charge-offs to loans and leases, total (percent).	1.19	0.46	0.59	0.97	0.78	0.56	0.49	0.39	0.59
Net charge-off rate, credit card loans (percent). . .	3.39	3.39	4.37	5.47	5.75	4.99	4.74	3.44	4.06
CONDITION RATIOS									
Equity capital to assets (percent).	6.16	8.16	8.49	9.20	9.15	10.28	10.28	10.52	10.37
Noncurrent assets plus other real estate owned to assets [6] (percent)	3.16	0.92	0.71	0.90	0.75	0.53	0.50	0.54	0.94
Percentage of banks losing money	16.5	3.1	7.5	6.7	6.0	6.0	6.2	7.9	11.6
Number of problem institutions	1,492	193	94	136	116	80	52	50	76
Assets of problem institutions	640	31	24	39	30	28	7	8	22
Number of failed/assisted institutions	169	6	7	11	3	4	–	–	3

– Represents zero. [1] Net operating revenue equals net interest income plus noninterest income. [2] Net income (including securities transactions and nonrecurring items) as a percentage of average total assets. [3] Net income as a percentage of average total equity capital. [4] Interest income less interest expense as a percentage of average earning assets (i.e. the profit margin a bank earns on its loans and investments). [5] Total loans and leases charged off (removed from balance sheet because of uncollectibility), less amounts recovered on loans and leases previously charged off. [6] Noncurrent assets: the sum of loans, leases, debt securities, and other assets that are 90 days or more past due, or in nonaccrual status. Other real estate owned: primarily foreclosed property.

Source: U.S. Federal Deposit Insurance Corporation, *Annual Report; Statistics on Banking*, annual; and *FDIC Quarterly Banking Profile*.

Table 1139. **FDIC-Insured Financial Institutions by Asset Size: 2007**

[(11,176 represents $11,176,000,000,000). Preliminary. See headnote, Table 1138]

Item	Unit	Total	Less than $100 million	$100 million to $1 billion	$1 billion to $10 billion	Greater than $10 billion
COMMERCIAL BANKS						
Institutions reporting	Number . . .	7,282	3,065	3,706	425	86
Assets, total	Bil. dol. . . .	11,176	163	1,062	1,113	8,838
Deposits	Bil. dol. . . .	7,309	134	855	792	5,528
Net income	Bil. dol. . . .	100	1	11	12	76
Return on assets	Percent . . .	0.95	0.82	1.06	1.08	0.92
Return on equity	Percent . . .	9.29	6.00	10.34	9.47	9.22
Equity capital to assets	Percent . . .	10.24	13.38	10.34	11.54	10.00
Noncurrent assets plus other real estate owned to assets	Percent . . .	0.85	0.94	1.10	1.05	0.80
Net charge-offs to loans and leases	Percent . . .	0.61	0.24	0.27	0.47	0.70
Percentage of banks losing money	Percent . . .	10.7	16.9	6.4	4.7	7.0
SAVINGS INSTITUTIONS						
Institutions reporting	Number . . .	1,251	375	719	124	33
Assets, total	Bil. dol. . . .	1,863	19	248	308	1,288
Deposits	Bil. dol. . . .	1,106	14	185	216	690
Net income	Bil. dol. . . .	6	(Z)	2	2	2
Return on assets	Percent . . .	0.32	0.21	0.68	0.71	0.21
Return on equity	Percent . . .	2.71	1.25	6.00	6.59	1.73
Equity capital to assets	Percent . . .	11.17	16.80	11.29	10.69	11.14
Noncurrent assets plus other real estate owned to assets	Percent . . .	1.45	1.07	0.89	1.13	1.60
Net charge-offs to loans and leases	Percent . . .	0.46	0.14	0.13	0.23	0.56
Percentage of banks losing money	Percent . . .	16.5	28.3	11.0	11.0	20.8

Z Less than $500 million.

Source: U.S. Federal Deposit Insurance Corporation, *Annual Report; Statistics on Banking*, annual; and *FDIC Quarterly Banking Profile*. See also <http://www.fdic.gov/bank/index.html>.

Table 1140. **FDIC-Insured Financial Institutions—Number and Assets by State and Island Areas: 2007**

[**In billions of dollars, except as indicated (13,038.8 represents $13,038,800,000,000). As of Dec. 31.** Information is obtained primarily from the Federal Financial Institutions Examination Council (FFIEC) Call Reports and the Office of Thrift Supervision's Thrift Financial Reports. Data are based on the location of each reporting institution's main office. Reported data may include assets located outside of the reporting institution's home state]

State or island area	Number of insti- tutions	Assets by asset size of bank				State or island area	Number of insti- tutions	Assets by asset size of bank			
		Total	Less than $1 bil.	$1 bil. to $10 bil.	Greater than $10 bil.			Total	Less than $1 bil.	$1 bil. to $10 bil.	Greater than $10 bil.
Total . . .	**8,533**	**13,038.8**	**1,492.0**	**1,420.3**	**10,126.5**	NV	44	1,684.4	5.4	25.6	1,653.5
						NH	24	9.9	7.9	2.0	–
AL	160	248.6	28.5	13.3	206.8	NJ	127	147.7	30.5	60.4	56.9
AK	6	4.4	1.1	3.3	–	NM	53	18.7	8.6	10.2	–
AZ	57	19.0	8.4	10.7	–	NY	195	509.1	39.9	110.6	358.6
AR	150	51.7	28.6	23.1	–	NC	111	2,184.2	26.2	24.5	2,133.5
CA	312	452.4	60.8	151.2	240.4	ND	97	20.4	12.2	8.2	–
CO	160	51.2	29.4	21.8	–	OH	265	2,008.9	41.6	27.7	1,939.6
CT	56	64.9	15.5	20.2	29.2	OK	259	72.9	32.6	12.6	27.6
DE	33	605.2	4.0	21.5	579.6	OR	40	37.7	7.5	15.6	14.7
DC	7	1.4	1.4	–	–	PA	246	478.8	57.4	87.4	334.0
FL	317	160.2	67.9	67.3	25.0	RI	13	172.0	2.3	5.1	164.6
GA	352	284.8	72.7	37.0	175.1	SC	93	53.0	22.4	16.8	13.8
HI	9	38.1	1.4	13.7	23.0	SD	89	571.6	12.0	12.8	546.8
ID	19	7.6	5.5	2.1	–	TN	203	94.3	42.3	15.3	36.7
IL	670	395.6	105.8	88.2	201.5	TX	659	345.9	96.6	93.9	155.4
IN	162	71.9	32.9	38.9	–	UT	67	365.4	12.4	25.6	327.3
IA	391	59.6	49.8	9.8	–	VT	16	8.2	3.7	4.6	–
KS	357	62.6	41.2	21.4	–	VA	119	375.4	31.8	24.2	319.4
KY	206	48.2	34.3	13.9	–	WA	97	75.1	24.2	28.5	22.3
LA	162	49.5	32.4	6.1	11.0	WV	68	23.0	9.8	13.3	–
ME	33	63.0	12.4	5.2	45.5	WI	296	152.3	54.3	23.0	75.1
MD	98	40.4	22.3	18.1	–	WY	43	7.8	6.7	1.1	–
MA	181	238.0	55.7	37.3	145.1	AS	1	0.1	0.1	–	–
MI	164	165.8	31.5	15.7	118.6	GU	3	1.1	1.1	–	–
MN	444	106.7	51.5	9.1	46.1	FM	1	0.1	0.1	–	–
MS	97	54.4	18.6	22.6	13.2	PR	10	100.8	–	39.9	60.9
MO	361	114.4	53.4	35.4	25.6	VI	3	0.2	0.2	–	–
MT	79	17.6	11.0	6.6	–						
NE	248	42.5	24.3	18.2	–						

– Represents zero.

Source: U.S. Federal Deposit Insurance Corporation, *Statistics on Banking*, annual.

U.S. Census Bureau, Statistical Abstract of the United States: 2009

Table 1141. **FDIC-Insured Financial Institutions—Number of Offices and Deposits by State: 2007**

[As of June 30 (6,702.2 represents $6,702,200,000,000). Includes insured U.S. branches of foreign banks. The term "offices" includes both main offices and branches. "Banking office" is defined to include all offices and facilities that actually hold deposits, and does not include loan production offices, computer centers, and other nondeposit installations, such as automated teller machines (ATMs). Several institutions have designated home offices that do not accept deposits; these have been included to provide a more complete listing of all offices. The figures for each geographical area only include deposits of offices located within that area. Based on the Summary of Deposits survey]

State	Number of offices	Total deposits (bil. dol.)	State	Number of offices	Total deposits (bil. dol.)	State	Number of offices	Total deposits (bil. dol.)
Total [1]	97,272	6,702.2	IA	1,630	56.6	NC	2,676	206.3
U.S.	96,622	6,636.0	KS	1,543	54.0	ND	442	13.9
			KY	1,814	63.2	OH	4,082	209.1
AL	1,496	74.3	LA	1,606	73.0	OK	1,349	57.4
AK	133	6.9	ME	517	20.0	OR	1,086	47.9
AZ	1,279	80.0	MD	1,805	95.0	PA	4,758	259.4
AR	1,490	47.4	MA	2,177	180.8	RI	246	25.5
CA	7,122	751.0	MI	3,137	154.7	SC	1,370	64.1
CO	1,612	81.3	MN	1,842	106.2	SD	481	63.3
CT	1,285	81.0	MS	1,180	41.6	TN	2,270	107.2
DE	269	160.2	MO	2,376	102.6	TX	6,573	450.0
DC	228	25.6	MT	374	14.6	UT	615	181.7
FL	5,599	373.9	NE	1,067	36.0	VT	273	9.9
GA	2,813	177.9	NV	565	188.1	VA	2,593	182.2
HI	288	26.8	NH	432	21.5	WA	1,898	105.7
ID	522	17.7	NJ	3,351	222.5	WV	653	25.9
IL	4,951	338.9	NM	505	21.9	WI	2,366	109.7
IN	2,390	88.6	NY	5,267	722.8	WY	226	10.6

[1] Includes Puerto Rico and other areas, not shown separately.

Source: U.S. Federal Deposit Insurance Corporation, *Bank and Thrift Branch Office Data Book*, annual.

Table 1142. **U.S. Banking Offices of Foreign Banks—Summary: 1990 to 2007**

[In billions of dollars, except as indicated (791 represents $791,000,000,000). As of December. Data cover foreign-bank branches and agencies in the 50 states and the District of Columbia, New York investment companies (through September 1996); U.S. commercial banks of which more than 25 percent are owned by foreign banks, and International Banking Facilities. Foreign banks are those owned by institutions located outside of the United States and its affiliated insular areas. Beginning 2000, data include U.S. chartered entities that are completely or partially owned by foreign companies that are not banks themselves]

Item	1990	2000	2002	2003	2004	2005	2006	2007	Share [1] 1990	Share [1] 2000	Share [1] 2005	Share [1] 2007
Assets	791	1,303	1,392	1,431	1,712	2,025	2,404	2,754	21.4	20.1	21.7	23.7
Loans, total	398	535	500	478	603	746	852	986	18.0	13.8	14.0	15.0
Business	193	300	246	203	217	260	324	392	30.8	26.7	24.7	27.2
Deposits	384	708	705	724	919	1,049	1,244	1,488	14.5	17.7	18.2	21.8

[1] Percent of "domestically owned" commercial banks plus U.S. offices of foreign banks.

Source: Board of Governors of the Federal Reserve System, "Share Data for U.S. Offices of Foreign Banks"; published March 2008; <http://www.federalreserve.gov/releases/lba/Share/SHRTBL1.html>.

Table 1143. **Federal and State-Chartered Credit Unions—Summary: 1990 to 2007**

[Except as noted, as of December 31 (36,241 represents 36,241,000). Federal data include District of Columbia, Puerto Rico, Guam, and Virgin Islands. Excludes state-insured, privately insured, and noninsured state-chartered credit unions and corporate central credit unions, which have mainly other credit unions as members]

Year	Operating credit unions Federal	Operating credit unions State	Number of failed institutions [1]	Members (1,000) Federal	Members (1,000) State	Assets (mil. dol.) Federal	Assets (mil. dol.) State	Loans outstanding (mil. dol.) Federal	Loans outstanding (mil. dol.) State	Savings (mil. dol.) Federal	Savings (mil. dol.) State
1990	8,511	4,349	164	36,241	19,454	130,073	68,133	83,029	44,102	117,892	62,082
1995	7,329	4,358	26	42,163	24,927	193,781	112,860	120,514	71,606	170,300	99,838
2000	6,336	3,980	29	43,883	33,705	242,881	195,363	163,851	137,485	210,188	169,053
2001	6,118	3,866	22	43,817	35,560	270,123	231,432	170,326	152,112	235,201	201,923
2002	5,953	3,735	15	44,600	36,300	301,238	255,837	181,768	160,881	261,819	222,372
2003	5,776	3,593	13	46,153	36,287	336,611	273,572	202,898	173,236	291,484	236,856
2004	5,572	3,442	21	46,858	36,710	358,701	288,294	223,878	190,376	308,317	247,804
2005	5,393	3,302	27	47,612	36,895	377,804	300,868	249,515	208,728	321,820	255,804
2006	5,189	3,173	22	48,262	37,487	394,125	315,817	270,420	223,917	333,914	267,275
2007	5,036	3,065	17	48,474	38,363	417,578	335,885	289,169	237,755	349,100	283,298

[1] 1990 for year ending September 30; 1995 reflects 15-month period from October 1994 through December 1995; beginning 2000, reflects calendar year. A failed institution is defined as a credit union which has ceased operation because it was involuntarily liquidated or merged with assistance from the National Credit Union Share Insurance Fund.

Source: National Credit Union Administration, *Annual Report of the National Credit Union Administration*, and unpublished data.

Table 1144. Noncash Payments by Method of Payment and ATM Cash Withdrawals: 2003 and 2006

[81.4 represents 81,400,000,000. Based on two data collection efforts to estimate the annual number and value of significant types of noncash payments. Estimates of check payments and ATM withdrawals were based on findings from the Depository Institutions Payments Study (2007 DI study). Electronic payments volume estimates were based on findings from the Electronic Payments Study and supplemented by the 2007 DI study. The Depository Institutions Payments Study collected the number and value of different types of payments from deposit accounts at a representative, random sample of depository institutions. A total of 1,437 depository institutions (commercial banks, savings institutions, and credit unions) from a stratified random sample of 2,700 institutions provided data for the survey. The Electronic Payments Study estimated the number and value of electronic payments in the United States for calendar year 2006. Data were collected by surveying payment networks and card issuers. Of the 73 organizations asked to participate, 65 of the largest organizations provided data. Respondents to this study collectively accounted for an estimated 99.8 percent of the electronic transactions and 99.9 percent of the electronic payments value in the United States]

Method of payment	Transactions (bil.)		Value (tril. dol.)		Average value per transaction (dol.)	
	2003	2006	2003	2006	2003	2006
Noncash payments, total	**81.4**	**93.3**	**67.6**	**75.8**	**830**	**813**
Checks (paid)	37.3	30.6	41.1	41.7	1,104	1,366
Commercial checks	36.8	30.2	40.8	41.5	1,108	1,373
Commercial banks	29.7	25.2	38.4	39.0	1,293	1,551
Credit unions	4.2	2.7	0.9	0.9	219	326
Savings institutions	3.0	2.3	1.5	1.6	511	675
U.S. Treasury checks	0.3	0.2	0.3	0.2	1,154	1,203
Postal money orders.	0.2	0.2	(Z)	(Z)	146	164
Electronic payments.	44.1	62.7	26.4	34.1	599	544
Automated Clearing House (ACH).	8.8	14.6	24.1	31.0	2,754	2,122
Debit cards	15.6	25.3	0.6	1.0	40	39
Signature [1]	10.3	16.0	0.4	0.6	42	40
PIN [2]	5.3	9.4	0.2	0.3	38	37
Credit cards [3]	19.0	21.7	1.7	2.1	89	98
Electronic benefits transfer cards.	0.8	1.1	(Z)	(Z)	26	27
Memo:						
ATM cash withdrawals	**5.9**	**5.8**	**0.5**	**0.6**	**85**	**99**
Checks (written) [4].	37.6	33.1	41.2	42.4	1,096	1,280
Checks converted to ACH	0.3	2.6	0.1	0.7	187	267

Z Less than $50 billion.   [1] Signature debit card payments are made like credit card payments, but use funds from transaction deposit accounts.   [2] PIN debit card payments also use funds from transaction deposit accounts and typically enter the entry of the same personal identification number (PIN) used to access automated teller machines (ATMs). Excludes a portion estimated to have been returned to the customer as cash.   [3] Credit cards include both general purpose and private-label cards.   [4] Includes the use of checks as source documents to initiate electronic payments.

Source: Board of Governors of the Federal Reserve System, "The 2007 Federal Reserve Payments Study"; published 10 December 2007; <http://www.frbservices.org/files/communications/pdf/research/2007paymentsstudy.pdf>.

Table 1145. Percentage of Households Using Selected Electronic Banking Technologies: 1995 to 2004

[Covers only those households that access services (other than by check or credit card) at a bank, thrift institution, or credit union. Based on sample surveys. For details on the Survey of Consumer Finances, see Appendix III and the Web site of the Federal Reserve Board: <www.federalreserve.gov/boarddocs/surveys>. The Reuters/University of Michigan Survey of Consumers is based on data from approximately 1,000 respondents. For details, see the Web site of the University of Michigan: <www.umich.edu>]

Technology	Survey of Consumer Finances				Reuters/ University of Michigan Survey of Consumers	
	1995	1998	2001	2004	1999	2003
ELECTRONIC						
Direct deposit of any type.	53	67	71	75	65	70
ATM card	35	55	57	65	59	65
Debit card [1]	20	37	50	62	(NA)	54
Preauthorized debts	25	40	43	50	31	46
Automated phone system.	(NA)	26	22	20	40	44
Computer banking	4	7	19	34	10	32
Smart card [2]	1	2	3	(NA)	(NA)	6
Prepaid card [2]	(NA)	(NA)	(NA)	(NA)	(NA)	73
NONELECTRONIC						
In person	87	81	78	78	(NA)	(NA)
Mail	59	55	51	51	(NA)	(NA)
Phone (talk in person)	(NA)	43	42	42	(NA)	(NA)

NA Not available.   [1] A debit card is a card that automatically deducts the amount of a purchase from the money in an account.   [2] A smart card is a type of payment card containing a computer chip which is set to hold a sum of money. As the card is used, purchases are subtracted from that sum. Prepaid cards are cards that contain a stored value, or a value that has been paid up-front, allowing you to use the card much like cash. As you use the card, the prepaid value is drawn down. Examples are phone cards and gift cards. Smart cards are different from prepaid cards in that you can add money to the card at special machines designed for smart cards or sometimes at ATMs.

Source: Board of Governors of the Federal Reserve System, *Federal Reserve Bulletin*, winter 2004 and unpublished data.

U.S. Census Bureau, Statistical Abstract of the United States: 2009

Table 1146. Percent of U.S. Households That Use Selected Payment Instruments: 1995 and 2004

[In percent. Based on Survey of Consumer Finances conducted by the Board of Governors of the Federal Reserve System; see Appendix III]

Age and education of head of household	Any of these instruments		ATM [1]		Debit card		Direct deposit		Automatic bill paying		Software [2]	
	1995	2004	1995	2004	1995	2004	1995	2004	1995	2004	2001	2004
All households	**77.7**	**90.4**	**62.5**	**74.4**	**17.6**	**59.3**	**46.7**	**71.2**	**21.8**	**47.4**	**18.0**	**19.3**
Under 30 years old.	76.3	87.3	72.3	83.0	24.4	74.4	31.0	54.0	17.7	36.5	17.0	20.4
30 to 60 years old	78.7	90.3	68.6	82.3	19.7	67.6	42.8	68.2	24.4	50.3	22.0	21.9
61 years old and over . . .	76.1	91.9	44.2	51.6	9.6	32.5	63.3	87.0	18.2	46.5	9.0	12.8
No college degree	71.4	86.2	54.7	67.4	14.3	54.9	40.3	64.3	18.1	39.5	10.9	12.4
College degree	91.8	97.5	80.4	86.4	25.2	67.0	61.0	83.2	30.1	61.1	31.8	31.3

[1] The question on ATMs asked whether any member of the household had an ATM card, not whether the member used it. The other questions asked about usage of other instruments. [2] The question on software asked whether the respondent or spouse/partner uses any type of computer software to help in managing their money.

Source: Mester, Loretta J., "Changes in the Use of Electronic Means of Payment: 1995–2004," *Business Review*, Second Quarter 2006, published by Federal Reserve Bank of Philadelphia. See also <http://www.philadelphiafed.org/files/br/brq2-2006-4changes-electronic-means.pdf>.

Table 1147. Debit Cards—Holders, Number, Transactions, and Volume, 2000 and 2006, and Projections, 2010

[176 represents 176,000,000]

Type of debit card	Cardholders (mil.)		Number of cards (mil.)			Number of point-of-sale transactions (mil.)			Purchase volume (bil. dol.)		
	2006	2010, proj.	2000	2006	2010, proj.	2000	2006	2010, proj.	2000	2006	2010, proj.
Total [1]	176	185	235	354	484	8,291	26,053	40,953	311	1,025	1,643
Bank [2]	156	164	137	313	440	5,290	16,323	26,183	210	657	1,021
EFT systems [3]	175	184	223	271	281	2,979	9,712	14,723	100	366	619
Other [4]	11	13	11	11	13	22	17	48	1	1	2

[1] Cardholders may hold more than one type of card. Bank cards and EFT cards are the same pieces of plastic that carry multiple brands. The total card figure shown does not include any duplication. [2] Visa and MasterCard debit cards. [3] Cards issued by financial institution members of regional and national switches such as Star, Interlink, Pulse, Nyce, etc. EFT = Electronic funds transfer. [4] Retail cards such as those issued by supermarkets.

Source: The Nilson Report, Carpinteria, CA, Twice-monthly newsletter. (Copyright used by permission.)

Table 1148. Credit Cards—Holders, Number, Spending, and Debt, 2000 and 2006, and Projections, 2010

[159 represents 159,000,000]

Type of credit card	Cardholders (mil.)			Number of cards (mil.)			Credit card purchase volume (bil. dol.)			Credit card debt outstanding (bil. dol.)		
	2000	2006	2010, proj.	2000	2006	2010, proj.	2000	2006	2010, proj.	2000	2006	2010, proj.
Total [1]	159	173	181	1,425	1,488	1,618	1,242	1,950	2,747	680	886	1,177
Bank [2]	(NA)	(NA)	(NA)	455	561	698	768	1,251	1,720	480	641	838
Store	114	114	114	597	574	569	120	142	160	92	98	110
Oil company	76	59	55	98	77	76	45	55	70	5	8	10
Other [3]	132	122	113	275	276	275	308	503	798	103	139	219

NA Not available. [1] Cardholders may hold more than one type of card. [2] Visa and MasterCard credit cards. [3] Includes Universal Air Travel Plan (UATP), phone cards, automobile rental, and miscellaneous cards; credit card purchase volume excludes phone cards. Except for data on cardholders, also includes Discover and American Express.

Source: The Nilson Report, Carpinteria, CA, Twice-monthly newsletter. (Copyright used by permission.)

Table 1149. Usage of General Purpose Credit Cards by Families: 1995 to 2004

[General purpose credit cards include Mastercard, Visa, Optima, and Discover cards. Excludes cards used only for business purposes. All dollar figures are given in constant 2004 dollars based on consumer price index data as published by U.S. Bureau of Labor Statistics. Families include one-person units; for definition of family, see text, Section 1. Based on Survey of Consumer Finances; see Appendix III. For definition of median, see Guide to Tabular Presentation]

Age of family head and family income	Percent having a general purpose credit card	Median number of cards	Median new charges on last month's bills (dol.)	Percent having a balance after last month's bills	Median balance (dol.) [1]	Percent of cardholding families who—		
						Almost always pay off the balance	Some-times pay off the balance	Hardly ever pay off the balance
1995, total	66.5	2	200	56.0	1,800	52.4	20.1	27.5
1998, total	67.5	2	200	54.7	2,200	53.8	19.3	26.9
2001, total	72.7	2	200	53.7	1,900	55.3	19.1	25.6
2004, total	**71.5**	**2**	**300**	**56.2**	**2,100**	**55.7**	**20.3**	**24.0**
Under 35 years old	60.6	2	200	66.1	1,500	49.0	20.4	30.6
35 to 44 years old	73.3	2	300	70.8	2,400	41.6	26.2	32.2
45 to 54 years old	77.5	2	300	61.2	3,000	49.3	23.9	26.8
55 to 64 years old	78.2	2	400	46.1	2,500	66.8	16.8	16.5
65 to 74 years old	75.5	2	300	37.7	2,300	70.7	13.4	15.9
75 years old and over	65.4	2	200	32.2	1,100	77.5	12.9	9.7
Less than $10,000	31.5	1	100	59.4	1,200	50.9	17.3	31.9
$10,000 to $24,999	48.6	1	100	59.7	1,200	49.9	17.0	33.1
$25,000 to $49,999	71.2	2	200	64.3	2,000	46.9	20.3	32.8
$50,000 to $99,999	88.2	2	300	56.1	2,800	56.1	22.0	21.8
$100,000 and more	96.6	2	1,200	42.8	3,400	71.1	20.2	8.7

[1] Among families having a balance.

Source: Board of Governors of the Federal Reserve System, unpublished data.

Table 1150. Consumer Credit Outstanding and Finance Rates: 1990 to 2007

[In billions of dollars, except percent (808 represents $808,000,000,000). Covers most short- and intermediate-term credit extended to individuals, excluding loans secured by real estate. Estimated amounts of seasonally adjusted credit outstanding as of end of year; finance rates, annual averages]

Type of credit	1990	1995	2000	2001	2002	2003	2004	2005	2006	2007
Total	**808**	**1,141**	**1,722**	**1,872**	**1,984**	**2,078**	**2,191**	**2,285**	**2,387**	**2,518**
Revolving	239	444	683	716	749	771	800	825	875	942
Nonrevolving [1]	570	698	1,039	1,155	1,235	1,308	1,391	1,460	1,512	1,576
FINANCE RATES (percent)										
Commercial banks:										
New automobiles (48 months)	11.78	9.57	9.34	8.50	7.62	6.93	6.60	7.08	7.72	7.77
Other consumer goods (24 months)	15.46	13.94	13.90	13.22	12.54	11.95	11.89	12.05	12.41	12.39
Credit card plans	18.17	15.99	15.78	14.87	13.40	12.30	12.72	12.51	13.21	13.38
Finance companies:										
New automobiles	12.54	11.19	6.61	5.65	4.29	3.40	4.36	5.46	4.96	4.54
Used automobiles	15.99	14.48	13.55	12.18	10.74	9.72	8.96	9.03	9.67	9.42

[1] Comprises automobile loans and all other loans not included in revolving credit, such as loans for mobile homes, education, boats, trailers, or vacations. These loans may be secured or unsecured.

Source: Board of Governors of the Federal Reserve System, *Statistical Supplement to the Federal Reserve Bulletin*, monthly.

Table 1151. Consumer Credit by Type of Holder: 1990 to 2007

[In billions of dollars (824 represents $824,000,000,000). As of December 31. Not seasonally adjusted]

Type of holder	1990	1995	2000	2001	2002	2003	2004	2005	2006	2007
Total	**824**	**1,168**	**1,741**	**1,892**	**2,000**	**2,104**	**2,219**	**2,314**	**2,418**	**2,551**
Nonfinancial corporations	67	85	81	73	75	58	59	59	57	55
U.S. government	–	9	60	72	80	82	86	90	92	98
Commercial banking	382	502	551	568	603	669	704	707	741	805
Savings institutions	50	40	65	71	69	78	91	109	96	91
Credit unions	92	132	184	190	196	206	215	229	235	239
Government-sponsored enterprises	19	34	37	39	37	21	–	–	–	–
Asset-backed securities issuers	77	213	528	598	633	597	571	604	664	682
Finance companies	138	152	234	280	308	393	492	517	534	580

– Represents or rounds to zero.

Source: Board of Governors of the Federal Reserve System, "Federal Reserve Statistical Release, Z.1, Flow of Funds Accounts of the United States"; published: 6 March 2008; <http://www.federalreserve.gov/releases/z1/20080306/>.

Banking, Finance, and Insurance 725

Table 1152. **Mortgage Debt Outstanding by Type of Property and Holder: 1990 to 2007**

[In billions of dollars (3,798 represents $3,798,000,000,000). As of December 31]

Type of property and holder	1990	1995	2000	2001	2002	2003	2004	2005	2006	2007
Total mortgages [1]	**3,798**	**4,545**	**6,786**	**7,494**	**8,399**	**9,395**	**10,665**	**12,096**	**13,500**	**14,557**
Home [2]	2,621	3,459	5,127	5,678	6,437	7,228	8,271	9,374	10,444	11,136
Multifamily residential	288	276	405	446	485	565	618	688	741	831
Commercial	821	739	1,171	1,281	1,381	1,508	1,680	1,933	2,207	2,473
Farm	68	72	85	89	95	94	97	102	109	117
Household sector	139	111	100	105	113	118	126	132	135	141
State and local government	110	114	131	130	124	133	141	150	158	167
Commercial banking	849	1,090	1,660	1,790	2,058	2,256	2,596	2,958	3,403	3,633
Savings institutions	802	597	723	758	781	871	1,057	1,153	1,074	1,095
Credit unions	50	66	125	141	159	183	213	246	277	311
Life insurance companies	268	213	236	243	250	261	273	285	304	323
Government-sponsored enterprises (GSE)	156	250	264	297	357	622	629	589	607	641
Agency- and GSE-backed mortgage pools	1,020	1,571	2,493	2,832	3,159	3,327	3,375	3,542	3,837	4,443
Asset-backed securities issuers	68	248	618	740	851	1,022	1,460	2,129	2,721	2,893
Finance companies	114	105	238	258	330	370	476	541	594	533
Real estate investment trusts	8	14	19	18	30	50	119	159	171	148
HOME MORTGAGES [2]										
Total [1]	**2,621**	**3,459**	**5,127**	**5,678**	**6,437**	**7,228**	**8,271**	**9,374**	**10,444**	**11,136**
Household sector	129	96	87	94	100	106	112	119	125	131
Commercial banking	433	650	970	1,028	1,227	1,356	1,581	1,793	2,082	2,201
Savings institutions	600	482	594	620	631	703	874	954	868	879
Credit unions	50	66	125	141	159	183	213	246	277	311
Government-sponsored enterprises (GSE)	119	209	210	231	277	515	508	455	457	445
Agency- and GSE-backed mortgage pools	991	1,543	2,426	2,749	3,064	3,211	3,256	3,420	3,711	4,302
Asset-backed securities issuers	55	194	386	463	544	664	1,050	1,608	2,092	2,117
Finance companies	80	66	187	210	286	320	422	490	538	474
Real estate investment trusts	–	7	9	9	20	38	104	135	131	104
Memo:										
Home equity loans included above [1, 3]	215	237	408	439	501	593	773	912	1,059	1,120
Commercial banking	115	140	235	259	303	366	484	549	654	692
Savings institutions	60	51	73	78	78	96	121	152	138	177

– Represents or rounds to zero. [1] Includes other holders not shown separately. [2] Mortgages on one- to four-family properties. [3] Loans made under home equity lines of credit and home equity loans secured by junior liens. Excludes home equity loans held by individuals.

Source: Board of Governors of the Federal Reserve System, "Federal Reserve Statistical Release, Z.1, Flow of Funds Accounts of the United States"; published: 6 March 2008; <http://www.federalreserve.gov/releases/z1/20080306/>.

Table 1153. **Characteristics of Conventional First Mortgage Loans for Purchase of Single-Family Homes: 2000 to 2007**

[In percent, except as indicated (234.9 represents $234,900). Annual averages. Covers fully amortized conventional mortgage loans used to purchase single-family nonfarm homes. Excludes refinancing loans, nonamortized and balloon loans, loans insured by the Federal Housing Administration, and loans guaranteed by the Veterans Administration. Based on a sample of mortgage lenders, including savings and loans associations, savings banks, commercial banks, and mortgage companies]

Loan characteristics	New homes						Previously occupied homes					
	2000	2003	2004	2005	2006	2007	2000	2003	2004	2005	2006	2007
Contract interest rate, [1] all loans	7.4	5.7	5.7	5.9	6.5	6.3	7.9	5.7	5.7	5.8	6.5	6.5
Fixed-rate loans	8.0	5.9	6.0	6.1	6.6	6.3	8.2	5.8	6.0	6.0	6.5	6.5
Adjustable-rate loans [2]	6.5	5.1	5.4	5.3	6.2	6.2	7.2	5.0	5.1	5.6	6.4	6.3
Initial fees, charges [3]	0.69	0.63	0.50	0.54	0.67	0.81	0.66	0.32	0.37	0.33	0.33	0.40
Effective interest rate, [4] all loans	7.5	5.8	5.8	5.9	6.6	6.4	8.1	5.7	5.7	5.9	6.6	6.5
Fixed-rate loans	8.2	6.0	6.0	6.2	6.7	6.4	8.3	5.9	6.0	6.0	6.6	6.5
Adjustable-rate loans [2]	6.5	5.2	5.4	5.4	6.2	6.3	7.2	5.0	5.2	5.6	6.4	6.4
Term to maturity (years)	29.2	28.7	28.8	29.2	29.5	29.4	28.6	26.5	27.7	28.3	28.9	29.3
Purchase price ($1,000)	234.9	275.3	293.6	328.5	346.4	360.4	191.8	237.0	253.2	291.3	295.9	286.2
Loan-to-price ratio	77.4	77.9	76.0	75.2	75.4	77.1	77.9	72.6	74.6	74.6	76.9	79.9
Percent of number of loans with adjustable rates	40	21	42	29	21	11	21	17	33	30	22	11

[1] Initial interest rate paid by the borrower as specified in the loan contract. [2] Loans with a contractual provision for periodic adjustments in the contract interest rate. [3] Includes all fees, commissions, discounts, and "points" paid by the borrower, or seller, in order to obtain the loan. Excludes those charges for mortgage, credit, life, or property insurance; for property transfer; and for title search and insurance. [4] Contract interest rate plus fees and charges amortized over a 10-year period.

Source: U.S. Federal Housing Finance Board, *Rates & Terms on Conventional Home Mortgages, Annual Summary.*

Table 1154. Mortgage Originations and Delinquency and Foreclosure Rates: 1990 to 2007

[In percent, except as indicated (459 represents $459,000,000,000). Covers one- to four-family residential nonfarm mortgage loans. Mortgage origination is the making of a new mortgage, including all steps taken by a lender to attract and qualify a borrower, process the mortgage loan, and place it on the lender's books. Based on the National Delinquency Survey which covers 46 million loans on one- to four-unit properties, representing over 80 percent of all 'first-lien' residential mortgage loans outstanding. Loans surveyed were reported by approximately 120 lenders, including mortgage bankers, commercial banks, and thrifts]

Item	1990	2000	2001	2002	2003	2004	2005	2006	2007
MORTGAGE ORIGINATIONS									
Total (bil. dol.)	**459**	**1,139**	**2,243**	**2,854**	**3,812**	**2,773**	**2,908**	**2,726**	**2,330**
Purchase (bil. dol.)	389	905	960	1,097	1,280	1,309	1,512	1,399	1,161
Refinance (bil. dol.)	70	234	1,283	1,757	2,532	1,463	1,397	1,326	1,169
DELINQUENCY RATES [1]									
Total	**4.7**	**4.4**	**5.1**	**5.1**	**4.7**	**4.5**	**4.5**	**4.6**	**5.3**
Prime conventional loans	(NA)	2.3	2.7	2.6	2.5	2.3	2.3	2.4	2.9
Subprime conventional loans	(NA)	11.9	14.0	14.3	12.2	10.8	10.8	12.3	15.6
Federal Housing Administration loans	6.7	9.1	10.8	11.5	12.2	12.2	12.5	12.7	12.7
Veterans Administration loans	6.3	6.8	7.7	7.9	8.0	7.3	7.0	6.7	6.4
FORECLOSURE RATES									
Total loans in foreclosure process [2]	**0.9**	**1.2**	**1.5**	**1.5**	**1.3**	**1.2**	**1.0**	**1.2**	**2.0**
Prime conventional loans	(NA)	0.4	0.5	0.5	0.6	0.5	0.4	0.5	1.0
Subprime conventional loans	(NA)	9.4	9.4	8.0	5.6	3.8	3.3	4.5	8.7
Federal Housing Administration loans	1.3	1.7	2.2	2.8	2.9	2.7	2.3	1.9	2.3
Veterans Administration loans	1.2	1.2	1.3	1.6	1.6	1.5	1.1	1.0	1.1
Loans entering foreclosure process [3]:									
Prime conventional loans	(NA)	0.6	0.8	0.8	0.8	0.8	0.7	0.8	1.3
Subprime conventional loans	(NA)	9.2	9.3	8.5	6.6	5.9	5.6	7.3	11.7
Federal Housing Administration loans	1.7	2.3	2.8	3.3	3.6	3.9	3.4	3.3	3.6
Veterans Administration loans	1.6	1.5	1.7	1.8	1.9	2.0	1.5	1.4	1.6

NA Not available. [1] Number of loans delinquent 30 days or more as percentage of mortgage loans serviced in survey. Annual average of quarterly figures. [2] Percentage of loans in the foreclosure process at year-end, not seasonally adjusted. [3] Percentage of loans entering foreclosure process at year-end, not seasonally adjusted.

Source: Mortgage Bankers Association of America, Washington, DC, "1–4 Family Mortgage Originations 1990–2005"; <http://www.mbaa.org/ResearchandForecasts/MarketEnvironment/1-4FamilyMortgageOriginations1990-2005.htm>; accessed 16 June 2006; *National Delinquency Survey*, quarterly and unpublished data.

Table 1155. Delinquency Rates and Charge-Off Rates on Loans at Insured Commercial Banks: 1990 to 2007

[In percent. Annual averages of quarterly figures, not seasonally adjusted. Delinquent loans are those past due 30 days or more and still accruing interest as well as those in nonaccrual status. They are measured as a percentage of end-of-period loans. Charge-offs, which are the value of loans removed from the books and charged against loss reserves, are measured net of recoveries as a percentage of average loans and annualized]

Type of loan	1990	2000	2001	2002	2003	2004	2005	2006	2007
DELINQUENCY RATES									
Total loan	**5.33**	**2.18**	**2.61**	**2.69**	**2.33**	**1.80**	**1.57**	**1.57**	**2.06**
Real estate	6.10	1.89	2.13	1.99	1.76	1.44	1.37	1.48	2.28
Residential [1]	(NA)	2.11	2.29	2.11	1.83	1.55	1.55	1.73	2.57
Commercial [2]	(NA)	1.49	1.79	1.71	1.54	1.20	1.07	1.12	1.94
Consumer	3.83	3.55	3.67	3.51	3.28	3.08	2.81	2.90	3.13
Credit cards	(NA)	4.50	4.86	4.87	4.47	4.11	3.70	4.01	4.25
Other	(NA)	2.98	3.03	2.79	2.67	2.46	2.24	2.21	2.46
Leases	1.97	1.59	2.11	2.24	1.91	1.33	1.28	1.26	1.20
Commercial and industrial	5.34	2.22	3.08	3.84	3.34	2.19	1.51	1.27	1.23
Agricultural	3.84	2.54	2.63	2.51	2.50	1.68	1.30	1.11	1.21
CHARGE-OFF RATES									
Total loan	**1.44**	**0.66**	**0.95**	**1.07**	**0.86**	**0.60**	**0.54**	**0.42**	**0.60**
Real estate	0.85	0.10	0.19	0.16	0.17	0.09	0.06	0.09	0.23
Residential [1]	(NA)	0.12	0.24	0.16	0.19	0.10	0.08	0.11	0.26
Commercial [2]	(NA)	0.05	0.13	0.15	0.13	0.07	0.05	0.06	0.19
Consumer	1.82	2.36	2.75	3.17	2.91	2.68	2.75	2.05	2.48
Credit cards	3.46	4.46	5.46	6.22	5.64	4.87	4.84	3.64	3.99
Other	1.03	1.14	1.28	1.48	1.44	1.34	1.38	1.06	1.55
Leases	0.66	0.31	0.66	1.08	0.86	0.42	0.58	0.17	0.24
Commercial and industrial	1.29	0.76	1.43	1.75	1.24	0.53	0.26	0.29	0.49
Agricultural	0.21	0.25	0.63	0.45	0.35	0.19	0.07	0.10	0.10

NA Not available. [1] Residential real estate loans include loans secured by one- to four-family properties, including home equity lines of credit. [2] Commercial real estate loans include construction and land development loans, loans secured by multifamily residences, and loans secured by nonfarm, nonresidential real estate.

Source: Federal Financial Institutions Examination Council (FFIEC), *Consolidated Reports of Condition and Income* (1990–2000: FFIEC 031 through 034; beginning 2001: FFIEC 031 & 041).

Table 1156. Money Stock: 1990 to 2007

[In billions of dollars (825 represents $825,000,000,000). As of December. Seasonally adjusted averages of daily figures]

Item	1990	1995	2000	2001	2002	2003	2004	2005	2006	2007
M1, total	**825**	**1,127**	**1,088**	**1,182**	**1,219**	**1,306**	**1,376**	**1,375**	**1,367**	**1,364**
Currency [1]	246	372	531	581	626	663	698	724	749	759
Travelers' checks [2]	8	9	8	8	8	8	8	7	7	6
Demand deposits [3]	277	389	310	336	306	325	343	325	306	293
Other checkable deposits [4]	294	357	238	257	279	310	328	319	305	306
M2, total	**3,279**	**3,641**	**4,931**	**5,451**	**5,801**	**6,062**	**6,422**	**6,692**	**7,036**	**7,447**
M1	825	1,127	1,088	1,182	1,219	1,306	1,376	1,375	1,367	1,364
Non-M1 components of M2	2,454	2,514	3,844	4,269	4,582	4,756	5,045	5,317	5,669	6,083
Retail money funds	358	448	921	982	910	777	697	700	799	976
Savings deposits (including MMDAs [5])	923	1,134	1,878	2,313	2,779	3,169	3,518	3,622	3,699	3,890
Commercial banks	581	775	1,424	1,739	2,061	2,337	2,631	2,772	2,906	3,035
Thrift institutions	342	360	454	573	718	831	887	850	793	855
Small time deposits [6]	1,173	931	1,045	975	892	810	830	996	1,170	1,217
Commercial banks	611	575	700	635	590	537	551	645	758	815
Thrift institutions	563	357	345	340	302	274	279	351	412	402

[1] Currency outside U.S. Treasury, Federal Reserve Banks, and the vaults of depository institutions. [2] Outstanding amount of U.S. dollar-denominated travelers' checks of nonbank issuers. Travelers' checks issued by depository institutions are included in demand deposits. [3] Demand deposits at domestically chartered commercial banks, U.S. branches and agencies of foreign banks, and Edge Act corporations (excluding those amounts held by depository institutions, the U.S. government, and foreign banks and official institutions) less cash items in the process of collection and Federal Reserve float. [4] Negotiable order of withdrawal (NOW) and automatic transfer service (ATS) balances at domestically chartered commercial banks, U.S. branches and agencies of foreign banks, Edge Act corporations, and thrift institutions, credit union share draft balances, and demand deposits at thrift institutions. [5] Money market deposit accounts (MMDAs). [6] Small-denomination time deposits are those issued in amounts of less than $100,000. All Individual Retirement Account (IRA) and Keogh account balances at commercial banks and thrift institutions are subtracted from small time deposits.

Source: Board of Governors of the Federal Reserve System, *Statistical Supplement to the Federal Reserve Bulletin*, monthly, and *Money Stock Measures, Federal Reserve Statistical Release H.6*, weekly.

Table 1157. Money Market Interest Rates and Mortgage Rates: 1980 to 2007

[Percent per year. Annual averages of monthly data, except as indicated]

Type	1980	1990	1995	2000	2001	2002	2003	2004	2005	2006	2007
Federal funds, effective rate	13.35	8.10	5.83	6.24	3.88	1.67	1.13	1.35	3.22	4.97	5.02
Prime rate charged by banks	15.26	10.01	8.83	9.23	6.91	4.67	4.12	4.34	6.19	7.96	8.05
Discount rate [1]	11.77	6.98	5.21	5.73	3.40	1.17	2.12	2.34	4.19	5.96	5.86
Eurodollar deposits, 3-month	14.00	8.16	5.93	6.45	3.70	1.73	1.14	1.55	3.51	5.19	5.32
Large negotiable CDs:											
3-month, secondary market	13.02	8.15	5.92	6.46	3.71	1.73	1.15	1.57	3.51	5.16	5.27
6-month, secondary market	12.94	8.17	5.98	6.59	3.66	1.81	1.17	1.74	3.73	5.24	5.23
Taxable money market funds [2]	12.68	7.82	5.48	5.89	3.67	1.29	0.64	0.82	2.66	4.51	4.70
Tax-exempt money market funds [2]	(NA)	5.45	3.39	3.54	2.24	0.94	0.53	0.66	1.87	2.90	3.13
Certificates of deposit (CDs): [3]											
6-month	(NA)	7.79	4.92	5.09	3.43	1.67	1.02	1.14	2.37	3.29	3.46
1-year	(NA)	7.92	5.39	5.46	3.60	1.98	1.20	1.45	2.77	3.64	3.65
2½-year	(NA)	7.96	5.69	5.64	3.97	2.74	1.77	2.21	3.18	3.75	3.65
5-year	(NA)	8.06	6.00	5.97	4.58	3.96	2.93	3.34	3.75	4.02	3.89
U.S. government securities: [4]											
Secondary market:											
3-month Treasury bill	11.39	7.50	5.49	5.82	3.40	1.61	1.01	1.37	3.15	4.73	4.36
6-month Treasury bill	11.32	7.46	5.56	5.90	3.34	1.68	1.05	1.58	3.39	4.81	4.44
Auction average: [5]											
3-month Treasury bill	11.51	7.51	5.51	5.85	3.45	1.62	1.02	1.38	3.16	4.73	4.41
Home mortgages:											
New-home mortgage yields [6]	12.66	10.05	7.87	7.52	7.00	6.43	5.80	5.77	5.94	6.60	6.40
Conventional, 15 yr. fixed [3]	(NA)	9.73	7.39	7.76	6.53	6.02	5.25	5.23	5.50	6.13	6.11
Conventional, 30 yr. fixed [3]	(NA)	9.97	7.86	8.08	7.01	6.56	5.89	5.86	5.93	6.47	6.40

NA Not available. [1] Rate for the Federal Reserve Bank of New York. Beginning 2003, the rate charged for discounts made and advances extended under the Federal Reserve's primary credit discount window program, which became effective January 9, 2003. The rate replaced that for adjustment credit, which was discontinued after January 8, 2003. [2] 12-month return for period ending December 31. Source: iMoneyNet, Inc., Westborough, MA, *Money Market Insight*, monthly, <http://www.imoneynet.com> (copyright). [3] Annual averages. Source: Bankrate, Inc., North Palm Beach, FL, *Bank Rate Monitor*, weekly (copyright); <http://www.bankrate.com>. [4] Averages based on daily closing bid yields in secondary market, bank discount basis. [5] Averages computed on an issue-date basis; bank discount basis. Source: U.S. Council of Economic Advisors, *Economic Indicators*, monthly. [6] Effective rate (in the primary market) on conventional mortgages, reflecting fees and charges as well as contract rate and assumed, on the average, repayment at end of ten years. Source: U.S. Federal Housing Finance Board, *Rates & Terms on Conventional Home Mortgages, Annual Summary*.

Source: Except as noted, Board of Governors of the Federal Reserve System, *Statistical Supplement to the Federal Reserve Bulletin*, monthly.

Table 1158. **Bond Yields: 1980 to 2007**

[**Percent per year**. Annual averages of daily figures, except as indicated]

Type	1980	1990	1995	2000	2001	2002	2003	2004	2005	2006	2007
U.S. Treasury, constant maturities: [1,2]											
1-year	12.00	7.89	5.94	6.11	3.49	2.00	1.24	1.89	3.62	4.94	4.53
2-year	11.73	8.16	6.15	6.26	3.83	2.64	1.65	2.38	3.85	4.82	4.36
3-year	11.51	8.26	6.25	6.22	4.09	3.10	2.10	2.78	3.93	4.77	4.35
5-year	11.45	8.37	6.38	6.16	4.56	3.82	2.97	3.43	4.05	4.75	4.43
7-year	11.40	8.52	6.50	6.20	4.88	4.30	3.52	3.87	4.15	4.76	4.51
10-year	11.43	8.55	6.57	6.03	5.02	4.61	4.01	4.27	4.29	4.80	4.63
20-year	(NA)	(NA)	6.95	6.23	5.63	5.43	4.96	5.04	4.64	5.00	4.91
State and local govt. bonds, Aaa rating [3]	7.84	6.96	5.79	5.58	5.01	4.87	4.52	4.51	4.28	4.15	4.13
State and local govt. bonds, Baa rating [3]	8.99	7.30	6.05	6.19	5.75	5.63	5.20	5.09	4.86	4.71	4.59
Municipal (Bond Buyer, 20 bonds)	8.55	7.27	5.95	5.71	5.15	5.04	4.75	4.68	4.40	4.40	4.40
High-grade municipal bonds (Standard & Poor's) [4]	8.51	7.25	5.95	5.77	5.19	5.05	4.73	4.63	4.29	4.42	4.42
Corporate Aaa rating seasoned [3,5]	11.94	9.32	7.59	7.62	7.08	6.49	5.66	5.63	5.23	5.59	5.56
Corporate Baa rating seasoned [3]	13.67	10.36	8.20	8.37	7.95	7.80	6.76	6.39	6.06	6.48	6.48
Corporate seasoned, all industries [3]	12.75	9.77	7.83	7.98	7.49	7.10	6.24	6.00	5.57	5.98	6.01

NA Not available. [1] Yields on actively traded non-inflation-indexed issues adjusted to constant maturities. Data from U.S. Treasury. [2] Through 1995, yields are based on closing bid prices quoted by at least five dealers. Beginning 2000, yields are based on closing indicative prices quoted by secondary market participants. [3] Data from Moody's Investors Service, New York, NY. [4] Source: U.S. Council of Economic Advisors, *Economic Indicators*, monthly. [5] Moody's Aaa rates through December 6, 2001, are average of Aaa utility and Aaa industrial bond rates. As of December 7, 2001, these rates are averages of Aaa industrial bonds only.

Source: Except as noted, Board of Governors of the Federal Reserve System, *Statistical Supplement to the Federal Reserve Bulletin*, monthly.

Table 1159. **Volume of Debt Markets by Type of Security: 1990 to 2007**

[**In billions of dollars (1,081 represents $1,081,000,000,000)**. Covers debt markets as represented by the source]

Type of security	1990	1995	2000	2003	2004	2005	2006	2007
NEW ISSUE VOLUME [1]								
Total	**1,081**	**1,640**	**2,569**	**6,743**	**5,524**	**5,715**	**6,221**	**6,122**
U.S. Treasury securities [2]	398	511	312	745	853	746	789	752
Federal agency debt [3]	55	228	447	1,268	882	669	747	942
Municipal	128	160	201	283	360	408	387	429
Mortgage-backed securities [4]	380	348	684	3,071	1,779	1,967	1,988	2,027
Asset-backed securities [5]	44	113	337	600	870	1,172	1,253	865
Corporate debt [6]	77	280	588	776	781	753	1,059	1,106
DAILY TRADING VOLUME								
Total	**111**	**246**	**358**	**750**	**815**	**916**	**890**	**1,008**
U.S. Treasury securities [2,7]	111	193	207	434	499	555	525	567
Federal agency debt [7]	(NA)	24	73	82	79	79	74	83
Municipal [8]	(NA)	(NA)	9	13	15	17	23	25
Mortgage-backed securities [4,7]	(NA)	29	70	206	207	252	255	320
Corporate [6]	(NA)	(NA)	(NA)	16	15	14	14	13
VOLUME OF SECURITIES OUTSTANDING								
Total	**7,745**	**11,229**	**16,961**	**22,023**	**23,693**	**25,270**	**27,383**	**29,729**
U.S. Treasury securities [2]	2,196	3,307	2,967	3,575	3,944	4,166	4,323	4,517
Federal agency debt [9]	435	845	1,855	2,637	2,745	2,614	2,660	2,946
Municipal	1,184	1,294	1,481	1,901	2,031	2,226	2,403	2,617
Mortgage-backed securities [4]	1,333	2,352	3,566	5,239	5,456	5,916	6,492	7,210
Asset-backed securities [5,9]	90	316	1,072	1,694	1,828	1,955	2,130	2,472
Money market instruments [10]	1,157	1,177	2,663	2,520	2,904	3,434	4,008	4,140
Corporate debt [6,9]	1,350	1,938	3,358	4,458	4,785	4,960	5,365	5,825

NA Not available. [1] Covers only long-term issuance. [2] Marketable public debt. [3] Includes overnight discount notes. [4] Includes only Government National Mortgage Association (GNMA), Federal National Mortgage Association (FNMA), Federal Home Loan Mortgage Corporation (FHLMC) mortgage-backed securities (MBS) and collateralized mortgage obligations (CMOs) and private-label MBS/CMOs. [5] Excludes mortgage-backed assets. [6] Includes nonconvertible corporate debt, Yankee bonds, and MTNs (Medium-Term Notes), but excludes all issues with maturities of one year or less, agency debt, and all certificates of deposit. [7] Primary dealer transactions. [8] Includes customer-to-dealer and dealer-to-dealer transactions. [9] The Securities Industry and Financial Markets Association estimates. [10] Commercial paper, bankers acceptances, and large time deposits.

Source: The Securities Industry and Financial Markets Association, New York, NY. Copyright. Based on data supplied by Board of Governors of the Federal Reserve System, U.S. Dept. of Treasury, Thompson Financial Securities Data Company, Inside MBS & ABS, FHLMC, FNMA, GNMA, Federal Home Loan Banks, Student Loan Marketing Association, Federal Farm Credit Banks, Tennessee Valley Authority, Bloomberg, and Municipal Securities Rulemaking Board.

U.S. Census Bureau, Statistical Abstract of the United States: 2009

Table 1160. **Total Returns of Stocks, Bonds, and Treasury Bills: 1980 to 2007**

[**In percent**. Average annual percent change. Stock return data are based on the Standard & Poor's 500 index. Minus sign (−) indicates loss]

| Period | Stocks | | | | Treasury bills, total return | Bonds (10-year), total return |
	Total return	Capital gains	Dividends and reinvestment	Total return after inflation		
1980 to 1989	17.55	12.59	4.40	11.85	9.13	13.01
1990 to 1999	18.21	15.31	2.51	14.85	4.95	8.02
2000 to 2006	1.13	−0.49	1.63	−1.10	3.07	6.76
2001	−11.89	−13.04	1.32	−13.68	3.32	5.51
2002	−22.10	−23.37	1.65	−23.91	1.61	15.15
2003	28.68	26.38	1.82	26.31	1.03	0.54
2004	10.88	8.99	1.73	7.38	1.43	4.59
2005	4.91	3.00	1.85	1.45	3.30	3.16
2006	15.80	13.62	1.91	11.97	4.97	2.36
2007	5.49	3.53	1.89	1.35	4.52	10.17

Source: Global Financial Data, Los Angeles, CA, "GFD Guide to Total Returns"; <http://www.globalfindata.com/articles/total _return_worksheet.xls>; and unpublished data. (copyright).

Table 1161. **Equities, Corporate Bonds, and Treasury Securities—Holdings and Net Purchases by Type of Investor: 2000 to 2007**

[**In billions of dollars (17,627 represents $17,627,000,000,000). Holdings as of Dec. 31**. Minus sign (−) indicates net sales]

| Type of investor | Holdings | | | | | Net purchases | | | | |
	2000	2004	2005	2006	2007	2000	2004	2005	2006	2007
EQUITIES [1]										
Total [2]	**17,627**	**17,389**	**18,512**	**20,909**	**21,464**	**5.4**	**67.7**	**−149.3**	**−417.2**	**−567.1**
Household sector [3]	8,199	5,938	5,875	6,178	5,447	−637.7	−269.3	−467.4	−761.0	−988.6
Rest of the world [4]	1,483	1,905	2,039	2,455	2,806	199.7	25.0	56.9	120.2	182.1
Life insurance companies	892	1,054	1,162	1,365	1,518	111.3	51.5	65.9	71.4	88.6
Private pension funds	1,971	2,334	2,537	2,755	2,767	62.8	11.2	−18.5	−9.9	−100.2
State and local government retirement funds	1,299	1,601	1,716	1,928	1,981	11.6	1.9	−5.6	−41.2	−25.1
Mutual funds	3,227	3,694	4,176	4,990	5,443	193.1	158.5	129.6	131.3	91.7
Exchange-traded funds	66	219	286	402	574	42.4	52.6	50.0	68.3	137.2
CORPORATE & FOREIGN BONDS										
Total [2]	**4,798**	**7,870**	**8,597**	**9,761**	**10,723**	**344.8**	**803.9**	**800.9**	**1,162.1**	**961.9**
Household sector [3]	618	1,255	1,286	1,469	1,505	78.2	43.9	−24.9	193.9	66.0
Rest of the world [4]	842	1,559	1,764	2,251	2,583	168.2	259.5	328.5	438.9	301.4
Commercial banking	266	564	687	780	979	56.0	82.4	123.4	93.3	198.5
Property-casualty insurance companies	188	245	263	277	289	6.4	26.4	17.5	14.2	12.4
Life insurance companies	1,222	1,768	1,841	1,842	1,910	49.0	147.8	78.9	36.1	68.4
Private pension funds	303	305	325	334	351	−76.3	−7.7	20.9	8.9	16.1
State and local government retirement funds	314	213	228	266	249	4.2	6.0	14.5	37.6	−16.9
Money market mutual funds	180	261	263	368	377	27.3	2.3	2.2	105.1	8.8
Mutual funds	362	623	699	813	972	−6.2	74.5	74.5	114.1	159.0
Government−sponsored enterprises. .	135	415	466	483	465	23.3	137.4	50.9	17.1	−17.9
Brokers and dealers	113	252	338	397	440	19.3	23.9	85.4	59.5	42.5
TREASURY SECURITIES										
Total [2]	**3,358**	**4,371**	**4,678**	**4,862**	**5,099**	**−294.9**	**362.5**	**307.3**	**183.7**	**237.5**
Household sector [3]	605	555	550	490	309	−213.6	46.5	−95.7	−68.6	−181.4
State and local governments	310	389	463	498	525	5.5	24.9	74.0	34.6	27.2
Rest of the world [4]	1,021	1,814	1,984	2,115	2,324	−70.5	347.4	260.7	139.7	209.0
Monetary authority	512	718	744	779	741	33.7	51.2	26.4	34.7	−38.3

[1] Excludes mutual fund shares; see Table 1175. [2] Includes other types not shown separately. [3] Includes nonprofit organizations. [4] Holdings and net purchases of U.S. issues by foreign residents.

Source: Board of Governors of the Federal Reserve System, "Federal Reserve Statistical Release, Z.1, Flow of Funds Accounts of the United States"; published 6 March 2008; <http://www.federalreserve.gov/releases/z1/20080306/>.

Table 1162. **New Security Issues of Corporations by Type of Offering: 2000 to 2007**

[**In billions of dollars (1,082 represents $1,082,000,000,000)**. Represents gross proceed of issues maturing in more than one year. Figures are the principal amount or the number of units multiplied by the offering price. Excludes secondary offerings, employee stock plans, investment companies other than closed-end, intracorporate transactions, and Yankee bonds. Stock data include ownership securities issued by limited partnerships]

Type of offering	2000	2005	2006	2007	Type of offering	2000	2005	2006	2007
Total.	**1,082**	**2,439**	**2,710**	**2,448**	Nonfinancial	259	216	344	412
					Financial.	688	2,108	2,247	1,867
Bonds, total	947	2,324	2,591	2,279	Stocks, total	135	115	119	169
Sold in the U.S.	825	2,141	2,318	2,030	Nonfinancial	118	55	56	65
Sold abroad	123	182	273	249	Financial.	17	61	63	103

Source: Board of Governors of the Federal Reserve System, *Statistical Supplement to the Federal Reserve Bulletin*, monthly.

Table 1163. **U.S. Purchases and Sales of Foreign Bonds and Stocks, 1990 to 2007, and by Selected Country, 2007**

[In billions of dollars (31.2 represents $31,200,000,000). Covers transactions in all types of long-term foreign securities by foreigners as reported to the Treasury International Capital Reporting System by banks, brokers, and other entities in the United States. Data cover new issues of securities, transactions in outstanding issues, and redemptions of securities. Includes transactions executed in the United States for the account of foreigners, and transactions executed abroad for the account of reporting institutions and their domestic customers. Data by country show the country of location of the foreign buyers and sellers who deal directly with reporting institutions in the United States. The data do not necessarily indicate the country of beneficial owner or issuer. The term "foreigner" covers all institutions and individuals domiciled outside the United States, including U.S. citizens domiciled abroad, and the foreign branches, subsidiaries, and other affiliates abroad of U.S. banks and businesses; the central governments, central banks, and other official institutions of foreign countries; and international and regional organizations. "Foreigner" also includes persons in the United States to the extent that they are known by reporting institutions to be acting on behalf of foreigners. Excludes acquisitions of foreign stocks through mergers that involve stock swaps. Including stock swaps, net purchases of foreign securities was $235 billion in 2007. Minus sign (−) indicates net sales by U.S. investors or a net inflow of capital into the United States]

Year and country	Net purchases			Total transactions [1]			Bonds		Stocks	
	Total	Bonds	Stocks	Total	Bonds	Stocks	Purchases	Sales	Purchases	Sales
1990	31.2	21.9	9.2	907	652	255	337	315	132	123
1995	98.7	48.4	50.3	2,569	1,827	741	938	890	396	346
2000	17.1	4.1	13.1	5,539	1,922	3,617	963	959	1,815	1,802
2001	19.6	−30.5	50.1	5,135	2,290	2,845	1,130	1,160	1,448	1,398
2002	−27.0	−28.5	1.5	5,253	2,716	2,537	1,344	1,372	1,269	1,268
2003	56.5	−32.0	88.6	5,580	2,883	2,698	1,425	1,457	1,393	1,305
2004	152.8	67.9	85.0	6,399	2,986	3,413	1,527	1,459	1,749	1,664
2005	172.4	45.1	127.3	7,572	2,965	4,608	1,505	1,460	2,367	2,240
2006	250.9	144.5	106.5	11,283	3,904	7,379	2,024	1,880	3,743	3,636
2007, total [2]	**223.5**	**128.6**	**94.9**	**16,578**	**6,052**	**10,525**	**3,090**	**2,962**	**5,310**	**5,215**
United Kingdom	154.6	87.9	66.7	5,090	1,638	3,452	863	775	1,760	1,693
Cayman Islands	5.2	13.2	−8.0	2,490	428	2,062	220	207	1,027	1,035
Ireland	3.0	5.9	−2.9	2,265	2,190	75	1,098	1,092	36	39
Japan	−3.8	−5.6	1.7	1,058	148	910	71	77	456	454
Canada	10.6	5.0	5.5	939	492	447	249	244	226	221
Hong Kong	−9.5	−2.8	−6.7	675	20	655	8	11	324	331
Bermuda	10.5	2.4	8.1	583	75	509	39	36	258	250
Bahamas, The	−0.4	−0.8	0.5	319	181	138	90	91	69	69
France	11.2	5.0	6.1	306	69	236	37	32	121	115
British Virgin Islands	(Z)	0.8	−0.8	279	54	225	27	27	112	113
Australia	3.5	1.2	2.3	250	42	208	22	20	105	103
Netherlands	−6.9	−0.6	−6.2	191	35	156	17	18	75	81
Sweden	−3.4	0.5	−3.9	190	19	171	10	9	83	87
Germany	−5.9	−14.8	8.9	187	93	94	39	54	52	43

Z Less than $50 million.   [1] Total purchases plus total sales.   [2] Includes other countries not shown separately.

Source: U.S. Dept. of Treasury, *Treasury Bulletin*, quarterly.

Table 1164. **U.S. Holdings of Foreign Stocks and Bonds by Country: 2005 to 2007**

[In billions of dollars (3,317.7 represents $3,317,700,000,000). See also Table 1249]

Country	Stocks			Country	Bonds		
	2005	2006	2007, prel.		2005	2006	2007, prel.
Total holdings	**3,317.7**	**4,329.0**	**5,170.6**	**Total holdings**	**1,011.6**	**1,275.5**	**1,478.1**
Europe [1]	1,614.0	2,191.1	2,550.7	Europe [1]	474.8	646.9	798.3
United Kingdom	544.5	689.1	797.0	United Kingdom	193.9	256.1	340.4
France	205.1	306.9	350.5	Belgium & Luxembourg	33.5	42.8	104.1
Germany	158.0	220.4	306.3	Netherlands	51.8	67.9	70.8
Switzerland	191.9	262.9	275.1	France	43.9	58.9	65.4
Netherlands	132.8	161.5	186.0	Germany	45.7	58.2	44.1
Spain	63.5	85.6	108.5	Ireland	16.9	38.3	47.2
Italy	63.9	92.7	94.6	Spain	5.7	24.2	34.5
Finland	44.4	55.9	82.7	Canada	157.5	162.1	170.5
Sweden	40.5	59.4	55.7	Caribbean financial centers [1]	137.1	199.0	250.4
Canada	247.8	298.1	393.5	Cayman Islands	118.4	177.9	224.8
Caribbean financial centers [1]	330.1	418.1	468.6	Latin America, excluding			
Bermuda	173.8	191.9	220.5	Caribbean financial centers [1]	87.0	82.1	80.7
Cayman Islands	102.6	160.6	175.3	Mexico	28.2	23.8	22.6
Latin America, excluding				Brazil	21.7	18.2	16.8
Caribbean financial centers [1]	154.3	207	315.2	Asia [1]	75.5	93.4	79.1
Brazil	68.6	92.0	180.5	Japan	25.6	35.5	30.7
Mexico	57.9	84.6	92.2	Africa [1]	6.4	6.7	3.8
Asia [1]	849.9	1,050.2	1,231.4	South Africa	2.6	3.0	3.3
Japan	493.3	543.5	518.0	Other countries [1]	73.3	85.4	95.3
Korea, South	110.3	114.2	151.7	Australia	48.6	61.6	66.3
China [2]	26.9	73.9	123.3				
Hong Kong	44.5	85.8	112.8				
Taiwan [2]	57.1	74.2	79.6				
Africa [1]	39.9	49.4	61.9				
South Africa	31.6	39.6	47.2				
Other countries [1]	81.7	115.1	149.3				
Australia	71.1	102.0	132.2				

[1] Includes other countries not shown separately.   [2] See footnote 3, Table 1166.

Source: U.S. Bureau of Economic Analysis, *Survey of Current Business*, July 2008.

Table 1165. Foreign Purchases and Sales of U.S. Securities by Type of Security, 1990 to 2007, and by Selected Country, 2007

[In billions of dollars (18.7 represents $18,700,000,000). Covers transactions in all types of long-term domestic securities by foreigners as reported to the Treasury International Capital Reporting System by banks, brokers, and other entities in the United States (except nonmarketable U.S. Treasury notes, foreign series; and nonmarketable U.S. Treasury bonds and notes, foreign currency series). See headnote, Table 1163. Excludes U.S. equities acquired through mergers and reincorporations that involve stock swaps. Also excludes principal repayment flows on foreign holdings of U.S. government agency and corporate asset-backed securities (ABS). Including stock swaps and accounting for ABS repayment flows, net purchases of U.S. securities was $830 billion in 2007. Minus sign (–) indicates net sales by foreigners or a net outflow of capital from the United States]

Year and country	Net purchases					Total transactions [4]				
	Total	Treasury bonds and notes [1]	U.S. govt. corpo- rations [2] bonds	Corpo- rate bonds [3]	Corpo- rate stocks	Total	Treasury bonds and notes [1]	U.S. govt. corpo- rations [2] bonds	Corpo- rate bonds [3]	Corpo- rate stocks
1990	18.7	17.9	6.3	9.7	–15.1	4,204	3,620	104	117	362
1995	231.9	134.1	28.7	57.9	11.2	7,243	5,828	222	278	915
2000	457.8	–54.0	152.8	184.1	174.9	16,910	7,795	1,305	775	7,036
2001	520.8	18.5	164.0	222.0	116.4	20,003	10,517	2,239	1,260	5,986
2002	547.6	119.9	195.1	182.3	50.2	25,498	14,409	3,261	1,459	6,369
2003	719.9	263.6	155.8	265.7	34.7	26,332	15,739	2,725	1,694	6,174
2004	916.5	352.1	226.4	309.5	28.5	29,441	17,520	2,192	2,033	7,696
2005	1,011.5	338.1	219.3	372.2	82.0	33,303	19,764	1,976	2,182	9,382
2006	1,143.2	195.5	286.5	510.8	150.4	41,011	21,720	2,858	2,846	13,587
2007, total [5] . . .	**1,005.8**	**201.1**	**226.1**	**383.1**	**195.5**	**58,372**	**29,972**	**3,875**	**3,442**	**21,084**
United Kingdom . . .	546.3	208.1	60.3	208.5	69.5	21,512	15,545	779	1,547	3,640
Cayman Islands . . .	82.4	–2.8	13.1	31.9	40.2	13,819	3,556	1,095	806	8,361
France	21.8	–6.2	4.3	4.3	19.5	5,352	2,699	31	53	2,570
Bermuda	–16.1	–4.2	–25.5	8.3	5.5	3,136	974	178	112	1,872
Canada	21.2	–2.6	3.2	12.4	8.1	1,868	1,308	63	86	411
Ireland	11.5	1.7	1.1	8.7	(Z)	1,777	1,532	81	70	94
Japan	0.3	–47.4	14.1	38.6	–5.0	1,371	950	219	98	103
Bahamas, The	11.3	9.4	0.6	1.5	–0.1	900	497	12	29	362
Germany	5.0	–1.3	0.3	5.4	0.6	800	219	25	36	520
Norway	–8.3	–27.3	8.2	4.7	6.1	593	369	149	23	52
China [6]	111.4	–8.0	73.7	41.7	4.0	546	224	246	59	17
Netherlands	7.1	1.5	–0.6	–0.7	6.9	446	168	36	17	226
Hong Kong	80.9	2.0	30.7	12.8	35.4	386	142	101	25	118
Switzerland	–3.9	–2.6	–1.9	3.6	–3.0	328	57	25	43	203

Z Less than $50 million.   [1] Marketable bonds and notes.   [2] Includes federally sponsored agencies.   [3] Includes transactions in directly placed issues abroad by U.S. corporations and issues of states and municipalities.   [4] Total purchases plus total sales.   [5] Includes other countries not shown separately.   [6] See footnote 3, Table 1166.
Source: U.S. Dept. of Treasury, *Treasury Bulletin*, quarterly.

Table 1166. Foreign Holdings of U.S. Securities by Country: 2005 to 2007

[In billions of dollars (1,984.4 represents $1,984,400,000,000). Covers only private holdings of U.S. securities, except as noted. See also Table 1249]

Type of security and country	2005	2006	2007, prel.	Type of security and country	2005	2006	2007, prel.
U.S. Treasury securities [1, 2]	**1,984.4**	**2,126.2**	**2,432.1**	Hong Kong	24.5	26.2	31.6
Japan	659.1	636.4	606.8	Africa	2.8	3.1	2.7
China [3]	327.1	445.2	479.8	Other countries	23.3	32.7	43.8
United Kingdom	80.9	13.6	157.5	Australia	13.9	22.7	31.2
Brazil	28.9	53.0	134.5				
OPEC Asia [4]	69.5	101.5	118.9	**Corporate stocks**	**2,109.9**	**2,547.5**	**2,833.1**
Belgium and Luxembourg	61.3	72.8	85.5	Europe [2]	1,162.4	1,397.1	1,533.7
Cayman Islands	27.4	33.8	59.0	United Kingdom	291.4	377.8	444.5
Hong Kong	40.5	53.2	53.5	Belgium and Luxembourg . .	191.9	243.5	246.6
Switzerland	36.3	37.4	42.5	Netherlands	163.1	167.6	178.6
Singapore	33.2	33.0	41.2	Switzerland	139.8	162.2	168.6
				France	82.9	116.1	135.8
Corporate and agency bonds	**2,243.1**	**2,824.9**	**3,299.3**	Germany	80.2	84.3	97.0
Europe [2]	1,396.1	1,762.4	2,095.0	Ireland	63.4	75.3	79.1
United Kingdom	482.8	593.4	767.4	Sweden	47.7	50.6	53.0
Belgium and Luxembourg . .	542.7	648.3	720.3	Denmark	26.4	31.1	31.5
Ireland	69.8	120.8	160.3	Italy	30.2	29.1	24.1
Germany	70.6	90.4	114.3	Canada	253.6	318.4	348.8
Netherlands	83.1	103.3	107.5	Caribbean financial centers [2] . .	317.2	391.8	456.7
Switzerland	63.8	88.6	101.4	Cayman Islands	164.8	220.8	272.7
France	31.5	54.6	64.7	Bermuda	59.9	72.0	84.2
Canada . . . . [2] . .	63.8	77.3	87.1	Netherlands Antilles	25.8	25.3	18.5
Caribbean financial centers [2] . .	356.4	503.9	568.1	Latin America, excluding Caribbean financial centers . .	33.9	40.4	43.5
Cayman Islands	228.9	353.7	431.8	Asia [2]	268.0	310.1	349.3
Bermuda	96.5	110.8	96.6	Japan	187.6	213.3	213.9
Latin America, excluding Caribbean financial centers . .	30.0	38.3	46.6	Singapore	32.0	45.5	45.5
Asia [2]	370.7	407.2	456.0	Hong Kong	13.1	11.1	41.8
Japan	241.2	253.3	288.5	Africa	4.7	5.5	5.8
China [3]	48.9	65.6	59.5	Other countries [2]	69.7	84.2	95.3
				Australia	61.2	74.8	86.4

[1] Includes foreign official holdings.   [2] Includes other countries not shown separately.   [3] With the establishment of diplomatic relations with China on January 1, 1979, the U.S. government recognized the People's Republic of China as the sole legal government of China and acknowledged the Chinese position that there is only one China and that Taiwan is part of China.   [4] Comprises Indonesia, Iran, Iraq, Kuwait, Qatar, Saudi Arabia, and the United Arab Emirates.
Source: U.S. Bureau of Economic Analysis, *Survey of Current Business*, July 2008.

Table 1167. **Stock Prices and Yields: 2000 to 2007**

[Closing values as of end of December, except as noted]

Index	2000	2002	2003	2004	2005	2006	2007
STOCK PRICES							
Standard & Poor's indices: [1]							
S&P 500 composite (1941–43 = 10).	1,320	880	1,112	1,212	1,248	1,418	1,468
S&P 400 MidCap Index (1982 = 100).	517	430	576	663	738	804	858
S&P 600 SmallCap Index (Dec. 31, 1993 = 100)	220	197	270	329	351	400	395
S&P 500/Barra Value Index (Dec. 31, 1974 = 35)	636	428	552	626	648	764	761
S&P 500/Barra Growth Index (Dec. 31, 1974 = 35) . . .	688	449	556	582	597	653	703
Russell indices: [2]							
Russell 1000 (Dec. 31, 1986 = 130).	700	466	595	651	679	770	800
Russell 2000 (Dec. 31, 1986 = 135).	484	383	557	652	673	788	766
Russell 3000 (Dec. 31, 1986 = 140).	726	490	630	694	723	822	849
N.Y. Stock Exchange common stock index:							
Composite (Dec. 31, 2002 = 5000).	6,946	5,000	6,440	7,250	7,754	9,139	9,740
Yearly high.	7,165	6,445	6,470	7,373	7,868	9,188	10,387
Yearly low	6,095	4,452	4,419	6,211	6,903	7,708	8,344
American Stock Exchange Composite Index (Dec. 29, 1995 = 550)	898	824	1,174	1,434	1,759	2,056	2,410
NASDAQ Composite Index (Feb. 5, 1971 = 100)	2,471	1,336	2,003	2,175	2,205	2,415	2,653
Nasdaq-100 (Jan. 31, 1985 = 125).	2,342	984	1,468	1,621	1,645	1,757	2,085
Industrial (Feb. 5, 1971 = 100)	1,483	1,030	1,604	1,858	1,860	2,090	2,179
Banks (Feb. 5, 1971 = 100)	1,939	2,231	2,899	3,218	3,078	3,417	2,663
Computers (Oct. 29, 1993 = 200).	1,295	623	935	965	992	1,053	1,283
Transportation (Feb. 5, 1971 = 100)	1,160	1,298	1,754	2,229	2,438	2,582	2,673
Telecommunications (Oct. 29, 1993 = 200)	463	109	184	198	184	235	257
Biotech (Oct. 29, 1993 = 200)	1,085	497	724	769	790	798	835
Dow-Jones and Co., Inc.:							
Composite (65 stocks).	3,317	2,375	3,001	3,396	3,638	4,121	4,385
Industrial (30 stocks)	10,787	8,342	10,454	10,783	10,718	12,463	13,266
Transportation (20 stocks).	2,947	2,310	3,007	3,797	4,196	4,560	4,571
Utility (15 stocks).	412	215	267	335	405	457	533
Dow Jones Wilshire 5000 Composite Index [3] (Dec. 31, 1980 = 1404.596)	12,176	8,343	10,799	11,971	12,518	14,258	14,820
COMMON STOCK YIELDS (percent)							
Standard & Poor's Composite Index (500 stocks): [4]							
Dividend-price ratio [5].	1.15	1.61	1.77	1.72	1.83	1.87	1.86
Earnings-price ratio [6].	3.63	2.92	3.84	4.89	5.36	5.78	5.29

[1] Standard & Poor's Indices are market-value weighted and are chosen for market size, liquidity, and industry group representation. The S&P 500 index represents 500 large publicly-traded companies. The S&P MidCap Index tracks mid-cap companies. The S&P SmallCap Index consists of 600 domestic small-cap stocks. [2] The Russell 1000 and 3000 indices show respectively the 1000 and 3000 largest capitalization stocks in the United States. The Russell 2000 index shows the 2000 largest capitalization stocks in the United States after the first 1000. [3] The Dow Jones Wilshire 5000 Composite Index measures the performance of all U.S. headquartered equity securities with readily available prices. Source: Dow Jones & Company, Inc., New York, NY, *Dow Jones Indexes*, (copyright). [4] Source: U.S. Council of Economic Advisors, *Economic Indicators*, monthly. [5] Aggregate cash dividends (based on latest known annual rate) divided by aggregate market value based on Wednesday closing prices. Averages of monthly figures. [6] Averages of quarterly ratios which are ratio of earnings (after taxes) for 4 quarters ending with particular quarter-to-price index for last day of that quarter.

Source: Except as noted, Global Financial Data, Los Angeles, CA, <http://www.globalfindata.com/> (copyright).

Table 1168. **Dow Jones U.S. Total Market Index by Industry: 2000 to 2007**

[As of end of year]

Industry	2000	2002	2003	2004	2005	2006	2007
U.S. Total Market Index, total	**306.88**	**204.51**	**262.68**	**289.38**	**302.37**	**343.25**	**357.48**
Basic materials.	154.49	136.97	181.10	200.33	205.79	236.22	307.92
Consumer goods	219.82	198.48	240.91	266.44	265.88	298.60	320.39
Consumer services	279.11	212.34	280.07	306.85	298.62	338.32	310.76
Oil and gas	272.96	200.29	246.08	319.76	422.12	510.72	679.31
Financial	440.91	346.36	445.96	492.54	510.02	592.98	474.23
Health care	360.18	242.87	286.04	295.22	315.50	332.38	354.89
Industrials	276.11	179.78	235.69	272.24	280.72	314.41	351.44
Technology	749.01	327.84	493.02	499.78	513.48	561.85	645.98
Telecommunications	210.38	115.04	119.12	136.84	126.90	168.11	179.65
Utilities	177.80	95.75	114.54	136.79	152.41	178.78	204.52

Source: Dow Jones & Company, Inc., New York, NY, *Dow Jones Indexes* (copyright).

U.S. Census Bureau, Statistical Abstract of the United States: 2009

Table 1169. Transaction Activity in Equities, Options, and Security Futures, 1990 to 2007, and by Exchange, 2007

[In billions of dollars (2,229 represents $2,229,000,000,000). Market value of all sales of equities and options listed on an exchange or subject to last-sale reporting. Also reported are the value of such options that were exercised and the value of single-stock futures that were delivered. Excludes options and futures on indexes]

Year and exchange	Total	Equity trading	Option trading	Option exercises and futures deliveries
1990	2,229	2,154	27	48
1995	6,321	6,208	51	63
2000	36,275	35,557	485	233
2001	26,138	25,636	278	224
2002	23,028	22,658	161	209
2003	22,737	22,292	164	282
2004	27,876	27,158	223	495
2005	34,567	33,222	350	995
2006	43,939	41,796	531	1,611
2007, total [1]	**66,136**	**63,064**	**861**	**2,211**
American Stock Exchange	716	454	71	191
Chicago Board Options Exchange	821	78	216	527
Chicago Stock Exchange	400	400	–	–
FINRA [2]	15,758	15,758	–	–
International Securities Exchange	1,015	314	200	501
NASDAQ Stock Market	17,112	17,112	–	–
National Stock Exchange	320	320	–	–
New York Stock Exchange	17,289	17,289	–	–
NYSE Arca [3]	11,873	11,240	175	458
Philadelphia Stock Exchange	643	64	163	416

– Represents zero.   [1] Includes other exchanges not shown separately.   [2] Financial Industry Regulatory Authority.
[3] NYSE Arca, formerly Archipelago, is a fully electronic stock exchange.

Source: U.S. Securities and Exchange Commission, "Select SEC and Market Data"; <http://www.sec.gov/about.shtml>.

Table 1170. Volume of Trading on New York Stock Exchange: 1990 to 2007

[39,946 represents 39,946,000,000. *Round lot:* A unit of trading or a multiple thereof. On the NYSE, the unit of trading is generally 100 shares in stocks. For some inactive stocks, the unit of trading is 10 shares. *Odd lot:* An amount of stock less than the established 100-share unit or 10-share unit of trading]

Item	Unit	1990	1995	2000	2002	2003	2004	2005	2006	2007
Shares traded	Million	**39,946**	**87,873**	**265,499**	**369,069**	**356,767**	**372,718**	**523,811**	**597,720**	**706,029**
Round lots [1]	Million	39,665	87,218	262,478	363,136	352,398	367,099	516,743	588,127	698,646
Average daily shares	Million	157	346	1,042	1,441	1,398	1,457	2,051	2,343	2,783
High day	Million	292	653	1,561	2,813	1,886	2,690	3,628	3,853	5,800
Low day	Million	57	118	403	462	360	509	694	797	999
Odd lots	Million	282	656	3,021	5,933	4,370	5,619	7,068	9,593	7,383
Value of shares traded	Bil. dol.	**1,336**	**3,110**	**11,205**	**10,491**	**9,847**	**11,841**	**18,174**	**22,247**	**30,287**
Round lots [1]	Bil. dol.	1,325	3,083	11,060	10,278	9,692	11,618	17,858	21,790	29,909
Odd lots	Bil. dol.	11	27	145	213	154	223	316	458	378

[1] Beginning 2005, reflects trades of NYSE Group.

Source: New York Stock Exchange, Inc., New York, NY, "Facts & Figures"; <http://www.nysedata.com/factbook> (copyright).

Table 1171. Household Ownership of Equities: 2005

[56.9 represents 56,900,000. Based on a national probability sample of 4,927 household financial decision-makers. Further questions about equity ownership were asked of those 2,476 decision-makers who indicated they owned equities]

Type of holding	Households owning equities		Number of individual investors (mil.)
	Number (mil.)	Percent of all households	
Any type of equity (net) [1]	56.9	50.3	91.1
Any equity inside employer-sponsored retirement plans	37.6	33.2	48.8
Any equity outside employer-sponsored retirement plans	39.3	34.7	58.9
Individual stock (net) [1]	28.4	25.1	42.6
Individual stock inside employer-sponsored retirement plans	7.6	6.7	9.9
Individual stock outside employer-sponsored retirement plans	23.3	20.6	35.0
Stock mutual funds (net) [1]	51.8	45.8	77.7
Stock mutual funds inside employer-sponsored retirement plans	36.0	31.8	46.8
Stock mutual funds outside employer-sponsored retirement plans	31.1	27.5	46.7

[1] Net figure adjusted for multiple responses.

Source: Investment Company Institute, Washington, DC, and Securities Industry Association, New York, NY, *Equity Ownership in America, Fall 2005* (copyright).

Table 1172. Households Owning Mutual Funds by Age and Income: 2000 and 2007

[In percent. Ownership includes money market, stock, bond, and hybrid mutual funds, variable annuities, and mutual funds owned through Individual Retirement Accounts (IRAs), Keoghs, and employer-sponsored retirement plans. In 2007, an estimated 50,600,000 households own mutual funds. The May 2007 survey included a sample of 3,977 randomly selected households; for details, see source. For definition of mutual fund, see headnote, Table 1174]

Age of household head and household income	Percent distribution, 2007	As percent of all households		Age of household head and household income	Percent distribution, 2007	As percent of all households	
		2000	2007			2000	2007
Total	**100**	**45**	**44**	Less than $25,000.	8	13	13
Less than 35 years old. . .	18	36	34	$25,000 to $34,999	6	33	25
35 to 44 years old	22	55	48	$35,000 to $49,999	12	46	37
45 to 54 years old	24	59	51	$50,000 to $74,999	24	66	57
55 to 64 years old	20	50	53	$75,000 to $99,999	17	75	66
65 years old and over . . .	16	26	34	$100,000 and over	33	78	74

Source: Investment Company Institute, Washington, DC, *Fundamentals, Investment Company Institute Research in Brief*, Vol. 16, No. 5, November 2007 (copyright).

Table 1173. Characteristics of Mutual Fund Owners: 2007

[In percent, except as indicated. Mutual fund ownership includes holdings of money market, stock, bond, and hybrid mutual funds; and funds owned through variable annuities, Individual Retirement Accounts (IRAs), Keoghs, and employer-sponsored retirement plans. Based on a national probability sample of 1,733 primary financial decision-makers in households with mutual fund investments. For definition of mutual fund, see headnote, Table 1174. For definition of median, see Guide to Tabular Presentation]

Characteristic	Total	Age			Household income			
		Under 40 years old	40 to 64 years old	65 years old and over	Less than $50,000	$50,000 to $99,999	$100,000 to $149,999	$150,000 or more
Median household income (dol.) . . .	74,000	70,000	80,000	49,000	33,000	70,000	111,500	185,000
Median household financial assets [1] (dol.)	175,000	75,000	250,000	375,000	55,000	130,000	300,000	600,000
Own an IRA	68	56	72	75	58	67	77	80
Household with defined contribution retirement plan(s) [2] . . .	76	86	77	50	58	80	86	80
401(k) plan	62	76	64	30	44	66	72	68
403(b), state, local, or federal government plan	32	31	34	31	27	32	36	38
Median mutual fund assets (dol.). . .	100,000	48,000	115,000	150,000	30,000	75,000	150,000	350,000
Own:								
Equity funds.	80	80	82	73	70	82	86	84
Bond funds	45	41	49	41	37	43	49	60
Own mutual funds bought:								
Outside employer-sponsored retirement plan(s)	74	63	75	88	70	70	79	89
Inside employer-sponsored retirement plan(s)	66	73	69	40	53	68	76	69

[1] Includes assets in employer-sponsored retirement plans but excludes value of primary residence.   [2] For definition of defined contribution plan, see headnote, Table 533.

Source: Investment Company Institute, Washington, DC, *Profile of Mutual Fund Shareholders*, Spring 2008 (copyright).

Table 1174. Mutual Funds—Summary: 1990 to 2007

[Number of funds and assets as of December 31 (1,065 represents $1,065,000,000,000). A mutual fund is an open-end investment company that continuously issues and redeems shares that represent an interest in a pool of financial assets. Excludes data for funds that invest in other mutual funds. Minus sign (−) indicates net redemptions]

Type of fund	Unit	1990	2000	2001	2002	2003	2004	2005	2006	2007
Number of funds, total	**Number**. . .	**3,079**	**8,155**	**8,305**	**8,244**	**8,126**	**8,041**	**7,975**	**8,118**	**8,029**
Equity funds	Number . . .	1,099	4,385	4,716	4,747	4,599	4,547	4,586	4,769	4,767
Hybrid funds	Number . . .	193	523	483	473	508	510	505	508	488
Bond funds	Number . . .	1,046	2,208	2,091	2,035	2,045	2,041	2,013	1,993	1,967
Money market funds, taxable [1] . . .	Number . . .	506	703	689	679	662	639	595	575	548
Money market funds, tax-exempt [2]. . .	Number . . .	235	336	326	310	312	304	276	273	259
Assets, total	**Bil. dol.** . . .	**1,065**	**6,965**	**6,975**	**6,390**	**7,414**	**8,107**	**8,905**	**10,412**	**12,021**
Equity funds	Bil. dol. . . .	239	3,962	3,418	2,662	3,684	4,384	4,940	5,911	6,521
Hybrid funds	Bil. dol. . . .	36	346	346	325	430	519	567	653	713
Bond funds	Bil. dol. . . .	291	811	925	1,130	1,248	1,290	1,357	1,494	1,679
Money market funds, taxable [1] . . .	Bil. dol. . . .	415	1,607	2,013	1,997	1,764	1,603	1,707	1,988	2,642
Money market funds, tax-exempt [2]. . .	Bil. dol. . . .	84	238	272	275	288	310	334	366	465
Net sales:										
Equity, hybrid and bond funds	Bil. dol. . . .	51	300	206	206	282	293	303	369	403
Money market funds, taxable [1] . . .	Bil. dol. . . .	36	192	386	−63	−252	−157	67	257	629
Money market funds, tax-exempt [2]. . .	Bil. dol. . . .	7	31	31	14	7	16	24	33	90

[1] Funds invest in short-term, high-grade securities sold in the money market.   [2] Funds invest in municipal securities with relatively short maturities.

Source: Investment Company Institute, Washington, DC, *Mutual Fund Fact Book*, annual (copyright).

Table 1175. **Mutual Fund Shares—Holdings and Net Purchases by Type of Investor: 2000 to 2007**

[In billions of dollars (4,433 represents $4,433,000,000,000). Holdings as of Dec. 31. For definition of mutual fund, see headnote, Table 1174. Excludes money market mutual funds. Minus sign (–) indicates net sales]

Type of investor	Holdings					Net purchases				
	2000	2004	2005	2006	2007	2000	2004	2005	2006	2007
Total	4,433	5,436	6,049	7,068	7,798	237.6	298.2	260.2	336.8	367.9
Households, nonprofit organizations	2,704	3,417	3,840	4,536	5,082	66.7	216.4	228.5	236.7	307.1
Nonfinancial corporate business. . .	122	140	156	207	250	3.5	1.4	6.7	32.9	32.9
State and local governments	31	28	29	31	33	1.2	–1.3	0.4	–2.0	0.2
Rest of the world.	149	196	242	296	326	–9.2	32.7	32.2	25.3	15.4
Commercial banking	15	18	17	25	30	2.5	–0.9	–1.8	3.9	3.7
Credit unions	2	3	2	2	2	–0.3	–0.9	–1.0	–0.1	–
Property-casualty insurance companies	3	5	6	7	8	0.4	0.5	0.3	0.5	0.4
Life insurance companies	97	114	109	149	161	5.6	12.8	–9.9	26.9	8.0
Private pension funds	1,132	1,278	1,399	1,529	1,611	117.3	36.1	10.2	11.4	4.1
State and local government retirement funds	178	236	248	288	296	49.9	1.5	–5.5	1.3	–3.7

– Represents or rounds to zero.

Source: Board of Governors of the Federal Reserve System, "Federal Reserve Statistical Release, Z.1, Flow of Funds Accounts of the United States"; published: 6 March 2008; <http://www.federalreserve.gov/releases/z1/20080306/>.

Table 1176. **Retirement Assets by Type of Asset: 1990 to 2007**

[In billions of dollars, except as indicated (3,921 represents $3,921,000,000,000). As of December 31. Estimated]

Type of asset	1990	2000	2002	2003	2004	2005	2006	2007
Retirement assets, total	3,921	11,690	10,550	12,545	13,778	14,862	16,509	17,619
IRA assets	637	2,629	2,533	2,993	3,299	3,652	4,220	4,747
Bank and thrift deposits [1]	266	250	263	268	268	278	313	340
Life insurance companies [2]	40	203	268	285	282	308	318	336
Mutual funds . . . . [3]	138	1,231	1,043	1,309	1,491	1,664	1,977	2,243
Securities held in brokerage accounts [3] . . .	192	945	959	1,131	1,257	1,402	1,612	1,827
Traditional.	(NA)	2,407	2,322	2,719	2,957	3,259	3,749	4,208
Roth	(X)	78	78	106	140	160	195	225
SEP and SAR-SEP [4]	(NA)	134	117	145	169	191	223	253
SIMPLE [5]	(NA)	10	16	23	34	42	53	61
Defined contribution plans	892	2,969	2,472	3,043	3,335	3,620	4,119	4,472
401(k) plans	(NA)	1,725	1,573	1,922	2,189	2,396	2,770	3,047
403(b) plans	(NA)	517	433	533	571	616	687	739
457 plans	(NA)	110	98	117	130	143	158	173
Other defined contribution plans [6]	(NA)	618	368	472	446	465	503	513
State and local government pension plans . . .	739	2,335	1,980	2,399	2,626	2,765	3,087	3,186
Private defined benefit plans	922	2,009	1,670	2,025	2,162	2,310	2,397	2,360
Federal pension plans [7]	340	797	894	958	1,023	1,072	1,141	1,197
Annuities [8]	391	951	1,001	1,125	1,332	1,443	1,545	1,658
Memo:								
Mutual fund retirement assets	205	2,485	2,089	2,666	3,074	3,441	4,081	4,578
Percent of total retirement assets	5	21	20	21	22	23	25	26
Percent of all mutual funds	19	36	33	36	38	39	39	38

NA Not available. X Not applicable. [1] Includes Keogh deposits. [2] Annuities held by IRAs, excluding variable annuity mutual fund IRA assets. [3] Excludes mutual fund assets held through brokerage accounts, which are included in mutual funds. [4] Simplified Employee Pension IRAs and salary reduction (SAR) SEP IRAs. [5] Savings Incentive Match Plan for Employees (SIMPLE) IRAs. [6] Includes Keoghs and other defined contribution plans (profit-sharing, thrift-savings, stock bonus, and money purchase) without 401(k) features. [7] Federal pension plans include U.S. Treasury security holdings of the civil service retirement and disability fund, the military retirement fund, the judicial retirement fund, the Railroad Retirement Board, and the foreign service retirement and disability fund. These plans also include securities held in the National Railroad Retirement Investment Trust and Federal Employees Retirement System (FERS) Thrift Savings Plan (TSP). [8] Annuities include all fixed and variable annuity reserves at life insurance companies less annuities held by IRAs, 403(b) plans, 457 plans, and private pension funds. Some of these annuity reserves represent assets of individuals held outside retirement plan arrangements and IRAs; however, information to separate out such reserves is not available.

Source: Investment Company Institute, Washington, DC, *Research Fundamentals, "The U.S. Retirement Market, 2007"*; Vol. 17, No. 3, July 2008 and *Research Fundamentals, "Appendix: Additional Data on the U.S. Retirement Market, 2007"*; Vol. 17, No. 3A, July 2008. (Copyright)

Table 1177. **Assets of Private and Public Pension Funds by Type of Fund: 1990 to 2007**

[In billions of dollars (3,291 represents $3,291,000,000,000). As of end of year. Except for corporate equities, represents book value. Excludes social security trust funds; see Table 528]

Type of pension fund	1990	1995	2000	2002	2003	2004	2005	2006	2007
Total, all types.	**3,291**	**5,680**	**9,106**	**8,128**	**9,653**	**10,566**	**11,308**	**12,249**	**12,717**
Private funds	2,221	3,812	6,016	5,304	6,345	6,965	7,515	8,058	8,367
Insured [1]	570	891	1,526	1,605	1,803	2,028	2,197	2,356	2,525
Noninsured [2, 3]	1,651	2,921	4,490	3,699	4,542	4,937	5,318	5,701	5,842
Credit market instruments [3] . . .	486	631	644	599	669	668	713	727	761
Agency- and GSE-backed securities [4] . . .	138	218	202	188	226	238	256	255	269
Corporate and foreign bonds	195	279	303	291	312	305	325	334	351
Corporate equities	606	1,257	1,971	1,589	2,097	2,334	2,537	2,755	2,767
Mutual fund shares	40	357	1,132	932	1,127	1,278	1,399	1,529	1,611
Unallocated insurance contracts [5]	215	322	308	250	317	328	338	364	355
State and local government employee retirement funds [3]	730	1,327	2,293	1,930	2,349	2,578	2,721	3,050	3,152
Credit market instruments [3]	402	510	743	639	658	675	693	770	796
Agency- and GSE-backed securities [4]	63	63	179	193	235	259	258	295	319
Corporate equities	285	704	1,299	1,057	1,421	1,601	1,716	1,928	1,981
Mutual fund shares	8	63	178	167	208	236	248	288	296
Federal government retirement funds [6]	340	541	797	894	958	1,023	1,072	1,141	1,197

[1] Annuity reserves held by life insurance companies, excluding unallocated contracts held by private pension funds. [2] Private defined benefit plans and defined contribution plans (including 401(k) type plans). [3] Includes other types of assets not shown separately. [4] GSE = Government-sponsored enterprises. [5] Assets held at life insurance companies (e.g., guaranteed investment contracts (GICs), variable annuities). [6] Includes the Federal Employees Thrift Savings Plan, the National Railroad Retirement Investment Trust, and nonmarketable government securities held by federal government retirement funds.

Source: Board of Governors of the Federal Reserve System, "Federal Reserve Statistical Release, Z.1, Flow of Funds Accounts of the United States"; published 6 March 2008; <http://www.federalreserve.gov/releases/z1/20080306/>.

Table 1178. **Annual Revenues of Selected Securities Industries: 2000 to 2006**

[In millions of dollars (384,992 represents $384,992,000,000). Covers taxable and tax-exempt employer firms only. Based on the North American Industry Classification System (NAICS), 2002; see text, Section 15. Based on Service Annual Survey. Estimates have been adjusted to the results of the 2002 Economic Census. See Appendix III]

Kind of business	2002 NAICS code	2000	2003	2004	2005	2006
Total	523x	**384,992**	**311,525**	**349,166**	**406,374**	**499,162**
Securities and commodity contracts intermediation and brokerage	5231	296,045	225,299	250,080	293,096	365,667
Investment banking & securities dealing	52311	145,416	108,306	127,257	154,040	198,851
Securities brokerage	52312	144,631	110,689	115,626	131,101	156,490
Commodity contracts dealing	52313	2,945	3,329	3,858	4,142	4,946
Commodity contracts brokerage	52314	3,053	2,975	3,339	3,813	5,380
Other financial investment activities [1]	5239x	88,947	86,226	99,086	113,278	133,495
Portfolio management	52392	75,349	71,535	80,872	91,120	107,066
Investment advice	52393	13,598	14,691	18,214	22,158	26,429

[1] Excludes NAICS 52391 (miscellaneous intermediation) and NAICS 52399 (all other financial investment activities).

Source: U.S. Census Bureau, *Service Annual Survey: 2006*.

Table 1179. **Securities Industry—Financial Summary: 1990 to 2006**

[In billions of dollars, except as indicated. (71.4 represents $71,400,000,000)]

Type	1990	1995	2000	2001	2002	2003	2004	2005	2006
Number of firms	8,437	7,722	7,258	7,002	6,768	6,565	6,284	6,016	5,808
Revenues, total	**71.4**	**143.4**	**349.5**	**280.1**	**221.8**	**219.0**	**242.9**	**332.5**	**458.5**
Commissions	12.0	23.2	54.1	44.8	45.0	45.5	47.6	46.8	49.7
Trading/investment gains	15.7	29.0	70.8	39.0	24.2	38.8	30.7	30.7	55.2
Underwriting profits	3.7	8.9	18.7	16.9	14.7	17.2	19.1	19.9	23.6
Margin interest	3.2	6.5	24.5	13.9	6.4	5.3	7.0	13.3	23.7
Mutual fund sales	3.2	7.4	19.4	16.4	15.7	16.2	18.5	20.7	23.3
Other	33.4	68.5	161.9	149.1	115.8	96.0	120.1	201.2	282.9
Expenses, total	**70.6**	**132.1**	**310.4**	**260.7**	**206.5**	**193.3**	**219.7**	**311.3**	**419.9**
Interest expense	28.1	56.9	131.9	98.9	56.4	44.4	59.7	140.2	226.1
Compensation	22.9	41.5	95.2	83.5	74.9	77.4	83.5	88.8	103.4
Commissions/clearance paid	3.0	5.7	15.5	14.0	15.0	16.3	17.4	18.6	22.0
Other	16.6	28.0	67.8	64.2	60.3	55.1	59.2	63.6	68.4
Net income, pretax	**0.8**	**11.3**	**39.1**	**19.4**	**15.3**	**25.7**	**23.2**	**21.2**	**38.6**
Pre-tax profit margin (percent)	1.1	7.9	11.2	6.9	6.9	11.7	9.5	6.4	8.4
Pre-tax return on equity (percent) . . .	2.2	20.1	31.1	13.8	10.7	17.6	15.0	13.1	22.1
Assets	657	1,494	2,866	3,371	3,261	3,980	4,831	5,215	6,222
Liabilities	623	1,435	2,728	3,227	3,119	3,831	4,671	5,051	6,037
Ownership equity	34	59	138	144	142	149	160	164	185

Source: U.S. Securities and Exchange Commission, "Select SEC and Market Data Fiscal 2007"; <http://www.sec.gov/about/secstats2007.pdf>.

U.S. Census Bureau, Statistical Abstract of the United States: 2009

Table 1180. **Life Insurance in Force and Purchases in the United States—Summary: 1990 to 2006**

[As of December 31 or calendar year, as applicable (389 represents 389,000,000). Covers life insurance with life insurance companies only. Represents all life insurance in force on lives of U.S. residents whether issued by U.S. or foreign companies]

Year	Number of policies, total (mil.)	Life insurance in force — Value (bil. dol.) Total [1]	Individual	Group	Life insurance purchases [2] — Number (1,000) Total	Individual	Group	Life insurance purchases [2] — Amount (bil. dol.) Total	Individual	Group
1990	389	9,393	5,391	3,754	28,791	14,199	14,592	1,529	1,070	459
1995	370	11,696	6,890	4,605	31,999	12,595	19,404	1,577	1,039	538
1999	367	15,496	9,172	6,110	38,584	11,673	26,912	2,367	1,400	967
2000	369	15,953	9,376	6,376	34,882	13,345	21,537	2,515	1,594	921
2001	377	16,290	9,346	6,765	40,095	14,059	26,036	2,773	1,600	1,172
2002	375	16,346	9,312	6,876	38,713	14,692	24,020	2,767	1,753	1,014
2003	379	17,044	9,655	7,236	35,767	13,821	21,946	2,823	1,773	1,050
2004	373	17,508	9,717	7,631	38,453	12,581	25,872	2,948	1,846	1,102
2005	373	18,399	9,970	8,263	34,519	11,407	23,112	2,836	1,796	1,040
2006	375	19,112	10,057	8,906	29,287	10,908	18,378	2,835	1,813	1,022

[1] Includes other types of policies not shown separately. [2] Excludes revivals, increases, dividend additions, and reinsurance acquired. Includes long-term credit insurance (life insurance on loans of more than 10 years' duration).

Source: American Council of Life Insurers, Washington, DC, *Life Insurers Fact Book*, annual (copyright).

Table 1181. **U.S. Life Insurance Companies—Summary: 1990 to 2006**

[As of December 31 or calendar year, as applicable (402.2 represents $402,200,000,000). Covers domestic and foreign business of U.S. companies. Beginning 1995, includes annual statement data for companies that primarily are health insurance companies]

Item	Unit	1990	1995	1999	2000	2001	2002	2003	2004	2005	2006
U.S. companies [1]	Number .	2,195	1,650	1,347	1,269	1,341	1,284	1,227	1,179	1,119	1,072
Income	**Bil. dol.**	**402.2**	**528.1**	**726.9**	**811.5**	**724.4**	**734.0**	**727.0**	**756.8**	**779.0**	**883.6**
Life insurance premiums	Bil. dol . .	76.7	102.8	120.3	130.6	125.3	134.5	127.3	139.7	142.3	149.2
Annuity considerations [2]	Bil. dol . .	129.1	158.4	270.2	306.7	251.3	269.3	268.6	276.7	277.1	302.7
Health insurance premiums. . . .	Bil. dol . .	58.3	90.0	100.0	105.6	103.4	108.7	115.8	125.8	118.3	141.2
Investment and other.	Bil. dol . .	138.2	176.9	236.4	268.5	244.5	221.5	215.3	214.7	241.4	290.4
Payments under life insurance and annuity contracts	Bil. dol . .	88.4	227.6	355.3	375.2	304.9	301.3	307.1	331.7	365.7	422.7
Payments to life insurance beneficiaries.	Bil. dol . .	24.6	34.5	41.4	44.1	46.5	48.2	51.7	51.6	53.0	55.7
Surrender values under life insurance [3]	Bil. dol . .	18.0	19.5	32.8	27.2	30.7	32.9	35.9	35.5	39.2	38.5
Surrender values under annuity contracts [3,4]	Bil. dol . .	(NA)	105.4	198.3	214.0	151.3	142.9	140.3	162.9	190.3	237.8
Policyholder dividends	Bil. dol . .	12.0	17.8	19.1	20.0	20.0	21.0	20.8	19.0	17.9	18.4
Annuity payments [4]	Bil. dol . .	32.6	48.5	62.5	68.7	55.2	55.0	57.1	61.2	63.9	71.1
Matured endowments	Bil. dol . .	0.7	1.0	0.5	0.6	0.5	0.6	0.6	0.6	0.6	0.6
Other payments	Bil. dol . .	0.6	0.9	0.6	0.6	0.6	0.6	0.7	0.9	0.7	0.6
Health insurance benefit payments	Bil. dol . .	40.0	64.7	74.5	78.8	76.3	78.7	81.9	88.5	79.6	97.0
BALANCE SHEET											
Assets	**Bil. dol.**	**1,408**	**2,144**	**3,071**	**3,182**	**3,269**	**3,380**	**3,887**	**4,253**	**4,482**	**4,823**
Government bonds	Bil. dol . .	211	409	362	364	377	481	538	563	590	579
Corporate securities	Bil. dol . .	711	1,241	2,180	2,238	2,263	2,266	2,666	2,965	3,136	3,413
Percent of total assets . . .	Percent .	50	58	71	70	69	67	69	70	70	71
Bonds	Bil. dol .	583	869	1,190	1,241	1,354	1,475	1,644	1,785	1,850	1,882
Stocks	Bil. dol .	128	372	990	997	909	791	1,022	1,180	1,285	1,531
Mortgages	Bil. dol .	270	212	230	237	244	251	269	283	295	314
Real estate	Bil. dol .	43	52	38	36	32	33	31	31	33	33
Policy loans	Bil. dol .	63	96	99	102	104	105	107	109	110	113
Other	Bil. dol .	110	133	163	204	248	244	276	303	319	371
Interest earned on assets [5]	Percent .	8.89	7.41	6.71	7.05	6.31	5.38	5.03	4.80	4.90	5.35
Obligations and surplus funds [6] . .	Bil. dol . .	1,408	2,144	3,071	3,182	3,269	3,380	3,888	4,253	4,482	4,823
Policy reserves	**Bil. dol.**	**1,197**	**1,812**	**2,610**	**2,712**	**2,446**	**2,507**	**2,895**	**3,160**	**3,360**	**3,608**
Annuities [7]	Bil. dol . .	798	1,213	1,781	1,841	1,516	1,550	1,835	2,024	2,174	2,328
Group	Bil. dol . .	516	619	907	960	571	570	662	712	758	807
Individual	Bil. dol . .	282	594	874	881	945	980	1,173	1,312	1,415	1,521
Supplementary contracts [8] . .	Bil. dol . .	17	25	32	34	13	14	15	16	16	17
Life insurance	Bil. dol . .	349	511	705	742	816	833	921	988	1,029	1,110
Health insurance	Bil. dol . .	33	63	92	96	101	111	123	134	141	153
Liabilities for deposit-type contracts [9]	Bil. dol . .	18	20	21	21	338	364	405	445	456	487
Capital and surplus	Bil. dol . .	91	151	181	188	191	202	231	250	256	266

NA Not available. [1] Beginning 1995, includes life insurance companies that sell accident and health insurance. [2] Beginning 2001, excludes certain deposit-type funds from income due to codification. [3] Beginning with 1995, "surrender values" include annuity withdrawals of funds, which were not included in prior years. [4] Beginning 2001, excludes payments under deposit-type contracts. [5] Net rate. [6] Includes other obligations not shown separately. [7] Beginning 2001, excludes reserves for guaranteed interest contracts (GICs). [8] Through 2000, includes reserves for contracts with and without life contingencies; beginning 2001, includes only reserves for contracts with life contingencies. [9] Policyholder dividend accumulations for all years. Beginning 2001, also includes liabilities for guaranteed interest contracts, supplementary contracts without life contingencies, and premium and other deposits.

Source: American Council of Life Insurers, Washington, DC, *Life Insurers Fact Book*, annual (copyright).

Table 1182. **Property and Casualty Insurance—Summary: 2000 to 2006**

[In billions of dollars (305.1 represents $305,100,000,000). Minus sign (−) indicates loss]

Item	2000	2001	2002	2003	2004	2005	2006
Premiums, net written [1]	**305.1**	**327.8**	**373.1**	**407.5**	**425.7**	**427.6**	**447.7**
Automobile, private [2]	120.0	128.1	139.6	151.3	157.6	159.6	160.4
Automobile, commercial [2]	19.8	21.8	24.6	25.5	26.7	26.8	26.7
Fire	(NA)	5.1	7.4	8.4	8.1	7.9	9.4
Homeowners' multiple peril	32.7	35.4	40.2	46.0	50.0	53.0	55.8
Commercial multiple peril	(NA)	22.5	25.4	27.4	29.1	29.7	31.8
Marine, inland and ocean	8.3	8.7	9.4	10.4	10.8	11.2	12.3
Accident and health	14.5	15.6	15.6	11.9	9.8	9.6	6.7
Workers' compensation	26.2	27.1	30.6	32.9	36.7	39.7	41.8
Medical malpractice	(NA)	6.3	7.4	8.8	9.1	9.7	10.4
Other liability [3]	(NA)	20.0	29.3	36.1	39.8	39.4	42.2
Reinsurance	(NA)	11.8	15.1	15.5	13.7	6.6	12.9
Losses and expenses	321.3	361.8	377.4	389.4	407.7	421.2	401.2
Underwriting gain/loss	−27.3	−52.6	−30.8	−4.9	4.3	−5.6	31.2
Net investment income	41.5	38.6	39.5	39.8	40.3	49.7	53.3
Operating earnings after taxes	4.4	−13.6	4.3	23.5	29.4	34.4	60.4

NA Not available. [1] Excludes state funds. [2] Includes premiums for automobile liability and physical damage. [3] Coverages protecting against legal liability resulting from negligence, carelessness, or failure to act.

Source: Insurance Information Institute, New York, NY, *The III Insurance Fact Book*, annual; and *Financial Services Fact Book*, annual (copyright). Data from ISO and Highline Data LLC. See also <http://www.iii.org>.

Table 1183. **Automobile Insurance—Average Expenditures Per Insured Vehicle by State: 2000 to 2005**

[In dollars. Average expenditure equals total premiums written divided by liability car-years. A car-year is equal to 365 days of insured coverage for a single vehicle. The average expenditures for automobile insurance in a state are affected by a number of factors, including the underlying rate structure, the coverages purchased, the deductibles and limits selected, the types of vehicles insured, and the distribution of driver characteristics. The NAIC does not rank state average expenditures and does not endorse any conclusions drawn from this data]

State	2000	2004	2005	State	2000	2004	2005	State	2000	2004	2005
U.S.	**690**	**838**	**829**	KS	540	603	590	ND	477	562	554
				KY	616	758	750	OH	579	680	669
AL	594	677	678	LA	806	1,062	1,076	OK	603	690	678
AK	770	974	962	ME	528	650	644	OR	625	753	737
AZ	792	931	926	MD	757	947	945	PA	699	843	849
AR	606	708	693	MA	946	1,113	1,113	RI	825	1,034	1,059
CA	672	833	845	MI	702	980	931	SC	620	763	753
CO	755	850	827	MN	696	829	791	SD	482	587	565
CT	871	991	991	MS	654	749	745	TN	592	666	659
DE	849	1,022	1,028	MO	612	702	685	TX	678	847	845
DC	996	1,185	1,182	MT	530	683	685	UT	620	722	706
FL	781	1,062	1,063	NE	533	637	621	VT	568	693	699
GA	674	779	784	NV	829	939	983	VA	576	702	698
HI	702	817	843	NH	665	798	792	WA	722	839	840
ID	505	590	583	NJ	977	1,221	1,184	WV	680	875	857
IL	652	760	743	NM	674	728	727	WI	545	636	615
IN	570	671	657	NY	939	1,172	1,122	WY	496	629	639
IA	479	580	555	NC	564	597	602				

Source: National Association of Insurance Commissioners (NAIC), Kansas City, MO, *Auto Insurance Database Report*, annual (copyright). Reprinted with permission of the NAIC. Further reprint or distribution strictly prohibited without prior written permission of the NAIC.

Table 1184. **Renters and Homeowners Insurance—Average Premiums by State: 2005**

[In dollars. Average premium equals premiums divided by exposure per house-years. A house-year is equal to 365 days of insured coverage for a single dwelling and is the standard measurement for homeowners insurance. The NAIC does not rank state average expenditures and does not endorse any conclusions drawn from these data]

State	Renters [1]	Homeowners [2]	State	Renters [1]	Homeowners [2]	State	Renters [1]	Homeowners [2]
U.S.	**193**	**764**	KS	173	836	ND	128	736
			KY	163	628	OH	166	531
AL	225	847	LA	244	1,144	OK	242	996
AK	184	837	ME	147	553	OR	168	491
AZ	219	635	MD	163	696	PA	150	624
AR	218	775	MA	220	827	RI	193	849
CA	257	895	MI	173	734	SC	189	817
CO	174	807	MN	150	790	SD	124	622
CT	199	823	MS	253	939	TN	209	692
DE	158	498	MO	173	688	TX [3]	269	1,372
DC	188	963	MT	163	663	UT	146	477
FL	202	1,083	NE	157	767	VT	159	646
GA	214	672	NV	211	671	VA	149	641
HI	215	837	NH	157	636	WA	173	589
ID	157	457	NJ	179	682	WV	177	640
IL	174	660	NM	203	605	WI	126	495
IN	177	639	NY	223	842	WY	158	649
IA	139	594	NC	153	644			

[1] Based on the HO-4 renters insurance policy for tenants. Includes broad named-peril coverage for the personal property of tenants. [2] Based on the HO-3 homeowner package policy for owner-occupied dwellings, 1–4 family units. Provides "all risks" coverage (except those specifically excluded in the policy) on buildings, broad named-peril coverage on personal property, and is the most common package written. [3] The Texas Insurance Commissioner promulgates residential policy forms which are similar but not identical to the standard forms.

Source: National Association of Insurance Commissioners (NAIC), Kansas City, MO, *Dwelling Fire, Homeowners Owner-Occupied, and Homeowners Tenant and Condominium/Cooperative Unit Owners Insurance* (copyright). Reprinted with permission of the NAIC. Further reprint or distribution strictly prohibited without prior written permission of the NAIC.

Banking, Finance, and Insurance 739

Table 1185. Real Estate and Rental and Leasing—Nonemployer Establishments and Receipts by Kind of Business: 2000 to 2005

[1,696 represents 1,696,000. Includes only firms subject to federal income tax. Nonemployers are businesses with no paid employees. Data originate chiefly from administrative records of the Internal Revenue Service; see Appendix III. Data for 2000 based on the North American Industry Classification System (NAICS), 1997; beginning 2004, based on NAICS 2002. See text, Section 15]

Kind of business	NAICS code	Establishments (1,000)			Receipts (mil. dol.)		
		2000	2004	2005	2000	2004	2005
Real estate & rental & leasing, total . . .	**53**	**1,696**	**2,218**	**2,442**	**133,398**	**189,905**	**207,688**
Real estate	531	1,616	2,135	2,357	127,862	183,662	201,075
Lessors of real estate	5311	714	820	869	86,934	110,672	117,430
Offices of real estate agents & brokers	5312	522	703	808	22,623	34,288	39,346
Activities related to real estate	5313	380	612	680	18,305	38,701	44,299
Rental & leasing services	532	79	82	83	5,440	6,102	6,465
Automotive equipment rental & leasing	5321	19	20	20	995	974	1,023
Consumer goods rental	5322	17	18	18	766	811	837
General rental centers	5323	3	4	4	252	338	375
Commercial/industrial equipment rental & leasing	5324	41	40	41	3,426	3,979	4,230
Lessors of other nonfinancial intangible assets	533	1	1	2	96	141	152

Source: U.S. Census Bureau, "Nonemployer Statistics"; <http://www.census.gov/epcd/nonemployer/>.

Table 1186. Real Estate and Rental and Leasing—Establishments, Employees, and Payroll: 2000 and 2005

[300.2 represents 300,200. Covers establishments with payroll. Kind-of-business classification for 2000 based on North American Industry Classification System (NAICS) 1997; data for 2005 based on NAICS 2002. See text, Section 15, Business Enterprise. Employees are for the week including March 12. Most government employees are excluded. For statement on methodology, see Appendix III]

Kind of business	NAICS code	Establishments (1,000)		Employees (1,000)		Payroll (bil. dol.)	
		2000	2005	2000	2005	2000	2005
Real estate & rental & leasing, total . . .	**53**	**300.2**	**370.7**	**1,942**	**2,144**	**59.2**	**81.8**
Real estate	531	234.9	302.5	1,280	1,480	40.4	59.7
Lessors of real estate	5311	108.2	117.0	501	530	12.5	17.0
Offices of real estate agents & brokers	5312	65.1	107.2	271	346	10.6	17.6
Activities related to real estate	5313	61.6	78.3	507	604	17.3	25.0
Rental & leasing services	532	63.2	65.9	636	635	17.2	19.9
Automotive equipment rental & leasing	5321	11.1	13.1	182	182	5.1	6.1
Passenger car rental & leasing	53211	5.2	7.0	129	127	3.4	4.0
Truck, utility trailer & RV rental & leasing	53212	5.8	6.1	53	54	1.7	2.1
Consumer goods rental [1]	5322	33.1	33.6	255	264	4.2	5.3
Video tape & disk rental	53223	19.6	18.7	152	154	1.6	1.8
General rental centers	5323	6.4	5.5	42	35	1.2	1.1
Commercial/industrial equipment rental & leasing	5324	12.6	13.7	157	153	6.7	7.4
Lessors of other nonfinancial intangible assets	533	2.1	2.3	26	29	1.6	2.2

[1] Includes other kinds of business not shown separately.

Source: U.S. Census Bureau, "County Business Patterns"; <http://www.census.gov/epcd/cbp/view/cbpview.html>.

Table 1187. Rental and Leasing Services—Revenue by Kind of Business: 2000 to 2006

[In millions of dollars (98,504 represents $98,504,000,000). Based on the North American Industry Classification System (NAICS) 2002; see text, Section 15. Covers taxable and tax-exempt employer firms. Estimates have been adjusted using the results of the 2002 Economic Census. Based on Service Annual Survey; see Appendix III]

Kind of business	2002 NAICS code	2000	2002	2003	2004	2005	2006
Rental & leasing services	**532**	**98,504**	**95,108**	**96,387**	**102,863**	**108,489**	**117,669**
Automotive equipment rental & leasing	5321	37,231	35,779	37,007	41,126	43,643	46,053
Passenger car rental & leasing	53211	22,949	22,683	23,007	24,793	25,958	27,539
Truck, utility trailer, & RV rental & leasing. . .	53212	14,282	13,096	14,000	16,333	17,685	18,514
Consumer goods rental [1]	5322	20,159	20,701	21,923	23,412	22,723	23,163
Video tape & disk rental	53223	9,569	9,364	10,053	10,604	9,507	9,833
General rental centers	5323	3,636	3,387	3,611	3,710	3,790	4,089
Commercial/industrial equip. rental & leasing . .	5324	37,478	35,241	33,846	34,615	38,333	44,364

[1] Includes other kinds of business not shown separately.

Source: U.S. Census Bureau, "Service Annual Survey: 2006"; published December 2007; <http://www.census.gov/econ/www/servmenu.html>.

Section 26
Arts, Recreation, and Travel

This section presents data on the arts, entertainment, and recreation economic sector of the economy, and personal recreational activities, the arts and humanities, and domestic and foreign travel.

Arts, Entertainment, and Recreation Industry—The U.S. Census Bureau's *Service Annual Survey, Arts, Entertainment, and Recreation Sector,* provides estimates of operation revenue of taxable firms and revenues and expenses of firms exempt from federal taxes for industries in this sector of the economy. Data beginning 1998 are based on the North American Industry Classification System (NAICS). Most establishments were previously classified in the Standard Industrial Classification (SIC) in services, some in retail trade.

This new sector is comprised of industries which existed previously, were revised from previous industry definitions, or are completely new industries. Among those which existed previously are amusement and theme parks. Revised industries include museums. New industries include theater companies and dinner theaters. The following URL contains detailed information about NAICS and provides a comparison of the SIC and NAICS <http://www.census.gov/epcd/www/naics.html>. See also the text in Section 15, Business Enterprise.

The Economic Census, conducted every 5 years, for the years ending "2" and "7," provides information on the number of establishments, receipts, payroll, and paid employees for the U.S. and various geographic levels.

Recreation and leisure activities—Data on the participation in various recreation and leisure time activities are based on several sample surveys. Data on participation in fishing, hunting, and other forms of wildlife-associated recreation are published periodically by the U.S. Department of Interior, Fish and Wildlife Service. The most recent data are from the 2006 survey. Data on participation in various sports recreation activities are published by the National Sporting Goods Association. Mediamark, Inc. also conducts periodic surveys on sports and leisure activities, as well as other topics.

Parks and recreation—The Department of the Interior has responsibility for administering the national parks. The National Park Service publishes information on visits to national park areas in its annual report, *National Park Statistical Abstract. The National Parks: Index (year)* is an annual report which contains brief descriptions, with acreages and visits for each area administered by the service, plus certain "related" areas. This information can be found at: <http://www.nature.nps.gov/stats>. Statistics for state parks are compiled by the National Association of State Park Directors.

Travel—Statistics on arrivals and departures to the United States are reported by the International Trade Administration (ITA), Office of Travel & Tourism Industries (OTTI). Data on domestic travel, business receipts and employment of the travel industry, and travel expenditures are published by the research department of the Travel Industry Association (TIA). Other data on household transportation characteristics are in Section 23, Transportation.

Statistical reliability—For a discussion of statistical collection and estimation, sampling procedures, and measures of statistical reliability applicable to Census Bureau data, see Appendix III.

U.S. Census Bureau, Statistical Abstract of the United States: 2009

Table 1188. Arts, Entertainment, and Recreation Services—Estimated Revenue: 2000 to 2006

[In millions of dollars (127,394 represents $127,394,000,000), except percent. For taxable and tax-exempt employer firms. Except where indicated, estimates adjusted using the results of the 2002 Economic Census. Based on the Service Annual Survey, see Appendix III]

Industry	2002 NAICS code [1]	2000	2002	2003	2004	2005	2006
Arts, entertainment, and recreation	71	127,394	141,902	149,360	158,557	165,808	177,910
Performing arts, spectator sports, and related industries	711	51,149	58,285	60,367	62,796	64,912	70,001
Performing arts companies	7111	10,746	10,864	11,070	11,554	12,028	11,871
Spectator sports	7112	19,339	22,313	22,445	23,659	24,559	26,615
Sports teams and clubs	711211	10,739	13,025	13,257	14,115	14,080	15,766
Racetracks	711212	6,349	6,702	6,582	7,022	7,570	7,759
Other spectator sports	711219	2,251	2,586	2,606	2,522	2,909	3,090
Promoters of performing arts, sports, and similar events	7113	10,098	12,168	12,872	13,571	14,045	16,365
Agents and managers for artists, athletes, entertainers and other public figures	7114	3,184	3,602	3,604	3,819	3,672	3,565
Independent artists, writers, and performers	7115	7,782	9,338	10,376	10,193	10,608	11,585
Museums, historical sites, and similar institutions . . .	712	9,350	8,607	9,082	9,688	10,115	11,547
Amusement, gambling, and recreation industries	713	66,895	75,010	79,911	86,073	90,781	96,362
Amusement parks and arcades	7131	9,441	9,443	9,930	10,561	11,072	11,098
Amusement and theme parks	71311	8,245	8,174	8,737	9,344	9,882	9,963
Amusement arcades	71312	1,196	1,269	1,193	1,217	1,190	1,135
Gambling industries	7132	14,621	18,893	22,370	25,698	27,994	30,614
Casinos (except casino hotels)	71321	9,592	12,387	14,601	16,664	18,068	19,876
Other gambling industries	71329	5,029	6,506	7,769	9,034	9,926	10,738
Other amusement and recreation industries	7139	42,833	46,674	47,611	49,814	51,715	54,650
Golf courses and country clubs	71391	16,692	17,533	16,987	17,880	18,533	19,267
Skiing facilities	71392	1,551	1,801	1,839	1,980	2,049	2,234
Marinas	71393	3,379	3,352	3,382	3,393	3,670	3,898
Fitness and recreational sports centers	71394	12,543	14,987	16,130	16,839	17,545	18,447
Bowling centers	71395	2,762	3,075	3,293	3,505	3,415	3,609
All other amusement and recreation	71399	5,906	5,926	5,980	6,217	6,503	7,195

[1] Based on the North American Industry Classification System (NAICS) 2002; see text, this section and Section 15.

Source: U.S. Census Bureau, "2006 Service Annual Survey, Arts, Entertainment, and Recreation Services." See <http://www.census.gov/econ/www/servmenu.html>; (released December 2007).

Table 1189. Arts, Entertainment, and Recreation—Establishments, Revenue, Payroll, and Employees by Kind of Business (1997 NAICS Basis): 1997 and 2002

[(104,715 represents $104,715,000,000) For establishments with payroll. Data are based on the 1997 and 2002 economic censuses which are subject to nonsampling error. For details on survey methodology, sampling and nonsampling errors, see Appendix III. Based on the North American Industry Classification System (NAICS) 1997 codes, see text, section 15]

Kind of business	1997 NAICS code	Number of establishments		Revenue (mil. dol.)		Annual payroll (mil. dol.)		Paid employees (1,000)	
		1997	2002	1997	2002	1997	2002	1997	2002
Arts, entertainment, and recreation, total.	71	99,099	110,324	104,715	141,923	32,787	45,175	1,588	1,849
Performing arts, spectator sports, and related industries [1]	711	30,566	37,737	37,619	58,286	14,456	21,232	327	423
Performing arts companies.	7111	9,199	9,303	8,570	10,864	2,725	3,267	122	138
Spectator sports.	7112	3,881	4,072	13,656	22,313	6,151	10,206	92	108
Promoters of performing arts, sports, and similar events.	7113	3,941	4,521	6,622	11,698	1,401	2,020	72	99
Agents and managers for artists, athletes, entertainers, and others. . .	7114	2,532	3,977	2,410	4,073	911	1,415	13	21
Museums, historical sites, and similar institutions [1]	712	5,580	6,664	6,764	8,609	1,837	2,936	92	123
Amusement, gambling, and recreation industries [1]	713	62,914	65,923	58,463	75,028	20,792	21,007	1,146	1,303
Amusement parks and arcades.	7131	3,344	3,015	8,418	9,443	1,962	2,069	139	122
Gambling industries	7132	2,060	2,075	13,673	18,902	2,728	3,599	146	158
Other amusement and recreation services	7139	57,510	60,833	36,372	46,682	11,310	15,339	862	1,023

[1] Includes other industries not shown separately.

Source: U.S. Census Bureau, "2002 Economic Census, Comparative Statistics for United States; Arts, Entertainment and Recreation"; (accessed 14 June 2007) and <http://www.census.gov/econ/census02/data/comparative/USCS71.HTM>; (accessed 14 June 2007).

Table 1190. **Arts, Entertainment, and Recreation—Nonemployer Establishments and Receipts by Kind of Business (NAICS Basis): 2000 to 2005**

[**(781.7 represents 781,700)**. Includes only firms subject to federal income tax. Nonemployers are businesses with no paid employees]

Kind of business	2002 NAICS code [1]	Establishments (1,000)			Receipts (mil. dol.)		
		2000	2004	2005	2000	2004	2005
Arts, entertainment, and recreation	**71**	**781.7**	**923.1**	**972.5**	**17,713**	**22,448**	**23,704**
Performing arts, spectator sports, and related industries	711	645.4	781.8	828.8	13,008	16,637	17,741
Performing arts companies	7111	19.3	29.3	30.0	576	766	827
Spectator sports	7112	67.3	91.0	91.6	1,481	1,894	1,877
Promoters of performing arts, sports, and similar events	7113	23.1	33.9	35.5	851	1,292	1,434
Agents/managers for artists, athletes, and other public figures	7114	27.1	31.8	32.6	857	1,111	1,183
Independent artists, writers, and performers	7115	508.6	595.8	639.1	9,244	11,573	12,419
Museums, historical sites, and similar institutions	712	3.6	5.5	5.6	52	80	91
Amusement, gambling, and recreation industries	713	132.7	135.8	138.1	4,653	5,732	5,873
Amusement parks and arcades	7131	5.4	5.7	5.4	291	372	346
Gambling industries.	7132	5.9	7.8	8.4	532	1,049	1,064
Other amusement and recreation services . . .	7139	121.3	122.4	124.2	3,830	4,311	4,463

[1] Based on the 2002 North American Industry Classification System (NAICS); see text, Section 15.
Source: U.S. Census Bureau, Nonemployer Statistics; released June 2007. See <http://www.census.gov/epcd/nonemployer/index.html>.

Table 1191. **Arts, Entertainment, and Recreation—Establishments, Employees, and Payroll by Kind of Business (NAICS Basis): 2000 and 2005**

[**(1,741.5 represents 1,741,500)**. For establishments with payroll. See Appendix III]

Kind of business	2002 NAICS code [1]	Establishments		Paid employees [2] (1,000)		Annual payroll (mil. dol.)	
		2000	2005	2000	2005	2000	2005
Arts, entertainment, and recreation	**71**	**103,816**	**121,777**	**1,741.5**	**1,936.5**	**43,204**	**52,936**
Performing arts, spectator sports	711	33,859	41,675	351.9	412.1	19,090	24,074
Performing arts companies	7111	9,253	9,209	126.4	134.4	3,251	3,720
Theater companies and dinner theaters	71111	3,367	3,544	63.4	73.4	1,469	1,842
Dance companies	71112	584	593	10.7	9.2	216	211
Musical groups and artists	71113	4,497	4,526	44.0	44.5	1,341	1,429
Other performing arts companies.	71119	805	546	8.3	7.3	226	239
Spectator sports	7112	4,461	4,502	100.2	114.8	9,215	11,671
Sports teams and clubs	711211	684	775	36.3	46.7	7,587	9,659
Racetracks	711212	899	739	45.8	48.4	994	1,172
Other spectator sports	711219	2,878	2,988	18.1	19.7	633	839
Promoters of performing arts, sports, and similar events	7113	4,394	5,651	71.8	101.1	1,917	2,415
Promoters of performing arts, sports, and similar events with facilities.	71131	1,107	2,050	44.3	75.7	787	1,315
Promoters of performing arts, sports, and similar events without facilities.	71132	3,287	3,601	27.6	25.4	1,130	1,100
Agents/managers for artists, athletes, and other public figures	7114	3,048	3,469	16.0	19.4	1,117	1,633
Independent artists, writers, and performers . . .	7115	12,703	18,844	37.5	42.5	3,589	4,635
Museums, historical sites, & similar institutions . . .	712	5,777	6,980	110.4	120.9	2,549	3,175
Museums.	71211	3,988	4,763	75.4	79.9	1,765	2,132
Historical sites.	71212	892	982	8.3	9.6	143	208
Zoos and botanical gardens.	71213	414	605	20.5	26.0	509	694
Nature parks and other similar institutions	71219	483	630	6.2	5.4	133	140
Amusement, gambling, & recreation industries . . .	713	64,180	73,122	1,279.2	1,403.4	21,564	25,687
Amusement parks and arcades	7131	2,879	2,917	124.0	144.6	2,277	2,825
Amusement and theme parks	71311	716	584	102.8	118.1	2,011	2,471
Amusement arcades	71312	2,163	2,333	21.3	26.5	266	355
Gambling industries	7132	2,191	2,440	202.6	195.2	4,757	5,227
Casinos (except casino hotels)	71321	537	508	150.2	136.3	3,592	3,697
Other gambling industries	71329	1,654	1,932	52.4	59.0	1,165	1,530
Other amusement and recreation services	7139	59,110	67,765	952.6	1,063.5	14,531	17,635
Golf courses and country clubs	71391	11,885	11,978	297.9	304.6	6,243	7,432
Skiing facilities.	71392	389	390	56.9	73.8	452	587
Marinas	71393	4,126	4,143	24.8	27.5	640	840
Fitness and recreational sports centers.	71394	23,003	31,988	382.8	488.8	4,499	6,126
Bowling centers	71395	5,234	4,666	87.9	82.5	888	943
All other amusement and recreation industries	71399	14,473	14,600	102.4	86.3	1,808	1,708

[1] North American Industry Classification System code (NAICS); see text, this section and Section 15.   [2] For employees on the payroll for the period including March 12.
Source: U.S. Census Bureau, County Business Patterns; annual. See <http://www.census.gov/epcd/cbp/view/cbpview.html>.

Arts, Recreation, and Travel   743

Table 1192. **Expenditures Per Consumer Unit for Entertainment and Reading: 1985 to 2006**

[**Data are annual averages. In dollars, except as indicated.** Based on Consumer Expenditure Survey (CE); see text in Section 13, for description of survey. See also headnote, Table 664. For composition of regions, see map, inside front cover]

Year and characteristic	Entertainment and reading		Entertainment				Reading
	Total	Percent of total expenditures	Total	Fees and admissions	Audio and visual equipment, and services	Other entertainment supplies, equipment, and services [1]	
1985............	1,311	5.6	1,170	320	371	479	141
1990............	1,575	5.6	1,422	371	454	597	153
1991............	1,635	5.5	1,472	378	468	627	163
1992............	1,662	5.6	1,500	379	492	629	162
1993............	1,792	5.8	1,626	414	590	621	166
1994............	1,732	5.5	1,567	439	533	595	165
1995............	1,775	5.5	1,612	433	542	637	163
1996............	1,993	5.9	1,834	459	561	814	159
1997............	1,977	5.7	1,813	471	577	766	164
1998............	1,907	5.4	1,746	449	535	762	161
1999............	2,050	5.5	1,891	459	608	824	159
2000............	2,009	5.3	1,863	515	622	727	146
2001............	2,094	5.3	1,953	526	660	767	141
2002............	2,218	5.5	2,079	542	692	845	139
2003............	2,187	5.4	2,060	494	730	835	127
2004............	2,348	5.4	2,218	528	788	903	130
2005............	2,514	5.4	2,388	588	888	912	126
2006, total.............	**2,493**	**5.2**	**2,376**	**606**	**906**	**863**	**117**
Age of reference person:							
Under 25 years old.........	1,394	4.9	1,348	280	672	396	46
25 to 34 years old	2,319	4.9	2,237	475	969	793	82
35 to 44 years old	3,078	5.4	2,966	839	1,052	1,075	112
45 to 54 years old	2,903	5.0	2,770	757	1,020	992	133
55 to 64 years old	2,813	5.5	2,666	605	906	1,155	147
65 to 74 years old	2,192	5.4	2,049	559	791	699	143
75 years old and over........	1,228	4.2	1,099	300	523	277	129
Hispanic or Latino Origin of reference person:							
Hispanic..................	1,611	3.7	1,568	401	772	395	43
Non-Hispanic	2,608	5.3	2,481	633	924	924	127
Race of reference person:							
White, Asian, and all other races....	2,667	5.3	2,540	663	928	950	127
Black....................	1,218	3.5	1,172	192	747	234	46
Region of residence:							
Northeast.................	2,478	5.0	2,346	662	919	765	132
Midwest..................	2,390	5.3	2,261	599	830	832	129
South	2,181	4.9	2,096	442	890	765	85
West	3,114	5.4	2,970	829	1,001	1,139	144
Size of consumer unit:							
One person	1,555	5.3	1,464	363	631	469	91
Two or more persons	2,886	5.1	2,758	708	1,022	1,028	128
Two persons	2,721	5.4	2,576	631	934	1,011	145
Three persons	2,691	4.8	2,580	595	1,053	932	111
Four persons.............	3,359	5.3	3,232	911	1,175	1,145	127
Five persons or more	3,062	4.7	2,965	860	1,043	1,062	97
Income before taxes: Quintiles of income:							
Lowest 20 percent	930	4.6	879	163	476	241	51
Second 20 percent	1,344	4.4	1,271	230	632	409	73
Third 20 percent...........	1,996	4.8	1,898	391	876	630	98
Fourth 20 percent..........	2,851	5.1	2,720	637	1,040	1,042	131
Highest 20 percent	5,337	5.7	5,105	1,607	1,505	1,993	232
Education:							
Less than a high school graduate ...	1,177	4.1	1,134	147	596	391	43
High school graduate	1,918	4.9	1,842	327	799	716	76
High school graduate with some college................	2,354	5.1	2,250	492	891	867	104
Associate's degree.............	2,664	5.1	2,542	633	1,013	896	122
Bachelor's degree	3,537	5.5	3,366	1,075	1,153	1,137	171
Master's, professional, doctoral degree..................	4,191	5.6	3,933	1,395	1,131	1,407	258

[1] Other equipment and services include pets, toys, and playground equipment; sports, exercise, and photographic equipment; and recreational vehicles.

Source: U.S. Bureau of Labor Statistics, *Consumer Expenditure Survey,* annual and Current Standard Tables. See also <http://www.bls.gov/cex/home/htm>.

Table 1193. Personal Consumption Expenditures for Recreation: 1990 to 2006

[In billions of dollars (290.2 represents $290,200,000,000), except percent. Represents market value of purchases of goods and services by individuals and nonprofit institutions]

Type of product or service	1990	2000	2002	2003	2004	2005	2006
Total recreation expenditures	**290.2**	**585.7**	**629.9**	**659.9**	**707.8**	**746.9**	**791.1**
Percent of total personal consumption [1]	7.6	8.7	8.6	8.6	8.7	8.6	8.6
Books and maps	16.2	33.7	37.1	38.7	40.4	41.8	43.4
Magazines, newspapers, and sheet music	21.6	35.0	35.1	36.3	39.4	42.1	45.0
Nondurable toys and sport supplies	32.8	56.6	59.2	60.6	63.3	66.5	71.4
Wheel goods, sports, and photographic equipment [2]	29.7	57.6	61.4	65.6	71.3	76.2	78.9
Video and audio products, computer equipment, and musical instruments	53.0	116.6	120.0	123.1	133.3	142.3	151.5
Video and audio goods, including musical instruments	44.1	72.8	75.4	76.5	81.7	85.8	90.1
Computers, peripherals, and software	8.9	43.8	44.6	46.6	51.6	56.5	61.4
Radio and television repair	3.2	4.2	4.1	4.1	4.6	4.8	5.4
Flowers, seeds, and potted plants	10.9	18.0	18.0	17.9	18.3	19.2	19.9
Admissions to specified spectator amusements	15.1	30.4	34.8	36.0	37.6	38.7	39.9
Motion picture theaters	5.1	8.6	9.6	9.9	9.9	9.5	9.3
Legitimate theaters and opera, and entertainments of nonprofit institutions [3]	5.2	10.3	11.7	11.9	12.5	13.2	13.4
Spectator sports [4]	4.8	11.5	13.5	14.3	15.3	16.0	17.2
Clubs and fraternal organizations except insurance [5]	13.5	19.0	21.1	22.2	22.3	23.7	23.9
Commercial participant amusements [6]	25.2	75.8	83.7	91.2	100.9	106.8	115.3
Parimutuel net receipts	3.5	5.0	5.3	5.2	5.7	6.2	6.6
Other [7]	65.4	133.9	150.0	158.9	170.8	178.7	190.0

[1] See Table 655.   [2] Includes boats and pleasure aircraft.   [3] Except athletic.   [4] Consists of admissions to professional and amateur athletic events and to racetracks, including horse, dog, and auto.   [5] Consists of current expenditures (including consumption of fixed capital) of nonprofit clubs and fraternal organizations and dues and fees paid to proprietary clubs.   [6] Consists of billiard parlors; bowling alleys; dancing, riding, shooting, skating, and swimming places; amusement devices and parks; golf courses; sightseeing buses and guides; private flying operations; casino gambling; and other commercial participant amusements.   [7] Consists of net receipts of lotteries and expenditures for purchases of pets and pet care services, cable TV, film processing, photographic studios, sporting and recreation camps, video cassette rentals, and recreational services not elsewhere classified.

Source: U.S. Bureau of Economic Analysis, *Survey of Current Business*; accessed 7 February 2008. See also <http://www.bea.gov/bea/dn/nipaweb/index.asp>.

Table 1194. Performing Arts—Selected Data: 1990 to 2006

[Sales, receipts, and expenditures in millions of dollars (282 represents $282,000,000). For season ending in year shown, except as indicated]

Item	1990	1995	1999	2000	2001	2002	2003	2004	2005	2006
Legitimate theater: [1]										
Broadway shows:										
New productions	40	33	39	37	28	37	36	39	39	39
Attendance (mil.)	8.0	9.0	11.7	11.4	11.9	11.0	11.4	11.6	11.5	12.0
Playing weeks [2, 3]	1,070	1,120	1,441	1,464	1,484	1,434	1,544	1,451	1,494	1,501
Gross ticket sales	282	406	588	603	666	643	721	771	769	862
Broadway road tours: [4]										
Attendance (mil.)	11.1	15.6	14.6	11.7	11.0	11.7	12.4	12.9	18.2	17.1
Playing weeks	944	1,242	1,082	888	823	863	877	1,060	1,389	1,377
Gross ticket sales	367	701	707	572	541	593	642	714	934	915
Nonprofit professional theatres: [5]										
Companies reporting [6]	185	215	313	262	363	1,146	1,274	1,477	1,490	1,893
Gross income	308	444	740	791	961	1,436	1,481	1,571	1,647	1,791
Earned income	188	281	442	466	555	761	787	856	845	923
Contributed income	119	163	298	325	407	675	694	715	802	868
Gross expenses	306	445	701	708	924	1,405	1,476	1,464	1,530	1,667
Productions	2,265	2,646	3,921	3,241	4,787	10,000	13,000	11,000	12,000	14,000
Performances	46,131	56,608	64,556	66,123	81,828	157,000	170,000	169,000	169,000	172,000
Total attendance (mil.)	15.2	18.6	18.0	22.0	21.1	32.2	34.3	32.1	32.5	30.5
OPERA America professional member companies: [7]										
Number of companies reporting [8]	98	88	95	98	96	86	89	95	93	110
Expenses [8]	321	435	591	637	685	684	692	678	755	849
Performances [9]	2,336	6,500...	2,200	2,153	2,031	1,868.0	1,730	1,946	2,097	2,032
Total attendance (mil.) [9, 10]	7.5	6.5	6.6	6.7	6.5	4.9	5.9	5.1	5.1	5.3
Main season attendance (mil.) [9, 11]	4.1	3.9	4.0	4.3	4.2	3.2	3.1	3.4	3.3	3.7
Symphony orchestras: [12]										
Concerts	18,931	29,328	31,549	33,154	36,437	37,118	38,182	37,263	37,196	36,731
Attendance (mil.)	24.7	30.9	30.8	31.7	31.5	30.3	27.8	27.7	26.5	29.1
Gross revenue	378	536	672	734	775	764	781	827	812	945
Operating expenses	622	859	1,088	1,126	1,286	1,312	1,315	1,483	1,513	1,603
Support	258	351	486	521	560	580	576	639	626	713

[1] Source: The League of American Theaters and Producers, Inc, New York, NY. For season ending in year shown.   [2] All shows (new productions and holdovers from previous seasons).   [3] Eight performances constitute one playing week.   [4] North American Tours include U.S. and Canadian companies.   [5] Source: Theatre Communications Group, New York, NY. For years ending on or prior to Aug. 31.   [6] Beginning in 2002, nonprofit theatre data is based on survey responses and extrapolated data from IRS Form 990.   [7] Source: OPERA America, New York, NY. For years ending on or prior to Aug 31.   [8] U.S. companies.   [9] Prior to 1993, and for 1999, U.S. and Canadian companies; 1993 to 1998 and 2000 to 2006, U.S. companies only.   [10] Includes educational performances, outreach, etc.   [11] For paid performances.   [12] Source: American Symphony Orchestra League, Inc., New York, NY. For years ending Aug. 31. Prior to 1995, represents 254 U.S. orchestras; beginning 1995, represents all U.S. orchestras, excluding college/university and youth orchestras. Also, beginning 1995, data based on 1,200 orchestras.

Source: Compiled from sources listed in footnotes. See also <http://www.livebroadway.com>; <http://www.tcg.org>; <http://www.operaamerica.org/>; and <http://www.symphony.org>.

Arts, Recreation, and Travel   745

Table 1195. **Arts and Humanities—Selected Federal Aid Programs: 1990 to 2006**

[In millions of dollars (170.8 represents $170,800,000), except as indicated. For fiscal year ending September 30]

Type of fund and program	1990	1995	2000	2001	2002	2003	2004	2005	2006
National Endowment for the Arts:									
Funds available [1]	170.8	152.1	85.2	94.0	98.6	101.0	105.5	108.8	112.8
Program appropriation [2]	124.3	109.0	66.0	86.7	95.8	95.1	99.3	99.5	100.7
Grants awarded (number) [2]	4,475	3,685	1,882	2,093	2,138	1,925	2,150	2,161	2,293
Funds obligated [3, 4]	157.6	147.9	83.5	92.5	96.2	99.3	102.6	104.4	107.0
National Endowment for the Humanities:									
Funds available [1]	140.6	152.3	102.6	106.8	110.1	111.6	127.1	119.8	121.5
Program appropriation	114.2	125.7	82.7	86.4	89.9	89.3	98.7	99.9	102.2
Matching funds [5]	26.3	25.7	15.1	15.6	16.1	16.0	15.9	15.9	15.2
Grants awarded (number)	2,195	1,871	1,230	1,290	1,252	963	1,246	1,174	1,282
Funds obligated [3]	141.0	151.8	100.0	105.7	106.1	100.1	125.1	117.8	120.3
Education programs	16.3	19.2	13.0	12.1	12.1	11.3	17.4	14.6	14.4
State programs	29.6	32.0	30.6	32.1	32.8	33.0	36.3	36.9	38.7
Research grants	22.5	22.2	6.9	7.0	7.0	7.9	8.4	7.1	8.7
Fellowship program	15.3	16.5	6.1	7.0	7.7	6.9	8.1	8.9	7.2
Challenge [6]	14.6	13.8	10.8	11.9	13.4	8.3	12.6	12.7	10.5
Public programs	25.4	25.8	11.8	16.3	13.2	12.7	18.3	14.4	15.5
Preservation and access	17.5	22.2	20.7	19.2	19.8	20.7	23.7	22.4	24.5

[1] Includes other funds not shown separately. Excludes administrative funds. [2] Excludes cooperative agreements and interagency agreements. [3] Includes obligations for new grants, supplemental awards on previous years' grants, and program contracts. [4] Beginning with 1997 data, the grantmaking structure changed from discipline-based categories to thematic ones. [5] Represents federal funds obligated only upon receipt or certification by endowment of matching nonfederal gifts. [6] Program designed to stimulate new sources and higher levels of giving to institutions for the purpose of guaranteeing long-term stability and financial independence. Program usually requires a match of at least 3 private dollars to each federal dollar. Funds for challenge grants are not allocated by program area because they are awarded on a grant-by-grant basis.

Source: U.S. National Endowment for the Arts, *Annual Report;* and U.S. National Endowment for the Humanities, *Annual Report.* See also <http://arts.endow.gov/> and <http://www.neh.gov/>.

Table 1196. **Budgets for Selected U.S. Federal and Quasi-Governmental Organizations Funding Arts and Culture: 2004 and 2006**

[In millions of dollars (489 represents $489,000,000). Independent of the Arts Endowment and its state and regional partners, other public agencies also support arts and culture, along with legislative earmarks]

Organization	2004	2006	Organization	2004	2006
Smithsonian Institution [1]	489	517	Department of Education (Arts in Education Model Development Program)	10	13
Corporation for Public Broadcasting	377	460	Commission of Fine Arts	8	2
Institute of Museum and Library Services	262	247	National Capital Planning Commission	8	8
National Endowment for the Humanities	135	142	General Services Administration (Art-in-architecture Program)	5	7
National Endowment for the Arts	121	124			
National Gallery of Art	88	95	Advisory Council on Historic Preservation	4	5
Department of Interior (Save America's Treasures)	30	28	Department of State (Bureau of Education and Cultural Affairs' cultural exchanges, presentations, and diplomacy)	(NA)	5
Kennedy Center for the Performing Arts	17	18			

NA Not available. [1] Exclusive of buildings and facilities capital.
Source: National Endowment for the Arts, *How the United States Funds the Arts. Other Public Support for the Arts and Culture.* See also <http://www.nea.gov/pub/how.pdf>.

Table 1197. **Total State Arts Agency Legislative Appropriations: 2007 to 2008**

[For fiscal year ending September 30. In thousands of dollars (350,122 represents $350,122,000). The National Assembly of State Arts Agencies (NASAA) is the membership organization of the nations' state and jurisdictional arts agencies. Legislative appropriations include funds designated to the state arts agency by state legislatures. These include line items, which are not controlled by the agency but passed through to designated entities. State arts agencies also receive monies from other sources including other state funds, the federal government (primarily the National Endowment for the Arts), private funds, and legislative earmarks. Minus sign (–) indicates decrease in spending]

State	Legislative appropriation including line items 2007	Legislative appropriation including line items 2008	Percent change 2007 to 2008	State	Legislative appropriation including line items 2007	Legislative appropriation including line items 2008	Percent change 2007 to 2008	State	Legislative appropriation including line items 2007	Legislative appropriation including line items 2008	Percent change 2007 to 2008
U.S.	**350,122**	**359,615**	**2.7**	KY	4,203	4,195	–0.2	OH	11,238	12,488	11.1
AL	4,879	5,824	19.4	LA	4,968	6,715	35.2	OK	4,443	5,151	15.9
AK	601	601	–0.1	ME	757	804	6.1	OR	714	2,115	196.1
AZ	1,888	2,112	11.9	MD	14,351	15,190	5.9	PA	15,225	15,225	–
AR	1,524	1,557	2.2	MA	12,121	12,268	1.2	RI	2,689	2,778	3.3
CA	4,024	4,002	–0.5	MI	6,508	7,488	15.1	SC	5,409	5,445	0.7
CO	1,500	1,531	2.1	MN	8,593	10,215	18.9	SD	610	636	4.3
CT	7,362	9,880	34.2	MS	1,826	1,856	1.6	TN	6,715	7,262	8.2
DE	2,063	2,085	1.1	MO	4,845	10,665	120.1	TX	3,917	4,216	7.6
DC	9,368	9,380	0.1	MT	396	544	37.3	UT	3,028	4,342	43.4
FL	40,935	15,576	–61.9	NE	1,351	1,468	8.7	VT	570	546	–4.2
GA	4,135	4,189	1.3	NV	1,541	2,225	44.4	VA	4,873	6,183	26.9
HI	7,089	7,661	8.1	NH	740	844	14.1	WA	2,368	2,578	8.9
ID	899	957	6.4	NJ	24,312	28,498	17.2	WV	2,424	2,572	6.1
IL	19,799	15,205	–23.2	NM	1,846	2,250	21.9	WI	2,420	2,470	2.1
IN	3,632	3,993	9.9	NY	45,232	51,793	14.5	WY	807	1,019	26.3
IA	1,213	1,246	2.8	NC	8,541	9,990	17.0				
KS	1,561	1,659	6.2	ND	500	585	16.9				

– Represents zero.

Source: National Assembly of State Arts Agencies, *"Legislative Appropriations Annual Survey,"* February 2008. See also <http://www.nasaa-arts.org/nasaanews/nn_contents.shtml>.

746   Arts, Recreation, and Travel

Table 1198. **Attendance Rates for Various Arts Activities: 2002**

[In percent. For persons 18 years old and over. Represents attendance at least once in the prior 12 months. Excludes elementary and high school performances. Based on the 2002 household survey *Public Participation in the Arts*. See also Table 1199]

Item	Jazz	Classical music	Musicals	Non-musical plays	Ballet	Art museums/ galleries	Art/craft fairs and festivals	Historic sites [1]	Literature [2]
Total	**10.8**	**11.6**	**17.1**	**12.3**	**3.9**	**26.5**	**33.4**	**31.6**	**46.7**
Sex: Male	10.7	10.3	14.0	10.3	2.5	24.6	27.0	30.5	37.6
Female	10.8	12.7	20.0	14.2	5.1	28.2	39.2	32.5	55.1
Race and Ethnicity:									
White alone	11.4	13.7	20.1	14.2	4.7	29.5	38.0	36.0	51.4
African American alone	12.7	4.5	10.3	7.1	1.5	14.8	9.7	17.8	37.1
Other alone	7.3	10.3	11.9	10.0	2.3	32.7	25.8	30.4	43.7
Hispanic	6.2	5.5	6.9	6.2	1.6	16.1	20.3	17.2	26.5
Age:									
18 to 24 years old	10.5	7.8	14.8	11.4	2.6	23.7	29.2	28.3	42.8
25 to 34 years old	10.8	9.0	15.4	10.7	3.5	26.7	33.5	33.3	47.7
35 to 44 years old	13.0	10.7	19.1	13.0	4.9	27.4	37.2	35.8	46.6
45 to 54 years old	13.9	15.2	19.3	15.2	5.1	32.9	38.8	38.0	51.6
55 to 64 years old	8.8	15.6	19.7	13.8	3.3	27.8	35.1	31.6	48.9
65 to 74 years old	7.6	12.5	16.6	13.0	3.3	23.4	31.1	24.2	45.3
75 years old and older	3.9	9.5	10.1	5.4	2.2	13.4	15.7	12.8	36.7
Education:									
Grade school	0.9	1.5	1.6	1.1	–	4.5	8.4	6.3	14.0
Some high school	2.7	1.9	4.1	3.7	0.8	7.7	14.0	11.4	23.4
High school graduate	5.3	4.5	9.1	5.7	1.2	14.2	25.7	20.2	37.7
Some college	12.2	11.5	19.4	12.7	3.9	29.0	38.2	36.5	52.9
College graduate	19.4	21.9	30.2	22.5	7.2	46.6	49.3	51.2	63.1
Graduate school	24.0	34.1	37.6	31.8	12.9	58.6	51.9	56.8	74.3
Income:									
Less than $10,000	5.1	6.7	7.6	5.3	1.5	12.4	19.7	14.1	32.1
$10,000 to $19,999	5.4	5.2	8.2	5.4	1.9	14.0	21.4	14.9	37.5
$20,000 to $29,999	6.3	6.3	8.6	6.0	2.4	16.2	24.5	20.8	37.5
$30,000 to $39,999	10.9	10.3	13.6	10.0	2.8	23.3	33.2	28.6	44.1
$40,000 to $49,999	10.3	12.9	16.1	12.2	3.6	25.3	34.6	32.7	47.9
$50,000 to $74,999	11.2	12.4	21.5	14.0	4.3	30.4	40.3	39.1	52.3
$75,000 or More	18.2	19.9	29.3	21.8	7.2	44.6	46.5	50.9	60.8

– Represents or rounds to zero.   [1] Parks, historic buildings, neighborhoods.   [2] Read a book (literature) during the previous twelve months. Includes novels, short stories, poetry, and/or plays.

Source: U.S. National Endowment for the Arts, Research Division Report #45, *2002 Survey of Public Participation in the Arts.* See also <http://www.nea.gov/research/ResearchReports_chrono.html>.

Table 1199. **Participation in Various Leisure Activities: 2002**

[In percent, except as indicated (205.9 represents 205,900,000). For persons 18 years old and over. Covers activities engaged in at least once in the prior 12 months. See headnote, Table 1198]

Item	Adult population (mil.)	Attendance at—			Participation in—				
		Movies	Sports events	Amusement park	Exercise program	Playing sports	Charity work	Home improvement/ repair	Gardening
Total	**205.9**	**60.0**	**35.0**	**41.7**	**55.1**	**30.4**	**29.0**	**42.4**	**47.3**
Sex:									
Male	98.7	59.5	41.4	40.4	55.0	38.8	25.6	46.3	37.1
Female	107.2	60.5	29.2	42.9	55.1	22.7	32.1	38.9	56.7
Race and Ethnicity:									
White alone	150.1	63.0	38.4	42.8	59.1	33.0	32.5	47.7	52.3
African American alone	23.7	49.2	27.0	36.6	46.1	23.1	22.7	26.3	30.3
Other alone	9.5	58.1	22.3	43.9	50.4	26.9	22.5	33.8	41.3
Hispanic	22.7	52.5	26.4	38.9	40.1	22.3	15.3	28.0	34.8
Age:									
18 to 24 years old	26.8	82.8	46.0	57.6	61.3	49.4	25.3	21.1	20.7
25 to 34 years old	36.9	73.3	41.8	56.2	60.2	39.6	26.0	41.1	41.4
35 to 44 years old	44.2	68.0	42.2	53.3	59.5	36.6	33.2	53.0	51.8
45 to 54 years old	39.0	60.4	35.8	37.1	58.6	28.6	33.4	54.9	55.4
55 to 64 years old	25.9	46.6	25.5	27.1	48.4	16.0	28.1	44.8	56.6
65 to 74 years old	17.6	32.2	19.7	18.4	47.0	13.7	28.8	38.4	57.2
75 years old and over	15.5	19.5	11.1	9.6	31.3	6.0	21.3	22.1	47.9
Education:									
Grade school	11.6	19.5	9.4	17.2	21.0	6.9	8.2	19.5	32.5
Some high school	20.1	39.4	17.4	30.6	32.7	17.2	12.5	24.9	31.2
High school graduate	63.8	51.7	28.3	37.9	45.6	22.6	20.2	35.6	43.8
Some college	56.9	68.7	39.9	48.9	62.3	35.2	33.1	46.5	49.6
College graduate	36.1	77.1	51.0	50.1	73.2	45.2	42.6	56.0	56.1
Graduate school	17.4	77.5	48.3	44.0	77.3	43.6	53.1	61.6	63.3
Income:									
Less than $10,000	14.4	38.7	16.5	30.4	36.5	15.0	16.2	19.7	32.2
$10,000 to $19,999	22.7	41.8	20.1	30.7	42.0	18.5	18.8	23.5	38.8
$20,000 to $29,999	25.0	48.3	23.0	34.7	45.2	21.4	20.7	28.4	40.9
$30,000 to $39,999	24.2	57.5	30.0	39.3	53.3	26.6	27.4	42.0	46.6
$40,000 to $49,999	17.6	63.1	34.8	42.6	55.0	29.3	29.1	46.0	49.1
$50,000 to $74,999	34.7	69.3	44.8	50.2	63.0	36.0	35.3	53.6	54.4
$75,000 or more	45.8	79.4	53.3	54.0	72.5	48.0	41.5	61.2	56.3
Not reported	21.5	51.0	28.4	31.4	45.1	22.6	23.2	33.6	42.9

Source: U.S. National Endowment for the Arts, Research Division Report #45, 2002 *Survey of Public Participation in the Arts.* See <http://www.nea.gov/research/ResearchReports_chrono.html>.

Arts, Recreation, and Travel   747

Table 1200. **Adult Participation in Selected Leisure Activities by Frequency: 2007**

[In thousands (13,462 represents 13,462,000), except percent. For fall 2007. Based on sample and subject to sampling error; see source]

| Activity | Participated in the last 12 months [1] | | Frequency of participation | | | | | | | |
| | | | Two or more times a week | | Once a week | | Two to three times a month | | Once a month | |
	Number	Percent	Number	Percent	Number	Percent	Number	Percent	Number	Percent
Adult education courses	13,462	6.1	2,765	1.3	2,415	1.1	538	0.2	768	0.4
Attend auto shows	17,311	7.8	180	0.1	300	0.1	482	0.2	1,129	0.5
Attend art galleries or shows	8,624	3.9	50	(Z)	102	0.1	287	0.1	771	0.4
Attend classical music/opera performances.	9,350	4.2	91	(Z)	121	0.1	371	0.2	1,167	0.5
Attend country music performances...	11,310	5.1	39	(Z)	43	(Z)	262	0.1	542	0.3
Attend dance performances	9,070	4.1	138	0.1	190	0.1	249	0.1	572	0.3
Attend horse races	5,939	2.7	222	0.1	260	0.1	413	0.2	226	0.1
Attend other music performances [2] ...	23,824	10.8	317	0.1	276	0.1	1,080	0.5	2,056	0.9
Attend rock music performances	21,368	9.7	139	0.1	233	0.1	449	0.2	1,185	0.5
Backgammon	3,675	1.7	408	0.2	211	0.1	446	0.2	422	0.2
Baking...................	47,647	21.6	8,832	4.0	7,019	3.2	11,448	5.2	7,145	3.2
Barbecuing	77,941	35.3	12,557	5.7	12,661	5.7	18,441	8.4	10,120	4.6
Billiards/pool	21,071	9.5	1,983	0.9	1,577	0.7	2,716	1.2	1,993	0.9
Bird watching...............	12,498	5.7	6,106	2.8	992	0.5	1,112	0.5	612	0.3
Board games...............	38,188	17.3	3,638	1.7	3,689	1.7	6,702	3.0	7,400	3.4
Book clubs	6,370	2.9	310	0.1	184	0.1	543	0.3	2,719	1.2
Chess	7,363	3.3	648	0.3	387	0.2	783	0.4	900	0.4
Concerts on radio.............	6,997	3.2	1,304	0.6	777	0.4	794	0.4	625	0.3
Cooking for fun	44,912	20.3	15,207	6.9	7,933	3.6	7,373	3.3	3,669	1.7
Crossword puzzles	30,959	14.0	13,901	6.3	3,490	1.6	2,959	1.3	2,116	1.0
Dance/go dancing	20,698	9.4	2,139	1.0	1,994	0.9	3,023	1.4	2,540	1.2
Dining out.................	107,456	48.7	22,697	10.3	24,354	11.0	24,731	11.2	13,409	6.1
Electronic games (not TV)	18,995	8.6	6,637	3.0	2,491	1.1	2,642	1.2	1,301	0.6
Entertain friends or relatives at home. .	90,197	40.8	7,838	3.6	11,671	5.3	18,046	8.2	19,365	8.8
Fantasy sports league...........	6,192	2.8	2,059	0.9	1,380	0.6	229	0.1	231	0.1
Fly kites	5,219	2.4	4	–	96	(Z)	138	0.1	355	0.2
Furniture refinishing	6,253	2.8	241	0.1	43	(Z)	308	0.1	560	0.3
Go to bars/night clubs..........	40,762	18.5	3,685	1.7	4,867	2.2	6,571	3.0	5,703	2.6
Go to beach	52,463	23.8	3,319	1.5	2,327	1.1	5,039	2.3	4,834	2.2
Go to live theater	29,082	13.2	273	0.1	687	0.3	1,042	0.5	3,205	1.5
Go to museums..............	27,039	12.2	136	0.1	212	0.1	543	0.3	2,736	1.2
Home decoration and furnishing	27,696	12.5	1,640	0.7	1,114	0.5	2,928	1.3	5,128	2.3
Karaoke	9,142	4.1	608	0.3	440	0.2	754	0.3	969	0.4
Model making	3,501	1.6	199	0.1	134	0.1	264	0.1	428	0.2
Painting, drawing	15,146	6.9	2,865	1.3	1,505	0.7	2,029	0.9	1,537	0.7
PC/computer games...........	44,287	20.1	21,141	9.6	4,975	2.3	4,627	2.1	3,498	1.6
Photo album/scrap book	17,782	8.1	1,394	0.6	1,436	0.7	2,410	1.1	2,909	1.3
Photography	28,340	12.8	4,787	2.2	3,508	1.6	5,854	2.7	4,109	1.9
Picnic...................	22,426	10.2	229	0.1	616	0.3	1,630	0.7	2,607	1.2
Play bingo.................	9,795	4.4	778	0.4	1,337	0.6	552	0.3	1,184	0.5
Play cards.................	50,325	22.8	6,065	2.8	5,615	2.5	7,599	3.4	8,615	3.9
Play musical instrument.	17,108	7.8	5,902	2.7	1,844	0.8	2,125	1.0	1,443	0.7
Read books	86,715	39.3	47,385	21.5	8,769	4.0	7,157	3.2	5,635	2.6
Read comic books	4,305	2.0	1,281	0.6	341	0.2	355	0.2	185	0.1
Trivia games	12,977	5.9	2,579	1.2	1,478	0.7	1,633	0.7	1,300	0.6
Video games...............	26,119	11.8	9,765	4.4	3,380	1.5	2,906	1.3	2,084	0.9
Woodworking...............	10,296	4.7	2,155	1.0	933	0.4	1,748	0.8	1,171	0.5
Word games	20,621	9.3	7,186	3.3	2,185	1.0	2,975	1.4	1,834	0.8
Zoo attendance	27,081	12.3	258	0.1	172	0.1	756	0.3	1,463	0.7

– Represents or rounds to zero.   Z represents less than 0.05.   [1] Includes those participating less than once a month not shown separately.   [2] Excluding country and rock.

Source: Mediamark Research, Inc., New York, NY, *Top-line Reports* (copyright). See also <http://www.mediamark.com/mri/docs/TopLineReports.html>.

Table 1201. **Household Pet Ownership: 2006**

[Based on a sample survey of 47,000 households in 2006; For definition of mean and other details, see source]

Item	Unit	Dogs	Cats	Birds	Horses
Total companion pet population [1]	Million	72.1	81.7	11.2	7.3
Number of households owning pets...................	Million	43.0	37.5	4.5	2.1
Percent of households owning companion pets [1]	Percent ...	37.2	32.4	3.9	1.8
Average number owned per household...............	Number ...	1.7	2.2	2.5	3.5
PERCENT OF HOUSEHOLDS OWNING PETS					
Annual household income:					
Under $20,000	Percent ...	30.7	30.1	4.4	1.5
$20,000 to $34,999........................	Percent ...	37.3	33.6	4.2	1.7
$35,000 to $54,999........................	Percent ...	39.8	34.1	4.4	2.1
$55,000 to $84,999........................	Percent ...	42.8	35.5	3.7	1.9
$85,000 and over	Percent ...	42.1	33.3	3.7	2.3
Household size: [1]					
One person	Percent ...	21.9	24.7	2.1	0.8
Two persons	Percent ...	37.6	33.4	3.9	1.7
Three persons	Percent ...	47.5	39.1	5.1	2.3
Four persons	Percent ...	51.9	38.5	5.4	2.7
Five or more persons.......................	Percent ...	54.3	40.0	6.6	3.6

[1] As of December 31, 2006.

Source: American Veterinary Medical Association, Schaumburg, IL, *U.S. Pet Ownership and Demographics Sourcebook, 2007* (copyright). *U.S. Pet Ownership and Demographics Sourcebook, 2007* (copyright). See also <http://www.avma.org/>.

Table 1202. Retail Sales and Household Participation in Lawn and Garden Activities: 2003 to 2007

[(38,371 represents $38,371,000,000). For calendar year. Subject to sampling variability; see source]

Activity	Retail sales (mil. dol.)					Percent households engaged in activity				
	2003	2004	2005	2006	2007	2003	2004	2005	2006	2007
Total	38,371	36,778	35,208	34,077	35,102	78	75	83	74	71
Lawn care	10,413	8,887	9,657	8,558	10,754	54	48	54	48	48
Indoor houseplants	1,571	1,495	1,464	1,156	988	41	39	42	35	31
Flower gardening	3,025	2,735	3,003	2,572	2,386	38	36	41	33	30
Insect control	2,053	1,823	1,869	1,746	2,103	30	28	30	26	25
Shrub care	1,042	1,027	1,109	840	913	27	26	31	25	23
Vegetable gardening	1,408	1,058	1,154	1,164	1,421	24	22	25	22	22
Tree care	2,359	3,067	2,820	2,322	2,192	25	24	26	21	18
Landscaping	10,507	11,346	9,078	10,893	9,874	33	33	31	30	27
Flower bulbs	1,036	892	945	786	811	26	26	29	22	20
Fruit trees	635	589	507	640	477	12	11	13	11	10
Container gardening	1,219	1,196	1,295	948	927	24	21	26	18	18
Raising transplants [1]	230	258	237	257	320	10	9	11	9	7
Herb gardening	345	367	371	296	451	14	14	17	12	13
Growing berries	345	141	151	121	144	6	6	8	6	5
Ornamental gardening	831	769	678	493	561	9	9	12	7	6
Water gardening	1,565	1,128	870	1,285	780	15	13	11	14	11

[1] Starting plants in advance of planting in ground.

Source: The National Gardening Association, Burlington, VT, *National Gardening Survey,* annual (copyright). See also <http://www.garden.org/home>.

Table 1203. Selected Recreational Activities: 1990 to 2007

[41 represents 41,000,000]

Activity	Unit	1990	1995	2000	2003	2004	2005	2006	2007
Softball, amateur: [1]									
Total participants [2]	Million . . .	41	42	31	30	28	27	25	(NA)
Youth participants	1,000 . . .	1,100	1,350	1,370	1,351	1,356	1,447	1,459	(NA)
Adult teams [3]	1,000 . . .	188	187	155	119	132	128	127	(NA)
Youth teams [3]	1,000 . . .	46	74	81	79	80	85	86	(NA)
Golf facilities [4]	Number . .	12,846	14,074	15,489	15,899	16,057	16,052	15,990	15,970
Tennis players [5]	1,000 . . .	21,000	17,820	22,900	24,100	24,000	24,720	24,200	25,130
Tenpin bowling [6]									
Establishments	Number . .	7,611	7,049	6,247	5,811	5,761	5,818	5,566	5,498
Membership, total [7]	1,000 . . .	6,588	4,925	3,756	3,246	3,112	2,896	2,728	2,608
Skiing: [8]									
Skier visits [9]	Million . . .	50.0	52.7	52.2	57.6	57.1	56.9	58.9	60.1
Operating resorts	Number . .	591	520	503	490	494	492	478	481
Motion picture screens [10]	1,000 . . .	24	28	37	36	37	39	39	39
Receipts, box office	Mil. dol . .	5,022	5,494	7,468	9,165	9,215	8,832	9,137	9,629
Attendance	Million . . .	1,189	1,263	1,385	1,520	1,484	1,378	1,395	1,400
Boating: [11]									
People participating in recreational boating [12, 13] . . .	Million . . .	59.9	62.3	60.0	56.0	56.4	51.5	53.6	59.1
Retail expenditures on boating [14]	Mil. dol . . .	13,731	17,226	27,065	30,283	32,953	37,317	39,493	37,483
Recreational boats in use by boat type [15]	Million . . .	16.0	15.4	16.8	17.2	17.4	17.7	16.9	16.9
Outboard	Million . . .	(NA)	(NA)	8.3	8.4	8.4	8.5	8.3	8.3
Inboard	Million . . .	(NA)	(NA)	1.0	1.1	1.1	1.1	1.1	1.1
Sterndrive	Million . . .	(NA)	(NA)	1.6	1.6	1.7	1.7	1.6	1.7
Personal watercraft	Million . . .	(NA)	(NA)	1.2	1.2	1.3	1.2	1.2	1.2
Sailboats	Million . . .	(NA)	(NA)	1.6	1.6	1.6	1.6	1.6	1.6
Other	Million . . .	(NA)	(NA)	3.1	3.4	3.4	3.6	3.1	3.0

NA Not available. [1] Source: Amateur Softball Association, Oklahoma City, OK. [2] Amateur Softball Association teams and other amateur softball teams. [3] Amateur Softball Association teams only. [4] Source: National Golf Foundation, Jupiter, FL. [5] Source: Tennis Industry Association, Hilton Head, SC. Players for persons 12 years old and over who played at least once. [6] Source: United States Bowling Congress, Greendale, WI. [7] Membership totals are for U.S., Canada, and for U.S. military personnel worldwide. [8] Source: National Ski Areas Association, Kottke National End of Season Survey Report (copyright). [9] Represents one person visiting a ski area for all or any part of a day or night, and includes full-and half-day, night, complimentary, adult, child, season, and other types of tickets. Data are estimated and are for the season ending in the year shown. 2007 data are preliminary. [10] Source: Motion Picture Association of America, Inc., Encino, CA. [11] Source: National Marine Manufacturers Association, Chicago, IL. (copyright). [12] People participating are now measured as adults 18 years and older. [13] Data for 1990–2006 have been revised, see report. [14] Represents estimated expenditures for new and used boats, motors and engines, accessories, safety equipment, fuel, insurance, docking, maintenance, launching, storage, repairs, and other expenses. [15] 2007 data are estimated.

Source: Compiled from sources listed in footnotes.

Table 1204. College and Professional Football Summary: 1990 to 2007

[35,330 represents 35,330,000. For definition of median, see Guide to Tabular Presentation]

Sport	Unit	1990	1995	2000	2003	2004	2005	2006	2007
NCAA college: [1]									
Teams	Number.	533	565	606	617	612	615	615	619
Attendance	1,000 ..	35,330	35,638	39,059	46,145	43,106	43,487	47,909	48,752
National Football League: [2]									
Teams	Number.	28	30	31	32	32	32	32	32
Attendance, total [3]	1,000 ..	17,666	19,203	20,954	21,639	21,709	21,792	22,200	22,256
Regular season	1,000 ..	13,960	15,044	16,387	16,914	17,001	17,012	17,341	17,345
Average per game	Number.	62,321	62,682	66,078	66,328	66,409	66,455	67,738	67,755
Postseason games [4]	1,000 ..	848	(NA)	809	806	789	802	776	792
Players' salaries: [5]									
Average	$1,000 .	354	584	787	1,259	1,331	1,400	1,700	1,750
Median base salary	$1,000 .	275	301	441	534	537	569	722	772

NA Not available. [1] Source: National Collegiate Athletic Assn., Indianapolis, IN; <http://www.ncaasports.com> (copyright). [2] Source: National Football League, New York, NY; <http://www.nfl.com/>. [3] Preseason attendance data are not shown. [4] Includes Pro Bowl (a nonchampionship game) and Super Bowl. [5] Source: National Football League Players Association, Washington, DC.; <http://www.nflpa.org/>.

Source: Compiled from sources listed in footnotes.

Table 1205. Selected Spectator Sports: 1990 to 2007

[55,512 represents 55,512,000]

Sport	Unit	1990	1995	2000	2003	2004	2005	2006	2007
Baseball, major leagues: [1]									
Attendance	1,000 ...	55,512	51,288	74,339	69,501	74,822	76,286	77,524	80,803
Regular season	1,000 ...	54,824	50,469	72,748	67,568	73,023	74,926	76,043	79,503
Playoffs [2]	1,000 ...	479	533	1,314	1,568	1,625	1,191	1,218	1,083
World Series	1,000 ...	209	286	277	365	174	168	225	173
Players' salaries: [3]									
Average	$1,000 ..	598	1,111	1,896	2,372	2,313	2,476	2,699	2,825
Basketball: [4, 5]									
NCAA—Men's college:									
Teams	Number. .	767	868	932	967	981	983	984	982
Attendance	1,000 ...	28,741	28,548	29,025	30,124	30,761	30,569	30,940	32,836
NCAA—Women's college:									
Teams	Number. .	782	864	956	1,009	1,008	1,036	1,018	1,003
Attendance [6]	1,000 ...	2,777	4,962	8,698	10,164	10,016	9,940	9,903	10,878
National Hockey League: [7]									
Regular season attendance	1,000 ...	12,580	9,234	18,800	20,409	20,356	([8])	20,854	20,862
Playoffs attendance	1,000 ...	1,356	1,329	1,525	1,636	1,709	([8])	1,530	1,497
Professional rodeo: [9]									
Rodeos	Number. .	754	739	688	657	671	662	649	592
Performances	Number. .	2,159	2,217	2,081	1,949	1,982	1,940	1,884	1,733
Members	Number. .	5,693	6,894	6,255	6,158	6,247	6,127	5,892	5,528
Permit-holders (rookies)	Number. .	3,290	3,835	3,249	3,121	2,990	2,701	2,468	2,186
Total prize money	Mil. dol..	18.2	24.5	32.3	34.3	35.5	36.6	36.2	40.5

[1] Source: Major League Baseball (previously, The National League of Professional Baseball Clubs), New York, NY, National League Green Book; and The American League of Professional Baseball Clubs, New York, NY, American League Red Book. [2] Beginning 1997, two rounds of playoffs were played. Prior years had one round. [3] Source: Major League Baseball Players Association, New York, NY. [4] Season ending in year shown. [5] Source: National Collegiate Athletic Association, Indianapolis, IN (copyright). [6] For women's attendance total, excludes double-headers with men's teams. [7] For season ending in year shown. Source: National Hockey League, Montreal, Quebec. [8] In September 2004, franchise owners locked out their players upon the expiration of the collective bargaining agreement. The entire season was cancelled in February 2005. [9] Source: Professional Rodeo Cowboys Association, Colorado Springs, CO., Official Professional Rodeo Media Guide, annual (copyright).

Source: Compiled from sources listed in footnotes.

Table 1206. Adult Attendance at Sports Events by Frequency: 2007

[In thousands (2,343 represents 2,343,000), except percent. For fall 2007. Based on survey and subject to sampling error; see source]

Event	Attend one or more times a month Number	Attend one or more times a month Percent	Attend less than once a month Number	Attend less than once a month Percent	Event	Attend one or more times a month Number	Attend one or more times a month Percent	Attend less than once a month Number	Attend less than once a month Percent
Auto racing—NASCAR	2,343	1.1	10,209	4.6	Weekend				
Auto racing—Other	2,384	1.1	7,443	3.4	professional games	4,007	1.8	11,787	5.3
Baseball	7,591	3.4	20,664	9.4	Golf	1,499	0.7	6,122	2.8
Basketball:					High school sports	10,850	4.9	10,557	4.8
College games	3,812	1.7	9,830	4.5	Horse racing:				
Professional games	3,280	1.5	10,996	5.0	Flats, runners	1,279	0.6	5,860	2.7
Bowling	1,602	0.7	5,460	2.5	Trotters/harness	629	0.3	4,906	2.2
Boxing	990	0.5	5,012	2.3	Ice hockey	1,872	0.9	8,499	3.9
Equestrian events	475	0.2	5,177	2.3	Motorcycle racing	854	0.4	5,127	2.3
Figure skating	391	0.2	5,044	2.3	Pro beach volleyball	403	0.2	4,729	2.1
Fishing tournaments	740	0.3	4,933	2.2	Rodeo/bull riding	744	0.3	6,333	2.9
Football:					Soccer	3,437	1.6	6,497	2.9
College games	5,759	2.6	12,705	5.8	Tennis	901	0.4	5,527	2.5
Monday night					Truck and tractor pull/				
professional games	2,165	1.0	6,821	3.1	mud racing	904	0.4	5,895	2.7
					Wrestling—professional	943	0.4	5,562	2.5

Source: Mediamark Research, Inc., New York, NY, Top-line Reports (copyright). See also <http://www.mediamark.com/mri/docs/TopLineReports.html>.

Table 1207. Participation in NCAA Sports: 2006 to 2007

[For the academic year]

Sport	Male			Female		
	Teams	Athletes	Average squad	Teams	Athletes	Average squad
Total [1]	**8,341**	**233,830**	**(X)**	**9,372**	**174,534**	**(X)**
Baseball	897	29,486	32.9	(X)	(X)	(X)
Basketball	1,022	16,640	16.3	1,050	15,152	14.4
Bowling [2]	2	29	14.5	49	439	9.0
Cross country	898	12,202	13.6	967	13,303	13.8
Equestrian [2,3]	8	92	11.5	48	1,348	28.1
Fencing [3]	36	629	17.5	45	694	15.4
Field hockey	(X)	(X)	(X)	259	5,500	21.2
Football	625	62,459	99.9	(X)	(X)	(X)
Golf [3]	782	8,318	10.6	512	4,122	8.1
Gymnastics	19	324	17.1	86	1,472	17.1
Ice hockey	136	3,957	29.1	79	1,828	23.1
Lacrosse	226	8,353	37.0	286	6,411	22.4
Rifle [3]	29	181	6.2	36	230	6.4
Rowing [2]	63	2,430	38.6	144	7,210	50.1
Rugby [2]	3	97	32.3	5	143	28.6
Sailing [2]	26	469	18.0	(X)	(X)	(X)
Skiing [3]	40	529	13.2	44	542	12.3
Soccer	763	20,481	26.8	941	22,077	23.5
Softball	(X)	(X)	(X)	942	16,997	18.0
Squash [2]	27	445	16.5	27	360	13.3
Swimming/diving [3]	390	8,056	20.7	504	11,128	22.1
Synchronized swimming [2] . . .	(X)	(X)	(X)	8	100	12.5
Tennis	745	7,625	10.2	895	8,784	9.8
Track, indoor [3]	575	19,779	34.4	641	19,704	30.7
Track, outdoor [3]	678	22,898	33.8	732	21,516	29.4
Volleyball	80	1,222	15.3	1,007	14,277	14.2
Water polo	41	893	21.8	61	1,148	18.8
Wrestling	229	6,227	27.2	(X)	(X)	(X)

X Not applicable.   [1] Includes other sports not shown separately.   [2] Sport recognized by the NCAA but does not have an NCAA championship.   [3] Co-ed championship sport.

Source: The National Collegiate Athletic Association (NCAA), Indianapolis, IN, *2006–07 Participation Study* (copyright). See <http://www.ncaa.org/wps/portal>.

Table 1208. Participation in High School Athletic Programs by Sex: 1979 to 2007

[Data based on number of state associations reporting and may underrepresent the number of schools with and participants in athletic programs]

Year	Participant [1]		Sex and sport	Most popular sports, 2006–2007 [2]	
	Male	Female		School	Participant
1979–80	3,517,829	1,750,264			
1984–85	3,354,284	1,757,884	MALE		
1985–86	3,344,275	1,807,121	Football (11-player)	13,922	1,104,548
1986–87	3,364,082	1,836,356	Basketball	17,762	556,269
1987–88	3,425,777	1,849,684	Track & field (outdoor)	15,709	544,180
1988–89	3,416,844	1,839,352	Baseball	15,458	477,430
1989–90	3,398,192	1,858,659	Soccer	11,066	377,999
1990–91	3,406,355	1,892,316	Wrestling	9,445	257,246
1991–92	3,429,853	1,940,801	Cross country	13,354	216,085
1992–93	3,416,389	1,997,489	Golf	13,541	159,747
1993–94	3,472,967	2,130,315	Tennis	9,438	156,944
1994–95	3,536,359	2,240,461	Swimming & diving	6,358	106,738
1995–96	3,634,052	2,367,936			
1996–97	3,706,225	2,474,043	FEMALE		
1997–98	3,763,120	2,570,333	Basketball	17,458	456,967
1998–99	3,832,352	2,652,726	Track & field (outdoor)	15,578	444,181
1999–20	3,861,749	2,675,874	Volleyball	14,881	405,832
2000–01	3,921,069	2,784,154	Softball (fast pitch)	14,968	373,448
2001–02	3,960,517	2,806,998	Soccer	10,503	337,632
2002–03	3,988,738	2,856,358	Cross country	13,146	183,376
2003–04	4,038,253	2,865,299	Tennis	9,678	176,696
2004–05	4,110,319	2,908,390	Swimming & diving	6,708	143,639
2005–06	4,206,549	2,953,355	Competitive spirit squads	3,743	95,177
2006–07	4,321,103	3,021,807	Golf	9,046	66,283

[1] A participant is counted in the number of sports participated in.   [2] Ten most popular sports for each sex in terms of number of participants.

Source: National Federation of State High School Associations, Indianapolis, IN, *The 2006–2007 High School Athletics Participation Survey* (copyright). See <http://www.nfhs.org/>.

Arts, Recreation, and Travel   **751**

Table 1209. **Participation in Selected Sports Activities: 2006**

[In thousands (263,410 represents 263,410,000), except rank. For persons 7 years of age or older. Except as indicated, a participant plays a sport more than once in the year]

Activity	All persons Number	All persons Rank	Sex Male	Sex Female	Age 7–11 years	Age 12–17 years	Age 18–24 years	Age 25–34 years	Age 35–44 years	Age 45–54 years	Age 55–64 years	Age 65 years and over	Household income Under 15,000	Household income 15,000–24,999	Household income 25,000–34,999	Household income 35,000–49,000	Household income 50,000–74,999	Household income 75,000 and over
SERIES I SPORTS																		
Total	**263,410**	**(X)**	**128,098**	**135,042**	**19,436**	**25,360**	**28,724**	**36,945**	**42,285**	**42,700**	**30,872**	**36,818**	**28,316**	**25,856**	**30,508**	**40,652**	**54,258**	**83,550**
Number participated in—																		
Aerobic exercising[1]	33,689	9	9,744	23,945	1,003	2,455	4,826	8,004	5,874	5,255	3,746	2,525	1,692	2,317	3,161	4,916	6,811	14,791
Backpacking[2]	13,304	19	7,677	5,627	1,228	1,962	1,986	3,023	2,513	1,497	716	379	1,055	1,209	1,178	2,114	2,790	4,958
Baseball	14,646	17	11,449	3,198	3,689	3,910	1,950	1,691	1,384	958	579	485	1,162	838	1,034	2,474	3,492	5,646
Basketball	26,735	14	17,937	8,799	5,417	7,230	4,033	4,035	2,912	1,933	727	448	1,570	2,229	2,412	4,333	6,378	9,814
Bicycle riding[1]	35,621	8	19,476	16,146	7,855	6,328	2,017	4,622	6,036	4,392	2,782	1,590	2,715	1,837	3,325	5,599	7,227	14,917
Billiards	31,830	11	19,706	12,124	1,168	3,352	5,973	8,349	6,533	4,074	1,703	678	3,032	2,638	3,540	5,289	6,477	10,853
Bowling[3]	44,779	5	22,704	22,076	5,061	7,596	8,266	7,502	7,478	5,217	2,012	1,646	3,212	3,052	4,540	7,100	10,507	16,369
Camping[3]	48,609	4	24,803	23,806	5,373	6,328	4,830	8,932	9,491	7,430	3,916	2,310	2,846	4,025	5,785	8,777	10,972	16,205
Exercise walking[1]	87,469	1	35,035	52,434	3,901	4,711	7,238	14,820	15,335	16,941	12,306	12,217	6,796	7,650	9,194	14,162	17,098	32,570
Exercising with equipment[1]	52,392	3	25,491	26,901	1,205	4,532	7,437	9,964	10,028	9,176	5,739	4,310	2,677	3,005	4,794	7,668	10,616	23,632
Fishing (net)	40,608	6	27,027	13,580	4,573	4,355	5,181	7,360	6,759	5,611	3,523	3,246	3,569	3,829	4,637	6,687	8,827	13,059
Fishing—fresh water	36,637	7	24,407	12,230	4,478	4,069	4,547	6,840	6,152	4,940	2,869	2,742	3,242	3,410	4,403	6,135	7,876	11,571
Fishing—salt water	10,367	23	7,258	3,109	515	998	1,345	1,752	1,896	1,585	1,279	997	694	802	687	1,680	2,567	3,937
Football—tackle	11,888	21	10,261	1,627	2,199	4,150	2,627	870	910	622	210	301	1,038	1,208	1,375	1,798	2,498	3,970
Golf	24,428	15	18,553	5,875	875	2,139	2,269	4,336	5,317	3,990	2,962	2,542	845	879	1,728	2,962	5,916	12,099
Hiking	30,970	12	15,737	15,234	3,178	2,992	3,395	6,377	6,027	4,888	2,724	1,389	1,967	2,444	2,585	5,214	5,792	12,968
Hunting with firearms	17,817	16	15,449	2,368	864	1,932	2,586	3,149	3,332	3,146	1,615	1,194	1,373	1,690	1,792	3,286	4,250	5,427
Running/jogging[1]	28,787	13	15,038	13,749	2,056	5,235	5,600	6,154	4,748	3,044	1,402	547	1,737	1,532	2,324	4,875	5,454	12,895
Soccer	14,024	18	7,722	6,302	4,790	4,102	1,717	1,626	1,133	226	136	296	396	845	898	2,263	3,657	5,964
Softball[1]	12,442	20	5,608	6,834	2,342	2,825	1,735	2,386	1,551	961	454	187	710	784	913	2,611	2,847	4,577
Swimming[1]	56,463	2	25,340	31,123	9,208	9,360	5,841	8,211	9,090	7,348	3,917	3,490	3,555	3,590	5,157	8,680	11,737	23,744
Tennis	10,356	24	5,296	5,060	786	2,218	1,052	1,888	1,615	1,591	668	538	324	572	377	1,175	1,978	5,930
Volleyball	11,062	22	4,464	6,598	1,094	3,977	1,348	1,741	1,419	1,157	189	137	790	840	1,034	1,444	2,470	4,484
Weightlifting	32,878	10	21,313	11,565	399	4,509	6,469	7,116	5,926	5,049	2,194	1,216	2,030	1,609	2,832	4,840	6,805	14,762
Wrestling	3,801	25	3,126	675	394	1,035	939	292	435	347	300	59	548	466	247	533	929	1,077

See footnotes at end of table.

Table 1209. **Participation in Selected Sports Activities: 2006—Con.**

[See headnote, page 752]

Activity	All persons Number	Rank	Sex Male	Female	Age 7–11 years	12–17 years	18–24 years	25–34 years	35–44 years	45–54 years	55–64 years	65 years and over	Household income (dol.) Under 15,000	15,000–24,999	25,000–34,999	35,000–49,999	50,000–74,999	75,000 and over
Total	263,138	(X)	128,097	135,041	19,435	25,361	28,723	36,947	42,285	42,699	30,872	36,817	27,905	26,639	30,079	40,562	55,882	82,071
SERIES II SPORTS																		
Number participating in—																		
Boating—motor/power	29,258	2	16,592	12,665	1,912	3,055	3,940	5,875	5,221	4,890	2,448	1,918	1,114	1,599	2,338	3,753	6,509	13,945
Canoeing	7,111	9	3,930	3,182	448	995	633	1,140	1,370	1,463	758	304	514	279	672	1,061	1,682	2,903
Cheerleading	3,814	16	245	3,568	1,731	1,480	430	39	49	39	–	45	264	204	230	811	985	1,319
Hockey (ice)	2,559	19	2,007	552	431	336	434	590	362	312	35	59	19	103	199	387	669	1,183
Hunting with bow and arrow	5,853	12	5,108	745	194	423	752	1,174	1,571	838	583	320	353	553	494	1,432	1,552	1,469
In-line roller skating	10,497	4	4,990	5,506	3,101	3,054	1,245	1,397	899	607	82	112	590	776	1,302	1,834	2,748	3,247
Mountain biking—off road	8,543	7	5,494	3,049	864	1,002	635	1,986	1,713	1,595	505	242	346	535	712	1,395	2,215	3,340
Muzzleloading	3,742	17	3,507	234	57	130	581	659	973	578	421	342	300	377	312	1,012	936	805
Paintball games	8,002	8	6,296	1,706	559	3,194	2,202	813	720	342	76	96	474	669	900	1,281	1,736	2,941
Racquetball	3,966	15	2,507	1,460	64	634	643	1,272	554	505	180	114	100	113	446	841	955	1,512
Scooter riding	9,530	6	5,409	4,120	5,123	2,477	236	660	360	299	241	135	666	785	1,337	1,198	2,179	3,365
Skateboarding	9,731	5	7,415	2,316	2,907	4,440	1,362	655	202	18	28	118	902	885	1,540	903	2,524	2,977
Skiing—alpine	6,394	10	4,026	2,368	424	880	1,099	1,328	1,057	1,279	146	182	40	445	410	474	1,496	3,529
Skiing—cross country	2,560	18	1,297	1,263	216	257	347	362	374	586	196	223	–	144	274	319	479	1,344
Snowboarding	5,232	14	3,816	1,416	860	1,688	1,413	752	271	125	40	84	146	313	456	829	1,217	2,272
Target shoot	17,090	3	13,594	3,497	855	1,493	2,391	3,652	3,499	2,862	1,510	829	1,186	1,626	1,735	3,151	3,716	5,677
Target shoot—airgun	5,610	13	4,547	1,063	1,002	1,613	753	523	584	606	336	194	227	455	1,225	930	1,114	1,660
Water skiing	6,283	11	3,614	2,670	433	1,132	1,487	1,074	1,086	828	99	145	187	123	276	833	1,541	3,324
Work-out at club	36,978	1	16,502	20,476	583	2,689	6,053	8,009	7,296	6,056	2,948	3,343	1,440	1,578	2,986	4,546	9,113	17,315

– Represents or rounds to zero. X Not applicable. [1] Participant engaged in activity at least six times in the year. [2] Includes wilderness camping. [3] Vacation/overnight.

Source: National Sporting Goods Association, Mt. Prospect, IL, Sports Participation in 2006: Series I and Series II (copyright). See <http://www.nsga.org/public/pages/index.cfm?pageid=864>.

Table 1210. Sporting Goods Sales by Product Category: 1990 to 2006, and Projection, 2007

[In millions of dollars (50,725 represents $50,725,000,000), except percent. Based on a sample survey of consumer purchases of 80,000 households, (100,000 beginning 2000), except recreational transport, which was provided by industry associations. Excludes Alaska and Hawaii. Minus sign (–) indicates decrease]

Selected product category	1990	2000	2001	2002	2003	2004	2005	2006	2007, proj.
Sales, all products	**50,725**	**74,442**	**74,337**	**77,726**	**79,779**	**85,811**	**88,434**	**90,511**	**90,767**
Annual percent change [1]	(NA)	4.6	–0.1	4.6	2.6	7.6	3.1	2.3	0.3
Percent of retail sales	(NA)	2.5	2.4	2.5	2.4	2.5	2.4	2.3	(NA)
Athletic and sport clothing [2]	10,130	11,030	10,217	9,801	10,543	11,201	10,898	10,699	10,999
Athletic and sport footwear [2]	11,654	13,026	13,814	14,144	14,446	14,752	15,719	16,902	17,497
Aerobic shoes	611	292	281	239	222	237	261	262	268
Basketball shoes	918	786	761	789	890	877	878	964	987
Cross training shoes	679	1,528	1,476	1,421	1,407	1,327	1,437	1,516	1,561
Golf shoes	226	226	223	243	222	230	259	232	233
Gym shoes, sneakers	2,536	1,871	2,004	2,042	2,059	2,221	2,314	2,434	2,531
Jogging and running shoes	1,110	1,638	1,670	1,733	1,802	1,989	2,157	2,260	2,337
Tennis shoes	740	533	505	503	544	508	528	505	510
Walking shoes [2]	2,950	3,317	3,280	3,415	3,468	3,496	3,673	4,091	4,294
Athletic and sport equipment [2]	14,439	21,608	21,594	21,699	22,394	23,328	23,735	24,520	25,245
Archery	265	259	276	279	320	332	372	398	410
Baseball and softball	217	319	316	334	340	352	372	388	402
Billiards and indoor games	192	516	528	574	625	622	572	571	568
Camping	1,072	1,354	1,371	1,442	1,487	1,531	1,447	1,535	1,571
Exercise	1,824	3,610	3,889	4,378	4,957	5,074	5,177	5,226	5,383
Fishing tackle	1,910	2,030	2,058	2,024	1,981	2,026	2,139	2,219	2,263
Golf	2,514	3,805	3,871	3,258	3,046	3,198	3,466	3,662	3,809
Hunting and firearms	2,202	2,274	2,206	2,449	2,654	3,175	3,563	3,709	3,798
Optics	438	729	783	826	847	859	887	1,014	1,115
Skin diving and scuba	294	355	348	348	338	351	358	369	376
Snow skiing [3]	475	495	515	527	462	452	643	615	633
Tennis	333	383	371	358	343	362	397	420	441
Recreational transport	14,502	28,779	28,712	32,083	32,397	36,531	38,082	38,389	37,035
Bicycles and supplies	2,423	5,131	4,725	4,961	4,736	4,898	5,343	5,161	5,393
Pleasure boats, motors, & accessories	7,644	13,224	14,558	15,382	14,705	16,054	17,634	17,811	17,454
Recreational vehicles	4,113	9,529	8,598	10,960	12,058	14,753	14,366	14,732	13,475
Snowmobiles	322	894	831	779	898	826	739	685	713

NA Not available. [1] Represents change from immediate prior year. [2] Includes other products not shown separately.
[3] Data through 2004 categorized as "Skiing Downhill."

Source: National Sporting Goods Association, Mt. Prospect, IL, *The Sporting Goods Market in 2007*; and prior issues (copyright). See <http://www.nsga.org/i4a/pages/index.cfm?pageid=3345>.

Table 1211. Consumer Purchases of Sporting Goods by Consumer Characteristics: 2006

[In percent. Based on sample survey of consumer purchases of 100,000 households. Excludes Alaska and Hawaii]

Characteristic	Total house-holds	Footwear					Equipment				
		Aero-bic shoes	Gym shoes/ sneak-ers	Jog-ging/ run-ning shoes	Hiking shoes/ boots	Walk-ing shoes	Multi-pur-pose home gyms	Rod/ reel combi-nation	Golf club sets	Rifles	Soccer balls
Total	**100**	**100**	**100**	**100**	**100**	**100**	**100**	**100**	**100**	**100**	**100**
Age of user:											
Under 14 years old	19.0	7.6	43.4	8.4	8.3	5.4	0.4	5.8	5.7	0.7	55.8
14 to 17 years old	5.8	4.6	9.8	7.3	4.8	2.7	0.4	3.2	4.4	2.1	16.0
18 to 24 years old	9.9	7.1	6.2	10.3	9.3	3.8	2.2	6.4	9.0	12.5	7.0
25 to 34 years old	13.5	15.1	12.7	25.8	20.5	11.8	22.1	22.0	16.6	14.9	4.6
35 to 44 years old	14.8	23.6	10.9	21.1	25.7	14.8	31.5	19.2	27.0	31.1	6.4
45 to 64 years old	24.6	35.6	13.2	23.9	27.9	41.1	24.7	33.4	22.0	16.1	4.1
65 years old and over	12.4	6.4	3.8	3.2	3.5	20.4	3.4	5.4	15.3	18.5	1.5
Multiple ages	–	–	–	–	–	–	15.3	4.6	–	4.1	4.6
Sex of user:											
Male	49.3	22.2	52.8	47.9	67.7	35.1	63.2	76.7	71.2	89.5	58.8
Female	50.7	77.8	47.2	52.1	32.3	64.9	21.4	12.9	28.8	7.1	35.2
Household use	–	–	–	–	–	–	15.4	10.4	–	3.4	6.0
Annual household income:											
Under $15,000	13.3	3.6	7.9	3.3	7.2	7.8	2.6	6.9	1.3	10.3	6.5
$15,000 to $24,999	13.6	10.2	11.3	5.3	6.8	11.8	9.3	10.1	6.8	3.7	3.8
$25,000 to $34,999	12.5	11.9	10.8	9.4	13.2	12.7	15.0	12.9	1.7	7.4	6.9
$35,000 to $49,999	14.9	14.3	16.4	13.0	16.6	14.7	11.0	16.4	7.6	17.4	10.7
$50,000 to $74,999	18.0	17.4	17.2	19.9	21.0	19.8	13.1	16.6	20.1	30.3	20.7
$75,000 to $99,999	12.8	21.8	17.3	19.7	15.5	13.5	15.2	16.0	17.3	5.8	20.3
$100,000 and over	14.9	20.8	19.1	29.4	19.7	19.7	33.8	21.1	45.2	25.1	31.1

– Represents or rounds to zero.

Source: National Sporting Goods Association, Mt. Prospect, IL, *The Sporting Goods Market in 2007* (copyright). See <http://www.nsga.org.public/pages/index.cfm?pageid=869>.

Table 1212. National Park System—Summary: 1990 to 2007

[For year ending September 30, except as noted. (986 represents $986,000,000). Includes data for five areas in Puerto Rico and Virgin Islands, one area in American Samoa, and one area in Guam]

Item	1990	1995	2000	2003	2004	2005	2006	2007
Finances (mil. dol.): [1]								
Expenditures reported	986	1,445	1,833	2,315	2,371	2,451	2,463	2,412
Salaries and wages	459	633	799	934	956	984	998	1,005
Improvements, maintenance	160	234	299	344	332	361	389	381
Construction	109	192	215	293	354	381	300	280
Other	259	386	520	744	729	725	776	746
Funds available	1,506	2,225	3,316	4,099	4,087	4,218	4,242	4,266
Appropriations	1,053	1,325	1,881	3,298	2,388	2,425	2,450	2,484
Other [2]	453	900	1,435	1,801	1,699	1,793	1,792	1,782
Revenue from operations	79	106	234	274	264	286	308	346
Recreation visits (millions): [3]								
All areas	258.7	269.6	285.9	266.1	276.9	273.5	272.6	275.6
National parks [4]	57.7	64.8	66.1	63.4	63.8	63.5	60.4	62.3
National monuments	23.9	23.5	23.8	20.0	19.8	20.9	19.6	19.7
National historical, commemorative, archaeological [5]	57.5	56.9	72.2	66.6	77.0	74.9	73.6	75.1
National parkways	29.1	31.3	34.0	31.1	31.7	31.7	32.6	31.1
National recreation areas [4]	47.2	53.7	50.0	47.7	46.6	46.8	47.8	48.9
National seashores and lakeshores	23.3	22.5	22.5	22.6	21.3	21.7	19.6	19.9
National Capital Parks	7.5	5.5	5.4	3.5	4.7	4.3	6.2	4.9
Recreation overnight stays (millions)	17.6	16.8	15.4	14.2	13.7	13.5	13.2	13.8
In commercial lodgings	3.9	3.8	3.7	3.5	3.5	3.4	3.4	3.6
In Park Service campgrounds	7.9	7.1	5.9	5.7	5.4	5.2	5.0	5.1
In backcountry	1.7	2.2	1.9	1.8	1.7	1.7	1.7	1.7
Other	4.2	3.7	3.8	3.2	3.1	3.2	3.1	3.4
Land (1,000 acres): [6, 7]								
Total	76,362	77,355	78,153	79,006	79,023	79,048	78,810	78,845
Parks	46,089	49,307	49,785	49,823	49,892	49,910	49,912	49,911
Recreation areas	3,344	3,353	3,388	3,391	3,391	3,391	3,391	3,413
Other	26,929	24,695	24,980	25,792	25,740	25,747	25,507	25,521
Acquisition, net	21	27	186	138	12	17	15	22

[1] Financial data are those associated with the National Park System. Certain other functions of the National Park Service (principally the activities absorbed from the former Heritage Conservation and Recreation Service in 1981) are excluded. [2] Includes funds carried over from prior years. [3] For calendar year. Includes other areas not shown separately. [4] For 1990, combined data for North Cascades National Park and two adjacent National Recreation Areas are included in National Parks total. [5] Includes military areas. [6] Federal land only, as of Dec. 31. Federal land acreages, in addition to National Park Service administered lands, also include lands within national park system area boundaries but under the administration of other agencies. Year-to-year changes in the federal lands figures includes changes in the acreages of these other lands and hence often differ from "net acquisition." [7] The decrease in the 2006 land total reflects acreage by the Bureau of Land Management and not by the National Park Service.

Source: U.S. National Park Service, *National Park Statistical Abstract,* annual; and unpublished data. See also <http://www2.nature.nps.gov/stats/>.

Table 1213. State Parks and Recreation Areas by State: 2006

[For year ending June 30 (13,883 represents 13,883,000). Data are shown as reported by state park directors. In some states, park agency has under its control forests, fish and wildlife areas, and/or other areas. In other states, agency is responsible for state parks only]

State	Acreage (1,000)	Visitors (1,000) [1]	Revenue Total ($1,000)	Revenue Percent of operating expenditures	State	Acreage (1,000)	Visitors (1,000) [1]	Revenue Total ($1,000)	Revenue Percent of operating expenditures
United States	**13,883**	**730,067**	**876,706**	**38.7**	Missouri	202	15,475	7,697	27.1
					Montana	55	5,704	4,992	61.9
Alabama	48	5,160	22,280	69.3	Nebraska	135	9,685	16,044	85.2
Alaska	3,354	4,875	2,773	38.6	Nevada	128	3,394	2,794	23.8
Arizona	64	2,298	13,501	44.4	New Hampshire	232	3,825	10,959	100.2
Arkansas	54	8,857	21,632	50.9	New Jersey	423	16,042	9,843	25.3
California	1,560	79,782	88,330	18.9	New Mexico	93	4,075	4,544	16.7
Colorado	410	11,305	20,585	68.9	New York	1,346	55,255	72,405	34.2
Connecticut	205	6,273	4,589	30.1	North Carolina	195	13,248	5,949	17.8
Delaware	26	4,399	11,340	53.7	North Dakota	18	917	1,524	50.7
Florida	699	19,519	42,034	51.7	Ohio	174	49,878	17,998	25.0
Georgia	85	11,011	34,752	55.9	Oklahoma	72	12,188	22,048	53.5
Hawaii	32	1,088	2,004	24.3	Oregon	97	43,810	16,246	37.8
Idaho	46	(NA)	3,805	24.9	Pennsylvania	291	36,237	16,023	19.5
Illinois	538	46,005	7,063	13.5	Rhode Island	9	6,489	3,916	40.7
Indiana	178	18,144	40,711	84.0	South Carolina	84	6,904	20,315	77.1
Iowa	68	14,055	3,924	27.7	South Dakota	103	7,327	9,959	75.5
Kansas	33	6,378	5,855	57.9	Tennessee	144	31,135	37,120	47.7
Kentucky	59	7,052	54,410	62.2	Texas	588	9,243	35,625	55.0
Louisiana	42	1,678	6,781	20.5	Utah	150	905	11,527	39.3
Maine	100	2,063	2,940	33.8	Vermont	69	1,050	6,476	92.8
Maryland	138	10,561	15,332	47.5	Virginia	66	7,184	12,511	43.8
Massachusetts	337	33,717	9,461	13.3	Washington	120	39,297	12,871	20.4
Michigan	273	22,350	38,768	95.4	West Virginia	177	6,912	20,390	59.1
Minnesota	279	8,116	15,533	46.3	Wisconsin	139	14,516	17,011	80.4
Mississippi	24	2,382	10,264	94.8	Wyoming	122	2,304	1,252	17.3

NA Not available. [1] Includes overnight visitors.

Source: The National Association of State Park Directors, Raleigh, NC, *2008 Annual Information Exchange.* See <http://www.naspd.org/>.

Table 1214. **National Park Service Visits and Acreage by State and Island Area: 2007**

[See headnote, Table 1215]

State and island area	Recreation visits [1]	Gross area acres	Federal land			Nonfederal land	
			NPS fee acres [2]	NPS/OTFED less than fee acres [3]	Other federal fee acres [4]	Other public acres	Private acres
Total.........	275,581,547	84,323,151	78,127,018	276,481	441,082	1,192,573	4,285,997
Alabama........	881,594	21,081	16,715	202	–	3,295	869
Alaska.........	2,636,540	54,638,803	51,084,827	27,885	8	189,087	3,336,997
American Samoa....	6,774	9,000	–	–	–	4,500	4,500
Arizona.........	10,666,670	2,962,853	2,618,735	115	76,937	57,067	209,999
Arkansas........	2,741,053	104,976	98,404	3,309	6	2,736	522
California........	34,396,905	8,107,244	7,560,432	22,437	13,061	313,492	197,822
Colorado........	5,563,458	673,296	609,625	6,859	42,451	862	13,499
Connecticut	12,536	7,782	5,719	1,055	–	874	133
District of Columbia ..	31,738,969	7,088	6,951	7	–	126	4
Florida.........	8,014,147	2,637,755	2,436,995	1,330	45,907	129,192	24,332
Georgia.........	6,321,158	62,923	39,645	46	1,461	16,775	4,996
Guam	209,661	2,037	958	–	–	872	208
Hawaii.........	5,122,853	364,999	353,661	1	11	11,228	98
Idaho..........	551,552	517,904	507,425	627	3,960	901	4,991
Illinois	358,809	13	12	–	–	–	1
Indiana	2,215,500	15,317	10,516	498	–	3,280	1,023
Iowa	206,566	2,713	2,708	–	–	5	1
Kansas	95,828	11,792	461	269	–	39	11,023
Kentucky	1,872,559	95,415	94,382	137	–	844	52
Louisiana	383,010	21,126	14,536	–	–	2,456	4,134
Maine	2,202,228	90,257	66,768	11,120	22	10,646	1,701
Maryland	3,359,005	71,857	39,508	5,975	395	23,269	2,711
Massachusetts	9,902,441	57,897	32,946	972	40	21,866	2,072
Michigan	1,591,808	718,187	631,716	732	42	58,515	27,183
Minnesota	621,593	301,333	139,509	3,193	141	98,811	59,678
Mississippi	6,037,460	117,629	103,698	5,261	–	45	8,625
Missouri.........	4,411,018	83,471	54,338	9,262	–	14,070	5,801
Montana	4,169,221	1,274,374	1,214,184	1,233	6,137	1,464	51,355
Nebraska........	275,045	29,748	5,650	494	–	36	23,567
Nevada	5,797,968	778,512	774,509	–	2,508	81	1,415
New Hampshire.....	29,091	15,897	8,362	1,556	5,772	162	45
New Jersey	5,502,356	99,096	35,216	81	3,208	59,000	1,592
New Mexico	1,622,257	391,029	376,528	5	2,524	3,365	8,607
New York	15,824,023	72,426	33,475	3,920	164	19,812	15,056
North Carolina......	19,325,848	405,793	362,741	12,272	20,782	3,289	6,709
North Dakota	491,551	72,581	71,252	258	151	56	865
Ohio	2,730,125	34,157	19,403	1,329	84	8,203	5,138
Oklahoma	1,382,734	10,241	10,008	9	189	8	27
Oregon	905,008	199,087	192,015	1,404	4,975	182	512
Pennsylvania	9,172,347	136,745	48,427	2,511	387	19,627	65,793
Puerto Rico	1,025,407	75	53	–	–	22	–
Rhode Island	49,348	5	5	–	–	–	–
South Carolina	1,438,888	32,618	30,131	61	5	51	2,370
South Dakota	3,621,584	307,377	141,317	122,327	–	79	43,653
Tennessee	7,889,132	383,545	352,962	1,679	9,629	3,616	15,658
Texas	5,593,186	1,236,625	1,191,216	85	1,013	5,079	39,233
Utah	8,164,441	2,117,038	2,097,106	833	1,142	12,803	5,155
Vermont.........	32,179	22,178	8,830	3,874	8,809	544	120
Virgin Islands	720,662	48,604	14,034	3	18,135	14,677	1,754
Virginia	22,815,437	362,554	306,884	6,228	21,260	6,973	21,209
Washington	6,891,951	1,965,395	1,832,279	2,108	100,187	12,691	18,129
West Virginia	1,762,748	92,604	63,802	308	314	6,894	21,285
Wisconsin........	442,061	133,754	61,742	11,481	802	47,628	12,101
Wyoming	5,785,254	2,396,340	2,343,697	1,126	48,462	1,380	1,675

– Represents zero. [1] See Table 1215, for footnotes 1, 2, 3, and 4.

Source: U.S. National Park Service, *Statistical Abstract, and unpublished data. See also <http://www2.nature.nps.gov/stats/>.*

Table 1215. **National Park Service Visits and Acreage by Type of Area: 2007**

[Includes data for five areas in Puerto Rico and Virgin Islands, one area in American Samoa, and one area in Guam]

Type of area	Recreation visits [1]	Gross area acres	Federal land			Nonfederal land	
			NPS fee acres [2]	NPS/OTFED less than fee acres [3]	Other federal fee acres [4]	Other public acres	Private acres
Total [5]...........	275,581,547	84,323,151	78,127,018	276,481	441,082	1,192,573	4,285,997
National historic sites.....	9,801,452	37,663	22,886	784	51	922	13,019
National historical parks...	26,593,375	172,870	123,364	3,045	360	28,510	17,592
National memorials	29,967,770	10,583	7,962	8	149	63	2,402
National monuments	19,740,736	2,027,865	1,802,847	14,830	30,671	19,777	159,740
National parks	62,274,038	52,090,325	49,711,580	149,927	49,499	498,131	1,681,188
National recreation areas ..	48,917,566	3,700,018	3,146,341	23,621	243,101	106,121	180,835
National seashores	16,186,543	595,014	403,188	14,890	61,226	106,131	9,579
National parkways.......	31,139,216	176,960	157,886	8,520	125	294	10,135

[1] Recreation visit represents the entry of a person onto lands or waters administered by the National Park Service (NPS) for recreational purposes excluding government personnel, through traffic (commuters), trades-persons, and persons residing within park boundaries. [2] Fee represents complete federal ownership of all rights in the land. [3] Represents federal ownership of some rights in the land. [4] NPS acreage lies under the jurisdiction of another federal agency (such as Bureau of Land Management). [5] Includes other "type of areas" not shown separately.

Source: U.S. National Park Service, Statistical Abstract. See also <http://www2.nature.nps.gov/stats/>.

Table 1216. **Participants in Wildlife-Related Recreation Activities: 2006**

[In thousands (33,916 represents 33,916,000). For persons 16 years old and over engaging in activity at least once in 2006. Based on survey and subject to sampling error; see source for details]

Participant	Number	Days of partici- pation	Trips	Participant	Number	Days of partici- pation
Total sportspersons [1] . . .	**33,916**	**736,707**	**588,891**	**Wildlife watchers** [1] . . .	**71,132**	**(X)**
Total anglers	29,952	516,781	403,492	Away from home [2]	22,977	352,070
Freshwater	25,431	433,337	336,528	Observe wildlife	21,546	291,027
Excluding Great Lakes . . .	25,035	419,942	323,265	Photograph wildlife	11,708	103,872
Great Lakes	1,420	18,016	13,264	Feed wildlife	7,084	77,329
Saltwater.	7,717	85,663	66,963			
				Around home [3]	67,756	(X)
Total hunters	12,510	219,925	185,399	Observe wildlife	44,467	(X)
Big game	10,682	164,061	115,255	Photograph wildlife	18,763	(X)
Small game	4,797	52,395	40,856	Feed wild birds	55,512	(X)
Migratory birds	2,293	19,770	16,390	Visit public parks	13,271	(X)
Other animals.	1,128	15,205	12,898	Maintain plantings or natural areas	14,508	(X)

X Not applicable. [1] Detail does not add to total due to multiple responses and nonresponse. [2] Persons taking a trip of at least 1 mile from home for activity. [3] Activity within 1 mile of home.

Source: U.S. Fish and Wildlife Service, *2006 National Survey of Fishing, Hunting, and Wildlife Associated Recreation,* October 2007. See <http://wsfrprograms.fws.gov/Subpages/NationalSurvey/nat_survey2006_final.pdf> and <http://federalaid.fws.gov/surveys/surveys.html>.

Table 1217. **Expenditures for Wildlife-Related Recreation Activities: 2006**

[In millions (42,011 represents $42,011,000,000). For persons 16 years old and over. Based on survey and subject to sampling error; see source for details]

Expenditure item	Fishing Expen- ditures (mil.dol.)	Fishing Spenders Number (1,000)	Fishing Spenders Per- cent of an- glers	Hunting Expen- ditures (mil.dol.)	Hunting Spenders Number (1,000)	Hunting Spenders Per- cent of hunt- ers	Wildlife watching Expen- ditures (mil.dol.)	Wildlife watching Spenders Number (1,000)	Wildlife watching Spenders Per- cent of watch- ers [2]
Total, all items [1]	**42,011**	**28,307**	**95**	**22,893**	**12,153**	**97**	**45,655**	**55,979**	**79**
TRIP-RELATED EXPENDITURES									
Total trip-related [3]	17,879	26,318	88	6,679	10,828	87	12,875	19,443	85
Food and lodging	6,303	22,572	75	2,791	9,567	76	7,516	16,415	71
Food	4,327	22,415	75	2,177	9,533	76	4,298	16,261	71
Lodging	1,975	5,304	18	614	1,599	13	3,218	6,624	29
Transportation	4,962	22,361	75	2,697	10,064	80	4,456	18,329	80
Public	524	1,163	4	214	401	3	1,567	2,902	13
Private.	4,438	21,979	73	2,483	9,982	80	2,889	17,447	76
Other trip costs.	6,614	22,275	74	1,190	3,416	27	903	7,681	33
EQUIPMENT AND OTHER EXPENDITURES									
Total equipment and other expenditures . .	24,133	25,355	85	16,215	11,745	94	32,780	52,178	73
Equipment.	5,332	19,082	64	5,366	9,287	74	9,870	49,040	69
Auxiliary equipment.	779	3,837	13	1,330	4,196	34	1,033	4,848	7
Special equipment [4]	12,646	1,818	6	4,035	505	4	12,271	1,914	3
Other expenditures [5]	5,375	20,638	69	5,483	10,632	85	9,606	19,070	27
Magazines, books	115	2,944	10	84	1,767	14	360	9,490	13
Licenses, stamps, tags, and permits .	503	16,259	54	743	9,862	79	(X)	(X)	(X)

X Not applicable. [1] Total not adjusted for multiple responses or nonresponse. [2] Percent of wildlife-watching participants column is based on away-from-home participants for trip-related expenditures. For equipment and other expenditures, the percent of wildlife-watching participants is based on total participants. [3] Information on trip-related expenditures for wildlife watching was collected for away-from-home participants only. Equipment and other expenditures for wildlife watching are based on information collected from both away-from-home and around-the-home participants. [4] Special equipment includes boats, campers, cabins, trail bikes, etc. [5] Other expenditures not shown.

Source: U.S. Fish and Wildlife Service, *2006 National Survey of Fishing, Hunting, and Wildlife-Associated Recreation,* October 2007. See <http://wsfrprograms.fws.gov/Subpages/NationalSurvey/natsurvey2006final.pdf>.

Table 1218. **Tribal Gaming Revenues: 2002 to 2007**

[In millions (14,497 represents $14,497,000,000). For year ending September 30]

	2002 Num- ber of opera- tions	2002 Rev- enue	2003 Num- ber of opera- tions	2003 Rev- enue	2004 Num- ber of opera- tions	2004 Rev- enue	2005 Num- ber of opera- tions	2005 Rev- enue	2006 Num- ber of opera- tions	2006 Rev- enue	2007 Num- ber of opera- tions	2007 Rev- enue
Total [1]	**330**	**14,497**	**358**	**16,826**	**375**	**19,479**	**392**	**22,579**	**394**	**24,889**	**382**	**26,016**
Region I	47	1,196	46	1,441	45	1,602	49	1,829	46	2,080	43	2,208
Region II.	51	3,594	54	4,700	54	5,822	57	6,993	56	7,675	58	7,796
Region III	40	1,782	43	1,899	45	2,160	48	2,529	45	2,719	44	2,841
Region IV	109	3,524	109	3,597	117	3,816	118	3,984	122	4,070	109	4,218
Region V	79	581	82	867	87	1,259	92	1,730	98	2,126	100	2,553
Region VI	22	3,820	24	4,322	27	4,821	28	5,514	27	6,219	28	6,400

[1] Region 1: Alaska, Idaho, Oregon, and Washington. Region 2: California and Northern Nevada. Region 3: Arizona, Colorado, New Mexico, and Southern Nevada. Region 4: Iowa, Michigan, Minnesota, Montana, North Dakota, Nebraska, South Dakota, Wisconsin, and Wyoming. Data for Montana not included for years 2004 and earlier. Region 5: Kansas, Oklahoma, and Texas. Region 6: Alabama, Connecticut, Florida, Louisiana, Mississippi, North Carolina, and New York.

Source: National Indian Gaming Commission, *Tribal Gaming Revenues,* Annual. See also <http://www.nigc.gov>.

Arts, Recreation, and Travel **757**

Table 1219. Gaming Revenue by Industry: 2000 to 2006

[In millions of dollars (62,154 represents $62,154,000,000). Data shown are for gross revenue. Gross gambling revenue (GGR) is the amount wagered minus the winnings returned to players, a true measure of the economic value of gambling. GGR is the figure used to determine what an operation earns before taxes, salaries, and other expenses are paid]

Industry	2000	2001	2002	2003	2004	2005	2006
Total [2]	62,154	65,174	68,783	73,062	78,589	84,433	90,931
Card rooms	949	992	811	979	989	1,025	1,104
Commercial casinos	26,455	27,318	28,144	28,669	[1]30,595	[1]31,775	[1]34,113
Charitable games and bingo [3]	2,466	2,591	2,671	2,331	2,336	2,338	2,237
Legal bookmaking	131	126	116	128	116	130	191
Lotteries	17,277	17,475	18,658	20,283	21,405	22,898	24,631
Parimutuel wagering	3,935	3,936	3,912	3,847	3,740	3,689	3,580

[1] Amount includes deepwater cruise ships, curises-to-nowhere and noncasino devises. [2] Includes industry not shown separately. [3] Data are estimated.
Source: Christiansen Capital Advisors LLC. Prepared for the American Gaming Association (AGA). Industry Information, Fact Sheets, *Gaming Revenue: Current-Year Data (Copyright)*. See also <http://www.americangaming.org/Industry/factsheets/index.cfm> and <www.cca-i.com>.

Table 1220. North America Cruise Industry in the United States: 2002 to 2006

[The North American passenger cruise industry is defined as those cruise lines that primarily market their cruises in North America. These cruise lines offer cruises with destinations throughout the globe. While most of these cruises originate in ports throughout North America, cruises also originate at ports in other continents]

Item	Unit	2002	2003	2004	2005	2006
Capacity Measures:						
Number of ships	Number	123	134	144	145	151
Lower berths [1]	Number	197,553	212,004	225,714	230,891	249,691
Passenger embarkations: [2]						
Global	1,000	9,220	9,830	10,850	11,500	12,000
United States	1,000	6,500	7,113	8,100	8,612	9,001
Florida	1,000	4,413	4,676	4,724	4,843	5,018
California	1,000	600	807	1,095	1,301	1,241
New York	1,000	326	438	547	370	536
Other U.S. ports	1,000	1,056	1,192	1,734	2,098	2,206
Canada	1,000	527	482	454	455	423
San Juan	1,000	298	325	450	581	555
Rest of world	1,000	1,895	1,910	1,846	1,852	2,021
United States expenditures of the North American cruise industry:	Bil. dol.	11.95	12.92	14.70	16.18	17.64
U.S. purchases of the cruise line goods and services	Bil. dol.	8.84	9.49	10.70	11.76	12.89
Passenger and crew expenditures [3]	Bil. dol.	2.06	2.36	2.88	3.23	3.48
Wages & taxes paid by cruise lines	Bil. dol.	1.05	1.07	1.12	1.19	1.27

[1] Single beds. [2] Port of departure. [3] Consist of the expenditures made by the cruise lines and their crew and passengers during the course of providing or taking cruises. These included cruise expenditures for headquarters operations, food and beverages provided aboard cruise ships and businesses services such as, advertising and marketing. Additionally, cruise passengers and crew purchase a variety of goods and services including clothing, shore excursions, and lodging as part of their cruise vacation or as part of a pre- or post-cruise stay.
Source: Business Research & Economic Advisors (BREA), Exton, PA. The Contribution of the North American Cruise Industry to the U.S. Economy in 2006. Prepared for the Cruise Lines International Association, August 2007. See also <http://www.cruising.org>.

Table 1221. Top States and Cities Visited by Overseas Travelers: 2000 to 2007

[25,975 represents 25,975,000. Includes travelers for business and pleasure, international travelers in transit through the United States, and students. Excludes travel by international personnel and international businessmen employed in the United States. Starting with the 2006 data, the statistical policy for visitation estimates of international travelers to the U.S. has changed. For more information, go to <http://tinet.ita.doc.gov/outreachpages/2007_statistical_policy.html/>. **States and Cities are ranked by the latest overseas traveler data**]

State and other area	Overseas visitors [1] (1,000)				City	Overseas visitors [1] (1,000)			
	2000	2005	2006	2007		2000	2005	2006	2007
Total overseas travelers [2],[3]	25,975	21,679	21,668	23,892	New York City, NY	5,714	5,810	6,219	7,646
New York	5,922	6,092	6,414	7,908	Los Angeles, CA	3,533	2,580	2,514	2,652
California	6,364	4,791	4,615	5,185	Orlando, FL	2,935	2,081	1,972	2,341
Florida	6,026	4,379	4,117	4,683	San Francisco, CA	2,831	2,124	1,993	2,270
Hawaii	2,727	2,255	2,058	1,864	Orlando, FL	3,013	2,016	1,993	2,055
Nevada	2,364	1,821	1,690	1,768	Las Vegas, NV	2,260	1,778	1,647	1,720
Massachusetts	1,429	867	1,105	1,171	Oahu/Honolulu, HI	2,234	1,821	1,733	1,553
Illinois	1,377	1,149	1,083	1,171	Washington, DC	1,481	1,106	1,062	1,195
Guam	1,325	1,127	1,170	1,099	Chicago, IL	1,351	1,084	1,062	1,147
Texas	1,169	954	975	1,003	Boston, MA	1,325	802	997	1,075
New Jersey	909	997	845	956	San Diego, CA	701	499	650	645
Pennsylvania	649	629	672	812	Philadelphia, PA	390	434	(B)	550
Arizona	883	564	563	573	Atlanta, GA	701	564	477	478
Georgia	(B)	(B)	520	526	Houston, TX	442	369	455	478
Washington	(B)	(B)	390	454	Anaheim, CA	494	390	303	430
North Carolina	(B)	(B)	(B)	358	San Jose, CA	494	347	412	430
Colorado	(B)	(B)	(B)	311	Seattle, WA	416	347	325	406
Connecticut	(B)	(B)	(B)	311	Dallas/Ft. Worth, TX	494	347	(B)	358

B Figure too small to meet statistical standards for reliability of a derived figure. [1] Excludes Canada and Mexico. [2] A person is counted in each area visited, but only once in the total. [3] Includes other states and cities, not shown separately.
Source: U.S. Department of Commerce; International Trade Administration; Office of Travel and Tourism Industries and Bureau of Economic Analysis (BEA); released: May 2008. See <http://www.tinet.ita.doc.gov>.

758   Arts, Recreation, and Travel

Table 1222. Domestic Travel by U.S. Resident Households—Summary: 1999 to 2005

[In millions (995.5 represents 995,500,000). See headnote, Table 1223]

Type of trip	1999	2000	2001	2002	2003	2004	2005
All travel: [1]							
Household trips	995.5	1,008.9	993.8	994.9	978.2	1,002.6	1,019.1
Person-trips	1,856.7	1,892.1	1,869.9	1,919.1	1,890.3	1,953.3	1,992.4
All overnight travel:							
Household trips	488.5	493.0	480.7	475.2	470.5	482.2	499.0
Person-trips	873.4	895.6	878.3	884.1	903.2	941.8	968.3
Business travel:							
Household trips	400.5	401.0	393.0	364.8	346.8	349.5	345.7
Person-trips	559.9	566.6	545.3	512.0	502.1	513.0	510.0
Leisure travel: [2]							
Household trips	595.1	607.9	600.8	630.1	631.4	653.1	673.5
Person-trips	1,296.8	1,325.4	1,324.6	1,407.1	1,388.2	1,440.4	1,482.5

[1] Includes personal and other trips (e.g. medical, funerals, weddings) not shown separately.   All domestic travel included. Ninety-five percent of U.S. resident person-trips are domestic.   [2] Includes visiting friends/relatives, outdoor recreation, entertainment, and travel for other pleasure/personal reasons, etc.

Source: Travel Industry Association of America, Washington, DC, *TravelScope,* annual (copyright). See also <http://www.tia.org/index.html>.

Table 1223. Characteristics of Domestic Overnight Leisure Trips by U.S. Resident Households: 2000 to 2005

[In millions except as indicated (317.4 represents 317,400,000). Represents household trips to destinations 50 miles or more, one-way, away from home, and including one or more overnights. "Leisure" includes visiting friends/relatives, outdoor recreation, entertainment, and travel for other pleasure/personal reasons etc. Other pleasure/personal trips are trips such as for medical reasons, funerals, weddings, etc. Based on a monthly mail panel survey of 25,000 U.S. households. For details, see source]

Characteristic	Unit	2000	2001	2002	2003	2004	2005
Total overnight leisure trips	Millions...	317.4	300.8	312.0	318.1	322.5	349.3
Average nights per trip	Number...	4.4	4.3	4.1	4.1	4.3	4.4
Traveled primarily by auto, truck, RV, or rental car	Percent...	80.1	80.1	81.4	81.4	81.3	81.7
Traveled primarily by air	Percent...	17.1	16.7	15.3	15.1	15.3	14.8
Stayed in a hotel/motel/B&B while on trip	Percent...	44.0	41.3	42.5	43.0	43.9	43.0
Household income:							
Less than $50,000	Percent...	43.6	41.6	39.5	37.1	38.5	35.2
$50,000 or more	Percent...	56.4	58.4	60.5	62.9	61.5	64.8

Source: Travel Industry Association of America, Washington, DC, *TravelScope,* annual (copyright). See also <http://www.tia.org/index.html>.

Table 1224. Domestic Travel Expenditures by State: 2005

[572,037 represents $572,037,000,000. Represents U.S. spending on domestic overnight trips and day trips of 50 miles or more, one way, away from home. Excludes spending by foreign visitors and by U.S. residents in U.S. territories and abroad]

State	Total (mil. dol.)	Percent distri- bution	Rank	State	Total (mil. dol.)	Percent distri- bution	Rank	State	Total (mil. dol.)	Percent distri- bution	Rank
U.S., total...	**572,037**	**100.0**	**(X)**	IN	7,612	1.3	27	NV	28,221	4.9	5
				KS	4,475	0.8	38	NY	33,039	5.8	4
				KY	6,385	1.1	29	OH	13,929	2.4	12
AL	6,546	1.1	28	LA	7,889	1.4	25	OK	4,925	0.9	34
AK	1,552	0.3	48	MA	11,692	2.0	15	OR	6,358	1.1	30
AR	4,747	0.8	36	MD	10,289	1.8	18	PA	17,155	3.0	7
AZ	11,122	1.9	16	ME	2,170	0.4	43	RI	1,574	0.3	47
CA	71,314	12.5	1	MI	13,460	2.4	13	SC	8,526	1.5	23
CO	10,771	1.9	17	MN	9,016	1.6	21	SD	1,806	0.3	46
CT	7,791	1.4	26	MO	10,179	1.8	19	TN	12,084	2.1	14
DC	5,385	0.9	32	MS	5,881	1.0	31	TX	37,245	6.5	3
DE	1,259	0.2	51	MT	2,393	0.4	42	UT	4,622	0.8	37
FL	49,982	8.7	2	NC	14,216	2.5	11	VA	16,480	2.9	10
GA	16,572	2.9	9	ND	1,424	0.2	50	VT	1,511	0.3	49
HI	8,663	1.5	22	NE	3,232	0.6	39	WA	9,262	1.6	20
IA	5,364	0.9	33	NH	3,048	0.5	40	WI	8,043	1.4	24
ID	2,703	0.5	41	NJ	16,663	2.9	8	WV	2,116	0.4	44
IL	24,505	4.3	6	NM	4,769	0.8	35	WY	2,074	0.4	45

X Not applicable.

Source: Travel Industry Association of America, Washington, DC, *TravelScope/Directions,* annual (copyright). See also *Impact of Travel on State Economies, 2005* (copyright) at <http://www.tia.org/home.asp>.

U.S. Census Bureau, Statistical Abstract of the United States: 2009

Table 1225. **Travel Forecast Summary: 2005 to 2011**

[In billions of dollars (11,049 represents $11,049,000,000,000)]

Measurement	Unit	2005	2006	2007 [1]	2008 [2]	2009 [2]	2010 [2]	2011 [2]
Real GDP................	Billions ...	11,049	11,366	11,590	11,826	12,173	12,511	12,824
Unemployment rate	Percent ...	5.1	4.6	4.6	5.0	4.9	4.7	4.5
Consumer price index (CPI) [3]....	Percent ...	195.3	201.6	207.3	216.2	223.0	227.7	232.3
Travel price index (TPI) [3]	Percent ...	219.5	230.4	242.6	273.5	279.3	274.4	273.7
Total travel expenditures in U.S. ...	Billions ...	653.8	699.8	739.4	775.9	806.2	849.7	894.9
U.S. residents	Billions ...	572.1	614.1	642.7	674.6	701.1	739.5	778.9
International visitors [4]	Billions ...	81.7	85.7	96.7	101.3	105.1	110.2	116.0
Total international visitors to the United States	Millions ...	49.2	51.0	53.6	55.6	57.6	59.5	61.9
Total domestic person trips [5]	Millions ...	1,992	2,001	2,008	1,984	1,996	2,040	2,078

[1] Projected. [2] Forecast. [3] 1982 through 1984 = 100. [4] Excludes international visitors' spending on traveling to the U.S. on U.S. flag carriers, and other misc. transportation. [5] One person on one trip 50 miles or more, one way, away from home, or including one or more nights away from home.

Source: TIA's Travel Forecast Model; TravelScope/Directions (copyright); Data from <http://www.tia.org/researchpubs/index.html>; Bureau of Labor Statistics; U.S. Department of Commmerce, Bureau of Economic Analysis, Office of Travel and Tourism Industries.

Table 1226. **Chain-Type Price Indexes for Direct Tourism Output: 1998 to 2007**

[Index numbers, 2000 = 100. See headnote, Table 1227. For explanation of chain-type price indexes, see text Section 13]

Tourism goods and services group	1998	1999	2000	2001	2002	2003	2004	2005	2006	2007
Traveler accommodations	93.1	96.8	100.0	102.0	101.2	102.8	108.7	114.2	119.4	125.5
Transportation................	91.9	93.8	100.0	97.8	95.1	98.9	101.6	108.0	115.4	118.4
Passenger air transportation......	95.2	95.8	100.0	95.8	90.3	93.2	92.1	94.8	99.7	100.8
All other transportation-related commodities...............	88.9	91.9	100.0	99.9	99.4	103.3	108.8	118.1	127.6	132.1
Food services and drinking places....	95.8	97.3	100.0	103.2	106.0	108.2	111.4	115.0	118.7	122.9
Recreation, entertainment, and shopping.................	94.9	97.3	100.0	102.5	104.0	105.4	107.7	110.3	112.8	115.5
Recreation and entertainment.....	93.0	96.1	100.0	103.4	105.9	108.6	111.7	115.5	119.0	122.3
Shopping..................	96.3	98.2	100.0	101.8	102.6	103.1	104.9	106.5	108.3	110.6
All tourism goods and services	93.6	95.8	100.0	100.6	100.4	102.8	106.0	110.7	115.7	119.4

Source: U.S. Department of Commerce, Bureau of Economic Analysis, Office of Travel and Tourism Industries, *United States Travel and Tourism Satellite Accounts (TTSAs)*. See <http://www.bea.gov/bea/dn2/home/tourism.htm>.

Table 1227. **Tourism Sales by Commodity Group and Tourism Employment by Industry Group: 2001 to 2007**

[Sales in billions of dollars (524 represents $524,000,000,000). Employment in thousands (5,756 represents 5,756,000). Direct tourism-related sales comprise all output consumed directly by visitors (e.g., traveler accommodations, passenger air transportation, souvenirs). Direct tourism-related employment comprises all jobs where the workers are engaged in the production of direct tourism-related output (e.g., hotel staff, airline pilots, and souvenir sellers)]

Tourism commodity group	Direct tourism sales (bil. dol.)				Tourism industry group	Direct tourism employment			
	2001	2005	2006	2007		2001	2005	2006	2007
All commodities [1]	**524**	**658**	**707**	**747**	**All industries**	**5,756**	**5,739**	**5,772**	**5,869**
Traveler accommodations	91	113	120	128	Traveler accommodations.....	1,377	1,353	1,356	1,376
Transportation.............	205	253	278	294	Transportation	1,327	1,108	1,110	1,125
Passenger air transportation..	85	97	105	110	Air transportation services....	592	450	446	454
All other transportation-related commodities......	120	157	173	183	All other transportation-related industries	735	658	664	671
Food services and drinking places	84	110	117	123	Food and beverage services....	1,608	1,847	1,869	1,909
Recreation, entertainment, and shopping	143	181	192	202	Recreation, entertainment, and shopping	1,190	1,179	1,174	1,192
Recreation and entertainment	60	79	82	86	Recreation and entertainment	596	624	618	633
Shopping	83	103	110	116	Shopping	594	555	556	559
					All other industries	254	251	263	266

[1] Commodities that are typically purchased by visitors from the producer: such as airline passenger fares, meals, or hotel services.

Source: U.S. Bureau of Economic Analysis, "Industry Economic Accounts, Satellite Industry Accounts, Travel and Tourism." See <http://www.bea.gov/bea/dn2/home/tourism.htm>.

Table 1228. **International Travelers and Payments: 1990 to 2007**

[**(47,880 represents $47,880,000,000).** For coverage, see Table 1229. Some traveler data revised since originally issued]

Year	Travel and passenger fare (mil. dol.)				U.S. net travel and passenger receipts (mil. dol.)	U.S. travelers to international countries (1,000)	International travelers to the U.S. (1,000)
	Payments by U.S. travelers		Receipts from international visitors				
	Total [1]	Travel payments	Total [1]	Travel receipts			
1990	47,880	37,349	58,305	43,007	10,425	44,624	39,363
1995	59,579	44,916	82,304	63,395	22,725	51,285	43,491
2000	88,979	64,705	103,087	82,400	14,108	61,327	51,238
2001	82,833	60,200	89,819	71,893	6,986	59,442	46,927
2002	78,684	58,715	83,651	66,605	4,967	58,065	43,581
2003	78,436	57,447	80,250	64,359	1,814	56,250	41,218
2004	90,468	65,750	93,397	74,546	2,929	61,809	46,086
2005	95,119	68,970	102,769	81,799	7,650	63,503	49,206
2006	99,605	72,104	107,756	85,720	8,151	63,662	51,063
2007 [2]	104,653	76,167	122,298	96,712	17,645	64,052	55,986

[1] Includes passenger fares not shown separately. [2] Preliminary estimates for the receipts payment figures, and U.S. travelers to International countries.

Source: U.S. Department of Commerce; International Trade Administration; Office of Travel and Tourism Industries and Bureau of Economic Analysis (BEA); released May 2008. See <http://www.tinet.ita.doc.gov>.

Table 1229. **International Travel: 1990 to 2007**

[**In thousands (44,619 represents 44,619,000).** U.S. travelers cover residents of the United States, its territories and possessions. International travelers to the U.S. include travelers for business and pleasure, excludes travel by international personnel and international businessmen employed in the United States. Some traveler data revised since originally issued]

Item and area	1990	1995	2000	2003	2004	2005	2006	2007
U.S. travelers to international countries [1,2]	**44,619**	**51,285**	**61,327**	**56,250**	**61,809**	**63,503**	**63,662**	**64,052**
Canada	12,252	13,005	15,188	14,232	15,088	14,391	13,855	13,371
Mexico.	16,377	19,221	19,285	17,566	19,370	20,325	19,659	19,453
Total overseas.	15,990	19,059	26,853	24,452	27,351	28,787	30,148	31,228
Europe	8,043	8,596	13,373	10,319	11,679	11,976	12,029	12,304
International travelers to the U.S. . . .	**39,363**	**43,491**	**51,238**	**41,218**	**46,086**	**49,206**	**51,063**	**55,986**
Canada	17,263	14,663	14,667	12,666	13,857	14,862	15,992	17,761
Mexico.	7,041	8,189	10,596	10,526	11,907	12,665	13,317	14,333
Total overseas.	15,059	20,639	25,975	18,026	20,322	21,679	21,668	23,892
Europe	6,659	8,793	11,597	8,639	9,686	10,313	10,136	11,406
Asia	4,360	6,616	7,554	5,003	5,802	6,198	6,152	6,377
South America	1,328	2,449	2,941	1,522	1,645	1,820	1,928	2,274
Caribbean	1,137	1,044	1,331	998	1,095	1,135	1,198	1,317
Oceania	662	588	731	525	660	737	756	834
Central America	412	509	822	656	692	696	694	786
Middle East	365	454	702	447	502	527	553	620
Africa	137	186	295	236	241	252	253	278

[1] A person is counted in each area visited but only once in the total. [2] 2007 U.S. outbound totals are preliminary estimates.

Source: U.S. Department of Commerce; International Trade Administration; Office of Travel and Tourism Industries and Bureau of Economic Analysis (BEA); released May 2008. See <http://www.tinet.ita.doc.gov>.

Table 1230. **Top 20 U.S. Gateways for Nonstop International Air Travel: 2005 and 2006**

[**150,110 represents 150,110,000.** International passengers are residents of any country traveling nonstop to and from the United States on U.S. and foreign carriers. The data cover all passengers arriving and departing from U.S. airports on nonstop commercial international flights with 60 seats or more]

Gateway airport	2005 [1]	2006	Percent change 2005–2006	Gateway airport	2005 [1]	2006	Percent change 2005–2006
Total	150,110	154,351	2.8	Dallas-Ft. Worth, TX	5,051	5,216	3.3
Total, top 20	131,182	135,191	3.1	Washington (Dulles), DC	4,792	5,176	8.0
Top 20, percentage of total	87.4	87.6	(X)	Honolulu, HI	4,410	4,049	−8.2
				Boston, MA	3,902	3,776	−3.2
New York (JFK), NY.	18,469	19,351	4.8	Detroit, MI	3,823	3,685	−3.6
Los Angeles, CA	16,836	16,498	−2.0	Philadelphia, PA	3,693	3,515	−4.8
Miami, FL	14,621	14,852	1.6	Minneapolis-St. Paul, MN	2,456	2,649	7.9
Chicago (O'Hare), IL	11,013	11,516	4.6	Guam Island, GU	2,595	2,476	−4.6
Newark, NJ	9,128	9,926	8.7	Seattle-Tacoma, WA	2,187	2,420	10.7
San Francisco, CA	7,295	8,302	13.8	Fort Lauderdale, FL.	2,285	2,260	−1.1
Atlanta, GA	7,839	8,164	4.1	Orlando, FL	2,039	2,137	4.8
Houston (Bush), TX	6,570	7,147	8.8	San Juan, PR.	2,179	2,075	−4.8

X Not applicable. [1] Data have been revised.

Source: U.S. Department of Transportation, Bureau of Transportation Statistics, Office of Airline Information, T-100 Segment data, February 2008. See also <http://www.bts.gov/publications/pocket_guide_to_transportation/2008/>.

Table 1231. Selected U.S.-Canadian and U.S.-Mexican Border Land— Passenger Gateways: 2006

[(30,038 represents 30,038,000)]

Item and gateway	Entering the U.S. (1,000)	Item and gateway	Entering the U.S. (1,000)
All U.S.-Canadian land gateways [1]		**All U.S.-Mexican land gateways** [1]	
Personal vehicles	30,038	Personal vehicles	88,296
Personal vehicle passengers	62,986	Personal vehicle passengers	179,255
Buses	129	Buses	263
Bus passengers	3,499	Bus passengers	3,187
Train passengers	245	Train passengers	22
Pedestrians	532	Pedestrians	46,251
Selected top five gateways:		**Selected top five gateways:**	
Personal vehicles		Personal vehicles	
Buffalo-Niagara Falls, NY	6,026	San Ysidro, CA	17,135
Detroit, MI	5,634	El Paso, TX	15,603
Blaine, WA	2,597	Brownsville, TX	6,967
Port Huron, MI	1,976	Hidalgo, TX	6,480
Calais, ME	1,174	Calexico, CA	6,110
Personal vehicle passengers		Personal vehicle passengers	
Buffalo-Niagara Falls, NY	13,515	San Ysidro, CA	31,869
Detroit, MI	9,932	El Paso, TX	28,000
Blaine, WA	5,276	Laredo, TX	14,244
Port Huron, MI	4,107	Brownsville, TX	14,023
Champlain-Rouses Point, NY	2,921	Hidalgo, TX	12,632
Pedestrians		Pedestrians	
Buffalo-Niagara Falls, NY	346	San Ysidro, CA	7,812
Calais, ME	29	Nogales, AZ	7,726
Sumas, WA	22	El Paso, TX	7,500
International Falls, MN	20	Laredo, TX	4,246
Point Roberts, WA	15	Calexico, CA	4,049

[1] Data reflects all personal vehicles, buses, passengers, and pedestrians entering the U.S.-Canadian border, and U.S.-Mexican border, regardless of nationality.

Source: U.S. Department of Transportation, Bureau of Transportation Statistics, special tabulations, June 2007. Based on the following primary data source: U.S. Department of Homeland Security, Customs and Border Protection, Office of Field Operations, Operations Management Database (Washington, D.C. 2006). See <http://www.bts.gov/programs/international/border_crossing_entry_data/>.

Table 1232. Foreign Visitors for Pleasure Admitted by Country of Citizenship: 1990 to 2006

[In thousands (13,418 represents 13,418,000). For years ending September 30. Represents non-U.S. citizens (also known as nonimmigrants) admitted to the country for a temporary period of time]

Country	1990	2000 [1]	2005	2006	Country	1990	2000 [1]	2005	2006
All countries [2]	13,418	30,511	23,815	24,888	Singapore	32	131	57	59
					Thailand	25	76	37	40
Europe [3]	5,383	11,806	10,016	9,749	Turkey	20	93	57	59
Austria	87	182	116	115	United Arab Emirates	7	36	3	4
Belgium	95	254	154	153	Africa [3]	105	327	212	211
Czech Republic	(X)	44	26	27	Egypt	16	44	19	20
Denmark	75	150	153	166	Nigeria	11	27	40	37
Finland	83	95	76	75	South Africa	26	114	64	65
France	566	1,113	1,007	875	Oceania [3]	562	748	723	765
Germany [4]	969	1,925	1,248	1,215	Australia	380	535	527	562
Greece	43	60	40	38	New Zealand [6]	153	170	184	192
Hungary	15	58	30	30	North America [3],[7]	2,463	6,501	5,546	6,839
Iceland	10	27	34	41	Canada	119	277	23	29
Ireland	81	325	398	417	Mexico	1,061	3,972	4,070	5,262
Italy	308	626	636	579	Caribbean [3]	963	1,404	876	978
Netherlands	214	559	483	480	Aruba	10	24	([8])	([8])
Norway	80	144	117	123	Barbados	34	57	41	43
Poland	55	116	119	121	Haiti	57	72	65	56
Portugal	30	86	81	85	Jamaica	132	240	152	186
Russia	(X)	74	53	58	Costa Rica	62	172	109	105
Spain	183	370	402	432	El Salvador	46	175	147	139
Sweden	230	321	249	248	Guatemala	91	177	135	136
Switzerland	236	400	207	217	Honduras	52	87	75	75
United Kingdom	1,899	4,671	4,232	4,088	Nicaragua	13	47	33	35
Asia [3]	3,830	7,853	5,688	5,636	Panama	43	106	64	65
China [5]	187	656	221	248	South America [3]	1,016	2,867	1,498	1,583
India	75	253	247	265	Argentina	136	515	145	162
Indonesia	28	62	42	43	Bolivia	14	48	18	18
Israel	128	319	220	220	Brazil	300	706	385	431
Japan	2,846	4,946	3,758	3,620	Chile	54	194	82	86
Korea, South	120	606	528	570	Colombia	122	411	282	310
Malaysia	27	64	32	32	Ecuador	57	122	119	121
Pakistan	27	47	34	30	Peru	97	190	142	126
Philippines	76	163	144	142	Uruguay	16	66	24	24
Saudi Arabia	33	67	10	10	Venezuela	199	570	270	276

X Not applicable. [1] Due to the temporary expiration of the Visa Waiver Program from May through October 2000, data for business and pleasure not available separately for 2000 and 2001. [2] Includes "other" countries and countries "unknown" not shown separately. [3] Total includes all countries for the region. [4] Data for 1990 are for former West Germany. [5] See Table 1288, footnote 2. [6] Prior to fiscal year 1995, data for Niue are included in New Zealand. [7] The majority of short-term admissions from Canada and Mexico are excluded. [8] Netherlands total includes Aruba.

Source: U.S. Dept. of Homeland Security, Office of Immigration Statistics, *2006 Yearbook of Immigration Statistics, Nonimmigrant Admissions*. See also <http://www.dhs.gov/ximgtn/statistics/publications/yearbook.shtm>.

Section 27
Accommodation, Food Services, and Other Services

This section presents statistics relating to services other than those covered in the previous few sections (22 to 26) on wholesale and retail trade, transportation, communications, financial services, and recreation services. Data shown for services are classified by kind of business and cover sales or receipts, establishments, employees, payrolls, and other items. The principal sources of these data are from the Census Bureau and include the *2002 Economic Census*, annual surveys, and the *County Business Patterns* program. These data are supplemented by data from several sources such as the National Restaurant Association on food and drink sales (Table 1243), the American Hotel & Lodging Association on lodging (Table 1242), and Universal McCann on advertising (Table 1239).

Data on these services also appear in several other sections. For instance, labor force employment and earnings data appear in Section 12, Labor Force, Employment, and Earnings; gross domestic product of the industry (Table 648) appears in Section 13, Income, Expenditures, Poverty, and Wealth; and financial data (several tables) from the quarterly *Statistics of Income Bulletin,* published by the Internal Revenue Service, appear in Section 15, Business Enterprise.

Censuses—Limited coverage of the service industries started in 1933. Beginning with the 1967 census, legislation provides for a census of each area to be conducted every 5 years (for years ending in "2" and "7"). For more information on the most current census, see the Economic Census, *Guide to Economic Census*, found at <http://www.census.gov/econ /census02/guide/index.html>. The industries covered in the censuses and surveys of business are defined in the *North American Industry Classification System* (NAICS). For information on NAICS, see the Census Web site at <http://www .census.gov/epcd/www/naics.html>.

In general, the 2002 Economic Census has two final series of publications for these sectors: 1) subject series with reports such as product lines, and establishment and firm sizes and 2) geographic reports with individual reports for each state. For information on these series, see the Census Bureau Web site at <http: //www.census.gov/econ/census02>.

Current surveys—The Service Annual Survey provides annual estimates of nationwide receipts for selected personal, business, leasing and repair, amusement and entertainment, social and health, and other professional service industries in the United States. For selected social, health, and other professional service industries, separate estimates are developed for receipts of taxable firms and revenue and expenses for firms and organizations exempt from federal income taxes. Several service sectors from this survey are covered in other sections of this publication. The estimates for tax exempt firms in these industries are derived from a sample of employer firms only. Estimates obtained from annual and monthly surveys are based on sample data and are not expected to agree exactly with results that would be obtained from a complete census of all establishments. Data include estimates for sampling units not reporting.

Statistical reliability—For a discussion of statistical collection and estimation, sampling procedures, and measures of statistical reliability applicable to Census Bureau data, see Appendix III.

U.S. Census Bureau, Statistical Abstract of the United States: 2009

Table 1233. Selected Service-Related Industries—Establishments, Sales, Payroll, and Employees by Kind of Business: 2002

[886,801 represents $886,801,000,000. Covers only establishments with payroll. For statement on methodology, see Appendix III]

Kind of business	2002 NAICS code [1]	Estab-lishments (number)	Sales or receipts (mil. dol.)	Annual payroll (mil. dol.)	Paid employ-ees [2] (1,000)
Professional, scientific, and technical services	**54**	**771,305**	**886,801**	**376,090**	**7,244**
Professional, scientific, and technical services	541	771,305	886,801	376,090	7,244
Legal services	5411	179,420	182,098	69,869	1,160
Accounting, tax preparation, bookkeeping, & payroll services	5412	112,240	84,072	41,272	1,317
Architectural, engineering, & related services	5413	107,386	161,835	68,015	1,267
Specialized design services	5414	30,484	17,075	4,952	117
Computer systems design & related services	5415	105,710	173,414	72,368	1,107
Management, scientific and tech consulting services	5416	116,159	105,452	42,825	739
Scientific research & development services	5417	15,334	64,481	43,526	618
Advertising and related services	5418	38,047	56,681	19,484	409
Other professional, scientific, and technical services	5419	66,525	41,693	13,779	508
Management of companies and enterprises	**55**	**49,308**	**107,064**	**178,996**	**2,605**
Administrative and support and waste management and remediation services	**56**	**350,583**	**432,578**	**206,439**	**8,742**
Administrative and support services	561	331,921	381,268	194,207	8,410
Office administrative services	5611	22,611	32,081	14,578	366
Facilities support services	5612	3,568	12,957	4,915	146
Employment services	5613	41,552	128,662	94,936	4,166
Business support services	5614	34,735	43,979	17,617	770
Travel arrangement & reservation services	5615	28,470	25,535	8,051	265
Investigation & security services	5616	22,957	31,375	16,004	761
Services to buildings and dwellings	5617	156,555	75,316	29,134	1,584
Other support services	5619	21,473	31,363	8,973	353
Waste management and remediation services	562	18,662	51,309	12,232	332
Waste collection	5621	8,669	28,205	6,388	172
Waste treatment & disposal	5622	2,527	10,834	2,174	50
Remediation & other waste management services	5629	7,466	12,270	3,671	109
Accommodation and food services	**72**	**565,590**	**449,499**	**127,554**	**10,121**
Accommodation	721	60,949	128,098	34,955	1,813
Traveler accommodation	7211	50,982	123,900	33,910	1,761
RV (recreational vehicle) parks & recreational camps	7212	7,353	3,467	883	39
Rooming & boarding houses	7213	2,614	731	162	13
Food services and drinking places	722	504,641	321,401	92,599	8,308
Full-service restaurants	7221	195,659	144,650	46,064	3,905
Limited-service eating places	7222	228,789	135,324	35,442	3,526
Special food services	7223	31,337	26,525	7,729	541
Drinking places (alcoholic beverages)	7224	48,856	14,902	3,364	336
Other services (except public administration)	**81**	**537,576**	**307,049**	**82,955**	**3,475**
Repair and maintenance	811	231,043	118,306	35,118	1,285
Automotive repair and maintenance	8111	166,821	75,219	21,592	871
Electronic & precision equipment repair & maintenance	8112	14,567	14,983	4,965	128
Commercial and industrial machinery and equipment repair and maintenance [3]	8113	24,519	19,485	5,891	173
Personal and household goods repair and maintenance	8114	25,136	8,619	2,669	113
Personal and laundry services	812	201,019	72,220	22,908	1,297
Personal care services	8121	99,454	20,217	8,180	535
Death care services	8122	22,477	14,280	3,830	148
Drycleaning & laundry services	8123	41,906	20,444	6,667	371
Other personal services	8129	37,182	17,279	4,232	242
Religious, grantmaking, civic, professional, and similar organizations	813	105,514	116,523	24,929	893
Grantmaking & giving services	8132	14,626	46,276	5,102	137
Social advocacy organizations	8133	12,469	12,059	3,162	104
Civic & social organizations	8134	31,658	14,679	4,427	321
Business, professional, labor, political, and similar organizations	8139	46,761	43,509	12,238	332

[1] North American Industrial Classification System, 2002; see text, Section 15. [2] For employees on the payroll during the pay period including March 12. [3] Excludes automotive and electronic equipment.

Source: U.S. Census Bureau, "2002 Economic Census, Geographic Area Series," August 2005; <http://www.census.gov/econ/census02/guide/02ECUS.HTM>.

Table 1234. **Selected Service-Related Industries—Nonemployer Establishments and Receipts by Kind of Business: 2002 to 2005**

[2,553 **represents** 2,553,000. Includes only firms subject to federal income tax. Nonemployers are businesses with no paid employees. Data originate chiefly from administrative records of the Internal Revenue Service; see Appendix III]

Kind of business	2002 NAICS code [1]	Establishments (1,000)			Receipts (mil. dol.)		
		2002	2004	2005	2002	2004	2005
Professional, scientific, and technical services. . . .	**54**	**2,553**	**2,725**	**2,854**	**96,395**	**110,596**	**118,575**
Professional, scientific, and technical services.	541	2,553	2,725	2,854	96,395	110,596	118,577
Legal services	5411	227	244	247	12,899	14,457	15,087
Accounting, tax preparation, bookkeeping, and payroll services	5412	325	340	338	6,423	7,159	7,371
Offices of certified public accountants	541211	38	37	37	1,619	1,721	1,795
Tax preparation services.	541213	79	83	84	1,133	1,313	1,401
Payroll services.	541214	4	4	4	87	106	106
Other accounting services.	541219	204	216	212	3,585	4,020	4,069
Architectual, engineering [2]	5413	209	236	231	8,560	10,206	10,807
Specialized design services	5414	146	167	166	5,073	5,944	6,356
Computer systems design [2]	5415	279	312	282	10,491	12,084	12,029
Management, scientific and technical consulting. .	5416	465	416	580	18,637	20,157	24,232
Scientific research and development services . . .	5417	25	29	28	799	956	987
Advertising and related services	5418	108	115	112	5,495	6,211	6,414
Other	5419	770	867	871	28,018	33,421	35,294
Administrative and support and waste management and remediation services	**56**	**1,263**	**1,337**	**1,417**	**26,910**	**30,932**	**33,028**
Administrative and support services.	561	1,244	1,319	1,398	25,826	29,685	31,666
Office administrative services	5611	127	172	180	1,886	2,517	2,667
Facilities support services	5612	21	25	25	633	730	761
Employment services	5613	30	21	19	1,013	1,128	1,179
Business support services	5614	176	183	185	4,460	5,102	5,274
Travel arrangement and reservation services. . . .	5615	33	31	31	1,433	1,510	1,543
Investigations and security services	5616	70	63	64	1,123	1,161	1,184
Services to buildings and dwellings	5617	722	750	816	13,261	15,189	16,548
Exterminating and pest control services.	56171	8	8	8	315	371	398
Janitorial services	56172	428	431	470	5,899	6,433	6,895
Landscaping services.	56173	209	226	249	4,811	5,749	6,387
Carpet and upholstery cleaning services	56174	22	24	25	666	745	776
Other	56179	56	61	65	1,570	1,890	2,093
Other support services	5619	65	75	77	2,016	2,348	2,511
Waste management and remediation services.	562	18	18	19	1,084	1,247	1,364
Accommodation and food services	**72**	**242**	**275**	**279**	**14,178**	**15,510**	**15,307**
Accommodation.	721	52	56	56	3,766	3,976	3,823
Traveler accommodation	7211	34	36	36	3,150	3,284	3,100
RV (recreational vehicle) parks and recreational camps	7212	7	7	7	333	348	365
Rooming and boarding houses	7213	11	14	14	284	345	358
Food services and drinking places	722	190	219	223	10,412	11,534	11,483
Full-service restaurants	7221	34	37	37	3,561	3,964	3,815
Limited-service eating places	7222	43	48	47	2,978	3,238	3,168
Special food services	7223	90	109	115	2,358	2,755	2,917
Drinking places (alcoholic beverages).	7224	23	24	25	1,515	1,576	1,583
Other services (except public administration).	**81**	**2,459**	**2,800**	**2,873**	**60,468**	**70,299**	**74,025**
Repair and maintenance	811	643	695	691	22,817	25,466	26,465
Automotive repair and maintenance	8111	271	287	289	12,182	13,266	13,706
Automotive, mechanical and electrical repair [3]	81111	135	141	143	6,214	6,771	6,972
Automotive body, paint, interior, and glass repair	81112	74	80	78	3,401	3,660	3,736
Other automotive repair and maintenance	81119	62	66	68	2,567	2,835	2,998
Electronic and precision equipment repair [3]	8112	46	47	45	1,468	1,566	1,572
Commercial and industrial machinery and equipment repair and maintenance [4]	8113	52	56	55	2,335	2,651	2,790
Personal and household goods repair [3]	8114	274	305	302	6,831	7,983	8,397
Personal and laundry services	812	1,642	1,924	1,996	35,127	42,151	44,809
Personal care services	8121	666	776	827	13,582	16,354	17,707
Hair, nail, and skin care services	81211	572	660	703	11,969	14,304	15,472
Barber shops	812111	81	91	91	1,671	1,854	1,878
Beauty salons	812112	400	449	480	8,357	9,661	10,304
Nail salons	812113	90	120	132	1,942	2,788	3,289
Other	81219	94	117	124	1,613	2,050	2,236
Death care services	8122	14	15	15	746	791	816
Drycleaning and laundry services	8123	37	36	36	1,741	1,865	1,884
Other personal services.	8129	925	1,097	1,118	19,057	23,141	24,401
Pet care (except veterinary) services	81291	39	46	49	762	941	1,034
Photofinishing.	81292	12	14	15	298	315	326
Parking lots and garages	81293	4	4	4	221	261	271
Other	81299	871	1,034	1,050	17,777	21,625	22,770
Religious, grantmaking, civic, professonal, and similar organizations	813	174	181	186	2,524	2,682	2,752

[1] Based on the North American Industry Classification System, 2002, see text, Section 15. [2] Includes related services. [3] Includes maintenance. [4] Except automotive and electronic.

Source: U.S. Census Bureau, "Nonemployer Statistics"; <http://www.census.gov/epcd/nonemployer/index.html> (accessed 10 July 2007).

Table 1235. Selected Service-Related Industries—Establishments, Employees, and Payroll by Industry: 2004 and 2005

[805 represents 805,000. Covers establishments with payroll. Excludes most government employees, railroad employees, and self-employed persons. Kind-of-business classification based on North American Industry Classification System, 2002 (NAICS); see text, Section 15. For statement on methodology, see Appendix III]

Kind of business	2002 NAICS code	Establishments (1,000)		Employees (1,000) [1]		Annual payroll (bil. dol.)	
		2004	2005	2004	2005	2004	2005
Professional, scientific, and technical services	**54**	**805**	**826**	**7,570**	**7,689**	**426.7**	**456.5**
Professional, scientific, and technical services	541	805	826	7,570	7,689	426.7	456.5
Legal services	5411	185	188	1,218	1,199	78.1	81.3
Offices of lawyers	54111	173	175	1,123	1,103	74.1	77.0
Accounting, tax preparation, bookkeeping, and payroll services	5412	117	119	1,390	1,330	46.6	48.6
Tax preparation services	541213	22	23	198	205	2.0	2.2
Architectural, engineering, & related services [2]	5413	109	112	1,265	1,298	75.9	81.7
Architectural services	54131	24	25	181	186	10.5	11.5
Engineering services	54133	55	56	858	882	56.0	59.7
Specialized design services [2]	5414	32	33	119	121	5.2	5.6
Graphic design services	54143	16	17	60	60	2.7	2.8
Computer systems design & related services [2]	5415	106	108	1,105	1,132	77.7	82.0
Custom computer programming services	541511	47	48	435	460	31.9	34.8
Computer systems design services	541512	43	44	458	457	31.7	32.2
Management, scientific, & technical consulting services [2]	5416	129	138	880	957	55.5	61.8
Management consulting services	54161	103	108	755	814	48.3	53.2
Environmental consulting services	54162	9	9	60	62	3.0	3.3
Scientific research & development services	5417	16	17	641	661	51.4	54.5
Research & development in the physical engineering & life sciences	54172	14	14	587	603	47.8	50.7
Advertising & related services [2]	5418	39	39	390	414	19.6	22.5
Advertising agencies	54181	13	13	139	156	9.3	11.4
Direct mail advertising	54186	4	3	71	71	2.7	2.9
Other professional, scientific, & tech services	5419	72	73	562	578	16.8	18.4
Veterinary services	54194	27	27	267	270	6.8	7.3
Management of companies and enterprises	**55**	**46**	**48**	**2,825**	**2,856**	**222.5**	**243.3**
Admin/support & waste mgmt & remediation service	**56**	**359**	**370**	**8,708**	**9,280**	**235.5**	**255.4**
Administrative & support services [2]	561	340	350	8,364	8,947	222.1	241.7
Employment services	5613	41	41	4,028	4,580	106.5	118.1
Temporary help services	56132	27	28	2,326	2,615	54.7	58.5
Business support services [2]	5614	35	36	774	764	19.8	20.8
Telephone call centers	56142	5	5	392	383	8.0	8.3
Collection agencies	56144	5	5	141	138	4.2	4.2
Credit bureaus	56145	1	1	26	22	1.5	1.5
Travel arrangement & reservation services	5615	24	24	270	254	10.3	10.9
Travel agencies	56151	18	17	132	127	4.6	5.0
Investigation & security services	5616	23	24	755	767	17.4	18.7
Investigation, guard, & armored car services	56161	13	14	636	651	13.1	14.1
Security systems services	56162	10	10	118	116	4.2	4.7
Services to buildings & dwellings	5617	166	173	1,604	1,624	33.3	35.4
Waste management & remediation services	562	19	19	344	333	13.4	13.7
Waste collection	5621	9	9	179	172	6.9	6.8
Waste treatment & disposal	5622	3	3	55	54	2.5	2.6
Remediation & other waste mgmt services	5629	8	8	109	108	4.0	4.3
Accommodation & food services	**72**	**591**	**603**	**10,750**	**11,026**	**147.2**	**156.0**
Accommodation	721	62	63	1,845	1,854	39.5	41.8
Traveler accommodation	7211	52	53	1,794	1,805	38.3	40.6
Hotels (except casino hotels) & motels	72111	48	48	1,407	1,414	27.5	29.2
RV (recreational vehicle) parks & recreational camps	7212	7	7	38	38	1.0	1.0
Rooming & boarding houses	7213	2	2	14	12	0.2	0.2
Food services & drinking places	722	529	541	8,905	9,171	107.7	114.2
Full-service restaurants	7221	206	210	4,263	4,340	55.2	58.1
Limited-service eating places	7222	242	250	3,772	3,927	40.4	42.8
Special food services	7223	32	33	508	552	8.1	9.2
Drinking places (alcoholic beverages)	7224	48	47	361	352	4.0	4.1
Other services (except public administration)	**81**	**735**	**740**	**5,416**	**5,391**	**122.5**	**127.5**
Repair & maintenance [2]	811	229	228	1,320	1,295	38.4	39.5
Automotive repair & maintenance	8111	166	166	905	880	23.2	23.7
Personal & household goods repair & maintenance	8114	25	24	109	104	2.8	2.8
Personal & laundry services [2]	812	208	210	1,333	1,337	25.0	26.4
Personal care services	8121	106	108	580	589	9.4	9.9
Death care services	8122	20	22	126	138	3.5	4.0
Drycleaning & laundry services	8123	43	43	390	382	7.6	7.9
Religious/grantmaking/civic/professional [3]	813	297	302	2,763	2,759	59.1	61.6
Religious organizations	8131	171	173	1,649	1,632	26.4	27.2
Grantmaking & giving services	8132	16	16	140	145	5.6	6.0
Social advocacy organizations	8133	13	14	115	121	3.6	3.9
Civic & social organizations	8134	32	32	323	327	4.7	5.0
Business/professional/labor/political [3]	8139	66	67	535	534	18.8	19.5
Labor unions [3]	81393	16	16	179	177	4.6	4.8

[1] Includes employees on the payroll for the pay period including March 12. [2] Includes other kinds of business not shown separately. [3] And similar organizations.

Source: U.S. Census Bureau, "County Business Patterns"; <http://www.census.gov/epcd/cbp/view/cbpview.html>.

Table 1236. Selected Service-Related Industries—Establishments, Employees, and Annual Payroll by State: 2005

[7,689 represents 7,689,000. Covers establishments with payroll. Excludes most government employees, railroad employees, and self-employed persons. Based on the North American Industry Classification System, 2002 (NAICS); see text, Section 15. For statement on methodology, see Appendix III]

State	Professional, scientific, & technical services (NAICS 54)			Admin./ support waste mgt./ remediation services (NAICS 56)			Accommodation and food services (NAICS 72)		
	Estab-lish-ments	Employ-ees[1] (1,000)	Annual payroll (mil. dol.)	Estab-lish-ments	Employ-ees[1] (1,000)	Annual payroll (mil. dol.)	Estab-lish-ments	Employ-ees[1] (1,000)	Annual payroll (mil. dol.)
United States ...	**826,101**	**7,689**	**456,456**	**369,507**	**9,280**	**255,399**	**603,435**	**11,026**	**156,041**
Alabama.	9,180	96	4,919	4,024	118	2,616	7,529	145	1,591
Alaska	1,832	12	676	1,003	17	650	1,966	24	483
Arizona.	15,426	119	6,193	7,712	221	5,837	10,688	239	3,238
Arkansas	5,474	36	1,456	2,427	50	986	4,878	87	891
California	108,411	1,192	74,611	41,386	1,061	31,253	71,625	1,285	19,888
Colorado.	21,670	155	9,458	7,757	171	5,258	11,697	222	3,136
Connecticut.	10,224	100	6,581	5,386	102	3,185	7,579	129	2,374
Delaware	2,460	27	1,896	1,274	25	654	1,722	31	484
District of Columbia .	4,579	88	8,207	1,004	30	993	1,956	49	1,162
Florida	65,901	423	21,899	31,055	1,240	33,734	33,049	725	10,739
Georgia	26,284	210	11,816	11,308	318	8,824	17,218	337	4,341
Hawaii	3,257	25	1,218	1,723	38	973	3,393	100	2,309
Idaho	3,805	35	1,412	1,967	47	965	3,256	52	572
Illinois	38,478	350	22,464	15,649	443	11,483	25,595	447	6,278
Indiana.	12,797	110	5,023	6,925	166	4,152	12,316	245	2,934
Iowa	6,103	42	1,760	3,397	63	1,387	6,771	108	1,105
Kansas.	7,087	57	2,419	3,342	66	1,695	5,776	102	1,102
Kentucky	8,004	61	2,396	3,670	89	1,742	6,965	147	1,677
Louisiana	11,047	85	3,535	4,388	107	2,409	7,886	180	2,194
Maine.	3,503	22	1,029	1,958	25	697	3,909	45	718
Maryland	19,132	221	13,707	7,811	165	4,779	10,230	189	2,711
Massachusetts.	22,073	244	18,514	9,152	187	6,409	15,562	241	4,045
Michigan.	22,701	291	18,336	12,040	319	9,170	19,297	331	3,861
Minnesota.	16,534	128	7,495	7,138	137	4,103	10,812	215	2,768
Mississippi	4,597	32	1,256	2,199	45	891	4,649	115	1,598
Missouri	13,570	133	6,969	7,227	145	3,568	11,811	235	2,868
Montana	3,274	22	728	1,519	13	262	3,375	42	475
Nebraska	4,139	45	1,998	2,416	62	1,455	4,108	67	697
Nevada	7,477	53	2,855	3,879	97	3,158	4,915	291	7,733
New Hampshire. . . .	4,032	30	1,716	2,030	40	1,191	3,369	56	803
New Jersey.	31,669	305	20,505	13,326	293	8,771	18,872	275	4,979
New Mexico	4,704	36	1,720	1,834	38	897	3,944	77	934
New York	58,105	578	39,540	23,760	485	16,926	42,300	558	10,007
North Carolina.	21,169	175	9,504	10,820	262	6,433	16,903	315	3,894
North Dakota.	1,397	12	418	861	11	237	1,795	29	291
Ohio	25,597	245	12,704	13,644	336	8,294	23,337	430	4,800
Oklahoma.	8,926	66	2,719	3,958	98	2,360	6,676	121	1,279
Oregon.	10,983	76	3,693	5,119	93	2,249	9,433	141	1,945
Pennsylvania.	29,777	304	18,452	14,136	296	7,640	26,115	405	5,054
Rhode Island.	3,114	23	1,142	1,679	23	563	2,901	43	611
South Carolina.	9,140	77	3,778	5,322	130	2,914	8,913	174	2,150
South Dakota	1,703	10	332	933	10	191	2,285	35	384
Tennessee	11,082	111	5,320	6,151	180	4,376	10,892	220	2,724
Texas.	55,618	519	31,442	23,521	787	21,371	39,989	801	10,305
Utah	7,460	64	2,761	3,524	94	2,268	4,360	88	1,016
Vermont	2,099	16	588	974	8	201	1,963	30	403
Virginia.	25,836	355	24,260	9,964	230	6,647	14,670	285	3,928
Washington.	18,399	148	9,141	8,396	131	4,773	14,963	215	3,182
West Virginia.	3,035	23	844	1,443	29	638	3,501	59	653
Wisconsin.	11,492	97	4,752	6,563	132	3,014	13,972	220	2,383
Wyoming	1,745	8	301	813	7	158	1,749	26	345

[1] For employees on the payroll for the pay period including March 12.

Source: U.S. Census Bureau, "County Business Patterns"; <http://www.census.gov/epcd/cbp/view/cbpview.html>.

Table 1237. Professional, Scientific, and Technical Services—Estimated Revenue: 2000 to 2006

[In millions of dollars (803,527 represents $803,527,000,000). For taxable employer firms. Estimates have been adjusted to the results of the 2002 Economic Census. Based on the Service Annual Survey; see Appendix III]

Kind of business	2002 NAICS code [1]	2000	2002	2003	2004	2005	2006
Professional, scientific, and technical services (except notaries)	**54**	**803,527**	**846,056**	**879,725**	**966,645**	**1,055,970**	**1,126,947**
Legal services (except notaries)	5411	160,619	180,042	199,915	209,475	221,752	236,166
Offices of lawyers	54111	152,834	170,808	187,819	197,385	207,833	221,821
Other legal services	54119	7,785	9,234	12,096	12,090	13,919	14,345
Accounting, tax preparation, bookkeeping and payroll services	5412	79,361	84,073	87,791	92,884	100,414	105,146
Offices of certified public accountants	541211	45,773	48,498	47,835	50,679	54,346	57,748
Tax preparation services	541213	3,347	4,129	4,468	4,944	5,472	5,837
Payroll services	541214	21,394	21,418	24,366	25,359	27,426	28,154
Other accounting services	541219	8,847	10,028	11,122	11,902	13,170	13,407
Architectural, engineering, & related services	5413	150,269	158,266	160,917	184,292	209,487	221,836
Architectural services	54131	25,021	25,240	26,851	28,609	31,939	34,709
Landscape architectural services	54132	(X)	(X)	(X)	4,218	4,575	5,018
Engineering services	54133	111,929	116,887	117,509	132,814	152,497	160,657
Testing laboratories	54138	7,128	8,771	8,849	9,908	10,412	11,098
Other related services	54134,5,6,7	6,191	7,368	7,708	8,742	10,065	10,354
Specialized design services	5414	17,889	17,076	18,090	19,617	21,484	22,846
Interior design services	54141	6,798	7,018	7,497	8,061	8,822	9,745
Graphic design services	54143	8,962	8,096	8,269	8,528	9,190	9,211
All other design services	54142,9	(X)	(X)	(X)	3,028	3,472	3,890
Computer systems design and services	5415	186,402	173,414	171,393	173,525	188,490	200,695
Custom computer programming services	541511	70,004	60,126	58,140	58,303	64,418	67,986
Computer systems design services	541512	82,763	78,335	76,992	77,042	84,877	90,569
Computer facilities management services	541513	21,816	22,279	22,518	23,422	22,748	24,077
Other computer-related services	541519	11,819	12,674	13,743	14,758	16,447	18,063
Management, scientific, and technical consulting services	5416	90,129	105,452	108,783	121,709	137,329	147,981
Management consulting services	54161	78,250	90,914	92,129	102,452	115,850	124,687
Environmental consulting services	54162	5,578	6,933	7,902	8,748	9,083	10,171
Other scientific and technical consulting services	54169	6,301	7,605	8,752	10,509	12,396	13,123
Scientific research and development services	5417	35,587	45,983	48,142	54,272	59,548	67,340
Research and development in physical, engineering and life sciences	54171	34,029	44,089	46,104	51,994	57,069	64,941
Research and development in social sciences and humanities	54172	1,558	1,894	2,038	2,278	2,479	2,399
Advertising and related services	5418	59,680	56,681	58,629	63,585	66,705	71,923
Advertising agencies	54181	21,584	21,104	22,396	24,551	25,195	27,581
Public relations agencies	54182	6,501	6,205	6,305	6,954	7,573	8,485
Media buying agencies	54183	1,036	1,150	1,063	1,405	1,468	1,698
Media representatives	54184	3,247	2,729	2,712	2,096	2,267	2,360
Display advertising	54185	4,752	4,617	4,925	5,440	6,182	6,678
Direct mail advertising	54186	10,351	10,544	10,648	11,570	12,174	12,215
All other advertising	54187,9	(X)	(X)	(X)	11,568	11,845	12,906
Other professional, scientific, and technical services	5419	23,591	25,069	26,065	47,289	50,761	53,015
Marketing research and public opinion polling	54191	11,683	10,890	11,118	11,851	12,702	12,740
Photographic services	54192	6,613	6,538	6,758	6,984	7,256	7,206
Photography studios, portrait	541921	4,642	4,752	4,879	5,031	5,258	5,143
Commercial photography	541922	1,971	1,786	1,879	1,953	1,998	2,063
Translation and interpretation services	54193	810	876	968	1,093	1,121	1,157
Veterinary services	54194	(X)	(X)	(X)	19,274	20,744	22,882
All other professional, scientific, and technical services	54199	4,485	6,765	7,221	8,008	8,938	9,028

X Not applicable.   [1] Based on the North American Industry Classification System, 2002; see Section 15.

Source: U.S. Census Bureau, "2006 Service Annual Survey, Professional, Scientific, and Technical Sector Services"; <http://www.census.gov/econ/www/servmenu.html> (released 30 March 2008).

Table 1238. Selected Service Industries—E-Commerce Revenue: 2005 and 2006

[98,837 represents $98,837,000,000). Includes data only for businesses with paid employees, except for accommodation and food services, which also includes businesses with and without paid employees. Except as noted, based on the Service Annual Survey]

Kind of business	2002 NAICS code [1]	E-commerce revenue (mil. dol.) 2005	E-commerce revenue (mil. dol.) 2006	E-commerce revenue as percent of total revenue, 2006	E-commerce revenue, percent distribution, 2006
Selected service industries, total [2]	(X)	**98,837**	**113,540**	**1.8**	**100.0**
Selected transportation and warehousing [2]	(X)	6,147	7,526	2.3	6.4
Truck transportation	484	5,387	6,392	2.9	5.6
Couriers and messengers	492	(S)	(S)	(S)	(S)
Warehousing and storage	493	703	801	3.8	0.7
Information	51	29,215	31,194	3.0	27.5
Publishing industries	511	12,146	13,344	4.8	11.8
Online information services	51811	4,147	4,045	14.6	3.6
Selected finance [3]	(X)	6,093	7,344	1.5	6.5
Securities and commodity contracts intermediation and brokerage	5231	5,820	7,220	2.0	6.4
Rental and leasing services	532	5,427	6,347	5.4	5.6
Selected professional, scientific, and technical services [4]	(X)	23,057	24,719	2.1	21.8
Computer systems design and related services	5415	3,194	3,798	1.9	3.4
Administrative and support and waste management and remediation services	56	13,214	14,495	2.6	12.8
Travel arrangements and reservation services	5615	8,328	8,441	27.2	7.4
Health care and social assistance services	62	(S)	(S)	(S)	(S)
Arts, entertainment, and recreation services	71	1,925	2,346	1.3	2.1
Accommodation and food services [5]	72	7,735	9,512	1.6	8.4
Selected other services [6]	(X)	4,484	6,304	1.6	5.6
Repair and maintenance	811	957	990	0.7	0.9
Religious, grantmaking, civic, professional, and similar organizations	813	2,237	3,427	2.1	3.0

S Data do not meet publication standards.   X Not applicable.   [1] North American Industry Classification System (NAICS), 2002; see text Section 15.   [2] Excludes NAICS 481 (air transportation), 482 (rail transportation), 484 (water transportation), 485 (transit and good passenger transportation), 486 (pipeline transportation), 487 (scenic and sightseeing transportation), 488 (support activities for transportation) and 491 (postal service).   [3] Excludes NAICS 521 (monetary authorities-central bank), 522 (credit intermediation and related activities), 5232 (securities and commodity exchanges), NAICS 52391 (miscellaneous intermediation), 52399 (all other financial investment activities), 524 (insurance carriers and related activities) and 525 (funds and trusts).   [4] Excludes NAICS 54112 (offices of notaries).   [5] Based on 2006 Annual Retail Trade Survey.   [6] Excludes NAICS 81311 (religious organizations), 81393 (labor and similar organizations), 81394 (political organizations) and 814 (private households).

Source: U.S. Census Bureau, Internet site E-Stats (released 16 May 2008); <http://www.census.gov/eos/www/ebusiness614.htm>.

Table 1239. Advertising—Estimated Expenditures by Medium: 1990 to 2007

[In millions of dollars (129,968 represents $129,968,000,000). See source for definitions of types of advertising]

Medium	1990	2000	2001	2002	2003	2004	2005	2006	2007 [1]
Total	**129,968**	**247,472**	**231,287**	**236,875**	**245,477**	**263,766**	**271,074**	**281,653**	**279,612**
National	73,638	151,664	141,797	145,429	152,482	167,096	172,797	182,483	185,280
Local	56,330	95,808	89,490	91,446	92,995	96,670	98,277	99,170	94,332
Newspapers	32,281	49,050	44,255	44,031	44,843	46,614	47,335	46,555	42,133
National	3,867	7,229	6,615	6,806	7,357	7,629	7,465	7,084	6,609
Local	28,414	41,821	37,640	37,225	37,486	38,985	39,870	39,471	35,524
Magazines	6,803	12,370	11,095	10,995	11,435	12,247	12,847	13,168	13,787
Broadcast TV	26,616	44,802	38,881	42,068	41,932	46,264	44,293	46,880	44,521
Four TV networks	9,863	15,888	14,300	15,000	15,030	16,713	16,128	16,676	16,643
Syndication	1,109	3,108	3,102	3,034	3,434	3,674	3,865	3,691	3,329
Spot (national)	7,788	12,264	9,223	10,920	9,948	11,370	10,040	11,626	10,138
Spot (local)	7,856	13,542	12,256	13,114	13,520	14,507	14,260	14,887	14,411
Cable TV	2,631	15,455	15,736	16,297	18,814	21,527	23,654	25,025	26,319
Cable TV networks	2,000	11,765	11,777	12,071	13,954	16,424	18,296	19,320	20,614
Spot (local)	631	3,690	3,959	4,226	4,860	5,103	5,358	5,705	5,705
Radio	8,726	19,295	17,861	18,877	19,100	19,581	19,640	19,643	19,152
Network	482	780	711	775	798	836	814	798	830
Spot (national)	1,635	3,668	2,956	3,340	3,540	3,540	3,469	3,642	3,423
Spot (local)	6,609	14,847	14,194	14,762	14,762	15,205	15,357	15,203	14,899
Yellow Pages	8,926	13,228	13,592	13,776	13,896	14,002	14,229	14,393	14,250
National	1,132	2,093	2,087	2,087	2,114	2,110	2,163	2,206	2,185
Local	7,794	11,135	11,505	11,689	11,782	11,892	12,066	12,187	12,065
Direct mail	23,370	44,591	44,725	46,067	48,370	52,191	55,218	58,642	60,225
Business papers	2,875	4,915	4,468	3,976	4,004	4,072	4,170	4,195	4,111
Out-of-home [2]	1,084	5,176	5,134	5,175	5,443	5,770	6,232	6,731	7,202
National	640	2,068	2,051	2,061	2,298	2,530	2,736	2,955	3,027
Local	444	3,108	3,083	3,114	3,145	3,240	3,496	3,776	4,175
Internet [3]	(NA)	6,507	5,645	4,883	5,650	6,853	7,764	9,100	10,529
Miscellaneous [4]	16,656	32,083	29,895	30,730	31,990	34,645	35,692	37,321	37,383
National	12,074	24,418	23,042	23,414	24,550	26,907	27,822	29,380	29,830
Local	4,582	7,665	6,853	7,316	7,440	7,738	7,870	7,941	7,553

NA Not available.   [1] Preliminary data.   [2] Prior to 2000, represents only "outdoor" billboards. Beginning 2000, includes other forms of outdoor advertising (i.e. transportation vehicles, bus shelters, telephone kiosks, etc.) previously covered under "Miscellaneous."   [3] Excludes search revenue.   [4] Beginning 2000, part of miscellaneous now included under Out-of-home advertising. See footnote 2.

Source: Universal McCann, New York, N.Y. (copyright). See also <http://www.universalmccann.com>.

Table 1240. Administrative and Support and Waste Management and Remediation Services—Estimated Revenue: 2000 to 2006

[**In millions of dollars (396,499 represents $396,499,000,000).** For taxable and tax-exempt employer firms. Estimates have been adjusted to results of the 2002 Economic Census. Based on the Service Annual Survey; see Appendix III]

Kind of business	2002 NAICS code [1]	2000	2002	2003	2004	2005	2006
Administrative and support and waste management and remediation services . . .	**56**	**396,499**	**397,408**	**414,988**	**484,037**	**528,432**	**561,317**
Administrative and support services	561	345,302	346,099	360,434	425,394	464,588	490,696
Office administrative services.	56111	26,288	32,081	34,556	38,014	43,071	47,021
Facilities support services	56121	13,211	12,957	12,158	12,520	14,005	15,661
Employment services	5613	144,242	128,662	133,833	145,717	159,098	170,316
Employment placement agencies	56131	4,985	5,940	5,874	6,513	6,765	7,077
Temporary help services	56132	79,622	68,190	69,910	77,660	84,828	89,652
Professional employer organizations	56133	59,635	54,532	58,049	61,544	67,505	73,587
Business support services.	5614	41,203	43,981	46,111	48,166	50,881	52,249
Document preparation services.	56141	1,920	2,419	2,500	2,483	2,642	2,606
Telephone call centers	56142	14,805	13,394	13,273	13,843	14,574	14,977
Telephone answering services.	561421	2,135	2,109	1,897	1,783	1,887	1,801
Telemarketing bureaus.	561422	12,670	11,285	11,376	12,060	12,687	13,176
Business service centers.	56143	8,257	8,234	8,335	8,469	8,372	8,504
Private mail centers.	561431	1,692	1,957	2,187	2,274	2,226	2,460
Other business service centers (including copy shops).	561439	6,565	6,277	6,148	6,195	6,146	6,044
Collection agencies	56144	7,300	8,852	9,830	10,860	11,411	11,336
Credit bureaus.	56145	3,741	4,591	5,230	5,516	6,332	6,405
Other business support services	56149	5,180	6,491	6,943	6,995	7,550	8,421
Repossession services	561491	418	552	549	534	543	564
Court reporting and stenotype services.	561492	1,250	1,638	1,715	1,792	1,847	1,994
All other business support services	561499	3,512	4,301	4,679	4,669	5,160	5,863
Travel arrangement and reservation services	5615	26,119	25,535	26,594	28,140	29,639	29,679
Travel agencies	56151	11,639	9,387	9,759	10,046	10,586	10,942
Tour operators.	56152	3,564	3,190	3,212	3,510	3,701	3,636
Other travel arrangement and reservation services	56159	10,916	12,958	13,623	14,584	15,352	15,101
Convention and visitors bureaus	561591	1,020	1,128	1,227	1,256	1,314	1,387
All other travel arrangement and reservation services.	561599	9,896	11,830	12,396	13,328	14,038	13,714
Investigation and security services	5616	27,594	31,375	32,325	33,723	37,278	38,540
Investigation, guard, and armored car services	56161	17,581	19,468	20,920	21,754	24,593	25,615
Investigation services	561611	2,350	2,586	3,090	3,345	3,593	3,541
Security guards and patrol services	561612	13,393	14,763	15,551	16,321	18,624	19,578
Armored car services.	561613	1,838	2,119	2,279	2,088	2,376	2,496
Security systems services	56162	10,013	11,907	11,405	11,969	12,685	12,925
Security systems services (except locksmiths)	561621	8,683	10,592	9,987	10,488	11,083	11,157
Locksmiths	561622	1,330	1,315	1,418	1,481	1,602	1,768
Services to buildings and dwellings.	5617	35,790	40,144	43,697	85,799	93,445	97,603
Exterminating and pest control services	56171	5,723	6,597	7,206	7,673	8,118	8,301
Janitorial services.	56172	24,593	27,009	29,303	30,288	32,020	32,728
Landscaping services	56173	(X)	(X)	(X)	40,171	44,491	46,804
Carpet and upholstery cleaning services	56174	2,463	2,719	2,808	2,964	3,386	3,596
Other services to buildings and dwellings	56179	3,011	3,819	4,380	4,703	5,428	6,174
Other support services.	5619	30,855	31,364	31,160	33,315	37,171	39,627
Packaging and labeling services.	56191	4,432	4,916	5,021	5,591	6,698	7,104
Convention and trade show organizers	56192	8,410	8,562	9,083	9,517	10,647	11,409
All other support services	56199	18,013	17,886	17,056	18,207	19,826	21,114
Waste management and remediation services	562	51,197	51,309	54,554	58,643	63,844	70,621
Waste collection	5621	28,820	28,206	30,272	32,430	34,477	37,832
Solid waste collection	562111	27,032	26,416	28,363	30,436	32,273	35,307
Hazardous waste collection	562112	1,249	1,325	1,445	1,565	1,720	1,941
Other waste collection.	562119	539	465	464	429	484	584
Waste treatment and disposal	5622	11,025	10,834	11,173	11,398	12,636	13,189
Hazardous waste treatment and disposal	562211	3,155	3,642	3,351	3,264	3,845	4,163
Solid waste landfill	562212	5,965	5,272	5,802	6,168	6,446	6,821
Solid waste combustors and incinerators	562213	1,261	1,365	1,442	1,303	1,565	1,349
Other nonhazardous waste treatment and disposal	562219	644	555	578	663	780	856
Remediation and other waste management services.	5629	11,352	12,269	13,109	14,815	16,731	19,600
Remediation services	56291	6,750	7,640	7,745	8,834	10,252	12,704
Materials recovery facility.	56292	1,593	1,800	2,222	2,633	2,740	2,788
All other waste management services	56299	3,009	2,829	3,142	3,348	3,739	4,108
Septic tank and related services	562991	2,197	1,973	2,049	2,132	2,374	2,575
All other miscellaneous waste management services	562998	812	856	1,093	1,216	1,365	1,533

X Not applicable.　[1] North American Industry Classification System, 2002; see text, Section 15.

Source: U.S. Census Bureau, "2006 Service Annual Survey, Administrative & Support, and Waste Management and Remediation Services"; <http://www.census.gov/econ/www/servmenu.html> (released 30 March 2008).

Table 1241. Estimated Accommodation and Food Services Sales by Kinds of Business: 2000 to 2006

[In millions of dollars (443,642 represents 443,642,000,000). Estimates are based on data from the Annual Retail Trade Survey and administrative records and have been adjusted to the results of the 2002 Economic Census]

Kind of business	NAICS code [1]	2000	2001	2002	2003	2004	2005	2006
Accommodation and food services, total ..	72	443,642	451,300	463,678	484,174	516,580	545,713	578,949
Accommodation	721	138,181	133,448	131,864	134,481	144,604	152,080	158,582
Traveler accommodation.	7211	133,582	128,591	127,050	129,610	139,731	147,014	153,070
RV parks and recreational camps.	7212	3,608	3,838	3,799	3,884	3,863	4,004	4,335
Rooming and boarding houses.	7213	991	1,019	1,015	987	1,010	1,062	1,177
Food services and drinking places [2]	722	305,461	317,852	331,814	349,693	371,976	393,633	420,367
Full service restaurants.	7221	134,204	140,682	148,211	155,085	163,834	171,660	183,102
Limited service eating places.	7222	127,879	132,924	138,302	147,087	158,699	169,175	179,872
Drinking places	7224	15,415	15,769	16,417	17,580	18,168	19,120	21,005

[1] North American Industry Classification System, 2002; see text, Section 15.   [2] Includes other kinds of business not shown separately.

Source: U.S. Census Bureau, "Annual Accommodation and Food Services-2005;" <http://www.census.gov/svsd/www /artstbl.html> (accessed 23 May 2008).

Table 1242. Lodging Industry Summary: 1990 to 2006

Year	Average occupancy rate (percent)	Average room rate (dol.)	Room size of property	2006 Establishments	2006 Rooms (mil.)	Item	2006 Business traveler	2006 Leisure traveler
1990	63.3	57.96	Total	47,135	4.4	Typical night:		
1995	65.5	66.65				Made reservations		
2000	63.7	85.89	Percent:			(percent)	90	86
2002	59.1	83.54	Under 75 rooms . .	57.0	26.1	Amount paid (dol.)	$112.00	$103.00
2003	61.6	82.52	75–149 rooms . . .	30.9	35.1	Length of stay (percent):		
2004	61.3	86.24	150–299 rooms . .	8.7	18.8	One night	35	42
2005	63.1	90.88	300–500 rooms . .	2.3	9.1	Two nights	26	30
2006	63.3	97.78	Over 500 rooms . .	1.1	10.9	Three or more	39	28

Source: American Hotel & Lodging Association, Washington, DC Lodging Industry Profile, annual (copyright). See also <http://www.ahla.com>.

Table 1243. Commercial and Noncommercial Groups—Food and Drink Establishments and Sales: 1990 to 2008

[(238,149 represents $238,149,000,000). Excludes military. Data refer to sales to consumers of food and alcoholic beverages. Sales are estimated. For details, see source]

Type of group	Establishments, 2005	Sales (mil. dol.) 1990	1995	2000	2005	2006 [1]	2007 [1]	2008 [1]
Total.	914,513	238,149	294,631	377,652	486,425	509,350	532,826	556,305
Commercial restaurant services [2, 3]	713,478	211,606	265,910	345,345	445,009	466,747	488,291	510,430
Eating places [2]	451,475	155,552	198,293	259,743	329,528	345,124	360,722	376,739
Full-service restaurants.	198,330	77,811	96,396	133,834	165,170	172,769	179,680	187,406
Limited-service restaurants [4]	197,400	[5]69,798	[5]92,901	107,147	136,903	142,932	150,217	156,827
Snack and nonalcoholic beverage bars	41,140	(5)	(5)	12,867	17,150	18,532	19,604	20,938
Bars and taverns [6]	48,856	9,533	9,948	12,412	15,002	15,303	15,961	16,456
Managed services [2]	20,693	14,149	18,186	24,841	32,030	34,000	36,162	38,282
Manufacturing and industrial plants. . .	(NA)	3,856	4,814	6,223	6,570	6,905	7,163	7,401
Colleges and universities	(NA)	2,788	3,989	5,879	9,283	10,034	10,949	11,908
Lodging places	14,841	13,568	15,561	19,438	23,854	25,444	26,262	27,598
Retail hosts [2, 7]	134,399	9,513	12,589	14,869	22,502	23,788	24,865	26,154
Department store restaurants.	4,014	876	1,038	903	490	(NA)	(NA)	(NA)
Grocery store restaurants [7]	61,115	5,432	6,624	7,116	12,032	(NA)	(NA)	(NA)
Gasoline service stations	53,251	1,718	2,520	4,693	6,137	(NA)	(NA)	(NA)
Recreation and sports	36,132	2,871	3,866	4,772	11,397	11,916	12,735	13,226
Noncommercial restaurant services [2]	201,035	26,543	28,722	32,307	41,416	42,603	44,535	45,875
Employee restaurant services	3,470	1,864	1,364	986	548	470	472	465
Industrial, commercial organizations . .	1,005	1,603	1,129	717	260	(NA)	(NA)	(NA)
Educational restaurant services	104,880	7,671	9,059	9,977	11,007	11,083	11,395	11,607
Elementary and secondary schools. . .	100,704	3,700	4,533	5,039	5,320	5,383	5,582	5,738
Hospitals.	5,736	8,968	9,219	9,982	12,332	12,634	13,454	13,844
Miscellaneous	50,009	2,892	3,673	4,898	9,703	(NA)	(NA)	(NA)
Clubs	26,689	1,993	2,278	3,164	7,555	(NA)	(NA)	(NA)

NA Not available.   [1] Projection.   [2] Includes other types of groups, not shown separately.   [3] Data for establishments with payroll.   [4] Fast-food restaurants.   [5] Snack and nonalcoholic beverage bars included in limited service restaurants, prior to 1997.   [6] For establishments serving food.   [7] Includes a portion of delicatessen sales in grocery stores.

Source: National Restaurant Association, Washington, DC, Restaurant Numbers: 25 Year History, 1970–1995, 1998; Restaurant Industry in Review, annual; and National Restaurant Association 2008 Restaurant Industry Forecast, December 2007, (copyright).

Table 1244. Other Services—Estimated Revenue for Employer Firms by Kind of Business: 2000 to 2006

[In millions of dollars (302,783 represents $302,783,000,000). For employer firms. Estimates have been adjusted to the results of the 2002 Economic Census. Based on the Service Annual Survey; see Appendix III]

Kind of business	2002 NAICS code [1]	2000	2004	2005	2006
Other services	81	302,783	338,022	360,688	387,009
Repair and maintenance [2]	811	112,719	127,939	136,920	141,562
Automotive repair and maintenance	8111	73,219	81,116	85,447	87,616
Automotive mechanical and electrical repair and maintenance	81111	37,879	42,154	44,011	45,011
General automotive repair	811111	30,988	35,547	37,233	38,103
Automotive body, paint, interior, and glass repair	81112	25,766	27,693	29,152	29,458
Automotive body, paint, and interior repair and maintenance	811121	22,018	24,283	25,477	25,621
Other automotive repair and maintenance	81119	9,574	11,269	12,284	13,147
Electronic and precision equipment repair and maintenance	8112	14,419	16,514	17,625	18,759
Commercial and industrial machinery and equipment (except automotive and electronic) repair and maintenance	8113	16,687	21,231	24,432	25,128
Personal and household goods repair and maintenance	8114	8,394	9,078	9,416	10,059
Home and garden equipment and appliance repair and maintenance	81141	3,866	4,285	4,354	4,695
Personal and laundry services [2]	812	67,140	76,169	80,883	83,049
Personal care services	8121	18,264	23,178	25,291	26,493
Hair, nail, and skin care services	81211	15,553	18,932	20,141	20,641
Barber shops	812111	479	522	521	527
Beauty salons	812112	14,445	17,191	18,058	18,354
Nail salons	812113	629	1,219	1,562	1,760
Other personal care services	81219	2,711	4,246	5,150	5,852
Death care services	8122	13,707	15,080	15,665	15,182
Funeral homes and funeral services	81221	10,279	11,705	12,140	12,487
Cemeteries and crematories	81222	3,428	3,375	3,525	2,695
Drycleaning and laundry services	8123	19,950	20,040	21,094	22,261
Coin-operated laundries and drycleaners	81231	3,359	3,235	3,244	3,311
Drycleaning and laundry services (except coin-operated)	81232	7,846	7,581	7,901	8,417
Linen and uniform supply	81233	8,745	9,224	9,949	10,533
Other personal services	8129	15,219	17,873	18,833	19,114
Pet care (except veterinary) services	81291	(X)	1,689	1,981	2,223
Photofinishing	81292	3,809	3,173	2,609	2,287
Parking lots and garages	81293	6,389	7,121	7,588	7,711
All other personal services	81299	5,021	5,890	6,656	6,894
Religious, grantmaking, civic, professional, and similar organizations (except religious, labor, and political organizations) [3]	813	122,924	133,913	142,885	162,399
Grantmaking and giving services	8132	57,465	56,408	61,362	73,822
Social advocacy organizations	8133	10,852	13,424	13,957	14,905
Civic and social organizations	8134	13,703	16,694	17,116	18,605
Business, professional, and other organizations (except labor and political organizations)	8139	40,904	47,387	50,450	55,067

X Not applicable.   [1] Based on the North American Industry Classification System, 2002; see Section 15.   [2] For taxable firms only.   [3] For tax-exempt firms only.

Source: U.S. Census Bureau, "2006 Service Annual Survey, Other Services"; <http://www.census.gov/econ/www/servmenu.html>. (released 30 March 2008).

Table 1245. National Nonprofit Associations—Number by Type: 1980 to 2007

[Data compiled during last few months of year previous to year shown and the beginning months of year shown]

Type	1980	1990	2000	2001	2002	2003	2004	2005	2006	2007 [1]
Total	14,726	22,289	21,840	22,449	22,141	22,464	22,659	22,720	23,772	25,048
Trade, business, commercial	3,118	3,918	3,880	3,922	3,883	3,818	3,812	3,789	3,942	4,072
Agriculture and environment	677	940	1,103	1,120	1,125	1,137	1,140	1,170	1,286	1,353
Legal, governmental, public admin., military	529	792	790	807	814	832	839	868	887	938
Scientific, engineering, technical	1,039	1,417	1,302	1,317	1,309	1,326	1,354	1,354	1,396	1,505
Educational	[2]2,376	1,291	1,297	1,346	1,307	1,301	1,313	1,318	1,365	1,471
Cultural	([2])	1,886	1,786	1,812	1,766	1,749	1,735	1,733	1,782	1,881
Social welfare	994	1,705	1,829	1,925	1,917	1,941	1,972	2,072	2,218	2,307
Health, medical	1,413	2,227	2,495	2,574	2,601	2,808	2,921	2,982	3,089	3,383
Public affairs	1,068	2,249	1,776	1,857	1,808	1,836	1,881	1,854	1,938	1,951
Fraternal, nationality, ethnic	435	573	525	537	529	557	547	550	567	580
Religious	797	1,172	1,123	1,160	1,154	1,155	1,157	1,147	1,162	1,204
Veteran, hereditary, patriotic	208	462	835	834	785	802	803	774	790	774
Hobby, avocational	910	1,475	1,330	1,408	1,380	1,435	1,449	1,433	1,525	1,615
Athletic sports	504	840	717	762	730	760	755	762	863	960
Labor unions	235	253	232	233	218	211	213	208	209	227
Chambers of Commerce [3]	105	168	143	142	141	139	136	135	137	169
Greek and non-Greek letter societies	318	340	296	312	301	309	305	349	302	335
Fan clubs	(NA)	581	381	381	373	348	327	314	314	323

NA Not available.   [1] The increase in the number of associations comes from the increase in newly discovered and established associations.   [2] Data for cultural associations included with educational associations.   [3] National and binational. Includes trade and tourism organizations.

Source: ENCYCLOPEDIA OF ASSOCIATIONS V1, 39E © 2003 Gale, a part of Cengage Learning, Inc. Reproduced by permission. www.cengage.com/permissions.

Section 28
Foreign Commerce and Aid

This section presents data on the flow of goods, services, and capital between the United States and other countries; changes in official reserve assets of the United States; international investments; and foreign assistance programs.

The Bureau of Economic Analysis publishes current figures on U.S. international transactions and the U.S. international investment position in its monthly *Survey of Current Business*. Statistics for the foreign aid programs are presented by the Agency for International Development (AID) in its annual *U.S. Overseas Loans and Grants and Assistance from International Organizations*.

The principal source of merchandise import and export data is the U.S. Census Bureau. Current data are presented monthly in *U.S. International Trade in Goods and Services* report Series FT 900. The *Guide to Foreign Trade Statistics*, found on the Census Bureau Web site at <http://www.census.gov/foreign-trade /guide/index.html>, lists the Bureau's monthly and annual products and services in this field. In addition, the International Trade Administration and the Bureau of Economic Analysis present summary as well as selected commodity and country data for U.S. foreign trade on their Web sites: <http://ita.doc.gov/td /industry/otea/> and <http://www.bea .gov/international/index>, respectively. The merchandise trade data published by the Bureau of Economic Analysis in the *Survey of Current Business* and on the Web include balance of payments adjustments to the Census Bureau data. The U.S. Treasury Department's *Monthly Treasury Statement of Receipts and Outlays of the United States Government* contains information on import duties. The International Trade Commission, U.S. Department of Agriculture (agricultural products), U.S. Department of Energy (mineral fuels, like petroleum and coal), and the U.S. Geological Survey (minerals) release various reports and specialized products on U.S. trade.

International accounts—The international transactions tables (Tables 1246 to 1248) show, for given time periods, the transfer of goods, services, grants, and financial assets and liabilities between the United States and the rest of the world. The international investment position table (Table 1249) presents, for specific dates, the value of U.S. investments abroad and of foreign investments in the United States. The movement of foreign and U.S. capital as presented in the balance of payments is not the only factor affecting the total value of foreign investments. Among the other factors are changes in the valuation of assets or liabilities, including changes in prices of securities, defaults, expropriations, and write-offs.

Direct investment abroad means the ownership or control, directly or indirectly, by one person of 10 percent or more of the voting securities of an incorporated business enterprise or an equivalent interest in an unincorporated business enterprise. Direct investment position is the value of U.S. parents' claims on the equity of and receivables due from foreign affiliates, less foreign affiliates' receivables due from their U.S. parents. Income consists of parents' shares in the earnings of their affiliates plus net interest received by parents on intercompany accounts, less withholding taxes on dividends and interest.

Foreign aid—Foreign assistance is divided into three major categories— grants (military supplies and services and other grants), credits, and other assistance (through net accumulation of foreign currency claims from the sale of agricultural commodities). *Grants* are transfers for which no payment is expected (other than a limited percentage of the foreign currency "counterpart" funds generated by the grant), or which at most involve an obligation on the part of the receiver to extend aid to the United States or other countries to achieve a

U.S. Census Bureau, Statistical Abstract of the United States: 2009

common objective. *Credits* are loan disbursements or transfers under other agreements which give rise to specific obligations to repay, over a period of years, usually with interest. All known returns to the U.S. government stemming from grants and credits (reverse grants, returns of grants, and payments of principal) are taken into account in net grants and net credits, but no allowance is made for interest or commissions. *Other assistance* represents the transfer of U.S. farm products in exchange for foreign currencies (plus, since enactment of Public Law 87-128, currency claims from principal and interest collected on credits extended under the farm products program), less the government's disbursements of the currencies as grants, credits, or for purchases. The net acquisition of currencies represents net transfers of resources to foreign countries under the agricultural programs, in addition to those classified as grants or credits.

In 1952, economic, technical, and military aid programs were combined under the Mutual Security Act, which in turn was followed by the Foreign Assistance Act passed in 1961. Appropriations to provide military assistance were also made in the Department of Defense Appropriation Act (rather than the Foreign Assistance Appropriation Act) beginning in 1966 for certain countries in Southeast Asia and in other legislation concerning programs for specific countries (such as Israel). Figures on activity under the Foreign Assistance Act as reported in the *Foreign Grants and Credits* series differ from data published by AID or its immediate predecessors, due largely to differences in reporting, timing, and treatment of particular items.

Exports—The Census Bureau compiles export data primarily from Shipper's Export Declarations required to be filed with customs officials for shipments leaving the United States. They include U.S. exports under mutual security programs and exclude shipments to U.S. Armed Forces for their own use.

The value reported in the export statistics is generally equivalent to a free alongside ship (f.a.s.) value at the U.S. port of export, based on the transaction price, including inland freight, insurance, and

other charges incurred in placing the merchandise alongside the carrier at the U.S. port of exportation. This value, as defined, excludes the cost of loading merchandise aboard the exporting carrier and also excludes freight, insurance, and any other charges or transportation and other costs beyond the U.S. port of exportation. The country of destination is defined as the country of ultimate destination or country where the merchandise is to be consumed, further processed, or manufactured, as known to the shipper at the time of exportation. When ultimate destination is not known, the shipment is statistically credited to the last country to which the shipper knows the merchandise will be shipped in the same form as exported.

Effective January 1990, the United States began substituting Canadian import statistics for U.S. exports to Canada. As a result of the data exchange between the United States and Canada, the United States has adopted the Canadian import exemption level for its export statistics based on shipments to Canada.

Data are estimated for shipments valued under $2,501 to all countries, except Canada, using factors based on the ratios of low-valued shipments to individual country totals.

Prior to 1989, exports were based on Schedule B, Statistical Classification of Domestic and Foreign Commodities Exported from the United States. Beginning in 1989, Schedule B classifications are based on the Harmonized System and coincide with the Standard International Trade Classification, Revision 3. This revision will affect the comparability of most export series beginning with the 1989 data for commodities.

Imports—The Census Bureau compiles import data from various customs forms required to be filed with customs officials. Data on import values are presented on two valuations bases in this section: The c.i.f. (cost, insurance, and freight) and the customs import value (as appraised by the U.S. Customs Service in accordance with legal requirements of the Tariff Act of 1930, as amended). This latter valuation, primarily used for collection of import duties, frequently does not reflect the actual transaction value. Country of origin is defined as country where the merchandise was grown, mined, or manufactured. If country of origin is unknown, country of shipment is reported.

Imports are classified either as "General imports" or "Imports for consumption." *General imports* are a combination of entries for immediate consumption, entries into customs bonded warehouses, and entries into U.S. Foreign Trade Zones, thus generally reflecting total arrivals of merchandise. *Imports for consumption* are a combination of entries for immediate consumption, withdrawals from warehouses for consumption, and entries of merchandise into U.S. customs territory from U.S. Foreign Trade Zones, thus generally reflecting the total of the commodities entered into U.S. consumption channels.

Beginning in 1989, import statistics are based on the Harmonized Tariff Schedule of the United States, which coincides with import Standard International Trade Classification, Revision 3. This revision will affect the comparability of most import series beginning with the 1989 data.

Area coverage—Except as noted, the geographic area covered by the export and import trade statistics is the United States Customs area (includes the 50 states, the District of Columbia, and Puerto Rico), the U.S. Virgin Islands (effective January 1981), and U.S. Foreign Trade Zones (effective July 1982). Data for selected tables and total values for 1980 have been revised to reflect the U.S. Virgin Islands' trade with foreign countries, where possible.

Statistical reliability—For a discussion of statistical collection and estimation, sampling procedures, and measures of statistical reliability applicable to Census Bureau data, see Appendix III.

U.S. Census Bureau, Statistical Abstract of the United States: 2009

Table 1246. **U.S. International Transactions by Type of Transaction: 1990 to 2007**

[In millions of dollars (706,975 represents $706,975,000,000). Minus sign (–) indicates debits. N.i.e. = Not included elsewhere]

Type of transaction	1990	1995	1999	2000	2001	2002	2003	2004	2005	2006	2007
Exports of goods and services and income receipts	**706,975**	**1,004,631**	**1,259,809**	**1,421,515**	**1,295,693**	**1,255,663**	**1,338,213**	**1,574,326**	**1,819,016**	**2,142,164**	**2,463,505**
Exports of goods and services	535,233	794,387	965,884	1,070,597	1,004,896	974,721	1,017,757	1,160,588	1,283,753	1,457,015	1,645,726
Goods, balance of payments basis [1]	387,401	575,204	683,965	771,994	718,712	682,422	713,415	807,516	894,631	1,023,109	1,148,481
Services [2]	147,832	219,183	281,919	298,603	286,184	292,299	304,342	353,072	389,122	433,905	497,245
Transfers under U.S. military agency sales contracts [3]	9,932	14,643	15,928	13,790	12,539	11,943	13,315	15,781	19,539	17,430	16,052
Travel	43,007	63,395	74,801	82,400	71,893	66,605	64,359	74,546	81,799	85,720	96,712
Passenger fares	15,298	18,909	19,785	20,687	17,926	17,046	15,891	18,851	20,970	22,036	25,586
Other transportation	22,042	26,081	26,916	29,803	28,442	29,195	31,416	36,957	41,281	46,323	51,586
Royalties and license fees [4]	16,634	30,289	39,670	43,233	40,696	44,508	46,988	56,715	64,395	72,191	82,614
Other private services [4]	40,251	65,048	103,934	107,904	113,857	122,207	131,563	149,262	160,051	189,050	223,483
U.S. government miscellaneous services	668	818	885	786	831	795	810	959	1,087	1,155	1,212
Income receipts	171,742	210,244	293,925	350,918	290,797	280,942	320,456	413,739	535,263	685,150	817,779
Income receipts on U.S.-owned assets abroad	170,570	208,065	291,177	348,083	287,918	278,131	317,643	410,917	532,373	682,270	814,807
Direct investment receipts	65,973	95,260	131,626	151,839	128,665	145,590	186,417	250,606	294,538	328,543	368,275
Other private receipts	94,072	108,092	156,354	192,398	155,692	129,238	126,529	157,313	235,120	351,327	444,299
U.S. government receipts	10,525	4,713	3,197	3,846	3,561	3,303	4,697	2,998	2,715	2,400	2,233
Compensation of employees	1,172	2,179	2,748	2,835	2,879	2,811	2,813	2,822	2,890	2,880	2,972
Imports of goods and services and income payments	**-759,290**	**-1,080,124**	**-1,511,011**	**-1,780,296**	**-1,629,097**	**-1,651,990**	**-1,789,819**	**-2,114,837**	**-2,458,225**	**-2,838,254**	**-3,082,014**
Imports of goods and services	-616,097	-890,771	-1,230,974	-1,450,432	-1,370,022	-1,398,446	-1,514,672	-1,768,318	-1,995,320	-2,210,298	-2,345,984
Goods, balance of payments basis [1]	-498,438	-749,374	-1,031,784	-1,226,684	-1,148,231	-1,167,377	-1,264,307	-1,477,094	-1,681,780	-1,861,380	-1,967,853
Services [2]	-117,659	-141,397	-199,190	-223,748	-221,791	-231,069	-250,365	-291,224	-313,540	-348,918	-378,130
Direct defense expenditures	-17,531	-10,043	-13,335	-13,473	-14,835	-19,101	-25,296	-29,299	-30,075	-31,032	-32,820
Travel	-37,349	-44,916	-58,963	-64,705	-60,200	-58,715	-57,447	-65,750	-68,970	-72,104	-76,167
Passenger fares	-10,531	-14,663	-21,315	-24,274	-22,633	-19,969	-20,989	-24,718	-26,149	-27,501	-28,486
Other transportation	-24,966	-27,034	-34,139	-41,425	-38,682	-38,407	-44,705	-54,161	-61,937	-65,262	-67,050
Royalties and license fees [4]	-3,135	-6,919	-13,107	-16,468	-16,538	-19,353	-19,033	-23,266	-24,612	-23,777	-25,048
Other private services [4]	-22,229	-35,199	-55,510	-60,520	-66,021	-72,604	-79,764	-90,252	-97,818	-125,221	-144,375
U.S. government miscellaneous services	-1,919	-2,623	-2,821	-2,883	-2,882	-2,920	-3,131	-3,778	-3,979	-4,021	-4,184
Income payments	-143,192	-189,353	-280,037	-329,864	-259,075	-253,544	-275,147	-346,519	-462,905	-627,956	-736,030
Income payments on foreign-owned assets in the U.S.	-139,728	-183,090	-272,082	-322,345	-250,989	-245,164	-266,635	-337,556	-453,615	-618,466	-726,031
Direct investment payments	-3,450	-30,318	-53,437	-56,910	-12,783	-43,244	-73,750	-99,754	-121,333	-144,397	-134,414
Other private payments	-95,508	-97,149	-138,120	-180,918	-159,825	-127,012	-119,051	-155,266	-228,408	-339,088	-426,515
U.S. government payments	-40,770	-55,623	-80,525	-84,517	-78,381	-74,908	-73,834	-82,536	-103,874	-134,981	-165,102
Compensation of employees	-3,464	-6,263	-7,955	-7,519	-8,086	-8,380	-8,512	-8,963	-9,290	-9,489	-9,999
Unilateral current transfers, net	**-26,654**	**-38,074**	**-50,428**	**-58,645**	**-51,295**	**-64,948**	**-71,794**	**-84,482**	**-89,784**	**-92,027**	**-112,705**
U.S. government grants [3]	-10,359	-11,190	-13,774	-16,714	-11,517	-17,097	-22,173	-23,634	-33,039	-27,142	-33,237
U.S. government pensions and other transfers	-3,224	-3,451	-4,406	-4,705	-5,798	-5,125	-5,341	-6,264	-6,303	-6,508	-7,323
Private remittances and other transfers [5]	-13,070	-23,433	-32,248	-37,226	-33,980	-42,726	-44,280	-54,584	-50,442	-58,377	-72,145

See footnotes at end of table.

Table 1246. **U.S. International Transactions by Type of Transaction: 1990 to 2007**—Con.

[See headnote, page 776]

Type of transaction	1990	1995	1999	2000	2001	2002	2003	2004	2005	2006	2007
Capital account transactions, net	-6,579	-927	-4,939	-1,010	-1,270	-1,470	-3,480	-2,369	-4,036	-3,880	-1,843
U.S. assets abroad, net (increase/financial outflow (–))	**-81,234**	**-352,264**	**-504,062**	**-560,523**	**-382,616**	**-294,646**	**-325,424**	**-1,000,870**	**-546,631**	**-1,251,749**	**-1,289,854**
U.S. official reserve assets, net	-2,158	-9,742	8,747	-290	-4,911	-3,681	1,523	2,805	14,096	2,374	-122
Special drawing rights	-192	-808	10	-722	-630	-475	601	-398	4,511	-223	-154
Reserve position in the International Monetary Fund	731	-2,466	5,484	2,308	-3,600	-2,632	1,494	3,826	10,200	3,331	1,021
Foreign currencies	-2,697	-6,468	3,253	-1,876	-681	-574	-572	-623	-615	-734	-989
U.S. Government assets, other than official reserve assets, net	2,317	-984	2,750	-941	-486	345	537	1,710	5,539	5,346	-22,273
U.S. credits and other long-term assets	-8,410	-4,859	-6,175	-5,182	-4,431	-5,251	-7,279	-3,044	-2,255	-2,992	-2,475
Repayments on U.S. credits and other long-term assets [6]	10,856	4,125	9,559	4,265	3,873	5,701	7,981	4,716	5,603	8,329	4,104
U.S. foreign currency holdings and U.S. short-term assets, net	-130	-250	-634	-24	72	-105	-165	38	2,191	9	-23,902
U.S. private assets, net	-81,393	-341,538	-515,559	-559,292	-377,219	-291,310	-327,484	-1,005,385	-566,266	-1,259,469	-1,267,459
Direct investment	-37,183	-98,750	-224,934	-159,212	-142,349	-154,460	-149,564	-316,223	-36,235	-241,244	-333,271
Foreign securities	-28,765	-122,394	-122,236	-127,908	-90,644	-48,568	-146,722	-170,549	-251,199	-365,204	-288,731
U.S. claims on unaffiliated foreigners reported by U.S. nonbanking concerns	-27,824	-45,286	-97,704	-138,790	-8,520	-50,022	-18,184	-152,566	-71,207	-164,597	-706
U.S. claims reported by U.S. banks, n.i.e.	12,379	-75,108	-70,685	-133,382	-135,706	-38,260	-13,014	-366,047	-207,625	-488,424	-644,751
Foreign-owned assets in the United States, net (increase/financial inflow (+))	**139,357**	**435,102**	**742,210**	**1,038,224**	**782,870**	**795,161**	**858,303**	**1,533,201**	**1,247,347**	**2,061,113**	**2,057,703**
Foreign official assets in the U.S., net	33,910	109,880	43,543	42,758	28,059	115,945	278,069	397,755	259,268	487,939	411,058
U.S. Government securities	30,243	72,712	32,527	35,710	54,620	90,971	224,874	314,941	213,334	428,401	230,330
Other U.S. Government liabilities	1,868	-105	-2,863	-1,825	-2,309	137	-723	-134	-421	2,816	5,342
U.S. liabilities reported by U.S. banks, n.i.e.	3,385	34,008	12,964	5,746	-29,978	21,221	48,643	69,245	26,260	22,365	108,695
Other foreign official assets	-1,586	3,265	915	3,127	5,726	3,616	5,275	13,703	20,095	34,357	66,691
Other foreign assets in the U.S., net	105,447	325,222	698,667	995,466	754,811	679,216	580,234	1,135,446	988,079	1,573,174	1,646,645
Direct investments in U.S	48,494	57,776	289,444	321,274	167,021	84,372	63,750	145,966	112,638	241,961	237,542
U.S. Treasury securities	-2,534	91,544	-44,497	-69,983	-14,378	100,403	91,455	93,608	132,300	-58,204	156,825
U.S. securities other than U.S. Treasury securities	1,592	77,249	298,834	459,889	393,885	283,299	220,705	381,493	450,386	683,363	573,850
U.S. currency flows	16,586	8,840	24,407	-3,357	23,794	18,861	10,591	13,301	8,447	2,227	-10,675
U.S. liabilities reported by U.S. nonbanking concerns	45,133	59,637	76,247	170,672	66,110	95,871	96,526	165,872	69,572	242,727	156,290
U.S. liabilities reported by U.S. banks, n.i.e.	-3,824	30,176	54,232	116,971	118,379	96,410	97,207	335,206	214,736	461,100	532,813
Financial derivatives, net	(NA)	(NA)	(NA)	(NA)	(NA)	(NA)	(NA)	(NA)	(NA)	**29,710**	**6,496**
Statistical discrepancy	27,425	31,656	68,421	-59,265	-14,285	-37,770	-6,000	95,030	32,313	-47,078	-41,287
Balance on goods	-111,037	-174,170	-347,819	-454,690	-429,519	-484,955	-550,892	-669,578	-787,149	-838,270	-819,373
Balance on services	30,173	77,786	82,729	74,855	64,393	61,230	53,977	61,848	75,582	84,987	119,115
Balance on income	28,550	20,891	13,888	21,054	31,722	27,398	45,309	67,219	72,358	57,194	81,749
Balance on current account [7]	-78,968	-113,567	-301,630	-417,426	-384,699	-461,275	-523,400	-624,993	-728,993	-788,116	-731,214

NA Not available. [1] Excludes exports of goods under U.S. military agency sales contracts identified in census export documents, excludes imports of goods under direct defense expenditures identified in census import documents, and reflects various other adjustments (for valuation, coverage, and timing) of census statistics to balance of payments basis. [2] Includes some goods: Mainly military equipment; major equipment, other materials, supplies, and petroleum products purchased abroad by U.S. military agencies; and fuels purchased by airline and steamship operators. [3] Includes transfers of goods and services under U.S. military grant programs. [4] These lines are presented on a gross basis. The definition of exports is revised to exclude U.S. parents' payments to foreign affiliates and to include U.S. affiliates' receipts from foreign parents. The definition of imports is revised to include U.S. parents' payments to foreign affiliates and to exclude U.S. affiliates' receipts from foreign parents. [5] The "other transfers" component includes taxes paid by U.S. private residents to foreign governments and taxes paid by private nonresidents to the U.S. government. [6] Includes sales of foreign obligations to foreigners. [7] Conceptually, "Balance on current account" is equal to "net foreign investment" in the national income and product accounts (NIPAs). However, the foreign transactions account in the NIPAs (a) includes adjustments to the international transactions accounts for the treatment of gold, (b) includes adjustments for the different geographical treatment of transactions with U.S. territories and Puerto Rico, and (c) includes services furnished without payment by financial pension plans except life insurance carriers and private noninsured pension plans.

Source: U.S. Bureau of Economic Analysis, *Survey of Current Business*, July 2008. See also <http://www.bea.gov/international/bp_web/list.cfm?anon=71&registered=0>; (released 17 June 2008).

Table 1247. U.S. Balances on International Transactions by Area and Selected Country: 2006 and 2007

[In millions of dollars (–838,270 represents –$838,270,000,000). Minus sign (–) indicates debits]

Area or country	2006, balance on—				2007, balance on—			
	Goods [1]	Services	Income	Current account	Goods [1]	Services	Income	Current account
All areas	**–838,270**	**84,987**	**57,194**	**–788,116**	**–819,373**	**119,115**	**81,749**	**–731,214**
Europe	–142,538	23,419	19,670	–105,824	–130,334	40,501	48,510	–53,246
European Union	–120,212	21,749	12,570	–86,878	–113,936	36,700	39,584	–42,365
Euro Area	–93,166	7,323	23,238	–66,804	–90,445	20,151	39,534	–39,247
Germany	–48,494	–6,489	–4,351	–59,227	–45,255	–5,985	1,225	–51,203
Italy	–20,388	70	3,651	–17,068	–21,134	810	4,762	–16,002
Netherlands	13,587	1,955	15,977	31,823	14,299	3,105	21,135	38,726
United Kingdom	–8,971	12,282	–11,900	–4,374	–7,634	16,534	–2,247	11,178
Canada	–75,083	13,337	15,468	–45,967	–70,611	18,120	16,919	–37,305
Latin America, other Western Hemisphere	–112,579	12,746	30,812	–100,056	–105,316	22,770	27,086	–85,476
Mexico	–67,302	6,787	156	–72,469	–77,589	8,008	1,597	–80,512
Venezuela	–28,157	2,491	1,251	–24,475	–29,717	3,213	524	–25,956
Asia and Pacific	–409,766	33,024	–41,501	–433,574	–410,314	33,121	–47,541	–445,692
Australia	9,005	4,054	3,772	16,904	10,067	4,893	3,742	18,879
China [2]	–233,087	3,752	–26,318	–257,896	–256,611	5,413	–36,083	–289,703
Hong Kong	9,589	–1,257	2,293	10,602	12,997	–1,133	4,149	15,956
India	–11,854	–772	1,130	–13,756	–6,586	–157	1,841	–7,470
Japan [3]	–90,967	16,436	–38,399	–111,141	–85,139	14,950	–41,222	–110,251
Korea, South	–14,393	4,827	–132	–10,246	–13,901	4,752	–199	–9,950
Singapore	6,543	4,206	10,740	21,476	7,451	3,177	13,559	24,203
Taiwan [2]	–15,769	1,304	–3,301	–18,096	–12,528	363	–2,683	–15,293
Middle East	–36,112	–125	–2,621	–51,094	–33,759	126	–3,301	–48,977
Africa	–62,192	3,890	5,789	–58,835	–69,039	4,845	5,758	–67,318
International and unallocated	(X)	–1,304	29,576	7,232	(X)	–368	34,318	6,800

X Not applicable. [1] Adjusted to balance of payments basis; excludes exports under U.S. military sales contracts and imports under direct defense expenditures. [2] See footnote 2, Table 1288. [3] Includes Ryukyu Islands.

Source: U.S. Bureau of Economic Analysis, *Survey of Current Business,* July 2008. See also <http://www.bea.gov/bea/international/bp_web/list.cfm?anon=71&registered=0>; (released June 17, 2008).

Table 1248. Private International Service Transactions by Selected Type of Service and Selected Country: 2000 to 2007

[In millions of dollars (284,027 represents $284,027,000,000). For all transactions, see Table 1246]

Type of service and country	Exports				Imports			
	2000	2005	2006	2007	2000	2005	2006	2007
Private services, total	**284,027**	**368,496**	**415,321**	**479,980**	**207,392**	**279,486**	**313,865**	**341,126**
TYPE OF SERVICE								
Travel	82,400	81,799	85,720	96,712	64,705	68,970	72,104	76,167
Passenger fares	20,687	20,970	22,036	25,586	24,274	26,149	27,501	28,486
Other transportation	29,803	41,281	46,323	51,586	41,425	61,937	65,262	67,050
Freight	12,547	16,470	17,408	19,596	27,388	43,920	45,700	45,576
Port services	17,256	24,811	28,915	31,990	14,037	18,017	19,562	21,474
Royalties and license fees	43,233	64,395	72,191	82,614	16,468	24,612	23,777	25,048
Affiliated	30,479	48,496	52,469	58,880	12,536	20,331	18,161	19,653
Unaffiliated	12,754	15,900	19,723	23,733	3,932	4,281	5,617	5,396
Industrial processes	4,662	6,480	7,829	7,931	1,692	2,843	3,111	3,637
Other	8,093	9,420	11,893	15,802	2,241	1,438	2,506	1,758
Other private services	107,904	160,051	189,050	223,483	60,520	97,818	125,221	144,375
Affiliated	34,970	48,002	57,664	73,290	27,176	37,826	49,631	57,063
Unaffiliated	72,934	112,050	131,386	150,193	33,344	59,992	75,590	87,312
Education	10,348	14,021	14,645	15,732	2,032	3,992	4,465	4,523
Financial services	16,026	31,004	37,046	45,974	4,840	6,420	8,211	11,455
Insurance services	3,631	7,566	10,095	10,286	11,284	28,710	37,373	42,761
Telecommunications	3,884	4,748	5,111	4,915	5,429	4,519	4,794	5,179
Business, professional, and technical services	25,319	40,454	47,327	56,355	9,130	14,810	19,298	21,893
Other unaffiliated services	13,730	14,257	17,162	16,929	632	1,541	1,449	1,500
AREA AND COUNTRY								
Europe	107,650	153,262	172,000	205,029	89,825	122,723	138,968	154,390
European Union	94,232	133,633	149,752	179,235	77,876	105,745	119,062	133,137
Euro Area	56,735	77,827	86,046	105,610	45,625	61,553	70,263	76,050
France	10,553	12,929	14,055	16,035	10,642	12,309	14,752	14,612
Germany	15,928	21,217	21,407	25,371	12,400	18,977	21,125	24,186
Italy	5,459	7,135	7,395	8,971	5,061	6,172	6,426	7,101
Netherlands	7,057	8,689	10,306	12,332	5,698	7,768	8,422	9,286
United Kingdom	31,973	45,125	52,187	60,661	28,304	35,240	38,685	42,965
Canada	24,559	32,671	37,228	42,890	17,711	21,809	23,648	24,578
Latin America, other Western Hemisphere	54,417	61,622	71,910	85,207	38,092	51,747	59,443	62,400
Mexico	14,334	20,366	21,639	23,758	11,023	14,184	14,704	15,602
Asia and Pacific	79,386	99,882	111,568	119,307	51,798	68,832	76,587	83,872
Australia	5,575	7,527	8,587	10,446	3,494	4,670	4,885	5,948
China [1]	5,211	9,015	11,453	14,180	3,259	6,627	7,689	8,756
India	2,546	5,173	6,822	9,350	1,892	5,031	7,647	9,601
Japan	33,411	41,513	41,148	40,227	17,405	22,276	23,747	24,470
Korea, South	7,287	10,466	12,224	12,711	4,617	6,036	6,430	6,552
Taiwan [1]	4,856	6,390	7,491	6,975	4,221	6,531	6,892	7,160
Middle East	6,852	9,279	11,226	14,110	3,310	5,271	5,380	6,059
Africa	4,957	6,321	7,588	9,282	2,710	3,950	4,609	5,200
International organizations and unallocated	6,206	5,458	3,800	4,156	3,946	5,155	5,230	4,625

[1] See footnote 2, Table 1288.

Source: U.S. Bureau of Economic Analysis, *Survey of Current Business,* July 2008.

Table 1249. International Investment Position by Type of Investment: 2000 to 2007

[In billions of dollars (–1,331 represents –$1,331,000,000,000). Estimates for end of year; subject to considerable error due to nature of basic data. Unless otherwise specified, types below refer to current-cost method. For information on current-cost method and market value, see article cited in source]

Type of investment	2000	2002	2003	2004	2005	2006	2007, prel.
Net international investment position	**–1,331**	**–2,038**	**–2,087**	**–2,245**	**–1,925**	**–2,226**	**–2,442**
Financial derivatives, net [1]	(X)	(X)	(X)	(X)	58	60	84
Net international investment position, excluding financial derivatives	–1,331	–2,038	–2,087	–2,245	–1,983	–2,286	–2,525
U.S.-owned assets abroad	**6,239**	**6,649**	**7,638**	**9,341**	**11,962**	**14,381**	**17,640**
Financial derivatives, gross positive fair value [1]	(X)	(X)	(X)	(X)	1,190	1,239	2,285
U.S.-owned assets abroad, excluding financial derivatives	6,239	6,649	7,638	9,341	10,772	13,142	15,355
U.S. official reserve assets	128	159	184	190	188	220	277
Gold	72	91	109	114	134	165	218
Special drawing rights	11	12	13	14	8	9	9
Reserve position in the International Monetary Fund	15	22	23	20	8	5	4
Foreign currencies	31	34	40	42	38	41	45
U.S. government assets, other	85	85	85	83	78	72	94
U.S. credits and other long-term assets	83	83	82	80	77	72	70
U.S. foreign currency holdings and U.S. short-term assets	3	3	3	3	1	1	24
U.S. private assets	6,025	6,405	7,370	9,068	10,506	12,850	14,984
Direct investment at current cost	1,532	1,867	2,054	2,498	2,652	2,936	3,333
Foreign securities	2,426	2,077	2,948	3,545	4,329	5,604	6,649
Bonds	573	703	869	985	1,012	1,276	1,478
Corporate stocks	1,853	1,374	2,079	2,560	3,318	4,329	5,171
U.S. claims on unaffiliated foreigners [2]	837	902	594	794	1,018	1,163	1,176
U.S. claims reported by U.S. banks [3]	1,232	1,559	1,773	2,231	2,507	3,147	3,826
Foreign-owned assets in the United States	**7,569**	**8,687**	**9,725**	**11,586**	**13,887**	**16,607**	**20,082**
Financial derivatives, gross negative fair value [1]	(X)	(X)	(X)	(X)	1,132	1,179	2,201
Foreign-owned assets in the United States, excluding financial derivatives	7,569	8,687	9,725	11,586	12,755	15,428	17,881
Foreign official assets in the United States	1,031	1,251	1,563	2,012	2,306	2,826	3,337
U.S. government securities	756	970	1,187	1,510	1,725	2,167	2,503
U.S. Treasury securities	640	812	986	1,252	1,341	1,558	1,697
Other	116	158	200	258	385	609	805
Other U.S. government liabilities	19	17	16	16	16	19	24
U.S. liabilities reported by U.S. banks [3]	153	156	201	270	297	297	406
Other foreign official assets	102	108	159	215	269	343	404
Other foreign assets	6,539	7,436	8,162	9,574	10,448	12,602	14,544
Direct investment at current cost	1,421	1,500	1,581	1,743	1,906	2,152	2,423
U.S. Treasury securities	382	474	527	562	644	568	735
U.S. securities other than U.S. Treasury securities	2,623	2,779	3,423	3,996	4,353	5,372	6,132
Corporate and other bonds	1,069	1,531	1,711	2,035	2,243	2,825	3,299
Corporate stocks	1,554	1,248	1,712	1,960	2,110	2,547	2,833
U.S. currency	205	248	259	272	280	283	272
U.S. liabilities to unaffiliated foreigners [2]	739	897	451	600	658	797	960
U.S. liabilities reported by U.S. banks [3]	1,169	1,538	1,921	2,402	2,607	3,430	4,022
Memoranda:							
Direct investment abroad at market value	2,694	2,023	2,729	3,363	3,638	4,455	5,148
Direct investment in the United States at market value	2,783	2,022	2,455	2,717	2,818	3,294	3,524

X Not applicable.   [1] A break in series in 2005 reflects the introduction of U.S. Department of the Treasury data on financial derivatives.   [2] Reported by U.S. nonbanking concerns.   [3] Not included elsewhere.

Source: U.S. Bureau of Economic Analysis, *Survey of Current Business*, July 2008.

Table 1250. U.S. Reserve Assets: 1990 to 2007

[In billions of dollars (83.3 represents $83,300,000,000). As of end of year, except as indicated]

Type	1990	2000	2001	2002	2003	2004	2005	2006	2007
Total	83.3	67.6	68.7	79.0	85.9	86.8	65.1	65.9	70.6
Gold stock	11.1	11.0	11.0	11.0	11.0	11.0	11.0	11.0	11.0
Special drawing rights	11.0	10.5	10.8	12.2	12.6	13.6	8.2	8.9	9.5
Foreign currencies	52.2	31.2	29.0	33.8	39.7	42.7	37.8	40.9	45.8
Reserve position in IMF [1]	9.1	14.8	17.9	22.0	22.5	19.5	8.0	5.0	4.2

[1] International Monetary Fund.

U.S. Department of the Treasury, *Treasury Bulletin,* quarterly. For latest issue, see <http://www.fms.treas.gov/bulletin/index.html>.

Table 1251. Foreign Direct Investment Position in the United States on a Historical-Cost Basis by Selected Country, 2000 to 2007, and by Industry, 2007

[In millions of dollars (1,256,867 represents $1,256,867,000,000)]

Country	2000	2004	2005	2006	2007 Total [1]	2007 Manufac-turing	2007 Whole-sale	2007 Finance [2] and insurance
All countries..........	1,256,867	1,520,316	1,634,121	1,843,885	2,093,049	709,545	278,353	263,993
Canada.............	114,309	125,276	165,667	175,198	213,224	43,118	10,177	71,218
Europe [3]...............	887,014	1,078,782	1,154,048	1,324,355	1,482,978	557,115	139,133	160,130
Austria..............	3,007	3,572	2,425	2,453	2,512	1,711	(D)	(D)
Belgium..............	14,787	12,581	10,024	11,248	19,520	9,369	1,881	1,248
Denmark.............	4,025	5,064	6,117	7,348	4,120	3,124	333	(D)
Finland..............	8,875	5,639	5,938	7,315	5,998	3,986	(D)	1
France..............	125,740	137,927	114,260	147,046	168,576	79,636	8,999	29,144
Germany.............	122,412	164,921	177,176	204,708	202,648	61,901	10,772	34,148
Ireland.............	25,523	16,446	17,465	28,553	33,557	15,742	174	2,691
Italy...............	6,576	6,889	7,725	9,175	15,482	2,766	1,511	(D)
Luxembourg..........	58,930	116,479	79,680	103,944	134,310	61,886	1,296	6,884
Netherlands..........	138,894	159,601	156,602	173,265	209,449	94,998	21,444	36,766
Norway.............	2,665	2,862	9,810	10,736	7,952	−853	2,817	1
Spain..............	5,068	5,818	7,472	14,442	27,606	3,357	132	1,093
Sweden.............	21,991	22,292	22,269	18,499	31,857	12,878	7,442	264
Switzerland..........	64,719	122,165	133,387	134,193	155,696	98,672	7,865	29,388
United Kingdom.......	277,613	267,209	371,350	406,337	410,787	92,682	72,240	16,023
Latin America and other Western Hemisphere	**53,691**	**76,268**	**57,175**	**62,685**	**62,955**	**9,694**	**8,687**	**7,479**
South and Central America [3]..	13,384	25,001	22,507	24,563	26,467	3,434	6,836	(D)
Brazil..............	882	1,195	2,051	1,014	1,356	90	(D)	(D)
Mexico..............	7,462	7,592	3,595	5,332	5,954	3,339	1,283	72
Panama.............	3,819	10,408	10,983	12,182	12,903	123	−5	(D)
Venezuela...........	792	5,009	5,292	5,391	6,059	94	(D)	−1
Other Western Hemisphere [3]..	40,307	51,268	34,668	38,122	36,488	6,260	1,851	(D)
Bermuda.............	18,336	6,626	2,147	8,367	−519	4,150	186	−10,715
Netherlands Antilles.......	3,807	3,532	5,531	5,021	5,806	−202	239	(Z)
U.K. islands, Caribbean....	15,191	21,702	23,063	24,790	32,807	3,384	1,120	7,742
Africa................	**2,700**	**1,859**	**2,341**	**1,814**	**1,124**	**−450**	**592**	**(D)**
Middle East [3]............	**6,506**	**7,899**	**8,306**	**9,342**	**12,937**	**2,028**	**5,908**	**(D)**
Israel..............	3,012	3,921	4,231	(D)	5,307	1,933	336	(D)
Saudi Arabia..........	(D)	(D)	(D)	(D)	(D)	8	(D)	2
Asia and Pacific [3]..........	**192,647**	**230,231**	**246,585**	**270,490**	**319,832**	**98,040**	**113,857**	**24,916**
Australia.............	18,775	40,107	36,392	39,730	49,100	4,656	2,349	4,605
Hong Kong...........	1,493	2,744	3,467	3,181	3,209	1,530	1,059	(D)
Japan..............	159,690	174,490	189,851	204,833	233,148	79,951	97,827	17,753
Korea, South.........	3,110	5,270	6,077	9,101	13,057	(D)	9,371	161
Singapore...........	5,087	1,733	3,338	5,368	10,217	(D)	94	(D)
Taiwan [4]............	3,174	3,209	3,731	4,126	4,368	1,523	1,321	19

D Suppressed to avoid disclosure of data of individual companies.   Z Less than $500,000.   [1] Includes other industries not shown separately.   [2] Excludes depository institutions.   [3] Includes other countries not shown separately.   [4] See footnote 2, Table 1288.

Source: U.S. Bureau of Economic Analysis, *Survey of Current Business*, July 2008, and previous issues. For most recent copy and previous issues, see <http://www.bea.gov/bea/pubs.htm>.

Table 1252. U.S. Majority-Owned Affiliates of Foreign Companies—Assets, Sales, Employment, Value, Exports, and Imports by Industry: 2005

[5,883,782 represents $5,883,782,000,000. Preliminary. A U.S. affiliate is a U.S. business enterprise in which one foreign owner (individual, branch, partnership, association, trust, corporation, or government) has a direct or indirect voting interest of 10 percent or more. Estimates cover the universe of nonbank affiliates]

Industry	2002 NAICS code [1]	Total assets (mil. dol.)	Sales [2] (mil. dol.)	Employ-ment [3] (1,000)	Employee compen-sation (mil. dol.)	Gross book value, P & E [4] (mil. dol.)	Merchan-dise exports [5] (mil. dol.)	Merchan-dise imports [5] (mil. dol.)
All industries..............	(X)	5,883,782	2,495,380	5,085.7	335,870	1,092,128	169,238	452,968
Manufacturing [6]...............	31–33	1,095,936	1,001,845	1,986.6	146,591	483,477	97,333	160,323
Petroleum and coal products......	324	(D)	(D)	30.1	4,248	(D)	(D)	23,235
Chemicals.................	325	233,534	182,227	276.6	28,248	91,581	18,438	25,889
Computers and electronic products..	334	55,176	57,621	143.2	10,514	21,854	(D)	14,405
Transportation equipment........	336	254,736	235,015	387.9	26,981	117,499	29,022	58,815
Wholesale trade..............	42	519,722	791,488	567.8	46,637	215,604	65,443	279,847
Retail trade.................	44–45	64,097	128,959	531.1	16,696	38,625	177	4,721
Information................	51	208,519	77,078	211.9	18,836	34,694	1,382	(D)
Finance (except depository institutions) and insurance	52, exc. 521,522	3,313,319	191,610	200.7	35,117	30,814	–	1
Real estate and rental and leasing....	53	98,663	25,708	48.1	2,942	83,548	(D)	568
Professional, scientific, and technical services...................	54	87,830	54,172	197.1	16,369	11,134	(D)	(D)
Other industries.............		495,696	224,520	1,342	52,682	194,232	4,903	(D)

– Represents or rounds to zero.   D Withheld to avoid disclosure of data of individual companies.   [1] North American Industry Classification System, 2002.   [2] Excludes returns, discounts, allowances, and sales and excise taxes.   [3] Average number of full-time and part-time employees.   [4] Plant and equipment (P & E). Includes mineral rights and minor amounts of property other than land.   [5] F.a.s. value at port of exportation. Goods shipped by/to affiliates.   [6] Includes industries not shown separately.

Source: U.S. Bureau of Economic Analysis, *Survey of Current Business*, August 2007 and *Foreign Direct Investment in the United States: Operations of U.S. Affiliates of Foreign Companies*, annual.

Table 1253. Foreign Direct Investment in the United States—Gross Book Value and Employment of U.S. Affiliates of Foreign Companies by State: 2000 to 2005

[**1,175,628 represents $1,175,628,000,000.** A U.S. affiliate is a U.S. business enterprise in which one foreign owner (individual, branch, partnership, association, trust corporation, or government) has a direct or indirect voting interest of 10 percent or more. Estimates cover the universe of nonbank U.S. affiliates. Beginning 2002, data are on a majority-owned basis and not strictly comparable with 2000 data]

State and other area	Gross book value of property, plant, and equipment (mil. dol.)				Total employment			2005	
	2000	2003	2004	2005	2002 (1,000)	2003 (1,000)	2004 (1,000)	Total (1,000)	Percent of all businesses
Total	1,175,628	1,047,010	1,060,181	1,092,128	5,425.4	5,244.4	5,131.5	5,085.7	(X)
United States.....	1,070,422	(D)	931,238	961,405	5,398.6	5,214.4	5,102.1	5,055.9	4.4
Alabama	16,646	15,704	16,857	17,882	75.1	72.6	72.4	63.2	3.9
Alaska............	28,964	30,526	31,121	31,633	12.6	11.7	12.2	12.1	5.1
Arizona	10,716	9,720	9,333	10,989	57.5	58.0	64.2	64.4	3.0
Arkansas	4,613	4,779	4,913	5,819	35.7	32.2	31.5	33.9	3.4
California.........	121,040	86,133	90,622	93,733	612.6	558.0	541.8	542.6	4.2
Colorado	15,319	13,721	16,115	16,921	77.7	72.3	71.7	72.2	3.7
Connecticut	13,604	12,113	12,517	12,833	111.0	105.5	102.1	100.9	6.9
Delaware..........	6,114	5,733	4,508	4,754	22.4	28.1	27.5	27.2	7.2
District of Columbia . . .	4,247	4,052	4,518	4,262	17.4	15.8	15.1	15.6	3.3
Florida............	38,755	27,431	26,819	26,369	252.1	247.8	237.6	226.0	3.2
Georgia...........	29,510	26,089	23,574	23,389	191.2	183.9	177.5	170.3	4.9
Hawaii............	10,369	7,496	6,948	6,545	36.7	35.2	31.1	30.3	6.1
Idaho	2,749	2,171	2,187	2,623	12.5	11.6	13.2	12.2	2.3
Illinois...........	48,425	40,719	39,276	40,352	262.9	252.5	232.4	226.4	4.4
Indiana	30,179	29,977	30,904	34,358	133.2	134.7	133.7	139.9	5.4
Iowa	7,186	6,109	6,391	6,469	36.6	38.7	37.4	37.3	2.9
Kansas	9,036	5,143	5,322	5,761	34.9	31.4	31.9	32.9	2.9
Kentucky	22,091	25,852	26,919	25,728	88.4	87.9	86.1	86.0	5.6
Louisiana..........	31,160	28,927	27,962	28,016	50.5	49.2	50.4	52.3	3.3
Maine	5,087	5,910	5,313	5,415	31.7	29.4	28.4	23.7	4.6
Maryland	13,157	10,667	11,172	11,938	105.4	102.9	100.6	102.7	4.8
Massachusetts	23,875	23,243	22,834	21,279	196.9	188.4	182.0	167.5	5.8
Michigan	39,238	38,683	38,886	40,677	202.9	204.6	202.4	202.3	5.3
Minnesota	13,472	10,355	10,926	11,156	88.1	85.5	85.2	85.6	3.6
Mississippi........	4,121	5,874	6,777	6,599	25.8	21.7	25.4	25.2	2.7
Missouri...........	15,773	14,375	16,027	16,798	91.5	87.2	84.0	85.1	3.6
Montana	3,099	2,097	2,233	2,974	5.9	5.5	6.5	6.7	1.9
Nebraska..........	2,737	1,699	2,021	2,051	18.7	19.0	19.8	18.7	2.4
Nevada	10,128	5,580	6,530	7,236	25.8	26.1	26.7	30.1	2.7
New Hampshire	5,124	(D)	4,693	5,136	41.1	41.7	40.8	34.2	6.1
New Jersey	35,115	32,426	33,846	35,759	228.3	224.0	218.4	214.0	6.2
New Mexico........	5,801	3,963	3,792	4,218	12.8	11.6	12.7	13.6	2.2
New York..........	68,522	59,904	60,572	62,086	386.8	384.2	380.5	378.0	5.2
North Carolina	29,931	25,088	23,917	23,813	214.8	203.8	199.2	192.2	5.7
North Dakota	1,824	1,512	1,416	1,125	7.4	7.8	6.3	7.1	2.5
Ohio.............	37,530	32,759	32,898	35,396	214.2	208.0	207.8	213.8	4.5
Oklahoma	7,635	8,297	8,222	7,698	33.9	34.5	32.9	34.8	2.9
Oregon	13,178	10,029	11,749	12,050	50.9	47.9	47.1	47.4	3.3
Pennsylvania	34,106	31,248	30,237	31,970	235.8	233.1	226.5	233.2	4.6
Rhode Island	3,394	3,279	3,381	3,934	27.5	26.1	26.3	22.9	5.3
South Carolina	23,563	20,520	21,844	22,814	133.0	126.8	121.9	110.4	7.0
South Dakota	1,011	743	750	872	7.6	6.5	5.6	7.1	2.2
Tennessee.........	20,842	17,919	19,890	19,496	130.1	128.5	129.5	125.9	5.2
Texas	110,032	83,192	83,739	85,426	352.8	340.3	338.2	344.6	4.2
Utah	14,340	11,837	11,402	11,997	32.3	34.0	30.6	31.7	3.2
Vermont	2,146	1,321	1,357	1,883	11.1	10.3	11.0	11.3	4.3
Virginia	23,570	16,607	16,422	17,112	141.9	138.9	134.8	138.8	4.5
Washington	22,257	17,378	17,477	18,629	84.5	83.7	85.9	85.9	3.6
West Virginia	7,061	6,092	5,716	5,836	22.7	21.4	18.4	21.3	3.6
Wisconsin	13,961	15,882	15,949	15,959	107.1	95.6	87.9	85.3	3.5
Wyoming..........	8,072	10,956	12,444	13,637	8.5	8.4	9.0	9.1	4.5
Puerto Rico.......	2,169	2,684	2,613	2,593	16.6	16.6	16.6	17.4	(NA)
Other territories and offshore	34,105	39,142	36,125	43,494	9.9	12.9	10.5	10.9	(NA)
Foreign	2,406	(D)	1,515	1,763	0.3	0.4	2.2	1.5	(NA)
Unspecified [1]	66,526	86,645	88,688	82,875	(NA)	(NA)	(NA)	(NA)	(NA)

D Data withheld to avoid disclosure. NA Not available. X Not applicable. [1] Covers property, plant, and equipment not located in a particular state, including aircraft, railroad rolling stock, satellites, undersea cable, and trucks engaged in interstate transportation.

Source: U.S. Bureau of Economic Analysis, *Survey of Current Business*, August 2007 and *Foreign Direct Investment in the United States, Operations of U.S. Affiliates of Foreign Companies*, annual.

Table 1254. U.S. Businesses Acquired or Established by Foreign Direct Investors—Investment Outlays by Industry of U.S. Business Enterprise and Country of Ultimate Beneficial Owner: 2000 to 2007

[In millions of dollars (335,629 represents $335,629,000,000). Foreign direct investment is the ownership or control directly or indirectly, by one foreign individual branch, partnership, association, trust, corporation, or government of 10 percent or more of the voting securities of a U.S. business enterprise or an equivalent interest in an unincorporated one. Data represent number and full cost of acquisitions of existing U.S. business enterprises, including business segments or operating units of existing U.S. business enterprises and establishments of new enterprises. Investments may be made by the foreign direct investor itself, or indirectly by an existing U.S. affiliate of the foreign direct investor. Covers investments in U.S. business enterprises with assets of over $1 million, or ownership of 200 acres of U.S. land]

Industry and country	2000	2001	2002	2003	2004	2005	2006	2007, prel.
Total [1]	335,629	147,109	54,519	63,591	86,219	91,390	165,603	276,835
By type of investment:								
U.S. businesses acquired	322,703	138,091	43,442	50,212	72,738	73,997	148,604	254,972
U.S. businesses established	12,926	9,017	11,077	13,379	13,481	17,393	16,999	21,863
By type of investor:								
Foreign direct investors	105,151	23,134	13,650	27,866	34,184	40,304	44,129	102,339
U.S. affiliates	230,478	123,975	40,869	35,725	52,035	51,086	121,474	174,496
INDUSTRY [2]								
Manufacturing	143,285	37,592	16,446	10,750	18,251	34,036	56,330	135,194
Wholesale trade	8,561	3,982	871	1,086	(D)	3,489	8,273	6,046
Retail trade	1,672	1,913	551	941	3,073	1,262	1,295	8,359
Information	67,932	27,599	14,181	9,236	4,315	8,487	10,341	9,694
Depository institutions	2,636	5,709	613	4,864	(D)	7,973	7,547	15,255
Finance (except depository institutions) and insurance	44,420	40,780	4,344	23,511	26,234	5,529	33,776	24,251
Real estate and rental and leasing	4,526	3,572	5,266	2,817	6,335	8,756	12,441	20,631
Professional, scientific, and technical services	32,332	7,044	4,012	1,955	(D)	6,407	8,923	9,984
Other industries	30,264	18,917	8,234	8,429	10,121	15,453	26,677	47,422
COUNTRY [3]								
Canada	28,346	16,646	4,333	9,157	31,502	13,640	12,121	41,072
Europe [1]	249,167	78,328	39,644	39,024	43,815	56,416	106,732	146,471
France	26,149	5,772	15,196	2,955	6,415	5,608	18,140	17,090
Germany	18,452	12,733	3,067	8,830	4,788	7,239	20,514	13,999
Netherlands	47,686	14,879	3,476	1,077	461	2,609	4,769	8,886
Switzerland	22,789	16,468	2,656	649	6,505	2,332	12,401	3,531
United Kingdom	110,208	17,095	12,188	20,373	23,288	30,420	26,261	67,524
Latin America and other Western Hemisphere	15,400	15,274	3,487	1,607	2,629	5,042	(D)	6,692
South and Central America	5,334	431	373	182	1,382	980	2,273	5,624
Other Western Hemisphere	10,066	14,843	3,144	1,425	1,247	4,062	(D)	1,067
Africa	(D)	(D)	(D)	(D)	(D)	(D)	(D)	97
Middle East	947	(D)	(D)	1,738	1,318	5,068	11,755	27,408
Asia and Pacific [1]	40,282	11,383	5,131	11,469	6,015	10,924	15,759	36,933
Australia	(D)	4,869	1,565	9,032	3,850	4,713	5,650	15,222
Japan	26,044	5,345	3,275	1,544	1,027	4,245	8,350	8,541

D Suppressed to avoid disclosure of data of individual companies. [1] Includes other countries not shown separately. [2] Based on 1997 North American Industry Classification System (NAICS). Beginning 2002, based on NAICS 2002; see text, Section 15. [3] For investments in which more than one investor participated, each investor and each investor's outlays are classified by country of each ultimate beneficial owner.

Source: U.S. Bureau of Economic Analysis, *Survey of Current Business*, June 2008. For most recent copy and historical issues, see <http://www.bea.gov/bea/pubs.htm>.

Table 1255. U.S. Direct Investment Position Abroad, Capital Outflows, and Income by Industry of Foreign Affiliates: 2000 to 2007

[In millions of dollars (1,316,247 represents $1,316,247,000,000). See footnote 2, Table 1254 and headnote, Table 1256]

Industry	Direct investment position on a historical-cost basis			Capital outflows [inflows (–)]			Income [1]		
	2000	2006	2007	2000	2006	2007	2000	2006	2007
All industries, total [2]	1,316,247	2,454,674	2,791,269	142,627	221,664	313,787	133,692	308,963	348,791
Mining	72,111	129,625	147,319	2,174	19,547	16,335	13,164	31,073	31,585
Manufacturing [2]	343,899	466,688	531,315	43,002	46,719	55,249	42,230	55,465	65,127
Food	23,497	30,202	33,766	2,014	2,623	1,142	2,681	4,024	4,210
Chemicals	75,807	108,567	117,963	3,812	9,846	10,527	(D)	14,561	16,580
Primary and fabricated metals	21,644	25,372	28,685	1,233	4,235	2,668	1,536	2,481	3,203
Machinery	22,229	32,248	37,063	2,659	3,644	4,260	2,257	3,182	5,334
Computer and electronic products	59,909	58,800	69,912	17,303	13,256	7,415	8,860	10,003	9,926
Electrical equipment, appliances and components	10,005	17,172	18,429	2,100	1,709	1,836	1,079	1,791	1,516
Transportation equipment	49,887	52,888	65,053	7,814	1,201	11,768	4,107	3,911	5,370
Wholesale trade	93,936	158,090	183,038	11,938	20,124	26,385	14,198	28,108	30,238
Information	52,345	93,355	111,866	16,531	-4,773	19,120	-964	10,728	13,376
Finance and insurance	217,086	497,266	531,933	21,659	23,295	35,324	15,210	32,520	40,137
Professional, scientific, and technical services	32,868	69,118	63,791	5,441	10,167	10,256	3,548	10,191	8,367
Holding companies (nonbank)	(NA)	794,586	927,578	(NA)	96,794	115,260	(NA)	122,785	136,875

D Withheld to avoid disclosure of individual company data. NA Not available. [1] Prior to 2006, income is shown net of withholding taxes. Starting 2006, income is shown gross of withholding taxes. [2] Includes other industries not shown separately.

Source: U.S. Bureau of Economic Analysis, *Survey of Current Business*, September 2008. For most recent copy and historical issues, see <http://www.bea.gov/bea/pubs.htm>.

Table 1256. U.S. Direct Investment Position Abroad on a Historical-Cost Basis by Selected Country: 2000 to 2007

[In millions of dollars (1,316,247 represents $1,316,247,000,000). U.S. investment abroad is the ownership or control by one U.S. person of 10 percent or more of the voting securities of an incorporated foreign business enterprise or an equivalent interest in an unincorporated foreign business enterprise. Negative position can occur when a U.S. parent company's liabilities to the foreign affiliate are greater than its equity in and loans to the foreign affiliate]

Country	2000	2001	2002	2003	2004	2005	2006	2007
All countries	1,316,247	1,460,352	1,616,548	1,769,613	2,160,844	2,241,656	2,454,674	2,791,269
Canada [1]	132,472	152,601	166,473	187,953	214,931	231,836	230,045	257,058
Europe [1]	687,320	771,936	859,378	976,889	1,180,130	1,210,679	1,341,116	1,551,165
Austria	2,872	3,964	4,011	6,366	9,264	11,236	17,909	20,490
Belgium	17,973	22,589	25,727	27,415	41,840	49,306	51,137	54,464
Czech Republic	1,228	1,179	1,264	1,668	2,444	2,729	3,424	3,782
Denmark	5,270	5,160	6,184	5,597	6,815	6,914	6,979	7,903
Finland	1,342	1,686	1,722	1,677	2,208	1,950	2,499	2,683
France	42,628	40,125	43,348	51,229	63,359	60,526	62,003	68,454
Germany	55,508	63,396	61,073	72,262	79,467	100,473	96,243	107,351
Greece	795	835	981	1,431	1,899	1,884	1,985	1,829
Hungary	1,920	2,033	2,503	2,856	3,024	2,795	3,957	4,886
Ireland	35,903	39,541	51,598	60,604	72,907	55,173	71,065	87,023
Italy	23,484	22,883	23,771	23,092	25,184	24,528	26,342	28,408
Luxembourg	27,849	50,771	62,181	68,298	83,634	79,937	94,554	113,611
Netherlands	115,429	147,687	158,415	186,366	219,384	240,205	280,514	370,160
Norway	4,379	4,446	6,045	7,511	8,491	8,533	10,330	11,650
Poland	3,884	4,573	4,231	4,382	7,256	5,575	6,464	8,278
Portugal	2,664	2,746	3,093	2,402	1,915	2,138	2,864	3,702
Russia	1,147	883	1,135	2,511	6,088	9,363	10,699	12,986
Spain	21,236	28,174	38,001	41,119	48,409	50,197	50,759	55,894
Sweden	25,959	26,374	30,114	27,004	29,730	30,153	33,057	36,372
Switzerland	55,377	63,768	74,229	92,750	121,790	100,692	115,216	127,709
Turkey	1,826	1,641	1,869	2,213	2,682	2,563	2,576	4,905
United Kingdom	230,762	228,230	247,952	277,246	330,416	351,513	375,348	398,836
Latin America and other Western Hemisphere	266,576	279,611	289,413	297,222	351,709	379,582	427,397	471,953
South America [1]	84,220	76,809	64,603	66,256	68,685	73,311	79,846	93,373
Argentina	17,488	15,535	11,288	10,663	9,201	10,103	13,867	14,868
Brazil	36,717	32,027	27,598	29,553	29,485	30,882	33,090	41,552
Chile	10,052	10,526	8,928	9,021	10,804	11,127	11,356	12,632
Colombia	3,693	3,122	2,622	2,773	2,991	4,292	4,622	5,603
Ecuador	832	579	809	975	881	941	554	673
Peru	3,130	3,197	3,310	3,401	4,773	5,542	4,815	6,811
Venezuela	10,531	10,069	8,671	8,438	9,109	8,934	10,066	9,974
Central America [1]	73,841	60,716	65,395	64,647	73,214	82,496	93,480	104,533
Costa Rica	1,716	1,835	1,803	840	2,687	1,598	3,252	3,508
Honduras	399	227	181	272	755	821	1,001	968
Mexico	39,352	52,544	56,303	56,851	63,384	73,687	83,219	91,663
Panama	30,758	5,141	5,842	5,409	4,919	4,826	4,714	6,243
Other Western Hemisphere [1]	108,515	142,086	159,416	166,319	209,810	223,775	254,070	274,047
Bahamas, The	3,291	5,533	7,645	8,643	11,255	13,451	10,652	12,239
Barbados	2,141	2,240	1,817	984	3,249	3,881	4,217	2,909
Bermuda	60,114	84,969	89,473	84,508	100,856	113,222	134,613	148,633
Dominican Republic	1,143	1,116	983	816	1,028	815	907	933
Jamaica	2,483	2,957	3,097	3,406	3,551	1,018	973	739
Netherlands Antilles	3,579	5,695	4,753	2,926	4,712	5,607	9,017	13,292
Trinidad and Tobago	1,550	2,025	2,326	2,392	2,577	2,219	3,041	3,829
U.K. Islands, Caribbean	33,451	36,443	48,305	61,882	82,159	83,164	90,060	90,803
Africa [1]	11,891	15,574	16,040	19,835	20,356	22,756	25,074	27,764
Egypt	1,998	2,557	2,682	3,524	4,526	5,475	6,511	7,513
Nigeria	470	260	901	1,100	1,936	1,105	190	-828
South Africa	3,562	3,070	3,334	3,580	3,913	3,969	4,118	4,839
Middle East [1]	10,863	13,212	15,158	16,885	18,963	21,115	25,540	29,370
Israel	3,735	5,690	5,726	7,020	6,171	7,978	9,427	10,119
Saudi Arabia	3,661	3,570	4,930	3,140	3,657	3,830	4,737	5,345
United Arab Emirates	683	834	1,087	1,934	2,962	2,285	3,621	3,846
Asia and Pacific [1]	207,125	227,418	270,086	270,830	374,754	375,689	405,502	453,959
Australia	34,838	27,778	39,074	48,447	(D)	75,669	68,484	79,027
China [2]	11,140	12,081	10,570	11,261	17,616	19,016	23,405	28,298
Hong Kong	27,447	32,494	40,329	36,426	32,735	36,415	41,019	47,431
India	2,379	2,496	4,232	4,868	7,658	7,162	9,226	13,633
Indonesia	8,904	10,511	(D)	(D)	(D)	8,603	9,864	10,049
Japan	57,091	55,651	66,468	57,794	71,005	81,175	92,383	101,607
Korea, South	8,968	9,977	11,856	13,063	17,747	19,760	24,609	27,151
Malaysia	7,910	7,489	7,101	7,057	8,909	11,097	12,557	15,699
New Zealand	4,271	4,273	3,926	3,859	4,620	5,191	5,974	5,385
Philippines	3,638	5,436	5,964	6,390	6,176	6,522	7,149	6,684
Singapore	24,133	40,764	50,955	51,053	61,076	76,390	78,436	82,623
Taiwan [2]	7,836	9,301	10,144	11,983	(D)	14,356	16,374	16,374
Thailand	5,824	6,176	7,774	6,886	7,499	10,352	10,911	14,983

D Suppressed to avoid disclosure of data of individual companies.   [1] Includes other countries not shown separately.   [2] See footnote 2, Table 1288.

Source: U.S. Bureau of Economic Analysis, *Survey of Current Business*, July 2008. For most recent copy and historical issues, see <http://www.bea.gov/bea/pubs.htm>.

Table 1257. U.S. Government Foreign Grants and Credits by Country: 2000 to 2007

[In millions of dollars (17,858 represents $17,858,000,000). See text, this section. Negative figures (–) occur when the total of grant returns, principal repayments, and/or foreign currencies disbursed by the U.S. government exceeds new grants and new credits utilized and/or acquisitions of foreign currencies through new sales of farm products]

Country	2000	2001	2002	2003	2004	2005	2006	2007
Total, net	17,858	12,601	17,213	23,131	22,335	31,729	23,304	31,779
Investment in financial institutions.	1,500	1,702	1,486	1,434	1,994	1,263	2,024	1,651
Western Europe [1]	429	615	485	706	348	345	98	231
Ireland.	–	–	–	44	50	–	30	–
Spain.	–19	–19	–19	–19	–19	–19	–205	–
Yugoslavia . . . . [2]	1	–	–54	231	13	4	–73	–2
Bosnia and Herzegovina [2]	52	115	64	47	66	72	49	46
Macedonia [2] . . . . [2]	50	29	15	58	42	67	30	2
Former Yugoslavia – Regional [2] . . .	63	87	131	66	38	66	120	45
Other [3] and unspecified [2].	478	395	314	221	69	49	45	50
Eastern Europe [1]	2,220	1,352	1,689	1,492	1,273	–70	257	1,062
Albania.	26	38	40	42	43	53	31	36
Romania.	38	43	48	66	34	57	41	41
Armenia	20	52	54	74	66	85	61	68
Azerbaijan.	8	15	32	35	47	74	52	44
Georgia	36	49	97	66	113	169	75	87
Kazakhstan	42	58	52	50	56	69	40	43
Kyrgyzstan	15	32	36	35	39	60	50	26
Moldova	32	60	28	23	27	38	26	20
Russia	797	280	266	192	251	–681	–920	–41
Tajikistan.	8	34	18	25	40	61	35	33
Ukraine.	138	195	118	96	114	145	119	69
Former Soviet Union—Regional [2] . .	501	295	510	364	372	456	470	461
Other [4] and unspecified [2]	419	62	232	214	107	153	76	73
Near East and South Asia [1]	3,304	1,445	1,632	2,268	3,544	5,259	4,500	9,659
Afghanistan	5	6	140	555	1,222	2,076	3,560	7,262
Bangladesh	43	89	45	29	50	48	45	81
Egypt.	3,091	1,296	1,689	2,055	2,689	2,827	149	1,761
Greece	–169	–153	–218	–287	–457	–114	–103	–74
India	–64	–56	–122	–150	–40	–70	61	46
Nepal	15	27	28	43	37	50	57	63
Pakistan.	366	170	145	223	230	530	703	526
Turkey	–86	–5	–138	–322	–299	–228	–194	–296
UNRWA [5]	97	77	71	124	27	48	137	135
Other and unspecified [2]	21	–	2	14	79	54	47	117
Africa [1]	1,058	1,613	2,085	3,909	2,450	2,199	1,342	3,523
Algeria.	–53	182	–73	–123	–146	–173	–1,324	–19
Burundi	3	6	3	18	27	6	37	18
Congo (Kinshasa)	9	17	33	1,078	229	135	131	94
Ethiopia	142	98	86	138	234	308	233	278
Ghana.	40	86	48	50	67	53	54	55
Guinea.	19	45	41	30	33	36	29	15
Kenya	44	108	50	58	82	91	186	178
Liberia	19	19	10	13	50	40	61	81
Madagascar	21	63	36	31	34	35	44	48
Malawi	45	41	46	42	54	46	61	68
Mali.	50	9	49	50	45	55	52	43
Mozambique	119	133	105	107	105	64	92	106
Nigeria.	–17	17	45	472	41	67	–178	123
Rwanda	26	57	32	36	35	47	55	71
Senegal	27	51	42	45	53	39	34	39
Somalia	7	1	6	10	16	7	33	40
South Africa	68	119	98	115	332	103	106	155
Sudan	17	13	11	41	120	130	390	363
Tanzania	15	50	44	49	66	62	75	104
Uganda	92	55	71	86	120	148	154	183
Zambia	44	42	34	52	56	90	89	105
Zimbabwe.	23	24	21	23	31	27	32	69
Other and unspecified [2]	164	215	181	278	407	513	621	1,060
Far East and Pacific [1]	544	599	105	712	–129	42	–106	141
Cambodia.	23	42	35	32	44	58	56	61
Hong Kong	–15	–24	–20	–23	–28	–28	–28	–28
Indonesia	270	488	196	821	–157	–8	–71	–18
Korea, South.	–132	–215	–134	–137	–110	–43	–43	–40
Malaysia.	134	184	11	2	–45	–46	–45	–185
Philippines	20	–17	–46	–35	–15	–36	–28	46
Thailand.	–102	–118	–27	–37	11	4	–67	–
Pacific Islands, Trust Territory of the [6].	145	206	193	103	204	190	174	195
Other and unspecified [2]	19	11	15	22	40	47	39	182

See footnotes at end of table.

U.S. Census Bureau, Statistical Abstract of the United States: 2009

Table. 1257. **U.S. Government Foreign Grants and Credits by Country: 2000 to 2007**—Con.

[**In millions of dollars.** See headnote, page 784]

Country	2000	2001	2002	2003	2004	2005	2006	2007
Western Hemisphere [1]	**1,621**	**1,698**	**1,590**	**1,658**	**1,986**	**2,164**	**1,537**	**1,409**
Bolivia	136	189	152	212	217	159	142	155
Brazil	195	119	106	−78	−136	−93	−344	−181
Colombia	33	71	76	328	467	598	613	771
Ecuador	14	38	75	39	36	59	80	73
El Salvador	27	78	45	56	104	52	27	40
Guatemala	49	106	54	42	40	21	34	25
Haiti	63	106	66	64	83	118	154	164
Honduras	100	258	85	51	84	70	60	75
Mexico	−123	14	−13	5	14	40	30	50
Nicaragua	53	152	60	41	28	36	53	71
Panama [7]	−13	−9	(Z)	5	14	7	11	6
Peru	87	133	109	93	167	127	71	−258
Other [8] and unspecified [2]	1,100	608	925	868	806	815	510	447
Middle East [1]	**4,345**	**553**	**3,736**	**7,745**	**8,384**	**16,326**	**9,882**	**9,260**
Iraq [9]	(Z)	1	(Z)	3,235	5,011	10,481	8,822	6,102
Israel	3,932	82	3,061	2,761	2,163	4,953	390	2,373
Jordan	317	298	483	1,420	800	582	462	424
Lebanon	22	60	28	24	30	37	45	146
Yemen	16	7	1	17	31	24	30	40
West Bank-Gaza Regional	64	115	143	195	171	179	128	152
Other international organizations	**2,837**	**3,024**	**4,405**	**3,207**	**2,485**	**4,201**	**3,770**	**4,843**

– Represents zero. Z Less than $500,000. [1] Includes other countries not shown separately. [2] In recent years, significant amounts of foreign assistance has been reported on a regional, interregional, and worldwide basis. Country totals in this table may understate actual assistance to many countries. [3] Includes European Atomic Energy Community, European Coal and Steel Community, European Payments Union, European Productivity Agency, North Atlantic Treaty Organization, and Organization for European Economic Cooperation. [4] In 1992, some successor countries assumed portions of outstanding credits of the former Yugoslavia (assignment of the remaining portions is pending). Subsequent negative totals reflect payments to the United States on these assumed credits which were greater than the extension of new credits and grants to these countries. [5] United Nations Relief and Works Agency for Palestine refugees. [6] Excludes transactions with Commonwealth of the Northern Mariana Islands after October 1986; includes transactions with Federated States of Micronesia, Republic of the Marshall Islands, and Republic of Palau. [7] Includes transfer of Panama Canal to the Republic of Panama on Dec. 1999. [8] Includes Andean Development Corporation, Caribbean Development Bank, Central American Bank for Economic Integration, Eastern Caribbean Central Bank, Inter-American Institute of Agricultural Science, Organizations of American States, and Pan American Health Organization. [9] Foreign assistance to Iraq in 1991–96 was direct humanitarian assistance to ethnic minorities of Northern Iraq after the conflict in the Persian Gulf. Foreign assistance to Iraq in 2003, 2004, 2005, 2006, and 2007 includes Iraq Reconstruction and humanitarian assistance.

Source: U.S. Bureau of Economic Analysis, press releases, and unpublished data.

Table 1258. **U.S. Foreign Economic and Military Aid Programs: 1980 to 2006**

[**In millions of dollars (9,694 represents $9,694,000,000). For years ending September 30.** Economic aid shown here represents U.S. economic aid—not just aid under the Foreign Assistance Act. Major components in recent years include AID, Food for Peace, Peace Corps, and paid-in subscriptions to international financial institutions. Annual figures are gross unadjusted program figures]

Year and region	Total foreign assistance	Military assistance	Economic assistance, by funding agency					
			Total	U.S. Agency for International Development	U.S. Department of Agriculture	State Department	Other U.S. agencies	Multilateral organizations
1980	9,694	2,122	7,572	4,062	1,437	459	137	1,478
1990	16,015	4,971	11,044	6,964	1,643	590	377	1,469
1995	16,520	4,121	12,398	7,281	1,517	763	1,056	1,781
2000	16,762	4,838	11,924	5,907	1,941	1,578	1,387	1,110
2001	17,959	3,843	14,116	6,972	2,071	2,441	1,486	1,147
2002	20,392	4,611	15,781	8,850	1,433	2,335	1,572	1,591
2003	26,486	6,627	19,859	10,534	2,676	2,179	3,833	637
2004	34,156	6,141	28,015	11,414	2,226	4,062	7,428	2,885
2005	35,627	7,411	28,217	10,273	2,306	5,015	8,908	1,715
2006, total	**39,039**	**12,070**	**26,969**	**9,827**	**2,033**	**5,343**	**8,275**	**1,492**
Asia	6,016	2,158	3,858	2,683	307	229	541	99
Central Asia	2,581	70	2,511	627	43	103	1,738	–
Eastern Europe	598	113	485	374	–	29	81	1
Latin America and Caribbean	3,445	123	3,322	654	219	1,814	625	11
Middle East and North Africa	15,301	9,266	6,035	2,041	67	327	3,600	–
Oceania	258	2	256	–	–	–	256	–
Sub-Saharan Africa	5,159	239	4,920	1,559	1,326	1,496	403	138
Western Europe	51	19	32	26	–	5	1	–
Canada	23	–	23	–	–	–	23	–
World not specified	5,608	81	5,526	1,863	72	1,342	1,007	1,243

– Represents or rounds to zero.

Source: U.S. Agency for International Development, *U.S. Overseas Loans, Grants, Obligations, and Loan Authorizations,* annual. See also <http://qesdb.cdie.org/gbk/index.html>.

U.S. Census Bureau, Statistical Abstract of the United States: 2009

Table 1259. U.S. Foreign Economic and Military Aid by Major Recipient Country: 2000 to 2006

[In millions of dollars (16,762.1 represents $16,762,100,000), except as indicated. For years ending Sept. 30]

Recipient country	2000	2003	2004	2005	2006 Total	2006 Economic aid	2006 Military aid
Total [1]	16,762.1	26,486.3	34,156.3	35,627.4	39,039.2	26,968.8	12,070.4
Afghanistan	42.9	1,089.2	2,116.5	2,514.4	3,739.8	1,932.8	1,807.0
Albania	69.4	58.9	65.1	49.7	46.5	41.8	4.8
Angola	105.3	161.1	116.0	66.9	52.4	51.9	0.5
Armenia	103.9	104.6	97.5	95.6	326.7	320.8	5.9
Azerbaijan	54.2	72.7	68.7	75.9	53.2	47.9	5.3
Bangladesh	78.3	102.4	92.9	87.1	82.2	80.2	1.9
Bolivia	241.1	209.3	182.8	161.8	223.6	223.6	–
Bosnia and Herzegovina	170.2	92.7	94.5	56.0	72.1	62.2	9.9
Bulgaria	48.8	60.7	49.7	50.2	42.0	30.5	11.5
Burundi	7.4	43.6	49.4	59.0	49.3	49.1	0.1
Cambodia	27.0	63.4	90.6	97.4	70.6	69.5	1.0
Chad	4.1	7.3	57.8	63.6	83.7	83.4	0.3
Colombia	1,159.6	681.5	758.1	823.5	1,348.5	1,257.8	90.8
Congo (Kinshasa) [2]	30.9	111.6	117.2	125.3	170.8	170.5	0.3
Ecuador	77.4	88.7	91.1	86.8	76.4	76.4	–
Egypt	2,076.1	1,716.4	1,957.6	1,563.2	1,786.5	498.3	1,288.2
El Salvador	35.0	62.4	70.5	59.6	66.4	54.7	11.7
Eritrea	37.0	106.2	86.2	133.2	6.2	6.2	–
Ethiopia	277.6	602.4	436.1	693.5	322.0	319.4	2.6
Georgia	–	–	0.6	0.1	0.0	0.0	–
Ghana	16.7	5.3	0.6	1.2	0.6	–	0.6
Guatemala	33.4	49.5	55.1	43.9	36.3	36.0	0.4
Haiti	41.4	71.1	66.0	273.1	87.1	85.0	2.1
Honduras	8.1	23.2	13.2	12.5	7.3	3.1	4.2
India	242.3	201.4	160.7	591.0	267.4	265.4	1.9
Indonesia	–	1.5	10.3	1.2	3.3	3.3	–
Iraq	0.1	49.8	–	36.7	–	–	–
Israel	–	–	–	0.2	0.1	0.1	–
Jamaica	448.3	1,681.0	638.4	682.8	562.2	351.3	210.9
Jordan	53.4	81.2	83.4	71.4	106.9	101.2	5.7
Kazakhstan	90.1	125.8	187.1	244.0	390.5	390.5	–
Kenya	1.1	1.1	1.3	1.2	1.1	1.1	–
Kosovo	–	–	–	1.0	0.7	0.7	–
Kyrgyzstan	7.3	6.8	5.4	6.8	3.0	3.0	–
Liberia	–	–	–	0.1	25.1	25.1	–
Macedonia	27.4	47.2	47.5	155.6	55.4	55.2	0.2
Madagascar	44.4	39.4	52.9	84.3	73.9	73.5	0.4
Malawi	1.0	3.4	2.0	9.3	4.6	3.7	0.9
Mali	0.6	5.8	0.4	–	0.5	0.5	–
Marshall Islands	3.8	20.4	12.6	20.9	12.6	12.6	–
Mexico	81.0	99.5	94.7	94.4	99.5	99.5	–
Micronesia, Federated States of	48.6	51.3	50.8	31.6	26.7	24.2	2.5
Morocco	87.6	92.8	113.4	127.8	157.6	157.3	0.3
Mozambique	15.5	31.6	31.4	49.7	63.9	63.9	–
Namibia	21.8	54.7	55.4	62.5	59.8	59.2	0.6
Nepal	–	–	0.1	0.1	–	–	–
Nicaragua	6.3	14.2	19.7	27.1	33.5	33.5	–
Nigeria	–	–	–	–	–	–	–
Pakistan	19.3	597.0	440.3	766.5	942.1	643.0	299.0
Peru	204.2	230.5	272.6	190.6	338.4	338.4	–
Philippines	82.2	224.7	238.3	177.8	212.6	179.9	32.6
Poland	84.8	32.8	37.4	81.5	33.8	2.0	31.8
Romania	46.1	72.0	53.9	65.3	52.9	38.5	14.4
Russia	710.4	780.0	951.4	1,263.6	1,208.6	1,207.6	1.0
Rwanda	37.7	47.6	59.4	77.0	103.2	102.9	0.3
Senegal	37.4	50.7	52.9	47.5	65.0	63.4	1.6
Serbia and Montenegro [3]	354.1	253.3	258.3	226.1	5.8	5.8	–
South Africa	54.9	86.6	122.5	174.6	261.4	261.4	–
Sri Lanka	9.2	39.2	39.4	164.2	46.7	45.1	1.5
Sudan	50.9	187.8	482.3	1,042.5	908.2	758.4	149.8
Tajikistan	36.1	64.9	53.5	70.7	53.2	51.7	1.5
Tanzania	42.8	80.4	99.6	134.7	185.9	185.9	–
Turkey	5.4	28.5	50.3	53.7	23.2	5.3	17.9
Uganda	76.4	179.6	218.7	269.8	279.5	279.2	0.3
Ukraine	199.5	86.1	159.8	170.6	173.8	158.0	15.8
Uzbekistan	34.0	167.5	49.6	44.3	49.1	49.1	–
West Bank/Gaza	122.0	190.7	138.8	349.6	139.3	139.3	–
Zambia	20.9	31.2	32.8	60.5	29.8	29.8	–
Zimbabwe	20.9	34.0	31.6	45.9	–	–	–

– Represents or rounds to zero.   [1] Includes other countries not shown separately.   [2] See footnote 3, Table 1288.   [3] See footnote 3, Table 1339.

Source: U.S. Agency for International Development, *U.S. Overseas Loans, Grants, Obligations, and Loan Authorizations*, annual. See also <http://qesdb.cdie.org/gbk/index.html>.

Table 1260. U.S. International Trade in Goods and Services: 2000 to 2007

[In millions of dollars (-379,835 represents -$379,835,000,000). Data presented on a balance of payments basis and will not agree with the following merchandise trade Tables 1261 to 1271]

Category	2000	2001	2002	2003	2004	2005	2006	2007
TRADE BALANCE								
Total	**-379,835**	**-365,126**	**-423,725**	**-496,915**	**-607,730**	**-711,567**	**-753,283**	**-700,258**
Goods	-454,690	-429,519	-484,955	-550,892	-669,578	-787,149	-838,270	-819,373
Services	74,855	64,393	61,230	53,977	61,848	75,582	84,987	119,115
Travel	17,695	11,693	7,890	6,912	8,796	12,829	13,616	20,545
Passenger fares	-3,587	-4,707	-2,923	-5,098	-5,867	-5,179	-5,465	-2,900
Other transportation	-11,622	-10,240	-9,212	-13,289	-17,204	-20,656	-18,939	-15,464
Royalties, license fees	26,765	24,158	25,155	27,955	33,449	39,783	48,414	57,566
Other private services	47,384	47,836	49,603	51,799	59,010	62,233	63,829	79,108
Other [1]	317	-2,296	-7,158	-11,981	-13,518	-10,536	-13,602	-16,768
U.S. govt misc. services	-2,097	-2,051	-2,125	-2,321	-2,819	-2,892	-2,866	-2,972
EXPORTS								
Total	**1,070,597**	**1,004,896**	**974,721**	**1,017,757**	**1,160,588**	**1,283,753**	**1,457,014**	**1,645,726**
Goods	771,994	718,712	682,422	713,415	807,516	894,631	1,023,109	1,148,481
Services	298,603	286,184	292,299	304,342	353,072	389,122	433,905	497,245
Travel	82,400	71,893	66,605	64,359	74,546	81,799	85,720	96,712
Passenger fares	20,687	17,926	17,046	15,891	18,851	20,970	22,036	25,586
Other transportation	29,803	28,442	29,195	31,416	36,957	41,281	46,323	51,586
Royalties, license fees	43,233	40,696	44,508	46,988	56,715	64,395	72,191	82,614
Other private services	107,904	113,857	122,207	131,563	149,262	160,051	189,050	223,483
Other [1]	13,790	12,539	11,943	13,315	15,781	19,539	17,430	16,052
U.S. govt misc. services	786	831	795	810	959	1,087	1,155	1,212
IMPORTS								
Total	**1,450,432**	**1,370,022**	**1,398,446**	**1,514,672**	**1,768,318**	**1,995,320**	**2,210,298**	**2,345,983**
Goods	1,226,684	1,148,231	1,167,377	1,264,307	1,477,094	1,681,780	1,861,380	1,967,853
Services	223,748	221,791	231,069	250,365	291,224	313,540	348,918	378,130
Travel	64,705	60,200	58,715	57,447	65,750	68,970	72,104	76,167
Passenger fares	24,274	22,633	19,969	20,989	24,718	26,149	27,501	28,486
Other transportation	41,425	38,682	38,407	44,705	54,161	61,937	65,262	67,050
Royalties, license fees	16,468	16,538	19,353	19,033	23,266	24,612	23,777	25,048
Other private services	60,520	66,021	72,604	79,764	90,252	97,818	125,221	144,375
Other [1]	13,473	14,835	19,101	25,296	29,299	30,075	31,032	32,820
U.S. govt misc. services	2,883	2,882	2,920	3,131	3,778	3,979	4,021	4,184

[1] Represents transfers under U.S. military sales contracts for exports and direct defense expenditures for imports.

Source: U.S. Census Bureau, *U.S. International Trade in Goods and Services, Annual Revision for 2007*, Series FT-900(07-04) and previous reports. See also <http://www.census.gov/foreign-trade/Press-Release/2007pr/final_revisions/07final.pdf> (released 10 June 2008).

Table 1261. U.S. International Trade in Goods by Related Parties: 2000 to 2007

[In millions of dollars (1,205,339 represents $1,205,339,000,000). "Related party trade" is trade by U.S. companies with their subsidiaries abroad as well as trade by U.S. subsidiaries of foreign companies with their parent companies. Based on the North American Industry Classification System (NAICS), 2002; see text, Section 15]

Country and commodity	2002 NAICS code	2000	2004	2005	2006	2007
IMPORTS FOR CONSUMPTION						
Total imports	(X)	1,205,339	1,460,160	1,662,380	1,845,053	1,942,863
Related party trade, total [1]	**(X)**	**563,084**	**697,561**	**775,730**	**862,657**	**920,369**
Canada	(X)	100,689	116,261	127,719	139,490	146,906
Japan	(X)	108,290	102,207	108,322	116,690	116,304
Mexico	(X)	89,068	94,716	99,709	114,504	120,551
China [2]	(X)	18,061	53,172	62,716	70,701	82,404
Germany	(X)	37,781	46,959	30,792	54,972	61,318
Transportation equipment	336	161,150	181,805	188,445	200,855	207,668
Computer & electronic products	334	166,279	168,554	176,719	189,046	196,933
Chemicals	325	45,452	76,268	84,459	96,919	109,734
Machinery, except electrical	333	39,918	50,013	56,804	62,975	61,272
Oil & gas	211	13,241	31,694	48,725	61,758	69,394
EXPORTS						
Total exports	(X)	780,418	817,936	904,380	1,037,143	1,162,708
Related party trade, domestic exports, total [1]	**(X)**	**196,596**	**218,688**	**245,712**	**279,832**	**301,314**
Canada	(X)	64,133	69,029	76,331	80,687	88,396
Mexico	(X)	34,249	38,602	44,570	49,801	52,470
Japan	(X)	20,313	16,200	17,427	18,332	17,486
Netherlands	(X)	6,845	8,064	9,308	13,835	12,812
Germany	(X)	6,751	8,778	9,250	13,779	16,185
Transportation equipment	336	46,288	48,687	52,513	58,379	63,885
Chemicals	325	26,374	42,495	48,121	55,349	58,343
Computer & electronic products	334	51,210	39,309	41,863	47,140	47,127
Machinery, except electrical	333	19,831	23,061	25,492	27,627	30,231
Electrical equipment, appliances & components	335	7,575	8,675	9,888	11,642	12,205

X Not applicable.   [1] Includes other countries and other commodities not shown separately.   [2] See footnote 2, Table 1288.

Source: U.S. Census Bureau, "Related Party Trade—2007"; published 9 May 2008. See <http://www.census.gov/foreign-trade/Press-Release/2007pr/aip/related_party>.

Foreign Commerce and Aid   787

Table 1262. U.S. Exports and Imports for Consumption of Merchandise by Customs District: 2000 to 2007

[In billions of dollars (780.0 represents $780,000,000,000). Exports are f.a.s. (free alongside ship) value all years; imports are on customs-value basis. These data may differ from those in Tables 1261, 1266, and 1267. For methodology, see Foreign Trade Statistics in Appendix III]

Customs district	Exports					Imports for consumption				
	2000	2004	2005	2006	2007	2000	2004	2005	2006	2007
Total [1]	780.0	817.9	904.4	1,037.1	1,162.7	1,205.6	1,460.2	1,662.4	1,845.1	1,942.9
Anchorage, AK	5.9	8.7	12.1	14.9	14.1	13.4	10.5	10.2	11.4	11.1
Baltimore, MD	6.2	7.2	9.0	10.0	14.4	18.6	26.7	29.5	29.6	30.3
Boston, MA	7.0	9.7	9.9	10.5	11.4	18.7	19.2	21.4	22.6	24.4
Buffalo, NY [2]	38.2	33.6	34.7	37.8	41.0	38.4	40.9	42.1	44.3	44.4
Charleston, SC [2]	12.6	15.4	16.1	16.2	20.0	16.9	26.0	30.9	32.4	34.0
Chicago, IL	21.7	25.9	30.0	32.2	34.3	51.1	69.1	78.5	88.5	98.3
Cleveland, OH	22.7	19.0	20.8	21.4	22.1	36.5	44.6	51.2	59.0	64.2
Dallas/Fort Worth, TX	11.5	16.4	17.8	20.6	20.7	18.8	27.8	32.0	38.3	40.5
Detroit, MI	79.4	93.4	105.7	112.6	119.8	97.6	112.2	122.8	126.0	127.3
Duluth, MN	1.5	1.8	1.9	2.0	2.1	7.0	9.0	9.4	7.0	7.3
El Paso, TX	18.0	19.3	19.9	22.0	20.9	24.1	27.8	27.7	29.5	33.7
Great Falls, MT	5.0	6.1	9.7	12.4	14.8	14.3	21.5	26.8	27.8	28.8
Honolulu, HI	0.7	1.8	2.4	3.2	4.8	2.9	2.2	2.9	4.2	4.2
Houston/Galveston, TX	29.7	39.5	46.7	58.1	72.3	40.9	64.4	89.4	104.9	112.4
Laredo, TX	57.7	56.0	60.3	67.3	71.0	62.7	74.4	78.2	88.8	95.8
Los Angeles, CA	77.6	70.8	78.4	90.4	100.2	150.1	191.0	213.5	236.0	247.3
Miami, FL	31.0	30.0	34.1	39.6	45.5	23.3	27.8	30.4	30.8	31.4
Milwaukee, WI	0.1	0.1	0.2	0.2	0.2	1.5	1.5	1.5	1.7	1.5
Minneapolis, MN	1.4	1.7	2.3	2.5	3.3	4.3	5.8	6.9	12.0	13.0
Mobile, AL [2]	4.0	5.0	4.9	6.0	6.1	7.9	11.0	13.7	16.7	16.4
New Orleans, LA	35.9	36.8	32.4	39.9	52.1	54.0	76.2	94.2	110.0	120.1
New York, NY	79.5	80.8	90.8	106.3	123.7	145.6	163.6	176.3	188.4	200.1
Nogales, AZ	7.3	5.9	6.9	8.3	8.0	14.1	12.5	13.6	17.0	17.2
Norfolk, VA [2]	12.4	13.4	16.7	18.1	22.1	13.6	20.0	23.5	26.4	28.1
Ogdensburg, NY	12.4	11.9	13.2	14.3	15.3	23.7	24.2	27.8	30.1	30.2
Pembina, ND	8.7	11.0	13.6	16.1	17.9	11.0	11.1	12.8	14.1	15.2
Philadelphia, PA	6.0	9.0	10.1	13.1	14.3	28.3	38.6	47.5	55.5	59.8
Port Arthur, TX	1.2	2.0	2.1	3.0	3.1	10.9	18.0	21.3	23.9	24.9
Portland, ME	2.6	2.8	2.8	3.1	3.3	8.7	9.3	10.9	10.9	10.9
Portland, OR	7.2	6.7	6.3	7.6	9.9	12.5	13.9	14.2	16.3	18.4
Providence, RI	(Z)	0.1	0.1	0.1	0.2	1.3	3.3	4.4	5.8	4.7
San Diego, CA	12.7	14.0	15.0	16.0	16.0	22.2	25.4	28.2	34.5	37.9
San Francisco, CA	58.3	38.2	36.6	41.4	43.3	68.6	54.9	61.8	69.2	68.4
San Juan, PR	4.8	9.7	9.7	11.8	14.9	11.8	19.1	19.4	20.5	21.1
Savannah, GA	15.9	21.6	24.6	27.9	33.5	26.1	38.4	47.6	54.2	59.9
Seattle, WA	40.4	43.5	48.9	65.2	74.0	40.5	43.2	51.0	54.1	57.9
St Albans, VT	4.5	3.6	4.2	3.6	3.3	9.4	10.5	12.6	11.3	10.9
St Louis, MO	1.3	0.7	1.3	1.7	2.1	7.9	9.1	10.1	11.1	12.0
Tampa, FL	4.8	7.5	10.0	12.7	13.5	14.7	15.4	19.7	25.5	22.9
Virgin Islands, U.S.	0.3	0.5	0.5	0.6	0.6	4.8	6.8	9.0	10.3	10.9
Washington, DC	2.8	2.8	3.7	5.2	5.4	2.6	3.3	3.7	7.3	6.9
Wilmington, NC	2.5	1.9	2.2	2.3	2.8	10.6	13.9	15.5	16.4	17.0

Z Less than $50 million. [1] Totals shown for exports reflect the value of estimated parcel post and Special Category shipments, and adjustments for undocumented exports to Canada are not distributed by coastal area or customs district. The value of bituminous coal exported through Norfolk, VA; Charleston, SC; and Mobile, AL, is reflected in the total but not distributed by district. [2] Excludes exports of bituminous coal.

Source: U.S. Census Bureau, U.S. Highlights of Export and Import Trade, series FT 990; U.S. Merchandise Trade: Selected Highlights, series FT 920; 1991–2004, U.S. Export History and U.S. Import History on compact disc; beginning 2005, U.S. Merchandise Trade: Selected Highlights, series FT920, December issues. See also <http://www.census.gov/foreign-trade/Press-Release/ft920_index.html>.

Table 1263. Export and Import Unit Value Indexes—Selected Countries: 2003 to 2007

[Indexes in U.S. dollars, 2000 = 100. A unit value is an implicit price derived from value and quantity data]

Country	Export unit value					Import unit value				
	2003	2004	2005	2006	2007	2003	2004	2005	2006	2007
United States	**99.7**	**103.6**	**106.9**	**110.7**	**116.1**	**96.9**	**102.3**	**110.0**	**115.4**	**120.2**
Australia	109.9	129.1	152.9	174.3	194.7	103.8	111.1	116.6	119.8	127.8
Belgium	120.4	134.9	142.0	149.1	(NA)	119.8	136.1	142.8	150.5	(NA)
Canada	103.8	117.1	130.2	139.7	150.2	101.9	105.5	112.7	120.7	125.1
France	130.7	127.3	126.6	127.1	138.7	118.7	122.5	121.7	124.3	136.8
Germany	118.3	128.9	129.7	134.8	(NA)	110.4	120.3	123.2	139.5	(NA)
Greece	133.4	154.1	160.1	168.2	186.8	(NA)	(NA)	(NA)	(NA)	(NA)
Ireland	114.7	115.4	119.1	118.2	(NA)	111.1	119.6	120.7	125.2	(NA)
Italy	129.6	148.6	158.3	170.3	(NA)	124.8	143.8	156.6	174.5	(NA)
Japan	90.9	96.1	96.1	93.9	94.8	93.1	103.9	115.4	124.3	132.1
Korea, South	85.1	91.5	92.7	92.4	93.8	95.6	107.3	117.3	126.3	133.6
Netherlands	115.9	126.3	133.1	139.4	(NA)	117.5	130.9	132.8	138.7	(NA)
Norway	104.3	126.8	160.9	193.4	216.5	116.1	126.5	132.4	138.9	158.2
Spain	120.1	133.4	139.9	147.8	(NA)	115.9	130.6	137.4	142.8	(NA)
Sweden	110.3	121.1	124.1	130.8	148.2	116.2	131.2	138.4	148.4	165.9
Switzerland	123.5	137.2	139.4	143.1	156.1	121.5	135.3	142.1	148.5	161.2
United Kingdom	108.0	121.5	125.5	130.9	144.1	103.6	115.6	119.6	125.5	138.3

NA Not available.
Source: International Monetary Fund, Washington, DC, *International Financial Statistics,* monthly, (copyright).

Table 1264. **U.S. Exports of Goods by State of Origin: 2000 to 2007**

[**In millions of dollars (782,429 represents $782,429,000,000), except as indicated.** Exports are on a f.a.s. value basis. Exports are based on origin of movement]

State and other area	2000	2006	2007 Total	2007 Rank	State and other area	2000	2006	2007 Total	2007 Rank
Total	782,429	1,036,635	1,162,479	(X)	Montana	541	900	1,134	48
					Nebraska	2,511	3,633	4,266	37
United States.	712,055	982,193	1,104,699	(X)	Nevada.	1,482	5,494	5,714	32
					New Hampshire	2,373	2,817	2,914	42
Alabama	7,317	13,899	14,407	24					
Alaska	2,464	4,046	4,010	39	New Jersey	18,638	27,231	30,836	9
Arizona	14,334	18,299	19,228	18	New Mexico.	2,391	2,895	2,585	44
Arkansas.	2,599	4,264	4,887	34	New York	42,846	59,132	71,116	3
California.	119,640	127,771	134,319	2	North Carolina	17,946	21,286	23,356	15
Colorado.	6,593	7,955	7,352	31	North Dakota	626	1,520	2,047	45
Connecticut	8,047	12,248	13,799	25	Ohio.	26,322	38,161	42,562	8
Delaware.	2,197	3,897	4,024	38	Oklahoma	3,072	4,395	4,579	36
District of Columbia. . .	1,003	1,040	1,082	(X)	Oregon	11,441	15,303	16,531	23
Florida	26,543	38,558	44,858	6	Pennsylvania	18,792	26,359	29,195	11
					Rhode Island	1,186	1,532	1,649	46
Georgia	14,925	20,113	23,366	14					
Hawaii	387	693	560	50	South Carolina	8,565	13,620	16,575	22
Idaho	3,559	3,727	4,703	35	South Dakota.	679	1,192	1,510	47
Illinois.	31,438	42,135	48,896	5	Tennessee.	11,592	21,648	21,865	16
Indiana	15,386	22,666	25,956	12	Texas	103,866	150,890	168,229	1
Iowa.	4,466	8,428	9,656	28	Utah.	3,221	6,801	7,815	30
Kansas.	5,145	8,636	10,277	27	Vermont	4,097	3,874	3,685	41
Kentucky.	9,612	17,254	19,652	17	Virginia	11,698	14,155	16,864	21
Louisiana	16,814	23,477	30,319	10	Washington	32,215	53,058	66,370	4
Maine.	1,779	2,642	2,750	43	West Virginia	2,219	3,240	3,987	40
					Wisconsin	10,508	17,174	18,825	19
Maryland.	4,593	7,600	8,949	29	Wyoming.	503	834	802	49
Massachusetts.	20,514	24,057	25,351	13					
Michigan	33,845	40,500	44,555	7	Puerto Rico	9,735	15,213	18,078	(X)
Minnesota	10,303	16,349	18,062	20	Virgin Islands	174	585	808	(X)
Mississippi.	2,726	4,484	5,184	33	Other [1]	60,810	36,176	38,894	(X)
Missouri	6,497	12,781	13,484	26	Timing adjustments .	−346	(X)	(X)	(X)

X Not applicable.   [1] Includes unreported, not specified, special category, estimated shipments, and re-exports.

Source: U.S. Census Bureau, *U.S. International Trade in Goods and Services,* series FT-900, December issues. See <http://www.census.gov/foreign-trade/Press-Release/2007pr/12/>; (released 13 February 2008).

Table 1265. **U.S. Agricultural Exports by State: 2000 to 2007**

[**In millions of dollars (50,762 represents $50,762,000,000).** For years ending September 30]

State	2000	2004	2005	2006	2007	State	2000	2004	2005	2006	2007
U.S.	50,762	62,409	62,516	68,593	81,947						
						NE	2,816	2,944	2,816	3,216	4,047
AL	401	558	564	568	616	NV	39	38	42	37	43
AK	2	3	3	3	4	NH.	14	17	15	17	19
AZ	391	442	417	464	506	NJ	150	188	192	220	245
AR	1,210	1,778	1,686	1,923	2,165						
CA	6,298	8,714	9,465	10,609	11,302	NM.	82	143	153	236	269
CO	894	748	714	806	1,119	NY	515	570	622	723	867
CT	140	88	84	98	116	NC	1,525	1,804	1,801	2,046	2,101
DE	127	130	134	134	160	ND	1,475	1,795	1,739	1,895	2,565
FL	1,469	1,578	1,542	1,619	1,892	OH	1,348	1,590	1,563	1,734	2,175
GA	908	1,105	1,125	1,328	1,469	OK	534	856	765	668	871
						OR	749	898	902	987	1,195
HI	81	89	95	93	88	PA	989	1,084	1,123	1,299	1,474
ID	803	884	898	932	1,179	RI	7	10	11	11	12
IL.	2,951	3,778	3,289	3,847	4,719	SC	333	424	382	467	436
IN	1,501	1,942	1,824	2,005	2,415						
IA	2,944	3,926	4,007	4,190	5,247	SD	1,094	1,321	1,233	1,096	1,850
KS	2,929	2,971	2,892	3,112	3,835	TN	561	833	816	927	770
KY	806	951	1,074	1,096	1,214	TX	2,877	3,876	3,622	3,624	5,199
LA	426	557	553	647	695	UT	246	237	249	290	344
ME	61	76	71	88	97	VT	14	26	16	35	47
MD	273	302	286	311	358	VA	490	584	575	561	622
						WA	1,595	1,808	1,943	2,202	2,649
MA	120	169	151	204	201	WV	36	37	39	40	46
MI	813	904	934	1,080	1,237	WI	1,283	1,325	1,518	1,716	2,102
MN.	2,230	2,523	2,770	2,926	3,582	WY	48	44	50	51	61
MS.	571	1,027	916	943	1,134						
MO	1,204	1,552	1,249	1,489	2,064	Unallo-					
MT.	319	557	583	555	723	cated	2,072	2,605	3,007	3,423	3,807

Source: U.S. Dept. of Agriculture, Economic Research Service, "State Export Data"; published 29 June 2008. See <http://www.ers.usda.gov/data/stateexports/>.

Table 1266. U.S. Exports, Imports, and Merchandise Trade Balance, by Country: 2003 to 2007

[In millions of dollars (724,771 represents $724,771,000,000). Includes silver ore and bullion. Country totals include exports of special category commodities, if any. Data include nonmonetary gold and include trade of Virgin Islands with foreign countries. For methodology, see Foreign Trade Statistics in Appendix III. Minus sign (−) denotes an excess of imports over exports]

Country	Exports, domestic and foreign					General imports					Merchandise trade balance				
	2003	2004	2005	2006	2007	2003	2004	2005	2006	2007	2003	2004	2005	2006	2007
Total [1]	724,771	818,775	905,978	1,036,635	1,162,479	1,257,121	1,469,704	1,673,455	1,853,938	1,956,962	−532,350	−650,930	−767,477	−817,304	−794,483
Afghanistan	61	150	262	417	495	56	25	67	45	74	5	126	195	372	421
Albania	10	20	18	28	34	4	11	37	24	10	5	9	−19	4	25
Algeria	487	972	1,167	1,102	1,652	4,748	7,410	10,446	15,456	17,816	−4,261	−6,438	−9,279	−14,354	−16,164
Angola	491	594	929	1,550	1,280	4,267	4,521	8,484	11,719	12,508	−3,776	−3,927	−7,555	−10,169	−11,228
Anguilla	22	21	32	43	93	1	1	4	4	5	20	20	28	39	88
Antigua and Barbuda	127	126	190	194	240	13	4	4	6	9	115	121	186	188	232
Argentina	2,437	3,388	4,122	4,776	5,856	3,170	3,746	4,584	3,979	4,487	−733	−357	−462	797	1,369
Armenia	103	91	66	80	111	38	46	46	47	33	65	45	19	34	78
Aruba	355	384	559	511	529	955	1,776	2,920	2,845	2,995	−600	−1,392	−2,361	−2,335	−2,466
Australia	13,088	14,225	15,828	17,779	19,212	6,414	7,546	7,342	8,204	8,615	6,674	6,680	8,486	9,575	10,597
Austria	1,768	1,946	2,593	2,986	3,172	4,492	5,798	6,103	8,304	10,669	−2,724	−3,853	−3,510	−5,318	−7,497
Azerbaijan	120	159	133	231	178	10	45	45	716	1,887	110	121	87	−485	−1,710
Bahamas, The	1,075	1,186	1,787	2,282	2,468	479	638	700	453	504	595	548	1,087	1,830	1,965
Bahrain	508	302	351	475	591	378	405	432	632	625	130	−104	−81	−158	−33
Bangladesh	226	289	320	333	456	2,074	2,303	2,693	3,271	3,432	−1,848	−2,013	−2,373	−2,938	−2,976
Barbados	300	348	395	443	457	43	37	32	34	38	257	312	363	409	419
Belarus	84	33	35	75	102	215	336	345	539	1,033	−131	−303	−310	−465	−932
Belgium	15,236	16,871	18,691	21,340	25,290	10,141	12,446	13,023	14,405	15,281	5,095	4,425	5,668	6,935	10,009
Belize	199	152	218	239	234	101	107	98	147	105	97	45	119	92	129
Benin	30	46	72	116	289	1	2	1	1	5	30	44	72	115	284
Bermuda	401	472	491	638	660	15	25	87	16	24	386	447	403	622	636
Bolivia	183	194	220	215	278	185	260	293	362	363	−2	−67	−74	−147	−85
Bosnia and Herzegovina	21	28	18	52	20	12	11	71	26	25	9	17	−53	26	−5
Botswana	26	54	67	27	54	14	74	178	252	188	12	−19	−111	−225	−134
Brazil	11,211	13,897	15,372	19,231	24,626	17,910	21,160	24,436	26,367	25,644	−6,699	−7,263	−9,064	−7,136	−1,019
Brunei	38	48	50	48	140	423	406	563	550	405	−385	−358	−513	−502	−265
Bulgaria	156	172	268	293	306	441	507	454	458	426	−286	−335	−186	−165	−120
Cambodia	58	59	70	75	139	1,262	1,497	1,767	2,188	2,463	−1,204	−1,439	−1,697	−2,114	−2,325
Cameroon	91	100	117	120	133	214	308	158	273	297	−123	−209	−41	−153	−164
Canada	169,924	189,880	211,899	230,656	248,888	221,595	256,360	290,384	302,438	317,057	−51,671	−66,480	−78,486	−71,782	−68,169
Cayman Islands	309	400	681	632	640	13	15	54	15	21	297	387	627	617	619
Chad	64	41	54	61	66	23	756	1,498	1,918	2,145	42	−715	−1,444	−1,857	−2,079
Chile	2,715	3,606	5,223	6,786	8,315	3,705	4,732	6,664	9,565	8,999	−990	−1,126	−1,442	−2,779	−684
China [2]	28,368	34,744	41,925	55,186	65,236	152,436	196,682	243,470	287,774	321,443	−124,068	−161,938	−201,545	−232,589	−256,207
Colombia	3,756	4,505	5,462	6,709	8,558	6,385	7,256	8,849	9,266	9,434	−2,629	−2,751	−3,387	−2,557	−876
Congo (Brazzaville) [3]	79	66	104	138	140	433	858	1,623	3,097	3,071	−354	−792	−1,519	−2,959	−2,931
Congo (Kinshasa) [3]	31	67	65	71	113	175	124	264	85	207	−144	−57	−199	−14	−94
Costa Rica	3,414	3,306	3,599	4,132	4,581	3,364	3,333	3,415	3,844	3,942	49	−27	183	288	639
Cote d'Ivoire	103	118	124	148	162	490	715	1,198	702	600	−387	−597	−1,074	−554	−439
Croatia	197	130	159	147	247	181	291	364	353	332	16	−161	−206	−207	−85
Cuba	259	404	369	341	447	−	−	−	−	−	259	400	369	340	447
Cyprus	212	96	84	240	169	25	26	31	51	17	187	70	54	189	152
Czech Republic	672	827	1,054	1,123	1,262	1,394	1,756	2,193	2,349	2,431	−722	−929	−1,139	−1,227	−1,168

See footnotes at end of table.

Table 1266. **U.S. Exports, Imports, and Merchandise Trade Balance, by Country: 2003 to 2007**—Con.

[See headnote, page 790]

Country	Exports, domestic and foreign					General imports					Merchandise trade balance				
	2003	2004	2005	2006	2007	2003	2004	2005	2006	2007	2003	2004	2005	2006	2007
Denmark	1,548	2,147	1,918	2,269	2,930	3,708	3,876	5,144	5,540	6,064	-2,161	-1,730	-3,226	-3,272	-3,135
Djibouti	32	44	48	48	59	1	1	3	3	5	31	43	47	44	54
Dominica	34	36	62	68	84	5	3	3	3	2	29	33	58	65	82
Dominican Republic	4,205	4,358	4,719	5,351	6,084	4,455	4,527	4,604	4,532	4,216	-250	-169	115	818	1,869
Ecuador	1,447	1,669	1,964	2,727	2,936	2,722	4,283	5,759	7,094	6,135	-1,275	-2,615	-3,795	-4,367	-3,199
Egypt	2,607	3,078	3,159	4,133	5,347	1,143	1,284	2,091	2,396	2,377	1,464	1,794	1,068	1,737	2,970
El Salvador	1,821	1,868	1,854	2,152	2,313	2,020	2,052	1,989	1,857	2,044	-199	-185	-135	295	270
Equatorial Guinea	336	215	282	552	236	904	1,170	1,561	1,733	1,777	-568	-955	-1,280	-1,182	-1,541
Estonia	121	134	145	221	242	182	393	511	526	296	-61	-259	-366	-305	-54
Ethiopia	409	355	510	137	168	31	41	62	81	88	379	314	448	56	79
Fiji	20	25	28	33	30	175	214	170	146	153	-156	-188	-141	-113	-123
Finland	1,713	2,069	2,254	2,648	3,133	3,602	3,887	4,342	4,974	5,266	-1,889	-1,818	-2,088	-2,326	-2,133
France	17,053	21,263	22,410	24,217	27,413	29,219	31,606	33,842	37,040	41,553	-12,166	-10,342	-11,432	-12,822	-14,140
French Guiana	156	228	27	33	31	3			1	—	152	228	27	33	31
French Polynesia	92	93	112	108	124	48	67	60	58	62	44	26	52	50	62
Gabon	63	93	99	135	478	1,970	2,467	2,816	1,361	2,182	-1,907	-2,374	-2,717	-1,226	-1,704
Georgia	131	227	214	264	364	54	78	194	105	212	77	149	20	158	153
Germany	28,832	31,416	34,184	41,319	49,651	68,113	77,266	84,751	89,082	94,164	-39,281	-45,850	-50,567	-47,763	-44,513
Ghana	209	310	337	290	416	82	145	158	192	199	127	164	179	97	218
Gibraltar	14	138	163	286	594	3	2	5		3	11	136	159	285	591
Greece	2,507	2,063	1,192	1,555	2,110	614	724	884	966	1,192	1,893	1,340	309	589	918
Grenada	68	70	82	74	83	8	5	6	5	8	61	65	77	70	75
Guadeloupe	46	38	55	65	139	3	3	2		5	43	35	52	63	134
Guatemala	2,263	2,551	2,835	3,511	4,065	2,947	3,154	3,137	3,102	3,026	-683	-603	-302	409	1,039
Guinea	36	59	94	65	74	69	64	75	94	99	-33	-5	19	-29	-26
Guyana	117	138	177	179	188	119	122	120	125	123	-2	16	57	54	65
Haiti	639	673	710	817	680	332	371	447	496	488	307	302	262	321	192
Honduras	2,826	3,078	3,254	3,687	4,461	3,313	3,640	3,749	3,718	3,912	-486	-562	-495	-30	549
Hong Kong	13,521	15,827	16,351	17,776	20,118	8,851	9,314	8,892	7,947	7,026	4,669	6,514	7,459	9,829	13,092
Hungary	933	1,143	1,023	1,188	1,292	2,701	2,573	2,561	2,584	2,828	-1,767	-1,430	-1,538	-1,397	-1,536
Iceland	242	309	512	366	630	282	274	269	228	206	-40	35	243	138	424
India	4,980	6,109	7,989	10,056	17,589	13,055	15,572	18,804	21,831	24,073	-8,076	-9,463	-10,815	-11,775	-6,485
Indonesia	2,516	2,671	3,054	3,079	4,235	9,515	10,811	12,014	13,425	14,301	-6,999	-8,139	-8,960	-10,346	-10,067
Iran	99	85	96	86	145	161	152	175	157	173	-62	-67	-79	-71	-28
Iraq	310	857	1,374	1,491	1,560	4,585	8,514	9,054	11,546	11,396	-4,275	-7,657	-7,680	-10,055	-9,835
Ireland	7,696	8,167	9,336	8,516	9,009	25,747	27,448	28,733	28,526	30,445	-18,051	-19,281	-19,397	-20,010	-21,436
Israel	6,892	9,169	9,737	10,965	13,019	12,769	14,552	16,831	19,167	20,794	-5,877	-5,382	-7,093	-8,202	-7,775
Italy	10,561	10,685	11,524	12,546	14,150	25,414	28,097	31,009	32,655	35,028	-14,854	-17,413	-19,485	-20,109	-20,878
Jamaica	1,470	1,431	1,701	2,036	2,316	423	320	376	528	720	1,047	1,111	1,325	1,508	1,596
Japan	52,004	54,243	55,485	59,613	62,704	118,037	129,805	138,004	148,181	145,463	-66,032	-75,562	-82,519	-88,568	-82,760
Jordan	492	552	644	650	856	674	1,093	1,267	1,422	1,329	-181	-542	-623	-772	-473
Kazakhstan	168	320	538	646	753	393	539	1,101	961	1,252	-224	-218	-563	-314	-499
Kenya	197	394	633	526	578	249	352	348	354	325	-53	42	285	172	253
Korea, South	24,073	26,413	27,765	32,442	34,645	37,229	46,168	43,781	45,804	47,562	-13,157	-19,755	-16,016	-13,362	-12,918

See footnotes at end of table.

U.S. Census Bureau, Statistical Abstract of the United States: 2009

Country	Exports, domestic and foreign					General imports					Merchandise trade balance				
	2003	2004	2005	2006	2007	2003	2004	2005	2006	2007	2003	2004	2005	2006	2007
Kuwait	1,507	1,519	1,975	2,087	2,484	2,277	3,231	4,335	3,981	4,119	-770	-1,712	-2,360	-1,894	-1,635
Kyrgyzstan	39	29	31	71	49	11	11	5	4	2	28	19	27	67	47
Latvia	124	121	178	246	381	377	365	362	299	334	-254	-244	-185	-53	47
Lebanon	314	464	466	931	826	92	75	86	89	104	222	390	379	842	722
Lesotho	5	6	4	4	8	393	467	404	408	443	-388	-461	-400	-404	-436
Liberia	33	61	69	68	76	60	84	91	140	115	-26	-23	-22	-72	-39
Libya	—	39	84	435	511	—	332	1,590	2,472	3,385	—	-292	-1,507	-2,037	-2,874
Liechtenstein	16	11	20	16	16	262	286	296	324	284	246	-276	-276	-309	-268
Lithuania	162	295	390	567	720	347	482	634	570	456	-185	-187	-244	-4	265
Luxembourg	279	705	782	581	1,001	265	290	389	534	526	14	414	394	47	475
Macau	55	86	102	200	226	1,356	1,487	1,249	1,230	1,095	-1,301	-1,401	-1,147	-1,030	-869
Macedonia	26	21	32	22	34	61	78	48	42	73	-35	-57	-17	-20	-39
Madagascar	46	36	28	45	32	384	470	324	281	338	-337	-434	-295	-236	-306
Malawi	17	22	28	46	52	77	61	116	60	59	-60	-39	-88	-14	-8
Malaysia	10,914	10,921	10,461	12,544	11,680	25,440	28,179	33,685	36,533	32,629	-14,526	-17,258	-23,224	-23,989	-20,948
Mali	31	43	43	43	32	2	4	4	8	10	29	39	29	35	22
Malta	202	181	194	163	207	373	383	283	371	329	-171	-202	-89	-208	-122
Martinique	22	28	35	32	194	1	2	22	42	7	21	26	13	-9	187
Mauritania	35	34	86	90	103	1	7	1	51	1	34	27	85	39	102
Mauritius	32	28	31	36	50	298	270	222	219	187	-266	-242	-191	-183	-138
Mexico	97,412	110,835	120,365	133,979	136,092	138,060	155,902	170,109	198,253	210,714	-40,648	-45,067	-49,744	-64,274	-74,622
Moldova	25	40	40	30	53	43	49	50	50	23	-18	-10	-10	-7	30
Monaco	50	18	17	34	43	22	23	38	32	21	29	-5	-21	2	21
Mongolia	21	28	22	23	26	183	239	144	114	84	-163	-211	-122	-91	-58
Morocco	469	526	525	878	1,343	385	515	446	521	610	83	11	79	357	733
Mozambique	62	77	63	64	115	8	11	12	16	5	54	66	51	49	110
Namibia	28	75	112	127	128	123	238	130	116	220	-95	-164	-17	11	-92
Nepal	16	25	25	17	29	171	143	111	99	90	-155	-118	-87	-83	-61
Netherlands	20,695	24,289	26,485	31,129	32,963	10,953	12,451	14,862	17,342	18,403	9,742	11,839	11,623	13,787	14,560
Netherlands Antilles	747	824	1,138	1,485	2,082	632	435	922	1,119	782	115	390	215	366	1,300
New Caledonia	43	45	38	44	58	13	19	27	51	79	31	26	11	-7	-22
New Zealand	1,848	2,073	2,652	2,929	2,814	2,403	2,968	3,155	3,116	3,113	-555	-895	-503	-188	-299
Nicaragua	502	592	626	752	890	770	990	1,181	1,526	1,604	-268	-398	-555	-774	-714
Niger	34	34	79	129	69	4	27	66	124	10	30	7	13	5	60
Nigeria	1,017	1,554	1,621	2,234	2,778	10,394	16,249	24,239	27,863	32,770	-9,377	-14,694	-22,618	-25,630	-29,992
Norway	1,466	1,604	1,942	2,394	3,062	5,232	6,509	6,776	7,085	7,318	-3,766	-4,904	-4,834	-4,691	-4,256
Oman	322	330	595	829	1,059	695	418	555	909	1,041	-372	-88	40	-80	18
Pakistan	843	1,814	1,252	1,989	2,035	2,531	2,875	3,253	3,672	3,578	-1,688	-1,061	-2,002	-1,683	-1,543
Panama	1,849	1,835	2,162	2,701	3,740	301	316	327	379	365	1,547	1,519	1,835	2,322	3,375
Papua New Guinea	30	43	55	44	66	66	54	59	84	109	-36	-12	-3	-40	-43
Paraguay	484	623	896	911	1,237	53	59	52	58	68	430	564	844	853	1,169
Peru	1,699	2,101	2,309	2,927	4,120	2,409	3,702	5,119	5,880	5,272	-710	-1,601	-2,810	-2,954	-1,152
Philippines	7,987	7,087	6,895	7,617	7,712	10,059	9,137	9,250	9,694	9,408	-2,072	-2,050	-2,355	-2,077	-1,696
Poland	758	929	1,268	1,961	3,123	1,324	1,822	1,949	2,253	2,226	-566	-892	-681	-292	897
Portugal	863	1,046	1,132	1,471	2,479	1,967	2,243	2,329	3,060	3,049	-1,105	-1,197	-1,197	-1,590	-571
Qatar	408	455	987	1,279	2,757	331	387	448	262	477	76	68	539	1,017	2,280
Romania	367	525	609	554	677	730	853	1,208	1,119	1,054	-363	-328	-599	-565	-378

See footnotes at end of table.

U.S. Census Bureau, Statistical Abstract of the United States: 2009

Table 1266. U.S. Exports, Imports, and Merchandise Trade Balance, by Country: 2003 to 2007—Con.

[See headnote, page 790]

Country	Exports, domestic and foreign					General imports					Merchandise trade balance				
	2003	2004	2005	2006	2007	2003	2004	2005	2006	2007	2003	2004	2005	2006	2007
Russia	2,447	2,961	3,962	4,701	7,365	8,618	11,891	15,307	19,828	19,314	-6,171	-8,930	-11,344	-15,127	-11,949
Saudi Arabia	4,596	5,257	6,813	7,640	10,396	18,069	20,959	27,193	31,689	35,626	-13,473	-15,702	-20,380	-24,050	-25,230
Senegal	102	89	159	97	150	5	3	4	21	19	97	86	155	76	132
Serbia and Montenegro [4]	50	143	133	147	155	15	92	55	68	64	35	51	78	79	91
Sierra Leone	28	41	38	39	55	7	11	9	36	48	22	30	29	3	7
Singapore	16,560	19,609	20,642	24,684	26,284	15,138	15,370	15,110	17,768	18,394	1,422	4,238	5,532	6,916	7,891
Slovakia	115	132	150	510	680	1,009	1,211	961	1,405	1,505	-894	-1,080	-811	-895	-825
Slovenia	140	192	234	239	297	484	510	413	483	488	-345	-318	-179	-244	-192
South Africa	2,819	3,179	3,907	4,462	5,521	4,624	5,945	5,886	7,501	9,054	-1,805	-2,766	-1,979	-3,039	-3,533
Spain	5,930	6,638	6,914	7,426	9,862	6,677	7,350	8,615	9,778	10,498	-747	-712	-1,701	-2,352	-636
Sri Lanka	155	164	198	237	227	1,808	1,957	2,083	2,146	2,065	-1,653	-1,793	-1,885	-1,909	-1,838
St. Kitts and Nevis	59	60	94	127	111	45	42	50	50	54	14	19	44	77	57
St. Lucia	120	105	135	149	165	13	14	32	30	33	107	91	103	119	132
St. Vincent and the Grenadines	46	46	45	58	69	4	4	16	2	1	42	41	30	56	68
Sudan	26	68	108	77	79	3	4	14	6	8	23	65	95	71	72
Suriname	193	179	246	259	304	140	141	165	165	130	53	38	80	94	174
Swaziland	8	12	12	12	29	162	199	199	156	145	-154	-186	-187	-144	-116
Sweden	3,223	3,267	3,715	4,126	4,494	11,119	12,683	13,821	13,870	13,024	-7,896	-9,416	-10,106	-9,745	-8,530
Switzerland	8,656	9,280	10,720	14,375	17,039	10,685	11,628	13,000	14,230	14,760	-2,029	-2,348	-2,280	145	2,279
Syria [2]	214	213	155	224	361	246	268	324	214	111	-32	-55	-169	11	251
Taiwan [2]	17,448	21,744	22,069	23,047	26,309	31,599	34,624	34,826	38,212	38,278	-14,152	-12,879	-12,757	-15,165	-11,968
Tajikistan	50	56	29	43	7	7	7	241	35	46	43	48	-212	-18	53
Tanzania	65	128	96	161	174	24	24	34	35	46	41	103	63	126	128
Thailand	5,835	6,368	7,257	8,147	8,455	15,179	17,579	19,890	22,466	22,755	-9,343	-11,211	-12,633	-14,320	-14,300
Togo	15	24	28	108	288	6	2	6	4	5	9	22	22	105	283
Trinidad and Tobago	1,063	1,208	1,417	1,615	1,780	4,334	5,842	7,891	8,362	8,790	-3,271	-4,635	-6,474	-6,748	-7,010
Tunisia	171	258	261	363	403	102	209	264	470	458	68	49	-3	-107	-55
Turkey	2,900	3,362	4,269	5,724	6,590	3,788	4,934	5,182	5,359	4,601	-888	-1,572	-913	365	1,989
Turkmenistan	34	295	237	113	185	76	81	135	76	219	-42	-214	102	37	-34
Turks and Caicos Islands	72	137	238	366	396	6	7	9	12	13	66	130	228	354	383
Uganda	42	63	63	51	80	35	26	26	22	27	7	38	37	29	54
Ukraine	231	399	533	756	1,342	262	800	1,098	1,640	1,220	-32	-400	-565	-884	122
United Arab Emirates	3,508	4,086	8,482	11,648	11,605	1,128	1,143	1,468	1,385	1,338	2,380	2,943	7,014	10,263	10,267
United Kingdom	33,828	36,000	38,588	45,410	50,229	42,795	46,274	51,033	53,513	56,858	-8,967	-10,274	-12,445	-8,103	-6,629
Uruguay	327	326	357	482	641	256	580	732	512	492	71	-254	-376	-30	149
Uzbekistan	256	230	74	54	89	84	88	96	152	165	173	142	-22	-98	-76
Venezuela	2,831	4,767	6,421	9,002	10,201	17,136	24,921	33,978	37,134	39,910	-14,305	-20,153	-27,557	-28,132	-29,709
Vietnam	1,324	1,164	1,193	1,100	1,903	4,555	5,275	6,631	8,567	10,633	-3,231	-4,111	-5,438	-7,466	-8,730
Virgin Islands, British	71	97	125	217	176	35	17	34	26	43	36	79	91	191	133
Yemen	191	232	219	255	66	62	279	447	125	171	129	-47	-228	130	-105
Zambia	20	26	29	52	69	13	33	32	28	49	7	-7	-3	23	21
Zimbabwe	42	47	46	48	105	57	76	94	103	73	-15	-29	-48	-56	33

- Represents or rounds to zero. [1] Includes timing adjustment and unidentified countries not shown separately. [2] See footnote 2, Table 1288. [3] See footnote 3, Table 1288. [4] See footnote 3, Table 1339.

Source: U.S. Census Bureau, U.S. International Trade in Goods and Services, Series FT-900(07-04), and previous final reports. See also <http://www.census.gov/foreign-trade/Press-Release/2007pr/final_revisions/>; (released 10 June 2008).

Table 1267. U.S. Exports and General Imports by Selected SITC Commodity Groups: 2000 to 2007

[In millions of dollars (781,918 represents $781,918,000,000). SITC = Standard International Trade Classification. For methodology, see Foreign Trade Statistics in Appendix III. N.e.s. = not elsewhere specified]

Selected commodities	Exports [1]				General imports [2]			
	2000	2005	2006	2007	2000	2005	2006	2007
Total.....................	781,918	905,978	1,036,635	1,162,479	1,218,022	1,673,455	1,853,938	1,956,962
Agricultural commodities [3]	**51,296**	**63,139**	**70,912**	**89,921**	**39,186**	**59,530**	**65,459**	**72,067**
Animal feeds................	3,780	4,029	4,534	5,506	597	699	828	1,008
Cereal flour.................	1,310	2,015	2,339	2,839	1,753	3,010	3,357	3,774
Corn......................	4,695	5,062	7,251	10,095	160	125	179	257
Cotton, raw and linters.........	1,893	3,929	4,514	4,589	28	20	15	14
Meat and preparations.........	7,004	6,669	7,257	9,131	3,841	5,747	5,231	5,355
Soybeans	5,284	6,282	6,949	10,002	31	63	56	97
Vegetables and fruits..........	7,477	10,259	11,071	12,125	9,286	14,082	15,455	17,671
Wheat.....................	3,374	4,410	4,205	8,328	229	174	311	501
Manufactured goods [3]..........	**625,894**	**685,398**	**785,599**	**868,297**	**1,012,855**	**1,287,376**	**1,416,302**	**1,479,971**
ADP equipment, office machinery ..	46,595	29,800	31,091	29,914	92,133	98,584	106,416	101,602
Airplane parts...............	15,062	17,538	20,515	21,666	5,572	5,592	6,771	8,434
Airplanes..................	24,777	30,291	43,933	51,854	12,412	10,734	10,604	13,286
Alcoholic beverages, distilled......	424	726	844	984	2,946	4,360	4,912	5,521
Aluminum	3,780	4,483	5,596	5,806	6,949	11,931	14,919	13,947
Artwork/antiques.............	1,387	1,858	3,250	4,335	5,864	5,512	6,633	8,740
Basketware, etc	3,309	5,612	6,200	6,995	4,840	8,585	9,093	10,810
Chemicals, cosmetics	5,292	8,059	9,100	10,120	3,539	7,922	8,333	8,872
Chemicals, dyeing............	4,089	4,901	5,337	5,807	2,667	2,971	3,054	3,115
Chemicals, fertilizers	2,249	2,990	2,941	3,339	1,684	3,701	3,438	4,981
Chemicals, inorganic..........	5,359	7,698	9,074	10,807	6,108	10,165	11,414	13,349
Chemicals, medicinal..........	12,893	25,012	28,431	32,755	14,685	39,176	45,746	53,798
Chemicals, n.e.s.............	12,264	15,846	17,860	20,730	5,725	8,939	9,477	10,851
Chemicals, organic	17,990	26,765	29,839	33,869	28,578	38,009	42,212	42,178
Chemicals, plastics	19,519	28,861	32,617	37,129	10,647	17,385	18,813	18,248
Clothing	8,191	4,129	3,849	3,209	64,296	76,383	79,149	81,176
Copper	1,425	2,118	3,266	3,489	4,471	7,040	12,888	11,532
Cork, wood, lumber...........	4,320	4,038	4,273	4,412	8,227	10,939	10,386	8,282
Crude fertilizers	1,724	1,702	1,947	2,009	1,401	1,698	1,825	1,854
Electrical machinery	89,917	74,286	83,228	81,452	108,747	99,121	109,721	113,613
Fish and preparations	2,806	3,864	4,012	4,044	9,907	11,915	13,176	13,519
Footwear..................	663	508	572	578	14,842	17,932	19,160	19,408
Furniture and bedding	4,744	4,415	4,877	5,123	18,923	30,633	32,788	33,853
Gem diamonds..............	1,289	2,578	3,884	5,305	12,068	16,238	17,285	18,937
General industrial machinery.....	33,094	38,902	44,089	48,641	34,667	52,333	59,710	63,940
Glass	2,502	2,696	3,041	3,350	2,248	2,782	2,956	2,885
Gold, nonmonetary...........	5,898	5,533	8,790	13,344	2,657	4,430	5,633	4,670
Iron and steel mill products......	5,715	10,430	11,799	14,018	15,807	24,632	32,904	30,890
Jewelry...................	1,574	3,029	4,033	4,538	6,459	9,696	11,222	11,193
Lighting, plumbing...........	1,384	1,694	1,868	2,090	5,104	7,591	8,069	8,111
Metal manufactures, n.e.s.	13,453	13,510	15,860	17,315	16,204	24,777	27,893	29,929
Metal ores; scrap	4,234	11,057	16,617	22,999	3,817	5,335	6,533	7,549
Metalworking machinery.........	6,191	6,457	8,228	5,351	7,726	7,530	8,644	7,723
Nickel....................	401	752	1,038	1,379	1,425	2,178	3,348	4,903
Optical goods...............	3,246	3,076	3,173	3,210	4,019	3,789	4,378	4,698
Paper and paperboard.........	10,640	11,457	12,337	13,480	15,185	17,561	18,503	17,913
Photographic equipment........	4,236	3,343	3,590	3,612	6,896	4,481	4,506	2,760
Plastic articles, n.e.s...........	7,607	8,036	8,915	9,427	8,034	13,633	14,823	15,348
Platinum	888	610	1,739	1,615	5,566	3,916	5,833	7,716
Power generating machinery......	32,743	41,296	44,036	49,933	33,773	41,263	44,742	50,191
Printed materials.............	4,776	5,445	5,748	6,190	3,680	4,917	5,142	5,548
Pulp and waste paper	4,576	5,093	5,738	6,906	3,381	3,049	3,181	3,734
Records/magnetic media	5,395	5,142	4,912	5,088	5,172	7,258	7,095	7,382
Rubber articles, n.e.s.	1,673	1,598	1,787	1,953	1,962	2,925	3,039	3,212
Rubber tires and tubes	2,379	2,778	3,007	3,517	4,785	7,725	8,662	9,380
Scientific instruments...........	30,984	34,544	39,278	42,315	22,007	30,242	32,297	35,604
Ships, boats...............	1,070	1,913	2,575	3,062	1,178	1,719	1,548	1,921
Specialized industrial machinery ...	30,959	33,144	37,469	48,357	22,711	31,076	33,010	35,761
Television, VCR, etc...........	27,921	20,974	22,515	24,735	70,468	104,079	115,327	129,796
Textile yarn, fabric...........	10,534	11,830	12,106	11,861	15,171	21,249	22,184	22,759
Toys/games/sporting goods.......	3,609	3,756	4,172	5,039	20,011	25,069	26,547	31,807
Travel goods	351	379	461	436	4,430	6,183	6,882	7,625
Vehicles	57,421	71,747	83,472	95,187	161,544	195,926	211,946	210,431
Watches/clocks/parts..........	348	256	304	392	3,481	3,939	4,082	4,454
Wood manufactures...........	1,842	1,818	2,007	2,125	7,228	12,847	12,539	10,390
Mineral fuel [3]	**13,179**	**26,488**	**34,711**	**41,725**	**135,367**	**289,723**	**332,500**	**364,987**
Coal.....................	2,162	3,471	3,663	4,288	805	2,418	2,639	2,451
Crude oil..................	463	595	853	1,015	89,876	182,944	225,156	245,771
Petroleum preparations	5,746	14,782	22,078	26,522	25,673	59,698	66,197	74,108
Liquified propane/butane	663	587	805	1,048	1,508	4,371	4,419	4,024
Natural gas	411	3,094	2,226	3,130	12,594	34,911	28,268	31,938
Mineral fuels, other mineral.......	3,734	3,191	4,435	4,708	4,911	3,055	3,942	3,717
Reexports..................	68,203	101,125	108,070	117,177	(X)	(X)	(X)	(X)

X Not applicable.   [1] F.a.s. basis. Exports by commodity are only for domestic exports.   [2] Customs value basis.   [3] Includes other commodities not shown separately.

Source: U.S. Census Bureau, *U.S. International Trade in Goods and Services*, Series FT-900(07-04), and previous final reports. See also <http://www.census.gov/foreign-trade/Press-Release/2007pr/final_revisions/>; (released 10 June 2008).

Table 1268. **United States Total and Aerospace Foreign Trade: 1990 to 2006**

[In millions of dollars (–101,718 represents –$101,718,000,000), except percent. Data are reported as exports of domestic merchandise, including Department of Defense shipments and undocumented exports to Canada, f.a.s. (free alongside ship) basis, and imports for consumption, customs value basis. Minus sign (–) indicates deficit]

Year	Merchandise trade			Aerospace trade						
						Exports				
								Civil		
	Trade balance	Imports	Exports	Trade balance	Imports	Total	Percent of U.S. exports	Total	Trans-ports	Military
1990	–101,718	495,311	393,592	27,282	11,801	39,083	9.9	31,517	16,691	7,566
1991	–66,723	488,453	421,730	30,785	13,003	43,788	10.4	35,548	20,881	8,239
1992	–84,501	532,665	448,164	31,356	13,662	45,018	10.0	36,906	22,379	8,111
1993	–115,568	580,659	465,091	27,235	12,183	39,418	8.5	31,823	18,146	7,596
1994	–150,630	663,256	512,626	25,010	12,363	37,373	7.3	30,050	15,931	7,322
1995	–158,801	743,543	584,742	21,562	11,509	33,071	5.7	25,079	10,606	7,991
1996	–170,214	795,289	625,075	26,602	13,668	40,270	6.4	29,477	13,624	10,792
1997	–180,522	869,704	689,182	32,240	18,134	50,374	7.3	40,075	21,028	10,299
1998	–229,758	911,896	682,138	40,961	23,110	64,071	9.4	51,999	29,168	12,072
1999	–328,821	1,024,618	695,797	37,381	25,063	62,444	9.0	50,624	25,694	11,820
2000	–436,104	1,218,022	781,918	26,735	27,944	54,679	7.0	45,566	19,615	9,113
2001	–411,899	1,140,999	729,100	26,035	32,473	58,508	8.0	49,371	22,151	9,137
2002	–468,263	1,161,366	693,103	29,514	27,241	56,775	8.2	47,348	21,661	9,427
2003	–532,350	1,257,121	724,771	27,111	25,393	52,504	7.2	44,060	19,434	8,445
2004	–650,930	1,469,704	818,775	31,002	25,815	56,817	6.9	47,325	18,577	9,492
2005	–767,477	1,673,455	905,978	39,783	27,649	67,433	7.4	57,225	21,888	10,207
2006	–817,304	1,853,938	1,036,635	54,809	30,453	85,262	8.2	71,857	32,897	13,404

Source: Aerospace Industries Association of America, Washington, DC, *Aerospace Facts and Figures,* annual.

Table 1269. **U.S. High Technology Exports by Industry and Selected Major Country: 2000 to 2007**

[In billions of dollars (222.5 represents $222,500,000,000)]

Selected industries	2000	2006	2007	Selected countries	2000	2006	2007
Total exports	222.5	220.2	214.1	Total exports	222.5	220.2	214.1
Computers and office equipment. . .	57.8	49.7	47.0	Canada	34.4	30.1	28.8
Consumer electronics	10.0	11.0	8.8	China [1]	4.6	14.1	14.5
Communications equipment	26.9	27.3	29.7	Japan	19.9	13.9	11.9
Electronic components	22.1	17.4	17.5	Korea, South	12.1	10.6	8.9
Semiconductors	60.0	52.4	49.8	Malaysia	7.8	8.5	7.4
Industrial electronics	30.5	40.4	38.9	Mexico	30.0	29.6	26.4
Electromedical equipment	8.1	15.3	16.6	Taiwan [1]	10.4	8.9	8.4
Photonics	7.1	6.6	5.9	European Union 27	51.5	46.1	46.3

[1] See footnote 2, Table 1288.

Source: AeA (formerly the American Electronics Association), *Cyberstates 2008,* annual (copyright). See <http://www.aeanet.org>.

Table 1270. **U.S. Exporting Companies Profile by Employment-Size Class: 2000 and 2006**

[(668,310 represents $668,310,000,000.) Based on data from export trade documents and the Business Register. For information on data limitations, see the Techical Documentation in the source]

Employment-size class	Number of exporters		Known export value [1] (mil. dol.)		Percent of—			
					Number of exporters		Known export value	
	2000	2006	2000	2006	2000	2006	2000	2006
All companies, total . . .	246,452	245,945	668,310	910,465	100.0	100.0	100.0	100.0
No employees	74,772	76,115	47,024	63,022	30.3	30.9	7.0	6.9
1 to 19 employees	96,268	101,254	45,272	61,850	39.1	41.2	6.8	6.8
20 to 49 employees	31,362	30,178	21,262	30,714	12.7	12.3	3.2	3.4
50 to 99 employees	16,988	15,524	19,711	27,335	6.9	6.3	2.9	3.0
100 to 249 employees.	13,685	11,775	32,192	44,170	5.6	4.8	4.8	4.9
250 to 499 employees.	5,454	4,441	27,397	35,908	2.2	1.8	4.1	3.9
500 or more employees	7,923	6,658	475,453	647,466	3.2	2.7	71.1	71.1

[1] Known value is defined as the value of exports by known exporters, i.e., those export transactions that could be matched to specific companies. Export values are on f.a.s. or "free alongside ship basis."

Source: U.S. Census Bureau, *A Profile of U.S. Exporting Companies, 2000* and *2005–2006*. See also <http://www.census.gov /foreign-trade/Press-Release/edb/2006/edb-3a.pdf>; (released 11 January 2008).

Foreign Commerce and Aid   795

Table 1271. **Domestic Exports and Imports for Consumption of Merchandise by Selected NAICS Product Category: 2000 to 2007**

[In millions of dollars (712,285 represents $712,285,000,000). Includes nonmonetary gold. For methodology, see Foreign Trade Statistics in Appendix III. NAICS = North American Industry Classification System; see text, Section 15]

Product category	2000	2003	2004	2005	2006	2007
Domestic exports, total	**712,285**	**651,713**	**729,425**	**803,920**	**929,811**	**1,046,825**
Agricultural, forestry, and fishery products	29,153	34,699	37,830	37,013	41,503	53,519
Agricultural products, total	23,596	29,194	31,949	30,611	34,770	46,451
Livestock and livestock products	1,255	1,177	963	1,123	1,283	1,362
Forestry products not elsewhere specified	1,644	1,462	1,653	1,667	1,698	1,916
Fish, fresh or chilled; and other marine products	2,658	2,866	3,265	3,612	3,753	3,791
Mining, total	6,187	6,117	8,677	12,550	13,970	16,881
Oil and gas	1,706	2,143	3,001	4,453	4,229	5,556
Minerals and ores	4,481	3,973	5,676	8,098	9,741	11,325
Manufacturing, total	644,440	577,789	645,104	711,420	821,855	911,160
Food and kindred products	24,966	26,795	25,952	28,849	32,201	38,746
Beverages and tobacco products	5,568	3,648	3,644	3,400	3,847	4,191
Textiles and fabrics	7,010	7,557	8,363	8,471	8,520	8,242
Textile mill products	2,236	1,881	2,072	2,343	2,561	2,628
Apparel and accessories	8,104	4,923	4,350	4,069	3,789	3,124
Leather and allied products	2,322	2,035	2,190	2,295	2,450	2,353
Wood products	4,854	3,818	4,249	4,445	4,913	4,960
Paper products	15,539	13,965	15,168	16,565	17,985	19,669
Printed, publishing, and similar products	4,869	4,706	4,983	5,495	5,798	6,278
Petroleum and coal products	8,862	9,349	12,579	17,788	25,959	30,846
Chemicals	77,649	88,384	105,238	114,214	129,504	147,364
Plastics and rubber products	16,970	15,661	17,316	18,787	20,575	22,077
Nonmetallic mineral products	7,830	6,069	6,596	6,911	7,766	8,588
Primary metal products	20,126	17,877	21,159	27,423	37,079	44,592
Fabricated metal products	21,737	18,848	20,821	23,296	27,238	29,800
Machinery, except electrical	85,038	69,285	86,264	96,760	109,364	122,488
Computers and electronic products	161,449	115,883	122,161	123,926	135,025	136,597
Electrical equipment, appliances and components	25,401	20,632	23,606	26,551	31,360	33,495
Transportation equipment	121,701	122,246	129,907	147,244	177,990	202,165
Furniture and fixtures	2,882	2,349	2,633	2,829	3,158	3,494
Miscellaneous manufactured commodities	19,327	21,591	24,795	29,831	34,449	38,998
Special classification provisions	32,505	33,109	37,814	42,936	52,482	65,265
Waste and scrap	4,948	6,456	8,548	10,357	15,843	22,460
Used or second-hand merchandise	1,950	1,808	2,108	2,742	4,359	5,831
Goods returned or reimported	333	205	152	62	55	35
Special classification provision not elsewhere specified	25,274	24,640	27,006	29,776	32,225	36,940
Imports for consumption, total	**1,205,339**	**1,250,097**	**1,460,161**	**1,662,380**	**1,845,053**	**1,942,863**
Agricultural, forestry, and fishery products	24,378	26,197	27,814	30,751	34,641	37,700
Agricultural products, total	11,771	13,035	14,356	15,803	17,342	19,688
Livestock and livestock products	3,085	2,782	2,498	3,276	4,104	4,692
Forestry products not elsewhere specified	1,409	1,612	2,019	2,250	2,771	2,745
Fish, fresh or chilled; and other marine products	8,113	8,768	8,942	9,422	10,424	10,575
Mining, total	79,841	105,662	138,427	188,942	222,412	237,624
Oil and gas	76,166	101,800	133,606	182,473	214,738	229,495
Minerals and ores	3,675	3,862	4,821	6,469	7,674	8,129
Manufacturing, total	1,040,329	1,060,349	1,231,005	1,373,160	1,512,175	1,585,605
Food and kindred products	18,944	23,769	27,740	29,759	31,802	34,720
Beverages and tobacco products	8,350	10,925	11,652	12,845	14,611	15,948
Textiles and fabrics	7,042	6,791	7,387	7,453	7,361	7,456
Textile mill products	7,347	9,857	11,707	13,508	14,680	15,412
Apparel and accessories	62,928	66,499	70,533	74,473	77,010	78,962
Leather and allied products	21,463	22,627	24,541	26,554	28,473	29,404
Wood products	15,388	16,581	22,869	23,652	22,730	18,547
Paper products	19,080	18,414	20,645	22,120	23,461	23,484
Printed, publishing, and similar products	4,197	4,699	5,148	5,601	5,806	6,351
Petroleum and coal products	40,156	39,161	54,544	81,402	92,968	102,176
Chemicals	76,606	102,078	115,246	132,031	146,751	160,251
Plastics and rubber products	17,362	20,504	24,085	28,087	30,564	32,047
Nonmetallic mineral products	14,740	14,428	16,531	18,455	20,285	19,675
Primary metal products	43,833	34,065	56,498	64,642	88,616	88,866
Fabricated metal products	27,974	30,068	35,976	41,065	45,963	50,042
Machinery, except electrical	79,366	77,344	94,402	109,589	121,285	121,361
Computers and electronic products	250,694	212,201	248,033	269,986	295,375	312,868
Electrical equipment, appliances and components	39,567	41,914	48,781	55,179	62,252	67,130
Transportation equipment	213,110	223,304	239,565	252,199	269,390	277,816
Furniture and fixtures	15,607	19,636	22,560	25,096	27,020	27,684
Miscellaneous manufactured commodities	56,577	65,484	72,563	79,465	85,775	95,405
Special classification provisions	60,791	57,889	62,915	69,526	75,826	81,934
Waste and scrap	1,875	1,810	3,054	3,206	4,788	5,027
Used or second-hand merchandise	6,345	4,752	5,710	6,013	7,155	9,000
Goods returned or reimported	33,851	33,605	34,223	37,057	38,586	39,624
Special classification provision not elsewhere specified	18,720	17,723	19,928	23,250	25,298	28,282

Source: U.S. Census Bureau, *U.S. International Trade in Goods and Services,* series FT-900, December issues. For most recent, see <http://www.census.gov/foreign-trade/Press-Release/2007pr/12/#exhibits>; (released 14 February 2008); and previous December or final reports.

This section presents summary economic and social statistics for Puerto Rico, the U.S. Virgin Islands, Guam, American Samoa, and the Northern Mariana Islands. Primary sources are the decennial censuses of population and housing, county business patterns, and the Puerto Rico Community Survey conducted by the U.S. Census Bureau; the annual *Vital Statistics of the United States,* issued by the National Center for Health Statistics; and the annual *Income and Product* of the Puerto Rico Planning Board.

Jurisdiction—The United States gained jurisdiction over these areas as follows: the islands of *Puerto Rico* and *Guam,* surrendered by Spain to the United States in December 1898, were ceded to the United States by the Treaty of Paris, ratified in 1899. Puerto Rico became a commonwealth on July 25, 1952, thereby achieving a high degree of local autonomy under its own constitution. The *U.S. Virgin Islands,* comprising 50 islands and cays, was purchased by the United States from Denmark in 1917. *American Samoa,* a group of seven islands, was acquired by the United States in accordance with a convention among the United States, Great Britain, and Germany, ratified in 1900 (Swains Island was annexed in 1925). By an agreement approved by the Security Council and the United States, the Northern Mariana Islands, previously under Japanese mandate, was administered by the United States between 1947 and 1986 under the United Nations trusteeship system. The Northern Mariana Islands became a commonwealth in 1986.

Censuses—Because characteristics of the Puerto Rico and the Island Areas differ, the presentation of census data for them is not uniform. The 1960 Census of Population covered all of the places listed above except the Northern Mariana Islands (their census was conducted in April 1958 by the Office of the High Commissioner), while the 1960 Census of Housing also excluded American Samoa. The 1970, 1980, 1990, and 2000 Censuses of Population and Housing covered all five areas. Beginning in 1967, Congress authorized the economic censuses, to be taken at 5-year intervals, for years ending in "2" and "7." Prior economic censuses were conducted in Puerto Rico for 1949, 1954, 1958, and 1963 and in Guam and the U.S. Virgin Islands for 1958 and 1963. In 1967, the census of construction industries was added for the first time in Puerto Rico; in 1972, the U.S. Virgin Islands and Guam were covered; and in 1982, the economic census was taken for the first time for the Northern Mariana Islands.

Puerto Rico Community Survey—The Puerto Rico Community Survey (PRCS) began in 2005 and is a critical element in the Census Bureau's reengineered 2010 census plan. The American Community Survey is the equivalent of the PRCS for the United States (50 states, and District of Columbia). The PRCS collects and produces population and housing information every year instead of every 10 years. About 36,000 households are surveyed each year from across every municipio in Puerto Rico.

Information in other sections—In addition to the statistics presented in this section, other data are included as integral parts of many tables showing distribution by states in various sections of the *Abstract.* See "Puerto Rico and the Island Areas" in the Index. For definition and explanation of terms used, see Sections 1, 2, 4, 17, 20, 21, and 22.

Table 1272. **Estimated Resident Population With Projections: 1980 to 2025**

[In thousands (3,210 represents 3,210,000). Population as of July 1. Population data generally are de-facto figures for the present territory. Data for 1990 to 2000 are adjusted to the 2000 Census of Population for Puerto Rico only. See text, Section 30, for general comments regarding the data. For details of methodology, coverage, and reliability, see source]

Area	1980	1990	2000	2005	2007	2008	Projected 2010	2015	2020	2025
Puerto Rico.	3,210	3,537	3,816	3,912	3,943	3,958	3,986	4,044	4,080	4,092
American Samoa	32	47	58	62	64	65	66	71	75	79
Guam	107	134	155	169	173	176	181	192	203	213
Virgin Islands.	98	104	109	110	110	110	110	109	109	107
Northern Mariana Islands.	17	44	70	80	85	87	91	100	109	116

Source: U.S. Census Bureau, International Data Base. See Internet site: <http://www.census.gov/ipc/www/idb/index.html>.

Table 1273. **Vital Statistics—Specified Areas: 1980 to 2006**

[Births, deaths, and infant deaths by place of residence. Rates for 1980, 1990, and 2000 based on population enumerated as of **April 1;** for other years, on population estimated as of **July 1**]

Area and year	Births Number	Rate [1]	Deaths Number	Rate [1]	Infant deaths Number	Rate [2]
Puerto Rico:						
1980.	72,986	22.8	20,413	6.4	1,351	18.5
1990.	66,417	18.8	25,957	7.3	888	13.4
1995.	63,425	17.0	30,032	8.1	804	12.7
2000. [3]	59,333	15.2	28,369	7.2	574	9.7
2005 [3]	50,564	12.9	29,531	7.5	466	9.2
2006 [3]	48,590	12.4	28,413	7.2	(NA)	(NA)
Guam:						
1980.	2,945	27.8	393	3.7	43	14.6
1990.	3,839	28.6	520	3.9	31	8.1
1995.	4,180	29.0	592	4.1	38	9.4
2000.	3,766	24.4	648	4.2	22	5.8
2005. [3]	3,187	18.9	677	4.0	34	10.7
2006 [3]	(NA)	(NA)	679	4.0	(NA)	(NA)
Virgin Islands:						
1980.	2,504	25.9	504	5.2	61	24.4
1990.	2,267	21.8	480	4.6	33	14.6
1995.	2,063	18.1	664	5.8	34	16.6
2000.	1,564	12.9	641	5.3	21	13.4
2005.	1,605	14.8	663	6.1	11	(B)
2006 [3]	1,431	13.2	629	5.8	(NA)	(NA)
American Samoa:						
1997.	1,634	27.1	257	4.3	17	(B)
2002.	1,627	28.2	294	5.1	25	(NA)
2005. [3]	1,720	27.6	272	4.4	12	(B)
2006 [3]	1,442	25.0	266	4.6	(NA)	(NA)
Northern Marianas:						
1998.	1,462	21.9	162	2.4	13	(B)
2002.	1,290	17.4	163	2.2	9	(NA)
2005. [3]	1,335	16.6	186	2.3	6	(B)
2006 [3]	1,422	17.2	170	2.1	(NA)	(NA)

B Base figure too small to meet statistical standards of reliability.   NA Not available.   [1] Per 1,000 population.   [2] Rates are infant deaths (under 1 year) per 1,000 live births.   [3] Data for 2006 are preliminary.

Source: U.S. National Center for Health Statistics, National Vital Statistics Reports (NVSR) Births: Preliminary Data for 2006, Vol. 56, No. 7, December 5, 2007, and Deaths: Preliminary Data for 2006, Vol. 56, No. 16, June 11, 2008. See <http://www.cdc.gov/nchs/nvss.htm>.

Table 1274. **Public Elementary and Secondary Schools by Area: 2005**

[For school year ending in year shown, unless otherwise indicated. (2,865,945 represents $2,865,945,000)]

Item	Puerto Rico	Guam	U.S. Virgin Islands	American Samoa	Item	Puerto Rico	Guam	U.S. Virgin Islands	American Samoa
Enrollment, fall	563,490	30,986	16,750	16,399	Teachers	42,036	1,804	1,434	971
Elementary (kindergarten–grade 8)	399,384	21,946	11,728	11,996	Student support staff.	3,742	65	174	218
Secondary (grades 9–12 and post graduates)	164,106	9,040	5,022	4,403	Other support services staff.	18,510	215	299	101
Staff, fall	75,023	3,455	2,664	1,872	Current expenditures [1] ($1,000)	2,865,945	(NA)	137,793	58,163
School district staff .	2,180	285	206	189	Per pupil [2] (dol.)	5,304	(NA)	8,698	3,801
School staff	50,591	2,890	1,985	1,364					

[1] Public elementary and secondary day schools.   [2] Per pupil expenditures include current expenditures, capital expenditures, and interest on school debt and excludes "other current expenditures" such as community services, private school programs, adult education, and other programs not allocable to expenditures per pupil in public schools.

Source: U.S. National Center for Education Statistics, *Digest of Education Statistics,* annual; and unpublished data. See Internet site <http://nces.ed.gov/annuals>.

Table 1275. Occupational Employment and Average Annual Wages in Guam, Puerto Rico, and Virgin Islands: 2007

[The Occupational Employment Survey (OES) program conducts a semiannual mail survey designed to produce estimates of employment and wages for specific occupations. For more details on the survey, see <http://www.bls.gov/oes/oesemp.htm#scope>]

Selected occupations	SOC code [1]	Guam		Puerto Rico		Virgin Islands	
		Employ-ment	Average annual wages	Employ-ment	Average annual wages	Employ-ment	Average annual wages
Total, all occupations [2,3]	(X)	57,920	28,860	1,014,970	23,910	46,870	32,300
Management	11	4,310	55,620	36,230	64,800	1,930	72,530
Business and financial operations	13	2,070	41,340	38,990	34,800	1,490	44,830
Computer and mathematical	15	360	44,280	9,190	42,520	330	48,890
Architecture and engineering	17	920	46,290	13,790	46,930	440	55,520
Life, physical, and social science	19	420	41,260	10,040	40,010	250	48,810
Community and social services	21	710	31,820	17,990	25,550	470	33,770
Legal	23	(NA)	71,010	4,640	56,010	510	69,270
Education, training, and library	25	4,130	37,210	70,320	30,900	4,120	42,400
Arts, design, entertainment sports	27	520	26,750	6,890	29,490	330	38,370
Healthcare practitioner and technical	29	1,540	54,430	44,590	29,440	(NA)	48,950
Healthcare support	31	550	21,990	11,640	16,560	420	20,130
Protective service	33	2,470	26,690	65,650	21,580	2,510	29,510
Food preparation and serving related	35	5,920	16,020	68,430	14,800	4,170	19,650
Buildings and grounds cleaning and maintenance	37	3,420	17,250	43,870	15,760	3,130	19,980
Personal care and service	39	2,410	28,790	16,260	16,100	1,060	21,420
Sales and related occupations	41	5,540	19,920	110,720	19,570	4,610	24,250
Office and administrative support	43	10,760	25,660	193,440	21,000	8,370	25,780
Farming, fishing, and forestry	45	(NA)	27,360	1,700	18,440	(NA)	(NA)
Construction and extraction	47	3,730	26,520	65,380	18,200	4,030	34,210
Installation, maintenance, and repair	49	2,990	27,280	37,050	24,930	2,710	34,370
Production	51	1,500	24,930	84,490	19,960	2,130	37,030
Transportation and material moving	53	3,390	21,960	63,670	17,330	2,590	26,030

NA Not available.   X Not applicable.   [1] Office of Management and Budget's Standard Occupational Classification (SOC) is used to define occupations. SOC categorizes workers into 1 of 801 detailed occupations and aggregates; the detailed occupations into 23 major occupational groups.   [2] Estimates for detailed occupations do not sum to the totals because the totals include occupations not shown separately.   [3] Estimates do not include self-employed workers.

Source: U.S. Department of Labor, Bureau of Labor Statistics; *Occupational Employment and Wages*, May 2007; <http://www.bls.gov/oes/home.htm>.

Table 1276. Prisoners in Custody of Correctional Authorities in U.S. Territories and Commonwealths: 2005 and 2006

[As of December 31. Minus sign (–) indicates decrease]

Jurisdiction	Total inmates			Sentenced to more than 1 year			
	2005	2006	Percent change 2005–2006	2005	2006	Percent change 2005–2006	Incar-ceration rate, 2006 [1]
Total	15,735	15,205	–3.4	12,399	11,743	–5.3	270
American Samoa	222	210	–5.4	174	113	–35.1	196
Guam	505	495	–2.0	238	337	41.6	197
Northern Mariana Islands	149	126	–15.4	83	76	–8.4	92
Puerto Rico	14,263	13,788	–3.3	11,469	10,789	–5.9	275
U.S. Virgin Islands	596	586	–1.7	435	428	–1.6	394

[1] The number of prisoners with a sentence of more than 1 year per 100,000 persons in the resident population.

Source: U.S. Department of Justice, Office of Justice Programs, Bureau of Justice Statistics, *Prisoners in 2006*, December 2007, NCJ 219416. See also <http://www.ojp.usdoj.gov/bjs/abstract/p06.htm>.

Table 1277. Federal Direct Payments: 2006

[In thousands of dollars (6,355,179 represents $6,355,179,000). For fiscal years ending September 30]

Selected program payment	Puerto Rico	Guam	Virgin Islands	American Samoa	Northern Mariana Islands
Direct payments to individuals for retirement and disability [1]	6,355,179	250,023	181,624	48,352	27,088
Social security:					
Retirement insurance	2,636,964	79,875	104,787	12,553	6,614
Survivors' insurance	1,153,214	34,960	27,202	12,726	5,166
Disability insurance	1,736,038	19,984	22,250	11,923	1,755
Federal retirement and disability:					
Civilian [2]	244,069	54,609	15,747	1,555	6,453
Military	92,350	40,615	5,435	3,335	1,549
Veterans' benefits:					
Service-connected disability	275,183	15,683	3,610	4,803	813
Other	43,344	2,143	471	738	75

[1] Includes other payments, not shown separately.   [2] Includes retirement and disability payments to former U.S. Postal Service employees.

Source: U.S. Census Bureau, *Consolidated Federal Funds Report for Fiscal Year, 2006* (issued April 2008). See also <http://www.census.gov/govs/www/cffr04.html>.

Table 1278. **Tenure by Household Type in Puerto Rico: 2006**

[The Puerto Rico Community Survey universe includes the household population and the population living in institutions, college dormitories, and other group quarters. Based on a sample and subject to sampling variability; see text, this section and Appendix III]

Household type	Owner Occu- pied	Renter Occu- pied	Household type	Owner Occu- pied	Renter Occu- pied
Total households.	**919,418**	**321,038**	Householder 15 to 34 years	22,910	46,303
Family households.	716,285	223,315	Householder 35 to 64 years	106,043	57,360
Married-couple family	491,662	96,208	Householder 65 years and over. .	49,393	6,235
Householder 15 to 34 years	55,409	37,417	Nonfamily households	203,133	97,723
Householder 35 to 64 years	319,170	49,711	Householder living alone	180,288	82,970
Householder 65 years and over . . .	117,083	9,080	Householder 15 to 34 years	12,047	14,680
Other family	224,623	127,107	Householder 35 to 64 years	84,614	44,342
Male householder, no wife present. .	46,277	17,209	Householder 65 years and over. .	83,627	23,948
Householder 15 to 34 years	6,590	7,078	Householder not living alone	22,845	14,753
Householder 35 to 64 years	26,129	8,845	Householder 15 to 34 years	3,632	7,446
Householder 65 years and over . .	13,558	1,286	Householder 35 to 64 years	14,063	6,510
Female householder, no husband present	178,346	109,898	Householder 65 years and over . .	5,150	797

Source: U.S. Census Bureau, 2006 Puerto Rico Community Survey; B25011.Tenure by Household Type and Age of Householder. using American FactFinder®; <http://factfinder.census.gov/>; (accessed: 4 January 2008).

Table 1279. **Selected Social, Demographic, and Housing Characteristics in Puerto Rico: 2006**

[The Puerto Rico Community Survey universe includes the household population and the population living in institutions, college dormitories, and other group quarters. Based on a sample and subject to sampling variability; see text, this section and Appendix III]

Characteristic	Estimate	Per- cent	Characteristic	Estimate	Per- cent
Total	**3,927,776**	**100.0**	Now married, except separated	656,925	40.3
			Separated	73,136	4.5
SEX AND AGE			Widowed	181,109	11.1
Male.	1,887,087	48.0	Divorced	211,713	13.0
Female	2,040,689	52.0			
			HOUSEHOLDS		
Under 5 years	251,606	6.4			
5 to 9 years	279,325	7.1	**Total households**	**1,240,456**	**100.0**
10 to 14 years	308,248	7.8	Family households (families)	939,600	75.7
15 to 19 years	295,908	7.5	With own children under 18 years . . .	396,968	32.0
20 to 24 years	291,542	7.4	Married-couple families.	587,870	47.4
25 to 34 years	550,504	14.0	With own children under 18 years . . .	231,678	18.7
35 to 44 years	530,802	13.5	Male householder, no wife present	63,486	5.1
45 to 54 years	490,341	12.5	With own children under 18 years . . .	21,095	1.7
55 to 59 years	226,424	5.8	Female householder, no husband		
60 to 64 years	199,190	5.1	present	288,244	23.2
65 to 74 years	285,199	7.3	With own children under 18 years . . .	144,195	11.6
75 to 84 years	158,267	4.0	Nonfamily households	300,856	24.3
85 years and over	60,420	1.5	Householder living alone	263,258	21.2
			65 years and over	107,575	8.7
MARITAL STATUS					
			Average household size	3.13	(X)
Males 15 years and over	1,457,880	37.1	Average family size	3.64	(X)
Never married	562,450	38.6			
Now married, except separated	667,471	45.8	DISABILITY STATUS OF THE CIVILIAN		
Separated	45,677	3.1	NONINSTITUTIONALIZED POPULATION		
Widowed	44,415	3.0			
Divorced	137,867	9.5	Population 5 years and over	3,646,609	100.0
Females 15 years and over	1,630,717	41.5	With a disability.	946,419	26.0
Never married	507,834	31.1			

X Not applicable.

Source: U.S. Census Bureau, 2006 Puerto Rico Community Survey; Table DP-2 PR Selected Social Charecteristics Puerto Rico: 2006 using American FactFinder®; <http://factfinder.census.gov/>; (accessed: 4 January 2008).

Table 1280. Puerto Rico—Summary: 1980 to 2007

[3,184.0 represents 3,184,000]

Item	Unit	1980	1990	2000	2003	2004	2005	2006	2007
POPULATION									
Total [1]	1,000	3,184.0	3,512.4	3,808.0	3,869.0	3,886.7	3,903.5	3,919.8	3,934.6
Persons per family	Number	4.3	3.7	3.4	3.3	3.3	3.3	3.2	3.2
EDUCATION [2]									
Enrollment, total	1,000	941.4	953.0	971.5	1,172.3	(NA)	(NA)	(NA)	(NA)
Public (except public colleges or universities)	1,000	716.1	651.2	612.3	596.3	584.9	575.9	563.5	548.1
College and university	1,000	130.1	156.0	175.5	199.8	207.1	208.0	209.5	(NA)
Expenses	Mil. dol.	825.0	1,686.4	4,254.1	4,962.3	5,534.8	6,017.3	(NA)	(NA)
As percent of GNP	Percent	7.5	7.8	10.3	10.5	11.2	(NA)	(NA)	(NA)
Public	Mil. dol.	612.2	1,054.2	3,160.4	3,617.0	3,945.5	4,389.5	(NA)	(NA)
Private	Mil. dol.	212.8	644.2	1,093.7	1,345.3	1,589.3	1,627.8	1,686.3	1,709.3
LABOR FORCE [3]									
Total [4]	1,000	907	1,124	1,303	1,352	1,360	1,385	1,422	1,409
Employed [5]	1,000	753	963	1,159	1,188	1,206	1,238	1,256	1,263
Agriculture [6]	1,000	38	36	24	24	25	26	22	16
Manufacturing	1,000	143	168	159	134	136	138	136	135
Trade	1,000	138	185	239	252	253	261	271	260
Government	1,000	184	222	249	269	268	274	280	296
Unemployed	1,000	154	161	143	164	155	147	166	147
Unemployment rate [7]	Rate	17.0	14.0	11.0	12.1	11.4	10.6	11.7	10.4
Compensation of employees	Mil. dol.	7,200	13,639	23,504	26,183	27,769	29,372	30,342	31,050
Average compensation	Dollar	9,563	14,854	20,280	22,039	23,026	23,725	24,158	24,584
Salary and wages	Mil. dol.	7,200	13,639	23,504	22,670	24,016	25,393	26,181	26,894
INCOME [8]									
Personal income:									
Current dollars	Mil. dol.	11,002	21,105	38,856	44,216	45,566	48,820	51,090	53,084
Constant (1954) dollars	Mil. dol.	3,985	5,551	8,491	9,155	9,289	9,611	9,619	9,698
Disposable personal income:									
Current dollars	Mil. dol.	10,403	19,914	36,239	41,120	42,476	45,488	47,582	49,684
Constant (1954) dollars	Mil. dol.	3,768	5,238	7,919	8,514	8,659	8,955	8,958	9,077
Average family income:									
Current dollars	Dollar	14,858	22,232	34,693	37,716	38,688	41,273	41,707	43,173
Constant (1954) dollars	Dollar	5,381	5,847	7,581	7,809	7,887	8,125	7,852	7,887
BANKING [9]									
Assets	Mil. dol.	10,223	27,902	58,813	74,315	94,427	109,292	112,658	(NA)
TOURISM [8]									
Number of visitors	1,000	2,140	3,426	4,566	4,402	4,889	5,073	5,022	5,062
Visitor expenditures	Mil. dol.	619	1,366	2,388	2,677	3,024	3,239	3,369	3,414
Average per visitor	Dollar	289	399	523	608	619	638	671	674
Net income from tourism	Mil. dol.	202	383	615	678	735	771	806	830

NA Not available. [1] 1980, 1990, and 2000 enumerated as of April 1; all other years estimated as of July 1. [2] Enrollment for the first school month. Expenses for school year ending in year shown. "Public" includes: Public Preschool, Public Elementary, Public Intermediate, Public High School, Public Post-High School, Public Technological, Public Adult Education, Public Vocational Education, and Public Special Education. "College and university" includes both public and private colleges and universities. [3] Annual average of monthly figures. For fiscal years. [4] For population 16 years old and over. [5] Includes other employment not shown separately. [6] Includes forestry and fisheries. [7] Percent unemployed of the labor force. [8] For fiscal years. [9] As of June 30. Does not include federal savings banks and international banking entities.

Source: Puerto Rico Planning Board, San Juan, PR, Economic Report of the Governor, annual; <http://www.gobierno.pr/gprportal/inicio>.

Table 1281. Puerto Rico—Economic Summary by Industry: 2005

[In thousands of dollars, (15,863,227 represents $15,863,227,000). Covers establishments with payroll. Employees are for the pay period including March 12. See headnote, Table 736. Based on the County Business Patterns (CBP). This annual series is used as a benchmark for statistical series, surveys, and databases between economic censuses. For a description of CBP; see Appendix III. Starting with the 2003 CBP series, the data are tabulated using the 2002 North American Industial Classification System (NAICS)]

Industry	2002 NAICS code [1]	Total number of establishments	Number of employees	Annual payroll (1,000)
Establishments, total [2]	(X)	**46,853**	**761,672**	**15,863,227**
Construction	23	2,920	62,181	1,008,863
Manufacturing	31–33	2,170	116,539	3,443,299
Wholesale trade	42	2,355	37,315	1,099,652
Retail trade	44–45	11,137	135,203	1,977,541
Transportation and warehousing	48–49	1,093	16,610	398,824
Information	51	592	22,137	768,337
Finance and insurance	52	1,806	36,577	1,273,184
Real estate and rental and leasing	53	1,817	16,760	315,911
Professional, scientific, and technical services	54	4,230	31,058	864,348
Management of companies and enterprises	55	97	6,461	225,250
Admin/support waste mgt/remediation services	56	1,787	67,134	1,055,641
Educational services	61	746	33,194	602,140
Health care and social assistance	62	6,735	72,414	1,346,325
Arts, entertainment, and recreation	71	429	3,892	60,675
Accommodation and food services	72	4,108	74,910	913,128

X Not applicable. [1] See text, Section 12 for more information on NAICS. [2] Includes other industries not shown separately.

Source: U.S. Census Bureau, "County Business Patterns"; <http://www.census.gov/epcd/cbp/view/cbppr.html>.

Table 1282. Puerto Rico—Gross Product and Net Income: 1990 to 2007

[**In millions of dollars (21,619 represents $21,619,000,000). For fiscal years ending June 30**. Data for 2007 are preliminary. Minus sign (–) indicates decrease]

Item	1990	1995	2000	2004	2005	2006	2007
Gross product	**21,619**	**28,452**	**41,419**	**50,709**	**53,752**	**56,733**	**58,712**
Agriculture	434	318	529	414	375	385	441
Manufacturing	12,126	17,867	24,079	33,267	34,534	36,547	36,717
Contract construction and mining [1]	720	1,006	1,875	1,905	1,848	1,807	1,875
Transportation & other public services [2]	2,468	3,276	4,237	5,343	5,309	5,701	5,971
Trade	4,728	5,989	8,340	9,802	10,217	10,709	11,061
Finance, insurance, real estate	3,896	5,730	9,977	13,029	14,267	14,998	16,336
Services	3,015	4,724	6,603	7,646	7,965	8,241	8,529
Government	3,337	4,440	5,478	7,389	8,151	8,424	8,586
Commonwealth	2,884	3,793	4,601	6,362	7,032	7,204	7,282
Municipalities	453	647	877	1,026	1,118	1,220	1,304
Rest of the world	–8,985	–14,195	–20,283	–28,501	–29,056	–30,210	–30,989
Statistical discrepancy	–121	–703	585	415	144	131	186
Net income	**17,941**	**23,653**	**32,610**	**40,517**	**43,484**	**45,585**	**46,664**
Agriculture	486	442	669	697	670	650	710
Manufacturing	11,277	16,685	22,348	31,405	32,443	34,240	34,343
Mining	26	30	41	42	50	59	59
Contract construction	679	903	1,691	1,706	1,654	1,609	1,662
Transportation & other public services [2]	1,778	2,360	2,968	3,649	3,707	3,952	4,248
Trade	3,420	4,108	5,752	6,804	7,277	7,612	7,780
Finance, insurance, and real estate	3,280	4,735	8,264	10,787	11,750	12,220	12,948
Services	2,643	4,146	5,682	6,539	6,840	7,028	7,317
Commonwealth government [3]	3,337	4,440	5,478	7,389	8,151	8,424	8,586
Rest of the world	–8,985	–14,195	–20,283	–28,501	–29,056	–30,210	–30,989

[1] Mining includes only quarries. [2] Includes other public utilities, and radio and television broadcasting. [3] Includes public enterprises not elsewhere classified.

Source: Puerto Rico Planning Board, San Juan, PR, *Economic Report of the Governor,* annual; <http://www.gobierno.pr/gprportal/inicio>.

Table 1283. Puerto Rico—Transfer Payments: 1990 to 2007

[**In millions of dollars (4,871 represents $4,871,000,000).** Data represent transfer payments between federal and state governments and other nonresidents. Data for 2007 are preliminary. Minus sign (–) indicates decrease]

Item	1990	1995	2000	2004	2005	2006	2007
Total receipts	**4,871**	**6,236**	**8,659**	**10,087**	**10,551**	**11,210**	**12,024**
Federal government	4,649	5,912	7,966	9,273	9,673	10,190	10,963
Transfers to individuals [1]	4,577	5,838	7,868	9,161	9,547	10,066	10,829
Veterans benefits	349	440	491	521	491	592	624
Medicare	368	661	1,196	1,844	1,825	2,056	2,317
Old age, disability, survivors (social security)	2,055	2,912	3,863	4,810	5,118	5,423	5,746
Nutritional assistance	880	1,063	1,193	1,241	1,306	1,352	1,472
Industry subsidies	72	74	98	112	127	124	135
U.S. state governments	18	18	15	16	15	18	23
Other nonresidents	205	307	679	797	863	1,003	1,038
Total payments	**1,801**	**2,301**	**2,763**	**3,471**	**3,583**	**3,742**	**3,763**
Federal government	1,756	2,132	2,693	3,350	3,516	3,688	3,709
Transfers from individuals	817	1,052	1,326	1,700	1,792	1,869	1,889
Contribution to Medicare	97	162	191	258	303	340	362
Employee contribution for social security	720	888	1,133	1,438	1,483	1,524	1,520
Transfers from industries	16	49	51	49	74	115	98
Unemployment insurance	247	184	234	219	221	230	231
Employer contribution for social security	675	847	1,081	1,382	1,429	1,473	1,491
Other nonresidents [2]	45	164	70	121	67	54	53
Net balance	**3,070**	**3,935**	**5,897**	**6,616**	**6,968**	**7,468**	**8,262**
Federal government	2,893	3,780	5,273	5,923	6,157	6,502	7,254
U.S. state governments	16	13	10	–21	10	15	20
Other nonresidents	162	143	614	714	801	952	988

[1] Includes other receipts and payments not shown separately. [2] Includes U.S. state governments.

Source: Puerto Rico Planning Board, San Juan, PR, *Economic Report of the Governor,* annual. <http://www.gobierno.pr/gprportal/inicio>.

Table 1284. Puerto Rico—Merchandise Imports and Exports: 1980 to 2007

[**In millions of dollars (9,018 represents $9,018,000,000).** Imports are imports for consumption; see text, Section 28]

Item	1980	1985	1990	1995	2000	2001	2002	2003	2004	2005	2006	2007
Imports	9,018	10,162	16,200	18,969	27,199	27,690	30,511	35,945	37,252	40,418	42,462	43,496
From U.S.	5,345	6,130	10,792	12,213	15,171	14,718	15,675	16,949	18,124	20,994	21,982	22,402
From other	3,673	4,032	5,408	6,756	11,834	12,972	14,824	18,996	19,128	19,424	20,480	21,094
Exports	6,576	11,087	20,402	23,573	43,191	46,689	50,641	55,814	54,982	56,843	59,218	62,398
To U.S.	5,643	9,873	17,915	20,986	38,335	40,981	44,907	46,880	45,311	47,121	47,452	47,507
To other	933	1,214	2,487	2,587	4,856	5,708	5,734	8,934	9,671	9,722	11,766	14,891

Source: U.S. Census Bureau, *Foreign Commerce and Navigation of the United States,* annual; *U.S. Trade with Puerto Rico and U.S. Possessions, FT 895;* and, through 1985, *Highlights of U.S. Export and Import Trade, FT990;* thereafter, *FT920.* <http://www.census.gov/foreign-trade/statistics/index.html>.

Section 30
International Statistics

This section presents statistics for the world as a whole and for many countries on a comparative basis with the United States. Data are shown for population, births and deaths, social and industrial indicators, finances, agriculture, communication, and military affairs.

Statistics of the individual nations may be found primarily in official national publications, generally in the form of yearbooks, issued by most of the nations at various intervals in their own national languages and expressed in their own or customary units of measure. (For a listing of selected publications, see Guide to Sources.) For handier reference, especially for international comparisons, the United Nations Statistics Division compiles data as submitted by member countries and issues a number of international summary publications, generally in English and French. Among these are the *Statistical Yearbook*; the *Demographic Yearbook*; *International Trade Statistics Yearbook*; *National Accounts Statistics: Main Aggregates and Detailed Tables*; *Population and Vital Statistics Reports* (quarterly); the *Monthly Bulletin of Statistics*; and the *Energy Statistics Yearbook*. Specialized agencies of the United Nations also issue international summary publications on agricultural, labor, health, and education statistics. Among these are the *Production Yearbook* and *Trade Yearbook* issued by the Food and Agriculture Organization, the *Yearbook of Labour Statistics* issued by the International Labour Office, *World Health Statistics* issued by the World Health Organization, and the *Statistical Yearbook* issued by the Educational, Scientific, and Cultural Organization.

The U.S. Census Bureau presents estimates and projections of basic demographic measures for countries and regions of the world in the *World Population Reports* (WP) series. The *International Population Reports* (Series IPC), and *International Briefs* (Series IB) also present population figures for many foreign countries. Detailed population statistics are also available from the Census Bureau's International Data Base (http://www.census.gov/ipc/www/idb/>.

The International Monetary Fund (IMF) and the Organization for Economic Cooperation and Development (OECD) also compile data on international statistics. The IMF publishes a series of reports relating to financial data. These include *International Financial Statistics, Direction of Trade*, and *Balance of Payments Yearbook*, published in English, French, and Spanish. The OECD publishes a vast number of statistical publications in various fields such as economics, health, and education. Among these are *OECD in Figures, Main Economic Indicators, Economic Outlook, National Accounts, Labour Force Statistics, OECD Health Data*, and *Education at a Glance*.

Statistical coverage, country names, and classifications—Problems of space and availability of data limit the number of countries and the extent of statistical coverage shown. The list of countries included and the spelling of country names are based almost entirely on the list of independent nations, dependencies, and areas of special sovereignty provided by the U.S. Department of State.

In recent years, several important changes took place in the status of the world's nations. In 1991, the Soviet Union broke up into 15 independent countries: Armenia, Azerbaijan, Belarus, Estonia, Georgia, Kazakhstan, Kyrgyzstan, Latvia, Lithuania, Moldova, Russia, Tajikistan, Turkmenistan, Ukraine, and Uzbekistan.

In the South Pacific, the Marshall Islands, Micronesia, and Palau gained full independence from the U.S. in 1991.

Following the breakup of the Socialist Federal Republic of Yugoslavia in 1992, the United States recognized Bosnia and Herzegovina, Croatia, Slovenia, and Macedonia as independent countries.

U.S. Census Bureau, Statistical Abstract of the United States: 2009

The Treaty of Maastricht created the European Union (EU) in 1992 with 12 member countries. The EU is not a state intended to replace existing states, but it is more than just an international organization. Its member states have set up common institutions to which they delegate some of their sovereignty so that decisions on specific matters of joint interest can be made democratically at a European level. This pooling of sovereignty is also called "European integration." The EU has grown in size with successive waves of accessions in 1995, 2004, and 2007. The 27 current members of the EU are: Austria, Belgium, Bulgaria, Cyprus, Czech Republic, Denmark, Estonia, Finland, France, Germany, Greece, Hungary, Ireland, Italy, Latvia, Lithuania, Luxembourg, Malta, the Netherlands, Poland, Portugal, Romania, Slovakia, Slovenia, Spain, Sweden, and the United Kingdom.

In 1992, the EU decided to establish economic and monetary union (EMU), with the introduction of a single European currency managed by a European Central Bank. The single currency—the euro—became a reality on January 1, 2002, when euro notes and coins replaced national currencies in 12 of the then 15 countries of the European Union (Belgium, Germany, Greece, Spain, France, Ireland, Italy, Luxembourg, the Netherlands, Austria, Portugal, and Finland). Since then, 12 countries have become members of the EU, but Slovenia, Malta, and Cyprus have been the only new members of the EU to adopt the euro as the national currency.

On January 1, 1993, Czechoslovakia was succeeded by two independent countries: the Czech Republic and Slovakia. Eritrea announced its independence from Ethiopia in April 1993 and was subsequently recognized as an independent nation by the United States. In May of 2002, Timor-Leste won independence from Indonesia.

Serbia and Montenegro, both former republics of Yugoslavia, became independent of one another on May 31, 2006. This separation is seen in the population estimates tables (Tables 1288, 1290, and 1305), but some tables still show both countries as combined. On February 17, 2008, Kosovo declared its independence from Serbia, making it the world's newest independent state.

The population estimates and projections used in Tables 1285–1288, 1290, and 1295 were prepared by the Census Bureau. For each country, the data on population, by age and sex, fertility, mortality, and international migration were evaluated and, where necessary, adjusted for inconsistencies and errors in the data. In most instances, comprehensive projections were made by the component method, resulting in distributions of the population by age and sex and requiring an assessment of probable future trends of fertility, mortality, and international migration.

Economic associations—The Organization for European Economic Co-Operation (OEEC), a regional grouping of Western European countries established in 1948 for the purpose of harmonizing national economic policies and conditions, was succeeded on September 30, 1961, by the Organization for Economic Cooperation and Development (OECD). The member nations of the OECD are Australia, Austria, Belgium, Canada, Czech Republic, Denmark, Finland, France, Germany, Greece, Hungary, Iceland, Ireland, Italy, Japan, Luxembourg, Mexico, the Netherlands, New Zealand, Norway, Poland, Portugal, Slovakia, South Korea, Spain, Sweden, Switzerland, Turkey, the United Kingdom, and the United States.

Quality and comparability of the data—The quality and comparability of the data presented here are affected by a number of factors:

(1) The year for which data are presented may not be the same for all subjects for a particular country or for a given subject for different countries, though the data shown are the most recent available. All such variations have been noted. The data shown are for calendar years except as otherwise specified.

(2) The bases, methods of estimating, methods of data collection, extent of coverage, precision of definition, scope of territory, and margins of error may vary for different items within a particular country, and for like items for different countries. Footnotes and headnotes to the tables give a few of the major time-periods and coverage qualifications

attached to the figures; considerably more detail is presented in the source publications. Many of the measures shown are, at best, merely rough indicators of magnitude.

(3) Figures shown in this section for the United States may not always agree with figures shown in the preceding sections. Disagreements may be attributable to the use of differing original sources, a difference in the definition of geographic limits (the 50 states, conterminous United States only, or the United States including certain outlying areas and possessions), or to possible adjustments made in the United States' figures by other sources in order to make them more comparable with figures from other countries.

International comparisons of national accounts data—In order to compare national accounts data for different countries, it is necessary to convert each country's data into a common unit of currency, usually the U.S. dollar. The market exchange rates, which are often used in converting national currencies, do not necessarily reflect the relative purchasing power in the various countries. It is necessary that the goods and services produced in different countries be valued consistently if the differences observed are meant to reflect real differences in the volumes of goods and services produced. The use of purchasing power parities (see Tables 1305, 1306, and 1347) instead of exchange rates is intended to achieve this objective.

The method used to present the data shown in Table 1306 is to construct volume measures directly by revaluing the goods and services sold in different countries at a common set of international prices. By dividing the ratio of the gross domestic products of two countries expressed in their own national currencies by the corresponding ratio calculated at constant international prices, it is possible to derive the implied purchasing power parity (PPP) between the two currencies concerned. PPPs show how many units of currency are needed in one country to buy the same amount of goods and services that one unit of currency will buy in the other country. For further information, see *National Accounts, Main Aggregates, Volume I,* issued annually by the Organisation for Economic Cooperation and Development, Paris, France.

International Standard Industrial Classification—The original version of the International Standard Industrial Classification of All Economic Activities (ISIC) was adopted in 1948. Wide use has been made both nationally and internationally in classifying data according to kind of economic activity in the fields of production, employment, national income, and other economic statistics. A number of countries have utilized the ISIC as the basis for devising their industrial classification scheme.

Substantial comparability has been attained between the industrial classifications of many other countries, including the United States and the ISIC by ensuring, as far as practicable, that the categories at detailed levels of classification in national schemes fitted into only one category of the ISIC. The United Nations, the International Labour Organization, the Food and Agriculture Organization, and other international bodies have utilized the ISIC in publishing and analyzing statistical data. Revisions of the ISIC were issued in 1958, 1968, and 1989.

International maps—A series of regional world maps is provided on pages 806–812. References are included in Table 1288 for easy location of individual countries on the maps. The Robinson map projection is used for this series of maps. A map projection is used to portray all or part of the round Earth on a flat surface, but this cannot be done without some distortion. For the Robinson projection, distortion is very low along the Equator and within 45 degrees of the center but is greatest near the poles. For additional information on map projections and maps, please contact the Earth Science Information Center, U.S. Geological Survey, 507 National Center, Reston, VA 22092.

U.S. Census Bureau, Statistical Abstract of the United States: 2009

S5 (Asia and Russia)

S6 (Australia, SE Asia, and Pacific Islands)

S4 (Africa)

S3 (Europe)

S2 (South America)

S1 (North and Central America)

806 International Statistics

S1 (North and Central America)

U.S. Census Bureau, Statistical Abstract of the United States: 2009

Caribbean Sea

Venezuela

Guyana
Suriname
French Guiana
(France)

Colombia

Ecuador

Galapagos Islands
(Ecuador)

Peru

Brazil

Bolivia

Pacific Ocean

Paraguay

Atlantic Ocean

Uruguay

Chile — Argentina

Falkland Islands
(United Kingdom)

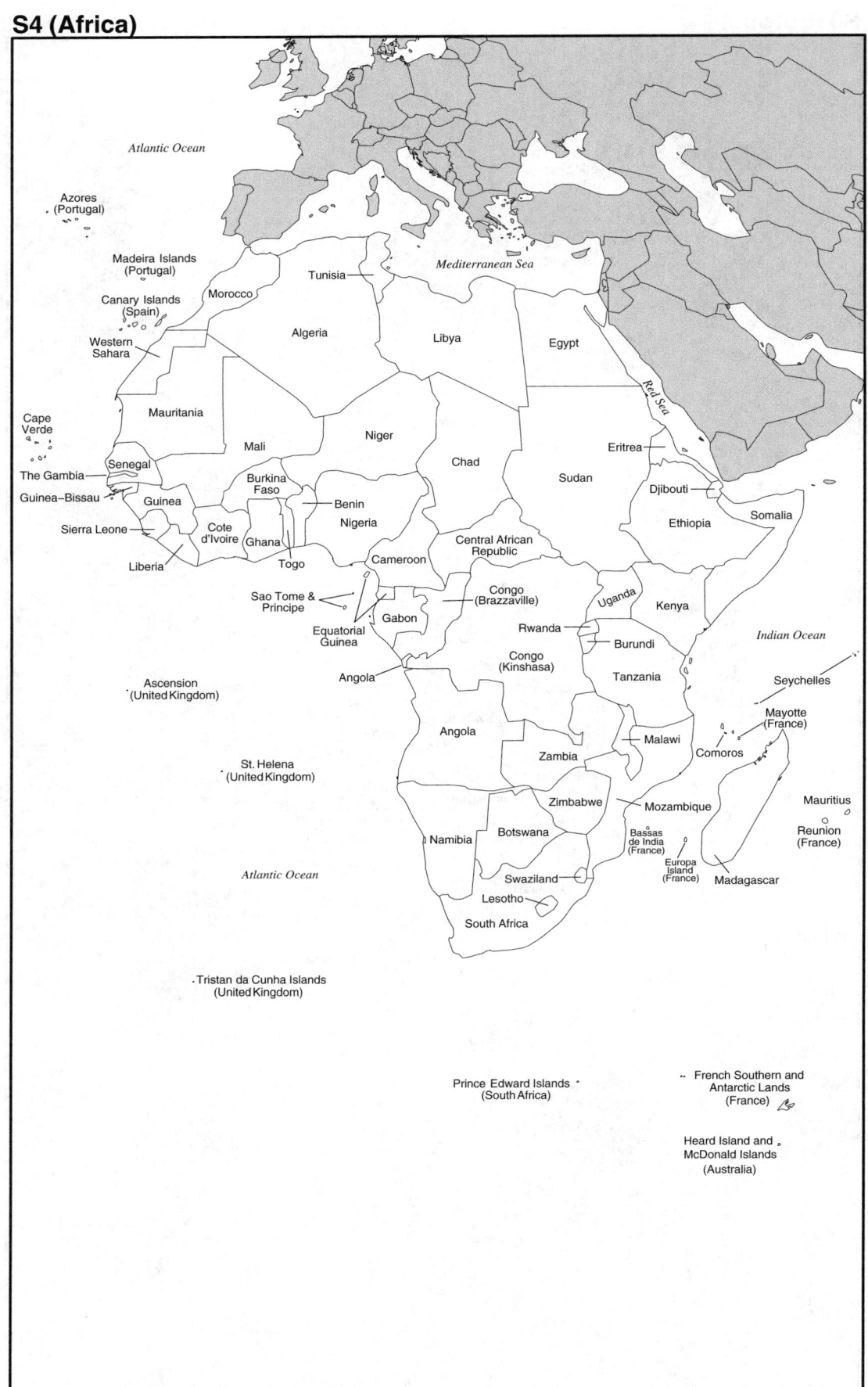

Atlantic Ocean

Azores
(Portugal)

Madeira Islands
(Portugal)

Canary Islands
(Spain)

Western
Sahara

Morocco

Tunisia

Mediterranean Sea

Algeria

Libya

Egypt

Red Sea

Cape
Verde

Mauritania

Mali

Niger

Chad

Sudan

Eritrea

Djibouti

The Gambia
Senegal
Guinea–Bissau
Guinea
Sierra Leone
Liberia

Burkina
Faso
Benin
Nigeria
Cote
d'Ivoire
Ghana
Togo
Cameroon

Central African
Republic

Ethiopia

Somalia

Sao Tome &
Principe

Equatorial
Guinea

Gabon

Congo
(Brazzaville)

Uganda

Kenya

Indian Ocean

Rwanda
Burundi

Ascension
(United Kingdom)

Angola

Congo
(Kinshasa)

Tanzania

Seychelles

Mayotte
(France)

Comoros

St. Helena
(United Kingdom)

Angola

Zambia

Malawi

Mauritius

Reunion
(France)

Atlantic Ocean

Namibia

Botswana

Zimbabwe

Mozambique

Bassas
de India
(France)
Europa
Island
(France)

Madagascar

Swaziland

Lesotho

South Africa

Tristan da Cunha Islands
(United Kingdom)

Prince Edward Islands
(South Africa)

French Southern and
Antarctic Lands
(France)

Heard Island and
McDonald Islands
(Australia)

Pacific Ocean

Arctic Ocean

North Korea
South Korea
Japan

Taiwan

Macau
Hong Kong
China

Russia

Mongolia

China

Bhutan

Bangladesh

Sri
Lanka

Indian Ocean

Nepal

India

Maldives

Kazakhstan

Kyrgyzstan

Uzbekistan

Tajikistan

Afghanistan

Pakistan

Turkmenistan

Socotra
(Yemen)

Caspian Sea

Iran

Azerbaijan

Oman

Georgia

Bahrain

Qatar

United Arab
Emirates

Armenia

Iraq

Kuwait

Yemen

Turkey

Syria

Jordan

Saudi
Arabia

Black Sea

Cyprus

Lebanon
West Bank
Gaza Strip
Israel

Red Sea

U.S. Census Bureau, Statistical Abstract of the United States: 2009

Pitcairn Islands (U.K.)

Pacific Ocean

French Polynesia (France)

Kingman Reef (U.S.)

Palmyra Atoll (U.S.)

Jarvis Island (U.S.)

Kiribati

Cook Islands (New Zealand)

Johnston Atoll (U.S.)

Midway Islands (U.S.)

Howland Island (U.S.)

Baker Island (U.S.)

Kiribati

Tokelau (New Zealand)

Samoa

American Samoa (U.S.)

Niue (New Zealand)

Tonga

Tuvalu

Wallis and Futuna (France)

Fiji

Wake Island (U.S.)

Kiribati

Nauru

Marshall Islands

Vanuatu

New Caledonia (France)

New Zealand

Northern Mariana Islands (U.S.)

Guam (U.S.)

Federated States of Micronesia

Solomon Islands

Papua New Guinea

Australia

Palau

Philippines

East Timor

Indonesia

Australia

Vietnam

Brunei

Malaysia

Singapore

Laos

Cambodia

Thailand

Burma

Indian Ocean

Table 1285. **Total World Population: 1980 to 2050**

[As of midyear (**4,453 represents 4,453,000,000**)]

Year	Population (mil.)	Average annual [1] Growth rate (percent)	Average annual [1] Population change (mil.)	Year	Population (mil.)	Average annual [1] Growth rate (percent)	Average annual [1] Population change (mil.)
1980	4,453	1.7	76.2	2015	7,270	1.1	79.3
1990	5,282	1.6	83.3	2020	7,659	1.0	75.5
1995	5,691	1.4	80.4	2025	8,027	0.9	70.8
2000	6,085	1.3	77.4	2030	8,373	0.8	66.6
2007	6,628	1.2	79.4	2035	8,699	0.7	62.6
2008	6,707	1.2	79.8	2040	9,003	0.6	58.2
2009	6,787	1.2	80.1	2045	9,284	0.6	53.1
2010	6,867	1.2	80.6	2050	9,539	(NA)	(NA)

NA Not available. [1] Represents change from year shown to immediate succeeding year.
Source: U.S. Census Bureau, International Data Base, "Total Midyear Population for the World: 1950–2050," updated 18 June 2008; <http://www.census.gov/ipc/www/idb/>.

Table 1286. **Population by Continent: 1980 to 2050**

[**In millions, except percent (4,453 represents 4,453,000,000). As of midyear**]

Year	World	Africa [1]	North America [1]	South America [1]	Asia	Europe [1]	Oceania
1980	4,453	478	371	242	2,644	695	23
1990	5,282	633	423	297	3,180	722	27
2000	6,085	810	485	349	3,678	731	31
2010	6,867	1,017	539	398	4,149	729	35
2020	7,659	1,252	592	444	4,611	720	40
2030	8,373	1,508	644	483	4,993	702	44
2040	9,003	1,784	691	512	5,291	679	47
2050	9,539	2,073	732	531	5,503	649	50
PERCENT DISTRIBUTION							
1980	100.0	10.7	8.3	5.4	59.4	15.6	0.5
2000	100.0	13.3	8.0	5.7	60.5	12.0	0.5
2050	100.0	21.7	7.7	5.6	57.7	6.8	0.5

[1] Estimates and projections for France now include the 4 overseas departments of French Guiana, Guadeloupe, Martinique, and Reunion in the national total. These areas will now be included in the same regions as France (Europe) and not in the regions where they were included in prior releases (French Guiana in South America, Guadeloupe and Martinique in North America, and Reunion in Africa). Saint Barthelemy and Saint Martin recently voted to become French overseas collectivities apart from Guadeloupe and are included in the totals for North America.
Source: U.S. Census Bureau, "International Data Base" (as of 18 June 2008); <http://www.census.gov/ipc/www/idb/>.

Table 1287. **Population and Population Change, by Development Status: 1950 to 2050**

[**(2,556 represents 2,556,000,000). As of midyear**. Minus sign (–) indicates decrease. The "less developed" countries include all of Africa, all of Asia except Japan, the Transcaucasian and Central Asian republics of the New Independent States, all of Latin America and the Caribbean, and all of Oceania except Australia, New Zealand, and Hawaii. This category matches the "less developed country" classification employed by the United Nations]

Year	Number (mil.) World	Number (mil.) Less developed countries [1]	Number (mil.) More developed countries [1]	Percent of world Less developed countries [1]	Percent of world More developed countries [1]
POPULATION					
1950	2,556	1,749	807	68.4	31.6
1960	3,042	2,130	911	70.0	30.0
1970	3,712	2,707	1,004	72.9	27.1
1980	4,453	3,371	1,082	75.7	24.3
1990	5,282	4,138	1,144	78.3	21.7
2000	6,085	4,890	1,195	80.4	19.6
2010	6,867	5,642	1,224	82.2	17.8
2020	7,659	6,417	1,243	83.8	16.2
2030	8,373	7,124	1,249	85.1	14.9
2040	9,003	7,756	1,248	86.1	13.9
2050	9,539	8,301	1,238	87.0	13.0
POPULATION CHANGE					
1950–1960	486	382	104	78.6	21.4
1960–1970	670	577	93	86.1	13.9
1970–1980	741	663	78	89.5	10.5
1980–1990	830	767	62	92.5	7.5
1990–2000	803	752	50	93.8	6.2
2000–2010	782	752	30	96.2	3.8
2010–2020	792	774	18	97.7	2.3
2020–2030	714	707	7	99.1	0.9
2030–2040	630	632	–2	100.3	–0.3
2040–2050	536	545	–9	101.8	–1.8

[1] See footnote 1, Table 1286.
Source: U.S. Census Bureau, "International Data Base" (as of 18 June 2008); <http://www.census.gov/ipc/www/idb/>.

Table 1288. **Population by Country or Area: 1990 to 2010**

[5,282,372 represents 5,282,372,000. Population data generally are de facto figures for the present territory. Population estimates were derived from information available as of winter 2007–08. See text of this section for general comments concerning the data. For details of methodology, coverage, and reliability, see coverage, and reliability, see source. Minus sign (–) indicates decrease]

Country or area	Map reference, see p. 806–812	Midyear population (1,000)				Population rank, 2008	Annual rate of growth,[1] 2000–2010 (percent)	Population per sq. mile, 2008	Area (sq. mile)
		1990	2000	2008	2010, proj.				
World	S0	**5,282,372**	**6,084,908**	**6,706,993**	**6,866,880**	(X)	**1.2**	**133**	**50,464,436**
Afghanistan	S5	14,669	23,898	32,738	34,505	38	3.7	131	250,000
Albania	S3	3,251	3,474	3,620	3,660	129	0.5	342	10,579
Algeria	S4	25,089	30,429	33,770	34,586	36	1.3	37	919,591
Andorra	S3	53	65	83	85	198	2.6	475	174
Angola	S4	8,297	10,377	12,531	13,068	69	2.3	26	481,351
Antigua and Barbuda	S1	64	75	85	87	197	1.4	494	171
Argentina	S2	33,036	37,336	40,482	41,343	30	1.0	38	1,056,637
Armenia	S5	3,377	3,043	2,969	2,967	137	–0.3	271	10,965
Australia	S6	16,956	19,053	21,007	21,516	54	1.2	7	2,941,285
Austria	S3	7,723	8,113	8,206	8,214	92	0.1	258	31,832
Azerbaijan	S5	7,200	7,809	8,178	8,304	93	0.6	246	33,243
Bahamas, The	S1	257	290	307	311	175	0.7	79	3,888
Bahrain	S4	500	634	718	737	161	1.5	2,798	257
Bangladesh	S5	109,897	130,407	153,547	159,765	7	2.0	2,970	51,703
Barbados	S1	263	273	282	284	179	0.4	1,698	166
Belarus	S3	10,201	10,034	9,686	9,613	84	–0.4	121	80,154
Belgium	S3	9,969	10,264	10,404	10,423	76	0.2	890	11,690
Belize	S1	191	248	301	315	177	2.4	34	8,803
Benin	S4	4,705	6,619	8,533	9,056	91	3.1	200	42,710
Bhutan	S5	615	606	682	700	162	1.4	38	18,147
Bolivia	S2	6,574	8,153	9,248	9,499	87	1.5	22	418,683
Bosnia and Herzegovina	S3	4,424	4,035	4,590	4,622	119	1.4	233	19,741
Botswana	S4	1,263	1,639	1,842	1,893	146	1.4	8	226,012
Brazil	S2	151,170	176,320	196,343	201,103	5	1.3	60	3,265,061
Brunei	S6	253	325	381	395	174	1.9	187	2,035
Bulgaria	S3	8,894	7,818	7,263	7,149	96	–0.9	170	42,683
Burkina Faso	S4	8,361	11,588	15,265	16,242	62	3.4	144	105,714
Burma	S5	39,243	44,301	47,758	48,511	26	0.9	188	253,954
Burundi	S4	5,505	6,621	8,691	9,281	90	3.4	878	9,903
Cambodia	S5	9,345	12,396	14,242	14,753	63	1.7	209	68,154
Cameroon	S4	11,884	15,343	18,468	19,294	58	2.3	102	181,251
Canada	S1	27,791	31,100	33,213	33,760	37	0.8	9	3,511,006
Cape Verde	S1	349	402	427	432	170	0.7	274	1,556
Central African Republic	S4	3,085	3,940	4,444	4,579	121	1.5	18	240,533
Chad	S4	5,841	7,943	10,111	10,543	81	2.8	21	486,178
Chile	S2	13,129	15,156	16,454	16,746	60	1.0	57	289,112
China [2]	S5	1,148,364	1,268,853	1,330,045	1,347,563	1	0.6	369	3,600,930
Colombia	S2	32,957	39,817	45,014	46,271	28	1.5	112	401,042
Comoros	S4	429	579	732	773	160	2.9	873	838
Congo (Brazzaville) [3]	S4	2,265	3,102	3,903	4,124	128	2.8	30	131,853
Congo (Kinshasa) [3]	S4	39,047	51,849	66,515	70,916	18	3.1	76	875,521
Costa Rica	S2	3,027	3,711	4,196	4,311	123	1.5	215	19,560
Cote d'Ivoire	S4	12,491	16,885	20,180	21,059	55	2.2	164	122,780
Croatia	S3	4,508	4,411	4,492	4,487	120	0.2	206	21,781
Cuba	S1	10,513	11,106	11,424	11,477	72	0.3	267	42,803
Cyprus	S5	681	758	793	801	158	0.5	222	3,568
Czech Republic	S3	10,310	10,270	10,221	10,202	78	–0.1	343	29,836
Denmark	S3	5,141	5,337	5,485	5,516	110	0.3	335	16,368
Djibouti	S4	366	431	506	526	167	2.0	60	8,486
Dominica	S1	70	71	73	73	201	0.3	250	290
Dominican Republic	S1	7,083	8,410	9,507	9,794	86	1.5	509	18,680
Ecuador	S2	10,318	12,505	13,928	14,245	65	1.3	130	106,888
Egypt	S4	56,683	70,512	81,714	84,440	16	1.8	213	384,344
El Salvador	S1	5,100	6,126	7,066	7,304	99	1.8	883	8,000
Equatorial Guinea	S4	371	491	616	651	164	2.8	57	10,830
Eritrea	S4	3,138	4,197	5,502	5,793	109	3.2	117	46,842
Estonia	S3	1,569	1,380	1,308	1,291	151	–0.7	78	16,684
Ethiopia	S4	48,397	64,165	82,545	88,013	14	3.2	191	432,310
Fiji	S6	738	833	932	958	156	1.4	132	7,054
Finland	S3	4,986	5,169	5,245	5,255	113	0.2	45	117,557
France [4]	S3	58,168	61,137	64,058	64,768	21	0.6	259	247,125
Gabon	S4	938	1,236	1,486	1,545	150	2.2	15	99,486
Gambia, The	S4	949	1,368	1,735	1,831	147	2.9	449	3,861
Georgia [5]	S5	5,426	4,777	4,631	4,601	116	–0.4	172	26,911
Germany [5]	S3	79,380	82,188	82,370	82,283	15	(Z)	611	134,835
Ghana	S4	15,414	19,736	23,383	24,279	48	2.1	262	89,166
Greece	S3	10,130	10,559	10,723	10,750	74	0.2	212	50,502
Grenada	S2	92	89	90	91	195	0.2	680	133
Guatemala	S1	8,966	11,085	13,002	13,550	67	2.0	311	41,865
Guinea	S4	6,118	8,350	9,807	10,324	83	2.1	103	94,927
Guinea-Bissau	S4	996	1,279	1,503	1,565	148	2.0	139	10,811
Guyana	S2	751	755	771	774	159	0.2	10	76,004
Haiti	S1	6,131	7,444	8,925	9,386	89	2.3	839	10,641
Honduras	S1	4,792	6,348	7,639	7,944	94	2.2	177	43,201
Hungary	S3	10,372	10,137	9,931	9,880	82	–0.3	279	35,653
Iceland	S1	255	281	304	309	176	0.9	8	38,707
India	S5	838,159	1,004,124	1,147,996	1,184,090	2	1.6	1,000	1,147,950
Indonesia	S6	181,770	213,829	237,512	242,968	4	1.3	337	705,189
Iran	S5	56,669	63,273	65,875	67,038	19	0.6	104	631,660

See footnotes at end of table.

U.S. Census Bureau, Statistical Abstract of the United States: 2009

Table 1288. **Population by Country or Area: 1990 to 2010**—Con.

[See headnote, page 814]

Country or area	Map refer- ence	Midyear population (1,000)				Popu- lation rank, 2008	Annual rate of growth, [1] 2000– 2010 (percent)	Popula- tion per sq. mile, 2008	Area (sq. mile)
		1990	2000	2008	2010, proj.				
Iraq	S5	18,135	22,676	28,221	29,672	42	2.7	169	166,858
Ireland	S3	3,508	3,792	4,156	4,250	125	1.1	156	26,598
Israel	S4	4,478	6,115	7,112	7,354	98	1.8	906	7,849
Italy	S3	56,743	57,719	58,145	58,091	23	0.1	512	113,521
Jamaica	S1	2,347	2,616	2,804	2,847	138	0.8	671	4,181
Japan	S5	123,537	126,729	127,288	126,804	10	(Z)	880	144,689
Jordan	S4	3,262	4,999	6,199	6,486	104	2.6	175	35,510
Kazakhstan	S5	16,398	15,032	15,341	15,460	61	0.3	15	1,030,811
Kenya	S4	23,354	30,508	37,954	40,047	34	2.7	173	219,788
Kiribati	S6	71	92	110	115	190	2.3	352	313
Korea, North	S5	20,019	21,648	23,479	23,802	47	0.9	505	46,490
Korea, South	S5	42,869	46,839	48,379	48,636	25	0.4	1,276	37,911
Kuwait	S5	2,142	1,974	2,597	2,788	139	3.5	377	6,880
Kyrgyzstan	S5	4,382	4,851	5,357	5,509	112	1.3	73	73,861
Laos	S5	4,210	5,498	6,678	6,994	102	2.4	75	89,112
Latvia	S3	2,664	2,376	2,245	2,218	141	−0.7	91	24,552
Lebanon	S4	3,150	3,581	3,972	4,061	126	1.3	1,006	3,950
Lesotho	S4	1,721	2,068	2,128	2,133	142	0.3	182	11,718
Liberia	S4	2,117	2,695	3,335	3,534	133	2.7	90	37,189
Libya	S4	4,140	5,115	6,174	6,447	105	2.3	9	679,359
Liechtenstein	S3	29	32	34	35	210	0.8	555	62
Lithuania	S5	3,695	3,654	3,565	3,545	130	−0.3	142	25,174
Luxembourg	S3	383	439	486	498	168	1.3	487	998
Macedonia	S3	1,861	2,015	2,061	2,072	144	0.3	215	9,597
Madagascar	S4	11,633	15,742	20,043	21,282	56	3.0	89	224,533
Malawi	S4	9,536	11,560	13,932	14,613	64	2.3	384	36,324
Malaysia	S6	17,507	21,804	25,274	26,160	46	1.8	199	126,853
Maldives	S5	217	300	386	396	173	2.8	3,332	116
Mali	S4	8,085	10,049	12,324	13,025	70	2.6	26	471,042
Malta	S4	359	390	404	407	171	0.4	3,307	122
Marshall Islands	S6	46	53	63	66	205	2.2	904	70
Mauritania	S4	1,984	2,668	3,365	3,561	132	2.9	8	397,838
Mauritius	S4	1,062	1,186	1,274	1,294	152	0.9	1,626	784
Mexico	S1	84,914	99,927	109,955	112,469	11	1.2	148	742,486
Micronesia, Federated States of	S6	109	108	108	107	192	−0.1	397	271
Moldova	S5	4,394	4,391	4,324	4,317	122	−0.2	332	13,012
Monaco	S3	30	32	33	33	211	0.4	42,471	1
Mongolia	S5	2,218	2,664	2,996	3,087	136	1.5	5	603,906
Montenegro	S3	583	732	678	667	163	−0.9	127	5,333
Morocco	S4	24,735	30,184	34,343	35,373	35	1.6	199	172,317
Mozambique	S4	12,667	18,125	21,285	22,061	52	2.0	70	302,737
Namibia	S4	1,471	1,893	2,089	2,128	143	1.2	7	318,694
Nauru	S6	9	12	14	14	220	1.9	1,698	8
Nepal	S5	19,325	24,702	29,519	30,758	40	2.2	534	55,282
Netherlands	S3	14,952	15,908	16,645	16,783	59	0.5	1,272	13,082
New Zealand	S6	3,414	3,802	4,173	4,252	124	1.1	40	103,483
Nicaragua	S2	3,685	4,935	5,786	5,996	108	1.9	125	46,430
Niger	S4	7,945	10,516	13,273	14,054	66	2.9	27	489,073
Nigeria	S4	96,604	123,179	146,255	152,217	8	2.1	416	351,649
Norway	S3	4,242	4,492	4,644	4,676	115	0.4	39	118,865
Oman	S5	1,773	2,534	3,312	3,526	134	3.3	40	82,031
Pakistan	S5	114,607	146,405	172,800	179,659	6	2.0	575	300,664
Palau	S6	15	19	21	22	217	1.4	119	177
Panama	S2	2,393	2,900	3,310	3,411	135	1.6	113	29,340
Papua New Guinea	S6	3,828	4,934	5,932	6,182	106	2.3	34	174,849
Paraguay	S2	4,244	5,592	6,831	7,162	101	2.5	45	153,398
Peru	S2	21,600	26,087	29,181	29,907	41	1.4	59	494,208
Philippines	S6	65,088	81,222	96,062	99,900	12	2.1	834	115,124
Poland	S3	38,119	38,654	38,501	38,464	33	(Z)	328	117,554
Portugal	S3	9,923	10,336	10,677	10,736	75	0.4	301	35,502
Qatar	S5	446	627	825	841	157	2.9	187	4,416
Romania	S5	22,866	22,452	22,247	22,181	51	−0.1	250	88,934
Russia	S5	147,973	146,710	140,702	139,390	9	−0.5	21	6,562,083
Rwanda	S4	6,982	8,278	10,186	10,769	79	2.6	1,057	9,633
Saint Kitts and Nevis	S1	42	39	40	40	209	0.4	395	101
Saint Lucia	S1	138	153	160	161	187	0.5	682	234
Saint Vincent and the Grenadines	S1	107	115	118	119	189	0.3	789	150
Samoa	S0	172	197	217	223	182	1.3	192	1,133
San Marino	S3	23	27	30	31	212	1.3	1,294	23
Sao Tome and Principe	S4	119	160	206	219	185	3.2	533	386
Saudi Arabia	S4	16,061	23,147	28,147	29,207	43	2.3	34	829,996
Senegal	S4	7,846	10,332	12,853	13,516	68	2.7	173	74,131
Serbia	S3	9,348	10,118	10,159	10,173	80	0.1	298	34,116
Seychelles	S4	73	79	82	83	199	0.4	467	176
Sierra Leone	S4	4,226	4,816	6,295	6,589	103	3.1	228	27,653
Singapore	S6	3,047	4,037	4,608	4,701	118	1.5	17,500	263
Slovakia	S3	5,263	5,400	5,455	5,470	111	0.1	290	18,842
Slovenia	S3	1,991	2,011	2,008	2,003	145	(Z)	258	7,780
Solomon Islands	S6	335	466	581	610	165	2.7	55	10,633
Somalia	S4	6,692	7,386	9,559	10,112	85	3.1	39	242,216
South Africa	S4	38,476	45,064	48,783	49,109	24	0.9	104	471,008

See footnotes at end of table.

U.S. Census Bureau, Statistical Abstract of the United States: 2009

Table 1288. **Population by Country or Area: 1990 to 2010**—Con.

[See headnote, page 814]

Country or area	Map reference	Mid-year population (1,000)				Population rank, 2008	Annual rate of growth,[1] 2000–2010 (percent)	Population per sq. mile, 2008	Area (sq. mile)
		1990	2000	2008	2010, proj.				
Spain	S3	39,351	40,016	40,491	40,549	29	0.1	210	192,873
Sri Lanka	S5	17,365	19,436	21,129	21,514	53	1.0	845	24,996
Sudan	S4	26,050	34,194	40,218	41,980	31	2.1	44	917,375
Suriname	S2	395	432	476	487	169	1.2	8	62,344
Swaziland	S4	885	1,110	1,129	1,119	153	0.1	170	6,641
Sweden	S3	8,601	8,924	9,045	9,074	88	0.2	57	158,662
Switzerland	S3	6,837	7,267	7,582	7,623	95	0.5	494	15,355
Syria	S4	12,436	16,306	19,748	20,606	57	2.3	278	71,062
Tajikistan	S5	5,272	6,230	7,212	7,487	97	1.8	131	55,097
Tanzania	S4	25,214	33,712	40,213	41,893	32	2.2	118	342,100
Thailand	S5	55,197	61,863	65,493	66,303	20	0.7	331	197,595
Timor-Leste	S6	746	847	1,109	1,155	154	3.1	197	5,641
Togo	S4	3,505	4,712	5,859	6,185	107	2.7	279	20,998
Tonga	S0	92	102	119	123	188	1.8	430	277
Trinidad and Tobago	S2	1,198	1,118	1,047	1,029	155	−0.8	529	1,980
Tunisia	S4	8,211	9,568	10,384	10,589	77	1.0	173	59,985
Turkey	S5	56,085	65,667	71,893	73,322	17	1.1	242	297,591
Turkmenistan	S5	3,659	4,520	5,180	5,345	114	1.7	27	188,456
Tuvalu	S6	9	11	12	13	222	1.5	1,213	10
Uganda	S4	17,456	23,956	31,368	33,399	39	3.3	407	77,108
Ukraine	S5	51,622	49,005	45,994	45,416	27	−0.8	197	233,089
United Arab Emirates	S5	1,826	3,219	4,621	4,976	117	4.4	144	32,000
United Kingdom	S3	57,493	59,522	60,944	61,285	22	0.3	653	93,278
United States	S1	250,132	282,339	303,825	309,163	3	0.9	86	3,537,421
Uruguay	S2	3,110	3,328	3,478	3,510	131	0.5	52	67,035
Uzbekistan	S5	20,530	25,042	27,345	27,866	44	1.1	166	164,247
Vanuatu	S6	154	190	215	222	184	1.5	46	4,710
Venezuela	S2	19,325	23,493	26,415	27,223	45	1.5	78	340,560
Vietnam	S5	67,283	79,060	86,117	87,814	13	1.1	686	125,622
Yemen	S5	12,416	17,495	23,013	24,658	49	3.4	113	203,849
Zambia	S4	7,978	10,205	11,670	12,057	71	1.7	41	285,994
Zimbabwe	S4	10,156	11,820	11,350	11,652	73	−0.1	76	149,293
OTHER									
Taiwan [2]	S5	20,278	22,183	22,921	23,025	50	0.4	1,840	12,456
AREAS OF SPECIAL SOVEREIGNTY AND DEPENDENCIES									
American Samoa	S0	47	58	65	66	204	1.4	844	77
Anguilla	S1	8	11	14	15	219	2.6	358	39
Aruba	S1	63	90	102	105	193	1.5	1,363	75
Bermuda	S1	58	63	67	67	202	0.7	3,251	20
Cayman Islands	S1	26	38	48	50	208	2.7	477	100
Cook Islands	S0	18	16	12	11	221	−3.5	132	93
Faroe Islands	S3	47	46	49	49	207	0.7	90	541
French Polynesia	S0	202	249	283	291	178	1.6	200	1,413
Gaza Strip [6]	S4	646	1,130	1,500	1,604	149	3.5	10,793	139
Gibraltar	S3	29	28	28	28	214	0.2	12,088	2
Greenland	S1	56	57	58	58	206	0.1	(Z)	131,931
Guam	S6	134	155	176	181	186	1.5	842	209
Guernsey	S3	63	64	66	66	203	0.3	2,182	30
Hong Kong	S5	5,688	6,659	7,019	7,090	100	0.6	17,446	402
Isle of Man	S3	69	73	76	77	200	0.5	345	221
Jersey	S3	84	89	92	92	194	0.3	2,026	45
Macau	S6	352	432	546	568	166	2.7	50,475	11
Mayotte	S4	90	156	216	231	183	3.9	1,490	145
Montserrat	S1	11	4	5	5	226	2.6	132	39
Netherlands Antilles	S2	189	210	225	229	180	0.8	607	371
New Caledonia	S6	168	202	225	230	181	1.3	31	7,172
Northern Mariana Islands	S6	44	70	87	91	196	2.6	470	184
Puerto Rico	S1	3,537	3,816	3,958	3,986	127	0.4	1,156	3,425
Saint Barthelemy [4]	S1	5	7	7	7	224	0.4	924	8
Saint Helena	S4	7	7	8	8	223	0.6	48	159
Saint Martin [4]	S1	30	28	29	30	213	0.6	1,409	21
Saint Pierre and Miquelon	S1	6	7	7	7	225	0.2	76	93
Turks and Caicos Islands	S1	12	18	22	24	216	3.0	135	166
Virgin Islands	S1	104	109	110	110	191	0.1	822	134
Virgin Islands, British	S1	16	20	24	25	215	2.0	415	58
Wallis and Futuna	S6	13	15	15	15	218	0.5	144	106
West Bank [6]	S4	1,253	1,980	2,408	2,515	140	2.4	1,105	2,178
Western Sahara	S4	221	309	394	417	172	3.0	4	102,703

X Not applicable.   Z Less than 0.05 percent or less than one person per square mile.   [1] Computed by the exponential method. For explanation of average annual percent change, see Guide to Tabular Presentation.   [2] With the establishment of diplomatic relations with China on January 1, 1979, the U.S. government recognized the People's Republic of China as the sole legal government of China and acknowledged the Chinese position that there is only one China and that Taiwan is part of China.   [3] "Congo" is the official short-form name for both the Republic of Congo and the Democratic Republic of the Congo. To distinguish one from the other the U.S. Dept. of State adds the capital in parentheses. This practice is unofficial and provisional.   [4] Data for France include the overseas departments of French Guiana, Guadeloupe, Martinique, and Reunion. Saint Barthelemy and Saint Martin recently voted to become French overseas collectivities apart from Guadeloupe and are now listed individually.   [5] Data for 1990 are for former West Germany and East Germany combined.   [6] The Gaza Strip and West Bank are Israeli occupied with interim status subject to Israeli/Palestinian negotiations. The final status is yet to be determined.

Source: U.S. Census Bureau, "International Data Base" (as of 18 June 2008); <http://www.census.gov/ipc/www/idb/>.

Table 1289. **Foreign or Foreign-Born Population, Labor Force, and Net Migration in Selected OECD Countries: 2000 and 2005**

[**31,108 represents 31,108,000.** In Australia and the United States the data refer to people present in the country who are foreign born. In the European countries and Japan they generally refer to foreigners and represent the nationalities of residents]

Country	Foreign population [1]				Foreign labor force [2]				Average net migration 1990– 2005 [3] (per 1,000 popu- lation)
	Number (1,000)		Percent of total population		Number (1,000)		Percent of total labor force		
	2000	2005	2000	2005	2000	2005	2000	2005	
United States	**31,108**	**38,343**	**11.0**	**12.9**	**18,029**	**22,422**	**12.9**	**15.2**	**4.4**
Australia	4,418	4,830	23.0	23.8	2,373	2,604	24.7	24.9	5.2
Austria	702	802	8.8	9.7	(NA)	633	(NA)	14.8	3.9
Belgium	862	901	8.4	8.6	388	435	8.6	9.1	3.1
Denmark	259	270	4.8	5.0	(NA)	167	(NA)	6.1	2.1
France	(NA)	(NA)	(NA)	(NA)	1,578	1,456	6.0	5.3	1.2
Germany [4]	7,297	6,756	8.9	8.8	3,546	3,823	8.8	9.3	4.2
Italy [5]	1,380	2,671	2.4	4.6	838	(NA)	3.9	(NA)	3.5
Japan [6]	1,686	2,012	1.3	1.6	155	181	0.2	0.3	(Z)
Luxembourg	165	182	37.3	39.6	153	196	57.3	62.6	8.3
Netherlands	668	691	4.2	4.2	300	288	3.9	3.4	3.1
Spain [7]	896	2,739	2.2	6.2	455	1,689	2.5	8.1	6.0
Sweden	477	480	5.4	5.3	446	(NA)	10.5	(NA)	2.7
Switzerland [8]	1,384	1,512	19.3	20.3	717	830	20.1	20.9	4.2
United Kingdom [9]	2,342	3,035	4.0	5.2	1,107	1,504	4.0	5.4	1.4

NA Not available. [1] Data are from population registers of foreigners except for France, Greece, Mexico, and Poland (census), Ireland and the United Kingdom (Labour Force Survey), Portugal (residence permits), Australia (inter- and post-censal estimates), and the United States (Current Population Survey). [2] Includes unemployed except for Belgium, Greece, Norway, Luxembourg, Netherlands, and the United Kingdom. Germany, Luxembourg, and Netherlands include cross-border workers. Belgium and Italy include the self-employed. Data for Austria, Germany, and Luxembourg are from social security registers, and for Denmark, from the register of population. Data for Italy, Spain, and Switzerland are from residence or work permits. Figures for Japan and Netherlands are estimates. Data for other countries are from labor force surveys. [3] Or latest period available. [4] Labor force data are for western Germany only. [5] Children under 18 who are registered on their parents' permit are not counted. [6] Data are based on registered foreign nationals which include foreigners staying in Japan for more than 90 days. [7] Number of foreigners with a residence permit. Permits of short duration (less than 6 months) as well as students are excluded. [8] Number of foreigners with an annual residence permit or with a settlement permit (permanent permit). Seasonal and frontier workers are excluded. [9] Estimated from the annual labour force survey. Fluctuations from year to year may be due to sampling error.

Source: Organization for Economic Cooperation and Development, Paris, France, *International Migration Outlook* (2007 edition) (copyright).

Table 1290. **Age Distribution by Country or Area: 2008 and 2010**

[**In percent.** Covers countries with 13 million or more population in 2008]

Country or area	2008		2010, proj.		Country or area	2008		2010, proj.	
	Under 15 years old	65 years old and over	Under 15 years old	65 years old and over		Under 15 years old	65 years old and over	Under 15 years old	65 years old and over
World	**27.3**	**7.6**	**26.9**	**7.7**	Korea, South	17.4	10.5	16.2	11.1
					Madagascar	43.7	3.1	43.3	3.0
Afghanistan	44.6	2.4	44.4	2.4	Malawi	46.0	2.7	45.6	2.7
Algeria	26.3	5.0	24.7	5.1	Malaysia	31.8	4.9	31.0	5.1
Argentina	25.8	10.8	25.5	10.9	Mexico	29.6	6.1	28.7	6.4
Australia	18.8	13.3	18.4	13.7	Morocco	30.5	5.2	29.6	5.3
Bangladesh	33.4	3.5	33.8	3.7	Mozambique	44.5	2.8	44.1	2.9
Bolivia	33.5	4.7	32.1	4.9	Nepal	38.0	3.8	37.3	3.9
Brazil	27.0	6.3	26.5	6.6	Netherlands	17.6	14.6	17.2	15.2
Burkina Faso	46.3	2.5	46.0	2.5	Niger	47.0	2.4	46.9	2.4
Burma	25.7	5.4	24.9	5.5	Nigeria	41.7	3.0	41.2	3.1
Cambodia	33.2	3.6	32.2	3.7	Pakistan	37.8	4.2	36.6	4.2
Cameroon	41.1	3.2	40.7	3.3	Peru	29.7	5.6	28.5	5.8
Canada	16.3	14.9	15.9	15.5	Philippines	35.5	4.1	34.9	4.2
Chile	23.6	8.8	22.7	9.3	Poland	15.2	13.4	14.8	13.5
China [1]	20.1	8.0	19.6	8.3	Romania	15.6	14.7	15.5	14.7
Colombia . . . . [2]	29.4	5.5	28.5	5.8	Russia	14.6	14.1	15.0	13.3
Congo (Kinshasa) [2] . .	47.1	2.5	46.7	2.5	Saudi Arabia	38.0	2.4	38.0	2.5
Cote d'Ivoire	40.9	2.8	40.2	2.9	South Africa	29.2	5.3	28.6	5.5
Ecuador	32.1	5.2	31.0	5.4	Spain	14.4	17.9	14.5	18.4
Egypt	31.8	4.7	31.0	4.9	Sri Lanka	24.1	7.9	23.6	8.3
Ethiopia	46.0	2.7	46.2	2.7	Sudan	41.1	2.5	40.2	2.5
France [3]	18.6	16.3	18.6	16.5	Syria	36.2	3.3	35.5	3.4
Germany	13.8	20.0	13.5	20.4	Taiwan [1]	17.3	10.5	16.2	10.8
Ghana	37.8	3.6	36.9	3.6	Tanzania	43.5	2.8	42.5	2.9
Guatemala	40.1	3.7	38.7	3.8	Thailand	21.2	8.5	20.4	8.9
India	31.5	5.2	30.7	5.4	Turkey	24.4	7.0	23.5	7.3
Indonesia	28.4	5.8	27.7	6.1	Uganda	50.0	2.2	50.0	2.1
Iran	22.3	5.4	21.3	5.4	Ukraine	13.9	16.1	13.7	15.5
Iraq	39.2	3.0	38.5	3.0	United Kingdom	16.9	16.0	16.5	16.4
Italy	13.6	20.0	13.4	20.3	**United States**	**20.1**	**12.7**	**20.0**	**13.0**
Japan	13.7	21.6	13.3	22.6	Uzbekistan	29.0	5.0	27.3	4.7
Kazakhstan	22.1	8.2	21.6	7.6	Venezuela	31.0	5.1	30.0	5.3
Kenya	42.2	2.6	42.3	2.7	Vietnam	25.6	5.8	24.3	5.7
Korea, North	22.9	8.8	22.2	9.5	Yemen	46.2	2.6	46.1	2.5

[1] See footnote 2, Table 1288. [2] See footnote 3, Table 1288. [3] See footnote 4, Table 1288.
Source: U.S. Census Bureau, "International Data Base" (as of 18 June 2008); <http://www.census.gov/ipc/www/idb/>.

Table 1291. **Births to Unmarried Women by Country: 1980 to 2006**
[Percent of all live births]

Country	1980	1990	2000	2004	2005	2006
United States [1]	**18.4**	**28.0**	**33.2**	**35.8**	**36.9**	**38.5**
Canada	12.8	24.4	28.3	25.6	25.6	(NA)
Japan	0.8	1.1	1.6	2.0	2.0	2.1
Denmark	33.2	46.4	44.6	45.4	45.7	46.4
France	11.4	30.1	43.6	47.4	48.4	50.5
Germany [2]	(NA)	15.1	23.4	27.9	29.2	30.0
Ireland	5.9	14.6	31.5	31.9	32.0	33.2
Italy	4.3	6.5	9.7	(NA)	15.4	(NA)
Netherlands	4.1	11.4	24.9	32.5	34.9	37.1
Spain	3.9	9.6	17.7	25.1	26.6	28.4
Sweden	39.7	47.0	55.3	55.4	55.4	55.5
United Kingdom	11.5	27.9	39.5	42.3	42.9	43.7

NA Not available. [1] Marital status is inferred from a comparison of the child's and parents' surnames on the birth certificate for those states that do not report on marital status. No estimates are included for misstatements on birth records or failures to register births. [2] Data are for 1991 instead of 1990.

Source: U.S. Bureau of Labor Statistics, updated and revised from "Families and Work Transition in 12 Countries 1980–2001," *Monthly Labor Review*, September 2003, with national sources, some of which may be unpublished.

Table 1292. **Marriage and Divorce Rates by Country: 1980 to 2006**
[Per 1,000 population aged 15–64 years]

Country	Marriage rate				Divorce rate			
	1980	1990	2000	2006	1980	1990	2000	2006
United States [1]	**15.9**	**14.9**	**12.5**	**10.2**	**7.9**	**7.2**	**6.2**	**5.1**
Canada	11.5	10.0	7.5	6.6	3.7	4.2	3.4	(NA)
Japan	9.8	8.4	9.3	(NA)	1.8	1.8	3.1	(NA)
Denmark	8.0	9.1	10.8	10.1	4.1	4.0	4.0	4.0
France	9.7	7.7	7.9	6.9	2.4	2.8	3.0	3.5
Germany [2]	(NA)	8.2	7.6	6.8	(NA)	2.5	3.5	3.5
Ireland [3]	10.9	8.3	7.6	(NA)	(NA)	(NA)	1.0	(NA)
Italy	8.7	8.2	7.3	6.3	0.3	0.7	1.0	(NA)
Netherlands	9.6	9.3	8.2	6.5	2.7	2.8	3.2	2.9
Spain	9.4	8.6	7.9	7.0	(NA)	0.9	1.4	(NA)
Sweden	7.1	7.4	7.0	7.7	3.7	3.5	3.8	3.4
United Kingdom	11.6	10.0	8.0	(NA)	4.1	4.1	4.0	(NA)

NA Not available. [1] Marriage rates include unlicensed marriages in California; exclude data for Louisiana in 2006. Divorce rates exclude data for California, Georgia, Hawaii, Indiana, and Louisiana in 2004; and California, Georgia, Hawaii, Indiana, Louisiana, and Minnesota in 2005 and 2006. [2] Data are for 1991 instead of 1990. [3] Divorce not allowed by law prior to 1997.

Source: U.S. Bureau of Labor Statistics, updated and revised from "Families and Work in Transition in 13 Countries, 1980-2001," *Monthly Labor Review*, September 2003, with national sources, some of which may be unpublished.

Table 1293. **Single-Parent Households: 1980 to 2007**
[In thousands (6,061 represents 6,061,000). For the United Kingdom in 1981, children are defined as those under 15 and those who are 15, 16, or 17 and attended school full-time; for later years, children are defined as those under 16 and those who are 16 or 17 and attend school full-time. For Ireland, children are defined as those under 15. For France, children are defined as those under 25. For Canada for 2001 onward and for Germany for 1995 onward, children are of all ages. For all other countries, children are defined as children living at home, or away at school, under 18. Data are generally for the entire year, but in some instances they are only for a particular month within the year]

Country and year	Number	Percent of all households with children	Country and year	Number	Percent of all households with children
United States:			Germany:		
1980	6,061	19.5	1991	1,429	15.2
1990	7,752	24.0	1995 [1]	2,496	18.8
2000	9,357	27.0	2000 [1]	2,274	17.6
2006	10,484	28.8	2006	2,608	21.1
Canada:			Ireland: [2]		
1981	437	12.7	1981	30	7.2
1991	572	16.2	1991	44	10.7
2001 [1]	1,184	23.5	2002	50	17.4
2006	1,276	24.6	2006	78	22.6
Japan:			Netherlands:		
1980	796	4.9	1988	179	9.6
1990	934	6.5	2000	240	13.0
2000	996	8.3	2007	301	18.4
2005	1,163	10.2	Sweden:		
Denmark: [2]			1985	117	11.2
1980	99	13.4	1995 [1]	189	17.4
1990	117	17.8	2000	233	21.4
2001	120	18.4	2005	242	22.0
2007	140	20.7	United Kingdom: [3]		
France:			1981	1,010	13.9
1982	887	10.2	1991	1,344	19.4
1990	1,175	13.2	2000	1,434	20.7
1999	1,494	17.4	2007	1,708	25.0
2005 [1]	1,725	19.8			

[1] Break in series. [2] Data are from family-based, rather than household-based, statistics. [3] Great Britain only (excludes Northern Ireland).

Source: U.S. Bureau of Labor Statistics, updated and revised from "Families and Work in Transition in 12 Countries, 1980–2001," *Monthly Labor Review*, September 2003, with national sources, some of which may be unpublished.

Table 1294. **Percent Distribution of Households by Type and Country: 1980 to 2007**

[Data are generally for the entire year, but in some instances they are only for a particular month within the year]

Year	Total	Married-couple households [1]			Single parent [2]	One person	Other [3]
		Total	With children [2]	Without children [2]			
United States:							
1980	100.0	60.8	30.9	29.9	7.5	22.7	9.0
1990	100.0	56.0	26.3	29.8	8.3	24.6	11.0
1995	100.0	54.4	25.5	28.9	9.1	25.0	11.5
2000	100.0	52.8	24.1	28.7	8.9	25.5	12.7
2006	100.0	50.9	22.7	28.1	9.2	26.6	13.3
Canada:							
1981	100.0	66.8	36.3	30.5	5.3	20.3	7.6
1991	100.0	62.8	29.6	33.2	5.7	22.9	8.6
2001 [4]	100.0	58.5	33.4	25.2	10.2	25.7	5.5
2006	100.0	57.4	31.4	26.1	10.3	26.8	5.5
Japan:							
1980	100.0	68.4	42.9	25.6	2.2	19.8	9.5
1990	100.0	65.2	33.1	32.1	2.3	23.1	9.4
1995	100.0	62.8	27.4	35.4	2.0	25.6	9.6
2000	100.0	60.3	23.6	36.7	2.1	27.6	10.0
2005	100.0	57.6	20.8	36.8	2.4	29.5	10.5
Denmark: [5]							
1980	100.0	50.3	25.0	25.3	3.9	44.9	1.0
1990	100.0	45.6	19.5	26.1	4.2	49.6	0.6
1995	100.0	44.9	18.2	26.6	4.2	50.4	0.5
2001	100.0	45.7	18.5	27.2	4.2	49.6	0.6
2007	100.0	44.9	18.2	26.7	4.8	49.8	0.6
France:							
1982	100.0	67.5	39.8	27.7	4.5	24.6	3.4
1990	100.0	64.0	35.9	28.1	5.5	27.1	3.4
1999	100.0	59.3	29.9	29.4	6.3	31.0	3.4
2005 [4]	100.0	56.4	27.2	29.2	6.7	32.8	4.1
Germany:							
1991	100.0	55.3	31.6	23.7	7.1	33.6	4.0
1995	100.0	53.3	29.2	24.0	6.8	34.9	5.1
2000 [4]	100.0	56.8	28.0	28.8	6.0	36.1	1.2
2005	100.0	54.7	25.5	29.1	6.4	37.5	1.4
2006	100.0	53.1	24.5	28.6	6.6	38.8	1.5
Ireland:							
1981	100.0	(NA)	(NA)	(NA)	(NA)	16.9	(NA)
1991	100.0	61.6	47.9	13.7	10.6	20.2	7.6
1996	100.0	59.6	44.5	15.1	11.2	21.5	7.7
2002	100.0	59.2	41.4	17.7	11.7	21.6	7.6
2006	100.0	57.3	37.4	20.0	11.6	22.4	8.7
Netherlands:							
1988	100.0	64.7	37.3	27.4	5.4	28.7	1.2
1993	100.0	63.1	33.3	29.9	5.0	30.9	1.0
2000	100.0	60.2	30.6	29.6	5.6	33.4	0.7
2006	100.0	58.0	29.1	28.9	6.3	35.0	0.7
2007	100.0	57.7	28.7	28.9	6.4	35.3	0.7
Sweden:							
1985	100.0	54.8	23.8	31.0	3.2	36.1	5.9
1990	100.0	52.1	21.9	30.2	3.9	39.6	4.4
1995 [4]	100.0	50.7	21.2	29.4	4.6	42.3	2.4
2000	100.0	45.8	19.1	26.7	5.3	46.5	2.3
2005	100.0	45.4	18.8	26.6	5.4	46.3	2.8
United Kingdom: [6]							
1981	100.0	65.0	31.0	34.0	5.0	22.0	8.0
1991	100.0	61.0	25.0	36.0	6.0	27.0	6.0
1994–95	100.0	58.0	25.0	33.0	7.0	27.0	8.0
2000	100.0	58.0	23.0	35.0	6.0	29.0	7.0
2007	100.0	56.0	21.0	35.0	7.0	29.0	8.0

NA Not available. [1] May include unmarried cohabiting couples. Such couples are explicitly included under married couples in Canada, Denmark, Ireland, France, the Netherlands, and Sweden. In Germany, cohabitants are grouped with married couples beginning in 2000. In other countries, some unmarried cohabitants are included as married couples, while some are classified under "other households." [2] Children are defined as unmarried children living at home according to the following age limits: under 18 years old in the United States, Canada (1981–96), Japan, Denmark, Sweden, and the United Kingdom, except that the United Kingdom includes 15-, 16-, and 17-year-olds in 1981 and 16- and 17-year-olds thereafter only if they are attending school full-time; under 25 years old in France; and children of all ages in Canada (2001 onward), Germany, Ireland, and the Netherlands. [3] Includes both family and nonfamily households not elsewhere classified. These households comprise, for example, siblings residing together, other households composed of relatives, and households made up of roommates. Some unmarried cohabitating couples may also be included in the "other" group. See footnote 1. [4] Break in series. [5] From family-based statistics. However, one person living alone constitutes a family in Denmark. In this respect, the Danish data are closer to household statistics. [6] Great Britain only (excludes Northern Ireland).

Source: U.S. Bureau of Labor Statistics, updated and revised from "Families and Work in Transition in 12 Countries, 1980–2001," *Monthly Labor Review*, September 2003, with national sources, some of which may be unpublished.

International Statistics **819**

Table 1295. **Births, Deaths, and Life Expectancy, by Country or Area: 2008 and 2010**

[Covers countries with 12 million or more population in 2008]

Country or area	Crude birth rate [1]		Crude death rate [2]		Expectation of life at birth (years)		Infant mortality rate [3]		Total fertility rate per woman [4]	
	2008	2010, proj.	2008	2010, proj.	2008	2010, proj.	2008	2010, proj.	2008	2010, proj.
United States......	**14.2**	**14.2**	**8.3**	**8.3**	**78.1**	**78.4**	**6.3**	**6.2**	**2.10**	**2.11**
Afghanistan	45.8	45.1	19.6	18.8	44.2	45.1	154.7	149.3	6.58	6.47
Algeria..........	17.0	16.7	4.6	4.7	73.8	74.3	28.8	26.8	1.82	1.76
Angola..........	44.1	43.3	24.4	23.7	37.9	38.5	182.3	178.1	6.20	6.05
Argentina........	18.1	17.8	7.4	7.4	76.4	76.8	11.8	11.1	2.37	2.33
Australia........	12.6	12.4	6.7	6.8	81.5	81.7	4.8	4.7	1.78	1.78
Bangladesh	28.9	27.8	8.0	7.7	63.2	63.9	57.5	54.3	3.08	3.04
Brazil..........	18.7	18.1	6.4	6.4	71.7	72.3	23.3	21.9	2.22	2.19
Burkina Faso	44.7	44.0	13.6	13.0	52.6	53.3	86.0	83.0	6.34	6.21
Burma..........	17.2	16.7	9.2	9.1	62.9	63.8	49.1	46.2	1.92	1.86
Cambodia........	25.7	25.8	8.2	8.0	61.7	62.5	56.6	53.0	3.08	3.00
Cameroon	34.6	33.6	12.4	12.0	53.3	54.0	64.6	62.2	4.41	4.25
Canada.........	10.3	10.3	7.6	7.9	81.2	81.3	5.1	5.0	1.57	1.58
Chile	14.8	14.5	5.8	5.9	77.2	77.5	7.9	7.5	1.95	1.90
China [5]	13.7	14.3	7.0	7.1	73.2	73.8	21.2	19.4	1.77	1.80
Colombia........	19.9	19.3	5.5	5.5	72.5	73.1	19.5	18.3	2.49	2.44
Congo (Kinshasa) [6] ..	43.0	42.3	11.9	11.4	54.0	54.7	83.1	79.4	6.28	6.11
Cote d'Ivoire......	32.7	31.5	11.2	10.4	54.6	56.2	69.8	66.4	4.23	4.01
Ecuador.........	21.5	20.8	4.2	4.2	76.8	77.2	21.4	19.9	2.59	2.50
Egypt..........	22.1	21.3	5.1	5.1	71.9	72.4	28.4	26.2	2.72	2.61
Ethiopia.........	44.0	43.3	11.8	11.3	55.0	55.8	82.6	79.0	6.17	6.07
France [7].........	12.7	12.4	8.5	8.7	80.9	81.1	3.4	3.3	1.98	1.97
Germany	8.2	8.2	10.8	11.0	79.1	79.4	4.0	4.0	1.41	1.42
Ghana..........	29.2	27.9	9.4	9.1	59.5	60.2	52.3	49.9	3.78	3.57
Guatemala.......	28.6	27.4	5.2	5.0	70.0	70.6	28.8	26.9	3.59	3.36
India	22.2	21.3	6.4	6.1	69.3	70.5	32.3	28.1	2.76	2.67
Indonesia........	19.2	18.5	6.2	6.3	70.5	71.1	31.0	28.9	2.34	2.28
Iran...........	16.9	17.3	5.7	5.8	70.9	71.4	36.9	34.7	1.71	1.70
Iraq...........	30.8	29.4	5.1	4.9	69.6	70.3	45.4	42.2	3.97	3.76
Italy...........	8.4	8.0	10.6	10.8	80.1	80.3	5.6	5.4	1.30	1.32
Japan..........	7.9	7.4	9.3	9.8	82.1	82.2	2.8	2.8	1.22	1.20
Kazakhstan	16.4	16.7	9.4	9.4	67.6	68.2	26.6	24.9	1.88	1.87
Kenya..........	37.9	35.1	10.3	9.3	56.6	58.8	56.0	53.5	4.70	4.38
Korea, North	14.6	13.8	7.3	7.5	72.2	72.7	21.9	20.5	2.00	1.90
Korea, South	9.1	8.7	5.7	6.2	78.6	78.8	4.3	4.2	1.20	1.22
Madagascar	38.4	37.9	8.3	8.0	62.5	63.3	55.6	52.8	5.19	5.09
Malawi.........	41.8	41.2	17.9	17.4	43.5	44.1	90.6	87.6	5.67	5.51
Malaysia	22.4	22.1	5.0	5.0	73.0	73.6	16.4	15.4	2.98	2.92
Mali...........	49.4	48.9	16.2	15.5	49.9	50.8	103.8	100.3	7.34	7.25
Mexico.........	20.0	19.4	4.8	4.8	75.8	76.3	19.0	17.8	2.37	2.31
Morocco.........	21.3	20.6	5.5	5.4	71.5	72.1	38.2	35.6	2.57	2.46
Mozambique......	38.2	37.8	20.3	19.8	41.0	41.4	107.8	103.8	5.24	5.13
Nepal..........	29.9	28.8	9.0	8.7	60.9	61.7	62.0	58.7	3.91	3.73
Netherlands	10.5	10.3	8.7	8.8	79.3	79.6	4.8	4.7	1.66	1.66
Niger..........	49.6	48.6	20.3	19.6	44.3	44.8	115.4	112.6	7.29	7.11
Nigeria.........	37.2	36.1	16.9	16.3	46.5	47.2	95.7	93.0	5.01	4.82
Pakistan.........	28.4	26.9	7.9	7.5	64.1	64.9	66.9	63.4	3.73	3.46
Peru	19.8	19.0	6.2	6.1	70.4	71.0	29.5	27.7	2.42	2.32
Philippines	26.4	25.7	5.2	5.1	70.8	71.4	21.2	19.9	3.32	3.23
Poland..........	10.0	10.0	10.0	10.1	75.4	75.9	6.9	6.7	1.27	1.29
Romania........	10.6	10.4	11.8	11.9	72.2	72.7	23.7	22.1	1.38	1.40
Russia.........	11.0	11.1	16.1	16.0	65.9	66.2	10.8	10.3	1.40	1.41
Saudi Arabia......	28.9	28.2	2.5	2.5	76.1	76.5	11.9	11.2	3.89	3.77
Senegal.........	36.5	34.7	10.7	10.3	57.1	57.9	58.9	56.6	4.86	4.60
South Africa	20.2	19.6	16.9	17.0	48.9	49.2	45.1	43.8	2.43	2.33
Spain	9.9	9.5	9.9	10.1	79.9	80.2	4.3	4.2	1.30	1.32
Sri Lanka........	16.6	15.9	6.1	6.2	75.0	75.3	19.0	18.1	2.02	1.96
Sudan	34.3	33.3	13.6	12.3	50.3	52.5	87.0	78.1	4.58	4.37
Syria	26.6	25.2	4.7	4.6	70.9	71.5	26.8	25.0	3.21	3.02
Taiwan [5]	9.0	9.0	6.7	6.9	77.8	78.2	5.5	5.3	1.13	1.15
Tanzania	35.1	33.4	12.9	12.3	51.5	52.5	70.5	68.1	4.62	4.31
Thailand........	13.6	13.2	7.2	7.3	72.8	73.4	18.2	17.1	1.64	1.65
Turkey.........	16.2	15.6	6.0	6.1	73.1	73.7	37.0	34.3	1.87	1.82
Uganda	48.2	47.6	12.3	11.9	52.3	53.0	66.0	63.7	6.81	6.73
Ukraine	9.6	9.6	15.9	15.7	68.1	68.5	9.2	8.7	1.25	1.27
United Kingdom.....	10.7	10.7	10.1	10.0	78.9	79.2	4.9	4.8	1.66	1.66
Uzbekistan	18.0	17.5	5.3	5.3	71.7	72.2	24.2	22.7	2.01	1.92
Venezuela	20.9	20.3	5.1	5.1	73.5	73.8	22.0	21.1	2.52	2.45
Vietnam.........	16.5	16.1	6.2	6.2	71.3	71.9	23.6	22.2	1.86	1.80
Yemen..........	42.4	41.8	7.8	7.4	62.9	63.6	56.3	53.2	6.41	6.23

[1] Number of births during 1 year per 1,000 persons (based on midyear population).   [2] Number of deaths during 1 year per 1,000 persons (based on midyear population).   [3] Number of deaths of children under 1 year of age per 1,000 live births in a calendar year.   [4] Average number of children that would be born if all women lived to the end of their childbearing years and, at each year of age, they experienced the birth rates occurring in the specified year.   [5] See footnote 2, Table 1288.   [6] See footnote 3, Table 1288.   [7] France now includes the overseas departments of French Guiana, Guadeloupe, Martinique, and Reunion. Saint Barthelemy and Saint Martin voted to become French overseas collectivities apart from Guadeloupe and are now listed individually.

Source: U.S. Census Bureau, "International Data Base" (as of 18 June 2008); <http://www.census.gov/ipc/www/idb/>.

Table 1296. Life Expectancy at Birth and at Age 65, by Sex—Selected Countries: 1980 and 2005

| Country | Life expectancy at birth | | | | Life expectancy at age 65 | | | |
| | Females | | Males | | Females | | Males | |
	1980	2005	1980	2005	1980	2005	1980	2005
United States [1] . . .	**77.4**	**80.4**	**70.0**	**75.2**	**18.3**	**20.0**	**14.1**	**17.1**
Australia	78.1	83.3	71.0	78.5	17.9	21.4	13.7	18.1
Austria	76.1	82.2	69.0	76.7	16.3	20.3	12.9	17.0
Belgium	76.8	81.6	70.0	75.8	16.9	20.0	13.0	16.3
Canada	78.9	(NA)	71.7	(NA)	18.9	21.0	14.5	17.7
Czech Republic	73.9	79.1	66.8	72.9	14.3	17.3	11.2	13.9
Denmark	77.3	80.2	71.2	75.6	17.6	18.6	13.6	15.5
Finland	77.6	82.3	69.2	75.5	16.5	21.1	12.5	17.0
France	78.4	83.8	70.2	76.7	18.2	21.4	13.6	17.1
Germany	76.1	81.8	69.6	76.2	16.7	19.6	13.0	16.1
Greece	76.8	81.7	72.2	76.8	16.8	19.4	14.6	17.2
Hungary	72.7	76.9	65.5	68.6	14.6	16.9	11.6	13.1
Iceland	79.7	83.1	73.7	79.2	19.1	20.7	15.8	18.0
Ireland	75.6	81.8	70.1	77.1	15.7	18.9	12.6	15.7
Italy	77.4	83.2	70.6	77.6	17.1	20.7	13.3	16.7
Japan	78.8	85.5	73.4	78.6	17.7	23.2	14.6	18.1
Luxembourg	75.9	82.3	69.1	76.2	16.0	19.0	12.3	15.5
Mexico	70.2	77.9	64.1	73.0	17.0	18.7	15.4	17.1
Netherlands	79.2	81.6	72.5	77.2	18.0	20.0	13.7	16.4
New Zealand	76.3	81.7	70.0	77.5	17.0	20.4	13.2	17.5
Norway	79.2	82.5	72.3	77.7	18.0	20.1	14.3	16.7
Poland	74.4	79.4	66.0	70.8	15.5	18.6	12.0	14.4
Portugal	75.2	81.4	67.7	74.9	16.5	18.9	12.9	15.6
Slovakia	74.3	77.9	66.8	70.1	15.4	16.9	12.3	13.2
Spain	78.6	83.9	72.5	77.4	17.9	20.7	14.8	16.8
Sweden	78.8	82.8	72.8	78.4	17.9	20.7	14.3	17.4
Switzerland	79.6	83.9	72.8	78.7	(NA)	21.0	(NA)	17.5
Turkey	60.3	73.8	55.8	68.9	12.8	15.0	11.7	13.1
United Kingdom	76.2	81.1	70.2	76.9	16.6	19.1	12.6	16.1

NA Not available. [1] Source of 2005 life expectancy of birth data: U.S. National Center for Health Statistics, *National Vital Statistics Reports (NVSR), Deaths: Final Data for 2005.*

Source: Organization for Economic Cooperation and Development, Paris, France, *OECD Health Data 2007* (copyright). See also <http://www.oecd.org/health/healthdata>.

Table 1297. People Infected With HIV and AIDS-Related Deaths, by Region: 2001 and 2007

[**In thousands (29,000 represents 29,000,000)**. Estimates are based on ranges, called 'plausibility bounds,' which reflect the certainty associated with each estimate and define the boundaries within which the actual numbers lie]

| Region | Adults and children living with HIV | | Adults and children newly infected with HIV | | Adult prevalence (percent) | | Adult and child deaths due to AIDS | |
	2001	2007	2001	2007	2001	2007	2001	2007
Total	**29,000**	**33,200**	**3,200**	**2,500**	**0.8**	**0.8**	**1,700**	**2,100**
Sub-Saharan Africa	20,900	22,500	2,200	1,700	5.8	5.0	1,400	1,600
North Africa and Middle East	300	380	41	35	0.3	0.3	22	25
South and South-East Asia	3,500	4,000	450	340	0.3	0.3	170	270
East Asia	420	800	77	92	(Z)	0.1	12	32
Oceania	26	75	4	14	0.2	0.4	(Z)	1,200
Latin America	1,300	1,600	130	100	0.4	0.5	51	58
Caribbean	190	230	20	17	1.0	1.0	14	11
Eastern Europe and Central Asia . . .	630	1,600	230	150	0.4	0.9	8	55
Western and Central Europe	620	760	32	31	0.2	0.3	10	12
North America	1,100	1,300	44	46	0.6	0.6	21	21

Z Less than 0.1 percent or 500 deaths.

Source: Joint United Nations Programme on HIV/AIDS (UNAIDS) and World Health Organization (WHO), *AIDS Epidemic Update: December 2007 (copyright)*. See also <http://data.unaids.org/pub/EPISlides/2007/2007_epiupdate_en.pdf>.

Table 1298. Percentage of the Adult Population Considered to be Obese: 2005

[Obesity rates are defined as the percentage of the population with a Body Mass Index (BMI) over 30 kg/m². The BMI is a single number that evaluates an individual's weight status in relation to height (weight/height², with weight in kilograms and height in meters). For Australia, the United Kingdom, and the United States, figures are based on health examinations, rather than self-reported information. Obesity estimates derived from health examinations are generally higher and more reliable than those coming from self-reports because they preclude any misreporting of people's height and weight. However, health examinations are only conducted regularly in a few countries. For more information on methods by country, see <http://www.irdes.fr/EspaceAnglais/home.html>]

Country	2005	Country	2005	Country	2005
United States	[1]**32.2**	France	[1]9.5	Luxembourg	18.6
Australia	[2]21.7	Germany	13.6	Mexico	30.2
Austria	[2]9.1	Greece	[3]21.9	New Zealand	[3]20.9
Belgium	[1]12.7	Hungary	[3]18.8	Norway	9.0
Canada	18.0	Ireland	[4]13.0	Spain	[3]13.1
Czech Republic	17.0	Italy	9.9	Sweden	10.7
Denmark	11.4	Japan	[1]3.0	Switzerland	[4]7.7
Finland	14.1	Korea, South	3.5	United Kingdom	23.0

[1] 2004 data. [2] 1999 data. [3] 2003 data. [4] 2002 data.

Source: Organization for Economic Cooperation and Development, Paris, France, *OECD Factbook*, 2008 (copyright). See also <http://lysander.sourceoecd.org/vl=3837252/cl=39/nw=1/rpsv/factbook/>.

Table 1299. Daily Tobacco Consumption by Country and Sex: 1980 and 2005

[Smokers as percent of population. Includes tobacco forms consumed by smoking only]

Country	Total		Females		Males	
	1980	2005	1980	2005	1980	2005
United States.	**33.5**	**16.9**	**29.3**	**14.9**	**37.6**	**19.1**
Australia.	36.0	17.7	31.1	16.5	41.1	18.9
Canada	(NA)	17.3	(NA)	15.5	(NA)	19.1
Denmark.	50.5	26.0	44.0	23.0	57.0	29.0
Finland.	26.1	21.8	16.6	18.2	35.2	26.0
France	30.0	23.0	16.0	19.0	44.0	28.0
Greece.	(NA)	38.6	(NA)	31.3	(NA)	46.0
Iceland	(NA)	19.5	(NA)	19.5	(NA)	19.5
Ireland	(NA)	27.0	34.1	26.0	(NA)	28.0
Italy	35.5	22.3	16.7	16.4	54.3	28.7
Japan	42.3	29.2	14.4	13.8	70.2	45.8
Luxembourg	(NA)	23.0	(NA)	19.0	(NA)	27.0
Netherlands	43.0	31.0	34.0	26.0	52.0	35.0
New Zealand.	(NA)	22.5	(NA)	22.5	(NA)	22.5
Norway.	36.0	25.0	30.0	24.0	42.0	26.0
Poland	(NA)	26.3	(NA)	19.3	(NA)	33.9
Sweden	32.4	15.9	28.7	18.0	36.3	13.9
United Kingdom	39.0	24.0	37.0	23.0	42.0	25.0

NA Not available.

Source: Organization for Economic Cooperation and Development, Paris, France, *OECD Health Data 2007* (copyright).

Table 1300. Medical Doctors and Inpatient Care—Selected Countries: 1990 to 2005

Country	Medical doctors per 1,000 population			Inpatient care					
				Acute care beds per 1,000 population			Average length of stay (days)		
	1990	2000	2005	1990	2000	2005	1990	2000	2005 [5]
United States	**2.1**	**2.3**	**2.4**	**3.7**	**2.9**	**2.7**	**9.1**	**6.8**	**5.6**
Australia	2.2	2.5	[4]2.7	4.8	3.8	[4]3.6	(NA)	16.0	6.1
Austria	2.2	3.1	3.5	7.5	6.6	6.1	12.8	8.6	5.9
Belgium	3.3	3.9	4.0	5.2	5.0	4.4	13.8	(NA)	7.1
Canada	2.1	2.1	2.2	4.0	3.2	[4]2.9	13.0	(NA)	7.3
Czech Republic.	2.7	3.4	3.6	8.6	6.6	5.7	15.4	11.4	8.0
Denmark	2.9	3.3	[4]3.6	4.1	3.5	[4]3.1	8.2	6.0	3.5
Finland	2.0	2.3	2.4	4.3	3.2	2.9	18.2	10.3	4.8
France	3.1	3.3	3.4	5.2	4.1	3.7	15.1	13.2	5.4
Germany	[1]2.8	3.3	3.4	8.3	6.8	6.4	(NA)	11.4	8.6
Greece	3.4	4.3	[4]4.9	(NA)	3.8	[4]3.8	9.9	8.4	6.0
Hungary	2.8	3.1	3.0	7.1	6.3	5.5	12.6	8.9	6.3
Iceland	2.8	3.4	3.7	4.3	(NA)	(NA)	18.3	(NA)	5.4
Ireland	[2]2.0	2.2	2.8	3.2	3.0	2.8	7.9	7.4	6.6
Italy	[3]3.8	4.1	3.8	6.2	4.2	3.3	11.7	7.7	6.8
Japan	1.7	1.9	[4]2.0	12.3	9.6	8.2	50.5	39.1	19.8
Korea, South	0.8	1.3	1.6	2.7	5.2	6.5	13.0	14.0	10.6
Luxembourg	2.0	2.1	2.5	6.7	5.9	5.2	17.6	(NA)	7.3
Mexico	1.0	1.6	1.8	1.0	1.0	1.0	(NA)	4.2	4.0
Netherlands	2.5	3.2	3.7	3.8	3.1	3.1	16.0	12.9	6.8
New Zealand	1.9	2.2	[4]2.2	(NA)	(NA)	(NA)	9.4	8.0	(NA)
Norway	[1]2.6	2.9	3.7	3.8	3.1	3.0	(NA)	8.9	5.2
Poland	2.1	2.2	2.1	6.3	5.2	4.7	12.5	8.9	6.5
Portugal	2.8	3.1	3.4	3.4	3.3	3.0	10.8	9.2	7.1
Slovakia	(NA)	3.1	[4]3.1	(NA)	6.5	5.0	(NA)	10.4	7.3
Spain	(NA)	3.2	3.8	3.6	3.0	[4]2.6	12.2	9.0	6.7
Sweden.	2.9	3.1	[4]3.4	4.1	2.4	2.2	18.0	6.4	4.6
Switzerland	3.0	3.5	3.8	6.5	4.1	3.6	(NA)	12.8	8.5
Turkey.	0.9	1.3	[4]1.5	2.0	2.2	2.0	6.9	5.9	5.2
United Kingdom	[3]1.6	2.0	2.4	(NA)	3.8	3.1	17.6	8.4	6.1

NA Not available. [1] 1991 data. [2] 1992 data. [3] 1993 data. [4] 2004 data. [5] Acute care only.

Source: Organization for Economic Cooperation and Development, Paris, France, *OECD Health Data 2007* (copyright).

Table 1301. Health Expenditures as Percent of GDP by Country: 1980 to 2005

[In percent. GDP = gross domestic product; for explanation, see text, Section 13]

Country	Total health expenditures					Public health expenditures				
	1980	1990	2000	2004	2005	1980	1990	2000	2004	2005
United States	**8.8**	**11.9**	**13.3**	**15.3**	**15.3**	**3.6**	**4.7**	**5.8**	**6.9**	**6.9**
Australia	6.8	7.5	8.8	(NA)	9.5	4.3	5.1	6.0	(NA)	6.4
Austria	7.5	7.0	9.4	9.6	10.2	5.1	5.1	6.6	6.8	7.7
Belgium	6.3	7.2	8.6	(NA)	10.3	(NA)	(NA)	6.5	(NA)	7.4
Canada	7.1	9.0	8.9	9.9	9.8	5.4	6.7	6.3	6.9	6.9
Czech Republic	(NA)	4.7	6.7	7.3	7.2	(NA)	4.6	6.1	6.5	6.4
Denmark	8.9	8.3	8.3	8.9	9.1	7.9	6.9	6.8	(NA)	7.7
Finland	6.3	7.8	6.7	7.5	7.5	5.0	6.3	5.0	5.7	5.9
France	7.0	8.4	9.2	10.5	11.1	5.6	6.4	7.0	8.3	8.9
Germany [1]	8.7	8.5	10.4	(NA)	10.7	6.8	6.5	8.2	(NA)	8.2
Greece	6.6	7.4	9.9	10.0	10.1	3.7	4.0	5.2	5.3	4.3
Hungary	(NA)	(NA)	7.1	8.3	8.1	(NA)	(NA)	5.0	6.0	5.7
Iceland	6.2	7.9	9.2	10.2	9.5	5.5	6.9	7.6	8.5	7.9
Ireland	8.3	6.1	6.3	7.1	7.5	6.8	4.4	4.6	5.7	5.8
Italy	(NA)	7.7	7.9	8.4	8.9	(NA)	6.1	5.8	6.4	6.8
Japan	6.5	5.9	7.6	(NA)	8.0	4.6	4.6	6.1	(NA)	6.6
Korea, South	(NA)	4.4	4.8	5.6	6.0	(NA)	1.7	2.2	2.9	3.2
Luxembourg	5.2	5.4	5.8	8.0	8.3	4.8	5.0	5.2	7.3	7.5
Mexico	(NA)	4.8	5.6	6.5	6.4	(NA)	2.0	2.6	3.0	2.9
Netherlands	7.2	7.7	7.9	9.2	9.2	5.0	5.2	5.0	5.7	5.7
New Zealand	5.9	6.9	7.7	8.4	9.0	5.1	5.7	6.0	6.5	7.0
Norway	7.0	7.7	8.5	9.7	9.1	5.9	6.4	7.0	8.1	7.6
Poland	(NA)	4.9	5.7	6.5	6.2	(NA)	4.5	4.0	4.5	4.3
Portugal	5.6	6.2	9.4	10.0	10.2	3.6	4.1	6.8	7.2	7.4
Slovakia	(NA)	(NA)	5.5	(NA)	7.1	(NA)	(NA)	4.9	(NA)	5.3
Spain	5.3	6.5	7.2	8.1	8.2	4.2	5.1	5.2	5.7	5.9
Sweden	9.0	8.3	8.4	9.1	9.1	8.3	7.5	7.1	7.7	7.7
Switzerland	7.4	8.3	10.4	11.6	11.6	(NA)	4.3	5.8	6.8	6.9
Turkey	3.3	3.6	6.6	7.7	7.6	1.0	2.2	4.2	5.5	5.4
United Kingdom	5.6	6.0	7.3	8.3	8.3	5.0	5.0	5.9	7.1	7.2

NA Not available. [1] Data prior to 1991 are for former West Germany.

Source: Organization for Economic Cooperation and Development, Paris, France, *OECD Health Data 2007* (copyright).

Table 1302. Educational Performance: 2005 and 2006

[Tertiary-type A includes education leading to a BA, Master's, or equivalent degree, and advanced research programs. Performance figures were gathered from the Program for International Student Assessment (PISA), an internationally standardized assessment jointly developed by participating countries, which takes place in 3-yearly cycles. To implement PISA, each of the participating countries selects a nationally representative sample of 15-year-olds, regardless of grade level. Tests are typically administered to between 4,500 and 10,000 students in each country]

Country	Student performance on the combined reading, scientific, and mathematical literacy scales (2006)			Educational attainment of adult population and current graduation rates (2005) (percent)	
	Mean score on the combined reading literacy scale [1]	Mean score on the mathematical literacy scale [2]	Mean score on the scientific literacy scale [3]	Upper secondary or higher attainment (25–64-year-olds) [4]	Tertiary type A attainment (25–64-year-olds)
Australia	513	520	527	65	23
Austria	490	505	511	81	9
Canada	527	527	534	85	23
Czech Republic	483	510	513	90	[5]13
Finland	547	548	563	79	18
France	488	496	495	66	15
Germany	495	504	516	83	15
Greece	460	459	473	57	15
Italy	469	462	475	50	[5]12
Japan	498	523	531	(NA)	22
Korea	556	547	522	76	23
Luxembourg	479	490	486	66	17
Mexico	410	406	410	21	14
Poland	508	495	498	51	[5]17
Spain	461	480	488	49	20
Sweden	507	502	503	84	21
Switzerland	499	530	512	83	19
United Kingdom	495	495	515	67	21
United States	**(NA)**	**474**	**489**	**88**	**30**
OECD mean	492	498	500	68	19

NA Not available. [1] Reading literacy is understanding, using, and reflecting on written texts in order to achieve one's goals, to develop one's knowledge and potential, and to participate in society. [2] Mathematical literacy is an individual's capacity to identify and understand the role that mathematics plays in the world, to make well-founded judgments, and to use and engage with mathematics in ways that meet the needs of that individual's life. [3] Scientific literacy is the capacity to use scientific knowledge to identify questions and to draw evidence-based conclusions in order to understand and help make decisions about the natural world and the changes made to it through human activity. [4] Excluding ISCED 3C short programs. [5] All tertiary levels: type A and type B (focus on practical, technical, or occupational skills).

Source: Organization for Economic Cooperation and Development, Paris, France, *OECD Factbook*, 2008 and *Education at a Glance*, 2007 (copyright). See also <http://oberon.sourceoecd.org/vl=2046809/cl=18/nw=1/rpsv/factbook/>.

Table 1303. Average Temperatures and Precipitation—Selected International Cities

[In degrees Fahrenheit, except as noted. Data are generally based on a standard 30-year period; for details, see source. For data on U.S. cities, see Tables 373–377. Minus sign (–) indicates degrees below zero]

City	January Average high	Average low	Warmest	Coldest	Average precipitation (inches)	July Average high	Average low	Warmest	Coldest	Average precipitation (inches)
Amsterdam, Netherlands...	41	34	57	3	3.1	69	55	90	39	2.9
Athens, Greece.........	55	44	70	28	1.9	89	73	108	61	0.2
Baghdad, Iraq..........	58	38	75	25	1.1	110	78	122	61	–
Bangkok, Thailand.......	89	71	95	54	0.4	90	78	99	72	6.2
Beijing, China........	34	17	54	1	0.2	86	72	104	63	8.8
Berlin, Germany........	35	26	58	−11	(NA)	73	56	95	41	(NA)
Bogota, Colombia.......	66	43	84	27	1.9	64	47	82	32	1.8
Brasilia, Brazil.........	81	64	95	54	(NA)	79	52	97	37	(NA)
Buenos Aires, Argentina ...	85	64	104	44	4.2	58	41	88	23	2.3
Cairo, Egypt..........	65	49	86	32	0.2	93	72	108	63	–
Frankfurt, Germany......	38	30	56	−4	1.8	75	57	97	38	2.4
Geneva, Switzerland......	39	29	57	−2	2.2	77	56	96	41	2.8
Hong Kong, China.......	67	58	79	43	1.1	89	81	97	70	14.3
Istanbul, Turkey........	46	37	64	16	3.7	82	66	100	50	0.7
Jakarta, Indonesia	83	75	92	72	(NA)	88	74	92	67	(NA)
Karachi, Pakistan.......	76	55	93	39	0.3	89	83	109	68	3.5
Lagos, Nigeria.........	82	79	93	64	(NA)	79	76	88	70	(NA)
London, England.......	45	36	61	15	2.4	72	56	93	45	1.8
Madrid, Spain.........	51	32	68	14	1.8	90	61	104	46	0.4
Manila, Philippines.......	86	71	95	61	0.8	88	76	99	70	15.9
Mexico City, Mexico......	70	45	86	26	0.3	74	56	86	37	5.1
Montreal, Canada.......	21	7	52	−31	2.8	79	61	93	43	3.4
Moscow, Russia	21	11	46	−33	1.4	71	55	95	41	3.2
Nairobi, Kenya.........	77	58	88	45	1.8	71	54	85	43	0.5
New Delhi, India.......	68	48	85	32	0.9	93	81	111	70	7.9
Paris, France	43	34	59	1	(NA)	75	58	95	41	(NA)
Rio De Janeiro, Brazil.....	91	74	109	64	5.3	81	64	102	52	1.8
Rome, Italy..........	55	39	64	19	3.2	83	66	100	55	0.6
Seoul, Korea..........	33	21	55	−1	(NA)	82	71	97	55	(NA)
Singapore, Singapore.....	85	73	100	66	9.4	86	76	99	70	5.9
Sydney, Australia.......	79	65	109	49	4.0	62	44	80	32	2.5
Tel Aviv, Israel..........	62	46	84	32	(NA)	87	69	100	50	(NA)
Tokyo, Japan	48	35	66	25	2.0	82	71	95	55	5.3
Toronto, Canada	28	15	59	−24	1.9	79	60	99	45	2.8

– Represents zero.   NA Not available.

Source: U.S. National Oceanic and Atmospheric Administration, *Climates of the World*. See also <http://www.ncdc.noaa.gov/oa/oldpubs/>.

Table 1304. Carbon Dioxide Emissions From Consumption of Fossil Fuels by Country: 1990 to 2005

[In million metric tons of carbon dioxide (21,394.9 represents 21,394,900,000). Includes carbon dioxide emissions from the consumption of petroleum, natural gas, and coal, and the flaring of natural gas]

Country	1990	1995	2000	2001	2002	2003	2004	2005
World, total [1].....	**21,394.9**	**21,989.9**	**23,751.0**	**24,011.5**	**24,545.9**	**25,779.8**	**27,185.9**	**28,192.7**
Australia..........	263.3	285.3	352.6	366.7	374.6	375.3	381.2	406.6
Brazil	218.7	285.1	342.1	346.2	343.8	343.1	352.7	360.6
Canada...........	468.9	505.9	558.4	565.6	586.4	613.4	626.3	631.3
China [2]..........	2,241.2	2,844.6	2,912.6	3,050.9	3,376.2	3,983.1	4,753.3	5,322.7
France	366.5	369.5	399.0	402.5	398.6	405.2	412.5	415.3
Germany..........	(X)	876.7	848.0	868.6	841.3	865.2	867.3	844.2
India............	574.6	862.2	994.1	1,016.7	1,014.7	1,029.1	1,128.9	1,165.7
Indonesia	150.9	213.3	271.0	296.8	311.4	314.9	341.6	359.5
Iran	201.8	260.2	318.6	332.0	362.5	384.3	403.9	450.7
Italy	413.1	427.9	444.5	441.6	448.5	470.3	465.6	466.6
Japan...........	1,009.1	1,075.5	1,190.2	1,177.7	1,185.8	1,234.2	1,241.9	1,230.4
Korea, South	241.1	378.0	440.0	446.1	465.2	479.4	488.1	499.6
Mexico	300.2	318.8	380.6	377.4	383.8	389.4	381.9	398.2
Netherlands........	206.2	221.6	249.5	275.6	256.5	258.8	267.8	269.7
Poland	330.7	305.3	289.7	273.7	271.9	284.6	289.5	284.6
Russia	(X)	1,622.9	1,580.2	1,569.5	1,569.4	1,627.4	1,668.7	1,696.0
Saudi Arabia	207.8	233.9	289.3	299.9	309.6	344.8	385.8	412.4
South Africa.......	295.5	344.2	383.4	390.7	377.1	409.4	438.1	423.8
Spain	235.3	248.1	323.1	327.8	344.9	353.3	373.7	387.1
Taiwan [2]	117.8	180.9	248.5	245.2	269.4	285.6	281.9	284.4
Thailand	83.8	144.0	160.6	170.9	185.7	204.2	223.7	234.2
Turkey	128.8	151.9	200.3	182.7	193.0	204.4	208.8	230.0
Ukraine..........	(X)	418.3	322.5	314.5	322.3	352.6	342.1	342.6
United Kingdom	598.5	555.8	554.6	565.4	556.2	566.7	576.3	577.2
United States.......	5,001.7	5,289.3	5,823.5	5,723.1	5,763.1	5,812.8	5,935.5	5,957.0

X Not applicable.   [1] Includes other countries not shown separately.   [2] See footnote 2, Table 1288.

Source: U.S. Energy Information Administration, "International Energy Annual, 2005"; <http://www.eia.doe.gov/pub/international/iealf/tableh1co2.xls> (released 18 September 2007).

Table 1305. Gross National Income (GNI) by Country: 2000 and 2006

[**48 represents $48,000,000,000**. GNI measures the total domestic and foreign value added claimed by residents. GNI comprises GDP plus net receipts of primary income (compensation of employees and property income) from nonresident sources]

Country	Gross national income [1]				GNI on purchasing power parity basis [2]			
	Total (bil. dol.)		Per capita (dol.)		Total (bil. dol.)		Per capita (dol.)	
	2000	2006	2000	2006	2000	2006	2000	2006
Algeria	48	101	1,580	3,030	157	[3]198	5,150	[3]5,940
Argentina	276	201	7,690	5,150	438	457	11,820	11,670
Australia	385	742	20,080	35,860	488	703	25,430	33,940
Bangladesh	50	71	380	450	211	192	1,610	1,230
Belarus	14	34	1,380	3,470	48	94	4,810	9,700
Belgium	255	405	24,900	38,460	277	357	26,990	33,860
Brazil	621	893	3,650	4,710	1,220	1,648	7,170	8,700
Bulgaria	13	31	1,580	3,990	50	79	6,070	10,270
Burkina Faso	3	6	250	440	11	16	1,010	1,130
Cambodia	4	7	290	490	21	22	1,770	1,550
Cameroon	9	18	580	990	26	37	1,750	2,060
Canada	668	1,197	21,720	36,650	836	1,184	27,180	36,280
Chile	73	112	4,810	6,810	135	186	8,890	11,300
China [4]	1,064	2,621	840	2,000	4,817	6,119	3,810	4,660
Colombia	87	142	2,050	3,120	252	279	5,960	6,130
Congo (Kinshasa) [5] . . .	2	8	510	130	2	16	680	270
Cote d'Ivoire	11	17	690	880	23	30	1,480	1,580
Czech Republic	54	131	5,250	12,790	140	215	13,620	20,920
Ecuador	16	39	1,330	2,910	38	90	3,060	6,810
Egypt	95	101	1,490	1,360	229	367	3,580	4,940
Ethiopia	7	13	110	170	45	49	700	630
France	1,453	[6]2,307	23,990	[6]36,560	1,503	1,975	25,530	32,240
Germany	2,067	3,033	25,150	36,810	2,133	2,692	25,950	32,680
Ghana	6	12	330	510	37	28	1,910	1,240
Greece	124	305	11,700	27,390	178	344	16,860	30,870
Guatemala	19	34	1,700	2,590	45	[3]67	3,920	5,120
Hong Kong	179	199	26,830	29,040	175	269	26,310	39,200
Hungary	48	110	4,770	10,870	120	171	11,930	16,970
India	456	909	450	820	2,439	2,726	2,400	2,460
Indonesia	118	316	570	1,420	585	737	2,840	3,310
Iran	105	205	1,650	2,930	378	687	5,940	9,800
Iraq	(NA)	(NA)	(NA)	([7])	(NA)	(NA)	(NA)	(NA)
Italy	1,164	1,883	20,170	31,990	1,427	1,705	24,730	28,970
Japan	4,492	4,935	35,400	38,630	3,337	4,196	26,300	32,840
Kazakhstan	19	59	1,250	3,870	65	133	4,310	8,700
Kenya	11	21	350	580	30	54	990	1,470
Korea, South	423	857	9,010	17,690	712	1,113	15,140	22,990
Madagascar	4	5	250	280	13	17	810	870
Malawi	2	3	170	230	6	9	590	690
Malaysia	79	147	3,390	5,620	191	317	8,210	12,160
Mexico	500	816	5,100	7,830	852	1,249	8,690	11,990
Morocco	34	66	1,180	2,160	97	118	3,390	3,860
Mozambique	4	7	210	310	15	14	820	660
Nepal	5	9	230	320	31	28	1,330	1,010
Netherlands	403	704	25,330	43,050	435	620	27,340	37,940
Niger	2	4	180	270	8	9	740	630
Nigeria	34	90	270	620	100	204	790	1,410
Pakistan	62	127	450	800	260	383	1,880	2,410
Peru	53	82	2,050	2,980	120	179	4,620	6,490
Philippines	79	120	1,030	1,390	319	296	4,170	3,430
Poland	164	313	4,230	8,210	381	543	9,850	14,250
Portugal	112	189	11,090	17,850	171	211	16,930	19,960
Romania	38	104	1,680	4,830	127	219	5,670	10,150
Russia	250	822	1,720	5,770	1,027	1,815	7,050	12,740
Saudi Arabia	168	331	8,120	13,980	261	528	12,610	22,300
Senegal	5	9	500	760	14	19	1,460	1,560
Singapore	92	129	22,780	28,730	96	194	23,780	43,300
South Africa	131	255	2,980	5,390	406	422	9,220	8,900
Spain	599	1,206	14,790	27,340	800	1,244	19,760	28,200
Sri Lanka	16	26	890	1,310	63	74	3,400	3,730
Sudan	11	30	340	800	49	67	1,560	1,780
Sweden	254	395	28,680	43,530	216	312	24,340	34,310
Switzerland	284	435	39,610	58,050	222	306	30,910	40,840
Syria	16	30	960	1,560	52	80	3,190	4,110
Tanzania	9	[8]13	270	[8]350	17	39	510	980
Thailand	122	194	2,010	3,050	381	472	6,270	7,440
Turkey	201	394	2,980	5,400	425	614	6,300	8,410
Uganda	6	9	270	300	29	26	1,240	880
Ukraine	34	91	690	1,940	197	286	3,980	6,110
United Kingdom	1,485	2,456	25,220	40,560	1,462	2,037	24,840	33,650
United States	**9,697**	**13,387**	**34,360**	**44,710**	**9,791**	**13,196**	**34,690**	**44,070**
Uzbekistan	9	16	360	610	37	[3]58	1,490	2,190
Venezuela	104	164	4,310	6,070	135	296	5,580	10,970
Vietnam	30	59	380	700	156	194	1,990	2,310
Yemen	7	16	420	760	13	46	760	2,090
Zimbabwe	6	5	440	340	32	2	2,500	170

NA Not available. [1] Gross national income calculated using the World Bank Atlas method; for details, see source. [2] For explanation of Purchasing Power Parity, see headnote, Table 1306. [3] The estimate is based on regression; others are extrapolated from the latest International Comparison Program benchmark estimates. [4] See footnote 2, Table 1288. [5] See footnote 3, Table 1288. [6] Include the French overseas departments of French Guiana, Guadeloupe, Martinique, and Reunion. [7] Estimated to be lower middle income ($906–$3,595). [8] Data refer to mainland Tanzania only.

Source: Copyright the International Bank for Reconstruction and Development/The World Bank, Washington, DC, *World Development Indicators*, annual (copyright).

Table 1306. Real GDP per Capita and per Employed Persons by Country: 1980 to 2006

[U.S. figures based on the System of National Income and Product Accounts (NIPA) from the Bureau of Economic Analysis. All other countries, based on the 1993 United Nations System of National Accounts. Per capita data based on total resident population. Real GDP is a macroeconomic measure of the size of an economy adjusted for price changes and inflation. Employed data include people serving in the armed forces for some countries. Real dollars are calculated based on 2002 Purchasing Power Parities (PPPs). PPPs are currency conversion rates used to convert GDPs expressed in different currencies to a common value [U.S. dollars in this case]. A PPP for a given country is the number of national currency units needed to buy the specific basket of goods and services that one unit of currency will buy in the United States. See text, this section]

Country	Real GDP per capita (2002 U.S. dollars)						Real GDP per employed person (2002 U.S. dollars)					
	1980	1990	2000	2004	2005	2006	1980	1990	2000	2004	2005	2006
United States	23,615	29,620	36,225	37,934	38,778	39,682	53,033	61,263	73,944	79,127	80,289	81,454
Canada	20,842	24,242	29,174	30,846	31,447	31,991	46,518	51,309	60,642	61,877	62,816	63,311
Australia	18,863	22,287	27,885	30,212	30,663	31,053	43,610	47,871	59,084	62,390	62,131	62,482
Japan	17,450	24,325	26,824	27,887	28,420	29,030	34,878	46,857	52,174	55,961	56,806	57,794
Korea, South	4,980	10,226	16,828	19,748	20,535	21,489	13,877	24,241	37,391	42,058	43,250	44,831
Austria	19,603	24,113	29,729	30,684	31,088	31,900	38,993	47,826	57,780	60,603	61,557	62,684
Belgium	18,132	21,857	28,903	30,246	30,402	31,233	46,972	56,293	72,389	76,153	75,223	77,071
Denmark	19,828	24,245	30,166	30,916	31,771	32,678	40,336	47,770	59,277	61,714	63,149	63,954
France	19,673	23,631	27,522	28,539	28,855	29,253	48,832	60,126	68,714	71,351	72,248	73,134
Germany	(NA)	(NA)	26,872	27,388	27,650	28,426	(NA)	(NA)	56,421	58,124	58,731	59,870
Italy	18,343	23,151	26,996	27,325	27,148	27,536	48,433	58,079	67,039	65,537	65,388	65,477
Netherlands	20,499	24,262	31,106	31,752	32,159	32,907	51,541	57,209	63,351	65,550	66,443	67,324
Norway	21,483	26,531	36,051	38,295	39,057	39,869	45,037	54,657	69,801	75,688	76,957	76,825
Spain	13,859	17,876	22,599	23,925	24,349	24,948	38,862	46,595	53,679	54,043	53,901	54,314
Sweden	19,728	23,687	27,656	29,758	30,499	31,621	38,573	44,511	57,610	62,204	63,755	65,412
United Kingdom	17,765	22,632	27,946	30,458	30,853	31,618	39,624	47,924	59,657	63,775	64,419	65,684

NA Not available.

Source: U.S. Bureau of Labor Statistics, "Comparative Real Gross Domestic Product per Capita and per Employed Person, Sixteen Countries, 1960–2006," 11 July 2007; <http://www.bls.gov/fls/flsgdp.pdf>.

Table 1307. **Average Annual Percent Changes in International Economic Composite Indexes by Country: 1990 to 2007**

[**Change from previous year**; derived from indexes with base 2000 = 100. The coincident index changes are for calendar years and the leading index changes are for years ending June 30 because they lead the coincident indexes by about 6 months, on average. The G-7 countries are United States, Canada, France, Germany, Italy, United Kingdom, and Japan. Minus sign (–) indicates decrease]

Country	Leading index						Coincident index					
	1990	2000	2004	2005	2006	2007	1990	2000	2004	2005	2006	2007
Total, 13 countries	2.1	6.3	7.5	4.6	4.8	3.1	4.5	5.0	3.7	2.4	4.0	3.7
12 countries, excluding U.S.	3.8	7.7	7.4	5.7	5.1	4.5	6.8	5.4	3.6	2.1	4.6	5.1
G-7 countries	2.0	6.0	7.5	4.6	4.7	3.0	4.5	4.8	3.5	2.2	3.9	3.5
North America	–0.9	4.1	7.4	2.8	4.3	0.9	–0.2	4.8	3.9	2.7	3.0	1.2
United States	–1.0	3.9	7.8	2.8	4.2	0.6	–0.1	4.4	3.8	2.7	2.8	0.9
Canada.	–1.1	7.1	3.1	3.1	5.1	4.2	–1.7	9.7	4.8	3.5	3.7	3.6
Four European countries	1.8	4.4	4.7	5.0	4.8	4.4	5.9	9.8	2.5	1.4	5.9	6.9
France	1.5	1.5	5.0	6.8	5.9	3.1	5.7	14.4	1.4	2.0	4.4	5.3
Germany.	4.5	6.2	6.8	6.7	6.7	7.2	7.2	7.9	1.2	–1.3	5.8	8.7
Italy	0.2	7.2	1.6	2.7	4.4	5.1	9.3	16.2	5.0	4.2	10.8	9.1
United Kingdom	–0.3	2.5	3.3	1.8	0.4	0.4	0.9	4.0	4.8	3.3	3.7	4.2
Seven Pacific region countries . .	6.1	11.2	10.5	6.5	5.4	4.6	8.1	1.2	4.5	2.7	3.4	3.5
Australia	–1.4	8.2	4.5	3.1	2.8	0.7	–0.4	5.1	7.9	4.7	4.6	7.5
Taiwan [1]	4.9	8.5	11.5	6.7	5.2	4.9	5.1	4.9	8.3	4.3	3.4	2.9
Thailand	12.1	9.5	13.8	5.7	5.8	3.8	11.6	9.4	8.2	6.5	2.7	2.6
Japan.	6.6	11.3	11.1	7.0	5.1	4.6	8.6	–0.5	4.0	2.3	3.1	3.2
Korea, South	6.5	15.9	8.9	7.1	11.9	7.5	9.9	13.7	4.6	4.3	5.8	5.5
Malaysia	5.0	19.8	12.2	9.0	7.9	8.1	9.1	11.1	5.6	2.9	4.6	3.1
New Zealand	0.8	4.6	5.5	2.7	2.1	3.3	–1.2	2.7	9.3	5.1	1.8	4.7

[1] See footnote 2, Table 1288.

Source: Foundation for International Business and Economic Research, New York, NY, *International Economic Indicators,* monthly.

Table 1308. **Sectoral Contributions to Gross Value Added: 1995 and 2005**

[**In percent**. According to the 1993 System of National Accounts (SNA) and the International Standard Industrial Classification (ISIC), Revision 3. Value added is estimated at basic prices and includes financial intermediation services indirectly measured (FISIM). It represents an industry's contribution to national GDP and is calculated as the difference between production and intermediate inputs. Value added comprises labor costs, consumption of fixed capital, indirect taxes less subsidies, and net operating surplus and mixed income]

Country	Agriculture		Industry						Services	
			Total		Manufacturing					
	1995	2005	1995	2005	1995	2005			1995	2005
United States [1] . .	1.6	1.2	[2]26.4	[2]22.8	[3]17.6	[3]13.4			[4]72.0	[4]76.0
Australia.	3.8	3.1	28.4	28.0	14.6	11.0			67.8	68.9
Austria	2.7	1.6	30.4	29.8	19.3	19.4			66.9	68.6
Belgium	1.5	1.1	28.3	24.1	20.2	17.1			70.2	74.8
Canada	2.9	[5]2.1	30.7	[5]31.2	18.4	[5]16.5			66.4	[5]66.7
Czech Republic	5.0	2.9	38.3	38.3	24.3	25.9			56.7	58.8
Denmark.	3.5	1.5	25.1	25.5	17.1	14.2			71.5	73.0
Finland.	4.4	2.9	32.8	31.4	25.3	23.1			62.8	65.7
France	3.4	2.3	24.8	20.7	[6]16.1	13.2			72.6	77.0
Germany	1.3	1.0	32.2	29.3	22.6	23.2			66.6	69.7
Greece.	7.7	4.0	21.3	19.4	[7]10.3	9.5			70.0	76.6
Hungary.	8.5	4.3	30.3	30.1	[7]23.5	22.2			61.9	65.6
Iceland [8].	11.0	[9]6.7	28.2	[9]24.7	[10]16.4	[9]12.5			60.9	[9]68.7
Ireland	7.0	2.1	38.0	36.1	30.2	24.5			55.0	61.9
Italy	3.3	2.2	30.3	26.6	22.2	18.2			66.4	71.2
Japan [11]	1.9	1.4	33.2	28.7	[12]22.4	20.2			64.9	69.1
Korea.	6.4	3.4	41.9	40.3	27.6	28.4			51.8	56.3
Luxembourg	1.0	0.4	21.7	16.2	13.7	8.8			77.2	83.4
Mexico	5.2	[9]3.8	26.5	[9]26.0	19.8	[9]17.9			68.3	[9]70.2
Netherlands	3.5	2.2	27.4	24.2	17.4	14.1			69.2	73.7
New Zealand [13]	7.2	[14]7.0	26.0	[14]23.9	17.9	[14]15.6			66.9	[14]69.1
Norway.	3.1	1.6	34.2	43.0	13.2	9.6			62.8	55.4
Poland	8.0	4.6	35.2	30.8	21.1	18.5			56.8	64.6
Portugal	5.7	2.7	28.4	25.0	18.6	[5]15.7			65.9	72.2
Slovakia	5.9	4.4	37.8	35.7	26.8	23.4			56.3	59.9
Spain.	4.5	3.3	29.4	29.3	[7]18.6	15.5			66.1	67.5
Sweden	2.7	1.2	30.3	28.2	22.3	[9]19.7			67.0	70.6
Switzerland.	2.0	1.2	29.8	26.5	20.0	[9]18.6			68.2	72.3
Turkey [13, 15]	15.7	10.5	31.9	30.3	22.6	21.2			52.4	59.2
United Kingdom	1.9	0.9	30.7	23.2	20.9	13.0			67.5	75.9

[1] Value added is estimated at factor cost. [2] Sanitary and similar services are included under industry. [3] Contribution to GDP instead of value added. [4] Includes government enterprises. [5] 2003. [6] 1999. [7] 2000. [8] Value added estimated at factor cost. [9] 2004. [10] 1997. [11] Value added is estimated approximately at market prices. [12] 1996. [13] Value added is estimated at producer's prices. [14] 2002. [15] According to the 1968 System of National Accounts.

Source: Organization for Economic Cooperation and Development, Paris, France, *OECD in Figures,* 2007 (copyright). See also <http://oberon.sourceoecd.org/vl=7506974/cl=15/nw=1/rpsv/~6676/v2007n7/s1/p1l>.

International Statistics 827

Table 1309. **Index of Industrial Production by Country: 1980 to 2007**

[**Annual averages of monthly data**. Industrial production index measures output in the manufacturing, mining, electric, gas, and water utilities industries. Minus sign (–) indicates decrease]

Country	Index (2000 = 100)								Annual percent change				
	1980	1990	1995	2000	2004	2005	2006	2007	2000–2001	2003–2004	2004–2005	2005–2006	2006–2007
OECD, total.	**62.1**	**78.1**	**83.4**	**100.0**	**102.8**	**105.0**	**108.8**	**111.9**	**–2.4**	**3.4**	**2.1**	**3.6**	**2.8**
Australia.	61.9	80.4	87.0	100.0	103.7	105.0	105.7	108.5	0.1	0.3	1.3	0.7	4.9
Austria	52.6	69.0	74.5	100.0	112.3	117.3	125.9	132.1	2.8	6.3	4.5	7.3	2.6
Belgium [1]	70.6	85.9	86.5	100.0	104.3	103.9	109.2	112.0	–1.0	3.2	–0.4	5.1	–
Canada	55.8	69.1	78.6	100.0	100.1	101.3	100.9	100.9	–4.0	2.0	1.2	–0.4	8.2
Czech Republic [1] . . .	(X)	119.9	90.6	100.0	125.7	134.0	149.0	161.2	6.7	9.6	6.6	11.2	0.4
Denmark.	57.5	75.8	86.5	100.0	103.2	104.9	108.6	109.0	1.6	–	1.6	3.5	4.4
Finland.	45.5	60.3	69.1	100.0	108.4	108.7	119.3	124.5	–0.2	5.0	0.3	9.8	1.6
France . . [2]	75.9	86.5	87.0	100.0	102.1	102.3	102.9	104.5	1.2	2.5	0.2	0.6	6.1
Germany [2]	75.2	90.7	87.4	100.0	102.6	106.0	112.2	119.1	0.2	3.0	3.3	5.8	2.0
Greece.	75.6	83.2	81.7	100.0	100.2	99.5	100.1	102.1	–1.8	0.9	–0.7	0.6	8.1
Hungary [1]	69.3	67.6	59.4	100.0	121.5	129.9	142.9	154.5	3.6	7.3	6.9	10.0	7.2
Ireland	16.8	30.9	49.6	100.0	123.8	127.6	134.1	143.8	10.0	0.2	3.1	5.1	2.7
Italy	76.6	86.4	93.0	100.0	96.3	95.9	98.2	98.0	–1.0	–0.6	–0.4	2.4	–0.2
Japan [1]	66.8	98.5	95.5	100.0	100.5	101.2	105.8	108.7	–6.3	5.3	0.7	4.5	2.7
Korea, South [1]	14.3	43.1	64.9	100.0	126.3	134.6	145.9	155.8	0.7	10.2	6.6	8.4	6.8
Luxembourg	55.4	79.5	81.3	100.0	117.8	125.2	122.6	117.6	3.1	6.4	6.3	–2.1	–4.1
Mexico [3]	56.6	67.3	70.4	100.0	100.3	100.5	105.9	107.9	–3.5	4.2	0.2	5.4	1.9
Netherlands	76.3	83.9	90.9	100.0	102.6	103.5	104.7	107.9	0.6	2.5	0.9	1.2	3.1
New Zealand.	(X)	83.1	94.9	100.0	111.6	110.3	108.5	110.2	–0.4	3.1	–1.2	–1.6	1.6
Norway.	46.3	71.5	90.3	100.0	97.4	96.8	94.5	93.7	–1.3	2.0	–0.6	–2.4	–0.8
Poland	(NA)	61.0	69.7	100.0	124.8	129.9	145.5	159.5	0.4	12.7	4.1	12.0	9.6
Portugal	54.7	87.2	84.7	100.0	100.0	100.3	103.1	104.9	3.1	–2.5	0.3	2.8	1.7
Spain.	66.9	80.6	83.7	100.0	101.6	102.4	106.4	108.4	–1.4	1.5	0.8	3.9	1.9
Sweden [4, 5]	51.7	69.1	83.4	100.0	105.4	107.3	112.0	(NA)	–1.1	5.2	1.8	4.4	(NA)
Switzerland.	64.9	79.1	82.2	100.0	98.4	101.0	108.8	(NA)	–0.7	4.1	2.6	7.7	(NA)
Turkey	(NA)	70.5	82.5	100.0	119.3	125.7	133.1	140.2	–8.7	9.8	5.4	5.9	5.3
United Kingdom	71.5	87.7	93.2	100.0	97.1	95.2	95.4	95.7	–1.5	0.8	–2.0	0.2	0.3
United States	**54.2**	**66.3**	**77.0**	**100.0**	**100.0**	**103.4**	**105.7**	**107.4**	**–3.5**	**2.5**	**3.4**	**2.2**	**1.6**

– Represents or rounds to zero. NA Not available. X Not applicable. [1] Not adjusted for unequal number of working days in the month. [2] Data prior to 1991 are for former West Germany. [3] Including construction. [4] Mining and manufacturing. [5] Annual figures correspond to official annual figures and differ from the average of the monthly figures.

Source: Organization for Economic Cooperation and Development, Paris, France, *Main Economic Indicators,* monthly (copyright).

Table 1310. **Annual Percent Change in Labor Productivity and Hours Worked by Country: 1995 to 2007**

[**Change for period shown**. For OECD countries and Eastern Europe, labor productivity growth refers to the growth in gross domestic product per hour worked. Data are derived from an annual database maintained by the Groningen Growth and Development Centre at the University of Groningen, Netherlands, in association with The Conference Board. Growth for regional aggregates is calculated based on the sum of gross domestic product divided by the sum of total hours worked. Gross domestic product for each country was converted based on the 2005 OECD benchmark for purchasing power parities and updated to 2007 using the aggregate inflation rate for each country relative to U.S. inflation. Minus sign (–) indicates decrease]

Country	Labor productivity		Total hours worked		Country	Labor productivity		Total hours worked	
	1995–2000	2000–2007	1995–2000	2000–2007		1995–2000	2000–2007	1995–2000	2000–2007
All OECD	**2.0**	**1.7**	**1.3**	**0.6**	**European Union (EU-12, new)** [3] **. . . . . .**	3.3	4.4	–0.2	0.4
All OECD, excl.					Bulgaria	–0.9	3.5	0.1	2.0
United States	1.8	1.6	1.1	0.7	Cyprus	1.9	0.3	1.9	3.1
United States	**2.1**	**2.0**	**1.9**	**0.4**	Czech Republic	1.9	4.4	–0.4	–0.1
					Estonia.	7.9	6.6	–1.7	1.9
European Union					Hungary	2.4	2.2	1.6	1.7
(EU-27, enlarged) [1] . .	2.1	1.6	0.8	0.7	Latvia.	5.9	7.1	–0.4	1.8
					Lithuania.	4.5	6.6	0.1	1.2
European Union					Malta	2.0	0.7	1.0	0.7
(EU-15, old) [2] **. . . . . .**	1.7	1.2	1.1	0.8	Poland	5.5	3.3	–0.1	0.6
Austria	3.7	1.4	–0.7	0.6	Slovakia	5.0	5.1	–1.5	0.6
Belgium	2.2	0.9	0.5	1.0	Slovenia	4.7	3.9	–0.3	0.4
Denmark.	1.1	0.8	1.7	0.9	Romania	–0.6	7.4	–0.7	–1.3
Finland	2.8	2.3	2.0	0.8	Other OECD members. .	1.5	1.8	1.2	0.6
France	2.1	1.3	0.7	0.4	Japan.	1.7	1.9	–0.7	–0.4
Germany.	2.0	1.4	(Z)	–0.2	Australia	2.2	1.6	1.6	1.7
Greece.	1.4	3.1	2.1	1.2	Canada.	1.7	1.1	2.4	1.4
Ireland	5.5	2.5	4.0	2.7	Iceland	2.3	2.4	2.5	1.2
Italy	1.1	0.3	0.8	0.7	Mexico	0.9	0.6	4.6	1.8
Luxembourg	2.6	0.9	3.4	2.9	New Zealand	1.4	1.1	1.1	2.1
Netherlands.	1.8	1.2	2.3	0.5	Norway	2.3	1.8	1.4	0.5
Portugal	3.6	0.3	0.4	0.7	South Korea	4.7	4.5	–0.4	0.2
Spain	–0.3	–	4.5	3.4	Switzerland	1.3	1.1	0.7	0.5
Sweden	2.4	2.6	0.8	0.2	Turkey	2.0	4.1	1.9	0.6
U.K.	2.2	2.3	1.0	0.3					

– Represents zero. Z Less than .05 percent. [1] Referring to all members of the European Union as of 1 May 2004, and including Bulgaria and Romania, who joined on 1 January 2007. [2] Referring to membership of the European Union until 30 April 2004. [3] Referring to new membership of the European Union as of 1 May 2004, and including Bulgaria and Romania, who joined on 1 January 2007.

Source: The Conference Board, New York, NY, *Performance 2008: Productivity, Employment, and Growth in the World's Economies,* by Bart van Ark, 2008 (copyright). See also <http://www.conference-board.org/economics/research.cfm>.

828 International Statistics

Table 1311. **Annual Percent Changes in Consumer Prices, by Country: 2000 to 2007**

[**Change from previous year**. See text of this section for general comments concerning the data. For additional qualifications of the data for individual countries, see source. Minus sign (–) indicates decrease]

Country	2000	2004	2005	2006	2007	Country	2000	2004	2005	2006	2007
United States	**3.4**	**2.7**	**3.4**	**3.2**	**2.9**	Kenya	10.0	11.6	10.3	14.5	9.8
Argentina	−0.9	4.4	9.6	10.9	8.8	Korea, South	2.2	3.6	2.8	2.3	2.5
Australia	4.5	2.3	2.7	3.5	2.3	Malaysia	1.5	1.5	3.0	3.6	2.0
Austria	2.4	2.1	2.3	1.5	2.2	Mexico	9.5	4.7	4.0	3.6	4.0
Bangladesh	2.4	9.2	7.0	6.8	9.1	Netherlands	2.5	1.2	1.7	1.1	1.6
Belgium	2.5	2.1	2.8	1.8	1.8	Nigeria	14.5	15.0	17.9	8.2	5.4
Bolivia	4.6	4.4	5.4	4.3	8.7	Norway	3.1	0.5	1.5	2.3	0.7
Brazil	7.0	6.6	6.9	4.2	3.6	Pakistan	4.4	7.4	9.1	7.9	7.6
Canada	2.7	1.9	2.2	2.0	2.1	Peru	3.8	3.7	1.6	2.0	1.8
Chile	3.8	1.1	3.1	3.4	4.4	Philippines	4.4	6.0	7.6	6.2	2.8
Colombia	9.2	5.9	5.1	4.3	5.5	Portugal	2.8	2.4	2.3	2.7	2.8
Egypt	2.7	11.3	4.9	7.6	9.3	Romania	45.7	11.9	9.0	6.6	4.8
France	1.7	2.1	1.8	1.6	1.5	Russia	20.8	10.9	12.7	9.7	9.0
Germany	1.5	1.7	2.0	1.7	2.1	South Africa	5.4	1.4	3.4	4.6	7.1
Ghana	25.2	12.6	15.1	10.9	(NA)	Spain	3.4	3.0	3.4	3.5	2.8
Greece	3.1	2.9	3.6	3.2	2.9	Sri Lanka	6.2	7.6	11.6	13.7	(NA)
Guatemala	6.0	7.4	8.4	6.5	6.5	Sweden	0.9	0.4	0.5	1.4	2.2
India	4.0	3.8	4.3	5.8	6.4	Switzerland	1.5	0.8	1.2	1.1	0.7
Indonesia	4.5	6.2	10.5	13.1	6.4	Thailand	1.6	2.8	4.5	4.6	2.2
Iran	14.5	14.8	13.4	11.9	(NA)	Turkey	54.9	10.6	10.1	10.5	8.8
Israel	1.1	−0.4	1.3	2.1	0.5	United Kingdom	2.9	3.0	2.8	3.2	4.3
Italy	2.5	2.2	2.0	2.1	1.8	Venezuela	16.2	21.8	16.0	13.7	18.7
Japan	−0.7	0.0	−0.3	0.2	0.1						

NA Not available.

Source: International Monetary Fund, Washington, DC, *International Financial Statistics,* monthly (copyright).

Table 1312. **Comparative Price Levels—Selected OECD Countries: 2008**

[Purchasing power parities (PPPs) are the rates of currency conversion that eliminate the differences in price levels between countries. Comparative price levels are defined as the ratios of PPPs to exchange rates. The PPPs are given in national currency units per U.S. dollar. The table is to be read vertically. Each column shows the number of specified monetary units needed in each of the countries listed to buy the same representative basket of consumer goods and services. In each case the representative basket costs a hundred units in the country whose currency is specified. Example of data: An item that costs $1.00 in the United States would cost $1.28 (U.S. dollars) in Japan]

Country	United States (U.S. dollar)	Canada (Canadian dollar)	Mexico (Mexican peso)	Japan (yen)	France (euro)	Germany (euro)	Italy (euro)	United Kingdom (pound)
United States	**100**	**84**	**162**	**78**	**70**	**73**	**72**	**79**
Australia [1]	136	114	184	106	95	99	98	107
Austria	136	114	184	106	96	99	98	107
Belgium	143	119	193	112	100	104	103	113
Canada	120	100	162	94	84	87	86	95
Czech Republic	97	81	131	76	68	71	70	77
Denmark	187	156	252	146	131	136	134	148
Finland	166	139	224	130	117	121	120	131
France	142	119	192	111	100	104	103	113
Germany	138	115	186	108	97	100	99	109
Greece	123	102	165	96	86	89	88	97
Hungary	92	77	124	72	65	67	66	73
Iceland	157	132	213	123	111	115	113	124
Ireland	176	148	238	138	124	128	127	139
Italy	139	116	187	109	98	101	100	110
Japan	128	107	173	100	90	93	92	101
Korea, South	88	74	119	69	62	64	63	70
Luxembourg	139	116	188	109	98	101	100	110
Mexico	74	62	100	58	52	54	53	59
Netherlands	138	115	186	108	97	100	99	109
New Zealand [1]	125	104	168	98	88	91	90	99
Norway	187	156	252	146	131	136	134	147
Poland	96	81	130	75	68	70	69	76
Portugal	116	97	156	91	81	84	83	92
Slovakia	93	78	125	73	65	67	67	73
Spain	127	106	172	100	89	93	92	101
Sweden	156	131	211	122	110	114	112	123
Switzerland	174	146	235	136	122	127	126	138
Turkey	91	76	123	72	64	66	66	72
United Kingdom	127	106	171	99	89	92	91	100

[1] Estimates based on quarterly consumer prices.

Source: Organization for Economic Cooperation and Development, Paris, France, *Main Economic Indicators,* April 2008 (copyright). See also <http://www.oecd.org/dataoecd/48/18/18598721.pdf>.

Table 1313. Indexes of Living Costs Abroad: 2008

[As of January 2008. Washington, D.C. = 100. Indexes compare the costs in dollars of representative goods and services (excluding housing and education) purchased at the foreign location and the cost of comparable goods and services in the Washington, D.C. area. The indexes are computed for private American employees and exclude special advantages that may be available only to U.S. government employees. The indexes are place-to-place comparisons at specific times and currency exchange rates. They cannot be used for measuring cost changes over time at a foreign location. Since the indexes reflect only the expenditure pattern and living costs of American families, they should not be used to compare living costs of Americans in the United States with the living costs of foreign nationals living in their own country]

Country	City	Survey date	Relative living costs [1]	Country	City	Survey date	Relative living costs [1]
Algeria	Algiers	5/1/2007	109	Kenya	Nairobi	4/30/2007	138
Angola	Luanda	5/15/2005	141	Korea	Seoul	3/7/2006	139
Argentina	Buenos Aires	1/5/2005	84	Kuwait	Kuwait City	10/10/2005	116
Armenia	Yerevan	1/30/2007	136	Laos	Vientiane	12/30/2005	95
Australia	Canberra	6/27/2006	130	Latvia	Riga	5/30/2007	131
Austria	Vienna	1/20/2006	158	Lebanon	Beirut	6/19/2006	106
Azerbaijan	Baku	6/14/2007	140	Liberia	Monrovia	12/1/2007	128
Bahamas	Nassau	11/26/2005	148	Lithuania	Vilnius	4/27/2007	123
Bahrain	Bahrain	8/26/2007	113	Luxembourg		8/13/2004	154
Bangladesh	Dhaka	3/6/2006	84	Macedonia	Skopje	4/23/2007	130
Belarus	Minsk	3/15/2007	136	Madagascar	Antananarivo	1/17/2006	110
Belgium	Brussels	7/25/2005	160		Kuala		
Belize	Belize City	6/5/2005	121	Malaysia	Lumpur	1/20/2006	99
Bolivia	La Paz	3/5/2007	74	Mexico	Mexico City	3/7/2007	114
Bosnia-				Moldova	Chisinau	3/9/2006	87
Herzegovina	Sarajevo	10/17/2006	109	Mongolia	Ulaanbaatar	5/12/2005	93
Botswana	Gaborone	5/1/2006	103	Morocco	Rabat	3/17/2005	138
	Rio de			Mozambique	Maputo	8/22/2005	124
Brazil	Janeiro	11/20/2005	123	Namibia	Windhoek	4/20/2006	117
Bulgaria	Sofia	5/15/2006	107	Nepal	Kathmandu	6/22/2007	100
Burma	Rangoon	3/4/2006	121	Netherlands	The Hague	3/31/2006	149
Burundi	Bujumbura	1/6/2006	133	New Zealand	Wellington	10/6/2005	145
Cambodia	Phnom Penh	1/3/2005	116	Nicaragua	Managua	5/2/2006	84
Cameroon	Yaounde	3/27/2006	143	Niger	Niamey	7/28/2005	122
Canada	Montreal	1/12/2007	133	Nigeria	Abuja	5/23/2006	145
Central African				Norway	Oslo	2/12/2007	185
Republic	Bangui	3/1/2001	139	Oman	Muscat	4/1/2006	119
Chad	Ndjamena	8/1/2006	144	Pakistan	Islamabad	12/10/2004	98
Chile [2]	Santiago	5/26/2006	113	Panama	Panama City	8/21/2006	99
China [2]	Beijing	7/27/2007	124	Paraguay	Asuncion	2/27/2006	90
Colombia	Bogota	2/10/2006	86	Peru	Lima	12/7/2005	117
Congo [3]	Brazzaville	7/31/2007	177	Philippines	Manila	4/16/2007	94
Costa Rica	San Jose	8/15/2006	103	Poland	Warsaw	3/17/2006	129
Cote DIvoire	Abidjan	12/10/2006	149	Portugal	Lisbon	5/18/2006	124
Croatia	Zagreb	3/22/2007	141	Qatar	Doha	8/15/2007	125
Cuba	Havana	8/1/2005	143	Romania	Bucharest	11/27/2006	114
Cyprus	Nicosia	5/23/2007	138	Russia	Moscow	12/20/2006	162
Czech Republic	Prague	9/15/2005	137	Rwanda	Kigali	2/25/2007	128
Denmark	Copenhagen	6/28/2006	163	Saudi Arabia	Riyadh	5/8/2006	108
Djibouti	Djibouti City	4/10/2004	145	Serbia	Belgrade	5/11/2007	112
Ecuador	Quito	1/17/2005	123	Sierra Leone	Freetown	10/20/2006	125
Egypt	Cairo	3/13/2006	91	Singapore		4/9/2007	140
El Salvador	San Salvador	1/25/2007	100	Slovakia	Bratislava	5/31/2007	135
Estonia	Tallinn	1/17/2007	128	South Africa	Johannesburg	7/20/2007	119
Ethiopia	Addis Ababa	4/10/2006	113	Spain	Madrid	4/17/2006	152
Finland	Helsinki	3/21/2007	181	Sri Lanka	Colombo	2/23/2006	82
France	Paris	4/19/2007	192	Sudan	Khartoum	10/17/2004	118
Gabon	Libreville	5/2/2007	171	Sweden	Stockholm	3/19/2006	164
Georgia	Tbilisi	10/8/2004	125	Switzerland	Geneva	3/30/2006	178
Germany	Berlin	3/6/2006	149	Syria	Damascus	2/23/2006	88
Ghana	Accra	10/4/2007	125	Taiwan [4]	Taipei	3/6/2007	131
Greece	Athens	7/20/2005	154	Tajikistan	Dushande	10/1/1997	93
	Guatemala				Dar es		
Guatemala	City	4/23/2007	108	Tanzania	Salaam	12/14/2005	116
Guinea	Conakry	5/7/2007	145	Thailand	Bangkok	2/3/2006	90
Guyana	Georgetown	1/15/2007	93	Timor Leste	Timor Leste	7/11/2007	120
	Port-au-			Turkey	Istanbul	2/11/2007	162
Haiti	Prince	1/6/2005	118	Turkmenistan	Ashgabat	6/1/2005	108
Honduras	Tegucigalpa	6/10/2007	79	Uganda	Kampala	3/1/2007	119
Hong Kong		7/13/2007	157	Ukraine	Kyiv	10/13/2006	125
Hungary	Budapest	6/30/2005	133	United Arab			
Iceland	Reykjavik	7/31/2006	179	Emirates	Dubai	4/15/2007	119
India	New Delhi	10/16/2006	93	United Kingdom	London	10/18/2006	177
Indonesia	Jakarta	5/18/2006	115	Uruguay	Montevideo	6/30/2005	106
Ireland	Dublin	5/9/2005	170	Uzbekistan	Tashkent	8/15/2007	94
Israel	Tel Aviv	11/15/2006	139	Venezuela	Caracas	8/15/2007	111
Italy	Rome	2/27/2007	190	Vietnam	Hanoi	1/31/2005	96
Jamaica	Kingston	3/1/2007	101	Yemen	Sanaa	12/10/2005	123
Japan	Okinawa	5/24/2002	140	Zambia	Lusaka	3/16/2007	127
Jordan	Amman	5/20/2007	115	Zimbabwe	Harare	1/10/2006	195
Kazakhstan	Almaty	5/30/2007	140				

[1] The relative living cost measures living costs for private American citizens living abroad. It is a comparison of goods and services prices between the foreign post and Washington, D.C., with the price ratios weighted by the pattern of expenditure in Washington, D.C. Consequently, the relative living cost is a straight comparison of price levels between the post and Washington, D.C., but not necessarily a comparison of the cost of living abroad. [2] See footnote 2, Table 1288. [3] See footnote 3, Table 1288. [4] There are no U.S. Government employees in Taiwan. The figures listed in this column represent a living cost comparison for American employees of the American Institute in Taiwan, who have some duty-free and other special benefits that may not be available to other Americans in Taiwan.

Source: U.S. Department of State, Bureau of Administration, "Indexes of Living Costs Abroad, Quarters Allowances, and Hardship Differentials," January 2008; <http://aoprals.state.gov/content.asp?content_id=186&menu_id=81>.

Table 1314. Percent of Household Final Consumption Expenditures Spent on Food, Alcohol, and Tobacco Consumed at Home, by Selected Countries: 2006

Country/Territory	Food [1]	Alcoholic beverages and tobacco	Country/Territory	Food [1]	Alcoholic beverages and tobacco
United States	**7.2**	**2.0**	Lithuania	24.9	6.4
Algeria	43.7	2.0	Malaysia	15.0	1.2
Australia	11.2	4.1	Mexico	24.5	2.5
Austria	11.1	2.6	Morocco	44.8	1.5
Azerbaijan	51.6	2.4	Netherlands	10.4	3.0
Belarus	47.3	6.3	New Zealand	12.5	4.4
Belgium	13.2	3.7	Nigeria	40.7	2.5
Bolivia	29.1	2.2	Norway	12.8	4.3
Brazil	24.7	1.9	Pakistan	41.5	2.5
Bulgaria	29.5	4.2	Peru	29.6	2.0
Canada	9.3	3.8	Philippines	27.4	2.1
Chile	23.7	0.8	Poland	22.1	7.4
China [2]	27.8	2.2	Portugal	18.0	4.0
Colombia	25.5	4.4	Romania	34.6	5.0
Croatia	33.9	4.1	Russia	31.4	2.5
Czech Republic	17.0	8.0	Saudi Arabia	21.4	1.1
Ecuador	28.5	5.8	Singapore	8.1	2.3
Egypt	41.5	2.5	Slovakia	19.2	4.9
Estonia	18.4	8.6	Slovenia	15.9	4.4
Finland	12.4	4.8	South Africa	21.4	4.6
France	13.9	3.1	Spain	14.6	3.3
Germany	11.2	3.5	Sweden	11.9	3.5
Hong Kong	13.0	0.8	Switzerland	10.4	3.6
Hungary	17.8	8.2	Taiwan [2]	23.9	2.1
Indonesia	26.7	2.0	Thailand	25.8	5.6
Ireland	8.2	5.0	Tunisia	36.7	1.0
Israel	18.1	1.7	Turkey	28.7	5.1
Italy	14.9	2.8	Turkmenistan	32.7	2.7
Japan	14.3	3.1	Ukraine	43.1	6.4
Jordan	43.6	5.1	United Arab Emirates . . .	10.1	0.6
Kazakhstan	36.6	3.5	United Kingdom	8.7	3.6
Korea, South	15.1	2.6	Venezuela	29.4	3.1
Kuwait	12.0	1.3	Vietnam	39.7	2.9
Latvia	19.0	6.3			

[1] Includes nonalcoholic beverages.   [2] See footnote 2, Table 1288.

Source: U.S. Department of Agriculture, Economic Research Service; Food, CPI, Prices and Expenditures: Expenditure Tables; <http://www.ers.usda.gov/Briefing/CPIFoodAndExpenditures/Data/>.

Table 1315. Gross Public Debt, Expenditures, and Receipts by Country: 1990 to 2007

[Percent of nominal gross domestic product. Gross debt includes one-off revenues from the sale of the mobile telephone licenses. Expenditures and receipts refer to the general government sector, which is a consolidation of accounts for the central, state, and local governments plus social security. Expenditures, or total outlays, are defined as current outlays plus capital outlays. Receipts cover current receipts, but exclude capital receipts. Nontax receipts consist of property income (including dividends and other transfers from public enterprises), fees, charges, sales, fines, capital transfers received by the general government, etc.). Minus sign (–) indicates deficit]

Country	Gross debt			Expenditures			Receipts		
	1990	2000	2007	1990	2000	2007	1990	2000	2007
United States [1] **. . . . . . .**	**–4.2**	**1.6**	**–3.0**	**37.1**	**34.2**	**37.4**	**32.8**	**35.8**	**34.4**
Australia	–2.0	[2]0.9	0.7	35.7	[2]35.2	34.7	33.7	36.1	35.4
Austria	–2.5	[2]–1.6	–0.7	51.5	[2]51.5	48.2	48.9	49.6	47.5
Belgium	–6.7	(Z)	–0.2	52.2	49.1	48.7	45.5	49.1	48.5
Canada	–5.8	2.9	1.0	48.8	41.1	39.0	43.0	44.1	40.0
Czech Republic	(X)	–3.7	–1.6	(X)	41.7	41.8	(X)	37.9	40.3
Denmark	–1.3	2.3	4.5	55.9	53.3	50.3	54.6	55.5	54.8
Finland	5.4	6.9	5.3	47.9	48.4	47.5	53.2	55.3	52.8
France	–2.4	–1.5	–2.7	49.4	51.6	52.4	47.0	50.1	49.7
Germany	–1.9	[2]1.3	0.0	43.6	[2]45.1	43.8	41.7	46.4	43.8
Greece	–14.0	–4.1	–3.1	44.9	46.7	43.3	30.9	43.0	40.2
Hungary	(NA)	–3.0	–5.5	(NA)	46.5	50.1	(NA)	43.6	44.6
Iceland	–3.3	2.4	5.2	41.5	41.9	43.1	38.3	43.6	48.3
Ireland	–2.8	4.6	0.3	42.9	31.5	36.7	40.1	36.3	37.0
Italy	–11.4	[2]–0.9	–1.9	52.9	[2]46.1	48.5	41.5	45.3	46.6
Japan [3]	2.1	–7.7	–2.4	32.0	39.0	35.8	34.0	31.4	33.4
Korea, South	3.1	5.4	4.6	20.0	23.9	30.7	23.1	29.3	35.3
Netherlands	–5.3	[2]2.0	0.4	54.9	[2]44.2	45.9	49.6	46.1	46.3
New Zealand	–4.6	[2]1.6	3.8	53.2	[2]39.6	41.7	48.7	41.2	45.4
Norway	2.2	15.6	17.3	53.3	42.3	40.6	55.5	57.7	57.9
Portugal	–6.1	[2]–3.0	–2.7	40.5	[2]43.1	45.8	34.5	40.2	43.1
Spain	–4.1	[2]–0.9	2.2	42.8	[2]39.1	38.7	38.7	38.1	41.0
Sweden	3.3	5.0	3.4	59.7	57.0	51.3	63.1	60.7	54.7
United Kingdom	–1.8	[2]4.0	–3.0	41.9	[2]37.0	44.7	40.1	41.0	41.7

NA Not available.   X Not applicable.   Z Less than 0.05 percent.   [1] Receipts exclude the operating surpluses of public enterprises, while expenditures include them.   [2] Includes substantial one-off revenues from the sale of the mobil telephone licenses.   [3] The 2000 expenditures include capital transfers to the Deposit Insurance Company. Receipts include deferred tax payments on postal savings accounts in 2000.

Source: Organization for Economic Cooperation and Development, Paris, France, *OECD Economic Outlook*, June 2008 (copyright).

Table 1316. Percent of Women in National Parliaments by Country: 2008

[Compiled on the basis of information provided by National Parliaments as of May 31, 2008]

Country	Lower or single House Election year	Lower or single House Percent women	Upper House or Senate Election year	Upper House or Senate Percent women	Country	Lower or single House Election year	Lower or single House Percent women	Upper House or Senate Election year	Upper House or Senate Percent women
Afghanistan	2005	27.7	2005	21.6	Kazakhstan	2007	15.9	2005	4.3
Argentina	2007	40.0	2007	38.9	Korea, South	2008	13.7	(X)	(X)
Australia	2007	26.7	2007	35.5	Mexico	2006	23.2	2006	18.0
Austria	2006	32.8	(1)	24.6	Namibia	2004	26.9	2004	26.9
Belarus	2004	29.1	2004	31.0	Netherlands	2006	39.3	2007	34.7
Belgium	2007	35.3	2007	38.0	Nicaragua	2006	18.5	(X)	(X)
Bolivia	2005	16.9	2005	3.7	Pakistan	2008	22.5	2006	17.0
Bosnia and Herzegovina	2006	11.9	2007	13.3	Philippines	2007	20.5	2007	17.4
Cambodia	2003	19.5	2006	14.8	Poland	2007	20.2	2007	8.0
Canada	2006	21.3	(1)	34.4	Russia	2007	14.0	(1)	4.7
Chile	2005	15.0	2005	5.3	Rwanda	2003	48.8	2003	34.6
China[2]	2008	21.3	(X)	(X)	Saudi Arabia	2005	–	(X)	(X)
Czech Republic	2006	15.5	2006	13.6	Slovenia	2004	12.2	2002	2.5
Dominican Republic	2006	19.7	2006	3.1	South Africa[3]	2004	33.0	2004	40.7
Ethiopia	2005	21.9	2005	18.8	Spain	2008	36.3	2008	28.3
France	2007	18.2	2004	18.2	Sudan	2005	18.1	2005	6.0
Gabon	2001	16.7	2003	15.4	Switzerland	2007	28.5	2007	21.7
Germany	2005	31.6	(1)	21.7	Thailand	2007	11.7	2008	16.0
Iran	2008	2.8	(X)	(X)	United Kingdom	2005	19.5	(1)	19.7
Iraq	2005	25.5	(X)	(X)	**United States**	**2006**	**16.8**	**2006**	**16.0**
Ireland	2007	13.3	2007	21.7	Uruguay	2004	12.1	2004	12.9
Italy	2008	21.1	2008	18.0	Uzbekistan	2004	17.5	2005	15.0
Japan	2005	9.4	2007	18.2	Zimbabwe	2008	13.5	2008	(NA)

– Represents zero. NA Not available. X Not applicable. [1] Term of the chamber is not fixed (i.e., renewals do not take place on the same date, but rather when individual mandates expire). [2] With the establishment of diplomatic relations with China on January 1, 1979, the U.S. government recognized the People's Republic of China as the sole legal government of China and acknowledged the Chinese position that there is only one China and that Taiwan is part of China. [3] The Upper House figures on the distribution of seats do not include the 36 special rotating delegates appointed on an ad hoc basis, and all percentages given are therefore calculated on the basis of the 55 permanent seats.

Source: Inter-Parliamentary Union, Geneva, Switzerland, "Women in National Parliaments"; <http://www.ipu.org/wmn-e/classif.htm> (released 31 May 2008).

Table 1317. Percent Distribution of Tax Receipts by Country: 1990 to 2006

Country	Total[1]	Income and profits taxes[2] Total[3]	Income and profits taxes[2] Individual	Income and profits taxes[2] Corporate	Social security contributions Total[4]	Social security contributions Employees	Social security contributions Employers	Taxes on goods and services[5] Total[3]	Taxes on goods and services[5] General consumption taxes[6]	Taxes on goods and services[5] Taxes on specific goods and services[7]
United States:										
1990	100.0	45.4	37.7	7.7	25.9	11.0	13.4	17.3	8.0	7.1
2000	100.0	50.7	41.9	8.7	23.2	10.4	11.6	16.1	7.6	6.3
2006	100.0	48.5	36.3	12.3	24.0	10.5	12.3	16.5	7.7	6.1
Canada:										
1990	100.0	48.6	40.8	7.0	12.2	4.4	7.6	25.8	14.1	10.3
2000	100.0	50.1	36.8	12.2	13.6	5.5	7.8	24.2	14.3	8.5
2006	100.0	48.7	36.7	10.6	14.6	5.8	8.3	24.4	14.2	8.7
France:										
1990	100.0	17.2	11.8	5.3	44.1	13.2	27.2	28.4	18.8	8.7
2000	100.0	24.9	18.0	6.9	36.0	8.9	24.8	25.7	16.9	8.2
2006	100.0	24.3	17.5	6.8	36.8	9.3	24.8	24.9	16.9	7.3
Germany:										
1990	100.0	32.4	27.6	4.8	37.5	16.2	19.1	26.7	16.6	9.2
2000	100.0	30.1	25.3	4.8	39.0	17.2	19.2	28.1	18.4	8.8
2006	100.0	30.3	24.4	5.9	38.5	16.9	18.4	28.4	17.9	9.4
Italy:										
1990	100.0	36.5	26.3	10.0	32.9	6.3	23.6	28.0	14.7	10.6
2000	100.0	33.2	24.9	6.8	28.6	5.4	19.9	27.8	15.4	9.7
2006	100.0	32.8	25.3	8.0	29.9	5.4	20.6	26.0	14.7	8.8
Japan:										
1990	100.0	48.5	26.9	21.6	29.0	11.0	15.0	13.2	4.3	7.3
2000	100.0	34.8	21.1	13.8	35.1	14.7	16.4	19.3	9.1	8.0
2006	100.0	56.5	29.4	27.1	(NA)	(NA)	(NA)	29.1	14.3	11.5
United Kingdom:										
1990	100.0	38.3	27.1	11.2	16.7	6.5	9.7	30.5	16.4	12.4
2000	100.0	39.1	29.3	9.7	16.9	6.8	9.5	32.0	18.3	12.3
2006	100.0	39.9	29.1	10.8	18.2	7.5	10.1	29.1	18.2	9.8

NA Not available. [1] Includes property taxes, employer payroll taxes other than social security contributions, and miscellaneous taxes not shown separately. [2] Includes taxes on capital gains. [3] Includes other taxes not shown separately. [4] Includes contributions of self-employed not shown separately. [5] Taxes on the production, sales, transfer, leasing, and delivery of goods and services and rendering of services. [6] Primary value-added and sales taxes. [7] For example, excise taxes on alcohol, tobacco, and gasoline.

Source: Organization for Economic Cooperation and Development, Paris, France, *Revenue Statistics,* annual (copyright).

Table 1318. Household Tax Burden by Country: 2007

[**Percent of gross wage earnings of the average production worker**. The tax burden reflects income tax plus employee social security contributions less cash benefits. Minus sign (–) indicates tax credit]

Country	Single person without children	One earner family with two children	Country	Single person without children	One earner family with two children
Australia	23.4	10.0	Korea, South	11.9	9.5
Austria	33.5	19.8	Luxembourg	29.1	2.8
Belgium	42.0	22.4	Mexico	5.2	5.2
Canada	23.3	10.6	Netherlands	35.4	26.9
Czech Republic	22.9	-6.3	New Zealand	21.5	2.8
Denmark	41.0	29.3	Norway	29.5	21.5
Finland	30.1	22.9	Poland	31.1	24.7
France	27.8	17.5	Portugal	22.5	10.3
Germany	42.8	23.9	Slovakia	22.4	4.4
Greece	26.1	26.5	Spain	20.4	12.4
Hungary	38.7	24.4	Sweden	27.6	19.8
Iceland	24.4	6.7	Switzerland	21.8	9.3
Ireland	13.9	-12.0	Turkey	30.3	30.3
Italy	28.5	12.5	United Kingdom	27.0	20.6
Japan	20.1	13.9	**United States**	**24.5**	**11.8**

Source: Organization for Economic Cooperation and Development, Paris, France, *Taxing Wages, 2006–2007*, (copyright).

Table 1319. Civilian Labor Force, Employment, and Unemployment by Country: 1990 to 2007

[**125,840 represents 125,840,000**. Data based on U.S. labor force definitions (see source) except that minimum age for population base varies as follows: United States, Canada, France, Sweden, and United Kingdom, 16 years; Australia, Japan, Netherlands, Germany, and Italy (beginning 1993), 15 years; and Italy (prior to 1993) 14 years]

Year	United States	Canada	Aus-tralia	Japan	France	Ger-many [1]	Italy	Nether-lands	Swe-den	United King-dom
Civilian labor force (1,000):										
1990	[2]125,840	14,047	8,440	63,050	24,159	29,410	22,670	6,767	4,594	28,766
2000	[2]142,583	15,637	9,590	66,990	26,099	[2]39,302	[2]23,361	[2]8,052	4,482	28,952
2005	149,320	17,108	10,506	65,850	27,092	[2]40,760	24,179	8,459	[2]4,694	30,126
2006	151,428	17,351	10,699	65,960	27,322	41,250	24,395	8,541	4,748	30,586
2007	153,124	17,696	10,948	66,080	27,509	(NA)	24,459	8,686	4,823	30,774
Labor force participation rate: [3]										
1990	[2]66.5	67.4	64.7	62.6	[2]55.7	55.3	47.2	57.0	67.3	64.3
2000	67.1	66.0	64.4	62.0	56.6	56.7	48.1	[2]63.4	63.7	62.9
2005	66.0	67.4	65.3	60.0	56.5	[2]57.6	48.7	64.7	[2]64.8	63.1
2006	66.2	67.4	65.6	60.0	56.6	58.2	48.9	65.1	65.0	63.5
2007	66.0	67.7	66.0	60.0	56.7	(NA)	48.6	65.9	65.3	63.4
Civilian employment (1,000):										
1990	[2]118,793	12,964	7,877	61,700	22,075	27,950	21,080	6,251	4,513	26,713
2000	[2]136,891	14,681	8,989	63,790	23,714	36,236	20,973	[2]7,813	4,222	27,368
2005	141,730	16,080	9,975	62,910	24,493	[2]36,185	22,290	8,056	[2]4,334	28,665
2006	144,427	16,393	10,186	63,210	24,717	36,978	22,721	8,205	4,416	28,917
2007	146,047	16,767	10,470	63,510	25,135	(NA)	22,953	8,408	4,530	29,120
Employment-population ratio: [4]										
1990	[2]62.8	62.2	60.4	61.3	[2]50.9	52.6	43.9	52.7	66.1	59.8
2000	64.4	62.0	60.3	59.0	51.4	52.2	43.2	[2]61.5	60.0	59.4
2005	62.7	63.4	62.0	57.3	51.1	[2]51.2	44.9	61.6	[2]59.9	60.1
2006	63.1	63.6	62.5	57.5	51.2	52.2	45.5	62.5	60.4	60.1
2007	63.0	64.2	63.1	57.6	51.8	(NA)	45.6	63.8	61.3	60.0
Unemployment rate:										
1990	[2]5.6	7.7	6.7	2.1	[2]8.6	5.0	7.0	7.6	1.8	7.1
2000	4.0	6.1	6.3	4.8	9.1	7.8	10.2	[2]3.0	5.8	5.5
2005	5.1	6.0	5.1	4.5	9.6	[2]11.2	7.8	4.8	[2]7.7	4.9
2006	4.6	5.5	4.8	4.2	9.5	10.4	6.9	3.9	7.0	5.5
2007	4.6	5.3	4.4	3.9	8.6	8.7	6.2	3.2	6.1	5.4
Under 25 years old	10.5	10.1	9.4	7.8	20.0	(NA)	20.6	6.0	19.1	14.5
Teenagers [5]	15.7	13.6	13.8	8.8	27.2	(NA)	31.7	8.6	29.7	21.3
20 to 24 years old	8.2	8.0	6.3	7.6	17.9	(NA)	18.2	3.9	13.8	10.5
25 years old and over	3.6	4.3	3.2	3.5	7.3	(NA)	5.0	2.7	4.3	3.7

NA Not available. [1] Unified Germany for 1991 onward. Prior to 1991, data relate to the former West Germany. [2] Break in series. Data not comparable with prior years. [3] Civilian labor force as a percent of the civilian working-age population. Germany and Japan include the institutionalized population as part of the working-age population. [4] Civilian employment as a percent of the civilian working-age population. Germany and Japan include the institutionalized population as part of the working-age population. [5] 16- to 19-year-olds in the United States, Canada, France, Sweden, and the United Kingdom; 15- to 19-year-olds in Australia, Japan, Germany, Italy, and the Netherlands.

Source: U.S. Bureau of Labor Statistics, *Comparative Civilian Labor Force Statistics, 10 Countries, 1960–2007*, 18 April 2008. See also <http://www.bls.gov/fls/flscomparelf.htm>.

U.S. Census Bureau, Statistical Abstract of the United States: 2009

Table 1320. Percent of Persons Not in Education or at Work: 2005

[Represents those persons not in education and either unemployed or not in the labor force]

Country	15 to 19 years old			20 to 24 years old		
	Total	Unemployed	Not in the labor force	Total	Unemployed	Not in the labor force
Australia	7.4	3.8	3.6	11.7	4.4	7.3
Belgium	6.2	1.8	4.4	18.3	11.0	7.3
Canada.	6.1	2.8	3.3	13.2	6.1	7.1
Czech Republic	5.3	3.8	1.5	16.6	8.9	7.7
Denmark.	4.3	1.8	2.5	8.3	3.8	4.5
Finland	5.3	2.0	3.3	13.1	7.0	6.1
France	6.2	3.2	3.0	16.5	10.6	5.9
Germany.	4.4	2.4	2.0	18.7	10.3	8.4
Greece	9.8	2.8	7.0	20.1	11.8	8.3
Hungary	6.4	1.9	4.5	18.9	7.1	11.8
Israel	24.7	1.8	22.9	40.3	7.1	33.2
Italy	11.1	3.9	7.2	24.1	10.5	13.6
Mexico	17.1	2.2	14.9	27.4	3.2	24.2
Netherlands.	3.9	1.3	2.6	9.1	3.9	5.2
Poland	1.7	0.7	1.0	20.1	14.3	5.8
Portugal	8.4	3.1	5.3	14.1	8.8	5.3
Spain	8.5	4.1	4.4	15.5	8.9	6.6
Sweden	4.7	2.1	2.6	13.4	8.7	4.7
Switzerland	7.2	2.5	4.7	11.0	5.2	5.8
United States	**6.1**	**1.9**	**4.2**	**15.5**	**4.9**	**10.6**

Source: Organization for Economic Cooperation and Development, Paris, France, *Education at a Glance 2007* (copyright).

Table 1321. Unemployment Rates by Country: 2000 to 2007

[**Annual averages.** The standardized unemployment rates shown here are calculated as the number of unemployed persons as a percentage of the civilian labor force. The unemployed are persons of working age who, in the reference period, are without work, available for work, and have taken specific steps to find work]

Country	2000	2005	2006	2007	Country	2000	2005	2006	2007
OECD, total	**6.2**	**6.7**	**6.1**	**5.6**	Ireland	4.3	4.3	4.4	4.6
Euro area [1]	(NA)	8.8	8.2	7.4	Italy	10.1	7.7	6.8	6.1
					Japan.	4.7	4.4	4.1	3.9
United States	**4.0**	**5.1**	**4.6**	**4.6**	Korea, South	4.4	3.7	3.5	3.2
Australia.	6.3	5.1	4.8	4.4	Luxembourg	2.3	4.5	4.8	4.7
Austria	3.6	5.2	4.8	4.4	Netherlands.	2.8	4.7	3.9	3.2
Belgium	6.9	8.5	8.2	7.5	New Zealand	6.0	3.7	3.8	3.6
Canada.	6.8	6.8	6.3	6.0	Norway.	3.4	4.6	3.5	2.6
Czech Republic . . .	8.7	7.9	7.1	5.3	Poland	16.1	17.7	13.8	9.6
Denmark.	4.3	4.8	3.9	3.8	Portugal	4.0	7.6	7.7	8.0
Finland	9.7	8.3	7.7	6.8	Spain	11.1	9.2	8.5	8.3
France	9.1	9.3	9.2	8.3	Sweden	5.6	7.3	7.0	6.1
Germany.	7.2	10.6	9.8	8.4	Switzerland	2.7	4.4	4.0	3.6
Hungary	6.4	7.2	7.5	7.4	United Kingdom . . .	5.4	4.8	5.3	5.3

NA Not available. [1] Euro area refers to European Union member countries that have adopted the Euro as the common currency as of January 1, 2001, (Austria, Belgium, Finland, France, Germany, Greece, Ireland, Italy, Luxembourg, Netherlands, Portugal, and Spain).

Source: Organization for Economic Cooperation and Development, Paris, France, *Main Economic Indicators*, April 2007 and earlier releases.

Table 1322. Female Labor Force Participation Rates by Country: 1980 to 2006

[**In percent**. Female labor force of all ages divided by female population 15–64 years old]

Country	1980	1990	2000	2006	Country	1980	1990	2000	2006
Australia	52.7	62.1	66.1	69.8	Korea, South	(NA)	51.2	54.9	58.5
Austria	48.7	55.4	62.2	67.6	Luxembourg	39.9	50.7	52.0	58.3
Belgium	47.0	52.4	56.9	59.3	Mexico	33.7	(NA)	42.2	46.0
Canada.	57.8	67.6	71.0	74.5	Netherlands.	35.5	[1]53.1	65.6	69.8
Czech Republic	(X)	69.1	64.2	62.9	New Zealand	44.6	[1]63.0	68.3	73.0
Denmark.	(NA)	78.5	76.3	77.5	Norway.	62.3	71.2	77.5	76.0
Finland	70.1	73.8	72.3	73.9	Poland	(NA)	(NA)	61.1	57.6
France	54.4	57.8	61.9	64.7	Portugal	54.3	62.9	67.5	72.3
Germany [2].	52.8	56.7	63.7	69.3	Slovakia	(NA)	(NA)	63.3	61.0
Greece	33.0	43.6	50.5	55.6	Spain	32.2	41.2	53.2	61.4
Hungary	(NA)	(NA)	52.9	55.8	Sweden	74.1	[1]80.4	77.3	78.7
Iceland	(NA)	65.6	85.7	86.4	Switzerland	54.1	65.7	73.3	76.2
Ireland	36.3	43.8	56.2	62.1	Turkey	(NA)	36.7	29.0	27.3
Italy	39.6	45.9	46.8	51.2	United Kingdom	58.3	66.5	69.8	71.5
Japan.	54.8	60.3	63.8	66.0	**United States . . . . . .**	**59.7**	**[1]68.5**	**72.7**	**71.7**

NA Not available. X Not applicable. [1] Break in series. Data not comparable with prior years. [2] Prior to 1991, data are for former West Germany.

Source: Organization for Economic Cooperation and Development, Paris, France, *OECD in Figures*, 2007 (copyright). See also <http://lysander.sourceoecd.org/vl=1229955/cl=16/nw=1/rpsv/~6676/v2007n7/s1/p1l>.

Table 1323. Civilian Employment-Population Ratio: 1990 to 2007

[Civilian employment as a percent of the civilian working-age population. See headnote, Table 1319]

Country	Women					Men				
	1990	1995	2000	2006	2007	1990	1995	2000	2006	2007
United States [1]**. . .**	**54.3**	**55.6**	**57.5**	**56.6**	**56.6**	**72.0**	**70.8**	**71.9**	**70.1**	**69.8**
Canada	54.1	52.7	56.0	58.9	59.7	70.6	66.1	68.2	68.6	68.8
Australia.	49.5	50.5	52.5	55.5	56.2	71.4	68.2	68.4	69.6	70.2
Japan	48.0	47.7	46.4	46.0	46.1	75.4	75.0	72.5	69.8	70.0
France.	41.5	41.9	44.5	45.8	46.7	61.4	57.4	59.0	57.1	57.4
Germany [1,2,3,4] . .	40.9	42.7	44.4	46.0	(NA)	65.6	63.1	60.6	58.8	(NA)
Italy [1]	29.2	29.1	31.6	34.7	34.9	60.0	56.2	55.8	57.3	57.3
Netherlands [1,3] . .	39.4	44.4	52.0	55.2	56.8	66.5	66.7	71.4	70.0	71.0
Sweden	[4]61.8	54.7	56.1	56.4	57.3	70.6	62.0	64.1	64.5	65.5
United Kingdom. . .	50.3	49.8	52.5	53.9	53.7	70.0	64.7	66.9	66.7	66.7

NA Not available.   [1] Break in series between 1990 and 1995.   [2] Unified Germany for 1991 onward. Prior to 1991, data relate to the former West Germany.   [3] Break in series between 1995 and 2000.   [4] Break in series between 2000 and 2005.

Source: U.S. Bureau of Labor Statistics, *Comparative Civilian Labor Force Statistics, 10 Countries, 1960–2007*, 18 April 2008. See also <http://www.bls.gov/fls/flscomparelf.htm>.

Table 1324. Civilian Employment by Industry and Country: 2000 and 2007

[**136,891 represents 136,891,000**. Civilian employment as a percent of the civilian working-age population. See headnote, Table 1319]

Industry	United States [1,2]	Canada [1]	Aus-tralia	Japan	France	Ger-many [2]	Italy	Swe-den [2]	United Kingdom
TOTAL EMPLOYMENT (1,000)									
2000, total	**136,891**	**14,764**	**8,989**	**63,790**	**23,714**	**36,238**	**20,973**	**4,222**	**27,058**
Agriculture, forestry, fishing [3] . . .	2,464	487	446	3,070	922	952	1,120	122	419
Industry [4]	30,050	3,220	1,901	19,710	5,506	11,898	6,634	1,000	6,637
Manufacturing	19,644	2,249	1,129	13,180	4,087	8,647	4,944	762	4,612
Services [5]	104,377	11,057	6,642	41,010	17,286	23,388	13,219	3,100	20,002
2007, total	**146,047**	**16,866**	**10,470**	**63,510**	**(NA)**	**(NA)**	**22,953**	**4,530**	**(NA)**
Agriculture, forestry, fishing [3] . . .	2,095	422	359	2,580	(NA)	(NA)	920	101	(NA)
Industry [4]	28,894	3,433	2,165	17,140	(NA)	(NA)	6,860	956	(NA)
Manufacturing	16,302	2,045	1,080	11,620	(NA)	(NA)	4,867	660	(NA)
Services [5]	115,058	13,011	7,946	43,790	(NA)	(NA)	15,173	3,473	(NA)
PERCENT DISTRIBUTION									
2000, total	**100.0**	**100.0**	**100.0**	**100.0**	**100.0**	**100.0**	**100.0**	**100.0**	**100.0**
Agriculture, forestry, fishing [3] . . .	1.8	3.3	5.0	4.8	3.9	2.6	5.3	2.9	1.5
Industry [4]	22.0	21.8	21.1	30.9	23.2	32.8	31.6	23.7	24.5
Manufacturing	14.4	15.2	12.6	20.7	17.2	23.9	23.6	18.0	17.0
Services [5]	76.2	74.9	73.9	64.3	72.9	64.5	63.0	73.4	73.9
2007, total	**100.0**	**100.0**	**100.0**	**100.0**	**(NA)**	**(NA)**	**100.0**	**100.0**	**(NA)**
Agriculture, forestry, fishing [3] . . .	1.4	2.5	3.4	4.1	(NA)	(NA)	4.0	2.2	(NA)
Industry [4]	19.8	20.4	20.7	27.0	(NA)	(NA)	29.9	21.1	(NA)
Manufacturing	11.2	12.1	10.3	18.3	(NA)	(NA)	21.2	14.6	(NA)
Services [5]	78.8	77.1	75.9	68.9	(NA)	(NA)	66.1	76.7	(NA)

NA Not available.   [1] Data for the United States and Canada are based on the 2002 North American Industry Classification System (NAICS).   [2] Break in series between 2000 and 2007.   [3] Includes hunting.   [4] Includes manufacturing, mining, and construction.   [5] Transportation, communication, public utilities, trade, finance, public administration, private household services, and miscellaneous services.

Source: U.S. Bureau of Labor Statistics, *Comparative Civilian Labor Force Statistics, 10 Countries, 1960–2007*, 18 April 2008. See also <http://www.bls.gov/fls/flscomparelf.htm>.

U.S. Census Bureau, Statistical Abstract of the United States: 2009

Table 1325. **World Supply and Utilization of Major Crops, Livestock, and Products: 1995 to 2007**

[In millions of units (214.3 represents 214,300,000). For major crops, data ending in year shown. For meat and dairy, calendar year data, selected countries]

Commodity	1995	2000	2001	2002	2003	2004	2005	2006	2007 [1]
Wheat									
Area (hectares)	214.3	215.4	217.6	214.7	214.6	209.6	217.7	218.4	211.9
Production (metric tons)	523.1	585.8	581.5	581.2	568.4	554.4	626.8	621.5	593.7
Exports (metric tons) [2]	101.5	113.4	101.5	105.7	105.6	108.4	110.7	116.2	110.7
Consumption (metric tons) [3]	545.0	585.1	584.2	585.4	603.7	588.4	608.6	624.4	616.9
Ending stocks (metric tons) [4]	160.2	208.5	205.8	201.6	166.3	132.4	150.6	147.6	124.4
Coarse grains									
Area (hectares)	323.6	299.7	296.8	301.5	293.2	306.4	299.7	300.7	303.6
Production (metric tons)	869.7	877.7	862.5	894.1	875.3	916.0	1,015.7	977.8	980.6
Exports (metric tons) [2]	98.6	104.9	104.1	102.0	102.1	103.2	100.9	107.1	115.2
Consumption (metric tons) [3]	858.8	882.3	884.2	906.9	903.0	945.7	978.2	991.6	1,008.8
Ending stocks (metric tons) [4]	190.8	232.8	211.2	198.3	170.6	140.9	178.4	164.6	136.5
Rice, milled									
Area (hectares)	147.4	155.3	151.7	150.6	145.9	148.2	150.5	152.6	152.9
Production (metric tons)	363.6	408.9	398.8	399.3	377.8	391.5	400.4	417.6	417.6
Exports (metric tons)	20.7	22.8	24.1	26.9	28.7	27.4	28.5	30.2	29.2
Consumption (metric tons) [3]	365.2	399.7	395.0	413.1	407.5	413.0	408.1	415.5	418.9
Ending stocks (metric tons) [4]	118.3	143.5	147.3	133.6	103.9	82.4	74.7	76.9	75.6
Total grains [5]									
Area (hectares)	685.3	670.4	666.1	666.8	653.8	664.2	667.9	671.6	668.4
Production (metric tons)	1,756.4	1,872.4	1,842.8	1,874.6	1,821.6	1,861.9	2,043.0	2,016.8	1,991.9
Exports (metric tons) [2]	220.8	241.1	229.7	234.6	236.4	239.0	240.0	253.4	255.2
Consumption (metric tons) [3]	1,769.0	1,867.2	1,863.4	1,905.4	1,914.3	1,947.1	1,994.9	2,031.4	2,044.7
Ending stocks (metric tons) [4]	469.3	584.9	564.3	533.5	440.8	355.7	403.8	389.2	336.4
Oilseeds									
Crush (metric tons)	238.3	246.3	253.9	264.5	268.8	278.4	302.6	318.3	331.5
Production (metric tons)	299.5	304.3	313.9	324.9	330.2	335.1	381.6	391.6	406.3
Exports (metric tons)	47.5	59.2	66.8	62.2	69.6	67.0	74.4	76.0	83.2
Ending stocks (metric tons)	28.1	38.2	39.6	41.8	48.1	44.4	56.8	64.4	70.8
Meals [6]									
Production (metric tons)	166.2	167.9	174.7	182.6	185.4	190.0	206.5	215.6	225.2
Exports (metric tons)	61.5	46.7	48.5	52.8	53.7	58.6	60.0	65.3	68.5
Oils [7]									
Production (metric tons)	73.4	86.0	89.7	92.7	95.8	102.5	111.3	118.1	122.2
Exports (metric tons)	27.3	28.7	30.9	33.0	35.8	38.9	42.4	47.1	48.9
Cotton									
Area (hectares)	32.2	32.3	32.0	33.7	30.4	32.1	35.8	34.9	34.7
Production (bales) [8]	85.9	87.9	89.1	98.7	88.4	95.3	122.1	117.7	122.1
Exports (bales) [8]	28.4	27.2	26.3	29.1	30.3	33.2	35.0	44.5	37.3
Consumption (bales) [8]	84.4	90.5	90.8	93.5	97.6	97.2	107.5	114.7	121.4
Ending stocks (bales) [8]	29.9	51.1	49.3	54.8	45.4	44.3	57.4	60.2	60.8
Beef and Pork									
Production (metric tons)	124.2	132.1	134.6	139.3	140.6	144.1	148.6	152.2	149.2
Consumption (metric tons)	123.2	131.0	133.3	138.3	139.3	142.0	146.1	149.4	146.4
Exports (metric tons) [2]	7.6	8.9	9.0	10.1	10.5	11.1	12.0	12.4	12.7
Broilers and Turkeys									
Production (metric tons)	43.6	55.8	57.9	60.1	59.9	61.3	64.6	65.5	68.0
Consumption (metric tons)	43.1	54.7	56.4	58.6	58.4	59.5	62.8	64.2	66.2
Exports (metric tons) [2]	5.0	5.2	6.0	6.1	6.5	6.5	7.3	7.0	7.7
Dairy									
Milk production (metric tons)	(NA)	389.4	394.4	405.3	409.6	415.7	421.4	427.8	435.7

NA Not available.　[1] Forecast for crops, preliminary for meat and dairy.　[2] Excludes intra-EU (European Union) trade but includes intra-FSU (Former Soviet Union) trade.　[3] Where stocks data are not available, consumption includes stock changes. [4] Stocks data are based on differing marketing years and do not represent levels at a given date. Data not available for all countries.　[5] Wheat, coarse grains, and rice.　[6] Includes the following types of meals: copra, cottonseed, fishmeal, palm kernel, rapeseed, sunflower, soybean, and peanut.　[7] Includes the following types of oils: coconut, cottonseed, olive, palm, palm kernel, peanut, sunflower, rapeseed, and soybean.　[8] 480-pound bales.

Source: U.S. Dept. of Agriculture, Economic Research Service, "Agricultural Outlook: Statistical Indicators" (published January 2008); <http://www.ers.usda.gov/publications/agoutlook/aotables/>.

Table 1326. **World Crop Production Summary: 2006 to 2008**

[In millions of metric tons, (596.0 represents 596,000,000), except as indicated]

Country	Wheat		Coarse Grains		Rice (milled)		Oilseeds [1]		Cotton [2]	
	2006– 2007	2007– 2008, prel.	2006– 2007	2007– 2008, prel.	2006– 2007	2007– 2008, prel.	2006– 2007	2007– 2008, prel.	2006– 2007	2007– 2008, prel.
World	**596.0**	**610.8**	**988.5**	**1075.7**	**420.1**	**427.7**	**403.3**	**387.7**	**122.1**	**120.1**
United States . . .	**49.3**	**56.2**	**280.1**	**351.1**	**6.2**	**6.3**	**96.6**	**80.0**	**21.6**	**19.2**
Canada.	25.3	20.1	23.1	27.8	([3])	([3])	12.6	11.6	([3])	([3])
Mexico	3.2	3.5	29.1	29.8	0.2	0.2	0.6	0.6	0.7	0.6
EU-27 [4]	124.8	119.5	138.3	137.6	1.7	1.7	24.3	24.3	1.6	1.5
Russia	44.9	49.4	30.2	29.3	0.4	0.5	8.1	6.9	([3])	([3])
Ukraine	14.0	13.9	19.2	14.6	0.1	0.1	6.8	6.0	([3])	([3])
China	108.5	109.9	159.1	159.0	127.2	129.8	54.3	52.2	35.5	35.8
India.	69.4	75.8	32.5	38.2	93.4	95.7	29.9	33.9	21.8	25.3
Indonesia	([3])	([3])	6.7	7.5	35.3	35.5	7.9	8.2	–	–
Pakistan	21.3	23.3	3.6	3.6	5.2	5.5	5.3	4.6	9.9	8.9
Thailand	([3])	([3])	3.9	3.9	18.3	18.5	0.6	0.6	–	–
Argentina	15.2	16.0	27.5	27.0	0.7	0.8	53.2	52.3	0.8	0.7
Brazil	2.2	3.8	53.2	60.4	7.7	8.1	62.0	64.1	7.0	7.2
Australia	10.6	13.1	6.6	9.9	0.1	–	1.0	1.4	1.4	0.6
South Africa.	2.1	1.8	7.8	12.0	([3])	([3])	0.6	1.3	0.1	0.1
Turkey	17.5	15.5	10.9	10.0	0.4	0.4	2.3	2.0	3.9	3.2
All others	87.7	88.9	156.6	153.8	123.3	124.6	37.2	37.9	17.9	17.0

– Represents zero. [1] Includes soybean, cottonseed, peanut (in shell), sunflower seed, rapeseed for individual countries. Copra and palm kernel are added to world totals. [2] In millions of 480 pound bales. [3] Indicates no reported or insignificant production. [4] See footnote 1, Table 1327.

Source: U.S. Department of Agriculture, Foreign Agricultural Service, *World Agricultural Production*, June 2008. See also <http://www.fas.usda.gov/wap/circular/2008/08-07/wapfull0607.pdf>.

Table 1327. **Wheat, Rice, and Corn—Exports and Imports of Leading Countries: 2000 to 2007**

[In thousands of metric tons (28,027 represents 28,027,000). Wheat data are for trade year beginning in July of year shown; rice data are for calendar year; corn data are for trade year beginning in October of year shown. Countries listed are the ten leading exporters or importers in 2007]

Leading exporters	Exports			Leading importers	Imports		
	2000	2005	2007 [1]		2000	2005	2007 [1]
WHEAT				**WHEAT**			
United States	28,027	27,424	33,500	Brazil	7,453	6,194	7,000
Canada.	17,351	15,616	14,500	Egypt	6,050	7,771	7,000
Russia	696	10,664	12,500	EU [2]	3,536	6,758	6,500
Argentina	11,396	8,301	10,000	Japan	5,885	5,469	5,500
EU [2]	15,675	15,694	9,000	Indonesia.	4,069	4,981	5,300
Australia	16,682	15,213	8,000	Algeria	5,600	5,469	4,400
China [3]	623	1,397	2,500	Morocco	3,632	2,418	4,000
Turkey	1,601	2,900	1,500	Mexico	3,066	3,549	3,600
Ukraine.	78	6,461	1,500	Korea, South	3,127	3,884	3,000
Pakistan	253	50	1,000	Nigeria	1,913	3,656	3,000
RICE				**RICE**			
Thailand	7,521	7,376	9,000	Philippines	1,175	1,791	1,900
Vietnam	3,528	4,705	5,000	Indonesia.	1,500	539	1,600
India.	1,936	4,537	3,500	Nigeria	1,906	1,600	1,600
United States	2,541	3,306	3,500	EU [2]	1,295	1,083	1,100
Pakistan	2,417	3,579	2,900	Iraq	959	1,306	1,100
China [3]	1,847	1,216	1,300	Saudi Arabia	1,053	1,448	1,015
Egypt	705	958	950	Bangladesh	401	531	1,000
Uruguay	806	812	800	South Africa	572	764	925
Argentina	368	487	500	Iran	765	1,251	900
Cambodia	–	350	450	Brazil	670	691	800
CORN				**CORN**			
United States	48,329	56,084	62,000	Japan	16,340	16,617	16,300
Argentina	12,229	10,707	14,500	EU [2]	3,689	2,634	10,500
Brazil	3,741	2,826	10,500	Mexico	6,017	6,787	9,700
South Africa.	1,415	1,406	1,500	Korea, South	8,728	8,488	8,800
Ukraine.	397	2,464	1,500	Egypt	5,268	4,397	5,000
India.	92	497	700	Taiwan [3]	4,924	4,533	4,300
China [3]	7,276	3,727	500	Colombia	1,857	3,151	3,500
Canada.	127	239	400	Iran	1,265	2,300	2,700
EU [2]	585	449	300	Malaysia	2,588	2,517	2,500
Serbia and Montenegro [4] . .	6	1,274	200	Algeria	1,500	2,061	2,400

[1] Estimates. [2] European Union (EU) has been updated to EU-27 for 1999–2007, but 1995–98 remains EU-15 data. EU15: Austria, Belgium, Denmark, Finland, France, Germany, Greece, Ireland, Italy, Luxembourg, Netherlands, Portugal, Spain, Sweden, and United Kingdom. EU-25 added: Poland, Czech Republic, Hungary, Slovakia, Slovenia, Latvia, Lithuania, Estonia, Cyprus, and Malta. EU-27 added: Romania, Bulgaria. [3] See footnote 2, Table 1288. [4] As of June 2006, Serbia and Montenegro are separate countries.

Source: U.S. Department of Agriculture, Economic Research Service, unpublished data from the PS&D (Production, supply, and distribution) database.

Table 1328. Fisheries—Commercial Catch by Country: 1990 to 2005

[In thousands of metric tons, live weight (97,852 represents 97,852,000). Catch of fish, crustaceans, mollusks (including weight of shells). Includes aquaculture (the farming of aquatic organisms), but not marine mammals and aquatic plants]

Country	1990	2000	2004	2005	Country	1990	2000	2004	2005
World [1]	97,852	130,957	140,288	141,403	Norway	1,754	3,191	3,161	3,050
China [2]	31,136	41,568	47,505	49,467	Philippines	2,209	2,291	2,728	2,804
Peru	6,874	10,665	9,627	9,416	Burma	743	1,169	1,987	2,217
India	3,800	5,609	6,186	6,319	Bangladesh	846	1,661	2,102	2,216
Indonesia	3,022	4,909	5,687	5,578	Korea, South	2,843	2,118	1,981	2,075
United States	5,871	5,174	5,566	5,361	Iceland	1,508	1,986	1,737	1,669
Chile	5,195	4,692	5,584	5,029	Mexico	1,383	1,369	1,363	1,422
Japan	10,361	5,751	5,088	4,819	Malaysia	1,005	1,441	1,507	1,390
Thailand	2,790	3,736	4,100	3,743	Taiwan [2]	1,444	1,338	1,298	1,322
Vietnam	939	1,949	3,078	3,367	Canada	1,685	1,125	1,321	1,235
Russia	7,604	4,048	3,051	3,306					

[1] Includes other countries not shown separately.   [2] See footnote 2, Table 1288.

Source: U.S. National Oceanic and Atmospheric Administration, National Marine Fisheries Service, *Fisheries of the United States,* annual. Data from Food and Agriculture Organization of the United Nations, Rome, Italy.

Table 1329. Meat Production by Type and Country: 2005 and 2006

[In thousands of metric tons (52,454 represents 52,454,000). Carcass weight basis for beef, veal, and pork. Excludes offals and rabbit]

Country	Beef and veal		Country	Pork [1]		Country	Poultry meat	
	2005	2006, prel.		2005	2006, prel.		2005	2006, prel.
World [2]	52,454	53,734	World [2]	96,139	98,504	World [2]	59,645	60,538
United States	11,318	11,981	China [3]	50,106	51,972	United States	15,870	16,043
Brazil	8,592	9,020	European Union [4]	21,676	21,677	China [3]	10,200	10,350
European Union [4]	8,090	8,060	United States	9,392	9,559	Brazil	9,350	9,355
China [3]	7,115	7,492	Brazil	2,710	2,830	European Union [4]	8,169	7,803
Argentina	3,200	3,100	Canada	1,920	1,898	Mexico	2,498	2,592
India	2,250	2,375	Russia	1,735	1,805	India	1,900	2,000
Mexico	2,125	2,175	Vietnam	1,602	1,713	Japan	1,166	1,227
Australia	2,102	2,183	Japan	1,245	1,247	Argentina	1,030	1,200
Russia	1,525	1,430	Mexico	1,195	1,200	Russia	900	1,180
Canada	1,523	1,391	Philippines	1,175	1,215	Thailand	950	1,100

[1] Includes edible pork fat, but excludes lard and inedible greases (except United States).   [2] Includes other countries not shown separately.   [3] See footnote 2, Table 1288.   [4] See footnote 2, Table 1327.

Source: U.S. Department of Agriculture, National Agricultural Statistics Service, *Agricultural Statistics,* annual.

Table 1330. Meat Consumption by Type and Country: 2006 to 2007

[In thousands of metric tons (12,834 represents 12,834,000). Carcass weight basis for beef, veal, and pork. Broiler (chicken, 16-week-old) weight based on ready-to-cook equivalent]

Country	Beef and veal		Country	Pork		Country	Poultry meat	
	2006	2007 [1]		2006	2007 [1]		2006	2007 [1]
World	58,711	59,985	World	98,138	95,514	World	63,651	67,592
United States	12,834	12,830	China [2]	48,246	44,048	United States	13,671	13,624
European Union [3]	8,649	8,674	European Union [3]	20,631	21,257	China [2]	10,371	11,624
China [2]	6,967	7,404	United States	8,640	8,964	European Union [3]	7,661	8,128
Brazil	6,964	7,311	Russia	2,639	2,803	Brazil	6,853	7,384
Argentina	2,553	2,673	Japan	2,452	2,472	Mexico	3,016	3,121
Mexico	2,519	2,568	Brazil	2,191	2,260	Russia	2,373	2,581
Russia	2,361	2,392	Vietnam	1,731	1,855	India	2,000	2,300
India [4]	1,694	1,765	Mexico	1,488	1,514	Japan	1,939	1,936
Japan	1,159	1,182	Korea, South	1,420	1,506	Argentina	1,123	1,226
Canada	1,086	1,099	Philippines	1,239	1,270	South Africa	1,141	1,182
Pakistan	1,090	1,119	Canada	971	984	Iran	1,152	1,194
Other countries	10,835	10,968	Other countries	6,490	6,581	Other countries	12,351	13,292

[1] Preliminary data.   [2] See footnote 2, Table 1288.   [3] European Union-27: Austria, Belgium, Bulgaria, Cyprus, Czech Republic, Denmark, Estonia, Finland, France, Germany, Greece, Hungary, Ireland, Italy, Latvia, Lithuania, Luxembourg, Malta, Netherlands, Poland, Portugal, Romania, Slovakia, Slovenia, Spain, Sweden, and United Kingdom.   [4] Includes buffalo.

Source: U.S. Department of Agriculture, Foreign Agricultural Service, *Livestock and Poultry: World Markets and Trade,* annual. See also <http://www.fas.usda.gov/dlp/circular/2008/livestock_poultry_04-2008.pdf>.

Table 1331. **EU and U.S. Organic Land, Farm Sector, and Sales: 2005 and 2006**

[EU numbers for land and farms include those certified organic and in-conversion; U.S. numbers include only certified organic farms and land. For definition of "certified organic" in the United States, see headnote, Table 798. 1 hectare = 2.47 acres]

Country	2005			2006		
	Total organic land (hectares)	Organic farms (number)	Farmland under organic production (percent)	Total organic land (hectares)	Organic farms (number)	Farmland under organic production (percent)
Austria	360,396	20,310	13.0	361,487	20,162	13.0
Belgium	22,996	693	1.7	29,308	783	2.1
Denmark.	147,482	2,892	5.7	138,079	2,794	5.3
Finland	147,587	4,296	6.5	144,558	3,966	6.4
France	560,838	11,402	2.0	552,824	11,640	2.0
Germany.	807,406	17,020	4.7	825,539	17,557	4.9
Greece	288,255	14,614	7.2	302,256	23,900	7.6
Ireland	35,266	978	0.8	39,947	1,104	1.0
Italy	1,067,102	44,733	8.4	1,148,162	45,115	9.0
Luxembourg	3,243	72	2.5	3,630	72	2.8
Netherlands.	48,765	1,468	2.5	48,424	1,448	2.5
Portugal	212,728	1,623	5.8	269,374	1,696	7.3
Spain	807,569	15,693	3.3	926,390	17,214	3.7
Sweden	222,268	2,951	7.0	225,385	2,380	7.1
United Kingdom	619,852	4,285	3.9	604,571	4,485	3.8
European Union	5,351,753	143,030	4.2	5,619,934	154,316	4.4
United States	1,642,044	8,493	0.4	(NA)	(NA)	(NA)

NA Not available.

Source: U.S. Department of Agriculture, Economic Research Service, "Market-Led Versus Government Facilitated Growth: Development of the U.S. and EU Organic Agricultural Sectors," August 2005; and unpublished data. See also <http://www.ers.usda.gov/Publications/WRS0505/>.

Table 1332. **World Production of Major Mineral Commodities: 1990 to 2006**

[5,354 represents 5,354,000,000]

Commodity	Unit	1990	2000	2005	2006	Leading producers, **2005**
MINERAL FUELS						
Coal.	Mil. short tons	5,354	4,949	6,490	(NA)	China [3], United States, India
Dry natural gas.	Tril. cu. ft.	73.6	88.3	101.5	(NA)	Russia, United States, Canada
Natural gas plant liquids [1] . . .	Mil. barrels [2]	4,640	6,466	7,638	(NA)	United States, Saudi Arabia, Canada
Petroleum, crude	Mil. barrels [2]	22,079	25,001	26,940	(NA)	Saudi Arabia, Russia, United States
NONMETALLIC MINERALS						
Cement, hydraulic.	Mil. metric tons . . .	1,160	1,600	2,360	2,560	China [3], India, United States
Diamond, gem and industrial. .	Mil. carats	111	(NA)	178	171	Australia, Russia, Botswana
Nitrogen in ammonia	Mil. metric tons . . .	97.5	109.0	122.0	124.0	China [3], India, Russia
Phosphate rock, marketable . .	Mil. metric tons . . .	162	133	147	142	United States, China [3], Morocco and Western Sahara
Potash, marketable	Mil. metric tons . . .	28.0	25.3	31.0	29.0	Canada, Russia, Belarus
Salt	Mil. metric tons . . .	183	214	238	251	United States, China [3], Germany
Sulfur, elemental basis.	Mil. metric tons . . .	58.0	57.2	66.0	66.0	United States, Canada, China [3]
METALS						
Aluminum [4]	Mil. metric tons . . .	19.3	24.0	32.0	34.0	China [3], Russia, Canada
Bauxite, gross weight	Mil. metric tons . . .	113	135	172	178	Australia, Brazil, China [3]
Chromite, gross weight	1,000 metric tons . .	13,200	14,400	19,300	19,600	South Africa, Kazakhstan, India
Copper, metal content [5]	1,000 metric tons . .	8,950	13,200	15,000	15,100	Chile, United States, Indonesia
Gold, metal content.	Metric tons	2,180	2,550	2,470	2,460	South Africa, Australia, United States
Iron ore, gross weight [6]	Mil. metric tons . . .	983	1,060	1,540	1,800	China [3], Brazil, Australia
Lead, metal content [5]	1,000 metric tons . .	3,370	3,100	3,450	3,470	China [3], Australia, United States
Nickel, metal content [5].	1,000 metric tons . .	974	1,250	1,480	1,580	Russia, Canada, Australia
Tin, metal content [5].	1,000 metric tons . .	220	238	290	302	China [3], Indonesia, Peru

NA Not available. [1] Excludes China [3]. [2] 42-gallon barrels. [3] See footnote 2, Table 1288. [4] Unalloyed ingot metal. [5] Mine output. [6] Includes iron ore concentrates and iron ore agglomerates.

Source: Mineral fuels, U.S. Energy Information Administration, *International Energy Annual, 2005* (accessed 9 July 2008); nonmetallic minerals and metals, 1990, U.S. Bureau of Mines, thereafter, U.S. Geological Survey, *Minerals Yearbook; Annual Reports;* and *Mineral Commodity Summaries, 2007.*

U.S. Census Bureau, Statistical Abstract of the United States: 2009

Table 1333. **World Primary Energy Production by Region and Type: 1980 to 2005**

[**In quadrillion Btu (287.6 represents 287,600,000,000,000,000).** Btu = British thermal unit. For Btu conversion factors, see source]

Region and type	1980	1985	1990	1995	2000	2001	2002	2003	2004	2005 [1]
World total [2]	**287.6**	**307.3**	**349.8**	**363.9**	**396.3**	**403.2**	**406.9**	**422.7**	**444.5**	**460.1**
North America	83.2	87.7	92.0	96.2	99.0	99.7	100.3	98.9	99.5	99.0
United States	67.2	67.8	70.9	71.3	71.5	71.9	70.9	70.3	70.4	69.6
Central and South America	12.1	13.6	16.7	21.1	26.0	26.0	25.3	25.8	27.2	28.4
Europe	40.3	47.8	47.0	49.1	50.9	51.5	51.3	50.7	50.7	49.1
Eurasia [3]	56.5	65.3	72.1	52.3	56.0	57.9	59.7	63.5	66.8	68.6
Middle East.	42.3	25.8	41.0	48.3	57.5	56.2	54.2	57.6	62.1	65.2
Africa	17.4	18.4	21.6	24.1	27.8	28.0	28.0	30.1	32.0	34.7
Asia and Oceania	35.9	48.7	59.4	72.9	79.1	83.9	88.1	96.1	106.1	115.2
Petroleum	133.1	121.2	136.2	141.8	156.5	155.7	153.8	159.2	166.5	169.3
Dry natural gas	54.7	64.2	75.9	80.3	91.3	93.7	96.7	98.9	102.0	105.3
Coal.	71.3	82.3	91.0	88.5	90.4	95.9	97.8	105.5	114.4	122.2
Hydroelectric power	17.9	20.4	22.4	25.3	27.0	26.4	26.4	26.8	27.7	29.0
Nuclear electric power. . .	7.6	15.3	20.4	23.3	25.7	26.4	26.7	26.4	27.4	27.5
Geothermal, solar, wind, wood, and waste	0.5	0.8	1.7	2.2	3.0	3.1	3.4	3.7	4.0	4.3

[1] Preliminary.   [2] Includes geothermal, solar, and wood and waste energy produced in the United States and not used for generating electricity, not shown separately by type.   [3] Prior to 1992, data were for the former U.S.S.R. only.
Source: U.S. Energy Information Administration, "International Energy Annual, 2005"; <http://www.eia.doe.gov/emeu/iea/contents.html> (accessed 9 July 2008).

Table 1334. **World Primary Energy Consumption by Region and Type: 1980 to 2005**

[**In quadrillion Btu (283.5 represents 283,500,000,000,000,000).** Btu = British thermal unit. For Btu conversion factors, see source]

Region and type	1980	1985	1990	1995	2000	2001	2002	2003	2004	2005 [1]
World total [2]	**283.5**	**308.5**	**347.4**	**365.0**	**398.1**	**402.3**	**410.7**	**426.6**	**447.6**	**462.8**
North America	91.6	91.1	100.7	108.8	118.2	115.6	117.5	118.4	120.9	121.9
United States	78.1	76.5	84.7	91.2	99.0	96.3	97.9	98.2	100.4	100.7
Central and South America	11.5	12.3	14.5	17.6	20.9	21.2	21.2	21.6	22.5	23.4
Europe	71.9	73.2	76.4	76.7	81.4	82.7	82.4	84.2	85.8	86.3
Eurasia [3]	46.7	55.7	61.0	42.8	40.8	41.2	41.8	43.6	44.8	45.8
Middle East.	5.8	8.6	11.2	13.8	17.3	17.9	19.0	19.8	20.9	22.9
Africa	6.8	8.5	9.5	10.6	12.0	12.6	12.7	13.3	14.0	14.4
Asia and Oceania	49.1	59.2	74.2	94.9	107.5	111.1	116.1	125.6	138.8	148.1
Petroleum	131.0	123.1	136.4	142.4	155.3	156.6	157.8	161.0	166.5	169.4
Dry natural gas	54.0	63.6	75.2	81.0	91.3	92.7	96.0	99.5	103.5	107.6
Coal.	70.3	82.4	89.2	88.5	93.5	95.1	98.4	107.0	116.2	122.6
Hydroelectric power	17.9	20.4	22.4	25.3	27.0	26.4	26.4	26.8	27.7	29.0
Nuclear electric power. . .	7.6	15.3	20.4	23.3	25.7	26.4	26.7	26.4	27.4	27.5
Geothermal, solar, wind, wood, and waste	0.5	0.8	1.7	2.2	3.0	3.1	3.4	3.7	4.0	4.3

[1] Preliminary.   [2] See footnote 2, Table 1333.   [3] Prior to 1992, data were for the former U.S.S.R. only.
Source: U.S. Energy Information Administration, "International Energy Annual, 2005"; <http://www.eia.doe.gov/emeu/iea/contents.html> (accessed 9 July 2008).

Table 1335. **World Energy Consumption by Region and Energy Source, 1990 to 2004, and Projections, 2010 to 2025**

[**In quadrillion Btu (347.3 represents 347,300,000,000,000,000).** Btu = British thermal units. For Btu conversion factors, see source. Energy totals include net imports of coal coke and electricity generated from biomass in the United States. Totals may not equal sum of components due to independent rounding. The electricity portion of the national consumption values consists of generation for domestic use plus an adjustment for electricity trade based on a fuel's share of total generation in the exporting country]

Region and energy source	1990	2003	2004	Projections			
				2010	2015	2020	2025
World, total	**347.3**	**425.7**	**446.7**	**511.1**	**559.4**	**607.0**	**653.7**
North America	100.8	118.3	120.9	130.3	137.4	145.1	153.0
United States [1]	84.7	98.3	100.7	106.5	112.3	118.2	124.4
Western Europe.	69.9	79.5	81.1	84.1	85.8	86.1	87.5
Industrialized Asia.	26.6	36.9	37.8	39.9	42.1	43.9	45.4
Eastern Europe and former Soviet Union . . .	67.2	47.9	49.7	54.7	59.4	64.4	68.7
Developing Asia.	47.5	88.2	99.9	131.0	154.7	178.8	202.5
Middle East	11.3	19.9	21.1	26.3	29.5	32.6	35.5
Africa	9.5	13.3	13.7	16.9	19.2	21.2	23.1
Central and South America.	14.5	21.7	22.5	27.7	31.5	34.8	38.0
Oil	136.2	161.9	168.2	183.9	197.6	210.6	224.1
Natural gas	75.2	99.8	103.4	120.6	134.3	147.0	158.5
Coal.	89.4	105.6	114.5	136.4	151.6	167.2	182.9
Nuclear.	20.4	26.4	27.5	29.8	32.5	35.7	38.1
Other	26.2	32.1	33.2	40.4	43.4	46.5	50.1

[1] Includes the 50 states and the District of Columbia.
Source: U.S. Energy Information Administration (EIA), *International Energy Outlook 2007.* See also <http://www.eia.doe.gov/oiaf/ieo/ieorefcase.html>.

840   International Statistics

Table 1336. Energy Consumption by Country: 2000 and 2005

[**398.1 represents 398,100,000,000,000,000.** See text of this section for general comments about the data. For data qualifications for countries and Btu conversion factors, see source]

Country	Total (quad. Btu) 2000	Total (quad. Btu) 2005, prel.	Per capita (mil. Btu) 2000	Per capita (mil. Btu) 2005, prel.	Country	Total (quad. Btu) 2000	Total (quad. Btu) 2005, prel.	Per capita (mil. Btu) 2000	Per capita (mil. Btu) 2005, prel.
World total	**398.1**	**462.8**	**65.6**	**71.8**	Japan	22.3	22.6	175.8	177.0
United States	**99.0**	**100.7**	**350.6**	**340.5**	Korea, North	0.9	0.9	39.7	40.9
Algeria	1.2	1.4	40.7	43.8	Korea, South	7.9	9.3	166.6	190.7
Argentina	2.7	2.9	71.1	74.2	Kuwait	0.9	1.2	460.9	498.3
Australia	4.9	5.5	253.2	273.4	Libya	0.6	0.8	123.1	135.3
Austria	1.4	1.5	170.5	188.3	Malaysia	1.9	2.5	86.0	106.3
Bahrain	0.4	0.5	575.2	665.8	Mexico	6.3	6.9	63.3	64.8
Bangladesh	0.5	0.7	3.9	4.8	Morocco	0.4	0.6	14.8	17.1
Belarus	1.1	1.1	104.9	111.2	Netherlands	3.8	4.2	238.5	258.5
Belgium	2.7	2.6	262.4	249.2	New Zealand	0.9	0.9	223.9	211.3
Brazil	8.6	9.3	48.8	50.1	Nigeria	0.8	1.1	7.1	8.3
Bulgaria	0.9	0.9	111.3	121.8	Norway	2.0	2.1	435.4	455.7
Burma	0.2	0.3	3.5	5.4	Pakistan	1.9	2.3	12.9	14.2
Canada	12.9	14.3	413.5	436.2	Peru	0.5	0.6	20.3	22.8
Chile	1.0	1.3	67.0	78.4	Philippines	1.3	1.3	15.7	15.2
China [1]	37.5	67.1	29.5	51.4	Poland	3.6	3.7	93.8	94.9
Colombia	1.2	1.3	29.4	29.1	Portugal	1.1	1.1	103.6	105.1
Congo (Kinshasa) [2]	0.1	0.1	1.7	1.6	Romania	1.6	1.7	70.6	77.6
Cuba	0.5	0.5	41.2	40.4	Russia	27.7	30.3	188.9	212.2
Czech Republic	1.6	1.8	156.8	173.7	Saudi Arabia	4.9	6.7	209.6	252.0
Denmark	0.9	0.8	163.9	153.0	Serbia and Montenegro [3]	0.6	0.8	57.8	69.8
Ecuador	0.3	0.4	27.6	29.8	South Africa	4.6	5.0	104.2	113.7
Egypt	2.0	2.8	28.4	35.5	Spain	5.6	6.6	140.4	163.3
Finland	1.2	1.3	236.2	241.5	Sweden	2.2	2.3	246.5	259.9
France	10.9	11.4	177.3	181.5	Switzerland	1.3	1.3	178.1	169.7
Germany	14.3	14.5	173.5	176.0	Syria	0.8	0.8	48.0	42.9
Greece	1.3	1.4	126.7	133.1	Taiwan [1]	3.8	4.5	170.1	198.1
Hong Kong	0.8	1.0	121.0	150.4	Thailand	2.6	3.6	41.7	56.5
Hungary	1.0	1.2	101.3	115.2	Trinidad and Tobago	0.4	0.7	376.1	613.1
India	13.5	16.2	13.4	14.8	Tunisia	0.3	0.4	31.5	35.7
Indonesia	4.1	5.4	18.9	23.4	Turkey	3.2	3.7	48.2	53.7
Iran	5.0	7.3	79.2	112.2	Ukraine	5.8	6.2	117.4	132.2
Iraq	1.1	1.2	47.8	47.7	United Arab Emirates	1.9	2.3	579.7	563.6
Ireland	0.6	0.7	158.3	164.1	United Kingdom	9.7	10.0	163.1	165.7
Israel	0.8	0.9	138.9	135.9	Venezuela	2.8	3.1	117.9	124.2
Italy	7.6	8.1	132.2	138.9	Vietnam	0.7	1.2	9.3	14.7

[1] See footnote 2, Table 1288.   [2] See footnote 3, Table 1288.   [3] As of June 2006, Serbia and Montenegro are separate countries.

Source: U.S. Energy Information Administration, "International Energy Annual, 2005"; <http://www.eia.doe.gov/emeu/iea/contents.html> (accessed 9 July 2008).

Table 1337. World Daily Crude Oil Production by Major Producing Country: 1980 to 2005

[In thousands of barrels per day (59,558 barrels represents 59,558,000 barrels)]

Country	1980	1990	1995	2000	2001	2002	2003	2004	2005
World, total [1]	**59,558**	**60,492**	**62,385**	**68,495**	**68,101**	**67,168**	**69,448**	**72,512**	**73,807**
Saudi Arabia	9,900	6,410	8,231	8,404	8,031	7,634	8,775	9,101	9,550
Russia	(X)	(X)	5,995	6,479	6,917	7,408	8,132	8,805	9,043
United States	**8,597**	**7,355**	**6,560**	**5,822**	**5,801**	**5,746**	**5,681**	**5,419**	**5,178**
Iran	1,662	3,088	3,643	3,696	3,724	3,444	3,743	4,001	4,139
China [2]	2,114	2,774	2,990	3,249	3,300	3,390	3,409	3,485	3,609
Mexico	1,936	2,553	2,618	3,012	3,127	3,177	3,371	3,383	3,334
Norway	486	1,630	2,766	3,222	3,226	3,131	3,042	2,954	2,698
Nigeria	2,055	1,810	1,993	2,165	2,256	2,118	2,275	2,329	2,627
Venezuela	2,168	2,137	2,750	3,155	3,010	2,604	2,335	2,557	2,565
United Arab Emirates	1,709	2,117	2,233	2,368	2,205	2,082	2,348	2,478	2,535
Kuwait	1,656	1,175	2,057	2,079	1,998	1,894	2,136	2,376	2,529
Canada	1,435	1,553	1,805	1,977	2,029	2,171	2,306	2,398	2,369
Iraq	2,514	2,040	560	2,571	2,390	2,023	1,308	2,011	1,878
Algeria	1,106	1,175	1,202	1,254	1,310	1,306	1,611	1,677	1,797
United Kingdom	1,622	1,820	2,489	2,275	2,282	2,292	2,093	1,845	1,649
Brazil	182	631	695	1,269	1,295	1,455	1,496	1,477	1,634
Libya	1,787	1,375	1,390	1,410	1,367	1,319	1,421	1,515	1,633
Kazakhstan	(X)	(X)	414	718	815	939	1,027	1,203	1,288
Angola	150	475	646	746	742	896	903	1,052	1,250
Indonesia	1,577	1,462	1,503	1,428	1,340	1,249	1,155	1,096	1,067
Qatar	472	406	442	737	714	679	715	783	835
Oman	282	685	851	970	913	897	819	751	774
Argentina	491	483	715	761	802	799	783	733	704
India	182	660	703	646	642	665	660	683	665
Egypt	595	873	920	768	720	715	713	673	658
Malaysia	283	619	682	690	659	698	738	755	631
Ecuador	204	285	392	395	412	393	411	528	532
Colombia	126	440	585	691	625	577	541	529	526
Australia	380	575	562	722	657	626	512	436	446
Yemen	–	193	345	438	441	439	429	404	400

– Represents zero.   X Not applicable.   [1] Includes countries not shown separately.   [2] See footnote 2, Table 1288.

Source: U.S. Energy Information Administration, "International Energy Annual, 2005"; <http://www.eia.doe.gov/pub/international/iealf/table22.xls> (accessed 9 July 2008).

U.S. Census Bureau, Statistical Abstract of the United States: 2009

Table 1338. **World Dry Natural Gas Production by Major Producing Country: 1980 to 2005**

[In trillion cubic feet (53.35 represents 53,350,000,000,000)]

Country	1980	1990	1995	2000	2001	2002	2003	2004	2005
World total [1]	53.35	73.57	77.96	88.30	90.45	92.21	95.39	98.53	101.53
Russia	(X)	(X)	21.01	20.63	20.51	21.03	21.77	22.39	22.62
United States	**19.40**	**17.81**	**18.60**	**19.18**	**19.62**	**18.93**	**19.10**	**18.59**	**18.07**
Canada	2.76	3.85	5.60	6.47	6.60	6.63	6.45	6.48	6.56
Iran	0.25	0.84	1.25	2.13	2.33	2.65	2.86	2.96	3.56
Algeria	0.41	1.79	2.05	2.94	2.79	2.80	2.85	2.83	3.11
United Kingdom	1.32	1.75	2.67	3.83	3.69	3.66	3.63	3.39	3.10
Norway.	0.92	0.98	1.08	1.87	1.95	2.41	2.70	2.95	3.07
Netherlands	3.40	2.69	2.98	2.56	2.75	2.68	2.57	3.04	2.78
Indonesia	0.63	1.53	2.24	2.36	2.34	2.48	2.61	2.66	2.61
Saudi Arabia	0.33	1.08	1.34	1.76	1.90	2.00	2.12	2.32	2.52
Malaysia	0.06	0.65	1.02	1.50	1.66	1.71	2.01	2.20	2.24
Turkmenistan.	(X)	(X)	1.14	1.64	1.70	1.89	2.09	2.07	2.22
Uzbekistan	(X)	(X)	1.70	1.99	2.23	2.04	2.03	2.11	2.11
China [2].	0.51	0.51	0.60	0.96	1.07	1.15	1.21	1.44	1.76
United Arab Emirates	0.20	0.78	1.11	1.36	1.39	1.53	1.58	1.63	1.66
Qatar	0.18	0.28	0.48	1.03	0.95	1.04	1.11	1.38	1.62
Argentina	0.28	0.63	0.88	1.32	1.31	1.28	1.45	1.58	1.61
Mexico	0.90	0.90	0.96	1.31	1.30	1.33	1.40	1.46	1.52
Egypt	0.03	0.29	0.44	0.65	0.87	0.88	1.06	1.15	1.50
Australia	0.31	0.72	1.03	1.16	1.19	1.23	1.27	1.31	1.42
Pakistan	0.29	0.48	0.65	0.86	0.77	0.81	0.89	0.97	1.09
Trinidad and Tobago	0.08	0.18	0.27	0.49	0.54	0.61	0.87	0.99	1.07
India	0.05	0.40	0.63	0.79	0.85	0.93	0.96	1.00	1.06
Venezuela.	0.52	0.76	0.89	0.96	1.12	1.00	0.86	0.96	1.01
Kazakhstan.	(X)	(X)	0.17	0.31	0.36	0.46	0.49	0.72	0.93
Thailand	–	0.21	0.37	0.66	0.66	0.71	0.77	0.79	0.84
Nigeria	0.04	0.13	0.18	0.44	0.53	0.50	0.72	0.77	0.79
Germany	(X)	(X)	0.74	0.78	0.79	0.79	0.78	0.73	0.70
Oman	0.03	0.10	0.15	0.32	0.49	0.53	0.56	0.61	0.70
Ukraine	(X)	(X)	0.62	0.64	0.64	0.65	0.69	0.68	0.69

– Represents or rounds to zero.   X Not applicable.   [1] Includes countries not shown separately.   [2] See footnote 2, Table 1288.

Source: U. S. Energy Information Administration, "International Energy Annual, 2005"; <http://www.eia.doe.gov/pub/international/iealf/table24.xls> (accessed 9 July 2008).

Table 1339. **World Coal Production by Major Producing Country: 1980 to 2005**

[In millions of short tons (4,188.0 represents 4,188,000,000)]

Country	1980	1990	1995	2000	2001	2002	2003	2004	2005
World, total [1]	4,188.0	5,353.9	5,105.0	4,949.5	5,242.6	5,268.3	5,656.8	6,096.8	6,489.6
China [2].	683.6	1,190.4	1,537.0	1,314.4	1,458.7	1,521.2	1,837.6	2,156.4	2,430.3
United States	**829.7**	**1,029.1**	**1,033.0**	**1,073.6**	**1,127.7**	**1,094.3**	**1,071.8**	**1,112.1**	**1,131.5**
India	125.8	247.6	320.6	370.0	388.7	401.1	425.9	455.2	473.2
Australia	116.1	225.8	266.5	338.1	362.9	376.8	377.2	390.7	414.0
Russia	(X)	(X)	291.0	276.4	285.4	273.2	295.8	298.9	320.6
South Africa	131.9	193.2	227.3	248.9	250.8	245.8	263.8	267.7	270.1
Germany	(X)	(X)	274.2	226.0	227.1	232.6	229.1	234.8	229.2
Poland	253.5	237.1	220.9	179.2	180.0	178.2	180.3	178.3	175.0
Indonesia	0.6	11.6	45.4	84.5	102.1	114.0	127.1	145.9	167.8
Kazakhstan.	(X)	(X)	93.1	81.7	87.2	81.3	93.6	95.8	95.4
Greece	25.6	57.2	63.6	70.4	73.1	77.7	75.3	77.2	76.5
Canada	40.4	75.3	82.7	76.2	77.6	73.4	68.5	72.7	72.0
Czech Republic	(X)	(X)	82.6	71.8	72.9	70.4	71.0	68.6	68.9
Ukraine	(X)	(X)	79.7	68.8	68.0	67.9	70.8	65.7	66.5
Colombia	4.5	22.6	28.4	42.0	47.9	43.6	55.1	59.2	65.1
Turkey	20.8	52.3	60.7	69.7	68.5	59.5	53.5	51.1	64.3
Serbia and Montenegro [3]. . .	(X)	(X)	44.7	40.8	40.0	42.2	44.3	45.3	44.5
Vietnam	5.8	5.1	9.2	12.8	14.3	17.5	18.4	28.1	35.7
Korea, North	48.6	51.0	34.5	32.8	33.7	31.9	32.5	33.2	35.1
Romania	38.8	42.1	45.3	32.3	36.7	33.5	36.4	35.0	34.3
Bulgaria	33.3	34.9	30.6	29.2	29.4	28.7	30.1	29.2	27.2
Spain	36.8	46.7	37.1	30.8	29.7	28.9	27.0	26.7	25.8
Thailand	1.6	13.7	20.3	19.6	21.6	21.6	20.8	22.1	23.6
United Kingdom	143.8	104.1	52.5	33.7	34.7	32.6	30.6	27.0	22.1
Estonia	(X)	(X)	13.7	12.9	13.0	13.7	16.4	15.4	16.1
Mexico.	4.0	8.6	10.3	12.5	12.5	12.1	10.6	10.9	11.9
Hungary	28.7	19.7	16.1	15.5	15.3	14.4	14.7	12.4	10.5
Mongolia.	5.3	7.9	5.5	5.5	5.8	6.2	6.2	7.6	8.2
Venezuela.	(Z)	2.4	4.5	8.7	8.4	8.1	7.3	7.4	7.9
Macedonia	(X)	(X)	8.0	8.3	8.9	8.4	8.1	8.0	7.6

X Not applicable.   Z Less than 50,000 short tons.   [1] Includes countries not shown separately.   [2] See footnote 2, Table 1288.   [3] As of June 2006, Serbia and Montenegro are separate countries.

Source: U.S. Energy Information Administration, "International Energy Annual, 2005"; <http://www.eia.doe.gov/pub/international/iealf/table25.xls> (accessed 9 July 2008).

Table 1340. Net Electricity Generation by Type and Country: 2004

[16,650.2 represents 16,650,200,000,000. kWh = kilowatt hours]

Country	Total [1] (bil. kWh)	Thermal [2]	Hydro	Nuclear	Country	Total [1] (bil. kWh)	Thermal [2]	Hydro	Nuclear
World, total [3]	**16,650.2**	**66.7**	**16.6**	**15.7**	Norway	109.0	0.4	98.9	–
United States	**3,979.0**	**71.0**	**6.7**	**19.8**	Venezuela	96.1	27.9	72.1	–
China [4]	2,079.7	81.8	15.8	2.3	Egypt	95.9	86.4	13.1	–
Japan	1,014.7	62.2	9.2	26.4	Argentina	95.7	59.5	31.6	7.6
Russia	886.3	64.4	19.9	15.5	Netherlands	94.7	89.4	0.1	3.8
India	631.8	83.4	13.3	2.4	Finland	81.5	42.7	18.3	26.5
Canada	582.2	25.7	58.0	14.7	Pakistan	81.1	66.3	31.3	2.4
Germany	576.5	61.9	3.6	27.5	Belgium	79.8	40.8	0.4	56.3
France	542.0	9.4	10.9	78.6	Czech Republic	79.1	65.0	2.5	31.6
Brazil	380.9	9.1	83.4	3.0	Malaysia	78.2	92.6	7.4	–
United Kingdom	367.9	75.5	1.3	20.0	Kazakhstan	62.3	87.2	12.8	–
Korea, South	346.1	62.8	1.2	35.9	Switzerland	62.0	1.7	53.9	41.3
Italy	277.6	81.1	14.1	–	Austria	59.7	34.4	60.4	–
Spain	260.2	57.7	12.0	23.2	Greece	55.5	89.3	8.3	–
South Africa	227.3	93.3	0.3	6.3	Romania	54.0	60.0	30.3	9.8
Australia	225.3	92.0	6.9	–	Philippines	53.1	65.6	16.0	–
Mexico [4]	212.1	80.0	11.8	4.1	Paraguay	51.4	(Z)	100.0	–
Taiwan [4]	202.0	78.0	3.2	18.8	Chile	49.9	50.5	46.5	–
Ukraine	172.7	45.3	6.8	47.9	United Arab Emirates	49.3	100.0	–	–
Iran	155.7	93.2	6.8	–	Colombia	49.2	18.4	80.6	–
Saudi Arabia	150.3	100.0	–	–	Uzbekistan	48.3	86.6	13.4	–
Sweden	146.4	3.3	40.6	50.3	Israel	46.2	99.9	0.1	–
Turkey	144.0	68.1	31.7	–	Portugal	42.7	71.1	22.9	–
Poland	143.5	97.7	1.4	–	Bulgaria	39.1	51.5	8.5	39.9
Thailand	119.2	92.2	5.0	–	Denmark	38.1	74.6	0.1	–
Indonesia	113.5	86.0	8.4	–					

– Represents zero.   Z Less than 0.05 percent.   [1] Includes thermal, hydro, nuclear, and geothermal, solar, wind, and wood and waste generation.   [2] Electricity generated from coal, oil, and gas.   [3] Includes countries not shown separately.   [4] See footnote 2, Table 1288.

Source: U.S. Energy Information Administration, "International Energy Annual 2005"; <http://www.eia.doe.gov/pub/international/iea2005/table63.xls> (accessed 9 July 2008).

Table 1341. Commercial Nuclear Power Generation by Country: 1990 to 2007

[Generation for calendar years; other data as of December (1,743.9 represents 1,743,900,000,000). kWh = kilowatt-hours. kW = kilowatts]

Country	Reactors 1990	2005	2006	2007	Gross electricity generated (bil. kWh) 1990	2005	2006	2007	Gross capacity (1,000 kW) 1990	2005	2006	2007
Total	**368**	**446**	**444**	**439**	**1,743.9**	**2,690.4**	**2,792.9**	**2,666.9**	**301,745**	**391,366**	**394,973**	**395,644**
United States	**112**	**104**	**103**	**104**	**606.4**	**815.8**	**823.2**	**843.0**	**105,998**	**104,235**	**105,077**	**106,476**
Argentina	2	2	2	2	7.0	6.9	7.7	7.2	1,005	1,005	1,005	1,005
Armenia	(NA)	1	1	1	(NA)	2.7	2.6	2.5	(NA)	408	408	408
Belgium	7	7	7	7	42.7	47.6	46.6	48.2	5,740	6,101	6,101	6,101
Brazil	1	2	2	2	2.0	9.8	13.8	12.4	657	2,007	2,007	2,007
Bulgaria	(NA)	4	4	2	(NA)	18.7	19.5	(NA)	(NA)	2,880	2,880	2,000
Canada	19	21	21	21	74.0	92.5	98.4	94.0	13,855	15,341	15,341	15,367
China [1]	(NA)	9	8	9	(NA)	53.1	54.9	62.9	(NA)	7,014	8,014	9,014
Czech Republic	(NA)	6	6	6	(NA)	24.7	25.9	26.1	(NA)	3,760	3,760	3,760
Finland	4	4	4	4	18.9	23.3	22.9	23.4	2,400	2,760	2,800	2,800
France	58	59	59	58	314.1	451.5	450.2	439.1	58,862	66,042	66,130	65,880
Germany	22	18	17	17	147.2	163.0	167.4	140.5	23,973	21,723	21,366	21,457
Great Britain	42	23	23	19	68.8	(NA)	(NA)	(NA)	15,274	13,760	13,760	12,540
Hungary	4	4	4	4	13.6	13.8	13.5	14.7	1,760	1,866	1,866	1,910
India	6	15	16	17	6.0	17.6	17.6	17.8	1,330	3,310	3,900	4,120
Italy	2	(NA)	(NA)	(NA)	(NA)	(NA)	(NA)	(NA)	1,132	(NA)	(NA)	(NA)
Japan	40	54	55	55	191.9	287.9	303.2	278.7	31,645	48,222	49,580	49,580
Korea, South	9	20	20	20	52.8	145.6	148.7	142.9	7,616	17,768	18,393	18,393
Lithuania	(NA)	1	1	1	(NA)	10.9	8.6	9.8	(NA)	1,500	1,500	1,500
Mexico	1	2	2	2	2.1	10.8	10.9	10.4	675	1,350	1,350	1,350
Netherlands	2	1	1	1	3.4	3.9	3.5	4.2	540	480	512	512
Pakistan	1	2	2	2	0.4	2.6	2.7	2.5	137	462	462	462
Romania	(NA)	1	1	2	(NA)	5.5	5.6	7.0	(NA)	706	706	1,412
Russia	(NA)	31	31	31	(NA)	146.8	154.5	158.3	(NA)	23,266	23,266	23,266
Slovakia	(NA)	6	6	5	(NA)	17.7	18.0	(NA)	(NA)	2,640	2,640	2,200
Slovenia	1	1	1	1	4.6	5.9	5.5	5.7	664	707	707	727
South Africa	2	2	2	2	8.9	12.8	10.6	13.2	1,930	1,930	1,930	1,930
Spain	10	9	9	8	54.3	57.5	60.1	55.0	7,984	7,895	7,895	7,735
Sweden	12	11	10	10	68.2	72.5	67.7	66.9	10,344	9,852	9,241	9,356
Switzerland	5	5	5	5	23.6	23.2	27.6	27.7	3,079	3,352	3,352	3,352
Taiwan [1]	6	6	6	6	32.9	39.9	39.9	40.6	5,146	5,144	5,144	5,144
Ukraine	(NA)	15	15	15	(NA)	88.8	90.2	47.7	(NA)	13,880	13,880	13,880

– Represents zero.   NA Not available.   [1] See footnote 2, Table 1288.

Source: Platts Energy, A Division of The McGraw-Hill Companies Inc., New York, NY, *Nucleonics Week,* February issue (copyright).

U.S. Census Bureau, Statistical Abstract of the United States: 2009

[1992 = 100. Data relate to employees (wage and salary earners) in Belgium, and to all employed persons (employees, self-employed workers, and unpaid family workers) in the other countries. Minus sign (–) indicates decrease. For explanation of average annual percent change, see Guide to Tabular Presentation]

Index	United States	Can-ada	Japan	Bel-gium	France	Ger-many	Italy	Nether-lands	Nor-way	Swe-den	United King-dom
Output per hour:											
1990	93.5	94.7	94.4	96.8	95.3	(NA)	97.3	98.0	98.3	96.4	90.1
1995	112.3	111.7	111.0	112.7	114.9	110.2	111.1	117.7	98.7	126.3	105.0
2000	147.1	134.7	131.2	130.5	143.7	132.0	116.1	138.6	105.9	175.9	117.2
2004	185.3	136.5	152.1	145.8	162.3	146.8	110.4	156.3	128.8	226.8	140.0
2005	189.4	141.7	162.0	150.3	169.2	152.3	110.3	161.7	133.3	241.0	145.0
2006	193.2	141.6	165.1	153.6	175.4	163.1	111.8	166.8	137.7	255.2	151.5
Average annual percent change:											
1995–2000	5.5	3.8	3.4	3.0	4.6	3.7	0.9	3.3	1.4	6.8	2.2
2004–2005	2.2	3.8	6.5	3.1	4.3	3.7	–0.1	3.5	3.5	6.2	3.6
2005–2006	2.0	–0.1	1.9	2.2	3.7	7.1	1.4	3.1	3.3	5.9	4.5
Compensation per hour, national currency basis: [1]											
1990	90.5	89.2	90.6	90.1	88.5	(NA)	87.7	89.8	92.3	87.9	88.7
1995	107.3	106.6	108.3	108.6	110.7	117.0	112.0	111.8	109.2	105.3	108.9
2000	134.7	123.0	114.7	120.1	127.0	136.3	128.7	132.1	140.5	133.0	133.8
2004	161.5	139.8	115.5	138.7	144.6	148.0	145.7	158.1	169.7	157.6	165.1
2005	168.3	146.6	116.5	143.5	143.7	149.8	150.2	161.3	177.7	163.0	172.3
2006	172.4	149.4	114.9	146.5	147.5	155.9	152.9	165.8	185.8	169.2	184.2
Average annual percent change:											
1995–2000	4.7	2.9	1.2	2.0	2.8	3.1	2.8	3.4	5.2	4.8	4.2
2004–2005	4.2	4.9	0.8	3.5	–0.6	1.2	3.0	2.0	4.7	3.4	4.4
2005–2006	2.5	1.9	–1.4	2.1	2.6	4.1	1.8	2.8	4.5	3.8	6.9
Real hourly compensation: [2]											
1990	96.1	95.6	95.2	95.2	93.8	(NA)	98.1	95.6	97.7	97.6	97.5
1995	100.1	102.3	106.3	101.8	104.8	107.3	98.0	104.0	102.8	96.6	101.2
2000	112.0	108.0	111.0	103.6	113.2	117.4	99.8	110.3	118.0	117.0	108.9
2004	122.4	111.8	113.9	110.8	119.4	120.0	102.2	118.7	132.6	128.9	122.5
2005	123.4	114.7	115.2	111.5	116.5	119.1	103.3	119.1	136.9	132.9	124.3
2006	122.5	114.5	113.3	111.8	117.7	121.9	103.0	121.1	139.8	135.2	128.8
Average annual percent change:											
1995–2000	2.3	1.1	0.9	0.4	1.6	1.8	0.4	1.2	2.8	3.9	1.5
2004–2005	0.8	2.6	1.1	0.6	–2.4	–0.8	1.1	0.3	3.2	3.1	1.5
2005–2006	–0.7	–0.2	–1.6	0.3	1.0	2.4	–0.3	1.7	2.1	1.7	3.6
Unit labor costs, national currency: [1]											
1990	96.7	94.2	95.9	93.0	92.8	(NA)	90.2	91.7	93.9	91.2	98.5
1995	95.5	95.4	97.6	96.4	96.3	106.2	100.8	95.0	110.7	83.4	103.7
2000	91.6	91.3	87.4	92.0	88.4	103.3	110.9	95.3	132.7	75.6	114.2
2004	87.2	102.4	76.0	95.1	89.1	100.8	132.0	101.2	131.7	69.5	117.9
2005	88.9	103.4	71.9	95.5	85.0	98.3	136.2	99.8	133.3	67.7	118.8
2006	89.3	105.5	69.6	95.4	84.1	95.6	136.7	99.4	134.9	66.3	121.6
Average annual percent change:											
1995–2000	–0.8	–0.9	–2.2	–0.9	–1.7	–0.5	1.9	0.1	3.7	–1.9	2.0
2004–2005	1.9	1.0	–5.4	0.4	–4.7	–2.5	3.1	–1.4	1.2	–2.6	0.8
2005–2006	0.5	2.0	–3.2	–0.1	–1.0	–2.8	0.4	–0.3	1.2	–2.0	2.3
Unit labor costs, U.S. dollar basis: [1, 3]											
1990	96.7	97.5	83.9	89.5	90.2	(NA)	92.7	88.5	93.3	89.7	99.5
1995	95.5	84.0	131.7	105.2	102.2	115.8	76.2	104.1	108.6	68.0	92.7
2000	91.6	74.3	102.8	67.7	65.8	76.2	65.1	70.2	93.6	48.0	98.0
2004	87.2	95.1	89.0	94.3	89.5	100.1	104.5	100.4	121.4	55.1	122.4
2005	88.9	103.2	82.8	94.7	85.4	97.8	107.9	99.1	128.6	52.8	122.5
2006	89.3	112.4	75.8	95.5	85.3	95.9	109.3	99.7	130.8	52.4	126.9
Average annual percent change:											
1995–2000	–0.8	–2.4	–4.8	–8.4	–8.4	–8.0	–3.1	–7.6	–2.9	–6.7	1.1
2004–2005	1.9	8.5	–7.0	0.5	–4.6	–2.4	3.2	–1.3	5.9	–4.2	0.1
2005–2006	0.5	9.0	–8.4	0.8	–0.1	–1.9	1.3	0.6	1.7	–0.7	3.6
Employment:											
1990	105.4	112.7	97.5	102.5	105.2	(NA)	104.2	100.0	105.1	117.2	115.0
1995	102.8	104.7	90.1	91.9	92.6	86.1	94.6	92.1	107.0	98.1	101.6
2000	102.7	116.7	81.4	89.3	91.2	82.7	93.5	92.5	107.9	99.0	94.9
2004	85.6	112.9	72.1	82.5	85.7	77.9	93.9	84.0	95.2	90.6	78.5
2005	85.0	111.7	71.5	81.5	83.5	76.6	92.3	81.5	95.2	89.6	74.9
2006	84.6	110.6	72.6	80.7	81.8	75.9	93.4	80.8	96.3	89.0	73.0
Average annual percent change:											
1995–2000	–	2.2	–2.0	–0.6	–0.3	–0.8	–0.2	0.1	0.2	0.2	–1.4
2004–2005	–0.6	–1.1	–0.8	–1.2	–2.6	–1.7	–1.7	–3.0	0.1	–1.1	–4.5
2005–2006	–0.5	–1.0	1.5	–1.1	–2.0	–0.9	1.2	–0.8	1.1	–0.7	–2.6
Aggregate hours:											
1990	104.9	112.6	102.9	104.3	105.5	(NA)	103.3	100.4	103.4	114.8	116.9
1995	104.4	106.3	89.1	92.4	91.6	85.3	98.2	92.3	106.6	105.6	102.7
2000	103.8	118.9	80.0	92.1	86.8	79.4	97.2	92.2	106.4	108.1	98.1
2004	85.4	115.4	71.5	83.6	79.7	74.2	96.4	83.5	94.2	99.7	80.7
2005	84.4	112.9	70.6	80.9	77.5	72.5	94.1	80.8	95.1	98.2	77.0
2006	85.1	112.0	72.3	81.3	75.9	71.7	96.2	80.2	96.1	97.5	74.7
Average annual percent change:											
1995–2000	–0.1	2.3	–2.1	–0.1	–1.1	–1.4	–0.2	–	–	0.5	–0.9
2004–2005	–1.2	–2.1	–1.3	–3.2	–2.8	–2.2	–2.4	–3.3	1.0	–1.5	–4.6
2005–2006	0.9	–0.9	2.4	0.5	–2.0	–1.2	2.3	–0.8	1.0	–0.7	–2.9

– Represents or rounds to zero.   NA Not available.   [1] In Canada, France, Sweden, and the United Kingdom, compensation adjusted for employment taxes and government subsidies to estimate the actual labor cost to employers.   [2] Index of hourly compensation divided by the index of consumer prices to adjust for changes in purchasing power.   [3] Indexes in national currency adjusted for changes in prevailing exchange rates.

Source: U.S. Bureau of Labor Statistics, *International Comparisons of Manufacturing Productivity and Unit Labor Cost Trends, Supplementary Tables, 1950–2006*, revised, 28 February 2008. See also <http://www.bls.gov/fls/prodsupptabletoc.htm>.

Table 1343. **Indexes of Hourly Compensation Costs for Production Workers in Manufacturing by Country: 1980 to 2006**

[**United States = 100.** Compensation costs include pay for time worked, other direct pay (including holiday and vacation pay, bonuses, other direct payments, and the cost of pay in kind), employer expenditures for legally required insurance programs and contractual and private benefit plans, and for some countries, other labor taxes. Data adjusted for exchange rates. Area averages are trade-weighted to account for difference in countries' relative importance to U.S. trade in manufactured goods. The trade weights used to compute the average compensation cost measures for selected economic groups are based on the relative dollar value of U.S. trade in manufactured commodities (exports plus imports) with each country or area in 2004; see source for detail]

Area or country	1980	1985	1990	1995	1996	1997	1998	1999	2000	2001	2002	2003	2004	2005	2006
United States	**100**	**100**	**100**	**100**	**100**	**100**	**100**	**100**	**100**	**100**	**100**	**100**	**100**	**100**	**100**
Total [1]	**68**	**52**	**80**	**87**	**82**	**76**	**72**	**72**	**69**	**65**	**64**	**72**	**78**	**79**	**82**
OECD [2,3]	73	56	85	92	88	82	77	78	74	69	69	78	85	86	90
Europe [3]	99	61	114	124	120	107	106	103	91	87	91	107	117	117	121
Euro Area [4]	101	62	117	132	127	111	108	105	92	88	92	109	119	119	123
Asian newly industrial-izing economies [5]	12	13	25	39	40	39	32	35	36	33	33	33	35	37	42
Brazil	(NA)	(NA)	(NA)	(NA)	32	32	30	18	18	14	12	12	14	17	21
Canada	92	88	110	96	96	93	86	85	84	79	78	87	94	101	108
Mexico	23	12	11	10	9	10	9	10	11	11	12	11	11	11	12
Australia	88	64	88	89	96	92	82	84	73	65	71	88	101	105	110
Hong Kong [6]	16	14	22	28	29	30	29	28	28	28	26	25	24	24	24
Israel	35	29	52	55	57	59	59	56	58	59	51	52	52	52	54
Japan	57	49	85	137	115	104	95	108	112	94	86	90	95	90	85
Korea, South	10	10	25	42	46	43	31	39	42	38	41	43	47	54	62
New Zealand	56	36	57	60	64	62	51	50	43	39	42	52	59	63	61
Philippines	(NA)	(NA)	(NA)	5	6	5	4	4	4	4	4	4	4	4	4
Singapore	16	20	26	45	46	45	40	37	37	34	31	32	32	31	36
Sri Lanka	2	2	2	3	3	3	3	2	2	2	2	2	2	2	(NA)
Taiwan [7]	11	12	26	35	34	33	29	31	32	30	26	25	26	27	27
Austria	92	60	120	147	139	120	119	114	97	93	96	113	123	123	128
Belgium	122	65	120	150	142	122	122	117	102	97	101	118	130	129	134
Czech Republic	(X)	(X)	(X)	15	17	15	16	16	15	15	18	21	24	25	28
Denmark	112	63	123	146	142	127	128	127	109	106	111	132	146	145	149
Finland	89	65	141	132	125	110	105	104	91	88	91	108	120	119	126
France	92	59	104	112	107	94	93	90	79	76	78	92	101	101	105
Germany	(X)	(X)	(X)	175	167	143	136	130	115	110	113	133	143	140	144
Greece	39	29	45	53	54	50	48	45	39	39	30	53	63	64	68
Hungary	(NA)	(NA)	(NA)	16	15	15	15	15	14	15	18	21	25	26	26
Ireland	67	49	82	82	82	78	77	76	68	69	73	88	98	101	109
Italy	84	60	119	96	102	93	90	86	74	71	75	90	102	102	105
Luxembourg	119	58	107	137	127	108	106	103	89	83	86	102	113	115	116
Netherlands	125	69	121	140	130	114	115	113	98	97	103	122	133	134	136
Norway	123	82	147	145	143	133	132	131	115	115	129	146	157	165	172
Poland	(NA)	(NA)	(NA)	(NA)	(NA)	15	16	15	14	16	15	16	17	19	21
Portugal	21	12	24	30	30	28	28	27	23	22	23	28	30	31	32
Spain	61	36	76	74	75	66	65	63	54	53	56	67	75	75	79
Sweden	129	75	140	126	137	123	121	117	105	93	98	118	130	128	133
Switzerland	114	75	139	168	157	131	130	123	107	105	110	124	131	128	129
United Kingdom	78	49	84	80	80	86	92	92	86	82	85	95	107	108	114

NA Not available.   X Not applicable.   [1] For 1980–1990, the trade-weighted measure includes all 33 foreign economies except for Brazil, Czech Republic, Hungary, Poland, and the Philippines. For 1995, it includes all but Brazil and Poland. For 1996, it includes all but Poland. For 1997 onward, the measure includes all 33 economies.   [2] Organization for Economic Cooperation and Development; see text of this section.   [3] Data for Czech Republic and Hungary 1980–1990; and Poland 1980–1996 not included.   [4] Euro area refers to European Union member countries that have adopted the Euro as the common currency as of January 1, 2001, (Austria, Belgium, Finland, France, Germany, Greece, Ireland, Italy, Luxembourg, Netherlands, Portugal, and Spain).   [5] Hong Kong, South Korea, Singapore, and Taiwan.   [6] Hong Kong Special Administrative Region of China. Index based on the average of selected manufacturing industries.   [7] See footnote 2, Table 1288.

Source: U.S. Bureau of Labor Statistics, *International Comparisons of Hourly Compensation Costs in Manufacturing, 2006*, 25 January 2008. See also <ftp://ftp.bls.gov/pub/special.requests/ForeignLabor/ichccpwsuppt01.txt>.

U.S. Census Bureau, Statistical Abstract of the United States: 2009

Table 1344. **Key Global Telecom Indicators for the World Telecommunication Service Sector: 1995 to 2006**

[In billions U.S. dollars (779 represents $779,000,000,000), except as indicated. All data were converted by annual average exchange rates. Country fiscal year data was aggregated to obtain calendar year estimates]

Indicators	1995	2000	2002	2003	2004	2005	2006
Telecom market total revenue (bil. dol.)	779	1,210	1,314	1,426	(NA)	(NA)	(NA)
Telecom telephone services revenue [1] (bil. dol.). . .	428	477	478	475	552	(NA)	(NA)
Other statistics:							
Main telephone lines [2] (mil.)	689	983	1,086	1,140	1,207	1,261	1,270
Mobile cellular subscribers (mil.)	91	740	1,166	1,414	1,766	2,221	2,685
International telephone traffic minutes [3] (bil.)	63	118	131	142	145	167	183
Personal computers (mil.).	235	500	615	650	775	808	885
Internet users (mil.).	40	399	619	724	870	1,006	1,131

NA Not available. [1] Revenue from installation, subscription and local, trunk and international call charges for fixed telephone service. [2] See footnote 1, Table 1345. [3] Including traffic between countries of former Soviet Union.

Source: International Telecommunication Union, Geneva Switzerland, 2007; <http://www.itu.int/ITU-D/ict/statistics/at_glance /KeyTelecom99.html>. Reproduced with the kind permission of ITU.

Table 1345. **Telephones, Cellular Phones, and Computers by Country: 2006**

[Rates per 100 persons. For data qualifications for countries, see source]

Country	Telephone main lines [1]	Cellular phone subscribers	Personal computers [2]	Country	Telephone main lines [1]	Cellular phone subscribers	Personal computers [2]
Afghanistan	0.29	8.11	0.32	Lebanon	18.85	30.61	11.62
Argentina	24.17	80.52	(NA)	Malaysia	16.83	75.45	23.41
Australia	48.81	97.02	(NA)	Mexico	18.33	52.63	13.85
Austria	43.40	112.81	(NA)	Netherlands	45.61	105.91	91.22
Bahamas	40.18	77.27	(NA)	New Zealand	44.06	93.99	54.15
Belgium	45.21	92.55	42.16	Nigeria	1.26	24.05	(NA)
Brazil	20.54	52.90	(NA)	Norway	44.27	108.57	63.13
Canada	64.49	57.57	94.58	Pakistan	3.34	21.98	(NA)
China [3]	27.79	34.83	5.60	Peru	8.46	30.91	(NA)
Colombia.	16.98	64.31	5.38	Poland	29.81	95.45	16.77
Cuba	8.61	1.35	3.54	Portugal	40.15	115.95	17.06
Czech Republic . . .	28.28	121.54	(NA)	Russia	30.80	105.71	13.33
Egypt	14.33	23.86	4.19	Saudi Arabia	15.68	78.05	13.89
Finland	36.30	107.76	(NA)	Singapore	42.32	109.34	72.61
France	55.82	85.08	65.87	South Africa	9.88	83.33	(NA)
Germany.	65.94	103.55	65.28	Spain	45.81	106.39	36.88
Greece	55.39	98.56	9.38	Sudan	2.07	11.59	11.45
Hungary	33.37	98.95	31.78	Sweden	59.52	105.92	88.20
India.	3.64	14.83	2.76	Switzerland	66.89	99.04	88.30
Indonesia	6.57	28.30	2.00	Syria	16.62	23.96	6.66
Iran	32.11	23.92	10.53	Thailand	10.92	62.88	(NA)
Ireland	49.93	112.59	58.91	Turkey	25.39	71.00	5.93
Israel	43.88	122.74	(NA)	United Kingdom . . .	56.15	116.57	81.21
Italy	46.25	135.14	(NA)	**United States**	**57.15**	**77.40**	**79.89**
Japan	43.02	79.32	(NA)	Venezuela	15.49	69.04	(NA)
Korea, South	49.82	83.77	54.44	Vietnam	32.23	18.17	2.34

NA Not available. [1] Fixed telephone lines refer to telephone lines connecting a customer's terminal equipment (e.g. telephone set, facsimile machine) to the public switched telephone network (PSTN) and which have a dedicated port on a telephone exchange. Fixed telephone lines per 100 inhabitants is calculated by dividing the number of fixed telephone lines by the population and multiplying by 100. [2] In many countries mainframe computers are used extensively, and thousands of users can be connected to a single mainframe computer; thus the number of PCs understates the total use of computers. [3] See footnote 2, Table 1288.

Source: International Telecommunications Union, Geneva, Switzerland, *World Telecommunication Indicators*, (copyright). See also <http://www.itu.int/itu-d/icteye/Indicators/Indicators.aspx>. Reproduced with the kind permission of ITU.

Table 1346. **Patents by Country: 2007**

[Includes only U.S. patents granted to residents of areas outside of the United States and its territories. See also Table 748]

Country	Total [1]	Inventions	Designs	Country	Total [1]	Inventions	Designs
Total	**89,236**	**77,756**	**10,569**	Netherlands	1,595	1,250	124
				Australia	1,546	1,266	241
Japan	35,942	33,354	2,417	Switzerland	1,280	1,035	240
Germany.	10,012	9,051	810	Sweden	1,278	1,061	207
Taiwan [2]	7,491	6,128	1,355	Israel	1,219	1,107	80
Korea, South	7,264	6,295	957	Finland	943	850	92
United Kingdom	4,030	3,292	676	Belgium	624	520	90
Canada	3,970	3,318	632	Austria	553	456	93
France	3,720	3,130	556	Denmark.	511	388	63
Italy	1,836	1,302	524	Other countries	5,422	3,953	1,412

[1] Includes patents for botanical plants and reissues, not shown separately. [2] See footnote 2, Table 1288.

Source: U.S. Patent and Trademark Office, Technology Assessment and Forecast Database.

Table 1347. Research and Development (R&D) Expenditures, by Country

[Figures are for 2005 or latest year available. GDP = gross domestic product; for explanation, see text, Section 13]

Country	Gross domestic expenditure on R&D (GERD)				Government budget		Business enterprise							Higher education expenditure on R&D (HERD)	
		Percent financed by—		Per capita at current U.S. dollars, PPPs[1]				Percent financed by—		Percent of R&D expenditure (BERD) performed in—					
	Percent of GDP	Government	Industry		Percent of GDP	Percent defense R&D	Percent of GERD	Government	Industry	High-tech indus-tries[2]	Medium high-tech indus-tries[3]	Medium low-tech and low-tech indus-tries[4]	Service industries	Percent of GERD	Percent of GDP
OECD total	**2.25**	**30.20**	**62.10**	**659**	**0.80**	**32.6**	**67.9**	**6.9**	**89.4**	**(NA)**	**(NA)**	**(NA)**	**(NA)**	**17.7**	**0.4**
EU-27[5]	1.74	35.72	53.49	470	0.71	13.0	62.5	7.9	82.0	(NA)	(NA)	(NA)	(NA)	22.7	0.4
Australia[6]	1.76	39.84	51.64	574	0.54	6.5	53.5	4.3	91.4	12.1	17.9	15.6	41.1	27.2	0.5
Austria[6]	2.42	36.46	45.47	831	0.70	0.0	67.7	6.4	67.2	39.2	23.7	16.2	18.0	26.7	0.6
Belgium	1.82	23.55	60.31	601	0.60	0.3	68.3	5.8	81.8	38.8	23.5	16.1	17.8	22.8	0.4
Brazil	0.91	57.88	39.88	76	0.53	1.2	40.2	0.8	99.2	(NA)	(NA)	(NA)	(NA)	38.4	0.4
Canada[6]	1.98	32.93	47.85	675	0.57	3.6	53.9	2.2	82.4	37.5	9.5	11.3	37.9	36.4	0.7
China[7,8]	1.34	26.34	67.04	88	(NA)	(NA)	68.3	4.6	91.2	(NA)	(NA)	(NA)	(NA)	9.9	0.1
Czech Republic	1.42	40.87	54.09	293	0.57	2.8	64.5	14.7	80.8	11.5	40.8	9.0	36.9	16.4	0.2
Denmark	2.45	27.10	59.89	834	0.76	0.6	68.3	2.4	85.6	37.9	17.4	10.2	33.3	23.8	0.6
Finland	3.48	25.65	66.86	1,077	0.99	2.4	70.8	3.8	90.9	55.2	16.2	11.7	14.5	19.0	0.7
France	2.13	37.56	51.73	644	0.93	22.3	61.9	9.3	79.9	44.7	30.0	11.6	9.4	19.5	0.4
Germany	2.46	30.52	66.56	758	0.77	6.4	69.3	5.9	91.8	30.6	53.4	7.1	8.3	16.9	0.4
Greece	0.49	46.42	28.23	144	0.29	0.5	29.3	4.4	75.9	32.4	18.1	13.3	34.2	49.3	0.2
Hungary	0.94	49.41	39.45	165	0.37	0.1	43.2	3.9	77.8	55.4	18.0	5.7	18.9	25.1	0.2
Ireland	1.26	32.43	57.25	491	0.48	–	65.3	4.1	86.1	38.2	13.6	9.1	38.7	27.0	0.3
Italy	1.10	50.80	43.00	305	0.62	1.4	47.8	13.8	75.0	34.8	30.7	9.3	24.4	32.8	0.4
Japan[8]	3.33	16.76	76.12	1,023	0.70	5.1	76.4	1.2	98.3	38.0	39.0	11.9	9.1	13.4	0.4
Korea	2.99	23.02	74.96	662	0.92	16.6	76.9	4.6	94.4	53.0	26.1	8.9	6.9	9.9	0.3
Mexico	0.50	45.34	46.49	54	0.21	0.0	49.5	5.7	92.6	39.4	21.8	35.1	32.6	27.4	0.1
Netherlands	1.78	36.23	51.06	598	0.73	2.0	57.8	3.4	81.6	15.6	28.5	9.4	18.3	27.9	0.5
Norway	1.52	41.91	49.23	735	0.70	5.6	53.7	8.9	80.6	19.4	16.0	17.8	35.3	30.7	0.5
Poland	0.57	57.71	33.35	79	0.29	1.3	31.8	13.7	83.0	19.4	30.6	13.5	24.7	31.6	0.3
Portugal	0.80	60.11	31.73	160	0.77	0.6	36.2	5.3	89.2	(NA)	(NA)	(NA)	(NA)	39.1	0.3
Russia	1.07	61.95	30.00	116	0.36	52.1	68	53.6	37.3	7.7	5.1	3.4	78.6	5.8	0.1
South Africa	0.86	35.61	48.62	96	(NA)	(NA)	56.3	7.7	74.5	(NA)	(NA)	(NA)	(NA)	21.1	0.2
Spain	1.12	41.01	48.04	306	0.84	16.4	54.4	12.5	82.1	24.7	26.9	17.1	25.6	28.6	0.3
Sweden	3.89	23.45	64.97	1,250	0.87	16.9	74	5.9	85.9	51.4	30.0	6.5	10.4	19.6	0.8
Switzerland	2.93	22.71	69.73	1,017	0.76	0.4	73.7	1.5	90.9	25.4	38.2	22.9	11.6	22.9	0.7
Turkey	0.67	56.96	37.92	49	(NA)	(NA)	24.2	4.2	95.0	(NA)	(NA)	(NA)	(NA)	67.9	0.5
United Kingdom[6,9,10]	1.78	32.76	42.10	584	0.72	31.0	61.6	8.6	64.4	47.9	21.6	7.1	21.1	25.6	0.5
United States	**2.62**	**30.37**	**63.97**	**1,094**	**1.03**	**57.9**	**69.6**	**9.7**	**90.3**	**40.3**	**16.6**	**6.4**	**36.1**	**14.1**	**0.4**

NA Not available or not applicable.   [1] Purchasing Power Parities, see headnote, Table 1306.   [2] Aerospace; office and computing equipment; pharmaceuticals; radio, TV, and communication equipment; medical, precision and optical instruments.   [3] Motor vehicles; chemicals; electrical machinery; other transport; machinery and equipment.   [4] Rubber and plastics; nonmetallic mineral products; shipbuilding; ferrous and nonferrous metals; metal products; petroleum; other manufacturing industries.   [5] See footnote 2, Table 1327.   [6] Government budget appropriations for R&D; federal government only.   [7] See footnote 2, Table 1288.   [8] Percent of GERD/BERD financed by government or industry; the sum of the breakdown does not add to the total.   [9] GERD, BERD: Excluding most or all capital expenditures.   [10] HERD: Excluding most or all capital expenditures.

Source: Organization for Economic Cooperation and Development, Paris, France, OECD In Figures, 2007 (copyright). See also <http://www.oecd.org/document/19/0,3343,en_2649_34489_39503891_1_1_1_1,00.html>.

Table 1348. Dow-Jones World Stock Index by Country and Industry: 2000 to 2007

[Index figures shown are as of December 31. 1991 = 100. Based on share prices denominated in U.S. dollars. Stocks in countries that impose significant restrictions on foreign ownership are included in the world index in the same proportion that shares are available to foreign investors]

Country and industry	2000	2005	2006	2007	Country and industry	2000	2005	2006	2007
World, total	**210.9**	**234.1**	**277.5**	**300.9**	Asia/Pacific	93.0	132.0	146.2	158.1
Americas.	299.1	307.3	351.7	376.9	Australia	156.0	312.5	400.6	500.1
United States	306.9	302.4	343.2	357.5	Hong Kong.	245.6	273.6	378.0	546.5
Canada	225.3	369.4	425.7	541.7	Indonesia.	31.2	79.0	128.0	179.4
Mexico	132.2	360.1	501.0	555.8	Japan	88.3	113.5	115.8	108.9
Europe	241.2	267.4	349.7	385.7	Malaysia	88.5	119.5	158.9	229.7
Austria	86.2	335.5	400.6	469.5	New Zealand	96.7	227.3	259.5	261.9
Belgium.	196.9	321.2	427.5	449.5	Singapore	135.2	176.3	249.4	319.0
Denmark	220.1	375.1	505.7	607.5	Thailand	27.2	76.7	81.3	112.9
Finland	1,537.8	948.5	1,206.6	1,691.7					
France	252.9	273.3	365.7	406.9	Basic materials.	117.6	213.8	273.5	372.8
Germany	219.1	224.3	302.8	398.2	Consumer goods	183.8	241.9	290.4	325.1
Ireland.	312.3	470.4	672.0	532.0	Consumer services	192.8	214.4	245.3	240.9
Italy	192.2	213.8	280.6	286.2	Oil and gas	230.7	383.3	450.7	590.3
Netherlands	335.7	309.6	401.8	448.9	Financial.	207.1	259.8	314.2	287.7
Norway	151.8	276.1	402.4	521.3	Healthcare.	329.9	310.6	340.5	353.4
Spain	193.5	288.6	422.1	497.0	Industrial.	167.1	192.4	226.4	258.0
Sweden	339.0	378.3	542.6	526.7	Technology	552.7	375.1	412.7	459.2
Switzerland	388.8	452.5	577.6	606.3	Telecommunications . . .	273.3	201.6	260.1	313.4
United Kingdom	199.8	217.6	278.3	290.1	Utilities	156.0	176.9	233.0	276.0

Source: Dow Jones & Company, Inc., New York, NY, *Dow Jones Indexes*, (copyright).

Table 1349. Foreign Stock Market Activity—Morgan Stanley Capital International Indexes: 2000 to 2007

[Index figures shown are as of December 31. January 1, 1970 = 100, except as noted. Minus sign (–) indicates decrease. Based on share prices denominated in U.S. dollars. EM = Emerging Markets]

Index and country	Index			Percent change [1]		Index and country	Index			Percent change [1]	
	2000	2006	2007	2006	2007		2000	2006	2007	2006	2007
ALL COUNTRY (AC) INDEXES						Sweden.	4,240	6,839	6,746	40.5	–1.4
						Switzerland	2,695	4,079	4,237	25.9	3.9
AC World index [2]	290.1	367.8	403.3	18.8	9.6	United Kingdom	1,146	1,522	1,593	26.2	4.7
AC World index except USA [2]	193.5	292.7	333.9	23.8	14.1	Hong Kong	5,475	7,250	9,967	26.3	37.5
AC Asia Pacific [2].	89.6	140.5	157.8	14.5	12.3	Japan	2,552	3,208	3,034	5.1	–5.4
AC Europe [2].	376.5	531.5	594.0	30.3	11.8	Singapore	2,081	3,400	4,213	41.9	23.9
European Union [2]	361.5	494.1	551.7	30.6	11.7	**EMERGING MARKETS**					
DEVELOPED MARKETS						EM Far East index [4].	127.9	327.1	437.1	27.6	33.6
						India [6].	114.5	390.6	668.9	48.9	71.2
World index	1,221	1,484	1,589	18.0	7.1	Indonesia.	77.8	449.3	677.6	69.6	50.8
EAFE index [3]	1,492	2,074	2,253	23.5	8.6	Korea, South	78.7	336.7	437.5	11.2	30.0
Europe index	1,378	1,912	2,121	30.2	11.0	Malaysia	160.7	288.6	408.6	33.1	41.5
Pacific index.	1,832	2,577	2,668	10.4	3.5	Pakistan [6]	44.6	141.2	187.1	–1.7	32.5
Far East index	2,583	3,287	3,246	7.4	–1.2	Philippines	146.7	263.2	363.4	55.4	38.0
						Sri Lanka [6].	36.3	183.2	155.4	42.8	–15.1
United States	1,250	1,336	1,391	13.2	4.1	Taiwan [7]	191.7	278.8	294.0	16.3	5.4
Canada.	832.5	1,513	1,930	16.2	27.6	Thailand	58.9	189.7	267.4	6.8	40.9
Australia	317.7	799.0	998.8	27.1	25.0	EM Latin America. . .	915.6	2,996	4,400	39.3	46.9
New Zealand [4]	56.4	147.9	153.9	10.0	4.0	Argentina.	1,233	3,084	2,919	66.1	–5.4
Austria	708.3	3,249	3,273	34.8	0.7	Brazil	763.2	2,205	3,867	40.5	75.3
Belgium.	1,222	2,261	2,142	33.3	–5.3	Chile	605	1,492	1,803	26.4	20.8
Denmark	2,201	4,859	6,037	36.8	24.2	Colombia [6].	42.1	549.8	619.3	10.9	12.6
Finland [4]	921.8	679.3	985.1	27.2	45.0	Mexico [6]	1,464.9	5,483	5,992	39.0	9.3
France	1,509	2,052	2,275	31.7	10.9	Peru [6].	125.0	671.4	1,249	52.1	86.0
Germany	1,436	1,902	2,521	33.0	32.5	Venezuela [6]	106.1	174.1	163.4	62.2	–6.2
Greece [4]	475.8	801.7	1,036	31.6	29.2	Czech Republic [8]	79.9	546.5	828.9	29.6	51.7
Ireland [4]	308.4	565.4	441.8	43.9	–21.9	Hungary [8]	233.6	1,003	1,137	31.1	13.4
Italy	447.2	636.0	653.0	28.1	2.7	Jordan [6].	55.1	209.1	252.9	–32.5	20.9
Luxembourg [5].	491.9	(NA)	(NA)	(NA)	(NA)	Poland [6]	499.0	1,223	1,501	35.3	22.7
Netherlands	2,177	2,487	2,923	28.2	17.5	Russia [8]	155.2	1,250	1,536	53.7	22.9
Norway [4]	1,181	3,386	4,349	41.6	28.4	South Africa [6]	157.6	443.1	508.3	17.3	14.7
Portugal [4]	127.8	193.3	234.0	43.4	21.0	Turkey [6]	247.7	441.7	751.1	–9.2	70.0
Spain	347.1	716.0	864.0	44.8	20.7						

NA Not available. [1] Percent change during calendar year (e.g. December 31, 2006 through December 31, 2007). Adjusted for foreign exchange fluctuations relative to U.S. dollar. [2] January 1, 1988 = 100. [3] Europe, Australasia, Far East Index. Comprises all European and Far East countries listed under developed markets plus Australia and New Zealand. [4] January 1, 1988 = 100. [5] MSCI Luxembourg Index discontinued as of March 29, 2002. [6] January 1, 1993 = 100. [7] See footnote 2, Table 1288. [8] January 1, 1995 = 100.

Source: MSCI Barra. This information is the exclusive property of MSCI Inc. ("MSCI") and may not be reproduced or redisseminated in any form or used to create any financial products or indices without MSCI's prior written permission. This information is provided "as is" and none of MSCI, its affiliates or any other person involved in or related to the compilation of this information (collectively, the "MSCI Parties" makes any express or implied warranties or representations with respect to the information or the results to be obtained by the use thereof, and the MSCI Parties hereby expressly disclaim all implied warranties (including without limitation, the implied warranties of merchantability and fitness for a particular purpose) with respect to this information. In no event shall any MSCI Party have any liability of any kind to any persons or entity arising from or related to this information.

Table 1350. Foreign Stock Market Indices: 1980 to 2007

[**As of year end**. The DAX-30 index is a total return index which includes dividends, whereas the other foreign indices are price indices which exclude dividends]

Year	London FTSE 100	Tokyo Nikkei 225	Hong Kong Hang Seng	Germany DAX-30	Paris CAC-40	Dow Jones Europe STOXX 50
1980	647	7,116	1,477	481	(X)	(X)
1985	1,413	13,113	1,752	1,366	(X)	(X)
1990	2,144	23,849	3,025	1,398	1,518	835
1993	3,418	17,417	11,888	2,267	2,268	1,429
1994	3,066	19,723	8,191	2,107	1,881	1,299
1995	3,689	19,868	10,073	2,254	1,872	1,538
1996	4,119	19,361	13,452	2,889	2,316	1,850
1997	5,136	15,259	10,723	4,250	2,999	2,634
1998	5,883	13,842	9,507	5,002	3,943	3,320
1999	6,930	18,934	16,962	6,958	5,958	4,742
2000	6,223	13,786	15,096	6,434	5,926	4,557
2001	5,217	10,543	11,397	5,160	4,625	3,707
2002	3,940	8,579	9,321	2,893	3,064	2,408
2003	4,477	10,677	12,576	3,965	3,558	2,660
2004	4,814	11,489	14,230	4,256	3,821	2,775
2005	5,619	16,111	14,876	5,408	4,715	3,349
2006	6,221	17,226	19,965	6,597	5,542	3,697
2007	6,457	15,308	27,813	8,067	5,614	3,684

X Not applicable.

Source: Global Financial Data, Los Angeles, CA, <http://www.globalfinancialdata.com>, unpublished data (copyright).

Table 1351. United States and Foreign Stock Markets—Market Capitalization and Value of Shares Traded: 2000 to 2007

[**In billions of U.S. dollars (15,104.0 represents $15,104,000,000,000)**. Market capitalization is the market value of all domestic listed companies at the end of the year. The market value of a company is the share price times the number of shares outstanding. Value of shares traded is the annual total turnover of listed company shares]

Country	Market capitalization				Value of shares traded			
	2000	2005	2006	2007	2000	2005	2006	2007
United States	**15,104.0**	**16,970.9**	**19,425.9**	**19,947.3**	**31,862.5**	**21,510.0**	**33,267.6**	**42,613.2**
Argentina	166.1	61.5	79.7	86.7	6.0	16.4	4.5	8.3
Australia	372.8	804.1	1,095.9	1,298.4	226.3	616.1	826.3	1,322.8
Austria	29.9	124.4	191.3	228.7	9.4	45.9	79.6	121.4
Belgium	182.5	288.5	396.2	386.4	38.0	125.7	165.9	255.7
Brazil	226.2	474.6	711.1	1,370.4	101.3	154.2	254.5	585.0
Canada	841.4	1,480.9	1,700.7	2,186.6	634.7	845.0	1,290.2	1,645.5
Chile	60.4	136.4	174.6	212.9	6.1	18.9	28.8	44.5
China [1]	581.0	780.8	2,426.3	6,226.3	721.5	586.3	1,635.1	7,791.7
Denmark	107.7	178.0	231.0	277.7	91.6	152.0	176.7	242.2
Egypt	28.7	79.7	93.5	139.3	11.1	25.4	47.5	53.1
Finland	293.6	209.5	265.5	369.2	206.6	273.5	356.8	543.3
France	1,446.6	1,758.7	2,428.6	2,771.2	1,083.3	1,526.1	2,504.7	3,418.9
Germany	1,270.2	1,221.3	1,637.8	2,105.5	1,069.1	1,763.2	2,486.7	3,363.1
Greece	110.8	145.0	208.3	264.9	95.1	65.3	107.5	151.5
Hong Kong	623.4	1,055.0	1,715.0	1,162.6	377.9	460.1	830.7	916.9
India	148.1	553.1	818.9	1,819.1	509.8	433.9	638.5	1,107.6
Indonesia	26.8	81.4	138.9	211.7	14.3	41.9	48.8	112.9
Iran	34.0	38.7	37.9	45.6	5.0	8.2	4.9	8.2
Ireland	81.9	114.1	163.4	144.0	14.4	64.7	79.9	136.6
Israel	64.1	120.1	173.3	236.4	23.4	59.9	88.8	113.5
Italy	768.4	798.2	1,026.6	1,072.7	778.4	1,115.2	1,366.1	2,313.5
Japan	3,157.2	4,736.5	4,726.3	4,453.5	2,693.9	4,997.4	6,252.5	6,497.2
Korea, South	171.6	718.2	835.2	1,123.6	1,067.7	1,203.0	1,340.1	1,974.0
Luxembourg	34.0	51.3	79.5	166.1	1.2	0.2	0.2	0.2
Malaysia	116.9	181.2	235.4	325.7	58.5	50.0	66.9	150.0
Mexico	125.2	239.1	348.3	397.7	45.3	52.7	80.1	115.6
Morocco	10.9	27.2	49.4	75.5	1.1	4.1	13.5	26.3
Netherlands	640.5	592.9	779.6	956.5	677.2	835.8	1,096.1	1,803.4
New Zealand	18.6	43.4	44.9	47.5	10.8	17.4	19.8	21.7
Norway	65.0	191.0	281.1	357.4	60.1	194.8	351.0	471.9
Philippines	51.6	40.2	68.4	103.2	8.2	7.0	11.2	29.3
Poland	31.3	93.9	149.1	207.3	14.6	30.0	55.0	84.6
Portugal	60.7	67.0	104.2	132.3	54.4	41.6	70.2	144.5
Russia	38.9	548.6	1,057.2	1,503.0	20.3	159.3	514.4	754.5
Saudi Arabia	67.2	646.1	326.9	515.1	17.3	1,103.5	1,403.0	679.8
Singapore	152.8	316.7	276.3	353.5	91.5	119.8	184.4	384.2
Sweden	328.3	403.9	573.3	612.5	390.0	464.0	677.1	968.8
Switzerland	792.3	938.6	1,212.5	1,274.5	609.1	883.3	1,286.8	1,777.8
Taiwan [1]	247.6	516.0	654.9	723.7	983.5	716.5	894.6	1,272.4
Thailand	29.5	124.9	141.1	196.0	23.3	89.3	100.8	108.2
Turkey	69.7	161.5	162.4	286.6	179.2	201.3	227.6	302.4
United Kingdom	2,580.0	3,058.2	3,794.3	3,858.5	1,835.3	4,167.0	4,242.1	10,324.5

[1] See footnote 2, Table 1288.

Source: Standard and Poor's, New York, NY, *Standard & Poor's Emerging Stock Markets Factbook 2008* (copyright).

U.S. Census Bureau, Statistical Abstract of the United States: 2009

Table 1352. **Foreign Exchange Rates: 2007**

[**Foreign currency units per U.S. dollar**. Rates shown include market, official, principal, and secondary rates]

Country	Currency	2007	Country	Currency	2007
Afghanistan [1]	Afghanis	(NA)	Laos	Kip	9,658.00
Albania	Leks	92.67	Latvia	Lats	0.52
Algeria	Algerian dinars	69.90	Lebanon	Lebanese pounds	1,507.50
Antigua and Barbuda	E. Caribbean dollars	2.70	Lesotho	Maloti	7.25
Argentina	Argentine pesos	3.11	Liberia	Liberian dollars	(NA)
Armenia	Drams	344.06	Libya [1]	Libyan dinars	1.26
Aruba	Aruban florins	(NA)	Lithuania	Litai	2.54
Australia	Australian dollars	1.21	Luxembourg [2]	Euro	0.73
Austria [2]	Euro	0.73	Macedonia	Denars	44.73
Bahamas, The	Bahamian dollars	1.00	Madagascar	Malagasy ariary	1,880.00
Bahrain	Bahrain dinars	0.38	Malaysia	Ringgit	3.46
Bangladesh	Taka	69.89	Mali	CFA francs	493.51
Barbados	Barbados dollars	(NA)	Malta	Maltese liri	0.31
Belarus	Belarusian rubel	2,145.00	Mauritania	Ouguiyas	(NA)
Belgium [2]	Euro	0.73	Mauritius	Mauritian rupees	31.80
Belize	Belize dollars	2.00	Mexico	Mexican pesos	10.80
Benin	CFA francs	493.51	Moldova	Lei	12.18
Bolivia	Bolivianos	7.86	Mongolia	Togrogs	1,170.00
Botswana	Pula	6.20	Morocco	Dirhams	8.36
Brazil	Reals	1.85	Mozambique	Meticais	26.26
Bulgaria	Leva	1.44	Namibia	Namibia dollars	7.18
Burkina Faso	CFA francs	493.51	Nepal	Nepalese rupees	(NA)
Burma [1]	Kyats	1,296.00	Netherlands [2]	Euro	0.73
Cambodia	Riel	4,006.00	Netherlands Antilles	Guilders	(NA)
Cameroon	CFA francs	493.51	New Zealand	New Zealand dollars	1.38
Canada	Canadian dollars	1.07	Nicaragua	Cordobas	18.46
Central African Republic	CFA francs	481.80	Niger	CFA francs	493.51
Chad	CFA francs	480.10	Nigeria	Naira	127.46
Chile	Chilean pesos	526.25	Norway	Norwegian kroner	5.84
China [3]	Yuan	7.61	Oman	Rials omani	0.38
Colombia	Colombian pesos	2,013.80	Pakistan	Pakistan rupees	60.63
Comoros	Comorian francs	361.40	Panama	Balboas	1.00
Congo (Brazzaville) [4]	CFA francs	483.60	Papua New Guinea	Kina	3.03
Costa Rica	Colones	519.53	Paraguay	Guaranies	5,031.00
Cote d'Ivoire	CFA francs	481.83	Peru	Nuevos soles	3.17
Croatia	Kunas	5.37	Philippines	Philippine pesos	46.15
Cyprus	Cyprus pounds	0.43	Poland	Zlotys	2.81
Czech Republic	Koruny	20.53	Portugal [2]	Euro	0.73
Denmark	Kroner	5.48	Qatar	Qatar riyals	3.64
Djibouti	Djibouti francs	177.71	Romania	Lei	2.43
Dominica	E. Caribbean dollars	2.70	Russia	Russian rubles	25.66
Dominican Republic	Dominican pesos	33.11	Rwanda	Rwanda francs	585.00
Ecuador	U.S. dollars	1.00	Saint Kitts and Nevis	E. Caribbean dollars	2.70
Egypt	Egyptian pounds	5.67	Saint Lucia	E. Caribbean dollars	2.70
El Salvador	U.S. dollars	1.00	Saint Vincent and the		
Equatorial Guinea	CFA francs	481.83	Grenadines	E. Caribbean dollars	2.70
Estonia	Krooni	11.54	Saudi Arabia	Saudi A. riyals	3.75
Ethiopia [1]	Birr	8.96	Senegal	CFA francs	481.83
Euro area (EMU-11) [2]	Euro	0.73	Sierra Leone	Leones	(NA)
Fiji	Fiji dollars	(NA)	Singapore	Singapore dollar	1.51
Finland [2]	Euro	0.73	Slovakia	Koruny	24.92
France [2]	Euro	0.73	Slovenia	Tolars	0.73
Gabon	CFA francs	481.83	South Africa	Rand	7.05
Georgia	Lari	1.70	Spain [2]	Euro	0.73
Germany [2]	Euro	0.73	Sri Lanka	Sri Lanka rupees	110.78
Greece [2]	Euro	0.73	Sudan	Sudanese dinars	2.06
Guatemala	Quetzales	7.68	Suriname [1]	Suriname dollar	2.75
Guyana	Guyana dollars	201.89	Swaziland	Emalangeni	7.40
Haiti	Gourdes	37.14	Sweden	Swedish kronor	6.76
Honduras	Lempiras	18.90	Switzerland	Swiss francs	1.20
Hong Kong	Hong Kong dollars	7.80	Syria	Syrian pounds	50.01
Hungary	Forint	186.16	Tanzania	Tanzania shillings	1,255.00
Iceland	Kronur	63.39	Thailand	Baht	33.60
India	Indian rupees	41.49	Togo	CFA francs	482.71
Indonesia	Rupiah	9,056.00	Trinidad and Tobago	Tt dollars	6.33
Iran	Rials	9,407.50	Tunisia	Tunisian dinars	1.28
Iraq	Dinars	1,255.00	Turkey	Liras	1.32
Ireland [2]	Euro	0.73	Uganda	Uganda shillings	1,685.80
Israel	New sheqalim	4.14	Ukraine	Hryvnias	5.05
Italy [2]	Euro	0.73	United Arab Emirates	Dirhams	3.67
Jamaica	Jamaica dollars	69.03	United Kingdom	Pounds sterling	0.50
Japan	Yen	117.99	Uruguay	Uruguayan pesos	23.95
Jordan	Jordinian dinars	0.71	Vanuatu	Vatu	(NA)
Kazakhstan	Tenge	122.55	Venezuela	Bolivares	2,147.00
Kenya	Kenya shillings	68.31	Yemen	Yemeni rials	199.14
Korea, South	Won	929.20	Zambia	Zambian kwacha	3,990.20
Kuwait	Kuwaiti dinars	0.28	Zimbabwe	Zimbabwe dollar	30,000.00
Kyrgyzstan	Soms	37.75			

NA Not available. [1] End-of year values were used if annual averages were unavailable. Some values were estimated using partial year data. [2] The euro became the official currency of the 11 Euro Area (EMU) nations on January 1, 1999, Greece in 2001, and Slovenia in 2007. [3] See footnote 2, Table 1288. [4] See footnote 3, Table 1288.

Source: Central Intelligence Agency, *The World Factbook, 2008*. See also <https://www.cia.gov/library/publications/the-world-factbook/index.html/>.

Table 1353. Reserve Assets and International Transaction Balances by Country: 2000 to 2007

[In millions of U.S. dollars (56,600 represents $56,600,000,000). Assets include holdings of convertible foreign currencies, special drawing rights, and reserve position in International Monetary Fund and exclude gold holdings. Minus sign (–) indicates debits]

Country	Total reserve assets				Current account balance			Merchandise trade balance		
			2007							
	2000	2006	Total	Currency holdings [1]	2000	2006	2007	2000	2006	2007
United States......	56,600	54,850	59,520	45,800	–415,150	–811,490	(NA)	–449,780	–834,550	(NA)
Algeria..........	12,024	77,914	110,318	110,180	(NA)	(NA)	(NA)	(NA)	(NA)	(NA)
Argentina........	25,147	30,903	44,682	44,175	–8,981	8,092	(NA)	2,452	13,872	(NA)
Australia.........	18,118	53,448	24,768	24,237	–14,763	–41,046	(NA)	–4,862	–9,596	(NA)
Austria..........	14,319	7,010	10,689	10,261	–4,864	8,836	(NA)	–2,737	286	(NA)
Bangladesh.......	1,486	3,806	5,420	5,419	–306	1,196	(NA)	–1,654	–2,890	(NA)
Belgium [2]........	9,994	8,783	10,384	9,298	11,381	(NA)	(NA)	2,591	(NA)	(NA)
Brazil............	32,488	85,156	179,433	179,431	–24,225	13,620	(NA)	–698	46,458	(NA)
Burma...........	223	1,236	(NA)	(NA)	–212	802	(NA)	–504	2,211	(NA)
Cameroon........	212	1,716	2,909	2,903	–249	(NA)	(NA)	502	(NA)	(NA)
Canada..........	32,102	34,994	40,991	39,314	19,622	20,797	12,815	45,047	45,146	45,838
Chile .3..........	15,035	19,392	16,837	16,695	–898	5,256	(NA)	2,119	22,213	(NA)
China [3].........	168,278	1,068,493	1,530,282	1,528,249	20,518	249,866	(NA)	34,474	217,746	(NA)
Colombia.........	8,916	15,296	20,767	20,096	764	–3,057	(NA)	2,633	322	(NA)
Congo (Brazzaville) [4] ..	222	1,841	2,197	2,196	648	(NA)	(NA)	2,037	(NA)	(NA)
Cote d'Ivoire......	668	1,798	2,519	2,517	–241	529	(NA)	1,486	3,152	(NA)
Denmark.........	15,108	[5]29,724	32,534	32,029	2,262	7,439	3,168	6,641	2,699	–1,044
Ecuador..........	947	1,490	2,816	2,765	921	1,503	(NA)	1,395	1,729	(NA)
Egypt	13,118	24,462	30,188	30,054	–971	2,635	(NA)	–8,321	–8,438	(NA)
Finland	7,977	6,494	7,063	6,689	10,526	10,978	(NA)	13,684	11,177	(NA)
France..........	37,039	42,652	45,710	43,587	18,580	–28,310	(NA)	–3,620	–37,690	(NA)
Germany	56,890	41,687	44,327	40,768	–31,960	151	(NA)	55,460	197,220	(NA)
Ghana..........	232	2,090	(NA)	(NA)	–387	–1,040	(NA)	–830	–3,027	(NA)
Greece	13,424	566	631	518	–9,820	–29,565	(NA)	–20,239	–44,285	(NA)
Hungary.........	11,190	21,527	23,970	23,773	–4,004	–7,421	(NA)	–2,913	–1,146	(NA)
India	37,902	170,738	266,988	266,553	–4,601	–9,415	(NA)	–10,640	–43,078	(NA)
Indonesia........	28,502	41,103	54,976	54,737	7,992	9,937	(NA)	25,042	29,646	(NA)
Ireland..........	5,360	720	779	591	–516	–9,095	(NA)	25,010	31,888	(NA)
Israel...........	23,281	29,153	28,519	28,406	–854	7,990	(NA)	–3,540	–3,233	(NA)
Italy............	25,567	25,662	28,385	27,319	–5,781	47,312	(NA)	9,549	–11,690	(NA)
Japan...........	354,902	879,682	952,784	948,356	119,660	170,520	(NA)	116,720	81,300	(NA)
Kenya	898	2,416	3,355	3,335	–199	–526	(NA)	–1,262	–3,266	(NA)
Korea, South	96,131	238,882	262,150	261,771	12,251	5,385	5,954	16,954	27,905	29,409
Kuwait..........	7,082	12,566	16,660	16,286	14,679	50,996	(NA)	13,027	44,288	(NA)
Malaysia	28,330	82,132	101,024	100,640	8,488	25,488	(NA)	20,827	36,698	(NA)
Mexico..........	35,509	76,271	87,109	86,309	–18,707	–2,008	(NA)	–8,337	–6,133	(NA)
Morocco.........	4,823	20,341	(NA)	(NA)	–501	1,778	(NA)	–3,235	–9,416	(NA)
Nepal	945	(NA)	(NA)	(NA)	–299	–10	(NA)	–814	–1,592	(NA)
Netherlands	9,643	10,802	10,270	8,749	7,264	55,795	(NA)	17,800	45,195	(NA)
Nigeria..........	9,911	42,299	51,334	51,333	7,429	(NA)	(NA)	10,415	(NA)	(NA)
Norway..........	27,597	56,842	60,840	60,294	25,851	58,323	(NA)	25,975	59,856	(NA)
Pakistan.........	1,513	11,543	14,044	13,829	–85	–6,750	(NA)	–1,157	–9,647	(NA)
Peru	8,374	16,733	26,857	26,853	–1,526	2,589	(NA)	–411	8,934	(NA)
Philippines	13,090	20,025	30,211	30,071	–2,225	5,897	(NA)	–5,971	–6,817	(NA)
Poland..........	26,562	46,371	62,967	62,720	–9,981	11,084	(NA)	–12,307	–7,004	(NA)
Portugal.........	8,909	2,064	1,258	1,044	–11,748	–18,281	(NA)	–14,532	–20,872	(NA)
Romania	2,470	28,066	37,195	37,194	–1,355	–12,785	(NA)	–1,684	–14,836	(NA)
Saudi Arabia.......	19,585	27,523	33,760	32,308	14,317	99,066	(NA)	49,777	147,391	(NA)
Singapore	80,132	136,259	162,957	162,517	10,728	36,326	(NA)	13,956	44,747	(NA)
South Africa	6,083	23,057	29,589	29,234	–191	–16,487	(NA)	4,698	–6,101	(NA)
Spain	30,989	10,822	11,480	10,792	–23,185	–106,344	(NA)	–37,087	–100,729	(NA)
Sri Lanka	1,039	2,837	(NA)	(NA)	–1,044	–1,434	(NA)	–1,044	–2,345	(NA)
Sudan	138	1,660	1,378	1,378	–557	–5,110	(NA)	440	–1,448	(NA)
Sweden	14,863	24,778	27,044	26,382	6,617	28,413	(NA)	15,215	21,415	(NA)
Switzerland........	32,272	38,094	44,474	43,867	33,562	54,849	(NA)	2,071	5,038	(NA)
Syria	(NA)	(NA)	(NA)	(NA)	1,061	890	(NA)	1,423	886	(NA)
Thailand.........	32,016	65,291	85,221	85,110	9,313	2,175	(NA)	11,701	13,936	(NA)
Trinidad and Tobago. .	1,386	6,570	(NA)	(NA)	544	(NA)	(NA)	969	(NA)	(NA)
Turkey..........	22,488	60,892	73,384	73,156	–9,822	–32,774	(NA)	–21,959	–41,238	(NA)
United Kingdom.....	38,770	40,700	48,960	47,500	–37,360	–75,550	(NA)	–49,850	–142,900	(NA)
Venezuela	13,088	29,417	24,196	23,686	11,853	27,149	(NA)	16,664	32,712	(NA)

NA Not available.   [1] Holdings of convertible foreign currencies.   [2] Balance of payments current account and trade balance data for 2000 are for Belgium–Luxembourg. Thereafter, data is for Belgium only.   [3] See footnote 2, Table 1288.   [4] See footnote 3, Table 1288.   [5] Break in series. Data not comparable to earlier years.

Source: International Monetary Fund, Washington, DC, *International Financial Statistics,* monthly, (copyright).

U.S. Census Bureau, Statistical Abstract of the United States: 2009

Table 1354. Foreign Trade—Destination of Exports and Source of Imports for Selected Countries: 2005

[In millions of dollars (4,945 represents $4,945,000,000). Data represent all goods which add to or subtract from the stock of material resources of a country by entering (imports) or leaving (exports) its economic territory. Goods transported through a country (goods in transit) or temporarily admitted or withdrawn are not included. Countries use one of two trade systems—general or specific. A country uses the general trade system when its statistical territory coincides with its economic territory. Special trade systems cover goods that cross the customs frontier plus goods that are imported into and exported from custom-bonded areas. In this case, the statistical territory comprises only a particular part of the economic territory. For more information, see source]

Country	United States Imports	United States Exports	Canada Imports	Canada Exports	Japan Imports	Japan Exports	France Imports	France Exports	Germany Imports	Germany Exports	United Kingdom Imports	United Kingdom Exports
Argentina	4,945	4,100	374	144	327	543	581	756	1,197	1,261	495	307
Australia	7,657	15,771	1,443	1,351	24,513	12,418	1,297	3,032	1,474	6,153	3,658	4,581
Austria	6,275	2,596	1,066	373	1,324	1,076	4,300	4,233	30,771	51,780	3,968	2,398
Belgium	13,398	18,602	1,481	1,880	2,120	7,122	38,450	32,745	38,063	53,519	24,238	20,172
Brazil	26,221	15,345	2,926	912	4,421	2,713	3,457	2,773	7,075	6,609	3,203	1,527
Canada [1]	291,866	211,417	(NA)	(NA)	8,924	8,806	2,477	3,011	3,191	6,569	6,654	5,967
China [1]	259,829	41,835	24,365	5,835	108,478	80,074	25,957	7,206	49,308	26,132	31,461	5,131
Colombia	9,424	5,415	481	369	370	793	349	340	729	826	551	214
Czech Republic	2,306	1,051	251	116	391	1,439	3,984	3,205	21,538	23,084	3,265	1,925
Denmark	5,304	1,913	1,293	240	2,369	868	3,791	3,244	11,109	14,929	6,943	4,164
Egypt	2,221	3,169	117	257	115	790	2,930	1,765	798	2,075	605	994
Finland	4,532	2,248	1,006	358	1,231	1,887	5,002	2,106	9,285	10,091	4,313	2,724
France	34,772	22,538	4,122	2,095	8,529	7,860	(NA)	(NA)	67,512	97,635	37,328	35,974
Germany	86,934	34,141	8,476	2,668	17,823	18,646	81,728	63,123	(NA)	(NA)	68,551	41,580
Hungary	2,633	1,022	182	59	565	1,820	2,988	2,858	17,756	16,750	3,254	1,481
India	19,875	7,958	1,476	895	3,192	3,518	2,619	2,287	4,184	5,068	5,138	5,110
Indonesia	12,947	3,045	789	569	20,817	9,214	1,429	556	2,978	1,730	1,775	680
Ireland	28,770	9,335	1,698	347	3,762	1,932	8,953	3,471	19,137	5,933	18,226	29,410
Israel	17,129	9,732	670	355	837	1,220	1,186	1,283	1,458	2,916	1,720	2,466
Italy	32,417	11,512	3,780	1,583	6,863	5,725	41,109	39,864	43,854	66,131	22,167	15,897
Japan	141,950	55,400	12,211	7,543	(NA)	(NA)	12,894	6,733	26,437	16,106	16,160	6,926
Luxembourg	410	782	73	60	43	224	1,919	2,009	3,184	4,499	1,505	382
Mexico	172,481	120,048	12,047	2,690	2,535	6,930	869	2,063	2,518	7,282	1,841	1,159
Netherlands	15,503	26,496	1,263	1,811	2,130	13,123	19,670	17,889	61,395	56,911	34,785	22,939
Norway	7,112	1,935	5,004	1,281	1,139	1,088	8,032	1,713	10,531	6,987	21,655	4,136
Poland	2,074	1,267	440	220	228	998	4,802	5,770	19,843	26,832	3,911	2,949
Russia	16,150	3,942	1,427	466	6,184	4,488	10,071	2,054	19,923	21,144	8,952	3,413
Saudi Arabia	28,966	6,830	1,424	361	28,722	4,174	4,465	2,342	1,686	4,973	2,379	2,905
South Africa	6,062	3,882	577	374	5,538	3,274	1,280	2,009	3,966	8,005	6,139	3,787
Spain	9,128	6,994	992	987	1,763	5,186	33,848	44,267	22,204	49,222	17,566	19,277
Sweden	14,228	3,709	1,895	383	2,165	1,959	6,012	5,439	13,889	21,036	9,531	8,275
Switzerland	13,153	10,730	1,755	883	5,046	2,154	10,910	12,695	28,034	35,082	5,211	9,318
Thailand	21,035	7,233	1,637	397	15,558	22,451	1,885	2,009	3,012	2,488	3,140	1,166
United Kingdom	52,369	38,621	8,588	6,819	6,703	15,073	27,875	38,244	47,708	74,397	6,610	(NA)
United States	**(NA)**	**(NA)**	**177,671**	**302,204**	**65,404**	**135,947**	**28,109**	**31,118**	**49,246**	**84,676**	**41,356**	**56,611**

NA Not available.   1 See footnote 2, Table 1288.

Source: Organization for Economic Cooperation and Development, Paris, France, OECD International Trade by Commodity Statistics, 2001–2006.

Table 1355. International Tourism Arrivals, Expenditures, and Receipts—Leading Countries: 2000 to 2006

[Arrivals in thousands of nonresident tourists at national borders, excluding same-day visitors (77,190 represents 77,190,000); expenditures and receipts in millions of dollars. Receipts are dollars spent by foreign tourists on travel inside the country shown. Expenditures are dollars visitors (same-day visitors and tourists) from a given country of origin spend on travel outside their country of residence. Excludes international transport receipts]

Country	Arrivals					Expenditures				Receipts				
	2000	2003	2004	2005	2006	2000	2004	2005	2006	2000	2003	2004	2005	2006
France	77,190	75,048	75,121	75,908	79,083	17,715	28,703	30,458	31,264	30,641	36,619	44,895	43,942	46,499
Spain	47,898	50,854	52,430	55,914	58,190	5,922	12,153	15,046	16,697	29,802	39,634	45,067	47,789	51,292
United States	51,238	41,218	46,086	49,206	50,978	67,043	69,627	73,290	76,807	97,943	83,316	94,537	102,124	106,736
China [1]	31,229	32,970	41,761	46,809	49,913	13,114	19,149	21,759	24,322	16,231	17,406	25,739	29,296	33,949
Italy	41,181	39,604	37,071	36,513	41,058	15,685	20,460	22,370	23,152	27,493	31,247	35,378	35,319	38,257
United Kingdom [2]	23,212	22,787	25,678	28,039	30,654	38,262	56,444	59,532	63,319	21,769	22,668	28,202	30,573	33,888
Germany [3]	18,983	18,399	20,137	21,500	23,569	52,824	71,187	74,189	74,123	18,611	23,125	27,613	29,121	32,846
Russia	21,169	22,521	22,064	22,201	22,486	8,848	15,285	17,434	18,235	3,429	4,502	5,530	5,870	7,628
Mexico	20,641	18,665	20,618	21,915	21,353	5,499	6,959	7,600	8,108	8,294	9,362	10,796	11,803	12,177
Austria [3]	17,982	19,078	19,373	19,952	20,261	8,463	11,834	10,994	9,348	9,998	13,842	15,290	15,589	16,510
Turkey	9,586	13,341	16,826	20,273	18,916	1,713	2,524	2,872	2,743	7,636	13,203	15,888	18,152	16,853
Ukraine	6,431	12,514	15,629	17,631	18,900	470	2,463	2,805	2,834	394	935	2,560	3,125	3,485
Canada	19,627	17,534	19,145	18,770	18,265	12,438	15,914	18,174	20,538	10,778	10,602	12,847	13,768	14,678
Malaysia	10,222	10,577	15,703	16,431	17,547	2,075	3,178	3,711	4,020	5,011	5,901	8,203	8,846	10,427
Greece	13,096	13,969	13,313	14,765	16,039	4,558	2,872	3,039	2,997	9,219	10,766	12,715	13,334	14,461
Hong Kong	8,814	9,676	13,655	14,773	15,821	12,502	13,270	13,305	13,974	5,868	7,072	8,918	10,179	11,461
Poland	17,400	13,720	14,290	15,200	15,670	3,313	3,841	4,341	5,760	5,677	4,069	5,833	6,274	7,239
Thailand	9,579	10,082	11,737	11,567	13,822	2,772	4,514	3,800	4,632	7,483	7,856	10,043	9,577	13,394
Portugal	12,097	11,707	10,639	10,612	11,282	2,228	2,763	3,050	3,298	5,243	6,622	7,672	7,676	8,388
Netherlands [3]	10,003	9,181	9,646	10,012	10,739	12,191	16,348	16,140	17,087	7,197	9,163	10,308	10,446	11,381
Macao [4]	5,197	6,309	8,324	9,014	10,683	(NA)	(NA)	(NA)	(NA)	3,205	5,303	7,344	7,757	9,337
Hungary	(NA)	(NA)	12,212	9,979	9,259	1,651	2,848	2,382	2,126	3,733	4,061	4,034	4,120	4,254
Croatia [3]	5,831	7,409	7,912	8,467	8,659	568	848	754	737	2,758	6,310	6,727	7,370	7,990
Egypt	5,116	5,746	7,795	8,244	8,646	1,072	1,257	1,629	1,784	4,345	4,584	6,125	6,851	7,591
Saudi Arabia [5]	6,585	7,332	8,599	8,037	8,620	(NA)	4,428	3,975	1,804	(NA)	3,418	(NA)	(NA)	(NA)
South Africa	5,872	6,505	6,678	7,369	8,396	2,085	3,157	3,373	3,384	2,677	5,571	6,322	7,335	7,876
Ireland	6,646	6,764	6,953	7,333	8,001	2,525	5,177	6,074	6,862	2,615	3,862	4,375	4,782	5,369
Switzerland [6]	7,821	6,530	(NA)	7,229	7,863	5,419	8,104	8,837	9,919	6,652	8,617	9,600	10,095	10,640
Singapore	6,062	4,703	6,553	7,080	7,588	4,535	9,242	9,947	10,384	5,142	3,783	5,226	5,903	7,069
Japan	4,757	5,212	6,138	6,728	7,334	31,884	38,252	37,565	26,876	3,373	8,848	11,265	12,430	8,470
Belgium [3]	6,457	6,690	6,710	6,747	6,995	9,429	13,956	14,948	15,482	6,592	8,193	9,208	9,845	10,242
Morocco	4,278	4,761	5,477	5,843	6,558	426	574	612	703	2,039	3,221	3,922	4,610	5,984
Tunisia	5,058	5,114	5,998	6,378	6,550	263	340	374	410	1,682	1,583	1,970	2,143	2,275
Czech Republic	4,666	5,076	6,061	6,336	6,435	1,276	2,280	2,405	2,670	2,973	3,566	4,187	4,659	5,026
Korea, South [2]	5,322	4,753	5,818	6,023	6,155	7,132	12,350	15,406	18,241	6,834	5,358	6,069	5,806	5,322
Romania [2]	5,264	5,595	6,600	5,839	6,037	425	539	925	1,310	359	449	503	1,052	1,308
Bulgaria	2,785	4,048	4,630	4,837	5,158	538	1,363	1,309	1,474	1,074	1,621	2,202	2,412	2,610
Australia	4,530	4,354	4,774	5,020	5,064	6,387	10,242	11,253	11,690	9,289	12,438	15,214	16,868	17,854
Brazil	5,313	4,133	4,794	5,358	5,019	3,894	2,871	4,720	5,764	1,810	2,479	3,222	3,861	4,316
Indonesia	5,064	4,467	5,321	5,002	4,871	3,197	3,507	3,584	3,600	4,975	4,037	4,798	4,522	4,448

NA Not available. [1] See footnote 2, Table 1288. [2] Arrivals are of nonresident visitors at national borders, including tourists and same-day visitors. [3] Arrivals are of nonresident tourists in all types of accomodation establishments. [4] Expenditures and receipts include both travel and passenger transport. [5] Receipts include both travel and passenger transport. [6] Arrivals of nonresident tourists in hotels and similar establishments.

Source: World Tourism Organization, Madrid, Spain, *World Tourism Barometer*, March 2008 (copyright). ©UNWTO, 9284404808

Table 1356. **Household Expenditure on Recreation and Culture as a Percentage of GDP: 1970 to 2006**

[Household expenditure on recreation and culture includes purchases of audio-visual, photographic, and computer equipment; CDs and DVDs; musical instruments; camper vans; caravans; sports equipment; toys; domestic pets and related products; gardening tools and plants; newspapers; tickets to sporting matches, cinemas and theatres; and spending on gambling (including lottery tickets) less any winnings. It excludes expenditures on restaurants, hotels, and travel and holiday homes but includes package holidays]

Country	1980	1990	1995	2000	2001	2002	2003	2004	2005	2006
Australia	5.8	6.1	7.2	7.3	7.1	7.2	7.2	7.1	6.9	(NA)
Austria	5.0	6.5	6.4	6.9	6.9	6.9	6.8	6.7	6.6	6.5
Belgium	(NA)	(NA)	4.8	5.2	5.2	4.8	4.8	4.7	4.7	4.7
Canada	4.4	5.1	5.5	5.7	5.7	5.8	5.7	5.6	5.5	(NA)
Czech Republic	(NA)	(NA)	5.5	6.1	6.2	6.0	6.2	6.0	5.9	5.6
Denmark	4.8	4.9	5.1	5.2	5.1	5.1	5.3	5.4	5.3	(NA)
Finland	5.2	5.4	5.3	5.4	5.3	5.3	5.5	5.5	5.7	5.7
France	4.8	4.8	4.8	5.1	5.1	5.2	5.2	5.2	5.2	5.2
Germany	(NA)	(NA)	5.1	5.6	5.6	5.4	5.3	5.3	5.3	5.2
Hungary	(NA)	(NA)	(NA)	4.1	4.2	4.2	4.2	4.2	4.3	4.3
Iceland	(NA)	6.1	7.2	7.1	6.9	6.9	6.7	6.5	6.5	6.3
Ireland	(NA)	(NA)	4.0	3.4	3.4	3.0	3.0	3.1	3.1	(NA)
Italy	4.1	4.4	4.2	4.5	4.4	4.3	4.2	4.3	4.1	4.1
Japan	(NA)	(NA)	(NA)	6.1	6.2	6.2	6.2	6.2	6.1	(NA)
Korea	2.2	3.9	4.3	4.1	4.2	4.4	4.0	3.6	3.7	3.7
Luxembourg	(NA)	(NA)	3.9	3.6	3.8	3.9	3.6	3.5	3.4	3.1
Mexico	(NA)	2.2	1.9	2.0	2.0	1.9	1.9	2.0	(NA)	(NA)
Netherlands	(NA)	5.6	5.2	5.5	5.4	5.3	5.1	5.0	4.8	4.8
New Zealand	(NA)	5.3	6.3	7.2	7.1	(NA)	(NA)	(NA)	(NA)	(NA)
Norway	(NA)	(NA)	5.4	5.2	5.3	5.5	5.6	5.5	5.1	(NA)
Poland	(NA)	(NA)	4.8	5.2	4.6	4.5	4.6	4.6	4.0	(NA)
Portugal	(NA)	(NA)	3.6	4.2	4.1	4.1	4.1	4.2	(NA)	(NA)
Slovakia	(NA)	(NA)	4.0	4.7	5.4	5.2	4.8	4.7	5.0	4.9
Spain	(NA)	(NA)	5.2	5.7	5.7	5.6	5.5	5.5	5.5	(NA)
Sweden	(NA)	(NA)	5.0	5.6	5.6	5.5	5.5	5.4	5.3	(NA)
Switzerland	(NA)	5.2	5.4	5.1	5.1	5.1	5.1	5.0	4.9	4.7
United Kingdom	5.5	6.3	6.8	7.3	7.3	7.5	7.5	7.7	7.7	(NA)
United States	**4.5**	**5.4**	**6.1**	**6.4**	**6.4**	**6.4**	**6.4**	**6.4**	**6.4**	**6.4**
Israel	(NA)	3.4	3.9	4.1	4.0	3.9	4.0	4.1	4.4	4.4
Slovenia	(NA)	(NA)	4.9	5.4	5.4	5.3	5.4	5.5	5.5	5.5

NA Not available.

Source: Organization for Economic Cooperation and Development, Paris, France, *OECD Factbook, 2008* (copyright). See also <http://titania.sourceoecd.org/vl=3566958/cl=17/nw=1/rpsv/factbook/>.

Table 1357. **Development Assistance, by Country: 2005 and 2006**

[2,128 represents $2,128,000,000]

Country	Official development aid (ODA) 2006 [1]			Multilateral grants by NGO's aid [4] 2005	
	Million U.S. dollars	Percent of GNI [2]	Percent of Total DAC ODA [3]	Percent of ODA	Percent of GNI
Australia	2,128	0.30	2.0	13.8	0.12
Austria	1,513	0.48	1.5	21.7	0.05
Belgium	1,968	0.50	1.9	33.4	0.07
Canada	3,713	0.30	3.6	24.6	0.09
Denmark	2,234	0.80	2.1	35.6	0.03
Finland	826	0.39	0.8	33.8	0.01
France	10,448	0.47	10.1	27.8	(NA)
Germany	10,351	0.36	10.0	26.1	0.05
Greece	384	0.16	0.4	46.3	–
Ireland	997	0.53	1.0	32.9	0.18
Italy	3,672	0.20	3.5	55.4	0.01
Japan	11,608	0.25	11.2	20.8	0.01
Luxembourg	291	0.89	0.3	27.1	0.03
Netherlands	5,452	0.81	5.2	28.0	0.07
New Zealand	257	0.27	0.2	18.2	0.09
Norway	2,946	0.89	2.8	27.0	(NA)
Portugal	391	0.21	0.4	42.1	–
Spain	3,801	0.32	3.7	38.3	(NA)
Sweden	3,967	1.03	3.8	32.9	0.01
Switzerland	1,647	0.39	1.6	20.8	0.08
United Kingdom	12,607	0.52	12.1	24.2	0.03
United States	**22,739**	**0.17**	**21.9**	**8.5**	**0.07**
EU-15 [5]	58,902	0.43	56.7	30.9	0.03
DAC total	103,940	0.30	100.0	23.1	0.05

NA Not available. – Represents zero. [1] Preliminary. [2] Gross National Income. See headnote, Table 1305. [3] DAC: OECD Development Assistance Committee. [4] NGO: Nongovernmental organizations. [5] See footnote 2, Table 1327.

Source: Organization for Economic Cooperation and Development, Paris, France, OECD in Figures, 2007 (copyright). See also <http://www.oecd.org/document/19/0,3343,en_2649_34489_39503891_1_1_1_1,00.html>.

Table 1358. Net Flow of Financial Resources to Developing Countries and Multilateral Organizations: 1995 to 2005

[**165,182 represents $165,182,000,000.** Net flow covers loans, grants, and grant-like flows minus amortization on loans. Military flows are excluded. Developing countries are designated by Development Assistance Committee as developing. GNI = gross national income. For explanation of GNI, see headnote, Table 1305. Minus sign (–) indicates net inflow]

Type of aid and country	Amount (mil. dol.)					Percent of GNI		
	1995	2000	2003	2004	2005	1995	2000	2005
Total net flows	165,182	134,485	125,551	160,356	305,019	0.75	0.56	0.94
United States	46,984	25,252	37,860	32,283	104,410	0.65	0.25	0.84
Australia.	2,536	1,961	3,010	2,466	5,366	0.76	0.53	0.79
Austria	906	1,135	1,445	1,352	4,215	0.39	0.61	1.40
Belgium	–234	2,281	1,221	816	3,142	–0.09	1.00	0.84
Canada	5,724	6,483	4,949	5,986	13,373	1.04	0.95	1.20
Denmark.	1,799	2,176	1,896	2,634	2,215	1.07	1.39	0.85
Finland.	604	1,087	–44	1,338	1,642	0.50	0.91	0.84
France	12,477	5,557	6,936	12,599	15,744	0.81	0.41	0.74
Germany	21,197	12,331	5,224	15,251	30,059	0.87	0.66	1.07
Greece.	–	229	403	328	709	–	0.20	0.32
Ireland	247	740	2,334	3,851	5,298	0.46	0.93	3.09
Italy	2,800	10,846	4,218	3,239	4,103	0.26	1.01	0.23
Japan	42,295	11,423	6,335	11,368	23,259	0.82	0.24	0.50
Luxembourg	72	129	201	242	265	0.40	0.75	0.84
Netherlands	6,795	6,947	15,196	14,106	22,781	1.71	1.85	3.65
New Zealand.	166	142	208	271	401	0.31	0.32	0.40
Norway.	1,670	1,437	3,306	2,785	2,791	1.16	0.87	0.94
Portugal	395	4,622	1,145	676	1,109	0.38	4.45	0.62
Spain	2,025	23,471	6,667	12,762	6,801	0.37	4.25	0.61
Sweden	2,224	3,952	1,255	2,954	3,545	1.00	1.76	0.99
Switzerland	1,118	2,054	3,225	1,372	7,474	0.35	0.80	1.87
United Kingdom	13,382	10,230	18,561	31,680	46,318	1.19	0.72	2.03

– Represents zero.

Source: Organization for Economic Cooperation and Development, Paris, France, *Annual Reports of the Development Assistance Committee* (copyright).

Table 1359. External Debt by Country: 1990 to 2006

[**In billions of dollars (28.1 represents $28,100,000,000).** Total external debt is debt owed to nonresidents repayable in foreign currency, goods, or services. Total external debt is the sum of public, publicly guaranteed, and private nonguaranteed long-term debt, use of IMF credit, and short-term debt. Short-term debt includes all debt having an original maturity of one year or less and interest in arrears on long-term debt]

Country	1990	2000	2005	2006	Country	1990	2000	2005	2006
Algeria	28.1	25.3	16.9	5.6	Mexico	104.4	150.3	167.2	160.7
Angola	8.6	9.4	11.8	9.6	Morocco	25.0	20.7	16.8	18.5
Argentina	62.2	145.9	114.3	122.2	Nigeria	33.4	31.4	22.2	7.7
Bangladesh.	12.4	15.7	18.9	20.5	Pakistan	20.7	32.8	33.7	35.9
Brazil	120.0	238.8	188.0	194.2	Panama	6.5	7.0	9.8	10.0
Bulgaria	(NA)	10.2	16.8	20.9	Peru	20.0	28.7	28.7	28.2
Cameroon.	6.4	9.3	7.2	3.2	Philippines	30.6	57.4	61.5	60.3
Chile [1]	19.2	37.0	45.2	48.0	Poland	49.4	63.3	98.8	125.8
China [1]	55.3	145.7	281.6	322.8	Romania.	1.1	10.5	38.7	55.1
Colombia . . . . . . [2] .	17.2	33.9	37.7	39.7	Russia [3]	(NA)	160.0	229.0	251.1
Congo (Kinshasa) [2] .	10.3	4.9	10.6	6.1	Serbia and				
Cote d'Ivoire	17.3	12.1	10.7	13.8	Montenegro [4, 5] . . .	(NA)	11.9	16.3	13.8
Croatia	(NA)	11.3	30.2	37.5	Slovakia	(NA)	12.1	23.7	27.1
Czech Republic	(NA)	21.5	(NA)	(NA)	South Africa	(NA)	24.9	30.6	35.5
Ecuador	12.1	13.7	17.1	16.5	Sri Lanka	5.9	9.2	11.4	11.4
Egypt	33.0	29.2	34.1	29.3	Sudan	14.8	15.7	18.5	19.2
Ghana	3.7	6.6	6.7	3.2	Syria	17.3	21.7	6.5	6.5
Hungary	21.2	29.5	66.1	107.7	Tanzania.	6.5	7.4	7.8	4.2
India	83.6	99.1	123.1	153.1	Thailand	28.1	79.7	52.3	55.2
Indonesia	69.9	144.4	138.3	131.0	Tunisia	7.7	10.6	17.8	18.5
Iran	9.0	8.0	21.3	20.1	Turkey	49.4	117.4	171.1	207.9
Jordan	8.3	7.4	7.7	8.0	Ukraine	(NA)	12.2	33.3	49.9
Kazakhstan.	(NA)	11.8	43.4	74.1	Uruguay	4.4	8.2	14.6	9.8
Lebanon	1.8	9.9	22.4	24.0	Venezuela.	33.2	38.2	44.2	44.6
Malaysia.	15.3	41.9	51.0	52.5	Vietnam	23.3	12.8	19.3	20.2

NA Not available. [1] See footnote 2, Table 1288. [2] See footnote 3, Table 1288. [3] The debt of the former Soviet Union is included in Russia's data after 1990 on the assumption that 100 percent of all outstanding external debt as of December 1991 has become a liability of Russia. Beginning in 2000, the data for Russia has also been revised to include obligations to members of the former Council for Mutual Economic Assistance and other countries in the form of trade-related credits amounting to $15.4 billion as of the end of 1996. [4] External debt obligations, excluding IBRD, IMF, and short-term, of Bosnia and Herzegovina before 2000 are included under Serbia and Montenegro. Data from 2000 onwards are estimates and also reflect borrowing by the former Yugoslavia that are not yet allocated to the successor republics. [5] As of June 2006, Serbia and Montenegro are separate countries (formerly Yugoslavia). Starting 2006, data exclude Montenegro.

Source: Copyright the International Bank for Reconstruction and Development/The World Bank, Washington, DC, *2008 World Development Indicators* (copyright).

Table 1360. **Foreign Direct Investment Flows in OECD Countries: 2000 to 2006**

[In billions of dollars (1,068.6 represents $1,068,600,000,000). Data are converted to U.S. dollars using the yearly average exchange rate]

Country	Inflows				Outflows			
	2000	2005	2006 [1]	Cumulative, 1994–2006	2000	2005	2006 [1]	Cumulative, 1994–2006
OECD, total.....	**1,068.6**	**745.3**	**948.2**	**6,983.3**	**1,022.0**	**870.2**	**1,128.3**	**7,356.8**
Australia.........	14.0	–35.0	24.5	112.8	3.2	–34.3	21.0	38.2
Austria.........	8.8	9.0	0.2	54.1	5.7	10.0	4.1	52.5
Belgium.........	(NA)	34.0	71.5	196.8	(NA)	31.8	62.6	115.4
Canada........	66.8	33.8	66.6	312.4	44.7	34.1	42.1	314.8
Czech Republic....	5.0	11.7	6.0	60.0	(Z)	(Z)	1.3	2.2
Denmark........	31.3	13.1	7.0	96.5	23.1	15.0	8.2	82.6
Finland........	8.8	4.5	3.7	57.8	24.0	4.5	(Z)	80.8
France.........	43.3	81.0	81.1	542.0	177.5	120.9	115.1	827.2
Germany........	198.3	35.8	42.9	498.9	56.6	55.5	79.5	539.4
Greece.........	1.1	0.6	5.4	17.4	2.1	1.5	4.2	6.6
Hungary........	2.8	7.6	6.1	50.4	0.6	2.3	3.0	7.4
Iceland.........	0.2	3.1	3.2	8.2	0.4	7.1	4.2	11.4
Ireland.........	25.8	–31.1	12.8	93.4	4.6	13.6	22.1	69.9
Italy..........	13.4	20.0	16.6	139.3	12.3	41.8	42.1	173.4
Japan.........	8.3	2.8	–6.5	54.5	31.5	45.8	50.2	344.8
Korea, South......	9.3	6.3	36.5	93.2	5.0	4.3	7.1	46.5
Luxembourg	(NA)	116.3	97.0	497.0	(NA)	124.0	81.6	433.9
Mexico.........	17.6	19.6	19.0	213.2	(NA)	6.5	5.8	17.5
Netherlands	63.9	41.4	4.4	335.2	75.6	142.8	22.7	560.2
New Zealand......	1.3	3.1	1.6	28.4	0.6	–0.3	–1.6	3.3
Norway.........	6.9	5.1	6.8	51.6	8.6	21.8	20.5	66.4
Poland.........	9.4	9.5	13.9	88.6	(Z)	3.1	4.1	4.8
Portugal........	6.6	4.0	7.4	46.7	8.1	2.1	3.5	43.2
Spain.........	39.6	25.0	20.0	262.1	58.2	41.8	89.7	344.9
Sweden........	23.4	10.2	27.8	219.2	41.0	26.5	24.1	209.2
Switzerland......	19.3	–1.3	25.1	112.1	44.7	54.2	81.5	276.1
Turkey.........	1.0	9.8	20.2	44.8	0.9	1.1	0.9	5.5
United Kingdom....	118.8	193.7	139.6	850.8	233.5	83.7	79.5	1,075.7
United States.....	**321.3**	**109.8**	**183.6**	**1,827.6**	**159.2**	**9.1**	**248.9**	**1,602.3**

NA Not available.　　Z Less than $50 million.　　[1] Preliminary.
Source: Organization for Economic Cooperation and Development, Paris, France, *OECD Factbook, 2008*. See also <http://oberon.sourceoecd.org/vl=344130/cl=12/nw=1/rpsv/factbook/>.

Table 1361. **Military Expenditures, 2006, and Manpower, 2008, by Country**

[8,181 represents 8,181,000. Manpower covers males and females deemed fit for military service, ages 15–49]

Country	Expenditures (percent of GDP [1])	Manpower (1,000)	Country	Expenditures (percent of GDP [1])	Manpower (1,000)
Afghanistan	1.9	8,181	Israel	7.3	2,837
Albania	[2]1.5	1,566	Italy	[2]1.8	21,966
Algeria...........	3.3	16,358	Japan.............	0.8	22,157
Argentina..........	[2]1.3	16,719	Kazakhstan	[6]0.9	6,422
Australia..........	2.4	8,160	Korea, North........	(NA)	10,281
Austria	[2]0.9	3,201	Korea, South	2.7	21,966
Bahrain	4.5	314	Kuwait............	5.3	1,393
Belarus	[2]1.4	3,821	Laos	0.5	2,045
Belgium...........	[2]1.3	3,889	Lebanon	[2]3.1	1,883
Bolivia............	1.9	3,416	Libya	[2]3.9	2,822
Bosnia and Herzegovina..	[2]4.5	1,959	Malaysia	[2]2.0	10,691
Brazil	2.6	83,373	Mexico	0.5	47,073
Bulgaria...........	[2]2.6	2,765	Morocco	[7]5.0	15,383
Burma............	[2]2.1	18,428	Netherlands	[2]1.6	6,375
Cambodia..........	[2]3.0	5,257	New Zealand	[2]1.0	1,656
Canada...........	[2]1.1	13,064	Nicaragua	0.6	2,538
Chile.............	2.7	7,043	Nigeria	1.5	35,845
China [3]	4.3	609,273	Norway	[2]1.9	1,750
Colombia..........	[2]3.4	17,976	Oman	[2]11.4	1,207
Congo (Brazzaville) [4] ...	3.1	1,029	Pakistan	[5]3.0	63,823
Cote d'Ivoire........	[2]1.6	4,775	Peru	1.5	12,014
Croatia	[2]2.4	1,627	Philippines	[2]0.9	38,060
Cuba	3.8	5,025	Poland	[2]1.7	15,888
Czech Republic......	[5]1.3	4,119	Russia............	[2]3.9	50,250
Denmark	[5]1.3	2,009	Saudi Arabia	[2]10.0	12,924
Ecuador	2.8	6,069	Singapore	[2]4.9	1,039
Egypt	[2]3.4	35,559	South Africa	1.7	11,514
El Salvador	5.0	2,688	Spain	[2]1.2	16,219
Ethiopia...........	3.0	19,915	Sudan............	[2]3.0	11,265
Finland	[2]2.0	1,888	Sweden...........	[2]1.5	3,337
France	[2]2.6	23,961	Switzerland	[2]1.0	2,993
Germany	[2]1.5	30,958	Syria.............	[2]5.9	8,461
Greece	[2]4.3	4,150	Thailand	[2]1.8	27,027
Honduras..........	0.6	2,731	Turkey............	[2]5.3	33,445
Hungary	[2]1.8	3,834	Ukraine	[2]1.4	16,571
India	2.5	467,795	United Arab Emirates....	[2]3.1	2,765
Indonesia..........	[2]3.0	104,497	United Kingdom	[2]2.4	23,738
Iran	2.5	34,344	**United States ....**	[2]**4.1**	**118,601**
Iraq	8.6	11,899	Venezuela	[2]1.2	11,050
Ireland	[2]0.9	1,708	Vietnam...........	[2]2.5	39,425

NA Not available.　　[1] GDP calculated on an exchange rate basis.　　[2] 2005 data.　　[3] See footnote 2, Table 1288.　　[4] See footnote 3, Table 1288.　　[5] 2007 data.　　[6] 2002 data.　　[7] 2003 data.
Source: Central Intelligence Agency, *The World Factbook, 2008*. See also <https://www.cia.gov/library/publications/the-world-factbook/index.html> (accessed 23 June 2008).

856　International Statistics

Appendix I

Guide to Sources of Statistics, State Statistical Abstracts, and Foreign Statistical Abstracts

Alphabetically arranged, this guide contains references to important primary sources of statistical information for the United States and other countries. Secondary sources have been included if the information contained in them is presented in a particularly convenient form or if primary sources are not readily available. Nonrecurrent publications presenting compilations or estimates for years later than 2000, or types of data not available in regular series, are also included. Data are also available in press releases.

Valuable information may also be found in state reports, foreign statistical abstracts, which are included at the end of this appendix, and in reports for particular commodities, industries, or similar segments of our economic and social structures, many of which are not included here.

Publications listed under each subject are divided into two main groups: "U.S. Government" and "Nongovernment." The location of the publisher of each report is given except for federal agencies located in Washington, DC. Most federal publications may be purchased from the Superintendent of Documents, U.S. Government Printing Office, Washington, DC, tel. 202-512-1800, (Web site <http://bookstore.gpo.gov>). In some cases, federal publications may be obtained from the issuing agency.

Title	Frequency	Paper	Internet PDF	Internet Other formats
U.S. GOVERNMENT				
Administrative Office of the United States Courts <http://www.uscourts.gov>				
Calendar Year Reports on Authorized Wiretaps (state and federal)	Annual	X	X	X
Federal Court Management Statistics	Annual	X		X
Federal Judicial Caseload Statistics	Annual	X		
Judicial Business of the United States Courts	Annual	X	X	
Statistical Tables for the Federal Judiciary	Semiannual	X		X
Agency for International Development <http://www.usaid.gov>				
U.S. Overseas Loans and Grants: Obligations and Loan Authorizations	Annual	X	X	X
Army Corps of Engineers <http://www.usace.army.mil>				
Waterborne Commerce of the United States (in five parts)	Annual	X		X
Board of Governors of the Federal Reserve System <http://www.federalreserve.gov>				
Assets and Liabilities of Commercial Banks in the United States H.8	Weekly	X	X	X
Consumer Credit G.19	Monthly	X	X	X
Federal Reserve Bulletin	Annual	X	X	X
Foreign Exchange Rates H.10	Daily			X
Flow of Funds Accounts of the United States Z.1	Quarterly	X	X	X
Industrial Production and Capacity Utilization G.17	Monthly	X	X	X
Money Stock and Debt Measures H.6	Weekly	X	X	X
Statistical Supplement to the Federal Reserve Bulletin	Monthly	X	X	X
Bureau of Economic Analysis <http://www.bea.gov>				
Survey of Current Business	Monthly	X	X	X
Bureau of Justice Statistics <http://www.ojp.usdoj.gov/bjs>				
American Indians and Crime: A BJS Statistical Profile, December 2004	Periodic	X	X	X
Background Checks for Firearm Transfers	Annual	X	X	X
Capital Punishment, 2006, December 2007	Annual		X	X
Carjacking, 1993–2002, July 2004	Periodic		X	X
Census of Publicly Funded Forensic Crime Laboratories, February 2005	Periodic	X	X	X
Census of State and Federal Correctional Facilities, 2000, August 2003	Periodic	X	X	X
Civil Rights Complaints in U.S. District Courts, July 2002	Periodic	X	X	X
Civil Trial Cases and Verdicts in Large Counties, 2001, April 2004	Periodic	X	X	X
Compendium of Federal Justice Statistics, 2004, December 2006	Annual	X	X	X
Contacts Between Police and Public: Findings from the 2005 National Survey, April 2007	Periodic	X	X	X

Appendix I 857

U.S. Census Bureau, Statistical Abstract of the United States: 2009

Title	Frequency	Paper	PDF	Other formats
Bureau of Justice Statistics—Con.				
Contract Trials and Verdicts in Large Counties, 2001, February 2005	Periodic	X	X	X
Crime and the Nation's Households, 2005, April 2007	Annual	X	X	X
Crimes Against Persons Age 65 or Older, 1993–2002, January 2005	Periodic	X	X	X
Criminal Victimization in the United States, 2006, December 2007	Annual	X	X	X
Cross-National Studies in Crime and Justice, September 2004	Periodic	X	X	X
Defense Counsel in Criminal Cases, November 2000	Periodic	X	X	X
Education and Correctional Populations, January 2003	Periodic	X	X	X
Family Violence Statistics	Periodic	X	X	X
Federal Criminal Case Processing, 2002, January 2005	Periodic	X	X	X
Federal Law Enforcement Officers, 2004, August 2006	Biennial	X	X	X
Felony Defendants in Large Urban Counties, 2004, April 2008	Biennial		X	X
Felony Sentences in State Courts, 2004, July 2007	Biennial	X	X	X
Firearm Use by Offenders, November 2001	Periodic	X	X	X
Hepatitis Testing and Treatment in State Prisons, April 2004	Periodic	X	X	X
Hispanic Victims of Violent Crime, 1993–2000, April 2002	Periodic	X	X	X
HIV in Prisons 2006	Annual		X	X
Homicide Trends in the United States	Annual	X	X	X
Identity Theft, 2005, November 2007	Periodic	X	X	X
Immigration Offenders in the Federal Criminal Justice System, August 2002	Periodic	X	X	X
Incarcerated Parents and Their Children, August 2000	Periodic	X	X	X
Indicators of School Crime and Safety	Annual	X	X	X
Intimate Partner Violence, 1993 to 2001, February 2003	Periodic	X	X	X
Jails in Indian Country, 2004, November 2006	Annual	X	X	X
Justice Expenditure and Employment Extract Series, 2005, August 2007	Annual			X
Juvenile Offenders and Victims	Periodic	X	X	X
Juvenile Victimization and Offending, 1993–2003	Periodic	X	X	X
Law Enforcement Management and Administrative Statistics 2000: Data for Individual State and Local Agencies With 100 or More Officers	Periodic	X	X	X
Local Police Departments, 2003, May 2006	Periodic	X	X	X
Medical Malpractice Trials and Verdicts in Large Counties, April 2004	Periodic	X	X	X
Money Laundering Offenders, 1994–2001, July 2003	Periodic	X	X	X
Prevalence of Imprisonment in the U.S. Population, 1974–2001, August 2003	Periodic	X	X	X
Prison and Jail Inmates at Midyear, 2006, June 2007	Annual	X	X	X
Prisoners in 2006, December 2007	Annual	X	X	X
Probation and Parole in the United States	Annual	X	X	X
Profile of Jail Inmates, 2002, July 2004	Periodic	X	X	X
Prosecutors in State Courts, 2001, May 2002	Biennial	X	X	X
Rape and Sexual Assault: Reporting to Police and Medical Attention, August 2002	Periodic	X	X	X
Reentry Trends in the United States Current Data Electronic	Periodic		X	X
Sheriff's Offices, 2003, April 2006	Periodic	X	X	X
Sourcebook of Criminal Justice Statistics	Annual	X	X	X
State Court Prosecutors in Large Districts, December 2001	Periodic	X	X	X
State Court Prosecutors in Small Districts, 2001, January 2003	Periodic	X	X	X
State Court Sentencing of Convicted Felons, 2004, July 2007	Biennial		X	X
State Prison Expenditures, 2001, June 2004	Periodic	X	X	X
Summary of State Sex Offender Registries, 2001, March 2002	Periodic	X	X	X
Survey of DNA Crime Laboratories, 2001, January 2002	Periodic	X	X	X
Survey of State Criminal History Information Systems, September 2003	Biennial	X	X	X
Survey of State Procedures Related to Firearm Sales, 2005, November 2006	Periodic	X	X	X
Tort Trials and Verdicts in Large Counties, November 2004	Periodic	X	X	X
Traffic Stop Data Collection Policies for State Police, 2004, June 2005	Periodic	X	X	X
Violent Victimization of College Students, 1995–2002, January 2005	Periodic	X	X	X
Weapon Use and Violent Crime, 1993–2001, September 2003	Periodic	X	X	X
Bureau of Labor Statistics <http://www.bls.gov>				
100 Years of U.S. Consumer Spending: Data for the Nation, New York City, and Boston, Report 991	Periodic	X	X	
College Enrollment and Work Activity of High School Graduates	Annual	X	X	
Comparative Labor Force Statistics, Ten Countries	Semiannual	X	X	X
Compensation and Working Conditions	Quarterly		X	X
Consumer Expenditure Survey, Integrated Diary and Interview Survey Data	Annual	X	X	X
Consumer Prices: Energy and Food	Monthly	X	X	X
CPI Detailed Report	Monthly		X	X
Employer Costs for Employee Compensation	Annual	X	X	X
Employment and Earnings	Monthly		X	X
Employment and Wages	Annual	X	X	X
Employment Characteristics of Families	Annual	X	X	X
Employment Cost Index	Quarterly	X	X	X
Employment Cost Indexes and Levels	Annual	X	X	X
The Employment Situation	Monthly	X	X	X
Geographic Profile of Employment and Unemployment	Annual	X	X	X
International Comparisons of Hourly Compensation Costs for Production Workers in Manufacturing	Annual	X	X	X
International Comparisons of Manufacturing Productivity and Unit Labor Cost Trends	Annual	X	X	X
Metropolitan Area Employment and Unemployment	Monthly	X	X	X
Monthly Labor Review	Monthly		X	X
National Compensation Survey	Annual	X	X	X
Occupational Injuries and Illnesses in the United States by Industry	Annual	X	X	X
Occupational Projections and Training Data	Biennial	X	X	X
Producer Price Indexes Detailed Report	Monthly		X	X
Productivity and Costs by Industry	Periodic	X	X	X
Selected Service-Providing and Mining Industries, 2005	Annual	X	X	X
Manufacturing, 2005	Annual	X	X	X
Wholesale Trade, Retail Trade, and Food Services and Drinking Places, 2005	Annual	X	X	X
Real Earnings	Monthly	X	X	X
Regional and State Employment and Unemployment	Monthly	X	X	X

858 Appendix I

U.S. Census Bureau, Statistical Abstract of the United States: 2009

Title	Frequency	Paper	Internet PDF	Internet Other formats
Bureau of Labor Statistics—Con.				
Relative Importance of Components in the Consumer Price Indexes	Annual	X	X	X
Union Members	Annual	X	X	X
U.S. Import and Export Price Indexes	Monthly	X	X	X
Usual Weekly Earnings of Wage and Salary Workers	Quarterly	X	X	X
Work Experience of the Population	Annual	X	X	X
Bureau of Land Management				
<http://www.blm.gov/wo/st/en.html>				
Public Land Statistics	Annual	X	X	
Census Bureau				
<http://www.census.gov>				
2002 Economic Census				
Comparative Statistics	Quinquennial	X	X	X
Bridge Between NAICS and SIC	Quinquennial	X	X	X
Business Expenses	Quinquennial	X	X	X
Industry/Geography	Quinquennial		X	X
2002 Economic Census, Company Statistics Series, Survey of Business Owners	Quinquennial	X	X	X
American Indian- and Alaska Native-Owned Firms	Quinquennial	X	X	X
Asian-Owned Firms	Quinquennial	X	X	X
Black-Owned Firms	Quinquennial	X	X	X
Hispanic-Owned Firms	Quinquennial	X	X	X
Native Hawaiian- and Other Pacific Islander-Owned Firms	Quinquennial	X	X	X
American Community Survey Annual Earnings and Poverty Report, 2006	Annual	X	X	
Annual Revision of Monthly Retail and Food Services: Sales and Inventories	Annual		X	
Annual Revision of Monthly Wholesale Distributors: Sales and Inventories	Annual		X	X
Annual Survey of Manufactures	Annual		X	
Census of Governments	Quinquennial	X	X	
Volume 3, No. 2 Compendium of Public Employment	Quinquennial	X	X	
Volume 4, No. 6 Employee-Retirement Systems of State and Local Governments	Quinquennial	X	X	
Volume 3, No. 1 Employment of Major Local Governments	Quinquennial	X	X	
Volume 4, No. 3 Finances of County Governments	Quinquennial	X	X	
Volume 1, No. 1 Government Organization	Quinquennial	X	X	
Volume 4, No. 1 Public Education Finances	Quinquennial	X	X	
Census of Housing Decennial (2000, most recent)	Decennial	X	X	X
Census of Population Decennial (2000, most recent)	Decennial	X	X	X
Consolidated Federal Funds Report (CFFR)	Annual	X	X	X
State and County Areas	Annual	X	X	X
County Business Patterns	Annual		X	X
Current Construction Reports:				
New Residential Construction and New Residential Sales	Annual		X	
Value of Construction Put in Place, C30	Monthly		X	
Residential Improvements and Repairs, C50	Monthly		X	
Current Housing Reports:				
Housing Vacancies, H111	Quarterly		X	X
Who Could Afford to Buy a Home in 2002, H121	Occasional	X	X	X
Survey of Market Absorption of Apartments (SOMA)	Quarterly		X	X
Characteristics of Apartments Completed, H131	Annual	X	X	X
American Housing Survey for the United States, H150	Biennial	X	X	X
American Housing Survey for Selected Metropolitan Areas, H170	Biennial	X	X	X
Current Industrial Reports			X	
Current Population Reports (Series P20 and P23)		X	X	X
Consumer Income and Poverty, P60, and Household Economic Studies, P70		X	X	
Alternative Poverty Estimates in the United States: 2003	Periodic	X	X	
Alternative Income Estimates in the United States: 2003	Periodic	X	X	
Income, Poverty, and Health Insurance Coverage in the United States, 2007	Annual	X	X	X
Economic Census of Outlying Areas	Quinquennial	X	X	
Federal Aid to States (FAS) for Fiscal Year	Annual	X	X	X
Global Population Profile: 2002 (Series WP)		X	X	X
International Briefs (Series IB)		X	X	
International Data Base				X
International Population Reports (Series P95)		X	X	
Manufacturer's Shipments, Inventories, and Orders	Monthly		X	
Manufacturer's Shipments, Inventories, and Orders: 1992–2005	Annual		X	
New York City Housing and Vacancy Survey, 2005	Every 3 years		X	X
Nonemployer Statistics	Annual		X	X
Population Estimates and Projections				X
Quarterly Financial Report for Manufacturing, Mining, and Trade Corporations	Quarterly		X	
Residential Finance Survey, 2001	Every 10 years	X	X	X
Service Annual Survey Report	Annual		X	
Survey of Plant Capacity Utilization (Current Industrial Reports MQ-C1)	Annual		X	
U.S. International Trade in Goods and Services: includes cumulative data			X	X
U.S. Trade With Puerto Rico and U.S. Possessions (FT 895)	Monthly		X	
Vehicle Inventory and Use Survey (discontinued)	Quinquennial	X	X	X
Centers for Disease Control and Prevention, Atlanta, GA				
<http://www.cdc.gov>				
CDC Injury Fact Book		X	X	X
Morbidity and Mortality Weekly Report	Annual	X	X	X
Centers for Medicare and Medicaid Services (CMS)				
<http://www.cms.hhs.gov>				
CMS Statistics	Annual	X	X	
Data Compendium	Annual	X	X	
Health Care Financing Review Medicare and Medicaid Statistical Supplement	Quarterly	X	X	
Health Care Financing Review	Quarterly	X	X	
Trustees' Report	Annual	X	X	
Central Intelligence Agency				
<http://www.cia.gov>				
World Factbook	Annual	X	X	X

Title	Frequency	Paper	Internet PDF	Internet Other formats
Coast Guard (See Department of Homeland Security)				
Comptroller of the Currency <http://www.occ.treas.gov>				
Quarterly Journal	Quarterly		X	X
Office of the Clerk U.S. House of Representatives <http://clerk.house.gov>				
Statistics of the Presidential and Congressional Election	Biennial		X	X
Council of Economic Advisers <http://www.whitehouse.gov>				
Economic Indicators	Monthly	X	X	X
Economic Report of the President	Annual	X	X	
Department of Agriculture, Economic Research Service <http://www.ers.usda.gov>				
Agricultural Income and Finance (Situation and Outlook Report)	Annual		X	
Agricultural Price Reports	Annual	X	X	X
Amber Waves	Periodic	X	X	X
America's Diverse Family Farms: Structure and Finances	Annual	X	X	
Cotton Ginnings	Periodic	X	X	X
Cotton and Wool Yearbook	Annual		X	X
Dairy Yearbook	Periodic	X	X	
Feedgrains Yearbook	Annual	X	X	
Food Spending in American Households (Statistical Bulletin No. 824)	Annual	X	X	
Food Marketing Review, (Agricultural Economic Report No. 743)	Annual	X	X	
Fruit and Tree Nut Yearbook	Annual		X	X
Oil Crops Yearbook	Annual	X	X	
Poultry Yearbook	Annual			X
Red Meat Yearbook	Annual			X
Rice Yearbook	Annual		X	X
Sugar and Sweeteners Yearbook	Annual			X
Situation and Outlook Reports issued for agricultural exports, cotton and wool, dairy, feed, fruit and tree nuts, livestock and poultry, oil crops, rice, sugar and sweeteners, vegetables, wheat, and world agriculture	Periodic	X	X	
Structure and Finances of U.S. Farms: Family Farm Report	Annual	X	X	
Vegetable and Melons Yearbook	Annual		X	X
World Agricultural Supply and Demand Estimates	Monthly	X	X	X
Department of Agriculture, Food and Nutrition Service <http://www.fns.usda.gov/fns/default.htm>				
Characteristics of Food Stamp Households	Annual	X	X	
Food and Consumer Service Programs	Monthly			X
Department of Agriculture, Foreign Agricultural Service <http://www.fas.usda.gov>				
Livestock and Poultry World Markets and Trade	Biannual	X	X	
Department of Agriculture, National Agricultural Statistics Service <http://www.nass.usda.gov>				
Agricultural Chemical Usage	Periodic	X	X	X
Agricultural Statistics	Annual	X	X	
Catfish Production	Annual	X	X	X
Cattle	Biennial	X	X	X
Census of Agriculture	Quinquennial	X	X	
Cherry Production	Annual	X	X	X
Chickens and Eggs	Annual	X	X	X
Citrus Fruits	Annual	X	X	X
Cranberries	Annual	X	X	X
Crop Production Reports	Monthly	X	X	X
Crop Values Report	Annual	X	X	X
Dairy Products	Annual	X	X	X
Farm Labor	Quarterly	X	X	X
Farms, Land in Farms, and Livestock Operations	Annual	X	X	X
Floriculture Crops	Annual	X	X	X
Land Values and Cash Rents	Annual	X	X	X
Livestock Slaughter	Annual	X	X	X
Meat Animals: Production, Disposition, and Income	Annual	X	X	X
Milk Production	Annual	X	X	X
Noncitrus Fruits and Nuts	Biennial	X	X	X
Poultry: Production and Value Summary	Annual	X	X	X
Stock Reports. Stocks of grain, peanuts, potatoes, and rice	Periodic	X	X	X
Trout Production	Annual	X	X	X
Turkeys: Hatchery and Raised	Annual	X	X	X
Usual Planting and Harvesting Dates	Periodic	X	X	X
Vegetable Reports	Periodic	X	X	X
Weekly Weather and Crop Bulletin Report	Weekly	X	X	
Winter Wheat Seedlings	Monthly	X	X	X
Department of Agriculture, Natural Resources and Conservation Service <http://www.nrcs.usda.gov>				
National Resources Inventory	Periodic	X		X
Department of Defense <http://www.defenselink.mil/pubs>				
Foreign Military Sales and Military Assistance Facts	Annual			X
Personnel Statistics	Annual		X	
Department of Education <http://www.ed.gov/index.jhtml>				
Department of Education, Rehabilitation Services Administration				
Caseload Statistics of State Vocational Rehabilitation Agencies in Fiscal Year	Annual	X	X	X
Department of Health and Human Services <http://www.os.hhs.gov>				

Title	Frequency	Paper	Internet PDF	Internet Other formats
Department of Health and Human Services—Con.				
Annual Report.	Annual	X		
Department of Homeland Security (DHS)				
<http://www.dhs.gov/index.shtm>				
Budget in Brief.	Annual	X	X	
Department of Homeland Security, Coast Guard				
<http://www.uscg.mil/default.asp>				
Fact File.		X	X	X
Department of Homeland Security, Office of Immigration Statistics				
<http://www.dhs.gov/ximgtn/statistics/>				
Yearbook of Immigration Statistics.	Annual	X	X	
Department of Housing and Urban Development				
<http://www.hud.gov>				
Survey of Mortgage Lending Activity	Monthly	X		X
Department of Labor				
<http://www.dol.gov>				
Annual Report of the Secretary.	Annual	X	X	X
Department of State				
<http://www.state.gov>				
United States Contribution to International Organizations.	Annual			X
Department of Transportation				
<http://www.dot.gov>				
Air Travel Consumer Report.	Monthly	X	X	X
Airport Activity Statistics of Certified Route Air Carriers	Annual	X		X
Transportation Safety Information Report	Quarterly	X		X
U.S. International Air Travel Statistics.	Quarterly	X	X	X
Wage Statistics of Class I Railroads in the United States.	Annual	X	X	
Department of the Treasury, Alcohol and Tobacco Tax and Trade Bureau				
<http://www.atf.treas.gov>				
Alcohol and Tobacco Summary Statistics	Annual	X		
Tobacco Products Monthly Statistical Releases		X		
Department of the Treasury, Bureau of Public Debt				
<http://www.publicdebt.treas.gov>				
Monthly Statement of the Public Debt of the United States.	Monthly	X	X	X
Department of the Treasury, Financial Management Services				
<http://www.fms.treas.gov>				
Active Foreign Credits of the United States Government	Quarterly	X		
Combined Statement of Receipts, Outlays, and Balances	Annual	X	X	X
Monthly Treasury Statement of Receipts and Outlays of the United States Government	Monthly	X	X	X
Treasury Bulletin	Quarterly	X	X	X
Financial Report of the United States Government	Annual	X	X	
Department of Veterans Affairs				
<http://www.va.gov>				
Disability Compensation, Pension, and Death Pension Data.	Annual			X
Government Life Insurance Programs for Veterans and Members of the Service	Annual			X
Selected Compensation and Pension Data by State of Residence.	Annual			X
Veterans Affairs Annual Accountability Report	Annual	X	X	X
Drug Enforcement Administration				
<http://www.whitehousedrugpolicy.gov>				
Drug Abuse and Law Enforcement Statistics	Irregular	X	X	X
Employment and Training Administration				
<http://www.doleta.gov>				
Unemployment Insurance Claims	Weekly			X
Energy Information Administration				
<http://www.eia.doe.gov>				
Annual Energy Outlook.	Annual	X	X	X
Annual Energy Review.	Annual	X	X	X
Annual Coal Report.	Annual		X	X
Electric Power Annual.	Annual		X	X
Electric Power Monthly.	Monthly		X	X
Electric Sales, Revenue and Retail Price	Annual			X
Emissions of Greenhouse Gases in the U.S.	Annual		X	X
International Energy Annual.	Annual			X
International Energy Outlook.	Annual	X	X	X
Monthly Energy Review.	Monthly		X	X
Performance Profiles of Major Energy Producers	Annual		X	X
Petroleum Marketing Annual.	Monthly		X	X
Petroleum Supply Annual Volume 1.	Annual		X	X
Petroleum Supply Annual Volume 2 (Web only)	Annual		X	X
Petroleum Supply Monthly.	Monthly		X	X
Quarterly Coal Report.	Quarterly		X	X
Renewable Energy Annual.	Annual		X	
Residential Energy Consumption Survey	Quadrennial		X	X
State Electricity Profiles.	Annual		X	X
State Energy Data Report.	Annual		X	X
State Energy Price and Expenditure Report	Annual		X	X
U.S. Crude Oil, Natural Gas, and Natural Gas Liquids Reserves.	Annual		X	X
Weekly Coal Production, Web only	Weekly		X	X
Environmental Protection Agency				
<http://www.epa.gov/>				
Air Quality Data.	Annual			X
Drinking Water Infrastructure Needs Survey	Periodic	X	X	

U.S. Census Bureau, Statistical Abstract of the United States: 2009

Title	Frequency	Paper	Internet PDF	Internet Other formats
Environmental Protection Agency—Con.				
Needs Survey, Conveyance and Treatment of Municipal Wastewater Summaries of Technical Data	Biennial		X	
Toxics Release Inventory	Annual		X	X
National Water Quality Inventory: 2000 Report (EPA-841-T-01-001)	Biennial	X	X	
Export-Import Bank of the United States <http://www.exim.gov/>				
Annual Report	Annual	X	X	
Report to the U.S. Congress on Export Credit Competition and the Export-Import Bank of the United States	Annual	X	X	
Farm Credit Administration <http://www.fca.gov/FCA-HomePage.htm>				
Annual Report on the Farm Credit System	Annual	X	X	
Federal Bureau of Investigation <http://www.fbi.gov/ucr/ucr.htm>				
Crime in the United States	Annual		X	X
Hate Crime Statistics	Annual		X	X
Law Enforcement Officers Killed and Assaulted	Annual		X	X
Federal Communications Commission <http://www.fcc.gov/>				
Annual Report	Annual	X	X	
Statistics of Communications Common Carriers	Annual	X	X	
Telecommunications Industry Revenue	Annual	X	X	
Trends in Telephone Service	Annual	X	X	
Trends in the International Telecommunications Industry	Annual	X	X	
High-Speed Services for Internet Access	Annual	X	X	
Federal Deposit Insurance Corporation <http://www.fdic.gov/>				
Annual Report	Annual	X	X	
FDIC Quarterly	Quarterly	X	X	
Historical Statistics on Banking	Annual		X	
Quarterly Banking Profile	Quarterly	X	X	X
Statistics on Banking	Quarterly			X
Summary of Deposits	Annual			X
Federal Highway Administration <http://www.fhwa.dot.gov>				
Highway Statistics	Annual	X	X	
Federal Railroad Administration <http://www.fra.dot.gov> <http://safetydata.fra.dot.gov/officeofsafety>				
Railroad Safety Statistics	Annual	X	X	X
Fish and Wildlife Service <http://www.fws.gov/>				
Federal Aid in Fish and Wildlife Restoration	Annual	X	X	
National Survey of Fishing, Hunting, and Wildlife Associated Recreation	Quinquennial	X	X	
Forest Service <http://www.fs.fed.us/>				
An Analysis of the Timber Situation in the United States 1996–2050	Periodic			X
Land Areas of the National Forest System	Annual	X		X
U.S. Timber Production, Trade, Consumption, and Price Statistics 2001	Biennial	X	X	
General Services Administration, Federal Real Property Council <http://www.gsa.gov/Portal/gsa/ep/home.do?tabId=5>				
Federal Real Property Profile	Annual		X	X
Geological Survey <http://ask.usgs.gov>				
A Statistical Summary of Data from the U.S. Geological Surveys National Water Quality Networks (Open-File Report 83-533)		X		
Estimated Use of Water in the United States in 2000	Quinquennial	X	X	X
Mineral Commodity Summaries	Annual	X		X
Mineral Industry Surveys	Monthly	X	X	X
Minerals Yearbook	Monthly	X	X	X
Internal Revenue Service <http://www.irs.gov>				
Corporation Income Tax Returns	Annual	X	X	X
Individual Income Tax Returns	Annual	X	X	X
IRS Data Book	Annual	X	X	X
Statistics of Income Bulletin	Quarterly	X	X	X
International Trade Administration, Office of Travel and Tourism Industries <http://www.tinet.ita.doc.gov>				
Travel Data reports			X	
International Trade Commission <http://www.usitc.gov>				
Recent Trends in U.S. Services	Periodic	X	X	
Synthetic Organic Chemicals, U.S. Production and Sales	Annual	X	X	
Library of Congress <http://www.loc.gov/index.html>				
Annual Report	Annual	X	X	
Maritime Administration <http://www.marad.dot.gov>				
Annual Report	Annual	X	X	
Cargo-Carrying U.S. Flag Fleet by Area of Operation	Semiannual	X	X	X
Merchant Fleet Ocean-Going Vessels 1,000 Gross Tons and Over	Quarterly			X
Seafaring Wage Rates	Biennial	X	X	

862 Appendix I

Title	Frequency	Paper	Internet PDF	Internet Other formats
Mine Safety and Health Administration <http://www.msha.gov>				
Informational Reports by Mining Industry: Coal; Metallic Minerals; Nonmetallic Minerals (except stone and coal); Stone, Sand, and Gravel	Annual			X
Mine Injuries and Worktime (Some preliminary data)	Quarterly	X		X
National Aeronautics and Space Administration <http://ifmp.nasa.gov>				
Annual Procurement Report	Annual	X	X	
The Civil Service Work Force		X	X	
National Center for Education Statistics <http://nces.ed.gov>				
Characteristics of the 100 Largest Public Elementary and Secondary School Districts in the United States	Annual	X	X	X
Characteristics of Private Schools in the United States, 2005–2006	Periodic	X	X	
College and University Library Survey				X
Computer and Internet Use by Students	Biennial	X	X	
The Condition of Education	Annual	X	X	
Digest of Education Statistics	Annual	X	X	
Enrollment in Postsecondary Institutions, Graduation Rates, and Financial Statistics	Annual		X	
Indicators of School Crime and Safety	Annual	X	X	
National Education Statistics Quarterly (last edition 4th quarter 2005)	Quarterly			X
The Nation's Report Card: Civics 2006	Periodic	X	X	
The Nation's Report Card: Economics 2006	Periodic	X	X	
The Nation's Report Card: History 2006	Periodic	X	X	
The Nation's Report Card: Mathematics 2007	Periodic	X	X	
The Nation's Report Card: Reading 2007	Periodic	X	X	
The Nation's Report Card: Science 2005	Periodic	X	X	
The Nation's Report Card: Writing 2007	Periodic	X	X	
Projections of Education Statistics	Annual	X	X	X
School and Staffing Survey:	Quadrennial			X
Characteristics of Schools, Districts, Teachers, Principals, and School Libraries in the United States	Annual	X	X	
Status and Trends in the Education of Racial and Ethnic Minorities		X	X	
National Center for Health Statistics <http://www.cdc.gov/nchs/>				
Ambulatory Care Visits to Physician Offices, Hospital Outpatient Departments, and Emergency Departments	Annual	X	X	
Health: United States	Annual	X	X	
Health Characteristics of Adults 55 Years of Age and Over	Periodic	X	X	
Fertility, Family Planning, and Reproductive Health of U.S. Women: Data from the 2002 National Survey of Family Growth	Periodic		X	X
National Hospital Discharge Survey: Annual Summary	Annual		X	
National Vital Statistics Reports (NVSR)	Monthly		X	
Vital and Health Statistics			X	
Series 10: Health Interview Survey Statistics	Annual	X	X	
Series 11: Health and Nutrition Examination Survey Statistics	Irregular	X	X	
Series 13: Data from National Health Care Survey	Irregular	X	X	
Series 14: Data on Health Resources: Manpower and Facilities	Irregular	X	X	
Series 20: Mortality Data	Irregular	X	X	
Series 21: Natality, Marriage, and Divorce Data	Irregular	X	X	
Series 23: Data from the National Survey of Family Growth	Irregular	X	X	
National Credit Union Administration <http://www.ncua.gov>				
Annual Report	Annual	X	X	
Yearend Statistics	Annual	X	X	
National Endowment for the Arts <http://www.nea.gov>				
National Endowment for the Arts, Annual Report	Annual			X
The Performing Arts in the GDP, 2002	Periodic	X	X	
Artist Labor Force by State, 2000	Periodic	X	X	
Artist Employment, 2000–2002	Periodic	X	X	
The Arts in the GDP	Periodic	X	X	
Demographic Characteristics of Art Attendance, 2002	Periodic	X	X	
2002 Survey of Public Participation in the Arts	Periodic	X	X	
National Endowment for the Humanities <ttp://www.neh.gov>				
Budget Request	Annual	X		X
National Guard Bureau <http://www.ngb.army.mil/default.aspx>				
Annual Review of the Chief	Annual	X	X	
National Highway Traffic Safety Administration <http://www.nhtsa.dot.gov>				
Traffic Safety Facts	Annual	X	X	
National Oceanic and Atmospheric Administration <http://www.lib.noaa.gov>				
Climates of the World, HCS 6-4	Monthly			X
Comparative Climatic Data	Annual		X	X
Daily Normals of Temp, Precip, HDD, & CDD/Clim 84	Periodic			X
Fisheries of the United States	Annual	X	X	
General Summary of Tornadoes	Annual			X
Hourly Precipitation Data Monthly with annual summary; for each state	Monthly			X
Local Climatological Data Monthly with annual summary; for major cities	Monthly			X
Monthly Climatic Data for the World	Monthly			X
Monthly Normals of Temp, Precip, HDD, & CDD/Clim 84	Periodic		X	X

Title	Frequency	Paper	Internet PDF	Internet Other formats
National Oceanic and Atmospheric Administration—Con.				
Our Living Oceans	Periodic	X	X	
Storm Data	Monthly			X
U.S. Climate Normals	Daily	X	X	X
Weekly Weather and Crop Bulletin National Summary	Weekly	X	X	
National Park Service				
<http://www.nps.gov/>				
Federal Recreation Fee Report	Annual	X		
National Park Statistical Abstract	Annual	X	X	
National Science Foundation				
<http://www.nsf.gov/statistics/>				
Academic Institutional Profiles	Annual		X	X
Academic Research and Development Expenditures	Annual		X	X
Characteristics of Doctoral Scientists and Engineers in the United States	Biennial		X	X
Characteristics of Recent Science/Engineering Graduates	Biennial		X	X
Federal Funds for Research and Development	Annual		X	X
Federal Research and Development Funding by Budget Function	Annual		X	X
Federal Science and Engineering Support to Universities, Colleges, and Nonprofit Institutions	Annual		X	X
Graduate Students and Postdoctorates in Science and Engineering	Annual		X	X
National Patterns of Research & Development Resources	Annual		X	X
Research and Development in Industry	Annual		X	X
Science and Engineering Degrees	Annual		X	X
Science and Engineering Degrees, by Race/Ethnicity of Recipients	Annual		X	X
Science and Engineering Doctorate Awards	Annual		X	X
Science and Engineering Indicators	Biennial	X	X	X
Science and Engineering State Profiles	Annual		X	X
Science Resources Statistics Info Briefs (various topics)	Frequent	X	X	X
Scientific and Engineering Research Facilities at Universities and Colleges	Biennial		X	X
Women, Minorities, and Persons with Disabilities in Science and Engineering	Biennial		X	X
National Transportation Safety Board				
<http://www.ntsb.gov>				
Annual Review of Aircraft Accident Data: U.S. Air Carriers Operations	Annual		X	
Annual Review of Aircraft Accident Data: U.S. General Aviation	Annual		X	
Office of Juvenile Justice and Delinquency Prevention				
<http://ojjdp.ncjrs.org/>				
Highlights of the 2006 National Youth Gang Survey (FS-200805)	Annual		X	X
Juvenile Arrests 2004 (Bulletin, NCJ 214563)	Annual	X	X	X
Victims of Violent Juvenile Crime (Bulletin, NCJ 201628)	Periodic	X	X	X
Office of Management and Budget				
<http://www.whitehouse.gov/omb>				
The Budget of the United States Government	Annual	X	X	
Office of Personnel Management				
<http://www.opm.gov>				
Demographic Profile of the Federal Workforce	Biennial		X	X
Employment and Trends	Bimonthly		X	X
The Fact Book	Annual		X	X
Statistical Abstract for the Federal Employee Benefit Programs	Annual			X
Work Years and Personnel Costs	Annual		X	X
Patent and Trademark Office				
<http://www.uspto.gov>				
Technology Assessment and Forecast Reports		X	X	X
All Technologies (Utility Patents)	Annual	X	X	X
Patent Counts by Country/State and Year, Utility Patents Report	Annual	X	X	X
Patenting Trends in the United States	Annual	X		
Railroad Retirement Board, Chicago, IL				
<http://www.rrb.gov/default.asp>				
Annual Report	Annual		X	
Quarterly Benefit Statistics	Quarterly		X	
Securities and Exchange Commission				
<http://www.sec.gov/about.shtml>				
Select SEC and Market Data	Annual		X	
Small Business Administration				
<http://www.sba.gov>				
Annual Report	Annual	X		X
Handbook of Small Business Data		X	X	
Quarterly Indicators	Annual	X	X	X
Small Business and Micro Business Lending	Annual	X	X	X
State and Territory Small Business Profiles	Annual	X	X	X
The Small Business Economy	Annual	X	X	X
The State of Small Business	Annual	X	X	
Social Security Administration				
<http://www.ssa.gov>				
Annual Statistical Report on the Social Security Disability Insurance Program	Annual	X	X	X
Annual Statistical Supplement to the Social Security Bulletin	Annual	X	X	X
Children Receiving SSI	Annual	X	X	X
Congressional Statistics	Annual	X	X	X
Fast Facts & Figures about Social Security	Annual	X	X	X
Income of the Population 55 and over	Biennially	X	X	X
OASDI Beneficiaries by State and County	Annual	X	X	X
Social Security Bulletin	Quarterly	X	X	X
State Assistance Programs for SSI Recipients	Annual	X	X	X
SSI Annual Statistical Report	Annual	X	X	X
SSI Disabled Recipients Who Work	Annual	X	X	X
SSI Recipients by State and County	Annual	X	X	X

Title	Frequency	Paper	Internet	
			PDF	Other formats
Substance Abuse and Mental Health Services Administration <http://www.samhsa.gov/>				
National Survey on Drug Use and Health	Annual	X	X	X
National Survey on Substance Abuse Treatment Services (N-SSATS)	Annual	X	X	X

NONGOVERNMENT

Title	Frequency	Paper	PDF	Other formats
Aerospace Industries Association, Washington, DC <http://www.aia-aerospace.org>				
Aerospace Facts and Figures	Annual	X	X	X
Aerospace Industry Year-End Review and Forecast	Annual		X	
Commercial Helicopter Shipments	Annual		X	
Employment in the Aerospace Industry	Quarterly		X	
Exports of Aerospace Products	Quarterly		X	
Imports of Aerospace Products	Quarterly		X	
Manufacturing Production, Capacity, and Utilization in Aerospace and Aircraft and Parts	Quarterly		X	
Orders, Shipments, Backlog, and Inventories for Aircraft, Missiles, and Parts	Quarterly		X	
Air Transport Association of America, Inc., Washington, DC <http://www.airlines.org>				
Air Transport Association, Annual Report	Annual		X	
The Alan Guttmacher Institute, New York, NY <http://www.guttmacher.org>				
Perspectives on Sexual and Reproductive Health	Quarterly	X	X	X
American Bureau of Metal Statistics, Inc., Secaucus, NJ <http://www.abms.com>				
Non-Ferrous Metal Yearbook	Annual	X		X
American Council of Life Insurers, Washington, DC <http://www.acli.com/ACLI/DefaultNotLoggedIn.htm>				
Life Insurers Fact Book	Annual	X	X	
American Dental Association, Chicago, IL <http://www.ada.org>				
Dental Students Register	Annual	X		
Distribution of Dentists in the United States by Region and State	Triennial	X		
Survey of Dental Practice	Annual	X		
American Forest & Paper Association, Washington, DC <http://www.afandpa.org>				
Annual Statistical Summary of Recovered Paper Utilization	Annual	X	X	
Statistics of Paper, Paperboard, and Wood Pulp	Monthly	X	X	
American Gas Association, Washington, DC <http://www.aga.org>				
Gas Facts	Annual	X	X	X
American Iron and Steel Institute, Washington, DC <http://www.steel.org/AM/Template.cfm?Section=Home>				
Annual Statistical Report	Annual	X		
American Jewish Committee, New York, NY <http://www.ajc.org/site/c.ijITI2PHKoG/b.685761/k.CB97/Home.htm>				
American Jewish Year Book	Annual	X	X	
American Medical Association, Chicago, IL <http://www.ama-assn.org>				
Physician Characteristics and Distribution in the U.S.	Annual	X		
State Medical Licensure Statistics, and License Requirements	Annual	X		
American Osteopathic Association, Chicago, IL <http://www.osteopathic.org/index.cfm>				
American Osteopathic Association Fact Sheet	Biennial	X	X	
American Petroleum Institute, Washington, DC <http://www.api.org>				
The Basic Petroleum Data Book (online subscription)	Annual	X		
Joint Association Survey on Drilling Costs (JA5)	Annual	X		
Petroleum Industry Environmental Report	Annual	X		X
Quarterly Well Completion Report (online subscription)	Quarterly	X	X	
American Public Transportation Association, Washington, DC <http://www.apta.com>				
Public Transportation Fact Book	Annual	X	X	
Association for Manufacturing Technology, McLean, VA <http://www.amtonline.org>				
Economic Handbook of the Machine Tool Industry 2003–2004 (online version by subscription only)	Annual		X	
Association of American Railroads, Washington, DC <http://www.aar.org>				
Analysis of Class I Railroads	Annual	X	X	X
Cars of Revenue Freight Loaded	Weekly		X	X
Freight Commodity Statistics, Class I Railroads in the United States	Annual	X	X	X
Yearbook of Railroad Facts	Annual	X	X	
Association of Racing Commissioners International, Inc., Lexington, KY <http://www.arci.com>				
Statistical Reports on Greyhound Racing in the United States	Annual	X		
Statistical Reports on Horse Racing in the United States	Annual	X		
Statistical Reports on Jai Alai in the United States	Annual	X		
Book Industry Study Group, Inc., New York, NY <http://www.bisg.org>				
Book Industry Trends	Annual	X		

U.S. Census Bureau, Statistical Abstract of the United States: 2009

Title	Frequency	Paper	Internet PDF	Internet Other formats
Book Industry Study Group, Inc., New York, NY—Con.				
Used-Book Sales.	Periodic	X		
Boy Scouts of America, Irving, TX				
<http://www.scouting.org>				
Annual Report	Annual	X		X
The Bureau of National Affairs, Inc., Washington, DC				
<http://www.bna.com>				
Basic Patterns in Union Contracts	Annual	X		
BNA's Employment Outlook	Quarterly	X		
BNA's Job Absence and Turnover	Quarterly	X		
Directory of U.S. Labor Organizations	Annual	X		
National Labor Relations Board Election Statistics	Annual	X		
Union Membership & Earnings Data Book	Annual	X		
Source Book on Collective Bargaining	Annual	X		
Carl H. Pforzheimer & Co, New York, NY				
Comparative Oil Company Statistics Annual	Annual	X		
Chronicle of Higher Education, Inc., Washington, DC				
<http://chronicle.com>				
Almanac.	Annual	X		X
College Board, New York, NY				
<http://www.collegeboard.com>				
2007 College-Bound Seniors Total Group Profile Report	Annual	X	X	
Commodity Research Bureau, Logical Systems, Inc., Chicago, IL				
<http://www.crbtrader.com>				
Commodity Year Book Update CD	Quarterly			
CRB Commodity Index Report	Weekly	X		
CRB Commodity Year Book	Annual	X		
CRB Futures Perspective.	Weekly	X	X	
Electronic Futures Trend Analyzer	Daily			X
Final Markets-End-of-Day Data	Daily			X
Futures Market Service	Weekly		X	
The Conference Board, New York, NY				
<http://www.conference-board.org>				
<http://www.conference-board.org/economics>				
<http://www.conference-board.org/economics/bci>				
Business Cycle Indicators	Monthly	X	X	
Corporate Contributions.	Annual	X	X	
Productivity, Employment, and Income in the World's Economies	Annual	X	X	
CQ Press, Washington, DC				
<http://www.cqpress.com/gethome.asp>				
America Votes.	Biennial	X		
Consumer Electronics Association (Electronic Industries Alliance), Arlington, VA				
<http://www.ce.org>				
Consumer Electronics Association (CEA) Sales and Forecasts	Semiannual	X	X	
The Council of State Governments, Lexington, KY				
<http://www.csg.org>				
The Book of the States	Annual	X	X	
State Administrative Officials Classified by Function	Annual	X		
State Elective Officials and the Legislatures	Annual	X		
State Legislative Leadership, Committees, and Staff	Annual	X		
Credit Union National Association, Inc., Madison, WI				
<http://www.cuna.org>				
The Credit Union Ranking Report	Annual	X		
Credit Union Services Profile	Annual	X		
Operating Ratios and Spreads	Semiannual	X		
Dow Jones & Co., New York, NY.				
<http://online.wsj.com/public/us?>				
Wall Street Journal.	Daily	X		X
Edison Electric Institute, Washington, DC				
<http://www.eei.org>				
Statistical Yearbook of the Electric Power Industry	Annual	X	X	X
Editor & Publisher Co., New York, NY				
<http://www.editorandpublisher.com/eandp/index.jsp>				
Editor & Publisher	Monthly	X		
International Year Book	Annual	X		X
Market Guide.	Annual	X		
Euromonitor International, London, England				
<http://www.euromonitor.com>				
Consumer Asia	Annual	X		
Consumer China	Annual	X		
Consumer Eastern Europe	Annual	X		
Consumer Europe	Annual	X		
Consumer International	Annual	X		
Consumer Latin America	Annual	X		
European Marketing Data and Statistics	Annual	X		
International Marketing Data and Statistics	Annual	X		
Latin America Marketing Data and Statistics	Annual	X		
World Consumer Expenditure Patterns	Annual	X		
World Consumer Income Patterns	Annual	X		
World Economic Factbook	Annual	X		
World Retail Data and Statistics	Annual	X		

866 Appendix I

Title	Frequency	Paper	Internet PDF	Other formats
Federal National Mortgage Association, Washington, DC <http://www.fanniemae.com>				
Annual Report	Annual	X	X	
Food and Agriculture Organization of the United Nations, Rome, Italy <http://www.fao.org>				
Fertilizer Yearbook	Annual	X		
Production Yearbook.	Annual	X		
Trade Yearbook	Annual	X		
Yearbook of Fishery Statistics	Annual	X		
Yearbook of Forest Products	Annual	X		
The Foundation Center, New York, NY <http://www.foundationcenter.org>				
Foundation Yearbook	Annual	X		
FC Stats.	Annual			X
General Aviation Manufacturers Association, Washington, DC <http://www.gama.aero/home.php>				
Shipment Report	Quarterly	X		X
Statistical Databook	Annual	X	X	
Girl Scouts of the USA, New York, NY <http://www.girlscouts.org>				
Annual Report	Annual	X	X	
Giving Institute (previously AAFRC), Indianapolis, IN <http://www.aafrc.org>				
Giving USA	Annual	X		X
Health Forum, an American Hospital Association Company, Chicago, IL <http://www.ahadata.com>				
Annual Report	Annual	X		
AHA Hospital Statistics	Annual	X		X
Independent Petroleum Association of America, Washington, DC <http://www.ipaa.org>				
Domestic Oil and Gas Trends.	Monthly	X		
Oil & Natural Gas Production in Your State	Annual	X	X	X
U.S. Petroleum Statistics	Annual	X	X	X
Information Today, Inc., Medford, NJ <http://www.infotoday.com>				
American Library Directory	Annual	X		
Bowker Annual Library and Book Trade Almanac . . .	Annual	X		
Institute for Criminal Justice Ethics, New York, NY <http://www.lib.jjay.cuny.edu/cje>				
Criminal Justice Ethics	Semiannual	X		
Insurance Information Institute, New York, NY <http://www.iii.org>				
The I.I.I. Insurance Fact Book.	Annual	X		X
Inter-American Development Bank, Washington, DC <http://www.iadb.org>				
Annual Report	Annual	X	X	
Economic and Social Progress in Latin America. . . .	Annual	X		
International Air Transport Association <http://www.iata.org/index.htm>				
World Air Transport Statistics	Annual	X	X	X
International City Management Association, Washington, DC <http://www.icma.org>				
Compensation: An Annual Report on Local Government Executive Salaries and Fringe Benefits.	Annual			X
Municipal Year Book	Annual	X		
International Labour Organization, Geneva, Switzerland <http://www.ilo.org/global/lang—en/index.htm>				
Yearbook of Labour Statistics	Annual	X		X
International Monetary Fund, Washington, DC <http://www.imf.org>				
Annual Report	Annual	X	X	X
Balance of Payments Statistics.	Monthly	X		
Direction of Trade Statistics.	Monthly	X		
Government Finance Statistics Yearbook	Annual	X		
International Financial Statistics	Monthly	X		
International Telecommunication Union, Geneva, Switzerland <http://www.itu.int/home/index.html>				
ITU Yearbook of Statistics	Annual	X		
World Telecommunication Indicators	Annual	X		
Investment Company Institute, Washington, DC <http://www.ici.org>				
Mutual Fund Fact Book	Annual	X	X	
Jane's Information Group, Coulsdon, UK, and Alexandria, VA <http://www.janes.com>				
Jane's Air-Launched Weapons	Monthly	X		X
Jane's All the World's Aircraft	Annual	X		X
Jane's Armour and Artillery.	Annual	X		X
Jane's Avionics	Annual	X		X
Jane's Fighting Ships	Annual	X		X
Jane's Infantry Weapons	Annual	X		X
Jane's Merchant Ships	Annual	X		X
Jane's Military Communications	Annual	X		X
Jane's Military Logistics.	Annual	X		X

U.S. Census Bureau, Statistical Abstract of the United States: 2009

Title	Frequency	Paper	PDF	Other formats
			Internet	
Jane's Information Group, Coulsdon, UK, and Alexandria, VA—Con.				
Jane's Military Training Systems	Annual	X		X
Jane's NATO Handbook	Annual	X		X
Jane's Spaceflight Directory	Annual	X		X
Joint Center for Housing Studies of Harvard University, Cambridge, MA <http://www.jchs.harvard.edu/>				
The State of the Nation's Housing	Annual	X	X	X
Joint Center for Political and Economic Studies, Washington, DC <http://www.jointcenter.org>				
Black Elected Officials: A Statistical Summary	Annual	X	X	
McGraw-Hill Construction Dodge, a Division of the McGraw-Hill Companies, New York, NY <http://www.construction.com> <http://www.dodge.construction.com/Analytics/>				
Dodge Construction Potential (online subscription)	Monthly	X	X	X
National Academy of Sciences, Washington, DC <http://www.pnas.org>				
Summary Report Doctorate Recipients From United States' Universities	Annual	X		
National Academy of Social Insurance, Washington, DC <http://www.nasi.org>				
Workers' Compensation, Benefits, Coverage, and Costs	Annual	X	X	
National Association of Home Builders, Washington, DC <http://www.nahb.org>				
Home Builders Forecast (online subscription)	Monthly			X
Housing Economics (online subscription)	Monthly			X
Housing Market Statistics (online subscription)	Monthly			X
National Association of Latino Elected and Appointed Officials, Washington, DC <http://www.naleo.org>				
National Directory of Latino Elected Officials	Annual		X	X
National Association of Realtors, Washington, DC <http://www.realtor.org>				
Real Estate Outlook: Market Trends & Insights. (discontinued)	Monthly	X		X
Real Estate Insights	Monthly		X	X
Research Update				
Economist's Commentary	Daily			X
Profile of Home Buyer and Sellers	Annual	X		
Investment and Vacation Home Buyers Survey	Annual		X	
NAR Member Survey	Annual	X		
National Association of State Budget Officers, Washington, DC <http://www.nasbo.org>				
State Expenditure Report	Annual	X	X	
Fiscal Survey of the States	Semiannual	X	X	
National Association of State Park Directors, Raleigh, NC <http://www.naspd.org>				
Annual Information Exchange	Annual		X	X
National Catholic Educational Association, Washington, DC <http://www.ncea.org>				
Catholic Schools in America	Annual		X	X
United States Catholic Elementary and Secondary Schools Staffing and Enrollment	Annual	X		X
U.S. Catholic Elementary Schools and Their Finances	Biennial			
U.S. Catholic Secondary Schools and Their Finances	Biennial	X		
National Council of Churches USA, New York, NY <http://www.ncccusa.org>				
Yearbook of American and Canadian Churches	Annual	X		X
National Education Association, Washington, DC <http://www.nea.org/index.html>				
Rankings of the States and Estimates of School Statistics	Annual	X	X	
Status of the American Public School Teacher, 2000–2001	Quinquennial	X	X	
National Fire Protection Association, Quincy, MA <http://www.nfpa.org>				
NFPA Journal	Bimonthly			X
National Golf Foundation, Jupiter, FL <http://www.ngf.org/cgi/home.asp>				
Golf Consumer Profile	Annual		X	
Golf Facilities in the U.S.	Annual	X	X	
National Marine Manufacturers Association, Chicago, IL <http://www.nmma.org>				
Boating (A Statistical Report on America's Top Family Sport)	Annual	X		X
U.S. Recreational Boat Registration Statistics	Annual	X	X	
National Restaurant Association, Washington, DC <http://www.restaurant.org>				
Quick-Service Restaurant Trends	Annual	X		
Restaurant Economic Trends (online subscriptions)	Monthly			X
Restaurant Industry Forecast	Annual	X		
Restaurant Industry in Review	Annual	X	X	X
Restaurant Industry Operations Report	Annual	X		
Restaurant Industry Pocket Factbook	Annual			
Restaurant Industry 2015, 2005	Annual	X		
Restaurant Performance Index	Monthly	X		X
Restaurant Spending	Annual	X		
State of the Restaurant Industry Work Force	Annual	X		
Tableservice Restaurant Trends	Annual	X		

868   Appendix I

Title	Frequency	Paper	Internet PDF	Internet Other formats

Title	Frequency	Paper	PDF	Other formats
National Restaurant Association, Washington, DC—Con.				
The Economic Impact of the Nation's Eating and Drinking Places	Annual	X		
Hourly Wages for Food Service Occupations	Annual	X		
Research News and Numbers	Monthy	X		
National Safety Council, Itasca, IL				
<http://www.nsc.org>				
Injury Facts	Annual	X		X
National Sporting Goods Association, Mt. Prospect, IL				
<http://www.nsga.org/				
The Sporting Goods Market in 2008	Annual	X	X	
Sports Participation in 2007	Annual	X	X	
New York Stock Exchange, Inc., New York, NY				
<http://www.nyse.com>				
Fact Book (online subscription)	Annual	X	X	
The New York Times Almanac, 2008	Annual	X		
Organisation for Economic Cooperation and Development, Paris, France				
<http://caliban.sourceoecd.org/vl=2166835/cl=28/nw=1/rpsv/home.htm>				
OECD-FAO Agricultural Outlook	Annual	X		X
Bank Profitability: Financial Statements of Banks, 1924–2003	Biannual	X		X
Central Government Debt: Statistical Yearbook, 1996–2005	Annual	X		X
Coal Information	Annual	X		X
CO$_2$ Emissions From Fuel Combustion, 1971–2004	Annual	X		X
Communications Outlook	Biannual	X		X
DAC Journal	Quarterly	X	X	
Education at a Glance: OECD Indicators	Annual	X		X
Electricity Information	Annual	X		X
Energy Balances of Non-OECD Countries	Annual	X		X
Energy Balances of OECD Countries	Annual	X		X
Energy Prices and Taxes	Quarterly	X	X	
Energy Statistics of Non-OECD Countries	Annual	X	X	X
Energy Statistics of OECD Countries	Annual	X	X	X
Environmental Data Compendium	Annual	X		X
Environmental Outlook	Sporadic	X	X	
Financial Market Trends	Triennial	X	X	
Geographical Distribution of Financial Flows to Aid Recipients	Annual	X		
Historical Statistics, 1970–2000. 2001 Edition (discontinued as of 2001)		X	X	X
Information Technology Outlook, 2002 Edition	Biennial	X	X	X
Insurance Statistics Yearbook	Annual	X	X	X
International Development Statistics	Annual			X
Internal Migration Outlook	Annual	X	X	
International Trade by Commodity Statistics	Annual	X	X	
Iron and Steel Industry in 2002, 2004 Edition	Annual			
Labor Force Statistics	Annual	X	X	
Main Economic Indicators	Monthly	X	X	
Main Science and Technology Indicators, Vol. 2003	Biennial	X	X	
Measuring Globalisation: The Role of Multinationals in OECD Countries	One time			
Monthly Statistics of International Trade	Monthly	X	X	
National Accounts of OECD Countries	Annual			
Volume I: Main Aggregates		X	X	X
Volume II: Detailed Tables		X	X	X
Volume IIIa: Financial Accounts	Annual		X	X
Volume IIIb: Financial Balance Sheets	Annual		X	X
Volume IV: Summary of General Aggregates and Balances			X	X
Natural Gas Information	Annual	X	X	X
Nuclear Energy Data	Annual	X		
OECD Economic Outlook	Biennial	X		X
OECD Economic Studies	Annual	X		X
OECD Economic Surveys	Annual	X		X
OECD Employment Outlook	Annual	X		X
OECD Factbook	Annual	X	X	X
OECD Health Data	Annual	X	X	X
OECD Science, Technology, and Industry Outlook	Biennial	X	X	X
OECD Territorial Reviews	Quarterly	X	X	
Organisation for Economic Cooperation and Development (OECD) in Figures	Bimonthly	X		X
Oil Information 2003 Edition	Annual	X	X	
Oil, Gas, Coal, and Electricity Quarterly Statistics	Quarterly	X	X	
Quarterly Labour Force Statistics (discontinued as of 4th quarter 2004)	Quarterly	X	X	
Quarterly National Accounts	Quarterly	X	X	
Research and Development Statistics	Annual	X	X	X
Revenue Statistics 1965–2005, 2006 Edition	Annual	X	X	
Review of Fisheries in OECD Member Countries	Annual	X	X	
Structural Statistics for Industry and Services	Annual	X	X	
Taxing Wages	Annual	X	X	
Trends in International Migration 2004 Edition	Annual	X	X	
Trends in the Transport Sector	Annual	X	X	
Uranium Resources Production and Demand, 2001	Biennial	X	X	
World Energy Outlook	Annual	X	X	
PennWell Corporation, Tulsa, OK				
<http://www.pennwell.com>				
Offshore (online subscription)	Monthly	X	X	
Oil and Gas Journal (online subscription)	Weekly	X	X	
Population Association of America, Washington, DC				
<http://www.popassoc.org>				
Demography	Quarterly	X	X	X
Puerto Rico Planning Board, San Juan, PR				
<http://www.jp.gobierno.pr>				

Appendix I 869

Title	Frequency	Paper	Internet PDF	Internet Other formats
Puerto Rico Planning Board, San Juan, PR—Con.				
Activity Index	Monthly	X		X
Balance of Payments Puerto Rico	Annual	X		
Economic Report to the Governor	Annual	X		
External Trade Statistics 2007	Annual	X		X
Income and Product	Annual	X		
Projections	Annual	X		
Selected Statistics on Construction Industry	Annual	X		
Statistical Appendix–Economic Report to the Governor	Annual	X		X
Radio Advertising Bureau, New York, NY				
<http://www.rab.com>				
Media Facts	Annual		X	
Radio Marketing Guide and Fact Book	Quarterly		X	
Reed Business Information, New York, NY				
<http://www.reedbusiness.com/index.html>				
Library Journal	Semimonthly	X		X
Publishers Weekly	Weekly	X		X
School Library Journal	Monthly	X		X
Regional Airline Association, Washington, DC				
<http://www.raa.org>				
Statistical Report	Annual	X	X	X
Securities Industry Association, New York, NY				
<http://www.sia.com>				
Foreign Activity Report	Quarterly	X		
Securities Industry Trends	Periodic	X		
Securities Industry Yearbook	Annual	X		X
Standard and Poor's Corporation, New York, NY				
<http://www.standardandpoors.com>				
Analysts' Handbook	Monthly	X		
Corporation Records	Daily	X		
Daily Stock Price Records	Quarterly	X		
Standard and Poor's Global Stock Market Factbook	Annual	X		
United Nations Statistics Division, New York, NY				
<http://unstats.un.org/unsd/default.htm>				
Compendium of Human Settlements Statistics (Series N)	Annual	X		
Demographic Yearbook (Series R)	Annual	X	X	X
Energy Balances and Electricity Profiles (Series W)	Annual	X	X	
Energy Statistics Yearbook (Series J)	Annual	X	X	
Industrial Statistics Yearbook (Series P)				
Commodity Production Statistics	Annual	X		
International Trade Statistics Yearbook (Series G)	Annual	X		
Monthly Bulletin of Statistics (Series Q)	Monthly	X		
National Accounts Statistics (Series X)				
Main Aggregates and Detailed Tables	Annual	X		
Analysis of Main Aggregates	Annual	X		
Population and Vital Statistics Report (Series A)	Quarterly	X		
Social Statistics and Indicators (Series K)	Occasional	X		X
The World's Women: Progress in Statistics, 2005		X	X	X
Statistical Yearbook (Series; also available in CD-ROM, Series S/CD)	Annual	X		X
World Statistics Pocketbook (Series V)	Annual	X		
United Nations Conference on Trade and Development, Geneva, Switzerland				
<http://www.unctad.org/Templates/StartPage.asp?intItemID=2068&lang=1>				
Development and Globalization: Facts and Figures	Annual	X	X	X
Handbook of Statistics	Annual	X	X	X
United States Telecom Association, Washington, DC				
<http://www.usta.org>				
Statistics of the Local Exchange Carriers	Annual		X	X
University of Michigan, Center for Political Studies, Institute for Social Research, Ann Arbor, MI				
<http://www.umich.edu>				
National Election Studies Cumulative Datafile	Biennial	X		X
Warren Communications News, Washington, DC				
<http://www.warren-news.com>				
Cable and Station Coverage Atlas	Annual			X
Television and Cable Factbook	Annual	X		X
World Almanac, New York, NY				
<http://www.worldalmanac.com>				
The World Almanac and Book of Facts	Annual	X		X
The World Bank Group, Washington, DC				
<http://www.worldbank.org>				
Global Development Finance, 2008	Annual	X	X	
The Little Data Book, 2008	Annual	X	X	
Atlas of Global Development	Annual	X	X	
World Development Indicators, 2008	Annual	X		X
World Health Organization, Geneva, Switzerland				
<http://www.who.int/en/>				
AIDS Epidemic Update	Annual	X	X	
World Health Statistics Report	Annual	X	X	
World Trade Organization				
<http://www.wto.org>				
International Trade Statistics	Annual	X	X	X

Guide to State Statistical Abstracts

This bibliography includes the most recent statistical abstracts for states published since 2000, plus those that will be issued in late 2008. For some states, a near equivalent has been listed in substitution for, or in addition to, a statistical abstract. All sources contain statistical tables on a variety of subjects for the state as a whole, its component parts, or both. Internet sites also contain statistical data.

Alabama

University of Alabama, Center for Business and Economic Research, Box 870221, Tuscaloosa, AL 35487-0221. 205-348-6191. Fax: 205-348-2951. Internet site <http://cber.cba.ua.edu/>.

Alabama Economic Outlook, 2008. Revised annually.

Alaska

Department of Commerce, Community, and Economic Development, Division of Community Advocacy, P.O. Box 110001, Juneau, Alaska 99811-0001. 907-465-3500. Fax 907-465-3532. Internet site <http://www.dced.state.ak.us/dca/misc_resources.htm>.

The Alaska Economic Performance Report, 2006. Online.

Arizona

Economic and Business Research Center, University of Arizona, 1130 East Helen Street, McClelland Hall, Rm. 103, P.O. Box 210108, Tucson, AZ 85721-0108. 520-621-2155. Fax: 520-621-2150. Internet site <http://www.ebr.eller.arizona.edu/>.

Arizona Statistical Abstract, 2003.

Arizona's Economy. Quarterly newsletter, 2008.

Arizona Economic Indicators Databook, 2007. Semiannual. Online.

Arkansas

University of Arkansas at Little Rock, Institute for Economic Advancement, Economic Research, 2801 South University Avenue, Little Rock, AR 72204-1099. 501-569-8519. Fax: 501-5698538. Internet site <http://www.aiea.ualr.edu/default.html>.

Arkansas State and County Economic Data, 2006.

Arkansas Personal Income Handbook, 2006.

Arkansas Statistical Abstract, 2006. Revised biennially.

California

Department of Finance, 915 L Street, Sacramento, CA 95814. 916-445-3878. Internet site <http://www.dof.ca.gov/default.asp>.

California Statistical Abstract, 2007. Annual. Online only.

Colorado

University of Colorado, University Libraries, 184 UCB, 1720 Pleasant St., Boulder, CO 80309-0184. 303-492-8705. Internet site <http://www.colorado.edu/libraries/govpubs/online.htm>.

Colorado by the Numbers. Online only.

Colorado Office of Economic Development and International Trade, 1625 Broadway, Suite 2700, Denver, CO 80202. 303-892-3840. Fax: 303-892-3848. Internet site <http://www.state.co.us/oed/>.

Colorado Data Book. Online only.

Connecticut

Connecticut Department of Economic & Community Development, 505 Hudson St., Hartford, CT 06106-7106. 860-270-8000. Internet site <http://www.ct.gov/ecd/site/default.asp>.

Connecticut Town Profiles, 2008.

Delaware

Delaware Economic Development Office, 99 Kings Highway, Dover, DE 19901-7305. 302-739-4271. Fax: 302-739-5749. Internet site <http://dedo.delaware.gov>.

Delaware Statistical Overview, 2008. Online only.

District of Columbia

Business Resource Center, John A. Wilson Building, 1350 Pennsylvania Avenue, NW, Washington, DC 20004. 202-727-1000. Internet site <http://brc.dc.gov/resources/facts.asp>.

Market Facts and Statistics. Online only.

Florida

University of Florida, Bureau of Economic and Business Research, P.O. Box 117145, 221 Matherly Hall, Gainesville, FL 32611-7145. 352-392-0171, ext. 219. Internet site <http://www.bebr.ufl.edu/>.

Florida Statistical Abstract, 2007. Annual. Also available on CD-ROM.

Florida County Perspective, 2007. One profile for each county. Annual. Also available on CD-ROM.

Florida County Rankings, 2007. Annual. Also available on CD-ROM.

Georgia

University of Georgia, Selig Center for Economic Growth, Terry College of Business, Athens, GA 30602. 706-542-8100. Internet site <http://www.selig.uga.edu/>.

Georgia Statistical Abstract, 2006–07.

U.S. Census Bureau, Statistical Abstract of the United States: 2009

Georgia—Con.

University of Georgia, Center for Agribusiness and Economic Development, 301 Lumpkin House, Athens, GA 30602-7509. 706-542-2434. Fax: 706-542-0770. Internet site <http://www.georgiastats.uga.edu/>.

The Georgia County Guide, 2008. Annual.

Hawaii

Hawaii State Department of Business, and Economic Development & Tourism, Research and Economic Analysis Division, Statistics and Data Support Branch, P.O. Box 2359, Honolulu, HI 96804. 808-586-2423. Fax: 808-587-2790. Internet site <http://www.hawaii.gov/dbedt/>.

The State of Hawaii Data Book 2006. Annual. Periodically updated.

Idaho

Idaho Commerce & Labor, 317 West Main St., Boise, ID 83735. 208-332-3570. Fax. 208-334-6300. Internet site <http://labor.idaho.gov/dnn/default.aspx?alias=labor.idaho.gov/dnn/idl/>.

County Profiles Idaho. Online.

Idaho Community Profiles. Online.

Illinois

Institute of Government and Public Affairs, 1007 W. Nevada Street, Urbana, IL 61801. 217-333-3340. Internet site <http://www.igpa.uiuc.edu/>.

Indiana

Indiana University, Indiana Business Research Center, Kelley School of Business, Ste 3110, 1275 E. 10th Street, Bloomington, IN 47405. 812-855-5507. Internet site <http://www.stats.indiana.edu/>.

STATS Indiana. Online only.

Iowa

Office of Social and Economic Trend Analysis, 303 East Hall, Ames, IA 50010-1070. 515-294-9903. Fax: 515-294-0592. Internet site <http://www.seta.iastate.edu/>.

State Library of Iowa, State Data Center, Ola Babcock Miller Building, 1112E Grand, Des Moines, IA 50319-0233. 800-248-4483. Fax: 515-242-6543. Internet site <http://www.iowadatacenter.org>.

Kansas

University of Kansas, Policy Research Institute, 1541 Lilac Lane, 607 Blake Hall, Lawrence, KS 66044-3177. 785-864-3701. Fax: 785-864-3683. Internet site <http://www.ipsr.ku.edu/>.

Kansas Statistical Abstract, 2006. 41st ed. Online only.

Kentucky

Kentucky Cabinet for Economic Development, Division of Research, 300 West Broadway, Frankfort, KY 40601. 800-626-2930. Internet site <http://www.thinkkentucky.com/>.

Kentucky Deskbook of Economic Statistics. Online only.

Louisiana

Louisiana State Census Data Center, Office of Electronic Services, P.O. Box 94095, Baton Rouge, LA 70804. 225-219-4025. Fax: 225-219-4027. Internet site <http://www.louisiana.gov/explore/demographics_and_geography>.

Maine

Maine State Planning Office, 38 State House Station, 184 State Street, Augusta, ME 04333. 800-662-4545. Fax: 207-287-6489. Internet site <http://www.maine.gov/spo/>.

Maryland

RESI, Towson University, 8000 York Road, Towson, MD 21252-0001. 410-704-7374. Fax 410-704-4115. Internet site <http://wwwnew.towson.edu/>.

Maryland Statistical Abstract, 2006.

Massachusetts

MassCHIP, Massachusetts Department of Public Health, 250 Washington Street, Boston, MA 02108-4619. 617-624-6000. Internet site <http://masschip.state.ma.us/>.

Instant Topics. Online only.

Michigan

Michigan Economic Development Corporation, 300 North Washington Square, Lansing, MI 48913. 1-888-784-7328. Internet site <http://www.michigan.org/medc/miinfo>.

Minnesota

Minnesota Department of Employment and Economic Development, 1st National Bank Building, 332 Minnesota Street Suite E200, Saint Paul, MN 55101-1351. 800-657-3858. Internet site <http://www.deed.state.mn.us/facts/index.htm>.

Compare Minnesota: Profiles of Minnesota's Economy & Population. Online only.

Minnesota State Demographic Center, 658 Cedar Street, Saint Paul, MN 55155. Room 300. 651-296-2557. Internet site <http://www.demography.state.mn.us/>.

Mississippi

Mississippi State University, College of Business and Industry, Office of Business Research and Services, P.O. Box 5288, Mississippi State, MS 39762. 662-325-3817. Internet site <http://www.cbi.msstate.edu/dept/bizserv/abstract/>.

Mississippi Statistical Abstract, 2007. 40th ed. Also available on CD-ROM.

Missouri

University of Missouri, Economic and Policy Analysis Research Center, 10 Professional Building, Columbia, MO 65211. 573-882-4805. Fax: 573-882-5563. Internet site <http://econ.missouri.edu/eparc/>.

Statistical Abstract for Missouri, 2003. 13th ed. Biennial. Online only.

Montana

Census and Economic Information Center, Montana Department of Commerce, 301 S. Park Ave., P.O. Box 200505, Helena, MT 59620-0505. 406-841-2740. Fax: 406-841-2731. Internet site <http://ceic.commerce.state.mt.us/>.

Nebraska

Nebraska Department of Economic Development, P. O. Box 94666, 301 Centennial Mall South, Lincoln, NE 68509-4666. 800-426-6505. Fax 402-471-3778. Internet site <http://info.neded.org/>.

Nevada

Department of Administration, Budget and Planning Division, 209 East Musser Street, Room 200, Carson City, NV 89701. 775-684-0222. Fax: 775-684-0260. Internet site <http://www.budget.state.nv.us/>.

Nevada Statistical Abstract. Online only.

New Hampshire

New Hampshire Office of Energy and Planning, 4 Chenell Drive, Concord, NH 03301-8519. 603-271-2155. Fax 603-271-2615. Internet site <http://www.nh.gov/oep/index.htm>.

New Jersey

New Jersey State Data Center, NJ Department of Labor and Workforce Development, 1 John Fitch Plaza, Trenton, NJ 08625-0110. 609-984-2595. Fax: 609-984-6833. Internet site <http://www.state.nj.us/labor/lra/>.

Labor Market Information. Online only.

New Mexico

University of New Mexico, Bureau of Business and Economic Research, MSC06 3510, 1 University of New Mexico, Albuquerque, NM 87131-0001. 505-277-6626. Fax 505-277-2773. Internet site <http://www.unm.edu/~bber/>.

New Mexico Business, Current Economic Report Monthly.

FOR-UNM Bulletin. Quarterly.

New York

Nelson A. Rockefeller Institute of Government, 411 State Street, Albany, NY 12203-1003. 518-443-5522. Fax: 518-443-5788. Internet site <http://www.rockinst.org/>.

New York State Statistical Yearbook, 2007 32nd ed.

North Carolina

Office of State Budget and Management, 116 West Jones Street, Raleigh, NC 27603-8005. 919-807-4700. Fax 919-733-0640. Internet site <http://www.osbm.state.nc.us/osbm/>.

How North Carolina Ranks, 2008. Online only.

North Dakota

University of North Dakota, Bureau of Business and Economic Research, P.O. Box 8369, Grand Forks, ND 58202. 800-225-5863. Fax 701-777-3365. Internet site <http://business.und.edu/bber/>.

North Dakota Statistical Abstract. Online only.

Ohio

Office of Strategic Research, Ohio Department of Development, 77 S. High Street, P.O. Box 1001, Columbus, OH 43216-1001. 614-466-2116. Internet site <http://www.odod.state.oh.us/research>.

Research products and services. Updated continuously.

Ohio County Profiles, 2006.

Ohio County Indicators. Updated periodically.

Oklahoma

University of Oklahoma, Center for Economic and Management Research, Michael F. Price College of Business, 307 West Brooks, Room 4, Norman OK 73019. 405-325-2931, Fax: 405-325-7688. Internet site <http://cemr.ou.edu/academics/cntremrcontact.aspx>.

Statistical Abstract of Oklahoma, 2005.

Oregon

Secretary of State, Archives Division, Archives Bldg., 800 Summer Street, NE, Salem, OR 97310. 503-373-0701. Fax: 503-373-0953. Internet site <http://www.sos.state.or.us/bbook>.

Oregon Blue Book. 2007–2008. Biennial.

Pennsylvania

Pennsylvania State Data Center, Institute of State and Regional Affairs, Penn State Harrisburg, 777 West Harrisburg Pike, Middletown, PA 17057-4898. 717-948-6336. Fax: 717-948-6754 Internet site <http://pasdc.hbg.psu.edu>.

Pennsylvania Statistical Abstract, 2007.

Rhode Island

Rhode Island Economic Development Corporation, 315 Iron Horse Way, Suite 101, Providence, RI 02908. 401-278-9100. Fax 401-273-8270. Internet site <http://www.riedc.com/r/index.html>.

RI Databank. Online only.

Appendix I   873

South Carolina

Budget and Control Board, Office of Research and Statistics, 1919 Blanding Street, Columbia 29201. 803-898-9949. Internet site <http://www.ors2.state.sc.us/abstract/index.asp>.

South Carolina Statistical Abstract, 2007. Also available on CD-Rom.

South Dakota

South Dakota State Data Center, Business Research Bureau, The University of South Dakota, 414 E. Clark Street,132 Patterson Hall, Vermillion, SD 57069. 605-677-5287. Fax: 605-677-5427. Internet site <http://www.usd.edu/brbinfo/>.

2006 South Dakota Community Abstracts.

Tennessee

College of Business Administration, The University of Tennessee, Temple Court, Suite 100, 804 Volunteer Blvd., Knoxville, Tennessee 37996-4334. 865-974-5441. Fax: 865-974-3100. Internet site <http://cber.bus.utk.edu/Default.htm>.

Tennessee Statistical Abstract, 2003. Last printed edition.

Texas

Dallas Morning News, Communications Center, P.O. Box 655237, Dallas, TX 75265-5237. 214-977-8262. Internet site <http://www.texasalmanac.com/>.

Texas Almanac, 2008–2009. 64th ed.

Texas State Data Center and Office of the State Demographer, Institute for Demographic and Socioeconomic Research, University of Texas at San Antonio, One UTSA Circle, San Antonio, TX 78249-0704. 210-458-6543. Fax: 210-458-6541. Internet site <http://txsdc.utsa.edu/>.

Utah

Governor's Office of Planning and Budget, Demographic & Economic Analysis, Suite 150 P.O. Box 132210, Salt Lake City, UT 84114. 801-538-1027. Fax: 801-538-1547. Internet site <http://www.governor.utah.gov/dea/>.

2008 Economic Report to the Governor. Annual.

Utah Data Guide Newsletter. Quarterly.

Vermont

Department of Labor, Labor Market Information, P.O. Box 488, Montpelier, VT 05601-0488. 802-828-4202. Fax: 802-828-4050. Internet site <http://www.vtlmi.info/>.

Vermont Economic-Demographic Profile, 2007. Annual.

Virginia

Weldon Cooper Center for Public Service, P.O. Box 400206, Charlottesville, VA 22904-4206. 434-982-5582. Fax: 434-982-5524. Internet site <http://www.coopercenter.org/>.

VaStat. Online only.

Washington

Washington State Office of Financial Management, Forecasting Division, P.O. Box 43113, Olympia, WA 98504-3113. 360-902-0555. Internet site <http://www.ofm.wa.gov/>.

Washington State Data Book, 2005. Online only.

West Virginia

West Virginia University, College of Business and Economics, Bureau of Business and Economic Research, P.O. Box 6025, Morgantown, WV 26506-6025. 304-293-4092. Fax: 304-2935652. Internet site <http://www.be.wvu.edu/bber/index.htm>.

2006 West Virginia County Data Profiles.

West Virginia Economic Outlook, 2008. Annual.

Wisconsin

Wisconsin Legislative Reference Bureau, One East Main Street, Suite 200, Madison, WI 53701-2037. 608-266-3561. Internet site <http://www.legis.state.wi.us/lrb/pubs/bluebook.htm/>.

2005–2006 Wisconsin Blue Book. Biennial.

Wyoming

Department of Administration and Information, Economic Analysis Division, 1807 Capitol Avenue, Suite 206, Cheyenne, WY 82002-0060. 307-777-7504. Fax: 307-632-1819. Internet site <http://eadiv.state.wy.us/>.

The Equality State Almanac, 2007.

Guide to Foreign Statistical Abstracts

This bibliography presents recent statistical abstracts for member nations of the Organization for Economic Cooperation and Development and Russia. All sources contain statistical tables on a variety of subjects for the individual countries. Many of the following publications provide text in English as well as in the national language(s). For further information on these publications, contact the named statistical agency which is responsible for editing the publication.

Australia

Australian Bureau of Statistics, Canberra. <http://www.abs.gov.au>.

Year Book Australia. Annual. 2007. With CD-ROM. (In English.)

Austria

Statistik Austria, 1110 Wien. <http://www.statistik.at/index.shtml>.

Statistisches Jahrbuch Osterreichs. Annual. 2008. With CD-ROM. (In German.) With English translations of table headings.

Belgium

Institut National de Statistique, Rue de Louvain; 44-1000 Bruxelles. <http://statbel.fgov.be/info/links_en.asp>.

Annuaire statistique de la Belgique. Annual. 1995. (In French.)

Canada

Statistics Canada, Ottawa, Ontario, KIA OT6. <http://www.statcan.ca/start.html>.

Canada Yearbook: A review of economic, social, and political developments in Canada. 2001. Irregular. (In English.)

Czech Republic

Czech Statistical Office, Na padesatem 81, Praha 10; <http://www.czso.cz/>.

Statisticka Rocenka Ceske Republiky 2007. With CD-ROM. (In English and Czech.)

Denmark

Danmarks Statistik, Sejrogade 11, 2100 Kobenhavn O. <http://www.dst.dk>.

Statistisk ARBOG. 2008. Annual. English version available only on Internet and is free of charge at: <www.dst.dk/yearbook>. (Printed version—In Danish only.)

Finland

Statistics Finland, Helsinki. <http://www.stat.fi/comment.

Statistical Yearbook of Finland, Annual. 2007. With CD-ROM. (In English, Finnish, and Swedish.)

France

Institut National de la Statistique et des Etudes Economiques, Paris 18, Bld. Adolphe Pinard, 75675 Paris (Cedex 14). <http://www.insee.fr/fr/home/home_page.asp>.

Annuaire Statistique de la France. Annual. 2003. (In French.) 2005. CD-ROM only.

Germany

Statistische Bundesamt, D-65180 Wiesbaden. <http://www.destatis.de>.

Statistisches Jahrbuch fur die Bundesrepublic Deutschland. Annual. 2006. (In German.)

Statistisches Jahrbuch fur das Ausland. 2005. Statistisches Jahrbuch 2006 Fur die Bundesreublik Deutschland und fur das Ausland CDROM.

Greece

National Statistical Service of Greece, Athens. <http:// www.statistics.gr/>.

Concise Statistical Yearbook 2006. (In English and Greek.)

Statistical Yearbook of Greece. Annual. 2006. (In English and Greek.)

Hungary

Hungarian Central Statistical Office, 1024 Budapest. <http://www.ksh.hu>.

Statistical Yearbook of Hungary, 2006. With CD-ROM. (In English and Hungarian.)

Iceland

Hagstofa Islands/Statistics Iceland; <http://www.hagstofa.is/template41.asp?PageID=251>.

Statistical Yearbook of Iceland. 2007 (In English and Icelandic.)

Ireland

Central Statistics Office, Skehard Road, Cork. <http://www.cso.ie>.

Statistical Yearbook of Ireland. Annual. 2007. (In English.)

Italy

Istituto Nazionale Statistica; <http://www.istat.it>. Via Cesare Balbo 16 Roma.

Annuario Statistico Italiano. Annual. 2007. With CD-ROM. (In Italian.)

Japan

Statistics Bureau, Ministry of Internal Affairs and Communications, Statistical Research and Training Institute, Ministry of Internal Affairs and Communications, Japan. <http://www.stat.go.jp/english/data/index.htm>.

Japan Statistical Yearbook. Annual. 2008. (In English and Japanese.)

Korea, South

National Statistical Office, Government Complex, #920 Dunsan-dong Seo-gu Daejeon 302-701. <http://www.nso.go.kr/>.

Korea Statistical Yearbook. Annual. 2007. (In Korean and English.)

Luxembourg

Statec Centre Administratif Pierre Werner, 13 rue Erasme, B.P. 304, L-2013, Luxembourg. <www.statec.lu/>.

Annuaire Statistique du Luxembourg. 2007. (In French.) (Alphabetical numbering system).

Mexico

Instituto Nacional de Estadistica Geografia e Informatica, Av. Heroe Nacozari Num. 2301 Sur Fracc. Jardines del Parque, CP 20270 Aguascalientes, Ags. <http://www.inegi.gob.mx/difusion/ingles/fiest.html>.

Anuario estadistico de los Estados Unidos Mexicanos. Annual. 1998. Also on disc. (In Spanish.) *Agenda Estadistica 1999.*

Netherlands

Statistics Netherlands, R L Vellekoop. Prinses Beatrixiaan 428, 2273 X Z Voorburg; <http://www.cbs.nl/en/>. *Statistical Yearbook 2008 of the Netherlands.* (In English.)

Statistisch Jaarboek 2008.

New Zealand

Department of Statistics, Wellington. <http://www.stats.govt.nz/>.

New Zealand Official Yearbook. Annual. 2006. (In English.)

Norway

Statistics Norway, Oslo/Kongsvinger. <http://www.ssb.no/english/subjects/>.

Statistical Yearbook. Annual. 2007. (In English.)

Poland

Central Statistical Office al. Niepodleglosci 208, 00-925 Warsaw. <http://www.stat.gov.pl/english/index.htm>. *Concise Statistical Yearbook 2005.* CD-ROM only. (In Polish and English.) *Statistical Yearbook of the Republic of Poland 2007.* CD-ROM only. (In Polish and English.)

Portugal

INE (Instituto Nacional de Estatistica.) <http://www.ine.pt/index_eng.htm>. Avenida Antonio Jose de Almeida P-1000-043 Lisboa.

Anuario Estatistico de Portugal. 2001. (In Portuguese and English.)

Russia

State Committee of Statistics of Russia, Moscow. <http://www.gks.ru/eng/>.

Statistical Yearbook. 2007. (In Russian.)

Slovakia

Statistical Office of the Slovak Republic, Dubravska Cesta 9, 845 02 Bratislava 45. <http://www.statistics.sk/webdata/english/index2_a.htm>.

Statisticka Rocenka Slovenskej Republiky. 2007. (In English and Slovak.) With CD-ROM.

Spain

INE (Instituto Nacional de Estadistica); Paseo de la Castellana, 183, Madrid 16. <http://www.ine.es/welcoing.htm>.

Anuario Estadistico de Espana. 2008. CD-ROM only. (In Spanish.)

Sweden

Statistics Sweden, SE-104 51 Stockholm. <http://www.scb.se/indexeng.asp>.

Statistisk Arsbok for Sverige. Annual. 2008. (In English and Swedish.)

Switzerland

Bundesamt fur Statistik, Hallwylstrasse 15, CH-3003, Bern.

Statistisches Jahrbuch der Schweiz. Annual. 2008. With CD-ROM. (In French and German.)

Turkey

State Institute of Statistics, Prime Ministry, Necatibey Cad/Ankara. No. 114 06100.

Statistical Yearbook of Turkey. 2004. With CD-ROM. (In English and Turkish.)

Turkey in Statistics. 1999. (In English only.)

United Kingdom

The Stationary Office; P.O. Box 29, Norwich, NR3 1GN. <http://www.statistics.gov.uk/>.

Annual Abstract of Statistics. Annual. 2002. (In English.)

Metropolitan and Micropolitan Statistical Areas: Concepts, Components, and Population

The United States Office of Management and Budget (OMB) defines metropolitan and micropolitan statistical areas according to published standards that are applied to U.S. Census Bureau data. The general concept of a metropolitan or micropolitan statistical area is that of a core area containing a substantial population nucleus, together with adjacent communities having a high degree of economic and social integration with that core. Currently defined metropolitan and micropolitan statistical areas are based on application of 2000 standards (which appeared in the Federal Register on December 27, 2000) to 2000 decennial census data. Current metropolitan and micropolitan statistical area definitions were announced by OMB effective June 6, 2003, and subsequently updated as of December 2003, November 2004, December 2005, December 2006, and November 2007.

Standard definitions of metropolitan areas were first issued in 1949 by the then Bureau of the Budget (predecessor of OMB), under the designation "standard metropolitan area" (SMA). The term was changed to "standard metropolitan statistical area" (SMSA) in 1959 and to "metropolitan statistical area" (MSA) in 1983. The term "metropolitan area" (MA) was adopted in 1990 and referred collectively to metropolitan statistical areas (MSAs), consolidated metropolitan statistical areas (CMSAs), and primary metropolitan statistical areas (PMSAs). The term "core-based statistical area" (CBSA) became effective in 2000 and refers collectively to metropolitan and micropolitan statistical areas.

OMB has been responsible for the official metropolitan areas since they were first defined, except for the period 1977 to 1981, when they were the responsibility of the Office of Federal Statistical Policy and Standards, U.S. Department of Commerce. The standards for defining metropolitan areas were modified in 1958, 1971, 1975, 1980, 1990, and 2000.

Defining Metropolitan and Micropolitan Statistical Areas—The 2000 standards provide that each CBSA must contain at least one urban area of 10,000 or more population. Each metropolitan statistical area must have at least one urbanized area of 50,000 or more inhabitants. Each micropolitan statistical area must have at least one urban cluster of at least 10,000 but less than 50,000 population.

Under the standards, the county (or counties) in which at least 50 percent of the population resides within urban areas of 10,000 or more population, or that contain at least 5,000 people residing within a single urban area of 10,000 or more population, is identified as a "central county" (counties). Additional "outlying counties" are included in the CBSA if they meet specified requirements of commuting to or from the central counties. Counties or equivalent entities form the geographic "building blocks" for metropolitan and micropolitan statistical areas throughout the United States and Puerto Rico.

If specified criteria are met, a metropolitan statistical area containing a single core with a population of 2.5 million or more may be subdivided to form smaller groupings of counties referred to as "metropolitan divisions."

As of November 2007, there are 363 metropolitan statistical areas and 577 micropolitan statistical areas in the United States. In addition, there are eight metropolitan statistical areas and five micropolitan statistical areas in Puerto Rico.

Principal Cities and Metropolitan and Micropolitan Statistical Area Titles— The largest city in each metropolitan or micropolitan statistical area is designated a "principal city." Additional cities qualify if specified requirements are met concerning population size and employment. The title of each metropolitan or micropolitan statistical area consists of the names of up to three of its principal cities and the name of each state into which the metropolitan or micropolitan statistical area extends. Titles of metropolitan divisions also typically are based on principal city names, but in certain cases consist of county names.

Defining New England City and Town Areas—In view of the importance of cities and towns in New England, the 2000 standards also provide for a set of geographic areas that are defined using cities and towns in the six New England states. The New England city and town areas (NECTAs) are defined using the same criteria as metropolitan and micropolitan statistical areas and are identified as either metropolitan or micropolitan, based, respectively, on the presence of either an urbanized area of 50,000 or more population or an urban cluster of at least 10,000 but less than 50,000 population. If the specified criteria are met, a NECTA containing a single core with a population of at least 2.5 million may be subdivided to form smaller groupings of cities and towns referred to as New England city and town area divisions.

Changes in Definitions Over Time—Changes in the definitions of these statistical areas since the 1950 census have consisted chiefly of (1) the recognition of new areas as they reached the minimum required city or urbanized area population and (2) the addition of counties (or cities and towns in New England) to existing areas as new decennial census data showed them to qualify.

In some instances, formerly separate areas have been merged, components of an area have been transferred from one area to another, or components have been dropped from an area. The large majority of changes have taken place on the basis of decennial census data. However, Census Bureau data serve as the basis for intercensal updates in specified circumstances.

Because of these historical changes in geographic definitions, users must be cautious in comparing data for these statistical areas from different dates. For some purposes, comparisons of data for areas as defined at given dates may be appropriate; for other purposes, it may be preferable to maintain consistent area definitions. Historical metropolitan area definitions are available for 1999, 1993, 1990, 1983, 1981, 1973, 1970, 1963, 1960, and 1950.

Excluding Tables 19 through 23 in the Population section; Table 574 in the Labor Force section; Table 661 in the Income section, and the tables that follow in this appendix, the tables presenting data for metropolitan areas in this edition of the *Statistical Abstract* are based on the 1999 or earlier metropolitan area definitions. For a list of component counties according to the 1999 definition, see Appendix II in the 2002 edition of the *Statistical Abstract* or <http://www.census.gov /population /www/estimates/pastmetro .html>.

U.S. Census Bureau, Statistical Abstract of the United States: 2009

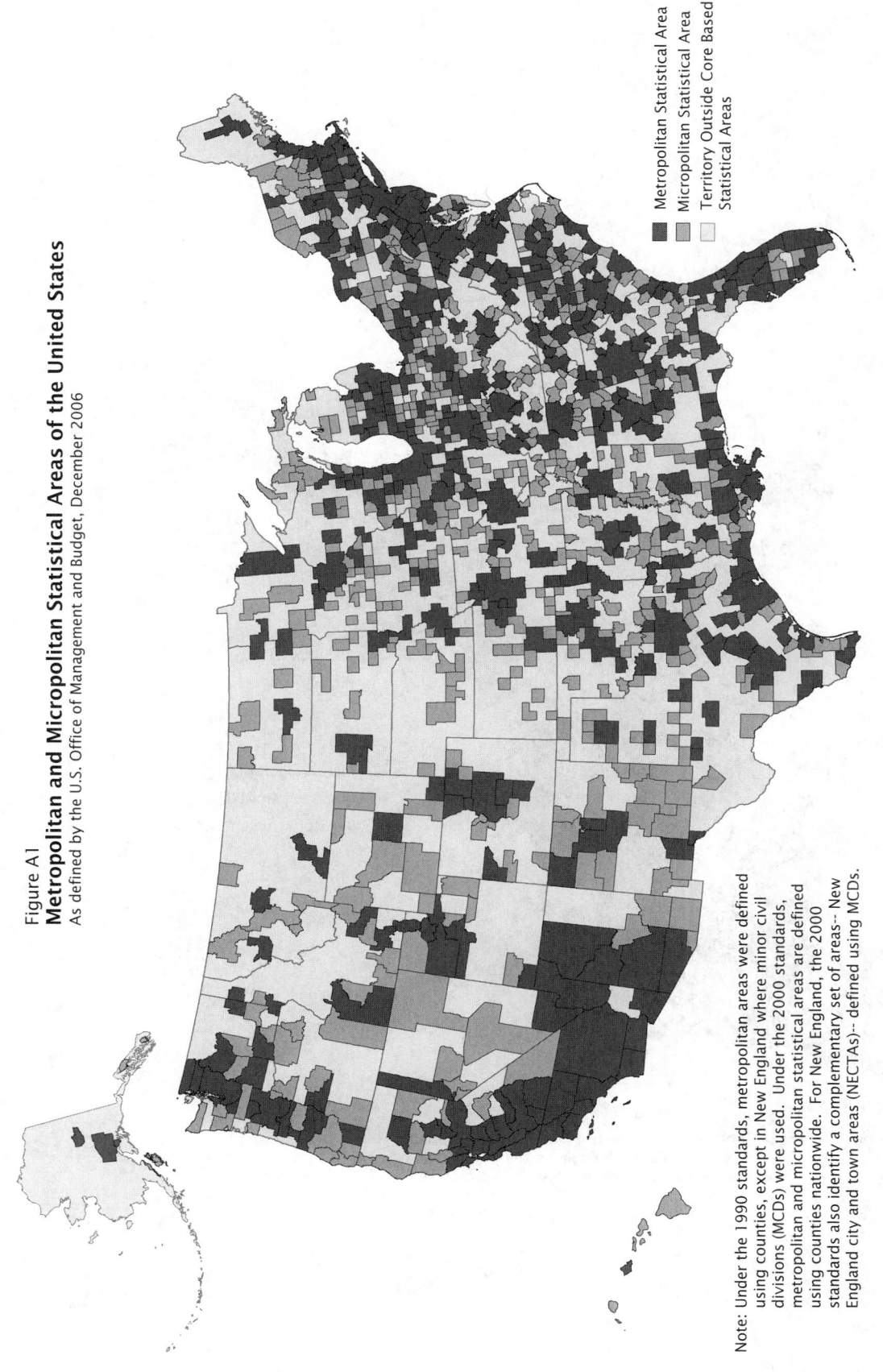

Figure A1
Metropolitan and Micropolitan Statistical Areas of the United States
As defined by the U.S. Office of Management and Budget, December 2006

Metropolitan Statistical Area
Micropolitan Statistical Area
Territory Outside Core Based
Statistical Areas

Note: Under the 1990 standards, metropolitan areas were defined
using counties, except in New England where minor civil
divisions (MCDs) were used. Under the 2000 standards,
metropolitan and micropolitan statistical areas are defined
using counties nationwide. For New England, the 2000
standards also identify a complementary set of areas-- New
England city and town areas (NECTAs)-- defined using MCDs.

Metropolitan and Micropolitan New England City and Town Areas (NECTAs)
As defined by the U.S. Office of Management and Budget, December 2006

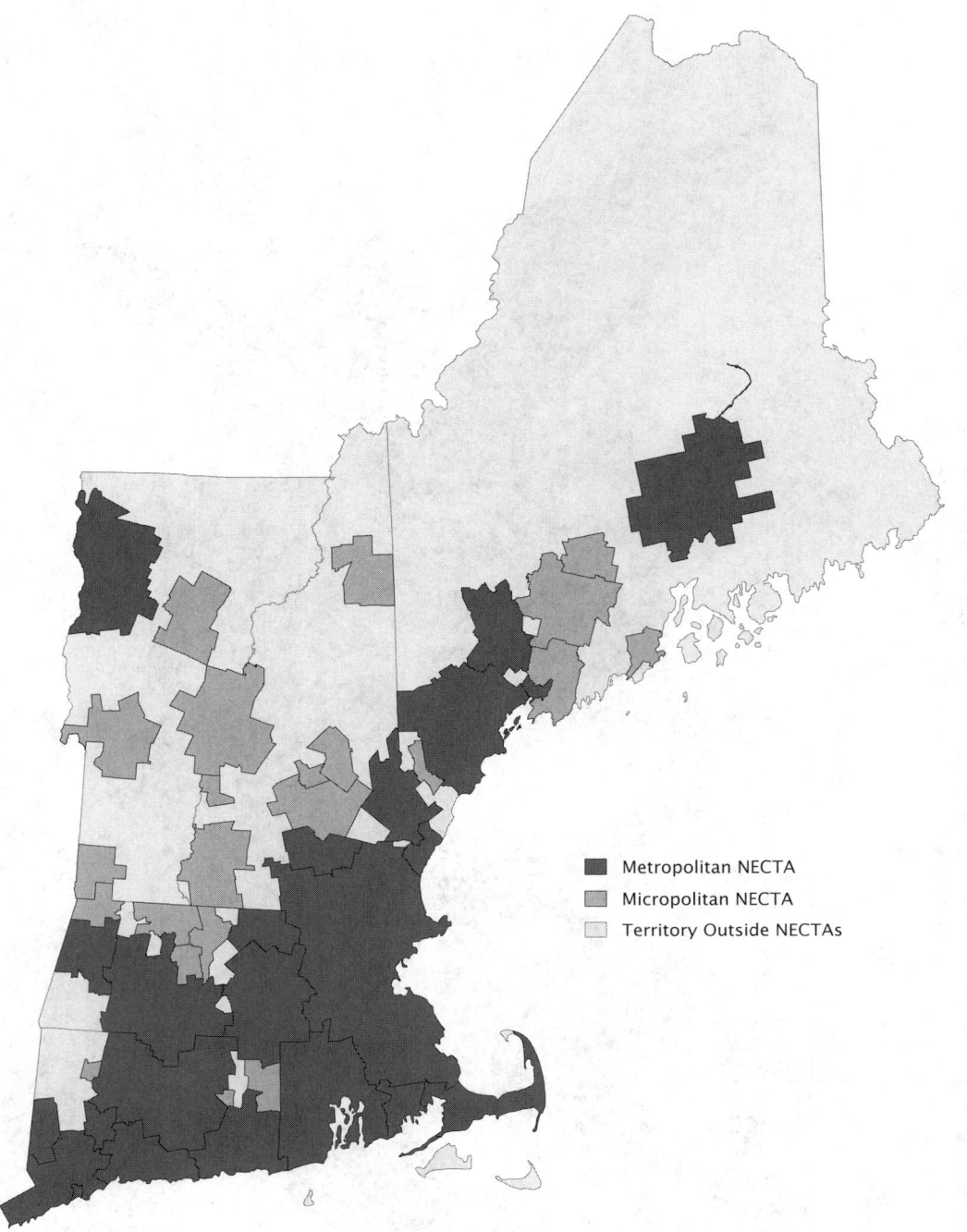

Metropolitan NECTA

Micropolitan NECTA

Territory Outside NECTAs

Note: Under the 2000 standards, metropolitan and micropolitan statistical areas are defined using
        counties nationwide. For New England, the 2000 standards also identify a complementary
        set of areas-- New England city and town areas (NECTAs) -- defined using MCDs.

Table A. **Metropolitan Statistical Areas and Components— Population: 2007**

[Population as of **July 2007. (159 represents 159,000.)** Metropolitan statistical areas as defined by the U.S. Office of Management and Budget as of December 2006. All geographic boundaries for 2007 population estimates are defined as of January 1, 2007. All metropolitan areas are arranged alphabetically]

Metropolitan statistical area Metropolitan division Component county	Population, 2007 (1,000)	Metropolitan statistical area Metropolitan division Component county	Population, 2007 (1,000)	Metropolitan statistical area Metropolitan division Component county	Population, 2007 (1,000)
Abilene, TX	**159**	**Asheville, NC**—Con.		**Bangor, ME**	**149**
Callahan County, TX	14	Haywood County, NC	56	Penobscot County, ME	149
Jones County, TX	19	Henderson County, NC	101		
Taylor County, TX	127	Madison County, NC	20	**Barnstable Town, MA**	**222**
				Barnstable County, MA	222
Akron, OH	**699**	**Athens-Clarke County, GA**	**187**		
Portage County, OH	156	Clarke County, GA	114	**Baton Rouge, LA**	**770**
Summit County, OH	543	Madison County, GA	28	Ascension Parish, LA	99
		Oconee County, GA	31	East Baton Rouge	
Albany, GA	**164**	Oglethorpe County, GA	14	Parish, LA	430
Baker County, GA	4			East Feliciana Parish,	
Dougherty County, GA	96	**Atlanta-Sandy Springs-**		LA	21
Lee County, GA	33	**Marietta, GA**	**5,279**	Iberville Parish, LA	33
Terrell County, GA	10	Barrow County, GA	67	Livingston Parish, LA	117
Worth County, GA	21	Bartow County, GA	93	Pointe Coupee Parish,	
		Butts County, GA	24	LA	22
Albany-Schenectady-Troy,		Carroll County, GA	112	St. Helena Parish, LA	11
NY	**853**	Cherokee County, GA	204	West Baton Rouge	
Albany County, NY	299	Clayton County, GA	272	Parish, LA	23
Rensselaer County, NY	155	Cobb County, GA	692	West Feliciana Parish,	
Saratoga County, NY	216	Coweta County, GA	119	LA	15
Schenectady County,		Dawson County, GA	21		
NY	151	DeKalb County, GA	737	**Battle Creek, MI**	**137**
Schoharie County, NY	32	Douglas County, GA	124	Calhoun County, MI	137
		Fayette County, GA	106		
Albuquerque, NM	**835**	Forsyth County, GA	159	**Bay City, MI**	**108**
Bernalillo County, NM	629	Fulton County, GA	992	Bay County, MI	108
Sandoval County, NM	118	Gwinnett County, GA	776		
Torrance County, NM	17	Haralson County, GA	29	**Beaumont-Port Arthur, TX**	**376**
Valencia County, NM	71	Heard County, GA	11	Hardin County, TX	52
		Henry County, GA	186	Jefferson County, TX	242
Alexandria, LA	**150**	Jasper County, GA	14	Orange County, TX	83
Grant Parish, LA	20	Lamar County, GA	17		
Rapides Parish, LA	130	Meriwether County, GA	23	**Bellingham, WA**	**193**
		Newton County, GA	96	Whatcom County, WA	193
Allentown-Bethlehem-		Paulding County, GA	128		
Easton, PA-NJ	**804**	Pickens County, GA	30	**Bend, OR**	**154**
Warren County, NJ	110	Pike County, GA	17	Deschutes County, OR	154
Carbon County, PA	63	Rockdale County, GA	82		
Lehigh County, PA	337	Spalding County, GA	63	**Billings, MT**	**150**
Northampton County,		Walton County, GA	83	Carbon County, MT	10
PA	294			Yellowstone County, MT	140
		Atlantic City, NJ	**271**		
Altoona, PA	**126**	Atlantic County, NJ	271	**Binghamton, NY**	**246**
Blair County, PA	126			Broome County, NY	196
		Auburn-Opelika, AL	**131**	Tioga County, NY	50
Amarillo, TX	**242**	Lee County, AL	131		
Armstrong County, TX	2			**Birmingham-Hoover, AL**	**1,108**
Carson County, TX	6	**Augusta-Richmond County,**		Bibb County, AL	22
Potter County, TX	121	**GA-SC**	**529**	Blount County, AL	57
Randall County, TX	113	Burke County, GA	23	Chilton County, AL	42
		Columbia County, GA	109	Jefferson County, AL	659
Ames, IA	**85**	McDuffie County, GA	22	St. Clair County, AL	78
Story County, IA	85	Richmond County, GA	197	Shelby County, AL	182
		Aiken County, SC	152	Walker County, AL	69
Anchorage, AK	**362**	Edgefield County, SC	25		
Anchorage Municipality,				**Bismarck, ND**	**103**
AK	280	**Austin-Round Rock, TX**	**1,598**	Burleigh County, ND	77
Matanuska-Susitna		Bastrop County, TX	72	Morton County, ND	26
Borough, AK	83	Caldwell County, TX	37		
		Hays County, TX	141	**Blacksburg-Christiansburg-**	
Anderson, IN	**131**	Travis County, TX	974	**Radford, VA**	**158**
Madison County, IN	131	Williamson County, TX	373	Giles County, VA	17
				Montgomery County, VA	89
Anderson, SC	**180**	**Bakersfield, CA**	**791**	Pulaski County, VA	35
Anderson County, SC	180	Kern County, CA	791	Radford city, VA	16
Ann Arbor, MI	**350**	**Baltimore-Towson, MD**	**2,668**	**Bloomington, IN**	**184**
Washtenaw County, MI	350	Anne Arundel County,		Greene County, IN	33
		MD	512	Monroe County, IN	129
Anniston-Oxford, AL	**113**	Baltimore County, MD	789	Owen County, IN	22
Calhoun County, AL	113	Carroll County, MD	169		
		Harford County, MD	240	**Bloomington-Normal, IL**	**164**
Appleton, WI	**218**	Howard County, MD	274	McLean County, IL	164
Calumet County, WI	44	Queen Anne's County,			
Outagamie County, WI	174	MD	47	**Boise City-Nampa, ID**	**588**
		Baltimore city, MD	637	Ada County, ID	373
Asheville, NC	**404**			Boise County, ID	8
Buncombe County, NC	227			Canyon County, ID	179

U.S. Census Bureau, Statistical Abstract of the United States: 2009

Metropolitan statistical area Metropolitan division Component county	Popu- lation, 2007 (1,000)	Metropolitan statistical area Metropolitan division Component county	Popu- lation, 2007 (1,000)	Metropolitan statistical area Metropolitan division Component county	Popu- lation, 2007 (1,000)
Boise City-Nampa, ID—Con.		**Charleston-North Charles-**		**Cleveland-Elyria-Mentor,**	
Gem County, ID	16	**ton, SC . . . .**	630	**OH . . . .**	2,096
Owyhee County, ID	11	Berkeley County, SC . . .	164	Cuyahoga County, OH . .	1,296
		Charleston County, SC. .	343	Geauga County, OH . . .	95
Boston-Cambridge-Quincy,		Dorchester County, SC. .	124	Lake County, OH.	233
MA-NH	4,483			Lorain County, OH.	302
Boston-Quincy, MA	1,858	**Charlotte-Gastonia-**		Medina County, OH	170
Norfolk County, MA . . .	655	**Concord, NC-SC . . . .**	1,652		
Plymouth County, MA. . .	490	Anson County, NC	25	**Coeur d'Alene, ID . . . .**	134
Suffolk County, MA	713	Cabarrus County, NC . . .	163	Kootenai County, ID. . . .	134
Cambridge-Newton-		Gaston County, NC	203		
Framingham, MA	1,473	Mecklenburg County,		**College Station-Bryan, TX . .**	203
Middlesex County, MA . .	1,473	NC.	867	Brazos County, TX.	171
Peabody, MA.	733	Union County, NC	185	Burleson County, TX . . .	17
Essex County, MA	733	York County, SC	209	Robertson County, TX . .	16
Rockingham County-					
Strafford County, NH . . .	418	**Charlottesville, VA . . . .**	193	**Colorado Springs, CO. . . . .**	609
Rockingham County,		Albemarle County, VA . .	93	El Paso County, CO. . . .	587
NH.	297	Fluvanna County, VA . . .	25	Teller County, CO	22
Strafford County, NH . . .	122	Greene County, VA	18		
		Nelson County, VA.	15	**Columbia, MO. . . . .**	162
Boulder, CO	290	Charlottesville city, VA . .	41	Boone County, MO	152
Boulder County, CO. . . .	290			Howard County, MO . . .	10
		Chattanooga, TN-GA	515		
Bowling Green, KY	116	Catoosa County, GA . . .	62	**Columbia, SC . . . .**	716
Edmonson County, KY. . .	12	Dade County, GA	16	Calhoun County, SC . . .	15
Warren County, KY	104	Walker County, GA	65	Fairfield County, SC. . . .	23
		Hamilton County, TN . . .	330	Kershaw County, SC . . .	58
Bremerton-Silverdale, WA . .	237	Marion County, TN.	28	Lexington County, SC . . .	243
Kitsap County, WA.	237	Sequatchie County, TN. .	13	Richland County, SC . . .	358
				Saluda County, SC	19
Bridgeport-Stamford-		**Cheyenne, WY . . . .**	86		
Norwalk, CT	895	Laramie County, WY . . .	86	**Columbus, GA-AL. . . . .**	283
Fairfield County, CT. . . .	895			Russell County, AL	50
		Chicago-Naperville-Joliet,		Chattahoochee County,	
Brownsville-Harlingen, TX . .	387	**IL . . . .**	9,525	GA.	9
Cameron County, TX . . .	387	**Chicago-Naperville-Joliet,**		Harris County, GA	29
		IL	7,953	Marion County, GA	7
Brunswick, GA	102	Cook County, IL	5,285	Muscogee County, GA . .	187
Brantley County, GA . . .	15	DeKalb County, IL	104		
Glynn County, GA	75	DuPage County, IL	929	**Columbus, IN . . . .**	75
McIntosh County, GA. . .	11	Grundy County, IL	47	Bartholomew County, IN. .	75
		Kane County, IL	501		
Buffalo-Niagara Falls, NY . .	1,128	Kendall County, IL	97	**Columbus, OH . . . .**	1,754
Erie County, NY	913	McHenry County, IL. . . .	316	Delaware County, OH . .	161
Niagara County, NY. . . .	215	Will County, IL.	674	Fairfield County, OH . . .	141
		Gary, IN.	699	Franklin County, OH . . .	1,118
Burlington, NC	145	Jasper County, IN	32	Licking County, OH	157
Alamance County, NC . .	145	Lake County, IN	492	Madison County, OH . . .	41
		Newton County, IN.	14	Morrow County, OH. . . .	35
Burlington-South Burling-		Porter County, IN.	161	Pickaway County, OH . . .	54
ton, VT	207	**Lake County-Kenosha**		Union County, OH	47
Chittenden County, VT. .	152	**County, IL-WI. . . . .**	873		
Franklin County, VT	48	Lake County, IL.	710	**Corpus Christi, TX . . . .**	414
Grand Isle County, VT . .	8	Kenosha County, WI . . .	163	Aransas County, TX. . . .	25
				Nueces County, TX	321
Canton-Massillon, OH	407	**Chico, CA. . . . .**	219	San Patricio County, TX .	69
Carroll County, OH	29	Butte County, CA.	219		
Stark County, OH	379			**Corvallis, OR . . . .**	81
		Cincinnati-Middletown,		Benton County, OR	81
Cape Coral-Fort Myers, FL .	591	**OH-KY-IN . . . .**	2,134		
Lee County, FL	591	Dearborn County, IN . . .	50	**Cumberland, MD-WV. . . . . .**	99
		Franklin County, IN	23	Allegany County, MD . . .	73
Carson City, NV	55	Ohio County, IN.	6	Mineral County, WV. . . .	27
Carson City, NV	55	Boone County, KY.	112		
		Bracken County, KY. . . .	9	**Dallas-Fort Worth-Arlington,**	
Casper, WY.	72	Campbell County, KY. . .	87	**TX . . . .**	6,145
Natrona County, WY . . .	72	Gallatin County, KY	8	**Dallas-Plano-Irving, TX . . .**	4,112
		Grant County, KY	25	Collin County, TX.	731
Cedar Rapids, IA.	253	Kenton County, KY.	157	Dallas County, TX	2,367
Benton County, IA	27	Pendleton County, KY . .	15	Delta County, TX.	5
Jones County, IA	20	Brown County, OH.	44	Denton County, TX	612
Linn County, IA	206	Butler County, OH	358	Ellis County, TX.	143
		Clermont County, OH . . .	193	Hunt County, TX	83
Champaign-Urbana, IL	221	Hamilton County, OH . . .	842	Kaufman County, TX . . .	96
Champaign County, IL . .	190	Warren County, OH	204	Rockwall County, TX . . .	74
Ford County, IL	14			**Fort Worth-Arlington, TX .**	2,034
Piatt County, IL	16	**Clarksville, TN-KY. . . . .**	262	Johnson County, TX. . . .	150
		Christian County, KY . . .	81	Parker County, TX.	109
Charleston, WV.	304	Trigg County, KY	13	Tarrant County, TX.	1,717
Boone County, WV	25	Montgomery County, TN. .	154	Wise County, TX	58
Clay County, WV	10	Stewart County, TN	13		
Kanawha County, WV . .	191			**Dalton, GA . . . .**	134
Lincoln County, WV	22	**Cleveland, TN . . . .**	111	Murray County, GA	41
Putnam County, WV . . .	55	Bradley County, TN	95	Whitfield County, GA . . .	93
		Polk County, TN	16		

882 Appendix II

Metropolitan statistical area Metropolitan division Component county	Popu- lation, 2007 (1,000)
Danville, IL	81
Vermilion County, IL	81
Danville, VA	106
Pittsylvania County, VA	61
Danville city, VA	45
Davenport-Moline-Rock Island, IA-IL	376
Henry County, IL	50
Mercer County, IL	16
Rock Island County, IL	147
Scott County, IA	163
Dayton, OH	836
Greene County, OH	155
Miami County, OH	101
Montgomery County, OH	538
Preble County, OH	42
Decatur, AL	149
Lawrence County, AL	34
Morgan County, AL	115
Decatur, IL	109
Macon County, IL	109
Deltona-Daytona Beach-Ormond Beach, FL	500
Volusia County, FL	500
Denver-Aurora, CO	2,465
Adams County, CO	422
Arapahoe County, CO	545
Broomfield County, CO	54
Clear Creek County, CO	9
Denver County, CO	588
Douglas County, CO	272
Elbert County, CO	23
Gilpin County, CO	5
Jefferson County, CO	529
Park County, CO	17
Des Moines-West Des Moines, IA	547
Dallas County, IA	57
Guthrie County, IA	11
Madison County, IA	15
Polk County, IA	418
Warren County, IA	45
Detroit-Warren-Livonia, MI	4,468
Detroit-Livonia-Dearborn, MI	1,985
Wayne County, MI	1,985
Warren-Troy-Farmington Hills, MI	2,482
Lapeer County, MI	92
Livingston County, MI	183
Macomb County, MI	831
Oakland County, MI	1,206
St. Clair County, MI	170
Dothan, AL	139
Geneva County, AL	26
Henry County, AL	17
Houston County, AL	97
Dover, DE	152
Kent County, DE	152
Dubuque, IA	92
Dubuque County, IA	92
Duluth, MN-WI	274
Carlton County, MN	34
St. Louis County, MN	197
Douglas County, WI	44
Durham, NC	480
Chatham County, NC	61
Durham County, NC	257
Orange County, NC	124
Person County, NC	37

Metropolitan statistical area Metropolitan division Component county	Popu- lation, 2007 (1,000)
Eau Claire, WI	158
Chippewa County, WI	60
Eau Claire County, WI	97
El Centro, CA	162
Imperial County, CA	162
Elizabethtown, KY	112
Hardin County, KY	98
Larue County, KY	14
Elkhart-Goshen, IN	198
Elkhart County, IN	198
Elmira, NY	88
Chemung County, NY	88
El Paso, TX	735
El Paso County, TX	735
Erie, PA	279
Erie County, PA	279
Eugene-Springfield, OR	344
Lane County, OR	344
Evansville, IN-KY	350
Gibson County, IN	33
Posey County, IN	26
Vanderburgh County, IN	174
Warrick County, IN	57
Henderson County, KY	45
Webster County, KY	14
Fairbanks, AK	97
Fairbanks North Star Borough, AK	97
Fargo, ND-MN	192
Clay County, MN	55
Cass County, ND	138
Farmington, NM	122
San Juan County, NM	122
Fayetteville, NC	349
Cumberland County, NC	307
Hoke County, NC	42
Fayetteville-Springdale-Rogers, AR-MO	436
Benton County, AR	203
Madison County, AR	15
Washington County, AR	194
McDonald County, MO	23
Flagstaff, AZ	127
Coconino County, AZ	127
Flint, MI	435
Genesee County, MI	435
Florence, SC	199
Darlington County, SC	67
Florence County, SC	132
Florence-Muscle Shoals, AL	143
Colbert County, AL	55
Lauderdale County, AL	89
Fond du Lac, WI	99
Fond du Lac County, WI	99
Fort Collins-Loveland, CO	288
Larimer County, CO	288
Fort Smith, AR-OK	290
Crawford County, AR	59
Franklin County, AR	18
Sebastian County, AR	122
Le Flore County, OK	50
Sequoyah County, OK	41
Fort Walton Beach-Crestview-Destin, FL	181
Okaloosa County, FL	181

Metropolitan statistical area Metropolitan division Component county	Popu- lation, 2007 (1,000)
Fort Wayne, IN	410
Allen County, IN	349
Wells County, IN	28
Whitley County, IN	33
Fresno, CA	899
Fresno County, CA	899
Gadsden, AL	103
Etowah County, AL	103
Gainesville, FL	257
Alachua County, FL	240
Gilchrist County, FL	17
Gainesville, GA	180
Hall County, GA	180
Glens Falls, NY	129
Warren County, NY	66
Washington County, NY	63
Goldsboro, NC	114
Wayne County, NC	114
Grand Forks, ND-MN	98
Polk County, MN	31
Grand Forks County, ND	67
Grand Junction, CO	139
Mesa County, CO	139
Grand Rapids-Wyoming, MI	777
Barry County, MI	59
Ionia County, MI	64
Kent County, MI	604
Newaygo County, MI	49
Great Falls, MT	82
Cascade County, MT	82
Greeley, CO	244
Weld County, CO	244
Green Bay, WI	301
Brown County, WI	243
Kewaunee County, WI	21
Oconto County, WI	37
Greensboro-High Point, NC	698
Guilford County, NC	466
Randolph County, NC	140
Rockingham County, NC	92
Greenville, NC	172
Greene County, NC	20
Pitt County, NC	152
Greenville-Mauldin-Easley, SC	614
Greenville County, SC	428
Laurens County, SC	70
Pickens County, SC	116
Gulfport-Biloxi, MS	232
Hancock County, MS	40
Harrison County, MS	176
Stone County, MS	16
Hagerstown-Martinsburg, MD-WV	261
Washington County, MD	145
Berkeley County, WV	100
Morgan County, WV	16
Hanford-Corcoran, CA	149
Kings County, CA	149
Harrisburg-Carlisle, PA	529
Cumberland County, PA	228
Dauphin County, PA	256
Perry County, PA	45

Appendix II **883**

Metropolitan statistical area Metropolitan division Component county	Population, 2007 (1,000)	Metropolitan statistical area Metropolitan division Component county	Population, 2007 (1,000)	Metropolitan statistical area Metropolitan division Component county	Population, 2007 (1,000)
Harrisonburg, VA	**118**	**Ithaca, NY**	**101**	**Killeen-Temple-Fort Hood,**	
Rockingham County, VA.	74	Tompkins County, NY. . .	101	**TX**—Con.	
Harrisonburg city, VA . . .	44			Lampasas County, TX . .	21
		Jackson, MI	**163**		
Hartford-West Hartford-East		Jackson County, MI	163	**Kingsport-Bristol-Bristol,**	
Hartford, CT	**1,189**			**TN-VA**	**304**
Hartford County, CT. . . .	877	**Jackson, MS**	**534**	Hawkins County, TN . . .	57
Middlesex County, CT . .	164	Copiah County, MS	29	Sullivan County, TN	154
Tolland County, CT	148	Hinds County, MS	249	Scott County, VA	23
		Madison County, MS . . .	89	Washington County, VA .	53
Hattiesburg, MS	**138**	Rankin County, MS	138	Bristol city, VA	18
Forrest County, MS	78	Simpson County, MS . . .	28		
Lamar County, MS.	48			**Kingston, NY**	**182**
Perry County, MS	12	**Jackson, TN**	**113**	Ulster County, NY	182
		Chester County, TN	16		
Hickory-Lenoir-Morganton,		Madison County, TN . . .	97	**Knoxville, TN**	**682**
NC	**360**			Anderson County, TN. . .	73
Alexander County, NC . .	36	**Jacksonville, FL**	**1,301**	Blount County, TN	120
Burke County, NC	89	Baker County, FL	26	Knox County, TN	424
Caldwell County, NC . . .	79	Clay County, FL	182	Loudon County, TN	45
Catawba County, NC . . .	156	Duval County, FL.	849	Union County, TN	19
		Nassau County, FL	68		
Hinesville-Fort Stewart, GA .	**72**	St. Johns County, FL . . .	175	**Kokomo, IN**	**100**
Liberty County, GA	61			Howard County, IN	84
Long County, GA.	11	**Jacksonville, NC**	**163**	Tipton County, IN.	16
		Onslow County, NC	163		
Holland-Grand Haven, MI . .	**259**			**La Crosse, WI-MN**	**131**
Ottawa County, MI.	259	**Janesville, WI**	**160**	Houston County, MN . . .	20
		Rock County, WI	160	La Crosse County, WI . .	111
Honolulu, HI	**906**				
Honolulu County, HI. . . .	906	**Jefferson City, MO**	**146**	**Lafayette, IN**	**192**
		Callaway County, MO. . .	43	Benton County, IN	9
Hot Springs, AR	**96**	Cole County, MO.	74	Carroll County, IN	20
Garland County, AR. . . .	96	Moniteau County, MO . .	15	Tippecanoe County, IN. .	163
		Osage County, MO	13		
Houma-Bayou Cane-				**Lafayette, LA**	**256**
Thibodaux, LA	**201**	**Johnson City, TN**	**194**	Lafayette Parish, LA . . .	205
Lafourche Parish, LA . . .	93	Carter County, TN	59	St. Martin Parish, LA . . .	52
Terrebonne Parish, LA . .	108	Unicoi County, TN	18		
		Washington County, TN .	117	**Lake Charles, LA**	**192**
Houston-Sugar Land-				Calcasieu Parish, LA . . .	185
Baytown, TX	**5,628**	**Johnstown, PA**	**145**	Cameron Parish, LA . . .	7
Austin County, TX	27	Cambria County, PA. . . .	145		
Brazoria County, TX. . . .	294			**Lake Havasu City-Kingman,**	
Chambers County, TX . .	29	**Jonesboro, AR**	**116**	**AZ**	**195**
Fort Bend County, TX . .	510	Craighead County, AR . .	92	Mohave County, AZ	195
Galveston County, TX . .	284	Poinsett County, AR. . . .	25		
Harris County, TX	3,936			**Lakeland, FL**	**575**
Liberty County, TX	75	**Joplin, MO**	**171**	Polk County, FL.	575
Montgomery County, TX .	413	Jasper County, MO	115		
San Jacinto County, TX .	25	Newton County, MO. . . .	56	**Lancaster, PA**	**498**
Waller County, TX	36			Lancaster County, PA. . .	498
		Kalamazoo-Portage, MI	**323**		
Huntington-Ashland,		Kalamazoo County, MI. .	245	**Lansing-East Lansing, MI** . .	**456**
WV-KY-OH	**284**	Van Buren County, MI . .	78	Clinton County, MI.	70
Boyd County, KY.	48			Eaton County, MI.	107
Greenup County, KY . . .	37	**Kankakee-Bradley, IL**	**111**	Ingham County, MI	279
Lawrence County, OH . .	63	Kankakee County, IL . . .	111		
Cabell County, WV	94			**Laredo, TX**	**233**
Wayne County, WV	41	**Kansas City, MO-KS**	**1,985**	Webb County, TX	233
		Franklin County, KS. . . .	26		
Huntsville, AL	**387**	Johnson County, KS . . .	526	**Las Cruces, NM**	**199**
Limestone County, AL . .	74	Leavenworth County,		Dona Ana County, NM . .	199
Madison County, AL. . . .	313	KS.	74		
		Linn County, KS	10	**Las Vegas-Paradise, NV** . . .	**1,836**
Idaho Falls, ID	**119**	Miami County, KS	31	Clark County, NV.	1,836
Bonneville County, ID. . .	97	Wyandotte County, KS . .	154		
Jefferson County, ID . . .	23	Bates County, MO	17	**Lawrence, KS**	**113**
		Caldwell County, MO . . .	9	Douglas County, KS. . . .	113
Indianapolis-Carmel, IN	**1,695**	Cass County, MO	97		
Boone County, IN	54	Clay County, MO.	212	**Lawton, OK**	**114**
Brown County, IN	15	Clinton County, MO	21	Comanche County, OK. .	114
Hamilton County, IN. . . .	262	Jackson County, MO . . .	667		
Hancock County, IN. . . .	66	Lafayette County, MO . .	33	**Lebanon, PA**	**128**
Hendricks County, IN . . .	135	Platte County, MO	85	Lebanon County, PA . . .	128
Johnson County, IN	136	Ray County, MO	23		
Marion County, IN	877			**Lewiston, ID-WA**	**60**
Morgan County, IN.	70	**Kennewick-Richland-Pasco,**		Nez Perce County, ID . .	39
Putnam County, IN	37	**WA**	**229**	Asotin County, WA.	21
Shelby County, IN	44	Benton County, WA	159		
		Franklin County, WA . . .	70	**Lewiston-Auburn, ME**	**107**
Iowa City, IA	**147**			Androscoggin County,	
Johnson County, IA	126	**Killeen-Temple-Fort Hood,**		ME.	107
Washington County, IA. .	21	**TX**	**370**		
		Bell County, TX	277	**Lexington-Fayette, KY**	**447**
		Coryell County, TX.	72	Bourbon County, KY . . .	20
				Clark County, KY.	36

Metropolitan statistical area Metropolitan division Component county	Population, 2007 (1,000)	Metropolitan statistical area Metropolitan division Component county	Population, 2007 (1,000)	Metropolitan statistical area Metropolitan division Component county	Population, 2007 (1,000)
Lexington-Fayette, KY—Con.		**Manchester-Nashua, NH . . .**	402	**Montgomery, AL . . . .**	366
Fayette County, KY	279	Hillsborough County, NH	402	Autauga County, AL. . . .	50
Jessamine County, KY . .	46			Elmore County, AL. . . .	78
Scott County, KY	43	**Mansfield, OH. . . . .**	126	Lowndes County, AL . . .	13
Woodford County, KY. . .	24	Richland County, OH. . .	126	Montgomery County, AL .	226
Lima, OH	105	**McAllen-Edinburg-Mission,**		**Morgantown, WV . . . .**	118
Allen County, OH.	105	**TX . . . .**	711	Monongalia County, WV. .	88
		Hidalgo County, TX	711	Preston County, WV . . .	30
Lincoln, NE.	292				
Lancaster County, NE . .	276	**Medford, OR . . . .**	199	**Morristown, TN . . . .**	135
Seward County, NE	17	Jackson County, OR . . .	199	Grainger County, TN . . .	23
				Hamblen County, TN . . .	62
Little Rock-North Little		**Memphis, TN-MS-AR. . . . . .**	1,281	Jefferson County, TN . . .	50
Rock-Conway, AR	666	Crittenden County, AR . .	52		
Faulkner County, AR . . .	105	DeSoto County, MS. . . .	149	**Mount Vernon-Anacortes,**	
Grant County, AR	17	Marshall County, MS . . .	37	**WA . . . .**	116
Lonoke County, AR	64	Tate County, MS	27	Skagit County, WA.	116
Perry County, AR.	10	Tunica County, MS	10		
Pulaski County, AR	374	Fayette County, TN	37	**Muncie, IN . . . .**	115
Saline County, AR	96	Shelby County, TN.	910	Delaware County, IN . . .	115
		Tipton County, TN	58		
Logan, UT-ID.	121			**Muskegon-Norton Shores,**	
Franklin County, ID	12	**Merced, CA. . . . .**	246	**MI. . . . .**	174
Cache County, UT.	109	Merced County, CA	246	Muskegon County, MI . .	174
Longview, TX	204	**Miami-Fort Lauderdale-**		**Myrtle Beach-Conway-North**	
Gregg County, TX	117	**Pompano Beach, FL . . . . .**	5,413	**Myrtle Beach, SC . . . . . .**	250
Rusk County, TX	49	**Fort Lauderdale-**		Horry County, SC	250
Upshur County, TX	38	**Pompano Beach-**			
		Deerfield Beach, FL. . . .	1,760	**Napa, CA . . . .**	133
Longview, WA.	100	Broward County, FL. . . .	1,760	Napa County, CA	133
Cowlitz County, WA	100	**Miami-Miami Beach-**			
		Kendall, FL	2,387	**Naples-Marco Island, FL . . .**	316
Los Angeles-Long Beach-		Miami-Dade County, FL .	2,387	Collier County, FL	316
Santa Ana, CA	12,876	**West Palm Beach-Boca**			
Los Angeles-Long		**Raton-Boynton Beach,**		**Nashville-Davidson–**	
Beach-Glendale, CA. . . .	9,879	**FL. . . . .**	1,266	**Murfreesboro–Franklin,**	
Los Angeles County, CA.	9,879	Palm Beach County, FL .	1,266	**TN . . . .**	1,521
Santa Ana-Anaheim-				Cannon County, TN	13
Irvine, CA	2,997	**Michigan City-La Porte, IN. .**	110	Cheatham County, TN . .	39
Orange County, CA	2,997	LaPorte County, IN	110	Davidson County, TN . . .	620
				Dickson County, TN	47
Louisville/Jefferson County,		**Midland, TX . . . .**	126	Hickman County, TN . . .	24
KY-IN	1,234	Midland County, TX	126	Macon County, TN.	22
Clark County, IN	105			Robertson County, TN . .	63
Floyd County, IN	73	**Milwaukee-Waukesha-West**		Rutherford County, TN . .	241
Harrison County, IN	37	**Allis, WI . . . .**	1,544	Smith County, TN	19
Washington County, IN. .	28	Milwaukee County, WI . .	951	Sumner County, TN	153
Bullitt County, KY.	74	Ozaukee County, WI . . .	86	Trousdale County, TN . .	8
Henry County, KY	16	Washington County, WI .	128	Williamson County, TN. .	166
Jefferson County, KY . . .	709	Waukesha County, WI . .	379	Wilson County, TN.	106
Meade County, KY.	27				
Nelson County, KY	43	**Minneapolis-St. Paul-**		**New Haven-Milford, CT . . . .**	845
Oldham County, KY	56	**Bloomington, MN-WI . . . . .**	3,208	New Haven County, CT .	845
Shelby County, KY.	40	Anoka County, MN.	326		
Spencer County, KY . . .	17	Carver County, MN	88	**New Orleans-Metairie-**	
Trimble County, KY. . . .	9	Chisago County, MN . . .	50	**Kenner, LA . . . .**	1,030
		Dakota County, MN	390	Jefferson Parish, LA . . .	424
Lubbock, TX	267	Hennepin County, MN . .	1,137	Orleans Parish, LA	239
Crosby County, TX	6	Isanti County, MN	39	Plaquemines Parish, LA .	22
Lubbock County, TX. . . .	261	Ramsey County, MN . . .	500	St. Bernard Parish, LA . .	20
		Scott County, MN	127	St. Charles Parish, LA . .	52
Lynchburg, VA	244	Sherburne County, MN. .	86	St. John the Baptist	
Amherst County, VA. . . .	32	Washington County, MN.	226	Parish, LA.	48
Appomattox County, VA .	14	Wright County, MN	117	St. Tammany Parish, LA.	227
Bedford County, VA	67	Pierce County, WI	40		
Campbell County, VA . . .	53	St. Croix County, WI . . .	81	**New York-Northern New**	
Bedford city, VA.	6			**Jersey-Long Island,**	
Lynchburg city, VA	71	**Missoula, MT . . . .**	106	**NY-NJ-PA . . . .**	18,816
		Missoula County, MT . . .	106	**Edison, NJ . . . .**	2,320
Macon, GA	230			Middlesex County, NJ . .	789
Bibb County, GA	155	**Mobile, AL . . . .**	404	Monmouth County, NJ . .	642
Crawford County, GA . . .	12	Mobile County, AL	404	Ocean County, NJ	565
Jones County, GA	27			Somerset County, NJ. . .	324
Monroe County, GA	25	**Modesto, CA. . . . .**	511	**Nassau-Suffolk, NY . . . . .**	2,760
Twiggs County, GA	10	Stanislaus County, CA . .	511	Nassau County, NY	1,307
				Suffolk County, NY	1,453
Madera, CA.	147	**Monroe, LA. . . . .**	172	**Newark-Union, NJ-PA . . . .**	2,129
Madera County, CA	147	Ouachita Parish, LA. . . .	150	Essex County, NJ	776
		Union Parish, LA.	23	Hunterdon County, NJ . .	129
Madison, WI	556			Morris County, NJ	488
Columbia County, WI . . .	55	**Monroe, MI . . . .**	154	Sussex County, NJ	151
Dane County, WI.	477	Monroe County, MI	154	Union County, NJ	525
Iowa County, WI	24			Pike County, PA	59

U.S. Census Bureau, Statistical Abstract of the United States: 2009

Metropolitan statistical area / Metropolitan division / Component county	Population, 2007 (1,000)
New York-Northern New Jersey-Long Island, NY-NJ-PA—Con.	
New York-White Plains-Wayne, NY-NJ	**11,608**
Bergen County, NJ	896
Hudson County, NJ	598
Passaic County, NJ	492
Bronx County, NY	1,374
Kings County, NY	2,528
New York County, NY. . .	1,621
Putnam County, NY . . .	99
Queens County, NY. . . .	2,270
Richmond County, NY . .	482
Rockland County, NY. . .	296
Westchester County, NY.	951
Niles-Benton Harbor, MI . . .	**160**
Berrien County, MI.	160
Norwich-New London, CT . .	**267**
New London County, CT.	267
Ocala, FL	**325**
Marion County, FL.	325
Ocean City, NJ	**96**
Cape May County, NJ . .	96
Odessa, TX.	**130**
Ector County, TX.	130
Ogden-Clearfield, UT.	**518**
Davis County, UT	288
Morgan County, UT	8
Weber County, UT.	222
Oklahoma City, OK	**1,193**
Canadian County, OK . .	104
Cleveland County, OK . .	236
Grady County, OK	51
Lincoln County, OK	32
Logan County, OK.	36
McClain County, OK . . .	32
Oklahoma County, OK. .	702
Olympia, WA.	**239**
Thurston County, WA. . .	239
Omaha-Council Bluffs, NE-IA	**830**
Harrison County, IA	15
Mills County, IA.	15
Pottawattamie County, IA	89
Cass County, NE.	26
Douglas County, NE . . .	497
Sarpy County, NE	147
Saunders County, NE. . .	20
Washington County, NE .	20
Orlando-Kissimmee, FL. . . .	**2,032**
Lake County, FL	301
Orange County, FL	1,066
Osceola County, FL. . . .	256
Seminole County, FL . . .	410
Oshkosh-Neenah, WI	**162**
Winnebago County, WI. .	162
Owensboro, KY.	**112**
Daviess County, KY. . . .	94
Hancock County, KY . . .	9
McLean County, KY	10
Oxnard-Thousand Oaks-Ventura, CA	**798**
Ventura County, CA. . . .	798
Palm Bay-Melbourne-Titusville, FL.	**536**
Brevard County, FL	536
Palm Coast, FL.	**88**
Flagler County, FL.	88

Metropolitan statistical area / Metropolitan division / Component county	Population, 2007 (1,000)
Panama City-Lynn Haven, FL.	**164**
Bay County, FL	164
Parkersburg-Marietta-Vienna, WV-OH	**161**
Washington County, OH .	62
Pleasants County, WV . .	7
Wirt County, WV	6
Wood County, WV.	86
Pascagoula, MS	**152**
George County, MS. . . .	22
Jackson County, MS . . .	130
Pensacola-Ferry Pass-Brent, FL	**453**
Escambia County, FL. . .	306
Santa Rosa County, FL .	147
Peoria, IL	**371**
Marshall County, IL	13
Peoria County, IL.	183
Stark County, IL.	6
Tazewell County, IL	131
Woodford County, IL . . .	38
Philadelphia-Camden-Wilmington, PA-NJ-DE-MD.	**5,828**
Camden, NJ	**1,246**
Burlington County, NJ . .	447
Camden County, NJ. . . .	514
Gloucester County, NJ . .	286
Philadelphia, PA	**3,888**
Bucks County, PA	621
Chester County, PA	486
Delaware County, PA . . .	554
Montgomery County, PA.	776
Philadelphia County, PA .	1,450
Wilmington, DE-MD-NJ . .	**694**
New Castle County, DE .	528
Cecil County, MD.	100
Salem County, NJ	66
Phoenix-Mesa-Scottsdale, AZ	**4,179**
Maricopa County, AZ . . .	3,880
Pinal County, AZ	299
Pine Bluff, AR.	**101**
Cleveland County, AR . .	9
Jefferson County, AR . . .	79
Lincoln County, AR	14
Pittsburgh, PA	**2,356**
Allegheny County, PA. . .	1,219
Armstrong County, PA . .	69
Beaver County, PA	173
Butler County, PA	182
Fayette County, PA	145
Washington County, PA .	206
Westmoreland County, PA	362
Pittsfield, MA	**130**
Berkshire County, MA . .	130
Pocatello, ID.	**88**
Bannock County, ID. . . .	80
Power County, ID	8
Portland-South Portland-Biddeford, ME.	**513**
Cumberland County, ME.	275
Sagadahoc County, ME .	36
York County, ME	201
Portland-Vancouver-Beaverton, OR-WA	**2,175**
Clackamas County, OR .	376
Columbia County, OR . .	49
Multnomah County, OR .	702
Washington County, OR.	523
Yamhill County, OR	97
Clark County, WA	418
Skamania County, WA . .	11

Metropolitan statistical area / Metropolitan division / Component county	Population, 2007 (1,000)
Port St. Lucie, FL	**400**
Martin County, FL	139
St. Lucie County, FL . . .	261
Poughkeepsie-Newburgh-Middletown, NY.	**670**
Dutchess County, NY. . .	293
Orange County, NY	377
Prescott, AZ	**213**
Yavapai County, AZ	213
Providence-New Bedford-Fall River, RI-MA	**1,601**
Bristol County, MA	543
Bristol County, RI.	50
Kent County, RI.	169
Newport County, RI	83
Providence County, RI . .	629
Washington County, RI. .	127
Provo-Orem, UT	**493**
Juab County, UT	10
Utah County, UT	484
Pueblo, CO.	**155**
Pueblo County, CO	155
Punta Gorda, FL	**153**
Charlotte County, FL . . .	153
Racine, WI	**195**
Racine County, WI.	195
Raleigh-Cary, NC	**1,048**
Franklin County, NC. . . .	57
Johnston County, NC. . .	157
Wake County, NC	833
Rapid City, SD	**120**
Meade County, SD	24
Pennington County, SD .	96
Reading, PA	**402**
Berks County, PA	402
Redding, CA	**179**
Shasta County, CA	179
Reno-Sparks, NV	**410**
Storey County, NV.	4
Washoe County, NV. . . .	406
Richmond, VA.	**1,213**
Amelia County, VA.	13
Caroline County, VA. . . .	27
Charles City County, VA. .	7
Chesterfield County, VA .	300
Cumberland County, VA .	10
Dinwiddie County, VA. . .	26
Goochland County, VA . .	21
Hanover County, VA. . . .	99
Henrico County, VA	290
King and Queen County, VA	7
King William County, VA .	16
Louisa County, VA	32
New Kent County, VA. . .	17
Powhatan County, VA . .	28
Prince George County, VA	36
Sussex County, VA	12
Colonial Heights city, VA.	18
Hopewell city, VA.	23
Petersburg city, VA. . . .	33
Richmond city, VA	200
Riverside-San Bernardino-Ontario, CA.	**4,081**
Riverside County, CA. . .	2,074
San Bernardino County, CA.	2,008
Roanoke, VA.	**297**
Botetourt County, VA . . .	32
Craig County, VA.	5

U.S. Census Bureau, Statistical Abstract of the United States: 2009

Metropolitan statistical area Metropolitan division Component county	Population, 2007 (1,000)
Roanoke, VA—Con.	
Franklin County, VA	51
Roanoke County, VA	90
Roanoke city, VA	93
Salem city, VA	25
Rochester, MN	**181**
Dodge County, MN	20
Olmsted County, MN	140
Wabasha County, MN	22
Rochester, NY	**1,030**
Livingston County, NY	63
Monroe County, NY	730
Ontario County, NY	104
Orleans County, NY	42
Wayne County, NY	91
Rockford, IL	**352**
Boone County, IL	54
Winnebago County, IL	299
Rocky Mount, NC	**146**
Edgecombe County, NC	53
Nash County, NC	93
Rome, GA	**96**
Floyd County, GA	96
Sacramento–Arden-Arcade–Roseville, CA	**2,091**
El Dorado County, CA	176
Placer County, CA	333
Sacramento County, CA	1,387
Yolo County, CA	196
Saginaw-Saginaw Township North, MI	**202**
Saginaw County, MI	202
St. Cloud, MN	**186**
Benton County, MN	40
Stearns County, MN	146
St. George, UT	**134**
Washington County, UT	134
St. Joseph, MO-KS	**123**
Doniphan County, KS	8
Andrew County, MO	17
Buchanan County, MO	86
DeKalb County, MO	12
St. Louis, MO-IL [1]	**2,804**
Bond County, IL	18
Calhoun County, IL	5
Clinton County, IL	36
Jersey County, IL	22
Macoupin County, IL	48
Madison County, IL	267
Monroe County, IL	32
St. Clair County, IL	261
Franklin County, MO	100
Jefferson County, MO	216
Lincoln County, MO	52
St. Charles County, MO	344
St. Louis County, MO	995
Warren County, MO	30
Washington County, MO	24
St. Louis city, MO	351
Salem, OR	**387**
Marion County, OR	311
Polk County, OR	75
Salinas, CA	**408**
Monterey County, CA	408
Salisbury, MD	**120**
Somerset County, MD	26
Wicomico County, MD	94
Salt Lake City, UT	**1,100**
Salt Lake County, UT	1,010
Summit County, UT	36
Tooele County, UT	55

Metropolitan statistical area Metropolitan division Component county	Population, 2007 (1,000)
San Angelo, TX	**108**
Irion County, TX	2
Tom Green County, TX	106
San Antonio, TX	**1,991**
Atascosa County, TX	44
Bandera County, TX	20
Bexar County, TX	1,594
Comal County, TX	105
Guadalupe County, TX	113
Kendall County, TX	31
Medina County, TX	44
Wilson County, TX	39
San Diego-Carlsbad-San Marcos, CA	**2,975**
San Diego County, CA	2,975
Sandusky, OH	**77**
Erie County, OH	77
San Francisco-Oakland-Fremont, CA	**4,204**
Oakland-Fremont-Hayward, CA	**2,484**
Alameda County, CA	1,464
Contra Costa County, CA	1,020
San Francisco-San Mateo-Redwood City, CA	**1,720**
Marin County, CA	248
San Francisco County, CA	765
San Mateo County, CA	707
San Jose-Sunnyvale-Santa Clara, CA	**1,804**
San Benito County, CA	55
Santa Clara County, CA	1,749
San Luis Obispo-Paso Robles, CA	**262**
San Luis Obispo County, CA	262
Santa Barbara-Santa Maria-Goleta, CA	**404**
Santa Barbara County, CA	404
Santa Cruz-Watsonville, CA	**252**
Santa Cruz County, CA	252
Santa Fe, NM	**143**
Santa Fe County, NM	143
Santa Rosa-Petaluma, CA	**464**
Sonoma County, CA	464
Sarasota-Bradenton-Venice, FL	**687**
Manatee County, FL	315
Sarasota County, FL	372
Savannah, GA	**329**
Bryan County, GA	30
Chatham County, GA	248
Effingham County, GA	51
Scranton–Wilkes-Barre, PA	**549**
Lackawanna County, PA	209
Luzerne County, PA	312
Wyoming County, PA	28
Seattle-Tacoma-Bellevue, WA	**3,309**
Seattle-Bellevue-Everett, WA	**2,536**
King County, WA	1,859
Snohomish County, WA	677
Tacoma, WA	**773**
Pierce County, WA	773
Sebastian-Vero Beach, FL	**132**
Indian River County, FL	132

Metropolitan statistical area Metropolitan division Component county	Population, 2007 (1,000)
Sheboygan, WI	**115**
Sheboygan County, WI	115
Sherman-Denison, TX	**119**
Grayson County, TX	119
Shreveport-Bossier City, LA	**388**
Bossier Parish, LA	109
Caddo Parish, LA	253
De Soto Parish, LA	26
Sioux City, IA-NE-SD	**143**
Woodbury County, IA	102
Dakota County, NE	20
Dixon County, NE	6
Union County, SD	14
Sioux Falls, SD	**227**
Lincoln County, SD	38
McCook County, SD	6
Minnehaha County, SD	175
Turner County, SD	8
South Bend-Mishawaka, IN-MI	**317**
St. Joseph County, IN	266
Cass County, MI	51
Spartanburg, SC	**276**
Spartanburg County, SC	276
Spokane, WA	**456**
Spokane County, WA	456
Springfield, IL	**207**
Menard County, IL	12
Sangamon County, IL	194
Springfield, MA	**683**
Franklin County, MA	72
Hampden County, MA	458
Hampshire County, MA	153
Springfield, MO	**420**
Christian County, MO	73
Dallas County, MO	17
Greene County, MO	264
Polk County, MO	30
Webster County, MO	36
Springfield, OH	**140**
Clark County, OH	140
State College, PA	**145**
Centre County, PA	145
Stockton, CA	**671**
San Joaquin County, CA	671
Sumter, SC	**104**
Sumter County, SC	104
Syracuse, NY	**645**
Madison County, NY	70
Onondaga County, NY	454
Oswego County, NY	121
Tallahassee, FL	**352**
Gadsden County, FL	47
Jefferson County, FL	14
Leon County, FL	261
Wakulla County, FL	30
Tampa-St. Petersburg-Clearwater, FL	**2,724**
Hernando County, FL	169
Hillsborough County, FL	1,175
Pasco County, FL	463
Pinellas County, FL	917
Terre Haute, IN	**169**
Clay County, IN	27
Sullivan County, IN	21
Vermillion County, IN	16

U.S. Census Bureau, Statistical Abstract of the United States: 2009

Metropolitan statistical area Metropolitan division Component county	Population, 2007 (1,000)	Metropolitan statistical area Metropolitan division Component county	Population, 2007 (1,000)	Metropolitan statistical area Metropolitan division Component county	Population, 2007 (1,000)
Terre Haute, IN—Con.		**Virginia Beach-Norfolk-**		**Weirton-Steubenville,**	
Vigo County, IN	105	**Newport News, VA-NC**	1,659	**WV-OH**	123
		Currituck County, NC . . .	24	Jefferson County, OH . . .	69
Texarkana, TX-Texarkana,		Gloucester County, VA . .	38	Brooke County, WV	24
AR	134	Isle of Wight County, VA .	35	Hancock County, WV . . .	30
Miller County, AR	43	James City County, VA . .	61		
Bowie County, TX	92	Mathews County, VA . . .	9	**Wenatchee, WA.**	107
		Surry County, VA	7	Chelan County, WA	71
Toledo, OH	651	York County, VA	61	Douglas County, WA . . .	36
Fulton County, OH	43	Chesapeake city, VA . . .	219		
Lucas County, OH	442	Hampton city, VA	146	**Wheeling, WV-OH**	145
Ottawa County, OH	41	Newport News city, VA . .	179	Belmont County, OH . . .	68
Wood County, OH	125	Norfolk city, VA	236	Marshall County, WV . . .	33
		Poquoson city, VA	12	Ohio County, WV.	44
Topeka, KS	229	Portsmouth city, VA	102		
Jackson County, KS. . . .	13	Suffolk city, VA	81	**Wichita, KS.**	596
Jefferson County, KS . . .	18	Virginia Beach city, VA . .	435	Butler County, KS	63
Osage County, KS.	16	Williamsburg city, VA . . .	12	Harvey County, KS	33
Shawnee County, KS . . .	173			Sedgwick County, KS. . .	476
Wabaunsee County, KS .	7	**Visalia-Porterville, CA**	422	Sumner County, KS	24
		Tulare County, CA	422		
Trenton-Ewing, NJ	365			**Wichita Falls, TX.**	148
Mercer County, NJ.	365	**Waco, TX**	228	Archer County, TX	9
		McLennan County, TX . .	228	Clay County, TX	11
Tucson, AZ	967			Wichita County, TX	128
Pima County, AZ	967	**Warner Robins, GA.**	131		
		Houston County, GA . . .	131	**Williamsport, PA**	117
Tulsa, OK	906			Lycoming County, PA. . .	117
Creek County, OK	69	**Washington-Arlington-**			
Okmulgee County, OK . .	39	**Alexandria, DC-VA-MD-WV.**	5,307	**Wilmington, NC.**	340
Osage County, OK.	46	**Bethesda-Gaithersburg-**		Brunswick County, NC . .	99
Pawnee County, OK	16	**Frederick, MD**	1,156	New Hanover County,	
Rogers County, OK	83	Frederick County, MD . .	225	NC.	190
Tulsa County, OK	585	Montgomery County,		Pender County, NC	50
Wagoner County, OK. . .	67	MD	931		
		Washington-Arlington-		**Winchester, VA-WV**	121
Tuscaloosa, AL.	205	**Alexandria, DC-VA-MD-**		Frederick County, VA . . .	73
Greene County, AL	9	**WV**	4,151	Winchester city, VA	26
Hale County, AL	18	District of Columbia, DC.	588	Hampshire County, WV .	23
Tuscaloosa County, AL. .	178	Calvert County, MD. . . .	88		
		Charles County, MD. . . .	140	**Winston-Salem, NC.**	463
Tyler, TX.	199	Prince George's County,		Davie County, NC	41
Smith County, TX	199	MD	829	Forsyth County, NC	339
		Arlington County, VA . . .	205	Stokes County, NC	46
Utica-Rome, NY	295	Clarke County, VA	14	Yadkin County, NC	38
Herkimer County, NY . . .	63	Fairfax County, VA.	1,010		
Oneida County, NY	232	Fauquier County, VA . . .	66	**Worcester, MA**	781
		Loudoun County, VA . . .	279	Worcester County, MA . .	781
Valdosta, GA.	130	Prince William County,			
Brooks County, GA	16	VA	360	**Yakima, WA**	233
Echols County, GA	4	Spotsylvania County, VA.	119	Yakima County, WA. . . .	233
Lanier County, GA.	8	Stafford County, VA	121		
Lowndes County, GA . . .	102	Warren County, VA	36	**York-Hanover, PA**	421
		Alexandria city, VA	140	York County, PA	421
Vallejo-Fairfield, CA	409	Fairfax city, VA	23		
Solano County, CA	409	Falls Church city, VA . . .	11	**Youngstown-Warren-**	
		Fredericksburg city, VA. .	22	**Boardman, OH-PA.**	571
Victoria, TX.	114	Manassas city, VA	35	Mahoning County, OH . .	240
Calhoun County, TX. . . .	20	Manassas Park city, VA .	11	Trumbull County, OH . . .	213
Goliad County, TX	7	Jefferson County, WV . .	51	Mercer County, PA.	117
Victoria County, TX	86				
		Waterloo-Cedar Falls, IA . . .	163	**Yuba City, CA**	164
Vineland-Millville-Bridgeton,		Black Hawk County, IA. .	127	Sutter County, CA	92
NJ	156	Bremer County, IA.	24	Yuba County, CA.	72
Cumberland County, NJ .	156	Grundy County, IA.	12		
				Yuma, AZ	191
		Wausau, WI	130	Yuma County, AZ	191
		Marathon County, WI . . .	130		

[1] The portion of Sullivan city in Crawford County, Missouri, is legally part of the St. Louis, MO-IL Metropolitan Statistical Area. The estimate shown here for the St. Louis, MO-IL Metropolitan Statistical Area does not include this area.

Source: U.S. Census Bureau, "CBSA-EST2007-alldata: Population Estimates and Estimated Components of Change for Metropolitan and Micropolitan Statistical Areas and Their Geographic Components: April 1, 2000 to July 1, 2007"; <http://www.census.gov/population/estimates/metrogeneral/2007/CBSA-EST2007-alldata.csv>; and unpublished data.

Table B. **Micropolitan Statistical Areas and Components—Population: 2007**

[Population as of **July 2007. (56 represents 56,000.)** Micropolitan statistical areas as defined by the U.S. Office of Management and Budget as of December 2006. All geographic boundaries for 2007 population estimates are defined as of January 1, 2007. All micropolitan areas are arranged alphabetically]

Micropolitan statistical area Component county	Popu-lation, 2007 (1,000)	Micropolitan statistical area Component county	Popu-lation, 2007 (1,000)	Micropolitan statistical area Component county	Popu-lation, 2007 (1,000)
Abbeville, LA	56	**Astoria, OR**	37	**Big Rapids, MI**	42
Vermilion Parish, LA	56	Clatsop County, OR.	37	Mecosta County, MI.	42
Aberdeen, SD	39	**Atchison, KS**	17	**Big Spring, TX**	32
Brown County, SD.	35	Atchison County, KS	17	Howard County, TX.	32
Edmunds County, SD	4	**Athens, OH**	63	**Bishop, CA**	17
Aberdeen, WA	71	Athens County, OH	63	Inyo County, CA	17
Grays Harbor County, WA .	71	**Athens, TN**	52	**Blackfoot, ID**	43
Ada, OK	37	McMinn County, TN.	52	Bingham County, ID	43
Pontotoc County, OK.	37	**Athens, TX**	79	**Bloomsburg-Berwick, PA** . .	83
Adrian, MI	101	Henderson County, TX. . . .	79	Columbia County, PA.	65
Lenawee County, MI	101	**Auburn, IN**	42	Montour County, PA	18
Alamogordo, NM	63	DeKalb County, IN	42	**Bluefield, WV-VA**	105
Otero County, NM.	63	**Auburn, NY**	80	Tazewell County, VA	44
Albany-Lebanon, OR	113	Cayuga County, NY.	80	Mercer County, WV	61
Linn County, OR	113	**Augusta-Waterville, ME**. . . .	121	**Blytheville, AR**	47
Albemarle, NC	59	Kennebec County, ME. . . .	121	Mississippi County, AR . . .	47
Stanly County, NC.	59	**Austin, MN**	38	**Bogalusa, LA**	45
Albert Lea, MN	31	Mower County, MN	38	Washington Parish, LA . . .	45
Freeborn County, MN	31	**Bainbridge, GA**	29	**Bonham, TX**	33
Albertville, AL	88	Decatur County, GA	29	Fannin County, TX	33
Marshall County, AL	88	**Baraboo, WI**	58	**Boone, IA**	26
Alexander City, AL	52	Sauk County, WI.	58	Boone County, IA	26
Coosa County, AL.	11	**Barre, VT**	59	**Boone, NC**	45
Tallapoosa County, AL. . . .	41	Washington County, VT . . .	59	Watauga County, NC.	45
Alexandria, MN	36	**Bartlesville, OK**	50	**Borger, TX**	22
Douglas County, MN	36	Washington County, OK. . .	50	Hutchinson County, TX . . .	22
Alice, TX	41	**Bastrop, LA**	29	**Bozeman, MT**	87
Jim Wells County, TX	41	Morehouse Parish, LA. . . .	29	Gallatin County, MT.	87
Allegan, MI	113	**Batavia, NY**	58	**Bradford, PA**	44
Allegan County, MI	113	Genesee County, NY.	58	McKean County, PA	44
Alma, MI	42	**Batesville, AR**	35	**Brainerd, MN**	90
Gratiot County, MI.	42	Independence County, AR .	35	Cass County, MN	29
Alpena, MI	30	**Bay City, TX**	37	Crow Wing County, MN . . .	62
Alpena County, MI.	30	Matagorda County, TX. . . .	37	**Branson, MO**	77
Altus, OK	26	**Beatrice, NE**	23	Stone County, MO.	32
Jackson County, OK	26	Gage County, NE	23	Taney County, MO	46
Americus, GA	37	**Beaver Dam, WI**	88	**Brenham, TX**	32
Schley County, GA	4	Dodge County, WI.	88	Washington County, TX . . .	32
Sumter County, GA	33	**Beckley, WV**	79	**Brevard, NC**	30
Amsterdam, NY	49	Raleigh County, WV	79	Transylvania County, NC . .	30
Montgomery County, NY . .	49	**Bedford, IN**	46	**Brigham City, UT**	48
Andrews, TX	13	Lawrence County, IN	46	Box Elder County, UT	48
Andrews County, TX	13	**Beeville, TX**	33	**Brookhaven, MS**	35
Angola, IN	33	Bee County, TX	33	Lincoln County, MS	35
Steuben County, IN.	33	**Bellefontaine, OH**	46	**Brookings, OR**	22
Arcadia, FL	35	Logan County, OH	46	Curry County, OR	22
DeSoto County, FL	35	**Bemidji, MN**	44	**Brookings, SD**	29
Ardmore, OK	57	Beltrami County, MN	44	Brookings County, SD	29
Carter County, OK.	48	**Bennettsville, SC**	29	**Brownsville, TN**	19
Love County, OK.	9	Marlboro County, SC	29	Haywood County, TN.	19
Arkadelphia, AR	24	**Bennington, VT**	36	**Brownwood, TX**	39
Clark County, AR	24	Bennington County, VT . . .	36	Brown County, TX.	39
Ashland, OH	55	**Berlin, NH-VT**	39	**Bucyrus, OH**	44
Ashland County, OH	55	Coos County, NH	33	Crawford County, OH	44
Ashtabula, OH	101	Essex County, VT	6	**Burley, ID**	40
Ashtabula County, OH	101			Cassia County, ID.	21

Appendix II   889

Micropolitan statistical area Component county	Population, 2007 (1,000)
Burley, ID—Con.	
Minidoka County, ID	19
Burlington, IA-IL	48
Henderson County, IL	8
Des Moines County, IA . . .	41
Butte-Silver Bow, MT	33
Silver Bow County, MT . . .	33
Cadillac, MI.	47
Missaukee County, MI	15
Wexford County, MI.	32
Calhoun, GA.	52
Gordon County, GA.	52
Cambridge, MD.	32
Dorchester County, MD . . .	32
Cambridge, OH.	40
Guernsey County, OH	40
Camden, AR	32
Calhoun County, AR	6
Ouachita County, AR	26
Campbellsville, KY	24
Taylor County, KY	24
Canon City, CO.	47
Fremont County, CO	47
Canton, IL.	37
Fulton County, IL.	37
Cape Girardeau-Jackson, MO-IL	93
Alexander County, IL.	8
Bollinger County, MO.	12
Cape Girardeau County, MO	73
Carbondale, IL	59
Jackson County, IL	59
Carlsbad-Artesia, NM	51
Eddy County, NM	51
Cedar City, UT	44
Iron County, UT	44
Cedartown, GA	41
Polk County, GA	41
Celina, OH	41
Mercer County, OH	41
Central City, KY	31
Muhlenberg County, KY . . .	31
Centralia, IL	40
Marion County, IL	40
Centralia, WA	74
Lewis County, WA.	74
Chambersburg, PA	142
Franklin County, PA.	142
Charleston-Mattoon, IL	62
Coles County, IL	51
Cumberland County, IL . . .	11
Chester, SC	33
Chester County, SC.	33
Chillicothe, OH	75
Ross County, OH	75
City of The Dalles, OR.	24
Wasco County, OR	24
Claremont, NH	43
Sullivan County, NH	43

Micropolitan statistical area Component county	Population, 2007 (1,000)
Clarksburg, WV.	92
Doddridge County, WV . . .	7
Harrison County, WV.	68
Taylor County, WV	16
Clarksdale, MS	28
Coahoma County, MS	28
Clearlake, CA	65
Lake County, CA.	65
Cleveland, MS.	38
Bolivar County, MS	38
Clewiston, FL	40
Hendry County, FL	40
Clinton, IA	49
Clinton County, IA.	49
Clovis, NM	45
Curry County, NM	45
Coffeyville, KS	35
Montgomery County, KS . .	35
Coldwater, MI	46
Branch County, MI	46
Columbia, TN	80
Maury County, TN.	80
Columbus, MS	60
Lowndes County, MS.	60
Columbus, NE	32
Platte County, NE	32
Concord, NH.	148
Merrimack County, NH. . . .	148
Connersville, IN	24
Fayette County, IN	24
Cookeville, TN	102
Jackson County, TN	11
Overton County, TN.	21
Putnam County, TN	70
Coos Bay, OR.	64
Coos County, OR	64
Corbin, KY	38
Whitley County, KY	38
Cordele, GA	22
Crisp County, GA	22
Corinth, MS	36
Alcorn County, MS	36
Cornelia, GA.	42
Habersham County, GA . . .	42
Corning, NY	97
Steuben County, NY	97
Corsicana, TX.	49
Navarro County, TX.	49
Cortland, NY.	48
Cortland County, NY	48
Coshocton, OH.	36
Coshocton County, OH . . .	36
Crawfordsville, IN	38
Montgomery County, IN . . .	38
Crescent City, CA	29
Del Norte County, CA	29
Crossville, TN.	53
Cumberland County, TN. . .	53
Crowley, LA	60
Acadia Parish, LA	60

Micropolitan statistical area Component county	Population, 2007 (1,000)
Cullman, AL	81
Cullman County, AL.	81
Culpeper, VA.	46
Culpeper County, VA	46
Danville, KY	54
Boyle County, KY	29
Lincoln County, KY	25
Daphne-Fairhope-Foley, AL .	172
Baldwin County, AL.	172
Decatur, IN	34
Adams County, IN.	34
Defiance, OH	39
Defiance County, OH.	39
Del Rio, TX.	48
Val Verde County, TX	48
Deming, NM	27
Luna County, NM	27
De Ridder, LA	35
Beauregard Parish, LA . . .	35
Dickinson, ND.	23
Billings County, ND	1
Stark County, ND	22
Dillon, SC.	31
Dillon County, SC	31
Dixon, IL.	35
Lee County, IL	35
Dodge City, KS	33
Ford County, KS	33
Douglas, GA	48
Atkinson County, GA	8
Coffee County, GA	40
Dublin, GA	57
Johnson County, GA	10
Laurens County, GA	48
DuBois, PA.	81
Clearfield County, PA.	81
Dumas, TX	20
Moore County, TX.	20
Duncan, OK	43
Stephens County, OK	43
Dunn, NC	109
Harnett County, NC.	109
Durango, CO.	50
La Plata County, CO	50
Durant, OK	40
Bryan County, OK.	40
Dyersburg, TN	38
Dyer County, TN	38
Eagle Pass, TX	52
Maverick County, TX	52
East Liverpool-Salem, OH . .	109
Columbiana County, OH . .	109
Easton, MD.	36
Talbot County, MD.	36
East Stroudsburg, PA	165
Monroe County, PA.	165
Edwards, CO	59
Eagle County, CO	51
Lake County, CO	8

U.S. Census Bureau, Statistical Abstract of the United States: 2009

Micropolitan statistical area Component county	Popu- lation, 2007 (1,000)	Micropolitan statistical area Component county	Popu- lation, 2007 (1,000)	Micropolitan statistical area Component county	Popu- lation, 2007 (1,000)
Effingham, IL	34	**Fort Leonard Wood, MO**	44	**Grants Pass, OR**	81
Effingham County, IL	34	Pulaski County, MO	44	Josephine County, OR	81
El Campo, TX	41	**Fort Madison-Keokuk,**		**Great Bend, KS**	28
Wharton County, TX	41	**IA-MO**	43	Barton County, KS	28
El Dorado, AR	43	Lee County, IA	36	**Greeneville, TN**	66
Union County, AR	43	Clark County, MO	7	Greene County, TN	66
Elizabeth City, NC	63	**Fort Morgan, CO**	28	**Greensburg, IN**	25
Camden County, NC	9	Morgan County, CO	28	Decatur County, IN	25
Pasquotank County, NC	41	**Fort Payne, AL**	68	**Greenville, MS**	56
Perquimans County, NC	12	DeKalb County, AL	68	Washington County, MS	56
Elk City, OK	20	**Fort Polk South, LA**	47	**Greenville, OH**	52
Beckham County, OK	20	Vernon Parish, LA	47	Darke County, OH	52
Elko, NV	49	**Fort Valley, GA**	26	**Greenwood, MS**	45
Elko County, NV	47	Peach County, GA	26	Carroll County, MS	10
Eureka County, NV	2	**Frankfort, IN**	34	Leflore County, MS	35
Ellensburg, WA	39	Clinton County, IN	34	**Greenwood, SC**	68
Kittitas County, WA	39	**Frankfort, KY**	70	Greenwood County, SC	68
Emporia, KS	39	Anderson County, KY	21	**Grenada, MS**	23
Chase County, KS	3	Franklin County, KY	48	Grenada County, MS	23
Lyon County, KS	36	**Fredericksburg, TX**	24	**Guymon, OK**	20
Enid, OK	58	Gillespie County, TX	24	Texas County, OK	20
Garfield County, OK	58	**Freeport, IL**	47	**Hammond, LA**	115
Enterprise-Ozark, AL	95	Stephenson County, IL	47	Tangipahoa Parish, LA	115
Coffee County, AL	47	**Fremont, NE**	36	**Hannibal, MO**	38
Dale County, AL	48	Dodge County, NE	36	Marion County, MO	28
Escanaba, MI	37	**Fremont, OH**	61	Ralls County, MO	10
Delta County, MI	37	Sandusky County, OH	61	**Harriman, TN**	53
Espanola, NM	41	**Gaffney, SC**	54	Roane County, TN	53
Rio Arriba County, NM	41	Cherokee County, SC	54	**Harrisburg, IL**	26
Eufaula, AL-GA	31	**Gainesville, TX**	38	Saline County, IL	26
Barbour County, AL	28	Cooke County, TX	38	**Harrison, AR**	45
Quitman County, GA	3	**Galesburg, IL**	69	Boone County, AR	37
Eureka-Arcata-Fortuna, CA	129	Knox County, IL	52	Newton County, AR	8
Humboldt County, CA	129	Warren County, IL	17	**Hastings, NE**	39
Evanston, WY	20	**Gallup, NM**	70	Adams County, NE	33
Uinta County, WY	20	McKinley County, NM	70	Clay County, NE	6
Fairmont, MN	20	**Garden City, KS**	38	**Havre, MT**	17
Martin County, MN	20	Finney County, KS	38	Hill County, MT	17
Fairmont, WV	57	**Gardnerville Ranchos, NV**	45	**Hays, KS**	27
Marion County, WV	57	Douglas County, NV	45	Ellis County, KS	27
Fallon, NV	25	**Georgetown, SC**	60	**Heber, UT**	21
Churchill County, NV	25	Georgetown County, SC	60	Wasatch County, UT	21
Faribault-Northfield, MN	62	**Gettysburg, PA**	101	**Helena, MT**	71
Rice County, MN	62	Adams County, PA	101	Jefferson County, MT	11
Farmington, MO	63	**Gillette, WY**	40	Lewis and Clark County,	
St. Francois County, MO	63	Campbell County, WY	40	MT	60
Fergus Falls, MN	57	**Glasgow, KY**	51	**Henderson, NC**	43
Otter Tail County, MN	57	Barren County, KY	41	Vance County, NC	43
Fernley, NV	52	Metcalfe County, KY	10	**Hereford, TX**	18
Lyon County, NV	52	**Gloversville, NY**	55	Deaf Smith County, TX	18
Findlay, OH	74	Fulton County, NY	55	**Hilo, HI**	173
Hancock County, OH	74	**Granbury, TX**	57	Hawaii County, HI	173
Fitzgerald, GA	28	Hood County, TX	49	**Hilton Head Island-**	
Ben Hill County, GA	18	Somervell County, TX	8	**Beaufort, SC**	169
Irwin County, GA	10	**Grand Island, NE**	70	Beaufort County, SC	147
Forest City, NC	63	Hall County, NE	56	Jasper County, SC	22
Rutherford County, NC	63	Howard County, NE	7	**Hobbs, NM**	58
Forrest City, AR	27	Merrick County, NE	8	Lea County, NM	58
St. Francis County, AR	27	**Grants, NM**	27	**Homosassa Springs, FL**	140
Fort Dodge, IA	39	Cibola County, NM	27	Citrus County, FL	140
Webster County, IA	39				

U.S. Census Bureau, Statistical Abstract of the United States: 2009

Micropolitan statistical area Component county	Population, 2007 (1,000)	Micropolitan statistical area Component county	Population, 2007 (1,000)	Micropolitan statistical area Component county	Population, 2007 (1,000)
Hood River, OR	**21**	**Kearney, NE**	**52**	**Levelland, TX**	**22**
Hood River County, OR . . .	21	Buffalo County, NE	45	Hockley County, TX.	22
		Kearney County, NE	7		
Hope, AR	**33**			**Lewisburg, PA**	**44**
Hempstead County, AR . . .	23	**Keene, NH**	**78**	Union County, PA	44
Nevada County, AR.	9	Cheshire County, NH.	78		
				Lewisburg, TN	**29**
Houghton, MI	**37**	**Kendallville, IN**	**48**	Marshall County, TN	29
Houghton County, MI.	35	Noble County, IN.	48		
Keweenaw County, MI. . . .	2			**Lewistown, PA**	**47**
		Kennett, MO	**32**	Mifflin County, PA	47
Hudson, NY	**62**	Dunklin County, MO	32		
Columbia County, NY	62			**Lexington, NE**.	**27**
		Kerrville, TX	**48**	Dawson County, NE	25
Humboldt, TN	**49**	Kerr County, TX	48	Gosper County, NE.	2
Gibson County, TN	49				
		Ketchikan, AK.	**13**	**Lexington Park, MD**	**100**
Huntingdon, PA	**46**	Ketchikan Gateway		St. Mary's County, MD. . . .	100
Huntingdon County, PA . . .	46	Borough, AK.	13		
				Liberal, KS	**23**
Huntington, IN	**38**	**Key West, FL**	**73**	Seward County, KS.	23
Huntington County, IN	38	Monroe County, FL	73		
				Lincoln, IL	**30**
Huntsville, TX.	**64**	**Kill Devil Hills, NC**	**34**	Logan County, IL.	30
Walker County, TX	64	Dare County, NC.	34		
				Lincolnton, NC	**73**
Huron, SD.	**16**	**Kingsville, TX**	**31**	Lincoln County, NC	73
Beadle County, SD	16	Kenedy County, TX	(Z)		
		Kleberg County, TX.	30	**Lock Haven, PA**	**37**
Hutchinson, KS.	**63**			Clinton County, PA	37
Reno County, KS	63	**Kinston, NC**	**57**		
		Lenoir County, NC.	57	**Logansport, IN**	**39**
Hutchinson, MN	**37**			Cass County, IN	39
McLeod County, MN	37	**Kirksville, MO**	**29**		
		Adair County, MO	25	**London, KY**	**57**
Indiana, PA.	**88**	Schuyler County, MO.	4	Laurel County, KY.	57
Indiana County, PA	88				
		Klamath Falls, OR.	**67**	**Los Alamos, NM**	**19**
Indianola, MS	**31**	Klamath County, OR	67	Los Alamos County, NM. . .	19
Sunflower County, MS. . . .	31				
		Kodiak, AK.	**13**	**Lufkin, TX**.	**83**
Iron Mountain, MI-WI.	**32**	Kodiak Island Borough, AK.	13	Angelina County, TX	83
Dickinson County, MI.	27				
Florence County, WI	5	**Laconia, NH**	**61**	**Lumberton, NC**	**128**
		Belknap County, NH	61	Robeson County, NC.	128
Jackson, WY-ID	**28**				
Teton County, ID	8	**La Follette, TN**	**41**	**Macomb, IL**.	**32**
Teton County, WY.	20	Campbell County, TN	41	McDonough County, IL . . .	32
Jacksonville, IL.	**40**	**La Grande, OR**	**25**	**Madison, IN**	**33**
Morgan County, IL.	35	Union County, OR.	25	Jefferson County, IN	33
Scott County, IL	5				
		LaGrange, GA.	**64**	**Madisonville, KY**.	**46**
Jacksonville, TX	**48**	Troup County, GA	64	Hopkins County, KY	46
Cherokee County, TX	48				
		Lake City, FL	**68**	**Magnolia, AR**	**24**
Jamestown, ND.	**20**	Columbia County, FL.	68	Columbia County, AR	24
Stutsman County, ND	20				
		Lamesa, TX	**14**	**Malone, NY**.	**50**
Jamestown-Dunkirk-		Dawson County, TX.	14	Franklin County, NY	50
Fredonia, NY.	**134**				
Chautauqua County, NY . . .	134	**Lancaster, SC**	**73**	**Manhattan, KS**	**114**
		Lancaster County, SC	73	Geary County, KS.	25
Jasper, IN.	**54**			Pottawatomie County, KS. .	19
Dubois County, IN.	41	**Laramie, WY**.	**32**	Riley County, KS.	69
Pike County, IN.	13	Albany County, WY	32		
				Manitowoc, WI	**81**
Jennings, LA	**31**	**Las Vegas, NM**	**29**	Manitowoc County, WI. . . .	81
Jefferson Davis Parish, LA.	31	San Miguel County, NM. . .	29		
				Mankato-North Mankato,	
Jesup, GA.	**29**	**Laurel, MS**	**85**	**MN**	**91**
Wayne County, GA	29	Jasper County, MS	18	Blue Earth County, MN . . .	60
		Jones County, MS.	67	Nicollet County, MN.	32
Juneau, AK.	**31**				
Juneau City and Borough,		**Laurinburg, NC**.	**36**	**Marinette, WI-MI**	**67**
AK.	31	Scotland County, NC.	36	Menominee County, MI . . .	24
				Marinette County, WI.	43
Kahului-Wailuku, HI	**142**	**Lawrenceburg, TN**	**41**		
Maui County, HI	142	Lawrence County, TN	41	**Marion, IN**.	**69**
				Grant County, IN.	69
Kalispell, MT	**87**	**Lebanon, MO**	**35**		
Flathead County, MT.	87	Laclede County, MO	35	**Marion, OH**	**65**
				Marion County, OH	65
Kapaa, HI	**63**	**Lebanon, NH-VT**	**171**		
Kauai County, HI.	63	Grafton County, NH.	86	**Marion-Herrin, IL**.	**65**
		Orange County, VT	29	Williamson County, IL	65
		Windsor County, VT	57		

892   Appendix II

Micropolitan statistical area Component county	Population, 2007 (1,000)
Marquette, MI	65
Marquette County, MI	65
Marshall, MN	25
Lyon County, MN	25
Marshall, MO	23
Saline County, MO	23
Marshall, TX	64
Harrison County, TX	64
Marshalltown, IA	39
Marshall County, IA	39
Marshfield-Wisconsin Rapids, WI	74
Wood County, WI	74
Martin, TN	33
Weakley County, TN	33
Martinsville, VA	70
Henry County, VA	56
Martinsville city, VA	15
Maryville, MO	22
Nodaway County, MO	22
Mason City, IA	52
Cerro Gordo County, IA	44
Worth County, IA	8
Mayfield, KY	38
Graves County, KY	38
Maysville, KY	31
Lewis County, KY	14
Mason County, KY	17
McAlester, OK	45
Pittsburg County, OK	45
McComb, MS	53
Amite County, MS	13
Pike County, MS	40
McMinnville, TN	40
Warren County, TN	40
McPherson, KS	29
McPherson County, KS	29
Meadville, PA	89
Crawford County, PA	89
Menomonie, WI	42
Dunn County, WI	42
Meridian, MS	105
Clarke County, MS	17
Kemper County, MS	10
Lauderdale County, MS	77
Merrill, WI	30
Lincoln County, WI	30
Mexico, MO	26
Audrain County, MO	26
Miami, OK	32
Ottawa County, OK	32
Middlesborough, KY	29
Bell County, KY	29
Midland, MI	83
Midland County, MI	83
Milledgeville, GA	56
Baldwin County, GA	46
Hancock County, GA	10
Minden, LA	41
Webster Parish, LA	41

Micropolitan statistical area Component county	Population, 2007 (1,000)
Mineral Wells, TX	27
Palo Pinto County, TX	27
Minot, ND	63
McHenry County, ND	5
Renville County, ND	2
Ward County, ND	56
Mitchell, SD	23
Davison County, SD	19
Hanson County, SD	4
Moberly, MO	26
Randolph County, MO	26
Monroe, WI	36
Green County, WI	36
Montrose, CO	40
Montrose County, CO	40
Morehead City, NC	63
Carteret County, NC	63
Morgan City, LA	51
St. Mary Parish, LA	51
Moscow, ID	36
Latah County, ID	36
Moses Lake, WA	83
Grant County, WA	83
Moultrie, GA	45
Colquitt County, GA	45
Mountain Home, AR	42
Baxter County, AR	42
Mountain Home, ID	29
Elmore County, ID	29
Mount Airy, NC	72
Surry County, NC	72
Mount Pleasant, MI	67
Isabella County, MI	67
Mount Pleasant, TX	29
Titus County, TX	29
Mount Sterling, KY	44
Bath County, KY	12
Menifee County, KY	7
Montgomery County, KY	25
Mount Vernon, IL	48
Hamilton County, IL	8
Jefferson County, IL	40
Mount Vernon, OH	59
Knox County, OH	59
Murray, KY	36
Calloway County, KY	36
Muscatine, IA	54
Louisa County, IA	12
Muscatine County, IA	42
Muskogee, OK	71
Muskogee County, OK	71
Nacogdoches, TX	62
Nacogdoches County, TX	62
Natchez, MS-LA	51
Concordia Parish, LA	19
Adams County, MS	32
Natchitoches, LA	39
Natchitoches Parish, LA	39
New Bern, NC	119
Craven County, NC	97
Jones County, NC	10
Pamlico County, NC	13

Micropolitan statistical area Component county	Population, 2007 (1,000)
Newberry, SC	38
Newberry County, SC	38
New Castle, IN	47
Henry County, IN	47
New Castle, PA	91
Lawrence County, PA	91
New Iberia, LA	75
Iberia Parish, LA	75
New Philadelphia-Dover, OH	91
Tuscarawas County, OH	91
Newport, TN	35
Cocke County, TN	35
Newton, IA	37
Jasper County, IA	37
New Ulm, MN	26
Brown County, MN	26
Nogales, AZ	43
Santa Cruz County, AZ	43
Norfolk, NE	48
Madison County, NE	34
Pierce County, NE	7
Stanton County, NE	6
North Platte, NE	37
Lincoln County, NE	36
Logan County, NE	1
McPherson County, NE	1
North Vernon, IN	28
Jennings County, IN	28
North Wilkesboro, NC	67
Wilkes County, NC	67
Norwalk, OH	60
Huron County, OH	60
Oak Harbor, WA	81
Island County, WA	81
Oak Hill, WV	46
Fayette County, WV	46
Ocean Pines, MD	49
Worcester County, MD	49
Ogdensburg-Massena, NY	110
St. Lawrence County, NY	110
Oil City, PA	55
Venango County, PA	55
Okeechobee, FL	40
Okeechobee County, FL	40
Olean, NY	80
Cattaraugus County, NY	80
Oneonta, NY	62
Otsego County, NY	62
Ontario, OR-ID	54
Payette County, ID	23
Malheur County, OR	31
Opelousas-Eunice, LA	91
St. Landry Parish, LA	91
Orangeburg, SC	90
Orangeburg County, SC	90
Oskaloosa, IA	22
Mahaska County, IA	22
Ottawa-Streator, IL	154
Bureau County, IL	35
LaSalle County, IL	113

U.S. Census Bureau, Statistical Abstract of the United States: 2009

Micropolitan statistical area / Component county	Popu-lation, 2007 (1,000)	Micropolitan statistical area / Component county	Popu-lation, 2007 (1,000)	Micropolitan statistical area / Component county	Popu-lation, 2007 (1,000)
Ottawa-Streator, IL—Con.		**Plymouth, IN**	47	**Roseburg, OR**	104
Putnam County, IL	6	Marshall County, IN	47	Douglas County, OR	104
Ottumwa, IA	36	**Point Pleasant, WV-OH**	56	**Roswell, NM**	63
Wapello County, IA	36	Gallia County, OH	31	Chaves County, NM	63
Owatonna, MN	36	Mason County, WV	26	**Ruidoso, NM**	21
Steele County, MN	36	**Ponca City, OK**	46	Lincoln County, NM	21
Owosso, MI	72	Kay County, OK	46	**Russellville, AR**	81
Shiawassee County, MI	72	**Pontiac, IL**	38	Pope County, AR	59
Oxford, MS	43	Livingston County, IL	38	Yell County, AR	22
Lafayette County, MS	43	**Poplar Bluff, MO**	41	**Ruston, LA**	58
Paducah, KY-IL	98	Butler County, MO	41	Jackson Parish, LA	15
Massac County, IL	15	**Portales, NM**	19	Lincoln Parish, LA	43
Ballard County, KY	8	Roosevelt County, NM	19	**Rutland, VT**	63
Livingston County, KY	10	**Port Angeles, WA**	70	Rutland County, VT	63
McCracken County, KY	65	Clallam County, WA	70	**Safford, AZ**	43
Pahrump, NV	44	**Portsmouth, OH**	76	Graham County, AZ	35
Nye County, NV	44	Scioto County, OH	76	Greenlee County, AZ	8
Palatka, FL	74	**Pottsville, PA**	147	**St. Marys, GA**	49
Putnam County, FL	74	Schuylkill County, PA	147	Camden County, GA	49
Palestine, TX	57	**Price, UT**	20	**St. Marys, PA**	33
Anderson County, TX	57	Carbon County, UT	20	Elk County, PA	33
Pampa, TX	23	**Prineville, OR**	23	**Salina, KS**	61
Gray County, TX	22	Crook County, OR	23	Ottawa County, KS	6
Roberts County, TX	1	**Pullman, WA**	41	Saline County, KS	55
Paragould, AR	40	Whitman County, WA	41	**Salisbury, NC**	137
Greene County, AR	40	**Quincy, IL-MO**	77	Rowan County, NC	137
Paris, TN	32	Adams County, IL	67	**Sanford, NC**	58
Henry County, TN	32	Lewis County, MO	10	Lee County, NC	58
Paris, TX	49	**Raymondville, TX**	21	**Sault Ste. Marie, MI**	39
Lamar County, TX	49	Willacy County, TX	21	Chippewa County, MI	39
Parsons, KS	22	**Red Bluff, CA**	61	**Sayre, PA**	61
Labette County, KS	22	Tehama County, CA	61	Bradford County, PA	61
Payson, AZ	52	**Red Wing, MN**	46	**Scottsbluff, NE**	37
Gila County, AZ	52	Goodhue County, MN	46	Banner County, NE	1
Pecos, TX	11	**Rexburg, ID**	49	Scotts Bluff County, NE	36
Reeves County, TX	11	Fremont County, ID	13	**Scottsboro, AL**	53
Pella, IA	33	Madison County, ID	37	Jackson County, AL	53
Marion County, IA	33	**Richmond, IN**	68	**Scottsburg, IN**	24
Pendleton-Hermiston, OR	85	Wayne County, IN	68	Scott County, IN	24
Morrow County, OR	11	**Richmond-Berea, KY**	98	**Seaford, DE**	184
Umatilla County, OR	73	Madison County, KY	81	Sussex County, DE	184
Peru, IN	37	Rockcastle County, KY	17	**Searcy, AR**	73
Miami County, IN	37	**Rio Grande City-Roma, TX**	62	White County, AR	73
Phoenix Lake-Cedar Ridge, CA	56	Starr County, TX	62	**Sebring, FL**	99
Tuolumne County, CA	56	**Riverton, WY**	37	Highlands County, FL	99
Picayune, MS	57	Fremont County, WY	37	**Sedalia, MO**	41
Pearl River County, MS	57	**Roanoke Rapids, NC**	76	Pettis County, MO	41
Pierre, SD	20	Halifax County, NC	55	**Selinsgrove, PA**	38
Hughes County, SD	17	Northampton County, NC	21	Snyder County, PA	38
Stanley County, SD	3	**Rochelle, IL**	55	**Selma, AL**	43
Pierre Part, LA	23	Ogle County, IL	55	Dallas County, AL	43
Assumption Parish, LA	23	**Rockingham, NC**	46	**Seneca, SC**	71
Pittsburg, KS	39	Richmond County, NC	46	Oconee County, SC	71
Crawford County, KS	39	**Rockland, ME**	41	**Seneca Falls, NY**	34
Plainview, TX	36	Knox County, ME	41	Seneca County, NY	34
Hale County, TX	36	**Rock Springs, WY**	39	**Sevierville, TN**	84
Platteville, WI	49	Sweetwater County, WY	39	Sevier County, TN	84
Grant County, WI	49	**Rolla, MO**	43	**Seymour, IN**	42
Plattsburgh, NY	82	Phelps County, MO	43	Jackson County, IN	42
Clinton County, NY	82				

894   Appendix II

Micropolitan statistical area Component county	Population, 2007 (1,000)	Micropolitan statistical area Component county	Population, 2007 (1,000)	Micropolitan statistical area Component county	Population, 2007 (1,000)
Shawnee, OK	69	**Sulphur Springs, TX**	34	**Union, SC**	28
Pottawatomie County, OK	69	Hopkins County, TX	34	Union County, SC	28
Shelby, NC	98	**Summerville, GA**	27	**Union City, TN-KY**	38
Cleveland County, NC	98	Chattooga County, GA	27	Fulton County, KY	7
Shelbyville, TN	44	**Sunbury, PA**	91	Obion County, TN	32
Bedford County, TN	44	Northumberland County, PA	91	**Urbana, OH**	40
Shelton, WA	56	**Susanville, CA**	35	Champaign County, OH	40
Mason County, WA	56	Lassen County, CA	35	**Uvalde, TX**	27
Sheridan, WY	28	**Sweetwater, TX**	15	Uvalde County, TX	27
Sheridan County, WY	28	Nolan County, TX	15	**Valley, AL**	35
Sidney, OH	49	**Tahlequah, OK**	45	Chambers County, AL	35
Shelby County, OH	49	Cherokee County, OK	45	**Van Wert, OH**	29
Sierra Vista-Douglas, AZ	128	**Talladega-Sylacauga, AL**	80	Van Wert County, OH	29
Cochise County, AZ	128	Talladega County, AL	80	**Vermillion, SD**	13
Sikeston, MO	41	**Tallulah, LA**	12	Clay County, SD	13
Scott County, MO	41	Madison Parish, LA	12	**Vernal, UT**	29
Silver City, NM	30	**Taos, NM**	32	Uintah County, UT	29
Grant County, NM	30	Taos County, NM	32	**Vernon, TX**	14
Silverthorne, CO	27	**Taylorville, IL**	35	Wilbarger County, TX	14
Summit County, CO	27	Christian County, IL	35	**Vicksburg, MS**	49
Snyder, TX	16	**The Villages, FL**	72	Warren County, MS	49
Scurry County, TX	16	Sumter County, FL	72	**Vidalia, GA**	37
Somerset, KY	60	**Thomaston, GA**	28	Montgomery County, GA	9
Pulaski County, KY	60	Upson County, GA	28	Toombs County, GA	28
Somerset, PA	78	**Thomasville, GA**	45	**Vincennes, IN**	38
Somerset County, PA	78	Thomas County, GA	45	Knox County, IN	38
Southern Pines-Pinehurst, NC	84	**Thomasville-Lexington, NC**	157	**Wabash, IN**	33
Moore County, NC	84	Davidson County, NC	157	Wabash County, IN	33
Spearfish, SD	23	**Tiffin, OH**	57	**Wahpeton, ND-MN**	23
Lawrence County, SD	23	Seneca County, OH	57	Wilkin County, MN	6
Spencer, IA	17	**Tifton, GA**	42	Richland County, ND	16
Clay County, IA	17	Tift County, GA	42	**Walla Walla, WA**	58
Spirit Lake, IA	17	**Toccoa, GA**	25	Walla Walla County, WA	58
Dickinson County, IA	17	Stephens County, GA	25	**Walterboro, SC**	39
Starkville, MS	44	**Torrington, CT**	188	Colleton County, SC	39
Oktibbeha County, MS	44	Litchfield County, CT	188	**Wapakoneta, OH**	46
Statesboro, GA	66	**Traverse City, MI**	142	Auglaize County, OH	46
Bulloch County, GA	66	Benzie County, MI	18	**Warren, PA**	41
Statesville-Mooresville, NC	151	Grand Traverse County, MI	85	Warren County, PA	41
Iredell County, NC	151	Kalkaska County, MI	17	**Warrensburg, MO**	52
Staunton-Waynesboro, VA	116	Leelanau County, MI	22	Johnson County, MO	52
Augusta County, VA	71	**Troy, AL**	30	**Warsaw, IN**	76
Staunton city, VA	24	Pike County, AL	30	Kosciusko County, IN	76
Waynesboro city, VA	22	**Truckee-Grass Valley, CA**	97	**Washington, IN**	30
Stephenville, TX	36	Nevada County, CA	97	Daviess County, IN	30
Erath County, TX	36	**Tullahoma, TN**	99	**Washington, NC**	46
Sterling, CO	21	Coffee County, TN	52	Beaufort County, NC	46
Logan County, CO	21	Franklin County, TN	41	**Washington, OH**	28
Sterling, IL	59	Moore County, TN	6	Fayette County, OH	28
Whiteside County, IL	59	**Tupelo, MS**	132	**Watertown, SD**	32
Stevens Point, WI	68	Itawamba County, MS	23	Codington County, SD	26
Portage County, WI	68	Lee County, MS	80	Hamlin County, SD	6
Stillwater, OK	80	Pontotoc County, MS	29	**Watertown-Fort Atkinson, WI**	80
Payne County, OK	80	**Tuskegee, AL**	22	Jefferson County, WI	80
Storm Lake, IA	20	Macon County, AL	22	**Watertown-Fort Drum, NY**	117
Buena Vista County, IA	20	**Twin Falls, ID**	93	Jefferson County, NY	117
Sturgis, MI	62	Jerome County, ID	20	**Wauchula, FL**	29
St. Joseph County, MI	62	Twin Falls County, ID	73	Hardee County, FL	29
		Ukiah, CA	86		
		Mendocino County, CA	86		

Appendix II   895

U.S. Census Bureau, Statistical Abstract of the United States: 2009

Micropolitan statistical area Component county	Population, 2007 (1,000)	Micropolitan statistical area Component county	Population, 2007 (1,000)	Micropolitan statistical area Component county	Population, 2007 (1,000)
Waycross, GA	**54**	**Williston, ND**	**20**	**Woodward, OK**	**20**
Pierce County, GA	18	Williams County, ND	20	Woodward County, OK	20
Ware County, GA	36				
		Willmar, MN	**41**	**Wooster, OH**	**114**
West Helena, AR	**22**	Kandiyohi County, MN	41	Wayne County, OH	114
Phillips County, AR	22				
		Wilmington, OH	**43**	**Worthington, MN**	**20**
West Plains, MO	**39**	Clinton County, OH	43	Nobles County, MN	20
Howell County, MO	39				
		Wilson, NC	**77**	**Yankton, SD**	**22**
West Point, MS	**21**	Wilson County, NC	77	Yankton County, SD	22
Clay County, MS	21				
		Winfield, KS	**34**	**Yazoo City, MS**	**27**
Whitewater, WI	**101**	Cowley County, KS	34	Yazoo County, MS	27
Walworth County, WI	101				
		Winona, MN	**50**	**Zanesville, OH**	**85**
Willimantic, CT	**117**	Winona County, MN	50	Muskingum County, OH	85
Windham County, CT	117				

Z Less than 500.

Source: U.S. Census Bureau, "CBSA-EST2007-alldata: Population Estimates and Estimated Components of Change for Metropolitan and Micropolitan Statistical Areas and Their Geographic Components: April 1, 2000 to July 1, 2007"; <http://www.census.gov/population/estimates/metrogeneral/2007/CBSA-EST2007-alldata.csv>; and unpublished data.

U.S. Census Bureau, Statistical Abstract of the United States: 2009

Appendix III
Limitations of the Data

Introduction—The data presented in this *Statistical Abstract* came from many sources. The sources include not only federal statistical bureaus and other organizations that collect and issue statistics as their principal activity, but also governmental administrative and regulatory agencies, private research bodies, trade associations, insurance companies, health associations, and private organizations such as the National Education Association and philanthropic foundations. Consequently, the data vary considerably as to reference periods, definitions of terms and, for ongoing series, the number and frequency of time periods for which data are available.

The statistics presented were obtained and tabulated by various means. Some statistics are based on complete enumerations or censuses while others are based on samples. Some information is extracted from records kept for administrative or regulatory purposes (school enrollment, hospital records, securities registration, financial accounts, social security records, income tax returns, etc.), while other information is obtained explicitly for statistical purposes through interviews or by mail. The estimation procedures used vary from highly sophisticated scientific techniques, to crude "informed guesses."

Each set of data relates to a group of individuals or units of interest referred to as the *target universe* or *target population*, or simply as the *universe* or *population*. Prior to data collection the target universe should be clearly defined. For example, if data are to be collected for the universe of households in the United States, it is necessary to define a "household." The target universe may not be completely tractable. Cost and other considerations may restrict data collection to a *survey universe* based on some available list, such list may be inaccurate or out of date. This list is called a *survey frame* or *sampling frame*.

The data in many tables are based on data obtained for all population units, *a census,* or on data obtained for only a portion, or *sample,* of the population units. When the data presented are based on a sample, the sample is usually a scientifically selected *probability sample.* This is a sample selected from a list or sampling frame in such a way that every possible sample has a known chance of selection and usually each unit selected can be assigned a number, greater than zero and less than or equal to one, representing its likelihood or probability of selection.

For large-scale sample surveys, the probability sample of units is often selected as a multistage sample. The first stage of a multistage sample is the selection of a probability sample of large groups of population members, referred to as primary sampling units (PSUs). For example, in a national multistage household sample, PSUs are often counties or groups of counties. The second stage of a multistage sample is the selection, within each PSU selected at the first stage, of smaller groups of population units, referred to as secondary sampling units. In subsequent stages of selection, smaller and smaller nested groups are chosen until the ultimate sample of population units is obtained. To qualify a multistage sample as a probability sample, all stages of sampling must be carried out using probability sampling methods.

Prior to selection at each stage of a multistage (or a single stage) sample, a list of the sampling units or sampling frame for that stage must be obtained. For example, for the first stage of selection of a national household sample, a list of the counties and county groups that form the PSUs must be obtained. For the final stage of selection, lists of households, and sometimes persons within the households, have to be compiled in the field. For surveys of economic entities and for the economic censuses the Bureau generally uses a frame constructed from the Bureau's Business Register. The Business Register contains all establishments with payroll in the United States including small single establishment firms as well as large multi-establishment firms.

Wherever the quantities in a table refer to an entire universe, but are constructed from data collected in a sample survey, the table quantities are referred to as *sample estimates.* In constructing a sample estimate, an attempt is made to come as close as is feasible to the corresponding universe quantity that would be obtained from a complete census of the universe. Estimates based on a sample will, however, generally differ from the hypothetical census figures. Two classifications of errors are associated with estimates based on sample surveys: (1) *sampling error*—the error arising from the use of a sample, rather than a census, to estimate population quantities and (2) *nonsampling error*—those errors arising from nonsampling sources. As discussed below, the magnitude of the sampling error for an estimate can usually be estimated from the sample data. However, the magnitude of the nonsampling error for an estimate can rarely be estimated. Consequently, actual error in an estimate exceeds the error that can be estimated.

The particular sample used in a survey is only one of a large number of possible samples of the same size which could have been selected using the same sampling procedure. Estimates derived from the different samples would, in general, differ from each other. The *standard error* (SE) is a measure of the variation among the estimates derived from all possible samples. The standard error is the most commonly used measure of the sampling error of an estimate. Valid estimates of the standard errors of survey estimates can usually be calculated from the data collected in a probability sample. For convenience, the standard error is sometimes expressed as a percent of the estimate and is called the relative standard error or *coefficient of variation* (CV). For example, an estimate of 200 units with an estimated standard error of 10 units has an estimated CV of 5 percent.

A sample estimate and an estimate of its standard error or CV can be used to construct interval estimates that have a prescribed confidence that the interval includes the average of the estimates derived from all possible samples with a known probability. To illustrate, if all possible samples were selected under essentially the same general conditions, and using the same sample design, and if an estimate and its estimated standard error were calculated from each sample, then: 1) approximately 68 percent of the intervals from one standard error below the estimate to one standard error above the estimate would include the average estimate derived from all possible samples; 2) approximately 90 percent of the intervals from 1.6 standard errors below the estimate to 1.6 standard errors above the estimate would include the average estimate derived from all possible samples; and 3) approximately 95 percent of the intervals from two standard errors below the estimate to two standard errors above the estimate would include the average estimate derived from all possible samples.

Thus, for a particular sample, one can say with the appropriate level of confidence (e.g., 90 percent or 95 percent) that the average of all possible samples is included in the constructed interval. Example of a confidence interval: An estimate is 200 units with a standard error of 10 units. An approximately 90 percent confidence interval (plus or minus 1.6 standard errors) is from 184 to 216.

All surveys and censuses are subject to nonsampling errors. Nonsampling errors are of two kinds—*random* and *nonrandom.* Random nonsampling errors arise because of the varying interpretation of questions (by respondents or interviewers) and varying actions of coders, keyers, and other processors. Some randomness is also introduced when respondents must estimate. Nonrandom nonsampling errors result from total nonresponse (no usable data obtained for a sampled unit), partial or item nonresponse (only a portion of a response may be usable), inability or unwillingness on the part of respondents to provide correct information, difficulty interpreting questions, mistakes

U.S. Census Bureau, Statistical Abstract of the United States: 2009

in recording or keying data, errors of collection or processing, and coverage problems (overcoverage and undercoverage of the target universe). Random nonresponse errors usually, but not always, result in an understatement of sampling errors and thus an overstatement of the precision of survey estimates. Estimating the magnitude of nonsampling errors would require special experiments or access to independent data and, consequently, the magnitudes are seldom available.

Nearly all types of nonsampling errors that affect surveys also occur in complete censuses. Since surveys can be conducted on a smaller scale than censuses, nonsampling errors can presumably be controlled more tightly. Relatively more funds and effort can perhaps be expended toward eliciting responses, detecting and correcting response error, and reducing processing errors. As a result, survey results can sometimes be more accurate than census results.

To compensate for suspected nonrandom errors, adjustments of the sample estimates are often made. For example, adjustments are frequently made for nonresponse, both total and partial. Adjustments made for either type of nonresponse are often referred to as *imputations*. Imputation for total nonresponse is usually made by substituting for the questionnaire responses of the nonrespondents the "average" questionnaire responses of the respondents. These imputations usually are made separately within various groups of sample members, formed by attempting to place respondents and nonrespondents together that have "similar" design or ancillary characteristics. Imputation for item nonresponse is usually made by substituting for a missing item the response to that item of a respondent having characteristics that are "similar" to those of the nonrespondent.

For an estimate calculated from a sample survey, the *total error* in the estimate is composed of the sampling error, which can usually be estimated from the sample, and the nonsampling error, which usually cannot be estimated from the sample. The total error present in a population quantity obtained from a complete census is composed of only nonsampling errors. Ideally, estimates of the total error associated with data given in the *Statistical Abstract* tables should be given. However, due to the unavailability of estimates of nonsampling errors, only estimates of the levels of sampling errors, in terms of estimated standard errors or coefficients of variation, are available. To obtain estimates of the estimated standard errors from the sample of interest, obtain a copy of the referenced report which appears at the end of each table.

Source of Additional Material: The Federal Committee on Statistical Methodology (FCSM) is an interagency committee dedicated to improving the quality of federal statistics <http://fcsm.ssd.census.gov>.

Principal data bases—Beginning below are brief descriptions of 35 of the sample surveys and censuses that provide a substantial portion of the data contained in this *Abstract.*

U.S. DEPARTMENT OF AGRICULTURE, National Agriculture Statistics Service

Basic Area Frame Sample

Universe, Frequency, and Types of Data: June agricultural survey collects data on planted acreage and livestock inventories on all land in the 48 contiguous states and Hawaii. The survey also serves to measure list incompleteness and is subsampled for multiple frame surveys.

Type of Data Collection Operation: Stratified probability sample of about 11,000 land area units of about 1 sq. mile (range from 0.1 sq. mile in cities to several sq. miles in open grazing areas). Sample includes 42,000 parcels of agricultural land. About 20 percent of the sample replaced annually.

Data Collection and Imputation Procedures: Data collection is by personal enumeration. Imputation is based on enumerator observation or data reported by respondents having similar agricultural characteristics.

Estimates of Sampling Error: Estimated CVs range from 1 percent to 2 percent for regional estimates to 3 percent to

6 percent for state estimates of major crop acres and livestock inventories.

Other (nonsampling) Errors: Minimized through rigid quality controls on the collection process and careful review of all reported data.

Sources of Additional Material: U.S. Department of Agriculture, National Agricultural Statistics Service, USDA's National Agricultural Statistics Service: The Fact Finders of Agriculture, March 2007.

Multiple Frame Surveys

Universe, Frequency, and Types of Data: Surveys of U.S. farm operators to obtain data on major livestock inventories, selected crop acreage and production, grain stocks, and farm labor characteristics, farm economic data, and chemical use data. Estimates are made quarterly, semi-annually, or annually depending on the data series.

Type of Data Collection Operation: Primary frame is obtained from general or special purpose lists, supplemented by a probability sample of land areas used to estimate for list incompleteness.

Data Collection and Imputation Procedures: Mail, telephone, or personal interviews used for initial data collection. Mail nonrespondent follow-up by phone and personal interviews. Imputation based on average of respondents.

Estimates of Sampling Error: Estimated CVs range from 1 percent to 2 percent at the U.S. level for crop and livestock data series and 3 to 5 percent for economic data. Regional CVs range from 3 to 6 percent, while state estimate CVs run 5 to 10 percent.

Other (nonsampling) Errors: In addition to above, replicated sampling procedures used to monitor effects of changes in survey procedures.

Sources of Additional Material: U.S. Department of Agriculture, National Agricultural Statistics Service), USDA's National Agricultural Statistics Service: The Fact Finders of Agriculture, March 2007.

Objective Yield Surveys

Universe, Frequency, and Types of Data: Monthly surveys during the growing season of corn, cotton, potatoes, soybeans, and wheat fields in top producing states for forecasting and estimating yield per acre.

Type of Data Collection Operation: Random location of plots in probability sample. Corn, cotton, soybeans, spring wheat, and durum wheat selected in June from Basic Area Frame Sample (see above). Winter wheat and potatoes selected from March and June multiple frame surveys, respectively.

Data Collection and Imputation Procedures: Enumerators count and measure plant characteristics in sample fields. Production measured from plots at harvest. Harvest loss measured from post harvest gleanings.

Estimates of Sampling Error: CVs for national estimates of production are about 2 to 3 percent.

Other (nonsampling) Errors: In addition to above, replicated sampling procedures used to monitor effects of changes in survey procedures.

Sources of Additional Material: U.S. Department of Agriculture, National Agricultural Statistics Service), USDA's National Agricultural Statistics Service: The Fact Finders of Agriculture, March 2007.

U.S. BUREAU OF JUSTICE STATISTICS (BJS)

National Crime Victimization Survey

Universe, Frequency, and Types of Data: Monthly survey of individuals and households in the United States to obtain data on criminal victimization of those units for compilation of annual estimates.

Type of Data Collection Operation: National probability sample survey of about 42,000 interviewed households in 203 PSUs selected from a list of addresses from the 1990 census, supplemented by new construction permits and an area sample where permits are not required.

Data Collection and Imputation Procedures: Interviews are conducted every 6 months for 3 years for each household in the sample; 7,000 households are interviewed monthly. Personal interviews are used in the first interview; the intervening interviews are conducted by telephone whenever possible.

Estimates of Sampling Error: CVs for 2005 estimates are: 4.1 percent for personal crimes (includes all crimes of violence plus purse snatching crimes), 4.2 percent for crimes of violence; 16.2 percent for estimate of rape/sexual assault counts; 9.7 percent for robbery counts; 4.4 percent for assault counts; 15.1 percent for purse snatching/pocket picking; 2.2 percent for property crimes; 4.2 percent for burglary counts; 2.5 percent for theft (of property); and 6.6 percent for motor vehicle theft counts.

Other (nonsampling) Errors: Respondent recall errors which may include reporting incidents for other than the reference period; interviewer coding and processing errors; and possible mistaken reporting or classifying of events. Adjustment is made for a household noninterview rate of about 9 percent and for a within-household noninterview rate of 16 percent.

Sources of Additional Material: U.S. Bureau of Justice Statistics, *Criminal Victimization in the United States*, annual.

U.S. Bureau of Labor Statistics

Consumer Expenditure Survey (CE)

Universe, Frequency and Types of Data: Consists of two continuous components: a quarterly interview survey and a weekly diary or recordkeeping survey. They are nationwide surveys that collect data on consumer expenditures, income, characteristics, and assets and liabilities. Samples are national probability samples of households that are representative of the civilian noninstitutional population. The surveys have been ongoing since 1980.

Type of Data Collection Operation: The Interview Survey is a panel rotation survey. Each panel is interviewed for five quarters and then dropped from the survey. About 7,000 consumer units are

interviewed each quarter. The Diary Survey sample is new each year and consists of about 7,000 consumer units. Data are collected on an ongoing basis in 91 areas of the country.

Data Collection and Imputation Procedures: For the Interview Survey, data are collected by personal interview with each consumer unit interviewed once per quarter for five consecutive quarters. Designed to collect information that respondents can recall for 3 months or longer, such as large or recurring expenditures. For the Diary Survey, respondents record all their expenditures in a self-reporting diary for two consecutive one-week periods. Designed to pick up items difficult to recall over a long period, such as detailed food expenditures. Missing or invalid attributes, expenditures, or incomes are imputed. Assets and liabilities are not imputed. The U.S. Census Bureau collects the data for the Bureau of Labor Statistics.

Estimates of Sampling Error: Standard error tables are available since 2000.

Other (nonsampling) Errors: Includes incorrect information given by respondents, data processing errors, interviewer errors, and so on. They occur regardless of whether data are collected from a sample or from the entire population.

Sources of Additional Material: Bureau of Labor Statistics, see Internet site <http://www.bls.gov/cex>.

Consumer Price Index (CPI)

Universe, Frequency, and Types of Data: A monthly survey of price changes of all types of consumer goods and services purchased by urban wage earners and clerical workers prior to 1978, and urban consumers thereafter. Both indexes continue to be published.

Type of Data Collection Operation: Prior to 1978, and since 1998, sample of various consumer items in 87 urban areas; from 1978–1997, in 85 PSUs, except from January 1987 through March 1988, when 91 areas were sampled.

Data Collection and Imputation Procedures: Prices of consumer items are obtained each month from about 25,500 retail outlets and from about 4,000

U.S. Census Bureau, Statistical Abstract of the United States: 2009

housing units in 87 areas. Prices of food, fuel, and a few other items are obtained monthly; prices of most other commodities and services are collected every month in the three largest geographic areas and every other month in others.

Estimates of Sampling Error: Estimates of standard errors are available.

Other (nonsampling) Errors: Errors result from inaccurate reporting, difficulties in defining concepts and their operational implementation, and introduction of product quality changes and new products.

Sources of Additional Material: U.S. Bureau of Labor Statistics, Internet site <http://www.bls.gov/cpi/home.htm> and *BLS Handbook of Methods*, Chapter 17, see Internet site <http://www.bls.gov/opub/hom/pdf/homch17.pdf>.

Current Employment Statistics (CES) Program

Universe, Frequency, and Types of Data: Monthly survey drawn from a sampling frame of over 8 million unemployment insurance tax accounts in order to obtain data by industry on employment, hours, and earnings.

Type of Data Collection Operation: In 2006, the CES sample included about 160,000 businesses and government agencies, which represent approximately 400,000 individual worksites.

Data Collection and Imputation Procedures: Each month, the state agencies cooperating with BLS, as well as BLS Data Collection Centers, collect data through various automated collection modes and mail. BLS Washington staff prepares national estimates of employment, hours, and earnings while states use the data to develop state and area estimates.

Estimates of Sampling Errors: The relative standard error for total nonfarm employment is 0.1 percent. From April 2002 to March 2003, the cumulative net birth/death model added 469,000.

Other (nonsampling) Errors: Estimates of employment adjusted annually to reflect complete universe. Average adjustment is 0.2 percent over the last decade, with an absolute range from less than 0.05 percent to 0.6 percent.

Sources of Additional Material: U.S. Bureau of Labor Statistics, Employment and Earnings, monthly, Explanatory Notes and Estimates of Errors, Tables 2-A through 2-F. See <http://www.bls.gov/web/cestntab.htm>.

National Compensation Survey (NCS)

Universe, Frequency, and Types of Data: NCS collects data from establishments of all employment-size classes in private industries as well as state and local governments. The survey stratifies its data by geographic area and industry. NCS collects data on work schedules, wages, salaries, and employer costs for employee benefits. For approximately 80 metropolitan areas and the nation, NCS produces information on workers' earnings and benefits in a variety of occupations at different work levels. NCS is also responsible for two quarterly releases: the Employment Cost Index (ECI), which measures percent changes in the cost of employment, and the Employer Costs for Employee Compensation (ECEC), which measures costs per hour worked for individual benefits. The survey provides data by industry sector, industry division, occupational group, bargaining status, metropolitan area status, census region, and census division. ECEC also provides data by establishment-size class.

Type of Data Collection Operation: Establishments are selected for the survey based on a probability-proportionate-to-employment technique. NCS replaces its sample on a continual basis. Private industry establishments are in the survey for approximately 5 years.

Data Collection and Imputation Procedures: A personal visit to the establishment is the initial source for collecting data. Communication via mail, fax, and telephone provide quarterly updates. Imputation is done for individual benefits.

Estimates of Sampling Error: NCS uses standard errors to evaluate published series. These standard errors are available at <http://www.bls.gov/ncs/ect/home.htm>.

Other (nonsampling) Errors: Nonsampling errors have a number of potential sources. The primary sources are

(1) survey nonresponse and (2) data collection and processing errors. Nonsampling errors are not measured. The use of quality assurance programs reduces the potential for nonsampling errors. These programs include the use of reinterviews, interview observations, and the systematic professional review of reports. The programs also serve as a training device that provides feedback on errors for field economists (or data collectors). Quality assurance programs also provide information on sources of error. This information is used to improve procedures that result in fewer errors. NCS also conducts extensive training of field economists to maintain high standards in data collection.

Sources of Additional Material: Bureau of Labor Statistics, *BLS Handbook of Methods*, Chapter 8 <http://www.bls.gov /opub/hom/pdf/homch8.pdf>.

Producer Price Index (PPI)

Universe, Frequency, and Types of Data: Monthly survey of producing companies to determine price changes of all commodities and services produced in the United States for sale in commercial transactions. Data on agriculture, forestry, fishing, manufacturing, mining, gas, electricity, construction, public utilities, wholesale trade, retail trade, transportation, healthcare, and other services.

Type of Data Collection Operation: Probability sample of approximately 30,000 establishments that result in about 100,000 price quotations per month.

Data Collection and Imputation Procedures: Data are collected by mail and facsimile. Missing prices are estimated by those received for similar products or services. Some prices are obtained from trade publications, organized exchanges, and government agencies. To calculate index, price changes are multiplied by their relative weights taken from the Census Bureau's 2002 shipment values from their Census of Industries.

Estimates of Sampling Error: Not applicable.

Other (nonsampling) Errors: Not available at present.

Sources of Additional Material: U.S. Bureau of Labor Statistics, *BLS Handbook of Methods*, Chapter 14, Bulletin 2490. U.S. Bureau of Labor Statistics Internet site <http://stats.bls.gov/ppi/>.

BOARD OF GOVERNORS OF THE FEDERAL RESERVE SYSTEM

Survey of Consumer Finances

Universe, Frequency, and Types of Data: Periodic sample survey of families. In this survey a given household is divided into a primary economic unit and other economic units. The primary economic unit, which may be a single individual, is generally chosen as the person or couple who either holds the title to the home or is listed on the lease, along with all other people in the household who are financially dependent on that person or couple. The primary economic unit is used as the reference family. The survey collects detailed data on the composition of family balance sheets, the terms of loans, and relationships with financial institutions. It also gathers information on the employment history and pension rights of the survey respondent and the spouse or partner of the respondent.

Type of Data Collection Operation: The survey employs a two-part strategy for sampling families. Some families are selected by standard multistage area probability sampling methods applied to all 50 states. The remaining families in the survey are selected using statistical records derived from tax returns, under the strict rules governing confidentiality and the rights of potential respondents to refuse participation.

Data Collection and Imputation Procedures: National Opinion Research Center (NORC) at the University of Chicago has collected data for the survey since 1992. Since 1995, the survey has used computer-assisted personal interviewing. Adjustments for nonresponse are made through multiple imputation of unanswered questions and through weighting adjustments based on data used in the sample design for families that refused participation.

Estimates of Sampling Error: Because of the complex design of the survey, the estimation of potential sampling errors is not straightforward. A replicate-based procedure is available.

Other (nonsampling) Errors: The survey aims to complete 4,500 interviews, with about two thirds of that number deriving from the area-probability sample. The response rate is typically about 70 percent for the area-probability sample and about 35 percent over all strata in the tax-data sample. Proper training and monitoring of interviewers, careful design of questionnaires, and systematic editing of the resulting data were used to control inaccurate survey responses.

Sources of Additional Material: Board of Governors of the Federal Reserve System, "Recent Changes in U.S. Family Finances: Evidence from the 2001 and 2004 Survey of Consumer Finances," *Federal Reserve Bulletin*, 2006, <http://www.federalreserve.gov/Pubs/Bulletin>.

U.S. CENSUS BUREAU

2002 Economic Census
(Industry Series, Geographic Area Series and Subject Series Reports) (for NAICS sectors 22, 42, 44–45, 48–49, and 51–81).

Universe, Frequency, and Types of Data: Conducted every 5 years to obtain data on number of establishments, number of employees, total payroll size, total sales/receipts/revenue, and other industry-specific statistics. In 2002, the universe was all employer and nonemployer establishments excluding agriculture, forestry, fishing and hunting, and government.

Type of Data Collection Operation: All large employer firms were surveyed (i.e., all employer firms above payroll-size cutoffs established to separate large from small employers) plus a 5 percent to 25 percent sample of the small employer firms. Firms with no employees were not sent a census return.

Data Collection and Imputation Procedures: Mail questionnaires were used with both mail and telephone follow-ups for nonrespondents. Businesses also had the option to respond electronically. Data for nonrespondents and for small employer firms not mailed a questionnaire were obtained from administrative records of other federal agencies or imputed. Nonemployer data were obtained exclusively from IRS 2002 income tax returns.

Estimates of Sampling Error: Not applicable for basic data such as sales, revenue, receipts, payroll, etc. Other (nonsampling) errors: establishment response rates by NAICS sector in 2002 ranged from 80 percent to 89 percent. Item response rates generally ranged from 50 percent to 90 percent with lower rates for the more detailed questions. Nonsampling errors may occur during the collection, reporting, and keying of data, and due to industry misclassification.

Sources of Additional Material: U.S. Census Bureau, *2002 Economic Census: Industry Series, Geographic Area Series* and *Subject Series Reports* (by NAICS sector), Appendix C and <http://www.census.gov/econ/census02/guide/index.html>.

American Community Survey (ACS)

Universe, Frequency, and Types of Data: Nationwide survey to obtain data about demographic, social, economic, and housing characteristics of people, households, and housing units. Covers the household population and, for the first time in 2006, also includes the population living in institutions, college dormitories, and other group quarters.

Type of Data Collection Operation: First-phase sampling is performed during both Main and Supplemental sampling for approximately 3,000,000 housing units in the U.S. and 36,000 in Puerto Rico (PR). First stage sampling defines the universe for the second stage of sampling through two steps. First, all addresses that were in a first-stage sample within the past four years are excluded from eligibility. This ensures that no address is in sample more than once in any 5-year period. The second step is to select a 20 percent systematic sample of "new" units, i.e. those units that have never appeared on a previous Master Address File (MAF) extract. Each new address is systematically assigned to either the current year or to one of four back-samples. This procedure maintains five equal partitions of the universe. Sampling is performed separately on small (15 persons or fewer) and large (more than 15 persons) group quarters, but the target rate for both is a 2.5% sample of the group quarters population. Approximately 200,000 group quarters were selected in the U.S., and an additional 1,000 in Puerto Rico.

Data Collection and Imputation Procedures: The American Community Survey is conducted every month on independent samples. Each housing unit in the independent monthly samples is mailed a prenotice letter announcing the selection of the address to participate, a survey questionnaire package, and a reminder postcard. These sample units receive a second (replacement) questionnaire package if the initial questionnaire has not been returned by a scheduled date. In the mail-out/mailback sites, sample units for which a questionnaire is not returned in the mail and for which a telephone number is available are defined as the telephone nonresponse follow-up universe. Interviewers attempt to contact and interview these mail nonresponse cases. Sample units from all sites that are still unresponsive two months after the mailing of the survey questionnaires and directly after the completion of the telephone follow-up operation are subsampled at rates between 1 in 2 and 1 in 3. The selected nonresponse units are assigned to Field Representatives (FRs), who visit the units, verify their existence or declare them nonexistent, determine their occupancy status, and conduct interviews. Collection of group quarters data is conducted by field representatives. Their methods include completing the questionnaire while speaking to the resident in person or over the telephone, conducting a personal interview with a proxy, such as a relative or guardian, or leaving paper questionnaires for residents to complete for themselves and then pick them up later. This last option is used for data collection in federal prisons. After data collection is completed, any remaining incomplete or inconsistent information was imputed during the final automated edit of the collected data.

Estimates of Sampling Error: The data in the ACS products are estimates of the actual figures that would have been obtained by interviewing the entire population using the same methodology. The estimates from the chosen sample also differ from other samples of housing units and persons within those housing units.

Other (nonsampling) Errors: Nonsampling Error—In addition to sampling error, data users should realize that other types of errors may be introduced during any of the various complex operations used to collect and process survey data. An important goal of the ACS is to minimize the amount of nonsampling error introduced through nonresponse for sample housing units. One way of accomplishing this is by following up on mail nonrespondents.

Sources of Additional Material: U.S. Census Bureau, American Community Survey Web site available on Internet, <http://www.census.gov/acs/www/index.html> U.S. Census Bureau, American Community Survey Accuracy of the Data documents available on the Internet, <http://www.census.gov/acs/www/UseData/Accuracy/Accuracy1.htm>.

American Housing Survey

Universe, Frequency, and Types of Data: Conducted nationally in odd numbered years to obtain data on the approximately 124 million occupied or vacant housing units in the United States (group quarters are excluded). Data include characteristics of occupied housing units, vacant units, new housing and mobile home units, financial characteristics, recent mover households, housing and neighborhood quality indicators, and energy characteristics.

Type of Data Collection Operation: The national sample was a multistage probability sample with about 57,000 units eligible for interview in 2005. Sample units, selected within 394 PSUs, were surveyed over a 4-month period.

Data Collection and Imputation Procedures: For 2005, the survey was conducted by personal interviews. The interviewers obtained the information from the occupants or, if the unit was vacant, from informed persons such as landlords, rental agents, or knowledgeable neighbors.

U.S. Census Bureau, Statistical Abstract of the United States: 2009

Estimates of Sampling Error: For the national sample, illustrations of the Standard Error (SE) of the estimates are provided in the Appendix D of the 2005 report.

Other (nonsampling) Errors: Response rate was about 90 percent. Nonsampling errors may result from incorrect or incomplete responses, errors in coding and recording, and processing errors. Appendix D of the 2005 report has a complete discussion of the errors.

Sources of Additional Material: U.S. Census Bureau, *Current Housing Reports*, Series H-150 and H-170, *American Housing Survey* see <http://www.census.gov/hhes/www/ahs.html>.

Annual Survey of Government Employment and Payroll

Universe, Frequency, and Types of Data: The survey measures the number of state, local, and federal civilian government employees and their gross payrolls for the pay period including March 12, 2006. The survey is conducted annually except in years ending in '2' and '7' when a census of all state and local governments is done. The survey provides data on full-time and part-time employment, part-time hours worked, full-time equivalent employment, and payroll statistics by governmental function (elementary and secondary education, higher education, police protection, fire protection, financial administration, central staff services, judicial and legal, highways, public welfare, solid waste management, sewerage, parks and recreation, health, hospitals, water supply, electric power, gas supply, transit, natural resources, correction, libraries, air transportation, water transport and terminals, other education, state liquor stores, social insurance administration, and housing and community development).

Type of Data Collection Operations: The survey sample is taken from the 2002 Census of Governments and contains approximately 11,000 local government units. These units were sampled from a sampling frame that contained 83,767 local governments (county, city, township, special district, school districts) in addition to 50 state governments and the District of Columbia. This frame was slightly different from the Annual Finance Survey sampling frame. Forty-two of the state governments provided data from central payroll records for all or most of their agencies/institutions. Data for agencies and institutions for the remaining state governments were obtained by mail canvass questionnaires. Local governments were also canvassed using a mail questionnaire. However, elementary and secondary school system data in Florida, North Dakota, and Washington were supplied by special arrangements with the state education agency in each of these states. All respondents receiving the mail questionnaire had the option of responding using the employment Web site developed for reporting data. Approximately 25% of the state agency and local government respondents chose to respond on the Web.

Editing and Imputation Procedures: Editing: Editing is a process that ensures survey data are accurate, complete, and consistent. Efforts are made at all phases of collection, processing, and tabulation to minimize errors. Although some edits are built into the Internet data collection instrument and the data entry programs, the majority of the edits are performed after the case has been loaded into the Census Bureau's database. Edits consist primarily of two types: consistency and a ratio of the current year's reported value to the prior year's value. The consistency edits check the logical relationships of data items reported on the form. For example, if a value exists for employees for a function then a value must exist for payroll also. If part-time employees and payroll are reported then part-time hours must be reported and vice versa. The current year/prior year edits compare data for the number of employees, the function reported for the employees, and the average salary between reporting years. If data falls out of acceptable tolerance levels, the item is flagged for review. Some additional checks are made comparing data from the Annual Finance Survey to data reported on the Annual Survey of Government Employment and Payroll to verify that employees reported on the Annual Survey of Government Employment and Payroll at a particular function have a corresponding expenditure on the Finance Survey. For both types of edits, the edit results are reviewed by analysts and adjusted when needed. When the analyst is unable to resolve or accept the edit failure, contact is made with the respondent to verify or correct the reported data.

Imputation: Not all respondents answer every item on the questionnaire. There are also questionnaires that are not returned despite efforts to gain a response. Imputation is the process of filling in missing or invalid data with reasonable values in order to have a complete data set. For general purpose governments and for schools, the imputations were based on recent historical data from either a prior year annual survey or the most recent Census of Governments, if it was available. These data were adjusted by a growth rate that was determined by the growth of units that were similar (in size, geography, and type of government) to the nonrespondent. If there was no recent historical data available, the imputations were based on the data from a randomly selected donor that was similar to the nonrespondent. This donor's data was adjusted by dividing each data item by the population (or enrollment) of the donor and multiplying the result by the nonrespondent's population (or enrollment). For special districts, if prior year data are available, the data are brought forward with a national level growth rate applied. Otherwise, the data are imputed to be zero. In cases where good secondary data sources exist, the data from those sources were used.

Estimates of Sampling Error: Estimated relative standard errors for all variables are given in tabulations on the Web site. For U.S. and state-and-local government-level estimates of total full-time equivalents and total payroll, most relative standard errors are generally less than one percent, but vary considerably for detailed characteristics.

Other (nonsampling) Errors: Although every effort is made in all phases of collection, processing, and tabulation to minimize errors, the sample data are subject to nonsampling errors such as inability to obtain data for every variable from all units in the sample, inaccuracies in classification, response errors, misinterpretation of questions, mistakes in keying and coding, and coverage errors. These same errors may be evident in census collections and may affect the Census of Governments data used to adjust the sample during the estimation phase and used in the imputation process.

Sources of Additional Material: <http://www.census.gov/govs/www/apes.html> and <http://www.census.gov/govs/www/apesstl06.html>.

Annual Survey of Government Finances

Universe, Frequency, and Types of Data: The United States Census Bureau conducts an Annual Survey of Government Finances, as authorized by law under Title 13, United States Code, Section 182. Alternatively, every five years, in years ending in a '2' or '7,' a Census of Governments, including a Finance portion, is conducted under Title 13, Section 161. The survey coverage includes all state and local governments in the United States. For both the Census and annual survey, the finance detail data is equivalent, encompassing the entire range of government finance activities —revenue, expenditure, debt, and assets.

Type of Data Collection Operations: The data collection phase for the annual survey made use of three methods to obtain data: mail canvass, internet collection, and central collection from state sources. In 28 states, all or part of the general purpose finance data for local governments was obtained from cooperative arrangements between the Census Bureau and a state government agency. These usually involved a data collection effort carried out to meet the needs of both agencies—the state agency for purposes of audit, oversight, or information, and the Census Bureau for statistical purposes. Data for the balance of local governments in this annual survey were obtained via mail questionnaires sent directly to county, municipal, township, special district, and school district governments. School district data were collected via cooperative arrangements with state education

U.S. Census Bureau, Statistical Abstract of the United States: 2009

agencies. Data for state governments were compiled by analysts of the Census Bureau, usually with the cooperation and assistance of state officials. The data were compiled from state government audits, budgets, and other financial reports, either in printed or electronic format. The compilation generally involved recasting the state financial records into the classification categories used for reporting by the Census Bureau.

Data Collection and Imputation Procedures: Survey is conducted by mail with mail follow-ups of nonrespondents. Imputation for all nonresponse items is based on previous year reports or, for new governments, on data from similar donors.

Estimates of Sampling Error: The local government statistics in this survey are developed from a sample survey. Therefore, the local totals, as well as aggregates of state and local government data, are considered estimated amounts subject to sampling error. State government finance data are not subject to sampling. Consequently, state-local aggregates shown here are more reliable (on a relative standard error basis) than the local government estimates they include. Estimates of major United States totals for local governments are subject to a computed sampling variability of less than one-half of 1 percent. State and local government totals are generally subject to sampling variability of less than 3 percent.

Other (nonsampling) Errors: The estimates are also subject to the inaccuracies in classification, response, and processing. Efforts were made at all phases of collection, processing, and tabulation to minimize errors. However, the data are still subject to errors from estimating for missing data, errors from misreported data, errors from miscoding, and difficulties in identifying every unit that should be included in the report. Every effort was made to keep such errors to a minimum through care in examining, editing, and tabulating the data reported by government officials.

Sources of Additional Material: <http://www.census.gov/govs/www /financegen.html> and <http://www

.census.gov/govs/www /05censustechdoc.html>.

Annual Survey of Manufactures (ASM)

Universe, Frequency, and Types of Data: The Annual Survey of Manufactures is conducted annually, except for years ending in '2' and '7' for all manufacturing establishments having one or more paid employees. The purpose of the ASM is to provide key intercensal measures of manufacturing activity, products, and location for the public and private sectors. The ASM provides statistics on employment, payroll, worker hours, payroll supplements, cost of materials, value added by manufacturing, capital expenditures, inventories, and energy consumption. It also provides estimates of value of shipments for 1,800 classes of manufactured products.

Type of Data Collection Operation: The ASM includes approximately 50,000 establishments selected from the census universe of 346,000 manufacturing establishments. Approximately 24,000 large establishments are selected with certainty, and the remaining 26,000 other establishments are selected with probability proportional to a composite measure of establishment size. The survey is updated from two sources: Internal Revenue Service administrative records are used to include new single-unit manufacturers and the Company Organization Survey identifies new establishments of multiunit forms.

Data Collection and Imputation Procedures: Survey is conducted by mail with phone and mail follow-ups of nonrespondents. Imputation (for all nonresponse items) is based on previous year reports, or for new establishments in survey, on industry averages.

Estimates of Sampling Error: Estimated relative standard errors for number of employees, new expenditures, and for value added totals are given in annual publications. For U.S. level industry statistics, most estimated relative standard errors are 2 percent or less, but vary considerably for detailed characteristics.

Other (nonsampling) Errors: The unit response rate is about 85 percent. Nonsampling errors include those due to collection, reporting, and transcription errors, many of which are corrected through computer and clerical checks.

Sources of Additional Material: U.S. Census Bureau, *Annual Survey of Manufactures*, and Technical Paper 24.

Census of Population

Universe, Frequency, and Types of Data: Complete count of U.S. population conducted every 10 years since 1790. Data obtained on number and characteristics of people in the U.S.

Type of Data Collection Operation: In the 1990, and 2000 censuses the 100 percent items included: age, date of birth, sex, race, Hispanic origin, and relationship to householder. In 1980, approximately 19 percent of the housing units were included in the sample; in 1990 and 2000, approximately 17 percent.

Data Collection and Imputation Procedures: In 1980, 1990, and 2000, mail questionnaires were used extensively with personal interviews in the remainder. Extensive telephone and personal follow-up for nonrespondents was done in the censuses. Imputations were made for missing characteristics.

Estimates of Sampling Error: Sampling errors for data are estimated for all items collected by sample and vary by characteristic and geographic area. The coefficients of variation (CVs) for national and state estimates are generally very small.

Other (nonsampling) Errors: Since 1950, evaluation programs have been conducted to provide information on the magnitude of some sources of nonsampling errors such as response bias and undercoverage in each census. Results from the evaluation program for the 1990 census indicated that the estimated net undercoverage amounted to about 1.5 percent of the total resident population. For Census 2000, the evaluation program indicated a net overcount of 0.5 percent of the resident population.

Sources of Additional Material: U.S. Census Bureau, The Coverage of Population in the 1980 Census, PHC80-E4; *Content Reinterview Study: Accuracy of Data for Selected Population and Housing Characteristics as Measured by Reinterview,* PHC80-E2; *1980 Census of Population,* Vol. 1, (PC80-1), Appendixes B, C, and D. *Content Reinterview Survey: Accuracy of Data for Selected Population and Housing Characteristics as Measured by Reinterview,* 1990, CPH-E-1; Effectiveness of Quality Assurance, CPH-E-2; Programs to Improve Coverage in the 1990 Census, 1990, CPH-E-3. For Census 2000 evaluations, see <http://www.census.gov/pred/www>.

County Business Patterns

Universe, Frequency, and Types of Data: County Business Patterns is an annual tabulation of basic data items extracted from the Business Register, a file of all known single- and multilocation employer companies maintained and updated by the U.S. Census Bureau. Data include number of establishments, number of employees, first quarter and annual payrolls, and number of establishments by employment size class. Data are excluded for self-employed individuals, private households, railroad employees, agricultural production workers, and most government employees.

Type of Data Collection Operation: The annual Company Organization Survey provides individual establishment data for multilocation companies. Data for single establishment companies are obtained from various Census Bureau programs, such as the Annual Survey of Manufactures and Current Business Surveys, as well as from administrative records of the Internal Revenue Service, the Social Security Administration, and the Bureau of Labor Statistics.

Estimates of Sampling Error: Not applicable.

Other (nonsampling) Errors: The data are subject to nonsampling errors, such as inability to identify all cases in the universe; definition and classification difficulties; differences in interpretation of questions; errors in recording or coding the data obtained; and estimation of employers who reported too late to be included in the tabulations and for records with missing or misreported data.

Sources of Additional Materials: U. S. Census Bureau, County Business Patterns

Current Population Survey (CPS)

Universe, Frequency, and Types of Data: Nationwide monthly sample designed primarily to produce national and state estimates of labor force characteristics of the civilian noninstitutionalized population 16 years of age and older.

Type of Data Collection Operation: Multistage probability sample that currently includes 72,000 households from 824 sample areas. Sample size increased in some states to improve data reliability for those areas on an annual average basis. A continual sample rotation system is used. Households are in sample 4 months, out for 8 months, and in for 4 more. Month-to-month overlap is 75 percent; year-to-year overlap is 50 percent.

Data Collection and Imputation Procedures: For first and fifth months that a household is in sample, personal interviews; other months, approximately 85 percent of the data collected by phone. Imputation is done for item nonresponse. Adjustment for total nonresponse is done by a predefined cluster of units, by MSA size and residence; for item nonresponse imputation varies by subject matter.

Estimates of Sampling Error: The national total estimates of the civilian labor force and of employment have monthly CVs of about .2 percent and annual average CVs of about .125 percent. Unemployment is a much smaller characteristic and consequently has substantially larger CVs than the civilian labor force or employment. The national unemployment rate, the most important CPS statistic, has a monthly CV of about 2 percent and an annual average CV of about 1 percent. The CVs for states vary since more populous states have larger samples (and smaller CVs) than states with smaller populations. Assuming a 6 percent unemployment rate, the smallest states have monthly CVs of about 17 percent and annual average CVs of about 8 percent. The estimated CVs for family income and poverty rate for all persons in 2005 are .4 percent and 1.2 percent, respectively. CVs for subnational areas, such as states, tend to be larger and vary by area.

Other (nonsampling) Errors: Estimates of response bias on unemployment are available. Estimates of unemployment rate from reinterviews range from −2.4 percent to 1.0 percent of the basic CPS unemployment rate (over a 30-month span from January 2004 through June 2006). Eligible CPS households are approximately 82 percent of the assigned households, with a corresponding response rate of 91 percent.

Sources of Additional Material: U.S. Census Bureau and Bureau of Labor Statistics, Current Population Survey: Design and Methodology, (Technical Paper 66), available on the Internet <http://www.census.gov/prod/2006pubs/tp-66.pdf> and the Bureau of Labor Statistics, <http://www.bls.gov/cps/> and the *BLS Handbook of Methods*, Chapter 1, available on the Internet at <http://www.bls.gov/opub/hom/homch1a.htm>.

Foreign Trade—Export Statistics

Universe, Frequency, and Types of Data: The export declarations collected by U.S. Bureau of Customs and Border Protection are processed each month to obtain data on the movement of U.S. merchandise exports to foreign countries. Data obtained include value, quantity, and shipping weight of exports by commodity, country of destination, district of exportation, and mode of transportation.

Type of Data Collection Operation: Shipper's Export Declarations (paper and electronic) are generally required to be filed for the exportation of merchandise valued over $2,500. U.S. Bureau of Customs and Border Protection officials collect and transmit the documents to the Census Bureau on a flow basis for data compilation. Data for shipments valued under $2,501 are estimated, based on established percentages of individual country totals.

Data Collection and Imputation Procedures: Statistical copies of Shipper's Export Declarations are received on a daily basis from ports throughout the country and subjected to a monthly processing cycle. They are fully processed to the extent they reflect items valued over $2,500. Estimates for shipments

910   Appendix III

valued at $2,500 or less are made, based on established percentages of individual country totals.

Estimates of Sampling Error: Not applicable.

Other (nonsampling) Errors: The goods data are a complete enumeration of documents collected by the U.S. Bureau of Customs and Border Protection and are not subject to sampling errors; but they are subject to several types of nonsampling errors. Quality assurance procedures are performed at every stage of collection, processing and tabulation; however the data are still subject to several types of nonsampling errors. The most significant of these include reporting errors, undocumented shipments, timeliness, data capture errors, and errors in the estimation of low-valued transactions. Additional information on errors affecting export data can be found at <http://www.census.gov /foreign-trade/Press-Release /currentpressrelease/explain.pdf>.

Sources of Additional Material: U.S. Census Bureau, FT 900 U.S. International Trade in Goods and Services, FT 895 U.S. Trade with Puerto Rico and U.S. Possessions, FT 920 U.S. Merchandise trade: selected highlights, and Information Section on Goods and Services at <http://www.census.gov/ft900>.

Foreign Trade—Import Statistics

Universe, Frequency, and Types of Data: The import entry documents collected by U.S. Bureau of Customs and Border Protection are processed each month to obtain data on the movement of merchandise imported into the United States. Data obtained include value, quantity, and shipping weight by commodity, country of origin, district of entry, and mode of transportation.

Type of Data Collection Operation: Import entry documents, either paper or electronic, are required to be filed for the importation of goods into the United States valued over $2,000 or for articles which must be reported on formal entries. U.S. Bureau of Customs and Border Protection officials collect and transmit statistical copies of the documents to the Census Bureau on a flow basis for

data compilation. Estimates for shipments valued under $2,001 and not reported on formal entries are based on estimated established percentages for individual country totals.

Data Collection and Imputation Procedures: Statistical copies of import entry documents, received on a daily basis from ports of entry throughout the country, are subjected to a monthly processing cycle. They are fully processed to the extent they reflect items valued at $2,001 and over or items which must be reported on formal entries.

Estimates of Sampling Error: Not applicable.

Other (nonsampling) Errors: The goods data are a complete enumeration of documents collected by the U.S. Bureau of Customs and Border Protection and are not subject to sampling errors; but they are subject to several types of nonsampling errors. Quality assurance procedures are performed at every stage of collection, processing, and tabulation; however the data are still subject to several types of nonsampling errors. The most significant of these include reporting errors, undocumented shipments, timeliness, data capture errors, and errors in the estimation of low-valued transactions. Additional information on errors affecting import data can be found at <http://www.census.gov /foreign-trade/Press-Release /currentpressrelease/explain.pdf>.

Sources of Additional Material: U.S. Census Bureau, FT 900 U.S. International Trade in Goods and Services, FT 895 U.S. Trade with Puerto Rico and U.S. Possessions, FT920 U.S. Merchandise Trade: selected highlights, and Information Section on Goods and Services at <http://www.census.gov/ft900>.

Monthly Retail Trade and Food Service Survey

Universe, Frequency, and Types of Data: Provides monthly estimates of retail and food service sales by kind of business and end of month inventories of retail stores.

Type of Data Collection Operation: Probability sample of all firms from a list frame. The list frame is the Bureau's Business Register updated quarterly for recent birth Employer Identification (EI) Numbers issued by the Internal Revenue Service and assigned a kind of business code by the Social Security Administration. The largest firms are included monthly; a sample of others is included every month also.

Data Collection and Imputation Procedures: Data are collected by mail questionnaire with telephone follow-ups and fax reminders for nonrespondents. Imputation is made for each nonresponse item and each item failing edit checks.

Estimates of Sampling Error: For the 2006 monthly surveys, CVs are about 0.4 percent for estimated total retail sales and 0.7 percent for estimated total retail inventories. Sampling errors are shown in monthly publications.

Other (nonsampling) Errors: Imputation rates are about 22 percent for monthly retail and food service sales, and 29 percent for monthly retail inventories.

Sources of Additional Material: U.S. Census Bureau, Current Business Reports, Annual Revision of Monthly Retail and Food Services: Sales and Inventories.

Monthly Survey of Construction

Universe, Frequency, and Types of Data: Survey conducted monthly of newly constructed housing units (excluding mobile homes). Data are collected on the start, completion, and sale of housing. (Annual figures are aggregates of monthly estimates.)

Type of Data Collection Operation: A multistage probability sample of approximately 900 of the 20,000 permit-issuing jurisdictions in the U.S. was selected. Each month in each of these permit offices, field representatives list and select a sample of permits for which to collect data. To obtain data in areas where building permits are not required, a multistage probability sample of 70 land areas (census tracts or subsections of census tracts) was selected. All roads in these areas are canvassed and data are collected on all new residential construction found. Sampled buildings are followed up until they are completed (and sold, if for sale).

Data Collection and Imputation Procedures: Data are obtained by telephone inquiry and/or field visit. Nonresponse/undercoverage adjustment factors are used to account for late reported data.

Estimates of Sampling Error: Estimated CV of 3 percent to 4 percent for estimates of national totals of units started, but may be higher than 20 percent for estimated totals of more detailed characteristics, such as housing units in multiunit structures.

Other (nonsampling) Errors: Response rate is over 90 percent for most items. Nonsampling errors are attributed to definitional problems, differences in interpretation of questions, incorrect reporting, inability to obtain information about all cases in the sample, and processing errors.

Sources of Additional Material: All data are available on the Internet at <http://www.census.gov/const/www/newressalesindex.html> or <http://www.census.gov/const/www/newsresconstindex.html>. Further documentation of the survey is also available at those sites.

Nonemployer Statistics

Universe, Frequency, and Types of Data: Nonemployer statistics are an annual tabulation of economic data by industry for active businesses without paid employees that are subject to federal income tax. Data showing the number of firms and receipts by industry are available for the U.S., states, counties, and metropolitan areas. Most types of businesses covered by the Census Bureau's economic statistics programs are included in the nonemployer statistics. Tax-exempt and agricultural-production businesses are excluded from nonemployer statistics.

Type of Data Collection Operation: The universe of nonemployer firms is created annually as a byproduct of the Census Bureau's Business Register processing for employer establishments. If a business is active but without paid employees, then it becomes part of the potential nonemployer universe. Industry classification and receipts are available for each potential nonemployer

912 Appendix III

business. These data are obtained primarily from the annual business income tax returns of the Internal Revenue Service (IRS). The potential nonemployer universe undergoes a series of complex processing, editing, and analytical review procedures at the Census Bureau to distinguish nonemployers from employers, and to correct and complete data items used in creating the data tables.

Estimates of Sampling Error: Not applicable.

Other (nonsampling) Errors: The data are subject to nonsampling errors, such as industry misclassification as well as errors of response, keying, nonreporting, and coverage.

Sources of Additional Material: U. S. Census Bureau, Nonemployer Statistics

Service Annual Survey

Universe, Frequency, and Types of Data: The U.S. Census Bureau conducts the Service Annual Survey to provide nationwide estimates of revenues and expenses for selected service industries. Estimates are summarized by industry classification based on the 2002 North American Industry Classification System (NAICS). Selected service industries covered by the Service Annual Survey include all or part of the following NAICS sectors: Transportation and Warehousing (NAICS 48–49); Information (NAICS 51); Finance and Insurance (NAICS 52); Real Estate and Rental and Leasing (NAICS 53); Professional, Scientific, and Technical Services (NAICS 54); Administrative and Support and Waste Management and Remediation Services (NAICS 56); Health Care and Social Assistance (NAICS 62); Arts, Entertainment, and Recreation (NAICS 71); and Other Services, except Public Administration (NAICS 81). Data collected include total revenue, total expenses, detailed expenses, revenue from e-commerce transactions; and for selected industries, revenue from detailed service products, revenue from exported services, and inventories. For industries with a significant nonprofit component, separate estimates are developed for taxable firms and firms and organizations exempt from federal income taxes. Questionnaires are mailed in January and request annual data for the prior year. Estimates are published approximately 12 months after the initial survey mailing.

Type of Data Collection Operation: The Service Annual Survey estimates are developed from a probability sample of employer firms and administrative records for nonemployers. Service Annual Survey questionnaires are mailed to a probability sample that is periodically reselected from a universe of firms located in the United States and having paid employees. The sample includes firms of all sizes and covers both taxable firms and firms exempt from federal income taxes. Updates to the sample are made on a quarterly basis to account for new businesses. Firms without paid employees, or nonemployers, are included in the estimates through imputation and/or administrative records data provided by other federal agencies. Links to additional information about confidentiality protection, sampling error, nonsampling error, sample design, definitions, and copies of the questionnaires may be found on the Internet at <http://www.census.gov/econ/www/servmenu.html>.

Estimates of Sampling Error: Coefficients of variation (CVs) for the 2005 Service Annual Survey estimates range from 0.4 percent to 1.8 percent for total revenue estimates computed at the NAICS sector (2-digit NAICS code) level. The full 2005 Service Annual Survey results, including coefficients of variations (CVs), can be found at <http://www.census.gov/econ/www/servmenu.html>. Links to additional information regarding sampling error may be found at: <http://www.census.gov/svsd/www/cv.html>.

Other (Nonsampling) Errors: Data are imputed for unit nonresponse, item nonresponse, and for reported data that fails edits. The percent of imputed data for total revenue for the 2005 Service Annual Survey is approximately 9 percent.

Sources of Additional Material: U.S. Census Bureau, Current Business Reports, Service Annual Survey, Census Bureau Web site: <http://www.census.gov/econ/www/servmenu.html>.

Survey of Business Owners (SBO)

Universe, Frequency, and Types of Data: The Survey of Business Owners (SBO), formerly known as the Surveys of Minority- and Women-Owned Business Enterprises (SMOBE/SWOBE), provides statistics that describe the composition of U.S. businesses by gender, Hispanic or Latino origin, and race. Data are presented for businesses owned by American Indians and Alaska Natives, Asians, Blacks, Hispanics, Native Hawaiians and Other Pacific Islanders, and Women. All U.S. firms operating during 2002 with receipts of $1,000 or more, which are classified by the North American Industry Classification System (NAICS) codes 11 through 99, are represented, except for the following: NAICS 111, 112, 4811 (part), 482, 491, 525 (part), 813, 814, and 92. The lists of all firms (or sample frames) are compiled from a combination of business tax returns and data collected on other economic census reports. The published data include the number of firms, gross receipts, number of paid employees, and annual payroll. Data are presented by industry classifications and/or geographic area (states, metropolitan and micropolitan statistical areas, counties, and corporate municipalities (places) including cities, towns, townships, villages, and boroughs), and size of firm (employment and receipts).

Type of Data Collection Operation: The survey is based on a stratified probability sample of approximately 2.3 million firms from a universe of approximately 23 million firms. There were 5.5 million firms with paid employees and 17.4 million firms with no paid employees. The data are based on the entire firm rather than on individual locations of a firm.

Data Collection and Imputation Procedures: Data were collected through a mailout/mailback operation. Compensation for missing data is addressed through reweighting, edit correction, and standard statistical imputation methods.

Estimates of Sampling Error: Sampling error is present in these estimates because they are based on the results of a sample survey and not on an enumeration of the entire universe. Since these estimates are based on a probability sample, it is possible to estimate the sampling variability of the survey estimates. The standard error (SE) provides a measure of the variation. The relative standard error or coefficient of variation (CV) provides a measure of the magnitude of the variation relative to the estimate and is calculated as 100 multiplied by the ratio of the estimate to the SE. The CVs for number of firms and receipts at the national level typically range from 0 to 4 percent.

Other (nonsampling) Error: Nonsampling errors are attributed to many sources: inability to obtain information for all cases in the universe, adjustments to the weights of respondents to compensate for nonrespondents, imputation for missing data, data errors and biases, mistakes in recording or keying data, errors in collection or processing, and coverage problems. Explicit measures of the effects of these nonsampling errors are not available. However, it is believed that most of the important operational and data errors were detected and corrected through an automated data edit designed to review the data for reasonableness and consistency. Quality control techniques were used to verify that operating procedures were carried out as specified.

Sources of Additional Materials: U.S. Census Bureau, Guide to the 2002 Economic Census and Related Statistics; <http://www.census.gov/econ/census02/guide/index.html>.

U.S. DEPARTMENT OF EDUCATION National Center for Education Statistics

Integrated Postsecondary Education Data Survey (IPEDS), Completions

Universe, Frequency, and Types of Data: Annual survey of all institutions and branches listed in the Education Directory, Colleges and Universities to obtain data on earned degrees and other formal awards, conferred by field of study, level of degree, sex, and by racial/ethnic characteristics (every other year prior to 1989, then annually).

Type of Data Collection Operation: Complete census.

Data Collection and Imputation Procedures: Data are collected through a Web-based survey in the fall of every year. Missing data are imputed by using data of similar institutions.

Estimates of Sampling Error: Not applicable.

Other (nonsampling Errors: For 2005–06, the response rate for degree-granting institutions was 100.0 percent.

Sources of Additional Material: U.S. Department of Education, National Center for Education Statistics, *Postsecondary Institutions in the United States: Fall 2006 and Degrees and Other Awards Conferred: 2005–06*. See <http://www.nces.ed.gov/ipeds/>.

National Household Education Surveys (NHES) Program

Universe, Frequency, and Types of Data: The National Household Education Surveys Program is a system of telephone surveys of the noninstitutionalized civilian population of the United States. Surveys in NHES have varying universes of interest depending on the particular survey. Specific topics covered by each survey are at the NHES Web site <http://nces.ed.gov/nhes>. A list of the surveys fielded as part of NHES, each universe, and the years they were fielded is provided below. 1) Adult Education—Interviews were conducted with a representative sample of civilian, noninstitutionalized persons age 16 and older who were not enrolled in grade 12 or below (1991, 1995, 1999, 2001, 2003, 2005). 2) After-School Programs and Activities—Interviews were conducted with parents of a representative sample of students in grades K through 8 (1999, 2001, 2005). 3) Civic Involvement—Interviews were conducted with representative samples of parents, youth, and adults (1996, 1999). 4) Early Childhood Program Participation —Interviews were conducted with parents of a representative sample of children from birth through grade 3, with the specific age groups varying by survey year (1991, 1995, 1999, 2001, 2005). 5) Parent and Family Involvement in Education—Interviews were conducted with parents of a representative sample of children age 3 through grade 12 or in grades K through 12 depending on the survey year (1996, 1999, 2003, and 2007 forthcoming). 6) School Readiness—Interviews were conducted with parents of a representative sample of 3-to-7-year-old children (1993 and 1999) and of 3-to-5-year-old children, not yet in kindergarten, 2007 forthcoming).

Type of Data Collection Operation: NHES uses telephone interviews to collect data.

Data Collection and Imputation Procedures: Telephone numbers are selected using random digit dialing (RDD) techniques. Approximately 45,000 to 64,000 households are contacted in order to identify persons eligible for the surveys. Data are collected using computer-assisted telephone interviewing (CATI) procedures. Missing data are imputed using hot-deck imputation procedures.

Estimates of Sampling Error: Unweighted sample sizes range between 2,250 and 55,708. The average root design effects of the surveys in NHES range from 1.1 to 1.5.

Other (nonsampling) Errors: Because of unit nonresponse and because the samples are drawn from households with telephone instead of all households, nonresponse and/or coverage bias may exist for some estimates. However, both sources of potential bias are adjusted for in the weighting process. Analyses of both potential sources of bias in the NHES collections have been studied and no significant bias has been detected.

Sources of Additional Material: Please see the NHES Web site at <http://nces.ed.gov/nhes>.

Schools and Staffing Survey (SASS)

Universe, frequency and Types of Data: NCES designed the SASS survey system to emphasize teacher demand and shortage, teacher and administrator characteristics, school programs, and general conditions in schools. SASS also collects data on many other topics, including principals' and teachers' perceptions of school climate and problems in their schools; teacher compensation; district hiring practices and basic characteristics of the student population.

The SASS has had four core components: the School Questionnaire, the Teacher Questionnaire, the Principal Questionnaire, and the School District Questionnaire. For the 2003–04 SASS, a sample of public charter schools is included in the sample as part of the public school questionnaire. Since 1987–88, the SASS is the largest, most extensive survey of K through 12 school districts, schools, teachers, and administrators in the U.S. Surveys have been conducted every 3 to 4 years depending on budgetary constraints. The SASS includes data from public, private, and Bureau of Indian Affairs school sectors. Therefore, the SASS provides a multitude of opportunities for analysis and reporting on elementary and secondary educational issues

Type of Data Collection Operation: The U.S. Census Bureau performs the data collection and begins by sending advance letters to the sampled Local Education Agencies (LEAs) and schools in August and September of collection years. Beginning in October, questionnaires are delivered by U.S. Census Bureau field representatives. The sampling frame for the public school sample is the most recent Common Core of Data (CCD) school file. CCD is a universe file that includes all elementary and secondary schools in the United States. Schools operated by the Department of Defense or those that offered only kindergarten or prekindergarten or adult education were excluded from the SASS sample. The list frame used for the private school sample is the most recent Private School Universe Survey (PSS) list, updated with association lists. An area frame supplement is based on the canvassing of private schools within specific geographical areas. A separate universe of schools funded by the Bureau of Indian Affairs (BIA) is drawn from the Program Education Directory maintained by the BIA. To avoid duplicates in the BIA files, BIA schools in the CCD school file are treated as public schools.

Estimates of Sampling Error: Sample errors can be calculated using replicate weights and Balanced Repeated Replication complex survey design methodology. Errors depend on cell sizes and range from less than 1 percent to over 5 percent (for reasonable cell sizes).

Other (nonsampling) Errors: Because of unit nonresponse, bias may exist in some sample cells. However, bias has been adjusted for in the weighting process. Analysis of bias has been studied and no significant bias has been detected.

Sources of Additional Material: Please see the SASS Web site at <http://nces.ed.gov/surveys/sass/>.

U.S. DEPARTMENT OF JUSTICE, FEDERAL BUREAU OF INVESTIGATION

Uniform Crime Reporting (UCR) Program

Universe, Frequency, and Types of Data: Monthly reports on the number of criminal offenses that become known to law enforcement agencies. Data are also collected on crimes cleared by arrest or exceptional means; age, sex, and race of arrestees and for victims and offenders for homicides, number of law enforcement employees, on fatal and nonfatal assaults against law enforcement officers, and on hate crimes reported.

Type of Data Collection Operation: Crime statistics are based on reports of crime data submitted either directly to the FBI by contributing law enforcement agencies or through cooperating state UCR Programs.

Data Collection and Imputation Procedures: States with UCR programs collect data directly from individual law enforcement agencies and forward reports, prepared in accordance with UCR standards, to the FBI. Accuracy and consistency edits are performed by the FBI.

Estimates of Sampling Error: Not applicable.

Other (nonsampling) Errors: During 2006, law enforcement agencies active in the UCR Program represented 94.2 percent of the total population. The coverage amounted to 95.6 percent of the United States population in Metropolitan Statistical Areas, 86.3 percent of the population in cities outside metropolitan areas, and 88.1 percent in nonmetropolitan counties.

Sources of Additional Material: U.S. Department of Justice, Federal Bureau of Investigation, *Crime in the United States, annual, Hate Crime Statistics,* annual, *Law Enforcement Officers Killed and Assaulted,* annual, <http://www.fbi.gov/ucr/ucr.htm>.

U.S. INTERNAL REVENUE SERVICE

Corporation Income Tax Returns

Universe, Frequency, and Types of Data: Annual study of unaudited corporation income tax returns, Forms 1120, 1120-A, 1120-F, 1120-L, 1120-PC, 1120-REIT, 1120-RIC, and 1120S, filed by corporations or businesses legally defined as corporations. Data provided on various financial characteristics by industry and size of total assets, and business receipts.

Type of Data Collection Operation: Stratified probability sample of approximately 110,000 returns for Tax Year 2005, allocated to sample classes which are based on type of return, size of total assets, size of net income or deficit, and selected business activity. Sampling rates for sample classes varied from .25 percent to 100 percent.

Data Collection and Imputation Procedures: Computer selection of sample of tax return records. Data adjusted during editing for incorrect, missing, or inconsistent entries to ensure consistency with other entries on return and to comply with statistical definitions.

Estimates of Sampling Error: Estimated CVs for Tax Year 2005: Returns with assets over $10 million are self-representing. Coefficients of variation are published in the 2005 Statistics of Income Corporation Income Tax Returns, Table 1, by industry group.

Other (nonsampling) Errors: Nonsampling errors include coverage errors, processing errors, and response errors.

Sources of Additional Material: U.S. Internal Revenue Service, *Statistics of Income, Corporation Income Tax Returns,* annual.

Individual Income Tax Returns

Universe, Frequency, and Types of Data: Annual study of unaudited individual income tax returns, Forms 1040, 1040A, and 1040EZ, filed by U.S. citizens and residents. Data provided on various financial characteristics by size of adjusted gross income, marital status, and by taxable and nontaxable returns. Data by state, based on the population of returns filed, also include returns from 1040NR, filed by nonresident aliens plus certain self employment tax returns.

Type of Data Collection Operation: Stratified probability sample of 292,966 returns for tax year 2005. The sample is classified into sample strata based on the larger of total income or total loss amounts, the size of business plus farm receipts, and other criteria such as the potential usefulness of the return for tax policy modeling. Sampling rates for sample strata varied from 0.01 percent to 100 percent.

Data Collection and Imputation Procedures: Computer selection of sample of tax return records. Data adjusted during editing for incorrect, missing, or inconsistent entries to ensure consistency with other entries on return.

Estimates of Sampling Error: Estimated CVs for tax year 2005: Adjusted gross income less deficit 0.08 percent; salaries and wages 0.16 percent; and tax exempt interest received 1.45 percent. (State data not subject to sampling error.)

Other (nonsampling) Errors: Processing errors and errors arising from the use of tolerance checks for the data.

Sources of Additional Material: U.S. Internal Revenue Service, *Statistics of Income, Individual Income Tax Returns,* annual, (Publication 1304).

Partnership Income Tax Returns

Universe, Frequency, and Types of Data: Annual study of preaudited income tax returns of partnerships related to financial and tax-related activity during calendar years 2003 to 2006 and reported on

Forms 1065 and 1065B to the IRS in calendar year 2007. Data are provided by industry, based on the NAICS industry coding used by IRS.

Type of Data Collection Operation: Stratified probability sample of approximately 45,000 partnership returns from a population of 3.2 million filed during calendar year 2007. The sample is classified based on combinations of industry code, gross receipts, net income or loss, and total assets. Sampling rates vary from 0.07 percent to 100 percent.

Data Collection and Imputation Procedures: The sample of tax return records are selected via computer after data are transcribed by IRS and placed on an administrative file. Data are manually adjusted during editing for incorrect, missing, or inconsistent entries to ensure consistency with other entries on return. Data not available due to regulations are handled with weighting adjustments.

Estimates of Sampling Error: Some of the estimated Coefficients of Variation (the estimated standard error of the total divided by the estimated total) for tax year 2006: For number of partnerships, 0.36 percent; business receipts, 0.18 percent; net income, 0.73 percent; and ordinary business income; 0.53 percent.

Other (nonsampling) Errors: The potential exists for coverage error due to unavailable returns; processing errors; and taxpayer reporting errors, since data are preaudit.

Sources of Additional Material: U.S. Internal Revenue Service, *Statistics of Income, Partnership Returns and Statistics of Income Bulletin*, Vol. 27, No. 2 (Fall 2007).

Sole Proprietorship Income Tax Returns

Universe, Frequency, and Types of Data: Annual study of unaudited income tax returns of nonfarm sole proprietorships, Form 1040 with business schedules. Data provided on various financial characteristics by industry.

Type of Data Collection Operation: Stratified probability sample of 82,689 sole proprietorships for tax year 2005. The sample is classified based on presence

or absence of certain business schedules; the larger of total income or loss; size of business plus farm receipts, and other criteria such as the potential usefulness of the return for tax policy modeling. Sampling rates vary from 0.1 percent to 100 percent.

Data Collection and Imputation Procedures: Computer selection of sample of tax return records. Data adjusted during editing for incorrect, missing, or inconsistent entries to ensure consistency with other entries on return.

Estimates of Sampling Error: Estimated CVs for tax year 2005 are available. For sole proprietorships, business receipts, 0.56 percent; depreciation 1.26 percent.

Other (nonsampling) Errors: Processing errors and errors arising from the use of tolerance checks for the data.

Sources of Additional Material: U.S. Internal Revenue Service, *Statistics of Income, Sole Proprietorship Returns* (for years 1980 through 1983) and *Statistics of Income Bulletin*, Vol. 27, No. 1 (Summer 2007, as well as bulletins for earlier years).

U.S. NATIONAL CENTER FOR HEALTH STATISTICS (NCHS)

National Health Interview Survey (NHIS)

Universe, Frequency, and Types of Data: Continuous data collection covering the civilian noninstitutional population to obtain information on demographic characteristics, conditions, injuries, impairments, use of health services, health behaviors, and other health topics.

Type of Data Collection Operation: Multistage probability sample of 49,000 households (in 198 PSUs) from 1985 to 1994; 36–40,000 households (358 design PSUs or 449 effective PSUs when divided by state boundaries) from 1995 to 2005; an estimated completed 35,000 households (428 effective PSUs) beginning in 2006.

Data Collection and Imputation Procedures: Some missing data items (e.g., race, ethnicity) are imputed using a hot deck imputation value. Sequential regression models are used to create multiple imputation files for family income. Unit nonresponse is compensated for by an adjustment to the survey weights.

Estimates of Sampling Error: For 2006 medically attended injury episodes rates in the past 12 months by falling for: females 49.93 (4.44), and males 38.83 (4.59) per 1,000 population; for 2006 injury episodes rates during the past 12 months inside the home—34.89 (2.81) per 1,000 population.

Other (nonsampling) Errors: The response rate was 93.8 percent in 1996; in 2006, the total household response rate was 87.3 percent, with the final family response rate of 87.0 percent, and the final sample adult response rate of 70.8 percent. (Note: the NHIS questionnaire was redesigned in 1997, and a new sample design was instituted in 2006).

Sources of Additional Material: National Center for Health Statistics, Summary Health Statistics for the U.S. Population: National Health Interview Survey, 2006, Vital and Health Statistics, Series 10 #236; National Center for Health Statistics, Summary Health Statistics for U.S. Children: National Health Interview Survey, 2006, Vital and Health Statistics, Series 10 #234; National Center for Health Statistics, Summary Health Statistics for U.S. Adults: National Health Interview Survey, 2006, Vital and Health Statistics, Series 10 #235; U.S. National Center for Health Statistics, Design and Estimation for the National Health Interview Survey, 1995-2004, Vital and Health Statistics, Series 2 #130.

National Survey of Family Growth (NSFG)

Universe, Frequency, and Types of Data: Periodic survey of men and women 15–44 years of age in the household population of the United States. Interviews were conducted in 2002 in person by trained female interviewers. Interview topics covered include births and pregnancies, marriage, divorce, and cohabitation, sexual activity, contraceptive use, and medical care. For men, data on father involvement with children were collected. The most sensitive data—on sexual behavior related to HIV and Sexually Transmitted Disease

risk—were collected in a self-administered form in which the data are entered into a computer.

Type of Data Collection Operation: In the 2002 (Cycle 6) NSFG, the sample was a multistage area probability sample of men and women 15–44 years of age in the household population of the United States. Only one person 15–44 was selected from households with one or more persons 15–44. Data were collected and entered into laptop (notebook) computers. In the self-administered portion, the respondent entered his or her own answers into the computer. Sample included 12,571 interviews. The response rate was 79 percent. Hispanic and Black persons, as well as those 15–19 years of age, were sampled at higher rates than White adults. All percentages and other statistics shown for the NSFG are weighted to make national estimates. The weights adjust for the different rates of sampling for each group, and for nonresponse.

Data Collection and Imputation Procedures: When interviews are received, they are reviewed for consistency and quality, and analysis variables (recodes) are created. Missing data on these recodes were imputed using multiple regression techniques and checked again for consistency. Variables indicating whether a value has been imputed ("imputation flags") are included on the data file.

Estimates of Sampling Error: Sampling error codes are included on the data file so that users can estimate sampling errors for their own analyses. Sampling error estimates for nine illustrative analyses are shown on the NSFG Web site at <http://www.cdc.gov/nchs/nsfg.htm>. Sampling error estimates are also shown in most NCHS reports.

Other (nonsampling) Errors: In any survey, errors can occur because the respondent (the person being interviewed) does not recall the specific fact or event being asked about. The NSFG questionnaire in 2002 was programmed to check the consistency of many variables during the interview, so that the interviewer and respondent had a chance to correct any inconsistent information. Further checking occurred after

U.S. Census Bureau, Statistical Abstract of the United States: 2009

the interview and during recoding and imputation. Typically, less than 1 percent of cases need imputation because of missing data.

Sources of Additional Material: The following references can be found at <http://www.cdc.gov/nchs/nsfg.htm>. "National Survey of Family Growth, Cycle 6: Sample Design, Weighting, and Variance Estimation." Vital and Health Statistics, Series 2, Number 142, July 2006. "Plan and Operation of Cycle 6 of the National Survey of Family Growth." Vital and Health Statistics, Series 1, No. 42. August 2005. "Sexual Behavior and Selected Health Measures: Men and Women 15–44 Years of Age, United States, 2002." *Advance Data from Vital and Health Statistics*, No. 362, Sept 15, 2005.

National Vital Statistics System

Universe, Frequency, and Types of Data: Annual data on births and deaths in the United States.

Type of Data Collection Operation: Mortality data based on complete file of death records, except 1972, based on 50 percent sample. Natality statistics 1951–1971, based on 50 percent sample of birth certificates, except a 20 percent to 50 percent sample in 1967, received by NCHS.

Data Collection and Imputation Procedures: Reports based on records from registration offices of all states, District of Columbia, New York City, Puerto Rico, Virgin Islands, Guam, American Samoa, and Northern Marianas.

Estimates of Sampling Error: For recent years, there is no sampling for these files; the files are based on 100 percent of events registered.

Other (nonsampling) Errors: It is believed that more than 99 percent of the births and deaths occurring in this country are registered.

Sources of Additional Material: U.S. National Center for Health Statistics, *Vital Statistics of the United States*, Vol. I and Vol. II, annual, and the *National Vital Statistics Reports*. See the NCHS Web site at <http://www.cdc.gov/nchs/nvss.htm>.

National Highway Traffic Safety Administration (NHTSA)

Fatality Analysis Reporting System (FARS)

Universe, Frequency, and Types of Data: FARS is a census of all fatal motor vehicle traffic crashes that occur throughout the United States including the District of Columbia and Puerto Rico on roadways customarily open to the public. The crash must be reported to the state/jurisdiction and at least one directly related fatality must occur within thirty days of the crash.

Type of Data Collection Operation: One or more analysts, in each state, extract data from the official documents and enter the data into a standardized electronic database.

Data Collection and Imputation Procedures: Detailed data describing the characteristics of the fatal crash, the vehicles and persons involved are obtained from police crash reports, driver and vehicle registration records, autopsy reports, highway department, etc. Computerized edit checks monitor the accuracy and completeness of the data. The FARS incorporates a sophisticated mathematical multiple imputation procedure to develop a probability distribution of missing blood alcohol concentration (BAC) levels in the database for drivers, pedestrians, and cyclists.

Estimates of Sampling Error: Since this is census data, there are no sampling errors.

Other (nonsampling) Errors: FARS represents a census of all police-reported crashes and captures all data reported at the state level. FARS data undergo a rigorous quality control process to prevent inaccurate reporting. However, these data are highly dependent on the accuracy of the police accident reports. Errors or omissions within police accident reports may not be detected.

Sources of Additional Material: The FARS Coding and Validation Manual, ANSI D16.1 Manual on Classification of Motor Vehicle Traffic Accidents (Sixth Edition).

Appendix IV
Weights and Measures

For assistance on metric usage, call or write:

Elizabeth J. Gentry
NIST
Weights and Measures Division
100 Bureau Drive – Mail Stop 2600
Gaithersburg, MD 20899-2600

Telephone: 301-975-3690 or 4004   FAX: 301-975-8091

E-mail: TheSI@nist.gov

Internet site: <http://www.nist.gov/metric>

[Conversions provided in table are approximate]

Symbol	When you know conventional	Multiply by	To find metric	Symbol
in	inches	2.54	centimeters	cm
ft	feet	30.48	centimeters	cm
yd	yards	0.91	meters	m
mi	miles	1.61	kilometers	km
in^2	square inches	6.45	square centimeters	cm^2
ft^2	square feet	0.09	square meters	m^2
yd^2	square yards	0.84	square meters	m^2
mi^2	square miles	2.59	square kilometers	km^2
	acre	0.41	hectare	ha
oz	ounces [1]	28.35	grams	g
lb	pounds[1]	0.45	kilograms	kg
oz (troy)	ounces [2]	31.10	grams	g
	short tons (2,000 lb)	0.91	metric tons	t
	long tons (2,240 lb)	1.02	metric tons	t
fl oz	fluid ounces	29.57	milliliters	mL
c	cups	0.24	liters	L
pt	pints	0.47	liters	L
qt	quarts	0.95	liters	L
gal	gallons	3.78	liters	L
ft^3	cubic feet	0.03	cubic meters	m^3
yd^3	cubic yards	0.76	cubic meters	m^3
°F	degrees Fahrenheit (subtract 32)	0.55	degrees Celsius	°C

Symbol	When you know metric	Multiply by	To find conventional	Symbol
cm	centimeters	0.39	inches	in
cm	centimeters	0.03	feet	ft
m	meters	1.09	yards	yd
km	kilometers	0.62	miles	mi
cm^2	square centimeters	0.15	square inches	in^2
m^2	square meters	10.76	square feet	ft^2
m^2	square meters	1.20	square yards	yd^2
km^2	square kilometers	0.39	square miles	mi^2
ha	hectares	2.47	acre	
g	grams	0.04	ounces [1]	oz
kg	kilograms	2.21	pounds[2]	lb
g	grams	0.04	ounces [2]	oz (troy)
t	metric tons	1.10	short tons (2,000 lb)	
t	metric tons	0.98	long tons (2,240 lb)	
mL	milliliters	0.03	fluid ounces	fl oz
L	liter	4.23	cups	c
L	liters	2.13	pints (liquid)	pt
L	liters	1.05	quarts (liquid)	qt
L	liters	0.26	gallons	gal
m^3	cubic meters	35.32	cubic feet	ft^3
m^3	cubic meters	1.32	cubic yards	yd^3
°C	degrees Celsius (after multiplying, add 32)	1.80	degrees Fahrenheit	°F

[1] For weighing ordinary commodities.   [2] For weighing precious metals, jewels, etc.

U.S. Census Bureau, Statistical Abstract of the United States: 2009

Appendix V

Tables Deleted From the
2008 Edition of the Statistical Abstract

2008
number

Sec. 1. POPULATION

19   Resident Population by Region, Race, and Hispanic Origin: 2000
68   Families by Size and Presence of Children: 1990 to 2006
74   Self-Described Religious Identification of Adult Population: 1990 and 2001

Sec. 2. VITAL STATISTICS

93   Contraceptive Use by Women, 15 to 44 Years of Age, Who Have Ever Had Sexual Intercourse: 1982 to 2002

Sec. 3. HEALTH AND NUTRITION

131   Prescription Drug Use in the Past Month, by Sex, Age, Race, and Hispanic Origin: 1988–1994 and 1999–2002

Sec. 4. EDUCATION

226   Type of School Attended by Student and Household Characteristics: 1993 and 2003
228   Students Who are Homeschooled by Selected Characteristics: 2003
238   Public Schools Using Selected Safety and Security Measures, by School Characteristics: 2003–04
250   Public Schools With Broadband and Wireless Connections: 2000 to 2005
251   Public Schools Providing Hand-held Computers to Students or Teachers for Instructional Purposes, by School Characteristics: 2002 to 2005
254   Distance Education in Public Elementary and Secondary Schools: 2002–2003
261   Public High Schools Offering Dual Credit and Exam-Based Courses and Course Enrollments: 2002–2003
262   Foreign Language Enrollment in Public High Schools: 1970 to 2000
281   Average Amount of Aid Received by Aided Undergraduates: 2003–2004
282   Average Out-of-Pocket Net Price of Attendance for Undergraduates: 2003–04

Sec. 5. LAW ENFORCEMENT, COURTS, AND PRISONS

320   Drug Use by Arrestees in Major U.S. Cities by Type of Drug and Sex: 2003

Sec. 6. GEOGRAPHY AND ENVIRONMENT

349   Total and Federally Owned Land by State: 2004
351   Developed Land by Type: 1982 to 2001
370   Federal Funding for the Superfund, Brownfields, and Related Programs: 1995 to 2005

Sec. 8. STATE AND LOCAL GOVERNMENT FINANCES AND EMPLOYMENT

427   State and Local Governments—Per Capita Summary of Finances by State: 2004

Sec. 11. SOCIAL INSURANCE AND HUMAN SERVICES

560   Licensed Child Care Centers and Family Child Care Providers by State and Other Areas: 2005
563   Foundations—Number and Finances: 1990 to 2005

Sec. 12. LABOR FORCE, EMPLOYMENT, AND EARNINGS

618   Adults in Selected Work-Related Informal Learning Activities: 2002–03

Sec. 15. BUSINESS ENTERPRISE

744   Women-Owned Firms by Kind of Business and Receipts Size: 2002

U.S. Census Bureau, Statistical Abstract of the United States: 2009

2008
number

Sec. 15. **BUSINESS ENTERPRISE**—Con.

745   Hispanic- or Latino-Owned Firms by Kind of Business and Receipts Size: 2002
747   Black-Owned Firms by Kind of Business and Receipts: 2002
748   American Indian- and Alaska Native-Owned Firms by Kind of Business and Receipts Size: 2002
749   Asian-Owned Firms by Kind of Business and Receipts Size: 2002
750   Native Hawaiian- and Other Pacific Islander-Owned Firms by Kind of Business and Receipts Size: 2002

Sec. 16. **SCIENCE AND TECHNOLOGY**

784   College Graduates by Education and Occupation: 1993 and 2003
785   Profile of Employed College Graduates by Employment Sector and Occupation Group: 2003
794   Space Vehicle Systems—Net Sales and Backlog Orders: 1970 to 2005
798   Nobel Prize Laureates in Selected Sciences: 1901 to 2004

Sec. 17. **AGRICULTURE**

828   Greenhouse and Nursery Crops—Value of Production, Trade, and Consumption: 1990 to 2005

Sec. 18. **NATURAL RESOURCES**

875   U.S. Petroleum Balance: 1980 to 2005
881   Liquefied Petroleum Gases—Summary: 1980 to 2006

Sec. 20. **CONSTRUCTION AND HOUSING**

926   Construction—Establishments, Employees, Payroll, Value of Construction, Costs, and Capital Expenditures by Kind of Business (NAICS Basis): 2002

Sec. 22. **WHOLESALE AND RETAIL TRADE**

1009   Wholesale and Retail Trade—Establishments, Sales, Payroll, and Employees: 2002
1030   Shopping Centers—Number, Gross Leasable Area, and Retail Sales by Gross Leasable Area: 1990 to 2005
1031   Shopping Centers—Gross Leasable Area and Retail Sales, by State: 2005

Sec. 23. **TRANSPORTATION**

1091   Line Haul Railroads—Producer Price Indexes: 2000 to 2006

Sec. 24. **INFORMATION AND COMMUNICATIONS**

1124   Academic Libraries—Summary: 2004

Sec. 25. **BANKING, FINANCE, AND INSURANCE**

1141   Flow of Funds Accounts—Liabilities of Households: 1990 to 2006
1143   Amount of Debt Held by Families—Percent Distribution: 2001 and 2004
1144   Ratios of Debt Payments to Family Income: 1995 to 2004
1180   Securities Listed on New York Stock Exchange: 1990 to 2006
1181   Stock Ownership by Age of Head of Family and Family Income: 1995 to 2004
1183   Characteristics of Equity Owners: 2005
1188   Mutual Fund Retirement Assets: 1990 to 2005

Sec. 26. **ARTS, ENTERTAINMENT, AND RECREATION**

1210   Participation in Various Arts Activities: 2002
1239   Impact of International Travel on States' Economies: 2004

Sec. 30. **INTERNATIONAL STATISTICS**

1316   Gross Domestic Product (GDP) by Country: 1995 to 2004
1326   Income Tax and Social Security Contributions as Percent of Labor Costs: 2004

Index

Table

Abortions 97, 98, 99
Accidents and fatalities . 192, 193, 1032, 1063,
1064, 1071, 1080
   Age of driver 1073
   Aircraft 1032, 1036, 1037
   Alcohol involvement 1069, 1070, 1072
   Costs 194
   Deaths and death rates . 112, 113, 114, 115,
116, 1063, 1064, 1080
   Fires 194, 343
   Industrial 635, 636, 637, 638
   Injuries 192, 193, 861
   Mining 861
   Motor vehicles . 112, 113, 115, 1032, 1063,
1064, 1065, 1066, 1067, 1068, 1071, 1072,
1073
   Motorcycle 1063, 1065, 1072
   Police officers assaulted, killed 319
   Railroad 1032, 1080
   Transportation 1032
   Vehicle rollovers 1067
   Work fatalities/injuries .. 636, 637, 638, 644
   Work time lost 636
Accommodation and food services industry:
   Capital 749, 751, 753, 755
   Earnings 610, 612, 621, 734, 737, 740,
1233, 1235, 1236
   Electronic commerce 1238
   Employees . 610, 612, 734, 1227, 1233, 1235,
1236
   Equipment and software expenditures .. 753
   Establishments . 734, 735, 740, 1233, 1234,
1235, 1236
   Finances 724, 727
   Gross domestic product 648
   Hires and separations 615
   Hours 610
   Nonemployers 735, 1234
   Occupational safety 638
   Productivity 619
   Profits 763
   Sales .. 724, 727, 732, 733, 734, 735, 1227,
1233, 1234, 1241, 1243
Accountants and auditors 596, 598
Accounting, tax preparation, bookkeeping, and
payroll services:
   Earnings 612, 1233, 1235
   Employees 612, 1235
   Establishments 1233, 1234, 1235
   Finances 724
   Nonemployers 1234
   Receipts 724, 1233, 1234, 1237
Acquired immuno-deficiency syndrome (AIDS) ..
175, 176, 177, 178, 1297
Activities of daily living (ADLs) 186
Activity limitation caused by chronic conditions .
185, 186
Administrative & support & waste management
& remediation services industry:
   Capital 751, 753, 755
   Earnings 610, 612, 621, 734, 737, 740,
1233, 1235, 1236

Table

Administrative & support & waste management
& remediation services industry:—Con.
   Electronic commerce 1238
   Employees . 610, 612, 734, 737, 740, 1233,
1235, 1236
   Equipment and software expenditures .. 753
   Establishments . 734, 735, 737, 1233, 1234,
1235, 1236
   Finance 724, 727
   Gross domestic product 648
   Hours 610
   Nonemployers 735, 1234
   Occupational safety 638
   Payroll 1235
   Productivity 619
   Profits 734
   Sales, shipments, receipts ... 724, 727, 732,
733, 734, 735, 1233, 1234, 1240
Adopted children 560
Adult education 294, 1302
Advertising and related services:
   Earnings 612, 1235
   Employees 612, 1235
   Establishments 1235
   Expenditures 1239
   Productivity 619
Aerobics 1209, 1211
Aeronautics, civil. (See Air transportation.)
Aerospace engineering, degrees conferred . 785
Aerospace industry:
   Earnings 612, 738, 787, 967
   Employees 612, 738, 787, 967, 1042
   Foreign trade 1267, 1268
   Industrial production 759
   New orders, backlog 999
   Productivity 619
   Research and development 774, 775
   Sales 999, 1002
   Shipments 967, 999, 1000, 1001, 1002
Afghanistan. (See Foreign countries.)
Africa. (See Foreign countries.)
African American. (See Black population.)
After-school activities 256, 257
Age of population. (See Population.)
Aggravated assault 295, 296, 297, 298
Agricultural loans. (See Farm mortgage loans.)
Agricultural products. (See Farms and individual
products.)
Agricultural sciences:
   Degrees conferred 290, 291, 292, 782
   Enrollment 779
Agriculture (see also Farms, and Farmers and
farm workers):
   Employees 596
   Federal aid to state and local governments ..
415
   Foreign trade . 719, 809, 810, 811, 813, 814,
815, 816, 1265
   Government payments 800, 801, 804
   Value added 801
Agriculture, construction, and mining machin-
ery manufacturing (see also Machine tools,
and Machinery manufacturing) . 612, 619, 967

NOTE: Index citations refer to **table** numbers, not page numbers.

U.S. Census Bureau, Statistical Abstract of the United States: 2009

Agriculture, forestry, and fishing industry:
  Capital 751, 755
  Earnings 621, 737, 837, 838
  Employees 600, 737, 837, 838
  Establishments 737, 833, 837, 838
  Finances 722, 724, 727
  Gross domestic product 648, 836
  Occupational safety 635, 638
  Profits 722, 763
  Sales, shipments, receipts ... 722, 724, 727,
                                732, 733, 763, 837
Aid to families with dependent children. (See
  Temporary assistance for needy families pro-
  gram.)
AIDS (acquired immuno-deficiency syndrome) ..
      115, 121, 175, 176, 177, 178, 1297
Air conditioning, homes with 946
Air Force, personnel 492, 494
Air pollution:
  Air pollution control equipment 368
  Emissions ... 357, 358, 359, 360, 364, 365,
                                366, 913, 1304
    Greenhouse gases 360
    Industry 368
    Toxic chemicals 364, 365, 366
Air transportation:
  Accidents and deaths 1032, 1036, 1037
  Airline markets 1035
  Airport summary 1034, 1039
    Flight on-time performance 1039
    International travel 1230
  Carrier delays, cancellations 1038
  Civil aviation 1042
  Consumer complaints 1040
  Cost indexes 1033
  Employees 1030
  Federal outlays 455
  Finances 1030
  Fleet size 1027, 1042
  Freight 1028, 1030
  Manufacturing orders booked/announced . 1000
  Passenger screening 517
  Price indexes 705, 717
  Regional airlines 1041
  Traffic carried 517, 1030, 1041, 1230
Air transportation industry:
  Capital 751
  Earnings 612, 1029, 1031, 1235
  Employees .. 612, 1025, 1029, 1031, 1227,
                                        1235
  Establishments 1029, 1031, 1235
  Finances 1030, 1033
  Gross domestic product 648
  Occupational safety 638
  Productivity 619
  Profits 1030
  Revenues 1029, 1030
Aircraft manufacturing. (See Aerospace indus-
  try.)
Airline operations (see also Air transportation) ..
                                        1030, 1035
Airplanes 1267
Airports or airfields 1042
  Federal aid to state and local government ...
                                            415
    Serving regional airlines 1041
    Traffic 1034, 1039, 1230
Alaska Native. (See American Indian, Alaska
  Native population.)

Alcoholic beverages (see also Beer, wine, and
  liquor stores, and Liquors and beverages):
  Alcoholism treatment 170, 198
  Consumer expenditures . 662, 664, 665, 1023,
                                            1314
  Consumption 199, 207
    "Binge" use 199, 200
  Foreign trade 1267
  Price indexes 705, 713
  Sales 1014, 1023
Alcohol-induced deaths 113
Alcohol involvement in fatal crashes . 1069, 1070,
                                            1072
Alcoholism treatment 170, 198
Aleut population. (See American Indian, Alaska
  Native population.)
Algeria. (See Foreign countries.)
Aliens deported 512, 513
Alimony 472, 473, 523
Almonds 803, 824, 825, 845
Alternative fueled vehicles 1057
Alternative minimum tax 468
Altitudes, geographical 349
Aluminum:
  Consumption 863
  Employment 863
  Foreign trade 720, 721, 863, 868, 1267
  Prices 713, 720, 721, 863
  Production 987
  Recycling 362, 363
  World production 867
Alzheimer's disease, deaths . 113, 114, 115, 116
Ambulatory health care services industry:
  Capital 751
  Earnings 152, 612, 734
  Employees 612, 734
  Establishments 734
  Finances 724
  Gross domestic product 648
  Sales, receipts 724, 734
American College Testing Program (ACT) ... 259
American Indian, Alaska Native population . 5, 6,
                                        8, 9, 11, 18
  Age and/or sex 6, 8, 9, 11
  Births, birth rates .. 5, 79, 81, 82, 83, 84, 85
  Business owners 744, 745
  Cancer deaths 119
  Charter schools 230
  Children 8, 9, 11
  College enrollment 270
  Computer use 253
  Crime 312
  Deaths, death rates . 5, 104, 105, 106, 117,
                                119, 120, 121
  Degrees conferred 289, 782
  Educational attainment 35
  Elderly 8, 9, 11
  Food stamp participants 554
  Gaming revenue 1218
  Grandparents living with grandchildren .. 69
  Health care visits to professionals . 158, 159
  Heart disease, deaths 117
  HIV disease 121
  Hospital visits 159, 169
  Housing tenure 35
  Immunization of children 183
  Internet usage 1118
  Metropolitan area population 21
  Migration 5

NOTE: Index citations refer to **table** numbers, not page numbers.

U.S. Census Bureau, Statistical Abstract of the United States: 2009

American Indian, Alaska Native population—Con.
Occupation 35
Poverty 35
Reservation and trust lands population .. 37
States 18
Suicides, death 120
Teachers 245
Tribes 36
Veterans 504
American Samoa. (See Island areas of the U.S.)
American sign language 275
American Stock Exchange 1169
Composite index 1167
AMTRAK 1080
Amusement and recreation services. (See Arts, recreation, and travel.)
Amusement, gambling, and recreation industry:
Capital 751
Earnings 612, 734, 1189, 1190, 1191
Employees 612, 734, 1189
Establishments 734, 1190, 1191
Gross domestic product 648
Nonemployer establishments 1190
Occupational safety 638
Productivity 619
Receipts, revenue 734, 1189, 1190
Gaming revenue 1218, 1219
Amusement parks 1188, 1189, 1190, 1191, 1199
Analgesics 199
Ancestry 51
Andorra. (See Foreign countries.)
Anemias, deaths 112, 113
Anesthesiologists 157
Angiocardiography 162
Angola. (See Foreign countries.)
Anguilla. (See Foreign countries.)
Animal oils and fats. (See Oils, animal.)
Animal slaughtering and processing industry ... 612, 619
Animals, domestic (see also individual classes):
Charitable contributions 564
Inventory and production 827
Pets 612, 1201, 1244
Annuities. (See Pensions and retirement benefits.)
Antigua and Barbuda. (See Foreign countries.)
Antimony 863
Apparel goods (see also Clothing accessory stores):
Consumer expenditures 662, 664, 665
Foreign trade 1267
Prices 703, 704, 705, 713, 717
Sales 1014, 1015, 1016
Apparel manufacturing:
Capital 751
Earnings 612, 965, 967, 973
Electronic commerce 969
Employees 612, 965, 967, 971, 973
Establishments 967
Finances 764
Foreign trade 1271
Industrial production index 759
Gross domestic product 648, 964
Occupational safety 638
Productivity 619
Profits 764
Shipments 967, 969
Toxic chemical releases 365

Apples 210, 709, 798, 803, 824
Appliances, household:
Consumer expenditures 664, 665
Homes with 946
Price indexes 705, 713
Sales and shipments 1003, 1014, 1016
Appliances (household) manufacturing:
Inventories 976
Shipments 976
Apricots 824
Aquaculture 803, 855, 856, 857
Archery 1209, 1210
Architects and engineers 596
Architectural services. (See Engineering and architectural services.)
Area of:
Developed land 350, 351
Foreign countries 1288
Forest land 350, 351, 352, 841
Island areas of the U.S. 344
Lakes 347
Parks 1212, 1213, 1214, 1215
States 344
Timberland 841
United States 1, 344, 1288
Water 1, 344
World 1288
Argentina. (See Foreign countries.)
Arizona. (See State data.)
Arkansas. (See State data.)
Armed Forces ... 492, 493, 494, 495, 496, 499, 501
Foreign countries 493, 495, 1361
Retirement system 497
Armenia. (See Foreign countries.)
Army personnel 492, 494
Arrests (see also Law enforcement) ... 312, 313, 316
Arson 312, 343
Arteriography 162
Arthritis 188
Artists 596
Funding 1197
Arts and humanities:
After-school activities 256, 257
Aid to 1195, 1196
Attendance 1194, 1198
Charitable contributions 561, 564
Federal aid 1195, 1196
Grants, foundations 564
Philanthropy 561, 564
States 1197
Arts, recreation, and travel:
Capital 751, 753, 755
Earnings 610, 612, 621, 734, 737, 740, 1189, 1190
Employees . 610, 612, 734, 737, 740, 1189, 1190, 1191
Equipment and software expenditures .. 753
Establishments . 734, 735, 737, 1189, 1190, 1191
Finances 724, 727, 1188, 1190
Gaming 1218, 1219
Gross domestic product 648
Hires and separations 615
Hours 610
Nonemployers 735, 1191
Occupational safety 638
Payroll 1189, 1191

NOTE: Index citations refer to **table** numbers, not page numbers.

U.S. Census Bureau, Statistical Abstract of the United States: 2009

Arts, recreation, and travel—Con.
Productivity 619
Profits 763
Receipts, revenue . 724, 727, 732, 733, 734, 735, 1188, 1189, 1190, 1191
Aruba. (See Foreign countries.)
Asbestos 322, 863, 864, 867, 868
Asia. (See Foreign countries.)
Asian and Pacific Islander population:
After-school activities 256, 257
Births 79, 81, 82, 83, 84, 85
Cancer, deaths 119
Charter school enrollment 230
Congress, members of 390
Consumer expenditures 664
Deaths, death rates 104, 105, 106, 117, 119, 120, 121
Disabled students 277
Doctorates 782
Educational attainment 221, 222
Health insurance coverage 146, 148
Heart disease, deaths 117
Hospital visits 159, 169
HIV disease 121
Income 671, 672, 682, 683
Language 227
Overweight 203
Poverty 689, 690, 693
Science doctorates 782
States 18
Suicides, deaths 120
Work-related learning activities 617
Asian population 5, 6, 8, 9, 11, 35, 43
Adoption 560
After-school activities 256, 257
Births 5
Business owners 744, 745
Children 8, 9, 11, 68
College costs 278
College enrollment 274
Computer use 253
Deaths 5
Educational attainment 35, 221, 222
Elderly 8, 9, 11
Family type 66
Food stamp participants 554
Foreign-born population 220
Foster care 560
Grandparents living with grandchildren .. 69
Health care visits to professionals 158
Health insurance coverage 146, 148
Hospital visits 159
Households 61, 66, 63, 65
Housing tenure 35
Immunization of children 183
Income 35, 671, 672, 679, 682, 683
Internet usage 1118
Labor force .. 568, 569, 570, 572, 575, 579, 596, 602, 607, 626, 631, 643
Class of worker 584
Industry 600
Job search 603
Multiple job holders 589
Occupation 35, 599
Public assistance 524, 554, 555
Living arrangements 57
Marital status 55
Metropolitan area population 21

Asian population—Con.
Migration 5
Occupation 35
Poverty 35, 689, 690, 691, 693, 694
School enrollment 220, 241, 274
Students with weapons 239
Veterans 504
Asparagus 210
Asphalt 713
Assault 295, 296, 297, 298, 304, 305, 306
Asset-backed securities . 730, 1129, 1130, 1151, 1159
Assets, personal 698, 699, 700, 1133
Assistance, public. (See Public aid, assistance.)
Associations, national, nonprofit . 561, 562, 563, 564, 1245
Asthma 112, 113, 114, 116, 160, 170
Adults 190
Children 184
Astronomy 785
Athletic goods. (See Sporting and athletic goods.)
ATMs (automated teller machines) .. 1144, 1145
Attention deficit disorder 160, 179
Audio equipment 717
Auditing. (See Accounting, tax preparation, bookkeeping, and payroll services.)
Australia. (See Foreign countries.)
Austria. (See Foreign countries.)
Authors 596
Automatic bill paying 1145
Automobile dealers:
Earnings 612, 1007, 1008
Employees 612, 1007, 1008
Establishments 1007, 1008
Inventories 1012
Productivity 619
Sales 1009
Automobile loans 1150
Automobile rentals and leasing. (See Automotive equipment rental and leasing and Rental and leasing services.)
Automobiles (see also Motor vehicles):
Consumer expenditures . 662, 663, 664, 665, 666
Expenditure per new car 1021
Foreign trade 1267
Imports 1021
Insurance 10, 655
Lease 705
Price indexes 705, 713
Production 1021
Sales 1021
Automotive equipment rental and leasing . 612, 619
Automotive products. (See Motor vehicles, Tires and tubes, etc.)
Automotive repair and maintenance service:
Earnings 612
Employees 612
Establishments 1235
Nonemployers 1234
Productivity 619
Receipts/revenue 1234, 1244
Avocados 824
Azerbaijan. (See Foreign countries.)

B

Backpacking 1209
Bacon 709

NOTE: Index citations refer to **table** numbers, not page numbers.

U.S. Census Bureau, Statistical Abstract of the United States: 2009

Bahamas, The. (See Foreign countries.)
Bahrain. (See Foreign countries.)
Bakeries and tortilla manufacturing .. 612, 619, 967
Bakery products 664, 665, 705, 713
Balance of payments 1246, 1247, 1260
Balance sheet 728, 729, 731
Ballet 1198
Bananas 210, 709
Bangladesh. (See Foreign countries.)
Bankruptcies 742, 746, 747
Banks, commercial:
    Consumer credit 1150, 1151
    Credit cards 1137, 1148
    Debit cards 1147
    Delinquency rates, repossessions, loans . 1155
    Deposits 1137, 1142
    Earnings 612, 1128
    Employees 612, 1128
    Establishments 1128, 1136, 1137
    Finances ... 1129, 1130, 1136, 1137, 1138, 1139, 1140, 1141, 1142, 1152, 1156, 1175
    Flow of funds 1129, 1130, 1175
    Foreign banking offices in United States . 1142
    Gross domestic product 648, 1125
    Individual Retirement Accounts (IRAs); 401(k) plans 535, 538, 1176
    Insured banks 1136, 1140
    Loans 1137
    Productivity 619
    Profits 1138, 1139
    Robbery 308
    Service charges 655
    State data 1140, 1141
    Stock and bond prices and yields 1167
Barbados. (See Foreign countries.)
Barbecuing 1200
Barber shops 655, 1234, 1244
Barite 863, 864, 867, 868
Barley 798, 803
Bars. (See Food Services and drinking places.)
Base, military closings 492
Baseball . 1203, 1205, 1206, 1207, 1208, 1209, 1210
Basketball . 1205, 1206, 1207, 1208, 1209, 1210
Bass 855
Bauxite 864, 867
    Prices 864, 868
    World production 867, 1332
Beans 210, 798, 803, 806, 822
Beauty shops 1244
Beef (see also Meat and meat products):
    Consumer expenditures 662, 664, 665
    Consumption 209, 826, 1325, 1330
        Foreign countries 1330
    Foreign trade 810, 826
    Price indexes 705
    Prices 705, 709, 713
    Production 826
        Foreign countries 1325, 1329
    Supply 826
Beer. (See Malt beverages.)
Beer, wine, and liquor stores:
    Earnings 612, 1008
    Employees 612, 1008
    Establishments 1008
    Productivity 619
    Sales 1009, 1023
Belarus. (See Foreign countries.)

Belgium. (See Foreign countries.)
Belize. (See Foreign countries.)
Benin. (See Foreign countries.)
Bermuda. (See Foreign countries.)
Beryllium 863
Beverages (see also Alcoholic beverages):
    Consumption 207
    Expenditure 664, 665
    Price indexes . 703, 704, 705, 717, 720, 721
Beverages and tobacco product manufacturing:
    Earnings 612, 965, 967
    Employees 612, 965, 967, 971
    Finances 764
    Gross domestic product 648
    Industrial production index 759
    Productivity 619
    Profits 764
    Shipments 967, 975, 976
Bhutan. (See Foreign countries.)
Bicycles 308, 705, 1209, 1210
Billiards 1209
Biological sciences:
    Degrees conferred 782, 785
    Employment 596
    Enrollment 779
Bird ownership 1201
Birth and birth rates . 4, 5, 77, 78, 79, 80, 81, 82, 84, 86, 87, 90, 91
    American Indian, Eskimo, and Aleut population 5, 79, 81, 82, 83, 84, 85
    Asian and Pacific Islander population . 79, 81, 82, 83, 84, 90
    Asian population 5
    Assisted reproductive technology 96
    Births to single or unmarried women . 84, 90, 1291
    Births to teenage mothers 83, 85, 90
    Birth weight 87
    Black, African-American population ... 5, 78, 79, 80, 81, 82, 83, 84, 85, 86, 90
    Cesarean section deliveries 86, 162
    Characteristics of mother . 79, 83, 84, 85, 86, 90, 91
    Delivery procedures 86, 162
    First births 89, 90, 91
    Foreign countries 1291, 1295
    Hispanic population .. 5, 78, 81, 82, 83, 84, 85, 86, 90
    Island areas of the U.S. 81, 87, 1273
    Life expectancy .. 100, 101, 102, 103, 1296
    Native Hawaiian, Other Pacific Islander 5
    Race .. 5, 78, 79, 80, 81, 82, 83, 84, 85, 86
    States 15, 81, 87
Birth control 94, 95
Birth weights 87
Bismuth 863
Black, African-American population .. 5, 6, 8, 9, 11, 18, 35, 41
    Abortions 97, 98
    Activity limitation 185, 186
    Adoption 560
    Adult education 294
    After-school activities 256, 257
    Age and/or sex 6, 7, 9, 11
    AIDS 178
    Birth and birth rates ... 5, 78, 79, 81, 85, 90
        Births to teenage mothers 83, 85
        Births to unmarried women 84
    Breastfeeding 88

NOTE: Index citations refer to **table** numbers, not page numbers.

Black, African-American population—Con.
  Business owners 744, 745
  Cancer 119, 173
  Child care 559
  Children under 18 years old . 2, 8, 9, 11, 68
      Literacy activities 226, 229
      Poverty 690, 691
      School readiness 226, 229
  Cigarette smoking 196
  Community service 256
  Computer use 253
  Congress, members of 390
  Consumer expenditures 664
  Contraceptive use 94, 95
  Crime 309, 312
  Criminal victimizations 309
  Deaths and death rates ... 5, 104, 105, 106,
            110, 111, 117, 119, 120, 121
  Degrees conferred 289, 782
  Disabled persons 277, 541
  Educational attainment ... 35, 221, 222, 223
      Earnings 224
  Elderly 8, 9, 11, 691
  Elected officials 390, 398
  Elections, voter registrations and turnout ...
                                           400
  Families, characteristics 35, 63, 65, 66
  Fertility, fertility rate 82
  Food stamp participants 541, 554
  Foreign-born population 220
  Foster care 560
  Grandparents living with grandchildren .. 69
  Health care, visits to professionals . 158, 159
  Health insurance coverage ... 139, 146, 148
  Heart disease, deaths 117
  High school graduates and dropouts ... 262,
                                          264
  HIV disease 121, 178
  Homicides 300, 301, 302
  Hospital use 159, 169
  Households, characteristics 61, 63, 65
  Housing 35, 949, 953, 956, 957, 959
  Immunization of children 183
  Income .. 35, 523, 668, 669, 671, 672, 673,
                   674, 679, 682, 683
  Infant deaths 110, 111
  Internet access/use 253, 1118, 1121
  Jail inmates 335
  Job search 603
  Labor force 568, 569, 570, 572
      Class of worker 584
      Displaced workers 593
      Earnings 446, 626
      Employed . 446, 569, 586, 587, 589, 590,
                       596, 599, 600
      Employment status 569, 570
          Educational attainment 572, 607
          High school graduates and dropouts,
            employment status 265, 575
          School enrollment, persons 16 to 24
            years old 575
          Unemployed 602, 607
      Job search 603
      Persons working at home 586
      Work-related learning activity 617
  Life expectancy 100, 102, 103
  Living arrangements 57, 68
  Marital status 55

Black, African-American population—Con.
  Metropolitan area population 21
  Migration 5
  Minimum wage workers 631
  Nurses 596
  Occupation 35, 596, 599
  Overweight 203
  Pension plan coverage 523
  Physical activity 204
  Poverty 35, 689, 690, 691, 694
  Projections 11
  Property owners 953, 956, 957, 959
  Public assistance 524, 541, 554, 555
  Recreation activities 1198, 1199
  School dropouts, high school 263, 265
  Schools and education:
      Adult education 294
      American College Testing Program (ACT) .
                                          259
      Attainment 221, 222, 223
      Enrollment 216, 220, 241, 274
          Charter schools 230
          College costs 278
          College enrollment 270, 271, 272
          Disability 277
          Preprimary enrollment 228
      High school dropouts 262, 263, 265
      High school graduates 265
      Higher education institutions:
          Degrees conferred 782
          Enrollment 220, 270, 271, 272
      Scholastic Assessment Test (SAT) 258
      Students with weapons 239
      Teachers 243, 245, 248, 255, 596
  Senior citizen communities 957
  Sexual activity 92
  States 18
  Suicides 120
  Union membership 643
  Veterans 504
  Volunteers 256
  Voter registration and turnout 400
Black lung benefit program 524, 542, 543
Blackberries 824
Blast furnace and basic steel products. (See Iron
  and steel products.)
Blind persons 544
      Medicaid payments and recipients 140
Blood alcohol concentration . 1069, 1070, 1072
Blueberries 803, 824
BMI. (See Body Mass Index.)
Boats. (See Ships.)
Body Mass Index (BMI) 203
Bolivia. (See Foreign countries.)
Bolts, nuts, etc. (See Iron and steel products.)
Bonds:
  Foreign 1163, 1164
  Holdings by sector . 700, 1130, 1131, 1132,
                      1161, 1164, 1166
  Life insurance companies 1161, 1181
  New issues 1162
  Prices, yields, sales, and issues .. 460, 1158,
                        1160, 1163, 1165
  Rating 427, 428
  U.S. savings 460, 1133
Book, periodical, and music stores ... 612, 619,
                      1008, 1009, 1017
Book publishing industry 1086, 1087, 1098

NOTE: Index citations refer to **table** numbers, not page numbers.

Bookkeeping. (See Accounting, tax preparation, bookkeeping, and payroll services.)
Books (see also Information industry, Libraries and librarians, and Publishing industry):
   Reading 1089
   Sales 1014, 1015, 1016, 1097
Boots. (See Footwear.)
Border Lengths, Canada and Mexico 345
Border Patrol activities 512
Boron 864, 865
Bosnia and Herzegovina. (See Foreign countries.)
Botox 171
Botswana. (See Foreign countries.)
Botulism 175
Bowling 1203, 1206, 1209, 1210
Bowling center industry . 619, 1188, 1190, 1191
Boxing 1206
Brazil. (See Foreign countries.)
Bread 705, 709
Breastfeeding 88
Bridge inventory 1050
British Virgin Islands. (See Foreign countries.)
Broadcasting industry:
   Capital 751
   Earnings 612, 734, 1086, 1088
   Employees 612, 734, 1086, 1088
   Establishments 734, 1086, 1088
   Finances 724, 1087
   Gross domestic product 648
   Multinational companies 766, 767
   Productivity 619
   Receipts, revenue 724, 734, 1087, 1088
   World 1344
Broadway and off-Broadway shows 1194
Broccoli 210, 803, 822
Broilers (see also Poultry) .. 713, 798, 802, 803, 826, 834, 835
Bromine 863, 864
Bronchitis, acute or chronic respiratory disease, emphysema, etc. ... 112, 113, 114, 115, 116, 160, 161, 190
Brunei. (See Foreign countries.)
Buddhist population. (See Religion.)
Budget, federal:
   Debt 452
   Outlays 451, 453, 454, 455
   Receipts 451, 457
   Tax expenditures 459
   Taxes 457
Building construction:
   Earnings 612, 919
   Employees 612, 919
   Establishments 919
   Occupational safety 638
Building materials, and garden supplies, retail stores:
   Earnings 612, 734, 1008
   Electronic commerce 1013
   Employees 612, 734, 1008
   Establishments 734, 1008, 1017
   Inventories 1012
   Nonemployers 1017
   Productivity 619
   Sales 734, 1009, 1011, 1020, 1017
Building permits. (See Construction industry, and Housing and housing units.)
Buildings (see also Construction industry, and Housing and housing units):
   Characteristics 963
   Construction value 921, 922, 923, 924

Buildings (see also Construction industry, and Housing and housing units)—Con.
   Energy consumption and expenditures . 887
   Federal 484
   Fires and property loss 342, 343
   Floorspace 484, 887, 963
   Principal activity 887, 963
Bulgaria. (See Foreign countries.)
Burglary 295, 296, 297, 298, 308, 309, 312
Burkina Faso. (See Foreign countries.)
Burma. (See Foreign countries.)
Burundi. (See Foreign countries.)
Buses and bus transportation. (See Passenger transit and Motor vehicles.)
Business enterprise (see also individual types of business and industry):
   American Indian- and Alaska Native-owned businesses 744, 745
   Asian-owned businesses 744, 745
   Bankruptcies filed 742, 746, 747
   Black-owned businesses 744, 745
   Capital, fixed by industry 751
   Corporations:
      Philanthropy 561
      Profits and sales 725
   Corporations, partnerships, and proprietorships . 722, 724, 725, 726, 727, 732, 733
   Cycles 756
   Economic indicators 757
   Employees 736, 737, 738, 741, 765
      Coastal counties 25
   Establishments 734, 736, 737, 738
      Coastal counties 25
   Failures and starts 739, 742
   Finances . 722, 725, 726, 728, 729, 762, 764, 766, 767, 979, 980
   Firms 738, 741
   Flow of funds 1129
   Foreign investment in the U.S. . 1251, 1252, 1253, 1254
   Hispanic-owned businesses 744, 745
   Leading indicators 757
   Loans to minority-operated small businesses 743
   Multinational companies . 765, 766, 767, 768
   Native Hawaiian and Other Pacific Islander-owned business 744, 745
   Patents 748, 749, 1346
   Payroll 736, 738, 741
   Profits 761, 762, 763, 764, 979, 980
   Sales, shipments, receipts ... 974, 976, 977, 980
   Small business 738, 739, 741, 743
   Women-owned businesses 744, 745
Business management, degrees conferred . 290, 291, 292
   Salary offers 287
Butane 870
Butter 209, 709, 832
Butylene 870

C

Cabbage 822
Cable and other pay television services 705, 1090
   Advertising expenditures 1239
   Price indexes 705
   Viewing 1089, 1091

NOTE: Index citations refer to **table** numbers, not page numbers.

U.S. Census Bureau, Statistical Abstract of the United States: 2009

Cable and other program distribution:
    Earnings 612, 1086
    Employees 612, 1086
    Establishments 1086
    Finances 1087
    Revenue 1087, 1114
Cable and other subscription programming:
    Earnings 612, 1086
    Employees 612, 1086
    Establishments 1086
    Finances 1087, 1106
    Revenue 1087, 1106
Cadmium 864, 867
Cafeterias. (See Eating and drinking places.)
Calcium, dietary 208
California. (See State data.)
Calves 803, 826, 827, 830
Cambodia. (See Foreign countries.)
Cameras 995
Cameroon. (See Foreign countries.)
Campaigns, fundraising ... 404, 405, 406, 407,
                                                  408, 409
Camping 1209, 1210
Canada. (See Foreign countries.)
Cancer (malignancies) 160, 170, 173, 174
    Deaths .. 112, 113, 114, 115, 116, 119, 174
Candy 705
Cantaloupe 210, 822
Capacity utilization, index 760
Cape Verde. (See Foreign countries.)
Capital (see also individual industries):
    Banking 1137, 1138
    Expenditures 752, 753, 754, 755, 967
    New security issues 1162
    Residential 960
    Stocks 751, 974
    Utilities 911, 914, 1110
Capital equipment, producer price indexes . 713
Capital gains 467
Capital punishment 339, 340
Carbon dioxide emissions 360, 913, 1304
Cardiac catheterization 162
Cardiovascular disease. (See Heart disease.)
Carp 855
Carrots 210, 803, 822
Cars. (See Automobiles.)
Casualty insurance 1182
Catalog and mail order sales . 1009, 1013, 1014,
                                                     1017
Catfish 803, 855, 857
Catholic population. (See Religion.)
Cat ownership 1201
CAT scan 162
Cattle:
    Farm marketings, sales 802, 803
    Imports 810
    Number on farms 827, 828, 830
    Organic 798
    Prices 713, 827
    Production 827, 830
    Slaughter 830
    Value on farms 827
Cauliflower 210, 822
Cayman Islands. (See Foreign countries.)
Celery 210, 822
Cellular and other wireless telecommunications .
                         1086, 1087, 1113
Cellular telephones (see also Telephone carri-
    ers.) 1111, 1344

Cement (see also Nonmetallic mineral product
    manufacturing) 863, 864
    Earnings 612
    Employment 612, 864
    Prices 713, 864
    Productivity 619
    World production 1332
Central African Republic. (See Foreign coun-
    tries.)
Central America. (See Foreign countries.)
Central and South American population (His-
    panic origin) 38, 78, 85
Cereal and bakery products:
    Expenditures, prices 664, 665, 705
    Per capita consumption 209
Cerebrovascular diseases, deaths . 112, 113, 114,
                           115, 116, 161, 170
Certificates of deposit 1133, 1157
Cesarean section deliveries 86, 162
Chad. (See Foreign countries.)
Charitable contributions (see also Philanthropy) .
           471, 473, 561, 563, 564, 565
Charter schools 230
Checks 1144
Cheese (see also Dairy products) . 209, 709, 832
Chemical engineering, degrees conferred .. 785
Chemical products:
    Foreign trade 1261, 1267, 1271
    Price indexes 713, 720, 721
    Production 759, 986
Chemicals manufacturing (see also individual
    chemicals):
    Capital 751
    Earnings 612, 965, 967, 973
    Electronic commerce 969
    Employees 612, 965, 967, 971, 973
    Establishments 965
    Finances 764
    Foreign trade 1271
    Gross domestic product 648, 964
    Industrial production index 759
    Inventories 975, 976
    Multinational companies 766, 767, 768
    Productivity 619
    Profits 762, 764
    Research and development 774, 775
    Shipments 967, 975, 976
    Toxic chemical releases 364, 365, 366
Chemistry (see also Physical sciences):
    Degrees conferred 785
    Employment 596
    Salary offers 287
Cherries 803, 824
Chicken pox 175
Chickens. (See Poultry.)
Child abuse 329, 330
Child care 559, 596, 598, 601, 705, 957
    Expenditures for 667
    Tax credit 473, 474
Child day care services:
    Earnings 612
    Employees 596, 612
    Finances 557
Child labor violations 630
Child support 523, 549, 550
Children (see also Birth, Death, Divorce, Mar-
    riage, and Population):
    Activity limitation 185
    Adopted 560
    Age and/or sex 7, 8, 9, 10, 11, 16, 17

NOTE: Index citations refer to **table** numbers, not page numbers.

Children (see also Birth, Death, Divorce, Mar-
 riage, and Population)—Con.
  Aid, social welfare programs . 521, 523, 526,
    546, 547, 548, 549, 550, 551, 554, 555,
    557, 558
  AIDS 177, 178, 1297
  Alcohol use 199
  American Indian, Alaska Native population ..
    8, 9, 11
  Asian population 8, 9, 11, 68
  Asthma 184
  Attention Deficit Disorder 179
  Black, African-American population . 8, 9, 11,
    68
  Child abuse 329, 330
  Child day care 559, 705
  Child labor violations 630
  Child support 523, 549, 550
  Cigarette smoking 199
  Computer use 252, 253
  Congenital abnormalities 170
  Cost of raising 667
  Crime, arrests 313
  Deaths and death rates . 109, 110, 111, 114,
    115
  Disability status 180
  Drug use 199
  Families with 63, 64, 65, 66, 67
  Food cost 708
  Food insecurity 206
  Food stamp program 553, 554
  Foreign-born population 41, 42
  Foreign country ... 1290, 1293, 1294, 1295,
    1297, 1302
  Foster care 560
  Grandparents living with grandchildren .. 69
  Head Start program 555
  Health insurance coverage .. 139, 142, 146,
    147, 148
  High school dropouts 262, 263
  High school graduates 261, 267
  Hispanic-origin population 8, 9, 11
  HIV 1297
  Hospital use 160, 161, 169, 170
  Hunger 206
  Immigrants 47
  Immunization against diseases 183
  Income, families with children 676
  Injuries 192
  Internet access 253
  Juvenile delinquency institutions 327
  Labor force (16 to 19 years old), ... 568
    Employed 581, 584, 589, 591
    Employment status 575
    Minimum wage workers 631
    Multiple job holders 589
    Participation rates 576
    Sex 568, 571
    Unemployed 602, 603, 608
  Language proficiency 227
  Literacy activities, skills 226, 229
  Literacy, comparative 1302
  Living arrangements 68
  Metropolitan areas 22
  Mobility status 29
  Mothers in the labor force, by age of chil-
    dren 90, 91, 578, 579
  Music purchases 1103

Children (see also Birth, Death, Divorce, Mar-
 riage, and Population)—Con.
  Native Hawaiian, Other Pacific Islander
    population 8, 9, 11
  Physician visits 158, 159, 160
  Pneumonia 170
  Poverty 690, 691
  Projections 10, 11, 17
  Respiratory infection, acute 160, 161
  School enrollment . 211, 213, 215, 216, 217,
    218, 219, 232, 236
    Preprimary school enrollment 228
    Projections 211
  School readiness 229
  Social security beneficiaries and payments ..
    526
  States 16, 17
  Special education 181
  Stay-at-home parents 67
  Suicides 114
  Two-or-more-races population 8, 9, 11
Chile. (See Foreign countries.)
China. (See Foreign countries.)
Chinese population 85
Chiropractors' offices 152
Chocolate. (See Cocoa.)
Cholera 175
Cholelithiases, deaths 113
Christian population. (See Religion.)
Christmas trees 803
Chromite 1332
Chromium 868
Churches (see also Religion):
  Construction value 924
  Grants, foundations 561, 564
  Number and membership 75
  Volunteers 566
Cigar usage 199
Cigarettes (see also Tobacco):
  Consumption 981, 1299, 1314
  Foreign trade 981
  Price indexes 714
  Production 981
  Smokers and use 196, 197, 199, 200
Circuit boards 992
Circulation of newspapers and periodicals . 1090,
    1093, 1094, 1095
Circulatory diseases 189
Cirrhosis of liver, deaths 114, 115
Cities (see also Metropolitan areas):
  Climate . 373, 374, 375, 376, 377, 378, 379
    Foreign cities 1303
  Crime 298
  Debt 440
  Employees, earnings, payrolls 449
  Finances of city governments 439, 440
  Foreign born 40
  Foreign travel to 1221
  Governmental units 410, 411, 412
  Income 686
  Language spoken at home 54
  Officials elected 398, 399
  Population 26, 27
  Poverty 686
  Property tax rates 430
  Taxes paid, by family income level 429
Citrus fruits:
  Consumption 210, 823
  Foreign trade 823

NOTE: Index citations refer to **table** numbers, not page numbers.

U.S. Census Bureau, Statistical Abstract of the United States: 2009

Citrus fruits—Con.
   Production 823, 824
Civil and architectural engineering 785
Civil aviation. (See Air transportation.)
Civil cases, U.S. District Courts 322
Civil service employees. (See Government.)
Clams 854, 855, 858, 859
Cleaning supplies 664, 665
Clergymen 596
Climate, selected cities 373, 374, 375, 376,
                  377, 378, 379, 1303
   Precipitation 376, 377, 378, 1303
   Temperature 372, 373, 374, 375, 1303
Clocks and watches 705, 717
Clothing and accessory stores, retail:
   Earnings 612, 1008
   Electronic commerce 1013
   Employees 612, 734, 1008
   Establishments 734, 1008, 1017
   Finances 764
   Inventories 1012
   Nonemployers 1017
   Price indexes 705, 717
   Productivity 619
   Profits 764
   Sales 734, 1009, 1011, 1020, 1017
Clubs, after-school 256
Coal (see also Coal mining, and Petroleum and
  coal product manufacturing):
   Car loadings 1082, 1081,
   Consumption . 877, 883, 884, 886, 889, 903,
                       1334, 1335
   Emissions 913
   Expenditures 890
   Foreign trade . 877, 878, 884, 893, 894, 1267
   Net generation 903
   Net summer capacity 904
   Prices 713, 865, 877, 878
   Production 878, 883, 884
     World production . 867, 878, 1332, 1333,
                           1339
   Reserves 879, 880
Coal mining:
   Earnings 838, 860
   Employment 838, 860, 861, 878
   Establishments 838
   Fatalities 861
   Gross domestic product 648
   Injuries 861
   Inspections 861
   Mines 861, 878
   Output 862, 883
   Productivity 862, 878
   Safety 861
   Shipments 860
   Supply 877
Coast Guard 355, 511
Coastal population 24, 25
Coastlines 346
Cobalt 864
Cocaine (see also Drugs (illegal), arrests and
  use) 199, 316, 317
Cocoa 209, 810
Cod 854, 859
Coffee:
   Consumption 207, 209
   Foreign trade 808, 810
   Price indexes 705
   Prices 705, 709, 713

Cogeneration of electricity (combined-heat-and-
  power) 885, 903
Cohabitation, unmarried 62, 92
Coke. (See Coal.)
College:
   Costs 278
   Enrollment .. 211, 217, 218, 219, 268, 269,
            270, 271, 273, 274, 275
   Federal obligations 778
   Freshmen 276
   Price index 279, 705
   Research & development 777
   Science & engineering 779, 781
   State appropriations 281
   Tuition 282
Colleges and universities. (See Education,
  higher education institutions.)
Colombia. (See Foreign countries.)
Colorado. (See State data.)
Commerce:
   Domestic, by rail 1081, 1082
   Domestic, by water 1043, 1044
   Foreign. (See Foreign trade.)
Commerce and housing credit 453
Commercial buildings:
   Characteristics 887, 963
   Construction value 924
   Crime incidents 306
   Energy characteristics 887
   Floorspace 924
   Inventory 963
Commercial energy ... 885, 886, 887, 889, 890,
      891, 892, 905, 908, 909, 910, 913, 915
Commercial paper 729
Commodities. (See individual types of commodi-
  ties.)
Commodity flow 1048
Communicable diseases 175
Communications:
   Degrees conferred 290, 291, 292
   Price indexes 703
Communications equipment manufacturing:
   Earnings 612, 787, 965, 967
   Employees 612, 787, 965, 967
   Establishments 965
   Foreign trade 1269
   Inventories 976
   Productivity 619
   Shipments 967, 976, 996
Communications industry. (See Information
  industry.)
Community development 436, 455
Community food, housing services 557
Community service 256, 566
Commuting to work 634, 1060
Comoros. (See Foreign countries.)
Compact disks (CD-ROM) 1102
Computer:
   After-school activities 257
   Consumer expenditures 717
   Foreign trade 1261, 1269, 1271
   Sales 753, 1014, 1015, 1016
   Use 252, 253, 1089, 1090, 1091, 1120,
                  1121, 1344, 1345
Computer programming and data processing
  services:
   Earnings and employees 612
Computer sales 995

NOTE: Index citations refer to **table** numbers, not page numbers.

Computer specialists:
    Degrees conferred . 290, 291, 292, 779, 782,
        785
    Labor force 596, 598, 786
    Research & development . 772, 777, 789, 774
    Salary offers 287
Computer systems design:
    Capital 751
    Earnings 1233, 1235
    Employees 1233, 1234, 1235
    Establishments 1235
    Gross domestic product 648
    Receipts 1233, 1234, 1237
    Research and development 774, 775
Computerized axial tomography (CAT scan) . 162
Computers and electronic product manufacturing:
    Capital 751
    Earnings 612, 787, 965, 967
    Electronic commerce 969
    Employees 612, 787, 965, 967, 971
    Establishments 965
    Finances 764
    Foreign trade 1271
    Gross domestic product 648
    Industrial production index 759
    Inventories 975, 976
    Multinational companies 766, 767
    Productivity 619
    Profits 764
    Research and development 775
    Shipments 967, 969, 975, 976, 993, 994
Concerts, symphony orchestras 1194
Condensed and evaporated milk 209, 832
Congestion on road 1059
Congo (Brazzaville). (See Foreign countries.)
Congo (Kinshasa). (See Foreign countries.)
Congress, U.S.:
    Asian, Pacific Islander members 390
    Bills, acts, resolutions 391, 392
    Black members 390
    Campaign finances 408, 409
    Composition 388, 389
    Congressional districts candidates, votes
       cast 387
    Hispanic members 390
    Members, characteristics 390
    Representatives, vote cast ... 386, 387, 403
    Senators, vote cast 385
    Seniority 390
    Time in session 391
    Women members 390
Connecticut. (See State data.)
Construction industry (see also Building materials, and Highways):
    Building authorized 926
    Building permits, value 926
    Capital 751, 753, 755
    Construction contracts 924, 925
    Earnings . 610, 612, 621, 622, 734, 737, 740,
        919
    Employees .. 586, 600, 610, 611, 612, 639,
        734, 737, 740, 786, 919
    Equipment and software expenditures .. 753
    Establishments 734, 735, 737, 919
    Finances 724, 727, 1282
    Gross domestic product 648, 1282
    Hires and separations 615
    Hours 610

Construction industry (see also Building materials, and Highways)—Con.
    Nonemployers 735
    Occupational safety 635, 638
    Producer price indexes 920
    Profits 722, 763
    Residential 926, 927, 928, 929
    Shipments, receipts 722, 724, 727, 732,
        733, 734, 735
    Unions 643
    Value, work 921, 922, 923
Construction machinery, manufacturing:
    Earnings 612, 967
    Employees 612, 967
    Productivity 619
    Shipments 967
Construction materials. (See Building materials.)
Consumer:
    Consumer complaints against airlines . 1040
    Consumer goods 713
    Credit . 729, 1132, 1134, 1135, 1148, 1149,
        1150, 1151
       Delinquency rates 1155
    Electronics 1015
    Expenditures ., 662, 663, 664, 665, 666, 717
       Books 1097
       Communications 1089
       Entertainment 664, 665, 1192
       Food ....., 662, 663, 664, 665, 666, 807
       Housing ...., 662, 663, 664, 665, 666
       Medical care .. 126, 127, 129, 130, 133,
        662, 663, 664, 665, 666
       Metropolitan areas 663
       Reading material 664, 665, 1192
       Sporting goods 1210
       Transportation 664, 665
Consumer price indexes 702, 703, 704, 705
    By commodity group 703, 705
    Foreign countries 1311, 1313
    Medical care 132, 703, 705
    Purchasing power of the dollar 702
    Year-to-year changes 703, 704
Consumption. (See individual commodities.)
Contraception use 94, 95
Convenience stores 1008, 1022
Cook Islands. (See Foreign countries.)
Cookies 705
Cooking oils consumption 209
Copper:
    Consumption 864
    Foreign trade 864
    Prices 713, 720, 721, 864, 865
    Production and value 864
       World production 867, 1332
Copyrights, registration 750
Corn:
    Acreage 818, 819
       Organic 798
    Consumption 209, 210
    Ethanol 818
    Farm marketings, sales 802, 803
    Foreign trade 812, 814, 815, 818, 1267,
        1327
    Prices 713, 720, 818, 819
    Production 812, 818, 819, 822
       World production 812
    Supply and disappearance 818
Coronary procedures 162
Corporate business sector 729, 730

NOTE: Index citations refer to **table** numbers, not page numbers.

U.S. Census Bureau, Statistical Abstract of the United States: 2009

Corporate business sector—Con.
Political action committees 404, 405
Corporations:
Capital 731
Dividend payments 761
Finances . 722, 723, 724, 725, 726, 727, 729,
730, 731, 732, 733, 1129, 1130, 1175
Manufacturing 979
Nonfinancial 729, 730
Philanthropy 561
Profits .. 722, 761, 762, 763, 764, 978, 979
Receipts 722
Sales 727, 732, 733, 978
Stocks and bonds 1158, 1159
Taxes:
Corporate income tax 418, 433, 435,
437, 761
Returns 722, 723, 731
Correctional institutions (see also Prisons and
prisoners):
Employment 447, 596
Expenditures 433, 436
Per capita 331
Prisoners 332, 333, 1276
Cosmetic surgery 171
Cosmetics, perfume, etc., foreign trade 705,
713
Costa Rica. (See Foreign countries.)
Cost-of-living indexes 706, 1313
Cote d'Ivoire. (See Foreign countries.)
Cotton:
Acreage 818, 1325
Consumption 982, 1325
Farm marketings, sales 801, 803, 805
Foreign trade . 808, 812, 814, 815, 818, 1267
Prices 713, 806, 818, 819
Production 812, 818, 819
World 812, 1325, 1326
Supply and disappearance 818
Country data (See Foreign countries.)
County governments 410, 411, 412
Debt 442
Elected officials 398, 399
Employees, earnings, payroll 450
Finances of county government ... 441, 442
Couriers and messengers:
Earnings 612, 1029, 1031
Employees 612, 1025, 1029, 1031
Establishments 1029, 1031
Occupational safety 638
Revenue 1029, 1078
Courts 321, 322, 323
Criminal appeals 324
Criminal matters: investigated 315
District courts, U.S. 322, 323
Juvenile court cases handled 327
Public officials, prosecutions 326
Sentencing 323
Supreme Court, U.S. 321
Cows (see also Cattle and Dairy products) . 828,
831, 832
Crabs 854, 855, 858, 859
Crack cocaine 199
Cranberries 824
Crappie 855
Crawfish 855
Credit cards ... 1134, 1144, 1148, 1149, 1150,
1155

Credit intermediation industry:
Capital 751
Earnings 1126, 1128
Employees 1126, 1128
Establishments 1126, 1127, 1128
Nonemployers 1127
Receipts 1126, 1127
Credit markets 1130, 1150
Credit unions:
Consumer credit 1151
Earnings 1128
Employees 1128
Establishments 1128, 1136, 1143
Finances ... 1129, 1136, 1143, 1150, 1152,
1175
Individual Retirement Accounts (IRAs) . 1176
Crews 1207
Crime (see also Criminal victimization, and Law
enforcement):
Assault 295, 296, 297, 298, 304
Average value lost 308
Burglary . 295, 296, 297, 298, 304, 308, 309
Child abuse and neglect 329, 330
Drug abuse violations 316, 323
Hate crimes 310, 311
Homicides, race, and sex 300, 301, 302
Larceny-theft 295, 296, 297, 298, 308
Motor vehicle theft . 295, 296, 297, 298, 308,
309
Murder, murder circumstances 295, 296,
297, 298, 299
Place and time of occurrence 306
Police officers assaulted, killed 319
Property crime ... 295, 296, 297, 298, 309
Rape, forcible . 295, 296, 297, 298, 303, 304
Robbery 295, 296, 297, 298, 304, 308
Schools 237, 306
Shoplifting 308
Violent crime . 295, 296, 297, 298, 299, 307
Workplace 514, 639
Criminal victimization 304, 305, 306, 309
Households 309
Place of occurrence 309
Violent 304, 306, 307
Weapons involved 306
Workplace 639
Croaker 854
Croatia. (See Foreign countries.)
Crops (see also Farms, and individual crops):
Acreage 817, 818, 1325
Farm marketings, sales 801, 803, 805
Foreign trade 813, 815, 818, 1325
Prices 806, 818
Production 818, 1325, 1326
Productivity 817
Supply and disappearance 818, 1325
Cross country (running) 1207, 1208
Crossword puzzles 1200
Crude materials:
Futures price index 716
Prices 712, 713
Crude oil (see also Petroleum and products):
Foreign trade . 869, 870, 884, 894, 895, 896
Prices 710, 713, 714, 865, 869, 888
Production ... 863, 869, 870, 873, 883, 896
World production 1337
Cruise industry 1220
Crustaceans 854, 855, 856, 858, 859
Cryptosporidiosis 175

NOTE: Index citations refer to **table** numbers, not page numbers.

U.S. Census Bureau, Statistical Abstract of the United States: 2009

Cuba. (See Foreign countries.)
Cuban population 38
    Births, birth rates 78, 85
    Educational attainment 38, 221
    Labor force 38, 569
Cucumbers 210, 822
Cultural expenditures 1356
Currency:
    Foreign exchange rate 1352
    Personal saving component 656
    Supply 1156
Customs regions, imports and exports 1262
Cyprus. (See Foreign countries.)
Czech Republic. (See Foreign countries.)

D

Dairy products (see also individual products):
    Consumer expenditures 662, 665
    Consumption 207, 209, 1325
    Farm marketings, sales 801, 803, 832
    Foreign trade 810, 813
    Manufacture 832
    Prices 713, 806
    Production 832, 1325
Dairy products manufacturing 619, 967
Dance 1198
Data processing services. (See Computer pro-
    gramming and data processing services.)
Dates 824
Day care. (See Child day care services.)
Death and death rates (see also Accidents and
    fatalities):
    Age and sex . 102, 103, 104, 105, 106, 114,
                          115, 117, 122
    AIDS 112, 178, 1297
    American Indian, Alaska Native population . 5
    Asian population 5
    Black, African-American population . 5, 102,
        103, 104, 105, 106, 110, 111, 117, 119,
                          120, 121
    Cancer 112, 114, 116, 119, 122
    Cause .. 112, 113, 114, 115, 116, 117, 118,
                    119, 120, 121, 1032, 1080
    Fetal and neonatal 109, 110, 111
    Foreign countries 1295
    Heart disease . 112, 114, 115, 116, 117, 122
    Hispanic or Latino origin .. 5, 104, 106, 107,
                          119, 120, 121
    Industrial 635, 636
    Infant 109, 110, 111
    Injuries 113
    Island areas of the U.S. . 108, 111, 116, 1273
    Maternal 110
    Military deaths 498
    Native Hawaiian, Other Pacific Islander
        population 5
    Race . 5, 102, 103, 104, 106, 110, 111, 117,
                          119, 120, 121
    States 15, 108, 111, 116
    Suicide 112, 114, 115, 120
    Summary 77
    Traffic fatalities ... 1032, 1063, 1064, 1065,
                    1066, 1068, 1069, 1070
    Weather related 371
    Workers' deaths 635, 636, 639, 861
Death care services 612, 705, 1233, 1234,
                          1235, 1244
Death penalty 339, 340
Debit cards 1144, 1145, 1147

Debt (see also Loans and mortgages):
    City 440
    Consumer 1135, 1150
    County governments 442
    Farm 799
    Federal government 452
    Foreign countries 1359
    Households 1130, 1134
    Local governments 421, 438
    State and local government . 421, 425, 433,
                          436
        Highways 1054
    State government 433, 436
Deductions (taxes) 471, 472, 473
    Businesses 725, 726, 727, 731
Defense, Department of (see also Air Force,
    Army, Marine Corps, and Navy):
    Budget authority, outlays . 453, 455, 485, 486
    Contract and grant awards 489, 490
    Employees, civilian 489, 491, 492
    Expenditures 489, 490, 491
        Health and medical care 125, 128
    Military bases 491, 492
    Military personnel . 489, 491, 492, 493, 494,
                          495, 496
    Military reserve and national guard 499,
                          500, 501
    Military retirees 490, 497, 523, 529
Defined contribution plans 1129, 1176
Degrees conferred (see also individual field) ....
    288, 289, 290, 291, 292, 293, 781, 782, 783,
                          785, 780
    Salary offers 287
Delaware. (See State data.)
Delinquency. (See Juveniles.)
Denmark. (See Foreign countries.)
Dentists 154, 596
    Charges and expenditures for 126, 127,
                          130, 132, 717
    Dental schools, students, and graduates . 293
    Medicaid payments, recipients 140
    Offices 152, 153
Department stores:
    Earnings 612, 1008, 1011
    Employees 612, 1008, 1011
    Establishments 1008, 1011
    Inventories 1012
    Productivity 619
    Sales 1009, 1011, 1012, 1020, 1243
Deposits. (See Banks.)
Dermatologists 157
Development aid 1357
Diabetes 112, 114, 115, 116, 160, 188
Diagnostic health procedures 162
Diamonds 864, 1332
    World production 1332
Diatomite 863, 864
Dietitians and nutritionists 596
DVDs 995
Diphtheria 183
Direct deposit 1145
Direct mail advertising expenditures 1239
Direct mail advertising industry 1235, 1237
Directory and mailing list publications industry .
                          1086, 1087, 1099
Disability 182
    Beneficiaries 523, 526
    Benefits paid 526, 528
    Elderly 34

NOTE: Index citations refer to **table** numbers, not page numbers.

U.S. Census Bureau, Statistical Abstract of the United States: 2009

Disability—Con.
Food stamp participants 553, 554
Government transfer payments ... 520, 521, 522
Labor force status 594
Medicaid payments and or recipients .. 140, 541
Military retirement system 497
Payments 528
Persons with disability 541
Poverty 693
Public assistance recipients and/or payments 541, 544
Social security recipients 526, 527
Students with disabilities 180, 181, 277
Supplemental security income recipients and payments 544
Transit buses equipped 1075
Veterans receiving compensation 505
Disability Insurance Trust Fund (Social Security) . 528
Disasters (tornadoes, floods, etc.) . 370, 371, 844
Discount rates, Federal Reserve Bank of New York 1157
Diseases (see also Death and death rates, and specific diseases) 170, 175, 188
Deaths from . 112, 114, 115, 116, 117, 118, 121
Dishwashers 946
Disposable personal income (see also Income, and National income) 656, 657, 660, 1135
District Courts, U.S. ... 314, 315, 322, 323, 324
District of Columbia. (See State data.)
Dividends:
Corporation 761
Individual income tax returns 465
National and/or personal income components 656
Persons receiving income 523
Railroad stock 1080
Divorce. (See Marriage and divorce, and Marital status.)
Djibouti. (See Foreign countries.)
Doctorates:
Conferred 288, 289, 780, 782
Field 292, 782, 785
Non U.S. citizen 780, 782, 783, 785
Sex 288, 783
State 781, 782
Doctors, M.D.s. (See Physicians.)
Dog ownership 1201
Dominica. (See Foreign countries.)
Dominican Republic. (See Foreign countries.)
Dow-Jones stock index 1167, 1168
Dress codes, schools 240
Drinking places. (See Food services and drinking places.)
Driving (see also Motor vehicles, and Transportation):
Crashes 1067, 1071
Fatal accidents 1032, 1063, 1064, 1065
Intoxicated 312, 1069, 1070, 1072
Licensed drivers 1058
Traffic offense 312
Drowning, accidental deaths 113
Drug stores and proprietary stores. (See Pharmacies and drug stores.)
Drugs (illegal):
Arrests 312, 314, 316
Court cases 315, 323, 324

Drugs (illegal)—Con.
Deaths 113
Enforcement activities 317
Juveniles 327
Seizures 317
Testing, schools 240
Usage 199, 200, 316
Drugs and medicines (see also Pharmaceutical and medicine manufacturing):
Consumer price indexes 132, 705
Expenditures for .. 124, 126, 127, 128, 130, 131, 133, 151
Foreign trade 1267
Medicaid payments 140
Number of prescriptions 151
Price indexes 132, 705, 717
Retail sales 151, 1014
Drunk driving, arrests 312
Dry-cleaning and laundry services:
Earnings 612, 1233, 1235
Employees 612, 1233, 1235
Establishments 1233, 1234, 1235
Expenditures 664, 665
Productivity 619
Receipts 1233, 1234, 1244
Dryers, clothes 946
Dwellings. (See Housing and housing units, and Households or families.)

E

Earnings 624, 625
Agriculture, forestry, fisheries . 621, 737, 837, 838
Airlines 1030
American Indian and Alaska Native-owned businesses 744, 745
Asian-owned businesses 744, 745
Black-owned businesses 745
College faculty 284
College graduates, salaries 287
Construction industry 737, 740
Educational attainment 224, 681
Employment covered by social insurance 525, 540, 542
Family type 676, 677
Foreign-born population 41
Government employees:
Federal ... 443, 444, 478, 479, 621, 624
State and local . 443, 444, 448, 621, 624
Hispanic or Latino origin-owned businesses . 744, 745
Income tax returns (reported totals) 465, 466
Industry 621, 737, 740
Manufacturing 737, 740, 837, 838, 965, 967, 972
Mineral industries 860
Minimum wage workers 629, 631
Mining industry 737
Minority-owned businesses 744, 745
Municipal employees 449
Native Hawaiian and Other Pacific Islander-owned businesses 744, 745
Occupations 623, 626, 627, 628
Personal income ... 656, 658, 659, 660, 661
Private employer firms . 624, 625, 738, 740, 741
Railroads 1080
Retail trade 737, 740

NOTE: Index citations refer to **table** numbers, not page numbers.

Earnings—Con.
    School teachers 232, 243, 244, 255
    Science & engineering . 776, 777, 779, 780,
                    781, 782, 783, 785
    States 625
    Telephone systems, employees . 1108, 1110
    Transportation 737, 740
    Union members 623, 643
    Wholesale trade 737, 740
    Women-owned businesses 744, 745
Earth sciences, degrees conferred 782, 785
Eating and drinking places. (See Food services
   and drinking places.)
E coli 0157:H7 175
E-commerce. (See Electronic commerce.)
Economic assistance, foreign 1258
Economic growth rates 646
Economic indicators 756, 757, 1307
    Foreign countries 1307, 1308
Ecuador. (See Foreign countries.)
Education:
    Adult education 294, 1302
    After-school activities 256, 257
    After-school care 257
    Arts 256, 257
    Alternative school 234
    American College Testing (ACT) Program ....
                             259
    Attainment 33, 35, 221, 222, 223, 225,
                            1302
        American Indian, Alaska Native popula-
          tion 35
        Asian population 35
        Asian and Pacific Islander population . 221,
                             222
        Black, African-American population .. 35,
            221, 222, 223, 263, 264
        Elderly 33
        Foreign born 41, 42
        Foreign countries 1302
        General Education Development certifi-
          cates (GEDs) 266
        Hispanic-origin population . 35, 38, 221,
           222, 223, 263, 271
        Income 670, 676
        Internet access/use ... 1091, 1120, 1121
        Island areas of the U.S. 1274
        Labor force status 572, 607
        Media users 1091
        Native Hawaiian, Other Pacific Islander
          population 35
        Occupation 599
        Poverty 694
        Race 35, 264
        Recreation activities 1199
        States 225
        Women 218, 222, 223
    Catholic schools 254
    Charitable contributions 564
    Charter schools 230
    Club activities 256, 257
    Computer use in schools ... 252, 256, 257
    Construction, value 922, 923
    Crime incidents 237, 306
    Degrees conferred . 288, 289, 290, 291, 292,
                 293, 782, 785, 780
        Nonresident aliens 289
        Salary offers 287
    Disabled students 180, 277

Education—Con.
    Disciplinary problems 238
    Dress code 240
    Drug testing 240
    Employment, state and local government ...
                             447
    Employment status of high school graduates
      and dropouts 265
    Enrollment .. 211, 213, 215, 216, 217, 218,
      219, 228, 231, 232, 236, 241, 268, 269,
                 271, 274, 779
        Catholic schools 254
        Foreign-born students 220
        Island areas of U.S. 1274, 1280
        Preprimary schools 217, 228
        States 236, 271
    Expenditures (see also Finances):
        City government 440
        Control 212
        County government 442
        Local government 438
        Private 212
        State and local government ... 417, 433,
                           436
    Federal aid .. 214, 280, 415, 416, 520, 521,
            522, 769, 770, 777, 778
    Foreign countries 1302
    Foreign language 227
    Games, after-school 256, 257
    General Education Development (GEDs) . 266
    Grants to institutions from foundations . 564
    Handicapped students 180
    Higher education institutions:
        Beginning salary offers, college gradu-
          ates 287
        Charges for room and board 282
        Costs 278
        Degrees conferred .. 213, 288, 289, 290,
          291, 292, 293, 781, 782, 785, 780
          Nonresident aliens ... 289, 782, 780,
                             784
        Dormitory charges 282
        Enrollment 211, 213, 217, 218, 219,
          268, 269, 270, 271, 273, 779
          College freshmen 276
          Disabled 277
          Foreign-born students 220, 784
          Foreign languages 275
          Foreign students 270, 273
          Projections 211, 213
          States 271
        Expenditures 212, 213
          Price indexes 279
          Scientific purposes 777, 1347
        Faculty 269, 284, 285, 286
        Finances 212, 213, 281
        Financial aid 280
        Libraries 1116
        Number 269, 271
        Price indexes 279, 705
        Research and development 769, 770,
                  777, 778, 1347
        Tuition and fees 282
        State appropriations 281
        Voluntary financial support 283
    High school dropouts ... 225, 263, 264, 265
    Homework 257
    Internet access 252

NOTE: Index citations refer to **table** numbers, not page numbers.

U.S. Census Bureau, Statistical Abstract of the United States: 2009

Education—Con.
    Island areas of the U.S. 1274, 1280
    Language spoken at home 227
    Literacy 1302
    Loans and grants, federal government .. 280
    Math 1302
    Metal detectors 240
    Montessori schools 254
    Music activities 256, 257
    Philanthropy 561, 564
    Price indexes 703, 705, 718
    Private elementary and secondary schools:
        Computer use 252
        Enrollment . 211, 212, 217, 219, 242, 254
        Expenditures 212
        Internet access 252
        Number 242, 254
        Teachers 245, 254, 255
    Program for International Student Assesss-
        ment (PISA) 1302
    Public elementary and secondary schools:
        After-school activities 256, 257
        Alternative education 234
        Charter schools 230
        Clubs 256
        Computer use 252, 257
        Crimes against students 237
        Disciplinary problems 238
        Dress code 240
        Drug testing 240
        Enrollment . 211, 213, 217, 219, 232, 236
            Projections 211, 213
            Size 231
            States 236
        Finances 212, 213, 249, 250, 251
        High school graduates 213, 261
        Metal detectors 240
        Number 231
        Personnel 248
            Salaries 247
        Religious activities 256
        Safety and security measures 240
        School districts 235, 411
        Scouts 256
        Security measures 240
        Special education programs ... 234, 180,
                                            181
        Teachers 213, 232, 243, 244, 248
            Tutoring 256
            Mobility 245, 246
            Projections 213
        Vocational education 234
    Reading 1302
    Religious activities 256
    Research and development .. 769, 770, 777,
                                            778
    Safety and security measures 240
    Scouts, after school 256
    Scholastic Assessment Test (SAT) 258
    School districts 235, 411
    School type 229, 230, 231
    School years completed. (See Education
        attainment.)
    Science and/or engineering . 777, 779, 780,
                            781, 782, 784, 785, 1302
    Special education programs .. 180, 181, 254
    Sports activities 256, 257

Education—Con.
    State data:
        Elementary and secondary . 234, 236, 244,
                                        251, 261
        Higher education 271, 281
    Student language spoken at home 227
    Students with weapons 239
    Teachers:
        Catholic schools 254
        Elementary and secondary . 232, 242, 244,
                                            254
        Employment projections 213, 598
        Higher education 269, 284
        Mobility 245, 246
    Television, after school 257
    Tests:
        American College Testing (ACT) Program .
                                            259
        National Assessment of Educational
            Progress (NAEP) Tests 260
        Program for International Student
            Assessment (PISA) 1302
        Scholastic Assessment Tests (SAT) ... 258
    Tutoring 256
    Vocational education 234
    Volunteers 256, 566
    Work, after school 257
Education and health services:
    Earnings 610, 612, 622
    Employees 610, 611, 612
    Hires and separations 615
    Hours 610
Educational expense indexes 705
Educational performance 1302
Educational services:
    Capital 751, 753, 755
    Earnings 621, 734, 737, 740
    Employees ... 601, 610, 612, 734, 737, 740
    Equipment and software expenditures .. 753
    Establishments 734, 735, 737, 740
    Finances 724, 727
    Gross domestic product (GDP) 648
    Hires and separations 615
    Industry 734
    Nonemployers 735
    Occupational safety 638
    Profits 763
    Receipts 724, 727, 732, 733, 734, 735
Eggs (see also Poultry):
    Consumption 209
    Farm marketings, sales 803
    Prices 705, 709, 713, 834
    Production 834
Egypt. (See Foreign countries.)
Elderly (see also Population):
    Activity limitation 185, 186
    Adult education 294
    Age and/or sex .. 7, 8, 9, 10, 11, 16, 17, 33
    AIDS 178
    Asian population 8, 9, 11
    Assets 699, 1133
    Black, African-American population . 8, 9, 11
    Cancer 114, 115, 170
    Cerebrovascular disease 115, 170
    Cigarette smoking 196
    Computer use 1091, 1120, 1121, 1123
    Deaths and death rates . 105, 107, 115, 117,
                            118, 119, 120, 121, 122
    Disability population 34, 182

NOTE: Index citations refer to **table** numbers, not page numbers.

Elderly (see also Population)—Con.
Education, attainment 33, 223
Elections, voter registration and turnout . 400
Food stamps, programs 553, 554
Foreign-born population 41
Grandparents living with grandchildren .. 69
Health care expenditures 133
Health insurance coverage ... 139, 146, 148
Heart disease 114, 117, 170
Height distribution 201
Hispanic-origin population 8, 9, 11, 38
Homeownership .. 941, 950, 953, 956, 957, 959
Hospital use 160, 161, 169, 170
Households 61, 70, 71
Immigrants 48
Income 523
Internet access/use 1091, 1121
Individual Retirement Accounts (IRAs) .. 535
Job search 603, 1120, 1122, 1123
Labor force 568, 571, 576, 602
    Disabled 594
    Displaced workers 593
    Employed 581, 584, 587, 589, 591
    Participation rates 568, 576
    Reason not in 595
    Tenure with employer 591
    Unemployed 602
Living arrangements 34, 57
Marital status 33, 56
Media users 1091
Medicaid payments and recipients . 139, 140
Medicare program 135, 136, 137
Metropolitan areas 22
Mobility status 29
Mutual fund owners 1172, 1173
Native Hawaiian, Other Pacific Islander
    population 8, 9, 11
Nursing homes 187, 714, 717
Overweight 203
Persons living alone (one-person house-
    holds) 71
Physical activity 204
Physician visits 158, 159, 160, 161
Pneumonia 114, 115, 170
Poverty 33, 691
Projections 10, 11, 17
Property owners 950, 956
Public assistance 523
Recreation activities . 1192, 1198, 1199, 1209, 1211
Senior citizens' communities 957
States 16, 17
Suicide 114
TV viewing 1091
Two-or-more-races population 8, 9
Victimization 305
Voter registration and turnout 400
Weight distribution 202
Elections:
Black elected officials 398
Campaign finances . 404, 406, 407, 408, 409
Congressional 386, 387, 402, 403
Foreign countries 1316
Gubernatorial 394
Hispanic-origin officials 399
Political action committees (PAC) . 404, 405, 409

Elections—Con.
Presidential .. 380, 381, 382, 383, 384, 402, 403, 406, 407
State legislatures 395, 396, 397
Voter registration 400, 401, 402, 403
Voter turnout 400, 401, 403
Votes cast ... 380, 381, 383, 384, 385, 386, 387, 394, 401
Voting-age population 400, 401, 403
Women in public office 397, 1316
**Electric light and power industry (see also Elec-
tricity, and Utilities):**
Capital expenditures 752, 754
Customers 910, 915
Emissions 359, 360, 913
Finances 911
General capacity 906, 907
Industrial production index 759
Multinational companies 767
Peak load 907
Water use 881, 882, 903, 904
Electrical engineering 785, 786
**Electrical equipment, appliances, and compo-
nents manufacturing (see also Computers and
electronic product manufacturing):**
Capital 751
Earnings 612, 965, 967, 973
Electronic commerce 969
Employees ... 612, 965, 967, 968, 971, 973
Establishments 965
Finances 764
Foreign trade 1271
Gross domestic product 648, 964
Industrial production index 759
Inventories 975, 976
Multinational companies 767
Occupational safety 638
Productivity 619
Profits 764
Research and development 774, 775
Shipments 967, 969, 975, 976
Toxic chemical releases 365
Value added 967, 976
**Electricity (see also Electric light and power
industry):**
Capability 906, 907
Commercial buildings 887
Consumption 887, 908, 910
Emissions 913
Expenditures 664, 665, 889, 890, 893
Foreign countries 1340, 1341
Hydroelectric power 883, 912, 1340
Nuclear 883, 899, 900, 1340, 1341
Price indexes 705, 717
Prices 710, 713, 905, 909
Production 903, 906, 910
    World production 1340
Renewable sources 892, 903, 904, 912
Residential 910
Sales 908, 910
Service, class of 909
Electronic benefits transfer cards 1144
Electronic commerce (e-commerce):
Business sales 1013
Consumer sales 1014, 1015, 1016
Establishments 1008
Manufacturing 969
Nonemployer 1017
Retail trade 1013, 1014, 1015, 1016

NOTE: Index citations refer to **table** numbers, not page numbers.

Electronic commerce (e-commerce)—Con.
    Services 1238
    Wholesale 1005
Electronic goods:
    Foreign trade 1267, 1269
    Sales, shipments, receipts, prices . 713, 992,
        993, 994, 996, 1014
Electronic instruments manufacturing . 612, 619
Electronic shopping and mail order houses . 612,
        619, 1009, 1014
Electronics and appliance stores:
    Earnings 612, 734, 1008
    Electronic commerce 1013
    Employees 612, 734, 1008
    Establishments 734, 1008
    Productivity 619
    Sales 734, 1009, 1011, 1013
El Salvador. (See Foreign countries.)
Emergency medicine, departments ... 157, 159,
        161
Emergency shelters 556
Emissions. (See Air pollution.)
Emphysema 113, 114, 190
Employee benefits 149, 150, 519, 633, 634
    Government employees 445
Employees. (See Business enterprise, and indi-
    vidual industries.)
Employment service industry:
    Earnings 612, 1233
    Employees 612, 1233, 1235
    Establishments 1233, 1234, 1235
    Nonemployers 1234
    Receipts 1233, 1234
Endangered species 369
Energy (see also Electric light and power indus-
    try, and various fuel types):
    Air pollutant emissions . 357, 358, 359, 360,
        913
        Foreign countries 1304
    Commercial buildings 887, 963
    Consumption . 883, 885, 886, 887, 891, 1334
        End-use sector 885, 886
        Foreign countries 1334, 1335, 1336
        Renewable sources . 883, 884, 891, 892,
            901, 903, 904, 912
        Source 883, 886
    Electric . 881, 882, 886, 887, 889, 890, 899,
        900, 902, 903, 904, 905, 906, 907, 908,
        909, 910, 911, 912
    End-use sector 885, 886, 889
    Expenditures 889, 890
        Commercial 890, 963
        Residential 890
    Federal outlays 455
    Price indexes:
        Consumer 703, 704, 705
        Futures 715
        Producer 713, 715
    Prices 710, 888, 905
    Solar collectors, manufacturer's shipments ..
        901
Engineering and architectural services:
    Earnings 612, 787, 1233, 1235
    Employees 612, 787, 1233, 1234, 1235
    Establishments 1235
    Nonemployers 1234
    Receipts 1233, 1234, 1237
    Research and development 774

Engineers and scientists (see also individual
    fields):
    Degrees conferred . 290, 291, 292, 781, 782,
        785, 780
    Employment 596, 786, 788, 789
    Research and development .. 774, 777, 789
    Salary offers 287
English, ability to speak 54, 227
Entertainment:
    Consumer expenditures . 664, 665, 995, 1192
    Consumer price indexes 705
    Gaming 995, 1219
    Personal expenditures . 655, 664, 665, 1192
Environment (see also Pollution):
    Charitable contributions 564
    Environmental industry, agencies 368
    Volunteers 566
    Wetlands 351, 353
Environmental Protection Agency 481
Environmental science:
    Degrees conferred 779, 785
    Research & development 772, 777
Equatorial Guinea. (See Foreign countries.)
Eritrea. (See Foreign countries.)
Eskimo population. (See American Indian,
    Alaska Native population.)
Establishments. (See Business enterprise, and
    individual industries.)
Estate and gift taxes 462
Estonia. (See Foreign countries.)
Ethane 870, 892
Ethanol 818, 892
Ethiopia. (See Foreign countries.)
Ethylene 870
Europe. (See Foreign countries.)
European Union. (See Foreign countries.)
Evaporated and condensed milk 209, 832
Exchange-traded funds 1129, 1161
Excise taxes 457, 462
Executions 339, 340
Executive Office of the President (federal) .. 481
Exercise equipment 1193, 1210, 1211
Expectation of life (average lifetime) . 100, 102,
        103
        Foreign countries 1295
        Life years lost 122
        Projections 100
Expenditures. (See individual subjects).
Expenditures of state and local government.
    (See individual governmental units.)
Expenditures of U.S. government . 414, 415, 416,
        455, 654, 1052, 1257, 1258, 1259
    Aid to the arts and humanities .. 1195, 1196
    Aid to Island areas 416, 1277
    Aid to state and local government . 414, 415,
        416
        By function 415, 792
        Highway trust fund 416, 1052
    Budget outlays 451, 453, 454, 455, 456
        By function 455
        By source of funds 457
    Contract awards 489, 490, 491
    Education. (See Federal aid to education.)
    Food programs, federal 551, 552
    Health 124, 125, 126, 127, 128
    Homeland security 507, 508, 509
    Hospitals 163
    Military personnel 489, 491
    National defense 485, 486, 718
    Outlays 451, 452, 453

NOTE: Index citations refer to **table** numbers, not page numbers.

Expenditures of U.S. government—Con.
    Agency 454
      Function 455
      Payments for individuals 456
    Payrolls 443, 444, 478, 479, 480
    Price indexes 718
    Public debt 452
    Public roads 416, 1052
    Research and development .. 769, 770, 771, 773, 1347
    Retirement benefits 519
    Schools 214
    Science/space 790
    Veterans benefits. (See Veterans affairs.)
Exports. (See Foreign trade.)
Express mail 1084, 1085

F

Fabricated metal product manufacturing:
    Capital 751, 1255
    Earnings 612, 965, 967, 973
    Electronic commerce 969
    Employees 612, 965, 967, 971, 973
    Establishments 965
    Finance 764, 988
    Foreign trade 988, 1271
    Gross domestic product 648, 964
    Industrial production index 759
    Occupational safety 638
    Productivity 619
    Profits 762, 764
    Research and development 774
    Shipments 967, 969, 975, 976
    Toxic chemical releases 365
Fabrics. (See Textile mill products.)
Falls, accidental deaths 113, 114
Families. (See Households.)
Family and consumer sciences, degrees conferred 290, 291, 292
Farm mortgage loans 1152
Farmers and farm workers:
    Employment 596
    Unemployment 606
Farms:
    Acreage 793, 794, 795, 796, 797, 798
      Cropland 350, 352, 798, 817
      Crops harvested (see also individual crops) .. 817, 818, 819, 820, 821, 822, 1325
    Agrichemicals 801, 806
    Agricultural products:
      Exports 1327
      Foreign countries, production . 1326, 1329
      Prices. (See Prices received by farmers.)
      Railroad car loadings 1081, 1082
      Waterborne commerce 1044
      World production 1325, 1326, 1329
    Assets and liabilities 799, 1129
    Capital stocks, farm housing 960
    Corporate 793, 795
    Crops (see also individual crops):
      Acreage 817, 818
      Fruits and nuts 823, 824, 825
      Income 803, 805
      Production 812, 817, 818
        World 1325, 1326, 1329
      Vegetables 822
    Debt 799
      Mortgages outstanding 1152

Farms—Con.
    Expenses 801
    Family or individual 793, 795
    Farm products sold, marketing receipts . 800, 801, 802, 803, 805
    Government payments to farmers . 800, 801, 804, 805
    Gross farm product 648, 800
    Housing, rental value 801
    Income 800, 801, 803, 804, 805
    Inventories, change in 800
    Labor expenses 801, 806
    Machinery and motor vehicles 799, 801
    Mortgage loans 1152
    National income, origin in 800
    Number of farms .. 793, 794, 795, 796, 797
    Organic acreage, livestock 798, 1331
    Parity ratio 806
    Partnerships 793, 795
    Prices:
      Crops 806, 818
      Livestock and products 806, 827
    Taxes 800, 806
    Tenure of operator 795
    Value:
      Farm land and buildings 795, 799
      Farm products sold, marketing receipts . 795, 800, 801, 803, 805
Faroe Islands. (See Foreign countries.)
Fat, nutrient 208
Fatalities. (See Accidents and fatalities.)
Fats. (See Lard, Margarine, and Oils.)
Federal agency debt 1159
Federal aid to education 214, 415, 416, 417
    Elementary and secondary education ... 214
    Higher education institutions 214
    Research and development 770, 778
    Science and engineering 777
Federal aid to state and local government . 414, 415, 416, 417
Federal budget. (See Expenditures of U.S. government.)
Federal debt 452
Federal employees retirement trust fund. (See Government.)
Federal funds, summary distribution by state ... 461
Federal government. (See Government.)
Federal government finances. (See Receipts and Expenditures of U.S. government.)
Federal Housing Administration, mortgage loans 1154
Federal trust funds 458
Feed. (See Grain.)
Feldspar 863, 864, 867
Female householder. (See Households or families.)
Female population. (See Women.)
Fencing 1207
Fertility rate 78, 79, 81, 82
Fertilizers:
    Farm expenditures for 801
    Foreign trade 1267
    Prices 713, 806
    Shipments 986
Fetal deaths (neonatal) 109, 110
Fiber, dietary 208
Fibers 713, 716, 982
Field hockey 1207
Figure skating 1206

NOTE: Index citations refer to **table** numbers, not page numbers.

Fiji. (See Foreign countries.)
Filberts (hazelnuts) 824, 825
Filling stations. (See Gasoline stations.)
Finance and insurance industry:
    Capital 751, 753, 755, 1162
    Earnings . 610, 612, 621, 622, 734, 737, 740,
        1126, 1128
    Employees .. 584, 586, 600, 610, 611, 612,
        734, 737, 740, 1126, 1128
    Equipment and software expenditures .. 753
    Establishments . 734, 735, 737, 1126, 1127,
        1128
    Finances . 724, 727, 1129, 1136, 1150, 1282
    Foreign investments in U.S. 1252
    Gross domestic product 648, 650, 1125,
        1282
    Hires and separations 615
    Hours 610
    Multinational companies 766, 767
    Nonemployers 735, 1127
    Occupational safety 638
    Profits 763
    Sales or receipts .. 724, 727, 732, 733, 734,
        735, 1126, 1127
    Union membership 643
Finance companies 1129, 1130
    Consumer credit 1150, 1151
    Corporate funds 730
Financial institution. (See Banks, commercial;
    Credit unions; and Savings institutions.)
Finished consumer goods, producer price
    indexes 713
Finland. (See Foreign countries.)
Fire departments. (See Public safety.)
Fire insurance 1182
Firearms 308, 318, 1209, 1210
Fires 844
Fires and property loss 341, 342, 343, 844
Firms. (See Business enterprise, and individual
    types of business and industry.)
Fish (see also individual species):
    Aquaculture 803, 855, 856, 857
    Canning and preserving 859
    Catch, quantity, value . 852, 853, 854, 1328
    Consumer expenditures 664, 665
    Consumption 209
    Farms 855
    Foreign trade 852, 1271
    Prices 705, 713, 720, 721, 853
    Production and value, processed products ..
        857, 859
    Sales 855, 856
    Supply 852
Fishing, commercial:
    Catch, quantity, value . 852, 853, 854, 1328
    Foreign trade 852
    Products 852, 859
Fishing and hunting 836, 838, 1209, 1210,
    1216, 1230
Flax, organic acreage 798
Floods 370, 371
Floriculture 803
Florida. (See State data.)
Florists:
    Earnings 612, 1008
    Employees 612, 1008
    Establishments 1008
    Productivity 619
Flounder 854, 859
Flour 209, 709, 713

Flowers 1202
Flu (influenza) 112, 114
Fluorspar 863, 864, 867
Food (see also individual commodities and
    industry data below):
    Car loadings 1081
    Commercial vegetables 822
    Consumption 208, 209, 210
    Expenditures . 662, 664, 665, 666, 667, 807,
        1023, 1314
    Fish products . 705, 709, 713, 714, 852, 853,
        854, 857, 858, 859
    Food costs 706, 708, 709, 1015, 1016
    Hunger, insecurity 206
    Prices (see also individual commodities) . 703,
      704, 705, 708, 709, 712, 713, 714, 716,
      717, 720, 721, 1015, 1016
    Sales 1014
    World production 1325, 1326, 1329
Food and beverage stores:
    Earnings 612, 734, 1008
    Employees 612, 734, 1008
    Establishments 734, 1008, 1017, 1022
    Finances 724
    Inventories 1012
    Nonemployers 1017
    Productivity 619
    Profits 764
    Sales ... 724, 734, 1007, 1009, 1011, 1012,
        1017, 1020, 1022, 1023
        Prescription drugs 151
Food insecurity 206
Food manufacturing:
    Capital 751
    Earnings 612, 965, 967, 973
    Employees .. 612, 965, 967, 971, 973, 1227
    Establishments 965
    Finances 764
    Foreign trade 1271
    Gross domestic product 648, 964
    Industrial production index 759
    Occupational safety 638
    Profits 764
    Research and development 774
    Sales or shipments 967, 969, 975, 976
    Toxic chemical releases 365
Food services and drinking places:
    Capital 751
    Earnings 612, 734, 1233, 1235
    Employees 612, 734, 1233, 1234, 1235
    Establishments . 734, 1007, 1233, 1234, 1235,
        1243
    Finances 724
    Nonemployers 1234
    Productivity 619, 1233, 1234
    Sales ... 724, 734, 1009, 1011, 1020, 1023,
        1227, 1241, 1243
Food stamps, programs 521, 524, 551, 552,
    553, 554
Football 1204, 1206, 1207, 1208
Footwear:
    Consumer expenditures 664, 665
    Foreign trade 984, 1267
    Prices 705, 713, 721
    Production 984
    Sport footwear 1210
Foreign aid or assistance 1257, 1259, 1357,
    1358
Foreign-born population 39, 41, 42, 43

NOTE: Index citations refer to **table** numbers, not page numbers.

Foreign-born population—Con.
Age 41, 42
Cities 40
Doctorates 780, 782
Earnings 41
Educational attainment 41, 42
Employment 570, 584, 1289
Foreign countries 1289
Households 41
Income 41, 42
Marital status 41
Poverty status 41
States 39
Foreign companies, U.S. affiliates .. 1252, 1253,
                                            1254

Foreign countries:
Age distribution 1290
Agriculture . 1308, 1325, 1326, 1327, 1331
Agricultural trade 811, 816, 1265
Aid to developing countries 1257, 1258,
                            1259, 1357, 1358
AIDS 1297
Alcohol 1314
Area 1288
Armed Forces personnel 1361
Balance of payments 1353
Births and birth rates 1291, 1295
Border crossings 1231
Border lengths 345
Carbon dioxide emissions 1304
Cellular phones 1345
Cigarettes 1299, 1314
Coal production 878, 1333, 1334, 1335,
                                            1339
College students enrolled in U.S. 273
Communications 1344, 1345
Consumer prices 1311, 1312
Consumption expenditures 1314
Corn 1327
Cost of living 1313
Cotton 812, 1325, 1326
Crude oil 894, 895, 1335, 1337
Cultural expenditures 1356
Dairy 1325
Death and death rates 1295
Debt 1315, 1359
Developing countries 1287, 1358
Development aid 1357
Doctorates 780
Doctors 1300
Economic indicators 1307, 1308, 1309
Economic sectoral contributions 1308
Education 1302
Electricity generation 1340
Elected officials 1316
Emissions 1304
Employment and labor force ... 1307, 1319,
        1320, 1321, 1322, 1323, 1324, 1342, 1343
Energy production and consumption . 1333,
                            1334, 1335, 1336
Exchange rates 1352
Exports and imports 1264, 1327, 1354
Fertility 1295
Financial assets, liabilities (flow of funds) ...
                                            1131
Fish catches 1328
Food consumption 1314, 1325, 1330
Food production 1325, 1331

Foreign countries—Con.
Foreign born 1289
Foreign direct investment 1360
Foreign population 1289
Gas 1332, 1333, 1334, 1335, 1338
Geothermal energy 1333, 1334
Government finances 1306, 1315, 1317
Grain 812, 1325, 1326
Gross domestic product 1308
Gross national income 1305
Health care expenditures 1301
HIV infection 1297
Hours worked 1310
Households and families . 1293, 1294, 1314,
                                            1356
Hydroelectric power 1333, 1334, 1340
Immigrant population 1289
Immigration to U.S. 46, 49, 50
Income tax 1317, 1318
Industry 1308, 1309, 1324, 1348
Infant mortality 1295
Inpatient care 1300
International transactions, balances .. 1247,
                                1248, 1353
Investment in U.S. . 1131, 1165, 1166, 1249,
                    1251, 1252, 1253, 1254
Labor costs 1342, 1343
Labor force 1289, 1319, 1322, 1323
Labor productivity 1310
Life expectancy 1295, 1296
Living costs 1313
Manufacturing 1308, 1324, 1343
    Productivity 1342
Marriage and divorce 1292, 1294
Meat 1325, 1329, 1330
Merchandise trade balance 1353
Migration 1289
Military manpower 1361
Military personnel, U.S. on active duty . 493,
                                            495
Military sales 488
Minerals 1332
Multilateral grants 1359
Multinational companies 768
Natural gas . 1333, 1334, 1335, 1336, 1338
Nongovernmental organizations 1357
Nuclear power generation . 1333, 1334, 1335,
                                1340, 1341
Obesity 1298
Oil 894, 895, 1335, 1337
Oil seeds 812, 1325, 1326
Organic farms 1331
Parliament 1316
Patents 1346
Petroleum production ... 1333, 1334, 1335,
                                            1337
Physicians 1300
Population 1288, 1289, 1290
Poultry 1325, 1329, 1330
Precipitation (cities) 1303
Prices 1311, 1312
Production:
    Crops 812, 1325, 1326
    Industrial 1309
    Meat 1329
    Minerals 867, 1332
Productivity, labor 1310
Purchasing power parity 1305, 1306

NOTE: Index citations refer to **table** numbers, not page numbers.

U.S. Census Bureau, Statistical Abstract of the United States: 2009

Foreign countries—Con.
  Rainfall (cities) 1303
  Recreation spending 1356
  Refugees admitted to U.S. 50
  Research and development expenditures . 771,
                                            1347
  Reserve assets 1353
  Rice 812, 1325, 1326, 1327
  Sales and assistance by U.S. military ... 487,
                                             488
  Single-parent households 1293, 1294
  Social security contributions 1317
  Stocks and bonds . 1163, 1164, 1165, 1166,
                     1348, 1349, 1350, 1351
  Tax burden 1317, 1318
  Taxes (revenue) 1315, 1317
  Telephones 1344, 1345
  Temperature (cities) 1303
  Tobacco 1299, 1314
  Tourism 1355
  Trade with United States ... 814, 816, 1248,
                                1266, 1354
  Travelers and expenditures . 1221, 1228, 1229
  Unemployment 1319, 1320, 1321
  Unmarried women 1291
  U.S. investment abroad .. 1163, 1164, 1256
  Visitors from 1232
  Vital statistics 1295
  Weather 1303
  Wheat 812, 1320, 1325, 1326, 1327
  Women 1291, 1316, 1322
Foreign currency holdings 1353
Foreign exchange rates 1352
Foreign grants and credits, U.S. government ....
                                            1257
Foreign investments .. 1131, 1165, 1251, 1252,
                          1253, 1255
Foreign languages:
  Degrees conferred 290, 291, 292
  Persons speaking 52, 53, 54, 227
  Students enrolled 275
Foreign sales and assistance by U.S. govern-
  ment 1258, 1259
  Economic assistance 1259
  Military sales and assistance . 487, 488, 1259
Foreign students, college 273
Foreign trade (see also Foreign aid, Foreign
  countries, and individual commodities) . 1261,
          1262, 1263, 1264, 1265, 1266, 1271
  Aerospace products 1267, 1268
  Agricultural products .. 808, 809, 810, 811,
          812, 813, 815, 816, 823, 825, 1265
  Aircraft and aircraft parts 1000, 1267
  Automobiles 1267
  Balance of trade 1246, 1247, 1266
  Chemicals 1261, 1267, 1271
  Coal 878, 893, 894
  Companies exporting 1270
  Computer and electronic products 1261,
                                         1271
  Countries 1266, 1354
  Crude oil 870, 894, 895, 896
  Customs districts 1262
  Electrical equipment, appliances and compo-
    nents 1261, 1267, 1271
  Fish products 852
  High technology exports 1269
  Indexes, unit value 1263

Foreign trade (see also Foreign aid, Foreign
  countries, and individual commodities)—Con.
  Industry 1271
  International transactions, balances, U.S. . 1246,
                          1247, 1248, 1260
  Mineral imports 868
  Oil and gas 870, 1261, 1271
  Petroleum products 870
  Price indexes 718, 719, 720
  Puerto Rico 1284
  Related party trade 1261
  Services 1246, 1248
  Timber products 845, 846, 1267
  Transportation equipment . 1261, 1267, 1268,
                                           1271
  U.S. affiliates of foreign companies 1252
Forest products (see also individual products):
  Car loadings 1081, 1082
  Consumption 845
  Farm income 803
  Foreign trade 845, 846
  Growth 842
  Industry . 836, 837, 838, 839, 840, 846, 847,
                                    848, 850
  Prices 713, 714, 720, 721, 849
  Removal 842, 843
  Sales 801
  Volume 842
Forests:
  Land, acreage and ownership 350, 352
  National 841
Forgery and counterfeiting (arrests) 312
Foster care 560
Foundations, philanthropic . 561, 562, 563, 564
Foundries 612, 619
401(k) plans 532, 538, 1176
France. (See Foreign countries.)
Franchised establishments 1018
Freight traffic. (See Air transportation, Railroads,
  Rivers, and Waterways.)
French Guiana. (See Foreign countries.)
French Polynesia. (See Foreign countries.)
Fruit and vegetable preserving manufacturing ..
                                  612, 619, 967
Fruit juices 207, 210, 808
Fruits:
  Consumer expenditures 662, 664, 665
  Consumption 210, 823
  Farm marketings and sales 801, 803
  Foreign trade 808, 813, 815, 823, 1267
  Prices 705, 709, 713, 720, 806
  Production 823, 824
Fuel (see also Energy, and individual types):
  Commercial building use 887, 890, 963
  Consumer expenditures 664, 665
  Consumption, motor vehicles 1062
  Electricity generated by . 891, 892, 899, 900,
                            903, 904, 912
  Prices .. 703, 704, 705, 710, 712, 713, 720,
              721, 806, 865, 888, 890, 905
    Retail 710
  Production and value 867, 870, 883
  Renewable. (See Energy.)
  Residential use 890, 891, 892, 916
  World production 867
Funds, trusts, and other financial vehicles . 612,
                                      751, 1128
Funeral service and crematories. (See Death care
  services.)

NOTE: Index citations refer to **table** numbers, not page numbers.

U.S. Census Bureau, Statistical Abstract of the United States: 2009

Furniture .. 664, 665, 705, 713, 717, 721, 1267
Furniture and home furnishing stores:
   Earnings 612, 734, 1008
   Employees 612, 734, 1008
   Establishments 734, 1008, 1017
   Inventories 1012
   Nonemployers 1017
   Productivity 619
   Sales .. 734, 1009, 1011, 1012, 1014, 1017
Furniture and related product manufacturing:
   Capital 751
   Earnings 612, 965, 967, 973
   Electronic commerce 969
   Employees 612, 965, 967, 973
   Establishments 965
   Finances 764
   Foreign trade 1271
   Gross domestic product 648, 964
   Industrial production index 759
   Occupational safety 638
   Productivity 619
   Profits 764
   Shipments 967, 969, 975, 976
   Toxic chemical releases 365
Futures price indexes, selected commodities ....
   715

G

Gabon. (See Foreign countries.)
Gallbladder disorders, deaths 113
Gambia, The. (See Foreign countries.)
Gambling 312, 1191
Gaming 995, 1218, 1219
Garages. (See Gasoline stations, and Automobile
  repair and maintenance service.)
Garden activities and equipment . 705, 713, 1202
Garden supplies. (See Building materials and
  garden supplies.)
Garlic 822
Garnet (industrial) 863, 864
Gas (see also Gas utility industry, Gasoline, and
  Petroleum):
   Liquefied petroleum gases 870
   Natural 860, 865, 870, 875
     Consumption 875, 883
     Energy expenditures 889, 890
     Foreign trade 884, 893, 894, 1271
     Offshore lease revenues 873
     Prices 710, 711, 713, 717, 888
     Production and value 870, 875, 883,
                  1332, 1333
       Foreign countries 1332, 1338
       Indexes 862
     Reserves 872, 875
     Residential 916
     World production 1332, 1333, 1338
   Natural gas plant liquids 870, 876
   Price indexes 705
Gas and electric utilities. (See Utilities.)
Gas utility industry (see also Utilities):
   Accidents and deaths 1032
   Construction expenditures 915
   Customers 915, 916
   End users 915
   Finances 914
   Mains, mileage 915
   Prices 915
   Revenues 882, 914, 915, 916
   Sales 915, 916

Gasoline (see also Motor fuel):
   Blending components 884
   Consumer expenditures . 662, 663, 664, 665,
                  666
   Excise taxes 1053
   Finished motor gasoline 869, 870
   Prices 710, 711, 717
Gasoline stations, retail:
   Earnings 612, 734, 1008
   Employees 612, 734, 1008
   Establishments 734, 1008
   Finances 724
   Productivity 619
   Sales 724, 734, 1009, 1011, 1020, 1243
Gastroenterology 157
Gaza Strip. (See Foreign countries.)
Gemstones 864
General merchandise stores:
   Earnings 612, 734, 1008
   Electronic commerce 1013
   Employees 612, 734, 1008
   Establishments 734, 1008
   Finances 764
   Inventories 1012
   Productivity 619
   Profits 764
   Sales .. 734, 1009, 1011, 1013, 1020, 1243
Geography and cartography. (See Land.)
Georgia. (See Foreign countries.)
Georgia, state of. (See State data.)
Geothermal energy . 891, 892, 903, 904, 1333,
                        1334
Germanium 864
Germany. (See Foreign countries.)
Germany DAX-30 stock market index 1350
Ghana. (See Foreign countries.)
Gibraltar. (See Foreign countries.)
Gift, novelty, and souvenir stores 1008
Gift and estate taxes 418, 462
Glass 361, 362, 363, 713
Gold:
   Consumption 864
   Employment 860, 862, 864
   Foreign trade 864, 1267
   Prices 713, 864, 865
   Production and value 863, 864
     World production 867, 1332
   Reserve assets 1250
Golf . 957, 1203, 1206, 1207, 1208, 1209, 1210,
                        1211
Golf courses, industry 1188, 1191
Gonorrhea 175
Government (see also Expenditures of U.S. gov-
  ernment, Receipts, and individual governmen-
  tal units):
   Buildings 484
   Capital stock 701
   Consumer credit holdings 1151
   Earnings 448, 610, 621, 624
   Employees ... 483, 610, 611, 612, 624, 786
     Benefits 445
     City government 449
     County government 450
     Federal, civilian . 443, 444, 480, 481, 482
     Salaries 443, 444, 479
     Local government ... 443, 444, 447, 448
     Retirement systems . 523, 529, 530, 531
     State government ... 443, 444, 447, 448
   Employment cost index 628

NOTE: Index citations refer to **table** numbers, not page numbers.

U.S. Census Bureau, Statistical Abstract of the United States: 2009

Government (see also Expenditures of U.S. government, Receipts, and individual governmental units)—Con.
  Expenditures:
    Capital outlay 419, 420
    City government 440, 445, 449
    Consumption 412, 654, 718
    County government 442, 450
    Federal 451, 453, 455, 457, 459
      Agriculture 800, 801, 804
      Aid to state and local government ....
        414, 415, 417, 1052
      Capital outlay 419, 420
    Local government ... 419, 420, 437, 438
    State and local government ... 417, 418,
        419, 420
    State government .. 418, 419, 420, 426,
        433, 436
    Transfer payments 520, 521, 522
  Federally owned land 484
  Flow of funds 1129, 1130
  Highways . 425, 436, 438, 1047, 1051, 1052,
        1053, 1054, 1055
  Hires and separations 615
  Hospitals 163
  Insurance. (See Social insurance.)
  Land. (See Public lands.)
  Local government:
    Cities:
      Employees, earnings, payroll 449
      Finances 439, 440
    Counties:
      Employees, earnings, payroll 450
      Finances 441, 442
    Employees 443, 444, 447, 448, 624
    Number, by type 410, 411
    Payroll 443, 444, 448, 449, 450
    Population, by size-group 412
  Number of units, by type of government ....
        410, 411
  Occupational safety 635
  Payrolls 443, 444, 449, 450
  Purchases of goods and services .. 645, 646
  Salaries and wages (see also Income, and
    individual industries):
    Federal 478
    National income component 621
    State and local government employees ..
        232, 447, 448
  Securities 422, 1157, 1158, 1165
    Bond ratings 427, 428
  State and local government:
    Benefits 445
    Employees 443, 444, 447, 448
    Federal aid 414, 415, 416, 1052
    Finances . 416, 417, 418, 419, 420, 421,
        424, 425
    Payroll 443, 444, 447, 448
    Revenue from parimutuel and amuse-
      ment taxes and lotteries 431
  State government . 426, 434, 435, 436, 624
  Strategic and critical materials, summary ....
        818
Government National Mortgage Association
  loans 1152
Governors, number and vote cast 393, 394
Graduates:
  College 288, 291, 292, 293, 782, 785

Graduates—Con.
  High school 213, 261, 264, 265, 267
Grain (see also individual classes):
  Car loadings 1082
  Consumption 209, 1325
  Farm marketings, sales 803
  Foreign trade 808, 810, 812, 813, 815
  Prices 715, 806
  Production 801, 812, 818, 1325, 1326
Grandparents living with grandchildren 69
Grants, by foundations 561, 562, 563, 564
Grapefruit 210, 709, 824
Grapes 210, 709, 798, 803, 824
Graphite 864
Great Britain. (See Foreign countries.)
Great Lakes:
  Area 347
  Commerce 1043
Greece. (See Foreign countries.)
Greenhouse and nursery crops 803
Greenhouse gases 360
Greenland. (See Foreign countries.)
Grenada. (See Foreign countries.)
Grocery stores (See also Food and beverage
  stores):
  Earnings 612, 1008
  Employees 612, 1008
  Establishments 1008, 1017, 1022
  Nonemployers 1017
  Productivity 619
  Sales 1009, 1017, 1020, 1022
Gross domestic product (GDP):
  Components, annual growth rates . 645, 646,
        647, 1024
  Foreign countries 1306
  Implicit price deflators for 645
  Industry 648
  National defense outlays 485
  Per capita 657, 1306
  Per employed person 1306
  Price indexes 718
  Relation to national and personal income ....
        651
  Sectoral contributions 1308
  State 649, 650
Gross national product 657
  Foreign countries 1305
Gross private domestic investment ... 645, 646,
        718
Gross value added 1308
Ground water used 354
Group health insurance plans 144
Group quarters population 73
Guadeloupe. (See Foreign countries.)
Guam. (See Island areas of the U.S.)
Guamanian population 1272
Guatemala. (See Foreign countries.)
Guernsey. (See Foreign countries.)
Guinea. (See Foreign countries.)
Guinea-Bissau. (See Foreign countries.)
Guns. (See Firearms.)
Guyana. (See Foreign countries.)
Gymnastics 1207
Gypsum and gypsum products .. 713, 863, 864,
        867, 920

H

Haddock 859
Haemophilus influenza 175
Haiti. (See Foreign countries.)

NOTE: Index citations refer to **table** numbers, not page numbers.

Table

Hake, Pacific whiting, imports 854
Halibut 854
Hallucinogenic drugs 199
Ham prices 709
Handguns 299, 318
Handicapped. (See Disability.)
Hawaii. (See State data.)
Hawaiian population. (See Native Hawaiian and
  Other Pacific Islander population.)
Hay 803, 818
Hazardous shipments 1048
Hazardous waste/materials:
  Generation 356
  State data 356, 367
  Transportation 1032
Hazelnuts (filberts) 824, 825
Head Start program 555
Health and education service industries ... 611,
                                            643

Health and personal care stores:
  Earnings 612, 734, 1008
  Employees 612, 734, 1008
  Establishments 734, 1008, 1017
  Nonemployers 1017
  Productivity 619
  Sales 734, 1009, 1011, 1012, 1017
Health care and social assistance industry:
  Capital 751, 753
  Earnings 610, 621, 734, 737, 740, 1235
  Electronic commerce 1238
  Employees .. 152, 610, 737, 740, 734, 1235
  Equipment and software expenditures .. 753
  Establishments 734, 735, 737
  Finances 724, 727
  Gross domestic product 648
  Hires and separations 615
  Hours 610
  Nonemployers 735
  Profits 763
  Receipts 724, 727, 732, 733, 734, 735
Health insurance (see also Health services,
  Insurance carriers, Medicaid, Medicare, and
  SCHIP):
  Contributions 150
  Coverage 139, 142, 144, 146, 147, 148,
                                      149, 150
  Enrollment and payments ... 135, 140, 141,
                                 142, 143, 145
  Expenditures . 124, 125, 126, 127, 128, 129,
    130, 131, 133, 142, 150, 519, 662, 663,
                            664, 665, 666, 717
  Premiums and policy reserves, life insurance
    companies 1181
  State Children's Health Insurance program ..
                                          142
Health insurance industry, employment 154
Health Maintenance Organizations 144, 145
Health sciences, degrees conferred ... 290, 291,
                                      292, 293
Health services:
  Buildings and floor space 963
  Charitable contributions 561, 564
  Construction, value 922, 923
  Coverage 135, 136, 139, 141, 146, 506
  Expenditures:
    Private expenditures . 124, 125, 126, 127,
                     129, 130, 131, 133, 664
    Public expenditures . 124, 125, 126, 127,
                      128, 129, 130, 131

Table

Health services—Con.
  State and local government ... 131, 417,
                                 418, 425
    City government 440
    County government 442
    State government 433, 436
  Foreign countries 1301
  Government employment and payrolls . 444
  Government expenditures:
    Federal government . 131, 415, 416, 456
  Hospitals . 163, 164, 165, 166, 167, 169, 170
  Industry:
    Capital expenditures 751
    Earnings 612
    Employees 154, 612
    Occupational safety 638
  Medicaid . 131, 139, 140, 141, 143, 146, 415,
                                            456
  Medicare . 125, 128, 131, 134, 135, 136, 137,
                       138, 146, 456, 528
  Nursing homes 126, 127, 130, 187
  Occupations 156, 157, 596
  Philanthropy 561
  Price indexes 132, 705
  Veterans' health care 125, 128
  Volunteers 566
Heart disease 112, 114, 116, 117, 160, 170
  Deaths 112, 114, 115, 116
Heat pumps 946
Heating and plumbing equipment . 901, 929, 946
Heating oil 710
Heavy and civil engineering construction .. 612,
                                        638, 919
HVAC and commercial refrigeration equipment
  manufacturing 612, 619
Heights, average, by age and sex 201
Helium 863
Hepatitis 115, 175
Heroin 199, 316, 317
Herring, sea 854
Highways:
  Accidents 1063, 1067, 1071
  Bridge inventory 1050
  Debt, state and local government 1054
  Employees, government 444, 447
  Expenditures:
    City government 440
    County government 442
    Local government 438
    State and local government ... 416, 417,
                             418, 419, 420, 425
    State government 433, 436
    U.S. government ... 415, 416, 417, 1052
  Federal-aid systems 1047, 1052
  Interstate mileage 1049
  Mileage 1047, 1049
  Motor fuel consumption 1062
  Motor fuel tax 1053
  Type and control 1047, 1049
  Types of roads traveled 1049
  Value of new construction 923
Hiking 1209
Hindu population. (See Religion.)
Hispanic- or Latino- origin population . 5, 6, 8, 9,
                                      11, 18, 38
  Activity limitation 185, 186
  Adoption 560
  Adult education 294

NOTE: Index citations refer to **table** numbers, not page numbers.

U.S. Census Bureau, Statistical Abstract of the United States: 2009

Hispanic- or Latino- origin population—Con.
    After-school activities 256, 257
    Age and/or sex 6, 8, 9, 11, 38
    AIDS 178
    Births and birth rates . 5, 78, 80, 81, 82, 83,
                                84, 85, 86, 90
    Breastfeeding 88
    Business owners 744, 745
    Cancer, deaths 119
    Child care 559
    Children under 18 years old . 6, 8, 9, 11, 38,
                                    68
        Literacy activities 226, 229, 253
    College costs 278
    College enrollment 270
    Community service 256
    Computer use 253
    Congress, members of 390
    Consumer expenditure 664
    Contraceptive use 94, 95
    Criminal victimization rates 305, 309
    Deaths 5, 106, 107, 117, 119, 120, 121
    Degrees conferred 289, 782
    Disability status 277, 541
    Educational attainment ... 35, 38, 221, 222,
                                   223
        Earnings 224
    Elderly 6, 8, 9, 11, 691
    Elected officials 390, 399
    Elections, voter registration and turnout . 400
    Families, characteristics 38, 63, 65, 66
    Food stamp participants 554
    Foreign-born populations 42, 220, 570
    Foster care 560
    Grandparents living with grandchildren .. 69
    Health insurance coverage ... 139, 146, 148
    Heart disease, deaths 117
    High school dropouts 262, 263, 264
    HIV disease 121
    Household or family characteristics . 38, 59,
                               61, 63, 65, 66
    Housing ... 35, 38, 949, 953, 956, 957, 959
    Immunization of children 183
    Income:
        Family 35, 672, 673, 674, 676
        Household 668, 669, 670, 671
        Persons 35, 679, 682, 683
    Internet access/use 253, 1118
    Jail inmates 335
    Job search 603
    Labor force and employment . 568, 569, 570,
                                 572, 575
        Displaced workers 593
        Earnings 626
        Employed . 38, 569, 570, 572, 584, 586,
                587, 589, 590, 596, 600
            By industry, occupation 596, 599,
                              600
            Minimum wage workers 631
        Job search 603
        Persons working at home 586
        Unemployed 38, 569, 602, 603
        Union membership 643
    Living arrangements 57, 68
    Marital status 55
    Metropolitan area population 21
    Migration 5
    Nurses 596

Hispanic- or Latino- origin population—Con.
    Occupation 35, 596, 599
    Overweight 203
    Pension plan coverage 523
    Physical activity 204
    Poverty 35, 38, 139, 689, 690, 691, 694
    Projections 11
    Public assistance 541, 554, 555
    School enrollment . 216, 220, 241, 264, 270,
                               274, 575
        Adult education 294
        Charter schools 230
        College costs 278
        Preprimary school 228
        Students with weapons 239
        Teachers 243, 245, 255, 596
    Senior citizen communities 957
    Sexual activity 92
    Sports participation 205
    States 18
    Suicides, deaths 120
    Teachers 243, 255
    Union membership 256
    Volunteers 643
    Voter registration and turnout 400
HIV infection (see also AIDS) . 114, 115, 121, 177,
                             178, 1297
Hockey 1207, 1209
Hogs 713, 798, 803, 826, 827, 828, 829
Home equity loans/lines of credit ... 956, 1134,
                           1137, 1152
Home furnishings. (See Appliances.)
Home furnishings stores . 612, 619, 1008, 1009
Home health care 134, 596, 598
Home health care services:
    Earnings 612
    Employees 612
    Expenditures 126, 127, 128, 130
    Finances 152
Home remodeling 961
Homeland Security, Department of (see also
  National Security, and Veterans Affairs):
    Employees 509
    Expenditures 509
    Funding 507, 508
    Grants by state 510
    National workload statistics 516
    Outlays 454
Homeless, assistance and shelter 556
Homeowners' insurance 1182, 1184
Homes. (See Housing and housing units.)
Homework 257
Homicides . 113, 114, 115, 295, 296, 297, 298,
                      299, 300, 301, 302
Honduras. (See Foreign countries.)
Hong Kong. (See Foreign countries.)
Hong Kong Hong Seng stock market index . 1350
Horses:
    Ownership 1201
    Racing 1206
    Riding 1206
Horses and mules 803
Hospices 134
Hospitals:
    Average daily patient care 164, 165
    Beds 163, 165, 1300
    Capital 751
    Charges and personal expenditure for . 126,
             127, 128, 129, 130, 131, 140

NOTE: Index citations refer to **table** numbers, not page numbers.

U.S. Census Bureau, Statistical Abstract of the United States: 2009

Hospitals—Con.
Construction 924
Consumer price index 132
Cost to hospital per patient 164, 165
Diagnostic procedures 162
Discharges from 167, 168, 169, 170
Earnings 612, 734
Emergency departments 159, 161
Employees 154, 163, 447, 612, 734
Establishments 163, 165, 734
Finances 152, 153, 163, 1243
Gross domestic product 648
Medicare program 134, 136, 137, 138
Mental hospitals 163, 166
National expenditures . 124, 125, 126, 127,
128, 129, 130, 131
Outpatient visits ... 159, 160, 163, 165, 166
Patients 163, 164, 165
Prices 705, 717
Public expenditures 125, 126, 127, 129,
130, 131
City governments 440
County governments 442
State governments 433, 436
Receipts 152, 153, 734
States 165
Surgery 162
Organ transplants 172
Use, admissions, and patient days . 163, 165,
166, 167, 169, 170
Hotels and other lodging places (see also Accommodation and food services):
Buildings and floor space 963
Earnings 612
Employees 612
Establishments 1242
New construction 935
Occupancy rate 1242
Occupational safety 638
Prices 705
Productivity 619
Receipts 1243
House of Representatives .. 386, 387, 388, 389,
390, 391
Households or families (see also Housing and housing units) . 57, 58, 60, 61, 64, 65, 66, 70,
71
Adoption 560
Age of householder . 61, 65, 670, 1133, 1134,
1172
Asian population 61, 63, 65, 66
Assets . 700, 1129, 1132, 1133, 1161, 1175
Automobiles, ownership 959
Balance sheet 700
Black, African-American population . 61, 63,
65, 66, 668, 669, 671, 672, 673, 677
Characteristics .. 60, 61, 62, 63, 64, 65, 66,
70, 670
Children under 18 years . 63, 64, 65, 66, 67,
68, 667, 678
Computer use 253, 1091, 1120
Consumer expenditures . 662, 663, 664, 665,
666
Criminal victimization 309
Culture 1356
Debt 700, 1132, 1134, 1135
Educational attainment 670, 676
Elderly 61, 65, 70, 71, 670

Households or families (see also Housing and housing units)—Con.
Employment of parents 580
Expenditures 1356
Female householder . 58, 60, 61, 62, 63, 64,
65, 66, 70, 71
Finances, financial services . 1129, 1130, 1132,
1133, 1152, 1161, 1172, 1175
Flow of funds 1129, 1130, 1132
Food costs 708
Food insecurity 206
Food stamp program 553, 554
Foreign-born population 41
Foster care 560
Hispanic-origin population .. 35, 38, 59, 61,
63, 65, 66
Hunger 206
Income .. 35, 668, 669, 670, 671, 672, 673,
674, 676, 677, 678, 1133, 1134, 1172
Individual retirement accounts (IRAs) ... 535
Internet access 253, 1089, 1091
Interracial married couples 59
Language spoken at home 227
Living arrangements 34, 57, 68
Male householder 60, 62, 64, 65
Marital status of householder . 65, 70, 1291,
1292, 1293, 1294
Married couples with or without own children 58, 59, 60, 61, 63, 64, 65
Media users 1091
Mobility status 31
Mutual fund ownership 1172
Net worth 698, 699, 700
Nonfamily 58, 60, 70, 71
One-person households .. 58, 60, 61, 70, 71
Persons living alone (one-person households) 57, 58, 60, 61, 70, 71
Poverty 35, 694
Asian population 35, 694
Black, African-American population .. 35,
694
Hispanic-origin population .. 35, 38, 694
Public assistance to families 524
Race 65
Recreation 1356
Region of householder 676
Single parent . 58, 63, 64, 65, 66, 1291, 1293,
1294
Size 41, 58, 61
Stay-at-home parents 67
Stock ownership 1133
Taxes paid 476, 477
Telephones 1090
Tenure 35
Unmarried partners 62
Wealth 698, 699
Housekeeping supplies expenditures . 664, 665
Housing and household operations, price indexes 705, 717
Housing and housing units (see also Households or families):
Age of housing stocks 946, 962
Amenities 929, 959
Appliances 705
Building permit value 926
Capital 960
Coastal counties 25
Condominiums 938

NOTE: Index citations refer to **table** numbers, not page numbers.

U.S. Census Bureau, Statistical Abstract of the United States: 2009

Housing and housing units (see also House-
holds or families)—Con.
  Construction:
    Apartments completed and rented .. 939
    New units 926, 927, 928
    Time to completion 930
    Value 921, 924
  Consumer expenditures . 662, 663, 664, 665,
                                           666
  Consumer price indexes 703, 704, 705
  Cost of living index 706
  Costs 953
  Deficiencies 959
  Elderly 950, 953, 959
  Energy:
    Characteristics 929
    Consumption 885
    Expenditures 889, 890
  Fires and property loss 342
  Floorspace 929
  Government expenditures ... 417, 418, 433,
                                 440, 442, 455
  Heating equipment used 929, 946, 958
  Homeless 556
  Improvements 961, 962
  Kitchen equipment 946
  Loans and mortgages . 932, 956, 1152, 1153,
                                          1154
    Federal Housing Administration (FHA) ...
                                      932, 956
    Veterans Administration (VA) .. 929, 932,
                                           956
  Lot size 948
  Maintenance and repair expenditures .. 664,
                                      665, 962
  Metropolitan area data 936
  Mobile homes 713, 934, 946, 947
  Neighborhood indicators 957
  New privately owned homes, characteristics .
                                           929
  Ownership .. 29, 35, 38, 41, 670, 940, 941,
    943, 946, 949, 950, 951, 952, 953, 954,
                                          1178
  Plumbing 946
  Price indexes 704, 707, 931
  Prices, or costs ... 933, 934, 935, 936, 938,
                                      952, 953
  Public housing, low rent units 541
    Federal aid to state and local govern-
      ments 415, 416
  Puerto Rico 1278
  Remodeling 961
  Rent, rental value 952, 953
  Rooms 948
  Sales 932, 935, 937
  Secured communities 957
  Senior citizen communities 957
  Shelters 556
  Square footage 948
  State data 951
  Structural type 927, 942, 946, 947
  Supportive 556
  Tenure . 29, 35, 38, 41, 670, 698, 699, 940,
    941, 943, 944, 945, 946, 949, 950, 951,
                      952, 953, 954, 1178, 1278
  Transitional 556
  Vacancies 940, 942, 943, 946
  Value 700, 952, 954

Housing and housing units (see also House-
holds or families)—Con.
  Year built 946, 950
Housing and Urban Development, Dept. of:
  Employment 481
  Federal aid to state and local governments ..
                                      415, 416
Housing assistance 524, 556
Human immunodeficiency virus (HIV) infection
  (see also AIDS) . 114, 115, 121, 177, 178, 1297
Human services:
  Charitable contributions 564, 565
  Homeless shelters 556
Hungary. (See Foreign countries.)
Hunger 206
Hunting and fishing 836, 838, 1209, 1210,
                               1216, 1230
Hurricanes 370, 371
Hydroelectric power 891, 912
  Capacity 912
  Consumption 883, 886, 891, 903, 1334
  Net generation 906, 912
  Net summer capacity 904
  Production 883, 1333, 1340
Hydrogen-powered vehicles 1057
Hypertension 160
Hysterectomy 162

                    I

Ice cream 209, 709, 832
Ice hockey 1206, 1207, 1209
Ice skating 1209
Iceland. (See Foreign countries.)
Idaho. (See State data.)
Identity theft 320
Illegal immigration. (See Immigrants.)
Illinois. (See State data.)
Immigrants (see also Foreign-born population) ..
                                44, 47, 49, 50
  Class of admission 47, 48
  Country of birth 48, 49, 50
  Deported 512, 513
  Doctorates 780, 782
  Foreign countries 1289
  Interdiction 511
  Investigations 514
  Refugees 47, 48, 50
  Unauthorized 46
Immigration and customs enforcement 332,
                                           514
Immunization of children 183
Imports. (See Foreign trade.)
Income (see also Consumer expenditures, Earn-
  ings, and Poverty):
  Adult education 294
  Aggregate income 675
  American Indian, Alaska Native population ..
                                           35
  Asian and Pacific Islander population .. 669,
                                      673, 674
  Asian population ... 35, 671, 672, 673, 674,
                            679, 682, 683, 694
  Black, African-American population . 35, 523,
                       673, 674, 676, 679, 682, 694
  City 686
  Consumer expenditures 666
  Corporate 722, 724, 731, 732
  Disposable personal 656, 657, 660
  Distribution 668, 670, 673, 676, 680

NOTE: Index citations refer to **table** numbers, not page numbers.

Income (see also Consumer expenditures, Earnings, and Poverty)—Con.
    Families 33, 35, 38, 672, 673, 674, 676, 677, 685, 686
        American Indian, Alaska Native 35
        Asian 35, 672
        Black, African-American 35, 672
        Computer use 253
        Hispanic-origin 35, 672
        Island areas 1280
        Native Hawaiian, Other Pacific Islander .. 35
        Type of family 673, 674, 676, 677
    Farm 800, 803, 804, 805
    Foreign born 41, 42
    Hispanic-origin population . 35, 38, 523, 668, 669, 671, 672, 679, 682, 683
    Household 668, 669, 670, 671
        After-school activities 256, 257
        Age 670, 681
        Asian population 671
        Black, African-American population . 668, 669, 671
        Computer use 1120
        Educational attainment 670, 681
        Elderly 670
        Hispanic-origin population . 668, 669, 671
        Internet access/use 1121
        Mobility status 31
        Recreation activities, physical activity . 204, 1209, 1211
        Stock, mutual fund ownership 1173
        Taxes 1318
        Tenure 670
    Millionaires 697
    National income ... 645, 646, 647, 651, 657
        By type of income 651
        Originating in farming 800
    Native Hawaiian, Other Pacific Islander population 35
    Per capita 657, 682
    Personal 656, 658, 659, 661
    Persons 41, 679, 680, 682, 683
        Educational attainment 680, 681
        Source of income 523
    Savings 652, 653
    Sports participation, goods 1209, 1211
    State data:
        Gross domestic product 649, 650
        Family 685
        Household 684
        Personal income 658, 659, 660
Income tax (see also Tax receipts):
    Alternative minimum tax 468
    Average tax by income level 463, 470
    Capital gains 467
    Corporation 462, 463, 731
    Deductions 471, 472, 473
    Foreign countries 1317
    Individual ... 463, 464, 466, 467, 468, 469, 470, 471, 472, 473, 475, 476, 477
    Rates 476, 477
    Tax credits 474
Index numbers. (See individual subjects.)
India. (See Foreign countries.)
Indian, American population. (See American Indian, Alaska Native population.)
Indian, Asian population. (See Asian Indian population.)

Indiana. (See State data.)
Individual retirement accounts (IRAs) . 472, 473, 535, 536, 537, 1173, 1176
Indo-European languages 227
Indonesia. (See Foreign countries.)
Industrial energy . 885, 886, 889, 890, 891, 892, 905, 908, 909, 910, 913, 915
Industrial minerals 863
Industrial production indexes 759
    Foreign countries 1309
Industry. (See Corporations, and individual industries.)
Infant deaths (see also Death and death rates) .. 77, 110, 111
    Foreign countries 1295
    Island areas of the U.S. 1273
Inflation. (See Consumer price indexes, and Prices.)
Information and communications technology equipment 703, 753
Information industry:
    Capital 751, 752, 753, 755
    Earnings . 610, 612, 621, 622, 656, 734, 737, 740, 1086, 1088, 1235
    Electronic commerce 1238
    Employees .. 610, 611, 612, 734, 737, 740, 786, 1086, 1088, 1235
    Equipment and software expenditures .. 753
    Establishments .. 734, 735, 737, 965, 1086, 1088, 1235
    Finances 724, 727, 1087
    Foreign countries 1344
    Gross domestic product 648, 650
    Hires and separations 615
    Hours 610
    Multinational companies 766, 767
    Nonemployers 735
    Occupational safety 638
    Productivity 619
    Profits 724, 762, 763
    Research and development 775
    Shipments, revenue 724, 727, 732, 733, 734, 735, 1087, 1088
Influenza 112, 114, 116, 175
Infrastructure expenditures. (See Government.)
Inhalants, persons using 199
Injuries (see also Accidents, and Occupational safety) 122, 161, 170, 192, 1032, 1080
    Consumer products 193
    Costs 194
    Crime victimization 304
    Industrial 635, 636, 637, 638
    Mining 861
    Work time lost 636
Inmates (see also Correctional institutions) . 335, 336
Installment loans (see also Loans and mortgages) 1134, 1150
Institutional care facilities (see also Hospitals, and Nursing and residential care facilities) 163, 166
Institutions of higher education. (See Education.)
Instruments and related products, manufacturing:
    Earnings 612, 973
    Employees 612, 973
    Foreign trade 720, 721, 1271
    Gross domestic product 964
    Productivity 619

NOTE: Index citations refer to **table** numbers, not page numbers.

U.S. Census Bureau, Statistical Abstract of the United States: 2009

Instruments and related products,
  manufacturing—Con.
    Profits 764
    Toxic chemical releases 365
Insurance. (See individual forms of insurance.)
Insurance agents, brokers, and service:
    Earnings 1128
    Employees 1128
    Establishments 1128, 1137
    Finances 1161, 1182
    Gross domestic product 1125
    Prices 705, 717
Insurance carriers:
    Capital 751
    Earnings 612, 1126, 1128
    Employees 612, 1126, 1128
    Establishments 1126, 1127, 1128
    Finances 1129, 1182
    Gross domestic product 1125
    Nonemployers 1127
    Occupational safety 638
    Profits 1182
    Receipts 1126, 1127
Insurance, government. (See Social insurance.)
Insurance, medical care 125, 129, 130
Interest:
    Payments, federal government 455
    Persons receiving income 523
    Receipts, by source:
      Individual income tax returns 465
      National and personal income compo-
        nent 656
Interest rates 1157
    Mortgages 1153, 1157
Intermediate goods, price indexes, producer ....
                           713
Internal revenue collections (see also Tax
  receipts) 462
Internal waterways, traffic 1043
International affairs:
    Charitable organizations 564
    Commerce 1262, 1263, 1266, 1284
    Development aid 1357, 1358, 1360
    Federal outlays 455
    Foreign exchange rates 1352
    Foreign investments in U.S. 1165, 1166,
                          1249, 1251
    International transactions, U.S. . 1246, 1247,
                     1248, 1249, 1250
    U.S. government aid 1257, 1258, 1259
    U.S. investments .. 1163, 1164, 1246, 1256
International data (See Foreign countries, or
  World summary statistics.)
International investment position, U.S. ... 1246,
                          1249, 1256
International mail (U.S. postal) 1084
Internet access/use .. 1089, 1091, 1103, 1120,
                          1200, 1344
    Activities 1122, 1123, 1124
    Connection type 1119, 1121, 1124
    Public libraries 1117
    Schools 252, 253
Internet publishing and broadcasting:
    Earnings 612, 1086
    Employees 612, 1086
    Establishments 1086
    Finances 1087
    Revenue 1087, 1107

Internet service providers, Web search portals,
  data processing:
    Earnings 612, 1086
    Employees 612, 1086
    Establishments 1086
    Finances 1087
    Revenue 1087, 1115
Interracial married couples 59
Inventories (see also Commodities, and Stocks) .
    974, 975, 976, 977, 1006, 1012, 1018
    Business (GDP) 645
Investments (see also Capital stock, and Securi-
  ties):
    Foreign, in U.S. ... 1165, 1166, 1246, 1249,
            1251, 1253, 1254, 1255, 1360
    Private domestic, gross 645, 652, 718
    U.S. government obligations 1137
    U.S. international . 1163, 1164, 1246, 1249,
                              1256
Iowa. (See State data.)
Iran. (See Foreign countries.)
Iraq. (See Foreign countries.)
Ireland (Eire). (See Foreign countries.)
Iron (nutritional) 208
Iron (see also Steel):
    Foreign trade 868, 1267
    Mining industry 860
       Productivity 619
    Prices 713, 864
    Production 863, 864, 867, 935
       World production 867, 1332
Iron and steel mills (see also Primary metal
  manufacturing):
    Capital 988
    Earnings 612, 965, 967
    Electronic commerce 969
    Employees 612, 965, 967, 988
    Establishments 965
    Foreign trade 988
    Shipments 967, 969, 988
Iron and steel products 867, 989
    Foreign trade 720, 721, 864, 868, 1267
    Production and value 864
    Scrap 863
Irrigation 354
Islamic population. (See Religion.)
Island areas of the U.S.:
    Aid by U.S. government 1277
    Area 344
    Banks and banking 1280
    Births 81, 1273
    Climate (Puerto Rico) ... 374, 375, 376, 377,
                          378, 379
    Commerce 1282, 1284
    Deaths 108, 111, 116
    Economic summary 1281
    Education 1274, 1280
    Employees 1281
    Establishments 1281
    Federal payments 461, 1277
    Finances 1282, 1283
    Foreign investment 1253
    Foreign trade 1284
    Geography 344
    Gross product 1282
    Income 1280
    Industry 1281, 1282
    Labor force and employment 1280
    Occupations 1275

NOTE: Index citations refer to **table** numbers, not page numbers.

Island areas of the U.S.—Con.
 Payroll by industry 1281
 Population and/or area ... 344, 1272, 1280,
  1288
 Prisoners in 1276
 Public aid 545, 1277
 Social insurance 527
 Tourism 1280
 Unemployment insurance 540
 Vital statistics 1273
Isle of Man. (See Foreign countries.)
Isobutane 870
Israel. (See Foreign countries.)
Italy. (See Foreign countries.)
Itemized deductions (taxes) 471, 472, 473

J

Jails 334, 335
Jamaica. (See Foreign countries.)
Japan. (See Foreign countries.)
Jazz 1198
Jersey. (See Foreign countries.)
Jet fuel 870
Jewelry, luggage, and leather goods stores . 612,
  619
Jewelry price indexes 705, 713, 717
Jewelry sales 1009
Jewish population. (See Religion.)
Job gains and losses 613, 614
Job search methods 603
Jogging 1209, 1210, 1211
Jordan. (See Foreign countries.)
Judicial service (federal):
 Employees and payrolls 478
 Federal outlays 455
Juices 207, 705
Juveniles:
 Arrest 313
 Court cases 327, 328

K

Kansas. (See State data.)
Karaoke 1199
Kazakhstan. (See Foreign countries.)
Kentucky. (See State data.)
Kenya. (See Foreign countries.)
Keogh plans 473, 1133
Kerosene 870
Kidney disease and infections, deaths (see also
 Nephritis) 112, 188
Kiribati. (See Foreign countries.)
Korea. (See Foreign countries.)
Kuwait. (See Foreign countries.)
Kyrgyzstan. (See Foreign countries.)

L

Laboratories, medical and dental 152
Labor force, employment, and earnings (see
 also individual industries or occupations):
 Accidents and fatalities . 635, 636, 637, 638,
  639
  Work time lost 636
 Adult education 294
 Average pay, states 625
 Back wages 630
 Child labor violations 630
 Commuting to work 1060
 City government 449
 Civilian labor force:
  Asian and Pacific Islander population . 568,
   569, 572, 602, 607, 626

Labor force, employment, and earnings (see
 also individual industries or
 occupations)—Con.
  Asian population ... 568, 569, 570, 572,
   575, 586, 587, 589, 591, 593, 596, 599,
    600, 602, 603, 607, 626, 631, 643
  Black, African-American population . 568,
   569, 572, 575, 586, 587, 596, 607
  Displaced workers 593
  Educational attainment ... 572, 599, 607
  Employed . 567, 569, 570, 573, 574, 575,
   578, 580, 582, 584, 586, 587, 588, 589,
    590, 592, 599, 600
  Female ... 569, 570, 571, 572, 573, 575,
   576, 577, 578, 579, 586, 587, 588, 607
   Age of children 578, 579, 580
   Marital status 576, 577, 578
   Multiple job holders 589
  Foreign-born population 41, 570
  High school graduates, dropouts 265
  Hispanic-origin population . 38, 568, 569,
    586, 587, 596, 600
  Home-based work 586
  Hours worked per day 618
  Married couples with children 580
  Metropolitan areas 574
  Minimum wage workers 631
  Multiple job holders 589, 618
  Not at work 583
  Part-time 592
  Participation rates .. 568, 569, 572, 573,
    576, 577, 578, 579
   Selected countries 1319, 1322
   Wives, by age of youngest child . 579
  Projections 568, 598, 601
  Race . 568, 569, 572, 575, 586, 587, 596,
    607
  Reason not in 595
  School enrollment, persons 16 to 24
   years old 575
  Self-employed workers 584, 585
  States 573
  Unemployed .. 567, 569, 573, 574, 575,
   578, 602, 603, 604, 605, 606, 607, 608,
    609
  Women who gave birth in previous year .
    90, 91, 579
  Work-related learning 617
 Computer use 1091
 Disabled persons 541, 594
 Displaced workers 593
 Earnings 621, 624, 625, 626, 627
 Educational attainment 223, 572, 607
 Elderly ... 33, 568, 570, 571, 576, 581, 602
 Employee benefits . 149, 150, 533, 633, 634
  Government employees 445
 Employees ... 610, 611, 612, 624, 788, 971
  States 611
 Employer costs 632, 970
 Employment cost index ... 628, 1342, 1343
 Employment taxes and contributions ... 457
 Family and Medical Leave Act (FMLA) ... 630
 Female . 569, 571, 572, 573, 575, 576, 577,
  578, 579, 596, 600, 603, 604, 605, 607,
    608, 626, 627
 Flexible schedules 587
 Foreign countries . 1310, 1319, 1321, 1322,
    1323, 1324

NOTE: Index citations refer to **table** numbers, not page numbers.

U.S. Census Bureau, Statistical Abstract of the United States: 2009

Labor force, employment, and earnings (see also individual industries or occupations)—Con.

Foreign-owned firms 1252, 1253
Government. (See Government.)
High school graduates and dropouts 265
Hispanic-origin population . 35, 38, 568, 569, 600, 602
Hires and separations 615
Hours 1310, 1342
Hours worked per day 618
Indexes of compensation 620, 1343
Internet access 1091, 1120
Job gains and losses 613, 614
Job search 603
Metropolitan areas 574
Minimum wage workers 629, 631
Mobility status 29
Occupational groups. (See Occupations, and individual occupations.)
Occupational safety . 635, 636, 637, 638, 639
Part-time work 584, 591, 594, 620, 632, 633, 634
Persons working at home 586
Poverty status 692
Production workers 967, 968
Productivity 620, 1310, 1342
Projections 568, 598, 601
Self-employed 584, 585, 786
Social insurance coverage 525
State data 573, 597, 609, 625
Students 257
Tenure with employer 591
Unemployed workers:
Age 575, 602
Asian and Pacific Islander population . 569, 602, 607
Asian population ... 569, 575, 602, 603, 607
Black, African-American population . 569, 575, 602, 603, 607
Educational attainment 223, 607
Foreign-born population 41
Foreign countries 1319, 1321
High school graduates and dropouts . 265
Hispanic-origin population . 38, 569, 602, 603, 607
Industry 605
Job search activities 603
Occupation 606
Race 569, 575, 602, 603, 607
Reason 604, 608
Sex . 569, 573, 575, 578, 602, 603, 604, 605, 606, 607, 608
States 573, 609
Union membership 642, 643, 644
Violations 630
Work arrangements 587, 588
Work-related learning 617
Work stoppages 641
Workplace deaths/injuries ... 635, 636, 637, 638, 639
Workplace violence/security measures .. 640
Labor organizations or unions:
Membership 642, 643, 644
Political action committees (PAC) .. 404, 405
Labor strikes 641
Lacrosse 1207

Lakes 344, 347, 353, 355
Lamb and mutton (see also Meat and meat products) 209, 826
Lambs. (See Sheep and lambs.)
Land (see also Farms, and Public lands):
Area:
Border lengths 345
Coastal 24, 346
Foreign countries 1288
Island areas 344
National parks 1212, 1214, 1215
States 344
United States 1, 344
Farmland . 350, 352, 793, 794, 795, 796, 797
Federal land 350, 841
Foreign investors 1252, 1253
Forest, area and ownership .. 350, 351, 352, 841
Parks 1212, 1213, 1214, 1215
Shoreline 346
Use 350, 351, 352
Wetlands 351, 353
Landfills (see also Solid waste) 361, 912
Languages spoken at home 52, 53, 54, 227
Laos. (See Foreign countries.)
Larceny, larceny-theft . 295, 296, 297, 298, 304, 308, 309
Lard 209
Latex. (See Rubber.)
Latvia. (See Foreign countries.)
Laundry, cleaning, and garment services. (See Dry-cleaning and laundry services.)
Law degrees conferred 290, 291, 292, 293
Law enforcement (see also Correctional institutions, Courts, and Crime):
Arrests 312, 314, 316
Drug enforcement 316, 317
Employees 444
Expenditures 417, 418, 433, 436
Handgun checks 318
Marshall service 314
Police officers 319, 444, 596
Wiretaps 325
Workplace violence 639
Lawn care 705, 713, 1202
Lawyers (see also Legal services) 596
Lead 863, 864
Air quality 357, 358
Consumption 864
Employment 864
Foreign trade 864
Prices 864, 865
Production and value 864
World production 867, 1332
Learning disability 179
Leasing. (See Real estate, Rental and leasing industry.)
Leather and allied product, manufacturing (see also Footwear, and Hides and skins):
Capital 751
Earnings 612, 965, 967, 973
Electronic commerce 969
Employees 612, 965, 967, 971, 973
Establishments 965
Foreign trade 1271
Gross domestic product 648, 964
Industrial production index 759
Prices 713
Shipments 969, 976
Toxic chemical releases 365

NOTE: Index citations refer to **table** numbers, not page numbers.

	Table

Lebanon. (See Foreign countries.)
Legal assistants 596
Legal, governmental, public administrative
   associations 1245
Legal services:
   Capital 751
   Earnings 612, 1233, 1235
   Employees 612, 1233, 1235
   Establishments 1233, 1234, 1235, 1237
   Finances 724
   Gross domestic product 648
   Prices 705, 717
   Nonemployers 1234
   Receipts 724, 1233, 1234, 1237
Legionellosis 175
Legislatures, state party composition . 395, 396
Leisure activities. (See Recreation.)
Leisure and hospitality industry:
   Earnings 610, 612, 622
   Employees 610, 611, 612
   Hires and separations 615
   Hours 610
   Occupational safety 638
Lemons 709, 803, 824
Lesotho. (See Foreign countries.)
Letters (postal) 1084, 1085
Lettuce 210, 709, 798, 803, 822
Liberia. (See Foreign countries.)
Libraries and librarians 1116, 1117
   Degrees conferred 290, 292
   Employees 596, 1116
   Internet use 1117
Libya. (See Foreign countries.)
Licenses, permits, etc.:
   Taxes 433
Liechtenstein. (See Foreign countries.)
Life expectancy 100, 101, 102, 103
   Foreign countries 1295, 1296
   Projections 100, 1295
Life insurance 1180, 1181
   Capital 1181
   Cash value 1133
   Consumer expenditures 662, 664, 717
   Establishments 1181
   Finances 519, 1129, 1152, 1161, 1175,
                                       1181
   Flow of funds 1161, 1175
   In force 1180
   Individual Retirement Accounts (IRAs) . 1176
   Mortgage loans outstanding 1152
   Purchases, policies 1180
   Reserves 700, 1132, 1181
   Sales 1180, 1181
Life sciences 772, 777, 782
   Degrees conferred 290, 291, 292
   Employment 786
Life table 100, 101, 102, 103
   Life years lost 122
Light and power. (See Electric light and power
   industry.)
Lightning 370
Lime 863, 864
Liposuction 171
Liquor stores, retail. (See Beer, wine, and liquor
   stores.)
Liquors and beverages:
   Alcoholism treatment 198
   Consumption 199, 207
   Government revenues .. 417, 418, 424, 433,
                                      434, 437

Literacy activities 226, 229
Literacy, comparative 1302
Lithuania. (See Foreign countries.)
Livestock and livestock products (see also Ani-
   mals, domestic, and individual classes):
   Commodity futures trading 715
   Consumption 209, 826, 1330
   Farm marketings, sales 801, 803, 805
   Foreign trade . 808, 810, 813, 815, 826, 1271
   Number on farms 827, 828, 829, 831
   Prices 716, 721, 806, 827
   Production 826, 827, 829, 830, 1329
   Purchases 801
   Supply 826
   Value on farms 827
Living cost. (See Consumer price indexes and
   Prices.)
Loans and mortgages (see also Debt):
   Automobile loans 1150
   Banks, commercial 1137, 1155
   Consumer credit .. 1132, 1134, 1135, 1137,
                       1147, 1150, 1155
   Credit market, flow of funds 1130, 1132
   Credit unions 1128
   Delinquency rates 1154, 1155
   Farm. (See Farm mortgage loans.)
   Federal Housing Administration (FHA) . 1154
   Foreclosure rates 1154
   Home mortgage/equity loans . 696, 700, 956,
                 1134, 1135, 1152, 1155
   Installment loans 1134
   Interest rates 1153, 1157
   Life insurance 1181
   Minority-operated small businesses 743
   Mortgage-backed securities 1159
   Mortgage pools 1130
   Mortgages . 700, 728, 729, 1130, 1132, 1134,
                                        1152
   Personal loans 1150
   Savings institutions 1143
   Veterans Administration (VA) 1154
Lobsters 854, 855, 858
Local and suburban transit. (See Passenger tran-
   sit industry.)
Local government. (See State and local govern-
   ment, and individual governmental units.)
Locomotives (railroad) 1080
Lodging industries. (See Hotels and other lodg-
   ing places.)
London FTSE 100 stock market index 1350
Long-term care insurance 634
Lotteries 431, 432
Louisiana. (See State data.)
Low birth weight 85, 87
LSD usage 199
Lumber (see also Forest products, and Wood
   products manufacturing):
   Consumption 845, 847
   Foreign trade 845, 846
   Prices 713, 849
   Production 845
   Railroad car loadings 1081, 1082
   Waterborne commerce 1044
Luxembourg. (See Foreign countries.)
Lyme disease 175

M

Macadamia nuts 824
Macau. (See Foreign countries.)
Macedonia. (See Foreign countries.)

NOTE: Index citations refer to **table** numbers, not page numbers.

U.S. Census Bureau, Statistical Abstract of the United States: 2009

Machine tools 705, 713, 991, 1006
Machinery manufacturing:
  Capital 751
  Earnings 612, 965, 967
  Employees 612, 965, 967, 971
  Establishments 965
  Finances 764
  Foreign trade 720, 721
  Gross domestic product 648, 964
  Industrial production index 759
  Inventories 976
  Productivity 619
  Profits 764
  Research and development 774, 775
  Shipments 967, 969, 975, 976
  Toxic chemical releases 365
Madagascar. (See Foreign countries.)
Magazines:
  Advertising expenditures 1239
  Reading 1089
  Recycling 363
Magnesium 864, 867
Mail 1084, 1085
Mail order houses (including electronic shop-
  ping):
  Earnings 612, 1008
  Employees 612, 1008
  Establishments 1008, 1017
  Productivity 619
  Sales 1009, 1013, 1014, 1017
Maine. (See State data.)
Malaria 175
Malawi. (See Foreign countries.)
Malaysia. (See Foreign countries.)
Maldives. (See Foreign countries.)
Male householder. (See Households or families.)
Mali. (See Foreign countries.)
Malt beverages (see also Beverages) .. 207, 705,
                                       808, 810
Malta. (See Foreign countries.)
Mammography testing 195
Managed care health plans 134, 143
Management of companies and enterprises:
  Capital 751, 753, 755
  Earnings 612, 737, 1233, 1235
  Employees 612, 737, 1233, 1235
  Establishments 737, 1233, 1234, 1235
  Equipment and software expenditures .. 753
  Finances 724, 727, 732
  Gross domestic product 648
  Profits 734
  Receipts ... 724, 727, 732, 733, 1233, 1234
  Research and development 774
Managers. (See Proprietors, etc.)
Manganese 864, 868
Manganiferous ore 863
Manufactured fibers (see also Foreign trade, and
  specific items) 982
Manufacturers' excise taxes 462
Manufacturing industry (see also individual
  industries):
  Capital 751, 753, 755, 1162
  Earnings . 610, 612, 621, 622, 734, 737, 740,
                                       967, 972
  Economic indicators 757
  Electronic commerce 969
  Employees .. 586, 600, 610, 611, 612, 722,
                    734, 737, 740, 786, 968, 971
  Employer costs 970
  Equipment and software expenditures .. 753

Manufacturing industry (see also individual
  industries)—Con.
  Establishments 734, 735, 737, 967, 972
  Finances 724, 727, 764, 979, 980, 1282
  Foreign countries 1342, 1343
  Foreign investments in U.S. 1251
  Form of organization 967
  Gross domestic product . 648, 650, 964, 1282
  Hires and separations 615
  Hours 610
  Industrial production index 759
  Inventories 975, 976
  Investment abroad 1256
  Island areas of the United States 1281
  Multinational companies 766, 767, 768
  Nonemployers 735
  Occupational safety 635, 638
  Productivity 619, 620, 760
      Foreign countries 1342
  Profits 722, 762, 764, 980
  Sales, shipments, receipts ... 722, 724, 727,
      732, 733, 734, 735, 967, 972, 974, 975,
                                       976, 980
  State data 966, 968, 972
  Toxic chemical releases 365
  Union membership 643
  Value added 972
Maple syrup, organic acreage trees 802
Margarine 209, 709
Marijuana (see also Drugs (illegal)):
  Arrests, seizures 316, 317
  Use 199, 200
Marine Corps 492, 494
Marital status of population 55, 56
  Asian population 55
  Black, African-American population 55
  Computer use 1120
  Contraceptive use 94, 95
  Couples with or without own household . 58
  Elderly 33, 56
  Employed persons 578, 580
  Female householder 65, 1291
  Foreign-born population 41
  Foreign countries 1294
  Hispanic-origin population 55
  Householder status 65, 1293, 1294
  Internet access 1120
  Labor force participation rates 576, 577,
                                       578, 579
  Male householder 65
  Nonfamily householder 70
  Scientists and engineers 784
  Sexual activity 92
  Unmarried partners 62
  Women in the labor force 577, 578
  Work schedules 587
Marriage and divorce (see also Marital status) ...
                                       77, 123
  Foreign countries 1292
Married couples. (See Households or families.)
Married persons. (See Marital status.)
Marshall Islands. (See Foreign countries.)
Martial arts 1209
Martinique. (See Foreign countries.)
Maryland. (See State data.)
Massachusetts. (See State data.)
Maternal and child health service, expenditures
  for 125

NOTE: Index citations refer to **table** numbers, not page numbers.

Mathematics:
 Degrees conferred . 290, 291, 292, 779, 782,
  785
 Employment 786
 Literacy 1302
 Research & development 772, 777
 Salary offers 287
Mauritania. (See Foreign countries.)
Mauritius. (See Foreign countries.)
Mayotte. (See Foreign countries.)
Measles 175, 183
Measuring, analyzing, and controlling instru-
 ments. (See Instruments and related products,
 manufacturing.)
Meat and meat products (see also Food manu-
 facturing, and individual meats):
 Consumer expenditures 664, 665
 Consumption 209, 826, 1325, 1330
 Farm marketings 801, 803
 Foreign trade 808, 813, 815, 826, 1267
 Price indexes . 705, 709, 713, 715, 716, 721
 Production 826, 1325, 1329
 Supply 826
Mechanical engineering 785
Media (see also individual medium) . 1089, 1090,
  1091
Medicaid:
 Coverage, recipients ... 139, 140, 141, 143,
  146, 524
 Expenditures 131, 140, 141, 153
 Federal payments 456
 Nursing homes 140
 State data 141, 143
Medical care (see also Health services):
 Expenditures for .. 125, 126, 127, 128, 129,
  130, 131, 520, 521, 522, 662, 664, 665,
  1301
 Insurance benefits 125, 126, 129
 Price indexes, consumer . 132, 703, 704, 705,
  717
Medical equipment and supplies manufacturing .
  612, 619, 967
Medical malpractice insurance 1182
Medical research 125
Medical schools 293
 International graduates 157
 Number, students, graduates 293
Medical sciences, employment 154, 596
Medical services. (See Health services.)
Medicare:
 Ambulatory care visits 159
 Benefit payments, expenditures .. 125, 130,
  131, 137, 138, 153, 519, 521
 Contributions 138
 Enrollees 135, 136
 Federal payments 456
 Hospital visits 159
 State data 135
 Trust funds 138
 Utilization and charges 134, 137
Medicines (see Drugs and medicines, and Phar-
 maceutical and medicine manufacturing):
Melons 210, 822
Members of Congress. (See Congress, U.S.)
Membership organizations:
 Charitable contributions 564
 Earnings 612
 Employees 612
 Establishments 1235
 Revenue 1244

Menhaden 854
Meningitis 175
Mental hospitals 163, 166
Mercury 863, 864, 867
Metal detectors 240
Metal ore mining industry:
 Capital 860
 Earnings 860
 Employees 860
 Establishments 860
 Gross domestic product 648
 Occupational safety 861
 Production indexes 862
 Shipments 860
 Value added 860
Metals 860, 863, 864, 865, 867, 868, 1081
 Foreign trade 1267, 1271
 Prices 713, 715, 720
 Production and value 863, 864
  Indexes of production 862
 Railroad, car loadings of 1081, 1082
 Spot market price indexes 716
 World production 867, 1332
Metalworking manufacturing 612, 619, 967
Methamphetamine, illegal use 199
Methane gases 360
Metropolitan statistical areas:
 Airline markets 1035
 American Indian and Alaska Native popula-
  tion 21
 Asian population 21
 Black population 21
 Civilian labor force 574
 Components of change 20
 Consumer expenditures 663
 Consumer price index 706
 Elderly 22
 Hispanic-origin population 21
 Housing prices 936
 Income 661
 Migration 20
 Native Hawaiian and Other Pacific Islander
  population 21
 Population 19, 21, 22
 States 23
Mexican-origin population 38
 Births and birth rates 78, 85
 Breastfeeding 88
 Educational attainment 221
 Labor force 569
Mexico. (See Foreign countries.)
Mica 867, 868
 Foreign trade (sheet) 868
 Production and value 863, 864
 World production 867
Mica, scrap and flake 863
Michigan. (See State data.)
Microcomputers (See Computers.)
Micronesia, Federated States of. (See Foreign
 countries.)
Migraine headaches 191
Migration 4, 5, 13, 29, 30, 31, 32, 1289
Military bases 491, 492
Military manpower ... 491, 492, 493, 495, 1361
Military outlays 485, 486
Military sciences, degrees conferred 290
Military services:
 Casualties 498
 Contract and grant awards ... 489, 490, 491

NOTE: Index citations refer to **table** numbers, not page numbers.

U.S. Census Bureau, Statistical Abstract of the United States: 2009

Military services—Con.
  Expenditures 489, 490, 491, 519
  National guard 501
  Pay grades 496
  Payroll 489, 491
  Personnel 489, 491, 492, 493, 494, 495,
                                            496
        Foreign countries 493, 495
        Rank 496
  Reserves 499, 500
  Retirees 489
  Retirement system 497, 519, 529
Milk, cream, and other dairy products:
  Consumption 209, 833
  Prices 709, 713
  Production 831, 832, 833
  Sales 832
Millet, organic acreage 798
Mine safety 861
Mineral fuels 720, 721, 863, 865
Mineral leases 873
Minerals and mineral products (see also Mining,
    and individual minerals):
  Foreign trade 868
      Waterborne commerce 1044
    Imports as percent of consumption 868
    Price indexes 720, 721
    Prices 864
    Production and value ... 863, 864, 866, 867
      Foreign countries 1332
    World production 867, 1332
Mining industry (see also Minerals and mineral
    products, and individual minerals):
  Capital 751
      Expenditures 753, 755
  Earnings . 612, 621, 734, 737, 837, 838, 860
  Employees .. 586, 600, 612, 734, 737, 786,
                                      837, 838, 860
  Equipment and software expenditures .. 753
  Establishments ... 734, 735, 737, 837, 838,
                                            860
  Finances 724, 727, 764, 1282
  Gross domestic product 648, 1282
  Industrial production index 759
  Multinational companies . 766, 767, 768, 1255
  Nonemployers 735
  Occupational safety 635, 638, 861
  Productivity 619
  Profits 722, 764
  Receipts . 722, 724, 727, 732, 733, 734, 735,
                                            837
  Safety 861
  Sales 837
  Union membership 643
Mining machinery, manufacturing 612, 967
Minnesota. (See State data.)
Mississippi. (See State data.)
Mississippi River traffic 1043
Missouri. (See State data.)
Mobile homes 713, 934, 946, 947
Mobility status of population 29, 30, 31, 32
Moldova. (See Foreign countries.)
Molybdenum 864, 867
Monaco. (See Foreign countries.)
Monetary authorities, flow of funds . 1129, 1161
Money market accounts, funds . 728, 1129, 1131,
                                      1132, 1159
      Families using 1133, 1173
Money market rates 1157

Money orders 1085
Money supply (stock) 1156
Mongolia. (See Foreign countries.)
Montana. (See State data.)
Montenegro. (See Foreign countries.)
Montserrat. (See Foreign countries.)
Morocco. (See Foreign countries.)
Mortality costs 122
Mortgage pools and trusts ... 1129, 1130, 1152
Mortgages. (See Loans and mortgages.)
Motels. (See Hotels.)
Motion picture and sound recording industry:
  Attendance 1203
  Capital 751
  Earnings 612, 734, 1086, 1088
  Employees 612, 734, 1086, 1088
  Establishments 734, 1086, 1088
  Finances 1087, 1101
  Gross domestic product 648
  Productivity 612
  Receipts, revenue .. 734, 1087, 1088, 1101,
                                            1203
Motor freight transportation and warehousing
    (See Trucking and warehousing.)
Motor fuel taxes 433, 1053, 1062
Motor vehicle and parts dealers, retail:
  Earnings 612, 734, 1008, 1018
  Electronic commerce 1013
  Employees 612, 734, 1008, 1018
  Establishments . 734, 1007, 1008, 1017, 1018
  Finances 724, 1018
  Franchises 1018
  Inventories 1012, 1018
  Nonemployers 1017
  Price indexes 705, 713, 717
  Profits 1018
  Sales ... 724, 734, 1007, 1009, 1011, 1013,
                              1017, 1018, 1020
Motor vehicle manufacturing:
  Capital 751
  Earnings 612, 973
  Employees 612, 971, 973, 997, 998
  Foreign trade 1271
  Gross domestic product 648, 964
  Industrial production index 759
  Inventories 976
  Productivity 619
  Research and development 774, 775
  Sales, shipments, receipts ... 967, 977, 989,
                                      997, 998, 1019
  State data 998
Motor vehicles:
  Accidents/deaths .. 116, 1032, 1063, 1065,
                                            1071
  Air pollutant emissions 359
  Alternative fueled vehicles 1057
  Common carriers 1074
  Consumer expenditures . 662, 663, 664, 665
  Crashes 1067
  Drivers' licenses 1058
  Expenditure per new car 1021
  Foreign trade 720, 721, 1267
  Fuel consumed 1062
  Imports 1021
  Insurance 655, 1182
  Miles of travel 1061
  Number 1027
  Ownership 959
  Price indexes 705, 713, 717, 720, 721

NOTE: Index citations refer to **table** numbers, not page numbers.

Motor vehicles—Con.
   Production 1021
   Railroad car loadings 1082
   Registrations 1056, 1058
   Sales 1021
   Service and repair shops. (See Automotive
      repair and maintenance service.)
   Taxes, licenses and motor fuel 418, 424,
                           435, 436
   Theft ... 295, 296, 297, 298, 308, 309, 312
   Traffic fatalities ... 1063, 1064, 1065, 1066,
                  1068, 1069, 1070
   Trucks 1061, 1062
Motorcycles 1058, 1063
   Accidents and deaths 1063
   Racing 1206
Mountain biking 1209
Movie theaters 1089, 1101, 1199, 1203
Mozambique. (See Foreign countries.)
Multilateral grants 1359
Multinational companies ... 765, 766, 767, 768,
                               1255
Multiple births 80
Multiple jobholders 589, 618
Mumps 175
Municipal and state bonds . 427, 428, 728, 729,
         1130, 1132, 1158, 1159, 1167
Municipal waste 361, 362, 363, 892
Municipalities. (See Cities and Metropolitan
   areas.)
Murders . 295, 296, 297, 298, 299, 300, 302, 312
Museums 1196, 1198
Museums, historical sites:
   Earnings 612, 734
   Employees 612, 734, 1189, 1190, 1191
   Establishments 734, 1190, 1191
   Federal aid 1195, 1196
   Finances 1190
   Nonemployers 1191
   Receipts, revenue .. 734, 1188, 1189, 1190,
                             1191
Mushrooms 803, 822
Music:
   After-school activities 256, 257
   Industry receipts 1102
   Listening and expenditures . 1014, 1016, 1089,
                      1103, 1198
Musicians and composers 596
Muslim population. (See Religion.)
Mussels 855
Mutton (see also Meat and meat products) . 209,
                               826
Mutual funds 729, 730, 1129, 1131, 1132,
1133, 1161, 1171, 1172, 1173, 1174, 1175,
                         1176, 1179

N

Nail salons 1244
National Aeronautics and Space Administration
   (NASA), budget 792
National Association of Securities Dealers (NAS-
   DAQ) 1167
National College Athletic Association (NCAA)
   sports participation 1207
National debt. (See Debt.)
National forests. (See Forests.)
National Guard 501
National health expenditures 124, 125, 126,
         127, 128, 129, 130, 131

National income (see also Gross domestic prod-
   uct) 657
National Security. (See Department of Defense,
   Department of Homeland Security, and indi-
   vidual military services.)
Native Hawaiian and Other Pacific Islander . 5, 6,
                                8, 9,
   Births 5, 85
   Business owners 744, 745
   Children 8, 9
   College costs 278
   Deaths 5
   Educational attainment 35
   Elderly 8, 9
   Grandparents living with grandchildren .. 69
   Head Start 555
   Housing tenure 35
   Income 35
   Metropolitan area population 21
   Migration 5
   Minority businesses 744, 745
   Occupation 35
   Poverty 35
   Veterans 504
Natural gas:
   Consumption . 883, 884, 886, 887, 903, 1334,
                             1335
   Electricity generation 906
   Expenditures 890
   Foreign trade 884, 893, 894, 1267
   Prices 705, 864, 875, 888
   Production 870, 871, 883, 884
      World . 867, 875, 1332, 1333, 1336, 1338
   Reserves 872, 875
Natural gas distribution industry 612, 619
Natural gas plant liquids 870, 871
   Reserves 870, 872
   Supply 869, 870
Natural resources (see also Forest products,
   Minerals and mineral products, Paper and
   paperboard products, Timber, Wood products
   manufacturing, and individual resources and
   minerals):
   Federal outlays 455
   Fisheries and fish products .. 852, 853, 854,
                           857, 858, 859
   Forests and timberland 841, 842, 843
   Governmental finances 418
      Aid to state and local governments . 415
      Government employment and payrolls ...
                             444
      Governmental revenue 418
      State and local governments ... 417, 425
      State governments 433
   Minerals 860, 865
   Coal 877, 878, 879
   Consumption 864
   Employment 864
   Mining 638, 861, 862
   Natural gas 871, 872, 873, 874, 875,
                             876
   Petroleum 869, 871, 872, 873, 874
   Price 864
   Production 863, 864, 866, 867, 1332
   Products 865
   Trade 864, 868
   Uranium 880
Paper products 846, 849, 850, 851
Wildfires 844

NOTE: Index citations refer to **table** numbers, not page numbers.

U.S. Census Bureau, Statistical Abstract of the United States: 2009

Natural resources (see also Forest products, Minerals and mineral products, Paper and paperboard products, Timber, Wood products manufacturing, and individual resources and minerals)—Con.
  Wood products 845, 846, 847, 849, 850
Natural resource-related industry (see also Mining industry, Oil and gas extraction. and individual industries):
  Employment 612, 837, 838
    Hires and separations 615
  Establishments 837, 838
  Gross Domestic Product 836
  Mineral industry 860
  Oil and gas extraction 874
  Payroll and earnings 612, 837, 838
  Petroleum industry 869
  Sales and revenue 837
  Timber-related industry 839, 840
Nauru. (See Foreign countries.)
Navy; personnel 492, 494
Nebraska. (See State data.)
Nectarines 210, 824
Neonatal deaths (see also Death and death rates) 110
Nepal. (See Foreign countries.)
Nephritis, nephrotic syndrome, and nephrosis (See Kidney disease) . 112, 113, 114, 115, 116
Netherlands. (See Foreign countries.)
Netherlands Antilles. (See Foreign countries.)
Neurologists 157
Nevada. (See State data.)
New Caledonia. (See Foreign countries.)
New Hampshire. (See State data.)
New Jersey. (See State data.)
New Mexico. (See State data.)
New York. (See State data.)
New York Stock Exchange 1167, 1169
New Zealand. (See Foreign countries.)
Newspaper, book, and directory publishers:
  Earnings 612, 1086
  Employees 612, 1086
  Establishments 1086
  Finances 1087, 1092
  Productivity 619
  Revenue 1087, 1092
Newspapers (See also Publishing industry):
  Advertising expenditures 1239
  Expenditures, consumer 1089, 1193
  Number and circulation .. 1090, 1093, 1094
  Online-news 1124
  Reading 1089, 1090, 1091
  Receipts 1088
  Recycling 363
Newsprint 851
  Producer prices 849
Nicaragua. (See Foreign countries.)
Nickel 863, 864, 867, 868
  Consumption 864
  Employment 864
  Foreign trade 864, 868
  Prices 864
  Production and value 863, 864, 867
  World production 867, 1332
Niger. (See Foreign countries.)
Nigeria. (See Foreign countries.)
Nitrogen in ammonia, world production ... 863, 1332
Nonalcoholic beverages 664, 665
Nonemployer establishments ... 558, 735, 839, 1017, 1127, 1185, 1190, 1234

Nonmetallic mineral mining and quarrying, except fuels:
  Capital 751, 860
  Earnings 860
  Employees 860
  Establishments 860
  Finances 764
  Gross domestic product 836
  Occupational safety 861
  Productivity 619
  Shipments, receipts 860
  Value added 860
Nonmetallic mineral product manufacturing (see also Metals and metal products):
  Earnings 612, 965, 967, 973
  Electronic commerce 969
  Employees 612, 965, 967, 971, 973
  Establishments 965
  Foreign trade 1271
  Gross domestic product 648, 964
  Occupational safety 638
  Productivity 619
  Profits 764
  Sales, shipments, receipts ... 967, 969, 975, 976
  Stone, clay, and glass 1081, 1082
  Toxic chemical releases 365
Nonprofit organizations ... 561, 562, 563, 564, 612, 1244, 1245
Nongovernmental organizations 1357
North Carolina. (See State data.)
North Dakota. (See State data.)
North Korea. (See Foreign countries.)
Northern Mariana Islands. (See Island areas of the U.S.)
Norway. (See Foreign countries.)
Nuclear power 899, 900, 902
  Capacity 899, 900, 1341
  Commercial generation, by country ... 1341
  Consumption 883, 884, 1334, 1335
  Production . 899, 900, 906, 1333, 1340, 1341
  Reactors 900, 1341
  State data 899, 900, 906
  Waste discharged fuel 902
Nursery and greenhouse products 803
Nursing and residential care facilities:
  Capital 751
  Earnings 612, 734
  Employees 154, 187, 612, 734
  Establishments 187, 734
  Expenditures . 124, 126, 127, 128, 130, 131
    Consumer 126, 127
  Occupational safety 638
  Receipts 152, 153, 734
  Residents 187
Nursing personnel 156
  Employment 596
    Projections 598
Nutrients and nutritional intake 208
Nutritional deficiencies, deaths 111
Nuts:
  Cash receipts, marketing 803
  Consumption 825
  Foreign trade 813, 815, 825
  Organic acreage 798
  Production 825

O

Oats 798

NOTE: Index citations refer to **table** numbers, not page numbers.

Obesity 203, 1298
Obstetricians (see also Physicians) 157
Occupational safety 637, 638, 861
Occupations (see also individual occupations):
    American Indian, Alaska Native population ..
                                            35
    Asian population 35, 596, 599
    Black, African-American population . 35, 596,
                                           599
    Earnings 623, 626, 627
    Employment 586, 587, 596, 597, 599
        Employee benefits 634
        Flexible schedules 587
        Home-based work 586
        Projections 596
        Race 35, 596
        Sex 596, 600
        State data 597
    Employment cost index 628
    Hispanic-origin population 35, 596
    Island areas 1283
    Mobility status 29
    Native Hawaiian, Other Pacific Islander
      population 35
    Pension plan/health plan coverage 633
    Science and engineering 786, 787, 788
    White-collar and blue-collar workers 628
Office buildings. (See Commercial buildings.)
Office equipment. (See Computer and office
  equipment.)
Office supplies, stationery, and gift stores . 612,
                                 619, 1008
Offshore leases 873
Ohio. (See State data.)
Oil. (See Petroleum and products.)
Oil and gas extraction industry:
    Capital 751
    Earnings 612, 734, 837, 838, 860
    Employees ... 612, 734, 837, 838, 860, 874
    Establishments 734, 837, 838, 860, 874
    Gross domestic product 648, 836
    Output 862
    Payroll 874
    Production indexes 862
    Productivity 619
    Sales 842
    Shipments, receipts 734
    Value added 860
Oil crops 801, 806, 808, 810
Oil spills 355
Oils:
    Animal (oils and fats) 209
    Prices 709, 713, 716
    Vegetable:
        Consumption 209
        Foreign trade 808, 813, 1267
        Production, consumption, and stocks . 209,
                                       812
Oilseeds 715, 720, 808, 1325, 1326
Oklahoma. (See State data.)
Old-age pensions. (See Pensions.)
Old-age, survivors, disability, and health insur-
  ance. (See Social insurance.)
Olives 824
Oman. (See Foreign countries.)
Onions 210, 803, 822
Opera 1194
Operations performed, medical 162
Ophthalmologists 157

Optometrists 152
Oranges 210, 709, 803, 824
Oregon. (See State data.)
Ores, crude (see also individual ores):
    Foreign trade 1267
Organ transplants 172
Organic farmland, livestock 798, 1331
Osteopaths (see also Physicians) 155
Otolaryngology 157
Outdoor recreation activities (see also Recre-
  ation, and specific forms of recreation) . 1199,
                                      1209, 1216
Outlays, federal budget 451, 452, 453
    Agency 454
    Function 455
    Payments for individuals 456
    Science and engineering 790
Outpatient care centers industry 152
Outpatient hospital visits 159, 163, 165
Overweight persons 202, 203, 1298
Oysters 854, 855, 858, 859

P

Pain, lower back, neck, and face 191
Pain relievers, illegal use 199
Pakistan. (See Foreign countries.)
Palau. (See Foreign countries.)
Panama. (See Foreign countries.)
Paper and paperboard products:
    Foreign trade 1267
    Prices 713, 720, 849
    Production 850, 851
    Railroad car loadings 1081, 1082
    Recycling 362, 363
Paper products, manufacturing:
    Capital 751
    Earnings . 612, 837, 838, 839, 840, 965, 967,
                                         973
    Electronic commerce 969
    Employees .. 612, 837, 838, 839, 840, 965,
                               967, 971, 973
    Establishments 837, 838, 839, 965
    Finances 764
    Foreign trade 1271
    Gross domestic product 648, 836, 964
    Industrial production index 759
    Output 851
    Productivity 619
    Profits 764
    Research and development 774
    Sales, shipments, receipts ... 824, 837, 839,
                     840, 967, 969, 975, 976
    Toxic chemical releases 365
Papua New Guinea. (See Foreign countries.)
Paraguay. (See Foreign countries.)
Paris CAC-40 stock market index 1350
Parkinson's disease, deaths 113, 114
Parks 1212, 1213
    Finances 1212, 1213
    Government employment and payrolls . 444
    National 1212, 1214, 1215
    State 1213
Parliament, foreign 1316
Parolees (see also Correctional institutions, and
  Prisons and prisoners) 334
Parties, political. (See Political parties.)
Partnerships, establishments and finances . 722,
                     723, 724, 726, 727

NOTE: Index citations refer to **table** numbers, not page numbers.

U.S. Census Bureau, Statistical Abstract of the United States: 2009

Passenger transit industry (see also Passengers):
    Earnings 612
    Employees 619
    Expenditures 717
Passengers (see also Passenger transit industry,
    and various transportation modes):
    Arriving from overseas .. 1221, 1228, 1229,
                                               1230
    Border crossings 516, 1231
    Carrier operation, summary 1030, 1074,
                                               1080
        Air 1030, 1041
        Rail 1080
    Passenger traffic, volume 516
    Railroads 1080
Pasta, prices 709, 713
Patents and trademarks 748, 749, 1346
Pathologists 157
Payrolls. (See Earnings, and individual indus-
    tries.)
PCP usage 199
Peaches 210, 803, 824
Peanut butter 709
Peanuts 209, 802, 803
Pears 210, 709, 824
Peat 863, 864
Pecans 824, 825
Pediatricians (see also Physicians) 157
Pennsylvania. (See State data.)
Pensions and retirement benefits (see also
    Social insurance):
    Annuities 1176, 1181
    Expenditures 519, 529, 662
    Families receiving 523, 535
    Funds (flow of funds) 1129, 1132, 1177
    Government employees . 523, 529, 530, 531
    Plans 534, 538, 1176
    Railroad 523
    Retirement and pension plans 529, 532,
                                        533, 1161, 1175, 1176
    Veterans 502, 523
Pentanes plus 870
Peppers 803, 822
Perch 855, 859
Performing arts 1191, 1194, 1198
Performing arts, spectator sports industry:
    Capital 751
    Earnings 612, 734, 1190
    Employees 612, 734, 1189, 1191
    Establishments 734, 1189, 1190, 1191
    Nonemployers 1190
    Occupational safety 638
    Receipts, revenue ... 734, 1188, 1189, 1190
Periodical publishing 1086, 1087, 1096
Perlite 863, 864
Personal and laundry services:
    Earnings 612, 734, 1233, 1235
    Employees 612, 734, 1233, 1235
    Establishments 734, 1233, 1234, 1235
    Finances 724
    Productivity 619
    Receipts 724, 734, 1233, 1234, 1244
Personal care price indexes 705
Personal care workers 596
Personal computers. (See Computers.)
Personal consumption expenditures .. 645, 646,
                                        657, 717, 718
    Chain-type price indexes 718
    Recreation 1193

Personal health care expenditures 126, 127,
                                        129, 130
Personal income 656, 658, 659, 660, 661
Personal savings 652, 653
Pertussis 175
Peru. (See Foreign countries.)
Pesticides 801
Pet and pet supplies stores 1008
Pet ownership 1201
Pet products and services 705
Petroleum and coal product manufacturing:
    Capital 751
    Earnings 612, 837, 965, 973
    Employees 612, 837, 965, 971, 973
    Establishments 837, 965
    Finances 764, 898
    Foreign investments in U.S. 1251, 1252,
                                               1254
    Foreign trade 1271
    Gross domestic product 648, 964
    Industrial production index 759
    Multinational companies 766, 767
    Productivity 619
    Profits 762, 764, 897, 898
    Research and development 774, 775
    Sales, shipments 837, 860, 975, 976
    Toxic chemical releases 365
Petroleum and natural gas extraction 874
Petroleum and products:
    Consumption . 868, 883, 884, 886, 903, 1334,
                                               1335
    Disposition 870
    Electricity generation 906
    Emissions 913
    Expenditures 889
    Foreign trade . 868, 870, 884, 893, 894, 895,
                        896, 897, 914, 1261, 1271
    Net summer capacity 904
    Oilspills 355
    Prices 710, 713, 719, 865, 888
    Production ... 863, 867, 870, 873, 883, 884
        World 867, 1332, 1333, 1337
    Railroad car loadings of 1081, 1082
    Refineries 870
    Reserves 872, 873
    Stocks 870, 896
    Strategic reserve 870, 896
    Value 869, 871
    Wells 869, 873
        Drilling costs 869
        Leases and production 873
Pharmaceutical and medicine manufacturing:
    Earnings 612, 965, 967
    Employees 612, 965, 967
    Productivity 619
    Shipments 967, 985
Pharmacies and drug stores:
    Earnings 1008, 1011
    Employees 1008, 1011
    Establishments 1008, 1011
    Prescription sales 151, 1009, 1011
    Retail 151
Pharmacists 596
Pike, northern 855
Philanthropy 561, 562, 563, 564, 565
Philippines. (See Foreign countries.)
Phosphate rock:
    Consumption 864
    Employment 864

NOTE: Index citations refer to **table** numbers, not page numbers.

Phosphate rock—Con.
    Foreign trade 864
    Prices 864
    Production and value 863, 864
    World production 867, 1332
Photographic equipment and supplies 1267
Physical activity 204, 205
Physical sciences:
    Degrees conferred . 290, 291, 292, 779, 782,
                                                785
    Employees 596
    Research & development expenditures . 772,
                                                779
Physicians 154, 156, 157
    Degrees conferred 293
    Employment 156, 157, 596
    Expenditures for .. 124, 126, 127, 128, 129,
                                          130, 131
    Foreign countries 1300
    International medical school graduates . 157
    Medical schools, students and graduates ....
                                                293
    Offices 152, 153
    Osteopaths 155
    Price index 132, 705, 717
    Specialty and professional activity 157
    State data 156
    Type of practice 155, 157
    Visits to 158, 159, 160
Physics (see also Physical sciences):
    Degrees conferred 785
    Enrollment 779
    Salary offers 287
Pig iron. (See Iron.)
Pigs. (See Hogs.)
Pilchard. (See Sardines.)
Pineapples 210, 824
Pipe (smoking), usage 199
Pipeline, freight and mileage 1026, 1083
Pipelines, transportation industry:
    Capital 751, 1083
    Earnings 612, 1029, 1031
    Employees 612, 1025, 1029, 1031
    Establishments 1029, 1031
    Finances 1083
    Gross domestic product 648
    Output 1083
    Revenue 1029
Pistachios 803, 824, 825
Pistols. (See Firearms.)
Plague 175
Plants 1202
Plastic and rubber products manufacturing:
    Capital 751
    Earnings 612, 965, 967, 973
    Electronic commerce 969
    Employees ... 586, 612, 965, 967, 971, 973
    Establishments 965
    Finances 764
    Foreign trade 1271
    Gross domestic product 648, 964
    Industrial production index 759
    Inventories 976
    Occupational safety 638
    Prices 713, 720, 721
    Productivity 619
    Profits 764
    Research and development 774

Plastic and rubber products
  manufacturing—Con.
    Sales, shipments, receipts ... 967, 969, 975,
                                                976
    Toxic chemical releases 365
Plastic surgeons 157
Plastics 361, 362, 363
Platinum-group metals 863
    Consumption 863
    Employment 863
    Foreign trade 863, 868
    Prices 713, 863, 864, 865
    Production 863
Plums and prunes 210, 824
Plural births 80
Plywood:
    Consumption 845
    Foreign trade 845, 846
    Industry 838, 839, 840
    Output 845
    Producer price indexes 849
Pneumonia 112, 114, 115, 161, 170
Poland. (See Foreign countries.)
Police. (See Law enforcement and Public safety.)
Poliomyelitis 183
Political action committees (PAC) . 404, 405, 409
Political parties, organizations:
    Campaign finances 407, 408, 409
        Political action committees (PAC) 409
    Congress, composition of 388, 389
    Congressional districts 387
    Governors, by party affiliation 393
    State legislatures, composition of . 395, 396,
                                                397
    Volunteers 566
    Votes ... 380, 382, 383, 384, 385, 387, 394
Political science 785
Pollock 854, 859
Pollution:
    Air 357, 358, 359, 360
    Hazardous waste sites 367
    Industry 365
    Motor vehicle emissions 359
    Oilspills 355
    Toxic releases 364, 365, 366
    Wastewater treatment 918
Poor persons. (See Income and Poverty.)
Population (see also Birth, Death, Divorce, and
  Marriage):
    Adopted children 560
    Age:
        American Indian, Alaska Native popula-
            tion 8, 9, 11
        Asian population 8, 9, 11
        Black, African-American population . 8, 9,
                                                11
        Distribution 7, 8, 9, 10, 11, 16, 41
        Foreign born 41, 42
        Hispanic-origin population .. 8, 9, 11, 38
        Metropolitan areas 22
        Native Hawaiian, Other Pacific Islander
            population 8, 9
        Race 7, 8, 9, 11
        School enrollment 215, 216
        Sex 7, 10, 33
        State 16, 17
        Voting-age population 400, 403
    American Indian, Alaska Native. (See Ameri-
      can Indian, Alaska Native population.)

NOTE: Index citations refer to **table** numbers, not page numbers.

U.S. Census Bureau, Statistical Abstract of the United States: 2009

Population (see also Birth, Death, Divorce, and
  Marriage)—Con.
  Ancestry 51
  Asian, Pacific Islander population. (See
    Asian, Pacific Islander population.)
  Asian population. (See Asian population.)
  Black. (See Black, African-American popula-
    tion.)
  Cities 26, 27
  Civilian 2
  Coastal 24, 25
  Components of change 4, 5, 15, 20
  Continents 1286
  Density 1, 13
    Foreign countries 1288
  Developed countries 1287
  Elderly 7, 8, 9, 10, 11, 16, 33, 71
  Ethnic origin 51
  Fertility 82
  Foreign born 39, 40, 41, 42, 43, 1289
    Students 220
  Foreign countries 1287, 1288, 1290
  Foster children 560
  Group quarters 73
  Hispanic origin. (See Hispanic-origin popula-
    tion.)
  Households and/or families. (See House-
    holds or families.)
  Immigrants .. 39, 40, 41, 42, 43, 44, 45, 46,
                                    47, 49, 50
  Island areas of the U.S. 1272, 1280
  Labor force. (See Labor force, employment
    and earnings.)
  Less developed countries 1287
  Life expectancy 1295, 1296
  Marital status. (See Marital status of popula-
    tion.)
  Metropolitan areas 19, 20, 21, 22
  Migration 4, 5, 20, 29, 30, 31, 32, 1289
  Mobility 20, 29, 30, 31, 32
  Native Hawaiian, Other Pacific Islander
    population. (See Native Hawaiian, Other
    Pacific Islander population.)
  Nativity 39, 41
  Obesity 203, 1298
  Place of birth 39
  Projections 3, 4, 10, 11
  Race 5, 6, 8, 9, 11, 14, 17
    States 18
  Resident 1, 2, 3, 4, 7, 12, 24
  Rural 28
  Sex 7, 10, 41
  States 12, 13, 15, 16, 18
    American Indian, Alaska Native popula-
      tion 18
    Asian population 18
    Black, African-American population ... 18
    Density 13
    Hispanic-origin population 18
    Native Hawaiian, Other Pacific Islander
      population 18
    Projections 14, 17
    Race 18
    Voting age 400, 403
  Total, including Armed Forces overseas ... 2
  Townships and special districts 412
  Urban 28
  Veterans 504

Population (see also Birth, Death, Divorce, and
  Marriage)—Con.
  World 1285, 1287, 1288, 1290
Pork (see also Meat and meat products):
  Consumption 209, 826, 1330
  Foreign trade 810, 826
  Prices 705, 713
  Production 826, 827, 1325, 1329
  Supply 826
Pork chops 709
Portland cement 863
Ports, U.S. 1045, 1046
Portugal. (See Foreign countries.)
Postal rates 1084
Postal Service 1085
  Productivity 619
Potash (potassium salts) 863, 867, 868
Potatoes:
  Acreage 818, 822
  Consumption 210, 823
  Farm marketings, sales 803
  Foreign trade 823
  Prices 709, 806, 818
  Production 818, 822, 823
Poultry (see also Eggs):
  Consumer expenditures 664, 665
  Consumption 209, 826, 1325, 1330
  Farm marketings, sales 802, 803
  Foreign trade 813, 815, 826
  Number on farms 834
  Organic 798
  Prices 705, 709, 713, 806, 834
  Production and sales 826, 834, 835
    Foreign countries 1325, 1329
  Value 834
Poverty:
  Asian and Pacific Islander population .. 524,
                                   689, 690, 693
  Asian population ... 35, 524, 689, 690, 691,
                                       693, 695
  Black, African-American population:
    Families 35, 686, 687, 694, 695
    Households 524
    Persons 35, 689, 690, 691, 693, 695
  Children 690, 691
  Families 35, 693, 694
    American Indian, Alaska Native popula-
      tion 35
    Asian and Pacific Islander population . 693
    Asian population 35, 693, 694, 695
    Black, African-American population .. 35,
                                     693, 694, 695
    Elderly 676
    Hispanic-origin population . 35, 38, 694,
                                           695
    Housing 524, 920
    Labor force 692, 694
    Native Hawaiian, Other Pacific Islander
      population 35
  Foreign born 41
  Hispanic-origin population:
    Families 35, 38, 694, 695
    Households 524
    Persons 35, 38, 689, 690, 691, 695
  Native Hawaiian, Other Pacific Islander
    population 35
  Persons 686
    Age 691, 692

NOTE: Index citations refer to **table** numbers, not page numbers.

U.S. Census Bureau, Statistical Abstract of the United States: 2009

Poverty—Con.
American Indian, Alaska Native popula-
tion 35
Asian population 35, 695
Black, African-American population .. 35,
689, 690, 691, 693, 695
Children 690, 691
City 686
Elderly 33, 691
Hispanic-origin population . 35, 38, 689,
690, 691, 695
Native Hawaiian and Other Pacific
Islander population 35
State 687
Threshold 688
Power (see also Electric light and power indus-
try):
Electric 903, 906, 907, 908, 910, 911
Hydro 912
Nuclear 899, 1341
Prices 710, 713, 890
Water (see hydroelectric power) 912
Power generation and supply industry . 612, 619
Power plants. (See Electric light and power
industry.)
Prawns 855
Precipitation, selected cities 376, 377, 378,
1303
Pregnancies 96, 160
Teen pregnancies 79, 83, 84, 85, 87
Prescription drugs 124, 126, 127, 128, 129,
130, 131, 132, 151, 705
President, U.S., elections for . 380, 381, 382, 383,
384, 403
Campaign finances 406, 407
Prices (see also individual commodities):
Bonds 1167
Electricity 710, 890, 905, 909
Energy 888
Fish 853
Food 708, 709
Foreign countries 1311, 1312, 1313
Fuel 710
Gas 711
Housing 707, 933, 934, 935, 936, 938
Indexes:
Airline cost 1033
Construction materials 920
Consumer price 703, 705, 1311
Foreign countries 1311, 1313
Medical care 132
Metropolitan areas 704, 706
Exports 718, 720
Futures price index 715
Gross domestic product 718
Housing price index 707
Imports 718, 721
Producer prices 702, 712, 713, 714
Construction materials 920
Stage-of-processing 712
Timber 849
Purchasing power of the dollar 702
Received by farmers 806
School expenditures 279
Spot market price 716
Tourism commodities 1226
Living abroad 1313
Lumber and stumpage 848

Prices (see also individual commodities)—Con.
Mineral products (see also individual miner-
als) 864
Received by farmers:
Crops 818
Indexes 806
Livestock and products, poultry . 827, 834
Stocks 1167
Primaries, Presidential preference 407
Primary metal manufacturing:
Capital 751
Earnings 612, 965, 967, 973
Electronic commerce 969
Employees 612, 965, 967, 971, 973
Establishments 965
Finance 764, 988
Foreign trade 988, 1271
Gross domestic product 648, 964
Industrial production index 759
Occupational safety 638
Productivity 619
Profits 762, 764
Research and development 774
Shipments 967, 969, 975, 976, 989, 990
Toxic chemical releases 365
Printing and related support activities. (See Pub-
lishing industry.)
Prisons and prisoners (see also Correctional
institutions) ... 333, 334, 336, 337, 338, 339,
340, 1276
Death sentence 337, 338, 339, 340
Executions 339, 340
Expenditures 433, 436
Per capita 331
Inmate characteristics 334
Sentence, by offense 323
Probation 334
Producer price indexes 712, 713, 714
Construction materials 920
Stage-of-processing 712
Timber 849
Productivity (see also individual industries):
Capacity utilization 760
Farm output 817
Labor 619, 620, 1310, 1342, 1343
Mining industries 878
Professional and business services:
Earnings 612, 622
Employees 611, 612
Hires and separations 615
Professional, scientific and technical services:
Capital 751, 753, 755
Earnings ... 610, 612, 734, 737, 740, 1233,
1237
E-commerce 1015, 1016, 1238
Employees . 610, 612, 734, 737, 740, 1233,
1234, 1235, 1236
Equipment and software expenditures .. 753
Establishments . 734, 735, 737, 1233, 1234,
1236
Finances 724, 727
Gross domestic product 648
Hours 610
Multinational companies 766, 767, 768
Nonemployers 735, 1234
Occupational safety 638
Profits 763
Sales, receipts . 724, 727, 732, 733, 734, 735,
1233, 1234, 1237

NOTE: Index citations refer to **table** numbers, not page numbers.

U.S. Census Bureau, Statistical Abstract of the United States: 2009

Profits 731, 1018, 1138, 1139, 1179, 1182
   Corporations . 652, 722, 761, 762, 763, 764, 978
   Partnerships and proprietorships . 722, 725, 726
Projections:
   Births 1295
   College enrollment 211, 213
   Deaths 1295
   Degrees conferred 213
   Employment 598, 601
   Emissions 913
   Energy 884
   Health expenditures 124, 126, 129
   High school graduates 213
   Island areas 1272
   Labor force 568, 598, 601
   Life expectancy 100, 1295
   Population ... 3, 10, 11, 14, 17, 1272, 1285, 1286, 1287, 1288
   School enrollment 211, 213
   Teachers 213
Propane 870
Property and casualty insurance ... 1161, 1175, 1182
   Fire losses 341, 342, 343
Property tax 418, 433
   Rates, selected cities 430
   State and local government 417, 418
Proprietors' income 656
Proprietorships 722, 724, 725
Propylene 870
Prostitution and commercialized vice, arrests ... 312
Protective service workers. (See Public safety.)
Protein available for consumption 208
Protestants. (See Religion.)
Prunes and plums 210, 824
Psychiatric care and institutions. (See Mental hospitals.)
Psychology:
   Degrees conferred . 290, 291, 292, 782, 785
   Employment 596
   Enrollment 779
   Research, U.S. government obligations for .. 772
Psychotherapeutic drugs, nonmedical use .. 199
Public administration. (See Government.)
Public aid, assistance 545
   Benefits paid 519, 545
   Federal aid to state and local governments .. 415, 416
   Federal expenditures ... 125, 126, 128, 129, 135, 140, 141, 546, 547
   Health expenditures 125, 126, 128, 129, 135, 140, 141
   Homeless 556
   Means-tested 524
   Program participation of household 524
   Recipients 523, 545, 546, 547
Public domain. (See Public lands.)
Public housing 416, 527, 556
Public lands (see also Forests):
   Area 350, 352, 841, 1214, 1215
   Leases, permits, licenses 873
   National forests 841
   National park system 1212, 1214, 1215
   Ownership 841
   Recreation 1212, 1214, 1215

Public officials, prosecutions 326
Public roads. (See Highways.)
Public safety (see also Law enforcement):
   Employment 596
      City government 449
      Fire protection 444, 447
      Police protection and correction 444, 447
   Expenditures:
      City government 440
      Construction, value 922, 923
      County government 442
      Local government 438
      State and local government 417, 453
      State government 433, 436
   Volunteers 566
Public schools. (See Education.)
Public transportation 664, 665, 705
Public welfare 425, 433, 436, 438
Publishing. (see also Books, Newspapers, and Printing.):
   Books 713, 1097
   Newspapers 1093, 1094, 1095
Publishing industry:
   Capital 751
   Earnings 612, 734, 1086, 1088
   Employees 612, 734, 1086, 1088
   Establishments 734, 1086, 1088
   Finances 764, 1087
   Gross domestic product 648, 964
   Industrial production index 759
   Profit 764
   Receipts, revenue 734, 1087, 1088
Puerto Rican population (see also Hispanic-origin population) 38, 1273, 1280
   Births, birth rates 78, 85, 1274
   Educational attainment 222
   Households 1278, 1279
   Labor force 545, 572
   Population 38, 1273, 1280
   Tenure 1279
Puerto Rico. (See Island areas of the U.S.)
Pulmonary diseases (see also Respiratory diseases) 112, 113, 114, 116, 170, 175
Pulp manufacturing 838, 839, 840
Pulpwood 843, 845, 846, 850
Pulses 210
Pumice and pumicite 863, 864
Purchasing power of the dollar 702
Pyrites 865

Q

Qatar. (See Foreign countries.)
Quarries. (See Mining industries.)
Quicksilver (mercury) 863, 864

R

Rabies 175
Racquetball 1209
Radio advertising expenditures 1239
Radio broadcasting industry (see also Broadcasting, and Telecommunications):
   Earnings 612, 1086, 1088
   Employees 612, 1086, 1088
   Establishments 1086, 1088
   Finances 1087, 1104
   Productivity 619
   Revenue 1087, 1088, 1104
   Stations 1090

NOTE: Index citations refer to **table** numbers, not page numbers.

Radiologists 157
Radios:
  Audience characteristics 1089, 1091
  Households with 1090
  Listening 1089
Rail transportation industry (see also Railroads):
  Capital 751
  Earnings 612, 1080
  Employees 612, 1025, 1080
  Finances 1080
  Gross domestic product 648
  Productivity 619, 1080
Railroad employees' retirement funds . 519, 521
Railroads:
  AMTRAK 1080
  Carloadings, by commodity 1081, 1082
  Equipment in service 1080
  Freight traffic 1080, 1081, 1082
  Mileage owned and operated 1080
  Occupational safety 1032, 1080
  Passenger traffic and revenue .. 1080, 1231
  Vehicles 1027
Rainfall, selected cities 376, 377, 1303
Raisins 803
Rankings:
  Airport traffic 1034, 1230
  Cities:
    Population 26
    Residential property tax 430
  Countries:
    Agricultural exports and imports .. 1327
    Consumption of beef, pork, poultry . 1330
    Population 1288
  Federal R&D obligations to higher education .
                                          778
  Sports participation 1208, 1209
  State:
    Domestic travel expenditures 1224
    Exports 1264
    Farm marketings 805
    Foreign trade 1264
    Government finances 434
    Personal income per capita 659
    Population 13
    Public elementary/secondary school
      finances 251
Rape, forcible ... 295, 296, 297, 298, 303, 304,
                                    305, 306
Raspberries 824
Raw materials. (See Crude materials.)
Reading (see also Books, and Libraries) 664,
                                  665, 1192, 1200
  Literacy 226, 1302
Real estate (see also Housing) 696
Real estate and rental and leasing industry:
  Capital 751, 753, 755
  Earnings ... 610, 612, 621, 734, 737, 1126,
                                        1186
  Employees . 596, 610, 612, 734, 737, 1126,
                                        1186
  Equipment and software expenditures .. 753
  Establishments . 734, 735, 737, 1126, 1185,
                                        1186
  Finances 724, 727
  Gross domestic product 648, 650, 1125
  Hires and separations 615
  Hours 610
  Nonemployers 735, 1185
  Productivity 619

Real estate and rental and leasing
  industry—Con.
  Receipts 724, 727, 732, 733, 734, 735,
                                  1126, 1185, 1186
Real estate investment trust (REITs) . 1129, 1130,
                                          1152
Receipts (see also Tax receipts, and individual
  industries):
  American Indian and Alaska Native-owned
    businesses 744, 745
  Asian-owned businesses 744, 745
  Black-owned businesses 744, 745
  Corporations, partnerships, and proprietor-
    ships . 722, 723, 724, 725, 726, 727, 731,
                                      732, 733
  Hispanic- or Latino-owned businesses . 744,
                                          745
  International transportation 1246
  Minority-owned businesses 744, 745
  Native Hawaiian and Other Pacific Islander-
    owned businesses 744, 745
  Revenue:
    Local governments 418, 437
      City governments 439
      County governments 441
    State and local governments combined ..
                                      417, 424
    State governments .. 418, 426, 433, 434
      Tax collections 435
    United States government ... 418, 451, 457,
                                          462
  Women-owned businesses 744, 745
Recreation (see also Arts, recreation, and travel,
  and Sports):
  Activities 204, 1089, 1194, 1198, 1199,
            1200, 1202, 1203, 1209, 1212, 1213
  Building construction, value 924
  Consumer expenditures . 1089, 1097, 1193,
                              1210, 1211, 1356
  Consumer price indexes 705, 717
  Employment and expenditures, government .
                                          455
    All governments 440, 444, 447
    County governments 442
  Foreign countries 1356
  Parks:
    Government expenditures 417, 419
    National 1212, 1214, 1215
    Visits 1212, 1213, 1214, 1215
  Performing arts 1194
  Travel . 1222, 1223, 1224, 1228, 1229, 1230,
                                          1231
  Volunteers 566
Recreational vehicles (RVs) 1203, 1210
  RV parks and recreational camps . 612, 1235,
                                          1241
Recycling waste 361, 362, 363, 364
Refrigerators and refrigeration equipment . 1003
Refinery production 870
Refugees 45, 47, 48, 50
Refuse collection 705
Religion 74, 75, 76
  After-school activities 256, 257
  Charitable contributions 564
  Philanthropy 561, 564
  Theology degrees 293
Religious building construction 963

NOTE: Index citations refer to **table** numbers, not page numbers.

U.S. Census Bureau, Statistical Abstract of the United States: 2009

Religious, grantmaking, civic, professional orga-
  nizations:
    Employees 734, 1235
    Establishments 734, 1235
    Revenues 734, 1244
    Volunteers 566
Religious identification 74
Renewable energy (See Energy.)
Rental and leasing services:
    Capital 751
    Earnings 1126, 1186
    Electronic commerce 1238
    Employees 1126, 1186
    Establishments 1126, 1186, 1235
    Revenues 1126, 1187, 1238
Renters' insurance 1184
Rents 705, 955
Repair services. (See Automobile repair and
  maintenance service.)
Representatives, U.S. (See Congress, U.S.)
Research and development:
    Employment 789
    Expenditures:
        College and universities . 769, 770, 777,
                                        1347
        Federal .. 769, 770, 771, 772, 773, 778,
                                        1347
        Foreign countries 771, 1347
        Industry 769, 770, 774, 775, 1347
        Manufacturing 774
        National defense 769, 1347
        Nonprofit 769, 770
        Space related 769, 773
        State 776
Residential buildings. (See Construction indus-
  try, and Housing and housing units.)
Residential capital 960
Residential energy 713, 885, 886, 889, 890,
        891, 892, 905, 908, 909, 910, 913, 915
Respiratory conditions (see also Pulmonary dis-
  eases) 184, 190
Restaurants. (See Food services and drinking
  places.)
Retail trade:
    Capital expenditures 751, 753, 755
    Earnings 610, 612, 621, 734, 737, 740,
                                        1007
    Electronic commerce 1015, 1016
    Employees .. 600, 610, 612, 734, 737, 740,
                                1007, 1227, 1281
    Equipment and software expenditures .. 753
    Establishments . 734, 735, 737, 1007, 1017,
                                        1281
    Finances 724, 727, 764, 1150
    Foreign investments in the U.S. 1252
    Gross domestic product 648, 650
    Hires and separations 615
    Hours 610
    Inventories 758, 1012
    Multinational companies 766, 767
    Nonemployers 735, 1017
    Occupational safety 638
    Productivity 619
    Profits 764
    Sales, receipts . 724, 727, 732, 733, 734, 735,
        1007, 1009, 1010, 1012, 1015, 1016, 1017,
                                1020, 1227
Retirement systems:
    Benefits paid 519, 529
    Civil service 529, 530, 1177
Retirement systems—Con.
    Defined benefit retirement plans . 534, 1176
    Defined contribution plans 1129, 1176
    Federal government . 529, 530, 1129, 1176,
                                        1177
    Government transfer payments ... 520, 521,
                                        522
    Military retirement system 497
    Old-age, survivors, disability, and health
      insurance. (See Social insurance.)
    Pension plans ... 519, 529, 533, 1176, 1177
    Public employees 519, 529
    Railroad 1177
    Social security trust funds 528
    State and local government . 425, 433, 1176,
                                        1177
Reunion. (See Foreign countries.)
Revolvers. (See Firearms.)
Rhode Island. (See State data.)
Rice:
    Acreage 798, 1325
    Consumption 209, 1325
    Farm marketings, sales 803
    Foreign trade 808, 812
    Prices 709, 713
    Production 812, 1325, 1326
    World 812
Rifle (NCAA) 1207
Rivers, canals, harbors, etc.:
    Commerce, domestic and foreign 1043
    Drainage area and flow 348
    Length of principal rivers 348
Roads, public. (See Highways.)
Roadway congestion 1059
Robbery ... 295, 296, 297, 298, 304, 305, 306,
                                        308
Rockfish 859
Rodeos 1206
Roller skating 1209
Romania. (See Foreign countries.)
Roth IRAs 535, 536, 537, 1176
Rowing 1207
Rubber, crude natural 808, 810
Rubber and misc. plastics manufacturing. (See
  Plastics and rubber products manufacturing.)
Rubber products 713, 1267
Rubella 175, 183
Rugs 713, 982
Running/jogging 1209
Rural population. 28
Russell stock index 1167
Russia. (See Foreign countries.)
Rwanda. (See Foreign countries.)

                    S

Safety:
    Mine 638, 861
    Schools 240
Sailing 1209
Saint Kitts and Nevis. (See Foreign countries.)
Saint Lucia. (See Foreign countries.)
Saint Vincent and the Grenadines. (See Foreign
  countries.)
Salad and cooking oils, consumption 209
Salaries and wages. (See Earnings.)
Sales. (See individual commodities and indus-
  tries.)
Salesworkers 596, 606, 626, 627
Salmon 854, 855, 858, 859
Salmonellosis 175

NOTE: Index citations refer to **table** numbers, not page numbers.

Salt (common), production/value . 863, 864, 1332
Samoa. (See Foreign countries.)
Samoa, American. (See Island areas of the U.S.)
Samoan population 1272
San Marino. (See Foreign countries.)
Sand and gravel industry (see also Mining
   industry) 713, 863
Sanitation. (See Health and Sewage treatment.)
Sao Tome and Principe. (See Foreign countries.)
Sardines 859
Satellites 791
Saudi Arabia. (See Foreign countries.)
Savings:
   Credit unions 1143
   Deposits 653, 1132
   Gross savings, sources and uses 652
   Personal 652, 656
Savings banks. (See Savings institutions.)
Savings bonds 460, 1133
Savings institutions:
   Consumer credit 1151
   Earnings 1128
   Employees 1128
   Establishments 1128, 1136, 1137
   Finances ... 1129, 1130, 1136, 1139, 1152,
                                            1156
   Individual Retirement Accounts (IRAs) . 1176
   Service charges 655
Saw logs 845, 849
Saw mills 838, 839, 840
Scallops 854, 858
Scenic and sightseeing transportation industry:
   Earnings 612, 1029, 1031
   Employees 612, 1025, 1029, 1031
   Establishments 1029, 1031
   Revenue 1029
SCHIP (See State Childrens Health Insurance Pro-
   gram.)
Scholastic Assessment Test (SAT) 258
Schools (see also Education):
   After-school activities 256, 257
   Alternative 234
   Boards, elected officials 398, 399
   Charter schools 230
   Districts 232, 411
   Dress code 240
   Drug testing 240
   Internet access 252
   Lunch programs 551
   Metal detectors 240
   Number 231, 254, 269, 271
   Safety and security measures 240
   Special education 180, 181, 234
   Types 230, 231, 234
   Violence 239
   Vocational 234
Science literacy 1302
Scientific instruments. (See Instruments.)
Scientific research. (See Research and develop-
   ment.)
Scientists and engineers (see also individual
   fields):
   Characteristics 784
   Degrees conferred . 290, 291, 292, 780, 781,
                                  782, 785
   Employment 596, 786, 788, 789
   Non-U.S. citizens 780, 782, 784
   Occupation 786, 787, 788
Scrap metal. (See individual commodities.)
Scuba diving 1209, 1210

Seafoods 854, 858, 859
Securities:
   Brokerage charges 655
   Foreign holdings .. 1131, 1166, 1246, 1249,
                                        1351
   Foreign purchases and sales ... 1163, 1165,
                       1348, 1349, 1351
   Government 422, 728, 729, 1131, 1159,
                       1165, 1166
   Held by life insurance 1181
   Holdings of banks 728, 729, 1137
   Holdings of individuals and businesses . 1132
   New issues 1159, 1162
   Prices, indexes, yields, and issues 1158,
                       1167, 1168, 1349
   Sales, stocks and bonds . 1159, 1163, 1165,
                       1348, 1349, 1351
   Savings of individuals 653
   State and local government . 422, 700, 728,
                                   729, 1159
Securities, commodity contracts, and invest-
   ments (industry):
   Capital 751
   Earnings 612, 1126, 1128
   Electronic commerce 1238
   Employees 612, 1126, 1128
   Establishments 1126, 1127, 1128
   Finances 1129, 1178, 1179
   Gross domestic product 1125
   Nonemployers 1127
   Profits 1179
   Receipts 1126, 1127
Sedatives, persons using 199
Seeds 801
Selenium, dietary 208
Semiconductors (see also Computer and elec-
   tronic product components) .. 787, 992, 1269
Senators, U.S. 385, 388, 389, 390
Senegal. (See Foreign countries.)
Septicemia 112, 113, 114, 115
Serbia (See Foreign countries.)
Service industries (see also specific sectors):
   Capital 751, 753
   Earnings 612, 621, 622, 1233, 1235
   Electronic commerce 1238
   Employees . 154, 586, 600, 611, 612, 1233,
                                    1235, 1281
   Equipment and software expenditures .. 753
   Establishments 1281
   Finances 734, 735, 737
   Foreign trade 1246, 1248, 1260
   Gross domestic product 650, 1282
   Industry 734
   Multinational companies 766, 767
   Occupational safety 635, 638
   Price indexes 703
   Productivity 619
   Profits 722, 763
   Sales or receipts 734, 735, 1233, 1234
Service occupations:
   Benefits 149, 633
   Earnings 626, 627
   Employment 596
      Projections 598
      States 597
   Unemployment 606
   Union membership 643
Service stations. (See Gasoline service stations.)

NOTE: Index citations refer to **table** numbers, not page numbers.

U.S. Census Bureau, Statistical Abstract of the United States: 2009

Service workers. (See Service industries, and Service occupations.)
Sewage treatment systems 881, 882, 918
    Construction 420
    Expenditures 417, 418, 419, 420
    Prices 705
    Residences 946, 950
Sexual activity 92, 93
Sexual assault. (See Rape and assault.)
Seychelles. (See Foreign countries.)
Sheep and lambs 798, 803, 826, 827
Shellfish:
    Canned, quantity and value 859
    Catch, quantity and value 854
    Consumption 209
    Prices 713
    Sales 855, 856
Shelter (see also Consumer price indexes, and Housing and housing units), ... 703, 705
    Homeless 556
Shigellosis 175
Ship and boat building and repairing 619
Shipments, manufacturers' (see also individual industries or products) ... 967, 968, 976, 977
Shipping. (See Merchant vessels and Tonnage, U.S. Flag Fleet.)
Ships 713, 1220
Shoe stores 612, 619, 1009
Shoes. (See Footwear.)
Shoplifting 308
Shortening 209, 709, 713
Shoreline 346
Shrimp 854, 858, 859
Sickness. (See Illness.)
Sierra Leone. (See Foreign countries.)
Silicon 863
Silver 863, 867, 868, 873
    Consumption 864
    Employment 864
    Foreign trade 864, 868
    Prices 864, 865
    Production and value 864, 867, 873
    World production 867
Silverware. (See Jewelry.)
Singapore. (See Foreign countries.)
Single-parent households ... 58, 63, 64, 65, 66, 1291, 1293, 1294
Single persons. (See Marital status.)
Sinusitis 190
Skateboarding 1209
Skiing 1203, 1207, 1209, 1210
Skilled nursing facilities, services 134, 187
Skins. (See Hides, etc.)
Slaughtering and meat-packing industry. (See Meat and meat products.)
Slovakia. (See Foreign countries.)
Slovenia. (See Foreign countries.)
Small business:
    Employees 738, 739, 740, 741
    Firms 738, 739, 740, 741
    Loans 743
    Payroll 738, 740, 741
Smart card 1145
Smoking 196, 197, 199
Snow and ice pellets, selected cities 378
Snowboarding 1209
Snowmobiles 1210
Soap 713
Soccer 1206, 1207, 1208, 1209
Social assistance industry:
    Capital 751

Social assistance industry—Con.
    Earnings 612, 734
    Employees 612, 734
    Establishments 558, 734
    Gross domestic product 648
    Nonemployers 558
    Receipts 152, 557, 558, 734
Social insurance (see also Medicare, Retirement systems, and Social Security):
    Employment covered 525
    Expenditures 520, 521, 522
    Government insurance trust funds 418
        Federal receipts and expenditures .. 528
        State and local receipts, expenditures 417, 433, 531
    Government transfer payments ... 520, 521, 522
    Individual programs:
        Beneficiaries and benefits 526, 527
        Coverage 525, 531
        Federal retirement insurance . 530, 1129, 1177
            Civil service 530
        Old-age, survivors, disability, and health insurance:
            Contributions 528
            Coverage, workers and earnings . 525
            Payments 521, 526, 527, 528
            Tax collections 462
            Trust funds 528
    Railroad insurance 521
    State and local government retirement systems 531, 1129, 1177
    Trust funds 1177
    Unemployment insurance (federal and state) . 520, 521, 522, 539, 540
    Workers' compensation . 125, 128, 521, 542, 543
Social sciences:
    Degrees conferred . 290, 291, 292, 779, 782, 785
    Employment 596, 786
    Enrollment 779
    Research & development 772, 777
    Salary offers 287
Social Security (old-age survivors, disability, and health insurance) (see also Social insurance):
    Beneficiaries and payments 526, 527
    Contributions, rates 528
        Foreign countries 1317
    Coverage, workers and earnings 525
    Families receiving 523
    Federal government outlays 455, 456
    Food stamp participants 554
    Payments 519, 521, 526, 527
    Trust funds 528
Social services:
    Capital expenditures 752
    Earnings 612
    Employees 612
    Occupational safety 638
Social welfare (see also Public aid, assistance, and individual programs):
    Charitable contributions 561, 564
    Employees (state and local government) . 447
    Expenditures:
        City government 440
        County government 442
    Program participation 524

NOTE: Index citations refer to **table** numbers, not page numbers.

U.S. Census Bureau, Statistical Abstract of the United States: 2009

Social welfare (see also Public aid, assistance, and individual programs)—Con.
    State and local government 417
    State government 433, 436
    Volunteers 566
Sodium, dietary 208
Sodium carbonate 863, 864
Sodium sulfate 863, 864
Soft drinks (see also Beverages) . 207, 705, 713
Softball 1203, 1207, 1208, 1209
Software publishing industry (see also Publishing):
    Earnings 612, 1086
    Employees 612, 1086
    Establishments 1086
    Finances 1087, 1100
    Inventory 1100
    Productivity 619
    Research and development 774
    Revenue 1087, 1100
Software sales, expenditures 753
Solar energy 891, 892, 901, 903, 904
Solid waste:
    Disposal 356, 361, 362
    Expenditures 420, 438
    Industry 368
    Landfills 356, 361, 363
    Recycling 362
Solomon Islands. (See Foreign countries.)
Somalia. (See Foreign countries.)
South Africa. (See Foreign countries.)
South Carolina. (See State data.)
South Dakota. (See State data.)
South Korea. (See Foreign countries.)
Soybeans:
    Acreage 818, 820
      Organic 798
    Farm marketings, sales 803
    Foreign trade 812, 814, 815, 818, 1267
    Prices 713, 818, 820
    Production 812, 818, 820
      World production 812
    Supply and disappearance 818
Space industry, commercial 791
Space program:
    Finances 790, 792
    NASA 792
    Space shuttle 792
Space research and technology, federal outlays .
                     455, 790, 1002
Spain. (See Foreign countries.)
Spanish speakers 52, 54, 227
Special education 180, 181
Specialty trade contractors 612, 638, 919
Speeding 1068
Spices 705
Sporting and athletic goods (see also Retail trade, and Sports) 1210, 1211, 1267
    Consumer price indexes 705
    Producer prices 713
    Sales 1014, 1210, 1211
Sporting goods, hobby, book, and music stores:
    Earnings 612, 734, 1008
    Electronic commerce 1013
    Employees 612, 734, 1008
    Establishments 734, 1008, 1017
    Nonemployers 1017
    Productivity 619
    Sales .. 734, 1009, 1011, 1012, 1013, 1017

Sports ... 1200, 1203, 1204, 1205, 1206, 1207, 1208
    After-school activities 256, 257
    Expenditures 1193, 1210
    NCAA 1204, 1205, 1207
    Volunteers 566
Sports associations 1245
Sports industry 1188, 1189, 1190, 1191
Spot market price index 716
Squash (NCAA) 1207
Squash (vegetable) 822
Squid 854
Sri Lanka. (See Foreign countries.)
Stamps, postage, receipts from 1085
Standard & Poor's stock indices 1167
State and local governments, combined data (see also individual governmental units):
    Debt 417, 418, 421
      Highways 1054
    Employees 443, 444, 447, 448
      Benefits 445, 519
    Employer costs 632
    Expenditures (see also Finances) .. 281, 417, 418, 419, 420, 422, 425
      By type 418, 419
      Capital outlay 419, 420
      Construction, value 923
      Hospitals and medical care 128, 163, 425
    Federal aid 414, 415, 416, 453
      By function 415
    Finances 418
      Intergovernmental .. 415, 417, 418, 424
      Mortgage debt 1152
    Flow of funds 1129, 1130
    Gross domestic product 648
    Hospitals 163, 164
    Mortgage holdings 1152
    Number of units 410
    Payrolls 443, 444
    Purchases of goods and services .. 645, 647
    Receipts by source 418
    Retirement systems ... 519, 529, 531, 1129, 1161, 1175, 1176, 1177
    Securities issued 422
    Treasury securities holdings 1161
    Women holding public office 397
State Children's Health Insurance Program (SCHIP) 142
State data:
    Abortion 99
    Agriculture:
      Farms 797
      Income, farm 804, 805
    AIDS 176
    Alcohol use 200
    Altitudes 349
    American Indian, Alaska Native population .. 18
    Apparel and accessory stores, sales ... 1020
    Aquaculture 856
    Area 344
    Arts, funding 1197
    Asian population 18
    Automobile insurance expenditures ... 1183
    Automotive dealers 1020
    Average pay 625
    Bankruptcies 747

NOTE: Index citations refer to **table** numbers, not page numbers.

U.S. Census Bureau, *Statistical Abstract of the United States: 2009*

State data—Con.

Births and birth rates 15, 81
  Birth weight 87
  Births to single or unmarried women . 87
Black, African-American population 18
Black elected officials 398
Blood alcohol concentration (BAC) 1070
Border crossings 1231
Border lengths 345
Building materials and garden supplies,
  sales 1020
Building permits 926
Cancer 174
Capital punishment 340
Charitable contributions 565
Child abuse cases 330
Cigarette smoking 197, 200
Civilian labor force 573
Climate 374, 375, 376, 377, 378, 379
Coal and coke production 878
Coastal population 25
Coastline 346
Commuting to work 1060
Congress, U.S., composition 389
Construction contracts 925
Corrections 433, 447
Crime rates 297
Crops, principal 819, 820, 821
Deaths and death rates .. 15, 108, 111, 116
  Infant 111
Defense contracts 490
Department stores, sales 1020
Doctorates 777
Domestic travel expenditures 1224
Drivers' licenses 1058
Drug use 200
Earnings 625, 966, 1007
Eating and drinking places, sales 1020
Elections . 383, 384, 385, 387, 389, 394, 395,
                                     401, 403
  Voter registration 401
Electrical power 906, 908, 909
Elevations 349
Employees .. 447, 448, 480, 611, 741, 788,
            966, 968, 998, 1007, 1236
Energy consumption 886
Energy expenditures 889
Energy, renewable 912
Establishments 966, 1007, 1236
Exports 1264, 1265
Farms 797
  Government payments 804
  Income 804, 805
Federal funds 461
Financial institutions 1140, 1141
Fire protection 436
Fish 856
Food stamp program 552
Food stores 1020
Foreign born 39
Foreign investment in the U.S. 1253
Foreign trade 1264, 1265
Foreign travel to 1221
Forest land 841
Fuel production 871
Furniture, home furnishings stores 1020
Gas utility industry 916
Gasoline service stations 1020

State data—Con.

Gasoline tax rates 1053
General merchandise stores, sales 1020
Government finances:
  Agricultural payments 804
  Federal aid to state and local govern-
    ments 416
  Federal (income tax returns) 475
  Grants 510
  Local government 437
  State and local governments ... 424, 425
  State governments .. 426, 433, 434, 436
  Tax collections 431, 435
  Transfer payments 522
Governors, vote cast 394
Gross domestic product 649, 650
Hazardous waste 356, 366
Health insurance coverage 147
Health maintenance organizations (HMO) . 145
Highway funds 1055
Highway mileage 1049
Highway trust fund 1052
Hispanic elected officials 399
Hispanic-origin population 18
Hospitals 165, 425, 447
Housing . 707, 926, 928, 937, 943, 947, 951,
                                     954, 955
  Sold 937
Immigrants, unauthorized 46
Income 804
  Disposable personal 658, 660
  Family 685
  Household 684
  Personal 658, 659
Income tax returns 475
Internet usage/connection 1119
Lakes 347
Language spoken at home 53
Legislatures, composition 395, 396
Livestock 830, 831
Local government units 411, 412
Lotteries, revenue from 431
Manufactures, summary statistics 972
Marriage and divorce 123
Medicaid 141
Medicare 135
Metropolitan area population 23
Migration 15, 32
Milk production 831
Millionaires 697
Mining, mineral production value 866
Motor fuel tax 1053
Motor vehicle dealers 1020
Motor vehicle manufacturing 998
Motor vehicle registrations 1058
Motorcycles 1058
Native Hawaiian, Other Pacific Islander
  population 18
Newspapers, number and circulation .. 1095
Nurses 156
Occupations 597, 788
Parks 1213, 1214, 1215
Patents 749
Philanthropy 565
Physicians 156
Police protection 436, 447
Population 12, 13, 15, 16, 18
  Age distribution 16, 17

NOTE: Index citations refer to **table** numbers, not page numbers.

U.S. Census Bureau, Statistical Abstract of the United States: 2009

State data—Con.
    American Indian, Alaska Native population 18
    Asian population 18
    Black, African-American population ... 18
    Components of change 15
    Density 13
    Hispanic-origin population 18
    Metropolitan area population 23
    Native Hawaiian, Other Pacific Islander population 18
    Projections 14, 17
Poultry 835
Poverty 384, 687
President, vote cast 383, 384
Prisons and prisoners 333
Public aid 545
Public road and street mileage 1049
Recreational areas 1213
Representatives, U.S. vote cast for 386
Retail trade, sales 1007, 1020
Roads and highways 1049, 1052, 1055
Rural population 28
Sales 1007, 1020
Schools and education:
    Colleges, number 271
    Educational attainment 225
    Elementary/secondary teachers, public .. 244
    Enrollment:
        Elementary and secondary . 234, 236
        Higher education 271
    Finances, elementary and secondary, public 251
    High school graduates, public 261
    Higher education appropriations 281
    Teachers 244
    Test scores 260
Science and engineering 783, 788
Senators, vote cast for 385
Services industry 1236
Shorelines 346
Small businesses 741
Social Security program 527
State children's health insurance 142
Supplemental Security Income 545
Taxation 434, 435, 475
Temperatures (highs and lows) 372
Temporary assistance for needy families program (TANF) 547, 548
Toxic chemical releases 366
Traffic fatalities 1064, 1070
Travel expenditures 1224
Unemployment 573, 609
Unemployment insurance 522, 540
Union membership 644
Urban population 28
Vehicle miles of travel 1058
Veterans, number and expenditures 502, 522
Voter registration 401
Voter turnout 403
Votes cast ... 382, 383, 384, 385, 386, 387, 394, 402, 403
Voting age population 401, 403
Water, sewage, and other services 918
Wealth 697
Women holding public office 397

State data—Con.
    Workforce 788
State government (see also State and local governments):
    Debt 418, 421, 433, 436
        Public highways 1054
    Employees and payrolls . 443, 444, 447, 448
    Finances 418, 420, 426, 433, 436
        Revenue from lotteries 431
        Tax collections 434, 435
    Highway funds, disbursements of 1055
    Hires and separations 615
    National Park systems 1213, 1214
    Receipts, highways 1051
    Taxes 434, 435
State highways. (See Highways.)
State park systems 1213
Stationery 664, 665
Stay-at-home parents 67
Steak 705, 709
Steam engines and turbines, electric, locomotive (railroad) 1080
Steel (see also Iron and steel) . 713, 867, 988, 989
    Scrap 988
    World production 867
Steel works and rolling mills. (See Iron and steel.)
Stimulants, persons using 199
Stock exchanges:
    Prices 1167
    Volume of trading 1169, 1170
Stockholders' equity, profit rates on 1138
Stocks:
    Corporate, flow of funds 1129, 1161
    Foreign 1164, 1165
    Foreign market indices 1350
    Holdings by sector . 1131, 1133, 1161, 1164, 1166
    Households 698
    Life insurance 1161, 1181
    New issues 1162
    Ownership 1171
    Prices, yield, sales, issues, etc. . 1158, 1160, 1167, 1169, 1348, 1349, 1351
Stone 864
Stone, clay, and concrete products manufacturing. (See Nonmetallic mineral product manufacturing.)
Stone, clay, and glass products . 720, 721, 1081, 1082,
Stone (crushed) 713, 863
Stoves or ranges 1003
Strategic petroleum reserves 875
Strawberries 803, 824
Strokes (see also Cerebrovascular diseases) . 112, 114, 116, 170
Strontium, foreign trade 868
Students. (See Education, enrollment.)
Sturgeon 855
Subprime loans 1154
Subways and urban railways . 1074, 1076, 1077
Sudan. (See Foreign countries.)
Sugar and sugar cane (see also Food, and kindred products):
    Beet 803
    Consumption 209
    Expenditure 664, 665
    Farm marketings 803
    Foreign trade 810
    Prices 705, 709, 713

NOTE: Index citations refer to **table** numbers, not page numbers.

U.S. Census Bureau, Statistical Abstract of the United States: 2009

Suicides 112, 114, 115
Sulfur:
    Consumption 864
    Employment 864
    Foreign trade 864
    Prices 864
    Production and value 864, 867
    World production 1332
Sunfish 855
Superfund environmental program 367
Supermarkets. (See Grocery stores.)
Supplemental Security Income .. 521, 523, 544,
                                 545, 554
    States 545
Supreme Court, U.S. 321
Surgical procedures 162
    Cosmetic 171
    Organ transplants, facilities 172
Suriname. (See Foreign countries.)
Swaziland. (See Foreign countries.)
Sweden. (See Foreign countries.)
Sweet potatoes 210, 822
Swimming 1207, 1208, 1209
Swine. (See Hogs.)
Switzerland. (See Foreign countries.)
Symphony orchestras 1194
Synagogues. (See Religion.)
Syphilis 175, 176
Syria. (See Foreign countries.)

T

Taiwan. (See Foreign countries.)
Tajikistan. (See Foreign countries.)
Talc, pyrophyllite, and soapstone 863, 864
Tangerines 824
Tantalum 868
Tanzania. (See Foreign countries.)
Target shooting 1209
Tariff. (See Customs receipts.)
Taxes:
    Corporate 723, 731, 761
    Deductions 471, 472, 473
    Individual income . 463, 464, 466, 467, 468,
         469, 470, 471, 472, 473, 474
    Partnerships 726
    Proprietorships 725
Tax burden, expenditures, revenue loss esti-
  mates 459, 1318
Tax receipts:
    Foreign countries 1315, 1317
    Governmental revenue, by type of tax .. 418
    Motor-fuel taxes and motor-vehicle fees . 1053
    National (internal revenue) 462
        Adjusted gross income 470
        Collections by source 462
        Corporation income tax:
            Federal budget receipts 457
            Internal revenue collections . 462, 463
            Tax liabilities 731
            Tax returns filed 731
        Employment taxes 457, 462, 463
        Estate and gift taxes 457, 462, 463
        Excise taxes ... 424, 433, 434, 435, 457,
                                   462
        Individual income tax 418, 424, 433,
      434, 435, 457, 462, 463, 464, 465, 466,
      467, 468, 469, 470, 471, 472, 473, 474,
                                  475
           Average tax by income level 470
           Rates 476, 477

Tax receipts—Con.
    Property tax:
        City government 439
        County government 441
        Rates, selected cities 430
        State and local government ... 417, 418,
                            424, 435
    State and local government:
        By households 429
        By type of tax 417, 418, 424
        City government 430, 439
        County government 441
        Local government 437
        State government 433, 434, 436
Tea 207, 705
Teachers:
    Catholic schools 254
    Degrees conferred 289, 290, 291, 292
    Employment . 232, 242, 269, 285, 286, 596
        Projections 213, 598
    Higher education institutions 269
    Private schools 254, 255
    Public schools 213, 232, 244
        Experience, and degrees held .. 243, 255
        Number 213, 232, 242, 243, 244
        Salaries 232, 244
    States 244
Technicians 786
Teenagers:
    Abortions 98
    AIDS 178
    Alcohol use 199
    American Indian, Alaska Native population ..
                                  8, 9, 11
    Asian population 8, 9, 11
    Births/birth rates 79, 83, 84, 85, 87, 89
    Black, African-American population . 8, 9, 11
    Child abuse 329
    Cigarette smoking 199
    Computer use 253
    Contraception use 94, 95
    Cost of raising 667
    Crimes, arrests 305, 313
        Homicide rates 300
    Disabled 277
    Drug use 199
    Education:
        College costs 278
        College freshmen, characteristics ... 276
        Enrollment 211, 213, 215, 216, 217,
        218, 232, 236, 241, 254, 267, 268, 274
           Projections 211, 213
        High school dropouts 262, 263
        High school graduates 232, 261, 267
        Test scores 258, 259, 1302
    Health insurance coverage 146
    Hispanic-origin population 8, 9, 11
    Juvenile delinquency 327, 328
    Labor force 568
        Employed 581, 584, 587, 589, 591
        Minimum wage workers 631
        Multiple job holders 589
        Participation rates 576
        School enrollment status 575, 1320
        Sex 568, 571
        Unemployed 602, 603, 608
    Life expectancy 103
    Marital status 56

NOTE: Index citations refer to **table** numbers, not page numbers.

Teenagers—Con.
　Mobility status 29
　Music purchases 1103
　Native Hawaiian, Other Pacific Islander
　　population 8, 9, 11
　Population 7, 8, 9, 11
　　Projections 10, 11
　　Race 8, 9, 11
　Sexual activity 92, 93
　Sports activity participation 1208, 1209
　Sporting goods purchasers 1211
　Suicides 114
　Victimization 305
Telecommunications 996, 1108, 1344
Telecommunications industry (See also Broad-
　casting):
　Earnings 612, 1086, 1088
　Employees 612, 1086, 1088
　Establishments 1086, 1088
　Finances 724, 1087, 1088, 1108, 1109,
　　　　　　　　　　　　　　　　　　1113
　Productivity 619
　Receipts 724, 1087, 1109, 1113
Telemarketers 596
Telephone carriers 1108
　Cellular 1111, 1112, 1345
Telephone communication:
　Earnings 612, 1108, 1110
　Employees 612, 1110, 1112
　Finances 1110, 1112
　Price indexes 705
　Productivity 619
　Receipts 1110
Telephones (see also Telegraph, etc.):
　Access lines 1110, 1344
　Calls 1110, 1344
　Consumer expenditures 664, 665, 1111
　Households with service . 1090, 1110, 1111
　Number 1110
　　Foreign countries 1345
　Sales or shipments 996
Television broadcasting (see also Cable and
　other pay TV services):
　Advertising expenditures 1239
Television broadcasting industry:
　Earnings 612, 1086
　Employees 612, 1086
　Finances 1086, 1105
　Productivity 619
　Revenue 1087, 1104
Televisions:
　Consumer expenditures .. 1089, 1192, 1193
　Households with 1090
　Injuries associated 193
　Sales or shipments 995
　Viewing 1089, 1091
Temperature:
　Cities 373, 374, 375, 376, 379
　Foreign cities 1303
　States (highs and lows) 372
Temporary assistance for needy families pro-
　gram (TANF) ... 416, 456, 521, 523, 546, 547,
　　　　　　　　　　　　548, 550, 554
Tennessee. (See State data.)
Tennis ... 1203, 1206, 1207, 1208, 1209, 1210
Tenure. (See Housing and housing units and
　Farms.)
Tetanus 175
Texas. (See State data.)

Textile mill products:
　End-use 982
　Foreign trade 983, 1267, 1271
　Prices 716, 720
　Production 983
Textile mills and product manufacturing:
　Capital 751
　Earnings 612, 965, 967, 973
　Electronic commerce 969
　Employees 612, 965, 967, 971, 973
　Establishments 965
　Finances 764
　Foreign trade 1271
　Gross domestic product 648, 964
　Industrial production index 759
　Inventories 976
　Occupational safety 638
　Profits 764
　Shipments 967, 969, 975, 976
　Toxic chemical releases 365
Textiles 664, 665
Thailand. (See Foreign countries.)
Theaters:
　Attendance and receipts 1194, 1200
　Federal aid 1195, 1196
Theft. (See Crime and criminals.)
Theology, degrees conferred 293
Thread. (See Yarn, thread, etc.)
Thrift Savings Plan 529
Tilapia 855
Timber (see also Forest products, Lumber, and
　Wood products):
　Area 841
　Consumption 845
　Growth 841
　Foreign trade 845, 846
　Ownership 841
　Producer prices 848, 849
　Production 845
　Manufacturing 836, 838, 839, 840
　Removals 841, 843
　Roundwood products 843, 845
　Volume 841
Tin:
　Foreign trade 868
　Prices 865
　Production 867
　　World 1332
Tires and tubes 713, 717, 1267
Titanium:
　Imports 868
　Production 863, 864, 867
　World production 867
Tobacco (see also Cigarettes, and Tobacco
　manufacturing):
　Consumer expenditures . 662, 664, 665, 717,
　　　　　　　　　　　　　　981, 1314
　Consumption and use .. 196, 197, 199, 981,
　　　　　　　　　　　　　　　1299
　Farm marketings, sales 801, 803
　Foreign countries 1299
　Foreign trade 720, 721, 808, 981, 1267
　Prices 705, 713, 717, 720, 721, 806
　Production 981
Tobacco manufacturing (see also Beverage and
　tobacco product manufacturing):
　Capital 751
　Earnings 973
　Employees 973
　Foreign trade 1271

NOTE: Index citations refer to **table** numbers, not page numbers.

U.S. Census Bureau, Statistical Abstract of the United States: 2009

Tobacco manufacturing (see also Beverage and tobacco product manufacturing)—Con.
  Inventories 976
  Price indexes 705, 714
  Shipments 975, 976
  Toxic chemical releases 365
Togo. (See Foreign countries.)
Toilet articles and preparations 655
Tokyo Nikkei 225 stock market index 1350
Tomatoes 210, 709, 803, 822
Tonga. (See Foreign countries.)
Tools. (See Machine tools.)
Tornadoes 370
Tourism, domestic and foreign (see also Travel) .
1220, 1221, 1222, 1223, 1224, 1225, 1226,
    1227, 1228, 1229, 1230, 1231, 1232, 1355
Townships and special districts 410, 411
Toxic-shock syndrome 175
Toys and sporting goods:
  Consumer expenditures 1193
  Foreign trade 1267
  Price indexes 705, 713
Track and field 1207, 1208
Trade (business). (See Commerce, Foreign trade,
  Retail trade, and Wholesale trade.)
Trade, transportation and utilities:
  Earnings 612, 622
  Employees 611, 612
  Hires and separations 615
  Occupational safety 638
Traffic fatalities . 1032, 1063, 1064, 1065, 1066,
                    1068, 1069, 1070
Tranquilizers 199
Transfer payments (See Public aid, assistance.)
Transit and ground transportation industry. (See
  also Passenger transit industry):
  Capital 751
  Earnings 612, 1029, 1031
  Employees 612, 1025, 1029, 1031
  Establishments 1029, 1031
  Gross domestic product 648
  Revenue 1029
Transit systems:
  Characteristics 1076
  Cities served 1076
  Consumer expenditures 717
  Mileage 1026
  Trips taken 1077
  Vehicles 1027
Transportation (see also Motor vehicles, and
  individual modes):
  Accidents 1032, 1036, 1037
  Alternative fueled vehicles 1057
  Carriers of passengers .. 1030, 1074, 1080,
                          1230
  Carriers of property 1081, 1082
  Commodity shipments 1048
  Commuting to work 1060
  Construction, value 922, 923
  Consumer complaints 1040
  Consumer expenditures . 662, 663, 664, 665,
                          666
  Consumer price indexes . 703, 704, 705, 717
    Motor fuel 705
    New cars and new trucks 705
  Cost indexes 706
    Airlines 1033
    Tourism commodities 1226
  Energy .. 885, 886, 890, 891, 892, 905, 913
  Expenditures 655

Transportation (see also Motor vehicles, and
  individual modes)—Con.
  Federal government:
    Aid to state and local governments . 415,
                                        416
    Outlays 455, 773
  Freight 1028
  Government employees and payrolls ... 444
  Government finances .. 417, 418, 419, 420,
                      433, 434, 436, 455
  Hazardous shipments 1048
  Metropolitan areas 1035
  Occupations 596, 606
  Port traffic 1045
  Producer prices 714
  Stock and bond prices and yields 1167
  System mileage 1026
  Travel trends 1225
  Travel volume 1030, 1041
Transportation and warehousing:
  Capital 751, 753, 755
  Earnings 610, 612, 622, 734, 737, 740,
                      1029, 1031
  Employees .. 586, 610, 612, 734, 737, 740,
                      1025, 1029, 1031
  Equipment and software expenditures .. 753
  Establishments . 734, 735, 737, 1029, 1031
  Finances 724, 727
  Hires and separations 615
  Hours 610
  Nonemployers 735
  Occupational safety 638
  Productivity 619
  Revenue 1029, 1078
  Sales, receipts . 724, 727, 732, 733, 734, 735
Transportation equipment manufacturing (see
  also Aerospace, and Motor vehicles):
  Earnings 612, 965, 967, 973
  Electronic commerce 969
  Employees 612, 965, 967, 971, 973
  Establishments 965
  Finances 764
  Gross domestic product 648
  Inventories 976
  Multinational companies 766, 767, 768
  Occupational safety 638
  Producer prices 714
  Productivity 619
  Profits 764
  Research and development 774
  Shipments 967, 969, 975, 976
  Toxic chemical releases 365
Transportation, communications, and utilities
  industry (see also Energy, Information, Trans-
  portation and warehousing, and Utilities):
  Earnings 881, 882
  Employees 881, 882, 918
  Profits 881, 911, 914, 915, 916
Transportation support services industry . 1025,
                          1029, 1031
Travel (see also Arts, recreation, and travel):
  Accidents 1032, 1228
    Air carriers 1036, 1037
  Border crossings 516, 1231
  Business, pleasure travelers 1222, 1223,
                                  1232
  Cruise ships 1220
  Domestic expenditures by state 1224
  Forecast 1225

NOTE: Index citations refer to **table** numbers, not page numbers.

U.S. Census Bureau, Statistical Abstract of the United States: 2009

Travel (see also Arts, recreation, and
  travel)—Con.
    Foreign 1221, 1228, 1229, 1355
    Highway mileage 1047, 1049
    Household trips 1222, 1223
    International expenditures 1225, 1228
    Passengers . 1026, 1030, 1041, 1228, 1229,
                                              1230
    Person trips 1213, 1222, 1225
    Price index 1226
    Recreation 1222, 1223
    Services 1260
    Tourists 1221, 1228, 1229, 1230, 1355
    Volume 1030, 1041
Travel accommodations industry . 612, 619, 1226,
                                      1227, 1235
Travel arrangement industry:
    Earnings 612, 1233, 1235
    Employees 612, 1233, 1235
    Establishments 1233, 1234, 1235
    Nonemployers 1234
    Receipts 1233, 1234, 1240
Travel in the United States 345, 1225, 1231
Travelers' checks 1156
Treasury bonds:
    Purchases and holdings . 1159, 1161, 1165,
                                            1166
    Yields 1158
Trichinosis 175
Trinidad and Tobago. (See Foreign countries.)
Trips. (See Travel.)
Trout 855, 857
Truck and tractor pull 1206
Truck transportation industry:
    Capital 751
    Commodities handled 1079
    Earnings 612, 1029, 1031
    Employees 612, 1025, 1029, 1031
    Establishments 1029, 1031
    Finances 1078
    Gross domestic product 648
    Occupational safety 638
    Productivity 619
    Revenue 1029, 1078, 1079
Trucks:
    Factory sales (trucks and buses) 1021
    Imports 1021
    Motor-fuel consumption 1062
    Registration (trucks and buses) 1058
Tuberculosis 175, 176
    Hospitals 163
Tuition 282
    Consumer price indexes 705
Tuna 854, 858, 859
Tungsten:
    Foreign trade 868
    Production and value 863, 864
    World production 867
Tunisia. (See Foreign countries.)
Turbines. (See Steam engines.)
Turkey. (See Foreign countries.)
Turkeys 709, 713, 798, 803, 826, 835
Turkmenistan. (See Foreign countries.)
Turks and Caicos Islands. (See Foreign coun-
    tries.)
Tutoring 256
Tuvalu. (See Foreign countries.)
Typhoid fever 175

U

Uganda (See Foreign countries.)
Ukraine (See Foreign countries.)
Ulcers 188
Ultrasound, diagnostic 162
Unemployment. (See Labor force, unemployed
    workers.)
Unemployment insurance:
    Beneficiaries 523, 539, 540
    Coverage, workers and earnings 540
    Governmental finances 417, 433, 457
    Payments 519, 520, 521, 522, 539, 540
Union membership 642, 643, 644
    Employee benefits 634
United Arab Emirates. (See Foreign countries.)
United Kingdom. (See Foreign countries.)
United States securities (see also Debt):
    Purchases and holdings . 1132, 1137, 1159,
                                      1161, 1165, 1166
    Yields 1157, 1158
Universities. (See Education, higher education
    institutions.)
Unmarried-partner households 62
Unmarried women, births 84, 85, 87, 1291
Uranium (see also Nuclear power) . 863, 880, 902
Urban population 28
Uruguay (See Foreign countries.)
Utah. (See State data.)
Utilities (see also Electric light power industry,
    and Gas utility industry):
    Capital 751, 753, 755
    Cost of living 706
    Customers and bills 910
    Earnings . 610, 612, 621, 622, 734, 737, 740,
                                              881, 882
    Employees ... 610, 612, 734, 737, 881, 882
    Equipment and software expenditures .. 753
    Establishments 734, 735, 737, 882
    Expense 911
    Finances 724, 727
    Gross domestic product 648
    Hours 610
    Income 911
    Industrial production index 759
    Industry 734, 881, 882, 907
    Investor owned 911
    Multinational companies 766, 767
    Net generation 907, 910
    Net summer capacity 907
    Nonemployers 735
    Occupational safety 638
    Price indexes 704
    Productivity 619
    Revenue 910, 911
    Sales, shipments, receipts ... 724, 727, 732,
                                      733, 734, 735
    States 909
Urban transit systems industry 1031
Uzbekistan. (See Foreign countries.)

V

Vacancy rates, housing . 940, 942, 943, 944, 945
Vanadium 867, 868
Vanuatu. (See Foreign countries.)
Veal (see also Beef, and Meat and meat prod-
    ucts) 209, 713, 826, 1330
Vegetable oils. (See Oils.)
Vegetables (see also individual commodities):
    Acreage 822
    Consumer expenditures 664, 665

NOTE: Index citations refer to **table** numbers, not page numbers.

U.S. Census Bureau, Statistical Abstract of the United States: 2009

Vegetables (see also individual commodities)—Con.
    Consumption 210, 823
    Farm marketings, sales 801, 803
    Foreign trade . 808, 810, 813, 815, 823, 1267
    Gardens 1202
    Prices 705, 713, 714, 720, 806
    Production 822, 823
Vehicles. (See Motor vehicles, Tractors, etc.)
Veneer, wood products 838, 839, 840, 852
Venereal diseases (see also AIDS) 175
Venezuela. (See Foreign countries.)
Vermiculite 863, 864
Vermont. (See State data.)
Vessels. (See Ships.)
Veterans:
    Characteristics 504
    Number 502, 503
    Pensions and other benefits:
        Service-connected compensation . 505, 506
        Disbursements 485, 506, 519, 521
        Federal aid to state and local govern-
           ments 415
        Federal payments 456
        Health expenditures 125, 128
        Veterans or dependents receiving .. 505, 523
Veterans Affairs, Dept. of:
    Expenditures . 125, 128, 505, 506, 520, 521, 522
        Hospital, medical care 125
        Home loans 1154
Vetoed bills, Congressional 392
VCRs 1089, 1090
Video games 257, 1015, 1089
Vietnam. (See Foreign countries.)
Violent crime. (See Crime.)
Virgin Islands. (See Island areas of the U.S.)
Virginia. (See State data.)
Visa holders, doctorates 780
Vital statistics (see also Birth, Death, Divorce, and Marriage):
    Fertility and fertility rate 82
    Foreign countries 1295
    Island areas 1273
    Life expectancy 100, 102, 103
    Marriage and divorce 77, 123
    Rates, summary 77
    World 1295
Vitamins 208
Vocational rehabilitation 125, 557
Volleyball 1207, 1208, 1209
Volunteer activities 256, 566, 1199
Voter registration 400, 401
Voter turnout 400, 401, 403
Votes:
    Congressional 385, 386, 387, 403
    Gubernatorial 394
    Presidential .. 380, 381, 382, 383, 384, 403
Voting-age population 400, 401, 403

              W

Wage earners. (See Labor force, employment, and earnings, and individual industries.)
Wages and wage rates. (See Earnings.)
Walleye 855
Wallis and Futuna. (See Foreign countries.)
Walnuts 803, 824, 825
Warehouse clubs and superstores . 1008, 1009, 1022

Warehouses (see also Trucking and warehousing) 963
Warehousing and storage industry:
    Capital 751
    Earnings 612, 1029, 1031
    Employees 612, 1025, 1029, 1031
    Establishments 1029, 1031
    Gross domestic product 648
    Occupational safety 638
    Revenue 1029, 1078
Washing machines, homes with 946
Washington. (See State data.)
Waste management & remediation services:
    Capital 751
    Earnings 734
    Employees 734
    Establishments 734
    Receipts 734
Wastepaper 713, 849
Wastewater treatment 881, 882, 918
Watches. (See Clocks and watches, etc.)
Water (see also Wastewater treatment, and Water transportation industry):
    Area 1, 344
    Consumption 354
    Freight 1043, 1044
    Lakes 347
    Pollution:
        Oil spills 355
        Rivers and streams 355
        Toxic releases 364, 366
    Power 912
    Public supply 354, 917, 946
    Vessels 1027, 1203
Water heater 1003
Water polo 1207
Water skiing 1209
Water transportation industry:
    Capital 751
    Earnings 612, 1029, 1031
    Employees 612, 1025, 1029, 1031
    Establishments 1029, 1031
    Foreign trade 1044
    Freight 1028, 1043, 1044
    Gross domestic product 648
    Occupational safety 1032
    Outlays 455
    Revenue 1029
Water utility 664, 665, 705, 881, 882, 917
Water, sewage and other systems . 612, 881, 882, 918
Watermelons 822
Waterways 1043
Wealth:
    Business 701
    Families 698, 699
    Government 701
    Households 701
    Millionaires 697
    Persons 696, 697
Weather 370, 371, 372, 373, 374, 375, 376, 377, 378, 379
    Foreign countries 1303
Weight 202
Welfare services. (See Public aid, assistance; Social welfare; and individual programs.)
West Bank. (See Foreign countries.)
West Virginia. (See State data.)
Western Sahara. (See Foreign countries.)
Wetlands 351, 353

NOTE: Index citations refer to **table** numbers, not page numbers.

Wheat:
    Acreage 818, 821, 1325
        Organic 798
    Farm marketings, sales 803
    Farm prices 818, 821
    Foreign trade 805, 808, 815, 818, 1267, 1327
    Price index 713, 720
    Production 812, 818, 821
        World production 1325, 1326
    Supply and disappearance 818
Wheat flour 209
Whiting, quantity and value of catch 854
Wholesale trade:
    Capital expenditures 751, 753, 755
    Earnings 610, 612, 621, 734, 737, 740, 1004
    Employees .. 586, 600, 610, 612, 734, 737, 740, 1004, 1281
    Equipment and software expenditures .. 753
    Establishments . 734, 735, 737, 1004, 1281
    Finances 724, 727, 764
    Foreign investments in U.S. 1252, 1254
    Gross domestic product 648, 650
    Hires and separations 615
    Hours 610
    Inventories 1006
    Multinational companies 766, 767, 768
    Nonemployers 735
    Occupational safety 638
    Productivity 619
    Profits 764
    Sales, receipts . 724, 727, 732, 733, 734, 735, 1006, 1015
Whooping cough (pertussis) 175
Wildfires 844
Wildlife:
    Endangered species 369
    Related recreation activities 1216, 1230
Wilshire equity index 1167
Wind:
    Energy source 891, 892, 903, 904
    Selected cities 379
Wines (see also Alcoholic beverages) . 207, 705, 808, 810
Wiretaps 325
Wisconsin. (See State data.)
Women:
    Abortions 97, 98
    Activity limitation 185, 186
    Adult education 294
    Age 7, 10
    AIDS 177, 178
    American Indian, Alaska Native population . 6
    Apparel 664, 665
    Asian population 6
    Births and birth rates . 77, 78, 79, 84, 86, 90, 91, 1295
        Births to single women .. 84, 85, 87, 90, 1291
        Breastfeeding 88
        Cesarean section deliveries 86, 162
        Characteristics, selected 79, 90, 91
        First births 90
    Black, African-American population 6
    Body Mass Index (BMI) 203
    Business owners 744, 745
    Cancer 119, 173
    Cerebrovasular diseases, deaths 118

Women—Con.
    Child day care 559
    Child support 549
    Cigarette smoking 196, 197
    Community service 256, 566
    Computer use 1091, 1120
    Contraceptive use 94, 95
    Cosmetic surgery 171
    Criminal victimization 305, 307
    Deaths and death rates . 104, 105, 106, 109, 110, 117, 118, 119, 120, 121
    Delivery procedures, births 86, 162
    Education:
        Adult education 294
        American College Testing program .. 259
        Attainment 221, 223, 264, 265, 267
            Earnings 224
        College costs 278
        College enrollment . 213, 218, 267, 268, 269, 270, 779
            By age 268
            By state 271
            Disabled 277
        Degrees conferred .. 288, 290, 291, 292, 293, 781, 782
        Enrollment by level 218, 241, 274
        High school dropouts 262, 264, 265
        Teachers 243, 245, 255, 285, 596
        SAT tests 258
        Students with weapons 239
    Elected officials 390, 397, 1316
    Elections, voter registration and turnout . 400
    Fertility, fertility rate 82
    Food cost 708
    Food stamp participants 554
    Foreign parliaments 1316
    Gynecological services 160, 162
    Health insurance coverage 146, 148
    Heart disease, deaths 117
    Height distribution 201
    Hispanic-origin population 6
    HIV disease 121
    Homicides 302
    Hospital use 160, 161, 162, 167, 170
    Householders . 58, 60, 61, 63, 64, 65, 70, 71
    Illness/injury 192
    Income 679, 680, 681
    Injuries 192
    Internet access/use 1091, 1120, 1121
    Job search 603
    Labor force and employment:
        Age 568, 571
        Children 89, 90, 91
        Displaced workers 593
        Earnings 626, 627
        Educational attainment ... 572, 590, 607
        Employed . 569, 573, 575, 578, 584, 586, 587, 589, 591, 596, 600
        Foreign born 570
        Foreign countries 1320, 1322, 1323
        Hours worked per day 618
        Industry 600
        Marital status 576, 577, 578, 579
        Occupation 596, 627
        Participation rates .. 568, 569, 572, 573, 576, 577, 578, 579
        Persons working at home 586
        Projections 568

NOTE: Index citations refer to **table** numbers, not page numbers.

U.S. Census Bureau, Statistical Abstract of the United States: 2009

Women—Con.
Reason not in 595
School enrollment 575
States 573
Tenure with employer 591
Unemployed .. 569, 573, 575, 578, 602,
604, 605, 606, 607, 608
Union membership 643
Work-related learning 617
Life expectancy .. 100, 101, 102, 103, 1296
Mammography 195
Marital status 55, 56, 59
Marriage and divorce 123, 1292
Military personnel 494, 500, 501
Music purchases 1103
Native Hawaiian, Other Pacific Islander
population 6
Overweight 203
Persons living alone (one-person house-
holds) 71
Physical activity 204
Physicians 157
Visits to 158, 159, 160
Pilots 1042
Population 6, 7, 10
Property owners 950
Public assistance 524, 525, 541, 554
Race 6
Rape 295, 296, 297, 298, 303, 312
Recreational activities .. 1198, 1199, 1209,
1211
Science & engineering 779, 781, 782
Sexual activity 92, 93
Social security beneficiaries and payments ..
526
Sports participation in school ... 1207, 1208
Suicides 120
Surgical procedures 162
Tobacco consumption 1299
Unemployment ... 569, 573, 575, 578, 602,
604, 605, 606, 607, 608
Age 602
Reason 604, 608
Union membership 643
Unmarried-partner households 62
Volunteers 256, 566
Voter registration and turnout 400
Weight 202
Wood and wood products. (See Forest products,
and Lumber.)
Wood products manufacturing:
Capital 751
Earnings . 612, 837, 838, 839, 840, 965, 967,
973
Electronic commerce 969
Employees .. 612, 837, 838, 839, 840, 965,
967, 971, 973, 1253
Establishments ... 837, 838, 839, 965, 1253
Finances 764
Foreign trade 1271
Gross domestic product 648, 836, 964

Wood products manufacturing—Con.
Industrial production index 759
Prices 849
Productivity 619
Profits 764
Railroad car loadings 1081, 1082
Receipts 837
Renewable energy 912
Shipments 837, 839, 840, 967, 969
Toxic chemical releases 365
Woodpulp (see also Paper and paperboard prod-
ucts):
Foreign trade 846
Producer price indexes 849
Production 850
Work stoppages 641
Workplace deaths/injuries . 635, 636, 637, 638,
639
Workplace violence/security measures 640
Workers. (See Employment, and Labor force.)
Workers' compensation program . 125, 153, 519,
521, 523, 542, 543
Workstations. (See Computer.)
World. (See Foreign countries, International
Affairs, and World summary statistics)
World summary statistics:
Age distribution 1290
Agriculture 1325, 1326
Communications 1344
Comparative data (area, population, etc.) ....
1288, 1290
Emissions 1304
Energy . 1333, 1334, 1335, 1336, 1340, 1341
Farm commodities 812, 1326
Fisheries 1328
HIV and AIDS 1297
Labor 1343
Mineral production 875, 878
Minerals 1332
Natural resources (oil, gas, coal) . 1337, 1338,
1339
Patents 1346
Population 1285, 1286, 1288, 1290
Stock market 1348, 1349
Telecommunication service sector 1344
Wrestling 1206, 1208, 1207
Wyoming. (See State data.)

Y

Yarn and thread 713
Yemen. (See Foreign countries.)
Yogurt consumption/production 209, 832

Z

Zambia. (See Foreign countries.)
Zimbabwe. (See Foreign countries.)
Zinc:
Foreign trade 864, 868
Mining industry 862
Prices 864, 865
Production and value (mine and smelter) ....
863, 864, 867
World 867, 1332

NOTE: Index citations refer to **table** numbers, not page numbers.

U.S. Census Bureau, Statistical Abstract of the United States: 2009